SELECTED COMMERCIAL STATUTES

FOR SECURED TRANSACTIONS COURSES

2023 Edition

Advisory Panel

CAROL L. CHOMSKY
Professor of Law
University of Minnesota Law School

CHRISTINA L. KUNZ
Professor Emerita
Mitchell Hamline School of Law

ELIZABETH R. SCHILTZ
Herrick Professor of Law
University of St. Thomas School of Law

ANNE LAWTON
Professor Emerita
Michigan State University College of Law

WEST ACADEMIC PUBLISHING

The publisher is not engaged in rendering legal or other professional advice, and this publication is not a substitute for the advice of an attorney. If you require legal or other expert advice, you should seek the services of a competent attorney or other professional.

COPYRIGHT © 2009–2012 Thomson Reuters
© 2013 LEG, Inc. d/b/a West Academic Publishing
© 2014–2022 LEG, Inc. d/b/a West Academic
© 2023 LEG, Inc. d/b/a West Academic
    860 Blue Gentian Road, Suite 350
    Eagan, MN 55121
    1-877-888-1330

Printed in the United States of America

ISBN: 979-8-88786-015-2

[No claim of copyright is made for official U.S. government statutes, rules or regulations.]

PREFACE

As commercial law professors who use statutory law supplements in our own classes, the four of us on the Advisory Panel welcome the opportunity to continue shaping this mainstay of commercial law teaching to serve the evolving needs of students and teachers. Although the statutes and codes included in the volume are available electronically, a one-volume annotatable hard-copy resource remains a valuable tool for teaching and learning the provisions. From our experience updating the compilation each year, we also know the amount of work involved in creating a usable, reliable, and up-to-date statutory reference tool, making the continued publication of the supplements a worthwhile endeavor.

Our goal is to offer a set of supplements that will meet the needs of the teachers of most commercial law subjects. We reconsider decisions on content each year, so we hope that you will let us know how this version served you. We thank faculty who provided feedback in the survey we conducted in early 2019, the results of which are reflected in our decisions about what to include or omit in these volumes.

In 2023, West Academic is publishing a comprehensive statutory supplement (a useful tool for students who will take more than one commercial law course) as well as abridged volumes appropriate for use in courses on secured transactions, sales and contracts, or payment systems. The materials in each volume reflect changes through the dates noted for each provision. We have indicated where to find changes in law adopted after those dates. Where we have identified typographical errors or outdated cross-references still included in a provision, we have marked the corrections in square brackets and italics, e.g., [*unrevised Article 1*].

As we determine what to include or exclude from the comprehensive supplement and how to maximize its usability, we are constrained by publishing parameters that limit that volume's maximum size. Page thickness, margin size, and font size must be chosen to avoid or minimize increasing the size of the comprehensive volume. The price of the book must also stay competitive and within the reach of law students; dividing the comprehensive supplement into multiple volumes to make it physically easier to handle (as has been suggested to us) would result in increased cost. This year, the need to include extensive revisions and additions to the UCC created additional challenges. While the comprehensive supplement necessarily remains long and somewhat bulky, the abridged volumes are slimmer and more transportable. We periodically trim from the abridged volumes material that we think is not used by most teachers of the targeted subjects, to make them more practical and convenient for students who do not need a volume for multiple courses.

With these constraints in mind and based on our own judgments and discussions with other commercial law professors, we have made the following selection decisions:

- The comprehensive volume contains the entire UCC and Official Comments. The abridged volumes omit portions of the UCC not typically taught in the targeted courses, to make those volumes slimmer for easier handling.

- The volumes contain the 2022 amendments to the UCC, which affect almost every Article. At the time of publication, some jurisdictions were already considering legislation to adopt the 2022 amendments, and it is useful for students to have access to the 2022 changes, to prepare for likely changes in the UCC in their own and other jurisdictions.

- This year, we omitted the names of members of the UCC drafting committees and advisors as well as the concordances and conversion tables for superseded versions of UCC Articles. That information may be found on the ULC website for those interested in that historical information.

- The comprehensive volume contains only the PEB Commentaries that have continuing relevance to current versions of the UCC, and each abridged volume contains a subset of that collection.

- Where appropriate, the volumes also contain older versions of some UCC Articles. The comprehensive and Payments volumes include both the pre-1990 version of and the 2002 amendments to Articles 3 and 4, because each of the three versions (pre-1990, 1990 with the 2002 amendments, and 1990 unamended) is in effect in at least one enacting jurisdiction. The Sales and Contracts volume contains the 2000 version of Article 1 because so many older Article 2 cases contain references to that unrevised version.

- None of the volumes contain the 2003 amendments to Articles 2 and 2A that were withdrawn by the ULC and the ALI in May 2011. The amendments are available on Westlaw for historical reference.

- Professors differ widely on which international sources they teach, if any. We omit some suggested sources (for instance, the ICC's Incoterms) because copyright permission fees would make the book too expensive. Some less frequently used international sources (for instance, UNIDROIT and UNCITRAL) are readily available online and should be accessed there, to keep the book less expensive and less unwieldy for its users. For online access to those materials, see:

   www.uncitral.org
   www.unidroit.org
   www.iccwbo.org

- These statutory supplements cannot include the wide variety of material treated in consumer law classes without becoming too bulky for other use. The supplements will nonetheless be adequate for use with consumer law books that have incorporated much of the non-commercial law material directly into their texts.

- We have included links to, rather than full text of, lengthy material previously incorporated that we think is used infrequently (e.g., Regulation CC Commentary and Official Interpretations of Regulation E) to reduce the length of the volume without sacrificing critical content.

- For teachers who cover bankruptcy topics in their commercial law courses, the comprehensive supplement and the Secured Transactions volume include the bankruptcy statute; the comprehensive volume also includes the bankruptcy rules. For the bankruptcy forms, we refer the user to a site for electronic access, where the forms may be completed electronically and are updated to reflect any changes made in the annual revision cycle.

Advisory Panel:

Prof. Carol L. Chomsky, University of Minnesota Law School, Minneapolis, MN

Prof. Emerita Christina L. Kunz, Mitchell Hamline School of Law, Saint Paul, MN

Prof. Elizabeth R. Schiltz, University of St. Thomas School of Law, Minneapolis, MN

Prof. Emerita Anne Lawton, Michigan State University College of Law, East Lansing, MI

April 2023

GUIDE TO USING THE UCC

The Uniform Commercial Code (UCC) was first promulgated in the 1950s by the Uniform Law Commission (ULC) and the American Law Institute (ALI). Since then, the UCC has been widely enacted throughout the states and territories of the United States. The UCC is not a static product, however. The Permanent Editorial Board (PEB) for the Uniform Commercial Code, composed of representatives from the ULC and the ALI, advises those organizations on further changes needed in the UCC and prepares PEB Commentaries to interpret UCC provisions.

Frequent consideration of revisions and amendments keeps the UCC current with new developments in commercial practices, including concerns related to electronic commerce and consumer protection. In the years since the UCC was first promulgated, the following changes have been made:

- The original nine UCC Articles were supplemented by additional Articles on emerging areas of law (Article 2A on leases of goods in 1987, Article 4A on funds transfers in 1989, Article 12 on Controllable Electronic Records in 2022). In 1989, Article 6 on bulk sales was recommended for deletion as no longer necessary in light of modern commercial realities.

- Some Articles were "revised" (completely rewritten) to modernize the law (Article 3 on negotiable instruments and Article 4 on bank deposits and collections in 1990, Article 8 on investment securities in 1994, Article 5 on letters of credit in 1995, Article 9 on secured transactions in 1998, Article 1 containing definitions and rules applicable throughout the UCC in 2001, Article 7 on documents of title in 2003).

- Some individual UCC sections were "amended" (edited) to eliminate ambiguities and gaps in coverage or to bring those sections in conformity with changes in amendments or revisions in other Articles.

- In 2022, an extensive set of amendments was adopted to accommodate emerging technologies such as artificial intelligence, distributed ledger technology, and virtual currency. These amendments added new Articles 12 (Controllable Electronic Records) and A (transitional provisions for the 2022 amendments) and made changes, small and large, to every UCC Article.

While most revisions and amendments have been enacted by many or all jurisdictions, not all changes to the UCC are successful or lasting. In 2003, the ULC and ALI wrote and approved a set of amendments to Article 2 (sales) and Article 2A (leases), but the amendments were withdrawn from the Official Text in 2011 after no state legislatures enacted them. The withdrawn amendments are not included in this volume, although they remain of historical interest.

Even successful revisions and amendments take time to be adopted, so a particular jurisdiction's version of the UCC may not match the current UCC text as promulgated by the ALI and the ULC. That is particularly true this year, as the 2022 amendments are too recent for many adoptions before the publication of this 2023 edition. It is nonetheless important to include these amendments, to acquaint students with the changes on the horizon.

To effectively use the UCC and other uniform acts in this volume, you should be aware of the following choices about the substance and format:

- The uniform acts in these volumes (including the UCC) are current through April 2023. Any revisions and amendments approved at the 2023 annual meetings of the ALI (in May) and the ULC (in July) may be found at www.ali.org and www.uniformlaws.org. The latter website also contains information on the history of uniform acts, as well as pending legislation and enactments of uniform acts in states and territories.

- The comprehensive volume contains the entire UCC and Official Comments. The abridged volumes contain only the UCC Articles and Official Comments generally used in the related courses.

- Because the 2022 amendments are so new, they are included in ~~strikeout~~/underline format so that users of the volume can see both the language likely still being used in most jurisdictions and the new language proposed by the amendments and being considered for adoption in many locations. For Articles 1 through 8, the amendments are incorporated into the UCC Articles themselves in ~~strikeout~~/<u>underline</u> format. For Article 9, the amendments are so extensive that they are instead included in Appendix F, making the new and old versions more readable. New Article 12 (Controllable Electronic Records) and new Article A (Transitional Provisions for Uniform Commercial Code Amendments) are included, but not in ~~strikeout~~/<u>underline</u> format, so that they are more readable.

- Older versions of UCC Articles are included in Appendices to the UCC in relevant volumes if they are still enacted in some jurisdictions (Articles 3 and 4) or if the older version is referenced in many judicial opinions that are likely to be used in teaching (Article 1).

- The first page of each UCC Article indicates the history of the Article's approval, amendment, and revision; it also shows where in the UCC Appendices in this volume to find earlier or later versions, revisions, and amendments, if included. Each section of the UCC and its Comments are accompanied by a notation indicating the years in which that section or set of Comments was amended.

- Commentaries written by the Permanent Editorial Board (PEB) of the UCC are included in an Appendix to the UCC. The comprehensive volume contains all PEB Commentaries except those that have been made unnecessary by subsequent revisions and amendments to the UCC. The abridged volumes contain only the Commentaries related to provisions typically covered in the relevant courses.

TABLE OF CONTENTS

PREFACE..iii

GUIDE TO USING THE UCC v

Uniform Commercial Code 1
    UCC Article 1. General Provisions 21
    UCC Article 2. Sales 51
    UCC Article 2A. Leases 179
    UCC Article 3. Negotiable Instruments 271
    UCC Article 4. Bank Deposits and Collections 371
    UCC Article 4A. Funds Transfers 415
    UCC Article 5. Letters of Credit 473
    UCC Article 6. Bulk Transfers...503
    UCC Article 7. Documents of Title...531
    UCC Article 8. Investment Securities 583
    UCC Article 9. Secured Transactions 685
    UCC Article 12. Controllable Electronic Records 921
    UCC Article A. Transitional Provisions for Uniform Commercial Code Amendments
        (2022)...943
    Appendix A. [Omitted]
    Appendix B. [Omitted]
    Appendix C. [Omitted]
    Appendix D. PEB Commentaries and Reports on the Uniform Commercial Code
        [Selected Provisions] 953
    Appendix E. Prefatory Note to 2022 UCC Amendments.......................................1033
    Appendix F. 2022 Amendments to UCC Article 9 1037

Other Uniform Acts
    Uniform Voidable Transactions Act..1117

Federal Statutes and Regulations
    Food Security Act of 1985 1125
    Federal Trade Commission Credit Practices Regulations 1131
    Federal Tax Lien Statute 1135

Bankruptcy Materials
    Bankruptcy Code...1143
    Official Bankruptcy Forms 1363

UNIFORM COMMERCIAL CODE*

The American Law Institute
and the
Uniform Law Commission

* Copyright © 2023 by The American Law Institute and the Uniform Law Commission. Reproduced with permission. All rights reserved.

UNIFORM COMMERCIAL CODE

Prefatory Note to 2022 amendments appears in Appendix E.

2022 amendments to Articles 1–8 appear in ~~strikeout~~/<u>underline</u> format in each Article.

2022 amendments to Article 9 appear in Appendix F.

Articles 12 and A added by 2022 amendments appear after Article 9.

Current through April 2023

For updates, see www.uniformlaws.org

ARTICLE 1. GENERAL PROVISIONS

PART 1. GENERAL PROVISIONS

1–101. Short Titles.
1–102. Scope of Article.
1–103. Construction of [Uniform Commercial Code] to Promote Its Purposes and Policies; Applicability of Supplemental Principles of Law.
1–104. Construction Against Implied Repeal.
1–105. Severability.
1–106. Use of Singular and Plural; Gender.
1–107. Section Captions.
1–108. Relation to Electronic Signatures in Global and National Commerce Act.

PART 2. GENERAL DEFINITIONS AND PRINCIPLES OF INTERPRETATION

1–201. General Definitions.
1–202. Notice; Knowledge.
1–203. Lease Distinguished From Security Interest.
1–204. Value.
1–205. Reasonable Time; Seasonableness.
1–206. Presumptions.

PART 3. TERRITORIAL APPLICABILITY AND GENERAL RULES

1–301. Territorial Applicability; Parties' Power to Choose Applicable Law.
1–302. Variation by Agreement.
1–303. Course of Performance, Course of Dealing, and Usage of Trade.
1–304. Obligation of Good Faith.
1–305. Remedies to Be Liberally Administered.
1–306. Waiver or Renunciation of Claim or Right After Breach.
1–307. Prima Facie Evidence by Third-Party Documents.
1–308. Performance or Acceptance Under Reservation of Rights.
1–309. Option to Accelerate at Will.
1–310. Subordinated Obligations.

ARTICLE 2. SALES

PART 1. SHORT TITLE, GENERAL CONSTRUCTION AND SUBJECT MATTER

2–101. Short Title.

UNIFORM COMMERCIAL CODE

2–102.   Scope; Certain Security and Other Transactions Excluded from this Article.

2–103.   Definitions and Index of Definitions.

2–104.   Definitions: "Merchant"; "Between Merchants"; "Financing Agency".

2–105.   Definitions: Transferability; "Goods"; "Future" Goods; "Lot"; "Commercial Unit".

2–106.   Definitions: "Contract"; "Agreement"; "Contract for Sale"; "Sale"; "Present Sale"; "Conforming" to Contract; "Termination"; "Cancellation"; "Hybrid Transaction".

2–107.   Goods to Be Severed from Realty: Recording.

PART 2.   FORM, FORMATION AND READJUSTMENT OF CONTRACT

2–201.   Formal Requirements; Statute of Frauds.

2–202.   Final Written Expression: Parol or Extrinsic Evidence.

2–203.   Seals Inoperative.

2–204.   Formation in General.

2–205.   Firm Offers.

2–206.   Offer and Acceptance in Formation of Contract.

2–207.   Additional Terms in Acceptance or Confirmation.

2–208.   [Reserved.] [Course of Performance or Practical Construction.]

2–209.   Modification, Rescission and Waiver.

2–210.   Delegation of Performance; Assignment of Rights.

PART 3.   GENERAL OBLIGATION AND CONSTRUCTION OF CONTRACT

2–301.   General Obligations of Parties.

2–302.   Unconscionable Contract or Clause.

2–303.   Allocation or Division of Risks.

2–304.   Price Payable in Money, Goods, Realty, or Otherwise.

2–305.   Open Price Term.

2–306.   Output, Requirements and Exclusive Dealings.

2–307.   Delivery in Single Lot or Several Lots.

2–308.   Absence of Specified Place for Delivery.

2–309.   Absence of Specific Time Provisions; Notice of Termination.

2–310.   Open Time for Payment or Running of Credit; Authority to Ship Under Reservation.

2–311.   Options and Cooperation Respecting Performance.

2–312.   Warranty of Title and Against Infringement; Buyer's Obligation Against Infringement.

2–313.   Express Warranties by Affirmation, Promise, Description, Sample.

2–314.   Implied Warranty: Merchantability; Usage of Trade.

2–315.   Implied Warranty: Fitness for Particular Purpose.

2–316.   Exclusion or Modification of Warranties.

2–317.   Cumulation and Conflict of Warranties Express or Implied.

2–318.   Third Party Beneficiaries of Warranties Express or Implied.

2–319.   F.O.B. and F.A.S. Terms.

2–320.   C.I.F. and C. & F. Terms.

2–321.   C.I.F. or C. & F.: "Net Landed Weights"; "Payment on Arrival"; Warranty of Condition on Arrival.

2–322.   Delivery "Ex-Ship".

2–323.   Form of Bill of Lading Required in Overseas Shipment; "Overseas".

2–324.   "No Arrival, No Sale" Term.

2–325.   "Letter of Credit" Term; "Confirmed Credit".

2–326.   Sale on Approval and Sale or Return; Rights of Creditors.

2–327.   Special Incidents of Sale on Approval and Sale or Return.

2–328.   Sale by Auction.

UNIFORM COMMERCIAL CODE

PART 4.   TITLE, CREDITORS AND GOOD FAITH PURCHASERS

2–401.   Passing of Title; Reservation for Security; Limited Application of This Section.
2–402.   Rights of Seller's Creditors Against Sold Goods.
2–403.   Power to Transfer; Good Faith Purchase of Goods; "Entrusting".

PART 5.   PERFORMANCE

2–501.   Insurable Interest in Goods; Manner of Identification of Goods.
2–502.   Buyer's Right to Goods on Seller's Repudiation, Failure to Deliver, or Insolvency.
2–503.   Manner of Seller's Tender of Delivery.
2–504.   Shipment by Seller.
2–505.   Seller's Shipment Under Reservation.
2–506.   Rights of Financing Agency.
2–507.   Effect of Seller's Tender; Delivery on Condition.
2–508.   Cure by Seller of Improper Tender or Delivery; Replacement.
2–509.   Risk of Loss in the Absence of Breach.
2–510.   Effect of Breach on Risk of Loss.
2–511.   Tender of Payment by Buyer; Payment by Check.
2–512.   Payment by Buyer Before Inspection.
2–513.   Buyer's Right to Inspection of Goods.
2–514.   When Documents Deliverable on Acceptance; When on Payment.
2–515.   Preserving Evidence of Goods in Dispute.

PART 6.   BREACH, REPUDIATION AND EXCUSE

2–601.   Buyer's Rights on Improper Delivery.
2–602.   Manner and Effect of Rightful Rejection.
2–603.   Merchant Buyer's Duties as to Rightfully Rejected Goods.
2–604.   Buyer's Options as to Salvage of Rightfully Rejected Goods.
2–605.   Waiver of Buyer's Objections by Failure to Particularize.
2–606.   What Constitutes Acceptance of Goods.
2–607.   Effect of Acceptance; Notice of Breach; Burden of Establishing Breach After Acceptance; Notice of Claim or Litigation to Person Answerable Over.
2–608.   Revocation of Acceptance in Whole or in Part.
2–609.   Right to Adequate Assurance of Performance.
2–610.   Anticipatory Repudiation.
2–611.   Retraction of Anticipatory Repudiation.
2–612.   "Installment Contract"; Breach.
2–613.   Casualty to Identified Goods.
2–614.   Substituted Performance.
2–615.   Excuse by Failure of Presupposed Conditions.
2–616.   Procedure on Notice Claiming Excuse.

PART 7.   REMEDIES

2–701.   Remedies for Breach of Collateral Contracts Not Impaired.
2–702.   Seller's Remedies on Discovery of Buyer's Insolvency.
2–703.   Seller's Remedies in General.
2–704.   Seller's Right to Identify Goods to the Contract Notwithstanding Breach or to Salvage Unfinished Goods.
2–705.   Seller's Stoppage of Delivery in Transit or Otherwise.
2–706.   Seller's Resale Including Contract for Resale.
2–707.   "Person in the Position of a Seller".

2–708. Seller's Damages for Non-acceptance or Repudiation.

2–709. Action for the Price.

2–710. Seller's Incidental Damages.

2–711. Buyer's Remedies in General; Buyer's Security Interest in Rejected Goods.

2–712. "Cover"; Buyer's Procurement of Substitute Goods.

2–713. Buyer's Damages for Non-delivery or Repudiation.

2–714. Buyer's Damages for Breach in Regard to Accepted Goods.

2–715. Buyer's Incidental and Consequential Damages.

2–716. Buyer's Right to Specific Performance or Replevin.

2–717. Deduction of Damages From the Price.

2–718. Liquidation or Limitation of Damages; Deposits.

2–719. Contractual Modification or Limitation of Remedy.

2–720. Effect of "Cancellation" or "Rescission" on Claims for Antecedent Breach.

2–721. Remedies for Fraud.

2–722. Who Can Sue Third Parties for Injury to Goods.

2–723. Proof of Market Price: Time and Place.

2–724. Admissibility of Market Quotations.

2–725. Statute of Limitations in Contracts for Sale.

ARTICLE 2A. LEASES

PART 1. GENERAL PROVISIONS

2A–101. Short Title.

2A–102. Scope.

2A–103. Definitions and Index of Definitions.

2A–104. Leases Subject to Other Law.

2A–105. Territorial Application of Article to Goods Covered by Certificate of Title.

2A–106. Limitation on Power of Parties to Consumer Lease to Choose Applicable Law and Judicial Forum.

2A–107. Waiver or Renunciation of Claim or Right After Default.

2A–108. Unconscionability.

2A–109. Option to Accelerate at Will.

PART 2. FORMATION AND CONSTRUCTION OF LEASE CONTRACT

2A–201. Statute of Frauds.

2A–202. Final Written Expression: Parol or Extrinsic Evidence.

2A–203. Seals Inoperative.

2A–204. Formation in General.

2A–205. Firm Offers.

2A–206. Offer and Acceptance in Formation of Lease Contract.

2A–207. [Reserved.] [Course of Performance or Practical Construction.]

2A–208. Modification, Rescission and Waiver.

2A–209. Lessee Under Finance Lease as Beneficiary of Supply Contract.

2A–210. Express Warranties.

2A–211. Warranties Against Interference and Against Infringement; Lessee's Obligation Against Infringement.

2A–212. Implied Warranty of Merchantability.

2A–213. Implied Warranty of Fitness for Particular Purpose.

2A–214. Exclusion or Modification of Warranties.

2A–215. Cumulation and Conflict of Warranties Express or Implied.

2A–216. Third-Party Beneficiaries of Express and Implied Warranties.

2A–217. Identification.

UNIFORM COMMERCIAL CODE

2A–218. Insurance and Proceeds.

2A–219. Risk of Loss.

2A–220. Effect of Default on Risk of Loss.

2A–221. Casualty to Identified Goods.

PART 3. EFFECT OF LEASE CONTRACT

2A–301. Enforceability of Lease Contract.

2A–302. Title to and Possession of Goods.

2A–303. Alienability of Party's Interest Under Lease Contract or of Lessor's Residual Interest in Goods; Delegation of Performance; Transfer of Rights.

2A–304. Subsequent Lease of Goods by Lessor.

2A–305. Sale or Sublease of Goods by Lessee.

2A–306. Priority of Certain Liens Arising by Operation of Law.

2A–307. Priority of Liens Arising by Attachment or Levy on, Security Interests in, and Other Claims to Goods.

2A–308. Special Rights of Creditors.

2A–309. Lessor's and Lessee's Rights When Goods Become Fixtures.

2A–310. Lessor's and Lessee's Rights When Goods Become Accessions.

2A–311. Priority Subject to Subordination.

PART 4. PERFORMANCE OF LEASE CONTRACT: REPUDIATED, SUBSTITUTED AND EXCUSED

2A–401. Insecurity: Adequate Assurance of Performance.

2A–402. Anticipatory Repudiation.

2A–403. Retraction of Anticipatory Repudiation.

2A–404. Substituted Performance.

2A–405. Excused Performance.

2A–406. Procedure on Excused Performance.

2A–407. Irrevocable Promises: Finance Leases.

PART 5. DEFAULT

A. IN GENERAL

2A–501. Default: Procedure.

2A–502. Notice After Default.

2A–503. Modification or Impairment of Rights and Remedies.

2A–504. Liquidation of Damages.

2A–505. Cancellation and Termination and Effect of Cancellation, Termination, Rescission, or Fraud on Rights and Remedies.

2A–506. Statute of Limitations.

2A–507. Proof of Market Rent: Time and Place.

B. DEFAULT BY LESSOR

2A–508. Lessee's Remedies.

2A–509. Lessee's Rights on Improper Delivery; Rightful Rejection.

2A–510. Installment Lease Contracts: Rejection and Default.

2A–511. Merchant Lessee's Duties as to Rightfully Rejected Goods.

2A–512. Lessee's Duties as to Rightfully Rejected Goods.

2A–513. Cure by Lessor of Improper Tender or Delivery; Replacement.

2A–514. Waiver of Lessee's Objections.

2A–515. Acceptance of Goods.

2A–516.   Effect of Acceptance of Goods; Notice of Default; Burden of Establishing Default After Acceptance; Notice of Claim or Litigation to Person Answerable Over.

2A–517.   Revocation of Acceptance of Goods.

2A–518.   Cover; Substitute Goods.

2A–519.   Lessee's Damages for Non-delivery, Repudiation, Default, and Breach of Warranty in Regard to Accepted Goods.

2A–520.   Lessee's Incidental and Consequential Damages.

2A–521.   Lessee's Right to Specific Performance or Replevin.

2A–522.   Lessee's Right to Goods on Lessor's Insolvency.

C.   DEFAULT BY LESSEE

2A–523.   Lessor's Remedies.

2A–524.   Lessor's Right to Identify Goods to Lease Contract.

2A–525.   Lessor's Right to Possession of Goods.

2A–526.   Lessor's Stoppage of Delivery in Transit or Otherwise.

2A–527.   Lessor's Rights to Dispose of Goods.

2A–528.   Lessor's Damages for Non-acceptance, Failure to Pay, Repudiation, or Other Default.

2A–529.   Lessor's Action for the Rent.

2A–530.   Lessor's Incidental Damages.

2A–531.   Standing to Sue Third Parties for Injury to Goods.

2A–532.   Lessor's Rights to Residual Interest.

ARTICLE 3.   NEGOTIABLE INSTRUMENTS

PART 1.   GENERAL PROVISIONS AND DEFINITIONS

3–101.   Short Title.

3–102.   Subject Matter.

3–103.   Definitions.

3–104.   Negotiable Instrument.

3–105.   Issue of Instrument.

3–106.   Unconditional Promise or Order.

3–107.   Instrument Payable in Foreign Money.

3–108.   Payable on Demand or at Definite Time.

3–109.   Payable to Bearer or to Order.

3–110.   Identification of Person to Whom Instrument Is Payable.

3–111.   Place of Payment.

3–112.   Interest.

3–113.   Date of Instrument.

3–114.   Contradictory Terms of Instrument.

3–115.   Incomplete Instrument.

3–116.   Joint and Several Liability; Contribution.

3–117.   Other Agreements Affecting Instrument.

3–118.   Statute of Limitations.

3–119.   Notice of Right to Defend Action.

PART 2.   NEGOTIATION, TRANSFER, AND INDORSEMENT

3–201.   Negotiation.

3–202.   Negotiation Subject to Rescission.

3–203.   Transfer of Instrument; Rights Acquired by Transfer.

3–204.   Indorsement.

3–205.   Special Indorsement; Blank Indorsement; Anomalous Indorsement.

3–206.   Restrictive Indorsement.

3–207.   Reacquisition.

PART 3.   ENFORCEMENT OF INSTRUMENTS

3–301.   Person Entitled to Enforce Instrument.

3–302.   Holder in Due Course.

3–303.   Value and Consideration.

3–304.   Overdue Instrument.

3–305.   Defenses and Claims in Recoupment.

3–306.   Claims to an Instrument.

3–307.   Notice of Breach of Fiduciary Duty.

3–308.   Proof of Signatures and Status as Holder in Due Course.

3–309.   Enforcement of Lost, Destroyed, or Stolen Instrument.

3–310.   Effect of Instrument on Obligation for Which Taken.

3–311.   Accord and Satisfaction by Use of Instrument.

3–312.   Lost, Destroyed, or Stolen Cashier's Check, Teller's Check, or Certified Check.

PART 4.   LIABILITY OF PARTIES

3–401.   Signature <u>Necessary for Liability on Instrument</u>.

3–402.   Signature by Representative.

3–403.   Unauthorized Signature.

3–404.   Impostors; Fictitious Payees.

3–405.   Employer's Responsibility for Fraudulent Indorsement by Employee.

3–406.   Negligence Contributing to Forged Signature or Alteration of Instrument.

3–407.   Alteration.

3–408.   Drawee Not Liable on Unaccepted Draft.

3–409.   Acceptance of Draft; Certified Check.

3–410.   Acceptance Varying Draft.

3–411.   Refusal to Pay Cashier's Checks, Teller's Checks, and Certified Checks.

3–412.   Obligation of Issuer of Note or Cashier's Check.

3–413.   Obligation of Acceptor.

3–414.   Obligation of Drawer.

3–415.   Obligation of Indorser.

3–416.   Transfer Warranties.

3–417.   Presentment Warranties.

3–418.   Payment or Acceptance by Mistake.

3–419.   Instruments Signed for Accommodation.

3–420.   Conversion of Instrument.

PART 5.   DISHONOR

3–501.   Presentment.

3–502.   Dishonor.

3–503.   Notice of Dishonor.

3–504.   Excused Presentment and Notice of Dishonor.

3–505.   Evidence of Dishonor.

PART 6.   DISCHARGE AND PAYMENT

3–601.   Discharge and Effect of Discharge.

3–602.   Payment.

3–603.   Tender of Payment.

UNIFORM COMMERCIAL CODE

3–604.   Discharge by Cancellation or Renunciation.
3–605.   Discharge of Secondary Obligors.

ARTICLE 4.   BANK DEPOSITS AND COLLECTIONS

PART 1.   GENERAL PROVISIONS AND DEFINITIONS

4–101.   Short Title.
4–102.   Applicability.
4–103.   Variation by Agreement; Measure of Damages; Action Constituting Ordinary Care.
4–104.   Definitions and Index of Definitions.
4–105.   Definitions of Types of Banks.
4–106.   Payable Through or Payable at Bank: Collecting Bank.
4–107.   Separate Office of Bank.
4–108.   Time of Receipt of Items.
4–109.   Delays.
4–110.   Electronic Presentment.
4–111.   Statute of Limitations.

PART 2.   COLLECTION OF ITEMS: DEPOSITARY AND COLLECTING BANKS

4–201.   Status of Collecting Bank as Agent and Provisional Status of Credits; Applicability of Article; Item Indorsed "Pay Any Bank".
4–202.   Responsibility for Collection or Return; When Action Timely.
4–203.   Effect of Instructions.
4–204.   Methods of Sending and Presenting; Sending Directly to Payor Bank.
4–205.   Depositary Bank Holder of Unindorsed Item.
4–206.   Transfer Between Banks.
4–207.   Transfer Warranties.
4–208.   Presentment Warranties.
4–209.   Encoding and Retention Warranties.
4–210.   Security Interest of Collecting Bank in Items, Accompanying Documents and Proceeds.
4–211.   When Bank Gives Value for Purposes of Holder in Due Course.
4–212.   Presentment by Notice of Item Not Payable by, Through, or at Bank; Liability of Drawer or Indorser.
4–213.   Medium and Time of Settlement by Bank.
4–214.   Right of Charge-Back or Refund; Liability of Collecting Bank; Return of Item.
4–215.   Final Payment of Item by Payor Bank; When Provisional Debits and Credits Become Final; When Certain Credits Become Available for Withdrawal.
4–216.   Insolvency and Preference.

PART 3.   COLLECTION OF ITEMS: PAYOR BANKS

4–301.   Deferred Posting; Recovery of Payment by Return of Items; Time of Dishonor; Return of Items by Payor Bank.
4–302.   Payor Bank's Responsibility for Late Return of Item.
4–303.   When Items Subject to Notice, Stop-Payment Order, Legal Process, or Setoff; Order in Which Items May Be Charged or Certified.

PART 4.   RELATIONSHIP BETWEEN PAYOR BANK AND ITS CUSTOMER

4–401.   When Bank May Charge Customer's Account.
4–402.   Bank's Liability to Customer for Wrongful Dishonor; Time of Determining Insufficiency of Account.
4–403.   Customer's Right to Stop Payment; Burden of Proof of Loss.
4–404.   Bank Not Obliged to Pay Check More Than Six Months Old.
4–405.   Death or Incompetence of Customer.

UNIFORM COMMERCIAL CODE

4–406.　Customer's Duty to Discover and Report Unauthorized Signature or Alteration.
4–407.　Payor Bank's Right to Subrogation on Improper Payment.

PART 5.　COLLECTION OF DOCUMENTARY DRAFTS

4–501.　Handling of Documentary Drafts; Duty to Send for Presentment and to Notify Customer of Dishonor.
4–502.　Presentment of "On Arrival" Drafts.
4–503.　Responsibility of Presenting Bank for Documents and Goods; Report of Reasons for Dishonor; Referee in Case of Need.
4–504.　Privilege of Presenting Bank to Deal With Goods; Security Interest for Expenses.

ARTICLE 4A.　FUNDS TRANSFERS

PART 1.　SUBJECT MATTER AND DEFINITIONS

4A–101.　Short Title.
4A–102.　Subject Matter.
4A–103.　Payment Order—Definitions.
4A–104.　Funds Transfer—Definitions.
4A–105.　Other Definitions.
4A–106.　Time Payment Order Is Received.
4A–107.　Federal Reserve Regulations and Operating Circulars.
4A–108.　Relationship to Electronic Fund Transfer Act.

PART 2.　ISSUE AND ACCEPTANCE OF PAYMENT ORDER

4A–201.　Security Procedure.
4A–202.　Authorized and Verified Payment Orders.
4A–203.　Unenforceability of Certain Verified Payment Orders.
4A–204.　Refund of Payment and Duty of Customer to Report With Respect to Unauthorized Payment Order.
4A–205.　Erroneous Payment Orders.
4A–206.　Transmission of Payment Order Through Funds-Transfer or Other Communication System.
4A–207.　Misdescription of Beneficiary.
4A–208.　Misdescription of Intermediary Bank or Beneficiary's Bank.
4A–209.　Acceptance of Payment Order.
4A–210.　Rejection of Payment Order.
4A–211.　Cancellation and Amendment of Payment Order.
4A–212.　Liability and Duty of Receiving Bank Regarding Unaccepted Payment Order.

PART 3.　EXECUTION OF SENDER'S PAYMENT ORDER BY RECEIVING BANK

4A–301.　Execution and Execution Date.
4A–302.　Obligations of Receiving Bank in Execution of Payment Order.
4A–303.　Erroneous Execution of Payment Order.
4A–304.　Duty of Sender to Report Erroneously Executed Payment Order.
4A–305.　Liability for Late or Improper Execution or Failure to Execute Payment Order.

PART 4.　PAYMENT

4A–401.　Payment Date.
4A–402.　Obligation of Sender to Pay Receiving Bank.
4A–403.　Payment by Sender to Receiving Bank.
4A–404.　Obligation of Beneficiary's Bank to Pay and Give Notice to Beneficiary.
4A–405.　Payment by Beneficiary's Bank to Beneficiary.
4A–406.　Payment by Originator to Beneficiary; Discharge of Underlying Obligation.

PART 5. MISCELLANEOUS PROVISIONS

4A–501. Variation by Agreement and Effect of Funds-Transfer System Rule.
4A–502. Creditor Process Served on Receiving Bank; Setoff by Beneficiary's Bank.
4A–503. Injunction or Restraining Order With Respect to Funds Transfer.
4A–504. Order in Which Items and Payment Orders May Be Charged to Account; Order of Withdrawals From Account.
4A–505. Preclusion of Objection to Debit of Customer's Account.
4A–506. Rate of Interest.
4A–507. Choice of Law.

ARTICLE 5. LETTERS OF CREDIT

5–101. Short Title.
5–102. Definitions.
5–103. Scope.
5–104. Formal Requirements.
5–105. Consideration.
5–106. Issuance, Amendment, Cancellation, and Duration.
5–107. Confirmer, Nominated Person, and Adviser.
5–108. Issuer's Rights and Obligations.
5–109. Fraud and Forgery.
5–110. Warranties.
5–111. Remedies.
5–112. Transfer of Letter of Credit.
5–113. Transfer by Operation of Law.
5–114. Assignment of Proceeds.
5–115. Statute of Limitations.
5–116. Choice of Law and Forum.
5–117. Subrogation of Issuer, Applicant, and Nominated Person.
5–118. Security Interest of Issuer or Nominated Person.

ARTICLE 6. BULK TRANSFERS

ALTERNATIVE A

1. Repeal.
2. Amendment.
3. Amendment.
4. Savings Clause.

ALTERNATIVE B

6–101. Short Title.
6–102. Definitions and Index of Definitions.
6–103. Applicability of Article.
6–104. Obligations of Buyer.
6–105. Notice to Claimants.
6–106. Schedule of Distribution.
6–107. Liability for Noncompliance.
6–108. Bulk Sales by Auction; Bulk Sales Conducted by Liquidator.
6–109. What Constitutes Filing; Duties of Filing Officer; Information From Filing Officer.
6–110. Limitation of Actions.

UNIFORM COMMERCIAL CODE

ARTICLE 7.   DOCUMENTS OF TITLE

PART 1.   GENERAL

7–101.   Short Title.
7–102.   Definitions and Index of Definitions.
7–103.   Relation of Article to Treaty or Statute.
7–104.   Negotiable and Nonnegotiable Document of Title.
7–105.   Reissuance in Alternative Medium.
7–106.   Control of Electronic Document of Title.

PART 2.   WAREHOUSE RECEIPTS: SPECIAL PROVISIONS

7–201.   Person That May Issue a Warehouse Receipt; Storage Under Bond.
7–202.   Form of Warehouse Receipt; Effect of Omission.
7–203.   Liability for Nonreceipt or Misdescription.
7–204.   Duty of Care; Contractual Limitation of Warehouse's Liability.
7–205.   Title Under Warehouse Receipt Defeated in Certain Cases.
7–206.   Termination of Storage at Warehouse's Option.
7–207.   Goods Must Be Kept Separate; Fungible Goods.
7–208.   Altered Warehouse Receipts.
7–209.   Lien of Warehouse.
7–210.   Enforcement of Warehouse's Lien.

PART 3.   BILLS OF LADING: SPECIAL PROVISIONS

7–301.   Liability for Nonreceipt or Misdescription; "Said to Contain"; "Shipper's Weight, Load, and Count"; Improper Handling.
7–302.   Through Bills of Lading and Similar Documents of Title.
7–303.   Diversion; Reconsignment; Change of Instructions.
7–304.   Tangible Bills of Lading in a Set.
7–305.   Destination Bills.
7–306.   Altered Bills of Lading.
7–307.   Lien of Carrier.
7–308.   Enforcement of Carrier's Lien.
7–309.   Duty of Care; Contractual Limitation of Carrier's Liability.

PART 4.   WAREHOUSE RECEIPTS AND BILLS OF LADING: GENERAL OBLIGATIONS

7–401.   Irregularities in Issue of Receipt or Bill or Conduct of Issuer.
7–402.   Duplicate Document of Title; Overissue.
7–403.   Obligation of Bailee to Deliver; Excuse.
7–404.   No Liability for Good-Faith Delivery Pursuant to Document of Title.

PART 5.   WAREHOUSE RECEIPTS AND BILLS OF LADING: NEGOTIATION AND TRANSFER

7–501.   Form of Negotiation and Requirements of Due Negotiation.
7–502.   Rights Acquired by Due Negotiation.
7–503.   Document of Title to Goods Defeated in Certain Cases.
7–504.   Rights Acquired in Absence of Due Negotiation; Effect of Diversion; Stoppage of Delivery.
7–505.   Indorser Not Guarantor for Other Parties.
7–506.   Delivery Without Indorsement: Right to Compel Indorsement.

7–507. Warranties on Negotiation or Delivery of Document of Title.
7–508. Warranties of Collecting Bank as to Documents of Title.
7–509. Adequate Compliance with Commercial Contract.

PART 6. WAREHOUSE RECEIPTS AND BILLS OF
LADING: MISCELLANEOUS PROVISIONS

7–601. Lost, Stolen, or Destroyed Documents of Title.
7–602. Judicial Process Against Goods Covered by Negotiable Document of Title.
7–603. Conflicting Claims; Interpleader.

PART 7. MISCELLANEOUS PROVISIONS

7–701. Effective Date.
7–702. Repeals.
7–703. Applicability.
7–704. Savings Clause.

ARTICLE 8. INVESTMENT SECURITIES

PART 1. SHORT TITLE AND GENERAL MATTERS

8–101. Short Title.
8–102. Definitions.
8–103. Rules for Determining Whether Certain Obligations and Interests are Securities or Financial Assets.
8–104. Acquisition of Security or Financial Asset or Interest Therein.
8–105. Notice of Adverse Claim.
8–106. Control.
8–107. Whether Indorsement, Instruction, or Entitlement Order is Effective.
8–108. Warranties in Direct Holding.
8–109. Warranties in Indirect Holding.
8–110. Applicability; Choice of Law.
8–111. Clearing Corporation Rules.
8–112. Creditor's Legal Process.
8–113. Statute of Frauds Inapplicable.
8–114. Evidentiary Rules Concerning Certificated Securities.
8–115. Securities Intermediary and Others Not Liable to Adverse Claimant.
8–116. Securities Intermediary as Purchaser for Value.

PART 2. ISSUE AND ISSUER

8–201. Issuer.
8–202. Issuer's Responsibility and Defenses; Notice of Defect or Defense.
8–203. Staleness as Notice of Defect or Defense.
8–204. Effect of Issuer's Restriction on Transfer.
8–205. Effect of Unauthorized Signature on Security Certificate.
8–206. Completion or Alteration of Security Certificate.
8–207. Rights and Duties of Issuer with Respect to Registered Owners.
8–208. Effect of Signature of Authenticating Trustee, Registrar, or Transfer Agent.
8–209. Issuer's Lien.
8–210. Overissue.

PART 3. TRANSFER OF CERTIFICATED AND UNCERTIFICATED SECURITIES

8–301. Delivery.
8–302. Rights of Purchaser.

UNIFORM COMMERCIAL CODE

8–303. Protected Purchaser.

8–304. Indorsement.

8–305. Instruction.

8–306. Effect of Guaranteeing Signature, Indorsement, or Instruction.

8–307. Purchaser's Right to Requisites for Registration of Transfer.

PART 4.   REGISTRATION

8–401. Duty of Issuer to Register Transfer.

8–402. Assurance that Indorsement or Instruction is Effective.

8–403. Demand that Issuer Not Register Transfer.

8–404. Wrongful Registration.

8–405. Replacement of Lost, Destroyed, or Wrongfully Taken Security Certificate.

8–406. Obligation to Notify Issuer of Lost, Destroyed, or Wrongfully Taken Security Certificate.

8–407. Authenticating Trustee, Transfer Agent, and Registrar.

PART 5.   SECURITY ENTITLEMENTS

8–501. Securities Account; Acquisition of Security Entitlement from Securities Intermediary.

8–502. Assertion of Adverse Claim Against Entitlement Holder.

8–503. Property Interest of Entitlement Holder in Financial Asset Held by Securities Intermediary.

8–504. Duty of Securities Intermediary to Maintain Financial Asset.

8–505. Duty of Securities Intermediary with Respect to Payments and Distributions.

8–506. Duty of Securities Intermediary to Exercise Rights as Directed by Entitlement Holder.

8–507. Duty of Securities Intermediary to Comply with Entitlement Order.

8–508. Duty of Securities Intermediary to Change Entitlement Holder's Position to Other Form of Security Holding.

8–509. Specification of Duties of Securities Intermediary by Other Statute or Regulation; Manner of Performance of Duties of Securities Intermediary and Exercise of Rights of Entitlement Holder.

8–510. Rights of Purchaser of Security Entitlement from Entitlement Holder.

8–511. Priority Among Security Interests and Entitlement Holders.

ARTICLE 9.   SECURED TRANSACTIONS

PART 1.   GENERAL PROVISIONS

[SUBPART 1.   SHORT TITLE, DEFINITIONS, AND GENERAL CONCEPTS]

9–101. Short Title.

9–102. Definitions and Index of Definitions.

9–103. Purchase-Money Security Interest; Application of Payments; Burden of Establishing.

9–104. Control of Deposit Account.

9–105. Control of Electronic Chattel Paper.

9–106. Control of Investment Property.

9–107. Control of Letter-of-Credit Right.

9–108. Sufficiency of Description.

[SUBPART 2.   APPLICABILITY OF ARTICLE]

9–109. Scope.

9–110. Security Interests Arising Under Article 2 or 2A.

UNIFORM COMMERCIAL CODE

PART 2. EFFECTIVENESS OF SECURITY AGREEMENT; ATTACHMENT OF SECURITY INTEREST; RIGHTS OF PARTIES TO SECURITY AGREEMENT

[SUBPART 1. EFFECTIVENESS AND ATTACHMENT]

9–201. General Effectiveness of Security Agreement.
9–202. Title to Collateral Immaterial.
9–203. Attachment and Enforceability of Security Interest; Proceeds; Supporting Obligations; Formal Requisites.
9–204. After-Acquired Property; Future Advances.
9–205. Use or Disposition of Collateral Permissible.
9–206. Security Interest Arising in Purchase or Delivery of Financial Asset.

[SUBPART 2. RIGHTS AND DUTIES]

9–207. Rights and Duties of Secured Party Having Possession or Control of Collateral.
9–208. Additional Duties of Secured Party Having Control of Collateral.
9–209. Duties of Secured Party if Account Debtor Has Been Notified of Assignment.
9–210. Request for Accounting; Request Regarding List of Collateral or Statement of Account.

PART 3. PERFECTION AND PRIORITY

[SUBPART 1. LAW GOVERNING PERFECTION AND PRIORITY]

9–301. Law Governing Perfection and Priority of Security Interests.
9–302. Law Governing Perfection and Priority of Agricultural Liens.
9–303. Law Governing Perfection and Priority of Security Interests in Goods Covered by a Certificate of Title.
9–304. Law Governing Perfection and Priority of Security Interests in Deposit Accounts.
9–305. Law Governing Perfection and Priority of Security Interests in Investment Property.
9–306. Law Governing Perfection and Priority of Security Interests in Letter-of-Credit Rights.
9–307. Location of Debtor.

[SUBPART 2. PERFECTION]

9–308. When Security Interest or Agricultural Lien Is Perfected; Continuity of Perfection.
9–309. Security Interest Perfected Upon Attachment.
9–310. When Filing Required to Perfect Security Interest or Agricultural Lien; Security Interests and Agricultural Liens to Which Filing Provisions Do Not Apply.
9–311. Perfection of Security Interests in Property Subject to Certain Statutes, Regulations, and Treaties.
9–312. Perfection of Security Interests in Chattel Paper, Deposit Accounts, Documents, Goods Covered by Documents, Instruments, Investment Property, Letter-of-Credit Rights, and Money; Perfection by Permissive Filing; Temporary Perfection Without Filing or Transfer of Possession.
9–313. When Possession by or Delivery to Secured Party Perfects Security Interest Without Filing.
9–314. Perfection by Control.
9–315. Secured Party's Rights on Disposition of Collateral and in Proceeds.
9–316. Effect of Change in Governing Law.

[SUBPART 3. PRIORITY]

9–317. Interests That Take Priority Over or Take Free of Security Interest or Agricultural Lien.
9–318. No Interest Retained in Right to Payment That Is Sold; Rights and Title of Seller of Account or Chattel Paper With Respect to Creditors and Purchasers.
9–319. Rights and Title of Consignee With Respect to Creditors and Purchasers.
9–320. Buyer of Goods.
9–321. Licensee of General Intangible and Lessee of Goods in Ordinary Course of Business.
9–322. Priorities Among Conflicting Security Interests in and Agricultural Liens on Same Collateral.

9–323. Future Advances.

9–324. Priority of Purchase-Money Security Interests.

9–325. Priority of Security Interests in Transferred Collateral.

9–326. Priority of Security Interests Created by New Debtor.

9–327. Priority of Security Interests in Deposit Account.

9–328. Priority of Security Interests in Investment Property.

9–329. Priority of Security Interests in Letter-of-Credit Right.

9–330. Priority of Purchaser of Chattel Paper or Instrument.

9–331. Priority of Rights of Purchasers of Instruments, Documents, and Securities Under Other Articles; Priority of Interests in Financial Assets and Security Entitlements Under Article 8.

9–332. Transfer of Money; Transfer of Funds From Deposit Account.

9–333. Priority of Certain Liens Arising by Operation of Law.

9–334. Priority of Security Interests in Fixtures and Crops.

9–335. Accessions.

9–336. Commingled Goods.

9–337. Priority of Security Interests in Goods Covered by Certificate of Title.

9–338. Priority of Security Interest or Agricultural Lien Perfected by Filed Financing Statement Providing Certain Incorrect Information.

9–339. Priority Subject to Subordination.

[SUBPART 4.   RIGHTS OF BANK]

9–340. Effectiveness of Right of Recoupment or Set-Off Against Deposit Account.

9–341. Bank's Rights and Duties With Respect to Deposit Account.

9–342. Bank's Right to Refuse to Enter Into or Disclose Existence of Control Agreement.

PART 4.   RIGHTS OF THIRD PARTIES

9–401. Alienability of Debtor's Rights.

9–402. Secured Party Not Obligated on Contract of Debtor or in Tort.

9–403. Agreement Not to Assert Defenses Against Assignee.

9–404. Rights Acquired by Assignee; Claims and Defenses Against Assignee.

9–405. Modification of Assigned Contract.

9–406. Discharge of Account Debtor; Notification of Assignment; Identification and Proof of Assignment; Restrictions on Assignment of Accounts, Chattel Paper, Payment Intangibles, and Promissory Notes Ineffective.

9–407. Restrictions on Creation or Enforcement of Security Interest in Leasehold Interest or in Lessor's Residual Interest.

9–408. Restrictions on Assignment of Promissory Notes, Health-Care-Insurance Receivables, and Certain General Intangibles Ineffective.

9–409. Restrictions on Assignment of Letter-of-Credit Rights Ineffective.

PART 5.   FILING

[SUBPART 1. FILING OFFICE; CONTENTS AND
EFFECTIVENESS OF FINANCING STATEMENT]

9–501. Filing Office.

9–502. Contents of Financing Statement; Record of Mortgage as Financing Statement; Time of Filing Financing Statement.

9–503. Name of Debtor and Secured Party.

9–504. Indication of Collateral.

9–505. Filing and Compliance With Other Statutes and Treaties for Consignments, Leases, Other Bailments, and Other Transactions.

9–506. Effect of Errors or Omissions.

9–507. Effect of Certain Events on Effectiveness of Financing Statement.
9–508. Effectiveness of Financing Statement if New Debtor Becomes Bound by Security Agreement.
9–509. Persons Entitled to File a Record.
9–510. Effectiveness of Filed Record.
9–511. Secured Party of Record.
9–512. Amendment of Financing Statement.
9–513. Termination Statement.
9–514. Assignment of Powers of Secured Party of Record.
9–515. Duration and Effectiveness of Financing Statement; Effect of Lapsed Financing Statement.
9–516. What Constitutes Filing; Effectiveness of Filing.
9–517. Effect of Indexing Errors.
9–518. Claim Concerning Inaccurate or Wrongfully Filed Record.

[SUBPART 2. DUTIES AND OPERATION OF FILING OFFICE]

9–519. Numbering, Maintaining, and Indexing Records; Communicating Information Provided in Records.
9–520. Acceptance and Refusal to Accept Record.
9–521. Uniform Form of Written Financing Statement and Amendment.
9–522. Maintenance and Destruction of Records.
9–523. Information From Filing Office; Sale or License of Records.
9–524. Delay by Filing Office.
9–525. Fees.
9–526. Filing-Office Rules.
9–527. Duty to Report.

PART 6. DEFAULT

[SUBPART 1. DEFAULT AND ENFORCEMENT OF SECURITY INTEREST]

9–601. Rights After Default; Judicial Enforcement; Consignor or Buyer of Accounts, Chattel Paper, Payment Intangibles, or Promissory Notes.
9–602. Waiver and Variance of Rights and Duties.
9–603. Agreement on Standards Concerning Rights and Duties.
9–604. Procedure if Security Agreement Covers Real Property or Fixtures.
9–605. Unknown Debtor or Secondary Obligor.
9–606. Time of Default for Agricultural Lien.
9–607. Collection and Enforcement by Secured Party.
9–608. Application of Proceeds of Collection or Enforcement; Liability for Deficiency and Right to Surplus.
9–609. Secured Party's Right to Take Possession After Default.
9–610. Disposition of Collateral After Default.
9–611. Notification Before Disposition of Collateral.
9–612. Timeliness of Notification Before Disposition of Collateral.
9–613. Contents and Form of Notification Before Disposition of Collateral: General.
9–614. Contents and Form of Notification Before Disposition of Collateral: Consumer-Goods Transaction.
9–615. Application of Proceeds of Disposition; Liability for Deficiency and Right to Surplus.
9–616. Explanation of Calculation of Surplus or Deficiency.
9–617. Rights of Transferee of Collateral.
9–618. Rights and Duties of Certain Secondary Obligors.
9–619. Transfer of Record or Legal Title.
9–620. Acceptance of Collateral in Full or Partial Satisfaction of Obligation; Compulsory Disposition of Collateral.
9–621. Notification of Proposal to Accept Collateral.
9–622. Effect of Acceptance of Collateral.

9–623.   Right to Redeem Collateral.
9–624.   Waiver.

[SUBPART 2.   NONCOMPLIANCE WITH ARTICLE]

9–625.   Remedies for Secured Party's Failure to Comply With Article.
9–626.   Action in Which Deficiency or Surplus Is in Issue.
9–627.   Determination of Whether Conduct Was Commercially Reasonable.
9–628.   Nonliability and Limitation on Liability of Secured Party; Liability of Secondary Obligor.

PART 7.   TRANSITION RULES [Omitted]

PART 8.   TRANSITION PROVISIONS FOR 2010 AMENDMENTS [Omitted]

ARTICLE 10. [Omitted]

ARTICLE 11. [Omitted]

ARTICLE 12. CONTROLLABLE ELECTRONIC RECORDS

12–101.   Title.
12–102.   Definitions.
12–103.   Relation to Article 9 and Consumer Laws.
12–104.   Rights in Controllable Account, Controllable Electronic Record, and Controllable Payment Intangible.
12–105.   Control of Controllable Electronic Record.
12–106.   Discharge of Account Debtor on Controllable Account or Controllable Payment Intangible.
12–107.   Governing Law

Article A. TRANSITIONAL PROVISIONS FOR
UNIFORM COMMERCIAL CODE AMENDMENTS (2022)

PART 1. GENERAL PROVISIONS AND DEFINITIONS

A–101.   Short Title.
A–102.   Definitions.

PART 2. GENERAL TRANSITIONAL PROVISION

A–201.   Saving Clause.

PART 3. TRANSITIONAL PROVISIONS FOR ARTICLES 9 AND 12

A–301.   Saving Clause
A–302.   Security Interest Perfected Before Effective Date.
A–303.   Security Interest Unperfected Before Effective Date.
A–304.   Effectiveness of Actions Taken Before Effective Date.
A–305.   Priority.
A–306.   Priority of Claims When Priority Rules of Article 9 Do Not Apply.

PART 4. EFFECTIVE DATE

A–401.   Effective Date.

UCC ARTICLE 1

GENERAL PROVISIONS

Article 1 was revised in 2001 and amended in 2017 and 2022.
2022 Amendments appear in ~~strikeout~~/<u>underline</u> format.
Prefatory Note to 2022 amendments appears in Appendix E.
Current through April 2023
For updates, see www.uniformlaws.org

PART 1.   GENERAL PROVISIONS

1–101. Short Titles.
1–102. Scope of Article.
1–103. Construction of [Uniform Commercial Code] to Promote Its Purposes and Policies; Applicability of Supplemental Principles of Law.
1–104. Construction Against Implied Repeal.
1–105. Severability.
1–106. Use of Singular and Plural; Gender.
1–107. Section Captions.
1–108. Relation to Electronic Signatures in Global and National Commerce Act.

PART 2.   GENERAL DEFINITIONS AND PRINCIPLES OF INTERPRETATION

1–201. General Definitions.
1–202. Notice; Knowledge.
1–203. Lease Distinguished From Security Interest.
1–204. Value.
1–205. Reasonable Time; Seasonableness.
1–206. Presumptions.

PART 3.   TERRITORIAL APPLICABILITY AND GENERAL RULES

1–301. Territorial Applicability; Parties' Power to Choose Applicable Law.
1–302. Variation by Agreement.
1–303. Course of Performance, Course of Dealing, and Usage of Trade.
1–304. Obligation of Good Faith.
1–305. Remedies to Be Liberally Administered.
1–306. Waiver or Renunciation of Claim or Right After Breach.
1–307. Prima Facie Evidence by Third-Party Documents.
1–308. Performance or Acceptance Under Reservation of Rights.
1–309. Option to Accelerate at Will.
1–310. Subordinated Obligations.

Article 1 Concordance

Unrevised	Revised
1–101	1–101(a)
1–102(1, 2)	1–103(a)
1–102(3, 4)	1–302[1]
1–102(5)	1–106
1–103	1–103(b)
1–104	1–104
1–105	1–301
1–106	1–305
1–107	1–306
1–108	1–105
1–109	1–107
1–201(25, 26, 27)	1–202
1–201(37)	1–201(b)(35), 1–203
1–201(44)	1–204
1–201 (all other)	1–201
1–202	1–307
1–203	1–304
1–204(1)	1–302(b)[2]
1–204(2, 3)	1–205
1–205, 2–208	1–303
1–206	deleted
1–207	1–308
1–208	1–309
1–209	1–310

PART 1

GENERAL PROVISIONS

§ 1–101.   Short Titles.

(a)   This [Act] may be cited as the Uniform Commercial Code.

(b)   This article may be cited as Uniform Commercial Code-General Provisions.

Official Comment

Source: Former Section 1–101.

Changes from former law: Subsection (b) is new. It is added in order to make the structure of Article 1 parallel with that of the other articles of the Uniform Commercial Code.

Each other article of the Uniform Commercial Code (except Articles 10 and 11) may also be cited by its own short title. See Sections 2–101, 2A–101, 3–101, 4–101, 4A–101, 5–101, 6–101, 7–101, 8–101, and 9–101, 12–101, and A–101.

As amended in 2022.

---

[1]   Except last sentence of (b).
[2]   Last sentence.

§ 1–102. Scope of Article.

This article applies to a transaction to the extent that it is governed by another article of [the Uniform Commercial Code].

Official Comment

Source: New.

1.   This section is intended to resolve confusion that has occasionally arisen as to the applicability of the substantive rules in this article. This section makes clear what has always been the case—the rules in Article 1 apply to transactions to the extent that those transactions are governed by one of the other articles of the Uniform Commercial Code. See also Comment 1 to Section 1–301.

§ 1–103. Construction of [Uniform Commercial Code] to Promote Its Purposes and Policies; Applicability of Supplemental Principles of Law.

(a)   [The Uniform Commercial Code] must be liberally construed and applied to promote its underlying purposes and policies, which are:

(1)   to simplify, clarify, and modernize the law governing commercial transactions;

(2)   to permit the continued expansion of commercial practices through custom, usage, and agreement of the parties; and

(3)   to make uniform the law among the various jurisdictions.

(b)   Unless displaced by the particular provisions of [the Uniform Commercial Code], the principles of law and equity, including the law merchant and the law relative to capacity to contract, principal and agent, estoppel, fraud, misrepresentation, duress, coercion, mistake, bankruptcy, and other validating or invalidating cause supplement its provisions.

Official Comment

Source: Former Section 1–102(1)–(2); Former Section 1–103.

Changes from former law: This section is derived from subsections (1) and (2) of former Section 1–102 and from former Section 1–103. Subsection (a) of this section combines subsections (1) and (2) of former Section 1–102. Except for changing the form of reference to the Uniform Commercial Code and minor stylistic changes, its language is the same as subsections (1) and (2) of former Section 1–102. Except for changing the form of reference to the Uniform Commercial Code and minor stylistic changes, subsection (b) of this section is identical to former Section 1–103. The provisions have been combined in this section to reflect the interrelationship between them.

1.   The Uniform Commercial Code is drawn to provide flexibility so that, since it is intended to be a semi-permanent and infrequently-amended piece of legislation, it will provide its own machinery for expansion of commercial practices. It is intended to make it possible for the law embodied in the Uniform Commercial Code to be applied by the courts in the light of unforeseen and new circumstances and practices. The proper construction of the Uniform Commercial Code requires, of course, that its interpretation and application be limited to its reason.

Even prior to the enactment of the Uniform Commercial Code, courts were careful to keep broad acts from being hampered in their effects by later acts of limited scope. See *Pacific Wool Growers v. Draper & Co.*, 158 Or. 1, 73 P.2d 1391 (1937), and compare Section 1–104. The courts have often recognized that the policies embodied in an act are applicable in reason to subject-matter that was not expressly included in the language of the act, *Commercial Nat. Bank of New Orleans v. Canal-Louisiana Bank & Trust Co.*, 239 U.S. 520, 36 S.Ct. 194, 60 L.Ed. 417 (1916) (bona fide purchase policy of Uniform Warehouse Receipts Act extended to case not covered but of equivalent nature), and did the same where reason and policy so required, even where the subject-matter had been intentionally excluded from the act in general. *Agar v. Orda*, 264 N.Y. 248, 190 N.E. 479 (1934) (Uniform Sales Act change in seller's remedies applied to contract for sale of choses in action even though the general coverage of that Act was intentionally limited to goods "other than things in action.") They implemented a statutory policy with liberal and useful remedies not provided in the statutory text. They disregarded a statutory limitation of remedy where the reason of the limitation did not apply. *Fiterman v. J. N. Johnson & Co.*, 156 Minn. 201, 194 N.W. 399 (1923) (requirement of return of the goods as a condition to rescission for breach of warranty; also, partial rescission allowed). Nothing in the Uniform Commercial Code stands in the way of the continuance of such action by the courts.

The Uniform Commercial Code should be construed in accordance with its underlying purposes and policies. The text of each section should be read in the light of the purpose and policy of the rule or principle in question, as also of the Uniform Commercial Code as a whole, and the application of the language should be construed narrowly or broadly, as the case may be, in conformity with the purposes and policies involved.

2. **Applicability of supplemental principles of law.** Subsection (b) states the basic relationship of the Uniform Commercial Code to supplemental bodies of law. The Uniform Commercial Code was drafted against the backdrop of existing bodies of law, including the common law and equity, and relies on those bodies of law to supplement it provisions in many important ways. At the same time, the Uniform Commercial Code is the primary source of commercial law rules in areas that it governs, and its rules represent choices made by its drafters and the enacting legislatures about the appropriate policies to be furthered in the transactions it covers. Therefore, while principles of common law and equity may *supplement* provisions of the Uniform Commercial Code, they may not be used to *supplant* its provisions, or the purposes and policies those provisions reflect, unless a specific provision of the Uniform Commercial Code provides otherwise. In the absence of such a provision, the Uniform Commercial Code preempts principles of common law and equity that are inconsistent with either its provisions or its purposes and policies.

The language of subsection (b) is intended to reflect both the concept of supplementation and the concept of preemption. Some courts, however, had difficulty in applying the identical language of former Section 1–103 to determine when other law appropriately may be applied to supplement the Uniform Commercial Code, and when that law has been displaced by the Code. Some decisions applied other law in situations in which that application, while not inconsistent with the text of any particular provision of the Uniform Commercial Code, clearly was inconsistent with the underlying purposes and policies reflected in the relevant provisions of the Code. *See, e.g., Sheerbonnet, Ltd. v. American Express Bank, Ltd.*, 951 F. Supp. 403 (S.D.N.Y. 1995). In part, this difficulty arose from Comment 1 to former Section 1–103, which stated that "this section indicates the continued applicability to commercial contracts of all supplemental bodies of law except insofar as they are explicitly displaced by this Act." The "explicitly displaced" language of that Comment did not accurately reflect the proper scope of Uniform Commercial Code preemption, which extends to displacement of other law that is inconsistent with the purposes and policies of the Uniform Commercial Code, as well as with its text.

The supplemental principles of law and equity to which subsection (b) refers may evolve over time to take into account developments in technology. These developments may include, for example, developing case law on contract formation in an electronic environment and the use of automated transactions and arrangements that are sometimes referred to as "electronic agents" (which may or may not actually reflect or create agency relationships under the applicable law of agency). See generally Uniform Electronic Transactions Act (UETA); Restatement (Third) of Agency § 1.04, Reporter's Note to Comment *e* (2006) (discussing the relationship between "electronic agents" and the law of principal and agent). The supplementation recognized by subsection (b) should reflect this evolution.

3. **Application of subsection (b) to statutes.** The primary focus of Section 1–103 is on the relationship between the Uniform Commercial Code and principles of common law and equity as developed by the courts. State law, however, increasingly is statutory. Not only are there a growing number of state statutes addressing specific issues that come within the scope of the Uniform Commercial Code, but in some States many general principles of common law and equity have been codified. When the other law relating to a matter within the scope of the Uniform Commercial Code is a statute, the principles of subsection (b) remain relevant to the court's analysis of the relationship between that statute and the Uniform Commercial Code, but other principles of statutory interpretation that specifically address the interrelationship between statutes will be relevant as well. In some situations, the principles of subsection (b) still will be determinative. For example, the mere fact that an equitable principle is stated in statutory form rather than in judicial decisions should not change the court's analysis of whether the principle can be used to supplement the Uniform Commercial Code—under subsection (b), equitable principles may supplement provisions of the Uniform Commercial Code only if they are consistent with the purposes and policies of the Uniform Commercial Code as well as its text. In other situations, however, other interpretive principles addressing the interrelationship between statutes may lead the court to conclude that the other statute is controlling, even though it conflicts with the Uniform Commercial Code. This, for example, would be the result in a situation where the other statute was specifically intended to provide additional protection to a class of individuals engaging in transactions covered by the Uniform Commercial Code.

4. **Listing not exclusive.** The list of sources of supplemental law in subsection (b) is intended to be merely illustrative of the other law that may supplement the Uniform Commercial Code, and is not exclusive. No listing could be exhaustive. Further, the fact that a particular section of the Uniform Commercial Code makes express reference to other law is not intended to suggest the negation of the general application of the principles

of subsection (b). Note also that the word "bankruptcy" in subsection (b), continuing the use of that word from former Section 1–103, should be understood not as a specific reference to federal bankruptcy law but, rather as a reference to general principles of insolvency, whether under federal or state law.

As amended in 2022.

§ 1–104.   Construction Against Implied Repeal.

[The Uniform Commercial Code] being a general act intended as a unified coverage of its subject matter, no part of it shall be deemed to be impliedly repealed by subsequent legislation if such construction can reasonably be avoided.

Official Comment

Source: Former Section 1–104.

Changes from former law: Except for changing the form of reference to the Uniform Commercial Code, this section is identical to former Section 1–104.

1.   This section embodies the policy that an act that bears evidence of carefully considered permanent regulative intention should not lightly be regarded as impliedly repealed by subsequent legislation. The Uniform Commercial Code, carefully integrated and intended as a uniform codification of permanent character covering an entire "field" of law, is to be regarded as particularly resistant to implied repeal.

§ 1–105.   Severability.

If any provision or clause of [the Uniform Commercial Code] or its application to any person or circumstance is held invalid, the invalidity does not affect other provisions or applications of [the Uniform Commercial Code] which can be given effect without the invalid provision or application, and to this end the provisions of [the Uniform Commercial Code] are severable.

Official Comment

Source: Former Section 1–108.

Changes from former law: Except for changing the form of reference to the Uniform Commercial Code, this section is identical to former Section 1–108.

1.   This is the model severability section recommended by the National Conference of Commissioners on Uniform State Laws for inclusion in all acts of extensive scope.

§ 1–106.   Use of Singular and Plural; Gender.

In [the Uniform Commercial Code], unless the statutory context otherwise requires:

(1)   words in the singular number include the plural, and those in the plural include the singular; and

(2)   words of any gender also refer to any other gender.

Official Comment

Source: Former Section 1–102(5). See also 1 U.S.C. Section 1.

Changes from former law: Other than minor stylistic changes, this section is identical to former Section 1–102(5).

1.   This section makes it clear that the use of singular or plural in the text of the Uniform Commercial Code is generally only a matter of drafting style—singular words may be applied in the plural, and plural words may be applied in the singular. Only when it is clear from the statutory context that the use of the singular or plural does not include the other is this rule inapplicable. *See, e.g.,* Section 9–322.

§ 1–107.   Section Captions.

Section captions are part of [the Uniform Commercial Code].

Official Comment

Source: Former Section 1–109.

Changes from former law: None.

1.   Section captions are a part of the text of the Uniform Commercial Code, and not mere surplusage. This is not the case, however, with respect to subsection headings appearing in ~~Article 9~~Articles 9, 12, and A (Transitional Provisions). See ~~Comment 3 to~~ Section 9–101, Comment 3 ("subsection headings are not a part of the official text itself and have not been approved by the sponsors."); Section 12–101, Comment; Section A–101, Comment.

As amended in 2022.

§ 1–108.   Relation to Electronic Signatures in Global and National Commerce Act.

This article modifies, limits, and supersedes the Federal Electronic Signatures in Global and National Commerce Act, 15 U.S.C. § 7001 *et seq.*, except that nothing in this article modifies, limits, or supersedes section 7001(c) of that act or authorizes electronic delivery of any of the notices described in section 7003(b) of that Act.

Official Comment

Source: New

1.   The federal Electronic Signatures in Global and National Commerce Act, 15 U.S.C. Section 7001 *et seq.* became effective in 2000. Section 102(a) of that Act provides that a State statute may modify, limit, or supersede the provisions of section 101 of that Act with respect to state law if such statute, *inter alia*, specifies the alternative procedures or requirements for the use or acceptance (or both) of electronic records or electronic signatures to establish the legal effect, validity, or enforceability of contracts or other records, and (i) such alternative procedures or requirements are consistent with Titles I and II of that Act, (ii) such alternative procedures or requirements do not require, or accord greater legal status or effect to, the implementation or application of a specific technology or technical specification for performing the functions of creating, storing, generating, receiving, communicating, or authenticating electronic records or electronic signatures; and (iii) if enacted or adopted after the date of the enactment of that Act, makes specific reference to that Act. Article 1 fulfills the first two of those three criteria; this Section fulfills the third criterion listed above.

2.   As stated in this section, however, Article 1 does not modify, limit, or supersede Section 101(c) of the Electronic Signatures in Global and National Commerce Act (requiring affirmative consent from a consumer to electronic delivery of transactional disclosures that are required by state law to be in writing); nor does it authorize electronic delivery of any of the notices described in Section 103(b) of that Act.

PART 2

GENERAL DEFINITIONS AND PRINCIPLES OF INTERPRETATION

§ 1–201.   General Definitions.

(a)   Unless the context otherwise requires, words or phrases defined in this section, or in the additional definitions contained in other articles of [the Uniform Commercial Code] that apply to particular articles or parts thereof, have the meanings stated.

(b)   Subject to definitions contained in other articles of [the Uniform Commercial Code] that apply to particular articles or parts thereof:

(1)   "Action", in the sense of a judicial proceeding, includes recoupment, counterclaim, set-off, suit in equity, and any other proceeding in which rights are determined.

(2)   "Aggrieved party" means a party entitled to pursue a remedy.

(3)   "Agreement", as distinguished from "contract", means the bargain of the parties in fact, as found in their language or inferred from other circumstances, including course of performance, course of dealing, or usage of trade as provided in Section 1–303.

(4)   "Bank" means a person engaged in the business of banking and includes a savings bank, savings and loan association, credit union, and trust company.

(5) "Bearer" means a person in control of a negotiable electronic document of title or a person in possession of a negotiable instrument, negotiable tangible document of title, or certificated security that is payable to bearer or indorsed in blank.

(6) "Bill of lading" means a document of title evidencing the receipt of goods for shipment issued by a person engaged in the business of directly or indirectly transporting or forwarding goods. The term does not include a warehouse receipt.

(7) "Branch" includes a separately incorporated foreign branch of a bank.

(8) "Burden of establishing" a fact means the burden of persuading the trier of fact that the existence of the fact is more probable than its nonexistence.

(9) "Buyer in ordinary course of business" means a person that buys goods in good faith, without knowledge that the sale violates the rights of another person in the goods, and in the ordinary course from a person, other than a pawnbroker, in the business of selling goods of that kind. A person buys goods in the ordinary course if the sale to the person comports with the usual or customary practices in the kind of business in which the seller is engaged or with the seller's own usual or customary practices. A person that sells oil, gas, or other minerals at the wellhead or minehead is a person in the business of selling goods of that kind. A buyer in ordinary course of business may buy for cash, by exchange of other property, or on secured or unsecured credit, and may acquire goods or documents of title under a preexisting contract for sale. Only a buyer that takes possession of the goods or has a right to recover the goods from the seller under Article 2 may be a buyer in ordinary course of business. "Buyer in ordinary course of business" does not include a person that acquires goods in a transfer in bulk or as security for or in total or partial satisfaction of a money debt.

(10) "Conspicuous", with reference to a term, means so written, displayed, or presented that, based on the totality of the circumstances, a reasonable person against which it is to operate ought to have noticed it. Whether a term is "conspicuous" or not is a decision for the court. ~~Conspicuous terms include the following:~~

    (A) ~~a heading in capitals equal to or greater in size than the surrounding text, or in contrasting type, font, or color to the surrounding text of the same or lesser size; and~~

    (B) ~~language in the body of a record or display in larger type than the surrounding text, or in contrasting type, font, or color to the surrounding text of the same size, or set off from surrounding text of the same size by symbols or other marks that call attention to the language.~~

(11) "Consumer" means an individual who enters into a transaction primarily for personal, family, or household purposes.

(12) "Contract", as distinguished from "agreement", means the total legal obligation that results from the parties' agreement as determined by [the Uniform Commercial Code] as supplemented by any other applicable laws.

(13) "Creditor" includes a general creditor, a secured creditor, a lien creditor, and any representative of creditors, including an assignee for the benefit of creditors, a trustee in bankruptcy, a receiver in equity, and an executor or administrator of an insolvent debtor's or assignor's estate.

(14) "Defendant" includes a person in the position of defendant in a counterclaim, cross-claim, or third-party claim.

(15) "Delivery", with respect to an electronic document of title means voluntary transfer of control and with respect to an instrument, a tangible document of title, or an authoritative tangible copy of a record evidencing chattel paper, means voluntary transfer of possession.

(16) "Document of title" means a record (i) that in the regular course of business or financing is treated as adequately evidencing that the person in possession or control of the record is entitled to receive, control, hold, and dispose of the record and the goods the record covers and (ii) that purports to be issued by or addressed to a bailee and to cover goods in the bailee's possession which are either identified or are fungible portions of an identified mass. The term includes a bill

of lading, transport document, dock warrant, dock receipt, warehouse receipt, and order for delivery of goods. An electronic document of title means a document of title evidenced by a record consisting of information stored in an electronic medium. A tangible document of title means a document of title evidenced by a record consisting of information that is inscribed on a tangible medium.

(16A) "Electronic" means relating to technology having electrical, digital, magnetic, wireless, optical, electromagnetic, or similar capabilities.

(17) "Fault" means a default, breach, or wrongful act or omission.

(18) "Fungible goods" means:

    (A) goods of which any unit, by nature or usage of trade, is the equivalent of any other like unit; or

    (B) goods that by agreement are treated as equivalent.

(19) "Genuine" means free of forgery or counterfeiting.

(20) "Good faith," except as otherwise provided in Article 5, means honesty in fact and the observance of reasonable commercial standards of fair dealing.

(21) "Holder" means:

    (A) the person in possession of a negotiable instrument that is payable either to bearer or to an identified person that is the person in possession;

    (B) the person in possession of a negotiable tangible document of title if the goods are deliverable either to bearer or to the order of the person in possession; or

    (C) the person in control, other than pursuant to Section 7–106(g), of a negotiable electronic document of title.

(22) "Insolvency proceeding" includes an assignment for the benefit of creditors or other proceeding intended to liquidate or rehabilitate the estate of the person involved.

(23) "Insolvent" means:

    (A) having generally ceased to pay debts in the ordinary course of business other than as a result of bona fide dispute;

    (B) being unable to pay debts as they become due; or

    (C) being insolvent within the meaning of federal bankruptcy law.

(24) "Money" means a medium of exchange that is currently authorized or adopted by a domestic or foreign government. The term includes a monetary unit of account established by an intergovernmental organization or by agreement between two or more countries. The term does not include an electronic record that is a medium of exchange recorded and transferable in a system that existed and operated for the medium of exchange before the medium of exchange was authorized or adopted by the government.

(25) "Organization" means a person other than an individual.

(26) "Party", as distinguished from "third party", means a person that has engaged in a transaction or made an agreement subject to [the Uniform Commercial Code].

(27) "Person" means an individual, corporation, business trust, estate, trust, partnership, limited liability company, association, joint venture, government, governmental subdivision, agency, or instrumentality, public corporation, or any other legal or commercial entity. The term includes a protected series, however denominated, of an entity if the protected series is established under law other than [the Uniform Commercial Code] that limits, or limits if conditions specified under the law are satisfied, the ability of a creditor of the entity or of any other protected series of the entity to satisfy a claim from assets of the protected series.

(28) "Present value" means the amount as of a date certain of one or more sums payable in the future, discounted to the date certain by use of either an interest rate specified by the parties if that rate is not manifestly unreasonable at the time the transaction is entered into or, if an interest rate is not so specified, a commercially reasonable rate that takes into account the facts and circumstances at the time the transaction is entered into.

(29) "Purchase" means taking by sale, lease, discount, negotiation, mortgage, pledge, lien, security interest, issue or reissue, gift, or any other voluntary transaction creating an interest in property.

(30) "Purchaser" means a person that takes by purchase.

(31) "Record" means information that is inscribed on a tangible medium or that is stored in an electronic or other medium and is retrievable in perceivable form.

(32) "Remedy" means any remedial right to which an aggrieved party is entitled with or without resort to a tribunal.

(33) "Representative" means a person empowered to act for another, including an agent, an officer of a corporation or association, and a trustee, executor, or administrator of an estate.

(34) "Right" includes remedy.

(35) "Security interest" means an interest in personal property or fixtures which secures payment or performance of an obligation. "Security interest" includes any interest of a consignor and a buyer of accounts, chattel paper, a payment intangible, or a promissory note in a transaction that is subject to Article 9. "Security interest" does not include the special property interest of a buyer of goods on identification of those goods to a contract for sale under Section 2–401, but a buyer may also acquire a "security interest" by complying with Article 9. Except as otherwise provided in Section 2–505, the right of a seller or lessor of goods under Article 2 or 2A to retain or acquire possession of the goods is not a "security interest", but a seller or lessor may also acquire a "security interest" by complying with Article 9. The retention or reservation of title by a seller of goods notwithstanding shipment or delivery to the buyer under Section 2–401 is limited in effect to a reservation of a "security interest." Whether a transaction in the form of a lease creates a "security interest" is determined pursuant to Section 1–203.

(36) "Send", in connection with a ~~writing,~~ record, or ~~notice~~ notification, means:

    (A) to deposit in the mail, ~~or~~ deliver for transmission, or transmit by any other usual means of communication, with postage or cost of transmission provided for, ~~and properly addressed and, in the case of an instrument, to an address specified thereon or otherwise agreed, or if there be none~~ addressed to any address reasonable under the circumstances; or

    (B) ~~in any other way to cause to be received any record or notice within the time it would have arrived if properly sent~~ to cause the record or notification to be received within the time it would have been received if properly sent under subparagraph (A).

(37) ~~"Signed" includes using any symbol executed or adopted with present intention to adopt or accept a writing.~~ "Sign" means, with present intent to authenticate or adopt a record:

(A)   execute or adopt a tangible symbol; or

(B)   attach to or logically associate with the record an electronic symbol, sound, or process.

"Signed", "signing", and "signature" have corresponding meanings.

(38) "State" means a State of the United States, the District of Columbia, Puerto Rico, the United States Virgin Islands, or any territory or insular possession subject to the jurisdiction of the United States.

(39) "Surety" includes a guarantor or other secondary obligor.

(40) "Term" means a portion of an agreement that relates to a particular matter.

(41) "Unauthorized signature" means a signature made without actual, implied, or apparent authority. The term includes a forgery.

(42) "Warehouse receipt" means a document of title issued by a person engaged in the business of storing goods for hire.

(43) "Writing" includes printing, typewriting, or any other intentional reduction to tangible form. "Written" has a corresponding meaning.

Legislative Note:

A state should review and amend any statute or regulation that relies on or refers to the definition of "money" in subsection (b)(24) to account for the amendment to that definition.

A state should enact the amendment to subsection (b)(27) whether the state has enacted the Uniform Protected Series Act (2017) or otherwise recognizes a protected series under its law. Because the amendment applies only under the enacting state's Uniform Commercial Code, inclusion of the amendment does not require the enacting state to recognize a limit on liability of a protected series organized under the law of another jurisdiction or a limit on liability of the entity that established the protected series. The amendment clarifies the status of a protected series as a "person" under the choice-of-law and substantive law rules of the enacting state's Uniform Commercial Code.

As amended in 2003 and 2022.

Official Comment

Source: Former Section 1–201.

Changes from former law: In order to make it clear that all definitions in the Uniform Commercial Code (not just those appearing in Article 1, as stated in former Section 1–201, but also those appearing in other Articles) do not apply if the context otherwise requires, a new subsection (a) to that effect has been added, and the definitions now appear in subsection (b). The reference in subsection (a) to the "context" is intended to refer to the context in which the defined term is used in the Uniform Commercial Code. In other words, the definition applies whenever the defined term is used unless the context in which the defined term is used in the statute indicates that the term was not used in its defined sense. Consider, for example, Sections 3–103(a)(9) [*version before 2002 revision*] (defining "promise," in relevant part, as "a written undertaking to pay money signed by the person undertaking to pay") and 3–303(a)(1) (indicating that an instrument is issued or transferred for value if "the instrument is issued or transferred for a promise of performance, to the extent that the promise has been performed"). It is clear from the statutory context of the use of the word "promise" in Section 3–303(a)(1) that the term was not used in the sense of its definition in Section 3–103(a)(9) [*version before 2002 revision*]. Thus, the Section 3–103(a)(9) [*version before 2002 revision*] definition should not be used to give meaning to the word "promise" in Section 3–303(a).

Some definitions in former Section 1–201 have been reformulated as substantive provisions and have been moved to other sections. See Sections 1–202 (explicating concepts of notice and knowledge formerly addressed in Sections 1–201(25)–(27)), 1–204 (determining when a person gives value for rights, replacing the definition of "value" in former Section 1–201(44)), and 1–206 (addressing the meaning of presumptions, replacing the definitions of "presumption" and "presumed" in former Section 1–201(31)). Similarly, the portion of the definition of "security interest" in former Section 1–201(37) which explained the difference between a security interest and a lease has been relocated to Section 1–203.

Two definitions in former Section 1–201 have been deleted. The definition of "honor" in former Section 1–201(21) has been moved to Section 2–103(1)(b), inasmuch as the definition only applies to the use of the word in Article 2. [*Note from West Advisory Panel: This sentence appears to be in error because, although "honor" was deleted from Article 1, no conforming amendment to Section 2–103(1) was made as part of the Article 1 revision.*] The definition of "telegram" in former Section 1–201(41) has been deleted because that word no longer appears in the definition of "conspicuous."

Other than minor stylistic changes and renumbering, the remaining definitions in this section are as in former Article 1 except as noted below.

1. "Action." Unchanged from former Section 1–201, which was derived from similar definitions in Section 191, Uniform Negotiable Instruments Law; Section 76, Uniform Sales Act; Section 58, Uniform Warehouse Receipts Act; Section 53, Uniform Bills of Lading Act.

2. "Aggrieved party." Unchanged from former Section 1–201.

3. "Agreement." Derived from former Section 1–201. As used in the Uniform Commercial Code the word is intended to include full recognition of usage of trade, course of dealing, course of performance and the

surrounding circumstances as effective parts thereof, and of any agreement permitted under the provisions of the Uniform Commercial Code to displace a stated rule of law. Whether an agreement has legal consequences is determined by applicable provisions of the Uniform Commercial Code and, to the extent provided in Section 1–103, by the law of contracts. Concerning developments in technology, including, for example, contract formation in electronic environments, automated transactions, and electronic agents, see Section 1–103, Comment 2.

4. "Bank." Derived from Section 4A–104.

5. "Bearer." Unchanged, except in one respect, from former section 1–201, which was derived from Section 191, Uniform Negotiable Instruments Law. The term bearer applies to negotiable documents of title and has been broadened to include a person in control of an electronic negotiable document of title. Control of an electronic document of title is defined in Article 7 (Section 7–106).

6. "Bill of Lading." Derived from former Section 1–201. The reference to, and definition of, an "airbill" has been deleted as no longer necessary. A bill of lading is one type of document of title as defined in subsection (16). This definition should be read in conjunction with the definition of carrier in Article 7 (Section 7–102).

7. "Branch." Unchanged from former Section 1–201.

8. "Burden of establishing a fact." Unchanged from former Section 1–201.

9. "Buyer in ordinary course of business." Except for minor stylistic changes, identical to former Section 1–201 (as amended in conjunction with the 1999 revisions to Article 9). The major significance of the phrase lies in Section 2–403 and in the Article on Secured Transactions (Article 9).

The first sentence of paragraph (9) makes clear that a buyer from a pawnbroker cannot be a buyer in ordinary course of business. The second sentence explains what it means to buy "in the ordinary course." The penultimate sentence prevents a buyer that does not have the right to possession as against the seller from being a buyer in ordinary course of business. Concerning when a buyer obtains possessory rights, see Sections 2–502 and 2–716. However, the penultimate sentence is not intended to affect a buyer's status as a buyer in ordinary course of business in cases (such as a "drop shipment") involving delivery by the seller to a person buying from the buyer or a donee from the buyer. The requirement relates to whether *as against the seller* the buyer or one taking through the buyer has possessory rights.

10. "Conspicuous." Derived from former Section 1–201(10). This definition states the general standard that to be conspicuous a term ought to be noticed by a reasonable person against which the term is to operate. Whether a term is conspicuous is an issue for the court. ~~Subparagraphs (A) and (B) set out several methods for making a term conspicuous. Requiring that a term be conspicuous blends a notice function (the term ought to be noticed) and a planning function (giving guidance to the party relying on the term regarding how that result can be achieved). Although these paragraphs indicate some of the methods for making a term attention-calling, the test is whether attention can reasonably be expected to be called to it. The statutory language should not be construed to permit a result that is inconsistent with that test.~~ Whether the appearance and presentation of a particular term satisfy this standard is determined by reference to the totality of the circumstances and requires a case-by-case analysis.

Historically, contract terms were presented in writing, making the use of standards that relate to the size and appearance of type relevant to the determination of conspicuousness. Today terms in a record are frequently communicated electronically. New technologies have created opportunities for terms to be displayed or presented in novel ways, such as by the use of pop-up windows, text balloons, dynamically expanding or dynamically magnifying text, and non-visual elements such as vibrations, to name a few.

The definition has been revised in the Uniform Commercial Code Amendments (2022) (2022 Amendments) by deleting the statutory examples relating to the appearance of type and instead indicating in these comments a broader universe of factors that are applicable to both written and electronic presentations. This approach is intended to be both more protective of consumers and more useful to drafters by providing more clarity and flexibility in the methods that may be used to call attention to a term.

The attributes of a reasonable person against which a term is to operate can vary depending upon the nature of the transaction and the market in which the transaction occurs. For example, assume that a merchant of goods wishes to enter into a transaction for the sale or lease of goods which does not include an implied warranty of merchantability or fitness for particular purpose. Depending on the particular transaction, the person against which the term excluding implied warranties is to operate may be a large business buyer or lessee, a small business, or a consumer. Similarly, the determination of whether a term is conspicuous may, depending on the context, yield a different conclusion when the term is used in a standard form agreement than when terms of the agreement are the subject of negotiation or discussion.

Terms presented in an online record raise issues that differ in some respects from the issues associated with presenting the same terms in a writing. For example, how a term appears depends to some extent on the equipment and settings used by the person presented with the term.

The test of whether a term is conspicuous remains constant notwithstanding the different contexts referenced above. A term is conspicuous if its appearance and presentation are such that it ought to be noticed by a reasonable person against which the term is to operate. If the term is in a standard form intended for use in many agreements, the determination of whether the term is conspicuous may be made with reference to typical likely parties to the agreements, taking into account all aspects of the transaction, the range of likely equipment and settings used by such parties, and the education, sophistication, disabilities, and other attributes of such parties. If the term is not in a standard form, the determination of whether it is conspicuous should be made with reference to a reasonable person in the position of the actual person against which it is to operate.

Factors relevant to whether a term is conspicuous include, but are not limited to, the following:

(i)   The use of headings and text that contrast with the surrounding text. For example, a term is likely to be conspicuous if it is introduced by a heading in uppercase letters equal to or greater in size than the surrounding text. Similarly, a term is likely to be conspicuous if set out in language in the body of a record or display in larger type than the surrounding text, or in contrasting type, font, or color to the surrounding text of the same size, or set off from surrounding text of the same size by symbols or other marks that call attention to the language. However, even with those characteristics, for a term to be conspicuous the overall statutory test must always be met. For example, even if in bold, uppercase letters, a term might not be conspicuous if placed among other terms also in bold, uppercase letters so there is no contrast with the surrounding text or if the application of other factors causes the term not to be provided such that a reasonable person against which it is to operate ought to have noticed it.

(ii)   The placement of the term in the record. A term appearing at, or hyperlinked from, text at the beginning of a record, or near the place where the person against which the term is to operate must signify assent, is more likely to be conspicuous than a term in the middle of a lengthy record absent the use of a method reasonably designed to draw the person's attention to the term in middle of the record (for example, by providing separate reasonable notice of the term before presenting the record containing the term to the person for assent or forcing the person to stop on a screen highlighting the term during the presentation of the record for assent).

(iii)   If terms are available only through the use of a hyperlink, in addition to the placement of the hyperlink as described above, factors to be considered include whether there is language drawing attention to the hyperlink and describing its function, and the size and color of the text used for the hyperlink and any related language.

(iv)   The language of the heading, if any. A misleading heading—such as the heading "Warranty" for a paragraph that contains a disclaimer of warranties—might cause a reasonable person to fail to notice the language that would disclaim warranties, so that the term would not be conspicuous.

(v)   The effort needed to access the term. The process and flow of the display and presentation is also relevant. For example, a term accessible only by triggering multiple hyperlinks is less likely to be conspicuous than a term accessible from a single hyperlink.

(vi)   Whether the person against which the term is to operate must separately assent to or acknowledge the term. Obtaining separate assent or acknowledgment of a term is generally sufficient to make the term conspicuous.

As noted above, the evolution of technology has led to an evolution in the ways in which terms in an electronic record are displayed or presented. A term displayed or presented in a novel way utilizing emerging technologies is, of course, conspicuous if the effect of the display or presentation is that a reasonable person against which the term is to operate ought to have noticed it.

This definition deals only with requirements that a term be conspicuous (or noted conspicuously) that are stated in particular provisions of the Uniform Commercial Code. Other protective doctrines designed to assure that assent is meaningful that are found in law outside the UCC may also apply. See Section 1–103(b).

11.   "Consumer." Derived from Section 9–102(a)(25).

12.   "Contract." Except for minor stylistic changes, identical to former Section 1–201.

13.   "Creditor." Unchanged from former Section 1–201.

14. "Defendant." Except for minor stylistic changes, identical to former Section 1–201, which was derived from Section 76, Uniform Sales Act.

15. "Delivery." Derived from former Section 1–201. The reference to certificated securities has been in a pre-2022 version was deleted in light of the more specific treatment of the matter in Section 8–301. The definition has been also was revised to accommodate electronic documents of title. Control of an electronic document of title is defined in Article 7 (Section 7–106). Another revision in the 2022 Amendments conformed the reference to chattel paper to the revised definition of that term and the revised methods of perfection. See Sections 9–102(a)(11) (defining "chattel paper"); 9–314A (perfection by possession and control of chattel paper).

16. "Document of title." Derived from former Section 1–201, which was derived from Section 76, Uniform Sales Act. This definition makes explicit that the obligation or designation of a third party as "bailee" is essential to a document of title and clearly rejects any such result as obtained in *Hixson v. Ward*, 254 Ill.App. 505 (1929), which treated a conditional sales contract as a document of title. Also the definition is left open so that new types of documents may be included, including documents which gain commercial recognition in the international arena. See UNCITRAL Draft Instrument on the Carriage of Goods By Sea. It is unforeseeable what documents may one day serve the essential purpose now filled by warehouse receipts and bills of lading. The definition is stated in terms of the function of the documents with the intention that any document which gains commercial recognition as accomplishing the desired result shall be included within its scope. Fungible goods are adequately identified within the language of the definition by identification of the mass of which they are a part.

Dock warrants were within the Sales Act definition of document of title apparently for the purpose of recognizing a valid tender by means of such paper. In current commercial practice a dock warrant or receipt is a kind of interim certificate issued by shipping companies upon delivery of the goods at the dock, entitling a designated person to be issued a bill of lading. The receipt itself is invariably nonnegotiable in form although it may indicate that a negotiable bill is to be forthcoming. Such a document is not within the general compass of the definition, although trade usage may in some cases entitle such paper to be treated as a document of title. If the dock receipt actually represents a storage obligation undertaken by the shipping company, then it is a warehouse receipt within this Section regardless of the name given to the instrument.

The goods must be "described," but the description may be by marks or labels and may be qualified in such a way as to disclaim personal knowledge of the issuer regarding contents or condition. However, baggage and parcel checks and similar "tokens" of storage which identify stored goods only as those received in exchange for the token are not covered by this Article. The definition is broad enough to include an airway bill.

A document of title may be either tangible or electronic. Tangible Paper documents of title should be construed to mean traditional paper documents. are "tangible documents of title." Electronic documents of title are documents that are stored in an electronic medium instead of in tangible form. The concept of an electronic medium should be construed liberally to include electronic, digital, magnetic, optical, electromagnetic, or any other current or similar emerging technologies. "Electronic" is defined in paragraph 16A. As to reissuing a document of title in an alternative medium, see Article 7, Section 7–105. Control for electronic documents of title is defined in Article 7 (Section 7–106).

16A. "Electronic." The basic nature of most modern technologies and the need for a recognized, single term warrants the use of "electronic" as the defined term, even though not all technologies listed may be technically "electronic" in nature. The definition is intended to be applied broadly as new technologies develop. The term must be construed broadly in light of developing technologies in order to validate commercial transactions regardless of the medium used by the parties to document them. See generally Uniform Electronic Transactions Act, Section 2, Comment 4.

17. "Fault." Derived from former Section 1–201. "Default" has been added to the list of events constituting fault.

18. "Fungible goods." Derived from former Section 1–201. References to securities have been deleted because Article 8 no longer uses the term "fungible" to describe securities. Accordingly, this provision now defines the concept only in the context of goods.

19. "Genuine." Unchanged from former Section 1–201.

20. "Good faith." Former Section 1–201(19) defined "good faith" simply as honesty in fact; the definition contained no element of commercial reasonableness. Initially, that definition applied throughout the Code with only one exception. Former Section 2–103(1)(b) provided that "in that Article . . . good faith in the case of a merchant means honesty in fact and the observance of reasonable commercial standards of fair dealing in the

trade." This alternative definition was limited in applicability though, because it applied only to transactions within the scope of Article 2 and it applied only to merchants.

Over time, however, amendments to the Uniform Commercial Code brought the Article 2 merchant concept of good faith (subjective honesty and objective commercial ~~reasonableness~~ standards of fair dealing) into other Articles. First, Article 2A explicitly incorporated the Article 2 standard. ~~See Section 2A–103(7).~~ Then, other Articles broadened the applicability of that standard by adopting it for all parties rather than just for merchants. ~~See, e.g., Sections 3–103(a)(4) [version before 2002 revision], 4A–105(a)(6), 7–102(a)(6), 8–102(a)(10), and 9–102(a)(43).~~ Finally, Articles 2 and 2A were amended ~~so as~~ to apply the standard to non-merchants as well as merchants. ~~See Sections 2–103(1)(j), 2A–103(1)(m).~~ All of these definitions are comprised of two elements—honesty in fact *and* the observance of reasonable commercial standards of fair dealing. Only revised Article 5 ~~defines~~ continued to define "good faith" solely in terms of subjective honesty, and ~~only~~ Article 6 (in the few states that have not chosen to delete the Article) is without a definition of good faith. (It should be noted that, while revised Article 6 did not define good faith, Comment 2 to revised Section 6–102 states that "this Article adopts the definition of 'good faith' in Article 1 in all cases, even when the buyer is a merchant.")

Thus, the definition of "good faith" in this section merely confirms what has been the case for a number of years as Articles of the UCC have been amended or revised—the obligation of "good faith," applicable in each Article, is to be interpreted in the context of all Articles except for Article 5 as including both the subjective element of honesty in fact and the objective element of the observance of reasonable commercial standards of fair dealing. As a result, both the subjective and objective elements are part of the standard of "good faith," whether that obligation is specifically referenced in another Article of the Code (other than Article 5) or is provided by this Article.

Of course, as noted in the statutory text, the definition of "good faith" in this section does not apply when the narrower definition of "good faith" in revised Article 5 is applicable.

As noted above, the definition of "good faith" in this section requires not only honesty in fact but also "observance of reasonable commercial standards of fair dealing." Although "fair dealing" is a broad term that must be defined in context, it is clear that it is concerned with the fairness of conduct rather than the care with which an act is performed. This is an entirely different concept than whether a party exercised ordinary care in conducting a transaction. Both concepts are to be determined in the light of reasonable commercial standards, but those standards in each case are directed to different aspects of commercial conduct. See e.g., Sections 3–103(a)(9) [*version before 2002 revision*] and 4–104(c) and Comment 4 to Section 3–103.

21.   "Holder." ~~Derived from former Section 1–201.~~ The definition has been reorganized for clarity and amended to provide for electronic negotiable documents of title. <u>The definition excludes persons who have control of an electronic document of title pursuant to Section 7–106(g) through the acknowledgment by a person in control. This ensures that an issuer of a document can ascertain who is entitled to delivery from the document itself or from the system in which the document is recorded, without any obligation to look behind the document or the system to ascertain the identity of an undisclosed principal.</u>

22.   "Insolvency proceedings." Unchanged from former Section 1–201.

23.   "Insolvent." Derived from former Section 1–201. The three tests of insolvency—"generally ceased to pay debts in the ordinary course of business other than as a result of a bona fide dispute as to them," "unable to pay debts as they become due," and "insolvent within the meaning of the federal bankruptcy law"—are expressly set up as alternative tests and must be approached from a commercial standpoint.

24.   "Money." ~~Substantively identical to former Section 1–201. The test is that of sanction of government, whether by authorization before issue or adoption afterward, which recognizes the circulating medium as a part of the official currency of that government. The narrow view that money is limited to legal tender is rejected.~~ <u>The definition of "money" applies to the term only as used in the Uniform Commercial Code. The definition does not determine whether an asset constitutes "money" for other purposes. Only something currently authorized or adopted as a medium of exchange by a government can be money. As further elaborated in the second sentence of the definition, adoption by a government may occur through establishment by an intergovernmental organization or pursuant to an agreement between governments. Coins and paper currency previously, but not currently, authorized or adopted as a medium of exchange by a government, and currently owned and traded only for their numismatic or historical value, are not money.</u>

<u>An electronic medium of exchange established pursuant to a country's law and that is recorded and transferable in a system that did not exist and did not operate for that medium of exchange before the electronic medium of exchange was authorized or adopted by the country's government also constitutes money. This is so</u>

even if ownership is established or maintained through a system not operated by the government. In contrast, an existing medium of exchange created or distributed by one or more private persons is not money solely because the government of one or more countries later authorizes or adopts the pre-existing medium of exchange.

Although the term "money" is used in several articles, the definition is particularly significant under Article 9. Under the pre-2022 version of this definition, money was generally understood to include only tangible coins, bills, notes, and the like, although the statutory text did not explicitly so limit the term. This worked well under Article 9, which provided that the only method of perfecting a security interest in money as original collateral was by taking possession of it. See pre-2022 Section 9–312(b)(3). The 2022 revised definition of money in Section 1–201(b)(24) is broader and includes both "tangible money" and "electronic money" (new defined types of collateral under the 2022 revisions to Article 9). As under the pre-2022 Article 9, a security interest in tangible money as original collateral may be perfected only by possession. Section 9–312(b)(3). A security interest in electronic money as original collateral may be perfected only by control. Section 9–102(a)(31A) (defining "electronic money"); 9–312(b)(4) (perfection by control for electronic money). Note that the definition of "money" in Section 9–102(a)(54A) is narrower in two respects than the definition in this section—the Article 9 definition excludes deposit accounts and money in electronic form that cannot be subjected to control under Section 9–105A. See Section 9–102(a)(54A).

Examples: The following examples illustrate the definition of "money."

Example 1: Nation A enacts legislation authorizing or adopting an existing cryptocurrency (spitcoin), created on a private blockchain, as a medium of exchange. Because spitcoin was recorded and transferable in a system that existed and operated for that cryptocurrency before the electronic record was authorized or adopted by Nation A, spitcoin does not become "money" under this definition as a result of Nation A's legislation.

Example 2: Nation B creates a new cryptocurrency (beebuck) and authorizes or adopts it as a medium of exchange. Beebuck is "money." Beebuck is not recorded and transferable in a system that existed and operated for that cryptocurrency before the electronic record was authorized or adopted by Nation B.

Example 3: Nation C enacts legislation authorizing or adopting as a medium of exchange beebuck, the cryptocurrency previously adopted by Nation B in Example 2. Although beebuck *is* recorded and transferable in a system that existed and operated for beebuck before it was authorized or adopted by Nation C, beebuck was *already* money when authorized or adopted by Nation C. Consequently, beebuck is "money." Nation C's action had no relevance or effect on the characterization of beebuck as money.

25. "Organization." The former definition of this word has been replaced with the standard definition used in acts prepared by the National Conference of Commissioners on Uniform State Laws.

26. "Party." Substantively identical to former Section 1–201. Mention of a party includes, of course, a person acting through an agent. However, where an agent comes into opposition or contrast to the principal, particular account is taken of that situation.

27. "Person." ~~The former definition of this word~~ A previous definition of this term ~~has been~~ was replaced with the standard ~~definition~~ language used in acts prepared by the National Conference of Commissioners on Uniform State Laws. ~~A protected series formed under the Uniform Protected Series Act (2017) is a "person." See PEB Commentary No. 23, dated February 24, 2021. The Commentary is available at https://www.ali.org/peb-ucc.~~ This definition recognizes the wide range of subjects that can enjoy legal rights and possess legal duties, including the catchall residual category of "any other legal or commercial entity." See, e.g., John Chipman Gray, The Nature and Sources of the Law 27 (Roland Gray rev., 2d ed., The MacMillan Co. 1931) ("a 'person' is a subject of legal rights and duties"). For additional authorities, see PEB Commentary No. 23, n. 5. The reference to a "public corporation" in the pre-2022 text of the definition has been deleted as unnecessary and duplicative of other examples in the definition of entities that are persons.

The second sentence of the definition provides needed clarity as to the status of a protected series for purposes of the Uniform Commercial Code. See PEB Commentary No. 23. Several states have enacted statutes that provide for protected series within a limited liability company or other unincorporated organization. These statutes afford rights and impose duties upon a protected series and generally empower a protected series to conduct its own activities under its own name. The types of protected series that are included as persons under the definition include, but are not limited to, those established under the Uniform Protected Series Act.

Providing that a protected series is a "person" for purposes of the enacting state's Uniform Commercial Code will expressly permit a protected series, whether created under the law of the enacting state or of another jurisdiction, to be a "seller" or a "buyer" under Article 2, a "lessor" or a "lessee" under Article 2A, or an "organization." It also permits a protected series to be a "debtor" under Article 9, and, if the law under which the protected series is organized requires a public filing for the protected series to be recognized under that law, a "registered organization" under Article 9.

28.   "Present value." This definition was formerly contained within the definition of "security interest" in former Section 1–201(37).

29.   "Purchase." Derived from former Section 1–201. The form of definition has been changed from "includes" to "means."

30.   "Purchaser." Unchanged from former Section 1–201.

31.   "Record." Derived from Section 9–102(a)(69).

32.   "Remedy." Unchanged from former Section 1–201. The purpose is to make it clear that both remedy and right (as defined) include those remedial rights of "self help" which are among the most important bodies of rights under the Uniform Commercial Code, remedial rights being those to which an aggrieved party may resort on its own.

33.   "Representative." ~~Derived from former Section 1–201. Reorganized, and form changed from "includes" to "means."~~ Concerning developments in technology, including, for example, contract formation in electronic environments, automated transactions, and electronic agents, see Section 1–103, Comment 2.

34.   "Right." Except for minor stylistic changes, identical to former Section 1–201.

35.   "Security Interest." The definition is the first paragraph of the definition of "security interest" in former Section 1–201, with minor stylistic changes. The remaining portion of that definition has been moved to Section 1–203. Note that, because of the scope of Article 9, the term includes the interest of certain outright buyers of certain kinds of property.

36.   "Send." ~~Derived from former Section 1–201. Compare "notifies".~~ The definition of "send" adopts pre-2022 Section 9–102(a)(75). The explicit statement in the previous text of this definition on the appropriateness of sending to an agreed-upon address or to an "address reasonable under the circumstances" was limited to "the case of an instrument." The definition no longer includes that limitation relating to an instrument. Moreover, it is common for parties to rely on their agreement as to appropriate addresses for purposes of notifications and communications. Nothing in the definition or in the Uniform Commercial Code limits the effectiveness of sending a record or notification to an address that has been agreed upon by affected persons. See generally Sections 1–103 and 1–302.

37.   "Signed." "Sign." ~~Derived from former Section 1–201. Former Section 1–201 referred to "intention to authenticate"; because other articles now use the term "authenticate," the language has been changed to "intention to adopt or accept." The latter formulation is derived from the definition of "authenticate" in Section 9–102(a)(7). This provision refers only to writings, because the term "signed," as used in some articles, refers only to writings.~~ The definition of "sign" adopted in the 2022 Amendments is broad—it encompasses the authentication or adoption of all records, not just writings. The definition replaces the definition of "signed" in pre-2022 texts of this Article. This ~~provision~~ definition also makes it clear that, as the ~~term~~ terms "sign," "signed," ~~is~~ and "signature" are used in the Uniform Commercial Code, a complete signature is not necessary. ~~The~~ A symbol may be printed, ~~stamped~~ stamped, or written on or electronically attached or associated with, a record.~~; it~~ It may be by initials or by thumbprint or by electronic symbol, sound, or process. It may be on any part of ~~the document~~ a writing or other record and in appropriate cases may be found in a billhead or letterhead. No catalog of possible situations can be complete and the court must use common sense and commercial experience in passing upon these matters. The question always is whether the symbol, sound, or process was executed or adopted by the party with present intention to authenticate or ~~adopt or accept~~ the ~~writing~~ record.

A "writing," which necessarily is in tangible form, must exist at the time it is signed and must be signed by the execution or adoption of a tangible symbol to qualify as a signed writing. A writing adopted only by use of an electronic symbol, sound, or process would not be a signed writing until and unless it results in a tangible symbol being on or affixed to the writing. Moreover, if an electronic record is electronically signed and subsequently printed in tangible form, the resulting writing would not constitute a signed writing unless and until some action is taken with "present intent to authenticate or adopt" the writing.

Concerning developments in technology, including, for example, contract formation in electronic environments, automated transactions, and electronic agents, see also Section 1–103, Comment 2.

38.   "State." This is the standard definition of the term used in acts prepared by the National Conference of Commissioners on Uniform State Laws.

39. "Surety." This definition makes it clear that "surety" includes all secondary obligors, not just those whose obligation refers to the person obligated as a surety. As to the nature of secondary obligations generally, see Restatement (Third), Suretyship and Guaranty Section 1 (1996).

40. "Term." Unchanged from former Section 1–201.

41. "Unauthorized signature." Unchanged from former Section 1–201.

42. "Warehouse receipt." Derived from former Section 1–201, which was derived from Section 76(1), Uniform Sales Act; Section 1, Uniform Warehouse Receipts Act. Receipts issued by a field warehouse are included, provided the warehouseman and the depositor of the goods are different persons. The definition makes clear that the receipt must qualify as a document of title under subsection (16).

43. "Written" or "writing." ~~Unchanged from former Section 1–201.~~ Several amendments to the Uniform Commercial Code over the years have replaced the terms "written" and "writing" with the term "record," defined in paragraph (31) and also in some other Articles. Pursuant to the 2022 Amendments, additional references to the terms "writing," "writings," and "written" have been replaced by "record." For example, the 2022 revisions to Articles 2 and 2A made these changes in provisions where an affected party may be assumed to have assented to the use of a record that is not a writing. Where references to those terms remain in Articles 2 and 2A, the use by parties of a record other than a writing may be given effect for purposes of those Articles under law other than the Uniform Commercial Code, such as the Electronic Signatures in Global and National Commerce Act, 15 U.S.C. Section 7001 *et seq.*, and the Uniform Electronic Transactions Act. See Sections 2–207, Comment 8; 2A–102, Comment (g).

As amended in 2003, 2005, 2021, and 2022.

§ 1–202.   Notice; Knowledge.

(a)   Subject to subsection (f), a person has "notice" of a fact if the person:

(1)   has actual knowledge of it;

(2)   has received a notice or notification of it; or

(3)   from all the facts and circumstances known to the person at the time in question, has reason to know that it exists.

(b)   "Knowledge" means actual knowledge. "Knows" has a corresponding meaning.

(c)   "Discover", "learn", or words of similar import refer to knowledge rather than to reason to know.

(d)   A person "notifies" or "gives" a notice or notification to another person by taking such steps as may be reasonably required to inform the other person in ordinary course, whether or not the other person actually comes to know of it.

(e)   Subject to subsection (f), a person "receives" a notice or notification when:

(1)   it comes to that person's attention; or

(2)   it is duly delivered in a form reasonable under the circumstances at the place of business through which the contract was made or at another location held out by that person as the place for receipt of such communications.

(f)   Notice, knowledge, or a notice or notification received by an organization is effective for a particular transaction from the time it is brought to the attention of the individual conducting that transaction and, in any event, from the time it would have been brought to the individual's attention if the organization had exercised due diligence. An organization exercises due diligence if it maintains reasonable routines for communicating significant information to the person conducting the transaction and there is reasonable compliance with the routines. Due diligence does not require an individual acting for the organization to communicate information unless the communication is part of the individual's regular duties or the individual has reason to know of the transaction and that the transaction would be materially affected by the information.

Official Comment

Source: Derived from former Section 1–201(25)–(27).

Changes from former law: These provisions are substantive rather than purely definitional. Accordingly, they have been relocated from Section 1–201 to this section. The reference to the "forgotten notice" doctrine has been deleted.

    1.   Under subsection (a), a person has notice of a fact when, *inter alia*, the person has received a notification of the fact in question.

    2.   As provided in subsection (d), the word "notifies" is used when the essential fact is the proper dispatch of the notice, not its receipt. Compare "Send." When the essential fact is the other party's receipt of the notice, that is stated. Subsection (e) states when a notification is received.

    3.   Subsection (f) makes clear that notice, knowledge, or a notification, although "received," for instance, by a clerk in Department A of an organization, is effective for a transaction conducted in Department B only from the time when it was or should have been communicated to the individual conducting that transaction.

§ 1–203.   Lease Distinguished From Security Interest.

    (a)   Whether a transaction in the form of a lease creates a lease or security interest is determined by the facts of each case.

    (b)   A transaction in the form of a lease creates a security interest if the consideration that the lessee is to pay the lessor for the right to possession and use of the goods is an obligation for the term of the lease and is not subject to termination by the lessee, and:

    (1)   the original term of the lease is equal to or greater than the remaining economic life of the goods;

    (2)   the lessee is bound to renew the lease for the remaining economic life of the goods or is bound to become the owner of the goods;

    (3)   the lessee has an option to renew the lease for the remaining economic life of the goods for no additional consideration or for nominal additional consideration upon compliance with the lease agreement; or

    (4)   the lessee has an option to become the owner of the goods for no additional consideration or for nominal additional consideration upon compliance with the lease agreement.

    (c)   A transaction in the form of a lease does not create a security interest merely because:

    (1)   the present value of the consideration the lessee is obligated to pay the lessor for the right to possession and use of the goods is substantially equal to or is greater than the fair market value of the goods at the time the lease is entered into;

    (2)   the lessee assumes risk of loss of the goods;

    (3)   the lessee agrees to pay, with respect to the goods, taxes, insurance, filing, recording, or registration fees, or service or maintenance costs;

    (4)   the lessee has an option to renew the lease or to become the owner of the goods;

    (5)   the lessee has an option to renew the lease for a fixed rent that is equal to or greater than the reasonably predictable fair market rent for the use of the goods for the term of the renewal at the time the option is to be performed; or

    (6)   the lessee has an option to become the owner of the goods for a fixed price that is equal to or greater than the reasonably predictable fair market value of the goods at the time the option is to be performed.

    (d)   Additional consideration is nominal if it is less than the lessee's reasonably predictable cost of performing under the lease agreement if the option is not exercised. Additional consideration is not nominal if:

    (1)   when the option to renew the lease is granted to the lessee, the rent is stated to be the fair market rent for the use of the goods for the term of the renewal determined at the time the option is to be performed; or

(2)   when the option to become the owner of the goods is granted to the lessee, the price is stated to be the fair market value of the goods determined at the time the option is to be performed.

(e)   The "remaining economic life of the goods" and "reasonably predictable" fair market rent, fair market value, or cost of performing under the lease agreement must be determined with reference to the facts and circumstances at the time the transaction is entered into.

Official Comment

Source: Former Section 1–201(37).

Changes from former law: This section is substantively identical to those portions of former Section 1–201(37) that distinguished "true" leases from security interests, except that the definition of "present value" formerly embedded in Section 1–201(37) has been placed in Section 1–201(28) [*unrevised Article 1; see Concordance, p. 22*].

1.   An interest in personal property or fixtures which secures payment or performance of an obligation is a "security interest." See Section 1–201(37) [*unrevised Article 1; see Concordance, p. 22*]. Security interests are sometimes created by transactions in the form of leases. Because it can be difficult to distinguish leases that create security interests from those that do not, this section provides rules that govern the determination of whether a transaction in the form of a lease creates a security interest.

2.   One of the reasons it was decided to codify the law with respect to leases was to resolve an issue that created considerable confusion in the courts: what is a lease? The confusion existed, in part, due to the last two sentences of the definition of security interest in the 1978 Official Text of the Act, Section 1–201(37). The confusion was compounded by the rather considerable change in the federal, state and local tax laws and accounting rules as they relate to leases of goods. The answer is important because the definition of lease determines not only the rights and remedies of the parties to the lease but also those of third parties. If a transaction creates a lease and not a security interest, the lessee's interest in the goods is limited to its leasehold estate; the residual interest in the goods belongs to the lessor. This has significant implications to the lessee's creditors. "On common law theory, the lessor, since he has not parted with title, is entitled to full protection against the lessee's creditors and trustee in bankruptcy. . . ." 1 G. Gilmore, *Security Interests in Personal Property* Section 3.6, at 76 (1965).

Under pre-UCC chattel security law there was generally no requirement that the lessor file the lease, a financing statement, or the like, to enforce the lease agreement against the lessee or any third party; the Article on Secured Transactions (Article 9) did not change the common law in that respect. Coogan, *Leasing and the Uniform Commercial Code*, in Equipment Leasing—Leveraged Leasing 681, 700 n.25, 729 n.80 (2d ed. 1980). The Article on Leases (Article 2A) did not change the law in that respect, except for leases of fixtures. Section 2A–309. An examination of the common law will not provide an adequate answer to the question of what is a lease. The definition of security interest in Section 1–201(37) of the 1978 Official Text of the Act provided that the Article on Secured Transactions (Article 9) governs security interests disguised as leases, *i.e.*, leases intended as security; however, the definition became vague and outmoded.

Lease is defined in Article 2A as a transfer of the right to possession and use of goods for a term, in return for consideration. Section 2A–103(1)(j). The definition continues by stating that the retention or creation of a security interest is not a lease. Thus, the task of sharpening the line between true leases and security interests disguised as leases continues to be a function of this Article.

This section begins where Section ~~1–201(35)~~ 1–201(b)(35) leaves off. It draws a sharper line between leases and security interests disguised as leases to create greater certainty in commercial transactions.

Prior to enactment of the rules now codified in this section, the 1978 Official Text of Section 1–201(37) provided that whether a lease was intended as security (*i.e.*, a security interest disguised as a lease) was to be determined from the facts of each case; however, (a) the inclusion of an option to purchase did not itself make the lease one intended for security, and (b) an agreement that upon compliance with the terms of the lease the lessee would become, or had the option to become, the owner of the property for no additional consideration, or for a nominal consideration, did make the lease one intended for security.

Reference to the intent of the parties to create a lease or security interest led to unfortunate results. In discovering intent, courts relied upon factors that were thought to be more consistent with sales or loans than leases. Most of these criteria, however, were as applicable to true leases as to security interests. Examples include the typical net lease provisions, a purported lessor's lack of storage facilities or its character as a financing party rather than a dealer in goods. Accordingly, this section contains no reference to the parties' intent.

Subsections (a) and (b) were originally taken from Section 1(2) of the Uniform Conditional Sales Act (act withdrawn 1943), modified to reflect current leasing practice. Thus, reference to the case law prior to the incorporation of those concepts in this article will provide a useful source of precedent. Gilmore, *Security Law, Formalism and Article 9*, 47 Neb.L.Rev. 659, 671 (1968). Whether a transaction creates a lease or a security interest continues to be determined by the facts of each case. Subsection (b) further provides that a transaction creates a security interest if the lessee has an obligation to continue paying consideration for the term of the lease, if the obligation is not terminable by the lessee (thus correcting early statutory gloss, *e.g.*, *In re Royer's Bakery, Inc.*, 1 U.C.C. Rep.Serv. (Callaghan) 342 (Bankr.E.D.Pa. 1963)) and if one of four additional tests is met. The first of these four tests, subparagraph (1), is that the original lease term is equal to or greater than the remaining economic life of the goods. The second of these tests, subparagraph (2), is that the lessee is either bound to renew the lease for the remaining economic life of the goods or to become the owner of the goods. *In re Gehrke Enters.*, 1 Bankr. 647, 651–52 (Bankr.W.D.Wis. 1979). The third of these tests, subparagraph (3), is whether the lessee has an option to renew the lease for the remaining economic life of the goods for no additional consideration or for nominal additional consideration, which is defined later in this section. *In re Celeryvale Transp.*, 44 Bankr. 1007, 1014–15 (Bankr.E.D.Tenn. 1984). The fourth of these tests, subparagraph (4), is whether the lessee has an option to become the owner of the goods for no additional consideration or for nominal additional consideration. All of these tests focus on economics, not the intent of the parties. *In re Berge*, 32 Bankr. 370, 371–73 (Bankr.W.D.Wis. 1983).

The focus on economics is reinforced by subsection (c). It states that a transaction does not create a security interest merely because the transaction has certain characteristics listed therein. Subparagraph (1) has no statutory derivative; it states that a full payout lease does not *per se* create a security interest. *Rushton v. Shea*, 419 F.Supp. 1349, 1365 (D.Del. 1976). Subparagraphs (2) and (3) provide the same regarding the provisions of the typical net lease. *Compare All-States Leasing Co. v. Ochs*, 42 Or.App. 319, 600 P.2d 899 (Ct.App. 1979), *with In re Tillery*, 571 F.2d 1361 (5th Cir. 1978). Subparagraph (4) restates and expands the provisions of the 1978 Official Text of Section 1–201(37) to make clear that the option can be to buy or renew. Subparagraphs (5) and (6) treat fixed price options and provide that fair market value must be determined at the time the transaction is entered into. *Compare Arnold Mach. Co. v. Balls*, 624 P.2d 678 (Utah 1981), *with Aoki v. Shepherd Mach. Co.*, 665 F.2d 941 (9th Cir. 1982).

The relationship of subsection (b) to subsection (c) deserves to be explored. The fixed price purchase option provides a useful example. A fixed price purchase option in a lease does not of itself create a security interest. This is particularly true if the fixed price is equal to or greater than the reasonably predictable fair market value of the goods at the time the option is to be performed. A security interest is created only if the option price is nominal and the conditions stated in the introduction to the second paragraph of this subsection are met. There is a set of purchase options whose fixed price is less than fair market value but greater than nominal that must be determined on the facts of each case to ascertain whether the transaction in which the option is included creates a lease or a security interest.

It was possible to provide for various other permutations and combinations with respect to options to purchase and renew. For example, this section could have stated a rule to govern the facts of *In re Marhoefer Packing Co.*, 674 F.2d 1139 (7th Cir. 1982). This was not done because it would unnecessarily complicate the definition. Further development of this rule is left to the courts.

Subsections (d) and (e) provide definitions and rules of construction.

As amended in 2022.

§ 1–204.   Value.

Except as otherwise provided in Articles 3, 4, [and] 5, [and 6], [6,] and 12, a person gives value for rights if the person acquires them:

(1)   in return for a binding commitment to extend credit or for the extension of immediately available credit, whether or not drawn upon and whether or not a charge-back is provided for in the event of difficulties in collection;

(2)   as security for, or in total or partial satisfaction of, a preexisting claim;

(3)   by accepting delivery under a preexisting contract for purchase; or

(4)   in return for any consideration sufficient to support a simple contract.

As amended in 2022.

Official Comment

Source: Former Section 1–201(44).

Changes from former law: Unchanged from former Section 1–201, which was derived from Sections 25, 26, 27, 191, Uniform Negotiable Instruments Law; Section 76, Uniform Sales Act; Section 53, Uniform Bills of Lading Act; Section 58, Uniform Warehouse Receipts Act; Section 22(1), Uniform Stock Transfer Act; Section 1, Uniform Trust Receipts Act. These provisions are substantive rather than purely definitional. Accordingly, they have been relocated from former Section 1–201 to this section.

1. ~~All the~~ Historically, most Uniform Acts in the commercial law field ~~(except the Uniform Conditional Sales Act)~~ have carried definitions of "value." ~~All those~~ Those definitions provided that value was any consideration sufficient to support a simple contract, including the taking of property in satisfaction of or as security for a pre-existing claim. Subsections (1), (2), and (4) in substance continue the definitions of "value" in the earlier acts. Subsection (3) makes explicit that "value" is also given in a third situation: where a buyer by taking delivery under a pre-existing contract converts a contingent into a fixed obligation.

This definition is not applicable to Articles 3 and 4, but the express inclusion of immediately available credit as value follows the separate definitions in those Articles. See Sections 4–208, 4–209, 3–303. A bank or other financing agency which in good faith makes advances against property held as collateral becomes a bona fide purchaser of that property even though provision may be made for charge-back in case of trouble. Checking credit is "immediately available" within the meaning of this section if the bank would be subject to an action for slander of credit in case checks drawn against the credit were dishonored, and when a charge-back is not discretionary with the bank, but may only be made when difficulties in collection arise in connection with the specific transaction involved. Article 12 adopts the substance of the Article 3 definition. See Section 12–102(a)(4).

As amended in 2022.

§ 1–205.   Reasonable Time; Seasonableness.

(a)   Whether a time for taking an action required by [the Uniform Commercial Code] is reasonable depends on the nature, purpose, and circumstances of the action.

(b)   An action is taken seasonably if it is taken at or within the time agreed or, if no time is agreed, at or within a reasonable time.

Official Comment

Source: Former Section 1–204(2)–(3).

Changes from former law: This section is derived from subsections (2) and (3) of former Section 1–204. Subsection (1) of that section is now incorporated in Section 1–302(b).

1.   Subsection (a) makes it clear that requirements that actions be taken within a "reasonable" time are to be applied in the transactional context of the particular action.

2.   Under subsection (b), the agreement that fixes the time need not be part of the main agreement, but may occur separately. Notice also that under the definition of "agreement" (Section 1–201) the circumstances of the transaction, including course of dealing or usages of trade or course of performance may be material. On the question what is a reasonable time these matters will often be important.

§ 1–206.   Presumptions.

Whenever [the Uniform Commercial Code] creates a "presumption" with respect to a fact, or provides that a fact is "presumed," the trier of fact must find the existence of the fact unless and until evidence is introduced that supports a finding of its nonexistence.

Legislative Note: Former Section 1–206, a Statute of Frauds for sales of "kinds of personal property not otherwise covered," has been deleted. The other articles of the Uniform Commercial Code make individual determinations as to requirements for memorializing transactions within their scope, so that the primary effect of former Section 1–206 was to impose a writing requirement on sales transactions not otherwise governed by the UCC. Deletion of former Section 1–206 does not constitute a recommendation to legislatures as to whether such sales transactions should be covered by a Statute of Frauds; rather, it reflects a determination that there is no need for uniform commercial law to resolve that issue.

Official Comment

Source: Former Section 1–201(31).

Changes from former law. None, other than stylistic changes.

1.   Several sections of the Uniform Commercial Code state that there is a "presumption" as to a certain fact, or that the fact is "presumed." This section, derived from the definition appearing in former Section 1–201(31), indicates the effect of those provisions on the proof process.

PART 3

TERRITORIAL APPLICABILITY AND GENERAL RULES

§ 1–301.   Territorial Applicability; Parties' Power to Choose Applicable Law.

(a)   Except as otherwise provided in this section, when a transaction bears a reasonable relation to this state and also to another state or nation the parties may agree that the law either of this state or of such other state or nation shall govern their rights and duties.

(b)   In the absence of an agreement effective under subsection (a), and except as provided in subsection (c), [the Uniform Commercial Code] applies to transactions bearing an appropriate relation to this state.

(c)   If one of the following provisions of [the Uniform Commercial Code] specifies the applicable law, that provision governs and a contrary agreement is effective only to the extent permitted by the law so specified:

(1)   Section 2–402;

(2)   Sections 2A–105 and 2A–106;

(3)   Section 4–102;

(4)   Section 4A–507;

(5)   Section 5–116;

[(6)   Section 6–103;]

(7)   Section 8–110;

(8)   Sections 9–301 through 9–307.

(9)   Section 12–107.

As amended in 2008 and 2022.

Official Comment

Source: Former Section 1–105.

Changes from former law: This section is substantively identical to former Section 1–105. Changes in language are stylistic only.

1.   Subsection (a) states affirmatively the right of the parties to a multi-state transaction or a transaction involving foreign trade to choose their own law. That right is subject to the firm rules stated in the sections listed in subsection (c), and is limited to jurisdictions to which the transaction bears a "reasonable relation." In general, the test of "reasonable relation" is similar to that laid down by the Supreme Court in *Seeman v. Philadelphia Warehouse Co.*, 274 U.S. 403, 47 S.Ct. 626, 71 L.Ed. 1123 (1927). Ordinarily the law chosen must be that of a jurisdiction where a significant enough portion of the making or performance of the contract is to occur or occurs. But an agreement as to choice of law may sometimes take effect as a shorthand expression of the intent of the parties as to matters governed by their agreement, even though the transaction has no significant contact with the jurisdiction chosen.

2.   Where there is no agreement as to the governing law, the Act is applicable to any transaction having an "appropriate" relation to any state which enacts it. Of course, the Act applies to any transaction which takes place in its entirety in a state which has enacted the Act. But the mere fact that suit is brought in a state does not

make it appropriate to apply the substantive law of that state. Cases where a relation to the enacting state is not "appropriate" include, for example, those where the parties have clearly contracted on the basis of some other law, as where the law of the place of contracting and the law of the place of contemplated performance are the same and are contrary to the law under the Code.

3. Where a transaction has significant contacts with a state which has enacted the Act and also with other jurisdictions, the question what relation is "appropriate" is left to judicial decision. In deciding that question, the court is not strictly bound by precedents established in other contexts. Thus a conflict-of-laws decision refusing to apply a purely local statute or rule of law to a particular multi-state transaction may not be valid precedent for refusal to apply the Code in an analogous situation. Application of the Code in such circumstances may be justified by its comprehensiveness, by the policy of uniformity, and by the fact that it is in large part a reformulation and restatement of the law merchant and of the understanding of a business community which transcends state and even national boundaries. *Compare Global Commerce Corp. v. Clark-Babbitt Industries, Inc.*, 239 F.2d 716, 719 (2d Cir. 1956). In particular, where a transaction is governed in large part by the Code, application of another law to some detail of performance because of an accident of geography may violate the commercial understanding of the parties.

4. Subsection (c) spells out essential limitations on the parties' right to choose the applicable law. Especially in Article 9 parties taking a security interest or asked to extend credit which may be subject to a security interest must have sure ways to find out whether and where to file and where to look for possible existing filings.

5. Sections 9–301 through 9–307 should be consulted as to the rules for perfection of security interests and agricultural liens and the effect of perfection and nonperfection and priority. In transactions to which the Hague Securities Convention applies, the requirements for foreclosure and the like, the characterization of a transfer as being outright or by way of security, and certain other issues will generally be governed by the law specified in the account agreement. See PEB Commentary No. 19, dated April 11, 2017.

6. This section is subject to Section 1–102, which states the scope of Article 1. As that section indicates, the rules of Article 1, including this section, apply to a transaction to the extent that transaction is governed by one of the other Articles of the Uniform Commercial Code.

As amended in 2008, 2017, and 2022.

§ 1–302. Variation by Agreement.

(a) Except as otherwise provided in subsection (b) or elsewhere in [the Uniform Commercial Code], the effect of provisions of [the Uniform Commercial Code] may be varied by agreement.

(b) The obligations of good faith, diligence, reasonableness, and care prescribed by [the Uniform Commercial Code] may not be disclaimed by agreement. The parties, by agreement, may determine the standards by which the performance of those obligations is to be measured if those standards are not manifestly unreasonable. Whenever [the Uniform Commercial Code] requires an action to be taken within a reasonable time, a time that is not manifestly unreasonable may be fixed by agreement.

(c) The presence in certain provisions of [the Uniform Commercial Code] of the phrase "unless otherwise agreed", or words of similar import, does not imply that the effect of other provisions may not be varied by agreement under this section.

Official Comment

Source: Former Sections 1–102(3)–(4) and 1–204(1).

Changes: This section combines the rules from subsections (3) and (4) of former Section 1–102 and subsection (1) of former Section 1–204. No substantive changes are made.

1. Subsection (a) states affirmatively at the outset that freedom of contract is a principle of the Uniform Commercial Code: "the effect" of its provisions may be varied by "agreement." The meaning of the statute itself must be found in its text, including its definitions, and in appropriate extrinsic aids; it cannot be varied by agreement. But the Uniform Commercial Code seeks to avoid the type of interference with evolutionary growth found in pre-Code cases such as *Manhattan Co. v. Morgan*, 242 N.Y. 38, 150 N.E. 594 (1926). Thus, private parties cannot make an instrument negotiable within the meaning of Article 3 except as provided in Section 3–104; nor can they change the meaning of such terms as "bona fide purchaser," "holder in due course," or "due negotiation," as used in the Uniform Commercial Code. But an agreement can change the legal consequences that would otherwise flow from the provisions of the Uniform Commercial Code. "Agreement" here includes the effect given

to course of dealing, usage of trade and course of performance by Sections 1–201 and 1–303; the effect of an agreement on the rights of third parties is left to specific provisions of the Uniform Commercial Code and to supplementary principles applicable under Section 1–103. The rights of third parties under Section 9–317 when a security interest is unperfected, for example, cannot be destroyed by a clause in the security agreement.

This principle of freedom of contract is subject to specific exceptions found elsewhere in the Uniform Commercial Code and to the general exception stated here. The specific exceptions vary in explicitness: the statute of frauds found in Section 2–201, for example, does not explicitly preclude oral waiver of the requirement of a writing, but a fair reading denies enforcement to such a waiver as part of the "contract" made unenforceable; Section 9–602, on the other hand, is a quite explicit limitation on freedom of contract. Under the exception for "the obligations of good faith, diligence, reasonableness and care prescribed by [the Uniform Commercial Code]," provisions of the Uniform Commercial Code prescribing such obligations are not to be disclaimed. However, the section also recognizes the prevailing practice of having agreements set forth standards by which due diligence is measured and explicitly provides that, in the absence of a showing that the standards manifestly are unreasonable, the agreement controls. In this connection, Section 1–303 incorporating into the agreement prior course of dealing and usages of trade is of particular importance.

Subsection (b) also recognizes that nothing is stronger evidence of a reasonable time than the fixing of such time by a fair agreement between the parties. However, provision is made for disregarding a clause which whether by inadvertence or overreaching fixes a time so unreasonable that it amounts to eliminating all remedy under the contract. The parties are not required to fix the most reasonable time but may fix any time which is not obviously unfair as judged by the time of contracting.

2.　　An agreement that varies the effect of provisions of the Uniform Commercial Code may do so by stating the rules that will govern in lieu of the provisions varied. Alternatively, the parties may vary the effect of such provisions by stating that their relationship will be governed by recognized bodies of rules or principles applicable to commercial transactions. Such bodies of rules or principles may include, for example, those that are promulgated by intergovernmental authorities such as UNCITRAL or UNIDROIT (*see, e.g.*, UNIDROIT Principles of International Commercial Contracts), or non-legal codes such as trade codes.

3.　　Subsection (c) is intended to make it clear that, as a matter of drafting, phrases such as "unless otherwise agreed" have been used to avoid controversy as to whether the subject matter of a particular section does or does not fall within the exceptions to subsection (b), but absence of such words contains no negative implication since under subsection (b) the general and residual rule is that the effect of all provisions of the Uniform Commercial Code may be varied by agreement.

§ 1–303.　　Course of Performance, Course of Dealing, and Usage of Trade.

(a)　A "course of performance" is a sequence of conduct between the parties to a particular transaction that exists if:

(1)　the agreement of the parties with respect to the transaction involves repeated occasions for performance by a party; and

(2)　the other party, with knowledge of the nature of the performance and opportunity for objection to it, accepts the performance or acquiesces in it without objection.

(b)　A "course of dealing" is a sequence of conduct concerning previous transactions between the parties to a particular transaction that is fairly to be regarded as establishing a common basis of understanding for interpreting their expressions and other conduct.

(c)　A "usage of trade" is any practice or method of dealing having such regularity of observance in a place, vocation, or trade as to justify an expectation that it will be observed with respect to the transaction in question. The existence and scope of such a usage must be proved as facts. If it is established that such a usage is embodied in a trade code or similar record, the interpretation of the record is a question of law.

(d)　A course of performance or course of dealing between the parties or usage of trade in the vocation or trade in which they are engaged or of which they are or should be aware is relevant in ascertaining the meaning of the parties' agreement, may give particular meaning to specific terms of the agreement, and may supplement or qualify the terms of the agreement. A usage of trade applicable in the place in which part of the performance under the agreement is to occur may be so utilized as to that part of the performance.

(e)   Except as otherwise provided in subsection (f), the express terms of an agreement and any applicable course of performance, course of dealing, or usage of trade must be construed whenever reasonable as consistent with each other. If such a construction is unreasonable:

(1)   express terms prevail over course of performance, course of dealing, and usage of trade;

(2)   course of performance prevails over course of dealing and usage of trade; and

(3)   course of dealing prevails over usage of trade.

(f)   Subject to Section 2–209, a course of performance is relevant to show a waiver or modification of any term inconsistent with the course of performance.

(g)   Evidence of a relevant usage of trade offered by one party is not admissible unless that party has given the other party notice that the court finds sufficient to prevent unfair surprise to the other party.

Official Comment

Source: Former Sections 1–205, 2–208, and Section 2A–207.

Changes from former law: This section integrates the "course of performance" concept from Articles 2 and 2A into the principles of former Section 1–205, which deals with course of dealing and usage of trade. In so doing, the section slightly modifies the articulation of the course of performance rules to fit more comfortably with the approach and structure of former Section 1–205. There are also slight modifications to be more consistent with the definition of "agreement" in former Section 1–201(3). It should be noted that a course of performance that might otherwise establish a defense to the obligation of a party to a negotiable instrument is not available as a defense against a holder in due course who took the instrument without notice of that course of performance.

1.   The Uniform Commercial Code rejects both the "lay-dictionary" and the "conveyancer's" reading of a commercial agreement. Instead the meaning of the agreement of the parties is to be determined by the language used by them and by their action, read and interpreted in the light of commercial practices and other surrounding circumstances. The measure and background for interpretation are set by the commercial context, which may explain and supplement even the language of a formal or final writing.

2.   "Course of dealing," as defined in subsection (b), is restricted, literally, to a sequence of conduct between the parties previous to the agreement. A sequence of conduct after or under the agreement, however, is a "course of performance." "Course of dealing" may enter the agreement either by explicit provisions of the agreement or by tacit recognition.

3.   The Uniform Commercial Code deals with "usage of trade" as a factor in reaching the commercial meaning of the agreement that the parties have made. The language used is to be interpreted as meaning what it may fairly be expected to mean to parties involved in the particular commercial transaction in a given locality or in a given vocation or trade. By adopting in this context the term "usage of trade," the Uniform Commercial Code expresses its intent to reject those cases which see evidence of "custom" as representing an effort to displace or negate "established rules of law." A distinction is to be drawn between mandatory rules of law such as the Statute of Frauds provisions of Article 2 on Sales whose very office is to control and restrict the actions of the parties, and which cannot be abrogated by agreement, or by a usage of trade, and those rules of law (such as those in Part 3 of Article 2 on Sales) which fill in points which the parties have not considered and in fact agreed upon. The latter rules hold "unless otherwise agreed" but yield to the contrary agreement of the parties. Part of the agreement of the parties to which such rules yield is to be sought for in the usages of trade which furnish the background and give particular meaning to the language used, and are the framework of common understanding controlling any general rules of law which hold only when there is no such understanding.

4.   A usage of trade under subsection (c) must have the "regularity of observance" specified. The ancient English tests for "custom" are abandoned in this connection. Therefore, it is not required that a usage of trade be "ancient or immemorial," "universal," or the like. Under the requirement of subsection (c) full recognition is thus available for new usages and for usages currently observed by the great majority of decent dealers, even though dissidents ready to cut corners do not agree. There is room also for proper recognition of usage agreed upon by merchants in trade codes.

5.   The policies of the Uniform Commercial Code controlling explicit unconscionable contracts and clauses (Sections 1–304, 2–302) apply to implicit clauses that rest on usage of trade and carry forward the policy underlying the ancient requirement that a custom or usage must be "reasonable." However, the emphasis is shifted. The very fact of commercial acceptance makes out a *prima facie* case that the usage is reasonable, and the burden is no longer on the usage to establish itself as being reasonable. But the anciently established policing of

usage by the courts is continued to the extent necessary to cope with the situation arising if an unconscionable or dishonest practice should become standard.

6.   Subsection (d), giving the prescribed effect to usages of which the parties "are or should be aware," reinforces the provision of subsection (c) requiring not universality but only the described "regularity of observance" of the practice or method. This subsection also reinforces the point of subsection (c) that such usages may be either general to trade or particular to a special branch of trade.

7.   Although the definition of "agreement" in Section 1–201 includes the elements of course of performance, course of dealing, and usage of trade, the fact that express reference is made in some sections to those elements is not to be construed as carrying a contrary intent or implication elsewhere. Compare Section 1–302(c).

8.   In cases of a well established line of usage varying from the general rules of the Uniform Commercial Code where the precise amount of the variation has not been worked out into a single standard, the party relying on the usage is entitled, in any event, to the minimum variation demonstrated. The whole is not to be disregarded because no particular line of detail has been established. In case a dominant pattern has been fairly evidenced, the party relying on the usage is entitled under this section to go to the trier of fact on the question of whether such dominant pattern has been incorporated into the agreement.

9.   Subsection (g) is intended to insure that this Act's liberal recognition of the needs of commerce in regard to usage of trade shall not be made into an instrument of abuse.

§ 1–304.   Obligation of Good Faith.

Every contract or duty within [the Uniform Commercial Code] imposes an obligation of good faith in its performance and enforcement.

Official Comment

Source: Former Section 1–203.

Changes from former law: Except for changing the form of reference to the Uniform Commercial Code, this section is identical to former Section 1–203.

1.   This section sets forth a basic principle running throughout the Uniform Commercial Code. The principle is that in commercial transactions good faith is required in the performance and enforcement of all agreements or duties. While this duty is explicitly stated in some provisions of the Uniform Commercial Code, the applicability of the duty is broader than merely these situations and applies generally, as stated in this section, to the performance or enforcement of every contract or duty within this Act. It is further implemented by Section 1–303 on course of dealing, course of performance, and usage of trade. This section does not support an independent cause of action for failure to perform or enforce in good faith. Rather, this section means that a failure to perform or enforce, in good faith, a specific duty or obligation under the contract, constitutes a breach of that contract or makes unavailable, under the particular circumstances, a remedial right or power. This distinction makes it clear that the doctrine of good faith merely directs a court towards interpreting contracts within the commercial context in which they are created, performed, and enforced, and does not create a separate duty of fairness and reasonableness which can be independently breached.

2.   "Performance and enforcement" of contracts and duties within the Uniform Commercial Code include the exercise of rights created by the Uniform Commercial Code.

§ 1–305.   Remedies to Be Liberally Administered.

(a)   The remedies provided by [the Uniform Commercial Code] must be liberally administered to the end that the aggrieved party may be put in as good a position as if the other party had fully performed but neither consequential or special damages nor penal damages may be had except as specifically provided in [the Uniform Commercial Code] or by other rule of law.

(b)   Any right or obligation declared by [the Uniform Commercial Code] is enforceable by action unless the provision declaring it specifies a different and limited effect.

Official Comment

Source: Former Section 1–106.

Changes from former law: Other than changes in the form of reference to the Uniform Commercial Code, this section is identical to former Section 1–106.

1.   Subsection (a) is intended to effect three propositions. The first is to negate the possibility of unduly narrow or technical interpretation of remedial provisions by providing that the remedies in the Uniform Commercial Code are to be liberally administered to the end stated in this section. The second is to make it clear that compensatory damages are limited to compensation. They do not include consequential or special damages, or penal damages; and the Uniform Commercial Code elsewhere makes it clear that damages must be minimized. Cf. Sections 1–304, 2–706(1), and 2–712(2). The third purpose of subsection (a) is to reject any doctrine that damages must be calculable with mathematical accuracy. Compensatory damages are often at best approximate: they have to be proved with whatever definiteness and accuracy the facts permit, but no more. Cf. Section 2–204(3).

2.   Under subsection (b), any right or obligation described in the Uniform Commercial Code is enforceable by action, even though no remedy may be expressly provided other than in this section, unless a particular provision specifies a different and limited effect. Whether specific performance or other equitable relief is available in a particular case is determined not by this section but by specific provisions and by supplementary principles. Cf. Sections 1–103, 2–716.

3.   "Consequential" or "special" damages and "penal" damages are not defined in the Uniform Commercial Code; rather, these terms are used in the sense in which they are used outside the Uniform Commercial Code.

As amended in 2022.

§ 1–306.   Waiver or Renunciation of Claim or Right After Breach.

A claim or right arising out of an alleged breach may be discharged in whole or in part without consideration by agreement of the aggrieved party in ~~an authenticated~~ a signed record.

As amended in 2022.

Official Comment

Source: Former Section 1–107.

Changes from former law: ~~This section changes former law in two respects. First, former~~ Former Section 1–107, requiring the "delivery" of a "written waiver or renunciation" ~~merges~~ merged the separate concepts of the aggrieved party's agreement to forego rights and the manifestation of that agreement. This section separates those concepts, and explicitly requires *agreement* of the aggrieved party. ~~Second, the revised section reflects developments in electronic commerce by providing for memorialization in an authenticated record. In this context, a party may "authenticate" a record by (i) signing a record that is a writing or (ii) attaching to or logically associating with a record that is not a writing an electronic sound, symbol or process with the present intent to adopt or accept the record. See Sections 1–201(b)(37) and 9–102(a)(7).~~

1.   This section makes consideration unnecessary to the effective renunciation or waiver of rights or claims arising out of an alleged breach of a ~~commercial~~ contract where the agreement effecting such renunciation is memorialized in a record ~~authenticated~~ signed by the aggrieved party. Its provisions, however, must be read in conjunction with the section imposing an obligation of good faith. (Section 1–304).

2.   Consistent with the revised definition of "sign" in Section 1–201, the cognate term "signed" replaces the reference to "authenticated" in the pre-2022 text of this section.

As amended in 2022.

§ 1–307.   Prima Facie Evidence by Third-Party Documents.

A document in due form purporting to be a bill of lading, policy or certificate of insurance, official weigher's or inspector's certificate, consular invoice, or any other document authorized or required by the contract to be issued by a third party is prima facie evidence of its own authenticity and genuineness and of the facts stated in the document by the third party.

Official Comment

Source: Former Section 1–202.

Changes from former law: Except for minor stylistic changes, this Section is identical to former Section 1–202.

1.   This section supplies judicial recognition for documents that are relied upon as trustworthy by commercial parties.

2.   This section is concerned only with documents that have been given a preferred status by the parties themselves who have required their procurement in the agreement, and for this reason the applicability of the section is limited to actions arising out of the contract that authorized or required the document. The list of documents is intended to be illustrative and not exclusive.

3.   The provisions of this section go no further than establishing the documents in question as prima facie evidence and leave to the court the ultimate determination of the facts where the accuracy or authenticity of the documents is questioned. In this connection the section calls for a commercially reasonable interpretation.

4.   Documents governed by this section need not be writings if records in another medium are generally relied upon in the context.

§ 1–308.   Performance or Acceptance Under Reservation of Rights.

(a)   A party that with explicit reservation of rights performs or promises performance or assents to performance in a manner demanded or offered by the other party does not thereby prejudice the rights reserved. Such words as "without prejudice," "under protest," or the like are sufficient.

(b)   Subsection (a) does not apply to an accord and satisfaction.

Official Comment

Source: Former Section 1–207.

Changes from former law: This section is identical to former Section 1–207.

1.   This section provides machinery for the continuation of performance along the lines contemplated by the contract despite a pending dispute, by adopting the mercantile device of going ahead with delivery, acceptance, or payment "without prejudice," "under protest," "under reserve," "with reservation of all our rights," and the like. All of these phrases completely reserve all rights within the meaning of this section. The section therefore contemplates that limited as well as general reservations and acceptance by a party may be made "subject to satisfaction of our purchaser," "subject to acceptance by our customers," or the like.

2.   This section does not add any new requirement of language of reservation where not already required by law, but merely provides a specific measure on which a party can rely as that party makes or concurs in any interim adjustment in the course of performance. It does not affect or impair the provisions of this Act such as those under which the buyer's remedies for defect survive acceptance without being expressly claimed if notice of the defects is given within a reasonable time. Nor does it disturb the policy of those cases which restrict the effect of a waiver of a defect to reasonable limits under the circumstances, even though no such reservation is expressed.

The section is not addressed to the creation or loss of remedies in the ordinary course of performance but rather to a method of procedure where one party is claiming as of right something which the other believes to be unwarranted.

3.   Subsection (b) states that this section does not apply to an accord and satisfaction. Section 3–311 governs if an accord and satisfaction is attempted by tender of a negotiable instrument as stated in that section. If Section 3–311 does not apply, the issue of whether an accord and satisfaction has been effected is determined by the law of contract. Whether or not Section 3–311 applies, this section has no application to an accord and satisfaction.

§ 1–309.   Option to Accelerate at Will.

A term providing that one party or that party's successor in interest may accelerate payment or performance or require collateral or additional collateral "at will" or when the party "deems itself insecure," or words of similar import, means that the party has power to do so only if that party in good faith believes that the prospect of payment or performance is impaired. The burden of establishing lack of good faith is on the party against which the power has been exercised.

Official Comment

Source: Former Section 1–208.

Changes from former law: Except for minor stylistic changes, this section is identical to former Section 1–208.

1.   The common use of acceleration clauses in many transactions governed by the Uniform Commercial Code, including sales of goods on credit, notes payable at a definite time, and secured transactions, raises an issue as to the effect to be given to a clause that seemingly grants the power to accelerate at the whim and caprice of one party. This section is intended to make clear that despite language that might be so construed and which further might be held to make the agreement void as against public policy or to make the contract illusory or too indefinite for enforcement, the option is to be exercised only in the good faith belief that the prospect of payment or performance is impaired.

Obviously this section has no application to demand instruments or obligations whose very nature permits call at any time with or without reason. This section applies only to an obligation of payment or performance which in the first instance is due at a future date.

§ 1–310.   Subordinated Obligations.

An obligation may be issued as subordinated to performance of another obligation of the person obligated, or a creditor may subordinate its right to performance of an obligation by agreement with either the person obligated or another creditor of the person obligated. Subordination does not create a security interest as against either the common debtor or a subordinated creditor.

Official Comment

Source: Former Section 1–209.

Changes from former law: This section is substantively identical to former Section 1–209. The language in that section stating that it "shall be construed as declaring the law as it existed prior to the enactment of this section and not as modifying it" has been deleted.

1.   Billions of dollars of subordinated debt are held by the public and by institutional investors. Commonly, the subordinated debt is subordinated on issue or acquisition and is evidenced by an investment security or by a negotiable or non-negotiable note. Debt is also sometimes subordinated after it arises, either by agreement between the subordinating creditor and the debtor, by agreement between two creditors of the same debtor, or by agreement of all three parties. The subordinated creditor may be a stockholder or other "insider" interested in the common debtor; the subordinated debt may consist of accounts or other rights to payment not evidenced by any instrument. All such cases are included in the terms "subordinated obligation," "subordination," and "subordinated creditor."

2.   Subordination agreements are enforceable between the parties as contracts; and in the bankruptcy of the common debtor dividends otherwise payable to the subordinated creditor are turned over to the superior creditor. This "turn-over" practice has on occasion been explained in terms of "equitable lien," "equitable assignment," or "constructive trust," but whatever the label the practice is essentially an equitable remedy and does not mean that there is a transaction "that creates a security interest in personal property . . . by contract" or a "sale of accounts, chattel paper, payment intangibles, or promissory notes" within the meaning of Section 9–109. On the other hand, nothing in this section prevents one creditor from assigning his rights to another creditor of the same debtor in such a way as to create a security interest within Article 9, where the parties so intend.

3.   The enforcement of subordination agreements is largely left to supplementary principles under Section 1–103. If the subordinated debt is evidenced by a certificated security, Section 8–202(a) authorizes enforcement against purchasers on terms stated or referred to on the security certificate. If the fact of subordination is noted on a negotiable instrument, a holder under Sections 3–302 and 3–306 is subject to the term because notice precludes him from taking free of the subordination. Sections 3–302(3)(a) [*unrevised Article 3 (Appendix A)*], 3–306, and 8–317 [*unrevised Article 8*] severely limit the rights of levying creditors of a subordinated creditor in such cases.

UCC ARTICLE 2

SALES

Article 2 was amended in 1966, 1972, 1988, 1990, 1994, 1995, 1999, 2000, 2003, 2019, and 2022.

2022 Amendments appear in ~~strikeout~~/<u>underline</u> format.

Prefatory Note to 2022 amendments appears in Appendix E.

Current through April 2023

For updates, see www.uniformlaws.org

PART 1. SHORT TITLE, GENERAL CONSTRUCTION AND SUBJECT MATTER

2–101. Short Title.
2–102. Scope; Certain Security and Other Transactions Excluded from this Article.
2–103. Definitions and Index of Definitions.
2–104. Definitions: "Merchant"; "Between Merchants"; "Financing Agency".
2–105. Definitions: Transferability; "Goods"; "Future" Goods; "Lot"; "Commercial Unit".
2–106. Definitions: "Contract"; "Agreement"; "Contract for Sale"; "Sale"; "Present Sale"; "Conforming" to Contract; "Termination"; "Cancellation"; <u>"Hybrid Transaction"</u>.
2–107. Goods to Be Severed from Realty: Recording.

PART 2. FORM, FORMATION AND READJUSTMENT OF CONTRACT

2–201. Formal Requirements; Statute of Frauds.
2–202. Final ~~Written~~ Expression: Parol or Extrinsic Evidence.
2–203. Seals Inoperative.
2–204. Formation in General.
2–205. Firm Offers.
2–206. Offer and Acceptance in Formation of Contract.
2–207. Additional Terms in Acceptance or Confirmation.
2–208. [Reserved.] [Course of Performance or Practical Construction.]
2–209. Modification, Rescission and Waiver.
2–210. Delegation of Performance; Assignment of Rights.

PART 3. GENERAL OBLIGATION AND CONSTRUCTION OF CONTRACT

2–301. General Obligations of Parties.
2–302. Unconscionable Contract or Clause.
2–303. Allocation or Division of Risks.
2–304. Price Payable in Money, Goods, Realty, or Otherwise.
2–305. Open Price Term.
2–306. Output, Requirements and Exclusive Dealings.
2–307. Delivery in Single Lot or Several Lots.
2–308. Absence of Specified Place for Delivery.
2–309. Absence of Specific Time Provisions; Notice of Termination.
2–310. Open Time for Payment or Running of Credit; Authority to Ship Under Reservation.
2–311. Options and Cooperation Respecting Performance.

2–312.   Warranty of Title and Against Infringement; Buyer's Obligation Against Infringement.
2–313.   Express Warranties by Affirmation, Promise, Description, Sample.
2–314.   Implied Warranty: Merchantability; Usage of Trade.
2–315.   Implied Warranty: Fitness for Particular Purpose.
2–316.   Exclusion or Modification of Warranties.
2–317.   Cumulation and Conflict of Warranties Express or Implied.
2–318.   Third Party Beneficiaries of Warranties Express or Implied.
2–319.   F.O.B. and F.A.S. Terms.
2–320.   C.I.F. and C. & F. Terms.
2–321.   C.I.F. or C. & F.: "Net Landed Weights"; "Payment on Arrival"; Warranty of Condition on Arrival.
2–322.   Delivery "Ex-Ship".
2–323.   Form of Bill of Lading Required in Overseas Shipment; "Overseas".
2–324.   "No Arrival, No Sale" Term.
2–325.   "Letter of Credit" Term; "Confirmed Credit".
2–326.   Sale on Approval and Sale or Return; Rights of Creditors.
2–327.   Special Incidents of Sale on Approval and Sale or Return.
2–328.   Sale by Auction.

PART 4.   TITLE, CREDITORS AND GOOD FAITH PURCHASERS

2–401.   Passing of Title; Reservation for Security; Limited Application of This Section.
2–402.   Rights of Seller's Creditors Against Sold Goods.
2–403.   Power to Transfer; Good Faith Purchase of Goods; "Entrusting".

PART 5.   PERFORMANCE

2–501.   Insurable Interest in Goods; Manner of Identification of Goods.
2–502.   Buyer's Right to Goods on Seller's Repudiation, Failure to Deliver, or Insolvency.
2–503.   Manner of Seller's Tender of Delivery.
2–504.   Shipment by Seller.
2–505.   Seller's Shipment Under Reservation.
2–506.   Rights of Financing Agency.
2–507.   Effect of Seller's Tender; Delivery on Condition.
2–508.   Cure by Seller of Improper Tender or Delivery; Replacement.
2–509.   Risk of Loss in the Absence of Breach.
2–510.   Effect of Breach on Risk of Loss.
2–511.   Tender of Payment by Buyer; Payment by Check.
2–512.   Payment by Buyer Before Inspection.
2–513.   Buyer's Right to Inspection of Goods.
2–514.   When Documents Deliverable on Acceptance; When on Payment.
2–515.   Preserving Evidence of Goods in Dispute.

PART 6.   BREACH, REPUDIATION AND EXCUSE

2–601.   Buyer's Rights on Improper Delivery.
2–602.   Manner and Effect of Rightful Rejection.
2–603.   Merchant Buyer's Duties as to Rightfully Rejected Goods.
2–604.   Buyer's Options as to Salvage of Rightfully Rejected Goods.
2–605.   Waiver of Buyer's Objections by Failure to Particularize.
2–606.   What Constitutes Acceptance of Goods.
2–607.   Effect of Acceptance; Notice of Breach; Burden of Establishing Breach After Acceptance; Notice of Claim or Litigation to Person Answerable Over.
2–608.   Revocation of Acceptance in Whole or in Part.
2–609.   Right to Adequate Assurance of Performance.

2–610. Anticipatory Repudiation.

2–611. Retraction of Anticipatory Repudiation.

2–612. "Installment Contract"; Breach.

2–613. Casualty to Identified Goods.

2–614. Substituted Performance.

2–615. Excuse by Failure of Presupposed Conditions.

2–616. Procedure on Notice Claiming Excuse.

PART 7. REMEDIES

2–701. Remedies for Breach of Collateral Contracts Not Impaired.

2–702. Seller's Remedies on Discovery of Buyer's Insolvency.

2–703. Seller's Remedies in General.

2–704. Seller's Right to Identify Goods to the Contract Notwithstanding Breach or to Salvage Unfinished Goods.

2–705. Seller's Stoppage of Delivery in Transit or Otherwise.

2–706. Seller's Resale Including Contract for Resale.

2–707. "Person in the Position of a Seller".

2–708. Seller's Damages for Non-acceptance or Repudiation.

2–709. Action for the Price.

2–710. Seller's Incidental Damages.

2–711. Buyer's Remedies in General; Buyer's Security Interest in Rejected Goods.

2–712. "Cover"; Buyer's Procurement of Substitute Goods.

2–713. Buyer's Damages for Non-delivery or Repudiation.

2–714. Buyer's Damages for Breach in Regard to Accepted Goods.

2–715. Buyer's Incidental and Consequential Damages.

2–716. Buyer's Right to Specific Performance or Replevin.

2–717. Deduction of Damages From the Price.

2–718. Liquidation or Limitation of Damages; Deposits.

2–719. Contractual Modification or Limitation of Remedy.

2–720. Effect of "Cancellation" or "Rescission" on Claims for Antecedent Breach.

2–721. Remedies for Fraud.

2–722. Who Can Sue Third Parties for Injury to Goods.

2–723. Proof of Market Price: Time and Place.

2–724. Admissibility of Market Quotations.

2–725. Statute of Limitations in Contracts for Sale.

PART 1

SHORT TITLE, GENERAL CONSTRUCTION AND SUBJECT MATTER

§ 2–101. Short Title.

This Article shall be known and may be cited as Uniform Commercial Code—Sales.

Official Comment

This Article is a complete revision and modernization of the Uniform Sales Act which was promulgated by the National Conference of Commissioners on Uniform State Laws in 1906 and has been adopted in 34 states and Alaska, the District of Columbia and Hawaii.

The coverage of the present Article is much more extensive than that of the old Sales Act and extends to the various bodies of case law which have been developed both outside of and under the latter.

The arrangement of the present Article is in terms of contract for sale and the various steps of its performance. The legal consequences are stated as following directly from the contract and action taken under it without resorting to the idea of when property or title passed or was to pass as being the determining factor. The purpose is to avoid making practical issues between practical men turn upon the location of an intangible something, the passing of which no man can prove by evidence and to substitute for such abstractions proof of words and actions of a tangible character.

§ 2–102. Scope; Certain Security and Other Transactions Excluded from this Article.

~~Unless the context otherwise requires, this Article applies to transactions in goods; it does not apply to any transaction which although in the form of an unconditional contract to sell or present sale is intended to operate only as a security transaction nor does this Article impair or repeal any statute regulating sales to consumers, farmers or other specified classes of buyers.~~

(1)   Unless the context otherwise requires, and except as provided in subsection (3), this Article applies to transactions in goods and, in the case of a hybrid transaction, it applies to the extent provided in subsection (2).

(2)   In a hybrid transaction:

(a)   If the sale-of-goods aspects do not predominate, only the provisions of this Article which relate primarily to the sale-of-goods aspects of the transaction apply, and the provisions that relate primarily to the transaction as a whole do not apply.

(b)   If the sale-of-goods aspects predominate, this Article applies to the transaction but does not preclude application in appropriate circumstances of other law to aspects of the transaction which do not relate to the sale of goods.

(3)   This Article does not:

(a)   apply to a transaction that, even though in the form of an unconditional contract to sell or present sale, operates only to create a security interest; or

(b)   impair or repeal a statute regulating sales to consumers, farmers, or other specified classes of buyers.

As amended in 2022.

Official Comment

Prior Uniform Statutory Provision: Section 75, Uniform Sales Act.

Changes: Section 75 has been rephrased.

Purposes ~~of Changes and New Matter:~~

1.   ~~To make it clear that: The Article leaves substantially unaffected the law relating to purchase money security such as conditional sale or chattel mortgage though it regulates the general sales aspects of such transactions. "Security transaction" is used in the same sense as in the Article on Secured Transactions (Article 9).~~ Subsection (3) makes it clear that this Article does not govern aspects of a transaction that, although in the form of a sale or contract to sell, create a security interest. See Sections 1–201(b)(35); 9–109(a)(1). Of course, this Article does apply to any sales aspects of such a transaction.

2.   Many ordinary transactions involve both a sale of goods and the provision of services, a lease of other goods, or a sale, lease, or license of property other than goods. In its original formulation, Article 2 provided no guidance on whether or to what extent the Article applied to such a hybrid transaction, although by defining a "sale" as "the passing of title [to goods] from the seller to the buyer for a price." Section 1–206 arguably regarded such transactions as sales. This section was substantially revised to address hybrid transactions pursuant to the Uniform Commercial Code Amendments (2022) (2022 Amendments). See Section 2–106(5) (defining "hybrid transaction").

In dealing with the issue of whether and to what extent, under the pre-2022 version of this section, Article 2 applied to hybrid transactions, most courts used some version of a "predominant purpose" test. Under those tests, Article 2 applied either in full or not at all, depending on whether the hybrid transaction, at its inception, was predominantly about the goods. In some cases, courts looked instead to the "gravamen of the claim," applying Article 2 to issues relating to the goods and applying other law to issues relating to other aspects of the transaction.

Still other courts used what was sometimes referred to as the "bifurcation approach," under which Article 2 applied to the sale-of-goods aspect of a hybrid transaction and other law applied to the other aspects of the transaction. The bifurcation approach was similar to the gravamen of the claim, but instead of applying all of Article 2 to some, but not all, types of claims relating to a hybrid transaction, it distinguished the provisions in Article 2 that deal with the goods from those that deal with the transaction as a whole, and applied only the former in a hybrid transaction.

Subsection (2) codifies aspects of the predominant purpose test and the bifurcation approach, establishing a two-tiered test. If the sale-of-goods aspects of a hybrid transaction predominate, then Article 2 applies. If the other aspects of the hybrid transaction predominate, then the provisions of Article 2 which relate primarily to the sale of goods, as opposed to those that relate to the transaction as a whole, apply. This approach has the benefit, for example, of ensuring that a person acquiring ownership of goods in a transaction in which the sale-of-goods aspects do not predominate is a buyer that benefits from the warranty provisions of this Article and may have a right to recover the goods from the seller and thereby may qualify as a buyer in ordinary course of business under Section 1–201(b)(9).

3.   It is important to note that, in contrast to the frequent reference (under prior case law in many states) to the predominant *purpose* of a hybrid transaction, subsection (2) focuses on which aspect of the transaction predominates without requiring a finding of the "purpose" of either or both parties (although that purpose, when evident, may be a relevant factor in deciding which aspect predominates). The determination of which aspect of a hybrid transaction predominates is left to the court, which should evaluate each transaction on a case-by-case basis without the necessity of applying any particular formula. Factors that may be relevant to that determination include, but are not limited to, the language of the agreement, the portion of the total price that is attributable to the sale of goods (as to which an agreed-upon allocation will ordinarily be binding on the parties), the purposes of the parties in entering into the transaction (when that is ascertainable), and the nature of the businesses of the parties (such as whether the seller is in the business of selling goods of that kind). Because the definition of "goods" expressly includes "specially manufactured goods," services involved in manufacturing goods are normally attributable to the sale-of-goods aspects of the transaction. Services in designing specially manufactured goods, however, would not normally be attributable to the sale-of-goods aspects of the transaction.

4.   If the sale-of-goods aspects of a hybrid transaction predominate, then this Article applies to the transaction. However, the application of this Article to a hybrid transaction does not preclude the application of principles of law and equity to supplement the provisions of this Article, see Section 1–103(b), nor does it preclude, in appropriate circumstances, the application of other law to the non-sale-of-goods aspects of the transaction. Whether it is appropriate to apply such other law will depend in part on what purposes the other law is designed to achieve and whether application of the other law would be likely to interfere with the application of this Article.

Example 1. Owner hires Contractor to replace the roof on a structure. As part of the transaction, Contractor promises to remove the existing shingles and install new shingles, which Contractor is providing. The transaction is a hybrid transaction because it involves the passing of title to the new shingles and the provision of services. If the sale-of-goods aspects of the transaction predominate, this Article applies to the transaction.

Example 2. Same facts as in Example 1. Even if the sale-of-goods aspects of the transaction predominate, other law might apply to the services aspects of the transaction. For example, if applicable law regulates the provision of roofing services, such as by requiring the roofer to be licensed, requiring specified disclosures, requiring or implying a warranty with respect to the quality of services, or giving the property owner a brief period of time to cancel the contract, such other law might apply.

Example 3. In a single transaction, Seller agrees to sell a warehouse full of goods to Buyer. The transaction includes the goods contained in the warehouse, the warehouse itself, and the real property on which the warehouse is situated. Assume the goods aspects of the transaction predominate. The application of this Article to the transaction does not preclude the application of real property law to the real-property aspects of the transaction. Accordingly, whether the sale of the real property complies with the applicable requirements of real property law is determined by law other than this Article. Other law will also determine whether consummation of the sale of the real property is a condition to the parties' obligations to buy and sell the goods.

5.   If the sale-of-goods aspects of a hybrid transaction do not predominate, under subsection (2), the provisions of this Article relating primarily to the sale of goods, as opposed to the transaction as a whole, apply. These provisions include those relating to warranties under Sections 2–312, 2–313, 2–314, 2–315, 2–316, 2–317, 2–318; tender of delivery and risk of loss under Sections 2–503, 2–504, 2–509, 2–510; acceptance, rejection, and

cure under Sections 2–508, 2–601, 2–602, 2–603, 2–604, 2–605, 2–606; and remedies for non-delivery of the goods or for tender of nonconforming goods under Sections 2–711, 7–712, 7–713, 2–714, 2–715, 2–716. In contrast, the provisions of this Article dealing with the transaction as a whole do not apply. These provisions include those relating to: the requirement of a signed record, Section 2–201; contract formation, Sections 2–204 through 2–207; and whether consideration is needed to modify the agreement, Section 2–209.

Example 4. Owner sends a purchase order to Contractor offering to enter into a contract with Contractor to replace the roof on a structure. The proposed transaction involves Contractor removing the existing shingles and installing new shingles, which Contractor is to provide. Contractor responds with a confirmation purporting to accept but containing additional and different terms. The transaction is a hybrid transaction because it involves the passing of title to the new shingles and the provision of services. If the sale-of-goods aspects of the transaction do not predominate, this Article does not apply to determine whether a contract was formed. That issue is governed by other law.

Example 5. Under the facts of Example 1, assume that the sale-of-goods aspects of the transaction do not predominate. The agreement provides that the job will be completed by December 31. Due to unforeseen circumstances affecting the availability of supplies and labor, the job is not completed by the agreed-upon deadline. Whether Contractor's failure to perform on time is excused is determined by general contract law, rather than by this Article (Section 2–615).

Example 6. Under the facts of Example 1, assume that the sale-of-goods aspects of the transaction do not predominate. A dispute between the parties arises and during litigation one party seeks to admit evidence of usage of trade to supplement or explain the parties' written agreement. If the proffered evidence relates to the sale-of-goods aspects of the transaction, the parol evidence rule in this Article, Section 2–202 applies. If the proffered evidence relates to the other aspects of the transaction or to the transaction as a whole, other law will govern the admissibility of the evidence.

Example 7. Restaurateur hires Remodeler to remodel Restaurateur's kitchen. The transaction requires Remodeler to supply a new oven meeting detailed specifications, but the services aspects of the transaction predominate. The oven supplied does not meet a minor aspect of those specifications (but does substantially satisfy the specifications as a whole). Whether Restaurateur may reject the oven (or must retain it subject to price adjustment), whether Restaurateur has a right to cover by purchasing a substitute oven, and the measure of Restaurateur's damages for the oven's nonconformity to the specifications are determined by this Article.

Example 8. Restaurateur hires Remodeler to remodel Restaurateur's kitchen by a specified completion date. The transaction requires Remodeler to supply a new oven, but the services aspects of the transaction predominate. Remodeler breaches by failing to complete the project by the specified date. The measure of Restaurateur's damages for Remodeler's failure to timely complete the project is not determined by this Article.

6.   The rules of subsections (1) and (2) are essentially gap fillers that apply when the parties' agreement is silent on what legal rules govern the different aspects of their transaction. In general, parties are free to preclude the application of this Article to the aspects of their transaction that are not about the sale of goods.

Example 9. Robotics Manufacturer contracts to design, build, and sell customized robotics to Car Maker. The transaction includes a sale of goods and the provision of services and is therefore a hybrid transaction. Assume that the sale-of-goods aspects predominate. The parties may, in their agreement, provide that Article 2 does not govern the services aspects of the transaction.

As Example 9 illustrates, parties may agree that Article 2 will not govern non-goods aspects of a hybrid transaction, even though the sale-of-goods aspects predominate. But, when sale-of-goods aspects predominate, the parties cannot agree that Article 2 does not govern matters that relate to the transaction as a whole, such as contract formation and enforceability. For example, in a situation such as Example 9, if the requirements of the Section 2–201 statute of frauds are not satisfied, it would make little sense to hold that the services aspects of the transaction are enforceable when the provision of services is clearly dependent on the existence of the sale-of-goods aspects. Of course, even when this article applies, its provisions may be varied by agreement to the extent provided in section 1–302.

Cross Reference:

Article 9.

Definitional Cross References:

"Contract". Section 1–201.
"Contract for sale". Section 2–106.
"Present sale". Section 2–106.
"Sale". Section 2–106.

As amended in 2022.

§ 2–103. Definitions and Index of Definitions.

(1) In this Article unless the context otherwise requires

(a) "Buyer" means a person who buys or contracts to buy goods.

(b) [Reserved.] ["Good faith" in the case of a merchant means honesty in fact and the observance of reasonable commercial standards of fair dealing in the trade.] [*Note from West Advisory Panel: This subsection will be deleted if the jurisdiction adopts the definition of good faith in revised Article 1 (2001).*]

(c) "Receipt" of goods means taking physical possession of them.

(d) "Seller" means a person who sells or contracts to sell goods.

(2) Other definitions applying to this Article or to specified Parts thereof, and the sections in which they appear are:

"Acceptance". Section 2–606.
"Banker's credit". Section 2–325.
"Between merchants". Section 2–104.
"Cancellation". Section 2–106(4).
"Commercial unit". Section 2–105.
"Confirmed credit". Section 2–325.
"Conforming to contract". Section 2–106.
"Contract for sale". Section 2–106.
"Cover". Section 2–712.
"Entrusting". Section 2–403.
"Financing agency". Section 2–104.
"Future goods". Section 2–105.
"Goods". Section 2–105.
"Identification". Section 2–501.
"Installment contract". Section 2–612.
"Letter of Credit". Section 2–325.
"Lot". Section 2–105.
"Merchant". Section 2–104.
"Overseas". Section 2–323.
"Person in position of seller". Section 2–707.
"Present sale". Section 2–106.
"Sale". Section 2–106.
"Sale on approval". Section 2–326.
"Sale or return". Section 2–326.
"Termination". Section 2–106.

(3) "Control" as provided in Section 7–106 and the following definitions in other Articles apply to this Article:

"Check". Section 3–104.
"Consignee". Section 7–102.
"Consignor". Section 7–102.

"Consumer goods". Section 9–102.
"Dishonor". Section 3–502.
"Draft". Section 3–104.

(4)   In addition Article 1 contains general definitions and principles of construction and interpretation applicable throughout this Article.

As amended in 1994, 1999, and 2003.

Official Comment

Prior Uniform Statutory Provision: Subsection (1): Section 76, Uniform Sales Act.

Changes:

The definitions of "buyer" and "seller" have been slightly rephrased, the reference in Section 76 of the prior Act to "any legal successor in interest of such person" being omitted. The definition of "receipt" is new.

Purposes of Changes and New Matter:

1.   The phrase "any legal successor in interest of such person" has been eliminated since Section 2–210 of this Article, which limits some types of delegation of performance on assignment of a sales contract, makes it clear that not every such successor can be safely included in the definition. In every ordinary case, however, such successors are as of course included.

2.   "Receipt" must be distinguished from delivery particularly in regard to the problems arising out of shipment of goods, whether or not the contract calls for making delivery by way of documents of title, since the seller may frequently fulfill his obligations to "deliver" even though the buyer may never "receive" the goods. Delivery with respect to documents of title is defined in Article 1 and requires transfer of physical delivery of a tangible document of title and transfer of control of an electronic document of title. Otherwise the many divergent incidents of delivery are handled incident by incident.

Cross References:

Point 1: See Section 2–210 and Comment thereon.
Point 2: Section 1–201.

Definitional Cross Reference:

"Person". Section 1–201.

As amended in 2003.

§ 2–104.   Definitions: "Merchant"; "Between Merchants"; "Financing Agency".

(1)   "Merchant" means a person who deals in goods of the kind or otherwise by his occupation holds himself out as having knowledge or skill peculiar to the practices or goods involved in the transaction or to whom such knowledge or skill may be attributed by his employment of an agent or broker or other intermediary who by his occupation holds himself out as having such knowledge or skill.

(2)   "Financing agency" means a bank, finance company or other person who in the ordinary course of business makes advances against goods or documents of title or who by arrangement with either the seller or the buyer intervenes in ordinary course to make or collect payment due or claimed under the contract for sale, as by purchasing or paying the seller's draft or making advances against it or by merely taking it for collection whether or not documents of title accompany or are associated with the draft. "Financing agency" includes also a bank or other person who similarly intervenes between persons who are in the position of seller and buyer in respect to the goods (Section 2–707).

(3)   "Between merchants" means in any transaction with respect to which both parties are chargeable with the knowledge or skill of merchants.

As amended in 2003.

Official Comment

Prior Uniform Statutory Provision: None. But see Sections 15(2), (5), 16(c), 45(2) and 71, Uniform Sales Act, and Sections 35 and 37, Uniform Bills of Lading Act for examples of the policy expressly provided for in this Article.

Purposes:

1. This Article assumes that transactions between professionals in a given field require special and clear rules which may not apply to a casual or inexperienced seller or buyer. It thus adopts a policy of expressly stating rules applicable "between merchants" and "as against a merchant", wherever they are needed instead of making them depend upon the circumstances of each case as in the statutes cited above. This section lays the foundation of this policy by defining those who are to be regarded as professionals or "merchants" and by stating when a transaction is deemed to be "between merchants".

2. The term "merchant" as defined here roots in the "law merchant" concept of a professional in business. The professional status under the definition may be based upon specialized knowledge as to the goods, specialized knowledge as to business practices, or specialized knowledge as to both and which kind of specialized knowledge may be sufficient to establish the merchant status is indicated by the nature of the provisions.

The special provisions as to merchants appear only in this Article and they are of three kinds. Sections 2–201(2), 2–205, 2–207 and 2–209 dealing with the statute of frauds, firm offers, confirmatory memoranda and modification rest on normal business practices which are or ought to be typical of and familiar to any person in business. For purposes of these sections almost every person in business would, therefore, be deemed to be a "merchant" under the language "who . . . by his occupation holds himself out as having knowledge or skill peculiar to the practices . . . involved in the transaction . . ." since the practices involved in the transaction are non-specialized business practices such as answering mail. In this type of provision, banks or even universities, for example, well may be "merchants." But even these sections only apply to a merchant in his mercantile capacity; a lawyer or bank president buying fishing tackle for his own use is not a merchant.

On the other hand, in Section 2–314 on the warranty of merchantability, such warranty is implied only "if the seller is a merchant with respect to goods of that kind." Obviously this qualification restricts the implied warranty to a much smaller group than everyone who is engaged in business and requires a professional status as to particular kinds of goods. The exception in Section 2–402(2) for retention of possession by a merchant-seller falls in the same class; as does Section 2–403(2) on entrusting of possession to a merchant "who deals in goods of that kind".

A third group of sections includes 2–103(1)(b), which provides that in the case of a merchant "good faith" includes observance of reasonable commercial standards of fair dealing in the trade; 2–327(1)(c), 2–603 and 2–605, dealing with responsibilities of merchant buyers to follow seller's instructions, etc.; 2–509 on risk of loss, and 2–609 on adequate assurance of performance. This group of sections applies to persons who are merchants under either the "practices" or the "goods" aspect of the definition of merchant.

3. The "or to whom such knowledge or skill may be attributed by his employment of an agent or broker. . ." clause of the definition of merchant means that even persons such as universities, for example, can come within the definition of merchant if they have regular purchasing departments or business personnel who are familiar with business practices and who are equipped to take any action required.

Cross References:

Point 1: See Sections 1–102 and 1–203 [*unrevised Article 1; see Concordance, p. 22*].

Point 2: See Sections 2–314, 2–315 and 2–320 to 2–325, of this Article, and Article 9.

Definitional Cross References:

"Bank". Section 1–201.
"Buyer". Section 2–103.
"Contract for sale". Section 2–106.
"Document of title". Section 1–201.
"Draft". Section 3–104.
"Goods". Section 2–105.
"Person". Section 1–201.
"Purchase". Section 1–201.
"Seller". Section 2–103.

§ 2–105.   Definitions: Transferability; "Goods"; "Future" Goods; "Lot"; "Commercial Unit".

(1)   "Goods" means all things (including specially manufactured goods) which are movable at the time of identification to the contract for sale other than the money in which the price is to be paid, investment securities (Article 8) and things in action. "Goods" also includes the unborn young of animals and growing crops and other identified things attached to realty as described in the section on goods to be severed from realty (Section 2–107).

(2)   Goods must be both existing and identified before any interest in them can pass. Goods which are not both existing and identified are "future" goods. A purported present sale of future goods or of any interest therein operates as a contract to sell.

(3)   There may be a sale of a part interest in existing identified goods.

(4)   An undivided share in an identified bulk of fungible goods is sufficiently identified to be sold although the quantity of the bulk is not determined. Any agreed proportion of such a bulk or any quantity thereof agreed upon by number, weight or other measure may to the extent of the seller's interest in the bulk be sold to the buyer who then becomes an owner in common.

(5)   "Lot" means a parcel or a single article which is the subject matter of a separate sale or delivery, whether or not it is sufficient to perform the contract.

(6)   "Commercial unit" means such a unit of goods as by commercial usage is a single whole for purposes of sale and division of which materially impairs its character or value on the market or in use. A commercial unit may be a single article (as a machine) or a set of articles (as a suite of furniture or an assortment of sizes) or a quantity (as a bale, gross, or carload) or any other unit treated in use or in the relevant market as a single whole.

Official Comment

Prior Uniform Statutory Provision: Subsections (1), (2), (3) and (4)—Sections 5, 6 and 76, Uniform Sales Act; Subsections (5) and (6)—none.

Changes: Rewritten.

Purposes of Changes and New Matter:

1.   Subsection (1) on "goods": The phraseology of the prior uniform statutory provision has been changed so that:

The definition of goods is based on the concept of movability and the term "chattels personal" is not used. It is not intended to deal with things which are not fairly identifiable as movables before the contract is performed.

Growing crops are included within the definition of goods since they are frequently intended for sale. The concept of "industrial" growing crops has been abandoned, for under modern practices fruit, perennial hay, nursery stock and the like must be brought within the scope of this Article. The young of animals are also included expressly in this definition since they, too, are frequently intended for sale and may be contracted for before birth. The period of gestation of domestic animals is such that the provisions of the section on identification can apply as in the case of crops to be planted. The reason of this definition also leads to the inclusion of a wool crop or the like as "goods" subject to identification under this Article.

The exclusion of "money in which the price is to be paid" from the definition of goods does not mean that foreign currency which is included in the definition of money may not be the subject matter of a sales transaction. Goods is intended to cover the sale of money when money is being treated as a commodity but not to include it when money is the medium of payment.

As to contracts to sell timber, minerals, or structures to be removed from the land Section 2–107(1) (Goods to be severed from Realty: recording) controls.

The use of the word "fixtures" is avoided in view of the diversity of definitions of that term. This Article in including within its scope "things attached to realty" adds the further test that they must be capable of severance without material harm thereto. As between the parties any identified things which fall within that definition become "goods" upon the making of the contract for sale.

"Investment securities" are expressly excluded from the coverage of this Article. It is not intended by this exclusion, however, to prevent the application of a particular section of this Article by analogy to securities (as was done with the Original Sales Act in *Agar v. Orda*, 264 N.Y. 248, 190 N.E. 479, 99 A.L.R. 269 (1934)) when the reason of that section makes such application sensible and the situation involved is not covered by the Article of this Act dealing specifically with such securities (Article 8).

2.   References to the fact that a contract for sale can extend to future or contingent goods and that ownership in common follows the sale of a part interest have been omitted here as obvious without need for expression; hence no inference to negate these principles should be drawn from their omission.

3.   Subsection (4) does not touch the question of how far an appropriation of a bulk of fungible goods may or may not satisfy the contract for sale.

4.   Subsections (5) and (6) on "lot" and "commercial unit" are introduced to aid in the phrasing of later sections.

5.   The question of when an identification of goods takes place is determined by the provisions of Section 2–501 and all that this section says is what kinds of goods may be the subject of a sale.

Cross References:

Point 1: Sections 2–107, 2–201, 2–501 and Article 8.
Point 5: Section 2–501.
See also Section 1–201.

Definitional Cross References:

"Buyer". Section 2–103.
"Contract". Section 1–201.
"Contract for sale". Section 2–106.
"Fungible". Section 1–201.
"Money". Section 1–201.
"Present sale". Section 2–106.
"Sale". Section 2–106.
"Seller". Section 2–103.

§ 2–106.   Definitions: "Contract"; "Agreement"; "Contract for Sale"; "Sale"; "Present Sale"; "Conforming" to Contract; "Termination"; "Cancellation"; "Hybrid Transaction".

(1)   In this Article unless the context otherwise requires "contract" and "agreement" are limited to those relating to the present or future sale of goods. "Contract for sale" includes both a present sale of goods and a contract to sell goods at a future time. A "sale" consists in the passing of title from the seller to the buyer for a price (Section 2–401). A "present sale" means a sale which is accomplished by the making of the contract.

(2)   Goods or conduct including any part of a performance are "conforming" or conform to the contract when they are in accordance with the obligations under the contract.

(3)   "Termination" occurs when either party pursuant to a power created by agreement or law puts an end to the contract otherwise than for its breach. On "termination" all obligations which are still executory on both sides are discharged but any right based on prior breach or performance survives.

(4)   "Cancellation" occurs when either party puts an end to the contract for breach by the other and its effect is the same as that of "termination" except that the cancelling party also retains any remedy for breach of the whole contract or any unperformed balance.

(5)   "Hybrid transaction" means a single transaction involving a sale of goods and:

(a)   the provision of services;

(b)   a lease of other goods; or

(c)   a sale, lease, or license of property other than goods.

As amended in 2022.

Official Comment

Prior Uniform Statutory Provision: Subsection (1)—Section 1(1) and (2), Uniform Sales Act; Subsection (2)—none, but subsection generally continues policy of Sections 11, 44 and 69, Uniform Sales Act; Subsections (3) and (4)—none.

Changes: Completely rewritten.

Purposes ~~of Changes and New Matter:~~

1.   Subsection (1): "Contract for sale" is used as a general concept throughout this Article, but the rights of the parties do not vary according to whether the transaction is a present sale or a contract to sell unless the Article expressly so provides.

2.   Subsection (2): It is in general intended to continue the policy of requiring exact performance by the seller of his obligations as a condition to his right to require acceptance. However, the seller is in part safeguarded against surprise as a result of sudden technicality on the buyer's part by the provisions of Section 2–508 on seller's cure of improper tender or delivery. Moreover usage of trade frequently permits commercial leeways in performance and the language of the agreement itself must be read in the light of such custom or usage and also, prior course of dealing, and in a long term contract, the course of performance.

3.   Subsections (3) and (4): These subsections are intended to make clear the distinction carried forward throughout this Article between termination and cancellation.

4.   In some transactions, the passing of title to goods from the seller to the buyer in return for a price is part of a larger transaction. The other aspects of the transaction might involve the seller providing services to the buyer, the seller leasing other goods to the buyer, or the seller transferring to the buyer rights to property other than goods. Such a transaction is a "hybrid transaction," as defined in subsection (5). Section 2–102 indicates the extent to which this Article applies to a hybrid transaction.

5.   A hybrid transaction is a single transaction. If contracting parties enter into separate agreements at the same time, each agreement creating a separate transaction, each transaction must be evaluated separately to determine if it is a hybrid transaction.

Example 1. To sell an ongoing business, Seller and Buyer enter into three separate written agreements: (i) a sale of goods used in the business; (ii) an agreement for Seller to provide consulting services to Buyer for a period of six months; and (iii) a sale of intangible assets associated with the business. Each agreement creates a separate transaction. None of those transactions involves both a sale of goods and the provision of services, the lease of other goods, or the sale, lease, or license of property other than goods. Thus, none of the separate transactions constitutes a hybrid transaction.

Example 2. To sell an ongoing business, Seller and Buyer enter into two separate written agreements: (i) a sale of goods and intangible assets used in the business; and (ii) an agreement for Seller to provide consulting services to Buyer for a period of six months, and not to compete with Buyer for a period of one year. The agreement to sell goods and intangible assets creates a hybrid transaction. The agreement for consulting services, a separate transaction, is not a hybrid transaction.

Even when contracting parties enter into a single agreement involving both a sale of goods and a sale, lease, or license of other property or the provision of services, the elements of the single agreement may be so independent that they create separate transactions. In that case, no hybrid transaction would exist merely because the separate transactions arose out of the same agreement.

Example 3. Farmer A and Farmer B sign a written agreement pursuant to which Farmer A will sell a tractor to Farmer B and Farmer A will board and feed Farmer B's cattle until the cattle are sold. The agreement specifies a price for the tractor, which is due upon delivery, and specifies a mechanism for determining the price for Farmer A's services, which is to be paid when the cattle are sold. The parties would have entered into an agreement to buy and sell the tractor even if they had not entered into an agreement to board and feed the cattle, and vice versa. Two separate transactions arise from the single agreement, neither of which is a hybrid transaction. Article 2 applies to the sale of the tractor. Other law applies to the agreement to board and feed the cattle.

Example 4. In a single record, Landscaper agrees to sell plants to Homeowner and to install the plants on Homeowner's property. The agreement specifies a total price but provides no mechanism for determining what portion of the price is allocable to the sale of plants and what portion is allocable to the installation services. Because the terms of the agreement relating to the sale of goods and those relating to services are not severable, the transaction is a hybrid transaction.

Cross References:

Point 2: Sections 1–203 [*unrevised Article 1; see Concordance, p. 22*], 1–205 [*unrevised Article 1; see Concordance, p. 22*], 2–208 and 2–508.

Definitional Cross References:

"Agreement". Section 1–201.
"Buyer". Section 2–103.
"Contract". Section 1–201.
"Goods". Section 2–105.
"Party". Section 1–201.
"Remedy". Section 1–201.
"Rights". Section 1–201.
"Seller". Section 2–103.

As amended in 2022.

§ 2–107.   Goods to Be Severed from Realty: Recording.

(1)   A contract for the sale of minerals or the like (including oil and gas) or a structure or its materials to be removed from realty is a contract for the sale of goods within this Article if they are to be severed by the seller but until severance a purported present sale thereof which is not effective as a transfer of an interest in land is effective only as a contract to sell.

(2)   A contract for the sale apart from the land of growing crops or other things attached to realty and capable of severance without material harm thereto but not described in subsection (1) or of timber to be cut is a contract for the sale of goods within this Article whether the subject matter is to be severed by the buyer or by the seller even though it forms part of the realty at the time of contracting, and the parties can by identification effect a present sale before severance.

(3)   The provisions of this section are subject to any third party rights provided by the law relating to realty records, and the contract for sale may be executed and recorded as a document transferring an interest in land and shall then constitute notice to third parties of the buyer's rights under the contract for sale.

As amended in 1972.

Official Comment

Prior Uniform Statutory Provision: See Section 76, Uniform Sales Act on prior policy; Section 7, Uniform Conditional Sales Act.

Purposes:

1.   Subsection (1).   Notice that this subsection applies only if the minerals or structures "are to be severed by the seller". If the buyer is to sever, such transactions are considered contracts affecting land and all problems of the Statute of Frauds and of the recording of land rights apply to them. Therefore, the Statute of Frauds section of this Article does not apply to such contracts though they must conform to the Statute of Frauds affecting the transfer of interests in land.

2.   Subsection (2).   "Things attached" to the realty which can be severed without material harm are goods within this Article regardless of who is to effect the severance. The word "fixtures" has been avoided because of the diverse definitions of this term, the test of "severance without material harm" being substituted.

The provision in subsection (3) for recording such contracts is within the purview of this Article since it is a means of preserving the buyer's rights under the contract of sale.

3.   The security phases of things attached to or to become attached to realty are dealt with in the Article on Secured Transactions (Article 9) and it is to be noted that the definition of goods in that Article differs from the definition of goods in this Article.

However, both Articles treat as goods growing crops and also timber to be cut under a contract of severance.

Cross References:

Point 1: Section 2–201.
Point 2: Section 2–105.
Point 3: Article 9 and Section 9–102(a)(44).

Definitional Cross References:

"Buyer". Section 2–103.
"Contract". Section 1–201.
"Contract for sale". Section 2–106.
"Goods". Section 2–105.
"Party". Section 1–201.
"Present sale". Section 2–106.
"Rights". Section 1–201.
"Seller". Section 2–103.

PART 2

FORM, FORMATION AND READJUSTMENT OF CONTRACT

§ 2–201.   Formal Requirements; Statute of Frauds.

(1)   Except as otherwise provided in this section a contract for the sale of goods for the price of $500 or more is not enforceable by way of action or defense unless there is ~~some writing~~ a record sufficient to indicate that a contract for sale has been made between the parties and signed by the party against whom enforcement is sought or by ~~his~~ the party's authorized agent or broker. A ~~writing~~ record is not insufficient because it omits or incorrectly states a term agreed upon but the contract is not enforceable under this ~~paragraph~~ subsection beyond the quantity of goods shown in such writing.

(2)   Between merchants if within a reasonable time a ~~writing~~ record in confirmation of the contract and sufficient against the sender is received and the party receiving it has reason to know its contents, it satisfies the requirements of subsection (1) against ~~such~~ the party unless ~~written~~ notice in a record of objection to its contents is given within 10 days after it is received.

(3)   A contract which does not satisfy the requirements of subsection (1) but which is valid in other respects is enforceable

    (a)   if the goods are to be specially manufactured for the buyer and are not suitable for sale to others in the ordinary course of the seller's business and the seller, before notice of repudiation is received and under circumstances which reasonably indicate that the goods are for the buyer, has made either a substantial beginning of their manufacture or commitments for their procurement; or

    (b)   if the party against whom enforcement is sought admits in his pleading, testimony or otherwise in court that a contract for sale was made, but the contract is not enforceable under this provision beyond the quantity of goods admitted; or

    (c)   with respect to goods for which payment has been made and accepted or which have been received and accepted (Section 2–606).

As amended in 2022.

Official Comment

Prior Uniform Statutory Provision: Section 4, Uniform Sales Act (which was based on Section 17 of the Statute of 29 Charles II).

Changes: Completely rephrased; restricted to sale of goods. See also Sections 1–206 [*unrevised Article 1; see Concordance, p. 22*], 8–319 [*unrevised Article 8*] and 9–203.

~~Purposes of Changes:~~ ~~The changed phraseology of this~~ Purposes: This section is intended to make it clear that:

1.   The required ~~writing~~ <u>record</u> need not contain all the material terms of the contract and such material terms as are stated need not be precisely stated. All that is required is that the ~~writing~~ <u>record</u> afford a basis for believing that the offered oral evidence rests on a real transaction. It may be written in lead pencil on a scratch pad <u>or another medium</u>. It need not indicate which party is the buyer and which the seller. The only term which must appear is the quantity term which need not be accurately stated but recovery is limited to the amount stated. The price, time and place of payment or delivery, the general quality of the goods, or any particular warranties may all be omitted.

Special emphasis must be placed on the permissibility of omitting the price term in view of the insistence of some courts on the express inclusion of this term even where the parties have contracted on the basis of a published price list. In many valid contracts for sale the parties do not mention the price in express terms, the buyer being bound to pay and the seller to accept a reasonable price which the trier of the fact may well be trusted to determine. Again, frequently the price is not mentioned since the parties have based their agreement on a price list or catalogue known to both of them and this list serves as an efficient safeguard against perjury. Finally, "market" prices and valuations that are current in the vicinity constitute a similar check. Thus if the price is not stated in the ~~memorandum~~ <u>record evidencing the contract</u> it can normally be supplied without danger of fraud. Of course if the "price" consists of goods rather than money the quantity of goods must be stated.

Only three definite and invariable requirements as to the ~~memorandum~~ <u>record</u> are made by this subsection. First, it must evidence a contract for the sale of goods; second, it must be "signed", a word which includes any authentication which identifies the party to be charged; and third, it must specify a quantity.

2.   "Partial performance" as a substitute for the required memorandum can validate the contract only for the goods which have been accepted or for which payment has been made and accepted.

Receipt and acceptance either of goods or of the price constitutes an unambiguous overt admission by both parties that a contract actually exists. If the court can make a just apportionment, therefore, the agreed price of any goods actually delivered can be recovered without a writing or, if the price has been paid, the seller can be forced to deliver an apportionable part of the goods. The overt actions of the parties make admissible evidence of the other terms of the contract necessary to a just apportionment. This is true even though the actions of the parties are not in themselves inconsistent with a different transaction such as a consignment for resale or a mere loan of money.

Part performance by the buyer requires the delivery of something by him that is accepted by the seller as such performance. Thus, part payment may be made by money or check, accepted by the seller. If the agreed price consists of goods or services, then they must also have been delivered and accepted.

3.   Between merchants, failure to answer a ~~written confirmation of~~ <u>record confirming</u> a contract within ten days of receipt is tantamount to a ~~writing~~ <u>record</u> under subsection (2) and is sufficient against both parties under subsection (1). The only effect, however, is to take away from the party who fails to answer the defense of the Statute of Frauds; the burden of persuading the trier of fact that a contract was in fact made orally prior to ~~the written confirmation~~ <u>giving a record confirming a contract</u> is unaffected. Compare the effect of a failure to reply under Section 2–207.

4.   Failure to satisfy the requirements of this section does not render the contract void for all purposes, but merely prevents it from being judicially enforced in favor of a party to the contract. For example, a buyer who takes possession of goods as provided in an oral contract which the seller has not meanwhile repudiated, is not a trespasser. Nor would the Statute of Frauds provisions of this section be a defense to a third person who wrongfully induces a party to refuse to perform an oral contract, even though the injured party cannot maintain an action for damages against the party so refusing to perform.

5.   The requirement of "signing" is discussed in the ~~Comment to~~ Section 1–201<u>, Comment 37</u>.

6.   ~~It~~ <u>For purposes of subsection (1), it</u> is not necessary that the ~~writing~~ <u>record</u> be delivered to anybody. It need not be signed or authenticated by both parties but it is, of course, not sufficient against one who has not signed it. Prior to a dispute no one can determine which party's signing of the memorandum may be necessary but from the time of contracting each party should be aware that to him it is signing by the other which is important.

7.   If the making of a contract is admitted in court, either in a written pleading, by stipulation or by oral statement before the court, no additional ~~writing~~ <u>record</u> is necessary for protection against fraud. Under this section it is no longer possible to admit the contract in court and still treat the Statute as a defense. However, the contract is not thus conclusively established. The admission so made by a party is itself evidential against him of the truth of the facts so admitted and of nothing more; as against the other party, it is not evidential at all.

8.   In furtherance of medium neutrality, references to "writing" and "written" in the pre-2022 text of this section have been changed to refer to a "record."

Cross References:

See Sections 1–201, 2–202, 2–207, 2–209 and 2–304.

Definitional Cross References:

"Action". Section 1–201.
"Between merchants". Section 2–104.
"Buyer". Section 2–103.
"Contract". Section 1–201.
"Contract for sale". Section 2–106.
"Goods". Section 2–105.
"Notice". Section 1–201 [*unrevised Article 1; see Concordance, p. 22*].
"Party". Section 1–201.
"Reasonable time". Section 1–204 [*unrevised Article 1; see Concordance, p. 22*].
"Sale". Section 2–106.
"Seller". Section 2–103.

As amended in 2022.

§ 2–202.   Final ~~Written~~ Expression: Parol or Extrinsic Evidence.

Terms with respect to which the confirmatory memoranda of the parties agree or which are otherwise set forth in a ~~writing~~ record intended by the parties as a final expression of their agreement with respect to such terms as are included therein may not be contradicted by evidence of any prior agreement or of a contemporaneous oral agreement but may be explained or supplemented

(a)   by course of performance, course of dealing, or usage of trade (Section 1–303); and

(b)   by evidence of consistent additional terms unless the court finds the ~~writing~~ record to have been intended also as a complete and exclusive statement of the terms of the agreement.

As amended in 2022.

Official Comment

Prior Uniform Statutory Provisions: None.

Purposes:

1.   This section definitely rejects:

(a)   Any assumption that because a ~~writing~~ record has been worked out which is final on some matters, it is to be taken as including all the matters agreed upon;

(b)   The premise that the language used has the meaning attributable to such language by rules of construction existing in the law rather than the meaning which arises out of the commercial context in which it was used; and

(c)   The requirement that a condition precedent to the admissibility of the type of evidence specified in paragraph (a) is an original determination by the court that the language used is ambiguous.

2.   Paragraph (a) makes admissible evidence of course of dealing, usage of trade and course of performance to explain or supplement the terms of any ~~writing~~ record stating the agreement of the parties in order that the true understanding of the parties as to the agreement may be reached. Such ~~writings~~ records are to be read on the assumption that the course of prior dealings between the parties and the usages of trade were taken for granted when the document was phrased. Unless carefully negated they have become an element of the meaning of the words used. Similarly, the course of actual performance by the parties is considered the best indication of what they intended the ~~writing~~ record to mean.

3.   Under paragraph (b) consistent additional terms, not reduced to ~~writing~~ a record, may be proved unless the court finds that the ~~writing~~ record was intended by both parties as a complete and exclusive statement of all

the terms. If the additional terms are such that, if agreed upon, they would certainly have been included in the ~~document~~ record in the view of the court, then evidence of their alleged making must be kept from the trier of fact.

4.   In furtherance of medium neutrality, references to a "writing" in the pre-2022 text of this section have been changed to refer to a "record."

Cross References:

Point 3: Sections 1–303, 2–207, 2–302 and 2–316.

Definitional Cross References:

"Agreed" and "agreement". Section 1–201.
"Course of dealing". Section 1–303.
"Course of performance". Section 1–303.
"Party". Section 1–201.
"Term". Section 1–201.
"Usage of trade". Section 1–303.
"Written" and "writing". Section 1–201.

As amended in 2022.

§ 2–203.   Seals Inoperative.

The affixing of a seal to a ~~writing~~ record evidencing a contract for sale or an offer to buy or sell goods does not constitute the ~~writing~~ record a sealed instrument and the law with respect to sealed instruments does not apply to such a contract or offer.

As amended in 2022.

Official Comment

Prior Uniform Statutory Provision: Section 3, Uniform Sales Act.

Changes: Portion pertaining to "seals" rewritten.

Purposes of Changes:

1.   This section makes it clear that every effect of the seal which relates to "sealed instruments" as such is wiped out insofar as contracts for sale are concerned. However, the substantial effects of a seal, except extension of the period of limitations, may be had by appropriate drafting as in the case of firm offers (see Section 2–205).

2.   This section leaves untouched any aspects of a seal which relate merely to signatures or to authentication of execution and the like. Thus, a statute providing that a purported signature gives prima facie evidence of its own authenticity or that a signature gives prima facie evidence of consideration is still applicable to sales transactions even though a seal may be held to be a signature within the meaning of such a statute. Similarly, the authorized affixing of a corporate seal bearing the corporate name to a contractual writing purporting to be made by the corporation may have effect as a signature without any reference to the law of sealed instruments.

3.   In furtherance of medium neutrality, the reference to a "writing" in the pre-2022 text of this section has been changed to refer to a "record."

Cross Reference:

Point 1: Section 2–205.

Definitional Cross References:

"Contract for sale". Section 2–106.
"Goods". Section 2–105.
"Writing". Section 1–201.

As amended in 2022.

§ 2–204.   Formation in General.

(1)   A contract for sale of goods may be made in any manner sufficient to show agreement, including conduct by both parties which recognizes the existence of such a contract.

(2)   An agreement sufficient to constitute a contract for sale may be found even though the moment of its making is undetermined.

(3)   Even though one or more terms are left open a contract for sale does not fail for indefiniteness if the parties have intended to make a contract and there is a reasonably certain basis for giving an appropriate remedy.

Official Comment

Prior Uniform Statutory Provision: Sections 1 and 3, Uniform Sales Act.

Changes: Completely rewritten by this and other sections of this Article.

Purposes of Changes:

Subsection (1) continues without change the basic policy of recognizing any manner of expression of agreement, oral, written or otherwise. The legal effect of such an agreement is, of course, qualified by other provisions of this Article.

Under subsection (1) appropriate conduct by the parties may be sufficient to establish an agreement. Subsection (2) is directed primarily to the situation where the interchanged correspondence does not disclose the exact point at which the deal was closed, but the actions of the parties indicate that a binding obligation has been undertaken.

Subsection (3) states the principle as to "open terms" underlying later sections of the Article. If the parties intend to enter into a binding agreement, this subsection recognizes that agreement as valid in law, despite missing terms, if there is any reasonably certain basis for granting a remedy. The test is not certainty as to what the parties were to do nor as to the exact amount of damages due the plaintiff. Nor is the fact that one or more terms are left to be agreed upon enough of itself to defeat an otherwise adequate agreement. Rather, commercial standards on the point of "indefiniteness" are intended to be applied, this Act making provision elsewhere for missing terms needed for performance, open price, remedies and the like.

The more terms the parties leave open, the less likely it is that they have intended to conclude a binding agreement, but their actions may be frequently conclusive on the matter despite the omissions.

Cross References:

Subsection (1): Sections 1–103, 2–201 and 2–302.
Subsection (2): Sections 2–205 through 2–209.
Subsection (3): See Part 3.

Definitional Cross References:

"Agreement". Section 1–201.
"Contract". Section 1–201.
"Contract for sale". Section 2–106.
"Goods". Section 2–105.
"Party". Section 1–201.
"Remedy". Section 1–201.
"Term". Section 1–201.

§ 2–205.   Firm Offers.

An offer by a merchant to buy or sell goods in a signed ~~writing~~ record which by its terms gives assurance that it will be held open is not revocable, for lack of consideration, during the time stated or if no time is stated for a reasonable time, but in no event may such period of irrevocability exceed three months; but any such term of assurance on a form supplied by the offeree must be separately signed by the offeror.

As amended in 2022.

Official Comment

Prior Uniform Statutory Provision: Sections 1 and 3, Uniform Sales Act.

Changes: Completely rewritten by this and other sections of this Article.

~~**Purposes of Changes**~~**Purposes:**

1.   This section is intended to modify the former rule which required that "firm offers" be sustained by consideration in order to bind, and to require instead that they must merely be characterized as such and expressed in signed ~~writings~~ records.

2.   The primary purpose of this section is to give effect to the deliberate intention of a merchant to make a current firm offer binding. The deliberation is shown in the case of an individualized document by the merchant's signature to the offer, and in the case of an offer included on a form supplied by the other party to the transaction by the separate signing of the particular clause which contains the offer. "Signed" here also includes authentication but the reasonableness of the authentication herein allowed must be determined in the light of the purpose of the section. The circumstances surrounding the signing may justify something less than a formal signature or initialing but typically the kind of authentication involved here would consist of a minimum of initialing of the clause involved. A handwritten memorandum on the writer's letterhead purporting in its terms to "confirm" a firm offer already made would be enough to satisfy this section, although not subscribed, since under the circumstances it could not be considered a memorandum of mere negotiation and it would adequately show its own authenticity. Similarly, an authorized telegram will suffice, and this is true even though the original draft contained only a typewritten signature. See generally Section 1–201(b)(37) (defining "sign") and Comment 37. However, despite settled courses of dealing or usages of the trade whereby firm offers are made by oral communication and relied upon without more evidence, such offers remain revocable under this Article since authentication by a writing is the essence of this section.

3.   This section is intended to apply to current "firm" offers and not to long term options, and an outside time limit of three months during which such offers remain irrevocable has been set. The three month period during which firm offers remain irrevocable under this section need not be stated by days or by date. If the offer states that it is "guaranteed" or "firm" until the happening of a contingency which will occur within the three month period, it will remain irrevocable until that event. A promise made for a longer period will operate under this section to bind the offeror only for the first three months of the period but may of course be renewed. If supported by consideration it may continue for as long as the parties specify. This section deals only with the offer which is not supported by consideration.

4.   Protection is afforded against the inadvertent signing of a firm offer when contained in a form prepared by the offeree by requiring that such a clause be separately authenticated. If the offer clause is called to the offeror's attention and he separately authenticates it, he will be bound; Section 2–302 may operate, however, to prevent an unconscionable result which otherwise would flow from other terms appearing in the form.

5.   Safeguards are provided to offer relief in the case of material mistake by virtue of the requirement of good faith and the general law of mistake.

6.   In furtherance of medium neutrality, the reference to a "writing" in the pre-2022 text of this section has been changed to refer to a "record."

Cross References:

Point 1: Section 1–102 [*unrevised Article 1; see Concordance, p. 22*].
Point 2: Section 1–102 [*unrevised Article 1; see Concordance, p. 22*].
Point 3: Section 2–201.
Point 5: Section 2–302.

Definitional Cross References:

"Goods". Section 2–105.
"Merchant". Section 2–104.
"Signed". Section 1–201.
"Writing". Section 1–201.

As amended in 2022.

§ 2–206.   Offer and Acceptance in Formation of Contract.

(1)   Unless otherwise unambiguously indicated by the language or circumstances

(a)   an offer to make a contract shall be construed as inviting acceptance in any manner and by any medium reasonable in the circumstances;

(b)   an order or other offer to buy goods for prompt or current shipment shall be construed as inviting acceptance either by a prompt promise to ship or by the prompt or current shipment of conforming or non-conforming goods, but such a shipment of non-conforming goods does not constitute an acceptance if the seller seasonably notifies the buyer that the shipment is offered only as an accommodation to the buyer.

(2)   Where the beginning of a requested performance is a reasonable mode of acceptance an offeror who is not notified of acceptance within a reasonable time may treat the offer as having lapsed before acceptance.

Official Comment

Prior Uniform Statutory Provision: Sections 1 and 3, Uniform Sales Act.

Changes: Completely rewritten in this and other sections of this Article.

Purposes of Changes: To make it clear that:

1.   Any reasonable manner of acceptance is intended to be regarded as available unless the offeror has made quite clear that it will not be acceptable. Former technical rules as to acceptance, such as requiring that telegraphic offers be accepted by telegraphed acceptance, etc., are rejected and a criterion that the acceptance be "in any manner and by any medium reasonable under the circumstances," is substituted. This section is intended to remain flexible and its applicability to be enlarged as new media of communication develop or as the more time-saving present day media come into general use.

2.   Either shipment or a prompt promise to ship is made a proper means of acceptance of an offer looking to current shipment. In accordance with ordinary commercial understanding the section interprets an order looking to current shipment as allowing acceptance either by actual shipment or by a prompt promise to ship and rejects the artificial theory that only a single mode of acceptance is normally envisaged by an offer. This is true even though the language of the offer happens to be "ship at once" or the like. "Shipment" is here used in the same sense as in Section 2–504; it does not include the beginning of delivery by the seller's own truck or by messenger. But loading on the seller's own truck might be a beginning of performance under subsection (2).

3.   The beginning of performance by an offeree can be effective as acceptance so as to bind the offeror only if followed within a reasonable time by notice to the offeror. Such a beginning of performance must unambiguously express the offeree's intention to engage himself. For the protection of both parties it is essential that notice follow in due course to constitute acceptance. Nothing in this section however bars the possibility that under the common law performance begun may have an intermediate effect of temporarily barring revocation of the offer, or at the offeror's option, final effect in constituting acceptance.

4.   Subsection (1)(b) deals with the situation where a shipment made following an order is shown by a notification of shipment to be referable to that order but has a defect. Such a non-conforming shipment is normally to be understood as intended to close the bargain, even though it proves to have been at the same time a breach. However, the seller by stating that the shipment is non-conforming and is offered only as an accommodation to the buyer keeps the shipment or notification from operating as an acceptance.

Definitional Cross References:

"Buyer". Section 2–103.
"Conforming". Section 2–106.
"Contract". Section 1–201.
"Goods". Section 2–105.
"Notifies". Section 1–201 [*unrevised Article 1; see Concordance, p. 22*].
"Reasonable time". Section 1–204 [*unrevised Article 1; see Concordance, p. 22*].

§ 2–207. Additional Terms in Acceptance or Confirmation.

(1) A definite and seasonable expression of acceptance or a written confirmation which is sent within a reasonable time operates as an acceptance even though it states terms additional to or different from those offered or agreed upon, unless acceptance is expressly made conditional on assent to the additional or different terms.

(2) The additional terms are to be construed as proposals for addition to the contract. Between merchants such terms become part of the contract unless:

(a) the offer expressly limits acceptance to the terms of the offer;

(b) they materially alter it; or

(c) notification of objection to them has already been given or is given within a reasonable time after notice of them is received.

(3) Conduct by both parties which recognizes the existence of a contract is sufficient to establish a contract for sale although the writings of the parties do not otherwise establish a contract. In such case the terms of the particular contract consist of those terms on which the writings of the parties agree, together with any supplementary terms incorporated under any other provisions of this Act.

Official Comment

Prior Uniform Statutory Provision: Sections 1 and 3, Uniform Sales Act.

Changes: Completely rewritten by this and other sections of this Article.

Purposes of Changes:

1. This section is intended to deal with two typical situations. The one is the written confirmation, where an agreement has been reached either orally or by informal correspondence between the parties and is followed by one or both of the parties sending formal memoranda embodying the terms so far as agreed upon and adding terms not discussed. The other situation is offer and acceptance, in which a wire or letter expressed and intended as an acceptance or the closing of an agreement adds further minor suggestions or proposals such as "ship by Tuesday," "rush," "ship draft against bill of lading inspection allowed," or the like. A frequent example of the second situation is the exchange of printed purchase order and acceptance (sometimes called "acknowledgment") forms. Because the forms are oriented to the thinking of the respective drafting parties, the terms contained in them often do not correspond. Often the seller's form contains terms different from or additional to those set forth in the buyer's form. Nevertheless, the parties proceed with the transaction.

2. Under this Article a proposed deal which in commercial understanding has in fact been closed is recognized as a contract. Therefore, any additional matter contained in the confirmation or in the acceptance falls within subsection (2) and must be regarded as a proposal for an added term unless the acceptance is made conditional on the acceptance of the additional or different terms.

3. Whether or not additional or different terms will become part of the agreement depends upon the provisions of subsection (2). If they are such as materially to alter the original bargain, they will not be included unless expressly agreed to by the other party. If, however, they are terms which would not so change the bargain they will be incorporated unless notice of objection to them has already been given or is given within a reasonable time.

4. Examples of typical clauses which would normally "materially alter" the contract and so result in surprise or hardship if incorporated without express awareness by the other party are: a clause negating such standard warranties as that of merchantability or fitness for a particular purpose in circumstances in which either warranty normally attaches; a clause requiring a guaranty of 90% or 100% deliveries in a case such as a contract by cannery, where the usage of the trade allows greater quantity leeways; a clause reserving to the seller the power to cancel upon the buyer's failure to meet any invoice when due; a clause requiring that complaints be made in a time materially shorter than customary or reasonable.

5. Examples of clauses which involve no element of unreasonable surprise and which therefore are to be incorporated in the contract unless notice of objection is seasonably given are: a clause setting forth and perhaps enlarging slightly upon the seller's exemption due to supervening causes beyond his control, similar to those covered by the provision of this Article on merchant's excuse by failure of presupposed conditions or a clause fixing in advance any reasonable formula of proration under such circumstances; a clause fixing a reasonable time for

complaints within customary limits, or in the case of a purchase for sub-sale, providing for inspection by the sub-purchaser; a clause providing for interest on overdue invoices or fixing the seller's standard credit terms where they are within the range of trade practice and do not limit any credit bargained for; a clause limiting the right of rejection for defects which fall within the customary trade tolerances for acceptance "with adjustment" or otherwise limiting remedy in a reasonable manner (see Sections 2–718 and 2–719).

6.　　If no answer is received within a reasonable time after additional terms are proposed, it is both fair and commercially sound to assume that their inclusion has been assented to. Where clauses on confirming forms sent by both parties conflict each party must be assumed to object to a clause of the other conflicting with one on the confirmation sent by himself. As a result the requirement that there be notice of objection which is found in subsection (2) is satisfied and the conflicting terms do not become a part of the contract. The contract then consists of the terms originally expressly agreed to, terms on which the confirmations agree, and terms supplied by this Act, including subsection (2). The written confirmation is also subject to Section 2–201. Under that section a failure to respond permits enforcement of a prior oral agreement; under this section a failure to respond permits additional terms to become part of the agreement.

7.　　In many cases, as where goods are shipped, accepted and paid for before any dispute arises, there is no question whether a contract has been made. In such cases, where the writings of the parties do not establish a contract, it is not necessary to determine which act or document constituted the offer and which the acceptance. See Section 2–204. The only question is what terms are included in the contract, and subsection (3) furnishes the governing rule.

8.　　Pursuant to the 2022 Amendments, some references in this Article to the terms "writing," "writings," or "written" have been changed to refer to a "record." These changes are made in provisions where an affected party may be assumed to have assented to the use of a record that is not a writing. For example, Section 2–201 involves a record signed by an affected party and Section 2–202 refers to a record intended by parties to be a final expression of their agreement. However, in this section and some other sections in this Article references to these terms remain. Where such references remain in this Article, the use by parties of a record other than a writing may be given effect for purposes of this Article under law other than the Uniform Commercial Code, such as the Electronic Signatures in Global and National Commerce Act, 15 U.S.C. Section 7001, *et seq.*, and the Uniform Electronic Transactions Act.

Cross References:

See generally Section 2–302.
Point 5: Sections 2–513, 2–602, 2–607, 2–609, 2–612, 2–614, 2–615, 2–616, 2–718 and 2–719.
Point 6: Sections 1–102 [*unrevised Article 1; see Concordance, p. 22*] and 2–104.

Definitional Cross References:

"Between merchants". Section 2–104.
"Contract". Section 1–201.
"Notification". Section 1–201 [*unrevised Article 1; see Concordance, p. 22*].
"Reasonable time". Section 1–204 [*unrevised Article 1; see Concordance, p. 22*].
"Seasonably". Section 1–204 [*unrevised Article 1; see Concordance, p. 22*].
"Send". Section 1–201.
"Term". Section 1–201.
"Written". Section 1–201.

As amended in 1966 and 2022.

§ 2–208.　　[Reserved.] [Course of Performance or Practical Construction.] [*Note from West Advisory Panel: This section will be repealed if the jurisdiction adopts revised Article 1 (2001).*]

[(1)　Where the contract for sale involves repeated occasions for performance by either party with knowledge of the nature of the performance and opportunity for objection to it by the other, any course of performance accepted or acquiesced in without objection shall be relevant to determine the meaning of the agreement.

(2)　The express terms of the agreement and any such course of performance, as well as any course of dealing and usage of trade, shall be construed whenever reasonable as consistent with each other; but when such construction is unreasonable, express terms shall control course of performance and course of performance shall control both course of dealing and usage of trade (Section 1–205) [*unrevised Article 1; see Concordance, p. 22*].

(3) Subject to the provisions of the next section on modification and waiver, such course of performance shall be relevant to show a waiver or modification of any term inconsistent with such course of performance.

Official Comment

Prior Uniform Statutory Provision: No such general provision but concept of this section recognized by terms such as "course of dealing", "the circumstances of the case," "the conduct of the parties," etc., in Uniform Sales Act.

Purposes:

1. The parties themselves know best what they have meant by their words of agreement and their action under that agreement is the best indication of what that meaning was. This section thus rounds out the set of factors which determines the meaning of the "agreement" and therefore also of the "unless otherwise agreed" qualification to various provisions of this Article.

2. Under this section a course of performance is always relevant to determine the meaning of the agreement. Express mention of course of performance elsewhere in this Article carries no contrary implication when there is a failure to refer to it in other sections.

3. Where it is difficult to determine whether a particular act merely sheds light on the meaning of the agreement or represents a waiver of a term of the agreement, the preference is in favor of "waiver" whenever such construction, plus the application of the provisions on the reinstatement of rights waived (see Section 2–209), is needed to preserve the flexible character of commercial contracts and to prevent surprise or other hardship.

4. A single occasion of conduct does not fall within the language of this section but other sections such as the ones on silence after acceptance and failure to specify particular defects can affect the parties' rights on a single occasion (see Sections 2–605 and 2–607).]

Cross References:

Point 1: Section 1–201.
Point 2: Section 2–202.
Point 3: Sections 2–209, 2–601 and 2–607.
Point 4: Sections 2–605 and 2–607.

§ 2–209.   Modification, Rescission and Waiver.

(1) An agreement modifying a contract within this Article needs no consideration to be binding.

(2) A signed agreement which excludes modification or rescission except by a signed writing <u>or other signed record</u> cannot be otherwise modified or rescinded, but except as between merchants such a requirement on a form supplied by the merchant must be separately signed by the other party.

(3) The requirements of the statute of frauds section of this Article (Section 2–201) must be satisfied if the contract as modified is within its provisions.

(4) Although an attempt at modification or rescission does not satisfy the requirements of subsection (2) or (3) it can operate as a waiver.

(5) A party who has made a waiver affecting an executory portion of the contract may retract the waiver by reasonable notification received by the other party that strict performance will be required of any term waived, unless the retraction would be unjust in view of a material change of position in reliance on the waiver.

As amended in 2022.

Official Comment

Prior Uniform Statutory Provision: Subsection (1)—Compare Section 1, Uniform Written Obligations Act; Subsections (2) to (5)—none.

Purposes of Changes and New Matter:

1.   This section seeks to protect and make effective all necessary and desirable modifications of sales contracts without regard to the technicalities which at present hamper such adjustments.

2.   Subsection (1) provides that an agreement modifying a sales contract needs no consideration to be binding.

However, modifications made thereunder must meet the test of good faith imposed by this Act. The effective use of bad faith to escape performance on the original contract terms is barred, and the extortion of a "modification" without legitimate commercial reason is ineffective as a violation of the duty of good faith. Nor can a mere technical consideration support a modification made in bad faith.

The test of "good faith" between merchants or as against merchants includes "observance of reasonable commercial standards of fair dealing in the trade" (Section 2–103), and may in some situations require an objectively demonstrable reason for seeking a modification. But such matters as a market shift which makes performance come to involve a loss may provide such a reason even though there is no such unforeseen difficulty as would make out a legal excuse from performance under Sections 2–615 and 2–616.

3.   Subsections (2) and (3) are intended to protect against false allegations of oral modifications. "Modification or rescission" includes abandonment or other change by mutual consent, contrary to the decision in *Green v. Doniger*, 300 N.Y. 238, 90 N.E.2d 56 (1949); it does not include unilateral "termination" or "cancellation" as defined in Section 2–106.

The Statute of Frauds provisions of this Article are expressly applied to modifications by subsection (3). Under those provisions the "delivery and acceptance" test is limited to the goods which have been accepted, that is, to the past. "Modification" for the future cannot therefore be conjured up by oral testimony if the price involved is $500.00 or more since such modification must be shown at least by an authenticated memo. And since a memo is limited in its effect to the quantity of goods set forth in it there is safeguard against oral evidence.

Subsection (2) permits the parties in effect to make their own Statute of Frauds as regards any future modification of the contract by giving effect to a clause in a signed agreement which expressly requires any modification to be by signed writing or other signed record. But note that if a consumer is to be held to such a clause on a form supplied by a merchant it must be separately signed.

4.   Subsection (4) is intended, despite the provisions of subsections (2) and (3), to prevent contractual provisions excluding modification except by a signed ~~writing~~ record from limiting in other respects the legal effect of the parties' actual later conduct. The effect of such conduct as a waiver is further regulated in subsection (5).

5.   In furtherance of medium neutrality, the reference to a signed "writing" in the pre-2022 text of this section has been supplemented to refer as well to a signed "record."

Cross References:

Point 1: Section 1–203 [*unrevised Article 1; see Concordance, p. 22*].
Point 2: Sections 1–201, 1–203 [*unrevised Article 1; see Concordance, p. 22*], 2–615 and 2–616.
Point 3: Sections 2–106, 2–201 and 2–202.
Point 4: Sections 2–202 and 2–208.

Definitional Cross References:

"Agreement". Section 1–201.
"Between merchants". Section 2–104.
"Contract". Section 1–201.
"Notification". Section 1–201 [*unrevised Article 1; see Concordance, p. 22*].
"Signed". Section 1–201.
"Term". Section 1–201.
"Writing". Section 1–201.

As amended in 2022.

§ 2–210.   Delegation of Performance; Assignment of Rights.

(1)   A party may perform his duty through a delegate unless otherwise agreed or unless the other party has a substantial interest in having his original promisor perform or control the acts required by the

contract. No delegation of performance relieves the party delegating of any duty to perform or any liability for breach.

(2)   Except as otherwise provided in Section 9–406, unless otherwise agreed, all rights of either seller or buyer can be assigned except where the assignment would materially change the duty of the other party, or increase materially the burden or risk imposed on him by his contract, or impair materially his chance of obtaining return performance. A right to damages for breach of the whole contract or a right arising out of the assignor's due performance of his entire obligation can be assigned despite agreement otherwise.

(3)   The creation, attachment, perfection, or enforcement of a security interest in the seller's interest under a contract is not a transfer that materially changes the duty of or increases materially the burden or risk imposed on the buyer or impairs materially the buyer's chance of obtaining return performance within the purview of subsection (2) unless, and then only to the extent that, enforcement actually results in a delegation of material performance of the seller. Even in that event, the creation, attachment, perfection, and enforcement of the security interest remain effective, but (i) the seller is liable to the buyer for damages caused by the delegation to the extent that the damages could not reasonably be prevented by the buyer, and (ii) a court having jurisdiction may grant other appropriate relief, including cancellation of the contract for sale or an injunction against enforcement of the security interest or consummation of the enforcement.

(4)   Unless the circumstances indicate the contrary a prohibition of assignment of "the contract" is to be construed as barring only the delegation to the assignee of the assignor's performance.

(5)   An assignment of "the contract" or of "all my rights under the contract" or an assignment in similar general terms is an assignment of rights and unless the language or the circumstances (as in an assignment for security) indicate the contrary, it is a delegation of performance of the duties of the assignor and its acceptance by the assignee constitutes a promise by him to perform those duties. This promise is enforceable by either the assignor or the other party to the original contract.

(6)   The other party may treat any assignment which delegates performance as creating reasonable grounds for insecurity and may without prejudice to his rights against the assignor demand assurances from the assignee (Section 2–609).

As amended in 1999.

Official Comment

Prior Uniform Statutory Provision: None.

Purposes:

1.   Generally, this section recognizes both delegation of performance and assignability as normal and permissible incidents of a contract for the sale of goods.

2.   Delegation of performance, either in conjunction with an assignment or otherwise, is provided for by subsection (1) where no substantial reason can be shown as to why the delegated performance will not be as satisfactory as personal performance.

3.   Under subsection (2) rights which are no longer executory such as a right to damages for breach may be assigned although the agreement prohibits assignment. In such cases no question of delegation of any performance is involved. Subsection (2) is subject to Section 9–406, which makes rights to payment for goods sold ("accounts"), whether or not earned, freely alienable notwithstanding a contrary agreement or rule of law.

4.   The nature of the contract or the circumstances of the case, however, may bar assignment of the contract even where delegation of performance is not involved. This Article and this section are intended to clarify this problem, particularly in cases dealing with output requirement and exclusive dealing contracts. In the first place the section on requirements and exclusive dealing removes from the construction of the original contract most of the "personal discretion" element by substituting the reasonably objective standard of good faith operation of the plant or business to be supplied. Secondly, the section on insecurity and assurances, which is specifically referred to in subsection (5) of this section, frees the other party from the doubts and uncertainty which may afflict him under an assignment of the character in question by permitting him to demand adequate assurance of due performance without which he may suspend his own performance. Subsection (5) is not in any way intended to limit the effect of the section on insecurity and assurances and the word "performance" includes the giving of orders under a requirements contract. Of course, in any case where a material personal discretion is sought to be transferred, effective assignment is barred by subsection (2).

5.   Subsection (4) lays down a general rule of construction distinguishing between a normal commercial assignment, which substitutes the assignee for the assignor both as to rights and duties, and a financing assignment in which only the assignor's rights are transferred.

This Article takes no position on the possibility of extending some recognition or power to the original parties to work out normal commercial readjustments of the contract in the case of financing assignments even after the original obligor has been notified of the assignment. This question is dealt with in the Article on Secured Transactions (Article 9).

6.   Subsection (5) recognizes that the non-assigning original party has a stake in the reliability of the person with whom he has closed the original contract, and is, therefore, entitled to due assurance that any delegated performance will be properly forthcoming.

7.   This section is not intended as a complete statement of the law of delegation and assignment but is limited to clarifying a few points doubtful under the case law. Particularly, neither this section nor this Article touches directly on such questions as the need or effect of notice of the assignment, the rights of successive assignees, or any question of the form of an assignment, either as between the parties or as against any third parties. Some of these questions are dealt with in Article 9.

Cross References:

Point 3: Articles 5 and 9.
Point 4: Sections 2–306 and 2–609.
Point 5: Article 9, Sections 9–402, 9–404, 9–405, and 9–406.
Point 7: Article 9.

Definitional Cross References:

"Agreement". Section 1–201.
"Buyer". Section 2–103.
"Contract". Section 1–201.
"Party". Section 1–201.
"Rights". Section 1–201.
"Seller". Section 2–103.
"Term". Section 1–201.

As amended in 1999.

PART 3

GENERAL OBLIGATION AND CONSTRUCTION OF CONTRACT

§ 2–301.   General Obligations of Parties.

The obligation of the seller is to transfer and deliver and that of the buyer is to accept and pay in accordance with the contract.

Official Comment

Prior Uniform Statutory Provision: Sections 11 and 41, Uniform Sales Act.

Changes: Rewritten.

Purposes of Changes:

This section uses the term "obligation" in contrast to the term "duty" in order to provide for the "condition" aspects of delivery and payment insofar as they are not modified by other sections of this Article such as those on cure of tender. It thus replaces not only the general provisions of the Uniform Sales Act on the parties' duties, but also the general provisions of that Act on the effect of conditions. In order to determine what is "in accordance with the contract" under this Article usage of trade, course of dealing and performance, and the general background of circumstances must be given due consideration in conjunction with the lay meaning of the words used to define the scope of the conditions and duties.

Cross References:

Section 1–106 [*unrevised Article 1; see Concordance, p. 22*]. See also Sections 1–205 [*unrevised Article 1; see Concordance, p. 22*], 2–208, 2–209, 2–508 and 2–612.

Definitional Cross References:

"Buyer". Section 2–103.
"Contract". Section 1–201.
"Party". Section 1–201.
"Seller". Section 2–103.

§ 2–302.   Unconscionable Contract or Clause.

(1)   If the court as a matter of law finds the contract or any clause of the contract to have been unconscionable at the time it was made the court may refuse to enforce the contract, or it may enforce the remainder of the contract without the unconscionable clause, or it may so limit the application of any unconscionable clause as to avoid any unconscionable result.

(2)   When it is claimed or appears to the court that the contract or any clause thereof may be unconscionable the parties shall be afforded a reasonable opportunity to present evidence as to its commercial setting, purpose and effect to aid the court in making the determination.

Official Comment

Prior Uniform Statutory Provision: None.

Purposes:

1.   This section is intended to make it possible for the courts to police explicitly against the contracts or clauses which they find to be unconscionable. In the past such policing has been accomplished by adverse construction of language, by manipulation of the rules of offer and acceptance or by determinations that the clause is contrary to public policy or to the dominant purpose of the contract. This section is intended to allow the court to pass directly on the unconscionability of the contract or particular clause therein and to make a conclusion of law as to its unconscionability. The basic test is whether, in the light of the general commercial background and the commercial needs of the particular trade or case, the clauses involved are so one-sided as to be unconscionable under the circumstances existing at the time of the making of the contract. Subsection (2) makes it clear that it is proper for the court to hear evidence upon these questions. The principle is one of the prevention of oppression and unfair surprise (Cf. *Campbell Soup Co. v. Wentz*, 172 F.2d 80, 3d Cir. 1948) and not of disturbance of allocation of risks because of superior bargaining power. The underlying basis of this section is illustrated by the results in cases such as the following:

Kansas City Wholesale Grocery Co. v. Weber Packing Corporation, 93 Utah 414, 73 P.2d 1272 (1937), where a clause limiting time for complaints was held inapplicable to latent defects in a shipment of catsup which could be discovered only by microscopic analysis; *Hardy v. General Motors Acceptance Corporation*, 38 Ga.App. 463, 144 S.E. 327 (1928), holding that a disclaimer of warranty clause applied only to express warranties, thus letting in a fair implied warranty; *Andrews Bros. v. Singer & Co.* (1934 CA) 1 K.B. 17, holding that where a car with substantial mileage was delivered instead of a "new" car, a disclaimer of warranties, including those "implied," left unaffected an "express obligation" on the description, even though the Sale of Goods Act called such an implied warranty; *New Prague Flouring Mill Co. v. G. A. Spears*, 194 Iowa 417, 189 N.W. 815 (1922), holding that a clause permitting the seller, upon the buyer's failure to supply shipping instructions, to cancel, ship, or allow delivery date to be indefinitely postponed 30 days at a time by the inaction, does not indefinitely postpone the date of measuring damages for the buyer's breach, to the seller's advantage; and *Kansas Flour Mills Co. v. Dirks*, 100 Kan. 376, 164 P. 273 (1917), where under a similar clause in a rising market the court permitted the buyer to measure his damages for non-delivery at the end of only one 30 day postponement; *Green v. Arcos*, Ltd. (1931 CA) 47 T.L.R. 336, where a blanket clause prohibiting rejection of shipments by the buyer was restricted to apply to shipments where discrepancies represented merely mercantile variations; *Meyer v. Packard Cleveland Motor Co.*, 106 Ohio St. 328, 140 N.E. 118 (1922), in which the court held that a "waiver" of all agreements not specified did not preclude implied warranty of fitness of a rebuilt dump truck for ordinary use as a dump truck; *Austin Co. v. J. H. Tillman Co.*, 104 Or. 541, 209 P. 131 (1922), where a clause limiting the buyer's remedy to return was held to be applicable only if the seller had delivered a machine needed for a construction job which reasonably met the contract description; *Bekkevold v. Potts*, 173 Minn. 87, 216 N.W. 790, 59 A.L.R. 1164 (1927), refusing to allow warranty of fitness for purpose imposed by law to be negated by clause excluding all warranties "made" by the seller; *Robert A. Munroe & Co. v. Meyer* (1930) 2 K.B. 312, holding that the warranty of description overrides a clause reading "with all faults and defects" where adulterated meat not up to the contract description was delivered.

2.   Under this section the court, in its discretion, may refuse to enforce the contract as a whole if it is permeated by the unconscionability, or it may strike any single clause or group of clauses which are so tainted or which are contrary to the essential purpose of the agreement, or it may simply limit unconscionable clauses so as to avoid unconscionable results.

3.   The present section is addressed to the court, and the decision is to be made by it. The commercial evidence referred to in subsection (2) is for the court's consideration, not the jury's. Only the agreement which results from the court's action on these matters is to be submitted to the general triers of the facts.

Definitional Cross Reference:

"Contract". Section 1–201.

§ 2–303.   Allocation or Division of Risks.

Where this Article allocates a risk or a burden as between the parties "unless otherwise agreed", the agreement may not only shift the allocation but may also divide the risk or burden.

Official Comment

Prior Uniform Statutory Provision: None.

Purposes:

1.   This section is intended to make it clear that the parties may modify or allocate "unless otherwise agreed" risks or burdens imposed by this Article as they desire, always subject, of course, to the provisions on unconscionability.

Compare Section 1–102(4) [*unrevised Article 1; see Concordance, p. 22*].

2.   The risk or burden may be divided by the express terms of the agreement or by the attending circumstances, since under the definition of "agreement" in this Act the circumstances surrounding the transaction as well as the express language used by the parties enter into the meaning and substance of the agreement.

Cross References:

Point 1: Sections 1–102 [*unrevised Article 1; see Concordance, p. 22*], 2–302.
Point 2: Section 1–201.

Definitional Cross References:

"Party". Section 1–201.
"Agreement". Section 1–201.

§ 2–304.   Price Payable in Money, Goods, Realty, or Otherwise.

(1)   The price can be made payable in money or otherwise. If it is payable in whole or in part in goods each party is a seller of the goods which he is to transfer.

(2)   Even though all or part of the price is payable in an interest in realty the transfer of the goods and the seller's obligations with reference to them are subject to this Article, but not the transfer of the interest in realty or the transferor's obligations in connection therewith.

Official Comment

Prior Uniform Statutory Provision: Subsections (2) and (3) of Section 9, Uniform Sales Act.

Changes: Rewritten.

Purposes of Changes:

1.   This section corrects the phrasing of the Uniform Sales Act so as to avoid misconstruction and produce greater accuracy in commercial result. While it continues the essential intent and purpose of the Uniform Sales Act it rejects any purely verbalistic construction in disregard of the underlying reason of the provisions.

2.   Under subsection (1) the provisions of this Article are applicable to transactions where the "price" of goods is payable in something other than money. This does not mean, however, that this whole Article applies automatically and in its entirety simply because an agreed transfer of title to goods is not a gift. The basic purposes and reasons of the Article must always be considered in determining the applicability of any of its provisions.

3.   Subsection (2) lays down the general principle that when goods are to be exchanged for realty, the provisions of this Article apply only to those aspects of the transaction which concern the transfer of title to goods but do not affect the transfer of the realty since the detailed regulation of various particular contracts which fall outside the scope of this Article is left to the courts and other legislation. However, the complexities of these situations may be such that each must be analyzed in the light of the underlying reasons in order to determine the applicable principles. Local statutes dealing with realty are not to be lightly disregarded or altered by language of this Article. In contrast, this Article declares definite policies in regard to certain matters legitimately within its scope though concerned with real property situations, and in those instances the provisions of this Article control.

Cross References:

Point 1: Section 1–102 [*unrevised Article 1; see Concordance, p. 22*].
Point 3: Sections 1–102 [*unrevised Article 1; see Concordance, p. 22*], 1–103, 1–104 and 2–107.

Definitional Cross References:

"Goods". Section 2–105.
"Money". Section 1–201.
"Party". Section 1–201.
"Seller". Section 2–103.

§ 2–305.   Open Price Term.

(1)   The parties if they so intend can conclude a contract for sale even though the price is not settled. In such a case the price is a reasonable price at the time for delivery if

(a)   nothing is said as to price; or

(b)   the price is left to be agreed by the parties and they fail to agree; or

(c)   the price is to be fixed in terms of some agreed market or other standard as set or recorded by a third person or agency and it is not so set or recorded.

(2)   A price to be fixed by the seller or by the buyer means a price for him to fix in good faith.

(3)   When a price left to be fixed otherwise than by agreement of the parties fails to be fixed through fault of one party the other may at his option treat the contract as cancelled or himself fix a reasonable price.

(4)   Where, however, the parties intend not to be bound unless the price be fixed or agreed and it is not fixed or agreed there is no contract. In such a case the buyer must return any goods already received or if unable so to do must pay their reasonable value at the time of delivery and the seller must return any portion of the price paid on account.

Official Comment

Prior Uniform Statutory Provision: Sections 9 and 10, Uniform Sales Act.

Changes: Completely rewritten.

Purposes of Changes:

1.   This section applies when the price term is left open on the making of an agreement which is nevertheless intended by the parties to be a binding agreement. This Article rejects in these instances the formula that "an agreement to agree is unenforceable" if the case falls within subsection (1) of this section, and rejects also defeating such agreements on the ground of "indefiniteness". Instead this Article recognizes the dominant intention of the parties to have the deal continue to be binding upon both. As to future performance, since this Article recognizes remedies such as cover (Section 2–712), resale (Section 2–706) and specific performance (Section 2–716) which go beyond any mere arithmetic as between contract price and market price, there is usually a

"reasonably certain basis for granting an appropriate remedy for breach" so that the contract need not fail for indefiniteness.

2.   Under some circumstances the postponement of agreement on price will mean that no deal has really been concluded, and this is made express in the preamble of subsection (1) ("The parties *if they so intend*") and in subsection (4). Whether or not this is so is, in most cases, a question to be determined by the trier of fact.

3.   Subsection (2), dealing with the situation where the price is to be fixed by one party rejects the uncommercial idea that an agreement that the seller may fix the price means that he may fix any price he may wish by the express qualification that the price so fixed must be fixed in good faith. Good faith includes observance of reasonable commercial standards of fair dealing in the trade if the party is a merchant. (Section 2–103). But in the normal case a "posted price" or a future seller's or buyer's "given price," "price in effect," "market price," or the like satisfies the good faith requirement.

4.   The section recognizes that there may be cases in which a particular person's judgment is not chosen merely as a barometer or index of a fair price but is an essential condition to the parties' intent to make any contract at all. For example, the case where a known and trusted expert is to "value" a particular painting for which there is no market standard differs sharply from the situation where a named expert is to determine the grade of cotton, and the difference would support a finding that in the one the parties did not intend to make a binding agreement if that expert were unavailable whereas in the other they did so intend. Other circumstances would of course affect the validity of such a finding.

5.   Under subsection (3), wrongful interference by one party with any agreed machinery for price fixing in the contract may be treated by the other party as a repudiation justifying cancellation, or merely as a failure to take cooperative action thus shifting to the aggrieved party the reasonable leeway in fixing the price.

6.   Throughout the entire section, the purpose is to give effect to the agreement which has been made. That effect, however, is always conditioned by the requirement of good faith action which is made an inherent part of all contracts within this Act. (Section 1–203) [*unrevised Article 1; see Concordance, p. 22*].

Cross References:

> Point 1: Sections 2–204(3), 2–706, 2–712 and 2–716.
> Point 3: Section 2–103.
> Point 5: Sections 2–311 and 2–610.
> Point 6: Section 1–203 [*unrevised Article 1; see Concordance, p. 22*].

Definitional Cross References:

> "Agreement". Section 1–201.
> "Burden of establishing". Section 1–201.
> "Buyer". Section 2–103.
> "Cancellation". Section 2–106.
> "Contract". Section 1–201.
> "Contract for sale". Section 2–106.
> "Fault". Section 1–201.
> "Goods". Section 2–105.
> "Party". Section 1–201.
> "Receipt of goods". Section 2–103.
> "Seller". Section 2–103.
> "Term". Section 1–201.

§ 2–306.   Output, Requirements and Exclusive Dealings.

(1)   A term which measures the quantity by the output of the seller or the requirements of the buyer means such actual output or requirements as may occur in good faith, except that no quantity unreasonably disproportionate to any stated estimate or in the absence of a stated estimate to any normal or otherwise comparable prior output or requirements may be tendered or demanded.

(2)   A lawful agreement by either the seller or the buyer for exclusive dealing in the kind of goods concerned imposes unless otherwise agreed an obligation by the seller to use best efforts to supply the goods and by the buyer to use best efforts to promote their sale.

Official Comment

Prior Uniform Statutory Provision: None.

Purposes:

1.   Subsection (1) of this section, in regard to output and requirements, applies to this specific problem the general approach of this Act which requires the reading of commercial background and intent into the language of any agreement and demands good faith in the performance of that agreement. It applies to such contracts of nonproducing establishments such as dealers or distributors as well as to manufacturing concerns.

2.   Under this Article, a contract for output or requirements is not too indefinite since it is held to mean the actual good faith output or requirements of the particular party. Nor does such a contract lack mutuality of obligation since, under this section, the party who will determine quantity is required to operate his plant or conduct his business in good faith and according to commercial standards of fair dealing in the trade so that his output or requirements will approximate a reasonably foreseeable figure. Reasonable elasticity in the requirements is expressly envisaged by this section and good faith variations from prior requirements are permitted even when the variation may be such as to result in discontinuance. A shut-down by a requirements buyer for lack of orders might be permissible when a shut-down merely to curtail losses would not. The essential test is whether the party is acting in good faith. Similarly, a sudden expansion of the plant by which requirements are to be measured would not be included within the scope of the contract as made but normal expansion undertaken in good faith would be within the scope of this section. One of the factors in an expansion situation would be whether the market price had risen greatly in a case in which the requirements contract contained a fixed price. Reasonable variation of an extreme sort is exemplified in *Southwest Natural Gas Co. v. Oklahoma Portland Cement Co.*, 102 F.2d 630 (C.C.A.10, 1939). This Article takes no position as to whether a requirements contract is a provable claim in bankruptcy.

3.   If an estimate of output or requirements is included in the agreement, no quantity unreasonably disproportionate to it may be tendered or demanded. Any minimum or maximum set by the agreement shows a clear limit on the intended elasticity. In similar fashion, the agreed estimate is to be regarded as a center around which the parties intend the variation to occur.

4.   When an enterprise is sold, the question may arise whether the buyer is bound by an existing output or requirements contract. That question is outside the scope of this Article, and is to be determined on other principles of law. Assuming that the contract continues, the output or requirements in the hands of the new owner continue to be measured by the actual good faith output or requirements under the normal operation of the enterprise prior to sale. The sale itself is not grounds for sudden expansion or decrease.

5.   Subsection (2), on exclusive dealing, makes explicit the commercial rule embodied in this Act under which the parties to such contracts are held to have impliedly, even when not expressly, bound themselves to use reasonable diligence as well as good faith in their performance of the contract. Under such contracts the exclusive agent is required, although no express commitment has been made, to use reasonable effort and due diligence in the expansion of the market or the promotion of the product, as the case may be. The principal is expected under such a contract to refrain from supplying any other dealer or agent within the exclusive territory. An exclusive dealing agreement brings into play all of the good faith aspects of the output and requirement problems of subsection (1). It also raises questions of insecurity and right to adequate assurance under this Article.

Cross References:

Point 4: Section 2–210.
Point 5: Sections 1–203 [*unrevised Article 1; see Concordance, p. 22*] and 2–609.

Definitional Cross References:

"Agreement". Section 1–201.
"Buyer". Section 2–103.
"Contract for sale". Section 2–106.
"Good faith". Section 1–201.
"Goods". Section 2–105.
"Party". Section 1–201.
"Term". Section 1–201.
"Seller". Section 2–103.

§ 2–307.   Delivery in Single Lot or Several Lots.

Unless otherwise agreed all goods called for by a contract for sale must be tendered in a single delivery and payment is due only on such tender but where the circumstances give either party the right to make or demand delivery in lots the price if it can be apportioned may be demanded for each lot.

Official Comment

Prior Uniform Statutory Provision: Section 45(1), Uniform Sales Act.

Changes: Rewritten and expanded.

Purposes of Changes:

1.   This section applies where the parties have not specifically agreed whether delivery and payment are to be by lots and generally continues the essential intent of original Act, Section 45(1) by assuming that the parties intended delivery to be in a single lot.

2.   Where the actual agreement or the circumstances do not indicate otherwise, delivery in lots is not permitted under this section and the buyer is properly entitled to reject for a deficiency in the tender, subject to any privilege in the seller to cure the tender.

3.   The "but" clause of this section goes to the case in which it is not commercially feasible to deliver or to receive the goods in a single lot as for example, where a contract calls for the shipment of ten carloads of coal and only three cars are available at a given time. Similarly, in a contract involving brick necessary to build a building the buyer's storage space may be limited so that it would be impossible to receive the entire amount of brick at once, or it may be necessary to assemble the goods as in the case of cattle on the range, or to mine them.

In such cases, a partial delivery is not subject to rejection for the defect in quantity alone, if the circumstances do not indicate a repudiation or default by the seller as to the expected balance or do not give the buyer ground for suspending his performance because of insecurity under the provisions of Section 2–609. However, in such cases the undelivered balance of goods under the contract must be forthcoming within a reasonable time and in a reasonable manner according to the policy of Section 2–503 on manner of tender of delivery. This is reinforced by the express provisions of Section 2–608 that if a lot has been accepted on the reasonable assumption that its nonconformity will be cured, the acceptance may be revoked if the cure does not seasonably occur. The section rejects the rule of *Kelly Construction Co. v. Hackensack Brick Co.*, 91 N.J.L. 585, 103 A. 417, 2 A.L.R. 685 (1918) and approves the result in *Lynn M. Ranger, Inc. v. Gildersleeve*, 106 Conn. 372, 138 A. 142 (1927) in which a contract was made for six carloads of coal then rolling from the mines and consigned to the seller but the seller agreed to divert the carloads to the buyer as soon as the car numbers became known to him. He arranged a diversion of two cars and then notified the buyer who then repudiated the contract. The seller was held to be entitled to his full remedy for the two cars diverted because simultaneous delivery of all of the cars was not contemplated by either party.

4.   Where the circumstances indicate that a party has a right to delivery in lots, the price may be demanded for each lot if it is apportionable.

Cross References:

Point 1: Section 1–201.
Point 2: Sections 2–508 and 2–601.
Point 3: Sections 2–503, 2–608 and 2–609.

Definitional Cross References:

"Contract for sale". Section 2–106.
"Goods". Section 2–105.
"Lot". Section 2–105.
"Party". Section 1–201.
"Rights". Section 1–201.

§ 2–308.   Absence of Specified Place for Delivery.

Unless otherwise agreed

(a)   the place for delivery of goods is the seller's place of business or if he has none his residence; but

(b) in a contract for sale of identified goods which to the knowledge of the parties at the time of contracting are in some other place, that place is the place for their delivery; and

(c) documents of title may be delivered through customary banking channels.

Official Comment

Prior Uniform Statutory Provision: Paragraphs (a) and (b)—Section 43(1), Uniform Sales Act; Paragraph (c)—none.

Changes: Slight modification in language.

Purposes of Changes and New Matter:

1. Paragraphs (a) and (b) provide for those noncommercial sales and for those occasional commercial sales where no place or means of delivery has been agreed upon by the parties. Where delivery by carrier is "required or authorized by the agreement", the seller's duties as to delivery of the goods are governed not by this section but by Section 2–504.

2. Under paragraph (b) when the identified goods contracted for are known to both parties to be in some location other than the seller's place of business or residence, the parties are presumed to have intended that place to be the place of delivery. This paragraph also applies (unless, as would be normal, the circumstances show that delivery by way of documents is intended) to a bulk of goods in the possession of a bailee. In such a case, however, the seller has the additional obligation to procure the acknowledgment by the bailee of the buyer's right to possession.

3. Where "customary banking channels" call only for due notification by the banker that the documents are available, leaving the buyer himself to see to the physical receipt of the goods, tender at the buyer's address is not required under paragraph (c). But that paragraph merely eliminates the possibility of a default by the seller if "customary banking channels" have been properly used in giving notice to the buyer. Where the bank has purchased a draft accompanied by or associated with documents or has undertaken its collection on behalf of the seller, Part 5 of Article 4 spells out its duties and relations to its customer. Where the documents move forward under a letter of credit the Article on Letters of Credit spells out the duties and relations between the bank, the seller and the buyer. Delivery in relationship to either tangible or electronic documents of title is defined in Article 1, Section 1–201.

4. The rules of this section apply only "unless otherwise agreed." The surrounding circumstances, usage of trade, course of dealing and course of performance, as well as the express language of the parties, may constitute an "otherwise agreement".

Cross References:

Point 1: Sections 2–504 and 2–505.
Point 2: Section 2–503.
Point 3: Section 2–512, Articles 4, Part 5, and 5.

Definitional Cross References:

"Contract for sale". Section 2–106.
"Delivery". Section 1–201.
"Document of title". Section 1–201.
"Goods". Section 2–105.
"Party". Section 1–201.
"Seller". Section 2–103.

As amended in 2003.

§ 2–309. Absence of Specific Time Provisions; Notice of Termination.

(1) The time for shipment or delivery or any other action under a contract if not provided in this Article or agreed upon shall be a reasonable time.

(2) Where the contract provides for successive performances but is indefinite in duration it is valid for a reasonable time but unless otherwise agreed may be terminated at any time by either party.

(3) Termination of a contract by one party except on the happening of an agreed event requires that reasonable notification be received by the other party and an agreement dispensing with notification is invalid if its operation would be unconscionable.

Official Comment

Prior Uniform Statutory Provision: Subsection (1)—see Sections 43(2), 45(2), 47(1) and 48, Uniform Sales Act, for policy continued under this Article; Subsection (2)—none; Subsection (3)—none.

Changes: Completely different in scope.

Purposes of Changes and New Matter:

1. Subsection (1) requires that all actions taken under a sales contract must be taken within a reasonable time where no time has been agreed upon. The reasonable time under this provision turns on the criteria as to "reasonable time" and on good faith and commercial standards set forth in Sections 1–203 [*unrevised Article 1; see Concordance, p. 22*], 1–204 [*unrevised Article 1; see Concordance, p. 22*] and 2–103. It thus depends upon what constitutes acceptable commercial conduct in view of the nature, purpose and circumstances of the action to be taken. Agreement as to a definite time, however, may be found in a term implied from the contractual circumstances, usage of trade or course of dealing or performance as well as in an express term. Such cases fall outside of this subsection since in them the time for action is "agreed" by usage.

2. The time for payment, where not agreed upon, is related to the time for delivery; the particular problems which arise in connection with determining the appropriate time of payment and the time for any inspection before payment which is both allowed by law and demanded by the buyer are covered in Section 2–513.

3. The facts in regard to shipment and delivery differ so widely as to make detailed provision for them in the text of this Article impracticable. The applicable principles, however, make it clear that surprise is to be avoided, good faith judgment is to be protected, and notice or negotiation to reduce the uncertainty to certainty is to be favored.

4. When the time for delivery is left open, unreasonably early offers of or demands for delivery are intended to be read under this Article as expressions of desire or intention, requesting the assent or acquiescence of the other party, not as final positions which may amount without more to breach or to create breach by the other side. See Sections 2–207 and 2–609.

5. The obligation of good faith under this Act requires reasonable notification before a contract may be treated as breached because a reasonable time for delivery or demand has expired. This operates both in the case of a contract originally indefinite as to time and of one subsequently made indefinite by waiver.

When both parties let an originally reasonable time go by in silence, the course of conduct under the contract may be viewed as enlarging the reasonable time for tender or demand of performance. The contract may be terminated by abandonment.

6. Parties to a contract are not required in giving reasonable notification to fix, at peril of breach, a time which is in fact reasonable in the unforeseeable judgment of a later trier of fact. Effective communication of a proposed time limit calls for a response, so that failure to reply will make out acquiescence. Where objection is made, however, or if the demand is merely for information as to when goods will be delivered or will be ordered out, demand for assurances on the ground of insecurity may be made under this Article pending further negotiations. Only when a party insists on undue delay or on rejection of the other party's reasonable proposal is there a question of flat breach under the present section.

7. Subsection (2) applies a commercially reasonable view to resolve the conflict which has arisen in the cases as to contracts of indefinite duration. The "reasonable time" of duration appropriate to a given arrangement is limited by the circumstances. When the arrangement has been carried on by the parties over the years, the "reasonable time" can continue indefinitely and the contract will not terminate until notice.

8. Subsection (3) recognizes that the application of principles of good faith and sound commercial practice normally call for such notification of the termination of a going contract relationship as will give the other party reasonable time to seek a substitute arrangement. An agreement dispensing with notification or limiting the time for the seeking of a substitute arrangement is, of course, valid under this subsection unless the results of putting it into operation would be the creation of an unconscionable state of affairs.

9. Justifiable cancellation for breach is a remedy for breach and is not the kind of termination covered by the present subsection.

10. The requirement of notification is dispensed with where the contract provides for termination on the happening of an "agreed event." "Event" is a term chosen here to contrast with "option" or the like.

Cross References:

Point 1: Sections 1–203 [*unrevised Article 1; see Concordance, p. 22*], 1–204 [*unrevised Article 1; see Concordance, p. 22*] and 2–103.

Point 2: Sections 2–320, 2–321, 2–504, and 2–511 through 2–514.

Point 5: Section 1–203 [*unrevised Article 1; see Concordance, p. 22*].

Point 6: Section 2–609.

Point 7: Section 2–204.

Point 9: Sections 2–106, 2–318, 2–610 and 2–703.

Definitional Cross References:

"Agreement". Section 1–201.

"Contract". Section 1–201.

"Notification". Section 1–201 [*unrevised Article 1; see Concordance, p. 22*].

"Party". Section 1–201.

"Reasonable time". Section 1–204 [*unrevised Article 1; see Concordance, p. 22*].

"Termination". Section 2–106.

§ 2–310. Open Time for Payment or Running of Credit; Authority to Ship Under Reservation.

Unless otherwise agreed

(a) payment is due at the time and place at which the buyer is to receive the goods even though the place of shipment is the place of delivery; and

(b) if the seller is authorized to send the goods he may ship them under reservation, and may tender the documents of title, but the buyer may inspect the goods after their arrival before payment is due unless such inspection is inconsistent with the terms of the contract (Section 2–513); and

(c) if delivery is authorized and made by way of documents of title otherwise than by subsection (b) then payment is due regardless of where the goods are received (i) at the time and place at which the buyer is to receive delivery of the tangible documents or (ii) at the time the buyer is to receive delivery of the electronic documents and at the seller's place of business or if none, the seller's residence; and

(d) where the seller is required or authorized to ship the goods on credit the credit period runs from the time of shipment but post-dating the invoice or delaying its dispatch will correspondingly delay the starting of the credit period.

As amended in 2003.

Official Comment

Prior Uniform Statutory Provision: Sections 42 and 47(2), Uniform Sales Act.

Changes: Completely rewritten in this and other sections.

Purposes of Changes: This section is drawn to reflect modern business methods of dealing at a distance rather than face to face. Thus:

1. Paragraph (a) provides that payment is due at the time and place "the buyer is to receive the goods" rather than at the point of delivery except in documentary shipment cases (paragraph (c)). This grants an opportunity for the exercise by the buyer of his preliminary right to inspection before paying even though under the delivery term the risk of loss may have previously passed to him or the running of the credit period has already started.

2. Paragraph (b) while providing for inspection by the buyer before he pays, protects the seller. He is not required to give up possession of the goods until he has received payment, where no credit has been contemplated by the parties. The seller may collect through a bank by a sight draft against an order bill of lading "hold until

arrival; inspection allowed." The obligations of the bank under such a provision are set forth in Part 5 of Article 4. Under subsection (c), in the absence of a credit term, the seller is permitted to ship under reservation and if he does payment is then due where and when the buyer is to receive delivery of the tangible documents of title. In the case of an electronic document of title, payment is due when the buyer is to receive delivery of the electronic document and at the seller's place of business, or if none, the seller's residence. Delivery as to documents of title is stated in Article 1, Section 1–201.

3.   Unless otherwise agreed, the place for the delivery of the documents and payment is the buyer's city but the time for payment is only after arrival of the goods, since under paragraph (b), and Sections 2–512 and 2–513 the buyer is under no duty to pay prior to inspection. Tender of a document of title requires that the seller be ready, willing and able to transfer possession of a tangible document of title or control of an electronic document of title to the buyer.

4.   Where the mode of shipment is such that goods must be unloaded immediately upon arrival, too rapidly to permit adequate inspection before receipt, the seller must be guided by the provisions of this Article on inspection which provide that if the seller wishes to demand payment before inspection, he must put an appropriate term into the contract. Even requiring payment against documents will not of itself have this desired result if the documents are to be held until the arrival of the goods. But under (b) and (c) if the terms are C.I.F., C.O.D., or cash against documents payment may be due before inspection.

5.   Paragraph (d) states the common commercial understanding that an agreed credit period runs from the time of shipment or from that dating of the invoice which is commonly recognized as a representation of the time of shipment. The provision concerning any delay in sending forth the invoice is included because such conduct results in depriving the buyer of his full notice and warning as to when he must be prepared to pay.

Cross References:

Generally: Part 5.
Point 1: Section 2–509.
Point 2: Sections 2–505, 2–511, 2–512, 2–513 and Article 4.
Point 3: Sections 2–308(b), 2–512 and 2–513.
Point 4: Section 2–513(3)(b).

Definitional Cross References:

"Buyer". Section 2–103.
"Delivery". Section 1–201.
"Document of title". Section 1–201.
"Goods". Section 2–105.
"Receipt of goods". Section 2–103.
"Seller". Section 2–103.
"Send". Section 1–201.
"Term". Section 1–201.

As amended in 2003.

§ 2–311.   Options and Cooperation Respecting Performance.

(1)   An agreement for sale which is otherwise sufficiently definite (subsection (3) of Section 2–204) to be a contract is not made invalid by the fact that it leaves particulars of performance to be specified by one of the parties. Any such specification must be made in good faith and within limits set by commercial reasonableness.

(2)   Unless otherwise agreed specifications relating to assortment of the goods are at the buyer's option and except as otherwise provided in subsections (1)(c) and (3) of Section 2–319 specifications or arrangements relating to shipment are at the seller's option.

(3)   Where such specification would materially affect the other party's performance but is not seasonably made or where one party's cooperation is necessary to the agreed performance of the other but is not seasonably forthcoming, the other party in addition to all other remedies

(a)   is excused for any resulting delay in his own performance; and

(b)   may also either proceed to perform in any reasonable manner or after the time for a material part of his own performance treat the failure to specify or to cooperate as a breach by failure to deliver or accept the goods.

Official Comment

Prior Uniform Statutory Provision: None.

Purposes:

1.   Subsection (1) permits the parties to leave certain detailed particulars of performance to be filled in by either of them without running the risk of having the contract invalidated for indefiniteness. The party to whom the agreement gives power to specify the missing details is required to exercise good faith and to act in accordance with commercial standards so that there is no surprise and the range of permissible variation is limited by what is commercially reasonable. The "agreement" which permits one party so to specify may be found as well in a course of dealing, usage of trade, or implication from circumstances as in explicit language used by the parties.

2.   Options as to assortment of goods or shipping arrangements are specifically reserved to the buyer and seller respectively under subsection (2) where no other arrangement has been made. This section rejects the test which mechanically and without regard to usage or the purpose of the option gave the option to the party "first under a duty to move" and applies instead a standard commercial interpretation to these circumstances. The "unless otherwise agreed" provision of this subsection covers not only express terms but the background and circumstances which enter into the agreement.

3.   Subsection (3) applies when the exercise of an option or cooperation by one party is necessary to or materially affects the other party's performance, but it is not seasonably forthcoming; the subsection relieves the other party from the necessity for performance or excuses his delay in performance as the case may be. The contract-keeping party may at his option under this subsection proceed to perform in any commercially reasonable manner rather than wait. In addition to the special remedies provided, this subsection also reserves "all other remedies". The remedy of particular importance in this connection is that provided for insecurity. Request may also be made pursuant to the obligation of good faith for a reasonable indication of the time and manner of performance for which a party is to hold himself ready.

4.   The remedy provided in subsection (3) is one which does not operate in the situation which falls within the scope of Section 2–614 on substituted performance. Where the failure to cooperate results from circumstances set forth in that Section, the other party is under a duty to proffer or demand (as the case may be) substitute performance as a condition to claiming rights against the noncooperating party.

Cross References:

    Point 1: Sections 1–201, 2–204 and 1–203. [*unrevised Article 1; see Concordance, p. 22*].
    Point 3: Sections 1–203 [*unrevised Article 1; see Concordance, p. 22*] and 2–609.
    Point 4: Section 2–614.

Definitional Cross References:

    "Agreement". Section 1–201.
    "Buyer". Section 2–103.
    "Contract for sale". Section 2–106.
    "Goods". Section 2–105.
    "Party". Section 1–201.
    "Remedy". Section 1–201.
    "Seasonably". Section 1–204 [*unrevised Article 1; see Concordance, p. 22*].
    "Seller". Section 2–103.

§ 2–312.   Warranty of Title and Against Infringement; Buyer's Obligation Against Infringement.

(1)   Subject to subsection (2) there is in a contract for sale a warranty by the seller that

(a)   the title conveyed shall be good, and its transfer rightful; and

(b)   the goods shall be delivered free from any security interest or other lien or encumbrance of which the buyer at the time of contracting has no knowledge.

(2)   A warranty under subsection (1) will be excluded or modified only by specific language or by circumstances which give the buyer reason to know that the person selling does not claim title in himself or that he is purporting to sell only such right or title as he or a third person may have.

(3)   Unless otherwise agreed a seller who is a merchant regularly dealing in goods of the kind warrants that the goods shall be delivered free of the rightful claim of any third person by way of infringement or the like but a buyer who furnishes specifications to the seller must hold the seller harmless against any such claim which arises out of compliance with the specifications.

Official Comment

Prior Uniform Statutory Provision: Section 13, Uniform Sales Act.

Changes: Completely rewritten, the provisions concerning infringement being new.

Purposes of Changes:

1.   Subsection (1) makes provision for a buyer's basic needs in respect to a title which he in good faith expects to acquire by his purchase, namely, that he receive a good, clean title transferred to him also in a rightful manner so that he will not be exposed to a lawsuit in order to protect it.

The warranty extends to a buyer whether or not the seller was in possession of the goods at the time the sale or contract to sell was made.

The warranty of quiet possession is abolished. Disturbance of quiet possession, although not mentioned specifically, is one way, among many, in which the breach of the warranty of title may be established.

The "knowledge" referred to in subsection 1(b) is actual knowledge as distinct from notice.

2.   The provisions of this Article requiring notification to the seller within a reasonable time after the buyer's discovery of a breach apply to notice of a breach of the warranty of title, where the seller's breach was innocent. However, if the seller's breach was in bad faith he cannot be permitted to claim that he has been misled or prejudiced by the delay in giving notice. In such case the "reasonable" time for notice should receive a very liberal interpretation. Whether the breach by the seller is in good or bad faith Section 2–725 provides that the cause of action accrues when the breach occurs. Under the provisions of that section the breach of the warranty of good title occurs when tender of delivery is made since the warranty is not one which extends to "future performance of the goods."

3.   When the goods are part of the seller's normal stock and are sold in his normal course of business, it is his duty to see that no claim of infringement of a patent or trademark by a third party will mar the buyer's title. A sale by a person other than a dealer, however, raises no implication in its circumstances of such a warranty. Nor is there such an implication when the buyer orders goods to be assembled, prepared or manufactured on his own specifications. If, in such a case, the resulting product infringes a patent or trademark, the liability will run from buyer to seller. There is, under such circumstances, a tacit representation on the part of the buyer that the seller will be safe in manufacturing according to the specifications, and the buyer is under an obligation in good faith to indemnify him for any loss suffered.

4.   This section rejects the cases which recognize the principle that infringements violate the warranty of title but deny the buyer a remedy unless he has been expressly prevented from using the goods. Under this Article "eviction" is not a necessary condition to the buyer's remedy since the buyer's remedy arises immediately upon receipt of notice of infringement; it is merely one way of establishing the fact of breach.

5.   Subsection (2) recognizes that sales by sheriffs, executors, certain foreclosing lienors and persons similarly situated may be so out of the ordinary commercial course that their peculiar character is immediately apparent to the buyer and therefore no personal obligation is imposed upon the seller who is purporting to sell only an unknown or limited right. This subsection does not touch upon and leaves open all questions of restitution arising in such cases, when a unique article so sold is reclaimed by a third party as the rightful owner.

Foreclosure sales under Article 9 are another matter. Section 9–610 provides that a disposition of collateral under that section includes warranties such as those imposed by this section on a voluntary disposition of property of the kind involved. Consequently, unless properly excluded under subsection (2) or under the special provisions for exclusion in Section 9–610, a disposition under Section 9–610 of collateral consisting of goods includes the warranties imposed by subsection (1) and, if applicable, subsection (3).

6. The warranty of subsection (1) is not designated as an "implied" warranty, and hence is not subject to Section 2–316(3). Disclaimer of the warranty of title is governed instead by subsection (2), which requires either specific language or the described circumstances.

Cross References:

Point 1: Section 2–403.
Point 2: Sections 2–607 and 2–725.
Point 3: Section 1–203 [*unrevised Article 1; see Concordance, p. 22*].
Point 4: Sections 2–609 and 2–725.
Point 6: Section 2–316.

Definitional Cross References:

"Buyer". Section 2–103.
"Contract for sale". Section 2–106.
"Goods". Section 2–105.
"Person". Section 1–201.
"Right". Section 1–201.
"Seller". Section 2–103.

As amended in 1999.

§ 2–313. Express Warranties by Affirmation, Promise, Description, Sample.

(1) Express warranties by the seller are created as follows:

(a) Any affirmation of fact or promise made by the seller to the buyer which relates to the goods and becomes part of the basis of the bargain creates an express warranty that the goods shall conform to the affirmation or promise.

(b) Any description of the goods which is made part of the basis of the bargain creates an express warranty that the goods shall conform to the description.

(c) Any sample or model which is made part of the basis of the bargain creates an express warranty that the whole of the goods shall conform to the sample or model.

(2) It is not necessary to the creation of an express warranty that the seller use formal words such as "warrant" or "guarantee" or that he have a specific intention to make a warranty, but an affirmation merely of the value of the goods or a statement purporting to be merely the seller's opinion or commendation of the goods does not create a warranty.

Official Comment

Prior Uniform Statutory Provision: Sections 12, 14 and 16, Uniform Sales Act.

Changes: Rewritten.

Purposes of Changes: To consolidate and systematize basic principles with the result that:

1. "Express" warranties rest on "dickered" aspects of the individual bargain, and go so clearly to the essence of that bargain that words of disclaimer in a form are repugnant to the basic dickered terms. "Implied" warranties rest so clearly on a common factual situation or set of conditions that no particular language or action is necessary to evidence them and they will arise in such a situation unless unmistakably negated.

This section reverts to the older case law insofar as the warranties of description and sample are designated "express" rather than "implied".

2. Although this section is limited in its scope and direct purpose to warranties made by the seller to the buyer as part of a contract for sale, the warranty sections of this Article are not designed in any way to disturb those lines of case law growth which have recognized that warranties need not be confined either to sales contracts or to the direct parties to such a contract. They may arise in other appropriate circumstances such as in the case of bailments for hire, whether such bailment is itself the main contract or is merely a supplying of containers under a contract for the sale of their contents. The provisions of Section 2–318 on third party beneficiaries expressly recognize this case law development within one particular area. Beyond that, the matter is left to the case law with the intention that the policies of this Act may offer useful guidance in dealing with further cases as they arise.

3.   The present section deals with affirmations of fact by the seller, descriptions of the goods or exhibitions of samples, exactly as any other part of a negotiation which ends in a contract is dealt with. No specific intention to make a warranty is necessary if any of these factors is made part of the basis of the bargain. In actual practice affirmations of fact made by the seller about the goods during a bargain are regarded as part of the description of those goods; hence no particular reliance on such statements need be shown in order to weave them into the fabric of the agreement. Rather, any fact which is to take such affirmations, once made, out of the agreement requires clear affirmative proof. The issue normally is one of fact.

4.   In view of the principle that the whole purpose of the law of warranty is to determine what it is that the seller has in essence agreed to sell, the policy is adopted of those cases which refuse except in unusual circumstances to recognize a material deletion of the seller's obligation. Thus, a contract is normally a contract for a sale of something describable and described. A clause generally disclaiming "all warranties, express or implied" cannot reduce the seller's obligation with respect to such description and therefore cannot be given literal effect under Section 2–316.

This is not intended to mean that the parties, if they consciously desire, cannot make their own bargain as they wish. But in determining what they have agreed upon good faith is a factor and consideration should be given to the fact that the probability is small that a real price is intended to be exchanged for a pseudo-obligation.

5.   Paragraph (1)(b) makes specific some of the principles set forth above when a description of the goods is given by the seller.

A description need not be by words. Technical specifications, blueprints and the like can afford more exact description than mere language and if made part of the basis of the bargain goods must conform with them. Past deliveries may set the description of quality, either expressly or impliedly by course of dealing. Of course, all descriptions by merchants must be read against the applicable trade usages with the general rules as to merchantability resolving any doubts.

6.   The basic situation as to statements affecting the true essence of the bargain is no different when a sample or model is involved in the transaction. This section includes both a "sample" actually drawn from the bulk of goods which is the subject matter of the sale, and a "model" which is offered for inspection when the subject matter is not at hand and which has not been drawn from the bulk of the goods.

Although the underlying principles are unchanged, the facts are often ambiguous when something is shown as illustrative, rather than as a straight sample. In general, the presumption is that any sample or model just as any affirmation of fact is intended to become a basis of the bargain. But there is no escape from the question of fact. When the seller exhibits a sample purporting to be drawn from an existing bulk, good faith of course requires that the sample be fairly drawn. But in mercantile experience the mere exhibition of a "sample" does not of itself show whether it is merely intended to "suggest" or to "be" the character of the subject-matter of the contract. The question is whether the seller has so acted with reference to the sample as to make him responsible that the whole shall have at least the values shown by it. The circumstances aid in answering this question. If the sample has been drawn from an existing bulk, it must be regarded as describing values of the goods contracted for unless it is accompanied by an unmistakable denial of such responsibility. If, on the other hand, a model of merchandise not on hand is offered, the mercantile presumption that it has become a literal description of the subject matter is not so strong, and particularly so if modification on the buyer's initiative impairs any feature of the model.

7.   The precise time when words of description or affirmation are made or samples are shown is not material. The sole question is whether the language or samples or models are fairly to be regarded as part of the contract. If language is used after the closing of the deal (as when the buyer when taking delivery asks and receives an additional assurance), the warranty becomes a modification, and need not be supported by consideration if it is otherwise reasonable and in order (Section 2–209).

8.   Concerning affirmations of value or a seller's opinion or commendation under subsection (2), the basic question remains the same: What statements of the seller have in the circumstances and in objective judgment become part of the basis of the bargain? As indicated above, all of the statements of the seller do so unless good reason is shown to the contrary. The provisions of subsection (2) are included, however, since common experience discloses that some statements or predictions cannot fairly be viewed as entering into the bargain. Even as to false statements of value, however, the possibility is left open that a remedy may be provided by the law relating to fraud or misrepresentation.

Cross References:

Point 1: Section 2–316.
Point 2: Sections 1–102(3) [*unrevised Article 1; see Concordance, p. 22*] and 2–318.

Point 3: Section 2–316(2)(b).
Point 4: Section 2–316.
Point 5: Sections 1–205(4) [*unrevised Article 1; see Concordance, p. 22*] and 2–314.
Point 6: Section 2–316.
Point 7: Section 2–209.
Point 8: Section 1–103 [*unrevised Article 1; see Concordance, p. 22*].

Definitional Cross References:

"Buyer". Section 2–103.
"Conforming". Section 2–106.
"Goods". Section 2–105.
"Seller". Section 2–103.

§ 2–314. Implied Warranty: Merchantability; Usage of Trade.

(1) Unless excluded or modified (Section 2–316), a warranty that the goods shall be merchantable is implied in a contract for their sale if the seller is a merchant with respect to goods of that kind. Under this section the serving for value of food or drink to be consumed either on the premises or elsewhere is a sale.

(2) Goods to be merchantable must be at least such as

(a) pass without objection in the trade under the contract description; and

(b) in the case of fungible goods, are of fair average quality within the description; and

(c) are fit for the ordinary purposes for which such goods are used; and

(d) run, within the variations permitted by the agreement, of even kind, quality and quantity within each unit and among all units involved; and

(e) are adequately contained, packaged, and labeled as the agreement may require; and

(f) conform to the promises or affirmations of fact made on the container or label if any.

(3) Unless excluded or modified (Section 2–316) other implied warranties may arise from course of dealing or usage of trade.

Official Comment

Prior Uniform Statutory Provision: Section 15(2), Uniform Sales Act.

Changes: Completely rewritten.

Purposes of Changes: This section, drawn in view of the steadily developing case law on the subject, is intended to make it clear that:

1. The seller's obligation applies to present sales as well as to contracts to sell subject to the effects of any examination of specific goods. (Subsection (2) of Section 2–316). Also, the warranty of merchantability applies to sales for use as well as to sales for resale.

2. The question when the warranty is imposed turns basically on the meaning of the terms of the agreement as recognized in the trade. Goods delivered under an agreement made by a merchant in a given line of trade must be of a quality comparable to that generally acceptable in that line of trade under the description or other designation of the goods used in the agreement. The responsibility imposed rests on any merchant-seller, and the absence of the words "grower or manufacturer or not" which appeared in Section 15(2) of the Uniform Sales Act does not restrict the applicability of this section.

3. A specific designation of goods by the buyer does not exclude the seller's obligation that they be fit for the general purposes appropriate to such goods. A contract for the sale of second-hand goods, however, involves only such obligation as is appropriate to such goods for that is their contract description. A person making an isolated sale of goods is not a "merchant" within the meaning of the full scope of this section and, thus, no warranty of merchantability would apply. His knowledge of any defects not apparent on inspection would, however, without need for express agreement and in keeping with the underlying reason of the present section and the provisions on good faith, impose an obligation that known material but hidden defects be fully disclosed.

4.   Although a seller may not be a "merchant" as to the goods in question, if he states generally that they are "guaranteed" the provisions of this section may furnish a guide to the content of the resulting express warranty. This has particular significance in the case of second-hand sales, and has further significance in limiting the effect of fine-print disclaimer clauses where their effect would be inconsistent with large-print assertions of "guarantee".

5.   The second sentence of subsection (1) covers the warranty with respect to food and drink. Serving food or drink for value is a sale, whether to be consumed on the premises or elsewhere. Cases to the contrary are rejected. The principal warranty is that stated in subsections (1) and (2)(c) of this section.

6.   Subsection (2) does not purport to exhaust the meaning of "merchantable" nor to negate any of its attributes not specifically mentioned in the text of the statute, but arising by usage of trade or through case law. The language used is "must be at least such as . . .," and the intention is to leave open other possible attributes of merchantability.

7.   Paragraphs (a) and (b) of subsection (2) are to be read together. Both refer, as indicated above, to the standards of that line of the trade which fits the transaction and the seller's business. "Fair average" is a term directly appropriate to agricultural bulk products and means goods centering around the middle belt of quality, not the least or the worst that can be understood in the particular trade by the designation, but such as can pass "without objection." Of course a fair percentage of the least is permissible but the goods are not "fair average" if they are all of the least or worst quality possible under the description. In cases of doubt as to what quality is intended, the price at which a merchant closes a contract is an excellent index of the nature and scope of his obligation under the present section.

8.   Fitness for the ordinary purposes for which goods of the type are used is a fundamental concept of the present section and is covered in paragraph (c). As stated above, merchantability is also a part of the obligation owing to the purchaser for use. Correspondingly, protection, under this aspect of the warranty, of the person buying for resale to the ultimate consumer is equally necessary, and merchantable goods must therefore be "honestly" resalable in the normal course of business because they are what they purport to be.

9.   Paragraph (d) on evenness of kind, quality and quantity follows case law. But precautionary language has been added as a remainder of the frequent usages of trade which permit substantial variations both with and without an allowance or an obligation to replace the varying units.

10.   Paragraph (e) applies only where the nature of the goods and of the transaction require a certain type of container, package or label. Paragraph (f) applies, on the other hand, wherever there is a label or container on which representations are made, even though the original contract, either by express terms or usage of trade, may not have required either the labelling or the representation. This follows from the general obligation of good faith which requires that a buyer should not be placed in the position of reselling or using goods delivered under false representations appearing on the package or container. No problem of extra consideration arises in this connection since, under this Article, an obligation is imposed by the original contract not to deliver mislabeled articles, and the obligation is imposed where mercantile good faith so requires and without reference to the doctrine of consideration.

11.   Exclusion or modification of the warranty of merchantability, or of any part of it, is dealt with in the section to which the text of the present section makes explicit precautionary references. That section must be read with particular reference to its subsection (4) on limitation of remedies. The warranty of merchantability, wherever it is normal, is so commonly taken for granted that its exclusion from the contract is a matter threatening surprise and therefore requiring special precaution.

12.   Subsection (3) is to make explicit that usage of trade and course of dealing can create warranties and that they are implied rather than express warranties and thus subject to exclusion or modification under Section 2–316. A typical instance would be the obligation to provide pedigree papers to evidence conformity of the animal to the contract in the case of a pedigreed dog or blooded bull.

13.   In an action based on breach of warranty, it is of course necessary to show not only the existence of the warranty but the fact that the warranty was broken and that the breach of the warranty was the proximate cause of the loss sustained. In such an action an affirmative showing by the seller that the loss resulted from some action or event following his own delivery of the goods can operate as a defense. Equally, evidence indicating that the seller exercised care in the manufacture, processing or selection of the goods is relevant to the issue of whether the warranty was in fact broken. Action by the buyer following an examination of the goods which ought to have indicated the defect complained of can be shown as matter bearing on whether the breach itself was the cause of the injury.

Cross References:

    Point 1: Section 2–316.
    Point 3: Sections 1–203 [*unrevised Article 1; see Concordance, p. 22*] and 2–104.
    Point 5: Section 2–315.
    Point 11: Section 2–316.
    Point 12: Sections 1–201, 1–205 [*unrevised Article 1; see Concordance, p. 22*] and 2–316.

Definitional Cross References:

    "Agreement". Section 1–201.
    "Contract". Section 1–201.
    "Contract for sale". Section 2–106.
    "Goods". Section 2–105.
    "Merchant". Section 2–104.
    "Seller". Section 2–103.

§ 2–315. Implied Warranty: Fitness for Particular Purpose.

Where the seller at the time of contracting has reason to know any particular purpose for which the goods are required and that the buyer is relying on the seller's skill or judgment to select or furnish suitable goods, there is unless excluded or modified under the next section an implied warranty that the goods shall be fit for such purpose.

Official Comment

Prior Uniform Statutory Provision: Section 15(1), (4), (5), Uniform Sales Act.

Changes: Rewritten.

Purposes of Changes:

1.   Whether or not this warranty arises in any individual case is basically a question of fact to be determined by the circumstances of the contracting. Under this section the buyer need not bring home to the seller actual knowledge of the particular purpose for which the goods are intended or of his reliance on the seller's skill and judgment, if the circumstances are such that the seller has reason to realize the purpose intended or that the reliance exists. The buyer, of course, must actually be relying on the seller.

2.   A "particular purpose" differs from the ordinary purpose for which the goods are used in that it envisages a specific use by the buyer which is peculiar to the nature of his business whereas the ordinary purposes for which goods are used are those envisaged in the concept of merchantability and go to uses which are customarily made of the goods in question. For example, shoes are generally used for the purpose of walking upon ordinary ground, but a seller may know that a particular pair was selected to be used for climbing mountains.

A contract may of course include both a warranty of merchantability and one of fitness for a particular purpose.

The provisions of this Article on the cumulation and conflict of express and implied warranties must be considered on the question of inconsistency between or among warranties. In such a case any question of fact as to which warranty was intended by the parties to apply must be resolved in favor of the warranty of fitness for particular purpose as against all other warranties except where the buyer has taken upon himself the responsibility of furnishing the technical specifications.

3.   In connection with the warranty of fitness for a particular purpose the provisions of this Article on the allocation or division of risks are particularly applicable in any transaction in which the purpose for which the goods are to be used combines requirements both as to the quality of the goods themselves and compliance with certain laws or regulations. How the risks are divided is a question of fact to be determined, where not expressly contained in the agreement, from the circumstances of contracting, usage of trade, course of performance and the like, matters which may constitute the "otherwise agreement" of the parties by which they may divide the risk or burden.

4.   The absence from this section of the language used in the Uniform Sales Act in referring to the seller, "whether he be the grower or manufacturer or not," is not intended to impose any requirement that the seller be a grower or manufacturer. Although normally the warranty will arise only where the seller is a merchant with the

appropriate "skill or judgment," it can arise as to non-merchants where this is justified by the particular circumstances.

5.   The elimination of the "patent or other trade name" exception constitutes the major extension of the warranty of fitness which has been made by the cases and continued in this Article. Under the present section the existence of a patent or other trade name and the designation of the article by that name, or indeed in any other definite manner, is only one of the facts to be considered on the question of whether the buyer actually relied on the seller, but it is not of itself decisive of the issue. If the buyer himself is insisting on a particular brand he is not relying on the seller's skill and judgment and so no warranty results. But the mere fact that the article purchased has a particular patent or trade name is not sufficient to indicate nonreliance if the article has been recommended by the seller as adequate for the buyer's purposes.

6.   The specific reference forward in the present section to the following section on exclusion or modification of warranties is to call attention to the possibility of eliminating the warranty in any given case. However it must be noted that under the following section the warranty of fitness for a particular purpose must be excluded or modified by a conspicuous writing.

Cross References:

>   Point 2: Sections 2–314 and 2–317.
>   Point 3: Section 2–303.
>   Point 6: Section 2–316.

Definitional Cross References:

>   "Buyer". Section 2–103.
>   "Goods". Section 2–105.
>   "Seller". Section 2–103.

§ 2–316.   Exclusion or Modification of Warranties.

(1)   Words or conduct relevant to the creation of an express warranty and words or conduct tending to negate or limit warranty shall be construed wherever reasonable as consistent with each other; but subject to the provisions of this Article on parol or extrinsic evidence (Section 2–202) negation or limitation is inoperative to the extent that such construction is unreasonable.

(2)   Subject to subsection (3), to exclude or modify the implied warranty of merchantability or any part of it the language must mention merchantability and in case of a writing must be conspicuous, and to exclude or modify any implied warranty of fitness the exclusion must be by a writing and conspicuous. Language to exclude all implied warranties of fitness is sufficient if it states, for example, that "There are no warranties which extend beyond the description on the face hereof."

(3)   Notwithstanding subsection (2)

(a)   unless the circumstances indicate otherwise, all implied warranties are excluded by expressions like "as is", "with all faults" or other language which in common understanding calls the buyer's attention to the exclusion of warranties and makes plain that there is no implied warranty; and

(b)   when the buyer before entering into the contract has examined the goods or the sample or model as fully as he desired or has refused to examine the goods there is no implied warranty with regard to defects which an examination ought in the circumstances to have revealed to him; and

(c)   an implied warranty can also be excluded or modified by course of dealing or course of performance or usage of trade.

(4)   Remedies for breach of warranty can be limited in accordance with the provisions of this Article on liquidation or limitation of damages and on contractual modification of remedy (Sections 2–718 and 2–719).

Official Comment

Prior Uniform Statutory Provision: None. See sections 15 and 71, Uniform Sales Act.

Purposes:

1.   This section is designed principally to deal with those frequent clauses in sales contracts which seek to exclude "all warranties, express or implied." It seeks to protect a buyer from unexpected and unbargained language of disclaimer by denying effect to such language when inconsistent with language of express warranty and permitting the exclusion of implied warranties only by conspicuous language or other circumstances which protect the buyer from surprise.

2.   The seller is protected under this Article against false allegations of oral warranties by its provisions on parol and extrinsic evidence and against unauthorized representations by the customary "lack of authority" clauses. This Article treats the limitation or avoidance of consequential damages as a matter of limiting remedies for breach, separate from the matter of creation of liability under a warranty. If no warranty exists, there is of course no problem of limiting remedies for breach of warranty. Under subsection (4) the question of limitation of remedy is governed by the sections referred to rather than by this section.

3.   Disclaimer of the implied warranty of merchantability is permitted under subsection (2), but with the safeguard that such disclaimers must mention merchantability and in case of a writing must be conspicuous.

4.   Unlike the implied warranty of merchantability, implied warranties of fitness for a particular purpose may be excluded by general language, but only if it is in writing and conspicuous.

5.   Subsection (2) presupposes that the implied warranty in question exists unless excluded or modified. Whether or not language of disclaimer satisfies the requirements of this section, such language may be relevant under other sections to the question whether the warranty was ever in fact created. Thus, unless the provisions of this Article on parol and extrinsic evidence prevent, oral language of disclaimer may raise issues of fact as to whether reliance by the buyer occurred and whether the seller had "reason to know" under the section on implied warranty of fitness for a particular purpose.

6.   The exceptions to the general rule set forth in paragraphs (a), (b) and (c) of subsection (3) are common factual situations in which the circumstances surrounding the transaction are in themselves sufficient to call the buyer's attention to the fact that no implied warranties are made or that a certain implied warranty is being excluded.

7.   Paragraph (a) of subsection (3) deals with general terms such as "as is," "as they stand," "with all faults," and the like. Such terms in ordinary commercial usage are understood to mean that the buyer takes the entire risk as to the quality of the goods involved. The terms covered by paragraph (a) are in fact merely a particularization of paragraph (c) which provides for exclusion or modification of implied warranties by usage of trade.

8.   Under paragraph (b) of subsection (3) warranties may be excluded or modified by the circumstances where the buyer examines the goods or a sample or model of them before entering into the contract. "Examination" as used in this paragraph is not synonymous with inspection before acceptance or at any other time after the contract has been made. It goes rather to the nature of the responsibility assumed by the seller at the time of the making of the contract. Of course if the buyer discovers the defect and uses the goods anyway, or if he unreasonably fails to examine the goods before he uses them, resulting injuries may be found to result from his own action rather than proximately from a breach of warranty. See Sections 2–314 and 2–715 and comments thereto.

In order to bring the transaction within the scope of "refused to examine" in paragraph (b), it is not sufficient that the goods are available for inspection. There must in addition be a demand by the seller that the buyer examine the goods fully. The seller by the demand puts the buyer on notice that he is assuming the risk of defects which the examination ought to reveal. The language "refused to examine" in this paragraph is intended to make clear the necessity for such demand.

Application of the doctrine of "caveat emptor" in all cases where the buyer examines the goods regardless of statements made by the seller is, however, rejected by this Article. Thus, if the offer of examination is accompanied by words as to their merchantability or specific attributes and the buyer indicates clearly that he is relying on those words rather than on his examination, they give rise to an "express" warranty. In such cases the question is one of fact as to whether a warranty of merchantability has been expressly incorporated in the agreement. Disclaimer of such an express warranty is governed by subsection (1) of the present section.

The particular buyer's skill and the normal method of examining goods in the circumstances determine what defects are excluded by the examination. A failure to notice defects which are obvious cannot excuse the buyer. However, an examination under circumstances which do not permit chemical or other testing of the goods would not exclude defects which could be ascertained only by such testing. Nor can latent defects be excluded by a simple examination. A professional buyer examining a product in his field will be held to have assumed the risk as to all defects which a professional in the field ought to observe, while a nonprofessional buyer will be held to have assumed the risk only for such defects as a layman might be expected to observe.

9.   The situation in which the buyer gives precise and complete specifications to the seller is not explicitly covered in this section, but this is a frequent circumstance by which the implied warranties may be excluded. The warranty of fitness for a particular purpose would not normally arise since in such a situation there is usually no reliance on the seller by the buyer. The warranty of merchantability in such a transaction, however, must be considered in connection with the next section on the cumulation and conflict of warranties. Under paragraph (c) of that section in case of such an inconsistency the implied warranty of merchantability is displaced by the express warranty that the goods will comply with the specifications. Thus, where the buyer gives detailed specifications as to the goods, neither of the implied warranties as to quality will normally apply to the transaction unless consistent with the specifications.

10.   As to the use of a record other than a writing and communications that are not written, see Section 2–207, Comment 8. Whether a term is conspicuous, including a term in a record other than a writing, is discussed in Section 1–201, Comment 10.

Cross References:

Point 2: Sections 2–202, 2–718 and 2–719.
Point 7: Sections 1–205 [*unrevised Article 1; see Concordance, p. 22*] and 2–208.

Definitional Cross References:

"Agreement". Section 1–201.
"Buyer". Section 2–103.
"Contract". Section 1–201.
"Course of dealing". Section 1–205 [*unrevised Article 1; see Concordance, p. 22*].
"Goods". Section 2–105.
"Remedy". Section 1–201.
"Seller". Section 2–103.
"Usage of trade". Section 1–205 [*unrevised Article 1; see Concordance, p. 22*].

As amended in 2022.

§ 2–317.   Cumulation and Conflict of Warranties Express or Implied.

Warranties whether express or implied shall be construed as consistent with each other and as cumulative, but if such construction is unreasonable the intention of the parties shall determine which warranty is dominant. In ascertaining that intention the following rules apply:

(a)   Exact or technical specifications displace an inconsistent sample or model or general language of description.

(b)   A sample from an existing bulk displaces inconsistent general language of description.

(c)   Express warranties displace inconsistent implied warranties other than an implied warranty of fitness for a particular purpose.

Official Comment

Prior Uniform Statutory Provision: On cumulation of warranties see Sections 14, 15, and 16, Uniform Sales Act.

Changes: Completely rewritten into one section.

Purposes of Changes:

1.   The present section rests on the basic policy of this Article that no warranty is created except by some conduct (either affirmative action or failure to disclose) on the part of the seller. Therefore, all warranties are made cumulative unless this construction of the contract is impossible or unreasonable.

This Article thus follows the general policy of the Uniform Sales Act except that in case of the sale of an article by its patent or trade name the elimination of the warranty of fitness depends solely on whether the buyer has relied on the seller's skill and judgment; the use of the patent or trade name is but one factor in making this determination.

2. The rules of this section are designed to aid in determining the intention of the parties as to which of inconsistent warranties which have arisen from the circumstances of their transaction shall prevail. These rules of intention are to be applied only where factors making for an equitable estoppel of the seller do not exist and where he has in perfect good faith made warranties which later turn out to be inconsistent. To the extent that the seller has led the buyer to believe that all of the warranties can be performed, he is estopped from setting up any essential inconsistency as a defense.

3. The rules in subsections (a), (b) and (c) are designed to ascertain the intention of the parties by reference to the factor which probably claimed the attention of the parties in the first instance. These rules are not absolute but may be changed by evidence showing that the conditions which existed at the time of contracting make the construction called for by the section inconsistent or unreasonable.

Cross Reference:

Point 1: Section 2–315.

Definitional Cross Reference:

"Party". Section 1–201.

§ 2–318. Third Party Beneficiaries of Warranties Express or Implied.

Note: *If this Act is introduced in the Congress of the United States this section should be omitted. (States to select one alternative.)*

ALTERNATIVE A

A seller's warranty whether express or implied extends to any natural person who is in the family or household of his buyer or who is a guest in his home if it is reasonable to expect that such person may use, consume or be affected by the goods and who is injured in person by breach of the warranty. A seller may not exclude or limit the operation of this section.

ALTERNATIVE B

A seller's warranty whether express or implied extends to any natural person who may reasonably be expected to use, consume or be affected by the goods and who is injured in person by breach of the warranty. A seller may not exclude or limit the operation of this section.

ALTERNATIVE C

A seller's warranty whether express or implied extends to any person who may reasonably be expected to use, consume or be affected by the goods and who is injured by breach of the warranty. A seller may not exclude or limit the operation of this section with respect to injury to the person of an individual to whom the warranty extends.

As amended in 1966.

Official Comment

Prior Uniform Statutory Provision: None.

Purposes:

1. The last sentence of this section does not mean that a seller is precluded from excluding or disclaiming a warranty which might otherwise arise in connection with the sale provided such exclusion or modification is permitted by Section 2–316. Nor does that sentence preclude the seller from limiting the remedies of his own buyer and of any beneficiaries, in any manner provided in Sections 2–718 or 2–719. To the extent that the contract of sale contains provisions under which warranties are excluded or modified, or remedies for breach are limited, such provisions are equally operative against beneficiaries of warranties under this section. What this last sentence forbids is exclusion of liability by the seller to the persons to whom the warranties which he has made to his buyer would extend under this section.

2. The purpose of this section is to give certain beneficiaries the benefit of the same warranty which the buyer received in the contract of sale, thereby freeing any such beneficiaries from any technical rules as to "privity." It seeks to accomplish this purpose without any derogation of any right or remedy resting on negligence.

It rests primarily upon the merchant-seller's warranty under this Article that the goods sold are merchantable and fit for the ordinary purposes for which such goods are used rather than the warranty of fitness for a particular purpose. Implicit in the section is that any beneficiary of a warranty may bring a direct action for breach of warranty against the seller whose warranty extends to him.

3.   The first alternative expressly includes as beneficiaries within its provisions the family, household and guests of the purchaser. Beyond this, the section in this form is neutral and is not intended to enlarge or restrict the developing case law on whether the seller's warranties, given to his buyer who resells, extend to other persons in the distributive chain.

The second alternative is designed for states where the case law has already developed further and for those that desire to expand the class of beneficiaries. The third alternative goes further, following the trend of modern decisions as indicated by Restatement of Torts 2d § 402A (Tentative Draft No. 10, 1965) in extending the rule beyond injuries to the person.

Cross References:

> Point 1: Sections 2–316, 2–718 and 2–719.
> Point 2: Section 2–314.

Definitional Cross References:

> "Buyer". Section 2–103.
> "Goods". Section 2–105.
> "Seller". Section 2–103.

As amended in 1966.

§ 2–319.   F.O.B. and F.A.S. Terms.

(1)   Unless otherwise agreed the term F.O.B. (which means "free on board") at a named place, even though used only in connection with the stated price, is a delivery term under which

(a)   when the term is F.O.B. the place of shipment, the seller must at that place ship the goods in the manner provided in this Article (Section 2–504) and bear the expense and risk of putting them into the possession of the carrier; or

(b)   when the term is F.O.B. the place of destination, the seller must at his own expense and risk transport the goods to that place and there tender delivery of them in the manner provided in this Article (Section 2–503);

(c)   when under either (a) or (b) the term is also F.O.B. vessel, car or other vehicle, the seller must in addition at his own expense and risk load the goods on board. If the term is F.O.B. vessel the buyer must name the vessel and in an appropriate case the seller must comply with the provisions of this Article on the form of bill of lading (Section 2–323).

(2)   Unless otherwise agreed the term F.A.S. vessel (which means "free alongside") at a named port, even though used only in connection with the stated price, is a delivery term under which the seller must

(a)   at his own expense and risk deliver the goods alongside the vessel in the manner usual in that port or on a dock designated and provided by the buyer; and

(b)   obtain and tender a receipt for the goods in exchange for which the carrier is under a duty to issue a bill of lading.

(3)   Unless otherwise agreed in any case falling within subsection (1)(a) or (c) or subsection (2) the buyer must seasonably give any needed instructions for making delivery, including when the term is F.A.S. or F.O.B. the loading berth of the vessel and in an appropriate case its name and sailing date. The seller may treat the failure of needed instructions as a failure of cooperation under this Article (Section 2–311). He may also at his option move the goods in any reasonable manner preparatory to delivery or shipment.

(4)   Under the term F.O.B. vessel or F.A.S. unless otherwise agreed the buyer must make payment against tender of the required documents and the seller may not tender nor the buyer demand delivery of the goods in substitution for the documents.

Official Comment

Prior Uniform Statutory Provision: None.

Purposes:

1.   This section is intended to negate the uncommercial line of decision which treats an "F.O.B." term as "merely a price term." The distinctions taken in subsection (1) handle most of the issues which have on occasion led to the unfortunate judicial language just referred to. Other matters which have led to sound results being based on unhappy language in regard to F.O.B. clauses are dealt with in this Act by Section 2–311(2) (seller's option re arrangements relating to shipment) and Sections 2–614 and 2–615 (substituted performance and seller's excuse).

2.   Subsection (1)(c) not only specifies the duties of a seller who engages to deliver "F.O.B. vessel," or the like, but ought to make clear that no agreement is soundly drawn when it looks to reshipment from San Francisco or New York, but speaks merely of "F.O.B." the place.

3.   The buyer's obligations stated in subsection (1)(c) and subsection (3) are, as shown in the text, obligations of cooperation. The last sentence of subsection (3) expressly, though perhaps unnecessarily, authorizes the seller, pending instructions, to go ahead with such preparatory moves as shipment from the interior to the named point of delivery. The sentence presupposes the usual case in which instructions "fail"; a prior repudiation by the buyer, giving notice that breach was intended, would remove the reason for the sentence, and would normally bring into play, instead, the second sentence of Section 2–704, which duly calls for lessening damages.

4.   The treatment of "F.O.B. vessel" in conjunction with F.A.S. fits, in regard to the need for payment against documents, with standard practice and case-law; but "F.O.B. vessel" is a term which by its very language makes express the need for an "on board" document. In this respect, that term is stricter than the ordinary overseas "shipment" contract (C.I.F., etc., Section 2–320).

Cross References:

Sections 2–311(3), 2–323, 2–503 and 2–504.

Definitional Cross References:

"Agreed". Section 1–201.
"Bill of lading". Section 1–201.
"Buyer". Section 2–103.
"Goods". Section 2–105.
"Seasonably". Section 1–204 [*unrevised Article 1; see Concordance, p. 22*].
"Seller". Section 2–103.
"Term". Section 1–201.

§ 2–320.   C.I.F. and C. & F. Terms.

(1)   The term C.I.F. means that the price includes in a lump sum the cost of the goods and the insurance and freight to the named destination. The term C. & F. or C.F. means that the price so includes cost and freight to the named destination.

(2)   Unless otherwise agreed and even though used only in connection with the stated price and destination, the term C.I.F. destination or its equivalent requires the seller at his own expense and risk to

(a)   put the goods into the possession of a carrier at the port for shipment and obtain a negotiable bill or bills of lading covering the entire transportation to the named destination; and

(b)   load the goods and obtain a receipt from the carrier (which may be contained in the bill of lading) showing that the freight has been paid or provided for; and

(c)   obtain a policy or certificate of insurance, including any war risk insurance, of a kind and on terms then current at the port of shipment in the usual amount, in the currency of the contract, shown to cover the same goods covered by the bill of lading and providing for payment of loss to the order of the buyer or for the account of whom it may concern; but the seller may add to the price the amount of the premium for any such war risk insurance; and

(d)   prepare an invoice of the goods and procure any other documents required to effect shipment or to comply with the contract; and

(e)   forward and tender with commercial promptness all the documents in due form and with any indorsement necessary to perfect the buyer's rights.

(3)   Unless otherwise agreed the term C. & F. or its equivalent has the same effect and imposes upon the seller the same obligations and risks as a C.I.F. term except the obligation as to insurance.

(4)   Under the term C.I.F. or C. & F. unless otherwise agreed the buyer must make payment against tender of the required documents and the seller may not tender nor the buyer demand delivery of the goods in substitution for the documents.

Official Comment

Prior Uniform Statutory Provisions: None.

Purposes: To make it clear that:

1.   The C.I.F. contract is not a destination but a shipment contract with risk of subsequent loss or damage to the goods passing to the buyer upon shipment if the seller has properly performed all his obligations with respect to the goods. Delivery to the carrier is delivery to the buyer for purposes of risk and "title". Delivery of possession of the goods is accomplished by delivery of the bill of lading, and upon tender of the required documents the buyer must pay the agreed price without awaiting the arrival of the goods and if they have been lost or damaged after proper shipment he must seek his remedy against the carrier or insurer. The buyer has no right of inspection prior to payment or acceptance of the documents.

2.   The seller's obligations remain the same even though the C.I.F. term is "used only in connection with the stated price and destination".

3.   The insurance stipulated by the C.I.F. term is for the buyer's benefit, to protect him against the risk of loss or damage to the goods in transit. A clause in a C.I.F. contract "insurance—for the account of sellers" should be viewed in its ordinary mercantile meaning that the sellers must pay for the insurance and not that it is intended to run to the seller's benefit.

4.   A bill of lading covering the entire transportation from the port of shipment is explicitly required but the provision on this point must be read in the light of its reason to assure the buyer of as full protection as the conditions of shipment reasonably permit, remembering always that this type of contract is designed to move the goods in the channels commercially available. To enable the buyer to deal with the goods while they are afloat the bill of lading must be one that covers only the quantity of goods called for by the contract. The buyer is not required to accept his part of the goods without a bill of lading because the latter covers a larger quantity, nor is he required to accept a bill of lading for the whole quantity under a stipulation to hold the excess for the owner. Although the buyer is not compelled to accept either goods or documents under such circumstances he may of course claim his rights in any goods which have been identified to his contract.

5.   The seller is given the option of paying or providing for the payment of freight. He has no option to ship "freight collect" unless the agreement so provides. The rule of the common law that the buyer need not pay the freight if the goods do not arrive is preserved.

Unless the shipment has been sent "freight collect" the buyer is entitled to receive documentary evidence that he is not obligated to pay the freight; the seller is therefore required to obtain a receipt "showing that the freight has been paid or provided for." The usual notation on the bill of lading that the freight has been prepaid is a sufficient receipt, as at common law. The phrase "provided for" is intended to cover the frequent situation in which the carrier extends credit to a shipper for the freight on successive shipments and receives periodical payments of the accrued freight charges from him.

6.   The requirement that unless otherwise agreed the seller must procure insurance "of a kind and on terms then current at the port for shipment in the usual amount, in the currency of the contract, sufficiently shown to cover the same goods covered by the bill of lading", applies to both marine and war risk insurance. As applied to marine insurance, it means such insurance as is usual or customary at the port for shipment with reference to the particular kind of goods involved, the character and equipment of the vessel, the route of the voyage, the port of destination and any other considerations that affect the risk. It is the substantial equivalent of the ordinary insurance in the particular trade and on the particular voyage and is subject to agreed specifications of type or extent of coverage. The language does not mean that the insurance must be adequate to cover all risks to which the goods may be subject in transit. There are some types of loss or damage that are not covered by the usual

marine insurance and are excepted in bills of lading or in applicable statutes from the causes of loss or damage for which the carrier or the vessel is liable. Such risks must be borne by the buyer under this Article.

Insurance secured in compliance with a C.I.F. term must cover the entire transportation of the goods to the named destination.

7.   An additional obligation is imposed upon the seller in requiring him to procure customary war risk insurance at the buyer's expense. This changes the common law on the point. The seller is not required to assume the risk of including in the C.I.F. price the cost of such insurance, since it often fluctuates rapidly, but is required to treat it simply as a necessary for the buyer's account. What war risk insurance is "current" or usual turns on the standard forms of policy or rider in common use.

8.   The C.I.F. contract calls for insurance covering the value of the goods at the time and place of shipment and does not include any increase in market value during transit or any anticipated profit to the buyer on a sale by him.

The contract contemplates that before the goods arrive at their destination they may be sold again and again on C.I.F. terms and that the original policy of insurance and bill of lading will run with the interest in the goods by being transferred to each successive buyer. A buyer who becomes the seller in such an intermediate contract for sale does not thereby, if his sub-buyer knows the circumstances, undertake to insure the goods again at an increased price fixed in the new contract or to cover the increase in price by additional insurance, and his buyer may not reject the documents on the ground that the original policy does not cover such higher price. If such a sub-buyer desires additional insurance he must procure it for himself.

Where the seller exercises an option to ship "freight collect" and to credit the buyer with the freight against the C.I.F. price, the insurance need not cover the freight since the freight is not at the buyer's risk. On the other hand, where the seller prepays the freight upon shipping under a bill of lading requiring prepayment and providing that the freight shall be deemed earned and shall be retained by the carrier "ship and/or cargo lost or not lost," or using words of similar import, he must procure insurance that will cover the freight, because notwithstanding that the goods are lost in transit the buyer is bound to pay the freight as part of the C.I.F. price and will be unable to recover it back from the carrier.

9.   Insurance "for the account of whom it may concern" is usual and sufficient. However, for a valid tender the policy of insurance must be one which can be disposed of together with the bill of lading and so must be "sufficiently shown to cover the same goods covered by the bill of lading". It must cover separately the quantity of goods called for by the buyer's contract and not merely insure his goods as part of a larger quantity in which others are interested, a case provided for in American mercantile practice by the use of negotiable certificates of insurance which are expressly authorized by this section. By usage these certificates are treated as the equivalent of separate policies and are good tender under C.I.F. contracts. The term "certificate of insurance", however, does not of itself include certificates or "cover notes" issued by the insurance broker and stating that the goods are covered by a policy. Their sufficiency as substitutes for policies will depend upon proof of an established usage or course of dealing. The present section rejects the English rule that not only brokers' certificates and "cover notes" but also certain forms of American insurance certificates are not the equivalent of policies and are not good tender under a C.I.F. contract.

The seller's failure to tender a proper insurance document is waived if the buyer refuses to make payment on other and untenable grounds at a time when proper insurance could have been obtained and tendered by the seller if timely objection had been made. Even a failure to insure on shipment may be cured by seasonable tender of a policy retroactive in effect; e.g., one insuring the goods "lost or not lost." The provisions of this Article on cure of improper tender and on waiver of buyer's objections by silence are applicable to insurance tenders under a C.I.F. term. Where there is no waiver by the buyer as described above, however, the fact that the goods arrive safely does not cure the seller's breach of his obligations to insure them and tender to the buyer a proper insurance document.

10.   The seller's invoice of the goods shipped under a C.I.F. contract is regarded as a usual and necessary document upon which reliance may properly be placed. It is the document which evidences points of description, quality and the like which do not readily appear in other documents. This Article rejects those statements to the effect that the invoice is a usual but not a necessary document under a C.I.F. term.

11.   The buyer needs all of the documents required under a C.I.F. contract, in due form and, if a tangible document of title, with necessary endorsements, so that before the goods arrive he may deal with them by negotiating the documents or may obtain prompt possession of the goods after their arrival. If the goods are lost or damaged in transit the documents are necessary to enable him promptly to assert his remedy against the carrier or insurer. The seller is therefore obligated to do what is mercantilely reasonable in the circumstances and should

make every reasonable exertion to send forward the documents as soon as possible after the shipment. The requirement that the documents be forwarded with "commercial promptness" expresses a more urgent need for action than that suggested by the phrase "reasonable time".

12.   Under a C.I.F. contract the buyer, as under the common law, must pay the price upon tender of the required documents without first inspecting the goods, but his payment in these circumstances does not constitute an acceptance of the goods nor does it impair his right of subsequent inspection or his options and remedies in the case of improper delivery. All remedies and rights for the seller's breach are reserved to him. The buyer must pay before inspection and assert his remedy against the seller afterward unless the nonconformity of the goods amounts to a real failure of consideration, since the purpose of choosing this form of contract is to give the seller protection against the buyer's unjustifiable rejection of the goods at a distant port of destination which would necessitate taking possession of the goods and suing the buyer there.

13.   A valid C.I.F. contract may be made which requires part of the transportation to be made on land and part on the sea, as where the goods are to be brought by rail from an inland point to a seaport and thence transported by vessel to the named destination under a "through" or combination bill of lading issued by the railroad company. In such a case shipment by rail from the inland point within the contract period is a timely shipment notwithstanding that the loading of the goods on the vessel is delayed by causes beyond the seller's control.

14.   Although subsection (2) stating the legal effects of the C.I.F. term is an "unless otherwise agreed" provision, the express language used in an agreement is frequently a precautionary, fuller statement of the normal C.I.F. terms and hence not intended as a departure or variation from them. Moreover, the dominant outlines of the C.I.F. term are so well understood commercially that any variation should, whenever reasonably possible, be read as falling within those dominant outlines rather than as destroying the whole meaning of a term which essentially indicates a contract for proper shipment rather than one for delivery at destination. Particularly careful consideration is necessary before a printed form or clause is construed to mean agreement otherwise and where a C.I.F. contract is prepared on a printed form designed for some other type of contract, the C.I.F. terms must prevail over printed clauses repugnant to them.

15.   Under subsection (4) the fact that the seller knows at the time of the tender of the documents that the goods have been lost in transit does not affect his rights if he has performed his contractual obligations. Similarly, the seller cannot perform under a C.I.F. term by purchasing and tendering landed goods.

16.   Under the C. & F. term, as under the C.I.F. term, title and risk of loss are intended to pass to the buyer on shipment. A stipulation in a C. & F. contract that the seller shall effect insurance on the goods and charge the buyer with the premium (in effect that he shall act as the buyer's agent for that purpose) is entirely in keeping with the pattern. On the other hand, it often happens that the buyer is in a more advantageous position than the seller to effect insurance on the goods or that he has in force an "open" or "floating" policy covering all shipments made by him or to him, in either of which events the C. & F. term is adequate without mention of insurance.

17.   It is to be remembered that in a French contract the term "C.A.F." does not mean "Cost and Freight" but has exactly the same meaning as the term "C.I.F." since it is merely the French equivalent of that term. The "A" does not stand for "and" but for "assurance" which means insurance.

Cross References:

>   Point 4: Section 2–323.
>   Point 6: Section 2–509(1)(a).
>   Point 9: Sections 2–508 and 2–605(1)(a).
>   Point 12: Sections 2–321(3), 2–512 and 2–513(3) and Article 5.

Definitional Cross References:

>   "Bill of lading". Section 1–201.
>   "Buyer". Section 2–103.
>   "Contract". Section 1–201.
>   "Goods". Section 2–105.
>   "Rights". Section 1–201.
>   "Seller". Section 2–103.
>   "Term". Section 1–201.

As amended in 2003.

§ 2–321. C.I.F. or C. & F.: "Net Landed Weights"; "Payment on Arrival"; Warranty of Condition on Arrival.

Under a contract containing a term C.I.F. or C. & F.

(1) Where the price is based on or is to be adjusted according to "net landed weights", "delivered weights", "out turn" quantity or quality or the like, unless otherwise agreed the seller must reasonably estimate the price. The payment due on tender of the documents called for by the contract is the amount so estimated, but after final adjustment of the price a settlement must be made with commercial promptness.

(2) An agreement described in subsection (1) or any warranty of quality or condition of the goods on arrival places upon the seller the risk of ordinary deterioration, shrinkage and the like in transportation but has no effect on the place or time of identification to the contract for sale or delivery or on the passing of the risk of loss.

(3) Unless otherwise agreed where the contract provides for payment on or after arrival of the goods the seller must before payment allow such preliminary inspection as is feasible; but if the goods are lost delivery of the documents and payment are due when the goods should have arrived.

Official Comment

Prior Uniform Statutory Provision: None.

Purposes:

This section deals with two variations of the C.I.F. contract which have evolved in mercantile practice but are entirely consistent with the basic C.I.F. pattern. Subsections (1) and (2), which provide for a shift to the seller of the risk of quality and weight deterioration during shipment, are designed to conform the law to the best mercantile practice and usage without changing the legal consequences of the C.I.F. or C. & F. term as to the passing of marine risks to the buyer at the point of shipment. Subsection (3) provides that where under the contract documents are to be presented for payment after arrival of the goods, this amounts merely to a postponement of the payment under the C.I.F. contract and is not to be confused with the "no arrival, no sale" contract. If the goods are lost, delivery of the documents and payment against them are due when the goods should have arrived. The clause for payment on or after arrival is not to be construed as such a condition precedent to payment that if the goods are lost in transit the buyer need never pay and the seller must bear the loss.

Cross Reference:

Section 2–324.

Definitional Cross References:

"Agreement". Section 1–201.
"Contract". Section 1–201.
"Delivery". Section 1–201.
"Goods". Section 2–105.
"Seller". Section 2–103.
"Term". Section 1–201.

§ 2–322. Delivery "Ex-Ship".

(1) Unless otherwise agreed a term for delivery of goods "ex-ship" (which means from the carrying vessel) or in equivalent language is not restricted to a particular ship and requires delivery from a ship which has reached a place at the named port of destination where goods of the kind are usually discharged.

(2) Under such a term unless otherwise agreed

(a) the seller must discharge all liens arising out of the carriage and furnish the buyer with a direction which puts the carrier under a duty to deliver the goods; and

(b) the risk of loss does not pass to the buyer until the goods leave the ship's tackle or are otherwise properly unloaded.

Prior Uniform Statutory Provision: None.

Purposes:

    1.   The delivery term, "ex-ship", as between seller and buyer, is the reverse of the f.a.s. term covered.

    2.   Delivery need not be made from any particular vessel under a clause calling for delivery "ex-ship", even though a vessel on which shipment is to be made originally is named in the contract, unless the agreement by appropriate language, restricts the clause to delivery from a named vessel.

    3.   The appropriate place and manner of unloading at the port of destination depend upon the nature of the goods and the facilities and usages of the port.

    4.   A contract fixing a price "ex-ship" with payment "cash against documents" calls only for such documents as are appropriate to the contract. Tender of a delivery order and of a receipt for the freight after the arrival of the carrying vessel is adequate. The seller is not required to tender a bill of lading as a document of title nor is he required to insure the goods for the buyer's benefit, as the goods are not at the buyer's risk during the voyage.

Cross Reference:

    Point 1: Section 2–319(2).

Definitional Cross References:

    "Buyer". Section 2–103.
    "Goods". Section 2–105.
    "Seller". Section 2–103.
    "Term". Section 1–201.

§ 2–323.   Form of Bill of Lading Required in Overseas Shipment; "Overseas".

    (1)   Where the contract contemplates overseas shipment and contains a term C.I.F. or C. & F. or F.O.B. vessel, the seller unless otherwise agreed must obtain a negotiable bill of lading stating that the goods have been loaded in board or, in the case of a term C.I.F. or C. & F., received for shipment.

    (2)   Where in a case within subsection (1) a tangible bill of lading has been issued in a set of parts, unless otherwise agreed if the documents are not to be sent from abroad the buyer may demand tender of the full set; otherwise only one part of the bill of lading need be tendered. Even if the agreement expressly requires a full set

    (a)   due tender of a single part is acceptable within the provisions of this Article on cure of improper delivery (subsection (1) of Section 2–508); and

    (b)   even though the full set is demanded, if the documents are sent from abroad the person tendering an incomplete set may nevertheless require payment upon furnishing an indemnity which the buyer in good faith deems adequate.

    (3)   A shipment by water or by air or a contract contemplating such shipment is "overseas" insofar as by usage of trade or agreement it is subject to the commercial, financing or shipping practices characteristic of international deep water commerce.

As amended in 2003.

Prior Uniform Statutory Provision: None.

Purposes:

    1.   Subsection (1) follows the "American" rule that a regular bill of lading indicating delivery of the goods at the dock for shipment is sufficient, except under a term "F.O.B. vessel." See Section 2–319 and comment thereto.

    2.   Subsection (2) deals with the problem of bills of lading covering deep water shipments, issued not as a single bill of lading but in a set of parts, each part referring to the other parts and the entire set constituting in commercial practice and at law a single bill of lading. Commercial practice in international commerce is to accept and pay against presentation of the first part of a set if the part is sent from overseas even though the contract of

the buyer requires presentation of a full set of bills of lading provided adequate indemnity for the missing parts is forthcoming. In accord with the amendment to Section 7–304, bills of lading in a set are limited to tangible bills.

This subsection codifies that practice as between buyer and seller. Article 5 (Section 5–113) [*unrevised Article 5*] authorizes banks presenting drafts under letters of credit to give indemnities against the missing parts, and this subsection means that the buyer must accept and act on such indemnities if he in good faith deems them adequate. But neither this subsection nor Article 5 decides whether a bank which has issued a letter of credit is similarly bound. The issuing bank's obligation under a letter of credit is independent and depends on its own terms. See Article 5.

Cross References:

Sections 2–508(2), 5–113 [*unrevised Article 5*].

Definitional Cross References:

"Bill of lading". Section 1–201.
"Buyer". Section 2–103.
"Contract". Section 1–201.
"Delivery". Section 1–201.
"Financing agency". Section 2–104.
"Person". Section 1–201.
"Seller". Section 2–103.
"Send". Section 1–201.
"Term". Section 1–201.

As amended in 2003.

§ 2–324.   "No Arrival, No Sale" Term.

Under a term "no arrival, no sale" or terms of like meaning, unless otherwise agreed,

(a)   the seller must properly ship conforming goods and if they arrive by any means he must tender them on arrival but he assumes no obligation that the goods will arrive unless he has caused the non-arrival; and

(b)   where without fault of the seller the goods are in part lost or have so deteriorated as no longer to conform to the contract or arrive after the contract time, the buyer may proceed as if there had been casualty to identified goods (Section 2–613).

Official Comment

Prior Uniform Statutory Provision: None.

Purposes:

1.   The "no arrival, no sale" term in a "destination" overseas contract leaves risk of loss on the seller but gives him an exemption from liability for non-delivery. Both the nature of the case and the duty of good faith require that the seller must not interfere with the arrival of the goods in any way. If the circumstances impose upon him the responsibility for making or arranging the shipment, he must have a shipment made despite the exemption clause. Further, the shipment made must be a conforming one, for the exemption under a "no arrival, no sale" term applies only to the hazards of transportation and the goods must be proper in all other respects.

The reason of this section is that where the seller is reselling goods bought by him as shipped by another and this fact is known to the buyer, so that the seller is not under any obligation to make the shipment himself, the seller is entitled under the "no arrival, no sale" clause to exemption from payment of damages for non-delivery if the goods do not arrive or if the goods which actually arrive are non-conforming. This does not extend to sellers who arrange shipment by their own agents, in which case the clause is limited to casualty due to marine hazards. But sellers who make known that they are contracting only with respect to what will be delivered to them by parties over whom they assume no control are entitled to the full quantum of the exemption.

2.   The provisions of this Article on identification must be read together with the present section in order to bring the exemption into application. Until there is some designation of the goods in a particular shipment or on a particular ship as being those to which the contract refers there can be no application of an exemption for their non-arrival.

3.   The seller's duty to tender the agreed or declared goods if they do arrive is not impaired because of their delay in arrival or by their arrival after transshipment.

4.   The phrase "to arrive" is often employed in the same sense as "no arrival, no sale" and may then be given the same effect. But a "to arrive" term, added to a C.I.F. or C. & F. contract, does not have the full meaning given by this section to "no arrival, no sale". Such a "to arrive" term is usually intended to operate only to the extent that the risks are not covered by the agreed insurance and the loss or casualty is due to such uncovered hazards. In some instances the "to arrive" term may be regarded as a time of payment term, or, in the case of the reselling seller discussed in point 1 above, as negating responsibility for conformity of the goods, if they arrive, to any description which was based on his good faith belief of the quality. Whether this is the intention of the parties is a question of fact based on all the circumstances surrounding the resale and in case of ambiguity the rules of Sections 2–316 and 2–317 apply to preclude dishonor.

5.   Paragraph (b) applies where goods arrive impaired by damage or partial loss during transportation and makes the policy of this Article on casualty to identified goods applicable to such a situation. For the term cannot be regarded as intending to give the seller an unforeseen profit through casualty; it is intended only to protect him from loss due to causes beyond his control.

Cross References:

Point 1: Section 1–203 [*unrevised Article 1; see Concordance, p. 22*].
Point 2: Section 2–501(a) and (c).
Point 5: Section 2–613.

Definitional Cross References:

"Buyer". Section 2–103.
"Conforming". Section 2–106.
"Contract". Section 1–201.
"Fault". Section 1–201.
"Goods". Section 2–105.
"Sale". Section 2–106.
"Seller". Section 2–103.
"Term". Section 1–201.

§ 2–325.   "Letter of Credit" Term; "Confirmed Credit".

(1)   Failure of the buyer seasonably to furnish an agreed letter of credit is a breach of the contract for sale.

(2)   The delivery to seller of a proper letter of credit suspends the buyer's obligation to pay. If the letter of credit is dishonored, the seller may on seasonable notification to the buyer require payment directly from him.

(3)   Unless otherwise agreed the term "letter of credit" or "banker's credit" in a contract for sale means an irrevocable credit issued by a financing agency of good repute and, where the shipment is overseas, of good international repute. The term "confirmed credit" means that the credit must also carry the direct obligation of such an agency which does business in the seller's financial market.

Official Comment

Prior Uniform Statutory Provision: None.

Purposes: To express the established commercial and banking understanding as to the meaning and effects of terms calling for "letters of credit" or "confirmed credit":

1.   Subsection (2) follows the general policy of this Article and Article 3 (Section 3–802) [*unrevised Article 3 (Appendix B)*] on conditional payment, under which payment by check or other short-term instrument is not ordinarily final as between the parties if the recipient duly presents the instrument and honor is refused. Thus the furnishing of a letter of credit does not substitute the financing agency's obligation for the buyer's, but the seller must first give the buyer reasonable notice of his intention to demand direct payment from him.

2. Subsection (3) requires that the credit be irrevocable and be a prime credit as determined by the standing of the issuer. It is not necessary, unless otherwise agreed, that the credit be a negotiation credit; the seller can finance himself by an assignment of the proceeds under Section 5–116(2) [*unrevised Article 5*].

3. The definition of "confirmed credit" is drawn on the supposition that the credit is issued by a bank which is not doing direct business in the seller's financial market; there is no intention to require the obligation of two banks both local to the seller.

Cross References:

Sections 2–403, 2–511(3) and 3–802 [*unrevised Article 3 (Appendix B)*] and Article 5.

Definitional Cross References:

"Buyer". Section 2–103.
"Contract for sale". Section 2–106.
"Draft". Section 3–104.
"Financing agency". Section 2–104.
"Notifies". Section 1–201 [*unrevised Article 1; see Concordance, p. 22*].
"Overseas". Section 2–323.
"Purchaser". Section 1–201.
"Seasonably". Section 1–204 [*unrevised Article 1; see Concordance, p. 22*].
"Seller". Section 2–103.
"Term". Section 1–201.

§ 2–326. Sale on Approval and Sale or Return; Rights of Creditors.

(1) Unless otherwise agreed, if delivered goods may be returned by the buyer even though they conform to the contract, the transaction is

(a) a "sale on approval" if the goods are delivered primarily for use, and

(b) a "sale or return" if the goods are delivered primarily for resale.

(2) Goods held on approval are not subject to the claims of the buyer's creditors until acceptance; goods held on sale or return are subject to such claims while in the buyer's possession.

(3) Any "or return" term of a contract for sale is to be treated as a separate contract for sale within the statute of frauds section of this Article (Section 2–201) and as contradicting the sale aspect of the contract within the provisions of this Article on parol or extrinsic evidence (Section 2–202).

As amended in 1999.

Official Comment

Prior Uniform Statutory Provision: Section 19(3), Uniform Sales Act.

Changes: Completely rewritten in this and the succeeding section.

Purposes of Changes: To make it clear that:

1. Both a "sale on approval" and a "sale or return" should be distinguished from other types of transactions with which they frequently have been confused. A "sale on approval," sometimes also called a sale "on trial" or "on satisfaction," deals with a contract under which the seller undertakes a risk in order to satisfy its prospective buyer with the appearance or performance of the goods that are sold. The goods are delivered to the proposed purchaser but they remain the property of the seller until the buyer accepts them. The price has already been agreed. The buyer's willingness to receive and test the goods is the consideration for the seller's engagement to deliver and sell. A "sale or return," on the other hand, typically is a sale to a merchant whose unwillingness to buy is overcome by the seller's engagement to take back the goods (or any commercial unit of goods) in lieu of payment if they fail to be resold. A sale or return is a present sale of goods which may be undone at the buyer's option. Accordingly, subsection (2) provides that goods delivered on approval are not subject to the prospective buyer's creditors until acceptance, and goods delivered in a sale or return are subject to the buyer's creditors while in the buyer's possession.

These two transactions are so strongly delineated in practice and in general understanding that every presumption runs against a delivery to a consumer being a "sale or return" and against a delivery to a merchant for resale being a "sale on approval."

2.   The right to return goods for failure to conform to the contract of sale does not make the transaction a "sale on approval" or "sale or return" and has nothing to do with this section or Section 2–327. This section is not concerned with remedies for breach of contract. It deals instead with a power given by the contract to turn back the goods even though they are wholly as warranted. This section nevertheless presupposes that a contract for sale is contemplated by the parties, although that contract may be of the particular character that this section addresses (i.e., a sale on approval or a sale or return).

If a buyer's obligation as a buyer is conditioned not on its personal approval but on the article's passing a described objective test, the risk of loss by casualty pending the test is properly the seller's and proper return is at its expense. On the point of "satisfaction" as meaning "reasonable satisfaction" when an industrial machine is involved, this Article takes no position.

3.   Subsection (3) resolves a conflict in the pre-UCC case law by recognizing that an "or return" provision is so definitely at odds with any ordinary contract for sale of goods that if a written agreement is involved the "or return" term must be contained in a written memorandum. The "or return" aspect of a sales contract must be treated as a separate contract under the Statute of Frauds section and as contradicting the sale insofar as questions of parol or extrinsic evidence are concerned.

4.   The transactions governed by this section are sales; the persons to whom the goods are delivered are buyers. This section has no application to transactions in which goods are delivered to a person who has neither bought the goods nor contracted to buy them. See PEB Commentary No. 20, dated January 24, 2019. Transactions in which a non-buyer takes delivery of goods for the purpose of selling them are bailments called consignments and are not "sale on approval" or "sale or return" transactions. Certain consignment transactions were dealt with in former pre-1998 Sections 2–326(3) and 9–114. These provisions have been deleted and have been replaced by new provisions in Article 9. See, e.g., Sections 9–109(a)(4); 9–103(d); 9–319.

Cross References:

> Point 2: Article 9.
> Point 3: Sections 2–201 and 2–202.

Definitional Cross References:

> "Between merchants". Section 2–104.
> "Buyer". Section 2–103.
> "Conform". Section 2–106.
> "Contract for sale". Section 2–106.
> "Creditor". Section 1–201.
> "Goods". Section 2–105.
> "Sale". Section 2–106.
> "Seller". Section 2–103.

As amended in 1999, 2000, 2019, and 2022.

§ 2–327.   Special Incidents of Sale on Approval and Sale or Return.

(1)   Under a sale on approval unless otherwise agreed

(a)   although the goods are identified to the contract the risk of loss and the title do not pass to the buyer until acceptance; and

(b)   use of the goods consistent with the purpose of trial is not acceptance but failure seasonably to notify the seller of election to return the goods is acceptance, and if the goods conform to the contract acceptance of any part is acceptance of the whole; and

(c)   after due notification of election to return, the return is at the seller's risk and expense but a merchant buyer must follow any reasonable instructions.

(2)   Under a sale or return unless otherwise agreed

(a) the option to return extends to the whole or any commercial unit of the goods while in substantially their original condition, but must be exercised seasonably; and

(b) the return is at the buyer's risk and expense.

Official Comment

Prior Uniform Statutory Provision: Section 19(3), Uniform Sales Act.

Changes: Completely rewritten in preceding and this section.

Purposes of Changes: To make it clear that:

1. In the case of a sale on approval:

If all of the goods involved conform to the contract, the buyer's acceptance of part of the goods constitutes acceptance of the whole. Acceptance of part falls outside the normal intent of the parties in the "on approval" situation and the policy of this Article allowing partial acceptance of a defective delivery has no application here. A case where a buyer takes home two dresses to select one commonly involves two distinct contracts; if not, it is covered by the words "unless otherwise agreed".

2. In the case of a sale or return, the return of any unsold unit merely because it is unsold is the normal intent of the "sale or return" provision, and therefore the right to return for this reason alone is independent of any other action under the contract which would turn on wholly different considerations. On the other hand, where the return of goods is for breach, including return of items resold by the buyer and returned by the ultimate purchasers because of defects, the return procedure is governed not by the present section but by the provisions on the effects and revocation of acceptance.

3. In the case of a sale on approval the risk rests on the seller until acceptance of the goods by the buyer, while in a sale or return the risk remains throughout on the buyer.

4. Notice of election to return given by the buyer in a sale on approval is sufficient to relieve him of any further liability. Actual return by the buyer to the seller is required in the case of a sale or return contract. What constitutes due "giving" of notice, as required in "on approval" sales, is governed by the provisions on good faith and notice. "Seasonable" is used here as defined in Section 1–204 [*unrevised Article 1; see Concordance, p. 22*]. Nevertheless, the provisions of both this Article and of the contract on this point must be read with commercial reason and with full attention to good faith.

Cross References:

Point 1: Sections 2–501, 2–601 and 2–603.
Point 2: Sections 2–607 and 2–608.
Point 4: Sections 1–201 and 1–204 [*unrevised Article 1; see Concordance, p. 22*].

Definitional Cross References:

"Agreed". Section 1–201.
"Buyer". Section 2–103.
"Commercial unit". Section 2–105.
"Conform". Section 2–106.
"Contract". Section 1–201.
"Goods". Section 2–105.
"Merchant". Section 2–104.
"Notifies". Section 1–201 [*unrevised Article 1; see Concordance, p. 22*].
"Notification". Section 1–201 [*unrevised Article 1; see Concordance, p. 22*].
"Sale on approval". Section 2–326.
"Sale or return". Section 2–326.
"Seasonably". Section 1–204 [*unrevised Article 1; see Concordance, p. 22*].
"Seller". Section 2–103.

§ 2–328. Sale by Auction.

(1) In a sale by auction if goods are put up in lots each lot is the subject of a separate sale.

(2)   A sale by auction is complete when the auctioneer so announces by the fall of the hammer or in other customary manner. Where a bid is made while the hammer is falling in acceptance of a prior bid the auctioneer may in his discretion reopen the bidding or declare the goods sold under the bid on which the hammer was falling.

(3)   Such a sale is with reserve unless the goods are in explicit terms put up without reserve. In an auction with reserve the auctioneer may withdraw the goods at any time until he announces completion of the sale. In an auction without reserve, after the auctioneer calls for bids on an article or lot, that article or lot cannot be withdrawn unless no bid is made within a reasonable time. In either case a bidder may retract his bid until the auctioneer's announcement of completion of the sale, but a bidder's retraction does not revive any previous bid.

(4)   If the auctioneer knowingly receives a bid on the seller's behalf or the seller makes or procures such a bid, and notice has not been given that liberty for such bidding is reserved, the buyer may at his option avoid the sale or take the goods at the price of the last good faith bid prior to the completion of the sale. This subsection shall not apply to any bid at a forced sale.

Official Comment

Prior Uniform Statutory Provision: Section 21, Uniform Sales Act.

Changes: Completely rewritten.

Purposes of Changes: To make it clear that:

1.   The auctioneer may in his discretion either reopen the bidding or close the sale on the bid on which the hammer was falling when a bid is made at that moment. The recognition of a bid of this kind by the auctioneer in his discretion does not mean a closing in favor of such a bidder, but only that the bid has been accepted as a continuation of the bidding. If recognized, such a bid discharges the bid on which the hammer was falling when it was made.

2.   An auction "with reserve" is the normal procedure. The crucial point, however, for determining the nature of an auction is the "putting up" of the goods. This Article accepts the view that the goods may be withdrawn before they are actually "put up," regardless of whether the auction is advertised as one without reserve, without liability on the part of the auction announcer to persons who are present. This is subject to any peculiar facts which might bring the case within the "firm offer" principle of this Article, but an offer to persons generally would require unmistakable language in order to fall within that section. The prior announcement of the nature of the auction either as with reserve or without reserve will, however, enter as an "explicit term" in the "putting up" of the goods and conduct thereafter must be governed accordingly. The present section continues the prior rule permitting withdrawal of bids in auctions both with and without reserve; and the rule is made explicit that the retraction of a bid does not revive a prior bid.

Cross Reference:

Point 2: Section 2–205.

Definitional Cross References:

"Buyer". Section 2–103.
"Good faith". Section 1–201.
"Goods". Section 2–105.
"Lot". Section 2–105.
"Notice". Section 1–201 [*unrevised Article 1; see Concordance, p. 22*].
"Sale". Section 2–106.
"Seller". Section 2–103.

PART 4

TITLE, CREDITORS AND GOOD FAITH PURCHASERS

§ 2–401.   Passing of Title; Reservation for Security; Limited Application of This
Section. *Despite language saying no security interest, a conditional sale is a secured transaction and it creates a security interest.*

Each provision of this Article with regard to the rights, obligations and remedies of the seller, the buyer, purchasers or other third parties applies irrespective of title to the goods except where the provision refers to such title. Insofar as situations are not covered by the other provisions of this Article and matters concerning title become material the following rules apply:

(1)   Title to goods cannot pass under a contract for sale prior to their identification to the contract (Section 2–501), and unless otherwise explicitly agreed the buyer acquires by their identification a special property as limited by this Act. Any retention or reservation by the seller of the title (property) in goods shipped or delivered to the buyer is limited in effect to a reservation of a security interest. Subject to these provisions and to the provisions of the Article on Secured Transactions (Article 9), title to goods passes from the seller to the buyer in any manner and on any conditions explicitly agreed on by the parties.

(2)   Unless otherwise explicitly agreed title passes to the buyer at the time and place at which the seller completes his performance with reference to the physical delivery of the goods, despite any reservation of a security interest and even though a document of title is to be delivered at a different time or place; and in particular and despite any reservation of a security interest by the bill of lading

(a)   if the contract requires or authorizes the seller to send the goods to the buyer but does not require him to deliver them at destination, title passes to the buyer at the time and place of shipment; but

(b)   if the contract requires delivery at destination, title passes on tender there.

(3)   Unless otherwise explicitly agreed where delivery is to be made without moving the goods,

(a)   if the seller is to deliver a tangible document of title, title passes at the time when and the place where he delivers such documents and if the seller is to deliver an electronic document of title, title passes when the seller delivers the document; or

(b)   if the goods are at the time of contracting already identified and no documents of title are to be delivered, title passes at the time and place of contracting.

(4)   A rejection or other refusal by the buyer to receive or retain the goods, whether or not justified, or a justified revocation of acceptance revests title to the goods in the seller. Such revesting occurs by operation of law and is not a "sale".

As amended in 2003.

Official Comment

Prior Uniform Statutory Provision: See generally, Sections 17, 18, 19 and 20, Uniform Sales Act.

Purposes: To make it clear that:

1.   This Article deals with the issues between seller and buyer in terms of step by step performance or non-performance under the contract for sale and not in terms of whether or not "title" to the goods has passed. That the rules of this section in no way alter the rights of either the buyer, seller or third parties declared elsewhere in the Article is made clear by the preamble of this section. This section, however, in no way intends to indicate which line of interpretation should be followed in cases where the applicability of "public" regulation depends upon a "sale" or upon location of "title" without further definition. The basic policy of this Article that known purpose and reason should govern interpretation cannot extend beyond the scope of its own provisions. It is therefore necessary to state what a "sale" is and when title passes under this Article in case the courts deem any public regulation to incorporate the defined term of the "private" law.

2.   "Future" goods cannot be the subject of a present sale. Before title can pass the goods must be identified in the manner set forth in Section 2–501. The parties, however, have full liberty to arrange by specific terms for the passing of title to goods which are existing.

3.   The "special property" of the buyer in goods identified to the contract is excluded from the definition of "security interest"; its incidents are defined in provisions of this Article such as those on the rights of the seller's creditors, on good faith purchase, on the buyer's right to goods on the seller's insolvency, and on the buyer's right to specific performance or replevin.

4.   The factual situations in subsections (2) and (3) upon which passage of title turn actually base the test upon the time when the seller has finally committed himself in regard to specific goods. Thus in a "shipment" contract he commits himself by the act of making the shipment. If shipment is not contemplated subsection (3) turns on the seller's final commitment, i.e. the delivery of documents or the making of the contract. As to delivery of an electronic document of title, see definition of delivery in Article 1, Section 1–201. This Article does not state a rule as to the place of title passage as to goods covered by an electronic document of title.

Cross References:

Point 2: Sections 2–102, 2–501 and 2–502.
Point 3: Sections 1–201, 2–402, 2–403, 2–502 and 2–716.

Definitional Cross References:

"Agreement". Section 1–201.
"Bill of lading". Section 1–201.
"Buyer". Section 2–103.
"Contract". Section 1–201.
"Contract for sale". Section 2–106.
"Delivery". Section 1–201.
"Document of title". Section 1–201.
"Good faith". Section 2–103.
"Goods". Section 2–105.
"Party". Section 1–201.
"Purchaser". Section 1–201.
"Receipt" of goods. Section 2–103.
"Remedy". Section 1–201.
"Rights". Section 1–201.
"Sale". Section 2–106.
"Security interest". Section 1–201.
"Seller". Section 2–103.
"Send". Section 1–201.

As amended in 2003.

§ 2–402.   Rights of Seller's Creditors Against Sold Goods.

(1)   Except as provided in subsections (2) and (3), rights of unsecured creditors of the seller with respect to goods which have been identified to a contract for sale are subject to the buyer's rights to recover the goods under this Article (Sections 2–502 and 2–716).

(2)   A creditor of the seller may treat a sale or an identification of goods to a contract for sale as void if as against him a retention of possession by the seller is fraudulent under any rule of law of the state where the goods are situated, except that retention of possession in good faith and current course of trade by a merchant-seller for a commercially reasonable time after a sale or identification is not fraudulent.

(3)   Nothing in this Article shall be deemed to impair the rights of creditors of the seller

(a)   under the provisions of the Article on Secured Transactions (Article 9); or

(b)   where identification to the contract or delivery is made not in current course of trade but in satisfaction of or as security for a pre-existing claim for money, security or the like and is made under circumstances which under any rule of law of the state where the goods are situated would apart from this Article constitute the transaction a fraudulent transfer or voidable preference.

Official Comment

Prior Uniform Statutory Provision: Subsection (2)—Section 26, Uniform Sales Act; Subsections (1) and (3)—none.

Changes: Rephrased.

Purposes of Changes and New Matter: To avoid confusion on ordinary issues between current sellers and buyers and issues in the field of preference and hindrance by making it clear that:

1. Local law on questions of hindrance of creditors by the seller's retention of possession of the goods are outside the scope of this Article, but retention of possession in the current course of trade is legitimate. Transactions which fall within the law's policy against improper preferences are reserved from the protection of this Article.

2. The retention of possession of the goods by a merchant seller for a commercially reasonable time after a sale or identification in current course is exempted from attack as fraudulent. Similarly, the provisions of subsection (3) have no application to identification or delivery made in the current course of trade, as measured against general commercial understanding of what a "current" transaction is.

Definitional Cross References:

"Contract for sale". Section 2–106.
"Creditor". Section 1–201.
"Good faith". Section 2–103.
"Goods". Section 2–105.
"Merchant". Section 2–104.
"Money". Section 1–201.
"Reasonable time". Section 1–204 [*unrevised Article 1; see Concordance, p. 22*].
"Rights". Section 1–201.
"Sale". Section 2–106.
"Seller". Section 2–103.

§ 2–403. Power to Transfer; Good Faith Purchase of Goods; "Entrusting".

(1) A purchaser of goods acquires all title which his transferor had or had power to transfer except that a purchaser of a limited interest acquires rights only to the extent of the interest purchased. A person with voidable title has power to transfer a good title to a good faith purchaser for value. When goods have been delivered under a transaction of purchase the purchaser has such power even though

(a) the transferor was deceived as to the identity of the purchaser, or

(b) the delivery was in exchange for a check which is later dishonored, or

(c) it was agreed that the transaction was to be a "cash sale", or

(d) the delivery was procured through fraud punishable as larcenous under the criminal law.

(2) Any entrusting of possession of goods to a merchant who deals in goods of that kind gives him power to transfer all rights of the entruster to a buyer in ordinary course of business.

(3) "Entrusting" includes any delivery and any acquiescence in retention of possession regardless of any condition expressed between the parties to the delivery or acquiescence and regardless of whether the procurement of the entrusting or the possessor's disposition of the goods have been such as to be larcenous under the criminal law.

> [*Publisher's Editorial Note: If a state adopts the repealer of Article 6—Bulk Transfers (Alternative A), subsec. (4) should read as follows:*]

(4) The rights of other purchasers of goods and of lien creditors are governed by the Articles on Secured Transactions (Article 9) and Documents of Title (Article 7).

> [*Publisher's Editorial Note: If a state adopts Revised Article 6—Bulk Sales (Alternative B), subsec. (4) should read as follows:*]

(4)   The rights of other purchasers of goods and of lien creditors are governed by the Articles on Secured Transactions (Article 9), Bulk Sales (Article 6) and Documents of Title (Article 7).

As amended in 1988.

> *For material relating to the changes made in text in 1988, see section 3 of Alternative A (Repealer of Article 6—Bulk Transfers) and Conforming Amendment to Section 2–403 following end of Alternative B (Revised Article 6—Bulk Sales).*

Official Comment

Prior Uniform Statutory Provision: Sections 20(4), 23, 24, 25, Uniform Sales Act; Section 9, especially 9(2), Uniform Trust Receipts Act; Section 9, Uniform Conditional Sales Act.

Changes: Consolidated and rewritten.

Purposes of Changes: To gather together a series of prior uniform statutory provisions and the case-law thereunder and to state a unified and simplified policy on good faith purchase of goods.

1.   The basic policy of our law allowing transfer of such title as the transferor has is generally continued and expanded under subsection (1). In this respect the provisions of the section are applicable to a person taking by any form of "purchase" as defined by this Act. Moreover the policy of this Act expressly providing for the application of supplementary general principles of law to sales transactions wherever appropriate joins with the present section to continue unimpaired all rights acquired under the law of agency or of apparent agency or ownership or other estoppel, whether based on statutory provisions or on case law principles. The section also leaves unimpaired the powers given to selling factors under the earlier Factors Acts. In addition subsection (1) provides specifically for the protection of the good faith purchaser for value in a number of specific situations which have been troublesome under prior law.

On the other hand, the contract of purchase is of course limited by its own terms as in a case of pledge for a limited amount or of sale of a fractional interest in goods.

2.   The many particular situations in which a buyer in ordinary course of business from a dealer has been protected against reservation of property or other hidden interest are gathered by subsections (2)–(4) into a single principle protecting persons who buy in ordinary course out of inventory. Consignors have no reason to complain, nor have lenders who hold a security interest in the inventory, since the very purpose of goods in inventory is to be turned into cash by sale.

The principle is extended in subsection (3) to fit with the abolition of the old law of "cash sale" by subsection (1)(c). It is also freed from any technicalities depending on the extended law of larceny; such extension of the concept of theft to include trick, particular types of fraud, and the like is for the purpose of helping conviction of the offender; it has no proper application to the long-standing policy of civil protection of buyers from persons guilty of such trick or fraud. Finally, the policy is extended, in the interest of simplicity and sense, to any entrusting by a bailor; this is in consonance with the explicit provisions of Section 7–205 on the powers of a warehouse who is also in the business of buying and selling fungible goods of the kind he stores. As to entrusting by a secured party, subsection (2) is limited by the more specific provisions of Section 9–320, which deny protection to a person buying farm products from a person engaged in farming operations.

3.   The definition of "buyer in ordinary course of business" (Section 1–201) ~~is effective~~ applies here and preserves the essence of the healthy limitations engrafted by the case-law on the older statutes. The older loose concept of good faith and wide definition of value combined to create apparent good faith purchasers in many situations in which the result outraged common sense; the court's solution was to protect the original title especially by use of "cash sale" or of over-technical construction of the enabling clauses of the statutes. But such rulings then turned into limitations on the proper protection of buyers in the ordinary market. Section ~~1–201(9)~~ 1–201(b)(9) cuts down the category of buyer in ordinary course in such fashion as to take care of the results of the cases, but with no price either in confusion or in injustice to proper dealings in the normal market.

4.   Except as provided in subsection (1), the rights of purchasers other than buyers in ordinary course are left to the Articles on Secured Transactions, Documents of Title, and Bulk Sales.

Cross References:

Point 1: Sections 1–103 [*unrevised Article 1; see Concordance, p. 22*] and 1–201.

Point 2: Sections 1–201, 2–402, 7–205 and 9–320.

Points 3 and 4: Sections 1–102 [*unrevised Article 1; see Concordance, p. 22*], 1–201, 2–104, 2–707 and Articles 6, 7 and 9.

Definitional Cross References:

"Buyer in ordinary course of business". Section 1–201.
"Good faith". Sections 1–201 and 2–103.
"Goods". Section 2–105.
"Person". Section 1–201.
"Purchaser". Section 1–201.
"Signed". Section 1–201.
"Term". Section 1–201.
"Value". Section 1–201 [*unrevised Article 1; see Concordance, p. 22*].

As amended in 2003 and 2022.

PART 5

PERFORMANCE

§ 2–501.   Insurable Interest in Goods; Manner of Identification of Goods.

(1)   The buyer obtains a special property and an insurable interest in goods by identification of existing goods as goods to which the contract refers even though the goods so identified are non-conforming and he has an option to return or reject them. Such identification can be made at any time and in any manner explicitly agreed to by the parties. In the absence of explicit agreement identification occurs

(a)   when the contract is made if it is for the sale of goods already existing and identified;

(b)   if the contract is for the sale of future goods other than those described in paragraph (c), when goods are shipped, marked or otherwise designated by the seller as goods to which the contract refers;

(c)   when the crops are planted or otherwise become growing crops or the young are conceived if the contract is for the sale of unborn young to be born within twelve months after contracting or for the sale of crops to be harvested within twelve months or the next normal harvest season after contracting whichever is longer.

(2)   The seller retains an insurable interest in goods so long as title to or any security interest in the goods remains in him and where the identification is by the seller alone he may until default or insolvency or notification to the buyer that the identification is final substitute other goods for those identified.

(3)   Nothing in this section impairs any insurable interest recognized under any other statute or rule of law.

Official Comment

Prior Uniform Statutory Provision: See Sections 17 and 19, Uniform Sales Act.

Purposes:

1.   The present section deals with the manner of identifying goods to the contract so that an insurable interest in the buyer and the rights set forth in the next section will accrue. Generally speaking, identification may be made in any manner "explicitly agreed to" by the parties. The rules of paragraphs (a), (b) and (c) apply only in the absence of such "explicit agreement".

2.   In the ordinary case identification of particular existing goods as goods to which the contract refers is unambiguous and may occur in one of many ways. It is possible, however, for the identification to be tentative or contingent. In view of the limited effect given to identification by this Article, the general policy is to resolve all doubts in favor of identification.

3.   The provision of this section as to "explicit agreement" clarifies the present confusion in the law of sales which has arisen from the fact that under prior uniform legislation all rules of presumption with reference to the passing of title or to appropriation (which in turn depended upon identification) were regarded as subject to the contrary intention of the parties or of the party appropriating. Such uncertainty is reduced to a minimum under this section by requiring "explicit agreement" of the parties before the rules of paragraphs (a), (b) and (c) are displaced—as they would be by a term giving the buyer power to select the goods. An "explicit" agreement,

however, need not necessarily be found in the terms used in the particular transaction. Thus, where a usage of the trade has previously been made explicit by reduction to a standard set of "rules and regulations" currently incorporated by reference into the contracts of the parties, a relevant provision of those "rules and regulations" is "explicit" within the meaning of this section.

4. In view of the limited function of identification there is no requirement in this section that the goods be in deliverable state or that all of the seller's duties with respect to the processing of the goods be completed in order that identification occur. For example, despite identification the risk of loss remains on the seller under the risk of loss provisions until completion of his duties as to the goods and all of his remedies remain dependent upon his not defaulting under the contract.

5. Undivided shares in an identified fungible bulk, such as grain in an elevator or oil in a storage tank, can be sold. The mere making of the contract with reference to an undivided share in an identified fungible bulk is enough under subsection (a) to effect an identification if there is no explicit agreement otherwise. The seller's duty, however, to segregate and deliver according to the contract is not affected by such an identification but is controlled by other provisions of this Article.

6. Identification of crops under paragraph (c) is made upon planting only if they are to be harvested within the year or within the next normal harvest season. The phrase "next normal harvest season" fairly includes nursery stock raised for normally quick "harvest," but plainly excludes a "timber" crop to which the concept of a harvest "season" is inapplicable.

Paragraph (c) is also applicable to a crop of wool or the young of animals to be born within twelve months after contracting. The product of a lumbering, mining or fishing operation, though seasonal, is not within the concept of "growing". Identification under a contract for all or part of the output of such an operation can be effected early in the operation.

Cross References:

> Point 1: Section 2–502.
> Point 4: Sections 2–509, 2–510 and 2–703.
> Point 5: Sections 2–105, 2–308, 2–503 and 2–509.
> Point 6: Sections 2–105(1), 2–107(1) and 2–402.

Definitional Cross References:

> "Agreement". Section 1–201.
> "Contract". Section 1–201.
> "Contract for sale". Section 2–106.
> "Future goods". Section 2–105.
> "Goods". Section 2–105.
> "Notification". Section 1–201 [unrevised Article 1; see Concordance, p. 22].
> "Party". Section 1–201.
> "Sale". Section 2–106.
> "Security interest". Section 1–201.
> "Seller". Section 2–103.

§ 2–502.　Buyer's Right to Goods on Seller's Repudiation, Failure to Deliver, or Insolvency.

(1) Subject to subsections (2) and (3) and even though the goods have not been shipped a buyer who has paid a part or all of the price of goods in which he has a special property under the provisions of the immediately preceding section may on making and keeping good a tender of any unpaid portion of their price recover them from the seller if:

(a) in the case of goods bought for personal, family, or household purposes, the seller repudiates or fails to deliver as required by the contract; or

(b) in all cases, the seller becomes insolvent within ten days after receipt of the first installment on their price.

(2)   The buyer's right to recover the goods under subsection (1)(a) vests upon acquisition of a special property, even if the seller had not then repudiated or failed to deliver.

(3)   If the identification creating his special property has been made by the buyer he acquires the right to recover the goods only if they conform to the contract for sale.

As amended in 1999.

Official Comment

Prior Uniform Statutory Provision: Compare Sections 17, 18 and 19, Uniform Sales Act.

Purposes:

1.   This section gives an additional right to the buyer as a result of identification of the goods to the contract in the manner provided in Section 2–501. The buyer is given a right to recover the goods, conditioned upon making and keeping good a tender of any unpaid portion of the price, in two limited circumstances. First, the buyer may recover goods bought for personal, family, or household purposes if the seller repudiates the contract or fails to deliver the goods. Second, in any case, the buyer may recover the goods if the seller becomes insolvent within 10 days after the seller receives the first installment on their price. The buyer's right to recover the goods under this section is an exception to the usual rule, under which the disappointed buyer must resort to an action to recover damages.

2.   The question of whether the buyer also acquires a security interest in identified goods and has rights to the goods when insolvency takes place after the ten-day period provided in this section depends upon compliance with the provisions of the Article on Secured Transactions (Article 9).

3.   Under subsection (2), the buyer's right to recover consumer goods under subsection (1)(a) vests upon acquisition of a special property, which occurs upon identification of the goods to the contract. See Section 2–501. Inasmuch as a secured party normally acquires no greater rights in its collateral that its debtor had or had power to convey, see Section 2–403(1) (first sentence), a buyer who acquires a right to recover under this section will take free of a security interest created by the seller if it attaches to the goods after the goods have been identified to the contract. The buyer will take free, even if the buyer does not buy in ordinary course and even if the security interest is perfected. Of course, to the extent that the buyer pays the price after the security interest attaches, the payments will constitute proceeds of the security interest.

4.   Subsection (3) is included to preclude the possibility of unjust enrichment, which would exist if the buyer were permitted to recover goods even though they were greatly superior in quality or quantity to that called for by the contract for sale.

Cross References:

Point 1: Sections 1–201 and 2–702.
Point 2: Article 9.

Definitional Cross References:

"Buyer". Section 2–103.
"Conform". Section 2–106.
"Contract for sale". Section 2–106.
"Goods". Section 2–105.
"Insolvent". Section 1–201.
"Rights". Section 1–201.
"Seller". Section 2–103.

As amended in 1999.

§ 2–503.   Manner of Seller's Tender of Delivery.

(1)   Tender of delivery requires that the seller put and hold conforming goods at the buyer's disposition and give the buyer any notification reasonably necessary to enable him to take delivery. The manner, time and place for tender are determined by the agreement and this Article, and in particular

(a)   tender must be at a reasonable hour, and if it is of goods they must be kept available for the period reasonably necessary to enable the buyer to take possession; but

(b)   unless otherwise agreed the buyer must furnish facilities reasonably suited to the receipt of the goods.

(2)   Where the case is within the next section respecting shipment tender requires that the seller comply with its provisions.

(3)   Where the seller is required to deliver at a particular destination tender requires that he comply with subsection (1) and also in any appropriate case tender documents as described in subsections (4) and (5) of this section.

(4)   Where goods are in the possession of a bailee and are to be delivered without being moved

(a)   tender requires that the seller either tender a negotiable document of title covering such goods or procure acknowledgment by the bailee of the buyer's right to possession of the goods; but

(b)   tender to the buyer of a non-negotiable document of title or of a record directing the bailee to deliver is sufficient tender unless the buyer seasonably objects, and except as otherwise provided in Article 9 receipt by the bailee of notification of the buyer's rights fixes those rights as against the bailee and all third persons; but risk of loss of the goods and of any failure by the bailee to honor the non-negotiable document of title or to obey the direction remains on the seller until the buyer has had a reasonable time to present the document or direction, and a refusal by the bailee to honor the document or to obey the direction defeats the tender.

(5)   Where the contract requires the seller to deliver documents

(a)   he must tender all such documents in correct form, except as provided in this Article with respect to bills of lading in a set (subsection (2) of Section 2–323); and

(b)   tender through customary banking channels is sufficient and dishonor of a draft accompanying or associated with the documents constitutes non-acceptance or rejection.

As amended in 2003.

Official Comment

Prior Uniform Statutory Provision: See Sections 11, 19, 20, 43(3) and (4), 46 and 51, Uniform Sales Act.

Changes: The general policy of the above sections is continued and supplemented but subsection (3) changes the rule of prior section 19(5) as to what constitutes a "destination" contract and subsection (4) incorporates a minor correction as to tender of delivery of goods in the possession of a bailee.

Purposes of Changes:

1.   The major general rules governing the manner of proper or due tender of delivery are gathered in this section. The term "tender" is used in this Article in two different senses. In one sense it refers to "due tender" which contemplates an offer coupled with a present ability to fulfill all the conditions resting on the tendering party and must be followed by actual performance if the other party shows himself ready to proceed. Unless the context unmistakably indicates otherwise this is the meaning of "tender" in this Article and the occasional addition of the word "due" is only for clarity and emphasis. At other times it is used to refer to an offer of goods or documents under a contract as if in fulfillment of its conditions even though there is a defect when measured against the contract obligation. Used in either sense, however, "tender" connotes such performance by the tendering party as puts the other party in default if he fails to proceed in some manner. These concepts of tender would apply to tender of either tangible or electronic documents of title.

2.   The seller's general duty to tender and deliver is laid down in Section 2–301 and more particularly in Section 2–507. The seller's right to a receipt if he demands one and receipts are customary is governed by Section 1–205 [*unrevised Article 1; see Concordance, p. 22*]. Subsection (1) of the present section proceeds to set forth two primary requirements of tender: first, that the seller "put and hold conforming goods at the buyer's disposition" and, second, that he "give the buyer any notice reasonably necessary to enable him to take delivery."

In cases in which payment is due and demanded upon delivery the "buyer's disposition" is qualified by the seller's right to retain control of the goods until payment by the provision of this Article on delivery on condition. However, where the seller is demanding payment on delivery he must first allow the buyer to inspect the goods in order to avoid impairing his tender unless the contract for sale is on C.I.F., C.O.D., cash against documents or similar terms negating the privilege of inspection before payment.

In the case of contracts involving documents the seller can "put and hold conforming goods at the buyer's disposition" under subsection (1) by tendering documents which give the buyer complete control of the goods under the provisions of Article 7 on due negotiation.

3. Under paragraph (a) of subsection (1) usage of the trade and the circumstances of the particular case determine what is a reasonable hour for tender and what constitutes a reasonable period of holding the goods available.

4. The buyer must furnish reasonable facilities for the receipt of the goods tendered by the seller under subsection (1), paragraph (b). This obligation of the buyer is no part of the seller's tender.

5. For the purposes of subsections (2) and (3) there is omitted from this Article the rule under prior uniform legislation that a term requiring the seller to pay the freight or cost of transportation to the buyer is equivalent to an agreement by the seller to deliver to the buyer or at an agreed destination. This omission is with the specific intention of negating the rule, for under this Article the "shipment" contract is regarded as the normal one and the "destination" contract as the variant type. The seller is not obligated to deliver at a named destination and bear the concurrent risk of loss until arrival, unless he has specifically agreed so to deliver or the commercial understanding of the terms used by the parties contemplates such delivery.

6. Paragraph (a) of subsection (4) continues the rule of the prior uniform legislation as to acknowledgment by the bailee. Paragraph (b) of subsection (4) adopts the rule that between the buyer and the seller the risk of loss remains on the seller during a period reasonable for securing acknowledgment of the transfer from the bailee, while as against all other parties the buyer's rights are fixed as of the time the bailee receives notice of the transfer.

7. Under subsection (5) documents are never "required" except where there is an express contract term or it is plainly implicit in the peculiar circumstances of the case or in a usage of trade. Documents may, of course, be "authorized" although not required, but such cases are not within the scope of this subsection. When documents are required, there are three main requirements of this subsection: (1) "All": each required document is essential to a proper tender; (2) "Such": the documents must be the ones actually required by the contract in terms of source and substance; (3) "Correct form": All documents must be in correct form. These requirements apply to both tangible and electronic documents of title. When tender is made through customary banking channels, a draft may accompany or be associated with a document of title. The language has been broadened to allow for drafts to be associated with an electronic document of title. Compare Section 2–104(2) definition of financing agency.

When a prescribed document cannot be procured, a question of fact arises under the provision of this Article on substituted performance as to whether the agreed manner of delivery is actually commercially impracticable and whether the substitute is commercially reasonable.

Cross References:

Point 2: Sections 1–205 [*unrevised Article 1; see Concordance, p. 22*], 2–301, 2–310, 2–507 and 2–513 and Article 7.

Point 5: Sections 2–308, 2–310 and 2–509.

Point 7: Section 2–614(1).

Specific matters involving tender are covered in many additional sections of this Article. See Sections 1–205 [*unrevised Article 1; see Concordance, p. 22*], 2–301, 2–306 to 2–319, 2–321(3), 2–504, 2–507(2), 2–511(1), 2–513, 2–612 and 2–614.

Definitional Cross References:

"Agreement". Section 1–201.

"Bill of lading". Section 1–201.

"Buyer". Section 2–103.

"Conforming". Section 2–106.

"Contract". Section 1–201.

"Delivery". Section 1–201.

"Dishonor". Section 3–508 [*unrevised Article 3 (Appendix B)*].

"Document of title". Section 1–201.

"Draft". Section 3–104.

"Goods". Section 2–105.

"Notification". Section 1–201 [*unrevised Article 1; see Concordance, p. 22*].

"Reasonable time". Section 1–204 [*unrevised Article 1; see Concordance, p. 22*].

"Receipt" of goods. Section 2–103.
"Rights". Section 1–201.
"Seasonably". Section 1–204 [*unrevised Article 1; see Concordance, p. 22*].
"Seller". Section 2–103.
"Written". Section 1–201.

As amended in 2003.

§ 2–504.   Shipment by Seller.

Where the seller is required or authorized to send the goods to the buyer and the contract does not require him to deliver them at a particular destination, then unless otherwise agreed he must

  (a)   put the goods in the possession of such a carrier and make such a contract for their transportation as may be reasonable having regard to the nature of the goods and other circumstances of the case; and

  (b)   obtain and promptly deliver or tender in due form any document necessary to enable the buyer to obtain possession of the goods or otherwise required by the agreement or by usage of trade; and

  (c)   promptly notify the buyer of the shipment.

Failure to notify the buyer under paragraph (c) or to make a proper contract under paragraph (a) is a ground for rejection only if material delay or loss ensues.

Official Comment

Prior Uniform Statutory Provision: Section 46, Uniform Sales Act.

Changes: Rewritten.

Purposes of Changes: To continue the general policy of the prior uniform statutory provision while incorporating certain modifications with respect to the requirement that the contract with the carrier be made expressly on behalf of the buyer and as to the necessity of giving notice of the shipment to the buyer, so that:

1.   The section is limited to "shipment" contracts as contrasted with "destination" contracts or contracts for delivery at the place where the goods are located. The general principles embodied in this section cover the special cases of F.O.B. point of shipment contracts and C.I.F. and C. & F. contracts. Under the preceding section on manner of tender of delivery, due tender by the seller requires that he comply with the requirements of this section in appropriate cases.

2.   The contract to be made with the carrier under paragraph (a) must conform to all express terms of the agreement, subject to any substitution necessary because of failure of agreed facilities as provided in the later provision on substituted performance. However, under the policies of this Article on good faith and commercial standards and on buyer's rights on improper delivery, the requirements of explicit provisions must be read in terms of their commercial and not their literal meaning. This policy is made express with respect to bills of lading in a set in the provision of this Article on form of bills of lading required in overseas shipment.

3.   In the absence of agreement, the provision of this Article on options and cooperation respecting performance gives the seller the choice of any reasonable carrier, routing and other arrangements. Whether or not the shipment is at the buyer's expense the seller must see to any arrangements, reasonable in the circumstances, such as refrigeration, watering of live stock, protection against cold, the sending along of any necessary help, selection of specialized cars and the like for paragraph (a) is intended to cover all necessary arrangements whether made by contract with the carrier or otherwise. There is, however, a proper relaxation of such requirements if the buyer is himself in a position to make the appropriate arrangements and the seller gives him reasonable notice of the need to do so. It is an improper contract under paragraph (a) for the seller to agree with the carrier to a limited valuation below the true value and thus cut off the buyer's opportunity to recover from the carrier in the event of loss, when the risk of shipment is placed on the buyer by his contract with the seller.

4.   Both the language of paragraph (b) and the nature of the situation it concerns indicate that the requirement that the seller must obtain and deliver promptly to the buyer in due form any document necessary to enable him to obtain possession of the goods is intended to cumulate with the other duties of the seller such as those covered in paragraph (a).

In this connection, in the case of pool car shipments a delivery order furnished by the seller on the pool car consignee, or on the carrier for delivery out of a larger quantity, satisfies the requirements of paragraph (b) unless the contract requires some other form of document.

5.   This Article, unlike the prior uniform statutory provision, makes it the seller's duty to notify the buyer of shipment in all cases. The consequences of his failure to do so, however, are limited in that the buyer may reject on this ground only where material delay or loss ensues.

A standard and acceptable manner of notification in open credit shipments is the sending of an invoice and in the case of documentary contracts is the prompt forwarding of the documents as under paragraph (b) of this section. It is also usual to send on a straight bill of lading but this is not necessary to the required notification. However, should such a document prove necessary or convenient to the buyer, as in the case of loss and claim against the carrier, good faith would require the seller to send it on request.

Frequently the agreement expressly requires prompt notification as by wire or cable. Such a term may be of the essence and the final clause of paragraph (c) does not prevent the parties from making this a particular ground for rejection. To have this vital and irreparable effect upon the seller's duties, such a term should be part of the "dickered" terms written in any "form," or should otherwise be called seasonably and sharply to the seller's attention.

6.   Generally, under the final sentence of the section, rejection by the buyer is justified only when the seller's dereliction as to any of the requirements of this section in fact is followed by material delay or damage. It rests on the seller, so far as concerns matters not within the peculiar knowledge of the buyer, to establish that his error has not been followed by events which justify rejection.

Cross References:

Point 1: Sections 2–319, 2–320 and 2–503(2).
Point 2: Sections 1–203 [*unrevised Article 1; see Concordance, p. 22*], 2–323(2), 2–601 and 2–614(1).
Point 3: Section 2–311(2).
Point 5: Section 1–203 [*unrevised Article 1; see Concordance, p. 22*].

Definitional Cross References:

"Agreement". Section 1–201.
"Buyer". Section 2–103.
"Contract". Section 1–201.
"Delivery". Section 1–201.
"Goods". Section 2–105.
"Notifies". Section 1–201 [*unrevised Article 1; see Concordance, p. 22*].
"Seller". Section 2–103.
"Send". Section 1–201.
"Usage of trade". Section 1–205 [*unrevised Article 1; see Concordance, p. 22*].

§ 2–505.   Seller's Shipment Under Reservation.

(1)   Where the seller has identified goods to the contract by or before shipment:

(a)   his procurement of a negotiable bill of lading to his own order or otherwise reserves in him a security interest in the goods. His procurement of the bill to the order of a financing agency or of the buyer indicates in addition only the seller's expectation of transferring that interest to the person named.

(b)   a non-negotiable bill of lading to himself or his nominee reserves possession of the goods as security but except in a case of conditional delivery (subsection (2) of Section 2–507) a non-negotiable bill of lading naming the buyer as consignee reserves no security interest even though the seller retains possession or control of the bill of lading.

(2)   When shipment by the seller with reservation of a security interest is in violation of the contract for sale it constitutes an improper contract for transportation within the preceding section but impairs

neither the rights given to the buyer by shipment and identification of the goods to the contract nor the seller's powers as a holder of a negotiable document of title.

As amended in 2003.

Official Comment

Prior Uniform Statutory Provision: Section 20(2), (3), (4), Uniform Sales Act.

Changes: Completely rephrased, the "powers" of the parties in cases of reservation being emphasized primarily rather than the "rightfulness" of reservation.

Purposes of Changes: To continue in general the policy of the prior uniform statutory provision with certain modifications of emphasis and language, so that:

1.   The security interest reserved to the seller under subsection (1) is restricted to securing payment or performance by the buyer and the seller is strictly limited in his disposition and control of the goods as against the buyer and third parties. Under this Article, the provision as to the passing of interest expressly applies "despite any reservation of security title" and also provides that the "rights, obligations and remedies" of the parties are not altered by the incidence of title generally. The security interest, therefore, must be regarded as a means given to the seller to enforce his rights against the buyer which is unaffected by and in turn does not affect the location of title generally. The rules set forth in subsection (1) are not to be altered by any apparent "contrary intent" of the parties as to passing of title, since the rights and remedies of the parties to the contract of sale, as defined in this Article, rest on the contract and its performance or breach and not on stereotyped presumptions as to the location of title.

This Article does not attempt to regulate local procedure in regard to the effective maintenance of the seller's security interest when the action is in replevin by the buyer against the carrier.

2.   Every shipment of identified goods under a negotiable bill of lading reserves a security interest in the seller under subsection (1) paragraph (a).

It is frequently convenient for the seller to make the bill of lading to the order of a nominee such as his agent at destination, the financing agency to which he expects to negotiate the document or the bank issuing a credit to him. In many instances, also, the buyer is made the order party. This Article does not deal directly with the question as to whether a bill of lading made out by the seller to the order of a nominee gives the carrier notice of any rights which the nominee may have so as to limit its freedom or obligation to honor the bill of lading in the hands of the seller as the original shipper if the expected negotiation fails. This is dealt with in the Article on Documents of Title (Article 7).

3.   A non-negotiable bill of lading taken to a party other than the buyer under subsection (1) paragraph (b) reserves possession of the goods as security in the seller but if he seeks to withhold the goods improperly the buyer can tender payment and recover them.

4.   In the case of a shipment by non-negotiable bill of lading taken to a buyer, the seller, under subsection (1) retains no security interest or possession as against the buyer and by the shipment he *de facto* loses control as against the carrier except where he rightfully and effectively stops delivery in transit. In cases in which the contract gives the seller the right to payment against delivery, the seller, by making an immediate demand for payment, can show that his delivery is conditional, but this does not prevent the buyer's power to transfer full title to a sub-buyer in ordinary course or other purchaser under Section 2–403.

5.   Under subsection (2) an improper reservation by the seller which would constitute a breach in no way impairs such of the buyer's rights as result from identification of the goods. The security title reserved by the seller under subsection (1) does not protect his retaining possession or control of the document or the goods for the purpose of exacting more than is due him under the contract.

Cross References:

Point 1: Section 1–201.
Point 2: Article 7.
Point 3: Sections 2–501(2) and 2–504.
Point 4: Sections 2–403, 2–507(2) and 2–705.
Point 5: Sections 2–310, 2–319(4), 2–320(4), 2–501 and 2–502 and Article 7.

Definitional Cross References:

"Bill of lading". Section 1–201.
"Buyer". Section 2–103.
"Consignee". Section 7–102.
"Contract". Section 1–201.
"Contract for sale". Section 2–106.
"Delivery". Section 1–201.
"Financing agency". Section 2–104.
"Goods". Section 2–105.
"Holder". Section 1–201.
"Person". Section 1–201.
"Security interest". Section 1–201.
"Seller". Section 2–103.

As amended in 2003.

§ 2–506.   Rights of Financing Agency.

(1)   A financing agency by paying or purchasing for value a draft which relates to a shipment of goods acquires to the extent of the payment or purchase and in addition to its own rights under the draft and any document of title securing it any rights of the shipper in the goods including the right to stop delivery and the shipper's right to have the draft honored by the buyer.

(2)   The right to reimbursement of a financing agency which has in good faith honored or purchased the draft under commitment to or authority from the buyer is not impaired by subsequent discovery of defects with reference to any relevant document which was apparently regular.

As amended in 2003.

Official Comment

Prior Uniform Statutory Provision: None.

Purposes:

1.   "Financing agency" is broadly defined in this Article to cover every normal instance in which a party aids or intervenes in the financing of a sales transaction. The term as used in subsection (1) is not in any sense intended as a limitation and covers any other appropriate situation which may arise outside the scope of the definition.

2.   "Paying" as used in subsection (1) is typified by the letter of credit, or "authority to pay" situation in which a banker, by arrangement with the buyer or other consignee, pays on his behalf a draft for the price of the goods. It is immaterial whether the draft is formally drawn on the party paying or his principal, whether it is a sight draft paid in cash or a time draft "paid" in the first instance by acceptance, or whether the payment is viewed as absolute or conditional. All of these cases constitute "payment" under this subsection. Similarly, "purchasing for value" is used to indicate the whole area of financing by the seller's banker, and the principle of subsection (1) is applicable without any niceties of distinction between "purchase," "discount," "advance against collection" or the like. But it is important to notice that the only right to have the draft honored that is acquired is that *against the buyer*; if any right against any one else is claimed it will have to be under some separate obligation of that other person. A letter of credit does not necessarily protect *purchasers* of drafts. See Article 5. And for the relations of the parties to documentary drafts see Part 5 of Article 4.

3.   Subsection (1) is made applicable to payments or advances against a draft which "relates to" a shipment of goods and this has been chosen as a term of maximum breadth. In particular the term is intended to cover the case of a draft against an invoice or against a delivery order. Further, it is unnecessary that there be an explicit assignment of the invoice attached to the draft to bring the transaction within the reason of this subsection.

4.   After shipment, "the rights of the shipper in the goods" are merely security rights and are subject to the buyer's right to force delivery upon tender of the price. The rights acquired by the financing agency are similarly limited and, moreover, if the agency fails to procure any outstanding negotiable document of title, it may find its exercise of these rights hampered or even defeated by the seller's disposition of the document to a third party. This section does not attempt to create any new rights in the financing agency against the carrier which

would force the latter to honor a stop order from the agency, a stranger to the shipment, or any new rights against a holder to whom a document of title has been duly negotiated under Article 7.

5. The deletion of the language "on its face" from subsection (2) is designed to accommodate electronic documents of title without changing the requirement of regularity of the document.

Cross References:

Point 1: Section 2–104(2) and Article 4.
Point 2: Part 5 of Article 4, and Article 5.
Point 4: Sections 2–501 and 2–502(1) and Article 7.

Definitional Cross References:

"Buyer". Section 2–103.
"Document of title". Section 1–201.
"Draft". Section 3–104.
"Financing agency". Section 2–104.
"Good faith". Section 2–103.
"Goods". Section 2–105.
"Honor". Section 1–201 [*unrevised Article 1; see Concordance, p. 22*].
"Purchase". Section 1–201.
"Rights". Section 1–201.
"Value". Section 1–201 [*unrevised Article 1; see Concordance, p. 22*].

As amended in 2003.

§ 2–507. Effect of Seller's Tender; Delivery on Condition.

(1) Tender of delivery is a condition to the buyer's duty to accept the goods and, unless otherwise agreed, to his duty to pay for them. Tender entitles the seller to acceptance of the goods and to payment according to the contract.

(2) Where payment is due and demanded on the delivery to the buyer of goods or documents of title, his right as against the seller to retain or dispose of them is conditional upon his making the payment due.

Official Comment

Prior Uniform Statutory Provision: See Sections 11, 41, 42 and 69, Uniform Sales Act.

Purposes:

1. Subsection (1) continues the policies of the prior uniform statutory provisions with respect to tender and delivery by the seller. Under this Article the same rules in these matters are applied to present sales and to contracts for sale. But the provisions of this subsection must be read within the framework of the other sections of this Article which bear upon the question of delivery and payment.

2. The "unless otherwise agreed" provision of subsection (1) is directed primarily to cases in which payment in advance has been promised or a letter of credit term has been included. Payment "according to the contract" contemplates immediate payment, payment at the end of an agreed credit term, payment by a time acceptance or the like. Under this Act, "contract" means the total obligation in law which results from the parties' agreement including the effect of this Article. In this context, therefore, there must be considered the effect in law of such provisions as those on means and manner of payment and on failure of agreed means and manner of payment.

3. Subsection (2) deals with the effect of a conditional delivery by the seller and in such a situation makes the buyer's "right as against the seller" conditional upon payment. These words are used as words of limitation to conform with the policy set forth in the bona fide purchase sections of this Article. Should the seller after making such a conditional delivery fail to follow up his rights, the condition is waived. This subsection (2) codifies the cash seller's right of reclamation which is in the nature of a lien. There is no specific time limit for a cash seller to exercise the right of reclamation. However, the right will be defeated by delay causing prejudice to the buyer, waiver, estoppel, or ratification of the buyer's right to retain possession. Common law rules and precedents governing such principles are applicable (Section 1–103). If third parties are involved, Section 2–403(1) protects good faith purchasers. See PEB Commentary No. 1, dated March 10, 1990.

Cross References:

> Point 1: Sections 2–310, 2–503, 2–511, 2–601 and 2–711 to 2–713.
> Point 2: Sections 1–201, 2–511 and 2–614.
> Point 3: Sections 2–401, 2–403, and 2–702(1)(b).

Definitional Cross References:

> "Buyer". Section 2–103.
> "Contract". Section 1–201.
> "Delivery". Section 1–201.
> "Document of title". Section 1–201.
> "Goods". Section 2–105.
> "Rights". Section 1–201.
> "Seller". Section 2–103.

As amended in 1990 and 2022.

§ 2–508. Cure by Seller of Improper Tender or Delivery; Replacement.

(1) Where any tender or delivery by the seller is rejected because non-conforming and the time for performance has not yet expired, the seller may seasonably notify the buyer of his intention to cure and may then within the contract time make a conforming delivery.

(2) Where the buyer rejects a non-conforming tender which the seller had reasonable grounds to believe would be acceptable with or without money allowance the seller may if he seasonably notifies the buyer have a further reasonable time to substitute a conforming tender.

Official Comment

Prior Uniform Statutory Provision: None.

Purposes:

1. Subsection (1) permits a seller who has made a non-conforming tender in any case to make a conforming delivery within the contract time upon seasonable notification to the buyer. It applies even where the seller has taken back the non-conforming goods and refunded the purchase price. He may still make a good tender within the contract period. The closer, however, it is to the contract date, the greater is the necessity for extreme promptness on the seller's part in notifying of his intention to cure, if such notification is to be "seasonable" under this subsection.

The rule of this subsection, moreover, is qualified by its underlying reasons. Thus if, after contracting for June delivery, a buyer later makes known to the seller his need for shipment early in the month and the seller ships accordingly, the "contract time" has been cut down by the supervening modification and the time for cure of tender must be referred to this modified time term.

2. Subsection (2) seeks to avoid injustice to the seller by reason of a surprise rejection by the buyer. However, the seller is not protected unless he had "reasonable grounds to believe" that the tender would be acceptable. Such reasonable grounds can lie in prior course of dealing, course of performance or usage of trade as well as in the particular circumstances surrounding the making of the contract. The seller is charged with commercial knowledge of any factors in a particular sales situation which require him to comply strictly with his obligations under the contract as, for example, strict conformity of documents in an overseas shipment or the sale of precision parts or chemicals for use in manufacture. Further, if the buyer gives notice either implicitly, as by a prior course of dealing involving rigorous inspections, or expressly, as by the deliberate inclusion of a "no replacement" clause in the contract, the seller is to be held to rigid compliance. If the clause appears in a "form" contract evidence that it is out of line with trade usage or the prior course of dealing and was not called to the seller's attention may be sufficient to show that the seller had reasonable grounds to believe that the tender would be acceptable.

3. The words "a further reasonable time to substitute a conforming tender" are intended as words of limitation to protect the buyer. What is a "reasonable time" depends upon the attending circumstances. Compare Section 2–511 on the comparable case of a seller's surprise demand for legal tender.

4. Existing trade usages permitting variations without rejection but with price allowance enter into the agreement itself as contractual limitations of remedy and are not covered by this section.

Cross References:

> Point 2: Section 2–302.
> Point 3: Section 2–511.
> Point 4: Sections 1–205 [*unrevised Article 1; see Concordance, p. 22*] and 2–721.

Definitional Cross References:

> "Buyer". Section 2–103.
> "Conforming". Section 2–106.
> "Contract". Section 1–201.
> "Money". Section 1–201.
> "Notifies". Section 1–201 [*unrevised Article 1; see Concordance, p. 22*].
> "Reasonable time". Section 1–204 [*unrevised Article 1; see Concordance, p. 22*].
> "Seasonably". Section 1–204 [*unrevised Article 1; see Concordance, p. 22*].
> "Seller". Section 2–103.

§ 2–509.   Risk of Loss in the Absence of Breach.

(1)   Where the contract requires or authorizes the seller to ship the goods by carrier

(a)   if it does not require him to deliver them at a particular destination, the risk of loss passes to the buyer when the goods are duly delivered to the carrier even though the shipment is under reservation (Section 2–505); but

(b)   if it does require him to deliver them at a particular destination and the goods are there duly tendered while in the possession of the carrier, the risk of loss passes to the buyer when the goods are there duly so tendered as to enable the buyer to take delivery.

(2)   Where the goods are held by a bailee to be delivered without being moved, the risk of loss passes to the buyer

(a)   on his receipt of possession or control of a negotiable document of title covering the goods; or

(b)   on acknowledgment by the bailee of the buyer's right to possession of the goods; or

(c)   after his receipt of possession or control of a non-negotiable document of title or other direction to deliver in a record, as provided in subsection (4)(b) of Section 2–503.

(3)   In any case not within subsection (1) or (2), the risk of loss passes to the buyer on his receipt of the goods if the seller is a merchant; otherwise the risk passes to the buyer on tender of delivery.

(4)   The provisions of this section are subject to contrary agreement of the parties and to the provisions of this Article on sale on approval (Section 2–327) and on effect of breach on risk of loss (Section 2–510).

As amended in 2003.

Official Comment

Prior Uniform Statutory Provision: Section 22, Uniform Sales Act.

Changes: Rewritten, subsection (3) of this section modifying prior law.

Purposes of Changes: To make it clear that:

1.   The underlying theory of these sections on risk of loss is the adoption of the contractual approach rather than an arbitrary shifting of the risk with the "property" in the goods. The scope of the present section, therefore, is limited strictly to those cases where there has been no breach by the seller. Where for any reason his delivery or tender fails to conform to the contract, the present section does not apply and the situation is governed by the provisions on effect of breach on risk of loss.

2.   The provisions of subsection (1) apply where the contract "requires or authorizes" shipment of the goods. This language is intended to be construed parallel to comparable language in the section on shipment by seller. In order that the goods be "duly delivered to the carrier" under paragraph (a) a contract must be entered into with the carrier which will satisfy the requirements of the section on shipment by the seller and the delivery must be made under circumstances which will enable the seller to take any further steps necessary to a due tender. The underlying reason of this subsection does not require that the shipment be made after contracting, but where, for

example, the seller buys the goods afloat and later diverts the shipment to the buyer, he must identify the goods to the contract before the risk of loss can pass. To transfer the risk it is enough that a proper shipment and a proper identification come to apply to the same goods although, aside from special agreement, the risk will not pass retroactively to the time of shipment in such a case.

3. Whether the contract involves delivery at the seller's place of business or at the situs of the goods, a merchant seller cannot transfer risk of loss and it remains upon him until actual receipt by the buyer, even though full payment has been made and the buyer has been notified that the goods are at his disposal. Protection is afforded him, in the event of breach by the buyer, under the next section.

The underlying theory of this rule is that a merchant who is to make physical delivery at his own place continues meanwhile to control the goods and can be expected to insure his interest in them. The buyer, on the other hand, has no control of the goods and it is extremely unlikely that he will carry insurance on goods not yet in his possession.

4. Where the agreement provides for delivery of the goods as between the buyer and seller without removal from the physical possession of a bailee, the provisions on manner of tender of delivery apply on the point of transfer of risk. Due delivery of a negotiable document of title covering the goods or acknowledgment by the bailee that he holds for the buyer completes the "delivery" and passes the risk. See definition of delivery in Article 1, Section 1–201 and the definition of control in Article 7, Section 7–106.

5. The provisions of this section are made subject by subsection (4) to the "contrary agreement" of the parties. This language is intended as the equivalent of the phrase "unless otherwise agreed" used more frequently throughout this Act. "Contrary" is in no way used as a word of limitation and the buyer and seller are left free to readjust their rights and risks as declared by this section in any manner agreeable to them. Contrary agreement can also be found in the circumstances of the case, a trade usage or practice, or a course of dealing or performance.

Cross References:

Point 1: Section 2–510(1).
Point 2: Sections 2–503 and 2–504.
Point 3: Sections 2–104, 2–503 and 2–510.
Point 4: Section 2–503(4).
Point 5: Section 1–201.

Definitional Cross References:

"Agreement". Section 1–201.
"Buyer". Section 2–103.
"Contract". Section 1–201.
"Delivery". Section 1–201.
"Document of title". Section 1–201.
"Goods". Section 2–105.
"Merchant". Section 2–104.
"Party". Section 1–201.
"Receipt" of goods. Section 2–103.
"Sale on approval". Section 2–326.
"Seller". Section 2–103.

As amended in 2003.

§ 2–510. Effect of Breach on Risk of Loss.

(1) Where a tender or delivery of goods so fails to conform to the contract as to give a right of rejection the risk of their loss remains on the seller until cure or acceptance.

(2) Where the buyer rightfully revokes acceptance he may to the extent of any deficiency in his effective insurance coverage treat the risk of loss as having rested on the seller from the beginning.

(3) Where the buyer as to conforming goods already identified to the contract for sale repudiates or is otherwise in breach before risk of their loss has passed to him, the seller may to the extent of any deficiency in his effective insurance coverage treat the risk of loss as resting on the buyer for a commercially reasonable time.

Official Comment

Prior Uniform Statutory Provision: None.

Purposes: To make clear that:

1.   Under subsection (1) the seller by his individual action cannot shift the risk of loss to the buyer unless his action conforms with all the conditions resting on him under the contract.

2.   The "cure" of defective tenders contemplated by subsection (1) applies only to those situations in which the seller makes changes in goods already tendered, such as repair, partial substitution, sorting out from an improper mixture and the like since "cure" by repossession and new tender has no effect on the risk of loss of the goods originally tendered. The seller's privilege of cure does not shift the risk, however, until the cure is completed.

Where defective documents are involved a cure of the defect by the seller or a waiver of the defects by the buyer will operate to shift the risk under this section. However, if the goods have been destroyed prior to the cure or the buyer is unaware of their destruction at the time he waives the defect in the documents, the risk of the loss must still be borne by the seller, for the risk shifts only at the time of cure, waiver of documentary defects or acceptance of the goods.

3.   In cases where there has been a breach of the contract, if the one in control of the goods is the aggrieved party, whatever loss or damage may prove to be uncovered by his insurance falls upon the contract breaker under subsections (2) and (3) rather than upon him. The word "effective" as applied to insurance coverage in those subsections is used to meet the case of supervening insolvency of the insurer. The "deficiency" referred to in the text means such deficiency in the insurance coverage as exists without subrogation. This section merely distributes the risk of loss as stated and is not intended to be disturbed by any subrogation of an insurer.

Cross Reference:

Section 2–509.

Definitional Cross References:

"Buyer". Section 2–103.
"Conform". Section 2–106.
"Contract for sale". Section 2–106.
"Goods". Section 2–105.
"Seller". Section 2–103.

§ 2–511.   Tender of Payment by Buyer; Payment by Check.

(1)   Unless otherwise agreed tender of payment is a condition to the seller's duty to tender and complete any delivery.

(2)   Tender of payment is sufficient when made by any means or in any manner current in the ordinary course of business unless the seller demands payment in legal tender and gives any extension of time reasonably necessary to procure it.

(3)   Subject to the provisions of this Act on the effect of an instrument on an obligation (Section 3–310), payment by check is conditional and is defeated as between the parties by dishonor of the check on due presentment.

As amended in 1994.

Official Comment

Prior Uniform Statutory Provision: Section 42, Uniform Sales Act.

Changes: Rewritten by this section and Section 2–507.

Purposes of Changes:

1.   The requirement of payment against delivery in subsection (1) is applicable to non-commercial sales generally and to ordinary sales at retail although it has no application to the great body of commercial contracts which carry credit terms. Subsection (1) applies also to documentary contracts in general and to contracts which look to shipment by the seller but contain no term on time and manner of payment, in which situations the payment may, in proper case, be demanded against delivery of appropriate documents.

In the case of specific transactions such as C.O.D. sales or agreements providing for payment against documents, the provisions of this subsection must be considered in conjunction with the special sections of the Article dealing with such terms. The provision that tender of payment is a condition to the seller's duty to tender and complete "any delivery" integrates this section with the language and policy of the section on delivery in several lots which call for separate payment. Finally, attention should be directed to the provision on right to adequate assurance of performance which recognizes, even before the time for tender, an obligation on the buyer not to impair the seller's expectation of receiving payment in due course.

2. Unless there is agreement otherwise the concurrence of the conditions as to tender of payment and tender of delivery requires their performance at a single place or time. This Article determines that place and time by determining in various other sections the place and time for tender of delivery under various circumstances and in particular types of transactions. The sections dealing with time and place of delivery together with the section on right to inspection of goods answer the subsidiary question as to when payment may be demanded before inspection by the buyer.

3. The essence of the principle involved in subsection (2) is avoidance of commercial surprise at the time of performance. The section on substituted performance covers the peculiar case in which legal tender is not available to the commercial community.

4. Subsection (3) is concerned with the rights and obligations as between the parties to a sales transaction when payment is made by check. This Article recognizes that the taking of a seemingly solvent party's check is commercially normal and proper and, if due diligence is exercised in collection, is not to be penalized in any way. The conditional character of the payment under this section refers only to the effect of the transaction "as between the parties" thereto and does not purport to cut into the law of "absolute" and "conditional" payment as applied to such other problems as the discharge of sureties or the responsibilities of a drawee bank which is at the same time an agent for collection.

The phrase "by check" includes not only the buyer's own but any check which does not effect a discharge under Article 3 (Section 3–802) [*unrevised Article 3 (Appendix B)*]. Similarly the reason of this subsection should apply and the same result should be reached where the buyer "pays" by sight draft on a commercial firm which is financing him.

5. Under subsection (3) payment by check is defeated if it is not honored upon due presentment. This corresponds to the provisions of article on Commercial Paper. (Section 3–802) [*unrevised Article 3 (Appendix B)*]. But if the seller procures certification of the check instead of cashing it, the buyer is discharged. (Section 3–411) [*unrevised Article 3 (Appendix B)*].

6. Where the instrument offered by the buyer is not a payment but a credit instrument such as a note or a check post-dated by even one day, the seller's acceptance of the instrument insofar as third parties are concerned, amounts to a delivery on credit and his remedies are set forth in the section on buyer's insolvency. As between the buyer and the seller, however, the matter turns on the present subsection and the section on conditional delivery and subsequent dishonor of the instrument gives the seller rights on it as well as for breach of the contract for sale.

Cross References:

Point 1: Sections 2–307, 2–310, 2–320, 2–325, 2–503, 2–513 and 2–609.
Point 2: Sections 2–307, 2–310, 2–319, 2–322, 2–503, 2–504 and 2–513.
Point 3: Section 2–614.
Point 5: Article 3, esp. Sections 3–802 [*unrevised Article 3 (Appendix B)*] and 3–411 [*unrevised Article 3 (Appendix B)*].
Point 6: Sections 2–507, 2–702, and Article 3.

Definitional Cross References:

"Buyer". Section 2–103.
"Check". Section 3–104.
"Dishonor". Section 3–508 [*unrevised Article 3 (Appendix B)*].
"Party". Section 1–201.
"Reasonable time". Section 1–204 [*unrevised Article 1; see Concordance, p. 22*].
"Seller". Section 2–103.

§ 2–512.   Payment by Buyer Before Inspection.

(1)   Where the contract requires payment before inspection non-conformity of the goods does not excuse the buyer from so making payment unless

     (a)   the non-conformity appears without inspection; or

     (b)   despite tender of the required documents the circumstances would justify injunction against honor under this Act (Section 5–109(b)).

(2)   Payment pursuant to subsection (1) does not constitute an acceptance of goods or impair the buyer's right to inspect or any of his remedies.

As amended in 1995.

Official Comment

Prior Uniform Statutory Provision: None, but see Sections 47 and 49, Uniform Sales Act.

Purposes:

1.   Subsection (1) of the present section recognizes that the essence of a contract providing for payment before inspection is the intention of the parties to shift to the buyer the risks which would usually rest upon the seller. The basic nature of the transaction is thus preserved and the buyer is in most cases required to pay first and litigate as to any defects later.

2.   "Inspection" under this section is an inspection in a manner reasonable for detecting defects in goods whose surface appearance is satisfactory.

3.   Clause (a) of this subsection states an exception to the general rule based on common sense and normal commercial practice. The apparent non-conformity referred to is one which is evident in the mere process of taking delivery.

4.   Clause (b) is concerned with contracts for payment against documents and incorporates the general clarification and modification of the case law contained in the section on excuse of a financing agency. Section 5–109(b).

5.   Subsection (2) makes explicit the general policy of the Uniform Sales Act that the payment required before inspection in no way impairs the buyer's remedies or rights in the event of a default by the seller. The remedies preserved to the buyer are all of his remedies, which include as a matter of reason the remedy for total non-delivery after payment in advance.

The provision on performance or acceptance under reservation of rights does not apply to the situations contemplated here in which payment is made in due course under the contract and the buyer need not pay "under protest" or the like in order to preserve his rights as to defects discovered upon inspection.

6.   This section applies to cases in which the contract requires payment before inspection either by the express agreement of the parties or by reason of the effect in law of that contract. The present section must therefore be considered in conjunction with the provision on right to inspection of goods which sets forth the instances in which the buyer is not entitled to inspection before payment.

Cross References:

     Point 4: Article 5.
     Point 5: Section 1–207 [*unrevised Article 1; see Concordance, p. 22*].
     Point 6: Section 2–513(3).

Definitional Cross References:

     "Buyer". Section 2–103.
     "Conform". Section 2–106.
     "Contract". Section 1–201.
     "Financing agency". Section 2–104.
     "Goods". Section 2–105.
     "Remedy". Section 1–201.
     "Rights". Section 1–201.

§ 2–513. Buyer's Right to Inspection of Goods.

(1)   Unless otherwise agreed and subject to subsection (3), where goods are tendered or delivered or identified to the contract for sale, the buyer has a right before payment or acceptance to inspect them at any reasonable place and time and in any reasonable manner. When the seller is required or authorized to send the goods to the buyer, the inspection may be after their arrival.

(2)   Expenses of inspection must be borne by the buyer but may be recovered from the seller if the goods do not conform and are rejected.

(3)   Unless otherwise agreed and subject to the provisions of this Article on C.I.F. contracts (subsection (3) of Section 2–321), the buyer is not entitled to inspect the goods before payment of the price when the contract provides

(a)   for delivery "C.O.D." or on other like terms; or

(b)   for payment against documents of title, except where such payment is due only after the goods are to become available for inspection.

(4)   A place or method of inspection fixed by the parties is presumed to be exclusive but unless otherwise expressly agreed it does not postpone identification or shift the place for delivery or for passing the risk of loss. If compliance becomes impossible, inspection shall be as provided in this section unless the place or method fixed was clearly intended as an indispensable condition failure of which avoids the contract.

Official Comment

Prior Uniform Statutory Provisions: Section 47(2), (3), Uniform Sales Act.

Changes: Rewritten, Subsections (2) and (3) being new.

Purposes of Changes and New Matter: To correspond in substance with the prior uniform statutory provision and to incorporate in addition some of the results of the better case law so that:

1.   The buyer is entitled to inspect goods as provided in subsection (1) unless it has been otherwise agreed by the parties. The phrase "unless otherwise agreed" is intended principally to cover such situations as those outlined in subsections (3) and (4) and those in which the agreement of the parties negates inspection before tender of delivery. However, no agreement by the parties can displace the entire right of inspection except where the contract is simply for the sale of "this thing." Even in a sale of boxed goods "as is" inspection is a right of the buyer, since if the boxes prove to contain some other merchandise altogether the price can be recovered back; nor do the limitations of the provision on effect of acceptance apply in such a case.

2.   The buyer's right of inspection is available to him upon tender, delivery or appropriation of the goods with notice to him. Since inspection is available to him on tender, where payment is due against delivery he may, unless otherwise agreed, make his inspection before payment of the price. It is also available to him after receipt of the goods and so may be postponed after receipt for a reasonable time. Failure to inspect before payment does not impair the right to inspect after receipt of the goods unless the case falls within subsection (4) on agreed and exclusive inspection provisions. The right to inspect goods which have been appropriated with notice to the buyer holds whether or not the sale was by sample.

3.   The buyer may exercise his right of inspection at any reasonable time or place and in any reasonable manner. It is not necessary that he select the most appropriate time, place or manner to inspect or that his selection be the customary one in the trade or locality. Any reasonable time, place or manner is available to him and the reasonableness will be determined by trade usages, past practices between the parties and the other circumstances of the case.

The last sentence of subsection (1) makes it clear that the place of arrival of shipped goods is a reasonable place for their inspection.

4.   Expenses of an inspection made to satisfy the buyer of the seller's performance must be assumed by the buyer in the first instance. Since the rule provides merely for an allocation of expense there is no policy to prevent the parties from providing otherwise in the agreement. Where the buyer would normally bear the expenses of the inspection but the goods are rightly rejected because of what the inspection reveals, demonstrable and reasonable costs of the inspection are part of his incidental damage caused by the seller's breach.

5. In the case of payment against documents, subsection (3) requires payment before inspection, since shipping documents against which payment is to be made will commonly be tendered while the goods are still in transit. This Article recognizes no exception in any peculiar case in which the goods happen to arrive before the documents are tendered. However, where by the agreement payment is to await the arrival of the goods, inspection before payment becomes proper since the goods are then "available for inspection."

Where by the agreement the documents are to be tendered after arrival of the goods the buyer is entitled to inspect before payment since the goods are then "available for inspection". Proof of usage is not necessary to establish this right, but if inspection before payment is disputed the contrary must be established by usage or by an explicit contract term to that effect.

For the same reason, that the goods are available for inspection, a term calling for payment against storage documents or a delivery order does not normally bar the buyer's right to inspection before payment under subsection (3)(b). This result is reinforced by the buyer's right under subsection (1) to inspect goods which have been appropriated with notice to him.

6. Under subsection (4) an agreed place or method of inspection is generally held to be intended as exclusive. However, where compliance with such an agreed inspection term becomes impossible, the question is basically one of intention. If the parties clearly intend that the method of inspection named is to be a necessary condition without which the entire deal is to fail, the contract is at an end if that method becomes impossible. On the other hand, if the parties merely seek to indicate a convenient and reliable method but do not intend to give up the deal in the event of its failure, any reasonable method of inspection may be substituted under this Article.

Since the purpose of an agreed place of inspection is only to make sure at that point whether or not the goods will be thrown back, the "exclusive" feature of the named place is satisfied under this Article if the buyer's failure to inspect there is held to be an acceptance with the knowledge of such defects as inspection would have revealed within the section on waiver of buyer's objections by failure to particularize. Revocation of the acceptance is limited to the situations stated in the section pertaining to that subject. The reasonable time within which to give notice of defects within the section on notice of breach begins to run from the point of the "acceptance."

7. Clauses on time of inspection are commonly clauses which limit the time in which the buyer must inspect and give notice of defects. Such clauses are therefore governed by the section of this Article which requires that such a time limitation must be reasonable.

8. Inspection under this Article is not to be regarded as a "condition precedent to the passing of title" so that risk until inspection remains on the seller. Under subsection (4) such an approach cannot be sustained. Issues between the buyer and seller are settled in this Article almost wholly by special provisions and not by the technical determination of the locus of the title. Thus "inspection as a condition to the passing of title" becomes a concept almost without meaning. However, in peculiar circumstances inspection may still have some of the consequences hitherto sought and obtained under that concept.

9. "Inspection" under this section has to do with the buyer's check-up on whether the seller's performance is in accordance with a contract previously made and is not to be confused with the "examination" of the goods or of a sample or model of them at the time of contracting which may affect the warranties involved in the contract.

Cross References:

Generally: Sections 2–310(b), 2–321(3) and 2–606(1)(b).
Point 1: Section 2–607.
Point 2: Sections 2–501 and 2–502.
Point 4: Section 2–715.
Point 5: Section 2–321(3).
Point 6: Sections 2–606 to 2–608.
Point 7: Section 1–204 [*unrevised Article 1; see Concordance, p. 22*].
Point 8: Comment to Section 2–401.
Point 9: Section 2–316(3)(b).

Definitional Cross References:

"Buyer". Section 2–103.
"Conform". Section 2–106.
"Contract". Section 1–201.
"Contract for sale". Section 2–106.

"Document of title". Section 1–201.
"Goods". Section 2–105.
"Party". Section 1–201.
"Presumed". Section 1–201 [*unrevised Article 1; see Concordance, p. 22*].
"Reasonable time". Section 1–204 [*unrevised Article 1; see Concordance, p. 22*].
"Rights". Section 1–201.
"Seller". Section 2–103.
"Send". Section 1–201.
"Term". Section 1–201.

As amended in 2003.

§ 2–514. When Documents Deliverable on Acceptance; When on Payment.

Unless otherwise agreed documents against which a draft is drawn are to be delivered to the drawee on acceptance of the draft if it is payable more than three days after presentment; otherwise, only on payment.

Official Comment

Prior Uniform Statutory Provision: Section 41, Uniform Bills of Lading Act.

Changes: Rewritten.

Purposes of Changes: To make the provision one of general application so that:

1. It covers any document against which a draft may be drawn, whatever may be the form of the document, and applies to interpret the action of a seller or consignor insofar as it may affect the rights and duties of any buyer, consignee or financing agency concerned with the paper. Supplementary or corresponding provisions are found in Sections 4–503 and 5–112 [*unrevised Article 5*].

2. An "arrival" draft is a sight draft within the purpose of this section.

Cross References:

Point 1: See Sections 2–502, 2–505(2), 2–507(2), 2–512, 2–513, 2–607 concerning protection of rights of buyer and seller, and 4–503 and 5–112 [*unrevised Article 5*] on delivery of documents.

Definitional Cross References:

"Delivery". Section 1–201.
"Draft". Section 3–104.

§ 2–515. Preserving Evidence of Goods in Dispute.

In furtherance of the adjustment of any claim or dispute

(a) either party on reasonable notification to the other and for the purpose of ascertaining the facts and preserving evidence has the right to inspect, test and sample the goods including such of them as may be in the possession or control of the other; and

(b) the parties may agree to a third party inspection or survey to determine the conformity or condition of the goods and may agree that the findings shall be binding upon them in any subsequent litigation or adjustment.

Official Comment

Prior Uniform Statutory Provision: None.

Purposes:

1. To meet certain serious problems which arise when there is a dispute as to the quality of the goods and thereby perhaps to aid the parties in reaching a settlement, and to further the use of devices which will promote certainty as to the condition of the goods, or at least aid in preserving evidence of their condition.

2. Under paragraph (a), to afford either party an opportunity for preserving evidence, whether or not agreement has been reached, and thereby to reduce uncertainty in any litigation and, in turn perhaps, to promote agreement.

Paragraph (a) does not conflict with the provisions on the seller's right to resell rejected goods or the buyer's similar right. Apparent conflict between these provisions which will be suggested in certain circumstances is to be resolved by requiring prompt action by the parties. Nor does paragraph (a) impair the effect of a term for payment before inspection. Short of such defects as amount to fraud or substantial failure of consideration, non-conformity is neither an excuse nor a defense to an action for non-acceptance of documents. Normally, therefore, until the buyer has made payment, inspected and rejected the goods, there is no occasion or use for the rights under paragraph (a).

3. Under paragraph (b), to provide for third party inspection upon the agreement of the parties, thereby opening the door to amicable adjustments based upon the findings of such third parties.

The use of the phrase "conformity or condition" makes it clear that the parties' agreement may range from a complete settlement of all aspects of the dispute by a third party to the use of a third party merely to determine and record the condition of the goods so that they can be resold or used to reduce the stake in controversy. "Conformity", at one end of the scale of possible issues, includes the whole question of interpretation of the agreement and its legal effect, the state of the goods in regard to quality and condition, whether any defects are due to factors which operate at the risk of the buyer, and the degree of non-conformity where that may be material. "Condition", at the other end of the scale, includes nothing but the degree of damage or deterioration which the goods show. Paragraph (b) is intended to reach any point in the gamut which the parties may agree upon.

The principle of the section on reservation of rights reinforces this paragraph in simplifying such adjustments as the parties wish to make in partial settlement while reserving their rights as to any further points. Paragraph (b) also suggests the use of arbitration, where desired, of any points left open, but nothing in this section is intended to repeal or amend any statute governing arbitration. Where any question arises as to the extent of the parties' agreement under the paragraph, the presumption should be that it was meant to extend only to the relation between the contract description and the goods as delivered, since that is what a craftsman in the trade would normally be expected to report upon. Finally, a written and authenticated report of inspection or tests by a third party, whether or not sampling has been practicable, is entitled to be admitted as evidence under this Act, for it is a third party document.

Cross References:

Point 2: Sections 2–513(3), 2–706 and 2–711(2) and Article 5.

Point 3: Sections 1–202 [*unrevised Article 1; see Concordance, p. 22*] and 1–207 [*unrevised Article 1; see Concordance, p. 22*].

Definitional Cross References:

"Conform". Section 2–106.
"Goods". Section 2–105.
"Notification". Section 1–201 [*unrevised Article 1; see Concordance, p. 22*].
"Party". Section 1–201.

PART 6

BREACH, REPUDIATION AND EXCUSE

§ 2–601.   Buyer's Rights on Improper Delivery.

Subject to the provisions of this Article on breach in installment contracts (Section 2–612) and unless otherwise agreed under the sections on contractual limitations of remedy (Sections 2–718 and 2–719), if the goods or the tender of delivery fail in any respect to conform to the contract, the buyer may

(a) reject the whole; or

(b) accept the whole; or

(c) accept any commercial unit or units and reject the rest.

Official Comment

Prior Uniform Statutory Provision: No one general equivalent provision but numerous provisions, dealing with situations of non-conformity where buyer may accept or reject, including Sections 11, 44 and 69(1), Uniform Sales Act.

Changes: Partial acceptance in good faith is recognized and the buyer's remedies on the contract for breach of warranty and the like, where the buyer has returned the goods after transfer of title, are no longer barred.

Purposes of Changes: To make it clear that:

1. A buyer accepting a non-conforming tender is not penalized by the loss of any remedy otherwise open to him. This policy extends to cover and regulate the acceptance of a part of any lot improperly tendered in any case where the price can reasonably be apportioned. Partial acceptance is permitted whether the part of the goods accepted conforms or not. The only limitation on partial acceptance is that good faith and commercial reasonableness must be used to avoid undue impairment of the value of the remaining portion of the goods. This is the reason for the insistence on the "commercial unit" in paragraph (c). In this respect, the test is not only what unit has been the basis of contract, but whether the partial acceptance produces so materially adverse an effect on the remainder as to constitute bad faith.

2. Acceptance made with the knowledge of the other party is final. An original refusal to accept may be withdrawn by a later acceptance if the seller has indicated that he is holding the tender open. However, if the buyer attempts to accept, either in whole or in part, after his original rejection has caused the seller to arrange for other disposition of the goods, the buyer must answer for any ensuing damage since the next section provides that any exercise of ownership after rejection is wrongful as against the seller. Further, he is liable even though the seller may choose to treat his action as acceptance rather than conversion, since the damage flows from the misleading notice. Such arrangements for resale or other disposition of the goods by the seller must be viewed as within the normal contemplation of a buyer who has given notice of rejection. However, the buyer's attempts in good faith to dispose of defective goods where the seller has failed to give instructions within a reasonable time are not to be regarded as an acceptance.

Cross References:

Sections 2–602(2)(a), 2–612, 2–718 and 2–719.

Definitional Cross References:

"Buyer". Section 2–103.
"Commercial unit". Section 2–105.
"Conform". Section 2–106.
"Contract". Section 1–201.
"Goods". Section 2–105.
"Installment contract". Section 2–612.
"Rights". Section 1–201.

§ 2–602.   Manner and Effect of Rightful Rejection.

(1)   Rejection of goods must be within a reasonable time after their delivery or tender. It is ineffective unless the buyer seasonably notifies the seller.

(2)   Subject to the provisions of the two following sections on rejected goods (Sections 2–603 and 2–604),

(a)   after rejection any exercise of ownership by the buyer with respect to any commercial unit is wrongful as against the seller; and

(b)   if the buyer has before rejection taken physical possession of goods in which he does not have a security interest under the provisions of this Article (subsection (3) of Section 2–711), he is under a duty after rejection to hold them with reasonable care at the seller's disposition for a time sufficient to permit the seller to remove them; but

(c)   the buyer has no further obligations with regard to goods rightfully rejected.

(3)   The seller's rights with respect to goods wrongfully rejected are governed by the provisions of this Article on Seller's remedies in general (Section 2–703).

Official Comment

Prior Uniform Statutory Provision: Section 50, Uniform Sales Act.

Changes: Rewritten.

Purposes of Changes: To make it clear that:

1.   A tender or delivery of goods made pursuant to a contract of sale, even though wholly non-conforming, requires affirmative action by the buyer to avoid acceptance. Under subsection (1), therefore, the buyer is given a reasonable time to notify the seller of his rejection, but without such seasonable notification his rejection is ineffective. The sections of this Article dealing with inspection of goods must be read in connection with the buyer's reasonable time for action under this subsection. Contract provisions limiting the time for rejection fall within the rule of the section on "Time" and are effective if the time set gives the buyer a reasonable time for discovery of defects. What constitutes a due "notifying" of rejection by the buyer to the seller is defined in Section 1–201 [*unrevised Article 1; see Concordance, p. 22*].

2.   Subsection (2) lays down the normal duties of the buyer upon rejection, which flow from the relationship of the parties. Beyond his duty to hold the goods with reasonable care for the buyer's [seller's] disposition, this section continues the policy of prior uniform legislation in generally relieving the buyer from any duties with respect to them, except when the circumstances impose the limited obligation of salvage upon him under the next section.

3.   The present section applies only to rightful rejection by the buyer. If the seller has made a tender which in all respects conforms to the contract, the buyer has a positive duty to accept and his failure to do so constitutes a "wrongful rejection" which gives the seller immediate remedies for breach. Subsection (3) is included here to emphasize the sharp distinction between the rejection of an improper tender and the non-acceptance which is a breach by the buyer.

4.   The provisions of this section are to be appropriately limited or modified when a negotiation is in process.

Cross References:

Point 1: Sections 1–201 [*unrevised Article 1; see Concordance, p. 22*], 1–204(1) and (3) [*unrevised Article 1; see Concordance, p. 22*], 2–512(2), 2–513(1) and 2–606(1)(b).

Point 2: Section 2–603(1).

Point 3: Section 2–703.

Definitional Cross References:

"Buyer". Section 2–103.
"Commercial unit". Section 2–105.
"Goods". Section 2–105.
"Merchant". Section 2–104.
"Notifies". Section 1–201 [*unrevised Article 1; see Concordance, p. 22*].
"Reasonable time". Section 1–204 [*unrevised Article 1; see Concordance, p. 22*].
"Remedy". Section 1–201.
"Rights". Section 1–201.
"Seasonably". Section 1–204 [*unrevised Article 1; see Concordance, p. 22*].
"Security interest". Section 1–201.
"Seller". Section 2–103.

§ 2–603.   Merchant Buyer's Duties as to Rightfully Rejected Goods.

(1)   Subject to any security interest in the buyer (subsection (3) of Section 2–711), when the seller has no agent or place of business at the market of rejection a merchant buyer is under a duty after rejection of goods in his possession or control to follow any reasonable instructions received from the seller with respect to the goods and in the absence of such instructions to make reasonable efforts to sell them for the seller's account if they are perishable or threaten to decline in value speedily. Instructions are not reasonable if on demand indemnity for expenses is not forthcoming.

(2)   When the buyer sells goods under subsection (1), he is entitled to reimbursement from the seller or out of the proceeds for reasonable expenses of caring for and selling them, and if the expenses include no

selling commission then to such commission as is usual in the trade or if there is none to a reasonable sum not exceeding ten per cent on the gross proceeds.

(3) In complying with this section the buyer is held only to good faith and good faith conduct hereunder is neither acceptance nor conversion nor the basis of an action for damages.

Official Comment

Prior Uniform Statutory Provision: None.

Purposes:

1. This section recognizes the duty imposed upon the merchant buyer by good faith and commercial practice to follow any reasonable instructions of the seller as to reshipping, storing, delivery to a third party, reselling or the like. Subsection (1) goes further and extends the duty to include the making of reasonable efforts to effect a salvage sale where the value of the goods is threatened and the seller's instructions do not arrive in time to prevent serious loss.

2. The limitations on the buyer's duty to resell under subsection (1) are to be liberally construed. The buyer's duty to resell under this section arises from commercial necessity and thus is present only when the seller has "no agent or place of business at the market of rejection". A financing agency which is acting in behalf of the seller in handling the documents rejected by the buyer is sufficiently the seller's agent to lift the burden of salvage resale from the buyer. (See provisions of Sections 4–503 and 5–112 [*unrevised Article 5*] on bank's duties with respect to rejected documents.) The buyer's duty to resell is extended only to goods in his "possession or control", but these are intended as words of wide, rather than narrow, import. In effect, the measure of the buyer's "control" is whether he can practicably effect control without undue commercial burden.

3. The explicit provisions for reimbursement and compensation to the buyer in subsection (2) are applicable and necessary only where he is not acting under instructions from the seller. As provided in subsection (1) the seller's instructions to be "reasonable" must on demand of the buyer include indemnity for expenses.

4. Since this section makes the resale of perishable goods an affirmative duty in contrast to a mere right to sell as under the case law, subsection (3) makes it clear that the buyer is liable only for the exercise of good faith in determining whether the value of the goods is sufficiently threatened to justify a quick resale or whether he has waited a sufficient length of time for instructions, or what a reasonable means and place of resale is.

5. A buyer who fails to make a salvage sale when his duty to do so under this section has arisen is subject to damages pursuant to the section on liberal administration of remedies.

Cross References:

Point 2: Sections 4–503 and 5–112 [*unrevised Article 5*].
Point 5: Section 1–106 [*unrevised Article 1; see Concordance, p. 22*]. Compare generally section 2–706.

Definitional Cross References:

"Buyer". Section 2–103.
"Good faith". Section 1–201.
"Goods". Section 2–105.
"Merchant". Section 2–104.
"Security interest". Section 1–201.
"Seller". Section 2–103.

§ 2–604. Buyer's Options as to Salvage of Rightfully Rejected Goods.

Subject to the provisions of the immediately preceding section on perishables if the seller gives no instructions within a reasonable time after notification of rejection the buyer may store the rejected goods for the seller's account or reship them to him or resell them for the seller's account with reimbursement as provided in the preceding section. Such action is not acceptance or conversion.

Official Comment

Prior Uniform Statutory Provision: None.

Purposes:

The basic purpose of this section is twofold: on the one hand it aims at reducing the stake in dispute and on the other at avoiding the pinning of a technical "acceptance" on a buyer who has taken steps towards realization on or preservation of the goods in good faith. This section is essentially a salvage section and the buyer's right to act under it is conditioned upon (1) non-conformity of the goods, (2) due notification of rejection to the seller under the section on manner of rejection, and (3) the absence of any instructions from the seller which the merchant-buyer has a duty to follow under the preceding section.

This section is designed to accord all reasonable leeway to a rightfully rejecting buyer acting in good faith. The listing of what the buyer may do in the absence of instructions from the seller is intended to be not exhaustive but merely illustrative. This is not a "merchant's" section and the options are pure options given to merchant and nonmerchant buyers alike. The merchant-buyer, however, may in some instances be under a duty rather than an option to resell under the provisions of the preceding section.

Cross References:

Sections 2–602(1), and 2–603(1) and 2–706.

Definitional Cross References:

"Buyer". Section 2–103.
"Notification". Section 1–201 [*unrevised Article 1; see Concordance, p. 22*].
"Reasonable time". Section 1–204 [*unrevised Article 1; see Concordance, p. 22*].
"Seller". Section 2–103.

§ 2–605.   Waiver of Buyer's Objections by Failure to Particularize.

(1)   The buyer's failure to state in connection with rejection a particular defect which is ascertainable by reasonable inspection precludes him from relying on the unstated defect to justify rejection or to establish breach

    (a)   where the seller could have cured it if stated seasonably; or

    (b)   between merchants when the seller has after rejection made a request in writing for a full and final written statement of all defects on which the buyer proposes to rely.

(2)   Payment against documents made without reservation of rights precludes recovery of the payment for defects apparent in the documents.

As amended in 2003.

Official Comment

Prior Uniform Statutory Provision: None.

Purposes:

1.   The present section rests upon a policy of permitting the buyer to give a quick and informal notice of defects in a tender without penalizing him for omissions in his statement, while at the same time protecting a seller who is reasonably misled by the buyer's failure to state curable defects.

2.   Where the defect in a tender is one which could have been cured by the seller, a buyer who merely rejects the delivery without stating his objections to it is probably acting in commercial bad faith and seeking to get out of a deal which has become unprofitable. Subsection (1)(a), following the general policy of this Article which looks to preserving the deal wherever possible, therefore insists that the seller's right to correct his tender in such circumstances be protected.

3.   When the time for cure is past, subsection (1)(b) makes it plain that a seller is entitled upon request to a final statement of objections upon which he can rely. What is needed is that he make clear to the buyer exactly what is being sought. A formal demand under paragraph (b) will be sufficient in the case of a merchant-buyer.

4.   Subsection (2) applies to the particular case of documents the same principle which the section on effects of acceptance applies to the case of goods. The matter is dealt with in this section in terms of "waiver" of objections rather than of right to revoke acceptance, partly to avoid any confusion with the problems of acceptance of goods and partly because defects in documents which are not taken as grounds for rejection are generally minor ones. The only defects concerned in the present subsection are defects in the documents which are apparent. This

138

rule applies to both tangible and electronic documents of title. Where payment is required against the documents they must be inspected before payment, and the payment then constitutes acceptance of the documents. Under the section dealing with this problem, such acceptance of the documents does not constitute an acceptance of the goods or impair any options or remedies of the buyer for their improper delivery. Where the documents are delivered without requiring such contemporary action as payment from the buyer, the reason of the next section on what constitutes acceptance of goods, applies. Their acceptance by non-objection is therefore postponed until after a reasonable time for their inspection. In either situation, however, the buyer "waives" only the defects apparent in the documents.

    5.   As to the use of a record other than a writing and communications that are not written, see Section 2–207, Comment 8.

Cross References:

    Point 2: Section 2–508.
    Point 4: Sections 2–512(2), 2–606(1)(b), 2–607(2).

Definitional Cross References:

    "Between merchants". Section 2–104.
    "Buyer". Section 2–103.
    "Seasonably". Section 1–204 [*unrevised Article 1; see Concordance, p. 22*].
    "Seller". Section 2–103.
    "Writing" and "written". Section 1–201.

As amended in 2003 and 2022.

§ 2–606.   What Constitutes Acceptance of Goods.

    (1)   Acceptance of goods occurs when the buyer

    (a)   after a reasonable opportunity to inspect the goods signifies to the seller that the goods are conforming or that he will take or retain them in spite of their non-conformity; or

    (b)   fails to make an effective rejection (subsection (1) of Section 2–602), but such acceptance does not occur until the buyer has had a reasonable opportunity to inspect them; or

    (c)   does any act inconsistent with the seller's ownership; but if such act is wrongful as against the seller it is an acceptance only if ratified by him.

    (2)   Acceptance of a part of any commercial unit is acceptance of that entire unit.

Official Comment

Prior Uniform Statutory Provision: Section 48, Uniform Sales Act.

Changes: Rewritten, the qualification in paragraph (c) and subsection (2) being new; otherwise the general policy of the prior legislation is continued.

Purposes of Changes and New Matter: To make it clear that:

    1.   Under this Article "acceptance" as applied to goods means that the buyer, pursuant to the contract, takes particular goods which have been appropriated to the contract as his own, whether or not he is obligated to do so, and whether he does so by words, action, or silence when it is time to speak. If the goods conform to the contract, acceptance amounts only to the performance by the buyer of one part of his legal obligation.

    2.   Under this Article acceptance of goods is always acceptance of identified goods which have been appropriated to the contract or are appropriated by the contract. There is no provision for "acceptance of title" apart from acceptance in general, since acceptance of title is not material under this Article to the detailed rights and duties of the parties. (See Section 2–401). The refinements of the older law between acceptance of goods and of title become unnecessary in view of the provisions of the sections on effect and revocation of acceptance, on effects of identification and on risk of loss, and those sections which free the seller's and buyer's remedies from the complications and confusions caused by the question of whether title has or has not passed to the buyer before breach.

3.   Under paragraph (a), payment made after tender is always one circumstance tending to signify acceptance of the goods but in itself it can never be more than one circumstance and is not conclusive. Also, a conditional communication of acceptance always remains subject to its expressed conditions.

4.   Under paragraph (c), any action taken by the buyer, which is inconsistent with his claim that he has rejected the goods, constitutes an acceptance. However, the provisions of paragraph (c) are subject to the sections dealing with rejection by the buyer which permit the buyer to take certain actions with respect to the goods pursuant to his options and duties imposed by those sections, without effecting an acceptance of the goods. The second clause of paragraph (c) modifies some of the prior case law and makes it clear that "acceptance" in law based on the wrongful act of the acceptor is acceptance only as against the wrongdoer and then only at the option of the party wronged.

In the same manner in which a buyer can bind himself, despite his insistence that he is rejecting or has rejected the goods, by an act inconsistent with the seller's ownership under paragraph (c), he can obligate himself by a communication of acceptance despite a prior rejection under paragraph (a). However, the sections on buyer's rights on improper delivery and on the effect of rightful rejection, make it clear that after he once rejects a tender, paragraph (a) does not operate in favor of the buyer unless the seller has re-tendered the goods or has taken affirmative action indicating that he is holding the tender open. See also Comment 2 to Section 2-601.

5.   Subsection (2) supplements the policy of the section on buyer's rights on improper delivery, recognizing the validity of a partial acceptance but insisting that the buyer exercise this right only as to whole commercial units.

Cross References:

Point 2: Sections 2-401, 2-509, 2-510, 2-607, 2-608 and Part 7.
Point 4: Sections 2-601 through 2-604.
Point 5: Section 2-601.

Definitional Cross References:

"Buyer". Section 2-103.
"Commercial unit". Section 2-105.
"Goods". Section 2-105.
"Seller". Section 2-103.

§ 2-607.   Effect of Acceptance; Notice of Breach; Burden of Establishing Breach After Acceptance; Notice of Claim or Litigation to Person Answerable Over.

(1)   The buyer must pay at the contract rate for any goods accepted.

(2)   Acceptance of goods by the buyer precludes rejection of the goods accepted and if made with knowledge of a non-conformity cannot be revoked because of it unless the acceptance was on the reasonable assumption that the non-conformity would be seasonably cured but acceptance does not of itself impair any other remedy provided by this Article for non-conformity.

(3)   Where a tender has been accepted

(a)   the buyer must within a reasonable time after he discovers or should have discovered any breach notify the seller of breach or be barred from any remedy; and

(b)   if the claim is one for infringement or the like (subsection (3) of Section 2-312) and the buyer is sued as a result of such a breach he must so notify the seller within a reasonable time after he receives notice of the litigation or be barred from any remedy over for liability established by the litigation.

(4)   The burden is on the buyer to establish any breach with respect to the goods accepted.

(5)   Where the buyer is sued for breach of a warranty or other obligation for which his seller is answerable over

(a)   he may give his seller written notice of the litigation. If the notice states that the seller may come in and defend and that if the seller does not do so he will be bound in any action against him by his buyer by any determination of fact common to the two litigations, then unless the seller after seasonable receipt of the notice does come in and defend he is so bound.

(b) if the claim is one for infringement or the like (subsection (3) of Section 2–312) the original seller may demand in writing that his buyer turn over to him control of the litigation including settlement or else be barred from any remedy over and if he also agrees to bear all expense and to satisfy any adverse judgment, then unless the buyer after seasonable receipt of the demand does turn over control the buyer is so barred.

(6) The provisions of subsections (3), (4) and (5) apply to any obligation of a buyer to hold the seller harmless against infringement or the like (subsection (3) of Section 2–312).

Official Comment

Prior Uniform Statutory Provision: Subsection (1)—Section 41, Uniform Sales Act; Subsections (2) and (3)—Sections 49 and 69, Uniform Sales Act.

Changes: Rewritten.

Purposes of Changes: To continue the prior basic policies with respect to acceptance of goods while making a number of minor though material changes in the interest of simplicity and commercial convenience so that:

1. Under subsection (1), once the buyer accepts a tender the seller acquires a right to its price on the contract terms. In cases of partial acceptance, the price of any part accepted is, if possible, to be reasonably apportioned, using the type of apportionment familiar to the courts in quantum valebant cases, to be determined in terms of "the contract rate," which is the rate determined from the bargain in fact (the agreement) after the rules and policies of this Article have been brought to bear.

2. Under subsection (2) acceptance of goods precludes their subsequent rejection. Any return of the goods thereafter must be by way of revocation of acceptance under the next section. Revocation is unavailable for a non-conformity known to the buyer at the time of acceptance, except where the buyer has accepted on the reasonable assumption that the non-conformity would be seasonably cured.

3. All other remedies of the buyer remain unimpaired under subsection (2). This is intended to include the buyer's full rights with respect to future installments despite his acceptance of any earlier non-conforming installment.

4. The time of notification is to be determined by applying commercial standards to a merchant buyer. "A reasonable time" for notification from a retail consumer is to be judged by different standards so that in his case it will be extended, for the rule of requiring notification is designed to defeat commercial bad faith, not to deprive a good faith consumer of his remedy.

The content of the notification need merely be sufficient to let the seller know that the transaction is still troublesome and must be watched. There is no reason to require that the notification which saves the buyer's rights under this section must include a clear statement of all the objections that will be relied on by the buyer, as under the section covering statements of defects upon rejection (Section 2–605). Nor is there reason for requiring the notification to be a claim for damages or of any threatened litigation or other resort to a remedy. The notification which saves the buyer's rights under this Article need only be such as informs the seller that the transaction is claimed to involve a breach, and thus opens the way for normal settlement through negotiation.

5. Under this Article various beneficiaries are given rights for injuries sustained by them because of the seller's breach of warranty. Such a beneficiary does not fall within the reason of the present section in regard to discovery of defects and the giving of notice within a reasonable time after acceptance, since he has nothing to do with acceptance. However, the reason of this section does extend to requiring the beneficiary to notify the seller that an injury has occurred. What is said above, with regard to the extended time for reasonable notification from the lay consumer after the injury is also applicable here; but even a beneficiary can be properly held to the use of good faith in notifying, once he has had time to become aware of the legal situation.

6. Subsection (4) unambiguously places the burden of proof to establish breach on the buyer after acceptance. However, this rule becomes one purely of procedure when the tender accepted was non-conforming and the buyer has given the seller notice of breach under subsection (3). For subsection (2) makes it clear that acceptance leaves unimpaired the buyer's right to be made whole, and that right can be exercised by the buyer not only by way of cross-claim for damages, but also by way of recoupment in diminution or extinction of the price.

7.   Subsections (3)(b) and (5)(b) give a warrantor against infringement an opportunity to defend or compromise third-party claims or be relieved of his liability. Subsection (5)(a) codifies for all warranties the practice of voucher to defend. Compare Section 3–803 [*unrevised Article 3 (Appendix B)*]. Subsection (6) makes these provisions applicable to the buyer's liability for infringement under Section 2–312.

8.   All of the provisions of the present section are subject to any explicit reservation of rights.

9.   As to the use of a record other than a writing and communications that are not written, see Section 2–207, Comment 8.

Cross References:

Point 1: Section 1–201.
Point 2: Section 2–608.
Point 4: Sections 1–204 [*unrevised Article 1; see Concordance, p. 22*] and 2–605.
Point 5: Section 2–318.
Point 6: Section 2–717.
Point 7: Sections 2–312 and 3–803 [*unrevised Article 3 (Appendix B)*].
Point 8: Section 1–207 [*unrevised Article 1; see Concordance, p. 22*].

Definitional Cross References:

"Burden of establishing". Section 1–201.
"Buyer". Section 2–103.
"Conform". Section 2–106.
"Contract". Section 1–201.
"Goods". Section 2–105.
"Notifies". Section 1–201 [*unrevised Article 1; see Concordance, p. 22*].
"Reasonable time". Section 1–204 [*unrevised Article 1; see Concordance, p. 22*].
"Remedy". Section 1–201.
"Seasonably". Section 1–204 [*unrevised Article 1; see Concordance, p. 22*].

As amended in 2022.

§ 2–608.   Revocation of Acceptance in Whole or in Part.

(1)   The buyer may revoke his acceptance of a lot or commercial unit whose non-conformity substantially impairs its value to him if he has accepted it

(a)   on the reasonable assumption that its non-conformity would be cured and it has not been seasonably cured; or

(b)   without discovery of such non-conformity if his acceptance was reasonably induced either by the difficulty of discovery before acceptance or by the seller's assurances.

(2)   Revocation of acceptance must occur within a reasonable time after the buyer discovers or should have discovered the ground for it and before any substantial change in condition of the goods which is not caused by their own defects. It is not effective until the buyer notifies the seller of it.

(3)   A buyer who so revokes has the same rights and duties with regard to the goods involved as if he had rejected them.

Official Comment

Prior Uniform Statutory Provision: Section 69(1)(d), (3), (4) and (5), Uniform Sales Act.

Changes: Rewritten.

Purposes of Changes: To make it clear that:

1.   Although the prior basic policy is continued, the buyer is no longer required to elect between revocation of acceptance and recovery of damages for breach. Both are now available to him. The non-alternative character of the two remedies is stressed by the terms used in the present section. The section no longer speaks of "rescission," a term capable of ambiguous application either to transfer of title to the goods or to the contract of sale and susceptible also of confusion with cancellation for cause of an executed or executory portion of the contract.

The remedy under this section is instead referred to simply as "revocation of acceptance" of goods tendered under a contract for sale and involves no suggestion of "election" of any sort.

2.   Revocation of acceptance is possible only where the non-conformity substantially impairs the value of the goods to the buyer. For this purpose the test is not what the seller had reason to know at the time of contracting; the question is whether the non-conformity is such as will in fact cause a substantial impairment of value to the buyer though the seller had no advance knowledge as to the buyer's particular circumstances.

3.   "Assurances" by the seller under paragraph (b) of subsection (1) can rest as well in the circumstances or in the contract as in explicit language used at the time of delivery. The reason for recognizing such assurances is that they induce the buyer to delay discovery. These are the only assurances involved in paragraph (b). Explicit assurances may be made either in good faith or bad faith. In either case any remedy accorded by this Article is available to the buyer under the section on remedies for fraud.

4.   Subsection (2) requires notification of revocation of acceptance within a reasonable time after discovery of the grounds for such revocation. Since this remedy will be generally resorted to only after attempts at adjustment have failed, the reasonable time period should extend in most cases beyond the time in which notification of breach must be given, beyond the time for discovery of non-conformity after acceptance and beyond the time for rejection after tender. The parties may by their agreement limit the time for notification under this section, but the same sanctions and considerations apply to such agreements as are discussed in the comment on manner and effect of rightful rejection.

5.   The content of the notice under subsection (2) is to be determined in this case as in others by considerations of good faith, prevention of surprise, and reasonable adjustment. More will generally be necessary than the mere notification of breach required under the preceding section. On the other hand the requirements of the section on waiver of buyer's objections do not apply here. The fact that quick notification of trouble is desirable affords good ground for being slow to bind a buyer by his first statement. Following the general policy of this Article, the requirements of the content of notification are less stringent in the case of a non-merchant buyer.

6.   Under subsection (2) the prior policy is continued of seeking substantial justice in regard to the condition of goods restored to the seller. Thus the buyer may not revoke his acceptance if the goods have materially deteriorated except by reason of their own defects. Worthless goods, however, need not be offered back and minor defects in the articles reoffered are to be disregarded.

7.   The policy of the section allowing partial acceptance is carried over into the present section and the buyer may revoke his acceptance, in appropriate cases, as to the entire lot or any commercial unit thereof.

Cross References:

    Point 3: Section 2–721.
    Point 4: Sections 1–204 [*unrevised Article 1; see Concordance, p. 22*], 2–602 and 2–607.
    Point 5: Sections 2–605 and 2–607.
    Point 7: Section 2–601.

Definitional Cross References:

    "Buyer". Section 2–103.
    "Commercial unit". Section 2–105.
    "Conform". Section 2–106.
    "Goods". Section 2–105.
    "Lot". Section 2–105.
    "Notifies". Section 1–201 [*unrevised Article 1; see Concordance, p. 22*].
    "Reasonable time". Section 1–204 [*unrevised Article 1; see Concordance, p. 22*].
    "Rights". Section 1–201.
    "Seasonably". Section 1–204 [*unrevised Article 1; see Concordance, p. 22*].
    "Seller". Section 2–103.

§ 2–609.   Right to Adequate Assurance of Performance.

(1)   A contract for sale imposes an obligation on each party that the other's expectation of receiving due performance will not be impaired. When reasonable grounds for insecurity arise with respect to the performance of either party the other may in writing demand adequate assurance of due performance and

until he receives such assurance may if commercially reasonable suspend any performance for which he has not already received the agreed return.

(2)   Between merchants the reasonableness of grounds for insecurity and the adequacy of any assurance offered shall be determined according to commercial standards.

(3)   Acceptance of any improper delivery or payment does not prejudice the aggrieved party's right to demand adequate assurance of future performance.

(4)   After receipt of a justified demand failure to provide within a reasonable time not exceeding thirty days such assurance of due performance as is adequate under the circumstances of the particular case is a repudiation of the contract.

Official Comment

Prior Uniform Statutory Provision: See Sections 53, 54(1)(b), 55 and 63(2), Uniform Sales Act.

Purposes:

1.   The section rests on the recognition of the fact that the essential purpose of a contract between commercial men is actual performance and they do not bargain merely for a promise, or for a promise plus the right to win a lawsuit and that a continuing sense of reliance and security that the promised performance will be forthcoming when due, is an important feature of the bargain. If either the willingness or the ability of a party to perform declines materially between the time of contracting and the time for performance, the other party is threatened with the loss of a substantial part of what he has bargained for. A seller needs protection not merely against having to deliver on credit to a shaky buyer, but also against having to procure and manufacture the goods, perhaps turning down other customers. Once he has been given reason to believe that the buyer's performance has become uncertain, it is an undue hardship to force him to continue his own performance. Similarly, a buyer who believes that the seller's deliveries have become uncertain cannot safely wait for the due date of performance when he has been buying to assure himself of materials for his current manufacturing or to replenish his stock of merchandise.

2.   Three measures have been adopted to meet the needs of commercial men in such situations. First, the aggrieved party is permitted to suspend his own performance and any preparation therefor, with excuse for any resulting necessary delay, until the situation has been clarified. "Suspend performance" under this section means to hold up performance pending the outcome of the demand, and includes also the holding up of any preparatory action. This is the same principle which governs the ancient law of stoppage and seller's lien, and also of excuse of a buyer from prepayment if the seller's actions manifest that he cannot or will not perform. (Original Act, Section 63(2).)

Secondly, the aggrieved party is given the right to require adequate assurance that the other party's performance will be duly forthcoming. This principle is reflected in the familiar clauses permitting the seller to curtail deliveries if the buyer's credit becomes impaired, which when held within the limits of reasonableness and good faith actually express no more than the fair business meaning of any commercial contract.

Third, and finally, this section provides the means by which the aggrieved party may treat the contract as broken if his reasonable grounds for insecurity are not cleared up within a reasonable time. This is the principle underlying the law of anticipatory breach, whether by way of defective part performance or by repudiation. The present section merges these three principles of law and commercial practice into a single theory of general application to all sales agreements looking to future performance.

3.   Subsection (2) of the present section requires that "reasonable" grounds and "adequate" assurance as used in subsection (1) be defined by commercial rather than legal standards. The express reference to commercial standards carries no connotation that the obligation of good faith is not equally applicable here.

Under commercial standards and in accord with commercial practice, a ground for insecurity need not arise from or be directly related to the contract in question. The law as to "dependence" or "independence" of promises within a single contract does not control the application of the present section.

Thus a buyer who falls behind in "his account" with the seller, even though the items involved have to do with separate and legally distinct contracts, impairs the seller's expectation of due performance. Again, under the same test, a buyer who requires precision parts which he intends to use immediately upon delivery, may have reasonable grounds for insecurity if he discovers that his seller is making defective deliveries of such parts to other buyers with similar needs. Thus, too, in a situation such as arose in *Jay Dreher Corporation v. Delco Appliance Corporation*, 93 F.2d 275 (C.C.A.2, 1937), where a manufacturer gave a dealer an exclusive franchise for the sale of his product but on two or three occasions breached the exclusive dealing clause, although there was no default in orders, deliveries or payments under the separate sales contract between the parties, the aggrieved dealer would be entitled to suspend his performance of the contract for sale under the present section and to demand assurance that the exclusive dealing contract would be lived up to. There is no need for an explicit clause tying the exclusive franchise into the contract for the sale of goods since the situation itself ties the agreements together.

The nature of the sales contract enters also into the question of reasonableness. For example, a report from an apparently trustworthy source that the seller had shipped defective goods or was planning to ship them would normally give the buyer reasonable grounds for insecurity. But when the buyer has assumed the risk of payment before inspection of the goods, as in a sales contract on C.I.F. or similar cash against documents terms, that risk is not to be evaded by a demand for assurance. Therefore no ground for insecurity would exist under this section unless the report went to a ground which would excuse payment by the buyer.

4.   What constitutes "adequate" assurance of due performance is subject to the same test of factual conditions. For example, where the buyer can make use of a defective delivery, a mere promise by a seller of good repute that he is giving the matter his attention and that the defect will not be repeated, is normally sufficient. Under the same circumstances, however, a similar statement by a known corner-cutter might well be considered insufficient without the posting of a guaranty or, if so demanded by the buyer, a speedy replacement of the delivery involved. By the same token where a delivery has defects, even though easily curable, which interfere with easy use by the buyer, no verbal assurance can be deemed adequate which is not accompanied by replacement, repair, money-allowance, or other commercially reasonable cure.

A fact situation such as arose in *Corn Products Refining Co. v. Fasola*, 94 N.J.L. 181, 109 A. 505 (1920) offers illustration both of reasonable grounds for insecurity and "adequate" assurance. In that case a contract for the sale of oils on 30 days' credit, 2% off for payment within 10 days, provided that credit was to be extended to the buyer only if his financial responsibility was satisfactory to the seller. The buyer had been in the habit of taking advantage of the discount but at the same time that he failed to make his customary 10 day payment, the seller heard rumors, in fact false, that the buyer's financial condition was shaky. Thereupon, the seller demanded cash before shipment or security satisfactory to him. The buyer sent a good credit report from his banker, expressed willingness to make payments when due on the 30 day terms and insisted on further deliveries under the contract. Under this Article the rumors, although false, were enough to make the buyer's financial condition "unsatisfactory" to the seller under the contract clause. Moreover, the buyer's practice of taking the cash discounts is enough, apart from the contract clause, to lay a commercial foundation for suspicion when the practice is suddenly stopped. These matters, however, go only to the justification of the seller's demand for security, or his "reasonable grounds for insecurity".

The adequacy of the assurance given is not measured as in the type of "satisfaction" situation affected with intangibles, such as in personal service cases, cases involving a third party's judgment as final, or cases in which the whole contract is dependent on one party's satisfaction, as in a sale on approval. Here, the seller must exercise good faith and observe commercial standards. This Article thus approves the statement of the court in *James B. Berry's Sons Co. of Illinois v. Monark Gasoline & Oil Co., Inc.*, 32 F.2d 74 (C.C.A.8, 1929), that the seller's satisfaction under such a clause must be based upon reason and must not be arbitrary or capricious; and rejects the purely personal "good faith" test of the Corn Products Refining Co. case, which held that in the seller's sole judgment, if for *any* reason he was dissatisfied, he was entitled to revoke the credit. In the absence of the buyer's failure to take the 2% discount as was his custom, the banker's report given in that case would have been "adequate" assurance under this Act, regardless of the language of the "satisfaction" clause. However, the seller is reasonably entitled to feel insecure at a sudden expansion of the buyer's use of a credit term, and should be entitled either to security or to a satisfactory explanation.

The entire foregoing discussion as to adequacy of assurance by way of explanation is subject to qualification when repeated occasions for the application of this section arise. This Act recognizes that repeated delinquencies must be viewed as cumulative. On the other hand, commercial sense also requires that if repeated claims for assurance are made under this section, the basis for these claims must be increasingly obvious.

5.   A failure to provide adequate assurance of performance and thereby to re-establish the security of expectation, results in a breach only "by repudiation" under subsection (4). Therefore, the possibility is continued of retraction of the repudiation under the section dealing with that problem, unless the aggrieved party has acted on the breach in some manner.

The thirty day limit on the time to provide assurance is laid down to free the question of reasonable time from uncertainty in later litigation.

6.   Clauses seeking to give the protected party exceedingly wide powers to cancel or readjust the contract when ground for insecurity arises must be read against the fact that good faith is a part of the obligation of the contract and not subject to modification by agreement and includes, in the case of a merchant, the reasonable observance of commercial standards of fair dealing in the trade. Such clauses can thus be effective to enlarge the protection given by the present section to a certain extent, to fix the reasonable time within which requested assurance must be given, or to define adequacy of the assurance in any commercially reasonable fashion. But any clause seeking to set up arbitrary standards for action is ineffective under this Article. Acceleration clauses are treated similarly in the Articles on Commercial Paper and Secured Transactions.

7.   As to the use of a record other than a writing and communications that are not written, see Section 2–207, Comment 8.

Cross References:

Point 3: Section 1–203 [*unrevised Article 1; see Concordance, p. 22*].
Point 5: Section 2–611.
Point 6: Sections 1–203 [*unrevised Article 1; see Concordance, p. 22*] and 1–208 [*unrevised Article 1; see Concordance, p. 22*] and Articles 3 and 9.

Definitional Cross References:

"Aggrieved party". Section 1–201.
"Between merchants". Section 2–104.
"Contract". Section 1–201.
"Contract for sale". Section 2–106.
"Party". Section 1–201.
"Reasonable time". Section 1–204 [*unrevised Article 1; see Concordance, p. 22*].
"Rights". Section 1–201.
"Writing". Section 1–201.

As amended in 2022.

§ 2–610.   Anticipatory Repudiation.

When either party repudiates the contract with respect to a performance not yet due the loss of which will substantially impair the value of the contract to the other, the aggrieved party may

(a)   for a commercially reasonable time await performance by the repudiating party; or

(b)   resort to any remedy for breach (Section 2–703 or Section 2–711), even though he has notified the repudiating party that he would await the latter's performance and has urged retraction; and

(c)   in either case suspend his own performance or proceed in accordance with the provisions of this Article on the seller's right to identify goods to the contract notwithstanding breach or to salvage unfinished goods (Section 2–704).

Official Comment

Prior Uniform Statutory Provision: See Sections 63(2) and 65, Uniform Sales Act.

Purposes: To make it clear that:

1.   With the problem of insecurity taken care of by the preceding section and with provision being made in this Article as to the effect of a defective delivery under an installment contract, anticipatory repudiation centers upon an overt communication of intention or an action which renders performance impossible or demonstrates a clear determination not to continue with performance.

Under the present section when such a repudiation substantially impairs the value of the contract, the aggrieved party may at any time resort to his remedies for breach, or he may suspend his own performance while he negotiates with, or awaits performance by, the other party. But if he awaits performance beyond a commercially reasonable time he cannot recover resulting damages which he should have avoided.

2.   It is not necessary for repudiation that performance be made literally and utterly impossible. Repudiation can result from action which reasonably indicates a rejection of the continuing obligation. And, a repudiation automatically results under the preceding section on insecurity when a party fails to provide adequate

assurance of due future performance within thirty days after a justifiable demand therefor has been made. Under the language of this section, a demand by one or both parties for more than the contract calls for in the way of counter-performance is not in itself a repudiation nor does it invalidate a plain expression of desire for future performance. However, when under a fair reading it amounts to a statement of intention not to perform except on conditions which go beyond the contract, it becomes a repudiation.

3. The test chosen to justify an aggrieved party's action under this section is the same as that in the section on breach in installment contracts—namely the substantial value of the contract. The most useful test of substantial value is to determine whether material inconvenience or injustice will result if the aggrieved party is forced to wait and receive an ultimate tender minus the part or aspect repudiated.

4. After repudiation, the aggrieved party may immediately resort to any remedy he chooses provided he moves in good faith (see Section 1-203) [unrevised Article 1; see Concordance, p. 22]. Inaction and silence by the aggrieved party may leave the matter open but it cannot be regarded as misleading the repudiating party. Therefore the aggrieved party is left free to proceed at any time with his options under this section, unless he has taken some positive action which in good faith requires notification to the other party before the remedy is pursued.

Cross References:

Point 1: Sections 2-609 and 2-612.
Point 2: Section 2-609.
Point 3: Section 2-612.
Point 4: Section 1-203 [unrevised Article 1; see Concordance, p. 22].

Definitional Cross References:

"Aggrieved party". Section 1-201.
"Contract". Section 1-201.
"Party". Section 1-201.
"Remedy". Section 1-201.

§ 2-611.   Retraction of Anticipatory Repudiation.

(1) Until the repudiating party's next performance is due he can retract his repudiation unless the aggrieved party has since the repudiation cancelled or materially changed his position or otherwise indicated that he considers the repudiation final.

(2) Retraction may be by any method which clearly indicates to the aggrieved party that the repudiating party intends to perform, but must include any assurance justifiably demanded under the provisions of this Article (Section 2-609).

(3) Retraction reinstates the repudiating party's rights under the contract with due excuse and allowance to the aggrieved party for any delay occasioned by the repudiation.

Official Comment

Prior Uniform Statutory Provision: None.

Purposes: To make it clear that:

1. The repudiating party's right to reinstate the contract is entirely dependent upon the action taken by the aggrieved party. If the latter has cancelled the contract or materially changed his position at any time after the repudiation, there can be no retraction under this section.

2. Under subsection (2) an effective retraction must be accompanied by any assurances demanded under the section dealing with right to adequate assurance. A repudiation is of course sufficient to give reasonable ground for insecurity and to warrant a request for assurance as an essential condition of the retraction. However, after a timely and unambiguous expression of retraction, a reasonable time for the assurance to be worked out should be allowed by the aggrieved party before cancellation.

Cross Reference:

Point 2: Section 2-609.

Definitional Cross References:

"Aggrieved party". Section 1-201.

"Cancellation". Section 2–106.
"Contract". Section 1–201.
"Party". Section 1–201.
"Rights". Section 1–201.

§ 2–612.   "Installment Contract"; Breach.

(1)   An "installment contract" is one which requires or authorizes the delivery of goods in separate lots to be separately accepted, even though the contract contains a clause "each delivery is a separate contract" or its equivalent.

(2)   The buyer may reject any installment which is non-conforming if the non-conformity substantially impairs the value of that installment and cannot be cured or if the non-conformity is a defect in the required documents; but if the non-conformity does not fall within subsection (3) and the seller gives adequate assurance of its cure the buyer must accept that installment.

(3)   Whenever non-conformity or default with respect to one or more installments substantially impairs the value of the whole contract there is a breach of the whole. But the aggrieved party reinstates the contract if he accepts a non-conforming installment without seasonably notifying of cancellation or if he brings an action with respect only to past installments or demands performance as to future installments.

Official Comment

Prior Uniform Statutory Provision: Section 45(2), Uniform Sales Act.

Changes: Rewritten.

Purposes of Changes: To continue prior law but to make explicit the more mercantile interpretation of many of the rules involved, so that:

1.   The definition of an installment contract is phrased more broadly in this Article so as to cover installment deliveries tacitly authorized by the circumstances or by the option of either party.

2.   In regard to the apportionment of the price for separate payment this Article applies the more liberal test of what can be apportioned rather than the test of what is clearly apportioned by the agreement. This Article also recognizes approximate calculation or apportionment of price subject to subsequent adjustment. A provision for separate payment for each lot delivered ordinarily means that the price is at least roughly calculable by units of quantity, but such a provision is not essential to an "installment contract." If separate acceptance of separate deliveries is contemplated, no generalized contrast between wholly "entire" and wholly "divisible" contracts has any standing under this Article.

3.   This Article rejects any approach which gives clauses such as "each delivery is a separate contract" their legalistically literal effect. Such contracts nonetheless call for installment deliveries. Even where a clause speaks of "a separate contract for all purposes", a commercial reading of the language under the section on good faith and commercial standards requires that the singleness of the document and the negotiation, together with the sense of the situation, prevail over any uncommercial and legalistic interpretation.

4.   One of the requirements for rejection under subsection (2) is non-conformity substantially impairing the value of the installment in question. However, an installment agreement may require accurate conformity in quality as a condition to the right to acceptance if the need for such conformity is made clear either by express provision or by the circumstances. In such a case the effect of the agreement is to define explicitly what amounts to substantial impairment of value impossible to cure. A clause requiring accurate compliance as a condition to the right to acceptance must, however, have some basis in reason, must avoid imposing hardship by surprise and is subject to waiver or to displacement by practical construction.

Substantial impairment of the value of an installment can turn not only on the quality of the goods but also on such factors as time, quantity, assortment, and the like. It must be judged in terms of the normal or specifically known purposes of the contract. The defect in required documents refers to such matters as the absence of insurance documents under a C.I.F. contract, falsity of a bill of lading, or one failing to show shipment within the contract period or to the contract destination. Even in such cases, however, the provisions on cure of tender apply if appropriate documents are readily procurable.

5.   Under subsection (2) an installment delivery must be accepted if the non-conformity is curable and the seller gives adequate assurance of cure. Cure of non-conformity of an installment in the first instance can usually

be afforded by an allowance against the price, or in the case of reasonable discrepancies in quantity either by a further delivery or a partial rejection. This Article requires reasonable action by a buyer in regard to discrepant delivery and good faith requires that the buyer make any reasonable minor outlay of time or money necessary to cure an overshipment by severing out an acceptable percentage thereof. The seller must take over a cure which involves any material burden; the buyer's obligation reaches only to cooperation. Adequate assurance for purposes of subsection (2) is measured by the same standards as under the section on right to adequate assurance of performance.

6. Subsection (3) is designed to further the continuance of the contract in the absence of an overt cancellation. The question arising when an action is brought as to a single installment only is resolved by making such action waive the right to cancellation. This involves merely a defect in one or more installments, as contrasted with the situation where there is a true repudiation within the section on anticipatory repudiation. Whether the non-conformity in any given installment justifies cancellation as to the future depends, not on whether such non-conformity indicates an intent or likelihood that the future deliveries will also be defective, but whether the non-conformity substantially impairs the value of the whole contract. If only the seller's security in regard to future installments is impaired, he has the right to demand adequate assurances of proper future performance but has not an immediate right to cancel the entire contract. It is clear under this Article, however, that defects in prior installments are cumulative in effect, so that acceptance does not wash out the defect "waived." Prior policy is continued, putting the rule as to buyer's default on the same footing as that in regard to seller's default.

7. Under the requirement of seasonable notification of cancellation under subsection (3), a buyer who accepts a non-conforming installment which substantially impairs the value of the entire contract should properly be permitted to withhold his decision as to whether or not to cancel pending a response from the seller as to his claim for cure or adjustment. Similarly, a seller may withhold a delivery pending payment for prior ones, at the same time delaying his decision as to cancellation. A reasonable time for notifying of cancellation, judged by commercial standard under the section on good faith, extends of course to include the time covered by any reasonable negotiation in good faith. However, during this period the defaulting party is entitled, on request, to know whether the contract is still in effect, before he can be required to perform further.

Cross References:

Point 2: Sections 2–307 and 2–607.
Point 3: Section 1–203 [*unrevised Article 1; see Concordance, p. 22*].
Point 5: Sections 2–208 and 2–609.
Point 6: Section 2–610.

Definitional Cross References:

"Action". Section 1–201.
"Aggrieved party". Section 1–201.
"Buyer". Section 2–103.
"Cancellation". Section 2–106.
"Conform". Section 2–106.
"Contract". Section 1–201.
"Lot". Section 2–105.
"Notifies". Section 1–201 [*unrevised Article 1; see Concordance, p. 22*].
"Seasonably". Section 1–204 [*unrevised Article 1; see Concordance, p. 22*].
"Seller". Section 2–103.

§ 2–613. Casualty to Identified Goods.

Where the contract requires for its performance goods identified when the contract is made, and the goods suffer casualty without fault of either party before the risk of loss passes to the buyer, or in a proper case under a "no arrival, no sale" term (Section 2–324) then

(a) if the loss is total the contract is avoided; and

(b) if the loss is partial or the goods have so deteriorated as no longer to conform to the contract the buyer may nevertheless demand inspection and at his option either treat the contract as avoided or accept the goods with due allowance from the contract price for the deterioration or the deficiency in quantity but without further right against the seller.

Prior Uniform Statutory Provision: Sections 7 and 8, Uniform Sales Act.

Changes: Rewritten, the basic policy being continued but the test of a "divisible" or "indivisible" sale or contract being abandoned in favor of adjustment in business terms.

Purposes of Changes:

1.   Where goods whose continued existence is presupposed by the agreement are destroyed without fault of either party, the buyer is relieved from his obligation but may at his option take the surviving goods at a fair adjustment. "Fault" is intended to include negligence and not merely wilful wrong. The buyer is expressly given the right to inspect the goods in order to determine whether he wishes to avoid the contract entirely or to take the goods with a price adjustment.

2.   The section applies whether the goods were already destroyed at the time of contracting without the knowledge of either party or whether they are destroyed subsequently but before the risk of loss passes to the buyer. Where under the agreement, including of course usage of trade, the risk has passed to the buyer before the casualty, the section has no application. Beyond this, the essential question in determining whether the rules of this section are to be applied is whether the seller has or has not undertaken the responsibility for the continued existence of the goods in proper condition through the time of agreed or expected delivery.

3.   The section on the term "no arrival, no sale" makes clear that delay in arrival, quite as much as physical change in the goods, gives the buyer the options set forth in this section.

Cross Reference:

Point 3: Section 2–324.

Definitional Cross References:

"Buyer". Section 2–103.
"Conform". Section 2–106.
"Contract". Section 1–201.
"Fault". Section 1–201.
"Goods". Section 2–105.
"Party". Section 1–201.
"Rights". Section 1–201.
"Seller". Section 2–103.

§ 2–614.   Substituted Performance.

(1)   Where without fault of either party the agreed berthing, loading, or unloading facilities fail or an agreed type of carrier becomes unavailable or the agreed manner of delivery otherwise becomes commercially impracticable but a commercially reasonable substitute is available, such substitute performance must be tendered and accepted.

(2)   If the agreed means or manner of payment fails because of domestic or foreign governmental regulation, the seller may withhold or stop delivery unless the buyer provides a means or manner of payment which is commercially a substantial equivalent. If delivery has already been taken, payment by the means or in the manner provided by the regulation discharges the buyer's obligation unless the regulation is discriminatory, oppressive or predatory.

Prior Uniform Statutory Provision: None.

Purposes:

1.   Subsection (1) requires the tender of a commercially reasonable substituted performance where agreed to facilities have failed or become commercially impracticable. Under this Article, in the absence of specific agreement, the normal or usual facilities enter into the agreement either through the circumstances, usage of trade or prior course of dealing.

This section appears between Section 2–613 on casualty to identified goods and the next section on excuse by failure of presupposed conditions, both of which deal with excuse and complete avoidance of the contract where the occurrence or non-occurrence of a contingency which was a basic assumption of the contract makes the expected performance impossible. The distinction between the present section and those sections lies in whether the failure or impossibility of performance arises in connection with an incidental matter or goes to the very heart of the agreement. The differing lines of solution are contrasted in a comparison of *International Paper Co. v. Rockefeller*, 161 App.Div. 180, 146 N.Y.S. 371 (1914) and *Meyer v. Sullivan*, 40 Cal.App. 723, 181 P. 847 (1919). In the former case a contract for the sale of spruce to be cut from a particular tract of land was involved. When a fire destroyed the trees growing on that tract the seller was held excused since performance was impossible. In the latter case the contract called for delivery of wheat "f.o.b. Kosmos Steamer at Seattle." The war led to cancellation of that line's sailing schedule after space had been duly engaged and the buyer was held entitled to demand substituted delivery at the warehouse on the line's loading dock. Under this Article, of course, the seller would also be entitled, had the market gone the other way, to make a substituted tender in that manner.

There must, however, be a true commercial impracticability to excuse the agreed to performance and justify a substituted performance. When this is the case a reasonable substituted performance tendered by either party should excuse him from strict compliance with contract terms which do not go to the essence of the agreement.

2.   The substitution provided in this section as between buyer and seller does not carry over into the obligation of a financing agency under a letter of credit, since such an agency is entitled to performance which is plainly adequate on its face and without need to look into commercial evidence outside of the documents. See Article 5, especially Sections 5–102, 5–103, 5–109, 5–110, 5–114 [*all sections are in unrevised Article 5*].

3.   Under subsection (2) where the contract is still executory on both sides, the seller is permitted to withdraw unless the buyer can provide him with a commercially equivalent return despite the governmental regulation. Where, however, only the debt for the price remains, a larger leeway is permitted. The buyer may pay in the manner provided by the regulation even though this may not be commercially equivalent provided that the regulation is not "discriminatory, oppressive or predatory."

Cross Reference:

Point 2: Article 5.

Definitional Cross References:

"Buyer". Section 2–103.
"Fault". Section 1–201.
"Party". Section 1–201.
"Seller". Section 2–103.

§ 2–615.   Excuse by Failure of Presupposed Conditions.

Except so far as a seller may have assumed a greater obligation and subject to the preceding section on substituted performance:

(a)   Delay in delivery or non-delivery in whole or in part by a seller who complies with paragraphs (b) and (c) is not a breach of his duty under a contract for sale if performance as agreed has been made impracticable by the occurrence of a contingency the non-occurrence of which was a basic assumption on which the contract was made or by compliance in good faith with any applicable foreign or domestic governmental regulation or order whether or not it later proves to be invalid.

(b)   Where the causes mentioned in paragraph (a) affect only a part of the seller's capacity to perform, he must allocate production and deliveries among his customers but may at his option include regular customers not then under contract as well as his own requirements for further manufacture. He may so allocate in any manner which is fair and reasonable.

(c)   The seller must notify the buyer seasonably that there will be delay or non-delivery and, when allocation is required under paragraph (b), of the estimated quota thus made available for the buyer.

Official Comment

Prior Uniform Statutory Provision: None.

Purposes:

1.   This section excuses a seller from timely delivery of goods contracted for, where his performance has become commercially impracticable because of unforeseen supervening circumstances not within the contemplation of the parties at the time of contracting. The destruction of specific goods and the problem of the use of substituted performance on points other than delay or quantity, treated elsewhere in this Article, must be distinguished from the matter covered by this section.

2.   The present section deliberately refrains from any effort at an exhaustive expression of contingencies and is to be interpreted in all cases sought to be brought within its scope in terms of its underlying reason and purpose.

3.   The first test for excuse under this Article in terms of basic assumption is a familiar one. The additional test of commercial impracticability (as contrasted with "impossibility," "frustration of performance" or "frustration of the venture") has been adopted in order to call attention to the commercial character of the criterion chosen by this Article.

4.   Increased cost alone does not excuse performance unless the rise in cost is due to some unforeseen contingency which alters the essential nature of the performance. Neither is a rise or a collapse in the market in itself a justification, for that is exactly the type of business risk which business contracts made at fixed prices are intended to cover. But a severe shortage of raw materials or of supplies due to a contingency such as war, embargo, local crop failure, unforeseen shutdown of major sources of supply or the like, which either causes a marked increase in cost or altogether prevents the seller from securing supplies necessary to his performance, is within the contemplation of this section. (See *Ford & Sons, Ltd. v. Henry Leetham & Sons, Ltd.*, 21 Com.Cas. 55 (1915, K.B.D.).)

5.   Where a particular source of supply is exclusive under the agreement and fails through casualty, the present section applies rather than the provision on destruction or deterioration of specific goods. The same holds true where a particular source of supply is shown by the circumstances to have been contemplated or assumed by the parties at the time of contracting. (See *Davis Co. v. Hoffmann-LaRoche Chemical Works*, 178 App.Div. 855, 166 N.Y.S. 179 (1917) and *International Paper Co. v. Rockefeller*, 161 App.Div. 180, 146 N.Y.S. 371 (1914).) There is no excuse under this section, however, unless the seller has employed all due measures to assure himself that his source will not fail. (See *Canadian Industrial Alcohol Co., Ltd. v. Dunbar Molasses Co.*, 258 N.Y. 194, 179 N.E. 383, 80 A.L.R. 1173 (1932) and *Washington Mfg. Co. v. Midland Lumber Co.*, 113 Wash. 593, 194 P. 777 (1921).)

In the case of failure of production by an agreed source for causes beyond the seller's control, the seller should, if possible, be excused since production by an agreed source is without more a basic assumption of the contract. Such excuse should not result in relieving the defaulting supplier from liability nor in dropping into the seller's lap an unearned bonus of damages over. The flexible adjustment machinery of this Article provides the solution under the provision on the obligation of good faith. A condition to his making good the claim of excuse is the turning over to the buyer of his rights against the defaulting source of supply to the extent of the buyer's contract in relation to which excuse is being claimed.

6.   In situations in which neither sense nor justice is served by either answer when the issue is posed in flat terms of "excuse" or "no excuse," adjustment under the various provisions of this Article is necessary, especially the sections on good faith, on insecurity and assurance and on the reading of all provisions in the light of their purposes, and the general policy of this Act to use equitable principles in furtherance of commercial standards and good faith.

7.   The failure of conditions which go to convenience or collateral values rather than to the commercial practicability of the main performance does not amount to a complete excuse. However, good faith and the reason of the present section and of the preceding one may properly be held to justify and even to require any needed delay involved in a good faith inquiry seeking a readjustment of the contract terms to meet the new conditions.

8.   The provisions of this section are made subject to assumption of greater liability by agreement and such agreement is to be found not only in the expressed terms of the contract but in the circumstances surrounding the contracting, in trade usage and the like. Thus the exemptions of this section do not apply when the contingency in question is sufficiently foreshadowed at the time of contracting to be included among the business risks which are fairly to be regarded as part of the dickered terms, either consciously or as a matter of reasonable, commercial interpretation from the circumstances. (See *Madeirense Do Brasil, S.A. v. Stulman-Emrick Lumber Co.*, 147 F.2d 399 (C.C.A., 2 Cir., 1945).) The exemption otherwise present through usage of trade under the present section may also be expressly negated by the language of the agreement. Generally, express agreements as to exemptions designed to enlarge upon or supplant the provisions of this section are to be read in the light of mercantile sense

and reason, for this section itself sets up the commercial standard for normal and reasonable interpretation and provides a minimum beyond which agreement may not go.

Agreement can also be made in regard to the consequences of exemption as laid down in paragraphs (b) and (c) and the next section on procedure on notice claiming excuse.

9.   The case of a farmer who has contracted to sell crops to be grown on designated land may be regarded as falling either within the section on casualty to identified goods or this section, and he may be excused, when there is a failure of the specific crop, either on the basis of the destruction of identified goods or because of the failure of a basic assumption of the contract.

Exemption of the buyer in the case of a "requirements" contract is covered by the "Output and Requirements" section both as to assumption and allocation of the relevant risks. But when a contract by a manufacturer to buy fuel or raw material makes no specific reference to a particular venture and no such reference may be drawn from the circumstances, commercial understanding views it as a general deal in the general market and not conditioned on any assumption of the continuing operation of the buyer's plant. Even when notice is given by the buyer that the supplies are needed to fill a specific contract of a normal commercial kind, commercial understanding does not see such a supply contract as conditioned on the continuance of the buyer's further contract for outlet. On the other hand, where the buyer's contract is in reasonable commercial understanding conditioned on a definite and specific venture or assumption as, for instance, a war procurement subcontract known to be based on a prime contract which is subject to termination, or a supply contract for a particular construction venture, the reason of the present section may well apply and entitle the buyer to the exemption.

10.   Following its basic policy of using commercial practicability as a test for excuse, this section recognizes as of equal significance either a foreign or domestic regulation and disregards any technical distinctions between "law," "regulation," "order" and the like. Nor does it make the present action of the seller depend upon the eventual judicial determination of the legality of the particular governmental action. The seller's good faith belief in the validity of the regulation is the test under this Article and the best evidence of his good faith is the general commercial acceptance of the regulation. However, governmental interference cannot excuse unless it truly "supervenes" in such a manner as to be beyond the seller's assumption of risk. And any action by the party claiming excuse which causes or colludes in inducing the governmental action preventing his performance would be in breach of good faith and would destroy his exemption.

11.   An excused seller must fulfill his contract to the extent which the supervening contingency permits, and if the situation is such that his customers are generally affected he must take account of all in supplying one. Subsections (a) and (b), therefore, explicitly permit in any proration a fair and reasonable attention to the needs of regular customers who are probably relying on spot orders for supplies. Customers at different stages of the manufacturing process may be fairly treated by including the seller's manufacturing requirements. A fortiori, the seller may also take account of contracts later in date than the one in question. The fact that such spot orders may be closed at an advanced price causes no difficulty, since any allocation which exceeds normal past requirements will not be reasonable. However, good faith requires, when prices have advanced, that the seller exercise real care in making his allocations, and in case of doubt his contract customers should be favored and supplies prorated evenly among them regardless of price. Save for the extra care thus required by changes in the market, this section seeks to leave every reasonable business leeway to the seller.

Cross References:

Point 1: Sections 2–613 and 2–614.

Point 2: Section 1–102 [*unrevised Article 1; see Concordance, p. 22*].

Point 5: Sections 1–203 [*unrevised Article 1; see Concordance, p. 22*] and 2–613.

Point 6: Sections 1–102 [*unrevised Article 1; see Concordance, p. 22*], 1–203 [*unrevised Article 1; see Concordance, p. 22*] and 2–609.

Point 7: Section 2–614.

Point 8: Sections 1–201, 2–302 and 2–616.

Point 9: Sections 1–102 [*unrevised Article 1; see Concordance, p. 22*], 2–306 and 2–613.

Definitional Cross References:

"Between merchants". Section 2–104.

"Buyer". Section 2–103.

"Contract". Section 1–201.

"Contract for sale". Section 2–106.

"Good faith". Section 1–201.
"Merchant". Section 2–104.
"Notifies". Section 1–201 [*unrevised Article 1; see Concordance, p. 22*].
"Seasonably". Section 1–201 [*unrevised Article 1; see Concordance, p. 22*].
"Seller". Section 2–103.

§ 2–616.   Procedure on Notice Claiming Excuse.

(1)   Where the buyer receives notification of a material or indefinite delay or an allocation justified under the preceding section he may by written notification to the seller as to any delivery concerned, and where the prospective deficiency substantially impairs the value of the whole contract under the provisions of this Article relating to breach of installment contracts (Section 2–612), then also as to the whole,

(a)   terminate and thereby discharge any unexecuted portion of the contract; or

(b)   modify the contract by agreeing to take his available quota in substitution.

(2)   If after receipt of such notification from the seller the buyer fails so to modify the contract within a reasonable time not exceeding thirty days the contract lapses with respect to any deliveries affected.

(3)   The provisions of this section may not be negated by agreement except in so far as the seller has assumed a greater obligation under the preceding section.

Official Comment

Prior Uniform Statutory Provision: None.

Purposes:

1.   This section seeks to establish simple and workable machinery for providing certainty as to when a supervening and excusing contingency "excuses" the delay, "discharges" the contract, or may result in a waiver of the delay by the buyer. When the seller notifies, in accordance with the preceding section, claiming excuse, the buyer may acquiesce, in which case the contract is so modified. No consideration is necessary in a case of this kind to support such a modification. If the buyer does not elect so to modify the contract, he may terminate it and under subsection (2) his silence after receiving the seller's claim of excuse operates as such a termination. Subsection (3) denies effect to any contract clause made in advance of trouble which would require the buyer to stand ready to take delivery whenever the seller is excused from delivery by unforeseen circumstances.

2.   As to the use of a record other than a writing and communications that are not written, see Section 2–207, Comment 8.

Cross References:

Point 1: Sections 2–209 and 2–615.

Definitional Cross References:

"Buyer". Section 2–103.
"Contract". Section 1–201.
"Installment contract". Section 2–612.
"Notification". Section 1–201 [*unrevised Article 1; see Concordance, p. 22*].
"Reasonable time". Section 1–204 [*unrevised Article 1; see Concordance, p. 22*].
"Seller". Section 2–103.
"Termination". Section 2–106.
"Written". Section 1–201.

As amended in 2022.

PART 7

REMEDIES

§ 2–701.   Remedies for Breach of Collateral Contracts Not Impaired.

Remedies for breach of any obligation or promise collateral or ancillary to a contract for sale are not impaired by the provisions of this Article.

Official Comment

Prior Uniform Statutory Provision: None.

Purposes:

Whether a claim for breach of an obligation collateral to the contract for sale requires separate trial to avoid confusion of issues is beyond the scope of this Article; but contractual arrangements which as a business matter enter vitally into the contract should be considered a part thereof in so far as cross-claims or defenses are concerned.

Definitional Cross References:

"Contract for sale". Section 2–106.
"Remedy". Section 1–201.

§ 2–702.   Seller's Remedies on Discovery of Buyer's Insolvency.

(1)   Where the seller discovers the buyer to be insolvent he may refuse delivery except for cash including payment for all goods theretofore delivered under the contract, and stop delivery under this Article (Section 2–705).

(2)   Where the seller discovers that the buyer has received goods on credit while insolvent he may reclaim the goods upon demand made within ten days after the receipt, but if misrepresentation of solvency has been made to the particular seller in writing within three months before delivery the ten day limitation does not apply. Except as provided in this subsection the seller may not base a right to reclaim goods on the buyer's fraudulent or innocent misrepresentation of solvency or of intent to pay.

(3)   The seller's right to reclaim under subsection (2) is subject to the rights of a buyer in ordinary course or other good faith purchaser under this Article (Section 2–403). Successful reclamation of goods excludes all other remedies with respect to them.

As amended in 1966.

Official Comment

Prior Uniform Statutory Provision: Subsection (1)—Sections 53(1)(b), 54(1)(c) and 57, Uniform Sales Act; Subsection (2)—none; Subsection (3)—Section 76(3), Uniform Sales Act.

Changes: Rewritten, the protection given to a seller who has sold on credit and has delivered goods to the buyer immediately preceding his insolvency being extended.

Purposes of Changes and New Matter: To make it clear that:

1.   The seller's right to withhold the goods or to stop delivery except for cash when he discovers the buyer's insolvency is made explicit in subsection (1) regardless of the passage of title, and the concept of stoppage has been extended to include goods in the possession of any bailee who has not yet attorned to the buyer.

2.   Subsection (2) takes as its base line the proposition that any receipt of goods on credit by an insolvent buyer amounts to a tacit business misrepresentation of solvency and therefore is fraudulent as against the particular seller. This Article makes discovery of the buyer's insolvency and demand within a ten day period a condition of the right to reclaim goods on this ground. The ten day limitation period operates from the time of receipt of the goods.

An exception to this time limitation is made when a written misrepresentation of solvency has been made to the particular seller within three months prior to the delivery. To fall within the exception the statement of solvency must be in writing, addressed to the particular seller and dated within three months of the delivery.

3.   Because the right of the seller to reclaim goods under this section constitutes preferential treatment as against the buyer's other creditors, subsection (3) provides that such reclamation bars all his other remedies as to the goods involved.

4.   As to the use of a record other than a writing and communications that are not written, see Section 2–207, Comment 8.

As amended in 1966 and 2022.

Cross References:

> Point 1: Sections 2–401 and 2–705.
> Compare Section 2–502.

Definitional Cross References:

> "Buyer". Section 2–103.
> "Buyer in ordinary course of business". Section 1–201.
> "Contract". Section 1–201.
> "Good faith". Section 1–201.
> "Goods". Section 2–105.
> "Insolvent". Section 1–201.
> "Person". Section 1–201.
> "Purchaser". Section 1–201.
> "Receipt" of goods. Section 2–103.
> "Remedy". Section 1–201.
> "Rights". Section 1–201.
> "Seller". Section 2–103.
> "Writing". Section 1–201.

§ 2–703.   Seller's Remedies in General.

Where the buyer wrongfully rejects or revokes acceptance of goods or fails to make a payment due on or before delivery or repudiates with respect to a part or the whole, then with respect to any goods directly affected and, if the breach is of the whole contract (Section 2–612), then also with respect to the whole undelivered balance, the aggrieved seller may

(a)   withhold delivery of such goods;

(b)   stop delivery by any bailee as hereafter provided (Section 2–705);

(c)   proceed under the next section respecting goods still unidentified to the contract;

(d)   resell and recover damages as hereafter provided (Section 2–706);

(e)   recover damages for non-acceptance (Section 2–708) or in a proper case the price (Section 2–709);

(f)   cancel.

Official Comment

Prior Uniform Statutory Provision: No comparable index section. See Section 53, Uniform Sales Act.

Purposes:

1.   This section is an index section which gathers together in one convenient place all of the various remedies open to a seller for any breach by the buyer. This Article rejects any doctrine of election of remedy as a fundamental policy and thus the remedies are essentially cumulative in nature and include all of the available remedies for breach. Whether the pursuit of one remedy bars another depends entirely on the facts of the individual case.

2.   The buyer's breach which occasions the use of the remedies under this section may involve only one lot or delivery of goods, or may involve all of the goods which are the subject matter of the particular contract. The right of the seller to pursue a remedy as to all the goods when the breach is as to only one or more lots is covered by the section on breach in installment contracts. The present section deals only with the remedies available after the goods involved in the breach have been determined by that section.

3.   In addition to the typical case of refusal to pay or default in payment, the language in the preamble, "fails to make a payment due," is intended to cover the dishonor of a check on due presentment, or the non-acceptance of a draft, and the failure to furnish an agreed letter of credit.

4.   It should also be noted that this Act requires its remedies to be liberally administered and provides that any right or obligation which it declares is enforceable by action unless a different effect is specifically prescribed (Section 1–106) [*unrevised Article 1; see Concordance, p. 22*].

Cross References:

Point 2: Section 2–612.
Point 3: Section 2–325.
Point 4: Section 1–106 [*unrevised Article 1; see Concordance, p. 22*].

Definitional Cross References:

"Aggrieved party". Section 1–201.
"Buyer". Section 2–103.
"Cancellation". Section 2–106.
"Contract". Section 1–201.
"Goods". Section 2–105.
"Remedy". Section 1–201.
"Seller". Section 2–103.

§ 2–704.   Seller's Right to Identify Goods to the Contract Notwithstanding Breach or to Salvage Unfinished Goods.

(1)   An aggrieved seller under the preceding section may

(a)   identify to the contract conforming goods not already identified if at the time he learned of the breach they are in his possession or control;

(b)   treat as the subject of resale goods which have demonstrably been intended for the particular contract even though those goods are unfinished.

(2)   Where the goods are unfinished an aggrieved seller may in the exercise of reasonable commercial judgment for the purposes of avoiding loss and of effective realization either complete the manufacture and wholly identify the goods to the contract or cease manufacture and resell for scrap or salvage value or proceed in any other reasonable manner.

Official Comment

Prior Uniform Statutory Provision: Sections 63(3) and 64(4), Uniform Sales Act.

Changes: Rewritten, the seller's rights being broadened.

Purposes of Changes:

1.   This section gives an aggrieved seller the right at the time of breach to identify to the contract any conforming finished goods, regardless of their resalability, and to use reasonable judgment as to completing unfinished goods. It thus makes the goods available for resale under the resale section, the seller's primary remedy, and in the special case in which resale is not practicable, allows the action for the price which would then be necessary to give the seller the value of his contract.

2.   Under this Article the seller is given express power to complete manufacture or procurement of goods for the contract unless the exercise of reasonable commercial judgment as to the facts as they appear at the time he learns of the breach makes it clear that such action will result in a material increase in damages. The burden is on the buyer to show the commercially unreasonable nature of the seller's action in completing manufacture.

Cross References:

Sections 2–703 and 2–706.

Definitional Cross References:

"Aggrieved party". Section 1–201.

"Conforming". Section 2–106.
"Contract". Section 1–201.
"Goods". Section 2–105.
"Rights". Section 1–201.
"Seller". Section 2–103.

§ 2–705.   Seller's Stoppage of Delivery in Transit or Otherwise.

(1)   The seller may stop delivery of goods in the possession of a carrier or other bailee when he discovers the buyer to be insolvent (Section 2–702) and may stop delivery of carload, truckload, planeload or larger shipments of express or freight when the buyer repudiates or fails to make a payment due before delivery or if for any other reason the seller has a right to withhold or reclaim the goods.

(2)   As against such buyer the seller may stop delivery until

(a)   receipt of the goods by the buyer; or

(b)   acknowledgment to the buyer by any bailee of the goods except a carrier that the bailee holds the goods for the buyer; or

(c)   such acknowledgment to the buyer by a carrier by reshipment or as a warehouseman; or

(d)   negotiation to the buyer of any negotiable document of title covering the goods.

(3)(a)   To stop delivery the seller must so notify as to enable the bailee by reasonable diligence to prevent delivery of the goods.

(b)   After such notification the bailee must hold and deliver the goods according to the directions of the seller but the seller is liable to the bailee for any ensuing charges or damages.

(c)   If a negotiable document of title has been issued for goods the bailee is not obliged to obey a notification to stop until surrender of possession or control of the document.

(d)   A carrier who has issued a non-negotiable bill of lading is not obliged to obey a notification to stop received from a person other than the consignor.

As amended in 2003.

Official Comment

Prior Uniform Statutory Provision: Sections 57–59, Uniform Sales Act; see also Sections 12, 14 and 42, Uniform Bills of Lading Act and Sections 9, 11 and 49, Uniform Warehouse Receipts Act.

Changes: This section continues and develops the above sections of the Uniform Sales Act in the light of the other uniform statutory provisions noted.

Purposes: To make it clear that:

1.   Subsection (1) applies the stoppage principle to other bailees as well as carriers.

It also expands the remedy to cover the situations, in addition to buyer's insolvency, specified in the subsection. But since stoppage is a burden in any case to carriers, and might be a very heavy burden to them if it covered all small shipments in all these situations, the right to stop for reasons other than insolvency is limited to carload, truckload, planeload or larger shipments. The seller shipping to a buyer of doubtful credit can protect himself by shipping C.O.D.

Where stoppage occurs for insecurity it is merely a suspension of performance, and if assurances are duly forthcoming from the buyer the seller is not entitled to resell or divert.

Improper stoppage is a breach by the seller if it effectively interferes with the buyer's right to due tender under the section on manner of tender of delivery. However, if the bailee obeys an unjustified order to stop he may also be liable to the buyer. The measure of his obligation is dependent on the provisions of the Documents of Title Article (Section 7–303). Subsection 3(b) therefore gives him a right of indemnity as against the seller in such a case.

2.   "Receipt by the buyer" includes receipt by the buyer's designated representative, the subpurchaser, when shipment is made direct to him and the buyer himself never receives the goods. It is entirely proper under

this Article that the seller, by making such direct shipment to the sub-purchaser, be regarded as acquiescing in the latter's purchase and as thus barred from stoppage of the goods as against him.

As between the buyer and the seller, the latter's right to stop the goods at any time until they reach the place of final delivery is recognized by this section.

Under subsection (3)(c) and (d), the carrier is under no duty to recognize the stop order of a person who is a stranger to the carrier's contract. But the seller's right as against the buyer to stop delivery remains, whether or not the carrier is obligated to recognize the stop order. If the carrier does obey it, the buyer cannot complain merely because of that circumstance; and the seller becomes obligated under subsection (3)(b) to pay the carrier any ensuing damages or charges.

3. A diversion of a shipment is not a "reshipment" under subsection (2)(c) when it is merely an incident to the original contract of transportation. Nor is the procurement of "exchange bills" of lading which change only the name of the consignee to that of the buyer's local agent but do not alter the destination of a reshipment.

Acknowledgment by the carrier as a "warehouse" within the meaning of this Article requires a contract of a truly different character from the original shipment, a contract not in extension of transit but as a warehouse.

4. Subsection (3)(c) makes the bailee's obedience of a notification to stop conditional upon the surrender of possession or control of any outstanding negotiable document.

5. Any charges or losses incurred by the carrier in following the seller's orders, whether or not he was obligated to do so, fall to the seller's charge.

6. After an effective stoppage under this section the seller's rights in the goods are the same as if he had never made a delivery.

Cross References:

Sections 2–702 and 2–703.
Point 1: Sections 2–503 and 2–609, and Article 7.
Point 2: Section 2–103 and Article 7.

Definitional Cross References:

"Buyer". Section 2–103.
"Contract for sale". Section 2–106.
"Document of title". Section 1–201.
"Goods". Section 2–105.
"Insolvent". Section 1–201.
"Notification". Section 1–201 [*unrevised Article 1; see Concordance, p. 22*].
"Receipt" of goods. Section 2–103.
"Rights". Section 1–201.
"Seller". Section 2–103.

As amended in 2003.

§ 2–706. Seller's Resale Including Contract for Resale.

(1) Under the conditions stated in Section 2–703 on seller's remedies, the seller may resell the goods concerned or the undelivered balance thereof. Where the resale is made in good faith and in a commercially reasonable manner the seller may recover the difference between the resale price and the contract price together with any incidental damages allowed under the provisions of this Article (Section 2–710), but less expenses saved in consequence of the buyer's breach.

(2) Except as otherwise provided in subsection (3) or unless otherwise agreed resale may be at public or private sale including sale by way of one or more contracts to sell or of identification to an existing contract of the seller. Sale may be as a unit or in parcels and at any time and place and on any terms but every aspect of the sale including the method, manner, time, place and terms must be commercially reasonable. The resale must be reasonably identified as referring to the broken contract, but it is not necessary that the goods be in existence or that any or all of them have been identified to the contract before the breach.

(3) Where the resale is at private sale the seller must give the buyer reasonable notification of his intention to resell.

(4)   Where the resale is at public sale

(a)   only identified goods can be sold except where there is a recognized market for a public sale of futures in goods of the kind; and

(b)   it must be made at a usual place or market for public sale if one is reasonably available and except in the case of goods which are perishable or threaten to decline in value speedily the seller must give the buyer reasonable notice of the time and place of the resale; and

(c)   if the goods are not to be within the view of those attending the sale the notification of sale must state the place where the goods are located and provide for their reasonable inspection by prospective bidders; and

(d)   the seller may buy.

(5)   A purchaser who buys in good faith at a resale takes the goods free of any rights of the original buyer even though the seller fails to comply with one or more of the requirements of this section.

(6)   The seller is not accountable to the buyer for any profit made on any resale. A person in the position of a seller (Section 2–707) or a buyer who has rightfully rejected or justifiably revoked acceptance must account for any excess over the amount of his security interest, as hereinafter defined (subsection (3) of Section 2–711).

Official Comment

Prior Uniform Statutory Provision: Section 60, Uniform Sales Act.

Changes: Rewritten.

Purposes of Changes: To simplify the prior statutory provision and to make it clear that:

1.   The only condition precedent to the seller's right of resale under subsection (1) is a breach by the buyer within the section on the seller's remedies in general or insolvency. Other meticulous conditions and restrictions of the prior uniform statutory provision are disapproved by this Article and are replaced by standards of commercial reasonableness. Under this section the seller may resell the goods after any breach by the buyer. Thus, an anticipatory repudiation by the buyer gives rise to any of the seller's remedies for breach, and to the right of resale. This principle is supplemented by subsection (2) which authorizes a resale of goods which are not in existence or were not identified to the contract before the breach.

2.   In order to recover the damages prescribed in subsection (1) the seller must act "in good faith and in a commercially reasonable manner" in making the resale. This standard is intended to be more comprehensive than that of "reasonable care and judgment" established by the prior uniform statutory provision. Failure to act properly under this section deprives the seller of the measure of damages here provided and relegates him to that provided in Section 2–708.

Under this Article the seller resells by authority of law, in his own behalf, for his own benefit and for the purpose of fixing his damages. The theory of a seller's agency is thus rejected.

3.   If the seller complies with the prescribed standard of duty in making the resale, he may recover from the buyer the damages provided for in subsection (1). Evidence of market or current prices at any particular time or place is relevant only on the question of whether the seller acted in a commercially reasonable manner in making the resale.

The distinction drawn by some courts between cases where the title had not passed to the buyer and the seller had resold as owner, and cases where the title had passed and the seller had resold by virtue of his lien on the goods, is rejected.

4.   Subsection (2) frees the remedy of resale from legalistic restrictions and enables the seller to resell in accordance with reasonable commercial practices so as to realize as high a price as possible in the circumstances. By "public" sale is meant a sale by auction. A "private" sale may be effected by solicitation and negotiation conducted either directly or through a broker. In choosing between a public and private sale the character of the goods must be considered and relevant trade practices and usages must be observed.

5.   Subsection (2) merely clarifies the common law rule that the time for resale is a reasonable time after the buyer's breach, by using the language "commercially reasonable." What is such a reasonable time depends upon the nature of the goods, the condition of the market and the other circumstances of the case; its length cannot be measured by any legal yardstick or divided into degrees. Where a seller contemplating resale receives a demand

from the buyer for inspection under the section of preserving evidence of goods in dispute, the time for resale may be appropriately lengthened.

On the question of the place for resale, subsection (2) goes to the ultimate test, the commercial reasonableness of the seller's choice as to the place for an advantageous resale. This Article rejects the theory that the seller is required to resell at the agreed place for delivery and that a resale elsewhere can be permitted only in exceptional cases.

6.   The purpose of subsection (2) being to enable the seller to dispose of the goods to the best advantage, he is permitted in making the resale to depart from the terms and conditions of the original contract for sale to any extent "commercially reasonable" in the circumstances.

7.   The provision of subsection (2) that the goods need not be in existence to be resold applies when the buyer is guilty of anticipatory repudiation of a contract for future goods, before the goods or some of them have come into existence. In such a case the seller may exercise the right of resale and fix his damages by "one or more contracts to sell" the quantity of conforming future goods affected by the repudiation. The companion provision of subsection (2) that resale may be made although the goods were not identified to the contract prior to the buyer's breach, likewise contemplates an anticipatory repudiation by the buyer but occurring after the goods are in existence. If the goods so identified conform to the contract, their resale will fix the seller's damages quite as satisfactorily as if they had been identified before the breach.

8.   Where the resale is to be by private sale, subsection (3) requires that reasonable notification of the seller's intention to resell must be given to the buyer. The length of notification of a private sale depends upon the urgency of the matter. Notification of the time and place of this type of sale is not required.

Subsection (4)(b) requires that the seller give the buyer reasonable notice of the time and place of a public resale so that he may have an opportunity to bid or to secure the attendance of other bidders. An exception is made in the case of goods "which are perishable or threaten to decline speedily in value."

9.   Since there would be no reasonable prospect of competitive bidding elsewhere, subsection (4) requires that a public resale "must be made at a usual place or market for public sale if one is reasonably available;" i.e., a place or market which prospective bidders may reasonably be expected to attend. Such a market may still be "reasonably available" under this subsection, though at a considerable distance from the place where the goods are located. In such a case the expense of transporting the goods for resale is recoverable from the buyer as part of the seller's incidental damages under subsection (1). However, the question of availability is one of commercial reasonableness in the circumstances and if such "usual" place or market is not reasonably available, a duly advertised public resale may be held at another place if it is one which prospective bidders may reasonably be expected to attend, as distinguished from a place where there is no demand whatsoever for goods of the kind.

Paragraph (a) of subsection (4) qualifies the last sentence of subsection (2) with respect to resales of unidentified and future goods at public sale. If conforming goods are in existence the seller may identify them to the contract after the buyer's breach and then resell them at public sale. If the goods have not been identified, however, he may resell them at public sale only as "future" goods and only where there is a recognized market for public sale of futures in goods of the kind.

The provisions of paragraph (c) of subsection (4) are intended to permit intelligent bidding.

The provision of paragraph (d) of subsection (4) permitting the seller to bid and, of course, to become the purchaser, benefits the original buyer by tending to increase the resale price and thus decreasing the damages he will have to pay.

10.   This Article departs in subsection (5) from the prior uniform statutory provision in permitting a good faith purchaser at resale to take a good title as against the buyer even though the seller fails to comply with the requirements of this section.

11.   Under subsection (6), the seller retains profit, if any, without distinction based on whether or not he had a lien since this Article divorces the question of passage of title to the buyer from the seller's right of resale or the consequences of its exercise. On the other hand, where "a person in the position of a seller" or a buyer acting under the section on buyer's remedies, exercises his right of resale under the present section he does so only for the limited purpose of obtaining cash for his "security interest" in the goods. Once that purpose has been accomplished any excess in the resale price belongs to the seller to whom an accounting must be made as provided in the last sentence of subsection (6).

Cross References:

Point 1: Sections 2–610, 2–702 and 2–703.
Point 2: Section 1–201.
Point 3: Sections 2–708 and 2–710.
Point 4: Section 2–328.
Point 8: Section 2–104.
Point 9: Section 2–710.
Point 11: Sections 2–401, 2–707 and 2–711(3).

Definitional Cross References:

"Buyer". Section 2–103.
"Contract". Section 1–201.
"Contract for sale". Section 2–106.
"Good faith". Section 2–103.
"Goods". Section 2–105.
"Merchant". Section 2–104.
"Notification". Section 1–201 [*unrevised Article 1; see Concordance, p. 22*].
"Person in position of seller". Section 2–707.
"Purchase". Section 1–201.
"Rights". Section 1–201.
"Sale". Section 2–106.
"Security interest". Section 1–201.
"Seller". Section 2–103.

§ 2–707.   "Person in the Position of a Seller".

(1)   A "person in the position of a seller" includes as against a principal an agent who has paid or become responsible for the price of goods on behalf of his principal or anyone who otherwise holds a security interest or other right in goods similar to that of a seller.

(2)   A person in the position of a seller may as provided in this Article withhold or stop delivery (Section 2–705) and resell (Section 2–706) and recover incidental damages (Section 2–710).

Official Comment

Prior Uniform Statutory Provision: Section 52(2), Uniform Sales Act.

Changes: Rewritten.

Purposes of Changes: To make it clear that:

In addition to following in general the prior uniform statutory provision, the case of a financing agency which has acquired documents by honoring a letter of credit for the buyer or by discounting a draft for the seller has been included in the term "a person in the position of a seller."

Cross Reference:

Article 5, Section 2–506.

Definitional Cross References:

"Consignee". Section 7–102.
"Consignor". Section 7–102.
"Goods". Section 2–105.
"Security interest". Section 1–201.
"Seller". Section 2–103.

§ 2–708.   Seller's Damages for Non-acceptance or Repudiation.

(1)   Subject to subsection (2) and to the provisions of this Article with respect to proof of market price (Section 2–723), the measure of damages for non-acceptance or repudiation by the buyer is the difference

between the market price at the time and place for tender and the unpaid contract price together with any incidental damages provided in this Article (Section 2–710), but less expenses saved in consequence of the buyer's breach.

(2)   If the measure of damages provided in subsection (1) is inadequate to put the seller in as good a position as performance would have done then the measure of damages is the profit (including reasonable overhead) which the seller would have made from full performance by the buyer, together with any incidental damages provided in this Article (Section 2–710), due allowance for costs reasonably incurred and due credit for payments or proceeds of resale.

Official Comment

Prior Uniform Statutory Provision: Section 64, Uniform Sales Act.

Changes: Rewritten.

Purposes of Changes: To make it clear that:

1.   The prior uniform statutory provision is followed generally in setting the current market price at the time and place for tender as the standard by which damages for non-acceptance are to be determined. The time and place of tender is determined by reference to the section on manner of tender of delivery, and to the sections on the effect of such terms as FOB, FAS, CIF, C. & F., Ex Ship and No Arrival, No Sale.

In the event that there is no evidence available of the current market price at the time and place of tender, proof of a substitute market may be made under the section on determination and proof of market price. Furthermore, the section on the admissibility of market quotations is intended to ease materially the problem of providing competent evidence.

2.   The provision of this section permitting recovery of expected profit including reasonable overhead where the standard measure of damages is inadequate, together with the new requirement that price actions may be sustained only where resale is impractical, are designed to eliminate the unfair and economically wasteful results arising under the older law when fixed price articles were involved. This section permits the recovery of lost profits in all appropriate cases, which would include all standard priced goods. The normal measure there would be list price less cost to the dealer or list price less manufacturing cost to the manufacturer. It is not necessary to a recovery of "profit" to show a history of earnings, especially of a new venture is involved.

3.   In all cases the seller may recover incidental damages.

Cross References:

Point 1: Sections 2–319 through 2–324, 2–503, 2–723 and 2–724.
Point 2: Section 2–709.
Point 3: Section 2–710.

Definitional Cross References:

"Buyer". Section 2–103.
"Contract". Section 1–201.
"Seller". Section 2–103.

§ 2–709.   Action for the Price.

(1)   When the buyer fails to pay the price as it becomes due the seller may recover, together with any incidental damages under the next section, the price

(a)   of goods accepted or of conforming goods lost or damaged within a commercially reasonable time after risk of their loss has passed to the buyer; and

(b)   of goods identified to the contract if the seller is unable after reasonable effort to resell them at a reasonable price or the circumstances reasonably indicate that such effort will be unavailing.

(2)   Where the seller sues for the price he must hold for the buyer any goods which have been identified to the contract and are still in his control except that if resale becomes possible he may resell them at any time prior to the collection of the judgment. The net proceeds of any such resale must be credited to the buyer and payment of the judgment entitles him to any goods not resold.

(3)   After the buyer has wrongfully rejected or revoked acceptance of the goods or has failed to make a payment due or has repudiated (Section 2–610), a seller who is held not entitled to the price under this section shall nevertheless be awarded damages for non-acceptance under the preceding section.

Official Comment

Prior Uniform Statutory Provision: Section 63, Uniform Sales Act.

Changes: Rewritten, important commercially needed changes being incorporated.

Purposes of Changes: To make it clear that:

1.   Neither the passing of title to the goods nor the appointment of a day certain for payment is now material to a price action.

2.   The action for the price is now generally limited to those cases where resale of the goods is impracticable except where the buyer has accepted the goods or where they have been destroyed after risk of loss has passed to the buyer.

3.   This section substitutes an objective test by action for the former "not readily resalable" standard. An action for the price under subsection (1)(b) can be sustained only after a "reasonable effort to resell" the goods "at reasonable price" has actually been made or where the circumstances "reasonably indicate" that such an effort will be unavailing.

4.   If a buyer is in default not with respect to the price, but on an obligation to make an advance, the seller should recover not under this section for the price as such, but for the default in the collateral (though coincident) obligation to finance the seller. If the agreement between the parties contemplates that the buyer will acquire, on making the advance, a security interest in the goods, the buyer on making the advance has such an interest as soon as the seller has rights in the agreed collateral. See Section 9–204.

5.   "Goods accepted" by the buyer under subsection (1)(a) include only goods as to which there has been no justified revocation of acceptance, for such a revocation means that there has been a default by the seller which bars his rights under this section. "Goods lost or damaged" are covered by the section on risk of loss. "Goods identified to the contract" under subsection (1)(b) are covered by the section on identification and the section on identification notwithstanding breach.

6.   This section is intended to be exhaustive in its enumeration of cases where an action for the price lies.

7.   If the action for the price fails, the seller may nonetheless have proved a case entitling him to damages for non-acceptance. In such a situation, subsection (3) permits recovery of those damages in the same action.

Cross References:

> Point 4: Section 1–106 [*unrevised Article 1; see Concordance, p. 22*].
> Point 5: Sections 2–501, 2–509, 2–510 and 2–704.
> Point 7: Section 2–708.

Definitional Cross References:

> "Action". Section 1–201.
> "Buyer". Section 2–103.
> "Conforming". Section 2–106.
> "Contract". Section 1–201.
> "Goods". Section 2–105.
> "Seller". Section 2–103.

§ 2–710.   Seller's Incidental Damages.

Incidental damages to an aggrieved seller include any commercially reasonable charges, expenses or commissions incurred in stopping delivery, in the transportation, care and custody of goods after the buyer's breach, in connection with return or resale of the goods or otherwise resulting from the breach.

Official Comment

Prior Uniform Statutory Provision: See Sections 64 and 70, Uniform Sales Act.

Purposes: To authorize reimbursement of the seller for expenses reasonably incurred by him as a result of the buyer's breach. The section sets forth the principal normal and necessary additional elements of damage flowing from the breach but intends to allow all commercially reasonable expenditures made by the seller.

Definitional Cross References:

"Aggrieved party". Section 1–201.
"Buyer". Section 2–103.
"Goods". Section 2–105.
"Seller". Section 2–103.

§ 2–711. Buyer's Remedies in General; Buyer's Security Interest in Rejected Goods.

(1)   Where the seller fails to make delivery or repudiates or the buyer rightfully rejects or justifiably revokes acceptance then with respect to any goods involved, and with respect to the whole if the breach goes to the whole contract (Section 2–612), the buyer may cancel and whether or not he has done so may in addition to recovering so much of the price as has been paid

(a)   "cover" and have damages under the next section as to all the goods affected whether or not they have been identified to the contract; or

(b)   recover damages for non-delivery as provided in this Article (Section 2–713).

(2)   Where the seller fails to deliver or repudiates the buyer may also

(a)   if the goods have been identified recover them as provided in this Article (Section 2–502); or

(b)   in a proper case obtain specific performance or replevy the goods as provided in this Article (Section 2–716).

(3)   On rightful rejection or justifiable revocation of acceptance a buyer has a security interest in goods in his possession or control for any payments made on their price and any expenses reasonably incurred in their inspection, receipt, transportation, care and custody and may hold such goods and resell them in like manner as an aggrieved seller (Section 2–706).

Official Comment

Prior Uniform Statutory Provision: No comparable index section; Subsection (3)—Section 69(5), Uniform Sales Act.

Changes: The prior uniform statutory provision is generally continued and expanded in Subsection (3).

Purposes of Changes and New Matter:

1.   To index in this section the buyer's remedies, subsection (1) covering those remedies permitting the recovery of money damages, and subsection (2) covering those which permit reaching the goods themselves. The remedies listed here are those available to a buyer who has not accepted the goods or who has justifiably revoked his acceptance. The remedies available to a buyer with regard to goods finally accepted appear in the section dealing with breach in regard to accepted goods. The buyer's right to proceed as to all goods when the breach is as to only some of the goods is determined by the section on breach in installment contracts and by the section on partial acceptance.

Despite the seller's breach, proper retender of delivery under the section on cure of improper tender or replacement can effectively preclude the buyer's remedies under this section, except for any delay involved.

2.   To make it clear in subsection (3) that the buyer may hold and resell rejected goods if he has paid a part of the price or incurred expenses of the type specified. "Paid" as used here includes acceptance of a draft or other time negotiable instrument or the signing of a negotiable note. His freedom of resale is coextensive with that of a seller under this Article except that the buyer may not keep any profit resulting from the resale and is limited to retaining only the amount of the price paid and the costs involved in the inspection and handling of the goods. The buyer's security interest in the goods is intended to be limited to the items listed in subsection (3), and the buyer is not permitted to retain such funds as he might believe adequate for his damages. The buyer's right to cover, or to have damages for non-delivery, is not impaired by his exercise of his right of resale.

3.   It should also be noted that this Act requires its remedies to be liberally administered and provides that any right or obligation which it declares is enforceable by action unless a different effect is specifically prescribed (Section 1–106) [*unrevised Article 1; see Concordance, p. 22*].

Cross References:

> Point 1: Sections 2–508, 2–601(c), 2–608, 2–612 and 2–714.
> Point 2: Section 2–706.
> Point 3: Section 1–106 [*unrevised Article 1; see Concordance, p. 22*].

Definitional Cross References:

> "Aggrieved party". Section 1–201.
> "Buyer". Section 2–103.
> "Cancellation". Section 2–106.
> "Contract". Section 1–201.
> "Cover". Section 2–712.
> "Goods". Section 2–105.
> "Notifies". Section 1–201 [*unrevised Article 1; see Concordance, p. 22*].
> "Receipt" of goods. Section 2–103.
> "Remedy". Section 1–201.
> "Security interest". Section 1–201.
> "Seller". Section 2–103.

§ 2–712.   "Cover"; Buyer's Procurement of Substitute Goods.

(1)   After a breach within the preceding section the buyer may "cover" by making in good faith and without unreasonable delay any reasonable purchase of or contract to purchase goods in substitution for those due from the seller.

(2)   The buyer may recover from the seller as damages the difference between the cost of cover and the contract price together with any incidental or consequential damages as hereinafter defined (Section 2–715), but less expenses saved in consequence of the seller's breach.

(3)   Failure of the buyer to effect cover within this section does not bar him from any other remedy.

Official Comment

Prior Uniform Statutory Provision: None.

Purposes:

1.   This section provides the buyer with a remedy aimed at enabling him to obtain the goods he needs thus meeting his essential need. This remedy is the buyer's equivalent of the seller's right to resell.

2.   The definition of "cover" under subsection (1) envisages a series of contracts or sales, as well as a single contract or sale; goods not identical with those involved but commercially usable as reasonable substitutes under the circumstances of the particular case; and contracts on credit or delivery terms differing from the contract in breach, but again reasonable under the circumstances. The test of proper cover is whether at the time and place the buyer acted in good faith and in a reasonable manner, and it is immaterial that hindsight may later prove that the method of cover used was not the cheapest or most effective.

The requirement that the buyer must cover "without unreasonable delay" is not intended to limit the time necessary for him to look around and decide as to how he may best effect cover. The test here is similar to that generally used in this Article as to reasonable time and seasonable action.

3.   Subsection (3) expresses the policy that cover is not a mandatory remedy for the buyer. The buyer is always free to choose between cover and damages for non-delivery under the next section.

However, this subsection must be read in conjunction with the section which limits the recovery of consequential damages to such as could not have been obviated by cover. Moreover, the operation of the section on specific performance of contracts for "unique" goods must be considered in this connection for availability of the goods to the particular buyer for his particular needs is the test for that remedy and inability to cover is made an express condition to the right of the buyer to replevy the goods.

4.   This section does not limit cover to merchants, in the first instance. It is the vital and important remedy for the consumer buyer as well. Both are free to use cover: the domestic or non-merchant consumer is required only to act in normal good faith while the merchant buyer must also observe all reasonable commercial standards of fair dealing in the trade, since this falls within the definition of good faith on his part.

Cross References:

Point 1: Section 2–706.
Point 2: Section 1–204 [*unrevised Article 1; see Concordance, p. 22*].
Point 3: Sections 2–713, 2–715 and 2–716.
Point 4: Section 1–203 [*unrevised Article 1; see Concordance, p. 22*].

Definitional Cross References:

"Buyer". Section 2–103.
"Contract". Section 1–201.
"Good faith". Section 2–103.
"Goods". Section 2–105.
"Purchase". Section 1–201.
"Remedy". Section 1–201.
"Seller". Section 2–103.

§ 2–713.   Buyer's Damages for Non-delivery or Repudiation.

(1)   Subject to the provisions of this Article with respect to proof of market price (Section 2–723), the measure of damages for non-delivery or repudiation by the seller is the difference between the market price at the time when the buyer learned of the breach and the contract price together with any incidental and consequential damages provided in this Article (Section 2–715), but less expenses saved in consequence of the seller's breach.

(2)   Market price is to be determined as of the place for tender or, in cases of rejection after arrival or revocation of acceptance, as of the place of arrival.

Official Comment

Prior Uniform Statutory Provision: Section 67(3), Uniform Sales Act.

Changes: Rewritten.

Purposes of Changes: To clarify the former rule so that:

1.   The general baseline adopted in this section uses as a yardstick the market in which the buyer would have obtained cover had he sought that relief. So the place for measuring damages is the place of tender (or the place of arrival if the goods are rejected or their acceptance is revoked after reaching their destination) and the crucial time is the time at which the buyer learns of the breach.

2.   The market or current price to be used in comparison with the contract price under this section is the price for goods of the same kind and in the same branch of trade.

3.   When the current market price under this section is difficult to prove the section on determination and proof of market price is available to permit a showing of a comparable market price or, where no market price is available, evidence of spot sale prices is proper. Where the unavailability of a market price is caused by a scarcity of goods of the type involved, a good case is normally made for specific performance under this Article. Such scarcity conditions, moreover, indicate that the price has risen and under the section providing for liberal administration of remedies, opinion evidence as to the value of the goods would be admissible in the absence of a market price and a liberal construction of allowable consequential damages should also result.

4.   This section carries forward the standard rule that the buyer must deduct from his damages any expenses saved as a result of the breach.

5.   The present section provides a remedy which is completely alternative to cover under the preceding section and applies only when and to the extent that the buyer has not covered.

Cross References:

Point 3: Sections 1–106 [*unrevised Article 1; see Concordance, p. 22*], 2–716 and 2–723.

Point 5: Section 2–712.

Definitional Cross References:

"Buyer". Section 2–103.
"Contract". Section 1–201.
"Seller". Section 2–103.

§ 2–714.   Buyer's Damages for Breach in Regard to Accepted Goods.

(1)   Where the buyer has accepted goods and given notification (subsection (3) of Section 2–607) he may recover as damages for any non-conformity of tender the loss resulting in the ordinary course of events from the seller's breach as determined in any manner which is reasonable.

(2)   The measure of damages for breach of warranty is the difference at the time and place of acceptance between the value of the goods accepted and the value they would have had if they had been as warranted, unless special circumstances show proximate damages of a different amount.

(3)   In a proper case any incidental and consequential damages under the next section may also be recovered.

Official Comment

Prior Uniform Statutory Provision: Section 69(6) and (7), Uniform Sales Act.

Changes: Rewritten.

Purposes of Changes:

1.   This section deals with the remedies available to the buyer after the goods have been accepted and the time for revocation of acceptance has gone by. In general this section adopts the rule of the prior uniform statutory provision for measuring damages where there has been a breach of warranty as to goods accepted, but goes further to lay down an explicit provision as to the time and place for determining the loss.

The section on deduction of damages from price provides an additional remedy for a buyer who still owes part of the purchase price, and frequently the two remedies will be available concurrently. The buyer's failure to notify of his claim under the section on effects of acceptance, however, operates to bar his remedies under either that section or the present section.

2.   The "non-conformity" referred to in subsection (1) includes not only breaches of warranties but also any failure of the seller to perform according to his obligations under the contract. In the case of such non-conformity, the buyer is permitted to recover for his loss "in any manner which is reasonable."

3.   Subsection (2) describes the usual, standard and reasonable method of ascertaining damages in the case of breach of warranty but it is not intended as an exclusive measure. It departs from the measure of damages for non-delivery in utilizing the place of acceptance rather than the place of tender. In some cases the two may coincide, as where the buyer signifies his acceptance upon the tender. If, however, the non-conformity is such as would justify revocation of acceptance, the time and place of acceptance under this section is determined as of the buyer's decision not to revoke.

4.   The incidental and consequential damages referred to in subsection (3), which will usually accompany an action brought under this section, are discussed in detail in the comment on the next section.

Cross References:

Point 1: Compare Section 2–711; Sections 2–607 and 2–717.
Point 2: Section 2–106.
Point 3: Sections 2–608 and 2–713.
Point 4: Section 2–715.

Definitional Cross References:

"Buyer". Section 2–103.
"Conform". Section 2–106.
"Goods". Section 1–201. [*Note from West Advisory Panel: This provision appears in § 2–105.*]

"Notification". Section 1–201 [*unrevised Article 1; see Concordance, p. 22*].
"Seller". Section 2–103.

§ 2–715. Buyer's Incidental and Consequential Damages.

(1) Incidental damages resulting from the seller's breach include expenses reasonably incurred in inspection, receipt, transportation and care and custody of goods rightfully rejected, any commercially reasonable charges, expenses or commissions in connection with effecting cover and any other reasonable expense incident to the delay or other breach.

(2) Consequential damages resulting from the seller's breach include

(a) any loss resulting from general or particular requirements and needs of which the seller at the time of contracting had reason to know and which could not reasonably be prevented by cover or otherwise; and

(b) injury to person or property proximately resulting from any breach of warranty.

Official Comment

Prior Uniform Statutory Provisions: Subsection (2)(b)—Sections 69(7) and 70, Uniform Sales Act.

Changes: Rewritten.

Purposes of Changes and New Matter:

1. Subsection (1) is intended to provide reimbursement for the buyer who incurs reasonable expenses in connection with the handling of rightfully rejected goods or goods whose acceptance may be justifiably revoked, or in connection with effecting cover where the breach of the contract lies in non-conformity or non-delivery of the goods. The incidental damages listed are not intended to be exhaustive but are merely illustrative of the typical kinds of incidental damage.

2. Subsection (2) operates to allow the buyer, in an appropriate case, any consequential damages which are the result of the seller's breach. The "tacit agreement" test for the recovery of consequential damages is rejected. Although the older rule at common law which made the seller liable for all consequential damages of which he had "reason to know" in advance is followed, the liberality of that rule is modified by refusing to permit recovery unless the buyer could not reasonably have prevented the loss by cover or otherwise. Subparagraph (2) carries forward the provisions of the prior uniform statutory provision as to consequential damages resulting from breach of warranty, but modifies the rule by requiring first that the buyer attempt to minimize his damages in good faith, either by cover or otherwise.

3. In the absence of excuse under the section on merchant's excuse by failure of presupposed conditions, the seller is liable for consequential damages in all cases where he had reason to know of the buyer's general or particular requirements at the time of contracting. It is not necessary that there be a conscious acceptance of an insurer's liability on the seller's part, nor is his obligation for consequential damages limited to cases in which he fails to use due effort in good faith.

Particular needs of the buyer must generally be made known to the seller while general needs must rarely be made known to charge the seller with knowledge.

Any seller who does not wish to take the risk of consequential damages has available the section on contractual limitation of remedy.

4. The burden of proving the extent of loss incurred by way of consequential damage is on the buyer, but the section on liberal administration of remedies rejects any doctrine of certainty which requires almost mathematical precision in the proof of loss. Loss may be determined in any manner which is reasonable under the circumstances.

5. Subsection (2)(b) states the usual rule as to breach of warranty, allowing recovery for injuries "proximately" resulting from the breach. Where the injury involved follows the use of goods without discovery of the defect causing the damage, the question of "proximate" cause turns on whether it was reasonable for the buyer to use the goods without such inspection as would have revealed the defects. If it was not reasonable for him to do so, or if he did in fact discover the defect prior to his use, the injury would not proximately result from the breach of warranty.

6.   In the case of sale of wares to one in the business of reselling them, resale is one of the requirements of which the seller has reason to know within the meaning of subsection (2)(a).

Cross References:

Point 1: Section 2–608.
Point 3: Sections 1–203 [*unrevised Article 1; see Concordance, p. 22*], 2–615 and 2–719.
Point 4: Section 1–106 [*unrevised Article 1; see Concordance, p. 22*].

Definitional Cross References:

"Cover". Section 2–712.
"Goods". Section 1–201. [*Note from West Advisory Panel: This provision appears in § 2–105.*]
"Person". Section 1–201.
"Receipt" of goods. Section 2–103.
"Seller". Section 2–103.

§ 2–716.   Buyer's Right to Specific Performance or Replevin.

(1)   Specific performance may be decreed where the goods are unique or in other proper circumstances.

(2)   The decree for specific performance may include such terms and conditions as to payment of the price, damages, or other relief as the court may deem just.

(3)   The buyer has a right of replevin for goods identified to the contract if after reasonable effort he is unable to effect cover for such goods or the circumstances reasonably indicate that such effort will be unavailing or if the goods have been shipped under reservation and satisfaction of the security interest in them has been made or tendered. In the case of goods bought for personal, family, or household purposes, the buyer's right of replevin vests upon acquisition of a special property, even if the seller had not then repudiated or failed to deliver.

As amended in 1999.

Official Comment

Prior Uniform Statutory Provision: Section 68, Uniform Sales Act.

Changes: Rephrased.

Purposes of Changes: To make it clear that:

1.   The present section continues in general prior policy as to specific performance and injunction against breach. However, without intending to impair in any way the exercise of the court's sound discretion in the matter, this Article seeks to further a more liberal attitude than some courts have shown in connection with the specific performance of contracts of sale.

2.   In view of this Article's emphasis on the commercial feasibility of replacement, a new concept of what are "unique" goods is introduced under this section. Specific performance is no longer limited to goods which are already specific or ascertained at the time of contracting. The test of uniqueness under this section must be made in terms of the total situation which characterizes the contract. Output and requirements contracts involving a particular or peculiarly available source or market present today the typical commercial specific performance situation, as contrasted with contracts for the sale of heirlooms or priceless works of art which were usually involved in the older cases. However, uniqueness is not the sole basis of the remedy under this section for the relief may also be granted "in other proper circumstances" and inability to cover is strong evidence of "other proper circumstances".

3.   The legal remedy of replevin is given to the buyer in cases in which cover is reasonably unavailable and goods have been identified to the contract. This is in addition to the buyer's right to recover identified goods under Section 2–502. For consumer goods, the buyer's right to replevin vests upon the buyer's acquisition of a special property, which occurs upon identification of the goods to the contract. See Section 2–501. Inasmuch as a secured party normally acquires no greater rights in its collateral that its debtor had or had power to convey, see Section 2–403(1) (first sentence), a buyer who acquires a right of replevin under subsection (3) will take free of a security interest created by the seller if it attaches to the goods after the goods have been identified to the contract. The buyer will take free, even if the buyer does not buy in ordinary course and even if the security interest is perfected.

Of course, to the extent that the buyer pays the price after the security interest attaches, the payments will constitute proceeds of the security interest.

4. This section is intended to give the buyer rights to the goods comparable to the seller's rights to the price.

5. If a negotiable document of title is outstanding, the buyer's right of replevin relates of course to the document not directly to the goods. See Article 7, especially Section 7–602.

Cross References:

Point 3: Section 2–502.
Point 4: Section 2–709.
Point 5: Article 7.

Definitional Cross References:

"Buyer". Section 2–103.
"Goods". Section 1–201 [*Note from West Advisory Panel: This provision appears in § 2–105.*]
"Rights". Section 1–201.

As amended in 1999.

§ 2–717. Deduction of Damages From the Price.

The buyer on notifying the seller of his intention to do so may deduct all or any part of the damages resulting from any breach of the contract from any part of the price still due under the same contract.

Official Comment

Prior Uniform Statutory Provision: See Section 69(1)(a), Uniform Sales Act.

Purposes:

1. This section permits the buyer to deduct from the price damages resulting from any breach by the seller and does not limit the relief to cases of breach of warranty as did the prior uniform statutory provision. To bring this provision into application the breach involved must be of the same contract under which the price in question is claimed to have been earned.

2. The buyer, however, must give notice of his intention to withhold all or part of the price if he wishes to avoid a default within the meaning of the section on insecurity and right to assurances. In conformity with the general policies of this Article, no formality of notice is required and any language which reasonably indicates the buyer's reason for holding up his payment is sufficient.

Cross Reference:

Point 2: Section 2–609.

Definitional Cross References:

"Buyer". Section 2–103.
"Notifies". Section 1–201 [*unrevised Article 1; see Concordance, p. 22*].

§ 2–718. Liquidation or Limitation of Damages; Deposits.

(1) Damages for breach by either party may be liquidated in the agreement but only at an amount which is reasonable in the light of the anticipated or actual harm caused by the breach, the difficulties of proof of loss, and the inconvenience or nonfeasibility of otherwise obtaining an adequate remedy. A term fixing unreasonably large liquidated damages is void as a penalty.

(2) Where the seller justifiably withholds delivery of goods because of the buyer's breach, the buyer is entitled to restitution of any amount by which the sum of his payments exceeds

(a) the amount to which the seller is entitled by virtue of terms liquidating the seller's damages in accordance with subsection (1), or

(b)   in the absence of such terms, twenty per cent of the value of the total performance for which the buyer is obligated under the contract or $500, whichever is smaller.

(3)   The buyer's right to restitution under subsection (2) is subject to offset to the extent that the seller establishes

(a)   a right to recover damages under the provisions of this Article other than subsection (1), and

(b)   the amount or value of any benefits received by the buyer directly or indirectly by reason of the contract.

(4)   Where a seller has received payment in goods their reasonable value or the proceeds of their resale shall be treated as payments for the purposes of subsection (2); but if the seller has notice of the buyer's breach before reselling goods received in part performance, his resale is subject to the conditions laid down in this Article on resale by an aggrieved seller (Section 2–706).

Official Comment

Prior Uniform Statutory Provision: None.

Purposes:

1.   Under subsection (1) liquidated damage clauses are allowed where the amount involved is reasonable in the light of the circumstances of the case. The subsection sets forth explicitly the elements to be considered in determining the reasonableness of a liquidated damage clause. A term fixing unreasonably large liquidated damages is expressly made void as a penalty. An unreasonably small amount would be subject to similar criticism and might be stricken under the section on unconscionable contracts or clauses.

2.   Subsection (2) refuses to recognize a forfeiture unless the amount of the payment so forfeited represents a reasonable liquidation of damages as determined under subsection (1). A special exception is made in the case of small amounts (20% of the price or $500, whichever is smaller) deposited as security. No distinction is made between cases in which the payment is to be applied on the price and those in which it is intended as security for performance. Subsection (2) is applicable to any deposit or down or part payment. In the case of a deposit or turn in of goods resold before the breach, the amount actually received on the resale is to be viewed as the deposit rather than the amount allowed the buyer for the trade in. However, if the seller knows of the breach prior to the resale of the goods turned in, he must make reasonable efforts to realize their true value, and this is assured by requiring him to comply with the conditions laid down in the section on resale by an aggrieved seller.

Cross References:

  Point 1: Section 2–302.
  Point 2: Section 2–706.

Definitional Cross References:

  "Aggrieved party". Section 1–201.
  "Agreement". Section 1–201.
  "Buyer". Section 2–103.
  "Goods". Section 2–105.
  "Notice". Section 1–201 [*unrevised Article 1; see Concordance, p. 22*].
  "Party". Section 1–201.
  "Remedy". Section 1–201.
  "Seller". Section 2–103.
  "Term". Section 1–201.

§ 2–719.   Contractual Modification or Limitation of Remedy.

(1)   Subject to the provisions of subsections (2) and (3) of this section and of the preceding section on liquidation and limitation of damages,

(a)   the agreement may provide for remedies in addition to or in substitution for those provided in this Article and may limit or alter the measure of damages recoverable under this Article, as by limiting the buyer's remedies to return of the goods and repayment of the price or to repair and replacement of non-conforming goods or parts; and

(b)   resort to a remedy as provided is optional unless the remedy is expressly agreed to be exclusive, in which case it is the sole remedy.

(2)   Where circumstances cause an exclusive or limited remedy to fail of its essential purpose, remedy may be had as provided in this Act.

(3)   Consequential damages may be limited or excluded unless the limitation or exclusion is unconscionable. Limitation of consequential damages for injury to the person in the case of consumer goods is prima facie unconscionable but limitation of damages where the loss is commercial is not.

Official Comment

Prior Uniform Statutory Provision: None.

Purposes:

1.   Under this section parties are left free to shape their remedies to their particular requirements and reasonable agreements limiting or modifying remedies are to be given effect.

However, it is of the very essence of a sales contract that at least minimum adequate remedies be available. If the parties intend to conclude a contract for sale within this Article they must accept the legal consequence that there be at least a fair quantum of remedy for breach of the obligations or duties outlined in the contract. Thus any clause purporting to modify or limit the remedial provisions of this Article in an unconscionable manner is subject to deletion and in that event the remedies made available by this Article are applicable as if the stricken clause had never existed. Similarly, under subsection (2), where an apparently fair and reasonable clause because of circumstances fails in its purpose or operates to deprive either party of the substantial value of the bargain, it must give way to the general remedy provisions of this Article.

2.   Subsection (1)(b) creates a presumption that clauses prescribing remedies are cumulative rather than exclusive. If the parties intend the term to describe the sole remedy under the contract, this must be clearly expressed.

3.   Subsection (3) recognizes the validity of clauses limiting or excluding consequential damages but makes it clear that they may not operate in an unconscionable manner. Actually such terms are merely an allocation of unknown or undeterminable risks. The seller in all cases is free to disclaim warranties in the manner provided in Section 2–316.

Cross References:

Point 1: Section 2–302.
Point 3: Section 2–316.

Definitional Cross References:

"Agreement". Section 1–201.
"Buyer". Section 2–103.
"Conforming". Section 2–106.
"Contract". Section 1–201.
"Goods". Section 2–105.
"Remedy". Section 1–201.
"Seller". Section 2–103.

§ 2–720.   Effect of "Cancellation" or "Rescission" on Claims for Antecedent Breach.

Unless the contrary intention clearly appears, expressions of "cancellation" or "rescission" of the contract or the like shall not be construed as a renunciation or discharge of any claim in damages for an antecedent breach.

Official Comment

Prior Uniform Statutory Provision: None.

Purpose:

This section is designed to safeguard a person holding a right of action from any unintentional loss of rights by the ill-advised use of such terms as "cancellation", "rescission", or the like. Once a party's rights have accrued they are not to be lightly impaired by concessions made in business decency and without intention to forego them. Therefore, unless the cancellation of a contract expressly declares that it is "without reservation of rights", or the like, it cannot be considered to be a renunciation under this section.

Cross Reference:

Section 1–107 [*unrevised Article 1; see Concordance, p. 22*].

Definitional Cross References:

"Cancellation". Section 2–106.
"Contract". Section 1–201.

§ 2–721.   Remedies for Fraud.

Remedies for material misrepresentation or fraud include all remedies available under this Article for non-fraudulent breach. Neither rescission or a claim for rescission of the contract for sale nor rejection or return of the goods shall bar or be deemed inconsistent with a claim for damages or other remedy.

Official Comment

Prior Uniform Statutory Provision: None.

Purposes: To correct the situation by which remedies for fraud have been more circumscribed than the more modern and mercantile remedies for breach of warranty. Thus the remedies for fraud are extended by this section to coincide in scope with those for non-fraudulent breach. This section thus makes it clear that neither rescission of the contract for fraud nor rejection of the goods bars other remedies unless the circumstances of the case make the remedies incompatible.

Definitional Cross References:

"Contract for sale". Section 2–106.
"Goods". Section 1–201. [*Note from West Advisory Panel: This provision appears in § 2–105.*]
"Remedy". Section 1–201.

§ 2–722.   Who Can Sue Third Parties for Injury to Goods.

Where a third party so deals with goods which have been identified to a contract for sale as to cause actionable injury to a party to that contract

(a)   a right of action against the third party is in either party to the contract for sale who has title to or a security interest or a special property or an insurable interest in the goods; and if the goods have been destroyed or converted a right of action is also in the party who either bore the risk of loss under the contract for sale or has since the injury assumed that risk as against the other;

(b)   if at the time of the injury the party plaintiff did not bear the risk of loss as against the other party to the contract for sale and there is no arrangement between them for disposition of the recovery, his suit or settlement is, subject to his own interest, as a fiduciary for the other party to the contract;

(c)   either party may with the consent of the other sue for the benefit of whom it may concern.

Official Comment

Prior Uniform Statutory Provision: None.

Purposes: To adopt and extend somewhat the principle of the statutes which provide for suit by the real party in interest. The provisions of this section apply only after identification of the goods. Prior to that time only the seller has a right of action. During the period between identification and final acceptance (except in the case of revocation of acceptance) it is possible for both parties to have the right of action. Even after final acceptance both parties may have the right of action if the seller retains possession or otherwise retains an interest.

Definitional Cross References:

"Action". Section 1–201.
"Buyer". Section 2–103.
"Contract for sale". Section 2–106.

"Goods". Section 2–105.
"Party". Section 1–201.
"Rights". Section 1–201.
"Security interest". Section 1–201.

§ 2–723. Proof of Market Price: Time and Place.

(1) If an action based on anticipatory repudiation comes to trial before the time for performance with respect to some or all of the goods, any damages based on market price (Section 2–708 or Section 2–713) shall be determined according to the price of such goods prevailing at the time when the aggrieved party learned of the repudiation.

(2) If evidence of a price prevailing at the times or places described in this Article is not readily available the price prevailing within any reasonable time before or after the time described or at any other place which in commercial judgment or under usage of trade would serve as a reasonable substitute for the one described may be used, making any proper allowance for the cost of transporting the goods to or from such other place.

(3) Evidence of a relevant price prevailing at a time or place other than the one described in this Article offered by one party is not admissible unless and until he has given the other party such notice as the court finds sufficient to prevent unfair surprise.

Official Comment

Prior Uniform Statutory Provision: None.

Purposes: To eliminate the most obvious difficulties arising in connection with the determination of market price, when that is stipulated as a measure of damages by some provision of this Article. Where the appropriate market price is not readily available the court is here granted reasonable leeway in receiving evidence of prices current in other comparable markets or at other times comparable to the one in question. In accordance with the general principle of this Article against surprise, however, a party intending to offer evidence of such a substitute price must give suitable notice to the other party.

This section is not intended to exclude the use of any other reasonable method of determining market price or of measuring damages if the circumstances of the case make this necessary.

Definitional Cross References:

"Action". Section 1–201.
"Aggrieved party". Section 1–201.
"Goods". Section 2–105.
"Notifies". Section 1–201 [*unrevised Article 1; see Concordance, p. 22*].
"Party". Section 1–201.
"Reasonable time". Section 1–204 [*unrevised Article 1; see Concordance, p. 22*].
"Usage of trade". Section 1–205 [*unrevised Article 1; see Concordance, p. 22*].

§ 2–724. Admissibility of Market Quotations.

Whenever the prevailing price or value of any goods regularly bought and sold in any established commodity market is in issue, reports in official publications or trade journals or in newspapers or periodicals of general circulation published as the reports of such market shall be admissible in evidence. The circumstances of the preparation of such a report may be shown to affect its weight but not its admissibility.

Official Comment

Prior Uniform Statutory Provision: None.

Purposes: To make market quotations admissible in evidence while providing for a challenge of the material by showing the circumstances of its preparation.

No explicit provision as to the weight to be given to market quotations is contained in this section, but such quotations, in the absence of compelling challenge, offer an adequate basis for a verdict.

Market quotations are made admissible when the price or value of goods traded "in any established market" is in issue. The reason of the section does not require that the market be closely organized in the manner of a produce exchange. It is sufficient if transactions in the commodity are frequent and open enough to make a market established by usage in which one price can be expected to affect another and in which an informed report of the range and trend of prices can be assumed to be reasonably accurate.

This section does not in any way intend to limit or negate the application of similar rules of admissibility to other material, whether by action of the courts or by statute. The purpose of the present section is to assure a minimum of mercantile administration in this important situation and not to limit any liberalizing trend in modern law.

Definitional Cross Reference:

"Goods". Section 2–105.

§ 2–725.   Statute of Limitations in Contracts for Sale.

(1) An action for breach of any contract for sale must be commenced within four years after the cause of action has accrued. By the original agreement the parties may reduce the period of limitation to not less than one year but may not extend it.

(2) A cause of action accrues when the breach occurs, regardless of the aggrieved party's lack of knowledge of the breach. A breach of warranty occurs when tender of delivery is made, except that where a warranty explicitly extends to future performance of the goods and discovery of the breach must await the time of such performance the cause of action accrues when the breach is or should have been discovered.

(3) Where an action commenced within the time limited by subsection (1) is so terminated as to leave available a remedy by another action for the same breach such other action may be commenced after the expiration of the time limited and within six months after the termination of the first action unless the termination resulted from voluntary discontinuance or from dismissal for failure or neglect to prosecute.

(4) This section does not alter the law on tolling of the statute of limitations nor does it apply to causes of action which have accrued before this Act becomes effective.

Official Comment

Prior Uniform Statutory Provision: None.

Purposes: To introduce a uniform statute of limitations for sales contracts, thus eliminating the jurisdictional variations and providing needed relief for concerns doing business on a nationwide scale whose contracts have heretofore been governed by several different periods of limitation depending upon the state in which the transaction occurred. This Article takes sales contracts out of the general laws limiting the time for commencing contractual actions and selects a four year period as the most appropriate to modern business practice. This is within the normal commercial record keeping period.

Subsection (1) permits the parties to reduce the period of limitation. The minimum period is set at one year. The parties may not, however, extend the statutory period.

Subsection (2), providing that the cause of action accrues when the breach occurs, states an exception where the warranty extends to future performance.

Subsection (3) states the saving provision included in many state statutes and permits an additional short period for bringing new actions, where suits begun within the four year period have been terminated so as to leave a remedy still available for the same breach.

Subsection (4) makes it clear that this Article does not purport to alter or modify in any respect the law on tolling of the Statute of Limitations as it now prevails in the various jurisdictions.

Definitional Cross References:

"Action". Section 1–201.
"Aggrieved party". Section 1–201.
"Agreement". Section 1–201.
"Contract for sale". Section 2–106.
"Goods". Section 2–105.

"Party". Section 1–201.
"Remedy". Section 1–201.
"Term". Section 1–201.
"Termination". Section 2–106.

UCC ARTICLE 2A

LEASES

Article 2A was amended in 1990, 1999, 2001, 2003, and 2010.
2022 Amendments appear in ~~strikeout~~/<u>underline</u> format.
Prefatory Note to 2022 amendments appears in Appendix E.
Current through April 2023
For updates, see www.uniformlaws.org

PART 1. GENERAL PROVISIONS

2A–101.   Short Title.
2A–102.   Scope.
2A–103.   Definitions and Index of Definitions.
2A–104.   Leases Subject to Other Law.
2A–105.   Territorial Application of Article to Goods Covered by Certificate of Title.
2A–106.   Limitation on Power of Parties to Consumer Lease to Choose Applicable Law and Judicial Forum.
2A–107.   Waiver or Renunciation of Claim or Right After Default.
2A–108.   Unconscionability.
2A–109.   Option to Accelerate at Will.

PART 2. FORMATION AND CONSTRUCTION OF LEASE CONTRACT

2A–201.   Statute of Frauds.
2A–202.   Final ~~Written~~ Expression: Parol or Extrinsic Evidence.
2A–203.   Seals Inoperative.
2A–204.   Formation in General.
2A–205.   Firm Offers.
2A–206.   Offer and Acceptance in Formation of Lease Contract.
2A–207.   [Reserved.] [Course of Performance or Practical Construction.]
2A–208.   Modification, Rescission and Waiver.
2A–209.   Lessee Under Finance Lease as Beneficiary of Supply Contract.
2A–210.   Express Warranties.
2A–211.   Warranties Against Interference and Against Infringement; Lessee's Obligation Against Infringement.
2A–212.   Implied Warranty of Merchantability.
2A–213.   Implied Warranty of Fitness for Particular Purpose.
2A–214.   Exclusion or Modification of Warranties.
2A–215.   Cumulation and Conflict of Warranties Express or Implied.
2A–216.   Third-Party Beneficiaries of Express and Implied Warranties.
2A–217.   Identification.
2A–218.   Insurance and Proceeds.
2A–219.   Risk of Loss.
2A–220.   Effect of Default on Risk of Loss.
2A–221.   Casualty to Identified Goods.

PART 3.   EFFECT OF LEASE CONTRACT

2A–301.   Enforceability of Lease Contract.
2A–302.   Title to and Possession of Goods.
2A–303.   Alienability of Party's Interest Under Lease Contract or of Lessor's Residual Interest in Goods; Delegation of Performance; Transfer of Rights.
2A–304.   Subsequent Lease of Goods by Lessor.
2A–305.   Sale or Sublease of Goods by Lessee.
2A–306.   Priority of Certain Liens Arising by Operation of Law.
2A–307.   Priority of Liens Arising by Attachment or Levy on, Security Interests in, and Other Claims to Goods.
2A–308.   Special Rights of Creditors.
2A–309.   Lessor's and Lessee's Rights When Goods Become Fixtures.
2A–310.   Lessor's and Lessee's Rights When Goods Become Accessions.
2A–311.   Priority Subject to Subordination.

PART 4.   PERFORMANCE OF LEASE CONTRACT: REPUDIATED, SUBSTITUTED AND EXCUSED

2A–401.   Insecurity: Adequate Assurance of Performance.
2A–402.   Anticipatory Repudiation.
2A–403.   Retraction of Anticipatory Repudiation.
2A–404.   Substituted Performance.
2A–405.   Excused Performance.
2A–406.   Procedure on Excused Performance.
2A–407.   Irrevocable Promises: Finance Leases.

PART 5.   DEFAULT

A.   IN GENERAL

2A–501.   Default: Procedure.
2A–502.   Notice After Default.
2A–503.   Modification or Impairment of Rights and Remedies.
2A–504.   Liquidation of Damages.
2A–505.   Cancellation and Termination and Effect of Cancellation, Termination, Rescission, or Fraud on Rights and Remedies.
2A–506.   Statute of Limitations.
2A–507.   Proof of Market Rent: Time and Place.

B.   DEFAULT BY LESSOR

2A–508.   Lessee's Remedies.
2A–509.   Lessee's Rights on Improper Delivery; Rightful Rejection.
2A–510.   Installment Lease Contracts: Rejection and Default.
2A–511.   Merchant Lessee's Duties as to Rightfully Rejected Goods.
2A–512.   Lessee's Duties as to Rightfully Rejected Goods.
2A–513.   Cure by Lessor of Improper Tender or Delivery; Replacement.
2A–514.   Waiver of Lessee's Objections.
2A–515.   Acceptance of Goods.
2A–516.   Effect of Acceptance of Goods; Notice of Default; Burden of Establishing Default After Acceptance; Notice of Claim or Litigation to Person Answerable Over.
2A–517.   Revocation of Acceptance of Goods.
2A–518.   Cover; Substitute Goods.
2A–519.   Lessee's Damages for Non-delivery, Repudiation, Default, and Breach of Warranty in Regard to Accepted Goods.

ARTICLE 2A

2A-520.   Lessee's Incidental and Consequential Damages.
2A-521.   Lessee's Right to Specific Performance or Replevin.
2A-522.   Lessee's Right to Goods on Lessor's Insolvency.

C.   DEFAULT BY LESSEE

2A-523.   Lessor's Remedies.
2A-524.   Lessor's Right to Identify Goods to Lease Contract.
2A-525.   Lessor's Right to Possession of Goods.
2A-526.   Lessor's Stoppage of Delivery in Transit or Otherwise.
2A-527.   Lessor's Rights to Dispose of Goods.
2A-528.   Lessor's Damages for Non-acceptance, Failure to Pay, Repudiation, or Other Default.
2A-529.   Lessor's Action for the Rent.
2A-530.   Lessor's Incidental Damages.
2A-531.   Standing to Sue Third Parties for Injury to Goods.
2A-532.   Lessor's Rights to Residual Interest.

FOREWORD

Article 2A of the Uniform Commercial Code, along with Conforming Amendments to Articles 1 and 9, is presented, upon the recommendation of the Permanent Editorial Board for the Uniform Commercial Code, by the National Conference of Commissioners on Uniform State Laws and the American Law Institute. It represents a major development in commercial law, addressing a type of business transaction, the leasing of personal property, that has long existed. Under present law, transactions of this type are governed partly by common law principles relating to personal property, partly by principles relating to real estate leases, and partly by reference to Articles 2 and 9 of the Uniform Commercial Code, dealing with Sales and Secured Transactions respectively. The legal rules and concepts derived from these sources imperfectly fit a transaction that involves personal property rather than realty, and a lease rather than either a sale or a security interest as such. A statute directly addressing the personal property lease is therefore appropriate.

Such a statute has become especially appropriate with the exponential expansion of the number and scale of personal property lease transactions. Article 2A will apply to transactions involving billions of dollars annually. It will apply to consumer's rental of automobiles or do-it-yourself equipment, on the one hand, and to leases of such items as commercial aircraft (to the extent not preempted by federal law) and industrial machinery, on the other. The text recognizes the differences between consumer and business leasing, while resting upon concepts that apply generally to any personal property lease transactions.

The final product represents an important undertaking of the Conference and the Institute. It has proceeded, following recommendations by the Conference's Study Committee in 1981, through preparation and review by the Conference's Drafting Committee first of a proposed free-standing Uniform Personal Property Leasing Act, which was approved by the Conference, and later of Article 2A, which proceeded through the Permanent Editorial Board, the Executive Committee of the Conference, the Conference, and the Council of the Institute and the Annual Meeting of the members of the Institute. Carrying the text through these several stages has required coordination of somewhat different procedures, and continued patience and mutual forbearance. At the same time, the text has been subjected to analysis and criticism from many points of view and thereby steadily improved.

The resulting product borrows from both Articles 2 and 9. These existing Articles of the Uniform Commercial Code have certain imperfections revealed by the long experience since their adoption. Article 2A cannot overcome those imperfections but seeks to minimize their significance as applied to leases. More fundamentally, there is important conceptual dissonance between Article 2 and Article 9. The formulation of Article 2A takes Articles 2 and 9 as they are for the time being and hence has required careful adjustment to this dissonance.

The drafting task has been complicated both as a matter of substance and as a matter of process. The Reporter, Ronald DeKoven, has been a master of substance and a steady and receptive principal in the

181

process. We join with the Conference and the Institute in expressing our admiration and appreciation for his contribution to this important field of law.

Geoffrey C. Hazard, Jr., *Chairman*
Permanent Editorial
Board for the Uniform
Commercial Code

October 1, 1987

PART 1

GENERAL PROVISIONS

§ 2A–101. Short Title.

This Article shall be known and may be cited as the Uniform Commercial Code—Leases.

Official Comment

Rationale for Codification:

There are several reasons for codifying the law with respect to leases of goods. An analysis of the case law as it applies to leases of goods suggests at least three significant issues to be resolved by codification. First, what is a lease? It is necessary to define lease to determine whether a transaction creates a lease or a security interest disguised as a lease. If the transaction creates a security interest disguised as a lease, the lessor will be required to file a financing statement or take other action to perfect its interest in the goods against third parties. There is no such requirement with respect to leases. Yet the distinction between a lease and a security interest disguised as a lease is not clear. Second, will the lessor be deemed to have made warranties to the lessee? If the transaction is a sale the express and implied warranties of Article 2 of the Uniform Commercial Code apply. However, the warranty law with respect to leases is uncertain. Third, what remedies are available to the lessor upon the lessee's default? If the transaction is a security interest disguised as a lease, the answer is stated in Part 5 of the Article on Secured Transactions (Article 9). There is no clear answer with respect to leases.

There are reasons to codify the law with respect to leases of goods in addition to those suggested by a review of the reported cases. The answer to this important question should not be limited to the issues raised in these cases. Is it not also proper to determine the remedies available to the lessee upon the lessor's default? It is, but that issue is not reached through a review of the reported cases. This is only one of the many issues presented in structuring, negotiating and documenting a lease of goods.

Statutory Analogue:

After it was decided to proceed with the codification project, the drafting committee of the National Conference of Commissioners on Uniform State Laws looked for a statutory analogue, gradually narrowing the focus to the Article on Sales (Article 2) and the Article on Secured Transactions (Article 9). A review of the literature with respect to the sale of goods reveals that Article 2 is predicated upon certain assumptions: Parties to the sales transaction frequently are without counsel; the agreement of the parties often is oral or evidenced by scant writings; obligations between the parties are bilateral; applicable law is influenced by the need to preserve freedom of contract. A review of the literature with respect to personal property security law reveals that Article 9 is predicated upon very different assumptions: Parties to a secured transaction regularly are represented by counsel; the agreement of the parties frequently is reduced to a writing, extensive in scope; the obligations between the parties are essentially unilateral; and applicable law seriously limits freedom of contract.

The lease is closer in spirit and form to the sale of goods than to the creation of a security interest. While parties to a lease are sometimes represented by counsel and their agreement is often reduced to a writing, the obligations of the parties are bilateral and the common law of leasing is dominated by the need to preserve freedom of contract. Thus the drafting committee concluded that Article 2 was the appropriate statutory analogue.

Issues: The drafting committee then identified and resolved several issues critical to codification:

Scope: The scope of the Article was limited to leases (Section 2A–102). There was no need to include leases intended as security, *i.e.*, security interests disguised as leases, as they are adequately treated in

Article 9. Further, even if leases intended as security were included, the need to preserve the distinction would remain, as policy suggests treatment significantly different from that accorded leases.

Definition of Lease: Lease was defined to exclude leases intended as security (Section 2A–103(1)(j)). Given the litigation to date a revised definition of security interest was suggested for inclusion in the Act. (Section 1–201(37))See pre-2001 Section 1–201(37). This revision Section 1–203 now sharpens the distinction between leases and security interests disguised as leases.

Filing: The lessor was not required to file a financing statement against the lessee or take any other action to protect the lessor's interest in the goods (Section 2A–301). The refined definition of security interest will more clearly signal the need to file to potential lessors of goods. Those lessors who are concerned will file a protective financing statement (Section 9–505).

Warranties: All of the express and implied warranties of the Article on Sales (Article 2) were included (Sections 2A–210 through 2A–216), revised to reflect differences in lease transactions. The lease of goods is sufficiently similar to the sale of goods to justify this decision. Further, many courts have reached the same decision.

Certificate of Title Laws: Many leasing transactions involve goods subject to certificate of title statutes. To avoid conflict with those statutes, this Article is subject to them (Section 2A–104(1)(a)).

Consumer Leases: Many leasing transactions involve parties subject to consumer protection statutes or decisions. To avoid conflict with those laws this Article is subject to them to the extent provided in (Section 2A–104(1)(c) and (2)). Further, certain consumer protections have been incorporated in the Article.

Finance Leases: Certain leasing transactions substitute the supplier of the goods for the lessor as the party responsible to the lessee with respect to warranties and the like. The definition of finance lease (Section 2A–103(1)(g)) was developed to describe these transactions. Various sections of the Article implement the substitution of the supplier for the lessor, including Sections 2A–209 and 2A–407. No attempt was made to fashion a special rule where the finance lessor is an affiliate of the supplier of goods; this is to be developed by the courts, case by case.

Sale and Leaseback: Sale and leaseback transactions are becoming increasingly common. A number of state statutes treat transactions where possession is retained by the seller as fraudulent *per se* or *prima facie* fraudulent. That position is not in accord with modern practice and thus is changed by the Article "if the buyer bought for value and in good faith" (Section 2A–308(3)).

Remedies: The Article has not only provided for lessor's remedies upon default by the lessee (Sections 2A–523 through 2A–531), but also for lessee's remedies upon default by the lessor (Sections 2A–508 through 2A–522). This is a significant departure from Article 9, which provides remedies only for the secured party upon default by the debtor. This difference is compelled by the bilateral nature of the obligations between the parties to a lease.

Damages: Many leasing transactions are predicated on the parties' ability to stipulate an appropriate measure of damages in the event of default. The rule with respect to sales of goods (Section 2–718) is not sufficiently flexible to accommodate this practice. Consistent with the common law emphasis upon freedom to contract, the Article has created a revised rule that allows greater flexibility with respect to leases of goods (Section 2A–504(1)).

History:

This Article is a revision of the Uniform Personal Property Leasing Act, which was approved by the National Conference of Commissioners on Uniform State Laws in August, 1985. However, it was believed that the subject matter of the Uniform Personal Property Leasing Act would be better treated as an article of this Act. Thus, although the Conference promulgated the Uniform Personal Property Leasing Act as a Uniform Law, activity was held in abeyance to allow time to restate the Uniform Personal Property Leasing Act as Article 2A.

In August, 1986 the Conference approved and recommended this Article (including conforming amendments to Article 1 and Article 9) for promulgation as an amendment to this Act. In December, 1986 the Council of the American Law Institute approved and recommended this Article (including conforming amendments to Article 1 and Article 9), with official comments, for promulgation as an amendment to this Act. In March, 1987 the Permanent Editorial Board for the Uniform Commercial Code approved and recommended this Article (including conforming amendments to Article 1 and Article 9), with official comments, for promulgation as an amendment to this Act. In May, 1987 the American Law Institute approved and recommended this Article (including conforming amendments to Article 1 and Article 9), with official comments, for promulgation as an amendment to this Act. In August, 1987 the Conference confirmed its approval of the final text of this Article.

Upon its initial promulgation, Article 2A was rapidly enacted in several states, was introduced in a number of other states, and underwent bar association, law revision commission and legislative study in still further states. In that process debate emerged, principally sparked by the study of Article 2A by the California Bar Association, California's non-uniform amendments to Article 2A, and articles appearing in a symposium on Article 2A published after its promulgation in the Alabama Law Review. The debate chiefly centered on whether Article 2A had struck the proper balance or was clear enough concerning the ability of a lessor to grant a security interest in its leasehold interest and in the residual, priority between a secured party and the lessee, and the lessor's remedy structure under Article 2A.

This debate over issues on which reasonable minds could and did differ began to affect the enactment effort for Article 2A in a deleterious manner. Consequently, the Standby Committee for Article 2A, composed predominantly of the former members of the drafting committee, reviewed the legislative actions and studies in the various states, and opened a dialogue with the principal proponents of the non-uniform amendments. Negotiations were conducted in conjunction with, and were facilitated by, a study of the uniform Article and the non-uniform Amendments by the New York Law Revision Commission. Ultimately, a consensus was reached, which has been approved by the membership of the Conference, the Permanent Editorial Board, and the Council of the Institute. Rapid and uniform enactment of Article 2A is expected as a result of the completed amendments. The Article 2A experience reaffirms the essential viability of the procedures of the Conference and the Institute for creating and updating uniform state law in the commercial law area.

Relationship of Article 2A to Other Articles:

The Article on Sales provided a useful point of reference for codifying the law of leases. Many of the provisions of that Article were carried over, changed to reflect differences in style, leasing terminology or leasing practices. Thus, the official comments to those sections of Article 2 whose provisions were carried over are incorporated by reference in Article 2A, as well; further, any case law interpreting those provisions should be viewed as persuasive but not binding on a court when deciding a similar issue with respect to leases. Any change in the sequence that has been made when carrying over a provision from Article 2 should be viewed as a matter of style, not substance. This is not to suggest that in other instances Article 2A did not also incorporate substantially revised provisions of Article 2, Article 9 or otherwise where the revision was driven by a concern over the substance; but for the lack of a mandate, the drafting committee might well have made the same or a similar change in the statutory analogue. Those sections in Article 2A include Sections 2A–104, 2A–105, 2A–106, 2A–108(2) and (4), 2A–109(2), 2A–208, 2A–214(2) and (3)(a), 2A–216, 2A–303, 2A–306, 2A–503, 2A–504(3)(b), 2A–506(2), and 2A–515. For lack of relevance or significance not all of the provisions of Article 2 were incorporated in Article 2A.

This codification was greatly influenced by the fundamental tenet of the common law as it has developed with respect to leases of goods: freedom of the parties to contract. Note that, like all other Articles of this Act, the principles of construction and interpretation contained in Article 1 are applicable throughout Article 2A (Section 2A–103(4)). These principles include the ability of the parties to vary the effect of the provisions of Article 2A, subject to certain limitations including those that relate to the obligations of good faith, diligence, reasonableness and care (Section 1–102(3)) [*unrevised Article 1; see Concordance, p. 22*]. Consistent with those principles no negative inference is to be drawn by the episodic use of the phrase "unless otherwise agreed" in certain provisions of Article 2A. Section 1–102(4) [*unrevised Article 1; see Concordance, p. 22*]. Indeed, the contrary is true, as the general rule in the Act, including this Article, is that the effect of the Act's provisions may be varied by agreement. Section 1–102(3) [*unrevised Article 1; see Concordance, p. 22*]. This conclusion follows even where the statutory analogue contains the phrase and the correlative provision in Article 2A does not.

As amended in 2022.

§ 2A–102. Scope.

(1)   This Article applies to any transaction, regardless of form, that creates a lease and, in the case of a hybrid lease, it applies to the extent provided in subsection (2).

(2)   In a hybrid lease:

(a)   if the lease-of-goods aspects do not predominate:

      (i)   only the provisions of this Article which relate primarily to the lease-of-goods aspects of the transaction apply, and the provisions that relate primarily to the transaction as a whole do not apply;

      (ii)   Section 2A–209 applies if the lease is a finance lease; and

      (iii)   Section 2A–407 applies to the promises of the lessee in a finance lease to the extent the promises are consideration for the right to possession and use of the leased goods; and

  (b)   if the lease-of-goods aspects predominate, this Article applies to the transaction, but does not preclude application in appropriate circumstances of other law to aspects of the lease which do not relate to the lease of goods.

As amended in 2022.

Official Comment

Uniform Statutory Source: Former Section 9–102(1) (now codified as Section 9–109). Throughout this Article, unless otherwise stated, references to "Section" are to other sections of this Act.

Changes: Substantially revised.

Purposes:

    1.   This Article governs transactions as diverse as the lease of a hand tool to an individual for a few hours and the leveraged lease of a complex line of industrial equipment to a multi-national organization for a number of years.

    To achieve that end it was necessary to provide that this Article applies to any transaction, regardless of form, that creates a lease. Since lease is defined as a transfer of an interest in goods (Section 2A–103(1)(j)) and goods is defined to include fixtures (Section 2A–103(1)(h)), application is limited to the extent the transaction relates to goods, including fixtures. Further, since the definition of lease does not include a sale (Section 2–106(1)) or retention or creation of a security interest (Section 1–201(37) 1–201(b)(35)), application is further limited; sales and security interests are governed by other Articles of this Act.

    2.   Finally, in In recognition of the diversity of the transactions to be governed, the sophistication of many of the parties to these transactions, and the common law tradition as it applies to the bailment for hire or lease, freedom of contract has been preserved. DeKoven, Proceedings After Default by the Lessee Under a True Lease of Equipment, in 1C P. Coogan, W. Hogan, D. Vagts, *Secured Transactions Under the Uniform Commercial Code*, § 29B.02[2] (1986). Thus, despite the extensive regulatory scheme established by this Article, the parties to a lease will be able to create private rules to govern their transaction. Sections 2A–103(4) and 1–102(3) [*unrevised Article 1; see Concordance, p. 22*]. However, there are special rules in this Article governing consumer leases, as well as other state and federal statutes, that may further limit freedom of contract with respect to consumer leases.

    3.   A court may apply this Article by analogy to any transaction, regardless of form, that creates a lease of personal property other than goods, taking into account the expressed intentions of the parties to the transaction and any differences between a lease of goods and a lease of other property. Such application has precedent as the provisions of the Article on Sales (Article 2) have been applied by analogy to leases of goods. *E.g.,* Hawkland, *The Impact of the Uniform Commercial Code on Equipment Leasing*, 1972 Ill.L.F. 446; Murray, *Under the Spreading Analogy of Article 2 of the Uniform Commercial Code*, 39 Fordham L.Rev. 447 (1971). Whether such application would be appropriate for other bailments of personal property, gratuitous or for hire, should be determined by the facts of each case. *See Mieske v. Bartell Drug Co.*, 92 Wash.2d 40, 46–48, 593 P.2d 1308, 1312 (1979).

    Further, parties to a transaction creating a lease of personal property other than goods, or a bailment of personal property, may provide by agreement that this Article applies. Upholding the parties' choice is consistent with the spirit of this Article.

    4.   If the lease-of-goods aspects of a hybrid lease do not predominate, under subsection (2)(a)(i) the provisions of this Article which relate primarily to the lease-of-goods aspects of the transaction apply and those that relate primarily to the transaction as a whole do not apply. Under subsection (2)(b), if the lease-of-goods aspects of a hybrid lease predominate, this Article applies to the transaction.

    5.   Relevant factors in determining whether the lease-of-goods aspects of a hybrid lease predominate include the language of the agreement and the portion of the total price that is attributable to the lease of goods, although neither is determinative. An agreed-upon allocation of a portion of the total price to the right to

possession and use of the goods is ordinarily binding on the parties, as is an agreement that the transaction includes or does not include a finance lease.

6. A finance lease, defined in Section 2A–103(1)(g), may be included in a hybrid lease in which the lease-of-goods aspects of the transaction do not predominate. In such a situation, subsection (2)(a)(ii) makes Section 2A–209 applicable and subsection (2)(a)(iii) addresses the application of Section 2A–407 to the promises made by the lessee under the finance lease. That latter section applies to those promises that are consideration for the lessee's right to possession and use of the leased goods. Whether a promise of a lessee so qualifies is a question of fact but an agreed-upon allocation of a portion of the total price to the right to possession and use of the leased goods is ordinarily binding on the parties. The fact that subsection (2)(a)(ii) and (iii) expressly make Sections 2A–209 and 2A–407 applicable if the lease is a finance lease does not prevent application of other provisions of this Article relating to finance leases pursuant to subsection (2)(b).

Example 1. Lessor and Customer enter into a contract that provides for Lessor to: (i) lease equipment to Customer; and (ii) provide to Customer a variety of maintenance and consulting services. The services aspects of the transaction predominate. Lessor did not select, manufacture, or supply the goods; instead, the goods were selected by Customer, and Lessor acquired the goods from Supplier for the sole purpose of leasing the goods to Customer. Assume that the lease aspects of the transaction involve a finance lease under Section 2A–103(1)(g). Pursuant to subsection (3)(a), Sections 2A–212 and 2A–213 apply. Under those sections, because the lease aspect of the transaction is a finance lease, Lessor makes no implied warranty of merchantability or implied warranty of fitness for particular purpose. Pursuant to subsection (2)(a)(ii), Section 2A–209 applies. Under that section, all warranties made by Supplier to Lessor extend to Customer.

Example 2. Same facts as Example 1. As consideration for Lessor's obligations under the contract, Customer promises to pay a single monthly fee of a specified amount. The contract does not indicate what portion of the monthly fee is consideration for the services or what portion is consideration for possession and use of the equipment. Section 2A–407 applies to the lessee's promises that are consideration for the lessee's right to possession and use of the equipment. In an action involving the application of Section 2A–407, the determination of what portion of the monthly fee is for the right to possession and use of the equipment is a question of fact.

Example 3. Same facts as Example 1 except that the lease-of-goods aspects of the transaction predominate. Section 2A–407 applies to all of the lessee's promises under the transaction.

7. Even if the lease-of-goods aspects of a hybrid lease predominate and this Article applies to the transaction, the application of this Article to a hybrid lease does not preclude the application of principles of law and equity to supplement the provisions of this Article, see Section 1–103(b), nor does it preclude, in appropriate circumstances, the application of other law to the non-lease-of-goods aspects of the transaction. Whether it is appropriate to apply such other law will depend in part on what purposes the other law is designed to achieve and whether application of the other law would be likely to interfere with the application of this Article.

Example 4. Same facts as Example 3 (the lease-of-goods aspects of the transaction predominate) except that the lease is not a finance lease. This Article applies to the transaction. Nevertheless, because principles of law and equity also apply unless displaced by particular provisions the Uniform Commercial Code, see Section 1–103(b), and this Article does not displace other law relating to whether Lessor's performance of services conforms to the contract, other law determines whether the services conform to the contract.

8. The rules of subsections (2)(a) and (2)(b) are essentially gap fillers that apply when the parties' agreement is silent on what legal rules govern the different aspects of their transaction. In general, parties are free to preclude the application of this Article to the aspects of their transaction that are not about the lease of goods. See Section 2–102, Comment 6.

Cross References:

Sections 1–102(3) [*unrevised Article 1; see Concordance, p. 22*], 1–201(37) [*unrevised Article 1; see Concordance, p. 22*], Article 2, esp. Section 2–106(1), and Sections 2A–103(1)(h), 2A–103(1)(j) and 2A–103(4).

Definitional Cross Reference:

"Lease". Section 2A–103(1)(j).

As amended in 2022.

§ 2A–103.   Definitions and Index of Definitions.

(1)   In this Article unless the context otherwise requires:

(a)   "Buyer in ordinary course of business" means a person who in good faith and without knowledge that the sale to him [or her] is in violation of the ownership rights or security interest or leasehold interest of a third party in the goods buys in ordinary course from a person in the business of selling goods of that kind but does not include a pawnbroker. "Buying" may be for cash or by exchange of other property or on secured or unsecured credit and includes acquiring goods or documents of title under a pre-existing contract for sale but does not include a transfer in bulk or as security for or in total or partial satisfaction of a money debt.

(b)   "Cancellation" occurs when either party puts an end to the lease contract for default by the other party.

(c)   "Commercial unit" means such a unit of goods as by commercial usage is a single whole for purposes of lease and division of which materially impairs its character or value on the market or in use. A commercial unit may be a single article, as a machine, or a set of articles, as a suite of furniture or a line of machinery, or a quantity, as a gross or carload, or any other unit treated in use or in the relevant market as a single whole.

(d)   "Conforming" goods or performance under a lease contract means goods or performance that are in accordance with the obligations under the lease contract.

(e)   "Consumer lease" means a lease that a lessor regularly engaged in the business of leasing or selling makes to a lessee who is an individual and who takes under the lease primarily for a personal, family, or household purpose[, if the total payments to be made under the lease contract, excluding payments for options to renew or buy, do not exceed $_____].

(f)   "Fault" means wrongful act, omission, breach, or default.

(g)   "Finance lease" means a lease with respect to which:

    (i)   the lessor does not select, manufacture, or supply the goods;

    (ii)   the lessor acquires the goods or the right to possession and use of the goods in connection with the lease; and

    (iii)   one of the following occurs:

        (A)   the lessee receives a copy of the contract by which the lessor acquired the goods or the right to possession and use of the goods before signing the lease contract;

        (B)   the lessee's approval of the contract by which the lessor acquired the goods or the right to possession and use of the goods is a condition to effectiveness of the lease contract;

        (C)   the lessee, before signing the lease contract, receives an accurate and complete statement designating the promises and warranties, and any disclaimers of warranties, limitations or modifications of remedies, or liquidated damages, including those of a third party, such as the manufacturer of the goods, provided to the lessor by the person supplying the goods in connection with or as part of the contract by which the lessor acquired the goods or the right to possession and use of the goods; or

        (D)   if the lease is not a consumer lease, the lessor, before the lessee signs the lease contract, informs the lessee in writing (a) of the identity of the person supplying the goods to the lessor, unless the lessee has selected that person and directed the lessor to acquire the goods or the right to possession and use of the goods from that person, (b) that the lessee is entitled under this Article to the promises and warranties, including those of any third party, provided to the lessor by the person supplying the goods in connection with or as part of the contract by which the lessor acquired the goods or the right to possession and use of the goods, and (c) that the lessee may communicate with the person supplying the goods to the lessor and receive an accurate and complete statement of those promises and warranties, including any disclaimers and limitations of them or of remedies.

(h)   "Goods" means all things that are movable at the time of identification to the lease contract, or are fixtures (Section 2A–309), but the term does not include money, documents, instruments, accounts, chattel paper, general intangibles, or minerals or the like, including oil and gas, before extraction. The term also includes the unborn young of animals.

(h.1) "Hybrid lease" means a single transaction involving a lease of goods and:

     (i)   the provision of services;

     (ii)   a sale of other goods; or

     (iii)   a sale, lease, or license of property other than goods.

(i)   "Installment lease contract" means a lease contract that authorizes or requires the delivery of goods in separate lots to be separately accepted, even though the lease contract contains a clause "each delivery is a separate lease" or its equivalent.

(j)   "Lease" means a transfer of the right to possession and use of goods for a term in return for consideration, but a sale, including a sale on approval or a sale or return, or retention or creation of a security interest is not a lease. Unless the context clearly indicates otherwise, the term includes a sublease.

(k)   "Lease agreement" means the bargain, with respect to the lease, of the lessor and the lessee in fact as found in their language or by implication from other circumstances including course of dealing or usage of trade or course of performance as provided in this Article. Unless the context clearly indicates otherwise, the term includes a sublease agreement.

(l)   "Lease contract" means the total legal obligation that results from the lease agreement as affected by this Article and any other applicable rules of law. Unless the context clearly indicates otherwise, the term includes a sublease contract.

(m)   "Leasehold interest" means the interest of the lessor or the lessee under a lease contract.

(n)   "Lessee" means a person who acquires the right to possession and use of goods under a lease. Unless the context clearly indicates otherwise, the term includes a sublessee.

(o)   "Lessee in ordinary course of business" means a person who in good faith and without knowledge that the lease to him [or her] is in violation of the ownership rights or security interest or leasehold interest of a third party in the goods, leases in ordinary course from a person in the business of selling or leasing goods of that kind but does not include a pawnbroker. "Leasing" may be for cash or by exchange of other property or on secured or unsecured credit and includes acquiring goods or documents of title under a pre-existing lease contract but does not include a transfer in bulk or as security for or in total or partial satisfaction of a money debt.

(p)   "Lessor" means a person who transfers the right to possession and use of goods under a lease. Unless the context clearly indicates otherwise, the term includes a sublessor.

(q)   "Lessor's residual interest" means the lessor's interest in the goods after expiration, termination, or cancellation of the lease contract.

(r)   "Lien" means a charge against or interest in goods to secure payment of a debt or performance of an obligation, but the term does not include a security interest.

(s)   "Lot" means a parcel or a single article that is the subject matter of a separate lease or delivery, whether or not it is sufficient to perform the lease contract.

(t)   "Merchant lessee" means a lessee that is a merchant with respect to goods of the kind subject to the lease.

(u)   "Present value" means the amount as of a date certain of one or more sums payable in the future, discounted to the date certain. The discount is determined by the interest rate specified by the parties if the rate was not manifestly unreasonable at the time the transaction was entered into;

otherwise, the discount is determined by a commercially reasonable rate that takes into account the facts and circumstances of each case at the time the transaction was entered into. [*Note from West Advisory Panel: Revised Article 1 (2001) adds a definition of "present value" in § 1–201(b)(28). The conforming amendments to Article 2A erroneously do not delete this definition.*]

(v) "Purchase" includes taking by sale, lease, mortgage, security interest, pledge, gift, or any other voluntary transaction creating an interest in goods.

(w) "Sublease" means a lease of goods the right to possession and use of which was acquired by the lessor as a lessee under an existing lease.

(x) "Supplier" means a person from whom a lessor buys or leases goods to be leased under a finance lease.

(y) "Supply contract" means a contract under which a lessor buys or leases goods to be leased.

(z) "Termination" occurs when either party pursuant to a power created by agreement or law puts an end to the lease contract otherwise than for default.

(2) Other definitions applying to this Article and the sections in which they appear are:

"Accessions". Section 2A–310(1).
"Construction mortgage". Section 2A–309(1)(d).
"Encumbrance". Section 2A–309(1)(e).
"Fixtures". Section 2A–309(1)(a).
"Fixture filing". Section 2A–309(1)(b).
"Purchase money lease". Section 2A–309(1)(c).

(3) The following definitions in other Articles apply to this Article:

"Account". Section 9–102(a)(2).
"Between merchants". Section 2–104(3).
"Buyer". Section 2–103(1)(a).
"Chattel paper". Section 9–102(a)(11).
"Consumer goods". Section 9–102(a)(23).
"Document". Section 9–102(a)(30).
"Entrusting". Section 2–403(3).
"General intangible". Section 9–102(a)(42).
["Good Faith". Section 2–103(1)(b).] [*Note from West Advisory Panel: This cross reference will be deleted if the jurisdiction adopts the definition of good faith in revised Article 1 (2001).*]
"Instrument". Section 9–102(a)(47).
"Merchant". Section 2–104(1).
"Mortgage". Section 9–102(a)(55).
"Pursuant to commitment". Section 9–102(a)(69).
"Receipt". Section 2–103(1)(c).
"Sale". Section 2–106(1).
"Sale on approval". Section 2–326.
"Sale or return". Section 2–326.
"Seller". Section 2–103(1)(d).

(4) In addition Article 1 contains general definitions and principles of construction and interpretation applicable throughout this Article.

As amended in 1990, 1999, 2001, 2003, 2010, and 2022.

Official Comment

(a) "Buyer in ordinary course of business". Section 1–201(b)(9).

(b) "Cancellation". Section 2–106(4). The effect of a cancellation is provided in Section 2A–505(1).

(c) "Commercial unit". Section 2–105(6).

(d)   "Conforming". Section 2–106(2).

(e)   "Consumer lease". New. This Article includes a subset of rules that applies only to consumer leases. Sections 2A–106, 2A–108(2), 2A–108(4), 2A–109(2), 2A–221, 2A–309, 2A–406, 2A–407, 2A–504(3)(b), and 2A–516(3)(b).

For a transaction to qualify as a consumer lease it must first qualify as a lease. Section 2A–103(1)(j). Note that this Article regulates the transactional elements of a lease, including a consumer lease; consumer protection statutes, present and future, and existing consumer protection decisions are unaffected by this Article. Section 2A–104(1)(c) and (2). Of course, Article 2A as state law also is subject to federal consumer protection law.

This definition is modeled after the definition of consumer lease in the Consumer Leasing Act, 15 U.S.C. § 1667 (1982), and in the Unif. Consumer Credit Code § 1.301(14), 7A U.L.A. 43 (1974). However, this definition of consumer lease differs from its models in several respects: the lessor can be a person regularly engaged either in the business of leasing or of selling goods, the lease need not be for a term exceeding four months, a lease primarily for an agricultural purpose is not covered, and whether there should be a limitation by dollar amount and its amount is left up to the individual states.

This definition focuses on the parties as well as the transaction. If a lease is within this definition, the lessor must be regularly engaged in the business of leasing or selling, and the lessee must be an individual, not an organization; note that a lease to two or more individuals having a common interest through marriage or the like is not excluded as a lease to an organization under Section ~~1–201(28)~~ 1–201(b)(25). The lessee must take the interest primarily for a personal, family or household purpose. If required by the enacting state, total payments under the lease contract, excluding payments for options to renew or buy, cannot exceed the figure designated.

(f)   "Fault". Section ~~1–201(16)~~ 1–201(b)(17).

(g)   "Finance Lease". New. This Article includes a subset of rules that applies only to finance leases. Sections 2A–209, 2A–211(2), 2A–212(1), 2A–213, 2A–219(1), 2A–220(1)(a), 2A–221, 2A–405(c), 2A–407, 2A–516(2) and 2A–517(1)(a) and (2).

For a transaction to qualify as a finance lease it must first qualify as a lease. Section 2A–103(1)(j). Unless the lessor is comfortable that the transaction will qualify as a finance lease, the lease agreement should include provisions giving the lessor the benefits created by the subset of rules applicable to the transaction that qualifies as a finance lease under this Article.

A finance lease is the product of a three party transaction. The supplier manufactures or supplies the goods pursuant to the lessee's specification, perhaps even pursuant to a purchase order, sales agreement or lease agreement between the supplier and the lessee. After the prospective finance lease is negotiated, a purchase order, sales agreement, or lease agreement is entered into by the lessor (as buyer or prime lessee) or an existing order, agreement or lease is assigned by the lessee to the lessor, and the lessor and the lessee then enter into a lease or sublease of the goods. Due to the limited function usually performed by the lessor, the lessee looks almost entirely to the supplier for representations, covenants and warranties. If a manufacturer's warranty carries through, the lessee may also look to that. Yet, this definition does not restrict the lessor's function solely to the supply of funds; if the lessor undertakes or performs other functions, express warranties, covenants and the common law will protect the lessee.

This definition focuses on the transaction, not the status of the parties; to avoid confusion it is important to note that in other contexts, *e.g.*, tax and accounting, the term finance lease has been used to connote different types of lease transactions, including leases that are disguised secured transactions. M. Rice, *Equipment Financing*, 62–71 (1981). A lessor who is a merchant with respect to goods of the kind subject to the lease may be a lessor under a finance lease. Many leases that are leases back to the seller of goods (Section 2A–308(3)) will be finance leases. This conclusion is easily demonstrated by a hypothetical. Assume that B has bought goods from C pursuant to a sales contract. After delivery to and acceptance of the goods by B, B negotiates to sell the goods to A and simultaneously to lease the goods back from A, on terms and conditions that, we assume, will qualify the transaction as a lease. Section 2A–103(1)(j). In documenting the sale and lease back, B assigns the original sales contract between B, as buyer, and C, as seller, to A. A review of these facts leads to the conclusion that the lease from A to B qualifies as a finance lease, as all three conditions of the definition are satisfied. Subparagraph (i) is satisfied as A, the lessor, had nothing to do with the selection, manufacture, or supply of the equipment. Subparagraph (ii) is satisfied as A, the lessor, bought the equipment at the same time that A leased the equipment to B, which certainly is in connection with the lease. Finally, subparagraph (iii)(A) is satisfied as A entered into the sales contract with B at the same time that A leased the equipment back to B. B, the lessee, will have received a copy of the sales contract in a timely fashion.

Subsection (i) requires the lessor to remain outside the selection, manufacture and supply of the goods; that is the rationale for releasing the lessor from most of its traditional liability. The lessor is not prohibited from possession, maintenance or operation of the goods, as policy does not require such prohibition. To insure the lessee's reliance on the supplier, and not on the lessor, subsection (ii) requires that the goods (where the lessor is the buyer of the goods) or that the right to possession and use of the goods (where the lessor is the prime lessee and the sublessor of the goods) be acquired in connection with the lease (or sublease) to qualify as a finance lease. The scope of the phrase "in connection with" is to be developed by the courts, case by case. Finally, as the lessee generally relies almost entirely upon the supplier for representations and covenants, and upon the supplier or a manufacturer, or both, for warranties with respect to the goods, subsection (iii) requires that one of the following occur: (A) the lessee receive a copy of the supply contract before signing the lease contract; (B) the lessee's approval of the supply contract is a condition to the effectiveness of the lease contract; (C) the lessee receive a statement describing the promises and warranties and any limitations relevant to the lessee before signing the lease contract; or (D) before signing the lease contract and except in a consumer lease, the lessee receive a writing identifying the supplier (unless the supplier was selected and required by the lessee) and the rights of the lessee under Section 2A–209, and advising the lessee a statement of promises and warranties is available from the supplier. Thus, even where oral supply orders or computer placed supply orders are compelled by custom and usage the transaction may still qualify as a finance lease if the lessee approves the supply contract before the lease contract is effective and such approval was a condition to the effectiveness of the lease contract. Moreover, where the lessor does not want the lessee to see the entire supply contract, including price information, the lessee may be provided with a separate statement of the terms of the supply contract relevant to the lessee; promises between the supplier and the lessor that do not affect the lessee need not be included. The statement can be a restatement of those terms or a copy of portions of the supply contract with the relevant terms clearly designated. Any implied warranties need not be designated, but a disclaimer or modification of remedy must be designated. A copy of any manufacturer's warranty is sufficient if that is the warranty provided. However, a copy of any Regulation M disclosure given pursuant to 12 C.F.R. § 213.4(g) concerning warranties in itself is not sufficient since those disclosures need only briefly identify express warranties and need not include any disclaimer of warranty.

If a transaction does not qualify as a finance lease, the parties may achieve the same result by agreement; no negative implications are to be drawn if the transaction does not qualify. Further, absent the application of special rules (fraud, duress, and the like), a lease that qualifies as a finance lease and is assigned by the lessor or the lessee to a third party does not lose its status as a finance lease under this Article. Finally, this Article creates no special rule where the lessor is an affiliate of the supplier; whether the transaction qualifies as a finance lease will be determined by the facts of each case.

Pursuant to the Uniform Commercial Code Amendments (2022) (2022 Amendments), some references in this Article to the terms "writing," "writings," or "written" have been changed to refer to a "record." These changes are made in provisions where an affected party may be assumed to have assented to the use of a record that is not a writing. For example, Section 2A–201 involves a record signed by an affected party and Section 2A–202 refers to a record intended by parties to be a final expression of their agreement. Where such references remain in this Article, the use by parties of a record other than a writing may be given effect for purposes of this Article under law other than the Uniform Commercial Code, such as the Electronic Signatures in Global and National Commerce Act, 15 U.S.C. Section 7001 *et seq.*, and the Uniform Electronic Transactions Act.

(h)   "Goods". Section 9–102(a)(44). See Section 2A–103(3) for reference to the definition of "Account", "Chattel paper", "Document", "General intangibles" and "Instrument". See Section 2A–217 for determination of the time and manner of identification.

(h.1) "Hybrid lease". In some transactions, the transfer of the right to possession and use of goods for a term in return for consideration (i.e., a lease), is part of a larger transaction. The other aspects of the transaction might involve the provision of services, a sale of other goods, or a transfer of rights to property other than goods. Such a transaction is a hybrid lease. Section 2A–102 indicates the extent to which this Article applies to a hybrid lease.

A hybrid lease is a single transaction. If contracting parties enter into separate agreements at the same time, each agreement must be evaluated separately to determine if it is a hybrid lease.

Example 1. Lessor and Customer A enter into a single agreement that provides for Lessor, in return for periodic payments from Customer A, to: (i) lease a photocopier to Customer A for twelve months; (ii) supply all the paper, staples, and toner needed to operate the copier during that period, and (iii) provide routine maintenance and repair services needed to keep the copier operating during that period. The transaction is a hybrid lease because it involves a lease of goods (the copier), a sale of goods (the paper, staples, and toner), and the provision of services.

Example 2. Lessor and Customer B enter into three separate written agreements at the same time: (i) a lease of a photocopier to Customer B for twelve months; (ii) a contract for Lessor to supply Customer B with all the paper, staples, and toner needed to operate the copier during that period, and (iii) a contract for Lessor to provide routine maintenance and repair services needed to keep the copier operating during that period. Because the parties executed three separate agreements, and the lease does not involve a sale, lease, or license of other property or the provision of services, the lease is not a hybrid lease.

Even when contracting parties enter into a single agreement involving both a lease of goods and a sale, lease, or license of other property or the provision of services, the agreement may involve separate transactions and not a single transaction. In that situation, the lease transaction would not be a hybrid lease if the lease of goods is unrelated to the other aspects of the agreement and the terms of the agreement relating to the lease of goods are readily severable from the terms of the agreement relating to the other transactions.

Example 3. Farmer A and Farmer B sign a written agreement pursuant to which Farmer A will lease a tractor to Farmer B for one year and Farmer B will board and feed Farmer A's cattle until the cattle are sold. The agreement specifies a rental payment for the tractor, which is due monthly, and a mechanism for determining the price for Farmer B's services, which is to be paid when the cattle are sold. The parties would have entered into an agreement to lease the tractor even if they had not entered into an agreement to board and feed the cattle, and vice versa. The transaction is not a hybrid lease. Article 2A applies to the lease of the tractor. Other law applies to the agreement to board and feed the cattle.

(i) "Installment lease contract". Section 2–612(1).

(j) "Lease". New. There are several reasons to codify the law with respect to leases of goods. An analysis of the case law as it applies to leases of goods suggests at least several significant issues to be resolved by codification. First and foremost is the definition of a lease. It is necessary to define lease to determine whether a transaction creates a lease or a security interest disguised as a lease. If the transaction creates a security interest disguised as a lease, the transaction will be governed by the Article on Secured Transactions (Article 9) and the lessor will be required to file a financing statement or take other action to perfect its interest in the goods against third parties. There is no such requirement with respect to leases under the common law and, except with respect to leases of fixtures (Section 2A–309), this Article imposes no such requirement. Yet the distinction between a lease and a security interest disguised as a lease is not clear from the case law at the time of the promulgation of this Article. DeKoven, *Leases of Equipment: Puritan Leasing Company v. August, A Dangerous Decision,* 12 U.S.F. L.Rev. 257 (1978).

At common law a lease of personal property is a bailment for hire. While there are several definitions of bailment for hire, all require a thing to be let and a price for the letting. Thus, in modern terms and as provided in this definition, a lease is created when the lessee agrees to furnish consideration for the right to the possession and use of goods over a specified period of time. Mooney, *Personal Property Leasing: A Challenge,* 36 Bus.Law. 1605, 1607 (1981). Further, a lease is neither a sale (Section 2–106(1)) nor a retention or creation of a security interest (Sections 1–201(b)(35) and 1–203). Due to extensive litigation to distinguish true leases from security interests, an amendment to former Section 1–201(37) (now codified as Section 1–203) was promulgated with this Article to create a sharper distinction.

This section as well as Section 1–203 must be examined to determine whether the transaction in question creates a lease or a security interest. The following hypotheticals indicate the perimeters of the issue. Assume that A has purchased a number of copying machines, new, for $1,000 each; the machines have an estimated useful economic life of three years. A advertises that the machines are available to rent for a minimum of one month and that the monthly rental is $100.00. A intends to enter into leases where A provides all maintenance, without charge to the lessee. Further, the lessee will rent the machine, month to month, with no obligation to renew. At the end of the lease term the lessee will be obligated to return the machine to A's place of business. This transaction qualifies as a lease under the first half of the definition, for the transaction includes a transfer by A to a prospective lessee of possession and use of the machine for a stated term, month to month. The machines are goods (Section 2A–103(1)(h)). The lessee is obligated to pay consideration in return, $100.00 for each month of the term.

However, the second half of the definition provides that a sale or a security interest is not a lease. Since there is no passing of title, there is no sale. Sections 2A–103(3) and 2–106(1). Under pre-Act security law this transaction would have created a bailment for hire or a true lease and not a conditional sale. *Da Rocha v. Macomber,* 330 Mass. 611, 614–15, 116 N.E.2d 139, 142 (1953). Under Section 1–203, the same result would follow. While the lessee is obligated to pay rent for the one month term of the lease, one of the other four conditions of Section 1–203(b) must be met and none is. The term of the lease is one month and the economic life of the machine is 36 months; thus, Section 1–203(b)(1) is not now satisfied. Considering the amount of the monthly rent, absent economic duress or coercion, the lessee is not bound either to renew the lease for the remaining economic life of the goods or to become the owner. If the lessee did lease the machine for 36 months, the lessee would have paid the lessor $3,600 for a machine that could have been purchased for $1,000; thus, Section 1–203(b)(2) is not satisfied. Finally, there are no options; thus, subparagraphs (3) and (4) of 1–203(b) are not satisfied. This transaction creates a lease, not a security interest. However, with each renewal of the lease the facts and circumstances at the time of each renewal must be examined to determine if that conclusion remains accurate, as it is possible that a transaction that first creates a lease, later creates a security interest.

Assume that the facts are changed and that A requires each lessee to lease the goods for 36 months, with no right to terminate. Under pre-Act security law this transaction would have created a conditional sale, and not a bailment for hire or true lease. *Hervey v. Rhode Island Locomotive Works*, 93 U.S. 664, 672–73 (1876). Under this subsection, and Section 1–203, the same result would follow. The lessee's obligation for the term is not subject to termination by the lessee and the term is equal to the economic life of the machine.

Between these extremes there are many transactions that can be created. Some of the transactions were not properly categorized by the courts in applying the 1978 and earlier Official Texts of former Section 1–201(37). This subsection, together with Section 1–203, draws a brighter line, which should create a clearer signal to the professional lessor and lessee.

(k) "Lease agreement". This definition is derived from Section 1–201(b)(3). Because the definition of lease is broad enough to cover future transfers, lease agreement includes an agreement contemplating a current or subsequent transfer. Thus it was not necessary to make an express reference to an agreement for the future lease of goods (Section 2–106(1)). This concept is also incorporated in the definition of lease contract. Note that the definition of lease does not include transactions in ordinary building materials that are incorporated into an improvement on land. Section 2A–309(2).

The provisions of this Article, if applicable, determine whether a lease agreement has legal consequences; otherwise the law of bailments and other applicable law determine the same. Sections 2A–103(4) and 1–103.

(*l*) "Lease contract". This definition is derived from the definition of contract in Section 1–201(b)(12). Note that a lease contract may be for the future lease of goods, since this notion is included in the definition of lease.

(m) "Leasehold interest". New.

(n) "Lessee". New.

(*o*) "Lessee in ordinary course of business". Section 1–201(b)(9).

(p) "Lessor". New.

(q) "Lessor's residual interest". New.

(r) "Lien". New. This term is used in Section 2A–307 (Priority of Liens Arising by Attachment or Levy on, Security Interests in, and Other Claims to Goods).

(s) "Lot". Section 2–105(5).

(t) "Merchant lessee". New. This term is used in Section 2A–511 (Merchant Lessee's Duties as to Rightfully Rejected Goods). A person may satisfy the requirement of dealing in goods of the kind subject to the lease as lessor, lessee, seller, or buyer.

[(u) "Present value". New. Authorities agree that present value should be used to determine fairly the damages payable by the lessor or the lessee on default. *E.g.*, *Taylor v. Commercial Credit Equip. Corp.*, 170 Ga.App. 322, 316 S.E.2d 788 (1984). Present value is defined to mean an amount that represents the discounted value as of a date certain of one or more sums payable in the future. This is a function of the economic principle that a dollar today is more valuable to the holder than a dollar payable in two years. While there is no question as to the principle, reasonable people would differ as to the rate of discount to apply in determining the value of that future dollar today. To minimize litigation, this Article allows the parties to specify the discount or interest rate, if the rate was not manifestly unreasonable at the time the transaction was entered into. In all other cases, the interest rate will be a commercially reasonable rate that takes into account the facts and circumstances of each case, as of the time the transaction was entered into.] [*Note from West Advisory Panel: Revised Article 1 (2001) adds a definition of "present value" in § 1–201(b)(28). The conforming amendments to Article 2A delete this comment, but erroneously do not delete the definition itself.*]

(v) "Purchase". Section 1–201(b)(29). This definition omits the reference to lien contained in the definition of purchase in Article 1 (Section 1–201(b)(29)). This should not be construed to exclude consensual liens from the definition of purchase in this Article; the exclusion was mandated by the scope of the definition of lien in Section 2A–103(1)(r). Further, the definition of purchaser in this Article adds a reference to lease; as purchase is defined in Section 1–201(b)(29) to include any other voluntary transaction creating an interest in property, this addition is not substantive.

(w)   "Sublease". New.

(x)   "Supplier". New.

(y)   "Supply contract". New.

(z)   "Termination". Section 2–106(3). The effect of a termination is provided in Section 2A–505(2).

As amended in 1999, 2001, and 2022.

§ 2A–104.   Leases Subject to Other Law.

(1)   A lease, although subject to this Article, is also subject to any applicable:

(a)   certificate of title statute of this State: (list any certificate of title statutes covering automobiles, trailers, mobile homes, boats, farm tractors, and the like);

(b)   certificate of title statute of another jurisdiction (Section 2A–105); or

(c)   consumer protection statute of this State, or final consumer protection decision of a court of this State existing on the effective date of this Article.

(2)   In case of conflict between this Article, other than Sections 2A–105, 2A–304(3), and 2A–305(3), and a statute or decision referred to in subsection (1), the statute or decision controls.

(3)   Failure to comply with an applicable law has only the effect specified therein.

As amended in 1990.

Official Comment

Uniform Statutory Source: Former Sections 9–203(4) and 9–302(3)(b) and (c) (now codified as Sections 9–201 and 9–311(a)(2) and (3)).

Changes: Substantially revised.

Purposes:

1.   This Article creates a comprehensive scheme for the regulation of transactions that create leases. Section 2A–102. Thus, the Article supersedes all prior legislation dealing with leases, except to the extent set forth in this Section.

2.   Subsection (1) states the general rule that a lease, although governed by the scheme of this Article, also may be governed by certain other applicable laws. This may occur in the case of a consumer lease. Section 2A–103(1)(e). Those laws may be state statutes existing prior to enactment of Article 2A or passed afterward. In this case, it is desirable for this Article to specify which statute controls. Or the law may be a pre-existing consumer protection decision. This Article preserves such decisions. Or the law may be a statute of the United States. Such a law controls without any statement in this Article under applicable principles of preemption.

An illustration of a statute of the United States that governs consumer leases is the Consumer Leasing Act, 15 U.S.C. §§ 1667–1667(e) (1982) and its implementing regulation, Regulation M, 12 C.F.R. § 213 (1986); the statute mandates disclosures of certain lease terms, delimits the liability of a lessee in leasing personal property, and regulates the advertising of lease terms. An illustration of a state statute that governs consumer leases and which if adopted in the enacting state prevails over this Article is the Unif. Consumer Credit Code, which includes many provisions similar to those of the Consumer Leasing Act, e.g. Unif. Consumer Credit Code §§ 3.202, 3.209, 3.401, 7A U.L.A. 108–09, 115, 125 (1974), as well as provisions in addition to those of the Consumer Leasing Act, e.g., Unif. Consumer Credit Code §§ 5.109–.111, 7A U.L.A. 171–76 (1974) (the right to cure a default). Such statutes may define consumer lease so as to govern transactions within and without the definition of consumer lease under this Article.

3.   Under subsection (2), subject to certain limited exclusions, in case of conflict a statute or a decision described in subsection (1) prevails over this Article. For example, a provision like Unif. Consumer Credit Code § 5.112, 7A U.L.A. 176 (1974), limiting self-help repossession, prevails over Section 2A–525(3). A consumer

protection decision rendered after the effective date of this Article may supplement its provisions. For example, in relation to Article 9 a court might conclude that an acceleration clause may not be enforced against an individual debtor after late payments have been accepted unless a prior notice of default is given. To the extent the decision establishes a general principle applicable to transactions other than secured transactions, it may supplement Section 2A–502.

4.   Consumer protection in lease transactions is primarily left to other law. However, several provisions of this Article do contain special rules that may not be varied by agreement in the case of a consumer lease. *E.g.*, Sections 2A–106, 2A–108, and 2A–109(2). Were that not so, the ability of the parties to govern their relationship by agreement together with the position of the lessor in a consumer lease too often could result in a one-sided lease agreement.

5.   In construing this provision the reference to statute should be deemed to include applicable regulations. A consumer protection decision is "final" on the effective date of this Article if it is not subject to appeal on that date or, if subject to appeal, is not later reversed on appeal. Of course, such a decision can be overruled by a later decision or superseded by a later statute.

Cross References:

Sections 2A–103(1)(e), 2A–106, 2A–108, 2A–109(2) and 2A–525(3).

Definitional Cross Reference:

"Lease". Section 2A–103(1)(j).

§ 2A–105.   Territorial Application of Article to Goods Covered by Certificate of Title.

Subject to the provisions of Sections 2A–304(3) and 2A–305(3), with respect to goods covered by a certificate of title issued under a statute of this State or of another jurisdiction, compliance and the effect of compliance or noncompliance with a certificate of title statute are governed by the law (including the conflict of laws rules) of the jurisdiction issuing the certificate until the earlier of (a) surrender of the certificate, or (b) four months after the goods are removed from that jurisdiction and thereafter until a new certificate of title is issued by another jurisdiction.

Official Comment

Uniform Statutory Source: Former Section 9–103(2)(a) and (b) (now codified as Sections 9–303 and 9–316).

Changes: Substantially revised. The provisions of the last sentence of former Section 9–103(2)(b) were not incorporated as they are superfluous in this context. The provisions of former Section 9–103(2)(d) were not incorporated because the problems dealt with are adequately addressed by this section and Sections 2A–304(3) and 305(3).

Purposes: The new certificate referred to in (b) must be permanent, not temporary. Generally, the lessor or creditor whose interest is indicated on the most recently issued certificate of title will prevail over interests indicated on certificates issued previously by other jurisdictions. This provision reflects a policy that it is reasonable to require holders of interests in goods covered by a certificate of title to police the goods or risk losing their interests when a new certificate of title is issued by another jurisdiction.

Cross References:

Sections 2A–304(3) and 2A–305(3); former Sections 9–103(2)(b) and 9–103(2)(d) (now codified as Sections 9–303, 9–316, and 9–337).

Definitional Cross Reference:

"Goods". Section 2A–103(1)(h).

§ 2A–106.   Limitation on Power of Parties to Consumer Lease to Choose Applicable Law and Judicial Forum.

(1)   If the law chosen by the parties to a consumer lease is that of a jurisdiction other than a jurisdiction in which the lessee resides at the time the lease agreement becomes enforceable or within 30 days thereafter or in which the goods are to be used, the choice is not enforceable.

(2)   If the judicial forum chosen by the parties to a consumer lease is a forum that would not otherwise have jurisdiction over the lessee, the choice is not enforceable.

Official Comment

Uniform Statutory Source: Unif. Consumer Credit Code § 1.201(8), 7A U.L.A. 36 (1974).

Changes: Substantially revised.

Purposes: There is a real danger that a lessor may induce a consumer lessee to agree that the applicable law will be a jurisdiction that has little effective consumer protection, or to agree that the applicable forum will be a forum that is inconvenient for the lessee in the event of litigation. As a result, this section invalidates these choice of law or forum clauses, except where the law chosen is that of the state of the consumer's residence or where the goods will be kept, or the forum chosen is one that otherwise would have jurisdiction over the lessee.

Subsection (1) limits potentially abusive choice of law clauses in consumer leases. The 30-day rule in subsection (1) was suggested by former Section 9–103(1)(c). This section has no effect on choice of law clauses in leases that are not consumer leases. Such clauses would be governed by other law.

Subsection (2) prevents enforcement of potentially abusive jurisdictional consent clauses in consumer leases. By using the term judicial forum, this section does not limit selection of a nonjudicial forum, such as arbitration. This section has no effect on choice of forum clauses in leases that are not consumer leases; such clauses are, as a matter of current law, "prima facie valid". *The Bremen v. Zapata Off-Shore Co.*, 407 U.S. 1, 10 (1972). Such clauses would be governed by other law, including the Model Choice of Forum Act (1968).

Cross Reference:

Former Section 9–103(1)(c).

Definitional Cross References:

"Consumer lease". Section 2A–103(1)(e).
"Lease agreement". Section 2A–103(1)(k).
"Lessee". Section 2A–103(1)(n).
"Goods". Section 2A–103(1)(h).
"Party". Section 1–201(29) [*unrevised Article 1; see Concordance, p. 22*].

§ 2A–107. Waiver or Renunciation of Claim or Right After Default.

Any claim or right arising out of an alleged default or breach of warranty may be discharged in whole or in part without consideration by a ~~written~~ waiver or renunciation in a signed ~~and~~ record delivered by the aggrieved party.

As amended in 2022.

Official Comment

Uniform Statutory Source: Section 1–107 [*unrevised Article 1; see Concordance, p. 22*].

Changes:

1.   Revised to reflect leasing practices and terminology. This clause is used throughout the official comments to this Article to indicate the scope of change in the provisions of the Uniform Statutory Source included in the section; these changes range from one extreme, *e.g.*, a significant difference in practice (a warranty as to merchantability is not implied in a finance lease (Section 2A–212)) to the other extreme, *e.g.*, a modest difference in style or terminology (the transaction governed is a lease not a sale (Section 2A–2032A–103) [Previous incorrect cross reference corrected by Permanent Editorial Board action November 1992]).

2.   In furtherance of medium neutrality, the reference to a signed "written" waiver or renunciation in the pre-2022 text of this section has been changed to refer to a waiver in a signed "record."

Cross References:

Sections 2A–103 and 2A–212.

Definitional Cross References:

"Aggrieved party". Section 1–201(2) [*unrevised Article 1; see Concordance, p. 22*].

"Delivery". Section 1–201(14) [*unrevised Article 1; see Concordance, p. 22*].
"Rights". Section 1–201(36) [*unrevised Article 1; see Concordance, p. 22*].
"Signed". Section 1–201(39) [*unrevised Article 1; see Concordance, p. 22*].
"Written". Section 1–201(46) [*unrevised Article 1; see Concordance, p. 22*].

As amended in 2022.

§ 2A–108. Unconscionability.

(1)   If the court as a matter of law finds a lease contract or any clause of a lease contract to have been unconscionable at the time it was made the court may refuse to enforce the lease contract, or it may enforce the remainder of the lease contract without the unconscionable clause, or it may so limit the application of any unconscionable clause as to avoid any unconscionable result.

(2)   With respect to a consumer lease, if the court as a matter of law finds that a lease contract or any clause of a lease contract has been induced by unconscionable conduct or that unconscionable conduct has occurred in the collection of a claim arising from a lease contract, the court may grant appropriate relief.

(3)   Before making a finding of unconscionability under subsection (1) or (2), the court, on its own motion or that of a party, shall afford the parties a reasonable opportunity to present evidence as to the setting, purpose, and effect of the lease contract or clause thereof, or of the conduct.

(4)   In an action in which the lessee claims unconscionability with respect to a consumer lease:

(a)   If the court finds unconscionability under subsection (1) or (2), the court shall award reasonable attorney's fees to the lessee.

(b)   If the court does not find unconscionability and the lessee claiming unconscionability has brought or maintained an action he [or she] knew to be groundless, the court shall award reasonable attorney's fees to the party against whom the claim is made.

(c)   In determining attorney's fees, the amount of the recovery on behalf of the claimant under subsections (1) and (2) is not controlling.

Official Comment

Uniform Statutory Source: Section 2–302 and Unif. Consumer Credit Code § 5.108, 7A U.L.A. 167–69 (1974).

Changes: Subsection (1) is taken almost verbatim from the provisions of Section 2–302(1). Subsection (2) is suggested by the provisions of Unif. Consumer Credit Code § 5.108(1), (2), 7A U.L.A. 167 (1974). Subsection (3), taken from the provisions of Section 2–302(2), has been expanded to cover unconscionable conduct. Unif. Consumer Credit Code § 5.108(3), 7A U.L.A. 167 (1974). The provision for the award of attorney's fees to consumers, subsection (4), covers unconscionability under subsection (1) as well as (2). Subsection (4) is modeled on the provisions of Unif. Consumer Credit Code § 5.108(6), 7A U.L.A. 169 (1974).

Purposes: Subsections (1) and (3) of this section apply the concept of unconscionability reflected in the provisions of Section 2–302 to leases. *See Dillman & Assocs. v. Capitol Leasing Co.*, 110 Ill.App.3d 335, 342, 442 N.E.2d 311, 316 (App.Ct. 1982). Subsection (3) omits the adjective "commercial" found in subsection 2–302(2) because subsection (3) is concerned with all leases and the relevant standard of conduct is determined by the context.

The balance of the section is modeled on the provisions of Unif. Consumer Credit Code § 5.108, 7A U.L.A. 167–69 (1974). Thus subsection (2) recognizes that a consumer lease or a clause in a consumer lease may not itself be unconscionable but that the agreement would never have been entered into if unconscionable means had not been employed to induce the consumer to agree. To make a statement to induce the consumer to lease the goods, in the expectation of invoking an integration clause in the lease to exclude the statement's admissibility in a subsequent dispute, may be unconscionable. Subsection (2) also provides a consumer remedy for unconscionable conduct, such as using or threatening to use force or violence, in the collection of a claim arising from a lease contract. These provisions are not exclusive. The remedies of this section are in addition to remedies otherwise available for the same conduct under other law, for example, an action in tort for abusive debt collection or under another statute of this State for such conduct. The reference to appropriate relief in subsection (2) is intended to foster liberal administration of this remedy. Sections 2A–103(4) and 1–106(1) [*unrevised Article 1; see Concordance, p. 22*].

Subsection (4) authorizes an award of reasonable attorney's fees if the court finds unconscionability with respect to a consumer lease under subsection (1) or (2). Provision is also made for recovery by the party against whom the claim was made if the court does not find unconscionability and does find that the consumer knew the action to be groundless. Further, subsection (4)(b) is independent of, and thus will not override, a term in the lease agreement that provides for the payment of attorney's fees.

Cross References:

Sections 1–106(1) [*unrevised Article 1; see Concordance, p. 22*], 2–302 and 2A–103(4).

Definitional Cross References:

"Action". Section 1–201(1) [*unrevised Article 1; see Concordance, p. 22*].
"Consumer lease". Section 2A–103(1)(e).
"Lease contract". Section 2A–103(1)(*l*).
"Lessee". Section 2A–103(1)(n).
"Party". Section 1–201(29) [*unrevised Article 1; see Concordance, p. 22*].

§ 2A–109.　Option to Accelerate at Will.

(1)　A term providing that one party or his [or her] successor in interest may accelerate payment or performance or require collateral or additional collateral "at will" or "when he [or she] deems himself [or herself] insecure" or in words of similar import must be construed to mean that he [or she] has power to do so only if he [or she] in good faith believes that the prospect of payment or performance is impaired.

(2)　With respect to a consumer lease, the burden of establishing good faith under subsection (1) is on the party who exercised the power; otherwise the burden of establishing lack of good faith is on the party against whom the power has been exercised.

Official Comment

Uniform Statutory Source: Section 1–208 [*unrevised Article 1; see Concordance, p. 22*] and Unif. Consumer Credit Code § 5.109(2), 7A U.L.A. 171 (1974).

Purposes: Subsection (1) reflects modest changes in style to the provisions of the first sentence of Section 1–208 [*unrevised Article 1; see Concordance, p. 22*].

Subsection (2), however, reflects a significant change in the provisions of the second sentence of Section 1–208 [*unrevised Article 1; see Concordance, p. 22*] by creating a new rule with respect to a consumer lease. A lease provision allowing acceleration at the will of the lessor or when the lessor deems itself insecure is of critical importance to the lessee. In a consumer lease it is a provision that is not usually agreed to by the parties but is usually mandated by the lessor. Therefore, where its invocation depends not on specific criteria but on the discretion of the lessor, its use should be regulated to prevent abuse. Subsection (1) imposes a duty of good faith upon its exercise. Subsection (2) shifts the burden of establishing good faith to the lessor in the case of a consumer lease, but not otherwise.

Cross Reference:

Section 1–208 [*unrevised Article 1; see Concordance, p. 22*].

Definitional Cross References:

"Burden of establishing". Section 1–201(8) [*unrevised Article 1; see Concordance, p. 22*].
"Consumer lease". Section 2A–103(1)(e).
"Good faith". Sections 1–201(19) [*unrevised Article 1; see Concordance, p. 22*] and 2–103(1)(b).
"Party". Section 1–201(29) [*unrevised Article 1; see Concordance, p. 22*].
"Term". Section 1–201(42) [*unrevised Article 1; see Concordance, p. 22*].

PART 2

FORMATION AND CONSTRUCTION
OF LEASE CONTRACT

§ 2A–201. Statute of Frauds.

(1) A lease contract is not enforceable by way of action or defense unless:

(a) the total payments to be made under the lease contract, excluding payments for options to renew or buy, are less than $1,000; or

(b) there is a ~~writing~~ record, signed by the party against whom enforcement is sought or by that party's authorized agent, sufficient to indicate that a lease contract has been made between the parties and to describe the goods leased and the lease term.

(2) Any description of leased goods or of the lease term is sufficient and satisfies subsection (1)(b), whether or not it is specific, if it reasonably identifies what is described.

(3) A ~~writing~~ record is not insufficient because it omits or incorrectly states a term agreed upon, but the lease contract is not enforceable under subsection (1)(b) beyond the lease term and the quantity of goods shown in the ~~writing~~ record.

(4) A lease contract that does not satisfy the requirements of subsection (1), but which is valid in other respects, is enforceable:

(a) if the goods are to be specially manufactured or obtained for the lessee and are not suitable for lease or sale to others in the ordinary course of the lessor's business, and the lessor, before notice of repudiation is received and under circumstances that reasonably indicate that the goods are for the lessee, has made either a substantial beginning of their manufacture or commitments for their procurement;

(b) if the party against whom enforcement is sought admits in that party's pleading, testimony or otherwise in court that a lease contract was made, but the lease contract is not enforceable under this provision beyond the quantity of goods admitted; or

(c) with respect to goods that have been received and accepted by the lessee.

(5) The lease term under a lease contract referred to in subsection (4) is:

(a) if there is a ~~writing~~ record signed by the party against whom enforcement is sought or by that party's authorized agent specifying the lease term, the term so specified;

(b) if the party against whom enforcement is sought admits in that party's pleading, testimony, or otherwise in court a lease term, the term so admitted; or

(c) a reasonable lease term.

As amended in 2022.

Official Comment

Uniform Statutory Source: Section 2–201; former Sections 9–203(1) and 9–110 (now codified as Sections 9–203(b) and 9–108).

Changes:

1. This section is modeled on Section 2–201, with changes to reflect the differences between a lease contract and a contract for the sale of goods. In particular, subsection (1)(b) adds a requirement that the ~~writing~~ record "describe the goods leased and the lease term", borrowing that concept, with revisions, from the provisions of former Section 9–203(1)(a) (now codified as Section 9–203(b)(3)(A)). Subsection (2), relying on the statutory analogue in former Section 9–110 (now codified as Section 9–108), sets forth the minimum criterion for satisfying that requirement.

2. In furtherance of medium neutrality, the references to a "writing" in the pre-2022 text of this section have been changed to refer to a "record."

Purposes: The changes in this section conform the provisions of Section 2–201 to custom and usage in lease transactions. Section 2–201(2), stating a special rule between merchants, was not included in this section as the number of such transactions involving leases, as opposed to sales, was thought to be modest. Subsection (4) creates no exception for transactions where payment has been made and accepted. This represents a departure from the analogue, Section 2–201(3)(c). The rationale for the departure is grounded in the distinction between sales and leases. Unlike a buyer in a sales transaction, the lessee does not tender payment in full for goods delivered, but only payment of rent for one or more months. It was decided that, as a matter of policy, this act of payment is not a sufficient substitute for the required memorandum. Subsection (5) was needed to establish the criteria for supplying the lease term if it is omitted, as the lease contract may still be enforceable under subsection (4).

Cross References:

Sections 2–201, 9–108 and 9–203(b)(3)(A).

Definitional Cross References:

"Action". Section 1–201(1) [*unrevised Article 1; see Concordance, p. 22*].
"Agreed". Section 1–201(3) [*unrevised Article 1; see Concordance, p. 22*].
"Buying". Section 2A–103(1)(a).
"Goods". Section 2A–103(1)(h).
"Lease". Section 2A–103(1)(j).
"Lease contract". Section 2A–103(1)(*l*).
"Lessee". Section 2A–103(1)(n).
"Lessor". Section 2A–103(1)(p).
"Notice". Section 1–201(25) [*unrevised Article 1; see Concordance, p. 22*].
"Party". Section 1–201(29) [*unrevised Article 1; see Concordance, p. 22*].
"Sale". Section 2–106(1).
"Signed". Section 1–201(39) [*unrevised Article 1; see Concordance, p. 22*].
"Term". Section 1–201(42) [*unrevised Article 1; see Concordance, p. 22*].
"Writing". Section 1–201(46) [*unrevised Article 1; see Concordance, p. 22*].

As amended in 2022.

§ 2A–202. Final ~~Written~~ Expression: Parol or Extrinsic Evidence.

Terms with respect to which the confirmatory memoranda of the parties agree or which are otherwise set forth in a ~~writing~~ record intended by the parties as a final expression of their agreement with respect to such terms as are included therein may not be contradicted by evidence of any prior agreement or of a contemporaneous oral agreement but may be explained or supplemented:

(a)   by course of dealing or usage of trade or by course of performance; and

(b)   by evidence of consistent additional terms unless the court finds the ~~writing~~ record to have been intended also as a complete and exclusive statement of the terms of the agreement.

As amended in 2022.

Official Comment

Changes: In furtherance of medium neutrality, the references to a "writing" have been changed to refer to a "record."

Uniform Statutory Source: Section 2–202.

Definitional Cross References:

"Agreement". Section 1–201(3) [*unrevised Article 1; see Concordance, p. 22*].
"Course of dealing". Section 1–205 [*unrevised Article 1; see Concordance, p. 22*].
"Party". Section 1–201(29) [*unrevised Article 1; see Concordance, p. 22*].
"Term". Section 1–201(42) [*unrevised Article 1; see Concordance, p. 22*].
"Usage of trade". Section 1–205 [*unrevised Article 1; see Concordance, p. 22*].
"Writing". Section 1–201(46) [*unrevised Article 1; see Concordance, p. 22*].

As amended in 2022.

§ 2A–203.   Seals Inoperative.

The affixing of a seal to a ~~writing~~ record evidencing a lease contract or an offer to enter into a lease contract does not render the ~~writing~~ record a sealed instrument and the law with respect to sealed instruments does not apply to the lease contract or offer.

As amended in 2022.

Official Comment

Uniform Statutory Source: Section 2–203.

Changes: Revised to reflect leasing practices and terminology. In furtherance of medium neutrality, the references to a "writing" have been changed to refer to a "record."

Definitional Cross References:

"Lease contract". Section 2A–103(1)(*l*).
"Writing". Section 1–201(46) [*unrevised Article 1; see Concordance, p. 22*].

As amended in 2022.

§ 2A–204.   Formation in General.

(1)   A lease contract may be made in any manner sufficient to show agreement, including conduct by both parties which recognizes the existence of a lease contract.

(2)   An agreement sufficient to constitute a lease contract may be found although the moment of its making is undetermined.

(3)   Although one or more terms are left open, a lease contract does not fail for indefiniteness if the parties have intended to make a lease contract and there is a reasonably certain basis for giving an appropriate remedy.

Official Comment

Uniform Statutory Source: Section 2–204.

Changes: Revised to reflect leasing practices and terminology.

Definitional Cross References:

"Agreement". Section 1–201(3) [*unrevised Article 1; see Concordance, p. 22*].
"Lease contract". Section 2A–103(1)(*l*).
"Party". Section 1–201(29) [*unrevised Article 1; see Concordance, p. 22*].
"Remedy". Section 1–201(34) [*unrevised Article 1; see Concordance, p. 22*].
"Term". Section 1–201(42) [*unrevised Article 1; see Concordance, p. 22*].

§ 2A–205.   Firm Offers.

An offer by a merchant to lease goods to or from another person in a signed ~~writing~~ record that by its terms gives assurance it will be held open is not revocable, for lack of consideration, during the time stated or, if no time is stated, for a reasonable time, but in no event may the period of irrevocability exceed 3 months. Any such term of assurance on a form supplied by the offeree must be separately signed by the offeror.

As amended in 2022.

Official Comment

Uniform Statutory Source: Section 2–205.

Changes: Revised to reflect leasing practices and terminology. In furtherance of medium neutrality, the reference to a signed "writing" in the pre-2022 text of this section has been changed to refer to a signed "record."

Definitional Cross References:

"Goods". Section 2A–103(1)(h).

"Lease". Section 2A–103(1)(j).

"Merchant". Section 2–104(1).

"Person". Section 1–201(30) [*unrevised Article 1; see Concordance, p. 22*].

"Reasonable time". Section 1–204(1) and (2) [*unrevised Article 1; see Concordance, p. 22*].

"Signed". Section 1–201(39) [*unrevised Article 1; see Concordance, p. 22*].

"Term". Section 1–201(42) [*unrevised Article 1; see Concordance, p. 22*].

"Writing". Section 1–201(46) [*unrevised Article 1; see Concordance, p. 22*].

As amended in 2022.

§ 2A–206. Offer and Acceptance in Formation of Lease Contract.

(1)   Unless otherwise unambiguously indicated by the language or circumstances, an offer to make a lease contract must be construed as inviting acceptance in any manner and by any medium reasonable in the circumstances.

(2)   If the beginning of a requested performance is a reasonable mode of acceptance, an offeror who is not notified of acceptance within a reasonable time may treat the offer as having lapsed before acceptance.

Official Comment

Uniform Statutory Source: Section 2–206(1)(a) and (2).

Changes: Revised to reflect leasing practices and terminology.

Definitional Cross References:

"Lease contract". Section 2A–103(1)(*l*).

"Notifies". Section 1–201(26).

"Reasonable time". Section 1–204(1) and (2) [*unrevised Article 1; see Concordance, p. 22*].

§ 2A–207. [Reserved.] [Course of Performance or Practical Construction.] [*Note from West Advisory Panel: This section will be repealed if the jurisdiction adopts revised Article 1.*]

[(1)   If a lease contract involves repeated occasions for performance by either party with knowledge of the nature of the performance and opportunity for objection to it by the other, any course of performance accepted or acquiesced in without objection is relevant to determine the meaning of the lease agreement.

(2)   The express terms of a lease agreement and any course of performance, as well as any course of dealing and usage of trade, must be construed whenever reasonable as consistent with each other; but if that construction is unreasonable, express terms control course of performance, course of performance controls both course of dealing and usage of trade, and course of dealing controls usage of trade.

(3)   Subject to the provisions of Section 2A–208 on modification and waiver, course of performance is relevant to show a waiver or modification of any term inconsistent with the course of performance.

Official Comment

Uniform Statutory Source: Sections 2–208 and 1–205(4) [*unrevised Article 1; see Concordance, p. 22*].

Changes: Revised to reflect leasing practices and terminology, except that subsection (2) was further revised to make the subsection parallel the provisions of Section 1–205(4) [*unrevised Article 1; see Concordance, p. 22*] by adding that course of dealing controls usage of trade.

Purposes: The section should be read in conjunction with Section 2A–208. In particular, although a specific term may control over course of performance as a matter of lease construction under subsection (2), subsection (3) allows the same course of dealing to show a waiver or modification, if Section 2A–208 is satisfied.

Cross References:

Sections 1–205(4) [*unrevised Article 1; see Concordance, p. 22*], 2–208 and 2A–208.

Definitional Cross References:

"Course of dealing". Section 1–205 [*unrevised Article 1; see Concordance, p. 22*].

"Knowledge". Section 1–201(25) [*unrevised Article 1; see Concordance, p. 22*].

"Lease agreement". Section 2A–103(1)(k).
"Lease contract". Section 2A–103(1)(*l*).
"Party". Section 1–201(29) [*unrevised Article 1; see Concordance, p. 22*].
"Term". Section 1–201(42) [*unrevised Article 1; see Concordance, p. 22*].
"Usage of trade". Section 1–205 [*unrevised Article 1; see Concordance, p. 22*].

§ 2A–208. Modification, Rescission and Waiver.

(1)   An agreement modifying a lease contract needs no consideration to be binding.

(2)   A signed lease agreement that excludes modification or rescission except by a signed ~~writing~~ record may not be otherwise modified or rescinded, but, except as between merchants, such a requirement on a form supplied by a merchant must be separately signed by the other party.

(3)   Although an attempt at modification or rescission does not satisfy the requirements of subsection (2), it may operate as a waiver.

(4)   A party who has made a waiver affecting an executory portion of a lease contract may retract the waiver by reasonable notification received by the other party that strict performance will be required of any term waived, unless the retraction would be unjust in view of a material change of position in reliance on the waiver.

As amended in 2022.

Official Comment

Uniform Statutory Source: Section 2–209.

Changes:

1.   Revised to reflect leasing practices and terminology, except that the provisions of subsection 2–209(3) were omitted.

2.   In furtherance of medium neutrality, the reference to a signed "writing" in the pre-2022 text of this section has been changed to refer to a signed "record."

Purposes:

Section 2–209(3) provides that "the requirements of the statute of frauds section of this Article (Section 2–201) must be satisfied if the contract as modified is within its provisions." This provision was not incorporated as it is unfair to allow an oral modification to make the entire lease contract unenforceable, *e.g.* if the modification takes it a few dollars over the dollar limit. At the same time, the problem could not be solved by providing that the lease contract would still be enforceable in its pre-modification state (if it then satisfied the statute of frauds) since in some cases that might be worse than no enforcement at all. Resolution of the issue is left to the courts based on the facts of each case.

Cross References:

Sections 2–201 and 2–209.

Definitional Cross References:

"Agreement". Section 1–201(3) [*unrevised Article 1; see Concordance, p. 22*].
"Between merchants". Section 2–104(3).
"Lease agreement". Section 2A–103(1)(k).
"Lease contract". Section 2A–103(1)(*l*).
"Merchant". Section 2–104(1).
"Notification". Section 1–201(26) [*unrevised Article 1; see Concordance, p. 22*].
"Party". Section 1–201(29) [*unrevised Article 1; see Concordance, p. 22*].
"Signed". Section 1–201(39) [*unrevised Article 1; see Concordance, p. 22*].
"Term". Section 1–201(42) [*unrevised Article 1; see Concordance, p. 22*].
"Writing". Section 1–201(46) [*unrevised Article 1: see Concordance, p. 22*].

As amended in 2022.

§ 2A-209. Lessee Under Finance Lease as Beneficiary of Supply Contract.

(1)   The benefit of a supplier's promises to the lessor under the supply contract and of all warranties, whether express or implied, including those of any third party provided in connection with or as part of the supply contract, extends to the lessee to the extent of the lessee's leasehold interest under a finance lease related to the supply contract, but is subject to the terms of the warranty and of the supply contract and all defenses or claims arising therefrom.

(2)   The extension of the benefit of a supplier's promises and of warranties to the lessee (Section 2A-209(1)) does not: (i) modify the rights and obligations of the parties to the supply contract, whether arising therefrom or otherwise, or (ii) impose any duty or liability under the supply contract on the lessee.

(3)   Any modification or rescission of the supply contract by the supplier and the lessor is effective between the supplier and the lessee unless, before the modification or rescission, the supplier has received notice that the lessee has entered into a finance lease related to the supply contract. If the modification or rescission is effective between the supplier and the lessee, the lessor is deemed to have assumed, in addition to the obligations of the lessor to the lessee under the lease contract, promises of the supplier to the lessor and warranties that were so modified or rescinded as they existed and were available to the lessee before modification or rescission.

(4)   In addition to the extension of the benefit of the supplier's promises and of warranties to the lessee under subsection (1), the lessee retains all rights that the lessee may have against the supplier which arise from an agreement between the lessee and the supplier or under other law.

As amended in 1990.

Official Comment

Uniform Statutory Source: None.

Changes: This section is modeled on former Section 9–318 (now codified as Sections 9–404 through 9–406), the Restatement (Second) of Contracts §§ 302–315 (1981), and leasing practices. *See Earman Oil Co. v. Burroughs Corp.*, 625 F.2d 1291, 1296–97 (5th Cir. 1980).

Purposes:

1.   The function performed by the lessor in a finance lease is extremely limited. Section 2A–103(1)(g). The lessee looks to the supplier of the goods for warranties and the like or, in some cases as to warranties, to the manufacturer if a warranty made by that person is passed on. That expectation is reflected in subsection (1), which is self-executing. As a matter of policy, the operation of this provision may not be excluded, modified or limited; however, an exclusion, modification, or limitation of any term of the supply contract or warranty, including any with respect to rights and remedies, and any defense or claim such as a statute of limitations, effective against the lessor as the acquiring party under the supply contract, is also effective against the lessee as the beneficiary designated under this provision. For example, the supplier is not precluded from excluding or modifying an express or implied warranty under a supply contract. Sections 2–312(2) and 2–316, or Section 2A–214. Further, the supplier is not precluded from limiting the rights and remedies of the lessor and from liquidating damages. Sections 2–718 and 2–719 or Sections 2A–503 and 2A–504. If the supply contract excludes or modifies warranties, limits remedies, or liquidates damages with respect to the lessor, such provisions are enforceable against the lessee as beneficiary. Thus, only selective discrimination against the beneficiaries designated under this section is precluded, i.e., exclusion of the supplier's liability to the lessee with respect to warranties made to the lessor. This section does not affect the development of other law with respect to products liability.

2.   Enforcement of this benefit is by action. Sections 2A–103(4) and 1–106(2) [*unrevised Article 1; see Concordance, p. 22*].

3.   The benefit extended by these provisions is not without a price, as this Article also provides in the case of a finance lease that is not a consumer lease that the lessee's promises to the lessor under the lease contract become irrevocable and independent upon the lessee's acceptance of the goods. Section 2A–407.

4.   Subsection (2) limits the effect of subsection (1) on the supplier and the lessor by preserving, notwithstanding the transfer of the benefits of the supply contract to the lessee, all of the supplier's and the lessor's rights and obligations with respect to each other and others; it further absolves the lessee of any duties with respect to the supply contract that might have been inferred from the extension of the benefits thereof.

5.　Subsections (2) and (3) also deal with difficult issues related to modification or rescission of the supply contract. Subsection (2) states a rule that determines the impact of the statutory extension of benefit contained in subsection (1) upon the relationship of the parties to the supply contract and, in a limited respect, upon the lessee. This statutory extension of benefit, like that contained in Sections 2A–216 and 2–318, is not a modification of the supply contract by the parties. Thus, subsection (3) states the rules that apply to a modification or rescission of the supply contract by the parties. Subsection (3) provides that a modification or rescission is not effective between the supplier and the lessee if, before the modification or rescission occurs, the supplier received notice that the lessee has entered into the finance lease. On the other hand, if the modification or rescission is effective, then to the extent of the modification or rescission of the benefit or warranty, the lessor by statutory dictate assumes an obligation to provide to the lessee that which the lessee would otherwise lose. For example, assume a reduction in an express warranty from four years to one year. No prejudice to the lessee may occur if the goods perform as agreed. If, however, there is a breach of the express warranty after one year and before four years pass, the lessor is liable. A remedy for any prejudice to the lessee because of the bifurcation of the lessee's recourse resulting from the action of the supplier and the lessor is left to resolution by the courts based on the facts of each case.

6.　Subsection (4) makes it clear that the rights granted to the lessee by this section do not displace any rights the lessee otherwise may have against the supplier.

Cross References:

　　Sections 2A–103(1)(g), 2A–407, 9–404, 9–405 and 9–406.

Definitional Cross References:

　　"Action". Section 1–201(1) [*unrevised Article 1; see Concordance, p. 22*].
　　"Finance lease". Section 2A–103(1)(g).
　　"Leasehold interest". Section 2A–103(1)(m).
　　"Lessee". Section 2A–103(1)(n).
　　"Lessor". Section 2A–103(1)(p).
　　"Notice". Section 1–201(25) [*unrevised Article 1; see Concordance, p. 22*].
　　"Party". Section 1–201(29) [*unrevised Article 1; see Concordance, p. 22*].
　　"Rights". Section 1–201(36) [*unrevised Article 1; see Concordance, p. 22*].
　　"Supplier". Section 2A–103(1)(x).
　　"Supply contract". Section 2A–103(1)(y).
　　"Term". Section 1–201(42) [*unrevised Article 1; see Concordance, p. 22*].

§ 2A–210.　Express Warranties.

(1)　Express warranties by the lessor are created as follows:

(a)　Any affirmation of fact or promise made by the lessor to the lessee which relates to the goods and becomes part of the basis of the bargain creates an express warranty that the goods will conform to the affirmation or promise.

(b)　Any description of the goods which is made part of the basis of the bargain creates an express warranty that the goods will conform to the description.

(c)　Any sample or model that is made part of the basis of the bargain creates an express warranty that the whole of the goods will conform to the sample or model.

(2)　It is not necessary to the creation of an express warranty that the lessor use formal words, such as "warrant" or "guarantee," or that the lessor have a specific intention to make a warranty, but an affirmation merely of the value of the goods or a statement purporting to be merely the lessor's opinion or commendation of the goods does not create a warranty.

Official Comment

Uniform Statutory Source: Section 2–313.

Changes: Revised to reflect leasing practices and terminology.

Purposes: All of the express and implied warranties of the Article on Sales (Article 2) are included in this Article, revised to reflect the differences between a sale of goods and a lease of goods. Sections 2A–210 through 2A–216. The lease of goods is sufficiently similar to the sale of goods to justify this decision. Hawkland, *The Impact of the*

Uniform Commercial Code on Equipment Leasing, 1972 Ill.L.F. 446, 459–60. Many state and federal courts have reached the same conclusion.

Value of the goods, as used in subsection (2), includes rental value.

Cross References:

Article 2, esp. Section 2–313, and Sections 2A–210 through 2A–216.

Definitional Cross References:

"Conforming". Section 2A–103(1)(d).
"Goods". Section 2A–103(1)(h).
"Lessee". Section 2A–103(1)(n).
"Lessor". Section 2A–103(1)(p).
"Value". Section 1–201(44) [*unrevised Article 1; see Concordance, p. 22*].

§ 2A–211. Warranties Against Interference and Against Infringement; Lessee's Obligation Against Infringement.

(1)   There is in a lease contract a warranty that for the lease term no person holds a claim to or interest in the goods that arose from an act or omission of the lessor, other than a claim by way of infringement or the like, which will interfere with the lessee's enjoyment of its leasehold interest.

(2)   Except in a finance lease there is in a lease contract by a lessor who is a merchant regularly dealing in goods of the kind a warranty that the goods are delivered free of the rightful claim of any person by way of infringement or the like.

(3)   A lessee who furnishes specifications to a lessor or a supplier shall hold the lessor and the supplier harmless against any claim by way of infringement or the like that arises out of compliance with the specifications.

Official Comment

Uniform Statutory Source: Section 2–312.

Changes: This section is modeled on the provisions of Section 2–312, with modifications to reflect the limited interest transferred by a lease contract and the total interest transferred by a sale. Section 2–312(2), which is omitted here, is incorporated in Section 2A–214. The warranty of quiet possession was abolished with respect to sales of goods. Section 2–312 official comment 1. Section 2A–211(1) reinstates the warranty of quiet possession with respect to leases. Inherent in the nature of the limited interest transferred by the lease—the right to possession and use of the goods—is the need of the lessee for protection greater than that afforded to the buyer. Since the scope of the protection is limited to claims or interests that arose from acts or omissions of the lessor, the lessor will be in position to evaluate the potential cost, certainly a far better position than that enjoyed by the lessee. Further, to the extent the market will allow, the lessor can attempt to pass on the anticipated additional cost to the lessee in the guise of higher rent.

Purposes: General language was chosen for subsection (1) that expresses the essence of the lessee's expectation: with an exception for infringement and the like, no person holding a claim or interest that arose from an act or omission of the lessor will be able to interfere with the lessee's use and enjoyment of the goods for the lease term. Subsection (2), like other similar provisions in later sections, excludes the finance lessor from extending this warranty; with few exceptions (Sections 2A–210 and 2A–211(1)), the lessee under a finance lease is to look to the supplier for warranties and the like or, in some cases as to warranties, to the manufacturer if a warranty made by that person is passed on. Subsections (2) and (3) are derived from Section 2–312(3). These subsections, as well as the analogue, should be construed so that applicable principles of law and equity supplement their provisions. Sections 2A–103(4) and 1–103.

Cross References:

Sections 2–312, 2–312(1), 2–312(2), 2–312 official comment 1, 2A–210, 2A–211(1) and 2A–214.

Definitional Cross References:

"Delivery". Section 1–201(14) [*unrevised Article 1; see Concordance, p. 22*].
"Finance lease". Section 2A–103(1)(g).

"Goods". Section 2A–103(1)(h).
"Lease". Section 2A–103(1)(j).
"Lease contract". Section 2A–103(1)(*l*).
"Leasehold interest". Section 2A–103(1)(m).
"Lessee". Section 2A–103(1)(n).
"Lessor". Section 2A–103(1)(p).
"Merchant". Section 2–104(1).
"Person". Section 1–201(30) [*unrevised Article 1; see Concordance, p. 22*].
"Supplier". Section 2A–103(1)(x).

§ 2A–212. Implied Warranty of Merchantability.

(1) Except in a finance lease, a warranty that the goods will be merchantable is implied in a lease contract if the lessor is a merchant with respect to goods of that kind.

(2) Goods to be merchantable must be at least such as

(a) pass without objection in the trade under the description in the lease agreement;

(b) in the case of fungible goods, are of fair average quality within the description;

(c) are fit for the ordinary purposes for which goods of that type are used;

(d) run, within the variation permitted by the lease agreement, of even kind, quality, and quantity within each unit and among all units involved;

(e) are adequately contained, packaged, and labeled as the lease agreement may require; and

(f) conform to any promises or affirmations of fact made on the container or label.

(3) Other implied warranties may arise from course of dealing or usage of trade.

Official Comment

Uniform Statutory Source: Section 2–314.

Changes: Revised to reflect leasing practices and terminology. *E.g., Glenn Dick Equip. Co. v. Galey Constr., Inc.,* 97 Idaho 216, 225, 541 P.2d 1184, 1193 (1975) (implied warranty of merchantability (Article 2) extends to lease transactions).

Definitional Cross References:

"Conforming". Section 2A–103(1)(d).
"Course of dealing". Section 1–205 [*unrevised Article 1; see Concordance, p. 22*].
"Finance lease". Section 2A–103(1)(g).
"Fungible". Section 1–201(17) [*unrevised Article 1; see Concordance, p. 22*].
"Goods". Section 2A–103(1)(h).
"Lease agreement". Section 2A–103(1)(k).
"Lease contract". Section 2A–103(1)(*l*).
"Lessor". Section 2A–103(1)(p).
"Merchant". Section 2–104(1).
"Usage of trade". Section 1–205 [*unrevised Article 1; see Concordance, p. 22*].

§ 2A–213. Implied Warranty of Fitness for Particular Purpose.

Except in a finance lease, if the lessor at the time the lease contract is made has reason to know of any particular purpose for which the goods are required and that the lessee is relying on the lessor's skill or judgment to select or furnish suitable goods, there is in the lease contract an implied warranty that the goods will be fit for that purpose.

Official Comment

Uniform Statutory Source: Section 2–315.

Changes: Revised to reflect leasing practices and terminology. *E.g.*, *All-States Leasing Co. v. Bass*, 96 Idaho 873, 879, 538 P.2d 1177, 1183 (1975) (implied warranty of fitness for a particular purpose (Article 2) extends to lease transactions).

Definitional Cross References:

"Finance lease". Section 2A–103(1)(g).
"Goods". Section 2A–103(1)(h).
"Knows". Section 1–201(25) [*unrevised Article 1; see Concordance, p. 22*].
"Lease contract". Section 2A–103(1)(*l*).
"Lessee". Section 2A–103(1)(n).
"Lessor". Section 2A–103(1)(p).

§ 2A–214.   Exclusion or Modification of Warranties.

(1)   Words or conduct relevant to the creation of an express warranty and words or conduct tending to negate or limit a warranty must be construed wherever reasonable as consistent with each other; but, subject to the provisions of Section 2A–202 on parol or extrinsic evidence, negation or limitation is inoperative to the extent that the construction is unreasonable.

(2)   Subject to subsection (3), to exclude or modify the implied warranty of merchantability or any part of it the language must mention "merchantability", be by a writing, and be conspicuous. Subject to subsection (3), to exclude or modify any implied warranty of fitness the exclusion must be by a writing and be conspicuous. Language to exclude all implied warranties of fitness is sufficient if it is in writing, is conspicuous and states, for example, "There is no warranty that the goods will be fit for a particular purpose".

(3)   Notwithstanding subsection (2), but subject to subsection (4),

(a)   unless the circumstances indicate otherwise, all implied warranties are excluded by expressions like "as is," or "with all faults," or by other language that in common understanding calls the lessee's attention to the exclusion of warranties and makes plain that there is no implied warranty, if in writing and conspicuous;

(b)   if the lessee before entering into the lease contract has examined the goods or the sample or model as fully as desired or has refused to examine the goods, there is no implied warranty with regard to defects that an examination ought in the circumstances to have revealed; and

(c)   an implied warranty may also be excluded or modified by course of dealing, course of performance, or usage of trade.

(4)   To exclude or modify a warranty against interference or against infringement (Section 2A–211) or any part of it, the language must be specific, be by a writing, and be conspicuous, unless the circumstances, including course of performance, course of dealing, or usage of trade, give the lessee reason to know that the goods are being leased subject to a claim or interest of any person.

Official Comment

Uniform Statutory Source: Sections 2–316 and 2–312(2).

Changes: Subsection (2) requires that a disclaimer of the warranty of merchantability be conspicuous and in writing as is the case for a disclaimer of the warranty of fitness; this is contrary to the rule stated in Section 2–316(2) with respect to the disclaimer of the warranty of merchantability. This section also provides that to exclude or modify the implied warranty of merchantability, fitness or against interference or infringement the language must be in writing and conspicuous. There are, however, exceptions to the rule. *E.g.*, course of dealing, course of performance, or usage of trade may exclude or modify an implied warranty. Section 2A–214(3)(c). The analogue of Section 2–312(2) has been moved to subsection (4) of this section for a more unified treatment of disclaimers; there is no policy with respect to leases of goods that would justify continuing certain distinctions found in the Article on Sales (Article 2) regarding the treatment of the disclaimer of various warranties. *Compare* Sections 2–312(2) and 2–316(2). Finally, the example of a disclaimer of the implied warranty of fitness stated in subsection (2) differs from the analogue stated in Section 2–316(2); this example should promote a better understanding of the effect of the disclaimer.

Purposes:

1.   These changes were made to reflect leasing practices. *E.g., FMC Finance Corp. v. Murphree,* 632 F.2d 413, 418 (5th Cir. 1980) (disclaimer of implied warranty under lease transactions must be conspicuous and in writing). The omission of the provisions of Section 2–316(4) was not substantive. Sections 2A–503 and 2A–504.

2.   As to the use of a record other than a writing and communications that are not written, see Section 2A–103, Comment (g). Whether a term is conspicuous, including a term in a record other than a writing, is discussed in Section 1–201, Comment 10.

Cross References:

Article 2, esp. Sections 2–312(2) and 2–316, and Sections 2A–503 and 2A–504.

Definitional Cross References:

"Conspicuous". Section 1–201(10) [*unrevised Article 1; see Concordance, p. 22*].
"Course of dealing". Section 1–205 [*unrevised Article 1; see Concordance, p. 22*].
"Fault". Section 2A–103(1)(f).
"Goods". Section 2A–103(1)(h).
"Knows". Section 1–201(25) [*unrevised Article 1; see Concordance, p. 22*].
"Lease". Section 2A–103(1)(j).
"Lease contract". Section 2A–103(1)(*l*).
"Lessee". Section 2A–103(1)(n).
"Person". Section 1–201(30) [*unrevised Article 1; see Concordance, p. 22*].
"Usage of trade". Section 1–205 [*unrevised Article 1; see Concordance, p. 22*].
"Writing". Section 1–201(46) [*unrevised Article 1; see Concordance, p. 22*].

As amended in 2022.

§ 2A–215.   Cumulation and Conflict of Warranties Express or Implied.

Warranties, whether express or implied, must be construed as consistent with each other and as cumulative, but if that construction is unreasonable, the intention of the parties determines which warranty is dominant. In ascertaining that intention the following rules apply:

(a)   Exact or technical specifications displace an inconsistent sample or model or general language of description.

(b)   A sample from an existing bulk displaces inconsistent general language of description.

(c)   Express warranties displace inconsistent implied warranties other than an implied warranty of fitness for a particular purpose.

Official Comment

Uniform Statutory Source: Section 2–317.

Definitional Cross Reference:

"Party". Section 1–201(29) [*unrevised Article 1; see Concordance, p. 22*].

§ 2A–216.   Third-Party Beneficiaries of Express and Implied Warranties.

ALTERNATIVE A

A warranty to or for the benefit of a lessee under this Article, whether express or implied, extends to any natural person who is in the family or household of the lessee or who is a guest in the lessee's home if it is reasonable to expect that such person may use, consume, or be affected by the goods and who is injured in person by breach of the warranty. This section does not displace principles of law and equity that extend a warranty to or for the benefit of a lessee to other persons. The operation of this section may not be excluded, modified, or limited, but an exclusion, modification, or limitation of the warranty, including any with respect to rights and remedies, effective against the lessee is also effective against any beneficiary designated under this section.

ALTERNATIVE B

A warranty to or for the benefit of a lessee under this Article, whether express or implied, extends to any natural person who may reasonably be expected to use, consume, or be affected by the goods and who is injured in person by breach of the warranty. This section does not displace principles of law and equity that extend a warranty to or for the benefit of a lessee to other persons. The operation of this section may not be excluded, modified, or limited, but an exclusion, modification, or limitation of the warranty, including any with respect to rights and remedies, effective against the lessee is also effective against the beneficiary designated under this section.

ALTERNATIVE C

A warranty to or for the benefit of a lessee under this Article, whether express or implied, extends to any person who may reasonably be expected to use, consume, or be affected by the goods and who is injured by breach of the warranty. The operation of this section may not be excluded, modified, or limited with respect to injury to the person of an individual to whom the warranty extends, but an exclusion, modification, or limitation of the warranty, including any with respect to rights and remedies, effective against the lessee is also effective against the beneficiary designated under this section.

Official Comment

Uniform Statutory Source: Section 2–318.

Changes: The provisions of Section 2–318 have been included in this section, modified in two respects: first, to reflect leasing practice, including the special practices of the lessor under a finance lease; second, to reflect and thus codify elements of the official comment to Section 2–318 with respect to the effect of disclaimers and limitations of remedies against third parties.

Purposes: Alternative A is based on the 1962 version of Section 2–318 and is least favorable to the injured person as the doctrine of privity imposed by other law is abrogated to only a limited extent. Alternatives B and C are based on later additions to Section 2–318 and are more favorable to the injured person. In determining which alternative to select, the state legislature should consider making its choice parallel to the choice it made with respect to Section 2–318, as interpreted by the courts.

The last sentence of each of Alternatives A, B and C does not preclude the lessor from excluding or modifying an express or implied warranty under a lease. Section 2A–214. Further, that sentence does not preclude the lessor from limiting the rights and remedies of the lessee and from liquidating damages. Sections 2A–503 and 2A–504. If the lease excludes or modifies warranties, limits remedies for breach, or liquidates damages with respect to the lessee, such provisions are enforceable against the beneficiaries designated under this section. However, this last sentence forbids selective discrimination against the beneficiaries designated under this section, *i.e.*, exclusion of the lessor's liability to the beneficiaries with respect to warranties made by the lessor to the lessee.

Other law, including the Article on Sales (Article 2), may apply in determining the extent to which a warranty to or for the benefit of the lessor extends to the lessee and third parties. This is in part a function of whether the lessor has bought or leased the goods.

This Article does not purport to change the development of the relationship of the common law, with respect to products liability, including strict liability in tort (as restated in Restatement (Second) of Torts, § 402A (1965)), to the provisions of this Act. *Compare Cline v. Prowler Indus. of Maryland*, 418 A.2d 968 (Del. 1980) and *Hawkins Constr. Co. v. Matthews Co.*, 190 Neb. 546, 209 N.W.2d 643 (1973) with *Dippel v. Sciano*, 37 Wis.2d 443, 155 N.W.2d 55 (1967).

Cross References:

Article 2, esp. Section 2–318, and Sections 2A–214, 2A–503 and 2A–504.

Definitional Cross References:

"Goods". Section 2A–103(1)(h).
"Lessee". Section 2A–103(1)(n).
"Person". Section 1–201(30) [*unrevised Article 1; see Concordance, p. 22*].
"Remedy". Section 1–201(34) [*unrevised Article 1; see Concordance, p. 22*].
"Rights". Section 1–201(36).

§ 2A–217. Identification.

Identification of goods as goods to which a lease contract refers may be made at any time and in any manner explicitly agreed to by the parties. In the absence of explicit agreement, identification occurs:

(a)   when the lease contract is made if the lease contract is for a lease of goods that are existing and identified;

(b)   when the goods are shipped, marked, or otherwise designated by the lessor as goods to which the lease contract refers, if the lease contract is for a lease of goods that are not existing and identified; or

(c)   when the young are conceived, if the lease contract is for a lease of unborn young of animals.

Official Comment

Uniform Statutory Source: Section 2–501.

Changes: This section, together with Section 2A–218, is derived from the provisions of Section 2–501, with changes to reflect lease terminology; however, this section omits as irrelevant to leasing practice the treatment of special property.

Purposes: With respect to subsection (b) there is a certain amount of ambiguity in the reference to when goods are designated, *e.g.*, when the lessor is both selling and leasing goods to the same lessee/buyer and has marked goods for delivery but has not distinguished between those related to the lease contract and those related to the sales contract. As in Section 2–501(1)(b), this issue has been left to be resolved by the courts, case by case.

Cross References:

Sections 2–501 and 2A–218.

Definitional Cross References:

"Agreement". Section 1–201(3) [*unrevised Article 1; see Concordance, p. 22*].
"Goods". Section 2A–103(1)(h).
"Lease". Section 2A–103(1)(j).
"Lease contract". Section 2A–103(1)(*l*).
"Lessor". Section 2A–103(1)(p).
"Party". Section 1–201(29) [*unrevised Article 1; see Concordance, p. 22*].

§ 2A–218. Insurance and Proceeds.

(1)   A lessee obtains an insurable interest when existing goods are identified to the lease contract even though the goods identified are nonconforming and the lessee has an option to reject them.

(2)   If a lessee has an insurable interest only by reason of the lessor's identification of the goods, the lessor, until default or insolvency or notification to the lessee that identification is final, may substitute other goods for those identified.

(3)   Notwithstanding a lessee's insurable interest under subsections (1) and (2), the lessor retains an insurable interest until an option to buy has been exercised by the lessee and risk of loss has passed to the lessee.

(4)   Nothing in this section impairs any insurable interest recognized under any other statute or rule of law.

(5)   The parties by agreement may determine that one or more parties have an obligation to obtain and pay for insurance covering the goods and by agreement may determine the beneficiary of the proceeds of the insurance.

Official Comment

Uniform Statutory Source: Section 2–501.

Changes: This section, together with Section 2A–217, is derived from the provisions of Section 2–501, with changes and additions to reflect leasing practices and terminology.

Purposes: Subsection (2) states a rule allowing substitution of goods by the lessor under certain circumstances, until default or insolvency of the lessor, or until notification to the lessee that identification is final. Subsection (3) states a rule regarding the lessor's insurable interest that, by virtue of the difference between a sale and a lease, necessarily is different from the rule stated in Section 2–501(2) regarding the seller's insurable interest. For this purpose the option to buy shall be deemed to have been exercised by the lessee when the resulting sale is closed, not when the lessee gives notice to the lessor. Further, subsection (5) is new and reflects the common practice of shifting the responsibility and cost of insuring the goods between the parties to the lease transaction.

Cross References:

Sections 2–501, 2–501(2) and 2A–217.

Definitional Cross References:

"Agreement". Section 1–201(3) [*unrevised Article 1; see Concordance, p. 22*].
"Buying". Section 2A–103(1)(a).
"Conforming". Section 2A–103(1)(d).
"Goods". Section 2A–103(1)(h).
"Insolvent". Section 1–201(23) [*unrevised Article 1; see Concordance, p. 22*].
"Lease contract". Section 2A–103(1)(*l*).
"Lessee". Section 2A–103(1)(n).
"Lessor". Section 2A–103(1)(p).
"Notification". Section 1–201(26) [*unrevised Article 1; see Concordance, p. 22*].
"Party". Section 1–201(29) [*unrevised Article 1; see Concordance, p. 22*].

§ 2A–219. Risk of Loss.

(1)   Except in the case of a finance lease, risk of loss is retained by the lessor and does not pass to the lessee. In the case of a finance lease, risk of loss passes to the lessee.

(2)   Subject to the provisions of this Article on the effect of default on risk of loss (Section 2A–220), if risk of loss is to pass to the lessee and the time of passage is not stated, the following rules apply:

(a)   If the lease contract requires or authorizes the goods to be shipped by carrier

    (i)   and it does not require delivery at a particular destination, the risk of loss passes to the lessee when the goods are duly delivered to the carrier; but

    (ii)   if it does require delivery at a particular destination and the goods are there duly tendered while in the possession of the carrier, the risk of loss passes to the lessee when the goods are there duly so tendered as to enable the lessee to take delivery.

(b)   If the goods are held by a bailee to be delivered without being moved, the risk of loss passes to the lessee on acknowledgment by the bailee of the lessee's right to possession of the goods.

(c)   In any case not within subsection (a) or (b), the risk of loss passes to the lessee on the lessee's receipt of the goods if the lessor, or, in the case of a finance lease, the supplier, is a merchant; otherwise the risk passes to the lessee on tender of delivery.

Official Comment

Uniform Statutory Source: Section 2–509(1) through (3).

Changes: Subsection (1) is new. The introduction to subsection (2) is new, but subparagraph (a) incorporates the provisions of Section 2–509(1); subparagraph (b) incorporates the provisions of Section 2–509(2) only in part, reflecting current practice in lease transactions.

Purposes: Subsection (1) states rules related to retention or passage of risk of loss consistent with current practice in lease transactions. The provisions of subsection (4) of Section 2–509 are not incorporated as they are not necessary. This section does not deal with responsibility for loss caused by the wrongful act of either the lessor or the lessee.

Cross References:

Sections 2–509(1), 2–509(2) and 2–509(4).

Definitional Cross References:

"Delivery". Section 1–201(14) [*unrevised Article 1; see Concordance, p. 22*].
"Finance lease". Section 2A–103(1)(g).
"Goods". Section 2A–103(1)(h).
"Lease contract". Section 2A–103(1)(*l*).
"Lessee". Section 2A–103(1)(n).
"Lessor". Section 2A–103(1)(p).
"Merchant". Section 2–104(1).
"Receipt". Section 2–103(1)(c).
"Rights". Section 1–201(36) [*unrevised Article 1; see Concordance, p. 22*].
"Supplier". Section 2A–103(1)(x).

§ 2A–220. Effect of Default on Risk of Loss.

(1) Where risk of loss is to pass to the lessee and the time of passage is not stated:

(a) If a tender or delivery of goods so fails to conform to the lease contract as to give a right of rejection, the risk of their loss remains with the lessor, or, in the case of a finance lease, the supplier, until cure or acceptance.

(b) If the lessee rightfully revokes acceptance, he [or she], to the extent of any deficiency in his [or her] effective insurance coverage, may treat the risk of loss as having remained with the lessor from the beginning.

(2) Whether or not risk of loss is to pass to the lessee, if the lessee as to conforming goods already identified to a lease contract repudiates or is otherwise in default under the lease contract, the lessor, or, in the case of a finance lease, the supplier, to the extent of any deficiency in his [or her] effective insurance coverage may treat the risk of loss as resting on the lessee for a commercially reasonable time.

Official Comment

Uniform Statutory Source: Section 2–510.

Changes: Revised to reflect leasing practices and terminology. The rule in Section (1)(b) does not allow the lessee under a finance lease to treat the risk of loss as having remained with the supplier from the beginning. This is appropriate given the limited circumstances under which the lessee under a finance lease is allowed to revoke acceptance. Section 2A–517 and Section 2A–516 official comment.

Definitional Cross References:

"Conforming". Section 2A–103(1)(d).
"Delivery". Section 1–201(14) [*unrevised Article 1; see Concordance, p. 22*].
"Finance lease". Section 2A–103(1)(g).
"Goods". Section 2A–103(1)(h).
"Lease contract". Section 2A–103(1)(*l*).
"Lessee". Section 2A–103(1)(n).
"Lessor". Section 2A–103(1)(p).
"Reasonable time". Section 1–204(1) and (2) [*unrevised Article 1; see Concordance, p. 22*].
"Rights". Section 1–201(36) [*unrevised Article 1; see Concordance, p. 22*].
"Supplier". Section 2A–103(1)(x).

§ 2A–221. Casualty to Identified Goods.

If a lease contract requires goods identified when the lease contract is made, and the goods suffer casualty without fault of the lessee, the lessor or the supplier before delivery, or the goods suffer casualty before risk of loss passes to the lessee pursuant to the lease agreement or Section 2A–219, then:

(a) if the loss is total, the lease contract is avoided; and

(b) if the loss is partial or the goods have so deteriorated as to no longer conform to the lease contract, the lessee may nevertheless demand inspection and at his [or her] option either treat the lease contract as avoided or, except in a finance lease that is not a consumer lease, accept the goods with due allowance from the rent payable for the balance of the lease term for the deterioration or the deficiency in quantity but without further right against the lessor.

Official Comment

Uniform Statutory Source: Section 2–613.

Changes: Revised to reflect leasing practices and terminology.

Purpose: Due to the vagaries of determining the amount of due allowance (Section 2–613(b)), no attempt was made in subsection (b) to treat a problem unique to lease contracts and installment sales contracts: determining how to recapture the allowance, *e.g.*, application to the first or last rent payments or allocation, *pro rata*, to all rent payments.

Cross References:

Section 2–613.

Definitional Cross References:

"Conforming". Section 2A–103(1)(d).
"Consumer lease". Section 2A–103(1)(e).
"Delivery". Section 1–201(14) [*unrevised Article 1; see Concordance, p. 22*].
"Fault". Section 2A–103(1)(f).
"Finance lease". Section 2A–103(1)(g).
"Goods". Section 2A–103(1)(h).
"Lease". Section 2A–103(1)(j).
"Lease agreement". Section 2A–103(1)(k).
"Lease contract". Section 2A–103(1)(*l*).
"Lessee". Section 2A–103(1)(n).
"Lessor". Section 2A–103(1)(p).
"Rights". Section 1–201(36) [*unrevised Article 1; see Concordance, p. 22*].
"Supplier". Section 2A–103(1)(x).

PART 3

EFFECT OF LEASE CONTRACT

§ 2A–301. Enforceability of Lease Contract.

Except as otherwise provided in this Article, a lease contract is effective and enforceable according to its terms between the parties, against purchasers of the goods and against creditors of the parties.

Official Comment

Uniform Statutory Source: Former Section 9–201 (now codified as Section 9–201).

Changes: The first sentence of former Section 9–201 was incorporated, modified to reflect leasing terminology. The second sentence of former Section 9–201 was eliminated as not relevant to leasing practices.

Purposes:

1.   This section establishes a general rule regarding the validity and enforceability of a lease contract. The lease contract is effective and enforceable between the parties and against third parties. Exceptions to this general rule arise where there is a specific rule to the contrary in this Article. Enforceability is, thus, dependent upon the lease contract meeting the requirements of the Statute of Frauds provisions of Section 2A–201. Enforceability is also a function of the lease contract conforming to the principles of construction and interpretation contained in the Article on General Provisions (Article 1). Section 2A–103(4).

2.   The effectiveness or enforceability of the lease contract is not dependent upon the lease contract or any financing statement or the like being filed or recorded; however, the priority of the interest of a lessor of fixtures with respect to the interests of certain third parties in such fixtures is subject to the provisions of the Article on Secured Transactions (Article 9). Section 2A–309. Prior to the adoption of this Article filing or recording was not

required with respect to leases, only <u>for nominal </u>leases ~~intended as security~~ <u>that created security interests</u>. ~~The definition of security interest, as amended concurrently with the adoption of this Article, more clearly delineates leases and leases intended as security and thus signals the need to file.~~ Section ~~1–201(37)~~ <u>1–203 now more clearly distinguishes leases from transactions that create security interests</u>. Those lessors who are concerned about whether the transaction creates a lease or a security interest will continue to file a protective financing statement. Section 9–505. ~~Coogan, Leasing and the Uniform Commercial Code, in~~ *~~Equipment Leasing Leveraged Leasing~~ 681, 744 46 (2d ed. 1980)*.

3.   **Hypothetical:**

(a)   In construing this section it is important to recognize its relationship to other sections in this Article. This is best demonstrated by reference to a hypothetical. Assume that on February 1 A, a manufacturer of combines and other farm equipment, leased a fleet of six combines to B, a corporation engaged in the business of farming, for a 12 month term. Under the lease agreement between A and B, A agreed to defer B's payment of the first two months' rent to April 1. On March 1 B recognized that it would need only four combines and thus subleased two combines to C for an 11 month term.

(b)   This hypothetical raises a number of issues that are answered by the sections contained in this part. Since lease is defined to include sublease (Section 2A–103(1)(j) and (w)), this section provides that the prime lease between A and B and the sublease between B and C are enforceable in accordance with their terms, except as otherwise provided in this Article; that exception, in this case, is one of considerable scope.

(c)   The separation of ownership, which is in A, and possession, which is in B with respect to four combines and which is in C with respect to two combines, is not relevant. Section 2A–302. A's interest in the six combines cannot be challenged simply because A parted with possession to B, who in turn parted with possession of some of the combines to C. Yet it is important to note that by the terms of Section 2A–302 this conclusion is subject to change if otherwise provided in this Article.

(d)   B's entering the sublease with C raises an issue that is treated by this part. In a dispute over the leased combines A may challenge B's right to sublease. The rule is permissive as to transfers of interests under a lease contract, including subleases. Section 2A–303(2). However, the rule has two significant qualifications. If the prime lease contract between A and B prohibits B from subleasing the combines, or makes such a sublease an event of default, Section 2A–303(2) applies; thus, while B's interest under the prime lease may be transferred under the sublease to C, A may have a remedy pursuant to Section 2A–303(5). Absent a prohibition or default provision in the prime lease contract A might be able to argue that the sublease to C materially increases A's risk; thus, while B's interest under the prime lease may be transferred under the sublease to C, A may have a remedy pursuant to Section 2A–303(5). Section 2A–303(5)(b)(ii).

(e)   Resolution of this issue is also a function of the section dealing with the sublease of goods by a prime lessee (Section 2A–305). Subsection (1) of Section 2A–305, which is subject to the rules of Section 2A–303 stated above, provides that C takes subject to the interest of A under the prime lease between A and B. However, there are two exceptions. First, if B is a merchant (Sections 2A–103(3) and 2–104(1)) dealing in goods of that kind and C is a sublessee in the ordinary course of business (Sections 2A–103(1)(o) and 2A–103(1)(n)), C takes free of the prime lease between A and B. Second, if B has rejected the six combines under the prime lease with A, and B disposes of the goods by sublease to C, C takes free of the prime lease if C can establish good faith. Section 2A–511(4).

(f)   If the facts of this hypothetical are expanded and we assume that the prime lease obligated B to maintain the combines, an additional issue may be presented. Prior to entering the sublease, B, in satisfaction of its maintenance covenant, brought the two combines that it desired to sublease to a local independent dealer of A's. The dealer did the requested work for B. C inspected the combines on the dealer's lot after the work was completed. C signed the sublease with B two days later. C, however, was prevented from taking delivery of the two combines as B refused to pay the dealer's invoice for the repairs. The dealer furnished the repair service to B in the ordinary course of the dealer's business. If under applicable law the dealer has a lien on repaired goods in the dealer's possession, the dealer's lien will take priority over B's and C's interests and also should take priority over A's interest, depending upon the terms of the lease contract and the applicable law. Section 2A–306.

(g)   Now assume that C is in financial straits and one of C's creditors obtains a judgment against C. If the creditor levies on C's subleasehold interest in the two combines, who will prevail? Unless the levying creditor also holds a lien covered by Section 2A–306, discussed above, the judgment creditor will take its interest subject to B's rights under the sublease and A's rights under the prime lease. Section 2A–307(1).

The hypothetical becomes more complicated if we assume that B is in financial straits and B's creditor holds the judgment. Here the judgment creditor takes subject to the sublease unless the lien attached to the two combines before the sublease contract became enforceable. Section 2A–307(2)(a). However, B's judgment creditor cannot prime A's interest in the goods because, with respect to A, the judgment creditor is a creditor of B in its capacity as lessee under the prime lease between A and B. Thus, here the judgment creditor's interest is subject to the lease between A and B. Section 2A–307(1).

(h)   Finally, assume that on April 1 B is unable to pay A the deferred rent then due under the prime lease, but that C is current in its payments under the sublease from B. What effect will B's default under the prime lease between A and B have on C's rights under the sublease between B and C? Section 2A–301 provides that a lease contract is effective against the creditors of either party. Since a lease contract includes a sublease contract (Section 2A–103(1)(*l*)), the sublease contract between B and C arguably could be enforceable against A, a prime lessor who has extended unsecured credit to B, the prime lessee/sublessor, if the sublease contract meets the requirements of Section 2A–201. However, the rule stated in Section 2A–301 is subject to other provisions in this Article. Under Section 2A–305, C, as sublessee, would take subject to the prime lease contract in most cases. Thus, B's default under the prime lease will in most cases lead to A's recovery of the goods from C. Section 2A–523. A and C could provide otherwise by agreement. Section 2A–311. C's recourse will be to assert a claim for damages against B. Sections 2A–211(1) and 2A–508.

4.   Relationship Between Sections:

(a)   As the analysis of the hypothetical demonstrates, Part 3 of the Article focuses on issues that relate to the enforceability of the lease contract (Sections 2A–301, 2A–302 and 2A–303) and to the priority of various claims to the goods subject to the lease contract (Sections 2A–304, 2A–305, 2A–306, 2A–307, 2A–308, 2A–309, 2A–310, and 2A–311).

(b)   This section states a general rule of enforceability, which is subject to specific rules to the contrary stated elsewhere in the Article. Section 2A–302 negates any notion that the separation of title and possession is fraudulent as a rule of law. Finally, Section 2A–303 states rules with respect to the transfer of the lessor's interest (as well as the residual interest in the goods) or the lessee's interest under the lease contract. Qualifications are imposed as a function of various issues, including whether the transfer is the creation or enforcement of a security interest or one that is material to the other party to the lease contract. In addition, a system of rules is created to deal with the rights and duties among assignor, assignee and the other party to the lease contract.

(c)   Sections 2A–304 and 2A–305 are twins that deal with good faith transferees of goods subject to the lease contract. Section 2A–304 creates a set of rules with respect to transfers by the lessor of goods subject to a lease contract; the transferee considered is a subsequent lessee of the goods. The priority dispute covered here is between the subsequent lessee and the original lessee of the goods (or persons claiming through the original lessee). Section 2A–305 creates a set of rules with respect to transfers by the lessee of goods subject to a lease contract; the transferees considered are buyers of the goods or sublessees of the goods. The priority dispute covered here is between the transferee and the lessor of the goods (or persons claiming through the lessor).

(d)   Section 2A–306 creates a rule with respect to priority disputes between holders of liens for services or materials furnished with respect to goods subject to a lease contract and the lessor or the lessee under that contract. Section 2A–307 creates a rule with respect to priority disputes between the lessee and creditors of the lessor and priority disputes between the lessor and creditors of the lessee.

(e)   Section 2A–308 creates a series of rules relating to allegedly fraudulent transfers and preferences. The most significant rule is that set forth in subsection (3) which validates sale-leaseback transactions if the buyer-lessor can establish that he or she bought for value and in good faith.

(f)   Sections 2A–309 and 2A–310 create a series of rules with respect to priority disputes between various third parties and a lessor of fixtures or accessions, respectively, with respect thereto.

(g)   Finally, Section 2A–311 allows parties to alter the statutory priorities by agreement.

Cross References:

Article 1, especially Section 1–201(37) [*unrevised Article 1; see Concordance, p. 22*], and Sections 2–104(1), 2A–103(1)(j), 2A–103(1)(*l*), 2A–103(1)(n), 2A–103(1)(*o*) and 2A–103(1)(w), 2A–103(3), 2A–103(4), 2A–201, 2A–301 through 2A–303, 2A–303(2), 2A–303(5), 2A–304 through 2A–307, 2A–307(1), 2A–307(2)(a), 2A–308 through 2A–311, 2A–508, 2A–511(4), 2A–523, Article 9, especially Sections 9–201 and 9–505.

Definitional Cross References:

"Creditor". Section 1–201(12) [*unrevised Article 1; see Concordance, p. 22*].
"Goods". Section 2A–103(1)(h).
"Lease contract". Section 2A–103(1)(*l*).
"Party". Section 1–201(29) [*unrevised Article 1; see Concordance, p. 22*].
"Purchaser". Section 1–201(33) [*unrevised Article 1; see Concordance, p. 22*].
"Term". Section 1–201(42) [*unrevised Article 1; see Concordance, p. 22*].

As amended in 2022.

§ 2A–302. Title to and Possession of Goods.

Except as otherwise provided in this Article, each provision of this Article applies whether the lessor or a third party has title to the goods, and whether the lessor, the lessee, or a third party has possession of the goods, notwithstanding any statute or rule of law that possession or the absence of possession is fraudulent.

Official Comment

Uniform Statutory Source: Former Section 9–202 (now codified as Section 9–202).

Changes: Former Section 9–202 was modified to reflect leasing terminology and to clarify the law of leases with respect to fraudulent conveyances or transfers.

Purposes: The separation of ownership and possession of goods between the lessor and the lessee (or a third party) has created problems under certain fraudulent conveyance statutes. *See, e.g., In re Ludlum Enters.*, 510 F.2d 996 (5th Cir. 1975); *Suburbia Fed. Sav. & Loan Ass'n v. Bel-Air Conditioning Co.*, 385 So.2d 1151 (Fla.Dist.Ct.App. 1980). This section provides, among other things, that separation of ownership and possession *per se* does not affect the enforceability of the lease contract. Sections 2A–301 and 2A–308.

Cross References:

Sections 2A–301, 2A–308 and 9–202.

Definitional Cross References:

"Goods". Section 2A–103(1)(h).
"Lessee". Section 2A–103(1)(n).
"Lessor". Section 2A–103(1)(p).

§ 2A–303. Alienability of Party's Interest Under Lease Contract or of Lessor's Residual Interest in Goods; Delegation of Performance; Transfer of Rights.

(1)   As used in this section, "creation of a security interest" includes the sale of a lease contract that is subject to Article 9, Secured Transactions, by reason of Section 9–109(a)(3).

(2)   Except as provided in subsection (3) and Section 9–407, a provision in a lease agreement which (i) prohibits the voluntary or involuntary transfer, including a transfer by sale, sublease, creation or enforcement of a security interest, or attachment, levy, or other judicial process, of an interest of a party under the lease contract or of the lessor's residual interest in the goods, or (ii) makes such a transfer an event of default, gives rise to the rights and remedies provided in subsection (4), but a transfer that is prohibited or is an event of default under the lease agreement is otherwise effective.

(3)   A provision in a lease agreement which (i) prohibits a transfer of a right to damages for default with respect to the whole lease contract or of a right to payment arising out of the transferor's due performance of the transferor's entire obligation, or (ii) makes such a transfer an event of default, is not enforceable, and such a transfer is not a transfer that materially impairs the prospect of obtaining return performance by, materially changes the duty of, or materially increases the burden or risk imposed on, the other party to the lease contract within the purview of subsection (4).

(4)   Subject to subsection (3) and Section 9–407:

(a) if a transfer is made which is made an event of default under a lease agreement, the party to the lease contract not making the transfer, unless that party waives the default or otherwise agrees, has the rights and remedies described in Section 2A–501(2);

(b) if paragraph (a) is not applicable and if a transfer is made that (i) is prohibited under a lease agreement or (ii) materially impairs the prospect of obtaining return performance by, materially changes the duty of, or materially increases the burden or risk imposed on, the other party to the lease contract, unless the party not making the transfer agrees at any time to the transfer in the lease contract or otherwise, then, except as limited by contract, (i) the transferor is liable to the party not making the transfer for damages caused by the transfer to the extent that the damages could not reasonably be prevented by the party not making the transfer and (ii) a court having jurisdiction may grant other appropriate relief, including cancellation of the lease contract or an injunction against the transfer.

(5) A transfer of "the lease" or of "all my rights under the lease", or a transfer in similar general terms, is a transfer of rights and, unless the language or the circumstances, as in a transfer for security, indicate the contrary, the transfer is a delegation of duties by the transferor to the transferee. Acceptance by the transferee constitutes a promise by the transferee to perform those duties. The promise is enforceable by either the transferor or the other party to the lease contract.

(6) Unless otherwise agreed by the lessor and the lessee, a delegation of performance does not relieve the transferor as against the other party of any duty to perform or of any liability for default.

(7) In a consumer lease, to prohibit the transfer of an interest of a party under the lease contract or to make a transfer an event of default, the language must be specific, by a writing, and conspicuous.

As amended in 1990 and 1999.

Official Comment

Uniform Statutory Source: Section 2–210; former Section 9–311 (now codified as Section 9–401).

Changes: The provisions of Section 2–210 and former Section 9–311 were incorporated in this section, with substantial modifications to reflect leasing terminology and practice and to harmonize the principles of the respective provisions, i.e. limitations on delegation of performance on the one hand and alienability of rights on the other. In addition, unlike Section 2–210 which deals only with voluntary transfers, this section deals with involuntary as well as voluntary transfers. Moreover, the principle of former Section 9–318(4) (now codified as Section 9–406) denying effectiveness to contractual terms prohibiting assignments of receivables due and to become due also is implemented.

Purposes:

1. Subsection (2) states a rule, consistent with Section 9–401(b), that voluntary and involuntary transfers of an interest of a party under the lease contract or of the lessor's residual interest, including by way of the creation or enforcement of a security interest, are effective, notwithstanding a provision in the lease agreement prohibiting the transfer or making the transfer an event of default. Although the transfers are effective, the provision in the lease agreement is nevertheless enforceable, but only as provided in subsection (4). Under subsection (4) the prejudiced party is limited to the remedies on "default under the lease contract" in this Article and, except as limited by this Article, as provided in the lease agreement, if the transfer has been made an event of default. Section 2A–501(2). Usually, there will be a specific provision to this effect or a general provision making a breach of a covenant an event of default. In those cases where the transfer is prohibited, but not made an event of default, the prejudiced party may recover damages; or, if the damage remedy would be ineffective adequately to protect that party, the court can order cancellation of the lease contract or enjoin the transfer. This rule that such provisions generally are enforceable is subject to subsection (3) and Section 9–407, which make such provisions unenforceable in certain instances.

2. Under Section 9–407, a provision in a lease agreement which prohibits the creation or enforcement of a security interest, including sales of lease contracts subject to Article 9 (Section 9–109(a)(3)), or makes it an event of default is generally not enforceable, reflecting the policy of Section 9–406 and former Section 9–318(4).

3. Subsection (3) is based upon Section 2–210(2) and Section 9–406. It makes unenforceable a prohibition against transfers of certain rights to payment or a provision making the transfer an event of default. It also provides that such transfers do not materially impair the prospect of obtaining return performance by, materially change the duty of, or materially increase the burden or risk imposed on, the other party to the lease contract so

as to give rise to the rights and remedies stated in subsection (4). Accordingly, a transfer of a right to payment cannot be prohibited or made an event of default, or be one that materially impairs performance, changes duties or increases risk, if the right is already due or will become due without further performance being required by the party to receive payment. Thus, a lessor can transfer the right to future payments under the lease contract, including by way of a grant of a security interest, and the transfer will not give rise to the rights and remedies stated in subsection (4) if the lessor has no remaining performance under the lease contract. The mere fact that the lessor is obligated to allow the lessee to remain in possession and to use the goods as long as the lessee is not in default does not mean that there is remaining performance on the part of the lessor. Likewise, the fact that the lessor has potential liability under a "non-operating" lease contract for breaches of warranty does not mean that there is remaining performance. In contrast, the lessor would have remaining performance under a lease contract requiring the lessor to regularly maintain and service the goods or to provide "upgrades" of the equipment on a periodic basis in order to avoid obsolescence. The basic distinction is between a mere potential duty to respond which is not remaining performance, and an affirmative duty to render stipulated performance. Although the distinction may be difficult to draw in some cases, it is instructive to focus on the difference between "operating" and "non-operating" leases as generally understood in the marketplace. Even if there is remaining performance under a lease contract, a transfer for security of a right to payment that is made an event of default or that is in violation of a prohibition against transfer does not give rise to the rights and remedies under subsection (4) if it does not constitute an actual delegation of a material performance under Section 9–407.

4.   The application of either the rule of Section 9–407 or the rule of subsection (3) to the grant by the lessor of a security interest in the lessor's right to future payment under the lease contract may produce the same result. Both provisions generally protect security transfers by the lessor in particular because the creation by the lessor of a security interest or the enforcement of that interest generally will not prejudice the lessee's rights if it does not result in a delegation of the lessor's duties. To the contrary, the receipt of loan proceeds or relief from the enforcement of an antecedent debt normally should enhance the lessor's ability to perform its duties under the lease contract. Nevertheless, there are circumstances where relief might be justified. For example, if ownership of the goods is transferred pursuant to enforcement of a security interest to a party whose ownership would prevent the lessee from continuing to possess the goods, relief might be warranted. See 49 U.S.C. § 1401(a) and (b) which places limitations on the operation of aircraft in the United States based on the citizenship or corporate qualification of the registrant.

5.   Relief on the ground of material prejudice when the lease agreement does not prohibit the transfer or make it an event of default should be afforded only in extreme circumstances, considering the fact that the party asserting material prejudice did not insist upon a provision in the lease agreement that would protect against such a transfer.

6.   Subsection (4) implements the rule of subsection (2). Subsection (2) provides that, even though a transfer is effective, a provision in the lease agreement prohibiting it or making it an event of default may be enforceable as provided in subsection (4). See *Brummund v. First National Bank of Clovis*, 656 P.2d 884, 35 U.C.C. Rep.Serv. (Callaghan) 1311 (N.Mex. 1983), stating the analogous rule for Section 9–311. If the transfer prohibited by the lease agreement is made an event of default, then, under subsection (4)(a), unless the default is waived or there is an agreement otherwise, the aggrieved party has the rights and remedies referred to in Section 2A–501(2), viz. those in this Article and, except as limited in the Article, those provided in the lease agreement. In the unlikely circumstance that the lease agreement prohibits the transfer without making a violation of the prohibition an event of default or, even if there is no prohibition against the transfer, and the transfer is one that materially impairs performance, changes duties, or increases risk (for example, a sublease or assignment to a party using the goods improperly or for an illegal purpose), then subsection (4)(b) is applicable. In that circumstance, unless the party aggrieved by the transfer has otherwise agreed in the lease contract, such as by assenting to a particular transfer or to transfers in general, or agrees in some other manner, the aggrieved party has the right to recover damages from the transferor and a court may, in appropriate circumstances, grant other relief, such as cancellation of the lease contract or an injunction against the transfer.

7.   If a transfer gives rise to the rights and remedies provided in subsection (4), the transferee as an alternative may propose, and the other party may accept, adequate cure or compensation for past defaults and adequate assurance of future due performance under the lease contract. Subsection (4) does not preclude any other relief that may be available to a party to the lease contract aggrieved by a transfer subject to an enforceable prohibition, such as an action for interference with contractual relations.

8.   Subsection (7) requires that a provision in a consumer lease prohibiting a transfer, or making it an event of default, must be specific, written and conspicuous. See Section 1–201(10) 1–201(b)(10). This assists in protecting a consumer lessee against surprise assertions of default.

9.   Subsection (5) is taken almost verbatim from the provisions of Section 2–210(5). The subsection states a rule of construction that distinguishes a commercial assignment, which substitutes the assignee for the assignor as to rights and duties, and an assignment for security or financing assignment, which substitutes the assignee for the assignor only as to rights. Note that the assignment for security or financing assignment is a subset of all security interests. Security interest is defined to include "any interest of a buyer of . . . chattel paper". Section 1–201(37) 1–201(b)(35). Chattel paper is defined to include a lease. Section 9–102. Thus, a buyer of leases is the holder of a security interest in the leases. That conclusion should not influence this issue, as the policy is quite different. Whether a buyer of leases is the holder of a commercial assignment, or an assignment for security or financing assignment should be determined by the language of the assignment or the circumstances of the assignment.

10.   As to the use of a record other than a writing and communications that are not written, see Section 2A–103, Comment (g).

Cross References:

Sections 1–201(11) [*unrevised Article 1; see Concordance, p. 22*], 1–201(37) [*unrevised Article 1; see Concordance, p. 22*], 2–210, 2A–401, 9–102(a)(11), 9–109(a)(3), 9–406, and 9–407.

Definitional Cross References:

"Agreed" and "Agreement". Section 1–201(3) [*unrevised Article 1; see Concordance, p. 22*].

"Conspicuous". Section 1–201(10) [*unrevised Article 1; see Concordance, p. 22*].

"Goods". Section 2A–103(1)(h).

"Lease". Section 2A–103(1)(j).

"Lease contract". Section 2A–103(1)(*l*).

"Lessee". Section 2A–103(1)(n).

"Lessor". Section 2A–103(1)(p).

"Lessor's residual interest". Section 2A–103(1)(q).

"Notice". Section 1–201(25) [*unrevised Article 1; see Concordance, p. 22*].

"Party". Section 1–201(29) [*unrevised Article 1; see Concordance, p. 22*].

"Person". Section 1–201(30) [*unrevised Article 1; see Concordance, p. 22*].

"Reasonable time". Section 1–204(1) and (2) [*unrevised Article 1; see Concordance, p. 22*].

"Rights". Section 1–201(36) [*unrevised Article 1; see Concordance, p. 22*].

"Term". Section 1–201(42) [*unrevised Article 1; see Concordance, p. 22*].

"Writing". Section 1–201(46) [*unrevised Article 1; see Concordance, p. 22*].

As amended in 1999 and 2022.

§ 2A–304. Subsequent Lease of Goods by Lessor.

(1)   Subject to Section 2A–303, a subsequent lessee from a lessor of goods under an existing lease contract obtains, to the extent of the leasehold interest transferred, the leasehold interest in the goods that the lessor had or had power to transfer, and except as provided in subsection (2) and Section 2A–527(4), takes subject to the existing lease contract. A lessor with voidable title has power to transfer a good leasehold interest to a good faith subsequent lessee for value, but only to the extent set forth in the preceding sentence. If goods have been delivered under a transaction of purchase, the lessor has that power even though:

(a)   the lessor's transferor was deceived as to the identity of the lessor;

(b)   the delivery was in exchange for a check which is later dishonored;

(c)   it was agreed that the transaction was to be a "cash sale"; or

(d)   the delivery was procured through fraud punishable as larcenous under the criminal law.

(2)   A subsequent lessee in the ordinary course of business from a lessor who is a merchant dealing in goods of that kind to whom the goods were entrusted by the existing lessee of that lessor before the interest of the subsequent lessee became enforceable against that lessor obtains, to the extent of the leasehold interest transferred, all of that lessor's and the existing lessee's rights to the goods, and takes free of the existing lease contract.

(3)   A subsequent lessee from the lessor of goods that are subject to an existing lease contract and are covered by a certificate of title issued under a statute of this State or of another jurisdiction takes no greater rights than those provided both by this section and by the certificate of title statute.

As amended in 1990.

Official Comment

Uniform Statutory Source: Section 2–403.

Changes: While Section 2–403 was used as a model for this section, the provisions of Section 2–403 were significantly revised to reflect leasing practices and to integrate this Article with certificate of title statutes.

Purposes:

1.   This section must be read in conjunction with, as it is subject to, the provisions of Section 2A–303, which govern voluntary and involuntary transfers of rights and duties under a lease contract, including the lessor's residual interest in the goods.

2.   This section must also be read in conjunction with Section 2–403. This section and Section 2A–305 are derived from Section 2–403, which states a unified policy on good faith purchases of goods. Given the scope of the definition of purchaser (Section 1–201(33) 1–201(b)(30)), a person who bought goods to lease as well as a person who bought goods subject to an existing lease from a lessor will take pursuant to Section 2–403. Further, a person who leases such goods from the person who bought them should also be protected under Section 2–403, first because the lessee's rights are derivative and second because the definition of purchaser should be interpreted to include one who takes by lease; no negative implication should be drawn from the inclusion of lease in the definition of purchase in this Article. Section 2A–103(1)(v).

3.   There are hypotheticals that relate to an entrustee's unauthorized lease of entrusted goods to a third party that are outside the provisions of Sections 2–403, 2A–304 and 2A–305. Consider a sale of goods by M, a merchant, to B, a buyer. After paying for the goods B allows M to retain possession of the goods as B is short of storage. Before B calls for the goods M leases the goods to L, a lessee. This transaction is not governed by Section 2–403(2) as L is not a buyer in the ordinary course of business. Section 1–201(9) 1–201(b)(9). Further, this transaction is not governed by Section 2A–304(2) as B is not an existing lessee. Finally, this transaction is not governed by Section 2A–305(2) as B is not M's lessor. Section 2A–307(2) resolves the potential dispute between B, M and L. By virtue of B's entrustment of the goods to M and M's lease of the goods to L, B has a cause of action against M under the common law. Sections 2A–103(4) and 1–103. *See, e.g.,* Restatement (Second) of Torts §§ 222A–243. Thus, B is a creditor of M. Sections 2A–103(4) and 1–201(12) 1–201(b)(13). Section 2A–307(2) provides that B, as M's creditor, takes subject to M's lease to L. Thus, if L does not default under the lease, L's enjoyment and possession of the goods should be undisturbed. However, B is not without recourse. B's action should result in a judgment against M providing, among other things, a turnover of all proceeds arising from M's lease to L, as well as a transfer of all of M's right, title and interest as lessor under M's lease to L, including M's residual interest in the goods. Section 2A–103(1)(q).

4.   Subsection (1) states a rule with respect to the leasehold interest obtained by a subsequent lessee from a lessor of goods under an existing lease contract. The interest will include such leasehold interest as the lessor has in the goods as well as the leasehold interest that the lessor had the power to transfer. Thus, the subsequent lessee obtains unimpaired all rights acquired under the law of agency, apparent agency, ownership or other estoppel, whether based upon statutory provisions or upon case law principles. Sections 2A–103(4) and 1–103. In general, the subsequent lessee takes subject to the existing lease contract, including the existing lessee's rights thereunder. Furthermore, the subsequent lease contract is, of course, limited by its own terms, and the subsequent lessee takes only to the extent of the leasehold interest transferred thereunder.

5.   Subsection (1) further provides that a lessor with voidable title has power to transfer a good leasehold interest to a good faith subsequent lessee for value. In addition, subsections (1)(a) through (d) provide specifically for the protection of the good faith subsequent lessee for value in a number of specific situations which have been troublesome under prior law.

6.   The position of an existing lessee who entrusts leased goods to its lessor is not distinguishable from the position of other entrusters. Thus, subsection (2) provides that the subsequent lessee in the ordinary course of business takes free of the existing lease contract between the lessor entrustee and the lessee entruster, if the lessor is a merchant dealing in goods of that kind. Further, the subsequent lessee obtains all of the lessor entrustee's and the lessee entruster's rights to the goods, but only to the extent of the leasehold interest transferred by the lessor entrustee. Thus, the lessor entrustee retains the residual interest in the goods. Section 2A–103(1)(q).

However, entrustment by the existing lessee must have occurred before the interest of the subsequent lessee became enforceable against the lessor. Entrusting is defined in Section 2–403(3) and that definition applies here. Section 2A–103(3).

7.   Subsection (3) states a rule with respect to a transfer of goods from a lessor to a subsequent lessee where the goods are subject to an existing lease and covered by a certificate of title. The subsequent lessee's rights are no greater than those provided by this section and the applicable certificate of title statute, including any applicable case law construing such statute. Where the relationship between the certificate of title statute and Section 2–403, the statutory analogue to this section, has been construed by a court, that construction is incorporated here. Sections 2A–103(4) and 1–102(1) and (2) [*unrevised Article 1; see Concordance, p. 22*]. The better rule is that the certificate of title statutes are in harmony with Section 2–403 and thus would be in harmony with this section. *E.g.*, *Atwood Chevrolet-Olds v. Aberdeen Mun. School Dist.*, 431 So.2d 926, 928 (Miss. 1983); *Godfrey v. Gilsdorf*, 476 P.2d 3, 6, 86 Nev. 714, 718 (1970); *Martin v. Nager*, 192 N.J.Super. 189, 197–98, 469 A.2d 519, 523 (Super.Ct.Ch.Div. 1983). Where the certificate of title statute is silent on this issue of transfer, this section will control.

Cross References:

Sections 1–102 [*unrevised Article 1; see Concordance, p. 22*], 1–103, 1–201(33) [*unrevised Article 1; see Concordance, p. 22*], 2–403, 2A–103(1)(v), 2A–103(3), 2A–103(4), 2A–303 and 2A–305.

Definitional Cross References:

"Agreed". Section 1–201(3) [*unrevised Article 1; see Concordance, p. 22*].
"Delivery". Section 1–201(14) [*unrevised Article 1; see Concordance, p. 22*].
"Entrusting". Section 2–403(3).
"Good faith". Sections 1–201(19) [*unrevised Article 1; see Concordance, p. 22*] and 2–103(1)(b).
"Goods". Section 2A–103(1)(h).
"Lease". Section 2A–103(1)(j).
"Lease contract". Section 2A–103(1)(*l*).
"Leasehold interest". Section 2A–103(1)(m).
"Lessee". Section 2A–103(1)(n).
"Lessee in the ordinary course of business". Section 2A–103(1)(o).
"Lessor". Section 2A–103(1)(p).
"Merchant". Section 2–104(1).
"Purchase". Section 2A–103(1)(v).
"Rights". Section 1–201(36) [*unrevised Article 1; see Concordance, p. 22*].
"Value". Section 1–201(44) [*unrevised Article 1; see Concordance, p. 22*].

As amended in 2022.

§ 2A–305.   Sale or Sublease of Goods by Lessee.

(1)   Subject to the provisions of Section 2A–303, a buyer or sublessee from the lessee of goods under an existing lease contract obtains, to the extent of the interest transferred, the leasehold interest in the goods that the lessee had or had power to transfer, and except as provided in subsection (2) and Section 2A–511(4), takes subject to the existing lease contract. A lessee with a voidable leasehold interest has power to transfer a good leasehold interest to a good faith buyer for value or a good faith sublessee for value, but only to the extent set forth in the preceding sentence. When goods have been delivered under a transaction of lease the lessee has that power even though:

(a)   the lessor was deceived as to the identity of the lessee;

(b)   the delivery was in exchange for a check which is later dishonored; or

(c)   the delivery was procured through fraud punishable as larcenous under the criminal law.

(2)   A buyer in the ordinary course of business or a sublessee in the ordinary course of business from a lessee who is a merchant dealing in goods of that kind to whom the goods were entrusted by the lessor obtains, to the extent of the interest transferred, all of the lessor's and lessee's rights to the goods, and takes free of the existing lease contract.

(3) A buyer or sublessee from the lessee of goods that are subject to an existing lease contract and are covered by a certificate of title issued under a statute of this State or of another jurisdiction takes no greater rights than those provided both by this section and by the certificate of title statute.

Official Comment

Uniform Statutory Source: Section 2–403.

Changes: While Section 2–403 was used as a model for this section, the provisions of Section 2–403 were significantly revised to reflect leasing practice and to integrate this Article with certificate of title statutes.

Purposes: This section, a companion to Section 2A–304, states the rule with respect to the leasehold interest obtained by a buyer or sublessee from a lessee of goods under an existing lease contract. *Cf.* Section 2A–304 official comment. Note that this provision is consistent with existing case law, which prohibits the bailee's transfer of title to a good faith purchaser for value under Section 2–403(1). *Rohweder v. Aberdeen Product. Credit Ass'n*, 765 F.2d 109 (8th Cir. 1985).

Subsection (2) is also consistent with existing case law. *American Standard Credit, Inc. v. National Cement Co.*, 643 F.2d 248, 269–70 (5th Cir. 1981); *but cf. Exxon Co., U.S.A. v. TLW Computer Indus.*, 37 U.C.C.Rep.Serv. (Callaghan) 1052, 1057–58 (D.Mass. 1983). Unlike Section 2A–304(2), this subsection does not contain any requirement with respect to the time that the goods were entrusted to the merchant. In Section 2A–304(2) the competition is between two customers of the merchant lessor; the time of entrusting was added as a criterion to create additional protection to the customer who was first in time: the existing lessee. In subsection (2) the equities between the competing interests were viewed as balanced.

There appears to be some overlap between Section 2–403(2) and Section 2A–305(2) with respect to a buyer in the ordinary course of business. However, an examination of this Article's definition of buyer in the ordinary course of business (Section 2A–103(1)(a)) makes clear that this reference was necessary to treat entrusting in the context of a lease.

Subsection (3) states a rule of construction with respect to a transfer of goods from a lessee to a buyer or sublessee, where the goods are subject to an existing lease and covered by a certificate of title. *Cf.* Section 2A–304 official comment.

Cross References:

Sections 2–403, 2A–103(1)(a), 2A–304 and 2A–305(2).

Definitional Cross References:

"Buyer". Section 2–103(1)(a).
"Buyer in the ordinary course of business". Section 2A–103(1)(a).
"Delivery". Section 1–201(14) [*unrevised Article 1; see Concordance, p. 22*].
"Entrusting". Section 2–403(3).
"Good faith". Sections 1–201(19) [*unrevised Article 1; see Concordance, p. 22*] and 2–103(1)(b).
"Goods". Section 2A–103(1)(h).
"Lease". Section 2A–103(1)(j).
"Lease contract". Section 2A–103(1)(*l*).
"Leasehold interest." Section 2A–103(1)(m).
"Lessee". Section 2A–103(1)(n).
"Lessee in the ordinary course of business". Section 2A–103(1)(*o*).
"Lessor". Section 2A–103(1)(p).
"Merchant". Section 2–104(1).
"Rights". Section 1–201(36) [*unrevised Article 1; see Concordance, p. 22*].
"Sale". Section 2–106(1).
"Sublease". Section 2A–103(1)(w).
"Value". Section 1–201(44) [*unrevised Article 1; see Concordance, p. 22*].

§ 2A–306. Priority of Certain Liens Arising by Operation of Law.

If a person in the ordinary course of his [or her] business furnishes services or materials with respect to goods subject to a lease contract, a lien upon those goods in the possession of that person given by statute or rule of law for those materials or services takes priority over any interest of the lessor or lessee under the lease contract or this Article unless the lien is created by statute and the statute provides otherwise or unless the lien is created by rule of law and the rule of law provides otherwise.

Official Comment

Uniform Statutory Source: Former Section 9–310 (now codified as Section 9–333).

Changes: The approach reflected in the provisions of former Section 9–310 was included, but revised to conform to leasing terminology and to expand the exception to the special priority granted to protected liens to cover liens created by rule of law as well as those created by statute.

Purposes: This section should be interpreted to allow a qualified lessor or a qualified lessee to be the competing lienholder if the statute or rule of law so provides. The reference to statute includes applicable regulations and cases; these sources must be reviewed in resolving a priority dispute under this section.

Cross Reference:

    Section 9–333.

Definitional Cross References:

    "Goods". Section 2A–103(1)(h).
    "Lease contract". Section 2A–103(1)(*l*).
    "Lessee". Section 2A–103(1)(n).
    "Lessor". Section 2A–103(1)(p).
    "Lien". Section 2A–103(1)(r).
    "Person". Section 1–201(30) [*unrevised Article 1; see Concordance, p. 22*].

§ 2A–307.   Priority of Liens Arising by Attachment or Levy on, Security Interests in, and Other Claims to Goods.

    (1)   Except as otherwise provided in Section 2A–306, a creditor of a lessee takes subject to the lease contract.

    (2)   Except as otherwise provided in subsection (3) and in Sections 2A–306 and 2A–308, a creditor of a lessor takes subject to the lease contract unless the creditor holds a lien that attached to the goods before the lease contract became enforceable.

    (3)   Except as otherwise provided in Sections 9–317, 9–321, and 9–323, a lessee takes a leasehold interest subject to a security interest held by a creditor of the lessor.

As amended in 1990 and 1999.

Official Comment

Uniform Statutory Source: None for subsection (1). The remainder of the Section was derived from former Sections 9–301 (now codified as Section 9–317) and 9–307(1) and (3) (now codified as Sections 9–320(a) and 9–323), respectively, and was substantially rewritten in conjunction with the 1998 revisions of Article 9.

Changes: The provisions of former Sections 9–301 and 9–307(1) and (3) were incorporated, and modified to reflect leasing terminology and the basic concepts reflected in this Article.

1998 Changes: Many of the substantive provisions of this Section were moved to Article 9 in conjunction with the 1998 revisions of Article 9.

Purposes:

    1.   Subsection (1) states a general rule of priority that a creditor of the lessee takes subject to the lease contract. The term lessee (Section 2A–103(1)(n)) includes sublessee. Therefore, this subsection not only covers disputes between the prime lessor and a creditor of the prime lessee but also disputes between the prime lessor, or the sublessor, and a creditor of the sublessee. Section 2A–301 ~~official comment~~ Comment 3(g). Further, by using the term creditor (Section~~1–201(12)~~ 1–201(b)(13)), this subsection will cover disputes with a general creditor, a secured creditor, a lien creditor and any representative of creditors. Section 2A–103(4).

    2.   Subsection (2) states a general rule of priority that a creditor of a lessor takes subject to the lease contract. Note the discussion above with regard to the scope of these rules. Section 2A–301 official comment 3(g).

Thus, the section will not only cover disputes between the prime lessee and a creditor of the prime lessor but also disputes between the prime lessee, or the sublessee, and a creditor of the sublessor.

3.   To take priority over the lease contract, and the interests derived therefrom, the creditor must come within the exception stated in subsection (2) or within one of the provisions of Article 9 mentioned in subsection (3). Subsection (2) provides that where the creditor holds a lien (Section 2A–103(1)(r)) that attached before the lease contract became enforceable (Section 2A–301), the creditor does not take subject to the lease. Subsection (3) provides that a lessee takes its leasehold interest subject to a security interest except as otherwise provided in Sections 9–317, 9–321, or 9–323.

4.   The rules of this section operate in favor of whichever party to the lease contract may enforce it, even if one party perhaps may not, e.g., under Section 2A–201(1)(b).

Cross References:

Sections 1–201(12) [*unrevised Article 1; see Concordance, p. 22*], 1–201(25) [*unrevised Article 1; see Concordance, p. 22*], 1–201(37) [*unrevised Article 1; see Concordance, p. 22*], 1–201(44) [*unrevised Article 1; see Concordance, p. 22*], 2A–103(1)(n), 2A–103(1)(o), 2A–103(1)(r), 2A–103(4), 2A–201(1)(b), 2A–301 official comment 3(g), Article 9, especially Sections 9–317, 9–321 and 9–323.

Definitional Cross References:

"Creditor". Section 1–201(12) [*unrevised Article 1; see Concordance, p. 22*].
"Goods". Section 2A–103(1)(h).
"Knowledge" and "Knows". Section 1–201(25) [*unrevised Article 1; see Concordance, p. 22*].
"Lease". Section 2A–103(1)(j).
"Lease contract". Section 2A–103(1)(*l*).
"Leasehold interest". Section 2A–103(1)(m).
"Lessee". Section 2A–103(1)(n).
"Lessee in the ordinary course of business". Section 2A–103(1)(o).
"Lessor". Section 2A–103(1)(p).
"Lien". Section 2A–103(1)(r).
"Party". Section 1–201(29) [*unrevised Article 1; see Concordance, p. 22*].
"Pursuant to commitment". Section 2A–103(3).
"Security interest". Section 1–201(37) [*unrevised Article 1; see Concordance, p. 22*].

As amended in 1999 and 2022.

§ 2A–308.   Special Rights of Creditors.

(1)   A creditor of a lessor in possession of goods subject to a lease contract may treat the lease contract as void if as against the creditor retention of possession by the lessor is fraudulent under any statute or rule of law, but retention of possession in good faith and current course of trade by the lessor for a commercially reasonable time after the lease contract becomes enforceable is not fraudulent.

(2)   Nothing in this Article impairs the rights of creditors of a lessor if the lease contract (a) becomes enforceable, not in current course of trade but in satisfaction of or as security for a pre-existing claim for money, security, or the like, and (b) is made under circumstances which under any statute or rule of law apart from this Article would constitute the transaction a fraudulent transfer or voidable preference.

(3)   A creditor of a seller may treat a sale or an identification of goods to a contract for sale as void if as against the creditor retention of possession by the seller is fraudulent under any statute or rule of law, but retention of possession of the goods pursuant to a lease contract entered into by the seller as lessee and the buyer as lessor in connection with the sale or identification of the goods is not fraudulent if the buyer bought for value and in good faith.

Official Comment

Uniform Statutory Source: Section 2–402(2) and (3)(b).

Changes: Rephrased and new material added to conform to leasing terminology and practice.

Purposes: Subsection (1) states a general rule of avoidance where the lessor has retained possession of goods if such retention is fraudulent under any statute or rule of law. However, the subsection creates an exception under certain circumstances for retention of possession of goods for a commercially reasonable time after the lease contract becomes enforceable.

Subsection (2) also preserves the possibility of an attack on the lease by creditors of the lessor if the lease was made in satisfaction of or as security for a pre-existing claim, and would constitute a fraudulent transfer or voidable preference under other law.

Finally, subsection (3) states a new rule with respect to sale-leaseback transactions, *i.e.*, transactions where the seller sells goods to a buyer but possession of the goods is retained by the seller pursuant to a lease contract between the buyer as lessor and the seller as lessee. Notwithstanding any statute or rule of law that would treat such retention as fraud, whether *per se, prima facie,* or otherwise, the retention is not fraudulent if the buyer bought for value (Section 1–201(44) 1–204) and in good faith (Sections 1–201(19) and 2–103(1)(b) 1–201(b)(20)). Section 2A–103(3) and (4). This provision overrides Section 2–402(2) to the extent it would otherwise apply to a sale-leaseback transaction.

Cross References:

Sections 1–201(19) [*unrevised Article 1; see Concordance, p. 22*]; 1–201(44) [*unrevised Article 1; see Concordance, p. 22*], 2–402(2) and 2A–103(4).

Definitional Cross References:

"Buyer". Section 2–103(1)(a).
"Contract". Section 1–201(11) [*unrevised Article 1; see Concordance, p. 22*].
"Creditor". Section 1–201(12) [*unrevised Article 1; see Concordance, p. 22*].
"Good faith". Sections 1–201(19) [*unrevised Article 1; see Concordance, p. 22*] and 2–103(1)(b).
"Goods". Section 2A–103(1)(h).
"Lease contract". Section 2A–103(1)(*l*).
"Lessee". Section 2A–103(1)(n).
"Lessor". Section 2A–103(1)(p).
"Money". Section 1–201(24) [*unrevised Article 1; see Concordance, p. 22*].
"Reasonable time". Section 1–204(1) and (2) [*unrevised Article 1; see Concordance, p. 22*].
"Rights". Section 1–201(36) [*unrevised Article 1; see Concordance, p. 22*].
"Sale". Section 2–106(1).
"Seller". Section 2–103(1)(d).
"Value". Section 1–201(44) [*unrevised Article 1; see Concordance, p. 22*].

As amended in 2022.

§ 2A–309. Lessor's and Lessee's Rights When Goods Become Fixtures.

(1) In this section:

(a) goods are "fixtures" when they become so related to particular real estate that an interest in them arises under real estate law;

(b) a "fixture filing" is the filing, in the office where a record of a mortgage on the real estate would be filed or recorded, of a financing statement covering goods that are or are to become fixtures and conforming to the requirements of Section 9–502(a) and (b);

(c) a lease is a "purchase money lease" unless the lessee has possession or use of the goods or the right to possession or use of the goods before the lease agreement is enforceable;

(d) a mortgage is a "construction mortgage" to the extent it secures an obligation incurred for the construction of an improvement on land including the acquisition cost of the land, if the recorded writing so indicates; and

(e) "encumbrance" includes real estate mortgages and other liens on real estate and all other rights in real estate that are not ownership interests.

(2) Under this Article a lease may be of goods that are fixtures or may continue in goods that become fixtures, but no lease exists under this Article of ordinary building materials incorporated into an improvement on land.

(3)   This Article does not prevent creation of a lease of fixtures pursuant to real estate law.

(4)   The perfected interest of a lessor of fixtures has priority over a conflicting interest of an encumbrancer or owner of the real estate if:

(a)   the lease is a purchase money lease, the conflicting interest of the encumbrancer or owner arises before the goods become fixtures, the interest of the lessor is perfected by a fixture filing before the goods become fixtures or within ten days thereafter, and the lessee has an interest of record in the real estate or is in possession of the real estate; or

(b)   the interest of the lessor is perfected by a fixture filing before the interest of the encumbrancer or owner is of record, the lessor's interest has priority over any conflicting interest of a predecessor in title of the encumbrancer or owner, and the lessee has an interest of record in the real estate or is in possession of the real estate.

(5)   The interest of a lessor of fixtures, whether or not perfected, has priority over the conflicting interest of an encumbrancer or owner of the real estate if:

(a)   the fixtures are readily removable factory or office machines, readily removable equipment that is not primarily used or leased for use in the operation of the real estate, or readily removable replacements of domestic appliances that are goods subject to a consumer lease, and before the goods become fixtures the lease contract is enforceable; or

(b)   the conflicting interest is a lien on the real estate obtained by legal or equitable proceedings after the lease contract is enforceable; or

(c)   the encumbrancer or owner has consented in writing to the lease or has disclaimed an interest in the goods as fixtures; or

(d)   the lessee has a right to remove the goods as against the encumbrancer or owner. If the lessee's right to remove terminates, the priority of the interest of the lessor continues for a reasonable time.

(6)   Notwithstanding subsection (4)(a) but otherwise subject to subsections (4) and (5), the interest of a lessor of fixtures, including the lessor's residual interest, is subordinate to the conflicting interest of an encumbrancer of the real estate under a construction mortgage recorded before the goods become fixtures if the goods become fixtures before the completion of the construction. To the extent given to refinance a construction mortgage, the conflicting interest of an encumbrancer of the real estate under a mortgage has this priority to the same extent as the encumbrancer of the real estate under the construction mortgage.

(7)   In cases not within the preceding subsections, priority between the interest of a lessor of fixtures, including the lessor's residual interest, and the conflicting interest of an encumbrancer or owner of the real estate who is not the lessee is determined by the priority rules governing conflicting interests in real estate.

(8)   If the interest of a lessor of fixtures, including the lessor's residual interest, has priority over all conflicting interests of all owners and encumbrancers of the real estate, the lessor or the lessee may (i) on default, expiration, termination, or cancellation of the lease agreement but subject to the agreement and this Article, or (ii) if necessary to enforce other rights and remedies of the lessor or lessee under this Article, remove the goods from the real estate, free and clear of all conflicting interests of all owners and encumbrancers of the real estate, but the lessor or lessee must reimburse any encumbrancer or owner of the real estate who is not the lessee and who has not otherwise agreed for the cost of repair of any physical injury, but not for any diminution in value of the real estate caused by the absence of the goods removed or by any necessity of replacing them. A person entitled to reimbursement may refuse permission to remove until the party seeking removal gives adequate security for the performance of this obligation.

(9)   Even though the lease agreement does not create a security interest, the interest of a lessor of fixtures, including the lessor's residual interest, is perfected by filing a financing statement as a fixture filing for leased goods that are or are to become fixtures in accordance with the relevant provisions of the Article on Secured Transactions (Article 9).

As amended in 1990 and 1999.

Official Comment

Uniform Statutory Source: Former Section 9–313.

Changes: Revised to reflect leasing terminology and to add new material.

Purposes:

1.   While former Section 9–313 (now codified as Sections 9–334 and 9–604) provided a model for this section, certain provisions were substantially revised.

2.   Section 2A–309(1)(c), which is new, defines purchase money lease to exclude leases where the lessee had possession or use of the goods or the right thereof before the lease agreement became enforceable. This term is used in subsection (4)(a) as one of the conditions that must be satisfied to obtain priority over the conflicting interest of an encumbrancer or owner of the real estate.

3.   Section 2A–309(4), which states one of several priority rules found in this section, deletes reference to office machines and the like (former Section 9–313(4)(c) (now codified as Section 9–334(e)(2)(A))) as well as certain liens (former Section 9–313(4)(d) (now codified as Section 9–334(e)(3))). However, these items are included in subsection (5), another priority rule that is more permissive than the rule found in subsection (4) as it applies whether or not the interest of the lessor is perfected. In addition, subsection (5)(a) expands the scope of the provisions of former Section 9–313(4)(c) (now codified as Section 9–334(e)(2)(A)) to include readily removable equipment not primarily used or leased for use in the operation of real estate; the qualifier is intended to exclude from the expanded rule equipment integral to the operation of real estate, *e.g.*, heating and air conditioning equipment.

4.   The rule stated in subsection (7) is more liberal than the rule stated in former Section 9–313(7) (now codified as Section 9–334(c)) in that issues of priority not otherwise resolved in this subsection are left for resolution by the priority rules governing conflicting interests in real estate, as opposed to the former Section 9–313(7) (now codified as Section 9–334(c)) automatic subordination of the security interest in fixtures. Note that, for the purpose of this section, where the interest of an encumbrancer or owner of the real estate is paramount to the interest of the lessor, the latter term includes the residual interest of the lessor.

5.   The rule stated in subsection (8) is more liberal than the rule stated in former Section 9–313(8) (now codified as Section 9–604) in that the right of removal is extended to both the lessor and the lessee and the occasion for removal includes expiration, termination or cancellation of the lease agreement, and enforcement of rights and remedies under this Article, as well as default. The new language also provides that upon removal the goods are free and clear of conflicting interests of owners and encumbrancers of the real estate.

6.   Finally, subsection (9) provides a mechanism for the lessor of fixtures to perfect its interest by filing a financing statement under the provisions of the Article on Secured Transactions (Article 9), even though the lease agreement does not create a security interest. See Section 1–201(37) 1–203. The relevant provisions of Article 9 must be interpreted permissively to give effect to this mechanism as it implicitly expands the scope of Article 9 so that its filing provisions apply to transactions that create a lease of fixtures, even though the lease agreement does not create a security interest. This mechanism is similar to that provided in Section 2–326(3)(c) for the seller of goods on consignment, even though the consignment is not "intended as security". Section 1–201(37). Given the lack of litigation with respect to the mechanism created for consignment sales, this new mechanism should prove effective.

7.   As to the use of a record other than a writing and communications that are not written, see Section 2A–103, Comment (g).

Cross References:

Sections 1–201(37) [*unrevised Article 1; see Concordance, p. 22*], 2A–309(1)(c), 2A–309(4), Article 9, especially Sections 9–334, 9–604 and 9–505.

Definitional Cross References:

"Agreed". Section 1–201(3).
"Cancellation". Section 2A–103(1)(b).
"Conforming". Section 2A–103(1)(d).
"Consumer lease". Section 2A–103(1)(e).
"Goods". Section 2A–103(1)(h).
"Lease". Section 2A–103(1)(j).

"Lease agreement". Section 2A–103(1)(k).

"Lease contract". Section 2A–103(1)(*l*).

"Lessee". Section 2A–103(1)(n).

"Lessor". Section 2A–103(1)(p).

"Lien". Section 2A–103(1)(r).

"Mortgage". Section 9–102(a)(55).

"Party". Section 1–201(29) [*unrevised Article 1; see Concordance, p. 22*].

"Person". Section 1–201(30) [*unrevised Article 1; see Concordance, p. 22*].

"Reasonable time". Section 1–204(1) and (2) [*unrevised Article 1; see Concordance, p. 22*].

"Remedy". Section 1–201(34) [*unrevised Article 1; see Concordance, p. 22*].

"Rights". Section 1–201(36) [*unrevised Article 1; see Concordance, p. 22*].

"Security interest". Section 1–201(37) [*unrevised Article 1; see Concordance, p. 22*].

"Termination". Section 2A–103(1)(z).

"Value". Section 1–201(44) [*unrevised Article 1; see Concordance, p. 22*].

"Writing". Section 1–201(46) [*unrevised Article 1; see Concordance, p. 22*].

As amended in 2022.

§ 2A–310. Lessor's and Lessee's Rights When Goods Become Accessions.

(1)   Goods are "accessions" when they are installed in or affixed to other goods.

(2)   The interest of a lessor or a lessee under a lease contract entered into before the goods became accessions is superior to all interests in the whole except as stated in subsection (4).

(3)   The interest of a lessor or a lessee under a lease contract entered into at the time or after the goods became accessions is superior to all subsequently acquired interests in the whole except as stated in subsection (4) but is subordinate to interests in the whole existing at the time the lease contract was made unless the holders of such interests in the whole have in writing consented to the lease or disclaimed an interest in the goods as part of the whole.

(4)   The interest of a lessor or a lessee under a lease contract described in subsection (2) or (3) is subordinate to the interest of

(a)   a buyer in the ordinary course of business or a lessee in the ordinary course of business of any interest in the whole acquired after the goods became accessions; or

(b)   a creditor with a security interest in the whole perfected before the lease contract was made to the extent that the creditor makes subsequent advances without knowledge of the lease contract.

(5)   When under subsections (2) or (3) and (4) a lessor or a lessee of accessions holds an interest that is superior to all interests in the whole, the lessor or the lessee may (a) on default, expiration, termination, or cancellation of the lease contract by the other party but subject to the provisions of the lease contract and this Article, or (b) if necessary to enforce his [or her] other rights and remedies under this Article, remove the goods from the whole, free and clear of all interests in the whole, but he [or she] must reimburse any holder of an interest in the whole who is not the lessee and who has not otherwise agreed for the cost of repair of any physical injury but not for any diminution in value of the whole caused by the absence of the goods removed or by any necessity for replacing them. A person entitled to reimbursement may refuse permission to remove until the party seeking removal gives adequate security for the performance of this obligation.

Official Comment

Uniform Statutory Source: Former Section 9–314 (now codified as Section 9–335).

Changes: Revised to reflect leasing terminology and to add new material.

Purposes: Subsection (1) defines "accessions." Subsection (2) adds leasing terminology to the priority rule that applies when the lease is entered into before the goods become accessions. Subsection (3) adds leasing terminology to the priority rule that applies when the lease is entered into on or after the goods become accessions.

Subsection (4) creates two exceptions to the priority rules stated in subsections (2) and (3).

Finally, subsection (5) is modeled on the provisions of former Section 9–314(4) (now codified as Section 9–335(d) and (e)) with respect to removal of accessions, restated to reflect the parallel changes in Section 2A–309(8).

Neither this section nor Section 9–335 governs where the accession to the goods is not subject to the interest of a lessor or a lessee under a lease contract and is not subject to the interest of a secured party under a security agreement. This issue is to be resolved by the courts, case by case.

As to the use of a record other than a writing and communications that are not written, see Section 2A–103, Comment (g).

Cross References:

Sections 2A–309(8), 9–102(a)(1), 9–335.

Definitional Cross References:

"Agreed". Section 1–201(3) [*unrevised Article 1; see Concordance, p. 22*].
"Buyer in the ordinary course of business". Section 2A–103(1)(a).
"Cancellation". Section 2A–103(1)(b).
"Creditor". Section 1–201(12) [*unrevised Article 1; see Concordance, p. 22*].
"Goods". Section 2A–103(1)(h).
"Holder". Section 1–201(20) [*unrevised Article 1; see Concordance, p. 22*].
"Knowledge". Section 1–201(25) [*unrevised Article 1; see Concordance, p. 22*].
"Lease". Section 2A–103(1)(j).
"Lease contract". Section 2A–103(1)(*l*).
"Lessee". Section 2A–103(1)(n).
"Lessee in the ordinary course of business". Section 2A–103(1)(o).
"Lessor". Section 2A–103(1)(p).
"Party". Section 1–201(29) [*unrevised Article 1; see Concordance, p. 22*].
"Person". Section 1–201(30) [*unrevised Article 1; see Concordance, p. 22*].
"Remedy". Section 1–201(34) [*unrevised Article 1; see Concordance, p. 22*].
"Rights". Section 1–201(36) [*unrevised Article 1; see Concordance, p. 22*].
"Security interest". Section 1–201(37) [*unrevised Article 1; see Concordance, p. 22*].
"Termination". Section 2A–103(1)(z).
"Value". Section 1–201(44) [*unrevised Article 1; see Concordance, p. 22*].
"Writing". Section 1–201(46) [*unrevised Article 1; see Concordance, p. 22*].

As amended in 2022.

§ 2A–311. Priority Subject to Subordination.

Nothing in this Article prevents subordination by agreement by any person entitled to priority.

As added in 1990.

Official Comment

Uniform Statutory Source: Former Section 9–316 (now codified as Section 9–339).

Purposes: The several preceding sections deal with questions of priority. This section is inserted to make it entirely clear that a person entitled to priority may effectively agree to subordinate the claim. Only the person entitled to priority may make such an agreement: the rights of such a person cannot be adversely affected by an agreement to which that person is not a party.

Cross References:

Sections 1–102 [*unrevised Article 1; see Concordance, p. 22*] and 2A–304 through 2A–310.

Definitional Cross References:

"Agreement". Section 1–201(3) [*unrevised Article 1; see Concordance, p. 22*].
"Person". Section 1–201(30) [*unrevised Article 1; see Concordance, p. 22*].

PART 4

PERFORMANCE OF LEASE CONTRACT: REPUDIATED, SUBSTITUTED AND EXCUSED

§ 2A–401. Insecurity: Adequate Assurance of Performance.

(1)   A lease contract imposes an obligation on each party that the other's expectation of receiving due performance will not be impaired.

(2)   If reasonable grounds for insecurity arise with respect to the performance of either party, the insecure party may demand in writing adequate assurance of due performance. Until the insecure party receives that assurance, if commercially reasonable the insecure party may suspend any performance for which he [or she] has not already received the agreed return.

(3)   A repudiation of the lease contract occurs if assurance of due performance adequate under the circumstances of the particular case is not provided to the insecure party within a reasonable time, not to exceed 30 days after receipt of a demand by the other party.

(4)   Between merchants, the reasonableness of grounds for insecurity and the adequacy of any assurance offered must be determined according to commercial standards.

(5)   Acceptance of any nonconforming delivery or payment does not prejudice the aggrieved party's right to demand adequate assurance of future performance.

Official Comment

Uniform Statutory Source: Section 2–609.

Changes: Revised to reflect leasing practices and terminology. Note that in the analogue to subsection (3) (Section 2–609(4)), the adjective "justified" modifies demand. The adjective was deleted here as unnecessary, implying no substantive change. As to the use of a record other than a writing and communications that are not written, see Section 2A–103, Comment (g).

Definitional Cross References:

"Aggrieved party". Section 1–201(2) [*unrevised Article 1; see Concordance, p. 22*].
"Agreed". Section 1–201(3) [*unrevised Article 1; see Concordance, p. 22*].
"Between merchants". Section 2–104(3).
"Conforming". Section 2A–103(1)(d).
"Delivery". Section 1–201(14) [*unrevised Article 1; see Concordance, p. 22*].
"Lease contract". Section 2A–103(1)(*l*).
"Party". Section 1–201(29) [*unrevised Article 1; see Concordance, p. 22*].
"Reasonable time". Section 1–204(1) and (2) [*unrevised Article 1; see Concordance, p. 22*].
"Receipt". Section 2–103(1)(c).
"Rights". Section 1–201(36) [*unrevised Article 1; see Concordance, p. 22*].
"Writing". Section 1–201(46) [*unrevised Article 1; see Concordance, p. 22*].

As amended in 2022.

§ 2A–402. Anticipatory Repudiation.

If either party repudiates a lease contract with respect to a performance not yet due under the lease contract, the loss of which performance will substantially impair the value of the lease contract to the other, the aggrieved party may:

(a)   for a commercially reasonable time, await retraction of repudiation and performance by the repudiating party;

(b)   make demand pursuant to Section 2A–401 and await assurance of future performance adequate under the circumstances of the particular case; or

(c) resort to any right or remedy upon default under the lease contract or this Article, even though the aggrieved party has notified the repudiating party that the aggrieved party would await the repudiating party's performance and assurance and has urged retraction. In addition, whether or not the aggrieved party is pursuing one of the foregoing remedies, the aggrieved party may suspend performance or, if the aggrieved party is the lessor, proceed in accordance with the provisions of this Article on the lessor's right to identify goods to the lease contract notwithstanding default or to salvage unfinished goods (Section 2A–524).

Official Comment

Uniform Statutory Source: Section 2–610.

Changes: Revised to reflect leasing practices and terminology.

Definitional Cross References:

"Aggrieved party". Section 1–201(2) [*unrevised Article 1; see Concordance, p. 22*].
"Goods". Section 2A–103(1)(h).
"Lease contract". Section 2A–103(1)(*l*).
"Lessor". Section 2A–103(1)(p).
"Notifies". Section 1–201(26) [*unrevised Article 1; see Concordance, p. 22*].
"Party". Section 1–201(29) [*unrevised Article 1; see Concordance, p. 22*].
"Reasonable time". Section 1–204(1) and (2) [*unrevised Article 1; see Concordance, p. 22*].
"Remedy". Section 1–201(34) [*unrevised Article 1; see Concordance, p. 22*].
"Rights". Section 1–201(36) [*unrevised Article 1; see Concordance, p. 22*].
"Value". Section 1–201(44) [*unrevised Article 1; see Concordance, p. 22*].

§ 2A–403. Retraction of Anticipatory Repudiation.

(1) Until the repudiating party's next performance is due, the repudiating party can retract the repudiation unless, since the repudiation, the aggrieved party has cancelled the lease contract or materially changed the aggrieved party's position or otherwise indicated that the aggrieved party considers the repudiation final.

(2) Retraction may be by any method that clearly indicates to the aggrieved party that the repudiating party intends to perform under the lease contract and includes any assurance demanded under Section 2A–401.

(3) Retraction reinstates a repudiating party's rights under a lease contract with due excuse and allowance to the aggrieved party for any delay occasioned by the repudiation.

Official Comment

Uniform Statutory Source: Section 2–611.

Changes: Revised to reflect leasing practices and terminology. Note that in the analogue to subsection (2) (Section 2–611(2)) the adjective "justifiably" modifies demanded. The adjective was deleted here (as it was in Section 2A–401) as unnecessary, implying no substantive change.

Definitional Cross References:

"Aggrieved party". Section 1–201(2) [*unrevised Article 1; see Concordance, p. 22*].
"Cancellation". Section 2A–103(1)(b).
"Lease contract". Section 2A–103(1)(*l*).
"Party". Section 1–201(29) [*unrevised Article 1; see Concordance, p. 22*].
"Rights". Section 1–201(36) [*unrevised Article 1; see Concordance, p. 22*].

§ 2A–404. Substituted Performance.

(1) If without fault of the lessee, the lessor and the supplier, the agreed berthing, loading, or unloading facilities fail or the agreed type of carrier becomes unavailable or the agreed manner of delivery otherwise becomes commercially impracticable, but a commercially reasonable substitute is available, the substitute performance must be tendered and accepted.

(2) If the agreed means or manner of payment fails because of domestic or foreign governmental regulation:

(a) the lessor may withhold or stop delivery or cause the supplier to withhold or stop delivery unless the lessee provides a means or manner of payment that is commercially a substantial equivalent; and

(b) if delivery has already been taken, payment by the means or in the manner provided by the regulation discharges the lessee's obligation unless the regulation is discriminatory, oppressive, or predatory.

Official Comment

Uniform Statutory Source: Section 2–614.

Changes: Revised to reflect leasing practices and terminology.

Definitional Cross References:

"Agreed". Section 1–201(3) [*unrevised Article 1; see Concordance, p. 22*].
"Delivery". Section 1–201(14) [*unrevised Article 1; see Concordance, p. 22*].
"Fault". Section 2A–103(1)(f).
"Lessee". Section 2A–103(1)(n).
"Lessor". Section 2A–103(1)(p).
"Supplier". Section 2A–103(1)(x).

§ 2A–405. Excused Performance.

Subject to Section 2A–404 on substituted performance, the following rules apply:

(a) Delay in delivery or nondelivery in whole or in part by a lessor or a supplier who complies with paragraphs (b) and (c) is not a default under the lease contract if performance as agreed has been made impracticable by the occurrence of a contingency the nonoccurrence of which was a basic assumption on which the lease contract was made or by compliance in good faith with any applicable foreign or domestic governmental regulation or order, whether or not the regulation or order later proves to be invalid.

(b) If the causes mentioned in paragraph (a) affect only part of the lessor's or the supplier's capacity to perform, he [or she] shall allocate production and deliveries among his [or her] customers but at his [or her] option may include regular customers not then under contract for sale or lease as well as his [or her] own requirements for further manufacture. He [or she] may so allocate in any manner that is fair and reasonable.

(c) The lessor seasonably shall notify the lessee and in the case of a finance lease the supplier seasonably shall notify the lessor and the lessee, if known, that there will be delay or nondelivery and, if allocation is required under paragraph (b), of the estimated quota thus made available for the lessee.

Official Comment

Uniform Statutory Source: Section 2–615.

Changes: Revised to reflect leasing practices and terminology.

Definitional Cross References:

"Agreed". Section 1–201(3) [*unrevised Article 1; see Concordance, p. 22*].
"Contract". Section 1–201(11) [*unrevised Article 1; see Concordance, p. 22*].
"Delivery". Section 1–201(14) [*unrevised Article 1; see Concordance, p. 22*].
"Finance lease". Section 2A–103(1)(g).
"Good faith". Sections 1–201(19) [*unrevised Article 1; see Concordance, p. 22*] and 2–103(1)(b).
"Knows". Section 1–201(25) [*unrevised Article 1; see Concordance, p. 22*].
"Lease". Section 2A–103(1)(j).
"Lease contract". Section 2A–103(1)(*l*).

"Lessee". Section 2A–103(1)(n).

"Lessor". Section 2A–103(1)(p).

"Notifies". Section 1–201(26) [*unrevised Article 1; see Concordance, p. 22*].

"Sale". Section 2–106(1).

"Seasonably". Section 1–204(3) [*unrevised Article 1; see Concordance, p. 22*].

"Supplier". Section 2A–103(1)(x).

§ 2A–406. Procedure on Excused Performance.

(1)   If the lessee receives notification of a material or indefinite delay or an allocation justified under Section 2A–405, the lessee may by written notification to the lessor as to any goods involved, and with respect to all of the goods if under an installment lease contract the value of the whole lease contract is substantially impaired (Section 2A–510):

(a)   terminate the lease contract (Section 2A–505(2)); or

(b)   except in a finance lease that is not a consumer lease, modify the lease contract by accepting the available quota in substitution, with due allowance from the rent payable for the balance of the lease term for the deficiency but without further right against the lessor.

(2)   If, after receipt of a notification from the lessor under Section 2A–405, the lessee fails so to modify the lease agreement within a reasonable time not exceeding 30 days, the lease contract lapses with respect to any deliveries affected.

Official Comment

Uniform Statutory Source: Section 2–616(1) and (2).

Changes:

1.   Revised to reflect leasing practices and terminology. Note that subsection 1(a) allows the lessee under a lease, including a finance lease, the right to terminate the lease for excused performance (Sections 2A–404 and 2A–405). However, subsection 1(b), which allows the lessee the right to modify the lease for excused performance, excludes a finance lease that is not a consumer lease. This exclusion is compelled by the same policy that led to codification of provisions with respect to irrevocable promises. Section 2A–407.

2.   As to the use of a record other than a writing and communications that are not written, see Section 2A–103, Comment (g).

Definitional Cross References:

"Consumer lease". Section 2A–103(1)(e).

"Delivery". Section 1–201(14) [*unrevised Article 1; see Concordance, p. 22*].

"Finance lease". Section 2A–103(1)(g).

"Goods". Section 2A–103(1)(h).

"Installment lease contract". Section 2A–103(1)(i).

"Lease agreement". Section 2A–103(1)(k).

"Lease contract". Section 2A–103(1)(*l*).

"Lessee". Section 2A–103(1)(n).

"Lessor". Section 2A–103(1)(p).

"Notice". Section 1–201(25) [*unrevised Article 1; see Concordance, p. 22*].

"Reasonable time". Section 1–204(1) and (2) [*unrevised Article 1; see Concordance, p. 22*].

"Receipt". Section 2–103(1)(c).

"Rights". Section 1–201(36) [*unrevised Article 1; see Concordance, p. 22*].

"Termination". Section 2A–103(1)(z).

"Value". Section 1–201(44) [*unrevised Article 1; see Concordance, p. 22*].

"Written". Section 1–201(46) [*unrevised Article 1; see Concordance, p. 22*].

As amended in 2022.

§ 2A–407.   Irrevocable Promises: Finance Leases.

(1)   In the case of a finance lease that is not a consumer lease the lessee's promises under the lease contract become irrevocable and independent upon the lessee's acceptance of the goods.

(2)   A promise that has become irrevocable and independent under subsection (1):

(a)   is effective and enforceable between the parties, and by or against third parties including assignees of the parties; and

(b)   is not subject to cancellation, termination, modification, repudiation, excuse, or substitution without the consent of the party to whom the promise runs.

(3)   This section does not affect the validity under any other law of a covenant in any lease contract making the lessee's promises irrevocable and independent upon the lessee's acceptance of the goods.

As amended in 1990.

Official Comment

Uniform Statutory Source: None.

Purposes:

1.   This section extends the benefits of the classic "hell or high water" clause to a finance lease that is not a consumer lease. This section is self-executing; no special provision need be added to the contract. This section makes covenants in a finance lease irrevocable and independent due to the function of the finance lessor in a three party relationship: the lessee is looking to the supplier to perform the essential covenants and warranties. Section 2A–209. Thus, upon the lessee's acceptance of the goods the lessee's promises to the lessor under the lease contract become irrevocable and independent. The provisions of this section remain subject to the obligation of good faith (Sections 2A–103(4) and 1–203 [*unrevised Article 1; see Concordance, p. 22*]), and the lessee's revocation of acceptance (Section 2A–517).

2.   The section requires the lessee to perform even if the lessor's performance after the lessee's acceptance is not in accordance with the lease contract; the lessee may, however, have and pursue a cause of action against the lessor, e.g., breach of certain limited warranties (Sections 2A–210 and 2A–211(1)). This is appropriate because the benefit of the supplier's promises and warranties to the lessor under the supply contract and, in some cases, the warranty of a manufacturer who is not the supplier, is extended to the lessee under the finance lease. Section 2A–209. Despite this balance, this section excludes a finance lease that is a consumer lease. That a consumer be obligated to pay notwithstanding defective goods or the like is a principle that is not tenable under case law (*Unico v. Owen*, 50 N.J. 101, 232 A.2d 405 (1967)), state statute (Unif.Consumer Credit Code §§ 3.403–.405, 7A U.L.A. 126–31 (1974)), or federal statute (15 U.S.C. § 1666i (1982)).

3.   The relationship of the three parties to a transaction that qualifies as a finance lease is best demonstrated by a hypothetical. A, the potential lessor, has been contacted by B, the potential lessee, to discuss the lease of an expensive line of equipment that B has recently placed an order for with C, the manufacturer of such goods. The negotiation is completed and A, as lessor, and B, as lessee, sign a lease of the line of equipment for a 60-month term. B, as buyer, assigns the purchase order with C to A. If this transaction creates a lease (Section 2A–103(1)(j)), this transaction should qualify as a finance lease. Section 2A–103(1)(g).

4.   The line of equipment is delivered by C to B's place of business. After installation by C and testing by B, B accepts the goods by signing a certificate of delivery and acceptance, a copy of which is sent by B to A and C. One year later the line of equipment malfunctions and B falls behind in its manufacturing schedule.

5.   Under this Article, because the lease is a finance lease, no warranty of fitness or merchantability is extended by A to B. Sections 2A–212(1) and 2A–213. Absent an express provision in the lease agreement, application of Section 2A–210 or Section 2A–211(1), or application of the principles of law and equity, including the law with respect to fraud, duress, or the like (Sections 2A–103(4) and 1–103), B has no claim against A. B's obligation to pay rent to A continues as the obligation became irrevocable and independent when B accepted the line of equipment (Section 2A–407(1)). B has no right of set-off with respect to any part of the rent still due under the lease. Section 2A–508(6). However, B may have another remedy. Despite the lack of privity between B and C (the purchase order with C having been assigned by B to A), B may have a claim against C. Section 2A–209(1).

6.   This section does not address whether a "hell or high water" clause, *i.e.*, a clause that is to the effect of this section, is enforceable if included in a finance lease that is a consumer lease or a lease that is not a finance lease. That issue will continue to be determined by the facts of each case and other law which this section does not

affect. Sections 2A–104, 2A–103(4), 9–403 and 9–404. However, with respect to finance leases that are not consumer leases courts have enforced "hell or high water" clauses. *In re O.P.M. Leasing Servs.*, 21 Bankr. 993, 1006 (Bankr.S.D.N.Y. 1982).

7.   Subsection (2) further provides that a promise that has become irrevocable and independent under subsection (1) is enforceable not only between the parties but also against third parties. Thus, the finance lease can be transferred or assigned without disturbing enforceability. Further, subsection (2) also provides that the promise cannot, among other things, be cancelled or terminated without the consent of the lessor.

Cross References:

Sections 1–103, 1–203 [*unrevised Article 1; see Concordance, p. 22*], 2A–103(1)(g), 2A–103(1)(j), 2A–103(4), 2A–104, 2A–209, 2A–209(1), 2A–210, 2A–211(1), 2A–212(1), 2A–213, 2A–517(1)(b), 9–403 and 9–404.

Definitional Cross References:

"Cancellation". Section 2A–103(1)(b).
"Consumer lease". Section 2A–103(1)(e).
"Finance lease". Section 2A–103(1)(g).
"Goods". Section 2A–103(1)(h).
"Lease contract". Section 2A–103(1)(*l*).
"Lessee". Section 2A–103(1)(n).
"Party". Section 1–201(29) [*unrevised Article 1; see Concordance, p. 22*].
"Termination". Section 2A–103(1)(z).

PART 5

DEFAULT

A.   IN GENERAL

§ 2A–501.   Default: Procedure.

(1)   Whether the lessor or the lessee is in default under a lease contract is determined by the lease agreement and this Article.

(2)   If the lessor or the lessee is in default under the lease contract, the party seeking enforcement has rights and remedies as provided in this Article and, except as limited by this Article, as provided in the lease agreement.

(3)   If the lessor or the lessee is in default under the lease contract, the party seeking enforcement may reduce the party's claim to judgment, or otherwise enforce the lease contract by self-help or any available judicial procedure or nonjudicial procedure, including administrative proceeding, arbitration, or the like, in accordance with this Article.

(4)   Except as otherwise provided in Section 1–305(a) or this Article or the lease agreement, the rights and remedies referred to in subsections (2) and (3) are cumulative.

(5)   If the lease agreement covers both real property and goods, the party seeking enforcement may proceed under this Part as to the goods, or under other applicable law as to both the real property and the goods in accordance with that party's rights and remedies in respect of the real property, in which case this Part does not apply.

As amended in 1990 and 2001.

Official Comment

Uniform Statutory Source: Former Section 9–501 (now codified as Sections 9–601 through 9–604).

Changes: Substantially revised.

Purposes:

1.   Subsection (1) is new and represents a departure from the Article on Secured Transactions (Article 9) as the subsection makes clear that whether a party to the lease agreement is in default is determined by this

Article as well as the agreement. Sections 2A–508 and 2A–523. It further departs from Article 9 in recognizing the potential default of either party, a function of the bilateral nature of the obligations between the parties to the lease contract.

2. Subsection (2) is a version of the first sentence of Section 9–601(a), revised to reflect leasing terminology.

3. Subsection (3), an expansive version of the second sentence of Section 9–601(a), lists the procedures that may be followed by the party seeking enforcement; in effect, the scope of the procedures listed in subsection (3) is consistent with the scope of the procedures available to the foreclosing secured party.

4. Subsection (4) establishes that the parties' rights and remedies are cumulative. DeKoven, *Leases of Equipment: Puritan Leasing Company v. August, A Dangerous Decision*, 12 U.S.F.L.Rev. 257, 276–80 (1978). Cumulation, and largely unrestricted selection, of remedies is allowed in furtherance of the general policy of the Commercial Code, stated in Section 1–305, that remedies be liberally administered to put the aggrieved party in as good a position as if the other party had fully performed. Therefore, cumulation of, or selection among, remedies is available to the extent necessary to put the aggrieved party in as good a position as it would have been in had there been full performance. However, cumulation of, or selection among, remedies is not available to the extent that the cumulation or selection would put the aggrieved party in a better position than it would have been in had there been full performance by the other party.

5. Section 9–602, which, among other things, states that certain rules, to the extent they give rights to the debtor and impose duties on the secured party, may not be waived or varied, is not incorporated in this Article. Given the significance of freedom of contract in the development of the common law as it applies to bailments for hire and the lessee's lack of an equity of redemption, there is no reason to impose that restraint.

Cross References:

Sections 1–305, 2A–508, 2A–523, Article 9, especially Sections 9–601 and 9–602.

Definitional Cross References:

"Goods". Section 2A–103(1)(h).
"Lease agreement". Section 2A–103(1)(k).
"Lease contract". Section 2A–103(1)(*l*).
"Lessee". Section 2A–103(1)(n).
"Lessor". Section 2A–103(1)(p).
"Party". Section 1–201(b)(26).
"Remedy". Section 1–201(b)(32).
"Rights". Section 1–201(b)(34).

As amended in 2001.

§ 2A–502. Notice After Default.

Except as otherwise provided in this Article or the lease agreement, the lessor or lessee in default under the lease contract is not entitled to notice of default or notice of enforcement from the other party to the lease agreement.

Official Comment

Uniform Statutory Source: None.

Purposes: This section makes clear that absent agreement to the contrary or provision in this Article to the contrary, *e.g.*, Section 2A–516(3)(a), the party in default is not entitled to notice of default or enforcement. While a review of Part 5 of Article 9 leads to the same conclusion with respect to giving notice of default to the debtor, it is never stated. Although Article 9 requires notice of disposition and strict foreclosure, the different scheme of lessors' and lessees' rights and remedies developed under the common law, and codified by this Article, generally does not require notice of enforcement; furthermore, such notice is not mandated by due process requirements. However, certain sections of this Article do require notice. *E.g.*, Section 2A–517(2) 2A–517(4) [Previous incorrect cross reference corrected by Permanent Editorial Board action, November 1992].

Cross References:

Sections 2A–516(3)(a), 2A–517(4), and Article 9, esp. Part 5.

Definitional Cross References:

"Lease agreement". Section 2A–103(1)(k).

"Lease contract". Section 2A–103(1)(*l*).

"Lessee". Section 2A–103(1)(n).

"Lessor". Section 2A–103(1)(p).

"Notice". Section 1–201(25) [*unrevised Article 1; see Concordance, p. 22*].

"Party". Section 1–201(29) [*unrevised Article 1; see Concordance, p. 22*].

§ 2A–503. Modification or Impairment of Rights and Remedies.

(1)   Except as otherwise provided in this Article, the lease agreement may include rights and remedies for default in addition to or in substitution for those provided in this Article and may limit or alter the measure of damages recoverable under this Article.

(2)   Resort to a remedy provided under this Article or in the lease agreement is optional unless the remedy is expressly agreed to be exclusive. If circumstances cause an exclusive or limited remedy to fail of its essential purpose, or provision for an exclusive remedy is unconscionable, remedy may be had as provided in this Article.

(3)   Consequential damages may be liquidated under Section 2A–504, or may otherwise be limited, altered, or excluded unless the limitation, alteration, or exclusion is unconscionable. Limitation, alteration, or exclusion of consequential damages for injury to the person in the case of consumer goods is prima facie unconscionable but limitation, alteration, or exclusion of damages where the loss is commercial is not prima facie unconscionable.

(4)   Rights and remedies on default by the lessor or the lessee with respect to any obligation or promise collateral or ancillary to the lease contract are not impaired by this Article.

As amended in 1990.

Official Comment

Uniform Statutory Source: Sections 2–719 and 2–701.

Changes: Rewritten to reflect lease terminology and to clarify the relationship between this section and Section 2A–504.

Purposes:

1.   A significant purpose of this Part is to provide rights and remedies for those parties to a lease who fail to provide them by agreement or whose rights and remedies fail of their essential purpose or are unenforceable. However, it is important to note that this implies no restriction on freedom to contract. Sections 2A–103(4) and 1–102(3) [*unrevised Article 1; see Concordance, p. 22*]. Thus, subsection (1), a revised version of the provisions of Section 2–719(1), allows the parties to the lease agreement freedom to provide for rights and remedies in addition to or in substitution for those provided in this Article and to alter or limit the measure of damages recoverable under this Article. Except to the extent otherwise provided in this Article (*e.g.*, Sections 2A–105, 106 and 108(1) and (2)), this Part shall be construed neither to restrict the parties' ability to provide for rights and remedies or to limit or alter the measure of damages by agreement, nor to imply disapproval of rights and remedy schemes other than those set forth in this Part.

2.   Subsection (2) makes explicit with respect to this Article what is implicit in Section 2–719 with respect to the Article on Sales (Article 2): if an exclusive remedy is held to be unconscionable, remedies under this Article are available. Section 2–719 official comment 1.

3.   Subsection (3), a revision of Section 2–719(3), makes clear that consequential damages may also be liquidated. Section 2A–504(1).

4.   Subsection (4) is a revision of the provisions of Section 2–701. This subsection leaves the treatment of default with respect to obligations or promises collateral or ancillary to the lease contract to other law. Sections 2A–103(4) and 1–103. An example of such an obligation would be that of the lessor to the secured creditor which has provided the funds to leverage the lessor's lease transaction; an example of such a promise would be that of the lessee, as seller, to the lessor, as buyer, in a sale-leaseback transaction.

Cross References:

Sections 1–102(3) [*unrevised Article 1; see Concordance, p. 22*], 1–103, Article 2, especially Sections 2–701, 2–719, 2–719(1), 2–719(3), 2–719 official comment 1, and Sections 2A–103(4), 2A–105, 2A–106, 2A–108(1), 2A–108(2), and 2A–504.

Definitional Cross References:

"Agreed". Section 1–201(3) [*unrevised Article 1; see Concordance, p. 22*].

"Consumer goods". Section 9–102(a)(23).

"Lease agreement". Section 2A–103(1)(k).

"Lease contract". Section 2A–103(1)(*l*).

"Lessee". Section 2A–103(1)(n).

"Lessor". Section 2A–103(1)(p).

"Person". Section 1–201(30) [*unrevised Article 1; see Concordance, p. 22*].

"Remedy". Section 1–201(34) [*unrevised Article 1; see Concordance, p. 22*].

"Rights". Section 1–201(36) [*unrevised Article 1; see Concordance, p. 22*].

§ 2A–504. Liquidation of Damages.

(1)   Damages payable by either party for default, or any other act or omission, including indemnity for loss or diminution of anticipated tax benefits or loss or damage to lessor's residual interest, may be liquidated in the lease agreement but only at an amount or by a formula that is reasonable in light of the then anticipated harm caused by the default or other act or omission.

(2)   If the lease agreement provides for liquidation of damages, and such provision does not comply with subsection (1), or such provision is an exclusive or limited remedy that circumstances cause to fail of its essential purpose, remedy may be had as provided in this Article.

(3)   If the lessor justifiably withholds or stops delivery of goods because of the lessee's default or insolvency (Section 2A–525 or 2A–526), the lessee is entitled to restitution of any amount by which the sum of his [or her] payments exceeds:

(a)   the amount to which the lessor is entitled by virtue of terms liquidating the lessor's damages in accordance with subsection (1); or

(b)   in the absence of those terms, 20 percent of the then present value of the total rent the lessee was obligated to pay for the balance of the lease term, or, in the case of a consumer lease, the lesser of such amount or $500.

(4)   A lessee's right to restitution under subsection (3) is subject to offset to the extent the lessor establishes:

(a)   a right to recover damages under the provisions of this Article other than subsection (1); and

(b)   the amount or value of any benefits received by the lessee directly or indirectly by reason of the lease contract.

Official Comment

Uniform Statutory Source: Sections 2–718(1), (2), (3) and 2–719(2).

Changes: Substantially rewritten.

Purposes: Many leasing transactions are predicated on the parties' ability to agree to an appropriate amount of damages or formula for damages in the event of default or other act or omission. The rule with respect to sales of goods (Section 2–718) may not be sufficiently flexible to accommodate this practice. Thus, consistent with the common law emphasis upon freedom to contract with respect to bailments for hire, this section has created a revised rule that allows greater flexibility with respect to leases of goods.

Subsection (1), a significantly modified version of the provisions of Section 2–718(1), provides for liquidation of damages in the lease agreement at an amount or by a formula. Section 2–718(1) does not by its express terms include liquidation by a formula; this change was compelled by modern leasing practice. Subsection (1), in a further expansion of Section 2–718(1), provides for liquidation of damages for default as well as any other act or omission.

A liquidated damages formula that is common in leasing practice provides that the sum of lease payments past due, accelerated future lease payments, and the lessor's estimated residual interest, less the net proceeds of disposition (whether by sale or re-lease) of the leased goods is the lessor's damages. Tax indemnities, costs, interest and attorney's fees are also added to determine the lessor's damages. Another common liquidated damages formula utilizes a periodic depreciation allocation as a credit to the aforesaid amount in mitigation of a lessor's damages. A third formula provides for a fixed number of periodic payments as a means of liquidating damages. Stipulated loss or stipulated damage schedules are also common. Whether these formulae are enforceable will be determined in the context of each case by applying a standard of reasonableness in light of the harm anticipated when the formula was agreed to. Whether the inclusion of these formulae will affect the classification of the transaction as a lease or a security interest is to be determined by the facts of each case. Section 1–201(37) 1–203. *E.g.*, *In re Noack*, 44 Bankr. 172, 174–75 (Bankr.E.D.Wis. 1984).

This section does not incorporate two other tests that under sales law determine enforceability of liquidated damages, *i.e.*, difficulties of proof of loss and inconvenience or nonfeasibility of otherwise obtaining an adequate remedy. The ability to liquidate damages is critical to modern leasing practice; given the parties' freedom to contract at common law, the policy behind retaining these two additional requirements here was thought to be outweighed. Further, given the expansion of subsection (1) to enable the parties to liquidate the amount payable with respect to an indemnity for loss or diminution of anticipated tax benefits resulted in another change: the last sentence of Section 2–718(1), providing that a term fixing unreasonably large liquidated damages is void as a penalty, was also not incorporated. The impact of local, state and federal tax laws on a leasing transaction can result in an amount payable with respect to the tax indemnity many times greater than the original purchase price of the goods. By deleting the reference to unreasonably large liquidated damages the parties are free to negotiate a formula, restrained by the rule of reasonableness in this section. These changes should invite the parties to liquidate damages. Peters, *Remedies for Breach of Contracts Relating to the Sale of Goods Under the Uniform Commercial Code: A Roadmap for Article Two*, 73 Yale L.J. 199, 278 (1963).

Subsection (2), a revised version of Section 2–719(2), provides that if the liquidated damages provision is not enforceable or fails of its essential purpose, remedy may be had as provided in this Article.

Subsection (3)(b) of this section differs from subsection (2)(b) of Section 2–718; in the absence of a valid liquidated damages amount or formula the lessor is permitted to retain 20 percent of the present value of the total rent payable under the lease. The alternative limitation of $500 contained in Section 2–718 is deleted as unrealistically low with respect to a lease other than a consumer lease.

Cross References:

Sections 1–201(37) [*unrevised Article 1; see Concordance, p. 22*], 2–718, 2–718(1), 2–718(2)(b) and 2–719(2).

Definitional Cross References:

"Consumer lease". Section 2A–103(1)(e).
"Delivery". Section 1–201(14) [*unrevised Article 1; see Concordance, p. 22*].
"Goods". Section 2A–103(1)(h).
"Insolvent". Section 1–201(23) [*unrevised Article 1; see Concordance, p. 22*].
"Lease agreement". Section 2A–103(1)(k).
"Lease contract". Section 2A–103(1)(*l*).
"Lessee". Section 2A–103(1)(n).
"Lessor". Section 2A–103(1)(p).
"Lessor's residual interest". Section 2A–103(1)(q).
"Party". Section 1–201(29) [*unrevised Article 1; see Concordance, p. 22*].
"Present value". Section 2A–103(1)(u).
"Remedy". Section 1–201(34) [*unrevised Article 1; see Concordance, p. 22*].
"Rights". Section 1–201(36) [*unrevised Article 1; see Concordance, p. 22*].
"Term". Section 1–201(42) [*unrevised Article 1; see Concordance, p. 22*].
"Value". Section 1–201(44) [*unrevised Article 1; see Concordance, p. 22*].

As amended in 2022.

§ 2A–505. Cancellation and Termination and Effect of Cancellation, Termination, Rescission, or Fraud on Rights and Remedies.

(1) On cancellation of the lease contract, all obligations that are still executory on both sides are discharged, but any right based on prior default or performance survives, and the cancelling party also retains any remedy for default of the whole lease contract or any unperformed balance.

(2) On termination of the lease contract, all obligations that are still executory on both sides are discharged but any right based on prior default or performance survives.

(3) Unless the contrary intention clearly appears, expressions of "cancellation," "rescission," or the like of the lease contract may not be construed as a renunciation or discharge of any claim in damages for an antecedent default.

(4) Rights and remedies for material misrepresentation or fraud include all rights and remedies available under this Article for default.

(5) Neither rescission nor a claim for rescission of the lease contract nor rejection or return of the goods may bar or be deemed inconsistent with a claim for damages or other right or remedy.

Official Comment

Uniform Statutory Source: Sections 2–106(3) and (4), 2–720 and 2–721.

Changes: Revised to reflect leasing practices and terminology.

Definitional Cross References:

"Cancellation". Section 2A–103(1)(b).
"Goods". Section 2A–103(1)(h).
"Lease contract". Section 2A–103(1)(*l*).
"Party". Section 1–201(29) [*unrevised Article 1; see Concordance, p. 22*].
"Remedy". Section 1–201(34) [*unrevised Article 1; see Concordance, p. 22*].
"Rights". Section 1–201(36) [*unrevised Article 1; see Concordance, p. 22*].
"Termination". Section 2A–103(1)(z).

§ 2A–506. Statute of Limitations.

(1) An action for default under a lease contract, including breach of warranty or indemnity, must be commenced within 4 years after the cause of action accrued. By the original lease contract the parties may reduce the period of limitation to not less than one year.

(2) A cause of action for default accrues when the act or omission on which the default or breach of warranty is based is or should have been discovered by the aggrieved party, or when the default occurs, whichever is later. A cause of action for indemnity accrues when the act or omission on which the claim for indemnity is based is or should have been discovered by the indemnified party, whichever is later.

(3) If an action commenced within the time limited by subsection (1) is so terminated as to leave available a remedy by another action for the same default or breach of warranty or indemnity, the other action may be commenced after the expiration of the time limited and within 6 months after the termination of the first action unless the termination resulted from voluntary discontinuance or from dismissal for failure or neglect to prosecute.

(4) This section does not alter the law on tolling of the statute of limitations nor does it apply to causes of action that have accrued before this Article becomes effective.

Official Comment

Uniform Statutory Source: Section 2–725.

Changes: Substantially rewritten.

Purposes: Subsection (1) does not incorporate the limitation found in Section 2–725(1) prohibiting the parties from extending the period of limitation. Breach of warranty and indemnity claims often arise in a lease transaction; with the passage of time such claims often diminish or are eliminated. To encourage the parties to commence litigation under these circumstances makes little sense.

Subsection (2) states two rules for determining when a cause of action accrues. With respect to default, the rule of Section 2–725(2) is not incorporated in favor of a more liberal rule of the later of the date when the default occurs or when the act or omission on which it is based is or should have been discovered. With respect to indemnity, a similarly liberal rule is adopted.

Cross References:

Sections 2–725(1) and 2–725(2).

Definitional Cross References:

"Action". Section 1–201(1) [*unrevised Article 1; see Concordance, p. 22*].
"Aggrieved party". Section 1–201(2) [*unrevised Article 1; see Concordance, p. 22*].
"Lease contract". Section 2A–103(1)(*l*).
"Party". Section 1–201(29) [*unrevised Article 1; see Concordance, p. 22*].
"Remedy". Section 1–201(34) [*unrevised Article 1; see Concordance, p. 22*].
"Termination". Section 2A–103(1)(z).

§ 2A–507.   Proof of Market Rent: Time and Place.

(1) Damages based on market rent (Section 2A–519 or 2A–528) are determined according to the rent for the use of the goods concerned for a lease term identical to the remaining lease term of the original lease agreement and prevailing at the times specified in Sections 2A–519 and 2A–528.

(2) If evidence of rent for the use of the goods concerned for a lease term identical to the remaining lease term of the original lease agreement and prevailing at the times or places described in this Article is not readily available, the rent prevailing within any reasonable time before or after the time described or at any other place or for a different lease term which in commercial judgment or under usage of trade would serve as a reasonable substitute for the one described may be used, making any proper allowance for the difference, including the cost of transporting the goods to or from the other place.

(3) Evidence of a relevant rent prevailing at a time or place or for a lease term other than the one described in this Article offered by one party is not admissible unless and until he [or she] has given the other party notice the court finds sufficient to prevent unfair surprise.

(4) If the prevailing rent or value of any goods regularly leased in any established market is in issue, reports in official publications or trade journals or in newspapers or periodicals of general circulation published as the reports of that market are admissible in evidence. The circumstances of the preparation of the report may be shown to affect its weight but not its admissibility.

As amended in 1990.

Official Comment

Uniform Statutory Source: Sections 2–723 and 2–724.

Changes: Revised to reflect leasing practices and terminology. Sections 2A–519 and 2A–528 specify the times as of which market rent is to be determined.

Definitional Cross References:

"Goods". Section 2A–103(1)(h).
"Lease". Section 2A–103(1)(j).
"Lease agreement". Section 2A–103(1)(k).
"Notice". Section 1–201(25) [*unrevised Article 1; see Concordance, p. 22*].
"Party". Section 1–201(29) [*unrevised Article 1; see Concordance, p. 22*].
"Reasonable time". Section 1–204(1) and (2) [*unrevised Article 1; see Concordance, p. 22*].
"Usage of trade". Section 1–205 [*unrevised Article 1; see Concordance, p. 22*].
"Value". Section 1–201(44) [*unrevised Article 1; see Concordance, p. 22*].

B. DEFAULT BY LESSOR

§ 2A–508. Lessee's Remedies.

(1) If a lessor fails to deliver the goods in conformity to the lease contract (Section 2A–509) or repudiates the lease contract (Section 2A–402), or a lessee rightfully rejects the goods (Section 2A–509) or justifiably revokes acceptance of the goods (Section 2A–517), then with respect to any goods involved, and with respect to all of the goods if under an installment lease contract the value of the whole lease contract is substantially impaired (Section 2A–510), the lessor is in default under the lease contract and the lessee may:

(a) cancel the lease contract (Section 2A–505(1));

(b) recover so much of the rent and security as has been paid and is just under the circumstances;

(c) cover and recover damages as to all goods affected whether or not they have been identified to the lease contract (Sections 2A–518 and 2A–520), or recover damages for nondelivery (Sections 2A–519 and 2A–520);

(d) exercise any other rights or pursue any other remedies provided in the lease contract.

(2) If a lessor fails to deliver the goods in conformity to the lease contract or repudiates the lease contract, the lessee may also:

(a) if the goods have been identified, recover them (Section 2A–522); or

(b) in a proper case, obtain specific performance or replevy the goods (Section 2A–521).

(3) If a lessor is otherwise in default under a lease contract, the lessee may exercise the rights and pursue the remedies provided in the lease contract, which may include a right to cancel the lease, and in Section 2A–519(3).

(4) If a lessor has breached a warranty, whether express or implied, the lessee may recover damages (Section 2A–519(4)).

(5) On rightful rejection or justifiable revocation of acceptance, a lessee has a security interest in goods in the lessee's possession or control for any rent and security that has been paid and any expenses reasonably incurred in their inspection, receipt, transportation, and care and custody and may hold those goods and dispose of them in good faith and in a commercially reasonable manner, subject to Section 2A–527(5).

(6) Subject to the provisions of Section 2A–407, a lessee, on notifying the lessor of the lessee's intention to do so, may deduct all or any part of the damages resulting from any default under the lease contract from any part of the rent still due under the same lease contract.

As amended in 1990.

Official Comment

Uniform Statutory Source: Sections 2–711 and 2–717.

Changes: Substantially rewritten.

Purposes:

1.   This section is an index to Sections 2A–509 through 522 which set out the lessee's rights and remedies after the lessor's default. The lessor and the lessee can agree to modify the rights and remedies available under this Article; they can, among other things, provide that for defaults other than those specified in subsection (1) the lessee can exercise the rights and remedies referred to in subsection (1); and they can create a new scheme of rights and remedies triggered by the occurrence of the default. Sections 2A–103(4) and 1–102(3) [*unrevised Article 1; see Concordance, p. 22*].

2.   Subsection (1), a substantially rewritten version of the provisions of Section 2–711(1), lists three cumulative remedies of the lessee where the lessor has failed to deliver conforming goods or has repudiated the contract, or the lessee has rightfully rejected or justifiably revoked. Sections 2A–501(2) and (4). Subsection (1) also allows the lessee to exercise any contractual remedy. This Article rejects any general doctrine of election of remedy. To determine if one remedy bars another in a particular case is a function of whether the lessee has been put in

as good a position as if the lessor had fully performed the lease agreement. Use of multiple remedies is barred only if the effect is to put the lessee in a better position than it would have been in had the lessor fully performed under the lease. Sections 2A–103(4), 2A–501(4), and 1–106(1) [*unrevised Article 1; see Concordance, p. 22*]. Subsection (1)(b), in recognition that no bright line can be created that would operate fairly in all installment lease cases and in recognition of the fact that a lessee may be able to cancel the lease (revoke acceptance of the goods) after the goods have been in use for some period of time, does not require that all lease payments made by the lessee under the lease be returned upon cancellation. Rather, only such portion as is just of the rent and security payments made may be recovered. If a defect in the goods is discovered immediately upon tender to the lessee and the goods are rejected immediately, then the lessee should recover all payments made. If, however, for example, a 36-month equipment lease is terminated in the 12th month because the lessor has materially breached the contract by failing to perform its maintenance obligations, it may be just to return only a small part or none of the rental payments already made.

3.   Subsection (2), a version of the provisions of Section 2–711(2) revised to reflect leasing terminology, lists two alternative remedies for the recovery of the goods by the lessee; however, each of these remedies is cumulative with respect to those listed in subsection (1).

4.   Subsection (3) is new. It covers defaults which do not deprive the lessee of the goods and which are not so serious as to justify rejection or revocation of acceptance under subsection (1). It also covers defaults for which the lessee could have rejected or revoked acceptance of the goods but elects not to do so and retains the goods. In either case, a lessee which retains the goods is entitled to recover damages as stated in Section 2A–519(3). That measure of damages is "the loss resulting in the ordinary course of events from the lessor's default as determined in any manner that is reasonable together with incidental and consequential damages, less expenses saved in consequence of the lessor's breach."

5.   Subsection (1)(d) and subsection (3) recognize that the lease agreement may provide rights and remedies in addition to or different from those which Article 2A provides. In particular, subsection (3) provides that the lease agreement may give the remedy of cancellation of the lease for defaults by the lessor that would not otherwise be material defaults which would justify cancellation under subsection (1). If there is a right to cancel, there is, of course, a right to reject or revoke acceptance of the goods.

6.   Subsection (4) is new and merely adds to the completeness of the index by including a reference to the lessee's recovery of damages upon the lessor's breach of warranty; such breach may not rise to the level of a default by the lessor justifying revocation of acceptance. If the lessee properly rejects or revokes acceptance of the goods because of a breach of warranty, the rights and remedies are those provided in subsection (1) rather than those in Section 2A–519(4).

7.   Subsection (5), a revised version of the provisions of Section 2–711(3), recognizes, on rightful rejection or justifiable revocation, the lessee's security interest in goods in its possession and control. Former Section 9–113 (now codified as Section 9–110), which recognized security interests arising under the Article on Sales (Article 2), was amended with the adoption of this Article to reflect the security interests arising under this Article. Pursuant to Section 2A–511(4), a purchaser who purchases goods from the lessee in good faith takes free of any rights of the lessor, or in the case of a finance lease, the supplier. Such goods, however, must have been rightfully rejected and disposed of pursuant to Section 2A–511 or 2A–512. However, Section 2A–517(5) provides that the lessee will have the same rights and duties with respect to goods where acceptance has been revoked as with respect to goods rejected. Thus, Section 2A–511(4) will apply to the lessee's disposition of such goods.

8.   Pursuant to Section 2A–527(5), the lessee must account to the lessor for the excess proceeds of such disposition, after satisfaction of the claim secured by the lessee's security interest.

9.   Subsection (6), a slightly revised version of the provisions of Section 2–717, sanctions a right of set-off by the lessee, subject to the rule of Section 2A–407 with respect to irrevocable promises in a finance lease that is not a consumer lease, and further subject to an enforceable "hell or high water" clause in the lease agreement. Section 2A–407 official comment. No attempt is made to state how the set-off should occur; this is to be determined by the facts of each case.

10.   There is no special treatment of the finance lease in this section. Absent supplemental principles of law and equity to the contrary, in the case of most finance leases, following the lessee's acceptance of the goods, the lessee will have no rights or remedies against the lessor, because the lessor's obligations to the lessee are minimal. Sections 2A–210 and 2A–211(1). Since the lessee will look to the supplier for performance, this is appropriate. Section 2A–209.

Cross References:

Sections 1–102(3) [*unrevised Article 1; see Concordance, p. 22*], 1–103, 1–106(1) [*unrevised Article 1; see Concordance, p. 22*], Article 2, especially Sections 2–711, 2–717 and Sections 2A–103(4), 2A–209, 2A–210, 2A–211(1), 2A–407, 2A–501(2), 2A–501(4), 2A–509 through 2A–522, 2A–511(3), 2A–517(5), 2A–527(5) and Section 9–110.

Definitional Cross References:

"Conforming". Section 2A–103(1)(d).
"Delivery". Section 1–201(14) [*unrevised Article 1; see Concordance, p. 22*].
"Good faith". Sections 1–201(19) [*unrevised Article 1; see Concordance, p. 22*] and 2–103(1)(b).
"Goods". Section 2A–103(1)(h).
"Installment lease contract". Section 2A–103(1)(i).
"Lease contract". Section 2A–103(1)(*l*).
"Lessee". Section 2A–103(1)(n).
"Lessor". Section 2A–103(1)(p).
"Notifies". Section 1–201(26) [*unrevised Article 1; see Concordance, p. 22*].
"Receipt". Section 2–103(1)(c).
"Remedy". Section 1–201(34) [*unrevised Article 1; see Concordance, p. 22*].
"Rights". Section 1–201(36) [*unrevised Article 1; see Concordance, p. 22*].
"Security interest". Section 1–201(37) [*unrevised Article 1; see Concordance, p. 22*].
"Value". Section 1–201(44) [*unrevised Article 1; see Concordance, p. 22*].

§ 2A–509. Lessee's Rights on Improper Delivery; Rightful Rejection.

(1)   Subject to the provisions of Section 2A–510 on default in installment lease contracts, if the goods or the tender or delivery fail in any respect to conform to the lease contract, the lessee may reject or accept the goods or accept any commercial unit or units and reject the rest of the goods.

(2)   Rejection of goods is ineffective unless it is within a reasonable time after tender or delivery of the goods and the lessee seasonably notifies the lessor.

Official Comment

Uniform Statutory Source: Sections 2–601 and 2–602(1).

Changes: Revised to reflect leasing practices and terminology.

Definitional Cross References:

"Commercial unit". Section 2A–103(1)(c).
"Conforming". Section 2A–103(1)(d).
"Delivery". Section 1–201(14) [*unrevised Article 1; see Concordance, p. 22*].
"Goods". Section 2A–103(1)(h).
"Installment lease contract". Section 2A–103(1)(i).
"Lease contract". Section 2A–103(1)(*l*).
"Lessee". Section 2A–103(1)(n).
"Lessor". Section 2A–103(1)(p).
"Notifies". Section 1–201(26) [*unrevised Article 1; see Concordance, p. 22*].
"Reasonable time". Section 1–204(1) and (2) [*unrevised Article 1; see Concordance, p. 22*].
"Rights". Section 1–201(36) [*unrevised Article 1; see Concordance, p. 22*].
"Seasonably". Section 1–204(3) [*unrevised Article 1; see Concordance, p. 22*].

§ 2A–510. Installment Lease Contracts: Rejection and Default.

(1)   Under an installment lease contract a lessee may reject any delivery that is nonconforming if the nonconformity substantially impairs the value of that delivery and cannot be cured or the nonconformity is a defect in the required documents; but if the nonconformity does not fall within subsection (2) and the lessor or the supplier gives adequate assurance of its cure, the lessee must accept that delivery.

(2)   Whenever nonconformity or default with respect to one or more deliveries substantially impairs the value of the installment lease contract as a whole there is a default with respect to the whole. But, the aggrieved party reinstates the installment lease contract as a whole if the aggrieved party accepts a nonconforming delivery without seasonably notifying of cancellation or brings an action with respect only to past deliveries or demands performance as to future deliveries.

Official Comment

Uniform Statutory Source: Section 2–612.

Changes: Revised to reflect leasing practices and terminology.

Definitional Cross References:

"Action". Section 1–201(1) [*unrevised Article 1; see Concordance, p. 22*].
"Aggrieved party". Section 1–201(2) [*unrevised Article 1; see Concordance, p. 22*].
"Cancellation". Section 2A–103(1)(b).
"Conforming". Section 2A–103(1)(d).
"Delivery". Section 1–201(14) [*unrevised Article 1; see Concordance, p. 22*].
"Installment lease contract". Section 2A–103(1)(i).
"Lessee". Section 2A–103(1)(n).
"Lessor". Section 2A–103(1)(p).
"Notifies". Section 1–201(26) [*unrevised Article 1; see Concordance, p. 22*].
"Seasonably". Section 1–204(3) [*unrevised Article 1; see Concordance, p. 22*].
"Supplier". Section 2A–103(1)(x).
"Value". Section 1–201(44) [*unrevised Article 1; see Concordance, p. 22*].

§ 2A–511. Merchant Lessee's Duties as to Rightfully Rejected Goods.

(1)   Subject to any security interest of a lessee (Section 2A–508(5)), if a lessor or a supplier has no agent or place of business at the market of rejection, a merchant lessee, after rejection of goods in his [or her] possession or control, shall follow any reasonable instructions received from the lessor or the supplier with respect to the goods. In the absence of those instructions, a merchant lessee shall make reasonable efforts to sell, lease, or otherwise dispose of the goods for the lessor's account if they threaten to decline in value speedily. Instructions are not reasonable if on demand indemnity for expenses is not forthcoming.

(2)   If a merchant lessee (subsection (1)) or any other lessee (Section 2A–512) disposes of goods, he [or she] is entitled to reimbursement either from the lessor or the supplier or out of the proceeds for reasonable expenses of caring for and disposing of the goods and, if the expenses include no disposition commission, to such commission as is usual in the trade, or if there is none, to a reasonable sum not exceeding 10 percent of the gross proceeds.

(3)   In complying with this section or Section 2A–512, the lessee is held only to good faith. Good faith conduct hereunder is neither acceptance or conversion nor the basis of an action for damages.

(4)   A purchaser who purchases in good faith from a lessee pursuant to this section or Section 2A–512 takes the goods free of any rights of the lessor and the supplier even though the lessee fails to comply with one or more of the requirements of this Article.

Official Comment

Uniform Statutory Source: Sections 2–603 and 2–706(5).

Changes: Revised to reflect leasing practices and terminology. ~~This section, by its terms, applies to merchants as well as others. Thus, in construing the section it is important to note that under this Act the term good faith is defined differently for merchants (Section 2–103(1)(b)) than for others (Section 1–201(19)). Section 2A–103(3) and (4).~~

Definitional Cross References:

"Action". Section 1–201(1) [*unrevised Article 1; see Concordance, p. 22*].
"Good faith". Sections 1–201(19) [*unrevised Article 1; see Concordance, p. 22*] and 2–103(1)(b).
"Goods". Section 2A–103(1)(h).

"Lease". Section 2A–103(1)(j).
"Lessee". Section 2A–103(1)(n).
"Lessor". Section 2A–103(1)(p).
"Merchant lessee". Section 2A–103(1)(t).
"Purchaser". Section 1–201(33) [*unrevised Article 1; see Concordance, p. 22*].
"Rights". Section 1–201(36) [*unrevised Article 1; see Concordance, p. 22*].
"Security interest". Section 1–201(37) [*unrevised Article 1; see Concordance, p. 22*].
"Supplier". Section 2A–103(1)(x).
"Value". Section 1–201(44) [*unrevised Article 1; see Concordance, p. 22*].

As amended in 2022.

§ 2A–512. Lessee's Duties as to Rightfully Rejected Goods.

(1) Except as otherwise provided with respect to goods that threaten to decline in value speedily (Section 2A–511) and subject to any security interest of a lessee (Section 2A–508(5)):

(a) the lessee, after rejection of goods in the lessee's possession, shall hold them with reasonable care at the lessor's or the supplier's disposition for a reasonable time after the lessee's seasonable notification of rejection;

(b) if the lessor or the supplier gives no instructions within a reasonable time after notification of rejection, the lessee may store the rejected goods for the lessor's or the supplier's account or ship them to the lessor or the supplier or dispose of them for the lessor's or the supplier's account with reimbursement in the manner provided in Section 2A–511; but

(c) the lessee has no further obligations with regard to goods rightfully rejected.

(2) Action by the lessee pursuant to subsection (1) is not acceptance or conversion.

Official Comment

Uniform Statutory Source: Sections 2–602(2)(b) and (c) and 2–604.

Changes: Substantially rewritten.

Purposes: The introduction to subsection (1) references goods that threaten to decline in value speedily and not perishables, the reference in Section 2–604, the statutory analogue. This is a change in style, not substance, as the first phrase includes the second. Subparagraphs (a) and (c) are revised versions of the provisions of Section 2–602(2)(b) and (c). Subparagraph (a) states the rule with respect to the lessee's treatment of goods in its possession following rejection; subparagraph (b) states the rule regarding such goods if the lessor or supplier then fails to give instructions to the lessee. If the lessee performs in a fashion consistent with subparagraphs (a) and (b), subparagraph (c) exonerates the lessee.

Cross References:

Sections 2–602(2)(b), 2–602(2)(c) and 2–604.

Definitional Cross References:

"Action". Section 1–201(1) [*unrevised Article 1; see Concordance, p. 22*].
"Goods". Section 2A–103(1)(h).
"Lessee". Section 2A–103(1)(n).
"Lessor". Section 2A–103(1)(p).
"Notification". Section 1–201(26) [*unrevised Article 1; see Concordance, p. 22*].
"Reasonable time". Section 1–204(1) and (2) [*unrevised Article 1; see Concordance, p. 22*].
"Seasonably". Section 1–204(3) [*unrevised Article 1; see Concordance, p. 22*].
"Security interest". Section 1–201(37) [*unrevised Article 1; see Concordance, p. 22*].
"Supplier". Section 2A–103(1)(x).
"Value". Section 1–201(44) [*unrevised Article 1; see Concordance, p. 22*].

§ 2A-513.   Cure by Lessor of Improper Tender or Delivery; Replacement.

(1)   If any tender or delivery by the lessor or the supplier is rejected because nonconforming and the time for performance has not yet expired, the lessor or the supplier may seasonably notify the lessee of the lessor's or the supplier's intention to cure and may then make a conforming delivery within the time provided in the lease contract.

(2)   If the lessee rejects a nonconforming tender that the lessor or the supplier had reasonable grounds to believe would be acceptable with or without money allowance, the lessor or the supplier may have a further reasonable time to substitute a conforming tender if he [or she] seasonably notifies the lessee.

Official Comment

Uniform Statutory Source: Section 2–508.

Changes: Revised to reflect leasing practices and terminology.

Definitional Cross References:

"Conforming". Section 2A–103(1)(d).
"Delivery". Section 1–201(14) [*unrevised Article 1; see Concordance, p. 22*].
"Lease contract". Section 2A–103(1)(*l*).
"Lessee". Section 2A–103(1)(n).
"Lessor". Section 2A–103(1)(p).
"Money". Section 1–201(24) [*unrevised Article 1; see Concordance, p. 22*].
"Notifies". Section 1–201(26) [*unrevised Article 1; see Concordance, p. 22*].
"Reasonable time". Section 1–204(1) and (2) [*unrevised Article 1; see Concordance, p. 22*].
"Seasonably". Section 1–204(3) [*unrevised Article 1; see Concordance, p. 22*].
"Supplier". Section 2A–103(1)(x).

§ 2A-514.   Waiver of Lessee's Objections.

(1)   In rejecting goods, a lessee's failure to state a particular defect that is ascertainable by reasonable inspection precludes the lessee from relying on the defect to justify rejection or to establish default:

(a)   if, stated seasonably, the lessor or the supplier could have cured it (Section 2A–513); or

(b)   between merchants if the lessor or the supplier after rejection has made a request in writing for a full and final written statement of all defects on which the lessee proposes to rely.

(2)   A lessee's failure to reserve rights when paying rent or other consideration against documents precludes recovery of the payment for defects apparent in the documents.

As amended in 2003.

Official Comment

Uniform Statutory Source: Section 2–605.

Changes: Revised to reflect leasing practices and terminology.

Purposes:

1.   The principles applicable to the commercial practice of payment against documents (subsection 2) are explained in official comment 4 to Section 2–605, the statutory analogue to this section.

2.   As to the use of a record other than a writing and communications that are not written, see Section 2A–103, Comment (g).

Cross Reference:

Section 2–605 official comment 4.

Definitional Cross References:

"Between merchants". Section 2–104(3).
"Goods". Section 2A–103(1)(h).
"Lessee". Section 2A–103(1)(n).

"Lessor". Section 2A–103(1)(p).

"Rights". Section 1–201(36) [*unrevised Article 1; see Concordance, p. 22*].

"Seasonably". Section 1–204(3) [*unrevised Article 1; see Concordance, p. 22*].

"Supplier". Section 2A–103(1)(x).

"Writing". Section 1–201(46) [*unrevised Article 1; see Concordance, p. 22*].

As amended in 2022.

§ 2A–515. Acceptance of Goods.

(1) Acceptance of goods occurs after the lessee has had a reasonable opportunity to inspect the goods and

(a) the lessee signifies or acts with respect to the goods in a manner that signifies to the lessor or the supplier that the goods are conforming or that the lessee will take or retain them in spite of their nonconformity; or

(b) the lessee fails to make an effective rejection of the goods (Section 2A–509(2)).

(2) Acceptance of a part of any commercial unit is acceptance of that entire unit.

Official Comment

Uniform Statutory Source: Section 2–606.

Changes: The provisions of Section 2–606(1)(a) were substantially rewritten to provide that the lessee's conduct may signify acceptance. Further, the provisions of Section 2–606(1)(c) were not incorporated as irrelevant given the lessee's possession and use of the leased goods.

Cross References:

Sections 2–606(1)(a) and 2–606(1)(c).

Definitional Cross References:

"Commercial unit". Section 2A–103(1)(c).

"Conforming". Section 2A–103(1)(d).

"Goods". Section 2A–103(1)(h).

"Lessee". Section 2A–103(1)(n).

"Lessor". Section 2A–103(1)(p).

"Supplier". Section 2A–103(1)(x).

§ 2A–516. Effect of Acceptance of Goods; Notice of Default; Burden of Establishing Default After Acceptance; Notice of Claim or Litigation to Person Answerable Over.

(1) A lessee must pay rent for any goods accepted in accordance with the lease contract, with due allowance for goods rightfully rejected or not delivered.

(2) A lessee's acceptance of goods precludes rejection of the goods accepted. In the case of a finance lease, if made with knowledge of a nonconformity, acceptance cannot be revoked because of it. In any other case, if made with knowledge of a nonconformity, acceptance cannot be revoked because of it unless the acceptance was on the reasonable assumption that the nonconformity would be seasonably cured. Acceptance does not of itself impair any other remedy provided by this Article or the lease agreement for nonconformity.

(3) If a tender has been accepted:

(a) within a reasonable time after the lessee discovers or should have discovered any default, the lessee shall notify the lessor and the supplier, if any, or be barred from any remedy against the party not notified;

(b) except in the case of a consumer lease, within a reasonable time after the lessee receives notice of litigation for infringement or the like (Section 2A–211) the lessee shall notify the lessor or be barred from any remedy over for liability established by the litigation; and

(c)   the burden is on the lessee to establish any default.

(4)   If a lessee is sued for breach of a warranty or other obligation for which a lessor or a supplier is answerable over the following apply:

(a)   The lessee may give the lessor or the supplier, or both, written notice of the litigation. If the notice states that the person notified may come in and defend and that if the person notified does not do so that person will be bound in any action against that person by the lessee by any determination of fact common to the two litigations, then unless the person notified after seasonable receipt of the notice does come in and defend that person is so bound.

(b)   The lessor or the supplier may demand in writing that the lessee turn over control of the litigation including settlement if the claim is one for infringement or the like (Section 2A–211) or else be barred from any remedy over. If the demand states that the lessor or the supplier agrees to bear all expense and to satisfy any adverse judgment, then unless the lessee after seasonable receipt of the demand does turn over control the lessee is so barred.

(5)   Subsections (3) and (4) apply to any obligation of a lessee to hold the lessor or the supplier harmless against infringement or the like (Section 2A–211).

As amended in 1990.

Official Comment

Uniform Statutory Source: Section 2–607.

Changes: Substantially revised.

Purposes:

1.   Subsection (2) creates a special rule for finance leases, precluding revocation if acceptance is made with knowledge of nonconformity with respect to the lease agreement, as opposed to the supply agreement; this is not inequitable as the lessee has a direct claim against the supplier. Section 2A–209(1). Revocation of acceptance of a finance lease is permitted if the lessee's acceptance was without discovery of the nonconformity (with respect to the lease agreement, not the supply agreement) and was reasonably induced by the lessor's assurances. Section 2A–517(1)(b). Absent exclusion or modification, the lessor under a finance lease makes certain warranties to the lessee. Sections 2A–210 and 2A–211(1). Revocation of acceptance is not prohibited even after the lessee's promise has become irrevocable and independent. Section 2A–407 official comment. Where the finance lease creates a security interest, the rule may be to the contrary. *General Elec. Credit Corp. of Tennessee v. Ger-Beck Mach. Co.,* 806 F.2d 1207 (3rd Cir. 1986).

2.   Subsection (3)(a) requires the lessee to give notice of default, within a reasonable time after the lessee discovered or should have discovered the default. In a finance lease, notice may be given either to the supplier, the lessor, or both, but remedy is barred against the party not notified. In a finance lease, the lessor is usually not liable for defects in the goods and the essential notice is to the supplier. While notice to the finance lessor will often not give any additional rights to the lessee, it would be good practice to give the notice since the finance lessor has an interest in the goods. Subsection (3)(a) does not use the term finance lease, but the definition of supplier is a person from whom a lessor buys or leases goods to be leased under a finance lease. Section 2A–103(1)(x). Therefore, there can be a "supplier" only in a finance lease. Subsection (4) applies similar notice rules as to lessors and suppliers if a lessee is sued for a breach of warranty or other obligation for which a lessor or supplier is answerable over.

3.   Subsection (3)(b) requires the lessee to give the lessor notice of litigation for infringement or the like. There is an exception created in the case of a consumer lease. While such an exception was considered for a finance lease, it was not created because it was not necessary—the lessor in a finance lease does not give a warranty against infringement. Section 2A–211(2). Even though not required under subsection (3)(b), the lessee who takes under a finance lease should consider giving notice of litigation for infringement or the like to the supplier, because the lessee obtains the benefit of the suppliers' promises subject to the suppliers' defenses or claims. Sections 2A–209(1) and 2–607(3)(b).

4.   As to the use of a record other than a writing and communications that are not written, see Section 2A–103, Comment (g).

Cross References:

Sections 2–607(3)(b), 2A–103(1)(x), 2A–209(1), 2A–210, 2A–211(1), 2A–211(2), 2A–407 official comment and 2A–517(1)(b).

Definitional Cross References:

"Action". Section 1–201(1) [*unrevised Article 1; see Concordance, p. 22*].
"Agreement". Section 1–201(3) [*unrevised Article 1; see Concordance, p. 22*].
"Burden of establishing". Section 1–201(8) [*unrevised Article 1; see Concordance, p. 22*].
"Conforming". Section 2A–103(1)(d).
"Consumer lease". Section 2A–103(1)(e).
"Delivery". Section 1–201(14) [*unrevised Article 1; see Concordance, p. 22*].
"Discover". Section 1–201(25) [*unrevised Article 1; see Concordance, p. 22*].
"Finance lease". Section 2A–103(1)(g).
"Goods". Section 2A–103(1)(h).
"Knowledge". Section 1–201(25) [*unrevised Article 1; see Concordance, p. 22*].
"Lease agreement". Section 2A–103(1)(k).
"Lease contract". Section 2A–103(1)(*l*).
"Lessee". Section 2A–103(1)(n).
"Lessor". Section 2A–103(1)(p).
"Notice". Section 1–201(25) [*unrevised Article 1; see Concordance, p. 22*].
"Notifies". Section 1–201(26) [*unrevised Article 1; see Concordance, p. 22*].
"Person". Section 1–201(30) [*unrevised Article 1; see Concordance, p. 22*].
"Reasonable time". Section 1–204(1) and (2) [*unrevised Article 1; see Concordance, p. 22*].
"Receipt". Section 2–103(1)(c).
"Remedy". Section 1–201(34) [*unrevised Article 1; see Concordance, p. 22*].
"Seasonably". Section 1–204(3) [*unrevised Article 1; see Concordance, p. 22*].
"Supplier". Section 2A–103(1)(x).
"Written". Section 1–201(46) [*unrevised Article 1; see Concordance, p. 22*].

As amended in 2022.

§ 2A–517. Revocation of Acceptance of Goods.

(1) A lessee may revoke acceptance of a lot or commercial unit whose nonconformity substantially impairs its value to the lessee if the lessee has accepted it:

(a) except in the case of a finance lease, on the reasonable assumption that its nonconformity would be cured and it has not been seasonably cured; or

(b) without discovery of the nonconformity if the lessee's acceptance was reasonably induced either by the lessor's assurances or, except in the case of a finance lease, by the difficulty of discovery before acceptance.

(2) Except in the case of a finance lease that is not a consumer lease, a lessee may revoke acceptance of a lot or commercial unit if the lessor defaults under the lease contract and the default substantially impairs the value of that lot or commercial unit to the lessee.

(3) If the lease agreement so provides, the lessee may revoke acceptance of a lot or commercial unit because of other defaults by the lessor.

(4) Revocation of acceptance must occur within a reasonable time after the lessee discovers or should have discovered the ground for it and before any substantial change in condition of the goods which is not caused by the nonconformity. Revocation is not effective until the lessee notifies the lessor.

(5) A lessee who so revokes has the same rights and duties with regard to the goods involved as if the lessee had rejected them.

As amended in 1990.

Official Comment

Uniform Statutory Source: Section 2–608.

Changes: Revised to reflect leasing practices and terminology. Note that in the case of a finance lease the lessee retains a limited right to revoke acceptance. Sections 2A–517(1)(b) and 2A–516 official comment. New subsections (2) and (3) added.

Purposes:

1.   The section states the situations under which the lessee may return the goods to the lessor and cancel the lease. Subsection (2) recognizes that the lessor may have continuing obligations under the lease and that a default as to those obligations may be sufficiently material to justify revocation of acceptance of the leased items and cancellation of the lease by the lessee. For example, a failure by the lessor to fulfill its obligation to maintain leased equipment or to supply other goods which are necessary for the operation of the leased equipment may justify revocation of acceptance and cancellation of the lease.

2.   Subsection (3) specifically provides that the lease agreement may provide that the lessee can revoke acceptance for defaults by the lessor which in the absence of such an agreement might not be considered sufficiently serious to justify revocation. That is, the parties are free to contract on the question of what defaults are so material that the lessee can cancel the lease.

Cross Reference:

Section 2A–516 official comment.

Definitional Cross References:

"Commercial unit". Section 2A–103(1)(c).
"Conforming". Section 2A–103(1)(d).
"Discover". Section 1–201(25) [*unrevised Article 1; see Concordance, p. 22*].
"Finance lease". Section 2A–103(1)(g).
"Goods". Section 2A–103(1)(h).
"Lessee". Section 2A–103(1)(n).
"Lessor". Section 2A–103(1)(p).
"Lot". Section 2A–103(1)(s).
"Notifies". Section 1–201(26) [*unrevised Article 1; see Concordance, p. 22*].
"Reasonable time". Section 1–204(1) and (2) [*unrevised Article 1; see Concordance, p. 22*].
"Rights". Section 1–201(36) [*unrevised Article 1; see Concordance, p. 22*].
"Seasonably". Section 1–204(3) [*unrevised Article 1; see Concordance, p. 22*].
"Value". Section 1–201(44) [*unrevised Article 1; see Concordance, p. 22*].

§ 2A–518.   Cover; Substitute Goods.

(1)   After a default by a lessor under the lease contract of the type described in Section 2A–508(1), or, if agreed, after other default by the lessor, the lessee may cover by making any purchase or lease of or contract to purchase or lease goods in substitution for those due from the lessor.

(2)   Except as otherwise provided with respect to damages liquidated in the lease agreement (Section 2A–504) or otherwise determined pursuant to agreement of the parties (Sections 1–302 and 2A–503), if a lessee's cover is by a lease agreement substantially similar to the original lease agreement and the new lease agreement is made in good faith and in a commercially reasonable manner, the lessee may recover from the lessor as damages (i) the present value, as of the date of the commencement of the term of the new lease agreement, of the rent under the new lease agreement applicable to that period of the new lease term which is comparable to the then remaining term of the original lease agreement minus the present value as of the same date of the total rent for the then remaining lease term of the original lease agreement, and (ii) any incidental or consequential damages, less expenses saved in consequence of the lessor's default.

(3)   If a lessee's cover is by lease agreement that for any reason does not qualify for treatment under subsection (2), or is by purchase or otherwise, the lessee may recover from the lessor as if the lessee had elected not to cover and Section 2A–519 governs.

As amended in 1990 and 2001.

Official Comment

Uniform Statutory Source: Section 2–712.

Changes: Substantially revised.

Purposes:

1.   Subsection (1) allows the lessee to take action to fix its damages after default by the lessor. Such action may consist of the lease of goods. The decision to cover is a function of commercial judgment, not a statutory mandate replete with sanctions for failure to comply. *Cf.* Section 9–625.

2.   Subsection (2) states a rule for determining the amount of lessee's damages provided that there is no agreement to the contrary. The lessee's damages will be established using the new lease agreement as a measure if the following three criteria are met: (i) the lessee's cover is by lease agreement, (ii) the lease agreement is substantially similar to the original lease agreement, and (iii) such cover was effected in good faith, and in a commercially reasonable manner. Thus, the lessee will be entitled to recover from the lessor the present value, as of the date of commencement of the term of the new lease agreement, of the rent under the new lease agreement applicable to that period which is comparable to the then remaining term of the original lease agreement less the present value of the rent reserved for the remaining term under the original lease, together with incidental or consequential damages less expenses saved in consequence of the lessor's default. Consequential damages may include loss suffered by the lessee because of deprivation of the use of the goods during the period between the default and the acquisition of the goods under the new lease agreement. If the lessee's cover does not satisfy the criteria of subsection (2), Section 2A–519 governs.

3.   Two of the three criteria to be met by the lessee are familiar, but the concept of the new lease agreement being substantially similar to the original lease agreement is not. Given the many variables facing a party who intends to lease goods and the rapidity of change in the market place, the policy decision was made not to draft with specificity. It was thought unwise to seek to establish certainty at the cost of fairness. Thus, the decision of whether the new lease agreement is substantially similar to the original will be determined case by case.

4.   While the section does not draw a bright line, it is possible to describe some of the factors that should be considered in finding that a new lease agreement is substantially similar to the original. First, the goods subject to the new lease agreement should be examined. For example, in a lease of computer equipment the new lease might be for more modern equipment. However, it may be that at the time of the lessor's breach it was not possible to obtain the same type of goods in the market place. Because the lessee's remedy under Section 2A–519 is intended to place the lessee in essentially the same position as if he had covered, if goods similar to those to have been delivered under the original lease are not available, then the computer equipment in this hypothetical should qualify as a commercially reasonable substitute. *See* Section 2–712(1).

5.   Second, the various elements of the new lease agreement should also be examined. Those elements include the presence or absence of options to purchase or release; the lessor's representations, warranties and covenants to the lessee, as well as those to be provided by the lessee to the lessor; and the services, if any, to be provided by the lessor or by the lessee. All of these factors allocate cost and risk between the lessor and the lessee and thus affect the amount of rent to be paid. If the differences between the original lease and the new lease can be easily valued, it would be appropriate for a court to adjust the difference in rental to take account of the difference between the two leases, find that the new lease is substantially similar to the old lease, and award cover damages under this section. If, for example, the new lease requires the lessor to insure the goods in the hands of the lessee, while the original lease required the lessee to insure, the usual cost of such insurance could be deducted from the rent due under the new lease before determining the difference in rental between the two leases.

6.   Having examined the goods and the agreement, the test to be applied is whether, in light of these comparisons, the new lease agreement is substantially similar to the original lease agreement. These findings should not be made with scientific precision, as they are a function of economics, nor should they be made independently with respect to the goods and each element of the agreement, as it is important that a sense of commercial judgment pervade the finding. To establish the new lease as a proper measure of damage under subsection (2), these factors, taken as a whole, must result in a finding that the new lease agreement is substantially similar to the original.

7.   A new lease can be substantially similar to the original lease even though its term extends beyond the remaining term of the original lease, so long as both (a) the lease terms are commercially comparable (e.g., it is highly unlikely that a one-month rental and a five-year lease would reflect similar commercial realities), and (b) the court can fairly apportion a part of the rental payments under the new lease to that part of the term of the new lease which is comparable to the remaining lease term under the original lease. Also, the lease term of the

new lease may be comparable to the term of the original lease even though the beginning and ending dates of the two leases are not the same. For example, a two-month lease of agricultural equipment for the months of August and September may be comparable to a two-month lease running from the 15th of August to the 15th of October if in the particular location two-month leases beginning on August 15th are basically interchangeable with two-month leases beginning August 1st. Similarly, the term of a one-year truck lease beginning on the 15th of January may be comparable to the term of a one-year truck lease beginning January 2d. If the lease terms are found to be comparable, the court may base cover damages on the entire difference between the costs under the two leases.

Cross References:

Sections 2–712(1), 2A–519 and 9–625.

Definitional Cross References:

"Agreement". Section 1–201(b)(3).
"Contract". Section 1–201(b)(12).
"Good faith". Section 1–201(b)(20).
"Goods". Section 2A–103(1)(h).
"Lease". Section 2A–103(1)(j).
"Lease agreement". Section 2A–103(1)(k).
"Lease contract". Section 2A–103(1)(*l*).
"Lessee". Section 2A–103(1)(n).
"Lessor". Section 2A–103(1)(p).
"Party". Section 1–201(b)(26).

"Present value". Section 2A–103(1)(u). [*Note from West Advisory Panel: Revised Article 1 (2001) defines "present value" in § 1–201(b)(28) for jurisdictions that adopt that version of Article 1. The conforming amendments to Article 2A delete the comment to the Article 2A definition of "present value" but erroneously do not delete the definition itself.*]

"Purchase". Section 2A–103(1)(v).

As amended in 2001.

§ 2A–519. Lessee's Damages for Non-delivery, Repudiation, Default, and Breach of Warranty in Regard to Accepted Goods.

(1)   Except as otherwise provided with respect to damages liquidated in the lease agreement (Section 2A–504) or otherwise determined pursuant to agreement of the parties (Sections 1–302 and 2A–503), if a lessee elects not to cover or a lessee elects to cover and the cover is by lease agreement that for any reason does not qualify for treatment under Section 2A–518(2), or is by purchase or otherwise, the measure of damages for non-delivery or repudiation by the lessor or for rejection or revocation of acceptance by the lessee is the present value, as of the date of the default, of the then market rent minus the present value as of the same date of the original rent, computed for the remaining lease term of the original lease agreement, together with incidental and consequential damages, less expenses saved in consequence of the lessor's default.

(2)   Market rent is to be determined as of the place for tender or, in cases of rejection after arrival or revocation of acceptance, as of the place of arrival.

(3)   Except as otherwise agreed, if the lessee has accepted goods and given notification (Section 2A–516(3)), the measure of damages for non-conforming tender or delivery or other default by a lessor is the loss resulting in the ordinary course of events from the lessor's default as determined in any manner that is reasonable together with incidental and consequential damages, less expenses saved in consequence of the lessor's default.

(4)   Except as otherwise agreed, the measure of damages for breach of warranty is the present value at the time and place of acceptance of the difference between the value of the use of the goods accepted and the value if they had been as warranted for the lease term, unless special circumstances show proximate damages of a different amount, together with incidental and consequential damages, less expenses saved in consequence of the lessor's default or breach of warranty.

As amended in 1990 and 2001.

Official Comment

Uniform Statutory Source: Sections 2–713 and 2–714.

Changes: Substantially revised.

Purposes:

1.   Subsection (1), a revised version of the provisions of Section 2–713(1), states the basic rule governing the measure of lessee's damages for non-delivery or repudiation by the lessor or for rightful rejection or revocation of acceptance by the lessee. This measure will apply, absent agreement to the contrary, if the lessee does not cover or if the cover does not qualify under Section 2A–518. There is no sanction for cover that does not qualify.

2.   The measure of damage is the present value, as of the date of default, of the market rent for the remaining term of the lease less the present value of the original rent for the remaining term of the lease, plus incidental and consequential damages less expenses saved in consequence of the default. Note that the reference in Section 2A–519(1) is to the date of default not to the date of an event of default. An event of default under a lease agreement becomes a default under a lease agreement only after the expiration of any relevant period of grace and compliance with any notice requirements under this Article and the lease agreement. American Bar Foundation, *Commentaries on Indentures*, § 5–1, at 216–217 (1971). Section 2A–501(1). This conclusion is also a function of whether, as a matter of fact or law, the event of default has been waived, suspended or cured. Sections 2A–103(4) and 1–103.

3.   Subsection (2), a revised version of the provisions of Section 2–713(2), states the rule with respect to determining market rent.

4.   Subsection (3), a revised version of the provisions of Section 2–714(1) and (3), states the measure of damages where goods have been accepted and acceptance is not revoked. The subsection applies both to defaults which occur at the inception of the lease and to defaults which occur subsequently, such as failure to comply with an obligation to maintain the leased goods. The measure in essence is the loss, in the ordinary course of events, flowing from the default.

5.   Subsection (4), a revised version of the provisions of Section 2–714(2), states the measure of damages for breach of warranty. The measure in essence is the present value of the difference between the value of the goods accepted and of the goods if they had been as warranted.

6.   Subsections (1), (3) and (4) specifically state that the parties may by contract vary the damages rules stated in those subsections.

Cross References:

Sections 2–713(1), 2–713(2), 2–714 and Section 2A–518.

Definitional Cross References:

"Conforming". Section 2A–103(1)(d).
"Delivery". Section 1–201(b)(15).
"Goods". Section 2A–103(1)(h).
"Lease". Section 2A–103(1)(j).
"Lease agreement". Section 2A–103(1)(k).
"Lessee". Section 2A–103(1)(n).
"Lessor". Section 2A–103(1)(p).
"Notification". Section 1–202.
"Present value". Section 2A–103(1)(u). [*Note from West Advisory Panel: Revised Article 1 (2001) defines "present value" in § 1–201(b)(28) for jurisdictions that adopt that version of Article 1. The conforming amendments to Article 2A delete the comment to the Article 2A definition of "present value" but erroneously do not delete the definition itself.*]
"Value". Section 1–204.

As amended in 2001.

§ 2A–520. Lessee's Incidental and Consequential Damages.

(1)   Incidental damages resulting from a lessor's default include expenses reasonably incurred in inspection, receipt, transportation, and care and custody of goods rightfully rejected or goods the acceptance

of which is justifiably revoked, any commercially reasonable charges, expenses or commissions in connection with effecting cover, and any other reasonable expense incident to the default.

(2) Consequential damages resulting from a lessor's default include:

(a) any loss resulting from general or particular requirements and needs of which the lessor at the time of contracting had reason to know and which could not reasonably be prevented by cover or otherwise; and

(b) injury to person or property proximately resulting from any breach of warranty.

Official Comment

Uniform Statutory Source: Section 2–715.

Changes: Revised to reflect leasing terminology and practices.

Purposes: Subsection (1), a revised version of the provisions of Section 2–715(1), lists some examples of incidental damages resulting from a lessor's default; the list is not exhaustive. Subsection (1) makes clear that it applies not only to rightful rejection, but also to justifiable revocation.

Subsection (2), a revised version of the provisions of Section 2–715(2), lists some examples of consequential damages resulting from a lessor's default; the list is not exhaustive.

Cross References:

Section 2–715.

Definitional Cross References:

"Goods". Section 2A–103(1)(h).
"Knows". Section 1–201(25) [*unrevised Article 1; see Concordance, p. 22*].
"Lessee". Section 2A–103(1)(n).
"Lessor". Section 2A–103(1)(p).
"Person". Section 1–201(30) [*unrevised Article 1; see Concordance, p. 22*].
"Receipt". Section 2–103(1)(c).

§ 2A–521. Lessee's Right to Specific Performance or Replevin.

(1) Specific performance may be decreed if the goods are unique or in other proper circumstances.

(2) A decree for specific performance may include any terms and conditions as to payment of the rent, damages, or other relief that the court deems just.

(3) A lessee has a right of replevin, detinue, sequestration, claim and delivery, or the like for goods identified to the lease contract if after reasonable effort the lessee is unable to effect cover for those goods or the circumstances reasonably indicate that the effort will be unavailing.

Official Comment

Uniform Statutory Source: Section 2–716.

Changes: Revised to reflect leasing practices and terminology, and to expand the reference to the right of replevin in subsection (3) to include other similar rights of the lessee.

Definitional Cross References:

"Delivery". Section 1–201(14) [*unrevised Article 1; see Concordance, p. 22*].
"Goods". Section 2A–103(1)(h).
"Lease contract". Section 2A–103(1)(*l*).
"Lessee". Section 2A–103(1)(n).
"Rights". Section 1–201(36) [*unrevised Article 1; see Concordance, p. 22*].
"Term". Section 1–201(42) [*unrevised Article 1; see Concordance, p. 22*].

§ 2A–522. Lessee's Right to Goods on Lessor's Insolvency.

(1)   Subject to subsection (2) and even though the goods have not been shipped, a lessee who has paid a part or all of the rent and security for goods identified to a lease contract (Section 2A–217) on making and keeping good a tender of any unpaid portion of the rent and security due under the lease contract may recover the goods identified from the lessor if the lessor becomes insolvent within 10 days after receipt of the first installment of rent and security.

(2)   A lessee acquires the right to recover goods identified to a lease contract only if they conform to the lease contract.

Official Comment

Uniform Statutory Source: Section 2–502.

Changes: Revised to reflect leasing practices and terminology.

Definitional Cross References:

"Conforming". Section 2A–103(1)(d).
"Goods". Section 2A–103(1)(h).
"Insolvent". Section 1–201(23) [*unrevised Article 1; see Concordance, p. 22*].
"Lease contract". Section 2A–103(1)(*l*).
"Lessee". Section 2A–103(1)(n).
"Lessor". Section 2A–103(1)(p).
"Receipt". Section 2–103(1)(c).
"Rights". Section 1–201(36) [*unrevised Article 1; see Concordance, p. 22*].

C.   DEFAULT BY LESSEE

§ 2A–523. Lessor's Remedies.

(1)   If a lessee wrongfully rejects or revokes acceptance of goods or fails to make a payment when due or repudiates with respect to a part or the whole, then, with respect to any goods involved, and with respect to all of the goods if under an installment lease contract the value of the whole lease contract is substantially impaired (Section 2A–510), the lessee is in default under the lease contract and the lessor may:

(a)   cancel the lease contract (Section 2A–505(1));

(b)   proceed respecting goods not identified to the lease contract (Section 2A–524);

(c)   withhold delivery of the goods and take possession of goods previously delivered (Section 2A–525);

(d)   stop delivery of the goods by any bailee (Section 2A–526);

(e)   dispose of the goods and recover damages (Section 2A–527), or retain the goods and recover damages (Section 2A–528), or in a proper case recover rent (Section 2A–529);

(f)   exercise any other rights or pursue any other remedies provided in the lease contract.

(2)   If a lessor does not fully exercise a right or obtain a remedy to which the lessor is entitled under subsection (1), the lessor may recover the loss resulting in the ordinary course of events from the lessee's default as determined in any reasonable manner, together with incidental damages, less expenses saved in consequence of the lessee's default.

(3)   If a lessee is otherwise in default under a lease contract, the lessor may exercise the rights and pursue the remedies provided in the lease contract, which may include a right to cancel the lease. In addition, unless otherwise provided in the lease contract:

(a)   if the default substantially impairs the value of the lease contract to the lessor, the lessor may exercise the rights and pursue the remedies provided in subsections (1) or (2); or

(b)   if the default does not substantially impair the value of the lease contract to the lessor, the lessor may recover as provided in subsection (2).

As amended in 1990.

Official Comment

Uniform Statutory Source: Section 2–703.

Changes: Substantially revised.

Purposes:

1.   Subsection (1) is an index to Sections 2A–524 through 2A–531 and states that the remedies provided in those sections are available for the defaults referred to in subsection (1): wrongful rejection or revocation of acceptance, failure to make a payment when due, or repudiation. In addition, remedies provided in the lease contract are available. Subsection (2) sets out a remedy if the lessor does not pursue to completion a right or actually obtain a remedy available under subsection (1), and subsection (3) sets out statutory remedies for defaults not specifically referred to in subsection (1). Subsection (3) provides that, if any default by the lessee other than those specifically referred to in subsection (1) is material, the lessor can exercise the remedies provided in subsection (1) or (2); otherwise the available remedy is as provided in subsection (3). A lessor who has brought an action seeking or has nonjudicially pursued one or more of the remedies available under subsection (1) may amend so as to claim or may nonjudicially pursue a remedy under subsection (2) unless the right or remedy first chosen has been pursued to an extent actually inconsistent with the new course of action. The intent of the provision is to reject the doctrine of election of remedies and to permit an alteration of course by the lessor unless such alteration would actually have an effect on the lessee that would be unreasonable under the circumstances. Further, the lessor may pursue remedies under both subsections (1) and (2) unless doing so would put the lessor in a better position than it would have been in had the lessee fully performed.

2.   The lessor and the lessee can agree to modify the rights and remedies available under the Article; they can, among other things, provide that for defaults other than those specified in subsection (1) the lessor can exercise the rights and remedies referred to in subsection (1), whether or not the default would otherwise be held to substantially impair the value of the lease contract to the lessor; they can also create a new scheme of rights and remedies triggered by the occurrence of the default. Sections 2A–103(4) and 1–102(3) [*unrevised Article 1; see Concordance, p. 22*].

3.   Subsection (1), a substantially rewritten version of Section 2–703, lists various cumulative remedies of the lessor where the lessee wrongfully rejects or revokes acceptance, fails to make a payment when due, or repudiates. Section 2A–501(2) and (4). The subsection also allows the lessor to exercise any contractual remedy.

4.   This Article rejects any general doctrine of election of remedy. Whether, in a particular case, one remedy bars another, is a function of whether lessor has been put in as good a position as if the lessee had fully performed the lease contract. Multiple remedies are barred only if the effect is to put the lessor in a better position than it would have been in had the lessee fully performed under the lease. Sections 2A–103(4), 2A–501(4), and 1–106(1) [*unrevised Article 1; see Concordance, p. 22*].

5.   **Hypothetical:** To better understand the application of subparagraphs (a) through (e), it is useful to review a hypothetical. Assume that A is a merchant in the business of selling and leasing new bicycles of various types. B is about to engage in the business of subleasing bicycles to summer residents of and visitors to an island resort. A, as lessor, has agreed to lease 60 bicycles to B. While there is one master lease, deliveries and terms are staggered. 20 bicycles are to be delivered by A to B's island location on June 1; the term of the lease of these bicycles is four months. 20 bicycles are to be delivered by A to B's island location on July 1; the term of the lease of these bicycles is three months. Finally, 20 bicycles are to be delivered by A to B's island location on August 1; the term of the lease of these bicycles is two months. B is obligated to pay rent to A on the 15th day of each month during the term for the lease. Rent is $50 per month, per bicycle. B has no option to purchase or release and must return the bicycles to A at the end of the term, in good condition, reasonable wear and tear excepted. Since the retail price of each bicycle is $400 and bicycles used in the retail rental business have a useful economic life of 36 months, this transaction creates a lease. Sections 2A–103(1)(j) and 1–201(37) 1–203.

6.   A's current inventory of bicycles is not large. Thus, upon signing the lease with B in February, A agreed to purchase 60 new bicycles from A's principal manufacturer, with special instructions to drop ship the bicycles to B's island location in accordance with the delivery schedule set forth in the lease.

7.   The first shipment of 20 bicycles was received by B on May 21. B inspected the bicycles, accepted the same as conforming to the lease and signed a receipt of delivery and acceptance. However, due to poor weather that summer, business was terrible and B was unable to pay the rent due on June 15. Pursuant to the lease A sent B notice of default and proceeded to enforce his rights and remedies against B.

8.   A's counsel first advised A that under Section 2A–510(2) and the terms of the lease B's failure to pay was a default with respect to the whole. Thus, to minimize A's continued exposure, A was advised to take possession of the bicycles. If A had possession of the goods A could refuse to deliver. Section 2A–525(1). However, the facts here are different. With respect to the bicycles in B's possession, A has the right to take possession of the bicycles, without breach of the peace. Section 2A–525(2). If B refuses to allow A access to the bicycles, A can proceed by action, including replevin or injunctive relief.

9.   With respect to the 40 bicycles that have not been delivered, this Article provides various alternatives. First, assume that 20 of the remaining 40 bicycles have been manufactured and delivered by the manufacturer to a carrier for shipment to B. Given the size of the shipment, the carrier was using a small truck for the delivery and the truck had not yet reached the island ferry when the manufacturer (at the request of A) instructed the carrier to divert the shipment to A's place of business. A's right to stop delivery is recognized under these circumstances. Section 2A–526(1). Second, assume that the 20 remaining bicycles were in the process of manufacture when B defaulted. A retains the right (as between A as lessor and B as lessee) to exercise reasonable commercial judgment whether to complete manufacture or to dispose of the unfinished goods for scrap. Since A is not the manufacturer and A has a binding contract to buy the bicycles, A elected to allow the manufacturer to complete the manufacture of the bicycles, but instructed the manufacturer to deliver the completed bicycles to A's place of business. Section 2A–524(2).

10.   Thus, so far A has elected to exercise the remedies referred to in subparagraphs (b) through (d) in subsection (1). None of these remedies bars any of the others because A's election and enforcement merely resulted in A's possession of the bicycles. Had B performed A would have recovered possession of the bicycles. Thus A is in the process of obtaining the benefit of his bargain. Note that A could exercise any other rights or pursue any other remedies provided in the lease contract (Section 2A–523(1)(f)), or elect to recover his loss due to the lessee's default under Section 2A–523(2).

11.   A's counsel next would determine what action, if any, should be taken with respect to the goods. As stated in subparagraph (e) and as discussed fully in Section 2A–527(1) the lessor may, but has no obligation to, dispose of the goods by a substantially similar lease (indeed, the lessor has no obligation whatsoever to dispose of the goods at all) and recover damages based on that action, but lessor will not be able to recover damages which put it in a better position than performance would have done, nor will it be able to recover damages for losses which it could have reasonably avoided. In this case, since A is in the business of leasing and selling bicycles, A will probably inventory the 60 bicycles for its retail trade.

12.   A's counsel then will determine which of the various means of ascertaining A's damages against B are available. Subparagraph (e) catalogues each relevant section. First, under Section 2A–527(2) the amount of A's claim is computed by comparing the original lease between A and B with any subsequent lease of the bicycles but only if the subsequent lease is substantially similar to the original lease contract. While the section does not define this term, the official comment does establish some parameters. If, however, A elects to lease the bicycles to his retail trade, it is unlikely that the resulting lease will be substantially similar to the original, as leases to retail customers are considerably different from leases to wholesale customers like B. If, however, the leases were substantially similar, the damage claim is for accrued and unpaid rent to the beginning of the new lease, plus the present value as of the same date, of the rent reserved under the original lease for the balance of its term less the present value as of the same date of the rent reserved under the replacement lease for a term comparable to the balance of the term of the original lease, together with incidental damages less expenses saved in consequence of the lessee's default.

13.   If the new lease is not substantially similar or if A elects to sell the bicycles or to hold the bicycles, damages are computed under Section 2A–528 or 2A–529.

14.   If A elects to pursue his claim under Section 2A–528(1) the damage rule is the same as that stated in Section 2A–528(2) except that damages are measured from default if the lessee never took possession of the goods or from the time when the lessor did or could have regained possession and that the standard of comparison is not the rent reserved under a substantially similar lease entered into by the lessor but a market rent, as defined in Section 2A–507. Further, if the facts of this hypothetical were more elaborate A may be able to establish that the measure of damage under subsection (1) is inadequate to put him in the same position that B's performance would have, in which case A can claim the present value of his lost profits.

15.   Yet another alternative for computing A's damage claim against B which will be available in some situations is recovery of the present value, as of entry of judgment, of the rent for the then remaining lease term under Section 2A–529. However, this formulation is not available if the goods have been repossessed or tendered back to A. For the 20 bicycles repossessed and the remaining 40 bicycles, A will be able to recover the present

value of the rent only if A is unable to dispose of them, or circumstances indicate the effort will be unavailing. If A has prevailed in an action for the rent, at any time up to collection of a judgment by A against B, A might dispose of the bicycles. In such case A's claim for damages against B is governed by Section 2A–527 or 2A–528. Section 2A–529(3). The resulting recalculation of claim should reduce the amount recoverable by A against B and the lessor is required to cause an appropriate credit to be entered against the earlier judgment. However, the nature of the post-judgment proceedings to resolve this issue, and the sanctions for a failure to comply, if any, will be determined by other law.

16.   Finally, if the lease agreement had so provided pursuant to subparagraph (f), A's claim against B would not be determined under any of these statutory formulae, but pursuant to a liquidated damages clause. Section 2A–504(1).

17.   These various methods of computing A's damage claim against B are alternatives subject to Section 2A–501(4). However, the pursuit of any one of these alternatives is not a bar to, nor has it been barred by, A's earlier action to obtain possession of the 60 bicycles. These formulae, which vary as a function of an overt or implied mitigation of damage theory, focus on allowing A a recovery of the benefit of his bargain with B. Had B performed, A would have received the rent as well as the return of the 60 bicycles at the end of the term.

18.   Finally, A's counsel should also advise A of his right to cancel the lease contract under subparagraph (a). Section 2A–505(1). Cancellation will discharge all existing obligations but preserve A's rights and remedies.

19.   Subsection (2) recognizes that a lessor who is entitled to exercise the rights or to obtain a remedy granted by subsection (1) may choose not to do so. In such cases, the lessor can recover damages as provided in subsection (2). For example, for non-payment of rent, the lessor may decide not to take possession of the goods and cancel the lease, but rather to merely sue for the unpaid rent as it comes due plus lost interest or other damages "determined in any reasonable manner." Subsection (2) also negates any loss of alternative rights and remedies by reason of having invoked or commenced the exercise or pursuit of any one or more rights or remedies.

20.   Subsection (3) allows the lessor access to a remedy scheme provided in this Article as well as that contained in the lease contract if the lessee is in default for reasons other than those stated in subsection (1). Note that the reference to this Article includes supplementary principles of law and equity, *e.g.*, fraud, misrepresentation and duress. Sections 2A–103(4) and 1–103.

21.   There is no special treatment of the finance lease in this section. Absent supplementary principles of law to the contrary, in most cases the supplier will have no rights or remedies against the defaulting lessee. Section 2A–209(2)(ii). Given that the supplier will look to the lessor for payment, this is appropriate. However, there is a specific exception to this rule with respect to the right to identify goods to the lease contract. Section 2A–524(2). The parties are free to create a different result in a particular case. Sections 2A–103(4) and 1–102(3) [*unrevised Article 1; see Concordance, p. 22*].

Cross References:

Sections 1–102(3) [*unrevised Article 1; see Concordance, p. 22*], 1–103, 1–106(1) [*unrevised Article 1; see Concordance, p. 22*], 1–201(37) [*unrevised Article 1; see Concordance, p. 22*], 2–703, 2A–103(1)(j), 2A–103(4), 2A–209(2)(ii), 2A–501(4), 2A–504(1), 2A–505(1), 2A–507, 2A–510(2), 2A–524 through 2A–531, 2A–524(2), 2A–525(1), 2A–525(2), 2A–526(1), 2A–527(1), 2A–527(2), 2A–528(1) and 2A–529(3).

Definitional Cross References:

"Delivery". Section 1–201(14) [*unrevised Article 1; see Concordance, p. 22*].

"Goods". Section 2A–103(1)(h).

"Installment lease contract". Section 2A–103(1)(i).

"Lease contract". Section 2A–103(1)(*l*).

"Lessee". Section 2A–103(1)(n).

"Lessor". Section 2A–103(1)(p).

"Remedy". Section 1–201(34) [*unrevised Article 1; see Concordance, p. 22*].

"Rights". Section 1–201(36) [*unrevised Article 1; see Concordance, p. 22*].

"Value". Section 1–201(44) [*unrevised Article 1; see Concordance, p. 22*].

As amended in 2022.

§ 2A–524. Lessor's Right to Identify Goods to Lease Contract.

(1)   After default by the lessee under the lease contract of the type described in Section 2A–523(1) or 2A–523(3)(a) or, if agreed, after other default by the lessee, the lessor may:

(a)   identify to the lease contract conforming goods not already identified if at the time the lessor learned of the default they were in the lessor's or the supplier's possession or control; and

(b)   dispose of goods (Section 2A–527(1)) that demonstrably have been intended for the particular lease contract even though those goods are unfinished.

(2)   If the goods are unfinished, in the exercise of reasonable commercial judgment for the purposes of avoiding loss and of effective realization, an aggrieved lessor or the supplier may either complete manufacture and wholly identify the goods to the lease contract or cease manufacture and lease, sell, or otherwise dispose of the goods for scrap or salvage value or proceed in any other reasonable manner.

As amended in 1990.

Official Comment

Uniform Statutory Source: Section 2–704.

Changes: Revised to reflect leasing practices and terminology.

Purposes: The remedies provided by this section are available to the lessor (i) if there has been a default by the lessee which falls within Section 2A–523(1) or 2A–523(3)(a), or (ii) if there has been any other default for which the lease contract gives the lessor the remedies provided by this section. Under "(ii)", the lease contract may give the lessor the remedies of identification and disposition provided by this section in various ways. For example, a lease provision might specifically refer to the remedies of identification and disposition, or it might refer to this section by number (*i.e.*, 2A–524), or it might do so by a more general reference such as "all rights and remedies provided by Article 2A for default by the lessee."

Definitional Cross References:

"Aggrieved party". Section 1–201(2) [*unrevised Article 1; see Concordance, p. 22*].
"Conforming". Section 2A–103(1)(d).
"Goods". Section 2A–103(1)(h).
"Learn". Section 1–201(25) [*unrevised Article 1; see Concordance, p. 22*].
"Lease". Section 2A–103(1)(j).
"Lease contract". Section 2A–103(1)(*l*).
"Lessor". Section 2A–103(1)(p).
"Rights". Section 1–201(36) [*unrevised Article 1; see Concordance, p. 22*].
"Supplier". Section 2A–103(1)(x).
"Value". Section 1–201(44) [*unrevised Article 1; see Concordance, p. 22*].

§ 2A–525. Lessor's Right to Possession of Goods.

(1)   If a lessor discovers the lessee to be insolvent, the lessor may refuse to deliver the goods.

(2)   After a default by the lessee under the lease contract of the type described in Section 2A–523(1) or 2A–523(3)(a) or, if agreed, after other default by the lessee, the lessor has the right to take possession of the goods. If the lease contract so provides, the lessor may require the lessee to assemble the goods and make them available to the lessor at a place to be designated by the lessor which is reasonably convenient to both parties. Without removal, the lessor may render unusable any goods employed in trade or business, and may dispose of goods on the lessee's premises (Section 2A–527).

(3)   The lessor may proceed under subsection (2) without judicial process if it can be done without breach of the peace or the lessor may proceed by action.

As amended in 1990.

Official Comment

Uniform Statutory Source: Section 2–702(1) and former Section 9–503 (now codified as Section 9–609).

Changes: Substantially revised.

Purposes:

1.   Subsection (1), a revised version of the provisions of Section 2–702(1), allows the lessor to refuse to deliver goods if the lessee is insolvent. Note that the provisions of Section 2–702(2), granting the unpaid seller certain rights of reclamation, were not incorporated in this section. Subsection (2) made this unnecessary.

2.   Subsection (2), a revised version of the provisions of former Section 9–503 (now codified as Section 9–609), allows the lessor, on a Section 2A–523(1) or 2A–523(3)(a) default by the lessee, the right to take possession of or reclaim the goods. Also, the lessor can contract for the right to take possession of the goods for other defaults by the lessee. Therefore, since the lessee's insolvency is an event of default in a standard lease agreement, subsection (2) is the functional equivalent of Section 2–702(2). Further, subsection (2) sanctions the classic crate and delivery clause obligating the lessee to assemble the goods and to make them available to the lessor. Finally, the lessor may leave the goods in place, render them unusable (if they are goods employed in trade or business), and dispose of them on the lessee's premises.

3.   Subsection (3), a revised version of the provisions of former Section 9–503 (now codified as Section 9–609), allows the lessor to proceed under subsection (2) without judicial process, absent breach of the peace, or by action. Sections 2A–501(3), 2A–103(4) and 1–201(1) [*unrevised Article 1; see Concordance, p. 22*]. In the appropriate case action includes injunctive relief. *Clark Equip. Co. v. Armstrong Equip. Co.*, 431 F.2d 54 (5th Cir. 1970), *cert. denied*, 402 U.S. 909 (1971). This Section, as well as a number of other Sections in this Part, are included in the Article to codify the lessor's common law right to protect the lessor's reversionary interest in the goods. Section 2A–103(1)(q). These Sections are intended to supplement and not displace principles of law and equity with respect to the protection of such interest. Sections 2A–103(4) and 1–103. Such principles apply in many instances, *e.g.*, loss or damage to goods if risk of loss passes to the lessee, failure of the lessee to return goods to the lessor in the condition stipulated in the lease, and refusal of the lessee to return goods to the lessor after termination or cancellation of the lease. See also Section 2A–532.

Cross References:

Sections 1–106(2) [*unrevised Article 1; see Concordance, p. 22*], 2–702(1), 2–702(2), 2A–103(4), 2A–501(3), 2A–532 and 9–609.

Definitional Cross References:

"Action". Section 1–201(1) [*unrevised Article 1; see Concordance, p. 22*].
"Delivery". Section 1–201(14) [*unrevised Article 1; see Concordance, p. 22*].
"Discover". Section 1–201(25) [*unrevised Article 1; see Concordance, p. 22*].
"Goods". Section 2A–103(1)(h).
"Insolvent". Section 1–201(23) [*unrevised Article 1; see Concordance, p. 22*].
"Lease contract". Section 2A–103(1)(*l*).
"Lessee". Section 2A–103(1)(n).
"Lessor". Section 2A–103(1)(p).
"Party". Section 1–201(29) [*unrevised Article 1; see Concordance, p. 22*].
"Rights". Section 1–201(36) [*unrevised Article 1; see Concordance, p. 22*].

§ 2A–526.   Lessor's Stoppage of Delivery in Transit or Otherwise.

(1)   A lessor may stop delivery of goods in the possession of a carrier or other bailee if the lessor discovers the lessee to be insolvent and may stop delivery of carload, truckload, planeload, or larger shipments of express or freight if the lessee repudiates or fails to make a payment due before delivery, whether for rent, security or otherwise under the lease contract, or for any other reason the lessor has a right to withhold or take possession of the goods.

(2)   In pursuing its remedies under subsection (1), the lessor may stop delivery until

(a)   receipt of the goods by the lessee;

(b)   acknowledgment to the lessee by any bailee of the goods, except a carrier, that the bailee holds the goods for the lessee; or

(c)   such an acknowledgment to the lessee by a carrier via reshipment or as a warehouse.

(3)(a)   To stop delivery, a lessor shall so notify as to enable the bailee by reasonable diligence to prevent delivery of the goods.

(b)   After notification, the bailee shall hold and deliver the goods according to the directions of the lessor, but the lessor is liable to the bailee for any ensuing charges or damages.

(c)   A carrier who has issued a nonnegotiable bill of lading is not obliged to obey a notification to stop received from a person other than the consignor.

As amended in 2003.

Official Comment

Uniform Statutory Source: Section 2–705.

Changes: Revised to reflect leasing practices and terminology.

Definitional Cross References:

"Bill of lading". Section 1–201(6) [*unrevised Article 1; see Concordance, p. 22*].
"Delivery". Section 1–201(14) [*unrevised Article 1; see Concordance, p. 22*].
"Discover". Section 1–201(25) [*unrevised Article 1; see Concordance, p. 22*].
"Goods". Section 2A–103(1)(h).
"Insolvent". Section 1–201(23) [*unrevised Article 1; see Concordance, p. 22*].
"Lease contract". Section 2A–103(1)(*l*).
"Lessee". Section 2A–103(1)(n).
"Lessor". Section 2A–103(1)(p).
"Notifies" and "Notification". Section 1–201(26) [*unrevised Article 1; see Concordance, p. 22*].
"Person". Section 1–201(30) [*unrevised Article 1; see Concordance, p. 22*].
"Receipt". Section 2–103(1)(c).
"Remedy". Section 1–201(34) [*unrevised Article 1; see Concordance, p. 22*].
"Rights". Section 1–201(36) [*unrevised Article 1; see Concordance, p. 22*].

§ 2A–527.   Lessor's Rights to Dispose of Goods.

(1)   After a default by a lessee under the lease contract of the type described in Section 2A–523(1) or 2A–523(3)(a) or after the lessor refuses to deliver or takes possession of goods (Section 2A–525 or 2A–526), or, if agreed, after other default by a lessee, the lessor may dispose of the goods concerned or the undelivered balance thereof by lease, sale, or otherwise.

(2)   Except as otherwise provided with respect to damages liquidated in the lease agreement (Section 2A–504) or otherwise determined pursuant to agreement of the parties (Sections 1–302 and 2A–503), if the disposition is by lease agreement substantially similar to the original lease agreement and the new lease agreement is made in good faith and in a commercially reasonable manner, the lessor may recover from the lessee as damages (i) accrued and unpaid rent as of the date of the commencement of the term of the new lease agreement, (ii) the present value, as of the same date, of the total rent for the then remaining lease term of the original lease agreement minus the present value, as of the same date, of the rent under the new lease agreement applicable to that period of the new lease term which is comparable to the then remaining term of the original lease agreement, and (iii) any incidental damages allowed under Section 2A–530, less expenses saved in consequence of the lessee's default.

(3)   If the lessor's disposition is by lease agreement that for any reason does not qualify for treatment under subsection (2), or is by sale or otherwise, the lessor may recover from the lessee as if the lessor had elected not to dispose of the goods and Section 2A–528 governs.

(4)   A subsequent buyer or lessee who buys or leases from the lessor in good faith for value as a result of a disposition under this section takes the goods free of the original lease contract and any rights of the original lessee even though the lessor fails to comply with one or more of the requirements of this Article.

(5)   The lessor is not accountable to the lessee for any profit made on any disposition. A lessee who has rightfully rejected or justifiably revoked acceptance shall account to the lessor for any excess over the amount of the lessee's security interest (Section 2A–508(5)).

As amended in 1990 and 2001.

Official Comment

Uniform Statutory Source: Section 2–706(1), (5) and (6).

Changes: Substantially revised.

Purposes:

1.   Subsection (1), a revised version of the first sentence of subsection 2–706(1), allows the lessor the right to dispose of goods after a statutory or other material default by the lessee (even if the goods remain in the lessee's possession—Section 2A–525(2)), after the lessor refuses to deliver or takes possession of the goods, or, if agreed, after other contractual default. The lessor's decision to exercise this right is a function of a commercial judgment, not a statutory mandate replete with sanctions for failure to comply. Cf. Section 9–625. As the owner of the goods, in the case of a lessor, or as the prime lessee of the goods, in the case of a sublessor, compulsory disposition of the goods is inconsistent with the nature of the interest held by the lessor or the sublessor and is not necessary because the interest held by the lessee or the sublessee is not protected by a right of redemption under the common law or this Article. Subsection 2A–527(5).

2.   The rule for determining the measure of damages recoverable by the lessor against the lessee is a function of several variables. If the lessor has elected to effect disposition under subsection (1) and such disposition is by lease that qualifies under subsection (2), the measure of damages set forth in subsection (2) will apply, absent agreement to the contrary. Sections 2A–504, 2A–103(4) and 1–302.

3.   The lessor's damages will be established using the new lease agreement as a measure if the following three criteria are satisfied: (i) the lessor disposed of the goods by lease, (ii) the lease agreement is substantially similar to the original lease agreement, and (iii) such disposition was in good faith, and in a commercially reasonable manner. Thus, the lessor will be entitled to recover from the lessee the accrued and unpaid rent as of the date of commencement of the term of the new lease, and the present value, as of the same date, of the rent, under the original lease for the then remaining term less the present value as of the same date of the rent under the new lease agreement applicable to the period of the new lease comparable to the remaining term under the original lease, together with incidental damages less expenses saved in consequence of the lessee's default. If the lessor's disposition does not satisfy the criteria of subsection (2), the lessor may calculate its claim against the lessee pursuant to Section 2A–528. Section 2A–523(1)(e).

4.   Two of the three criteria to be met by the lessor are familiar, but the concept of the new lease agreement that is substantially similar to the original lease agreement is not. Given the many variables facing a party who intends to lease goods and the rapidity of change in the market place, the policy decision was made not to draft with specificity. It was thought unwise to seek to establish certainty at the cost of fairness. The decision of whether the new lease agreement is substantially similar to the original will be determined case by case.

5.   While the section does not draw a bright line, it is possible to describe some of the factors that should be considered in a finding that a new lease agreement is substantially similar to the original. The various elements of the new lease agreement should be examined. Those elements include the options to purchase or release; the lessor's representations, warranties and covenants to the lessee as well as those to be provided by the lessee to the lessor; and the services, if any, to be provided by the lessor or by the lessee. All of these factors allocate cost and risk between the lessor and the lessee and thus affect the amount of rent to be paid. These findings should not be made with scientific precision, as they are a function of economics, nor should they be made independently, as it is important that a sense of commercial judgment pervade the finding. See Section 2A–507(2). To establish the new lease as a proper measure of damage under subsection (2), these various factors, taken as a whole, must result in a finding that the new lease agreement is substantially similar to the original. If the differences between the original lease and the new lease can be easily valued, it would be appropriate for a court to find that the new lease is substantially similar to the old lease, adjust the difference in the rent between the two leases to take account of the differences, and award damages under this section. If, for example, the new lease requires the lessor to insure the goods in the hands of the lessee, while the original lease required the lessee to insure, the usual cost of such insurance could be deducted from rent due under the new lease before the difference in rental between the two leases is determined.

6.   The following hypothetical illustrates the difficulty of providing a bright line. Assume that A buys a jumbo tractor for $1 million and then leases the tractor to B for a term of 36 months. The tractor is delivered to and is accepted by B on May 1. On June 1 B fails to pay the monthly rent to A. B returns the tractor to A, who immediately releases the tractor to C for a term identical to the term remaining under the lease between A and B. All terms and conditions under the lease between A and C are identical to those under the original lease between A and B, except that C does not provide any property damage or other insurance coverage, and B agreed to provide

complete coverage. Coverage is expensive and difficult to obtain. It is a question of fact whether it is so difficult to adjust the recovery to take account of the difference between the two leases as to insurance that the second lease is not substantially similar to the original.

7.   A new lease can be substantially similar to the original lease even though its term extends beyond the remaining term of the original lease, so long as both (a) the lease terms are commercially comparable (e.g., it is highly unlikely that a one-month rental and a five-year lease would reflect similar realities), and (b) the court can fairly apportion a part of the rental payments under the new lease to that part of the term of the new lease which is comparable to the remaining lease term under the original lease. Also, the lease term of the new lease may be comparable to the remaining term of the original lease even though the beginning and ending dates of the two leases are not the same. For example, a two-month lease of agricultural equipment for the months of August and September may be comparable to a two-month lease running from the 15th of August to the 15th of October if in the particular location two-month leases beginning on August 15th are basically interchangeable with two-month leases beginning August 1st. Similarly, the term of a one-year truck lease beginning on the 15th of January may be comparable to the term of a one-year truck lease beginning January 2d. If the lease terms are found to be comparable, the court may base cover damages on the entire difference between the costs under the two leases.

8.   Subsection (3), which is new, provides that if the lessor's disposition is by lease that does not qualify under subsection (2), or is by sale or otherwise, Section 2A–528 governs.

9.   Subsection (4), a revised version of subsection 2–706(5), applies to protect a subsequent buyer or lessee who buys or leases from the lessor in good faith and for value, pursuant to a disposition under this section. Note that by its terms, the rule in subsection 2A–304(1), which provides that the subsequent lessee takes subject to the original lease contract, is controlled by the rule stated in this subsection.

10.   Subsection (5), a revised version of subsection 2–706(6), provides that the lessor is not accountable to the lessee for any profit made by the lessor on a disposition. This rule follows from the fundamental premise of the bailment for hire that the lessee under a lease of goods has no equity of redemption to protect.

Cross References:

Sections 1–302, 2–706(1), 2–706(5), 2–706(6), 2A–103(4), 2A–304(1), 2A–504, 2A–507(2), 2A–523(1)(e), 2A–525(2), 2A–527(5), 2A–528 and 9–625.

Definitional Cross References:

"Buyer" and "Buying". Section 2–103(1)(a).
"Delivery". Section 1–201(b)(15).
"Good faith". Section 1–201(b)(20).
"Goods". Section 2A–103(1)(h).
"Lease". Section 2A–103(1)(j).
"Lease contract". Section 2A–103(1)(*l*).
"Lessee". Section 2A–103(1)(n).
"Lessor". Section 2A–103(1)(p).
"Present value". Section 2A–103(1)(u). [*Note from West Advisory Panel: Revised Article 1 (2001) defines "present value" in § 1–201(b)(28) for jurisdictions that adopt that version of Article 1. The conforming amendments to Article 2A delete the comment to the Article 2A definition of "present value" but erroneously do not delete the definition itself.*]
"Right". Section 1–201(b)(34).
"Sale". Section 2–106(1).
"Security interest". Sections 1–201(b)(35) and 1–203.
"Value". Section 1–204.

As amended in 2001.

§ 2A–528. Lessor's Damages for Non-acceptance, Failure to Pay, Repudiation, or Other Default.

(1)   Except as otherwise provided with respect to damages liquidated in the lease agreement (Section 2A–504) or otherwise determined pursuant to agreement of the parties (Sections 1–302 and 2A–503), if a lessor elects to retain the goods or a lessor elects to dispose of the goods and the disposition is by lease agreement that for any reason does not qualify for treatment under Section 2A–527(2), or is by sale or

otherwise, the lessor may recover from the lessee as damages for a default of the type described in Section 2A–523(1) or 2A–523(3)(a), or, if agreed, for other default of the lessee, (i) accrued and unpaid rent as of the date of default if the lessee has never taken possession of the goods, or, if the lessee has taken possession of the goods, as of the date the lessor repossesses the goods or an earlier date on which the lessee makes a tender of the goods to the lessor, (ii) the present value as of the date determined under clause (i) of the total rent for the then remaining lease term of the original lease agreement minus the present value as of the same date of the market rent at the place where the goods are located computed for the same lease term, and (iii) any incidental damages allowed under Section 2A–530, less expenses saved in consequence of the lessee's default.

(2)   If the measure of damages provided in subsection (1) is inadequate to put a lessor in as good a position as performance would have, the measure of damages is the present value of the profit, including reasonable overhead, the lessor would have made from full performance by the lessee, together with any incidental damages allowed under Section 2A–530, due allowance for costs reasonably incurred and due credit for payments or proceeds of disposition.

As amended in 1990 and 2001.

Official Comment

Uniform Statutory Source: Section 2–708.

Changes: Substantially revised.

Purposes:

1.   Subsection (1), a substantially revised version of Section 2–708(1), states the basic rule governing the measure of lessor's damages for a default described in Section 2A–523(1) or (3)(a), and, if agreed, for a contractual default. This measure will apply if the lessor elects to retain the goods (whether undelivered, returned by the lessee, or repossessed by the lessor after acceptance and default by the lessee) or if the lessor's disposition does not qualify under subsection 2A–527(2). Section 2A–527(3). Note that under some of these conditions, the lessor may recover damages from the lessee pursuant to the rule set forth in Section 2A–529. There is no sanction for disposition that does not qualify under subsection 2A–527(2). Application of the rule set forth in this section is subject to agreement to the contrary. Sections 2A–504, 2A–103(4) and 1–302.

2.   If the lessee has never taken possession of the goods, the measure of damage is the accrued and unpaid rent as of the date of default together with the present value, as of the date of default, of the original rent for the remaining term of the lease less the present value as of the same date of market rent, and incidental damages, less expenses saved in consequence of the default. Note that the reference in Section 2A–528(1)(i) and (ii) is to the date of default not to the date of an event of default. An event of default under a lease agreement becomes a default under a lease agreement only after the expiration of any relevant period of grace and compliance with any notice requirements under this Article and the lease agreement. American Bar Foundation, *Commentaries on Indentures,* § 5–1, at 216–217 (1971). Section 2A–501(1). This conclusion is also a function of whether, as a matter of fact or law, the event of default has been waived, suspended or cured. Sections 2A–103(4) and 1–103. If the lessee has taken possession of the goods, the measure of damages is the accrued and unpaid rent as of the earlier of the time the lessor repossesses the goods or the time the lessee tenders the goods to the lessor plus the difference between the present value, as of the same time, of the rent under the lease for the remaining lease term and the present value, as of the same time, of the market rent.

3.   Market rent will be computed pursuant to Section 2A–507.

4.   Subsection (2), a somewhat revised version of the provisions of subsection 2–708(2), states a measure of damages which applies if the measure of damages in subsection (1) is inadequate to put the lessor in as good a position as performance would have. The measure of damage is the lessor's profit, including overhead, together with incidental damages, with allowance for costs reasonably incurred and credit for payments or proceeds of disposition. In determining the amount of due credit with respect to proceeds of disposition a proper value should be attributed to the lessor's residual interest in the goods. Sections 2A–103(1)(q) and 2A–507(4).

5.   In calculating profit, a court should include any expected appreciation of the goods, *e.g.* the foal of a leased brood mare. Because this subsection is intended to give the lessor the benefit of the bargain, a court should consider any reasonable benefit or profit expected by the lessor from the performance of the lease agreement. *See Honeywell, Inc. v. Lithonia Lighting, Inc.,* 317 F.Supp. 406, 413 (N.D.Ga. 1970); *Locks v. Wade,* 36 N.J.Super. 128, 131, 114 A.2d 875, 877 (Super.Ct.App.Div. 1955). Further, in calculating profit the concept of present value must

be given effect. *Taylor v. Commercial Credit Equip. Corp.*, 170 Ga.App. 322, 316 S.E.2d 788 (Ct.App. 1984). *See generally* Section 2A–103(1)(u).

Cross References:

Sections 1–302, 2–708, 2A–103(1)(u), 2A–402, 2A–504, 2A–507, 2A–527(2) and 2A–529.

Definitional Cross References:

"Agreement". Section 1–201(b)(3).
"Goods". Section 2A–103(1)(h).
"Lease". Section 2A–103(1)(j).
"Lease agreement". Section 2A–103(1)(k).
"Lessee". Section 2A–103(1)(n).
"Lessor". Section 2A–103(1)(p).
"Party". Section 1–201(b)(26).
"Present value". Section 2A–103(1)(u). [*Note from West Advisory Panel: Revised Article 1 (2001) defines "present value" in § 1–201(b)(28) for jurisdictions that adopt that version of Article 1. The conforming amendments to Article 2A delete the comment to the Article 2A definition of "present value" but erroneously do not delete the definition itself.*]
"Sale". Section 2–106(1).

As amended in 2001.

§ 2A–529. Lessor's Action for the Rent.

(1)   After default by the lessee under the lease contract of the type described in Section 2A–523(1) or 2A–523(3)(a) or, if agreed, after other default by the lessee, if the lessor complies with subsection (2), the lessor may recover from the lessee as damages:

(a)   for goods accepted by the lessee and not repossessed by or tendered to the lessor, and for conforming goods lost or damaged within a commercially reasonable time after risk of loss passes to the lessee (Section 2A–219), (i) accrued and unpaid rent as of the date of entry of judgment in favor of the lessor, (ii) the present value as of the same date of the rent for the then remaining lease term of the lease agreement, and (iii) any incidental damages allowed under Section 2A–530, less expenses saved in consequence of the lessee's default; and

(b)   for goods identified to the lease contract if the lessor is unable after reasonable effort to dispose of them at a reasonable price or the circumstances reasonably indicate that effort will be unavailing, (i) accrued and unpaid rent as of the date of entry of judgment in favor of the lessor, (ii) the present value as of the same date of the rent for the then remaining lease term of the lease agreement, and (iii) any incidental damages allowed under Section 2A–530, less expenses saved in consequence of the lessee's default.

(2)   Except as provided in subsection (3), the lessor shall hold for the lessee for the remaining lease term of the lease agreement any goods that have been identified to the lease contract and are in the lessor's control.

(3)   The lessor may dispose of the goods at any time before collection of the judgment for damages obtained pursuant to subsection (1). If the disposition is before the end of the remaining lease term of the lease agreement, the lessor's recovery against the lessee for damages is governed by Section 2A–527 or Section 2A–528, and the lessor will cause an appropriate credit to be provided against a judgment for damages to the extent that the amount of the judgment exceeds the recovery available pursuant to Section 2A–527 or 2A–528.

(4)   Payment of the judgment for damages obtained pursuant to subsection (1) entitles the lessee to the use and possession of the goods not then disposed of for the remaining lease term of and in accordance with the lease agreement.

(5)   After default by the lessee under the lease contract of the type described in Section 2A–523(1) or Section 2A–523(3)(a) or, if agreed, after other default by the lessee, a lessor who is held not entitled to rent

under this section must nevertheless be awarded damages for non-acceptance under Section 2A–527 or Section 2A–528.

As amended in 1990.

Official Comment

Uniform Statutory Source: Section 2–709.

Changes: Substantially revised.

Purposes:

1.   Absent a lease contract provision to the contrary, an action for the full unpaid rent (discounted to present value as of the time of entry of judgment as to rent due after that time) is available as to goods not lost or damaged only if the lessee retains possession of the goods or the lessor is or apparently will be unable to dispose of them at a reasonable price after reasonable effort. There is no general right in a lessor to recover the full rent from the lessee upon holding the goods for the lessee. If the lessee tenders goods back to the lessor, and the lessor refuses to accept the tender, the lessor will be limited to the damages it would have suffered had it taken back the goods. The rule in Article 2 that the seller can recover the price of accepted goods is rejected here. In a lease, the lessor always has a residual interest in the goods which the lessor usually realizes upon at the end of a lease term by either sale or a new lease. Therefore, it is not a substantial imposition on the lessor to require it to take back and dispose of the goods if the lessee chooses to tender them back before the end of the lease term: the lessor will merely do earlier what it would have done anyway, sell or relet the goods. Further, the lessee will frequently encounter substantial difficulties if the lessee attempts to sublet the goods for the remainder of the lease term. In contrast to the buyer who owns the entire interest in goods and can easily dispose of them, the lessee is selling only the right to use the goods under the terms of the lease and the sublessee must assume a relationship with the lessor. In that situation, it is usually more efficient to eliminate the original lessee as a middleman by allowing the lessee to return the goods to the lessor who can then redispose of them.

2.   In some situations even where possession of the goods is reacquired, a lessor will be able to recover as damages the present value of the full rent due, not under this section, but under 2A–528(2) which allows a lost profit recovery if necessary to put the lessor in the position it would have been in had the lessee performed. Following is an example of such a case. A is a lessor of construction equipment and maintains a substantial inventory. B leases from A a backhoe for a period of two weeks at a rental of $1,000. After three days, B returns the backhoe and refuses to pay the rent. A has five backhoes in inventory, including the one returned by B. During the next 11 days after the return by B of the backhoe, A rents no more than three backhoes at any one time and, therefore, always has two on hand. If B had kept the backhoe for the full rental period, A would have earned the full rental on that backhoe, plus the rental on the other backhoes it actually did rent during that period. Getting this backhoe back before the end of the lease term did not enable A to make any leases it would not otherwise have made. The only way to put A in the position it would have been in had the lessee fully performed is to give the lessor the full rentals. A realized no savings at all because the backhoe was returned early and might even have incurred additional expense if it was paying for parking space for equipment in inventory. A has no obligation to relet the backhoe for the benefit of B rather than leasing that backhoe or any other in inventory for its own benefit. Further, it is probably not reasonable to expect A to dispose of the backhoe by sale when it is returned in an effort to reduce damages suffered by B. Ordinarily, the loss of a two-week rental would not require A to reduce the size of its backhoe inventory. Whether A would similarly be entitled to full rentals as lost profit in a one-year lease of a backhoe is a question of fact: in any event the lessor, subject to mitigation of damages rules, is entitled to be put in as good a position as it would have been had the lessee fully performed the lease contract.

3.   Under subsection (2) a lessor who is able and elects to sue for the rent due under a lease must hold goods not lost or damaged for the lessee. Subsection (3) creates an exception to the subsection (2) requirement. If the lessor disposes of those goods prior to collection of the judgment (whether as a matter of law or agreement), the lessor's recovery is governed by the measure of damages in Section 2A–527 if the disposition is by lease that is substantially similar to the original lease, or otherwise by the measure of damages in Section 2A–528. Section 2A–523 official comment.

4.   Subsection (4), which is new, further reinforces the requisites of Subsection (2). In the event the judgment for damages obtained by the lessor against the lessee pursuant to subsection (1) is satisfied, the lessee regains the right to use and possession of the remaining goods for the balance of the original lease term; a partial satisfaction of the judgment creates no right in the lessee to use and possession of the goods.

5.   The relationship between subsections (2) and (4) is important to understand. Subsection (2) requires the lessor to hold for the lessee identified goods in the lessor's possession. Absent agreement to the contrary,

whether in the lease or otherwise, under most circumstances the requirement that the lessor hold the goods for the lessee for the term will mean that the lessor is not allowed to use them. Sections 2A–103(4) and 1–203. Further, the lessor's use of the goods could be viewed as a disposition of the goods that would bar the lessor from recovery under this section, remitting the lessor to the two preceding sections for a determination of the lessor's claim for damages against the lessee.

6. Subsection (5), the analogue of subsection 2–709(3), further reinforces the thrust of subsection (3) by stating that a lessor who is held not entitled to rent under this section has not elected a remedy; the lessor must be awarded damages under Sections 2A–527 and 2A–528. This is a function of two significant policies of this Article—that resort to a remedy is optional, unless expressly agreed to be exclusive (Section 2A–503(2)) and that rights and remedies provided in this Article generally are cumulative. (Section 2A–501(2) and (4)).

Cross References:

Sections 1–203, 2–709, 2–709(3), 2A–103(4), 2A–501(2), 2A–501(4), 2A–503(2), 2A–504, 2A–523(1)(e), 2A–525(2), 2A–527, 2A–528 and 2A–529(2).

Definitional Cross References:

"Action". Section 1–201(1) [*unrevised Article 1; see Concordance, p. 22*].
"Conforming". Section 2A–103(1)(d).
"Goods". Section 2A–103(1)(h).
"Lease". Section 2A–103(1)(j).
"Lease agreement". Section 2A–103(1)(k).
"Lease contract". Section 2A–103(1)(*l*).
"Lessee". Section 2A–103(1)(n).
"Lessor". Section 2A–103(1)(p).
"Present value". Section 2A–103(1)(u). [*Note from West Advisory Panel: Revised Article 1 (2001) defines "present value" in § 1–201(b)(28) for jurisdictions that adopt that version of Article 1. The conforming amendments to Article 2A delete the comment to the Article 2A definition of "present value" but erroneously do not delete the definition itself.*]
"Reasonable time". Section 1–204(1) and (2) [*unrevised Article 1; see Concordance, p. 22*].

§ 2A–530. Lessor's Incidental Damages.

Incidental damages to an aggrieved lessor include any commercially reasonable charges, expenses, or commissions incurred in stopping delivery, in the transportation, care and custody of goods after the lessee's default, in connection with return or disposition of the goods, or otherwise resulting from the default.

Official Comment

Uniform Statutory Source: Section 2–710.

Changes: Revised to reflect leasing practices and terminology.

Definitional Cross References:

"Aggrieved party". Section 1–201(2) [*unrevised Article 1; see Concordance, p. 22*].
"Delivery". Section 1–201(14) [*unrevised Article 1; see Concordance, p. 22*].
"Goods". Section 2A–103(1)(h).
"Lessee". Section 2A–103(1)(n).
"Lessor". Section 2A–103(1)(p).

§ 2A–531. Standing to Sue Third Parties for Injury to Goods.

(1) If a third party so deals with goods that have been identified to a lease contract as to cause actionable injury to a party to the lease contract (a) the lessor has a right of action against the third party, and (b) the lessee also has a right of action against the third party if the lessee:

(i) has a security interest in the goods;

(ii) has an insurable interest in the goods; or

    (iii) bears the risk of loss under the lease contract or has since the injury assumed that risk as against the lessor and the goods have been converted or destroyed.

    (2)   If at the time of the injury the party plaintiff did not bear the risk of loss as against the other party to the lease contract and there is no arrangement between them for disposition of the recovery, his [or her] suit or settlement, subject to his [or her] own interest, is as a fiduciary for the other party to the lease contract.

    (3)   Either party with the consent of the other may sue for the benefit of whom it may concern.

Official Comment

Uniform Statutory Source: Section 2–722.

Changes: Revised to reflect leasing practices and terminology.

Definitional Cross References:

    "Action". Section 1–201(1) [*unrevised Article 1; see Concordance, p. 22*].
    "Goods". Section 2A–103(1)(h).
    "Lease contract". Section 2A–103(1)(*l*).
    "Lessee". Section 2A–103(1)(n).
    "Lessor". Section 2A–103(1)(p).
    "Party". Section 1–201(29) [*unrevised Article 1; see Concordance, p. 22*].
    "Rights". Section 1–201(36) [*unrevised Article 1; see Concordance, p. 22*].
    "Security interest". Section 1–201(37) [*unrevised Article 1; see Concordance, p. 22*].

§ 2A–532. Lessor's Rights to Residual Interest.

    In addition to any other recovery permitted by this Article or other law, the lessor may recover from the lessee an amount that will fully compensate the lessor for any loss of or damage to the lessor's residual interest in the goods caused by the default of the lessee.

As added in 1990.

Official Comment

Uniform Statutory Source: None.

Purposes: This section recognizes the right of the lessor to recover under this Article (as well as under other law) from the lessee for failure to comply with the lease obligations as to the condition of leased goods when returned to the lessor, for failure to return the goods at the end of the lease, or for any other default which causes loss or injury to the lessor's residual interest in the goods.

UCC ARTICLE 3

NEGOTIABLE INSTRUMENTS

Article 3 was revised in 1990 and amended in 2002 and 2022.

2022 Amendments appear in ~~strikeout~~/<u>underline</u> format.

Prefatory Note to 2022 amendments appears in Appendix E.

Current through April 2023

For updates, see www.uniformlaws.org

PART 1.   GENERAL PROVISIONS AND DEFINITIONS

3–101.   Short Title.
3–102.   Subject Matter.
3–103.   Definitions.
3–104.   Negotiable Instrument.
3–105.   Issue of Instrument.
3–106.   Unconditional Promise or Order.
3–107.   Instrument Payable in Foreign Money.
3–108.   Payable on Demand or at Definite Time.
3–109.   Payable to Bearer or to Order.
3–110.   Identification of Person to Whom Instrument Is Payable.
3–111.   Place of Payment.
3–112.   Interest.
3–113.   Date of Instrument.
3–114.   Contradictory Terms of Instrument.
3–115.   Incomplete Instrument.
3–116.   Joint and Several Liability; Contribution.
3–117.   Other Agreements Affecting Instrument.
3–118.   Statute of Limitations.
3–119.   Notice of Right to Defend Action.

PART 2.   NEGOTIATION, TRANSFER, AND INDORSEMENT

3–201.   Negotiation.
3–202.   Negotiation Subject to Rescission.
3–203.   Transfer of Instrument; Rights Acquired by Transfer.
3–204.   Indorsement.
3–205.   Special Indorsement; Blank Indorsement; Anomalous Indorsement.
3–206.   Restrictive Indorsement.
3–207.   Reacquisition.

PART 3.   ENFORCEMENT OF INSTRUMENTS

3–301.   Person Entitled to Enforce Instrument.
3–302.   Holder in Due Course.

3–303.   Value and Consideration.

3–304.   Overdue Instrument.

3–305.   Defenses and Claims in Recoupment.

3–306.   Claims to an Instrument.

3–307.   Notice of Breach of Fiduciary Duty.

3–308.   Proof of Signatures and Status as Holder in Due Course.

3–309.   Enforcement of Lost, Destroyed, or Stolen Instrument.

3–310.   Effect of Instrument on Obligation for Which Taken.

3–311.   Accord and Satisfaction by Use of Instrument.

3–312.   Lost, Destroyed, or Stolen Cashier's Check, Teller's Check, or Certified Check.

PART 4.   LIABILITY OF PARTIES

3–401.   Signature Necessary for Liability on Instrument.

3–402.   Signature by Representative.

3–403.   Unauthorized Signature.

3–404.   Impostors; Fictitious Payees.

3–405.   Employer's Responsibility for Fraudulent Indorsement by Employee.

3–406.   Negligence Contributing to Forged Signature or Alteration of Instrument.

3–407.   Alteration.

3–408.   Drawee Not Liable on Unaccepted Draft.

3–409.   Acceptance of Draft; Certified Check.

3–410.   Acceptance Varying Draft.

3–411.   Refusal to Pay Cashier's Checks, Teller's Checks, and Certified Checks.

3–412.   Obligation of Issuer of Note or Cashier's Check.

3–413.   Obligation of Acceptor.

3–414.   Obligation of Drawer.

3–415.   Obligation of Indorser.

3–416.   Transfer Warranties.

3–417.   Presentment Warranties.

3–418.   Payment or Acceptance by Mistake.

3–419.   Instruments Signed for Accommodation.

3–420.   Conversion of Instrument.

PART 5.   DISHONOR

3–501.   Presentment.

3–502.   Dishonor.

3–503.   Notice of Dishonor.

3–504.   Excused Presentment and Notice of Dishonor.

3–505.   Evidence of Dishonor.

PART 6.   DISCHARGE AND PAYMENT

3–601.   Discharge and Effect of Discharge.

3–602.   Payment.

3–603.   Tender of Payment.

3–604.   Discharge by Cancellation or Renunciation.

3–605.   Discharge of Secondary Obligors.

ARTICLE 3

PREFATORY NOTE

Revised Article 3 (with miscellaneous and conforming amendments to Articles 1 and 4) is a companion undertaking to Article 4A on funds transfers. Both efforts were undertaken for the purpose of accommodating modern technologies and practices in payment systems and with respect to negotiable instruments. Both efforts were drafted by the same committee over essentially the same period of time. The work on Article 4A was accorded priority and completed in 1989, and revised Article 3 was completed in 1990.

Revised Article 3 may, not inappropriately, be regarded as the latest effort in the progressive codification of the common law of negotiable instruments that began with the English Bills of Exchange Act enacted by Parliament in 1882. The Uniform Negotiable Instruments Law was promulgated by the Conference in 1896, and it in turn was reorganized and modernized by original Article 3—Commercial Paper as part of the Uniform Commercial Code jointly promulgated in 1952 by the Conference and the American Law Institute. Revised Article 3 in 1990 modernizes, reorganizes and clarifies the law.

Purpose of Drafting Effort

The original Articles 3 and 4 and their predecessors were based upon a paper payment system. Literally, there has been an explosion in the volume of paper to process since Articles 3 and 4 were first promulgated. In the early '50s, around 7 billion checks were processed annually. Correctly anticipating an increase in check volume as the result of a retail approach taken by bankers at that time, the American Bankers Association in 1954 placed a team on a research and development project to identify the most efficient method of processing checks mechanically. The eminently successful MICR line technology was the result. Upon its implementation, checks were processed at high rates of speed. In major part as a result of this technology, a seven-fold explosion in check volume has occurred between the '50s and 1988. In 1988, the Federal Reserve estimated check volume at 48 billion written annually. In 1987, Congress enacted the Expedited Funds Availability Act, and the Federal Reserve Board implemented it in 1988 with Regulation CC. Regulation CC covers many aspects of the forward check collection process and all aspects of the return process.

Present Articles 3 and 4, written for a paper-based system, do not adequately address the issues of responsibility and liability as they relate to modern technologies now employed and the procedures required by the current volume of checks and by the "Expedited Funds Availability Act" and Regulation CC. While agreements among parties to particular transactions have provided some relief, such stop-gap measures are no longer adequate.

In addition, practices have developed which are not easily accommodated within existing Article 3. For example, variable rate notes were unknown when Article 3 first was promulgated; they are common today. Questions about the "cash equivalency" of cashier's checks and money orders have arisen as banks have sought to raise defenses to the payment of these instruments.

The revision of Article 3 and Article 4 to update, improve and maintain the viability of it is necessary to accommodate these changing practices and modern technologies, the needs of a rapidly expanding national and international economy, the requirement for more rapid funds availability, and the need for more clarity and certainty. Absent such an update, further Federal preemption of state law may likely occur.

Uniformity is Essential

Traditionally, the legal structures for payments have been regulated by state law through the Uniform Commercial Code. In recent years, however, the Federal government has established regulations for credit and debit cards, and for the availability of funds in a way that regulates much of the check collection process.

With respect to wholesale funds transfers, on an average day two trillion dollars is transferred. Article 4A of the UCC promulgated in 1989 provides the governing comprehensive rules. In 1990, 12 states enacted Article 4A including California, New York and Illinois. In 1991, Article 4A has been introduced in the legislatures of most of the other states, and it is anticipated that most, if not all, will enact Article 4A uniformly. Within a short time, perhaps by 1992, the law of wholesale funds transfers should be uniform throughout the 50 states.

UNIFORM COMMERCIAL CODE

The law for payments through checks and which governs other negotiable instruments similarly should be uniform and up-to-date, either through state enactments or Federal preemption. Otherwise, checks as a viable payment system in international and national transactions will be severely hampered and the utility of other negotiable instruments impaired.

Process of Achieving Uniformity

The essence of uniform law revision is to obtain a sufficient consensus and balance among the interests of the various participants so that universal and uniform adoption by the legislatures of all 50 states may be achieved. As is the practice of the Conference, announcement of the drafting undertaking for Articles 3, 4 and 4A was widely circulated in 1985. Anyone who so requested, received notice of all meetings and was invited to attend. Upon request, names were put on a mailing list to receive copies of drafts as they progressed. In addition, the American Bar Association Ad Hoc Committee on Payments Systems closely followed the work of the Conference and widely circulated the drafts.

The Drafting Committee had 3 or 4 meetings each year and, by August 1990, had held 20 meetings. The drafting meetings began on Friday morning and ended on Sunday at noon. All the meetings were well attended, and the average attendance was 50 or more. The discussion of the drafts was open for comment by all those who attended. In addition, the reporters received a substantial amount of comment and suggestions by written and other communications between meetings of the drafting committee. The work product was read line for line at the annual meetings of the Conference three different years. In addition, the American Law Institute circulated the drafts two or three times to its entire membership. The ALI consultative group also held a meeting to comment and make suggestions on the draft. In addition, progress reports were published annually in *The Business Lawyer* from 1985 through 1990.

The consensus, balance and quality achieved in this lengthy deliberative process is a product not only of the fine work of the reporters and the drafting committee, but also the faithful and energetic participation of the advisors and participants in the drafting meetings. The advisors representing a variety of interests were [*Note from West Advisory Panel: We have deleted this list.*]

Balance Achieved

The consensus reflected in Revised Article 3 and in the conforming amendments to Articles 1 and 4 is supported by the participants from the banking community, the users, and the Federal regulators because it reflects a balance that each interest can reasonably embrace. Some of the benefits of the Revision include:

A. Benefits in the Public Interest

Certainty—Revised Articles 3 and 4 remove numerous uncertainties that exist in the current provisions and thus reduce risk to the payment system and allow appropriate planning by its users and operators.

Speed and Reliability—The Revision removes impediments to the use of automation, and better conforms to Regulation CC to expedite the availability of funds to customers and to reduce risks to banks.

Lower Costs—The Revision by providing for modern technologies, lowers costs to banks and thus to their customers.

Reduced Litigation—By clarification of troublesome issues, and by the provisions of Sections 3–404 through 3–406 which reform rules for allocation of loss from forgeries and alterations, the Revision should significantly reduce litigation.

B. Benefits to Users

"Good Faith"—The definition of good faith under Sections 3–103(a)(4) and 4–104(c) is expanded to include observance of reasonable commercial standards of fair dealing. This objective standard for good faith applies to the performance of all duties and obligations established under Articles 3 and 4.

Fiduciary Provisions—Section 3–307 protects drawers and persons owed a fiduciary responsibility by imposing stricter standards for obtaining holder in due course rights by a person dealing with the defaulting agent or fiduciary. It also spells out the circumstances under which a person receiving funds has notice of a breach of fiduciary duty, and resulting liability.

ARTICLE 3

Accord and Satisfaction—Under Section 3–311 payees can avoid the unintentional accord and satisfaction by returning the funds or by giving a notice that requires checks to be sent to a particular office where such proposals can be handled. On the other hand, the drawer of a full settlement check is protected from the instrument being indorsed with protest and thus losing the money and being liable on the balance of the claim.

Cashier's Checks—Section 3–411 and related provisions considerably improve the acceptability of bank obligations like cashier's checks as cash equivalents by providing disincentives to wrongful dishonor, such as the possible recovery of consequential damages.

Indorser Liability—Section 3–415 gives more time to hold a check before the user loses indorser liability.

Reporting Forgeries—Section 4–406 increases the outside time a customer has to report forged checks or alterations to thirty days. It also requires a bank truncating checks to retain the item or the capacity to furnish legible copies for seven years.

Individual Agent and Corporate Liability—Section 3–402, as to corporate instruments signed by agents without adequate indication and representation, (except as against a holder in due course), allows a representative to show the parties did not intend individual liability. It affords full protection to the agent that signs a corporate check, even though the check does not show representative status. Also, Section 3–403(b) makes it clear that a signature of an organization is considered unauthorized if more than one signature is required and it is missing.

Direct Suits—Section 3–420 allows a person whose indorsement is forged to sue the depositary bank directly, rather than each drawee of the checks involved.

C. Benefits to the Banking Community

Certainty—Section 3–104 and related provisions clarify what types of contracts are within Article 3 and how they are to be treated, thus promoting certainty of legal rules and reducing litigation costs and risks. Checks that may omit "words of negotiability" are included as fully negotiable; confusion over travelers checks is eliminated; variable rate instruments are included; and there is clarification of the impact of the FTC "Holder" Rule, clarification of the ability of parties to an instrument that is not included in Article 3 to contract for the application of its rules to their contract; and clarification of ordinary money orders as checks rather than bank obligations.

"Ordinary Care"—In Sections 3–103(a)(7) and 4–104(c), ordinary care is defined, making clear that financial institutions taking checks for processing or for payment by automated means need not manually handle each instrument if that is consistent with the institution's procedures and the procedures used do not vary unreasonably from the general usage of banks. This clarification is designed to accommodate and facilitate efficiency, thus lowering costs and lowering expedited funds availability risks. The definition of ordinary care relates to those specific instances in the Code where the standard of ordinary care is set forth.

Statute of Limitations—Sections 3–118 and 4–111 include statutory periods of limitations which will make the law uniform rather than leaving the topic to widely varying state laws.

Employee Fraud—Section 3–405 expands a per se negligence rule to the case of an indorsement forged by an employee whose duties involve handling checks. It also covers that of a faithless employee who supplies a name and then forges the indorsement, but does not require a precise match between the name of the payee and the indorsement.

Bank Definition—The definition of bank is expanded for the purposes of Articles 3 and 4 to clearly include savings and loans and credit unions so that their checks are directly governed by the Code. Section 4–104 clarifies that checks drawn on credit lines are subject to the rules for checks drawn on deposit accounts.

Truncation—Section 4–110 authorizes electronic presentment of items and related provisions remove impediments to truncation. Truncation will reduce risks from mandated funds availability and improve the check collection process. Section 4–406 allows an institution the benefit of its provisions even though it does not return the checks due to truncation. If both the customer and the institution fail to use ordinary care, a comparative negligence standard is used rather than placing the full loss on the institution.

_____

Table of Disposition of Sections in Former Article 3

The reference to a section in Revised Article 3 is to the section that refers to the issue addressed by the section in Former Article 3. If there is no comparable section in Revised Article 3 to a section in Former Article 3, that fact is indicated by the word "Omitted."

Former Article 3 Section	Revised Article 3 or 4 Section
3–101	3–101
3–102(1)(a)	3–105(a)
3–102(1)(b)	3–103(a)(6)
3–102(1)(c)	3–103(a)(9)
3–102(1)(d)	Omitted. See Comment 2 to 3–414.
3–102(1)(e)	3–104(b)
3–102(2)	3–103(b)
3–102(3)	3–103(c)
3–102(4)	3–103(d)
3–103(1)	3–102(a)
3–103(2)	3–102(b)
3–104(1)	3–104(a)
3–104(2)(a)	3–104(e)
3–104(2)(b)	3–104(f)
3–104(2)(c)	3–104(j)
3–104(2)(d)	3–104(e)
3–104(3)	Omitted.
3–105(1)(a)	3–106(a)
3–105(1)(b)	Omitted. See Comment 1 to 3–106.
3–105(1)(c)	Omitted. See Comment 1 to 3–106.
3–105(1)(d)	Omitted. See Comment 1 to 3–106.
3–105(1)(e)	Omitted. See Comment 1 to 3–106.
3–105(1)(f)	3–106(b)(ii)
3–105(1)(g)	3–106(b)(ii)
3–105(1)(h)	3–106(b)(ii)
3–105(2)(a)	3–106(a)(ii)
3–105(2)(b)	3–106(b)(ii)
3–106(1)	3–104(a)
3–106(2)	Omitted.
3–107(1)	Omitted. See Comment to 3–107.
3–107(2)	3–107
3–108	3–108(a)
3–109(1)	3–108(b)
3–109(2)	Omitted.
3–110(1)	3–109(b)
3–110(1)(a)	Omitted.
3–110(1)(b)	Omitted.
3–110(1)(c)	Omitted.
3–110(1)(d)	3–110(d)
3–110(1)(e)	3–110(c)(2)(i)
3–110(1)(f)	3–110(c)(2)(iv)
3–110(1)(g)	Omitted.
3–110(2)	Omitted.
3–110(3)	3–109(b)
3–111(a)	3–109(a)(1)
3–111(b)	3–109(a)(1)
3–111(c)	3–109(a)(3) and 3–205(b)
3–112(1)(a)	Omitted.

3–112(1)(b)............3–104(a)(3)(i)
3–112(1)(c)............3–104(a)(3)(i)
3–112(1)(d)............3–104(a)(3)(ii)
3–112(1)(e)............3–104(a)(3)(iii)
3–112(1)(f)............3–311
3–112(1)(g)............Omitted.
3–112(2)............Omitted.
3–113............Omitted.
3–114(1)............Omitted. See Comment to 3–113.
3–114(2)............3–113(a)
3–114(3)............Omitted. See Comment to 3–113.
3–115............3–115
3–116(a)............3–110(d)
3–116(b)............3–110(d)
3–117(a)............3–110(c)(2)(ii)
3–117(b)............3–110(c)(2)(i)
3–117(c)............Omitted.
3–118(a)............3–104(e) and 3–103(a)(6)
3–118(b)............3–114
3–118(c)............3–114
3–118(d)............3–112
3–118(e)............3–116(a)
3–118(f)............Omitted.
3–119............3–117 and 3–106(a) and (b)
3–120............4–106(a)
3–121............4–106(b)
3–122............Omitted. See Comment 1 to 3–118.
3–201(1)............3–203(b)
3–201(2)............3–204(c)
3–201(3)............3–203(c)
3–202(1)............3–201(a)
3–202(2)............3–204(a)
3–202(3)............3–203(d)
3–202(4)............Omitted.
3–203............3–204(d)
3–204(1)............3–205(a)
3–204(2)............3–205(b)
3–204(3)............3–205(c)
3–205............Omitted.
3–206(1)............3–206(a)
3–206(2)............3–206(c)(4) and (d)
3–206(3)............3–206(b), (c), and (e)
3–206(4)............3–206(d) and (e)
3–207(1)(a)............3–202(a)(i)
3–207(1)(b)............3–202(a)(ii)
3–207(1)(c)............3–202(a)(iii)
3–207(1)(d)............3–202(a)(iii)
3–207(2)............3–202(b)
3–208............3–207
3–301............Omitted. See Comment to 3–301.
3–302(1)............3–302(a)
3–302(2)............Omitted. See Comment 4 to 3–302.
3–302(3)(a)............3–302(c)(i)
3–302(3)(b)............3–302(c)(iii)
3–302(3)(c)............3–302(c)(ii)
3–302(4)............3–302(e)

3–303(a) ....3–303(a)(1) and (2)
3–303(b) ....3–303(a)(3)
3–303(c) ....3–303(a)(4) and (5)
3–304(1)(a) ....3–302(a)(1)
3–304(1)(b) ....Omitted.
3–304(2) ....3–307(b)
3–304(3)(a) ....3–302(a)(2)(iii); 3–304(b)(1)
3–304(3)(b) ....3–304(b)(3)
3–304(3)(c) ....3–304(a)(1), (2) and (3)
3–304(4)(a) ....Omitted.
3–304(4)(b) ....Omitted.
3–304(4)(c) ....Omitted.
3–304(4)(d) ....Omitted.
3–304(4)(e) 3–307
3–304(4)(f) ....3–304(c)
3–304(5) ....3–302(b)
3–304(6) ....Omitted.
3–305(1) 3–306
3–305(2)(a) ....3–305(a)(1)(i)
3–305(2)(b) ....3–305(a)(1)(ii)
3–305(2)(c) ....3–305(a)(1)(iii)
3–305(2)(d) ....3–305(a)(1)(iv)
3–305(2)(e) ....3–601(b)
3–306(a) 3–306
3–306(b) ....3–305(a)(2)
3–306(c) ....3–305(a)(2); 3–303(b); 3–105(b)
3–306(d) ....3–305(c)
3–307(1)(a) ....3–308(a)
3–307(1)(b) ....3–308(a)
3–307(2) ....3–308(b)
3–307(3) ....3–308(b)
3–401(1) ....3–401(a)
3–401(2) ....3–401(b)
3–402 ....3–204(a)
3–403(1) ....3–402(a)
3–403(2)(a) ....3–402(b)(2)
3–403(2)(b) ....3–402(b)(2)
3–403(3) ....3–402(b)(1)
3–404(1) ....3–403(a)
3–404(2) ....3–403(a)
3–405(1)(a) ....3–404(a)
3–405(1)(b) ....3–404(b)(i)
3–405(1)(c) 3–405
3–405(2) ....3–403(c)
3–406 3–406
3–407(1)(a) ....3–407(a)(i)
3–407(1)(b) ....3–407(a)(ii)
3–407(1)(c) ....3–407(a)(i)
3–407(2)(a) ....3–407(b)
3–407(2)(b) ....3–407(b)
3–407(3) ....3–407(c)
3–408 ....3–303(b)
3–409(1) 3–408
3–409(2) ....Omitted. See Comment 1 to 3–408.
3–410(1) ....3–409(a)
3–410(2) ....3–409(b)

3–410(3)..3–409(c)
3–411(1)..3–409(d); 3–414(c); 3–415(d)
3–411(2)..3–409(d)
3–411(3)..Omitted.
3–412(1)..3–410(a)
3–412(2)..3–410(b)
3–412(3)..3–410(c)
3–413(1)..3–412; 3–413(a)
3–413(2)..3–414(b) and (e)
3–413(3)..Omitted.
3–414(1)..3–415(a) and (b)
3–414(2)..Omitted.
3–415(1)..3–419(a)
3–415(2)..3–419(b)
3–415(3)..Omitted. See 3–605(h)
3–415(4)..3–419(c)
3–415(5)..3–419(e)
3–416(1)..Omitted.
3–416(2)..3–419(d)
3–416(3)..Omitted.
3–416(4)..3–419(c)
3–416(5)..Omitted.
3–416(6)..Omitted.
3–417(1)..3–417
3–417(2)..3–416
3–417(3)..Omitted.
3–417(4)..Omitted.
3–418..3–418
3–419(1)..3–420(a)
3–419(2)..3–420(b)
3–419(3)..3–420(c)
3–419(4)..3–206(c)(4) and (d)
3–501(1)(a)..3–414(b); 3–502(b)(3) and (4)
3–501(1)(b)..3–415(a); 3–502(a)(1) and (2); 3–502(b), (c), (d) and (e)
3–501(1)(c)..3–414(f); 3–415(e)
3–501(2)(a)..3–503(a)
3–501(2)(b)..Omitted. See Comment 2 to 3–414.
3–501(3)..Omitted. See Comment to 3–505.
3–501(4)..Omitted.
3–502(1)(a)..3–415(e)
3–502(1)(b)..3–414(f)
3–502(2)..Omitted. See Comment to 3–505.
3–503..Omitted. See Comment to 3–502.
3–504(1)..3–501(a)
3–504(2)(a)..3–501(b)(1)
3–504(2)(b)..3–501(b)(1)
3–504(2)(c)..3–501(b)(1); 3–111
3–504(3)(a)..3–501(b)(1)
3–504(3)(b)..Omitted.
3–504(4)..3–501(b)(1)
3–504(5)..Omitted.
3–505(1)(a)..3–501(b)(2)(i)
3–505(1)(b)..3–501(b)(2)(ii)
3–505(1)(c)..Omitted.
3–505(1)(d)..3–501(b)(2)(iii)
3–505(2)..Omitted.

3–506(1)..Omitted.
3–506(2)..Omitted.
3–507(1)..3–502
3–507(2)..Omitted.
3–507(3)..3–501(b)(3)(i)
3–507(4)..Omitted.
3–508(1)..3–503(b)
3–508(2)..3–503(c)
3–508(3)..3–503(b)
3–508(4)..Omitted.
3–508(5)..Omitted.
3–508(6)..Omitted.
3–508(7)..Omitted.
3–508(8)..3–503(b)
3–509(1)..3–505(b)
3–509(2)..3–505(b)
3–509(3)..3–505(b)
3–509(4)..Omitted.
3–509(5)..Omitted.
3–510(a)..3–505(a)(1)
3–510(b)..3–505(a)(2)
3–510(c)..3–505(a)(3)
3–511(1)..Omitted.
3–511(2)(a)..3–504(a)(iv)
3–511(2)(b)..3–504(a)(ii), (iv), and (v); 3–504(b)
3–511(2)(c)..3–504(a)(i)
3–511(3)(a)..3–504(a)(ii)
3–511(3)(b)..3–504(a)(ii)
3–511(4)..3–502(f)
3–511(5)..Omitted.
3–511(6)..Omitted.
3–601(1)..3–601(a)
3–601(2)..3–601(a)
3–601(3)..Omitted.
3–602 ....3–601(b)
3–603(1)..3–602(a) and (b)
3–603(1)(a)..3–602(b)(2)
3–603(1)(b)..Omitted. See 3–206(c)(3).
3–603(2)..Omitted.
3–604(1)..3–603(c)
3–604(2)..3–603(b)
3–604(3)..3–603(c)
3–605(1)(a)..3–604(a)(i)
3–605(1)(b)..3–604(a)(ii)
3–605(2)..3–604(b)
3–606(1)(a)..3–605(b) and (c)
3–606(1)(b)..3–605(e)
3–606(2)..Omitted.
3–701(1)..Omitted.
3–701(2)..Omitted.
3–701(3)..Omitted.
3–801(1)..Omitted.
3–801(2)..Omitted.
3–801(3)..Omitted.
3–801(4)..Omitted.
3–802(1)(a)..3–310(a) and (c)

3–802(1)(b)...3–310(b) and (c)
3–802(2) ....Omitted.
3–803 3–119
3–804 3–309
3–805 ....Omitted. See Comment 2 to 3–104.

PART 1

GENERAL PROVISIONS AND DEFINITIONS

§ 3–101.   Short Title.

This Article may be cited as Uniform Commercial Code—Negotiable Instruments.

§ 3–102.   Subject Matter.

(a)   This Article applies to negotiable instruments. It does not apply to money, to payment orders governed by Article 4A, or to securities governed by Article 8.

(b)   If there is conflict between this Article and Article 4 or 9, Articles 4 and 9 govern.

(c)   Regulations of the Board of Governors of the Federal Reserve System and operating circulars of the Federal Reserve Banks supersede any inconsistent provision of this Article to the extent of the inconsistency.

Official Comment

1.   Former Article 3 had no provision affirmatively stating its scope. Former Section 3–103 was a limitation on scope. In revised Article 3, Section 3–102 states that Article 3 applies to "negotiable instruments," defined in Section 3–104. Section 3–104(b) also defines the term "instrument" as a synonym for "negotiable instrument." In most places Article 3 uses the shorter term "instrument." This follows the convention used in former Article 3.

2.   The reference in former Section 3–103(1) to "documents of title" is omitted as superfluous because these documents contain no promise to pay money. The definition of "payment order" in Section 4A–103(a)(1)(iii) excludes drafts which are governed by Article 3. Section 3–102(a) makes clear that a payment order governed by Article 4A is not governed by Article 3. Thus, Article 3 and Article 4A are mutually exclusive.

Article 8 states in Section 8–103(d) that "A writing that is a security certificate is governed by this Article and not by Article 3, even though it also meets the requirements of that Article." Section 3–102(a) conforms to this provision. With respect to some promises or orders to pay money, there may be a question whether the promise or order is an instrument under Section 3–104(a) or a certificated security under Section 8–102(a)(4) and (15). Whether a writing is covered by Article 3 or Article 8 has important consequences. Among other things, under Section 8–207, the issuer of a certificated security may treat the registered owner as the owner for all purposes until the presentment for registration of a transfer. The issuer of a negotiable instrument, on the other hand, may discharge its obligation to pay the instrument only by paying a person entitled to enforce under Section 3–301. There are also important consequences to an indorser. An indorser of a security does not undertake the issuer's obligation or make any warranty that the issuer will honor the underlying obligation, while an indorser of a negotiable instrument becomes secondarily liable on the underlying obligation.

Ordinarily the distinction between instruments and certificated securities in non-bearer form should be relatively clear. A certificated security under Article 8 must be in registered form (Section 8–102(a)(13)) so that it can be registered on the issuer's records. By contrast, registration plays no part in Article 3. The distinction between an instrument and a certificated security in bearer form may be somewhat more difficult and will generally lie in the economic functions of the two writings. Ordinarily, negotiable instruments under Article 3 will be separate and distinct instruments, while certificated securities under Article 8 will be either one of a class or series or by their terms divisible into a class or series (Section 8–102(a)(15)(ii)). Thus, a promissory note in bearer form could come under either Article 3 if it were simply an individual note, or under Article 8 if it were one of a series of notes or divisible into a series. An additional distinction is whether the instrument is of the type commonly dealt in on securities exchanges or markets or commonly recognized as a medium for investment (Section 8–

102(a)(15)(iii)). Thus, a check written in bearer form (i.e., a check made payable to "cash") would not be a certificated security within Article 8 of the Uniform Commercial Code.

Occasionally, a particular writing may fit the definition of both a negotiable instrument under Article 3 and of an investment security under Article 8. In such cases, the instrument is subject exclusively to the requirements of Article 8. Section 8–103(d) and Section 3–102(a).

3.   Although the terms of Article 3 apply to transactions by Federal Reserve Banks, federal preemption would make ineffective any Article 3 provision that conflicts with federal law. The activities of the Federal Reserve Banks are governed by regulations of the Federal Reserve Board and by operating circulars issued by the Reserve Banks themselves. In some instances, the operating circulars are issued pursuant to a Federal Reserve Board regulation. In other cases, the Reserve Bank issues the operating circular under its own authority under the Federal Reserve Act, subject to review by the Federal Reserve Board. Section 3–102(c) states that Federal Reserve Board regulations and operating circulars of the Federal Reserve Banks supersede any inconsistent provision of Article 3 to the extent of the inconsistency. Federal Reserve Board regulations, being valid exercises of regulatory authority pursuant to a federal statute, take precedence over state law if there is an inconsistency. *Childs v. Federal Reserve Bank of Dallas*, 719 F.2d 812 (5th Cir. 1983), reh. den. 724 F.2d 127 (5th Cir. 1984). Section 3–102(c) treats operating circulars as having the same effect whether issued under the Reserve Bank's own authority or under a Federal Reserve Board regulation. Federal statutes may also preempt Article 3. For example, the Expedited Funds Availability Act, 12 U.S.C. § 4001 et seq., provides that the Act and the regulations issued pursuant to the Act supersede any inconsistent provisions of the UCC. 12 U.S.C. § 4007(b).

4.   In *Clearfield Trust Co. v. United States*, 318 U.S. 363 (1943), the Court held that if the United States is a party to an instrument, its rights and duties are governed by federal common law in the absence of a specific federal statute or regulation. In *United States v. Kimbell Foods, Inc.*, 440 U.S. 715 (1979), the Court stated a three-pronged test to ascertain whether the federal common-law rule should follow the state rule. In most instances courts under the *Kimbell* test have shown a willingness to adopt UCC rules in formulating federal common law on the subject. In *Kimbell* the Court adopted the priorities rules of Article 9.

5.   In 1989 the United Nations Commission on International Trade Law completed a Convention on International Bills of Exchange and International Promissory Notes. If the United States becomes a party to this Convention, the Convention will preempt state law with respect to international bills and notes governed by the Convention. Thus, an international bill of exchange or promissory note that meets the definition of instrument in Section 3–104 will not be governed by Article 3 if it is governed by the Convention. That Convention applies only to bills and notes that indicate on their face that they involve cross-border transactions. It does not apply at all to checks. Convention Articles 1(3), 2(1), 2(2). Moreover, because it applies only if the bill or note specifically calls for application of the Convention, Convention Article 1, there is little chance that the Convention will apply accidentally to a transaction that the parties intended to be governed by this Article.

As amended in 1995 and 2002.

§ 3–103.   Definitions.

(a)   In this Article:

(1)   "Acceptor" means a drawee who has accepted a draft.

(2)   "Consumer account" means an account established by an individual primarily for personal, family, or household purposes.

(3)   "Consumer transaction" means a transaction in which an individual incurs an obligation primarily for personal, family, or household purposes.

(4)   "Drawee" means a person ordered in a draft to make payment.

(5)   "Drawer" means a person who signs or is identified in a draft as a person ordering payment.

(6)   ["Good faith" means honesty in fact and the observance of reasonable commercial standards of fair dealing.] [*Note from West Advisory Panel: This subsection will be deleted if the jurisdiction adopts the definition of good faith in revised Article 1 (2001).*]

(7)   "Maker" means a person who signs or is identified in a note as a person undertaking to pay.

(8)   "Order" means a written instruction to pay money signed by the person giving the instruction. The instruction may be addressed to any person, including the person giving the instruction, or

to one or more persons jointly or in the alternative but not in succession. An authorization to pay is not an order unless the person authorized to pay is also instructed to pay.

(9) "Ordinary care" in the case of a person engaged in business means observance of reasonable commercial standards, prevailing in the area in which the person is located, with respect to the business in which the person is engaged. In the case of a bank that takes an instrument for processing for collection or payment by automated means, reasonable commercial standards do not require the bank to examine the instrument if the failure to examine does not violate the bank's prescribed procedures and the bank's procedures do not vary unreasonably from general banking usage not disapproved by this Article or Article 4.

(10) "Party" means a party to an instrument.

(11) "Principal obligor," with respect to an instrument, means the accommodated party or any other party to the instrument against whom a secondary obligor has recourse under this article.

(12) "Promise" means a written undertaking to pay money signed by the person undertaking to pay. An acknowledgment of an obligation by the obligor is not a promise unless the obligor also undertakes to pay the obligation.

(13) "Prove" with respect to a fact means to meet the burden of establishing the fact (Section 1–201(b)(8)).

(14) ["Record" means information that is inscribed on a tangible medium or that is stored in an electronic or other medium and is retrievable in perceivable form.]

(15) "Remitter" means a person who purchases an instrument from its issuer if the instrument is payable to an identified person other than the purchaser.

(16) "Remotely-created consumer item" means an item drawn on a consumer account, which is not created by the payor bank and does not bear a handwritten signature purporting to be the signature of the drawer.

(17) "Secondary obligor," with respect to an instrument, means (a) an indorser or an accommodation party, (b) a drawer having the obligation described in Section 3–414(d), or (c) any other party to the instrument that has recourse against another party to the instrument pursuant to Section 3–116(b).

(b) Other definitions applying to this Article and the sections in which they appear are:

"Acceptance" Section 3–409
"Accommodated party" Section 3–419
"Accommodation party" Section 3–419
"Account" Section 4–104
"Alteration" Section 3–407
"Anomalous indorsement" Section 3–205
"Blank indorsement" Section 3–205
"Cashier's check" Section 3–104
"Certificate of deposit" Section 3–104
"Certified check" Section 3–409
"Check" Section 3–104
"Consideration" Section 3–303
"Draft" Section 3–104
"Holder in due course" Section 3–302
"Incomplete instrument" Section 3–115
"Indorsement" Section 3–204
"Indorser" Section 3–204
"Instrument" Section 3–104
"Issue" Section 3–105
"Issuer" Section 3–105

"Negotiable instrument" Section 3–104

"Negotiation" Section 3–201

"Note" Section 3–104

"Payable at a definite time" Section 3–108

"Payable on demand" Section 3–108

"Payable to bearer" Section 3–109

"Payable to order" Section 3–109

"Payment" Section 3–602

"Person entitled to enforce" Section 3–301

"Presentment" Section 3–501

"Reacquisition" Section 3–207

"Special indorsement" Section 3–205

"Teller's check" Section 3–104

"Transfer of instrument" Section 3–203

"Traveler's check" Section 3–104

"Value" Section 3–303

(c)   The following definitions in other Articles apply to this Article:

"Banking day" Section 4–104

"Clearing house" Section 4–104

"Collecting bank" Section 4–105

"Depositary bank" Section 4–105

"Documentary draft" Section 4–104

"Intermediary bank" Section 4–105

"Item" Section 4–104

"Payor bank" Section 4–105

"Suspends payments" Section 4–104

(d)   In addition, Article 1 contains general definitions and principles of construction and interpretation applicable throughout this Article.

Legislative Note. A jurisdiction that enacts this statute that has not yet enacted the revised version of UCC Article 1 should add to Section 3–103 the definition of "good faith" that appears in the official version of Section 1–201(b)(20) and the definition of "record" that appears in the official version of Section 1–201(b)(31). Sections 3–103(a)(6) and (14) are reserved for that purpose. A jurisdiction that already has adopted or simultaneously adopts the revised Article 1 should not add those definitions, but should leave those numbers "reserved." If jurisdictions follow the numbering suggested here, the subsections will have the same numbering in all jurisdictions that have adopted these amendments (whether they have or have not adopted the revised version of UCC Article 1).

As amended in 2001 and 2002.

Official Comment

1.   Subsection (a) defines some common terms used throughout the Article that were not defined by former Article 3 and adds the definitions of "order" and "promise" found in former Section 3–102(1)(b) and (c).

2.   The definition of "order" includes an instruction given by the signer to itself. The most common example of this kind of order is a cashier's check: a draft with respect to which the drawer and drawee are the same bank or branches of the same bank. Former Section 3–118(a) treated a cashier's check as a note. It stated "a draft drawn on the drawer is effective as a note." Although it is technically more correct to treat a cashier's check as a promise by the issuing bank to pay rather than an order to pay, a cashier's check is in the form of a check and it is normally referred to as a check. Thus, revised Article 3 follows banking practice in referring to a cashier's check as both a draft and a check rather than a note. Some insurance companies also follow the practice of issuing drafts in which the drawer draws on itself and makes the draft payable at or through a bank. These instruments are also treated as drafts. The obligation of the drawer of a cashier's check or other draft drawn on the drawer is stated in Section 3–412.

284

An order may be addressed to more than one person as drawee either jointly or in the alternative. The authorization of alternative drawees follows former Section 3–102(1)(b) and recognizes the practice of drawers, such as corporations issuing dividend checks, who for commercial convenience name a number of drawees, usually in different parts of the country. Section 3–501(b)(1) provides that presentment may be made to any one of multiple drawees. Drawees in succession are not permitted because the holder should not be required to make more than one presentment. Dishonor by any drawee named in the draft entitles the holder to rights of recourse against the drawer or indorsers.

3. The last sentence of subsection (a)(12) is intended to make it clear that an I.O.U. or other written acknowledgment of indebtedness is not a note unless there is also an undertaking to pay the obligation.

4. This Article now uses the broadened definition of good faith in revised Article 1. The definition requires not only honesty in fact but also "observance of reasonable commercial standards of fair dealing." Although fair dealing is a broad term that must be defined in context, it is clear that it is concerned with the fairness of conduct rather than the care with which an act is performed. Failure to exercise ordinary care in conducting a transaction is an entirely different concept than failure to deal fairly in conducting the transaction. Both fair dealing and ordinary care, which is defined in Section 3–103(a)(9), are to be judged in the light of reasonable commercial standards, but those standards in each case are directed to different aspects of commercial conduct.

5. Subsection (a)(9) is a definition of ordinary care which is applicable not only to Article 3 but to Article 4 as well. See Section 4–104(c). The general rule is stated in the first sentence of subsection (a)(9) and it applies both to banks and to persons engaged in businesses other than banking. Ordinary care means observance of reasonable commercial standards of the relevant businesses prevailing in the area in which the person is located. The second sentence of subsection (a)(9) is a particular rule limited to the duty of a bank to examine an instrument taken by a bank for processing for collection or payment by automated means. This particular rule applies primarily to Section 4–406 and it is discussed in Comment 4 to that section. Nothing in Section 3–103(a)(9) is intended to prevent a customer from proving that the procedures followed by a bank are unreasonable, arbitrary, or unfair.

6. The definition of consumer account includes a joint account established by more than one individual. See Section 1–106(1) [*unrevised Article 1; see Concordance, p. 22*].

As amended in 2001 and 2002.

§ 3–104. Negotiable Instrument.

(a) Except as provided in subsections (c) and (d), "negotiable instrument" means an unconditional promise or order to pay a fixed amount of money, with or without interest or other charges described in the promise or order, if it:

(1) is payable to bearer or to order at the time it is issued or first comes into possession of a holder;

(2) is payable on demand or at a definite time; and

(3) does not state any other undertaking or instruction by the person promising or ordering payment to do any act in addition to the payment of money, but the promise or order may contain (i) an undertaking or power to give, maintain, or protect collateral to secure payment, (ii) an authorization or power to the holder to confess judgment or realize on or dispose of collateral, (iii) a waiver of the benefit of any law intended for the advantage or protection of an obligor, (iv) a term that specifies the law that governs the promise or order, or (v) an

undertaking to resolve in a specified forum a dispute concerning the promise or order.

(b) "Instrument" means a negotiable instrument.

(c) An order that meets all of the requirements of subsection (a), except paragraph (1), and otherwise falls within the definition of "check" in subsection (f) is a negotiable instrument and a check.

(d) A promise or order other than a check is not an instrument if, at the time it is issued or first comes into possession of a holder, it contains a conspicuous statement, however expressed, to the effect that the promise or order is not negotiable or is not an instrument governed by this Article.

(e) An instrument is a "note" if it is a promise and is a "draft" if it is an order. If an instrument falls within the definition of both "note" and "draft," a person entitled to enforce the instrument may treat it as either.

(f)   "Check" means (i) a draft, other than a documentary draft, payable on demand and drawn on a bank or (ii) a cashier's check or teller's check. An instrument may be a check even though it is described on its face by another term, such as "money order."

(g)   "Cashier's check" means a draft with respect to which the drawer and drawee are the same bank or branches of the same bank.

(h)   "Teller's check" means a draft drawn by a bank (i) on another bank, or (ii) payable at or through a bank.

(i)   "Traveler's check" means an instrument that (i) is payable on demand, (ii) is drawn on or payable at or through a bank, (iii) is designated by the term "traveler's check" or by a substantially similar term, and (iv) requires, as a condition to payment, a countersignature by a person whose specimen signature appears on the instrument.

(j)   "Certificate of deposit" means an instrument containing an acknowledgment by a bank that a sum of money has been received by the bank and a promise by the bank to repay the sum of money. A certificate of deposit is a note of the bank.

As amended in 2022.

Official Comment

1.   The definition of "negotiable instrument" defines the scope of Article 3 since Section 3–102 states: "This Article applies to negotiable instruments." The definition in Section 3–104(a) incorporates other definitions in Article 3. An instrument is either a "promise," defined in Section 3–103(a)(12), or "order," defined in Section 3–103(a)(8). A promise is a written undertaking to pay money signed by the person undertaking to pay. An order is a written instruction to pay money signed by the person giving the instruction. Thus, the term "negotiable instrument" is limited to a signed writing that orders or promises payment of money. "Money" is defined in Section 1–201(24) [*unrevised Article 1; see Concordance, p. 22*] and is not limited to United States dollars. It also includes a medium of exchange established by a foreign government or monetary units of account established by an intergovernmental organization or by agreement between two or more nations. Five other requirements are stated in Section 3–104(a): First, the promise or order must be "unconditional." The quoted term is explained in Section 3–106. Second, the amount of money must be "a fixed amount . . . with or without interest or other charges described in the promise or order." Section 3–112(b) relates to "interest." Third, the promise or order must be "payable to bearer or to order." The quoted phrase is explained in Section 3–109. An exception to this requirement is stated in subsection (c). Fourth, the promise or order must be payable "on demand or at a definite time." The quoted phrase is explained in Section 3–108. Fifth, the promise or order may not state "any other undertaking or instruction by the person promising or ordering payment to do any act in addition to the payment of money" with five exceptions. The quoted phrase is based on the first sentence of N.I.L. Section 5 which is the precursor of "no other promise, order, obligation or power given by the maker or drawer" appearing in former Section 3–104(1)(b). The words "instruction" and "undertaking" are used instead of "order" and "promise" that are used in the N.I.L. formulation because the latter words are defined terms that include only orders or promises to pay money. The first three exceptions stated in Section 3–104(a)(3) are based on and are intended to have the same meaning as former Section 3–112(1)(b), (c), (d), and (e), as well as N.I.L. § 5(1), (2), and (3). The final two exceptions stated in Section 3–104(a)(3), added pursuant to the Uniform Commercial Code Amendments (2022), deal with choice-of-law and choice-of-forum clauses. The latter of these includes an agreement to arbitrate. Subsection (b) states that "instrument" means a "negotiable instrument." This follows former Section 3–102(1)(e) which treated the two terms as synonymous.

2.   Unless subsection (c) applies, the effect of subsection (a)(1) and Section 3–102(a) is to exclude from Article 3 any promise or order that is not payable to bearer or to order. There is no provision in revised Article 3 that is comparable to former Section 3–805. The comment to former Section 3–805 states that the typical example of a writing covered by that section is a check reading "Pay John Doe." Such a check was governed by former Article 3 but there could not be a holder in due course of the check. Under Section 3–104(c) such a check is governed by revised Article 3 and there can be a holder in due course of the check. But subsection (c) applies only to checks. The comment to former Section 3–805 does not state any example other than the check to illustrate that section. Subsection (c) is based on the belief that it is good policy to treat checks, which are payment instruments, as negotiable instruments whether or not they contain the words "to the order of". These words are almost always pre-printed on the check form. Occasionally the drawer of a check may strike out these words before issuing the check. In the past some credit unions used check forms that did not contain the quoted words. Such check forms may still be in use but they are no longer common. Absence of the quoted words can easily be overlooked and

should not affect the rights of holders who may pay money or give credit for a check without being aware that it is not in the conventional form.

Total exclusion from Article 3 of other promises or orders that are not payable to bearer or to order serves a useful purpose. It provides a simple device to clearly exclude a writing that does not fit the pattern of typical negotiable instruments and which is not intended to be a negotiable instrument. If a writing could be an instrument despite the absence of "to order" or "to bearer" language and a dispute arises with respect to the writing, it might be argued that the writing is a negotiable instrument because the other requirements of subsection (a) are somehow met. Even if the argument is eventually found to be without merit it can be used as a litigation ploy. Words making a promise or order payable to bearer or to order are the most distinguishing feature of a negotiable instrument and such words are frequently referred to as "words of negotiability." Article 3 is not meant to apply to contracts for the sale of goods or services or the sale or lease of real property or similar writings that may contain a promise to pay money. The use of words of negotiability in such contracts would be an aberration. Absence of the words precludes any argument that such contracts might be negotiable instruments.

An order or promise that is excluded from Article 3 because of the requirements of Section 3–104(a) may nevertheless be similar to a negotiable instrument in many respects. Although such a writing cannot be made a negotiable instrument within Article 3 by contract or conduct of its parties, nothing in Section 3–104 or in Section 3–102 is intended to mean that in a particular case involving such a writing a court could not arrive at a result similar to the result that would follow if the writing were a negotiable instrument. For example, a court might find that the obligor with respect to a promise that does not fall within Section 3–104(a) is precluded from asserting a defense against a bona fide purchaser. The preclusion could be based on estoppel or ordinary principles of contract. It does not depend upon the law of negotiable instruments. An example is stated in the paragraph following Case # 2 in Comment 4 to Section 3–302.

Moreover, consistent with the principle stated in Section 1–102(2)(b) [*unrevised Article 1; see Concordance, p. 22*], the immediate parties to an order or promise that is not an instrument may provide by agreement that one or more of the provisions of Article 3 determine their rights and obligations under the writing. Upholding the parties' choice is not inconsistent with Article 3. Such an agreement may bind a transferee of the writing if the transferee has notice of it or the agreement arises from usage of trade and the agreement does not violate other law or public policy. An example of such an agreement is a provision that a transferee of the writing has the rights of a holder in due course stated in Article 3 if the transferee took rights under the writing in good faith, for value, and without notice of a claim or defense.

Even without an agreement of the parties to an order or promise that is not an instrument, it may be appropriate, consistent with the principles stated in Section 1–102(2) [*unrevised Article 1; see Concordance, p. 22*], for a court to apply one or more provisions of Article 3 to the writing by analogy, taking into account the expectations of the parties and the differences between the writing and an instrument governed by Article 3. Whether such application is appropriate depends upon the facts of each case.

3. Subsection (d) allows exclusion from Article 3 of a writing that would otherwise be an instrument under subsection (a) by a statement to the effect that the writing is not negotiable or is not governed by Article 3. For example, a promissory note can be stamped with the legend NOT NEGOTIABLE. The effect under subsection (d) is not only to negate the possibility of a holder in due course, but to prevent the writing from being a negotiable instrument for any purpose. Subsection (d) does not, however, apply to a check. If a writing is excluded from Article 3 by subsection (d), a court could, nevertheless, apply Article 3 principles to it by analogy as stated in Comment 2.

4. Instruments are divided into two general categories: drafts and notes. A draft is an instrument that is an order. A note is an instrument that is a promise. Section 3–104(e). The term "bill of exchange" is not used in Article 3. It is generally understood to be a synonym for the term "draft." Subsections (f) through (j) define particular instruments that fall within the categories of draft and note. The term "draft," defined in subsection (e), includes a "check" which is defined in subsection (f). "Check" includes a share draft drawn on a credit union payable through a bank because the definition of bank (Section 4–105) includes credit unions. However, a draft drawn on an insurance company payable through a bank is not a check because it is not drawn on a bank. "Money orders" are sold both by banks and non-banks. They vary in form and their form determines how they are treated in Article 3. The most common form of money order sold by banks is that of an ordinary check drawn by the purchaser except that the amount is machine impressed. That kind of money order is a check under Article 3 and is subject to a stop order by the purchaser-drawer as in the case of ordinary checks. The seller bank is the drawee and has no obligation to a holder to pay the money order. If a money order falls within the definition of a teller's check, the rules applicable to teller's checks apply. Postal money orders are subject to federal law. "Teller's check" is separately defined in subsection (h). A teller's check is always drawn by a bank and is usually drawn on another bank. In some cases a teller's check is drawn on a nonbank but is made payable at or through a bank. Article 3

treats both types of teller's check identically, and both are included in the definition of "check." A cashier's check, defined in subsection (g), is also included in the definition of "check." Traveler's checks are issued both by banks and nonbanks and may be in the form of a note or draft. Subsection (i) states the essential characteristics of a traveler's check. The requirement that the instrument be "drawn on or payable at or through a bank" may be satisfied without words on the instrument that identify a bank as drawee or paying agent so long as the instrument bears an appropriate routing number that identifies a bank as paying agent.

The definitions in Regulation CC § 229.2 of the terms "check," "cashier's check," "teller's check," and "traveler's check" are different from the definitions of those terms in Article 3.

Certificates of deposit are treated in former Article 3 as a separate type of instrument. In revised Article 3, Section 3–104(j) treats them as notes.

5.   There are some differences between the requirements of Article 3 and the requirements included in Article 3 of the Convention on International Bills of Exchange and International Promissory Notes. Most obviously, the Convention does not include the limitation on extraneous undertakings set forth in Section 3–104(a)(3), and does not permit documents payable to bearer that would be permissible under Section 3–104(a)(1) and Section 3–109. See Convention Article 3. In most respects, however, the requirements of Section 3–104 and Article 3 of the Convention are quite similar.

As amended in 2002 and 2022.

§ 3–105.   Issue of Instrument.

(a)   "Issue" means:

(1)   the first delivery of an instrument by the maker or drawer, whether to a holder or nonholder, for the purpose of giving rights on the instrument to any person; or

(2)   if agreed by the payee, the first transmission by the drawer to the payee of an image of an item and information derived from the item that enables the depositary bank to collect the item by transferring or presenting under federal law an electronic check.

(b)   An unissued instrument, or an unissued incomplete instrument that is completed, is binding on the maker or drawer, but nonissuance is a defense. An instrument that is conditionally issued or is issued for a special purpose is binding on the maker or drawer, but failure of the condition or special purpose to be fulfilled is a defense.

(c)   "Issuer" applies to issued and unissued instruments and means a maker or drawer of an instrument.

As amended in 2022.

Official Comment

1.   Under former Section 3–102(1)(a) "issue" was defined as the first delivery to a "holder or a remitter" but the term "remitter" was neither defined nor otherwise used. In revised Article 3, Section 3–105(a) defines "issue" more broadly to include the first delivery to anyone by the drawer or maker for the purpose of giving rights to anyone on the instrument. "Delivery" with respect to instruments is defined in Section 1–201(14) Section 1–201(b)(15) as meaning "voluntary transfer of possession." The reference in subsection (a)(2) to transmission of an image of an item and information derived from the item is derived from Section 4–110(a), dealing with electronic presentment.

Subsection (a) permits an instrument to be issued by an electronic transmission of an image of and information derived from the instrument by maker and drawer, rather than by delivery. Thus, for example, a drawer might, with the permission of the payee, write and sign a check, take a photograph of the check, send the photograph to the payee for processing electronically, and destroy the original check. If the electronic image and the information derived from it can be processed as an "electronic check" under Regulation CC, see 12 C.F.R. § 229.2(ggg), the check is "issued" and hence can be enforced pursuant to this Article.

2.   Subsection (b) continues the rule that nonissuance, conditional issuance or issuance for a special purpose is a defense of the maker or drawer of an instrument. Thus, the defense can be asserted against a person other than a holder in due course. The same rule applies to nonissuance of an incomplete instrument later completed.

3. Subsection (c) defines "issuer" to include the signer of an unissued instrument for convenience of reference in the statute.

As amended in 2022.

§ 3–106. Unconditional Promise or Order.

(a) Except as provided in this section, for the purposes of Section 3–104(a), a promise or order is unconditional unless it states (i) an express condition to payment, (ii) that the promise or order is subject to or governed by another record, or (iii) that rights or obligations with respect to the promise or order are stated in another record. A reference to another record does not of itself make the promise or order conditional.

(b) A promise or order is not made conditional (i) by a reference to another record for a statement of rights with respect to collateral, prepayment, or acceleration, or (ii) because payment is limited to resort to a particular fund or source.

(c) If a promise or order requires, as a condition to payment, a countersignature by a person whose specimen signature appears on the promise or order, the condition does not make the promise or order conditional for the purposes of Section 3–104(a). If the person whose specimen signature appears on an instrument fails to countersign the instrument, the failure to countersign is a defense to the obligation of the issuer, but the failure does not prevent a transferee of the instrument from becoming a holder of the instrument.

(d) If a promise or order at the time it is issued or first comes into possession of a holder contains a statement, required by applicable statutory or administrative law, to the effect that the rights of a holder or transferee are subject to claims or defenses that the issuer could assert against the original payee, the promise or order is not thereby made conditional for the purposes of Section 3–104(a); but if the promise or order is an instrument, there cannot be a holder in due course of the instrument.

As amended in 2002.

Official Comment

1. This provision replaces former Section 3–105. Its purpose is to define when a promise or order fulfills the requirement in Section 3–104(a) that it be an "unconditional" promise or order to pay. Under Section 3–106(a) a promise or order is deemed to be unconditional unless one of the two tests of the subsection make the promise or order conditional. If the promise or order states an express condition to payment, the promise or order is not an instrument. For example, a promise states, "I promise to pay $100,000 to the order of John Doe if he conveys title to Blackacre to me." The promise is not an instrument because there is an express condition to payment. However, suppose a promise states, "In consideration of John Doe's promise to convey title to Blackacre I promise to pay $100,000 to the order of John Doe." That promise can be an instrument if Section 3–104 is otherwise satisfied. Although the recital of the executory promise of Doe to convey Blackacre might be read as an implied condition that the promise be performed, the condition is not an express condition as required by Section 3–106(a)(i). This result is consistent with former Section 3–105(1)(a) and (b). Former Section 3–105(1)(b) is not repeated in Section 3–106 because it is not necessary. It is an example of an implied condition. Former Section 3–105(1)(d), (e), and (f) and the first clause of former Section 3–105(1)(c) are other examples of implied conditions. They are not repeated in Section 3–106 because they are not necessary. The law is not changed.

Section 3–106(a)(ii) and (iii) carry forward the substance of former Section 3–105(2)(a). The only change is the use of "writing" instead of "agreement" and a broadening of the language that can result in conditionality. For example, a promissory note is not an instrument defined by Section 3–104 if it contains any of the following statements: 1. "This note is subject to a contract of sale dated April 1, 1990 between the payee and maker of this note." 2. "This note is subject to a loan and security agreement dated April 1, 1990 between the payee and maker of this note." 3. "Rights and obligations of the parties with respect to this note are stated in an agreement dated April 1, 1990 between the payee and maker of this note." It is not relevant whether any condition to payment is or is not stated in the writing to which reference is made. The rationale is that the holder of a negotiable instrument should not be required to examine another document to determine rights with respect to payment. But subsection (b)(i) permits reference to a separate writing for information with respect to collateral, prepayment, or acceleration.

Many notes issued in commercial transactions are secured by collateral, are subject to acceleration in the event of default, or are subject to prepayment. A statement of rights and obligations concerning collateral, prepayment, or acceleration does not prevent the note from being an instrument if the statement is in the note itself. See Section 3–104(a)(3) and Section 3–108(b). In some cases it may be convenient not to include a statement concerning collateral, prepayment, or acceleration in the note, but rather to refer to an accompanying loan agreement, security agreement or mortgage for that statement. Subsection (b)(i) allows a reference to the appropriate writing for a statement of these rights. For example, a note would not be made conditional by the following statement: "This note is secured by a security interest in collateral described in a security agreement dated April 1, 1990 between the payee and maker of this note. Rights and obligations with respect to the collateral are [stated in] [governed by] the security agreement." The bracketed words are alternatives, either of which complies.

Subsection (b)(ii) addresses the issues covered by former Section 3–105(1)(f), (g), and (h) and Section 3–105(2)(b). Under Section 3–106(a) a promise or order is not made conditional because payment is limited to payment from a particular source or fund. This reverses the result of former Section 3–105(2)(b). There is no cogent reason why the general credit of a legal entity must be pledged to have a negotiable instrument. Market forces determine the marketability of instruments of this kind. If potential buyers don't want promises or orders that are payable only from a particular source or fund, they won't take them, but Article 3 should apply.

2.   Subsection (c) applies to traveler's checks or other instruments that may require a countersignature. Although the requirement of a countersignature is a condition to the obligation to pay, traveler's checks are treated in the commercial world as money substitutes and therefore should be governed by Article 3. The first sentence of subsection (c) allows a traveler's check to meet the definition of instrument by stating that the countersignature condition does not make it conditional for the purposes of Section 3–104. The second sentence states the effect of a failure to meet the condition. Suppose a thief steals a traveler's check and cashes it by skillfully imitating the specimen signature so that the countersignature appears to be authentic. The countersignature is for the purpose of identification of the owner of the instrument. It is not an indorsement. Subsection (c) provides that the failure of the owner to countersign does not prevent a transferee from becoming a holder. Thus, the merchant or bank that cashed the traveler's check becomes a holder when the traveler's check is taken. The forged countersignature is a defense to the obligation of the issuer to pay the instrument, and is included in defenses under Section 3–305(a)(2). These defenses may not be asserted against a holder in due course. Whether a holder has notice of the defense is a factual question. If the countersignature is a very bad forgery, there may be notice. But if the merchant or bank cashed a traveler's check and the countersignature appeared to be similar to the specimen signature, there might not be notice that the countersignature was forged. Thus, the merchant or bank could be a holder in due course.

3.   Subsection (d) concerns the effect of a statement to the effect that the rights of a holder or transferee are subject to claims and defenses that the issuer could assert against the original payee. The subsection applies only if the statement is required by statutory or administrative law. The prime example is the Federal Trade Commission Rule (16 C.F.R. Part 433) preserving consumers' claims and defenses in consumer credit sales. The intent of the FTC rule is to make it impossible for there to be a holder in due course of a note bearing the FTC legend and undoubtedly that is the result. But, under former Article 3, the legend may also have had the unintended effect of making the note conditional, thus excluding the note from former Article 3 altogether. Subsection (d) is designed to make it possible to preclude the possibility of a holder in due course without excluding the instrument from Article 3. Most of the provisions of Article 3 are not affected by the holder-in-due-course doctrine and there is no reason why Article 3 should not apply to a note bearing the FTC legend if holder-in-due-course rights are not involved. Under subsection (d) the statement does not make the note conditional. If the note otherwise meets the requirements of Section 3–104(a) it is a negotiable instrument for all purposes except that there cannot be a holder in due course of the note. No particular form of legend or statement is required by subsection (d). The form of a particular legend or statement may be determined by the other statute or administrative law. For example, the FTC legend required in a note taken by the seller in a consumer sale of goods or services is tailored to that particular transaction and therefore uses language that is somewhat different from that stated in subsection (d), but the difference in expression does not affect the essential similarity of the message conveyed. The effect of the FTC legend is to make the rights of a holder or transferee subject to claims or defenses that the issuer could assert against the original payee of the note.

§ 3–107.   Instrument Payable in Foreign Money.

Unless the instrument otherwise provides, an instrument that states the amount payable in foreign money may be paid in the foreign money or in an equivalent amount in dollars calculated by using the current bank-offered spot rate at the place of payment for the purchase of dollars on the day on which the instrument is paid.

Official Comment

The definition of instrument in Section 3–104 requires that the promise or order be payable in "money." That term is defined in Section 1–201(24) [*unrevised Article 1; see Concordance, p. 22*] and is not limited to United States dollars. Section 3–107 states than an instrument payable in foreign money may be paid in dollars if the instrument does not prohibit it. It also states a conversion rate which applies in the absence of a different conversion rate stated in the instrument. The reference in former Section 3–107(1) to instruments payable in "currency" or "current funds" has been dropped as superfluous.

§ 3–108. Payable on Demand or at Definite Time.

(a) A promise or order is "payable on demand" if it (i) states that it is payable on demand or at sight, or otherwise indicates that it is payable at the will of the holder, or (ii) does not state any time of payment.

(b) A promise or order is "payable at a definite time" if it is payable on elapse of a definite period of time after sight or acceptance or at a fixed date or dates or at a time or times readily ascertainable at the time the promise or order is issued, subject to rights of (i) prepayment, (ii) acceleration, (iii) extension at the option of the holder, or (iv) extension to a further definite time at the option of the maker or acceptor or automatically upon or after a specified act or event.

(c) If an instrument, payable at a fixed date, is also payable upon demand made before the fixed date, the instrument is payable on demand until the fixed date and, if demand for payment is not made before that date, becomes payable at a definite time on the fixed date.

Official Comment

This section is a restatement of former Section 3–108 and Section 3–109. Subsection (b) broadens former Section 3–109 somewhat by providing that a definite time includes a time readily ascertainable at the time the promise or order is issued. Subsection (b)(iii) and (iv) restates former Section 3–109(1)(d). It adopts the generally accepted rule that a clause providing for extension at the option of the holder, even without a time limit, does not affect negotiability since the holder is given only a right which the holder would have without the clause. If the extension is to be at the option of the maker or acceptor or is to be automatic, a definite time limit must be stated or the time of payment remains uncertain and the order or promise is not a negotiable instrument. If a definite time limit is stated, the effect upon certainty of time of payment is the same as if the instrument were made payable at the ultimate date with a term providing for acceleration.

§ 3–109. Payable to Bearer or to Order.

(a) A promise or order is payable to bearer if it:

(1) states that it is payable to bearer or to the order of bearer or otherwise indicates that the person in possession of the promise or order is entitled to payment;

(2) does not state a payee; or

(3) states that it is payable to or to the order of cash or otherwise indicates that it is not payable to an identified person.

(b) A promise or order that is not payable to bearer is payable to order if it is payable (i) to the order of an identified person or (ii) to an identified person or order. A promise or order that is payable to order is payable to the identified person.

(c) An instrument payable to bearer may become payable to an identified person if it is specially indorsed pursuant to Section 3–205(a). An instrument payable to an identified person may become payable to bearer if it is indorsed in blank pursuant to Section 3–205(b).

Official Comment

1. Under Section 3–104(a), a promise or order cannot be an instrument unless the instrument is payable to bearer or to order when it is issued or unless Section 3–104(c) applies. The terms "payable to bearer" and "payable to order" are defined in Section 3–109. The quoted terms are also relevant in determining how an instrument is negotiated. If the instrument is payable to bearer it can be negotiated by delivery alone. Section 3–201(b). An instrument that is payable to an identified person cannot be negotiated without the indorsement of the identified person. Section 3–201(b). An instrument payable to order is payable to an identified person. Section 3–

109(b). Thus, an instrument payable to order requires the indorsement of the person to whose order the instrument is payable.

2.   Subsection (a) states when an instrument is payable to bearer. An instrument is payable to bearer if it states that it is payable to bearer, but some instruments use ambiguous terms. For example, check forms usually have the words "to the order of" printed at the beginning of the line to be filled in for the name of the payee. If the drawer writes in the word "bearer" or "cash," the check reads "to the order of bearer" or "to the order of cash." In each case the check is payable to bearer. Sometimes the drawer will write the name of the payee "John Doe" but will add the words "or bearer." In that case the check is payable to bearer. Subsection (a). Under subsection (b), if an instrument is payable to bearer it can't be payable to order. This is different from former Section 3–110(3). An instrument that purports to be payable both to order and bearer states contradictory terms. A transferee of the instrument should be able to rely on the bearer term and acquire rights as a holder without obtaining the indorsement of the identified payee. An instrument is also payable to bearer if it does not state a payee. Instruments that do not state a payee are in most cases incomplete instruments. In some cases the drawer of a check may deliver or mail it to the person to be paid without filling in the line for the name of the payee. Under subsection (a) the check is payable to bearer when it is sent or delivered. It is also an incomplete instrument. This case is discussed in Comment 2 to Section 3–115. Subsection (a)(3) contains the words "otherwise indicates that it is not payable to an identified person." The quoted words are meant to cover uncommon cases in which an instrument indicates that it is not meant to be payable to a specific person. Such an instrument is treated like a check payable to "cash." The quoted words are not meant to apply to an instrument stating that it is payable to an identified person such as "ABC Corporation" if ABC Corporation is a nonexistent company. Although the holder of the check cannot be the nonexistent company, the instrument is not payable to bearer. Negotiation of such an instrument is governed by Section 3–404(b).

§ 3–110.   Identification of Person to Whom Instrument Is Payable.

(a)   The person to whom an instrument is initially payable is determined by the intent of the person, whether or not authorized, signing as, or in the name or behalf of, the issuer of the instrument. The instrument is payable to the person intended by the signer even if that person is identified in the instrument by a name or other identification that is not that of the intended person. If more than one person signs in the name or behalf of the issuer of an instrument and all the signers do not intend the same person as payee, the instrument is payable to any person intended by one or more of the signers.

(b)   If the signature of the issuer of an instrument is made by automated means, such as a check-writing machine, the payee of the instrument is determined by the intent of the person who supplied the name or identification of the payee, whether or not authorized to do so.

(c)   A person to whom an instrument is payable may be identified in any way, including by name, identifying number, office, or account number. For the purpose of determining the holder of an instrument, the following rules apply:

(1)   If an instrument is payable to an account and the account is identified only by number, the instrument is payable to the person to whom the account is payable. If an instrument is payable to an account identified by number and by the name of a person, the instrument is payable to the named person, whether or not that person is the owner of the account identified by number.

(2)   If an instrument is payable to:

(i)   a trust, an estate, or a person described as trustee or representative of a trust or estate, the instrument is payable to the trustee, the representative, or a successor of either, whether or not the beneficiary or estate is also named;

(ii)   a person described as agent or similar representative of a named or identified person, the instrument is payable to the represented person, the representative, or a successor of the representative;

(iii)   a fund or organization that is not a legal entity, the instrument is payable to a representative of the members of the fund or organization; or

(iv)   an office or to a person described as holding an office, the instrument is payable to the named person, the incumbent of the office, or a successor to the incumbent.

(d)   If an instrument is payable to two or more persons alternatively, it is payable to any of them and may be negotiated, discharged, or enforced by any or all of them in possession of the instrument. If an instrument is payable to two or more persons not alternatively, it is payable to all of them and may be negotiated, discharged, or enforced only by all of them. If an instrument payable to two or more persons is ambiguous as to whether it is payable to the persons alternatively, the instrument is payable to the persons alternatively.

Official Comment

1.   Section 3–110 states rules for determining the identity of the person to whom an instrument is initially payable if the instrument is payable to an identified person. This issue usually arises in a dispute over the validity of an indorsement in the name of the payee. Subsection (a) states the general rule that the person to whom an instrument is payable is determined by the intent of "the person, whether or not authorized, signing as, or in the name or behalf of, the issuer of the instrument." "Issuer" means the maker or drawer of the instrument. Section 3–105(c). If X signs a check as drawer of a check on X's account, the intent of X controls. If X, as President of Corporation, signs a check as President in behalf of Corporation as drawer, the intent of X controls. If X forges Y's signature as drawer of a check, the intent of X also controls. Under Section 3–103(a)(5), Y is referred to as the drawer of the check because the signing of Y's name identifies Y as the drawer. But since Y's signature was forged Y has no liability as drawer (Section 3–403(a)) unless some other provision of Article 3 or Article 4 makes Y liable. Since X, even though unauthorized, signed in the name of Y as issuer, the intent of X determines to whom the check is payable.

In the case of a check payable to "John Smith," since there are many people in the world named "John Smith" it is not possible to identify the payee of the check unless there is some further identification or the intention of the drawer is determined. Name alone is sufficient under subsection (a), but the intention of the drawer determines which John Smith is the person to whom the check is payable. The same issue is presented in cases of misdescriptions of the payee. The drawer intends to pay a person known to the drawer as John Smith. In fact that person's name is James Smith or John Jones or some other entirely different name. If the check identifies the payee as John Smith, it is nevertheless payable to the person intended by the drawer. That person may indorse the check in either the name John Smith or the person's correct name or in both names. Section 3–204(d). The intent of the drawer is also controlling in fictitious payee cases. Section 3–404(b). The last sentence of subsection (a) refers to rare cases in which the signature of an organization requires more than one signature and the persons signing on behalf of the organization do not all intend the same person as payee. Any person intended by a signer for the organization is the payee and an indorsement by that person is an effective indorsement.

Subsection (b) recognizes the fact that in a large number of cases there is no human signer of an instrument because the instrument, usually a check, is produced by automated means such as a check-writing machine. In that case, the relevant intent is that of the person who supplied the name of the payee. In most cases that person is an employee of the drawer, but in some cases the person could be an outsider who is committing a fraud by introducing names of payees of checks into the system that produces the checks. A check-writing machine is likely to be operated by means of a computer in which is stored information as to name and address of the payee and the amount of the check. Access to the computer may allow production of fraudulent checks without knowledge of the organization that is the issuer of the check. Section 3–404(b) is also concerned with this issue. See Case # 4 in Comment 2 to Section 3–404.

2.   Subsection (c) allows the payee to be identified in any way including the various ways stated. Subsection (c)(1) relates to instruments payable to bank accounts. In some cases the account might be identified by name and number, and the name and number might refer to different persons. For example, a check is payable to "X Corporation Account No. 12345 in Bank of Podunk." Under the last sentence of subsection (c)(1), this check is payable to X Corporation and can be negotiated by X Corporation even if Account No. 12345 is some other person's account or the check is not deposited in that account. In other cases the payee is identified by an account number and the name of the owner of the account is not stated. For example, Debtor pays Creditor by issuing a check drawn on Payor Bank. The check is payable to a bank account owned by Creditor but identified only by number. Under the first sentence of subsection (c)(1) the check is payable to Creditor and, under Section 1–201(20) [*unrevised Article 1; see Concordance, p. 22*], Creditor becomes the holder when the check is delivered. Under Section 3–201(b), further negotiation of the check requires the indorsement of Creditor. But under Section 4–205(a), if the check is taken by a depositary bank for collection, the bank may become a holder without the indorsement. Under Section 3–102(b), provisions of Article 4 prevail over those of Article 3. The depositary bank warrants that the amount of the check was credited to the payee's account.

3.   Subsection (c)(2) replaces former Section 3–117 and subsection (1)(e), (f), and (g) of former Section 3–110. This provision merely determines who can deal with an instrument as a holder. It does not determine

ownership of the instrument or its proceeds. Subsection (c)(2)(i) covers trusts and estates. If the instrument is payable to the trust or estate or to the trustee or representative of the trust or estate, the instrument is payable to the trustee or representative or any successor. Under subsection (c)(2)(ii), if the instrument states that it is payable to Doe, President of X Corporation, either Doe or X Corporation can be holder of the instrument. Subsection (c)(2)(iii) concerns informal organizations that are not legal entities such as unincorporated clubs and the like. Any representative of the members of the organization can act as holder. Subsection (c)(2)(iv) applies principally to instruments payable to public offices such as a check payable to County Tax Collector.

4.   Subsection (d) replaces former Section 3–116. An instrument payable to X or Y is governed by the first sentence of subsection (d). An instrument payable to X and Y is governed by the second sentence of subsection (d). If an instrument is payable to X or Y, either is the payee and if either is in possession that person is the holder and the person entitled to enforce the instrument. Section 3–301. If an instrument is payable to X and Y, neither X nor Y acting alone is the person to whom the instrument is payable. Neither person, acting alone, can be the holder of the instrument. The instrument is "payable to an identified person." The "identified person" is X and Y acting jointly. Section 3–109(b) and Section 1–102(5)(a) [*unrevised Article 1; see Concordance, p. 22*]. Thus, under Section 1–201(20) [*unrevised Article 1; see Concordance, p. 22*] X or Y, acting alone, cannot be the holder or the person entitled to enforce or negotiate the instrument because neither, acting alone, is the identified person stated in the instrument.

The third sentence of subsection (d) is directed to cases in which it is not clear whether an instrument is payable to multiple payees alternatively. In the case of ambiguity persons dealing with the instrument should be able to rely on the indorsement of a single payee. For example, an instrument payable to X and/or Y is treated like an instrument payable to X or Y.

§ 3–111.   Place of Payment.

Except as otherwise provided for items in Article 4, an instrument is payable at the place of payment stated in the instrument. If no place of payment is stated, an instrument is payable at the address of the drawee or maker stated in the instrument. If no address is stated, the place of payment is the place of business of the drawee or maker. If a drawee or maker has more than one place of business, the place of payment is any place of business of the drawee or maker chosen by the person entitled to enforce the instrument. If the drawee or maker has no place of business, the place of payment is the residence of the drawee or maker.

Official Comment

If an instrument is payable at a bank in the United States, Section 3–501(b)(1) states that presentment must be made at the place of payment, i.e. the bank. The place of presentment of a check is governed by Regulation CC § 229.36.

§ 3–112.   Interest.

(a)   Unless otherwise provided in the instrument, (i) an instrument is not payable with interest, and (ii) interest on an interest-bearing instrument is payable from the date of the instrument.

(b)   Interest may be stated in an instrument as a fixed or variable amount of money or it may be expressed as a fixed or variable rate or rates. The amount or rate of interest may be stated or described in the instrument in any manner and may require reference to information not contained in the instrument. If an instrument provides for interest, but the amount of interest payable cannot be ascertained from the description, interest is payable at the judgment rate in effect at the place of payment of the instrument and at the time interest first accrues.

Official Comment

1.   Under Section 3–104(a) the requirement of a "fixed amount" applies only to principal. The amount of interest payable is that described in the instrument. If the description of interest in the instrument does not allow for the amount of interest to be ascertained, interest is payable at the judgment rate. Hence, if an instrument calls for interest, the amount of interest will always be determinable. If a variable rate of interest is prescribed, the amount of interest is ascertainable by reference to the formula or index described or referred to in the instrument. The last sentence of subsection (b) replaces subsection (d) of former Section 3–118.

2. The purpose of subsection (b) is to clarify the meaning of "interest" in the introductory clause of Section 3–104(a). It is not intended to validate a provision for interest in an instrument if that provision violates other law.

§ 3–113. Date of Instrument.

(a) An instrument may be antedated or postdated. The date stated determines the time of payment if the instrument is payable at a fixed period after date. Except as provided in Section 4–401(c), an instrument payable on demand is not payable before the date of the instrument.

(b) If an instrument is undated, its date is the date of its issue or, in the case of an unissued instrument, the date it first comes into possession of a holder.

Official Comment

This section replaces former Section 3–114. Subsections (1) and (3) of former Section 3–114 are deleted as unnecessary. Section 3–113(a) is based in part on subsection (2) of former Section 3–114. The rule that a demand instrument is not payable before the date of the instrument is subject to Section 4–401(c) which allows the payor bank to pay a postdated check unless the drawer has notified the bank of the postdating pursuant to a procedure prescribed in that subsection. With respect to an undated instrument, the date is the date of issue.

§ 3–114. Contradictory Terms of Instrument.

If an instrument contains contradictory terms, typewritten terms prevail over printed terms, handwritten terms prevail over both, and words prevail over numbers.

Official Comment

Section 3–114 replaces subsections (b) and (c) of former Section 3–118.

§ 3–115. Incomplete Instrument.

(a) "Incomplete instrument" means a signed writing, whether or not issued by the signer, the contents of which show at the time of signing that it is incomplete but that the signer intended it to be completed by the addition of words or numbers.

(b) Subject to subsection (c), if an incomplete instrument is an instrument under Section 3–104, it may be enforced according to its terms if it is not completed, or according to its terms as augmented by completion. If an incomplete instrument is not an instrument under Section 3–104, but, after completion, the requirements of Section 3–104 are met, the instrument may be enforced according to its terms as augmented by completion.

(c) If words or numbers are added to an incomplete instrument without authority of the signer, there is an alteration of the incomplete instrument under Section 3–407.

(d) The burden of establishing that words or numbers were added to an incomplete instrument without authority of the signer is on the person asserting the lack of authority.

Official Comment

1. This section generally carries forward the rules set out in former Section 3–115. The term "incomplete instrument" applies both to an "instrument," i.e. a writing meeting all the requirements of Section 3–104, and to a writing intended to be an instrument that is signed but lacks some element of an instrument. The test in both cases is whether the contents show that it is incomplete and that the signer intended that additional words or numbers be added.

2. If an incomplete instrument meets the requirements of Section 3–104 and is not completed it may be enforced in accordance with its terms. Suppose, in the following two cases, that a note delivered to the payee is incomplete solely because a space on the pre-printed note form for the due date is not filled in:

Case # 1. If the incomplete instrument is never completed, the note is payable on demand. Section 3–108(a)(ii). However, if the payee and the maker agreed to a due date, the maker may have a defense under Section 3–117 if demand for payment is made before the due date agreed to by the parties.

Case # 2. If the payee completes the note by filling in the due date agreed to by the parties, the note is payable on the due date stated. However, if the due date filled in was not the date agreed to by the parties there is an alteration of the note. Section 3–407 governs the case.

Suppose Debtor pays Creditor by giving Creditor a check on which the space for the name of the payee is left blank. The check is an instrument but it is incomplete. The check is enforceable in its incomplete form and it is payable to bearer because it does not state a payee. Section 3–109(a)(2). Thus, Creditor is a holder of the check. Normally in this kind of case Creditor would simply fill in the space with Creditor's name. When that occurs the check becomes payable to the Creditor.

3.   In some cases the incomplete instrument does not meet the requirements of Section 3–104. An example is a check with the amount not filled in. The check cannot be enforced until the amount is filled in. If the payee fills in an amount authorized by the drawer the check meets the requirements of Section 3–104 and is enforceable as completed. If the payee fills in an unauthorized amount there is an alteration of the check and Section 3–407 applies.

4.   Section 3–302(a)(1) also bears on the problem of incomplete instruments. Under that section a person cannot be a holder in due course of the instrument if it is so incomplete as to call into question its validity. Subsection (d) of Section 3–115 is based on the last clause of subsection (2) of former Section 3–115.

§ 3–116.   Joint and Several Liability; Contribution.

(a)   Except as otherwise provided in the instrument, two or more persons who have the same liability on an instrument as makers, drawers, acceptors, indorsers who indorse as joint payees, or anomalous indorsers are jointly and severally liable in the capacity in which they sign.

(b)   Except as provided in Section 3–419(f) or by agreement of the affected parties, a party having joint and several liability who pays the instrument is entitled to receive from any party having the same joint and several liability contribution in accordance with applicable law.

As amended in 2002.

Official Comment

1.   Subsection (a) replaces subsection (e) of former Section 3–118. Subsection (b) states contribution rights of parties with joint and several liability by referring to applicable law. But subsection (b) is subject to Section 3–419(f). If one of the parties with joint and several liability is an accommodation party and the other is the accommodated party, Section 3–419(f) applies. Because one of the joint and several obligors may have recourse against the other joint and several obligor under subsection (b), each party that is jointly and severally liable under subsection (a) is a secondary obligor in part and a principal obligor in part, as those terms are defined in Section 3–103(a). Accordingly, Section 3–605 determines the effect of a release, an extension of time, or a modification of the obligation of one of the joint and several obligors, as well as the effect of an impairment of collateral provided by one of those obligors.

2.   Indorsers normally do not have joint and several liability. Rather, an earlier indorser has liability to a later indorser. But indorsers can have joint and several liability in two cases. If an instrument is payable to two payees jointly, both payees must indorse. The indorsement is a joint indorsement and the indorsers have joint and several liability and subsection (b) applies. The other case is that of two or more anomalous indorsers. The term is defined in Section 3–205(d). An anomalous indorsement normally indicates that the indorser signed as an accommodation party. If more than one accommodation party indorses a note as an accommodation to the maker, the indorsers have joint and several liability and subsection (b) applies.

As amended in 2002.

§ 3–117.   Other Agreements Affecting Instrument.

Subject to applicable law regarding exclusion of proof of contemporaneous or previous agreements, the obligation of a party to an instrument to pay the instrument may be modified, supplemented, or nullified by a separate agreement of the obligor and a person entitled to enforce the instrument, if the instrument is issued or the obligation is incurred in reliance on the agreement or as part of the same transaction giving rise to the agreement. To the extent an obligation is modified, supplemented, or nullified by an agreement under this section, the agreement is a defense to the obligation.

Official Comment

1.   The separate agreement might be a security agreement or mortgage or it might be an agreement that contradicts the terms of the instrument. For example, a person may be induced to sign an instrument under an agreement that the signer will not be liable on the instrument unless certain conditions are met. Suppose X requested credit from Creditor who is willing to give the credit only if an acceptable accommodation party will sign the note of X as co-maker. Y agrees to sign as co-maker on the condition that Creditor also obtain the signature of Z as co-maker. Creditor agrees and Y signs as co-maker with X. Creditor fails to obtain the signature of Z on the note. Under Sections 3–412 and 3–419(b), Y is obliged to pay the note, but Section 3–117 applies. In this case, the agreement modifies the terms of the note by stating a condition to the obligation of Y to pay the note. This case is essentially similar to a case in which a maker of a note is induced to sign the note by fraud of the holder. Although the agreement that Y not be liable on the note unless Z also signs may not have been fraudulently made, a subsequent attempt by Creditor to require Y to pay the note in violation of the agreement is a bad faith act. Section 3–117, in treating the agreement as a defense, allows Y to assert the agreement against Creditor, but the defense would not be good against a subsequent holder in due course of the note that took it without notice of the agreement. If there cannot be a holder in due course because of Section 3–106(d), a subsequent holder that took the note in good faith, for value and without knowledge of the agreement would not be able to enforce the liability of Y. This result is consistent with the risk that a holder not in due course takes with respect to fraud in inducing issuance of an instrument.

2.   The effect of merger or integration clauses to the effect that a writing is intended to be the complete and exclusive statement of the terms of the agreement or that the agreement is not subject to conditions is left to the supplementary law of the jurisdiction pursuant to Section 1–103. Thus, in the case discussed in Comment 1, whether Y is permitted to prove the condition to Y's obligation to pay the note is determined by that law. Moreover, nothing in this section is intended to validate an agreement which is fraudulent or void as against public policy, as in the case of a note given to deceive a bank examiner.

§ 3–118.   Statute of Limitations.

(a)   Except as provided in subsection (e), an action to enforce the obligation of a party to pay a note payable at a definite time must be commenced within six years after the due date or dates stated in the note or, if a due date is accelerated, within six years after the accelerated due date.

(b)   Except as provided in subsection (d) or (e), if demand for payment is made to the maker of a note payable on demand, an action to enforce the obligation of a party to pay the note must be commenced within six years after the demand. If no demand for payment is made to the maker, an action to enforce the note is barred if neither principal nor interest on the note has been paid for a continuous period of 10 years.

(c)   Except as provided in subsection (d), an action to enforce the obligation of a party to an unaccepted draft to pay the draft must be commenced within three years after dishonor of the draft or 10 years after the date of the draft, whichever period expires first.

(d)   An action to enforce the obligation of the acceptor of a certified check or the issuer of a teller's check, cashier's check, or traveler's check must be commenced within three years after demand for payment is made to the acceptor or issuer, as the case may be.

(e)   An action to enforce the obligation of a party to a certificate of deposit to pay the instrument must be commenced within six years after demand for payment is made to the maker, but if the instrument states a due date and the maker is not required to pay before that date, the six-year period begins when a demand for payment is in effect and the due date has passed.

(f)   An action to enforce the obligation of a party to pay an accepted draft, other than a certified check, must be commenced (i) within six years after the due date or dates stated in the draft or acceptance if the obligation of the acceptor is payable at a definite time, or (ii) within six years after the date of the acceptance if the obligation of the acceptor is payable on demand.

(g)   Unless governed by other law regarding claims for indemnity or contribution, an action (i) for conversion of an instrument, for money had and received, or like action based on conversion, (ii) for breach of warranty, or (iii) to enforce an obligation, duty, or right arising under this Article and not governed by this section must be commenced within three years after the [cause of action] accrues.

Official Comment

1.   Section 3–118 differs from former Section 3–122, which states when a cause of action accrues on an instrument. Section 3–118 does not define when a cause of action accrues. Accrual of a cause of action is stated in other sections of Article 3 such as those that state the various obligations of parties to an instrument. The only purpose of Section 3–118 is to define the time within which an action to enforce an obligation, duty, or right arising under Article 3 must be commenced. Section 3–118 does not attempt to state all rules with respect to a statute of limitations. For example, the circumstances under which the running of a limitations period may be tolled is left to other law pursuant to Section 1–103.

2.   The first six subsections apply to actions to enforce an obligation of any party to an instrument to pay the instrument. This changes present law in that indorsers who may become liable on an instrument after issue are subject to a period of limitations running from the same date as that of the maker or drawer. Subsections (a) and (b) apply to notes. If the note is payable at a definite time, a six-year limitations period starts at the due date of the note, subject to prior acceleration. If the note is payable on demand, there are two limitations periods. Although a note payable on demand could theoretically be called a day after it was issued, the normal expectation of the parties is that the note will remain outstanding until there is some reason to call it. If the law provides that the limitations period does not start until demand is made, the cause of action to enforce it may never be barred. On the other hand, if the limitations period starts when demand for payment may be made, i.e. at any time after the note was issued, the payee of a note on which interest or portions of principal are being paid could lose the right to enforce the note even though it was treated as a continuing obligation by the parties. Some demand notes are not enforced because the payee has forgiven the debt. This is particularly true in family and other noncommercial transactions. A demand note found after the death of the payee may be presented for payment many years after it was issued. The maker may be a relative and it may be difficult to determine whether the note represents a real or a forgiven debt. Subsection (b) is designed to bar notes that no longer represent a claim to payment and to require reasonably prompt action to enforce notes on which there is default. If a demand for payment is made to the maker, a six-year limitations period starts to run when demand is made. The second sentence of subsection (b) bars an action to enforce a demand note if no demand has been made on the note and no payment of interest or principal has been made for a continuous period of 10 years. This covers the case of a note that does not bear interest or a case in which interest due on the note has not been paid. This kind of case is likely to be a family transaction in which a failure to demand payment may indicate that the holder did not intend to enforce the obligation but neglected to destroy the note. A limitations period that bars stale claims in this kind of case is appropriate if the period is relatively long.

3.   Subsection (c) applies primarily to personal uncertified checks. Checks are payment instruments rather than credit instruments. The limitations period expires three years after the date of dishonor or 10 years after the date of the check, whichever is earlier. Teller's checks, cashier's checks, certified checks, and traveler's checks are treated differently under subsection (d) because they are commonly treated as cash equivalents. A great delay in presenting a cashier's check for payment in most cases will occur because the check was mislaid during that period. The person to whom traveler's checks are issued may hold them indefinitely as a safe form of cash for use in an emergency. There is no compelling reason for barring the claim of the owner of the cashier's check or traveler's check. Under subsection (d) the claim is never barred because the three-year limitations period does not start to run until demand for payment is made. The limitations period in subsection (d) in effect applies only to cases in which there is a dispute about the legitimacy of the claim of the person demanding payment.

4.   Subsection (e) covers certificates of deposit. The limitations period of six years doesn't start to run until the depositor demands payment. Most certificates of deposit are payable on demand even if they state a due date. The effect of a demand for payment before maturity is usually that the bank will pay, but that a penalty will be assessed against the depositor in the form of a reduction in the amount of interest that is paid. Subsection (e) also provides for cases in which the bank has no obligation to pay until the due date. In that case the limitations period doesn't start to run until there is a demand for payment in effect and the due date has passed.

5.   Subsection (f) applies to accepted drafts other than certified checks. When a draft is accepted it is in effect turned into a note of the acceptor. In almost all cases the acceptor will agree to pay at a definite time. Subsection (f) states that in that case the six-year limitations period starts to run on the due date. In the rare case in which the obligation of the acceptor is payable on demand, the six-year limitations period starts to run at the date of the acceptance.

6.   Subsection (g) covers warranty and conversion cases and other actions to enforce obligations or rights arising under Article 3. A three-year period is stated and subsection (g) follows general law in stating that the period runs from the time the cause of action accrues. Since the traditional term "cause of action" may have been

replaced in some states by "claim for relief" or some equivalent term, the words "cause of action" have been bracketed to indicate that the words may be replaced by an appropriate substitute to conform to local practice.

7.   One of the most significant differences between this Article and the Convention on International Bills of Exchange and International Promissory Notes is that the statute of limitation under the Convention generally is only four years, rather than the six years provided by this section. See Convention Article 84.

As amended in 2002.

§ 3–119.   Notice of Right to Defend Action.

In an action for breach of an obligation for which a third person is answerable over pursuant to this Article or Article 4, the defendant may give the third person notice of the litigation in a record, and the person notified may then give similar notice to any other person who is answerable over. If the notice states (i) that the person notified may come in and defend and (ii) that failure to do so will bind the person notified in an action later brought by the person giving the notice as to any determination of fact common to the two litigations, the person notified is so bound unless after seasonable receipt of the notice the person notified does come in and defend.

As amended in 2002.

Official Comment

This section is a restatement of former Section 3–803.

PART 2

NEGOTIATION, TRANSFER, AND INDORSEMENT

§ 3–201.   Negotiation.

(a)   "Negotiation" means a transfer of possession, whether voluntary or involuntary, of an instrument by a person other than the issuer to a person who thereby becomes its holder.

(b)   Except for negotiation by a remitter, if an instrument is payable to an identified person, negotiation requires transfer of possession of the instrument and its indorsement by the holder. If an instrument is payable to bearer, it may be negotiated by transfer of possession alone.

Official Comment

1.   Subsections (a) and (b) are based in part on subsection (1) of former Section 3–202. A person can become holder of an instrument when the instrument is issued to that person, or the status of holder can arise as the result of an event that occurs after issuance. "Negotiation" is the term used in Article 3 to describe this post-issuance event. Normally, negotiation occurs as the result of a voluntary transfer of possession of an instrument by a holder to another person who becomes the holder as a result of the transfer. Negotiation always requires a change in possession of the instrument because nobody can be a holder without possessing the instrument, either directly or through an agent. But in some cases the transfer of possession is involuntary and in some cases the person transferring possession is not a holder. In defining "negotiation" former Section 3–202(1) used the word "transfer," an undefined term, and "delivery," defined in Section 1–201(14) [*unrevised Article 1; see Concordance, p. 22*] to mean voluntary change of possession. Instead, subsections (a) and (b) use the term "transfer of possession" and, subsection (a) states that negotiation can occur by an involuntary transfer of possession. For example, if an instrument is payable to bearer and it is stolen by Thief or is found by Finder, Thief or Finder becomes the holder of the instrument when possession is obtained. In this case there is an involuntary transfer of possession that results in negotiation to Thief or Finder.

2.   In most cases negotiation occurs by a transfer of possession by a holder or remitter. Remitter transactions usually involve a cashier's or teller's check. For example, Buyer buys goods from Seller and pays for them with a cashier's check of Bank that Buyer buys from Bank. The check is issued by Bank when it is delivered to Buyer, regardless of whether the check is payable to Buyer or to Seller. Section 3–105(a). If the check is payable to Buyer, negotiation to Seller is done by delivery of the check to Seller after it is indorsed by Buyer. It is more common, however, that the check when issued will be payable to Seller. In that case Buyer is referred to as the "remitter." Section 3–103(a)(15). The remitter, although not a party to the check, is the owner of the check until ownership is transferred to Seller by delivery. This transfer is a negotiation because Seller becomes the holder of

the check when Seller obtains possession. In some cases Seller may have acted fraudulently in obtaining possession of the check. In those cases Buyer may be entitled to rescind the transfer to Seller because of the fraud and assert a claim of ownership to the check under Section 3–306 against Seller or a subsequent transferee of the check. Section 3–202(b) provides for rescission of negotiation, and that provision applies to rescission by a remitter as well as by a holder.

    3.   Other sections of Article 3 may modify the rule stated in the first sentence of subsection (b). See for example, Sections 3–404, 3–405 and 3–406.

§ 3–202. Negotiation Subject to Rescission.

    (a)   Negotiation is effective even if obtained (i) from an infant, a corporation exceeding its powers, or a person without capacity, (ii) by fraud, duress, or mistake, or (iii) in breach of duty or as part of an illegal transaction.

    (b)   To the extent permitted by other law, negotiation may be rescinded or may be subject to other remedies, but those remedies may not be asserted against a subsequent holder in due course or a person paying the instrument in good faith and without knowledge of facts that are a basis for rescission or other remedy.

Official Comment

    1.   This section is based on former Section 3–207. Subsection (2) of former Section 3–207 prohibited rescission of a negotiation against holders in due course. Subsection (b) of Section 3–202 extends this protection to payor banks.

    2.   Subsection (a) applies even though the lack of capacity or the illegality, is of a character which goes to the essence of the transaction and makes it entirely void. It is inherent in the character of negotiable instruments that any person in possession of an instrument which by its terms is payable to that person or to bearer is a holder and may be dealt with by anyone as a holder. The principle finds its most extreme application in the well settled rule that a holder in due course may take the instrument even from a thief and be protected against the claim of the rightful owner. The policy of subsection (a) is that any person to whom an instrument is negotiated is a holder until the instrument has been recovered from that person's possession. The remedy of a person with a claim to an instrument is to recover the instrument by replevin or otherwise; to impound it or to enjoin its enforcement, collection or negotiation; to recover its proceeds from the holder; or to intervene in any action brought by the holder against the obligor. As provided in Section 3–305(c), the claim of the claimant is not a defense to the obligor unless the claimant defends the action.

    3.   There can be no rescission or other remedy against a holder in due course or a person who pays in good faith and without notice, even though the prior negotiation may have been fraudulent or illegal in its essence and entirely void. As against any other party the claimant may have any remedy permitted by law. This section is not intended to specify what that remedy may be, or to prevent any court from imposing conditions or limitations such as prompt action or return of the consideration received. All such questions are left to the law of the particular jurisdiction. Section 3–202 gives no right that would not otherwise exist. The section is intended to mean that any remedies afforded by other law are cut off only by a holder in due course.

§ 3–203. Transfer of Instrument; Rights Acquired by Transfer.

    (a)   An instrument is transferred when it is delivered by a person other than its issuer for the purpose of giving to the person receiving delivery the right to enforce the instrument.

    (b)   Transfer of an instrument, whether or not the transfer is a negotiation, vests in the transferee any right of the transferor to enforce the instrument, including any right as a holder in due course, but the transferee cannot acquire rights of a holder in due course by a transfer, directly or indirectly, from a holder in due course if the transferee engaged in fraud or illegality affecting the instrument.

    (c)   Unless otherwise agreed, if an instrument is transferred for value and the transferee does not become a holder because of lack of indorsement by the transferor, the transferee has a specifically enforceable right to the unqualified indorsement of the transferor, but negotiation of the instrument does not occur until the indorsement is made.

(d)   If a transferor purports to transfer less than the entire instrument, negotiation of the instrument does not occur. The transferee obtains no rights under this Article and has only the rights of a partial assignee.

Official Comment

1.   Section 3–203 is based on former Section 3–201 which stated that a transferee received such rights as the transferor had. The former section was confusing because some rights of the transferor are not vested in the transferee unless the transfer is a negotiation. For example, a transferee that did not become the holder could not negotiate the instrument, a right that the transferor had. Former Section 3–201 did not define "transfer." Subsection (a) defines transfer by limiting it to cases in which possession of the instrument is delivered for the purpose of giving to the person receiving delivery the right to enforce the instrument.

Although transfer of an instrument might mean in a particular case that title to the instrument passes to the transferee, that result does not follow in all cases. The right to enforce an instrument and ownership of the instrument are two different concepts. A thief who steals a check payable to bearer becomes the holder of the check and a person entitled to enforce it, but does not become the owner of the check. If the thief transfers the check to a purchaser the transferee obtains the right to enforce the check. If the purchaser is not a holder in due course, the owner's claim to the check may be asserted against the purchaser. Ownership rights in instruments may be determined by principles of the law of property, independent of Article 3, which do not depend upon whether the instrument was transferred under Section 3–203. Moreover, a person who has an ownership right in an instrument might not be a person entitled to enforce the instrument. For example, suppose X is the owner and holder of an instrument payable to X. X sells the instrument to Y but is unable to deliver immediate possession to Y. Instead, X signs a document conveying all of X's right, title, and interest in the instrument to Y. Although the document may be effective to give Y a claim to ownership of the instrument, Y is not a person entitled to enforce the instrument until Y obtains possession of the instrument. No transfer of the instrument occurs under Section 3–203(a) until it is delivered to Y.

An instrument is a reified right to payment. The right is represented by the instrument itself. The right to payment is transferred by delivery of possession of the instrument "by a person other than its issuer for the purpose of giving to the person receiving delivery the right to enforce the instrument." The quoted phrase excludes issue of an instrument, defined in Section 3–105, and cases in which a delivery of possession is for some purpose other than transfer of the right to enforce. For example, if a check is presented for payment by delivering the check to the drawee, no transfer of the check to the drawee occurs because there is no intent to give the drawee the right to enforce the check.

2.   Subsection (b) states that transfer vests in the transferee any right of the transferor to enforce the instrument "including any right as a holder in due course." If the transferee is not a holder because the transferor did not indorse, the transferee is nevertheless a person entitled to enforce the instrument under Section 3–301 if the transferor was a holder at the time of transfer. Although the transferee is not a holder, under subsection (b) the transferee obtained the rights of the transferor as holder. Because the transferee's rights are derivative of the transferor's rights, those rights must be proved. Because the transferee is not a holder, there is no presumption under Section 3–308 that the transferee, by producing the instrument, is entitled to payment. The instrument, by its terms, is not payable to the transferee and the transferee must account for possession of the unindorsed instrument by proving the transaction through which the transferee acquired it. Proof of a transfer to the transferee by a holder is proof that the transferee has acquired the rights of a holder. At that point the transferee is entitled to the presumption under Section 3–308.

Under subsection (b) a holder in due course that transfers an instrument transfers those rights as a holder in due course to the purchaser. The policy is to assure the holder in due course a free market for the instrument. There is one exception to this rule stated in the concluding clause of subsection (b). A person who is party to fraud or illegality affecting the instrument is not permitted to wash the instrument clean by passing it into the hands of a holder in due course and then repurchasing it.

3.   Subsection (c) applies only to a transfer for value. It applies only if the instrument is payable to order or specially indorsed to the transferor. The transferee acquires, in the absence of a contrary agreement, the specifically enforceable right to the indorsement of the transferor. Unless otherwise agreed, it is a right to the general indorsement of the transferor with full liability as indorser, rather than to an indorsement without recourse. The question may arise if the transferee has paid in advance and the indorsement is omitted fraudulently or through oversight. A transferor who is willing to indorse only without recourse or unwilling to indorse at all should make those intentions clear before transfer. The agreement of the transferee to take less than an unqualified indorsement need not be an express one, and the understanding may be implied from conduct, from

301

past practice, or from the circumstances of the transaction. Subsection (c) provides that there is no negotiation of the instrument until the indorsement by the transferor is made. Until that time the transferee does not become a holder, and if earlier notice of a defense or claim is received, the transferee does not qualify as a holder in due course under Section 3–302.

4.   The operation of Section 3–203 is illustrated by the following cases. In each case Payee, by fraud, induced Maker to issue a note to Payee. The fraud is a defense to the obligation of Maker to pay the note under Section 3–305(a)(2).

Case # 1. Payee negotiated the note to X who took as a holder in due course. After the instrument became overdue X negotiated the note to Y who had notice of the fraud. Y succeeds to X's rights as a holder in due course and takes free of Maker's defense of fraud.

Case # 2. Payee negotiated the note to X who took as a holder in due course. Payee then repurchased the note from X. Payee does not succeed to X's rights as a holder in due course and is subject to Maker's defense of fraud.

Case # 3. Payee negotiated the note to X who took as a holder in due course. X sold the note to Purchaser who received possession. The note, however, was indorsed to X and X failed to indorse it. Purchaser is a person entitled to enforce the instrument under Section 3–301 and succeeds to the rights of X as holder in due course. Purchaser is not a holder, however, and under Section 3–308 Purchaser will have to prove the transaction with X under which the rights of X as holder in due course were acquired.

Case # 4. Payee sold the note to Purchaser who took for value, in good faith and without notice of the defense of Maker. Purchaser received possession of the note but Payee neglected to indorse it. Purchaser became a person entitled to enforce the instrument but did not become the holder because of the missing indorsement. If Purchaser received notice of the defense of Maker before obtaining the indorsement of Payee, Purchaser cannot become a holder in due course because at the time notice was received the note had not been negotiated to Purchaser. If indorsement by Payee was made after Purchaser received notice, Purchaser had notice of the defense when it became the holder.

5.   Subsection (d) restates former Section 3–202(3). The cause of action on an instrument cannot be split. Any indorsement which purports to convey to any party less than the entire amount of the instrument is not effective for negotiation. This is true of either "Pay A one-half," or "Pay A two-thirds and B one-third." Neither A nor B becomes a holder. On the other hand an indorsement reading merely "Pay A and B" is effective, since it transfers the entire cause of action to A and B as tenants in common. An indorsement purporting to convey less than the entire instrument does, however, operate as a partial assignment of the cause of action. Subsection (d) makes no attempt to state the legal effect of such an assignment, which is left to other law. A partial assignee of an instrument has rights only to the extent the applicable law gives rights, either at law or in equity, to a partial assignee.

6.   The rules for transferring instruments set out in this section are similar to the rules in Article 13 of the Convention on International Bills of Exchange and International Promissory Notes.

As amended in 2002.

§ 3–204.   Indorsement.

(a)   "Indorsement" means a signature, other than that of a signer as maker, drawer, or acceptor, that alone or accompanied by other words is made on an instrument for the purpose of (i) negotiating the instrument, (ii) restricting payment of the instrument, or (iii) incurring indorser's liability on the instrument, but regardless of the intent of the signer, a signature and its accompanying words is an indorsement unless the accompanying words, terms of the instrument, place of the signature, or other circumstances unambiguously indicate that the signature was made for a purpose other than indorsement. For the purpose of determining whether a signature is made on an instrument, a paper affixed to the instrument is a part of the instrument.

(b)   "Indorser" means a person who makes an indorsement.

(c)   For the purpose of determining whether the transferee of an instrument is a holder, an indorsement that transfers a security interest in the instrument is effective as an unqualified indorsement of the instrument.

(d)   If an instrument is payable to a holder under a name that is not the name of the holder, indorsement may be made by the holder in the name stated in the instrument or in the holder's name or both, but signature in both names may be required by a person paying or taking the instrument for value or collection.

Official Comment

1.   Subsection (a) is a definition of "indorsement," a term which was not defined in former Article 3. Indorsement is defined in terms of the purpose of the signature. If a blank or special indorsement is made to give rights as a holder to a transferee the indorsement is made for the purpose of negotiating the instrument. Subsection (a)(i). If the holder of a check has an account in the drawee bank and wants to be sure that payment of the check will be made by credit to the holder's account, the holder can indorse the check by signing the holder's name with the accompanying words "for deposit only" before presenting the check for payment to the drawee bank. In that case the purpose of the quoted words is to restrict payment of the instrument. Subsection (a)(ii). If X wants to guarantee payment of a note signed by Y as maker, X can do so by signing X's name to the back of the note as an indorsement. This indorsement is known as an anomalous indorsement (Section 3–205(d)) and is made for the purpose of incurring indorser's liability on the note. Subsection (a)(iii). In some cases an indorsement may serve more than one purpose. For example, if the holder of a check deposits it to the holder's account in a depositary bank for collection and indorses the check by signing the holder's name with the accompanying words "for deposit only" the purpose of the indorsement is both to negotiate the check to the depositary bank and to restrict payment of the check.

The "but" clause of the first sentence of subsection (a) elaborates on former Section 3–402. In some cases it may not be clear whether a signature was meant to be that of an indorser, a party to the instrument in some other capacity such as drawer, maker or acceptor, or a person who was not signing as a party. The general rule is that a signature is an indorsement if the instrument does not indicate an unambiguous intent of the signer not to sign as an indorser. Intent may be determined by words accompanying the signature, the place of signature, or other circumstances. For example, suppose a depositary bank gives cash for a check properly indorsed by the payee. The bank requires the payee's employee to sign the back of the check as evidence that the employee received the cash. If the signature consists only of the initials of the employee it is not reasonable to assume that it was meant to be an indorsement. If there was a full signature but accompanying words indicated that it was meant as a receipt for the cash given for the check, it is not an indorsement. If the signature is not qualified in any way and appears in the place normally used for indorsements, it may be an indorsement even though the signer intended the signature to be a receipt. To take another example, suppose the drawee of a draft signs the draft on the back in the space usually used for indorsements. No words accompany the signature. Since the drawee has no reason to sign a draft unless the intent is to accept the draft, the signature is effective as an acceptance. Custom and usage may be used to determine intent. For example, by long-established custom and usage, a signature in the lower right hand corner of an instrument indicates an intent to sign as the maker of a note or the drawer of a draft. Any similar clear indication of an intent to sign in some other capacity or for some other purpose may establish that a signature is not an indorsement. For example, if the owner of a traveler's check countersigns the check in the process of negotiating it, the countersignature is not an indorsement. The countersignature is a condition to the issuer's obligation to pay and its purpose is to provide a means of verifying the identify [should be "identity"] of the person negotiating the traveler's check by allowing comparison of the specimen signature and the countersignature. The countersignature is not necessary for negotiation and the signer does not incur indorser's liability. See Comment 2 to Section 3–106.

The last sentence of subsection (a) is based on subsection (2) of former Section 3–202. An indorsement on an allonge is valid even though there is sufficient space on the instrument for an indorsement.

2.   Assume that Payee indorses a note to Creditor as security for a debt. Under subsection (b) of Section 3–203 Creditor takes Payee's rights to enforce or transfer the instrument subject to the limitations imposed by Article 9. Subsection (c) of Section 3–204 makes clear that Payee's indorsement to Creditor, even though it mentions creation of a security interest, is an unqualified indorsement that gives to Creditor the right to enforce the note as its holder.

3.   Subsection (d) is a restatement of former Section 3–203. Section 3–110(a) states that an instrument is payable to the person intended by the person signing as or in the name or behalf of the issuer even if that person is identified by a name that is not the true name of the person. In some cases the name used in the instrument is a misspelling of the correct name and in some cases the two names may be entirely different. The payee may indorse in the name used in the instrument, in the payee's correct name, or in both. In each case the indorsement is effective. But because an indorsement in a name different from that used in the instrument may raise a question about its validity and an indorsement in a name that is not the correct name of the payee may raise a problem of

identifying the indorser, the accepted commercial practice is to indorse in both names. Subsection (d) allows a person paying or taking the instrument for value or collection to require indorsement in both names.

§ 3–205.   Special Indorsement; Blank Indorsement; Anomalous Indorsement.

(a)   If an indorsement is made by the holder of an instrument, whether payable to an identified person or payable to bearer, and the indorsement identifies a person to whom it makes the instrument payable, it is a "special indorsement." When specially indorsed, an instrument becomes payable to the identified person and may be negotiated only by the indorsement of that person. The principles stated in Section 3–110 apply to special indorsements.

(b)   If an indorsement is made by the holder of an instrument and it is not a special indorsement, it is a "blank indorsement." When indorsed in blank, an instrument becomes payable to bearer and may be negotiated by transfer of possession alone until specially indorsed.

(c)   The holder may convert a blank indorsement that consists only of a signature into a special indorsement by writing, above the signature of the indorser, words identifying the person to whom the instrument is made payable.

(d)   "Anomalous indorsement" means an indorsement made by a person who is not the holder of the instrument. An anomalous indorsement does not affect the manner in which the instrument may be negotiated.

Official Comment

1.   Subsection (a) is based on subsection (1) of former Section 3–204. It states the test of a special indorsement to be whether the indorsement identifies a person to whom the instrument is payable. Section 3–110 states rules for identifying the payee of an instrument. Section 3–205(a) incorporates the principles stated in Section 3–110 in identifying an indorsee. The language of Section 3–110 refers to language used by the issuer of the instrument. When that section is used with respect to an indorsement, Section 3–110 must be read as referring to the language used by the indorser.

2.   Subsection (b) is based on subsection (2) of former Section 3–204. An indorsement made by the holder is either a special or blank indorsement. If the indorsement is made by a holder and is not a special indorsement, it is a blank indorsement. For example, the holder of an instrument, intending to make a special indorsement, writes the words "Pay to the order of" without completing the indorsement by writing the name of the indorsee. The holder's signature appears under the quoted words. The indorsement is not a special indorsement because it does not identify a person to whom it makes the instrument payable. Since it is not a special indorsement it is a blank indorsement and the instrument is payable to bearer. The result is analogous to that of a check in which the name of the payee is left blank by the drawer. In that case the check is payable to bearer. See the last paragraphs of Comment 2 to Section 3–115.

A blank indorsement is usually the signature of the indorser on the back of the instrument without other words. Subsection (c) is based on subsection (3) of former Section 3–204. A "restrictive indorsement" described in Section 3–206 can be either a blank indorsement or a special indorsement. "Pay to T, in trust for B" is a restrictive indorsement. It is also a special indorsement because it identifies T as the person to whom the instrument is payable. "For deposit only" followed by the signature of the payee of a check is a restrictive indorsement. It is also a blank indorsement because it does not identify the person to whom the instrument is payable.

3.   The only effect of an "anomalous indorsement," defined in subsection (d), is to make the signer liable on the instrument as an indorser. Such an indorsement is normally made by an accommodation party. Section 3–419.

4.   Articles 14 and 16 of the Convention on International Bills of Exchange and International Promissory Notes includes similar rules for blank and special indorsements.

As amended in 2002.

§ 3–206.   Restrictive Indorsement.

(a)   An indorsement limiting payment to a particular person or otherwise prohibiting further transfer or negotiation of the instrument is not effective to prevent further transfer or negotiation of the instrument.

(b)   An indorsement stating a condition to the right of the indorsee to receive payment does not affect the right of the indorsee to enforce the instrument. A person paying the instrument or taking it for value or collection may disregard the condition, and the rights and liabilities of that person are not affected by whether the condition has been fulfilled.

(c)   If an instrument bears an indorsement (i) described in Section 4–201(b), or (ii) in blank or to a particular bank using the words "for deposit," "for collection," or other words indicating a purpose of having the instrument collected by a bank for the indorser or for a particular account, the following rules apply:

(1)   A person, other than a bank, who purchases the instrument when so indorsed converts the instrument unless the amount paid for the instrument is received by the indorser or applied consistently with the indorsement.

(2)   A depositary bank that purchases the instrument or takes it for collection when so indorsed converts the instrument unless the amount paid by the bank with respect to the instrument is received by the indorser or applied consistently with the indorsement.

(3)   A payor bank that is also the depositary bank or that takes the instrument for immediate payment over the counter from a person other than a collecting bank converts the instrument unless the proceeds of the instrument are received by the indorser or applied consistently with the indorsement.

(4)   Except as otherwise provided in paragraph (3), a payor bank or intermediary bank may disregard the indorsement and is not liable if the proceeds of the instrument are not received by the indorser or applied consistently with the indorsement.

(d)   Except for an indorsement covered by subsection (c), if an instrument bears an indorsement using words to the effect that payment is to be made to the indorsee as agent, trustee, or other fiduciary for the benefit of the indorser or another person, the following rules apply:

(1)   Unless there is notice of breach of fiduciary duty as provided in Section 3–307, a person who purchases the instrument from the indorsee or takes the instrument from the indorsee for collection or payment may pay the proceeds of payment or the value given for the instrument to the indorsee without regard to whether the indorsee violates a fiduciary duty to the indorser.

(2)   A subsequent transferee of the instrument or person who pays the instrument is neither given notice nor otherwise affected by the restriction in the indorsement unless the transferee or payor knows that the fiduciary dealt with the instrument or its proceeds in breach of fiduciary duty.

(e)   The presence on an instrument of an indorsement to which this section applies does not prevent a purchaser of the instrument from becoming a holder in due course of the instrument unless the purchaser is a converter under subsection (c) or has notice or knowledge of breach of fiduciary duty as stated in subsection (d).

(f)   In an action to enforce the obligation of a party to pay the instrument, the obligor has a defense if payment would violate an indorsement to which this section applies and the payment is not permitted by this section.

Official Comment

1.   This section replaces former Sections 3–205 and 3–206 and clarifies the law of restrictive indorsements.

2.   Subsection (a) provides that an indorsement that purports to limit further transfer or negotiation is ineffective to prevent further transfer or negotiation. If a payee indorses "Pay A only," A may negotiate the instrument to subsequent holders who may ignore the restriction on the indorsement. Subsection (b) provides that an indorsement that states a condition to the right of a holder to receive payment is ineffective to condition payment. Thus if a payee indorses "Pay A if A ships goods complying with our contract," the right of A to enforce the instrument is not affected by the condition. In the case of a note, the obligation of the maker to pay A is not affected by the indorsement. In the case of a check, the drawee can pay A without regard to the condition, and if the check is dishonored the drawer is liable to pay A. If the check was negotiated by the payee to A in return for a promise to perform a contract and the promise was not kept, the payee would have a defense or counterclaim against A if the check were dishonored and A sued the payee as indorser, but the payee would have that defense or counterclaim whether or not the condition to the right of A was expressed in the indorsement. Former Section 3–206 treated a conditional indorsement like indorsements for deposit or collection. In revised Article 3, Section

3–206(b) rejects that approach and makes the conditional indorsement ineffective with respect to parties other than the indorser and indorsee. Since the indorsements referred to in subsections (a) and (b) are not effective as restrictive indorsements, they are no longer described as restrictive indorsements.

3.　　　The great majority of restrictive indorsements are those that fall within subsection (c) which continues previous law. The depositary bank or the payor bank, if it takes the check for immediate payment over the counter, must act consistently with the indorsement, but an intermediary bank or payor bank that takes the check from a collecting bank is not affected by the indorsement. Any other person is also bound by the indorsement. For example, suppose a check is payable to X, who indorses in blank but writes above the signature the words "For deposit only." The check is stolen and is cashed at a grocery store by the thief. The grocery store indorses the check and deposits it in Depositary Bank. The account of the grocery store is credited and the check is forwarded to Payor Bank which pays the check. Under subsection (c), the grocery store and Depositary Bank are converters of the check because X did not receive the amount paid for the check. Payor Bank and any intermediary bank in the collection process are not liable to X. This Article does not displace the law of waiver as it may apply to restrictive indorsements. The circumstances under which a restrictive indorsement may be waived by the person who made it is not determined by this Article.

4.　　　Subsection (d) replaces subsection (4) of former Section 3–206. Suppose Payee indorses a check "Pay to T in trust for B." T indorses in blank and delivers it to (a) Holder for value; (b) Depositary Bank for collection; or (c) Payor Bank for payment. In each case these takers can safely pay T so long as they have no notice under Section 3–307 of any breach of fiduciary duty that T may be committing. For example, under subsection (b) of Section 3–307 these takers have notice of a breach of trust if the check was taken in any transaction known by the taker to be for T's personal benefit. Subsequent transferees of the check from Holder or Depositary Bank are not affected by the restriction unless they have knowledge that T dealt with the check in breach of trust.

5.　　　Subsection (f) allows a restrictive indorsement to be used as a defense by a person obliged to pay the instrument if that person would be liable for paying in violation of the indorsement.

§ 3–207.　　Reacquisition.

Reacquisition of an instrument occurs if it is transferred to a former holder, by negotiation or otherwise. A former holder who reacquires the instrument may cancel indorsements made after the reacquirer first became a holder of the instrument. If the cancellation causes the instrument to be payable to the reacquirer or to bearer, the reacquirer may negotiate the instrument. An indorser whose indorsement is canceled is discharged, and the discharge is effective against any subsequent holder.

Official Comment

Section 3–207 restates former Section 3–208. Reacquisition refers to cases in which a former holder reacquires the instrument either by negotiation from the present holder or by a transfer other than negotiation. If the reacquisition is by negotiation, the former holder reacquires the status of holder. Although Section 3–207 allows the holder to cancel all indorsements made after the holder first acquired holder status, cancellation is not necessary. Status of holder is not affected whether or not cancellation is made. But if the reacquisition is not the result of negotiation the former holder can obtain holder status only by striking the former holder's indorsement and any subsequent indorsements. The latter case is an exception to the general rule that if an instrument is payable to an identified person, the indorsement of that person is necessary to allow a subsequent transferee to obtain the status of holder. Reacquisition without indorsement by the person to whom the instrument is payable is illustrated by two examples:

Case # 1. X, a former holder, buys the instrument from Y, the present holder. Y delivers the instrument to X but fails to indorse it. Negotiation does not occur because the transfer of possession did not result in X's becoming holder. Section 3–201(a). The instrument by its terms is payable to Y, not to X. But X can obtain the status of holder by striking X's indorsement and all subsequent indorsements. When these indorsements are struck, the instrument by its terms is payable either to X or to bearer, depending upon how X originally became holder. In either case X becomes holder. Section 1–201(20) [unrevised Article 1; see Concordance, p. 22].

Case # 2. X, the holder of an instrument payable to X, negotiates it to Y by special indorsement. The negotiation is part of an underlying transaction between X and Y. The underlying transaction is rescinded by agreement of X and Y, and Y returns the instrument without Y's indorsement. The analysis is the same as that in Case # 1. X can obtain holder status by cancelling X's indorsement to Y.

In Case # 1 and Case # 2, X acquired ownership of the instrument after reacquisition, but X's title was clouded because the instrument by its terms was not payable to X. Normally, X can remedy the problem by obtaining Y's indorsement, but in some cases X may not be able to conveniently obtain that indorsement. Section 3–207 is a rule of convenience which relieves X of the burden of obtaining an indorsement that serves no substantive purpose. The effect of cancellation of any indorsement under Section 3–207 is to nullify it. Thus, the person whose indorsement is canceled is relieved of indorser's liability. Since cancellation is notice of discharge, discharge is effective even with respect to the rights of a holder in due course. Sections 3–601 and 3–604.

PART 3

ENFORCEMENT OF INSTRUMENTS

§ 3–301. Person Entitled to Enforce Instrument.

"Person entitled to enforce" an instrument means (i) the holder of the instrument, (ii) a nonholder in possession of the instrument who has the rights of a holder, or (iii) a person not in possession of the instrument who is entitled to enforce the instrument pursuant to Section 3–309 or 3–418(d). A person may be a person entitled to enforce the instrument even though the person is not the owner of the instrument or is in wrongful possession of the instrument.

Official Comment

This section replaces former Section 3–301 that stated the rights of a holder. The rights stated in former Section 3–301 to transfer, negotiate, enforce, or discharge an instrument are stated in other sections of Article 3. In revised Article 3, Section 3–301 defines "person entitled to enforce" an instrument. The definition recognizes that enforcement is not limited to holders. The quoted phrase includes a person enforcing a lost or stolen instrument. Section 3–309. It also includes a person in possession of an instrument who is not a holder. A nonholder in possession of an instrument includes a person that acquired rights of a holder by subrogation or under Section 3–203(a). It also includes both a remitter that has received an instrument from the issuer but has not yet transferred or negotiated the instrument to another person and also any other person who under applicable law is a successor to the holder or otherwise acquires the holder's rights.

As amended in 2002.

§ 3–302. Holder in Due Course.

(a) Subject to subsection (c) and Section 3–106(d), "holder in due course" means the holder of an instrument if:

(1) the instrument when issued or negotiated to the holder does not bear such apparent evidence of forgery or alteration or is not otherwise so irregular or incomplete as to call into question its authenticity; and

(2) the holder took the instrument (i) for value, (ii) in good faith, (iii) without notice that the instrument is overdue or has been dishonored or that there is an uncured default with respect to payment of another instrument issued as part of the same series, (iv) without notice that the instrument contains an unauthorized signature or has been altered, (v) without notice of any claim to the instrument described in Section 3–306, and (vi) without notice that any party has a defense or claim in recoupment described in Section 3–305(a).

(b) Notice of discharge of a party, other than discharge in an insolvency proceeding, is not notice of a defense under subsection (a), but discharge is effective against a person who became a holder in due course with notice of the discharge. Public filing or recording of a document does not of itself constitute notice of a defense, claim in recoupment, or claim to the instrument.

(c) Except to the extent a transferor or predecessor in interest has rights as a holder in due course, a person does not acquire rights of a holder in due course of an instrument taken (i) by legal process or by purchase in an execution, bankruptcy, or creditor's sale or similar proceeding, (ii) by purchase as part of a bulk transaction not in ordinary course of business of the transferor, or (iii) as the successor in interest to an estate or other organization.

(d) If, under Section 3–303(a)(1), the promise of performance that is the consideration for an instrument has been partially performed, the holder may assert rights as a holder in due course of the instrument only to the fraction of the amount payable under the instrument equal to the value of the partial performance divided by the value of the promised performance.

(e) If (i) the person entitled to enforce an instrument has only a security interest in the instrument and (ii) the person obliged to pay the instrument has a defense, claim in recoupment, or claim to the instrument that may be asserted against the person who granted the security interest, the person entitled to enforce the instrument may assert rights as a holder in due course only to an amount payable under the instrument which, at the time of enforcement of the instrument, does not exceed the amount of the unpaid obligation secured.

(f) To be effective, notice must be received at a time and in a manner that gives a reasonable opportunity to act on it.

(g) This section is subject to any law limiting status as a holder in due course in particular classes of transactions.

Official Comment

1. Subsection (a)(1) is a return to the N.I.L. rule that the taker of an irregular or incomplete instrument is not a person the law should protect against defenses of the obligor or claims of prior owners. This reflects a policy choice against extending the holder in due course doctrine to an instrument that is so incomplete or irregular "as to call into question its authenticity." The term "authenticity" is used to make it clear that the irregularity or incompleteness must indicate that the instrument may not be what it purports to be. Persons who purchase or pay such instruments should do so at their own risk. Under subsection (1) of former Section 3–304, irregularity or incompleteness gave a purchaser notice of a claim or defense. But it was not clear from that provision whether the claim or defense had to be related to the irregularity or incomplete aspect of the instrument. This ambiguity is not present in subsection (a)(1).

2. Subsection (a)(2) restates subsection (1) of former Section 3–302. Section 3–305(a) makes a distinction between defenses to the obligation to pay an instrument and claims in recoupment by the maker or drawer that may be asserted to reduce the amount payable on the instrument. Because of this distinction, which was not made in former Article 3, the reference in subsection (a)(2)(vi) is to both a defense and a claim in recoupment. Notice of forgery or alteration is stated separately because forgery and alteration are not technically defenses under subsection (a) of Section 3–305.

3. Discharge is also separately treated in the first sentence of subsection (b). Except for discharge in an insolvency proceeding, which is specifically stated to be a real defense in Section 3–305(a)(1), discharge is not expressed in Article 3 as a defense and is not included in Section 3–305(a)(2). Discharge is effective against anybody except a person having rights of a holder in due course who took the instrument without notice of the discharge. Notice of discharge does not disqualify a person from becoming a holder in due course. For example, a check certified after it is negotiated by the payee may subsequently be negotiated to a holder. If the holder had notice that the certification occurred after negotiation by the payee, the holder necessarily had notice of the discharge of the payee as indorser. Section 3–415(d). Notice of that discharge does not prevent the holder from becoming a holder in due course, but the discharge is effective against the holder. Section 3–601(b). Notice of a defense under Section 3–305(a)(1) of a maker, drawer or acceptor based on a bankruptcy discharge is different. There is no reason to give holder in due course status to a person with notice of that defense. The second sentence of subsection (b) is from former Section 3–304(5).

4. Professor Britton in his treatise *Bills and Notes* 309 (1961) stated: "A substantial number of decisions before the [N.I.L.] indicates that at common law there was nothing in the position of the payee as such which made it impossible for him to be a holder in due course." The courts were divided, however, about whether the payee of an instrument could be a holder in due course under the N.I.L. Some courts read N.I.L. § 52(4) to mean that a person could be a holder in due course only if the instrument was "negotiated" to that person. N.I.L. § 30 stated that "an instrument is negotiated when it is transferred from one person to another in such manner as to constitute the transferee the holder thereof." Normally, an instrument is "issued" to the payee; it is not transferred to the payee. N.I.L. § 191 defined "issue" as the "first delivery of the instrument . . . to a person who takes it as a holder." Thus, some courts concluded that the payee never could be a holder in due course. Other courts concluded that there was no evidence that the N.I.L. was intended to change the common law rule that the payee could be a holder in due course. Professor Britton states on p. 318: "The typical situations which raise the [issue] are those where the defense of a maker is interposed because of fraud by a [maker who is] principal debtor . . . against a surety co-

maker, or where the defense of fraud by a purchasing remitter is interposed by the drawer of the instrument against the good faith purchasing payee."

Former Section 3–302(2) stated: "A payee may be a holder in due course." This provision was intended to resolve the split of authority under the N.I.L. It made clear that there was no intent to change the common-law rule that allowed a payee to become a holder in due course. See Comment 2 to former Section 3–302. But there was no need to put subsection (2) in former Section 3–302 because the split in authority under the N.I.L. was caused by the particular wording of N.I.L. § 52(4). The troublesome language in that section was not repeated in former Article 3 nor is it repeated in revised Article 3. Former Section 3–302(2) has been omitted in revised Article 3 because it is surplusage and may be misleading. The payee of an instrument can be a holder in due course, but use of the holder-in-due-course doctrine by the payee of an instrument is not the normal situation.

The primary importance of the concept of holder in due course is with respect to assertion of defenses or claims in recoupment (Section 3–305) and of claims to the instrument (Section 3–306). The holder-in-due-course doctrine assumes the following case as typical. Obligor issues a note or check to Obligee. Obligor is the maker of the note or drawer of the check. Obligee is the payee. Obligor has some defense to Obligor's obligation to pay the instrument. For example, Obligor issued the instrument for goods that Obligee promised to deliver. Obligee never delivered the goods. The failure of Obligee to deliver the goods is a defense. Section 3–303(b). Although Obligor has a defense against Obligee, if the instrument is negotiated to Holder and the requirements of subsection (a) are met, Holder may enforce the instrument against Obligor free of the defense. Section 3–305(b). In the typical case the holder in due course is not the payee of the instrument. Rather, the holder in due course is an immediate or remote transferee of the payee. If Obligor in our example is the only obligor on the check or note, the holder-in-due-course doctrine is irrelevant in determining rights between Obligor and Obligee with respect to the instrument.

But in a small percentage of cases it is appropriate to allow the payee of an instrument to assert rights as a holder in due course. The cases are like those referred to in the quotation from Professor Britton referred to above, or other cases in which conduct of some third party is the basis of the defense of the issuer of the instrument. The following are examples:

Case # 1. Buyer pays for goods bought from Seller by giving to Seller a cashier's check bought from Bank. Bank has a defense to its obligation to pay the check because Buyer bought the check from Bank with a check known to be drawn on an account with insufficient funds to cover the check. If Bank issued the check to Buyer as payee and Buyer indorsed it over to Seller, it is clear that Seller can be a holder in due course taking free of the defense if Seller had no notice of the defense. Seller is a transferee of the check. There is no good reason why Seller's position should be any different if Bank drew the check to the order of Seller as payee. In that case, when Buyer took delivery of the check from Bank, Buyer became the owner of the check even though Buyer was not the holder. Buyer was a remitter. Section 3–103(a)(15). At that point nobody was the holder. When Buyer delivered the check to Seller, ownership of the check was transferred to Seller who also became the holder. This is a negotiation. Section 3–201. The rights of Seller should not be affected by the fact that in one case the negotiation to Seller was by a holder and in the other case the negotiation was by a remitter. Moreover, it should be irrelevant whether Bank delivered the check to Buyer and Buyer delivered it to Seller or whether Bank delivered it directly to Seller. In either case Seller can be a holder in due course that takes free of Bank's defense.

Case # 2. X fraudulently induces Y to join X in a spurious venture to purchase a business. The purchase is to be financed by a bank loan for part of the price. Bank lends money to X and Y by deposit in a joint account of X and Y who sign a note payable to Bank for the amount of the loan. X then withdraws the money from the joint account and absconds. Bank acted in good faith and without notice of the fraud of X against Y. Bank is payee of the note executed by Y, but its right to enforce the note against Y should not be affected by the fact that Y was induced to execute the note by the fraud of X. Bank can be a holder in due course that takes free of the defense of Y. Case # 2 is similar to Case # 1. In each case the payee of the instrument has given value to the person committing the fraud in exchange for the obligation of the person against whom the fraud was committed. In each case the payee was not party to the fraud and had no notice of it.

Suppose in Case # 2 that the note does not meet the requirements of Section 3–104(a) and thus is not a negotiable instrument covered by Article 3. In that case, Bank cannot be a holder in due course but the result should be the same. Bank's rights are determined by general principles of contract law. Restatement Second, Contracts § 164(2) governs the case. If Y is induced to enter into a contract with Bank by a fraudulent misrepresentation by X, the contract is voidable by Y unless Bank "in good faith and without reason to know of the misrepresentation either gives value or relies materially on the transaction." Comment e to § 164(2) states:

"This is the same principle that protects an innocent person who purchases goods or commercial paper in good faith, without notice and for value from one who obtained them from the original owner by a misrepresentation. See Uniform Commercial Code §§ 2–403(1), 3–305. In the cases that fall within [§ 164(2)], however, the innocent person deals directly with the recipient of the misrepresentation, which is made by one not a party to the contract."

The same result follows in Case # 2 if Y had been induced to sign the note as an accommodation party (Section 3–419). If Y signs as co-maker of a note for the benefit of X, Y is a surety with respect to the obligation of X to pay the note but is liable as maker of the note to pay Bank. Section 3–419(b). If Bank is a holder in due course, the fraud of X cannot be asserted against Bank under Section 3–305(b). But the result is the same without resort to holder-in-due-course doctrine. If the note is not a negotiable instrument governed by Article 3, general rules of suretyship apply. Restatement, Security § 119 states that the surety (Y) cannot assert a defense against the creditor (Bank) based on the fraud of the principal (X) if the creditor "without knowledge of the fraud . . . extended credit to the principal on the security of the surety's promise . . . ." The underlying principle of § 119 is the same as that of § 164(2) of Restatement Second, Contracts.

Case # 3. Corporation draws a check payable to Bank. The check is given to an officer of Corporation who is instructed to deliver it to Bank in payment of a debt owed by Corporation to Bank. Instead, the officer, intending to defraud Corporation, delivers the check to Bank in payment of the officer's personal debt, or the check is delivered to Bank for deposit to the officer's personal account. If Bank obtains payment of the check, Bank has received funds of Corporation which have been used for the personal benefit of the officer. Corporation in this case will assert a claim to the proceeds of the check against Bank. If Bank was a holder in due course of the check it took the check free of Corporation's claim. Section 3–306. The issue in this case is whether Bank had notice of the claim when it took the check. If Bank knew that the officer was a fiduciary with respect to the check, the issue is governed by Section 3–307.

Case # 4. Employer, who owed money to X, signed a blank check and delivered it to Secretary with instructions to complete the check by typing in X's name and the amount owed to X. Secretary fraudulently completed the check by typing in the name of Y, a creditor to whom Secretary owed money. Secretary then delivered the check to Y in payment of Secretary's debt. Y obtained payment of the check. This case is similar to Case # 3. Since Secretary was authorized to complete the check, Employer is bound by Secretary's act in making the check payable to Y. The drawee bank properly paid the check. Y received funds of Employer which were used for the personal benefit of Secretary. Employer asserts a claim to these funds against Y. If Y is a holder in due course, Y takes free of the claim. Whether Y is a holder in due course depends upon whether Y had notice of Employer's claim.

5. Subsection (c) is based on former Section 3–302(3). Like former Section 3–302(3), subsection (c) is intended to state existing case law. It covers a few situations in which the purchaser takes an instrument under unusual circumstances. The purchaser is treated as a successor in interest to the prior holder and can acquire no better rights. But if the prior holder was a holder in due course, the purchaser obtains rights of a holder in due course.

Subsection (c) applies to a purchaser in an execution sale or sale in bankruptcy. It applies equally to an attaching creditor or any other person who acquires the instrument by legal process or to a representative, such as an executor, administrator, receiver or assignee for the benefit of creditors, who takes the instrument as part of an estate. Subsection (c) applies to bulk purchases lying outside of the ordinary course of business of the seller. For example, it applies to the purchase by one bank of a substantial part of the paper held by another bank which is threatened with insolvency and seeking to liquidate its assets. Subsection (c) would also apply when a new partnership takes over for value all of the assets of an old one after a new member has entered the firm, or to a reorganized or consolidated corporation taking over the assets of a predecessor.

In the absence of controlling state law to the contrary, subsection (c) applies to a sale by a state bank commissioner of the assets of an insolvent bank. However, subsection (c) may be preempted by federal law if the Federal Deposit Insurance Corporation takes over an insolvent bank. Under the governing federal law, the FDIC and similar financial institution insurers are given holder in due course status and that status is also acquired by their assignees under the shelter doctrine.

6. Subsections (d) and (e) clarify two matters not specifically addressed by former Article 3:

Case # 5. Payee negotiates a $1,000 note to Holder who agrees to pay $900 for it. After paying $500, Holder learns that Payee defrauded Maker in the transaction giving rise to the note. Under subsection (d) Holder may assert rights as a holder in due course to the extent of $555.55 ($500 ÷ $900 = .555 × $1,000 = $555.55). This formula rewards Holder with a ratable portion of the bargained for profit.

Case # 6. Payee negotiates a note of Maker for $1,000 to Holder as security for payment of Payee's debt to Holder of $600. Maker has a defense which is good against Payee but of which Holder has no notice. Subsection (e) applies. Holder may assert rights as a holder in due course only to the extent of $600. Payee does not get the benefit of the holder-in-due-course status of Holder. With respect to $400 of the note, Maker may assert any rights that Maker has against Payee. A different result follows if the payee of a note negotiated it to a person who took it as a holder in due course and that person pledged the note as security for a debt. Because the defense cannot be asserted against the pledgor, the pledgee can assert rights as a holder in due course for the full amount of the note for the benefit of both the pledgor and the pledgee.

7. There is a large body of state statutory and case law restricting the use of the holder in due course doctrine in consumer transactions as well as some business transactions that raise similar issues. Subsection (g) subordinates Article 3 to that law and any other similar law that may evolve in the future. Section 3–106(d) also relates to statutory or administrative law intended to restrict use of the holder-in-due-course doctrine. See Comment 3 to Section 3–106.

8. The status of holder in due course resembles the status of protected holder under Article 29 of the Convention on International Bills of Exchange and International Promissory Notes. The requirements for being a protected holder under Article 29 generally track those of Section 3–302.

As amended in 2002.

§ 3–303. Value and Consideration.

(a) An instrument is issued or transferred for value if:

(1) the instrument is issued or transferred for a promise of performance, to the extent the promise has been performed;

(2) the transferee acquires a security interest or other lien in the instrument other than a lien obtained by judicial proceeding;

(3) the instrument is issued or transferred as payment of, or as security for, an antecedent claim against any person, whether or not the claim is due;

(4) the instrument is issued or transferred in exchange for a negotiable instrument; or

(5) the instrument is issued or transferred in exchange for the incurring of an irrevocable obligation to a third party by the person taking the instrument.

(b) "Consideration" means any consideration sufficient to support a simple contract. The drawer or maker of an instrument has a defense if the instrument is issued without consideration. If an instrument is issued for a promise of performance, the issuer has a defense to the extent performance of the promise is due and the promise has not been performed. If an instrument is issued for value as stated in subsection (a), the instrument is also issued for consideration.

Official Comment

1. Subsection (a) is a restatement of former Section 3–303 and subsection (b) replaces former Section 3–408. The distinction between value and consideration in Article 3 is a very fine one. Whether an instrument is taken for value is relevant to the issue of whether a holder is a holder in due course. If an instrument is not issued for consideration the issuer has a defense to the obligation to pay the instrument. Consideration is defined in subsection (b) as "any consideration sufficient to support a simple contract." The definition of value in Section 1–201(44) [*unrevised Article 1; see Concordance, p. 22*], which doesn't apply to Article 3, includes "any consideration sufficient to support a simple contract." Thus, outside Article 3, anything that is consideration is also value. A different rule applies in Article 3. Subsection (b) of Section 3–303 states that if an instrument is issued for value it is also issued for consideration.

Case # 1. X owes Y $1,000. The debt is not represented by a note. Later X issues a note to Y for the debt. Under subsection (a)(3) X's note is issued for value. Under subsection (b) the note is also issued for consideration whether or not, under contract law, Y is deemed to have given consideration for the note.

Case # 2. X issues a check to Y in consideration of Y's promise to perform services in the future. Although the executory promise is consideration for issuance of the check it is value only to the extent the promise is performed. Subsection (a)(1).

Case # 3. X issues a note to Y in consideration of Y's promise to perform services. If at the due date of the note Y's performance is not yet due, Y may enforce the note because it was issued for consideration. But if at the due date of the note, Y's performance is due and has not been performed, X has a defense. Subsection (b).

2.   Subsection (a), which defines value, has primary importance in cases in which the issue is whether the holder of an instrument is a holder in due course and particularly to cases in which the issuer of the instrument has a defense to the instrument. Suppose Buyer and Seller signed a contract on April 1 for the sale of goods to be delivered on May 1. Payment of 50% of the price of the goods was due upon signing of the contract. On April 1 Buyer delivered to Seller a check in the amount due under the contract. The check was drawn by X to Buyer as payee and was indorsed to Seller. When the check was presented for payment to the drawee on April 2, it was dishonored because X had stopped payment. At that time Seller had not taken any action to perform the contract with Buyer. If X has a defense on the check, the defense can be asserted against Seller who is not a holder in due course because Seller did not give value for the check. Subsection (a)(1). The policy basis for subsection (a)(1) is that the holder who gives an executory promise of performance will not suffer an out-of-pocket loss to the extent the executory promise is unperformed at the time the holder learns of dishonor of the instrument. When Seller took delivery of the check on April 1, Buyer's obligation to pay 50% of the price on that date was suspended, but when the check was dishonored on April 2 the obligation revived. Section 3–310(b). If payment for goods is due at or before delivery and the buyer fails to make the payment, the seller is excused from performing the promise to deliver the goods. Section 2–703. Thus, Seller is protected from an out-of-pocket loss even if the check is not enforceable. Holder-in-due-course status is not necessary to protect Seller.

3.   Subsection (a)(2) equates value with the obtaining of a security interest or a nonjudicial lien in the instrument. The term "security interest" covers Article 9 cases in which an instrument is taken as collateral as well as bank collection cases in which a bank acquires a security interest under Section 4–210. The acquisition of a common-law or statutory banker's lien is also value under subsection (a)(2). An attaching creditor or other person who acquires a lien by judicial proceedings does not give value for the purposes of subsection (a)(2).

4.   Subsection (a)(3) follows former Section 3–303(b) in providing that the holder takes for value if the instrument is taken in payment of or as security for an antecedent claim, even though there is no extension of time or other concession, and whether or not the claim is due. Subsection (a)(3) applies to any claim against any person; there is no requirement that the claim arise out of contract. In particular the provision is intended to apply to an instrument given in payment of or as security for the debt of a third person, even though no concession is made in return.

5.   Subsection (a)(4) and (5) restate former Section 3–303(c). They state generally recognized exceptions to the rule that an executory promise is not value. A negotiable instrument is value because it carries the possibility of negotiation to a holder in due course, after which the party who gives it is obliged to pay. The same reasoning applies to any irrevocable commitment to a third person, such as a letter of credit issued when an instrument is taken.

6.   The term "promise" in paragraph (a)(1) is used in the phrase "promise of performance" and for that reason does not have the specialized meaning given that term in Section 3–103(a)(12). See Section 1–201 ("Changes from Former Law"). No inference should be drawn from the decision to use the phrase "promise of performance," although the phrase does include the word "promise," which has the specialized definition set forth in Section 3–103. Indeed, that is true even though "undertaking" is used instead of "promise" in Section 3–104(a)(3). See Section 3–104 comment 1 (explaining the use of the term "undertaking" in Section 3–104 to avoid use of the defined term "promise").

As amended in 2002.

§ 3–304.   Overdue Instrument.

(a)   An instrument payable on demand becomes overdue at the earliest of the following times:

(1)   on the day after the day demand for payment is duly made;

(2)   if the instrument is a check, 90 days after its date; or

(3)   if the instrument is not a check, when the instrument has been outstanding for a period of time after its date which is unreasonably long under the circumstances of the particular case in light of the nature of the instrument and usage of the trade.

(b)   With respect to an instrument payable at a definite time the following rules apply:

(1) If the principal is payable in installments and a due date has not been accelerated, the instrument becomes overdue upon default under the instrument for nonpayment of an installment, and the instrument remains overdue until the default is cured.

(2) If the principal is not payable in installments and the due date has not been accelerated, the instrument becomes overdue on the day after the due date.

(3) If a due date with respect to principal has been accelerated, the instrument becomes overdue on the day after the accelerated due date.

(c) Unless the due date of principal has been accelerated, an instrument does not become overdue if there is default in payment of interest but no default in payment of principal.

Official Comment

1. To be a holder in due course, one must take without notice that an instrument is overdue. Section 3–302(a)(2)(iii). Section 3–304 replaces subsection (3) of former Section 3–304. For the sake of clarity it treats demand and time instruments separately. Subsection (a) applies to demand instruments. A check becomes stale after 90 days.

Under former Section 3–304(3)(c), a holder that took a demand note had notice that it was overdue if it was taken "more than a reasonable length of time after its issue." In substitution for this test, subsection (a)(3) requires the trier of fact to look at both the circumstances of the particular case and the nature of the instrument and trade usage. Whether a demand note is stale may vary a great deal depending on the facts of the particular case.

2. Subsections (b) and (c) cover time instruments. They follow the distinction made under former Article 3 between defaults in payment of principal and interest. In subsection (b) installment instruments and single payment instruments are treated separately. If an installment is late, the instrument is overdue until the default is cured.

§ 3–305. Defenses and Claims in Recoupment.

(a) Except as otherwise provided in this section, the right to enforce the obligation of a party to pay an instrument is subject to the following:

(1) a defense of the obligor based on (i) infancy of the obligor to the extent it is a defense to a simple contract, (ii) duress, lack of legal capacity, or illegality of the transaction which, under other law, nullifies the obligation of the obligor, (iii) fraud that induced the obligor to sign the instrument with neither knowledge nor reasonable opportunity to learn of its character or its essential terms, or (iv) discharge of the obligor in insolvency proceedings;

(2) a defense of the obligor stated in another section of this Article or a defense of the obligor that would be available if the person entitled to enforce the instrument were enforcing a right to payment under a simple contract; and

(3) a claim in recoupment of the obligor against the original payee of the instrument if the claim arose from the transaction that gave rise to the instrument; but the claim of the obligor may be asserted against a transferee of the instrument only to reduce the amount owing on the instrument at the time the action is brought.

(b) The right of a holder in due course to enforce the obligation of a party to pay the instrument is subject to defenses of the obligor stated in subsection (a)(1), but is not subject to defenses of the obligor stated in subsection (a)(2) or claims in recoupment stated in subsection (a)(3) against a person other than the holder.

(c) Except as stated in subsection (d), in an action to enforce the obligation of a party to pay the instrument, the obligor may not assert against the person entitled to enforce the instrument a defense, claim in recoupment, or claim to the instrument (Section 3–306) of another person, but the other person's claim to the instrument may be asserted by the obligor if the other person is joined in the action and personally asserts the claim against the person entitled to enforce the instrument. An obligor is not obliged to pay the instrument if the person seeking enforcement of the instrument does not have rights of a holder in due course and the obligor proves that the instrument is a lost or stolen instrument.

(d)   In an action to enforce the obligation of an accommodation party to pay an instrument, the accommodation party may assert against the person entitled to enforce the instrument any defense or claim in recoupment under subsection (a) that the accommodated party could assert against the person entitled to enforce the instrument, except the defenses of discharge in insolvency proceedings, infancy, and lack of legal capacity.

(e)   In a consumer transaction, if law other than this article requires that an instrument include a statement to the effect that the rights of a holder or transferee are subject to a claim or defense that the issuer could assert against the original payee, and the instrument does not include such a statement:

(1)   the instrument has the same effect as if the instrument included such a statement;

(2)   the issuer may assert against the holder or transferee all claims and defenses that would have been available if the instrument included such a statement; and

(3)   the extent to which claims may be asserted against the holder or transferee is determined as if the instrument included such a statement.

(f)   This section is subject to law other than this article that establishes a different rule for consumer transactions.

Legislative Note: If a consumer protection law in this state addresses the same issue as subsection (g), it should be examined for consistency with subsection (g) and, if inconsistent, should be amended. [Note from West Advisory Panel: So in original; should be (e).]

As amended in 2002.

Official Comment

1.   Subsection (a) states the defenses to the obligation of a party to pay the instrument. Subsection (a)(1) states the "real defenses" that may be asserted against any person entitled to enforce the instrument.

Subsection (a)(1)(i) allows assertion of the defense of infancy against a holder in due course, even though the effect of the defense is to render the instrument voidable but not void. The policy is one of protection of the infant even at the expense of occasional loss to an innocent purchaser. No attempt is made to state when infancy is available as a defense or the conditions under which it may be asserted. In some jurisdictions it is held that an infant cannot rescind the transaction or set up the defense unless the holder is restored to the position held before the instrument was taken which, in the case of a holder in due course, is normally impossible. In other states an infant who has misrepresented age may be estopped to assert infancy. Such questions are left to other law, as an integral part of the policy of each state as to the protection of infants.

Subsection (a)(1)(ii) covers mental incompetence, guardianship, ultra vires acts or lack of corporate capacity to do business, or any other incapacity apart from infancy. Such incapacity is largely statutory. Its existence and effect is left to the law of each state. If under the state law the effect is to render the obligation of the instrument entirely null and void, the defense may be asserted against a holder in due course. If the effect is merely to render the obligation voidable at the election of the obligor, the defense is cut off.

Duress, which is also covered by subsection (a)(ii), is a matter of degree. An instrument signed at the point of a gun is void, even in the hands of a holder in due course. One signed under threat to prosecute the son of the maker for theft may be merely voidable, so that the defense is cut off. Illegality is most frequently a matter of gambling or usury, but may arise in other forms under a variety of statutes. The statutes differ in their provisions and the interpretations given them. They are primarily a matter of local concern and local policy. All such matters are therefore left to the local law. If under that law the effect of the duress or the illegality is to make the obligation entirely null and void, the defense may be asserted against a holder in due course. Otherwise it is cut off.

Subsection (a)(1)(iii) refers to "real" or "essential" fraud, sometimes called fraud in the essence or fraud in the factum, as effective against a holder in due course. The common illustration is that of the maker who is tricked into signing a note in the belief that it is merely a receipt or some other document. The theory of the defense is that the signature on the instrument is ineffective because the signer did not intend to sign such an instrument at all. Under this provision the defense extends to an instrument signed with knowledge that it is a negotiable instrument, but without knowledge of its essential terms. The test of the defense is that of excusable ignorance of the contents of the writing signed. The party must not only have been in ignorance, but must also have had no reasonable opportunity to obtain knowledge. In determining what is a reasonable opportunity all relevant factors are to be taken into account, including the intelligence, education, business experience, and ability to read or understand English of the signer. Also relevant is the nature of the representations that were made, whether the signer had good reason to rely on the representations or to have confidence in the person making them, the presence or absence of any third person who might read or explain the instrument to the signer, or any other possibility of obtaining independent information, and the apparent necessity, or lack of it, for acting without delay. Unless the misrepresentation meets this test, the defense is cut off by a holder in due course.

Subsection (a)(1)(iv) states specifically that the defense of discharge in insolvency proceedings is not cut off when the instrument is purchased by a holder in due course. "Insolvency proceedings" is defined in Section 1–201(22) [*unrevised Article 1; see Concordance, p. 22*], and it includes bankruptcy whether or not the debtor is insolvent. Subsection (2)(e) of former Section 3–305 is omitted. The substance of that provision is stated in Section 3–601(b).

2. Subsection (a)(2) states other defenses that, pursuant to subsection (b), are cut off by a holder in due course. These defenses comprise those specifically stated in Article 3 and those based on common law contract principles. Article 3 defenses are nonissuance of the instrument, conditional issuance, and issuance for a special purpose (Section 3–105(b)); failure to countersign a traveler's check (Section 3–106(c)); modification of the obligation by a separate agreement (Section 3–117); payment that violates a restrictive indorsement (Section 3–206(f)); instruments issued without consideration or for which promised performance has not been given (Section 3–303(b)), and breach of warranty when a draft is accepted (Section 3–417(b)). The most prevalent common law defenses are fraud, misrepresentation or mistake in the issuance of the instrument. In most cases the holder in due course will be an immediate or remote transferee of the payee of the instrument. In most cases the holder-in-due-course doctrine is irrelevant if defenses are being asserted against the payee of the instrument, but in a small number of cases the payee of the instrument may be a holder in due course. Those cases are discussed in Comment 4 to Section 3–302.

Assume Buyer issues a note to Seller in payment of the price of goods that Seller fraudulently promises to deliver but which are never delivered. Seller negotiates the note to Holder who has no notice of the fraud. If Holder is a holder in due course, Holder is not subject to Buyer's defense of fraud. But in some cases an original party to the instrument is a holder in due course. For example, Buyer fraudulently induces Bank to issue a cashier's check to the order of Seller. The check is delivered by Bank to Seller, who has no notice of the fraud. Seller can be a holder in due course and can take the check free of Bank's defense of fraud. This case is discussed as Case # 1 in Comment 4 to Section 3–302. Former Section 3–305 stated that a holder in due course takes free of defenses of "any party to the instrument with whom the holder has not dealt." The meaning of this language was not at all clear and if read literally could have produced the wrong result. In the hypothetical case, it could be argued that Seller "dealt" with Bank because Bank delivered the check to Seller. But it is clear that Seller should take free of Bank's defense against Buyer regardless of whether Seller took delivery of the check from Buyer or from Bank. The quoted language is not included in Section 3–305. It is not necessary. If Buyer issues an instrument to Seller and Buyer has a defense against Seller, that defense can obviously be asserted. Buyer and Seller are the only people involved. The holder-in-due-course doctrine has no relevance. The doctrine applies only to cases in which more than two parties are involved. Its essence is that the holder in due course does not have to suffer the consequences of a defense of the obligor on the instrument that arose from an occurrence with a third party.

3. Subsection (a)(3) is concerned with claims in recoupment which can be illustrated by the following example. Buyer issues a note to the order of Seller in exchange for a promise of Seller to deliver specified equipment. If Seller fails to deliver the equipment or delivers equipment that is rightfully rejected, Buyer has a defense to the note because the performance that was the consideration for the note was not rendered. Section 3–303(b). This defense is included in Section 3–305(a)(2). That defense can always be asserted against Seller. This result is the same as that reached under former Section 3–408.

But suppose Seller delivered the promised equipment and it was accepted by Buyer. The equipment, however, was defective. Buyer retained the equipment and incurred expenses with respect to its repair. In this case, Buyer does not have a defense under Section 3–303(b). Seller delivered the equipment and the equipment was accepted. Under Article 2, Buyer is obliged to pay the price of the equipment which is represented by the note. But Buyer may have a claim against Seller for breach of warranty. If Buyer has a warranty claim, the claim may be asserted against Seller as a counterclaim or as a claim in recoupment to reduce the amount owing on the note. It is not relevant whether Seller is or is not a holder in due course of the note or whether Seller knew or had notice that Buyer had the warranty claim. It is obvious that holder-in-due-course doctrine cannot be used to allow Seller to cut off a warranty claim that Buyer has against Seller. Subsection (b) specifically covers this point by stating that a holder in due course is not subject to a "claim in recoupment . . . against a person other than the holder."

Suppose Seller negotiates the note to Holder. If Holder had notice of Buyer's warranty claim at the time the note was negotiated to Holder, Holder is not a holder in due course (Section 3–302(a)(2)(iv)) and Buyer may assert the claim against Holder (Section 3–305(a)(3)) but only as a claim in recoupment, i.e. to reduce the amount owed on the note. If the warranty claim is $1,000 and the unpaid note is $10,000, Buyer owes $9,000 to Holder. If the warranty claim is more than the unpaid amount of the note, Buyer owes nothing to Holder, but Buyer cannot recover the unpaid amount of the warranty claim from Holder. If Buyer had already partially paid the note, Buyer is not entitled to recover the amounts paid. The claim can be used only as an offset to amounts owing on the note. If Holder had no notice of Buyer's claim and otherwise qualifies as a holder in due course, Buyer may not assert the claim against Holder. Section 3–305(b).

The result under Section 3–305 is consistent with the result reached under former Article 3, but the rules for reaching the result are stated differently. Under former Article 3 Buyer could assert rights against Holder only if Holder was not a holder in due course, and Holder's status depended upon whether Holder had notice of a defense by Buyer. Courts have held that Holder had that notice if Holder had notice of Buyer's warranty claim. The rationale under former Article 3 was "failure of consideration." This rationale does not distinguish between cases in which the seller fails to perform and those in which the buyer accepts the performance of seller but makes a claim against the seller because the performance is faulty. The term "failure of consideration" is subject to varying interpretations and is not used in Article 3. The use of the term "claim in recoupment" in Section 3–305(a)(3) is a more precise statement of the nature of Buyer's right against Holder. The use of the term does not change the law because the treatment of a defense under subsection (a)(2) and a claim in recoupment under subsection (a)(3) is essentially the same.

Under former Article 3, case law was divided on the issue of the extent to which an obligor on a note could assert against a transferee who is not a holder in due course a debt or other claim that the obligor had against the original payee of the instrument. Some courts limited claims to those that arose in the transaction that gave rise to the note. This is the approach taken in Section 3–305(a)(3). Other courts allowed the obligor on the note to use any debt or other claim, no matter how unrelated to the note, to offset the amount owed on the note. Under current judicial authority and non-UCC statutory law, there will be many cases in which a transferee of a note arising from a sale transaction will not qualify as a holder in due course. For example, applicable law may require the use of a note to which there cannot be a holder in due course. See Section 3–106(d) and Comment 3 to Section 3–106. It is reasonable to provide that the buyer should not be denied the right to assert claims arising out of the sale transaction. Subsection (a)(3) is based on the belief that it is not reasonable to require the transferee to bear the risk that wholly unrelated claims may also be asserted. The determination of whether a claim arose from the transaction that gave rise to the instrument is determined by law other than this Article and thus may vary as local law varies.

4.   Subsection (c) concerns claims and defenses of a person other than the obligor on the instrument. It applies principally to cases in which an obligation is paid with the instrument of a third person. For example, Buyer buys goods from Seller and negotiates to Seller a cashier's check issued by Bank in payment of the price. Shortly after delivering the check to Seller, Buyer learns that Seller had defrauded Buyer in the sale transaction. Seller may enforce the check against Bank even though Seller is not a holder in due course. Bank has no defense to its obligation to pay the check and it may not assert defenses, claims in recoupment, or claims to the instrument of Buyer, except to the extent permitted by the "but" clause of the first sentence of subsection (c). Buyer may have a claim to the instrument under Section 3–306 based on a right to rescind the negotiation to Seller because of Seller's fraud. Section 3–202(b) and Comment 2 to Section 3–201. Bank cannot assert that claim unless Buyer is joined in the action in which Seller is trying to enforce payment of the check. In that case Bank may pay the amount of the check into court and the court will decide whether that amount belongs to Buyer or Seller. The last sentence of subsection (c) allows the issuer of an instrument such as a cashier's check to refuse payment in the rare case in which the issuer can prove that the instrument is a lost or stolen instrument and the person seeking enforcement does not have rights of a holder in due course.

5.   Subsection (d) applies to instruments signed for accommodation (Section 3–419) and this subsection equates the obligation of the accommodation party to that of the accommodated party. The accommodation party can assert whatever defense or claim the accommodated party had against the person enforcing the instrument. The only exceptions are discharge in bankruptcy, infancy and lack of capacity. The same rule does not apply to an indorsement by a holder of the instrument in negotiating the instrument. The indorser, as transferor, makes a warranty to the indorsee, as transferee, that no defense or claim in recoupment is good against the indorser. Section 3–416(a)(4). Thus, if the indorsee sues the indorser because of dishonor of the instrument, the indorser may not assert the defense or claim in recoupment of the maker or drawer against the indorsee.

Section 3–305(d) must be read in conjunction with Section 3–605, which provides rules (usually referred to as suretyship defenses) for determining when the obligation of an accommodation party is discharged, in whole or in part, because of some act or omission of a person entitled to enforce the instrument. To the extent a rule stated in Section 3–605 is inconsistent with Section 3–305(d), the Section 3–605 rule governs. For example, Section 3–605(a) provides rules for determining when and to what extent a discharge of the accommodated party under Section 3–604 will discharge the accommodation party. As explained in Comment 2 to Section 3–605, discharge of the accommodated party is normally part of a settlement under which the holder of a note accepts partial payment from an accommodated party who is financially unable to pay the entire amount of the note. If the holder then brings an action against the accommodation party to recover the remaining unpaid amount of the note, the accommodation party cannot use Section 3–305(d) to nullify Section 3–605(a) by asserting the discharge of the accommodated party as a defense. On the other hand, suppose the accommodated party is a buyer of goods who issued the note to the seller who took the note for the buyer's obligation to pay for the goods. Suppose the buyer has a claim for breach of warranty with respect to the goods against the seller and the warranty claim may be asserted against the holder of the note. The warranty claim is a claim in recoupment. If the holder and the accommodated party reach a settlement under which the holder accepts payment less than the amount of the note in full satisfaction of the note and the warranty claim, the accommodation party could defend an action on the note by the holder by asserting the accord and satisfaction under Section 3–305(d). There is no conflict with Section 3–605(a) because that provision is not intended to apply to settlement of disputed claims.

6. Subsection (e) is added to clarify the treatment of an instrument that omits the notice currently required by the Federal Trade Commission Rule related to certain consumer credit sales and consumer purchase money loans (16 C.F.R. Part 433). This subsection adopts the view that the instrument should be treated as if the language required by the FTC Rule were present. It is based on the language describing that rule in Section 3–106(d) and the analogous provision in Section 9–404(d).

7. Subsection (f) is modeled on Sections 9–403(e) and 9–404(c). It ensures that Section 3–305 is interpreted to accommodate relevant consumer-protection laws. The absence of such a provision from other sections in Article 3 should not justify any inference about the meaning of those sections.

8. Articles 28 and 30 of the Convention on International Bills of Exchange and International Promissory Notes includes a similar dichotomy, with a narrower group of defenses available against a protected holder under Articles 28(1) and 30 than are available under Article 28(2) against a holder that is not a protected holder.

As amended in 1994 and 2002.

§ 3–306. Claims to an Instrument.

A person taking an instrument, other than a person having rights of a holder in due course, is subject to a claim of a property or possessory right in the instrument or its proceeds, including a claim to rescind a negotiation and to recover the instrument or its proceeds. A person having rights of a holder in due course takes free of the claim to the instrument.

Official Comment

This section expands on the reference to "claims to" the instrument mentioned in former Sections 3–305 and 3–306. Claims covered by the section include not only claims to ownership but also any other claim of a property or possessory right. It includes the claim to a lien or the claim of a person in rightful possession of an instrument who was wrongfully deprived of possession. Also included is a claim based on Section 3–202(b) for rescission of a negotiation of the instrument by the claimant. Claims to an instrument under Section 3–306 are different from claims in recoupment referred to in Section 3–305(a)(3). The rule of this section is similar to the rule of Article 30(2) of the Convention on International Bills of Exchange and International Promissory Notes.

As amended in 2002.

§ 3–307. Notice of Breach of Fiduciary Duty.

(a) In this section:

(1) "Fiduciary" means an agent, trustee, partner, corporate officer or director, or other representative owing a fiduciary duty with respect to an instrument.

(2) "Represented person" means the principal, beneficiary, partnership, corporation, or other person to whom the duty stated in paragraph (1) is owed.

(b) If (i) an instrument is taken from a fiduciary for payment or collection or for value, (ii) the taker has knowledge of the fiduciary status of the fiduciary, and (iii) the represented person makes a claim to the instrument or its proceeds on the basis that the transaction of the fiduciary is a breach of fiduciary duty, the following rules apply:

(1)   Notice of breach of fiduciary duty by the fiduciary is notice of the claim of the represented person.

(2)   In the case of an instrument payable to the represented person or the fiduciary as such, the taker has notice of the breach of fiduciary duty if the instrument is (i) taken in payment of or as security for a debt known by the taker to be the personal debt of the fiduciary, (ii) taken in a transaction known by the taker to be for the personal benefit of the fiduciary, or (iii) deposited to an account other than an account of the fiduciary, as such, or an account of the represented person.

(3)   If an instrument is issued by the represented person or the fiduciary as such, and made payable to the fiduciary personally, the taker does not have notice of the breach of fiduciary duty unless the taker knows of the breach of fiduciary duty.

(4)   If an instrument is issued by the represented person or the fiduciary as such, to the taker as payee, the taker has notice of the breach of fiduciary duty if the instrument is (i) taken in payment of or as security for a debt known by the taker to be the personal debt of the fiduciary, (ii) taken in a transaction known by the taker to be for the personal benefit of the fiduciary, or (iii) deposited to an account other than an account of the fiduciary, as such, or an account of the represented person.

Official Comment

1.   This section states rules for determining when a person who has taken an instrument from a fiduciary has notice of a breach of fiduciary duty that occurs as a result of the transaction with the fiduciary. Former Section 3–304(2) and (4)(e) related to this issue, but those provisions were unclear in their meaning. Section 3–307 is intended to clarify the law by stating rules that comprehensively cover the issue of when the taker of an instrument has notice of breach of a fiduciary duty and thus notice of a claim to the instrument or its proceeds.

2.   Subsection (a) defines the terms "fiduciary" and "represented person" and the introductory paragraph of subsection (b) describes the transaction to which the section applies. The basic scenario is one in which the fiduciary in effect embezzles money of the represented person by applying the proceeds of an instrument that belongs to the represented person to the personal use of the fiduciary. The person dealing with the fiduciary may be a depositary bank that takes the instrument for collection or a bank or other person that pays value for the instrument. The section also covers a transaction in which an instrument is presented for payment to a payor bank that pays the instrument by giving value to the fiduciary. Subsections (b)(2), (3), and (4) state rules for determining when the person dealing with the fiduciary has notice of breach of fiduciary duty. Subsection (b)(1) states that notice of breach of fiduciary duty is notice of the represented person's claim to the instrument or its proceeds.

Under Section 3–306, a person taking an instrument is subject to a claim to the instrument or its proceeds, unless the taker has rights of a holder in due course. Under Section 3–302(a)(2)(v), the taker cannot be a holder in due course if the instrument was taken with notice of a claim under Section 3–306. Section 3–307 applies to cases in which a represented person is asserting a claim because a breach of fiduciary duty resulted in a misapplication of the proceeds of an instrument. The claim of the represented person is a claim described in Section 3–306. Section 3–307 states rules for determining when a person taking an instrument has notice of the claim which will prevent assertion of rights as a holder in due course. It also states rules for determining when a payor bank pays an instrument with notice of breach of fiduciary duty.

Section 3–307(b) applies only if the person dealing with the fiduciary "has knowledge of the fiduciary status of the fiduciary." Notice which does not amount to knowledge is not enough to cause Section 3–307 to apply. "Knowledge" is defined in Section 1–201(25) [*unrevised Article 1; see Concordance, p. 22*]. In most cases, the "taker" referred to in Section 3–307 will be a bank or other organization. Knowledge of an organization is determined by the rules stated in Section 1–201(27) [*unrevised Article 1; see Concordance, p. 22*]. In many cases, the individual who receives and processes an instrument on behalf of the organization that is the taker of the instrument "for payment or collection or for value" is a clerk who has no knowledge of any fiduciary status of the person from whom the instrument is received. In such cases, Section 3–307 doesn't apply because, under Section 1–201(27) [*unrevised Article 1; see Concordance, p. 22*], knowledge of the organization is determined by the knowledge of the "individual conducting that transaction," i.e. the clerk who receives and processes the instrument. Furthermore, paragraphs (2) and (4) each require that the person acting for the organization have knowledge of facts that indicate a breach of fiduciary duty. In the case of an instrument taken for deposit to an account, the knowledge is found in the fact that the deposit is made to an account other than that of the represented person or a fiduciary account for benefit of that person. In other cases the person acting for the organization must know that the instrument is taken in payment or as security for a personal debt of the fiduciary or for the personal benefit of the fiduciary. For example, if the instrument is being used to buy goods or services, the person acting for the organization must know that the goods or services are for the personal benefit of the fiduciary. The requirement that the taker have knowledge rather than notice is meant to limit Section 3–307 to relatively uncommon cases in which the person who deals with the fiduciary knows all the relevant facts: the fiduciary status and that the proceeds of the instrument are being used for the personal debt or benefit of the fiduciary or are being paid to an account that is not an account of the represented person or of the fiduciary, as such. Mere notice of these facts is not enough to put the taker on notice of the breach of fiduciary duty and does not give rise to any duty of investigation by the taker.

3. Subsection (b)(2) applies to instruments payable to the represented person or the fiduciary as such. For example, a check payable to Corporation is indorsed in the name of Corporation by Doe as its President. Doe gives the check to Bank as partial repayment of a personal loan that Bank had made to Doe. The check was indorsed either in blank or to Bank. Bank collects the check and applies the proceeds to reduce the amount owed on Doe's loan. If the person acting for Bank in the transaction knows that Doe is a fiduciary and that the check is being used to pay a personal obligation of Doe, subsection (b)(2) applies. If Corporation has a claim to the proceeds of the check because the use of the check by Doe was a breach of fiduciary duty, Bank has notice of the claim and did not take the check as a holder in due course. The same result follows if Doe had indorsed the check to himself before giving it to Bank. Subsection (b)(2) follows Uniform Fiduciaries Act § 4 in providing that if the instrument is payable to the fiduciary, as such, or to the represented person, the taker has notice of a claim if the instrument is negotiated for the fiduciary's personal debt. If fiduciary funds are deposited to a personal account of the fiduciary or to an account that is not an account of the represented person or of the fiduciary, as such, there is a split of authority concerning whether the bank is on notice of a breach of fiduciary duty. Subsection (b)(2)(iii) states that the bank is given notice of breach of fiduciary duty because of the deposit. The Uniform Fiduciaries Act § 9 states that the bank is not on notice unless it has knowledge of facts that makes its receipt of the deposit an act of bad faith.

The rationale of subsection (b)(2) is that it is not normal for an instrument payable to the represented person or the fiduciary, as such, to be used for the personal benefit of the fiduciary. It is likely that such use reflects an unlawful use of the proceeds of the instrument. If the fiduciary is entitled to compensation from the represented person for services rendered or for expenses incurred by the fiduciary the normal mode of payment is by a check drawn on the fiduciary account to the order of the fiduciary.

4. Subsection (b)(3) is based on Uniform Fiduciaries Act § 6 and applies when the instrument is drawn by the represented person or the fiduciary as such to the fiduciary personally. The term "personally" is used as it is used in the Uniform Fiduciaries Act to mean that the instrument is payable to the payee as an individual and not as a fiduciary. For example, Doe as President of Corporation writes a check on Corporation's account to the order of Doe personally. The check is then indorsed over to Bank as in Comment 3. In this case there is no notice of breach of fiduciary duty because there is nothing unusual about the transaction. Corporation may have owed Doe money for salary, reimbursement for expenses incurred for the benefit of Corporation, or for any other reason. If Doe is authorized to write checks on behalf of Corporation to pay debts of Corporation, the check is a normal way of paying a debt owed to Doe. Bank may assume that Doe may use the instrument for his personal benefit.

5. Subsection (b)(4) can be illustrated by a hypothetical case. Corporation draws a check payable to an organization. X, an officer or employee of Corporation, delivers the check to a person acting for the organization. The person signing the check on behalf of Corporation is X or another person. If the person acting for the organization in the transaction knows that X is a fiduciary, the organization is on notice of a claim by Corporation if it takes the instrument under the same circumstances stated in subsection (b)(2). If the organization is a bank and the check is taken in repayment of a personal loan of the bank to X, the case is like the case discussed in Comment 3. It is unusual for Corporation, the represented person, to pay a personal debt of Doe by issuing a check to the bank. It is more likely that the use of the check by Doe reflects an unlawful use of the proceeds of the check. The same analysis applies if the check is made payable to an organization in payment of goods or services. If the person acting for the organization knew of the fiduciary status of X and that the goods or services were for X's personal benefit, the organization is on notice of a claim by Corporation to the proceeds of the check. See the discussion in the last paragraph of Comment 2.

§ 3–308. Proof of Signatures and Status as Holder in Due Course.

(a) In an action with respect to an instrument, the authenticity of, and authority to make, each signature on the instrument is admitted unless specifically denied in the pleadings. If the validity of a

319

signature is denied in the pleadings, the burden of establishing validity is on the person claiming validity, but the signature is presumed to be authentic and authorized unless the action is to enforce the liability of the purported signer and the signer is dead or incompetent at the time of trial of the issue of validity of the signature. If an action to enforce the instrument is brought against a person as the undisclosed principal of a person who signed the instrument as a party to the instrument, the plaintiff has the burden of establishing that the defendant is liable on the instrument as a represented person under Section 3–402(a).

(b)   If the validity of signatures is admitted or proved and there is compliance with subsection (a), a plaintiff producing the instrument is entitled to payment if the plaintiff proves entitlement to enforce the instrument under Section 3–301, unless the defendant proves a defense or claim in recoupment. If a defense or claim in recoupment is proved, the right to payment of the plaintiff is subject to the defense or claim, except to the extent the plaintiff proves that the plaintiff has rights of a holder in due course which are not subject to the defense or claim.

Official Comment

1.   Section 3–308 is a modification of former Section 3–307. The first two sentences of subsection (a) are a restatement of former Section 3–307(1). The purpose of the requirement of a specific denial in the pleadings is to give the plaintiff notice of the defendant's claim of forgery or lack of authority as to the particular signature, and to afford the plaintiff an opportunity to investigate and obtain evidence. If local rules of pleading permit, the denial may be on information and belief, or it may be a denial of knowledge or information sufficient to form a belief. It need not be under oath unless the local statutes or rules require verification. In the absence of such specific denial the signature stands admitted, and is not in issue. Nothing in this section is intended, however, to prevent amendment of the pleading in a proper case.

The question of the burden of establishing the signature arises only when it has been put in issue by specific denial. "Burden of establishing" is defined in Section 1–201. The burden is on the party claiming under the signature, but the signature is presumed to be authentic and authorized except as stated in the second sentence of subsection (a). "Presumed" is defined in Section 1–201 [unrevised Article 1; see Concordance, p. 22] and means that until some evidence is introduced which would support a finding that the signature is forged or unauthorized, the plaintiff is not required to prove that it is valid. The presumption rests upon the fact that in ordinary experience forged or unauthorized signatures are very uncommon, and normally any evidence is within the control of, or more accessible to, the defendant. The defendant is therefore required to make some sufficient showing of the grounds for the denial before the plaintiff is required to introduce evidence. The defendant's evidence need not be sufficient to require a directed verdict, but it must be enough to support the denial by permitting a finding in the defendant's favor. Until introduction of such evidence the presumption requires a finding for the plaintiff. Once such evidence is introduced the burden of establishing the signature by a preponderance of the total evidence is on the plaintiff. The presumption does not arise if the action is to enforce the obligation of a purported signer who has died or become incompetent before the evidence is required, and so is disabled from obtaining or introducing it. "Action" is defined in Section 1–201 and includes a claim asserted against the estate of a deceased or an incompetent.

The last sentence of subsection (a) is a new provision that is necessary to take into account Section 3–402(a) that allows an undisclosed principal to be liable on an instrument signed by an authorized representative. In that case the person enforcing the instrument must prove that the undisclosed principal is liable.

2.   Subsection (b) restates former Section 3–307(2) and (3). Once signatures are proved or admitted a holder, by mere production of the instrument, proves "entitlement to enforce the instrument" because under Section 3–301 a holder is a person entitled to enforce the instrument. Any other person in possession of an instrument may recover only if that person has the rights of a holder. Section 3–301. That person must prove a transfer giving that person such rights under Section 3–203(b) or that such rights were obtained by subrogation or succession.

If a plaintiff producing the instrument proves entitlement to enforce the instrument, either as a holder or a person with rights of a holder, the plaintiff is entitled to recovery unless the defendant proves a defense or claim in recoupment. Until proof of a defense or claim in recoupment is made, the issue as to whether the plaintiff has rights of a holder in due course does not arise. In the absence of a defense or claim in recoupment, any person entitled to enforce the instrument is entitled to recover. If a defense or claim in recoupment is proved, the plaintiff may seek to cut off the defense or claim in recoupment by proving that the plaintiff is a holder in due course or that the plaintiff has rights of a holder in due course under Section 3–203(b) or by subrogation or succession. All elements of Section 3–302(a) must be proved.

Nothing in this section is intended to say that the plaintiff must necessarily prove rights as a holder in due course. The plaintiff may elect to introduce no further evidence, in which case a verdict may be directed for the plaintiff or the defendant, or the issue of the defense or claim in recoupment may be left to the trier of fact, according to the weight and sufficiency of the defendant's evidence. The plaintiff may elect to rebut the defense or claim in recoupment by proof to the contrary, in which case a verdict may be directed for either party or the issue may be for the trier of fact. Subsection (b) means only that if the plaintiff claims the rights of a holder in due course against the defense or claim in recoupment, the plaintiff has the burden of proof on that issue.

§ 3–309. Enforcement of Lost, Destroyed, or Stolen Instrument.

(a)   A person not in possession of an instrument is entitled to enforce the instrument if:

(1)   the person seeking to enforce the instrument:

    (A)   was entitled to enforce the instrument when loss of possession occurred; or

    (B)   has directly or indirectly acquired ownership of the instrument from a person who was entitled to enforce the instrument when loss of possession occurred;

(2)   the loss of possession was not the result of a transfer by the person or a lawful seizure; and

(3)   the person cannot reasonably obtain possession of the instrument because the instrument was destroyed, its whereabouts cannot be determined, or it is in the wrongful possession of an unknown person or a person that cannot be found or is not amenable to service of process.

(b)   A person seeking enforcement of an instrument under subsection (a) must prove the terms of the instrument and the person's right to enforce the instrument. If that proof is made, Section 3–308 applies to the case as if the person seeking enforcement had produced the instrument. The court may not enter judgment in favor of the person seeking enforcement unless it finds that the person required to pay the instrument is adequately protected against loss that might occur by reason of a claim by another person to enforce the instrument. Adequate protection may be provided by any reasonable means.

As amended in 2002.

Official Comment

1.   Section 3–309 is a modification of former Section 3–804. The rights stated are those of "a person entitled to enforce the instrument" at the time of loss rather than those of an "owner" as in former Section 3–804. Under subsection (b), judgment to enforce the instrument cannot be given unless the court finds that the defendant will be adequately protected against a claim to the instrument by a holder that may appear at some later time. The court is given discretion in determining how adequate protection is to be assured. Former Section 3–804 allowed the court to "require security indemnifying the defendant against loss." Under Section 3–309 adequate protection is a flexible concept. For example, there is substantial risk that a holder in due course may make a demand for payment if the instrument was payable to bearer when it was lost or stolen. On the other hand if the instrument was payable to the person who lost the instrument and that person did not indorse the instrument, no other person could be a holder of the instrument. In some cases there is risk of loss only if there is doubt about whether the facts alleged by the person who lost the instrument are true. Thus, the type of adequate protection that is reasonable in the circumstances may depend on the degree of certainty about the facts in the case.

2.   Subsection (a) is intended to reject the result in *Dennis Joslin Co. v. Robinson Broadcasting Corp.*, 977 F. Supp. 491 (D.D.C. 1997). A transferee of a lost instrument need prove only that its transferor was entitled to enforce, not that the transferee was in possession at the time the instrument was lost. The protections of subsection (a) should also be available when instruments are lost during transit, because whatever the precise status of ownership at the point of loss, either the sender or the receiver ordinarily would have been entitled to enforce the instrument during the course of transit. The amendments to subsection (a) are not intended to alter in any way the rules that apply to the preservation of checks in connection with truncation or any other expedited method of check collection or processing.

3.   A security interest may attach to the right of a person not in possession of an instrument to enforce the instrument. Although the secured party may not be the owner of the instrument, the secured party may nevertheless be entitled to exercise its debtor's right to enforce the instrument by resorting to its collection rights under the circumstances described in Section 9–607. This section does not address whether the person required to pay the instrument owes any duty to a secured party that is not itself the owner of the instrument.

4.   The destruction of a check in connection with a truncation process in which information is extracted from the check and an image of the check is made, and then such information and image are transmitted for payment does not, by itself, prevent application of this section. See Section 3–604, Comment 2.

Example: The payee of a check creates an image of the check, destroys the check, and transmits the image and information derived from the check for payment. Due to an error in transmission, the depositary bank never receives the transmission. The payee may be able to enforce the check if the payee can prove the terms of the check and otherwise satisfy the requirements of this section. The result would be different if there were no error in the transmission and the payor discharged its obligation on the check.

As amended in 2002 and 2022.

§ 3–310.   Effect of Instrument on Obligation for Which Taken.

(a)   Unless otherwise agreed, if a certified check, cashier's check, or teller's check is taken for an obligation, the obligation is discharged to the same extent discharge would result if an amount of money equal to the amount of the instrument were taken in payment of the obligation. Discharge of the obligation does not affect any liability that the obligor may have as an indorser of the instrument.

(b)   Unless otherwise agreed and except as provided in subsection (a), if a note or an uncertified check is taken for an obligation, the obligation is suspended to the same extent the obligation would be discharged if an amount of money equal to the amount of the instrument were taken, and the following rules apply:

(1)   In the case of an uncertified check, suspension of the obligation continues until dishonor of the check or until it is paid or certified. Payment or certification of the check results in discharge of the obligation to the extent of the amount of the check.

(2)   In the case of a note, suspension of the obligation continues until dishonor of the note or until it is paid. Payment of the note results in discharge of the obligation to the extent of the payment.

(3)   Except as provided in paragraph (4), if the check or note is dishonored and the obligee of the obligation for which the instrument was taken is the person entitled to enforce the instrument, the obligee may enforce either the instrument or the obligation. In the case of an instrument of a third person which is negotiated to the obligee by the obligor, discharge of the obligor on the instrument also discharges the obligation.

(4)   If the person entitled to enforce the instrument taken for an obligation is a person other than the obligee, the obligee may not enforce the obligation to the extent the obligation is suspended. If the obligee is the person entitled to enforce the instrument but no longer has possession of it because it was lost, stolen, or destroyed, the obligation may not be enforced to the extent of the amount payable on the instrument, and to that extent the obligee's rights against the obligor are limited to enforcement of the instrument.

(c)   If an instrument other than one described in subsection (a) or (b) is taken for an obligation, the effect is (i) that stated in subsection (a) if the instrument is one on which a bank is liable as maker or acceptor, or (ii) that stated in subsection (b) in any other case.

Official Comment

1.   Section 3–310 is a modification of former Section 3–802. As a practical matter, application of former Section 3–802 was limited to cases in which a check or a note was given for an obligation. Subsections (a) and (b) of Section 3–310 are therefore stated in terms of checks and notes in the interests of clarity. Subsection (c) covers the rare cases in which some other instrument is given to pay an obligation.

2.   Subsection (a) deals with the case in which a certified check, cashier's check or teller's check is given in payment of an obligation. In that case the obligation is discharged unless there is an agreement to the contrary. Subsection (a) drops the exception in former Section 3–802 for cases in which there is a right of recourse on the instrument against the obligor. Under former Section 3–802(1)(a) the obligation was not discharged if there was a right of recourse on the instrument against the obligor. Subsection (a) changes this result. The underlying obligation is discharged, but any right of recourse on the instrument is preserved.

3.   Subsection (b) concerns cases in which an uncertified check or a note is taken for an obligation. The typical case is that in which a buyer pays for goods or services by giving the seller the buyer's personal check, or in which the buyer signs a note for the purchase price. Subsection (b) also applies to the uncommon cases in which

a check or note of a third person is given in payment of the obligation. Subsection (b) preserves the rule under former Section 3–802(1)(b) that the buyer's obligation to pay the price is suspended, but subsection (b) spells out the effect more precisely. If the check or note is dishonored, the seller may sue on either the dishonored instrument or the contract of sale if the seller has possession of the instrument and is the person entitled to enforce it. If the right to enforce the instrument is held by somebody other than the seller, the seller can't enforce the right to payment of the price under the sales contract because that right is represented by the instrument which is enforceable by somebody else. Thus, if the seller sold the note or the check to a holder and has not reacquired it after dishonor, the only right that survives is the right to enforce the instrument. What that means is that even though the suspension of the obligation may end upon dishonor under paragraph (b)(1), the obligation is not revived in the circumstances described in paragraph (b)(4).

The last sentence of subsection (b)(3) applies to cases in which an instrument of another person is indorsed over to the obligee in payment of the obligation. For example, Buyer delivers an uncertified personal check of X payable to the order of Buyer to Seller in payment of the price of goods. Buyer indorses the check over to Seller. Buyer is liable on the check as indorser. If Seller neglects to present the check for payment or to deposit it for collection within 30 days of the indorsement, Buyer's liability as indorser is discharged. Section 3–415(e). Under the last sentence of Section 3–310(b)(3) Buyer is also discharged on the obligation to pay for the goods.

4. There was uncertainty concerning the applicability of former Section 3–802 to the case in which the check given for the obligation was stolen from the payee, the payee's signature was forged, and the forger obtained payment. The last sentence of subsection (b)(4) addresses this issue. If the payor bank pays a holder, the drawer is discharged on the underlying obligation because the check was paid. Subsection (b)(1). If the payor bank pays a person not entitled to enforce the instrument, as in the hypothetical case, the suspension of the underlying obligation continues because the check has not been paid. Section 3–602(a). The payee's cause of action is against the depositary bank or payor bank in conversion under Section 3–420 or against the drawer under Section 3–309. In the latter case, the drawer's obligation under Section 3–414(b) is triggered by dishonor which occurs because the check is unpaid. Presentment for payment to the drawee is excused under Section 3–504(a)(i) and, under Section 3–502(e), dishonor occurs without presentment if the check is not paid. The payee cannot merely ignore the instrument and sue the drawer on the underlying contract. This would impose on the drawer the risk that the check when stolen was indorsed in blank or to bearer.

A similar analysis applies with respect to lost instruments that have not been paid. If a creditor takes a check of the debtor in payment of an obligation, the obligation is suspended under the introductory paragraph of subsection (b). If the creditor then loses the check, what are the creditor's rights? The creditor can request the debtor to issue a new check and in many cases, the debtor will issue a replacement check after stopping payment on the lost check. In that case both the debtor and creditor are protected. But the debtor is not obliged to issue a new check. If the debtor refuses to issue a replacement check, the last sentence of subsection (b)(4) applies. The creditor may not enforce the obligation of debtor for which the check was taken. The creditor may assert only rights on the check. The creditor can proceed under Section 3–309 to enforce the obligation of the debtor, as drawer, to pay the check.

5. Subsection (c) deals with rare cases in which other instruments are taken for obligations. If a bank is the obligor on the instrument, subsection (a) applies and the obligation is discharged. In any other case subsection (b) applies.

As amended in 2002.

§ 3–311. Accord and Satisfaction by Use of Instrument.

(a) If a person against whom a claim is asserted proves that (i) that person in good faith tendered an instrument to the claimant as full satisfaction of the claim, (ii) the amount of the claim was unliquidated or subject to a bona fide dispute, and (iii) the claimant obtained payment of the instrument, the following subsections apply.

(b) Unless subsection (c) applies, the claim is discharged if the person against whom the claim is asserted proves that the instrument or an accompanying written communication contained a conspicuous statement to the effect that the instrument was tendered as full satisfaction of the claim.

(c) Subject to subsection (d), a claim is not discharged under subsection (b) if either of the following applies:

(1) The claimant, if an organization, proves that (i) within a reasonable time before the tender, the claimant sent a conspicuous statement to the person against whom the claim is asserted that

communications concerning disputed debts, including an instrument tendered as full satisfaction of a debt, are to be sent to a designated person, office, or place, and (ii) the instrument or accompanying communication was not received by that designated person, office, or place.

(2)　The claimant, whether or not an organization, proves that within 90 days after payment of the instrument, the claimant tendered repayment of the amount of the instrument to the person against whom the claim is asserted. This paragraph does not apply if the claimant is an organization that sent a statement complying with paragraph (1)(i).

(d)　A claim is discharged if the person against whom the claim is asserted proves that within a reasonable time before collection of the instrument was initiated, the claimant, or an agent of the claimant having direct responsibility with respect to the disputed obligation, knew that the instrument was tendered in full satisfaction of the claim.

Official Comment

1.　This section deals with an informal method of dispute resolution carried out by use of a negotiable instrument. In the typical case there is a dispute concerning the amount that is owed on a claim.

Case # 1. The claim is for the price of goods or services sold to a consumer who asserts that he or she is not obliged to pay the full price for which the consumer was billed because of a defect or breach of warranty with respect to the goods or services.

Case # 2. A claim is made on an insurance policy. The insurance company alleges that it is not liable under the policy for the amount of the claim.

In either case the person against whom the claim is asserted may attempt an accord and satisfaction of the disputed claim by tendering a check to the claimant for some amount less than the full amount claimed by the claimant. A statement will be included on the check or in a communication accompanying the check to the effect that the check is offered as full payment or full satisfaction of the claim. Frequently, there is also a statement to the effect that obtaining payment of the check is an agreement by the claimant to a settlement of the dispute for the amount tendered. Before enactment of revised Article 3, the case law was in conflict over the question of whether obtaining payment of the check had the effect of an agreement to the settlement proposed by the debtor. This issue was governed by a common law rule, but some courts hold that the common law was modified by former Section 1–207 which they interpreted as applying to full settlement checks.

2.　Comment d. to Restatement of Contracts, Section 281 discusses the full satisfaction check and the applicable common law rule. In a case like Case # 1, the buyer can propose a settlement of the disputed bill by a clear notation on the check indicating that the check is tendered as full satisfaction of the bill. Under the common law rule the seller, by obtaining payment of the check accepts the offer of compromise by the buyer. The result is the same if the seller adds a notation to the check indicating that the check is accepted under protest or in only partial satisfaction of the claim. Under the common law rule the seller can refuse the check or can accept it subject to the condition stated by the buyer, but the seller can't accept the check and refuse to be bound by the condition. The rule applies only to an unliquidated claim or a claim disputed in good faith by the buyer. The dispute in the courts was whether Section 1–207 [*unrevised Article 1; see Concordance, p. 22*] changed the common law rule. The Restatement states that section "need not be read as changing this well-established rule."

3.　As part of the revision of Article 3, Section 1–207 [*unrevised Article 1; see Concordance, p. 22*] has been amended to add subsection (2) stating that Section 1–207 [*unrevised Article 1; see Concordance, p. 22*] "does not apply to an accord and satisfaction." Because of that amendment and revised Article 3, Section 3–311 governs full satisfaction checks. Section 3–311 follows the common law rule with some minor variations to reflect modern business conditions. In cases covered by Section 3–311 there will often be an individual on one side of the dispute and a business organization on the other. This section is not designed to favor either the individual or the business organization. In Case # 1 the person seeking the accord and satisfaction is an individual. In Case # 2 the person seeking the accord and satisfaction is an insurance company. Section 3–311 is based on a belief that the common law rule produces a fair result and that informal dispute resolution by full satisfaction checks should be encouraged.

4.　Subsection (a) states three requirements for application of Section 3–311. "Good faith" in subsection (a)(i) is defined in Section 3–103(a)(6) as not only honesty in fact, but the observance of reasonable commercial standards of fair dealing. The meaning of "fair dealing" will depend upon the facts in the particular case. For example, suppose an insurer tenders a check in settlement of a claim for personal injury in an accident clearly covered by the insurance policy. The claimant is necessitous and the amount of the check is very small in relationship to the extent of the injury and the amount recoverable under the policy. If the trier of fact determines that the insurer was taking unfair advantage of the claimant, an accord and satisfaction would not result from payment of the check because of the absence of good faith by the insurer in making the tender. Another example of lack of good faith is found in the practice of some business debtors in routinely printing full satisfaction language on their check stocks so that all or a large part of the debts of the debtor are paid by checks bearing the full satisfaction language, whether or not there is any dispute with the creditor. Under such a practice the claimant cannot be sure whether a tender in full satisfaction is or is not being made. Use of a check on which full satisfaction language was affixed routinely pursuant to such a business practice may prevent an accord and satisfaction on the ground that the check was not tendered in good faith under subsection (a)(i).

Section 3–311 does not apply to cases in which the debt is a liquidated amount and not subject to a bona fide dispute. Subsection (a)(ii). Other law applies to cases in which a debtor is seeking discharge of such a debt by paying less than the amount owed. For the purpose of subsection (a)(iii) obtaining acceptance of a check is considered to be obtaining payment of the check.

The person seeking the accord and satisfaction must prove that the requirements of subsection (a) are met. If that person also proves that the statement required by subsection (b) was given, the claim is discharged unless subsection (c) applies. Normally the statement required by subsection (b) is written on the check. Thus, the canceled check can be used to prove the statement as well as the fact that the claimant obtained payment of the check. Subsection (b) requires a "conspicuous" statement that the instrument was tendered in full satisfaction of the claim. "Conspicuous" is defined in Section 1–201(10) [*unrevised Article 1; see Concordance, p. 22*]. The statement is conspicuous if "it is so written that a reasonable person against whom it is to operate ought to have noticed it." If the claimant can reasonably be expected to examine the check, almost any statement on the check should be noticed and is therefore conspicuous. In cases in which the claimant is an individual the claimant will receive the check and will normally indorse it. Since the statement concerning tender in full satisfaction normally will appear above the space provided for the claimant's indorsement of the check, the claimant "ought to have noticed" the statement.

5. Subsection (c)(1) is a limitation on subsection (b) in cases in which the claimant is an organization. It is designed to protect the claimant against inadvertent accord and satisfaction. If the claimant is an organization payment of the check might be obtained without notice to the personnel of the organization concerned with the disputed claim. Some business organizations have claims against very large numbers of customers. Examples are department stores, public utilities and the like. These claims are normally paid by checks sent by customers to a designated office at which clerks employed by the claimant or a bank acting for the claimant process the checks and record the amounts paid. If the processing office is not designed to deal with communications extraneous to recording the amount of the check and the account number of the customer, payment of a full satisfaction check can easily be obtained without knowledge by the claimant of the existence of the full satisfaction statement. This is particularly true if the statement is written on the reverse side of the check in the area in which indorsements are usually written. Normally, the clerks of the claimant have no reason to look at the reverse side of checks. Indorsement by the claimant normally is done by mechanical means or there may be no indorsement at all. Section 4–205(a). Subsection (c)(1) allows the claimant to protect itself by advising customers by a conspicuous statement that communications regarding disputed debts must be sent to a particular person, office, or place. The statement must be given to the customer within a reasonable time before the tender is made. This requirement is designed to assure that the customer has reasonable notice that the full satisfaction check must be sent to a particular place. The reasonable time requirement could be satisfied by a notice on the billing statement sent to the customer. If the full satisfaction check is sent to the designated destination and the check is paid, the claim is discharged. If the claimant proves that the check was not received at the designated destination the claim is not discharged unless subsection (d) applies.

6. Subsection (c)(2) is also designed to prevent inadvertent accord and satisfaction. It can be used by a claimant other than an organization or by a claimant as an alternative to subsection (c)(1). Some organizations may be reluctant to use subsection (c)(1) because it may result in confusion of customers that causes checks to be routinely sent to the special designated person, office, or place. Thus, much of the benefit of rapid processing of checks may be lost. An organization that chooses not to send a notice complying with subsection (c)(1)(i) may prevent an inadvertent accord and satisfaction by complying with subsection (c)(2). If the claimant discovers that it has obtained payment of a full satisfaction check, it may prevent an accord and satisfaction if, within 90 days of the payment of the check, the claimant tenders repayment of the amount of the check to the person against whom the claim is asserted.

7. Subsection (c) is subject to subsection (d). If a person against whom a claim is asserted proves that the claimant obtained payment of a check known to have been tendered in full satisfaction of the claim by "the

claimant or an agent of the claimant having direct responsibility with respect to the disputed obligation," the claim is discharged even if (i) the check was not sent to the person, office, or place required by a notice complying with subsection (c)(1), or (ii) the claimant tendered repayment of the amount of the check in compliance with subsection (c)(2).

A claimant knows that a check was tendered in full satisfaction of a claim when the claimant "has actual knowledge" of that fact. Section 1–201(25) [*unrevised Article 1; see Concordance, p. 22*]. Under Section 1–201(27) [*unrevised Article 1; see Concordance, p. 22*], if the claimant is an organization, it has knowledge that a check was tendered in full satisfaction of the claim when that fact is

"brought to the attention of the individual conducting that transaction, and in any event when it would have been brought to his attention if the organization had exercised due diligence. An organization exercises due diligence if it maintains reasonable routines for communicating significant information to the person conducting the transaction and there is reasonable compliance with the routines. Due diligence does not require an individual acting for the organization to communicate information unless such communication is part of his regular duties or unless he has reason to know of the transaction and that the transaction would be materially affected by the information."

With respect to an attempted accord and satisfaction the "individual conducting that transaction" is an employee or other agent of the organization having direct responsibility with respect to the dispute. For example, if the check and communication are received by a collection agency acting for the claimant to collect the disputed claim, obtaining payment of the check will result in an accord and satisfaction even if the claimant gave notice, pursuant to subsection (c)(1), that full satisfaction checks be sent to some other office. Similarly, if a customer asserting a claim for breach of warranty with respect to defective goods purchased in a retail outlet of a large chain store delivers the full satisfaction check to the manager of the retail outlet at which the goods were purchased, obtaining payment of the check will also result in an accord and satisfaction. On the other hand, if the check is mailed to the chief executive officer of the chain store subsection (d) would probably not be satisfied. The chief executive officer of a large corporation may have general responsibility for operations of the company, but does not normally have direct responsibility for resolving a small disputed bill to a customer. A check for a relatively small amount mailed to a high executive officer of a large organization is not likely to receive the executive's personal attention. Rather, the check would normally be routinely sent to the appropriate office for deposit and credit to the customer's account. If the check does receive the personal attention of the high executive officer and the officer is aware of the full-satisfaction language, collection of the check will result in an accord and satisfaction because subsection (d) applies. In this case the officer has assumed direct responsibility with respect to the disputed transaction.

If a full satisfaction check is sent to a lock box or other office processing checks sent to the claimant, it is irrelevant whether the clerk processing the check did or did not see the statement that the check was tendered as full satisfaction of the claim. Knowledge of the clerk is not imputed to the organization because the clerk has no responsibility with respect to an accord and satisfaction. Moreover, there is no failure of "due diligence" under Section 1–201(27) [*unrevised Article 1; see Concordance, p. 22*] if the claimant does not require its clerks to look for full satisfaction statements on checks or accompanying communications. Nor is there any duty of the claimant to assign that duty to its clerks. Section 3–311(c) is intended to allow a claimant to avoid an inadvertent accord and satisfaction by complying with either subsection (c)(1) or (2) without burdening the check-processing operation with extraneous and wasteful additional duties.

8.   In some cases the disputed claim may have been assigned to a finance company or bank as part of a financing arrangement with respect to accounts receivable. If the account debtor was notified of the assignment, the claimant is the assignee of the account receivable and the "agent of the claimant" in subsection (d) refers to an agent of the assignee.

§ 3–312.   Lost, Destroyed, or Stolen Cashier's Check, Teller's Check, or Certified Check.

(a)   In this section:

(1)   "Check" means a cashier's check, teller's check, or certified check.

(2)   "Claimant" means a person who claims the right to receive the amount of a cashier's check, teller's check, or certified check that was lost, destroyed, or stolen.

(3)   "Declaration of loss" means a statement, made in a record under penalty of perjury, to the effect that (i) the declarer lost possession of a check, (ii) the declarer is the drawer or payee of the check, in the case of a certified check, or the remitter or payee of the check, in the case of a cashier's check or teller's check, (iii) the loss of possession was not the result of a transfer by the declarer

or a lawful seizure, and (iv) the declarer cannot reasonably obtain possession of the check because the check was destroyed, its whereabouts cannot be determined, or it is in the wrongful possession of an unknown person or a person that cannot be found or is not amenable to service of process.

(4) "Obligated bank" means the issuer of a cashier's check or teller's check or the acceptor of a certified check.

(b) A claimant may assert a claim to the amount of a check by a communication to the obligated bank describing the check with reasonable certainty and requesting payment of the amount of the check, if (i) the claimant is the drawer or payee of a certified check or the remitter or payee of a cashier's check or teller's check, (ii) the communication contains or is accompanied by a declaration of loss of the claimant with respect to the check, (iii) the communication is received at a time and in a manner affording the bank a reasonable time to act on it before the check is paid, and (iv) the claimant provides reasonable identification if requested by the obligated bank. Delivery of a declaration of loss is a warranty of the truth of the statements made in the declaration. If a claim is asserted in compliance with this subsection, the following rules apply:

(1) The claim becomes enforceable at the later of (i) the time the claim is asserted, or (ii) the 90th day following the date of the check, in the case of a cashier's check or teller's check, or the 90th day following the date of the acceptance, in the case of a certified check.

(2) Until the claim becomes enforceable, it has no legal effect and the obligated bank may pay the check or, in the case of a teller's check, may permit the drawee to pay the check. Payment to a person entitled to enforce the check discharges all liability of the obligated bank with respect to the check.

(3) If the claim becomes enforceable before the check is presented for payment, the obligated bank is not obliged to pay the check.

(4) When the claim becomes enforceable, the obligated bank becomes obliged to pay the amount of the check to the claimant if payment of the check has not been made to a person entitled to enforce the check. Subject to Section 4–302(a)(1), payment to the claimant discharges all liability of the obligated bank with respect to the check.

(c) If the obligated bank pays the amount of a check to a claimant under subsection (b)(4) and the check is presented for payment by a person having rights of a holder in due course, the claimant is obliged to (i) refund the payment to the obligated bank if the check is paid, or (ii) pay the amount of the check to the person having rights of a holder in due course if the check is dishonored.

(d) If a claimant has the right to assert a claim under subsection (b) and is also a person entitled to enforce a cashier's check, teller's check, or certified check which is lost, destroyed, or stolen, the claimant may assert rights with respect to the check either under this section or Section 3–309.

As added in 1991 and amended in 2002.

Official Comment

1. This section applies to cases in which a cashier's check, teller's check, or certified check is lost, destroyed, or stolen. In one typical case a customer of a bank closes his or her account and takes a cashier's check or teller's check of the bank as payment of the amount of the account. The customer may be moving to a new area and the check is to be used to open a bank account in that area. In such a case the check will normally be payable to the customer. In another typical case a cashier's check or teller's check is bought from a bank for the purpose of paying some obligation of the buyer of the check. In such a case the check may be made payable to the customer and then negotiated to the creditor by indorsement. But often, the payee of the check is the creditor. In the latter case the customer is a remitter. The section covers loss of the check by either the remitter or the payee. The section also covers loss of a certified check by either the drawer or payee.

Under Section 3–309 a person seeking to enforce a lost, destroyed, or stolen cashier's check or teller's check may be required by the court to give adequate protection to the issuing bank against loss that might occur by reason of the claim by another person to enforce the check. This might require the posting of an expensive bond for the amount of the check. The purpose of Section 3–312 is to offer a person who loses such a check a means of getting refund of the amount of the check within a reasonable period of time without the expense of posting a bond and with full protection of the obligated bank.

2.   A claim to the amount of a lost, destroyed, or stolen cashier's check, teller's check, or certified check may be made under subsection (b) if the following requirements of that subsection are met. First, a claim may be asserted only by the drawer or payee of a certified check or the remitter or payee of a cashier's check or teller's check. An indorsee of a check is not covered because the indorsee is not an original party to the check or a remitter. Limitation to an original party or remitter gives the obligated bank the ability to determine, at the time it becomes obligated on the check, the identity of the person or persons who can assert a claim with respect to the check. The bank is not faced with having to determine the rights of some person who was not a party to the check at that time or with whom the bank had not dealt. If a cashier's check is issued to the order of the person who purchased it from the bank and that person indorses it over to a third person who loses the check, the third person may assert rights to enforce the check under Section 3–309 but has no rights under Section 3–312.

Second, the claim must be asserted by a communication to the obligated bank describing the check with reasonable certainty and requesting payment of the amount of the check. "Obligated bank" is defined in subsection (a)(4). Third, the communication must be received in time to allow the obligated bank to act on the claim before the check is paid, and the claimant must provide reasonable identification if requested. Subsections (b)(iii) and (iv). Fourth, the communication must contain or be accompanied by a declaration of loss described in subsection (b). This declaration is an affidavit or other writing made under penalty of perjury alleging the loss, destruction, or theft of the check and stating that the declarer is a person entitled to assert a claim, i.e. the drawer or payee of a certified check or the remitter or payee of a cashier's check or teller's check.

A claimant who delivers a declaration of loss makes a warranty of the truth of the statements made in the declaration. The warranty is made to the obligated bank and anybody who has a right to enforce the check. If the declaration of loss falsely alleges loss of a cashier's check that did not in fact occur, a holder of the check who was unable to obtain payment because subsection (b)(3) and (4) caused the obligated bank to dishonor the check would have a cause of action against the declarer for breach of warranty.

The obligated bank may not impose additional requirements on the claimant to assert a claim under subsection (b). For example, the obligated bank may not require the posting of a bond or other form of security. Section 3–312(b) states the procedure for asserting claims covered by the section. Thus, procedures that may be stated in other law for stating claims to property do not apply and are displaced within the meaning of Section 1–103.

3.   A claim asserted under subsection (b) does not have any legal effect, however, until the date it becomes enforceable, which cannot be earlier than 90 days after the date of a cashier's check or teller's check or 90 days after the date of acceptance of a certified check. Thus, if a lost check is presented for payment within the 90-day period, the bank may pay a person entitled to enforce the check without regard to the claim and is discharged of all liability with respect to the check. This ensures the continued utility of cashier's checks, teller's checks, and certified checks as cash equivalents. Virtually all such checks are presented for payment within 90 days.

If the claim becomes enforceable and payment has not been made to a person entitled to enforce the check, the bank becomes obligated to pay the amount of the check to the claimant. Subsection (b)(4). When the bank becomes obligated to pay the amount of the check to the claimant, the bank is relieved of its obligation to pay the check. Subsection (b)(3). Thus, any person entitled to enforce the check, including even a holder in due course, loses the right to enforce the check after a claim under subsection (b) becomes enforceable.

If the obligated bank pays the claimant under subsection (b)(4), the bank is discharged of all liability with respect to the check. The only exception is the unlikely case in which the obligated bank subsequently incurs liability under Section 4–302(a)(1) with respect to the check. For example, Obligated Bank is the issuer of a cashier's check and, after a claim becomes enforceable, it pays the claimant under subsection (b)(4). Later the check is presented to Obligated Bank for payment over the counter. Under subsection (b)(3), Obligated Bank is not obliged to pay the check and may dishonor the check by returning it to the person who presented it for payment. But the normal rules of check collection are not affected by Section 3–312. If Obligated Bank retains the check beyond midnight of the day of presentment without settling for it, it becomes accountable for the amount of the check under Section 4–302(a)(1) even though it had no obligation to pay the check.

An obligated bank that pays the amount of a check to a claimant under subsection (b)(4) is discharged of all liability on the check so long as the assertion of the claim meets the requirements of subsection (b) discussed in Comment 2. This is important in cases of fraudulent declarations of loss. For example, if the claimant falsely alleges a loss that in fact did not occur, the bank, subject to Section 1–203 [*unrevised Article 1; see Concordance, p. 22*], may rely on the declaration of loss. On the other hand, a claim may be asserted only by a person described in subsection (b)(i). Thus, the bank is discharged under subsection (a)(4) only if it pays such a person. Although it is highly unlikely, it is possible that more than one person could assert a claim under subsection (b) to the amount of a check. Such a case could occur if one of the claimants makes a false declaration of loss. The obligated bank is not required to determine whether a claimant who complies with subsection (b) is acting wrongfully. The bank may utilize procedures outside this Article, such as interpleader, under which the conflicting claims may be adjudicated.

Although it is unlikely that a lost check would be presented for payment after the claimant was paid by the bank under subsection (b)(4), it is possible for it to happen. Suppose the declaration of loss by the claimant fraudulently alleged a loss that in fact did not occur. If the claimant negotiated the check, presentment for payment would occur shortly after negotiation in almost all cases. Thus, a fraudulent declaration of loss is not likely to occur unless the check is negotiated after the 90-day period has already expired or shortly before expiration. In such a case the holder of the check, who may not have noticed the date of the check, is not entitled to payment from the obligated bank if the check is presented for payment after the claim becomes enforceable. Subsection (b)(3). The remedy of the holder who is denied payment in that case is an action against the claimant under subsection (c) if the holder is a holder in due course, or for breach of warranty under subsection (b). The holder would also have common law remedies against the claimant under the law of restitution or fraud.

4. The following cases illustrate the operation of Section 3–312:

Case # 1. Obligated Bank (OB) certified a check drawn by its customer, Drawer (D), payable to Payee (P). Two days after the check was certified, D lost the check and then asserted a claim pursuant to subsection (b). The check had not been presented for payment when D's claim became enforceable 90 days after the check was certified. Under subsection (b)(4), at the time D's claim became enforceable OB became obliged to pay D the amount of the check. If the check is later presented for payment, OB may refuse to pay the check and has no obligation to anyone to pay the check. Any obligation owed by D to P, for which the check was intended as payment, is unaffected because the check was never delivered to P.

Case # 2. Obligated Bank (OB) issued a teller's check to Remitter (R) payable to Payee (P). R delivered the check to P in payment of an obligation. P lost the check and then asserted a claim pursuant to subsection (b). To carry out P's order, OB issued an order pursuant to Section 4–403(a) to the drawee of the teller's check to stop payment of the check effective on the 90th day after the date of the teller's check. The check was not presented for payment. On the 90th day after the date of the teller's check P's claim becomes enforceable and OB becomes obliged to pay P the amount of the check. As in Case # 1, OB has no further liability with respect to the check to anyone. When R delivered the check to P, R's underlying obligation to P was discharged under Section 3–310. Thus, R suffered no loss. Since P received the amount of the check, P also suffered no loss except with respect to the delay in receiving the amount of the check.

Case # 3. Obligated Bank (OB) issued a cashier's check to its customer, Payee (P). Two days after issue, the check was stolen from P who then asserted a claim pursuant to subsection (b). Ten days after issue, the check was deposited by X in an account in Depositary Bank (DB). X had found the check and forged the indorsement of P. DB promptly presented the check to OB and obtained payment on behalf of X. On the 90th day after the date of the check P's claim becomes enforceable and P is entitled to receive the amount of the check from OB. Subsection (b)(4). Although the check was presented for payment before P's claim becomes enforceable, OB is not discharged. Because of the forged indorsement X was not a holder and neither was DB. Thus, neither is a person entitled to enforce the check (Section 3–301) and OB is not discharged under Section 3–602(a). Thus, under subsection (b)(4), because OB did not pay a person entitled to enforce the check, OB must pay P. OB's remedy is against DB for breach of warranty under Section 4–208(a)(1). As an alternative to the remedy under Section 3–312, P could recover from DB for conversion under Section 3–420(a).

Case # 4. Obligated Bank (OB) issued a cashier's check to its customer, Payee (P). P made an unrestricted blank indorsement of the check and mailed the check to P's bank for deposit to P's account. The check was never received by P's bank. When P discovered the loss, P asserted a claim pursuant to subsection (b). X found the check and deposited it in X's account in Depositary Bank (DB) after indorsing the check. DB presented the check for payment before the end of the 90-day period after its date. OB paid the check. Because of the unrestricted blank indorsement by P, X became a holder of the check. DB also became a holder. Since the check was paid before P's claim became enforceable and payment was made to a person entitled to enforce the check, OB is discharged of all liability with respect to the check. Subsection (b)(2). Thus, P is not entitled to payment from OB. Subsection (b)(4) doesn't apply.

Case # 5. Obligated Bank (OB) issued a cashier's check to its customer, Payee (P). P made an unrestricted blank indorsement of the check and mailed the check to P's bank for deposit to P's account. The check was never received by P's bank. When P discovered the loss, P asserted a claim pursuant to subsection (b). At the end of the 90-day period after the date of the check, OB paid the amount of the check to P under subsection (b)(4). X then found the check and deposited it to X's account in Depositary Bank (DB). DB presented the check to OB for payment. OB is not obliged to pay the check. Subsection (b)(4). If OB dishonors the check, DB's remedy is to charge back X's account. Section 4–214(a). Although P, as an indorser, would normally have liability to DB under Section 3–415(a) because the check was dishonored, P is released from that liability under Section 3–415(e) because collection of the check was initiated more than 30 days after the indorsement. DB has a remedy only against X. A depositary bank that takes a cashier's check that cannot be presented for payment before expiration of the 90-day period after its date is on notice that the check might not be paid because of the possibility of a claim asserted under subsection (b) which would excuse the issuer of the check from paying the check. Thus, the depositary bank cannot safely release funds with respect to the check until it has assurance that the check has been paid. DB cannot be a holder in due course of the check because it took the check when the check was overdue. Section 3–304(a)(2). Thus, DB has no action against P under subsection (c).

Case # 6. Obligated Bank (OB) issued a cashier's check payable to bearer and delivered it to its customer, Remitter (R). R held the check for 90 days and then wrongfully asserted a claim to the amount of the check under subsection (b). The declaration of loss fraudulently stated that the check was lost. R received payment from OB under subsection (b)(4). R then negotiated the check to X for value. X presented the check to OB for payment. Although OB, under subsection (b)(2), was not obliged to pay the check, OB paid X by mistake. OB's teller did not notice that the check was more than 90 days old and was not aware that OB was not obliged to pay the check. If X took the check in good faith, OB may not recover from X. Section 3–418(c). OB's remedy is to recover from R for fraud or for breach of warranty in making a false declaration of loss. Subsection (b).

As amended in 2004.

PART 4

LIABILITY OF PARTIES

§ 3–401.　Signature Necessary for Liability on Instrument.

(a) A person is not liable on an instrument unless (i) the person signed the instrument, or (ii) the person is represented by an agent or representative who signed the instrument and the signature is binding on the represented person under Section 3–402.

(b) A signature may be made (i) manually or by means of a device or machine, and (ii) by the use of any name, including a trade or assumed name, or by a word, mark, or symbol executed or adopted by a person with present intention to authenticate a writing.

As amended in 2022.

Official Comment

1. Obligation This section provides the fundamental rule that an obligation on an instrument depends on a signature that is binding on the obligor. The signature may be made by the obligor personally or by an agent or other representative authorized to act for the obligor. Signature by agents and other representatives is covered by Section 3–402. It is not necessary that the name of the obligor appear on the instrument, so long as there is a signature that binds the obligor. Signature includes an indorsement. These obligations include those on an "order" (Section 3–103(a)(6)) and a "promise" (Section 3–103(a)(9)) and those of an "issuer," "maker," or "drawer" (Sections 3–103(a)(5) and (7), 3–105(c), 3–412, and 3–414), an "acceptor" (Sections 3–409 and 3–413), and an indorser (Sections 3–204(b) and 3–415).

2. A signature may be handwritten, typed, printed or made in any other manner. It need not be subscribed, and may appear in the body of the instrument, as in the case of "I, John Doe, promise to pay . . ." without any other signature. It may be made by mark, or even by thumbprint. It may be made in any name, including any trade name or assumed name, however false and fictitious, which is adopted for the purpose. Parol evidence is admissible to identify the signer, and when the signer is identified the signature is effective. Indorsement in a name other than that of the indorser is governed by Section 3–204(d). Subsection (b) of the pre-2022 text of this section has been deleted as unnecessary in view of the 2022 revision of the definition of "sign." See Section 1–201(b)(37) and Comment 37. Although former subsection (b) had not proven to be problematic, its deletion eliminates any implication that the revised definition of "sign" is inadequate for purposes of this Article.

For example, former subsection (b) provided examples of the means of making a signature with the present intention of authenticating a writing, such as by means of a device or machine, by the use of a trade name or assumed name, or by the use of a word, mark, or symbol. These means now are encompassed by the broad, general terms of the revised definition of "sign." A signature may appear in the body of the instrument, as in the case of "I, John Doe, promise to pay * * *" without any other signature. It may be made in any name, including a name other than a designated payee. However, to be signed an instrument (a writing) must exist at the time it is signed by the execution or adoption of a tangible symbol on the instrument. The deletion of former subsection (b) effected no change in the law.

This section is not intended to affect any other law requiring a signature by mark to be witnessed, or any signature to be otherwise authenticated, or requiring any form of proof.

As amended in 2022.

§ 3–402. Signature by Representative.

(a) If a person acting, or purporting to act, as a representative signs an instrument by signing either the name of the represented person or the name of the signer, the represented person is bound by the signature to the same extent the represented person would be bound if the signature were on a simple contract. If the represented person is bound, the signature of the representative is the "authorized signature of the represented person" and the represented person is liable on the instrument, whether or not identified in the instrument.

(b) If a representative signs the name of the representative to an instrument and the signature is an authorized signature of the represented person, the following rules apply:

(1) If the form of the signature shows unambiguously that the signature is made on behalf of the represented person who is identified in the instrument, the representative is not liable on the instrument.

(2) Subject to subsection (c), if (i) the form of the signature does not show unambiguously that the signature is made in a representative capacity or (ii) the represented person is not identified in the instrument, the representative is liable on the instrument to a holder in due course that took the instrument without notice that the representative was not intended to be liable on the instrument. With respect to any other person, the representative is liable on the instrument unless the representative proves that the original parties did not intend the representative to be liable on the instrument.

(c) If a representative signs the name of the representative as drawer of a check without indication of the representative status and the check is payable from an account of the represented person who is identified on the check, the signer is not liable on the check if the signature is an authorized signature of the represented person.

Official Comment

1. Subsection (a) states when the represented person is bound on an instrument if the instrument is signed by a representative. If under the law of agency the represented person would be bound by the act of the representative in signing either the name of the represented person or that of the representative, the signature is the authorized signature of the represented person. Former Section 3–401(1) stated that "no person is liable on an instrument unless his signature appears thereon." This was interpreted as meaning that an undisclosed principal is not liable on an instrument. This interpretation provided an exception to ordinary agency law that binds an undisclosed principal on a simple contract.

It is questionable whether this exception was justified by the language of former Article 3 and there is no apparent policy justification for it. The exception is rejected by subsection (a) which returns to ordinary rules of agency. If P, the principal, authorized A, the agent, to borrow money on P's behalf and A signed A's name to a note without disclosing that the signature was on behalf of P, A is liable on the instrument. But if the person entitled to enforce the note can also prove that P authorized A to sign on P's behalf, why shouldn't P also be liable on the instrument? To recognize the liability of P takes nothing away from the utility of negotiable instruments. Furthermore, imposing liability on P has the merit of making it impossible to have an instrument on which nobody is liable even though it was authorized by P. That result could occur under former Section 3–401(1) if an authorized agent signed "as agent" but the note did not identify the principal. If the dispute was between the agent and the payee of the note, the agent could escape liability on the note by proving that the agent and the payee did not

331

intend that the agent be liable on the note when the note was issued. Former Section 3–403(2)(b). Under the prevailing interpretation of former Section 3–401(1), the principal was not liable on the note under former 3–401(1) because the principal's name did not appear on the note. Thus, nobody was liable on the note even though all parties knew that the note was signed by the agent on behalf of the principal. Under Section 3–402(a) the principal would be liable on the note.

2.   Subsection (b) concerns the question of when an agent who signs an instrument on behalf of a principal is bound on the instrument. The approach followed by former Section 3–403 was to specify the form of signature that imposed or avoided liability. This approach was unsatisfactory. There are many ways in which there can be ambiguity about a signature. It is better to state a general rule. Subsection (b)(1) states that if the form of the signature unambiguously shows that it is made on behalf of an identified represented person (for example, "P, by A, Treasurer") the agent is not liable. This is a workable standard for a court to apply. Subsection (b)(2) partly changes former Section 3–403(2). Subsection (b)(2) relates to cases in which the agent signs on behalf of a principal but the form of the signature does not fall within subsection (b)(1). The following cases are illustrative. In each case John Doe is the authorized agent of Richard Roe and John Doe signs a note on behalf of Richard Roe. In each case the intention of the original parties to the instrument is that Roe is to be liable on the instrument but Doe is not to be liable.

Case # 1. Doe signs "John Doe" without indicating in the note that Doe is signing as agent. The note does not identify Richard Roe as the represented person.

Case # 2. Doe signs "John Doe, Agent" but the note does not identify Richard Roe as the represented person.

Case # 3. The name "Richard Roe" is written on the note and immediately below that name Doe signs "John Doe" without indicating that Doe signed as agent.

In each case Doe is liable on the instrument to a holder in due course without notice that Doe was not intended to be liable. In none of the cases does Doe's signature unambiguously show that Doe was signing as agent for an identified principal. A holder in due course should be able to resolve any ambiguity against Doe.

But the situation is different if a holder in due course is not involved. In each case Roe is liable on the note. Subsection (a). If the original parties to the note did not intend that Doe also be liable, imposing liability on Doe is a windfall to the person enforcing the note. Under subsection (b)(2) Doe is prima facie liable because his signature appears on the note and the form of the signature does not unambiguously refute personal liability. But Doe can escape liability by proving that the original parties did not intend that he be liable on the note. This is a change from former Section 3–403(2)(a).

A number of cases under former Article 3 involved situations in which an agent signed the agent's name to a note, without qualification and without naming the person represented, intending to bind the principal but not the agent. The agent attempted to prove that the other party had the same intention. Some of these cases involved mistake, and in some there was evidence that the agent may have been deceived into signing in that manner. In some of the cases the court refused to allow proof of the intention of the parties and imposed liability on the agent based on former Section 3–403(2)(a) even though both parties to the instrument may have intended that the agent not be liable. Subsection (b)(2) changes the result of those cases, and is consistent with Section 3–117 which allows oral or written agreements to modify or nullify apparent obligations on the instrument.

Former Section 3–403 spoke of the represented person being "named" in the instrument. Section 3–402 speaks of the represented person being "identified" in the instrument. This change in terminology is intended to reject decisions under former Section 3–403(2) requiring that the instrument state the legal name of the represented person.

3.   Subsection (c) is directed at the check cases. It states that if the check identifies the represented person the agent who signs on the signature line does not have to indicate agency status. Virtually all checks used today are in personalized form which identify the person on whose account the check is drawn. In this case, nobody is deceived into thinking that the person signing the check is meant to be liable. This subsection is meant to overrule cases decided under former Article 3 such as Griffin v. Ellinger, 538 S.W.2d 97 (Texas 1976).

§ 3–403.   Unauthorized Signature.

(a)   Unless otherwise provided in this Article or Article 4, an unauthorized signature is ineffective except as the signature of the unauthorized signer in favor of a person who in good faith pays the instrument or takes it for value. An unauthorized signature may be ratified for all purposes of this Article.

(b)   If the signature of more than one person is required to constitute the authorized signature of an organization, the signature of the organization is unauthorized if one of the required signatures is lacking.

(c)   The civil or criminal liability of a person who makes an unauthorized signature is not affected by any provision of this Article which makes the unauthorized signature effective for the purposes of this Article.

Official Comment

1.   "Unauthorized" signature is defined in Section 1–201(43) [*unrevised Article 1; see Concordance, p. 22*] as one that includes a forgery as well as a signature made by one exceeding actual or apparent authority. Former Section 3–404(1) stated that an unauthorized signature was inoperative as the signature of the person whose name was signed unless that person "is precluded from denying it." Under former Section 3–406 if negligence by the person whose name was signed contributed to an unauthorized signature, that person "is precluded from asserting the . . . lack of authority." Both of these sections were applied to cases in which a forged signature appeared on an instrument and the person asserting rights on the instrument alleged that the negligence of the purported signer contributed to the forgery. Since the standards for liability between the two sections differ, the overlap between the sections caused confusion. Section 3–403(a) deals with the problem by removing the preclusion language that appeared in former Section 3–404.

2.   The except clause of the first sentence of subsection (a) states the generally accepted rule that the unauthorized signature, while it is wholly inoperative as that of the person whose name is signed, is effective to impose liability upon the signer or to transfer any rights that the signer may have in the instrument. The signer's liability is not in damages for breach of warranty of authority, but is full liability on the instrument in the capacity in which the signer signed. It is, however, limited to parties who take or pay the instrument in good faith; and one who knows that the signature is unauthorized cannot recover from the signer on the instrument.

3.   The last sentence of subsection (a) allows an unauthorized signature to be ratified. Ratification is a retroactive adoption of the unauthorized signature by the person whose name is signed and may be found from conduct as well as from express statements. For example, it may be found from the retention of benefits received in the transaction with knowledge of the unauthorized signature. Although the forger is not an agent, ratification is governed by the rules and principles applicable to ratification of unauthorized acts of an agent.

Ratification is effective for all purposes of this Article. The unauthorized signature becomes valid so far as its effect as a signature is concerned. Although the ratification may relieve the signer of liability on the instrument, it does not of itself relieve the signer of liability to the person whose name is signed. It does not in any way affect the criminal law. No policy of the criminal law prevents a person whose name is forged to assume liability to others on the instrument by ratifying the forgery, but the ratification cannot affect the rights of the state. While the ratification may be taken into account with other relevant facts in determining punishment, it does not relieve the signer of criminal liability.

4.   Subsection (b) clarifies the meaning of "unauthorized" in cases in which an instrument contains less than all of the signatures that are required as authority to pay a check. Judicial authority was split on the issue whether the one-year notice period under former Section 4–406(4) (now Section 4–406(f)) barred a customer's suit against a payor bank that paid a check containing less than all of the signatures required by the customer to authorize payment of the check. Some cases took the view that if a customer required that a check contain the signatures of both A and B to authorize payment and only A signed, there was no unauthorized signature within the meaning of that term in former Section 4–406(4) because A's signature was neither unauthorized nor forged. The other cases correctly pointed out that it was the customer's signature at issue and not that of A; hence, the customer's signature was unauthorized if all signatures required to authorize payment of the check were not on the check. Subsection (b) follows the latter line of cases. The same analysis applies if A forged the signature of B. Because the forgery is not effective as a signature of B, the required signature of B is lacking.

Subsection (b) refers to "the authorized signature of an organization." The definition of "organization" in Section 1–201(28) [*unrevised Article 1; see Concordance, p. 22*] is very broad. It covers not only commercial entities but also "two or more persons having a joint or common interest." Hence subsection (b) would apply when a husband and wife are both required to sign an instrument.

§ 3–404.   Impostors; Fictitious Payees.

(a)   If an impostor, by use of the mails or otherwise, induces the issuer of an instrument to issue the instrument to the impostor, or to a person acting in concert with the impostor, by impersonating the payee of the instrument or a person authorized to act for the payee, an indorsement of the instrument by any person in the name of the payee is effective as the indorsement of the payee in favor of a person who, in good faith, pays the instrument or takes it for value or for collection.

(b) If (i) a person whose intent determines to whom an instrument is payable (Section 3–110(a) or (b)) does not intend the person identified as payee to have any interest in the instrument, or (ii) the person identified as payee of an instrument is a fictitious person, the following rules apply until the instrument is negotiated by special indorsement:

(1) Any person in possession of the instrument is its holder.

(2) An indorsement by any person in the name of the payee stated in the instrument is effective as the indorsement of the payee in favor of a person who, in good faith, pays the instrument or takes it for value or for collection.

(c) Under subsection (a) or (b), an indorsement is made in the name of a payee if (i) it is made in a name substantially similar to that of the payee or (ii) the instrument, whether or not indorsed, is deposited in a depositary bank to an account in a name substantially similar to that of the payee.

(d) With respect to an instrument to which subsection (a) or (b) applies, if a person paying the instrument or taking it for value or for collection fails to exercise ordinary care in paying or taking the instrument and that failure substantially contributes to loss resulting from payment of the instrument, the person bearing the loss may recover from the person failing to exercise ordinary care to the extent the failure to exercise ordinary care contributed to the loss.

Official Comment

1. Under former Article 3, the impostor cases were governed by former Section 3–405(1)(a) and the fictitious payee cases were governed by Section 3–405(1)(b). Section 3–404 replaces former Section 3–405(1)(a) and (b) and modifies the previous law in some respects. Former Section 3–405 was read by some courts to require that the indorsement be in the exact name of the named payee. Revised Article 3 rejects this result. Section 3–404(c) requires only that the indorsement be made in a name "substantially similar" to that of the payee. Subsection (c) also recognizes the fact that checks may be deposited without indorsement. Section 4–205(a).

Subsection (a) changes the former law in a case in which the impostor is impersonating an agent. Under former Section 3–405(1)(a), if Impostor impersonated Smith and induced the drawer to draw a check to the order of Smith, Impostor could negotiate the check. If Impostor impersonated Smith, the president of Smith Corporation, and the check was payable to the order of Smith Corporation, the section did not apply. See the last paragraph of Comment 2 to former Section 3–405. In revised Article 3, Section 3–404(a) gives Impostor the power to negotiate the check in both cases.

2. Subsection (b) is based in part on former Section 3–405(1)(b) and in part on N.I.L. § 9(3). It covers cases in which an instrument is payable to a fictitious or nonexisting person and to cases in which the payee is a real person but the drawer or maker does not intend the payee to have any interest in the instrument. Subsection (b) applies to any instrument, but its primary importance is with respect to checks of corporations and other organizations. It also applies to forged check cases. The following cases illustrate subsection (b):

Case # 1. Treasurer is authorized to draw checks in behalf of Corporation. Treasurer fraudulently draws a check of Corporation payable to Supplier Co., a non-existent company. Subsection (b) applies because Supplier Co. is a fictitious person and because Treasurer did not intend Supplier Co. to have any interest in the check. Under subsection (b)(1) Treasurer, as the person in possession of the check, becomes the holder of the check. Treasurer indorses the check in the name "Supplier Co." and deposits it in Depositary Bank. Under subsection (b)(2) and (c)(i), the indorsement is effective to make Depositary Bank the holder and therefore a person entitled to enforce the instrument. Section 3–301.

Case # 2. Same facts as Case # 1 except that Supplier Co. is an actual company that does business with Corporation. If Treasurer intended to steal the check when the check was drawn, the result in Case # 2 is the same as the result in Case # 1. Subsection (b) applies because Treasurer did not intend Supplier Co. to have any interest in the check. It does not make any difference whether Supplier Co. was or was not a creditor of Corporation when the check was drawn. If Treasurer did not decide to steal the check until after the check was drawn, the case is covered by Section 3–405 rather than Section 3–404(b), but the result is the same. See Case # 6 in Comment 3 to Section 3–405.

Case # 3. Checks of Corporation must be signed by two officers. President and Treasurer both sign a check of Corporation payable to Supplier Co., a company that does business with Corporation from time to time but to which Corporation does not owe any money. Treasurer knows that no money is owed to Supplier Co. and does not intend that Supplier Co. have any interest in the check. President believes that money is owed to Supplier Co. Treasurer obtains possession of the check after it is signed. Subsection (b) applies because Treasurer is "a person whose intent determines to whom an instrument is payable" and Treasurer does not intend Supplier Co. to have any interest in the check. Treasurer becomes the holder of the check and may negotiate it by indorsing it in the name "Supplier Co."

Case # 4. Checks of Corporation are signed by a check-writing machine. Names of payees of checks produced by the machine are determined by information entered into the computer that operates the machine. Thief, a person who is not an employee or other agent of Corporation, obtains access to the computer and causes the check-writing machine to produce a check payable to Supplier Co., a non-existent company. Subsection (b)(ii) applies. Thief then obtains possession of the check. At that point Thief becomes the holder of the check because Thief is the person in possession of the instrument. Subsection (b)(1). Under Section 3–301 Thief, as holder, is the "person entitled to enforce the instrument" even though Thief does not have title to the check and is in wrongful possession of it. Thief indorses the check in the name "Supplier Co." and deposits it in an account in Depositary Bank which Thief opened in the name "Supplier Co." Depositary Bank takes the check in good faith and credits the "Supplier Co." account. Under subsection (b)(2) and (c)(i), the indorsement is effective. Depositary Bank becomes the holder and the person entitled to enforce the check. The check is presented to the drawee bank for payment and payment is made. Thief then withdraws the credit to the account. Although the check was issued without authority given by Corporation, the drawee bank is entitled to pay the check and charge Corporation's account if there was an agreement with Corporation allowing the bank to debit Corporation's account for payment of checks produced by the check-writing machine whether or not authorized. The indorsement is also effective if Supplier Co. is a real person. In that case subsection (b)(i) applies. Under Section 3–110(b) Thief is the person whose intent determines to whom the check is payable, and Thief did not intend Supplier Co. to have any interest in the check. When the drawee bank pays the check, there is no breach of warranty under Section 3–417(a)(1) or 4–208(a)(1) because Depositary Bank was a person entitled to enforce the check when it was forwarded for payment.

Case # 5. Thief, who is not an employee or agent of Corporation, steals check forms of Corporation. John Doe is president of Corporation and is authorized to sign checks on behalf of Corporation as drawer. Thief draws a check in the name of Corporation as drawer by forging the signature of Doe. Thief makes the check payable to the order of Supplier Co. with the intention of stealing it. Whether Supplier Co. is a fictitious person or a real person, Thief becomes the holder of the check and the person entitled to enforce it. The analysis is the same as that in Case # 4. Thief deposits the check in an account in Depositary Bank which Thief opened in the name "Supplier Co." Thief either indorses the check in a name other than "Supplier Co." or does not indorse the check at all. Under Section 4–205(a) a depositary bank may become holder of a check deposited to the account of a customer if the customer was a holder, whether or not the customer indorses. Subsection (c)(ii) treats deposit to an account in a name substantially similar to that of the payee as the equivalent of indorsement in the name of the payee. Thus, the deposit is an effective indorsement of the check. Depositary Bank becomes the holder of the check and the person entitled to enforce the check. If the check is paid by the drawee bank, there is no breach of warranty under Section 3–417(a)(1) or 4–208(a)(1) because Depositary Bank was a person entitled to enforce the check when it was forwarded for payment and, unless Depositary Bank knew about the forgery of Doe's signature, there is no breach of warranty under Section 3–417(a)(3) or 4–208(a)(3). Because the check was a forged check the drawee bank is not entitled to charge Corporation's account unless Section 3–406 or Section 4–406 applies.

3.   In cases governed by subsection (a) the dispute will normally be between the drawer of the check that was obtained by the impostor and the drawee bank that paid it. The drawer is precluded from obtaining recredit of the drawer's account by arguing that the check was paid on a forged indorsement so long as the drawee bank acted in good faith in paying the check. Cases governed by subsection (b) are illustrated by Cases # 1 through # 5 in Comment 2. In Cases # 1, # 2, and # 3 there is no forgery of the check, thus the drawer of the check takes the loss if there is no lack of good faith by the banks involved. Cases # 4 and # 5 are forged check cases. Depositary Bank is entitled to retain the proceeds of the check if it didn't know about the forgery. Under Section 3–418 the drawee bank is not entitled to recover from Depositary Bank on the basis of payment by mistake because Depositary Bank took the check in good faith and gave value for the check when the credit given for the check was withdrawn. And there is no breach of warranty under Section 3–417(a)(1) or (3) or 4–208(a)(1) or (3). Unless Section 3–406 applies the loss is taken by the drawee bank if a forged check is paid, and that is the result in Case # 5. In Case # 4 the loss is taken by Corporation, the drawer, because an agreement between Corporation and the drawee bank allowed the bank to debit Corporation's account despite the unauthorized use of the check-writing machine.

If a check payable to an impostor, fictitious payee, or payee not intended to have an interest in the check is paid, the effect of subsections (a) and (b) is to place the loss on the drawer of the check rather than on the drawee or the depositary bank that took the check for collection. Cases governed by subsection (a) always involve fraud, and fraud is almost always involved in cases governed by subsection (b). The drawer is in the best position to avoid the fraud and thus should take the loss. This is true in Case # 1, Case # 2, and Case # 3. But in some cases the person taking the check might have detected the fraud and thus have prevented the loss by the exercise of ordinary care. In those cases, if that person failed to exercise ordinary care, it is reasonable that that person bear loss to the extent the failure contributed to the loss. Subsection (d) is intended to reach that result. It allows the person who suffers loss as a result of payment of the check to recover from the person who failed to exercise ordinary care. In Case # 1, Case # 2, and Case # 3, the person suffering the loss is Corporation, the drawer of the check. In each case the most likely defendant is the depositary bank that took the check and failed to exercise ordinary care. In those cases, the drawer has a cause of action against the offending bank to recover a portion of the loss. The amount of loss to be allocated to each party is left to the trier of fact. Ordinary care is defined in Section 3–103(a)(9). An example of the type of conduct by a depositary bank that could give rise to recovery under subsection (d) is discussed in Comment 4 to Section 3–405. That comment addresses the last sentence of Section 3–405(b) which is similar to Section 3–404(d).

In Case # 1, Case # 2, and Case # 3, there was no forgery of the drawer's signature. But cases involving checks payable to a fictitious payee or a payee not intended to have an interest in the check are often forged check cases as well. Examples are Case # 4 and Case # 5. Normally, the loss in forged check cases is on the drawee bank that paid the check. Case # 5 is an example. In Case # 4 the risk with respect to the forgery is shifted to the drawer because of the agreement between the drawer and the drawee bank. The doctrine that prevents a drawee bank from recovering payment with respect to a forged check if the payment was made to a person who took the check for value and in good faith is incorporated into Section 3–418 and Sections 3–417(a)(3) and 4–208(a)(3). This doctrine is based on the assumption that the depositary bank normally has no way of detecting the forgery because the drawer is not that bank's customer. On the other hand, the drawee bank, at least in some cases, may be able to detect the forgery by comparing the signature on the check with the specimen signature that the drawee has on file. But in some forged check cases the depositary bank is in a position to detect the fraud. Those cases typically involve a check payable to a fictitious payee or a payee not intended to have an interest in the check. Subsection (d) applies to those cases. If the depositary bank failed to exercise ordinary care and the failure substantially contributed to the loss, the drawer in Case # 4 or the drawee bank in Case # 5 has a cause of action against the depositary bank under subsection (d). Comment 4 to Section 3–405 can be used as a guide to the type of conduct that could give rise to recovery under Section 3–404(d).

§ 3–405.   Employer's Responsibility for Fraudulent Indorsement by Employee.

(a)   In this section:

(1)   "Employee" includes an independent contractor and employee of an independent contractor retained by the employer.

(2)   "Fraudulent indorsement" means (i) in the case of an instrument payable to the employer, a forged indorsement purporting to be that of the employer, or (ii) in the case of an instrument with respect to which the employer is the issuer, a forged indorsement purporting to be that of the person identified as payee.

(3)   "Responsibility" with respect to instruments means authority (i) to sign or indorse instruments on behalf of the employer, (ii) to process instruments received by the employer for bookkeeping purposes, for deposit to an account, or for other disposition, (iii) to prepare or process instruments for issue in the name of the employer, (iv) to supply information determining the names or addresses of payees of instruments to be issued in the name of the employer, (v) to control the disposition of instruments to be issued in the name of the employer, or (vi) to act otherwise with respect to instruments in a responsible capacity. "Responsibility" does not include authority that merely allows an employee to have access to instruments or blank or incomplete instrument forms that are being stored or transported or are part of incoming or outgoing mail, or similar access.

(b)   For the purpose of determining the rights and liabilities of a person who, in good faith, pays an instrument or takes it for value or for collection, if an employer entrusted an employee with responsibility with respect to the instrument and the employee or a person acting in concert with the employee makes a fraudulent indorsement of the instrument, the indorsement is effective as the indorsement of the person to whom the instrument is payable if it is made in the name of that person. If the person paying the instrument or taking it for value or for collection fails to exercise ordinary care in paying or taking the instrument and that failure substantially contributes to loss resulting from the fraud, the person bearing the loss may recover from the person failing to exercise ordinary care to the extent the failure to exercise ordinary care contributed to the loss.

(c)   Under subsection (b), an indorsement is made in the name of the person to whom an instrument is payable if (i) it is made in a name substantially similar to the name of that person or (ii) the instrument, whether or not indorsed, is deposited in a depositary bank to an account in a name substantially similar to the name of that person.

Official Comment

1.   Section 3–405 is addressed to fraudulent indorsements made by an employee with respect to instruments with respect to which the employer has given responsibility to the employee. It covers two categories of fraudulent indorsements: indorsements made in the name of the employer to instruments payable to the employer and indorsements made in the name of payees of instruments issued by the employer. This section applies to instruments generally but normally the instrument will be a check. Section 3–405 adopts the principle that the risk of loss for fraudulent indorsements by employees who are entrusted with responsibility with respect to checks should fall on the employer rather than the bank that takes the check or pays it, if the bank was not negligent in the transaction. Section 3–405 is based on the belief that the employer is in a far better position to avoid the loss by care in choosing employees, in supervising them, and in adopting other measures to prevent forged indorsements on instruments payable to the employer or fraud in the issuance of instruments in the name of the employer. If the bank failed to exercise ordinary care, subsection (b) allows the employer to shift loss to the bank to the extent the bank's failure to exercise ordinary care contributed to the loss. "Ordinary care" is defined in Section 3–103(a)(9). The provision applies regardless of whether the employer is negligent.

The first category of cases governed by Section 3–405 are those involving indorsements made in the name of payees of instruments issued by the employer. In this category, Section 3–405 includes cases that were covered by former Section 3–405(1)(c). The scope of Section 3–405 in revised Article 3 is, however, somewhat wider. It covers some cases not covered by former Section 3–405(1)(c) in which the entrusted employee makes a forged indorsement to a check drawn by the employer. An example is Case # 6 in Comment 3. Moreover, a larger group of employees is included in revised Section 3–405. The key provision is the definition of "responsibility" in subsection (a)(1) which identifies the kind of responsibility delegated to an employee which will cause the employer to take responsibility for the fraudulent acts of that employee. An employer can insure this risk by employee fidelity bonds.

The second category of cases governed by Section 3–405—fraudulent indorsements of the name of the employer to instruments payable to the employer—were covered in former Article 3 by Section 3–406. Under former Section 3–406, the employer took the loss only if negligence of the employer could be proved. Under revised Article 3, Section 3–406 need not be used with respect to forgeries of the employer's indorsement. Section 3–405 imposes the loss on the employer without proof of negligence.

2.   With respect to cases governed by former Section 3–405(1)(c), Section 3–405 is more favorable to employers in one respect. The bank was entitled to the preclusion provided by former Section 3–405(1)(c) if it took the check in good faith. The fact that the bank acted negligently did not shift the loss to the bank so long as the bank acted in good faith. Under revised Section 3–405 the loss may be recovered from the bank to the extent the failure of the bank to exercise ordinary care contributed to the loss.

3.   Section 3–404(b) and Section 3–405 both apply to cases of employee fraud. Section 3–404(b) is not limited to cases of employee fraud, but most of the cases to which it applies will be cases of employee fraud. The following cases illustrate the application of Section 3–405. In each case it is assumed that the bank that took the check acted in good faith and was not negligent.

Case # 1. Janitor, an employee of Employer, steals a check for a very large amount payable to Employer after finding it on a desk in one of Employer's offices. Janitor forges Employer's indorsement on the check and obtains payment. Since Janitor was not entrusted with "responsibility" with respect to the check, Section 3–405 does not apply. Section 3–406 might apply to this case. The issue would be whether Employer was negligent in safeguarding the check. If not, Employer could assert that the indorsement was forged and bring an action for conversion against the depositary or payor bank under Section 3–420.

Case # 2. X is Treasurer of Corporation and is authorized to write checks on behalf of Corporation by signing X's name as Treasurer. X draws a check in the name of Corporation and signs X's name as Treasurer. The check is made payable to X. X then indorses the check and obtains payment. Assume that Corporation did not owe any money to X and did not authorize X to write the check. Although the writing of the check was not authorized, Corporation is bound as drawer of the check because X had authority to sign checks on behalf of Corporation. This result follows from agency law and Section 3–402(a). Section 3–405 does not apply in this case because there is no forged indorsement. X was payee of the check so the indorsement is valid. Section 3–110(a).

Case # 3. The duties of Employee, a bookkeeper, include posting the amounts of checks payable to Employer to the accounts of the drawers of the checks. Employee steals a check payable to Employer which was entrusted to Employee and forges Employer's indorsement. The check is deposited by Employee to an account in Depositary Bank which Employee opened in the same name as Employer, and the check is honored by the drawee bank. The indorsement is effective as Employer's indorsement because Employee's duties include processing checks for bookkeeping purposes. Thus, Employee is entrusted with "responsibility" with respect to the check. Neither Depositary Bank nor the drawee bank is liable to Employer for conversion of the check. The same result follows if Employee deposited the check in the account in Depositary Bank without indorsement. Section 4–205(a). Under subsection (c) deposit in a depositary bank in an account in a name substantially similar to that of Employer is the equivalent of an indorsement in the name of Employer.

Case # 4. Employee's duties include stamping Employer's unrestricted blank indorsement on checks received by Employer and depositing them in Employer's bank account. After stamping Employer's unrestricted blank indorsement on a check, Employee steals the check and deposits it in Employee's personal bank account. Section 3–405 doesn't apply because there is no forged indorsement. Employee is authorized by Employer to indorse Employer's checks. The fraud by Employee is not the indorsement but rather the theft of the indorsed check. Whether Employer has a cause of action against the bank in which the check was deposited is determined by whether the bank had notice of the breach of fiduciary duty by Employee. The issue is determined under Section 3–307.

Case # 5. The computer that controls Employer's check-writing machine was programmed to cause a check to be issued to Supplier Co. to which money was owed by Employer. The address of Supplier Co. was included in the information in the computer. Employee is an accounts payable clerk whose duties include entering information into the computer. Employee fraudulently changed the address of Supplier Co. in the computer data bank to an address of Employee. The check was subsequently produced by the check-writing machine and mailed to the address that Employee had entered into the computer. Employee obtained possession of the check, indorsed it in the name of Supplier Co, and deposited it to an account in Depositary Bank which Employee opened in the name "Supplier Co." The check was honored by the drawee bank. The indorsement is effective under Section 3–405(b) because Employee's duties allowed Employee to supply information determining the address of the payee of the check. An employee that is entrusted with duties that enable the employee to determine the address to which a check is to be sent controls the disposition of the check and facilitates forgery of the indorsement. The employer is held responsible. The drawee may debit the account of Employer for the amount of the check. There is no breach of warranty by Depositary Bank under Section 3–417(a)(1) or 4–208(a)(1).

Case # 6. Treasurer is authorized to draw checks in behalf of Corporation. Treasurer draws a check of Corporation payable to Supplier Co., a company that sold goods to Corporation. The check was issued to pay the price of these goods. At the time the check was signed Treasurer had no intention of stealing the check. Later, Treasurer stole the check, indorsed it in the name "Supplier Co." and obtained payment by depositing it to an account in Depositary Bank which Treasurer opened in the name "Supplier Co.". The indorsement is effective under Section 3–405(b). Section 3–404(b) does not apply to this case.

Case # 7. Checks of Corporation are signed by Treasurer in behalf of Corporation as drawer. Clerk's duties include the preparation of checks for issue by Corporation. Clerk prepares a check payable to the order of Supplier Co. for Treasurer's signature. Clerk fraudulently informs Treasurer that the check is needed to pay a debt owed to Supplier Co, a company that does business with Corporation. No money is owed to Supplier Co. and Clerk intends to steal the check. Treasurer signs it and returns it to Clerk for mailing. Clerk does not indorse the check but deposits it to an account in Depositary Bank which Clerk opened in the name "Supplier Co.". The check is honored by the drawee bank. Section 3–404(b)(i) does not apply to this case because Clerk, under Section 3–110(a), is not the person whose intent determines to whom the check is payable. But Section 3–405 does apply and it treats the deposit by Clerk as an effective indorsement by Clerk because Clerk was entrusted with responsibility with respect to the check. If Supplier Co. is a fictitious person Section 3–404(b)(ii) applies. But the result is the same. Clerk's deposit is treated as an effective indorsement of the check whether Supplier Co. is a fictitious or a real person or whether money was or was not owing to Supplier Co. The drawee bank may debit the account of Corporation for the amount of the check and there is no breach of warranty by Depositary Bank under Section 3–417(1)(a).

4.　The last sentence of subsection (b) is similar to subsection (d) of Section 3–404 which is discussed in Comment 3 to Section 3–404. In Case # 5, Case # 6, or Case # 7 the depositary bank may have failed to exercise ordinary care when it allowed the employee to open an account in the name "Supplier Co.," to deposit checks payable to "Supplier Co." in that account, or to withdraw funds from that account that were proceeds of checks payable to Supplier Co. Failure to exercise ordinary care is to be determined in the context of all the facts relating to the bank's conduct with respect to the bank's collection of the check. If the trier of fact finds that there was such a failure and that the failure substantially contributed to loss, it could find the depositary bank liable to the extent the failure contributed to the loss. The last sentence of subsection (b) can be illustrated by an example. Suppose in Case # 5 that the check is not payable to an obscure "Supplier Co." but rather to a well-known national corporation. In addition, the check is for a very large amount of money. Before depositing the check, Employee opens an account in Depositary Bank in the name of the corporation and states to the person conducting the transaction for the bank that Employee is manager of a new office being opened by the corporation. Depositary Bank opens the account without requiring Employee to produce any resolutions of the corporation's board of directors or other evidence of authorization of Employee to act for the corporation. A few days later, the check is deposited, the account is credited, and the check is presented for payment. After Depositary Bank receives payment, it allows Employee to withdraw the credit by a wire transfer to an account in a bank in a foreign country. The trier of fact could find that Depositary Bank did not exercise ordinary care and that the failure to exercise ordinary care contributed to the loss suffered by Employer. The trier of fact could allow recovery by Employer from Depositary Bank for all or part of the loss suffered by Employer.

As amended in 2005.

§ 3–406.　Negligence Contributing to Forged Signature or Alteration of Instrument.

(a)　A person whose failure to exercise ordinary care substantially contributes to an alteration of an instrument or to the making of a forged signature on an instrument is precluded from asserting the alteration or the forgery against a person who, in good faith, pays the instrument or takes it for value or for collection.

(b)　Under subsection (a), if the person asserting the preclusion fails to exercise ordinary care in paying or taking the instrument and that failure substantially contributes to loss, the loss is allocated between the person precluded and the person asserting the preclusion according to the extent to which the failure of each to exercise ordinary care contributed to the loss.

(c)　Under subsection (a), the burden of proving failure to exercise ordinary care is on the person asserting the preclusion. Under subsection (b), the burden of proving failure to exercise ordinary care is on the person precluded.

Official Comment

1.　Section 3–406(a) is based on former Section 3–406. With respect to alteration, Section 3–406 adopts the doctrine of *Young v. Grote*, 4 Bing. 253 (1827), which held that a drawer who so negligently draws an instrument as to facilitate its material alteration is liable to a drawee who pays the altered instrument in good faith. Under Section 3–406 the doctrine is expanded to apply not only to drafts but to all instruments. It includes in the protected class any "person who, in good faith, pays the instrument or takes it for value or for collection." Section 3–406 rejects decisions holding that the maker of a note owes no duty of care to the holder because at the time the instrument is issued there is no contract between them. By issuing the instrument and "setting it afloat upon a sea of strangers" the maker or drawer voluntarily enters into a relation with later holders which justifies imposition of a duty of care. In this respect an instrument so negligently drawn as to facilitate alteration does not differ in principle from an instrument containing blanks which may be filled. Under Section 3–407 a person paying an altered instrument or taking it for value, in good faith and without notice of the alteration may enforce rights with respect to the instrument according to its original terms. If negligence of the obligor substantially contributes to an alteration, this section gives the holder or the payor the alternative right to treat the altered instrument as though it had been issued in the altered form.

No attempt is made to define particular conduct that will constitute "failure to exercise ordinary care [that] substantially contributes to an alteration." Rather, "ordinary care" is defined in Section 3–103(a)(9) in general terms. The question is left to the court or the jury for decision in the light of the circumstances in the particular case including reasonable commercial standards that may apply.

Section 3–406 does not make the negligent party liable in tort for damages resulting from the alteration. If the negligent party is estopped from asserting the alteration the person taking the instrument is fully protected because the taker can treat the instrument as having been issued in the altered form.

2.　　Section 3–406 applies equally to a failure to exercise ordinary care that substantially contributes to the making of a forged signature on an instrument. Section 3–406 refers to "forged signature" rather than "unauthorized signature" that appeared in former Section 3–406 because it more accurately describes the scope of the provision. Unauthorized signature is a broader concept that includes not only forgery but also the signature of an agent which does not bind the principal under the law of agency. The agency cases are resolved independently under agency law. Section 3–406 is not necessary in those cases.

The "substantially contributes" test of former Section 3–406 is continued in this section in preference to a "direct and proximate cause" test. The "substantially contributes" test is meant to be less stringent than a "direct and proximate cause" test. Under the less stringent test the preclusion should be easier to establish. Conduct "substantially contributes" to a material alteration or forged signature if it is a contributing cause of the alteration or signature and a substantial factor in bringing it about. The analysis of "substantially contributes" in former Section 3–406 by the court in *Thompson Maple Products v. Citizens National Bank of Corry*, 234 A.2d 32 (Pa.Super.Ct. 1967), states what is intended by the use of the same words in revised Section 3–406(b). Since Section 3–404(d) and Section 3–405(b) also use the words "substantially contributes" the analysis of these words also applies to those provisions.

3.　　The following cases illustrate the kind of conduct that can be the basis of a preclusion under Section 3–406(a):

Case # 1. Employer signs checks drawn on Employer's account by use of a rubber stamp of Employer's signature. Employer keeps the rubber stamp along with Employer's personalized blank check forms in an unlocked desk drawer. An unauthorized person fraudulently uses the check forms to write checks on Employer's account. The checks are signed by use of the rubber stamp. If Employer demands that Employer's account in the drawee bank be recredited because the forged check was not properly payable, the drawee bank may defend by asserting that Employer is precluded from asserting the forgery. The trier of fact could find that Employer failed to exercise ordinary care to safeguard the rubber stamp and the check forms and that the failure substantially contributed to the forgery of Employer's signature by the unauthorized use of the rubber stamp.

Case # 2. An insurance company draws a check to the order of Sarah Smith in payment of a claim of a policyholder, Sarah Smith, who lives in Alabama. The insurance company also has a policyholder with the same name who lives in Illinois. By mistake, the insurance company mails the check to the Illinois Sarah Smith who indorses the check and obtains payment. Because the payee of the check is the Alabama Sarah Smith, the indorsement by the Illinois Sarah Smith is a forged indorsement. Section 3–110(a). The trier of fact could find that the insurance company failed to exercise ordinary care when it mailed the check to the wrong person and that the failure substantially contributed to the making of the forged indorsement. In that event the insurance company could be precluded from asserting the forged indorsement against the drawee bank that honored the check.

Case # 3. A company writes a check for $10. The figure "10" and the word "ten" are typewritten in the appropriate spaces on the check form. A large blank space is left after the figure and the word. The payee of the check, using a typewriter with a typeface similar to that used on the check, writes the word "thousand" after the word "ten" and a comma and three zeros after the figure "10". The drawee bank in good faith pays $10,000 when the check is presented for payment and debits the account of the drawer in that amount. The trier of fact could find that the drawer failed to exercise ordinary care in writing the check and that the failure substantially contributed to the alteration. In that case the drawer is precluded from asserting the alteration against the drawee if the check was paid in good faith.

4.　　Subsection (b) differs from former Section 3–406 in that it adopts a concept of comparative negligence. If the person precluded under subsection (a) proves that the person asserting the preclusion failed to exercise ordinary care and that failure substantially contributed to the loss, the loss may be allocated between the two parties on a comparative negligence basis. In the case of a forged indorsement the litigation is usually between the payee of the check and the depositary bank that took the check for collection. An example is a case like Case # 1 of Comment 3 to Section 3–405. If the trier of fact finds that Employer failed to exercise ordinary care in safeguarding the check and that the failure substantially contributed to the making of the forged indorsement, subsection (a) of Section 3–406 applies. If Employer brings an action for conversion against the depositary bank that took the checks from the forger, the depositary bank could assert the preclusion under subsection (a). But suppose the forger opened an account in the depositary bank in a name identical to that of Employer, the payee of the check, and then deposited the check in the account. Subsection (b) may apply. There may be an issue whether the depositary bank should have been alerted to possible fraud when a new account was opened for a corporation shortly before a very large check payable to a payee with the same name is deposited. Circumstances surrounding the opening of the account may have suggested that the corporation to which the check was payable may not be the same as the corporation for which the account was opened. If the trier of fact finds that collecting the check under these circumstances was a failure to exercise ordinary care, it could allocate the loss between the depositary bank and Employer, the payee.

§ 3–407.   Alteration.

(a)   "Alteration" means (i) an unauthorized change in an instrument that purports to modify in any respect the obligation of a party, or (ii) an unauthorized addition of words or numbers or other change to an incomplete instrument relating to the obligation of a party.

(b)   Except as provided in subsection (c), an alteration fraudulently made discharges a party whose obligation is affected by the alteration unless that party assents or is precluded from asserting the alteration. No other alteration discharges a party, and the instrument may be enforced according to its original terms.

(c)   A payor bank or drawee paying a fraudulently altered instrument or a person taking it for value, in good faith and without notice of the alteration, may enforce rights with respect to the instrument (i) according to its original terms, or (ii) in the case of an incomplete instrument altered by unauthorized completion, according to its terms as completed.

Official Comment

1.   This provision restates former Section 3–407. Former Section 3–407 defined a "material" alteration as any alteration that changes the contract of the parties in any respect. Revised Section 3–407 refers to such a change as an alteration. As under subsection (2) of former Section 3–407, discharge because of alteration occurs only in the case of an alteration fraudulently made. There is no discharge if a blank is filled in the honest belief that it is authorized or if a change is made with a benevolent motive such as a desire to give the obligor the benefit of a lower interest rate. Changes favorable to the obligor are unlikely to be made with any fraudulent intent, but if such an intent is found the alteration may operate as a discharge.

Discharge is a personal defense of the party whose obligation is modified and anyone whose obligation is not affected is not discharged. But if an alteration discharges a party there is also discharge of any party having a right of recourse against the discharged party because the obligation of the party with the right of recourse is affected by the alteration. Assent to the alteration given before or after it is made will prevent the party from asserting the discharge. The phrase "or is precluded from asserting the alteration" in subsection (b) recognizes the possibility of an estoppel or other ground barring the defense which does not rest on assent.

2.   Under subsection (c) a person paying a fraudulently altered instrument or taking it for value, in good faith and without notice of the alteration, is not affected by a discharge under subsection (b). The person paying or taking the instrument may assert rights with respect to the instrument according to its original terms or, in the case of an incomplete instrument that is altered by unauthorized completion, according to its terms as completed. If blanks are filled or an incomplete instrument is otherwise completed, subsection (c) places the loss upon the party who left the instrument incomplete by permitting enforcement in its completed form. This result is intended even though the instrument was stolen from the issuer and completed after the theft.

§ 3–408.   Drawee Not Liable on Unaccepted Draft.

A check or other draft does not of itself operate as an assignment of funds in the hands of the drawee available for its payment, and the drawee is not liable on the instrument until the drawee accepts it.

Official Comment

1.   This section is a restatement of former Section 3–409(1). Subsection (2) of former Section 3–409 is deleted as misleading and superfluous. Comment 3 says of subsection (2): "It is intended to make it clear that this section does not in any way affect any liability which may arise apart from the instrument." In reality subsection (2) did not make anything clear and was a source of confusion. If all it meant was that a bank that has not certified a check may engage in other conduct that might make it liable to a holder, it stated the obvious and was superfluous. Section 1–103 is adequate to cover those cases.

2. Liability with respect to drafts may arise under other law. For example, Section 4–302 imposes liability on a payor bank for late return of an item.

§ 3–409. Acceptance of Draft; Certified Check.

(a) "Acceptance" means the drawee's signed agreement to pay a draft as presented. It must be written on the draft and may consist of the drawee's signature alone. Acceptance may be made at any time and becomes effective when notification pursuant to instructions is given or the accepted draft is delivered for the purpose of giving rights on the acceptance to any person.

(b) A draft may be accepted although it has not been signed by the drawer, is otherwise incomplete, is overdue, or has been dishonored.

(c) If a draft is payable at a fixed period after sight and the acceptor fails to date the acceptance, the holder may complete the acceptance by supplying a date in good faith.

(d) "Certified check" means a check accepted by the bank on which it is drawn. Acceptance may be made as stated in subsection (a) or by a writing on the check which indicates that the check is certified. The drawee of a check has no obligation to certify the check, and refusal to certify is not dishonor of the check.

Official Comment

1. The first three subsections of Section 3–409 are a restatement of former Section 3–410. Subsection (d) adds a definition of certified check which is a type of accepted draft.

2. Subsection (a) states the generally recognized rule that the mere signature of the drawee on the instrument is a sufficient acceptance. Customarily the signature is written vertically across the face of the instrument, but since the drawee has no reason to sign for any other purpose a signature in any other place, even on the back of the instrument, is sufficient. It need not be accompanied by such words as "Accepted," "Certified," or "Good." It must not, however, bear any words indicating an intent to refuse to honor the draft. The last sentence of subsection (a) states the generally recognized rule that an acceptance written on the draft takes effect when the drawee notifies the holder or gives notice according to instructions.

3. The purpose of subsection (c) is to provide a definite date of payment if none appears on the instrument. An undated acceptance of a draft payable "thirty days after sight" is incomplete. Unless the acceptor writes in a different date the holder is authorized to complete the acceptance according to the terms of the draft by supplying a date of acceptance. Any date supplied by the holder is effective if made in good faith.

4. The last sentence of subsection (d) states the generally recognized rule that in the absence of agreement a bank is under no obligation to certify a check. A check is a demand instrument calling for payment rather than acceptance. The bank may be liable for breach of any agreement with the drawer, the holder, or any other person by which it undertakes to certify. Its liability is not on the instrument, since the drawee is not so liable until acceptance. Section 3–408. Any liability is for breach of the separate agreement.

§ 3–410. Acceptance Varying Draft.

(a) If the terms of a drawee's acceptance vary from the terms of the draft as presented, the holder may refuse the acceptance and treat the draft as dishonored. In that case, the drawee may cancel the acceptance.

(b) The terms of a draft are not varied by an acceptance to pay at a particular bank or place in the United States, unless the acceptance states that the draft is to be paid only at that bank or place.

(c) If the holder assents to an acceptance varying the terms of a draft, the obligation of each drawer and indorser that does not expressly assent to the acceptance is discharged.

Official Comment

1. This section is a restatement of former Section 3–412. It applies to conditional acceptances, acceptances for part of the amount, acceptances to pay at a different time from that required by the draft, or to the acceptance of less than all of the drawees. It applies to any other engagement changing the essential terms of the draft. If the drawee makes a varied acceptance the holder may either reject it or assent to it. The holder may reject by insisting on acceptance of the draft as presented. Refusal by the drawee to accept the draft as presented is dishonor. In that event the drawee is not bound by the varied acceptance and is entitled to have it canceled.

If the holder assents to the varied acceptance, the drawee's obligation as acceptor is according to the terms of the varied acceptance. Under subsection (c) the effect of the holder's assent is to discharge any drawer or indorser who does not also assent. The assent of the drawer or indorser must be affirmatively expressed. Mere failure to object within a reasonable time is not assent which will prevent the discharge.

2.   Under subsection (b) an acceptance does not vary from the terms of the draft if it provides for payment at any particular bank or place in the United States unless the acceptance states that the draft is to be paid only at such bank or place. Section 3–501(b)(1) states that if an instrument is payable at a bank in the United States presentment must be made at the place of payment (Section 3–111) which in this case is at the designated bank.

§ 3–411.   Refusal to Pay Cashier's Checks, Teller's Checks, and Certified Checks.

(a)   In this section, "obligated bank" means the acceptor of a certified check or the issuer of a cashier's check or teller's check bought from the issuer.

(b)   If the obligated bank wrongfully (i) refuses to pay a cashier's check or certified check, (ii) stops payment of a teller's check, or (iii) refuses to pay a dishonored teller's check, the person asserting the right to enforce the check is entitled to compensation for expenses and loss of interest resulting from the nonpayment and may recover consequential damages if the obligated bank refuses to pay after receiving notice of particular circumstances giving rise to the damages.

(c)   Expenses or consequential damages under subsection (b) are not recoverable if the refusal of the obligated bank to pay occurs because (i) the bank suspends payments, (ii) the obligated bank asserts a claim or defense of the bank that it has reasonable grounds to believe is available against the person entitled to enforce the instrument, (iii) the obligated bank has a reasonable doubt whether the person demanding payment is the person entitled to enforce the instrument, or (iv) payment is prohibited by law.

Official Comment

1.   In some cases a creditor may require that the debt be paid by an obligation of a bank. The debtor may comply by obtaining certification of the debtor's check, but more frequently the debtor buys from a bank a cashier's check or teller's check payable to the creditor. The check is taken by the creditor as a cash equivalent on the assumption that the bank will pay the check. Sometimes, the debtor wants to retract payment by inducing the obligated bank not to pay. The typical case involves a dispute between the parties to the transaction in which the check is given in payment. In the case of a certified check or cashier's check, the bank can safely pay the holder of the check despite notice that there may be an adverse claim to the check (Section 3–602). It is also clear that the bank that sells a teller's check has no duty to order the bank on which it is drawn not to pay it. A debtor using any of these types of checks has no right to stop payment. Nevertheless, some banks will refuse payment as an accommodation to a customer. Section 3–411 is designed to discourage this practice.

2.   The term "obligated bank" refers to the issuer of the cashier's check or teller's check and the acceptor of the certified check. If the obligated bank wrongfully refuses to pay, it is liable to pay for expenses and loss of interest resulting from the refusal to pay. There is no express provision for attorney's fees, but attorney's fees are not meant to be necessarily excluded. They could be granted because they fit within the language "expenses . . . resulting from the nonpayment." In addition the bank may be liable to pay consequential damages if it has notice of the particular circumstances giving rise to the damages.

3.   Subsection (c) provides that expenses or consequential damages are not recoverable if the refusal to pay is because of the reasons stated. The purpose is to limit that recovery to cases in which the bank refuses to pay even though its obligation to pay is clear and it is able to pay. Subsection (b) applies only if the refusal to honor the check is wrongful. If the bank is not obliged to pay there is no recovery. The bank may assert any claim or defense that it has, but normally the bank would not have a claim or defense. In the usual case it is a remitter that is asserting a claim to the check on the basis of a rescission of negotiation to the payee under Section 3–202. See Comment 2 to Section 3–201. The bank can assert that claim if there is compliance with Section 3–305(c), but the bank is not protected from damages under subsection (b) if the claim of the remitter is not upheld. In that case, the bank is insulated from damages only if payment is enjoined under Section 3–602(b)(1). Subsection (c)(iii) refers to cases in which the bank may have a reasonable doubt about the identity of the person demanding payment. For example, a cashier's check is payable to "Supplier Co." The person in possession of the check presents it for payment over the counter and claims to be an officer of Supplier Co. The bank may refuse payment until it has been given adequate proof that the presentment in fact is being made for Supplier Co., the person entitled to enforce the check.

§ 3–412.   Obligation of Issuer of Note or Cashier's Check.

The issuer of a note or cashier's check or other draft drawn on the drawer is obliged to pay the instrument (i) according to its terms at the time it was issued or, if not issued, at the time it first came into possession of a holder, or (ii) if the issuer signed an incomplete instrument, according to its terms when completed, to the extent stated in Sections 3–115 and 3–407. The obligation is owed to a person entitled to enforce the instrument or to an indorser who paid the instrument under Section 3–415.

Official Comment

1.   The obligations of the maker, acceptor, drawer, and indorser are stated in four separate sections. Section 3–412 states the obligation of the maker of a note and is consistent with former Section 3–413(1). Section 3–412 also applies to the issuer of a cashier's check or other draft drawn on the drawer. Under former Section 3–118(a), since a cashier's check or other draft drawn on the drawer was "effective as a note," the drawer was liable under former Section 3–413(1) as a maker. Under Sections 3–103(a)(8) and 3–104(f) a cashier's check or other draft drawn on the drawer is treated as a draft to reflect common commercial usage, but the liability of the drawer is stated by Section 3–412 as being the same as that of the maker of a note rather than that of the drawer of a draft. Thus, Section 3–412 does not in substance change former law.

2.   Under Section 3–105(b) nonissuance of either a complete or incomplete instrument is a defense by a maker or drawer against a person that is not a holder in due course.

3.   The obligation of the maker may be modified in the case of alteration if, under Section 3–406, the maker is precluded from asserting the alteration.

4.   The rule of this section is similar to the rule of Article 39 of the Convention on International Bills of Exchange and International Promissory Notes.

As amended in 2002.

§ 3–413.   Obligation of Acceptor.

(a)   The acceptor of a draft is obliged to pay the draft (i) according to its terms at the time it was accepted, even though the acceptance states that the draft is payable "as originally drawn" or equivalent terms, (ii) if the acceptance varies the terms of the draft, according to the terms of the draft as varied, or (iii) if the acceptance is of a draft that is an incomplete instrument, according to its terms when completed, to the extent stated in Sections 3–115 and 3–407. The obligation is owed to a person entitled to enforce the draft or to the drawer or an indorser who paid the draft under Section 3–414 or 3–415.

(b)   If the certification of a check or other acceptance of a draft states the amount certified or accepted, the obligation of the acceptor is that amount. If (i) the certification or acceptance does not state an amount, (ii) the amount of the instrument is subsequently raised, and (iii) the instrument is then negotiated to a holder in due course, the obligation of the acceptor is the amount of the instrument at the time it was taken by the holder in due course.

Official Comment

Subsection (a) is consistent with former Section 3–413(1). Subsection (b) has primary importance with respect to certified checks. It protects the holder in due course of a certified check that was altered after certification and before negotiation to the holder in due course. A bank can avoid liability for the altered amount by stating on the check the amount the bank agrees to pay. The subsection applies to other accepted drafts as well. The rule of this section is similar to the rule of Articles 41 of the Convention on International Bills of Exchange and International Promissory Notes. Articles 42 and 43 of the Convention include more detailed rules that in many respects do not have parallels in this Article.

As amended in 2002.

§ 3–414.   Obligation of Drawer.

(a)   This section does not apply to cashier's checks or other drafts drawn on the drawer.

(b)   If an unaccepted draft is dishonored, the drawer is obliged to pay the draft (i) according to its terms at the time it was issued or, if not issued, at the time it first came into possession of a holder, or (ii) if the drawer signed an incomplete instrument, according to its terms when completed, to the extent stated in

Sections 3–115 and 3–407. The obligation is owed to a person entitled to enforce the draft or to an indorser who paid the draft under Section 3–415.

(c)   If a draft is accepted by a bank, the drawer is discharged, regardless of when or by whom acceptance was obtained.

(d)   If a draft is accepted and the acceptor is not a bank, the obligation of the drawer to pay the draft if the draft is dishonored by the acceptor is the same as the obligation of an indorser under Section 3–415(a) and (c).

(e)   If a draft states that it is drawn "without recourse" or otherwise disclaims liability of the drawer to pay the draft, the drawer is not liable under subsection (b) to pay the draft if the draft is not a check. A disclaimer of the liability stated in subsection (b) is not effective if the draft is a check.

(f)   If (i) a check is not presented for payment or given to a depositary bank for collection within 30 days after its date, (ii) the drawee suspends payments after expiration of the 30-day period without paying the check, and (iii) because of the suspension of payments, the drawer is deprived of funds maintained with the drawee to cover payment of the check, the drawer to the extent deprived of funds may discharge its obligation to pay the check by assigning to the person entitled to enforce the check the rights of the drawer against the drawee with respect to the funds.

Official Comment

1.   Subsection (a) excludes cashier's checks because the obligation of the issuer of a cashier's check is stated in Section 3–412.

2.   Subsection (b) states the obligation of the drawer on an unaccepted draft. It replaces former Section 3–413(2). The requirement under former Article 3 of notice of dishonor or protest has been eliminated. Under revised Article 3, notice of dishonor is necessary only with respect to indorser's liability. The liability of the drawer of an unaccepted draft is treated as a primary liability. Under former Section 3–102(1)(d) the term "secondary party" was used to refer to a drawer or indorser. The quoted term is not used in revised Article 3. The effect of a draft drawn without recourse is stated in subsection (e).

3.   Under subsection (c) the drawer is discharged of liability on a draft accepted by a bank regardless of when acceptance was obtained. This changes former Section 3–411(1) which provided that the drawer is discharged only if the holder obtains acceptance. Holders that have a bank obligation do not normally rely on the drawer to guarantee the bank's solvency. A holder can obtain protection against the insolvency of a bank acceptor by a specific guaranty of payment by the drawer or by obtaining an indorsement by the drawer. Section 3–205(d).

4.   Subsection (d) states the liability of the drawer if a draft is accepted by a drawee other than a bank and the acceptor dishonors. The drawer of an unaccepted draft is the only party liable on the instrument. The drawee has no liability on the draft. Section 3–408. When the draft is accepted, the obligations change. The drawee, as acceptor, becomes primarily liable and the drawer's liability is that of a person secondarily liable as a guarantor of payment. The drawer's liability is identical to that of an indorser, and subsection (d) states the drawer's liability that way. The drawer is liable to pay the person entitled to enforce the draft or any indorser that pays pursuant to Section 3–415. The drawer in this case is discharged if notice of dishonor is required by Section 3–503 and is not given in compliance with that section. A drawer that pays has a right of recourse against the acceptor. Section 3–413(a).

5.   Subsection (e) does not permit the drawer of a check to avoid liability under subsection (b) by drawing the check without recourse. There is no legitimate purpose served by issuing a check on which nobody is liable. Drawing without recourse is effective to disclaim liability of the drawer if the draft is not a check. Suppose, in a documentary sale, Seller draws a draft on Buyer for the price of goods shipped to Buyer. The draft is payable upon delivery to the drawee of an order bill of lading covering the goods. Seller delivers the draft with the bill of lading to Finance Company that is named as payee of the draft. If Seller draws without recourse Finance Company takes the risk that Buyer will dishonor. If Buyer dishonors, Finance Company has no recourse against Seller but it can obtain reimbursement by selling the goods which it controls through the bill of lading.

6.   Subsection (f) is derived from former Section 3–502(1)(b). It is designed to protect the drawer of a check against loss resulting from suspension of payments by the drawee bank when the holder of the check delays collection of the check. For example, X writes a check payable to Y for $1,000. The check is covered by funds in X's account in the drawee bank. Y delays initiation of collection of the check for more than 30 days after the date of the check. The drawee bank suspends payments after the 30-day period and before the check is presented for payment. If the $1,000 of funds in X's account have not been withdrawn, X has a claim for those funds against the

drawee bank and, if subsection (e) were not in effect, X would be liable to Y on the check because the check was dishonored. Section 3–502(e). If the suspension of payments by the drawee bank will result in payment to X of less than the full amount of the $1,000 in the account or if there is a significant delay in payment to X, X will suffer a loss which would not have been suffered if Y had promptly initiated collection of the check. In most cases, X will not suffer any loss because of the existence of federal bank deposit insurance that covers accounts up to $100,000. Thus, subsection (e) has relatively little importance. There might be some cases, however, in which the account is not fully insured because it exceeds $100,000 or because the account doesn't qualify for deposit insurance. Subsection (f) retains the phrase "deprived of funds maintained with the drawee" appearing in former Section 3–502(1)(b). The quoted phrase applies if the suspension of payments by the drawee prevents the drawer from receiving the benefit of funds which would have paid the check if the holder had been timely in initiating collection. Thus, any significant delay in obtaining full payment of the funds is a deprivation of funds. The drawer can discharge drawer's liability by assigning rights against the drawee with respect to the funds to the holder.

7.   The obligation of the drawer under this section is similar to the obligation of the drawer under Article 38 of the Convention on International Bills of Exchange and International Promissory Notes.

As amended in 2002.

§ 3–415.   Obligation of Indorser.

(a)   Subject to subsections (b), (c), (d), (e) and to Section 3–419(d), if an instrument is dishonored, an indorser is obliged to pay the amount due on the instrument (i) according to the terms of the instrument at the time it was indorsed, or (ii) if the indorser indorsed an incomplete instrument, according to its terms when completed, to the extent stated in Sections 3–115 and 3–407. The obligation of the indorser is owed to a person entitled to enforce the instrument or to a subsequent indorser who paid the instrument under this section.

(b)   If an indorsement states that it is made "without recourse" or otherwise disclaims liability of the indorser, the indorser is not liable under subsection (a) to pay the instrument.

(c)   If notice of dishonor of an instrument is required by Section 3–503 and notice of dishonor complying with that section is not given to an indorser, the liability of the indorser under subsection (a) is discharged.

(d)   If a draft is accepted by a bank after an indorsement is made, the liability of the indorser under subsection (a) is discharged.

(e)   If an indorser of a check is liable under subsection (a) and the check is not presented for payment, or given to a depositary bank for collection, within 30 days after the day the indorsement was made, the liability of the indorser under subsection (a) is discharged.

As amended in 1993.

Official Comment

1.   Subsections (a) and (b) restate the substance of former Section 3–414(1). Subsection (2) of former Section 3–414 has been dropped because it is superfluous. Although notice of dishonor is not mentioned in subsection (a), it must be given in some cases to charge an indorser. It is covered in subsection (c). Regulation CC § 229.35(b) provides that a bank handling a check for collection or return is liable to a bank that subsequently handles the check to the extent the latter bank does not receive payment for the check. This liability applies whether or not the bank incurring the liability indorsed the check.

2.   Section 3–503 states when notice of dishonor is required and how it must be given. If required notice of dishonor is not given in compliance with Section 3–503, subsection (c) of Section 3–415 states that the effect is to discharge the indorser's obligation.

3.   Subsection (d) is similar in effect to Section 3–414(c) if the draft is accepted by a bank after the indorsement is made. See Comment 3 to Section 3–414. If a draft is accepted by a bank before the indorsement is made, the indorser incurs the obligation stated in subsection (a).

4.   Subsection (e) modifies former Sections 3–503(2)(b) and 3–502(1)(a) by stating a 30-day rather than a seven-day period, and stating it as an absolute rather than a presumptive period.

5.   As stated in subsection (a), the obligation of an indorser to pay the amount due on the instrument is generally owed not only to a person entitled to enforce the instrument but also to a subsequent indorser who paid

the instrument. But if the prior indorser and the subsequent indorser are both anomalous indorsers, this rule does not apply. In that case, Section 3–116 applies. Under Section 3–116(a), the anomalous indorsers are jointly and severally liable and if either pays the instrument the indorser who pays has a right of contribution against the other. Section 3–116(b). The right to contribution in Section 3–116(b) is subject to "agreement of the affected parties." Suppose the subsequent indorser can prove an agreement with the prior indorser under which the prior indorser agreed to treat the subsequent indorser as a guarantor of the obligation of the prior indorser. Rights of the two indorsers between themselves would be governed by the agreement. Under suretyship law, the subsequent indorser under such an agreement is referred to as a sub-surety. Under the agreement, if the subsequent indorser pays the instrument there is a right to reimbursement from the prior indorser; if the prior indorser pays the instrument, there is no right of recourse against the subsequent indorser. See PEB Commentary No. 11, dated February 10, 1994 [Appendix V, infra].

6. The rule of this section is similar to the rule of Article 44 of the Convention on International Bills of Exchange and International Promissory Notes.

As amended in 1994, 2002, and 2022.

§ 3–416. Transfer Warranties.

(a) A person who transfers an instrument for consideration warrants to the transferee and, if the transfer is by indorsement, to any subsequent transferee that:

(1) the warrantor is a person entitled to enforce the instrument;

(2) all signatures on the instrument are authentic and authorized;

(3) the instrument has not been altered;

(4) the instrument is not subject to a defense or claim in recoupment of any party which can be asserted against the warrantor;

(5) the warrantor has no knowledge of any insolvency proceeding commenced with respect to the maker or acceptor or, in the case of an unaccepted draft, the drawer; and

(6) with respect to a remotely-created consumer item, that the person on whose account the item is drawn authorized the issuance of the item in the amount for which the item is drawn.

(b) A person to whom the warranties under subsection (a) are made and who took the instrument in good faith may recover from the warrantor as damages for breach of warranty an amount equal to the loss suffered as a result of the breach, but not more than the amount of the instrument plus expenses and loss of interest incurred as a result of the breach.

(c) The warranties stated in subsection (a) cannot be disclaimed with respect to checks. Unless notice of a claim for breach of warranty is given to the warrantor within 30 days after the claimant has reason to know of the breach and the identity of the warrantor, the liability of the warrantor under subsection (b) is discharged to the extent of any loss caused by the delay in giving notice of the claim.

(d) A [cause of action] for breach of warranty under this section accrues when the claimant has reason to know of the breach.

As amended in 2002.

Official Comment

1. Subsection (a) is taken from subsection (2) of former Section 3–417. Subsections (3) and (4) of former Section 3–417 are deleted. Warranties under subsection (a) in favor of the immediate transferee apply to all persons who transfer an instrument for consideration whether or not the transfer is accompanied by indorsement. Any consideration sufficient to support a simple contract will support those warranties. If there is an indorsement the warranty runs with the instrument and the remote holder may sue the indorser-warrantor directly and thus avoid a multiplicity of suits.

2. Since the purpose of transfer (Section 3–203(a)) is to give the transferee the right to enforce the instrument, subsection (a)(1) is a warranty that the transferor is a person entitled to enforce the instrument (Section 3–301). Under Section 3–203(b) transfer gives the transferee any right of the transferor to enforce the instrument. Subsection (a)(1) is in effect a warranty that there are no unauthorized or missing indorsements that prevent the transferor from making the transferee a person entitled to enforce the instrument.

3.   The rationale of subsection (a)(4) is that the transferee does not undertake to buy an instrument that is not enforceable in whole or in part, unless there is a contrary agreement. Even if the transferee takes as a holder in due course who takes free of the defense or claim in recoupment, the warranty gives the transferee the option of proceeding against the transferor rather than litigating with the obligor on the instrument the issue of the holder-in-due-course status of the transferee. Subsection (3) of former Section 3–417 which limits this warranty is deleted. The rationale is that while the purpose of a "no recourse" indorsement is to avoid a guaranty of payment, the indorsement does not clearly indicate an intent to disclaim warranties.

4.   Under subsection (a)(5) the transferor does not warrant against difficulties of collection, impairment of the credit of the obligor or even insolvency. The transferee is expected to determine such questions before taking the obligation. If insolvency proceedings as defined in Section 1–201(22) [*unrevised Article 1; see Concordance, p. 22*] have been instituted against the party who is expected to pay and the transferor knows it, the concealment of that fact amounts to a fraud upon the transferee, and the warranty against knowledge of such proceedings is provided accordingly.

5.   Transfer warranties may be disclaimed with respect to any instrument except a check. Between the immediate parties disclaimer may be made by agreement. In the case of an indorser, disclaimer of transferor's liability, to be effective, must appear in the indorsement with words such as "without warranties" or some other specific reference to warranties. But in the case of a check, subsection (c) of Section 3–416 provides that transfer warranties cannot be disclaimed at all. In the check collection process the banking system relies on these warranties.

6.   Subsection (b) states the measure of damages for breach of warranty. There is no express provision for attorney's fees, but attorney's fees are not meant to be necessarily excluded. They could be granted because they fit within the phrase "expenses . . . incurred as a result of the breach." The intention is to leave to other state law the issue as to when attorney's fees are recoverable.

7.   Since the traditional term "cause of action" may have been replaced in some states by "claim for relief" or some equivalent term, the words "cause of action" in subsection (d) have been bracketed to indicate that the words may be replaced by an appropriate substitute to conform to local practice.

8.   Subsection (a)(6) is based on a number of nonuniform amendments designed to address concerns about certain kinds of check fraud. The provision implements a limited rejection of *Price v. Neal*, 97 Eng. Rep. 871 (K.B. 1762), so that in certain circumstances (those involving remotely-created consumer items) the payor bank can use a warranty claim to absolve itself of responsibility for honoring an unauthorized item. The provision rests on the premise that monitoring by depositary banks can control this type of fraud more effectively than any practices readily available to payor banks. The provision expressly includes both the case in which the consumer does not authorize the item at all and also the case in which the consumer authorizes the item but in an amount different from the amount in which the item is drawn. Similar provisions appear in Sections 3–417, 4–207, and 4–208.

The provision supplements applicable federal law, which requires telemarketers who submit instruments for payment to obtain the customer's "express verifiable authorization," which may be either in writing or tape recorded and must be made available upon request to the customer's bank. Federal Trade Commission's Telemarketing Sales Rule, 16 C.F.R. § 310.3(a)(3), implementing the Telemarketing and Consumer Fraud and Abuse Prevention Act, 15 U.S.C. §§ 6101–6108. Some states also have consumer-protection laws governing authorization of instruments in telemarketing transactions. *See, e.g.*, 9 Vt. Stat. Ann. § 2464.

9.   Article 45 of the Convention on International Bills of Exchange and International Promissory Notes includes warranties that are similar (except for the warranty in subsection (a)(6)).

As amended in 2002.

§ 3–417.   Presentment Warranties.

(a)   If an unaccepted draft is presented to the drawee for payment or acceptance and the drawee pays or accepts the draft, (i) the person obtaining payment or acceptance, at the time of presentment, and (ii) a previous transferor of the draft, at the time of transfer, warrant to the drawee making payment or accepting the draft in good faith that:

(1)   the warrantor is, or was, at the time the warrantor transferred the draft, a person entitled to enforce the draft or authorized to obtain payment or acceptance of the draft on behalf of a person entitled to enforce the draft;

(2)   the draft has not been altered;

(3)   the warrantor has no knowledge that the signature of the drawer of the draft is unauthorized; and

(4)   with respect to any remotely-created consumer item, that the person on whose account the item is drawn authorized the issuance of the item in the amount for which the item is drawn.

(b)   A drawee making payment may recover from any warrantor damages for breach of warranty equal to the amount paid by the drawee less the amount the drawee received or is entitled to receive from the drawer because of the payment. In addition, the drawee is entitled to compensation for expenses and loss of interest resulting from the breach. The right of the drawee to recover damages under this subsection is not affected by any failure of the drawee to exercise ordinary care in making payment. If the drawee accepts the draft, breach of warranty is a defense to the obligation of the acceptor. If the acceptor makes payment with respect to the draft, the acceptor is entitled to recover from any warrantor for breach of warranty the amounts stated in this subsection.

(c)   If a drawee asserts a claim for breach of warranty under subsection (a) based on an unauthorized indorsement of the draft or an alteration of the draft, the warrantor may defend by proving that the indorsement is effective under Section 3–404 or 3–405 or the drawer is precluded under Section 3–406 or 4–406 from asserting against the drawee the unauthorized indorsement or alteration.

(d)   If (i) a dishonored draft is presented for payment to the drawer or an indorser or (ii) any other instrument is presented for payment to a party obliged to pay the instrument, and (iii) payment is received, the following rules apply:

(1)   The person obtaining payment and a prior transferor of the instrument warrant to the person making payment in good faith that the warrantor is, or was, at the time the warrantor transferred the instrument, a person entitled to enforce the instrument or authorized to obtain payment on behalf of a person entitled to enforce the instrument.

(2)   The person making payment may recover from any warrantor for breach of warranty an amount equal to the amount paid plus expenses and loss of interest resulting from the breach.

(e)   The warranties stated in subsections (a) and (d) cannot be disclaimed with respect to checks. Unless notice of a claim for breach of warranty is given to the warrantor within 30 days after the claimant has reason to know of the breach and the identity of the warrantor, the liability of the warrantor under subsection (b) or (d) is discharged to the extent of any loss caused by the delay in giving notice of the claim.

(f)   A [cause of action] for breach of warranty under this section accrues when the claimant has reason to know of the breach.

As amended in 2002.

Official Comment

1.   This section replaces subsection (1) of former Section 3–417. The former provision was difficult to understand because it purported to state in one subsection all warranties given to any person paying any instrument. The result was a provision replete with exceptions that could not be readily understood except after close scrutiny of the language. In revised Section 3–417, presentment warranties made to drawees of uncertified checks and other unaccepted drafts are stated in subsection (a). All other presentment warranties are stated in subsection (d).

2.   Subsection (a) states three warranties. Subsection (a)(1) in effect is a warranty that there are no unauthorized or missing indorsements. "Person entitled to enforce" is defined in Section 3–301. Subsection (a)(2) is a warranty that there is no alteration. Subsection (a)(3) is a warranty of no knowledge that there is a forged drawer's signature. Subsection (a) states that the warranties are made to the drawee and subsections (b) and (c) identify the drawee as the person entitled to recover for breach of warranty. There is no warranty made to the drawer under subsection (a) when presentment is made to the drawee. Warranty to the drawer is governed by subsection (d) and that applies only when presentment for payment is made to the drawer with respect to a dishonored draft. In *Sun 'N Sand, Inc. v. United California Bank*, 582 P.2d 920 (Cal. 1978), the court held that under former Section 3–417(1) a warranty was made to the drawer of a check when the check was presented to the drawee for payment. The result in that case is rejected.

3.   Subsection (a)(1) retains the rule that the drawee does not admit the authenticity of indorsements and subsection (a)(3) retains the rule of *Price v. Neal*, 3 Burr. 1354 (1762), that the drawee takes the risk that the

349

drawer's signature is unauthorized unless the person presenting the draft has knowledge that the drawer's signature is unauthorized. Under subsection (a)(3) the warranty of no knowledge that the drawer's signature is unauthorized is also given by prior transferors of the draft.

4.   Subsection (d) applies to presentment for payment in all cases not covered by subsection (a). It applies to presentment of notes and accepted drafts to any party obliged to pay the instrument, including an indorser, and to presentment of dishonored drafts if made to the drawer or an indorser. In cases covered by subsection (d), there is only one warranty and it is the same as that stated in subsection (a)(1). There are no warranties comparable to subsections (a)(2) and (a)(3) because they are appropriate only in the case of presentment to the drawee of an unaccepted draft. With respect to presentment of an accepted draft to the acceptor, there is no warranty with respect to alteration or knowledge that the signature of the drawer is unauthorized. Those warranties were made to the drawee when the draft was presented for acceptance (Section 3–417(a)(2) and (3)) and breach of that warranty is a defense to the obligation of the drawee as acceptor to pay the draft. If the drawee pays the accepted draft the drawee may recover the payment from any warrantor who was in breach of warranty when the draft was accepted. Section 3–417(b). Thus, there is no necessity for these warranties to be repeated when the accepted draft is presented for payment. Former Section 3–417(1)(b)(iii) and (c)(iii) are not included in revised Section 3–417 because they are unnecessary. Former Section 3–417(1)(c)(iv) is not included because it is also unnecessary. The acceptor should know what the terms of the draft were at the time acceptance was made.

If presentment is made to the drawer or maker, there is no necessity for a warranty concerning the signature of that person or with respect to alteration. If presentment is made to an indorser, the indorser had itself warranted authenticity of signatures and that the instrument was not altered. Section 3–416(a)(2) and (3).

5.   The measure of damages for breach of warranty under subsection (a) is stated in subsection (b). There is no express provision for attorney's fees, but attorney's fees are not meant to be necessarily excluded. They could be granted because they fit within the language "expenses . . . resulting from the breach." Subsection (b) provides that the right of the drawee to recover for breach of warranty is not affected by a failure of the drawee to exercise ordinary care in paying the draft. This provision follows the result reached under former Article 3 in *Hartford Accident & Indemnity Co. v. First Pennsylvania Bank*, 859 F.2d 295 (3d Cir. 1988).

6.   Subsection (c) applies to checks and other unaccepted drafts. It gives to the warrantor the benefit of rights that the drawee has against the drawer under Section 3–404, 3–405, 3–406, or 4–406. If the drawer's conduct contributed to a loss from forgery or alteration, the drawee should not be allowed to shift the loss from the drawer to the warrantor.

7.   The first sentence of subsection (e) recognizes that checks are normally paid by automated means and that payor banks rely on warranties in making payment. Thus, it is not appropriate to allow disclaimer or warranties appearing on checks that normally will not be examined by the payor bank. The second sentence requires a breach of warranty claim to be asserted within 30 days after the drawee learns of the breach and the identity of the warrantor.

8.   Since the traditional term "cause of action" may have been replaced in some states by "claim for relief" or some equivalent term, the words "cause of action" in subsection (f) have been bracketed to indicate that the words may be replaced by an appropriate substitute to conform to local practice.

9.   For discussion of subsection (a)(4), see Comment 8 to Section 3–416.

As amended in 2002.

§ 3–418.   Payment or Acceptance by Mistake.

(a)   Except as provided in subsection (c), if the drawee of a draft pays or accepts the draft and the drawee acted on the mistaken belief that (i) payment of the draft had not been stopped pursuant to Section 4–403 or (ii) the signature of the drawer of the draft was authorized, the drawee may recover the amount of the draft from the person to whom or for whose benefit payment was made or, in the case of acceptance, may revoke the acceptance. Rights of the drawee under this subsection are not affected by failure of the drawee to exercise ordinary care in paying or accepting the draft.

(b)   Except as provided in subsection (c), if an instrument has been paid or accepted by mistake and the case is not covered by subsection (a), the person paying or accepting may, to the extent permitted by the law governing mistake and restitution, (i) recover the payment from the person to whom or for whose benefit payment was made or (ii) in the case of acceptance, may revoke the acceptance.

(c) The remedies provided by subsection (a) or (b) may not be asserted against a person who took the instrument in good faith and for value or who in good faith changed position in reliance on the payment or acceptance. This subsection does not limit remedies provided by Section 3–417 or 4–407.

(d) Notwithstanding Section 4–215, if an instrument is paid or accepted by mistake and the payor or acceptor recovers payment or revokes acceptance under subsection (a) or (b), the instrument is deemed not to have been paid or accepted and is treated as dishonored, and the person from whom payment is recovered has rights as a person entitled to enforce the dishonored instrument.

Official Comment

1. This section covers payment or acceptance by mistake and replaces former Section 3–418. Under former Article 3, the remedy of a drawee that paid or accepted a draft by mistake was based on the law of mistake and restitution, but that remedy was not specifically stated. It was provided by Section 1–103. Former Section 3–418 was simply a limitation on the unstated remedy under the law of mistake and restitution. Under revised Article 3, Section 3–418 specifically states the right of restitution in subsections (a) and (b). Subsection (a) allows restitution in the two most common cases in which the problem is presented: payment or acceptance of forged checks and checks on which the drawer has stopped payment. If the drawee acted under a mistaken belief that the check was not forged or had not been stopped, the drawee is entitled to recover the funds paid or to revoke the acceptance whether or not the drawee acted negligently. But in each case, by virtue of subsection (c), the drawee loses the remedy if the person receiving payment or acceptance was a person who took the check in good faith and for value or who in good faith changed position in reliance on the payment or acceptance. Subsections (a) and (c) are consistent with former Section 3–418 and the rule of *Price v. Neal*. The result in the two cases covered by subsection (a) is that the drawee in most cases will not have a remedy against the person paid because there is usually a person who took the check in good faith and for value or who in good faith changed position in reliance on the payment or acceptance.

2. If a check has been paid by mistake and the payee receiving payment did not give value for the check or did not change position in reliance on the payment, the drawee bank is entitled to recover the amount of the check under subsection (a) regardless of how the check was paid. The drawee bank normally pays a check by a credit to an account of the collecting bank that presents the check for payment. The payee of the check normally receives the payment by a credit to the payee's account in the depositary bank. But in some cases the payee of the check may have received payment directly from the drawee bank by presenting the check for payment over the counter. In those cases the payee is entitled to receive cash, but the payee may prefer another form of payment such as a cashier's check or teller's check issued by the drawee bank. Suppose Seller contracted to sell goods to Buyer. The contract provided for immediate payment by Buyer and delivery of the goods 20 days after payment. Buyer paid by mailing a check for $10,000 drawn on Bank payable to Seller. The next day Buyer gave a stop payment order to Bank with respect to the check Buyer had mailed to Seller. A few days later Seller presented Buyer's check to Bank for payment over the counter and requested a cashier's check as payment. Bank issued and delivered a cashier's check for $10,000 payable to Seller. The teller failed to discover Buyer's stop order. The next day Bank discovered the mistake and immediately advised Seller of the facts. Seller refused to return the cashier's check and did not deliver any goods to Buyer.

Under Section 4–215, Buyer's check was paid by Bank at the time it delivered its cashier's check to Seller. See Comment 3 to Section 4–215. Bank is obliged to pay the cashier's check and has no defense to that obligation. The cashier's check was issued for consideration because it was issued in payment of Buyer's check. Although Bank has no defense on its cashier's check it may have a right to recover $10,000, the amount of Buyer's check, from Seller under Section 3–418(a). Bank paid Buyer's check by mistake. Seller did not give value for Buyer's check because the promise to deliver goods to Buyer was never performed. Section 3–303(a)(1). And, on these facts, Seller did not change position in reliance on the payment of Buyer's check. Thus, the first sentence of Section 3–418(c) does not apply and Seller is obliged to return $10,000 to Bank. Bank is obliged to pay the cashier's check but it has a counterclaim against Seller based on its rights under Section 3–418(a). This claim can be asserted against Seller, but it cannot be asserted against some other person with rights of a holder in due course of the cashier's check. A person without rights of a holder in due course of the cashier's check would take subject to Bank's claim against Seller because it is a claim in recoupment. Section 3–305(a)(3).

If Bank recovers from Seller under Section 3–418(a), the payment of Buyer's check is treated as unpaid and dishonored. Section 3–418(d). One consequence is that Seller may enforce Buyer's obligation as drawer to pay the check. Section 3–414. Another consequence is that Seller's rights against Buyer on the contract of sale are also preserved. Under Section 3–310(b) Buyer's obligation to pay for the goods was suspended when Seller took Buyer's check and remains suspended until the check is either dishonored or paid. Under Section 3–310(b)(1) the obligation is discharged when the check is paid. Since Section 3–418(d) treats Buyer's check as unpaid and dishonored,

Buyer's obligation is not discharged and suspension of the obligation terminates. Under Section 3–310(b)(3), Seller may enforce either the contract of sale or the check subject to defenses and claims of Buyer.

If Seller had released the goods to Buyer before learning about the stop order, Bank would have no recovery against Seller under Section 3–418(a) because Seller in that case gave value for Buyer's check. Section 3–418(c). In this case Bank's sole remedy is under Section 4–407 by subrogation.

3. Subsection (b) covers cases of payment or acceptance by mistake that are not covered by subsection (a). It directs courts to deal with those cases under the law governing mistake and restitution. Perhaps the most important class of cases that falls under subsection (b), because it is not covered by subsection (a), is that of payment by the drawee bank of a check with respect to which the bank has no duty to the drawer to pay either because the drawer has no account with the bank or because available funds in the drawer's account are not sufficient to cover the amount of the check. With respect to such a case, under Restatement of Restitution § 29, if the bank paid because of a mistaken belief that there were available funds in the drawer's account sufficient to cover the amount of the check, the bank is entitled to restitution. But § 29 is subject to Restatement of Restitution § 33 which denies restitution if the holder of the check receiving payment paid value in good faith for the check and had no reason to know that the check was paid by mistake when payment was received.

The result in some cases is clear. For example, suppose Father gives Daughter a check for $10,000 as a birthday gift. The check is drawn on Bank in which both Father and Daughter have accounts. Daughter deposits the check in her account in Bank. An employee of Bank, acting under the belief that there were available funds in Father's account to cover the check, caused Daughter's account to be credited for $10,000. In fact, Father's account was overdrawn and Father did not have overdraft privileges. Since Daughter received the check gratuitously there is clear unjust enrichment if she is allowed to keep the $10,000 and Bank is unable to obtain reimbursement from Father. Thus, Bank should be permitted to reverse the credit to Daughter's account. But this case is not typical. In most cases the remedy of restitution will not be available because the person receiving payment of the check will have given value for it in good faith.

In some cases, however, it may not be clear whether a drawee bank should have a right of restitution. For example, a check-kiting scheme may involve a large number of checks drawn on a number of different banks in which the drawer's credit balances are based on uncollected funds represented by fraudulently drawn checks. No attempt is made in Section 3–418 to state rules for determining the conflicting claims of the various banks that may be victimized by such a scheme. Rather, such cases are better resolved on the basis of general principles of law and the particular facts presented in the litigation.

4. The right of the drawee to recover a payment or to revoke an acceptance under Section 3–418 is not affected by the rules under Article 4 that determine when an item is paid. Even though a payor bank may have paid an item under Section 4–215, it may have a right to recover the payment under Section 3–418. *National Savings & Trust Co. v. Park Corp.*, 722 F.2d 1303 (6th Cir. 1983), cert. denied, 466 U.S. 939 (1984), correctly states the law on the issue under former Article 3. Revised Article 3 does not change the previous law.

§ 3–419. Instruments Signed for Accommodation.

(a) If an instrument is issued for value given for the benefit of a party to the instrument ("accommodated party") and another party to the instrument ("accommodation party") signs the instrument for the purpose of incurring liability on the instrument without being a direct beneficiary of the value given for the instrument, the instrument is signed by the accommodation party "for accommodation."

(b) An accommodation party may sign the instrument as maker, drawer, acceptor, or indorser and, subject to subsection (d), is obliged to pay the instrument in the capacity in which the accommodation party signs. The obligation of an accommodation party may be enforced notwithstanding any statute of frauds and whether or not the accommodation party receives consideration for the accommodation.

(c) A person signing an instrument is presumed to be an accommodation party and there is notice that the instrument is signed for accommodation if the signature is an anomalous indorsement or is accompanied by words indicating that the signer is acting as surety or guarantor with respect to the obligation of another party to the instrument. Except as provided in Section 3–605, the obligation of an accommodation party to pay the instrument is not affected by the fact that the person enforcing the obligation had notice when the instrument was taken by that person that the accommodation party signed the instrument for accommodation.

(d)   If the signature of a party to an instrument is accompanied by words indicating unambiguously that the party is guaranteeing collection rather than payment of the obligation of another party to the instrument, the signer is obliged to pay the amount due on the instrument to a person entitled to enforce the instrument only if (i) execution of judgment against the other party has been returned unsatisfied, (ii) the other party is insolvent or in an insolvency proceeding, (iii) the other party cannot be served with process, or (iv) it is otherwise apparent that payment cannot be obtained from the other party.

(e)   If the signature of a party to an instrument is accompanied by words indicating that the party guarantees payment or the signer signs the instrument as an accommodation party in some other manner that does not unambiguously indicate an intention to guarantee collection rather than payment, the signer is obliged to pay the amount due on the instrument to a person entitled to enforce the instrument in the same circumstances as the accommodated party would be obliged, without prior resort to the accommodated party by the person entitled to enforce the instrument.

(f)   An accommodation party who pays the instrument is entitled to reimbursement from the accommodated party and is entitled to enforce the instrument against the accommodated party. In proper circumstances, an accommodation party may obtain relief that requires the accommodated party to perform its obligations on the instrument. An accommodated party that pays the instrument has no right of recourse against, and is not entitled to contribution from, an accommodation party.

As amended in 2002.

Official Comment

1.   Section 3–419 replaces former Section 3–415 and 3–416. An accommodation party is a person who signs an instrument to benefit the accommodated party either by signing at the time value is obtained by the accommodated party or later, and who is not a direct beneficiary of the value obtained. An accommodation party will usually be a co-maker or anomalous indorser. Subsection (a) distinguishes between direct and indirect benefit. For example, if X cosigns a note of Corporation that is given for a loan to Corporation, X is an accommodation party if no part of the loan was paid to X or for X's direct benefit. This is true even though X may receive indirect benefit from the loan because X is employed by Corporation or is a stockholder of Corporation, or even if X is the sole stockholder so long as Corporation and X are recognized as separate entities.

2.   It does not matter whether an accommodation party signs gratuitously either at the time the instrument is issued or after the instrument is in the possession of a holder. Subsection (b) of Section 3–419 takes the view stated in Comment 3 to former Section 3–415 that there need be no consideration running to the accommodation party: "The obligation of the accommodation party is supported by any consideration for which the instrument is taken before it is due. Subsection (2) is intended to change occasional decisions holding that there is no sufficient consideration where an accommodation party signs a note after it is in the hands of a holder who has given value. The [accommodation] party is liable to the holder in such a case even though there is no extension of time or other concession."

3.   As stated in Comment 1, whether a person is an accommodation party is a question of fact. But it is almost always the case that a co-maker who signs with words of guaranty after the signature is an accommodation party. The same is true of an anomalous indorser. In either case a person taking the instrument is put on notice of the accommodation status of the co-maker or indorser. This is relevant to Section 3–605(e). But, under subsection (c), signing with words of guaranty or as an anomalous indorser also creates a presumption that the signer is an accommodation party. A party challenging accommodation party status would have to rebut this presumption by producing evidence that the signer was in fact a direct beneficiary of the value given for the instrument.

An accommodation party is always a surety. A surety who is not a party to the instrument, however, is not an accommodation party. For example, if M issues a note payable to the order of P, and S signs a separate contract in which S agrees to pay P the amount of the instrument if it is dishonored, S is a surety but is not an accommodation party. In such a case, S's rights and duties are determined under the general law of suretyship. In unusual cases two parties to an instrument may have a surety relationship that is not governed by Article 3 because the requirements of Section 3–419(a) are not met. In those cases the general law of suretyship applies to the relationship. See PEB Commentary No. 11, dated February 10, 1994 [Appendix V, infra].

4.   Subsection (b) states that an accommodation party is liable on the instrument in the capacity in which the party signed the instrument. In most cases that capacity will be either that of a maker or indorser of a note. But subsection (d) provides a limitation on subsection (b). If the signature of the accommodation party is

accompanied by words indicating unambiguously that the party is guaranteeing collection rather than payment of the instrument, liability is limited to that stated in subsection (d), which is based on former Section 3–416(2).

Former Article 3 was confusing because the obligation of a guarantor was covered both in Section 3–415 and in Section 3–416. The latter section suggested that a signature accompanied by words of guaranty created an obligation distinct from that of an accommodation party. Revised Article 3 eliminates that confusion by stating in Section 3–419 the obligation of a person who uses words of guaranty. Portions of former Section 3–416 are preserved. Former Section 3–416(2) is reflected in Section 3–419(d) and former Section 3–416(4) is reflected in Section 3–419(c). Words added to an anomalous indorsement indicating that payment of the instrument is guaranteed by the indorser do not change the liability of the indorser as stated in Section 3–415. This is a change from former Section 3–416(5). See PEB Commentary No. 11, supra.

5.   Subsection (e) like former Section 3–415(5), provides that an accommodation party that pays the instrument is entitled to enforce the instrument against the accommodated party. Since the accommodation party that pays the instrument is entitled to enforce the instrument against the accommodated party, the accommodation party also obtains rights to any security interest or other collateral that secures payment of the instrument. Subsection (e) also provides that an accommodation party that pays the instrument is entitled to reimbursement from the accommodated party. See PEB Commentary No. 11, supra.

6.   In occasional cases, the accommodation party might pay the instrument even though the accommodated party had a defense to its obligation that was available to the accommodation party under Section 3–305(d). In such cases, the accommodation party's right to reimbursement may conflict with the accommodated party's right to raise its defense. For example, suppose the accommodation party pays the instrument without being aware of the defense. In that case the accommodation party should be entitled to reimbursement. Suppose the accommodation party paid the instrument with knowledge of the defense. In that case, to the extent of the defense, reimbursement ordinarily would not be justified, but under some circumstances reimbursement may be justified depending upon the facts of the case. The resolution of this conflict is left to the general law of suretyship. Section 1–103. See PEB Commentary No. 11, supra.

7.   Section 3–419, along with Section 3–116(a) and (b), Section 3–305(d) and Section 3–605, provides rules governing the rights of accommodation parties. In addition, except to the extent that it is displaced by provisions of this Article, the general law of suretyship also applies to the rights of accommodation parties. Section 1–103. See PEB Commentary No. 11, supra.

As amended in 1994, 2002, and 2022.

§ 3–420.   Conversion of Instrument.

(a)   The law applicable to conversion of personal property applies to instruments. An instrument is also converted if it is taken by transfer, other than a negotiation, from a person not entitled to enforce the instrument or a bank makes or obtains payment with respect to the instrument for a person not entitled to enforce the instrument or receive payment. An action for conversion of an instrument may not be brought by (i) the issuer or acceptor of the instrument or (ii) a payee or indorsee who did not receive delivery of the instrument either directly or through delivery to an agent or a co-payee.

(b)   In an action under subsection (a), the measure of liability is presumed to be the amount payable on the instrument, but recovery may not exceed the amount of the plaintiff's interest in the instrument.

(c)   A representative, other than a depositary bank, who has in good faith dealt with an instrument or its proceeds on behalf of one who was not the person entitled to enforce the instrument is not liable in conversion to that person beyond the amount of any proceeds that it has not paid out.

Official Comment

1.   Section 3–420 is a modification of former Section 3–419. The first sentence of Section 3–420(a) states a general rule that the law of conversion applicable to personal property also applies to instruments. Paragraphs (a) and (b) of former Section 3–419(1) are deleted as inappropriate in cases of noncash items that may be delivered for acceptance or payment in collection letters that contain varying instructions as to what to do in the event of nonpayment on the day of delivery. It is better to allow such cases to be governed by the general law of conversion that would address the issue of when, under the circumstances prevailing, the presenter's right to possession has been denied. The second sentence of Section 3–420(a) states that an instrument is converted if it is taken by transfer other than a negotiation from a person not entitled to enforce the instrument or taken for collection or payment from a person not entitled to enforce the instrument or receive payment. This covers cases in which a

depositary or payor bank takes an instrument bearing a forged indorsement. It also covers cases in which an instrument is payable to two persons and the two persons are not alternative payees, e.g. a check payable to John and Jane Doe. Under Section 3–110(d) the check can be negotiated or enforced only by both persons acting jointly. Thus, neither payee acting without the consent of the other, is a person entitled to enforce the instrument. If John indorses the check and Jane does not, the indorsement is not effective to allow negotiation of the check. If Depositary Bank takes the check for deposit to John's account, Depositary Bank is liable to Jane for conversion of the check if she did not consent to the transaction. John, acting alone, is not the person entitled to enforce the check because John is not the holder of the check. Section 3–110(d) and Comment 4 to Section 3–110. Depositary Bank does not get any greater rights under Section 4–205(1). If it acted for John as its customer, it did not become holder of the check under that provision because John, its customer, was not a holder.

Under former Article 3, the cases were divided on the issue of whether the drawer of a check with a forged indorsement can assert rights against a depositary bank that took the check. The last sentence of Section 3–420(a) resolves the conflict by following the rule stated in *Stone & Webster Engineering Corp. v. First National Bank & Trust Co.*, 184 N.E.2d 358 (Mass. 1962). There is no reason why a drawer should have an action in conversion. The check represents an obligation of the drawer rather than property of the drawer. The drawer has an adequate remedy against the payor bank for recredit of the drawer's account for unauthorized payment of the check.

There was also a split of authority under former Article 3 on the issue of whether a payee who never received the instrument is a proper plaintiff in a conversion action. The typical case was one in which a check was stolen from the drawer or in which the check was mailed to an address different from that of the payee and was stolen after it arrived at that address. The thief forged the indorsement of the payee and obtained payment by depositing the check to an account in a depositary bank. The issue was whether the payee could bring an action in conversion against the depositary bank or the drawee bank. In revised Article 3, under the last sentence of Section 3–420(a), the payee has no conversion action because the check was never delivered to the payee. Until delivery, the payee does not have any interest in the check. The payee never became the holder of the check nor a person entitled to enforce the check. Section 3–301. Nor is the payee injured by the fraud. Normally the drawer of a check intends to pay an obligation owed to the payee. But if the check is never delivered to the payee, the obligation owed to the payee is not affected. If the check falls into the hands of a thief who obtains payment after forging the signature of the payee as an indorsement, the obligation owed to the payee continues to exist after the thief receives payment. Since the payee's right to enforce the underlying obligation is unaffected by the fraud of the thief, there is no reason to give any additional remedy to the payee. The drawer of the check has no conversion remedy, but the drawee is not entitled to charge the drawer's account when the drawee wrongfully honored the check. The remedy of the drawee is against the depositary bank for breach of warranty under Section 3–417(a)(1) or 4–208(a)(1). The loss will fall on the person who gave value to the thief for the check.

The situation is different if the check is delivered to the payee. If the check is taken for an obligation owed to the payee, the last sentence of Section 3–310(b)(4) provides that the obligation may not be enforced to the extent of the amount of the check. The payee's rights are restricted to enforcement of the payee's rights in the instrument. In this event the payee is injured by the theft and has a cause of action for conversion.

The payee receives delivery when the check comes into the payee's possession, as for example when it is put into the payee's mailbox. Delivery to an agent is delivery to the payee. If a check is payable to more than one payee, delivery to one of the payees is deemed to be delivery to all of the payees. Occasionally, the person asserting a conversion cause of action is an indorsee rather than the original payee. If the check is stolen before the check can be delivered to the indorsee and the indorsee's indorsement is forged, the analysis is similar. For example, a check is payable to the order of A. A indorses it to B and puts it into an envelope addressed to B. The envelope is never delivered to B. Rather, Thief steals the envelope, forges B's indorsement to the check and obtains payment. Because the check was never delivered to B, the indorsee, B has no cause of action for conversion, but A does have such an action. A is the owner of the check. B never obtained rights in the check. If A intended to negotiate the check to B in payment of an obligation, that obligation was not affected by the conduct of Thief. B can enforce that obligation. Thief stole A's property not B's.

2. Subsection (2) of former Section 3–419 is amended because it is not clear why the former law distinguished between the liability of the drawee and that of other converters. Why should there be a conclusive presumption that the liability is face amount if a drawee refuses to pay or return an instrument or makes payment on a forged indorsement, while the liability of a maker who does the same thing is only presumed to be the face amount? Moreover, it was not clear under former Section 3–419(2) what face amount meant. If a note for $10,000 is payable in a year at 10% interest, it is common to refer to $10,000 as the face amount, but if the note is converted the loss to the owner also includes the loss of interest. In revised Article 3, Section 3–420(b), by referring to "amount payable on the instrument," allows the full amount due under the instrument to be recovered.

The "but" clause in subsection (b) addresses the problem of conversion actions in multiple payee checks. Section 3–110(d) states that an instrument cannot be enforced unless all payees join in the action. But an action for conversion might be brought by a payee having no interest or a limited interest in the proceeds of the check. This clause prevents such a plaintiff from receiving a windfall. An example is a check payable to a building contractor and a supplier of building material. The check is not payable to the payees alternatively. Section 3–110(d). The check is delivered to the contractor by the owner of the building. Suppose the contractor forges supplier's signature as an indorsement of the check and receives the entire proceeds of the check. The supplier should not, without qualification, be able to recover the entire amount of the check from the bank that converted the check. Depending upon the contract between the contractor and the supplier, the amount of the check may be due entirely to the contractor, in which case there should be no recovery, entirely to the supplier, in which case recovery should be for the entire amount, or part may be due to one and the rest to the other, in which case recovery should be limited to the amount due to the supplier.

3.   Subsection (3) of former Section 3–419 drew criticism from the courts, that saw no reason why a depositary bank should have the defense stated in the subsection. See *Knesz v. Central Jersey Bank & Trust Co.*, 477 A.2d 806 (N.J. 1984). The depositary bank is ultimately liable in the case of a forged indorsement check because of its warranty to the payor bank under Section 4–208(a)(1) and it is usually the most convenient defendant in cases involving multiple checks drawn on different banks. There is no basis for requiring the owner of the check to bring multiple actions against the various payor banks and to require those banks to assert warranty rights against the depositary bank. In revised Article 3, the defense provided by Section 3–420(c) is limited to collecting banks other than the depositary bank. If suit is brought against both the payor bank and the depositary bank, the owner, of course, is entitled to but one recovery.

PART 5

DISHONOR

§ 3–501.   Presentment.

(a)   "Presentment" means a demand made by or on behalf of a person entitled to enforce an instrument (i) to pay the instrument made to the drawee or a party obliged to pay the instrument or, in the case of a note or accepted draft payable at a bank, to the bank, or (ii) to accept a draft made to the drawee.

(b)   The following rules are subject to Article 4, agreement of the parties, and clearing-house rules and the like:

(1)   Presentment may be made at the place of payment of the instrument and must be made at the place of payment if the instrument is payable at a bank in the United States; may be made by any commercially reasonable means, including an oral, written, or electronic communication; is effective when the demand for payment or acceptance is received by the person to whom presentment is made; and is effective if made to any one of two or more makers, acceptors, drawees, or other payors.

(2)   Upon demand of the person to whom presentment is made, the person making presentment must (i) exhibit the instrument, (ii) give reasonable identification and, if presentment is made on behalf of another person, reasonable evidence of authority to do so, and (iii) sign a receipt on the instrument for any payment made or surrender the instrument if full payment is made.

(3)   Without dishonoring the instrument, the party to whom presentment is made may (i) return the instrument for lack of a necessary indorsement, or (ii) refuse payment or acceptance for failure of the presentment to comply with the terms of the instrument, an agreement of the parties, or other applicable law or rule.

(4)   The party to whom presentment is made may treat presentment as occurring on the next business day after the day of presentment if the party to whom presentment is made has established a cut-off hour not earlier than 2 p.m. for the receipt and processing of instruments presented for payment or acceptance and presentment is made after the cut-off hour.

Official Comment

Subsection (a) defines presentment. Subsection (b)(1) states the place and manner of presentment. Electronic presentment is authorized. The communication of the demand for payment or acceptance is effective when received. Subsection (b)(2) restates former Section 3–505. Subsection (b)(2)(i) allows the person to whom presentment is made to require exhibition of the instrument, unless the parties have agreed otherwise as in an electronic presentment agreement. Former Section 3–507(3) is the antecedent of subsection (b)(3)(i). Since a payor must decide whether to pay or accept on the day of presentment, subsection (b)(4) allows the payor to set a cut-off hour for receipt of instruments presented.

§ 3–502.   Dishonor.

(a)   Dishonor of a note is governed by the following rules:

(1)   If the note is payable on demand, the note is dishonored if presentment is duly made to the maker and the note is not paid on the day of presentment.

(2)   If the note is not payable on demand and is payable at or through a bank or the terms of the note require presentment, the note is dishonored if presentment is duly made and the note is not paid on the day it becomes payable or the day of presentment, whichever is later.

(3)   If the note is not payable on demand and paragraph (2) does not apply, the note is dishonored if it is not paid on the day it becomes payable.

(b)   Dishonor of an unaccepted draft other than a documentary draft is governed by the following rules:

(1)   If a check is duly presented for payment to the payor bank otherwise than for immediate payment over the counter, the check is dishonored if the payor bank makes timely return of the check or sends timely notice of dishonor or nonpayment under Section 4–301 or 4–302, or becomes accountable for the amount of the check under Section 4–302.

(2)   If a draft is payable on demand and paragraph (1) does not apply, the draft is dishonored if presentment for payment is duly made to the drawee and the draft is not paid on the day of presentment.

(3)   If a draft is payable on a date stated in the draft, the draft is dishonored if (i) presentment for payment is duly made to the drawee and payment is not made on the day the draft becomes payable or the day of presentment, whichever is later, or (ii) presentment for acceptance is duly made before the day the draft becomes payable and the draft is not accepted on the day of presentment.

(4)   If a draft is payable on elapse of a period of time after sight or acceptance, the draft is dishonored if presentment for acceptance is duly made and the draft is not accepted on the day of presentment.

(c)   Dishonor of an unaccepted documentary draft occurs according to the rules stated in subsection (b)(2), (3), and (4), except that payment or acceptance may be delayed without dishonor until no later than the close of the third business day of the drawee following the day on which payment or acceptance is required by those paragraphs.

(d)   Dishonor of an accepted draft is governed by the following rules:

(1)   If the draft is payable on demand, the draft is dishonored if presentment for payment is duly made to the acceptor and the draft is not paid on the day of presentment.

(2)   If the draft is not payable on demand, the draft is dishonored if presentment for payment is duly made to the acceptor and payment is not made on the day it becomes payable or the day of presentment, whichever is later.

(e)   In any case in which presentment is otherwise required for dishonor under this section and presentment is excused under Section 3–504, dishonor occurs without presentment if the instrument is not duly accepted or paid.

(f)   If a draft is dishonored because timely acceptance of the draft was not made and the person entitled to demand acceptance consents to a late acceptance, from the time of acceptance the draft is treated as never having been dishonored.

Official Comment

1. Section 3–415 provides that an indorser is obliged to pay an instrument if the instrument is dishonored and is discharged if the indorser is entitled to notice of dishonor and notice is not given. Under Section 3–414, the drawer is obliged to pay an unaccepted draft if it is dishonored. The drawer, however, is not entitled to notice of dishonor except to the extent required in a case governed by Section 3–414(d). Part 5 tells when an instrument is dishonored (Section 3–502) and what it means to give notice of dishonor (Section 3–503). Often dishonor does not occur until presentment (Section 3–501), and frequently presentment and notice of dishonor are excused (Section 3–504).

2. In the great majority of cases presentment and notice of dishonor are waived with respect to notes. In most cases a formal demand for payment to the maker of the note is not contemplated. Rather, the maker is expected to send payment to the holder of the note on the date or dates on which payment is due. If payment is not made when due, the holder usually makes a demand for payment, but in the normal case in which presentment is waived, demand is irrelevant and the holder can proceed against indorsers when payment is not received. Under former Article 3, in the small minority of cases in which presentment and dishonor were not waived with respect to notes, the indorser was discharged from liability (former Section 3–502(1)(a)) unless the holder made presentment to the maker on the exact day the note was due (former Section 3–503(1)(c)) and gave notice of dishonor to the indorser before midnight of the third business day after dishonor (former Section 3–508(2)). These provisions are omitted from Revised Article 3 as inconsistent with practice which seldom involves face-to-face dealings.

3. Subsection (a) applies to notes. Subsection (a)(1) applies to notes payable on demand. Dishonor requires presentment, and dishonor occurs if payment is not made on the day of presentment. There is no change from previous Article 3. Subsection (a)(2) applies to notes payable at a definite time if the note is payable at or through a bank or, by its terms, presentment is required. Dishonor requires presentment, and dishonor occurs if payment is not made on the due date or the day of presentment if presentment is made after the due date. Subsection (a)(3) applies to all other notes. If the note is not paid on its due date it is dishonored. This allows holders to collect notes in ways that make sense commercially without having to be concerned about a formal presentment on a given day.

4. Subsection (b) applies to unaccepted drafts other than documentary drafts. Subsection (b)(1) applies to checks. Except for checks presented for immediate payment over the counter, which are covered by subsection (b)(2), dishonor occurs according to rules stated in Article 4. Those rules contemplate four separate situations that warrant discussion. The first two situations arise in the normal course of affairs, in which the drawee bank makes settlement for the amount of the check to the presenting bank. In the first situation, the drawee bank under Section 4–301 recovers this settlement if it returns the check by its midnight deadline (Section 4–104). In that case the check is not paid and dishonor occurs under Section 3–502(b)(1). The second situation arises if the drawee bank has made such a settlement and does not return the check or give notice of dishonor or nonpayment within the midnight deadline. In that case, the settlement becomes final payment of the check under Section 4–215. Because the drawee bank already has paid such an item, it cannot be "accountable" for the item under the terms of Section 4–302(a)(1). Thus, no dishonor occurs regardless of whether the drawee bank retains the check indefinitely or for some reason returns the check after its midnight deadline.

The third and fourth situations arise less commonly, in cases in which the drawee bank does not settle for the check when it is received. Under Section 4–302 if the drawee bank is not also the depositary bank and retains the check without settling for it beyond midnight of the day it is presented for payment, the bank at that point becomes "accountable" for the amount of the check, i.e., it is obliged to pay the amount of the check. If the drawee bank is also the depositary bank, the bank becomes accountable for the amount of the check if the bank does not pay the check or return it or send notice of dishonor by its midnight deadline. Hence, if the drawee bank is also the depositary bank and does not either settle for the check when it is received (a settlement that would ripen into final payment if the drawee bank failed to take action to recover the settlement by its midnight deadline) or return the check or an appropriate notice by its midnight deadline, the drawee bank will become accountable for the amount of the check under Section 4–302. Thus, in all cases in which the drawee bank becomes accountable under Section 4–302, the check has not been paid (either by a settlement that became unrecoverable or otherwise) and thus, under Section 3–502(b)(1), the check is dishonored.

The fact that a bank that is accountable for the amount of the check under Section 4–302 is obliged to pay the check does not mean that the check has been paid. Indeed, because each of the paragraphs of Section 4–302(b) is limited by its terms to situations in which a bank has not paid the item, a drawee bank will be accountable under Section 4–302 only in situations in which it has not previously paid the check. Section 3–502(b)(1) reflects the view that a person presenting a check is entitled to payment, not just the ability to hold the drawee accountable under Section 4–302. If that payment is not made in a timely manner, the check is dishonored.

Regulation CC Section 229.36(d) provides that settlement between banks for the forward collection of checks is final. The relationship of that section to Articles 3 and 4 is discussed in the Commentary to that section.

Subsection (b)(2) applies to demand drafts other than those governed by subsection (b)(1). It covers checks presented for immediate payment over the counter and demand drafts other than checks. Dishonor occurs if presentment for payment is made and payment is not made on the day of presentment.

Subsection (b)(3) and (4) applies to time drafts. An unaccepted time draft differs from a time note. The maker of a note knows that the note has been issued, but the drawee of a draft may not know that a draft has been drawn on it. Thus, with respect to drafts, presentment for payment or acceptance is required. Subsection (b)(3) applies to drafts payable on a date stated in the draft. Dishonor occurs if presentment for payment is made and payment is not made on the day the draft becomes payable or the day of presentment if presentment is made after the due date. The holder of an unaccepted draft payable on a stated date has the option of presenting the draft for acceptance before the day the draft becomes payable to establish whether the drawee is willing to assume liability by accepting. Under subsection (b)(3)(ii) dishonor occurs when the draft is presented and not accepted. Subsection (b)(4) applies to unaccepted drafts payable on elapse of a period of time after sight or acceptance. If the draft is payable 30 days after sight, the draft must be presented for acceptance to start the running of the 30-day period. Dishonor occurs if it is not accepted. The rules in subsection (b)(3) and (4) follow former Section 3–501(1)(a).

5.   Subsection (c) gives drawees an extended period to pay documentary drafts because of the time that may be needed to examine the documents. The period prescribed is that given by Section 5–112 in cases in which a letter of credit is involved.

6.   Subsection (d) governs accepted drafts. If the acceptor's obligation is to pay on demand the rule, stated in subsection (d)(1), is the same as for that of a demand note stated in subsection (a)(1). If the acceptor's obligation is to pay at a definite time the rule, stated in subsection (d)(2), is the same as that of a time note payable at a bank stated in subsection (b)(2).

7.   Subsection (e) is a limitation on subsection (a)(1) and (2), subsection (b), subsection (c), and subsection (d). Each of those provisions states dishonor as occurring after presentment. If presentment is excused under Section 3–504, dishonor occurs under those provisions without presentment if the instrument is not duly accepted or paid.

8.   Under subsection (b)(3)(ii) and (4) if a draft is presented for acceptance and the draft is not accepted on the day of presentment, there is dishonor. But after dishonor, the holder may consent to late acceptance. In that case, under subsection (f), the late acceptance cures the dishonor. The draft is treated as never having been dishonored. If the draft is subsequently presented for payment and payment is refused dishonor occurs at that time.

As amended in 2002.

§ 3–503.   Notice of Dishonor.

(a)   The obligation of an indorser stated in Section 3–415(a) and the obligation of a drawer stated in Section 3–414(d) may not be enforced unless (i) the indorser or drawer is given notice of dishonor of the instrument complying with this section or (ii) notice of dishonor is excused under Section 3–504(b).

(b)   Notice of dishonor may be given by any person; may be given by any commercially reasonable means, including an oral, written, or electronic communication; and is sufficient if it reasonably identifies the instrument and indicates that the instrument has been dishonored or has not been paid or accepted. Return of an instrument given to a bank for collection is sufficient notice of dishonor.

(c)   Subject to Section 3–504(c), with respect to an instrument taken for collection by a collecting bank, notice of dishonor must be given (i) by the bank before midnight of the next banking day following the banking day on which the bank receives notice of dishonor of the instrument, or (ii) by any other person within 30 days following the day on which the person receives notice of dishonor. With respect to any other instrument, notice of dishonor must be given within 30 days following the day on which dishonor occurs.

Official Comment

1.   Subsection (a) is consistent with former Section 3–501(2)(a), but notice of dishonor is no longer relevant to the liability of a drawer except for the case of a draft accepted by an acceptor other than a bank. Comments 2 and 4 to Section 3–414. There is no reason why drawers should be discharged on instruments they draw until payment or acceptance. They are entitled to have the instrument presented to the drawee and dishonored (Section

3–414(b)) before they are liable to pay, but no notice of dishonor need be made to them as a condition of liability. Subsection (b), which states how notice of dishonor is given, is based on former Section 3–508(3).

2.   Subsection (c) replaces former Section 3–508(2). It differs from that section in that it provides a 30-day period for a person other than a collecting bank to give notice of dishonor rather than the three-day period allowed in former Article 3. Delay in giving notice of dishonor may be excused under Section 3–504(c).

§ 3–504.   Excused Presentment and Notice of Dishonor.

(a)   Presentment for payment or acceptance of an instrument is excused if (i) the person entitled to present the instrument cannot with reasonable diligence make presentment, (ii) the maker or acceptor has repudiated an obligation to pay the instrument or is dead or in insolvency proceedings, (iii) by the terms of the instrument presentment is not necessary to enforce the obligation of indorsers or the drawer, (iv) the drawer or indorser whose obligation is being enforced has waived presentment or otherwise has no reason to expect or right to require that the instrument be paid or accepted, or (v) the drawer instructed the drawee not to pay or accept the draft or the drawee was not obligated to the drawer to pay the draft.

(b)   Notice of dishonor is excused if (i) by the terms of the instrument notice of dishonor is not necessary to enforce the obligation of a party to pay the instrument, or (ii) the party whose obligation is being enforced waived notice of dishonor. A waiver of presentment is also a waiver of notice of dishonor.

(c)   Delay in giving notice of dishonor is excused if the delay was caused by circumstances beyond the control of the person giving the notice and the person giving the notice exercised reasonable diligence after the cause of the delay ceased to operate.

Official Comment

Section 3–504 is largely a restatement of former Section 3–511. Subsection (4) of former Section 3–511 is replaced by Section 3–502(f).

§ 3–505.   Evidence of Dishonor.

(a)   The following are admissible as evidence and create a presumption of dishonor and of any notice of dishonor stated:

(1)   a document regular in form as provided in subsection (b) which purports to be a protest;

(2)   a purported stamp or writing of the drawee, payor bank, or presenting bank on or accompanying the instrument stating that acceptance or payment has been refused unless reasons for the refusal are stated and the reasons are not consistent with dishonor;

(3)   a book or record of the drawee, payor bank, or collecting bank, kept in the usual course of business which shows dishonor, even if there is no evidence of who made the entry.

(b)   A protest is a certificate of dishonor made by a United States consul or vice consul, or a notary public or other person authorized to administer oaths by the law of the place where dishonor occurs. It may be made upon information satisfactory to that person. The protest must identify the instrument and certify either that presentment has been made or, if not made, the reason why it was not made, and that the instrument has been dishonored by nonacceptance or nonpayment. The protest may also certify that notice of dishonor has been given to some or all parties.

Official Comment

Protest is no longer mandatory and must be requested by the holder. Even if requested, protest is not a condition to the liability of indorsers or drawers. Protest is a service provided by the banking system to establish that dishonor has occurred. Like other services provided by the banking system, it will be available if market incentives, inter-bank agreements, or governmental regulations require it, but liabilities of parties no longer rest on it. Protest may be a requirement for liability on international drafts governed by foreign law which this Article cannot affect.

PART 6

DISCHARGE AND PAYMENT

§ 3–601. Discharge and Effect of Discharge.

(a)   The obligation of a party to pay the instrument is discharged as stated in this Article or by an act or agreement with the party which would discharge an obligation to pay money under a simple contract.

(b)   Discharge of the obligation of a party is not effective against a person acquiring rights of a holder in due course of the instrument without notice of the discharge.

Official Comment

Subsection (a) replaces subsections (1) and (2) of former Section 3–601. Subsection (b) restates former Section 3–602. Notice of discharge is not treated as notice of a defense that prevents holder in due course status. Section 3–302(b). Discharge is effective against a holder in due course only if the holder had notice of the discharge when holder in due course status was acquired. For example, if an instrument bearing a canceled indorsement is taken by a holder, the holder has notice that the indorser has been discharged. Thus, the discharge is effective against the holder even if the holder is a holder in due course.

§ 3–602. Payment.

(a)   Subject to subsection (e), an instrument is paid to the extent payment is made by or on behalf of a party obliged to pay the instrument, and to a person entitled to enforce the instrument.

(b)   Subject to subsection (e), a note is paid to the extent payment is made by or on behalf of a party obliged to pay the note to a person that formerly was entitled to enforce the note only if at the time of the payment the party obliged to pay has not received adequate notification that the note has been transferred and that payment is to be made to the transferee. A notification is adequate only if it is signed by the transferor or the transferee; reasonably identifies the transferred note; and provides an address at which payments subsequently are to be made. Upon request, a transferee shall seasonably furnish reasonable proof that the note has been transferred. Unless the transferee complies with the request, a payment to the person that formerly was entitled to enforce the note is effective for purposes of subsection (c) even if the party obliged to pay the note has received a notification under this paragraph.

(c)   Subject to subsection (e), to the extent of a payment under subsections (a) and (b), the obligation of the party obliged to pay the instrument is discharged even though payment is made with knowledge of a claim to the instrument under Section 3–306 by another person.

(d)   Subject to subsection (e), a transferee, or any party that has acquired rights in the instrument directly or indirectly from a transferee, including any such party that has rights as a holder in due course, is deemed to have notice of any payment that is made under subsection (b) after the date that the note is transferred to the transferee but before the party obliged to pay the note receives adequate notification of the transfer.

(e)   The obligation of a party to pay the instrument is not discharged under subsections (a) through (d) if:

(1)   a claim to the instrument under Section 3–306 is enforceable against the party receiving payment and (i) payment is made with knowledge by the payor that payment is prohibited by injunction or similar process of a court of competent jurisdiction, or (ii) in the case of an instrument other than a cashier's check, teller's check, or certified check, the party making payment accepted, from the person having a claim to the instrument, indemnity against loss resulting from refusal to pay the person entitled to enforce the instrument; or

(2)   the person making payment knows that the instrument is a stolen instrument and pays a person it knows is in wrongful possession of the instrument.

(f)   As used in this section, "signed," with respect to a record that is not a writing, includes the attachment to or logical association with the record of an electronic symbol, sound, or process with the present intent to adopt or accept the record.

As amended in 2002.

Official Comment

1.   This section replaces former Section 3–603(1). The phrase "claim to the instrument" in subsection (a) means, by reference to Section 3–306, a claim of ownership or possession and not a claim in recoupment. Subsection (e)(1)(ii) is added to conform to Section 3–411. Section 3–411 is intended to discourage an obligated bank from refusing payment of a cashier's check, certified check or dishonored teller's check at the request of a claimant to the check who provided the bank with indemnity against loss. See Comment 1 to Section 3–411. An obligated bank that refuses payment under those circumstances not only remains liable on the check but may also be liable to the holder of the check for consequential damages. Section 3–602(e)(1)(ii) and Section 3–411, read together, change the rule of former Section 3–603(1) with respect to the obligation of the obligated bank on the check. Payment to the holder of a cashier's check, teller's check, or certified check discharges the obligation of the obligated bank on the check to both the holder and the claimant even though indemnity has been given by the person asserting the claim. If the obligated bank pays the check in violation of an agreement with the claimant in connection with the indemnity agreement, any liability that the bank may have for violation of the agreement is not governed by Article 3, but is left to other law. This section continues the rule that the obligor is not discharged on the instrument if payment is made in violation of an injunction against payment. See Section 3–411(c)(iv).

2.   Subsection (a) covers payments made in a traditional manner, to the person entitled to enforce the instrument. Subsection (b), which provides an alternative method of payment, deals with the situation in which a person entitled to enforce the instrument transfers the instrument without giving notice to parties obligated to pay the instrument. If that happens and one of those parties subsequently makes a payment to the transferor, the payment is effective even though it is not made to the person entitled to enforce the instrument. Unlike the earlier version of Section 3–602, this rule is consistent with Section 9–406(a), Restatement of Mortgages § 5.5, and Restatement of Contracts § 338(1).

3.   In determining the party to whom a payment is made for purposes of this section, courts should look to traditional rules of agency. Thus, if the original payee of a note transfers ownership of the note to a third party but continues to service the obligation, the law of agency might treat payments made to the original payee as payments made to the third party.

4.   Subsection (d) assures that the discharge provided by subsection (c) is effective against the transferee and those whose rights derive from the transferee. By deeming those persons to have notice of any payment made under subsection (b), subsection (d) gives those persons "notice of the discharge" within the meaning of Section 3–302(b). Accordingly, the discharge is effective against those persons, even if any of them has the rights of a holder in due course. Compare Section 3–601(b). The deemed notice provided by subsection (d) does not, however, prevent a person from becoming or acquiring the rights of, a holder in due course. See Section 3–302(b). Thus, such a person does not become subject to other defenses described in Section 3–305(a)(2), claims in recoupment described in Section 3–305(a)(3), or claims to the instrument under Section 3–306. A transferee can prevent payment to the transferor from discharging the obligation on the note by assuring that each person who is obligated on the note receives adequate notification pursuant to subsection (b) prior to making a payment.

As amended in 2002 and 2003.

§ 3–603.   Tender of Payment.

(a)   If tender of payment of an obligation to pay an instrument is made to a person entitled to enforce the instrument, the effect of tender is governed by principles of law applicable to tender of payment under a simple contract.

(b)   If tender of payment of an obligation to pay an instrument is made to a person entitled to enforce the instrument and the tender is refused, there is discharge, to the extent of the amount of the tender, of the obligation of an indorser or accommodation party having a right of recourse with respect to the obligation to which the tender relates.

(c)   If tender of payment of an amount due on an instrument is made to a person entitled to enforce the instrument, the obligation of the obligor to pay interest after the due date on the amount tendered is discharged. If presentment is required with respect to an instrument and the obligor is able and ready to pay on the due date at every place of payment stated in the instrument, the obligor is deemed to have made tender of payment on the due date to the person entitled to enforce the instrument.

Official Comment

Section 3–603 replaces former Section 3–604. Subsection (a) generally incorporates the law of tender of payment applicable to simple contracts. Subsections (b) and (c) state particular rules. Subsection (b) replaces former Section 3–604(2). Under subsection (b) refusal of a tender of payment discharges any indorser or accommodation party having a right of recourse against the party making the tender. Subsection (c) replaces former Section 3–604(1) and (3).

§ 3–604. Discharge by Cancellation or Renunciation.

(a) A person entitled to enforce an instrument, with or without consideration, may discharge the obligation of a party to pay the instrument (i) by an intentional voluntary act, such as surrender of the instrument to the party, destruction, mutilation, or cancellation of the instrument, cancellation or striking out of the party's signature, or the addition of words to the instrument indicating discharge, or (ii) by agreeing not to sue or otherwise renouncing rights against the party by a signed record. The obligation of a party to pay a check is not discharged solely by destruction of the check in connection with a process in which information is extracted from the check and an image of the check is made and, subsequently, the information and image are transmitted for payment.

(b) Cancellation or striking out of an indorsement pursuant to subsection (a) does not affect the status and rights of a party derived from the indorsement.

(c) In this section, "signed," with respect to a record that is not a writing, includes the attachment to or logical association with the record of an electronic symbol, sound, or process with the present intent to adopt or accept the record.

As amended in 2002 and 2022.

Official Comment

1. Section 3–604 replaces former Section 3–605.

2. The destruction of a check in connection with a truncation process in which information is extracted from the check and an image of the check is made, and then such information and image are transmitted for payment is not within the scope of this section and does not by itself discharge the obligation of a party to pay the instrument. The destruction of the check also does not affect whether the check has been issued. See Section 3–105(a) and Comment 1.

3. Former subsection (c) has been deleted as unnecessary in view of the revised definition of "sign" in Section 1–201.

As amended in 2022.

§ 3–605. Discharge of Secondary Obligors.

(a) If a person entitled to enforce an instrument releases the obligation of a principal obligor in whole or in part, and another party to the instrument is a secondary obligor with respect to the obligation of that principal obligor, the following rules apply:

(1) Any obligations of the principal obligor to the secondary obligor with respect to any previous payment by the secondary obligor are not affected. Unless the terms of the release preserve the secondary obligor's recourse, the principal obligor is discharged, to the extent of the release, from any other duties to the secondary obligor under this article.

(2) Unless the terms of the release provide that the person entitled to enforce the instrument retains the right to enforce the instrument against the secondary obligor, the secondary obligor is discharged to the same extent as the principal obligor from any unperformed portion of its obligation on the instrument. If the instrument is a check and the obligation of the secondary obligor is based on an indorsement of the check, the secondary obligor is discharged without regard to the language or circumstances of the discharge or other release.

(3) If the secondary obligor is not discharged under paragraph (2), the secondary obligor is discharged to the extent of the value of the consideration for the release, and to the extent that the release would otherwise cause the secondary obligor a loss.

(b) If a person entitled to enforce an instrument grants a principal obligor an extension of the time at which one or more payments are due on the instrument and another party to the instrument is a secondary obligor with respect to the obligation of that principal obligor, the following rules apply:

(1) Any obligations of the principal obligor to the secondary obligor with respect to any previous payment by the secondary obligor are not affected. Unless the terms of the extension preserve the secondary obligor's recourse, the extension correspondingly extends the time for performance of any other duties owed to the secondary obligor by the principal obligor under this article.

(2) The secondary obligor is discharged to the extent that the extension would otherwise cause the secondary obligor a loss.

(3) To the extent that the secondary obligor is not discharged under paragraph (2), the secondary obligor may perform its obligations to a person entitled to enforce the instrument as if the time for payment had not been extended or, unless the terms of the extension provide that the person entitled to enforce the instrument retains the right to enforce the instrument against the secondary obligor as if the time for payment had not been extended, treat the time for performance of its obligations as having been extended correspondingly.

(c) If a person entitled to enforce an instrument agrees, with or without consideration, to a modification of the obligation of a principal obligor other than a complete or partial release or an extension of the due date and another party to the instrument is a secondary obligor with respect to the obligation of that principal obligor, the following rules apply:

(1) Any obligations of the principal obligor to the secondary obligor with respect to any previous payment by the secondary obligor are not affected. The modification correspondingly modifies any other duties owed to the secondary obligor by the principal obligor under this article.

(2) The secondary obligor is discharged from any unperformed portion of its obligation to the extent that the modification would otherwise cause the secondary obligor a loss.

(3) To the extent that the secondary obligor is not discharged under paragraph (2), the secondary obligor may satisfy its obligation on the instrument as if the modification had not occurred, or treat its obligation on the instrument as having been modified correspondingly.

(d) If the obligation of a principal obligor is secured by an interest in collateral, another party to the instrument is a secondary obligor with respect to that obligation, and a person entitled to enforce the instrument impairs the value of the interest in collateral, the obligation of the secondary obligor is discharged to the extent of the impairment. The value of an interest in collateral is impaired to the extent the value of the interest is reduced to an amount less than the amount of the recourse of the secondary obligor, or the reduction in value of the interest causes an increase in the amount by which the amount of the recourse exceeds the value of the interest. For purposes of this subsection, impairing the value of an interest in collateral includes failure to obtain or maintain perfection or recordation of the interest in collateral, release of collateral without substitution of collateral of equal value or equivalent reduction of the underlying obligation, failure to perform a duty to preserve the value of collateral owed, under Article 9 or other law, to a debtor or other person secondarily liable, and failure to comply with applicable law in disposing of or otherwise enforcing the interest in collateral.

(e) A secondary obligor is not discharged under subsections (a)(3), (b), (c), or (d) unless the person entitled to enforce the instrument knows that the person is a secondary obligor or has notice under Section 3–419(c) that the instrument was signed for accommodation.

(f) A secondary obligor is not discharged under this section if the secondary obligor consents to the event or conduct that is the basis of the discharge, or the instrument or a separate agreement of the party provides for waiver of discharge under this section specifically or by general language indicating that parties waive defenses based on suretyship or impairment of collateral. Unless the circumstances indicate otherwise, consent by the principal obligor to an act that would lead to a discharge under this section constitutes consent to that act by the secondary obligor if the secondary obligor controls the principal obligor or deals with the person entitled to enforce the instrument on behalf of the principal obligor.

(g) A release or extension preserves a secondary obligor's recourse if the terms of the release or extension provide that:

(1)   the person entitled to enforce the instrument retains the right to enforce the instrument against the secondary obligor; and

(2)   the recourse of the secondary obligor continues as if the release or extension had not been granted.

(h)   Except as otherwise provided in subsection (i), a secondary obligor asserting discharge under this section has the burden of persuasion both with respect to the occurrence of the acts alleged to harm the secondary obligor and loss or prejudice caused by those acts.

(i)   If the secondary obligor demonstrates prejudice caused by an impairment of its recourse, and the circumstances of the case indicate that the amount of loss is not reasonably susceptible of calculation or requires proof of facts that are not ascertainable, it is presumed that the act impairing recourse caused a loss or impairment equal to the liability of the secondary obligor on the instrument. In that event, the burden of persuasion as to any lesser amount of the loss is on the person entitled to enforce the instrument.

As amended in 2002.

Official Comment

1.   This section contains rules that are applicable when a secondary obligor (as defined in Section 3–103(a)(17)) is a party to an instrument. These rules essentially parallel modern interpretations of the law of suretyship and guaranty that apply when a secondary obligor is not a party to an instrument. See generally Restatement of the Law, Third, Suretyship and Guaranty (1996). Of course, the rules in this section do not resolve all possible issues concerning the rights and duties of the parties. In the event that a situation is presented that is not resolved by this section (or the other related sections of this Article), the resolution may be provided by the general law of suretyship because, pursuant to Section 1–103, that law is applicable unless displaced by provisions of this Act.

2.   Like the law of suretyship and guaranty, Section 3–605 provides secondary obligors with defenses that are not available to other parties to instruments. The general operation of Section 3–605, and its relationship to the law of suretyship and guaranty, can be illustrated by an example. Bank agrees to lend $10,000 to Borrower, but only if Backer also is liable for repayment of the loan. The parties could consummate that transaction in three different ways. First, if Borrower and Backer incurred those obligations with contracts not governed by this Article (such as a note that is not an instrument for purposes of this Article), the general law of suretyship and guaranty would be applicable. Under modern nomenclature, Bank is the "obligee," Borrower is the "principal obligor," and Backer is the "secondary obligor." See Restatement of Suretyship and Guaranty § 1. Then assume that Bank and Borrower agree to a modification of their rights and obligations after the note is signed. For example, they might agree that Borrower may repay the loan at some date after the due date, or that Borrower may discharge its repayment obligation by paying Bank $3,000 rather than $10,000. Alternatively, suppose that Bank releases collateral that Borrower has given to secure the loan. Under the law of suretyship and guaranty, the secondary obligor may be discharged under certain circumstances if these modifications of the obligations between Bank (the obligee) and Borrower (the principal obligor) are made without the consent of Backer (the secondary obligor). The rights that the secondary obligor has to a discharge of its liability in such cases commonly are referred to as suretyship defenses. The extent of the discharge depends upon the particular circumstances. See Restatement of Suretyship and Guaranty §§ 37, 39–44.

A second possibility is that the parties might decide to evidence the loan by a negotiable instrument. In that scenario, Borrower signs a note under which Borrower is obliged to pay $10,000 to the order of Bank on a due date stated in the note. Backer becomes liable for the repayment obligation by signing the note as a co-maker or indorser. In either case the note is signed for accommodation, Backer is an accommodation party, and Borrower is the accommodated party. See Section 3–419 (describing the obligations of accommodation parties). For purposes of Section 3–605, Backer is also a "secondary obligor" and Borrower is a "principal obligor," as those terms are defined in Section 3–103. Because Backer is a party to the instrument, its rights to a discharge based on any modification of obligations between Bank and Borrower are governed by Section 3–605 rather than by the general law of suretyship and guaranty. Within Section 3–605, subsection (a) describes the consequences of a release of Borrower, subsection (b) describes the consequences of an extension of time, and subsection (c) describes the consequences of other modifications.

The third possibility is that Borrower would use an instrument governed by this Article to evidence its repayment obligation, but Backer's obligation would be created in some way other than by becoming party to that instrument. In that case, Backer's rights are determined by suretyship and guaranty law rather than by this Article. See Comment 3 to Section 3–419.

A person also can acquire secondary liability without having been a secondary obligor at the time that the principal obligation was created. For example, a transferee of real or personal property that assumes the obligation of the transferor as maker of a note secured by the property becomes by operation of law a principal obligor, with the transferor becoming a secondary obligor. Restatement of Suretyship and Guaranty § 2(e); Restatement of Mortgages § 5.1. Article 3 does not determine the effect of the release of the transferee in that case because the assuming transferee is not a "party" to the instrument as defined in Section 3–103(a)(10). Section 3–605(a) does not apply then because the holder has not discharged the obligation of a "principal obligor," a term defined in Section 3–103(a)(11). Thus, the resolution of that question is governed by the law of suretyship. See Restatement of Suretyship and Guaranty § 39.

3.   Section 3–605 is not, however, limited to the conventional situation of the accommodation party discussed in Comment 2. It also applies in four other situations. First, it applies to indorsers of notes who are not accommodation parties. Unless an indorser signs without recourse, the indorser's liability under Section 3–415(a) is functionally similar to that of a guarantor of payment. For example, if Bank in the second hypothetical discussed in Comment 2 indorsed the note and transferred it to Second Bank, Bank is liable to Second Bank in the event of dishonor of the note by Borrower. Section 3–415(a). Because of that secondary liability as indorser, Bank qualifies as a "secondary obligor" under Section 3–103(a)(17) and has the same rights under Section 3–605 as an accommodation party.

Second, a similar analysis applies to the drawer of a draft that is accepted by a party that is not a bank. Under Section 3–414(d), that drawer has liability on the same terms as an indorser under Section 3–415(a). Thus, the drawer in that case is a "secondary obligor" under Section 3–103(a)(17) and has rights under Section 3–605 to that extent.

Third, a similar principle justifies application of Section 3–605 to persons who indorse a check. Assume that Drawer draws a check to the order of Payee. Payee then indorses the check and transfers it to Transferee. If Transferee presents the check and it is dishonored, Transferee may recover from Drawer under Section 3–414 or Payee under Section 3–415. Because of that secondary liability as an indorser, Payee is a secondary obligor under Section 3–103(a)(17). Drawer is a "principal obligor" under Section 3–103(a)(11). As noted in Comment 4, below, however, Section 3–605(a)(3) will discharge indorsers of checks in some cases in which other secondary obligors will not be discharged by this section.

Fourth, this section also deals with the rights of co-makers of instruments, even when those co-makers do not qualify as accommodation parties. The co-makers' rights of contribution under Section 3–116 make each co-maker a secondary obligor to the extent of that right of contribution.

4.   Subsection (a) is based on Restatement of Suretyship and Guaranty § 39. It addresses the effects of a release of the principal obligor by the person entitled to enforce the instrument. Paragraph (a)(1) governs the effect of that release on the principal obligor's duties to the secondary obligor; paragraphs (a)(2) and (a)(3) govern the effect of that release on the secondary obligor's duties to the person entitled to enforce the instrument.

With respect to the duties of the principal obligor, the release of course cannot affect obligations of the principal obligor with respect to payments that the secondary obligor already has made. But with respect to future payments by the secondary obligor, paragraph (a)(1) (based on Restatement of Suretyship and Guaranty § 39(a)) provides that the principal obligor is discharged, to the extent of the release, from any other duties to the secondary obligor. That rule is appropriate because otherwise the discharge granted to the principal obligor would be illusory: it would have obtained a release from a person entitled to enforce that instrument, but it would be directly liable for the same sum to the secondary obligor if the secondary obligor later complied with its secondary obligation to pay the instrument. This discharge does not occur, though, if the terms of the release effect a "preservation of recourse" as described in subsection (g). See Comment 10, below.

The discharge under paragraph (a)(1) of the principal obligor's duties to the secondary obligor is broad, applying to all duties under this article. This includes not only the principal obligor's liability as a party to an instrument (as a maker, drawer or indorser under Sections 3–412 through 3–415) but also obligations under Sections 3–116 and 3–419.

Paragraph (a)(2) is based closely on Restatement of Suretyship and Guaranty § 39(b). It articulates a default rule that the release of a principal obligor also discharges the secondary obligor, to the extent of the release granted to the principal obligor, from any unperformed portion of its obligation on the instrument. The discharge of the secondary obligor under paragraph (a)(2) is phrased more narrowly than the discharge of the principal obligor is phrased under paragraph (a)(1) because, unlike principal obligors, the only obligations of secondary obligors in Article 3 are "on the instrument" as makers or indorsers.

The parties can opt out of that rule by including a contrary statement in the terms of the release. The provision does not contemplate that any "magic words" are necessary. Thus, discharge of the secondary obligor under paragraph (a)(2) is avoided not only if the terms of the release track the statutory language (e.g., the person entitled to enforce the instrument "retains the right to enforce the instrument" against the secondary obligor), or if the terms of the release effect a preservation of recourse under subsection (g), but also if the terms of the release include a simple statement that the parties intend to "release the principal obligor but not the secondary obligor" or that the person entitled to enforce the instrument "reserves its rights" against the secondary obligor. At the same time, because paragraph (a)(2) refers to the "terms of the release," extrinsic circumstances cannot be used to establish that the parties intended the secondary obligor to remain obligated. If a release of the principal obligor includes such a provision, the secondary obligor is, nonetheless, discharged to the extent of the consideration that is paid for the release; that consideration is treated as a payment in partial satisfaction of the instrument.

Notwithstanding language in the release that prevents discharge of the secondary obligor under paragraph (a)(2), paragraph (a)(3) discharges the secondary obligor from its obligation to a person entitled to enforce the instrument to the extent that the release otherwise would cause the secondary obligor a loss. The rationale for that provision is that a release of the principal obligor changes the economic risk for which the secondary obligor contracted. This risk may be increased in two ways. First, by releasing the principal obligor, the person entitled to enforce the instrument has eliminated the likelihood of future payments by the principal obligor that would lessen the obligation of the secondary obligor. Second, unless the release effects a preservation of the secondary obligor's recourse, the release eliminates the secondary obligor's claims against the principal obligor with respect to any future payment by the secondary obligor. The discharge provided by this paragraph prevents that increased risk from causing the secondary obligor a loss. Moreover, permitting releases to be negotiated between the principal obligor and the person entitled to enforce the instrument without regard to the consequences to the secondary obligor would create an undue risk of opportunistic behavior by the obligee and principal obligor. That concern is lessened, and the discharge is not provided by paragraph (a)(3), if the secondary obligor has consented to the release or is deemed to have consented to it under subsection (f) (which presumes consent by a secondary obligor to actions taken by a principal obligor if the secondary obligor controls the principal obligor or deals with the person entitled to enforce the instrument on behalf of the principal obligor). See Comment 9, below.

Subsection (a) (and Restatement Section 39(b), the concepts of which it follows quite closely) is designed to facilitate negotiated workouts between a creditor and a principal obligor, so long as they are not at the expense of a secondary obligor who has not consented to the arrangement (either specifically or by waiving its rights to discharge under this section). Thus, for example, the provision facilitates an arrangement in which the principal obligor pays some portion of a guaranteed obligation, the person entitled to enforce the instrument grants a release to the principal obligor in exchange for that payment, and the person entitled to enforce the instrument pursues the secondary obligor for the remainder of the obligation. Under paragraph (a)(2), the person entitled to enforce the instrument may pursue the secondary obligor despite the release of the principal obligor so long as the terms of the release provide for this result. Under paragraph (a)(3), though, the secondary obligor will be protected against any loss it might suffer by reason of that release (if the secondary obligor has not waived discharge under subsection (f)). It should be noted that the obligee may be able to minimize the risk of such loss (and, thus, of the secondary obligor's discharge) by giving the secondary obligor prompt notice of the release even though such notice is not required.

The foregoing principles are illustrated by the following cases:

Case # 1. D borrows $1000 from C. The repayment obligation is evidenced by a note issued by D, payable to the order of C. S is an accommodation indorser of the note. As the due date of the note approaches, it becomes obvious that D cannot pay the full amount of the note and may soon be facing bankruptcy. C, in order to collect as much as possible from D and lessen the need to seek recovery from S, agrees to release D from its obligation under the note in exchange for $100 in cash. The agreement to release D is silent as to the effect of the release on S. Pursuant to Section 3–605(a)(2), the release of D discharges S from its obligations to C on the note.

Case # 2. Same facts as Case 1, except that the terms of the release provide that C retains its rights to enforce the instrument against S. D is discharged from its obligations to S pursuant to Section 3–605(a)(1), but S is not discharged from its obligations to C pursuant to Section 3–605(a)(2). However, if S could have recovered from D any sum it paid to C (had D not been discharged from its obligation to S), S has been harmed by the release and is discharged pursuant to Section 3–605(a)(3) to the extent of that harm.

Case # 3. Same facts as Case 1, except that the terms of the release provide that C retains its rights to enforce the instrument against S and that S retains its recourse against D. Under subsection (g), the release effects a preservation of recourse. Thus, S is not discharged from its obligations to C pursuant to Section 3–

605(a)(2) and D is not discharged from its obligations to S pursuant to Section 3–605(a)(1). Because S's claims against D are preserved, S will not suffer the kind of loss described in Case 2. If no other loss is suffered by S as a result of the release, S is not discharged pursuant to this section.

    Case # 4. Same facts as Case 3, except that D had made arrangements to work at a second job in order to earn the money to fulfill its obligations on the note. When C released D, however, D canceled the plans for the second job. While S still retains its recourse against D, S may be discharged from its obligation under the instrument to the extent that D's decision to forgo the second job causes S a loss because forgoing the job renders D unable to fulfill its obligations to S under Section 3–419.

    Subsection (a) reflects a change from former Section 3–605(b), which provided categorically that the release of a principal obligor by the person entitled to enforce the instrument did not discharge a secondary obligor's obligation on the instrument and assumed that the release also did not discharge the principal obligor's obligations to the secondary obligor under Section 3–419. The rule under subsection (a) is much closer to the policy of the Restatement of Suretyship and Guaranty than was former Section 3–605(b). The change, however, is likely to affect only a narrow category of cases. First, as discussed above, Section 3–605 applies only to transactions in which the payment obligation is represented by a negotiable instrument, and, within that set of transactions, only to those transactions in which the secondary obligation is incurred by indorsement or cosigning, not to transactions that involve a separate document of guaranty. See Comment 2, above. Second, as provided in subsection (f), secondary obligors cannot obtain a discharge under subsection (a) in any transaction in which they have consented to the challenged conduct. Thus, subsection (a) will not apply to any transaction that includes a provision waiving suretyship defenses (a provision that is almost universally included in commercial loan documentation) or to any transaction in which the creditor obtains the consent of the secondary obligor at the time of the release.

    The principal way in which subsection (a) goes beyond the policy of Restatement § 39 is with respect to the liability of indorsers of checks. Specifically, the last sentence of paragraph (a)(2) provides that a release of a principal obligor grants a complete discharge to the indorser of a check, without requiring the indorser to prove harm. In that particular context, it seems likely that continuing responsibility for the indorser often would be so inconsistent with the expectations of the parties as to create a windfall for the creditor and an unfair surprise for the indorser. Thus, the statute implements a simple rule that grants a complete discharge. The creditor, of course, can avoid that rule by contracting with the secondary obligor for a different result at the time that the creditor grants the release to the principal obligor.

    5.   Subsection (b) is based on Restatement of Suretyship and Guaranty § 40 and relates to extensions of the due date of the instrument. An extension of time to pay a note is often beneficial to the secondary obligor because the additional time may enable the principal obligor to obtain the funds to pay the instrument. In some cases, however, the extension may cause loss to the secondary obligor, particularly if deterioration of the financial condition of the principal obligor reduces the amount that the secondary obligor is able to recover on its right of recourse when default occurs. For example, suppose that the instrument is an installment note and the principal debtor is temporarily short of funds to pay a monthly installment. The payee agrees to extend the due date of the installment for a month or two to allow the debtor to pay when funds are available. Paragraph (b)(2) provides that an extension of time results in a discharge of the secondary obligor, but only to the extent that the secondary obligor proves that the extension caused loss. See subsection (h) (discussing the burden of proof under Section 3–605). Thus, if the extension is for a long period, the secondary obligor might be able to prove that during the period of extension the principal obligor became insolvent, reducing the value of the right of recourse of the secondary obligor. In such a case, paragraph (b)(2) discharges the secondary obligor to the extent of that harm. Although not required to notify the secondary obligor of the extension, the payee can minimize the risk of loss by the secondary obligor by giving the secondary obligor prompt notice of the extension; prompt notice can enhance the likelihood that the secondary obligor's right of recourse can remain valuable, and thus can limit the likelihood that the secondary obligor will suffer a loss because of the extension. See Restatement of Suretyship and Guaranty Section 38 comment b.

    If the secondary obligor is not discharged under paragraph (b)(2) (either because it would not suffer a loss by reason of the extension or because it has waived its right to discharge pursuant to subsection (f)), it is important to understand the effect of the extension on the rights and obligations of the secondary obligor. Consider the following cases:

    Case # 5. A borrows money from Lender and issues a note payable to the order of Lender that is due on April 1, 2002. B signs the note for accommodation at the request of Lender. B signed the note either as co-maker or as an anomalous indorser. In either case Lender subsequently makes an agreement with A extending the due date of A's obligation to pay the note to July 1, 2002. In either case B did not agree to the extension, and the extension did not address Lender's rights against B. Under paragraph (b)(1), A's obligations to B under this article are also extended to July 1, 2002. Under paragraph (b)(3), if B is not discharged, B may treat its obligations to Lender as also extended, or may pay the instrument on the original due date.

Case # 6. Same facts as Case 5, except that the extension agreement includes a statement that the Lender retains its right to enforce the note against B on its original terms. Under paragraph (b)(3), B is liable on the original due date, but under paragraph (b)(1), A's obligations to B under Section 3–419 are not due until July 1, 2002.

Case # 7. Same facts as Case 5, except that the extension agreement includes a statement that the Lender retains its right to enforce the note against B on its original terms and B retains its recourse against A as though no extension had been granted. Under paragraph (b)(3), B is liable on the original due date. Under paragraph (b)(1), A's obligations to B under Section 3–419 are not extended.

Under section 3–605(b), the results in Case 5 and Case 7 are identical to the results that follow from the law of suretyship and guaranty. See Restatement of Suretyship and Guaranty § 40. The situation in Case 6 is not specifically addressed in the Restatement, but the resolution in this Section is consistent with the concepts of suretyship and guaranty law as reflected in the Restatement. If the secondary obligor is called upon to pay on the due date, it may be difficult to quantify the extent to which the extension has impaired the right of recourse of the secondary obligor at that time. Still, the secondary obligor does have a right to make a claim against the obligee at that time. As a practical matter a suit making such a claim should establish the facts relevant to the extent of the impairment. See Restatement of Suretyship and Guaranty § 37(4).

As a practical matter, an extension of the due date will normally occur only when the principal obligor is unable to pay on the due date. The interest of the secondary obligor normally is to acquiesce in the willingness of the person entitled to enforce the instrument to wait for payment from the principal obligor rather than to pay right away and rely on an action against the principal obligor that may have little or no value. But in unusual cases the secondary obligor may prefer to pay the holder on the original due date so as to avoid continuing accrual of interest. In such cases, the secondary obligor may do so. See paragraph (b)(3). If the terms of the extension provide that the person entitled to enforce the instrument retains its right to enforce the instrument against the secondary obligor on the original due date, though, those terms are effective and the secondary obligor may not delay payment until the extended due date. Unless the extension agreement effects a preservation of recourse, however, the secondary obligor may not proceed against the principal obligor under Section 3–419 until the extended due date. See paragraph (b)(1). To the extent that delay causes loss to the secondary obligor it is discharged under paragraph (b)(2).

Even in those cases in which a secondary obligor does not have a duty to pay the instrument on the original due date, it always has the right to pay the instrument on that date, and perhaps minimize its loss by doing so. The secondary obligor is not precluded, however, from asserting its rights to discharge under Section 3–605(b)(2) if it does not exercise that option. The critical issue is whether the extension caused the secondary obligor a loss by increasing the difference between its cost of performing its obligation on the instrument and the amount recoverable from the principal obligor under this Article. The decision by the secondary obligor not to exercise its option to pay on the original due date may, under the circumstances, be a factor to be considered in the determination of that issue, especially if the secondary obligor has been given prompt notice of the extension (as discussed above).

6.   Subsection (c) is based on Restatement of Suretyship and Guaranty § 41. It is a residual provision, which applies to modifications of the obligation of the principal obligor that are not covered by subsections (a) and (b). Under subsection (c)(1), a modification of the obligation of the principal obligor on the instrument (other than a release covered by subsection (a) or an extension of the due date covered by subsection (b)), will correspondingly modify the duties of the principal obligor to the secondary obligor. Under subsection (c)(2), such a modification also will result in discharge of the secondary obligor to the extent the modification causes loss to the secondary obligor. To the extent that the secondary obligor is not discharged and the obligation changes the amount of money payable on the instrument, or the timing of such payment, subsection (c)(3) provides the secondary obligor with a choice: it may satisfy its obligation on the instrument as if the modification had not occurred, or it may treat its obligation to pay the instrument as having been modified in a manner corresponding to the modification of the principal obligor's obligation.

The following cases illustrate the application of subsection (c):

Case # 8. Corporation borrows money from Lender and issues a note payable to Lender. X signs the note as an accommodation party for Corporation. The note refers to a loan agreement under which the note was issued, which states various events of default that allow Lender to accelerate the due date of the note.

Among the events of default are breach of covenants not to incur debt beyond specified limits and not to engage in any line of business substantially different from that currently carried on by Corporation. Without consent of X, Lender agrees to modify the covenants to allow Corporation to enter into a new line of business that X considers to be risky, and to incur debt beyond the limits specified in the loan agreement to finance the new venture. This modification discharges X to the extent that the modification otherwise would cause X a loss.

Case # 9. Corporation borrows money from Lender and issues a note payable to Lender in the amount of $100,000. X signs the note as an accommodation party for Corporation. The note calls for 60 equal monthly payments of interest and principal. Before the first payment is made, Corporation and Lender agree to modify the note by changing the repayment schedule to require four annual payments of interest only, followed by a fifth payment of interest and the entire $100,000 principal balance. To the extent that the modification does not discharge X, X has the option of fulfilling its obligation on the note in accordance with the original terms or the modified terms.

7.   Subsection (d) is based on Restatement of Suretyship and Guaranty § 42 and deals with the discharge of secondary obligors by impairment of collateral. The last sentence of subsection (d) states four common examples of what is meant by impairment. Because it uses the term "includes," the provision allows a court to find impairment in other cases as well. There is extensive case law on impairment of collateral. The secondary obligor is discharged to the extent that the secondary obligor proves that impairment was caused by a person entitled to enforce the instrument. For example, assume that the payee of a secured note fails to perfect the security interest. The collateral is owned by the principal obligor who subsequently files in bankruptcy. As a result of the failure to perfect, the security interest is not enforceable in bankruptcy. If the payee were to obtain payment from the secondary obligor, the secondary obligor would be subrogated to the payee's security interest in the collateral under Section 3–419 and general principles of suretyship law. See Restatement of Suretyship and Guaranty § 28(1)(c). In this situation, though, the value of the security interest is impaired completely because the security interest is unenforceable. Thus, the secondary obligor is discharged from its obligation on the note to the extent of that impairment. If the value of the collateral impaired is as much or more than the amount of the note, and if there will be no recovery on the note as an unsecured claim, there is a complete discharge. Subsection (d) applies whether the collateral is personalty or realty, whenever the obligation in question is in the form of a negotiable instrument.

8.   Subsection (e) is based on the former Section 3–605(h). The requirement of knowledge in the first clause is consistent with Section 9–628. The requirement of notice in the second clause is consistent with Section 3–419(c).

9.   The importance of the suretyship defenses provided in Section 3–605 is greatly diminished by the fact that the right to discharge can be waived as provided in subsection (f). The waiver can be effectuated by a provision in the instrument or in a separate agreement. It is standard practice to include such a waiver of suretyship defenses in notes prepared by financial institutions or other commercial creditors. Thus, Section 3–605 will result in the discharge of an accommodation party on a note only in the occasional case in which the note does not include such a waiver clause and the person entitled to enforce the note nevertheless takes actions that would give rise to a discharge under this section without obtaining the consent of the secondary obligor.

Because subsection (f) by its terms applies only to a discharge "under this section," subsection (f) does not operate to waive a defense created by other law (such as the law governing enforcement of security interests under Article 9) that cannot be waived under that law. See, e.g., Section 9–602.

The last sentence of subsection (f) creates an inference of consent on the part of the secondary obligor whenever the secondary obligor controls the principal obligor or deals with the creditor on behalf of the principal obligor. That sentence is based on Restatement of Suretyship and Guaranty § 48(2).

10.   Subsection (g) explains the criteria for determining whether the terms of a release or extension preserve the secondary obligor's recourse, a concept of importance in the application of subsections (a) and (b). First, the terms of the release or extension must provide that the person entitled to enforce the instrument retains the right to enforce the instrument against the secondary obligor. Second, the terms of the release or extension must provide that the recourse of the secondary obligor against the principal obligor continues as though the release or extension had not been granted. Those requirements are drawn from Restatement of Suretyship and Guaranty § 38.

11.   Subsections (h) and (i) articulate rules for the burden of persuasion under Section 3–605. Those rules are based on Restatement of Suretyship and Guaranty § 49.

As amended in 2002.

UCC ARTICLE 4

BANK DEPOSITS AND COLLECTIONS

Article 4 was revised in 1990 and amended in 2002 and 2022.

2022 Amendments appear in ~~strikeout~~/*underline format.*

Prefatory Note to 2022 amendments appears in Appendix E.

Current through April 2023

For updates, see www.uniformlaws.org

PART 1.   GENERAL PROVISIONS AND DEFINITIONS

4–101.   Short Title.

4–102.   Applicability.

4–103.   Variation by Agreement; Measure of Damages; Action Constituting Ordinary Care.

4–104.   Definitions and Index of Definitions.

4–105.   Definitions of Types of Banks.

4–106.   Payable Through or Payable at Bank: Collecting Bank.

4–107.   Separate Office of Bank.

4–108.   Time of Receipt of Items.

4–109.   Delays.

4–110.   Electronic Presentment.

4–111.   Statute of Limitations.

PART 2.   COLLECTION OF ITEMS: DEPOSITARY AND COLLECTING BANKS

4–201.   Status of Collecting Bank as Agent and Provisional Status of Credits; Applicability of Article; Item Indorsed "Pay Any Bank".

4–202.   Responsibility for Collection or Return; When Action Timely.

4–203.   Effect of Instructions.

4–204.   Methods of Sending and Presenting; Sending Directly to Payor Bank.

4–205.   Depositary Bank Holder of Unindorsed Item.

4–206.   Transfer Between Banks.

4–207.   Transfer Warranties.

4–208.   Presentment Warranties.

4–209.   Encoding and Retention Warranties.

4–210.   Security Interest of Collecting Bank in Items, Accompanying Documents and Proceeds.

4–211.   When Bank Gives Value for Purposes of Holder in Due Course.

4–212.   Presentment by Notice of Item Not Payable by, Through, or at Bank; Liability of Drawer or Indorser.

4–213.   Medium and Time of Settlement by Bank.

4–214.   Right of Charge-Back or Refund; Liability of Collecting Bank; Return of Item.

4–215.   Final Payment of Item by Payor Bank; When Provisional Debits and Credits Become Final; When Certain Credits Become Available for Withdrawal.

4–216.   Insolvency and Preference.

PART 3.   COLLECTION OF ITEMS: PAYOR BANKS

4–301.   Deferred Posting; Recovery of Payment by Return of Items; Time of Dishonor; Return of Items by Payor Bank.
4–302.   Payor Bank's Responsibility for Late Return of Item.
4–303.   When Items Subject to Notice, Stop-Payment Order, Legal Process, or Setoff; Order in Which Items May Be Charged or Certified.

PART 4.   RELATIONSHIP BETWEEN PAYOR BANK AND ITS CUSTOMER

4–401.   When Bank May Charge Customer's Account.
4–402.   Bank's Liability to Customer for Wrongful Dishonor; Time of Determining Insufficiency of Account.
4–403.   Customer's Right to Stop Payment; Burden of Proof of Loss.
4–404.   Bank Not Obliged to Pay Check More Than Six Months Old.
4–405.   Death or Incompetence of Customer.
4–406.   Customer's Duty to Discover and Report Unauthorized Signature or Alteration.
4–407.   Payor Bank's Right to Subrogation on Improper Payment.

PART 5.   COLLECTION OF DOCUMENTARY DRAFTS

4–501.   Handling of Documentary Drafts; Duty to Send for Presentment and to Notify Customer of Dishonor.
4–502.   Presentment of "On Arrival" Drafts.
4–503.   Responsibility of Presenting Bank for Documents and Goods; Report of Reasons for Dishonor; Referee in Case of Need.
4–504.   Privilege of Presenting Bank to Deal With Goods; Security Interest for Expenses.

PART 1

GENERAL PROVISIONS AND DEFINITIONS

§ 4–101.   Short Title.

This Article may be cited as Uniform Commercial Code—Bank Deposits and Collections.

As amended in 1990.

Official Comment

1.   The great number of checks handled by banks and the country-wide nature of the bank collection process require uniformity in the law of bank collections. There is needed a uniform statement of the principal rules of the bank collection process with ample provision for flexibility to meet the needs of the large volume handled and the changing needs and conditions that are bound to come with the years. This Article meets that need.

2.   In 1950 at the time Article 4 was drafted, 6.7 billion checks were written annually. By the time of the 1990 revision of Article 4 annual volume was estimated by the American Bankers Association to be about 50 billion checks. The banking system could not have coped with this increase in check volume had it not developed in the late 1950s and early 1960s an automated system for check collection based on encoding checks with machine-readable information by Magnetic Ink Character Recognition (MICR). An important goal of the 1990 revision of Article 4 is to promote the efficiency of the check collection process by making the provisions of Article 4 more compatible with the needs of an automated system and, by doing so, increase the speed and lower the cost of check collection for those who write and receive checks. An additional goal of the 1990 revision of Article 4 is to remove any statutory barriers in the Article to the ultimate adoption of programs allowing the presentment of checks to payor banks by electronic transmission of information captured from the MICR line on the checks. The potential of these programs for saving the time and expense of transporting the huge volume of checks from depositary to payor banks is evident.

3.   Article 4 defines rights between parties with respect to bank deposits and collections. It is not a regulatory statute. It does not regulate the terms of the bank-customer agreement, nor does it prescribe what

constraints different jurisdictions may wish to impose on that relationship in the interest of consumer protection. The revisions in Article 4 are intended to create a legal framework that accommodates automation and truncation for the benefit of all bank customers. This may raise consumer problems which enacting jurisdictions may wish to address in individual legislation. For example, with respect to Section 4–401(c), jurisdictions may wish to examine their unfair and deceptive practices laws to determine whether they are adequate to protect drawers who postdate checks from unscrupulous practices that may arise on the part of persons who induce drawers to issue postdated checks in the erroneous belief that the checks will not be immediately payable. Another example arises from the fact that under various truncation plans customers will no longer receive their cancelled checks and will no longer have the cancelled check to prove payment. Individual legislation might provide that a copy of a bank statement along with a copy of the check is prima facie evidence of payment.

§ 4–102. Applicability.

(a)   To the extent that items within this Article are also within Articles 3 and 8, they are subject to those Articles. If there is conflict, this Article governs Article 3, but Article 8 governs this Article.

(b)   The liability of a bank for action or non-action with respect to an item handled by it for purposes of presentment, payment, or collection is governed by the law of the place where the bank is located. In the case of action or non-action by or at a branch or separate office of a bank, its liability is governed by the law of the place where the branch or separate office is located.

As amended in 1990.

Official Comment

1.   The rules of Article 3 governing negotiable instruments, their transfer, and the contracts of the parties thereto apply to the items collected through banking channels wherever no specific provision is found in this Article. In the case of conflict, this Article governs. See Section 3–102(b).

Bonds and like instruments constituting investment securities under Article 8 may also be handled by banks for collection purposes. Various sections of Article 8 prescribe rules of transfer some of which (see ~~Sections 8–304 and 8–306~~ Sections 8–108 and 8–304) [Amendments approved by the Permanent Editorial Board for Uniform Commercial Code November 4, 1995] may conflict with provisions of this Article (Sections 4–205, 4–207, and 4–208). In the case of conflict, Article 8 governs.

Section 4–210 deals specifically with overlapping problems and possible conflicts between this Article and Article 9. However, similar reconciling provisions are not necessary in the case of Articles 5 and 7. Sections 4–301 and 4–302 are consistent with Section 5–112 [*unrevised Article 5*]. In the case of Article 7 documents of title frequently accompany items but they are not themselves items. See Section 4–104(a)(9).

In *Clearfield Trust Co. v. United States*, 318 U.S. 363 (1943), the Court held that if the United States is a party to an instrument, its rights and duties are governed by federal common law in the absence of a specific federal statute or regulation. In *United States v. Kimbell Foods, Inc.*, 440 U.S. 715 (1979), the Court stated a three-pronged test to ascertain whether the federal common-law rule should follow the state rule. In most instances courts under the *Kimbell* test have shown a willingness to adopt UCC rules in formulating federal common law on the subject. In *Kimbell* the Court adopted the priorities rules of Article 9.

In addition, applicable federal law may supersede provisions of this Article. One federal law that does so is the Expedited Funds Availability Act, 12 U.S.C. § 4001 et seq., and its implementing Regulation CC, 12 CFR Pt. 229. In some instances this law is alluded to in the statute, e.g., Section 4–215(e) and (f). In other instances, although not referred to in this Article, the provisions of the EFAA and Regulation CC control with respect to checks. For example, except between the depositary bank and its customer, all settlements are final and not provisional (Regulation CC, Section 229.36(d)), and the midnight deadline may be extended (Regulation CC, Section 229.30(c)). The comments to this Article suggest in most instances the relevant Regulation CC provisions.

2.   Subsection (b) is designed to state a workable rule for the solution of otherwise vexatious problems of the conflicts of laws:

a.   The routine and mechanical nature of bank collections makes it imperative that one law govern the activities of one office of a bank. The requirement found in some cases that to hold an indorser notice must be given in accordance with the law of the place of indorsement, since that method of notice became an implied term of the indorser's contract, is more theoretical than practical.

b.   Adoption of what is in essence a tort theory of the conflict of laws is consistent with the general theory of this Article that the basic duty of a collecting bank is one of good faith and the exercise of ordinary care. Justification lies in the fact that, in using an ambulatory instrument, the drawer, payee, and indorsers must know that action will be taken with respect to it in other jurisdictions. This is especially pertinent with respect to the law of the place of payment.

c.   The phrase "action or non-action with respect to any item handled by it for purposes of presentment, payment, or collection" is intended to make the conflicts rule of subsection (b) apply from the inception of the collection process of an item through all phases of deposit, forwarding, presentment, payment and remittance or credit of proceeds. Specifically the subsection applies to the initial act of a depositary bank in receiving an item and to the incidents of such receipt. The conflicts rule of *Weissman v. Banque De Bruxelles*, 254 N.Y. 488, 173 N.E. 835 (1930), is rejected. The subsection applies to questions of possible vicarious liability of a bank for action or non-action of sub-agents (see Section 4–202(c)), and tests these questions by the law of the state of the location of the bank which uses the sub-agent. The conflicts rule of *St. Nicholas Bank of New York v. State Nat. Bank*, 128 N.Y. 26, 27 N.E. 849, 13 L.R.A. 241 (1891), is rejected. The subsection applies to action or non-action of a payor bank in connection with handling an item (see Sections 4–215(a), 4–301, 4–302, 4–303) as well as action or non-action of a collecting bank (Sections 4–201 through 4–216); to action or non-action of a bank which suspends payment or is affected by another bank suspending payment (Section 4–216); to action or non-action of a bank with respect to an item under the rule of Part 4 of Article 4.

d.   In a case in which subsection (b) makes this Article applicable, Section 4–103(a) leaves open the possibility of an agreement with respect to applicable law. This freedom of agreement follows the general policy of Section 1–105 [*unrevised Article 1; see Concordance, p. 22*].

§ 4–103.   Variation by Agreement; Measure of Damages; Action Constituting Ordinary Care.

(a)   The effect of the provisions of this Article may be varied by agreement, but the parties to the agreement cannot disclaim a bank's responsibility for its lack of good faith or failure to exercise ordinary care or limit the measure of damages for the lack or failure. However, the parties may determine by agreement the standards by which the bank's responsibility is to be measured if those standards are not manifestly unreasonable.

(b)   Federal Reserve regulations and operating circulars, clearing-house rules, and the like have the effect of agreements under subsection (a), whether or not specifically assented to by all parties interested in items handled.

(c)   Action or non-action approved by this Article or pursuant to Federal Reserve regulations or operating circulars is the exercise of ordinary care and, in the absence of special instructions, action or non-action consistent with clearing-house rules and the like or with a general banking usage not disapproved by this Article, is prima facie the exercise of ordinary care.

(d)   The specification or approval of certain procedures by this Article is not disapproval of other procedures that may be reasonable under the circumstances.

(e)   The measure of damages for failure to exercise ordinary care in handling an item is the amount of the item reduced by an amount that could not have been realized by the exercise of ordinary care. If there is also bad faith it includes any other damages the party suffered as a proximate consequence.

As amended in 1990.

Official Comment

1.   Section 1–102 states the general principles and rules for variation of the effect of this Act by agreement and the limitations to this power. Section 4–103 states the specific rules for variation of Article 4 by agreement and also certain standards of ordinary care. In view of the technical complexity of the field of bank collections, the enormous number of items handled by banks, the certainty that there will be variations from the normal in each day's work in each bank, the certainty of changing conditions and the possibility of developing improved methods of collection to speed the process, it would be unwise to freeze present methods of operation by mandatory statutory rules. This section, therefore, permits within wide limits variation of the effect of provisions of the Article by agreement.

2.   Subsection (a) confers blanket power to vary all provisions of the Article by agreements of the ordinary kind. The agreements may not disclaim a bank's responsibility for its own lack of good faith or failure to exercise ordinary care and may not limit the measure of damages for the lack or failure, but this subsection like Section 1–102(3) [*unrevised Article 1; see Concordance, p. 22*] approves the practice of parties determining by agreement the standards by which the responsibility is to be measured. In the absence of a showing that the standards manifestly are unreasonable, the agreement controls. Owners of items and other interested parties are not affected by agreements under this subsection unless they are parties to the agreement or are bound by adoption, ratification, estoppel or the like.

As here used "agreement" has the meaning given to it by Section 1–201(3) [*unrevised Article 1; see Concordance, p. 22*]. The agreement may be direct, as between the owner and the depositary bank; or indirect, as in the case in which the owner authorizes a particular type of procedure and any bank in the collection chain acts pursuant to such authorization. It may be with respect to a single item; or to all items handled for a particular customer, e.g., a general agreement between the depositary bank and the customer at the time a deposit account is opened. Legends on deposit tickets, collection letters and acknowledgments of items, coupled with action by the affected party constituting acceptance, adoption, ratification, estoppel or the like, are agreements if they meet the tests of the definition of "agreement." See Section 1–201(3) [*unrevised Article 1; see Concordance, p. 22*]. *First Nat. Bank of Denver v. Federal Reserve Bank*, 6 F.2d 339 (8th Cir. 1925) (deposit slip); *Jefferson County Bldg. Ass'n v. Southern Bank & Trust Co.*, 225 Ala. 25, 142 So. 66 (1932) (signature card and deposit slip); *Semingson v. Stock Yards Nat. Bank*, 162 Minn. 424, 203 N.W. 412 (1925) (passbook); *Farmers State Bank v. Union Nat. Bank*, 42 N.D. 449, 454, 173 N.W. 789, 790 (1919) (acknowledgment of receipt of item).

3.   Subsection (a) (subject to its limitations with respect to good faith and ordinary care) goes far to meet the requirements of flexibility. However, it does not by itself confer fully effective flexibility. Since it is recognized that banks handle a great number of items every business day and that the parties interested in each item include the owner of the item, the drawer (if it is a check), all nonbank indorsers, the payor bank and from one to five or more collecting banks, it is obvious that it is impossible, practically, to obtain direct agreements from all of these parties on all items. In total, the interested parties constitute virtually every adult person and business organization in the United States. On the other hand they may become bound to agreements on the principle that collecting banks acting as agents have authority to make binding agreements with respect to items being handled. This conclusion was assumed but was not flatly decided in *Federal Reserve Bank of Richmond v. Malloy*, 264 U.S. 160, at 167, 44 S.Ct. 296, at 298, 68 L.Ed. 617, 31 A.L.R. 1261 (1924).

To meet this problem subsection (b) provides that official or quasi-official rules of collection, that is Federal Reserve regulations and operating circulars, clearing-house rules, and the like, have the effect of agreements under subsection (a), whether or not specifically assented to by all parties interested in items handled. Consequently, such official or quasi-official rules may, standing by themselves but subject to the good faith and ordinary care limitations, vary the effect of the provisions of Article 4.

Federal Reserve regulations. Various sections of the Federal Reserve Act (12 U.S.C. § 221 et seq.) authorize the Board of Governors of the Federal Reserve System to direct the Federal Reserve banks to exercise bank collection functions. For example, Section 16 (12 U.S.C. § 248(*o*)) authorizes the Board to require each Federal Reserve bank to exercise the functions of a clearing house for its members and Section 13 (12 U.S.C. § 342) authorizes each Federal Reserve bank to receive deposits from nonmember banks solely for the purposes of exchange or of collection. Under this statutory authorization the Board has issued Regulation J (Subpart A— Collection of Checks and Other Items). Under the supremacy clause of the Constitution, federal regulations prevail over state statutes. Moreover, the Expedited Funds Availability Act, 12 U.S.C. Section 4007(b) provides that the Act and Regulation CC, 12 CFR 229, supersede "any provision of the law of any State, including the Uniform Commercial Code as in effect in such State, which is inconsistent with this chapter or such regulations." See Comment 1 to Section 4–102.

Federal Reserve operating circulars. The regulations of the Federal Reserve Board authorize the Federal Reserve banks to promulgate operating circulars covering operating details. Regulation J, for example, provides that "Each Reserve Bank shall receive and handle items in accordance with this subpart, and shall issue operating circulars governing the details of its handling of items and other matters deemed appropriate by the Reserve Bank." This Article recognizes that "operating circulars" issued pursuant to the regulations and concerned with operating details as appropriate may, within their proper sphere, vary the effect of the Article.

Clearing-House Rules. Local clearing houses have long issued rules governing the details of clearing; hours of clearing, media of remittance, time for return of mis-sent items and the like. The case law has recognized these rules, within their proper sphere, as binding on affected parties and as appropriate sources for the courts to look to in filling out details of bank collection law. Subsection (b) in recognizing clearing-house rules as a means of preserving flexibility continues the sensible approach indicated in the cases. Included in the term "clearing houses" are county and regional clearing houses as well as those within a single city or town. There is, of course, no intention of authorizing a local clearing house or a group of clearing houses to rewrite the basic law generally. The term "clearing-house rules" should be understood in the light of functions the clearing houses have exercised in the past.

And the like. This phrase is to be construed in the light of the foregoing. "Federal Reserve regulations and operating circulars" cover rules and regulations issued by public or quasi-public agencies under statutory authority. "Clearing-house rules" cover rules issued by a group of banks which have associated themselves to perform through a clearing house some of their collection, payment and clearing functions. Other agencies or associations of this kind may be established in the future whose rules and regulations could be appropriately looked on as constituting means of avoiding absolute statutory rigidity. The phrase "and the like" leaves open possibilities for future development. An agreement between a number of banks or even all the banks in an area simply because they are banks, would not of itself, by virtue of the phrase "and the like," meet the purposes and objectives of subsection (b).

4.   Under this Article banks come under the general obligations of the use of good faith and the exercise of ordinary care. "Good faith" is defined in Section 1–201(b)(20). The term "ordinary care" is defined in Section 3–103(a)(9). These definitions are made to apply to Article 4 by Section 4–104(c). Section 4–202 states respects in which collecting banks must use ordinary care. Subsection (c) of Section 4–103 provides that action or non-action approved by the Article or pursuant to Federal Reserve regulations or operating circulars constitutes the exercise of ordinary care. Federal Reserve regulations and operating circulars constitute an affirmative standard of ordinary care equally with the provisions of Article 4 itself.

Subsection (c) further provides that, absent special instructions, action or non-action consistent with clearing-house rules and the like or with a general banking usage not disapproved by the Article, prima facie constitutes the exercise of ordinary care. Clearing-house rules and the phrase "and the like" have the significance set forth above in these Comments. The term "general banking usage" is not defined but should be taken to mean a general usage common to banks in the area concerned. See Section 1–205(2) [*unrevised Article 1; see Concordance, p. 22*]. In a case in which the adjective "general" is used, the intention is to require a usage broader than a mere practice between two or three banks but it is not intended to require a usage broader than a mere practice between two or three banks but it is not intended to require anything as broad as a country-wide usage. A usage followed generally throughout a state, a substantial portion of a state, a metropolitan area or the like would certainly be sufficient. Consistently with the principle of Section 1–205(3) [*unrevised Article 1; see Concordance, p. 22*], action or non-action consistent with clearing-house rules or the like or with banking usages prima facie constitutes the exercise of ordinary care. However, the phrase "in the absence of special instructions" affords owners of items an opportunity to prescribe other standards and although there may be no direct supervision or control of clearing houses or banking usages by official supervisory authorities, the confirmation of ordinary care by compliance with these standards is prima facie only, thus conferring on the courts the ultimate power to determine ordinary care in any case in which it should appear desirable to do so. The prima facie rule does, however, impose on the party contesting the standards to establish that they are unreasonable, arbitrary or unfair as used by the particular bank.

5.   Subsection (d), in line with the flexible approach required for the bank collection process is designed to make clear that a novel procedure adopted by a bank is not to be considered unreasonable merely because that procedure is not specifically contemplated by this Article or by agreement, or because it has not yet been generally accepted as a bank usage. Changing conditions constantly call for new procedures and someone has to use the new procedure first. If this procedure is found to be reasonable under the circumstances, provided, of course, that it is not inconsistent with any provision of the Article or other law or agreement, the bank which has followed the new procedure should not be found to have failed in the exercise of ordinary care.

6.   Subsection (e) sets forth a rule for determining the measure of damages for failure to exercise ordinary care which, under subsection (a), cannot be limited by agreement. In the absence of bad faith the maximum recovery is the amount of the item concerned. The term "bad faith" is not defined; the connotation is the absence of good faith (Section 3–103). When it is established that some part or all of the item could not have been collected even by the use of ordinary care the recovery is reduced by the amount that would have been in any event uncollectible. This limitation on recovery follows the case law. Finally, if bad faith is established the rule opens to allow the recovery of other damages, whose "proximateness" is to be tested by the ordinary rules applied in comparable cases. Of course, it continues to be as necessary under subsection (e) as it has been under ordinary

common law principles that, before the damage rule of the subsection becomes operative, liability of the bank and some loss to the customer or owner must be established.

As amended in 2002.

§ 4–104.   Definitions and Index of Definitions.

(a)   In this Article, unless the context otherwise requires:

(1)   "Account" means any deposit or credit account with a bank, including a demand, time, savings, passbook, share draft, or like account, other than an account evidenced by a certificate of deposit;

(2)   "Afternoon" means the period of a day between noon and midnight;

(3)   "Banking day" means the part of a day on which a bank is open to the public for carrying on substantially all of its banking functions;

(4)   "Clearing house" means an association of banks or other payors regularly clearing items;

(5)   "Customer" means a person having an account with a bank or for whom a bank has agreed to collect items, including a bank that maintains an account at another bank;

(6)   "Documentary draft" means a draft to be presented for acceptance or payment if specified documents, certificated securities (Section 8–102) or instructions for uncertificated securities (Section 8–102), or other certificates, statements, or the like are to be received by the drawee or other payor before acceptance or payment of the draft;

(7)   "Draft" means a draft as defined in Section 3–104 or an item, other than an instrument, that is an order;

(8)   "Drawee" means a person ordered in a draft to make payment;

(9)   "Item" means an instrument or a promise or order to pay money handled by a bank for collection or payment. The term does not include a payment order governed by Article 4A or a credit or debit card slip;

(10)   "Midnight deadline" with respect to a bank is midnight on its next banking day following the banking day on which it receives the relevant item or notice or from which the time for taking action commences to run, whichever is later;

(11)   "Settle" means to pay in cash, by clearing-house settlement, in a charge or credit or by remittance, or otherwise as agreed. A settlement may be either provisional or final;

(12)   "Suspends payments" with respect to a bank means that it has been closed by order of the supervisory authorities, that a public officer has been appointed to take it over, or that it ceases or refuses to make payments in the ordinary course of business.

(b)   Other definitions applying to this Article and the sections in which they appear are:

"Agreement for electronic presentment" Section 4–110.
"Collecting bank" Section 4–105.
"Depositary bank" Section 4–105.
"Intermediary bank" Section 4–105.
"Payor bank" Section 4–105.
"Presenting bank" Section 4–105.
"Presentment notice" Section 4–110.

(c)   "Control" as provided in Section 7–106 and the following definitions in other Articles apply to this Article:

"Acceptance" Section 3–409.
"Alteration" Section 3–407.
"Cashier's check" Section 3–104.
"Certificate of deposit" Section 3–104.
"Certified check" Section 3–409.

"Check" Section 3–104.

["Good Faith" Section 3–103.] [*Note from West Advisory Panel: The definition of good faith in § 3–103 will be deleted if the jurisdiction adopts the definition of good faith in revised Article 1.*]

"Holder in due course" Section 3–302.

"Instrument" Section 3–104.

"Notice of dishonor" Section 3–503.

"Order" Section 3–103.

"Ordinary care" Section 3–103.

"Person entitled to enforce" Section 3–301.

"Presentment" Section 3–501.

"Promise" Section 3–103.

"Prove" Section 3–103.

"Record" Section 3–103.

"Remotely-Created consumer item" Section 3–103.

"Teller's check" Section 3–104.

"Unauthorized signature" Section 3–403.

(d) In addition, Article 1 contains general definitions and principles of construction and interpretation applicable throughout this Article.

As amended in 1990, 1994, 2001, 2002 and 2003.

Official Comment

1. Paragraph (a)(1): "Account" is defined to include both asset accounts in which a customer has deposited money and accounts from which a customer may draw on a line of credit. The limiting factor is that the account must be in a bank.

2. Paragraph (a)(3): "Banking day." Under this definition that part of a business day when a bank is open only for limited functions, e.g., to receive deposits and cash checks, but with loan, bookkeeping and other departments closed, is not part of a banking day.

3. Paragraph (a)(4): "Clearing house." Occasionally express companies, governmental agencies and other nonbanks deal directly with a clearing house; hence the definition does not limit the term to an association of banks.

4. Paragraph (a)(5): "Customer." It is to be noted that this term includes a bank carrying an account with another bank as well as the more typical nonbank customer or depositor.

5. Paragraph (a)(6): "Documentary draft" applies even though the documents do not accompany the draft but are to be received by the drawee or other payor before acceptance or payment of the draft. Documents may be either in electronic or tangible form. See Article 5, Section 5–102, Comment 2 and Article 1, Section 1–201 (definition of "document of title").

6. Paragraph (a)(7): "Draft" is defined in Section 3–104 as a form of instrument. Since Article 4 applies to items that may not fall within the definition of instrument, the term is defined here to include an item that is a written order to pay money, even though the item may not qualify as an instrument. The term "order" is defined in Section 3–103.

7. Paragraph (a)(8): "Drawee" is defined in Section 3–103 in terms of an Article 3 draft which is a form of instrument. Here "drawee" is defined in terms of an Article 4 draft which includes items that may not be instruments.

8. Paragraph (a)(9): "Item" is defined broadly to include an instrument, as defined in Section 3–104, as well as promises or orders that may not be within the definition of "instrument." The terms "promise" and "order" are defined in Section 3–103. A promise is a written undertaking to pay money. An order is a written instruction to pay money. But see Section 4–110(c). Since bonds and other investment securities under Article 8 may be within the term "instrument" or "promise," they are items and when handled by banks for collection are subject to this Article. See Comment 1 to Section 4–102. The functional limitation on the meaning of this term is the willingness of the banking system to handle the instrument, undertaking or instruction for collection or payment.

9. Paragraph (a)(10): "Midnight deadline." The use of this phrase is an example of the more mechanical approach used in this Article. Midnight is selected as a termination point or time limit to obtain greater uniformity

and definiteness than would be possible from other possible terminating points, such as the close of the banking day or business day.

10.   Paragraph (a)(11): The term "settle" has substantial importance throughout Article 4. In the American Bankers Association Bank Collection Code, in deferred posting statutes, in Federal Reserve regulations and operating circulars, in clearing-house rules, in agreements between banks and customers and in legends on deposit tickets and collection letters, there is repeated reference to "conditional" or "provisional" credits or payments. Tied in with this concept of creditors or payments being in some way tentative, has been a related but somewhat different problem as to when an item is "paid" or "finally paid" either to determine the relative priority of the item as against attachments, stop-payment orders and the like or in insolvency situations. There has been extensive litigation in the various states on these problems. To a substantial extent the confusion, the litigation and even the resulting court decisions fail to take into account that in the collection process some debits or credits are provisional or tentative and others are final and that very many debits or credits are provisional or tentative for awhile but later become final. Similarly, some cases fail to recognize that within a single bank, particularly a payor bank, each item goes through a series of processes and that in a payor bank most of these processes are preliminary to the basic act of payment or "final payment."

The term "settle" is used as a convenient term to characterize a broad variety of conditional, provisional, tentative and also final payments of items. Such a comprehensive term is needed because it is frequently difficult or unnecessary to determine whether a particular action is tentative or final or when a particular credit shifts from the tentative class to the final class. Therefore, its use throughout the Article indicates that in that particular context it is unnecessary or unwise to determine whether the debit or the credit or the payment is tentative or final. However, if qualified by the adjective "provisional" its tentative nature is intended, and if qualified by the adjective "final" its permanent nature is intended.

Examples of the various types of settlement contemplated by the term include payments in cash; the efficient but somewhat complicated process of payment through the adjustment and offsetting of balances through clearing houses; debit or credit entries in accounts between banks; the forwarding of various types of remittance instruments, sometimes to cover a particular item but more frequently to cover an entire group of items received on a particular day.

11.   Paragraph (a)(12): "Suspends payments." This term is designed to afford an objective test to determine when a bank is no longer operating as a part of the banking system.

As amended in 2003.

§ 4–105.   Definitions of Types of Banks.

In this Article:

(1)   ["Bank" means a person engaged in the business of banking, including a savings bank, savings and loan association, credit union, or trust company;]

(2)   "Depositary bank" means the first bank to take an item even though it is also the payor bank, unless the item is presented for immediate payment over the counter;

(3)   "Payor bank" means a bank that is the drawee of a draft;

(4)   "Intermediary bank" means a bank to which an item is transferred in course of collection except the depositary or payor bank;

(5)   "Collecting bank" means a bank handling an item for collection except the payor bank;

(6)   "Presenting bank" means a bank presenting an item except a payor bank.

Legislative Note: A jurisdiction that enacts this statute that has not yet enacted the revised version of UCC Article 1 should leave the definition of "Bank" in Section 4–105(1). Section 4–105(1) is reserved for that purpose. A jurisdiction that has adopted or simultaneously adopts the revised Article 1 should delete the definition of "Bank" from Section 4–105(1), but should leave those numbers "reserved." If jurisdictions follow the numbering suggested here, the subsections will have the same numbering in all jurisdictions that have adopted these amendments (whether they have or have not adopted the revised version of UCC Article 1). In either case, they should change the title of the section, as indicated in these revisions, so that all jurisdictions will have the same title for the section.

As amended in 1990 and 2002.

Official Comment

1.   The definitions in general exclude a bank to which an item is issued, as this bank does not take by transfer except in the particular case covered in which the item is issued to a payee for collection, as in the case in which a corporation is transferring balances from one account to another. Thus, the definition of "depositary bank" does not include the bank to which a check is made payable if a check is given in payment of a mortgage. This bank has the status of a payee under Article 3 on Negotiable Instruments and not that of a collecting bank.

2.   Paragraph (1): "Bank" is defined in Section 1–201(4)1–201(b)(4) as meaning "any person engaged in the business of banking." The definition in paragraph (1) makes clear that "bank" includes savings banks, savings and loan associations, credit unions and trust companies, in addition to the commercial banks commonly denoted by use of the term "bank."

3.   Paragraph (2): A bank that takes an "on us" item for collection, for application to a customer's loan, or first handles the item for other reasons is a depositary bank even though it is also the payor bank. However, if the holder presents the item for immediate payment over the counter, the payor bank is not a depositary bank.

4.   Paragraph (3): The definition of "payor bank" is clarified by use of the term "drawee." That term is defined in Section 4–104 as meaning "a person ordered in a draft to make payment." An "order" is defined in Section 3–103 as meaning "a written instruction to pay money. . . . An authorization to pay is not an order unless the person authorized to pay is also instructed to pay." The definition of order is incorporated into Article 4 by Section 4–104(c). Thus a payor bank is one instructed to pay in the item. A bank does not become a payor bank by being merely authorized to pay or by being given an instruction to pay not contained in the item.

5.   Paragraph (4): The term "intermediary bank" includes the last bank in the collection process if the drawee is not a bank. Usually the last bank is also a presenting bank.

As amended in 2022.

§ 4–106.   Payable Through or Payable at Bank: Collecting Bank.

(a)   If an item states that it is "payable through" a bank identified in the item, (i) the item designates the bank as a collecting bank and does not by itself authorize the bank to pay the item, and (ii) the item may be presented for payment only by or through the bank.

ALTERNATIVE A

(b)   If an item states that it is "payable at" a bank identified in the item, the item is equivalent to a draft drawn on the bank.

ALTERNATIVE B

(b)   If an item states that it is "payable at" a bank identified in the item, (i) the item designates the bank as a collecting bank and does not by itself authorize the bank to pay the item, and (ii) the item may be presented for payment only by or through the bank.

(c)   If a draft names a nonbank drawee and it is unclear whether a bank named in the draft is a co-drawee or a collecting bank, the bank is a collecting bank.

As added in 1990.

Official Comment

1.   This section replaces former Sections 3–120 and 3–121. Some items are made "payable through" a particular bank. Subsection (a) states that such language makes the bank a collecting bank and not a payor bank. An item identifying a "payable through" bank can be presented for payment to the drawee only by the "payable through" bank. The item cannot be presented to the drawee over the counter for immediate payment or by a collecting bank other than the "payable through" bank.

2.   Subsection (b) retains the alternative approach of the present law. Under Alternative A a note payable at a bank is the equivalent of a draft drawn on the bank and the midnight deadline provisions of Sections 4–301 and 4–302 apply. Under Alternative B a "payable at" bank is in the same position as a "payable through" bank under subsection (a).

3.   Subsection (c) rejects the view of some cases that a bank named below the name of a drawee is itself a drawee. The commercial understanding is that this bank is a collecting bank and is not accountable under Section

4–302 for holding an item beyond its deadline. The liability of the bank is governed by Sections 4–202(a) and 4–103(e).

§ 4–107.   Separate Office of Bank.

A branch or separate office of a bank is a separate bank for the purpose of computing the time within which and determining the place at or to which action may be taken or notices or orders shall be given under this Article and under Article 3.

As amended in 1962 and 1990.

Official Comment

1. A rule with respect to the status of a branch or separate office of a bank as a part of any statute on bank collections is highly desirable if not absolutely necessary. However, practices in the operations of branches and separate offices vary substantially in the different states and it has not been possible to find any single rule that is logically correct, fair in all situations and workable under all different types of practices. The decision not to draft the section with greater specificity leaves to the courts the resolution of the issues arising under this section on the basis of the facts of each case.

2. In many states and for many purposes a branch or separate office of the bank should be treated as a separate bank. Many branches function as separate banks in the handling and payment of items and require time for doing so similar to that of a separate bank. This is particularly true if branch banking is permitted throughout a state or in different towns and cities. Similarly, if there is this separate functioning a particular branch or separate office is the only proper place for various types of action to be taken or orders or notices to be given. Examples include the drawing of a check on a particular branch by a customer whose account is carried at that branch; the presentment of that same check at that branch; the issuance of an order to the branch to stop payment on the check.

3. Section 1 of the American Bankers Association Bank Collection Code provided simply: "A branch or office of any such bank shall be deemed a bank." Although this rule appears to be brief and simple, as applied to particular sections of the ABA Code it produces illogical and, in some cases, unreasonable results. For example, under Section 11 of the ABA Code it seems anomalous for one branch of a bank to have charged an item to the account of the drawer and another branch to have the power to elect to treat the item as dishonored. Similar logical problems would flow from applying the same rule to Article 4. Warranties by one branch to another branch under Sections 4–207 and 4–208 (each considered a separate bank) do not make sense.

4. Assuming that it is not desirable to make each branch a separate bank for all purposes, this section provides that a branch or separate office is a separate bank for certain purposes. In so doing the single legal entity of the bank as a whole is preserved, thereby carrying with it the liability of the institution as a whole on such obligations as it may be under. On the other hand, in cases in which the Article provides a number of time limits for different types of action by banks, if a branch functions as a separate bank, it should have the time limits available to a separate bank. Similarly if in its relations to customers a branch functions as a separate bank, notices and orders with respect to accounts of customers of the branch should be given at the branch. For example, whether a branch has notice sufficient to affect its status as a holder in due course of an item taken by it should depend upon what notice that branch has received with respect to the item. Similarly the receipt of a stop-payment order at one branch should not be notice to another branch so as to impair the right of the second branch to be a holder in due course of the item, although in circumstances in which ordinary care requires the communication of a notice or order to the proper branch of a bank, the notice or order would be effective at the proper branch from the time it was or should have been received. See Section 1–201(27) [*unrevised Article 1; see Concordance, p. 22*].

5. The bracketed language ("maintaining its own deposit ledger") in former Section 4–106 is deleted. Today banks keep records on customer accounts by electronic data storage. This has led most banks with branches to centralize to some degree their record keeping. The place where records are kept has little meaning if the information is electronically stored and is instantly retrievable at all branches of the bank. Hence, the inference to be drawn from the deletion of the bracketed language is that where record keeping is done is no longer an important factor in determining whether a branch is a separate bank.

§ 4–108.   Time of Receipt of Items.

(a) For the purpose of allowing time to process items, prove balances, and make the necessary entries on its books to determine its position for the day, a bank may fix an afternoon hour of 2 P.M. or later as a cutoff hour for the handling of money and items and the making of entries on its books.

(b)   An item or deposit of money received on any day after a cutoff hour so fixed or after the close of the banking day may be treated as being received at the opening of the next banking day.

As amended in 1990.

Official Comment

1.   Each of the huge volume of checks processed each day must go through a series of accounting procedures that consume time. Many banks have found it necessary to establish a cutoff hour to allow time for these procedures to be completed within the time limits imposed by Article 4. Subsection (a) approves a cutoff hour of this type provided it is not earlier than 2 P.M. Subsection (b) provides that if such a cutoff hour is fixed, items received after the cutoff hour may be treated as being received at the opening of the next banking day. If the number of items received either through the mail or over the counter tends to taper off radically as the afternoon hours progress, a 2 P.M. cutoff hour does not involve a large portion of the items received but at the same time permits a bank using such a cutoff hour to leave its doors open later in the afternoon without forcing into the evening the completion of its settling and proving process.

2.   The provision in subsection (b) that items or deposits received after the close of the banking day may be treated as received at the opening of the next banking day is important in cases in which a bank closes at twelve or one o'clock, e.g., on a Saturday, but continues to receive some items by mail or over the counter if, for example, it opens Saturday evening for the limited purpose of receiving deposits and cashing checks.

§ 4–109.   Delays.

(a)   Unless otherwise instructed, a collecting bank in a good faith effort to secure payment of a specific item drawn on a payor other than a bank, and with or without the approval of any person involved, may waive, modify, or extend time limits imposed or permitted by this [Act] for a period not exceeding two additional banking days without discharge of drawers or indorsers or liability to its transferor or a prior party.

(b)   Delay by a collecting bank or payor bank beyond time limits prescribed or permitted by this [Act] or by instructions is excused if (i) the delay is caused by interruption of communication or computer facilities, suspension of payments by another bank, war, emergency conditions, failure of equipment, or other circumstances beyond the control of the bank, and (ii) the bank exercises such diligence as the circumstances require.

As amended in 1990.

Official Comment

1.   Sections 4–202(b), 4–214, 4–301, and 4–302 prescribe various time limits for the handling of items. These are the limits of time within which a bank, in fulfillment of its obligation to exercise ordinary care, must handle items entrusted to it for collection or payment. Under Section 4–103 they may be varied by agreement or by Federal Reserve regulations or operating circular, clearing-house rules, or the like. Subsection (a) permits a very limited extension of these time limits. It authorizes a collecting bank to take additional time in attempting to collect drafts drawn on nonbank payors with or without the approval of any interested party. The right of a collecting bank to waive time limits under subsection (a) does not apply to checks. The two-day extension can only be granted in a good faith effort to secure payment and only with respect to specific items. It cannot be exercised if the customer instructs otherwise. Thus limited the escape provision should afford a limited degree of flexibility in special cases but should not interfere with the overall requirement and objective of speedy collections.

2.   An extension granted under subsection (a) is without discharge of drawers or indorsers. It therefore extends the times for presentment or payment as specified in Article 3.

3.   Subsection (b) is another escape clause from time limits. This clause operates not only with respect to time limits imposed by the Article itself but also time limits imposed by special instructions, by agreement or by Federal regulations or operating circulars, clearing-house rules or the like. The latter time limits are "permitted" by the Code. For example, a payor bank that fails to make timely return of a dishonored item may be accountable for the amount of the item. Subsection (b) excuses a bank from this liability when its failure to meet its midnight deadline resulted from, for example, a computer breakdown that was beyond the control of the bank, so long as the bank exercised the degree of diligence that the circumstances required. In *Port City State Bank v. American National Bank*, 486 F.2d 196 (10th Cir. 1973), the court held that a bank exercised sufficient diligence to be excused under this subsection. If delay is sought to be excused under this subsection, the bank has the burden of proof on

the issue of whether it exercised "such diligence as the circumstances require." The subsection is consistent with Regulation CC, Section 229.38(e).

§ 4–110.   Electronic Presentment.

(a)   "Agreement for electronic presentment" means an agreement, clearing-house rule, or Federal Reserve regulation or operating circular, providing that presentment of an item may be made by transmission of an image of an item or information describing the item ("presentment notice") rather than delivery of the item itself. The agreement may provide for procedures governing retention, presentment, payment, dishonor, and other matters concerning items subject to the agreement.

(b)   Presentment of an item pursuant to an agreement for presentment is made when the presentment notice is received.

(c)   If presentment is made by presentment notice, a reference to "item" or "check" in this Article means the presentment notice unless the context otherwise indicates.

As added in 1990.

Official Comment

1.   "An agreement for electronic presentment" refers to an agreement under which presentment may be made to a payor bank by a presentment notice rather than by presentment of the item. Under imaging technology now under development, the presentment notice might be an image of the item. The electronic presentment agreement may provide that the item may be retained by a depositary bank, other collecting bank, or even a customer of the depositary bank, or it may provide that the item will follow the presentment notice. The identifying characteristic of an electronic presentment agreement is that presentment occurs when the presentment notice is received. "An agreement for electronic presentment" does not refer to the common case of retention of items by payor banks because the item itself is presented to the payor bank in these cases. Payor bank check retention is a matter of agreement between payor banks and their customers. Provisions on payor bank check retention are found in Section 4–406(b).

2.   The assumptions under which the electronic presentment amendments are based are as follows: No bank will participate in an electronic presentment program without an agreement. These agreements may be either bilateral (Section 4–103(a)), under which two banks that frequently do business with each other may agree to depositary bank check retention, or multilateral (Section 4–103(b)), in which large segments of the banking industry may participate in such a program. In the latter case, federal or other uniform regulatory standards would likely supply the substance of the electronic presentment agreement, the application of which could be triggered by the use of some form of identifier on the item. Regulation CC, Section 229.36(c) authorizes truncation agreements but forbids them from extending return times or otherwise varying requirements of the part of Regulation CC governing check collection without the agreement of all parties interested in the check. For instance, an extension of return time could damage a depositary bank which must make funds available to its customers under mandatory availability schedules. The Expedited Funds Availability Act, 12 U.S.C. Section 4008(b)(2), directs the Federal Reserve Board to consider requiring that banks provide for check truncation.

3.   The parties affected by an agreement for electronic presentment, with the exception of the customer, can be expected to protect themselves. For example, the payor bank can probably be expected to limit its risk of loss from drawer forgery by limiting the dollar amount of eligible items (Federal Reserve program), by reconcilement agreements (ABA Safekeeping program), by insurance (credit union share draft program), or by other means. Because agreements will exist, only minimal amendments are needed to make clear that the UCC does not prohibit electronic presentment.

§ 4–111.   Statute of Limitations.

An action to enforce an obligation, duty, or right arising under this Article must be commenced within three years after the [cause of action] accrues.

As added in 1990.

Official Comment

This section conforms to the period of limitations set by Section 3–118(g) for actions for breach of warranty and to enforce other obligations, duties or rights arising under Article 3. Bracketing "cause of action" recognizes that some states use a different term, such as "claim for relief."

PART 2

COLLECTION OF ITEMS: DEPOSITARY AND COLLECTING BANKS

§ 4-201.   Status of Collecting Bank as Agent and Provisional Status of Credits; Applicability of Article; Item Indorsed "Pay Any Bank".

(a)   Unless a contrary intent clearly appears and before the time that a settlement given by a collecting bank for an item is or becomes final, the bank, with respect to an item, is an agent or sub-agent of the owner of the item and any settlement given for the item is provisional. This provision applies regardless of the form of indorsement or lack of indorsement and even though credit given for the item is subject to immediate withdrawal as of right or is in fact withdrawn; but the continuance of ownership of an item by its owner and any rights of the owner to proceeds of the item are subject to rights of a collecting bank, such as those resulting from outstanding advances on the item and rights of recoupment or setoff. If an item is handled by banks for purposes of presentment, payment, collection, or return, the relevant provisions of this Article apply even though action of the parties clearly establishes that a particular bank has purchased the item and is the owner of it.

(b)   After an item has been indorsed with the words "pay any bank" or the like, only a bank may acquire the rights of a holder until the item has been:

(1)   returned to the customer initiating collection; or

(2)   specially indorsed by a bank to a person who is not a bank.

As amended in 1990.

Official Comment

1.   This section states certain basic rules of the bank collection process. One basic rule, appearing in the last sentence of subsection (a), is that, to the extent applicable, the provisions of the Article govern without regard to whether a bank handling an item owns the item or is an agent for collection. Historically, much time has been spent and effort expended in determining or attempting to determine whether a bank was a purchaser of an item or merely an agent for collection. See discussion of this subject and cases cited in 11 A.L.R. 1043, 16 A.L.R. 1084, 42 A.L.R. 492, 68 A.L.R. 725, 99 A.L.R. 486. See also Section 4 of the American Bankers Association Bank Collection Code. The general approach of Article 4, similar to that of other articles, is to provide, within reasonable limits, rules or answers to major problems known to exist in the bank collection process without regard to questions of status and ownership but to keep general principles such as status and ownership available to cover residual areas not covered by specific rules. In line with this approach, the last sentence of subsection (a) says in effect that Article 4 applies to practically every item moving through banks for the purpose of presentment, payment or collection.

2.   Within this general rule of broad coverage, the first two sentences of subsection (a) state a rule of agency status. "Unless a contrary intent clearly appears" the status of a collecting bank is that of an agent or sub-agent for the owner of the item. Although as indicated in Comment 1 it is much less important under Article 4 to determine status than has been the case heretofore, status may have importance in some residual areas not covered by specific rules. Further, since status has been considered so important in the past, to omit all reference to it might cause confusion. The status of agency "applies regardless of the form of indorsement or lack of indorsement and even though credit given for the item is subject to immediate withdrawal as of right or is in fact withdrawn." Thus questions heretofore litigated as to whether ordinary indorsements "for deposit," "for collection" or in blank have the effect of creating an agency status or a purchase, no longer have significance in varying the prima facie rule of agency. Similarly, the nature of the credit given for an item or whether it is subject to immediate withdrawal as of right or is in fact withdrawn, does not alter the agency status. See A.L.R. references supra in Comment 1.

A contrary intent can change agency status but this must be clear. An example of a clear contrary intent would be if collateral papers established or the item bore a legend stating that the item was sold absolutely to the depositary bank.

3.   The prima facie agency status of collecting banks is consistent with prevailing law and practice today. Section 2 of the American Bankers Association Bank Collection Code so provided. Legends on deposit tickets,

collection letters and acknowledgments of items and Federal Reserve operating circulars consistently so provide. The status is consistent with rights of charge-back (Section 4–214 and Section 11 of the ABA Code) and risk of loss in the event of insolvency (Section 4–216 and Section 13 of the ABA Code). The right of charge-back with respect to checks is limited by Regulation CC, Section 226.36(d).

4.   Affirmative statement of a prima facie agency status for collecting banks requires certain limitations and qualifications. Under current practices substantially all bank collections sooner or later merge into bank credits, at least if collection is effected. Usually, this takes place within a few days of the initiation of collection. An intermediary bank receives final collection and evidences the result of its collection by a "credit" on its books to the depositary bank. The depositary bank evidences the results of its collection by a "credit" in the account of its customer. As used in these instances the term "credit" clearly indicates a debtor-creditor relationship. At some stage in the bank collection process the agency status of a collecting bank changes to that of debtor, a debtor of its customer. Usually at about the same time it also becomes a creditor for the amount of the item, a creditor of some intermediary, payor or other bank. Thus the collection is completed, all agency aspects are terminated and the identity of the item has become completely merged in bank accounts, that of the customer with the depositary bank and that of one bank with another.

Although Section 4–215(a) provides that an item is finally paid when the payor bank takes or fails to take certain action with respect to the item, the final payment of the item may or may not result in the simultaneous final settlement for the item in the case of all prior parties. If a series of provisional debits and credits for the item have been entered in accounts between banks, the final payment of the item by the payor bank may result in the automatic firming up of all these provisional debits and credits under Section 4–215(c), and the consequent receipt of final settlement for the item by each collecting bank and the customer of the depositary bank simultaneously with such action of the payor bank. However, if the payor bank or some intermediary bank accounts for the item with a remittance draft, the next prior bank usually does not receive final settlement for the item until the remittance draft finally clears. See Section 4–213(c). The first sentence of subsection (a) provides that the agency status of a collecting bank (whether intermediary or depositary) continues until the settlement given by it for the item is or becomes final. In the case of the series of provisional credits covered by Section 4–215(c), this could be simultaneously with the final payment of the item by the payor bank. In cases in which remittance drafts are used or in straight noncash collections, this would not be until the times specified in Sections 4–213(c) and 4–215(d). With respect to checks Regulation CC Sections 229.31(c), 229.32(b) and 229.36(d) provide that all settlements between banks are final in both the forward collection and return of checks.

Under Section 4–213(a) settlements for items may be made by any means agreed to by the parties. Since it is impossible to contemplate all the kinds of settlements that will be utilized, no attempt is made in Article 4 to provide when settlement is final in all cases. The guiding principle is that settlements should be final when the presenting person has received usable funds. Section 4–213(c) and (d) and Section 4–215(c) provide when final settlement occurs with respect to certain kinds of settlement, but these provisions are not intended to be exclusive.

A number of practical results flow from the rule continuing the agency status of a collecting bank until its settlement for the item is or becomes final, some of which are specifically set forth in this Article. One is that risk of loss continues in the owner of the item rather than the agent bank. See Section 4–214. Offsetting rights favorable to the owner are that pending such final settlement, the owner has the preference rights of Section 4–216 and the direct rights of Section 4–302 against the payor bank. It also follows from this rule that the dollar limitations of Federal Deposit Insurance are measured by the claim of the owner of the item rather than that of the collecting bank. With respect to checks, rights of the parties in insolvency are determined by Regulation CC Section 229.39 and the liability of a bank handling a check to a subsequent bank that does not receive payment because of suspension of payments by another bank is stated in Regulation CC Section 229.35(b).

5.   In those cases in which some period of time elapses between the final payment of the item by the payor bank and the time that the settlement of the collecting bank is or becomes final, e.g., if the payor bank or an intermediary bank accounts for the item with a remittance draft or in straight noncash collections, the continuance of the agency status of the collecting bank necessarily carries with it the continuance of the owner's status as principal. The second sentence of subsection (a) provides that whatever rights the owner has to proceeds of the item are subject to the rights of collecting banks for outstanding advances on the item and other valid rights, if any. The rule provides a sound rule to govern cases of attempted attachment of proceeds of a non-cash item in the hands of the payor bank as property of the absent owner. If a collecting bank has made an advance on an item which is still outstanding, its right to obtain reimbursement for this advance should be superior to the rights of the owner to the proceeds or to the rights of a creditor of the owner. An intentional crediting of proceeds of an item to the account of a prior bank known to be insolvent, for the purpose of acquiring a right of setoff, would not produce a valid setoff. See 8 Zollman, *Banks and Banking* (1936) Sec. 5443.

6.   This section and Article 4 as a whole represent an intentional abandonment of the approach to bank collection problems appearing in Section 4 of the American Bankers Association Bank Collection Code. Because the tremendous volume of items handled makes impossible the examination by all banks of all indorsements on all items and thus in fact this examination is not made, except perhaps by depositary banks, it is unrealistic to base the rights and duties of all banks in the collection chain on variations in the form of indorsements. It is anomalous to provide throughout the ABA Code that the prima facie status of collecting banks is that of agent or sub-agent but in Section 4 to provide that subsequent holders (sub-agents) shall have the right to rely on the presumption that the bank of deposit (the primary agent) is the owner of the item. It is unrealistic, particularly in this background, to base rights and duties on status of agent or owner. Thus Section 4–201 makes the pertinent provisions of Article 4 applicable to substantially all items handled by banks for presentment, payment or collection, recognizes the prima facie status of most banks as agents, and then seeks to state appropriate limits and some attributes to the general rules so expressed.

7.   Subsection (b) protects the ownership rights with respect to an item indorsed "pay any bank or banker" or in similar terms of a customer initiating collection or of any bank acquiring a security interest under Section 4–210, in the event the item is subsequently acquired under improper circumstances by a person who is not a bank and transferred by that person to another person, whether or not a bank. Upon return to the customer initiating collection of an item so indorsed, the indorsement may be cancelled (Section 3–207). A bank holding an item so indorsed may transfer the item out of banking channels by special indorsement; however, under Section 4–103(e), the bank would be liable to the owner of the item for any loss resulting therefrom if the transfer had been made in bad faith or with lack of ordinary care. If briefer and more simple forms of bank indorsements are developed under Section 4–206 (e.g., the use of bank transit numbers in lieu of present lengthy forms of bank indorsements), a depositary bank having the transit number "X100" could make subsection (b) operative by indorsements such as "Pay any bank—X100." Regulation CC Section 229.35(c) states the effect of an indorsement on a check by a bank.

§ 4–202.   Responsibility for Collection or Return; When Action Timely.

(a)   A collecting bank must exercise ordinary care in:

(1)   presenting an item or sending it for presentment;

(2)   sending notice of dishonor or nonpayment or returning an item other than a documentary draft to the bank's transferor after learning that the item has not been paid or accepted, as the case may be;

(3)   settling for an item when the bank receives final settlement; and

(4)   notifying its transferor of any loss or delay in transit within a reasonable time after discovery thereof.

(b)   A collecting bank exercises ordinary care under subsection (a) by taking proper action before its midnight deadline following receipt of an item, notice, or settlement. Taking proper action within a reasonably longer time may constitute the exercise of ordinary care, but the bank has the burden of establishing timeliness.

(c)   Subject to subsection (a)(1), a bank is not liable for the insolvency, neglect, misconduct, mistake, or default of another bank or person or for loss or destruction of an item in the possession of others or in transit.

As amended in 1990.

Official Comment

1.   Subsection (a) states the basic responsibilities of a collecting bank. Of course, under Section 1–203 [*unrevised Article 1; see Concordance, p. 22*] a collecting bank is subject to the standard requirement of good faith. By subsection (a) it must also use ordinary care in the exercise of its basic collection tasks. By Section 4–103(a) neither requirement may be disclaimed.

2.   If the bank makes presentment itself, subsection (a)(1) requires ordinary care with respect both to the time and manner of presentment. (Sections 3–501 and 4–212.) If it forwards the item to be presented the subsection requires ordinary care with respect to routing (Section 4–204), and also in the selection of intermediary banks or other agents.

3.   Subsection (a) describes types of basic action with respect to which a collecting bank must use ordinary care. Subsection (b) deals with the time for taking action. It first prescribes the general standard for timely action, namely, for items received on Monday, proper action (such as forwarding or presenting) on Monday or Tuesday is timely. Although under current "production line" operations banks customarily move items along on regular schedules substantially briefer than two days, the subsection states an outside time within which a bank may know it has taken timely action. To provide flexibility from this standard norm, the subsection further states that action within a reasonably longer time may be timely but the bank has the burden of proof. In the case of time items, action after the midnight deadline, but sufficiently in advance of maturity for proper presentation, is a clear example of a "reasonably longer time" that is timely. The standard of requiring action not later than Tuesday in the case of Monday items is also subject to possibilities of variation under the general provisions of Section 4–103, or under the special provisions regarding time of receipt of items (Section 4–108), and regarding delays (Section 4–109). This subsection (b) deals only with collecting banks. The time limits applicable to payor banks appear in Sections 4–301 and 4–302.

4.   At common law the so-called New York collection rule subjected the initial collecting bank to liability for the actions of subsequent banks in the collection chain; the so-called Massachusetts rule was that each bank, subject to the duty of selecting proper intermediaries, was liable only for its own negligence. Subsection (c) adopts the Massachusetts rule. But since this is stated to be subject to subsection (a)(1) a collecting bank remains responsible for using ordinary care in selecting properly qualified intermediary banks and agents and in giving proper instructions to them. Regulation CC Section 229.36(d) states the liability of a bank during the forward collection of checks.

§ 4–203.   Effect of Instructions.

Subject to Article 3 concerning conversion of instruments (Section 3–420) and restrictive indorsements (Section 3–206), only a collecting bank's transferor can give instructions that affect the bank or constitute notice to it, and a collecting bank is not liable to prior parties for any action taken pursuant to the instructions or in accordance with any agreement with its transferor.

As amended in 1990.

Official Comment

This section adopts a "chain of command" theory which renders it unnecessary for an intermediary or collecting bank to determine whether its transferor is "authorized" to give the instructions. Equally the bank is not put on notice of any "revocation of authority" or "lack of authority" by notice received from any other person. The desirability of speed in the collection process and the fact that, by reason of advances made, the transferor may have the paramount interest in the item requires the rule.

The section is made subject to the provisions of Article 3 concerning conversion of instruments (Section 3–420) and restrictive indorsements (Section 3–206). Of course instructions from or an agreement with its transferor does not relieve a collecting bank of its general obligation to exercise good faith and ordinary care. See Section 4–103(a). If in any particular case a bank has exercised good faith and ordinary care and is relieved of responsibility by reason of instructions of or an agreement with its transferor, the owner of the item may still have a remedy for loss against the transferor (another bank) if such transferor has given wrongful instructions.

The rules of the section are applied only to collecting banks. Payor banks always have the problem of making proper payment of an item; whether such payment is proper should be based upon all of the rules of Articles 3 and 4 and all of the facts of any particular case, and should not be dependent exclusively upon instructions from or an agreement with a person presenting the item.

§ 4–204.   Methods of Sending and Presenting; Sending Directly to Payor Bank.

(a)   A collecting bank shall send items by a reasonably prompt method, taking into consideration relevant instructions, the nature of the item, the number of those items on hand, the cost of collection involved, and the method generally used by it or others to present those items.

(b)   A collecting bank may send:

(1)   an item directly to the payor bank;

(2)   an item to a nonbank payor if authorized by its transferor; and

(3)   an item other than documentary drafts to a nonbank payor, if authorized by Federal Reserve regulation or operating circular, clearing-house rule, or the like.

(c)   Presentment may be made by a presenting bank at a place where the payor bank or other payor has requested that presentment be made.

As amended in 1962 and 1990.

Official Comment

1.   Subsection (a) prescribes the general standards applicable to proper sending or forwarding of items. Because of the many types of methods available and the desirability of preserving flexibility any attempt to prescribe limited or precise methods is avoided.

2.   Subsection (b)(1) codifies the practice of direct mail, express, messenger or like presentment to payor banks. The practice is now country-wide and is justified by the need for speed, the general responsibility of banks, Federal Deposit Insurance protection and other reasons.

3.   Full approval of the practice of direct sending is limited to cases in which a bank is a payor. Since nonbank drawees or payors may be of unknown responsibility, substantial risks may be attached to placing in their hands the instruments calling for payments from them. This is obviously so in the case of documentary drafts. However, in some cities practices have long existed under clearing-house procedures to forward certain types of items to certain nonbank payors. Examples include insurance loss drafts drawn by field agents on home offices. For the purpose of leaving the door open to legitimate practices of this kind, subsection (b)(3) affirmatively approves direct sending of any item other than documentary drafts to any nonbank payor, if authorized by Federal Reserve regulation or operating circular, clearing-house rule or the like.

On the other hand subsection (b)(2) approves sending any item directly to a nonbank payor if authorized by a collecting bank's transferor. This permits special instructions or agreements out of the norm and is consistent with the "chain of command" theory of Section 4–203. However, if a transferor other than the owner of the item, e.g., a prior collecting bank, authorizes a direct sending to a nonbank payor, such transferor assumes responsibility for the propriety or impropriety of such authorization.

4.   Section 3–501(b) provides where presentment may be made. This provision is expressly subject to Article 4. Section 4–204(c) specifically approves presentment by a presenting bank at any place requested by the payor bank or other payor. The time when a check is received by a payor bank for presentment is governed by Regulation CC Section 229.36(b).

§ 4–205.   Depositary Bank Holder of Unindorsed Item.

If a customer delivers an item to a depositary bank for collection:

(1)   the depositary bank becomes a holder of the item at the time it receives the item for collection if the customer at the time of delivery was a holder of the item, whether or not the customer indorses the item, and, if the bank satisfies the other requirements of Section 3–302, it is a holder in due course; and

(2)   the depositary bank warrants to collecting banks, the payor bank or other payor, and the drawer that the amount of the item was paid to the customer or deposited to the customer's account.

As amended in 1990.

Official Comment

Section 3–201(b) provides that negotiation of an instrument payable to order requires indorsement by the holder. The rule of former Section 4–205(1) was that the depositary bank may supply a missing indorsement of its customer unless the item contains the words "payee's indorsement required" or the like. The cases have differed on the status of the depositary bank as a holder if it fails to supply its customer's indorsement. *Marine Midland Bank, N.A. v. Price, Miller, Evans & Flowers*, 446 N.Y.S.2d 797 (N.Y.App.Div. 4th Dept. 1981), *rev'd*, 455 N.Y.S.2d 565 (N.Y. 1982). It is common practice for depositary banks to receive unindorsed checks under so-called "lockbox" agreements from customers who receive a high volume of checks. No function would be served by requiring a depositary bank to run these items through a machine that would supply the customer's indorsement except to afford the drawer and the subsequent banks evidence that the proceeds of the item reached the customer's account. Paragraph (1) provides that the depositary bank becomes a holder when it takes the item for deposit if the depositor is a holder. Whether it supplies the customer's indorsement is immaterial. Paragraph (2) satisfies the need for a receipt of funds by the depositary bank by imposing on that bank a warranty that it paid the customer or deposited the item to the customer's account. This warranty runs not only to collecting banks and to the payor bank or nonbank drawee but also to the drawer, affording protection to these parties that the depositary bank received the item and applied it to the benefit of the holder.

§ 4–206.   Transfer Between Banks.

Any agreed method that identifies the transferor bank is sufficient for the item's further transfer to another bank.

As amended in 1990.

Official Comment

This section is designed to permit the simplest possible form of transfer from one bank to another, once an item gets in the bank collection chain, provided only identity of the transferor bank is preserved. This is important for tracing purposes and if recourse is necessary. However, since the responsibilities of the various banks appear in the Article it becomes unnecessary to have liability or responsibility depend on more formal indorsements. Simplicity in the form of transfer is conducive to speed. If the transfer is between banks, this section takes the place of the more formal requirements of Section 3–201.

§ 4–207.   Transfer Warranties.

(a)   A customer or collecting bank that transfers an item and receives a settlement or other consideration warrants to the transferee and to any subsequent collecting bank that:

(1)   the warrantor is a person entitled to enforce the item;

(2)   all signatures on the item are authentic and authorized;

(3)   the item has not been altered;

(4)   the item is not subject to a defense or claim in recoupment (Section 3–305(a)) of any party that can be asserted against the warrantor;

(5)   the warrantor has no knowledge of any insolvency proceeding commenced with respect to the maker or acceptor or, in the case of an unaccepted draft, the drawer; and

(6)   with respect to any remotely-created consumer item, that the person on whose account the item is drawn authorized the issuance of the item in the amount for which the item is drawn.

(b)   If an item is dishonored, a customer or collecting bank transferring the item and receiving settlement or other consideration is obliged to pay the amount due on the item (i) according to the terms of the item at the time it was transferred, or (ii) if the transfer was of an incomplete item, according to its terms when completed as stated in Sections 3–115 and 3–407. The obligation of a transferor is owed to the transferee and to any subsequent collecting bank that takes the item in good faith. A transferor cannot disclaim its obligation under this subsection by an indorsement stating that it is made "without recourse" or otherwise disclaiming liability.

(c)   A person to whom the warranties under subsection (a) are made and who took the item in good faith may recover from the warrantor as damages for breach of warranty an amount equal to the loss suffered as a result of the breach, but not more than the amount of the item plus expenses and loss of interest incurred as a result of the breach.

(d)   The warranties stated in subsection (a) cannot be disclaimed with respect to checks. Unless notice of a claim for breach of warranty is given to the warrantor within 30 days after the claimant has reason to know of the breach and the identity of the warrantor, the warrantor is discharged to the extent of any loss caused by the delay in giving notice of the claim.

(e)   A cause of action for breach of warranty under this section accrues when the claimant has reason to know of the breach.

As added in 1990 and amended in 2002.

Official Comment

1.   Except for subsection (b), this section conforms to Section 3–416 and extends its coverage to items. The substance of this section is discussed in the Comment to Section 3–416. Subsection (b) provides that customers or collecting banks that transfer items, whether by indorsement or not, undertake to pay the item if the item is dishonored. This obligation cannot be disclaimed by a "without recourse" indorsement or otherwise. With respect to checks, Regulation CC Section 229.34 states the warranties made by paying and returning banks.

2.   For an explanation of subsection (a)(6), see comment 8 to Section 3–416.

3.   The warranties provided for in this section and in Sections 4–208 and 4–209 are supplemented by warranties created under federal law. For example, under Section 4–209(b), a person who undertakes to retain an item in connection with an agreement for electronic presentment makes a warranty that retention and presentment comply with the agreement. Under federal law, a person might also make a warranty that no person will be asked to make payment based on a check already paid. See 12 C.F.R. § 229.34(a).

As amended in 2002 and 2022.

§ 4–208.   Presentment Warranties.

(a)   If an unaccepted draft is presented to the drawee for payment or acceptance and the drawee pays or accepts the draft, (i) the person obtaining payment or acceptance, at the time of presentment, and (ii) a previous transferor of the draft, at the time of transfer, warrant to the drawee that pays or accepts the draft in good faith that:

(1)   the warrantor is, or was, at the time the warrantor transferred the draft, a person entitled to enforce the draft or authorized to obtain payment or acceptance of the draft on behalf of a person entitled to enforce the draft;

(2)   the draft has not been altered;

(3)   the warrantor has no knowledge that the signature of the purported drawer of the draft is unauthorized; and

(4)   with respect to any remotely-created consumer item, that the person on whose account the item is drawn authorized the issuance of the item in the amount for which the item is drawn.

(b)   A drawee making payment may recover from a warrantor damages for breach of warranty equal to the amount paid by the drawee less the amount the drawee received or is entitled to receive from the drawer because of the payment. In addition, the drawee is entitled to compensation for expenses and loss of interest resulting from the breach. The right of the drawee to recover damages under this subsection is not affected by any failure of the drawee to exercise ordinary care in making payment. If the drawee accepts the draft (i) breach of warranty is a defense to the obligation of the acceptor, and (ii) if the acceptor makes payment with respect to the draft, the acceptor is entitled to recover from a warrantor for breach of warranty the amounts stated in this subsection.

(c)   If a drawee asserts a claim for breach of warranty under subsection (a) based on an unauthorized indorsement of the draft or an alteration of the draft, the warrantor may defend by proving that the indorsement is effective under Section 3–404 or 3–405 or the drawer is precluded under Section 3–406 or 4–406 from asserting against the drawee the unauthorized indorsement or alteration.

(d)   If (i) a dishonored draft is presented for payment to the drawer or an indorser or (ii) any other item is presented for payment to a party obliged to pay the item, and the item is paid, the person obtaining payment and a prior transferor of the item warrant to the person making payment in good faith that the warrantor is, or was, at the time the warrantor transferred the item, a person entitled to enforce the item or authorized to obtain payment on behalf of a person entitled to enforce the item. The person making payment may recover from any warrantor for breach of warranty an amount equal to the amount paid plus expenses and loss of interest resulting from the breach.

(e)   The warranties stated in subsections (a) and (d) cannot be disclaimed with respect to checks. Unless notice of a claim for breach of warranty is given to the warrantor within 30 days after the claimant has reason to know of the breach and the identity of the warrantor, the warrantor is discharged to the extent of any loss caused by the delay in giving notice of the claim.

(f)   A cause of action for breach of warranty under this section accrues when the claimant has reason to know of the breach.

As added in 1990 and amended in 2002.

Official Comment

1.   This section conforms to Section 3–417 and extends its coverage to items. The substance of this section is discussed in the Comment to Section 3–417. "Draft" is defined in Section 4–104 as including an item that is an order to pay so as to make clear that the term "draft" in Article 4 may include items that are not instruments within Section 3–104.

2.   For an explanation of subsection (a)(4), see comment 8 to Section 3–416.

As amended in 2002.

§ 4–209.   Encoding and Retention Warranties.

(a)   A person who encodes information on or with respect to an item after issue warrants to any subsequent collecting bank and to the payor bank or other payor that the information is correctly encoded. If the customer of a depositary bank encodes, that bank also makes the warranty.

(b)   A person who undertakes to retain an item pursuant to an agreement for electronic presentment warrants to any subsequent collecting bank and to the payor bank or other payor that retention and presentment of the item comply with the agreement. If a customer of a depositary bank undertakes to retain an item, that bank also makes this warranty.

(c)   A person to whom warranties are made under this section and who took the item in good faith may recover from the warrantor as damages for breach of warranty an amount equal to the loss suffered as a result of the breach, plus expenses and loss of interest incurred as a result of the breach.

As added in 1990.

Official Comment

1.   Encoding and retention warranties are included in Article 4 because they are unique to the bank collection process. These warranties are breached only by the person doing the encoding or retaining the item and not by subsequent banks handling the item. Encoding and check retention may be done by customers who are payees of a large volume of checks; hence, this section imposes warranties on customers as well as banks. If a customer encodes or retains, the depositary bank is also liable for any breach of this warranty.

2.   A misencoding of the amount on the MICR line is not an alteration under Section 3–407(a) which defines alteration as changing the contract of the parties. If a drawer wrote a check for $2,500 and the depositary bank encoded $25,000 on the MICR line, the payor bank could debit the drawer's account for only $2,500. This subsection would allow the payor bank to hold the depositary bank liable for the amount paid out over $2,500 without first pursuing the person who received payment. Intervening collecting banks would not be liable to the payor bank for the depositary bank's error. If a drawer wrote a check for $25,000 and the depositary bank encoded $2,500, the payor bank becomes liable for the full amount of the check. The payor bank's rights against the depositary bank depend on whether the payor bank has suffered a loss. Since the payor bank can debit the drawer's account for $25,000, the payor bank has a loss only to the extent that the drawer's account is less than the full amount of the check. There is no requirement that the payor bank pursue collection against the drawer beyond the amount in the drawer's account as a condition to the payor bank's action against the depositary bank for breach of warranty. See *Georgia Railroad Bank & Trust Co. v. First National Bank & Trust*, 229 S.E.2d 482 (Ga.App. 1976), aff'd, 235 S.E.2d 1 (Ga. 1977), and *First National Bank of Boston v. Fidelity Bank, National Association*, 724 F.Supp. 1168 (E.D.Pa. 1989).

3.   A person retaining items under an electronic presentment agreement (Section 4–110) warrants that it has complied with the terms of the agreement regarding its possession of the item and its sending a proper presentment notice. If the keeper is a customer, its depositary bank also makes this warranty.

§ 4–210.   Security Interest of Collecting Bank in Items, Accompanying Documents and Proceeds.

(a)   A collecting bank has a security interest in an item and any accompanying documents or the proceeds of either:

(1)   in case of an item deposited in an account, to the extent to which credit given for the item has been withdrawn or applied;

(2)   in case of an item for which it has given credit available for withdrawal as of right, to the extent of the credit given, whether or not the credit is drawn upon or there is a right of charge-back; or

(3)   if it makes an advance on or against the item.

(b)   If credit given for several items received at one time or pursuant to a single agreement is withdrawn or applied in part, the security interest remains upon all the items, any accompanying documents or the proceeds of either. For the purpose of this section, credits first given are first withdrawn.

(c)   Receipt by a collecting bank of a final settlement for an item is a realization on its security interest in the item, accompanying documents, and proceeds. So long as the bank does not receive final settlement for the item or give up possession of the item or possession or control of the accompanying documents for purposes other than collection, the security interest continues to that extent and is subject to Article 9, but:

(1)   no security agreement is necessary to make the security interest enforceable (Section 9–203(b)(3)(A));

(2)   no filing is required to perfect the security interest; and

(3)   the security interest has priority over conflicting perfected security interests in the item, accompanying documents, or proceeds.

As amended in 1999 and 2003.

Official Comment

1.   Subsection (a) states a rational rule for the interest of a bank in an item. The customer of the depositary bank is normally the owner of the item and the several collecting banks are agents of the customer (Section 4–201). A collecting agent may properly make advances on the security of paper held for collection, and acquires at common law a possessory lien for these advances. Subsection (a) applies an analogous principle to a bank in the collection chain which extends credit on items in the course of collection. The bank has a security interest to the extent stated in this section. To the extent of its security interest it is a holder for value (Sections 3–303, 4–211) and a holder in due course if it satisfies the other requirements for that status (Section 3–302). Subsection (a) does not derogate from the banker's general common law lien or right of setoff against indebtedness owing in deposit accounts. See Section 1–103. Rather subsection (a) specifically implements and extends the principle as a part of the bank collection process.

2.   Subsection (b) spreads the security interest of the bank over all items in a single deposit or received under a single agreement and a single giving of credit. It also adopts the "first-in, first-out" rule.

3.   Collection statistics establish that the vast majority of items handled for collection are in fact collected. The first sentence of subsection (c) reflects the fact that in the normal case the bank's security interest is self-liquidating. The remainder of the subsection correlates the security interest with the provisions of Article 9, particularly for use in the cases of noncollection in which the security interest may be important.

§ 4–211.   When Bank Gives Value for Purposes of Holder in Due Course.

For purposes of determining its status as a holder in due course, a bank has given value to the extent it has a security interest in an item, if the bank otherwise complies with the requirements of Section 3–302 on what constitutes a holder in due course.

As amended in 1990.

Official Comment

The section completes the thought of the previous section and makes clear that a security interest in an item is "value" for the purpose of determining the holder's status as a holder in due course. The provision is in accord with the prior law (N.I.L. Section 27) and with Article 3 (Section 3–303). The section does not prescribe a security interest under Section 4–210 as a test of "value" generally because the meaning of "value" under other Articles is adequately defined in Section 1–201 [unrevised Article 1; see Concordance, p. 22].

§ 4–212. Presentment by Notice of Item Not Payable by, Through, or at Bank; Liability of Drawer or Indorser.

(a)   Unless otherwise instructed, a collecting bank may present an item not payable by, through, or at a bank by sending to the party to accept or pay a record providing notice that the bank holds the item for acceptance or payment. The notice must be sent in time to be received on or before the day when presentment is due and the bank must meet any requirement of the party to accept or pay under Section 3–501 by the close of the bank's next banking day after it knows of the requirement.

(b)   If presentment is made by notice and payment, acceptance, or request for compliance with a requirement under Section 3–501 is not received by the close of business on the day after maturity or, in the case of demand items, by the close of business on the third banking day after notice was sent, the presenting bank may treat the item as dishonored and charge any drawer or indorser by sending it notice of the facts.

As amended in 1990 and 2002.

Official Comment

1.   This section codifies a practice extensively followed in presentation of trade acceptances and documentary and other drafts drawn on nonbank payors. It imposes a duty on the payor to respond to the notice of the item if the item is not to be considered dishonored. Notice of such a dishonor charges drawers and indorsers. Presentment under this section is good presentment under Article 3. See Section 3–501.

2.   A drawee not receiving notice is not, of course, liable to the drawer for wrongful dishonor.

3.   A bank so presenting an instrument must be sufficiently close to the drawee to be able to exhibit the instrument on the day it is requested to do so or the next business day at the latest.

§ 4–213. Medium and Time of Settlement by Bank.

(a)   With respect to settlement by a bank, the medium and time of settlement may be prescribed by Federal Reserve regulations or circulars, clearing-house rules, and the like, or agreement. In the absence of such prescription:

(1)   the medium of settlement is cash or credit to an account in a Federal Reserve bank of or specified by the person to receive settlement; and

(2)   the time of settlement, is:

(i)   with respect to tender of settlement by cash, a cashier's check, or teller's check, when the cash or check is sent or delivered;

(ii)   with respect to tender of settlement by credit in an account in a Federal Reserve Bank, when the credit is made;

(iii) with respect to tender of settlement by a credit or debit to an account in a bank, when the credit or debit is made or, in the case of tender of settlement by authority to charge an account, when the authority is sent or delivered; or

(iv)   with respect to tender of settlement by a funds transfer, when payment is made pursuant to Section 4A–406(a) to the person receiving settlement.

(b)   If the tender of settlement is not by a medium authorized by subsection (a) or the time of settlement is not fixed by subsection (a), no settlement occurs until the tender of settlement is accepted by the person receiving settlement.

(c)   If settlement for an item is made by cashier's check or teller's check and the person receiving settlement, before its midnight deadline:

(1)   presents or forwards the check for collection, settlement is final when the check is finally paid; or

(2)   fails to present or forward the check for collection, settlement is final at the midnight deadline of the person receiving settlement.

(d)   If settlement for an item is made by giving authority to charge the account of the bank giving settlement in the bank receiving settlement, settlement is final when the charge is made by the bank receiving settlement if there are funds available in the account for the amount of the item.

As amended in 1990.

Official Comment

1.   Subsection (a) sets forth the medium of settlement that the person receiving settlement must accept. In nearly all cases the medium of settlement will be determined by agreement or by Federal Reserve regulations and circulars, clearing-house rules, and the like. In the absence of regulations, rules or agreement, the person receiving settlement may demand cash or credit in a Federal Reserve bank. If the person receiving settlement does not have an account in a Federal Reserve bank, it may specify the account of another bank in a Federal Reserve bank. In the unusual case in which there is no agreement on the medium of settlement and the bank making settlement tenders settlement other than cash or Federal Reserve bank credit, no settlement has occurred under subsection (b) unless the person receiving settlement accepts the settlement tendered. For example, if a payor bank, without agreement, tenders a teller's check, the bank receiving the settlement may reject the check and return it to the payor bank or it may accept the check as settlement.

2.   In several provisions of Article 4 the time that a settlement occurs is relevant. Subsection (a) sets out a general rule that the time of settlement, like the means of settlement, may be prescribed by agreement. In the absence of agreement, the time of settlement for tender of the common agreed media of settlement is that set out in subsection (a)(2). The time of settlement by cash, cashier's or teller's check or authority to charge an account is the time the cash, check or authority is sent, unless presentment is over the counter in which case settlement occurs upon delivery to the presenter. If there is no agreement on the time of settlement and the tender of settlement is not made by one of the media set out in subsection (a), under subsection (b) the time of settlement is the time the settlement is accepted by the person receiving settlement.

3.   Subsections (c) and (d) are special provisions for settlement by remittance drafts and authority to charge an account in the bank receiving settlement. The relationship between final settlement and final payment under Section 4-215 is addressed in subsection (b) of Section 4-215. With respect to settlement by cashier's checks or teller's checks, other than in response to over-the-counter presentment, the bank receiving settlement can keep the risk that the check will not be paid on the bank tendering the check in settlement by acting to initiate collection of the check within the midnight deadline of the bank receiving settlement. If the bank fails to initiate settlement before its midnight deadline, final settlement occurs at the midnight deadline, and the bank receiving settlement assumes the risk that the check will not be paid. If there is no agreement that permits the bank tendering settlement to tender a cashier's or teller's check, subsection (b) allows the bank receiving the check to reject it, and, if it does, no settlement occurs. However, if the bank accepts the check, settlement occurs and the time of final settlement is governed by subsection (c).

With respect to settlement by tender of authority to charge the account of the bank making settlement in the bank receiving settlement, subsection (d) provides that final settlement does not take place until the account charged has available funds to cover the amount of the item. If there is no agreement that permits the bank tendering settlement to tender an authority to charge an account as settlement, subsection (b) allows the bank receiving the tender to reject it. However, if the bank accepts the authority, settlement occurs and the time of final settlement is governed by subsection (d).

§ 4-214.   Right of Charge-Back or Refund; Liability of Collecting Bank; Return of Item.

(a)   If a collecting bank has made provisional settlement with its customer for an item and fails by reason of dishonor, suspension of payments by a bank, or otherwise to receive settlement for the item which is or becomes final, the bank may revoke the settlement given by it, charge back the amount of any credit given for the item to its customer's account, or obtain refund from its customer, whether or not it is able to return the item, if by its midnight deadline or within a longer reasonable time after it learns the facts it returns the item or sends notification of the facts. If the return or notice is delayed beyond the bank's midnight deadline or a longer reasonable time after it learns the facts, the bank may revoke the settlement, charge back the credit, or obtain refund from its customer, but it is liable for any loss resulting from the delay. These rights to revoke, charge back, and obtain refund terminate if and when a settlement for the item received by the bank is or becomes final.

(b)   A collecting bank returns an item when it is sent or delivered to the bank's customer or transferor or pursuant to its instructions.

(c)   A depositary bank that is also the payor may charge back the amount of an item to its customer's account or obtain refund in accordance with the section governing return of an item received by a payor bank for credit on its books (Section 4–301).

(d)   The right to charge back is not affected by:

(1)   previous use of a credit given for the item; or

(2)   failure by any bank to exercise ordinary care with respect to the item, but a bank so failing remains liable.

(e)   A failure to charge back or claim refund does not affect other rights of the bank against the customer or any other party.

(f)   If credit is given in dollars as the equivalent of the value of an item payable in foreign money, the dollar amount of any charge-back or refund must be calculated on the basis of the bank-offered spot rate for the foreign money prevailing on the day when the person entitled to the charge-back or refund learns that it will not receive payment in ordinary course.

As amended in 1990.

Official Comment

1.   Under current bank practice, in a major portion of cases banks make provisional settlement for items when they are first received and then await subsequent determination of whether the item will be finally paid. This is the principal characteristic of what are referred to in banking parlance as "cash items." Statistically, this practice of settling provisionally first and then awaiting final payment is justified because the vast majority of such cash items are finally paid, with the result that in this great preponderance of cases it becomes unnecessary for the banks making the provisional settlements to make any further entries. In due course the provisional settlements become final simply with the lapse of time. However, in those cases in which the item being collected is not finally paid or if for various reasons the bank making the provisional settlement does not itself receive final payment, provision is made in subsection (a) for the reversal of the provisional settlements, charge-back of provisional credits and the right to obtain refund.

2.   Various causes of a bank's not receiving final payment, with the resulting right of charge-back or refund, are stated or suggested in subsection (a). These include dishonor of the original item; dishonor of a remittance instrument given for it; reversal of a provisional credit for the item; suspension of payments by another bank. The causes stated are illustrative; the right of charge-back or refund is stated to exist whether the failure to receive final payment in ordinary course arises through one of them "or otherwise."

3.   The right of charge-back or refund exists if a collecting bank has made a provisional settlement for an item with its customer but terminates if and when a settlement received by the bank for the item is or becomes final. If the bank fails to receive such a final settlement the right of charge-back or refund must be exercised promptly after the bank learns the facts. The right exists (if so promptly exercised) whether or not the bank is able to return the item. The second sentence of subsection (a) adopts the view of *Appliance Buyers Credit Corp. v. Prospect National Bank*, 708 F.2d 290 (7th Cir. 1983), that if the midnight deadline for returning an item or giving notice is not met, a collecting bank loses its rights only to the extent of damages for any loss resulting from the delay.

4.   Subsection (b) states when an item is returned by a collecting bank. Regulation CC, Section 229.31 preempts this subsection with respect to checks by allowing direct return to the depositary bank. Because a returned check may follow a different path than in forward collection, settlement given for the check is final and not provisional except as between the depositary bank and its customer. Regulation CC Section 229.36(d). See also Regulations CC Sections 229.31(c) and 229.32(b). Thus owing to the federal preemption, this subsection applies only to noncheck items.

5.   The rule of subsection (d) relating to charge-back (as distinguished from claim for refund) applies irrespective of the cause of the nonpayment, and of the person ultimately liable for nonpayment. Thus charge-back is permitted even if nonpayment results from the depositary bank's own negligence. Any other rule would result in litigation based upon a claim for wrongful dishonor of other checks of the customer, with potential damages far in excess of the amount of the item. Any other rule would require a bank to determine difficult questions of fact. The customer's protection is found in the general obligation of good faith (Sections 1–203 [*unrevised Article 1; see Concordance, p. 22*] and 4–103). If bad faith is established the customer's recovery "includes other damages, if any, suffered by the party as a proximate consequence" (Section 4–103(e); see also Section 4–402).

6.   It is clear that the charge-back does not relieve the bank from any liability for failure to exercise ordinary care in handling the item. The measure of damages for such failure is stated in Section 4–103(e).

7.   Subsection (f) states a rule fixing the time for determining the rate of exchange if there is a charge-back or refund of a credit given in dollars for an item payable in a foreign currency. Compare Section 3–107. Fixing such a rule is desirable to avoid disputes. If in any case the parties wish to fix a different time for determining the rate of exchange, they may do so by agreement.

§ 4–215.   Final Payment of Item by Payor Bank; When Provisional Debits and Credits Become Final; When Certain Credits Become Available for Withdrawal.

(a)   An item is finally paid by a payor bank when the bank has first done any of the following:

(1)   paid the item in cash;

(2)   settled for the item without having a right to revoke the settlement under statute, clearing-house rule, or agreement; or

(3)   made a provisional settlement for the item and failed to revoke the settlement in the time and manner permitted by statute, clearing-house rule, or agreement.

(b)   If provisional settlement for an item does not become final, the item is not finally paid.

(c)   If provisional settlement for an item between the presenting and payor banks is made through a clearing house or by debits or credits in an account between them, then to the extent that provisional debits or credits for the item are entered in accounts between the presenting and payor banks or between the presenting and successive prior collecting banks seriatim, they become final upon final payment of the item by the payor bank.

(d)   If a collecting bank receives a settlement for an item which is or becomes final, the bank is accountable to its customer for the amount of the item and any provisional credit given for the item in an account with its customer becomes final.

(e)   Subject to (i) applicable law stating a time for availability of funds and (ii) any right of the bank to apply the credit to an obligation of the customer, credit given by a bank for an item in a customer's account becomes available for withdrawal as of right:

(1)   if the bank has received a provisional settlement for the item, when the settlement becomes final and the bank has had a reasonable time to receive return of the item and the item has not been received within that time;

(2)   if the bank is both the depositary bank and the payor bank, and the item is finally paid, at the opening of the bank's second banking day following receipt of the item.

(f)   Subject to applicable law stating a time for availability of funds and any right of a bank to apply a deposit to an obligation of the depositor, a deposit of money becomes available for withdrawal as of right at the opening of the bank's next banking day after receipt of the deposit.

As amended in 1990.

Official Comment

1.   By the definition and use of the term "settle" (Section 4–104(a)(11)) this Article recognizes that various debits or credits, remittances, settlements or payments given for an item may be either provisional or final, that settlements sometimes are provisional and sometimes are final and sometimes are provisional for awhile but later become final. Subsection (a) defines when settlement for an item constitutes final payment.

Final payment of an item is important for a number of reasons. It is one of several factors determining the relative priorities between items and notices, stop-payment orders, legal process and setoffs (Section 4–303). It is the "end of the line" in the collection process and the "turn around" point commencing the return flow of proceeds. It is the point at which many provisional settlements become final. See Section 4–215(c). Final payment of an item by the payor bank fixes preferential rights under Section 4–216.

2.   If an item being collected moves through several states, e.g., is deposited for collection in California, moves through two or three California banks to the Federal Reserve Bank of San Francisco, to the Federal Reserve Bank of Boston, to a payor bank in Maine, the collection process involves the eastward journey of the item from

California to Maine and the westward journey of the proceeds from Maine to California. Subsection (a) recognizes that final payment does not take place, in this hypothetical case, on the journey of the item eastward. It also adopts the view that neither does final payment occur on the journey westward because what in fact is journeying westward are *proceeds* of the item.

3.   Traditionally and under various decisions payment in cash of an item by a payor bank has been considered final payment. Subsection (a)(1) recognizes and provides that payment of an item in cash by a payor bank is final payment.

4.   Section 4–104(a)(11) defines "settle" as meaning "to pay in cash, by clearing-house settlement, in a charge or credit or by remittance, or otherwise as agreed. A settlement may be either provisional or final." Subsection (a)(2) of Section 4–215 provides that an item is finally paid by a payor bank when the bank has "settled for the item without having a right to revoke the settlement under statute, clearing-house rule or agreement." Former subsection (1)(b) is modified by subsection (a)(2) to make clear that a payor bank cannot make settlement provisional by unilaterally reserving a right to revoke the settlement. The right must come from a statute (e.g., Section 4–301), clearing-house rule or other agreement. Subsection (a)(2) provides in effect that if the payor bank finally settles for an item this constitutes final payment of the item. The subsection operates if nothing has occurred and no situation exists making the settlement provisional. If under statute, clearing-house rule or agreement, a right of revocation of the settlement exists, the settlement is provisional. Conversely, if there is an absence of a right to revoke under statute, clearing-house rule or agreement, the settlement is final and such final settlement constitutes final payment of the item.

A primary example of a statutory right on the part of the payor bank to revoke a settlement is the right to revoke conferred by Section 4–301. The underlying theory and reason for deferred posting statutes (Section 4–301) is to require a settlement on the date of receipt of an item but to keep that settlement provisional with the right to revoke prior to the midnight deadline. In any case in which Section 4–301 is applicable, any settlement by the payor bank is provisional solely by virtue of the statute, subsection (a)(2) of Section 4–215 does not operate, and such provisional settlement does not constitute final payment of the item. With respect to checks, Regulation CC Section 229.36(d) provides that settlement between banks for the forward collection of checks is final. The relationship of this provision to Article 4 is discussed in the Commentary to that section.

A second important example of a right to revoke a settlement is that arising under clearing-house rules. It is very common for clearing-house rules to provide that items exchanged and settled for in a clearing (e.g., before 10:00 a.m. on Monday) may be returned and the settlements revoked up to but not later than 2:00 p.m. on the same day (Monday) or under deferred posting at some hour on the next business day (e.g., 2:00 p.m. Tuesday). Under this type of rule the Monday morning settlement is provisional and being provisional does not constitute a final payment of the item.

An example of an agreement allowing the payor bank to revoke a settlement is a case in which the payor bank is also the depositary bank and has signed a receipt or duplicate deposit ticket or has made an entry in a passbook acknowledging receipt, for credit to the account of A, of a check drawn on it by B. If the receipt, deposit ticket, passbook or other agreement with A is to the effect that any credit so entered is provisional and may be revoked pending the time required by the payor bank to process the item to determine if it is in good form and there are funds to cover it, the agreement keeps the receipt or credit provisional and avoids its being either final settlement or final payment.

The most important application of subsection (a)(2) is that in which presentment of an item has been made over the counter for immediate payment. In this case Section 4–301(a) does not apply to make the settlement provisional, and final payment has occurred unless a rule or agreement provides otherwise.

5.   Former Section 4–213(1)(c) provided that final payment occurred when the payor bank completed the "process of posting." The term was defined in former Section 4–109. In the present Article, Section 4–109 has been deleted and the process-of-posting test has been abandoned in Section 4–215(a) for determining when final payment is made. Difficulties in determining when the events described in former Section 4–109 take place make the process-of-posting test unsuitable for a system of automated check collection or electronic presentment.

6.   The last sentence of former Section 4–213(1) is deleted as an unnecessary source of confusion. Initially the view that payor bank may be accountable for, that is, liable for the amount of, an item that it has already paid seems incongruous. This is particularly true in the light of the language formerly found in Section 4–302 stating that the payor bank can defend against liability for accountability by showing that it has already settled for the item. But, at least with respect to former Section 4–213(1)(c), such a provision was needed because under the process-of-posting test a payor bank may have paid an item without settling for it. Now that Article 4 has

abandoned the process-of-posting test, the sentence is no longer needed. If the payor bank has neither paid the item nor returned it within its midnight deadline, the payor bank is accountable under Section 4–302.

7.   Subsection (a)(3) covers the situation in which the payor bank makes a provisional settlement for an item, and this settlement becomes final at a later time by reason of the failure of the payor bank to revoke it in the time and manner permitted by statute, clearing-house rule or agreement. An example of this type of situation is the clearing-house settlement referred to in Comment 4. In the illustration there given if the time limit for the return of items received in the Monday morning clearing is 2:00 p.m. on Tuesday and the provisional settlement has not been revoked at that time in a manner permitted by the clearing-house rules, the provisional settlement made on Monday morning becomes final at 2:00 p.m. on Tuesday. Subsection (a)(3) provides specifically that in this situation the item is finally paid at 2:00 p.m. Tuesday. If on the other hand a payor bank receives an item in the mail on Monday and makes some provisional settlement for the item on Monday, it has until midnight on Tuesday to return the item or give notice and revoke any settlement under Section 4–301. In this situation subsection (a)(3) of Section 4–215 provides that if the provisional settlement made on Monday is not revoked before midnight on Tuesday as permitted by Section 4–301, the item is finally paid at midnight on Tuesday. With respect to checks, Regulation CC Section 229.30(c) allows an extension of the midnight deadline under certain circumstances. If a bank does not expeditiously return a check liability may accrue under Regulation CC Section 229.38. For the relationship of that liability to responsibility under this Article, see Regulation CC Sections 229.30 and 229.38.

8.   Subsection (b) relates final settlement to final payment under Section 4–215. For example, if a payor bank makes provisional settlement for an item by sending a cashier's or teller's check and that settlement fails to become final under Section 4–213(c), subsection (b) provides that final payment has not occurred. If the item is not paid, the drawer remains liable, and under Section 4–302(a) the payor bank is accountable unless it has returned the item before its midnight deadline. In this regard, subsection (b) is an exception to subsection (a)(3). Even if the payor bank has not returned an item by its midnight deadline there is still no final payment if provisional settlement had been made and settlement failed to become final. However, if presentment of the item was over the counter for immediate payment, final payment has occurred under Section 4–215(a)(2). Subsection (b) does not apply because the settlement was not provisional. Section 4–301(a). In this case the presenting person, often the payee of the item, has the right to demand cash or the cash equivalent of federal reserve credit. If the presenting person accepts another medium of settlement such as a cashier's or teller's check, the presenting person takes the risk that the payor bank may fail to pay a cashier's check because of insolvency or that the drawee of a teller's check may dishonor it.

9.   Subsection (c) states the country-wide usage that when the item is finally paid by the payor bank under subsection (a) this final payment automatically without further action "firms up" other provisional settlements made for it. However, the subsection makes clear that this "firming up" occurs only if the settlement between the presenting and payor banks was made either through a clearing house or by debits and credits in accounts between them. It does not take place if the payor bank remits for the item by sending some form of remittance instrument. Further, the "firming up" continues only to the extent that provisional debits and credits are entered seriatim in accounts between banks which are successive to the presenting bank. The automatic "firming up" is broken at any time that any collecting bank remits for the item by sending a remittance draft, because final payment to the remittee then usually depends upon final payment of the remittance draft.

10.   Subsection (d) states the general rule that if a collecting bank receives settlement for an item which is or becomes final, the bank is accountable to its customer for the amount of the item. One means of accounting is to remit to its customer the amount it has received on the item. If previously it gave to its customer a provisional credit for the item in an account its receipt of final settlement for the item "firms up" this provisional credit and makes it final. When this credit given by it so becomes final, in the usual case its agency status terminates and it becomes a debtor to its customer for the amount of the item. See Section 4–201(a). If the accounting is by a remittance instrument or authorization to charge further time will usually be required to complete its accounting (Section 4–213).

11.   Subsection (e) states when certain credits given by a bank to its customer become available for withdrawal as of right. Subsection (e)(1) deals with the situation in which a bank has given a credit (usually provisional) for an item to its customer and in turn has received a provisional settlement for the item from an intermediary or payor bank to which it has forwarded the item. In this situation before the provisional credit entered by the collecting bank in the account of its customer becomes available for withdrawal as of right, it is not only necessary that the provisional settlement received by the bank for the item becomes final but also that the collecting bank has a reasonable time to receive return of the item and the item has not been received within that time. How much time is "reasonable" for these purposes will of course depend on the distance the item has to travel

and the number of banks through which it must pass (having in mind not only travel time by regular lines of transmission but also the successive midnight deadlines of the several banks) and other pertinent facts. Also, if the provisional settlement received is some form of a remittance instrument or authorization to charge, the "reasonable" time depends on the identity and location of the payor of the remittance instrument, the means for clearing such instrument, and other pertinent facts. With respect to checks Regulation CC Sections 229.10–229.13 or similar applicable state law (Section 229.20) control. This is also time for the situation described in Comment 12.

12.   Subsection (e)(2) deals with the situation of a bank that is both a depositary bank and a payor bank. The subsection recognizes that if A and B are both customers of a depositary-payor bank and A deposits B's check on the depositary-payor in A's account on Monday, time must be allowed to permit the check under the deferred posting rules of Section 4–301 to reach the bookkeeper for B's account at some time on Tuesday, and, if there are insufficient funds in B's account, to reverse or charge back the provisional credit in A's account. Consequently this provisional credit in A's account does not become available for withdrawal as of right until the opening of business on Wednesday. If it is determined on Tuesday that there are insufficient funds in B's account to pay the check, the credit to A's account can be reversed on Tuesday. On the other hand if the item is in fact paid on Tuesday, the rule of subsection (e)(2) is desirable to avoid uncertainty and possible disputes between the bank and its customer as to exactly what hour within the day the credit is available.

§ 4–216.   Insolvency and Preference.

(a)   If an item is in or comes into the possession of a payor or collecting bank that suspends payment and the item has not been finally paid, the item must be returned by the receiver, trustee, or agent in charge of the closed bank to the presenting bank or the closed bank's customer.

(b)   If a payor bank finally pays an item and suspends payments without making a settlement for the item with its customer or the presenting bank which settlement is or becomes final, the owner of the item has a preferred claim against the payor bank.

(c)   If a payor bank gives or a collecting bank gives or receives a provisional settlement for an item and thereafter suspends payments, the suspension does not prevent or interfere with the settlement's becoming final if the finality occurs automatically upon the lapse of certain time or the happening of certain events.

(d)   If a collecting bank receives from subsequent parties settlement for an item, which settlement is or becomes final and the bank suspends payments without making a settlement for the item with its customer which settlement is or becomes final, the owner of the item has a preferred claim against the collecting bank.

As amended in 1990.

Official Comment

1.   The underlying purpose of the provisions of this section is not to confer upon banks, holders of items or anyone else preferential positions in the event of bank failures over general depositors or any other creditors of the failed banks. The purpose is to fix as definitely as possible the cut-off point of time for the completion or cessation of the collection process in the case of items that happen to be in the process at the time a particular bank suspends payments. It must be remembered that in bank collections as a whole and in the handling of items by an individual bank, items go through a whole series of processes. It must also be remembered that at any particular point of time a particular bank (at least one of any size) is functioning as a depositary bank for some items, as an intermediary bank for others, as a presenting bank for still others and as a payor bank for still others, and that when it suspends payments it will have close to its normal load of items working through its various processes. For the convenience of receivers, owners of items, banks, and in fact substantially everyone concerned, it is recognized that at the particular moment of time that a bank suspends payment, a certain portion of the items being handled by it have progressed far enough in the bank collection process that it is preferable to permit them to continue the remaining distance, rather than to send them back and reverse the many entries that have been made or the steps that have been taken with respect to them. Therefore, having this background and these purposes in mind, the section states what items must be turned backward at the moment suspension intervenes and what items have progressed far enough that the collection process with respect to them continues, with the resulting necessary statement of rights of various parties flowing from this prescription of the cut-off time.

2.   The rules stated are similar to those stated in the American Bankers Association Bank Collection Code, but with the abandonment of any theory of trust. On the other hand, some law previous to this Act may be relevant. See Note, *Uniform Commercial Code: Stopping Payment of an Item Deposited with an Insolvent Depositary Bank*, 40 Okla.L.Rev. 689 (1987). Although for practical purposes Federal Deposit Insurance affects materially the result of bank failures on holders of items and banks, no attempt is made to vary the rules of the section by reason of such insurance.

3.   It is recognized that in view of *Jennings v. United States Fidelity & Guaranty Co.*, 294 U.S. 216, 55 S.Ct. 394, 79 L.Ed. 869, 99 A.L.R. 1248 (1935), amendment of the National Bank Act would be necessary to have this section apply to national banks. But there is no reason why it should not apply to others. See Section 1–108 [*unrevised Article 1; see Concordance, p. 22*].

PART 3

COLLECTION OF ITEMS: PAYOR BANKS

§ 4–301.   Deferred Posting; Recovery of Payment by Return of Items; Time of Dishonor; Return of Items by Payor Bank.

(a)   If a payor bank settles for a demand item other than a documentary draft presented otherwise than for immediate payment over the counter before midnight of the banking day of receipt, the payor bank may revoke the settlement and recover the settlement if, before it has made final payment and before its midnight deadline, it

(1)   returns the item;

(2)   returns an image of the item, if the party to which the return is made has entered into an agreement to accept an image as a return of the item and the image is returned in accordance with that agreement; or

(3)   sends a record providing notice of dishonor or nonpayment if the item is unavailable for return.

(b)   If a demand item is received by a payor bank for credit on its books, it may return the item or send notice of dishonor and may revoke any credit given or recover the amount thereof withdrawn by its customer, if it acts within the time limit and in the manner specified in subsection (a).

(c)   Unless previous notice of dishonor has been sent, an item is dishonored at the time when for purposes of dishonor it is returned or notice sent in accordance with this section.

(d)   An item is returned:

(1)   as to an item presented through a clearing house, when it is delivered to the presenting or last collecting bank or to the clearing house or is sent or delivered in accordance with clearing-house rules; or

(2)   in all other cases, when it is sent or delivered to the bank's customer or transferor or pursuant to instructions.

As amended in 1990 and 2002.

Official Comment

1.   The term "deferred posting" appears in the caption of Section 4–301. This refers to the practice permitted by statute in most of the states before the UCC under which a payor bank receives items on one day but does not post the items to the customer's account until the next day. Items dishonored were then returned after the posting on the day after receipt. Under Section 4–301 the concept of "deferred posting" merely allows a payor bank that has settled for an item on the day of receipt to return a dishonored item on the next day before its midnight deadline, without regard to when the item was actually posted. With respect to checks Regulation CC Section 229.30(c) extends the midnight deadline under the UCC under certain circumstances. See the Commentary to Regulation CC Section 229.38(d) on the relationship between the UCC and Regulation CC on settlement.

2.   The function of this section is to provide the circumstances under which a payor bank that has made timely settlement for an item may return the item and revoke the settlement so that it may recover any settlement made. These circumstances are: (1) the item must be a demand item other than a documentary draft; (2) the item

must be presented otherwise than for immediate payment over the counter; and (3) the payor bank must return the item (or give notice if the item is unavailable for return) before its midnight deadline and before it has paid the item. With respect to checks, see Regulation CC Section 229.31(f) on notice in lieu of return and Regulation CC Section 229.33 as to the different requirement of notice of nonpayment. An instance of when an item may be unavailable for return arises under a collecting bank check retention plan under which presentment is made by a presentment notice and the item is retained by the collecting bank. Section 4–215(a)(2) provides that final payment occurs if the payor bank has settled for an item without a right to revoke the settlement under statute, clearinghouse rule or agreement. In any case in which Section 4–301(a) is applicable, the payor bank has a right to revoke the settlement by statute; therefore, Section 4–215(a)(2) is inoperable, and the settlement is provisional. Hence, if the settlement is not over the counter and the payor bank settles in a manner that does not constitute final payment, the payor bank can revoke the settlement by returning the item before its midnight deadline.

3.   The relationship of Section 4–301(a) to final settlement and final payment under Section 4–215 is illustrated by the following case. Depositary Bank sends by mail an item to Payor Bank with instructions to settle by remitting a teller's check drawn on a bank in the city where Depositary Bank is located. Payor Bank sends the teller's check on the day the item was presented. Having made timely settlement, under the deferred posting provisions of Section 4–301(a), Payor Bank may revoke that settlement by returning the item before its midnight deadline. If it fails to return the item before its midnight deadline, it has finally paid the item if the bank on which the teller's check was drawn honors the check. But if the teller's check is dishonored there has been no final settlement under Section 4–213(c) and no final payment under Section 4–215(b). Since the Payor Bank has neither paid the item nor made timely return, it is accountable for the item under Section 4–302(a).

4.   The time limits for action imposed by subsection (a) are adopted by subsection (b) for cases in which the payor bank is also the depositary bank, but in this case the requirement of a settlement on the day of receipt is omitted.

5.   Subsection (c) fixes a base point from which to measure the time within which notice of dishonor must be given. See Section 3–503.

6.   Subsection (d) leaves banks free to agree upon the manner of returning items but establishes a precise time when an item is "returned." For definition of "sent" as used in paragraphs (1) and (2) see Section 1–201(38) [*unrevised Article 1; see Concordance, p. 22*]. Obviously the subsection assumes that the item has not been "finally paid" under Section 4–215(a). If it has been, this provision has no operation.

7.   The fact that an item has been paid under proposed Section 4–215 does not preclude the payor bank from asserting rights of restitution or revocation under Section 3–418. *National Savings and Trust Co. v. Park Corp.*, 722 F.2d 1303 (6th Cir. 1983), cert. denied, 466 U.S. 939 (1984), is the correct interpretation of the present law on this issue.

8.   Paragraph (a)(2) is designed to facilitate electronic check-processing by authorizing the payor bank to return an image of the item instead of the actual item. It applies only when the payor bank and the party to which the return has been made have agreed that the payor bank can make such a return and when the return complies with the agreement. The purpose of the paragraph is to prevent third parties (such as the depositor of the check) from contending that the payor bank missed its midnight deadline because it failed to return the actual item in a timely manner. If the payor bank missed its midnight deadline, payment would have become final under Section 4–215 and the depositary bank would have lost its right of chargeback under Section 4–214. Of course, the depositary bank might enter into an agreement with its depositor to resolve that problem, but it is not clear that agreements by banks with their customers can resolve all such issues. In any event, paragraph (a)(2) should eliminate the need for such agreements. The provision rests on the premise that it is inappropriate to penalize a payor bank simply because it returns the actual item a few business days after the midnight deadline of the payor bank sent notice before that deadline to a collecting bank that had agreed to accept such notices.

Nothing in paragraph (a)(2) authorizes the payor bank to destroy the check.

As amended in 2002.

§ 4–302.   Payor Bank's Responsibility for Late Return of Item.

(a)   If an item is presented to and received by a payor bank, the bank is accountable for the amount of:

(1)   a demand item, other than a documentary draft, whether properly payable or not, if the bank, in any case in which it is not also the depositary bank, retains the item beyond midnight of the

banking day of receipt without settling for it or, whether or not it is also the depositary bank, does not pay or return the item or send notice of dishonor until after its midnight deadline; or

(2) any other properly payable item unless, within the time allowed for acceptance or payment of that item, the bank either accepts or pays the item or returns it and accompanying documents.

(b) The liability of a payor bank to pay an item pursuant to subsection (a) is subject to defenses based on breach of a presentment warranty (Section 4–208) or proof that the person seeking enforcement of the liability presented or transferred the item for the purpose of defrauding the payor bank.

As amended in 1990.

Official Comment

1. Subsection (a)(1) continues the former law distinguishing between cases in which the payor bank is not also the depositary bank and those in which the payor bank is also the depositary bank ("on us" items). For "on us" items the payor bank is accountable if it retains the item beyond its midnight deadline without settling for it. If the payor bank is not the depositary bank it is accountable if it retains the item beyond midnight of the banking day of receipt without settling for it. It may avoid accountability either by settling for the item on the day of receipt and returning the item before its midnight deadline under Section 4–301 or by returning the item on the day of receipt. This rule is consistent with the deferred posting practice authorized by Section 4–301 which allows the payor bank to make provisional settlement for an item on the day of receipt and to revoke that settlement by returning the item on the next day. With respect to checks, Regulation CC Section 229.36(d) provides that settlements between banks for forward collection of checks are final when made. See the Commentary on that provision for its effect on the UCC.

2. If the settlement given by the payor bank does not become final, there has been no payment under Section 4–215(b), and the payor bank giving the failed settlement is accountable under subsection (a)(1) of Section 4–302. For instance, the payor bank makes provisional settlement by sending a teller's check that is dishonored. In such a case settlement is not final under Section 4–213(c) and no payment occurs under Section 4–215(b). Payor bank is accountable on the item. The general principle is that unless settlement provides the presenting bank with usable funds, settlement has failed and the payor bank is accountable for the amount of the item. On the other hand, if the payor bank makes a settlement for the item that becomes final under Section 4–215, the item has been paid and thus the payor bank is not accountable for the item under this Section.

3. Subsection (b) is an elaboration of the deleted introductory language of former Section 4–302: "In the absence of a valid defense such as breach of a presentment warranty (subsection (1) of Section 4–207), settlement effected or the like. . . ." A payor bank can defend an action against it based on accountability by showing that the item contained a forged indorsement or a fraudulent alteration. Subsection (b) drops the ambiguous "or the like" language and provides that the payor bank may also raise the defense of fraud. Decisions that hold an accountable bank's liability to be "absolute" are rejected. A payor bank that makes a late return of an item should not be liable to a defrauder operating a check kiting scheme. In *Bank of Leumi Trust Co. v. Bally's Park Place Inc.*, 528 F.Supp. 349 (S.D.N.Y. 1981), and *American National Bank v. Foodbasket*, 497 P.2d 546 (Wyo. 1972), banks that were accountable under Section 4–302 for missing their midnight deadline were successful in defending against parties who initiated collection knowing that the check would not be paid. The "settlement effected" language is deleted as unnecessary. If a payor bank is accountable for an item it is liable to pay it. If it has made final payment for an item, it is no longer accountable for the item.

As amended in 2002.

§ 4–303. When Items Subject to Notice, Stop-Payment Order, Legal Process, or Setoff; Order in Which Items May Be Charged or Certified.

(a) Any knowledge, notice, or stop-payment order received by, legal process served upon, or setoff exercised by a payor bank comes too late to terminate, suspend, or modify the bank's right or duty to pay an item or to charge its customer's account for the item if the knowledge, notice, stop-payment order, or legal process is received or served and a reasonable time for the bank to act thereon expires or the setoff is exercised after the earliest of the following:

(1) the bank accepts or certifies the item;

(2) the bank pays the item in cash;

(3) the bank settles for the item without having a right to revoke the settlement under statute, clearing-house rule, or agreement;

(4) the bank becomes accountable for the amount of the item under Section 4–302 dealing with the payor bank's responsibility for late return of items; or

(5) with respect to checks, a cutoff hour no earlier than one hour after the opening of the next banking day after the banking day on which the bank received the check and no later than the close of that next banking day or, if no cutoff hour is fixed, the close of the next banking day after the banking day on which the bank received the check.

(b) Subject to subsection (a), items may be accepted, paid, certified, or charged to the indicated account of its customer in any order.

As amended in 1990.

Official Comment

1. While a payor bank is processing an item presented for payment, it may receive knowledge or a legal notice affecting the item, such as knowledge or a notice that the drawer has filed a petition in bankruptcy or made an assignment for the benefit of creditors; may receive an order of the drawer stopping payment on the item; may have served on it an attachment of the account of the drawer; or the bank itself may exercise a right of setoff against the drawer's account. Each of these events affects the account of the drawer and may eliminate or freeze all or part of whatever balance is available to pay the item. Subsection (a) states the rule for determining the relative priorities between these various legal events and the item.

2. The rule is that if any one of several things has been done to the item or if it has reached any one of several stages in its processing at the time the knowledge, notice, stop-payment order or legal process is received or served and a reasonable time for the bank to act thereon expires or the setoff is exercised, the knowledge, notice, stop-payment order, legal process or setoff comes too late, the item has priority and a charge to the customer's account may be made and is effective. With respect to the effect of the customer's bankruptcy, the bank's rights are governed by Bankruptcy Code Section 542(c) which codifies the result of *Bank of Marin v. England*, 385 U.S. 99 (1966). Section 4–405 applies to the death or incompetence of the customer.

3. Once a payor bank has accepted or certified an item or has paid the item in cash, the event has occurred that determines priorities between the item and the various legal events usually described as the "four legals." Paragraphs (1) and (2) of subsection (a) so provide. If a payor bank settles for an item presented over the counter for immediate payment by a cashier's check or teller's check which the presenting person agrees to accept, paragraph (3) of subsection (a) would control and the event determining priority has occurred. Because presentment was over the counter, Section 4–301(a) does not apply to give the payor bank the statutory right to revoke the settlement. Thus the requirements of paragraph (3) have been met unless a clearing-house rule or agreement of the parties provides otherwise.

4. In the usual case settlement for checks is by entries in bank accounts. Since the process-of-posting test has been abandoned as inappropriate for automated check collection, the determining event for priorities is a given hour on the day after the item is received. (Paragraph (5) of subsection (a).) The hour may be fixed by the bank no earlier than one hour after the opening on the next banking day after the bank received the check and no later than the close of that banking day. If an item is received after the payor bank's regular Section 4–108 cutoff hour, it is treated as received the next banking day. If a bank receives an item after its regular cutoff hour on Monday and an attachment is levied at noon on Tuesday, the attachment is prior to the item if the bank had not before that hour taken the action described in paragraphs (1), (2), and (3) of subsection (a). The Commentary to Regulation CC Section 229.36(d) explains that even though settlement by a paying bank for a check is final for Regulation CC purposes, the paying bank's right to return the check before its midnight deadline under the UCC is not affected.

5. Another event conferring priority for an item and a charge to the customer's account based upon the item is stated by the language "become accountable for the amount of the item under Section 4–302 dealing with the payor bank's responsibility for late return of items." Expiration of the deadline under Section 4–302 with resulting accountability by the payor bank for the amount of the item, establishes priority of the item over notices, stop-payment orders, legal process or setoff.

6. In the case of knowledge, notice, stop-payment orders and legal process the effective time for determining whether they were received too late to affect the payment of an item and a charge to the customer's account by reason of such payment, is receipt plus a reasonable time for the bank to act on any of these

communications. Usually a relatively short time is required to communicate to the accounting department advice of one of these events but certainly some time is necessary. Compare Sections 1–201(27) [*unrevised Article 1; see Concordance, p. 22*] and 4–403. In the case of setoff the effective time is when the setoff is actually made.

7.   As between one item and another no priority rule is stated. This is justified because of the impossibility of stating a rule that would be fair in all cases, having in mind the almost infinite number of combinations of large and small checks in relation to the available balance on hand in the drawer's account; the possible methods of receipt; and other variables. Further, the drawer has drawn all the checks, the drawer should have funds available to meet all of them and has no basis for urging one should be paid before another; and the holders have no direct right against the payor bank in any event, unless of course, the bank has accepted, certified or finally paid a particular item, or has become liable for it under Section 4–302. Under subsection (b) the bank has the right to pay items for which it is itself liable ahead of those for which it is not.

PART 4

RELATIONSHIP BETWEEN PAYOR BANK AND ITS CUSTOMER

§ 4–401.   When Bank May Charge Customer's Account.

(a)   A bank may charge against the account of a customer an item that is properly payable from the account even though the charge creates an overdraft. An item is properly payable if it is authorized by the customer and is in accordance with any agreement between the customer and bank.

(b)   A customer is not liable for the amount of an overdraft if the customer neither signed the item nor benefited from the proceeds of the item.

(c)   A bank may charge against the account of a customer a check that is otherwise properly payable from the account, even though payment was made before the date of the check, unless the customer has given notice to the bank of the postdating describing the check with reasonable certainty. The notice is effective for the period stated in Section 4–403(b) for stop-payment orders, and must be received at such time and in such manner as to afford the bank a reasonable opportunity to act on it before the bank takes any action with respect to the check described in Section 4–303. If a bank charges against the account of a customer a check before the date stated in the notice of postdating, the bank is liable for damages for the loss resulting from its act. The loss may include damages for dishonor of subsequent items under Section 4–402.

(d)   A bank that in good faith makes payment to a holder may charge the indicated account of its customer according to:

(1)   the original terms of the altered item; or

(2)   the terms of the completed item, even though the bank knows the item has been completed unless the bank has notice that the completion was improper.

As amended in 1990.

Official Comment

1.   An item is properly payable from a customer's account if the customer has authorized the payment and the payment does not violate any agreement that may exist between the bank and its customer. For an example of a payment held to violate an agreement with a customer, see *Torrance National Bank v. Enesco Federal Credit Union*, 285 P.2d 737 (Cal.App. 1955). An item drawn for more than the amount of a customer's account may be properly payable. Thus under subsection (a) a bank may charge the customer's account for an item even though payment results in an overdraft. An item containing a forged drawer's signature or forged indorsement is not properly payable. Concern has arisen whether a bank may require a customer to execute a stop-payment order when the customer notifies the bank of the loss of an unindorsed or specially indorsed check. Since such a check cannot be properly payable from the customer's account, it is inappropriate for a bank to require stop-payment order in such a case.

2. Subsection (b) adopts the view of case authority holding that if there is more than one customer who can draw on an account, the nonsigning customer is not liable for an overdraft unless that person benefits from the proceeds of the item.

3. Subsection (c) is added because the automated check collection system cannot accommodate postdated checks. A check is usually paid upon presentment without respect to the date of the check. Under the former law, if a payor bank paid a postdated check before its stated date, it could not charge the customer's account because the check was not "properly payable." Hence, the bank might have been liable for wrongfully dishonoring subsequent checks of the drawer that would have been paid had the postdated check not been prematurely paid. Under subsection (c) a customer wishing to postdate a check must notify the payor bank of its postdating in time to allow the bank to act on the customer's notice before the bank has to commit itself to pay the check. If the bank fails to act on the customer's timely notice, it may be liable for damages for the resulting loss which may include damages for dishonor of subsequent items. This Act does not regulate fees that banks charge their customers for a notice of postdating or other services covered by the Act, but under principles of law such as unconscionability or good faith and fair dealing, courts have reviewed fees and the bank's exercise of a discretion to set fees. *Perdue v. Crocker National Bank*, 38 Cal.3d 913 (1985) (unconscionability); *Best v. United Bank of Oregon*, 739 P.2d 554, 562–566 (1987) (good faith and fair dealing). In addition, Section 1–203 [*unrevised Article 1; see Concordance, p. 22*] provides that every contract or duty within this Act imposes an obligation of good faith in its performance or enforcement.

4. Section 3–407(c) states that a payor bank or drawee which pays a fraudulently altered instrument in good faith and without notice of the alteration may enforce rights with respect to the instrument according to its original terms or, in the case of an incomplete instrument altered by unauthorized completion, according to its terms as completed. Section 4–401(d) follows the rule stated in Section 3–407(c) by applying it to an altered item and allows the bank to enforce rights with respect to the altered item by charging the customer's account.

§ 4–402. Bank's Liability to Customer for Wrongful Dishonor; Time of Determining Insufficiency of Account.

(a) Except as otherwise provided in this Article, a payor bank wrongfully dishonors an item if it dishonors an item that is properly payable, but a bank may dishonor an item that would create an overdraft unless it has agreed to pay the overdraft.

(b) A payor bank is liable to its customer for damages proximately caused by the wrongful dishonor of an item. Liability is limited to actual damages proved and may include damages for an arrest or prosecution of the customer or other consequential damages. Whether any consequential damages are proximately caused by the wrongful dishonor is a question of fact to be determined in each case.

(c) A payor bank's determination of the customer's account balance on which a decision to dishonor for insufficiency of available funds is based may be made at any time between the time the item is received by the payor bank and the time that the payor bank returns the item or gives notice in lieu of return, and no more than one determination need be made. If, at the election of the payor bank, a subsequent balance determination is made for the purpose of reevaluating the bank's decision to dishonor the item, the account balance at that time is determinative of whether a dishonor for insufficiency of available funds is wrongful.

As amended in 1990.

Official Comment

1. Subsection (a) states positively what has been assumed under the original Article: that if a bank fails to honor a properly payable item it may be liable to its customer for wrongful dishonor. Under subsection (b) the payor bank's wrongful dishonor of an item gives rise to a statutory cause of action. Damages may include consequential damages. Confusion has resulted from the attempts of courts to reconcile the first and second sentences of former Section 4–402. The second sentence implied that the bank was liable for some form of damages other than those proximately caused by the dishonor if the dishonor was other than by mistake. But nothing in the section described what these noncompensatory damages might be. Some courts have held that in distinguishing between mistaken dishonors and nonmistaken dishonors, the so-called "trader" rule has been retained that allowed a "merchant or trader" to recover substantial damages for wrongful dishonor without proof of damages actually suffered. Comment 3 to former Section 4–402 indicated that this was not the intent of the drafters. White & Summers, Uniform Commercial Code, Section 18–4 (1988), states: "The negative implication is that when wrongful dishonors occur not 'through mistake' but willfully, the court may impose damages greater than 'actual damages'. . . . Certainly the reference to 'mistake' in the second sentence of 4–402 invites a court to

405

adopt the relevant pre-Code distinction." Subsection (b) by deleting the reference to mistake in the second sentence precludes any inference that Section 4–402 retains the "trader" rule. Whether a bank is liable for noncompensatory damages, such as punitive damages, must be decided by Section 1–103 and Section 1–106 [*unrevised Article 1; see Concordance, p. 22*] ("by other rule of law").

2.   Wrongful dishonor is different from "failure to exercise ordinary care in handling an item," and the measure of damages is that stated in this section, not that stated in Section 4–103(e). By the same token, if a dishonor comes within this section, the measure of damages of this section applies and not another measure of damages. If the wrongful refusal of the beneficiary's bank to make funds available from a funds transfer causes the beneficiary's check to be dishonored, no specific guidance is given as to whether recovery is under this section or Article 4A. In each case this issue must be viewed in its factual context, and it was thought unwise to seek to establish certainty at the cost of fairness.

3.   The second and third sentences of subsection (b) reject decisions holding that as a matter of law the dishonor of a check is not the "proximate cause" of the arrest and prosecution of the customer and leave to determination in each case as a question of fact whether the dishonor is or may be the "proximate cause."

4.   Banks commonly determine whether there are sufficient funds in an account to pay an item after the close of banking hours on the day of presentment when they post debit and credit items to the account. The determination is made on the basis of credits available for withdrawal as of right or made available for withdrawal by the bank as an accommodation to its customer. When it is determined that payment of the item would overdraw the account, the item may be returned at any time before the bank's midnight deadline the following day. Before the item is returned new credits that are withdrawable as of right may have been added to the account. Subsection (c) eliminates uncertainty under Article 4 as to whether the failure to make a second determination before the item is returned on the day following presentment is a wrongful dishonor if new credits were added to the account on that day that would have covered the amount of the check.

5.   Section 4–402 has been construed to preclude an action for wrongful dishonor by a plaintiff other than the bank's customer. *Loucks v. Albuquerque National Bank*, 418 P.2d 191 (N.Mex. 1966). Some courts have allowed a plaintiff other than the customer to sue when the customer is a business entity that is one and the same with the individual or individuals operating it. *Murdaugh Volkswagen, Inc. v. First National Bank*, 801 F.2d 719 (4th Cir. 1986) and *Karsh v. American City Bank*, 113 Cal.App.3d 419, 169 Cal.Rptr. 851 (1980). However, where the wrongful dishonor impugns the reputation of an operator of the business, the issue is not merely, as the court in *Koger v. East First National Bank*, 443 So.2d 141 (Fla.App. 1983), put it, one of a literal versus a liberal interpretation of Section 4–402. Rather the issue is whether the statutory cause of action in Section 4–402 displaces, in accordance with Section 1–103, any cause of action that existed at common law in a person who is not the customer whose reputation was damaged. See *Marcum v. Security Trust and Savings Co.*, 221 Ala. 419, 129 So. 74 (1930). While Section 4–402 should not be interpreted to displace the latter cause of action, the section itself gives no cause of action to other than a "customer," however that definition is construed, and thus confers no cause of action on the holder of a dishonored item. *First American National Bank v. Commerce Union Bank*, 692 S.W.2d 642 (Tenn.App. 1985).

§ 4–403.   Customer's Right to Stop Payment; Burden of Proof of Loss.

(a)   A customer or any person authorized to draw on the account if there is more than one person may stop payment of any item drawn on the customer's account or close the account by an order to the bank describing the item or account with reasonable certainty received at a time and in a manner that affords the bank a reasonable opportunity to act on it before any action by the bank with respect to the item described in Section 4–303. If the signature of more than one person is required to draw on an account, any of these persons may stop payment or close the account.

(b)   A stop-payment order is effective for six months, but it lapses after 14 calendar days if the original order was oral and was not confirmed in a record within that period. A stop-payment order may be renewed for additional six-month periods by a record given to the bank within a period during which the stop-payment order is effective.

(c)   The burden of establishing the fact and amount of loss resulting from the payment of an item contrary to a stop-payment order or order to close an account is on the customer. The loss from payment of an item contrary to a stop-payment order may include damages for dishonor of subsequent items under Section 4–402.

As amended in 1990 and 2002.

Official Comment

1.   The position taken by this section is that stopping payment or closing an account is a service which depositors expect and are entitled to receive from banks notwithstanding its difficulty, inconvenience and expense. The inevitable occasional losses through failure to stop or close should be borne by the banks as a cost of the business of banking.

2.   Subsection (a) follows the decisions holding that a payee or indorsee has no right to stop payment. This is consistent with the provision governing payment or satisfaction. See Section 3–602. The sole exception to this rule is found in Section 4–405 on payment after notice of death, by which any person claiming an interest in the account can stop payment.

3.   Payment is commonly stopped only on checks; but the right to stop payment is not limited to checks, and extends to any item payable by any bank. If the maker of a note payable at a bank is in a position analogous to that of a drawer (Section 4–106) the maker may stop payment of the note. By analogy the rule extends to drawees other than banks.

4.   A cashier's check or teller's check purchased by a customer whose account is debited in payment for the check is not a check drawn on the customer's account within the meaning of subsection (a); hence, a customer purchasing a cashier's check or teller's check has no right to stop payment of such a check under subsection (a). If a bank issuing a cashier's check or teller's check refuses to pay the check as an accommodation to its customer or for other reasons, its liability on the check is governed by Section 3–411. There is no right to stop payment after certification of a check or other acceptance of a draft, and this is true no matter who procures the certification. See Sections 3–411 and 4–303. The acceptance is the drawee's own engagement to pay, and it is not required to impair its credit by refusing payment for the convenience of the drawer.

5.   Subsection (a) makes clear that if there is more than one person authorized to draw on a customer's account any one of them can stop payment of any check drawn on the account or can order the account closed. Moreover, if there is a customer, such as a corporation, that requires its checks to bear the signatures of more than one person, any of these persons may stop payment on a check. In describing the item, the customer, in the absence of a contrary agreement, must meet the standard of what information allows the bank under the technology then existing to identify the item with reasonable certainty.

6.   Under subsection (b), a stop-payment order is effective after the order, whether written or oral, is received by the bank and the bank has a reasonable opportunity to act on it. If the order is written it remains in effect for six months from that time. If the order is oral it lapses after 14 days unless there is written confirmation. If there is written confirmation within the 14-day period, the six-month period dates from the giving of the oral order. A stop-payment order may be renewed any number of times by written notice given during a six-month period while a stop order is in effect. A new stop-payment order may be given after a six-month period expires, but such a notice takes effect from the date given. When a stop-payment order expires it is as though the order had never been given, and the payor bank may pay the item in good faith under Section 4–404 even though a stop-payment order had once been given.

7.   A payment in violation of an effective direction to stop payment is an improper payment, even though it is made by mistake or inadvertence. Any agreement to the contrary is invalid under Section 4–103(a) if in paying the item over the stop-payment order the bank has failed to exercise ordinary care. An agreement to the contrary which is imposed upon a customer as part of a standard form contract would have to be evaluated in the light of the general obligation of good faith. Sections 1–203 [unrevised Article 1; see Concordance, p. 22] and 4–104(c). The drawee is, however, entitled to subrogation to prevent unjust enrichment (Section 4–407); retains common law defenses, e.g., that by conduct in recognizing the payment the customer has ratified the bank's action in paying over a stop-payment order (Section 1–103); and retains common law rights, e.g., to recover money paid under a mistake under Section 3–418. It has sometimes been said that payment cannot be stopped against a holder in due course, but the statement is inaccurate. The payment can be stopped but the drawer remains liable on the instrument to the holder in due course (Sections 3–305, 3–414) and the drawee, if it pays, becomes subrogated to the rights of the holder in due course against the drawer. Section 4–407. The relationship between Sections 4–403 and 4–407 is discussed in the comments to Section 4–407. Any defenses available against a holder in due course remain available to the drawer, but other defenses are cut off to the same extent as if the holder were bringing the action.

§ 4–404.   Bank Not Obliged to Pay Check More Than Six Months Old.

A bank is under no obligation to a customer having a checking account to pay a check, other than a certified check, which is presented more than six months after its date, but it may charge its customer's account for a payment made thereafter in good faith.

Official Comment

This section incorporates a type of statute that had been adopted in 26 jurisdictions before the Code. The time limit is set at six months because banking and commercial practice regards a check outstanding for longer than that period as stale, and a bank will normally not pay such a check without consulting the depositor. It is therefore not required to do so, but is given the option to pay because it may be in a position to know, as in the case of dividend checks, that the drawer wants payment made.

Certified checks are excluded from the section because they are the primary obligation of the certifying bank (Sections 3–409 and 3–413). The obligation runs directly to the holder of the check. The customer's account was presumably charged when the check was certified.

§ 4–405.   Death or Incompetence of Customer.

(a)   A payor or collecting bank's authority to accept, pay, or collect an item or to account for proceeds of its collection, if otherwise effective, is not rendered ineffective by incompetence of a customer of either bank existing at the time the item is issued or its collection is undertaken if the bank does not know of an adjudication of incompetence. Neither death nor incompetence of a customer revokes the authority to accept, pay, collect, or account until the bank knows of the fact of death or of an adjudication of incompetence and has reasonable opportunity to act on it.

(b)   Even with knowledge, a bank may for 10 days after the date of death pay or certify checks drawn on or before that date unless ordered to stop payment by a person claiming an interest in the account.

As amended in 1990.

Official Comment

1.   Subsection (a) follows existing decisions holding that a drawee (payor) bank is not liable for the payment of a check before it has notice of the death or incompetence of the drawer. The justice and necessity of the rule are obvious. A check is an order to pay which the bank must obey under penalty of possible liability for dishonor. Further, with the tremendous volume of items handled any rule that required banks to verify the continued life and competency of drawers would be completely unworkable.

One or both of these same reasons apply to other phases of the bank collection and payment process and the rule is made wide enough to apply to these other phases. It applies to all kinds of "items"; to "customers" who own items as well as "customers" who draw or make them; to the function of collecting items as well as the function of accepting or paying them; to the carrying out of instructions to account for proceeds even though these may involve transfers to third parties; to depositary and intermediary banks as well as payor banks; and to incompetency existing at the time of the issuance of an item or the commencement of the collection or payment process as well as to incompetency occurring thereafter. Further, the requirement of actual knowledge makes inapplicable the rule of some cases that an adjudication of incompetency is constructive notice to all the world because obviously it is as impossible for banks to keep posted on such adjudications (in the absence of actual knowledge) as it is to keep posted as to death of immediate or remote customers.

2.   Subsection (b) provides a limited period after death during which a bank may continue to pay checks (as distinguished from other items) even though it has notice. The purpose of the provision, as of the existing statutes, is to permit holders of checks drawn and issued shortly before death to cash them without the necessity of filing a claim in probate. The justification is that these checks normally are given in immediate payment of an obligation, that there is almost never any reason why they should not be paid, and that filing in probate is a useless formality, burdensome to the holder, the executor, the court and the bank.

This section does not prevent an executor or administrator from recovering the payment from the holder of the check. It is not intended to affect the validity of any gift causa mortis or other transfer in contemplation of death, but merely to relieve the bank of liability for the payment.

3.   Any surviving relative, creditor or other person who claims an interest in the account may give a direction to the bank not to pay checks, or not to pay a particular check. Such notice has the same effect as a

direction to stop payment. The bank has no responsibility to determine the validity of the claim or even whether it is "colorable." But obviously anyone who has an interest in the estate, including the person named as executor in a will, even if the will has not yet been admitted to probate, is entitled to claim an interest in the account.

§ 4-406. Customer's Duty to Discover and Report Unauthorized Signature or Alteration.

(a)   A bank that sends or makes available to a customer a statement of account showing payment of items for the account shall either return or make available to the customer the items paid or provide information in the statement of account sufficient to allow the customer reasonably to identify the items paid. The statement of account provides sufficient information if the item is described by item number, amount, and date of payment.

(b)   If the items are not returned to the customer, the person retaining the items shall either retain the items or, if the items are destroyed, maintain the capacity to furnish legible copies of the items until the expiration of seven years after receipt of the items. A customer may request an item from the bank that paid the item, and that bank must provide in a reasonable time either the item or, if the item has been destroyed or is not otherwise obtainable, a legible copy of the item.

(c)   If a bank sends or makes available a statement of account or items pursuant to subsection (a), the customer must exercise reasonable promptness in examining the statement or the items to determine whether any payment was not authorized because of an alteration of an item or because a purported signature by or on behalf of the customer was not authorized. If, based on the statement or items provided, the customer should reasonably have discovered the unauthorized payment, the customer must promptly notify the bank of the relevant facts.

(d)   If the bank proves that the customer failed, with respect to an item, to comply with the duties imposed on the customer by subsection (c), the customer is precluded from asserting against the bank:

(1)   the customer's unauthorized signature or any alteration on the item, if the bank also proves that it suffered a loss by reason of the failure; and

(2)   the customer's unauthorized signature or alteration by the same wrongdoer on any other item paid in good faith by the bank if the payment was made before the bank received notice from the customer of the unauthorized signature or alteration and after the customer had been afforded a reasonable period of time, not exceeding 30 days, in which to examine the item or statement of account and notify the bank.

(e)   If subsection (d) applies and the customer proves that the bank failed to exercise ordinary care in paying the item and that the failure substantially contributed to loss, the loss is allocated between the customer precluded and the bank asserting the preclusion according to the extent to which the failure of the customer to comply with subsection (c) and the failure of the bank to exercise ordinary care contributed to the loss. If the customer proves that the bank did not pay the item in good faith, the preclusion under subsection (d) does not apply.

(f)   Without regard to care or lack of care of either the customer or the bank, a customer who does not within one year after the statement or items are made available to the customer (subsection (a)) discover and report the customer's unauthorized signature on or any alteration on the item is precluded from asserting against the bank the unauthorized signature or alteration. If there is a preclusion under this subsection, the payor bank may not recover for breach of warranty under Section 4-208 with respect to the unauthorized signature or alteration to which the preclusion applies.

As amended in 1990.

Revised Official Comment

1.   Under subsection (a), if a bank that has paid a check or other item for the account of a customer makes available to the customer a statement of account showing payment of the item, the bank must either return the item to the customer or provide a description of the item sufficient to allow the customer to identify it. Under subsection (c), the customer has a duty to exercise reasonable promptness in examining the statement or the returned item to discover any unauthorized signature of the customer or any alteration and to promptly notify the bank if the customer should reasonably have discovered the unauthorized signature or alteration.

The duty stated in subsection (c) becomes operative only if the "bank sends or makes available a statement of account or items pursuant to subsection (a)." A bank is not under a duty to send a statement of account or the paid items to the customer; but, if it does not do so, the customer does not have any duties under subsection (c).

Under subsection (a), a statement of account must provide information "sufficient to allow the customer reasonably to identify the items paid." If the bank supplies its customer with an image of the paid item, it complies with this standard. But a safe harbor rule is provided. The bank complies with the standard of providing "sufficient information" if "the item is described by item number, amount, and date of payment." This means that the customer's duties under subsection (c) are triggered if the bank sends a statement of account complying with the safe harbor rule without returning the paid items. A bank does not have to return the paid items unless it has agreed with the customer to do so. Whether there is such an agreement depends upon the particular circumstances. See Section 1–201(3) [*unrevised Article 1; see Concordance, p. 22*]. If the bank elects to provide the minimum information that is "sufficient" under subsection (a) and, as a consequence, the customer could not "reasonably have discovered the unauthorized payment," there is no preclusion under subsection (d). If the customer made a record of the issued checks on the check stub or carbonized copies furnished by the bank in the checkbook, the customer should usually be able to verify the paid items shown on the statement of account and discover any unauthorized or altered checks. But there could be exceptional circumstances. For example, if a check is altered by changing the name of the payee, the customer could not normally detect the fraud unless the customer is given the paid check or the statement of account discloses the name of the payee of the altered check. If the customer could not "reasonably have discovered the unauthorized payment" under subsection (c) there would not be a preclusion under subsection (d).

The safe harbor provided by subsection (a) serves to permit a bank, based on the state of existing technology, to trigger the customer's duties under subsection (c) by providing a "statement of account showing payment of items" without having to return the paid items, in any case in which the bank has not agreed with the customer to return the paid items. The safe harbor does not, however, preclude a customer under subsection (d) from asserting its unauthorized signature or an alteration against a bank in those circumstances in which under subsection (c) the customer should not "reasonably have discovered the unauthorized payment." Whether the customer has failed to comply with its duties under subsection (c) is determined on a case-by-case basis.

The provision in subsection (a) that a statement of account contains "sufficient information if the item is described by item number, amount, and date of payment" is based upon the existing state of technology. This information was chosen because it can be obtained by the bank's computer from the check's MICR line without examination of the items involved. The other two items of information that the customer would normally want to know—the name of the payee and the date of the item—cannot currently be obtained from the MICR line. The safe harbor rule is important in determining the feasibility of payor or collecting bank check retention plans. A customer who keeps a record of checks written, e.g., on the check stubs or carbonized copies of the checks supplied by the bank in the checkbook, will usually have sufficient information to identify the items on the basis of item number, amount, and date of payment. But customers who do not utilize these record-keeping methods may not. The policy decision is that accommodating customers who do not keep adequate records is not as desirable as accommodating customers who keep more careful records. This policy results in less cost to the check collection system and thus to all customers of the system. It is expected that technological advances such as image processing may make it possible for banks to give customers more information in the future in a manner that is fully compatible with automation or truncation systems. At that time the Permanent Editorial Board may wish to make recommendations for an amendment revising the safe harbor requirements in the light of those advances.

2.   Subsection (d) states the consequences of a failure by the customer to perform its duty under subsection (c) to report an alteration or the customer's unauthorized signature. Subsection (d)(1) applies to the unauthorized payment of the item to which the duty to report under subsection (c) applies. If the bank proves that the customer "should reasonably have discovered the unauthorized payment" (See Comment 1) and did not notify the bank, the customer is precluded from asserting against the bank the alteration or the customer's unauthorized signature if the bank proves that it suffered a loss as a result of the failure of the customer to perform its subsection (c) duty. Subsection (d)(2) applies to cases in which the customer fails to report an unauthorized signature or alteration with respect to an item in breach of the subsection (c) duty (See Comment 1) and the bank subsequently pays other items of the customer with respect to which there is an alteration or unauthorized signature of the customer and the same wrongdoer is involved. If the payment of the subsequent items occurred after the customer has had a reasonable time (not exceeding 30 days) to report with respect to the first item and before the bank received notice of the unauthorized signature or alteration of the first item, the customer is precluded from asserting the alteration or unauthorized signature with respect to the subsequent items.

If the customer is precluded in a single or multiple item unauthorized payment situation under subsection (d), but the customer proves that the bank failed to exercise ordinary care in paying the item or items and that the failure substantially contributed to the loss, subsection (e) provides a comparative negligence test for allocating loss between the customer and the bank. Subsection (e) also states that, if the customer proves that the bank did not pay the item in good faith, the preclusion under subsection (d) does not apply.

Subsection (d)(2) changes former subsection (2)(b) by adopting a 30-day period in place of a 14-day period. Although the 14-day period may have been sufficient when the original version of Article 4 was drafted in the 1950s, given the much greater volume of checks at the time of the revision, a longer period was viewed as more appropriate. The rule of subsection (d)(2) follows pre-Code case law that payment of an additional item or items bearing an unauthorized signature or alteration by the same wrongdoer is a loss suffered by the bank traceable to the customer's failure to exercise reasonable care (See Comment 1) in examining the statement and notifying the bank of objections to it. One of the most serious consequences of failure of the customer to comply with the requirements of subsection (c) is the opportunity presented to the wrongdoer to repeat the misdeeds. Conversely, one of the best ways to keep down losses in this type of situation is for the customer to promptly examine the statement and notify the bank of an unauthorized signature or alteration so that the bank will be alerted to stop paying further items. Hence, the rule of subsection (d)(2) is prescribed, and to avoid dispute a specific time limit, 30 days, is designated for cases to which the subsection applies. These considerations are not present if there are no losses resulting from the payment of additional items. In these circumstances, a reasonable period for the customer to comply with its duties under subsection (c) would depend on the circumstances (Section 1–204(2)) [unrevised Article 1; see Concordance, p. 22] and the subsection (d)(2) time limit should not be imported by analogy into subsection (c).

3. Subsection (b) applies if the items are not returned to the customer. Check retention plans may include a simple payor bank check retention plan or the kind of check retention plan that would be authorized by a truncation agreement in which a collecting bank or the payee may retain the items. Even after agreeing to a check retention plan, a customer may need to see one or more checks for litigation or other purposes. The customer's request for the check may always be made to the payor bank. Under subsection (b) retaining banks may destroy items but must maintain the capacity to furnish legible copies for seven years. A legible copy may include an image of an item. This Act does not define the length of the reasonable period of time for a bank to provide the check or copy of the check. What is reasonable depends on the capacity of the bank and the needs of the customer. This Act does not specify sanctions for failure to retain or furnish the items or legible copies; this is left to other laws regulating banks. See Comment 3 to Section 4–101. Moreover, this Act does not regulate fees that banks charge their customers for furnishing items or copies or other services covered by the Act, but under principles of law such as unconscionability or good faith and fair dealing, courts have reviewed fees and the bank's exercise of a discretion to set fees. *Perdue v. Crocker National Bank*, 38 Cal.3d 913 (1985) (unconscionability); *Best v. United Bank of Oregon*, 739 P.2d 554, 562–566 (1987) (good faith and fair dealing). In addition, Section 1–203 [*unrevised Article 1; see Concordance, p. 22*] provides that every contract or duty within this Act imposes an obligation of good faith in its performance or enforcement.

4. Subsection (e) replaces former subsection (3) and poses a modified comparative negligence test for determining liability. See the discussion on this point in the Comments to Sections 3–404, 3–405, and 3–406. The term "good faith" is defined in Section 1–201(b)(20) as including "observance of reasonable commercial standards of fair dealing." The connotation of this standard is fairness and not absence of negligence.

The term "ordinary care" used in subsection (e) is defined in Section 3–103(a)(7), made applicable to Article 4 by Section 4–104(c), to provide that sight examination by a payor bank is not required if its procedure is reasonable and is commonly followed by other comparable banks in the area. The case law is divided on this issue. The definition of "ordinary care" in Section 3–103 rejects those authorities that hold, in effect, that failure to use sight examination is negligence as a matter of law. The effect of the definition of "ordinary care" on Section 4–406 is only to provide that in the small percentage of cases in which a customer's failure to examine its statement or returned items has led to loss under subsection (d) a bank should not have to share that loss solely because it has adopted an automated collection or payment procedure in order to deal with the great volume of items at a lower cost to all customers.

5. Several changes are made in former Section 4–406(5). First, former subsection (5) is deleted and its substance is made applicable only to the one-year notice preclusion in former subsection (4) (subsection (f)). Thus if a drawer has not notified the payor bank of an unauthorized check or material alteration within the one-year period, the payor bank may not choose to recredit the drawer's account and pass the loss to the collecting banks on the theory of breach of warranty. Second, the reference in former subsection (4) to unauthorized indorsements is deleted. Section 4–406 imposes no duties on the drawer to look for unauthorized indorsements. Section 4–111

sets out a statute of limitations allowing a customer a three-year period to seek a credit to an account improperly charged by payment of an item bearing an unauthorized indorsement. Third, subsection (c) is added to Section 4–208 to assure that if a depositary bank is sued for breach of a presentment warranty, it can defend by showing that the drawer is precluded by Section 3–406 or Section 4–406(c) and (d).

As amended in 1991 and 2002.

§ 4–407.   Payor Bank's Right to Subrogation on Improper Payment.

If a payor bank has paid an item over the order of the drawer or maker to stop payment, or after an account has been closed, or otherwise under circumstances giving a basis for objection by the drawer or maker, to prevent unjust enrichment and only to the extent necessary to prevent loss to the bank by reason of its payment of the item, the payor bank is subrogated to the rights

(1)   of any holder in due course on the item against the drawer or maker;

(2)   of the payee or any other holder of the item against the drawer or maker either on the item or under the transaction out of which the item arose; and

(3)   of the drawer or maker against the payee or any other holder of the item with respect to the transaction out of which the item arose.

As amended in 1990.

Official Comment

1.   Section 4–403 states that a stop-payment order or an order to close an account is binding on a bank. If a bank pays an item over such an order it is prima facie liable, but under subsection (c) of Section 4–403 the burden of establishing the fact and amount of loss from such payment is on the customer. A defense frequently interposed by a bank in an action against it for wrongful payment over a stop-payment order is that the drawer or maker suffered no loss because it would have been liable to a holder in due course in any event. On this argument some cases have held that payment cannot be stopped against a holder in due course. Payment can be stopped, but if it is, the drawer or maker is liable and the sound rule is that the bank is subrogated to the rights of the holder in due course. The preamble and paragraph (1) of this section state this rule.

2.   Paragraph (2) also subrogates the bank to the rights of the payee or other holder against the drawer or maker either on the item or under the transaction out of which it arose. It may well be that the payee is not a holder in due course but still has good rights against the drawer. These may be on the check but also may not be as, for example, where the drawer buys goods from the payee and the goods are partially defective so that the payee is not entitled to the full price, but the goods are still worth a portion of the contract price. If the drawer retains the goods it is obligated to pay a part of the agreed price. If the bank has paid the check it should be subrogated to this claim of the payee against the drawer.

3.   Paragraph (3) subrogates the bank to the rights of the drawer or maker against the payee or other holder with respect to the transaction out of which the item arose. If, for example, the payee was a fraudulent salesman inducing the drawer to issue a check for defective securities, and the bank pays the check over a stop-payment order but reimburses the drawer for such payment, the bank should have a basis for getting the money back from the fraudulent salesman.

4.   The limitations of the preamble prevent the bank itself from getting any double recovery or benefits out of its subrogation rights conferred by the section.

5.   The spelling out of the affirmative rights of the bank in this section does not destroy other existing rights (Section 1–103). Among others these may include the defense of a payor bank that by conduct in recognizing the payment a customer has ratified the bank's action in paying in disregard of a stop-payment order or right to recover money paid under a mistake.

PART 5

COLLECTION OF DOCUMENTARY DRAFTS

§ 4–501. Handling of Documentary Drafts; Duty to Send for Presentment and to Notify Customer of Dishonor.

A bank that takes a documentary draft for collection shall present or send the draft and accompanying documents for presentment and, upon learning that the draft has not been paid or accepted in due course, shall seasonably notify its customer of the fact even though it may have discounted or bought the draft or extended credit available for withdrawal as of right.

As amended in 1990.

Official Comment

This section states the duty of a bank handling a documentary draft for a customer. "Documentary draft" is defined in Section 4–104. The duty stated exists even if the bank has bought the draft. This is because to the customer the draft normally represents an underlying commercial transaction, and if that is not going through as planned the customer should know it promptly. An electronic document of title may be presented through allowing access to the document or delivery of the document. Article 1, Section 1–201 (definition of "delivery").

As amended in 2003.

§ 4–502. Presentment of "On Arrival" Drafts.

If a draft or the relevant instructions require presentment "on arrival", "when goods arrive" or the like, the collecting bank need not present until in its judgment a reasonable time for arrival of the goods has expired. Refusal to pay or accept because the goods have not arrived is not dishonor; the bank must notify its transferor of the refusal but need not present the draft again until it is instructed to do so or learns of the arrival of the goods.

As amended in 1990.

Official Comment

The section is designed to establish a definite rule for "on arrival" drafts. The term includes not only drafts drawn payable "on arrival" but also drafts forwarded with instructions to present "on arrival." The term refers to the arrival of the relevant goods. Unless a bank has actual knowledge of the arrival of the goods, as for example, when it is the "notify" party on the bill of lading, the section only requires the exercise of such judgment in estimating time as a bank may be expected to have. Commonly the buyer-drawee will want the goods and will therefore call for the documents and take up the draft when they do arrive.

§ 4–503. Responsibility of Presenting Bank for Documents and Goods; Report of Reasons for Dishonor; Referee in Case of Need.

Unless otherwise instructed and except as provided in Article 5, a bank presenting a documentary draft:

(1) must deliver the documents to the drawee on acceptance of the draft if it is payable more than three days after presentment; otherwise, only on payment; and

(2) upon dishonor, either in the case of presentment for acceptance or presentment for payment, may seek and follow instructions from any referee in case of need designated in the draft or, if the presenting bank does not choose to utilize the referee's services, it must use diligence and good faith to ascertain the reason for dishonor, must notify its transferor of the dishonor and of the results of its effort to ascertain the reasons therefor, and must request instructions.

However the presenting bank is under no obligation with respect to goods represented by the documents except to follow any reasonable instructions seasonably received; it has a right to reimbursement for any expense incurred in following instructions and to prepayment of or indemnity for those expenses.

As amended in 1990.

Official Comment

1.   This section states the rules governing, in the absence of instructions, the duty of the presenting bank in case either of honor or of dishonor of a documentary draft. The section should be read in connection with Section 2–514 on when documents are deliverable on acceptance, when on payment. In the case of a dishonor of the draft, the bank, subject to Section 4–504, must return possession or control of the documents to its principal.

2.   If the draft is drawn under a letter of credit, Article 5 controls. See Sections 5–109 through 5–114 [*unrevised Article 5*].

As amended in 2003.

§ 4–504.   Privilege of Presenting Bank to Deal With Goods; Security Interest for Expenses.

(a)   A presenting bank that, following the dishonor of a documentary draft, has seasonably requested instructions but does not receive them within a reasonable time may store, sell, or otherwise deal with the goods in any reasonable manner.

(b)   For its reasonable expenses incurred by action under subsection (a) the presenting bank has a lien upon the goods or their proceeds, which may be foreclosed in the same manner as an unpaid seller's lien.

As amended in 1990.

Official Comment

The section gives the presenting bank, after dishonor, a privilege to deal with the goods in any commercially reasonable manner pending instructions from its transferor and, if still unable to communicate with its principal after a reasonable time, a right to realize its expenditures as if foreclosing on an unpaid seller's lien (Section 2–706). The provision includes situations in which storage of goods or other action becomes commercially necessary pending receipt of any requested instructions, even if the requested instructions are later received.

The "reasonable manner" referred to means one reasonable in the light of business factors and the judgment of a business man.

UCC ARTICLE 4A

FUNDS TRANSFERS

Article 4A was promulgated in 1989 and amended in 2012 and 2022.
2022 Amendments appear in ~~strikeout~~/<u>underline</u> format.
Prefatory Note to 2022 amendments appears in Appendix E.
Current through April 2023
For updates, see www.uniformlaws.org

PART 1.   SUBJECT MATTER AND DEFINITIONS

4A–101.   Short Title.
4A–102.   Subject Matter.
4A–103.   Payment Order—Definitions.
4A–104.   Funds Transfer—Definitions.
4A–105.   Other Definitions.
4A–106.   Time Payment Order Is Received.
4A–107.   Federal Reserve Regulations and Operating Circulars.
4A–108.   Relationship to Electronic Fund Transfer Act.

PART 2.   ISSUE AND ACCEPTANCE OF PAYMENT ORDER

4A–201.   Security Procedure.
4A–202.   Authorized and Verified Payment Orders.
4A–203.   Unenforceability of Certain Verified Payment Orders.
4A–204.   Refund of Payment and Duty of Customer to Report With Respect to Unauthorized Payment Order.
4A–205.   Erroneous Payment Orders.
4A–206.   Transmission of Payment Order Through Funds-Transfer or Other Communication System.
4A–207.   Misdescription of Beneficiary.
4A–208.   Misdescription of Intermediary Bank or Beneficiary's Bank.
4A–209.   Acceptance of Payment Order.
4A–210.   Rejection of Payment Order.
4A–211.   Cancellation and Amendment of Payment Order.
4A–212.   Liability and Duty of Receiving Bank Regarding Unaccepted Payment Order.

PART 3.   EXECUTION OF SENDER'S PAYMENT ORDER BY RECEIVING BANK

4A–301.   Execution and Execution Date.
4A–302.   Obligations of Receiving Bank in Execution of Payment Order.
4A–303.   Erroneous Execution of Payment Order.
4A–304.   Duty of Sender to Report Erroneously Executed Payment Order.
4A–305.   Liability for Late or Improper Execution or Failure to Execute Payment Order.

PART 4.   PAYMENT

4A–401.   Payment Date.
4A–402.   Obligation of Sender to Pay Receiving Bank.

4A–403. Payment by Sender to Receiving Bank.

4A–404. Obligation of Beneficiary's Bank to Pay and Give Notice to Beneficiary.

4A–405. Payment by Beneficiary's Bank to Beneficiary.

4A–406. Payment by Originator to Beneficiary; Discharge of Underlying Obligation.

PART 5.   MISCELLANEOUS PROVISIONS

4A–501. Variation by Agreement and Effect of Funds-Transfer System Rule.

4A–502. Creditor Process Served on Receiving Bank; Setoff by Beneficiary's Bank.

4A–503. Injunction or Restraining Order With Respect to Funds Transfer.

4A–504. Order in Which Items and Payment Orders May Be Charged to Account; Order of Withdrawals From Account.

4A–505. Preclusion of Objection to Debit of Customer's Account.

4A–506. Rate of Interest.

4A–507. Choice of Law.

PREFATORY NOTE

The National Conference of Commissioners on Uniform State laws and The American Law Institute have approved a new Article 4A to the Uniform Commercial Code. Comments that follow each of the sections of the statute are intended as official comments. They explain in detail the purpose and meaning of the various sections and the policy considerations on which they are based.

Description of transaction covered by Article 4A.

There are a number of mechanisms for making payments through the banking system. Most of these mechanisms are covered in whole or part by state or federal statutes. In terms of number of transactions, payments made by check or credit card are the most common payment methods. Payment by check is covered by Articles 3 and 4 of the UCC and some aspects of payment by credit card are covered by federal law. In recent years electronic funds transfers have been increasingly common in consumer transactions. For example, in some cases a retail customer can pay for purchases by use of an access or debit card inserted in a terminal at the retail store that allows the bank account of the customer to be instantly debited. Some aspects of these point-of-sale transactions and other consumer payments that are effected electronically are covered by a federal statute, the Electronic Fund Transfer Act (EFTA). If any part of a funds transfer is covered by EFTA, the entire funds transfer is excluded from Article 4A.

Another type of payment, commonly referred to as a wholesale wire transfer, is the primary focus of Article 4A. Payments that are covered by Article 4A are overwhelmingly between business or financial institutions. The dollar volume of payments made by wire transfer far exceeds the dollar volume of payments made by other means. The volume of payments by wire transfer over the two principal wire payment systems—the Federal Reserve wire transfer network (Fedwire) and the New York Clearing House Interbank Payments Systems (CHIPS)—exceeds one trillion dollars per day. Most payments carried out by use of automated clearing houses are consumer payments covered by EFTA and therefore not covered by Article 4A. There is, however, a significant volume of nonconsumer ACH payments that closely resemble wholesale wire transfers. These payments are also covered by Article 4A.

There is some resemblance between payments made by wire transfer and payments made by other means such as paper-based checks and credit cards or electronically-based consumer payments, but there are also many differences. Article 4A excludes from its coverage these other payment mechanisms. Article 4A follows a policy of treating the transaction that it covers—a "funds transfer"—as a unique method of payment that is governed by unique principles of law that address the operational and policy issues presented by this kind of payment.

The funds transfer that is covered by Article 4A is not a complex transaction and can be illustrated by the following example which is used throughout the Prefatory Note as a basis for discussion. X, a debtor, wants to pay an obligation owed to Y. Instead of delivering to Y a negotiable instrument such as a check or some other writing such as a credit card slip that enables Y to obtain payment from a bank, X transmits an instruction to X's bank to credit a sum of money to the bank account of Y. In most cases X's bank and Y's bank are different banks. X's bank may carry out X's instruction by instructing Y's bank to credit Y's account in the amount that X requested. The instruction that X issues to its bank is a "payment order." X is the "sender" of the payment order and X's bank is the "receiving bank" with respect to X's order. Y is the "beneficiary" of X's order. When X's bank issues an instruction to Y's bank to carry out X's payment order, X's bank "executes" X's order. The instruction of X's bank to Y's bank is also a payment order. With respect to that order, X's bank is the sender, Y's bank is the receiving bank, and Y is the beneficiary. The entire series of transactions by which X pays Y is known as the "funds transfer." With respect to the funds transfer, X is the "originator," X's bank is the "originator's bank," Y is the "beneficiary" and Y's bank is the "beneficiary's bank." In more complex transactions there are one or more additional banks known as "intermediary banks" between X's bank and Y's bank. In the funds transfer the instruction contained in the payment order of X to its bank is carried out by a series of payment orders by each bank in the transmission chain to the next bank in the chain until Y's bank receives a payment order to make the credit to Y's account. In most cases, the payment order of each bank to the next bank in the chain is transmitted electronically, and often the payment order of X to its bank is also transmitted electronically, but the means of transmission does not have any legal significance. A payment order may be transmitted by any means, and in some cases the payment order is transmitted by a slow means such as first class mail. To reflect this fact, the broader term "funds transfer" rather than the narrower term "wire transfer" is used in Article 4A to describe the overall payment transaction.

Funds transfers are divided into two categories determined by whether the instruction to pay is given by the person making payment or the person receiving payment. If the instruction is given by the person making the payment, the transfer is commonly referred to as a "credit transfer." If the instruction is given by the person receiving payment, the transfer is commonly referred to as a "debit transfer." Article 4A governs credit transfers and excludes debit transfers.

Why is Article 4A needed?

There is no comprehensive body of law that defines the rights and obligations that arise from wire transfers. Some aspects of wire transfers are governed by rules of the principal transfer systems. Transfers made by Fedwire are governed by Federal Reserve Regulation J and transfers over CHIPS are governed by the CHIPS rules. Transfers made by means of automated clearing houses are governed by uniform rules adopted by various associations of banks in various parts of the nation or by Federal Reserve rules or operating circulars. But the various funds transfer system rules apply to only limited aspects of wire transfer transactions. The resolution of the many issues that are not covered by funds transfer system rules depends on contracts of the parties, to the extent that they exist, or principles of law applicable to other payment mechanisms that might be applied by analogy. The result is a great deal of uncertainty. There is no consensus about the juridical nature of a wire transfer and consequently of the rights and obligations that are created. Article 4A is intended to provide the comprehensive body of law that we do not have today.

Characteristics of a funds transfer.

There are a number of characteristics of funds transfers covered by Article 4A that have influenced the drafting of the statute. The typical funds transfer involves a large amount of money. Multimillion dollar transactions are commonplace. The originator of the transfer and the beneficiary are typically sophisticated business or financial organizations. High speed is another predominant characteristic. Most funds transfers are completed on the same day, even in complex transactions in which there are several intermediary banks in the transmission chain. A funds transfer is a highly efficient substitute for payments made by the delivery of paper instruments. Another characteristic is extremely low cost. A transfer that involves many millions of dollars can be made for a price of a few dollars. Price does not normally vary very much or at all with the amount of the transfer. This system of pricing may not be feasible if the bank is exposed to very large liabilities in connection with the transaction. The pricing system assumes that the price reflects primarily the cost of the mechanical operation performed by the bank, but in fact, a bank may have more or less potential liability with respect to a funds transfer depending upon the amount of the transfer. Risk of loss to banks carrying out a funds transfer may arise from a variety of causes. In some funds transfers, there may be extensions of very large amounts of credit for short periods of time by the banks that carry out a funds transfer. If a payment order is issued to the beneficiary's bank, it is normal for the bank to release funds to the beneficiary immediately. Sometimes, payment to the beneficiary's bank by the bank that issued the order to the beneficiary's bank is delayed until the end of the day. If that payment is not received because of the insolvency of the bank that is obliged to pay, the beneficiary's bank may suffer a loss. There is also risk of loss if a bank fails to execute the payment order of a customer, or if the order is executed late. There also may be an error in the payment order issued by a bank that is executing the payment order of its customer. For example, the error might relate to the amount to be paid or to the identity of the person to be paid. Because the dollar amounts involved in funds transfers are so large, the risk of loss if something goes wrong in a transaction may also be very large. A major policy issue in the drafting of Article 4A is that of determining how risk of loss is to be allocated given the price structure in the industry.

Concept of acceptance and effect of acceptance by the beneficiary's bank.

Rights and obligations under Article 4A arise as the result of "acceptance" of a payment order by the bank to which the order is addressed. Section 4A–209. The effect of acceptance varies depending upon whether the payment order is issued to the beneficiary's bank or to a bank other than the beneficiary's bank. Acceptance by the beneficiary's bank is particularly important because it defines when the beneficiary's bank becomes obligated to the beneficiary to pay the amount of the payment order. Although Article 4A follows convention in using the term "funds transfer" to identify the payment from X to Y that is described above, no money or property right of X is actually transferred to Y. X pays Y by causing Y's bank to become indebted to Y in the amount of the payment. This debt arises when Y's bank accepts the payment order that X's bank issued to Y's bank to execute X's order. If the funds transfer was carried out by use of one or more intermediary banks between X's bank and Y's bank, Y's bank becomes indebted to Y when Y's bank accepts the payment order issued to it by an intermediary bank. The funds transfer is completed when this debt is incurred. Acceptance, the event that determines when the debt of Y's bank to Y arises, occurs (i) when Y's bank pays Y or notifies Y of receipt of the payment order, or (ii) when Y's bank receives payment from the bank that issued a payment order to Y's bank.

The only obligation of the beneficiary's bank that results from acceptance of a payment order is to pay the amount of the order to the beneficiary. No obligation is owed to either the sender of the payment order accepted by the beneficiary's bank or to the originator of the funds transfer. The obligation created by acceptance by the beneficiary's bank is for the benefit of the beneficiary. The purpose of the sender's payment order is to effect payment by the originator to the beneficiary and that purpose is achieved when the beneficiary's bank accepts the payment order. Section 4A–405 states rules for determining when the obligation of the beneficiary's bank to the beneficiary has been paid.

Acceptance by a bank other than the beneficiary's bank.

In the funds transfer described above, what is the obligation of X's bank when it receives X's payment order? Funds transfers by a bank on behalf of its customer are made pursuant to an agreement or arrangement that may or may not be reduced to a formal document signed by the parties. It is probably true that in most cases there is either no express agreement or the agreement addresses only some aspects of the transaction. Substantial risk is involved in funds transfers and a bank may not be willing to give this service to all customers, and may not be willing to offer it to any customer unless certain safeguards against loss such as security procedures are in effect. Funds transfers often involve the giving of credit by the receiving bank to the customer, and that also may involve an agreement. These considerations are reflected in Article 4A by the principle that, in the absence of a contrary agreement, a receiving bank does not incur liability with respect to a payment order until it accepts it. If X and X's bank in the hypothetical case had an agreement that obliged the bank to act on X's payment orders and the bank failed to comply with the agreement, the bank can be held liable for breach of the agreement. But apart from any obligation arising by agreement, the bank does not incur any liability with respect to X's payment order until the bank accepts the order. X's payment order is treated by Article 4A as a request by X to the bank to take action that will cause X's payment order to be carried out. That request can be accepted by X's bank by "executing" X's payment order. Execution occurs when X's bank sends a payment order to Y's bank intended by X's bank to carry out the payment order of X. X's bank could also execute X's payment order by issuing a payment order to an intermediary bank instructing the intermediary bank to instruct Y's bank to make the credit to Y's account. In that case execution and acceptance of X's order occur when the payment order of X's bank is sent to the intermediary bank. When X's bank executes X's payment order the bank is entitled to receive payment from X and may debit an authorized account of X. If X's bank does not execute X's order and the amount of the order is covered by a withdrawable credit balance in X's authorized account, the bank must pay X interest on the money represented by X's order unless X is given prompt notice of rejection of the order. Section 4A–210(b).

ARTICLE 4A

Bank error in funds transfers.

If a bank, other than the beneficiary's bank, accepts a payment order, the obligations and liabilities are owed to the originator of the funds transfer. Assume in the example stated above, that X's bank executes X's payment order by issuing a payment order to an intermediary bank that executes the order of X's bank by issuing a payment order to Y's bank. The obligations of X's bank with respect to execution are owed to X. The obligations of the intermediary bank with respect to execution are also owed to X. Section 4A–302 states standards with respect to the time and manner of execution of payment orders. Section 4A–305 states the measure of damages for improper execution. It also states that a receiving bank is liable for damages if it fails to execute a payment order that it was obliged by express agreement to execute. In each case consequential damages are not recoverable unless an express agreement of the receiving bank provides for them. The policy basis for this limitation is discussed in Comment 2 to Section 4A–305.

Error in the consummation of a funds transfer is not uncommon. There may be a discrepancy in the amount that the originator orders to be paid to the beneficiary and the amount that the beneficiary's bank is ordered to pay. For example, if the originator's payment order instructs payment of $100,000 and the payment order of the originator's bank instructs payment of $1,000,000, the originator's bank is entitled to receive only $100,000 from the originator and has the burden of recovering the additional $900,000 paid to the beneficiary by mistake. In some cases the originator's bank or an intermediary bank instructs payment to a beneficiary other than the beneficiary stated in the originator's payment order. If the wrong beneficiary is paid the bank that issued the erroneous payment order is not entitled to receive payment of the payment order that it executed and has the burden of recovering the mistaken payment. The originator is not obliged to pay its payment order. Section 4A–303 and Section 4A–207 state rules for determining the rights and obligations of the various parties to the funds transfer in these cases and in other typical cases in which error is made.

Pursuant to Section 4A–402(c) the originator is excused from the obligation to pay the originator's bank if the funds transfer is not completed, i.e. payment by the originator to the beneficiary is not made. Payment by the originator to the beneficiary occurs when the beneficiary's bank accepts a payment order for the benefit of the beneficiary of the originator's payment order. Section 4A–406. If for any reason that acceptance does not occur, the originator is not required to pay the payment order that it issued or, if it already paid, is entitled to refund of the payment with interest. This "money-back guarantee" is an important protection of the originator of a funds transfer. The same rule applies to any other sender in the funds transfer. Each sender's obligation to pay is excused if the beneficiary's bank does not accept a payment order for the benefit of the beneficiary of that sender's order. There is an important exception to this rule. It is common practice for the originator of a funds transfer to designate the intermediary bank or banks through which the funds transfer is to be routed. The originator's bank is required by Section 4A–302 to follow the instruction of the originator with respect to intermediary banks. If the originator's bank sends a payment order to the intermediary bank designated in the originator's order and the intermediary bank causes the funds transfer to miscarry by failing to execute the payment order or by instructing payment to the wrong beneficiary, the originator's bank is not required to pay its payment order and if it has already paid it is entitled to recover payment from the intermediary bank. This remedy is normally adequate, but if the originator's bank already paid its order and the intermediary bank has suspended payments or is not permitted by law to refund payment, the originator's bank will suffer a loss. Since the originator required the originator's bank to use the failed intermediary bank, Section 4A–402(e) provides that in this case the originator is obliged to pay its payment order and has a claim against the intermediary bank for the amount of the order. The same principle applies to any other sender that designates a subsequent intermediary bank.

Unauthorized payment orders.

An important issue addressed in Section 4A–202 and Section 4A–203 is how the risk of loss from unauthorized payment orders is to be allocated. In a large percentage of cases, the payment order of the originator of the funds transfer is transmitted electronically to the originator's bank. In these cases it may not be possible for the bank to know whether the electronic message has been authorized by its customer. To ensure that no unauthorized person is transmitting messages to the bank, the normal practice is to establish security procedures that usually involve the use of codes or identifying numbers or words. If the bank accepts a payment order that purports to be that of its customer after verifying its authenticity by complying with a security procedure agreed to by the customer and the bank, the customer is bound to pay the order even if it was not authorized. But there is an important limitation on this rule. The bank is entitled

419

to payment in the case of an unauthorized order only if the court finds that the security procedure was a commercially reasonable method of providing security against unauthorized payment orders. The customer can also avoid liability if it can prove that the unauthorized order was not initiated by an employee or other agent of the customer having access to confidential security information or by a person who obtained that information from a source controlled by the customer. The policy issues are discussed in the comments following Section 4A–203. If the bank accepts an unauthorized payment order without verifying it in compliance with a security procedure, the loss falls on the bank.

Security procedures are also important in cases of error in the transmission of payment orders. There may be an error by the sender in the amount of the order, or a sender may transmit a payment order and then erroneously transmit a duplicate of the order. Normally, the sender is bound by the payment order even if it is issued by mistake. But in some cases an error of this kind can be detected by a security procedure. Although the receiving bank is not obliged to provide a security procedure for the detection of error, if such a procedure is agreed to by the bank Section 4A–205 provides that if the error is not detected because the receiving bank does not comply with the procedure, any resulting loss is borne by the bank failing to comply with the security procedure.

Insolvency losses.

Some payment orders do not involve the granting of credit to the sender by the receiving bank. In those cases, the receiving bank accepts the sender's order at the same time the bank receives payment of the order. This is true of a transfer of funds by Fedwire or of cases in which the receiving bank can debit a funded account of the sender. But in some cases the granting of credit is the norm. This is true of a payment order over CHIPS. In a CHIPS transaction the receiving bank usually will accept the order before receiving payment from the sending bank. Payment is delayed until the end of the day when settlement is made through the Federal Reserve System. If the receiving bank is an intermediary bank, it will accept by issuing a payment order to another bank and the intermediary bank is obliged to pay that payment order. If the receiving bank is the beneficiary's bank, the bank usually will accept by releasing funds to the beneficiary before the bank has received payment. If a sending bank suspends payments before settling its liabilities at the end of the day, the financial stability of banks that are net creditors of the insolvent bank may also be put into jeopardy, because the dollar volume of funds transfers between the banks may be extremely large. With respect to two banks that are dealing with each other in a series of transactions in which each bank is sometimes a receiving bank and sometimes a sender, the risk of insolvency can be managed if amounts payable as a sender and amounts receivable as a receiving bank are roughly equal. But if these amounts are significantly out of balance, a net creditor bank may have a very significant credit risk during the day before settlement occurs. The Federal Reserve System and the banking community are greatly concerned with this risk, and various measures have been instituted to reduce this credit exposure. Article 4A also addresses this problem. A receiving bank can always avoid this risk by delaying acceptance of a payment order until after the bank has received payment. For example, if the beneficiary's bank credits the beneficiary's account it can avoid acceptance by not notifying the beneficiary of the receipt of the order or by notifying the beneficiary that the credit may not be withdrawn until the beneficiary's bank receives payment. But if the beneficiary's bank releases funds to the beneficiary before receiving settlement, the result in a funds transfer other than a transfer by means of an automated clearing house or similar provisional settlement system is that the beneficiary's bank may not recover the funds if it fails to receive settlement. This rule encourages the banking system to impose credit limitations on banks that issue payment orders. These limitations are already in effect. CHIPS has also proposed a loss-sharing plan to be adopted for implementation in the second half of 1990 under which CHIPS participants will be required to provide funds necessary to complete settlement of the obligations of one or more participants that are unable to meet settlement obligations. Under this plan, it will be a virtual certainty that there will be settlement on CHIPS in the event of failure by a single bank. Section 4A–403(b) and (c) are also addressed to reducing risks of insolvency. Under these provisions the amount owed by a failed bank with respect to payment orders it issued is the net amount owing after setting off amounts owed to the failed bank with respect to payment orders it received. This rule allows credit exposure to be managed by limitations on the net debit position of a bank.

International transfers.

The major international legal document dealing with the subject of electronic funds transfers is the Model Law on International Credit Transfers adopted in 1992 by the United Nations Commission on

International Trade Law. It covers basically the same type of transaction as does Article 4A, although it requires the funds transferred to have an international component. The Model Law and Article 4A basically live together in harmony, but to the extent there are differences they must be recognized and, to the extent possible, avoided or adjusted by agreement. See PEB Commentary No. 13, ~~dated February 16, 1994~~.

As amended in 1994 and 2022.

PART 1

SUBJECT MATTER AND DEFINITIONS

§ 4A–101. Short Title.

This Article may be cited as Uniform Commercial Code—Funds Transfers.

§ 4A–102. Subject Matter.

Except as otherwise provided in Section 4A–108, this Article applies to funds transfers defined in Section 4A–104.

Official Comment

Article 4A governs a specialized method of payment referred to in the Article as a funds transfer but also commonly referred to in the commercial community as a wholesale wire transfer. A funds transfer is made by means of one or more payment orders. The scope of Article 4A is determined by the definitions of "payment order" and "funds transfer" found in Section 4A–103 and Section 4A–104.

The funds transfer governed by Article 4A is in large part a product of recent and developing technological changes. Before this Article was drafted there was no comprehensive body of law—statutory or judicial—that defined the juridical nature of a funds transfer or the rights and obligations flowing from payment orders. Judicial authority with respect to funds transfers is sparse, undeveloped and not uniform. Judges have had to resolve disputes by referring to general principles of common law or equity, or they have sought guidance in statutes such as Article 4 which are applicable to other payment methods. But attempts to define rights and obligations in funds transfers by general principles or by analogy to rights and obligations in negotiable instrument law or the law of check collection have not been satisfactory.

In the drafting of Article 4A, a deliberate decision was made to write on a clean slate and to treat a funds transfer as a unique method of payment to be governed by unique rules that address the particular issues raised by this method of payment. A deliberate decision was also made to use precise and detailed rules to assign responsibility, define behavioral norms, allocate risks and establish limits on liability, rather than to rely on broadly stated, flexible principles. In the drafting of these rules, a critical consideration was that the various parties to funds transfers need to be able to predict risk with certainty, to insure against risk, to adjust operational and security procedures, and to price funds transfer services appropriately. This consideration is particularly important given the very large amounts of money that are involved in funds transfers.

Funds transfers involve competing interests—those of the banks that provide funds transfer services and the commercial and financial organizations that use the services, as well as the public interest. These competing interests were represented in the drafting process and they were thoroughly considered. The rules that emerged represent a careful and delicate balancing of those interests and are intended to be the exclusive means of determining the rights, duties and liabilities of the affected parties in any situation covered by particular provisions of the Article. Consequently, resort to principles of law or equity outside of Article 4A is not appropriate to create rights, duties and liabilities inconsistent with those stated in this Article.

§ 4A–103. Payment Order—Definitions.

(a) In this Article:

(1) "Payment order" means an instruction of a sender to a receiving bank, transmitted orally, ~~electronically, or in writing~~ or in a record, to pay, or to cause another bank to pay, a fixed or determinable amount of money to a beneficiary if:

    (i)   the instruction does not state a condition to payment to the beneficiary other than time of payment,

    (ii)   the receiving bank is to be reimbursed by debiting an account of, or otherwise receiving payment from, the sender, and

    (iii)   the instruction is transmitted by the sender directly to the receiving bank or to an agent, funds-transfer system, or communication system for transmittal to the receiving bank.

  (2)   "Beneficiary" means the person to be paid by the beneficiary's bank.

  (3)   "Beneficiary's bank" means the bank identified in a payment order in which an account of the beneficiary is to be credited pursuant to the order or which otherwise is to make payment to the beneficiary if the order does not provide for payment to an account.

  (4)   "Receiving bank" means the bank to which the sender's instruction is addressed.

  (5)   "Sender" means the person giving the instruction to the receiving bank.

  (b)   If an instruction complying with subsection (a)(1) is to make more than one payment to a beneficiary, the instruction is a separate payment order with respect to each payment.

  (c)   A payment order is issued when it is sent to the receiving bank.

As amended in 2022.

Official Comment

  <u>1.</u>   This section is discussed in the Comment following Section 4A–104.

  <u>2.   Pursuant to the Uniform Commercial Code Amendments (2022) and in furtherance of medium neutrality, the reference to "electronically, or in writing" in the pre-2022 text of this section has been changed to refer to "in a record."</u>

As amended in 2022.

§ 4A–104. Funds Transfer—Definitions.

In this Article:

  (a)   "Funds transfer" means the series of transactions, beginning with the originator's payment order, made for the purpose of making payment to the beneficiary of the order. The term includes any payment order issued by the originator's bank or an intermediary bank intended to carry out the originator's payment order. A funds transfer is completed by acceptance by the beneficiary's bank of a payment order for the benefit of the beneficiary of the originator's payment order.

  (b)   "Intermediary bank" means a receiving bank other than the originator's bank or the beneficiary's bank.

  (c)   "Originator" means the sender of the first payment order in a funds transfer.

  (d)   "Originator's bank" means (i) the receiving bank to which the payment order of the originator is issued if the originator is not a bank, or (ii) the originator if the originator is a bank.

Official Comment

  1.   Article 4A governs a method of payment in which the person making payment (the "originator") directly transmits an instruction to a bank either to make payment to the person receiving payment (the "beneficiary") or to instruct some other bank to make payment to the beneficiary. The payment from the originator to the beneficiary occurs when the bank that is to pay the beneficiary becomes obligated to pay the beneficiary. There are two basic definitions: "Payment order" stated in Section 4A–103 and "Funds transfer" stated in Section 4A–104. These definitions, other related definitions, and the scope of Article 4A can best be understood in the context of specific fact situations. Consider the following cases:

    Case # 1. X, which has an account in Bank A, instructs that bank to pay $1,000,000 to Y's account in Bank A. Bank A carries out X's instruction by making a credit of $1,000,000 to Y's account and notifying Y that the credit is available for immediate withdrawal. The instruction by X to Bank A is a "payment order" which was issued when it was sent to Bank A. Section 4A–103(a)(1) and (c). X is the "sender" of the payment order and Bank A is the "receiving bank." Section 4A–103(a)(5) and (a)(4). Y is the "beneficiary" of the payment order and Bank A is the "beneficiary's bank." Section 4A–103(a)(2) and (a)(3). When Bank A notified Y of receipt of the payment order, Bank A "accepted" the payment order. Section 4A–209(b)(1). When Bank A accepted the order it incurred an obligation to Y to pay the amount of the order. Section 4A–404(a). When Bank A accepted X's order, X incurred an obligation to pay Bank A the amount of the order. Section 4A–402(b). Payment from X to Bank A would normally be made by a debit to X's account in Bank A. Section 4A–403(a)(3). At the time Bank A incurred the obligation to pay Y, payment of $1,000,000 by X to Y was also made. Section 4A–406(a). Bank A paid Y when it gave notice to Y of a withdrawable credit of $1,000,000 to Y's account. Section 4A–405(a). The overall transaction, which comprises the acts of X and Bank A, in which the payment by X to Y is accomplished is referred to as the "funds transfer." Section 4A–104(a). In this case only one payment order was involved in the funds transfer. A one-payment-order funds transfer is usually referred to as a "book transfer" because the payment is accomplished by the receiving bank's debiting the account of the sender and crediting the account of the beneficiary in the same bank. X, in addition to being the sender of the payment order to Bank A, is the "originator" of the funds transfer. Section 4A–104(c). Bank A is the "originator's bank" in the funds transfer as well as the beneficiary's bank. Section 4A–104(d).

Case # 2. Assume the same facts as in Case # 1 except that X instructs Bank A to pay $1,000,000 to Y's account in Bank B. With respect to this payment order, X is the sender, Y is the beneficiary, and Bank A is the receiving bank. Bank A carries out X's order by instructing Bank B to pay $1,000,000 to Y's account. This instruction is a payment order in which Bank A is the sender, Bank B is the receiving bank, and Y is the beneficiary. When Bank A issued its payment order to Bank B, Bank A "executed" X's order. Section 4A–301(a). In the funds transfer, X is the originator, Bank A is the originator's bank, and Bank B is the beneficiary's bank. When Bank A executed X's order, X incurred an obligation to pay Bank A the amount of the order. Section 4A–402(c). When Bank B accepts the payment order issued to it by Bank A, Bank B incurs an obligation to Y to pay the amount of the order (Section 4A–404(a)) and Bank A incurs an obligation to pay Bank B. Section 4A–402(b). Acceptance by Bank B also results in payment of $1,000,000 by X to Y. Section 4A–406(a). In this case two payment orders are involved in the funds transfer.

Case # 3. Assume the same facts as in Case # 2 except that Bank A does not execute X's payment order by issuing a payment order to Bank B. One bank will not normally act to carry out a funds transfer for another bank unless there is a preexisting arrangement between the banks for transmittal of payment orders and settlement of accounts. For example, if Bank B is a foreign bank with which Bank A has no relationship, Bank A can utilize a bank that is a correspondent of both Bank A and Bank B. Assume Bank A issues a payment order to Bank C to pay $1,000,000 to Y's account in Bank B. With respect to this order, Bank A is the sender, Bank C is the receiving bank, and Y is the beneficiary. Bank C will execute the payment order of Bank A by issuing a payment order to Bank B to pay $1,000,000 to Y's account in Bank B. With respect to Bank C's payment order, Bank C is the sender, Bank B is the receiving bank, and Y is the beneficiary. Payment of $1,000,000 by X to Y occurs when Bank B accepts the payment order issued to it by Bank C. In this case the funds transfer involves three payment orders. In the funds transfer, X is the originator, Bank A is the originator's bank, Bank B is the beneficiary's bank, and Bank C is an "intermediary bank." Section 4A–104(b). In some cases there may be more than one intermediary bank, and in those cases each intermediary bank is treated like Bank C in Case # 3.

As the three cases demonstrate, a payment under Article 4A involves an overall transaction, the funds transfer, in which the originator, X, is making payment to the beneficiary, Y, but the funds transfer may encompass a series of payment orders that are issued in order to effect the payment initiated by the originator's payment order.

In some cases the originator and the beneficiary may be the same person. This will occur, for example, when a corporation orders a bank to transfer funds from an account of the corporation in that bank to another account of the corporation in that bank or in some other bank. In some funds transfers the first bank to issue a payment order is a bank that is executing a payment order of a customer that is not a bank. In this case the customer is the originator. In other cases, the first bank to issue a payment order is not acting for a customer, but is making a payment for its own account. In that event the first bank to issue a payment order is the originator as well as the originator's bank.

2. "Payment order" is defined in Section 4A–103(a)(1) as an instruction to a bank to pay, or to cause another bank to pay, a fixed or determinable amount of money. The bank to which the instruction is addressed is known as the "receiving bank." Section 4A–103(a)(4). "Bank" is defined in Section 4A–105(a)(2). The effect of this definition is to limit Article 4A to payments made through the banking system. A transfer of funds made by an entity outside the banking system is excluded. A transfer of funds through an entity other than a bank is usually

a consumer transaction involving relatively small amounts of money and a single contract carried out by transfers of cash or a cash equivalent such as a check. Typically, the transferor delivers cash or a check to the company making the transfer, which agrees to pay a like amount to a person designated by the transferor. Transactions covered by Article 4A typically involve very large amounts of money in which several transactions involving several banks may be necessary to carry out the payment. Payments are normally made by debits or credits to bank accounts. Originators and beneficiaries are almost always business organizations and the transfers are usually made to pay obligations. Moreover, these transactions are frequently done on the basis of very short-term credit granted by the receiving bank to the sender of the payment order. Wholesale wire transfers involve policy questions that are distinct from those involved in consumer-based transactions by nonbanks.

3.   Further limitations on the scope of Article 4A are found in the three requirements found in subparagraphs (i), (ii), and (iii) of Section 4A–103(a)(1). Subparagraph (i) states that the instruction to pay is a payment order only if it "does not state a condition to payment to the beneficiary other than time of payment." An instruction to pay a beneficiary sometimes is subject to a requirement that the beneficiary perform some act such as delivery of documents.

For eExample: aA New York bank may have issued a letter of credit in favor of X, a California seller of goods to be shipped to the New York bank's customer in New York. The terms of the letter of credit provide for payment to X if documents are presented to prove shipment of the goods. Instead of providing for presentment of the documents to the New York bank, the letter of credit states that they may be presented to a California bank that acts as an agent for payment. The New York bank sends an instruction to the California bank to pay X upon presentation of the required documents. The instruction is not covered by Article 4A because payment to the beneficiary is conditional upon receipt of shipping documents. The function of banks in a funds transfer under Article 4A is comparable to the role of banks in the collection and payment of checks in that it is essentially mechanical in nature. The low price and high speed that characterize funds transfers reflect this fact. Conditions to payment by the California bank other than time of payment impose responsibilities on that bank that go beyond those in Article 4A funds transfers. Although the payment by the New York bank to X under the letter of credit is not covered by Article 4A, if X is paid by the California bank, payment of the obligation of the New York bank to reimburse the California bank could be made by an Article 4A funds transfer. In such a case there is a distinction between the payment by the New York bank to X under the letter of credit and the payment by the New York bank to the California bank. For example, if the New York bank pays its reimbursement obligation to the California bank by a Fedwire naming the California bank as beneficiary (see Comment 1 to Section 4A–107), payment is made to the California bank rather than to X. That payment is governed by Article 4A and it could be made either before or after payment by the California bank to X. The payment by the New York bank to X under the letter of credit is not governed by Article 4A and it occurs when the California bank, as agent of the New York bank, pays X. No payment order was involved in that transaction. In this example, if the New York bank had erroneously sent an instruction to the California bank unconditionally instructing payment to X, the instruction would have been an Article 4A payment order. If the payment order was accepted (Section 4A–209(b)) by the California bank, a payment by the New York bank to X would have resulted (Section 4A–406(a)). But Article 4A would not prevent recovery of funds from X on the basis that X was not entitled to retain the funds under the law of mistake and restitution, letter of credit law or other applicable law.

An instruction to pay might be a component of a computer program or a transaction protocol intended to execute automatically under specified circumstances. The fact that the program or protocol itself is subject to a condition does not necessarily mean that an instruction to pay issued pursuant to that program or protocol "state[s] a condition to payment of the beneficiary" within the meaning of Section 4A–103(a)(1)(i). Whether the instruction does state such a condition depends on what the instruction says when it is received by the receiving bank. An instruction that neither grants discretion nor imposes a limitation on payment by the receiving bank does not state a condition to payment. What distinguishes the prior example is that the New York bank's instruction to the California bank did state a condition when the California bank received it.

Similarly, an instruction that is subject to a condition when received by Bank A, and which therefore does not constitute a payment order, does not become a payment order when the condition is satisfied. However, if, after the condition is satisfied, Bank A sends the instruction to Bank B without the stated condition, that second instruction could be a payment order if the instruction otherwise complies with Section 4A–103(a).

4.   Transfers of funds made through the banking system are commonly referred to as either "credit" transfers or "debit" transfers. In a credit transfer the instruction to pay is given by the person making payment. In a debit transfer the instruction to pay is given by the person receiving payment. The purpose of subparagraph (ii) of subsection (a)(1) of Section 4A–103 is to include credit transfers in Article 4A and to exclude debit transfers.

All of the instructions to pay in the three cases described in Comment 1 fall within subparagraph (ii). Take Case # 2 as an example. With respect to X's instruction given to Bank A, Bank A will be reimbursed by debiting X's account or otherwise receiving payment from X. With respect to Bank A's instruction to Bank B, Bank B will be reimbursed by receiving payment from Bank A. In a debit transfer, a creditor, pursuant to authority from the debtor, is enabled to draw on the debtor's bank account by issuing an instruction to pay to the debtor's bank. If the debtor's bank pays, it will be reimbursed by the debtor rather than by the person giving the instruction. For example, the holder of an insurance policy may pay premiums by authorizing the insurance company to order the policyholder's bank to pay the insurance company. The order to pay may be in the form of a draft covered by Article 3, or it might be an instruction to pay that is not an instrument under that Article. The bank receives reimbursement by debiting the policyholder's account. Or, a subsidiary corporation may make payments to its parent by authorizing the parent to order the subsidiary's bank to pay the parent from the subsidiary's account. These transactions are not covered by Article 4A because subparagraph (2) is not satisfied. Article 4A is limited to transactions in which the account to be debited by the receiving bank is that of the person in whose name the instruction is given.

If the beneficiary of a funds transfer is the originator of the transfer, the transfer is governed by Article 4A if it is a credit transfer in form. If it is in the form of a debit transfer it is not governed by Article 4A. For example, Corporation has accounts in Bank A and Bank B. Corporation instructs Bank A to pay to Corporation's account in Bank B. The funds transfer is governed by Article 4A. Sometimes, Corporation will authorize Bank B to draw on Corporation's account in Bank A for the purpose of transferring funds into Corporation's account in Bank B. If Corporation also makes an agreement with Bank A under which Bank A is authorized to follow instructions of Bank B, as agent of Corporation, to transfer funds from Customer's account in Bank A, the instruction of Bank B is a payment order of Customer and is governed by Article 4A. This kind of transaction is known in the wire-transfer business as a "drawdown transfer." If Corporation does not make such an agreement with Bank A and Bank B instructs Bank A to make the transfer, the order is in form a debit transfer and is not governed by Article 4A. These debit transfers are normally ACH transactions in which Bank A relies on Bank B's warranties pursuant to ACH rules, including the warranty that the transfer is authorized.

5. The principal effect of subparagraph (iii) of subsection (a) of Section 4A–103 is to exclude from Article 4A payments made by check or credit card. In those cases the instruction of the debtor to the bank on which the check is drawn or to which the credit card slip is to be presented is contained in the check or credit card slip signed by the debtor. The instruction is not transmitted by the debtor directly to the debtor's bank. Rather, the instruction is delivered or otherwise transmitted by the debtor to the creditor who then presents it to the bank either directly or through bank collection channels. These payments are governed by Articles 3 and 4 and federal law. There are, however, limited instances in which the paper on which a check is printed can be used as the means of transmitting a payment order that is covered by Article 4A. Assume that Originator instructs Originator's Bank to pay $10,000 to the account of Beneficiary in Beneficiary's Bank. Since the amount of Originator's payment order is small, if Originator's Bank and Beneficiary's Bank do not have an account relationship, Originator's Bank may execute Originator's order by issuing a teller's check payable to Beneficiary's Bank for $10,000 along with instructions to credit Beneficiary's account in that amount. The instruction to Beneficiary's Bank to credit Beneficiary's account is a payment order. The check is the means by which Originator's Bank pays its obligation as sender of the payment order. The instruction of Originator's Bank to Beneficiary's Bank might be given in a letter accompanying the check or it may be written on the check itself. In either case the instruction to Beneficiary's Bank is a payment order but the check itself (which is an order to pay addressed to the drawee rather than to Beneficiary's Bank) is an instrument under Article 3 and is not a payment order. The check can be both the means by which Originator's Bank pays its obligation under § 4A–402(b) to Beneficiary's Bank and the means by which the instruction to Beneficiary's Bank is transmitted.

6. Most payments covered by Article 4A are commonly referred to as wire transfers and usually involve some kind of electronic transmission, but the applicability of Article 4A does not depend upon the means used to transmit the instruction of the sender. Transmission may be by letter or other written communication, oral communication or electronic communication. An oral communication is normally given by telephone. Frequently the message is recorded by the receiving bank to provide evidence of the transaction, but apart from problems of proof there is no need to record the oral instruction. Transmission of an instruction may be a direct communication between the sender and the receiving bank or through an intermediary such as an agent of the sender, a communication system such as international cable, or a funds transfer system such as CHIPS, SWIFT or an automated clearing house.

As amended in 2022.

§ 4A-105.   Other Definitions.

(a)   In this Article:

(1)   "Authorized account" means a deposit account of a customer in a bank designated by the customer as a source of payment of payment orders issued by the customer to the bank. If a customer does not so designate an account, any account of the customer is an authorized account if payment of a payment order from that account is not inconsistent with a restriction on the use of that account.

(2)   "Bank" means a person engaged in the business of banking and includes a savings bank, savings and loan association, credit union, and trust company. A branch or separate office of a bank is a separate bank for purposes of this Article.

(3)   "Customer" means a person, including a bank, having an account with a bank or from whom a bank has agreed to receive payment orders.

(4)   "Funds-transfer business day" of a receiving bank means the part of a day during which the receiving bank is open for the receipt, processing, and transmittal of payment orders and cancellations and amendments of payment orders.

(5)   "Funds-transfer system" means a wire transfer network, automated clearing house, or other communication system of a clearing house or other association of banks through which a payment order by a bank may be transmitted to the bank to which the order is addressed.

(6)   [Reserved.] ["Good faith" means honesty in fact and the observance of reasonable commercial standards of fair dealing.] [*Note from West Advisory Panel: This subsection will be deleted if the jurisdiction adopts the definition of good faith in revised Article 1.*]

(7)   "Prove" with respect to a fact means to meet the burden of establishing the fact (Section 1–201(b)(8)).

(b)   Other definitions applying to this Article and the sections in which they appear are:

"Acceptance" Section 4A–209
"Beneficiary" Section 4A–103
"Beneficiary's bank" Section 4A–103
"Executed" Section 4A–301
"Execution date" Section 4A–301
"Funds transfer" Section 4A–104
"Funds-transfer system rule" Section 4A–501
"Intermediary bank" Section 4A–104
"Originator" Section 4A–104
"Originator's bank" Section 4A–104
"Payment by beneficiary's bank to beneficiary" Section 4A–405
"Payment by originator to beneficiary" Section 4A–406
"Payment by sender to receiving bank" Section 4A–403
"Payment date" Section 4A–401
"Payment order" Section 4A–103
"Receiving bank" Section 4A–103
"Security procedure" Section 4A–201
"Sender" Section 4A–103

(c)   The following definitions in Article 4 apply to this Article:

"Clearing house" Section 4–104
"Item" Section 4–104
"Suspends payments" Section 4–104

(d)   In addition Article 1 contains general definitions and principles of construction and interpretation applicable throughout this Article.

As amended in 2001.

1.   The definition of "bank" in subsection (a)(2) includes some institutions that are not commercial banks. The definition reflects the fact that many financial institutions now perform functions previously restricted to commercial banks, including acting on behalf of customers in funds transfers. Since many funds transfers involve payment orders to or from foreign countries the definition also covers foreign banks. The definition also includes Federal Reserve Banks. Funds transfers carried out by Federal Reserve Banks are described in Comments 1 and 2 to Section 4A–107.

2.   Funds transfer business is frequently transacted by banks outside of general banking hours. Thus, the definition of banking day in Section 4–104(1)(c) cannot be used to describe when a bank is open for funds transfer business. Subsection (a)(4) defines a new term, "funds transfer business day," which is applicable to Article 4A. The definition states, "is open for the receipt, processing, and transmittal of payment orders and cancellations and amendments of payment orders." In some cases it is possible to electronically transmit payment orders and other communications to a receiving bank at any time. If the receiving bank is not open for the processing of an order when it is received, the communication is stored in the receiving bank's computer for retrieval when the receiving bank is open for processing. The use of the conjunctive makes clear that the defined term is limited to the period during which all functions of the receiving bank can be performed, i.e., receipt, processing, and transmittal of payment orders, cancellations and amendments.

3.   Subsection (a)(5) defines "funds transfer system." The term includes a system such as CHIPS which provides for transmission of a payment order as well as settlement of the obligation of the sender to pay the order. It also includes automated clearing houses, operated by a clearing house or other association of banks, which process and transmit payment orders of banks to other banks. In addition the term includes organizations that provide only transmission services such as SWIFT. The definition also includes the wire transfer network and automated clearing houses of Federal Reserve Banks. Systems of the Federal Reserve Banks, however, are treated differently from systems of other associations of banks. Funds transfer systems other than systems of the Federal Reserve Banks are treated in Article 4A as a means of communication of payment orders between participating banks. Section 4A–206. The Comment to that section and the Comment to Section 4A–107 explain how Federal Reserve Banks function under Article 4A. Funds transfer systems are also able to promulgate rules binding on participating banks that, under Section 4A–501, may supplement or in some cases may even override provisions of Article 4A.

4.   Subsection (d) incorporates definitions stated in Article 1 as well as principles of construction and interpretation stated in that Article. Included is Section 1–103. The last paragraph of the Comment to Section 4A–102 is addressed to the issue of the extent to which general principles of law and equity should apply to situations covered by provisions of Article 4A.

§ 4A–106.   Time Payment Order Is Received.

(a)   The time of receipt of a payment order or communication cancelling or amending a payment order is determined by the rules applicable to receipt of a notice stated in Section 1–202. A receiving bank may fix a cut-off time or times on a funds-transfer business day for the receipt and processing of payment orders and communications cancelling or amending payment orders. Different cut-off times may apply to payment orders, cancellations, or amendments, or to different categories of payment orders, cancellations, or amendments. A cut-off time may apply to senders generally or different cut-off times may apply to different senders or categories of payment orders. If a payment order or communication cancelling or amending a payment order is received after the close of a funds-transfer business day or after the appropriate cut-off time on a funds-transfer business day, the receiving bank may treat the payment order or communication as received at the opening of the next funds-transfer business day.

(b)   If this Article refers to an execution date or payment date or states a day on which a receiving bank is required to take action, and the date or day does not fall on a funds-transfer business day, the next day that is a funds-transfer business day is treated as the date or day stated, unless the contrary is stated in this Article.

As amended in 2001.

Official Comment

The time that a payment order is received by a receiving bank usually defines the payment date or the execution date of a payment order. Section 4A–401 and Section 4A–301. The time of receipt of a payment order, or communication cancelling or amending a payment order is defined in subsection (a) by reference to the rules stated in Section 1–202. Thus, time of receipt is determined by the same rules that determine when a notice is received. Time of receipt, however, may be altered by a cut-off time.

As amended in 2001.

§ 4A–107. Federal Reserve Regulations and Operating Circulars.

Regulations of the Board of Governors of the Federal Reserve System and operating circulars of the Federal Reserve Banks supersede any inconsistent provision of this Article to the extent of the inconsistency.

Official Comment

1.   Funds transfers under Article 4A may be made, in whole or in part, by payment orders through a Federal Reserve Bank in what is usually referred to as a transfer by Fedwire. If Bank A, which has an account in Federal Reserve Bank X, wants to pay $1,000,000 to Bank B, which has an account in Federal Reserve Bank Y, Bank A can issue an instruction to Reserve Bank X requesting a debit of $1,000,000 to Bank A's Reserve account and an equal credit to Bank B's Reserve account. Reserve Bank X will debit Bank A's account and will credit the account of Reserve Bank Y. Reserve Bank X will issue an instruction to Reserve Bank Y requesting a debit of $1,000,000 to the account of Reserve Bank X and an equal credit to Bank B's account in Reserve Bank Y. Reserve Bank Y will make the requested debit and credit and will give Bank B an advice of credit. The definition of "bank" in Section 4A–105(a)(2) includes both Reserve Bank X and Reserve Bank Y. Bank A's instruction to Reserve Bank X to pay money to Bank B is a payment order under Section 4A–103(a)(1). Bank A is the sender and Reserve Bank X is the receiving bank. Bank B is the beneficiary of Bank A's order and of the funds transfer. Bank A is the originator of the funds transfer and is also the originator's bank. Section 4A–104(c) and (d). Reserve Bank X, an intermediary bank under Section 4A–104(b), executes Bank A's order by sending a payment order to Reserve Bank Y instructing that bank to credit the Federal Reserve account of Bank B. Reserve Bank Y is the beneficiary's bank.

Suppose the transfer of funds from Bank A to Bank B is part of a larger transaction in which Originator, a customer of Bank A, wants to pay Beneficiary, a customer of Bank B. Originator issues a payment order to Bank A to pay $1,000,000 to the account of Beneficiary in Bank B. Bank A may execute Originator's order by means of Fedwire which simultaneously transfers $1,000,000 from Bank A to Bank B and carries a message instructing Bank B to pay $1,000,000 to the account of Y. The Fedwire transfer is carried out as described in the previous paragraph, except that the beneficiary of the funds transfer is Beneficiary rather than Bank B. Reserve Bank X and Reserve Bank Y are intermediary banks. When Reserve Bank Y advises Bank B of the credit to its Federal Reserve account it will also instruct Bank B to pay to the account of Beneficiary. The instruction is a payment order to Bank B which is the beneficiary's bank. When Reserve Bank Y advises Bank B of the credit to its Federal Reserve account Bank B receives payment of the payment order issued to it by Reserve Bank Y. Section 4A–403(a)(1). The payment order is automatically accepted by Bank B at the time it receives the payment order of Reserve Bank Y. Section 4A–209(b)(2). At the time of acceptance by Bank B payment by Originator to Beneficiary also occurs. Thus, in a Fedwire transfer, payment to the beneficiary's bank, acceptance by the beneficiary's bank and payment by the originator to the beneficiary all occur simultaneously by operation of law at the time the payment order to the beneficiary's bank is received.

If Originator orders payment to the account of Beneficiary in Bank C rather than Bank B, the analysis is somewhat modified. Bank A may not have any relationship with Bank C and may not be able to make payment directly to Bank C. In that case, Bank A could send a Fedwire instructing Bank B to instruct Bank C to pay Beneficiary. The analysis is the same as the previous case except that Bank B is an intermediary bank and Bank C is the beneficiary's bank.

2.   A funds transfer can also be made through a Federal Reserve Bank in an automated clearing house transaction. In a typical case, Originator instructs Originator's Bank to pay to the account of Beneficiary in Beneficiary's Bank. Originator's instruction to pay a particular beneficiary is transmitted to Originator's Bank along with many other instructions for payment to other beneficiaries by many different beneficiary's banks. All of these instructions are contained in a magnetic tape or other electronic device. Transmission of instructions to the various beneficiary's banks requires that Originator's instructions be processed and repackaged with instructions of other originators so that all instructions to a particular beneficiary's bank are transmitted together to that bank. The repackaging is done in processing centers usually referred to as automated clearing houses.

Automated clearing houses are operated either by Federal Reserve Banks or by other associations of banks. If Originator's Bank chooses to execute Originator's instructions by transmitting them to a Federal Reserve Bank for processing by the Federal Reserve Bank, the transmission to the Federal Reserve Bank results in the issuance of payment orders by Originator's Bank to the Federal Reserve Bank, which is an intermediary bank. Processing by the Federal Reserve Bank will result in the issuance of payment orders by the Federal Reserve Bank to Beneficiary's Bank as well as payment orders to other beneficiary's banks making payments to carry out Originator's instructions.

3.   Although the terms of Article 4A apply to funds transfers involving Federal Reserve Banks, federal preemption would make ineffective any Article 4A provision that conflicts with federal law. The payments activities of the Federal Reserve Banks are governed by regulations of the Federal Reserve Board and by operating circulars issued by the Reserve Banks themselves. In some instances, the operating circulars are issued pursuant to a Federal Reserve Board regulation. In other cases, the Reserve Bank issues the operating circular under its own authority under the Federal Reserve Act, subject to review by the Federal Reserve Board. Section 4A–107 states that Federal Reserve Board regulations and operating circulars of the Federal Reserve Banks supersede any inconsistent provision of Article 4A to the extent of the inconsistency. Federal Reserve Board regulations, being valid exercises of regulatory authority pursuant to a federal statute, take precedence over state law if there is an inconsistency. *Childs v. Federal Reserve Bank of Dallas*, 719 F.2d 812 (5th Cir. 1983), reh. den. 724 F.2d 127 (5th Cir. 1984). Section 4A–107 treats operating circulars as having the same effect whether issued under the Reserve Bank's own authority or under a Federal Reserve Board regulation.

§ 4A–108.   Relationship to Electronic Fund Transfer Act.

(a)   Except as provided in subsection (b), this Article does not apply to a funds transfer any part of which is governed by the Electronic Fund Transfer Act of 1978 (Title XX, Public Law 95–630, 92 Stat. 3728, 15 U.S.C. sec. 1693 et. seq.) as amended from time to time.

(b)   This Article applies to a funds transfer that is a remittance transfer as defined in the Electronic Fund Transfer Act (15 U.S.C. sec. 1693o–1) as amended from time to time, unless the remittance transfer is an electronic fund transfer as defined in the Electronic Fund Transfer Act (15 U.S.C. sec. 1693a) as amended from time to time.

(c)   In a funds transfer to which this Article applies, in the event of an inconsistency between an applicable provision of this Article and an applicable provision of the Electronic Fund Transfer Act, the provision of the Electronic Fund Transfer Act governs to the extent of the inconsistency.

As amended in 2013.

Official Comment

1.   The Electronic Fund Transfer Act (EFTA), implemented by Regulation E, 12 C.F.R. Part 1005, is a federal statute that covers aspects of electronic fund transfers involving consumers. EFTA also governs remittance transfers, defined in 15 U.S.C. sec. 1693o–1, which involve transfers of funds through electronic means by consumers to recipients in another country through persons or financial institutions that provide such transfers in the normal course of their business. Not all "remittance transfers" as defined in EFTA, however, qualify as "electronic fund transfers" as defined under the EFTA, 15 U.S.C. sec. 1693a(7). While Section 4A–108(a) broadly states that Article 4A does not apply to any funds transfer that is governed in any part by EFTA, subsection (b) provides an exception. The purpose of Section 4A–108(b) is to allow this Article to apply to a funds transfer as defined in Section 4A–104(a) (see Section 4A–102) that also is a remittance transfer as defined in EFTA, so long as that remittance transfer is not an electronic fund transfer as defined in EFTA. If the resulting application of this Article to an EFTA-defined "remittance transfer" that is not an EFTA-defined "electronic fund transfer" creates an inconsistency between an applicable provision of this Article and an applicable provision of EFTA, then, as a matter of federal supremacy, the provision of EFTA governs to the extent of the inconsistency. Section 4A–108(c). Of course, in the case of a funds transfer that also relates to another jurisdiction, the forum's conflict of laws principles determine whether it will apply the law in effect in this State (including this Article and EFTA) or the law of another jurisdiction to all or any part of the funds transfer. See Section 4A–507.

2.   The following cases illustrate the relationship between EFTA and this Article pursuant to Section 4A–108.

Case # 1. A commercial customer of Bank A sends a payment order to Bank A, instructing Bank A to transfer funds from its account at Bank A to the account of a consumer at Bank B. The funds transfer is executed by a payment order from Bank A to an intermediary bank and is executed by the intermediary bank by means of an automated clearinghouse credit entry to the consumer's account at Bank B (the beneficiary's bank). The transfer into the consumer's account is an "electronic fund transfer" as defined in 15 U.S.C. sec. 1693a(7). Pursuant to Section 4A–108(a), Article 4A does not apply to any part of the funds transfer because EFTA governs part of the funds transfer. The transfer is not a "remittance transfer" as defined in 15 U.S.C. sec. 1693o–1 because the originator is not a consumer customer. Thus Section 4A–108(b) does not apply.

A court might, however, apply appropriate principles from Article 4A by analogy in analyzing any part of the funds transfer that is not subject to the provisions of EFTA or other law, such as the obligation of the intermediary bank to execute the payment order of the originator's bank (Section 4A–302), or whether the payment order of the commercial customer to Bank A is authorized or verified (Sections 4A–202 and 4A–203).

Case # 2. A consumer originates a payment order that is a remittance transfer as defined in 15 U.S.C. sec. 1693o–1 and provides the remittance transfer provider (Bank A) with cash in the amount of the transfer plus any relevant fees. The funds transfer is routed through an intermediary bank for final credit to the designated recipient's account at Bank B. Bank A's payment order identifies the designated recipient by both name and account number in Bank B, but the name and number provided identify different persons. This remittance transfer is not an "electronic fund transfer" as defined in 15 U.S.C. sec. 1693a(7) because it is not initiated by electronic means from a consumer's account, but does qualify as a "funds transfer" as defined in Section 4A–104. Both Article 4A and EFTA apply to the funds transfer. Sections 4A–102, 4A–108(a), (b). Article 4A's provision on mistakes in identifying the designated beneficiary, Section 4A–207, would apply as long as not inconsistent with the governing EFTA provisions. See 15 U.S.C. Sec. 1693o–1(d), Section 4A–108(c). See Comment 1 to this Section.

Case # 3. A consumer originates a payment order from the consumer's account at Bank A to the designated recipient's account at Bank B located outside the United States. Bank A uses the CHIPS system to execute that payment order. The funds transfer is a "remittance transfer" as defined in 15 U.S.C. sec. 1693o–1. This transfer is not an "electronic fund transfer" as defined in 15 U.S.C. Sec. 1693a(7) because of the exclusion for transfers through systems such as CHIPS in 15 U.S.C. Sec. 1693a(7)(B), but qualifies as a "funds transfer" as defined in Section 4A–104. Under Sections 4A–102 and 4A–108(b), both Article 4A and EFTA apply to the funds transfer. The EFTA will prevail to the extent of any inconsistency between EFTA and Article 4A. Section 4A–108(c). See Comment 1 to this Section. For example, if the consumer subsequently exercises a right under EFTA to cancel the remittance transfer and obtain a refund, Bank A would be required to comply with the EFTA rule even if Article 4A prevents Bank A from cancelling or reversing the payment order that Bank A sent to its receiving bank. Section 4A–211.

Case # 4. A person fraudulently originates an unauthorized payment order from a consumer's account through use of an online banking interface and the payment order is executed using a system that qualifies the transaction as an "electronic fund transfer" under EFTA. The funds transfer that results from execution of the unauthorized payment order is not governed by Article 4A. Section 4A–108(a). Whether the funds transfer also qualifies as a "remittance transfer" under EFTA has no bearing on the application of Article 4A.

Case # 5. A person fraudulently originates an unauthorized payment order from a consumer's account at Bank A through forging written documents that are provided in person to an employee of Bank A. This transaction is not an "electronic fund transfer" as defined in 15 U.S.C. Sec. 1693a(7) because it was not initiated by electronic means, but qualifies as a "funds transfer" as defined in Section 4A–104. Article 4A applies regardless of whether the funds transfer also qualifies as a "remittance transfer" under 15 U.S.C. sec. 1693o–1. If the funds transfer is not a remittance transfer, the provisions of Section 4A–108 are not implicated because the funds transfer does not fall under EFTA, and the general scope provision of Article 4A governs. Section 4A–102. If the funds transfer is a remittance transfer, and thus governed by EFTA, Section 4A–108(b) provides that Article 4A also applies. The provisions of Article 4A allocate the loss arising from the unauthorized payment order as long as those provisions are not inconsistent with the provisions of the EFTA applicable to remittance transfers. See 15 U.S.C. Sec. 1693o–1, Section 4A–108(c). See Comment 1 to this Section.

3.   Regulation J, 12 C.F.R. Part 210, of the Federal Reserve Board addresses the application of that regulation and EFTA to fund transfers made through Fedwire. Fedwire transfers are further described in Official Comments 1 and 2 to Section 4A–107. In addition, funds transfer system rules may be applicable pursuant to Section 4A–501.

Legislative Note: The reference to EFTA "as amended from time to time" means that the operation of this section at any particular time after enactment may depend on federal legislative action occurring after enactment. In states in which such an arrangement may constitute improper delegation, the language "as amended from time to time" may be deleted. In that case, however, the legislature should consider other mechanisms to assure that this section continues to operate harmoniously with EFTA as it may be subsequently amended.

PART 2

ISSUE AND ACCEPTANCE OF PAYMENT ORDER

§ 4A–201. Security Procedure.

"Security procedure" means a procedure established by agreement of a customer and a receiving bank for the purpose of (i) verifying that a payment order or communication amending or cancelling a payment order is that of the customer, or (ii) detecting error in the transmission or the content of the payment order or communication. A security procedure may impose an obligation on the receiving bank or the customer and may require the use of algorithms or other codes, identifying words, or numbers, symbols, sounds, biometrics, encryption, callback procedures, or similar security devices. Comparison of a signature on a payment order or communication with an authorized specimen signature of the customer or requiring a payment order to be sent from a known email address, IP address, or telephone number is not by itself a security procedure.

As amended in 2022.

Official Comment

1.   A large percentage of payment orders and communications amending or cancelling payment orders are transmitted electronically and it is standard practice to use security procedures that are designed to assure the authenticity of the message through steps designed to assure the identity of the sender, the integrity of the message, or both. Security procedures can also be used to detect error in the content of messages or to detect payment orders that are transmitted by mistake as in the case of multiple transmission of the same payment order. Security procedures might also apply to communications that are transmitted by telephone or in writing a record. Section 4A–201 defines these security procedures. The second sentence of the definition provides several examples of a security procedure, but this list is not exhaustive. The inclusion of the phrase "or similar security devices" means that, as new technologies emerge, what can be a security procedure will evolve. The definition of security procedure limits the term to a procedure "established by agreement of a customer and a receiving bank." The term does not apply to procedures that the receiving bank may follow unilaterally in processing payment orders. The question of whether loss that may result from the transmission of a spurious or erroneous payment order will be borne by the receiving bank or the sender or purported sender is affected by whether a security procedure was or was not in effect and whether there was or was not compliance with the procedure. Security procedures are referred to in Sections 4A–202 and 4A–203, which deal with authorized and verified payment orders, and Section 4A–205, which deals with erroneous payment orders.

Requiring that a payment order be sent from a known email, IP address or phone number is not by itself a "security procedure" within the meaning of this section because it is possible to make a payment order with a different origin appear to have been sent from such an address or phone number. However, requiring that a payment order have such an apparent origin in combination with other security protocols might be a security procedure.

2.   Several revisions to the pre-2022 text of this section were made in furtherance of medium neutrality. Other 2022 revisions were made for clarification.

As amended in 2022.

§ 4A–202. Authorized and Verified Payment Orders.

(a)   A payment order received by the receiving bank is the authorized order of the person identified as sender if that person authorized the order or is otherwise bound by it under the law of agency.

(b)   If a bank and its customer have agreed that the authenticity of payment orders issued to the bank in the name of the customer as sender will be verified pursuant to a security procedure, a payment order received by the receiving bank is effective as the order of the customer, whether or not authorized, if (i) the security procedure is a commercially reasonable method of providing security against unauthorized payment orders, and (ii) the bank proves that it accepted the payment order in good faith and in compliance with <u>the bank's obligations under</u> the security procedure and any ~~written~~ agreement or instruction of the customer<u>, evidenced by a record,</u> restricting acceptance of payment orders issued in the name of the customer. The bank is not required to follow an instruction that violates ~~a written~~ <u>an</u> agreement with the customer<u>, evidenced by a record,</u> or notice of which is not received at a time and in a manner affording the bank a reasonable opportunity to act on it before the payment order is accepted.

(c)   Commercial reasonableness of a security procedure is a question of law to be determined by considering the wishes of the customer expressed to the bank, the circumstances of the customer known to the bank, including the size, type, and frequency of payment orders normally issued by the customer to the bank, alternative security procedures offered to the customer, and security procedures in general use by customers and receiving banks similarly situated. A security procedure is deemed to be commercially reasonable if (i) the security procedure was chosen by the customer after the bank offered, and the customer refused, a security procedure that was commercially reasonable for that customer, and (ii) the customer expressly agreed in ~~writing~~ <u>a record</u> to be bound by any payment order, whether or not authorized, issued in its name and accepted by the bank in compliance with <u>the bank's obligations under</u> the security procedure chosen by the customer.

(d)   The term "sender" in this Article includes the customer in whose name a payment order is issued if the order is the authorized order of the customer under subsection (a), or it is effective as the order of the customer under subsection (b).

(e)   This section applies to amendments and cancellations of payment orders to the same extent it applies to payment orders.

(f)   Except as provided in this section and in Section 4A–203(a)(1), rights and obligations arising under this section or Section 4A–203 may not be varied by agreement.

As amended in 2022.

Official Comment

<u>1.</u>   This section is discussed in the Comment following Section 4A–203.

<u>2.   In furtherance of medium neutrality, references to "written" and "writing" have been changed to refer to a "evidenced by a record" and "a record." Other 2022 revisions were made for clarification.</u>

As amended in 2022.

§ 4A–203. Unenforceability of Certain Verified Payment Orders.

(a)   If an accepted payment order is not, under Section 4A–202(a), an authorized order of a customer identified as sender, but is effective as an order of the customer pursuant to Section 4A–202(b), the following rules apply:

(1)   By express ~~written~~ agreement <u>evidenced by a record</u>, the receiving bank may limit the extent to which it is entitled to enforce or retain payment of the payment order.

(2)   The receiving bank is not entitled to enforce or retain payment of the payment order if the customer proves that the order was not caused, directly or indirectly, by a person (i) entrusted at any time with duties to act for the customer with respect to payment orders or the security procedure, or (ii) who obtained access to transmitting facilities of the customer or who obtained, from a source controlled by the customer and without authority of the receiving bank, information facilitating breach of the security procedure, regardless of how the information was obtained or whether the customer was at fault. Information includes any access device, computer software, or the like.

(b)   This section applies to amendments of payment orders to the same extent it applies to payment orders.

As amended in 2022.

Official Comment

1.   Some person will always be identified as the sender of a payment order. Acceptance of the order by the receiving bank is based on a belief by the bank that the order was authorized by the person identified as the sender. If the receiving bank is the beneficiary's bank acceptance means that the receiving bank is obliged to pay the beneficiary. If the receiving bank is not the beneficiary's bank, acceptance means that the receiving bank has executed the sender's order and is obliged to pay the bank that accepted the order issued in execution of the sender's order. In either case the receiving bank may suffer a loss unless it is entitled to enforce payment of the payment order that it accepted. If the person identified as the sender of the order refuses to pay on the ground that the order was not authorized by that person, what are the rights of the receiving bank? In the absence of a statute or agreement that specifically addresses the issue, the question usually will be resolved by the law of agency. In some cases, the law of agency works well. For example, suppose the receiving bank executes a payment order given by means of a letter apparently written by a corporation that is a customer of the bank and apparently signed by an officer of the corporation. If the receiving bank acts solely on the basis of the letter, the corporation is not bound as the sender of the payment order unless the signature was that of the officer and the officer was authorized to act for the corporation in the issuance of payment orders, or some other agency doctrine such as apparent authority or estoppel causes the corporation to be bound. Estoppel can be illustrated by the following example. Suppose P is aware that A, who is unauthorized to act for P, has fraudulently misrepresented to T that A is authorized to act for P. T believes A and is about to rely on the misrepresentation. If P does not notify T of the true facts although P could easily do so, P may be estopped from denying A's lack of authority. A similar result could follow if the failure to notify T is the result of negligence rather than a deliberate decision. Restatement, Second, Agency § 8B. Other equitable principles such as subrogation or restitution might also allow a receiving bank to recover with respect to an unauthorized payment order that it accepted. In *Gatoil (U.S.A.), Inc. v. Forest Hill State Bank*, 1 U.C.C.Rep.Serv.2d 171 (D.Md. 1986), a joint venturer not authorized to order payments from the account of the joint venture, ordered a funds transfer from the account. The transfer paid a bona fide debt of the joint venture. Although the transfer was unauthorized the court refused to require recredit of the account because the joint venture suffered no loss. The result can be rationalized on the basis of subrogation of the receiving bank to the right of the beneficiary of the funds transfer to receive the payment from the joint venture.

But in most cases these legal principles give the receiving bank very little protection in the case of an authorized payment order. Cases like those just discussed are not typical of the way that most payment orders are transmitted and accepted, and such cases are likely to become even less common. Given the large amount of the typical payment order, a prudent receiving bank will be unwilling to accept a payment order unless it has assurance that the order is what it purports to be. This assurance is normally provided by security procedures described in Section 4A–201.

In a very large percentage of cases covered by Article 4A, transmission of the payment order is made electronically. The receiving bank may be required to act on the basis of a message that appears on a computer screen. Common law concepts of authority of agent to bind principal are not helpful. There is no way of determining the identity or the authority of the person who caused the message to be sent. The receiving bank is not relying on the authority of any particular person to act for the purported sender. The case is not comparable to payment of a check by the drawee bank on the basis of a signature that is forged. Rather, the receiving bank relies on a security procedure pursuant to which the authenticity of the message can be "tested" by various devices which are designed to provide certainty that the message is that of the sender identified in the payment order. In the wire transfer business the concept of "authorized" is different from that found in agency law. In that business a payment order is treated as the order of the person in whose name it is issued if it is properly tested pursuant to a security procedure and the order passes the test.

Section 4A–202 reflects the reality of the wire transfer business. A person in whose name a payment order is issued is considered to be the sender of the order if the order is "authorized" as stated in subsection (a) or if the order is "verified" pursuant to a security procedure in compliance with subsection (b). If subsection (b) does not apply, the question of whether the customer is responsible for the order is determined by the law of agency. The issue is one of actual or apparent authority of the person who caused the order to be issued in the name of the customer. In some cases the law of agency might allow the customer to be bound by an unauthorized order if conduct of the customer can be used to find an estoppel against the customer to deny that the order was unauthorized. If the customer is bound by the order under any of these agency doctrines, subsection (a) treats the order as authorized and thus the customer is deemed to be the sender of the order. In most cases, however, subsection (b) will apply. In that event there is no need to make an agency law analysis to determine authority. Under Section 4A–202, the issue of liability of the purported sender of the payment order will be determined by agency law only if the receiving bank did not comply with subsection (b).

2.   The scope of Section 4A–202 can be illustrated by the following cases. *Case # 1.* A payment order purporting to be that of Customer is received by Receiving Bank but the order was fraudulently transmitted by a person who had no authority to act for Customer. *Case # 2.* An authentic payment order was sent by Customer, but before the order was received by Receiving Bank the order was fraudulently altered by an unauthorized person to change the beneficiary. *Case # 3.* An authentic payment order was received by Receiving Bank, but before the order was executed by Receiving Bank a person who had no authority to act for Customer fraudulently sent a communication purporting to amend the order by changing the beneficiary. In each case Receiving Bank acted on the fraudulent communication by accepting the payment order. These cases are all essentially similar and they are treated identically by Section 4A–202. In each case Receiving Bank acted on a communication that it thought was authorized by Customer when in fact the communication was fraudulent. No distinction is made between Case # 1 in which Customer took no part at all in the transaction and Case # 2 and Case # 3 in which an authentic order was fraudulently altered or amended by an unauthorized person. If subsection (b) does not apply, each case is governed by subsection (a). If there are no additional facts on which an estoppel might be found, Customer is not responsible in Case # 1 for the fraudulently issued payment order, in Case # 2 for the fraudulent alteration or in Case # 3 for the fraudulent amendment. Thus, in each case Customer is not liable to pay the order and Receiving Bank takes the loss. The only remedy of Receiving Bank is to seek recovery from the person who received payment as beneficiary of the fraudulent order. If there was verification in compliance with subsection (b), Customer will take the loss unless Section 4A–203 applies.

3.   Subsection (b) of Section 4A–202 is based on the assumption that losses due to fraudulent payment orders can best be avoided by the use of commercially reasonable security procedures, and that the use of such procedures should be encouraged. The subsection is designed to protect both the customer and the receiving bank. A receiving bank needs to be able to rely on objective criteria to determine whether it can safely act on a payment order. Employees of the bank can be trained to "test" a payment order according to the various steps specified in the security procedure. The bank is responsible for the acts of these employees. Subsection (b)(ii) requires the bank to prove that it accepted the payment order in good faith and "in compliance with the bank's obligations under the security procedure." If the fraud was not detected because the bank's employee did not perform the acts required by the security procedure, the bank has not complied. Subsection (b)(ii) also requires the bank to prove that it complied with any agreement or instruction that restricts acceptance of payment orders issued in the name of the customer. If an agreement establishing a security procedure places obligations on both the sender and the receiving bank, the receiving bank need prove only that it complied with the obligations placed on the receiving bank. A customer may want to protect itself by imposing limitations on acceptance of payment orders by the bank. For example, the customer may prohibit the bank from accepting a payment order that is not payable from an authorized account, that exceeds the credit balance in specified accounts of the customer, or that exceeds some other amount. Another limitation may relate to the beneficiary. The customer may provide the bank with a list of authorized beneficiaries and prohibit acceptance of any payment order to a beneficiary not appearing on the list. Such limitations may be incorporated into the security procedure itself or they may be covered by a separate agreement or instruction. In either case, the bank must comply with the limitations if the conditions stated in subsection (b) are met. Normally limitations on acceptance would be incorporated into an agreement between the customer and the receiving bank, but in some cases the instruction might be unilaterally given by the customer. If standing instructions or an agreement state limitations on the ability of the receiving bank to act, provision must be made for later modification of the limitations. Normally this would be done by an agreement that specifies particular procedures to be followed. Thus, subsection (b) states that the receiving bank is not required to follow an instruction that violates ~~a written~~ an agreement evidenced by a record. The receiving bank is not bound by an instruction unless it has adequate notice of it. ~~Subsections (25), (26) and (27) of Section 1–201 apply~~ Section 1–202 applies.

Subsection (b)(i) assures that the interests of the customer will be protected by providing an incentive to a bank to make available to the customer a security procedure that is commercially reasonable. If a commercially reasonable security procedure is not made available to the customer, subsection (b) does not apply. The result is that subsection (a) applies and the bank acts at its peril in accepting a payment order that may be unauthorized. Prudent banking practice may require that security procedures be utilized in virtually all cases except for those in which personal contact between the customer and the bank eliminates the possibility of an unauthorized order. The burden of making available commercially reasonable security procedures is imposed on receiving banks because they generally determine what security procedures can be used and are in the best position to evaluate the efficacy of procedures offered to customers to combat fraud. The burden on the customer is to supervise its employees to assure compliance with the security procedure and to safeguard confidential security information and access to transmitting facilities so that the security procedure cannot be breached.

4. The principal issue that is likely to arise in litigation involving subsection (b) is whether the security procedure in effect when a fraudulent payment order was accepted was commercially reasonable. In considering this issue, a court will need to consider the totality of the security procedure, including each party's obligations under the procedure. The concept of what is commercially reasonable in a given case is flexible. Verification entails labor and equipment costs that can vary greatly depending upon the degree of security that is sought. A customer that transmits very large numbers of payment orders in very large amounts may desire and may reasonably expect to be provided with state-of-the-art procedures that provide maximum security. But the expense involved may make use of a state-of-the-art procedure infeasible for a customer that normally transmits payment orders infrequently or in relatively low amounts. Another variable is the type of receiving bank. It is reasonable to require large money center banks to make available state-of-the-art security procedures. On the other hand, the same requirement may not be reasonable for a small country bank. A receiving bank might have several security procedures that are designed to meet the varying needs of different customers. The type of payment order is another variable. For example, in a wholesale wire transfer, each payment order is normally transmitted electronically and individually. A testing procedure will be individually applied to each payment order. In funds transfers to be made by means of an automated clearing house many payment orders are incorporated into an electronic device such as a magnetic tape that is physically delivered. Testing of the individual payment orders is not feasible. Thus, a different kind of security procedure must be adopted to take into account the different mode of transmission.

The issue of whether a particular security procedure is commercially reasonable is a question of law. Whether the receiving bank complied with the procedure is a question of fact. It is appropriate to make the finding concerning commercial reasonability a matter of law because security procedures are likely to be standardized in the banking industry and a question of law standard leads to more predictability concerning the level of security that a bank must offer to its customers. The purpose of subsection (b) is to encourage banks to institute reasonable safeguards against fraud but not to make them insurers against fraud. A security procedure is not commercially unreasonable simply because another procedure might have been better or because the judge deciding the question would have opted for a more stringent procedure. For example, the use of a computer program to detect fraud is not commercially unreasonable merely because it does not detect all fraud or because another system or approach might be more successful at detecting fraud. The standard is not whether the security procedure is the best available. Rather it is whether the procedure is reasonable for the particular customer and the particular bank, which is a lower standard. What is reasonable for a particular customer requires the court to consider the circumstances of the customer known to the bank, including the size, type, and frequency of payment orders normally issued by the customer to the bank. Article 4A does not create an affirmative obligation on the receiving bank to obtain information about its customer. However, whatever knowledge the bank does have about the customer is relevant in determining the commercial reasonableness of the security procedure. On the other hand, aA security procedure that fails to meet prevailing standards of good banking practice applicable to the particular bank should not be held to be commercially reasonable. Subsection (c) states factors to be considered by the judge in making the determination of commercial reasonableness. The reasonableness of a security procedure is to be determined at the time that a payment order is processed, not at the time the customer and the bank agree to the security procedure. Accordingly, a security procedure that was reasonable when agreed to might become unreasonable as technologies emerge, prevailing practices change, or the bank acquires knowledge about the customer. Sometimes an informed customer refuses a security procedure that is commercially reasonable and suitable for that customer and insists on using a higher-risk procedure because it is more convenient or cheaper. In that case, under the last sentence of subsection (c), the customer has voluntarily assumed the risk of failure of the procedure and cannot shift the loss to the bank. But this result follows only if the customer expressly agrees in writing a record to assume that risk. It is implicit in the last sentence of subsection (c) that a bank that accedes to the wishes of its customer in this regard is not acting in bad faith by so doing so long as the customer is made aware of the risk. In all cases, however, a receiving bank cannot get the benefit of subsection (b) unless it has made available to the customer a security procedure that is commercially reasonable and suitable for use by that customer. In most cases, the mutual interest of bank and customer to protect against fraud should lead to agreement to a security procedure which is commercially reasonable.

4A. Subsection (b) generally allows a receiving bank to treat a payment order as authorized by the customer if the bank accepts the payment order in good faith and in compliance with the bank's obligations under a commercially reasonable, agreed-upon security procedure. For this purpose, "good faith" requires the exercise of reasonable commercial standards of fair dealing, see Section 4A–105(a)(6), not the absence of negligence. Consequently, the bank has no duty, beyond that to which the bank has agreed, to investigate suspicious activity or to advise its customer of such activity. However, a bank that obtains knowledge that a customer's operations have been infiltrated or knowledge that the customer is the victim of identity fraud might not be acting in good faith if the bank, without receiving some assurance from the customer that the issue has been remediated, thereafter accepts a payment order.

5.   The effect of Section 4A–202(b) is to place the risk of loss on the customer if an unauthorized payment order is accepted by the receiving bank after verification by the bank in compliance with a commercially reasonable security procedure. An exception to this result is provided by Section 4A–203(a)(2). The customer may avoid the loss resulting from such a payment order if the customer can prove that the fraud was not committed by a person described in that subsection. Breach of a commercially reasonable security procedure requires that the person committing the fraud have knowledge of how the procedure works and knowledge of codes, identifying devices, and the like. That person may also need access to transmitting facilities through an access device or other software in order to breach the security procedure. This confidential information must be obtained either from a source controlled by the customer or from a source controlled by the receiving bank. If the customer can prove that the person committing the fraud did not obtain the confidential information from an agent or former agent of the customer or from a source controlled by the customer, the loss is shifted to the bank. "Prove" is defined in Section 4A–105(a)(7). Because of bank regulation requirements, in this kind of case there will always be a criminal investigation as well as an internal investigation of the bank to determine the probable explanation for the breach of security. Because a funds transfer fraud usually will involve a very large amount of money, both the criminal investigation and the internal investigation are likely to be thorough. In some cases there may be an investigation by bank examiners as well. Frequently, these investigations will develop evidence of who is at fault and the cause of the loss. The customer will have access to evidence developed in these investigations and that evidence can be used by the customer in meeting its burden of proof.

6.   The effect of Section 4A–202(b) may also be changed by an agreement meeting the requirements of Section 4A–203(a)(1). Some customers may be unwilling to take all or part of the risk of loss with respect to unauthorized payment orders even if all of the requirements of Section 4A–202(b) are met. By virtue of Section 4A–203(a)(1), a receiving bank may assume all of the risk of loss with respect to unauthorized payment orders or the customer and bank may agree that losses from unauthorized payment orders are to be divided as provided in the agreement.

7.   In a large majority of cases the sender of a payment order is a bank. In many cases in which there is a bank sender, both the sender and the receiving bank will be members of a funds transfer system over which the payment order is transmitted. Since Section 4A–202(f) does not prohibit a funds transfer system rule from varying rights and obligations under Section 4A–202, a rule of the funds transfer system can determine how loss due to an unauthorized payment order from a participating bank to another participating bank is to be allocated. A funds transfer system rule, however, cannot change the rights of a customer that is not a participating bank. § 4A–501(b). Section 4A–202(f) also prevents variation by agreement except to the extent stated.

8.   In furtherance of medium neutrality, the reference to "written" in the pre-2022 text of this section has been changed to refer to "evidenced by a record."

As amended in 2022.

§ 4A–204. Refund of Payment and Duty of Customer to Report With Respect to Unauthorized Payment Order.

(a)   If a receiving bank accepts a payment order issued in the name of its customer as sender which is (i) not authorized and not effective as the order of the customer under Section 4A–202, or (ii) not enforceable, in whole or in part, against the customer under Section 4A–203, the bank shall refund any payment of the payment order received from the customer to the extent the bank is not entitled to enforce payment and shall pay interest on the refundable amount calculated from the date the bank received payment to the date of the refund. However, the customer is not entitled to interest from the bank on the amount to be refunded if the customer fails to exercise ordinary care to determine that the order was not authorized by the customer and to notify the bank of the relevant facts within a reasonable time not exceeding 90 days after the date the customer received notification from the bank that the order was accepted or that the customer's account was debited with respect to the order. The bank is not entitled to any recovery from the customer on account of a failure by the customer to give notification as stated in this section.

(b)   Reasonable time under subsection (a) may be fixed by agreement as stated in Section 1–302(b), but the obligation of a receiving bank to refund payment as stated in subsection (a) may not otherwise be varied by agreement.

As amended in 2001.

Official Comment

1.   With respect to unauthorized payment orders, in a very large percentage of cases a commercially reasonable security procedure will be in effect. Section 4A–204 applies only to cases in which (i) no commercially reasonable security procedure is in effect, (ii) the bank did not comply with a commercially reasonable security procedure that was in effect, (iii) the sender can prove, pursuant to Section 4A–203(a)(2), that the culprit did not obtain confidential security information controlled by the customer, or (iv) the bank, pursuant to Section 4A–203(a)(1) agreed to take all or part of the loss resulting from an unauthorized payment order. In each of these cases the bank takes the risk of loss with respect to an unauthorized payment order because the bank is not entitled to payment from the customer with respect to the order. The bank normally debits the customer's account or otherwise receives payment from the customer shortly after acceptance of the payment order. Subsection (a) of Section 4A–204 states that the bank must recredit the account or refund payment to the extent the bank is not entitled to enforce payment.

2.   Section 4A–204 is designed to encourage a customer to promptly notify the receiving bank that it has accepted an unauthorized payment order. Since cases of unauthorized payment orders will almost always involve fraud, the bank's remedy is normally to recover from the beneficiary of the unauthorized order if the beneficiary was party to the fraud. This remedy may not be worth very much and it may not make any difference whether or not the bank promptly learns about the fraud. But in some cases prompt notification may make it easier for the bank to recover some part of its loss from the culprit. The customer will routinely be notified of the debit to its account with respect to an unauthorized order or will otherwise be notified of acceptance of the order. The customer has a duty to exercise ordinary care to determine that the order was unauthorized after it has received notification from the bank, and to advise the bank of the relevant facts within a reasonable time not exceeding 90 days after receipt of notification. Reasonable time is not defined and it may depend on the facts of the particular case. If a payment order for $1,000,000 is wholly unauthorized, the customer should normally discover it in far less than 90 days. If a $1,000,000 payment order was authorized but the name of the beneficiary was fraudulently changed, a much longer period may be necessary to discover the fraud. But in any event, if the customer delays more than 90 days the customer's duty has not been met. The only consequence of a failure of the customer to perform this duty is a loss of interest on the refund payable by the bank. A customer that acts promptly is entitled to interest from the time the customer's account was debited or the customer otherwise made payment. The rate of interest is stated in Section 4A–506. If the customer fails to perform the duty, no interest is recoverable for any part of the period before the bank learns that it accepted an unauthorized order. But the bank is not entitled to any recovery from the customer based on negligence for failure to inform the bank. Loss of interest is in the nature of a penalty on the customer designed to provide an incentive for the customer to police its account. There is no intention to impose a duty on the customer that might result in shifting loss from the unauthorized order to the customer.

§ 4A–205.   Erroneous Payment Orders.

(a)   If an accepted payment order was transmitted pursuant to a security procedure for the detection of error and the payment order (i) erroneously instructed payment to a beneficiary not intended by the sender, (ii) erroneously instructed payment in an amount greater than the amount intended by the sender, or (iii) was an erroneously transmitted duplicate of a payment order previously sent by the sender, the following rules apply:

(1)   If the sender proves that the sender or a person acting on behalf of the sender pursuant to Section 4A–206 complied with the security procedure and that the error would have been detected if the receiving bank had also complied, the sender is not obliged to pay the order to the extent stated in paragraphs (2) and (3).

(2)   If the funds transfer is completed on the basis of an erroneous payment order described in clause (i) or (iii) of subsection (a), the sender is not obliged to pay the order and the receiving bank is entitled to recover from the beneficiary any amount paid to the beneficiary to the extent allowed by the law governing mistake and restitution.

(3)   If the funds transfer is completed on the basis of a payment order described in clause (ii) of subsection (a), the sender is not obliged to pay the order to the extent the amount received by the

beneficiary is greater than the amount intended by the sender. In that case, the receiving bank is entitled to recover from the beneficiary the excess amount received to the extent allowed by the law governing mistake and restitution.

(b)   If (i) the sender of an erroneous payment order described in subsection (a) is not obliged to pay all or part of the order, and (ii) the sender receives notification from the receiving bank that the order was accepted by the bank or that the sender's account was debited with respect to the order, the sender has a duty to exercise ordinary care, on the basis of information available to the sender, to discover the error with respect to the order and to advise the bank of the relevant facts within a reasonable time, not exceeding 90 days, after the bank's notification was received by the sender. If the bank proves that the sender failed to perform that duty, the sender is liable to the bank for the loss the bank proves it incurred as a result of the failure, but the liability of the sender may not exceed the amount of the sender's order.

(c)   This section applies to amendments to payment orders to the same extent it applies to payment orders.

Official Comment

1.   This section concerns error in the content or in the transmission of payment orders. It deals with three kinds of error. *Case # 1.* The order identifies a beneficiary not intended by the sender. For example, Sender intends to wire funds to a beneficiary identified only by an account number. The wrong account number is stated in the order. *Case # 2.* The error is in the amount of the order. For example, Sender intends to wire $1,000 to Beneficiary. Through error, the payment order instructs payment of $1,000,000. *Case # 3.* A payment order is sent to the receiving bank and then, by mistake, the same payment order is sent to the receiving bank again. In Case # 3, the receiving bank may have no way of knowing whether the second order is a duplicate of the first or is another order. Similarly, in Case # 1 and Case # 2, the receiving bank may have no way of knowing that the error exists. In each case, if this section does not apply and the funds transfer is completed, Sender is obliged to pay the order. Section 4A–402. Sender's remedy, based on payment by mistake, is to recover from the beneficiary that received payment.

Sometimes, however, transmission of payment orders of the sender to the receiving bank is made pursuant to a security procedure designed to detect one or more of the errors described above. Since "security procedure" is defined by Section 4A–201 as "a procedure established by agreement of a customer and a receiving bank for the purpose of . . . detecting error . . .," Section 4A–205 does not apply if the receiving bank and the customer did not agree to the establishment of a procedure for detecting error. A security procedure may be designed to detect an account number that is not one to which Sender normally makes payment. In that case, the security procedure may require a special verification that payment to the stated account number was intended. In the case of dollar amounts, the security procedure may require different codes for different dollar amounts. If a $1,000,000 payment order contains a code that is inappropriate for that amount, the error in amount should be detected. In the case of duplicate orders, the security procedure may require that each payment order be identified by a number or code that applies to no other order. If the number or code of each payment order received is registered in a computer base, the receiving bank can quickly identify a duplicate order. The three cases covered by this section are essentially similar. In each, if the error is not detected, some beneficiary will receive funds that the beneficiary was not intended to receive. If this section applies, the risk of loss with respect to the error of the sender is shifted to the bank which has the burden of recovering the funds from the beneficiary. The risk of loss is shifted to the bank only if the sender proves that the error would have been detected if there had been compliance with the procedure and that the sender (or an agent under Section 4A–206) complied. In the case of a duplicate order or a wrong beneficiary, the sender doesn't have to pay the order. In the case of an overpayment, the sender does not have to pay the order to the extent of the overpayment. If subsection (a)(1) applies, the position of the receiving bank is comparable to that of a receiving bank that erroneously executes a payment order as stated in Section 4A–303. However, failure of the sender to timely report the error is covered by Section 4A–205(b) rather than by Section 4A–304 which applies only to erroneous execution under Section 4A–303. A receiving bank to which the risk of loss is shifted by subsection (a)(1) or (2) is entitled to recover the amount erroneously paid to the beneficiary to the extent allowed by the law of mistake and restitution. Rights of the receiving bank against the beneficiary are similar to those of a receiving bank that erroneously executes a payment order as stated in Section 4A–303. Those rights are discussed in Comment 2 to Section 4A–303.

2.   A security procedure established for the purpose of detecting error is not effective unless both sender and receiving bank comply with the procedure. Thus, the bank undertakes a duty of complying with the procedure for the benefit of the sender. This duty is recognized in subsection (a)(1). The loss with respect to the sender's error is shifted to the bank if the bank fails to comply with the procedure and the sender (or an agent under Section 4A–206) does comply. Although the customer may have been negligent in transmitting the erroneous payment order,

the loss is put on the bank on a last-clear-chance theory. A similar analysis applies to subsection (b). If the loss with respect to an error is shifted to the receiving bank and the sender is notified by the bank that the erroneous payment order was accepted, the sender has a duty to exercise ordinary care to discover the error and notify the bank of the relevant facts within a reasonable time not exceeding 90 days. If the bank can prove that the sender failed in this duty it is entitled to compensation for the loss incurred as a result of the failure. Whether the bank is entitled to recover from the sender depends upon whether the failure to give timely notice would have made any difference. If the bank could not have recovered from the beneficiary that received payment under the erroneous payment order even if timely notice had been given, the sender's failure to notify did not cause any loss of the bank.

3.   Section 4A–205 is subject to variation by agreement under Section 4A–501. Thus, if a receiving bank and its customer have agreed to a security procedure for detection of error, the liability of the receiving bank for failing to detect an error of the customer as provided in Section 4A–205 may be varied as provided in an agreement of the bank and the customer.

§ 4A–206. Transmission of Payment Order Through Funds-Transfer or Other Communication System.

(a)   If a payment order addressed to a receiving bank is transmitted to a funds-transfer system or other third-party communication system for transmittal to the bank, the system is deemed to be an agent of the sender for the purpose of transmitting the payment order to the bank. If there is a discrepancy between the terms of the payment order transmitted to the system and the terms of the payment order transmitted by the system to the bank, the terms of the payment order of the sender are those transmitted by the system. This section does not apply to a funds-transfer system of the Federal Reserve Banks.

(b)   This section applies to cancellations and amendments of payment orders to the same extent it applies to payment orders.

Official Comment

1.   A payment order may be issued to a receiving bank directly by delivery of a ~~writing or electronic device~~ record or by an oral ~~or electronic~~ communication. If an agent of the sender is employed to transmit orders on behalf of the sender, the sender is bound by the order transmitted by the agent on the basis of agency law. Section 4A–206 is an application of that principle to cases in which a funds transfer or communication system acts as an intermediary in transmitting the sender's order to the receiving bank. The intermediary is deemed to be an agent of the sender for the purpose of transmitting payment orders and related messages for the sender. Section 4A–206 deals with error by the intermediary.

2.   Transmission by an automated clearing house of an association of banks other than the Federal Reserve Banks is an example of a transaction covered by Section 4A–206. Suppose Originator orders Originator's Bank to cause a large number of payments to be made to many accounts in banks in various parts of the country. These payment orders are electronically transmitted to Originator's Bank and stored in an electronic device that is held by Originator's Bank. Or, transmission of the various payment orders is made by delivery to Originator's Bank of an electronic device containing the instruction to the bank. In either case the terms of the various payment orders by Originator are determined by the information contained in the electronic device. In order to execute the various orders, the information in the electronic device must be processed. For example, if some of the orders are for payments to accounts in Bank X and some to accounts in Bank Y, Originator's Bank will execute these orders of Originator by issuing a series of payment orders to Bank X covering all payments to accounts in that bank, and by issuing a series of payment orders to Bank Y covering all payments to accounts in that bank. The orders to Bank X may be transmitted together by means of an electronic device, and those to Bank Y may be included in another electronic device. Typically, this processing is done by an automated clearing house acting for a group of banks including Originator's Bank. The automated clearing house is a funds transfer system. Section 4A–105(a)(5). Originator's Bank delivers Originator's electronic device or transmits the information contained in the device to the funds transfer system for processing into payment orders of Originator's Bank to the appropriate beneficiary's banks. The processing may result in an erroneous payment order. Originator's Bank, by use of Originator's electronic device, may have given information to the funds transfer system instructing payment of $100,000 to an account in Bank X, but because of human error or an equipment malfunction the processing may have converted that instruction into an instruction to Bank X to make a payment of $1,000,000. Under Section 4A–206, Originator's Bank issued a payment order for $1,000,000 to Bank X when the erroneous information was sent to Bank X. Originator's Bank is responsible for the error of the automated clearing house. The liability of the

funds transfer system that made the error is not governed by Article 4A. It is left to the law of contract, a funds transfer system rule, or other applicable law.

In the hypothetical case just discussed, if the automated clearing house is operated by a Federal Reserve Bank, the analysis is different. Section 4A–206 does not apply. Originator's Bank will execute Originator's payment orders by delivery or transmission of the electronic information to the Federal Reserve Bank for processing. The result is that Originator's Bank has issued payment orders to the Federal Reserve Bank which, in this case, is acting as an intermediary bank. When the Federal Reserve Bank has processed the information given to it by Originator's Bank it will issue payment orders to the various beneficiary's banks. If the processing results in an erroneous payment order, the Federal Reserve Bank has erroneously executed the payment order of Originator's Bank and the case is governed by Section 4A–303.

As amended in 2022.

§ 4A–207. Misdescription of Beneficiary.

(a) Subject to subsection (b), if, in a payment order received by the beneficiary's bank, the name, bank account number, or other identification of the beneficiary refers to a nonexistent or unidentifiable person or account, no person has rights as a beneficiary of the order and acceptance of the order cannot occur.

(b) If a payment order received by the beneficiary's bank identifies the beneficiary both by name and by an identifying or bank account number and the name and number identify different persons, the following rules apply:

(1) Except as otherwise provided in subsection (c), if the beneficiary's bank does not know that the name and number refer to different persons, it may rely on the number as the proper identification of the beneficiary of the order. The beneficiary's bank need not determine whether the name and number refer to the same person.

(2) If the beneficiary's bank pays the person identified by name or knows that the name and number identify different persons, no person has rights as beneficiary except the person paid by the beneficiary's bank if that person was entitled to receive payment from the originator of the funds transfer. If no person has rights as beneficiary, acceptance of the order cannot occur.

(c) If (i) a payment order described in subsection (b) is accepted, (ii) the originator's payment order described the beneficiary inconsistently by name and number, and (iii) the beneficiary's bank pays the person identified by number as permitted by subsection (b)(1), the following rules apply:

(1) If the originator is a bank, the originator is obliged to pay its order.

(2) If the originator is not a bank and proves that the person identified by number was not entitled to receive payment from the originator, the originator is not obliged to pay its order unless the originator's bank proves that the originator, before acceptance of the originator's order, had notice that payment of a payment order issued by the originator might be made by the beneficiary's bank on the basis of an identifying or bank account number even if it identifies a person different from the named beneficiary. Proof of notice may be made by any admissible evidence. The originator's bank satisfies the burden of proof if it proves that the originator, before the payment order was accepted, signed a ~~writing~~ record stating the information to which the notice relates.

(d) In a case governed by subsection (b)(1), if the beneficiary's bank rightfully pays the person identified by number and that person was not entitled to receive payment from the originator, the amount paid may be recovered from that person to the extent allowed by the law governing mistake and restitution as follows:

(1) If the originator is obliged to pay its payment order as stated in subsection (c), the originator has the right to recover.

(2) If the originator is not a bank and is not obliged to pay its payment order, the originator's bank has the right to recover.

As amended in 2022.

Official Comment

1. Subsection (a) deals with the problem of payment orders issued to the beneficiary's bank for payment to nonexistent or unidentifiable persons or accounts. Since it is not possible in that case for the funds transfer to be completed, subsection (a) states that the order cannot be accepted. Under Section 4A–402(c), a sender of a payment order is not obliged to pay its order unless the beneficiary's bank accepts a payment order instructing payment to the beneficiary of that sender's order. Thus, if the beneficiary of a funds transfer is nonexistent or unidentifiable, each sender in the funds transfer that has paid its payment order is entitled to get its money back.

2. Subsection (b), which takes precedence over subsection (a), deals with the problem of payment orders in which the description of the beneficiary does not allow identification of the beneficiary because the beneficiary is described by name and by an identifying number or an account number and the name and number refer to different persons. A very large percentage of payment orders issued to the beneficiary's bank by another bank are processed by automated means using machines capable of reading orders on standard formats that identify the beneficiary by an identifying number or the number of a bank account. The processing of the order by the beneficiary's bank and the crediting of the beneficiary's account are done by use of the identifying or bank account number without human reading of the payment order itself. The process is comparable to that used in automated payment of checks. The standard format, however, may also allow the inclusion of the name of the beneficiary and other information which can be useful to the beneficiary's bank and the beneficiary but which plays no part in the process of payment. If the beneficiary's bank has both the account number and name of the beneficiary supplied by the originator of the funds transfer, it is possible for the beneficiary's bank to determine whether the name and number refer to the same person, but if a duty to make that determination is imposed on the beneficiary's bank the benefits of automated payment are lost. Manual handling of payment orders is both expensive and subject to human error. If payment orders can be handled on an automated basis there are substantial economies of operation and the possibility of clerical error is reduced. Subsection (b) allows banks to utilize automated processing by allowing banks to act on the basis of the number without regard to the name if the bank does not know that the name and number refer to different persons. ~~"Know" is~~ "Knowledge" and "knows" are defined in Section ~~1–201(25)~~ 1–202(b) to mean actual knowledge, and Section ~~1–201(27)~~ 1–202(f) states rules for determining when an organization has knowledge of information received by the organization. The time of payment is the pertinent time at which knowledge or lack of knowledge must be determined.

Although the clear trend is for beneficiary's banks to process payment orders by automated means, Section 4A–207 is not limited to cases in which processing is done by automated means. A bank that processes by semi-automated means or even manually may rely on number as stated in Section 4A–207.

In cases covered by subsection (b) the erroneous identification would in virtually all cases be the identifying or bank account number. In the typical case the error is made by the originator of the funds transfer. The originator should know the name of the person who is to receive payment and can further identify that person by an address that would normally be known to the originator. It is not unlikely, however, that the originator may not be sure whether the identifying or account number refers to the person the originator intends to pay. Subsection (b)(1) deals with the typical case in which the beneficiary's bank pays on the basis of the account number and is not aware at the time of payment that the named beneficiary is not the holder of the account which was paid. In some cases the false number will be the result of error by the originator. In other cases fraud is involved. For example, Doe is the holder of shares in Mutual Fund. Thief, impersonating Doe, requests redemption of the shares and directs Mutual Fund to wire the redemption proceeds to Doe's account # 12345 in Beneficiary's Bank. Mutual Fund originates a funds transfer by issuing a payment order to Originator's Bank to make the payment to Doe's account # 12345 in Beneficiary's Bank. Originator's Bank executes the order by issuing a conforming payment order to Beneficiary's Bank which makes payment to account # 12345. That account is the account of Roe rather than Doe. Roe might be a person acting in concert with Thief or Roe might be an innocent third party. Assume that Roe is a gem merchant that agreed to sell gems to Thief who agreed to wire the purchase price to Roe's account in Beneficiary's Bank. Roe believed that the credit to Roe's account was a transfer of funds from Thief and released the gems to Thief in good faith in reliance on the payment. The case law is unclear on the responsibility of a beneficiary's bank in carrying out a payment order in which the identification of the beneficiary by name and number is conflicting. See *Securities Fund Services, Inc. v. American National Bank*, 542 F.Supp. 323 (N.D.Ill. 1982) and *Bradford Trust Co. v. Texas American Bank*, 790 F.2d 407 (5th Cir. 1986). Section 4A–207 resolves the issue.

If Beneficiary's Bank did not know about the conflict between the name and number, subsection (b)(1) applies. Beneficiary's Bank has no duty to determine whether there is a conflict and it may rely on the number as the proper identification of the beneficiary of the order. When it accepts the order, it is entitled to payment from Originator's Bank. Section 4A–402(b). On the other hand, if Beneficiary's Bank knew about the conflict between the name and number and nevertheless paid Roe, subsection (b)(2) applies. Under that provision, acceptance of the payment order of Originator's Bank did not occur because there is no beneficiary of that order. Since acceptance did not occur Originator's Bank is not obliged to pay Beneficiary's Bank. Section 4A–402(b). Similarly, Mutual Fund is excused from its obligation to pay Originator's Bank. Section 4A–402(c). Thus, Beneficiary's Bank takes the loss. Its only cause of action is against Thief. Roe is not obliged to return the payment to the beneficiary's bank because Roe received the payment in good faith and for value. Article 4A makes irrelevant the issue of whether Mutual Fund was or was not negligent in issuing its payment order.

    3.   Normally, subsection (b)(1) will apply to the hypothetical case discussed in Comment 2. Beneficiary's Bank will pay on the basis of the number without knowledge of the conflict. In that case subsection (c) places the loss on either Mutual Fund or Originator's Bank. It is not unfair to assign the loss to Mutual Fund because it is the person who dealt with the imposter and it supplied the wrong account number. It could have avoided the loss if it had not used an account number that it was not sure was that of Doe. Mutual Fund, however, may not have been aware of the risk involved in giving both name and number. Subsection (c) is designed to protect the originator, Mutual Fund, in this case. Under that subsection, the originator is responsible for the inconsistent description of the beneficiary if it had notice that the order might be paid by the beneficiary's bank on the basis of the number. If the originator is a bank, the originator always has that responsibility. The rationale is that any bank should know how payment orders are processed and paid. If the originator is not a bank, the originator's bank must prove that its customer, the originator, had notice. Notice can be proved by any admissible evidence, but the bank can always prove notice by providing the customer with a written statement of the required information and obtaining the customer's signature to the statement. That statement will then apply to any payment order accepted by the bank thereafter. The information need not be supplied more than once.

    In the hypothetical case if Originator's Bank made the disclosure stated in the last sentence of subsection (c)(2), Mutual Fund must pay Originator's Bank. Under subsection (d)(1), Mutual Fund has an action to recover from Roe if recovery from Roe is permitted by the law governing mistake and restitution. Under the assumed facts Roe should be entitled to keep the money as a person who took it in good faith and for value since it was taken as payment for the gems. In that case, Mutual Fund's only remedy is against Thief. If Roe was not acting in good faith, Roe has to return the money to Mutual Fund. If Originator's Bank does not prove that Mutual Fund had notice as stated in subsection (c)(2), Mutual Fund is not required to pay Originator's Bank. Thus, the risk of loss falls on Originator's Bank whose remedy is against Roe or Thief as stated above. Subsection (d)(2).

    4.   In furtherance of medium neutrality, the reference to a "writing" in the pre-2022 text of this section has been changed to refer to a "record."

As amended in 2022.

§ 4A–208. Misdescription of Intermediary Bank or Beneficiary's Bank.

    (a)   This subsection applies to a payment order identifying an intermediary bank or the beneficiary's bank only by an identifying number.

    (1)   The receiving bank may rely on the number as the proper identification of the intermediary or beneficiary's bank and need not determine whether the number identifies a bank.

    (2)   The sender is obliged to compensate the receiving bank for any loss and expenses incurred by the receiving bank as a result of its reliance on the number in executing or attempting to execute the order.

    (b)   This subsection applies to a payment order identifying an intermediary bank or the beneficiary's bank both by name and an identifying number if the name and number identify different persons.

    (1)   If the sender is a bank, the receiving bank may rely on the number as the proper identification of the intermediary or beneficiary's bank if the receiving bank, when it executes the sender's order, does not know that the name and number identify different persons. The receiving bank need not determine whether the name and number refer to the same person or whether the number refers to a bank. The sender is obliged to compensate the receiving bank for any loss and expenses incurred by the receiving bank as a result of its reliance on the number in executing or attempting to execute the order.

    (2)   If the sender is not a bank and the receiving bank proves that the sender, before the payment order was accepted, had notice that the receiving bank might rely on the number as the proper identification of the intermediary or beneficiary's bank even if it identifies a person different from

the bank identified by name, the rights and obligations of the sender and the receiving bank are governed by subsection (b)(1), as though the sender were a bank. Proof of notice may be made by any admissible evidence. The receiving bank satisfies the burden of proof if it proves that the sender, before the payment order was accepted, signed a ~~writing~~ record stating the information to which the notice relates.

(3) Regardless of whether the sender is a bank, the receiving bank may rely on the name as the proper identification of the intermediary or beneficiary's bank if the receiving bank, at the time it executes the sender's order, does not know that the name and number identify different persons. The receiving bank need not determine whether the name and number refer to the same person.

(4) If the receiving bank knows that the name and number identify different persons, reliance on either the name or the number in executing the sender's payment order is a breach of the obligation stated in Section 4A–302(a)(1).

As amended in 2022.

Official Comment

1.   This section addresses an issue similar to that addressed by Section 4A–207. Because of automation in the processing of payment orders, a payment order may identify the beneficiary's bank or an intermediary bank by an identifying number. The bank identified by number might or might not also be identified by name. The following two cases illustrate Section 4A–208(a) and (b):

Case # 1. Originator's payment order to Originator's Bank identifies the beneficiary's bank as Bank A and instructs payment to Account # 12345 in that bank. Originator's Bank executes Originator's order by issuing a payment order to Intermediary Bank. In the payment order of Originator's Bank the beneficiary's bank is identified as Bank A but is also identified by number, # 67890. The identifying number refers to Bank B rather than Bank A. If processing by Intermediary Bank of the payment order of Originator's Bank is done by automated means, Intermediary Bank, in executing the order, will rely on the identifying number and will issue a payment order to Bank B rather than Bank A. If there is an Account # 12345 in Bank B, the payment order of Intermediary Bank would normally be accepted and payment would be made to a person not intended by Originator. In this case, Section 4A–208(b)(1) puts the risk of loss on Originator's Bank. Intermediary Bank may rely on the number # 67890 as the proper identification of the beneficiary's bank. Intermediary Bank has properly executed the payment order of Originator's Bank. By using the wrong number to describe the beneficiary's bank, Originator's Bank has improperly executed Originator's payment order because the payment order of Originator's Bank provides for payment to the wrong beneficiary, the holder of Account # 12345 in Bank B rather than the holder of Account # 12345 in Bank A. Section 4A–302(a)(1) and Section 4A–303(c). Originator's Bank is not entitled to payment from Originator but is required to pay Intermediary Bank. Section 4A–303(c) and Section 4A–402(c). Intermediary Bank is also entitled to compensation for any loss and expenses resulting from the error by Originator's Bank.

If there is no Account # 12345 in Bank B, the result is that there is no beneficiary of the payment order issued by Originator's Bank and the funds transfer will not be completed. Originator's Bank is not entitled to payment from Originator and Intermediary Bank is not entitled to payment from Originator's Bank. Section 4A–402(c). Since Originator's Bank improperly executed Originator's payment order it may be liable for damages under Section 4A–305. As stated above, Intermediary Bank is entitled to compensation for loss and expenses resulting from the error by Originator's Bank.

Case # 2. Suppose the same payment order by Originator to Originator's Bank as in Case # 1. In executing the payment order Originator's Bank issues a payment order to Intermediary Bank in which the beneficiary's bank is identified only by number, # 67890. That number does not refer to Bank A. Rather, it identifies a person that is not a bank. If processing by Intermediary Bank of the payment order of Originator's Bank is done by automated means, Intermediary Bank will rely on the number # 67890 to identify the beneficiary's bank. Intermediary Bank has no duty to determine whether the number identifies a bank. The funds transfer cannot be completed in this case because no bank is identified as the beneficiary's bank. Subsection (a) puts the risk of loss on Originator's Bank. Originator's Bank is not entitled to payment from Originator. Section 4A–402(c). Originator's Bank has improperly executed Originator's payment order and may be liable for damages under Section 4A–305. Originator's Bank is obliged to compensate Intermediary Bank for loss and expenses resulting from the error by Originator's Bank.

Subsection (a) also applies if # 67890 identifies a bank, but the bank is not Bank A. Intermediary Bank may rely on the number as the proper identification of the beneficiary's bank. If the bank to which

Intermediary Bank sends its payment order accepts the order, Intermediary Bank is entitled to payment from Originator's Bank, but Originator's Bank is not entitled to payment from Originator. The analysis is similar to that in Case # 1.

2.   Subsection (b)(2) of Section 4A–208 addresses cases in which an erroneous identification of a beneficiary's bank or intermediary bank by name and number is made in a payment order of a sender that is not a bank. Suppose Originator issues a payment order to Originator's Bank that instructs that bank to use an intermediary bank identified as Bank A and by an identifying number, # 67890. The identifying number refers to Bank B. Originator intended to identify Bank A as intermediary bank. If Originator's Bank relied on the number and issued a payment order to Bank B the rights of Originator's Bank depend upon whether the proof of notice stated in subsection (b)(2) is made by Originator's Bank. If proof is made, Originator's Bank's rights are governed by subsection (b)(1) of Section 4A–208. Originator's Bank is not liable for breach of Section 4A–302(a)(1) and is entitled to compensation from Originator for any loss and expenses resulting from Originator's error. If notice is not proved, Originator's Bank may not rely on the number in executing Originator's payment order. Since Originator's Bank does not get the benefit of subsection (b)(1) in that case, Originator's Bank improperly executed Originator's payment order and is in breach of the obligation stated in Section 4A–302(a)(1). If notice is not given, Originator's Bank can rely on the name if it is not aware of the conflict in name and number. Subsection (b)(3).

3.   Although the principal purpose of Section 4A–208 is to accommodate automated processing of payment orders, Section 4A–208 applies regardless of whether processing is done by automation, semiautomated means or manually.

4.   In furtherance of medium neutrality, the reference to a "writing" in the pre-2022 text of this section has been changed to refer to a "record."

As amended in 2022.

§ 4A–209.   Acceptance of Payment Order.

(a)   Subject to subsection (d), a receiving bank other than the beneficiary's bank accepts a payment order when it executes the order.

(b)   Subject to subsections (c) and (d), a beneficiary's bank accepts a payment order at the earliest of the following times:

(1)   when the bank (i) pays the beneficiary as stated in Section 4A–405(a) or 4A–405(b), or (ii) notifies the beneficiary of receipt of the order or that the account of the beneficiary has been credited with respect to the order unless the notice indicates that the bank is rejecting the order or that funds with respect to the order may not be withdrawn or used until receipt of payment from the sender of the order;

(2)   when the bank receives payment of the entire amount of the sender's order pursuant to Section 4A–403(a)(1) or 4A–403(a)(2); or

(3)   the opening of the next funds-transfer business day of the bank following the payment date of the order if, at that time, the amount of the sender's order is fully covered by a withdrawable credit balance in an authorized account of the sender or the bank has otherwise received full payment from the sender, unless the order was rejected before that time or is rejected within (i) one hour after that time, or (ii) one hour after the opening of the next business day of the sender following the payment date if that time is later. If notice of rejection is received by the sender after the payment date and the authorized account of the sender does not bear interest, the bank is obliged to pay interest to the sender on the amount of the order for the number of days elapsing after the payment date to the day the sender receives notice or learns that the order was not accepted, counting that day as an elapsed day. If the withdrawable credit balance during that period falls below the amount of the order, the amount of interest payable is reduced accordingly.

(c)   Acceptance of a payment order cannot occur before the order is received by the receiving bank. Acceptance does not occur under subsection (b)(2) or (b)(3) if the beneficiary of the payment order does not have an account with the receiving bank, the account has been closed, or the receiving bank is not permitted by law to receive credits for the beneficiary's account.

(d)   A payment order issued to the originator's bank cannot be accepted until the payment date if the bank is the beneficiary's bank, or the execution date if the bank is not the beneficiary's bank. If the originator's bank executes the originator's payment order before the execution date or pays the beneficiary of the originator's payment order before the payment date and the payment order is subsequently canceled pursuant to Section 4A-211(b), the bank may recover from the beneficiary any payment received to the extent allowed by the law governing mistake and restitution.

Official Comment

1.   This section treats the sender's payment order as a request by the sender to the receiving bank to execute or pay the order and that request can be accepted or rejected by the receiving bank. Section 4A-209 defines when acceptance occurs. Section 4A-210 covers rejection. Acceptance of the payment order imposes an obligation on the receiving bank to the sender if the receiving bank is not the beneficiary's bank, or to the beneficiary if the receiving bank is the beneficiary's bank. These obligations are stated in Section 4A-302 and Section 4A-404.

2.   Acceptance by a receiving bank other than the beneficiary's bank is defined in Section 4A-209(a). That subsection states the only way that a bank other than the beneficiary's bank can accept a payment order. A payment order to a bank other than the beneficiary's bank is, in effect, a request that the receiving bank execute the sender's order by issuing a payment order to the beneficiary's bank or to an intermediary bank. Normally, acceptance occurs at the time of execution, but there is an exception stated in subsection (d) and discussed in Comment 9. Execution occurs when the receiving bank "issues a payment order intended to carry out" the sender's order. Section 4A-301(a). In some cases the payment order issued by the receiving bank may not conform to the sender's order. For example, the receiving bank might make a mistake in the amount of its order, or the order might be issued to the wrong beneficiary's bank or for the benefit of the wrong beneficiary. In all of these cases there is acceptance of the sender's order by the bank when the receiving bank issues its order intended to carry out the sender's order, even though the bank's payment order does not in fact carry out the instruction of the sender. Improper execution of the sender's order may lead to liability to the sender for damages or it may mean that the sender is not obliged to pay its payment order. These matters are covered in Section 4A-303, Section 4A-305, and Section 4A-402.

3.   A receiving bank has no duty to accept a payment order unless the bank makes an agreement, either before or after issuance of the payment order, to accept it, or acceptance is required by a funds transfer system rule. If the bank makes such an agreement it incurs a contractual obligation based on the agreement and may be held liable for breach of contract if a failure to execute violates the agreement. In many cases a bank will enter into an agreement with its customer to govern the rights and obligations of the parties with respect to payment orders issued to the bank by the customer or, in cases in which the sender is also a bank, there may be a funds transfer system rule that governs the obligations of a receiving bank with respect to payment orders transmitted over the system. Such agreements or rules can specify the circumstances under which a receiving bank is obliged to execute a payment order and can define the extent of liability of the receiving bank for breach of the agreement or rule. Section 4A-305(d) states the liability for breach of an agreement to execute a payment order.

4.   In the case of a payment order issued to the beneficiary's bank, acceptance is defined in Section 4A-209(b). The function of a beneficiary's bank that receives a payment order is different from that of a receiving bank that receives a payment order for execution. In the typical case, the beneficiary's bank simply receives payment from the sender of the order, credits the account of the beneficiary and notifies the beneficiary of the credit. Acceptance by the beneficiary's bank does not create any obligation to the sender. Acceptance by the beneficiary's bank means that the bank is liable to the beneficiary for the amount of the order. Section 4A-404(a). There are three ways in which the beneficiary's bank can accept a payment order which are described in the following comments.

5.   Under Section 4A-209(b)(1), the beneficiary's bank can accept a payment order by paying the beneficiary. In the normal case of crediting an account of the beneficiary, payment occurs when the beneficiary is given notice of the right to withdraw the credit, the credit is applied to a debt of the beneficiary, or "funds with respect to the order" are otherwise made available to the beneficiary. Section 4A-405(a). The quoted phrase covers cases in which funds are made available to the beneficiary as a result of receipt of a payment order for the benefit of the beneficiary but the release of funds is not expressed as payment of the order. For example, the beneficiary's bank might express a release of funds equal to the amount of the order as a "loan" that will be automatically repaid when the beneficiary's bank receives payment by the sender of the order. If the release of funds is designated as a loan pursuant to a routine practice of the bank, the release is conditional payment of the order rather than a loan, particularly if normal incidents of a loan such as the signing of a loan agreement or note and the payment of interest are not present. Such a release of funds is payment to the beneficiary under Section 4A-405(a). Under Section 4A-405(c) the bank cannot recover the money from the beneficiary if the bank does not receive payment from the sender of the payment order that it accepted. Exceptions to this rule are stated in § 4A-405(d) and (e). The beneficiary's bank may also accept by notifying the beneficiary that the order has been received. "Notifies" is

defined in Section 1–201(26)1–202(d). In some cases a beneficiary's bank will receive a payment order during the day but settlement of the sender's obligation to pay the order will not occur until the end of the day. If the beneficiary's bank wants to defer incurring liability to the beneficiary until the beneficiary's bank receives payment, it can do so. The beneficiary's bank incurs no liability to the beneficiary with respect to a payment order that it receives until it accepts the order. If the bank does not accept pursuant to subsection (b)(1), acceptance does not occur until the end of the day when the beneficiary's bank receives settlement. If the sender settles, the payment order will be accepted under subsection (b)(2) and the funds will be released to the beneficiary the next morning. If the sender doesn't settle, no acceptance occurs. In either case the beneficiary's bank suffers no loss.

6.   In most cases the beneficiary's bank will receive a payment order from another bank. If the sender is a bank and the beneficiary's bank receives payment from the sender by final settlement through the Federal Reserve System or a funds transfer system (Section 4A–403(a)(1)) or, less commonly, through credit to an account of the beneficiary's bank with the sender or another bank (Section 4A–403(a)(2)), acceptance by the beneficiary's bank occurs at the time payment is made. Section 4A–209(b)(2). A minor exception to this rule is stated in Section 4A–209(c). Section 4A–209(b)(2) results in automatic acceptance of payment orders issued to a beneficiary's bank by means of Fedwire because the Federal Reserve account of the beneficiary's bank is credited and final payment is made to that bank when the payment order is received.

Subsection (b)(2) would also apply to cases in which the beneficiary's bank mistakenly pays a person who is not the beneficiary of the payment order issued to the beneficiary's bank. For example, suppose the payment order provides for immediate payment to Account # 12345. The beneficiary's bank erroneously credits Account # 12346 and notifies the holder of that account of the credit. No acceptance occurs in this case under subsection (b)(1) because the beneficiary of the order has not been paid or notified. The holder of Account # 12345 is the beneficiary of the order issued to the beneficiary's bank. But acceptance will normally occur if the beneficiary's bank takes no other action, because the bank will normally receive settlement with respect to the payment order. At that time the bank has accepted because the sender paid its payment order. The bank is liable to pay the holder of Account # 12345. The bank has paid the holder of Account # 12346 by mistake, and has a right to recover the payment if the credit is withdrawn, to the extent provided in the law governing mistake and restitution.

7.   Subsection (b)(3) covers cases of inaction by the beneficiary's bank. It applies whether or not the sender is a bank and covers a case in which the sender and the beneficiary both have accounts with the receiving bank and payment will be made by debiting the account of the sender and crediting the account of the beneficiary. Subsection (b)(3) is similar to subsection (b)(2) in that it bases acceptance by the beneficiary's bank on payment by the sender. Payment by the sender is effected by a debit to the sender's account if the account balance is sufficient to cover the amount of the order. On the payment date (Section 4A–401) of the order the beneficiary's bank will normally credit the beneficiary's account and notify the beneficiary of receipt of the order if it is satisfied that the sender's account balance covers the order or is willing to give credit to the sender. In some cases, however, the bank may not be willing to give credit to the sender and it may not be possible for the bank to determine until the end of the day on the payment date whether there are sufficient good funds in the sender's account. There may be various transactions during the day involving funds going into and out of the account. Some of these transactions may occur late in the day or after the close of the banking day. To accommodate this situation, subsection (b)(3) provides that the status of the account is determined at the opening of the next funds transfer business day of the beneficiary's bank after the payment date of the order. If the sender's account balance is sufficient to cover the order, the beneficiary's bank has a source of payment and the result in almost all cases is that the bank accepts the order at that time if it did not previously accept under subsection (b)(1). In rare cases, a bank may want to avoid acceptance under subsection (b)(3) by rejecting the order as discussed in Comment 8.

8.   Section 4A–209 is based on a general principle that a receiving bank is not obliged to accept a payment order unless it has agreed or is bound by a funds transfer system rule to do so. Thus, provision is made to allow the receiving bank to prevent acceptance of the order. This principle is consistently followed if the receiving bank is not the beneficiary's bank. If the receiving bank is not the beneficiary's bank, acceptance is in the control of the receiving bank because it occurs only if the order is executed. But in the case of the beneficiary's bank acceptance can occur by passive receipt of payment under subsection (b)(2) or (3). In the case of a payment made by Fedwire acceptance cannot be prevented. In other cases the beneficiary's bank can prevent acceptance by giving notice of rejection to the sender before payment occurs under Section 4A–403(a)(1) or (2). A minor exception to the ability of the beneficiary's bank to reject is stated in Section 4A–502(c)(3).

Under subsection (b)(3) acceptance occurs at the opening of the next funds transfer business day of the beneficiary's bank following the payment date unless the bank rejected the order before that time or it rejects within one hour after that time. In some cases the sender and the beneficiary's bank may not be in the same time zone or the beginning of the business day of the sender and the funds transfer business day of the beneficiary's bank may not coincide. For example, the sender may be located in California and the beneficiary's bank in New York. Since in most cases notice of rejection would be communicated electronically or by telephone, it might not be feasible for the bank to give notice before one hour after the opening of the funds transfer business day in New York because at that hour, the sender's business day may not have started in California. For that reason, there are alternative deadlines stated in subsection (b)(3). In the case stated, the bank acts in time if it gives notice within one hour after the opening of the business day of the sender. But if the notice of rejection is received by the sender after the payment date, the bank is obliged to pay interest to the sender if the sender's account does not bear interest. In that case the bank had the use of funds of the sender that the sender could reasonably assume would be used to pay the beneficiary. The rate of interest is stated in Section 4A–506. If the sender receives notice on the day after the payment date the sender is entitled to one day's interest. If receipt of notice is delayed for more than one day, the sender is entitled to interest for each additional day of delay.

9. Subsection (d) applies only to a payment order by the originator of a funds transfer to the originator's bank and it refers to the following situation. On April 1, Originator instructs Bank A to make a payment on April 15 to the account of Beneficiary in Bank B. By mistake, on April 1, Bank A executes Originator's payment order by issuing a payment order to Bank B instructing immediate payment to Beneficiary. Bank B credited Beneficiary's account and immediately released the funds to Beneficiary. Under subsection (d) no acceptance by Bank A occurred on April 1 when Originator's payment order was executed because acceptance cannot occur before the execution date which in this case would be April 15 or shortly before that date. Section 4A–301(b). Under Section 4A–402(c), Originator is not obliged to pay Bank A until the order is accepted and that can't occur until the execution date. But Bank A is required to pay Bank B when Bank B accepted Bank A's order on April 1. Unless Originator and Beneficiary are the same person, in almost all cases Originator is paying a debt owed to Beneficiary and early payment does not injure Originator because Originator does not have to pay Bank A until the execution date. Section 4A–402(c). Bank A takes the interest loss. But suppose that on April 3, Originator concludes that no debt was owed to Beneficiary or that the debt was less than the amount of the payment order. Under Section 4A–211(b) Originator can cancel its payment order if Bank A has not accepted. If early execution of Originator's payment order is acceptance, Originator can suffer a loss because cancellation after acceptance is not possible without the consent of Bank A and Bank B. Section 4A–211(c). If Originator has to pay Bank A, Originator would be required to seek recovery of the money from Beneficiary. Subsection (d) prevents this result and puts the risk of loss on Bank A by providing that the early execution does not result in acceptance until the execution date. Since on April 3 Originator's order was not yet accepted, Originator can cancel it under Section 4A–211(b). The result is that Bank A is not entitled to payment from Originator but is obliged to pay Bank B. Bank A has paid Beneficiary by mistake. If Originator's payment order is cancelled, Bank A becomes the originator of an erroneous funds transfer to Beneficiary. Bank A has the burden of recovering payment from Beneficiary on the basis of a payment by mistake. If Beneficiary received the money in good faith in payment of a debt owed to Beneficiary by Originator, the law of mistake and restitution may allow Beneficiary to keep all or part of the money received. If Originator owed money to Beneficiary, Bank A has paid Originator's debt and, under the law of restitution, which applies pursuant to Section 1–103, Bank A is subrogated to Beneficiary's rights against Originator on the debt.

If Bank A is the Beneficiary's bank and Bank A credited Beneficiary's account and released the funds to Beneficiary on April 1, the analysis is similar. If Originator's order is cancelled, Bank A has paid Beneficiary by mistake. The right of Bank A to recover the payment from Beneficiary is similar to Bank A's rights in the preceding paragraph.

As amended in 2022.

§ 4A–210. Rejection of Payment Order.

(a) A payment order is rejected by the receiving bank by a notice of rejection transmitted to the sender orally, ~~electronically,~~ or in ~~writing~~ a record. A notice of rejection need not use any particular words and is sufficient if it indicates that the receiving bank is rejecting the order or will not execute or pay the order. Rejection is effective when the notice is given if transmission is by a means that is reasonable in the circumstances. If notice of rejection is given by a means that is not reasonable, rejection is effective when the notice is received. If an agreement of the sender and receiving bank establishes the means to be used to reject a payment order, (i) any means complying with the agreement is reasonable and (ii) any means not complying is not reasonable unless no significant delay in receipt of the notice resulted from the use of the noncomplying means.

(b) This subsection applies if a receiving bank other than the beneficiary's bank fails to execute a payment order despite the existence on the execution date of a withdrawable credit balance in an authorized account of the sender sufficient to cover the order. If the sender does not receive notice of rejection of the order on the execution date and the authorized account of the sender does not bear interest, the bank is obliged to pay interest to the sender on the amount of the order for the number of days elapsing after the execution date to the earlier of the day the order is canceled pursuant to Section 4A–211(d) or the day the sender receives notice or learns that the order was not executed, counting the final day of the period as an elapsed day. If the withdrawable credit balance during that period falls below the amount of the order, the amount of interest is reduced accordingly.

(c)   If a receiving bank suspends payments, all unaccepted payment orders issued to it are deemed rejected at the time the bank suspends payments.

(d)   Acceptance of a payment order precludes a later rejection of the order. Rejection of a payment order precludes a later acceptance of the order.

As amended in 2022.

Official Comment

1.   With respect to payment orders issued to a receiving bank other than the beneficiary's bank, notice of rejection is not necessary to prevent acceptance of the order. Acceptance can occur only if the receiving bank executes the order. Section 4A–209(a). But notice of rejection will routinely be given by such a bank in cases in which the bank cannot or is not willing to execute the order for some reason. There are many reasons why a bank doesn't execute an order. The payment order may not clearly instruct the receiving bank because of some ambiguity in the order or an internal inconsistency. In some cases, the receiving bank may not be able to carry out the instruction because of equipment failure, credit limitations on the receiving bank, or some other factor which makes proper execution of the order infeasible. In those cases notice of rejection is a means of informing the sender of the facts so that a corrected payment order can be transmitted or the sender can seek alternate means of completing the funds transfer. The other major reason for not executing an order is that the sender's account is insufficient to cover the order and the receiving bank is not willing to give credit to the sender. If the sender's account is sufficient to cover the order and the receiving bank chooses not to execute the order, notice of rejection is necessary to prevent liability to pay interest to the sender if the case falls within Section 4A–210(b) which is discussed in Comment 3.

2.   A payment order to the beneficiary's bank can be accepted by inaction of the bank. Section 4A–209(b)(2) and (3). To prevent acceptance under those provisions it is necessary for the receiving bank to send notice of rejection before acceptance occurs. Subsection (a) of Section 4A–210 states the rule that rejection is accomplished by giving notice of rejection. This incorporates the definitions in Section 1–201(26)1–202(d). Rejection is effective when notice is given if it is given by a means that is reasonable in the circumstances. Otherwise, it is effective when the notice is received. The question of when rejection is effective is important only in the relatively few cases under subsection (b)(2) and (3) in which a notice of rejection is necessary to prevent acceptance. The question of whether a particular means is reasonable depends on the facts in a particular case. In a very large percentage of cases the sender and the receiving bank will be in direct electronic contact with each other and in those cases a notice of rejection can be transmitted instantaneously. Since time is of the essence in a large proportion of funds transfers, some quick means of transmission would usually be required, but this is not always the case. The parties may specify by agreement the means by which communication between the parties is to be made.

3.   Subsection (b) deals with cases in which a sender does not learn until after the execution date that the sender's order has not been executed. It applies only to cases in which the receiving bank was assured of payment because the sender's account was sufficient to cover the order. Normally, the receiving bank will accept the sender's order if it is assured of payment, but there may be some cases in which the bank chooses to reject. Unless the receiving bank had obligated itself by agreement to accept, the failure to accept is not wrongful. There is no duty of the receiving bank to accept the payment order unless it is obliged to accept by express agreement. Section 4A–212. But even if the bank has not acted wrongfully, the receiving bank had the use of the sender's money that the sender could reasonably assume was to be the source of payment of the funds transfer. Until the sender learns that the order was not accepted the sender is denied the use of that money. Subsection (b) obliges the receiving bank to pay interest to the sender as restitution unless the sender receives notice of rejection on the execution date. The time of receipt of notice is determined pursuant to § 1–201(27)Section 1–202(e) and (f). The rate of interest is stated in Section 4A–506. If the sender receives notice on the day after the execution date, the sender is entitled to one day's interest. If receipt of notice is delayed for more than one day, the sender is entitled to interest for each additional day of delay.

4.   Subsection (d) treats acceptance and rejection as mutually exclusive. If a payment order has been accepted, rejection of that order becomes impossible. If a payment order has been rejected it cannot be accepted

later by the receiving bank. Once notice of rejection has been given, the sender may have acted on the notice by making the payment through other channels. If the receiving bank wants to act on a payment order that it has rejected it has to obtain the consent of the sender. In that case the consent of the sender would amount to the giving of a second payment order that substitutes for the rejected first order. If the receiving bank suspends payments (Section 4–104(1)(k)), subsection (c) provides that unaccepted payment orders are deemed rejected at the time suspension of payments occurs. This prevents acceptance by passage of time under Section 4A–209(b)(3).

5.   In furtherance of medium neutrality, the reference to "electronically" in the pre-2022 text of this section has been deleted as unnecessary and the reference to a "writing" in the pre-2022 text has been changed to refer to a "record."

As amended in 2022.

§ 4A–211. Cancellation and Amendment of Payment Order.

(a)   A communication of the sender of a payment order cancelling or amending the order may be transmitted to the receiving bank orally, ~~electronically,~~ or in ~~writing~~ a record. If a security procedure is in effect between the sender and the receiving bank, the communication is not effective to cancel or amend the order unless the communication is verified pursuant to the security procedure or the bank agrees to the cancellation or amendment.

(b)   Subject to subsection (a), a communication by the sender cancelling or amending a payment order is effective to cancel or amend the order if notice of the communication is received at a time and in a manner affording the receiving bank a reasonable opportunity to act on the communication before the bank accepts the payment order.

(c)   After a payment order has been accepted, cancellation or amendment of the order is not effective unless the receiving bank agrees or a funds-transfer system rule allows cancellation or amendment without agreement of the bank.

(1)   With respect to a payment order accepted by a receiving bank other than the beneficiary's bank, cancellation or amendment is not effective unless a conforming cancellation or amendment of the payment order issued by the receiving bank is also made.

(2)   With respect to a payment order accepted by the beneficiary's bank, cancellation or amendment is not effective unless the order was issued in execution of an unauthorized payment order, or because of a mistake by a sender in the funds transfer which resulted in the issuance of a payment order (i) that is a duplicate of a payment order previously issued by the sender, (ii) that orders payment to a beneficiary not entitled to receive payment from the originator, or (iii) that orders payment in an amount greater than the amount the beneficiary was entitled to receive from the originator. If the payment order is canceled or amended, the beneficiary's bank is entitled to recover from the beneficiary any amount paid to the beneficiary to the extent allowed by the law governing mistake and restitution.

(d)   An unaccepted payment order is canceled by operation of law at the close of the fifth funds-transfer business day of the receiving bank after the execution date or payment date of the order.

(e)   A canceled payment order cannot be accepted. If an accepted payment order is canceled, the acceptance is nullified and no person has any right or obligation based on the acceptance. Amendment of a payment order is deemed to be cancellation of the original order at the time of amendment and issue of a new payment order in the amended form at the same time.

(f)   Unless otherwise provided in an agreement of the parties or in a funds-transfer system rule, if the receiving bank, after accepting a payment order, agrees to cancellation or amendment of the order by the sender or is bound by a funds-transfer system rule allowing cancellation or amendment without the bank's agreement, the sender, whether or not cancellation or amendment is effective, is liable to the bank for any loss and expenses, including reasonable attorney's fees, incurred by the bank as a result of the cancellation or amendment or attempted cancellation or amendment.

(g)   A payment order is not revoked by the death or legal incapacity of the sender unless the receiving bank knows of the death or of an adjudication of incapacity by a court of competent jurisdiction and has reasonable opportunity to act before acceptance of the order.

(h)   A funds-transfer system rule is not effective to the extent it conflicts with subsection (c)(2).
As amended in 2022.

Official Comment

1.   This section deals with cancellation and amendment of payment orders. It states the conditions under which cancellation or amendment is both effective and rightful. There is no concept of wrongful cancellation or amendment of a payment order. If the conditions stated in this section are not met the attempted cancellation or amendment is not effective. If the stated conditions are met the cancellation or amendment is effective and rightful. The sender of a payment order may want to withdraw or change the order because the sender has had a change of mind about the transaction or because the payment order was erroneously issued or for any other reason. One common situation is that of multiple transmission of the same order. The sender that mistakenly transmits the same order twice wants to correct the mistake by cancelling the duplicate order. Or, a sender may have intended to order a payment of $1,000,000 but mistakenly issued an order to pay $10,000,000. In this case the sender might try to correct the mistake by cancelling the order and issuing another order in the proper amount. Or, the mistake could be corrected by amending the order to change it to the proper amount. Whether the error is corrected by amendment or cancellation and reissue the net result is the same. This result is stated in the last sentence of subsection (e).

2.   Subsection (a) allows a cancellation or amendment of a payment order to be communicated to the receiving bank "orally, ~~electronically,~~ or in ~~writing~~ a record." The quoted phrase is consistent with the language of Section 4A–103(a) applicable to payment orders. Cancellations and amendments are normally subject to verification pursuant to security procedures to the same extent as payment orders. Subsection (a) recognizes this fact by providing that in cases in which there is a security procedure in effect between the sender and the receiving bank the bank is not bound by a communication cancelling or amending an order unless verification has been made. This is necessary to protect the bank because under subsection (b) a cancellation or amendment can be effective by unilateral action of the sender. Without verification the bank cannot be sure whether the communication was or was not effective to cancel or amend a previously verified payment order.

3.   If the receiving bank has not yet accepted the order, there is no reason why the sender should not be able to cancel or amend the order unilaterally so long as the requirements of subsections (a) and (b) are met. If the receiving bank has accepted the order, it is possible to cancel or amend but only if the requirements of subsection (c) are met.

First consider the case of a receiving bank other than the beneficiary's bank. If the bank has not yet accepted the order, the sender can unilaterally cancel or amend. The communication amending or cancelling the payment order must be received in time to allow the bank to act on it before the bank issues its payment order in execution of the sender's order. The time that the sender's communication is received is governed by Section 4A–106. If a payment order does not specify a delayed payment date or execution date, the order will normally be executed shortly after receipt. Thus, as a practical matter, the sender will have very little time in which to instruct cancellation or amendment before acceptance. In addition, a receiving bank will normally have cut-off times for receipt of such communications, and the receiving bank is not obliged to act on communications received after the cut-off hour. Cancellation by the sender after execution of the order by the receiving bank requires the agreement of the bank unless a funds transfer rule otherwise provides. Subsection (c). Although execution of the sender's order by the receiving bank does not itself impose liability on the receiving bank (under Section 4A–402 no liability is incurred by the receiving bank to pay its order until it is accepted), it would commonly be the case that acceptance follows shortly after issuance. Thus, as a practical matter, a receiving bank that has executed a payment order will incur a liability to the next bank in the chain before it would be able to act on the cancellation request of its customer. It is unreasonable to impose on the receiving bank a risk of loss with respect to a cancellation request without the consent of the receiving bank.

The statute does not state how or when the agreement of the receiving bank must be obtained for cancellation after execution. The receiving bank's consent could be obtained at the time cancellation occurs or it could be based on a preexisting agreement. Or, a funds transfer system rule could provide that cancellation can be made unilaterally by the sender. By virtue of that rule any receiving bank covered by the rule is bound. Section 4A–501. If the receiving bank has already executed the sender's order, the bank would not consent to cancellation unless the bank to which the receiving bank has issued its payment order consents to cancellation of that order. It makes no sense to allow cancellation of a payment order unless all subsequent payment orders in the funds transfer that were issued because of the cancelled payment order are also cancelled. Under subsection (c)(1), if a receiving bank consents to cancellation of the payment order after it has executed, the cancellation is not effective unless the receiving bank also cancels the payment order issued by the bank.

4. With respect to a payment order issued to the beneficiary's bank, acceptance is particularly important because it creates liability to pay the beneficiary, it defines when the originator pays its obligation to the beneficiary, and it defines when any obligation for which the payment is made is discharged. Since acceptance affects the rights of the originator and the beneficiary it is not appropriate to allow the beneficiary's bank to agree to cancellation or amendment except in unusual cases. Except as provided in subsection (c)(2), cancellation or amendment after acceptance by the beneficiary's bank is not possible unless all parties affected by the order agree. Under subsection (c)(2), cancellation or amendment is possible only in the four cases stated. The following examples illustrate subsection (c)(2):

Case # 1. Originator's Bank executed a payment order issued in the name of its customer as sender. The order was not authorized by the customer and was fraudulently issued. Beneficiary's Bank accepted the payment order issued by Originator's Bank. Under subsection (c)(2) Originator's Bank can cancel the order if Beneficiary's Bank consents. It doesn't make any difference whether the payment order that Originator's Bank accepted was or was not enforceable against the customer under Section 4A–202(b). Verification under that provision is important in determining whether Originator's Bank or the customer has the risk of loss, but it has no relevance under Section 4A–211(c)(2). Whether or not verified, the payment order was not authorized by the customer. Cancellation of the payment order to Beneficiary's Bank causes the acceptance of Beneficiary's Bank to be nullified. Subsection (e). Beneficiary's Bank is entitled to recover payment from the beneficiary to the extent allowed by the law of mistake and restitution. In this kind of case the beneficiary is usually a party to the fraud who has no right to receive or retain payment of the order.

Case # 2. Originator owed Beneficiary $1,000,000 and ordered Bank A to pay that amount to the account of Beneficiary in Bank B. Bank A issued a complying order to Bank B, but by mistake issued a duplicate order as well. Bank B accepted both orders. Under subsection (c)(2)(i) cancellation of the duplicate order could be made by Bank A with the consent of Bank B. Beneficiary has no right to receive or retain payment of the duplicate payment order if only $1,000,000 was owed by Originator to Beneficiary. If Originator owed $2,000,000 to Beneficiary, the law of restitution might allow Beneficiary to retain the $1,000,000 paid by Bank B on the duplicate order. In that case Bank B is entitled to reimbursement from Bank A under subsection (f).

Case # 3. Originator owed $1,000,000 to X. Intending to pay X, Originator ordered Bank A to pay $1,000,000 to Y's account in Bank B. Bank A issued a complying payment order to Bank B which Bank B accepted by releasing the $1,000,000 to Y. Under subsection (c)(2)(ii) Bank A can cancel its payment order to Bank B with the consent of Bank B if Y was not entitled to receive payment from Originator. Originator can also cancel its order to Bank A with Bank A's consent. Subsection (c)(1). Bank B may recover the $1,000,000 from Y unless the law of mistake and restitution allows Y to retain some or all of the amount paid. If no debt was owed to Y, Bank B should have a right of recovery.

Case # 4. Originator owed Beneficiary $10,000. By mistake Originator ordered Bank A to pay $1,000,000 to the account of Beneficiary in Bank B. Bank A issued a complying order to Bank B which accepted by notifying Beneficiary of its right to withdraw $1,000,000. Cancellation is permitted in this case under subsection (c)(2)(iii). If Bank B paid Beneficiary it is entitled to recover the payment except to the extent the law of mistake and restitution allows Beneficiary to retain payment. In this case Beneficiary might be entitled to retain $10,000, the amount of the debt owed to Beneficiary. If Beneficiary may retain $10,000, Bank B would be entitled to $10,000 from Bank A pursuant to subsection (f). In this case Originator also cancelled its order. Thus Bank A would be entitled to $10,000 from Originator pursuant to subsection (f).

5. Unless constrained by a funds transfer system rule, a receiving bank may agree to cancellation or amendment of the payment order under subsection (c) but is not required to do so regardless of the circumstances. If the receiving bank has incurred liability as a result of its acceptance of the sender's order, there are substantial risks in agreeing to cancellation or amendment. This is particularly true for a beneficiary's bank. Cancellation or amendment after acceptance by the beneficiary's bank can be made only in the four cases stated and the beneficiary's bank may not have any way of knowing whether the requirements of subsection (c) have been met or whether it will be able to recover payment from the beneficiary that received payment. Even with indemnity the beneficiary's bank may be reluctant to alienate its customer, the beneficiary, by denying the customer the funds. Subsection (c) leaves the decision to the beneficiary's bank unless the consent of the beneficiary's bank is not required under a funds transfer system rule or other interbank agreement. If a receiving bank agrees to cancellation or amendment under subsection (c)(1) or (2), it is automatically entitled to indemnification from the sender under subsection (f). The indemnification provision recognizes that a sender has no right to cancel a payment order after it is accepted by the receiving bank. If the receiving bank agrees to cancellation, it is doing so as an accommodation to the sender and it should not incur a risk of loss in doing so.

6.   Acceptance by the receiving bank of a payment order issued by the sender is comparable to acceptance of an offer under the law of contracts. Under that law the death or legal incapacity of an offeror terminates the offer even though the offeree has no notice of the death or incapacity. Restatement Second, Contracts § 48. Comment a. to that section states that the "rule seems to be a relic of the obsolete view that a contract requires a 'meeting of minds,' and it is out of harmony with the modern doctrine that a manifestation of assent is effective without regard to actual mental assent." Subsection (g), which reverses the Restatement rule in the case of a payment order, is similar to Section 4–405(1) which applies to checks. Subsection (g) does not address the effect of the bankruptcy of the sender of a payment order before the order is accepted, but the principle of subsection (g) has been recognized in *Bank of Marin v. England*, 385 U.S. 99 (1966). Although Bankruptcy Code Section 542(c) may not have been drafted with wire transfers in mind, its language can be read to allow the receiving bank to charge the sender's account for the amount of the payment order if the receiving bank executed it in ignorance of the bankruptcy.

7.   Subsection (d) deals with stale payment orders. Payment orders normally are executed on the execution date or the day after. An order issued to the beneficiary's bank is normally accepted on the payment date or the day after. If a payment order is not accepted on its execution or payment date or shortly thereafter, it is probable that there was some problem with the terms of the order or the sender did not have sufficient funds or credit to cover the amount of the order. Delayed acceptance of such an order is normally not contemplated, but the order may not have been cancelled by the sender. Subsection (d) provides for cancellation by operation of law to prevent an unexpected delayed acceptance.

8.   A funds transfer system rule can govern rights and obligations between banks that are parties to payment orders transmitted over the system even if the rule conflicts with Article 4A. In some cases, however, a rule governing a transaction between two banks can affect a third party in an unacceptable way. Subsection (h) deals with such a case. A funds transfer system rule cannot allow cancellation of a payment order accepted by the beneficiary's bank if the rule conflicts with subsection (c)(2). Because rights of the beneficiary and the originator are directly affected by acceptance, subsection (c)(2) severely limits cancellation. These limitations cannot be altered by funds transfer system rule.

9.   In furtherance of medium neutrality, the reference to "electronically" in the pre-2022 text of this section has been deleted as unnecessary and the reference to a "writing" in the pre-2022 text has been changed to refer to a "record."

As amended in 2022.

§ 4A–212.   Liability and Duty of Receiving Bank Regarding Unaccepted Payment Order.

If a receiving bank fails to accept a payment order that it is obliged by express agreement to accept, the bank is liable for breach of the agreement to the extent provided in the agreement or in this Article, but does not otherwise have any duty to accept a payment order or, before acceptance, to take any action, or refrain from taking action, with respect to the order except as provided in this Article or by express agreement. Liability based on acceptance arises only when acceptance occurs as stated in Section 4A–209, and liability is limited to that provided in this Article. A receiving bank is not the agent of the sender or beneficiary of the payment order it accepts, or of any other party to the funds transfer, and the bank owes no duty to any party to the funds transfer except as provided in this Article or by express agreement.

Official Comment

With limited exceptions stated in this Article, the duties and obligations of receiving banks that carry out a funds transfer arise only as a result of acceptance of payment orders or of agreements made by receiving banks. Exceptions are stated in Section 4A–209(b)(3) and Section 4A–210(b). A receiving bank is not like a collecting bank under Article 4. No receiving bank, whether it be an originator's bank, an intermediary bank or a beneficiary's bank, is an agent for any other party in the funds transfer.

PART 3

EXECUTION OF SENDER'S PAYMENT ORDER BY RECEIVING BANK

§ 4A–301. Execution and Execution Date.

(a)   A payment order is "executed" by the receiving bank when it issues a payment order intended to carry out the payment order received by the bank. A payment order received by the beneficiary's bank can be accepted but cannot be executed.

(b)   "Execution date" of a payment order means the day on which the receiving bank may properly issue a payment order in execution of the sender's order. The execution date may be determined by instruction of the sender but cannot be earlier than the day the order is received and, unless otherwise determined, is the day the order is received. If the sender's instruction states a payment date, the execution date is the payment date or an earlier date on which execution is reasonably necessary to allow payment to the beneficiary on the payment date.

Official Comment

1.   The terms "executed," "execution" and "execution date" are used only with respect to a payment order to a receiving bank other than the beneficiary's bank. The beneficiary's bank can accept the payment order that it receives, but it does not execute the order. Execution refers to the act of the receiving bank in issuing a payment order "intended to carry out" the payment order that the bank received. A receiving bank has executed an order even if the order issued by the bank does not carry out the order received by the bank. For example, the bank may have erroneously issued an order to the wrong beneficiary, or in the wrong amount or to the wrong beneficiary's bank. In each of these cases execution has occurred but the execution is erroneous. Erroneous execution is covered in Section 4A–303.

2.   "Execution date" refers to the time a payment order should be executed rather than the day it is actually executed. Normally the sender will not specify an execution date, but most payment orders are meant to be executed immediately. Thus, the execution date is normally the day the order is received by the receiving bank. It is common for the sender to specify a "payment date" which is defined in Section 4A–401 as "the day on which the amount of the order is payable to the beneficiary by the beneficiary's bank." Except for automated clearing house transfers, if a funds transfer is entirely within the United States and the payment is to be carried out electronically, the execution date is the payment date unless the order is received after the payment date. If the payment is to be carried out through an automated clearing house, execution may occur before the payment date. In an ACH transfer the beneficiary is usually paid one or two days after issue of the originator's payment order. The execution date is determined by the stated payment date and is a day before the payment date on which execution is reasonably necessary to allow payment on the payment date. A funds transfer system rule could also determine the execution date of orders received by the receiving bank if both the sender and the receiving bank are participants in the funds transfer system. The execution date can be determined by the payment order itself or by separate instructions of the sender or an agreement of the sender and the receiving bank. The second sentence of subsection (b) must be read in the light of Section 4A–106 which states that if a payment order is received after the cut-off time of the receiving bank it may be treated by the bank as received at the opening of the next funds transfer business day.

3.   Execution on the execution date is timely, but the order can be executed before or after the execution date. Section 4A–209(d) and Section 4A–402(c) state the consequences of early execution and Section 4A–305(a) states the consequences of late execution.

§ 4A–302. Obligations of Receiving Bank in Execution of Payment Order.

(a)   Except as provided in subsections (b) through (d), if the receiving bank accepts a payment order pursuant to Section 4A–209(a), the bank has the following obligations in executing the order:

(1)   The receiving bank is obliged to issue, on the execution date, a payment order complying with the sender's order and to follow the sender's instructions concerning (i) any intermediary bank or funds-transfer system to be used in carrying out the funds transfer, or (ii) the means by which payment orders are to be transmitted in the funds transfer. If the originator's bank issues a payment order to an intermediary bank, the originator's bank is obliged to instruct the

intermediary bank according to the instruction of the originator. An intermediary bank in the funds transfer is similarly bound by an instruction given to it by the sender of the payment order it accepts.

(2)   If the sender's instruction states that the funds transfer is to be carried out telephonically or by wire transfer or otherwise indicates that the funds transfer is to be carried out by the most expeditious means, the receiving bank is obliged to transmit its payment order by the most expeditious available means, and to instruct any intermediary bank accordingly. If a sender's instruction states a payment date, the receiving bank is obliged to transmit its payment order at a time and by means reasonably necessary to allow payment to the beneficiary on the payment date or as soon thereafter as is feasible.

(b)   Unless otherwise instructed, a receiving bank executing a payment order may (i) use any funds-transfer system if use of that system is reasonable in the circumstances, and (ii) issue a payment order to the beneficiary's bank or to an intermediary bank through which a payment order conforming to the sender's order can expeditiously be issued to the beneficiary's bank if the receiving bank exercises ordinary care in the selection of the intermediary bank. A receiving bank is not required to follow an instruction of the sender designating a funds-transfer system to be used in carrying out the funds transfer if the receiving bank, in good faith, determines that it is not feasible to follow the instruction or that following the instruction would unduly delay completion of the funds transfer.

(c)   Unless subsection (a)(2) applies or the receiving bank is otherwise instructed, the bank may execute a payment order by transmitting its payment order by first class mail or by any means reasonable in the circumstances. If the receiving bank is instructed to execute the sender's order by transmitting its payment order by a particular means, the receiving bank may issue its payment order by the means stated or by any means as expeditious as the means stated.

(d)   Unless instructed by the sender, (i) the receiving bank may not obtain payment of its charges for services and expenses in connection with the execution of the sender's order by issuing a payment order in an amount equal to the amount of the sender's order less the amount of the charges, and (ii) may not instruct a subsequent receiving bank to obtain payment of its charges in the same manner.

Official Comment

1.   In the absence of agreement, the receiving bank is not obliged to execute an order of the sender. Section 4A-212. Section 4A-302 states the manner in which the receiving bank may execute the sender's order if execution occurs. Subsection (a)(1) states the residual rule. The payment order issued by the receiving bank must comply with the sender's order and, unless some other rule is stated in the section, the receiving bank is obliged to follow any instruction of the sender concerning which funds transfer system is to be used, which intermediary banks are to be used, and what means of transmission is to be used. The instruction of the sender may be incorporated in the payment order itself or may be given separately. For example, there may be a master agreement between the sender and receiving bank containing instructions governing payment orders to be issued from time to time by the sender to the receiving bank. In most funds transfers, speed is a paramount consideration. A sender that wants assurance that the funds transfer will be expeditiously completed can specify the means to be used. The receiving bank can follow the instructions literally or it can use an equivalent means. For example, if the sender instructs the receiving bank to transmit by telex, the receiving bank could use telephone instead. Subsection (c). In most cases the sender will not specify a particular means but will use a general term such as "by wire" or "wire transfer" or "as soon as possible." These words signify that the sender wants a same-day transfer. In these cases the receiving bank is required to use a telephonic or electronic communication to transmit its order and is also required to instruct any intermediary bank to which it issues its order to transmit by similar means. Subsection (a)(2). In other cases, such as an automated clearing house transfer, a same-day transfer is not contemplated. Normally the sender's instruction or the context in which the payment order is received makes clear the type of funds transfer that is appropriate. If the sender states a payment date with respect to the payment order, the receiving bank is obliged to execute the order at a time and in a manner to meet the payment date if that is feasible. Subsection (a)(2). This provision would apply to many ACH transfers made to pay recurring debts of the sender. In other cases, involving relatively small amounts, time may not be an important factor and cost may be a more important element. Fast means, such as telephone or electronic transmission, are more expensive than slow means such as mailing. Subsection (c) states that in the absence of instructions the receiving bank is given discretion to decide. It may issue its payment order by first class mail or by any means reasonable in the circumstances. Section 4A-305 states the liability of a receiving bank for breach of the obligations stated in Section 4A-302.

454

2.   Subsection (b) concerns the choice of intermediary banks to be used in completing the funds transfer, and the funds transfer system to be used. If the receiving bank is not instructed about the matter, it can issue an order directly to the beneficiary's bank or can issue an order to an intermediary bank. The receiving bank also has discretion concerning use of a funds transfer system. In some cases it may be reasonable to use either an automated clearing house system or a wire transfer system such as Fedwire or CHIPS. Normally, the receiving bank will follow the instruction of the sender in these matters, but in some cases it may be prudent for the bank not to follow instructions. The sender may have designated a funds transfer system to be used in carrying out the funds transfer, but it may not be feasible to use the designated system because of some impediment such as a computer breakdown which prevents prompt execution of the order. The receiving bank is permitted to use an alternate means of transmittal in a good faith effort to execute the order expeditiously. The same leeway is not given to the receiving bank if the sender designates an intermediary bank through which the funds transfer is to be routed. The sender's designation of that intermediary bank may mean that the beneficiary's bank is expecting to obtain a credit from that intermediary bank and may have relied on that anticipated credit. If the receiving bank uses another intermediary bank the expectations of the beneficiary's bank may not be realized. The receiving bank could choose to route the transfer to another intermediary bank and then to the designated intermediary bank if there were some reason such as a lack of a correspondent-bank relationship or a bilateral credit limitation, but the designated intermediary bank cannot be circumvented. To do so violates the sender's instructions.

3.   The normal rule, under subsection (a)(1), is that the receiving bank, in executing a payment order, is required to issue a payment order that complies as to amount with that of the sender's order. In most cases the receiving bank issues an order equal to the amount of the sender's order and makes a separate charge for services and expenses in executing the sender's order. In some cases, particularly if it is an intermediary bank that is executing an order, charges are collected by deducting them from the amount of the payment order issued by the executing bank. If that is done, the amount of the payment order accepted by the beneficiary's bank will be slightly less than the amount of the originator's payment order. For example, Originator, in order to pay an obligation of $1,000,000 owed to Beneficiary, issues a payment order to Originator's Bank to pay $1,000,000 to the account of Beneficiary in Beneficiary's Bank. Originator's Bank issues a payment order to Intermediary Bank for $1,000,000 and debits Originator's account for $1,000,010. The extra $10 is the fee of Originator's Bank. Intermediary Bank executes the payment order of Originator's Bank by issuing a payment order to Beneficiary's Bank for $999,990, but under § 4A–402(c) is entitled to receive $1,000,000 from Originator's Bank. The $10 difference is the fee of Intermediary Bank. Beneficiary's Bank credits Beneficiary's account for $999,990. When Beneficiary's Bank accepts the payment order of Intermediary Bank the result is a payment of $999,990 from Originator to Beneficiary. Section 4A–406(a). If that payment discharges the $1,000,000 debt, the effect is that Beneficiary has paid the charges of Intermediary Bank and Originator has paid the charges of Originator's Bank. Subsection (d) of Section 4A–302 allows Intermediary Bank to collect its charges by deducting them from the amount of the payment order, but only if instructed to do so by Originator's Bank. Originator's Bank is not authorized to give that instruction to Intermediary Bank unless Originator authorized the instruction. Thus, Originator can control how the charges of Originator's Bank and Intermediary Bank are to be paid. Subsection (d) does not apply to charges of Beneficiary's Bank to Beneficiary.

In the case discussed in the preceding paragraph the $10 charge is trivial in relation to the amount of the payment and it may not be important to Beneficiary how the charge is paid. But it may be very important if the $1,000,000 obligation represented the price of exercising a right such as an option favorable to Originator and unfavorable to Beneficiary. Beneficiary might well argue that it was entitled to receive $1,000,000. If the option was exercised shortly before its expiration date, the result could be loss of the option benefit because the required payment of $1,000,000 was not made before the option expired. Section 4A–406(c) allows Originator to preserve the option benefit. The amount received by Beneficiary is deemed to be $1,000,000 unless Beneficiary demands the $10 and Originator does not pay it.

§ 4A–303.   Erroneous Execution of Payment Order.

(a)   A receiving bank that (i) executes the payment order of the sender by issuing a payment order in an amount greater than the amount of the sender's order, or (ii) issues a payment order in execution of the sender's order and then issues a duplicate order, is entitled to payment of the amount of the sender's order under Section 4A–402(c) if that subsection is otherwise satisfied. The bank is entitled to recover from the beneficiary of the erroneous order the excess payment received to the extent allowed by the law governing mistake and restitution.

(b)   A receiving bank that executes the payment order of the sender by issuing a payment order in an amount less than the amount of the sender's order is entitled to payment of the amount of the sender's order under Section 4A–402(c) if (i) that subsection is otherwise satisfied and (ii) the bank corrects its mistake by issuing an additional payment order for the benefit of the beneficiary of the sender's order. If the error is not corrected, the issuer of the erroneous order is entitled to receive or retain payment from the sender of the order it accepted only to the extent of the amount of the erroneous order. This subsection does not apply if the receiving bank executes the sender's payment order by issuing a payment order in an amount less than the amount of the sender's order for the purpose of obtaining payment of its charges for services and expenses pursuant to instruction of the sender.

(c)   If a receiving bank executes the payment order of the sender by issuing a payment order to a beneficiary different from the beneficiary of the sender's order and the funds transfer is completed on the basis of that error, the sender of the payment order that was erroneously executed and all previous senders in the funds transfer are not obliged to pay the payment orders they issued. The issuer of the erroneous order is entitled to recover from the beneficiary of the order the payment received to the extent allowed by the law governing mistake and restitution.

Official Comment

1.   Section 4A–303 states the effect of erroneous execution of a payment order by the receiving bank. Under Section 4A–402(c) the sender of a payment order is obliged to pay the amount of the order to the receiving bank if the bank executes the order, but the obligation to pay is excused if the beneficiary's bank does not accept a payment order instructing payment to the beneficiary of the sender's order. If erroneous execution of the sender's order causes the wrong beneficiary to be paid, the sender is not required to pay. If erroneous execution causes the wrong amount to be paid the sender is not obliged to pay the receiving bank an amount in excess of the amount of the sender's order. Section 4A–303 takes precedence over Section 4A–402(c) and states the liability of the sender and the rights of the receiving bank in various cases of erroneous execution.

2.   Subsections (a) and (b) deal with cases in which the receiving bank executes by issuing a payment order in the wrong amount. If Originator ordered Originator's Bank to pay $1,000,000 to the account of Beneficiary in Beneficiary's Bank, but Originator's Bank erroneously instructed Beneficiary's Bank to pay $2,000,000 to Beneficiary's account, subsection (a) applies. If Beneficiary's Bank accepts the order of Originator's Bank, Beneficiary's Bank is entitled to receive $2,000,000 from Originator's Bank, but Originator's Bank is entitled to receive only $1,000,000 from Originator. Originator's Bank is entitled to recover the overpayment from Beneficiary to the extent allowed by the law governing mistake and restitution. Originator's Bank would normally have a right to recover the overpayment from Beneficiary, but in unusual cases the law of restitution might allow Beneficiary to keep all or part of the overpayment. For example, if Originator owed $2,000,000 to Beneficiary and Beneficiary received the extra $1,000,000 in good faith in discharge of the debt, Beneficiary may be allowed to keep it. In this case Originator's Bank has paid an obligation of Originator and under the law of restitution, which applies through Section 1–103, Originator's Bank would be subrogated to Beneficiary's rights against Originator on the obligation paid by Originator's Bank.

If Originator's Bank erroneously executed Originator's order by instructing Beneficiary's Bank to pay less than $1,000,000, subsection (b) applies. If Originator's Bank corrects its error by issuing another payment order to Beneficiary's Bank that results in payment of $1,000,000 to Beneficiary, Originator's Bank is entitled to payment of $1,000,000 from Originator. If the mistake is not corrected, Originator's Bank is entitled to payment from Originator only in the amount of the order issued by Originator's Bank.

3.   Subsection (a) also applies to duplicate payment orders. Assume Originator's Bank properly executes Originator's $1,000,000 payment order and then by mistake issues a second $1,000,000 payment order in execution of Originator's order. If Beneficiary's Bank accepts both orders issued by Originator's Bank, Beneficiary's Bank is entitled to receive $2,000,000 from Originator's Bank but Originator's Bank is entitled to receive only $1,000,000 from Originator. The remedy of Originator's Bank is the same as that of a receiving bank that executes by issuing an order in an amount greater than the sender's order. It may recover the overpayment from Beneficiary to the extent allowed by the law governing mistake and restitution and in a proper case as stated in Comment 2 may have subrogation rights if it is not entitled to recover from Beneficiary.

4.   Suppose Originator instructs Originator's Bank to pay $1,000,000 to Account # 12345 in Beneficiary's Bank. Originator's Bank erroneously instructs Beneficiary's Bank to pay $1,000,000 to Account # 12346 and Beneficiary's Bank accepted. Subsection (c) covers this case. Originator is not obliged to pay its payment order, but Originator's Bank is required to pay $1,000,000 to Beneficiary's Bank. The remedy of Originator's Bank is to recover $1,000,000 from the holder of Account # 12346 that received payment by mistake. Recovery based on the law of mistake and restitution is described in Comment 2.

§ 4A–304.   Duty of Sender to Report Erroneously Executed Payment Order.

If the sender of a payment order that is erroneously executed as stated in Section 4A–303 receives notification from the receiving bank that the order was executed or that the sender's account was debited with respect to the order, the sender has a duty to exercise ordinary care to determine, on the basis of information available to the sender, that the order was erroneously executed and to notify the bank of the relevant facts within a reasonable time not exceeding 90 days after the notification from the bank was received by the sender. If the sender fails to perform that duty, the bank is not obliged to pay interest on any amount refundable to the sender under Section 4A–402(d) for the period before the bank learns of the execution error. The bank is not entitled to any recovery from the sender on account of a failure by the sender to perform the duty stated in this section.

Official Comment

This section is identical in effect to Section 4A–204 which applies to unauthorized orders issued in the name of a customer of the receiving bank. The rationale is stated in Comment 2 to Section 4A–204.

§ 4A–305.   Liability for Late or Improper Execution or Failure to Execute Payment Order.

(a)   If a funds transfer is completed but execution of a payment order by the receiving bank in breach of Section 4A–302 results in delay in payment to the beneficiary, the bank is obliged to pay interest to either the originator or the beneficiary of the funds transfer for the period of delay caused by the improper execution. Except as provided in subsection (c), additional damages are not recoverable.

(b)   If execution of a payment order by a receiving bank in breach of Section 4A–302 results in (i) noncompletion of the funds transfer, (ii) failure to use an intermediary bank designated by the originator, or (iii) issuance of a payment order that does not comply with the terms of the payment order of the originator, the bank is liable to the originator for its expenses in the funds transfer and for incidental expenses and interest losses, to the extent not covered by subsection (a), resulting from the improper execution. Except as provided in subsection (c), additional damages are not recoverable.

(c)   In addition to the amounts payable under subsections (a) and (b), damages, including consequential damages, are recoverable to the extent provided in an express ~~written~~-agreement of the receiving bank, evidenced by a record.

(d)   If a receiving bank fails to execute a payment order it was obliged by express agreement to execute, the receiving bank is liable to the sender for its expenses in the transaction and for incidental expenses and interest losses resulting from the failure to execute. Additional damages, including consequential damages, are recoverable to the extent provided in an express ~~written~~-agreement of the receiving bank, evidenced by a record, but are not otherwise recoverable.

(e)   Reasonable attorney's fees are recoverable if demand for compensation under subsection (a) or (b) is made and refused before an action is brought on the claim. If a claim is made for breach of an agreement under subsection (d) and the agreement does not provide for damages, reasonable attorney's fees are recoverable if demand for compensation under subsection (d) is made and refused before an action is brought on the claim.

(f)   Except as stated in this section, the liability of a receiving bank under subsections (a) and (b) may not be varied by agreement.

As amended in 2022.

Official Comment

1.   Subsection (a) covers cases of delay in completion of a funds transfer resulting from an execution by a receiving bank in breach of Section 4A–302(a). The receiving bank is obliged to pay interest on the amount of the order for the period of the delay. The rate of interest is stated in Section 4A–506. With respect to wire transfers (other than ACH transactions) within the United States, the expectation is that the funds transfer will be completed the same day. In those cases, the originator can reasonably expect that the originator's account will be debited on the same day as the beneficiary's account is credited. If the funds transfer is delayed, compensation can be paid either to the originator or to the beneficiary. The normal practice is to compensate the beneficiary's bank to allow that bank to compensate the beneficiary by back-valuing the payment by the number of days of delay.

Thus, the beneficiary is in the same position that it would have been in if the funds transfer had been completed on the same day. Assume on Day 1, Originator's Bank issues its payment order to Intermediary Bank which is received on that day. Intermediary Bank does not execute that order until Day 2 when it issues an order to Beneficiary's Bank which is accepted on that day. Intermediary Bank complies with subsection (a) by paying one day's interest to Beneficiary's Bank for the account of Beneficiary.

2.   Subsection (b) applies to cases of breach of Section 4A–302 involving more than mere delay. In those cases the bank is liable for damages for improper execution but they are limited to compensation for interest losses and incidental expenses of the sender resulting from the breach, the expenses of the sender in the funds transfer and attorney's fees. This subsection reflects the judgment that imposition of consequential damages on a bank for commission of an error is not justified.

The leading common law case on the subject of consequential damages is *Evra Corp. v. Swiss Bank Corp.*, 673 F.2d 951 (7th Cir. 1982), in which Swiss Bank, an intermediary bank, failed to execute a payment order. Because the beneficiary did not receive timely payment the originator lost a valuable ship charter. The lower court awarded the originator $2.1 million for lost profits even though the amount of the payment order was only $27,000. The Seventh Circuit reversed, in part on the basis of the common law rule of *Hadley v. Baxendale* that consequential damages may not be awarded unless the defendant is put on notice of the special circumstances giving rise to them. Swiss Bank may have known that the originator was paying the shipowner for the hire of a vessel but did not know that a favorable charter would be lost if the payment was delayed. "Electronic payments are not so unusual as to automatically place a bank on notice of extraordinary consequences if such a transfer goes awry. Swiss Bank did not have enough information to infer that if it lost a $27,000 payment order it would face liability in excess of $2 million." 673 F.2d at 956.

If *Evra* means that consequential damages can be imposed if the culpable bank has notice of particular circumstances giving rise to the damages, it does not provide an acceptable solution to the problem of bank liability for consequential damages. In the typical case transmission of the payment order is made electronically. Personnel of the receiving bank that process payment orders are not the appropriate people to evaluate the risk of liability for consequential damages in relation to the price charged for the wire transfer service. Even if notice is received by higher level management personnel who could make an appropriate decision whether the risk is justified by the price, liability based on notice would require evaluation of payment orders on an individual basis. This kind of evaluation is inconsistent with the high-speed, low-price, mechanical nature of the processing system that characterizes wire transfers. Moreover, in *Evra* the culpable bank was an intermediary bank with which the originator did not deal. Notice to the originator's bank would not bind the intermediary bank, and it seems impractical for the originator's bank to convey notice of this kind to intermediary banks in the funds transfer. The success of the wholesale wire transfer industry has largely been based on its ability to effect payment at low cost and great speed. Both of these essential aspects of the modern wire transfer system would be adversely affected by a rule that imposed on banks liability for consequential damages. A banking industry amicus brief in *Evra* stated: "Whether banks can continue to make EFT services available on a widespread basis, by charging reasonable rates, depends on whether they can do so without incurring unlimited consequential risks. Certainly, no bank would handle for $3.25 a transaction entailing potential liability in the millions of dollars."

As the court in *Evra* also noted, the originator of the funds transfer is in the best position to evaluate the risk that a funds transfer will not be made on time and to manage that risk by issuing a payment order in time to allow monitoring of the transaction. The originator, by asking the beneficiary, can quickly determine if the funds transfer has been completed. If the originator has sent the payment order at a time that allows a reasonable margin for correcting error, no loss is likely to result if the transaction is monitored. The other published cases on this issue reach the *Evra* result. *Central Coordinates, Inc. v. Morgan Guaranty Trust Co.*, 40 U.C.C.Rep.Serv. 1340 (N.Y.Sup.Ct. 1985), and *Gatoil (U.S.A.), Inc. v. Forest Hill State Bank*, 1 U.C.C.Rep.Serv.2d 171 (D.Md. 1986).

Subsection (c) allows the measure of damages in subsection (b) to be increased by an express ~~written~~ agreement of the receiving bank, <u>evidenced by a record</u>. An originator's bank might be willing to assume additional responsibilities and incur additional liability in exchange for a higher fee.

3.   Subsection (d) governs cases in which a receiving bank has obligated itself by express agreement to accept payment orders of a sender. In the absence of such an agreement there is no obligation by a receiving bank to accept a payment order. Section 4A–212. The measure of damages for breach of an agreement to accept a payment order is the same as that stated in subsection (b). As in the case of subsection (b), additional damages, including consequential damages, may be recovered to the extent stated in an express ~~written~~ agreement of the receiving bank, <u>evidenced by a record</u>.

4. Reasonable attorney's fees are recoverable only in cases in which damages are limited to statutory damages stated in subsections (a), (b) and (d). If additional damages are recoverable because provided for by an express ~~written~~ agreement, evidenced by a record, attorney's fees are not recoverable. The rationale is that there is no need for statutory attorney's fees in the latter case, because the parties have agreed to a measure of damages which may or may not provide for attorney's fees.

5. The effect of subsection (f) is to prevent reduction of a receiving bank's liability under Section 4A–305.

6. In furtherance of medium neutrality, references to a "written" agreement have been changed to refer to an agreement "evidenced by a record."

As amended in 2022.

PART 4

PAYMENT

§ 4A–401. Payment Date.

"Payment date" of a payment order means the day on which the amount of the order is payable to the beneficiary by the beneficiary's bank. The payment date may be determined by instruction of the sender but cannot be earlier than the day the order is received by the beneficiary's bank and, unless otherwise determined, is the day the order is received by the beneficiary's bank.

Official Comment

"Payment date" refers to the day the beneficiary's bank is to pay the beneficiary. The payment date may be expressed in various ways so long as it indicates the day the beneficiary is to receive payment. For example, in ACH transfers the payment date is the equivalent of "settlement date" or "effective date." Payment date applies to the payment order issued to the beneficiary's bank, but a payment order issued to a receiving bank other than the beneficiary's bank may also state a date for payment to the beneficiary. In the latter case, the statement of a payment date is to instruct the receiving bank concerning time of execution of the sender's order. Section 4A–301(b).

§ 4A–402. Obligation of Sender to Pay Receiving Bank.

(a) This section is subject to Sections 4A–205 and 4A–207.

(b) With respect to a payment order issued to the beneficiary's bank, acceptance of the order by the bank obliges the sender to pay the bank the amount of the order, but payment is not due until the payment date of the order.

(c) This subsection is subject to subsection (e) and to Section 4A–303. With respect to a payment order issued to a receiving bank other than the beneficiary's bank, acceptance of the order by the receiving bank obliges the sender to pay the bank the amount of the sender's order. Payment by the sender is not due until the execution date of the sender's order. The obligation of that sender to pay its payment order is excused if the funds transfer is not completed by acceptance by the beneficiary's bank of a payment order instructing payment to the beneficiary of that sender's payment order.

(d) If the sender of a payment order pays the order and was not obliged to pay all or part of the amount paid, the bank receiving payment is obliged to refund payment to the extent the sender was not obliged to pay. Except as provided in Sections 4A–204 and 4A–304, interest is payable on the refundable amount from the date of payment.

(e) If a funds transfer is not completed as stated in subsection (c) and an intermediary bank is obliged to refund payment as stated in subsection (d) but is unable to do so because not permitted by applicable law or because the bank suspends payments, a sender in the funds transfer that executed a payment order in compliance with an instruction, as stated in Section 4A–302(a)(1), to route the funds transfer through that intermediary bank is entitled to receive or retain payment from the sender of the payment order that it accepted. The first sender in the funds transfer that issued an instruction requiring routing through that intermediary bank is subrogated to the right of the bank that paid the intermediary bank to refund as stated in subsection (d).

(f)   The right of the sender of a payment order to be excused from the obligation to pay the order as stated in subsection (c) or to receive refund under subsection (d) may not be varied by agreement.

Official Comment

1.   Subsection (b) states that the sender of a payment order to the beneficiary's bank must pay the order when the beneficiary's bank accepts the order. At that point the beneficiary's bank is obliged to pay the beneficiary. Section 4A–404(a). The last clause of subsection (b) covers a case of premature acceptance by the beneficiary's bank. In some funds transfers, notably automated clearing house transfers, a beneficiary's bank may receive a payment order with a payment date after the day the order is received. The beneficiary's bank might accept the order before the payment date by notifying the beneficiary of receipt of the order. Although the acceptance obliges the beneficiary's bank to pay the beneficiary, payment is not due until the payment date. The last clause of subsection (b) is consistent with that result. The beneficiary's bank is also not entitled to payment from the sender until the payment date.

2.   Assume that Originator instructs Bank A to order immediate payment to the account of Beneficiary in Bank B. Execution of Originator's payment ordered by Bank A is acceptance under Section 4A–209(a). Under the second sentence of Section 4A–402(c) the acceptance creates an obligation of Originator to pay Bank A the amount of the order. The last clause of that sentence deals with attempted funds transfers that are not completed. In that event the obligation of the sender to pay its payment order is excused. Originator makes payment to Beneficiary when Bank B, the beneficiary's bank, accepts a payment order for the benefit of Beneficiary. Section 4A–406(a). If that acceptance by Bank B does not occur, the funds transfer has miscarried because Originator has not paid Beneficiary. Originator doesn't have to pay its payment order, and if it has already paid it is entitled to refund of the payment with interest. The rate of interest is stated in Section 4A–506. This "money-back guarantee" is an important protection of Originator. Originator is assured that it will not lose its money if something goes wrong in the transfer. For example, risk of loss resulting from payment to the wrong beneficiary is borne by some bank, not by Originator. The most likely reason for noncompletion is a failure to execute or an erroneous execution of a payment order by Bank A or an intermediary bank. Bank A may have issued its payment order to the wrong bank or it may have identified the wrong beneficiary in its order. The money-back guarantee is particularly important to Originator if noncompletion of the funds transfer is due to the fault of an intermediary bank rather than Bank A. In that case Bank A must refund payment to Originator, and Bank A has the burden of obtaining refund from the intermediary bank that it paid.

Subsection (c) can result in loss if an intermediary bank suspends payments. Suppose Originator instructs Bank A to pay to Beneficiary's account in Bank B and to use Bank C as an intermediary bank. Bank A executes Originator's order by issuing a payment order to Bank C. Bank A pays Bank C. Bank C fails to execute the order of Bank A and suspends payments. Under subsections (c) and (d), Originator is not obliged to pay Bank A and is entitled to refund from Bank A of any payment that it may have made. Bank A is entitled to a refund from Bank C, but Bank C is insolvent. Subsection (e) deals with this case. Bank A was required to issue its payment order to Bank C because Bank C was designated as an intermediary bank by Originator. Section 4A–302(a)(1). In this case Originator takes the risk of insolvency of Bank C. Under subsection (e), Bank A is entitled to payment from Originator and Originator is subrogated to the right of Bank A under subsection (d) to refund of payment from Bank C.

3.   A payment order is not like a negotiable instrument on which the drawer or maker has liability. Acceptance of the order by the receiving bank creates an obligation of the sender to pay the receiving bank the amount of the order. That is the extent of the sender's liability to the receiving bank and no other person has any rights against the sender with respect to the sender's order.

§ 4A–403.   Payment by Sender to Receiving Bank.

(a)   Payment of the sender's obligation under Section 4A–402 to pay the receiving bank occurs as follows:

(1)   If the sender is a bank, payment occurs when the receiving bank receives final settlement of the obligation through a Federal Reserve Bank or through a funds-transfer system.

(2)   If the sender is a bank and the sender (i) credited an account of the receiving bank with the sender, or (ii) caused an account of the receiving bank in another bank to be credited, payment occurs when the credit is withdrawn or, if not withdrawn, at midnight of the day on which the credit is withdrawable and the receiving bank learns of that fact.

(3) If the receiving bank debits an account of the sender with the receiving bank, payment occurs when the debit is made to the extent the debit is covered by a withdrawable credit balance in the account.

(b) If the sender and receiving bank are members of a funds-transfer system that nets obligations multilaterally among participants, the receiving bank receives final settlement when settlement is complete in accordance with the rules of the system. The obligation of the sender to pay the amount of a payment order transmitted through the funds-transfer system may be satisfied, to the extent permitted by the rules of the system, by setting off and applying against the sender's obligation the right of the sender to receive payment from the receiving bank of the amount of any other payment order transmitted to the sender by the receiving bank through the funds-transfer system. The aggregate balance of obligations owed by each sender to each receiving bank in the funds-transfer system may be satisfied, to the extent permitted by the rules of the system, by setting off and applying against that balance the aggregate balance of obligations owed to the sender by other members of the system. The aggregate balance is determined after the right of setoff stated in the second sentence of this subsection has been exercised.

(c) If two banks transmit payment orders to each other under an agreement that settlement of the obligations of each bank to the other under Section 4A–402 will be made at the end of the day or other period, the total amount owed with respect to all orders transmitted by one bank shall be set off against the total amount owed with respect to all orders transmitted by the other bank. To the extent of the setoff, each bank has made payment to the other.

(d) In a case not covered by subsection (a), the time when payment of the sender's obligation under Section 4A–402(b) or 4A–402(c) occurs is governed by applicable principles of law that determine when an obligation is satisfied.

Official Comment

1. This section defines when a sender pays the obligation stated in Section 4A–402. If a group of two or more banks engage in funds transfers with each other, the participating banks will sometimes be senders and sometimes receiving banks. With respect to payment orders other than Fedwires, the amounts of the various payment orders may be credited and debited to accounts of one bank with another or to a clearing house account of each bank and amounts owed and amounts due are netted. Settlement is made through a Federal Reserve Bank by charges to the Federal Reserve accounts of the net debtor banks and credits to the Federal Reserve accounts of the net creditor banks. In the case of Fedwires the sender's obligation is settled by a debit to the Federal Reserve account of the sender and a credit to the Federal Reserve account of the receiving bank at the time the receiving bank receives the payment order. Both of these cases are covered by subsection (a)(1). When the Federal Reserve settlement becomes final the obligation of the sender under Section 4A–402 is paid.

2. In some cases a bank does not settle an obligation owed to another bank through a Federal Reserve Bank. This is the case if one of the banks is a foreign bank without access to the Federal Reserve payment system. In this kind of case, payment is usually made by credits or debits to accounts of the two banks with each other or to accounts of the two banks in a third bank. Suppose Bank B has an account in Bank A. Bank A advises Bank B that its account in Bank A has been credited $1,000,000 and that the credit is immediately withdrawable. Bank A also instructs Bank B to pay $1,000,000 to the account of Beneficiary in Bank B. This case is covered by subsection (a)(2). Bank B may want to immediately withdraw this credit. For example, it might do so by instructing Bank A to debit the account and pay some third party. Payment by Bank A to Bank B of Bank A's payment order occurs when the withdrawal is made. Suppose Bank B does not withdraw the credit. Since Bank B is the beneficiary's bank, one of the effects of receipt of payment by Bank B is that acceptance of Bank A's payment order automatically occurs at the time of payment. Section 4A–209(b)(2). Acceptance means that Bank B is obliged to pay $1,000,000 to Beneficiary. Section 4A–404(a). Subsection (a)(2) of Section 4A–403 states that payment does not occur until midnight if the credit is not withdrawn. This allows Bank B an opportunity to reject the order if it does not have time to withdraw the credit to its account and it is not willing to incur the liability to Beneficiary before it has use of the funds represented by the credit.

3. Subsection (a)(3) applies to a case in which the sender (bank or nonbank) has a funded account in the receiving bank. If Sender has an account in Bank and issues a payment order to Bank, Bank can obtain payment from Sender by debiting the account of Sender, which pays its Section 4A–402 obligation to Bank when the debit is made.

4. Subsection (b) deals with multilateral settlements made through a funds transfer system and is based on the CHIPS settlement system. In a funds transfer system such as CHIPS, which allows the various banks that

transmit payment orders over the system to settle obligations at the end of each day, settlement is not based on individual payment orders. Each bank using the system engages in funds transfers with many other banks using the system. Settlement for any participant is based on the net credit or debit position of that participant with all other banks using the system. Subsection (b) is designed to make clear that the obligations of any sender are paid when the net position of that sender is settled in accordance with the rules of the funds transfer system. This provision is intended to invalidate any argument, based on common-law principles, that multilateral netting is not valid because mutuality of obligation is not present. Subsection (b) dispenses with any mutuality of obligation requirements. Subsection (c) applies to cases in which two banks send payment orders to each other during the day and settle with each other at the end of the day or at the end of some other period. It is similar to subsection (b) in that it recognizes that a sender's obligation to pay a payment order is satisfied by a setoff. The obligations of each bank as sender to the other as receiving bank are obligations of the bank itself and not as representative of customers. These two sections are important in the case of insolvency of a bank. They make clear that liability under Section 4A–402 is based on the net position of the insolvent bank after setoff.

5. Subsection (d) relates to the uncommon case in which the sender doesn't have an account relationship with the receiving bank and doesn't settle through a Federal Reserve Bank. An example would be a customer that pays over the counter for a payment order that the customer issues to the receiving bank. Payment would normally be by cash, check or bank obligation. When payment occurs is determined by law outside Article 4A.

§ 4A–404. Obligation of Beneficiary's Bank to Pay and Give Notice to Beneficiary.

(a) Subject to Sections 4A–211(e), 4A–405(d), and 4A–405(e), if a beneficiary's bank accepts a payment order, the bank is obliged to pay the amount of the order to the beneficiary of the order. Payment is due on the payment date of the order, but if acceptance occurs on the payment date after the close of the funds-transfer business day of the bank, payment is due on the next funds-transfer business day. If the bank refuses to pay after demand by the beneficiary and receipt of notice of particular circumstances that will give rise to consequential damages as a result of nonpayment, the beneficiary may recover damages resulting from the refusal to pay to the extent the bank had notice of the damages, unless the bank proves that it did not pay because of a reasonable doubt concerning the right of the beneficiary to payment.

(b) If a payment order accepted by the beneficiary's bank instructs payment to an account of the beneficiary, the bank is obliged to notify the beneficiary of receipt of the order before midnight of the next funds-transfer business day following the payment date. If the payment order does not instruct payment to an account of the beneficiary, the bank is required to notify the beneficiary only if notice is required by the order. Notice may be given by first class mail or any other means reasonable in the circumstances. If the bank fails to give the required notice, the bank is obliged to pay interest to the beneficiary on the amount of the payment order from the day notice should have been given until the day the beneficiary learned of receipt of the payment order by the bank. No other damages are recoverable. Reasonable attorney's fees are also recoverable if demand for interest is made and refused before an action is brought on the claim.

(c) The right of a beneficiary to receive payment and damages as stated in subsection (a) may not be varied by agreement or a funds-transfer system rule. The right of a beneficiary to be notified as stated in subsection (b) may be varied by agreement of the beneficiary or by a funds-transfer system rule if the beneficiary is notified of the rule before initiation of the funds transfer.

Official Comment

1. The first sentence of subsection (a) states the time when the obligation of the beneficiary's bank arises. The second and third sentences state when the beneficiary's bank must make funds available to the beneficiary. They also state the measure of damages for failure, after demand, to comply. Since the Expedited Funds Availability Act, 12 U.S.C. 4001 et seq., also governs funds availability in a funds transfer, the second and third sentences of subsection (a) may be subject to preemption by that Act.

2. Subsection (a) provides that the beneficiary of an accepted payment order may recover consequential damages if the beneficiary's bank refuses to pay the order after demand by the beneficiary if the bank at that time had notice of the particular circumstances giving rise to the damages. Such damages are recoverable only to the extent the bank had "notice of the damages." The quoted phrase requires that the bank have notice of the general type or nature of the damages that will be suffered as a result of the refusal to pay and their general magnitude. There is no requirement that the bank have notice of the exact or even the approximate amount of the damages, but if the amount of damages is extraordinary the bank is entitled to notice of that fact. For example, in *Evra Corp. v. Swiss Bank Corp.*, 673 F.2d 951 (7th Cir. 1982), failure to complete a funds transfer of only $27,000

required to retain rights to a very favorable ship charter resulted in a claim for more than $2,000,000 of consequential damages. Since it is not reasonably foreseeable that a failure to make a relatively small payment will result in damages of this magnitude, notice is not sufficient if the beneficiary's bank has notice only that the $27,000 is necessary to retain rights on a ship charter. The bank is entitled to notice that an exceptional amount of damages will result as well. For example, there would be adequate notice if the bank had been made aware that damages of $1,000,000 or more might result.

3.   Under the last clause of subsection (a) the beneficiary's bank is not liable for damages if its refusal to pay was "because of a reasonable doubt concerning the right of the beneficiary to payment." Normally there will not be any question about the right of the beneficiary to receive payment. Normally, the bank should be able to determine whether it has accepted the payment order and, if it has been accepted, the first sentence of subsection (a) states that the bank is obliged to pay. There may be uncommon cases, however, in which there is doubt whether acceptance occurred. For example, if acceptance is based on receipt of payment by the beneficiary's bank under Section 4A–403(a)(1) or (2), there may be cases in which the bank is not certain that payment has been received. There may also be cases in which there is doubt about whether the person demanding payment is the person identified in the payment order as beneficiary of the order.

The last clause of subsection (a) does not apply to cases in which a funds transfer is being used to pay an obligation and a dispute arises between the originator and the beneficiary concerning whether the obligation is in fact owed. For example, the originator may try to prevent payment to the beneficiary by the beneficiary's bank by alleging that the beneficiary is not entitled to payment because of fraud against the originator or a breach of contract relating to the obligation. The fraud or breach of contract claim of the originator may be grounds for recovery by the originator from the beneficiary after the beneficiary is paid, but it does not affect the obligation of the beneficiary's bank to pay the beneficiary. Unless the payment order has been cancelled pursuant to Section 4A–211(c), there is no excuse for refusing to pay the beneficiary and, in a proper case, the refusal may result in consequential damages. Except in the case of a book transfer, in which the beneficiary's bank is also the originator's bank, the originator of a funds transfer cannot cancel a payment order to the beneficiary's bank, with or without the consent of that bank, because the originator is not the sender of that order. Thus, the beneficiary's bank may safely ignore any instruction by the originator to withhold payment to the beneficiary.

4.   Subsection (b) states the duty of the beneficiary's bank to notify the beneficiary of receipt of the order. If acceptance occurs under Section 4A–209(b)(1) the beneficiary is normally notified. Thus, subsection (b) applies primarily to cases in which acceptance occurs under Section 4A–209(b)(2) or (3). Notice under subsection (b) is not required if the person entitled to the notice agrees or a funds transfer system rule provides that notice is not required and the beneficiary is given notice of the rule. In ACH transactions the normal practice is not to give notice to the beneficiary unless notice is requested by the beneficiary. This practice can be continued by adoption of a funds transfer system rule. Subsection (a) is not subject to variation by agreement or by a funds transfer system rule.

§ 4A–405.   Payment by Beneficiary's Bank to Beneficiary.

(a)   If the beneficiary's bank credits an account of the beneficiary of a payment order, payment of the bank's obligation under Section 4A–404(a) occurs when and to the extent (i) the beneficiary is notified of the right to withdraw the credit, (ii) the bank lawfully applies the credit to a debt of the beneficiary, or (iii) funds with respect to the order are otherwise made available to the beneficiary by the bank.

(b)   If the beneficiary's bank does not credit an account of the beneficiary of a payment order, the time when payment of the bank's obligation under Section 4A–404(a) occurs is governed by principles of law that determine when an obligation is satisfied.

(c)   Except as stated in subsections (d) and (e), if the beneficiary's bank pays the beneficiary of a payment order under a condition to payment or agreement of the beneficiary giving the bank the right to recover payment from the beneficiary if the bank does not receive payment of the order, the condition to payment or agreement is not enforceable.

(d)   A funds-transfer system rule may provide that payments made to beneficiaries of funds transfers made through the system are provisional until receipt of payment by the beneficiary's bank of the payment order it accepted. A beneficiary's bank that makes a payment that is provisional under the rule is entitled to refund from the beneficiary if (i) the rule requires that both the beneficiary and the originator be given notice of the provisional nature of the payment before the funds transfer is initiated, (ii) the beneficiary, the beneficiary's bank and the originator's bank agreed to be bound by the rule, and (iii) the beneficiary's bank did not receive payment of the payment order that it accepted. If the beneficiary is obliged to refund payment to the beneficiary's bank, acceptance of the payment order by the beneficiary's bank is nullified and no payment by the originator of the funds transfer to the beneficiary occurs under Section 4A–406.

(e)   This subsection applies to a funds transfer that includes a payment order transmitted over a funds-transfer system that (i) nets obligations multilaterally among participants, and (ii) has in effect a loss-sharing agreement among participants for the purpose of providing funds necessary to complete settlement of the obligations of one or more participants that do not meet their settlement obligations. If the beneficiary's bank in the funds transfer accepts a payment order and the system fails to complete settlement pursuant to its rules with respect to any payment order in the funds transfer, (i) the acceptance by the beneficiary's bank is nullified and no person has any right or obligation based on the acceptance, (ii) the beneficiary's bank is entitled to recover payment from the beneficiary, (iii) no payment by the originator to the beneficiary occurs under Section 4A–406, and (iv) subject to Section 4A–402(e), each sender in the funds transfer is excused from its obligation to pay its payment order under Section 4A–402(c) because the funds transfer has not been completed.

Official Comment

1.   This section defines when the beneficiary's bank pays the beneficiary and when the obligation of the beneficiary's bank under Section 4A–404 to pay the beneficiary is satisfied. In almost all cases the bank will credit an account of the beneficiary when it receives a payment order. In the typical case the beneficiary is paid when the beneficiary is given notice of the right to withdraw the credit. Subsection (a)(i). In some cases payment might be made to the beneficiary not by releasing funds to the beneficiary, but by applying the credit to a debt of the beneficiary. Subsection (a)(ii). In this case the beneficiary gets the benefit of the payment order because a debt of the beneficiary has been satisfied. The two principal cases in which payment will occur in this manner are setoff by the beneficiary's bank and payment of the proceeds of the payment order to a garnishing creditor of the beneficiary. These cases are discussed in Comment 2 to Section 4A–502.

2.   If a beneficiary's bank releases funds to the beneficiary before it receives payment from the sender of the payment order, it assumes the risk that the sender may not pay the sender's order because of suspension of payments or other reason. Subsection (c). As stated in Comment 5 to Section 4A–209, the beneficiary's bank can protect itself against this risk by delaying acceptance. But if the bank accepts the order it is obliged to pay the beneficiary. If the beneficiary's bank has given the beneficiary notice of the right to withdraw a credit made to the beneficiary's account, the beneficiary has received payment from the bank. Once payment has been made to the beneficiary with respect to an obligation incurred by the bank under Section 4A–404(a), the payment cannot be recovered by the beneficiary's bank unless subsection (d) or (e) applies. Thus, a right to withdraw a credit cannot be revoked if the right to withdraw constituted payment of the bank's obligation. This principle applies even if funds were released as a "loan" (see Comment 5 to Section 4A–209), or were released subject to a condition that they would be repaid in the event the bank does not receive payment from the sender of the payment order, or the beneficiary agreed to return the payment if the bank did not receive payment from the sender.

3.   Subsection (c) is subject to an exception stated in subsection (d) which is intended to apply to automated clearing house transfers. ACH transfers are made in batches. A beneficiary's bank will normally accept, at the same time and as part of a single batch, payment orders with respect to many different originator's banks. Comment 2 to Section 4A–206. The custom in ACH transactions is to release funds to the beneficiary early on the payment date even though settlement to the beneficiary's bank does not occur until later in the day. The understanding is that payments to beneficiaries are provisional until the beneficiary's bank receives settlement. This practice is similar to what happens when a depositary bank releases funds with respect to a check forwarded for collection. If the check is dishonored the bank is entitled to recover the funds from the customer. ACH transfers are widely perceived as check substitutes. Section 4A–405(d) allows the funds transfer system to adopt a rule making payments to beneficiaries provisional. If such a rule is adopted, a beneficiary's bank that releases funds to the beneficiary will be able to recover the payment if it doesn't receive payment of the payment order that it accepted. There are two requirements with respect to the funds transfer system rule. The beneficiary, the beneficiary's bank and the originator's bank must all agree to be bound by the rule and the rule must require that both the beneficiary and the originator be given notice of the provisional nature of the payment before the funds transfer is initiated. There is no requirement that the notice be given with respect to a particular funds transfer. Once notice of the provisional nature of the payment has been given, the notice is effective for all subsequent payments to or from the person to whom the notice was given. Subsection (d) provides only that the funds transfer system rule must require notice to the beneficiary and the originator. The beneficiary's bank will know what the rule requires, but it has no way of knowing whether the originator's bank complied with the rule. Subsection (d) does not require proof that the originator received notice. If the originator's bank failed to give the required notice

and the originator suffered as a result, the appropriate remedy is an action by the originator against the originator's bank based on that failure. But the beneficiary's bank will not be able to get the benefit of subsection (d) unless the beneficiary had notice of the provisional nature of the payment because subsection (d) requires an agreement by the beneficiary to be bound by the rule. Implicit in an agreement to be bound by a rule that makes a payment provisional is a requirement that notice be given of what the rule provides. The notice can be part of the agreement or separately given. For example, notice can be given by providing a copy of the system's operating rules.

With respect to ACH transfers made through a Federal Reserve Bank acting as an intermediary bank, the Federal Reserve Bank is obliged under Section 4A–402(b) to pay a beneficiary's bank that accepts the payment order. Unlike Fedwire transfers, under current ACH practice a Federal Reserve Bank that processes a payment order does not obligate itself to pay if the originator's bank fails to pay the Federal Reserve Bank. It is assumed that the Federal Reserve will use its right of preemption which is recognized in Section 4A–107 to disclaim the Section 4A–402(b) obligation in ACH transactions if it decides to retain the provisional payment rule.

4.   Subsection (e) is another exception to subsection (c). It refers to funds transfer systems having loss-sharing rules described in the subsection. CHIPS has proposed a rule that fits the description. Under the CHIPS loss-sharing rule the CHIPS banks will have agreed to contribute funds to allow the system to settle for payment orders sent over the system during the day in the event that one or more banks are unable to meet their settlement obligations. Subsection (e) applies only if CHIPS fails to settle despite the loss-sharing rule. Since funds under the loss-sharing rule will be instantly available to CHIPS and will be in an amount sufficient to cover any failure that can be reasonably anticipated, it is extremely unlikely that CHIPS would ever fail to settle. Thus, subsection (e) addresses an event that should never occur. If that event were to occur, all payment orders made over the system would be cancelled under the CHIPS rule. Thus, no bank would receive settlement, whether or not a failed bank was involved in a particular funds transfer. Subsection (e) provides that each funds transfer in which there is a payment order with respect to which there is a settlement failure is unwound. Acceptance by the beneficiary's bank in each funds transfer is nullified. The consequences of nullification are that the beneficiary has no right to receive or retain payment by the beneficiary's bank, no payment is made by the originator to the beneficiary and each sender in the funds transfer is, subject to Section 4A–402(e), not obliged to pay its payment order and is entitled to refund under Section 4A–402(d) if it has already paid.

§ 4A–406.   Payment by Originator to Beneficiary; Discharge of Underlying Obligation.

(a)   Subject to Sections 4A–211(e), 4A–405(d), and 4A–405(e), the originator of a funds transfer pays the beneficiary of the originator's payment order (i) at the time a payment order for the benefit of the beneficiary is accepted by the beneficiary's bank in the funds transfer and (ii) in an amount equal to the amount of the order accepted by the beneficiary's bank, but not more than the amount of the originator's order.

(b)   If payment under subsection (a) is made to satisfy an obligation, the obligation is discharged to the same extent discharge would result from payment to the beneficiary of the same amount in money, unless (i) the payment under subsection (a) was made by a means prohibited by the contract of the beneficiary with respect to the obligation, (ii) the beneficiary, within a reasonable time after receiving notice of receipt of the order by the beneficiary's bank, notified the originator of the beneficiary's refusal of the payment, (iii) funds with respect to the order were not withdrawn by the beneficiary or applied to a debt of the beneficiary, and (iv) the beneficiary would suffer a loss that could reasonably have been avoided if payment had been made by a means complying with the contract. If payment by the originator does not result in discharge under this section, the originator is subrogated to the rights of the beneficiary to receive payment from the beneficiary's bank under Section 4A–404(a).

(c)   For the purpose of determining whether discharge of an obligation occurs under subsection (b), if the beneficiary's bank accepts a payment order in an amount equal to the amount of the originator's payment order less charges of one or more receiving banks in the funds transfer, payment to the beneficiary is deemed to be in the amount of the originator's order unless upon demand by the beneficiary the originator does not pay the beneficiary the amount of the deducted charges.

(d)   Rights of the originator or of the beneficiary of a funds transfer under this section may be varied only by agreement of the originator and the beneficiary.

Official Comment

1.   Subsection (a) states the fundamental rule of Article 4A that payment by the originator to the beneficiary is accomplished by providing to the beneficiary the obligation of the beneficiary's bank to pay. Since this obligation arises when the beneficiary's bank accepts a payment order, the originator pays the beneficiary at the time of acceptance and in the amount of the payment order accepted.

2.   In a large percentage of funds transfers, the transfer is made to pay an obligation of the originator. Subsection (a) states that the beneficiary is paid by the originator when the beneficiary's bank accepts a payment order for the benefit of the beneficiary. When that happens the effect under subsection (b) is to substitute the obligation of the beneficiary's bank for the obligation of the originator. The effect is similar to that under Article 3 if a cashier's check payable to the beneficiary had been taken by the beneficiary. Normally, payment by funds transfer is sought by the beneficiary because it puts money into the hands of the beneficiary more quickly. As a practical matter the beneficiary and the originator will nearly always agree to the funds transfer in advance. Under subsection (b) acceptance by the beneficiary's bank will result in discharge of the obligation for which payment was made unless the beneficiary had made a contract with respect to the obligation which did not permit payment by the means used. Thus, if there is no contract of the beneficiary with respect to the means of payment of the obligation, acceptance by the beneficiary's bank of a payment order to the account of the beneficiary can result in discharge.

3.   Suppose Beneficiary's contract stated that payment of an obligation owed by Originator was to be made by a cashier's check of Bank A. Instead, Originator paid by a funds transfer to Beneficiary's account in Bank B. Bank B accepted a payment order for the benefit of Beneficiary by immediately notifying Beneficiary that the funds were available for withdrawal. Before Beneficiary had a reasonable opportunity to withdraw the funds Bank B suspended payments. Under the unless clause of subsection (b) Beneficiary is not required to accept the payment as discharging the obligation owed by Originator to Beneficiary if Beneficiary's contract means that Beneficiary was not required to accept payment by wire transfer. Beneficiary could refuse the funds transfer as payment of the obligation and could resort to rights under the underlying contract to enforce the obligation. The rationale is that Originator cannot impose the risk of Bank B's insolvency on Beneficiary if Beneficiary had specified another means of payment that did not entail that risk. If Beneficiary is required to accept Originator's payment, Beneficiary would suffer a loss that would not have occurred if payment had been made by a cashier's check on Bank A, and Bank A has not suspended payments. In this case Originator will have to pay twice. It is obliged to pay the amount of its payment order to the bank that accepted it and has to pay the obligation it owes to Beneficiary which has not been discharged. Under the last sentence of subsection (b) Originator is subrogated to Beneficiary's right to receive payment from Bank B under Section 4A–404(a).

4.   Suppose Beneficiary's contract called for payment by a Fedwire transfer to Bank B, but the payment order accepted by Bank B was not a Fedwire transfer. Before the funds were withdrawn by Beneficiary, Bank B suspended payments. The sender of the payment order to Bank B paid the amount of the order to Bank B. In this case the payment by Originator did not comply with Beneficiary's contract, but the noncompliance did not result in a loss to Beneficiary as required by subsection (b)(iv). A Fedwire transfer avoids the risk of insolvency of the sender of the payment order to Bank B, but it does not affect the risk that Bank B will suspend payments before withdrawal of the funds by Beneficiary. Thus, the unless clause of subsection (b) is not applicable and the obligation owed to Beneficiary is discharged.

5.   Charges of receiving banks in a funds transfer normally are nominal in relationship to the amount being paid by the originator to the beneficiary. Wire transfers are normally agreed to in advance and the parties may agree concerning how these charges are to be divided between the parties. Subsection (c) states a rule that applies in the absence of agreement. In some funds transfers charges of banks that execute payment orders are collected by deducting the charges from the amount of the payment order issued by the bank, i.e. the bank issues a payment order that is slightly less than the amount of the payment order that is being executed. The process is described in Comment 3 to Section 4A–302. The result in such a case is that the payment order accepted by the beneficiary's bank will be slightly less than the amount of the originator's order. Subsection (c) recognizes the principle that a beneficiary is entitled to full payment of a debt paid by wire transfer as a condition to discharge. On the other hand, subsection (c) prevents a beneficiary from denying the originator the benefit of the payment by asserting that discharge did not occur because deduction of bank charges resulted in less than full payment. The typical case is one in which the payment is made to exercise a valuable right such as an option which is unfavorable to the beneficiary. Subsection (c) allows discharge notwithstanding the deduction unless the originator fails to reimburse the beneficiary for the deducted charges after demand by the beneficiary.

PART 5

MISCELLANEOUS PROVISIONS

§ 4A–501. Variation by Agreement and Effect of Funds-Transfer System Rule.

(a)   Except as otherwise provided in this Article, the rights and obligations of a party to a funds transfer may be varied by agreement of the affected party.

(b)   "Funds-transfer system rule" means a rule of an association of banks (i) governing transmission of payment orders by means of a funds-transfer system of the association or rights and obligations with respect to those orders, or (ii) to the extent the rule governs rights and obligations between banks that are parties to a funds transfer in which a Federal Reserve Bank, acting as an intermediary bank, sends a payment order to the beneficiary's bank. Except as otherwise provided in this Article, a funds-transfer system rule governing rights and obligations between participating banks using the system may be effective even if the rule conflicts with this Article and indirectly affects another party to the funds transfer who does not consent to the rule. A funds-transfer system rule may also govern rights and obligations of parties other than participating banks using the system to the extent stated in Sections 4A–404(c), 4A–405(d), and 4A–507(c).

Official Comment

1.   This section is designed to give some flexibility to Article 4A. Funds transfer system rules govern rights and obligations between banks that use the system. They may cover a wide variety of matters such as form and content of payment orders, security procedures, cancellation rights and procedures, indemnity rights, compensation rules for delays in completion of a funds transfer, time and method of settlement, credit restrictions with respect to senders of payment orders and risk allocation with respect to suspension of payments by a participating bank. Funds transfer system rules can be very effective in supplementing the provisions of Article 4A and in filling gaps that may be present in Article 4A. To the extent they do not conflict with Article 4A there is no problem with respect to their effectiveness. In that case they merely supplement Article 4A. Section 4A–501 goes further. It states that unless the contrary is stated, funds transfer system rules can override provisions of Article 4A. Thus, rights and obligations of a sender bank and a receiving bank with respect to each other can be different from that stated in Article 4A to the extent a funds transfer system rule applies. Since funds transfer system rules are defined as those governing the relationship between participating banks, a rule can have a direct effect only on participating banks. But a rule that affects the conduct of a participating bank may indirectly affect the rights of nonparticipants such as the originator or beneficiary of a funds transfer, and such a rule can be effective even though it may affect nonparticipants without their consent. For example, a rule might prevent execution of a payment order or might allow cancellation of a payment order with the result that a funds transfer is not completed or is delayed. But a rule purporting to define rights and obligations of nonparticipants in the system would not be effective to alter Article 4A rights because the rule is not within the definition of funds transfer system rule. Rights and obligations arising under Article 4A may also be varied by agreement of the affected parties, except to the extent Article 4A otherwise provides. Rights and obligations arising under Article 4A can also be changed by Federal Reserve regulations and operating circulars of Federal Reserve Banks. Section 4A–107.

2.   Subsection (b)(ii) refers to ACH transfers. Whether an ACH transfer is made through an automated clearing house of a Federal Reserve Bank or through an automated clearing house of another association of banks, the rights and obligations of the originator's bank and the beneficiary's bank are governed by uniform rules adopted by various associations of banks in various parts of the nation. With respect to transfers in which a Federal Reserve Bank acts as intermediary bank these rules may be incorporated, in whole or in part, in operating circulars of the Federal Reserve Bank. Even if not so incorporated these rules can still be binding on the association banks. If a transfer is made through a Federal Reserve Bank, the rules are effective under subsection (b)(ii). If the transfer is not made through a Federal Reserve Bank, the association rules are effective under subsection (b)(i).

§ 4A–502. Creditor Process Served on Receiving Bank; Setoff by Beneficiary's Bank.

(a)   As used in this section, "creditor process" means levy, attachment, garnishment, notice of lien, sequestration, or similar process issued by or on behalf of a creditor or other claimant with respect to an account.

(b)   This subsection applies to creditor process with respect to an authorized account of the sender of a payment order if the creditor process is served on the receiving bank. For the purpose of determining rights with respect to the creditor process, if the receiving bank accepts the payment order the balance in the authorized account is deemed to be reduced by the amount of the payment order to the extent the bank did not otherwise receive payment of the order, unless the creditor process is served at a time and in a manner affording the bank a reasonable opportunity to act on it before the bank accepts the payment order.

(c)   If a beneficiary's bank has received a payment order for payment to the beneficiary's account in the bank, the following rules apply:

(1)   The bank may credit the beneficiary's account. The amount credited may be set off against an obligation owed by the beneficiary to the bank or may be applied to satisfy creditor process served on the bank with respect to the account.

(2)   The bank may credit the beneficiary's account and allow withdrawal of the amount credited unless creditor process with respect to the account is served at a time and in a manner affording the bank a reasonable opportunity to act to prevent withdrawal.

(3)   If creditor process with respect to the beneficiary's account has been served and the bank has had a reasonable opportunity to act on it, the bank may not reject the payment order except for a reason unrelated to the service of process.

(d)   Creditor process with respect to a payment by the originator to the beneficiary pursuant to a funds transfer may be served only on the beneficiary's bank with respect to the debt owed by that bank to the beneficiary. Any other bank served with the creditor process is not obliged to act with respect to the process.

Official Comment

1.   When a receiving bank accepts a payment order, the bank normally receives payment from the sender by debiting an authorized account of the sender. In accepting the sender's order the bank may be relying on a credit balance in the account. If creditor process is served on the bank with respect to the account before the bank accepts the order but the bank employee responsible for the acceptance was not aware of the creditor process at the time the acceptance occurred, it is unjust to the bank to allow the creditor process to take the credit balance on which the bank may have relied. Subsection (b) allows the bank to obtain payment from the sender's account in this case. Under that provision, the balance in the sender's account to which the creditor process applies is deemed to be reduced by the amount of the payment order unless there was sufficient time for notice of the service of creditor process to be received by personnel of the bank responsible for the acceptance.

2.   Subsection (c) deals with payment orders issued to the beneficiary's bank. The bank may credit the beneficiary's account when the order is received, but under Section 4A–404(a) the bank incurs no obligation to pay the beneficiary until the order is accepted pursuant to Section 4A–209(b). Thus, before acceptance, the credit to the beneficiary's account is provisional. But under Section 4A–209(b) acceptance occurs if the beneficiary's bank pays the beneficiary pursuant to Section 4A–405(a). Under that provision, payment occurs if the credit to the beneficiary's account is applied to a debt of the beneficiary. Subsection (c)(1) allows the bank to credit the beneficiary's account with respect to a payment order and to accept the order by setting off the credit against an obligation owed to the bank or applying the credit to creditor process with respect to the account.

Suppose a beneficiary's bank receives a payment order for the benefit of a customer. Before the bank accepts the order, the bank learns that creditor process has been served on the bank with respect to the customer's account. Normally there is no reason for a beneficiary's bank to reject a payment order, but if the beneficiary's account is garnished, the bank may be faced with a difficult choice. If it rejects the order, the garnishing creditor's potential recovery of funds of the beneficiary is frustrated. It may be faced with a claim by the creditor that the rejection was a wrong to the creditor. If the bank accepts the order, the effect is to allow the creditor to seize funds of its customer, the beneficiary. Subsection (c)(3) gives the bank no choice in this case. It provides that it may not favor its customer over the creditor by rejecting the order. The beneficiary's bank may rightfully reject only if there is an independent basis for rejection.

3.   Subsection (c)(2) is similar to subsection (b). Normally the beneficiary's bank will release funds to the beneficiary shortly after acceptance or it will accept by releasing funds. Since the bank is bound by a garnishment order served before funds are released to the beneficiary, the bank might suffer a loss if funds were released without knowledge that a garnishment order had been served. Subsection (c)(2) protects the bank if it did not have adequate notice of the garnishment when the funds were released.

4. A creditor may want to reach funds involved in a funds transfer. The creditor may try to do so by serving process on the originator's bank, an intermediary bank or the beneficiary's bank. The purpose of subsection (d) is to guide the creditor and the court as to the proper method of reaching the funds involved in a funds transfer. A creditor of the originator can levy on the account of the originator in the originator's bank before the funds transfer is initiated, but that levy is subject to the limitations stated in subsection (b). The creditor of the originator cannot reach any other funds because no property of the originator is being transferred. A creditor of the beneficiary cannot levy on property of the originator and until the funds transfer is completed by acceptance by the beneficiary's bank of a payment order for the benefit of the beneficiary, the beneficiary has no property interest in the funds transfer which the beneficiary's creditor can reach. A creditor of the beneficiary that wants to reach the funds to be received by the beneficiary must serve creditor process on the beneficiary's bank to reach the obligation of the beneficiary's bank to pay the beneficiary which arises upon acceptance by the beneficiary's bank under Section 4A–404(a).

5. "Creditor process" is defined in subsection (a) to cover a variety of devices by which a creditor of the holder of a bank account or a claimant to a bank account can seize the account. Procedure and nomenclature varies widely from state to state. The term used in Section 4A–502 is a generic term.

§ 4A–503. Injunction or Restraining Order With Respect to Funds Transfer.

For proper cause and in compliance with applicable law, a court may restrain (i) a person from issuing a payment order to initiate a funds transfer, (ii) an originator's bank from executing the payment order of the originator, or (iii) the beneficiary's bank from releasing funds to the beneficiary or the beneficiary from withdrawing the funds. A court may not otherwise restrain a person from issuing a payment order, paying or receiving payment of a payment order, or otherwise acting with respect to a funds transfer.

Official Comment

This section is related to Section 4A–502(d) and to Comment 4 to Section 4A–502. It is designed to prevent interruption of a funds transfer after it has been set in motion. The initiation of a funds transfer can be prevented by enjoining the originator or the originator's bank from issuing a payment order. After the funds transfer is completed by acceptance of a payment order by the beneficiary's bank, that bank can be enjoined from releasing funds to the beneficiary or the beneficiary can be enjoined from withdrawing the funds. No other injunction is permitted. In particular, intermediary banks are protected, and injunctions against the originator and the originator's bank are limited to issuance of a payment order. Except for the beneficiary's bank, nobody can be enjoined from paying a payment order, and no receiving bank can be enjoined from receiving payment from the sender of the order that it accepted.

§ 4A–504. Order in Which Items and Payment Orders May Be Charged to Account; Order of Withdrawals From Account.

(a) If a receiving bank has received more than one payment order of the sender or one or more payment orders and other items that are payable from the sender's account, the bank may charge the sender's account with respect to the various orders and items in any sequence.

(b) In determining whether a credit to an account has been withdrawn by the holder of the account or applied to a debt of the holder of the account, credits first made to the account are first withdrawn or applied.

Official Comment

1. Subsection (a) concerns priority among various obligations that are to be paid from the same account. A customer may have written checks on its account with the receiving bank and may have issued one or more payment orders payable from the same account. If the account balance is not sufficient to cover all of the checks and payment orders, some checks may be dishonored and some payment orders may not be accepted. Although there is no concept of wrongful dishonor of a payment order in Article 4A in the absence of an agreement to honor by the receiving bank, some rights and obligations may depend on the amount in the customer's account. Section 4A–209(b)(3) and Section 4A–210(b). Whether dishonor of a check is wrongful also may depend upon the balance in the customer's account. Under subsection (a), the bank is not required to consider the competing items and payment orders in any particular order. Rather it may charge the customer's account for the various items and orders in any order. Suppose there is $12,000 in the customer's account. If a check for $5,000 is presented for payment and the bank receives a $10,000 payment order from the customer, the bank could dishonor the check and accept the payment order. Dishonor of the check is not wrongful because the account balance was less than

the amount of the check after the bank charged the account $10,000 on account of the payment order. Or, the bank could pay the check and not execute the payment order because the amount of the order is not covered by the balance in the account.

2.   Subsection (b) follows Section 4–208(b) in using the first-in-first-out rule for determining the order in which credits to an account are withdrawn.

§ 4A–505. Preclusion of Objection to Debit of Customer's Account.

If a receiving bank has received payment from its customer with respect to a payment order issued in the name of the customer as sender and accepted by the bank, and the customer received notification reasonably identifying the order, the customer is precluded from asserting that the bank is not entitled to retain the payment unless the customer notifies the bank of the customer's objection to the payment within one year after the notification was received by the customer.

Official Comment

This section is in the nature of a statute of repose for objecting to debits made to the customer's account. A receiving bank that executes payment orders of a customer may have received payment from the customer by debiting the customer's account with respect to a payment order that the customer was not required to pay. For example, the payment order may not have been authorized or verified pursuant to Section 4A–202 or the funds transfer may not have been completed. In either case the receiving bank is obliged to refund the payment to the customer and this obligation to refund payment cannot be varied by agreement. Section 4A–204 and Section 4A–402. Refund may also be required if the receiving bank is not entitled to payment from the customer because the bank erroneously executed a payment order. Section 4A–303. A similar analysis applies to that case. Section 4A–402(d) and (f) require refund and the obligation to refund may not be varied by agreement. Under 4A–505, however, the obligation to refund may not be asserted by the customer if the customer has not objected to the debiting of the account within one year after the customer received notification of the debit.

§ 4A–506. Rate of Interest.

(a)   If, under this Article, a receiving bank is obliged to pay interest with respect to a payment order issued to the bank, the amount payable may be determined (i) by agreement of the sender and receiving bank, or (ii) by a funds-transfer system rule if the payment order is transmitted through a funds-transfer system.

(b)   If the amount of interest is not determined by an agreement or rule as stated in subsection (a), the amount is calculated by multiplying the applicable Federal Funds rate by the amount on which interest is payable, and then multiplying the product by the number of days for which interest is payable. The applicable Federal Funds rate is the average of the Federal Funds rates published by the Federal Reserve Bank of New York for each of the days for which interest is payable divided by 360. The Federal Funds rate for any day on which a published rate is not available is the same as the published rate for the next preceding day for which there is a published rate. If a receiving bank that accepted a payment order is required to refund payment to the sender of the order because the funds transfer was not completed, but the failure to complete was not due to any fault by the bank, the interest payable is reduced by a percentage equal to the reserve requirement on deposits of the receiving bank.

Official Comment

1.   A receiving bank is required to pay interest on the amount of a payment order received by the bank in a number of situations. Sometimes the interest is payable to the sender and in other cases it is payable to either the originator or the beneficiary of the funds transfer. The relevant provisions are Section 4A–204(a), Section 4A–209(b)(3), Section 4A–210(b), Section 4A–305(a), Section 4A–402(d) and Section 4A–404(b). The rate of interest may be governed by a funds transfer system rule or by agreement as stated in subsection (a). If subsection (a) doesn't apply, the rate is determined under subsection (b). Subsection (b) is illustrated by the following example. A bank is obliged to pay interest on $1,000,000 for three days, July 3, July 4, and July 5. The published Fed Funds rate is .082 for July 3 and .081 for July 5. There is no published rate for July 4 because that day is not a banking day. The rate for July 3 applies to July 4. The applicable Fed Funds rate is .08167 (the average of .082, .082, and .081) divided by 360 which equals .0002268. The amount of interest payable is $1,000,000 × .0002268 × 3 = $680.40.

2.   In some cases, interest is payable in spite of the fact that there is no fault by the receiving bank. The last sentence of subsection (b) applies to those cases. For example, a funds transfer might not be completed because

the beneficiary's bank rejected the payment order issued to it by the originator's bank or an intermediary bank. Section 4A–402(c) provides that the originator is not obliged to pay its payment order and Section 4A–402(d) provides that the originator's bank must refund any payment received plus interest. The requirement to pay interest in this case is not based on fault by the originator's bank. Rather, it is based on restitution. Since the originator's bank had the use of the originator's money, it is required to pay the originator for the value of that use. The value of that use is not determined by multiplying the interest rate by the refundable amount because the originator's bank is required to deposit with the Federal Reserve a percentage of the bank's deposits as a reserve requirement. Since that deposit does not bear interest, the bank had use of the refundable amount reduced by a percentage equal to the reserve requirement. If the reserve requirement is 12%, the amount of interest payable by the bank under the formula stated in subsection (b) is reduced by 12%.

§ 4A–507. Choice of Law.

(a)   The following rules apply unless the affected parties otherwise agree or subsection (c) applies:

(1)   The rights and obligations between the sender of a payment order and the receiving bank are governed by the law of the jurisdiction in which the receiving bank is located.

(2)   The rights and obligations between the beneficiary's bank and the beneficiary are governed by the law of the jurisdiction in which the beneficiary's bank is located.

(3)   The issue of when payment is made pursuant to a funds transfer by the originator to the beneficiary is governed by the law of the jurisdiction in which the beneficiary's bank is located.

(b)   If the parties described in each paragraph of subsection (a) have made an agreement selecting the law of a particular jurisdiction to govern rights and obligations between each other, the law of that jurisdiction governs those rights and obligations, whether or not the payment order or the funds transfer bears a reasonable relation to that jurisdiction.

(c)   A funds-transfer system rule may select the law of a particular jurisdiction to govern (i) rights and obligations between participating banks with respect to payment orders transmitted or processed through the system, or (ii) the rights and obligations of some or all parties to a funds transfer any part of which is carried out by means of the system. A choice of law made pursuant to clause (i) is binding on participating banks. A choice of law made pursuant to clause (ii) is binding on the originator, other sender, or a receiving bank having notice that the funds-transfer system might be used in the funds transfer and of the choice of law by the system when the originator, other sender, or receiving bank issued or accepted a payment order. The beneficiary of a funds transfer is bound by the choice of law if, when the funds transfer is initiated, the beneficiary has notice that the funds-transfer system might be used in the funds transfer and of the choice of law by the system. The law of a jurisdiction selected pursuant to this subsection may govern, whether or not that law bears a reasonable relation to the matter in issue.

(d)   In the event of inconsistency between an agreement under subsection (b) and a choice-of-law rule under subsection (c), the agreement under subsection (b) prevails.

(e)   If a funds transfer is made by use of more than one funds-transfer system and there is inconsistency between choice-of-law rules of the systems, the matter in issue is governed by the law of the selected jurisdiction that has the most significant relationship to the matter in issue.

Official Comment

1.   Funds transfers are typically interstate or international in character. If part of a funds transfer is governed by Article 4A and another part is governed by other law, the rights and obligations of parties to the funds transfer may be unclear because there is no clear consensus in various jurisdictions concerning the juridical nature of the transaction. Unless all of a funds transfer is governed by a single law it may be very difficult to predict the result if something goes wrong in the transfer. Section 4A–507 deals with this problem. Subsection (b) allows parties to a funds transfer to make a choice-of-law agreement. Subsection (c) allows a funds transfer system to select the law of a particular jurisdiction to govern funds transfers carried out by means of the system. Subsection (a) states residual rules if no choice of law has occurred under subsection (b) or subsection (c).

2.   Subsection (a) deals with three sets of relationships. Rights and obligations between the sender of a payment order and the receiving bank are governed by the law of the jurisdiction in which the receiving bank is located. If the receiving bank is the beneficiary's bank the rights and obligations of the beneficiary are also governed by the law of the jurisdiction in which the receiving bank is located. Suppose Originator, located in

Canada, sends a payment order to Originator's Bank located in a state in which Article 4A has been enacted. The order is for payment to an account of Beneficiary in a bank in England. Under subsection (a)(1), the rights and obligations of Originator and Originator's Bank toward each other are governed by Article 4A if an action is brought in a court in the Article 4A state. If an action is brought in a Canadian court, the conflict of laws issue will be determined by Canadian law which might or might not apply the law of the state in which Originator's Bank is located. If that law is applied, the execution of Originator's order will be governed by Article 4A, but with respect to the payment order of Originator's Bank to the English bank, Article 4A may or may not be applied with respect to the rights and obligations between the two banks. The result may depend upon whether action is brought in a court in the state in which Originator's Bank is located or in an English court. Article 4A is binding only on a court in a state that enacts it. It can have extraterritorial effect only to the extent courts of another jurisdiction are willing to apply it. Subsection (c) also bears on the issues discussed in this Comment.

Under Section 4A–406 payment by the originator to the beneficiary of the funds transfer occurs when the beneficiary's bank accepts a payment order for the benefit of the beneficiary. A jurisdiction in which Article 4A is not in effect may follow a different rule or it may not have a clear rule. Under Section 4A–507(a)(3) the issue is governed by the law of the jurisdiction in which the beneficiary's bank is located. Since the payment to the beneficiary is made through the beneficiary's bank it is reasonable that the issue of when payment occurs be governed by the law of the jurisdiction in which the bank is located. Since it is difficult in many cases to determine where a beneficiary is located, the location of the beneficiary's bank provides a more certain rule.

3.   Subsection (b) deals with choice-of-law agreements and it gives maximum freedom of choice. Since the law of funds transfers is not highly developed in the case law there may be a strong incentive to choose the law of a jurisdiction in which Article 4A is in effect because it provides a greater degree of certainty with respect to the rights of various parties. With respect to commercial transactions, it is often said that "[u]niformity and predictability based upon commercial convenience are the prime considerations in making the choice of governing law . . . ." R. Leflar, *American Conflicts Law*, § 185 (1977). Subsection (b) is derived in part from recently enacted choice-of-law rules in the States of New York and California. N.Y.Gen. Obligations Law 5–1401 (McKinney's 1989 Supp.) and California Civil Code § 1646.5. This broad endorsement of freedom of contract is an enhancement of the approach taken by Restatement (Second) of Conflict of Laws § 187(b) (1971). The Restatement recognizes the basic right of freedom of contract, but the freedom granted the parties may be more limited than the freedom granted here. Under the formulation of the Restatement, if there is no substantial relationship to the jurisdiction whose law is selected and there is no "other" reasonable basis for the parties' choice, then the selection of the parties need not be honored by a court. Further, if the choice is violative of a fundamental policy of a state which has a materially greater interest than the chosen state, the selection could be disregarded by a court. Those limitations are not found in subsection (b).

4.   Subsection (c) may be the most important provision in regard to creating uniformity of law in funds transfers. Most rights stated in Article 4A regard parties who are in privity of contract such as originator and beneficiary, sender and receiving bank, and beneficiary's bank and beneficiary. Since they are in privity they can make a choice of law by agreement. But that is not always the case. For example, an intermediary bank that improperly executes a payment order is not in privity with either the originator or the beneficiary. The ability of a funds transfer system to make a choice of law by rule is a convenient way of dispensing with individual agreements and to cover cases in which agreements are not feasible. It is probable that funds transfer systems will adopt a governing law to increase the certainty of commercial transactions that are effected over such systems. A system rule might adopt the law of an Article 4A state to govern transfers on the system in order to provide a consistent, unitary, law governing all transfers made on the system. To the extent such system rules develop, individual choice-of-law agreements become unnecessary.

Subsection (c) has broad application. A system choice of law applies not only to rights and obligations between banks that use the system, but may also apply to other parties to the funds transfer so long as some part of the transfer was carried out over the system. The originator and any other sender or receiving bank in the funds transfer is bound if at the time it issues or accepts a payment order it had notice that the funds transfer involved use of the system and that the system chose the law of a particular jurisdiction. Under Section 4A–107, the Federal Reserve by regulation could make a similar choice of law to govern funds transfers carried out by use of Federal Reserve Banks. Subsection (d) is a limitation on subsection (c). If parties have made a choice-of-law agreement that conflicts with a choice of law made under subsection (c), the agreement prevails.

5.   Subsection (e) addresses the case in which a funds transfer involves more than one funds transfer system and the systems adopt conflicting choice-of-law rules. The rule that has the most significant relationship to the matter at issue prevails. For example, each system should be able to make a choice of law governing payment orders transmitted over that system with regard to a choice of law made by another system.

UCC ARTICLE 5

LETTERS OF CREDIT

Article 5 was revised in 1995 and amended in 2022.

2022 Amendments appear in ~~strikeout~~/<u>underline</u> format.

Prefatory Note to 2022 amendments appears in Appendix E.

Current through April 2023

For updates, see www.uniformlaws.org

5–101.   Short Title.
5–102.   Definitions.
5–103.   Scope.
5–104.   Formal Requirements.
5–105.   Consideration.
5–106.   Issuance, Amendment, Cancellation, and Duration.
5–107.   Confirmer, Nominated Person, and Adviser.
5–108.   Issuer's Rights and Obligations.
5–109.   Fraud and Forgery.
5–110.   Warranties.
5–111.   Remedies.
5–112.   Transfer of Letter of Credit.
5–113.   Transfer by Operation of Law.
5–114.   Assignment of Proceeds.
5–115.   Statute of Limitations.
5–116.   Choice of Law and Forum.
5–117.   Subrogation of Issuer, Applicant, and Nominated Person.
5–118.   Security Interest of Issuer or Nominated Person.

PREFATORY NOTE

Reason for Revision

When the original Article 5 was drafted 40 years ago, it was written for paper transactions and before many innovations in letters of credit. Now electronic and other media are used extensively. Since the 50's, standby letters of credit have developed and now nearly $500 billion standby letters of credit are issued annually worldwide, of which $250 billion are issued in the United States. The use of deferred payment letters of credit has also greatly increased. The customs and practices for letters of credit have evolved and are reflected in the Uniform Customs and Practice (UCP), usually incorporated into letters of credit, particularly international letters of credit, which have seen four revisions since the 1950's; the current version became effective in 1994 (UCP 500). Lastly, in a number of areas, court decisions have resulted in conflicting rules.

Prior to the appointment of a drafting committee, the ABA UCC Committee appointed a Task Force composed of knowledgeable practitioners and academics. The ABA Task Force studied the case law, evolving technologies and the changes in customs and practices. The Task Force identified a large number of issues which they discussed at some length, and made recommendations for revisions to Article 5. The Task Force stated in a foreword:

"As a result of these increases and changes in usage, practice, players, and pressure, it comes as no surprise that there has been a sizable increase in litigation. Indeed, the approximately 62 cases reported in the United States in 1987 constituted double the cumulative reported cases up to 1965. . . .

Moreover, almost forty years of hard use have revealed weaknesses, gaps and errors in the original statute which compromise its relevance. U.C.C. Article 5 was one of the few areas of the Uniform Commercial Code which did not benefit from prior codification and it should come as no surprise that it may require some revision. . . .

Measured in terms of these areas which are vital to any system of commercial law, the current combination of statute and case law is found wanting in major respects both as to predictability and certainty. What is at issue here are not matters of sophistry but important issues of substance which have not been resolved by the current case law/code method and which admit of little likelihood of such resolution." (45 Bus. Lawyer 1521, at 1532, 1535–6)

The Drafting Committee began its deliberations with the Task Force Report in hand. The final work of the Drafting Committee varies from many of the suggestions of the Task Force.

Need for Uniformity

Letters of Credit are a major instrument in international trade, as well as domestic transactions. To facilitate its usefulness and competitiveness, it is essential that U.S. law be in harmony with international rules and practices, as well as flexible enough to accommodate changes in technology and practices that have, and are, evolving. Not only should the rules be consistent within the United States, but they need to be substantively and procedurally consistent with international practices.

Thus, the goals of the drafting effort were:

- conforming the Article 5 rules to current customs and practices;

- accommodating new forms of Letters of Credit, changes in customs and practices, and evolving technology, particularly the use of electronic media;

- maintaining Letters of Credit as an inexpensive and efficient instrument facilitating trade; and

- resolving conflicts among reported decisions.

Process of Achieving Uniformity

The essence of uniform law revision is to obtain a sufficient consensus and balance among the interests of the various participants so that universal and uniform enactment by the various States may be achieved.

In part this is accomplished by extensive consultation on and broad circulation of the drafts from 1990, when the project began, until approval of the final draft by the American law Institute (ALI) and the National Conference of Commissioners on Uniform State Laws (NCCUSL).

Hundreds of groups were invited to participate in the drafting process. Twenty Advisors were appointed, representing a cross-section of interested parties. In addition 20 Observers regularly attended drafting meetings and over 100 were on the mailing list to receive all drafts of the revision.

The Drafting Committee meetings were open and all those who attended were afforded full opportunity to express their views and participate in the dialogue. The Advisors and Observers were a balanced group with ten representatives of users (Beneficiaries and Applicants); five representatives of governmental agencies; five representatives of the U.S. Council on International Banking (USCIB); seven from major banks in letter of credit transactions; eight from regional banks; and seven law professors who teach and write on Letters of Credit.

Nine Drafting Committee meetings were held that began Friday morning and ended Sunday noon. In addition, the draft was twice debated in full by NCCUSL, once by the ALI Council, once considered by the ALI Consultative Group and once by an ad hoc Committee of the Council; and reviewed and discussed by the ABA Subcommittee on Letters of Credit semi-annually and by several state and city bar association committees.

ARTICLE 5

The drafts were regularly reviewed and discussed in *The Business Lawyer, Letter of Credit Update*, and in other publications.

The consensus, balance and quality achieved in this lengthy deliberative process is a product of not only its Reporter and the Drafting Committee, but also the faithful and energetic participation of the following Advisors and active participants [*Note from West Advisory Panel: We have deleted the list of advisors, etc.*]

Balance of Benefits

Uniform laws can be enacted only if there is a consensus that the benefits achieved advance the public interest in a manner that can be embraced by all users of the law. It appears that as drafted, Revised Article 5 will enjoy substantial support by the participating interests in letter of credit transactions.

Benefits of Revised Article 5 in General

Independence Principle. Revised Article 5 clearly and forcefully states the independence of the letter of credit obligations from the underlying transactions that was unexpressed in, but was a fundamental predicate for, the original Article 5 (Sections 5–103(d) and 5–108(f)). Certainty of payment, independent of other claims, setoffs or other causes of action, is a core element of the commercial utility of letters of credit.

Clarifications. The revision authorizes the use of electronic technology (Sections 5–102(a)(14) and 5–104); expressly permits deferred payment letters of credit (Section 5–102(a)(8)) and two party letters of credit (Section 5–102(a)(10)); provides rules for unstated expiry dates (Section 5–106(c)), perpetual letters of credit (Section 5–106(d)), and non-documentary conditions (Section 5–108(g)); clarifies and establishes rules for successors by operation of law (Sections 5–102(a)(15) and 5–113); conforms to existing practice for assignment of proceeds (Section 5–114); and clarifies the rules where decisions have been in conflict (Section 5–106, Comment 1; Section 5–108, Comments 1, 3, 4, 7, and 9; Section 5–109, Comments 1 and 3; Section 5–113, Comment 1; and Section 5–117, Comment 1).

Harmonizes with International Practice

The UCP is used in most international letters of credit and in many domestic letters of credit. These international practices are well known and employed by the major issuers and users of letters of credit. Revisions have been made to Article 5 to coordinate the Article 5 rules with current international practice (e.g., deferred payment obligations, reasonable time to examine documents, preclusion, non-documentary conditions, return of documents, and irrevocable unless stated to be revocable).

Benefits of Revised Article 5 to Issuers

Consequential Damages. Section 5–111 precludes consequential and punitive damages. It, however, provides strong incentives for Issuers to honor, including provisions for attorneys fees and expenses of litigation, interest, and specific performance. If consequential and punitive damages were allowed, the cost of letters of credit could rise substantially.

Statute of Limitation. Section 5–115 establishes a one year statute of limitation from the expiration date or from accrual of the cause of action, whichever occurs later. Because it is usually obvious to all when there has been a breach, a short limitation period is fair to potential plaintiffs.

Choice of Law. Section 5–116 permits the issuer (or nominated party or adviser) to choose the law of the jurisdiction that will govern even if that law bears no relation to the transaction. Absent agreement, Section 5–116 states choice of law rules.

Assignment of Proceeds. Section 5–114 conforms more fully to existing practice and provides an orderly procedure for recording and accommodating assignments by consent of the issuer (or nominated party).

Subrogation. Section 5–117 clarifies the subrogation rights of an Issuer who has honored a letter of credit. These rights of subrogation also extend to an applicant who reimburses and a nominated party who pays or gives value.

Recognition of UCP. Section 5–116(c) expressly recognizes that if the UCP is incorporated by reference into the letter of credit, the agreement varies the provisions of Article 5 with which it may conflict except for the non-variable provisions of Article 5.

Benefits of Revised Article 5 to Applicants

Warranties. Section 5–110 specifies the warranties made by a beneficiary. It gives the applicant on a letter of credit which has been honored a direct cause of action if a drawing is fraudulent or forged or if a drawing violates any agreement augmented by a letter of credit.

Strict Compliance. Absent agreement to the contrary, the issuer must dishonor a presentation that does not strictly comply under standard practice with the terms and conditions of the letter of credit (Section 5–108).

Subrogation. New Section 5–117 clarifies the parties' rights of subrogation if the letter of credit is honored.

Limitations on General Disclaimers and Waivers. Section 5–103(c) limits the effect of general disclaimers and waivers in a letter of credit, or reimbursement or other agreement.

Benefits of Revised Article 5 to Beneficiaries

Irrevocable. A letter of credit is irrevocable unless the letter of credit expressly provides it is revocable (Section 5–106(a)).

Preclusion. Section 5–108(c) now provides that the Issuer is precluded from asserting any discrepancy not stated in its notice timely given, except for fraud, forgery or expiration.

Timely Examination. Section 5–108(b) requires examination and notice of any discrepancies within a reasonable time not to exceed the 7th business day after presentation of the documents.

Transfers by Operation of Law. New Section 5–113 allows a successor to a beneficiary by operation of law to make presentation and receive payment or acceptance.

Damages. The damages provided are expanded and clarified. They include attorneys fees and expenses of litigation and payment of the full amount of the wrongfully dishonored or repudiated demand, with interest, without an obligation of the beneficiary to mitigate damages (Section 5–111).

Revisions for Article 9 and Transition Provisions

[*Note from West Advisory Panel: We have deleted this section.*]

---

§ 5–101.   Short Title.

This article may be cited as Uniform Commercial Code—Letters of Credit.

Official Comment

The Official Comment to the original Section 5–101 was a remarkably brief inaugural address. Noting that letters of credit had not been the subject of statutory enactment and that the law concerning them had been developed in the cases, the Comment stated that Article 5 was intended "within its limited scope" to set an independent theoretical frame for the further development of letters of credit. That statement addressed accurately conditions as they existed when the statement was made, nearly half a century ago. Since Article 5 was originally drafted, the use of letters of credit has expanded and developed, and the case law concerning these developments is, in some respects, discordant.

Revision of Article 5 therefore has required reappraisal both of the statutory goals and of the extent to which particular statutory provisions further or adversely affect achievement of those goals.

The statutory goal of Article 5 was originally stated to be: (1) to set a substantive theoretical frame that describes the function and legal nature of letters of credit; and (2) to preserve procedural flexibility in order to accommodate further development of the efficient use of letters of credit. A letter of credit is an idiosyncratic form of undertaking that supports performance of an obligation incurred in a separate financial, mercantile, or other transaction or arrangement. The objectives of the original and revised Article 5 are best achieved (1) by defining the peculiar characteristics of a letter of credit that distinguish it and the legal consequences of its use from other forms of assurance such as secondary guarantees, performance bonds, and insurance policies, and from ordinary contracts, fiduciary engagements, and escrow arrangements; and (2) by preserving flexibility through variation by agreement in order to respond to and accommodate developments in custom and usage that are not inconsistent with the essential definitions and substantive mandates of the statute. No statute can, however, prescribe the manner in which such substantive rights and duties are to be enforced or imposed without risking stultification of wholesome developments in the letter of credit mechanism. Letter of credit law should remain responsive to commercial reality and in particular to the customs and expectations of the international banking and mercantile community. Courts should read the terms of this article in a manner consistent with these customs and expectations.

The subject matter in Article 5, letters of credit, may also be governed by an international convention that is now being drafted by UNCITRAL, the draft Convention on Independent Guarantees and Standby Letters of Credit. The Uniform Customs and Practice is an international body of trade practice that is commonly adopted by international and domestic letters of credit and as such is the "law of the transaction" by agreement of the parties. Article 5 is consistent with and was influenced by the rules in the existing version of the UCP. In addition to the UCP and the international convention, other bodies of law apply to letters of credit. For example, the federal bankruptcy law applies to letters of credit with respect to applicants and beneficiaries that are in bankruptcy; regulations of the Federal Reserve Board and the Comptroller of the Currency lay out requirements for banks that issue letters of credit and describe how letters of credit are to be treated for calculating asset risk and for the purpose of loan limitations. In addition there is an array of anti-boycott and other similar laws that may affect the issuance and performance of letters of credit. All of these laws are beyond the scope of Article 5, but in certain circumstances they will override Article 5.

§ 5–102. Definitions.

(a) In this article:

(1) "Adviser" means a person who, at the request of the issuer, a confirmer, or another adviser, notifies or requests another adviser to notify the beneficiary that a letter of credit has been issued, confirmed, or amended.

(2) "Applicant" means a person at whose request or for whose account a letter of credit is issued. The term includes a person who requests an issuer to issue a letter of credit on behalf of another if the person making the request undertakes an obligation to reimburse the issuer.

(3) "Beneficiary" means a person who under the terms of a letter of credit is entitled to have its complying presentation honored. The term includes a person to whom drawing rights have been transferred under a transferable letter of credit.

(4) "Confirmer" means a nominated person who undertakes, at the request or with the consent of the issuer, to honor a presentation under a letter of credit issued by another.

(5) "Dishonor" of a letter of credit means failure timely to honor or to take an interim action, such as acceptance of a draft, that may be required by the letter of credit.

(6) "Document" means a draft or other demand, document of title, investment security, certificate, invoice, or other record, statement, or representation of fact, law, right, or opinion (i) which is presented in a written or other medium permitted by the letter of credit or, unless prohibited by the letter of credit, by the standard practice referred to in Section 5–108(e) and (ii) which is capable of being examined for compliance with the terms and conditions of the letter of credit. A document may not be oral.

(7) "Good faith" means honesty in fact in the conduct or transaction concerned.

(8) "Honor" of a letter of credit means performance of the issuer's undertaking in the letter of credit to pay or deliver an item of value. Unless the letter of credit otherwise provides, "honor" occurs

(i) upon payment,

(ii) if the letter of credit provides for acceptance, upon acceptance of a draft and, at maturity, its payment, or

(iii) if the letter of credit provides for incurring a deferred obligation, upon incurring the obligation and, at maturity, its performance.

(9) "Issuer" means a bank or other person that issues a letter of credit, but does not include an individual who makes an engagement for personal, family, or household purposes.

(10) "Letter of credit" means a definite undertaking that satisfies the requirements of Section 5–104 by an issuer to a beneficiary at the request or for the account of an applicant or, in the case of a financial institution, to itself or for its own account, to honor a documentary presentation by payment or delivery of an item of value.

(11) "Nominated person" means a person whom the issuer (i) designates or authorizes to pay, accept, negotiate, or otherwise give value under a letter of credit and (ii) undertakes by agreement or custom and practice to reimburse.

(12) "Presentation" means delivery of a document to an issuer or nominated person for honor or giving of value under a letter of credit.

(13) "Presenter" means a person making a presentation as or on behalf of a beneficiary or nominated person.

(14) "Record" means information that is inscribed on a tangible medium, or that is stored in an electronic or other medium and is retrievable in perceivable form.

(15) "Successor of a beneficiary" means a person who succeeds to substantially all of the rights of a beneficiary by operation of law, including a corporation with or into which the beneficiary has been merged or consolidated, an administrator, executor, personal representative, trustee in bankruptcy, debtor in possession, liquidator, and receiver.

(b)   Definitions in other Articles applying to this article and the sections in which they appear are:

"Accept" or "Acceptance" Section 3–409
"Value" Sections 3–303, 4–211

(c)   Article 1 contains certain additional general definitions and principles of construction and interpretation applicable throughout this article.

Official Comment

1.   Since no one can be a confirmer unless that person is a nominated person as defined in Section 5–102(a)(11), those who agree to "confirm" without the designation or authorization of the issuer are not confirmers under Article 5. Nonetheless, the undertakings to the beneficiary of such persons may be enforceable by the beneficiary as letters of credit issued by the "confirmer" for its own account or as guarantees or contracts outside of Article 5.

2.   The definition of "document" contemplates and facilitates the growing recognition of electronic and other nonpaper media as "documents," however, for the time being, data in those media constitute documents only in certain circumstances. For example, a facsimile received by an issuer would be a document only if the letter of credit explicitly permitted it, if the standard practice authorized it and the letter did not prohibit it, or the agreement of the issuer and beneficiary permitted it. The fact that data transmitted in a nonpaper (unwritten) medium can be recorded on paper by a recipient's computer printer, facsimile machine, or the like does not under current practice render the data so transmitted a "document." A facsimile or S.W.I.F.T. message received directly by the issuer is in an electronic medium when it crosses the boundary of the issuer's place of business. One wishing to make a presentation by facsimile (an electronic medium) will have to procure the explicit agreement of the issuer (assuming that the standard practice does not authorize it). Article 5 contemplates that electronic documents may be presented under a letter of credit and the provisions of this Article should be read to apply to electronic documents as well as tangible documents. An electronic document of title is delivered through the voluntary transfer of control. Article 1, Section 1–201 (definition of "delivery"). See Article 7, Section 7–106 on control of an electronic document. Where electronic transmissions are authorized neither by the letter of credit nor by the practice, the beneficiary may transmit the data electronically to its agent who may be able to put it in written form and make a conforming presentation. Cf. Article 7, Section 7–105 on reissuing an electronic document in a tangible medium.

3.   "Good faith" continues in revised Article 5 to be defined as "honesty in fact." "Observance of reasonable standards of fair dealing" has not been added to the definition. The narrower definition of "honesty in fact" reinforces the "independence principle" in the treatment of "fraud," "strict compliance," "preclusion," and other tests affecting the performance of obligations that are unique to letters of credit. This narrower definition—which does not include "fair dealing"—is appropriate to the decision to honor or dishonor a presentation of documents specified in a letter of credit. The narrower definition is also appropriate for other parts of revised Article 5 where

greater certainty of obligations is necessary and is consistent with the goals of speed and low cost. It is important that U.S. letters of credit have continuing vitality and competitiveness in international transactions.

For example, it would be inconsistent with the "independence" principle if any of the following occurred: (i) the beneficiary's failure to adhere to the standard of "fair dealing" in the underlying transaction or otherwise in presenting documents were to provide applicants and issuers with an "unfairness" defense to dishonor even when the documents complied with the terms of the letter of credit; (ii) the issuer's obligation to honor in "strict compliance in accordance with standard practice" were changed to "reasonable compliance" by use of the "fair dealing" standard, or (iii) the preclusion against the issuer (Section 5–108(d)) were modified under the "fair dealing" standard to enable the issuer later to raise additional deficiencies in the presentation. The rights and obligations arising from presentation, honor, dishonor and reimbursement, are independent and strict, and thus "honesty in fact" is an appropriate standard.

The contract between the applicant and beneficiary is not governed by Article 5, but by applicable contract law, such as Article 2 or the general law of contracts. "Good faith" in that contract is defined by other law, such as Section 2–103(1)(b) [*The definition of good faith in 2–103(1)(b) will be deleted if the jurisdiction adopts the definition of good faith in revised Article 1*] or Restatement of Contracts 2d, § 205, which incorporate the principle of "fair dealing" in most cases, or a State's common law or other statutory provisions that may apply to that contract.

The contract between the applicant and the issuer (sometimes called the "reimbursement" agreement) is governed in part by this article (e.g., Sections 5–108(i), 5–111(b), and 5–103(c)) and partly by other law (e.g., the general law of contracts). The definition of good faith in Section 5–102(a)(7) applies only to the extent that the reimbursement contract is governed by provisions in this article; for other purposes good faith is defined by other law.

4. Payment and acceptance are familiar modes of honor. A third mode of honor, incurring an unconditional obligation, has legal effects similar to an acceptance of a time draft but does not technically constitute an acceptance. The practice of making letters of credit available by "deferred payment undertaking" as now provided in UCP 500 has grown up in other countries and spread to the United States. The definition of "honor" will accommodate that practice.

5. The exclusion of consumers from the definition of "issuer" is to keep creditors from using a letter of credit in consumer transactions in which the consumer might be made the issuer and the creditor would be the beneficiary. If that transaction were recognized under Article 5, the effect would be to leave the consumer without defenses against the creditor. That outcome would violate the policy behind the Federal Trade Commission Rule in 16 CFR Part 433. In a consumer transaction, an individual cannot be an issuer where that person would otherwise be either the principal debtor or a guarantor.

6. The label on a document is not conclusive; certain documents labelled "guarantees" in accordance with European (and occasionally, American) practice are letters of credit. On the other hand, even documents that are labelled "letter of credit" may not constitute letters of credit under the definition in Section 5–102(a). When a document labelled a letter of credit requires the issuer to pay not upon the presentation of documents, but upon the determination of an extrinsic fact such as applicant's failure to perform a construction contract, and where that condition appears on its face to be fundamental and would, if ignored, leave no obligation to the issuer under the document labelled letter of credit, the issuer's undertaking is not a letter of credit. It is probably some form of suretyship or other contractual arrangement and may be enforceable as such. See Sections 5–102(a)(10) and 5–103(d). Therefore, undertakings whose fundamental term requires an issuer to look beyond documents and beyond conventional reference to the clock, calendar, and practices concerning the form of various documents are not governed by Article 5. Although Section 5–108(g) recognizes that certain nondocumentary conditions can be included in a letter of credit without denying the undertaking the status of letter of credit, that section does not apply to cases where the nondocumentary condition is fundamental to the issuer's obligation. The rules in Sections 5–102(a)(10), 5–103(d), and 5–108(g) approve the conclusion in *Wichita Eagle & Beacon Publishing Co. v. Pacific Nat. Bank*, 493 F.2d 1285 (9th Cir. 1974).

The adjective "definite" is taken from the UCP. It approves cases that deny letter of credit status to documents that are unduly vague or incomplete. See, e.g., *Transparent Products Corp. v. Paysaver Credit Union*, 864 F.2d 60 (7th Cir. 1988). Note, however, that no particular phrase or label is necessary to establish a letter of credit. It is sufficient if the undertaking of the issuer shows that it is intended to be a letter of credit. In most cases the parties' intention will be indicated by a label on the undertaking itself indicating that it is a "letter of credit," but no such language is necessary.

A financial institution may be both the issuer and the applicant or the issuer and the beneficiary. Such letters are sometimes issued by a bank in support of the bank's own lease obligations or on behalf of one of its divisions as an applicant or to one of its divisions as beneficiary, such as an overseas branch. Because wide use of letters of credit in which the issuer and the applicant or the issuer and the beneficiary are the same would endanger the unique status of letters of credit, only financial institutions are authorized to issue them.

In almost all cases the ultimate performance of the issuer under a letter of credit is the payment of money. In rare cases the issuer's obligation is to deliver stock certificates or the like. The definition of letter of credit in Section 5-102(a)(10) contemplates those cases.

7.   Under the UCP any bank is a nominated bank where the letter of credit is "freely negotiable." A letter of credit might also nominate by the following: "We hereby engage with the drawer, indorsers, and bona fide holders of drafts drawn under and in compliance with the terms of this credit that the same will be duly honored on due presentation" or "available with any bank by negotiation." A restricted negotiation credit might be "available with x bank by negotiation" or the like.

Several legal consequences may attach to the status of nominated person. First, when the issuer nominates a person, it is authorizing that person to pay or give value and is authorizing the beneficiary to make presentation to that person. Unless the letter of credit provides otherwise, the beneficiary need not present the documents to the issuer before the letter of credit expires; it need only present those documents to the nominated person. Secondly, a nominated person that gives value in good faith has a right to payment from the issuer despite fraud. Section 5-109(a)(1).

8.   A "record" must be in or capable of being converted to a perceivable form. For example, an electronic message recorded in a computer memory that could be printed from that memory could constitute a record. Similarly, a tape recording of an oral conversation could be a record.

9.   Absent a specific agreement to the contrary, documents of a beneficiary delivered to an issuer or nominated person are considered to be presented under the letter of credit to which they refer, and any payment or value given for them is considered to be made under that letter of credit. As the court held in *Alaska Textile Co. v. Chase Manhattan Bank, N.A.*, 982 F.2d 813, 820 (2d Cir. 1992), it takes a "significant showing" to make the presentation of a beneficiary's documents for "collection only" or otherwise outside letter of credit law and practice.

10.   Although a successor of a beneficiary is one who succeeds "by operation of law," some of the successions contemplated by Section 5-102(a)(15) will have resulted from voluntary action of the beneficiary such as merger of a corporation. Any merger makes the successor corporation the "successor of a beneficiary" even though the transfer occurs partly by operation of law and partly by the voluntary action of the parties. The definition excludes certain transfers, where no part of the transfer is "by operation of law"—such as the sale of assets by one company to another.

11.   "Draft" in Article 5 does not have the same meaning it has in Article 3. For example, a document may be a draft under Article 5 even though it would not be a negotiable instrument, and therefore would not qualify as a draft under Section 3-104(e).

As amended in 2003.

§ 5-103.   Scope.

(a)   This article applies to letters of credit and to certain rights and obligations arising out of transactions involving letters of credit.

(b)   The statement of a rule in this article does not by itself require, imply, or negate application of the same or a different rule to a situation not provided for, or to a person not specified, in this article.

(c)   With the exception of this subsection, subsections (a) and (d), Sections 5-102(a)(9) and (10), 5-106(d), and 5-114(d), and except to the extent prohibited in Sections 1-302 and 5-117(d), the effect of this article may be varied by agreement or by a provision stated or incorporated by reference in an undertaking. A term in an agreement or undertaking generally excusing liability or generally limiting remedies for failure to perform obligations is not sufficient to vary obligations prescribed by this article.

(d)   Rights and obligations of an issuer to a beneficiary or a nominated person under a letter of credit are independent of the existence, performance, or nonperformance of a contract or arrangement out of which the letter of credit arises or which underlies it, including contracts or arrangements between the issuer and the applicant and between the applicant and the beneficiary.

As amended in 2001.

Official Comment

1.   Sections 5–102(a)(10) and 5–103 are the principal limits on the scope of Article 5. Many undertakings in commerce and contract are similar, but not identical to the letter of credit. Principal among those are "secondary," "accessory," or "suretyship" guarantees. Although the word "guarantee" is sometimes used to describe an independent obligation like that of the issuer of a letter of credit (most often in the case of European bank undertakings but occasionally in the case of undertakings of American banks), in the United States the word "guarantee" is more typically used to describe a suretyship transaction in which the "guarantor" is only secondarily liable and has the right to assert the underlying debtor's defenses. This article does not apply to secondary or accessory guarantees and it is important to recognize the distinction between letters of credit and those guarantees. It is often a defense to a secondary or accessory guarantor's liability that the underlying debt has been discharged or that the debtor has other defenses to the underlying liability. In letter of credit law, on the other hand, the independence principle recognized throughout Article 5 states that the issuer's liability is independent of the underlying obligation. That the beneficiary may have breached the underlying contract and thus have given a good defense on that contract to the applicant against the beneficiary is no defense for the issuer's refusal to honor. Only staunch recognition of this principle by the issuers and the courts will give letters of credit the continuing vitality that arises from the certainty and speed of payment under letters of credit. To that end, it is important that the law not carry into letter of credit transactions rules that properly apply only to secondary guarantees or to other forms of engagement.

2.   Like all of the provisions of the Uniform Commercial Code, Article 5 is supplemented by Section 1–103 and, through it, by many rules of statutory and common law. Because this article is quite short and has no rules on many issues that will affect liability with respect to a letter of credit transaction, law beyond Article 5 will often determine rights and liabilities in letter of credit transactions. Even within letter of credit law, the article is far from comprehensive; it deals only with "certain" rights of the parties. Particularly with respect to the standards of performance that are set out in Section 5–108, it is appropriate for the parties and the courts to turn to customs and practice such as the Uniform Customs and Practice for Documentary Credits, currently published by the International Chamber of Commerce as I.C.C. Pub. No. 500 (hereafter UCP). Many letters of credit specifically adopt the UCP as applicable to the particular transaction. Where the UCP are adopted but conflict with Article 5 and except where variation is prohibited, the UCP terms are permissible contractual modifications under Sections 1–302 and 5–103(c). See Section 5–116(c). Normally Article 5 should not be considered to conflict with practice except when a rule explicitly stated in the UCP or other practice is different from a rule explicitly stated in Article 5.

Except by choosing the law of a jurisdiction that has not adopted the Uniform Commercial Code, it is not possible entirely to escape the Uniform Commercial Code. Since incorporation of the UCP avoids only "conflicting" Article 5 rules, parties who do not wish to be governed by the nonconflicting provisions of Article 5 must normally either adopt the law of a jurisdiction other than a State of the United States or state explicitly the rule that is to govern. When rules of custom and practice are incorporated by reference, they are considered to be explicit terms of the agreement or undertaking.

Neither the obligation of an issuer under Section 5–108 nor that of an adviser under Section 5–107 is an obligation of the kind that is invariable under Section 1–102(3) [*unrevised Article 1; see Concordance, p. 22*]. Section 5–103(c) and Comment 1 to Section 5–108 make it clear that the applicant and the issuer may agree to almost any provision establishing the obligations of the issuer to the applicant. The last sentence of subsection (c) limits the power of the issuer to achieve that result by a nonnegotiated disclaimer or limitation of remedy.

What the issuer could achieve by an explicit agreement with its applicant or by a term that explicitly defines its duty, it cannot accomplish by a general disclaimer. The restriction on disclaimers in the last sentence of subsection (c) is based more on procedural than on substantive unfairness. Where, for example, the reimbursement agreement provides explicitly that the issuer need not examine any documents, the applicant understands the risk it has undertaken. A term in a reimbursement agreement which states generally that an issuer will not be liable unless it has acted in "bad faith" or committed "gross negligence" is ineffective under Section 5–103(c). On the other hand, less general terms such as terms that permit issuer reliance on an oral or electronic message believed in good faith to have been received from the applicant or terms that entitle an issuer to reimbursement when it honors a "substantially" though not "strictly" complying presentation, are effective. In each case the question is whether the disclaimer or limitation is sufficiently clear and explicit in reallocating a liability or risk that is allocated differently under a variable Article 5 provision.

Of course, no term in a letter of credit, whether incorporated by reference to practice rules or stated specifically, can free an issuer from a conflicting contractual obligation to its applicant. If, for example, an issuer promised its applicant that it would pay only against an inspection certificate of a particular company but failed to require such a certificate in its letter of credit or made the requirement only a nondocumentary condition that had to be disregarded, the issuer might be obliged to pay the beneficiary even though its payment might violate its contract with its applicant.

3.   Parties should generally avoid modifying the definitions in Section 5–102. The effect of such an agreement is almost inevitably unclear. To say that something is a "guarantee" in the typical domestic transaction is to say that the parties intend that particular legal rules apply to it. By acknowledging that something is a guarantee, but asserting that it is to be treated as a "letter of credit," the parties leave a court uncertain about where the rules on guarantees stop and those concerning letters of credit begin.

4.   Section 5–102(2) and (3) of Article 5 are omitted as unneeded; the omission does not change the law.

As amended in 2001.

§ 5–104.   Formal Requirements.

A letter of credit, confirmation, advice, transfer, amendment, or cancellation may be issued in any form that is a <u>signed</u> record ~~and is authenticated (i) by a signature or (ii) in accordance with the agreement of the parties or the standard practice referred to in Section 5–108(e)~~.

As amended in 2022.

Official Comment

1.   Neither Section 5–104 nor the definition of letter of credit in Section 5–102(a)(10) requires inclusion of all the terms that are normally contained in a letter of credit in order for an undertaking to be recognized as a letter of credit under Article 5. For example, a letter of credit will typically specify the amount available, the expiration date, the place where presentation should be made, and the documents that must be presented to entitle a person to honor. Undertakings that have the formalities required by Section 5–104 and meet the conditions specified in Section 5–102(a)(10) will be recognized as letters of credit even though they omit one or more of the items usually contained in a letter of credit.

2.   <u>This section was revised pursuant to the Uniform Commercial Code Amendments (2022). The reference in the pre-2022 text of this section to authentication by agreement of the parties or standard practice referred to in Section 5–108(e) is no longer necessary. Those forms of authentication are subsumed by the revised and expanded definition of "sign" in Section 1–201(b)(37), which is broad and flexible.</u> The ~~authentication~~ requirement that a record be signed as specified in this section is authentication <u>or adoption</u> only of the identity of the issuer, confirmer, or adviser.

~~An authentication agreement may be by system rule, by standard practice, or by direct agreement between the parties. The reference to practice is intended to incorporate future developments in the UCP and other practice rules as well as those that may arise spontaneously in commercial practice.~~

3.   Many banking transactions, including the issuance of many letters of credit, are now conducted mostly by electronic means. For example, S.W.I.F.T. is currently used to transmit letters of credit from issuing to advising banks. The letter of credit text so transmitted may be printed at the advising bank, stamped "original" and provided to the beneficiary in that form. The printed document may then be used as a way of controlling and recording payments and of recording and authorizing assignments of proceeds or transfers of rights under the letter of credit. Nothing in this section should be construed to conflict with that practice.

To be a record sufficient to serve as a letter of credit or other undertaking under this section, data must have a durability consistent with that function. Because consideration is not required for a binding letter of credit or similar undertaking (Section 5–105) yet those undertakings are to be strictly construed (Section 5–108), parties to a letter of credit transaction are especially dependent on the continued availability of the terms and conditions of the letter of credit or other undertaking. By declining to specify any particular medium in which the letter of credit must be established or communicated, Section 5–104 leaves room for future developments.

As amended in 2022.

§ 5–105.   Consideration.

Consideration is not required to issue, amend, transfer, or cancel a letter of credit, advice, or confirmation.

Official Comment

It is not to be expected that any issuer will issue its letter of credit without some form of remuneration. But it is not expected that the beneficiary will know what the issuer's remuneration was or whether in fact there was any identifiable remuneration in a given case. And it might be difficult for the beneficiary to prove the issuer's remuneration. This section dispenses with this proof and is consistent with the position of Lord Mansfield in *Pillans v. Van Mierop,* 97 Eng.Rep. 1035 (K.B. 1765) in making consideration irrelevant.

§ 5–106.   Issuance, Amendment, Cancellation, and Duration.

(a)   A letter of credit is issued and becomes enforceable according to its terms against the issuer when the issuer sends or otherwise transmits it to the person requested to advise or to the beneficiary. A letter of credit is revocable only if it so provides.

(b)   After a letter of credit is issued, rights and obligations of a beneficiary, applicant, confirmer, and issuer are not affected by an amendment or cancellation to which that person has not consented except to the extent the letter of credit provides that it is revocable or that the issuer may amend or cancel the letter of credit without that consent.

(c)   If there is no stated expiration date or other provision that determines its duration, a letter of credit expires one year after its stated date of issuance or, if none is stated, after the date on which it is issued.

(d)   A letter of credit that states that it is perpetual expires five years after its stated date of issuance, or if none is stated, after the date on which it is issued.

Official Comment

1.   This section adopts the position taken by several courts, namely that letters of credit that are silent as to revocability are irrevocable. See, e.g., *Weyerhaeuser Co. v. First Nat. Bank,* 27 UCC Rep.Serv. 777 (S.D. Iowa 1979); *West Va. Hous. Dev. Fund v. Sroka*, 415 F.Supp. 1107 (W.D.Pa. 1976). This is the position of the current UCP (500). Given the usual commercial understanding and purpose of letters of credit, revocable letters of credit offer unhappy possibilities for misleading the parties who deal with them.

2.   A person can consent to an amendment by implication. For example, a beneficiary that tenders documents for honor that conform to an amended letter of credit but not to the original letter of credit has probably consented to the amendment. By the same token an applicant that has procured the issuance of a transferable letter of credit has consented to its transfer and to performance under the letter of credit by a person to whom the beneficiary's rights are duly transferred. If some, but not all of the persons involved in a letter of credit transaction consent to performance that does not strictly conform to the original letter of credit, those persons assume the risk that other nonconsenting persons may insist on strict compliance with the original letter of credit. Under subsection (b) those not consenting are not bound. For example, an issuer might agree to amend its letter of credit or honor documents presented after the expiration date in the belief that the applicant has consented or will consent to the amendment or will waive presentation after the original expiration date. If that belief is mistaken, the issuer is bound to the beneficiary by the terms of the letter of credit as amended or waived, even though it may be unable to recover from the applicant.

In general, the rights of a recognized transferee beneficiary cannot be altered without the transferee's consent, but the same is not true of the rights of assignees of proceeds from the beneficiary. When the beneficiary makes a complete transfer of its interest that is effective under the terms for transfer established by the issuer, adviser, or other party controlling transfers, the beneficiary no longer has an interest in the letter of credit, and the transferee steps into the shoes of the beneficiary as the one with rights under the letter of credit. Section 5–102(a)(3). When there is a partial transfer, both the original beneficiary and the transferee beneficiary have an interest in performance of the letter of credit and each expects that its rights will not be altered by amendment unless it consents.

The assignee of proceeds under a letter of credit from the beneficiary enjoys no such expectation. Notwithstanding an assignee's notice to the issuer of the assignment of proceeds, the assignee is not a person protected by subsection (b). An assignee of proceeds should understand that its rights can be changed or completely extinguished by amendment or cancellation of the letter of credit. An assignee's claim is precarious, for it depends entirely upon the continued existence of the letter of credit and upon the beneficiary's preparation and presentation of documents that would entitle the beneficiary to honor under Section 5–108.

3.   The issuer's right to cancel a revocable letter of credit does not free it from a duty to reimburse a nominated person who has honored, accepted, or undertaken a deferred obligation prior to receiving notice of the amendment or cancellation. Compare UCP Article 8.

4.   Although all letters of credit should specify the date on which the issuer's engagement expires, the failure to specify an expiration date does not invalidate the letter of credit, or diminish or relieve the obligation of any party with respect to the letter of credit. A letter of credit that may be revoked or terminated at the discretion of the issuer by notice to the beneficiary is not "perpetual."

§ 5–107.   Confirmer, Nominated Person, and Adviser.

(a)   A confirmer is directly obligated on a letter of credit and has the rights and obligations of an issuer to the extent of its confirmation. The confirmer also has rights against and obligations to the issuer as if the issuer were an applicant and the confirmer had issued the letter of credit at the request and for the account of the issuer.

(b)   A nominated person who is not a confirmer is not obligated to honor or otherwise give value for a presentation.

(c)   A person requested to advise may decline to act as an adviser. An adviser that is not a confirmer is not obligated to honor or give value for a presentation. An adviser undertakes to the issuer and to the beneficiary accurately to advise the terms of the letter of credit, confirmation, amendment, or advice received by that person and undertakes to the beneficiary to check the apparent authenticity of the request to advise. Even if the advice is inaccurate, the letter of credit, confirmation, or amendment is enforceable as issued.

(d)   A person who notifies a transferee beneficiary of the terms of a letter of credit, confirmation, amendment, or advice has the rights and obligations of an adviser under subsection (c). The terms in the notice to the transferee beneficiary may differ from the terms in any notice to the transferor beneficiary to the extent permitted by the letter of credit, confirmation, amendment, or advice received by the person who so notifies.

Official Comment

1.   A confirmer has the rights and obligations identified in Section 5–108. Accordingly, unless the context otherwise requires, the terms "confirmer" and "confirmation" should be read into this article wherever the terms "issuer" and "letter of credit" appear.

A confirmer that has paid in accordance with the terms and conditions of the letter of credit is entitled to reimbursement by the issuer even if the beneficiary committed fraud (see Section 5–109(a)(1)(ii)) and, in that sense, has greater rights against the issuer than the beneficiary has. To be entitled to reimbursement from the issuer under the typical confirmed letter of credit, the confirmer must submit conforming documents, but the confirmer's presentation to the issuer need not be made before the expiration date of the letter of credit.

A letter of credit confirmation has been analogized to a guarantee of issuer performance, to a parallel letter of credit issued by the confirmer for the account of the issuer or the letter of credit applicant or both, and to a back-to-back letter of credit in which the confirmer is a kind of beneficiary of the original issuer's letter of credit. Like letter of credit undertakings, confirmations are both unique and flexible, so that no one of these analogies is perfect, but unless otherwise indicated in the letter of credit or confirmation, a confirmer should be viewed by the letter of credit issuer and the beneficiary as an issuer of a parallel letter of credit for the account of the original letter of credit issuer. Absent a direct agreement between the applicant and a confirmer, normally the obligations of a confirmer are to the issuer not the applicant, but the applicant might have a right to injunction against a confirmer under Section 5–109 or warranty claim under Section 5–110, and either might have claims against the other under Section 5–117.

2.   No one has a duty to advise until that person agrees to be an adviser or undertakes to act in accordance with the instructions of the issuer. Except where there is a prior agreement to serve or where the silence of the adviser would be an acceptance of an offer to contract, a person's failure to respond to a request to advise a letter of credit does not in and of itself create any liability, nor does it establish a relationship of issuer and adviser

between the two. Since there is no duty to advise a letter of credit in the absence of a prior agreement, there can be no duty to advise it timely or at any particular time. When the adviser manifests its agreement to advise by actually doing so (as is normally the case), the adviser cannot have violated any duty to advise in a timely way. This analysis is consistent with the result of *Sound of Market Street v. Continental Bank International*, 819 F.2d 384 (3d Cir. 1987) which held that there is no such duty. This section takes no position on the reasoning of that case, but does not overrule the result. By advising or agreeing to advise a letter of credit, the adviser assumes a duty to the issuer and to the beneficiary accurately to report what it has received from the issuer, but, beyond determining the apparent authenticity of the letter, an adviser has no duty to investigate the accuracy of the message it has received from the issuer. "Checking" the apparent authenticity of the request to advise means only that the prospective adviser must attempt to authenticate the message (e.g., by "testing" the telex that comes from the purported issuer), and if it is unable to authenticate the message must report that fact to the issuer and, if it chooses to advise the message, to the beneficiary. By proper agreement, an adviser may disclaim its obligation under this section.

3. An issuer may issue a letter of credit which the adviser may advise with different terms. The issuer may then believe that it has undertaken a certain engagement, yet the text in the hands of the beneficiary will contain different terms, and the beneficiary would not be entitled to honor if the documents it submitted did not comply with the terms of the letter of credit as originally issued. On the other hand, if the adviser also confirmed the letter of credit, then as a confirmer it will be independently liable on the letter of credit as advised and confirmed. If in that situation the beneficiary's ultimate presentation entitled it to honor under the terms of the confirmation but not under those in the original letter of credit, the confirmer would have to honor but might not be entitled to reimbursement from the issuer.

4. When the issuer nominates another person to "pay," "negotiate," or otherwise to take up the documents and give value, there can be confusion about the legal status of the nominated person. In rare cases the person might actually be an agent of the issuer and its act might be the act of the issuer itself. In most cases the nominated person is not an agent of the issuer and has no authority to act on the issuer's behalf. Its "nomination" allows the beneficiary to present to it and earns it certain rights to payment under Section 5–109 that others do not enjoy. For example, when an issuer issues a "freely negotiable credit," it contemplates that banks or others might take up documents under that credit and advance value against them, and it is agreeing to pay those persons but only if the presentation to the issuer made by the nominated person complies with the credit. Usually there will be no agreement to pay, negotiate, or to serve in any other capacity by the nominated person, therefore the nominated person will have the right to decline to take the documents. It may return them or agree merely to act as a forwarding agent for the documents but without giving value against them or taking any responsibility for their conformity to the letter of credit.

§ 5–108. Issuer's Rights and Obligations.

(a) Except as otherwise provided in Section 5–109, an issuer shall honor a presentation that, as determined by the standard practice referred to in subsection (e), appears on its face strictly to comply with the terms and conditions of the letter of credit. Except as otherwise provided in Section 5–113 and unless otherwise agreed with the applicant, an issuer shall dishonor a presentation that does not appear so to comply.

(b) An issuer has a reasonable time after presentation, but not beyond the end of the seventh business day of the issuer after the day of its receipt of documents:

(1) to honor,

(2) if the letter of credit provides for honor to be completed more than seven business days after presentation, to accept a draft or incur a deferred obligation, or

(3) to give notice to the presenter of discrepancies in the presentation.

(c) Except as otherwise provided in subsection (d), an issuer is precluded from asserting as a basis for dishonor any discrepancy if timely notice is not given, or any discrepancy not stated in the notice if timely notice is given.

(d) Failure to give the notice specified in subsection (b) or to mention fraud, forgery, or expiration in the notice does not preclude the issuer from asserting as a basis for dishonor fraud or forgery as described in Section 5–109(a) or expiration of the letter of credit before presentation.

(e)   An issuer shall observe standard practice of financial institutions that regularly issue letters of credit. Determination of the issuer's observance of the standard practice is a matter of interpretation for the court. The court shall offer the parties a reasonable opportunity to present evidence of the standard practice.

(f)   An issuer is not responsible for:

(1)   the performance or nonperformance of the underlying contract, arrangement, or transaction,

(2)   an act or omission of others, or

(3)   observance or knowledge of the usage of a particular trade other than the standard practice referred to in subsection (e).

(g)   If an undertaking constituting a letter of credit under Section 5–102(a)(10) contains nondocumentary conditions, an issuer shall disregard the nondocumentary conditions and treat them as if they were not stated.

(h)   An issuer that has dishonored a presentation shall return the documents or hold them at the disposal of, and send advice to that effect to, the presenter.

(i)   An issuer that has honored a presentation as permitted or required by this article:

(1)   is entitled to be reimbursed by the applicant in immediately available funds not later than the date of its payment of funds;

(2)   takes the documents free of claims of the beneficiary or presenter;

(3)   is precluded from asserting a right of recourse on a draft under Sections 3–414 and 3–415;

(4)   except as otherwise provided in Sections 5–110 and 5–117, is precluded from restitution of money paid or other value given by mistake to the extent the mistake concerns discrepancies in the documents or tender which are apparent on the face of the presentation; and

(5)   is discharged to the extent of its performance under the letter of credit unless the issuer honored a presentation in which a required signature of a beneficiary was forged.

Official Comment

1.   This section combines some of the duties previously included in Sections 5–114 and 5–109. Because a confirmer has the rights and duties of an issuer, this section applies equally to a confirmer and an issuer. See Section 5–107(a).

The standard of strict compliance governs the issuer's obligation to the beneficiary and to the applicant. By requiring that a "presentation" appear strictly to comply, the section requires not only that the documents themselves appear on their face strictly to comply, but also that the other terms of the letter of credit such as those dealing with the time and place of presentation are strictly complied with. Typically, a letter of credit will provide that presentation is timely if made to the issuer, confirmer, or any other nominated person prior to expiration of the letter of credit. Accordingly, a nominated person that has honored a demand or otherwise given value before expiration will have a right to reimbursement from the issuer even though presentation to the issuer is made after the expiration of the letter of credit. Conversely, where the beneficiary negotiates documents to one who is not a nominated person, the beneficiary or that person acting on behalf of the beneficiary must make presentation to a nominated person, confirmer, or issuer prior to the expiration date.

This section does not impose a bifurcated standard under which an issuer's right to reimbursement might be broader than a beneficiary's right to honor. However, the explicit deference to standard practice in Section 5–108(a) and (e) and elsewhere expands issuers' rights of reimbursement where that practice so provides. Also, issuers can and often do contract with their applicants for expanded rights of reimbursement. Where that is done, the beneficiary will have to meet a more stringent standard of compliance as to the issuer than the issuer will have to meet as to the applicant. Similarly, a nominated person may have reimbursement and other rights against the issuer based on this article, the UCP, bank-to-bank reimbursement rules, or other agreement or undertaking of the issuer. These rights may allow the nominated person to recover from the issuer even when the nominated person would have no right to obtain honor under the letter of credit.

The section adopts strict compliance, rather than the standard that commentators have called "substantial compliance," the standard arguably applied in *Banco Español de Credito v. State Street Bank and Trust Company*, 385 F.2d 230 (1st Cir. 1967) and *Flagship Cruises Ltd. v. New England Merchants Nat. Bank,* 569 F.2d 699 (1st

Cir. 1978). Strict compliance does not mean slavish conformity to the terms of the letter of credit. For example, standard practice (what issuers do) may recognize certain presentations as complying that an unschooled layman would regard as discrepant. By adopting standard practice as a way of measuring strict compliance, this article indorses the conclusion of the court in *New Braunfels Nat. Bank v. Odiorne,* 780 S.W.2d 313 (Tex.Ct.App. 1989) (beneficiary could collect when draft requested payment on "Letter of Credit No. 86–122–5" and letter of credit specified "Letter of Credit No. 86–122–S" holding strict compliance does not demand oppressive perfectionism). The section also indorses the result in *Tosco Corp. v. Federal Deposit Insurance Corp.,* 723 F.2d 1242 (6th Cir. 1983). The letter of credit in that case called for "drafts Drawn under Bank of Clarksville Letter of Credit Number 105." The draft presented stated "drawn under Bank of Clarksville, Clarksville, Tennessee letter of Credit No. 105." The court correctly found that despite the change of upper case "L" to a lower case "l" and the use of the word "No." instead of "Number," and despite the addition of the words "Clarksville, Tennessee," the presentation conformed. Similarly a document addressed by a foreign person to General Motors as "Jeneral Motors" would strictly conform in the absence of other defects.

Identifying and determining compliance with standard practice are matters of interpretation for the court, not for the jury. As with similar rules in Sections 4A–202(c) and 2–302, it is hoped that there will be more consistency in the outcomes and speedier resolution of disputes if the responsibility for determining the nature and scope of standard practice is granted to the court, not to a jury. Granting the court authority to make these decisions will also encourage the salutary practice of courts' granting summary judgment in circumstances where there are no significant factual disputes. The statute encourages outcomes such as *American Coleman Co. v. Intrawest Bank,* 887 F.2d 1382 (10th Cir. 1989), where summary judgment was granted.

In some circumstances standards may be established between the issuer and the applicant by agreement or by custom that would free the issuer from liability that it might otherwise have. For example, an applicant might agree that the issuer would have no duty whatsoever to examine documents on certain presentations (e.g., those below a certain dollar amount). Where the transaction depended upon the issuer's payment in a very short time period (e.g., on the same day or within a few hours of presentation), the issuer and the applicant might agree to reduce the issuer's responsibility for failure to discover discrepancies. By the same token, an agreement between the applicant and the issuer might permit the issuer to examine documents exclusively by electronic or electro-optical means. Neither those agreements nor others like them explicitly made by issuers and applicants violate the terms of Section 5–108(a) or (b) or Section 5–103(c).

2.   Section 5–108(a) balances the need of the issuer for time to examine the documents against the possibility that the examiner (at the urging of the applicant or for fear that it will not be reimbursed) will take excessive time to search for defects. What is a "reasonable time" is not extended to accommodate an issuer's procuring a waiver from the applicant. See Article 14c of the UCP.

Under both the UCC and the UCP the issuer has a reasonable time to honor or give notice. The outside limit of that time is measured in business days under the UCC and in banking days under the UCP, a difference that will rarely be significant. Neither business nor banking days are defined in Article 5, but a court may find useful analogies in Regulation CC, 12 CFR 229.2, in state law outside of the Uniform Commercial Code, and in Article 4.

Examiners must note that the seven-day period is not a safe harbor. The time within which the issuer must give notice is the lesser of a reasonable time or seven business days. Where there are few documents (as, for example, with the mine run standby letter of credit), the reasonable time would be less than seven days. If more than a reasonable time is consumed in examination, no timely notice is possible. What is a "reasonable time" is to be determined by examining the behavior of those in the business of examining documents, mostly banks. Absent prior agreement of the issuer, one could not expect a bank issuer to examine documents while the beneficiary waited in the lobby if the normal practice was to give the documents to a person who had the opportunity to examine those together with many others in an orderly process. That the applicant has not yet paid the issuer or that the applicant's account with the issuer is insufficient to cover the amount of the draft is not a basis for extension of the time period.

This section does not preclude the issuer from contacting the applicant during its examination; however, the decision to honor rests with the issuer, and it has no duty to seek a waiver from the applicant or to notify the applicant of receipt of the documents. If the issuer dishonors a conforming presentation, the beneficiary will be entitled to the remedies under Section 5–111, irrespective of the applicant's views.

Even though the person to whom presentation is made cannot conduct a reasonable examination of documents within the time after presentation and before the expiration date, presentation establishes the parties' rights. The beneficiary's right to honor or the issuer's right to dishonor arises upon presentation at the place provided in the letter of credit even though it might take the person to whom presentation has been made several days to determine whether honor or dishonor is the proper course. The issuer's time for honor or giving notice of dishonor may be extended or shortened by a term in the letter of credit. The time for the issuer's performance may be otherwise modified or waived in accordance with Section 5–106.

The issuer's time to inspect runs from the time of its "receipt of documents." Documents are considered to be received only when they are received at the place specified for presentation by the issuer or other party to whom presentation is made. "Receipt of documents" when documents of title are presented must be read in light of the definition of "delivery" in Article 1, Section 1–201 and the definition of "presentment" in Section 5–102(a)(12).

Failure of the issuer to act within the time permitted by subsection (b) constitutes dishonor. Because of the preclusion in subsection (c) and the liability that the issuer may incur under Section 5–111 for wrongful dishonor, the effect of such a silent dishonor may ultimately be the same as though the issuer had honored, i.e., it may owe damages in the amount drawn but unpaid under the letter of credit.

3.   The requirement that the issuer send notice of the discrepancies or be precluded from asserting discrepancies is new to Article 5. It is taken from the similar provision in the UCP and is intended to promote certainty and finality.

The section thus substitutes a strict preclusion principle for the doctrines of waiver and estoppel that might otherwise apply under Section 1–103. It rejects the reasoning in *Flagship Cruises Ltd. v. New England Merchants' Nat. Bank,* 569 F.2d 699 (1st Cir. 1978) and *Wing On Bank Ltd. v. American Nat. Bank & Trust Co.,* 457 F.2d 328 (5th Cir. 1972) where the issuer was held to be estopped only if the beneficiary relied on the issuer's failure to give notice.

Assume, for example, that the beneficiary presented documents to the issuer shortly before the letter of credit expired, in circumstances in which the beneficiary could not have cured any discrepancy before expiration. Under the reasoning of *Flagship* and *Wing On,* the beneficiary's inability to cure, even if it had received notice, would absolve the issuer of its failure to give notice. The virtue of the preclusion obligation adopted in this section is that it forecloses litigation about reliance and detriment.

Even though issuers typically give notice of the discrepancy of tardy presentation when presentation is made after the expiration of a credit, they are not required to give that notice and the section permits them to raise late presentation as a defect despite their failure to give that notice.

4.   To act within a reasonable time, the issuer must normally give notice without delay after the examining party makes its decision. If the examiner decides to dishonor on the first day, it would be obliged to notify the beneficiary shortly thereafter, perhaps on the same business day. This rule accepts the reasoning in cases such as *Datapoint Corp. v. M & I Bank,* 665 F.Supp. 722 (W.D.Wis. 1987) and *Esso Petroleum Canada, Div. of Imperial Oil, Ltd. v. Security Pacific Bank,* 710 F.Supp. 275 (D.Or. 1989).

The section deprives the examining party of the right simply to sit on a presentation that is made within seven days of expiration. The section requires the examiner to examine the documents and make a decision and, having made a decision to dishonor, to communicate promptly with the presenter. Nevertheless, a beneficiary who presents documents shortly before the expiration of a letter of credit runs the risk that it will never have the opportunity to cure any discrepancies.

5.   Confirmers, other nominated persons, and collecting banks acting for beneficiaries can be presenters and, when so, are entitled to the notice provided in subsection (b). Even nominated persons who have honored or given value against an earlier presentation of the beneficiary and are themselves seeking reimbursement or honor need notice of discrepancies in the hope that they may be able to procure complying documents. The issuer has the obligations imposed by this section whether the issuer's performance is characterized as "reimbursement" of a nominated person or as "honor."

6.   In many cases a letter of credit authorizes presentation by the beneficiary to someone other than the issuer. Sometimes that person is identified as a "payor" or "paying bank," or as an "acceptor" or "accepting bank," in other cases as a "negotiating bank," and in other cases there will be no specific designation. The section does not impose any duties on a person other than the issuer or confirmer, however a nominated person or other person may have liability under this article or at common law if it fails to perform an express or implied agreement with the beneficiary.

7.   The issuer's obligation to honor runs not only to the beneficiary but also to the applicant. It is possible that an applicant who has made a favorable contract with the beneficiary will be injured by the issuer's wrongful dishonor. Except to the extent that the contract between the issuer and the applicant limits that liability, the issuer will have liability to the applicant for wrongful dishonor under Section 5–111 as a matter of contract law.

A good faith extension of the time in Section 5–108(b) by agreement between the issuer and beneficiary binds the applicant even if the applicant is not consulted or does not consent to the extension.

The issuer's obligation to dishonor when there is no apparent compliance with the letter of credit runs only to the applicant. No other party to the transaction can complain if the applicant waives compliance with terms or conditions of the letter of credit or agrees to a less stringent standard for compliance than that supplied by this article. Except as otherwise agreed with the applicant, an issuer may dishonor a noncomplying presentation despite an applicant's waiver.

Waiver of discrepancies by an issuer or an applicant in one or more presentations does not waive similar discrepancies in a future presentation. Neither the issuer nor the beneficiary can reasonably rely upon honor over past waivers as a basis for concluding that a future defective presentation will justify honor. The reasoning of *Courtaulds of North America Inc. v. North Carolina Nat. Bank,* 528 F.2d 802 (4th Cir. 1975) is accepted and that expressed in *Schweibish v. Pontchartrain State Bank,* 389 So.2d 731 (La.App. 1980) and *Titanium Metals Corp. v. Space Metals, Inc.,* 529 P.2d 431 (Utah 1974) is rejected.

8.　The standard practice referred to in subsection (e) includes (i) international practice set forth in or referenced by the Uniform Customs and Practice, (ii) other practice rules published by associations of financial institutions, and (iii) local and regional practice. It is possible that standard practice will vary from one place to another. Where there are conflicting practices, the parties should indicate which practice governs their rights. A practice may be overridden by agreement or course of dealing. See Section 1–205(4) [*unrevised Article 1; see Concordance, p. 22*].

9.　The responsibility of the issuer under a letter of credit is to examine documents and to make a prompt decision to honor or dishonor based upon that examination. Nondocumentary conditions have no place in this regime and are better accommodated under contract or suretyship law and practice. In requiring that nondocumentary conditions in letters of credit be ignored as surplusage, Article 5 remains aligned with the UCP (see UCP 500 Article 13c), approves cases like *Pringle-Associated Mortgage Corp. v. Southern National Bank,* 571 F.2d 871, 874 (5th Cir. 1978), and rejects the reasoning in cases such as *Sherwood & Roberts, Inc. v. First Security Bank,* 682 P.2d 149 (Mont. 1984).

Subsection (g) recognizes that letters of credit sometimes contain nondocumentary terms or conditions. Conditions such as a term prohibiting "shipment on vessels more than 15 years old," are to be disregarded and treated as surplusage. Similarly, a requirement that there be an award by a "duly appointed arbitrator" would not require the issuer to determine whether the arbitrator had been "duly appointed." Likewise a term in a standby letter of credit that provided for differing forms of certification depending upon the particular type of default does not oblige the issuer independently to determine which kind of default has occurred. These conditions must be disregarded by the issuer. Where the nondocumentary conditions are central and fundamental to the issuer's obligation (as for example a condition that would require the issuer to determine in fact whether the beneficiary had performed the underlying contract or whether the applicant had defaulted) their inclusion may remove the undertaking from the scope of Article 5 entirely. See Section 5–102(a)(10) and Comment 6 to Section 5–102.

Subsection (g) would not permit the beneficiary or the issuer to disregard terms in the letter of credit such as place, time, and mode of presentation. The rule in subsection (g) is intended to prevent an issuer from deciding or even investigating extrinsic facts, but not from consulting the clock, the calendar, the relevant law and practice, or its own general knowledge of documentation or transactions of the type underlying a particular letter of credit.

Even though nondocumentary conditions must be disregarded in determining compliance of a presentation (and thus in determining the issuer's duty to the beneficiary), an issuer that has promised its applicant that it will honor only on the occurrence of those nondocumentary conditions may have liability to its applicant for disregarding the conditions.

10.　Subsection (f) condones an issuer's ignorance of "any usage of a particular trade"; that trade is the trade of the applicant, beneficiary, or others who may be involved in the underlying transaction. The issuer is expected to know usage that is commonly encountered in the course of document examination. For example, an issuer should know the common usage with respect to documents in the maritime shipping trade but would not be expected to understand synonyms used in a particular trade for product descriptions appearing in a letter of credit or an invoice.

11.　Where the issuer's performance is the delivery of an item of value other than money, the applicant's reimbursement obligation would be to make the "item of value" available to the issuer.

12.　An issuer is entitled to reimbursement from the applicant after honor of a forged or fraudulent drawing if honor was permitted under Section 5–109(a).

13.   The last clause of Section 5–108(i)(5) deals with a special case in which the fraud is not committed by the beneficiary, but is committed by a stranger to the transaction who forges the beneficiary's signature. If the issuer pays against documents on which a required signature of the beneficiary is forged, it remains liable to the true beneficiary. This principle is applicable to both electronic and tangible documents.

As amended in 2003.

§ 5–109.   Fraud and Forgery.

(a)   If a presentation is made that appears on its face strictly to comply with the terms and conditions of the letter of credit, but a required document is forged or materially fraudulent, or honor of the presentation would facilitate a material fraud by the beneficiary on the issuer or applicant:

(1)   the issuer shall honor the presentation, if honor is demanded by (i) a nominated person who has given value in good faith and without notice of forgery or material fraud, (ii) a confirmer who has honored its confirmation in good faith, (iii) a holder in due course of a draft drawn under the letter of credit which was taken after acceptance by the issuer or nominated person, or (iv) an assignee of the issuer's or nominated person's deferred obligation that was taken for value and without notice of forgery or material fraud after the obligation was incurred by the issuer or nominated person; and

(2)   the issuer, acting in good faith, may honor or dishonor the presentation in any other case.

(b)   If an applicant claims that a required document is forged or materially fraudulent or that honor of the presentation would facilitate a material fraud by the beneficiary on the issuer or applicant, a court of competent jurisdiction may temporarily or permanently enjoin the issuer from honoring a presentation or grant similar relief against the issuer or other persons only if the court finds that:

(1)   the relief is not prohibited under the law applicable to an accepted draft or deferred obligation incurred by the issuer;

(2)   a beneficiary, issuer, or nominated person who may be adversely affected is adequately protected against loss that it may suffer because the relief is granted;

(3)   all of the conditions to entitle a person to the relief under the law of this State have been met; and

(4)   on the basis of the information submitted to the court, the applicant is more likely than not to succeed under its claim of forgery or material fraud and the person demanding honor does not qualify for protection under subsection (a)(1).

Official Comment

1.   This recodification makes clear that fraud must be found either in the documents or must have been committed by the beneficiary on the issuer or applicant. See *Cromwell v. Commerce & Energy Bank*, 464 So.2d 721 (La. 1985).

Secondly, it makes clear that fraud must be "material." Necessarily courts must decide the breadth and width of "materiality." The use of the word requires that the fraudulent aspect of a document be material to a purchaser of that document or that the fraudulent act be significant to the participants in the underlying transaction. Assume, for example, that the beneficiary has a contract to deliver 1,000 barrels of salad oil. Knowing that it has delivered only 998, the beneficiary nevertheless submits an invoice showing 1,000 barrels. If two barrels in a 1,000 barrel shipment would be an insubstantial and immaterial breach of the underlying contract, the beneficiary's act, though possibly fraudulent, is not materially so and would not justify an injunction. Conversely, the knowing submission of those invoices upon delivery of only five barrels would be materially fraudulent. The courts must examine the underlying transaction when there is an allegation of material fraud, for only by examining that transaction can one determine whether a document is fraudulent or the beneficiary has committed fraud and, if so, whether the fraud was material.

Material fraud by the beneficiary occurs only when the beneficiary has no colorable right to expect honor and where there is no basis in fact to support such a right to honor. The section indorses articulations such as those stated in *Intraworld Indus. v. Girard Trust Bank*, 336 A.2d 316 (Pa. 1975), *Roman Ceramics Corp. v. People's Nat. Bank*, 714 F.2d 1207 (3d Cir. 1983), and similar decisions and embraces certain decisions under Section 5–114 that relied upon the phrase "fraud in the transaction." Some of these decisions have been summarized as follows in *Ground Air Transfer v. Westate's Airlines,* 899 F.2d 1269, 1272–73 (1st Cir. 1990):

> We have said throughout that courts may not "*normally*" issue an injunction because of an important exception to the general "no injunction" rule. The exception, as we also explained in *Itek*, 730 F.2d at 24–25, concerns "fraud" so serious as to make it obviously pointless and unjust to permit the beneficiary to obtain the money. Where the circumstances "*plainly*" show that the underlying contract forbids the beneficiary to call a letter of credit, *Itek*, 730 F.2d at 24; where they show that the contract deprives the beneficiary of even a "*colorable*" right to do so, id., at 25; where the contract and circumstances reveal that the beneficiary's demand for payment has "absolutely no basis in fact," id.; see *Dynamics Corp. of America*, 356 F.Supp. at 999; where the beneficiary's conduct has "so vitiated the entire transaction that the legitimate purposes of the independence of the issuer's obligation would no longer be served," Itek, 730 F.2d at 25 (quoting *Roman Ceramics Corp. v. Peoples National Bank,* 714 F.2d 1207, 1212 n.12, 1215 (3d Cir. 1983)(quoting Intraworld Indus., 336 A.2d at 324–25)); *then* a court may enjoin payment.

2.   Subsection (a)(2) makes clear that the issuer may honor in the face of the applicant's claim of fraud. The subsection also makes clear what was not stated in former Section 5–114, that the issuer may dishonor and defend that dishonor by showing fraud or forgery of the kind stated in subsection (a). Because issuers may be liable for wrongful dishonor if they are unable to prove forgery or material fraud, presumably most issuers will choose to honor despite applicant's claims of fraud or forgery unless the applicant procures an injunction. Merely because the issuer has a right to dishonor and to defend that dishonor by showing forgery or material fraud does not mean it has a duty to the applicant to dishonor. The applicant's normal recourse is to procure an injunction, if the applicant is unable to procure an injunction, it will have a claim against the issuer only in the rare case in which it can show that the issuer did not honor in good faith.

3.   Whether a beneficiary can commit fraud by presenting a draft under a clean letter of credit (one calling only for a draft and no other documents) has been much debated. Under the current formulation it would be possible but difficult for there to be fraud in such a presentation. If the applicant were able to show that the beneficiary were committing material fraud on the applicant in the underlying transaction, then payment would facilitate a material fraud by the beneficiary on the applicant and honor could be enjoined. The courts should be skeptical of claims of fraud by one who has signed a "suicide" or clean credit and thus granted a beneficiary the right to draw by mere presentation of a draft.

4.   The standard for injunctive relief is high, and the burden remains on the applicant to show, by evidence and not by mere allegation, that such relief is warranted. Some courts have enjoined payments on letters of credit on insufficient showing by the applicant. For example, in *Griffin Cos. v. First Nat. Bank,* 374 N.W.2d 768 (Minn.App. 1985), the court enjoined payment under a standby letter of credit, basing its decision on plaintiff's allegation, rather than competent evidence, of fraud.

There are at least two ways to prohibit injunctions against honor under this section after acceptance of a draft by the issuer. First is to define honor (see Section 5–102(a)(8)) in the particular letter of credit to occur upon acceptance and without regard to later payment of the acceptance. Second is explicitly to agree that the applicant has no right to an injunction after acceptance—whether or not the acceptance constitutes honor.

5.   Although the statute deals principally with injunctions against honor, it also cautions against granting "similar relief" and the same principles apply when the applicant or issuer attempts to achieve the same legal outcome by injunction against presentation (see *Ground Air Transfer Inc. v. Westates Airlines, Inc.,* 899 F.2d 1269 (1st Cir. 1990)), interpleader, declaratory judgment, or attachment. These attempts should face the same obstacles that face efforts to enjoin the issuer from paying. Expanded use of any of these devices could threaten the independence principle just as much as injunctions against honor. For that reason courts should have the same hostility to them and place the same restrictions on their use as would be applied to injunctions against honor. Courts should not allow the "sacred cow of equity to trample the tender vines of letter of credit law."

6.   Section 5–109(a)(1) also protects specified third parties against the risk of fraud. By issuing a letter of credit that nominates a person to negotiate or pay, the issuer (ultimately the applicant) induces that nominated person to give value and thereby assumes the risk that a draft drawn under the letter of credit will be transferred to one with a status like that of a holder in due course who deserves to be protected against a fraud defense.

7.   The "loss" to be protected against—by bond or otherwise under subsection (b)(2)—includes incidental damages. Among those are legal fees that might be incurred by the beneficiary or issuer in defending against an injunction action.

§ 5–110.   Warranties.

(a)   If its presentation is honored, the beneficiary warrants:

(1)   to the issuer, any other person to whom presentation is made, and the applicant that there is no fraud or forgery of the kind described in Section 5–109(a); and

(2)   to the applicant that the drawing does not violate any agreement between the applicant and beneficiary or any other agreement intended by them to be augmented by the letter of credit.

(b)   The warranties in subsection (a) are in addition to warranties arising under Article 3, 4, 7, and 8 because of the presentation or transfer of documents covered by any of those articles.

Official Comment

1.   Since the warranties in subsection (a) are not given unless a letter of credit has been honored, no breach of warranty under this subsection can be a defense to dishonor by the issuer. Any defense must be based on Section 5–108 or 5–109 and not on this section. Also, breach of the warranties by the beneficiary in subsection (a) cannot excuse the applicant's duty to reimburse.

2.   The warranty in Section 5–110(a)(2) assumes that payment under the letter of credit is final. It does not run to the issuer, only to the applicant. In most cases the applicant will have a direct cause of action for breach of the underlying contract. This warranty has primary application in standby letters of credit or other circumstances where the applicant is not a party to an underlying contract with the beneficiary. It is not a warranty that the statements made on the presentation of the documents presented are truthful nor is it a warranty that the documents strictly comply under Section 5–108(a). It is a warranty that the beneficiary has performed all the acts expressly and implicitly necessary under any underlying agreement to entitle the beneficiary to honor. If, for example, an underlying sales contract authorized the beneficiary to draw only upon "due performance" and the beneficiary drew even though it had breached the underlying contract by delivering defective goods, honor of its draw would break the warranty. By the same token, if the underlying contract authorized the beneficiary to draw only upon actual default or upon its or a third party's determination of default by the applicant and if the beneficiary drew in violation of its authorization, then upon honor of its draw the warranty would be breached. In many cases, therefore, the documents presented to the issuer will contain inaccurate statements (concerning the goods delivered or concerning default or other matters), but the breach of warranty arises not because the statements are untrue but because the beneficiary's drawing violated its express or implied obligations in the underlying transaction.

3.   The damages for breach of warranty are not specified in Section 5–111. Courts may find damage analogies in Section 2–714 in Article 2 and in warranty decisions under Articles 3 and 4.

Unlike wrongful dishonor cases—where the damages usually equal the amount of the draw—the damages for breach of warranty will often be much less than the amount of the draw, sometimes zero. Assume a seller entitled to draw only on proper performance of its sales contract. Assume it breaches the sales contract in a way that gives the buyer a right to damages but no right to reject. The applicant's damages for breach of the warranty in subsection (a)(2) are limited to the damages it could recover for breach of the contract of sale. Alternatively assume an underlying agreement that authorizes a beneficiary to draw only the "amount in default." Assume a default of $200,000 and a draw of $500,000. The damages for breach of warranty would be no more than $300,000.

§ 5–111.   Remedies.

(a)   If an issuer wrongfully dishonors or repudiates its obligation to pay money under a letter of credit before presentation, the beneficiary, successor, or nominated person presenting on its own behalf may recover from the issuer the amount that is the subject of the dishonor or repudiation. If the issuer's obligation under the letter of credit is not for the payment of money, the claimant may obtain specific performance or, at the claimant's election, recover an amount equal to the value of performance from the issuer. In either case, the claimant may also recover incidental but not consequential damages. The claimant is not obligated to take action to avoid damages that might be due from the issuer under this subsection. If, although not obligated to do so, the claimant avoids damages, the claimant's recovery from the issuer must be reduced by the amount of damages avoided. The issuer has the burden of proving the amount of damages avoided. In the case of repudiation the claimant need not present any document.

(b)   If an issuer wrongfully dishonors a draft or demand presented under a letter of credit or honors a draft or demand in breach of its obligation to the applicant, the applicant may recover damages resulting from the breach, including incidental but not consequential damages, less any amount saved as a result of the breach.

(c)   If an adviser or nominated person other than a confirmer breaches an obligation under this article or an issuer breaches an obligation not covered in subsection (a) or (b), a person to whom the obligation is owed may recover damages resulting from the breach, including incidental but not consequential damages, less any amount saved as a result of the breach. To the extent of the confirmation, a confirmer has the liability of an issuer specified in this subsection and subsections (a) and (b).

(d)   An issuer, nominated person, or adviser who is found liable under subsection (a), (b), or (c) shall pay interest on the amount owed thereunder from the date of wrongful dishonor or other appropriate date.

(e)   Reasonable attorney's fees and other expenses of litigation must be awarded to the prevailing party in an action in which a remedy is sought under this article.

(f)   Damages that would otherwise be payable by a party for breach of an obligation under this article may be liquidated by agreement or undertaking, but only in an amount or by a formula that is reasonable in light of the harm anticipated.

Official Comment

1.   The right to specific performance is new. The express limitation on the duty of the beneficiary to mitigate damages adopts the position of certain courts and commentators. Because the letter of credit depends upon speed and certainty of payment, it is important that the issuer not be given an incentive to dishonor. The issuer might have an incentive to dishonor if it could rely on the burden of mitigation falling on the beneficiary, (to sell goods and sue only for the difference between the price of the goods sold and the amount due under the letter of credit). Under the scheme contemplated by Section 5–111(a), the beneficiary would present the documents to the issuer. If the issuer wrongfully dishonored, the beneficiary would have no further duty to the issuer with respect to the goods covered by documents that the issuer dishonored and returned. The issuer thus takes the risk that the beneficiary will let the goods rot or be destroyed. Of course the beneficiary may have a duty of mitigation to the applicant arising from the underlying agreement, but the issuer would not have the right to assert that duty by way of defense or setoff. See Section 5–117(d). If the beneficiary sells the goods covered by dishonored documents or if the beneficiary sells a draft after acceptance but before dishonor by the issuer, the net amount so gained should be subtracted from the amount of the beneficiary's damages—at least where the damage claim against the issuer equals or exceeds the damage suffered by the beneficiary. If, on the other hand, the beneficiary suffers damages in an underlying transaction in an amount that exceeds the amount of the wrongfully dishonored demand (e.g., where the letter of credit does not cover 100 percent of the underlying obligation), the damages avoided should not necessarily be deducted from the beneficiary's claim against the issuer. In such a case, the damages would be the lesser of (i) the amount recoverable in the absence of mitigation (that is, the amount that is subject to the dishonor or repudiation plus any incidental damages) and (ii) the damages remaining after deduction for the amount of damages actually avoided.

A beneficiary need not present documents as a condition of suit for anticipatory repudiation, but if a beneficiary could never have obtained documents necessary for a presentation conforming to the letter of credit, the beneficiary cannot recover for anticipatory repudiation of the letter of credit. *Doelger v. Battery Park Bank,* 201 A.D. 515, 194 N.Y.S. 582 (1922) and *Decor by Nikkei Int'l, Inc. v. Federal Republic of Nigeria,* 497 F.Supp. 893 (S.D.N.Y. 1980), *aff'd,* 647 F.2d 300 (2d Cir. 1981), *cert. denied,* 454 U.S. 1148 (1982). The last sentence of subsection (c) does not expand the liability of a confirmer to persons to whom the confirmer would not otherwise be liable under Section 5–107.

Almost all letters of credit, including those that call for an acceptance, are "obligations to pay money" as that term is used in Section 5–111(a).

2.   What damages "result" from improper honor is for the courts to decide. Even though an issuer pays a beneficiary in violation of Section 5–108(a) or of its contract with the applicant, it may have no liability to an applicant. If the underlying contract has been fully performed, the applicant may not have been damaged by the issuer's breach. Such a case would occur when A contracts for goods at $100 per ton, but, upon delivery, the market value of conforming goods has decreased to $25 per ton. If the issuer pays over discrepancies, there should be no recovery by A for the price differential if the issuer's breach did not alter the applicant's obligation under the underlying contract, i.e., to pay $100 per ton for goods now worth $25 per ton. On the other hand, if the applicant intends to resell the goods and must itself satisfy the strict compliance requirements under a second letter of credit in connection with its sale, the applicant may be damaged by the issuer's payment despite discrepancies because the applicant itself may then be unable to procure honor on the letter of credit where it is the beneficiary, and may

be unable to mitigate its damages by enforcing its rights against others in the underlying transaction. Note that an issuer found liable to its applicant may have recourse under Section 5–117 by subrogation to the applicant's claim against the beneficiary or other persons.

One who inaccurately advises a letter of credit breaches its obligation to the beneficiary, but may cause no damage. If the beneficiary knows the terms of the letter of credit and understands the advice to be inaccurate, the beneficiary will have suffered no damage as a result of the adviser's breach.

3.　　Since the confirmer has the rights and duties of an issuer, in general it has an issuer's liability, see subsection (c). The confirmer is usually a confirming bank. A confirming bank often also plays the role of an adviser. If it breaks its obligation to the beneficiary, the confirming bank may have liability as an issuer or, depending upon the obligation that was broken, as an adviser. For example, a wrongful dishonor would give it liability as an issuer under Section 5–111(a). On the other hand a confirming bank that broke its obligation to advise the credit but did not commit wrongful dishonor would be treated under Section 5–111(c).

4.　　Consequential damages for breach of obligations under this article are excluded in the belief that these damages can best be avoided by the beneficiary or the applicant and out of the fear that imposing consequential damages on issuers would raise the cost of the letter of credit to a level that might render it uneconomic. *A fortiori* punitive and exemplary damages are excluded, however, this section does not bar recovery of consequential or even punitive damages for breach of statutory or common law duties arising outside of this article.

5.　　The section does not specify a rate of interest. It leaves the setting of the rate to the court. It would be appropriate for a court to use the rate that would normally apply in that court in other situations where interest is imposed by law.

6.　　The court must award attorney's fees to the prevailing party, whether that party is an applicant, a beneficiary, an issuer, a nominated person, or adviser. Since the issuer may be entitled to recover its legal fees and costs from the applicant under the reimbursement agreement, allowing the issuer to recover those fees from a losing beneficiary may also protect the applicant against undeserved losses. The party entitled to attorneys' fees has been described as the "prevailing party." Sometimes it will be unclear which party "prevailed," for example, where there are multiple issues and one party wins on some and the other party wins on others. Determining which is the prevailing party is in the discretion of the court. Subsection (e) authorizes attorney's fees in all actions where a remedy is sought "under this article." It applies even when the remedy might be an injunction under Section 5–109 or when the claimed remedy is otherwise outside of Section 5–111. Neither an issuer nor a confirmer should be treated as a "losing" party when an injunction is granted to the applicant over the objection of the issuer or confirmer; accordingly neither should be liable for fees and expenses in that case.

"Expenses of litigation" is intended to be broader than "costs." For example, expense of litigation would include travel expenses of witnesses, fees for expert witnesses, and expenses associated with taking depositions.

7.　　For the purposes of Section 5–111(f) "harm anticipated" must be anticipated at the time when the agreement that includes the liquidated damage clause is executed or at the time when the undertaking that includes the clause is issued. See Section 2A–504.

§ 5–112.　　Transfer of Letter of Credit.

(a)　　Except as otherwise provided in Section 5–113, unless a letter of credit provides that it is transferable, the right of a beneficiary to draw or otherwise demand performance under a letter of credit may not be transferred.

(b)　　Even if a letter of credit provides that it is transferable, the issuer may refuse to recognize or carry out a transfer if:

(1)　　the transfer would violate applicable law; or

(2)　　the transferor or transferee has failed to comply with any requirement stated in the letter of credit or any other requirement relating to transfer imposed by the issuer which is within the standard practice referred to in Section 5–108(e) or is otherwise reasonable under the circumstances.

Official Comment

1.　　In order to protect the applicant's reliance on the designated beneficiary, letter of credit law traditionally has forbidden the beneficiary to convey to third parties its right to draw or demand payment under the letter of credit. Subsection (a) codifies that rule. The term "transfer" refers to the beneficiary's conveyance of that right. Absent incorporation of the UCP (which make elaborate provision for partial transfer of a commercial letter of credit) or similar trade practice and absent other express indication in the letter of credit that the term is used to mean something else, a term in the letter of credit indicating that the beneficiary has the right to transfer should be taken to mean that the beneficiary may convey to a third party its right to draw or demand payment. Even in that case, the issuer or other person controlling the transfer may make the beneficiary's right to transfer subject to conditions, such as timely notification, payment of a fee, delivery of the letter of credit to the issuer or other person controlling the transfer, or execution of appropriate forms to document the transfer. A nominated person who is not a confirmer has no obligation to recognize a transfer.

The power to establish "requirements" does not include the right absolutely to refuse to recognize transfers under a transferable letter of credit. An issuer who wishes to retain the right to deny all transfers should not issue transferable letters of credit or should incorporate the UCP. By stating its requirements in the letter of credit an issuer may impose any requirement without regard to its conformity to practice or reasonableness. Transfer requirements of issuers and nominated persons must be made known to potential transferors and transferees to enable those parties to comply with the requirements. A common method of making such requirements known is to use a form that indicates the information that must be provided and the instructions that must be given to enable the issuer or nominated person to comply with a request to transfer.

2. The issuance of a transferable letter of credit with the concurrence of the applicant is *ipso facto* an agreement by the issuer and applicant to permit a beneficiary to transfer its drawing right and permit a nominated person to recognize and carry out that transfer without further notice to them. In international commerce, transferable letters of credit are often issued under circumstances in which a nominated person or adviser is expected to facilitate the transfer from the original beneficiary to a transferee and to deal with that transferee. In those circumstances it is the responsibility of the nominated person or adviser to establish procedures satisfactory to protect itself against double presentation or dispute about the right to draw under the letter of credit. Commonly such a person will control the transfer by requiring that the original letter of credit be given to it or by causing a paper copy marked as an original to be issued where the original letter of credit was electronic. By keeping possession of the original letter of credit the nominated person or adviser can minimize or entirely exclude the possibility that the original beneficiary could properly procure payment from another bank. If the letter of credit requires presentation of the original letter of credit itself, no other payment could be procured. In addition to imposing whatever requirements it considers appropriate to protect itself against double payment the person that is facilitating the transfer has a right to charge an appropriate fee for its activity.

"Transfer" of a letter of credit should be distinguished from "assignment of proceeds." The former is analogous to a novation or a substitution of beneficiaries. It contemplates not merely payment to but also performance by the transferee. For example, under the typical terms of transfer for a commercial letter of credit, a transferee could comply with a letter of credit transferred to it by signing and presenting its own draft and invoice. An assignee of proceeds, on the other hand, is wholly dependent on the presentation of a draft and invoice signed by the beneficiary.

By agreeing to the issuance of a transferable letter of credit, which is not qualified or limited, the applicant may lose control over the identity of the person whose performance will earn payment under the letter of credit.

§ 5–113. Transfer by Operation of Law.

(a) A successor of a beneficiary may consent to amendments, sign and present documents, and receive payment or other items of value in the name of the beneficiary without disclosing its status as a successor.

(b) A successor of a beneficiary may consent to amendments, sign and present documents, and receive payment or other items of value in its own name as the disclosed successor of the beneficiary. Except as otherwise provided in subsection (e), an issuer shall recognize a disclosed successor of a beneficiary as beneficiary in full substitution for its predecessor upon compliance with the requirements for recognition by the issuer of a transfer of drawing rights by operation of law under the standard practice referred to in Section 5–108(e) or, in the absence of such a practice, compliance with other reasonable procedures sufficient to protect the issuer.

(c) An issuer is not obliged to determine whether a purported successor is a successor of a beneficiary or whether the signature of a purported successor is genuine or authorized.

(d) Honor of a purported successor's apparently complying presentation under subsection (a) or (b) has the consequences specified in Section 5–108(i) even if the purported successor is not the successor of a beneficiary. Documents signed in the name of the beneficiary or of a disclosed successor by a person who is neither the beneficiary nor the successor of the beneficiary are forged documents for the purposes of Section 5–109.

(e) An issuer whose rights of reimbursement are not covered by subsection (d) or substantially similar law and any confirmer or nominated person may decline to recognize a presentation under subsection (b).

(f) A beneficiary whose name is changed after the issuance of a letter of credit has the same rights and obligations as a successor of a beneficiary under this section.

Official Comment

This section affirms the result in *Pastor v. Nat. Republic Bank of Chicago,* 76 Ill.2d 139, 390 N.E.2d 894 (Ill. 1979) and *Federal Deposit Insurance Co. v. Bank of Boulder,* 911 F.2d 1466 (10th Cir. 1990). Both electronic and tangible documents may be signed.

An issuer's requirements for recognition of a successor's status might include presentation of a certificate of merger, a court order appointing a bankruptcy trustee or receiver, a certificate of appointment as bankruptcy trustee, or the like. The issuer is entitled to rely upon such documents which on their face demonstrate that presentation is made by a successor of a beneficiary. It is not obliged to make an independent investigation to determine the fact of succession.

As amended in 2003.

§ 5–114. Assignment of Proceeds.

(a) In this section, "proceeds of a letter of credit" means the cash, check, accepted draft, or other item of value paid or delivered upon honor or giving of value by the issuer or any nominated person under the letter of credit. The term does not include a beneficiary's drawing rights or documents presented by the beneficiary.

(b) A beneficiary may assign its right to part or all of the proceeds of a letter of credit. The beneficiary may do so before presentation as a present assignment of its right to receive proceeds contingent upon its compliance with the terms and conditions of the letter of credit.

(c) An issuer or nominated person need not recognize an assignment of proceeds of a letter of credit until it consents to the assignment.

(d) An issuer or nominated person has no obligation to give or withhold its consent to an assignment of proceeds of a letter of credit, but consent may not be unreasonably withheld if the assignee possesses and exhibits the letter of credit and presentation of the letter of credit is a condition to honor.

(e) Rights of a transferee beneficiary or nominated person are independent of the beneficiary's assignment of the proceeds of a letter of credit and are superior to the assignee's right to the proceeds.

(f) Neither the rights recognized by this section between an assignee and an issuer, transferee beneficiary, or nominated person nor the issuer's or nominated person's payment of proceeds to an assignee or a third person affect the rights between the assignee and any person other than the issuer, transferee beneficiary, or nominated person. The mode of creating and perfecting a security interest in or granting an assignment of a beneficiary's rights to proceeds is governed by Article 9 or other law. Against persons other than the issuer, transferee beneficiary, or nominated person, the rights and obligations arising upon the creation of a security interest or other assignment of a beneficiary's right to proceeds and its perfection are governed by Article 9 or other law.

Official Comment

1. Subsection (b) expressly validates the beneficiary's present assignment of letter of credit proceeds if made after the credit is established but before the proceeds are realized. This section adopts the prevailing usage— "assignment of proceeds"—to an assignee. That terminology carries with it no implication, however, that an assignee acquires no interest until the proceeds are paid by the issuer. For example, an "assignment of the right to proceeds" of a letter of credit for purposes of security that meets the requirements of Section 9–203(b) would constitute the present creation of a security interest in a "letter-of-credit right." This security interest can be perfected by control (Section 9–107). Although subsection (a) explains the meaning of " 'proceeds' of a letter of credit," it should be emphasized that those proceeds also may be Article 9 proceeds of other collateral. For example,

if a seller of inventory receives a letter of credit to support the account that arises upon the sale, payments made under the letter of credit are Article 9 proceeds of the inventory, account, and any document of title covering the inventory. Thus, the secured party who had a perfected security interest in that inventory, account, or document has a perfected security interest in the proceeds collected under the letter of credit, so long as they are identifiable cash proceeds (Section 9–315(a), (d)). This perfection is continuous, regardless of whether the secured party perfected a security interest in the right to letter of credit proceeds.

2.   An assignee's rights to enforce an assignment of proceeds against an issuer and the priority of the assignee's rights against a nominated person or transferee beneficiary are governed by Article 5. Those rights and that priority are stated in subsections (c), (d), and (e). Note also that Section 4–210 gives first priority to a collecting bank that has given value for a documentary draft.

3.   By requiring that an issuer or nominated person consent to the assignment of proceeds of a letter of credit, subsections (c) and (d) follow more closely recognized national and international letter of credit practices than did prior law. In most circumstances, it has always been advisable for the assignee to obtain the consent of the issuer in order better to safeguard its right to the proceeds. When notice of an assignment has been received, issuers normally have required signatures on a consent form. This practice is reflected in the revision. By unconditionally consenting to such an assignment, the issuer or nominated person becomes bound, subject to the rights of the superior parties specified in subsection (e), to pay to the assignee the assigned letter of credit proceeds that the issuer or nominated person would otherwise pay to the beneficiary or another assignee.

Where the letter of credit must be presented as a condition to honor and the assignee holds and exhibits the letter of credit to the issuer or nominated person, the risk to the issuer or nominated person of having to pay twice is minimized. In such a situation, subsection (d) provides that the issuer or nominated person may not unreasonably withhold its consent to the assignment.

§ 5–115.   Statute of Limitations.

An action to enforce a right or obligation arising under this article must be commenced within one year after the expiration date of the relevant letter of credit or one year after the [claim for relief] [cause of action] accrues, whichever occurs later. A [claim for relief] [cause of action] accrues when the breach occurs, regardless of the aggrieved party's lack of knowledge of the breach.

Official Comment

1.   This section is based upon Sections 4–111 and 2–725(2).

2.   This section applies to all claims for which there are remedies under Section 5–111 and to other claims made under this article, such as claims for breach of warranty under Section 5–110. Because it covers all claims under Section 5–111, the statute of limitations applies not only to wrongful dishonor claims against the issuer but also to claims between the issuer and the applicant arising from the reimbursement agreement. These might be for reimbursement (issuer v. applicant) or for breach of the reimbursement contract by wrongful honor (applicant v. issuer).

3.   The statute of limitations, like the rest of the statute, applies only to a letter of credit issued on or after the effective date and only to transactions, events, obligations, or duties arising out of or associated with such a letter. If a letter of credit was issued before the effective date and an obligation on that letter of credit was breached after the effective date, the complaining party could bring its suit within the time that would have been permitted prior to the adoption of Section 5–115 and would not be limited by the terms of Section 5–115.

§ 5–116.   Choice of Law and Forum.

(a)   The liability of an issuer, nominated person, or adviser for action or omission is governed by the law of the jurisdiction chosen by an agreement in the form of a record signed or otherwise authenticated by the affected parties in the manner provided in Section 5–104 or by a provision in the person's letter of credit, confirmation, or other undertaking. The jurisdiction whose law is chosen need not bear any relation to the transaction.

(b)   Unless subsection (a) applies, the liability of an issuer, nominated person, or adviser for action or omission is governed by the law of the jurisdiction in which the person is located. The person is considered to be located at the address indicated in the person's undertaking. If more than one address is indicated, the person is considered to be located at the address from which the person's undertaking was issued.

(c) For the purpose of jurisdiction, choice of law, and recognition of interbranch letters of credit, but not enforcement of a judgment, all branches of a bank are considered separate juridical entities and a bank is considered to be located at the place where its relevant branch is considered to be located under ~~this~~ subsection (d).

(d) A branch of a bank is considered to be located at the address indicated in the branch's undertaking. If more than one address is indicated, the branch is considered to be located at the address from which the undertaking was issued.

~~(e)~~(e) Except as otherwise provided in this subsection, the liability of an issuer, nominated person, or adviser is governed by any rules of custom or practice, such as the Uniform Customs and Practice for Documentary Credits, to which the letter of credit, confirmation, or other undertaking is expressly made subject. If (i) this article would govern the liability of an issuer, nominated person, or adviser under subsection (a) or (b), (ii) the relevant undertaking incorporates rules of custom or practice, and (iii) there is conflict between this article and those rules as applied to that undertaking, those rules govern except to the extent of any conflict with the nonvariable provisions specified in Section 5–103(c).

~~(d)~~(f) If there is conflict between this article and Article 3, 4, 4A, or 9, this article governs.

~~(e)~~(g) The forum for settling disputes arising out of an undertaking within this article may be chosen in the manner and with the binding effect that governing law may be chosen in accordance with subsection (a).

As amended in 2022.

Official Comment

1. Subsection (a) refers to a record signed by the affected parties. The reference in the pre-2022 text of subsection (a) to an authentication pursuant to an agreement of the parties or standard practice is no longer necessary in view of the 2022 revision of "sign" in Section 1–201. See Section 5–104, Comment 2.

Although it would be possible for the parties to agree otherwise, the law normally chosen by agreement under subsection (a) and that provided in the absence of agreement under subsection (b) is the substantive law of a particular jurisdiction not including the choice of law principles of that jurisdiction. Thus, two parties, an issuer and an applicant, both located in Oklahoma might choose the law of New York. Unless they agree otherwise, the section anticipates that they wish the substantive law of New York to apply to their transaction and they do not intend that a New York choice of law principle might direct a court to Oklahoma law. By the same token, the liability of an issuer located in New York is governed by New York substantive law—in the absence of agreement—even in circumstances in which choice of law principles found in the common law of New York might direct one to the law of another State. Subsection (b) states the relevant choice of law principles and it should not be subordinated to some other choice of law rule. Within the States of the United States *renvoi* will not be a problem once every jurisdiction has enacted Section 5–116 because every jurisdiction will then have the same choice of law rule and in a particular case all choice of law rules will point to the same substantive law.

Subsection (b) does not state a choice of law rule for the "liability of an applicant." However, subsection (b) does state a choice of law rule for the liability of an issuer, nominated person, or adviser, and since some of the issues in suits by applicants against those persons involve the "liability of an issuer, nominated person, or adviser," subsection (b) states the choice of law rule for those issues. Because an issuer may have liability to a confirmer both as an issuer (Section 5–108(a), Comment 5 to Section 5–108) and as an applicant (Section 5–107(a), Comment 1 to Section 5–107, Section 5–108(i)), subsection (b) may state the choice of law rule for some but not all of the issuer's liability in a suit by a confirmer.

1A. The last sentence of pre-2022 subsection (b) is now in a new subsection (c) and a new subsection (d) has been added. These revisions were necessary to eliminate a potential ambiguity arising from the first sentence of subsection (b). The first sentence has been construed incorrectly as meaning that the last sentence, which recognizes the separateness of bank branches for the specified purposes, is inapplicable when a governing law has been chosen pursuant to subsection (a). These revisions reject that construction and reject decisions such as *Zeeco, Inc. v. JPMorgan Chase Bank*, Case No. 17–CV–384–JED–FHM, 2018 WL 1414119 (N.D. Okla. Mar. 21, 2018), *amending opinion dated March 20, 2018, both opinions vacated,* 2019 WL 3543081, 2019 U.S. Dist. LEXIS 133756 (Feb. 8, 2019).

2. Because the confirmer or other nominated person may choose different law from that chosen by the issuer or may be located in a different jurisdiction and fail to choose law, it is possible that a confirmer or

498

nominated person may be obligated to pay (under their law) but will not be entitled to payment from the issuer (under its law). Similarly, the rights of an unreimbursed issuer, confirmer, or nominated person against a beneficiary under Section 5–109, 5–110, or 5–117, will not necessarily be governed by the same law that applies to the issuer's or confirmer's obligation upon presentation. Because the UCP and other practice are incorporated in most international letters of credit, disputes arising from different legal obligations to honor have not been frequent. Since Section 5–108 incorporates standard practice, these problems should be further minimized—at least to the extent that the same practice is and continues to be widely followed.

3.   This section does not permit what is now authorized by the nonuniform Section 5–102(4) in New York. Under the current law in New York a letter of credit that incorporates the UCP is not governed in any respect by Article 5. Under revised Section 5–116 letters of credit that incorporate the UCP or similar practice will still be subject to Article 5 in certain respects. First, incorporation of the UCP or other practice does not override the nonvariable terms of Article 5. Second, where there is no conflict between Article 5 and the relevant provision of the UCP or other practice, both apply. Third, practice provisions incorporated in a letter of credit will not be effective if they fail to comply with Section 5–103(c). Assume, for example, that a practice provision purported to free a party from any liability unless it were "grossly negligent" or that the practice generally limited the remedies that one party might have against another. Depending upon the circumstances, that disclaimer or limitation of liability might be ineffective because of Section 5–103(c).

Even though Article 5 is generally consistent with UCP 500, it is not necessarily consistent with other rules or with versions of the UCP that may be adopted after Article 5's revision, or with other practices that may develop. The phrase in subsection 5–116(e), "rules of custom or practice, such as the Uniform Customs and Practice for Documentary Credits," includes the International Standby Practices and the Uniform Rules for Demand Guarantees, as well as the Supplement to the Uniform Customs and Practice for Documentary Credits for Electronic Presentation. Rules of practice incorporated in the letter of credit or other undertaking are those in effect when the letter of credit or other undertaking is issued. Except in the unusual cases discussed in the immediately preceding paragraph, practice adopted in a letter of credit will override the rules of Article 5 and the parties to letter of credit transactions must be familiar with practice (such as future versions of the UCP) that is explicitly adopted in letters of credit.

4.   In several ways Article 5 conflicts with and overrides similar matters governed by Articles 3 and 4. For example, "draft" is more broadly defined in letter of credit practice than under Section 3–104. The time allowed for honor and the required notification of reasons for dishonor are different in letter of credit practice than in the handling of documentary and other drafts under Articles 3 and 4.

5.   Subsection (e)(g) must be read in conjunction with existing law governing subject matter jurisdiction. If the local law restricts a court to certain subject matter jurisdiction not including letter of credit disputes, subsection (e)(g) does not authorize parties to choose that forum. For example, the parties' agreement under Section 5–116(e)5–116(g) would not confer jurisdiction on a probate court to decide a letter of credit case.

If the parties choose a forum under subsection (e)(g) and if—because of other law—that forum will not take jurisdiction, the parties' agreement or undertaking should then be construed (for the purpose of forum selection) as though it did not contain a clause choosing a particular forum. That result is necessary to avoid sentencing the parties to eternal purgatory where neither the chosen State nor the State which would have jurisdiction but for the clause will take jurisdiction—the former in disregard of the clause and the latter in honor of the clause.

As amended in 2022.

§ 5–117.   Subrogation of Issuer, Applicant, and Nominated Person.

(a)   An issuer that honors a beneficiary's presentation is subrogated to the rights of the beneficiary to the same extent as if the issuer were a secondary obligor of the underlying obligation owed to the beneficiary and of the applicant to the same extent as if the issuer were the secondary obligor of the underlying obligation owed to the applicant.

(b)   An applicant that reimburses an issuer is subrogated to the rights of the issuer against any beneficiary, presenter, or nominated person to the same extent as if the applicant were the secondary obligor of the obligations owed to the issuer and has the rights of subrogation of the issuer to the rights of the beneficiary stated in subsection (a).

(c)   A nominated person who pays or gives value against a draft or demand presented under a letter of credit is subrogated to the rights of:

(1) the issuer against the applicant to the same extent as if the nominated person were a secondary obligor of the obligation owed to the issuer by the applicant;

(2) the beneficiary to the same extent as if the nominated person were a secondary obligor of the underlying obligation owed to the beneficiary; and

(3) the applicant to same extent as if the nominated person were a secondary obligor of the underlying obligation owed to the applicant.

(d) Notwithstanding any agreement or term to the contrary, the rights of subrogation stated in subsections (a) and (b) do not arise until the issuer honors the letter of credit or otherwise pays and the rights in subsection (c) do not arise until the nominated person pays or otherwise gives value. Until then, the issuer, nominated person, and the applicant do not derive under this section present or prospective rights forming the basis of a claim, defense, or excuse.

Official Comment

1. By itself this section does not grant any right of subrogation. It grants only the right that would exist if the person seeking subrogation "were a secondary obligor." (The term "secondary obligor" refers to a surety, guarantor, or other person against whom or whose property an obligee has recourse with respect to the obligation of a third party. See Restatement of the Law Third, Suretyship and Guaranty § 1 (1996).) If the secondary obligor would not have a right to subrogation in the circumstances in which one is claimed under this section, none is granted by this section. In effect, the section does no more than to remove an impediment that some courts have found to subrogation because they conclude that the issuer's or other claimant's rights are "independent" of the underlying obligation. If, for example, a secondary obligor would not have a subrogation right because its payment did not fully satisfy the underlying obligation, none would be available under this section. The section indorses the position of Judge Becker in *Tudor Development Group, Inc. v. United States Fidelity and Guaranty*, 968 F.2d 357 (3rd Cir. 1991).

2. To preserve the independence of the letter of credit obligation and to insure that subrogation not be used as an offensive weapon by an issuer or others, the admonition in subsection (d) must be carefully observed. Only one who has completed its performance in a letter of credit transaction can have a right to subrogation. For example, an issuer may not dishonor and then defend its dishonor or assert a setoff on the ground that it is subrogated to another person's rights. Nor may the issuer complain after honor that its subrogation rights have been impaired by any good faith dealings between the beneficiary and the applicant or any other person. Assume, for example, that the beneficiary under a standby letter of credit is a mortgagee. If the mortgagee were obliged to issue a release of the mortgage upon payment of the underlying debt (by the issuer under the letter of credit), that release might impair the issuer's rights of subrogation, but the beneficiary would have no liability to the issuer for having granted that release.

§ 5–118.   Security Interest of Issuer or Nominated Person.

(a) An issuer or nominated person has a security interest in a document presented under a letter of credit to the extent that the issuer or nominated person honors or gives value for the presentation.

(b) So long as and to the extent that an issuer or nominated person has not been reimbursed or has not otherwise recovered the value given with respect to a security interest in a document under subsection (a), the security interest continues and is subject to Article 9, but:

(1) a security agreement is not necessary to make the security interest enforceable under Section 9–203(b)(3);

(2) if the document is presented in a medium other than a written or other tangible medium, the security interest is perfected; and

(3) if the document is presented in a written or other tangible medium and is not a certificated security, chattel paper, a document of title, an instrument, or a letter of credit, the security interest is perfected and has priority over a conflicting security interest in the document so long as the debtor does not have possession of the document.

As added in 1999.

Official Comment

1.   This section gives the issuer of a letter of credit or a nominated person thereunder an automatic perfected security interest in a "document" (as that term is defined in Section 5–102(a)(6)). The security interest arises only if the document is presented to the issuer or nominated person under the letter of credit and only to the extent of the value that is given. This security interest is analogous to that awarded to a collecting bank under Section 4–210. Subsection (b) contains special rules governing the security interest arising under this section. In all other respects, a security interest arising under this section is subject to Article 9. See Section 9–109. Thus, for example, a security interest arising under this section may give rise to a security interest in proceeds under Section 9–315.

2.   Subsection (b)(1) makes a security agreement unnecessary to the creation of a security interest under this section. Under subsection (b)(2), a security interest arising under this section is perfected if the document is presented in a medium other than a written or tangible medium. Documents that are written and that are not an otherwise-defined type of collateral under Article 9 (e.g., an invoice or inspection certificate) may be goods, in which an issuer or nominated person could perfect its security interest by possession. Because the definition of document in Section 5–102(a)(6) includes records (e.g., electronic records) that may not be goods, subsection (b)(2) provides for automatic perfection (i.e., without filing or possession).

Under subsection (b)(3), if the document (i) is in a written or tangible medium, (ii) is not a certificated security, chattel paper, a document of title, an instrument, or a letter of credit, and (iii) is not in the debtor's possession, the security interest is perfected and has priority over a conflicting security interest. If the document is a type of tangible collateral that subsection (b)(3) excludes from its perfection and priority rules, the issuer or nominated person must comply with the normal method of perfection (e.g., possession of an instrument) and is subject to the applicable Article 9 priority rules. Documents to which subsection (b)(3) applies may be important to an issuer or nominated person. For example, a confirmer who pays the beneficiary must be assured that its rights to all documents are not impaired. It will find it necessary to present all of the required documents to the issuer in order to be reimbursed. Moreover, when a nominated person sends documents to an issuer in connection with the nominated person's reimbursement, that activity is not a collection, enforcement, or disposition of collateral under Article 9.

One purpose of this section is to protect an issuer or nominated person from claims of a beneficiary's creditors. It is a fallback provision inasmuch as issuers and nominated persons frequently may obtain and perfect security interests under the usual Article 9 rules, and, in many cases, the documents will be owned by the issuer, nominated person, or applicant.

As added in 1999.

UCC ARTICLE 6

ALTERNATIVE A: REPEALER OF ARTICLE 6—
BULK TRANSFERS

ALTERNATIVE B: [REVISED] ARTICLE 6—
BULK SALES

(States To Select One Alternative)

Article 6 was revised in 1989.

Current through April 2023

For updates, see www.uniformlaws.org

ALTERNATIVE A

1.	Repeal.
2.	Amendment.
3.	Amendment.
4.	Savings Clause.

ALTERNATIVE B

6–101.	Short Title.
6–102.	Definitions and Index of Definitions.
6–103.	Applicability of Article.
6–104.	Obligations of Buyer.
6–105.	Notice to Claimants.
6–106.	Schedule of Distribution.
6–107.	Liability for Noncompliance.
6–108.	Bulk Sales by Auction; Bulk Sales Conducted by Liquidator.
6–109.	What Constitutes Filing; Duties of Filing Officer; Information From Filing Officer.
6–110.	Limitation of Actions.

PREFATORY NOTE

Background. Bulk sale legislation originally was enacted in response to a fraud perceived to be common around the turn of the century: a merchant would acquire his stock in trade on credit, then sell his entire inventory ("in bulk") and abscond with the proceeds, leaving creditors unpaid. The creditors had a right to sue the merchant on the unpaid debts, but that right often was of little practical value. Even if the merchant-debtor was found, in personam jurisdiction over him might not have been readily available. Those creditors who succeeded in obtaining a judgment often were unable to satisfy it because the defrauding seller had spent or hidden the sale proceeds. Nor did the creditors ordinarily have recourse to the merchandise sold. The transfer of the inventory to an innocent buyer effectively immunized the goods from the reach of the seller's creditors. The creditors of a bulk seller thus might be left without a means to satisfy their claims.

To a limited extent, the law of fraudulent conveyances ameliorated the creditors' plight. When the buyer in bulk was in league with the seller or paid less than full value for the inventory, fraudulent conveyance law enabled the defrauded creditors to avoid the sale and apply the transferred inventory toward the satisfaction of their claims against the seller. But fraudulent conveyance law provided no remedy against persons who bought in good faith, without reason to know of the seller's intention to pocket the proceeds and disappear, and for adequate value. In those cases, the only remedy for the seller's creditors was to attempt to recover from the absconding seller.

State legislatures responded to this perceived "bulk sale risk" with a variety of legislative enactments. Common to these statutes was the imposition of a duty on the buyer in bulk to notify the seller's creditors of the impending sale. The buyer's failure to comply with these and any other statutory duties generally afforded the seller's creditors a remedy analogous to the remedy for fraudulent conveyances: the creditors acquired the right to set aside the sale and reach the transferred inventory in the hands of the buyer.

Like its predecessors, Article 6 (1987 Official Text) is remarkable in that it obligates buyers in bulk to incur costs to protect the interests of the seller's creditors, with whom they usually have no relationship. Even more striking is that Article 6 affords creditors a remedy against a good faith purchaser for full value without notice of any wrongdoing on the part of the seller. The Article thereby impedes normal business transactions, many of which can be expected to benefit the seller's creditors. For this reason, Article 6 has been subjected to serious criticism. See, e.g., Rapson, *U.C.C. Article 6: Should It Be Revised or "Deep-Sixed"?* 38 Bus.Law. 1753 (1983).

In the legal context in which Article 6 (1987 Official Text) and its nonuniform predecessors were enacted, the benefits to creditors appeared to justify the costs of interfering with good faith transactions. Today, however, creditors are better able than ever to make informed decisions about whether to extend credit. Changes in technology have enabled credit reporting services to provide fast, accurate, and more complete credit histories at relatively little cost. A search of the public real estate and personal property records will disclose most encumbrances on a debtor's property with little inconvenience.

In addition, changes in the law now afford creditors greater opportunities to collect their debts. The development of "minimum contacts" with the forum state as a basis for *in personam* jurisdiction and the universal promulgation of state long-arm statutes and rules have greatly improved the possibility of obtaining personal jurisdiction over a debtor who flees to another state. Widespread enactment of the Uniform Enforcement of Foreign Judgments Act has facilitated nation-wide collection of judgments. And to the extent that a bulk sale is fraudulent and the buyer is a party to fraud, aggrieved creditors have a remedy under the Uniform Fraudulent Transfer Act. Moreover, creditors of a merchant no longer face the choice of extending unsecured credit or no credit at all. Retaining an interest in inventory to secure its price has become relatively simple and inexpensive under Article 9.

Finally, there is no evidence that, in today's economy, fraudulent bulk sales are frequent enough, or engender credit losses significant enough, to require regulation of all bulk sales, including the vast majority that are conducted in good faith. Indeed, the experience of the Canadian Province of British Columbia, which repealed its Sale of Goods in Bulk Act in 1985, and of the United Kingdom, which never has enacted bulk sales legislation, suggests that regulation of bulk sales no longer is necessary.

Recommendation. The National Conference of Commissioners on Uniform State Laws and the American Law Institute believe that changes in the business and legal contexts in which sales are conducted have made regulation of bulk sales unnecessary. The Conference and the Institute therefore withdraw their support for Article 6 of the Uniform Commercial Code and encourage those states that have enacted the Article to repeal it.

The Conference and the Institute recognize that bulk sales may present a particular problem in some states and that some legislatures may wish to continue to regulate bulk sales. They believe that existing Article 6 has become inadequate for that purpose. For those states that are disinclined to repeal Article 6, they have promulgated a revised version of Article 6. The revised Article is designed to afford better protection to creditors while minimizing the impediments to good-faith transactions.

The Official Comment to Section 6–101 explains the rationale underlying the revisions and highlights the major substantive changes reflected in them. Of particular interest is Section 6–103(1)(a), which limits the application of the revised Article to bulk sales by sellers whose principal business is the sale of inventory from stock. In approving this provision, the Conference and the Institute were mindful that some states have expanded the coverage of existing Article 6 to include bulk sales conducted by sellers whose principal business is the operation of a restaurant or tavern. Expansion of the scope of revised Article 6 is inconsistent with the recommendation that Article 6 be repealed. Nevertheless, the inclusion of restaurants and taverns within the scope of the revised Article as it is enacted in particular jurisdictions would not disturb the internal logic and structure of the revised Article.

[ALTERNATIVE A]

1.   Repeal.
2.   Amendment.
3.   Amendment.
4.   Savings Clause.

---

§ 1.   Repeal.

Article 6 and Section 9–111 [*unrevised Article 9*] of the Uniform Commercial Code are hereby repealed, effective _____.

§ 2.   Amendment.

Section 1–105(2) [*unrevised Article 1; see Concordance, p. 22*] of the Uniform Commercial Code is hereby amended to read as follows:

(2)   Where one of the following provisions of this Act specifies the applicable law, that provision governs and a contrary agreement is effective only to the extent permitted by the law (including the conflict of laws rules) so specified:

Rights of creditors against sold goods. Section 2–402.

Applicability of the Article on Leases. Sections 2A–105 and 2A–106.

Applicability of the Article on Bank Deposits and Collections. Section 4–102.

~~Bulk transfers subject to the Article on Bulk Transfers. Section 6–102.~~

Applicability of the Article on Investment Securities. Section 8–106 [*unrevised Article 8*].

Perfection provisions of the Article on Secured Transactions. Section 9–103 [*unrevised Article 9*].

§ 3.   Amendment.

Section 2–403(4) of the Uniform Commercial Code is hereby amended to read as follows:

(4)   The rights of other purchasers of goods and of lien creditors are governed by the Articles on Secured Transactions (Article 9)~~, Bulk Transfers (Article 6)~~ and Documents of Title (Article 7).

§ 4.   Savings Clause.

Rights and obligations that arose under Article 6 and Section 9–111 [*unrevised Article 9*] of the Uniform Commercial Code before their repeal remain valid and may be enforced as though those statutes had not been repealed.]

Legislative Note: To take account of differences between former Article 9 and revised Article 9, a State that repeals Article 6 after revised Article 9 takes effect must make the following changes to Alternative A. First, inasmuch as revised Article 9 contains no counterpart of former Section 9–111, the reference to that section in Section 1 of the repealer should be deleted, and Section 4 of the repeal bill should allude to former Section

9–111. Second, the last entry in Section 1–105(2) [unrevised Article 1; see Concordance, p. 22] should be amended as shown above in this Appendix.

[END OF ALTERNATIVE A]

[ALTERNATIVE B]

6–101.   Short Title.
6–102.   Definitions and Index of Definitions.
6–103.   Applicability of Article.
6–104.   Obligations of Buyer.
6–105.   Notice to Claimants.
6–106.   Schedule of Distribution.
6–107.   Liability for Noncompliance.
6–108.   Bulk Sales by Auction; Bulk Sales Conducted by Liquidator.
6–109.   What Constitutes Filing; Duties of Filing Officer; Information From Filing Officer.
6–110.   Limitation of Actions.

---

§ 6–101.   Short Title.

This Article shall be known and may be cited as Uniform Commercial Code—Bulk Sales.

Official Comment

Prior Uniform Statutory Provision: Section 6–101 (1987 Official Text).

Change: This Article applies only to sales, as defined in Section 2–103(1), and not to other transfers.

Purpose of Change: Transfers other than sales, *e.g.*, grants of security interests, do not present risks to creditors necessitating advance notice in accordance with the provisions of this Article. The Uniform Fraudulent Transfer Act affords a remedy to creditors who are injured by donative transfers.

Rationale for Revision of the Article:

Article 6 (1987 Official Text) imposes upon transferees in bulk several duties toward creditors of the transferor. These duties include the duty to notify the creditors of the impending bulk transfer and, in those jurisdictions that have adopted optional Section 6–106, the duty to assure that the new consideration for the transfer is applied to pay debts of the transferor.

Compliance with the provisions of Article 6 can be burdensome, particularly when the transferor has a large number of creditors. When the transferor is actively engaged in business at a number of locations, assembling a current list of creditors may not be possible. Mailing a notice to each creditor may prove costly. When the goods that are the subject of the transfer are located in several jurisdictions, the transferor may be obligated to comply with Article 6 as enacted in each jurisdiction. The widespread enactment of nonuniform amendments makes compliance with Article 6 in multiple-state transactions problematic. Moreover, the Article requires compliance even when there is no reason to believe that the transferor is conducting a fraudulent transfer, *e.g.*, when the transferor is scaling down the business but remaining available to creditors.

Article 6 imposes strict liability for noncompliance. Failure to comply with the provisions of the Article renders the transfer ineffective, even when the transferor has attempted compliance in good faith, and even when no creditor has been injured by the noncompliance. The potential liability for minor noncompliance may be high. If the transferor should enter bankruptcy before the expiration of the limitation period, Bankruptcy Code §§ 544(b), 550(a), 11 U.S.C. §§ 544(b), 550(a), may enable the transferor's bankruptcy trustee to set aside the entire transaction and recover from the noncomplying transferee all the goods transferred or their value. The trustee has this power even though the noncompliance was with respect to only a single creditor holding a small claim.

The benefits that compliance affords to creditors do not justify the substantial burdens and risks that the Article imposes upon good faith purchasers of business assets. The Article requires that notice be sent only ten days before the transferee takes possession of the goods or pays for them, whichever happens first. Given the delay between sending the notice and its receipt, creditors have scant opportunity to avail themselves of a judicial or nonjudicial remedy before the transfer has been consummated.

In some cases Article 6 may have the unintended effect of injuring, rather than aiding, creditors of the transferor. Those transferees who recognize the burdens and risks that Article 6 imposes upon them sometimes agree to purchase only at a reduced price. Others refuse to purchase at all, leaving the creditors to realize only the liquidation value, rather than the going concern value, of the business goods.

As a response to these inadequacies and others, the National Conference of Commissioners on Uniform State Laws has completely revised Article 6. This revision is designed to reduce the burdens and risks imposed upon good-faith buyers of business assets while increasing the protection afforded to creditors. Among the major changes it makes are the following:

—this Article applies only when the buyer has notice, or after reasonable inquiry would have had notice, that the seller will not continue to operate the same or a similar kind of business after the sale (Section 6–102(1)(c)).

—this Article does not apply to sales in which the value of the property otherwise available to creditors is less than $10,000 or those in which the value of the property is greater than $25,000,000 (Section 6–103(3)(*l*)).

—the choice-of-law provision (Sections 6–103(1)(b) and 6–103(2)) limits the applicable law to that of one jurisdiction.

—when the seller is indebted to a large number of persons, the buyer need neither obtain a list of those persons nor send individual notices to each person but instead may give notice by filing (Sections 6–105(2) and 6–104(2)).

—the notice period is increased from 10 days to 45 days (Section 6–105(5)), and the statute of limitations is extended from six months to one year (Section 6–110).

—the notice must include a copy of a "schedule of distribution," which sets forth how the net contract price is to be distributed (Sections 6–105(3) and 6–106(1)).

—a buyer who makes a good faith effort to comply with the requirements of this Article or to exclude the sale from the application of this Article, or who acts on the good faith belief that this Article does not apply to the sale, is not liable for noncompliance (Section 6–107(3)).

—a buyer's noncompliance does not render the sale ineffective or otherwise affect the buyer's title to the goods; rather, the liability of a noncomplying buyer is for damages caused by the noncompliance (Sections 6–107(1) and 6–107(8)).

In addition to making these and other major substantive changes, revised Article 6 resolves the ambiguities that three decades of law practice, judicial construction, and scholarly inquiry have disclosed.

§ 6–102.   Definitions and Index of Definitions.

(1)   In this Article, unless the context otherwise requires:

(a)   "Assets" means the inventory that is the subject of a bulk sale and any tangible and intangible personal property used or held for use primarily in, or arising from, the seller's business and sold in connection with that inventory, but the term does not include:

(i)   fixtures (section 9–102(a)(41)) other than readily removable factory and office machines;

(ii)   the lessee's interest in a lease of real property; or

(iii)   property to the extent it is generally exempt from creditor process under nonbankruptcy law.

(b)   "Auctioneer" means a person whom the seller engages to direct, conduct, control, or be responsible for a sale by auction.

(c)   "Bulk sale" means:

(i)   in the case of a sale by auction or a sale or series of sales conducted by a liquidator on the seller's behalf, a sale or series of sales not in the ordinary course of the seller's business of more than half of the seller's inventory, as measured by value on the date of the bulk-sale agreement, if on that date the auctioneer or liquidator has notice, or after reasonable inquiry would have had notice, that the seller will not continue to operate the same or a similar kind of business after the sale or series of sales; and

(ii)   in all other cases, a sale not in the ordinary course of the seller's business of more than half the seller's inventory, as measured by value on the date of the bulk-sale agreement, if on that date the buyer has notice, or after reasonable inquiry would have had notice, that the seller will not continue to operate the same or a similar kind of business after the sale.

(d)   "Claim" means a right to payment from the seller, whether or not the right is reduced to judgment, liquidated, fixed, matured, disputed, secured, legal, or equitable. The term includes costs of collection and attorney's fees only to the extent that the laws of this state permit the holder of the claim to recover them in an action against the obligor.

(e)   "Claimant" means a person holding a claim incurred in the seller's business other than:

   (i)   an unsecured and unmatured claim for employment compensation and benefits, including commissions and vacation, severance, and sick-leave pay;

   (ii)   a claim for injury to an individual or to property, or for breach of warranty, unless:

      (A)   a right of action for the claim has accrued;

      (B)   the claim has been asserted against the seller; and

      (C)   the seller knows the identity of the person asserting the claim and the basis upon which the person has asserted it; and

(States To Select One Alternative)

[ALTERNATIVE A]

[(iii) a claim for taxes owing to a governmental unit.]

[ALTERNATIVE B]

[(iii) a claim for taxes owing to a governmental unit, if:

      (A)   a statute governing the enforcement of the claim permits or requires notice of the bulk sale to be given to the governmental unit in a manner other than by compliance with the requirements of this Article; and

      (B)   notice is given in accordance with the statute.]

(f)   "Creditor" means a claimant or other person holding a claim.

(g)(i) "Date of the bulk sale" means:

      (A)   if the sale is by auction or is conducted by a liquidator on the seller's behalf, the date on which more than ten percent of the net proceeds is paid to or for the benefit of the seller; and

      (B)   in all other cases, the later of the date on which:

         (I)   more than ten percent of the net contract price is paid to or for the benefit of the seller; or

         (II)   more than ten percent of the assets, as measured by value, are transferred to the buyer.

   (ii)   For purposes of this subsection:

      (A)   Delivery of a negotiable instrument (Section 3–104(1) [*unrevised Article 3 (Appendix B)*]) to or for the benefit of the seller in exchange for assets constitutes payment of the contract price pro tanto;

      (B)   To the extent that the contract price is deposited in an escrow, the contract price is paid to or for the benefit of the seller when the seller acquires the unconditional right to receive the deposit or when the deposit is delivered to the seller or for the benefit of the seller, whichever is earlier; and

      (C)   An asset is transferred when a person holding an unsecured claim can no longer obtain through judicial proceedings rights to the asset that are superior to those of the buyer arising as a result of the bulk sale. A person holding an unsecured claim can obtain those superior rights to a tangible asset at least until the buyer has an unconditional right, under the bulk-sale agreement, to possess the asset, and a person holding an unsecured claim can obtain those superior rights to an intangible asset at least until the buyer has an unconditional right, under the bulk-sale agreement, to use the asset.

(h) "Date of the bulk-sale agreement" means:

(i) in the case of a sale by auction or conducted by a liquidator (subsection (c)(i)), the date on which the seller engages the auctioneer or liquidator; and

(ii) in all other cases, the date on which a bulk-sale agreement becomes enforceable between the buyer and the seller.

(i) "Debt" means liability on a claim.

(j) "Liquidator" means a person who is regularly engaged in the business of disposing of assets for businesses contemplating liquidation or dissolution.

(k) "Net contract price" means the new consideration the buyer is obligated to pay for the assets less:

(i) the amount of any proceeds of the sale of an asset, to the extent the proceeds are applied in partial or total satisfaction of a debt secured by the asset; and

(ii) the amount of any debt to the extent it is secured by a security interest or lien that is enforceable against the asset before and after it has been sold to a buyer. If a debt is secured by an asset and other property of the seller, the amount of the debt secured by a security interest or lien that is enforceable against the asset is determined by multiplying the debt by a fraction, the numerator of which is the value of the new consideration for the asset on the date of the bulk sale and the denominator of which is the value of all property securing the debt on the date of the bulk sale.

(l) "Net proceeds" means the new consideration received for assets sold at a sale by auction or a sale conducted by a liquidator on the seller's behalf less:

(i) commissions and reasonable expenses of the sale;

(ii) the amount of any proceeds of the sale of an asset, to the extent the proceeds are applied in partial or total satisfaction of a debt secured by the asset; and

(iii) the amount of any debt to the extent it is secured by a security interest or lien that is enforceable against the asset before and after it has been sold to a buyer. If a debt is secured by an asset and other property of the seller, the amount of the debt secured by a security interest or lien that is enforceable against the asset is determined by multiplying the debt by a fraction, the numerator of which is the value of the new consideration for the asset on the date of the bulk sale and the denominator of which is the value of all property securing the debt on the date of the bulk sale.

(m) A sale is "in the ordinary course of the seller's business" if the sale comports with usual or customary practices in the kind of business in which the seller is engaged or with the seller's own usual or customary practices.

(n) "United States" includes its territories and possessions and the Commonwealth of Puerto Rico.

(o) "Value" means fair market value.

(p) "Verified" means signed and sworn to or affirmed.

(2) The following definitions in other Articles apply to this Article:

(a) "Buyer." Section 2–103(1)(a).

(b) "Equipment." Section 9–102(a)(33).

(c) "Inventory." Section 9–102(a)(48).

(d) "Sale." Section 2–106(1).

(e) "Seller." Section 2–103(1)(d).

(3)   In addition, Article 1 contains general definitions and principles of construction and interpretation applicable throughout this Article.

As amended in 1999.

Official Comment

1.   (a) "Assets". New. The term generally includes only "personal property." Whether particular property is "personal property" is to be determined by law outside this Article; however, for purposes of this Article, (i) the term includes "readily removable factory and office machines" (compare Section 9–334(e)(2)(A)), even if they are covered by applicable real estate law and thus are "fixtures" as defined in Section 9–102(a)(41); (ii) the term does not include the lessee's interest in a lease of real property, even if that interest is considered to be personal property under other applicable law; and (iii) the term does not include property to the extent that it is "generally exempt from creditor process under nonbankruptcy law."

(b)   "Auctioneer". Compare Section 6–108(3) (1987 Official Text).

(c)   "Bulk Sale". Bulk sales are of two kinds. Subsection (1)(c)(i) describes bulk sales conducted by a professional intermediary (i.e., an auctioneer or liquidator), as to which sales Section 6–108 applies. If these indirect sales occur as a series of related sales, then the entire series is treated as a single "bulk sale" and the term applies to the sales in the aggregate. Sales made directly by the seller to the buyer, described in subsection (1)(c)(ii), include sales conducted by an auctioneer or liquidator for its own account.

The elements of both direct and indirect sales are the same. Some of these elements have been borrowed from the 1987 Official Text of Article 6 and restated. For example, the term includes only sales that are not "in the ordinary course of the seller's business" (subsection (1)(m)). The sale must be of "more than half of the seller's inventory, as measured by value [subsection (1)(o)] on the date of the bulk-sale agreement [subsection (1)(h)]." All inventory owned by the seller should be included in the calculation, regardless of where it is located. Inventory that is encumbered by a security interest or lien should be counted at its gross value, although the fact that it is encumbered may affect the applicability of this Article to the sale.

The determination whether a sale is a "bulk sale" and thus subject to this Article is not affected by whether other types of property are sold in connection with inventory. However, other provisions of this Article take account of the fact that other property may be sold in connection with inventory. For example, the availability of the exclusion in Section 6–103(3)(l) turns on the value of all the "assets," not just the inventory. Similarly, the notice required by Section 6–105 must describe the "assets," not just the inventory. And Section 6–107(4) measures the buyer's maximum cumulative liability for noncompliance by the value of the inventory and equipment sold in the bulk sale.

In an effort to limit its coverage to sales posing the greatest risks to creditors, this Article adds an additional element to the definition of "bulk sale." A sale is not a "bulk sale" unless the buyer, auctioneer, or liquidator has notice, or after a reasonable inquiry would have had notice, that the seller will not continue to operate the same or a similar kind of business after the sale. Whether a person has "notice" depends upon what the person knows and what the person would have known had the person conducted a reasonable inquiry. The issue of whether a transaction was a bulk sale is likely to be litigated only when the seller has absconded with the sale proceeds. This Article requires that the matters as to which the buyer, auctioneer, or liquidator had notice be determined only by reference to facts that the person knew or would have known at the date of the bulk-sale agreement. Reference to what actually occurred is inappropriate.

Whether an inquiry is "reasonable" depends on the facts and circumstances of each case. These facts and circumstances may include the identities of the buyer and seller and the type of assets being sold. In some cases, a reasonable inquiry may consist of no inquiry at all concerning the seller's future.

Not every change in business operations poses a substantial enough risk to creditors to justify the costs of compliance with this Article. Thus, in determining whether post-sale business is of a kind that is "the same" or "similar" to the business conducted before the sale, a court should consider whether, viewed from the perspective of the creditors of the seller, the change poses extraordinary risks or whether the change is a normal risk that creditors can be assumed to take. In particular, when the post-bulk sale business differs from the pre-bulk sale business only in the size of the business conducted, the seller should be considered to be continuing in the same or a similar kind of business and the sale should not be considered a bulk sale.

The seller must "continue to operate" the same or a similar kind of business as owner. If the owner sells the business assets to a buyer and continues to manage the business as an employee of the buyer, the seller is not continuing to operate the business within the meaning of this Article.

(d) "Claim". New. The first sentence derives from Bankruptcy Code § 101(4), 11 U.S.C. § 101(4). Changes, including the deletion of Section 101(4)(B), were made for stylistic purposes only.

(e) "Claimant". New. This term defines the category of claim holders who are the primary beneficiaries of the duties that this Article imposes. Compare "Creditor" (subsection (1)(f)).

States that choose not to afford taxing authorities the benefits of this Article should adopt Alternative A. Adoption of Alternative B would afford the benefits of this Article to taxing authorities except with respect to those taxes as to which there has been compliance with another statute requiring that notice of the bulk sale be given to the taxing authority.

(f) "Creditor". New. The term includes all holders of claims against the seller, even holders of claims arising from consumer transactions. Compare "Claimant" (subsection (1)(e)).

(g) "Date of the bulk sale". New. The parties are able to control the date of the bulk sale in several ways. They can keep the proceeds of the sale in escrow, thereby delaying the date of payment, or they can specifically agree that the assets remain subject to the reach of the seller's creditors, thereby delaying the date that the assets are transferred. By adjusting the time that the buyer acquires an unconditional right to possess tangible assets and the time the buyer acquires an unconditional right to use intangible assets, the parties may affect the substantive rights of creditors and thereby control the date the assets are transferred.

The connection between the time of transfer and the buyer's rights under the bulk-sale agreement appears only for purposes of sales to which this Article applies. Subsection (1)(g) does not purport to affect the rights of creditors of a seller of property for other purposes or under other circumstances.

(h) "Date of the bulk-sale agreement". New. Law outside this Article, including the provisions of Article 2, determines when an agreement for a bulk sale becomes enforceable between the buyer and the seller and when an auctioneer or liquidator is engaged.

(i) "Debt". New. This subsection is borrowed from Bankruptcy Code Section 101(11).

(j) "Liquidator". New. Although the definition of "liquidator" is quite broad, the term is used with respect to sales that are "conducted" by a liquidator on behalf of the seller. See subsection (1)(c)(i). Thus only those liquidators that "conduct" sales will be affected by this Article.

(k) "Net contract price". New. Consideration is not "new consideration" to the extent that it consists of the partial or total satisfaction of an antecedent debt owed to the buyer by the seller. When the buyer buys assets along with property other than assets, the "net contract price" is that portion of the new consideration allocable to the assets.

(l) "Net proceeds". New. The term appears, without definition, in Section 6–108 (1987 Official Text).

(m) "In the ordinary course of the seller's business". New.

(n) "United States". New. This subsection derives from former Section 9–103(3)(c).

(o) "Value". New. The definition in Section 1–201(44) [unrevised Article 1; see Concordance, p. 22] is not appropriate in the context of this Article.

(p) "Verified". New.

2. "Good faith". This Article adopts the definition of "good faith" in Article 1 in all cases, even when the buyer is a merchant.

Cross-References:

Point 1(a): Sections 9–102, 9–334.
Point 1(c): Sections 1–201 and 6–103.
Point 1(g): Article 2 generally.
Point 1(h): Section 2–201 and Article 2 generally.

As amended in 1999.

§ 6–103.   Applicability of Article.

(1) Except as otherwise provided in subsection (3), this Article applies to a bulk sale if:

(a) the seller's principal business is the sale of inventory from stock; and

(b) on the date of the bulk-sale agreement the seller is located in this state or, if the seller is located in a jurisdiction that is not a part of the United States, the seller's major executive office in the United States is in this state.

(2) A seller is deemed to be located at his [or her] place of business. If a seller has more than one place of business, the seller is deemed located at his [or her] chief executive office.

(3) This Article does not apply to:

(a) a transfer made to secure payment or performance of an obligation;

(b) a transfer of collateral to a secured party pursuant to Section 9–609;

(c) a disposition of collateral pursuant to Section 9–610;

(d) retention of collateral pursuant to Section 9–620;

(e) a sale of an asset encumbered by a security interest or lien if (i) all the proceeds of the sale are applied in partial or total satisfaction of the debt secured by the security interest or lien or (ii) the security interest or lien is enforceable against the asset after it has been sold to the buyer and the net contract price is zero;

(f) a general assignment for the benefit of creditors or to a subsequent transfer by the assignee;

(g) a sale by an executor, administrator, receiver, trustee in bankruptcy, or any public officer under judicial process;

(h) a sale made in the course of judicial or administrative proceedings for the dissolution or reorganization of an organization;

(i) a sale to a buyer whose principal place of business is in the United States and who:

    (i) not earlier than 21 days before the date of the bulk sale, (A) obtains from the seller a verified and dated list of claimants of whom the seller has notice three days before the seller sends or delivers the list to the buyer or (B) conducts a reasonable inquiry to discover the claimants;

    (ii) assumes in full the debts owed to claimants of whom the buyer has knowledge on the date the buyer receives the list of claimants from the seller or on the date the buyer completes the reasonable inquiry, as the case may be;

    (iii) is not insolvent after the assumption; and

    (iv) gives written notice of the assumption not later than 30 days after the date of the bulk sale by sending or delivering a notice to the claimants identified in subparagraph (ii) or by filing a notice in the office of the [Secretary of State];

(j) a sale to a buyer whose principal place of business is in the United States and who:

    (i) assumes in full the debts that were incurred in the seller's business before the date of the bulk sale;

    (ii) is not insolvent after the assumption; and

    (iii) gives written notice of the assumption not later than 30 days after the date of the bulk sale by sending or delivering a notice to each creditor whose debt is assumed or by filing a notice in the office of the [Secretary of State];

(k) a sale to a new organization that is organized to take over and continue the business of the seller and that has its principal place of business in the United States if:

    (i) the buyer assumes in full the debts that were incurred in the seller's business before the date of the bulk sale;

    (ii) the seller receives nothing from the sale except an interest in the new organization that is subordinate to the claims against the organization arising from the assumption; and

    (iii)   the buyer gives written notice of the assumption not later than 30 days after the date of the bulk sale by sending or delivering a notice to each creditor whose debt is assumed or by filing a notice in the office of the [Secretary of State];

(*l*)   a sale of assets having:

    (i)   a value, net of liens and security interests, of less than $10,000. If a debt is secured by assets and other property of the seller, the net value of the assets is determined by subtracting from their value an amount equal to the product of the debt multiplied by a fraction, the numerator of which is the value of the assets on the date of the bulk sale and the denominator of which is the value of all property securing the debt on the date of the bulk sale; or

    (ii)   a value of more than $25,000,000 on the date of the bulk-sale agreement; or

(m)   a sale required by, and made pursuant to, statute.

(4)   The notice under subsection (3)(i)(iv) must state: (i) that a sale that may constitute a bulk sale has been or will be made; (ii) the date or prospective date of the bulk sale; (iii) the individual, partnership, or corporate names and the addresses of the seller and buyer; (iv) the address to which inquiries about the sale may be made, if different from the seller's address; and (v) that the buyer has assumed or will assume in full the debts owed to claimants of whom the buyer has knowledge on the date the buyer receives the list of claimants from the seller or completes a reasonable inquiry to discover the claimants.

(5)   The notice under subsections (3)(j)(iii) and (3)(k)(iii) must state: (i) that a sale that may constitute a bulk sale has been or will be made; (ii) the date or prospective date of the bulk sale; (iii) the individual, partnership, or corporate names and the addresses of the seller and buyer; (iv) the address to which inquiries about the sale may be made, if different from the seller's address; and (v) that the buyer has assumed or will assume the debts that were incurred in the seller's business before the date of the bulk sale.

(6)   For purposes of subsection (3)(*l*), the value of assets is presumed to be equal to the price the buyer agrees to pay for the assets. However, in a sale by auction or a sale conducted by a liquidator on the seller's behalf, the value of assets is presumed to be the amount the auctioneer or liquidator reasonably estimates the assets will bring at auction or upon liquidation.

As amended in 1999.

Official Comment

Prior Uniform Statutory Provision: Sections 6–102 and 6–103 (1987 Official Text).

Changes: New choice-of-law provision; exclusions from the Article clarified, revised, and expanded.

Purposes of Changes and New Matter:

    1.   Subsection (1)(a) follows Section 6–102(3) of the 1987 Official Text and makes Article 6 applicable only when the seller's principal business is the sale of inventory from stock. This Article does not apply to a sale by a seller whose principal business is the sale of goods other than inventory, e.g., a farmer, is the sale of inventory not from stock, e.g., a manufacturer who produces goods to order, or is the sale of services, e.g., a dry cleaner, barber, or operator of a hotel, tavern, or restaurant.

    2.   The choice-of-law rule in subsections (1)(b) and (2) derives from former Section 9–103(3) (now codified as Sections 9–301 and 9–307). Any agreement between the buyer and the seller with regard to the law governing a bulk sale does not affect the choice-of-law rule in this Article.

    3.   Some of the transactions excluded by subsection (3), e.g., those excluded by subsection (3)(a), may not be bulk sales. This Article nevertheless specifically excludes them in order to allay any doubts about the Article's applicability. Certain transactions, e.g., the sale of fully encumbered inventory that remains subject to a security interest, may be excluded by more than one subsection.

    4.   Subsections (3)(a), (b), (c), (d), and (e) derive from subsections (1) and (3) of Section 6–103 (1987 Official Text).

    5.   Subsections (3)(f), (g), and (h) restate subsections (2), (4), and (5) of Section 6–103 with minor changes.

6.   Subsections (3)(i), (j), and (k) relate to sales in which the buyer assumes specified debts of the seller. A bulk sale does not fall within any of these subsections unless the buyer's assumption of debts is binding and irrevocable.

Subsection (3)(j) derives from subsection (6) of Section 6–103 (1987 Official Text) and is available to buyers who are not insolvent (as defined in Section 1–201(23)) [*unrevised Article 1; see Concordance, p. 22*], assume all the seller's business debts in full, and give notice of the assumption. Subsection (3)(k) derives from subsection (7) of Section 6–103 (1987 Official Text) and excludes transactions in which the risks to creditors are minimal. Like subsection (3)(j), this subsection applies only if the buyer assumes all the seller's business debts in full and gives notice of the assumption. In addition, the buyer must be a new organization that is organized to take over and continue the seller's business, the seller must receive nothing from the sale other than an interest in the new organization, and the seller's interest must be subordinate to the claims arising from the assumption. Sales that may qualify for the exclusion include the incorporation of a partnership or sole proprietorship.

Buyers often are reluctant to assume debts of which they have no knowledge. Subsection (3)(i), which is new, permits a qualifying buyer to exclude a sale from this Article by assuming only those debts owed to claimants of whom the buyer has knowledge after the buyer either conducts a reasonable inquiry to discover claimants or obtains a list of claimants from the seller. A buyer who takes a verified list from the seller is held to have knowledge of the claimants on the list and is entitled to rely in good faith on the list without making further inquiry. The protection afforded by the assumption of these debts, while not perfect, is sufficiently great to eliminate the need for compliance with Article 6.

7.   Subsection (3)(*l*) is new. Although the bulk sale of even a very small business may be of concern to some creditors, losses to creditors from sales of assets in which the seller's equity is less than $10,000 are not likely to justify the costs of complying with this Article. Sales of assets having a value of more than $25,000,000 have not presented serious risks to creditors. Publicity normally attends sales of that magnitude, and the sellers are unlikely to be able successfully to remove the proceeds from the reach of creditors. As used in this subsection, "price" includes all consideration for the assets, not only new consideration. Compare "Net contract price" (Section 6–102(1)(k)). If the auctioneer or liquidator does not make an estimation, then no presumption arises.

8.   Subsection (3)(m) is new. This Article assumes that creditors are aware of statutes that may require their debtors to conduct bulk sales under specified circumstances, *e.g.*, upon the termination of a franchise or of a contract between a dealer and supplier, and are able to take account of any risk that those sales may impose.

Cross-References:

Point 1: Sections 9–102(a)(23), (33), (34), (44), (48).
Point 2: Sections 1–105 [*unrevised Article 1; see Concordance, p. 22*], 9–301, and 9–307.
Point 3: Section 6–102.
Point 4: Sections 9–609, 9–610, and 9–620.
Point 6: Sections 1–201 and 1–203 [*unrevised Article 1; see Concordance, p. 22*].
Point 7: Section 6–102.

Definitional Cross-References:

"Asset". Section 6–102.
"Auctioneer". Section 6–102.
"Bulk sale". Section 6–102.
"Buyer". Section 2–103.
"Claimant". Section 6–102.
"Collateral". Section 9–102(a)(12).
"Date of the bulk sale". Section 6–102.
"Date of the bulk-sale agreement". Section 6–102.
"Debt". Section 6–102.
"Insolvent". Section 1–201.
"Inventory". Section 9–102(a)(48).
"Knowledge". Section 1–201 [*unrevised Article 1; see Concordance, p. 22*].
"Liquidator". Section 6–102.
"Net contract price". Section 6–102.
"Notice". Section 1–201 [*unrevised Article 1; see Concordance, p. 22*].
"Organization". Section 1–201.

"Presumed". Section 1–201 [*unrevised Article 1; see Concordance, p. 22*].

"Proceeds". Section 9–102(a)(64).

"Sale". Section 2–106.

"Secured party". Section 9–102(a)(72).

"Security interest". Section 1–201.

"Seller". Section 2–103.

"Send". Section 1–201.

"United States". Section 6–102.

"Value". Section 6–102.

"Verified". Section 6–102.

As amended in 1999.

§ 6–104.   Obligations of Buyer.

(1)   In a bulk sale as defined in Section 6–102(1)(c)(ii) the buyer shall:

(a)   obtain from the seller a list of all business names and addresses used by the seller within three years before the date the list is sent or delivered to the buyer;

(b)   unless excused under subsection (2), obtain from the seller a verified and dated list of claimants of whom the seller has notice three days before the seller sends or delivers the list to the buyer and including, to the extent known by the seller, the address of and the amount claimed by each claimant;

(c)   obtain from the seller or prepare a schedule of distribution (Section 6–106(1));

(d)   give notice of the bulk sale in accordance with Section 6–105;

(e)   unless excused under Section 6–106(4), distribute the net contract price in accordance with the undertakings of the buyer in the schedule of distribution; and

(f)   unless excused under subsection (2), make available the list of claimants (subsection (1)(b)) by:

(i)   promptly sending or delivering a copy of the list without charge to any claimant whose written request is received by the buyer no later than six months after the date of the bulk sale;

(ii)   permitting any claimant to inspect and copy the list at any reasonable hour upon request received by the buyer no later than six months after the date of the bulk sale; or

(iii)   filing a copy of the list in the office of the [Secretary of State] no later than the time for giving a notice of the bulk sale (Section 6–105(5)). A list filed in accordance with this subparagraph must state the individual, partnership, or corporate name and a mailing address of the seller.

(2)   A buyer who gives notice in accordance with Section 6–105(2) is excused from complying with the requirements of subsections (1)(b) and (1)(f).

Official Comment

Prior Uniform Statutory Provision: Section 6–104 (1987 Official Text).

Changes: Revised and rewritten.

Purposes of Changes and New Matter:

1.   Subsection (1) sets forth the buyer's duties in a bulk sale conducted by the seller. The buyer's failure to perform these duties may result in liability under Section 6–107. An auctioneer in a bulk sale by auction and a liquidator in a bulk sale that the liquidator conducts on the seller's behalf have similar duties but may face somewhat different liability. See Section 6–108(1). The buyer's duties are designed to afford the seller's claimants the opportunity to learn of the bulk sale before the seller has removed the assets from their reach and has received payment that is easily secreted.

2.   Section 6–104(3) (1987 Official Text) provides that "[r]esponsibility for the completeness and accuracy of the list of creditors rests on the transferor, and the transfer is not rendered ineffective by errors or omissions

516

therein unless the transferee is shown to have had knowledge." This sentence has been deleted as superfluous. Nothing in this Article suggests that the buyer is responsible for the completeness or accuracy of the list of claimants. The buyer's only obligations with respect to the list are to obtain it from the seller and to make it available. A buyer who sends or delivers notice of the bulk sale in accordance with Section 6–105(1) may rely in good faith on the list supplied by the seller unless, at the time the notice is sent or delivered, the buyer has knowledge of a claimant not on the list. A buyer who knows of a claimant not on the list is obligated to send notice of the bulk sale to that claimant.

3.   The buyer's only obligation with respect to the net contract price is to comply with the schedule of distribution. The schedule may provide for the buyer to pay the entire net contract price to the seller. If so, the buyer complies with the requirements of Section 6–104(1)(e) by paying the entire net contract price to the seller.

4.   The purpose of the list of claimants is to enable the buyer to give claimants notice of the bulk sale. If the buyer gives notice by filing in a public office (Section 6–105(2)), then the buyer need not obtain or preserve a list of the seller's claimants.

Cross-References:

Point 1: Sections 6–107 and 6–108.
Point 2: Sections 6–105 and 1–203.
Point 3: Section 6–106.
Point 4: Section 6–105.

Definitional Cross-References:

"Buyer". Section 2–103.
"Bulk sale". Section 6–102.
"Claimant". Section 6–102.
"Date of the bulk sale". Section 6–102.
"Net contract price". Section 6–102.
"Notice". Section 1–201 [*unrevised Article 1; see Concordance, p. 22*].
"Seller". Section 2–103.
"Verified". Section 6–102.

§ 6–105.   Notice to Claimants.

(1)   Except as otherwise provided in subsection (2), to comply with Section 6–104(1)(d), the buyer shall send or deliver a written notice of the bulk sale to each claimant on the list of claimants (Section 6–104(1)(b)) and to any other claimant of whom the buyer has knowledge at the time the notice of the bulk sale is sent or delivered.

(2)   A buyer may comply with Section 6–104(1)(d) by filing a written notice of the bulk sale in the office of the [Secretary of State] if:

(a)   on the date of the bulk-sale agreement the seller has 200 or more claimants, exclusive of claimants holding secured or matured claims for employment compensation and benefits, including commissions and vacation, severance, and sick-leave pay; or

(b)   the buyer has received a verified statement from the seller stating that, as of the date of the bulk-sale agreement, the number of claimants, exclusive of claimants holding secured or matured claims for employment compensation and benefits, including commissions and vacation, severance, and sick-leave pay, is 200 or more.

(3)   The written notice of the bulk sale must be accompanied by a copy of the schedule of distribution (Section 6–106(1)) and state at least:

(a)   that the seller and buyer have entered into an agreement for a sale that may constitute a bulk sale under the laws of the State of _____;

(b)   the date of the agreement;

(c)   the date on or after which more than ten percent of the assets were or will be transferred;

(d)   the date on or after which more than ten percent of the net contract price was or will be paid, if the date is not stated in the schedule of distribution;

(e)   the name and a mailing address of the seller;

(f)   any other business name and address listed by the seller pursuant to Section 6–104(1)(a);

(g)   the name of the buyer and an address of the buyer from which information concerning the sale can be obtained;

(h)   a statement indicating the type of assets or describing the assets item by item;

(i)   the manner in which the buyer will make available the list of claimants (Section 6–104(1)(f)), if applicable; and

(j)   if the sale is in total or partial satisfaction of an antecedent debt owed by the seller, the amount of the debt to be satisfied and the name of the person to whom it is owed.

(4)   For purposes of subsections (3)(e) and (3)(g), the name of a person is the person's individual, partnership, or corporate name.

(5)   The buyer shall give notice of the bulk sale not less than 45 days before the date of the bulk sale and, if the buyer gives notice in accordance with subsection (1), not more than 30 days after obtaining the list of claimants.

(6)   A written notice substantially complying with the requirements of subsection (3) is effective even though it contains minor errors that are not seriously misleading.

(7)   A form substantially as follows is sufficient to comply with subsection (3):

Notice of Sale

(1)   _____, whose address is _____, is described in this notice as the "seller."

(2)   _____, whose address is _____, is described in this notice as the "buyer."

(3)   The seller has disclosed to the buyer that within the past three years the seller has used other business names, operated at other addresses, or both, as follows: _____.

(4)   The seller and the buyer have entered into an agreement dated _____, for a sale that may constitute a bulk sale under the laws of the state of _____.

(5)   The date on or after which more than ten percent of the assets that are the subject of the sale were or will be transferred is _____, and [if not stated in the schedule of distribution] the date on or after which more than ten percent of the net contract price was or will be paid is _____.

(6)   The following assets are the subject of the sale: _____.

(7)   [If applicable] The buyer will make available to claimants of the seller a list of the seller's claimants in the following manner: _____.

(8)   [If applicable] The sale is to satisfy $_____ of an antecedent debt owed by the seller to _____.

(9)   A copy of the schedule of distribution of the net contract price accompanies this notice.

[End of Notice]

Official Comment

Prior Uniform Statutory Provision: Sections 6–105 and 6–107 (1987 Official Text).

Changes: Revised, alternative method of giving notice added, and form of notice added.

Purposes of Changes and New Matter:

1.   Subsection (1) sets forth the method by which the buyer may discharge the duty to notify the seller's claimants of the impending sale. The buyer "has knowledge" of a claimant only if the buyer has actual knowledge sufficient to enable the buyer to send a notice to the claimant. A buyer who knows only that the seller has other, unidentified claimants complies with this subsection by giving notice to the claimants on the seller's list.

2. Subsection (2) is new. It affords the buyer the opportunity to publish notice in cases in which the number of claimants—and thus the costs of compliance and risk of inadvertent noncompliance—are large. Although a filed notice will not inform every claimant of the impending sale, a filed notice is expected to inform a sufficient number of claimants (perhaps through credit reporting services) to enable them to stop an unfair or fraudulent transaction before it occurs.

The buyer may give notice by filing if the seller actually has 200 or more claimants or if the buyer receives a verified statement that the seller has 200 or more claimants. Claimants who hold secured or matured claims for employment compensation and benefits are not counted in determining the number of claimants for this purpose; however, they are entitled to receive notice of the bulk sale.

The duty to give notice must be performed in good faith. A buyer who receives a verified statement from the seller but knows the statement to be false does not act in good faith and thus does not comply with subsection (2)(b).

3. Subsection (3) prescribes the contents of the notice. The contents are the same regardless of whether notice is sent to each claimant or filed, except that the information in subsection (3)(i) is required only when notice is sent. The requirements of subsection (3) are the minimum; a notice that includes additional information is effective. The requirement in subsection (3)(h) for the description of assets is modeled on former Section 9–402(1) (now codified as Sections 9–108, 9–502, and 9–504). Neither the identification of assets by serial number nor an item-by-item list of assets is required.

Subsection (3)(j) applies when the sale satisfies a debt owed by the seller to the buyer or to a third party. Section 6–103(3) excludes certain sales of this kind from the application of this Article.

4. Subsection (4) requires that a notice give the proper name of the seller and the buyer. A trade name is insufficient. See Section 9–503(c). However, subsection (3)(f) requires that trade names be added when the seller has provided them to the buyer. The list need not include trade names or other names that the seller has used but not listed, even if the buyer knows of the names.

5. Subsection (5) requires that notice be given not less than 45 days before the date of the bulk sale. The period was extended from the 10 days afforded by the 1987 Official Text to provide ample time for claimants to receive or discover the notice and to take any action that the law permits to collect their claims from the seller. For example, depending upon the facts of each case and upon applicable law, claimants might seek to enjoin the sale, acquire a judicial lien on the assets or the proceeds, threaten to refuse to deal with the buyer unless the seller's debt is paid, or file an involuntary bankruptcy petition against the seller. The "date of the bulk sale" is defined in such a way as to permit the seller to transfer the assets to the buyer or the buyer to pay the price to the seller (but not both) before or during the 45 days.

6. Subsection (6) derives from former Section 9–402(8) (now codified as Section 9–506). The purpose of filing is to give notice to claimants. Whether an error in the seller's name is seriously misleading should depend upon whether a claimant searching under the seller's correct name could have found the filing. Whether an error other than in the seller's name is seriously misleading should depend upon whether the error prejudiced the ability of claimants to assert their rights.

Cross-References:

Point 1: Sections 1–201 [*unrevised Article 1; see Concordance, p. 22*] and 6–104.

Point 2: Sections 1–203 [*unrevised Article 1; see Concordance, p. 22*] and 6–104.

Point 3: Sections 6–102, 6–104, 9–108, 9–502 and 9–504.

Point 4: Sections 6–104 and 9–503.

Point 5: Sections 6–102.

Point 6: Sections 6–107 and 9–506.

Definitional Cross-References:

"Asset". Section 6–102.

"Bulk sale". Section 6–102.

"Buyer". Section 2–103.

"Claim". Section 6–102.

"Claimant". Section 6–102.

"Date of the bulk sale". Section 6–102.

"Date of the bulk-sale agreement". Section 6–102.

"Debt". Section 6–102.
"Knowledge". Section 1–201 [*unrevised Article 1; see Concordance, p. 22*].
"Net contract price". Section 6–102.
"Seller". Section 2–103.
"Send". Section 1–201.
"Verified". Section 6–102.
"Written". Section 1–201.

As amended in 1999.

§ 6–106.   Schedule of Distribution.

(1)   The seller and buyer shall agree on how the net contract price is to be distributed and set forth their agreement in a written schedule of distribution.

(2)   The schedule of distribution may provide for distribution to any person at any time, including distribution of the entire net contract price to the seller.

(3)   The buyer's undertakings in the schedule of distribution run only to the seller. However, a buyer who fails to distribute the net contract price in accordance with the buyer's undertakings in the schedule of distribution is liable to a creditor only as provided in Section 6–107(1).

(4)   If the buyer undertakes in the schedule of distribution to distribute any part of the net contract price to a person other than the seller, and, after the buyer has given notice in accordance with Section 6–105, some or all of the anticipated net contract price is or becomes unavailable for distribution as a consequence of the buyer's or seller's having complied with an order of court, legal process, statute, or rule of law, the buyer is excused from any obligation arising under this Article or under any contract with the seller to distribute the net contract price in accordance with the buyer's undertakings in the schedule if the buyer:

(a)   distributes the net contract price remaining available in accordance with any priorities for payment stated in the schedule of distribution and, to the extent that the price is insufficient to pay all the debts having a given priority, distributes the price pro rata among those debts shown in the schedule as having the same priority;

(b)   distributes the net contract price remaining available in accordance with an order of court;

(c)   commences a proceeding for interpleader in a court of competent jurisdiction and is discharged from the proceeding; or

(d)   reaches a new agreement with the seller for the distribution of the net contract price remaining available, sets forth the new agreement in an amended schedule of distribution, gives notice of the amended schedule, and distributes the net contract price remaining available in accordance with the buyer's undertakings in the amended schedule.

(5)   The notice under subsection (4)(d) must identify the buyer and the seller, state the filing number, if any, of the original notice, set forth the amended schedule, and be given in accordance with subsection (1) or (2) of Section 6–105, whichever is applicable, at least 14 days before the buyer distributes any part of the net contract price remaining available.

(6)   If the seller undertakes in the schedule of distribution to distribute any part of the net contract price, and, after the buyer has given notice in accordance with Section 6–105, some or all of the anticipated net contract price is or becomes unavailable for distribution as a consequence of the buyer's or seller's having complied with an order of court, legal process, statute, or rule of law, the seller and any person in control of the seller are excused from any obligation arising under this Article or under any agreement with the buyer to distribute the net contract price in accordance with the seller's undertakings in the schedule if the seller:

(a)   distributes the net contract price remaining available in accordance with any priorities for payment stated in the schedule of distribution and, to the extent that the price is insufficient to pay all the debts having a given priority, distributes the price pro rata among those debts shown in the schedule as having the same priority;

(b)   distributes the net contract price remaining available in accordance with an order of court;

(c) commences a proceeding for interpleader in a court of competent jurisdiction and is discharged from the proceeding; or

(d) prepares a written amended schedule of distribution of the net contract price remaining available for distribution, gives notice of the amended schedule, and distributes the net contract price remaining available in accordance with the amended schedule.

(7) The notice under subsection (6)(d) must identify the buyer and the seller, state the filing number, if any, of the original notice, set forth the amended schedule, and be given in accordance with subsection (1) or (2) of Section 6–105, whichever is applicable, at least 14 days before the seller distributes any part of the net contract price remaining available.

Official Comment

Purposes:

1. A principal purpose of bulk sales legislation has been to impair the ability of a seller to liquidate inventory and abscond with the proceeds, leaving creditors unpaid. Toward this end, a significant minority of jurisdictions adopted optional Section 6–106 (1987 Official Text), which imposes upon a transferee in bulk the duty to apply the new consideration for the transfer to the debts of the transferor pro rata. When one or more of these debts is unliquidated, disputed, or allegedly secured, making a pro rata distribution may prove quite difficult and distribution of the consideration may be delayed considerably. In addition, since preferences generally are permitted under state law, the appropriateness of mandating a pro rata distribution is questionable. Accordingly, this Article does not require the buyer to apply the consideration to payment of the seller's debts.

This Article recognizes, however, that the seller's claimants have an interest in learning what will happen to the net contract price. If the contemplated distribution is objectionable, claimants should be able to avail themselves of whatever remedies state law or federal law allows to prevent the sale or tie up the price. On the other hand, if the price is to be distributed in a manner that is favorable to creditors, then advance knowledge of that fact will facilitate the sale by obviating any need for claimants to interfere with it.

To afford advance notice of the intended distribution of the contract price, Section 6–105(3) requires the buyer to include with the notice of the sale a copy of the "schedule of distribution"—i.e., of the agreement between the buyer and the seller on how the net contract price is to be distributed.

2. This Article does not require the net contract price to be applied in any particular fashion. Rather, the buyer and the seller may agree to whatever they wish. They must, however, disclose their agreement in ample time before the date of the bulk sale. See Section 6–105(5). The terms of the schedule of distribution in any given sale will be a function of the negotiations between buyer and seller as affected by any applicable non-Code law (e.g., corporate dissolution statutes) imposing distribution requirements in sales of the kind conducted.

In formulating the schedule, the parties may be well advised to consider the likely reaction of claimants to the schedule. For example, a schedule that contemplates the distribution of the entire net contract price to the seller or to a single creditor may prompt the filing of an involuntary bankruptcy petition. A schedule that contemplates paying the net contract price into an escrow established for the benefit of the seller's claimants may be more favorably received.

The seller may incur additional debt between the time the schedule is published and the time the net contract price is paid. The schedule may provide for payment of those debts from the net contract price.

3. Unless otherwise agreed, the buyer's only liability to creditors for failure to comply with his undertakings in the schedule of distribution is set forth in Section 6–107(1). A creditor named in the schedule may not rely on the creation or publication of the schedule as the basis for imposing liability against the buyer on any other theory, including that of estoppel or third-party beneficiary.

The seller may wish to undertake to pay some of the price to creditors. The seller may, but need not, include this undertaking in the schedule of distribution. The buyer is not responsible for performance of the seller's undertakings. Thus, if the seller makes an undertaking with respect to payment of the net contract price and fails to perform in accordance with it, the buyer faces no liability. However, certain persons in control of the seller may be liable under those circumstances. See Section 6–107(11).

4. In some cases, the precise amount of the net contract price may be unknown at the time that the schedule of distribution is formulated and notice of the bulk sale is given. In other cases, the net contract price may prove to be less than originally anticipated. Parties who fail to provide for these contingencies in the schedule

of distribution and are unable to abide by the original schedule may be required to give a new notice with a new schedule.

The inability to abide by the schedule may be due to an external legal event, e.g., the suffering of a garnishment lien on the net contract price, the filing of a bankruptcy petition, or compliance with a corporate dissolution statute. If so, subsection (4), which applies to the extent that the net contract price is within the control of the buyer, may afford relief to the buyer, and subsection (6), which applies to the extent the net contract price is within the control of the seller, may afford relief to a person in control of the seller. Although this Article imposes no obligation on sellers with respect to distribution of the net contract price (or otherwise), a seller may incur an obligation of this kind by agreement with the buyer. Accordingly, subsection (6) provides the means by which the seller as well as a person in control of the seller may be excused from any such obligation.

Subsections (4)(a) and (6)(a) permit the buyer or seller respectively to distribute the net contract price remaining available in accordance with any priorities for payment. A schedule need not afford priority to particular debts. If the schedule contains no priorities, then the debts are treated as if they are all of the same priority, and the buyer or seller, as the case may be, may distribute the price pro rata in partial satisfaction of the debts set forth in the schedule. Law other than this Article determines whether a court order or a proceeding for interpleader is available for purposes of subsections (4)(b), (4)(c), (6)(b), and (6)(c).

Cross-References:

Point 1: Sections 6–104 and 6–105.

Point 2: Sections 6–105.

Point 3: Sections 1–102 [*unrevised Article 1; see Concordance, p. 22*] and 6–107.

Definitional Cross-References:

"Buyer". Section 2–103.

"Contract". Section 1–201.

"Creditor". Section 1–201.

"Debt". Section 6–102.

"Net contract price". Section 6–102.

"Person". Section 1–201.

"Seller". Section 2–103.

"Written". Section 1–201.

§ 6–107.   Liability for Noncompliance.

(1)   Except as provided in subsection (3), and subject to the limitation in subsection (4):

(a)   a buyer who fails to comply with the requirements of Section 6–104(1)(e) with respect to a creditor is liable to the creditor for damages in the amount of the claim, reduced by any amount that the creditor would not have realized if the buyer had complied; and

(b)   a buyer who fails to comply with the requirements of any other subsection of Section 6–104 with respect to a claimant is liable to the claimant for damages in the amount of the claim, reduced by any amount that the claimant would not have realized if the buyer had complied.

(2)   In an action under subsection (1), the creditor has the burden of establishing the validity and amount of the claim, and the buyer has the burden of establishing the amount that the creditor would not have realized if the buyer had complied.

(3)   A buyer who:

(a)   made a good faith and commercially reasonable effort to comply with the requirements of Section 6–104(1) or to exclude the sale from the application of this Article under Section 6–103(3); or

(b)   on or after the date of the bulk-sale agreement, but before the date of the bulk sale, held a good faith and commercially reasonable belief that this Article does not apply to the particular sale is not liable to creditors for failure to comply with the requirements of Section 6–104. The buyer has the burden of establishing the good faith and commercial reasonableness of the effort or belief.

(4)   In a single bulk sale the cumulative liability of the buyer for failure to comply with the requirements of Section 6–104(1) may not exceed an amount equal to:

(a) if the assets consist only of inventory and equipment, twice the net contract price, less the amount of any part of the net contract price paid to or applied for the benefit of the seller or a creditor; or

(b) if the assets include property other than inventory and equipment, twice the net value of the inventory and equipment less the amount of the portion of any part of the net contract price paid to or applied for the benefit of the seller or a creditor which is allocable to the inventory and equipment.

(5) For the purposes of subsection (4)(b), the "net value" of an asset is the value of the asset less (i) the amount of any proceeds of the sale of an asset, to the extent the proceeds are applied in partial or total satisfaction of a debt secured by the asset and (ii) the amount of any debt to the extent it is secured by a security interest or lien that is enforceable against the asset before and after it has been sold to a buyer. If a debt is secured by an asset and other property of the seller, the amount of the debt secured by a security interest or lien that is enforceable against the asset is determined by multiplying the debt by a fraction, the numerator of which is the value of the asset on the date of the bulk sale and the denominator of which is the value of all property securing the debt on the date of the bulk sale. The portion of a part of the net contract price paid to or applied for the benefit of the seller or a creditor that is "allocable to the inventory and equipment" is the portion that bears the same ratio to that part of the net contract price as the net value of the inventory and equipment bears to the net value of all of the assets.

(6) A payment made by the buyer to a person to whom the buyer is, or believes he [or she] is, liable under subsection (1) reduces pro tanto the buyer's cumulative liability under subsection (4).

(7) No action may be brought under subsection (1)(b) by or on behalf of a claimant whose claim is unliquidated or contingent.

(8) A buyer's failure to comply with the requirements of Section 6–104(1) does not (i) impair the buyer's rights in or title to the assets, (ii) render the sale ineffective, void, or voidable, (iii) entitle a creditor to more than a single satisfaction of his [or her] claim, or (iv) create liability other than as provided in this Article.

(9) Payment of the buyer's liability under subsection (1) discharges pro tanto the seller's debt to the creditor.

(10) Unless otherwise agreed, a buyer has an immediate right of reimbursement from the seller for any amount paid to a creditor in partial or total satisfaction of the buyer's liability under subsection (1).

(11) If the seller is an organization, a person who is in direct or indirect control of the seller, and who knowingly, intentionally, and without legal justification fails, or causes the seller to fail, to distribute the net contract price in accordance with the schedule of distribution is liable to any creditor to whom the seller undertook to make payment under the schedule for damages caused by the failure.

Official Comment

Prior Uniform Statutory Provision: None.

Purposes:

1. This section sets forth the consequences of noncompliance with the requirements of Section 6–104. Although other legal consequences may result from a bulk sale—*e.g.*, the buyer may be liable to the seller under Article 2 or to the seller's creditors under the Uniform Fraudulent Transfer Act—no other consequences may be imposed by reason of the buyer's failure to comply with the requirements of this Article.

The two subsections of Section 6–107(1) reflect the duties set forth in Section 6–104. The duties generally run only to claimants, but the duty to distribute the net contract price in accordance with the schedule of distribution (Section 6–104(1)(e)) may run also to certain creditors.

2. Article 6 (1987 Official Text), like many of its nonuniform predecessors, makes a noncomplying transfer ineffective against aggrieved creditors. In contrast, noncompliance with this Article neither renders the sale ineffective nor otherwise affects the buyer's rights in or title to the assets.

Liability under this Article is for breach of a statutory duty. The buyer's only liability is personal (*in personam*) liability. Aggrieved creditors may only recover money damages. *In rem* remedies, which are available upon noncompliance with Article 6 (1987 Official Text), are not available under this Article. Thus, aggrieved creditors no longer may treat the sale as if it had not occurred and use the judicial process to apply assets purchased by the buyer toward the satisfaction of their claims against the seller.

The change in the theory of liability and in the available remedy should be of particular significance if the seller enters bankruptcy after the sale is consummated. When an aggrieved creditor of the transferor has a nonbankruptcy right to avoid a transfer in whole or in part, as may be the case under Article 6 (1987 Official Text), the transferor's bankruptcy trustee may avoid the entire transfer. See Bankruptcy Code § 544(b), 11 U.S.C. § 544(b). Under this Article, a person who is aggrieved by the buyer's noncompliance may not avoid the sale. Rather, the person is entitled only to recover damages as provided in this section. Because no creditor has the right to avoid the transaction or to assert a remedy that is the functional equivalent of avoidance, the seller's bankruptcy trustee likewise should be unable to do so.

3.   This Article makes explicit what is implicit in Article 6 (1987 Official Text): only those persons as to whom there has been noncompliance are entitled to a remedy. For example, if notices are sent to each claimant other than claimant A, claimant B cannot recover. Similarly, a creditor who acquires a claim after notice is given has no remedy unless the buyer undertakes in the schedule of distribution to pay that creditor and the buyer fails to meet the obligation.

4.   Unlike Article 6 (1987 Official Text), which imposes strict liability upon a noncomplying transferee, this Article imposes liability for noncompliance only when the failure to comply actually has injured a creditor and only to the extent of the injury. Each creditor's damages are measured by the injury that the particular creditor sustained as a consequence of the buyer's failure to comply. This measure is stated as the amount of the debt reduced by any amount that the person would not have realized if the buyer had complied. Compare Section 4–103(5).

5.   A buyer is liable only for the buyer's own noncompliance with the requirements of Section 6–104. Under that section, the only step the buyer must take to discover the identity of the seller's claimants is to obtain a list of claimants from the seller. If the seller's list is incomplete and the buyer lacks knowledge of claimant C, then claimant C has no remedy under subsection (1)(b) of this section.

6.   The creditor has the burden of establishing the validity and amount of the debt owed by the seller as well as the fact of the buyer's noncompliance. In contesting the allegation of noncompliance, the buyer may introduce evidence tending to show either that the sale was not a bulk sale or that the sale was a bulk sale to which this Article does not apply. In contesting the validity and amount of the debt, the buyer may introduce evidence tending to show that the seller had a defense to the debt. The buyer has the burden of establishing the amount that the creditor would not have realized even if the buyer had complied. Implicit in subsection (2) is that certain failures to comply with the requirements of this Article will cause no injury and thus result in no liability.

The following examples illustrate the operation of subsection (2):

     Example 1:   The buyer fails to give notice of the bulk sale. Claimant D, who appears on seller's list of claimants, admits to having had actual knowledge of the impending sale two months before it occurred. The buyer is likely to be able to meet the burden of establishing that even had the buyer given notice of the sale, claimant D would not have recovered any more than the claimant actually recovered.

     Example 2:   The buyer failed to obtain a list of seller's business names (Section 6–104(1)(a)) or to make available the list of claimants (Section 6–104(1)(f)). In many cases, the buyer may be able to meet the burden of establishing that compliance with those subsections would not have enabled claimants to recover any more than they actually recovered.

7.   Subsection (3) may afford a complete defense to a noncomplying buyer. This defense is available to buyers who establish that they made a good faith effort to comply with the requirements of this Article or made a good faith effort to exclude the sale from the application of this Article (e.g., by assuming debts and attempting to comply with the notice requirements of Section 6–103(3)(i), (j), or (k)). When a buyer makes a good faith effort to comply with this Article or to exclude the transaction from its coverage, the injury caused by noncompliance is likely to be *de minimis*. In any event, the primary responsibility for satisfying claims rests with the creditors, and this Article imposes no greater duty upon buyers who attempt to comply with this Article or to exclude a sale from its application than to make a good faith effort to do so.

The defense of subsection (3) also is available to buyers who act on the good faith belief that this Article does not apply to the sale (e.g., because the sale is not a bulk sale or is excluded under Section 6–103). The good-faith-belief defense is an acknowledgement that reasonable people may disagree over whether a given transaction is or is not a bulk sale and over whether Section 6–103 excludes a particular transaction. A buyer acting in good faith should be protected from the liability that this Article otherwise would impose on buyers who may be completely innocent of wrongdoing. A buyer who is unaware of the requirements of this Article holds no belief concerning the applicability of the Article and so may not use the defense.

8. Even a buyer who completely fails to comply with this Article may not be liable in an amount equal to sum of the seller's debts. Subsection (4) limits the aggregate recovery for "any one bulk sale," which term includes a series of sales by a liquidator. The maximum cumulative liability for noncompliance with this Article parallels the maximum recovery generally available to creditors under the 1987 Official Text of Article 6. Under that Article, the noncomplying transferee may have to "pay twice" for the goods. First, the transferee may pay the purchase price to the transferor; then, the transferee may lose the goods to aggrieved creditors.

Under this Article, the maximum cumulative liability is an amount equal to twice the net contract price of the inventory and equipment (i.e., twice the amount that would be available to unsecured creditors from the inventory and equipment), less the amount of any portion of that net contract price paid to or applied for the benefit of the seller or a creditor of the seller. Unless the buyer receives credit for amounts paid to the seller (which amounts the creditors have a right to apply to payment of their claims), the buyer might wind up paying an amount equal to the net contract price three times (once to the seller and twice to aggrieved creditors). The grant of credit for amounts paid to the seller's creditors recognizes that ordinarily the seller has no obligation to pay creditors pro rata.

When the assets sold consist of only inventory and equipment, calculation of the maximum cumulative liability is relatively simple. But when the assets sold include property in addition to inventory and equipment, the calculation becomes more difficult. When inventory or equipment secures a debt that also is secured by other collateral and the aggregate value of the collateral exceeds the secured debt, a determination of the amount in clause (ii) of subsection (5) may require an allocation of the collateral to the debt in accordance with the statutory formula. In addition, one may need to determine which portion of payments of the net contract price is allocable to inventory and equipment. Subsection (5) directs that this allocation be made by multiplying the part of the net contract price paid to or applied for the benefit of the seller or a creditor by a fraction whose nominator is the net value of the inventory and equipment and whose denominator is the net value of all the assets.

Sometimes the seller may receive the net contract price and pay some or all of it to one or more creditors. In determining whether a payment to a creditor was made from the net contract price or from another source, courts are free to employ tracing rules. Amounts paid to secured parties usually are taken into account in determining the net contract price; if so, the buyer should not receive credit for them.

9. The buyer need not wait for judgment to be entered before paying a person believed to be a creditor of the seller. Indeed, the buyer is entitled to credit for amounts paid to persons who in fact may not be creditors of the seller, as long as the buyer acts with the belief that the seller is so indebted. As is the case with respect to all obligations under the Code, the buyer's belief must be held in good faith.

10. Any amounts paid by the buyer in satisfaction of the liability created by Section 6–107(1) reduce the seller's liability to the recipient pro tanto. Consequently, the buyer is entitled to immediate reimbursement of those amounts from the seller. The right of reimbursement is available only for amounts paid to actual creditors. Amounts paid to those whom the buyer incorrectly believes to be creditors ordinarily are not recoverable from the seller, although the buyer is entitled to credit for those amounts against the aggregate liability in subsection (4). Of course, the buyer and seller may vary the seller's reimbursement obligation by agreement.

11. Because of the difficulty in valuing claims that are unliquidated or contingent, persons holding claims of that kind may not bring an action under subsection (1)(b). If the claim remains unliquidated or contingent throughout the limitation period in Section 6–110, then these creditors have no remedy for noncompliance under that subsection. They may, however, be entitled to a remedy under subsection (1)(a) of (11) for failure to distribute the net contract price in accordance with the schedule of distribution.

12. In certain circumstances, subsection (11) imposes liability on a person in direct or indirect control of a seller that is an organization. Excuse under Section 6–106(6) is a "legal justification" that prevents liability from attaching under subsection (11). No special provision applies to the seller who fails to comply with the schedule. The seller already owes the debt to the creditor, and other law governs the consequences of a debtor who fails to pay a debt when promised.

Cross-References:

Point 1: Section 6–104.
Point 4: Section 4–103.
Point 5: Sections 6–104 and 6–105.
Point 6: Sections 1–201 [*unrevised Article 1; see Concordance, p. 22*], 6–102, 6–103, and 6–104.

Point 7: Sections 1–102 [*unrevised Article 1; see Concordance, p. 22*], 1–201 [*unrevised Article 1; see Concordance, p. 22*], 6–102 and 6–103.

Point 8: Section 6–102.

Point 9: Section 1–203 [*unrevised Article 1; see Concordance, p. 22*].

Point 10: Section 1–102 [*unrevised Article 1; see Concordance, p. 22*].

Point 11: Sections 6–102 and 6–110.

Point 12: Section 6–106.

Definitional Cross-References:

"Assets". Section 6–102.

"Bulk sale". Section 6–102.

"Burden of establishing". Section 1–201.

"Buyer". Section 2–103.

"Claim". Section 6–102.

"Claimant". Section 6–102.

"Creditor". Section 6–102.

"Date of the bulk sale". Section 6–102.

"Equipment". Section 6–102.

"Good faith". Section 6–102.

"Inventory". Section 9–102(a)(48).

"Net contract price". Section 6–102.

"Organization". Section 1–201.

"Person". Section 1–201.

"Proceeds". Section 9–102(a)(64).

"Security interest". Section 1–201.

"Seller". Section 2–103.

"Written". Section 1–201.

As amended in 1999.

§ 6–108. Bulk Sales by Auction; Bulk Sales Conducted by Liquidator.

(1)   Sections 6–104, 6–105, 6–106, and 6–107 apply to a bulk sale by auction and a bulk sale conducted by a liquidator on the seller's behalf with the following modifications:

(a)   "buyer" refers to auctioneer or liquidator, as the case may be;

(b)   "net contract price" refers to net proceeds of the auction or net proceeds of the sale, as the case may be;

(c)   the written notice required under Section 6–105(3) must be accompanied by a copy of the schedule of distribution (Section 6–106(1)) and state at least:

(i)   that the seller and the auctioneer or liquidator have entered into an agreement for auction or liquidation services that may constitute an agreement to make a bulk sale under the laws of the State of _____;

(ii)   the date of the agreement;

(iii)   the date on or after which the auction began or will begin or the date on or after which the liquidator began or will begin to sell assets on the seller's behalf;

(iv)   the date on or after which more than ten percent of the net proceeds of the sale were or will be paid, if the date is not stated in the schedule of distribution;

(v)   the name and a mailing address of the seller;

(vi)   any other business name and address listed by the seller pursuant to Section 6–104(1)(a);

(vii)   the name of the auctioneer or liquidator and an address of the auctioneer or liquidator from which information concerning the sale can be obtained;

(viii) a statement indicating the type of assets or describing the assets item by item;

(ix) the manner in which the auctioneer or liquidator will make available the list of claimants (Section 6–104(1)(f)), if applicable; and

(x) if the sale is in total or partial satisfaction of an antecedent debt owed by the seller, the amount of the debt to be satisfied and the name of the person to whom it is owed; and

(d) in a single bulk sale the cumulative liability of the auctioneer or liquidator for failure to comply with the requirements of this section may not exceed the amount of the net proceeds of the sale allocable to inventory and equipment sold less the amount of the portion of any part of the net proceeds paid to or applied for the benefit of a creditor which is allocable to the inventory and equipment.

(2) A payment made by the auctioneer or liquidator to a person to whom the auctioneer or liquidator is, or believes he [or she] is, liable under this section reduces pro tanto the auctioneer's or liquidator's cumulative liability under subsection (1)(d).

(3) A form substantially as follows is sufficient to comply with subsection (1)(c):

Notice of Sale

(1) _____, whose address is _____, is described in this notice as the "seller."

(2) _____, whose address is _____, is described in this notice as the "auctioneer" or "liquidator."

(3) The seller has disclosed to the auctioneer or liquidator that within the past three years the seller has used other business names, operated at other addresses, or both, as follows: _____.

(4) The seller and the auctioneer or liquidator have entered into an agreement dated _____ for auction or liquidation services that may constitute an agreement to make a bulk sale under the laws of the State of _____.

(5) The date on or after which the auction began or will begin or the date on or after which the liquidator began or will begin to sell assets on the seller's behalf is _____, and [if not stated in the schedule of distribution] the date on or after which more than ten percent of the net proceeds of the sale were or will be paid is _____.

(6) The following assets are the subject of the sale: _____.

(7) [If applicable] The auctioneer or liquidator will make available to claimants of the seller a list of the seller's claimants in the following manner: _____.

(8) [If applicable] The sale is to satisfy $_____ of an antecedent debt owed by the seller to _____.

(9) A copy of the schedule of distribution of the net proceeds accompanies this notice.

[End of Notice]

(4) A person who buys at a bulk sale by auction or conducted by a liquidator need not comply with the requirements of Section 6–104(1) and is not liable for the failure of an auctioneer or liquidator to comply with the requirements of this section.

Official Comment

Prior Uniform Statutory Provision: Section 6–108.

Changes: Revised, expanded to include sales conducted by a liquidator on the seller's behalf, and form of notice added.

Purposes of Changes and New Matter:

1. This section applies only to bulk sales by auction or conducted by a liquidator on the seller's behalf, as defined in Section 6–102(1)(c). Bulk sales conducted by an auctioneer or liquidator on its own behalf are treated as ordinary bulk sales and are not subject to this section.

2. Regardless of whether the assets are sold directly from the seller to the buyer, are sold to a variety of buyers at auction, or are sold on the seller's behalf by a liquidator to one or more buyers, a going-out-of-business sale of inventory presents similar risks to claimants. Auctioneers and liquidators are likely to be in a better

position to ascertain whether the sale they are conducting is, or is part of, a bulk sale than are their customers. Accordingly, buyers at auctions and from liquidators selling assets of others need not be concerned with complying with this Article. Instead, this section imposes upon auctioneers and liquidators duties and liabilities that are similar, but not always identical, to those of a buyer under Sections 6–104(1) and 6–107. Except to the extent that this section treats bulk sales by auctioneers and liquidators differently from those conducted by the seller on its own behalf, the Official Comments to Sections 6–104(1) and 6–107, as well as the Comments to Sections 6–105 and 6–106, which those sections incorporate by reference, are applicable to sales to which this section applies.

3.   Subsection (1)(d) sets forth the maximum cumulative liability for auctioneers and liquidators "in any one bulk sale," which term includes a series of sales by a liquidator. This liability is to be calculated in a manner similar to that set forth in Sections 6–107(4) and 6–107(5). The term "net proceeds of the auction or sale allocable to inventory and equipment" is analogous to the term "net value of the inventory and equipment"; however, the former takes into account the reasonable expenses of the auction or sale whereas the latter does not. Also, the latter is doubled whereas the former is not. The "amount of the portion of any part of the net proceeds paid to or applied for the benefit of a creditor which is allocable to inventory and equipment" is determined by multiplying the part of the net proceeds paid to or applied for the benefit of a creditor by a fraction whose numerator is the net proceeds of the sale allocable to inventory and equipment and whose denominator is the total net proceeds of the auction or sale. Because the amount of the net proceeds allocable to inventory and equipment is not doubled, the auctioneer or liquidator is not entitled to credit for payments made to the seller.

4.   Section 6–107(3) applies to all bulk sales. Accordingly, an auctioneer or liquidator who makes a good faith effort to comply with the requirements of this Article or to exclude the sale from this Article or who acts under a good faith belief that this Article does not apply to the sale faces no liability whatsoever.

Cross-References:

> Point 1: Section 6–102.
> Point 2: Sections 6–102, 6–104, 6–105, 6–106, and 6–107.
> Point 3: Sections 6–102 and 6–107.
> Point 4: Section 6–107.

Definitional Cross-References:

> "Assets". Section 6–102.
> "Auctioneer". Section 6–102.
> "Bulk sale". Section 6–102.
> "Claimants". Section 6–102.
> "Creditor". Section 6–102.
> "Debt". Section 6–102.
> "Equipment". Section 9–102(a)(33).
> "Inventory". Section 9–102(a)(48).
> "Liquidator". Section 6–102.
> "Net proceeds". Section 6–102.
> "Person". Section 1–201.
> "Seller". Section 2–103.
> "Written". Section 1–201.

As amended in 1999.

§ 6–109.   What Constitutes Filing; Duties of Filing Officer; Information From Filing Officer.

(1)   Presentation of a notice or list of claimants for filing and tender of the filing fee or acceptance of the notice or list by the filing officer constitutes filing under this Article.

(2)   The filing officer shall:

(a)   mark each notice or list with a file number and with the date and hour of filing;

(b)   hold the notice or list or a copy for public inspection;

(c) index the notice or list according to each name given for the seller and for the buyer; and

(d) note in the index the file number and the addresses of the seller and buyer given in the notice or list.

(3) If the person filing a notice or list furnishes the filing officer with a copy, the filing officer upon request shall note upon the copy the file number and date and hour of the filing of the original and send or deliver the copy to the person.

(4) The fee for filing and indexing and for stamping a copy furnished by the person filing to show the date and place of filing is $_____ for the first page and $_____ for each additional page. The fee for indexing each name more than two is $_____.

(5) Upon request of any person, the filing officer shall issue a certificate showing whether any notice or list with respect to a particular seller or buyer is on file on the date and hour stated in the certificate. If a notice or list is on file, the certificate must give the date and hour of filing of each notice or list and the name and address of each seller, buyer, auctioneer, or liquidator. The fee for the certificate is $_____ if the request for the certificate is in the standard form prescribed by the [Secretary of State] and otherwise is $_____. Upon request of any person, the filing officer shall furnish a copy of any filed notice or list for a fee of $_____.

(6) The filing officer shall keep each notice or list for two years after it is filed.

Official Comment

Prior Uniform Statutory Provision: None.

Purposes of New Matter:

This Article contemplates public filing of bulk sale notices and lists of claimants in a single filing office in each state. This section, which derives substantially from former Sections 9–403 and 9–407 (now codified as Sections 9–515, 9–516, 9–519, 9–522, 9–523, and 9–525), governs filing. The filing system is designed to enable one seeking information about a sale to discover any filed notices or lists by searching under either the seller's or the buyer's (but not the auctioneer's or liquidator's) individual, partnership, or corporate name.

Cross-References:

Sections 6–103, 6–105, 9–403 [*unrevised Article 9*], and 9–407 [*unrevised Article 9*].

Definitional Cross-References:

"Auctioneer". Section 6–102.
"Buyer". Section 2–103.
"Liquidator". Section 6–102.
"Person". Section 1–201.
"Seller". Section 2–103.
"Send". Section 1–201.

As amended in 1999.

§ 6–110. Limitation of Actions.

(1) Except as provided in subsection (2), an action under this Article against a buyer, auctioneer, or liquidator must be commenced within one year after the date of the bulk sale.

(2) If the buyer, auctioneer, or liquidator conceals the fact that the sale has occurred, the limitation is tolled and an action under this Article may be commenced within the earlier of (i) one year after the person bringing the action discovers that the sale has occurred or (ii) one year after the person bringing the action should have discovered that the sale has occurred, but no later than two years after the date of the bulk sale. Complete noncompliance with the requirements of this Article does not of itself constitute concealment.

(3) An action under Section 6–107(11) must be commenced within one year after the alleged violation occurs.

Official Comment

Prior Uniform Statutory Provision: Section 6–111 (1987 Official Text).

Changes: Statute of limitations extended and clarified.

Purposes of Changes and New Matter:

1.   This Article imposes liability upon only those who do not make a good faith and commercially reasonable effort to comply with the requirements of the Article or to exclude the sale from the application of the Article and who do not hold a good faith and commercially reasonable belief that the Article is inapplicable to the sale. Consequently, it extends the six-month limitation period of the 1987 Official Text, which applies to good faith transferees as well as those not in good faith, to one year. The period commences with the date of the bulk sale.

2.   Cases decided under the 1987 Official Text of Article 6 disagree over whether the complete failure to comply with the requirements of that Article constitutes a concealment that tolls the limitation. This Article adopts the view that noncompliance does not of itself constitute concealment.

3.   This Article does not contemplate tolling the limitation for actions against a person in control of the seller who fails to distribute the net contract price in accordance with the schedule of distribution. Those actions must be commenced within one year after the alleged violation occurs.

Cross-References:

Point 1: Sections 1–201, 6–102, 6–107 and 6–108.
Point 3: Section 6–107.

Definitional Cross-References:

"Action". Section 1–201.
"Auctioneer". Section 6–102.
"Buyer". Section 2–103.
"Date of the bulk sale". Section 6–102.
"Liquidator". Section 6–102.

[END OF ALTERNATIVE B]

CONFORMING AMENDMENT TO SECTION 1–105
[unrevised Article 1; see Concordance, p. 22]

States adopting Alternative B should amend Section 1–105(2) [unrevised Article 1; see Concordance, p. 22] of the Uniform Commercial Code to read as follows:

(2)   Where one of the following provisions of this Act specifies the applicable law, that provision governs and a contrary agreement is effective only to the extent permitted by the law (including the conflict of laws rules) so specified:

Rights of creditors against sold goods. Section 2–402.

Applicability of the Article on Leases. Sections 2A–105 and 2A–106.

Applicability of the Article on Bank Deposits and Collections. Section 4–102.

Bulk ~~transfers~~ sales subject to the Article on Bulk ~~Transfers~~ Sales. Section ~~6–102~~ 6–103.

Applicability of the Article on Investment Securities. Section 8–106 [unrevised Article 8].

Perfection provisions of the Article on Secured Transactions. Section 9–103 [unrevised Article 9].

CONFORMING AMENDMENT TO SECTION 2–403

States adopting Alternative B should amend Section 2–403(4) of the Uniform Commercial Code to read as follows:

(4)   The rights of other purchasers of goods and of lien creditors are governed by the Articles on Secured Transactions (Article 9), Bulk ~~Transfers~~ Sales (Article 6) and Documents of Title (Article 7).

UCC ARTICLE 7

DOCUMENTS OF TITLE

Article 7 was revised in 2003 and amended in 2022.

2022 Amendments appear in ~~strikeout~~/<u>underline</u> format.

Prefatory Note to 2022 amendments appears in Appendix E.

Current through April 2023

For updates, see www.uniformlaws.org

PART 1. GENERAL

7–101.	Short Title.
7–102.	Definitions and Index of Definitions.
7–103.	Relation of Article to Treaty or Statute.
7–104.	Negotiable and Nonnegotiable Document of Title.
7–105.	Reissuance in Alternative Medium.
7–106.	Control of Electronic Document of Title.

PART 2. WAREHOUSE RECEIPTS: SPECIAL PROVISIONS

7–201.	Person That May Issue a Warehouse Receipt; Storage Under Bond.
7–202.	Form of Warehouse Receipt; Effect of Omission.
7–203.	Liability for Nonreceipt or Misdescription.
7–204.	Duty of Care; Contractual Limitation of Warehouse's Liability.
7–205.	Title Under Warehouse Receipt Defeated in Certain Cases.
7–206.	Termination of Storage at Warehouse's Option.
7–207.	Goods Must Be Kept Separate; Fungible Goods.
7–208.	Altered Warehouse Receipts.
7–209.	Lien of Warehouse.
7–210.	Enforcement of Warehouse's Lien.

PART 3. BILLS OF LADING: SPECIAL PROVISIONS

7–301.	Liability for Nonreceipt or Misdescription; "Said to Contain"; "Shipper's Weight, Load, and Count"; Improper Handling.
7–302.	Through Bills of Lading and Similar Documents of Title.
7–303.	Diversion; Reconsignment; Change of Instructions.
7–304.	Tangible Bills of Lading in a Set.
7–305.	Destination Bills.
7–306.	Altered Bills of Lading.
7–307.	Lien of Carrier.
7–308.	Enforcement of Carrier's Lien.
7–309.	Duty of Care; Contractual Limitation of Carrier's Liability.

PART 4. WAREHOUSE RECEIPTS AND BILLS OF LADING: GENERAL OBLIGATIONS

7–401.   Irregularities in Issue of Receipt or Bill or Conduct of Issuer.
7–402.   Duplicate Document of Title; Overissue.
7–403.   Obligation of Bailee to Deliver; Excuse.
7–404.   No Liability for Good-Faith Delivery Pursuant to Document of Title.

PART 5. WAREHOUSE RECEIPTS AND BILLS OF LADING: NEGOTIATION AND TRANSFER

7–501.   Form of Negotiation and Requirements of Due Negotiation.
7–502.   Rights Acquired by Due Negotiation.
7–503.   Document of Title to Goods Defeated in Certain Cases.
7–504.   Rights Acquired in Absence of Due Negotiation; Effect of Diversion; Stoppage of Delivery.
7–505.   Indorser Not Guarantor for Other Parties.
7–506.   Delivery Without Indorsement: Right to Compel Indorsement.
7–507.   Warranties on Negotiation or Delivery of Document of Title.
7–508.   Warranties of Collecting Bank as to Documents of Title.
7–509.   Adequate Compliance with Commercial Contract.

PART 6. WAREHOUSE RECEIPTS AND BILLS OF LADING: MISCELLANEOUS PROVISIONS

7–601.   Lost, Stolen, or Destroyed Documents of Title.
7–602.   Judicial Process Against Goods Covered by Negotiable Document of Title.
7–603.   Conflicting Claims; Interpleader.

PART 7. MISCELLANEOUS PROVISIONS

7–701.   Effective Date.
7–702.   Repeals.
7–703.   Applicability.
7–704.   Savings Clause.

PREFATORY NOTE

Article 7 is the last of the articles of the Uniform Commercial Code to be revised. The genesis of this project is twofold: to provide a framework for the further development of electronic documents of title and to update the article for modern times in light of state, federal and international developments. Each section has been reviewed to determine its suitability given modern practice, the need for medium and gender neutrality, and modern statutory drafting.

To provide for electronic documents of title, several definitions in Article 1 were revised including "bearer," "bill of lading," "delivery," "document of title," "holder," and "warehouse receipt." The concept of an electronic document of title allows for commercial practice to determine whether records issued by bailees are "in the regular course of business or financing" and are "treated as adequately evidencing that the person in possession or control of the record is entitled to receive, control, hold, and dispose of the record and the goods the record covers." Rev. Section 1–201(b)(16). Such records in electronic form are electronic documents of title and in tangible form are tangible documents of title. Conforming amendments to other Articles of the UCC are also necessary to fully integrate electronic documents of title into the UCC. Conforming amendments to other Articles of the UCC are contained in Appendix I. [*Note from West Advisory Panel: Article 7 conforming amendments are incorporated in the affected sections so the referenced appendix is not included in this volume.*]

Key to the integration of the electronic document of title scheme is the concept of "control" defined in Section 7–106. This definition is adapted from the Uniform Electronic Transactions Act § 16 on

Transferrable Records and from Uniform Commercial Code § 9–105 concerning control of electronic chattel paper. Control of an electronic document of title is the conceptual equivalent to possession and indorsement of a tangible document of title. Of equal importance is the acknowledgment that parties may desire to substitute an electronic document of title for an already-issued paper document and vice versa. Section 7–105 sets forth the minimum requirements that need to be fulfilled in order to give effect to the substitute document issued in the alternate medium. To the extent possible, the rules for electronic documents of title are the same or as similar as possible to the rules for tangible documents of title. If a rule is meant to be limited to one medium or the other, that is clearly stated. Rules that reference documents of title, warehouse receipts, or bills of lading without a designation to "electronic" or "tangible" apply to documents of title in either medium. As with tangible negotiable documents of title, electronic negotiable documents of title may be negotiated and duly negotiated. Section 7–501.

Other changes that have been made are:

1. New definitions of "carrier," "good faith," "record", "sign" and "shipper" in Section 7–102.

2. Deletion of references to tariffs or filed classifications given the deregulation of the affected industries. See e.g. section 7–103 and 7–309.

3. Clarifying the rules regarding when a document is nonnegotiable. Section 7–104.

4. Making clear when rules apply just to warehouse receipts or bills of lading, thus eliminating the need for former section 7–105.

5. Clarifying that particular terms need not be included in order to have a valid warehouse receipt. Section 7–202.

6. Broadening the ability of the warehouse to make an effective limitation of liability in its warehouse receipt or storage agreement in accord with commercial practice. Section 7–204.

7. Allowing a warehouse to have a lien on goods covered by a storage agreement and clarifying the priority rules regarding the claim of a warehouse lien as against other interests. Section 7–209.

8. Conforming language usage to modern shipping practice. Sections 7–301 and 7–302.

9. Clarifying the extent of the carrier's lien. Section 7–307.

10. Adding references to Article 2A when appropriate. See e.g. Sections 7–503, 7–504, 7–509.

11. Clarifying that the warranty made by negotiation or delivery of a document of title should apply only in the case of a voluntary transfer of possession or control of the document. Section 7–507.

12. Providing greater flexibility to a court regarding adequate protection against loss when ordering delivery of the goods or issuance of a substitute document. Section 7–601.

13. Providing conforming amendments to the other Articles of the Uniform Commercial Code to accommodate electronic documents of title.

Legislative Note: All cross-references in this draft to Article 1 are to Revised Article 1 (2001). In the event a state has not enacted Revised Article 1, the cross-references should be changed to refer to the relevant sections in former Article 1.

PART 1

GENERAL

§ 7–101. Short Title.

This article may be cited as Uniform Commercial Code-Documents of Title.

Official Comment

Prior Uniform Statutory Provision: Former Section 7–101.

Changes: Revised for style only.

This Article is a revision of the 1962 Official Text with Comments as amended since 1962. The 1962 Official Text was a consolidation and revision of the Uniform Warehouse Receipts Act and the Uniform Bills of Lading Act, and embraced the provisions of the Uniform Sales Act relating to negotiation of documents of title.

This Article does not contain the substantive criminal provisions found in the Uniform Warehouse Receipts and Bills of Lading Acts. These criminal provisions are inappropriate to a Commercial Code, and for the most part duplicate portions of the ordinary criminal law relating to frauds. This revision deletes the former Section 7–105 that provided that courts could apply a rule from Parts 2 and 3 by analogy to a situation not explicitly covered in the provisions on warehouse receipts or bills of lading when it was appropriate. This is, of course, an unexceptional proposition and need not be stated explicitly in the statute. Thus former Section 7–105 has been deleted. Whether applying a rule by analogy to a situation is appropriate depends upon the facts of each case.

The Article does not attempt to define the tort liability of bailees, except to hold certain classes of bailees to a minimum standard of reasonable care. For important classes of bailees, liabilities in case of loss, damages or destruction, as well as other legal questions associated with particular documents of title, are governed by federal statutes, international treaties, and in some cases regulatory state laws, which supersede the provisions of this Article in case of inconsistency. See Section 7–103.

§ 7–102.   Definitions and Index of Definitions.

(a)   In this article, unless the context otherwise requires:

(1)   "Bailee" means a person that by a warehouse receipt, bill of lading, or other document of title acknowledges possession of goods and contracts to deliver them.

(2)   "Carrier" means a person that issues a bill of lading.

(3)   "Consignee" means a person named in a bill of lading to which or to whose order the bill promises delivery.

(4)   "Consignor" means a person named in a bill of lading as the person from which the goods have been received for shipment.

(5)   "Delivery order" means a record that contains an order to deliver goods directed to a warehouse, carrier, or other person that in the ordinary course of business issues warehouse receipts or bills of lading.

(6)   "Good faith" means honesty in fact and the observance of reasonable commercial standards of fair dealing.

(7)   "Goods" means all things that are treated as movable for the purposes of a contract for storage or transportation.

(8)   "Issuer" means a bailee that issues a document of title or, in the case of an unaccepted delivery order, the person that orders the possessor of goods to deliver. The term includes a person for which an agent or employee purports to act in issuing a document if the agent or employee has real or apparent authority to issue documents, even if the issuer did not receive any goods, the goods were misdescribed, or in any other respect the agent or employee violated the issuer's instructions.

(9)   "Person entitled under the document" means the holder, in the case of a negotiable document of title, or the person to which delivery of the goods is to be made by the terms of, or pursuant to instructions in a record under, a nonnegotiable document of title.

(10)   "Record" means information that is inscribed on a tangible medium or that is stored in an electronic or other medium and is retrievable in perceivable form. [Reserved.]

(11)   "Sign" means, with present intent to authenticate or adopt a record:

(A)   to execute or adopt a tangible symbol; or

(B)   to attach to or logically associate with the record an electronic sound, symbol, or process. [Reserved.]

(12) "Shipper" means a person that enters into a contract of transportation with a carrier.

(13) "Warehouse" means a person engaged in the business of storing goods for hire.

(b) Definitions in other articles applying to this article and the sections in which they appear are:

(1) "Contract for sale", Section 2–106.

(2) "Lessee in ordinary course", Section 2A–103.

(3) "Receipt" of goods, Section 2–103.

(c) In addition, Article 1 contains general definitions and principles of construction and interpretation applicable throughout this article.

As amended in 2022.

Legislative Note: If the state has enacted Revised Article 1, the definitions of "good faith" in subsection (a)(6) and "record" in (a)(10) need not be enacted in this section as they are contained in Article 1, Section 1–201. These subsections should be marked as "reserved" in order to provide for uniform numbering of subsections.

Official Comment

Prior Uniform Statutory Provision: Former Section 7–102.

Changes: New definitions of "carrier," "good faith," "record," "sign," and "shipper." Other definitions revised to accommodate electronic mediums.

Purposes:

1. "Bailee" is used in this Article as a blanket term to designate carriers, warehousemen and others who normally issue documents of title on the basis of goods which they have received. The definition does not, however, require actual possession of the goods. If a bailee acknowledges possession when it does not have possession, the bailee is bound by sections of this Article which declare the "bailee's" obligations. (See definition of "Issuer" in this section and Sections 7–203 and 7–301 on liability in case of non-receipt.) A "carrier" is one type of bailee and is defined as a person that issues a bill of lading. A "shipper" is a person who enters into the contract of transportation with the carrier. The definitions of "bailee," "consignee," "consignor," "goods", and "issuer", are unchanged in substance from prior law. "Document of title" is defined in Article 1, and may be in either tangible or electronic form.

2. The definition of warehouse receipt contained in the general definitions section of this Act (Section 1–201) does not require that the issuing warehouse be "lawfully engaged" in business or for profit. The warehouse's compliance with applicable state regulations such as the filing of a bond has no bearing on the substantive issues dealt with in this Article. Certainly the issuer's violations of law should not diminish its responsibility on documents the issuer has put in commercial circulation. But it is still essential that the business be storing goods "for hire" (Section 1–201 and this section). A person does not become a warehouse by storing its own goods.

3. When a delivery order has been accepted by the bailee it is for practical purposes indistinguishable from a warehouse receipt. Prior to such acceptance there is no basis for imposing obligations on the bailee other than the ordinary obligation of contract which the bailee may have assumed to the depositor of the goods. Delivery orders may be either electronic or tangible documents of title. See definition of "document of title" in Section 1–201.

4. The obligation of good faith imposed by this Article and by Article 1, Section 1–304 includes the observance of reasonable commercial standards of fair dealing.

5. ~~The definitions of "record" and "sign" are included to facilitate electronic mediums. See comment 9 to Section 9–102 discussing "record" and the comment to amended Section 2–103 discussing "sign".~~ <u>Pursuant to the Uniform Commercial Code Amendments (2022) (2022 Amendments), paragraphs (10) and (11) of subsection (a) have been deleted as unnecessary. Section 1–201 includes substantially equivalent definitions of "record" and "sign."</u>

6. "Person entitled under the document" is moved from former Section 7–403.

<u>In the case of a negotiable document of title, the person entitled is the holder. See Section 1–201(b)(21) (defining "holder"). For a nonnegotiable document of title, the person entitled is the person provided in the terms of the document or instructions under the document. A transferee of a nonnegotiable document to which the document has been delivered acquires the transferee's rights and rights that the transferor had actual authority</u>

to convey. Section 7–504(a). However, until but not after the bailee receives notice of a transfer, such a transferee's rights are subject to those of persons identified in Section 7–504(b), including "as against the bailee, by good faith dealings of the bailee with the transferor." Moreover, such a transferee is *not* a person entitled under the document unless so provided in the document or in instructions under the document.

Article 7 does not explain what constitutes an "instruction under" a nonnegotiable document, but instead leaves it to commercial practice, including usage of trade (Section 1–303(c)). In practice the term is generally understood to include a delivery order or other instruction to the bailee, by the person named in the document, to deliver the goods to a transferee of the document or to another person. A delivery order or other instruction under a nonnegotiable document should be distinguished from a mere "notice" or "notification" to the bailee of a transfer or security interest, as contemplated by Sections 7–504(b) and 9–312(d)(2). However, an instruction could, functionally, also constitute such a notice.

7.   These definitions apply in this Article unless the context otherwise requires. The "context" is intended to refer to the context in which the defined term is used in the Uniform Commercial Code. The definition applies whenever the defined term is used unless the context in which the defined term is used in the statute indicates that the term was not used in its defined sense. See comment to Section 1–201.

Cross References:

Point 1: Sections 1–201, 7–203 and 7–301.
Point 2: Sections 1–201 and 7–203.
Point 3: Section 1–201.
Point 4: Section 1–304.
Point 5: Section 9–102 and 2–103.
See general comment to document of title in Section 1–201.

Definitional Cross References:

"Bill of lading". Section 1–201.
"Contract". Section 1–201.
"Contract for sale". Section 2–106.
"Delivery". Section 1–201.
"Document of title". Section 1–201.
"Person". Section 1–201.
"Purchase". Section 1–201.
"Receipt of goods". Section 2–103.
"Right". Section 1–201.
"Warehouse receipt". Section 1–201.

As amended in 2022.

§ 7–103.   Relation of Article to Treaty or Statute.

(a)   This article is subject to any treaty or statute of the United States or regulatory statute of this state to the extent the treaty, statute, or regulatory statute is applicable.

(b)   This article does not modify or repeal any law prescribing the form or content of a document of title or the services or facilities to be afforded by a bailee, or otherwise regulating a bailee's business in respects not specifically treated in this article. However, violation of such a law does not affect the status of a document of title that otherwise is within the definition of a document of title.

(c)   This [act] modifies, limits, and supersedes the federal Electronic Signatures in Global and National Commerce Act (15 U.S.C. Section 7001, et. seq.) but does not modify, limit, or supersede Section 101(c) of that act (15 U.S.C. Section 7001(c)) or authorize electronic delivery of any of the notices described in Section 103(b) of that act (15 U.S.C. Section 7003(b)).

(d)   To the extent there is a conflict between [the Uniform Electronic Transactions Act] and this article, this article governs.

Legislative Note: In states that have not enacted the Uniform Electronic Transactions Act in some form, states should consider their own state laws to determine whether there is a conflict between the provisions of this article and those laws particularly as those other laws may affect electronic documents of title.

Official Comment

Prior Uniform Statutory Provision: Former Sections 7–103 and 10–104.

Changes: Deletion of references to tariffs and classifications; incorporation of former Section 10–104 into subsection (b), provide for intersection with federal and state law governing electronic transactions.

Purposes:

1.   To make clear what would of course be true without the Section, that applicable Federal law is paramount.

2.   To make clear also that regulatory state statutes (such as those fixing or authorizing a commission to fix rates and prescribe services, authorizing different charges for goods of different values, and limiting liability for loss to the declared value on which the charge was based) are not affected by the Article and are controlling on the matters which they cover unless preempted by federal law. The reference in former Section 7–103 to tariffs, classifications, and regulations filed or issued pursuant to regulatory state statutes has been deleted as inappropriate in the modern era of diminished regulation of carriers and warehouses. If a regulatory scheme requires a carrier or warehouse to issue a tariff or classification, that tariff or classification would be given effect via the state regulatory scheme that this Article recognizes as controlling. Permissive tariffs or classifications would not displace the provisions of this act, pursuant to this section, but may be given effect through the ability of parties to incorporate those terms by reference into their agreement.

3.   The document of title provisions of this act supplement the federal law and regulatory state law governing bailees. This Article focuses on the commercial importance and usage of documents of title. *State ex rel. Public Service Commission v. Gunkelman & Sons, Inc.*, 219 N.W.2d 853 (N.D. 1974).

4.   Subsection (c) is included to make clear the interrelationship between the federal Electronic Signatures in Global and National Commerce Act and this article and the conforming amendments to other articles of the Uniform Commercial Code promulgated as part of the revision of this article. Section 102 of the federal act allows a State statute to modify, limit, or supersede the provisions of Section 101 of the federal act. See the comments to Revised Article 1, Section 1–108.

5.   Subsection (d) makes clear that once this article is in effect, its provisions regarding electronic commerce and regarding electronic documents of title control in the event there is a conflict with the provisions of the Uniform Electronic Transactions Act or other applicable state law governing electronic transactions.

Cross References:

Sections 1–108, 7–201, 7–202, 7–204, 7–206, 7–309, 7–401, 7–403.

Definitional Cross Reference:

"Bill of lading". Section 1–201.

§ 7–104.   Negotiable and Nonnegotiable Document of Title.

(a)   Except as otherwise provided in subsection (c), a document of title is negotiable if by its terms the goods are to be delivered to bearer or to the order of a named person.

(b)   A document of title other than one described in subsection (a) is nonnegotiable. A bill of lading that states that the goods are consigned to a named person is not made negotiable by a provision that the goods are to be delivered only against an order in a record signed by the same or another named person.

(c)   A document of title is nonnegotiable if, at the time it is issued, the document has a conspicuous legend, however expressed, that it is nonnegotiable.

Official Comment

Prior Uniform Statutory Provision: Former Section 7–104.

Changes: Subsection (a) is revised to reflect modern style and trade practice. Subsection (b) is revised for style and medium neutrality. Subsection (c) is new.

Purposes:

1.   This Article deals with a class of commercial paper representing commodities in storage or transportation. This "commodity paper" is to be distinguished from what might be called "money paper" dealt with

in the Article of this Act on Commercial Paper (Article 3) and "investment paper" dealt with in the Article of this Act on Investment Securities (Article 8). The class of "commodity paper" is designated "document of title" following the terminology of the Uniform Sales Act Section 76. Section 1–201. The distinctions between negotiable and nonnegotiable documents in this section makes the most important subclassification employed in the Article, in that the holder of negotiable documents may acquire more rights than its transferor had (See Section 7–502). The former Section 7–104, which provided that a document of title was negotiable if it runs to a named person or assigns if such designation was recognized in overseas trade, has been deleted as not necessary in light of current commercial practice.

A document of title is negotiable only if it satisfies this section. "Deliverable on proper indorsement and surrender of this receipt" will not render a document negotiable. Bailees often include such provisions as a means of insuring return of nonnegotiable receipts for record purposes. Such language may be regarded as insistence by the bailee upon a particular kind of receipt in connection with delivery of the goods. Subsection (a) makes it clear that a document is not negotiable which provides for delivery to order or bearer only if written instructions to that effect are given by a named person. Either tangible or electronic documents of title may be negotiable if the document meets the requirement of this section.

2. Subsection (c) is derived from Section 3–104(d). Prior to issuance of the document of title, an issuer may stamp or otherwise provide by a notation on the document that it is nonnegotiable even if the document would otherwise comply with the requirement of subsection (a). Once issued as a negotiable document of title, the document cannot be changed from a negotiable document to a nonnegotiable document. A document of title that is nonnegotiable cannot be made negotiable by stamping or providing a notation that the document is negotiable. The only way to make a document of title negotiable is to comply with subsection (a). A negotiable document of title may fail to be duly negotiated if the negotiation does not comply with the requirements for "due negotiation" stated in Section 7–501.

Cross Reference:

Sections 7–501 and 7–502.

Definitional Cross References:

"Bearer". Section 1–201.
"Bill of lading". Section 1–201.
"Delivery". Section 1–201.
"Document of title". Section 1–201.
"Person". Section 1–201.
"Sign". Section 7–102
"Warehouse receipt". Section 1–201.

§ 7–105.   Reissuance in Alternative Medium.

(a) Upon request of a person entitled under an electronic document of title, the issuer of the electronic document may issue a tangible document of title as a substitute for the electronic document if:

(1) the person entitled under the electronic document surrenders control of the document to the issuer; and

(2) the tangible document when issued contains a statement that it is issued in substitution for the electronic document.

(b) Upon issuance of a tangible document of title in substitution for an electronic document of title in accordance with subsection (a):

(1) the electronic document ceases to have any effect or validity; and

(2) the person that procured issuance of the tangible document warrants to all subsequent persons entitled under the tangible document that the warrantor was a person entitled under the electronic document when the warrantor surrendered control of the electronic document to the issuer.

(c) Upon request of a person entitled under a tangible document of title, the issuer of the tangible document may issue an electronic document of title as a substitute for the tangible document if:

(1) the person entitled under the tangible document surrenders possession of the document to the issuer; and

(2) the electronic document when issued contains a statement that it is issued in substitution for the tangible document.

(d) Upon issuance of an electronic document of title in substitution for a tangible document of title in accordance with subsection (c):

(1) the tangible document ceases to have any effect or validity; and

(2) the person that procured issuance of the electronic document warrants to all subsequent persons entitled under the electronic document that the warrantor was a person entitled under the tangible document when the warrantor surrendered possession of the tangible document to the issuer.

Official Comment

Prior Uniform Statutory Provisions: None.

Other relevant law: UNCITRAL Draft Instrument on the Carriage of Goods by Sea Transport Law.

Purpose:

1. This section allows for documents of title issued in one medium to be reissued in another medium. This section applies to both negotiable and nonnegotiable documents. This section sets forth minimum requirements for giving the reissued document effect and validity. The issuer is not required to issue a document in an alternative medium and if the issuer chooses to do so, it may impose additional requirements. Because a document of title imposes obligations on the issuer of the document, it is imperative for the issuer to be the one who issues the substitute document in order for the substitute document to be effective and valid.

2. The request must be made to the issuer by the person entitled to enforce the document of title (Section 7–102(a)(9)) and that person must surrender possession or control of the original document to the issuer. The reissued document must have a notation that it has been issued as a substitute for the original document. These minimum requirements must be met in order to give the substitute document effect and validity. If these minimum requirements are not met for issuance of a substitute document of title, the original document of title continues to be effective and valid. Section 7–402. However, if the minimum requirements imposed by this section are met, in addition to any other requirements that the issuer may impose, the substitute document will be the document that is effective and valid.

3. To protect parties who subsequently take the substitute document of title, the person who procured issuance of the substitute document warrants that it was a person entitled under the original document at the time it surrendered possession or control of the original document to the issuer. This warranty is modeled after the warranty found in Section 4–209.

Cross Reference:

Sections 7–106, 7–402 and 7–601.

Definitional Cross Reference:

"Person entitled to enforce". Section 7–102.

§ 7–106. Control of Electronic Document of Title.

(a) A person has control of an electronic document of title if a system employed for evidencing the transfer of interests in the electronic document reliably establishes that person as the person to which the electronic document was issued or transferred.

(b) A system satisfies subsection (a), and a person ~~is deemed to have~~ has control of an electronic document of title, if the document is created, stored, and ~~assigned~~ transferred in ~~such~~ a manner that:

(1) a single authoritative copy of the document exists which is unique, identifiable, and, except as otherwise provided in paragraphs (4), (5), and (6), unalterable;

(2) the authoritative copy identifies the person asserting control as:

(A) the person to which the document was issued; or

(B)   if the authoritative copy indicates that the document has been transferred, the person to which the document was most recently transferred;

(3)   the authoritative copy is communicated to and maintained by the person asserting control or its designated custodian;

(4)   copies or amendments that add or change an identified ~~assignee~~ transferee of the authoritative copy can be made only with the consent of the person asserting control;

(5)   each copy of the authoritative copy and any copy of a copy is readily identifiable as a copy that is not the authoritative copy; and

(6)   any amendment of the authoritative copy is readily identifiable as authorized or unauthorized.

(c)   A system satisfies subsection (a), and a person has control of an electronic document of title, if an authoritative electronic copy of the document, a record attached to or logically associated with the electronic copy, or a system in which the electronic copy is recorded:

(1)   enables the person readily to identify each electronic copy as either an authoritative copy or a nonauthoritative copy;

(2)   enables the person readily to identify itself in any way, including by name, identifying number, cryptographic key, office, or account number, as the person to which each authoritative electronic copy was issued or transferred; and

(3)   gives the person exclusive power, subject to subsection (d), to:

(A)   prevent others from adding or changing the person to which each authoritative electronic copy has been issued or transferred; and

(B)   transfer control of each authoritative electronic copy.

(d)   Subject to subsection (e), a power is exclusive under subsection (c)(3)(A) and (B) even if:

(1)   the authoritative electronic copy, a record attached to or logically associated with the authoritative electronic copy, or a system in which the authoritative electronic copy is recorded limits the use of the document of title or has a protocol that is programmed to cause a change, including a transfer or loss of control; or

(2)   the power is shared with another person.

(e)   A power of a person is not shared with another person under subsection (d)(2) and the person's power is not exclusive if:

(1)   the person can exercise the power only if the power also is exercised by the other person; and

(2)   the other person:

(A)   can exercise the power without exercise of the power by the person; or

(B)   is the transferor to the person of an interest in the document of title.

(f)   If a person has the powers specified in subsection (c)(3)(A) and (B), the powers are presumed to be exclusive.

(g)   A person has control of an electronic document of title if another person, other than the transferor to the person of an interest in the document:

(1)   has control of the document and acknowledges that it has control on behalf of the person; or

(2)   obtains control of the document after having acknowledged that it will obtain control of the document on behalf of the person.

(h)   A person that has control under this section is not required to acknowledge that it has control on behalf of another person.

(i)   If a person acknowledges that it has or will obtain control on behalf of another person, unless the person otherwise agrees or law other than this article or Article 9 otherwise provides, the person does not owe any duty to the other person and is not required to confirm the acknowledgment to any other person.

As amended in 2022.

Official Comment

Prior Uniform Statutory Provision: Uniform Electronic Transactions Act Section 16.

~~Purpose:~~

1.   The 2022 revision of this section on control of electronic documents of title preserves subsection (a), the general rule, and subsection (b), the "safe harbor" from the pre-2022 section. The minor stylistic revisions are not substantive. The other revisions add a second "safe harbor" in subsection (c), explanatory provisions relating to exclusivity of powers in subsections (d) and (e), a presumption of exclusivity of powers in subsection (f), and a new subsection (g) on control through another person. The requirements for obtaining control under subsection (c) were inspired by Section 12–105 on control of controllable electronic records. See Section 12–105 and Comments.

~~The~~ This section defines "control" for electronic documents of title. Subsections (a) and (b) ~~and derives its rules~~ derive from the Uniform Electronic Transactions Act § Section 16 on transferrable records. Unlike under UETA § Section 16, however, a document of title may be reissued in an alternative medium pursuant to Section 7–105. At any point in time in which a document of title is in electronic form, the control concept of this section is relevant. As under UETA § Section 16, the control concept embodied in this section provides the legal framework for developing systems for electronic documents of title.

2.   Control of an electronic document of title substitutes for the concept of indorsement (for negotiable documents) and possession ~~in the tangible document of title context~~ (for tangible documents of title). See Section 7–501. A person with a tangible document of title delivers the document by voluntarily transferring possession and a person with an electronic document of title delivers the document by voluntarily transferring control. (Delivery is defined in Section 1–201(b)(15)).

3.   Subsection (a) sets forth the general rule that the "system employed for evidencing the transfer of interests in the electronic document reliably establishes that person as the person to which the electronic document was issued or transferred." The key to having a system that satisfies this test is that identity of *the* person to which the document was issued or transferred must be reliably established. Of great importance to the functioning of the control concept under subsection (a), as well as under the safe harbors in subsections (b) and (c), is to be able to demonstrate and identify, at any point in time, *the person* entitled under the electronic document. For example, a carrier may issue an electronic bill of lading by having the required information in a database that is encrypted and accessible by virtue of a password. If the computer system in which the required information is maintained identifies the person as *the* person to which the electronic bill of lading was issued or transferred, that person has control of the electronic document of title. That identification may be by virtue of passwords or other encryption methods. Registry systems may satisfy this test. For example, see the electronic warehouse receipt system established pursuant to 7 C.F.R. Part 735. This Article leaves to the market place the development of sufficient technologies and business practices that will meet the test.

An electronic document of title is evidenced by a record consisting of information stored in an electronic medium. Section 1–201(b)(16A) (defining "electronic") and (31) (defining "record"). For example, a record in a computer database could be an electronic document of title assuming that it otherwise meets the definition of document of title. To the extent that third parties wish to deal in paper mediums, Section 7–105 provides a mechanism for exiting the electronic environment by having the issuer reissue the document of title in a tangible medium. Thus if a person entitled to enforce an electronic document of title causes the information in the record to be printed onto paper without the issuer's involvement in issuing the document of title pursuant to Section 7–105, that paper is not a document of title.

4.   Subsection (a) sets forth the general test for control. ~~Subsection~~ Subsections (b) and (c) ~~sets~~ set forth ~~a~~ safe harbor ~~test~~ tests that, if satisfied, ~~results~~ result in control under the general test in subsection (a). The safe harbor in subsection (b) requires the existence of only one authoritative copy of the document but the safe harbor in subsection (c) allows for either a single authoritative copy or multiple authoritative copies.

~~The test in subsection (b) is also used in Section 9–105 although Section 9–105 does not include the general test of subsection (a).~~ Under subsection (b), at any point in time, a party should be able to identify the single authoritative copy which is unique and identifiable as the authoritative copy. This does not mean that once created ~~that~~ the authoritative copy need be static and never moved or copied from its original location. To the extent that backup systems exist which result in multiple copies, the key to this idea is that at any point in time, the one authoritative copy needs to be unique and identifiable.

~~Parties may not by contract provide that control exists. The test for control is a factual test that depends upon whether the general test in subsection (a) or the safe harbor in subsection (b) is satisfied.~~

5.　Article 7 has historically provided for rights under documents of title and rights of transferees of documents of title as those rights relate to the goods covered by the document. Third parties may possess or have control of documents of title. While misfeasance or negligence in failure to transfer or misdelivery of the document by those third parties may create serious issues, this Article has never dealt with those issues as it relates to tangible documents of title, preferring to leave those issues to the law of contracts, agency and tort law. In the electronic document of title regime, ~~third party~~ registry systems ~~are just beginning to develop. It is very difficult to write rules regulating those third parties without some definitive sense of how the third party registry systems will be structured. Systems that are evolving to date tend to be "closed" systems in which all participants must sign on to the master agreement which provides for rights as against the registry system as well as rights among the members. In those closed systems, the document of title never leaves the system so the parties rely upon the master agreement as to rights against the registry for its failures in dealing with the document. This article contemplates that those "closed" systems will continue to evolve and that the control mechanism in this statute provides a method for the participants in the closed system to achieve the benefits of obtaining control allowed by this article.~~

~~This article also contemplates that parties will evolve open systems where parties need not be subject to a master agreement. In an open system a party that is expecting to obtain rights through an electronic document may not be a party to the master agreement~~ continue to evolve. To the extent that ~~open~~ these systems evolve by use of the control ~~concept~~ concepts contained in this section, the law of contracts, agency, and torts as it applies to the registry's misfeasance or negligence concerning the transfer of control of the electronic document will allocate the risks and liabilities of the parties as that other law now does so for third parties who hold tangible documents and fail to deliver the documents.

6.　The subsection (c) "safe harbor" generally follows Section 12–105 for control of controllable electronic records as well as revised Section 9–105 on control of chattel paper evidenced by electronic records. See generally Sections 9–105 and 12–105 and Comments. It differs from subsection (b), which (as noted above) is based on a "single authoritative copy" of an electronic document of title and so is unavailable when the relevant record is maintained on a blockchain or another distributed ledger. The utility of distributed ledger technology depends on there being multiple authoritative copies of an electronic record. It is important to note that compliance with the conditions for control in subsection (c) also would satisfy the conditions provided in subsection (b). However, subsection (b) was retained out of an abundance of caution and to provide assurances that existing systems for control of electronic documents of title continue to be viable. The conditions for "control" in subsection (c) reflect the functions that possession serves with respect to writings, but in a more accurate and technologically flexible way than do the conditions in subsection (b).

7.　Under subsection (c), to obtain control of an electronic document of title a person must be able to identify each electronic copy as authoritative or nonauthoritative and identify itself as the person to which each authoritative electronic copy has been issued or transferred. As to the means of identification, see Section 12–105, Comment 7. In addition, the person must have the exclusive powers, first, to prevent others from adding or changing an identified person to which each authoritative electronic copy has been issued or transferred and, second, to transfer control of each authoritative copy. However, once it is established that a person has received those powers, subsection (f) provides a presumption of exclusivity. Consequently, a person asserting control need not prove exclusivity in order to make out a *prima facie* case. Application of the presumption will be governed also by Section 1–206 (effects of a presumption under the UCC) and applicable non-UCC law (including rules of procedure and evidence). In addition, subsection (d) contains two qualifications of the term "exclusive" as used in subsection (c)(3). A power can be "exclusive" under subsection (c)(3) even if one or both of these qualifications apply.

Subsection (e) provides that in certain circumstances a power is not shared within the meaning of subsection (d)(2), the relaxation of the exclusivity requirement provided by subsection (d)(2) does not apply, and, consequently, a person's power is not exclusive. Subsection (e) provides that a person does not share an exclusive power with another person if the person can exercise the power only with the other person's cooperation (subsection (e)(1)) but the other person either (i) can exercise of the power without the person's cooperation (subsection (e)(2)(A)) or (ii) is the transferor to the person (transferee) of an interest in the document of title (subsection (e)(2)(B)). It follows that a person to which subsection (e) applies does not have control based on its exclusive powers (although it might have control through another person under subsection (g), discussed below, or if another person having control is acting as the person's agent). As to the rationale for disqualifying a transferee (which includes a secured party in a secured transaction) from the benefit of shared control under subsection (d)(2), as provided in subsection (e)(2)(B), and for examples of the operation of subsection (e) (in the context of the similar provision in Section 12–105), see Section 12–105, Comments 5 and 9.

8. Subsection (g) provides for a person to obtain control through the control of another person. It follows revisions to the corresponding provisions for control of a security entitlement (Section 8–106(d)(3)), control of deposit accounts (Section 9–104(a)(4)), control of authoritative electronic copies of records evidencing chattel paper (Section 9–105(g)), control of electronic money (Section 9–105A(e)), and control of controllable electronic records (Section 12–105(e)). For a brief discussion and background, see Section 12–105, Comment 8. Under subsection (g) for an acknowledgment by another person to be effective to confer control on a person, the other person making the acknowledgment must be one "other than the transferor of an interest in the electronic record" to the person. The rationale for this limitation is discussed in Section 12–105, Comment 9. Control based on an acknowledgment under subsection (g) by another person having control continues only while the other person retains control. This result necessarily follows because such control derives solely from the other person's continued control.

Subsections (h) and (i) derive from Section 9–313(f) and (g). Subsection (h) makes clear that a person that has control under this section has no duty to acknowledge that it has or will obtain control on behalf of another person. Arrangements for a person to acknowledge that it has or will obtain control on behalf of another person are not standardized. Accordingly, subsection (i) leaves to the agreement of the parties and to any other applicable law (other than this Article or Article 9) any duties of a person that does acknowledge that it has or will obtain control on behalf of another person and provides that a person making an acknowledgment is not required to confirm the acknowledgment to another person. For example, subsection (g) would apply to give control to a person, Alpha, when another person, Beta, has control of each authoritative electronic document of title and acknowledges that it has control on behalf of Alpha. However, under subsection (h), Beta is not required to so acknowledge. And under subsection (i), even if Beta does so acknowledge, Beta owes no duty to Alpha, unless Beta agrees or other law so provides, and Beta is not required to confirm its acknowledgment to any other person.

9. This section applies to both negotiable and nonnegotiable electronic documents of title. For negotiable electronic documents of title, "delivery" is a necessary condition for negotiation, and therefore for due negotiation, under Section 7–501(b). "Delivery" of an electronic document of title is defined in Section 1–201(b)(15) as the "voluntary transfer of control." The person in control of a negotiable document, other than pursuant to subsection (g), also is a "holder," as defined in Section 1–201(b)(21)(C). Of course, nonnegotiable documents cannot be negotiated.

A security interest in an electronic document of title, whether negotiable or nonnegotiable, may be perfected by control. Section 9–314(a). But perfection of a security interest by control in a nonnegotiable document does not perfect a security interest in goods covered by the document and does not confer on a secured party or other purchaser the status of a person entitled under the document. See Section 7–102(a)(9) (defining "person entitled under the document") and Comment 6. This distinction arises from the differing rights conferred by a negotiable document and a nonnegotiable document. Both types serve as a receipt for the goods delivered to the bailee and a contract of storage (in the case of a warehouse receipt) or contract of carriage (in the case of a bill of lading). However, a negotiable document is also a representation of the goods themselves, whereas a nonnegotiable document confers only the right to receive possession of the goods. (On perfection of security interests in negotiable documents of title and goods covered by negotiable and nonnegotiable documents of title, see generally Section 9–312(a), (c), and (g) and Comment 7.)

Cross Reference:

Sections 7–105 and 7–501.

Definitional Cross References:

"Delivery". Section 1–201.
"Document of title". Section 1–201.

As amended in 2022.

PART 2

WAREHOUSE RECEIPTS: SPECIAL PROVISIONS

§ 7–201.   Person That May Issue a Warehouse Receipt; Storage Under Bond.

(a)   A warehouse receipt may be issued by any warehouse.

(b)   If goods, including distilled spirits and agricultural commodities, are stored under a statute requiring a bond against withdrawal or a license for the issuance of receipts in the nature of warehouse receipts, a receipt issued for the goods is deemed to be a warehouse receipt even if issued by a person that is the owner of the goods and is not a warehouse.

Official Comment

Prior Uniform Statutory Provision: Former Section 7–201.

Changes: Update for style only.

Purposes:

It is not intended by re-enactment of subsection (a) to repeal any provisions of special licensing or other statutes regulating who may become a warehouse. Limitations on the transfer of the receipts and criminal sanctions for violation of such limitations are not impaired. Section 7–103. Compare Section 7–401(4) on the liability of the issuer in such cases. Subsection (b) covers receipts issued by the owner for whiskey or other goods stored in bonded warehouses under such statutes as 26 U.S.C. Chapter 51.

Cross References:

Sections 7–103, 7–401.

Definitional Cross References:

"Warehouse receipt". Section 1–201.
"Warehouse". Section 7–102.

§ 7–202.   Form of Warehouse Receipt; Effect of Omission.

(a)   A warehouse receipt need not be in any particular form.

(b)   Unless a warehouse receipt provides for each of the following, the warehouse is liable for damages caused to a person injured by its omission:

(1)   a statement of the location of the warehouse facility where the goods are stored;

(2)   the date of issue of the receipt;

(3)   the unique identification code of the receipt;

(4)   a statement whether the goods received will be delivered to the bearer, to a named person, or to a named person or its order;

(5)   the rate of storage and handling charges, unless goods are stored under a field warehousing arrangement, in which case a statement of that fact is sufficient on a nonnegotiable receipt;

(6)   a description of the goods or the packages containing them;

(7)   the signature of the warehouse or its agent;

(8)   if the receipt is issued for goods that the warehouse owns, either solely, jointly, or in common with others, a statement of the fact of that ownership; and

(9)   a statement of the amount of advances made and of liabilities incurred for which the warehouse claims a lien or security interest, unless the precise amount of advances made or liabilities incurred, at the time of the issue of the receipt, is unknown to the warehouse or to its agent that issued the receipt, in which case a statement of the fact that advances have been made or liabilities incurred and the purpose of the advances or liabilities is sufficient.

(c)   A warehouse may insert in its receipt any terms that are not contrary to [the Uniform Commercial Code] and do not impair its obligation of delivery under Section 7–403 or its duty of care under Section 7–204. Any contrary provision is ineffective.

Official Comment

Prior Uniform Statutory Provision: Former Section 7–202.

Changes: Language is updated to accommodate electronic commerce and to reflect modern style.

Purposes:

1.   This section does not displace any particular legislation that requires other terms in a warehouse receipt or that may require a particular form of a warehouse receipt. This section does not require that a warehouse receipt be issued. A warehouse receipt that is issued need not contain any of the terms listed in subsection (b) in order to qualify as a warehouse receipt as long as the receipt falls within the definition of "warehouse receipt" in Article 1. Thus the title has been changed to eliminate the phrase "essential terms" as provided in prior law. The only consequence of a warehouse receipt not containing any term listed in subsection (b) is that a person injured by a term's omission has a right as against the warehouse for harm caused by the omission. Cases, such as *In re Celotex Corp.*, 134 B. R. 993 (Bankr. M.D. Fla. 1991), that held that in order to have a valid warehouse receipt all of the terms listed in this section must be contained in the receipt, are disapproved.

2.   The unique identification code referred to in subsection (b)(3) can include any combination of letters, number, signs, and/or symbols that provide a unique identification. Whether an electronic or tangible warehouse receipt contains a signature will be resolved with the definition of sign in Section 7–102.

Cross References:

Sections 7–103 and 7–401.

Definitional Cross References:

"Bearer". Section 1–201.
"Delivery". Section 1–201.
"Goods". Section 7–102.
"Person". Section 1–201.
"Security interest". Section 1–201.
"Sign". Section 7–102.
"Term". Section 1–201.
"Warehouse receipt". Section 1–201.
"Warehouse". Section 7–102.

§ 7–203.   Liability for Nonreceipt or Misdescription.

A party to or purchaser for value in good faith of a document of title, other than a bill of lading, that relies upon the description of the goods in the document may recover from the issuer damages caused by the nonreceipt or misdescription of the goods, except to the extent that:

(1)   the document conspicuously indicates that the issuer does not know whether all or part of the goods in fact were received or conform to the description, such as a case in which the description is in terms of marks or labels or kind, quantity, or condition, or the receipt or description is qualified by "contents, condition, and quality unknown", "said to contain", or words of similar import, if the indication is true; or

(2)   the party or purchaser otherwise has notice of the nonreceipt or misdescription.

Official Comment

Prior Uniform Statutory Provision: Former Section 7–203.

Changes: Changes to this section are for style only.

Purpose:

This section is a simplified restatement of existing law as to the method by which a bailee may avoid responsibility for the accuracy of descriptions which are made by or in reliance upon information furnished by the depositor. The issuer is liable on documents issued by an agent, contrary to instructions of its principal, without receiving goods. No disclaimer of the latter liability is permitted.

Cross Reference:

Section 7–301.

Definitional Cross References:

"Conspicuous". Section 1–201.
"Document of title". Section 1–201.
"Goods". Section 7–102.
"Good Faith". Section 1–201. [7–102]
"Issuer". Section 7–102.
"Notice". Section 1–202.
"Party". Section 1–201.
"Purchaser". Section 1–201.
"Receipt of goods". Section 2–103.
"Value". Section 1–204.

§ 7–204.   Duty of Care; Contractual Limitation of Warehouse's Liability.

(a) A warehouse is liable for damages for loss of or injury to the goods caused by its failure to exercise care with regard to the goods that a reasonably careful person would exercise under similar circumstances. Unless otherwise agreed, the warehouse is not liable for damages that could not have been avoided by the exercise of that care.

(b) Damages may be limited by a term in the warehouse receipt or storage agreement limiting the amount of liability in case of loss or damage beyond which the warehouse is not liable. Such a limitation is not effective with respect to the warehouse's liability for conversion to its own use. On request of the bailor in a record at the time of signing the storage agreement or within a reasonable time after receipt of the warehouse receipt, the warehouse's liability may be increased on part or all of the goods covered by the storage agreement or the warehouse receipt. In this event, increased rates may be charged based on an increased valuation of the goods.

(c) Reasonable provisions as to the time and manner of presenting claims and commencing actions based on the bailment may be included in the warehouse receipt or storage agreement.

[(d) This section does not modify or repeal [Insert reference to any statute that imposes a higher responsibility upon the warehouse or invalidates a contractual limitation that would be permissible under this Article].]

Legislative Note: Insert in subsection (d) a reference to any statute which imposes a higher responsibility upon the warehouse or invalidates a contractual limitation that would be permissible under this Article. If no such statutes exist, this section should be deleted.

Official Comment

Prior Uniform Statutory Provision: Former Section 7–204.

Changes: Updated to reflect modern, standard commercial practices.

Purposes of Changes:

1. Subsection (a) continues the rule without change from former Section 7–204 on the warehouse's obligation to exercise reasonable care.

2. Former Section 7–204(2) required that the term limiting damages do so by setting forth a specific liability per article or item or of a value per unit of weight. This requirement has been deleted as out of step with modern industry practice. Under subsection (b) a warehouse may limit its liability for damages for loss of or damage to the goods by a term in the warehouse receipt or storage agreement without the term constituting an impermissible disclaimer of the obligation of reasonable care. The parties cannot disclaim by contract the warehouse's obligation of care. Section 1–302. For example, limitations based upon per unit of weight, per package, per occurrence, or per receipt as well as limitations based upon a multiple of the storage rate may be commercially

appropriate. As subsection (d) makes clear, the states or the federal government may supplement this section with more rigid standards of responsibility for some or all bailees.

3.   Former Section 7–204(2) also provided that an increased rate can not be charged if contrary to a tariff. That language has been deleted. If a tariff is required under state or federal law, pursuant to Section 7–103(a), the tariff would control over the rule of this section allowing an increased rate. The provisions of a non-mandatory tariff may be incorporated by reference in the parties' agreement. See Comment 2 to Section 7–103. Subsection (c) deletes the reference to tariffs for the same reason that the reference has been omitted in subsection (b).

4.   As under former Section 7–204(2), subsection (b) provides that a limitation of damages is ineffective if the warehouse has converted the goods to its own use. A mere failure to redeliver the goods is not conversion to the warehouse's own use. See *Adams v. Ryan & Christie Storage, Inc.*, 563 F. Supp. 409 (E.D. Pa. 1983) aff'd 725 F.2d 666 (3rd Cir. 1983). Cases such as *I.C.C. Metals Inc. v. Municipal Warehouse Co.*, 409 N.E.2d 849 (N.Y. Ct. App. 1980) holding that mere failure to redeliver results in a presumption of conversion to the warehouse's own use are disapproved. "Conversion to its own use" is narrower than the idea of conversion generally. Cases such as *Lipman v. Peterson*, 575 P.2d 19 (Kan. 1978) holding to the contrary are disapproved.

5.   Storage agreements commonly establish the contractual relationship between warehouses and depositors who have an on-going relationship. The storage agreement may allow for the movement of goods into and out of a warehouse without the necessity of issuing or amending a warehouse receipt upon each entry or exit of goods from the warehouse.

Cross References:

   Sections 1–302, 7–103, 7–309 and 7–403.

Definitional Cross References:

   "Goods". Section 7–102.
   "Reasonable time". Section 1–204.
   "Sign". Section 7–102.
   "Term". Section 1–201.
   "Value". Section 1–204.
   "Warehouse receipt". Section 1–201.
   "Warehouse". Section 7–102.

§ 7–205.   Title Under Warehouse Receipt Defeated in Certain Cases.

   A buyer in ordinary course of business of fungible goods sold and delivered by a warehouse that is also in the business of buying and selling such goods takes the goods free of any claim under a warehouse receipt even if the receipt is negotiable and has been duly negotiated.

Official Comment

Prior Uniform Statutory Provision: Former Section 7–205.

Changes: Changes for style only.

Purposes:

1.   The typical case covered by this section is that of the warehouse-dealer in grain, and the substantive question at issue is whether in case the warehouse becomes insolvent the receipt holders shall be able to trace and recover grain shipped to farmers and other purchasers from the elevator. This was possible under the old acts, although courts were eager to find estoppels to prevent it. The practical difficulty of tracing fungible grain means that the preservation of this theoretical right adds little to the commercial acceptability of negotiable grain receipts, which really circulate on the credit of the warehouse. Moreover, on default of the warehouse, the receipt holders at least share in what grain remains, whereas retaking the grain from a good faith cash purchaser reduces the purchaser completely to the status of general creditor in a situation where there was very little the purchaser could do to guard against the loss. Compare 15 U.S.C. Section 714p enacted in 1955.

2.   This provision applies to both negotiable and nonnegotiable warehouse receipts. The concept of due negotiation is provided for in 7–501. The definition of "buyer in ordinary course" is in Article 1 and provides, among other things, that a buyer must either have possession or a right to obtain the goods under Article 2 in order to be a buyer in ordinary course. This section requires actual delivery of the fungible goods to the buyer in ordinary course. Delivery requires voluntary transfer of possession of the fungible goods to the buyer. See amended Section

2–103 [*2003 amendments to Article 2, withdrawn in 2011*]. This section is not satisfied by the delivery of the document of title to the buyer in ordinary course.

Cross References:

>   Sections 2–403 and 9–320.

Definitional Cross References:

>   "Buyer in ordinary course of business". Section 1–201.
>   "Delivery". Section 1–201.
>   "Duly negotiate". Section 7–501.
>   "Fungible" goods. Section 1–201.
>   "Goods". Section 7–102.
>   "Value". Section 1–204.
>   "Warehouse receipt". Section 1–201.
>   "Warehouse". Section 7–102.

§ 7–206.   Termination of Storage at Warehouse's Option.

(a)   A warehouse, by giving notice to the person on whose account the goods are held and any other person known to claim an interest in the goods, may require payment of any charges and removal of the goods from the warehouse at the termination of the period of storage fixed by the document of title or, if a period is not fixed, within a stated period not less than 30 days after the warehouse gives notice. If the goods are not removed before the date specified in the notice, the warehouse may sell them pursuant to Section 7–210.

(b)   If a warehouse in good faith believes that goods are about to deteriorate or decline in value to less than the amount of its lien within the time provided in subsection (a) and Section 7–210, the warehouse may specify in the notice given under subsection (a) any reasonable shorter time for removal of the goods and, if the goods are not removed, may sell them at public sale held not less than one week after a single advertisement or posting.

(c)   If, as a result of a quality or condition of the goods of which the warehouse did not have notice at the time of deposit, the goods are a hazard to other property, the warehouse facilities, or other persons, the warehouse may sell the goods at public or private sale without advertisement or posting on reasonable notification to all persons known to claim an interest in the goods. If the warehouse, after a reasonable effort, is unable to sell the goods, it may dispose of them in any lawful manner and does not incur liability by reason of that disposition.

(d)   A warehouse shall deliver the goods to any person entitled to them under this article upon due demand made at any time before sale or other disposition under this section.

(e)   A warehouse may satisfy its lien from the proceeds of any sale or disposition under this section but shall hold the balance for delivery on the demand of any person to which the warehouse would have been bound to deliver the goods.

Official Comment

Prior Uniform Statutory Provision: Former Section 7–206.

Changes: Changes for style.

Purposes:

1.   This section provides for three situations in which the warehouse may terminate storage for reasons other then [*should be "than"*] enforcement of its lien as permitted by Section 7–210. Most warehousing is for an indefinite term, the bailor being entitled to delivery on reasonable demand. It is necessary to define the warehouse's power to terminate the bailment, since it would be commercially intolerable to allow warehouses to order removal of the goods on short notice. The thirty day period provided where the document does not carry its own period of termination corresponds to commercial practice of computing rates on a monthly basis. The right to terminate under subsection (a) includes a right to require payment of "any charges", but does not depend on the existence of unpaid charges.

2. In permitting expeditious disposition of perishable and hazardous goods the pre-Code Uniform Warehouse Receipts Act, Section 34, made no distinction between cases where the warehouse knowingly undertook to store such goods and cases where the goods were discovered to be of that character subsequent to storage. The former situation presents no such emergency as justifies the summary power of removal and sale. Subsections (b) and (c) distinguish between the two situations. The reason of this section should apply if the goods become hazardous during the course of storage. The process for selling the goods described in Section 7–210 governs the sale of goods under this section except as provided in subsections (b) and (c) for the situations described in those subsections respectively.

3. Protection of its lien is the only interest which the warehouse has to justify summary sale of perishable goods which are not hazardous. This same interest must be recognized when the stored goods, although not perishable, decline in market value to a point which threatens the warehouse's security.

4. The right to order removal of stored goods is subject to provisions of the public warehousing laws of some states forbidding warehouses from discriminating among customers. Nor does the section relieve the warehouse of any obligation under the state laws to secure the approval of a public official before disposing of deteriorating goods. Such regulatory statutes and the regulations under them remain in force and operative. Section 7–103.

Cross References:

Sections 7–103 and 7–403.

Definitional Cross References:

"Delivery". Section 1–201.
"Document of title". Section 1–102.
"Good faith". Section 1–201 [7–102].
"Goods". Section 7–102.
"Notice". Section 1–202.
"Notification". Section 1–202.
"Person". Section 1–201.
"Reasonable time". Section 1–205.
"Value". Section 1–204.
"Warehouse". Section 7–102.

§ 7–207. Goods Must Be Kept Separate; Fungible Goods.

(a) Unless the warehouse receipt provides otherwise, a warehouse shall keep separate the goods covered by each receipt so as to permit at all times identification and delivery of those goods. However, different lots of fungible goods may be commingled.

(b) If different lots of fungible goods are commingled, the goods are owned in common by the persons entitled thereto and the warehouse is severally liable to each owner for that owner's share. If, because of overissue, a mass of fungible goods is insufficient to meet all the receipts the warehouse has issued against it, the persons entitled include all holders to which overissued receipts have been duly negotiated.

Official Comment

Prior Uniform Statutory Provision: Former Section 7–207.

Changes: Changes for style only.

Purposes:

No change of substance is made from former Section 7–207. Holders to whom overissued receipts have been duly negotiated shall share in a mass of fungible goods. Where individual ownership interests are merged into claims on a common fund, as is necessarily the case with fungible goods, there is no policy reason for discriminating between successive purchasers of similar claims.

Definitional Cross References:

"Delivery". Section 1–201.
"Duly negotiate". Section 7–501.
"Fungible goods". Section 1–201.

"Goods". Section 7–102.
"Holder". Section 1–201.
"Person". Section 1–201.
"Warehouse receipt". Section 1–201.
"Warehouse". Section 7–102.

§ 7–208.   Altered Warehouse Receipts.

If a blank in a negotiable tangible warehouse receipt has been filled in without authority, a good-faith purchaser for value and without notice of the lack of authority may treat the insertion as authorized. Any other unauthorized alteration leaves any tangible or electronic warehouse receipt enforceable against the issuer according to its original tenor.

Official Comment

Prior Uniform Statutory Provision: Former Section 7–208.

Changes: To accommodate electronic documents of title.

Purpose:

1.   The execution of tangible warehouse receipts in blank is a dangerous practice. As between the issuer and an innocent purchaser the risks should clearly fall on the former. The purchaser must have purchased the tangible negotiable warehouse receipt in good faith and for value to be protected under the rule of the first sentence which is a limited exception to the general rule in the second sentence. Electronic document of title systems should have protection against unauthorized access and unauthorized changes. See 7–106. Thus the protection for good faith purchasers found in the first sentence is not necessary in the context of electronic documents.

2.   Under the second sentence of this section, an unauthorized alteration whether made with or without fraudulent intent does not relieve the issuer of its liability on the warehouse receipt as originally executed. The unauthorized alteration itself is of course ineffective against the warehouse. The rule stated in the second sentence applies to both tangible and electronic warehouse receipts.

Definitional Cross References:

"Good faith". Section 1–201 [7–102].
"Issuer". Section 7–102.
"Notice". Section 1–202.
"Purchaser". Section 1–201.
"Value". Section 1–204.
"Warehouse receipt". Section 1–201.

§ 7–209.   Lien of Warehouse.

(a)   A warehouse has a lien against the bailor on the goods covered by a warehouse receipt or storage agreement or on the proceeds thereof in its possession for charges for storage or transportation, including demurrage and terminal charges, insurance, labor, or other charges, present or future, in relation to the goods, and for expenses necessary for preservation of the goods or reasonably incurred in their sale pursuant to law. If the person on whose account the goods are held is liable for similar charges or expenses in relation to other goods whenever deposited and it is stated in the warehouse receipt or storage agreement that a lien is claimed for charges and expenses in relation to other goods, the warehouse also has a lien against the goods covered by the warehouse receipt or storage agreement or on the proceeds thereof in its possession for those charges and expenses, whether or not the other goods have been delivered by the warehouse. However, as against a person to which a negotiable warehouse receipt is duly negotiated, a warehouse's lien is limited to charges in an amount or at a rate specified in the warehouse receipt or, if no charges are so specified, to a reasonable charge for storage of the specific goods covered by the receipt subsequent to the date of the receipt.

(b)   A warehouse may also reserve a security interest against the bailor for the maximum amount specified on the receipt for charges other than those specified in subsection (a), such as for money advanced and interest. The security interest is governed by Article 9.

(c)   A warehouse's lien for charges and expenses under subsection (a) or a security interest under subsection (b) is also effective against any person that so entrusted the bailor with possession of the goods that a pledge of them by the bailor to a good-faith purchaser for value would have been valid. However, the lien or security interest is not effective against a person that before issuance of a document of title had a legal interest or a perfected security interest in the goods and that did not:

(1)   deliver or entrust the goods or any document of title covering the goods to the bailor or the bailor's nominee with:

  (A)   actual or apparent authority to ship, store, or sell;

  (B)   power to obtain delivery under Section 7–403; or

  (C)   power of disposition under Sections 2–403, 2A–304(2), 2A–305(2), 9–320, or 9–321(c) or other statute or rule of law; or

(2)   acquiesce in the procurement by the bailor or its nominee of any document.

(d)   A warehouse's lien on household goods for charges and expenses in relation to the goods under subsection (a) is also effective against all persons if the depositor was the legal possessor of the goods at the time of deposit. In this subsection, "household goods" means furniture, furnishings, or personal effects used by the depositor in a dwelling.

(e)   A warehouse loses its lien on any goods that it voluntarily delivers or unjustifiably refuses to deliver.

Official Comment

Prior Uniform Statutory Provision: Former Sections 7–209 and 7–503.

Changes: Expanded to recognize warehouse lien when a warehouse receipt is not issued but goods are covered by a storage agreement.

Purposes:

1.   Subsection (a) defines the warehouse's statutory lien. Other than allowing a warehouse to claim a lien under this section when there is a storage agreement and not a warehouse receipt, this section remains unchanged in substance from former Section 7–209(1). Under the first sentence, a specific lien attaches automatically without express notation on the receipt or storage agreement with regard to goods stored under the receipt or the storage agreement. That lien is limited to the usual charges arising out of a storage transaction.

Example 1:   Bailor stored goods with a warehouse and the warehouse issued a warehouse receipt. A lien against those goods arose as set forth in subsection (a), the first sentence, for the charges for storage and the other expenses of those goods. The warehouse may enforce its lien under Section 7–210 as against the bailor. Whether the warehouse receipt is negotiable or nonnegotiable is not important to the warehouse's rights as against the bailor.

Under the second sentence, by notation on the receipt or storage agreement, the lien can be made a general lien extending to like charges in relation to other goods. Both the specific lien and general lien are as to goods in the possession of the warehouse and extend to proceeds from the goods as long as the proceeds are in the possession of the warehouse. The same rules apply whether the receipt is negotiable or non-negotiable.

Example 2:   Bailor stored goods (lot A) with a warehouse and the warehouse issued a warehouse receipt for those goods. In the warehouse receipt it is stated that the warehouse will also have a lien on goods covered by the warehouse receipt for storage charges and the other expenses for any other goods that are stored with the warehouse by the bailor. The statement about the lien on other goods does not specify an amount or a rate. Bailor then stored other goods (lot B) with the warehouse. Under subsection (a), first sentence, the warehouse has a lien on the specific goods (lot A) covered by the warehouse receipt. Under subsection (a), second sentence, the warehouse has a lien on the goods in lot A for the storage charges and the other expenses arising from the goods in lot B. That lien is enforceable as against the bailor regardless of whether the receipt is negotiable or nonnegotiable.

Under the third sentence, if the warehouse receipt is negotiable, the lien as against a holder of that receipt by due negotiation is limited to the amount or rate specified on the receipt for the specific lien or the general lien, or, if none is specified, to a reasonable charge for storage of the specific goods covered by the receipt for storage after the date of the receipt.

Example 3:   Same facts as Example 1 except that the warehouse receipt is negotiable and has been duly negotiated (Section 7–501) to a person other than the bailor. Under the last sentence of subsection (a), the warehouse may enforce its lien against the bailor's goods stored in the warehouse as against the person to whom the negotiable warehouse receipt has been duly negotiated. Section 7–502. That lien is limited to the charges or rates specified in the receipt or a reasonable charge for storage as stated in the last sentence of subsection (a).

Example 4:   Same facts as Example 2 except that the warehouse receipt is negotiable and has been duly negotiated (Section 7–501) to a person other than the bailor. Under the last sentence of subsection (a), the lien on lot A goods for the storage charges and the other expenses arising from storage of lot B goods is not enforceable as against the person to whom the receipt has been duly negotiated. Without a statement of a specified amount or rate for the general lien, the warehouse's general lien is not enforceable as against the person to whom the negotiable document has been duly negotiated. However, the warehouse lien for charges and expenses related to storage of lot A goods is still enforceable as against the person to whom the receipt was duly negotiated.

Example 5:   Same facts as Examples 2 and 4 except the warehouse had stated on the negotiable warehouse receipt a specified amount or rate for the general lien on other goods (lot B). Under the last sentence of subsection (a), the general lien on lot A goods for the storage charges and the other expenses arising from storage of lot B goods is enforceable as against the person to whom the receipt has been duly negotiated.

2.   Subsection (b) provides for a security interest based upon agreement. Such a security interest arises out of relations between the parties other than bailment for storage or transportation, as where the bailee assumes the role of financier or performs a manufacturing operation, extending credit in reliance upon the goods covered by the receipt. Such a security interest is not a statutory lien. Compare Sections 9–109 and 9–333. It is governed in all respects by Article 9, except that subsection (b) requires that the receipt specify a maximum amount and limits the security interest to the amount specified. A warehouse could also take a security interest to secure its charges for storage and the other expenses listed in subsection (a) to protect these claims upon the loss of the statutory possessory warehouse lien if the warehouse loses possession of the goods as provided in subsection (e).

Example 6:   Bailor stores goods with a warehouse and the warehouse issues a warehouse receipt that states that the warehouse is taking a security interest in the bailed goods for charges of storage, expenses, for money advanced, for manufacturing services rendered, and all other obligations that the bailor may owe the warehouse. That is a security interest covered in all respects by Article 9. Subsection (b). As allowed by this section, a warehouse may rely upon its statutory possessory lien to protect its charges for storage and the other expenses related to storage. For those storage charges covered by the statutory possessory lien, the warehouse is not required to use a security interest under subsection (b).

3.   Subsections (a) and (b) validate the lien and security interest "against the bailor." Under basic principles of derivative rights as provided in Section 7–504, the warehouse lien is also valid as against parties who obtain their rights from the bailor except as otherwise provided in subsection (a), third sentence, or subsection (c).

Example 7:   Bailor stores goods with a warehouse and the warehouse issues a nonnegotiable warehouse receipt that also claims a general lien in other goods stored with the warehouse. A lien on the bailed goods for the charges for storage and the other expenses arises under subsection (a). Bailor notifies the warehouse that the goods have been sold to Buyer and the bailee acknowledges that fact to the Buyer. Section 2–503. The warehouse lien for storage of those goods is effective against Buyer for both the specific lien and the general lien. Section 7–504.

Example 8:   Bailor stores goods with a warehouse and the warehouse issues a nonnegotiable warehouse receipt. A lien on the bailed goods for the charges for storage and the other expenses arises under subsection (a). Bailor grants a security interest in the goods while the goods are in the warehouse's possession to Secured Party (SP) who properly perfects a security interest in the goods. See Revised 9–312(d). The warehouse lien is superior in priority over SP's security interest. See Revised 9–203(b)(2) (debtor can grant a security interest to the extent of debtor's rights in the collateral).

Example 9:   Bailor stores goods with a warehouse and the warehouse issues a negotiable warehouse receipt. A lien on the bailed goods for the charges for storage and the other expenses arises under subsection (a). Bailor grants a security interest in the negotiable document to SP. SP properly perfects its interest in the negotiable document by taking possession through a "due negotiation." Revised 9–312(c). SP's security interest is subordinate to the warehouse lien. Section 7–209(a), third sentence. Given that bailor's rights are subject to the warehouse lien, the bailor cannot grant to the SP greater rights than the bailor has under Section 9–203(b)(2), perfection of the security interest in the negotiable document and the goods covered by the document through SP's filing of a financing statement should not give a different result.

As against third parties who have interests in the goods prior to the storage with the warehouse, subsection (c) continues the rule under the prior uniform statutory provision that to validate the lien or security interest of the warehouse, the owner must have entrusted the goods to the depositor, and that the circumstances must be such that a pledge by the depositor to a good faith purchaser for value would have been valid. Thus the owner's interest will not be subjected to a lien or security interest arising out of a deposit of its goods by a thief. The warehouse may be protected because of the actual, implied or apparent authority of the depositor, because of a Factor's Act, or because of other circumstances which would protect a bona fide pledgee, unless those circumstances are denied effect under the second sentence of subsection (c). The language of Section 7–503 is brought into subsection (c) for purposes of clarity. The comments to Section 7–503 are helpful in interpreting delivery, entrustment or acquiescence.

Where the third party is the holder of a security interest, obtained prior to the issuance of a negotiable warehouse receipt, the rights of the warehouse depend on the priority given to a hypothetical bona fide pledgee by Article 9, particularly Section 9–322. Thus the special priority granted to statutory liens by Section 9–333 does not apply to liens under subsection (a) of this section, since subsection (c), second sentence, "expressly provides otherwise" within the meaning of Section 9–333.

As to household goods, however, subsection (d) makes the warehouse's lien "for charges and expenses in relation to the goods" effective against all persons if the depositor was the legal possessor. The purpose of the exception is to permit the warehouse to accept household goods for storage in sole reliance on the value of the goods themselves, especially in situations of family emergency.

Example 10: Bailor grants a perfected security interest in the goods to SP prior to storage of the goods with the warehouse. Bailor then stores goods with the warehouse and the warehouse issues a warehouse receipt for the goods. A warehouse lien on the bailed goods for the charges for storage or other expenses arises under subsection (a). The warehouse lien is not effective as against SP unless SP entrusted the goods to the bailor with actual or apparent authority to ship store, or sell the goods or with power of disposition under subsection (c)(1) or acquiesced in the bailor's procurement of a document of title under subsection (c)(2). This result obtains whether the receipt is negotiable or nonnegotiable.

Example 11: Sheriff who had lawfully repossessed household goods in an eviction action stored the goods with a warehouse. A lien on the bailed goods arises under subsection (a). The lien is effective as against the owner of the goods. Subsection (d).

4. As under previous law, this section creates a statutory possessory lien in favor of the warehouse on the goods stored with the warehouse or on the proceeds of the goods. The warehouse loses its lien if it loses possession of the goods or the proceeds. Subsection (e).

5. Where goods have been stored under a non-negotiable warehouse receipt and are sold by the person to whom the receipt has been issued, frequently the goods are not withdrawn by the new owner. The obligations of the seller of the goods in this situation are set forth in Section 2–503(4) on tender of delivery and include procurement of an acknowledgment by the bailee of the buyer's right to possession of the goods. If a new receipt is requested, such an acknowledgment can be withheld until storage charges have been paid or provided for. The statutory lien for charges on the goods sold, granted by the first sentence of subsection (a), continues valid unless the bailee gives it up. See Section 7–403. But once a new receipt is issued to the buyer, the buyer becomes "the person on whose account the goods are held" under the second sentence of subsection (a); unless the buyer undertakes liability for charges in relation to other goods stored by the seller, there is no general lien against the buyer for such charges. Of course, the bailee may preserve the general lien in such a case either by an arrangement by which the buyer "is liable for" such charges, or by reserving a security interest under subsection (b).

6. A possessory warehouse lien arises as provided under subsection (a) if the parties to the bailment have a storage agreement or a warehouse receipt is issued. In the modern warehouse, the bailor and the bailee may enter into a master contract governing the bailment with the bailee and bailor keeping track of the goods stored pursuant to the master contract by notation on their respective books and records and the parties send notification via electronic communication as to what goods are covered by the master contract. Warehouse receipts are not issued. See Comment 4 to Section 7–204. There is no particular form for a warehouse receipt and failure to contain any of the terms listed in Section 7–202 does not deprive the warehouse of its lien that arises under subsection (a). See the comment to Section 7–202.

Cross References:

> Point 1: Sections 7–501 and 7–502.
> Point 2: Sections 9–109 and 9–333.
> Point 3: Sections 2–503, 7–503, 7–504, 9–203, 9–312, and 9–322.
> Point 4: Sections 2–503, 7–501, 7–502, 7–504, 9–312, 9–331, 9–333, 9–401.
> Point 5: Sections 2–503 and 7–403.
> Point 6: Sections 7–202 and 7–204.

Definitional Cross References:

> "Delivery". Section 1–201.
> "Document of Title". Section 1–201
> "Goods". Section 7–102.
> "Money". Section 1–201.
> "Person". Section 1–201.
> "Purchaser". Section 1–201.
> "Right". Section 1–201.
> "Security interest". Section 1–201.
> "Value". Section 1–204.
> "Warehouse receipt". Section 1–201.
> "Warehouse". Section 7–102.

§ 7–210.   Enforcement of Warehouse's Lien.

(a)   Except as otherwise provided in subsection (b), a warehouse's lien may be enforced by public or private sale of the goods, in bulk or in packages, at any time or place and on any terms that are commercially reasonable, after notifying all persons known to claim an interest in the goods. The notification must include a statement of the amount due, the nature of the proposed sale, and the time and place of any public sale. The fact that a better price could have been obtained by a sale at a different time or in a method different from that selected by the warehouse is not of itself sufficient to establish that the sale was not made in a commercially reasonable manner. The warehouse sells in a commercially reasonable manner if the warehouse sells the goods in the usual manner in any recognized market therefor, sells at the price current in that market at the time of the sale, or otherwise sells in conformity with commercially reasonable practices among dealers in the type of goods sold. A sale of more goods than apparently necessary to be offered to ensure satisfaction of the obligation is not commercially reasonable, except in cases covered by the preceding sentence.

(b)   A warehouse may enforce its lien on goods, other than goods stored by a merchant in the course of its business, only if the following requirements are satisfied:

(1)   All persons known to claim an interest in the goods must be notified.

(2)   The notification must include an itemized statement of the claim, a description of the goods subject to the lien, a demand for payment within a specified time not less than 10 days after receipt of the notification, and a conspicuous statement that unless the claim is paid within that time the goods will be advertised for sale and sold by auction at a specified time and place.

(3)   The sale must conform to the terms of the notification.

(4)   The sale must be held at the nearest suitable place to where the goods are held or stored.

(5)   After the expiration of the time given in the notification, an advertisement of the sale must be published once a week for two weeks consecutively in a newspaper of general circulation where the sale is to be held. The advertisement must include a description of the goods, the name of the person on whose account the goods are being held, and the time and place of the sale. The sale must take place at least 15 days after the first publication. If there is no newspaper of general circulation where the sale is to be held, the advertisement must be posted at least 10 days before the sale in not fewer than six conspicuous places in the neighborhood of the proposed sale.

(c)   Before any sale pursuant to this section, any person claiming a right in the goods may pay the amount necessary to satisfy the lien and the reasonable expenses incurred in complying with this section. In that event, the goods may not be sold but must be retained by the warehouse subject to the terms of the receipt and this article.

(d)   A warehouse may buy at any public sale held pursuant to this section.

(e)   A purchaser in good faith of goods sold to enforce a warehouse's lien takes the goods free of any rights of persons against which the lien was valid, despite the warehouse's noncompliance with this section.

(f)   A warehouse may satisfy its lien from the proceeds of any sale pursuant to this section but shall hold the balance, if any, for delivery on demand to any person to which the warehouse would have been bound to deliver the goods.

(g)   The rights provided by this section are in addition to all other rights allowed by law to a creditor against a debtor.

(h)   If a lien is on goods stored by a merchant in the course of its business, the lien may be enforced in accordance with subsection (a) or (b).

(i)   A warehouse is liable for damages caused by failure to comply with the requirements for sale under this section and, in case of willful violation, is liable for conversion.

Official Comment

Prior Uniform Statutory Provision: Former Section 7–210.

Changes: Update to accommodate electronic commerce and for style.

Purposes:

1.   Subsection (a) makes "commercial reasonableness" the standard for foreclosure proceedings in all cases except non-commercial storage with a warehouse. The latter category embraces principally storage of household goods by private owners; and for such cases the detailed provisions as to notification, publication and public sale are retained in subsection (b) with one change. The requirement in former Section 7–210(2)(b) that the notification must be sent in person or by registered or certified mail has been deleted. Notification may be sent by any reasonable means as provided in Section 1–202. The swifter, more flexible procedure of subsection (a) is appropriate to commercial storage. Compare seller's power of resale on breach by buyer under the provisions of the Article on Sales (Section 2–706). Commercial reasonableness is a flexible concept that allows for a wide variety of actions to satisfy the rule of this section, including electronic means of posting and sale.

2.   The provisions of subsections (d) and (e) permitting the bailee to bid at public sales and confirming the title of purchasers at foreclosure sales are designed to secure more bidding and better prices and remain unchanged from former Section 7–210.

3.   A warehouses may have recourse to an interpleader action in appropriate circumstances. See Section 7–603.

4.   If a warehouse has both a warehouse lien and a security interest, the warehouse may enforce both the lien and the security interest simultaneously by using the procedures of Article 9. Section 7–210 adopts as its touchstone "commercial reasonableness" for the enforcement of a warehouse lien. Following the procedures of Article 9 satisfies "commercial reasonableness."

Cross Reference:

Sections 2–706, 7–403, 7–603 and Part 6 of Article 9.

Definitional Cross References:

"Bill of lading". Section 1–201.
"Conspicuous". Section 1–201.
"Creditor". Section 1–201.
"Delivery". Section 1–201.
"Document of title". Section 1–201.
"Good faith". Section 1–201 [7–102].
"Goods". Section 7–102.

"Notification". Section 1–202.
"Notifies". Section 1–202.
"Person". Section 1–201.
"Purchaser". Section 1–201.
"Rights". Section 1–201.
"Term". Section 1–201.
"Warehouse". Section 7–102.

PART 3

BILLS OF LADING: SPECIAL PROVISIONS

§ 7–301.   Liability for Nonreceipt or Misdescription; "Said to Contain"; "Shipper's Weight, Load, and Count"; Improper Handling.

(a)   A consignee of a nonnegotiable bill of lading which has given value in good faith, or a holder to which a negotiable bill has been duly negotiated, relying upon the description of the goods in the bill or upon the date shown in the bill, may recover from the issuer damages caused by the misdating of the bill or the nonreceipt or misdescription of the goods, except to the extent that the bill indicates that the issuer does not know whether any part or all of the goods in fact were received or conform to the description, such as in a case in which the description is in terms of marks or labels or kind, quantity, or condition or the receipt or description is qualified by "contents or condition of contents of packages unknown", "said to contain", "shipper's weight, load, and count," or words of similar import, if that indication is true.

(b)   If goods are loaded by the issuer of a bill of lading;

(1)   the issuer shall count the packages of goods if shipped in packages and ascertain the kind and quantity if shipped in bulk; and

(2)   words such as "shipper's weight, load, and count," or words of similar import indicating that the description was made by the shipper are ineffective except as to goods concealed in packages.

(c)   If bulk goods are loaded by a shipper that makes available to the issuer of a bill of lading adequate facilities for weighing those goods, the issuer shall ascertain the kind and quantity within a reasonable time after receiving the shipper's request in a record to do so. In that case, "shipper's weight" or words of similar import are ineffective.

(d)   The issuer of a bill of lading, by including in the bill the words "shipper's weight, load, and count," or words of similar import, may indicate that the goods were loaded by the shipper, and, if that statement is true, the issuer is not liable for damages caused by the improper loading. However, omission of such words does not imply liability for damages caused by improper loading.

(e)   A shipper guarantees to an issuer the accuracy at the time of shipment of the description, marks, labels, number, kind, quantity, condition, and weight, as furnished by the shipper, and the shipper shall indemnify the issuer against damage caused by inaccuracies in those particulars. This right of indemnity does not limit the issuer's responsibility or liability under the contract of carriage to any person other than the shipper.

Official Comment

Prior Uniform Statutory Provision: Former Section 7–301.

Changes: Changes for clarity, style and to recognize deregulation in the transportation industry.

Purposes:

1.   This section continues the rules from former Section 7–301 with one substantive change. The obligations of the issuer of the bill of lading under former subsections (2) and (3) were limited to issuers who were common carriers. Subsections (b) and (c) apply the same rules to all issuers not just common carriers. This section is compatible with the policies stated in the federal Bills of Lading Act, 49 U.S.C. § 80113 (2000).

2.   The language of the pre-Code Uniform Bills of Lading Act suggested that a carrier is ordinarily liable for damage caused by improper loading, but may relieve itself of liability by disclosing on the bill that shipper

actually loaded. A more accurate statement of the law is that the carrier is not liable for losses caused by act or default of the shipper, which would include improper loading. *D. H. Overmyer Co. v. Nelson Brantley Glass Co.*, 168 S.E.2d 176 (Ga. Ct. App. 1969). There was some question whether under pre-Code law a carrier was liable even to a good faith purchaser of a negotiable bill for such losses, if the shipper's faulty loading in fact caused the loss. Subsection (d) permits the carrier to bar, by disclosure of shipper's loading, liability to a good faith purchaser. There is no implication that decisions such as *Modern Tool Corp. v. Pennsylvania R. Co.*, 100 F.Supp. 595 (D.N.J. 1951), are disapproved.

3.   This section is a restatement of existing law as to the method by which a bailee may avoid responsibility for the accuracy of descriptions which are made by or in reliance upon information furnished by the depositor or shipper. The wording in this section—"contents or condition of contents of packages unknown" or "shipper's weight, load and count"—to indicate that the shipper loaded the goods or that the carrier does not know the description, condition, or contents of the loaded packages continues to be appropriate as commonly understood in the transportation industry. The reasons for this wording are as important in 2002 as when the prior section initially was approved. The issuer is liable on documents issued by an agent, contrary to instructions of his principal, without receiving goods. No disclaimer of this liability is permitted since it is not a matter either of the care of the goods or their description.

4.   The shipper's erroneous report to the carrier concerning the goods may cause damage to the carrier. Subsection (e) therefore provides appropriate indemnity.

5.   The word "freight" in the former Section 7–301 has been changed to "goods" to conform to international and domestic land transport usage in which "freight" means the price paid for carriage of the goods and not the goods themselves. Hence, changing the word "freight" to the word "goods" is a clarifying change that fits both international and domestic practice.

Cross References:

Sections 7–203, 7–309 and 7–501.

Definitional Cross References:

"Bill of lading". Section 1–201.
"Consignee". Section 7–102.
"Document of title". Section 1–201.
"Duly negotiate". Section 7–501.
"Good faith". Section 1–201. [7–102].
"Goods". Section 7–102.
"Holder". Section 1–201.
"Issuer". Section 7–102.
"Notice". Section 1–202.
"Party". Section 1–201.
"Purchaser." Section 1–201.
"Receipt of goods". Section 2–103.
"Value". Section 1–204.

§ 7–302.   Through Bills of Lading and Similar Documents of Title.

(a)   The issuer of a through bill of lading, or other document of title embodying an undertaking to be performed in part by a person acting as its agent or by a performing carrier, is liable to any person entitled to recover on the bill or other document for any breach by the other person or the performing carrier of its obligation under the bill or other document. However, to the extent that the bill or other document covers an undertaking to be performed overseas or in territory not contiguous to the continental United States or an undertaking including matters other than transportation, this liability for breach by the other person or the performing carrier may be varied by agreement of the parties.

(b)   If goods covered by a through bill of lading or other document of title embodying an undertaking to be performed in part by a person other than the issuer are received by that person, the person is subject, with respect to its own performance while the goods are in its possession, to the obligation of the issuer. The person's obligation is discharged by delivery of the goods to another person pursuant to the bill or other document and does not include liability for breach by any other person or by the issuer.

(c)   The issuer of a through bill of lading or other document of title described in subsection (a) is entitled to recover from the performing carrier, or other person in possession of the goods when the breach of the obligation under the bill or other document occurred:

    (1)   the amount it may be required to pay to any person entitled to recover on the bill or other document for the breach, as may be evidenced by any receipt, judgment, or transcript of judgment; and

    (2)   the amount of any expense reasonably incurred by the issuer in defending any action commenced by any person entitled to recover on the bill or other document for the breach.

Official Comment

Prior Uniform Statutory Provision: Former Section 7–302.

Changes: To conform to current terminology and for style.

Purposes:

1.   This section continues the rules from former Section 7–302 without substantive change. The term "performing carrier" is substituted for the term "connecting carrier" to conform the terminology of this section with terminology used in recent UNCITRAL and OAS proposals concerning transportation and through bills of lading. This change in terminology is not substantive. This section is compatible with liability on carriers under federal law. See 49 U.S.C. §§ 11706, 14706 and 15906.

The purpose of this section is to subject the initial carrier under a through bill to suit for breach of the contract of carriage by any performing carrier and to make it clear that any such performing carrier holds the goods on terms which are defined by the document of title even though such performing carrier did not issue the document. Since the performing carrier does hold the goods on the terms of the document, it must honor a proper demand for delivery or a diversion order just as the original bailee would have to. Similarly it has the benefits of the excuses for non-delivery and limitations of liability provided for the original bailee who issued the bill. Unlike the original bailee-issuer, the performing carrier's responsibility is limited to the period while the goods are in its possession. The section does not impose any obligation to issue through bills.

2.   The reference to documents other than through bills looks to the possibility that multi-purpose documents may come into use, e.g., combination warehouse receipts and bills of lading. As electronic documents of title come into common usage, storage documents (e.g. warehouse receipts) and transportation documents (e.g. bills of lading) may merge seamlessly into one electronic document that can serve both the storage and transportation segments of the movement of goods.

3.   Under subsection (a) the issuer of a through bill of lading may become liable for the fault of another person. Subsection (c) gives the issuer appropriate rights of recourse.

4.   Despite the broad language of subsection (a), Section 7–302 is subject to preemption by federal laws and treaties. Section 7–103. The precise scope of federal preemption in the transportation sector is a question determined under federal law.

Cross reference:

Section 7–103.

Definitional Cross References:

"Agreement". Section 1–201.
"Bailee". Section 7–102.
"Bill of lading". Section 1–201.
"Delivery". Section 1–201.
"Document of title". Section 1–201.
"Goods". Section 7–102.
"Issuer". Section 7–102.
"Party". Section 1–201.
"Person". Section 1–201.

§ 7–303. Diversion; Reconsignment; Change of Instructions.

(a) Unless the bill of lading otherwise provides, a carrier may deliver the goods to a person or destination other than that stated in the bill or may otherwise dispose of the goods, without liability for misdelivery, on instructions from:

(1) the holder of a negotiable bill;

(2) the consignor on a nonnegotiable bill, even if the consignee has given contrary instructions;

(3) the consignee on a nonnegotiable bill in the absence of contrary instructions from the consignor, if the goods have arrived at the billed destination or if the consignee is in possession of the tangible bill or in control of the electronic bill; or

(4) the consignee on a nonnegotiable bill, if the consignee is entitled as against the consignor to dispose of the goods.

(b) Unless instructions described in subsection (a) are included in a negotiable bill of lading, a person to which the bill is duly negotiated may hold the bailee according to the original terms.

Official Comment

Prior Uniform Statutory Provision: Former Section 7–303.

Changes: To accommodate electronic documents and for style.

Purposes:

1. Diversion is a very common commercial practice which defeats delivery to the consignee originally named in a bill of lading. This section continues former Section 7–303's safe harbor rules for carriers in situations involving diversion and adapts those rules to electronic documents of title. This section works compatibly with Section 2–705. Carriers may as a business matter be willing to accept instructions from consignees in which case the carrier will be liable for misdelivery if the consignee was not the owner or otherwise empowered to dispose of the goods under subsection (a)(4). The section imposes no duty on carriers to undertake diversion. The carrier is of course subject to the provisions of mandatory filed tariffs as provided in Section 7–103.

2. It should be noted that the section provides only an immunity for carriers against liability for "misdelivery." It does not, for example, defeat the title to the goods which the consignee-buyer may have acquired from the consignor-seller upon delivery of the goods to the carrier under a non-negotiable bill of lading. Thus if the carrier, upon instructions from the consignor, returns the goods to the consignor, the consignee may recover the goods from the consignor or the consignor's insolvent estate. However, under certain circumstances, the consignee's title may be defeated by diversion of the goods in transit to a different consignee. The rights that arise between the consignor-seller and the consignee-buyer out of a contract for the sale of goods are governed by Article 2.

Cross References:

Point 1: Sections 2–705 and 7–103.
Point 2: Article 2, Sections 7–403 and 7–504(3).

Definitional Cross References:

"Bailee". Section 7–102.
"Bill of lading". Section 1–201.
"Carrier". Section 7–102
"Consignee". Section 7–102.
"Consignor". Section 7–102.
"Delivery". Section 1–201.
"Goods". Section 7–102.
"Holder". Section 1–201.
"Notice". Section 1–202.
"Person". Section 1–201.
"Purchaser". Section 1–201.
"Term". Section 1–201.

§ 7–304.   Tangible Bills of Lading in a Set.

(a)   Except as customary in international transportation, a tangible bill of lading may not be issued in a set of parts. The issuer is liable for damages caused by violation of this subsection.

(b)   If a tangible bill of lading is lawfully issued in a set of parts, each of which contains an identification code and is expressed to be valid only if the goods have not been delivered against any other part, the whole of the parts constitutes one bill.

(c)   If a tangible negotiable bill of lading is lawfully issued in a set of parts and different parts are negotiated to different persons, the title of the holder to which the first due negotiation is made prevails as to both the document of title and the goods even if any later holder may have received the goods from the carrier in good faith and discharged the carrier's obligation by surrendering its part.

(d)   A person that negotiates or transfers a single part of a tangible bill of lading issued in a set is liable to holders of that part as if it were the whole set.

(e)   The bailee shall deliver in accordance with Part 4 against the first presented part of a tangible bill of lading lawfully issued in a set. Delivery in this manner discharges the bailee's obligation on the whole bill.

Official Comment

Prior Uniform Statutory Provision: Former Section 7–304.

Changes: To limit bills in a set to tangible bills of lading and to use terminology more consistent with modern usage.

Purposes:

1.   Tangible bills of lading in a set are still used in some nations in international trade. Consequently, a tangible bill of lading part of a set could be at issue in a lawsuit that might come within Article 7. The statement of the legal effect of a lawfully issued set is in accord with existing commercial law relating to maritime and other international tangible bills of lading. This law has been codified in the Hague and Warsaw Conventions and in the Carriage of Goods by Sea Act, the provisions of which would ordinarily govern in situations where bills in a set are recognized by this Article. Tangible bills of lading in a set are prohibited in domestic trade.

2.   Electronic bills of lading in domestic or international trade will not be issued in a set given the requirements of control necessary to deliver the bill to another person. An electronic bill of lading will be a single, authoritative copy. Section 7–106. Hence, this section differentiates between electronic bills of lading and tangible bills of lading. This section does not prohibit electronic data messages about goods in transit because these electronic data messages are not the issued bill of lading. Electronic data messages contain information for the carrier's management and handling of the cargo but this information for the carrier's use is not the issued bill of lading.

Cross Reference:

Section 7–103, 7–303 and 7–106.

Definitional Cross References:

"Bailee". Section 7–102.
"Bill of lading". Section 1–201.
"Delivery". Section 1–201.
"Document of title". Section 1–201.
"Duly negotiate". Section 7–501.
"Good faith". Section 1–201. [7–102].
"Goods". Section 7–102.
"Holder". Section 1–201.
"Issuer". Section 7–102.
"Person". Section 1–201.
"Receipt of goods". Section 2–103.

§ 7–305.   Destination Bills.

(a)   Instead of issuing a bill of lading to the consignor at the place of shipment, a carrier, at the request of the consignor, may procure the bill to be issued at destination or at any other place designated in the request.

(b)   Upon request of any person entitled as against a carrier to control the goods while in transit and on surrender of possession or control of any outstanding bill of lading or other receipt covering the goods, the issuer, subject to Section 7–105, may procure a substitute bill to be issued at any place designated in the request.

Official Comment

Prior Uniform Statutory Provision: Former Section 7–305.

Changes: To accommodate electronic bills of lading and for style.

Purposes:

1.   Subsection (a) continues the rules of former Section 7–305(1) without substantive change. This proposal is designed to facilitate the use of order bills in connection with fast shipments. Use of order bills on high speed shipments is impeded by the fact that the goods may arrive at destination before the documents, so that no one is ready to take delivery from the carrier. This is especially inconvenient for carriers by truck and air, who do not have terminal facilities where shipments can be held to await the consignee's appearance. Order bills would be useful to take advantage of bank collection. This may be preferable to C.O.D. shipment in which the carrier, e.g. a truck driver, is the collecting and remitting agent. Financing of shipments under this plan would be handled as follows: seller at San Francisco delivers the goods to an airline with instructions to issue a bill in New York to a named bank. Seller receives a receipt embodying this undertaking to issue a destination bill. Airline wires its New York freight agent to issue the bill as instructed by the seller. Seller wires the New York bank a draft on buyer. New York bank indorses the bill to buyer when the buyer honors the draft. Normally seller would act through its own bank in San Francisco, which would extend credit in reliance on the airline's contract to deliver a bill to the order of its New York correspondent. This section is entirely permissive; it imposes no duty to issue such bills. Whether a performing carrier will act as issuing agent is left to agreement between carriers.

2.   Subsection (b) continues the rule from former Section 7–305(2) with accommodation for electronic bills of lading. If the substitute bill changes from an electronic to a tangible medium or vice versa, the issuance of the substitute bill must comply with Section 7–105 to give the substitute bill validity and effect.

Cross Reference:

Section 7–105.

Definitional Cross References:

"Bill of lading". Section 1–201.
"Consignor". Section 7–102.
"Goods". Section 7–102.
"Issuer". Section 7–102.
"Receipt of goods". Section 2–103.

§ 7–306.   Altered Bills of Lading.

An unauthorized alteration or filling in of a blank in a bill of lading leaves the bill enforceable according to its original tenor.

Official Comment

Prior Uniform Statutory Provision: Former Section 7–306.

Changes: None

Purposes:

An unauthorized alteration or filling in of a blank, whether made with or without fraudulent intent, does not relieve the issuer of its liability on the document as originally executed. This section applies to both tangible and electronic bills of lading, applying the same rule to both types of bills of lading. The control concept of Section 7–106 requires that any changes to the electronic document of title be readily identifiable as authorized or unauthorized. Section 7–306 should be compared to Section 7–208 where a different rule applies to the unauthorized filling in of a blank for tangible warehouse receipts.

Cross Reference:

Sections 7–106 and 7–208.

Definitional Cross References:

"Bill of lading". Section 1–201.
"Issuer". Section 7–102.

§ 7–307. Lien of Carrier.

(a) A carrier has a lien on the goods covered by a bill of lading or on the proceeds thereof in its possession for charges after the date of the carrier's receipt of the goods for storage or transportation, including demurrage and terminal charges, and for expenses necessary for preservation of the goods incident to their transportation or reasonably incurred in their sale pursuant to law. However, against a purchaser for value of a negotiable bill of lading, a carrier's lien is limited to charges stated in the bill or the applicable tariffs or, if no charges are stated, a reasonable charge.

(b) A lien for charges and expenses under subsection (a) on goods that the carrier was required by law to receive for transportation is effective against the consignor or any person entitled to the goods unless the carrier had notice that the consignor lacked authority to subject the goods to those charges and expenses. Any other lien under subsection (a) is effective against the consignor and any person that permitted the bailor to have control or possession of the goods unless the carrier had notice that the bailor lacked authority.

(c) A carrier loses its lien on any goods that it voluntarily delivers or unjustifiably refuses to deliver.

Official Comment

Prior Uniform Statutory Provision: Former Section 7–307.

Changes: Expanded to cover proceeds of the goods transported.

Purposes:

1. The section is intended to give carriers a specific statutory lien for charges and expenses similar to that given to warehouses by the first sentence of Section 7–209(a) and extends that lien to the proceeds of the goods as long as the carrier has possession of the proceeds. But because carriers do not commonly claim a lien for charges in relation to other goods or lend money on the security of goods in their hands, provisions for a general lien or a security interest similar to those in Section 7–209(a) and (b) are omitted. Carriers may utilize Article 9 to obtain a security interest and become a secured party or a carrier may agree to limit its lien rights in a transportation agreement with the shipper. As the lien given by this section is specific, and the storage or transportation often preserves or increases the value of the goods, subsection (b) validates the lien against anyone who permitted the bailor to have possession of the goods. Where the carrier is required to receive the goods for transportation, the owner's interest may be subjected to charges and expenses arising out of deposit of his goods by a thief. The crucial mental element is the carrier's knowledge or reason to know of the bailor's lack of authority. If the carrier does not know or have reason to know of the bailor's lack of authority, the carrier has a lien under this section against any person so long as the conditions of subsection (b) are satisfied. In light of the crucial mental element, Sections 7–307 and 9–333 combine to give priority to a carrier's lien over security interests in the goods. In this regard, the judicial decision in *In re Sharon Steel Corp.*, 25 U.C.C. Rep.2d 503, 176 B.R. 384 (W.D. Pa. 1995) is correct and is the controlling precedent.

2. The reference to charges in this section means charges relating to the bailment relationship for transportation. Charges does not mean that the bill of lading must state a specific rate or a specific amount. However, failure to state a specific rate or a specific amount has legal consequences under the second sentence of subsection (a).

3. The carrier's specific lien under this section is a possessory lien. See subsection (c). Part 3 of Article 7 does not require any particular form for a bill of lading. The carrier's lien arises when the carrier has issued a bill of lading.

Cross References:

Point 1: Sections 7–209, 9–109 and 9–333.

Point 3. Section 7–202 and 7–209.

Definitional Cross References:

"Bill of lading". Section 1–201.
"Carrier". Section 7–102.
"Consignor". Section 7–102.
"Delivery". Section 1–201.
"Goods". Section 7–102.
"Person". Section 1–201.
"Purchaser". Section 1–201.
"Value". Section 1–204.

§ 7–308. Enforcement of Carrier's Lien.

(a) A carrier's lien on goods may be enforced by public or private sale of the goods, in bulk or in packages, at any time or place and on any terms that are commercially reasonable, after notifying all persons known to claim an interest in the goods. The notification must include a statement of the amount due, the nature of the proposed sale, and the time and place of any public sale. The fact that a better price could have been obtained by a sale at a different time or in a method different from that selected by the carrier is not of itself sufficient to establish that the sale was not made in a commercially reasonable manner. The carrier sells goods in a commercially reasonable manner if the carrier sells the goods in the usual manner in any recognized market therefor, sells at the price current in that market at the time of the sale, or otherwise sells in conformity with commercially reasonable practices among dealers in the type of goods sold. A sale of more goods than apparently necessary to be offered to ensure satisfaction of the obligation is not commercially reasonable, except in cases covered by the preceding sentence.

(b) Before any sale pursuant to this section, any person claiming a right in the goods may pay the amount necessary to satisfy the lien and the reasonable expenses incurred in complying with this section. In that event, the goods may not be sold but must be retained by the carrier, subject to the terms of the bill of lading and this article.

(c) A carrier may buy at any public sale pursuant to this section.

(d) A purchaser in good faith of goods sold to enforce a carrier's lien takes the goods free of any rights of persons against which the lien was valid, despite the carrier's noncompliance with this section.

(e) A carrier may satisfy its lien from the proceeds of any sale pursuant to this section but shall hold the balance, if any, for delivery on demand to any person to which the carrier would have been bound to deliver the goods.

(f) The rights provided by this section are in addition to all other rights allowed by law to a creditor against a debtor.

(g) A carrier's lien may be enforced pursuant to either subsection (a) or the procedure set forth in Section 7–210(b).

(h) A carrier is liable for damages caused by failure to comply with the requirements for sale under this section and, in case of willful violation, is liable for conversion.

Official Comment

Prior Uniform Statutory Provision: Former Section 7–308.

Changes: To conform language to modern usage and for style.

Purposes:

This section is intended to give the carrier an enforcement procedure of its lien coextensive with that given the warehouse in cases other than those covering noncommercial storage by the warehouse. See Section 7–210 and comments.

Cross Reference:

Section 7–210.

Definitional Cross References:

"Bill of lading". Section 1–201.
"Carrier". Section 7–102.
"Creditor". Section 1–201.
"Delivery". Section 1–201.
"Good faith". Section 1–201. [7–102]
"Goods". Section 7–102.
"Notification". Section 1–202.
"Notifies". Section 1–202.
"Person". Section 1–201.
"Purchaser". Section 1–201.
"Rights". Section 1–201.
"Term". Section 1–201.

§ 7–309.   Duty of Care; Contractual Limitation of Carrier's Liability.

(a) A carrier that issues a bill of lading, whether negotiable or nonnegotiable, shall exercise the degree of care in relation to the goods which a reasonably careful person would exercise under similar circumstances. This subsection does not affect any statute, regulation, or rule of law that imposes liability upon a common carrier for damages not caused by its negligence.

(b) Damages may be limited by a term in the bill of lading or in a transportation agreement that the carrier's liability may not exceed a value stated in the bill or transportation agreement if the carrier's rates are dependent upon value and the consignor is afforded an opportunity to declare a higher value and the consignor is advised of the opportunity. However, such a limitation is not effective with respect to the carrier's liability for conversion to its own use.

(c) Reasonable provisions as to the time and manner of presenting claims and commencing actions based on the shipment may be included in a bill of lading or a transportation agreement.

Official Comment

Prior Uniform Statutory Provision: Former Section 7–309.

Changes: References to tariffs eliminated because of deregulation, adding reference to transportation agreements, and for style.

Purposes:

1. A bill of lading may also serve as the contract between the carrier and the bailor. Parties in their contract should be able to limit the amount of damages for breach of that contract including breach of the duty to take reasonable care of the goods. The parties cannot disclaim by contract the carrier's obligation of care. Section 1–302.

Federal statutes and treaties for air, maritime and rail transport may alter the standard of care. These federal statutes and treaties preempt this section when applicable. Section 7–103. Subsection (a) does not impair any rule of law imposing the liability of an insurer on a common carrier in intrastate commerce. Subsection (b), however, applies to the common carrier's liability as an insurer as well as to liability based on negligence. Subsection (b) allows the term limiting damages to appear either in the bill of lading or in the parties' transportation agreement. Compare 7–204(b). Subsection (c) allows the parties to agree to provisions regarding time and manner of presenting claims or commencing actions if the provisions are either in the bill of lading or the transportation agreement. Compare 7–204(c). Transportation agreements are commonly used to establish agreed terms between carriers and shippers that have an on-going relationship.

2. References to public tariffs in former Section 7–309(2) and (3) have been deleted in light of the modern era of deregulation. See Comment 2 to Section 7–103. If a tariff is required under state or federal law, pursuant to Section 7–103(a), the tariff would control over the rule of this section. As governed by contract law, parties may incorporate by reference the limits on the amount of damages or the reasonable provisions as to the time and manner of presenting claims set forth in applicable tariffs, e.g. a maximum unit value beyond which goods are not taken or a disclaimer of responsibility for undeclared articles of extraordinary value.

3.   As under former Section 7–309(2), subsection (b) provides that a limitation of damages is ineffective if the carrier has converted the goods to its own use. A mere failure to redeliver the goods is not conversion to the carrier's own use. "Conversion to its own use" is narrower than the idea of conversion generally. *Art Masters Associates, Ltd. v. United Parcel Service*, 77 N.Y.2d 200, 567 N.E.2d 226 (1990); *See, Kemper Ins. Co. v. Fed. Ex. Corp.*, 252 F.3d 509 (1st Cir.), *cert. denied* 534 U.S. 1020 (2001) (opinion interpreting federal law).

4.   As used in this section, damages may include damages arising from delay in delivery. Delivery dates and times are often specified in the parties' contract. See Section 7–403.

Cross Reference:

Sections 1–302, 7–103, 7–204, 7–403.

Definitional Cross References:

"Action". Section 1–201.
"Bill of lading". Section 1–201.
"Carrier". Section 7–102.
"Consignor". Section 7–102.
"Document of title". Section 1–201.
"Goods". Section 7–102.
"Value". Section 1–204.

PART 4

WAREHOUSE RECEIPTS AND BILLS OF LADING: GENERAL OBLIGATIONS

§ 7–401.   Irregularities in Issue of Receipt or Bill or Conduct of Issuer.

The obligations imposed by this article on an issuer apply to a document of title even if:

(1)   the document does not comply with the requirements of this article or of any other statute, rule, or regulation regarding its issuance, form, or content;

(2)   the issuer violated laws regulating the conduct of its business;

(3)   the goods covered by the document were owned by the bailee when the document was issued; or

(4)   the person issuing the document is not a warehouse but the document purports to be a warehouse receipt.

Official Comment

Prior Uniform Statutory Provision: Former Section 7–401.

Changes: Changes for style only.

Purposes:

The bailee's liability on its document despite non-receipt or misdescription of the goods is affirmed in Sections 7–203 and 7–301. The purpose of this section is to make it clear that regardless of irregularities a document which falls within the definition of document of title imposes on the issuer the obligations stated in this Article. For example, a bailee will not be permitted to avoid its obligation to deliver the goods (Section 7–403) or its obligation of due care with respect to them (Sections 7–204 and 7–309) by taking the position that no valid "document" was issued because it failed to file a statutory bond or did not pay stamp taxes or did not disclose the place of storage in the document. *Tate v. Action Moving & Storage, Inc.*, 383 S.E.2d 229 (N.C. App. 1989), rev. denied 389 S.E.2d 104 (N.C. 1990). Sanctions against violations of statutory or administrative duties with respect to documents should be limited to revocation of license or other measures prescribed by the regulation imposing the duty. See Section 7–103.

Cross References:

Sections 7–103, 7–203, 7–204, 7–301, 7–309.

Definitional Cross References:

"Bailee". Section 7–102.
"Document of title". Section 1–201.
"Goods". Section 7–102.
"Issuer". Section 7–102.
"Person". Section 1–201.
"Warehouse receipt". Section 1–201.
"Warehouse". Section 7–102.

§ 7–402. Duplicate Document of Title; Overissue.

A duplicate or any other document of title purporting to cover goods already represented by an outstanding document of the same issuer does not confer any right in the goods, except as provided in the case of tangible bills of lading in a set of parts, overissue of documents for fungible goods, substitutes for lost, stolen, or destroyed documents, or substitute documents issued pursuant to Section 7–105. The issuer is liable for damages caused by its overissue or failure to identify a duplicate document by a conspicuous notation.

Official Comment

Prior Uniform Statutory Provision: Former Section 7–402.

Changes: Changes to accommodate electronic documents.

Purposes:

1. This section treats a duplicate which is not properly identified as a duplicate like any other overissue of documents: a purchaser of such a document acquires no title but only a cause of action for damages against the person that made the deception possible, except in the cases noted in the section. But parts of a tangible bill lawfully issued in a set of parts are not "overissue" (Section 7–304). Of course, if the issuer has clearly indicated that a document is a duplicate so that no one can be deceived by it, and in fact the duplicate is a correct copy of the original, the issuer is not liable for preparing and delivering such a duplicate copy.

Section 7–105 allows documents of title to be reissued in another medium. Re-issuance of a document in an alternative medium under Section 7–105 requires that the original document be surrendered to the issuer in order to make the substitute document the effective document. If the substitute document is not issued in compliance with section 7–105, then the document should be treated as a duplicate under this section.

2. The section applies to nonnegotiable documents to the extent of providing an action for damages for one who acquires an unmarked duplicate from a transferor who knew the facts and would therefore have had no cause of action against the issuer of the duplicate. Ordinarily the transferee of a nonnegotiable document acquires only the rights of its transferor.

3. Overissue is defined so as to exclude the common situation where two valid documents of different issuers are outstanding for the same goods at the same time. Thus freight forwarders commonly issue bills of lading to their customers for small shipments to be combined into carload shipments for which the railroad will issue a bill of lading to the forwarder. So also a warehouse receipt may be outstanding against goods, and the holder of the receipt may issue delivery orders against the same goods. In these cases dealings with the subsequently issued documents may be effective to transfer title; e.g. negotiation of a delivery order will effectively transfer title in the ordinary case where no dishonesty has occurred and the goods are available to satisfy the orders. Section 7–503 provides for cases of conflict between documents of different issuers.

Cross References:

Point 1: Sections 7–105, 7–207, 7–304, and 7–601.
Point 3: Section 7–503.

Definitional Cross References:

"Bill of lading". Section 1–201.
"Conspicuous". Section 1–201.
"Document of title". Section 1–201.
"Fungible goods." Section 1–201.

"Goods". Section 7–102.

"Issuer". Section 7–102.

"Right". Section 1–201.

§ 7–403. Obligation of Bailee to Deliver; Excuse.

(a) A bailee shall deliver the goods to a person entitled under a document of title if the person complies with subsections (b) and (c), unless and to the extent that the bailee establishes any of the following:

(1) delivery of the goods to a person whose receipt was rightful as against the claimant;

(2) damage to or delay, loss, or destruction of the goods for which the bailee is not liable;

(3) previous sale or other disposition of the goods in lawful enforcement of a lien or on a warehouse's lawful termination of storage;

(4) the exercise by a seller of its right to stop delivery pursuant to Section 2–705 or by a lessor of its right to stop delivery pursuant to Section 2A–526;

(5) a diversion, reconsignment, or other disposition pursuant to Section 7–303;

(6) release, satisfaction, or any other personal defense against the claimant; or

(7) any other lawful excuse.

(b) A person claiming goods covered by a document of title shall satisfy the bailee's lien if the bailee so requests or if the bailee is prohibited by law from delivering the goods until the charges are paid.

(c) Unless a person claiming the goods is a person against which the document of title does not confer a right under Section 7–503(a):

(1) the person claiming under a document shall surrender possession or control of any outstanding negotiable document covering the goods for cancellation or indication of partial deliveries; and

(2) the bailee shall cancel the document or conspicuously indicate in the document the partial delivery or the bailee is liable to any person to which the document is duly negotiated.

Official Comment

Prior Uniform Statutory Provision: Former Section 7–403.

Changes: Definition in former Section 7–403(4) moved to Section 7–102; bracketed language in former Section 7–403(1)(b) deleted; added cross reference to Section 2A–526; changes for style.

Purposes:

1. The present section, following former Section 7–403, is constructed on the basis of stating what previous deliveries or other circumstances operate to excuse the bailee's normal obligation on the document. Accordingly, "justified" deliveries under the pre-Code uniform acts now find their place as "excuse" under subsection (a).

2. The principal case covered by subsection (a)(1) is delivery to a person whose title is paramount to the rights represented by the document. For example, if a thief deposits stolen goods in a warehouse facility and takes a negotiable receipt, the warehouse is not liable on the receipt if it has surrendered the goods to the true owner, even though the receipt is held by a good faith purchaser. See Section 7–503(a). However, if the owner entrusted the goods to a person with power of disposition, and that person deposited the goods and took a negotiable document, the owner receiving delivery would not be rightful as against a holder to whom the negotiable document was duly negotiated, and delivery to the owner would not give the bailee a defense against such a holder. See Sections 7–502(a)(2), 7–503(a)(1).

3. Subsection (a)(2) amounts to a cross reference to all the tort law that determines the varying responsibilities and standards of care applicable to commercial bailees. A restatement of this tort law would be beyond the scope of this Act. Much of the applicable law as to responsibility of bailees for the preservation of the goods and limitation of liability in case of loss has been codified for particular classes of bailees in interstate and foreign commerce by federal legislation and treaty and for intrastate carriers and other bailees by the regulatory state laws preserved by Section 7–103. In the absence of governing legislation the common law will prevail subject to the minimum standard of reasonable care prescribed by Sections 7–204 and 7–309 of this Article.

The bracketed language found in former Section 7–403(1)(b) has been deleted thereby leaving the allocations of the burden of going forward with the evidence and the burden of proof to the procedural law of the various states.

Subsection (a)(4) contains a cross reference to both the seller's and the lessor's rights to stop delivery under Article 2 and Article 2A respectively.

4.   As under former Section 7–403, there is no requirement that a request for delivery must be accompanied by a formal tender of the amount of the charges due. Rather, the bailee must request payment of the amount of its lien when asked to deliver, and only in case this request is refused is it justified in declining to deliver because of nonpayment of charges. Where delivery without payment is forbidden by law, the request is treated as implicit. Such a prohibition reflects a policy of uniformity to prevent discrimination by failure to request payment in particular cases. Subsection (b) must be read in conjunction with the priorities given to the warehouse lien and the carrier lien under Section 7–209 and 7–307, respectively. If the parties are in dispute about whether the request for payment of the lien is legally proper, the bailee may have recourse to interpleader. See Section 7–603.

5.   ~~Subsection (c)~~ In addition to compliance with subsection (b), subsection (c) conditions the bailee's duty to deliver the goods to a person entitled under a negotiable document on the surrender of possession or control of the document for cancellation or indication of partial deliveries. It also states the obvious duty of a bailee to take up a negotiable document or note partial deliveries conspicuously thereon, and the result of failure in that duty. It is subject to only one exception, that stated in subsection (a)(1) of this section and in Section 7–503(a). Subsection (c) is limited to cases of delivery to a claimant; it has no application, for example, where goods held under a negotiable document are lawfully sold to enforce the bailee's lien.

Subsection (c) does not specify any conditions on the duty of the bailee to deliver the goods covered by a nonnegotiable document to a person entitled, other than the conditions inherent in the definition of "person entitled under the document." See Sections 7–102(a)(9) (defining "person entitled under the document") and Comment 6; 7–504. In addition, the document itself may specify that the person entitled must present the document to the bailee in order to obtain delivery of the goods.

6.   When courts are considering subsection (a)(7), "any other lawful excuse," among others, refers to compliance with court orders under Sections 7–601, 7–602 and 7–603.

Cross References:

Point 2: Sections 7–502 and 7–503.
Point 3: Sections 2–705, 2A–526, 7–103, 7–204, and 7–309 and 10–103.
Point 4: Sections 7–209, 7–307 and 7–603.
Point 5: Section 7–503(1).
Point 6: Sections 7–601, 7–602, and 7–603.

Definitional Cross References:

"Bailee". Section 7–102.
"Conspicuous". Section 1–201.
"Delivery". Section 1–201.
"Document of title". Section 1–201.
"Duly negotiate". Section 7–501.
"Goods". Section 7–102.
"Lessor". Section 2A–103.
"Person". Section 1–201.
"Receipt of goods". Section 2–103.
"Right". Section 1–201.
"Terms". Section 1–201.
"Warehouse". Section 7–102.

As amended in 2022.

§ 7–404.   No Liability for Good-Faith Delivery Pursuant to Document of Title.

A bailee that in good faith has received goods and delivered or otherwise disposed of the goods according to the terms of a document of title or pursuant to this article is not liable for the goods even if:

(1) the person from which the bailee received the goods did not have authority to procure the document or to dispose of the goods; or

(2) the person to which the bailee delivered the goods did not have authority to receive the goods.

Official Comment

Prior Uniform Statutory Provision: Former Section 7–404.

Changes: Changes reflect the definition of good faith in Section 1–201 [7–102] and for style.

Purposes:

This section uses the test of good faith, as defined in Section 1–201 [7–102], to continue the policy of former Section 7–404. Good faith now means "honesty in fact and the observance of reasonable commercial standards of fair dealing." The section states explicitly that the common law rule of "innocent conversion" by unauthorized "intermeddling" with another's property is inapplicable to the operations of commercial carriers and warehousemen that in good faith perform obligations that they have assumed and that generally they are under a legal compulsion to assume. The section applies to delivery to a fraudulent holder of a valid document as well as to delivery to the holder of an invalid document. Of course, in appropriate circumstances, a bailee may use interpleader or other dispute resolution process. See Section 7–603.

Cross Reference:

Section 7–603.

Definitional Cross References:

"Bailee". Section 7–102.
"Delivery". Section 1–201.
"Document of title". Section 1–201.
"Good faith". Section 1–201. [7–102].
"Goods". Section 7–102.
"Person". Section 1–201.
"Receipt of goods". Section 2–103.
"Term". Section 1–201.

PART 5

WAREHOUSE RECEIPTS AND BILLS OF LADING: NEGOTIATION AND TRANSFER

§ 7–501. Form of Negotiation and Requirements of Due Negotiation.

(a) The following rules apply to a negotiable tangible document of title:

(1) If the document's original terms run to the order of a named person, the document is negotiated by the named person's indorsement and delivery. After the named person's indorsement in blank or to bearer, any person may negotiate the document by delivery alone.

(2) If the document's original terms run to bearer, it is negotiated by delivery alone.

(3) If the document's original terms run to the order of a named person and it is delivered to the named person, the effect is the same as if the document had been negotiated.

(4) Negotiation of the document after it has been indorsed to a named person requires indorsement by the named person and delivery.

(5) A document is duly negotiated if it is negotiated in the manner stated in this subsection to a holder that purchases it in good faith, without notice of any defense against or claim to it on the part of any person, and for value, unless it is established that the negotiation is not in the regular course of business or financing or involves receiving the document in settlement or payment of a monetary obligation.

(b) The following rules apply to a negotiable electronic document of title:

(1)   If the document's original terms run to the order of a named person or to bearer, the document is negotiated by delivery of the document to another person. Indorsement by the named person is not required to negotiate the document.

(2)   If the document's original terms run to the order of a named person and the named person has control of the document, the effect is the same as if the document had been negotiated.

(3)   A document is duly negotiated if it is negotiated in the manner stated in this subsection to a holder that purchases it in good faith, without notice of any defense against or claim to it on the part of any person, and for value, unless it is established that the negotiation is not in the regular course of business or financing or involves taking delivery of the document in settlement or payment of a monetary obligation.

(c)   Indorsement of a nonnegotiable document of title neither makes it negotiable nor adds to the transferee's rights.

(d)   The naming in a negotiable bill of lading of a person to be notified of the arrival of the goods does not limit the negotiability of the bill or constitute notice to a purchaser of the bill of any interest of that person in the goods.

Official Comment

Prior Uniform Statutory Provision: Former Section 7–501.

Changes: To accommodate negotiable electronic documents of title.

Purpose:

1.   Subsection (a) has been limited to tangible negotiable documents of title but otherwise remains unchanged in substance from the rules in former Section 7–501. Subsection (b) is new and applies to negotiable electronic documents of title. Delivery of a negotiable electronic document is through voluntary transfer of control. Section 1–201 definition of "delivery." The control concept as applied to negotiable electronic documents of title is the substitute for both possession and indorsement as applied to negotiable tangible documents of title. Section 7–106.

Article 7 does not separately define the term "duly negotiated." However, the elements of "duly negotiated" are set forth in subsection (a)(5) for tangible documents and (b)(3) for electronic documents. As under former Section 7–501, in order to effect a "due negotiation" the negotiation must be in the "regular course of business or financing" in order to transfer greater rights than those held by the person negotiating. The foundation of the mercantile doctrine of good faith purchase for value has always been, as shown by the case situations, the furtherance and protection of the regular course of trade. The reason for allowing a person, in bad faith or in error, to convey away rights which are not its own has from the beginning been to make possible the speedy handling of that great run of commercial transactions which are patently usual and normal.

There are two aspects to the usual and normal course of mercantile dealings, namely, the person making the transfer and the nature of the transaction itself. The first question which arises is: Is the transferor a person with whom it is reasonable to deal as having full powers? In regard to documents of title the only holder whose possession or control appears, commercially, to be in order is almost invariably a person in the trade. No commercial purpose is served by allowing a tramp or a professor to "duly negotiate" an order bill of lading for hides or cotton not their own, and since such a transfer is obviously not in the regular course of business, it is excluded from the scope of the protection of subsections (a)(5) or (b)(3).

The second question posed by the "regular course" qualification is: Is the transaction one which is normally proper to pass full rights without inquiry, even though the transferor itself may not have such rights to pass, and even though the transferor may be acting in breach of duty? In raising this question the "regular course" criterion has the further advantage of limiting, the effective wrongful disposition to transactions whose protection will really further trade. Obviously, the snapping up of goods for quick resale at a price suspiciously below the market deserves no protection as a matter of policy: it is also clearly outside the range of regular course.

Any notice on the document sufficient to put a merchant on inquiry as to the "regular course" quality of the transaction will frustrate a "due negotiation". Thus irregularity of the document or unexplained staleness of a bill of lading may appropriately be recognized as negating a negotiation in "regular" course.

A pre-existing claim constitutes value, and "due negotiation" does not require "new value." A usual and ordinary transaction in which documents are received as security for credit previously extended may be in "regular" course, even though there is a demand for additional collateral because the creditor "deems himself insecure." But the matter has moved out of the regular course of financing if the debtor is thought to be insolvent, the credit previously extended is in effect cancelled, and the creditor snatches a plank in the shipwreck under the guise of a demand for additional collateral. Where a money debt is "paid" in commodity paper, any question of "regular" course disappears, as the case is explicitly excepted from "due negotiation".

2.   Negotiation under this section may be made by any holder no matter how the holder acquired possession or control of the document.

3.   Subsections (a)(3) and (b)(2) make explicit a matter upon which the intent of the pre-Code law was clear but the language somewhat obscure: a negotiation results from a delivery to a banker or buyer to whose order the document has been taken by the person making the bailment. There is no presumption of irregularity in such a negotiation; it may very well be in "regular course."

4.   This Article does not contain any provision creating a presumption of due negotiation to, and full rights in, a holder of a document of title akin to that created by Uniform Commercial Code Article 3. But the reason of the provisions of this Act (Section 1–307) on the prima facie authenticity and accuracy of third party documents, joins with the reason of the present section to work such a presumption in favor of any person who has power to make a due negotiation. It would not make sense for this Act to authorize a purchaser to indulge the presumption of regularity if the courts were not also called upon to do so. Allocations of the burden of going forward with the evidence and the burden of proof are left to the procedural law of the various states.

5.   Subsections (c) and (d) are unchanged from prior law and apply to both tangible and electronic documents of title.

Cross References:

Sections 1–307, 7–502 and 7–503.

Definitional Cross References:

"Bearer". Section 1–201.
"Control". Section 7–106.
"Delivery". Section 1–201.
"Document of title". Section 1–201.
"Good faith". Section 1–201 [7–102].
"Holder". Section 1–201.
"Notice". Section 1–202.
"Person". Section 1–201.
"Purchase". Section 1–201.
"Rights". Section 1–201.
"Term". Section 1–201.
"Value". Section 1–204.

§ 7–502.   Rights Acquired by Due Negotiation.

(a)   Subject to Sections 7–205 and 7–503, a holder to which a negotiable document of title has been duly negotiated acquires thereby:

(1)   title to the document;

(2)   title to the goods;

(3)   all rights accruing under the law of agency or estoppel, including rights to goods delivered to the bailee after the document was issued; and

(4)   the direct obligation of the issuer to hold or deliver the goods according to the terms of the document free of any defense or claim by the issuer except those arising under the terms of the document or under this article, but in the case of a delivery order, the bailee's obligation accrues only upon the bailee's acceptance of the delivery order and the obligation acquired by the holder is that the issuer and any indorser will procure the acceptance of the bailee.

(b)   Subject to Section 7–503, title and rights acquired by due negotiation are not defeated by any stoppage of the goods represented by the document of title or by surrender of the goods by the bailee and are not impaired even if:

(1)   the due negotiation or any prior due negotiation constituted a breach of duty;

(2)   any person has been deprived of possession of a negotiable tangible document or control of a negotiable electronic document by misrepresentation, fraud, accident, mistake, duress, loss, theft, or conversion; or

(3)   a previous sale or other transfer of the goods or document has been made to a third person.

Official Comment

Prior Uniform Statutory Provision: Former Section 7–502.

Changes: To accommodate electronic documents of title and for style.

Purpose:

1.   This section applies to both tangible and electronic documents of title. The elements of duly negotiated, which constitutes a due negotiation, are set forth in Section 7–501. The several necessary qualifications of the broad principle that the holder of a document acquired in a due negotiation is the owner of the document and the goods have been brought together in the next section (Section 7–503).

2.   Subsection (a)(3) covers the case of "feeding" of a duly negotiated document by subsequent delivery to the bailee of such goods as the document falsely purported to cover; the bailee in such case is estopped as against the holder of the document.

3.   The explicit statement in subsection (a)(4) of the bailee's direct obligation to the holder precludes the defense that the document in question was "spent" after the carrier had delivered the goods to a previous holder. But the holder is subject to such defenses as non-negligent destruction even though not apparent on the document. The sentence on delivery orders applies only to delivery orders in negotiable form which have been duly negotiated. On delivery orders, see also Section 7–503(b) and Comment.

4.   Subsection (b) continues the law which gave full effect to the issuance or due negotiation of a negotiable document. The subsection adds nothing to the effect of the rules stated in subsection (a), but it has been included since such explicit reference was provided under former Section 7–502 to preserve the right of a purchaser by due negotiation. The listing is not exhaustive. The language "any stoppage" is included lest an inference be drawn that a stoppage of the goods before or after transit might cut off or otherwise impair the purchaser's rights.

Cross References:

Sections 7–103, 7–205, 7–403, 7–501, and 7–503.

Definitional Cross References:

"Bailee". Section 7–102.
"Control". Section 7–106.
"Delivery". Section 1–201.
"Delivery order". Section 7–102.
"Document of title". Section 1–201.
"Duly negotiate". Section 7–501.
"Fungible". Section 1–201.
"Goods". Section 7–102.
"Holder". Section 1–201.
"Issuer". Section 7–102.
"Person". Section 1–201.
"Rights". Section 1–201.
"Term". Section 1–201.
"Warehouse receipt". Section 1–201.

§ 7–503. Document of Title to Goods Defeated in Certain Cases.

(a) A document of title confers no right in goods against a person who that before issuance of the document had a legal interest or a perfected security interest in the goods and that did not:

(1) deliver or entrust the goods or any document of title covering the goods to the bailor or the bailor's nominee with:

(A) actual or apparent authority to ship, store, or sell;

(B) power to obtain delivery under Section 7–403; or

(C) power of disposition under Section 2–403, 2A–304(2), 2A–305(2), 9–320, or 9–321(c) or other statute or rule of law; or

(2) acquiesce in the procurement by the bailor or its nominee of any document.

(b) Title to goods based upon an unaccepted delivery order is subject to the rights of any person to which a negotiable warehouse receipt or bill of lading covering the goods has been duly negotiated. That title may be defeated under Section 7–504 to the same extent as the rights of the issuer or a transferee from the issuer.

(c) Title to goods based upon a bill of lading issued to a freight forwarder is subject to the rights of any person to which a bill issued by the freight forwarder is duly negotiated. However, delivery by the carrier in accordance with Part 4 pursuant to its own bill of lading discharges the carrier's obligation to deliver.

Official Comment

Prior Uniform Statutory Provision: Former Section 7–503.

Changes: Changes to cross-reference to Article 2A and for style.

Purposes:

1. In general it may be said that the title of a purchaser by due negotiation prevails over almost any interest in the goods which existed prior to the procurement of the document of title if the possession of the goods by the person obtaining the document derived from any action by the prior claimant which introduced the goods into the stream of commerce or carried them along that stream. A thief of the goods cannot indeed by shipping or storing them to the thief's own order acquire power to transfer them to a good faith purchaser. Nor can a tenant or mortgagor defeat any rights of a landlord or mortgagee which have been perfected under the local law merely by wrongfully shipping or storing a portion of the crop or other goods. However, "acquiescence" by the landlord or mortgagee does not require active consent under subsection (a)(2) and knowledge of the likelihood of storage or shipment with no objection or effort to control it is sufficient to defeat the landlord's or the mortgagee's rights as against one who takes by due negotiation of a negotiable document. *In re Sharon Steel*, 176 B.R. 384 (Bankr. W.D. Pa. 1995); *In re R.V. Segars Co*, 54 B.R. 170 (Bankr. S.C. 1985); *In re Jamestown Elevators, Inc.*, 49 B.R. 661 (Bankr. N.D. 1985).

On the other hand, where goods are delivered to a factor for sale, even though the factor has made no advances and is limited in its duty to sell for cash, the goods are "entrusted" to the factor "with actual . . . authority . . . to sell" under subsection (a)(1), and if the factor procures a negotiable document of title it can transfer the owner's interest to a purchaser by due negotiation. Further, where the factor is in the business of selling, goods entrusted to it simply for safekeeping or storage may be entrusted under circumstances which give the factor "apparent authority to ship, store or sell" under subsection (a)(1), or power of disposition under Section 2–403, 2A–304(2), 2A–305(2), 7–205, 9–320, or 9–321(c) or under a statute such as the earlier Factors Acts, or under a rule of law giving effect to apparent ownership. See Section 1–103.

Persons having an interest in goods also frequently deliver or entrust them to agents or servants other than factors for the purpose of shipping or warehousing or under circumstances reasonably contemplating such action. This Act is clear that such persons assume full risk that the agent to whom the goods are so delivered may ship or store in breach of duty, take a document to the agent's own order and then proceed to misappropriate the negotiable document of title that embodies the goods. This Act makes no distinction between possession or mere custody in such situations and finds no exception in the case of larceny by a bailee or the like. The safeguard in such situations lies in the requirement that a due negotiation can occur only "in the regular course of business or financing" and that the purchase be in good faith and without notice. See Section 7–501. Documents of title have no market among the commercially inexperienced and the commercially experienced do not take them without inquiry from persons known to be truck drivers or petty clerks even though such persons purport to be operating in their own names.

Again, where the seller allows a buyer to receive goods under a contract for sale, though as a "conditional delivery" or under "cash sale" terms and on explicit agreement for immediate payment, the buyer thereby acquires power to defeat the seller's interest by transfer of the goods to certain good faith purchasers. See Section 2–403. Both in policy and under the language of subsection (a)(1) that same power must be extended to accomplish the same result if the buyer procures a negotiable document of title to the goods and duly negotiates it.

This comment 1 should be considered in interpreting delivery, entrustment or acquiescence in application of Section 7–209.

2.   Under subsection (a) a delivery order issued by a person having no right in or power over the goods is ineffective unless the owner acts as provided in subsection (a)(1) or (2). Thus the rights of a transferee of a non-negotiable warehouse receipt can be defeated by a delivery order subsequently issued by the transferor only if the transferee "delivers or entrusts" to the "person procuring" the delivery order or "acquiesces" in that person's procurement. Similarly, a second delivery order issued by the same issuer for the same goods will ordinarily be subject to the first, both under this section and under Section 7–402. After a delivery order is validly issued but before it is accepted, it may nevertheless be defeated under subsection (b) in much the same way that the rights of a transferee may be defeated under Section 7–504. For example, a buyer in ordinary course from the issuer may defeat the rights of the holder of a prior delivery order if the bailee receives notification of the buyer's rights before notification of the holder's rights. Section 7–504(b)(2). But an accepted delivery order has the same effect as a document issued by the bailee.

3.   Under subsection (c) a bill of lading issued to a freight forwarder is subordinated to the freight forwarder's document of title, since the bill on its face gives notice of the fact that a freight forwarder is in the picture and the freight forwarder has in all probability issued a document of title. But the carrier is protected in following the terms of its own bill of lading.

Cross References:

> Point 1: Sections 1–103, 2–403, 2A–304(2), 2A–305(2), 7–205, 7–209, 7–501, 9–320, 9–321(c), and 9–331.
>
> Point 2: Sections 7–402 and 7–504.
>
> Point 3: Sections 7–402, 7–403 and 7–404.

Definitional Cross References:

> "Bill of lading". Section 1–201.
>
> "Contract for sale". Section 2–106.
>
> "Delivery". Section 1–201.
>
> "Delivery order". Section 7–102.
>
> "Document of title". Section 1–201.
>
> "Duly negotiate". Section 7–501.
>
> "Goods". Section 7–102.
>
> "Person". Section 1–201.
>
> "Right". Section 1–201.
>
> "Warehouse receipt". Section 1–201.

§ 7–504.   Rights Acquired in Absence of Due Negotiation; Effect of Diversion; Stoppage of Delivery.

(a)   A transferee of a document of title, whether negotiable or nonnegotiable, to which the document has been delivered but not duly negotiated, acquires the title and rights that its transferor had or had actual authority to convey.

(b)   In the case of a transfer of a nonnegotiable document of title, until but not after the bailee receives notice of the transfer, the rights of the transferee may be defeated:

(1)   by those creditors of the transferor which could treat the transfer as void under Section 2–402 or 2A–308;

(2)   by a buyer from the transferor in ordinary course of business if the bailee has delivered the goods to the buyer or received notification of the buyer's rights;

(3)   by a lessee from the transferor in ordinary course of business if the bailee has delivered the goods to the lessee or received notification of the lessee's rights; or

(4)   as against the bailee, by good-faith dealings of the bailee with the transferor.

(c)   A diversion or other change of shipping instructions by the consignor in a nonnegotiable bill of lading which causes the bailee not to deliver the goods to the consignee defeats the consignee's title to the goods if the goods have been delivered to a buyer in ordinary course of business or a lessee in ordinary course of business and, in any event, defeats the consignee's rights against the bailee.

(d)   Delivery of the goods pursuant to a nonnegotiable document of title may be stopped by a seller under Section 2–705 or a lessor under Section 2A–526, subject to the requirements of due notification in those sections. A bailee that honors the seller's or lessor's instructions is entitled to be indemnified by the seller or lessor against any resulting loss or expense.

Official Comment

Prior Uniform Statutory Provision: Former Section 7–504.

Changes: To include cross-references to Article 2A and for style.

Purposes:

1.   Under the general principles controlling negotiable documents, it is clear that in the absence of due negotiation a transferor cannot convey greater rights than the transferor has, even when the negotiation is formally perfect. This section recognizes the transferor's power to transfer rights which the transferor has or has "actual authority to convey." Thus, where a negotiable document of title is being transferred the operation of the principle of estoppel is not recognized, as contrasted with situations involving the transfer of the goods themselves. (Compare Section 2–403 on good faith purchase of goods.) This section applies to both tangible and electronic documents of title.

A necessary part of the price for the protection of regular dealings with negotiable documents of title is an insistence that no dealing which is in any way irregular shall be recognized as a good faith purchase of the document or of any rights pertaining to it. So, where the transfer of a negotiable document fails as a negotiation because a requisite indorsement is forged or otherwise missing, the purchaser in good faith and for value may be in the anomalous position of having less rights, in part, than if the purchaser had purchased the goods themselves. True, the purchaser's rights are not subject to defeat by attachment of the goods or surrender of them to the purchaser's transferor (contrast subsection (b)); but on the other hand, the purchaser cannot acquire enforceable rights to control or receive the goods over the bailee's objection merely by giving notice to the bailee. Similarly, a consignee who makes payment to its consignor against a straight bill of lading can thereby acquire the position of a good faith purchaser of goods under provisions of the Article of this Act on Sales (Section 2–403), whereas the same payment made in good faith against an unendorsed order bill would not have such effect. The appropriate remedy of a purchaser in such a situation is to regularize its status by compelling indorsement of the document (see Section 7–506).

2.   As in the case of transfer—as opposed to "due negotiation"—of negotiable documents, subsection (a) empowers the transferor of a nonnegotiable document to transfer only such rights as the transferor has or has "actual authority" to convey. In contrast to situations involving the goods themselves the operation of estoppel or agency principles is not here recognized to enable the transferor to convey greater rights than the transferor actually has. Subsection (b) makes it clear, however, that the transferee of a nonnegotiable document may acquire rights greater in some respects than those of his transferor by giving notice of the transfer to the bailee. ~~New subsection~~ Subsection (b)(3) provides for the rights of a lessee in the ordinary course.

Mere notice of a transfer of the document only prevents the persons identified in subsections (b)(1) through (4) from cutting off the rights of the transferee. For the transferee to become a "person entitled under the document," with a right to obtain delivery from the bailee under Section 7–403(a), either the document itself must provide for delivery to the transferee or the bailee must receive instructions in a record to deliver to the transferee. See Section 7–102(a)(9) (defining "person entitled under the document") and Comment 6.

Subsection (b)(2) ~~&~~ and (3) ~~require~~ requires delivery of the goods. Delivery of the goods means the voluntary transfer of physical possession of the goods. ~~See amended 2–103.~~

3.   Subsection (c) is in part a reiteration of the carrier's immunity from liability if it honors instructions of the consignor to divert, but there is added a provision protecting the title of the substituted consignee if the latter is a buyer in ordinary course of business. A typical situation would be where a manufacturer, having shipped a lot

of standardized goods to A on nonnegotiable bill of lading, diverts the goods to customer B who pays for them. Under pre-Code passage-of-title-by-appropriation doctrine A might reclaim the goods from B. However, no consideration of commercial policy supports this involvement of an innocent third party in the default of the manufacturer on his contract to A; and the common commercial practice of diverting goods in transit suggests a trade understanding in accordance with this subsection. The same result should obtain if the substituted consignee is a lessee in ordinary course. The extent of the lessee's interest in the goods is less than a buyer's interest in the goods. However, as against the first consignee and the lessee in ordinary course as the substituted consignee, the lessee's rights in the goods as granted under the lease are superior to the first consignee's rights.

4.   Subsection (d) gives the carrier an express right to indemnity where the carrier honors a seller's request to stop delivery.

5.   Section 1–202 gives the bailee protection, if due diligence is exercised where the bailee's organization has not had time to act on a notification.

Cross References:

Point 1: Sections 2–403 and 7–506.
Point 2: Sections 2–403 and 2A–304.
Point 3: Sections 7–303, 7–403(a)(5) and 7–404.
Point 4: Sections 2–705 and 7–403(a)(4).
Point 5: Section 1–202.

Definitional Cross References:

"Bailee". Section 7–102.
"Bill of lading". Section 1–201.
"Buyer in ordinary course of business". Section 1–201.
"Consignee". Section 7–102.
"Consignor". Section 7–102.
"Creditor". Section 1–201.
"Delivery". Section 1–201.
"Document of title". Section 1–201.
"Duly negotiate". Section 7–501.
"Good faith". Section 1–201. [7–102].
"Goods". Section 7–102.
"Honor". Section 1–201.
"Lessee in ordinary course". Section 2A–103.
"Notification" Section 1–202.
"Purchaser". Section 1–201.
"Rights". Section 1–201.

As amended in 2022.

§ 7–505.   Indorser Not Guarantor for Other Parties.

The indorsement of a tangible document of title issued by a bailee does not make the indorser liable for any default by the bailee or previous indorsers.

Official Comment

Prior Uniform Statutory Provision: Former Section 7–505.

Changes: Limited to tangible documents of title.

Purposes:

This section is limited to tangible documents of title as the concept of indorsement is irrelevant to electronic documents of title. Electronic documents of title will be transferred by delivery of control. Section 7–106. The indorsement of a tangible document of title is generally understood to be directed towards perfecting the transferee's rights rather than towards assuming additional obligations. The language of the present section, however, does not preclude the one case in which an indorsement given for value guarantees future action, namely, that in which the bailee has not yet become liable upon the document at the time of the indorsement. Under such circumstances the indorser, of course, engages that appropriate honor of the document by the bailee will occur. See Section 7–502(a)(4) as to negotiable delivery orders. However, even in such a case, once the bailee attorns to the transferee, the indorser's obligation has been fulfilled and the policy of this section excludes any continuing obligation on the part of the indorser for the bailee's ultimate actual performance.

Cross Reference:

Sections 7–106 and 7–502.

Definitional Cross References:

"Bailee". Section 7–102.
"Document of title". Section 1–201.
"Party". Section 1–201.

§ 7–506. Delivery Without Indorsement: Right to Compel Indorsement.

The transferee of a negotiable tangible document of title has a specifically enforceable right to have its transferor supply any necessary indorsement, but the transfer becomes a negotiation only as of the time the indorsement is supplied.

Official Comment

Prior Uniform Statutory Provision: Former Section 7–506.

Changes: Limited to tangible documents of title.

Purposes:

1. This section is limited to tangible documents of title as the concept of indorsement is irrelevant to electronic documents of title. Electronic documents of title will be transferred by delivery of control. Section 7–106. From a commercial point of view the intention to transfer a tangible negotiable document of title which requires an indorsement for its transfer, is incompatible with an intention to withhold such indorsement and so defeat the effective use of the document. Further, the preceding section and the Comment thereto make it clear that an indorsement generally imposes no responsibility on the indorser.

2. Although this section provides that delivery of a tangible document of title without the necessary indorsement is effective as a transfer, the transferee, of course, has not regularized its position until such indorsement is supplied. Until this is done the transferee cannot claim rights under due negotiation within the requirements of this Article (Section 7–501(a)(5)) on "due negotiation". Similarly, despite the transfer to the transferee of the transferor's title, the transferee cannot demand the goods from the bailee until the negotiation has been completed and the document is in proper form for surrender. See Section 7–403(c).

Cross References:

Point 1: Sections 7–106 and 7–505.
Point 2: Sections 7–501(a)(5) and 7–403(c).

Definitional Cross References:

"Document of title". Section 1–201.
"Rights". Section 1–201.

§ 7–507. Warranties on Negotiation or Delivery of Document of Title.

If a person negotiates or delivers a document of title for value, otherwise than as a mere intermediary under Section 7–508, unless otherwise agreed, the transferor, in addition to any warranty made in selling or leasing the goods, warrants to its immediate purchaser only that:

(1) the document is genuine;

(2) the transferor does not have knowledge of any fact that would impair the document's validity or worth; and

(3) the negotiation or delivery is rightful and fully effective with respect to the title to the document and the goods it represents.

Official Comment

Prior Uniform Statutory Provision: Former Section 7–507.

Changes: Substitution of the word "delivery" for the word "transfer," reference leasing transactions and style.

Purposes:

    1.   Delivery of goods by use of a document of title does not limit or displace the ordinary obligations of a seller or lessor as to any warranties regarding the goods that arises under other law. If the transfer of documents attends or follows the making of a contract for the sale or lease of goods, the general obligations on warranties as to the goods (Sections 2–312 through 2–318 and Sections 2A–210 through 2A–316) are brought to bear as well as the special warranties under this section.

    2.   The limited warranties of a delivering or collecting intermediary, including a collecting bank, are stated in Section 7–508.

Cross References:

    Point 1: Sections 2–312 through 2–318 and 2A–310 through 2A–316.
    Point 2: Section 7–508.

Definitional Cross References:

    "Delivery". Section 1–201.
    "Document of title". Section 1–201.
    "Genuine". Section 1–201.
    "Goods". Section 7–102.
    "Person". Section 1–201.
    "Purchaser". Section 1–201.
    "Value". Section 1–204.

§ 7–508.   Warranties of Collecting Bank as to Documents of Title.

    A collecting bank or other intermediary known to be entrusted with documents of title on behalf of another or with collection of a draft or other claim against delivery of documents warrants by the delivery of the documents only its own good faith and authority even if the collecting bank or other intermediary has purchased or made advances against the claim or draft to be collected.

Official Comment

Prior Uniform Statutory Provision: Former Section 7–508.

Changes: Changes for style only.

Purposes:

    1.   To state the limited warranties given with respect to the documents accompanying a documentary draft.

    2.   In warranting its authority a collecting bank or other intermediary only warrants its authority from its transferor. See Section 4–203. It does not warrant the genuineness or effectiveness of the document. Compare Section 7–507.

    3.   Other duties and rights of banks handling documentary drafts for collection are stated in Article 4, Part 5. On the meaning of draft, see Section 4–104 and Section 5–102, comment 11.

Cross References:

    Sections 4–104, 4–203, 4–501 through 4–504, 5–102, and 7–507.

Definitional Cross References:

    "Collecting bank". Section 4–105.
    "Delivery". Section 1–201.
    "Document of title". Section 1–102.
    "Documentary draft". Section 4–104.

"Intermediary bank". Section 4–105.
"Good faith". Section 1–201 [7–102.]

§ 7–509.   Adequate Compliance with Commercial Contract.

Whether a document of title is adequate to fulfill the obligations of a contract for sale, a contract for lease, or the conditions of a letter of credit is determined by Article 2, 2A, or 5.

Official Comment

Prior Uniform Statutory Provision: Former Section 7–509.

Changes: To reference Article 2A.

Purposes:

To cross-refer to the Articles of this Act which deal with the substantive issues of the type of document of title required under the contract entered into by the parties.

Cross References:

Articles 2, 2A and 5.

Definitional Cross References:

"Contract for sale". Section 2–106.
"Document of title". Section 1–201.
"Lease". Section 2A–103.

PART 6

WAREHOUSE RECEIPTS AND BILLS OF LADING: MISCELLANEOUS PROVISIONS

§ 7–601.   Lost, Stolen, or Destroyed Documents of Title.

(a)   If a document of title is lost, stolen, or destroyed, a court may order delivery of the goods or issuance of a substitute document and the bailee may without liability to any person comply with the order. If the document was negotiable, a court may not order delivery of the goods or issuance of a substitute document without the claimant's posting security unless it finds that any person that may suffer loss as a result of nonsurrender of possession or control of the document is adequately protected against the loss. If the document was nonnegotiable, the court may require security. The court may also order payment of the bailee's reasonable costs and attorney's fees in any action under this subsection.

(b)   A bailee that, without a court order, delivers goods to a person claiming under a missing negotiable document of title is liable to any person injured thereby. If the delivery is not in good faith, the bailee is liable for conversion. Delivery in good faith is not conversion if the claimant posts security with the bailee in an amount at least double the value of the goods at the time of posting to indemnify any person injured by the delivery which files a notice of claim within one year after the delivery.

Official Comment

Prior Uniform Statutory Provision: Former Section 7–601.

Changes: To accommodate electronic documents; to provide flexibility to courts similar to the flexibility in Section 3–309; to update to the modern era of deregulation; and for style.

Purposes:

1.   Subsection (a) authorizes courts to order compulsory delivery of the goods or compulsory issuance of a substitute document. Compare Section 7–402. Using language similar to that found in Section 3–309, courts are given discretion as to what is adequate protection when the lost, stolen or destroyed document was negotiable or whether security should be required when the lost, stolen or destroyed document was nonnegotiable. In determining whether a party is adequately protected against loss in the case of a negotiable document, the court should consider the likelihood that the party will suffer a loss. The court is also given discretion as to the bailee's

costs and attorney fees. The rights and obligations of a bailee under this section depend upon whether the document of title is lost, stolen or destroyed and is in addition to the ability of the bailee to bring an action for interpleader. See Section 7–603.

2.   Courts have the authority under this section to order a substitute document for either tangible or electronic documents. If the substitute document will be in a different medium than the original document, the court should fashion its order in light of the requirements of Section 7–105.

3.   Subsection (b) follows prior Section 7–601 in recognizing the legality of the well established commercial practice of bailees making delivery in good faith when they are satisfied that the claimant is the person entitled under a missing (i.e. lost, stolen, or destroyed) negotiable document. Acting without a court order, the bailee remains liable on the original negotiable document and, to avoid conversion liability, the bailee may insist that the claimant provide an indemnity bond. Cf. Section 7–403.

4.   Claimants on non-negotiable instruments are permitted to avail themselves of the subsection (a) procedure because straight (non-negotiable) bills of lading sometimes contain provisions that the goods shall not be delivered except upon production of the bill. If the carrier should choose to insist upon production of the bill, the consignee should have some means of compelling delivery on satisfactory proof of entitlement. Without a court order, a bailee may deliver, subject to Section 7–403, to a person claiming goods under a non-negotiable document that the same person claims is lost, stolen, or destroyed.

5.   The bailee's lien should be protected when a court orders delivery of the goods pursuant to this section.

Cross References:

Point 1: Sections 3–309, 7–402 and 7–603.
Point 2: Section 7–105.
Point 3: Section 7–403.
Point 4: Section 7–403.
Point 5: Sections 7–209 and 7–307.

Definitional Cross References:

"Bailee". Section 7–102.
"Delivery". Section 1–201.
"Document of title". Section 1–201.
"Good faith". Section 1–201 [7–102].
"Goods". Section 7–102.
"Person". Section 1–201.

§ 7–602.   Judicial Process Against Goods Covered by Negotiable Document of Title.

Unless a document of title was originally issued upon delivery of the goods by a person that did not have power to dispose of them, a lien does not attach by virtue of any judicial process to goods in the possession of a bailee for which a negotiable document of title is outstanding unless possession or control of the document is first surrendered to the bailee or the document's negotiation is enjoined. The bailee may not be compelled to deliver the goods pursuant to process until possession or control of the document is surrendered to the bailee or to the court. A purchaser of the document for value without notice of the process or injunction takes free of the lien imposed by judicial process.

Official Comment

Prior Uniform Statutory Provisions: Former Section 7–602.

Changes: Changes to accommodate electronic documents of title and for style.

Purposes:

1.   The purpose of the section is to protect the bailee from conflicting claims of the document of title holder and the judgment creditors of the person who deposited the goods. The rights of the former prevail unless, in effect, the judgment creditors immobilize the negotiable document of title through the surrender of possession of a tangible document or control of an electronic document. However, if the document of title was issued upon deposit of the goods by a person who had no power to dispose of the goods so that the document is ineffective to pass title, judgment liens are valid to the extent of the debtor's interest in the goods.

2.   The last sentence covers the possibility that the holder of a document who has been enjoined from negotiating it will violate the injunction by negotiating to an innocent purchaser for value. In such case the lien will be defeated.

Cross Reference:

Sections 7–106 and 7–501 through 7–503.

Definitional Cross References:

"Bailee". Section 7–102.
"Delivery". Section 1–201.
"Document of title". Section 1–201.
"Goods". Section 7–102.
"Notice". Section 1–202.
"Person". Section 1–201.
"Purchase". Section 1–201.
"Value". Section 1–204.

§ 7–603.   Conflicting Claims; Interpleader.

If more than one person claims title to or possession of the goods, the bailee is excused from delivery until the bailee has a reasonable time to ascertain the validity of the adverse claims or to commence an action for interpleader. The bailee may assert an interpleader either in defending an action for nondelivery of the goods or by original action.

Official Comment

Prior Uniform Statutory Provisions: Former Section 7–603.

Changes: Changes for style only.

Purposes:

1.   The section enables a bailee faced with conflicting claims to the goods to compel the claimants to litigate their claims with each other rather than with the bailee. The bailee is protected from legal liability when the bailee complies with court orders from the interpleader. *See e.g. Northwestern National Sales, Inc. v. Commercial Cold Storage, Inc.*, 162 Ga. App. 741, 293 S.E.2d. 30 (1982).

2.   This section allows the bailee to bring an interpleader action but does not provide an exclusive basis for allowing interpleader. If either state or federal procedural rules allow an interpleader in other situations, the bailee may commence an interpleader under those rules. Even in an interpleader to which this section applies, the state or federal process of interpleader applies to the bailee's action for interpleader. For example, state or federal interpleader statutes or rules may permit a bailee to protect its lien or to seek attorney's fees and costs in the interpleader action.

Cross reference:

Point 1: Section 7–403.

Definitional Cross References:

"Action". Section 1–201.
"Bailee". Section 7–102.
"Delivery". Section 1–201.
"Goods". Section 7–102.
"Person". Section 1–201.
"Reasonable time". Section 1–205.

PART 7

MISCELLANEOUS PROVISIONS

Legislative Note: The following provisions should be used to apply to both the Article 7 provisions and the conforming amendments to other articles of the Uniform Commercial Code.

[Note from West Advisory Panel: We have deleted these provisions on effective date, repeals, and other transition rules.]

UCC ARTICLE 8

INVESTMENT SECURITIES

Article 8 was revised in 1994 and amended in 2017 and 2022.
2022 Amendments appear in ~~strikeout~~/<u>underline</u> format.
Prefatory Note to 2022 amendments appears in Appendix E.
Current through April 2023
For updates, see www.uniformlaws.org

PART 1.   SHORT TITLE AND GENERAL MATTERS

8–101.   Short Title.
8–102.   Definitions.
8–103.   Rules for Determining Whether Certain Obligations and Interests are Securities or Financial Assets.
8–104.   Acquisition of Security or Financial Asset or Interest Therein.
8–105.   Notice of Adverse Claim.
8–106.   Control.
8–107.   Whether Indorsement, Instruction, or Entitlement Order is Effective.
8–108.   Warranties in Direct Holding.
8–109.   Warranties in Indirect Holding.
8–110.   Applicability; Choice of Law.
8–111.   Clearing Corporation Rules.
8–112.   Creditor's Legal Process.
8–113.   Statute of Frauds Inapplicable.
8–114.   Evidentiary Rules Concerning Certificated Securities.
8–115.   Securities Intermediary and Others Not Liable to Adverse Claimant.
8–116.   Securities Intermediary as Purchaser for Value.

PART 2.   ISSUE AND ISSUER

8–201.   Issuer.
8–202.   Issuer's Responsibility and Defenses; Notice of Defect or Defense.
8–203.   Staleness as Notice of Defect or Defense.
8–204.   Effect of Issuer's Restriction on Transfer.
8–205.   Effect of Unauthorized Signature on Security Certificate.
8–206.   Completion or Alteration of Security Certificate.
8–207.   Rights and Duties of Issuer with Respect to Registered Owners.
8–208.   Effect of Signature of Authenticating Trustee, Registrar, or Transfer Agent.
8–209.   Issuer's Lien.
8–210.   Overissue.

PART 3.   TRANSFER OF CERTIFICATED AND UNCERTIFICATED SECURITIES

8–301.   Delivery.
8–302.   Rights of Purchaser.
8–303.   Protected Purchaser.

8–304.   Indorsement.

8–305.   Instruction.

8–306.   Effect of Guaranteeing Signature, Indorsement, or Instruction.

8–307.   Purchaser's Right to Requisites for Registration of Transfer.

PART 4.   REGISTRATION

8–401.   Duty of Issuer to Register Transfer.

8–402.   Assurance that Indorsement or Instruction is Effective.

8–403.   Demand that Issuer Not Register Transfer.

8–404.   Wrongful Registration.

8–405.   Replacement of Lost, Destroyed, or Wrongfully Taken Security Certificate.

8–406.   Obligation to Notify Issuer of Lost, Destroyed, or Wrongfully Taken Security Certificate.

8–407.   Authenticating Trustee, Transfer Agent, and Registrar.

PART 5.   SECURITY ENTITLEMENTS

8–501.   Securities Account; Acquisition of Security Entitlement from Securities Intermediary.

8–502.   Assertion of Adverse Claim Against Entitlement Holder.

8–503.   Property Interest of Entitlement Holder in Financial Asset Held by Securities Intermediary.

8–504.   Duty of Securities Intermediary to Maintain Financial Asset.

8–505.   Duty of Securities Intermediary with Respect to Payments and Distributions.

8–506.   Duty of Securities Intermediary to Exercise Rights as Directed by Entitlement Holder.

8–507.   Duty of Securities Intermediary to Comply with Entitlement Order.

8–508.   Duty of Securities Intermediary to Change Entitlement Holder's Position to Other Form of Security Holding.

8–509.   Specification of Duties of Securities Intermediary by Other Statute or Regulation; Manner of Performance of Duties of Securities Intermediary and Exercise of Rights of Entitlement Holder.

8–510.   Rights of Purchaser of Security Entitlement from Entitlement Holder.

8–511.   Priority Among Security Interests and Entitlement Holders.

PREFATORY NOTE

The present version of Article 8 is the product of a major revision made necessary by the fact that the prior version of Article 8 did not adequately deal with the system of securities holding through securities intermediaries that has developed in the past few decades. Although the prior version of Article 8 did contain some provisions dealing with securities holding through securities intermediaries, these were engrafted onto a structure designed for securities practices of earlier times. The resulting legal uncertainties adversely affected all participants. The revision is intended to eliminate these uncertainties by providing a modern legal structure for current securities holding practices.

I.   EVOLUTION OF SECURITIES HOLDING SYSTEMS

A.   The Traditional Securities Holding System

The original version of Article 8, drafted in the 1940s and 1950s, was based on the assumption that possession and delivery of physical certificates are the key elements in the securities holding system. Ownership of securities was traditionally evidenced by possession of the certificates, and changes were accomplished by delivery of the certificates.

Transfer of securities in the traditional certificate-based system was a complicated, labor-intensive process. Each time securities were traded, the physical certificates had to be delivered from the seller to the buyer, and in the case of registered securities the certificates had to be surrendered to the issuer or its transfer agent for registration of transfer. As is well known, the mechanical problems of processing the paperwork for securities transfers reached crisis proportions in the late 1960s, leading to calls for the elimination of the physical certificate and development of modern electronic systems for recording ownership of securities and transfers of ownership. That was the focus of the revision effort that led to the promulgation of the 1978 amendments to Article 8 concerning uncertificated securities.

B. The Uncertificated Securities System Envisioned by the 1978 Amendments

In 1978, amendments to Article 8 were approved to establish the commercial law rules that were thought necessary to permit the evolution of a system in which issuers would no longer issue certificates. The Drafting Committee that produced the 1978 amendments was given a fairly limited charge. It was to draft the revisions that would be needed for uncertificated securities, but otherwise leave the Article 8 rules unchanged. Accordingly, the 1978 amendments primarily took the form of adding parallel provisions dealing with uncertificated securities to the existing rules of Article 8 on certificated securities.

The system of securities holding contemplated by the 1978 amendments differed from the traditional system only in that ownership of securities would not be evidenced by physical certificates. It was contemplated that changes in ownership would continue to be reflected by changes in the records of the issuer. The main difference would be that instead of surrendering an indorsed certificate for registration of transfer, an instruction would be sent to the issuer directing it to register the transfer. Although a system of the sort contemplated by the 1978 amendments may well develop in the coming decades, this has not yet happened for most categories of securities. Mutual funds shares have long been issued in uncertificated form, but virtually all other forms of publicly traded corporate securities are still issued in certificated form. Individual investors who wish to be recorded as registered owners on the issuers' books still obtain and hold physical certificates. The certificates representing the largest portion of the shares of publicly traded companies, however, are not held by the beneficial owners, but by clearing corporations. Settlement of securities trading occurs not by delivery of certificates or by registration of transfer on the records of the issuers or their transfer agents, but by computer entries in the records of clearing corporations and securities intermediaries. That is quite different from the system envisioned by the 1978 amendments.

C. Evolution of the Indirect Holding System

At the time of the "paperwork crunch" in the late 1960s, the trading volume on the New York Stock Exchange that so seriously strained the capacities of the clearance and settlement system was in the range of 10 million shares per day. Today, the system can easily handle trading volume on routine days of hundreds of millions of shares. This processing capacity could have been achieved only by the application of modern electronic information processing systems. Yet the legal rules under which the system operates are *not* the uncertificated securities provisions of Article 8. To understand why this is so, one must delve at least a bit deeper into the operations of the current system.

If one examines the shareholder records of large corporations whose shares are publicly traded on the exchanges or in the over the counter market, one would find that one entity—Cede & Co.—is listed as the shareholder of record of somewhere in the range of sixty to eighty per cent of the outstanding shares of all publicly traded companies. Cede & Co. is the nominee name used by The Depository Trust Company ("DTC"), a limited purpose trust company organized under New York law for the purpose of acting as a depository to hold securities for the benefit of its participants, some 600 or so broker-dealers and banks. Essentially all of the trading in publicly held companies is executed through the broker-dealers who are participants in DTC, and the great bulk of public securities—the sixty to eighty per cent figure noted above—are held by these broker-dealers and banks on behalf of their customers. If all of these broker-dealers and banks held physical certificates, then as trades were executed each day it would be necessary to deliver the certificates back and forth among these broker-dealers and banks. By handing all of their securities over to a common depository all of these deliveries can be eliminated. Transfers can be accomplished by adjustments to the participants' DTC accounts.

Although the use of a common depository eliminates the needs for physical deliveries, an enormous number of entries would still have to be made on DTC's books if each transaction between its participants were recorded one by one on DTC's books. Any two major broker-dealers may have executed numerous trades with each other in a given security on a single day. Significant processing efficiency has been achieved by netting all of the transactions among the participants that occur each day, so that entries need be made on the depository's books only for the net changes in the positions of each participant at the end of each day. This clearance and netting function might well be performed by the securities exchanges or by the same institution that acts as the depository, as is the case in many other securities markets around the world. In the United States, however, this clearance and netting function is carried out by a separate corporation, National Securities Clearing Corporation ("NSCC"). All that needs to be done to settle each day's trading is for NSCC to compute the net receive and deliver obligations and to instruct DTC to make the corresponding adjustments in the participants' accounts.

The broker-dealers and banks who are participants in the DTC-NSCC system in turn provide analogous clearance and settlement functions to their own customers. If Customer A buys 100 shares of XYZ Co. through Broker, and Customer B sells 100 shares of XYZ Co. through the same Broker, the trade can be settled by entries on Broker's books. Neither DTC's books showing Broker's total position in XYZ Co., nor XYZ Co.'s books showing DTC's total position in XYZ Co., need be changed to reflect the settlement of this trade. One can readily appreciate the significance of the settlement function performed at this level if one considers that a single major bank may be acting as securities custodian for hundreds or thousands of mutual funds, pension funds, and other institutional investors. On any given day, the customers of that bank may have entered into an enormous number of trades, yet it is possible that relatively little of this trading activity will result in any net change in the custodian bank's positions on the books of DTC.

Settlement of market trading in most of the major U.S. securities markets is now effected primarily through some form of netted clearance and depository system. Virtually all publicly traded corporate equity securities, corporate debt securities, and municipal debt securities are now eligible for deposit in the DTC system. Recently, DTC has implemented a similar depository settlement system for the commercial paper market, and could, but for limitations in present Article 8, handle other forms of short-term money market securities such as bankers' acceptances. For trading in mortgage-backed securities, such as Ginnie Mae's, a similar depository settlement system has been developed by Participants Trust Company. For trading in U.S. Treasury securities, a somewhat analogous book-entry system is operated under Treasury rules by the Federal Reserve System.

D. Need for Different Legal Rules for the Direct and Indirect Holding Systems

Both the traditional paper-based system, and the uncertificated system contemplated by the 1978 amendments, can be described as "direct" securities holding systems; that is, the beneficial owners of securities have a direct relationship with the issuer of the securities. For securities in bearer form, whoever has possession of the certificate thereby has a direct claim against the issuer. For registered securities, the registered owner, whether of certificated or uncertificated securities, has a direct relationship with the issuer by virtue of being recorded as the owner on the records maintained by the issuer or its transfer agent.

By contrast, the DTC depository system for corporate equity and debt securities can be described as an "indirect holding" system, that is, the issuer's records do not show the identity of all of the beneficial owners. Instead, a large portion of the outstanding securities of any given issue are recorded on the issuer's records as belonging to a depository. The depository's records in turn show the identity of the banks or brokers who are its members, and the records of those securities intermediaries show the identity of their customers.

Even after the 1978 amendments, the rules of Article 8 did not deal effectively with the indirect holding system. The rules of the 1978 version of Article 8 were based on the assumption that changes in ownership of securities would still be effected either by delivery of physical certificates or by registration of transfer on the books of the issuer. Yet in the indirect holding system, settlement of the vast majority of securities trades does not involve either of these events. For most, if not all, of the securities held through DTC, physical certificates representing DTC's total position do exist. These "jumbo certificates," however, are never delivered from person to person. Just as nothing ever happens to these certificates, virtually nothing happens to the official registry of stockholders maintained by the issuers or their transfer agents to reflect the great bulk of the changes in ownership of shares that occur each day.

The principal mechanism through which securities trades are settled today is not delivery of certificates or registration of transfers on the issuer's books, but netted settlement arrangements and accounting entries on the books of a multi-tiered pyramid of securities intermediaries. Herein is the basic problem. Virtually all of the rules of the prior version of Article 8 specifying how changes in ownership of securities are effected, and what happens if something goes awry in the process, were keyed to the concepts of a transfer of physical certificates or registration of transfers on the books of the issuers, yet that is not how changes in ownership are actually reflected in the modern securities holding system.

ARTICLE 8

II.   BRIEF OVERVIEW OF REVISED ARTICLE 8

A.   Drafting Approach—Neutrality Principle

One of the objectives of the revision of Article 8 is to devise a structure of commercial law rules for investment securities that will be sufficiently flexible to respond to changes in practice over the next few decades. If it were possible to predict with confidence how the securities holding and trading system would develop, one could produce a statute designed specifically for the system envisioned. Recent experience, however, shows the danger of that approach. The 1978 amendments to Article 8 were based on the assumption that the solution to the problems that plagued the paper-based securities trading system of the 1960s would be the development of uncertificated securities. Instead, the solution thus far has been the development of the indirect holding system.

If one thought that the indirect holding system would come to dominate securities holding, one might draft Article 8 rules designed primarily for the indirect holding system, giving limited attention to the traditional direct holding system of security certificates or any uncertificated version of a direct holding system that might develop in the future. It is, however, by no means clear whether the long-term evolution will be toward decreased or increased use of direct holdings. At present, investors in most equity securities can either hold their securities through brokers or request that certificates be issued in their own name. For the immediate future it seems likely that that situation will continue. One can imagine many plausible scenarios for future evolution. Direct holding might become less and less common as investors become more familiar and comfortable with book-entry systems and/or as market or regulatory pressures develop that discourage direct holding. One might note, for example, that major brokerage firms are beginning to impose fees for having certificates issued and that some observers have suggested that acceleration of the cycle for settlement of securities trades might be facilitated by discouraging customers from obtaining certificates. On the other hand, other observers feel that it is important for investors to retain the option of holding securities in certificated form, or at least in some form that gives them a direct relationship with the issuer and does not require them to hold through brokers or other securities intermediaries. Some groups within the securities industry are beginning to work on development of uncertificated systems that would preserve this option.

Revised Article 8 takes a neutral position on the evolution of securities holding practices. The revision was based on the assumption that the path of development will be determined by market and regulatory forces and that the Article 8 rules should not seek to influence that development in any specific direction. Although various drafting approaches were considered, it became apparent early in the revision process that the differences between the direct holding system and the indirect holding system are sufficiently significant that it is best to treat them as separate systems requiring different legal concepts. Accordingly, while the rules of the prior version of Article 8 have, in large measure, been retained for the direct holding system, a new Part 5 has been added, setting out the commercial law rules for the indirect securities holding system. The principle of neutrality does carry some implications for the design of specific Article 8 rules. At the very least, the Article 8 rules for all securities holding systems should be sufficiently clear and predictable that uncertainty about the governing law does not itself operate as a constraint on market developments. In addition, an effort has been made to identify and eliminate any Article 8 rules that might act as impediments to any of the foreseeable paths of development.

B.   Direct Holding System

With respect to securities held directly, Revised Article 8 retains the basic conceptual structure and rules of present law. Part 2, which is largely unchanged from former law, deals with certain aspects of the obligations of issuers. The primary purpose of the rules of Part 2 is to apply to investment securities the principles of negotiable instruments law that preclude the issuers of negotiable instruments from asserting defenses against subsequent purchasers. Part 3 deals with transfer for securities held directly. One of its principal purposes is to apply to investment securities the principles of negotiable instruments law that protect purchasers of negotiable instruments against adverse claims. Part 4 deals with the process of registration of transfer by the issuer or transfer agent.

Although the basic concepts of the direct holding system rules have been retained, there are significant changes in terminology, organization, and statement of the rules. Some of the major changes are as follows:

Simplification of Part 3. The addition of the new Part 5 on the indirect holding system makes unnecessary the rather elaborate provisions of former law, such as those in Section 8–313, that sought to fit the indirect holding system into the conceptual structure of the direct holding system. Thus, Part 3 of Revised Article 8 is, in many respects, more similar to the original version of Article 8 than to the 1978 version.

Protected purchaser. The prior version of Article 8 used the term "bona fide purchaser" to refer to those purchasers who took free from adverse claims, and it used the phrase "good faith" in stating the requirements for such status. In order to promote clarity, Revised Article 8 states the rules that protect purchasers against adverse claims without using the phrase "good faith" and uses the new term "protected purchaser" to refer to purchasers in the direct holding system who are protected against adverse claims. See Sections 8–105 and 8–303.

Certificated versus uncertificated securities. The rules of the 1978 version of Article 8 concerning uncertificated securities have been simplified considerably. The 1978 version added provisions on uncertificated securities parallel to the provisions of the original version of Article 8 dealing with securities represented by certificates. Thus, virtually every section had one set of rules on "certificated securities" and another on "uncertificated securities." The constant juxtaposition of "certificated securities" and "uncertificated securities" has probably led readers to overemphasize the differences. Revised Article 8 has a unitary definition of "security" in Section 8–102(a)(15) which refers to the underlying intangible interest or obligation. In Revised Article 8, the difference between certificated and uncertificated is treated not as an inherent attribute of the security but as a difference in the means by which ownership is evidenced. The terms "certificated" and "uncertificated" security are used in those sections where it is important to distinguish between these two means of evidencing ownership. Revised Article 8 also deletes the provisions of the 1978 version concerning "transaction statements" and "registered pledges." These changes are explained in the Revision Notes 3, 4, and 5, below.

Scope of Parts 2, 3, and 4. The rules of Parts 2, 3, and 4 deal only with the rights of persons who hold securities directly. In typical securities holding arrangements in the modern depository system, only the clearing corporation would be a direct holder of the securities. Thus, while the rules of Parts 2, 3, and 4 would apply to the relationship between the issuer and the clearing corporation, they have no application to relationships below the clearing corporation level. Under Revised Article 8, a person who holds a security through a broker or securities custodian has a security entitlement governed by the Part 5 rules but is not the direct holder of the security. Thus, the rules of Revised Section 8–303 on the rights of "protected purchasers," which are the analog of the bona fide purchaser rules of former Article 8, do not apply to persons who hold securities through brokers or securities custodians. Instead, Part 5 contains its own rules to protect investors in the indirect holding system against adverse claims. See Revised Section 8–502.

C.   Indirect Holding System

Although the Revised Article 8 provisions for the indirect holding system are somewhat complex, the basic approach taken can be summarized rather briefly. Revised Article 8 abandons the attempt to describe all of the complex relationships in the indirect holding system using the simple concepts of the traditional direct holding system. Instead, new rules specifically designed for the indirect holding system are added as Part 5 of Article 8. In a nutshell, the approach is to describe the core of the package of rights of a person who holds a security through a securities intermediary and then give that package of rights a name.

The starting point of Revised Article 8's treatment of the indirect holding system is the concept of "security entitlement." The term is defined in Section 8–102(a)(17) as "the rights and property interest of an entitlement holder with respect to a financial asset specified in Part 5." Like many legal concepts, however, the meaning of "security entitlement" is to be found less in any specific definition than in the matrix of rules that use the term. In a sense, then, the entirety of Part 5 is the definition of "security entitlement" because the Part 5 rules specify the rights and property interest that comprise a security entitlement.

Part 5 begins by specifying, in Section 8–501, when an entitlement holder acquires a security entitlement. The basic rule is very simple. A person acquires a security entitlement when the securities intermediary credits the financial asset to the person's account. The remaining sections of Part 5 specify the content of the security entitlement concept. Section 8–504 provides that a securities intermediary must maintain a sufficient quantity of financial assets to satisfy the claims of all of its entitlement holders. Section

ARTICLE 8

8–503 provides that these financial assets are held by the intermediary for the entitlement holders, are not the property of the securities intermediary, and are not subject to claims of the intermediary's general creditors. Thus, a security entitlement is itself a form of property interest not merely an *in personam* claim against the intermediary. The concept of a security entitlement does, however, include a package of *in personam* rights against the intermediary. Other Part 5 rules identify the core of this package of rights, subject to specification by agreement and regulatory law. See Sections 8–505 through 8–509.

To illustrate the basic features of the new rules, consider a simple example of two investors, John and Mary, each of whom owns 1000 shares of Acme, Inc., a publicly traded company. John has a certificate representing his 1000 shares and is registered on the books maintained by Acme's transfer agent as the holder of record of those 1000 shares. Accordingly, he has a direct claim against the issuer, he receives dividends and distributions directly from the issuer, and he receives proxies directly from the issuer for purposes of voting his shares. Mary has chosen to hold her securities through her broker. She does not have a certificate and is not registered on Acme's stock books as a holder of record. She enjoys the economic and corporate benefits of ownership but does so through her broker and any other intermediaries in the chain back to the issuer. John's interest in Acme common stock would be described under Revised Article 8 as a direct interest in a "security." Thus, if John grants a security interest in his investment position, the collateral would be described as a "security." Mary's interest in Acme common stock would be described under Revised Article 8 as a "security entitlement." Thus, if Mary grants a security interest in her investment position, the collateral would be described as a "security entitlement."

For many purposes, there is no need to differentiate among the various ways that an investor might hold securities. For example, for purposes of financial accounting, John and Mary would each be described as the owner of 1000 shares of Acme common stock. For those purposes it is irrelevant that John is the registered owner and has physical possession of a certificate, while Mary holds her position through an intermediary. Revised Article 8 recognizes this point in Section 8–104 which provides that acquiring a security entitlement and acquiring a security certificate are different ways of acquiring an interest in the underlying security.

D. Security Interests

Along with the revision of Article 8, significant changes have been made in the rules concerning security interests in securities. The revision returns to the pre-1978 structure in which the rules on security interests in investment securities are set out in Article 9, rather than in Article 8. The changes in Article 9 are, in part, conforming changes to adapt Article 9 to the new concept of a security entitlement. The Article 9 changes, however, go beyond that to establish a simplified structure for the creation and perfection of security interests in investment securities, whether held directly or indirectly.

The Revised Article 9 rules continue the long-established principle that a security interest in a security represented by a certificate can be perfected by a possessory pledge. The revised rules, however, do not require that all security interests in investment securities be implemented by procedures based on the conceptual structure of the common law pledge. Under the revised Article 9 rules, a security interest in securities can be created pursuant to Section 9–203 in the same fashion as a security interest in any other form of property, that is, by agreement between the debtor and secured party. There is no requirement of a "transfer," "delivery," or any similar action, physical or metaphysical, for the creation of an effective security interest. A security interest in securities is, of course, a form of property interest, but the only requirements for creation of this form of property interest are those set out in Section 9–203.

The perfection methods for security interests in investment securities are set out in Sections 9–309, 9–312, 9–313, and 9–314. The basic rule is that a security interest may be perfected by "control." The concept of control, defined in Section 8–106, plays an important role in both Article 8 and Article 9. In general, obtaining control means taking the steps necessary to place the lender in a position where it can have the collateral sold off without the further cooperation of the debtor. Thus, for certificated securities, a lender obtains control by taking possession of the certificate with any necessary indorsement. For securities held through a securities intermediary, the lender can obtain control in two ways. First, the lender obtains control if it becomes the entitlement holder; that is, has the securities positions transferred to an account in its own name. Second, the lender obtains control if the securities intermediary agrees to act on instructions from the secured party to dispose of the positions, even though the debtor remains the entitlement holder.

Such an arrangement suffices to give the lender control even though the debtor retains the right to trade and exercise other ordinary rights of an entitlement holder.

Except where the debtor is itself a securities firm, filing of an ordinary Article 9 financing statement is also a permissible alternative method of perfection. However, filing with respect to investment property does not assure the lender the same protections as for other forms of collateral, since the priority rules provide that a secured party who obtains control has priority over a secured party who does not obtain control.

The details of the new rules on security interests, as applied both to the retail level and to arrangements for secured financing of securities dealers, explained in the Official Comments to Sections 9–309, 9–312, 9–313, and 9–314.

III. SCOPE AND APPLICATION OF ARTICLE 8

A. Terminology

To understand the scope and application of the rules of Revised Article 8, and the related security interest rules of Article 9, it is necessary to understand some of the key defined terms:

Security, defined in Section 8–102(a)(15), has essentially the same meaning as under the prior version of Article 8. The difference in Revised Article 8 is that the definition of security does not determine the coverage of all of Article 8. Although the direct holding system rules in Parts 2, 3, and 4 apply only to securities, the indirect holding system rules of Part 5 apply to the broader category of "financial assets."

Financial asset, defined in Section 8–103(a)(9), is the term used to describe the forms of property to which the indirect holding system rules of Part 5 apply. The term includes not only "securities," but also other interests, obligations, or property that are held through securities accounts. The best illustration of the broader scope of the term financial asset is the treatment of money market instruments, discussed below.

Security entitlement, defined in Section 8–103(a)(17), is the term used to describe the property interest of a person who holds a security or other financial asset through a securities intermediary.

Securities intermediary, defined in Section 8–103(a)(14), is the term used for those who hold securities for others in the indirect holding system. It covers clearing corporations, banks acting as securities custodians, and brokers holding securities for their customers.

Entitlement holder, defined in Section 8–103(a)(7), is the term used for those who hold securities through intermediaries.

Securities account, defined in Section 8–501(a), describes the form of arrangement between a securities intermediary and an entitlement holder that gives rise to a security entitlement. As explained below, the definition of securities account plays a key role in setting the scope of the indirect holding system rules of Part 5.

Investment property, defined in Section 9–102(a)(49), determines the application of the new Article 9 rules for secured transactions. In addition to securities and security entitlements, the Article 9 term "investment property" is defined to include "securities account" in order to simplify the drafting of the Article 9 rules that permit debtors to grant security interests either in specific security entitlements or in an entire securities account. The other difference between the coverage of the Article 8 and Article 9 terms is that commodity futures contracts are excluded from Article 8, but are included within the Article 9 definition of "investment property." Thus, the new Article 9 rules apply to security interests in commodity futures positions as well as security interests in securities positions.

B. Notes on Scope of Article 8

Article 8 is in no sense a comprehensive codification of the law governing securities or transactions in securities. Although Article 8 deals with some aspects of the rights of securities holders against issuers, most of that relationship is governed not by Article 8, but by corporation, securities, and contract law. Although Article 8 deals with some aspects of the rights and duties of parties who transfer securities, it is not a codification of the law of contracts for the purchase or sale of securities. (The prior version of Article 8 did include a few miscellaneous rules on contracts for the sale of securities, but these have not been included in Revised Article 8). Although the new indirect holding system rules of Part 5 deal with some aspects of the relationship between brokers or other securities professionals and their customers, Article 8 is still not in any sense a comprehensive code of the law governing the relationship between broker-dealers or other securities intermediaries and their customers. Most of the law governing that relationship is the common law of contract and agency, supplemented or supplanted by regulatory law.

The distinction between the aspects of the broker-customer relationship that are and are not dealt with in this Article may be illuminated by considering the differing roles of the broker in a typical securities transaction, in which the broker acts as agent for the customer. When a customer directs a broker to buy or sell securities for the customer, and the broker executes that trade on a securities exchange or in the over the counter market, the broker is entering into a contract for the purchase or sale of the securities as agent of the customer. The rules of the exchange, practices of the market, or regulatory law will specify when and how that contract is to be performed. For example, today the terms of the standard contract for trades in most corporate securities require the seller to deliver the securities, and the buyer to pay for them, five business days after the date that the contract was made, although the SEC has recently promulgated a rule that will accelerate the cycle to require settlement in three business days. In the common speech of the industry, the transaction in which the broker enters into a contract for the purchase or sale of the securities is referred to as executing the trade, and the transaction in which the securities are delivered and paid for is referred to as settlement. Thus, the current settlement cycle is known as T+5, that is, settlement is required on the fifth business day after the date of the trade, and the new SEC rule will change it to T+3. One must be careful in moving from the jargon of the securities industry to the jargon of the legal profession. For most practical economic purposes, the trade date is the date that counts, because that is the time at which the price is set, the risk of price changes shifts, and the parties become bound to perform. For purposes of precise legal analysis, however, the securities phrase "trade" or "execute a trade" means enter into a contract for the purchase or sale of the securities. The transfer of property interests occurs not at the time the contract is made but at the time it is performed, that is, at settlement.

The distinction between trade and settlement is important in understanding the scope of Article 8. Article 8 deals with the settlement phase of securities transactions. It deals with the mechanisms by which interests in securities are transferred, and the rights and duties of those who are involved in the transfer process. It does not deal with the process of entering into contracts for the transfer of securities or regulate the rights and duties of those involved in the contracting process. To use securities parlance, Article 8 deals not with the trade, but with settlement of the trade. Indeed, Article 8 does not even deal with all aspects of settlement. In a netted clearance and settlement system such as the NSCC-DTC system, individual trades are not settled one-by-one by corresponding entries on the books of any depository. Rather, settlement of the individual trades occurs through the clearing arrangements, in accordance with the rules and agreements that govern those arrangements.

In the rules dealing with the indirect holding system, one must be particularly careful to bear in mind the distinction between trade and settlement. Under Revised Article 8, the property interest of a person who holds securities through an intermediary is described as a "security entitlement," which is defined in Revised Section 8–102(a)(17) as the package of rights and property interest of an entitlement holder specified in Part 5. Saying that the security entitlement is a package of rights against the broker does not mean that all of the customer's rights against the broker are part of the security entitlement and hence part of the subject matter of Article 8. The distinction between trade and settlement remains fundamental. The rules of this Article on the indirect holding system deal with brokers and other intermediaries as media through which investors hold their financial assets. Brokers are also media through which investors buy and sell their financial assets, but that aspect of their role is not the subject of this Article.

The principal goal of the Article 8 revision project is to provide a satisfactory framework for analysis of the indirect holding system. The technique used in Revised Article 8 is to acknowledge explicitly that the relationship between a securities intermediary and its entitlement holders is *sui generis*, and to state the applicable commercial law rules directly, rather than by inference from a categorization of the relationship based on legal concepts of a different era. One of the consequences of this drafting technique is that in order to provide content to the concept of security entitlement it becomes necessary to identify the core of the package of rights that make up a security entitlement. Sections 8–504 through 8–508 cover such basic matters as the duty of the securities intermediary to maintain a sufficient quantity of securities to satisfy all of its entitlement holders, the duty of the securities intermediary to pass through to entitlement holder the economic and corporate law rights of ownership of the security, and the duty of the securities intermediary to comply with authorized entitlement orders originated by the entitlement holder. These sections are best thought of as definitional; that is, a relationship which does not include these rights is not the kind of relationship that Revised Article 8 deals with. Because these sections take the form of statements of the duties of an intermediary toward its entitlement holders, one must be careful to avoid a distorted perspective on what Revised Article 8 is and is not designed to do. Revised Article 8 is not, and should not be, a comprehensive body of private law governing the relationship between brokers and their customers, nor a body of regulatory law to police against improper conduct by brokers or other intermediaries. Many, if not most, aspects of the relationship between brokers and customers are governed by the common law of contract and agency, supplemented or supplanted by federal and state regulatory law. Revised Article 8 does not take the place of this body of private and regulatory law. If there are gaps in the regulatory law, they should be dealt with as such; Article 8 is not the place to address them. Article 8 deals with how interests in securities are evidenced and how they are transferred. By way of a rough analogy, one might think of Article 8 as playing the role for the securities markets that real estate recording acts play for the real estate markets. Real estate recording acts do not regulate the conduct of parties to real estate transactions; Article 8 does not regulate the conduct of parties to securities transactions.

C. Application of Revised Articles 8 and 9 to Common Investments and Investment Arrangements

It may aid understanding to sketch briefly the treatment under Revised Articles 8 and 9 of a variety of relatively common products and arrangements.

1. Publicly traded stocks and bonds.

"Security" is defined in Revised Section 8–102(a)(15) in substantially the same terms as in the prior version of Article 8. It covers the ordinary publicly traded investment securities, such as corporate stocks and bonds. Parts 2, 3, and 4 govern the interests of persons who hold securities directly, and Part 5 governs the interest of those who hold securities indirectly.

Ordinary publicly traded securities provide a good illustration of the relationship between the direct and indirect holding system rules. The distinction between the direct and indirect holding systems is not an attribute of the securities themselves but of the way in which a particular person holds the securities. Thus, whether one looks to the direct holding system rules of Parts 2, 3, and 4 or the indirect holding system rules of Part 5 will depend on the level in the securities holding system being analyzed.

Consider, for example, corporate stock which is held through a depository, such as DTC. The clearing corporation, or its nominee, is the registered owner of all of the securities it holds on behalf of all of its participants. Thus the rules of Parts 2, 3, and 4 of Revised Article 8 apply to the relationship between the issuer and the clearing corporation. If, as is typically the case today, the securities are still represented by certificates, the clearing corporation will be the holder of the security certificate or certificates representing its total holdings. So far as Article 8 is concerned, the relationship between the issuer and the clearing corporation is no different from the relationship between the issuer and any other registered owner.

The relationship between the clearing corporation and its participants is governed by the indirect holding system rules of Part 5. At that level, the clearing corporation is the securities intermediary and the participant is the entitlement holder. If the participant is itself a securities intermediary, such as a broker holding for its customers or a bank acting as a securities custodian, the Part 5 rules apply to its relationship to its own customers. At that level the broker or bank custodian is the securities intermediary and the customer is the entitlement holder. Note that the broker or bank custodian is both an entitlement holder and a securities intermediary—but is so with respect to different security entitlements. For purposes of Article 8 analysis, the customer's security entitlement against the broker or bank custodian is a different item of property from the security entitlement of the broker or bank custodian against the clearing corporation.

For investors who hold their securities directly, it makes no difference that some other investors hold their interests indirectly. Many investors today choose to hold their securities directly, becoming the registered owners on the books of the issuer and obtaining certificates registered in their names. For such investors, the addition of the new indirect holding system rules to Article 8 is entirely irrelevant. They will continue to deal directly with the issuers, or their transfer agents, under essentially the same rules as in the prior version of Article 8.

ARTICLE 8

The securities holding options available to investors in a particular form of security may depend on the terms of the security. For example, direct holding is frequently not available for new issues of state and local government bonds. At one time, state and local government bonds were commonly issued in bearer form. Today, however, new issues of state and local government bonds must be in registered form and most are issued in what is known as "book-entry only" form; that is, the issuer specifies that the only person it will directly register as the registered owner is a clearing corporation. Thus, one of the inherent terms of the security is that investors can hold only in the indirect holding system.

2. Treasury securities.

U.S. government securities fall within the definition of security in Article 8 and therefore are governed by Article 8 in the same fashion as any other publicly held debt security, except insofar as Article 8 is preempted by applicable federal law or regulation.

New Treasury securities are no longer issued in certificated form; they can be held only through the book-entry systems established by the Treasury and Federal Reserve Banks. The Treasury offers a book-entry system, known as "Treasury Direct" which enables individual investors to have their positions recorded directly on the books of a Federal Reserve Bank, in a fashion somewhat similar to the uncertificated direct holding system contemplated by the 1978 version of Article 8. The governing law for the Treasury Direct system, however, is set out in the applicable Treasury regulations. The Treasury Direct system is not designed for active trading.

The great bulk of Treasury securities are held not through the Treasury Direct system but through a multi-tiered indirect holding system. The Federal Reserve Banks, acting as fiscal agent for the Treasury, maintain records of the holdings of member banks of the Federal Reserve System, and those banks in turn maintain records showing the extent to which they are holding for themselves or their own customers, including government securities dealers, institutional investors, or smaller banks who in turn may act as custodians for investors. The indirect holding system for Treasury securities was established under federal regulations promulgated in the 1970s. In the 1980s, Treasury released the proposed TRADES regulations that would have established a more comprehensive body of federal commercial law for the Treasury holding system. During the Article 8 revision process, Treasury withdrew these regulations, anticipating that once Revised Article 8 is enacted, it will be possible to base the law for the Treasury system on the new Article 8 rules.

3. Broker-customer relationships.

Whether the relationship between a broker and its customer is governed by the Article 8 Part 5 rules depends on the nature of the services that the broker performs for the customer.

Some investors use brokers only to purchase and sell securities. These customers take delivery of certificates representing the securities they purchase and hold them in their own names. When they wish to sell, they deliver the certificates to the brokers. The Article 8 Part 5 rules would not affect such customers, because the Part 5 rules deal with arrangements in which investors hold securities through securities intermediaries. The transaction between the customer and broker might be the traditional agency arrangement in which the broker buys or sells on behalf of the customer as agent for an undisclosed principal, or it might be a dealer transaction in which the "broker" as principal buys from or sells to the customer. In either case, if the customer takes delivery and holds the securities directly, she will become the "purchaser" of a "security" whose interest therein is governed by the rules of Parts 2, 3, and 4 of Article 8. If the customer meets the other requirements of Section 8–303(a), the customer who takes delivery can qualify as a "protected purchaser" who takes free from any adverse claims under Section 8–303(b). The broker's role in such transactions is primarily governed by non-Article 8 law. There are only a few provisions of Article 8 that affect the relationship between the customer and broker in such cases. See Section 8–108 (broker makes to the customer the warranties of a transferor) and 8–115 (broker not liable in conversion if customer was acting wrongfully against a third party in selling securities).

Many investors use brokers not only to purchase and sell securities, but also as the custodians through whom they hold their securities. The indirect holding system rules of Part 5 apply to the custodial aspect of this relationship. If a customer purchases a security through a broker and directs the broker to hold the security in an account for the customer, the customer will never become a "purchaser" of a "security" whose interest therein is governed by the rules of Parts 2, 3, and 4 of Article 8. Accordingly, the customer does not become a "protected purchaser" under Section 8–303. Rather, the customer becomes an "entitlement holder" who has a "security entitlement" to the security against the broker as "securities intermediary." See Section 8–501. It would make no sense to say that the customer in such a case takes an interest in the security free from all other claims, since the nature of the relationship is that the customer has an interest in common with other customers who hold positions in the same security through the same broker. Section 8–502, however, does protect an entitlement holder against adverse claims, in the sense that once the entitlement holder has acquired the package of rights that comprise a security entitlement no one else can take that package of rights away by arguing that the transaction that resulted in the customer's acquisition of the security entitlement was the traceable product of a transfer or transaction that was wrongful as against the claimant.

4.   Bank deposit accounts; brokerage asset management accounts.

An ordinary bank deposit account would not fall within the definition of "security" in Section 8–102(a)(15), so the rules of Parts 2, 3, and 4 of Article 8 do not apply to deposit accounts. Nor would the relationship between a bank and its depositors be governed by the rules of Part 5 of Article 8. The Part 5 rules apply to "security entitlements." Section 8–501(b) provides that a person has a security entitlement when a securities intermediary credits a financial asset to the person's "securities account." "Securities account" is defined in Section 8–501(a) as "an account to which a financial asset is or may be credited in accordance with an agreement under which the person maintaining the account undertakes to treat the person for whom the account is maintained as entitled to exercise the rights that comprise the financial asset." The definition of securities account plays a key role in setting the scope of Part 5 of Article 8. A person has a security entitlement governed by Part 5 only if the relationship in question falls within the definition of "securities account." The definition of securities account in Section 8–501(a) excludes deposit accounts from the Part 5 rules of Article 8. One of the basic elements of the relationship between a securities intermediary and an entitlement holder is that the securities intermediary has the duty to hold exactly the quantity of securities that it carries for the account of its customers. See Section 8–504. The assets that a securities intermediary holds for its entitlement holder are not assets that the securities intermediary can use in its own proprietary business. See Section 8–503. A deposit account is an entirely different arrangement. A bank is not required to hold in its vaults or in deposit accounts with other banks a sum of money equal to the claims of all of its depositors. Banks are permitted to use depositors' funds in their ordinary lending business; indeed, that is a primary function of banks. A deposit account, unlike a securities account, is simply a debtor-creditor relationship. Thus a bank or other financial institution maintaining deposit accounts is not covered by Part 5 of Article 8.

Today, it is common for brokers to maintain securities accounts for their customers which include arrangements for the customers to hold liquid "cash" assets in the form of money market mutual fund shares. Insofar as the broker is holding money market mutual fund shares for its customer, the customer has a security entitlement to the money market mutual fund shares. It is also common for brokers to offer their customers an arrangement in which the customer has access to those liquid assets via a deposit account with a bank, whereby shares of the money market fund are redeemed to cover checks drawn on the account. Article 8 applies only to the securities account; the linked bank account remains an account covered by other law. Thus the rights and duties of the customer and the bank are governed not by Article 8, but by the relevant payment system law, such as Article 4 or Article 4A.

5.   Trusts.

The indirect holding system rules of Part 5 of Article 8 are not intended to govern all relationships in which one person holds securities "on behalf of" another. Rather, the Part 5 rules come into play only if the relationship in question falls within the definition of securities account in Section 8–501(a). The definition of securities account serves the important function of ensuring that ordinary trust arrangements are not inadvertently swept into Part 5 of Article 8. Suppose that Bank serves as trustee of a trust for the benefit of Beneficiary. The corpus of the trust is invested in securities and other financial assets. Although Bank is, in some senses, holding securities for Beneficiary, the arrangement would not fall within the definition of securities account. Bank, as trustee, has not undertaken to treat Beneficiary as entitled to exercise all of the rights that comprise the portfolio securities. For instance, although Beneficiary receives the economic benefit of the portfolio securities, Beneficiary does not have the right to direct dispositions of individual trust assets or to exercise voting or other corporate law rights with respect to the individual securities. Thus Bank's obligations to Beneficiary as trustee are governed by ordinary trust law, not by Part 5 of Article 8.

Of course, if Bank, as trustee, holds the securities through an intermediary, Part 5 of Revised Article 8 would govern the relationship between Bank, as entitlement holder, and the intermediary through which Bank holds the securities. It is also possible that a different department of Bank acts as the intermediary through which Bank, as trustee, holds the securities. Bank, *qua* securities custodian, might be holding securities for a large number of customers, including Bank's own trust department. Insofar as Bank may be regarded as acting in different capacities, Part 5 of Article 8 may be relevant to the relationship between the two sides of Bank's business. However, the relationship between Bank as trustee and the beneficiaries of the trust would remain governed by trust law, not Article 8.

6. Mutual fund shares.

Shares of mutual funds are Article 8 securities, whether the fund is organized as a corporation, business trust, or other form of entity. See Sections 8–102(a)(15) and 8–103(b). Mutual funds commonly do not issue certificates. Thus, mutual fund shares are typically uncertificated securities under Article 8.

Although a mutual fund is, in a colloquial sense, holding the portfolio securities on behalf of the fund's shareholders, the indirect holding system rules of Part 5 do not apply to the relationship between the fund and its shareholders. The Part 5 rules apply to "security entitlements." Section 8–501(e) provides that issuance of a security is not establishment of a security entitlement. Thus, because mutual funds shares do fit within the Article 8 definition of security, the relationship between the fund and its shareholders is automatically excluded from the Part 5 rules.

Of course, a person might hold shares in a mutual fund through a brokerage account. Because mutual fund shares are securities, they automatically fall within the broader term "financial asset," so the Part 5 indirect holding system rules apply to mutual fund shares that are held through securities accounts. That is, a person who holds mutual fund shares through a brokerage account could have a security entitlement to the mutual fund shares, just as the person would have a security entitlement to any other security carried in the brokerage account.

7. Stock of closely held corporations.

Ordinary corporate stock falls within the Article 8 definition of security, whether or not it is publicly traded. See Sections 8–102(a)(15) and 8–103(a). There is nothing in the new indirect holding system rules of Article 8 that would preclude their application to shares of companies that are not publicly traded. The indirect holding system rules, however, would come into play only if the shares were in fact held through a securities account with a securities intermediary. Since that is typically not the case with respect to shares of closely held corporations, transactions involving those shares will continue to be governed by the traditional rules, as amended, that are set out in Parts 2, 3, and 4 of Article 8, and the corresponding provisions of Article 9. The simplification of the Article 8 rules on uncertificated securities may, however, make the alternative of dispensing with certificates more attractive for closely held corporations.

8. Partnership interests and limited liability company shares.

Interests in partnerships or shares of limited liability companies are not Article 8 securities unless they are in fact dealt in or traded on securities exchanges or in securities markets. See Section 8–103(c). The issuers, however, may if they wish explicitly "opt-in" by specifying that the interests or shares are securities governed by Article 8. Even though interests in partnerships or shares of limited liability companies do not generally fall within the category of "security" in Article 8, they would fall within the broader term "financial asset." Accordingly, if such interests are held through a securities account with a securities intermediary, the indirect holding system rules of Part 5 apply, and the interest of a person who holds them through such an account is a security entitlement.

9. Bankers' acceptances, commercial paper, and other money market instruments.

Money market instruments, such as commercial paper, bankers' acceptances, and certificates of deposit, are good examples of a form of property that may fall within the definition of "financial asset," even though they may not fall within the definition of "security." Section 8–103(d) provides that a writing that meets the definition of security certificate under Section 8–102(a)(15) is governed by Article 8, even though it also fits within the definition of "negotiable instrument" in Article 3.

Some forms of short term money market instruments may meet the requirements of an Article 8 security, while others may not. For example, the Article 8 definition of security requires that the obligation be in registered or bearer form. Bankers' acceptances are typically payable "to order," and thus do not qualify as Article 8 securities. Thus, the obligations of the immediate parties to a bankers' acceptance are governed by Article 3, rather than Article 8. That is an entirely appropriate classification, even for those bankers' acceptance that are handled as investment media in the securities markets, because Article 8, unlike Article 3, does not contain rules specifying the standardized obligations of parties to instruments. For example, the Article 3 rules on the obligations of acceptors and drawers of drafts are necessary to specify the obligations represented by bankers' acceptances, but Article 8 contains no provisions dealing with these issues.

Immobilization through a depository system is, however, just as important for money market instruments as for traditional securities. Under the prior version of Article 8, the rules on the depository system, set out in Section 8–320, applied only to Article 8 securities. Although some forms of money market instruments could be fitted within the language of the Article 8 definition of "security," this is not true for bankers' acceptances. Accordingly, it was not thought feasible to make bankers' acceptances eligible for deposit in clearing corporations under the prior version of Article 8. Revised Article 8 solves this problem by separating the coverage of the Part 5 rules from the definition of security. Even though a bankers' acceptance or other money market instrument is an Article 3 negotiable instrument rather than an Article 8 security, it would still fall within the definition of financial asset in Section 8–102(a)(9). Accordingly, if the instrument is held through a clearing corporation or other securities intermediary, the rules of Part 5 of Article 8 apply.

10. Repurchase agreement transactions.

Repurchase agreements are an important form of transaction in the securities business, particularly in connection with government securities. Repos and reverse repos can be used for a variety of purposes. The one that is of particular concern for purposes of commercial law rules is the use of repurchase agreements as a form of financing transaction for government securities dealers. Government securities dealers typically obtain intra-day financing from their clearing banks, and then at the end of the trading day seek overnight financing from other sources to repay that day's advances from the clearing bank. Repos are the principal source of this financing. The dealer ("repo seller") sells securities to the financing source ("repo buyer") for cash, and at the same time agrees to repurchase the same or like securities the following day, or at some other brief interval. The sources of the financing include a variety of entities seeking short term investments for surplus cash, such as pension funds, business corporations, money market funds, and banks. The pricing may be computed in various ways, but in essence the price at which the dealer agrees to repurchase the securities exceeds the price paid to the dealer by an amount equivalent to interest on the funds.

The transfer of the securities from a securities dealer as repo seller to a provider of funds as repo buyer can be effected in a variety of ways. The repo buyer might be willing to allow the repo seller to keep the securities "in its hands," relying on the dealer's representation that it will hold them on behalf of the repo buyer. In the jargon of the trade, these are known as "hold-in-custody repos" or "HIC repos." At the other extreme, the repo buyer might insist that the dealer "hand over" the securities so that in the event that the dealer fails and is unable to perform its obligation to repurchase them, the repo buyer will have the securities "in its hands." The jargon for these is "delivered-out repos." A wide variety of arrangements between these two extremes might be devised, in which the securities are "handed over" to a third party with powers concerning their disposition allocated between the repo seller and repo buyer in a variety of ways.

Specification of the rights of repo buyers is complicated by the fact that the transfer of the interest in securities from the repo seller to the repo buyer might be characterized as an outright sale or as the creation of a security interest. Article 8 does not attempt to specify any categorical rules on that issue.

Article 8 sets out rules on the rights of parties who have implemented securities transactions in certain ways. It does not, however, deal with the legal characterization of the transactions that are implemented through the Article 8 mechanisms. Rather, the Article 8 rules apply without regard to the characterization of transactions for other purposes. For example, the Article 8 rules for the direct holding system provide that a person who takes delivery of a duly indorsed security certificate for value and without notice of adverse claims takes free from any adverse claims. That rule applies without regard to the character of the transaction in which the security certificate was delivered. It applies both to delivery upon original issue and to delivery upon transfer. It applies to transfers in settlement of sales and to transfers in pledge.

Similarly, the Article 8 indirect holding system rules, such as the adverse claim cut-off rules in Sections 8–502 and 8–510, apply to the transactions that fall within their terms, whether those transactions were sales, secured transactions, or something else.

Repos involve transfers of interests in securities. The Article 8 rules apply to transfers of securities in repos, just as they apply to transfers of securities in any other form of transaction. The transfer of the interest in securities from the repo seller to the repo buyer might be characterized as an outright sale or as the creation of a security interest. Article 8 does not determine that question. The rules of Revised Article 8 have, however, been drafted to minimize the possibility that disputes over the characterization of the transfer in a repo would affect substantive questions that are governed by Article 8. See, e.g., Section 8–510 and Comment 4 thereto.

11. Securities lending transactions.

In a typical securities lending transaction, the owner of securities lends them to another person who needs the securities to satisfy a delivery obligation. For example, when a customer of a broker sells a security short, the broker executes an ordinary trade as seller and so must deliver the securities at settlement. The customer is "short" against the broker because the customer has an open obligation to deliver the securities to the broker, which the customer hopes to be able to satisfy by buying in the securities at a lower price. If the short seller's broker does not have the securities in its own inventory, the broker will borrow them from someone else. The securities lender delivers the securities to the borrowing broker, and the borrowing broker becomes contractually obligated to redeliver a like quantity of the same security. Securities borrowers are required to provide collateral, usually government securities, to assure performance of their redelivery obligation.

The securities lender does not retain any property interest in the securities that are delivered to the borrower. The transaction is an outright transfer in which the borrower obtains full title. The whole point of securities lending is that the borrower needs the securities to transfer them to someone else. It would make no sense to say that the lender retains any property interest in the securities it has lent. Accordingly, even if the securities borrower defaults on its redelivery obligation, the securities lender has no property interest in the original securities that could be asserted against any person to whom the securities borrower may have transferred them. One need not look to adverse claim cut-off rules to reach that result; the securities lender never had an adverse claim. The securities borrower's default is no different from any other breach of contract. The securities lender's protection is its right to foreclose on the collateral given to secure the borrower's redelivery obligation. Perhaps the best way to understand securities lending is to note that the word "loan" in securities lending transactions is used in the sense it carries in loans of money, as distinguished from loans of specific identifiable chattels. Someone who lends money does not retain any property interest in the money that is handed over to the borrower. To use civil law terminology, securities lending is *mutuum,* rather than *commodatum.* See Story on Bailments, §§ 6 and 47.

12. Traded stock options.

Stock options issued and cleared through the Options Clearing Corporation ("OCC") are a good example of a form of investment vehicle that is treated as a financial asset to which the Part 5 rules apply, but not as an Article 8 security to which Parts 2, 3, and 4 apply. OCC carries on its books the options positions of the brokerage firms which are clearing members of OCC. The clearing members in turn carry on their books the options positions of their customers. The arrangements are structurally similar to the securities depository system. In the options structure, however, there is no issuer separate from the clearing corporation. The financial assets held through the system are standardized contracts entitling the holder to purchase or sell a certain security at a set price. Rather than being an interest in or obligation of a separate issuer, an option is a contractual right against the counter-party. In order to assure performance of the options, OCC interposes itself as counter-party to each options trade. The rules of Parts 2, 3, and 4 of this Article, however, do not well describe the obligations and rights of OCC. On the other hand, the rules of Part 5, and the related Article 9 rules on security interests and priorities, do provide a workable legal framework for the commercial law analysis of the rights of the participants in the options market. Accordingly, publicly traded securities options are included within the definition of "financial asset," but not "security." See Section 8–103(e). Thus, although OCC would not be an issuer of a security for purposes of this Article, it would be a clearing corporation, against whom its clearing members have security entitlements to the options positions. Similarly, the clearing members' customers have security entitlements against the clearing members. Traded stock options are also a good illustration of the point that the classification issues under Article 8 are very different from classification under other law, such as the federal securities laws. See Section 8–102(d). Stock options are treated as securities for purposes of federal securities laws, but not for purposes of Article 8.

13. Commodity futures.

Section 8–103(f) provides that a "commodity contract" is not a security or a financial asset. Section 9–102(a)(15) defines commodity contract to include commodity futures contracts, commodity options, and options on commodity futures contracts that are traded on or subject to the rules of a board of trade that has been designated as a contract market for that contract pursuant to the federal commodities laws. Thus, commodity contracts themselves are not Article 8 securities to which the rules of Parts 2, 3, and 4 apply, nor is the relationship between a customer and a commodity futures commission merchant governed by the Part 5 rules of Article 8. Commodity contracts, however, are included within the Article 9 definition of "investment property." Thus security interests in commodity positions are governed by essentially the same set of rules as security interests in security entitlements.

14. "Whatever else they have or may devise."

The classification question posed by the above-captioned category of investment products and arrangements is among the most difficult—and important—issue raised by the Article 8 revision process. Rapid innovation is perhaps the only constant characteristic of the securities and financial markets. The rules of Revised Article 8 are intended to be sufficiently flexible to accommodate new developments.

A common mechanism by which new financial instruments are devised is that a financial institution that holds some security, financial instrument, or pool thereof, creates interests in that asset or pool which are sold to others. It is not possible to answer in the abstract the question of how such interests are treated under Article 8, because the variety of such products is limited only by human imagination and current regulatory structures. At this general level, however, one can note that there are at least three possible treatments under Article 8 of the relationship between the institution which creates the interests and the persons who hold them. (Again, it must be borne in mind that the Article 8 classification issue may be different from the classification question posed by federal securities law or other regulation.) First, creation of the new interests in the underlying assets may constitute issuance of a new Article 8 security. In that case the relationship between the institution that created the interest and the persons who hold them is not governed by the Part 5 rules, but by the rules of Parts 2, 3, and 4. See Section 8–501(e). That, for example, is the structure of issuance of mutual fund shares. Second, the relationship between the entity creating the interests and those holding them may fit within the Part 5 rules, so that the persons are treating as having security entitlements against the institution with respect to the underlying assets. That, for example, is the structure used for stock options. Third, it may be that the creation of the new interests in the underlying assets does not constitute issuance of a new Article 8 security, nor does the relationship between the entity creating the interests and those holding them fit within the Part 5 rules. In that case, the relationship is governed by other law, as in the case of ordinary trusts.

The first of these three possibilities—that the creation of the new interest is issuance of a new security for Article 8 purposes—is a fairly common pattern. For example, an American depositary receipt facility does not maintain securities accounts but issues securities called ADRs in respect of foreign securities deposited in such facility. Similarly, custodians of government securities which issue receipts, certificates, or the like representing direct interests in those securities (sometimes interests split between principal and income) do not maintain securities accounts but issue securities representing those interests. Trusts holding assets, in a variety of structured and securitized transactions, which issue certificates or the like representing "pass-through" or undivided beneficial interests in the trust assets, do not maintain securities accounts but issue securities representing those interests.

In analyzing these classification questions, courts should take care to avoid mechanical jurisprudence based solely upon exegesis of the wording of definitions in Article 8. The result of classification questions is that different sets of rules come into play. In order to decide the classification question it is necessary to understand fully the commercial setting and consider which set of rules best fits the transaction. Rather than letting the choice of rules turn on interpretation of the words of the definitions, the interpretation of the words of the definitions should turn on the suitability of the application of the substantive rules.

ARTICLE 8

B.   Revision Notes

1.   Provisions of former Article 8 on clearing corporations.

The keystone of the treatment of the indirect holding system in the prior version of Article 8 was the special provision on clearing corporations in Section 8–320. Section 8–320 was added to Article 8 in 1962, at the very end of the process that culminated in promulgation and enactment of the original version of the Code. The key concepts of the original version of Article 8 were "bona fide purchaser" and "delivery." Under Section 8–302 (1962) one could qualify as a "bona fide purchaser" only if one had taken delivery of a security, and Section 8–313 (1962) specified what counted as a delivery.

Section 8–320 was added to take account of the development of the system in which trades can be settled by netted book-entry movements at a depository without physical deliveries of certificates. Rather than reworking the basic concepts, however, Section 8–320 brought the depository system within Article 8 by definitional fiat. Subsection (a) of Section 8–320 (1962) stated that a transfer or pledge could be effected by entries on the books of a central depository, and subsection (b) stated that such an entry "has the effect of a delivery of a security in bearer form or duly indorsed in blank." In 1978, Section 8–320 was revised to conform it to the general substitution of the concept of "transfer" for "delivery," but the basic structure remained the same. Under the 1978 version of Article 8, the only book-entry transfers that qualified the transferee for bona fide purchaser rights were those made on the books of a clearing corporation. See Sections 8–302(1)(c), 8–313(1)(g), and 8–320. Thus, for practical purposes, the indirect holding system rules of the prior version of Article 8 required that the securities be held by a clearing corporation in accordance with the central depository rules of Section 8–320.

Some of the definitional provisions concerning clearing corporation in the prior version of Article 8 seem to have conflated the commercial law rules on the effect of book-entry transactions with issues about the regulation of entities that are acting as clearing corporations. For example, the Section 8–320 rules that gave effect to book-entry transfers applied only if the security was "in the custody of the clearing corporation, another clearing corporation, [or] a custodian bank." "Custodian bank" was defined in Section 8–102(4) as "a bank or trust company that is supervised and examined by state or federal authority having supervision over banks and is acting as custodian for a clearing corporation." Although this was probably inadvertent, these definitional provisions have operated as an obstacle to the development of clearing arrangements for global trading, since they effectively precluded clearing corporations from using foreign banks as custodians.

Revised Article 8 is based on the view that Article 8 is not the proper place for regulatory decisions about whether certain sorts of financial institutions should or should not be permitted to engage in a particular aspect of the securities business, such as acting as a clearing corporation, or how they should be permitted to conduct that business. Rather, Article 8 should deal only with the commercial law questions of what duties and rights flow from doing business as a clearing corporation, leaving it to other regulatory law to decide which entities should be permitted to act as clearing corporations, and to regulate their activities. Federal securities laws now establish a detailed regulatory structure for clearing corporations; there is no need for Article 8 to duplicate parts of that structure. Revised Article 8 deletes all provision of the prior version which had the effect of specifying how clearing corporations should conduct their operations. For example, Revised Article 8 deletes the definition of "custodian bank," which operated in the prior version only as a regulatory restriction on how clearing corporations could hold securities.

In general, the structure of Revised Article 8 is such that there is relatively little need for special provisions on clearing corporations. Book-entry transactions effected through clearing corporations are treated under the same rules in Part 5 as book-entry transactions effected through any other securities intermediary. Accordingly, Revised Article 8 has no direct analog of the special provisions in Section 8–320 on transfers on the books of clearing corporations.

2.   Former Section 8–313—"Transfer."

Section 8–313 of the 1978 version of Article was extremely complicated, because it attempted to cover many different issues. The following account of the evolution of Section 8–313 may assist in understanding why a different approach is taken in Revised Article 8. This explanation is, however, intended not as an actual account of historical events, but as a conceptual reconstruction, devised from the perspective of, and with the benefit of, hindsight.

UNIFORM COMMERCIAL CODE

The original objective of Article 8 was to ensure that certificates representing investment securities would be "negotiable" in the sense that purchasers would be protected by the bona fide purchaser rules. The requirements for bona fide purchaser status were that the purchaser had to (i) take delivery of the security and (ii) give value in good faith and without notice of adverse claims. Section 8–313 specified what counted as a "delivery," and Section 8–302 specified the other requirements.

The 1978 amendments added provisions on uncertificated securities, but the basic organizational pattern was retained. Section 8–302 continued to state the requirements of value, good faith, and lack of notice for good faith purchase, and Section 8–313 stated the mechanism by which the purchase had to be implemented. Delivery as defined in the original version of Section 8–313 had a meaning similar to the concept known in colloquial securities jargon as "good delivery"; that is, physical delivery with any necessary indorsement. Although the word "delivery" has now come to be used in securities parlance in a broader sense than physical delivery, when the provisions for uncertificated securities were added it was thought preferable to use another word. Thus, the word "transfer" was substituted for "delivery" in Section 8–313.

The 1978 amendments also moved the rules governing security interests in securities from Article 9 to Article 8, though the basic conceptual structure of the common law of pledge was retained. Since a pledge required a delivery, and since the term transfer had been substituted for delivery, the 1978 amendments provided that in order to create a security interest there must be a "transfer," in the defined Article 8 sense, from the debtor to the secured party. Accordingly, provisions had to be added to Section 8–313 so that any of the steps that should suffice to create a perfected security interest would be deemed to constitute a "transfer" within the meaning of Section 8–313. Thus, the Section 8–313 rules on "transfer," which had in the previous version dealt only with what counted as a delivery that qualified one for bona fide purchaser status, became the statutory locus for all of the rules on creation and perfection of security interests in securities. Accordingly the rather elaborate rules of subsections (1)(h), (1)(i), and (1)(j) were added.

Having expanded Section 8–313 to the point that it served as the rule specifying the formal requirements for transfer of all significant forms of interests in securities, it must have seemed only logical to take the next step and make the Section 8–313 rules the exclusive means of transferring interests in securities. Thus, while the prior version had stated that "Delivery to a purchaser occurs when . . .", the 1978 version stated that "Transfer of a security or a limited interest (including a security interest) therein to a purchaser occurs *only* . . . ." Having taken that step, however, it then became necessary to ensure that anyone who should be regarded as having an interest in a security would be covered by some provision of Section 8–313. Thus, the provisions of subsection (1)(d)(ii) and (iii) were added to make it possible to say that the customers of a securities intermediary who hold interests in securities held by the intermediary in fungible bulk received "transfers."

Section 8–313(1)(d) was the key provision in the 1978 version dealing with the indirect holding system at the level below securities depositories. It operated in essentially the same fashion as Section 8–320; that is, it stated that when a broker or bank holding securities in fungible bulk makes entries on its books identifying a quantity of the fungible bulk as belonging to the customer, that action is treated as a "transfer"—in the special Section 8–313 sense—of an interest in the security from the intermediary to the customer.

Revised Article 8 has no direct analog of the 1978 version of Section 8–313. The rules on secured transactions have been returned to Article 9, so subsections of Section 8–313 (1978) dealing with security interests are deleted from Article 8. Insofar as portions of Section 8–313 (1978) were designed to specify the formal requirements for transferees to qualify for protection against adverse claims, their place is taken by Revised Section 8–301, which defines "delivery," in a fashion somewhat akin to the pre-1978 version of Section 8–313. The descendant of the provisions of Section 8–313 (1978) dealing with the indirect holding system is Revised Section 8–501 which specifies when a person acquires a security entitlement. Section 8–501, however, is based on a different analysis of the transaction in which a customer acquires a position in the indirect holding system. The transaction is not described as a "transfer" of an interest in some portion of a fungible bulk of securities held by the securities intermediary but as the creation of a security entitlement. Accordingly, just as Revised Article 8 has no direct analog of the Section 8–320 rules on clearing corporation transfers, it has no direct analog of the Section 8–313(1) rules on "transfers" of interests in securities held in fungible bulk.

ARTICLE 8

3.　Uncertificated securities provisions.

Given the way that securities holding practices have evolved, the sharp distinction that the 1978 version of Article 8 drew between certificated securities and uncertificated securities has become somewhat misleading. Since many provisions of the 1978 version had separate subsections dealing first with certificated securities and then with uncertificated securities, and since people intuitively realize that the volume of trading in the modern securities markets could not possibly be handled by pushing around certificates, it was only natural for a reader of the statute to conclude that the uncertificated securities provisions of Article 8 were the basis of the book-entry system. That, however, is not the case. Although physical delivery of certificates plays little role in the settlement system, most publicly traded securities are still, in legal theory, certificated securities. To use clearance and settlement jargon, the book-entry securities holding system has used "immobilization" rather than "dematerialization."

The important legal and practical difference is between the direct holding system, in which the beneficial owners have a direct relationship with the issuer, and the indirect holding system, in which securities are held through tiers of securities intermediaries. Accordingly, in Revised Article 8 the contrast between certificated securities and uncertificated securities has been minimized or eliminated as much as possible in stating the substantive provisions.

4.　Transaction statements.

Although the 1978 provisions on uncertificated securities contemplated a system in which there would be no definitive certificates as reifications of the underlying interests or obligations, the 1978 amendments did not really dispense with all requirements of paper evidence of securities holding. The 1978 amendments required issuers of uncertificated securities to send paper "transaction statements" upon registration of transfer. Section 8–408 regulated the content and format of these transaction statements in considerable detail. The statements had to be in writing, include specific information, and contain a conspicuous legend stating that "This statement is merely a record of the rights of the addressee as of the time of its issuance. Delivery of this statement, of itself, confers no rights on the recipient. This statement is neither a negotiable instrument nor a security." Issuers were required to send statements when any transfer was registered (known as "initial transaction statements") and also were required to send periodic statements at least annually and also upon any security holder's reasonable request. Fees were regulated to some extent, in that Section 8–408(8) specified that if periodic statements were sent at least quarterly, the issuer could charge for statements requested by security holders at other times.

The detailed specification of reporting requirements for issuers of uncertificated securities was quite different from the treatment of securities intermediaries. Though the prior version of Article 8 did require non-clearing corporation securities intermediaries to send confirmations of transfers—a requirement deleted in Revised Article 8—it did not regulate their content or format. Article 8 has never imposed periodic reporting requirements on securities intermediaries. Thus, reporting requirements for the indirect holding system were left to agreements and regulatory authorities, while reporting requirements for a book-entry direct holding system were imposed by statute.

Securities holding systems based on transaction statements of the sort contemplated by the 1978 amendments have not yet evolved to any major extent—indeed, the statutory specification of the details of the information system may itself have acted as an impediment to the evolution of a book-entry direct system. Accordingly, Revised Article 8 drops the statutory requirements concerning transaction statements. The record keeping and reporting obligations of issuers of uncertificated securities would be left to agreement and other law, as is the case today for securities intermediaries.

In the 1978 version, the Part 2 rules concerning transfer restrictions, issuers' defenses, and the like were based on the assumption that transaction statements would be used in a fashion analogous to traditional security certificates. For example, Sections 8–202 and 8–204 specified that the terms of a security, or any restrictions on transfer imposed by the issuer, had to be noted on the transaction statement. Revised Article 8 deletes all such references to transaction statements. The terms of securities, or of restrictions of transfer, would be governed by whatever law or agreement specifies these matters, just as is the case for various other forms of business entities, such as partnerships, that have never issued certificates representing interests. Other Part 2 rules, such as Sections 8–205, 8–206, and 8–208, attempted to state rules on forgery and related matters for transactions statements. Since Revised Article 8 does not specify the format for information systems for uncertificated securities, there is no point in attempting to state rules on the consequences of wrongful information transmission in the particular format of written statements authenticated by signatures.

5. Deletion of provisions on registered pledges.

The 1978 version of Article 8 also added detailed provisions concerning "registered pledges" of uncertificated securities. Revised Article 8 adopts a new system of rules for security interests in securities, for both the direct and indirect holding systems that make it unnecessary to have special statutory provisions for registered pledges of uncertificated securities.

The reason that the 1978 version of Article 8 created this concept was that if the only means of creating security interests was the pledge, it seemed necessary to provide some substitute for the pledge in the absence of a certificate. The point of the registered pledge was, presumably, that it permitted a debtor to grant a perfected security interest in securities, yet still keep the securities in the debtor's own name for purposes of dividends, voting, and the like. The concept of registered pledge has, however, been thought troublesome by many legal commentators and securities industry participants. For example, in Massachusetts where many mutual funds have their headquarters, a non-uniform amendment was enacted to permit the issuer of an uncertificated security to refuse to register a pledge and instead issue a certificate to the owner that the owner could then pledge by ordinary means.

Under the 1978 version of Article 8, if an issuer chose to issue securities in uncertificated form, it was also required by statute to offer a registered pledge program. Revised Articles 8 and 9 take a different approach. All of the provisions dealing with registered pledges have been deleted. This does not mean, however, that issuers cannot offer such a service. The control rules of Revised Section 8–106 and the related priority provisions in Article 9 establish a structure that permits issuers to develop systems akin to the registered pledge device, without mandating that they do so, or legislating the details of the system. In essence, the registered pledge or control device amounts to a record keeping service. A debtor can always transfer securities to its lender. In a registered pledge or control agreement arrangement, the issuer keeps track of which securities the secured party holds for its own account outright, and which securities it holds in pledge from its debtors.

Under the rules of Revised Articles 8 and 9, the registered pledge issue can easily be left to resolution by the market. The concept of control is defined in such fashion that if an issuer or securities intermediary wishes to offer a service akin to the registered pledge device it can do so. The issuer or securities intermediary would offer to enter into agreements with the debtor and secured party under which it would hold the securities for the account of the debtor, but subject to instructions from the secured party. The secured party would thereby obtain control assuring perfection and priority of its lien.

Even if such arrangements are not offered by issuers, persons who hold uncertificated securities will have several options for using them as collateral for secured loans. Under the new rules, filing is a permissible method of perfection, for debtors other than securities firms. A secured party who relies on filing is, of course, exposed to the risk that the debtor will double finance and grant a later secured lender a security interest under circumstances that give that lender control and hence priority. If the lender is unwilling to run that risk, the debtor can transfer the securities outright to the lender on the books of the issuer, though between the parties the debtor would be the owner and the lender only a secured party. That, of course, requires that the debtor trust the secured party not to dispose of the collateral wrongfully, and the debtor may also need to make arrangements with the secured party to exercise benefits of ownership such as voting and receiving distributions.

It may well be that both lenders and borrowers would prefer to have some arrangement, such as the registered pledge device of current law, that permits the debtor to remain as the registered owner entitled to vote and receive dividends but gives the lender exclusive power to order their disposition. The approach taken in this revision is that if there is a genuine demand for such arrangements, it can be met by the market. The difficulty with the approach of present Article 8 is that it mandates that any issuer that wishes to issue securities in uncertificated form must also offer this record keeping service. That obligation may well have acted as a disincentive to the development of uncertificated securities. Thus, the deletion of the mandated registered pledge provisions is consistent with the principle of neutrality toward the evolution of securities holding practices.

6.   Former Section 8–403—Issuer's Duty as to Adverse Claims.

Section 8–403 of the prior version of Article 8 dealt with the obligations of issuers to adverse claimants. The starting point of American law on issuers' liability in such circumstances is the old case of *Lowry v. Commercial & Farmers' Bank,* 15 F. Cas. 1040 (C.C.D.Md. 1848) (No. 8551), under which issuers could be held liable for registering a transfer at the direction of a registered owner who was acting wrongfully as against a third person in making the transfer. The *Lowry* principle imposed onerous liability on issuers, particularly in the case of transfers by fiduciaries, such as executors and trustees. To protect against risk of such liability, issuers developed the practice of requiring extensive documentation for fiduciary stock transfers to assure themselves that the fiduciaries were acting rightfully. As a result, fiduciary stock transfers were cumbersome and time consuming.

In the present century, American law has gradually moved away from the *Lowry* principle. Statutes such as the Uniform Fiduciaries Act, the Model Fiduciary Stock Transfer Act, and the Uniform Act for the Simplification of Fiduciary Security Transfers sought to avoid the delays in stock transfers that could result from issuers' demands for documentation by limiting the issuer's responsibility for transfers in breach of the registered owner's duty to others. Although these statutes provided that issuers had no duty of inquiry to determine whether a fiduciary was acting rightfully, they all provided that an issuer could be liable if the issuer acted with notice of third party claims.

The prior version of Article 8 followed the same approach as the various fiduciary transfer statutes. Issuers were not required to seek out information from which they could determine whether a fiduciary was acting properly, but they were liable if they registered a transfer with notice that the fiduciary was acting improperly. Former Section 8–308(11) said that the failure of a fiduciary to comply with a controlling instrument or failure to obtain a court approval required under local law did not render the indorsement or instruction unauthorized. However, if a fiduciary was in fact acting improperly, then the beneficiary would be treated as an adverse claimant. See Section 8–302(2) (1978) and Comment 4. Former Section 8–403 specified that if written notice of an adverse claim had been sent to the issuer, the issuer "shall inquire into the adverse claim" before registering a transfer on the indorsement or instruction of the registered owner. The issuer could "discharge any duty of inquiry by any reasonable means," including by notifying the adverse claimant that the transfer would be registered unless the adverse claimant obtained a court order or gave an indemnity bond.

Revised Article 8 rejects the *Lowry* principle altogether. It provides that an issuer is not liable for wrongful registration if it acts on an effective indorsement or instruction, even though the issuer may have notice of adverse claims, so long as the issuer has not been served with legal process and is not acting in collusion with the wrongdoer in registering the transfer. See Revised Section 8–404 and Comments thereto. The provisions of prior Section 8–403 specifying that issuers had a duty to investigate adverse claims of which they had notice are deleted.

Revised Article 8 also deletes the provisions set out in Section 8–403(3) of prior law specifying that issuers did not have a duty to inquire into the rightfulness of transfers by fiduciaries. The omission of the rules formerly in Section 8–403(3) does not, of course, mean that issuers would be liable for acting on the instruction of fiduciaries in the circumstances covered by former Section 8–403(3). Former Section 8–403(3) assumed that issuers would be liable if they registered a transfer with notice of an adverse claim. Former Section 8–403(3) was necessary only to negate any inference that knowledge that a transfer was initiated by a fiduciary might give constructive notice of adverse claims. Under Section 8–404 of Revised Article 8, mere notice of adverse claims does not impose duties on the issuer. Accordingly the provisions included in former Section 8–403(3) are unnecessary.

Although the prior version of Article 8 included provisions similar or identical to those set out in the Uniform Act for the Simplification of Fiduciary Security Transfers and similar statutes, most states retained these statutes at the time the Uniform Commercial Code was adopted. These statutes are based on a premise different from Revised Article 8. The fiduciary simplification acts are predicated on the assumption that an issuer would be liable to an adverse claimant if the issuer had notice. These statutes seek only to preclude any inference that issuers have such notice when they register transfers on the instructions of a fiduciary. Revised Article 8 is based on the view that a third party should not be able to interfere with the relationship between an issuer and its registered shareholders unless the claimant obtains legal process. Since notice of an adverse claim does not impose duties on an issuer under Revised Article 8, the Uniform Act for the

Simplification of Fiduciary Security Transfers, or similar statutes, should be repealed upon enactment of Revised Article 8.

7. Former Section 8–319—Statute of Frauds.

Revised Article 8 deletes the special statute of frauds provision for securities contracts that was set out in former Section 8–319. See Revised Section 8–113. Most of the litigation involving the statute of frauds rule of the prior version of Article 8 involved informal transactions, rather than transactions on the organized securities markets. Typical cases were those in which an employee or former employee of a small enterprise sued to enforce an alleged promise that he or she would receive an equity interest in the business. The usual commercial policies relating to writings in contracts for the sale of personal property are at most tangentially implicated in such cases. There was a rather large and complex body of case law dealing with the applicability of Section 8–319 to cases of this sort. It seems doubtful that the cost of litigating these issues was warranted by whatever protections the statute of frauds offered against fraudulent claims.

Subsection (c) of former Section 8–319 provided that the statute of frauds bar did not apply if a written confirmation was sent and the recipient did not seasonably send an objection. That provision, however, presumably would not have had the effect of binding a broker's customer to the terms of a trade for which confirmation had been sent though the customer had not objected within 10 days. In the first place, the relationship between a broker and customer is ordinarily that of agent and principal; thus the broker is not seeking to enforce a contract for sale of a security, but to bind its principal for action taken by the broker as agent. Former Section 8–319 did not by its terms apply to the agency relationship. Moreover, even if former Section 8–319(c) applied, it is doubtful that it, of its own force, had the effect of precluding the customer from disputing whether there was a contract or what the terms of the contract were. Former Section 8–319(c) only removed the statute of frauds as a bar to enforcement; it did not say that there was a contract or that the confirmation had the effect of excluding other evidence of its terms. Thus, deletion of former Section 8–319 does not change the law one way or the other on whether a customer who fails to object to a written confirmation is precluded from denying the trade described in the confirmation, because that issue was never governed by former Section 8–319(c).

8. Miscellaneous.

Prior Section 8–105. Revised Article 8 deletes the statement found in Section 8–105(1) of the prior version that certificated securities "are negotiable instruments." This provision was added very late in the drafting process of the original Uniform Commercial Code. Apparently the thought was that it might be useful in dealing with potential transition problems arising out of the fact that bonds were then treated as negotiable instruments under the Uniform Negotiable Instruments Law. During that era, many other statutes, such as those specifying permissible categories of investments for regulated entities, might have used such phrases as "negotiable securities" or "negotiable instruments." Section 8–105 seems to have been included in the original version of Article 8 to avoid unfortunate interpretations of those other statutes once securities were moved from the Uniform Negotiable Instruments Law to UCC Article 8. Whether or not Section 8–105 was necessary at that time, it has surely outlived its purpose. The statement that securities "are negotiable instruments" is very confusing. As used in the Uniform Commercial Code, the term "negotiable instrument" means an instrument that is governed by Article 3; yet Article 8 securities are not governed by Article 3. Courts have occasionally cited Section 8–105(1) of prior law for the proposition that the rules that are generally thought of as characteristic of negotiability, such as the rule that bona fide purchasers take free from adverse claims, apply to certificated securities. Section 8–105(1), however, is unnecessary for that purpose, since the relevant rules are set out in specific provisions of Article 8.

Prior Sections 8–107 and 8–314. Article 8 has never been, and should not be, a comprehensive codification of the law of contracts for the purchase and sale of securities. The prior version of Article 8 did contain, however, a number of provisions dealing with miscellaneous aspects of the law of contracts as applied to contracts for the sale of securities. Section 8–107 dealt with one remedy for breach, and Section 8–314 dealt with certain aspects of performance. Revised Article 8 deletes these on the theory that inclusion of a few sections on issues of contract law is likely to cause more harm than good since inferences might be drawn from the failure to cover related issues. The deletion of these sections is not, however, intended as a rejection of the rules of contract law and interpretation that they expressed.

Prior Section 8–315. It is not entirely clear what the function of Section 8–315 of prior law was. The section specified that the owner of a security could recover it from a person to whom it had been transferred, if the transferee did not qualify as a bona fide purchaser. It seems to have been intended only to recognize that securities, like any other form of personal property, are governed by the general principle of property law that an owner can recover property from a person to whom it has been transferred under circumstances that did not cut off the owner's claim. Although many other Articles of the UCC deal with cut-off rules, Article 8 was the only one that included an affirmative statement of the rights of an owner to recover her property. It seems wiser to adopt the same approach as in Articles 2, 3, 7, and 9, and leave this point to other law. Accordingly, Section 8–315 is deleted in Revised Article 8, without, of course, implying rejection of the nearly self-evident rule that it sought to express.

Prior Section 8–407. This section, entitled "Exchangeability of Securities," seemed to say that holders of securities had the right to cause issuers to convert them back and forth from certificated to uncertificated form. The provision, however, applied only if the issuer "regularly maintains a system for issuing the class of securities involved under which both certificated and uncertificated securities are regularly issued to the category of owners, which includes the person in whose name the new security is to be registered." The provision seems unnecessary, since it applied only if the issuer decided that it should. The matter can be covered by agreement or corporate charter or by-laws.

V.   ACKNOWLEDGMENTS

[Note from West Advisory Panel: Section omitted.]

PART 1

SHORT TITLE AND GENERAL MATTERS

§ 8–101.   Short Title.

This Article may be cited as Uniform Commercial Code—Investment Securities.

§ 8–102.   Definitions.

(a)   In this Article:

(1)   "Adverse claim" means a claim that a claimant has a property interest in a financial asset and that it is a violation of the rights of the claimant for another person to hold, transfer, or deal with the financial asset.

(2)   "Bearer form," as applied to a certificated security, means a form in which the security is payable to the bearer of the security certificate according to its terms but not by reason of an indorsement.

(3)   "Broker" means a person defined as a broker or dealer under the federal securities laws, but without excluding a bank acting in that capacity.

(4)   "Certificated security" means a security that is represented by a certificate.

(5)   "Clearing corporation" means:

(i)   a person that is registered as a "clearing agency" under the federal securities laws;

(ii)   a federal reserve bank; or

(iii)   any other person that provides clearance or settlement services with respect to financial assets that would require it to register as a clearing agency under the federal securities laws but for an exclusion or exemption from the registration requirement, if its activities as a clearing corporation, including promulgation of rules, are subject to regulation by a federal or state governmental authority.

(6)   "Communicate" means to:

(i)   send a signed ~~writing~~ record; or

    (ii) transmit information by any mechanism agreed upon by the persons transmitting and receiving the information.

(7) "Entitlement holder" means a person identified in the records of a securities intermediary as the person having a security entitlement against the securities intermediary. If a person acquires a security entitlement by virtue of Section 8–501(b)(2) or (3), that person is the entitlement holder.

(8) "Entitlement order" means a notification communicated to a securities intermediary directing transfer or redemption of a financial asset to which the entitlement holder has a security entitlement.

(9) "Financial asset," except as otherwise provided in Section 8–103, means:

    (i) a security;

    (ii) an obligation of a person or a share, participation, or other interest in a person or in property or an enterprise of a person, which is, or is of a type, dealt in or traded on financial markets, or which is recognized in any area in which it is issued or dealt in as a medium for investment; or

    (iii) any property that is held by a securities intermediary for another person in a securities account if the securities intermediary has expressly agreed with the other person that the property is to be treated as a financial asset under this Article.

As context requires, the term means either the interest itself or the means by which a person's claim to it is evidenced, including a certificated or uncertificated security, a security certificate, or a security entitlement.

(10) [Reserved.] ["Good faith," for purposes of the obligation of good faith in the performance or enforcement of contracts or duties within this Article, means honesty in fact and the observance of reasonable commercial standards of fair dealing.] [*Note from West Advisory Panel: This subsection will be deleted if the jurisdiction adopts the definition of good faith in revised Article 1.*]

(11) "Indorsement" means a signature that alone or accompanied by other words is made on a security certificate in registered form or on a separate document for the purpose of assigning, transferring, or redeeming the security or granting a power to assign, transfer, or redeem it.

(12) "Instruction" means a notification communicated to the issuer of an uncertificated security which directs that the transfer of the security be registered or that the security be redeemed.

(13) "Registered form," as applied to a certificated security, means a form in which:

    (i) the security certificate specifies a person entitled to the security; and

    (ii) a transfer of the security may be registered upon books maintained for that purpose by or on behalf of the issuer, or the security certificate so states.

(14) "Securities intermediary" means:

    (i) a clearing corporation; or

    (ii) a person, including a bank or broker, that in the ordinary course of its business maintains securities accounts for others and is acting in that capacity.

(15) "Security," except as otherwise provided in Section 8–103, means an obligation of an issuer or a share, participation, or other interest in an issuer or in property or an enterprise of an issuer:

    (i) which is represented by a security certificate in bearer or registered form, or the transfer of which may be registered upon books maintained for that purpose by or on behalf of the issuer;

    (ii) which is one of a class or series or by its terms is divisible into a class or series of shares, participations, interests, or obligations; and

    (iii) which:

    (A) is, or is of a type, dealt in or traded on securities exchanges or securities markets; or

    (B) is a medium for investment and by its terms expressly provides that it is a security governed by this Article.

(16) "Security certificate" means a certificate representing a security.

(17) "Security entitlement" means the rights and property interest of an entitlement holder with respect to a financial asset specified in Part 5.

(18) "Uncertificated security" means a security that is not represented by a certificate.

(b) ~~Other~~ The following definitions ~~applying to~~ in this Article and ~~the sections in which they appear are~~ other Articles apply to this Article:

"Appropriate person". Section 8–107.
"Control". Section 8–106.
"Controllable account". Section 9–102.
"Controllable electronic record". Section 12–102.
"Controllable payment intangible". Section 9–102.
"Delivery". Section 8–301.
"Investment company security". Section 8–103.
"Issuer". Section 8–201.
"Overissue". Section 8–210.
"Protected purchaser". Section 8–303.
"Securities account". Section 8–501.

(c) In addition, Article 1 contains general definitions and principles of construction and interpretation applicable throughout this Article.

(d) The characterization of a person, business, or transaction for purposes of this Article does not determine the characterization of the person, business, or transaction for purposes of any other law, regulation, or rule.

As amended in 2001 and 2022.

Official Comment

1. "Adverse claim." The definition of the term "adverse claim" has two components. First, the term refers only to property interests. Second, the term means not merely that a person has a property interest in a financial asset but that it is a violation of the claimant's property interest for the other person to hold or transfer the security or other financial asset.

The term adverse claim is not, of course, limited to ownership rights, but extends to other property interests established by other law. A security interest, for example, would be an adverse claim with respect to a transferee from the debtor since any effort by the secured party to enforce the security interest against the property would be an interference with the transferee's interest.

The definition of adverse claim in the prior version of Article 8 might have been read to suggest that any wrongful action concerning a security, even a simple breach of contract, gave rise to an adverse claim. Insofar as such cases as *Fallon v. Wall Street Clearing Corp.,* 586 N.Y.S.2d 953, 182 A.D.2d 245 (1992) and *Pentech Intl. v. Wall St. Clearing Co.,* 983 F.2d 441 (2d Cir. 1993), were based on that view, they are rejected by the new definition which explicitly limits the term adverse claim to property interests. Suppose, for example, that A contracts to sell or deliver securities to B, but fails to do so and instead sells or pledges the securities to C. B, the promisee, has an action against A for breach of contract, but absent unusual circumstances the action for breach would not give rise to a property interest in the securities. Accordingly, B does not have an adverse claim. An adverse claim might, however, be based upon principles of equitable remedies that give rise to property claims. It would, for example, cover a right established by other law to rescind a transaction in which securities were transferred. Suppose, for example, that A holds securities and is induced by B's fraud to transfer them to B. Under the law of contract or restitution, A may have a right to rescind the transfer, which gives A a property claim to the securities. If so, A has an adverse claim to the securities in B's hands. By contrast, if B had committed no fraud, but had merely committed a breach of contract in connection with the transfer from A to B, A may have only a right to damages for breach, not a right to rescind. In that case, A would not have an adverse claim to the securities in B's hands.

2.   "Bearer form." The definition of "bearer form" has remained substantially unchanged since the early drafts of the original version of Article 8. The requirement that the certificate be payable to bearer by its terms rather than by an indorsement has the effect of preventing instruments governed by other law, such as chattel paper or Article 3 negotiable instruments, from being inadvertently swept into the Article 8 definition of security merely by virtue of blank indorsements. Although the other elements of the definition of security in Section 8–102(a)(14) probably suffice for that purpose in any event, the language used in the prior version of Article 8 has been retained.

3.   "Broker." Broker is defined by reference to the definitions of broker and dealer in the federal securities laws. The only difference is that banks, which are excluded from the federal securities law definition, are included in the Article 8 definition when they perform functions that would bring them within the federal securities law definition if it did not have the clause excluding banks. The definition covers both those who act as agents ("brokers" in securities parlance) and those who act as principals ("dealers" in securities parlance). Since the definition refers to persons "defined" as brokers or dealers under the federal securities law, rather than to persons required to "register" as brokers or dealers under the federal securities law, it covers not only registered brokers and dealers but also those exempt from the registration requirement, such as purely intrastate brokers. The only substantive rules that turn on the defined term broker are one provision of the section on warranties, Section 8–108(i), and the special perfection rule in Article 9 for security interests granted by brokers or securities intermediaries, Section 9–309(10).

4.   "Certificated security." The term "certificated security" means a security that is represented by a security certificate.

5.   "Clearing corporation." The definition of clearing corporation limits its application to entities that are subject to a rigorous regulatory framework. Accordingly, the definition includes only federal reserve banks, persons who are registered as "clearing agencies" under the federal securities laws (which impose a comprehensive system of regulation of the activities and rules of clearing agencies), and other entities subject to a comparable system of regulatory oversight.

6.   "Communicate." The term "communicate" assures that the Article 8 rules will be sufficiently flexible to adapt to changes in information technology. Sending a signed writing always suffices as a communication, but the parties can agree that a different means of transmitting information is to be used. Agreement is defined in Section 1–201(3) 1–201(b)(3) as "the bargain of the parties in fact as found in their language or by implication from other circumstances including course of dealing or usage of trade or course of performance." Thus, use of an information transmission method might be found to be authorized by agreement, even though the parties have not explicitly so specified in a formal agreement. The term communicate is used in Sections 8–102(a)(7) (definition of entitlement order), 8–102(a)(11) (definition of instruction), and 8–403 (demand that issuer not register transfer). Also in furtherance of medium neutrality, pursuant to the Uniform Commercial Code Amendments (2022) (2022 Amendments) the reference in paragraph (6)(i) to a "signed writing" has been changed to refer to a "signed record."

7.   "Entitlement holder." This term designates those who hold financial assets through intermediaries in the indirect holding system. Because many of the rules of Part 5 impose duties on securities intermediaries in favor of entitlement holders, the definition of entitlement holder is, in most cases, limited to the person specifically designated as such on the records of the intermediary. The last sentence of the definition covers the relatively unusual cases where a person may acquire a security entitlement under Section 8–501 even though the person may not be specifically designated as an entitlement holder on the records of the securities intermediary.

A person may have an interest in a security entitlement, and may even have the right to give entitlement orders to the securities intermediary with respect to it, even though the person is not the entitlement holder. For example, a person who holds securities through a securities account in its own name may have given discretionary trading authority to another person, such as an investment adviser. Similarly, the control provisions in Section 8–106 and the related provisions in Article 9 are designed to facilitate transactions in which a person who holds securities through a securities account uses them as collateral in an arrangement where the securities intermediary has agreed that if the secured party so directs the intermediary will dispose of the positions. In such arrangements, the debtor remains the entitlement holder but has agreed that the secured party can initiate entitlement orders. Moreover, an entitlement holder may be acting for another person as a nominee, agent, trustee, or in another capacity. Unless the entitlement holder is itself acting as a securities intermediary for the other person, in which case the other person would be an entitlement holder with respect to the securities entitlement, the relationship between an entitlement holder and another person for whose benefit the entitlement holder holds a securities entitlement is governed by other law.

8. "Entitlement order." This term is defined as a notification communicated to a securities intermediary directing transfer or redemption of the financial asset to which an entitlement holder has a security entitlement. The term is used in the rules for the indirect holding system in a fashion analogous to the use of the terms "indorsement" and "instruction" in the rules for the direct holding system. If a person directly holds a certificated security in registered form and wishes to transfer it, the means of transfer is an indorsement. If a person directly holds an uncertificated security and wishes to transfer it, the means of transfer is an instruction. If a person holds a security entitlement, the means of disposition is an entitlement order. An entitlement order includes a direction under Section 8–508 to the securities intermediary to transfer a financial asset to the account of the entitlement holder at another financial intermediary or to cause the financial asset to be transferred to the entitlement holder in the direct holding system (e.g., the delivery of a securities certificate registered in the name of the former entitlement holder). As noted in Comment 7, an entitlement order need not be initiated by the entitlement holder in order to be effective, so long as the entitlement holder has authorized the other party to initiate entitlement orders. See Section 8–107(b).

9. "Financial asset." The definition of "financial asset," in conjunction with the definition of "securities account" in Section 8–501, sets the scope of the indirect holding system rules of Part 5 of Revised Article 8. The Part 5 rules apply not only to securities held through intermediaries, but also to other financial assets held through intermediaries. The term financial asset is defined to include not only securities but also a broader category of obligations, shares, participations, and interests.

Having separate definitions of security and financial asset makes it possible to separate the question of the proper scope of the traditional Article 8 rules from the question of the proper scope of the new indirect holding system rules. Some forms of financial assets should be covered by the indirect holding system rules of Part 5, but not by the rules of Parts 2, 3, and 4. The term financial asset is used to cover such property. Because the term security entitlement is defined in terms of financial assets rather than securities, the rules concerning security entitlements set out in Part 5 of Article 8 and in Revised Article 9 apply to the broader class of financial assets.

The fact that something does or could fall within the definition of financial asset does not, without more, trigger Article 8 coverage. The indirect holding system rules of Revised Article 8 apply only if the financial asset is in fact held in a securities account, so that the interest of the person who holds the financial asset through the securities account is a security entitlement. Thus, questions of the scope of the indirect holding system rules cannot be framed as "Is such-and-such a 'financial asset' under Article 8?" Rather, one must analyze whether the relationship between an institution and a person on whose behalf the institution holds an asset falls within the scope of the term securities account as defined in Section 8–501. That question turns in large measure on whether it makes sense to apply the Part 5 rules to the relationship.

The term financial asset is used to refer both to the underlying asset and the particular means by which ownership of that asset is evidenced. Thus, with respect to a certificated security, the term financial asset may, as context requires, refer either to the interest or obligation of the issuer or to the security certificate representing that interest or obligation. Similarly, if a person holds a security or other financial asset through a securities account, the term financial asset may, as context requires, refer either to the underlying asset or to the person's security entitlement.

It is not necessary for all of the Part 5 rules to be relevant to a particular financial asset for the relevant property to qualify as a "financial asset" credited to a securities account. Many of the duties set forth in Part 5 will often be relevant to a digital asset such as a "controllable electronic record" (Section 12–102), or a "controllable account" or "controllable payment intangible" (Section 9–102) evidenced by a controllable electronic record, treated as a financial asset credited to a securities account. These duties include the duty to exercise rights as directed by the entitlement holder, comply with the entitlement holder's entitlement orders, and change the position to another form of holding.

If the parties agree to treat a digital asset as a financial asset under Article 8 and the digital asset is in fact held in a securities account for an entitlement holder, the rules applicable to controllable electronic records under Article 12 would not apply to the entitlement holder's security entitlement related to the financial asset. If the financial asset itself is a controllable electronic record, however, then the rules in Article 12 could apply to the securities intermediary's rights with respect to the controllable electronic record if the intermediary holds the asset directly.

10. "Good faith." Section 1–203 [*unrevised Article 1; see Concordance, p. 22*] provides that "Every contract or duty within [the Uniform Commercial Code] imposes an obligation of good faith in its performance or enforcement." Section 1–201(b)(20) defines "good faith" as "honesty in fact and the observance of reasonable commercial standards of fair dealing." The reference to commercial standards makes clear that assessments of

conduct are to be made in light of the commercial setting. The substantive rules of Article 8 have been drafted to take account of the commercial circumstances of the securities holding and processing system. For example, Section 8–115 provides that a securities intermediary acting on an effective entitlement order, or a broker or other agent acting as a conduit in a securities transaction, is not liable to an adverse claimant, unless the claimant obtained legal process or the intermediary acted in collusion with the wrongdoer. This, and other similar provisions, see Sections 8–404 and 8–503(e), do not depend on notice of adverse claims, because it would impair rather than advance the interest of investors in having a sound and efficient securities clearance and settlement system to require intermediaries to investigate the propriety of the transactions they are processing. The good faith obligation does not supplant the standards of conduct established in provisions of this kind.

In Revised Article 8, the definition of good faith is not germane to the question whether a purchaser takes free from adverse claims. The rules on such questions as whether a purchaser who takes in suspicious circumstances is disqualified from protected purchaser status are treated not as an aspect of good faith but directly in the rules of Section 8–105 on notice of adverse claims.

11. "Indorsement" is defined as a signature made on a security certificate or separate document for purposes of transferring or redeeming the security. The definition is adapted from the language of Section 8–308(1) of the prior version and from the definition of indorsement in the Negotiable Instruments Article, see Section 3–204(a). The definition of indorsement does not include the requirement that the signature be made by an appropriate person or be authorized. Those questions are treated in the separate substantive provision on whether the indorsement is effective, rather than in the definition of indorsement. See Section 8–107.

12. "Instruction" is defined as a notification communicated to the issuer of an uncertificated security directing that transfer be registered or that the security be redeemed. Instructions are the analog for uncertificated securities of indorsements of certificated securities.

13. "Registered form." The definition of "registered form" is substantially the same as in the prior version of Article 8. Like the definition of bearer form, it serves primarily to distinguish Article 8 securities from instruments governed by other law, such as Article 3.

Contrary to the holding in *Highland Capital Management LP v. Schneider*, 8 N.Y.3d 406 (2007), the registrability requirement in the definition of "registered form," and its parallel in the definition of "security," are satisfied only if books are maintained by or on behalf of the issuer for the purpose of registration of transfer, including the determination of rights under Section 8–207(a) (or if, in the case of a certificated security, the security certificate so states). It is not sufficient that the issuer records ownership, or records transfers thereof, for other purposes. Nor is it sufficient that the issuer, while not in fact maintaining books for the purpose of registration of transfer, could do so, for such is always the case.

14. "Securities intermediary." A "securities intermediary" is a person that in the ordinary course of its business maintains securities accounts for others and is acting in that capacity. The most common examples of securities intermediaries would be clearing corporations holding securities for their participants, banks acting as securities custodians, and brokers holding securities on behalf of their customers. However, a person need not be such an entity in order to be a securities intermediary. Because a "securities account" is an account to which a financial asset is or may be credited under Section 8–501(a) and the definition of "financial asset" is not limited to securities, a person may be a "securities intermediary" even if that person does not credit "securities" (as defined in Article 8) to the account. Rather, the securities accounts that a securities intermediary maintains may consist exclusively of financial assets described in Section 8–102(a)(9)(ii) and (iii). For example, a cryptocurrency exchange that holds only cryptocurrencies (and not securities) for customers might be a securities intermediary. Clearing corporations are listed separately as a category of securities intermediary in subparagraph (i) even though in most circumstances they would fall within the general definition in subparagraph (ii). The reason is to simplify the analysis of arrangements such as the NSCC-DTC system in which NSCC performs the comparison, clearance, and netting function, while DTC acts as the depository. Because NSCC is a registered clearing agency under the federal securities laws, it is a clearing corporation and hence a securities intermediary under Article 8, regardless of whether it is at any particular time or in any particular aspect of its operations holding securities on behalf of its participants.

The terms securities intermediary and broker have different meanings. Broker means a person engaged in the business of buying and selling securities, as agent for others or as principal. Securities intermediary means a person maintaining securities accounts for others. A stockbroker, in the colloquial sense, may or may not be acting as a securities intermediary.

The definition of securities intermediary includes the requirement that the person in question is "acting in the capacity" of maintaining securities accounts for others. This is to take account of the fact that a particular entity, such as a bank, may act in many different capacities in securities transactions. A bank may act as a transfer agent for issuers, as a securities custodian for institutional investors and private investors, as a dealer in government securities, as a lender taking securities as collateral, and as a provider of general payment and collection services that might be used in connection with securities transactions. A bank that maintains securities accounts for its customers would be a securities intermediary with respect to those accounts; but if it takes a pledge of securities from a borrower to secure a loan, it is not thereby acting as a securities intermediary with respect to the pledged securities, since it holds them for its own account rather than for a customer. In other circumstances, those two functions might be combined. For example, if the bank is a government securities dealer it may maintain securities accounts for customers and also provide the customers with margin credit to purchase or carry the securities, in much the same way that brokers provide margin loans to their customers.

The definition of securities intermediary includes the requirement that the person in question "in the ordinary course of its business maintain securities accounts for others". This "ordinary course" requirement does not have a fixed quantitative requirement and is determined by the facts of each case. Thus, a person need not necessarily satisfy a specified threshold of activity or necessarily have a minimum number of customers. Law other than the UCC may determine who may legally engage in such a business.

15. "Security." The definition of "security" has three components. First, there is the subparagraph (i) test that the interest or obligation be fully transferable, in the sense that the issuer either maintains transfer books or the obligation or interest is represented by a certificate in bearer or registered form. Second, there is the subparagraph (ii) test that the interest or obligation be divisible, that is, one of a class or series, as distinguished from individual obligations of the sort governed by ordinary contract law or by Article 3. Third, there is the subparagraph (iii) functional test, which generally turns on whether the interest or obligation is, or is of a type, dealt in or traded on securities markets or securities exchanges. There is, however, an "opt-in" provision in subparagraph (iii) which permits the issuer of any interest or obligation that is "a medium of investment" to specify that it is a security governed by Article 8.

The divisibility test of subparagraph (ii) applies to the security—that is, the underlying intangible interest— not the means by which that interest is evidenced. Thus, securities issued in book-entry only form meet the divisibility test because the underlying intangible interest is divisible via the mechanism of the indirect holding system. This is so even though the clearing corporation is the only eligible direct holder of the security.

The third component, the functional test in subparagraph (iii), provides flexibility while ensuring that the Article 8 rules do not apply to interests or obligations in circumstances so unconnected with the securities markets that parties are unlikely to have thought of the possibility that Article 8 might apply. Subparagraph (iii)(A) covers interests or obligations that either are dealt in or traded on securities exchanges or securities markets, or are of a type dealt in or traded on securities exchanges or securities markets. The "is dealt in or traded on" phrase eliminates problems in the characterization of new forms of securities which are to be traded in the markets, even though no similar type has previously been dealt in or traded in the markets. Subparagraph (iii)(B) covers the broader category of media for investment, but it applies only if the terms of the interest or obligation specify that it is an Article 8 security. This opt-in provision allows for deliberate expansion of the scope of Article 8.

Section 8–103 contains additional rules on the treatment of particular interests as securities or financial assets.

16. "Security certificate." The term "security" refers to the underlying asset, e.g., 1000 shares of common stock of Acme, Inc. The term "security certificate" refers to the paper certificates that have traditionally been used to embody the underlying intangible interest.

17. "Security entitlement" means the rights and property interest of a person who holds securities or other financial assets through a securities intermediary. A security entitlement is both a package of personal rights against the securities intermediary and an interest in the property held by the securities intermediary. A security entitlement is not, however, a specific property interest in any financial asset held by the securities intermediary or by the clearing corporation through which the securities intermediary holds the financial asset. See Sections 8–104(c) and 8–503. The formal definition of security entitlement set out in subsection (a)(16) of this section is a cross-reference to the rules of Part 5. In a sense, then, the entirety of Part 5 is the definition of security entitlement. The Part 5 rules specify the rights and property interest that comprise a security entitlement.

Rights and obligations relating to a security entitlement are enforceable by action. See Section 1–305(b) and PEB Commentary No. 25, dated August 12, 2022. The Commentary is available at https://www.ali.org/peb-ucc.

18. "Uncertificated security." The term "uncertificated security" means a security that is not represented by a security certificate—i.e., a paper certificate. This is so even if, for example, the organic documents relating to

the security refer to it as being "certificated" or refer to the electronic record evidencing the security as an "electronic certificate." For uncertificated securities, there is no need to draw any distinction between the underlying asset and the means by which a direct holder's interest in that asset is evidenced. Compare "certificated security" and "security certificate."

As discussed above in Comment 9, a controllable electronic record may be a "financial asset." However, a controllable electronic record is not itself a "security," defined in part in Section 8–102(a)(15) as "an obligation of an issuer or a share, participation, or other interest in an issuer or in property or an enterprise of an issuer." It also is not "a share or similar equity interest," an "investment company security," or "an interest in a partnership or limited liability company." See Section 8–103(a), (b), and (c). Of course, a controllable electronic record might be involved in the issuance and distribution of something that is a security for other, non-Article 8 purposes, including the federal securities laws. For example, a controllable electronic record (perhaps labeled as a "token" or "coin") might provide a mechanism for facilitating investments in such securities. As Section 8–102(d) makes clear, however, characterization under Article 8 does not determine characterization for other purposes. The converse is also true—characterization for other purposes does not determine characterization under Article 8.

Although not itself an Article 8 security, a controllable electronic record might play a role in the facilitating transactions in Article 8 securities. The following examples address situations in which controllable electronic records may have such a role as well as situations in which investment property is not involved.

Example 1 (corporate shares: Article 8 uncertificated securities; token as instruction). A Delaware corporation (D Corp) issues shares of stock and maintains books and records evidencing the registered ownership of the shares. Because the shares are not represented by security certificates, they are uncertificated securities. Pursuant to the applicable law and the organic documentation of D Corp, D Corp creates, or causes to be created, controllable electronic records (CERs)—"tokens"—to facilitate transfers of the shares. Also pursuant to that law and documentation, the transfer of control of a token on the platform on which the token is recorded constitutes an instruction to D Corp, as issuer, for the transfer of registration of the share(s) represented by the token to the transferee of control. Following receipt of the instruction upon transfer of control of a token, D Corp transfers registration of the share(s) on its books and records. See Sections 8–102(a)(12) (defining "instruction"); 8–401 (duty of issuer to register transfer). Although Article 12 governs the tokens (as CERs) and the transfer of control thereof, other law, including Delaware corporate law and Delaware Article 8 (and Article 9 of the relevant jurisdiction, if applicable) governs rights in the uncertificated securities and the transfer of registration. See Sections 8–110(a); 12–104(f).

Example 2 (LLC membership interests: Article 8 uncertificated securities; token as instruction). A Delaware limited liability company (LLC) issues membership interests that are dealt in or traded on securities exchanges or in securities markets and which by their terms are securities governed by Article 8. See Section 8–103(c). LLC maintains books and records evidencing the registered ownership of the interests. Because the interests are not represented by security certificates, they are uncertificated securities. Pursuant to the applicable law and the organic documentation of LLC, LLC creates, or causes to be created, controllable electronic records (CERs)—"tokens"—to facilitate transfers of the interests. Also pursuant to that law and documentation, the transfer of control of a token on the platform on which the token is recorded constitutes an instruction to LLC, as issuer, for the transfer of registration of the interest(s) represented by the token to the transferee of control. Following receipt of the instruction upon transfer of control of a token, LLC transfers registration of the interest(s) on its books and records. See Sections 8–102(a)(12) (defining "instruction"); 8–401 (duty of issuer to register transfer). Although Article 12 governs the tokens (as CERs) and the transfer of control thereof, other law, including Delaware LLC law and Delaware Article 8 (and Article 9 of the relevant jurisdiction, if applicable), governs rights in the uncertificated securities and the transfer of registration. See Sections 8–110(a); 12–104(f).

Example 3 (LLC membership interests not covered by Article 8; interests are general intangibles). A Delaware limited liability company issues membership interests that are not securities governed by UCC Article 8 and, consequently, are not investment property. See Section 8–103(c). Instead, the membership interests are general intangibles. LLC maintains books and records evidencing ownership of the interests. Pursuant to the applicable law and the organic documentation of LLC, LLC creates, or causes to be created, controllable electronic records (CERs)—"tokens"—to facilitate transfers of the interests. Also pursuant to that law and documentation, the transfer of control of a token on the platform on which the token is recorded constitutes a request to LLC, as issuer, for the transfer of the interest(s) related to the token. Following receipt of the request upon transfer of control of a token, LLC transfers the interest(s) on its books and records. Although Article 12 governs the tokens (as CERs) and the transfer of control, other law (including Article 9 or the relevant jurisdiction, if applicable, but not Article 8) governs rights in the interests (general intangibles). See Section 12–104(f).

Examples 1 and 2 posit that controllable electronic records function as instructions to the issuers. For an analogous example in another context, see Section 4A–104, Comment 3 ("An instruction to pay might be a component of a computer program or a transaction protocol intended to execute automatically under specified circumstances."). The central point is that the roles of the controllable electronic records must comply with the organic corporate and LLC laws and documentation as well as the Article 8 regime for uncertificated securities. Although controllable electronic records might be structured to functionally "represent" the underlying uncertificated securities, Article 8 makes no provision for such a "representation" for uncertificated securities (unlike the role of security certificates for certificated securities). Whether it would be possible and feasible to expand the structure contemplated in Examples 1 and 2 so that transfer of control of a controllable electronic record would, *ipso facto*, constitute a transfer of registration on the issuer's books and records would depend on the terms of and compliance with both the underlying organic laws and documentation for the uncertificated securities, the requirements of Article 8, and, where applicable, other law.

If the securities issued by D Corp or LLC in Examples 1 and 2 were payment obligations of the issuers that met the definition of "security" in Section 8–102(a)(15)—i.e., debt securities—the same analysis discussed in those examples as to the applicability and scope of Articles 8 and 12 would apply. However, if the debt obligations were not Article 8 securities (as in Example 3) but were obligations of account debtors on controllable accounts or controllable payment intangibles, then the relevant provisions of Articles 9 and 12, and not those of Article 8, would apply. See, e.g., Sections 9–107A; 9–306B; 9–314; 12–104(a), (b), and (e) and Comments 6–10; Article 12, Prefatory Note 4.

Definitional Cross References:

"Agreement". Section 1–201(b)(3).
"Bank". Section 1–201(b)(4).
"Person". Section 1–201(b)(27).
"Send". Section 1–201(b)(36).
"Signed". Section 1–201(b)(37).
"Writing". Section 1–201(b)(43).

As amended in 1999, 2001, 2010, and 2022.

§ 8–103. Rules for Determining Whether Certain Obligations and Interests are Securities or Financial Assets.

(a)   A share or similar equity interest issued by a corporation, business trust, joint stock company, or similar entity is a security.

(b)   An "investment company security" is a security. "Investment company security" means a share or similar equity interest issued by an entity that is registered as an investment company under the federal investment company laws, an interest in a unit investment trust that is so registered, or a face-amount certificate issued by a face-amount certificate company that is so registered. Investment company security does not include an insurance policy or endowment policy or annuity contract issued by an insurance company.

(c)   An interest in a partnership or limited liability company is not a security unless it is dealt in or traded on securities exchanges or in securities markets, its terms expressly provide that it is a security governed by this Article, or it is an investment company security. However, an interest in a partnership or limited liability company is a financial asset if it is held in a securities account.

(d)   A writing that is a security certificate is governed by this Article and not by Article 3, even though it also meets the requirements of that Article. However, a negotiable instrument governed by Article 3 is a financial asset if it is held in a securities account.

(e)   An option or similar obligation issued by a clearing corporation to its participants is not a security, but is a financial asset.

(f)   A commodity contract, as defined in Section 9–102(a)(15), is not a security or a financial asset.

(g)   A document of title is not a financial asset unless Section 8–102(a)(9)(iii) applies.

(h)   A controllable account, controllable electronic record, or controllable payment intangible is not a financial asset unless Section 8–102(a)(9)(iii) applies.

As amended in 1999, 2003, and 2022.

Official Comment

1.   This section contains rules that supplement the definitions of "financial asset" and "security" in Section 8–102. The Section 8–102 definitions are worded in general terms, because they must be sufficiently comprehensive and flexible to cover the wide variety of investment products that now exist or may develop. The rules in this section are intended to foreclose interpretive issues concerning the application of the general definitions to several specific investment products. No implication is made about the application of the Section 8–102 definitions to investment products not covered by this section.

2.   Subsection (a) establishes an unconditional rule that ordinary corporate stock is a security. That is so whether or not the particular issue is dealt in or traded on securities exchanges or in securities markets. Thus, shares of closely held corporations are Article 8 securities.

3.   Subsection (b) establishes that the Article 8 term "security" includes the various forms of the investment vehicles offered to the public by investment companies registered as such under the federal Investment Company Act of 1940, as amended. This clarification is prompted principally by the fact that the typical transaction in shares of open-end investment companies is an issuance or redemption, rather than a transfer of shares from one person to another as is the case with ordinary corporate stock. For similar reasons, the definitions of indorsement, instruction, and entitlement order in Section 8–102 refer to "redemptions" as well as "transfers," to ensure that the Article 8 rules on such matters as signature guaranties, Section 8–306, assurances, Sections 8–402 and 8–507, and effectiveness, Section 8–107, apply to directions to redeem mutual fund shares. The exclusion of insurance products is needed because some insurance company separate accounts are registered under the Investment Company Act of 1940, but these are not traded under the usual Article 8 mechanics.

4.   Subsection (c) is designed to foreclose interpretive questions that might otherwise be raised by the application of the "of a type" language of Section 8–102(a)(15)(iii) to partnership interests. Subsection (c) establishes the general rule that partnership interests or shares of limited liability companies are not Article 8 securities unless they are in fact dealt in or traded on securities exchanges or in securities markets. The issuer, however, may explicitly "opt-in" by specifying that the interests or shares are securities governed by Article 8. Partnership interests or shares of limited liability companies are included in the broader term "financial asset." Thus, if they are held through a securities account, the indirect holding system rules of Part 5 apply, and the interest of a person who holds them through such an account is a security entitlement.

5.   Subsection (d) deals with the line between Article 3 negotiable instruments and Article 8 investment securities. It continues the rule of the prior version of Article 8 that a writing that meets the Article 8 definition is covered by Article 8 rather than Article 3, even though it also meets the definition of negotiable instrument. However, subsection (d) provides that an Article 3 negotiable instrument is a "financial asset" so that the indirect holding system rules apply if the instrument is held through a securities intermediary. This facilitates making items such as money market instruments eligible for deposit in clearing corporations.

6.   Subsection (e) is included to clarify the treatment of investment products such as traded stock options, which are treated as financial assets but not securities. Thus, the indirect holding system rules of Part 5 apply, but the direct holding system rules of Parts 2, 3, and 4 do not.

7.   Subsection (f) excludes commodity contracts from all of Article 8. However, under Article 9, commodity contracts are included in the definition of "investment property." Therefore, the Article 9 rules on security interests in investment property do apply to security interests in commodity positions. See Section 9–102 and Comment 6 thereto. "Commodity contract" is defined in Section 9–102(a)(15).

8.   Subsection (g) allows a document of title to be a financial asset and thus subject to the indirect holding system rules of Part 5 only to the extent that the intermediary and the person entitled under the document so agree to do so pursuant to Section 8–102(a)(9)(iii). Subsection (h), added pursuant to the 2022 Amendments, adopts the same approach for a controllable account, controllable electronic record, or controllable payment intangible. This is to prevent the inadvertent application of the Part 5 rules to intermediaries who may hold either electronic or tangible documents of title or controllable accounts, controllable electronic records, or controllable payment intangibles.

Definitional Cross References:

"Clearing corporation". Section 8–102(a)(5).

614

"Commodity contract". Section 9–102(a)(15).
"Financial asset". Section 8–102(a)(9).
"Security". Section 8–102(a)(15).
"Security certificate". Section 8–102(a)(16).

As amended in 2003 and 2022.

§ 8–104. Acquisition of Security or Financial Asset or Interest Therein.

(a)   A person acquires a security or an interest therein, under this Article, if:

(1)   the person is a purchaser to whom a security is delivered pursuant to Section 8–301; or

(2)   the person acquires a security entitlement to the security pursuant to Section 8–501.

(b)   A person acquires a financial asset, other than a security, or an interest therein, under this Article, if the person acquires a security entitlement to the financial asset.

(c)   A person who acquires a security entitlement to a security or other financial asset has the rights specified in Part 5, but is a purchaser of any security, security entitlement, or other financial asset held by the securities intermediary only to the extent provided in Section 8–503.

(d)   Unless the context shows that a different meaning is intended, a person who is required by other law, regulation, rule, or agreement to transfer, deliver, present, surrender, exchange, or otherwise put in the possession of another person a security or financial asset satisfies that requirement by causing the other person to acquire an interest in the security or financial asset pursuant to subsection (a) or (b).

Official Comment

1.   This section lists the ways in which interests in securities and other financial assets are acquired under Article 8. In that sense, it describes the scope of Article 8. Subsection (a) describes the two ways that a person may acquire a security or interest therein under this Article: (1) by delivery (Section 8–301), and (2) by acquiring a security entitlement. Each of these methods is described in detail in the relevant substantive provisions of this Article. Part 3, beginning with the definition of "delivery" in Section 8–301, describes how interests in securities are acquired in the direct holding system. Part 5, beginning with the rules of Section 8–501 on how security entitlements are acquired, describes how interests in securities are acquired in the indirect holding system.

Subsection (b) specifies how a person may acquire an interest under Article 8 in a financial asset other than a security. This Article deals with financial assets other than securities only insofar as they are held in the indirect holding system. For example, a bankers' acceptance falls within the definition of "financial asset," so if it is held through a securities account the entitlement holder's right to it is a security entitlement governed by Part 5. The bankers' acceptance itself, however, is a negotiable instrument governed by Article 3, not by Article 8. Thus, the provisions of Parts 2, 3, and 4 of this Article that deal with the rights of direct holders of securities are not applicable. Article 3, not Article 8, specifies how one acquires a direct interest in a bankers' acceptance. If a bankers' acceptance is delivered to a clearing corporation to be held for the account of the clearing corporation's participants, the clearing corporation becomes the holder of the bankers' acceptance under the Article 3 rules specifying how negotiable instruments are transferred. The rights of the clearing corporation's participants, however, are governed by Part 5 of this Article.

2.   The distinction in usage in Article 8 between the term "security" (and its correlatives "security certificate" and "uncertificated security") on the one hand, and "security entitlement" on the other, corresponds to the distinction between the direct and indirect holding systems. For example, with respect to certificated securities that can be held either directly or through intermediaries, obtaining possession of a security certificate and acquiring a security entitlement are both means of holding the underlying security. For many other purposes, there is no need to draw a distinction between the means of holding. For purposes of commercial law analysis, however, the form of holding may make a difference. Where an item of property can be held in different ways, the rules on how one deals with it, including how one transfers it or how one grants a security interest in it, differ depending on the form of holding.

Although a security entitlement is means of holding the underlying security or other financial asset, a person who has a security entitlement does not have any direct claim to a specific asset in the possession of the securities intermediary. Subsection (c) provides explicitly that a person who acquires a security entitlement is a "purchaser" of any security, security entitlement, or other financial asset held by the securities intermediary only in the sense that under Section 8–503 a security entitlement is treated as a *sui generis* form of property interest.

3.   Subsection (d) is designed to ensure that parties will retain their expected legal rights and duties under Revised Article 8. One of the major changes made by the revision is that the rules for the indirect holding system are stated in terms of the "security entitlements" held by investors, rather than speaking of them as holding direct interests in securities. Subsection (d) is designed as a translation rule to eliminate problems of co-ordination of terminology, and facilitate the continued use of systems for the efficient handling of securities and financial assets through securities intermediaries and clearing corporations. The efficiencies of a securities intermediary or clearing corporation are, in part, dependent on the ability to transfer securities credited to securities accounts in the intermediary or clearing corporation to the account of an issuer, its agent, or other person by book entry in a manner that permits exchanges, redemptions, conversions, and other transactions (which may be governed by pre-existing or new agreements, constitutional documents, or other instruments) to occur and to avoid the need to withdraw from immobilization in an intermediary or clearing corporation physical securities in order to deliver them for such purposes. Existing corporate charters, indentures and like documents may require the "presentation," "surrender," "delivery," or "transfer" of securities or security certificates for purposes of exchange, redemption, conversion or other reason. Likewise, documents may use a wide variety of terminology to describe, in the context for example of a tender or exchange offer, the means of putting the offeror or the issuer or its agent in possession of the security. Subsection (d) takes the place of provisions of prior law which could be used to reach the legal conclusion that book-entry transfers are equivalent to physical delivery to the person to whose account the book entry is credited.

Definitional Cross References:

"Delivery". Section 8–301.
"Financial asset". Section 8–102(a)(9).
"Person". Section 1–201(30) [*unrevised Article 1; see Concordance, p. 22*].
"Purchaser". Sections 1–201(33) [*unrevised Article 1; see Concordance, p. 22*] & 8–116.
"Security". Section 8–102(a)(15).
"Security entitlement". Section 8–102(a)(17).

§ 8–105.   Notice of Adverse Claim.

(a)   A person has notice of an adverse claim if:

(1)   the person knows of the adverse claim;

(2)   the person is aware of facts sufficient to indicate that there is a significant probability that the adverse claim exists and deliberately avoids information that would establish the existence of the adverse claim; or

(3)   the person has a duty, imposed by statute or regulation, to investigate whether an adverse claim exists, and the investigation so required would establish the existence of the adverse claim.

(b)   Having knowledge that a financial asset or interest therein is or has been transferred by a representative imposes no duty of inquiry into the rightfulness of a transaction and is not notice of an adverse claim. However, a person who knows that a representative has transferred a financial asset or interest therein in a transaction that is, or whose proceeds are being used, for the individual benefit of the representative or otherwise in breach of duty has notice of an adverse claim.

(c)   An act or event that creates a right to immediate performance of the principal obligation represented by a security certificate or sets a date on or after which the certificate is to be presented or surrendered for redemption or exchange does not itself constitute notice of an adverse claim except in the case of a transfer more than:

(1)   one year after a date set for presentment or surrender for redemption or exchange; or

(2)   six months after a date set for payment of money against presentation or surrender of the certificate, if money was available for payment on that date.

(d)   A purchaser of a certificated security has notice of an adverse claim if the security certificate:

(1)   whether in bearer or registered form, has been indorsed "for collection" or "for surrender" or for some other purpose not involving transfer; or

(2) is in bearer form and has on it an unambiguous statement that it is the property of a person other than the transferor, but the mere writing of a name on the certificate is not such a statement.

(e) Filing of a financing statement under Article 9 is not notice of an adverse claim to a financial asset.

Official Comment

1. The rules specifying whether adverse claims can be asserted against persons who acquire securities or security entitlements, Sections 8–303, 8–502, and 8–510, provide that one is protected against an adverse claim only if one takes without notice of the claim. This section defines notice of an adverse claim.

~~The general Article 1 definition of "notice" in Section 1–201(25)   which provides that a person has notice of a fact if "from all the facts and circumstances known to him at the time in question he has reason to know that it exists"~~ Section 1–202(d), (e) and (f), on giving and receiving notice, does not apply to the interpretation of "notice of adverse claims." ~~The Section 1–201(25) definition of "notice"~~ Section 1–202(d), (e), and (f) does, however, apply to ~~usages of that term and its cognates in~~ giving and receiving notice under Article 8 in contexts other than notice of adverse claims.

2. This section must be interpreted in light of the definition of "adverse claim" in Section 8–102(a)(1). "Adverse claim" does not include all circumstances in which a third party has a property interest in securities, but only those situations where a security is transferred in violation of the claimant's property interest. Therefore, awareness that someone other than the transferor has a property interest is not notice of an adverse claim. The transferee must be aware that the transfer violates the other party's property interest. If A holds securities in which B has some form of property interest, and A transfers the securities to C, C may know that B has an interest, but infer that A is acting in accordance with A's obligations to B. The mere fact that C knew that B had a property interest does not mean that C had notice of an adverse claim. Whether C had notice of an adverse claim depends on whether C had sufficient awareness that A was acting in violation of B's property rights. The rule in subsection (b) is a particularization of this general principle.

3. Paragraph (a)(1) provides that a person has notice of an adverse claim if the person has knowledge of the adverse claim. Knowledge is defined in Section ~~1–201(25)~~ 1–202(b) as actual knowledge.

4. Paragraph (a)(2) provides that a person has notice of an adverse claim if the person is aware of a significant probability that an adverse claim exists and deliberately avoids information that might establish the existence of the adverse claim. This is intended to codify the "willful blindness" test that has been applied in such cases. See *May v. Chapman*, 16 M. & W. 355, 153 Eng.Rep. 1225 (1847); *Goodman v. Simonds*, 61 U.S. 343 (1857).

The first prong of the willful blindness test of paragraph (a)(2) turns on whether the person is aware facts sufficient to indicate that there is a significant probability that an adverse claim exists. The "awareness" aspect necessarily turns on the actor's state of mind. Whether facts known to a person make the person aware of a "significant probability" that an adverse claim exists turns on facts about the world and the conclusions that would be drawn from those facts, taking account of the experience and position of the person in question. A particular set of facts might indicate a significant probability of an adverse claim to a professional with considerable experience in the usual methods and procedures by which securities transactions are conducted, even though the same facts would not indicate a significant probability of an adverse claim to a non-professional.

The second prong of the willful blindness test of paragraph (a)(2) turns on whether the person "deliberately avoids information" that would establish the existence of the adverse claim. The test is the character of the person's response to the information the person has. The question is whether the person deliberately failed to seek further information because of concern that suspicions would be confirmed.

Application of the "deliberate avoidance" test to a transaction by an organization focuses on the knowledge and the actions of the individual or individuals conducting the transaction on behalf of the organization. Thus, an organization that purchases a security is not willfully blind to an adverse claim unless the officers or agents who conducted that purchase transaction are willfully blind to the adverse claim. Under the two prongs of the willful blindness test, the individual or individuals conducting a transaction must know of facts indicating a substantial probability that the adverse claim exists and deliberately fail to seek further information that might confirm or refute the indication. For this purpose, information known to individuals within an organization who are not conducting or aware of a transaction, but not forwarded to the individuals conducting the transaction, is not pertinent in determining whether the individuals conducting the transaction had knowledge of a substantial probability of the existence of the adverse claim. Cf. Section ~~1–201(27)~~ 1–202(f) (receipt of notice or knowledge by an organization). An organization may also "deliberately avoid information" if it acts to preclude or inhibit transmission of pertinent information to those individuals responsible for the conduct of purchase transactions.

5.   Paragraph (a)(3) provides that a person has notice of an adverse claim if the person would have learned of the adverse claim by conducting an investigation that is required by other statute or regulation. This rule applies only if there is some other statute or regulation that explicitly requires persons dealing with securities to conduct some investigation. The federal securities laws require that brokers and banks, in certain specified circumstances, check with a stolen securities registry to determine whether securities offered for sale or pledge have been reported as stolen. If securities that were listed as stolen in the registry are taken by an institution that failed to comply with requirement to check the registry, the institution would be held to have notice of the fact that they were stolen under paragraph (a)(3). Accordingly, the institution could not qualify as a protected purchaser under Section 8–303. The same result has been reached under the prior version of Article 8. See *First Nat'l Bank of Cicero v. Lewco Securities,* 860 F.2d 1407 (7th Cir. 1988).

6.   Subsection (b) provides explicitly for some situations involving purchase from one described or identifiable as a representative. Knowledge of the existence of the representative relation is not enough in itself to constitute "notice of an adverse claim" that would disqualify the purchaser from protected purchaser status. A purchaser may take a security on the inference that the representative is acting properly. Knowledge that a security is being transferred to an individual account of the representative or that the proceeds of the transaction will be paid into that account is not sufficient to constitute "notice of an adverse claim," but knowledge that the proceeds will be applied to the personal indebtedness of the representative is. See *State Bank of Binghamton v. Bache,* 162 Misc. 128, 293 N.Y.S. 667 (1937).

7.   Subsection (c) specifies whether a purchaser of a "stale" security is charged with notice of adverse claims, and therefore disqualified from protected purchaser status under Section 8–303. The fact of "staleness" is viewed as notice of certain defects after the lapse of stated periods, but the maturity of the security does not operate automatically to affect holders' rights. The periods of time here stated are shorter than those appearing in the provisions of this Article on staleness as notice of defects or defenses of an issuer (Section 8–203) since a purchaser who takes a security after funds or other securities are available for its redemption has more reason to suspect claims of ownership than issuer's defenses. An owner will normally turn in a security rather than transfer it at such a time. Of itself, a default never constitutes notice of a possible adverse claim. To provide otherwise would not tend to drive defaulted securities home and would serve only to disrupt current financial markets where many defaulted securities are actively traded. Unpaid or overdue coupons attached to a bond do not bring it within the operation of this subsection, though they may be relevant under the general test of notice of adverse claims in subsection (a).

8.   Subsection (d) provides the owner of a certificated security with a means of protection while a security certificate is being sent in for redemption or exchange. The owner may endorse it "for collection" or "for surrender," and this constitutes notice of the owner's claims, under subsection (d).

Definitional Cross References:

"Adverse claim". Section 8–102(a)(1).
"Bearer form". Section 8–102(a)(2).
"Certificated security". Section 8–102(a)(4).
"Financial asset". Section 8–102(a)(9).
"Knowledge". Section 1–201(25) [*unrevised Article 1; see Concordance, p. 22*].
"Person". Section 1–201(30) [*unrevised Article 1; see Concordance, p. 22*].
"Purchaser". Sections 1–201(33) [*unrevised Article 1; see Concordance, p. 22*] & 8–116.
"Registered form". Section 8–102(a)(13).
"Representative". Section 1–201(35) [*unrevised Article 1; see Concordance, p. 22*].
"Security certificate". Section 8–102(a)(16).

As amended in 2022.

§ 8–106.   Control.

(a)   A purchaser has "control" of a certificated security in bearer form if the certificated security is delivered to the purchaser.

(b)   A purchaser has "control" of a certificated security in registered form if the certificated security is delivered to the purchaser, and:

(1)   the certificate is indorsed to the purchaser or in blank by an effective indorsement; or

(2) the certificate is registered in the name of the purchaser, upon original issue or registration of transfer by the issuer.

(c) A purchaser has "control" of an uncertificated security if:

(1) the uncertificated security is delivered to the purchaser; or

(2) the issuer has agreed that it will comply with instructions originated by the purchaser without further consent by the registered owner.

(d) A purchaser has "control" of a security entitlement if:

(1) the purchaser becomes the entitlement holder;

(2) the securities intermediary has agreed that it will comply with entitlement orders originated by the purchaser without further consent by the entitlement holder; or

(3) another ~~person has control of the security entitlement on behalf of the purchaser or, having previously acquired control of the security entitlement, acknowledges that it has control on behalf of the purchaser.~~ person, other than the transferor to the purchaser of an interest in the security entitlement:

> (A) has control of the security entitlement and acknowledges that it has control on behalf of the purchaser; or

> (B) obtains control of the security entitlement after having acknowledged that it will obtain control of the security entitlement on behalf of the purchaser.

(e) If an interest in a security entitlement is granted by the entitlement holder to the entitlement holder's own securities intermediary, the securities intermediary has control.

(f) A purchaser who has satisfied the requirements of subsection (c) or (d) has control, even if the registered owner in the case of subsection (c) or the entitlement holder in the case of subsection (d) retains the right to make substitutions for the uncertificated security or security entitlement, to originate instructions or entitlement orders to the issuer or securities intermediary, or otherwise to deal with the uncertificated security or security entitlement.

(g) An issuer or a securities intermediary may not enter into an agreement of the kind described in subsection (c)(2) or (d)(2) without the consent of the registered owner or entitlement holder, but an issuer or a securities intermediary is not required to enter into such an agreement even though the registered owner or entitlement holder so directs. An issuer or securities intermediary that has entered into such an agreement is not required to confirm the existence of the agreement to another party unless requested to do so by the registered owner or entitlement holder.

(h) A person that has control under this section is not required to acknowledge that it has control on behalf of a purchaser.

(i) If a person acknowledges that it has or will obtain control on behalf of a purchaser, unless the person otherwise agrees or law other than this Article or Article 9 otherwise provides, the person does not owe any duty to the purchaser and is not required to confirm the acknowledgment to any other person.

As amended in 1999 and 2022.

Official Comment

1. The concept of "control" plays a key role in various provisions dealing with the rights of purchasers, including secured parties. See Sections 8–303 (protected purchasers); 8–503(e) (purchasers from securities intermediaries); 8–510 (purchasers of security entitlements from entitlement holders); 9–203(b)(3)(D) (attachment of security interests); 9–314 (perfection of security interests); 9–328 (priorities among conflicting security interests).

Obtaining "control" means that the purchaser has taken whatever steps are necessary, given the manner in which the securities or other financial assets are held, to place itself in a position where it can have the securities or other financial assets sold, without further action by the owner, registered owner, entitlement holder, transferor, or other person with an interest in the securities or other financial assets.

2.   Subsection (a) provides that a purchaser obtains "control" with respect to a certificated security in bearer form by taking "delivery," as defined in Section 8–301. Subsection (b) provides that a purchaser obtains "control" with respect to a certificated security in registered form by taking "delivery," as defined in Section 8–301, provided that the security certificate has been indorsed to the purchaser or in blank. Section 8–301 provides that delivery of a certificated security occurs when the purchaser obtains possession of the security certificate, or when an agent for the purchaser (other than a securities intermediary) either acquires possession or acknowledges that the agent holds for the purchaser.

3.   Subsection (c) specifies the means by which a purchaser can obtain control over uncertificated securities which the transferor holds directly. Two mechanisms are possible.

Under subsection (c)(1), securities can be "delivered" to a purchaser. Section 8–301(b) provides that "delivery" of an uncertificated security occurs when the purchaser becomes the registered holder. So far as the issuer is concerned, the purchaser would then be entitled to exercise all rights of ownership. See Section 8–207. As between the parties to a purchase transaction, however, the rights of the purchaser are determined by their contract. Cf. Section 9–202. Arrangements covered by this paragraph are analogous to arrangements in which bearer certificates are delivered to a secured party—so far as the issuer or any other parties are concerned, the secured party appears to be the outright owner, although it is in fact holding as collateral property that belongs to the debtor.

Under subsection (c)(2), a purchaser has control if the issuer has agreed to act on the instructions of the purchaser, even though the owner remains listed as the registered owner. The issuer, of course, would be acting wrongfully against the registered owner if it entered into such an agreement without the consent of the registered owner. Subsection (g) makes this point explicit. The subsection (c)(2) provision makes it possible for issuers to offer a service akin to the registered pledge device of the 1978 version of Article 8, without mandating that all issuers offer that service.

4.   Subsection (d) specifies the means by which a purchaser can obtain control of a security entitlement. Three mechanisms are possible, analogous to those provided in subsection (c) for uncertificated securities. Under subsection (d)(1), a purchaser has control if it is the entitlement holder. This subsection would apply whether the purchaser holds through the same intermediary that the debtor used, or has the securities position transferred to its own intermediary. Subsection (d)(2) provides that a purchaser has control if the securities intermediary has agreed to act on entitlement orders originated by the purchaser if no further consent by the entitlement holder is required. Under subsection (d)(2), control may be achieved even though the original entitlement holder remains as the entitlement holder. Finally, a purchaser may obtain control under subsection (d)(3) if another person has control and the person acknowledges that it has control on the purchaser's behalf. ~~Control~~ In general, control under subsection (d)(3) parallels the delivery of certificated securities and uncertificated securities under Section 8–301. ~~Of course, the acknowledging person cannot be the debtor.~~ See the discussion of subsection (d)(3) in Comment 4A, below.

~~This section~~ Subsection (d) specifies only the minimum requirements that such an arrangement must meet to confer "control" of a security entitlement; the details of the arrangement can be specified by agreement. The arrangement might cover all of the positions in a particular account or subaccount, or only specified positions. There is no requirement that the control party's right to give entitlement orders be exclusive. The arrangement might provide, for example, that only the control party can give entitlement orders, ~~or~~ that either the entitlement holder or the control party can give entitlement orders, that more than one person has unilateral control, or that two or more persons share control. The essential factor is whether a person may originate entitlement orders without further consent of the entitlement holder. See subsection (f).

The following examples illustrate the application of subsection (d):

     Example 1.   Debtor grants Alpha Bank a security interest in a security entitlement that includes 1000 shares of XYZ Co. stock that Debtor holds through an account with Able & Co. Alpha also has an account with Able. Debtor instructs Able to transfer the shares to Alpha, and Able does so by crediting the shares to Alpha's account. Alpha has control of the 1000 shares under subsection (d)(1). Although Debtor may have become the beneficial owner of the new securities entitlement, as between Debtor and Alpha, Able has agreed to act on Alpha's entitlement orders because, as between Able and Alpha, Alpha has become the entitlement holder. See Section 8–506.

     Example 2.   Debtor grants Alpha Bank a security interest in a security entitlement that includes 1000 shares of XYZ Co. stock that Debtor holds through an account with Able & Co. Alpha does not have an account with Able. Alpha uses Beta as its securities custodian. Debtor instructs Able to transfer the shares to Beta, for the account of Alpha, and Able does so. Alpha has control of the 1000 shares under subsection (d)(1). As in Example 1, although Debtor may have become the beneficial owner of the new securities entitlement, as between Debtor and Alpha, Beta has agreed to act on Alpha's entitlement orders because, as between Beta and Alpha, Alpha has become the entitlement holder.

Example 3.   Debtor grants Alpha Bank a security interest in a security entitlement that includes 1000 shares of XYZ Co. stock that Debtor holds through an account with Able & Co. Debtor, Able, and Alpha enter into an agreement under which Debtor will continue to receive dividends and distributions, and will continue to have the right to direct dispositions, but Alpha also has the right to direct dispositions. Alpha has control of the 1000 shares under subsection (d)(2).

Example 4.   Able & Co., a securities dealer, grants Alpha Bank a security interest in a security entitlement that includes 1000 shares of XYZ Co. stock that Able holds through an account with Clearing Corporation. Able causes Clearing Corporation to transfer the shares into Alpha's account at Clearing Corporation. As in Example 1, Alpha has control of the 1000 shares under subsection (d)(1).

Example 5.   Able & Co., a securities dealer, grants Alpha Bank a security interest in a security entitlement that includes 1000 shares of XYZ Co. stock that Able holds through an account with Clearing Corporation. Alpha does not have an account with Clearing Corporation. It holds its securities through Beta Bank, which does have an account with Clearing Corporation. Able causes Clearing Corporation to transfer the shares into Beta's account at Clearing Corporation. Beta credits the position to Alpha's account with Beta. As in Example 2, Alpha has control of the 1000 shares under subsection (d)(1).

Example 6.   Able & Co., a securities dealer, grants Alpha Bank a security interest in a security entitlement that includes 1000 shares of XYZ Co. stock that Able holds through an account with Clearing Corporation. Able causes Clearing Corporation to transfer the shares into a pledge account, pursuant to an agreement under which Able will continue to receive dividends, distributions, and the like, but Alpha has the right to direct dispositions. As in Example 3, Alpha has control of the 1000 shares under subsection (d)(2).

Example 7.   Able & Co., a securities dealer, grants Alpha Bank a security interest in a security entitlement that includes 1000 shares of XYZ Co. stock that Able holds through an account with Clearing Corporation. Able, Alpha, and Clearing Corporation enter into an agreement under which Clearing Corporation will act on instructions from Alpha with respect to the XYZ Co. stock carried in Able's account, but Able will continue to receive dividends, distributions, and the like, and will also have the right to direct dispositions. As in Example 3, Alpha has control of the 1000 shares under subsection (d)(2).

Example 8.   Able & Co., a securities dealer, holds a wide range of securities through its account at Clearing Corporation. Able enters into an arrangement with Alpha Bank pursuant to which Alpha provides financing to Able secured by securities identified as the collateral on lists provided by Able to Alpha on a daily or other periodic basis. Able, Alpha, and Clearing Corporation enter into an agreement under which Clearing Corporation agrees that if at any time Alpha directs Clearing Corporation to do so, Clearing Corporation will transfer any securities from Able's account at Alpha's instructions. Because Clearing Corporation has agreed to act on Alpha's instructions with respect to any securities carried in Able's account, at the moment that Alpha's security interest attaches to securities listed by Able, Alpha obtains control of those securities under subsection (d)(2). There is no requirement that Clearing Corporation be informed of which securities Able has pledged to Alpha.

Example 9.   Debtor grants Alpha Bank a security interest in a security entitlement that includes 1000 shares of XYZ Co. stock that Debtor holds through an account with Able & Co. Beta Bank agrees with Alpha to act as Alpha's collateral agent with respect to the security entitlement. Debtor, Able, and Beta enter into an agreement under which Debtor will continue to receive dividends and distributions, and will continue to have the right to direct dispositions, but Beta also has the right to direct dispositions. Because Able has agreed that it will comply with entitlement orders originated by Beta without further consent by Debtor, Beta has control of the security entitlement (see Example 3). Because Beta has <u>acknowledged that it has</u> control on behalf of Alpha, Alpha also has control under subsection (d)(3). It is not necessary for Able to enter into an agreement directly with Alpha or for Able to be aware of Beta's <s>agency</s> relationship with Alpha.

<u>4A.   Pursuant to the 2022 Amendments, subsection (d)(3) was revised to conform the provision for control through another person to the corresponding provisions for control of other types of assets. *See* Section 12–105, Comment 8; see also Sections 7–106(g) (control of electronic document of title); 9–104(a)(4) (control of deposit account); 9–105(g) (control of authoritative electronic copy of a record evidencing chattel paper); 9–105A(e) (control of electronic money). Control based on an acknowledgment under subsection (d)(3) by another person having control continues only while the other person retains control. This result necessarily follows because such control derives solely from the other person's continued control. Under subsection (d)(3), for an acknowledgment to be</u>

effective to confer control, it must be made by a person "other than the transferor of an interest in the security entitlement." See Section 12–105, Comment 9 (discussing the rationale for this requirement). Subsections (h) and (i) derive from Section 9–313(f) and (g). Subsection (h) makes clear that a person that has control under this section has no duty to acknowledge that it has or will obtain control on behalf of a purchaser. Arrangements for a person to acknowledge that it has or will obtain control on behalf of another person are not standardized. Accordingly, subsection (i) leaves to the agreement of the parties and to any other applicable law (other than this Article or Article 9) any duties of a person that does acknowledge that it has or will obtain control on behalf of a purchaser and provides that a person making an acknowledgment is not required to confirm the acknowledgment to any other person.

5.   For a purchaser to have "control" under subsection (c)(2) or (d)(2), it is essential that the issuer or securities intermediary, as the case may be, actually be a party to the agreement. If a debtor gives a secured party a power of attorney authorizing the secured party to act in the name of the debtor, but the issuer or securities intermediary does not specifically agree to this arrangement, the secured party does not have "control" within the meaning of subsection (c)(2) or (d)(2) because the issuer or securities intermediary is not a party to the agreement. The secured party does not have control under subsection (c)(1) or (d)(1) because, although the power of attorney might give the secured party authority to act on the debtor's behalf as an agent, the secured party has not actually become the registered owner or entitlement holder.

6.   Subsection (e) provides that if an interest in a security entitlement is granted by an entitlement holder to the securities intermediary through which the security entitlement is maintained, the securities intermediary has control. A common transaction covered by this provision is a margin loan from a broker to its customer.

7.   The term "control" is used in a particular defined sense. The requirements for obtaining control are set out in this section. The concept is not to be interpreted by reference to similar concepts in other bodies of law. In particular, the requirements for "possession" derived from the common law of pledge are not to be used as a basis for interpreting subsection (c)(2) or (d)(2). Those provisions are designed to supplant the concepts of "constructive possession" and the like. A principal purpose of the "control" concept is to eliminate the uncertainty and confusion that results from attempting to apply common law possession concepts to modern securities holding practices.

The key to the control concept is that the purchaser has the ability to have the securities sold or transferred without further action by the transferor. There is no requirement that the powers held by the purchaser be exclusive. For example, in a secured lending arrangement, if the secured party wishes, it can allow the debtor to retain the right to make substitutions, to direct the disposition of the uncertificated security or security entitlement, or otherwise to give instructions or entitlement orders. (As explained in Section 8–102, Comment 8, an entitlement order includes a direction under Section 8–508 to the securities intermediary to transfer a financial asset to the account of the entitlement holder at another financial intermediary or to cause the financial asset to be transferred to the entitlement holder in the direct holding system (e.g., by delivery of a securities certificate registered in the name of the former entitlement holder).) Subsection (f) is included to make clear the general point stated in subsections (c) and (d) that the test of control is whether the purchaser has obtained the requisite power, not whether the debtor has retained other powers. There is no implication that retention by the debtor of powers other than those mentioned in subsection (f) is inconsistent with the purchaser having control. Nor is there a requirement that the purchaser's powers be unconditional, provided that further consent of the entitlement holder is not a condition.

Example 10.   Debtor grants to Alpha Bank and to Beta Bank a security interest in a security entitlement that includes 1000 shares of XYZ Co. stock that Debtor holds through an account with Able & Co. By agreement among the parties, Alpha's security interest is senior and Beta's is junior. Able agrees to act on the entitlement orders of either Alpha or Beta. Alpha and Beta each has control under subsection (d)(2). Moreover, Beta has control notwithstanding a term of Able's agreement to the effect that Able's obligation to act on Beta's entitlement orders is conditioned on Alpha's consent. The crucial distinction is that Able's agreement to act on Beta's entitlement orders is not conditioned on Debtor's further consent.

Example 11.   Debtor grants to Alpha Bank a security interest in a security entitlement that includes 1000 shares of XYZ Co. stock that Debtor holds through an account with Able & Co. Able agrees to act on the entitlement orders of Alpha, but Alpha's right to give entitlement orders to the securities intermediary is conditioned on the Debtor's default. Alternatively, Alpha's right to give entitlement orders is conditioned upon Alpha's statement to Able that Debtor is in default. Because Able's agreement to act on *Beta's* Alpha's entitlement orders is not conditioned on Debtor's further consent, Alpha has control of the securities entitlement under either alternative. [Amendments in italics approved by the Permanent Editorial Board for Uniform Commercial Code January 15, 2000.]

In many situations, it will be better practice for both the securities intermediary and the purchaser to insist that any conditions relating in any way to the entitlement holder be effective only as between the purchaser and the entitlement holder. That practice would avoid the risk that the securities intermediary could be caught between conflicting assertions of the entitlement holder and the purchaser as to whether the conditions in fact have been met. Nonetheless, the existence of unfulfilled conditions effective against the intermediary would not preclude the purchaser from having control.

Definitional Cross References:

"Bearer form". Section 8–102(a)(2).

"Certificated security". Section 8–102(a)(4).

"Delivery". Section 8–301.

"Effective". Section 8–107.

"Entitlement holder". Section 8–102(a)(7).

"Entitlement order". Section 8–102(a)(8).

"Indorsement". Section 8–102(a)(11).

"Instruction". Section 8–102(a)(12).

"Purchaser". Sections 1–201(33) [*unrevised Article 1; see Concordance, p. 22*] & 8–116.

"Registered form". Section 8–102(a)(13).

"Securities intermediary". Section 8–102(a)(14).

"Security entitlement". Section 8–102(a)(17).

"Uncertificated security". Section 8–102(a)(18).

As amended in 1999, 2000, and 2022.

§ 8–107.   Whether Indorsement, Instruction, or Entitlement Order is Effective.

(a) "Appropriate person" means:

(1) with respect to an indorsement, the person specified by a security certificate or by an effective special indorsement to be entitled to the security;

(2) with respect to an instruction, the registered owner of an uncertificated security;

(3) with respect to an entitlement order, the entitlement holder;

(4) if the person designated in paragraph (1), (2), or (3) is deceased, the designated person's successor taking under other law or the designated person's personal representative acting for the estate of the decedent; or

(5) if the person designated in paragraph (1), (2), or (3) lacks capacity, the designated person's guardian, conservator, or other similar representative who has power under other law to transfer the security or financial asset.

(b) An indorsement, instruction, or entitlement order is effective if:

(1) it is made by the appropriate person;

(2) it is made by a person who has power under the law of agency to transfer the security or financial asset on behalf of the appropriate person, including, in the case of an instruction or entitlement order, a person who has control under Section 8–106(c)(2) or (d)(2); or

(3) the appropriate person has ratified it or is otherwise precluded from asserting its ineffectiveness.

(c) An indorsement, instruction, or entitlement order made by a representative is effective even if:

(1) the representative has failed to comply with a controlling instrument or with the law of the State having jurisdiction of the representative relationship, including any law requiring the representative to obtain court approval of the transaction; or

(2) the representative's action in making the indorsement, instruction, or entitlement order or using the proceeds of the transaction is otherwise a breach of duty.

(d) If a security is registered in the name of or specially indorsed to a person described as a representative, or if a securities account is maintained in the name of a person described as a representative, an indorsement, instruction, or entitlement order made by the person is effective even though the person is no longer serving in the described capacity.

(e)   Effectiveness of an indorsement, instruction, or entitlement order is determined as of the date the indorsement, instruction, or entitlement order is made, and an indorsement, instruction, or entitlement order does not become ineffective by reason of any later change of circumstances.

Official Comment

1.   This section defines two concepts, "appropriate person" and "effective." Effectiveness is a broader concept than appropriate person. For example, if a security or securities account is registered in the name of Mary Roe, Mary Roe is the "appropriate person," but an indorsement, instruction, or entitlement order made by John Doe is "effective" if, under agency or other law, Mary Roe is precluded from denying Doe's authority. Treating these two concepts separately facilitates statement of the rules of Article 8 that state the legal effect of an indorsement, instruction, or entitlement order. For example, a securities intermediary is protected against liability if it acts on an effective entitlement order, but has a duty to comply with an entitlement order only if it is originated by an appropriate person. See Sections 8–115 and 8–507.

One important application of the "effectiveness" concept is in the direct holding system rules on the rights of purchasers. A purchaser of a certificated security in registered form can qualify as a protected purchaser who takes free from adverse claims under Section 8–303 only if the purchaser obtains "control." Section 8–106 provides that a purchaser of a certificated security in registered form obtains control if there has been an "effective" indorsement.

2.   Subsection (a) provides that the term "appropriate person" covers two categories: (1) the person who is actually designated as the person entitled to the security or security entitlement, and (2) the successor or legal representative of that person if that person has died or otherwise lacks capacity. Other law determines who has power to transfer a security on behalf of a person who lacks capacity. For example, if securities are registered in the name of more than one person and one of the designated persons dies, whether the survivor is the appropriate person depends on the form of tenancy. If the two were registered joint tenants with right of survivorship, the survivor would have that power under other law and thus would be the "appropriate person." If securities are registered in the name of an individual and the individual dies, the law of decedents' estates determines who has power to transfer the decedent's securities. That would ordinarily be the executor or administrator, but if a "small estate statute" permits a widow to transfer a decedent's securities without administration proceedings, she would be the appropriate person. If the registration of a security or a securities account contains a designation of a death beneficiary under the Uniform Transfer on Death Security Registration Act or comparable legislation, the designated beneficiary would, under that law, have power to transfer upon the person's death and so would be the appropriate person. Article 8 does not contain a list of such representatives, because any list is likely to become outdated by developments in other law.

3.   Subsection (b) sets out the general rule that an indorsement, instruction, or entitlement order is effective if it is made by the appropriate person or by a person who has power to transfer under agency law or if the appropriate person is precluded from denying its effectiveness. The control rules in Section 8–106 provide for arrangements where a person who holds securities through a securities intermediary, or holds uncertificated securities directly, enters into a control agreement giving the secured party the right to initiate entitlement orders of instructions. Paragraph 2 of subsection (b) states explicitly that an entitlement order or instruction initiated by a person who has obtained such a control agreement is "effective."

Subsections (c), (d), and (e) supplement the general rule of subsection (b) on effectiveness. The term "representative," used in subsections (c) and (d), is defined in Section 1–201(35) 1–201(b)(33).

4.   Subsection (c) provides that an indorsement, instruction, or entitlement order made by a representative is effective even though the representative's action is a violation of duties. The following example illustrates this subsection:

   Example 1.   Certificated securities are registered in the name of John Doe. Doe dies and Mary Roe
   is appointed executor. Roe indorses the security certificate and transfers it to a purchaser in a transaction
   that is a violation of her duties as executor.

Roe's indorsement is effective, because Roe is the appropriate person under subsection (a)(4). This is so even though Roe's transfer violated her obligations as executor. The policies of free transferability of securities that underlie Article 8 dictate that neither a purchaser to whom Roe transfers the securities nor the issuer who registers transfer should be required to investigate the terms of the will to determine whether Roe is acting properly. Although Roe's indorsement is effective under this section, her breach of duty may be such that her beneficiary has an adverse claim to the securities that Roe transferred. The question whether that adverse claim can be asserted against purchasers is governed not by this section but by Section 8–303. Under Section 8–404, the issuer has no duties to an adverse claimant unless the claimant obtains legal process enjoining the issuer from registering transfer.

5. Subsection (d) deals with cases where a security or a securities account is registered in the name of a person specifically designated as a representative. The following example illustrates this subsection:

Example 2. Certificated securities are registered in the name of "John Jones, trustee of the Smith Family Trust." John Jones is removed as trustee and Martha Moe is appointed successor trustee. The securities, however, are not reregistered, but remain registered in the name of "John Jones, trustee of the Smith Family Trust." Jones indorses the security certificate and transfers it to a purchaser.

Subsection (d) provides that an indorsement by John Jones as trustee is effective even though Jones is no longer serving in that capacity. Since the securities were registered in the name of "John Jones, trustee of the Smith Family Trust," a purchaser, or the issuer when called upon to register transfer, should be entitled to assume without further inquiry that Jones has the power to act as trustee for the Smith Family Trust.

Note that subsection (d) does not apply to a case where the security or securities account is registered in the name of principal rather than the representative as such. The following example illustrates this point:

Example 3. Certificated securities are registered in the name of John Doe. John Doe dies and Mary Roe is appointed executor. The securities are not reregistered in the name of Mary Roe as executor. Later, Mary Roe is removed as executor and Martha Moe is appointed as her successor. After being removed, Mary Roe indorses the security certificate that is registered in the name of John Doe and transfers it to a purchaser.

Mary Roe's indorsement is not made effective by subsection (d), because the securities were not registered in the name of Mary Roe as representative. A purchaser or the issuer registering transfer should be required to determine whether Roe has power to act for John Doe. Purchasers and issuers can protect themselves in such cases by requiring signature guaranties. See Section 8–306.

6. Subsection (e) provides that the effectiveness of an indorsement, instruction, or entitlement order is determined as of the date it is made. The following example illustrates this subsection:

Example 4. Certificated securities are registered in the name of John Doe. John Doe dies and Mary Roe is appointed executor. Mary Roe indorses the security certificate that is registered in the name of John Doe and transfers it to a purchaser. After the indorsement and transfer, but before the security certificate is presented to the issuer for registration of transfer, Mary Roe is removed as executor and Martha Moe is appointed as her successor.

Mary Roe's indorsement is effective, because at the time Roe indorsed she was the appropriate person under subsection (a)(4). Her later removal as executor does not render the indorsement ineffective. Accordingly, the issuer would not be liable for registering the transfer. See Section 8–404.

Definitional Cross References:

"Entitlement order". Section 8–102(a)(8).
"Financial asset". Section 8–102(a)(9).
"Indorsement". Section 8–102(a)(11).
"Instruction". Section 8–102(a)(12).
"Representative". Section 1–201(35) [*unrevised Article 1; see Concordance, p. 22*].
"Securities account". Section 8–501.
"Security". Section 8–102(a)(15).
"Security certificate". Section 8–102(a)(16).
"Security entitlement". Section 8–102(a)(17).
"Uncertificated security". Section 8–102(a)(18).

As amended in 2022.

§ 8–108. Warranties in Direct Holding.

(a) A person who transfers a certificated security to a purchaser for value warrants to the purchaser, and an indorser, if the transfer is by indorsement, warrants to any subsequent purchaser, that:

(1) the certificate is genuine and has not been materially altered;

(2)   the transferor or indorser does not know of any fact that might impair the validity of the security;

(3)   there is no adverse claim to the security;

(4)   the transfer does not violate any restriction on transfer;

(5)   if the transfer is by indorsement, the indorsement is made by an appropriate person, or if the indorsement is by an agent, the agent has actual authority to act on behalf of the appropriate person; and

(6)   the transfer is otherwise effective and rightful.

(b)   A person who originates an instruction for registration of transfer of an uncertificated security to a purchaser for value warrants to the purchaser that:

(1)   the instruction is made by an appropriate person, or if the instruction is by an agent, the agent has actual authority to act on behalf of the appropriate person;

(2)   the security is valid;

(3)   there is no adverse claim to the security; and

(4)   at the time the instruction is presented to the issuer:

(i)   the purchaser will be entitled to the registration of transfer;

(ii)   the transfer will be registered by the issuer free from all liens, security interests, restrictions, and claims other than those specified in the instruction;

(iii)   the transfer will not violate any restriction on transfer; and

(iv)   the requested transfer will otherwise be effective and rightful.

(c)   A person who transfers an uncertificated security to a purchaser for value and does not originate an instruction in connection with the transfer warrants that:

(1)   the uncertificated security is valid;

(2)   there is no adverse claim to the security;

(3)   the transfer does not violate any restriction on transfer; and

(4)   the transfer is otherwise effective and rightful.

(d)   A person who indorses a security certificate warrants to the issuer that:

(1)   there is no adverse claim to the security; and

(2)   the indorsement is effective.

(e)   A person who originates an instruction for registration of transfer of an uncertificated security warrants to the issuer that:

(1)   the instruction is effective; and

(2)   at the time the instruction is presented to the issuer the purchaser will be entitled to the registration of transfer.

(f)   A person who presents a certificated security for registration of transfer or for payment or exchange warrants to the issuer that the person is entitled to the registration, payment, or exchange, but a purchaser for value and without notice of adverse claims to whom transfer is registered warrants only that the person has no knowledge of any unauthorized signature in a necessary indorsement.

(g)   If a person acts as agent of another in delivering a certificated security to a purchaser, the identity of the principal was known to the person to whom the certificate was delivered, and the certificate delivered by the agent was received by the agent from the principal or received by the agent from another person at the direction of the principal, the person delivering the security certificate warrants only that the delivering person has authority to act for the principal and does not know of any adverse claim to the certificated security.

(h)   A secured party who redelivers a security certificate received, or after payment and on order of the debtor delivers the security certificate to another person, makes only the warranties of an agent under subsection (g).

(i)   Except as otherwise provided in subsection (g), a broker acting for a customer makes to the issuer and a purchaser the warranties provided in subsections (a) through (f). A broker that delivers a security certificate to its customer, or causes its customer to be registered as the owner of an uncertificated security, makes to the customer the warranties provided in subsection (a) or (b), and has the rights and privileges of a purchaser under this section. The warranties of and in favor of the broker acting as an agent are in addition to applicable warranties given by and in favor of the customer.

Official Comment

1.   Subsections (a), (b), and (c) deal with warranties by security transferors to purchasers. Subsections (d) and (e) deal with warranties by security transferors to issuers. Subsection (f) deals with presentment warranties.

2.   Subsection (a) specifies the warranties made by a person who transfers a certificated security to a purchaser for value. Paragraphs (3), (4), and (5) make explicit several key points that are implicit in the general warranty of paragraph (6) that the transfer is effective and rightful. Subsection (b) sets forth the warranties made to a purchaser for value by one who originates an instruction. These warranties are quite similar to those made by one transferring a certificated security, subsection (a), the principal difference being the absolute warranty of validity. If upon receipt of the instruction the issuer should dispute the validity of the security, the burden of proving validity is upon the transferor. Subsection (c) provides for the limited circumstances in which an uncertificated security could be transferred without an instruction, see Section 8–301(b)(2). Subsections (d) and (e) give the issuer the benefit of the warranties of an indorser or originator on those matters not within the issuer's knowledge.

3.   Subsection (f) limits the warranties made by a purchaser for value without notice whose presentation of a security certificate is defective in some way but to whom the issuer does register transfer. The effect is to deny the issuer a remedy against such a person unless at the time of presentment the person had knowledge of an unauthorized signature in a necessary indorsement. The issuer can protect itself by refusing to make the transfer or, if it registers the transfer before it discovers the defect, by pursuing its remedy against a signature guarantor.

4.   Subsection (g) eliminates all substantive warranties in the relatively unusual case of a delivery of certificated security by an agent of a disclosed principal where the agent delivers the exact certificate that it received from or for the principal. Subsection (h) limits the warranties given by a secured party who redelivers a certificate. Subsection (i) specifies the warranties of brokers in the more common scenarios.

5.   Under Section 1–102(3) [*unrevised Article 1; see Concordance, p. 22*] the warranty provisions apply "unless otherwise agreed" and the parties may enter into express agreements to allocate the risks of possible defects. Usual estoppel principles apply with respect to transfers of both certificated and uncertificated securities whenever the purchaser has knowledge of the defect, and these warranties will not be breached in such a case.

Definitional Cross References:

"Adverse claim". Section 8–102(a)(1).

"Appropriate person". Section 8–107.

"Broker". Section 8–102(a)(3).

"Certificated security". Section 8–102(a)(4).

"Indorsement". Section 8–102(a)(11).

"Instruction". Section 8–102(a)(12).

"Issuer". Section 8–201.

"Person". Section 1–201(30) [*unrevised Article 1; see Concordance, p. 22*].

"Purchaser". Sections 1–201(33) [*unrevised Article 1; see Concordance, p. 22*] & 8–116.

"Secured party". Section 9–102(a)(72) [*Article 9 version prior to the 2010 Amendments*].

"Security". Section 8–102(a)(15).

"Security certificate". Section 8–102(a)(16).

"Uncertificated security". Section 8–102(a)(18).

"Value". Sections 1–201(44) [*unrevised Article 1; see Concordance, p. 22*] & 8–116.

§ 8–109.   Warranties in Indirect Holding.

(a)   A person who originates an entitlement order to a securities intermediary warrants to the securities intermediary that:

(1)   the entitlement order is made by an appropriate person, or if the entitlement order is by an agent, the agent has actual authority to act on behalf of the appropriate person; and

(2)   there is no adverse claim to the security entitlement.

(b)   A person who delivers a security certificate to a securities intermediary for credit to a securities account or originates an instruction with respect to an uncertificated security directing that the uncertificated security be credited to a securities account makes to the securities intermediary the warranties specified in Section 8–108(a) or (b).

(c)   If a securities intermediary delivers a security certificate to its entitlement holder or causes its entitlement holder to be registered as the owner of an uncertificated security, the securities intermediary makes to the entitlement holder the warranties specified in Section 8–108(a) or (b).

Official Comment

1.   Subsection (a) provides that a person who originates an entitlement order warrants to the securities intermediary that the order is authorized, and warrants the absence of adverse claims. Subsection (b) specifies the warranties that are given when a person who holds securities directly has the holding converted into indirect form. A person who delivers a certificate to a securities intermediary or originates an instruction for an uncertificated security gives to the securities intermediary the transfer warranties under Section 8–108. If the securities intermediary in turn delivers the certificate to a higher level securities intermediary, it gives the same warranties.

2.   Subsection (c) states the warranties that a securities intermediary gives when a customer who has been holding securities in an account with the securities intermediary requests that certificates be delivered or that uncertificated securities be registered in the customer's name. The warranties are the same as those that brokers make with respect to securities that the brokers sell to or buy on behalf of the customers. See Section 8–108(i).

3.   As with the Section 8–108 warranties, the warranties specified in this section may be modified by agreement under Section 1–102(3) [*unrevised Article 1; see Concordance, p. 22*].

Definitional Cross References:

"Adverse claim". Section 8–102(a)(1).
"Appropriate person". Section 8–107.
"Entitlement holder". Section 8–102(a)(7).
"Entitlement order". Section 8–102(a)(8).
"Instruction". Section 8–102(a)(12).
"Person". Section 1–201(30) [*unrevised Article 1; see Concordance, p. 22*].
"Securities account". Section 8–501.
"Securities intermediary". Section 8–102(a)(14).
"Security certificate". Section 8–102(a)(16).
"Uncertificated security". Section 8–102(a)(18).

§ 8–110.   Applicability; Choice of Law.

(a)   The local law of the issuer's jurisdiction, as specified in subsection (d), governs:

(1)   the validity of a security;

(2)   the rights and duties of the issuer with respect to registration of transfer;

(3)   the effectiveness of registration of transfer by the issuer;

(4)   whether the issuer owes any duties to an adverse claimant to a security; and

(5)   whether an adverse claim can be asserted against a person to whom transfer of a certificated or uncertificated security is registered or a person who obtains control of an uncertificated security.

(b)   The local law of the securities intermediary's jurisdiction, as specified in subsection (e), governs:

(1)　acquisition of a security entitlement from the securities intermediary;

(2)　the rights and duties of the securities intermediary and entitlement holder arising out of a security entitlement;

(3)　whether the securities intermediary owes any duties to an adverse claimant to a security entitlement; and

(4)　whether an adverse claim can be asserted against a person who acquires a security entitlement from the securities intermediary or a person who purchases a security entitlement or interest therein from an entitlement holder.

(c)　The local law of the jurisdiction in which a security certificate is located at the time of delivery governs whether an adverse claim can be asserted against a person to whom the security certificate is delivered.

(d)　"Issuer's jurisdiction" means the jurisdiction under which the issuer of the security is organized or, if permitted by the law of that jurisdiction, the law of another jurisdiction specified by the issuer. An issuer organized under the law of this State may specify the law of another jurisdiction as the law governing the matters specified in subsection (a)(2) through (5).

(e)　The following rules determine a "securities intermediary's jurisdiction" for purposes of this section:

(1)　If an agreement between the securities intermediary and its entitlement holder governing the securities account expressly provides that a particular jurisdiction is the securities intermediary's jurisdiction for purposes of this part, this article, or this [Act], that jurisdiction is the securities intermediary's jurisdiction.

(2)　If paragraph (1) does not apply and an agreement between the securities intermediary and its entitlement holder governing the securities account expressly provides that the agreement is governed by the law of a particular jurisdiction, that jurisdiction is the securities intermediary's jurisdiction.

(3)　If neither paragraph (1) nor paragraph (2) applies and an agreement between the securities intermediary and its entitlement holder governing the securities account expressly provides that the securities account is maintained at an office in a particular jurisdiction, that jurisdiction is the securities intermediary's jurisdiction.

(4)　If none of the preceding paragraphs applies, the securities intermediary's jurisdiction is the jurisdiction in which the office identified in an account statement as the office serving the entitlement holder's account is located.

(5)　If none of the preceding paragraphs applies, the securities intermediary's jurisdiction is the jurisdiction in which the chief executive office of the securities intermediary is located.

(f)　A securities intermediary's jurisdiction is not determined by the physical location of certificates representing financial assets, or by the jurisdiction in which is organized the issuer of the financial asset with respect to which an entitlement holder has a security entitlement, or by the location of facilities for data processing or other record keeping concerning the account.

(g)　The local law of the issuer's jurisdiction or the securities intermediary's jurisdiction governs a matter or transaction specified in subsection (a) or (b) even if the matter or transaction does not bear any relation to the jurisdiction.

As amended in 1999 and 2022.

Official Comment

1.　This section deals with applicability and choice of law issues concerning Article 8. The distinction between the direct and indirect holding systems plays a significant role in determining the governing law. An investor in the direct holding system is registered on the books of the issuer and/or has possession of a security certificate. Accordingly, the jurisdiction of incorporation of the issuer or location of the certificate determine the applicable law. By contrast, an investor in the indirect holding system has a security entitlement, which is a bundle of rights against the securities intermediary with respect to a security, rather than a direct interest in the underlying security. Accordingly, in the rules for the indirect holding system, the jurisdiction of incorporation of the issuer of the underlying security or the location of any certificates that might be held by the intermediary or a higher tier intermediary, do not determine the applicable law.

For securities in the indirect holding system, but not the direct holding system, this section's provisions are subject to the Convention on the Law Applicable to Certain Rights in Respect of Securities Held with an Intermediary (the "Convention" or "Hague Securities Convention"), to which the United States is a party. The Convention's primary rule is highly similar to this section, though there are potential differences as well. See Comments 3 and 5 through 7 below and PEB Commentary No. 19, dated April 11, 2017.

The Hague Securities Convention applies broadly to all instances "involving a choice between the laws of different [nations]", and can accordingly apply by reason of any of many elements, including without limitation a non-U.S. location of a party involved in the transaction, a non-U.S. party asserting an adverse claim, non-U.S. securities being credited to the securities account, or non-U.S. law being specified by the account agreement or other transaction document. Indeed one may wish to plan all indirect holding system transactions with the Hague Securities Convention as well as UCC Article 8 in mind, because even in transactions that appear wholly domestic, international factors may in fact be present (for example, if the securities intermediary holds securities for the entitlement holder through a non-U.S. intermediary) or may later become present (for example, if a non-U.S. party acquires an interest in or asserts an adverse claim to assets credited to the account).

In each of subsections (a), (b) and (c), the phrase "local law" refers to the law of a jurisdiction other than its conflict of laws rules. See Restatement (Second) of Conflict of Laws § 4.

2.   Subsection (a) provides that the law of an issuer's jurisdiction governs certain issues where the substantive rules of Article 8 determine the issuer's rights and duties. Paragraph (1) of subsection (a) provides that the law of the issuer's jurisdiction governs the validity of the security. This ensures that a single body of law will govern the questions addressed in Part 2 of Article 8, concerning the circumstances in which an issuer can and cannot assert invalidity as a defense against purchasers. Similarly, paragraphs (2), (3), and (4) of subsection (a) ensure that the issuer will be able to look to a single body of law on the questions addressed in Part 4 of Article 8, concerning the issuer's duties and liabilities with respect to registration of transfer.

Paragraph (5) of subsection (a) applies the law of an issuer's jurisdiction to the question whether an adverse claim can be asserted against a purchaser to whom transfer has been registered, or who has obtained control over an uncertificated security. Although this issue deals with the rights of persons other than the issuer, the law of the issuer's jurisdiction applies because the purchasers to whom the provision applies are those whose protection against adverse claims depends on the fact that their interests have been recorded on the books of the issuer.

The principal policy reflected in the choice of law rules in subsection (a) is that an issuer and others should be able to look to a single body of law on the matters specified in subsection (a), rather than having to look to the law of all of the different jurisdictions in which security holders may reside. The choice of law policies reflected in this subsection do not require that the body of law governing all of the matters specified in subsection (a) be that of the jurisdiction in which the issuer is incorporated. Thus, subsection (d) provides that the term "issuer's jurisdiction" means the jurisdiction in which the issuer is organized, or, if permitted by that law, the law of another jurisdiction selected by the issuer. Subsection (d) also provides that issuers organized under the law of a State which adopts this Article may make such a selection, except as to the validity issue specified in paragraph (1). The question whether an issuer can assert the defense of invalidity may implicate significant policies of the issuer's jurisdiction of incorporation. See, e.g., Section 8–202 and Comments thereto.

Although subsection (a) provides that the issuer's rights and duties concerning registration of transfer are governed by the law of the issuer's jurisdiction, other matters related to registration of transfer, such as appointment of a guardian for a registered owner or the existence of agency relationships, might be governed by another jurisdiction's law. Neither this section nor Section 1–105 (Revised Section 1–301) deals with what law governs the appointment of the administrator or executor; that question is determined under generally applicable choice of law rules.

3.   Subsection (b) and, where the Hague Securities Convention applies, article 2(1) thereof provide that the law governing the issues concerning the indirect holding system that are dealt with in Article 8 are principally determined by the agreement between the securities intermediary and the entitlement holder governing the securities account.

Paragraphs (1) and (2) and Hague Securities Convention article 2(1)(a) cover the matters dealt with in the Article 8 rules defining the concept of security entitlement and specifying the duties of securities intermediaries. Paragraph (3) and Convention article 2(1)(e) cover whether the intermediary owes any duties to an adverse claimant. Paragraph (4) and Convention article 2(1)(a) and (d) cover whether adverse claims can be asserted against entitlement holders and others.

Subsection (e) and Hague Securities Convention article 4 provide that the account agreement may effectively determine the applicable law for the foregoing issues in either of two ways. Most directly and doubtless most frequently, under both subsection (e)(2) and article 4(1), the law chosen by the parties to govern the account agreement determines the applicable law. Alternatively, subsection (e)(1) and article 4(1) provide mutually comparable rules that require slightly different phrasing in the agreement. Under subsection (e)(1), if the account agreement expressly provides that a particular jurisdiction is the securities intermediary's jurisdiction for purposes of UCC Article 8, then that provision determines the applicable law, even if the agreement's overall governing law clause (if any) is different. Under Convention article 4(1)'s comparable rule, if the account agreement expressly provides that a particular jurisdiction's law is applicable to all the issues specified in article 2(1) of the Hague Securities Convention, then that provision determines the applicable law, even if the agreement's overall governing law clause (if any) is different. The policy is to ensure that a securities intermediary and all of its entitlement holders can look to a single, readily-identifiable body of law to determine their rights and duties.

Where the Hague Securities Convention applies, the foregoing provisions of an account agreement effectively determine the applicable law only if the intermediary, at the time of the agreement, had an office in the designated jurisdiction (which may be anywhere in the United States if the account agreement specifies a state of the United States) that is engaged in a regular activity of maintaining securities accounts (a "Qualifying Office"). However, because the policy of this section and the Convention is to enable parties to determine, in advance and with certainty, what law will apply to transactions governed by this Article, the validation of the parties' selection of governing law by agreement is not conditioned upon a determination that the jurisdiction whose law is chosen bear a "reasonable relation" to a matter or the transaction. See Subsection (g) makes this explicit. See Comment 5A; see also Section 4A–507; compare Section 1–105(1) (Revised Section 1–301(a)). That is also true with respect to the similar provisions in subsection (d) of this section and in Section 9–305. The remaining paragraphs in subsection (e) and Convention article 5 contain additional default rules for determining the applicable law.

The Hague Securities Convention applies regardless of whether the law that it designates is that of a nation adhering thereto, though of course the Convention itself is the law only of adhering nations. The Convention applies to account agreements entered into before as well as after the Convention's effectiveness in the United States. However, for pre-Convention agreements that specify that a state of the United States is the securities intermediary's jurisdiction for purposes of UCC Article 8 and that do not expressly refer to the Convention, article 16(3) preserves the agreements' intended effect, by treating them as providing that the specified state's law is applicable to all the issues specified in article 2(1), if the Qualifying Office test is met. There is no doubt that the Convention, like UCC Article 8, applies to multiple tier holding arrangements, such as where the account holder holds through a broker which in turn holds through a clearing corporation.

Subsection (f) makes explicit a point that is implicit in the UCC Article 8 description of a security entitlement as a bundle of rights against the intermediary with respect to a security or other financial asset, rather than as a direct interest in the underlying security or other financial asset. The governing law for relationships in the indirect holding system is not determined by such matters as the jurisdiction of incorporation of the issuer of the securities held through the intermediary, or the location of any physical certificates held by the intermediary or a higher tier intermediary. Hague Securities Convention article 6 is in accord.

4. Subsection (c) provides a choice of law rule for adverse claim issues that may arise in connection with delivery of security certificates in the direct holding system. It applies the law of the place of delivery. If a certificated security issued by an Idaho corporation is sold, and the sale is settled by physical delivery of the certificate from Seller to Buyer in New York, under subsection (c), New York law determines whether Buyer takes free from adverse claims. The domicile of Seller, Buyer, and any adverse claimant is irrelevant.

5. The following examples illustrate how a forum applying these rules would determine the governing law:

Example 1. John Doe, a resident of Kansas, maintains a securities account with Able & Co. Able is incorporated in Delaware. Its chief executive offices are located in Illinois. The office where Doe transacts business with Able is located in Missouri. The agreement between Doe and Able provides that it is generally governed by the law of New York but also that Illinois is the securities intermediary's (Able's) jurisdiction for purposes of UCC Article 8 and that Illinois law is applicable to all the issues specified in article 2(1) of the Hague Securities Convention. Through the account, Doe holds securities of a Colorado corporation, which Able holds through Clearing Corporation. The rules of Clearing Corporation provide that the rights and duties of Clearing Corporation and its participants are governed by New York law. Subsection (a) specifies that a controversy concerning the rights and duties as between the issuer and Clearing Corporation is governed by Colorado law. Subsections (b) and (e) specify that a controversy concerning the rights and duties as between the Clearing Corporation and Able is governed by New York law, and that a controversy concerning the rights and duties as between Able and Doe is governed by Illinois law. Even if other facts cause the Hague Securities Convention to apply (see Comment 1), the Convention does not change the subsection (b) and (e) results, if at the time of the respective agreements Clearing Corporation and Able had offices in the United States engaged in a regular activity of maintaining securities accounts. The Convention does not apply to the subsection (a) result.

      Example 2.   Same facts as to Doe and Able as in Example 1. Through the account, Doe holds securities of a Senegalese corporation, which Able holds through Clearing Corporation. Clearing Corporation's operations are located in Belgium, and its rules and agreements with its participants provide that they are governed by Belgian law. Clearing Corporation holds the securities through a custodial account at the Paris branch office of Global Bank, which is organized under English law. The agreement between Clearing Corporation and Global Bank provides that it is governed by French law. Subsection (a) specifies that a controversy concerning the rights and duties as between the issuer and Global Bank is governed by Senegalese law. Prior to United States implementation of the Hague Securities Convention, subsections (b) and (e) had the effect in a U.S. forum that a controversy concerning the rights and duties as between Global Bank and Clearing Corporation was governed by French law, that a controversy concerning the rights and duties as between Clearing Corporation and Able was governed by Belgian law, and that a controversy concerning the rights and duties as between Able and Doe was governed by Illinois law. Under the Convention, the subsection (b) and (e) results are unchanged, if at the time of the respective agreements Global Bank, Clearing Corporation and Able had offices in France, Belgium and the United States, respectively, engaged in a regular activity of maintaining securities accounts. The Convention does not apply to the subsection (a) result.

      Example 3.   John Doe, a resident of Kansas, maintains a securities account with Able & Co. Able is organized in Switzerland and has its chief executive offices there. The agreement between Doe and Able provides that New York is the securities intermediary's jurisdiction for purposes of UCC Article 8. The agreement was entered into before the Hague Securities Convention's effectiveness in the United States, does not expressly provide that New York or any other law is applicable to all the issues specified in article 2(1) of the Hague Securities Convention, and does not otherwise expressly refer to the Convention. Through the account, Doe holds securities of a Japanese issuer. Roe, who lives in Japan, claims ownership of the securities and seeks to hold Able liable for not transferring the asset to Roe. Because the agreement between Doe and Able was entered into before the Convention's effectiveness in the United States, Convention article 16(3) specifies that the controversy between Roe and Able is governed by the law of New York, but only if at the time of the agreement between Doe and Able, Able had an office in the United States engaged in a regular activity of maintaining securities accounts.

    5A. Subsection (g) reflects what is stated in Comment 3—that the local law of the issuer's jurisdiction or securities intermediary's jurisdiction governs even if a matter or transaction bears no relation to that jurisdiction. This also is implicit in Section 1–301(c), which provides that the applicable law provided in this section (and other specified provisions) governs.

    6.   To the extent that this section or the Hague Securities Convention do not specify the governing law, general choice of law rules apply. For example, suppose that Examples 1 or 2 in the preceding Comment, Doe enters into an agreement with Roe in which Doe agrees to transfer all of his interests in the securities held through Able to Roe. Neither UCC Article 8 nor the Convention deals with whether such an agreement is enforceable or whether it gives Roe some interest in Doe's security entitlement. This section and the Convention specify what jurisdiction's law governs the issues that are dealt with in UCC Article 8 or listed in Convention article 2(1) respectively. UCC Article 8, however, does specify that securities intermediaries have only limited duties with respect to adverse claims. See Section 8–115. Subsection (b)(3) of this section and Convention article 2(1)(e) provide that Illinois law governs whether Able owes any duties to an adverse claimant. Thus, because Illinois has adopted Revised Article 8, Section 8–115 as enacted in Illinois determines whether Roe has any rights against Able.

    7.   The UCC choice of law provisions concerning security interests in securities and security entitlements are set out in Section 9–305, and within its scope the Hague Securities Convention also applies to such transactions.

Definitional Cross References:

    "Adverse claim". Section 8–102(a)(1).

"Agreement". Section 1–201(3) [*unrevised Article 1; see Concordance, p. 22*].

"Certificated security". Section 8–102(a)(4).

"Entitlement holder". Section 8–102(a)(7).

"Financial asset". Section 8–102(a)(9).

"Issuer". Section 8–201.

"Person". Section 1–201(30) [*unrevised Article 1; see Concordance, p. 22*].

"Purchase". Section 1–201(32) [*unrevised Article 1; see Concordance, p. 22*].

"Securities intermediary". Section 8–102(a)(14).

"Security". Section 8–102(a)(15).

"Security certificate". Section 8–102(a)(16).

"Security entitlement". Section 8–102(a)(17).

"Uncertificated security". Section 8–102(a)(18).

As amended in 1999, 2017, and 2022.

§ 8–111. Clearing Corporation Rules.

A rule adopted by a clearing corporation governing rights and obligations among the clearing corporation and its participants in the clearing corporation is effective even if the rule conflicts with this [Act] and affects another party who does not consent to the rule.

Official Comment

1. The experience of the past few decades shows that securities holding and settlement practices may develop rapidly, and in unforeseeable directions. Accordingly, it is desirable that the rules of Article 8 be adaptable both to ensure that commercial law can conform to changing practices and to ensure that commercial law does not operate as an obstacle to developments in securities practice. Even if practices were unchanging, it would not be possible in a general statute to specify in detail the rules needed to provide certainty in the operations of the clearance and settlement system.

The provisions of this Article and Article 1 on the effect of agreements provide considerable flexibility in the specification of the details of the rights and obligations of participants in the securities holding system by agreement. See Sections 8–504 through 8–509, and Section 1–102(3) and (4) [*unrevised Article 1; see Concordance, p. 22*]. Given the magnitude of the exposures involved in securities transactions, however, it may not be possible for the parties in developing practices to rely solely on private agreements, particularly with respect to matters that might affect others, such as creditors. For example, in order to be fully effective, rules of clearing corporations on the finality or reversibility of securities settlements must not only bind the participants in the clearing corporation but also be effective against their creditors. Section 8–111 provides that clearing corporation rules are effective even if they indirectly affect third parties, such as creditors of a participant. This provision does not, however, permit rules to be adopted that would govern the rights and obligations of third parties other than as a consequence of rules that specify the rights and obligations of the clearing corporation and its participants.

2. The definition of clearing corporation in Section 8–102 covers only federal reserve banks, entities registered as clearing agencies under the federal securities laws, and others subject to comparable regulation. The rules of registered clearing agencies are subject to regulatory oversight under the federal securities laws.

Definitional Cross References:

"Clearing corporation". Section 8–102(a)(5).

§ 8–112. Creditor's Legal Process.

(a) The interest of a debtor in a certificated security may be reached by a creditor only by actual seizure of the security certificate by the officer making the attachment or levy, except as otherwise provided in subsection (d). However, a certificated security for which the certificate has been surrendered to the issuer may be reached by a creditor by legal process upon the issuer.

(b) The interest of a debtor in an uncertificated security may be reached by a creditor only by legal process upon the issuer at its chief executive office in the United States, except as otherwise provided in subsection (d).

(c)   The interest of a debtor in a security entitlement may be reached by a creditor only by legal process upon the securities intermediary with whom the debtor's securities account is maintained, except as otherwise provided in subsection (d).

(d)   The interest of a debtor in a certificated security for which the certificate is in the possession of a secured party, or in an uncertificated security registered in the name of a secured party, or a security entitlement maintained in the name of a secured party, may be reached by a creditor by legal process upon the secured party.

(e)   A creditor whose debtor is the owner of a certificated security, uncertificated security, or security entitlement is entitled to aid from a court of competent jurisdiction, by injunction or otherwise, in reaching the certificated security, uncertificated security, or security entitlement or in satisfying the claim by means allowed at law or in equity in regard to property that cannot readily be reached by other legal process.

Official Comment

1.   In dealing with certificated securities the instrument itself is the vital thing, and therefore a valid levy cannot be made unless all possibility of the certificate's wrongfully finding its way into a transferee's hands has been removed. This can be accomplished only when the certificate is in the possession of a public officer, the issuer, or an independent third party. A debtor who has been enjoined can still transfer the security in contempt of court. See *Overlock v. Jerome-Portland Copper Mining Co.,* 29 Ariz. 560, 243 P. 400 (1926). Therefore, although injunctive relief is provided in subsection (e) so that creditors may use this method to gain control of the certificated security, the security certificate itself must be reached to constitute a proper levy whenever the debtor has possession.

2.   Subsection (b) provides that when the security is uncertificated and registered in the debtor's name, the debtor's interest can be reached only by legal process upon the issuer. The most logical place to serve the issuer would be the place where the transfer records are maintained, but that location might be difficult to identify, especially when the separate elements of a computer network might be situated in different places. The chief executive office is selected as the appropriate place by analogy to Section 9–307(b)(3). See Comment 2 to that section. This section indicates only how attachment is to be made, not when it is legally justified. For that reason there is no conflict between this section and *Shaffer v. Heitner,* 433 U.S. 186 (1977).

3.   Subsection (c) provides that a security entitlement can be reached only by legal process upon the debtor's security intermediary. Process is effective only if directed to the debtor's own security intermediary. If Debtor holds securities through Broker, and Broker in turn holds through Clearing Corporation, Debtor's property interest is a security entitlement against Broker. Accordingly, Debtor's creditor cannot reach Debtor's interest by legal process directed to the Clearing Corporation. See also Section 8–115.

4.   Subsection (d) provides that when a certificated security, an uncertificated security, or a security entitlement is controlled by a secured party, the debtor's interest can be reached by legal process upon the secured party. This section does not attempt to provide for rights as between the creditor and the secured party, as, for example, whether or when the secured party must liquidate the security.

Definitional Cross References:

"Certificated security". Section 8–102(a)(4).
"Issuer". Section 8–201.
"Secured party". Section 9–102(a)(72) [*Article 9 version prior to the 2010 Amendments*].
"Securities intermediary". Section 8–102(a)(14).
"Security certificate". Section 8–102(a)(16).
"Security entitlement". Section 8–102(a)(17).
"Uncertificated security". Section 8–102(a)(18).

§ 8–113.   Statute of Frauds Inapplicable.

A contract or modification of a contract for the sale or purchase of a security is enforceable whether or not there is a writing signed or record authenticated by a party against whom enforcement is sought, even if the contract or modification is not capable of performance within one year of its making.

Official Comment

This section provides that the statute of frauds does not apply to contracts for the sale of securities, reversing prior law which had a special statute of frauds in Section 8–319 (1978). With the increasing use of electronic means of communication, the statute of frauds is unsuited to the realities of the securities business. For securities transactions, whatever benefits a statute of frauds may play in filtering out fraudulent claims are outweighed by the obstacles it places in the development of modern commercial practices in the securities business.

Definitional Cross References:

"Action". Section 1–201(1) [*unrevised Article 1; see Concordance, p. 22*].
"Contract". Section 1–201(11) [*unrevised Article 1; see Concordance, p. 22*].
"Writing". Section 1–201(46) [*unrevised Article 1; see Concordance, p. 22*].

§ 8–114. Evidentiary Rules Concerning Certificated Securities.

The following rules apply in an action on a certificated security against the issuer:

(1) Unless specifically denied in the pleadings, each signature on a security certificate or in a necessary indorsement is admitted.

(2) If the effectiveness of a signature is put in issue, the burden of establishing effectiveness is on the party claiming under the signature, but the signature is presumed to be genuine or authorized.

(3) If signatures on a security certificate are admitted or established, production of the certificate entitles a holder to recover on it unless the defendant establishes a defense or a defect going to the validity of the security.

(4) If it is shown that a defense or defect exists, the plaintiff has the burden of establishing that the plaintiff or some person under whom the plaintiff claims is a person against whom the defense or defect cannot be asserted.

Official Comment

This section adapts the rules of negotiable instruments law concerning procedure in actions on instruments, see Section 3–308, to actions on certificated securities governed by this Article. An "action on a security" includes any action or proceeding brought against the issuer to enforce a right or interest that is part of the security, such as an action to collect principal or interest or a dividend, or to establish a right to vote or to receive a new security under an exchange offer or plan of reorganization. This section applies only to certificated securities; actions on uncertificated securities are governed by general evidentiary principles.

Definitional Cross References:

"Action". Section 1–201(1) [*unrevised Article 1; see Concordance, p. 22*].
"Burden of establishing". Section 1–201(8) [*unrevised Article 1; see Concordance, p. 22*].
"Certificated security". Section 8–102(a)(4).
"Indorsement". Section 8–102(a)(11).
"Issuer". Section 8–201.
"Presumed". Section 1–201(31) [*unrevised Article 1; see Concordance, p. 22*].
"Security". Section 8–102(a)(15).
"Security certificate". Section 8–102(a)(16).

§ 8–115. Securities Intermediary and Others Not Liable to Adverse Claimant.

A securities intermediary that has transferred a financial asset pursuant to an effective entitlement order, or a broker or other agent or bailee that has dealt with a financial asset at the direction of its customer or principal, is not liable to a person having an adverse claim to the financial asset, unless the securities intermediary, or broker or other agent or bailee:

(1) took the action after it had been served with an injunction, restraining order, or other legal process enjoining it from doing so, issued by a court of competent jurisdiction, and had a reasonable opportunity to act on the injunction, restraining order, or other legal process; or

(2) acted in collusion with the wrongdoer in violating the rights of the adverse claimant; or

(3) in the case of a security certificate that has been stolen, acted with notice of the adverse claim.

Official Comment

1.   Other provisions of Article 8 protect certain purchasers against adverse claims, both for the direct holding system and the indirect holding system. See Sections 8–303 and 8–502. This section deals with the related question of the possible liability of a person who acted as the "conduit" for a securities transaction. It covers both securities intermediaries—the "conduits" in the indirect holding system—and brokers or other agents or bailees—the "conduits" in the direct holding system. The following examples illustrate its operation:

Example 1.   John Doe is a customer of the brokerage firm of Able & Co. Doe delivers to Able a certificate for 100 shares of XYZ Co. common stock, registered in Doe's name and properly indorsed, and asks the firm to sell it for him. Able does so. Later, John Doe's spouse Mary Doe brings an action against Able asserting that Able's action was wrongful against her because the XYZ Co. stock was marital property in which she had an interest, and John Doe was acting wrongfully against her in transferring the securities.

Example 2.   Mary Roe is a customer of the brokerage firm of Baker & Co. and holds her securities through a securities account with Baker. Roe instructs Baker to sell 100 shares of XYZ Co. common stock that she carried in her account. Baker does so. Later, Mary Roe's spouse John Roe brings an action against Baker asserting that Baker's action was wrongful against him because the XYZ Co. stock was marital property in which he had an interest, and Mary Roe was acting wrongfully against him in transferring the securities.

Under common law conversion principles, Mary Doe might be able to assert that Able & Co. is liable to her in Example 1 for exercising dominion over property inconsistent with her rights in it. On that or some similar theory John Roe might assert that Baker is liable to him in Example 2. Section 8–115 protects both Able and Baker from liability.

2.   The policy of this section is similar to that of many other rules of law that protect agents and bailees from liability as innocent converters. If a thief steals property and ships it by mail, express service, or carrier, to another person, the recipient of the property does not obtain good title, even though the recipient may have given value to the thief and had no notice or knowledge that the property was stolen. Accordingly, the true owner can recover the property from the recipient or obtain damages in a conversion or similar action. An action against the postal service, express company, or carrier presents entirely different policy considerations. Accordingly, general tort law protects agents or bailees who act on the instructions of their principals or bailors. See Restatement (Second) of Torts § 235. See also UCC Section 7–404.

3.   Except as provided in paragraph 3, this section applies even though the securities intermediary, or the broker or other agent or bailee, had notice or knowledge that another person asserts a claim to the securities. Consider the following examples:

Example 3.   Same facts as in Example 1, except that before John Doe brought the XYZ Co. security certificate to Able for sale, Mary Doe telephoned or wrote to the firm asserting that she had an interest in all of John Doe's securities and demanding that they not trade for him.

Example 4.   Same facts as in Example 2, except that before Mary Roe gave an entitlement order to Baker to sell the XYZ Co. securities from her account, John Doe telephoned or wrote to the firm asserting that he had an interest in all of Mary Roe's securities and demanding that they not trade for her.

Section 8–115 protects Able and Baker from liability. The protections of Section 8–115 do not depend on the presence or absence of notice of adverse claims. It is essential to the securities settlement system that brokers and securities intermediaries be able to act promptly on the directions of their customers. Even though a firm has notice that someone asserts a claim to a customer's securities or security entitlements, the firm should not be placed in the position of having to make a legal judgment about the validity of the claim at the risk of liability either to its customer or to the third party for guessing wrong. Under this section, the broker or securities intermediary is privileged to act on the instructions of its customer or entitlement holder, unless it has been served with a restraining order or other legal process enjoining it from doing so. This is already the law in many jurisdictions. For example a section of the New York Banking Law provides that banks need not recognize any adverse claim to funds or securities on deposit with them unless they have been served with legal process. N.Y. Banking Law § 134. Other sections of the UCC embody a similar policy. See Sections 3–602, 5–114(2)(b) [*unrevised Article 5*].

Paragraph (1) of this section refers only to a court order enjoining the securities intermediary or the broker or other agent or bailee from acting at the instructions of the customer. It does not apply to cases where the adverse claimant tells the intermediary or broker that the customer has been enjoined, or shows the intermediary or broker a copy of a court order binding the customer.

Paragraph (3) takes a different approach in one limited class of cases, those where a customer sells stolen certificated securities through a securities firm. Here the policies that lead to protection of securities firms against assertions of other sorts of claims must be weighed against the desirability of having securities firms guard against the disposition of stolen securities. Accordingly, paragraph (3) denies protection to a broker, custodian, or other agent or bailee who receives a stolen security certificate from its customer, if the broker, custodian, or other agent or bailee had notice of adverse claims. The circumstances that give notice of adverse claims are specified in Section 8–105. The result is that brokers, custodians, and other agents and bailees face the same liability for selling stolen certificated securities that purchasers face for buying them.

4.   As applied to securities intermediaries, this section embodies one of the fundamental principles of the Article 8 indirect holding system rules—that a securities intermediary owes duties only to its own entitlement holders. The following examples illustrate the operation of this section in the multi-tiered indirect holding system:

Example 5.   Able & Co., a broker-dealer, holds 50,000 shares of XYZ Co. stock in its account at Clearing Corporation. Able acquired the XYZ shares from another firm, Baker & Co., in a transaction that Baker contends was tainted by fraud, giving Baker a right to rescind the transaction and recover the XYZ shares from Able. Baker sends notice to Clearing Corporation stating that Baker has a claim to the 50,000 shares of XYZ Co. in Able's account. Able then initiates an entitlement order directing Clearing Corporation to transfer the 50,000 shares of XYZ Co. to another firm in settlement of a trade. Under Section 8–115, Clearing Corporation is privileged to comply with Able's entitlement order, without fear of liability to Baker. This is so even though Clearing Corporation has notice of Baker's claim, unless Baker obtains a court order enjoining Clearing Corporation from acting on Able's entitlement order.

Example 6.   Able & Co., a broker-dealer, holds 50,000 shares of XYZ Co. stock in its account at Clearing Corporation. Able initiates an entitlement order directing Clearing Corporation to transfer the 50,000 shares of XYZ Co. to another firm in settlement of a trade. That trade was made by Able for its own account, and the proceeds were devoted to its own use. Able becomes insolvent, and it is discovered that Able has a shortfall in the shares of XYZ Co. stock that it should have been carrying for its customers. Able's customers bring an action against Clearing Corporation asserting that Clearing Corporation acted wrongfully in transferring the XYZ shares on Able's order because those were shares that should have been held by Able for its customers. Under Section 8–115, Clearing Corporation is not liable to Able's customers, because Clearing Corporation acted on an effective entitlement order of its own entitlement holder, Able. Clearing Corporation's protection against liability does not depend on the presence or absence of notice or knowledge of the claim by Clearing Corporation.

5.   If the conduct of a securities intermediary or a broker or other agent or bailee rises to a level of complicity in the wrongdoing of its customer or principal, the policies that favor protection against liability do not apply. Accordingly, paragraph (2) provides that the protections of this section do not apply if the securities intermediary or broker or other agent or bailee acted in collusion with the customer or principal in violating the rights of another person. The collusion test is intended to adopt a standard akin to the tort rules that determine whether a person is liable as an aider or abettor for the tortious conduct of a third party. See Restatement (Second) of Torts § 876.

Knowledge that the action of the customer is wrongful is a necessary but not sufficient condition of the collusion test. The aspect of the role of securities intermediaries and brokers that Article 8 deals with is the clerical or ministerial role of implementing and recording the securities transactions that their customers conduct. Faithful performance of this role consists of following the instructions of the customer. It is not the role of the record-keeper to police whether the transactions recorded are appropriate, so mere awareness that the customer may be acting wrongfully does not itself constitute collusion. That, of course, does not insulate an intermediary or broker from responsibility in egregious cases where its action goes beyond the ordinary standards of the business of implementing and recording transactions, and reaches a level of affirmative misconduct in assisting the customer in the commission of a wrong.

Definitional Cross References:

"Broker". Section 8–102(a)(3).
"Effective". Section 8–107.
"Entitlement order". Section 8–102(a)(8).
"Financial asset". Section 8–102(a)(9).
"Securities intermediary". Section 8–102(a)(14).
"Security certificate". Section 8–102(a)(16).

§ 8–116.   Securities Intermediary as Purchaser for Value.

A securities intermediary that receives a financial asset and establishes a security entitlement to the financial asset in favor of an entitlement holder is a purchaser for value of the financial asset. A securities intermediary that acquires a security entitlement to a financial asset from another securities intermediary acquires the security entitlement for value if the securities intermediary acquiring the security entitlement establishes a security entitlement to the financial asset in favor of an entitlement holder.

Official Comment

1.   This section is intended to make explicit two points that, while implicit in other provisions, are of sufficient importance to the operation of the indirect holding system that they warrant explicit statement. First, it makes clear that a securities intermediary that receives a financial asset and establishes a security entitlement in respect thereof in favor of an entitlement holder is a "purchaser" of the financial asset that the securities intermediary received. Second, it makes clear that by establishing a security entitlement in favor of an entitlement holder a securities intermediary gives value for any corresponding financial asset that the securities intermediary receives or acquires from another party, whether the intermediary holds directly or indirectly.

In many cases a securities intermediary that receives a financial asset will also be transferring value to the person from whom the financial asset was received. That, however, is not always the case. Payment may occur through a different system than settlement of the securities side of the transaction, or the securities might be transferred without a corresponding payment, as when a person moves an account from one securities intermediary to another. Even though the securities intermediary does not give value to the transferor, it does give value by incurring obligations to its own entitlement holder. Although the general definition of value in Section 1–201(44)(d)–1–204 should be interpreted to cover the point, this section is included to make this point explicit.

2.   The following examples illustrate the effect of this section:

Example 1.   Buyer buys 1000 shares of XYZ Co. common stock through Buyer's broker Able & Co. to be held in Buyer's securities account. In settlement of the trade, the selling broker delivers to Able a security certificate in street name, indorsed in blank, for 1000 shares XYZ Co. stock, which Able holds in its vault. Able credits Buyer's account for securities in that amount. Section 8–116 specifies that Able is a purchaser of the XYZ Co. stock certificate, and gave value for it. Thus, Able can obtain the benefit of Section 8–303, which protects purchasers for value, if it satisfies the other requirements of that section.

Example 2.   Buyer buys 1000 shares XYZ Co. common stock through Buyer's broker Able & Co. to be held in Buyer's securities account. The trade is settled by crediting 1000 shares XYZ Co. stock to Able's account at Clearing Corporation. Able credits Buyer's account for securities in that amount. When Clearing Corporation credits Able's account, Able acquires a security entitlement under Section 8–501. Section 8–116 specifies that Able acquired this security entitlement for value. Thus, Able can obtain the benefit of Section 8–502, which protects persons who acquire security entitlements for value, if it satisfies the other requirements of that section.

Example 3.   Thief steals a certificated bearer bond from Owner. Thief sends the certificate to his broker Able & Co. to be held in his securities account, and Able credits Thief's account for the bond. Section 8–116 specifies that Able is a purchaser of the bond and gave value for it. Thus, Able can obtain the benefit of Section 8–303, which protects purchasers for value, if it satisfies the other requirements of that section.

Definitional Cross References:

"Financial asset". Section 8–102(a)(9).

"Securities intermediary". Section 8–102(a)(14).

"Security entitlement". Section 8–102(a)(17).

"Entitlement holder". Section 8–102(a)(7).

As amended in 2022.

PART 2

ISSUE AND ISSUER

§ 8–201.   Issuer.

(a)   With respect to an obligation on or a defense to a security, an "issuer" includes a person that:

(1)   places or authorizes the placing of its name on a security certificate, other than as authenticating trustee, registrar, transfer agent, or the like, to evidence a share, participation, or other interest in its property or in an enterprise, or to evidence its duty to perform an obligation represented by the certificate;

(2)   creates a share, participation, or other interest in its property or in an enterprise, or undertakes an obligation, that is an uncertificated security;

(3)   directly or indirectly creates a fractional interest in its rights or property, if the fractional interest is represented by a security certificate; or

(4)   becomes responsible for, or in place of, another person described as an issuer in this section.

(b)   With respect to an obligation on or defense to a security, a guarantor is an issuer to the extent of its guaranty, whether or not its obligation is noted on a security certificate.

(c)   With respect to a registration of a transfer, issuer means a person on whose behalf transfer books are maintained.

Official Comment

1.   The definition of "issuer" in this section functions primarily to describe the persons whose defenses may be cut off under the rules in Part 2. In large measure it simply tracks the language of the definition of security in Section 8–102(a)(15).

2.   Subsection (b) distinguishes the obligations of a guarantor as issuer from those of the principal obligor. However, it does not exempt the guarantor from the impact of subsection (d) of Section 8–202. Whether or not the obligation of the guarantor is noted on the security is immaterial. Typically, guarantors are parent corporations, or stand in some similar relationship to the principal obligor. If that relationship existed at the time the security was originally issued the guaranty would probably have been noted on the security. However, if the relationship arose afterward, e.g., through a purchase of stock or properties, or through merger or consolidation, probably the notation would not have been made. Nonetheless, the holder of the security is entitled to the benefit of the obligation of the guarantor.

3.   Subsection (c) narrows the definition of "issuer" for purposes of Part 4 of this Article (registration of transfer). It is supplemented by Section 8–407.

Definitional Cross References:

"Person". Section 1–201(30) [*unrevised Article 1; see Concordance, p. 22*].
"Security". Section 8–102(a)(15).
"Security certificate". Section 8–102(a)(16).
"Uncertificated security". Section 8–102(a)(18).

§ 8–202.   Issuer's Responsibility and Defenses; Notice of Defect or Defense.

(a)   Even against a purchaser for value and without notice, the terms of a certificated security include terms stated on the certificate and terms made part of the security by reference on the certificate to another instrument, indenture, or document or to a constitution, statute, ordinance, rule, regulation, order, or the like, to the extent the terms referred to do not conflict with terms stated on the certificate. A reference under this subsection does not of itself charge a purchaser for value with notice of a defect going to the validity of the security, even if the certificate expressly states that a person accepting it admits notice. The terms of an uncertificated security include those stated in any instrument, indenture, or document or in a constitution, statute, ordinance, rule, regulation, order, or the like, pursuant to which the security is issued.

(b)   The following rules apply if an issuer asserts that a security is not valid:

(1)   A security other than one issued by a government or governmental subdivision, agency, or instrumentality, even though issued with a defect going to its validity, is valid in the hands of a purchaser for value and without notice of the particular defect unless the defect involves a violation of a constitutional provision. In that case, the security is valid in the hands of a purchaser for value and without notice of the defect, other than one who takes by original issue.

(2)   Paragraph (1) applies to an issuer that is a government or governmental subdivision, agency, or instrumentality only if there has been substantial compliance with the legal requirements governing the issue or the issuer has received a substantial consideration for the issue as a whole or for the particular security and a stated purpose of the issue is one for which the issuer has power to borrow money or issue the security.

(c)   Except as otherwise provided in Section 8–205, lack of genuineness of a certificated security is a complete defense, even against a purchaser for value and without notice.

(d)   All other defenses of the issuer of a security, including nondelivery and conditional delivery of a certificated security, are ineffective against a purchaser for value who has taken the certificated security without notice of the particular defense.

(e)   This section does not affect the right of a party to cancel a contract for a security "when, as and if issued" or "when distributed" in the event of a material change in the character of the security that is the subject of the contract or in the plan or arrangement pursuant to which the security is to be issued or distributed.

(f)   If a security is held by a securities intermediary against whom an entitlement holder has a security entitlement with respect to the security, the issuer may not assert any defense that the issuer could not assert if the entitlement holder held the security directly.

Official Comment

1.   In this Article the rights of the purchaser for value without notice are divided into two aspects, those against the issuer, and those against other claimants to the security. Part 2 of this Article, and especially this section, deal with rights against the issuer.

Subsection (a) states, in accordance with the prevailing case law, the right of the issuer (who prepares the text of the security) to include terms incorporated by adequate reference to an extrinsic source, so long as the terms so incorporated do not conflict with the stated terms. Thus, the standard practice of referring in a bond or debenture to the trust indenture under which it is issued without spelling out its necessarily complex and lengthy provisions is approved. Every stock certificate refers in some manner to the charter or articles of incorporation of the issuer. At least where there is more than one class of stock authorized applicable corporation codes specifically require a statement or summary as to preferences, voting powers and the like. References to constitutions, statutes, ordinances, rules, regulations or orders are not so common, except in the obligations of governments or governmental agencies or units; but where appropriate they fit into the rule here stated.

Courts have generally held that an issuer is estopped from denying representations made in the text of a security. *Delaware-New Jersey Ferry Co. v. Leeds,* 21 Del.Ch. 279, 186 A. 913 (1936). Nor is a defect in form or the invalidity of a security normally available to the issuer as a defense. *Bonini v. Family Theatre Corporation,* 327 Pa. 273, 194 A. 498 (1937); *First National Bank of Fairbanks v. Alaska Airmotive,* 119 F.2d 267 (C.C.A. Alaska 1941).

2.   The rule in subsection (a) requiring that the terms of a security be noted or referred to on the certificate is based on practices and expectations in the direct holding system for certificated securities. This rule does not express a general rule or policy that the terms of a security are effective only if they are communicated to beneficial owners in some particular fashion. Rather, subsection (a) is based on the principle that a purchaser who does obtain a certificate is entitled to assume that the terms of the security have been noted or referred to on the certificate. That policy does not come into play in a securities holding system in which purchasers do not take delivery of certificates.

The provisions of subsection (a) concerning notation of terms on security certificates are necessary only because paper certificates play such an important role for certificated securities that a purchaser should be protected against assertion of any defenses or rights that are not noted on the certificate. No similar problem exists with respect to uncertificated securities. The last sentence of subsection (a) is, strictly speaking, unnecessary, since it only recognizes the fact that the terms of an uncertificated security are determined by whatever other law or agreement governs the security. It is included only to preclude any inference that uncertificated securities are subject to any requirement analogous to the requirement of notation of terms on security certificates.

The rule of subsection (a) applies to the indirect holding system only in the sense that if a certificated security has been delivered to the clearing corporation or other securities intermediary, the terms of the security should be noted or referred to on the certificate. If the security is uncertificated, that principle does not apply even at the issuer-clearing corporation level. The beneficial owners who hold securities through the clearing corporation are bound by the terms of the security, even though they do not actually see the certificate. Since entitlement holders in an indirect holding system have not taken delivery of certificates, the policy of subsection (a) does not apply.

3.   The penultimate sentence of subsection (a) and all of subsection (b) embody the concept that it is the duty of the issuer, not of the purchaser, to make sure that the security complies with the law governing its issue. The penultimate sentence of subsection (a) makes clear that the issuer cannot, by incorporating a reference to a statute or other document, charge the purchaser with notice of the security's invalidity. Subsection (b) gives to a purchaser for value without notice of the defect the right to enforce the security against the issuer despite the presence of a defect that otherwise would render the security invalid. There are three circumstances in which a purchaser does not gain such rights: first, if the defect involves a violation of constitutional provisions, these rights accrue only to a subsequent purchaser, that is, one who takes other than by original issue. This Article leaves to the law of each particular State the rights of a purchaser on original issue of a security with a constitutional defect. No negative implication is intended by the explicit grant of rights to a subsequent purchaser.

Second, governmental issuers are distinguished in subsection (b) from other issuers as a matter of public policy, and additional safeguards are imposed before governmental issues are validated. Governmental issuers are estopped from asserting defenses only if there has been substantial compliance with the legal requirements governing the issue or if substantial consideration has been received and a stated purpose of the issue is one for which the issuer has power to borrow money or issue the security. The purpose of the substantial compliance requirement is to make certain that a mere technicality as, e.g., in the manner of publishing election notices, shall not be a ground for depriving an innocent purchaser of rights in the security. The policy is here adopted of such cases as *Tommie v. City of Gadsden,* 229 Ala. 521, 158 So. 763 (1935), in which minor discrepancies in the form of the election ballot used were overlooked and the bonds were declared valid since there had been substantial compliance with the statute.

A long and well established line of federal cases recognizes the principle of estoppel in favor of purchasers for value without notices where municipalities issue bonds containing recitals of compliance with governing constitutional and statutory provisions, made by the municipal authorities entrusted with determining such compliance. *Chaffee County v. Potter,* 142 U.S. 355 (1892); *Oregon v. Jennings,* 119 U.S. 74 (1886); *Gunnison County Commissioners v. Rollins,* 173 U.S. 255 (1898). This rule has been qualified, however, by requiring that the municipality have power to issue the security. *Anthony v. County of Jasper,* 101 U.S. 693 (1879); *Town of South Ottawa v. Perkins,* 94 U.S. 260 (1876). This section follows the case law trend, simplifying the rule by setting up two conditions for an estoppel against a governmental issuer: (1) substantial consideration given, and (2) power in the issuer to borrow money or issue the security for the stated purpose. As a practical matter the problem of policing governmental issuers has been alleviated by the present practice of requiring legal opinions as to the validity of the issue. The bulk of the case law on this point is nearly 100 years old and it may be assumed that the question now seldom arises.

Section 8-210, regarding overissue, provides the third exception to the rule that an innocent purchase for value takes a valid security despite the presence of a defect that would otherwise give rise to invalidity. See that section and its Comment for further explanation.

4.   Subsection (e) is included to make clear that this section does not affect the presently recognized right of either party to a "when, as and if" or "when distributed" contract to cancel the contract on substantial change.

5.   Subsection (f) has been added because the introduction of the security entitlement concept requires some adaptation of the Part 2 rules, particularly those that distinguish between purchasers who take by original issue and subsequent purchasers. The basic concept of Part 2 is to apply to investment securities the principle of negotiable instruments law that an obligor is precluded from asserting most defenses against purchasers for value without notice. Section 8-202 describes in some detail which defenses issuers can raise against purchasers for value and subsequent purchasers for value. Because these rules were drafted with the direct holding system in mind, some interpretive problems might be presented in applying them to the indirect holding. For example, if a municipality issues a bond in book-entry only form, the only direct "purchaser" of that bond would be the clearing corporation. The policy of precluding the issuer from asserting defenses is, however, equally applicable. Subsection

(f) is designed to ensure that the defense preclusion rules developed for the direct holding system will also apply to the indirect holding system.

Definitional Cross References:

"Certificated security". Section 8–102(a)(4).

"Notice". Section 1–201(25) [*unrevised Article 1; see Concordance, p. 22*].

"Purchaser". Sections 1–201(33) [*unrevised Article 1; see Concordance, p. 22*] & 8–116.

"Security". Section 8–102(a)(15).

"Uncertificated security". Section 8–102(a)(18).

"Value". Sections 1–201(44) [*unrevised Article 1; see Concordance, p. 22*] & 8–116.

§ 8–203. Staleness as Notice of Defect or Defense.

After an act or event, other than a call that has been revoked, creating a right to immediate performance of the principal obligation represented by a certificated security or setting a date on or after which the security is to be presented or surrendered for redemption or exchange, a purchaser is charged with notice of any defect in its issue or defense of the issuer, if the act or event:

(1) requires the payment of money, the delivery of a certificated security, the registration of transfer of an uncertificated security, or any of them on presentation or surrender of the security certificate, the money or security is available on the date set for payment or exchange, and the purchaser takes the security more than one year after that date; or

(2) is not covered by paragraph (1) and the purchaser takes the security more than two years after the date set for surrender or presentation or the date on which performance became due.

Official Comment

1. The problem of matured or called securities is here dealt with in terms of the effect of such events in giving notice of the issuer's defenses and not in terms of "negotiability". The substance of this section applies only to certificated securities because certificates may be transferred to a purchaser by delivery after the security has matured, been called, or become redeemable or exchangeable. It is contemplated that uncertificated securities which have matured or been called will merely be canceled on the books of the issuer and the proceeds sent to the registered owner. Uncertificated securities which have become redeemable or exchangeable, at the option of the owner, may be transferred to a purchaser, but the transfer is effectuated only by registration of transfer, thus necessitating communication with the issuer. If defects or defenses in such securities exist, the issuer will necessarily have the opportunity to bring them to the attention of the purchaser.

2. The fact that a security certificate is in circulation long after it has been called for redemption or exchange must give rise to the question in a purchaser's mind as to why it has not been surrendered. After the lapse of a reasonable period of time a purchaser can no longer claim "no reason to know" of any defects or irregularities in its issue. Where funds are available for the redemption the security certificate is normally turned in more promptly and a shorter time is set as the "reasonable period" than is set where funds are not available.

Defaulted certificated securities may be traded on financial markets in the same manner as unmatured and undefaulted instruments and a purchaser might not be placed upon notice of irregularity by the mere fact of default. An issuer, however, should at some point be placed in a position to determine definitely its liability on an invalid or improper issue, and for this purpose a security under this section becomes "stale" two years after the default. A different rule applies when the question is notice not of issuer's defenses but of claims of ownership. Section 8–105 and Comment.

3. Nothing in this section is designed to extend the life of preferred stocks called for redemption as "shares of stock" beyond the redemption date. After such a call, the security represents only a right to the funds set aside for redemption.

Definitional Cross References:

"Certificated security". Section 8–102(a)(4).

"Notice". Section 1–201(25) [*unrevised Article 1; see Concordance, p. 22*].

"Purchaser". Sections 1–201(33) [*unrevised Article 1; see Concordance, p. 22*] & 8–116.

"Security". Section 8–102(a)(15).

"Security certificate". Section 8–102(a)(16).

"Uncertificated security". Section 8–102(a)(18).

§ 8–204. Effect of Issuer's Restriction on Transfer.

A restriction on transfer of a security imposed by the issuer, even if otherwise lawful, is ineffective against a person without knowledge of the restriction unless:

(1) the security is certificated and the restriction is noted conspicuously on the security certificate; or

(2) the security is uncertificated and the registered owner has been notified of the restriction.

Official Comment

1. Restrictions on transfer of securities are imposed by issuers in a variety of circumstances and for a variety of purposes, such as to retain control of a close corporation or to ensure compliance with federal securities laws. Other law determines whether such restrictions are permissible. This section deals only with the consequences of failure to note the restriction on a security certificate.

This section imposes no bar to enforcement of a restriction on transfer against a person who has actual knowledge of it.

2. A restriction on transfer of a certificated security is ineffective against a person without knowledge of the restriction unless the restriction is noted conspicuously on the certificate. The word "noted" is used to make clear that the restriction need not be set forth in full text. Refusal by an issuer to register a transfer on the basis of an unnoted restriction would be a violation of the issuer's duty to register under Section 8–401.

3. The policy of this section is the same as in Section 8–202. A purchaser who takes delivery of a certificated security is entitled to rely on the terms stated on the certificate. That policy obviously does not apply to uncertificated securities. For uncertificated securities, this section requires only that the registered owner has been notified of the restriction. Suppose, for example, that A is the registered owner of an uncertificated security, and that the issuer has notified A of a restriction on transfer. A agrees to sell the security to B, in violation of the restriction. A completes a written instruction directing the issuer to register transfer to B, and B pays A for the security at the time A delivers the instruction to B. A does not inform B of the restriction, and B does not otherwise have notice or knowledge of it at the time B pays and receives the instruction. B presents the instruction to the issuer, but the issuer refuses to register the transfer on the grounds that it would violate the restriction. The issuer has complied with this section, because it did notify the registered owner A of the restriction. The issuer's refusal to register transfer is not wrongful. B has an action against A for breach of transfer warranty, see Section 8–108(b)(4)(iii). B's mistake was treating an uncertificated security transaction in the fashion appropriate only for a certificated security. The mechanism for transfer of uncertificated securities is registration of transfer on the books of the issuer; handing over an instruction only initiates the process. The purchaser should make arrangements to ensure that the price is not paid until it knows that the issuer has or will register transfer.

4. In the indirect holding system, investors neither take physical delivery of security certificates nor have uncertificated securities registered in their names. So long as the requirements of this section have been satisfied at the level of the relationship between the issuer and the securities intermediary that is a direct holder, this section does not preclude the issuer from enforcing a restriction on transfer. See Section 8–202(a) and Comment 2 thereto.

5. This section deals only with restrictions imposed by the issuer. Restrictions imposed by statute are not affected. See *Quiner v. Marblehead Social Co.,* 10 Mass. 476 (1813); *Madison Bank v. Price,* 79 Kan. 289, 100 P. 280 (1909); *Healey v. Steele Center Creamery Ass'n,* 115 Minn. 451, 133 N.W. 69 (1911). Nor does it deal with private agreements between stockholders containing restrictive covenants as to the sale of the security.

Definitional Cross References:

"Certificated security". Section 8–102(a)(4).

"Conspicuous". Section 1–201(10) [*unrevised Article 1; see Concordance, p. 22*].

"Issuer". Section 8–201.

"Knowledge". Section 1–201(25) [*unrevised Article 1; see Concordance, p. 22*].

"Notify". Section 1–201(25) [*unrevised Article 1; see Concordance, p. 22*].

"Purchaser". Sections 1–201(33) [*unrevised Article 1; see Concordance, p. 22*] & 8–116.

"Security". Section 8–102(a)(15).

"Security certificate". Section 8–102(a)(16).

"Uncertificated security". Section 8–102(a)(18).

§ 8–205.   Effect of Unauthorized Signature on Security Certificate.

An unauthorized signature placed on a security certificate before or in the course of issue is ineffective, but the signature is effective in favor of a purchaser for value of the certificated security if the purchaser is without notice of the lack of authority and the signing has been done by:

(1)   an authenticating trustee, registrar, transfer agent, or other person entrusted by the issuer with the signing of the security certificate or of similar security certificates, or the immediate preparation for signing of any of them; or

(2)   an employee of the issuer, or of any of the persons listed in paragraph (1), entrusted with responsible handling of the security certificate.

Official Comment

1.   The problem of forged or unauthorized signatures may arise where an employee of the issuer, transfer agent, or registrar has access to securities which the employee is required to prepare for issue by affixing the corporate seal or by adding a signature necessary for issue. This section is based upon the issuer's duty to avoid the negligent entrusting of securities to such persons. Issuers have long been held responsible for signatures placed upon securities by parties whom they have held out to the public as authorized to prepare such securities. See *Fifth Avenue Bank of New York v. The Forty-Second & Grand Street Ferry Railroad Co.,* 137 N.Y. 231, 33 N.E. 378, 19 L.R.A. 331, 33 Am.St.Rep. 712 (1893); *Jarvis v. Manhattan Beach Co.,* 148 N.Y. 652, 43 N.E. 68, 31 L.R.A. 776, 51 Am.St.Rep. 727 (1896). The "apparent authority" concept of some of the case-law, however, is here extended and this section expressly rejects the technical distinction, made by courts reluctant to recognize forged signatures, between cases where forgers sign signatures they are authorized to sign under proper circumstances and those in which they sign signatures they are never authorized to sign. *Citizens' & Southern National Bank v. Trust Co. of Georgia,* 50 Ga.App. 681, 179 S.E. 278 (1935). Normally the purchaser is not in a position to determine which signature a forger, entrusted with the preparation of securities, has "apparent authority" to sign. The issuer, on the other hand, can protect itself against such fraud by the careful selection and bonding of agents and employees, or by action over against transfer agents and registrars who in turn may bond their personnel.

2.   The issuer cannot be held liable for the honesty of employees not entrusted, directly or indirectly, with the signing, preparation, or responsible handling of similar securities and whose possible commission of forgery it has no reason to anticipate. The result in such cases as *Hudson Trust Co. v. American Linseed Co.,* 232 N.Y. 350, 134 N.E. 178 (1922), and *Dollar Savings Fund & Trust Co. v. Pittsburgh Plate Glass Co.,* 213 Pa. 307, 62 A. 916, 5 Ann.Cas. 248 (1906) is here adopted.

3.   This section is not concerned with forged or unauthorized indorsements, but only with unauthorized signatures of issuers, transfer agents, etc., placed upon security certificates during the course of their issue. The protection here stated is available to all purchasers for value without notice and not merely to subsequent purchasers.

Definitional Cross References:

"Certificated security". Section 8–102(a)(4).

"Issuer". Section 8–201.

"Notice". Section 1–201(25) [*unrevised Article 1; see Concordance, p. 22*].

"Purchaser". Sections 1–201(33) [*unrevised Article 1; see Concordance, p. 22*] & 8–116.

"Security certificate". Section 8–102(a)(14).

"Unauthorized signature". Section 1–201(43) [*unrevised Article 1; see Concordance, p. 22*].

§ 8–206.   Completion or Alteration of Security Certificate.

(a)   If a security certificate contains the signatures necessary to its issue or transfer but is incomplete in any other respect:

(1)   any person may complete it by filling in the blanks as authorized; and

(2)   even if the blanks are incorrectly filled in, the security certificate as completed is enforceable by a purchaser who took it for value and without notice of the incorrectness.

(b) A complete security certificate that has been improperly altered, even if fraudulently, remains enforceable, but only according to its original terms.

Official Comment

1. The problem of forged or unauthorized signatures necessary for the issue or transfer of a security is not involved here, and a person in possession of a blank certificate is not, by this section, given authority to fill in blanks with such signatures. Completion of blanks left in a transfer instruction is dealt with elsewhere (Section 8–305(a)).

2. Blanks left upon issue of a security certificate are the only ones dealt with here, and a purchaser for value without notice is protected. A purchaser is not in a good position to determine whether blanks were completed by the issuer or by some person not authorized to complete them. On the other hand the issuer can protect itself by not placing its signature on the writing until the blanks are completed or, if it does sign before all blanks are completed, by carefully selecting the agents and employees to whom it entrusts the writing after authentication. With respect to a security certificate that is completed by the issuer but later is altered, the issuer has done everything it can to protect the purchaser and thus is not charged with the terms as altered. However, it is charged according to the original terms, since it is not thereby prejudiced. If the completion or alteration is obviously irregular, the purchaser may not qualify as a purchaser who took without notice under this section.

3. Only the purchaser who physically takes the certificate is directly protected. However, a transferee may receive protection indirectly through Section 8–302(a).

4. The protection granted a purchaser for value without notice under this section is modified to the extent that an overissue may result where an incorrect amount is inserted into a blank (Section 8–210).

Definitional Cross References:

"Notice". Section 1–201(25) [*unrevised Article 1; see Concordance, p. 22*].
"Purchaser". Sections 1–201(33) [*unrevised Article 1; see Concordance, p. 22*] & 8–116.
"Security certificate". Section 8–102(a)(16).
"Unauthorized signature". Section 1–201(43) [*unrevised Article 1; see Concordance, p. 22*].
"Value". Sections 1–201(44) [*unrevised Article 1; see Concordance, p. 22*] & 8–116.

§ 8–207. Rights and Duties of Issuer with Respect to Registered Owners.

(a) Before due presentment for registration of transfer of a certificated security in registered form or of an instruction requesting registration of transfer of an uncertificated security, the issuer or indenture trustee may treat the registered owner as the person exclusively entitled to vote, receive notifications, and otherwise exercise all the rights and powers of an owner.

(b) This Article does not affect the liability of the registered owner of a security for a call, assessment, or the like.

Official Comment

1. Subsection (a) states the issuer's right to treat the registered owner of a security as the person entitled to exercise all the rights of an owner. This right of the issuer is limited by the provisions of Part 4 of this article. Once there has been due presentation for registration of transfer, the issuer has a duty to register ownership in the name of the transferee. Section 8–401. Thus its right to treat the old registered owner as exclusively entitled to the rights of ownership must cease.

The issuer may under this section make distributions of money or securities to the registered owners of securities without requiring further proof of ownership, provided that such distributions are distributable to the owners of all securities of the same issue and the terms of the security do not require surrender of a security certificate as a condition of payment or exchange. Any such distribution shall constitute a defense against a claim for the same distribution by a person, even if that person is in possession of the security certificate and is a protected purchaser of the security. See PEB Commentary No. 4, dated March 10, 1990.

2. Subsection (a) is permissive and does not require that the issuer deal exclusively with the registered owner. It is free to require proof of ownership before paying out dividends or the like if it chooses to. *Barbato v. Breeze Corporation*, 128 N.J.L. 309, 26 A.2d 53 (1942).

3.   This section does not operate to determine who is finally entitled to exercise voting and other rights or to receive payments and distributions. The parties are still free to incorporate their own arrangements as to these matters in seller-purchaser agreements which may be definitive as between them.

4.   No change in existing state laws as to the liability of registered owners for calls and assessments is here intended; nor is anything in this section designed to estop record holders from denying ownership when assessments are levied if they are otherwise entitled to do so under state law. See *State ex rel. Squire v. Murfey, Blosson & Co.,* 131 Ohio St. 289, 2 N.E.2d 866 (1936); *Willing v. Delaplaine,* 23 F.Supp. 579 (1937).

5.   No interference is intended with the common practice of closing the transfer books or taking a record date for dividend, voting, and other purposes, as provided for in by-laws, charters, and statutes.

Definitional Cross References:

"Certificated security". Section 8–102(a)(4).
"Instruction". Section 8–102(a)(12).
"Issuer". Section 8–201.
"Registered form". Section 8–102(a)(13).
"Security". Section 8–102(a)(15).
"Uncertificated security". Section 8–102(a)(18).

As amended in 1990 and 2022.

§ 8–208.   Effect of Signature of Authenticating Trustee, Registrar, or Transfer Agent.

(a)   A person signing a security certificate as authenticating trustee, registrar, transfer agent, or the like, warrants to a purchaser for value of the certificated security, if the purchaser is without notice of a particular defect, that:

(1)   the certificate is genuine;

(2)   the person's own participation in the issue of the security is within the person's capacity and within the scope of the authority received by the person from the issuer; and

(3)   the person has reasonable grounds to believe that the certificated security is in the form and within the amount the issuer is authorized to issue.

(b)   Unless otherwise agreed, a person signing under subsection (a) does not assume responsibility for the validity of the security in other respects.

Official Comment

1.   The warranties here stated express the current understanding and prevailing case law as to the effect of the signatures of authenticating trustees, transfer agents, and registrars. See *Jarvis v. Manhattan Beach Co.,* 148 N.Y. 652, 43 N.E. 68, 31 L.R.A. 776, 51 Am.St.Rep. 727 (1896). Although it has generally been regarded as the particular obligation of the transfer agent to determine whether securities are in proper form as provided by the by-laws and Articles of Incorporation, neither a registrar nor an authenticating trustee should properly place a signature upon a certificate without determining whether it is at least regular on its face. The obligations of these parties in this respect have therefore been made explicit in terms of due care. See *Feldmeier v. Mortgage Securities, Inc.,* 34 Cal.App.2d 201, 93 P.2d 593 (1939).

2.   Those cases which hold that an authenticating trustee is not liable for any defect in the mortgage or property which secures the bond or for any fraudulent misrepresentations made by the issuer are not here affected since these matters do not involve the genuineness or proper form of the security. *Ainsa v. Mercantile Trust Co.,* 174 Cal. 504, 163 P. 898 (1917); *Tschetinian v. City Trust Co.,* 186 N.Y. 432, 79 N.E. 401 (1906); *Davidge v. Guardian Trust Co. of New York,* 203 N.Y. 331, 96 N.E. 751 (1911).

3.   The charter or an applicable statute may affect the capacity of a bank or other corporation undertaking to act as an authenticating trustee, registrar, or transfer agent. See, for example, the Federal Reserve Act (U.S.C.A., Title 12, Banks and Banking, Section 248) under which the Board of Governors of the Federal Reserve Bank is authorized to grant special permits to National Banks permitting them to act as trustees. Such corporations are therefore held to certify as to their legal capacity to act as well as to their authority.

4.   Authenticating trustees, registrars, and transfer agents have normally been held liable for an issue in excess of the authorized amount. *Jarvis v. Manhattan Beach Co., supra; Mullen v. Eastern Trust & Banking Co.,*

108 Me. 498, 81 A. 948 (1911). In imposing upon these parties a duty of due care with respect to the amount they are authorized to help issue, this section does not necessarily validate the security, but merely holds persons responsible for the excess issue liable in damages for any loss suffered by the purchaser.

5.   Aside from questions of genuineness and excess issue, these parties are not held to certify as to the validity of the security unless they specifically undertake to do so. The case law which has recognized a unique responsibility on the transfer agent's part to testify as to the validity of any security which it countersigns is rejected.

6.   This provision does not prevent a transfer agent or issuer from agreeing with a registrar of stock to protect the registrar in respect of the genuineness and proper form of a security certificate signed by the issuer or the transfer agent or both. Nor does it interfere with proper indemnity arrangements between the issuer and trustees, transfer agents, registrars, and the like.

7.   An unauthorized signature is a signature for purposes of this section if and only if it is made effective by Section 8–205.

Definitional Cross References:

"Certificated security". Section 8–102(a)(4).
"Genuine". Section 1–201(18) [*unrevised Article 1; see Concordance, p. 22*].
"Issuer". Section 8–201.
"Notice". Section 1–201(25) [*unrevised Article 1; see Concordance, p. 22*].
"Purchaser". Sections 1–201(33) [*unrevised Article 1; see Concordance, p. 22*] & 8–116.
"Security". Section 8–102(a)(15).
"Security certificate". Section 8–102(a)(16).
"Uncertificated security". Section 8–102(a)(18).
"Value". Sections 1–201(44) [*unrevised Article 1; see Concordance, p. 22*] & 8–116.

§ 8–209.   Issuer's Lien.

A lien in favor of an issuer upon a certificated security is valid against a purchaser only if the right of the issuer to the lien is noted conspicuously on the security certificate.

Official Comment

This section is similar to Sections 8–202 and 8–204 which require that the terms of a certificated security and any restriction on transfer imposed by the issuer be noted on the security certificate. This section differs from those two sections in that the purchaser's knowledge of the issuer's claim is irrelevant. "Noted" makes clear that the text of the lien provisions need not be set forth in full. However, this would not override a provision of an applicable corporation code requiring statement in haec verba. This section does not apply to uncertificated securities. It applies to the indirect holding system in the same fashion as Sections 8–202 and 8–204, see Comment 2 to Section 8–202.

Definitional Cross References:

"Certificated security". Section 8–102(a)(4).
"Issuer". Section 8–201.
"Purchaser". Sections 1–201(33) [*unrevised Article 1; see Concordance, p. 22*] & 8–116.
"Security". Section 8–102(a)(15).
"Security certificate". Section 8–102(a)(16).

§ 8–210.   Overissue.

(a)   In this section, "overissue" means the issue of securities in excess of the amount the issuer has corporate power to issue, but an overissue does not occur if appropriate action has cured the overissue.

(b)   Except as otherwise provided in subsections (c) and (d), the provisions of this Article which validate a security or compel its issue or reissue do not apply to the extent that validation, issue, or reissue would result in overissue.

(c)   If an identical security not constituting an overissue is reasonably available for purchase, a person entitled to issue or validation may compel the issuer to purchase the security and deliver it if certificated or register its transfer if uncertificated, against surrender of any security certificate the person holds.

(d)   If a security is not reasonably available for purchase, a person entitled to issue or validation may recover from the issuer the price the person or the last purchaser for value paid for it with interest from the date of the person's demand.

Official Comment

1.   Deeply embedded in corporation law is the conception that "corporate power" to issue securities stems from the statute, either general or special, under which the corporation is organized. Corporation codes universally require that the charter or articles of incorporation state, at least as to capital shares, maximum limits in terms of number of shares or total dollar capital. Historically, special incorporation statutes are similarly drawn and sometimes similarly limit the face amount of authorized debt securities. The theory is that issue of securities in excess of the authorized amounts is prohibited. See, for example, *McWilliams v. Geddes & Moss Undertaking Co.,* 169 So. 894 (1936, La.); *Crawford v. Twin City Oil Co.,* 216 Ala. 216, 113 So. 61 (1927); *New York and New Haven R.R. Co. v. Schuyler,* 34 N.Y. 30 (1865). This conception persists despite modern corporation codes under which, by action of directors and stockholders, additional shares can be authorized by charter amendment and thereafter issued. This section does not give a person entitled to validation, issue, or reissue of a security, the right to compel amendment of the charter to authorize additional shares. Therefore, in a case where issue of an additional security would require charter amendment, the plaintiff is limited to the two alternate remedies set forth in subsections (c) and (d). The last clause of subsection (a), which is added in Revised Article 8, does, however, recognize that under modern conditions, overissue may be a relatively minor technical problem that can be cured by appropriate action under governing corporate law.

2.   Where an identical security is reasonably available for purchase, whether because traded on an organized market, or because one or more security owners may be willing to sell at a not unreasonable price, the issuer, although unable to issue additional shares, will be able to purchase them and may be compelled to follow that procedure. *West v. Tintic Standard Mining Co.,* 71 Utah 158, 263 P. 490 (1928).

3.   The right to recover damages from an issuer who has permitted an overissue to occur is well settled. *New York and New Haven R.R. Co. v. Schuyler,* 34 N.Y. 30 (1865). The measure of such damages, however, has been open to question, some courts basing them upon the value of stock at the time registration is refused; some upon the value at the time of trial; and some upon the highest value between the time of refusal and the time of trial. *Allen v. South Boston Railroad,* 150 Mass. 200, 22 N.E. 917, 5 L.R.A. 716, 15 Am.St.Rep. 185 (1889); *Commercial Bank v. Kortright,* 22 Wend. (N.Y.) 348 (1839). The purchase price of the security to the last purchaser who gave value for it is here adopted as being the fairest means of reducing the possibility of speculation by the purchaser. Interest may be recovered by the best available measure of compensation for delay.

Definitional Cross References:

"Issuer". Section 8–201.
"Security". Section 8–102(a)(15).
"Security certificate". Section 8–102(a)(16).
"Uncertificated security". Section 8–102(a)(18).

PART 3

TRANSFER OF CERTIFICATED AND UNCERTIFICATED SECURITIES

§ 8–301.   Delivery.   FOV 9-203 attachment

(a)   Delivery of a certificated security to a purchaser occurs when:

(1)   the purchaser acquires possession of the security certificate; *in registered form*

(2)   another person, other than a securities intermediary, either acquires possession of the security certificate on behalf of the purchaser or, having previously acquired possession of the certificate, acknowledges that it holds for the purchaser; or

(3)   a securities intermediary acting on behalf of the purchaser acquires possession of the security certificate, only if the certificate is in registered form and is (i) registered in the name of the purchaser, (ii) payable to the order of the purchaser, or (iii) specially indorsed to the purchaser by an effective indorsement and has not been indorsed to the securities intermediary or in blank.

(b)   Delivery of an uncertificated security to a purchaser occurs when:

(1)   the issuer registers the purchaser as the registered owner, upon original issue or registration of transfer; or

(2)   another person, other than a securities intermediary, either becomes the registered owner of the uncertificated security on behalf of the purchaser or, having previously become the registered owner, acknowledges that it holds for the purchaser.

As amended in 1999.

Official Comment

1.   This section specifies the requirements for "delivery" of securities. Delivery is used in Article 8 to describe the formal steps necessary for a purchaser to acquire a direct interest in a security under this Article. The concept of delivery refers to the implementation of a transaction, not the legal categorization of the transaction which is consummated by delivery. Issuance and transfer are different kinds of transaction, though both may be implemented by delivery. Sale and pledge are different kinds of transfers, but both may be implemented by delivery.

2.   Subsection (a) defines delivery with respect to certificated securities. Paragraph (1) deals with simple cases where purchasers themselves acquire physical possession of certificates. Paragraphs (2) and (3) of subsection (a) specify the circumstances in which delivery to a purchaser can occur although the certificate is in the possession of a person other than the purchaser. Paragraph (2) contains the general rule that a purchaser can take delivery through another person, so long as the other person is actually acting on behalf of the purchaser or acknowledges that it is holding on behalf of the purchaser. Paragraph (2) does not apply to acquisition of possession by a securities intermediary, because a person who holds securities through a securities account acquires a security entitlement, rather than having a direct interest. See Section 8–501. Subsection (a)(3) specifies the limited circumstances in which delivery of security certificates to a securities intermediary is treated as a delivery to the customer. Note that delivery is a method of perfecting a security interest in a certificated security. See Section 9–313(a), (e).

3.   Subsection (b) defines delivery with respect to uncertificated securities. Use of the term "delivery" with respect to uncertificated securities, does, at least on first hearing, seem a bit solecistic. The word "delivery" is, however, routinely used in the securities business in a broader sense than manual tradition. For example, settlement by entries on the books of a clearing corporation is commonly called "delivery," as in the expression "delivery versus payment." The diction of this section has the advantage of using the same term for uncertificated securities as for certificated securities, for which delivery is conventional usage. Paragraph (1) of subsection (b) provides that delivery occurs when the purchaser becomes the registered owner of an uncertificated security, either upon original issue or registration of transfer. Paragraph (2) provides for delivery of an uncertificated security through a third person, in a fashion analogous to subsection (a)(2).

Definitional Cross References:

"Certificated security". Section 8–102(a)(4).
"Effective". Section 8–107.
"Issuer". Section 8–201.
"Purchaser". Sections 1–201(33) [*unrevised Article 1; see Concordance, p. 22*] & 8–116.
"Registered form". Section 8–102(a)(13).
"Securities intermediary". Section 8–102(a)(14).
"Security certificate". Section 8–102(a)(16).
"Special indorsement". Section 8–304(a).
"Uncertificated security". Section 8–102(a)(18).

As amended in 1999.

§ 8–302.   Rights of Purchaser.

(a)   Except as otherwise provided in subsections (b) and (c), a purchaser of a certificated or uncertificated security acquires all rights in the security that the transferor had or had power to transfer.

(b)   A purchaser of a limited interest acquires rights only to the extent of the interest purchased.

(c)   A purchaser of a certificated security who as a previous holder had notice of an adverse claim does not improve its position by taking from a protected purchaser.

As amended in 1999.

Official Comment

1.   Subsection (a) provides that a purchaser of a certificated or uncertificated security acquires all rights that the transferor had or had power to transfer. This statement of the familiar "shelter" principle is qualified by the exceptions that a purchaser of a limited interest acquires only that interest, subsection (b), and that a person who does not qualify as a protected purchaser cannot improve its position by taking from a subsequent protected purchaser, subsection (c).

2.   Although this section provides that a purchaser acquires a property interest in a certificated or uncertificated security, it does not state that a person can acquire an interest in a security only by purchase. Article 8 also is not a comprehensive codification of all of the law governing the creation or transfer of interests in securities ~~by purchase~~. [Amendments in italics approved by the Permanent Editorial Board for Uniform Commercial Code January 15, 2000.]

For example, the grant of a security interest is a transfer of a property interest, but the formal steps necessary to effectuate such a transfer are governed by Article 9, not by Article 8. Under the Article 9 rules, a security interest in a certificated or uncertificated security can be created by execution of a security agreement under Section 9–203 and can be perfected by filing. A transfer of an Article 9 security interest can be implemented by an Article 8 delivery, but need not be.

Similarly, Article 8 does not determine whether a property interest in certificated or uncertificated security is acquired under other law, such as the law of gifts, trusts, or equitable remedies. Nor does Article 8 deal with transfers by operation of law. For example, transfers from decedent to administrator, from ward to guardian, and from bankrupt to trustee in bankruptcy are governed by other law as to both the time they occur and the substance of the transfer. The Article 8 rules do, however, determine whether the issuer is obligated to recognize the rights that a third party, such as a transferee, may acquire under other law. See Sections 8–207, 8–401, and 8–404.

Definitional Cross References:

"Certificated security". Section 8–102(a)(4).
"Notice of adverse claim". Section 8–105.
"Protected purchaser". Section 8–303.
"Purchaser". Sections 1–201(33) [*unrevised Article 1; see Concordance, p. 22*] & 8–116.
"Uncertificated security". Section 8–102(a)(18).
"Delivery". Section 8–301.

As amended in 1999 and 2000.

§ 8–303.   Protected Purchaser.

(a)   "Protected purchaser" means a purchaser of a certificated or uncertificated security, or of an interest therein, who:

(1)   gives value;

(2)   does not have notice of any adverse claim to the security; and

(3)   obtains control of the certificated or uncertificated security.

(b)   ~~In addition to acquiring the rights of a purchaser, a~~ A protected purchaser also acquires its interest in the security free of any adverse claim.

As amended in 2022.

Official Comment

1.   Subsection (a) lists the requirements that a purchaser must meet to qualify as a "protected purchaser." Subsection (b) provides that a protected purchaser takes its interest free from adverse claims. "Purchaser" is defined broadly in Section 1–201. A secured party as well as an outright buyer can qualify as a protected purchaser. Also, "purchase" includes taking by issue, so a person to whom a security is originally issued can qualify as a protected purchaser.

2.   To qualify as a protected purchaser under subsection (a), a purchaser must give value, take without notice of any adverse claim, and obtain control. Value is used in the broad sense defined in Section 1–201(44) 1–204. See also Section 8–116 (securities intermediary as purchaser for value). Adverse claim is defined in Section 8–102(a)(1). Section 8–105 specifies whether a purchaser has notice of an adverse claim. Control is defined in Section 8–106. To qualify as a protected purchaser under subsection (b), there must be a time at which all of the requirements are satisfied. Thus if a purchaser obtains notice of an adverse claim before giving value or satisfying the requirements for control, the purchaser cannot be a protected purchaser. See also Section 8–304(d).

The requirement that a protected purchaser obtain control expresses the point that to qualify for the adverse claim cut-off rule a purchaser must take through a transaction that is implemented by the appropriate mechanism. By contrast, the rules in Part 2 provide that any purchaser for value of a security without notice of a defense may take free of the issuer's defense based on that defense. See Section 8–202.

The reference to the acquisition of the rights of a purchaser in the pre-2022 text of subsection (b) has been deleted. However, because a protected purchaser acquires the rights of a purchaser under Section 8–302, the revised text does not diminish a protected purchaser's rights. That revision aligned the text more closely to that of Section 12–104(e) on the rights of a qualifying purchaser of a controllable electronic record, controllable account, or controllable payment intangible.

3.   The requirements for control differ depending on the form of the security. For securities represented by bearer certificates, a purchaser obtains control by delivery. See Sections 8–106(a) and 8–301(a). For securities represented by certificates in registered form, the requirements for control are: (1) delivery as defined in Section 8–301(b), plus (2) either an effective indorsement or registration of transfer by the issuer. See Section 8–106(b). Thus, a person who takes through a forged indorsement does not qualify as a protected purchaser by virtue of the delivery alone. If, however, the purchaser presents the certificate to the issuer for registration of transfer, and the issuer registers transfer over the forged indorsement, the purchaser can qualify as a protected purchaser of the new certificate. If the issuer registers transfer on a forged indorsement, the true owner will be able to recover from the issuer for wrongful registration, see Section 8–404, unless the owner's delay in notifying the issuer of a loss or theft of the certificate results in preclusion under Section 8–406.

For uncertificated securities, a purchaser can obtain control either by delivery, see Sections 8–106(c)(1) and 8–301(b), or by obtaining an agreement pursuant to which the issuer agrees to act on instructions from the purchaser without further consent from the registered owner, see Section 8–106(c)(2). The control agreement device of Section 8–106(c)(2) takes the place of the "registered pledge" concept of the 1978 version of Article 8. A secured lender who obtains a control agreement under Section 8–106(c)(2) can qualify as a protected purchaser of an uncertificated security.

4.   This section states directly the rules determining whether one takes free from adverse claims without using the phrase "good faith." Whether a person who takes under suspicious circumstances is disqualified is determined by the rules of Section 8–105 on notice of adverse claims. The term "protected purchaser," which replaces the term "bona fide purchaser" used in the prior version of Article 8, is derived from the term "protected holder" used in the Convention on International Bills and Notes prepared by the United Nations Commission on International Trade Law ("UNCITRAL").

Definitional Cross References:

"Adverse claim". Section 8–102(a)(1).
"Certificated security". Section 8–102(a)(4).
"Control". Section 8–106.
"Notice of adverse claim". Section 8–105.
"Purchaser". Sections 1–201(33) [*unrevised Article 1; see Concordance, p. 22*] & 8–116.
"Uncertificated security". Section 8–102(a)(18).
"Value". Sections 1–201(44) [*unrevised Article 1; see Concordance, p. 22*] & 8–116.

As amended in 2022.

§ 8–304.   Indorsement.

(a)   An indorsement may be in blank or special. An indorsement in blank includes an indorsement to bearer. A special indorsement specifies to whom a security is to be transferred or who has power to transfer it. A holder may convert a blank indorsement to a special indorsement.

(b)   An indorsement purporting to be only of part of a security certificate representing units intended by the issuer to be separately transferable is effective to the extent of the indorsement.

(c)   An indorsement, whether special or in blank, does not constitute a transfer until delivery of the certificate on which it appears or, if the indorsement is on a separate document, until delivery of both the document and the certificate.

(d)   If a security certificate in registered form has been delivered to a purchaser without a necessary indorsement, the purchaser may become a protected purchaser only when the indorsement is supplied. However, against a transferor, a transfer is complete upon delivery and the purchaser has a specifically enforceable right to have any necessary indorsement supplied.

(e)   An indorsement of a security certificate in bearer form may give notice of an adverse claim to the certificate, but it does not otherwise affect a right to registration that the holder possesses.

(f)   Unless otherwise agreed, a person making an indorsement assumes only the obligations provided in Section 8–108 and not an obligation that the security will be honored by the issuer.

Official Comment

1.   By virtue of the definition of indorsement in Section 8–102 and the rules of this section, the simplified method of indorsing certificated securities previously set forth in the Uniform Stock Transfer Act is continued. Although more than one special indorsement on a given security certificate is possible, the desire for dividends or interest, as the case may be, should operate to bring the certificate home for registration of transfer within a reasonable period of time. The usual form of assignment which appears on the back of a stock certificate or in a separate "power" may be filled up either in the form of an assignment, a power of attorney to transfer, or both. If it is not filled up at all but merely signed, the indorsement is in blank. If filled up either as an assignment or as a power of attorney to transfer, the indorsement is special.

2.   Subsection (b) recognizes the validity of a "partial" indorsement, e.g., as to fifty shares of the one hundred represented by a single certificate. The rights of a transferee under a partial indorsement to the status of a protected purchaser are left to the case law.

3.   Subsection (c) deals with the effect of an indorsement without delivery. There must be a voluntary parting with control in order to effect a valid transfer of a certificated security as between the parties. *Levey v. Nason,* 279 Mass. 268, 181 N.E. 193 (1932), and *National Surety Co. v. Indemnity Insurance Co. of North America,* 237 App.Div. 485, 261 N.Y.S. 605 (1933). The provision in Section 10 of the Uniform Stock Transfer Act that an attempted transfer without delivery amounts to a promise to transfer is omitted. Even under that Act the effect of such a promise was left to the applicable law of contracts, and this Article by making no reference to such situations intends to achieve a similar result. With respect to delivery there is no counterpart to subsection (d) on right to compel indorsement, such as is envisaged in *Johnson v. Johnson,* 300 Mass. 24, 13 N.E.2d 788 (1938), where the transferee under a written assignment was given the right to compel a transfer of the certificate.

4.   Subsection (d) deals with the effect of delivery without indorsement. As between the parties the transfer is made complete upon delivery, but the transferee cannot become a protected purchaser until indorsement is made. The indorsement does not operate retroactively, and notice may intervene between delivery and indorsement so as to prevent the transferee from becoming a protected purchaser. Although a purchaser taking without a necessary indorsement may be subject to claims of ownership, any issuer's defense of which the purchaser had no notice at the time of delivery will be cut off, since the provisions of this Article protect all purchasers for value without notice (Section 8–202).

The transferee's right to compel an indorsement where a security certificate has been delivered with intent to transfer is recognized in the case law. See *Coats v. Guaranty Bank & Trust Co.,* 170 La. 871, 129 So. 513 (1930). A proper indorsement is one of the requisites of transfer which a purchaser of a certificated security has a right to obtain (Section 8–307). A purchaser may not only compel an indorsement under that section but may also recover for any reasonable expense incurred by the transferor's failure to respond to the demand for an indorsement.

5.   Subsection (e) deals with the significance of an indorsement on a security certificate in bearer form. The concept of indorsement applies only to registered securities. A purported indorsement of bearer paper is normally of no effect. An indorsement "for collection," "for surrender" or the like, charges a purchaser with notice of adverse claims (Section 8–105(d)) but does not operate beyond this to interfere with any right the holder may otherwise possess to have the security registered.

6.   Subsection (f) makes clear that the indorser of a security certificate does not warrant that the issuer will honor the underlying obligation. In view of the nature of investment securities and the circumstances under which they are normally transferred, a transferor cannot be held to warrant as to the issuer's actions. As a transferor the indorser, of course, remains liable for breach of the warranties set forth in this Article (Section 8–108).

Definitional Cross References:

"Bearer form". Section 8–102(a)(2).
"Certificated security". Section 8–102(a)(4).
"Indorsement". Section 8–102(a)(11).
"Purchaser". Sections 1–201(33) [*unrevised Article 1; see Concordance, p. 22*] & 8–116.
"Registered form". Section 8–102(a)(13).
"Security certificate". Section 8–102(a)(16).

§ 8–305.   Instruction.

(a)   If an instruction has been originated by an appropriate person but is incomplete in any other respect, any person may complete it as authorized and the issuer may rely on it as completed, even though it has been completed incorrectly.

(b)   Unless otherwise agreed, a person initiating an instruction assumes only the obligations imposed by Section 8–108 and not an obligation that the security will be honored by the issuer.

Official Comment

1.   The term instruction is defined in Section 8–102(a)(12) as a notification communicated to the issuer of an uncertificated security directing that transfer be registered. Section 8–107 specifies who may initiate an effective instruction.

Functionally, presentation of an instruction is quite similar to the presentation of an indorsed certificate for registration. Note that instruction is defined in terms of "communicate," see Section 8–102(a)(6). Thus, the instruction may be in the form of a writing signed by the registered owner or in any other form agreed upon by the issuer and the registered owner. Allowing nonwritten forms of instructions will permit the development and employment of means of transmitting instructions electronically.

When a person who originates an instruction leaves a blank and the blank later is completed, subsection (a) gives the issuer the same rights it would have had against the originating person had that person completed the blank. This is true regardless of whether the person completing the instruction had authority to complete it. Compare Section 8–206 and its Comment, dealing with blanks left upon issue.

2.   Subsection (b) makes clear that the originator of an instruction, like the indorser of a security certificate, does not warrant that the issuer will honor the underlying obligation, but does make warranties as a transferor under Section 8–108.

Definitional Cross References:

"Appropriate person". Section 8–107.
"Instruction". Section 8–102(a)(12).
"Issuer". Section 8–201.

§ 8–306.   Effect of Guaranteeing Signature, Indorsement, or Instruction.

(a)   A person who guarantees a signature of an indorser of a security certificate warrants that at the time of signing:

(1)   the signature was genuine;

(2)   the signer was an appropriate person to indorse, or if the signature is by an agent, the agent had actual authority to act on behalf of the appropriate person; and

(3)   the signer had legal capacity to sign.

(b)   A person who guarantees a signature of the originator of an instruction warrants that at the time of signing:

(1)   the signature was genuine;

(2)   the signer was an appropriate person to originate the instruction, or if the signature is by an agent, the agent had actual authority to act on behalf of the appropriate person, if the person specified in the instruction as the registered owner was, in fact, the registered owner, as to which fact the signature guarantor does not make a warranty; and

(3)   the signer had legal capacity to sign.

(c)   A person who specially guarantees the signature of an originator of an instruction makes the warranties of a signature guarantor under subsection (b) and also warrants that at the time the instruction is presented to the issuer:

(1)   the person specified in the instruction as the registered owner of the uncertificated security will be the registered owner; and

(2)   the transfer of the uncertificated security requested in the instruction will be registered by the issuer free from all liens, security interests, restrictions, and claims other than those specified in the instruction.

(d)   A guarantor under subsections (a) and (b) or a special guarantor under subsection (c) does not otherwise warrant the rightfulness of the transfer.

(e)   A person who guarantees an indorsement of a security certificate makes the warranties of a signature guarantor under subsection (a) and also warrants the rightfulness of the transfer in all respects.

(f)   A person who guarantees an instruction requesting the transfer of an uncertificated security makes the warranties of a special signature guarantor under subsection (c) and also warrants the rightfulness of the transfer in all respects.

(g)   An issuer may not require a special guaranty of signature, a guaranty of indorsement, or a guaranty of instruction as a condition to registration of transfer.

(h)   The warranties under this section are made to a person taking or dealing with the security in reliance on the guaranty, and the guarantor is liable to the person for loss resulting from their breach. An indorser or originator of an instruction whose signature, indorsement, or instruction has been guaranteed is liable to a guarantor for any loss suffered by the guarantor as a result of breach of the warranties of the guarantor.

Official Comment

1.   Subsection (a) provides that a guarantor of the signature of the indorser of a security certificate warrants that the signature is genuine, that the signer is an appropriate person or has actual authority to indorse on behalf of the appropriate person, and that the signer has legal capacity. Subsection (b) provides similar, though not identical, warranties for the guarantor of a signature of the originator of an instruction for transfer of an uncertificated security.

Appropriate person is defined in Section 8–107(a) to include a successor or person who has power under other law to act for a person who is deceased or lacks capacity. Thus if a certificate registered in the name of Mary Roe is indorsed by Jane Doe as executor of Mary Roe, a guarantor of the signature of Jane Doe warrants that she has power to act as executor.

Although the definition of appropriate person in Section 8–107(a) does not itself include an agent, an indorsement by an agent is effective under Section 8–107(b) if the agent has authority to act for the appropriate person. Accordingly, this section provides an explicit warranty of authority for agents.

2.   The rationale of the principle that a signature guarantor warrants the authority of the signer, rather than simply the genuineness of the signature, was explained in the leading case of *Jennie Clarkson Home for*

Children v. Missouri, K. & T.R. Co., 182 N.Y. 47, 74 N.E. 571, 70 A.L.R. 787 (1905), which dealt with a guaranty of the signature of a person indorsing on behalf of a corporation. "If stock is held by an individual who is executing a power of attorney for its transfer, the member of the exchange who signs as a witness thereto guaranties not only the genuineness of the signature affixed to the power of attorney, but that the person signing is the individual in whose name the stock stands. With reference to stock standing in the name of a corporation, which can only sign a power of attorney through its authorized officers or agents, a different situation is presented. If the witnessing of the signature of the corporation is only that of the signature of a person who signs for the corporation, then the guaranty is of no value, and there is nothing to protect purchasers or the companies who are called upon to issue new stock in the place of that transferred from the frauds of persons who have signed the names of corporations without authority. If such is the only effect of the guaranty, purchasers and transfer agents must first go to the corporation in whose name the stock stands and ascertain whether the individual who signed the power of attorney had authority to do so. This will require time, and in many cases will necessitate the postponement of the completion of the purchase by the payment of the money until the facts can be ascertained. The broker who is acting for the owner has an opportunity to become acquainted with his customer, and may readily before sale ascertain, in case of a corporation, the name of the officer who is authorized to execute the power of attorney. It was therefore, we think, the purpose of the rule to cast upon the broker who witnesses the signature the duty of ascertaining whether the person signing the name of the corporation had authority to do so, and making the witness a guarantor that it is the signature of the corporation in whose name the stock stands."

3.   Subsection (b) sets forth the warranties that can reasonably be expected from the guarantor of the signature of the originator of an instruction, who, though familiar with the signer, does not have any evidence that the purported owner is in fact the owner of the subject uncertificated security. This is in contrast to the position of the person guaranteeing a signature on a certificate who can see a certificate in the signer's possession in the name of or indorsed to the signer or in blank. Thus, the warranty in paragraph (2) of subsection (b) is expressly conditioned on the actual registration's conforming to that represented by the originator. If the signer purports to be the owner, the guarantor under paragraph (2), warrants only the identity of the signer. If, however, the signer is acting in a representative capacity, the guarantor warrants both the signer's identity and authority to act for the purported owner. The issuer needs no warranty as to the facts of registration because those facts can be ascertained from the issuer's own records.

4.   Subsection (c) sets forth a "special guaranty of signature" under which the guarantor additionally warrants both registered ownership and freedom from undisclosed defects of record. The guarantor of the signature of an indorser of a security certificate effectively makes these warranties to a purchaser for value on the evidence of a clean certificate issued in the name of the indorser, indorsed to the indorser or indorsed in blank. By specially guaranteeing under subsection (c), the guarantor warrants that the instruction will, when presented to the issuer, result in the requested registration free from defects not specified.

5.   Subsection (d) makes clear that the warranties of a signature guarantor are limited to those specified in this section and do not include a general warranty of rightfulness. On the other hand subsections (e) and (f) provide that a person guaranteeing an indorsement or an instruction does warrant that the transfer is rightful in all respects.

6.   Subsection (g) makes clear what can be inferred from the combination of Sections 8–401 and 8–402, that the issuer may not require as a condition to transfer a guaranty of the indorsement or instruction nor may it require a special signature guaranty.

7.   Subsection (h) specifies to whom the warranties in this section run, and also provides that a person who gives a guaranty under this section has an action against the indorser or originator for any loss suffered by the guarantor.

Definitional Cross References:

"Appropriate person". Section 8–107.
"Genuine". Section 1–201(18) [*unrevised Article 1; see Concordance, p. 22*].
"Indorsement". Section 8–102(a)(11).
"Instruction". Section 8–102(a)(12).
"Issuer". Section 8–201.
"Security certificate". Section 8–102(a)(16).
"Uncertificated security". Section 8–102(a)(18).

§ 8–307.   Purchaser's Right to Requisites for Registration of Transfer.

Unless otherwise agreed, the transferor of a security on due demand shall supply the purchaser with proof of authority to transfer or with any other requisite necessary to obtain registration of the transfer of the security, but if the transfer is not for value, a transferor need not comply unless the purchaser pays the necessary expenses. If the transferor fails within a reasonable time to comply with the demand, the purchaser may reject or rescind the transfer.

Official Comment

1.   Because registration of the transfer of a security is a matter of vital importance, a purchaser is here provided with the means of obtaining such formal requirements for registration as signature guaranties, proof of authority, transfer tax stamps and the like. The transferor is the one in a position to supply most conveniently whatever documentation may be requisite for registration of transfer, and the duty to do so upon demand within a reasonable time is here stated affirmatively. If an essential item is peculiarly within the province of the transferor so that the transferor is the only one who can obtain it, the purchaser may specifically enforce the right to obtain it. Compare Section 8–304(d). If a transfer is not for value the transferor need not pay expenses.

2.   If the transferor's duty is not performed the transferee may reject or rescind the contract to transfer. The transferee is not bound to do so. An action for damages for breach of contract may be preferred.

Definitional Cross References:

"Purchaser". Sections 1–201(33) [*unrevised Article 1; see Concordance, p. 22*] & 8–116.
"Security". Section 8–102(a)(15).
"Value". Sections 1–201(44) [*unrevised Article 1; see Concordance, p. 22*] & 8–116.

PART 4

REGISTRATION

§ 8–401.   Duty of Issuer to Register Transfer.

(a)   If a certificated security in registered form is presented to an issuer with a request to register transfer or an instruction is presented to an issuer with a request to register transfer of an uncertificated security, the issuer shall register the transfer as requested if:

(1)   under the terms of the security the person seeking registration of transfer is eligible to have the security registered in its name;

(2)   the indorsement or instruction is made by the appropriate person or by an agent who has actual authority to act on behalf of the appropriate person;

(3)   reasonable assurance is given that the indorsement or instruction is genuine and authorized (Section 8–402);

(4)   any applicable law relating to the collection of taxes has been complied with;

(5)   the transfer does not violate any restriction on transfer imposed by the issuer in accordance with Section 8–204;

(6)   a demand that the issuer not register transfer has not become effective under Section 8–403, or the issuer has complied with Section 8–403(b) but no legal process or indemnity bond is obtained as provided in Section 8–403(d); and

(7)   the transfer is in fact rightful or is to a protected purchaser.

(b)   If an issuer is under a duty to register a transfer of a security, the issuer is liable to a person presenting a certificated security or an instruction for registration or to the person's principal for loss resulting from unreasonable delay in registration or failure or refusal to register the transfer.

Official Comment

1.   This section states the duty of the issuer to register transfers. A duty exists only if certain preconditions exist. If any of the preconditions do not exist, there is no duty to register transfer. If an indorsement on a security

656

certificate is a forgery, there is no duty. If an instruction to transfer an uncertificated security is not originated by an appropriate person, there is no duty. If there has not been compliance with applicable tax laws, there is no duty. If a security certificate is properly indorsed but nevertheless the transfer is in fact wrongful, there is no duty unless the transfer is to a protected purchaser (and the other preconditions exist).

This section does not constitute a mandate that the issuer must establish that all preconditions are met before the issuer registers a transfer. The issuer may waive the reasonable assurances specified in paragraph (a)(3). If it has confidence in the responsibility of the persons requesting transfer, it may ignore questions of compliance with tax laws. Although an issuer has no duty if the transfer is wrongful, the issuer has no duty to inquire into adverse claims, see Section 8–404.

2.   By subsection (b) the person entitled to registration may not only compel it but may hold the issuer liable in damages for unreasonable delay.

3.   Section 8–201(c) provides that with respect to registration of transfer, "issuer" means the person on whose behalf transfer books are maintained. Transfer agents, registrars or the like within the scope of their respective functions have rights and duties under this Part similar to those of the issuer. See Section 8–407.

Definitional Cross References:

"Appropriate person". Section 8–107.
"Certificated security". Section 8–102(a)(4).
"Genuine". Section 1–201(18) [*unrevised Article 1; see Concordance, p. 22*].
"Indorsement". Section 8–102(a)(11).
"Instruction". Section 8–102(a)(12).
"Issuer". Section 8–201.
"Protected purchaser". Section 8–303.
"Registered form". Section 8–102(a)(13).
"Uncertificated security". Section 8–102(a)(18).

§ 8–402.   Assurance that Indorsement or Instruction is Effective.

(a)   An issuer may require the following assurance that each necessary indorsement or each instruction is genuine and authorized:

(1)   in all cases, a guaranty of the signature of the person making an indorsement or originating an instruction including, in the case of an instruction, reasonable assurance of identity;

(2)   if the indorsement is made or the instruction is originated by an agent, appropriate assurance of actual authority to sign;

(3)   if the indorsement is made or the instruction is originated by a fiduciary pursuant to Section 8–107(a)(4) or (a)(5), appropriate evidence of appointment or incumbency;

(4)   if there is more than one fiduciary, reasonable assurance that all who are required to sign have done so; and

(5)   if the indorsement is made or the instruction is originated by a person not covered by another provision of this subsection, assurance appropriate to the case corresponding as nearly as may be to the provisions of this subsection.

(b)   An issuer may elect to require reasonable assurance beyond that specified in this section.

(c)   In this section:

(1)   "Guaranty of the signature" means a guaranty signed by or on behalf of a person reasonably believed by the issuer to be responsible. An issuer may adopt standards with respect to responsibility if they are not manifestly unreasonable.

(2)   "Appropriate evidence of appointment or incumbency" means:

(i)   in the case of a fiduciary appointed or qualified by a court, a certificate issued by or under the direction or supervision of the court or an officer thereof and dated within 60 days before the date of presentation for transfer; or

    (ii)   in any other case, a copy of a document showing the appointment or a certificate issued by or on behalf of a person reasonably believed by an issuer to be responsible or, in the absence of that document or certificate, other evidence the issuer reasonably considers appropriate.

Official Comment

1.   An issuer is absolutely liable for wrongful registration of transfer if the indorsement or instruction is ineffective. See Section 8–404. Accordingly, an issuer is entitled to require such assurance as is reasonable under the circumstances that all necessary indorsements are effective, and thus to minimize its risk. This section establishes the requirements the issuer may make in terms of documentation which, except in the rarest of instances, should be easily furnished. Subsection (b) provides that an issuer may require additional assurances if that requirement is reasonable under the circumstances, but if the issuer demands more than reasonable assurance that the instruction or the necessary indorsements are genuine and authorized, the presenter may refuse the demand and sue for improper refusal to register. Section 8–401(b).

2.   Under subsection (a)(1), the issuer may require in all cases a guaranty of signature. See Section 8–306. When an instruction is presented the issuer always may require reasonable assurance as to the identity of the originator. Subsection (c) allows the issuer to require that the person making these guaranties be one reasonably believed to be responsible, and the issuer may adopt standards of responsibility which are not manifestly unreasonable. Regulations under the federal securities laws, however, place limits on the requirements transfer agents may impose concerning the responsibility of eligible signature guarantors. See 17 CFR 240.17Ad–15.

3.   This section, by paragraphs (2) through (5) of subsection (a), permits the issuer to seek confirmation that the indorsement or instruction is genuine and authorized. The permitted methods act as a double check on matters which are within the warranties of the signature guarantor. See Section 8–306. Thus, an agent may be required to submit a power of attorney, a corporation to submit a certified resolution evidencing the authority of its signing officer to sign, an executor or administrator to submit the usual "shortform certificate," etc. But failure of a fiduciary to obtain court approval of the transfer or to comply with other requirements does not make the fiduciary's signature ineffective. Section 8–107(c). Hence court orders and other controlling instruments are omitted from subsection (a).

Subsection (a)(3) authorizes the issuer to require "appropriate evidence" of appointment or incumbency, and subsection (c) indicates what evidence will be "appropriate". In the case of a fiduciary appointed or qualified by a court that evidence will be a court certificate dated within sixty days before the date of presentation, subsection (c)(2)(i). Where the fiduciary is not appointed or qualified by a court, as in the case of a successor trustee, subsection (c)(2)(ii) applies. In that case, the issuer may require a copy of a trust instrument or other document showing the appointment, or it may require the certificate of a responsible person. In the absence of such a document or certificate, it may require other appropriate evidence. If the security is registered in the name of the fiduciary as such, the person's signature is effective even though the person is no longer serving in that capacity, see Section 8–107(d), hence no evidence of incumbency is needed.

4.   Circumstances may indicate that a necessary signature was unauthorized or was not that of an appropriate person. Such circumstances would be ignored at risk of absolute liability. To minimize that risk the issuer may properly exercise the option given by subsection (b) to require assurance beyond that specified in subsection (a). On the other hand, the facts at hand may reflect only on the rightfulness of the transfer. Such facts do not create a duty of inquiry, because the issuer is not liable to an adverse claimant unless the claimant obtains legal process. See Section 8–404.

Definitional Cross References:

    "Appropriate person". Section 8–107.
    "Genuine". Section 1–201(18) [unrevised Article 1; see Concordance, p. 22].
    "Indorsement". Section 8–102(a)(11).
    "Instruction". Section 8–102(a)(12).
    "Issuer". Section 8–201.

§ 8–403.   Demand that Issuer Not Register Transfer.

    (a)   A person who is an appropriate person to make an indorsement or originate an instruction may demand that the issuer not register transfer of a security by communicating to the issuer a notification that identifies the registered owner and the issue of which the security is a part and provides an address for communications directed to the person making the demand. The demand is effective only if it is received by the issuer at a time and in a manner affording the issuer reasonable opportunity to act on it.

(b) If a certificated security in registered form is presented to an issuer with a request to register transfer or an instruction is presented to an issuer with a request to register transfer of an uncertificated security after a demand that the issuer not register transfer has become effective, the issuer shall promptly communicate to (i) the person who initiated the demand at the address provided in the demand and (ii) the person who presented the security for registration of transfer or initiated the instruction requesting registration of transfer a notification stating that:

(1) the certificated security has been presented for registration of transfer or the instruction for registration of transfer of the uncertificated security has been received;

(2) a demand that the issuer not register transfer had previously been received; and

(3) the issuer will withhold registration of transfer for a period of time stated in the notification in order to provide the person who initiated the demand an opportunity to obtain legal process or an indemnity bond.

(c) The period described in subsection (b)(3) may not exceed 30 days after the date of communication of the notification. A shorter period may be specified by the issuer if it is not manifestly unreasonable.

(d) An issuer is not liable to a person who initiated a demand that the issuer not register transfer for any loss the person suffers as a result of registration of a transfer pursuant to an effective indorsement or instruction if the person who initiated the demand does not, within the time stated in the issuer's communication, either:

(1) obtain an appropriate restraining order, injunction, or other process from a court of competent jurisdiction enjoining the issuer from registering the transfer; or

(2) file with the issuer an indemnity bond, sufficient in the issuer's judgment to protect the issuer and any transfer agent, registrar, or other agent of the issuer involved from any loss it or they may suffer by refusing to register the transfer.

(e) This section does not relieve an issuer from liability for registering transfer pursuant to an indorsement or instruction that was not effective.

Official Comment

1. The general rule under this Article is that if there has been an effective indorsement or instruction, a person who contends that registration of the transfer would be wrongful should not be able to interfere with the registration process merely by sending notice of the assertion to the issuer. Rather, the claimant must obtain legal process. See Section 8–404. Section 8–403 is an exception to this general rule. It permits the registered owner— but not third parties—to demand that the issuer not register a transfer.

2. This section is intended to alleviate the problems faced by registered owners of certificated securities who lose or misplace their certificates. A registered owner who realizes that a certificate may have been lost or stolen should promptly report that fact to the issuer, lest the owner be precluded from asserting a claim for wrongful registration. See Section 8–406. The usual practice of issuers and transfer agents is that when a certificate is reported as lost, the owner is notified that a replacement can be obtained if the owner provides an indemnity bond. See Section 8–405. If the registered owner does not plan to transfer the securities, the owner might choose not to obtain a replacement, particularly if the owner suspects that the certificate has merely been misplaced.

Under this section, the owner's notification that the certificate has been lost would constitute a demand that the issuer not register transfer. No indemnity bond or legal process is necessary. If the original certificate is presented for registration of transfer, the issuer is required to notify the registered owner of that fact, and defer registration of transfer for a stated period. In order to prevent undue delay in the process of registration, the stated period may not exceed thirty days. This gives the registered owner an opportunity to either obtain legal process or post an indemnity bond and thereby prevent the issuer from registering transfer.

3. Subsection (e) makes clear that this section does not relieve an issuer from liability for registering a transfer pursuant to an ineffective indorsement. An issuer's liability for wrongful registration in such cases does not depend on the presence or absence of notice that the indorsement was ineffective. Registered owners who are confident that they neither indorsed the certificates, nor did anything that would preclude them from denying the

effectiveness of another's indorsement, see Sections 8–107(b) and 8–406, might prefer to pursue their rights against the issuer for wrongful registration rather than take advantage of the opportunity to post a bond or seek a restraining order when notified by the issuer under this section that their lost certificates have been presented for registration in apparently good order.

Definitional Cross References:

"Appropriate person". Section 8–107.
"Certificated security". Section 8–102(a)(4).
"Communicate". Section 8–102(a)(6).
"Effective". Section 8–107.
"Indorsement". Section 8–102(a)(11).
"Instruction". Section 8–102(a)(12).
"Issuer". Section 8–201.
"Registered form". Section 8–102(a)(13).
"Uncertificated security". Section 8–102(a)(18).

§ 8–404. Wrongful Registration.

(a) Except as otherwise provided in Section 8–406, an issuer is liable for wrongful registration of transfer if the issuer has registered a transfer of a security to a person not entitled to it, and the transfer was registered:

(1) pursuant to an ineffective indorsement or instruction;

(2) after a demand that the issuer not register transfer became effective under Section 8–403(a) and the issuer did not comply with Section 8–403(b);

(3) after the issuer had been served with an injunction, restraining order, or other legal process enjoining it from registering the transfer, issued by a court of competent jurisdiction, and the issuer had a reasonable opportunity to act on the injunction, restraining order, or other legal process; or

(4) by an issuer acting in collusion with the wrongdoer.

(b) An issuer that is liable for wrongful registration of transfer under subsection (a) on demand shall provide the person entitled to the security with a like certificated or uncertificated security, and any payments or distributions that the person did not receive as a result of the wrongful registration. If an overissue would result, the issuer's liability to provide the person with a like security is governed by Section 8–210.

(c) Except as otherwise provided in subsection (a) or in a law relating to the collection of taxes, an issuer is not liable to an owner or other person suffering loss as a result of the registration of a transfer of a security if registration was made pursuant to an effective indorsement or instruction.

Official Comment

1. Subsection (a)(1) provides that an issuer is liable if it registers transfer pursuant to an indorsement or instruction that was not effective. For example, an issuer that registers transfer on a forged indorsement is liable to the registered owner. The fact that the issuer had no reason to suspect that the indorsement was forged or that the issuer obtained the ordinary assurances under Section 8–402 does not relieve the issuer from liability. The reason that issuers obtain signature guaranties and other assurances is that they are liable for wrongful registration.

Subsection (b) specifies the remedy for wrongful registration. Pre-Code cases established the registered owner's right to receive a new security where the issuer had wrongfully registered a transfer, but some cases also allowed the registered owner to elect between an equitable action to compel issue of a new security and an action for damages. Cf. *Casper v. Kalt-Zimmers Mfg. Co.*, 159 Wis. 517, 149 N.W. 754 (1914). Article 8 does not allow such election. The true owner of a certificated security is required to take a new security except where an overissue would result and a similar security is not reasonably available for purchase. See Section 8–210. The true owner of an uncertificated security is entitled and required to take restoration of the records to their proper state, with a similar exception for overissue.

2.　Read together, subsections (c) and (a) have the effect of providing that an issuer has no duties to an adverse claimant unless the claimant serves legal process on the issuer to enjoin registration. Issuers, or their transfer agents, perform a record-keeping function for the direct holding system that is analogous to the functions performed by clearing corporations and securities intermediaries in the indirect holding system. This section applies to the record-keepers for the direct holding system the same standard that Section 8–115 applies to the record-keepers for the indirect holding system. Thus, issuers are not liable to adverse claimants merely on the basis of notice. As in the case of the analogous rules for the indirect holding system, the policy of this section is to protect the right of investors to have their securities transfers processed without the disruption or delay that might result if the record-keepers risked liability to third parties. It would be undesirable to apply different standards to the direct and indirect holding systems, since doing so might operate as a disincentive to the development of a book-entry direct holding system.

3.　This section changes prior law under which an issuer could be held liable, even though it registered transfer on an effective indorsement or instruction, if the issuer had in some fashion been notified that the transfer might be wrongful against a third party, and the issuer did not appropriately discharge its duty to inquire into the adverse claim. See Section 8–403 (1978).

The rule of former Section 8–403 was anomalous inasmuch as Section 8–207 provides that the issuer is entitled to "treat the registered owner as the person exclusively entitled to vote, receive notifications, and otherwise exercise all the rights and powers of an owner." Under Section 8–207, the fact that a third person notifies the issuer of a claim does not preclude the issuer from treating the registered owner as the person entitled to the security. See *Kerrigan v. American Orthodontics Corp.*, 960 F.2d 43 (7th Cir. 1992). The change made in the present version of Section 8–404 ensures that the rights of registered owners and the duties of issuers with respect to registration of transfer will be protected against third-party interference in the same fashion as other rights of registered ownership.

Definitional Cross References:

"Certificated security". Section 8–102(a)(4).
"Effective". Section 8–107.
"Indorsement". Section 8–102(a)(11).
"Instruction". Section 8–102(a)(12).
"Issuer". Section 8–201.
"Security". Section 8–102(a)(15).
"Uncertificated security". Section 8–102(a)(18).

§ 8–405.　Replacement of Lost, Destroyed, or Wrongfully Taken Security Certificate.

(a)　If an owner of a certificated security, whether in registered or bearer form, claims that the certificate has been lost, destroyed, or wrongfully taken, the issuer shall issue a new certificate if the owner:

(1)　so requests before the issuer has notice that the certificate has been acquired by a protected purchaser;

(2)　files with the issuer a sufficient indemnity bond; and

(3)　satisfies other reasonable requirements imposed by the issuer.

(b)　If, after the issue of a new security certificate, a protected purchaser of the original certificate presents it for registration of transfer, the issuer shall register the transfer unless an overissue would result. In that case, the issuer's liability is governed by Section 8–210. In addition to any rights on the indemnity bond, an issuer may recover the new certificate from a person to whom it was issued or any person taking under that person, except a protected purchaser.

Official Comment

1.　This section enables the owner to obtain a replacement of a lost, destroyed or stolen certificate, provided that reasonable requirements are satisfied and a sufficient indemnity bond supplied.

2.　Where an "original" security certificate has reached the hands of a protected purchaser, the registered owner—who was in the best position to prevent the loss, destruction or theft of the security certificate—is now deprived of the new security certificate issued as a replacement. This changes the pre-UCC law under which the original certificate was ineffective after the issue of a replacement except insofar as it might represent an action for damages in the hands of a purchaser for value without notice. *Keller v. Eureka Brick Mach. Mfg. Co.*, 43

Mo.App. 84, 11 L.R.A. 472 (1890). Where both the original and the new certificate have reached protected purchasers the issuer is required to honor both certificates unless an overissue would result and the security is not reasonably available for purchase. See Section 8–210. In the latter case alone, the protected purchaser of the original certificate is relegated to an action for damages. In either case, the issuer itself may recover on the indemnity bond.

Definitional Cross References:

"Bearer form". Section 8–102(a)(2).

"Certificated security". Section 8–102(a)(4).

"Issuer". Section 8–201.

"Notice". Section 1–201(25) [*unrevised Article 1; see Concordance, p. 22*].

"Overissue". Section 8–210.

"Protected purchaser". Section 8–303.

"Registered form". Section 8–102(a)(13).

"Security certificate". Section 8–102(a)(16).

§ 8–406. Obligation to Notify Issuer of Lost, Destroyed, or Wrongfully Taken Security Certificate.

If a security certificate has been lost, apparently destroyed, or wrongfully taken, and the owner fails to notify the issuer of that fact within a reasonable time after the owner has notice of it and the issuer registers a transfer of the security before receiving notification, the owner may not assert against the issuer a claim for registering the transfer under Section 8–404 or a claim to a new security certificate under Section 8–405.

Official Comment

An owner who fails to notify the issuer within a reasonable time after the owner knows or has reason to know of the loss or theft of a security certificate is estopped from asserting the ineffectiveness of a forged or unauthorized indorsement and the wrongfulness of the registration of the transfer. If the lost certificate was indorsed by the owner, then the registration of the transfer was not wrongful under Section 8–404, unless the owner made an effective demand that the issuer not register transfer under Section 8–403.

Definitional Cross References:

"Issuer". Section 8–201.

"Notify". Section 1–201(25) [*unrevised Article 1; see Concordance, p. 22*].

"Security certificate". Section 8–102(a)(16).

§ 8–407. Authenticating Trustee, Transfer Agent, and Registrar.

A person acting as authenticating trustee, transfer agent, registrar, or other agent for an issuer in the registration of a transfer of its securities, in the issue of new security certificates or uncertificated securities, or in the cancellation of surrendered security certificates has the same obligation to the holder or owner of a certificated or uncertificated security with regard to the particular functions performed as the issuer has in regard to those functions.

Official Comment

1. Transfer agents, registrars, and the like are here expressly held liable both to the issuer and to the owner for wrongful refusal to register a transfer as well as for wrongful registration of a transfer in any case within the scope of their respective functions where the issuer would itself be liable. Those cases which have regarded these parties solely as agents of the issuer and have therefore refused to recognize their liability to the owner for mere nonfeasance, i.e., refusal to register a transfer, are rejected. *Hulse v. Consolidated Quicksilver Mining Corp.,* 65 Idaho 768, 154 P.2d 149 (1944); *Nicholson v. Morgan,* 119 Misc. 309, 196 N.Y.Supp. 147 (1922); *Lewis v. Hargadine-McKittrick Dry Goods Co.,* 305 Mo. 396, 274 S.W. 1041 (1924).

2. The practice frequently followed by authenticating trustees of issuing certificates of indebtedness rather than authenticating duplicate certificates where securities have been lost or stolen became obsolete in view of the provisions of Section 8–405, which makes express provision for the issue of substitute securities. It is not a breach of trust or lack of due diligence for trustees to authenticate new securities. Cf. *Switzerland General Ins. Co. v. N.Y.C. & H.R.R. Co.,* 152 App.Div. 70, 136 N.Y.S. 726 (1912).

Definitional Cross References:

"Certificated security". Section 8–102(a)(4).
"Issuer". Section 8–201.
"Security". Section 8–102(a)(15).
"Security certificate". Section 8–102(a)(16).
"Uncertificated security". Section 8–102(a)(18).

PART 5

SECURITY ENTITLEMENTS

§ 8–501. Securities Account; Acquisition of Security Entitlement from Securities Intermediary.

(a)   "Securities account" means an account to which a financial asset is or may be credited in accordance with an agreement under which the person maintaining the account undertakes to treat the person for whom the account is maintained as entitled to exercise the rights that comprise the financial asset.

(b)   Except as otherwise provided in subsections (d) and (e), a person acquires a security entitlement if a securities intermediary:

(1)   indicates by book entry that a financial asset has been credited to the person's securities account;

(2)   receives a financial asset from the person or acquires a financial asset for the person and, in either case, accepts it for credit to the person's securities account; or

(3)   becomes obligated under other law, regulation, or rule to credit a financial asset to the person's securities account.

(c)   If a condition of subsection (b) has been met, a person has a security entitlement even though the securities intermediary does not itself hold the financial asset.

(d)   If a securities intermediary holds a financial asset for another person, and the financial asset is registered in the name of, payable to the order of, or specially indorsed to the other person, and has not been indorsed to the securities intermediary or in blank, the other person is treated as holding the financial asset directly rather than as having a security entitlement with respect to the financial asset.

(e)   Issuance of a security is not establishment of a security entitlement.

Official Comment

1.   Part 5 rules apply to security entitlements, and Section 8–501(b) provides that a person has a security entitlement when a financial asset has been credited to a "securities account." Thus, the term "securities account" specifies the type of arrangements between ~~institutions~~ intermediaries and their customers that are covered by Part 5. A securities account is a consensual arrangement in which the intermediary undertakes to treat the customer as entitled to exercise the rights that comprise the financial asset. The consensual aspect is covered by the requirement that the account be established pursuant to agreement. The term agreement is used in the broad sense defined in Section ~~1–201(3)~~ 1–201(b)(3). There is no requirement that a formal or written agreement be signed.

As the securities business is presently conducted, several significant relationships clearly fall within the definition of a securities account, including the relationship between a clearing corporation and its participants, a broker and customers who leave securities with the broker, and a bank acting as securities custodian and its custodial customers. Given the enormous variety of arrangements concerning securities that exist today, and the certainty that new arrangements will evolve in the future, it is not possible to specify all of the arrangements to which the term does and does not apply.

Whether an arrangement between ~~a firm~~ an intermediary and another person concerning a security or other financial asset is a "securities account" under this Article depends on whether the firm has undertaken to treat the other person as entitled to exercise the rights that comprise the security or other financial asset. Section ~~1–102~~ 1–103, however, states the fundamental principle of interpretation that the Code provisions should be construed and applied to promote their underlying purposes and policies. Thus, the question whether a given arrangement is a securities account should be decided not by dictionary analysis of the words of the definition taken out of context, but by considering whether it promotes the objectives of Article 8 to include the arrangement within the term securities account.

The effect of concluding that an arrangement is a securities account is that the rules of Part 5 apply. Accordingly, the definition of "securities account" must be interpreted in light of the substantive provisions in Part 5, which describe the core features of the type of relationship for which the commercial law rules of Revised Article 8 concerning security entitlements were designed. There are many arrangements between ~~institutions~~ intermediaries and other persons concerning securities or other financial assets which do not fall within the definition of "securities account" because the ~~institutions~~ intermediaries have not undertaken to treat the other persons as entitled to exercise the ordinary rights of an entitlement holder specified in the Part 5 rules. For example, the term securities account does not cover the relationship between a bank and its depositors or the relationship between a trustee and the beneficiary of an ordinary trust, because those are not relationships in which the holder of a financial asset has undertaken to treat the other as entitled to exercise the rights that comprise the financial asset in the fashion contemplated by the Part 5 rules.

In short, the primary factor in deciding whether an arrangement is a securities account is whether application of the Part 5 rules is consistent with the expectations of the parties to the relationship. Relationships not governed by Part 5 may be governed by other parts of Article 8 if the relationship gives rise to a new security, or may be governed by other law entirely.

2. Subsection (b) of this section specifies what circumstances give rise to security entitlements. Paragraph (1) of subsection (b) sets out the most important rule. It turns on the intermediary's conduct, reflecting a basic operating assumption of the indirect holding system that once a securities intermediary has acknowledged that it is carrying a position in a financial asset for its customer or participant, the intermediary is obligated to treat the customer or participant as entitled to the financial asset. Paragraph (1) does not attempt to specify exactly what accounting, record-keeping, or information transmission steps suffice to indicate that the intermediary has credited the account. That is left to agreement, trade practice, or rule in order to provide the flexibility necessary to accommodate varying or changing accounting and information processing systems. The point of paragraph (1) is that once an intermediary has acknowledged that it is carrying a position for the customer or participant, the customer or participant has a security entitlement. The precise form in which the intermediary manifests that acknowledgment is left to private ordering.

Paragraph (2) of subsection (b) sets out a different operational test, turning not on the intermediary's accounting system but on the facts that accounting systems are supposed to represent. Under paragraph (b)(2) a person has a security entitlement if the intermediary has received and accepted a financial asset for credit to the account of its customer or participant. For example, if a customer of a broker or bank custodian delivers a security certificate in proper form to the broker or bank to be held in the customer's account, the customer acquires a security entitlement. Paragraph (b)(2) also covers circumstances in which the intermediary receives a financial asset from a third person for credit to the account of the customer or participant. Paragraph (b)(2) is not limited to circumstances in which the intermediary receives security certificates or other financial assets in physical form. Paragraph (b)(2) also covers circumstances in which the intermediary acquires a security entitlement with respect to a financial asset which is to be credited to the account of the intermediary's own customer. For example, if a customer transfers her account from Broker A to Broker B, she acquires security entitlements against Broker B once the clearing corporation has credited the positions to Broker B's account. It should be noted, however, that paragraph (b)(2) provides that a person acquires a security entitlement when the intermediary not only receives but also accepts the financial asset for credit to the account. This limitation is included to take account of the fact that there may be circumstances in which an intermediary has received a financial asset but is not willing to undertake the obligations that flow from establishing a security entitlement. For example, a security certificate which is sent to an intermediary may not be in proper form, or may represent a type of financial asset which the intermediary is not willing to carry for others. It should be noted that in all but extremely unusual cases, the circumstances covered by paragraph (2) will also be covered by paragraph (1), because the intermediary will have credited the positions to the customer's account.

Paragraph (3) of subsection (b) sets out a residual test, to avoid any implication that the failure of an intermediary to make the appropriate entries to credit a position to a customer's securities account would prevent the customer from acquiring the rights of an entitlement holder under Part 5. As is the case with the paragraph (2) test, the paragraph (3) test would not be needed for the ordinary cases, since they are covered by paragraph (1).

3.   In a sense, Section 8–501(b) is analogous to the rules set out in the provisions of Sections 8–313(1)(d) and 8–320 of the prior version of Article 8 that specified what acts by a securities intermediary or clearing corporation sufficed as a transfer of securities held in fungible bulk. Unlike the prior version of Article 8, however, this section is not based on the idea that an entitlement holder acquires rights only by virtue of a "transfer" from the securities intermediary to the entitlement holder. In the indirect holding system, the significant fact is that the securities intermediary has undertaken to treat the customer as entitled to the financial asset. It is up to the securities intermediary to take the necessary steps to ensure that it will be able to perform its undertaking. It is, for example, entirely possible that a securities intermediary might make entries in a customer's account reflecting that customer's acquisition of a certain security at a time when the securities intermediary did not itself happen to hold any units of that security. The person from whom the securities intermediary bought the security might have failed to deliver and it might have taken some time to clear up the problem, or there may have been an operational gap in time between the crediting of a customer's account and the receipt of securities from another securities intermediary. The entitlement holder's rights against the securities intermediary do not depend on whether or when the securities intermediary acquired its interests. Subsection (c) is intended to make this point clear. Subsection (c) does not mean that the intermediary is free to create security entitlements without itself holding sufficient financial assets to satisfy its entitlement holders. The duty of a securities intermediary to maintain sufficient assets is governed by Section 8–504 and regulatory law. Subsection (c) is included only to make it clear the question whether a person has acquired a security entitlement does not depend on whether the intermediary has complied with that duty.

4.   Part 5 of Article 8 sets out a carefully designed system of rules for the indirect holding system. Persons who hold securities through brokers or custodians have security entitlements that are governed by Part 5, rather than being treated as the direct holders of securities. Subsection (d) specifies the limited circumstance in which a customer who leaves a financial asset with a broker or other securities intermediary has a direct interest in the financial asset, rather than a security entitlement.

The customer can be a direct holder only if the security certificate, or other financial asset, is registered in the name of, payable to the order of, or specially indorsed to the customer, and has not been indorsed by the customer to the securities intermediary or in blank. The distinction between those circumstances where the customer can be treated as direct owner and those where the customer has a security entitlement is essentially the same as the distinction drawn under the federal bankruptcy code between customer name securities and customer property. The distinction does not turn on any form of physical identification or segregation. A customer who delivers certificates to a broker with blank indorsements or stock powers is not a direct holder but has a security entitlement, even though the broker holds those certificates in some form of separate safe-keeping arrangement for that particular customer. The customer remains the direct holder only if there is no indorsement or stock power so that further action by the customer is required to place the certificates in a form where they can be transferred by the broker.

The rule of subsection (d) corresponds to the rule set out in Section 8–301(a)(3) specifying when acquisition of possession of a certificate by a securities intermediary counts as "delivery" to the customer.

Subsection (d) uses terminology applicable to conventional certificated securities (e.g., "indorsed") and contemplates the limited circumstances in which a securities intermediary (defined in Section 8–102(a)(14) to include only a clearing corporation or another person that in the ordinary course of its business maintains securities accounts for others and that is acting in that capacity) may hold a financial asset for a customer under a direct holding arrangement rather than as a security entitlement. However, assets such as controllable electronic records, controllable accounts, and controllable payment intangibles also might be associated with an intermediary as well as with its customer under a similar direct holding arrangement. For example, the intermediary and the customer might share control of the financial asset under an arrangement whereby the intermediary could exercise powers, such as the power to transfer control, only with the concurrent exercise of the powers by the customer. As with conventional certificated securities, whether an intermediary has created a security entitlement in favor of an entitlement holder or its customer is holding a financial asset directly depends on the nature of the relationship and the nature of the rights of the intermediary and the customer with respect to the financial asset. A securities intermediary and a customer wishing to establish the customer's direct holding status could avoid uncertainty by means of unambiguous contractual documentation of their relationship. Moreover, a person holding such an asset for the benefit of another may not be acting in the capacity of a securities intermediary at all, even if the person also regularly acts in that capacity. In such a case, subsection (d) would not apply and the relationship would be governed by the agreement of the parties and the application of law other than this Article.

5.   Subsection (e) is intended to make clear that Part 5 does not apply to an arrangement in which a security is issued representing an interest in underlying assets, as distinguished from arrangements in which the

underlying assets are carried in a securities account. A common mechanism by which new financial instruments are devised is that a financial institution that holds some security, financial instrument, or pool thereof, creates interests in that asset or pool which are sold to others. In many such cases, the interests so created will fall within the definition of "security" in Section 8–102(a)(15). If so, then by virtue of subsection (e) of Section 8–501, the relationship between the institution that creates the interests and the persons who hold them is not a security entitlement to which the Part 5 rules apply. Accordingly, an arrangement such as an American depositary receipt facility which creates freely transferable interests in underlying securities will be issuance of a security under Article 8 rather than establishment of a security entitlement to the underlying securities.

The subsection (e) rule can be regarded as an aspect of the definitional rules specifying the meaning of securities account and security entitlement. Among the key components of the definition of security in Section 8–102(a)(15) are the "transferability" and "divisibility" tests. Securities, in the Article 8 sense, are fungible interests or obligations that are intended to be tradable. The concept of security entitlement under Part 5 is quite different. A security entitlement is the package of rights that a person has against the person's own intermediary with respect to the positions carried in the person's securities account. That package of rights is not, as such, something that is traded. When a customer sells a security that she had held through a securities account, her security entitlement is terminated; when she buys a security that she will hold through her securities account, she acquires a security entitlement. In most cases, settlement of a securities trade will involve termination of one person's security entitlement and acquisition of a security entitlement by another person. That transaction, however, is not a "transfer" of the same entitlement from one person to another. That is not to say that an entitlement holder cannot transfer an interest in her security entitlement as such; granting a security interest in a security entitlement is such a transfer. On the other hand, the nature of a security entitlement is that the intermediary is undertaking duties only to the person identified as the entitlement holder.

6.   **Enforceability of Rights and Obligations.** Rights and obligations relating to a security entitlement are enforceable by action. See Section 1–305(b) and PEB Commentary No.25, dated August 12, 2022. The Commentary is available at https://www.ali.org/peb-ucc.

Definitional Cross References:

"Financial asset". Section 8–102(a)(9).
"Indorsement". Section 8–102(a)(11).
"Securities intermediary". Section 8–102(a)(14).
"Security". Section 8–102(a)(15).
"Security entitlement". Section 8–102(a)(17).

As amended in 2022.

§ 8–502.   Assertion of Adverse Claim Against Entitlement Holder.

An action based on an adverse claim to a financial asset, whether framed in conversion, replevin, constructive trust, equitable lien, or other theory, may not be asserted against a person who acquires a security entitlement under Section 8–501 for value and without notice of the adverse claim.

Official Comment

1.   The section provides investors in the indirect holding system with protection against adverse claims by specifying that no adverse claim can be asserted against a person who acquires a security entitlement under Section 8–501 for value and without notice of the adverse claim. It plays a role in the indirect holding system analogous to the rule of the direct holding system that protected purchasers take free from adverse claims (Section 8–303).

This section does not use the locution "takes free from adverse claims" because that could be confusing as applied to the indirect holding system. The nature of indirect holding system is that an entitlement holder has an interest in common with others who hold positions in the same financial asset through the same intermediary. Thus, a particular entitlement holder's interest in the financial assets held by its intermediary is necessarily "subject to" the interests of others. See Section 8–503. The rule stated in this section might have been expressed by saying that a person who acquires a security entitlement under Section 8–501 for value and without notice of adverse claims takes "that security entitlement" free from adverse claims. That formulation has not been used, however, for fear that it would be misinterpreted as suggesting that the person acquires a right to the underlying financial assets that could not be affected by the competing rights of others claiming through common or higher tier intermediaries. A security entitlement is a complex bundle of rights. This section does not deal with the question of what rights are in the bundle. Rather, this section provides that once a person has acquired the bundle, someone else cannot take it away on the basis of assertion that the transaction in which the security entitlement was created involved a violation of the claimant's rights.

2. Because securities trades are typically settled on a net basis by book-entry movements, it would ordinarily be impossible for anyone to trace the path of any particular security, no matter how the interest of parties who hold through intermediaries is described. Suppose, for example, that S has a 1000 share position in XYZ common stock through an account with a broker, Able & Co. S's identical twin impersonates S and directs Able to sell the securities. That same day, B places an order with Baker & Co., to buy 1000 shares of XYZ common stock. Later, S discovers the wrongful act and seeks to recover "her shares." Even if S can show that, at the stage of the trade, her sell order was matched with B's buy order, that would not suffice to show that "her shares" went to B. Settlement between Able and Baker occurs on a net basis for all trades in XYZ that day; indeed Able's net position may have been such that it received rather than delivered shares in XYZ through the settlement system.

In the unlikely event that this was the only trade in XYZ common stock executed in the market that day, one could follow the shares from S's account to B's account. The plaintiff in an action in conversion or similar legal action to enforce a property interest must show that the defendant has an item of property that belongs to the plaintiff. In this example, B's security entitlement is not the same item of property that formerly was held by S, it is a new package of rights that B acquired against Baker under Section 8–501. Principles of equitable remedies might, however, provide S with a basis for contending that if the position B received was the traceable product of the wrongful taking of S's property by S's twin, a constructive trust should be imposed on B's property in favor of S. See G. Palmer, The Law of Restitution § 2.14. Section 8–502 ensures that no such claims can be asserted against a person, such as B in this example, who acquires a security entitlement under Section 8–501 for value and without notice, regardless of what theory of law or equity is used to describe the basis of the assertion of the adverse claim.

In the above example, S would ordinarily have no reason to pursue B unless Able is insolvent and S's claim will not be satisfied in the insolvency proceedings. Because S did not give an entitlement order for the disposition of her security entitlement, Able must recredit her account for the 1000 shares of XYZ common stock. See Section 8–507(b).

3. The following examples illustrate the operation of Section 8–502.

Example 1. Thief steals bearer bonds from Owner. Thief delivers the bonds to Broker for credit to Thief's securities account, thereby acquiring a security entitlement under Section 8–501(b). Under other law, Owner may have a claim to have a constructive trust imposed on the security entitlement as the traceable product of the bonds that Thief misappropriated. Because Thief was himself the wrongdoer, Thief obviously had notice of Owner's adverse claim. Accordingly, Section 8–502 does not preclude Owner from asserting an adverse claim against Thief.

Example 2. Thief steals bearer bonds from Owner. Thief owes a personal debt to Creditor. Creditor has a securities account with Broker. Thief agrees to transfer the bonds to Creditor as security for or in satisfaction of his debt to Creditor. Thief does so by sending the bonds to Broker for credit to Creditor's securities account. Creditor thereby acquires a security entitlement under Section 8–501(b). Under other law, Owner may have a claim to have a constructive trust imposed on the security entitlement as the traceable product of the bonds that Thief misappropriated. Creditor acquired the security entitlement for value, since Creditor acquired it as security for or in satisfaction of Thief's debt to Creditor. See Section 1–201(44) 1–204. If Creditor did not have notice of Owner's claim, Section 8–502 precludes any action by Owner against Creditor, whether framed in constructive trust or other theory. Section 8–105 specifies what counts as notice of an adverse claim.

Example 3. Father, as trustee for Son, holds XYZ Co. shares in a securities account with Able & Co. In violation of his fiduciary duties, Father sells the XYZ Co. shares and uses the proceeds for personal purposes. Father dies, and his estate is insolvent. Assume—implausibly—that Son is able to trace the XYZ Co. shares and show that the "same shares" ended up in Buyer's securities account with Baker & Co. Section 8–502 precludes any action by Son against Buyer, whether framed in constructive trust or other theory, provided that Buyer acquired the security entitlement for value and without notice of adverse claims.

Example 4. Debtor holds XYZ Co. shares in a securities account with Able & Co. As collateral for a loan from Bank, Debtor grants Bank a security interest in the security entitlement to the XYZ Co. shares. Bank perfects by a method which leaves Debtor with the ability to dispose of the shares. See Section 9–312. In violation of the security agreement, Debtor sells the XYZ Co. shares and absconds with the proceeds. Assume—implausibly—that Bank is able to trace the XYZ Co. shares and show that the "same shares" ended up in Buyer's securities account with Baker & Co. Section 8–502 precludes any action by Bank against Buyer, whether framed in constructive trust or other theory, provided that Buyer acquired the security entitlement for value and without notice of adverse claims.

Example 5.   Debtor owns controlling interests in various public companies, including Acme and Ajax. Acme owns 60% of the stock of another public company, Beta. Debtor causes the Beta stock to be pledged to Lending Bank as collateral for Ajax's debt. Acme holds the Beta stock through an account with a securities custodian, C Bank, which in turn holds through Clearing Corporation. Lending Bank is also a Clearing Corporation participant. The pledge of the Beta stock is implemented by Acme instructing C Bank to instruct Clearing Corporation to debit C Bank's account and credit Lending Bank's account. Acme and Ajax both become insolvent. The Beta stock is still valuable. Acme's liquidator asserts that the pledge of the Beta stock for Ajax's debt was wrongful as against Acme and seeks to recover the Beta stock from Lending Bank. Because the pledge was implemented by an outright transfer into Lending Bank's account at Clearing Corporation, Lending Bank acquired a security entitlement to the Beta stock under Section 8–501. Lending Bank acquired the security entitlement for value, since it acquired it as security for a debt. See Section ~~1–201(44)~~ 1–204. If Lending Bank did not have notice of Acme's claim, Section 8–502 will preclude any action by Acme against Lending Bank, whether framed in constructive trust or other theory.

Example 6.   Debtor grants Alpha Co. a security interest in a security entitlement that includes 1000 shares of XYZ Co. stock that Debtor holds through an account with Able & Co. Alpha also has an account with Able. Debtor instructs Able to transfer the shares to Alpha, and Able does so by crediting the shares to Alpha's account. Alpha has control of the 1000 shares under Section 8–106(d). (The facts to this point are identical to those in Section 8–106, Comment 4, Example 1, except that Alpha Co. was Alpha Bank.) Alpha next grants Beta Co. a security interest in the 1000 shares included in Alpha's security entitlement. See Section 9–207(c)(3). Alpha instructs Able to transfer the shares to Gamma Co., Beta's custodian. Able does so, and Gamma credits the 1000 shares to Beta's account. Beta now has control under Section 8–106(d). By virtue of Debtor's explicit permission or by virtue of the permission inherent in Debtor's creation of a security interest in favor of Alpha and Alpha's resulting power to grant a security interest under Section 9–207, Debtor has no adverse claim to assert against Beta, assuming implausibly that Debtor could "trace" an interest to the Gamma account. Moreover, even if Debtor did hold an adverse claim, if Beta did not have notice of Debtor's claim, Section 8–502 will preclude any action by Debtor against Beta, whether framed in constructive trust or other theory.

4.   Although this section protects entitlement holders against adverse claims, it does not protect them against the risk that their securities intermediary will not itself have sufficient financial assets to satisfy the claims of all of its entitlement holders. Suppose that Customer A holds 1000 shares of XYZ Co. stock in an account with her broker, Able & Co. Able in turn holds 1000 shares of XYZ Co. through its account with Clearing Corporation, but has no other positions in XYZ Co. shares, either for other customers or for its own proprietary account. Customer B places an order with Able for the purchase of 1000 shares of XYZ Co. stock, and pays the purchase price. Able credits B's account with a 1000 share position in XYZ Co. stock, but Able does not itself buy any additional XYZ Co. shares. Able fails, having only 1000 shares to satisfy the claims of A and B. Unless other insolvency law establishes a different distributional rule, A and B would share the 1000 shares held by Able pro rata, without regard to the time that their respective entitlements were established. See Section 8–503(b). Section 8–502 protects entitlement holders, such as A and B, against adverse claimants. In this case, however, the problem that A and B face is not that someone is trying to take away their entitlements, but that the entitlements are not worth what they thought. The only role that Section 8–502 plays in this case is to preclude any assertion that A has some form of claim against B by virtue of the fact that Able's establishment of an entitlement in favor of B diluted A's rights to the limited assets held by Able.

Definitional Cross References:

"Adverse claim". Section 8–102(a)(1).
"Financial asset". Section 8–102(a)(9).
"Notice of adverse claim". Section 8–105.
"Security entitlement". Section 8–102(a)(17).
"Value". Sections 1–201(44) [*unrevised Article 1; see Concordance, p. 22*] & 8–116.

As amended in 1999 and 2022.

§ 8–503. **Property Interest of Entitlement Holder in Financial Asset Held by Securities Intermediary.**

(a)   To the extent necessary for a securities intermediary to satisfy all security entitlements with respect to a particular financial asset, all interests in that financial asset held by the securities intermediary are held by the securities intermediary for the entitlement holders, are not property of the securities intermediary, and are not subject to claims of creditors of the securities intermediary, except as otherwise provided in Section 8–511.

(b)   An entitlement holder's property interest with respect to a particular financial asset under subsection (a) is a pro rata property interest in all interests in that financial asset held by the securities intermediary, without regard to the time the entitlement holder acquired the security entitlement or the time the securities intermediary acquired the interest in that financial asset.

(c)   An entitlement holder's property interest with respect to a particular financial asset under subsection (a) may be enforced against the securities intermediary only by exercise of the entitlement holder's rights under Sections 8–505 through 8–508.

(d)   An entitlement holder's property interest with respect to a particular financial asset under subsection (a) may be enforced against a purchaser of the financial asset or interest therein only if:

(1)   insolvency proceedings have been initiated by or against the securities intermediary;

(2)   the securities intermediary does not have sufficient interests in the financial asset to satisfy the security entitlements of all of its entitlement holders to that financial asset;

(3)   the securities intermediary violated its obligations under Section 8–504 by transferring the financial asset or interest therein to the purchaser; and

(4)   the purchaser is not protected under subsection (e).

The trustee or other liquidator, acting on behalf of all entitlement holders having security entitlements with respect to a particular financial asset, may recover the financial asset, or interest therein, from the purchaser. If the trustee or other liquidator elects not to pursue that right, an entitlement holder whose security entitlement remains unsatisfied has the right to recover its interest in the financial asset from the purchaser.

(e)   An action based on the entitlement holder's property interest with respect to a particular financial asset under subsection (a), whether framed in conversion, replevin, constructive trust, equitable lien, or other theory, may not be asserted against any purchaser of a financial asset or interest therein who gives value, obtains control, and does not act in collusion with the securities intermediary in violating the securities intermediary's obligations under Section 8–504.

Official Comment

1.   This section specifies the sense in which a security entitlement is an interest in the property held by the securities intermediary. It expresses the ordinary understanding that securities that a firm holds for its customers are not general assets of the firm subject to the claims of creditors. Since securities intermediaries generally do not segregate securities in such fashion that one could identify particular securities as the ones held for customers, it would not be realistic for this section to state that "customers' securities" are not subject to creditors' claims. Rather subsection (a) provides that to the extent necessary to satisfy all customer claims, all units of that security held by the firm are held for the entitlement holders, are not property of the securities intermediary, and are not subject to creditors' claims, except as otherwise provided in Section 8–511.

An entitlement holder's property interest under this section is an interest with respect to a specific issue of securities or financial assets. For example, customers of a firm who have positions in XYZ common stock have security entitlements with respect to the XYZ common stock held by the intermediary, while other customers who have positions in ABC common stock have security entitlements with respect to the ABC common stock held by the intermediary.

Subsection (b) makes clear that the property interest described in subsection (a) is an interest held in common by all entitlement holders who have entitlements to a particular security or other financial asset. Temporal factors are irrelevant. One entitlement holder cannot claim that its rights to the assets held by the intermediary are superior to the rights of another entitlement holder by virtue of having acquired those rights before, or after, the other entitlement holder. Nor does it matter whether the intermediary had sufficient assets to satisfy all entitlement holders' claims at one point, but no longer does. Rather, all entitlement holders have a pro rata interest in whatever positions in that financial asset the intermediary holds.

Although this section describes the property interest of entitlement holders in the assets held by the intermediary, it does not necessarily determine how property held by a failed intermediary will be distributed in insolvency proceedings. If the intermediary fails and its affairs are being administered in an insolvency proceeding, the applicable insolvency law governs how the various parties having claims against the firm are treated. For example, the distributional rules for stockbroker liquidation proceedings under the Bankruptcy Code and Securities Investor Protection Act ("SIPA") provide that all customer property is distributed pro rata among all customers in proportion to the dollar value of their total positions, rather than dividing the property on an issue by issue basis. For intermediaries that are not subject to the Bankruptcy Code and SIPA, other insolvency law would determine what distributional rule is applied.

2.   Although this section recognizes that the entitlement holders of a securities intermediary have a property interest in the financial assets held by the intermediary, the incidents of this property interest are established by the rules of Article 8, not by common law property concepts. The traditional Article 8 rules on certificated securities were based on the idea that a paper certificate could be regarded as a nearly complete reification of the underlying right. The rules on transfer and the consequences of wrongful transfer could then be written using the same basic concepts as the rules for physical chattels. A person's claim of ownership of a certificated security is a right to a specific identifiable physical object, and that right can be asserted against any person who ends up in possession of that physical certificate, unless cut off by the rules protecting purchasers for value without notice. Those concepts do not work for the indirect holding system. A security entitlement is not a claim to a specific identifiable thing; it is a package of rights and interests that a person has against the person's securities intermediary and the property held by the intermediary. The idea that discrete objects might be traced through the hands of different persons has no place in the Revised Article 8 rules for the indirect holding system. The fundamental principles of the indirect holding system rules are that an entitlement holder's own intermediary has the obligation to see to it that the entitlement holder receives all of the economic and corporate rights that comprise the financial asset, and that the entitlement holder can look only to that intermediary for performance of the obligations. The entitlement holder cannot assert rights directly against other persons, such as other intermediaries through whom the intermediary holds the positions, or third parties to whom the intermediary may have wrongfully transferred interests, except in extremely unusual circumstances where the third party was itself a participant in the wrongdoing. Subsections (c) through (e) reflect these fundamental principles.

Subsection (c) provides that an entitlement holder's property interest can be enforced against the intermediary only by exercise of the entitlement holder's rights under Sections 8–505 through 8–508. These are the provisions that set out the duty of an intermediary to see to it that the entitlement holder receives all of the economic and corporate rights that comprise the security. If the intermediary is in insolvency proceedings and can no longer perform in accordance with the ordinary Part 5 rules, the applicable insolvency law will determine how the intermediary's assets are to be distributed.

Subsections (d) and (e) specify the limited circumstances in which an entitlement holder's property interest can be asserted against a third person to whom the intermediary transferred a financial asset that was subject to the entitlement holder's claim when held by the intermediary. Subsection (d) provides that the property interest of entitlement holders cannot be asserted against any transferee except in the circumstances therein specified. So long as the intermediary is solvent, the entitlement holders must look to the intermediary to satisfy their claims. If the intermediary does not hold financial assets corresponding to the entitlement holders' claims, the intermediary has the duty to acquire them. See Section 8–504. Thus, paragraphs (1), (2), and (3) of subsection (d) specify that the only occasion in which the entitlement holders can pursue transferees is when the intermediary is unable to perform its obligation, and the transfer to the transferee was a violation of those obligations. Even in that case, a transferee who gave value and obtained control is protected by virtue of the rule in subsection (e), unless the transferee acted in collusion with the intermediary.

Subsections (d) and (e) have the effect of protecting transferees from an intermediary against adverse claims arising out of assertions by the intermediary's entitlement holders that the intermediary acted wrongfully in transferring the financial assets. These rules, however, operate in a slightly different fashion than traditional adverse claim cut-off rules. Rather than specifying that a certain class of transferee takes free from all claims, subsections (d) and (e) specify the circumstances in which this particular form of claim can be asserted against a transferee. Revised Article 8 also contains general adverse claim cut-off rules for the indirect holding system. See Sections 8–502 and 8–510. The rule of subsections (d) and (e) takes precedence over the general cut-off rules of those sections, because Section 8–503 itself defines and sets limits on the assertion of the property interest of entitlement holders. Thus, the question whether entitlement holders' property interest can be asserted as an adverse claim against a transferee from the intermediary is governed by the collusion test of Section 8–503(e), rather than by the "without notice" test of Sections 8–502 and 8–510.

3.   The limitations that subsections (c) through (e) place on the ability of customers of a failed intermediary to recover securities or other financial assets from transferees are consistent with the fundamental policies of investor protection that underlie this Article and other bodies of law governing the securities business. The commercial law rules for the securities holding and transfer system must be assessed from the forward-looking perspective of their impact on the vast number of transactions in which no wrongful conduct occurred or will occur, rather than from the *post hoc* perspective of what rule might be most advantageous to a particular class of persons in litigation that might arise out of the occasional case in which someone has acted wrongfully. Although one can devise hypothetical scenarios where particular customers might find it advantageous to be able to assert rights against someone other than the customers' own intermediary, commercial law rules that permitted customers to do so would impair rather than promote the interest of investors and the safe and efficient operation of the clearance and settlement system. Suppose, for example, that Intermediary A transfers securities to B, that Intermediary A acted wrongfully as against its customers in so doing, and that after the transaction Intermediary A did not have sufficient securities to satisfy its obligations to its entitlement holders. Viewed solely from the standpoint of the customers of Intermediary A, it would seem that permitting the property to be recovered from B, would be good for investors. That, however, is not the case. B may itself be an intermediary with its own customers, or may be some other institution through which individuals invest, such as a pension fund or investment company. There is no reason to think that rules permitting customers of an intermediary to trace and recover securities that their intermediary wrongfully transferred work to the advantage of investors in general. To the contrary, application of such rules would often merely shift losses from one set of investors to another. The uncertainties that would result from rules permitting such recoveries would work to the disadvantage of all participants in the securities markets.

The use of the collusion test in Section 8–503(e) furthers the interests of investors generally in the sound and efficient operation of the securities holding and settlement system. The effect of the choice of this standard is that customers of a failed intermediary must show that the transferee from whom they seek to recover was affirmatively engaged in wrongful conduct, rather than casting on the transferee any burden of showing that the transferee had no awareness of wrongful conduct by the failed intermediary. The rule of Section 8–503(e) is based on the long-standing policy that it is undesirable to impose upon purchasers of securities any duty to investigate whether their sellers may be acting wrongfully.

Rather than imposing duties to investigate, the general policy of the commercial law of the securities holding and transfer system has been to eliminate legal rules that might induce participants to conduct investigations of the authority of persons transferring securities on behalf of others for fear that they might be held liable for participating in a wrongful transfer. The rules in Part 4 of Article 8 concerning transfers by fiduciaries provide a good example. Under *Lowry v. Commercial & Farmers' Bank,* 15 F.Cas. 1040 (C.C.D.Md. 1848) (No. 8581), an issuer could be held liable for wrongful transfer if it registered transfer of securities by a fiduciary under circumstances where it had any reason to believe that the fiduciary may have been acting improperly. In one sense that seems to be advantageous for beneficiaries who might be harmed by wrongful conduct by fiduciaries. The consequence of the *Lowry* rule, however, was that in order to protect against risk of such liability, issuers developed the practice of requiring extensive documentation for fiduciary stock transfers, making such transfers cumbersome and time consuming. Accordingly, the rules in Part 4 of Article 8, and in the prior fiduciary transfer statutes, were designed to discourage transfer agents from conducting investigations into the rightfulness of transfers by fiduciaries.

The rules of Revised Article 8 implement for the indirect holding system the same policies that the rules on protected purchasers and registration of transfer adopt for the direct holding system. A securities intermediary is, by definition, a person who is holding securities on behalf of other persons. There is nothing unusual or suspicious about a transaction in which a securities intermediary sells securities that it was holding for its customers. That is exactly what securities intermediaries are in business to do. The interests of customers of securities intermediaries would not be served by a rule that required counterparties to transfers from securities intermediaries to investigate whether the intermediary was acting wrongfully against its customers. Quite the contrary, such a rule would impair the ability of securities intermediaries to perform the function that customers want.

The rules of Section 8–503(c) through (e) apply to transferees generally, including pledgees. The reasons for treating pledgees in the same fashion as other transferees are discussed in the Comments to Section 8–511. The statement in subsection (a) that an intermediary holds financial assets for customers and not as its own property does not, of course, mean that the intermediary lacks power to transfer the financial assets to others. For example, although Article 9 provides that for a security interest to attach the debtor must either have "rights" in the collateral or the power to transfer "rights" in the collateral to a secured party, see Section 9–203, the fact that an intermediary is holding a financial asset in a form that permits ready transfer means that it has such rights, even if the intermediary is acting wrongfully against its entitlement holders in granting the security interest. The question whether the secured party takes subject to the entitlement holder's claim in such a case is governed by Section 8–511, which is an application to secured transactions of the general principles expressed in subsections (d) and (e) of this section.

Definitional Cross References:

"Control". Section 8–106.

"Entitlement holder". Section 8–102(a)(7).

"Financial asset". Section 8–102(a)(9).

"Insolvency proceedings". Section 1–201(22) [*unrevised Article 1; see Concordance, p. 22*].

"Purchaser". Sections 1–201(33) [*unrevised Article 1; see Concordance, p. 22*] & 8–116.

"Securities intermediary". Section 8–102(a)(14).

"Security entitlement". Section 8–102(a)(17).

"Value". Sections 1–201(44) [*unrevised Article 1; see Concordance, p. 22*] & 8–116.

§ 8–504. Duty of Securities Intermediary to Maintain Financial Asset.

(a) A securities intermediary shall promptly obtain and thereafter maintain a financial asset in a quantity corresponding to the aggregate of all security entitlements it has established in favor of its entitlement holders with respect to that financial asset. The securities intermediary may maintain those financial assets directly or through one or more other securities intermediaries.

(b) Except to the extent otherwise agreed by its entitlement holder, a securities intermediary may not grant any security interests in a financial asset it is obligated to maintain pursuant to subsection (a).

(c) A securities intermediary satisfies the duty in subsection (a) if:

(1) the securities intermediary acts with respect to the duty as agreed upon by the entitlement holder and the securities intermediary; or

(2) in the absence of agreement, the securities intermediary exercises due care in accordance with reasonable commercial standards to obtain and maintain the financial asset.

(d) This section does not apply to a clearing corporation that is itself the obligor of an option or similar obligation to which its entitlement holders have security entitlements.

Official Comment

1. This section expresses one of the core elements of the relationships for which the Part 5 rules were designed, to wit, that a securities intermediary undertakes to hold financial assets corresponding to the security entitlements of its entitlement holders. The locution "shall promptly obtain and shall thereafter maintain" is taken from the corresponding regulation under federal securities law, 17 C.F.R. § 240.15c3–3. This section recognizes the reality that as the securities business is conducted today, it is not possible to identify particular securities as belonging to customers as distinguished from other particular securities that are the firm's own property. Securities firms typically keep all securities in fungible form, and may maintain their inventory of a particular security in various locations and forms, including physical securities held in vaults or in transit to transfer agents, and book entry positions at one or more clearing corporations. Accordingly, this section states that a securities intermediary shall maintain a quantity of financial assets corresponding to the aggregate of all security entitlements it has established. The last sentence of subsection (a) provides explicitly that the securities intermediary may hold directly or indirectly. That point is implicit in the use of the term "financial asset," inasmuch as Section 8–102(a)(9) provides that the term "financial asset" may refer either to the underlying asset or the means by which it is held, including both security certificates and security entitlements.

2. Subsection (b) states explicitly a point that is implicit in the notion that a securities intermediary must maintain financial assets corresponding to the security entitlements of its entitlement holders, to wit, that it is wrongful for a securities intermediary to grant security interests in positions that it needs to satisfy customers' claims, except as authorized by the customers. This statement does not determine the rights of a secured party to

whom a securities intermediary wrongfully grants a security interest; that issue is governed by Sections 8–503 and 8–511.

Margin accounts are common examples of arrangements in which an entitlement holder authorizes the securities intermediary to grant security interests in the positions held for the entitlement holder. Securities firms commonly obtain the funds needed to provide margin loans to their customers by "rehypothecating" the customers' securities. In order to facilitate rehypothecation, agreements between margin customers and their brokers commonly authorize the broker to commingle securities of all margin customers for rehypothecation to the lender who provides the financing. Brokers commonly rehypothecate customer securities having a value somewhat greater than the amount of the loan made to the customer, since the lenders who provide the necessary financing to the broker need some cushion of protection against the risk of decline in the value of the rehypothecated securities. The extent and manner in which a firm may rehypothecate customers' securities are determined by the agreement between the intermediary and the entitlement holder and by applicable regulatory law. Current regulations under the federal securities laws require that brokers obtain the explicit consent of customers before pledging customer securities or commingling different customers' securities for pledge. Federal regulations also limit the extent to which a broker may rehypothecate customer securities to 110% of the aggregate amount of the borrowings of all customers.

3. The statement in this section that an intermediary must obtain and maintain financial assets corresponding to the aggregate of all security entitlements it has established is intended only to capture the general point that one of the key elements that distinguishes securities accounts from other relationships, such as deposit accounts, is that the intermediary undertakes to maintain a direct correspondence between the positions it holds and the claims of its customers. This section is not intended as a detailed specification of precisely how the intermediary is to perform this duty, nor whether there may be special circumstances in which an intermediary's general duty is excused. Accordingly, the general statement of the duties of a securities intermediary in this and the following sections is supplemented by two other provisions. First, each of Sections 8–504 through 8–508 contains an "agreement/due care" provision. Second, Section 8–509 sets out general qualifications on the duties stated in these sections, including the important point that compliance with corresponding regulatory provisions constitutes compliance with the Article 8 duties.

4. The "agreement/due care" provision in subsection (c) of this section is necessary to provide sufficient flexibility to accommodate the general duty stated in subsection (a) to the wide variety of circumstances that may be encountered in the modern securities holding system. For the most common forms of publicly traded securities, the modern depository-based indirect holding system has made the likelihood of an actual loss of securities remote, though correctable errors in accounting or temporary interruptions of data processing facilities may occur. Indeed, one of the reasons for the evolution of book-entry systems is to eliminate the risk of loss or destruction of physical certificates. There are, however, some forms of securities and other financial assets which must still be held in physical certificated form, with the attendant risk of loss or destruction. Risk of loss or delay may be a more significant consideration in connection with foreign securities. An American securities intermediary may well be willing to hold a foreign security in a securities account for its customer, but the intermediary may have relatively little choice of or control over foreign intermediaries through which the security must in turn be held. Accordingly, it is common for American securities intermediaries to disclaim responsibility for custodial risk of holding through foreign intermediaries.

Subsection (c)(1) provides that a securities intermediary satisfies the duty stated in subsection (a) if the intermediary acts with respect to that duty in accordance with the agreement between the intermediary and the entitlement holder. Subsection (c)(2) provides that if there is no agreement on the matter, the intermediary satisfies the subsection (a) duty if the intermediary exercises due care in accordance with reasonable commercial standards to obtain and maintain the financial asset in question. This formulation does not state that the intermediary has a universally applicable statutory duty of due care. Section 1–102(3) [*unrevised Article 1; see Concordance, p. 22*] provides that statutory duties of due care cannot be disclaimed by agreement, but the "agreement/due care" formula contemplates that there may be particular circumstances where the parties do not wish to create a specific duty of due care, for example, with respect to foreign securities. Under subsection (c)(1), compliance with the agreement constitutes satisfaction of the subsection (a) duty, whether or not the agreement provides that the intermediary will exercise due care.

In each of the sections where the "agreement/due care" formula is used, it provides that entering into an agreement and performing in accordance with that agreement is a method by which the securities intermediary may satisfy the statutory duty stated in that section. Accordingly, the general obligation of good faith performance of statutory and contract duties, see Sections 1–203 [*unrevised Article 1; see Concordance, p. 22*] and 8–102(a)(10), would apply to such an agreement. It would not be consistent with the obligation of good faith performance for an agreement to purport to establish the usual sort of arrangement between an intermediary and entitlement holder, yet disclaim altogether one of the basic elements that define that relationship. For example, an agreement stating that an intermediary assumes no responsibilities whatsoever for the safekeeping any of the entitlement holder's securities positions would not be consistent with good faith performance of the intermediary's duty to obtain and maintain financial assets corresponding to the entitlement holder's security entitlements.

To the extent that no agreement under subsection (c)(1) has specified the details of the intermediary's performance of the subsection (a) duty, subsection (c)(2) provides that the intermediary satisfies that duty if it exercises due care in accordance with reasonable commercial standards. The duty of care includes both care in the intermediary's own operations and care in the selection of other intermediaries through whom the intermediary holds the assets in question. The statement of the obligation of due care is meant to incorporate the principles of the common law under which the specific actions or precautions necessary to meet the obligation of care are determined by such factors as the nature and value of the property, the customs and practices of the business, and the like.

5.　　This section necessarily states the duty of a securities intermediary to obtain and maintain financial assets only at the very general and abstract level. For the most part, these matters are specified in great detail by regulatory law. Broker-dealers registered under the federal securities laws are subject to detailed regulation concerning the safeguarding of customer securities. See 17 C.F.R. § 240.15c3–3. Section 8–509(a) provides explicitly that if a securities intermediary complies with such regulatory law, that constitutes compliance with Section 8–503. In certain circumstances, these rules permit a firm to be in a position where it temporarily lacks a sufficient quantity of financial assets to satisfy all customer claims. For example, if another firm has failed to make a delivery to the firm in settlement of a trade, the firm is permitted a certain period of time to clear up the problem before it is obligated to obtain the necessary securities from some other source.

6.　　Subsection (d) is intended to recognize that there are some circumstances, where the duty to maintain a sufficient quantity of financial assets does not apply because the intermediary is not holding anything on behalf of others. For example, the Options Clearing Corporation is treated as a "securities intermediary" under this Article, although it does not itself hold options on behalf of its participants. Rather, it becomes the issuer of the options, by virtue of guaranteeing the obligations of participants in the clearing corporation who have written or purchased the options cleared through it. See Section 8–103(e). Accordingly, the general duty of an intermediary under subsection (a) does not apply, nor would other provisions of Part 5 that depend upon the existence of a requirement that the securities intermediary hold financial assets, such as Sections 8–503 and 8–508.

Definitional Cross References:

"Agreement". Section 1–201(3) [*unrevised Article 1; see Concordance, p. 22*].
"Clearing corporation". Section 8–102(a)(5).
"Entitlement holder". Section 8–102(a)(7).
"Financial asset". Section 8–102(a)(9).
"Securities intermediary". Section 8–102(a)(14).
"Security entitlement". Section 8–102(a)(17).

§ 8–505.　　Duty of Securities Intermediary with Respect to Payments and Distributions.

(a)　　A securities intermediary shall take action to obtain a payment or distribution made by the issuer of a financial asset. A securities intermediary satisfies the duty if:

(1)　the securities intermediary acts with respect to the duty as agreed upon by the entitlement holder and the securities intermediary; or

(2)　in the absence of agreement, the securities intermediary exercises due care in accordance with reasonable commercial standards to attempt to obtain the payment or distribution.

(b)　　A securities intermediary is obligated to its entitlement holder for a payment or distribution made by the issuer of a financial asset if the payment or distribution is received by the securities intermediary.

Official Comment

1.　　One of the core elements of the securities account relationships for which the Part 5 rules were designed is that the securities intermediary passes through to the entitlement holders the economic benefit of ownership of the financial asset, such as payments and distributions made by the issuer of the financial asset. Subsection (a) expresses the ordinary understanding that a securities intermediary will take appropriate action to see to it that any payments or distributions made by the issuer are received. One of the main reasons that investors make use of securities intermediaries is to obtain the services of a professional in performing the record-keeping and other functions necessary to ensure that payments and other distributions are received.

2. Subsection (a) incorporates the same "agreement/due care" formula as the other provisions of Part 5 dealing with the duties of a securities intermediary. See Comment 4 to Section 8–504. This formulation permits the parties to specify by agreement what action, if any, the intermediary is to take with respect to the duty to obtain payments and distributions. In the absence of specification by agreement, the intermediary satisfies the duty if the intermediary exercises due care in accordance with reasonable commercial standards. The provisions of Section 8–509 also apply to the Section 8–505 duty, so that compliance with applicable regulatory requirements constitutes compliance with the Section 8–505 duty.

3. Subsection (b) provides that a securities intermediary is obligated to its entitlement holder for those payments or distributions made by the issuer that are in fact received by the intermediary. It does not deal with the details of the time and manner of payment. Moreover, as with any other monetary obligation, the obligation to pay may be subject to other rights of the obligor, by way of set-off counterclaim or the like. Section 8–509(c) makes this point explicit.

4. This section applies to payments and distributions made by an issuer of a financial asset credited to a securities account. If a distribution is made to, or made available to, a securities intermediary on account of a financial asset as to which there is no issuer, the duties, if any, of the securities intermediary with respect to the distribution are subject to the agreement of the intermediary and the entitlement holder. However, in the absence of an agreement, this section may be applied by analogy in an appropriate case. If the securities intermediary is a secured party, Section 9–207(c) applies.

Definitional Cross References:

"Agreement". Section 1–201(3) [*unrevised Article 1; see Concordance, p. 22*].
"Entitlement holder". Section 8–102(a)(7).
"Financial asset". Section 8–102(a)(9).
"Securities intermediary". Section 8–102(a)(14).
"Security entitlement". Section 8–102(a)(17).

As amended in 2022.

§ 8–506. Duty of Securities Intermediary to Exercise Rights as Directed by Entitlement Holder.

A securities intermediary shall exercise rights with respect to a financial asset if directed to do so by an entitlement holder. A securities intermediary satisfies the duty if:

(1) the securities intermediary acts with respect to the duty as agreed upon by the entitlement holder and the securities intermediary; or

(2) in the absence of agreement, the securities intermediary either places the entitlement holder in a position to exercise the rights directly or exercises due care in accordance with reasonable commercial standards to follow the direction of the entitlement holder.

Official Comment

1. Another of the core elements of the securities account relationships for which the Part 5 rules were designed is that although the intermediary may, by virtue of the structure of the indirect holding system, be the party who has the power to exercise the corporate and other rights that come from holding the security, the intermediary exercises these powers as representative of the entitlement holder rather than at its own discretion. This characteristic is one of the things that distinguishes a securities account from other arrangements where one person holds securities "on behalf of" another, such as the relationship between a mutual fund and its shareholders or a trustee and its beneficiary.

2. The fact that the intermediary exercises the rights of security holding as representative of the entitlement holder does not, of course, preclude the entitlement holder from conferring discretionary authority upon the intermediary. Arrangements are not uncommon in which investors do not wish to have their intermediaries forward proxy materials or other information. Thus, this section provides that the intermediary shall exercise corporate and other rights "if directed to do so" by the entitlement holder. Moreover, as with the other Part 5 duties, the "agreement/due care" formulation is used in stating how the intermediary is to perform

this duty. This section also provides that the intermediary satisfies the duty if it places the entitlement holder in a position to exercise the rights directly. This is to take account of the fact that some of the rights attendant upon ownership of the security, such as rights to bring derivative and other litigation, are far removed from the matters that intermediaries are expected to perform.

3.   This section, and the two that follow, deal with the aspects of securities holding that are related to investment decisions. For example, one of the rights of holding a particular security that would fall within the purview of this section would be the right to exercise a conversion right for a convertible security. It is quite common for investors to confer discretionary authority upon another person, such as an investment adviser, with respect to these rights and other investment decisions. Because this section, and the other sections of Part 5, all specify that a securities intermediary satisfies the Part 5 duties if it acts in accordance with the entitlement holder's agreement, there is no inconsistency between the statement of duties of a securities intermediary and these common arrangements.

4.   Section 8–509 also applies to the Section 8–506 duty, so that compliance with applicable regulatory requirements constitutes compliance with this duty. This is quite important in this context, since the federal securities laws establish a comprehensive system of regulation of the distribution of proxy materials and exercise of voting rights with respect to securities held through brokers and other intermediaries. By virtue of Section 8–509(a), compliance with such regulatory requirement constitutes compliance with the Section 8–506 duty.

Definitional Cross References:

"Agreement". Section 1–201(3) [*unrevised Article 1; see Concordance, p. 22*].
"Entitlement holder". Section 8–102(a)(7).
"Financial asset". Section 8–102(a)(9).
"Securities intermediary". Section 8–102(a)(14).
"Security entitlement". Section 8–102(a)(17).

§ 8–507.   Duty of Securities Intermediary to Comply with Entitlement Order.

(a)   A securities intermediary shall comply with an entitlement order if the entitlement order is originated by the appropriate person, the securities intermediary has had reasonable opportunity to assure itself that the entitlement order is genuine and authorized, and the securities intermediary has had reasonable opportunity to comply with the entitlement order. A securities intermediary satisfies the duty if:

(1)   the securities intermediary acts with respect to the duty as agreed upon by the entitlement holder and the securities intermediary; or

(2)   in the absence of agreement, the securities intermediary exercises due care in accordance with reasonable commercial standards to comply with the entitlement order.

(b)   If a securities intermediary transfers a financial asset pursuant to an ineffective entitlement order, the securities intermediary shall reestablish a security entitlement in favor of the person entitled to it, and pay or credit any payments or distributions that the person did not receive as a result of the wrongful transfer. If the securities intermediary does not reestablish a security entitlement, the securities intermediary is liable to the entitlement holder for damages.

Official Comment

1.   Subsection (a) of this section states another aspect of duties of securities intermediaries that make up security entitlements—the securities intermediary's duty to comply with entitlement orders. One of the main reasons for holding securities through securities intermediaries is to enable rapid transfer in settlement of trades. Thus the right to have one's orders for disposition of the security entitlement honored is an inherent part of the relationship. Subsection (b) states the correlative liability of a securities intermediary for transferring a financial asset from an entitlement holder's account pursuant to an entitlement order that was not effective.

2.   The duty to comply with entitlement orders is subject to several qualifications. The intermediary has a duty only with respect to an entitlement order that is in fact originated by the appropriate person. Moreover, the intermediary has a duty only if it has had reasonable opportunity to assure itself that the order is genuine and authorized, and reasonable opportunity to comply with the order. The same "agreement/due care" formula is used in this section as in the other Part 5 sections on the duties of intermediaries, and the rules of Section 8–509 apply to the Section 8–507 duty.

3.   Appropriate person is defined in Section 8–107. In the usual case, the appropriate person is the entitlement holder, see Section 8–107(a)(3). Entitlement holder is defined in Section 8–102(a)(7) as the person "identified in the records of a securities intermediary as the person having a security entitlement." Thus, the general rule is that an intermediary's duty with respect to entitlement orders runs only to the person with whom the intermediary has established a relationship. One of the basic principles of the indirect holding system is that securities intermediaries owe duties only to their own customers. See also Section 8–115. The only situation in which a securities intermediary has a duty to comply with entitlement orders originated by a person other than the person with whom the intermediary established a relationship is covered by Section 8–107(a)(4) and (a)(5), which provide that the term "appropriate person" includes the successor or personal representative of a decedent, or the custodian or guardian of a person who lacks capacity. If the entitlement holder is competent, another person does not fall within the defined term "appropriate person" merely by virtue of having power to act as an agent for the entitlement holder. Thus, an intermediary is not required to determine at its peril whether a person who purports to be authorized to act for an entitlement holder is in fact authorized to do so. If an entitlement holder wishes to be able to act through agents, the entitlement holder can establish appropriate arrangements in advance with the securities intermediary.

One important application of this principle is that if an entitlement holder grants a security interest in its security entitlements to a third-party lender, the intermediary owes no duties to the secured party, unless the intermediary has entered into a "control" agreement in which it agrees to act on entitlement orders originated by the secured party. See Section 8–106. Even though the security agreement or some other document may give the secured party authority to act as agent for the debtor, that would not make the secured party an "appropriate person" to whom the security intermediary owes duties. If the entitlement holder and securities intermediary have agreed to such a control arrangement, then the intermediary's action in following instructions from the secured party would satisfy the subsection (a) duty. Although an agent, such as the secured party in this example, is not an "appropriate person," an entitlement order is "effective" if originated by an authorized person. See Section 8–107(a) and (b). Moreover, Section 8–507(a) provides that the intermediary satisfies its duty if it acts in accordance with the entitlement holder's agreement.

4.   Subsection (b) provides that an intermediary is liable for a wrongful transfer if the entitlement order was "ineffective." Section 8–107 specifies whether an entitlement order is effective. An "effective entitlement order" is different from an "entitlement order originated by an appropriate person." An entitlement order is effective under Section 8–107(b) if it is made by the appropriate person, or by a person who has power to act for the appropriate person under the law of agency, or if the appropriate person has ratified the entitlement order or is precluded from denying its effectiveness. Thus, although a securities intermediary does not have a duty to act on an entitlement order originated by the entitlement holder's agent, the intermediary is not liable for wrongful transfer if it does so.

Subsection (b), together with Section 8–107, has the effect of leaving to other law most of the questions of the sort dealt with by Article 4A for wire transfers of funds, such as allocation between the securities intermediary and the entitlement holder of the risk of fraudulent entitlement orders.

5.   The term entitlement order does not cover all directions that a customer might give a broker concerning securities held through the broker. Article 8 is not a codification of all of the law of customers and stockbrokers. Article 8 deals with the settlement of securities trades, not the trades. The term entitlement order does not refer to instructions to a broker to make trades, that is, enter into contracts for the purchase or sale of securities. Rather, the entitlement order is the mechanism of transfer for securities held through intermediaries, just as indorsements and instructions are the mechanism for securities held directly. In the ordinary case the customer's direction to the broker to deliver the securities at settlement is implicit in the customer's instruction to the broker to sell. The distinction is, however, significant in that this section has no application to the relationship between the customer and broker with respect to the trade itself. For example, assertions by a customer that it was damaged by a broker's failure to execute a trading order sufficiently rapidly or in the proper manner are not governed by this Article.

Definitional Cross References:

"Agreement". Section 1–201(3) [*unrevised Article 1; see Concordance, p. 22*].
"Appropriate person". Section 8–107.
"Effective". Section 8–107.
"Entitlement holder". Section 8–102(a)(7).
"Entitlement order". Section 8–102(a)(8).
"Financial asset". Section 8–102(a)(9).

"Securities intermediary". Section 8–102(a)(14).

"Security entitlement". Section 8–102(a)(17).

§ 8–508. Duty of Securities Intermediary to Change Entitlement Holder's Position to Other Form of Security Holding.

A securities intermediary shall act at the direction of an entitlement holder to change a security entitlement into another available form of holding for which the entitlement holder is eligible, or to cause the financial asset to be transferred to a securities account of the entitlement holder with another securities intermediary. A securities intermediary satisfies the duty if:

(1) the securities intermediary acts as agreed upon by the entitlement holder and the securities intermediary; or

(2) in the absence of agreement, the securities intermediary exercises due care in accordance with reasonable commercial standards to follow the direction of the entitlement holder.

Official Comment

1. This section states another aspect of the duties of securities intermediaries that make up security entitlements—the obligation of the securities intermediary to change an entitlement holder's position into any other form of holding for which the entitlement holder is eligible or to transfer the entitlement holder's position to an account at another intermediary. This section does not state unconditionally that the securities intermediary is obligated to turn over a certificate to the customer or to cause the customer to be registered on the books of the issuer, because the customer may not be eligible to hold the security directly. For example, municipal bonds are now commonly issued in "book-entry only" form, in which the only entity that the issuer will register on its own books is a depository.

If security certificates in registered form are issued for the security, and individuals are eligible to have the security registered in their own name, the entitlement holder can request that the intermediary deliver or cause to be delivered to the entitlement holder a certificate registered in the name of the entitlement holder or a certificate indorsed in blank or specially indorsed to the entitlement holder. If security certificates in bearer form are issued for the security, the entitlement holder can request that the intermediary deliver or cause to be delivered a certificate in bearer form. If the security can be held by individuals directly in uncertificated form, the entitlement holder can request that the security be registered in its name. The specification of this duty does not determine the pricing terms of the agreement in which the duty arises.

2. The same "agreement/due care" formula is used in this section as in the other Part 5 sections on the duties of intermediaries. So too, the rules of Section 8–509 apply to the Section 8–508 duty.

Definitional Cross References:

"Agreement". Section 1–201(3) [*unrevised Article 1; see Concordance, p. 22*].

"Entitlement holder". Section 8–102(a)(7).

"Financial asset". Section 8–102(a)(9).

"Securities intermediary". Section 8–102(a)(14).

"Security entitlement". Section 8–102(a)(17).

§ 8–509. Specification of Duties of Securities Intermediary by Other Statute or Regulation; Manner of Performance of Duties of Securities Intermediary and Exercise of Rights of Entitlement Holder.

(a) If the substance of a duty imposed upon a securities intermediary by Sections 8–504 through 8–508 is the subject of other statute, regulation, or rule, compliance with that statute, regulation, or rule satisfies the duty.

(b) To the extent that specific standards for the performance of the duties of a securities intermediary or the exercise of the rights of an entitlement holder are not specified by other statute, regulation, or rule or by agreement between the securities intermediary and entitlement holder, the securities intermediary shall perform its duties and the entitlement holder shall exercise its rights in a commercially reasonable manner.

(c)   The obligation of a securities intermediary to perform the duties imposed by Sections 8–504 through 8–508 is subject to:

(1)   rights of the securities intermediary arising out of a security interest under a security agreement with the entitlement holder or otherwise; and

(2)   rights of the securities intermediary under other law, regulation, rule, or agreement to withhold performance of its duties as a result of unfulfilled obligations of the entitlement holder to the securities intermediary.

(d)   Sections 8–504 through 8–508 do not require a securities intermediary to take any action that is prohibited by other statute, regulation, or rule.

Official Comment

This Article is not a comprehensive statement of the law governing the relationship between broker-dealers or other securities intermediaries and their customers. Most of the law governing that relationship is the common law of contract and agency, supplemented or supplanted by regulatory law. This Article deals only with the most basic commercial/property law principles governing the relationship. Although Sections 8–504 through 8–508 specify certain duties of securities intermediaries to entitlement holders, the point of these sections is to identify what it means to have a security entitlement, not to specify the details of performance of these duties.

For many intermediaries, regulatory law specifies in great detail the intermediary's obligations on such matters as safekeeping of customer property, distribution of proxy materials, and the like. To avoid any conflict between the general statement of duties in this Article and the specific statement of intermediaries' obligations in such regulatory schemes, subsection (a) provides that compliance with applicable regulation constitutes compliance with the duties specified in Sections 8–504 through 8–508.

Definitional Cross References:

"Agreement". Section 1–201(3) [*unrevised Article 1; see Concordance, p. 22*].
"Entitlement holder". Section 8–102(a)(7).
"Securities intermediary". Section 8–102(a)(14).
"Security agreement". Section 9–102(a)(73).
"Security interest". Section 1–201(37) [*unrevised Article 1; see Concordance, p. 22*].

§ 8–510.   Rights of Purchaser of Security Entitlement from Entitlement Holder.

(a)   In a case not covered by the priority rules in Article 9 or the rules stated in subsection (c), an action based on an adverse claim to a financial asset or security entitlement, whether framed in conversion, replevin, constructive trust, equitable lien, or other theory, may not be asserted against a person who purchases a security entitlement, or an interest therein, from an entitlement holder if the purchaser gives value, does not have notice of the adverse claim, and obtains control.

(b)   If an adverse claim could not have been asserted against an entitlement holder under Section 8–502, the adverse claim cannot be asserted against a person who purchases a security entitlement, or an interest therein, from the entitlement holder.

(c)   In a case not covered by the priority rules in Article 9, a purchaser for value of a security entitlement, or an interest therein, who obtains control has priority over a purchaser of a security entitlement, or an interest therein, who does not obtain control. Except as otherwise provided in subsection (d), purchasers who have control rank according to priority in time of:

(1)   the purchaser's becoming the person for whom the securities account, in which the security entitlement is carried, is maintained, if the purchaser obtained control under Section 8–106(d)(1);

(2)   the securities intermediary's agreement to comply with the purchaser's entitlement orders with respect to security entitlements carried or to be carried in the securities account in which the security entitlement is carried, if the purchaser obtained control under Section 8–106(d)(2); or

(3)   if the purchaser obtained control through another person under Section 8–106(d)(3), the time on which priority would be based under this subsection if the other person were the secured party.

(d)   A securities intermediary as purchaser has priority over a conflicting purchaser who has control unless otherwise agreed by the securities intermediary.

As amended in 1999.

Official Comment

1.   This section specifies certain rules concerning the rights of persons who purchase interests in security entitlements from entitlement holders. The rules of this section are provided to take account of cases where the purchaser's rights are derivative from the rights of another person who is and continues to be the entitlement holder.

2.   Subsection (a) provides that no adverse claim can be asserted against a purchaser of an interest in a security entitlement if the purchaser gives value, obtains control, and does not have notice of the adverse claim. The primary purpose of this rule is to give adverse claim protection to persons who take security interests in security entitlements and obtain control, but do not themselves become entitlement holders.

The following examples illustrate subsection (a):

Example 1.   X steals a certificated bearer bond from Owner. X delivers the certificate to Able & Co. for credit to X's securities account. Later, X borrows from Bank and grants bank a security interest in the security entitlement. Bank obtains control under Section 8–106(d)(2) by virtue of an agreement in which Able agrees to comply with entitlement orders originated by Bank. X absconds.

Example 2.   Same facts as in Example 1, except that Bank does not obtain a control agreement. Instead, Bank perfects by filing a financing statement.

In both of these examples, when X deposited the bonds X acquired a security entitlement under Section 8–501. Under other law, Owner may be able to have a constructive trust imposed on the security entitlement as the traceable product of the bonds that X misappropriated. X granted a security interest in that entitlement to Bank. Bank was a purchaser of an interest in the security entitlement from X. In Example 1, although Bank was not a person who acquired a security entitlement from the intermediary, Bank did obtain control. If Bank did not have notice of Owner's claim, Section 8–510(a) precludes Owner from asserting an adverse claim against Bank. In Example 2, Bank had a perfected security interest, but did not obtain control. Accordingly, Section 8–510(a) does not preclude Owner from asserting its adverse claim against Bank.

3.   Subsection (b) applies to the indirect holding system a limited version of the "shelter principle." The following example illustrates the relatively limited class of cases for which it may be needed:

Example 3.   Thief steals a certificated bearer bond from Owner. Thief delivers the certificate to Able & Co. for credit to Thief's securities account. Able forwards the certificate to a clearing corporation for credit to Able's account. Later Thief instructs Able to sell the positions in the bonds. Able sells to Baker & Co., acting as broker for Buyer. The trade is settled by book-entries in the accounts of Able and Baker at the clearing corporation, and in the accounts of Thief and Buyer at Able and Baker respectively. Owner may be able to reconstruct the trade records to show that settlement occurred in such fashion that the "same bonds" that were carried in Thief's account at Able are traceable into Buyer's account at Baker. Buyer later decides to donate the bonds to Alma Mater University and executes an assignment of its rights as entitlement holder to Alma Mater.

Buyer had a position in the bonds, which Buyer held in the form of a security entitlement against Baker. Buyer then made a gift of the position to Alma Mater. Although Alma Mater is a purchaser, Section 1–201(33) 1–201(b)(30), it did not give value. Thus, Alma Mater is a person who purchased a security entitlement, or an interest therein, from an entitlement holder (Buyer). Buyer was protected against Owner's adverse claim by the Section 8–502 rule. Thus, by virtue of Section 8–510(b), Owner is also precluded from asserting an adverse claim against Alma Mater.

4.   Subsection (c) specifies a priority rule for cases where an entitlement holder transfers conflicting interests in the same security entitlement to different purchasers. It follows the same principle as the Article 9 priority rule for investment property, that is, control trumps non-control. Indeed, the most significant category of conflicting "purchasers" may be secured parties. Priority questions for security interests, however, are governed by the rules in Article 9. Subsection (c) applies only to cases not covered by the Article 9 rules. It is intended primarily for disputes over conflicting claims arising out of repurchase agreement transactions that are not covered by the other rules set out in Articles 8 and 9.

The following example illustrates subsection (c):

> Example 4.   Dealer holds securities through an account at Alpha Bank. Alpha Bank in turns holds through a clearing corporation account. Dealer transfers securities to RP1 in a "hold in custody" repo transaction. Dealer then transfers the same securities to RP2 in another repo transaction. The repo to RP2 is implemented by transferring the securities from Dealer's regular account at Alpha Bank to a special account maintained by Alpha Bank for Dealer and RP2. The agreement among Dealer, RP2, and Alpha Bank provides that Dealer can make substitutions for the securities but RP2 can direct Alpha Bank to sell any securities held in the special account. Dealer becomes insolvent. RP1 claims a prior interest in the securities transferred to RP2.

In this example Dealer remained the entitlement holder but agreed that RP2 could initiate entitlement orders to Dealer's security intermediary, Alpha Bank. If RP2 had become the entitlement holder, the adverse claim rule of Section 8–502 would apply. Even if RP2 does not become the entitlement holder, the arrangement among Dealer, Alpha Bank, and RP2 does suffice to give RP2 control. Thus, under Section 8–510(c), RP2 has priority over RP1, because RP2 is a purchaser who obtained control, and RP1 is a purchaser who did not obtain control. The same result could be reached under Section 8–510(a) which provides that RP1's earlier in time interest cannot be asserted as an adverse claim against RP2. The same result would follow under the Article 9 priority rules if the interests of RP1 and RP2 are characterized as "security interests," see Section 9–328(1) [*Article 9 version prior to the 2010 Amendments*]. The main point of the rules of Section 8–510(c) is to ensure that there will be clear rules to cover the conflicting claims of RP1 and RP2 without characterizing their interests as Article 9 security interests.

The priority rules in Article 9 for conflicting security interests also include a default temporal priority rule for cases where multiple secured parties have obtained control but omitted to specify their respective rights by agreement. See Section 9–328(2) [*Article 9 version prior to the 2010 Amendments*] and Comment 5 to Section 9–328 [*Article 9 version prior to the 2010 Amendments*]. Because the purchaser priority rule in Section 8–510(c) is intended to track the Article 9 priority rules, it too has a temporal priority rule for cases where multiple non-secured party purchasers have obtained control but omitted to specify their respective rights by agreement. The rule is patterned on Section 9–328(2) [*Article 9 version prior to the 2010 Amendments*].

5.   If a securities intermediary itself is a purchaser, subsection (d) provides that it has priority over the interest of another purchaser who has control. Article 9 contains a similar rule. See Section 9–328(3) [*Article 9 version prior to the 2010 Amendments*].

Definitional Cross References:

"Adverse claim". Section 8–102(a)(1).
"Control". Section 8–106.
"Entitlement holder". Section 8–102(a)(7).
"Notice of adverse claim". Section 8–105.
"Purchase". Section 1–201(32) [*unrevised Article 1; see Concordance, p. 22*].
"Purchaser". Sections 1–201(33) [*unrevised Article 1; see Concordance, p. 22*] & 8–116.
"Securities intermediary". Section 8–102(a)(14).
"Security entitlement". Section 8–102(a)(17).
"Value". Sections 1–201(44) [*unrevised Article 1; see Concordance, p. 22*] & 8–116.

As amended in 1999 and 2022.

§ 8–511.   Priority Among Security Interests and Entitlement Holders.

(a)   Except as otherwise provided in subsections (b) and (c), if a securities intermediary does not have sufficient interests in a particular financial asset to satisfy both its obligations to entitlement holders who have security entitlements to that financial asset and its obligation to a creditor of the securities intermediary who has a security interest in that financial asset, the claims of entitlement holders, other than the creditor, have priority over the claim of the creditor.

(b)   A claim of a creditor of a securities intermediary who has a security interest in a financial asset held by a securities intermediary has priority over claims of the securities intermediary's entitlement holders who have security entitlements with respect to that financial asset if the creditor has control over the financial asset.

(c)　If a clearing corporation does not have sufficient financial assets to satisfy both its obligations to entitlement holders who have security entitlements with respect to a financial asset and its obligation to a creditor of the clearing corporation who has a security interest in that financial asset, the claim of the creditor has priority over the claims of entitlement holders.

Official Comment

1.　This section sets out priority rules for circumstances in which a securities intermediary fails leaving an insufficient quantity of securities or other financial assets to satisfy the claims of its entitlement holders and the claims of creditors to whom it has granted security interests in financial assets held by it. Subsection (a) provides that entitlement holders' claims have priority except as otherwise provided in subsection (b), and subsection (b) provides that the secured creditor's claim has priority if the secured creditor obtains control, as defined in Section 8–106. The following examples illustrate the operation of these rules.

　　Example 1.　Able & Co., a broker, borrows from Alpha Bank and grants Alpha Bank a security interest pursuant to a written agreement which identifies certain securities that are to be collateral for the loan, either specifically or by category. Able holds these securities in a clearing corporation account. Able becomes insolvent and it is discovered that Able holds insufficient securities to satisfy the claims of customers who have paid for securities that they held in accounts with Able and the collateral claims of Alpha Bank. Alpha Bank's security interest in the security entitlements that Able holds through the clearing corporation account may be perfected under the automatic perfection rule of Section 9–309(10), but Alpha Bank did not obtain control under Section 8–106. Thus, under Section 8–511(a) the entitlement holders' claims have priority over Alpha Bank's claim.

　　Example 2.　Able & Co., a broker, borrows from Beta Bank and grants Beta Bank a security interest in securities that Able holds in a clearing corporation account. Pursuant to the security agreement, the securities are debited from Alpha's account and credited to Beta's account in the clearing corporation account. Able becomes insolvent and it is discovered that Able holds insufficient securities to satisfy the claims of customers who have paid for securities that they held in accounts with Able and the collateral claims of Alpha Bank. Although the transaction between Able and Beta took the form of an outright transfer on the clearing corporation's books, as between Able and Beta, Able remains the owner and Beta has a security interest. In that respect the situation is no different than if Able had delivered bearer bonds to Beta in pledge to secure a loan. Beta's security interest is perfected, and Beta obtained control. See Sections 8–106 and 9–314. Under Section 8–511(b), Beta Bank's security interest has priority over claims of Able's customers.

The result in Example 2 is an application to this particular setting of the general principle expressed in Section 8–503, and explained in the Comments thereto, that the entitlement holders of a securities intermediary cannot assert rights against third parties to whom the intermediary has wrongfully transferred interests, except in extremely unusual circumstances where the third party was itself a participant in the transferor's wrongdoing. Under subsection (b) the claim of a secured creditor of a securities intermediary has priority over the claims of entitlement holders if the secured creditor has obtained control. If, however, the secured creditor acted in collusion with the intermediary in violating the intermediary's obligation to its entitlement holders, then under Section 8–503(e), the entitlement holders, through their representative in insolvency proceedings, could recover the interest from the secured creditor, that is, set aside the security interest.

2.　The risk that investors who hold through an intermediary will suffer a loss as a result of a wrongful pledge by the intermediary is no different than the risk that the intermediary might fail and not have the securities that it was supposed to be holding on behalf of its customers, either because the securities were never acquired by the intermediary or because the intermediary wrongfully sold securities that should have been kept to satisfy customers' claims. Investors are protected against that risk by the regulatory regimes under which securities intermediaries operate. Intermediaries are required to maintain custody, through clearing corporation accounts or in other approved locations, of their customers' securities and are prohibited from using customers' securities in their own business activities. Securities firms who are carrying both customer and proprietary positions are not permitted to grant blanket liens to lenders covering all securities which they hold, for their own account or for their customers. Rather, securities firms designate specifically which positions they are pledging. Under SEC Rules 8c–1 and 15c2–1, customers' securities can be pledged only to fund loans to customers, and only with the consent of the customers. Customers' securities cannot be pledged for loans for the firm's proprietary business; only proprietary positions can be pledged for proprietary loans. SEC Rule 15c3–3 implements these prohibitions in a fashion tailored to modern securities firm accounting systems by requiring brokers to maintain a sufficient inventory of securities, free from any liens, to satisfy the claims of all of their customers for fully paid and excess margin securities. Revised Article 8 mirrors that requirement, specifying in Section 8–504 that a securities intermediary must maintain a sufficient quantity of investment property to satisfy all security entitlements, and may not grant security interests in the positions it is required to hold for customers, except as authorized by the customers.

If a failed brokerage has violated the customer protection regulations and does not have sufficient securities to satisfy customers' claims, its customers are protected against loss from a shortfall by the Securities Investor Protection Act ("SIPA"). Securities firms required to register as brokers or dealers are also required to become members of the Securities Investor Protection Corporation ("SIPC"), which provides their customers with protection somewhat similar to that provided by FDIC and other deposit insurance programs for bank depositors. When a member firm fails, SIPC is authorized to initiate a liquidation proceeding under the provisions of SIPA. If the assets of the securities firm are insufficient to satisfy all customer claims, SIPA makes contributions to the estate from a fund financed by assessments on its members to protect customers against losses up to $500,000 for cash and securities held at member firms.

Article 8 is premised on the view that the important policy of protecting investors against the risk of wrongful conduct by their intermediaries is sufficiently treated by other law.

3.   Subsection (c) sets out a special rule for secured financing provided to enable clearing corporations to complete settlement. In order to permit clearing corporations to establish liquidity facilities where necessary to ensure completion of settlement, subsection (c) provides a priority for secured lenders to such clearing corporations. Subsection (c) does not turn on control because the clearing corporation may be the top tier securities intermediary for the securities pledged, so that there may be no practicable method for conferring control on the lender.

Definitional Cross References:

"Clearing corporation". Section 8–102(a)(5).
"Control". Section 8–106.
"Entitlement holder". Section 8–102(a)(7).
"Financial asset". Section 8–102(a)(9).
"Securities intermediary". Section 8–102(a)(14).
"Security entitlement". Section 8–102(a)(17).
"Security interest". Section 1–201(37) [*unrevised Article 1; see Concordance, p. 22*].
"Value". Sections 1–201(44) [*unrevised Article 1; see Concordance, p. 22*] & 8–116.

UCC ARTICLE 9

SECURED TRANSACTIONS

Article 9 was revised in 1999 and amended in 2010, 2017, 2018, 2019, and 2022.

2022 amendments to Article 9 appear in Appendix F.

Prefatory Note to 2022 amendments appears in Appendix E.

Text below current through June 2022

For updates, see www.uniformlaws.org

PART 1.   GENERAL PROVISIONS

[SUBPART 1.   SHORT TITLE, DEFINITIONS, AND GENERAL CONCEPTS]

9–101.   Short Title.
9–102.   Definitions and Index of Definitions.
9–103.   Purchase-Money Security Interest; Application of Payments; Burden of Establishing.
9–104.   Control of Deposit Account.
9–105.   Control of Electronic Chattel Paper.
9–106.   Control of Investment Property.
9–107.   Control of Letter-of-Credit Right.
9–108.   Sufficiency of Description.

[SUBPART 2.   APPLICABILITY OF ARTICLE]

9–109.   Scope.
9–110.   Security Interests Arising Under Article 2 or 2A.

PART 2.   EFFECTIVENESS OF SECURITY AGREEMENT; ATTACHMENT OF SECURITY INTEREST; RIGHTS OF PARTIES TO SECURITY AGREEMENT

[SUBPART 1.   EFFECTIVENESS AND ATTACHMENT]

9–201.   General Effectiveness of Security Agreement.
9–202.   Title to Collateral Immaterial.
9–203.   Attachment and Enforceability of Security Interest; Proceeds; Supporting Obligations; Formal Requisites.
9–204.   After-Acquired Property; Future Advances.
9–205.   Use or Disposition of Collateral Permissible.
9–206.   Security Interest Arising in Purchase or Delivery of Financial Asset.

[SUBPART 2.   RIGHTS AND DUTIES]

9–207.   Rights and Duties of Secured Party Having Possession or Control of Collateral.
9–208.   Additional Duties of Secured Party Having Control of Collateral.
9–209.   Duties of Secured Party if Account Debtor Has Been Notified of Assignment.
9–210.   Request for Accounting; Request Regarding List of Collateral or Statement of Account.

UNIFORM COMMERCIAL CODE

PART 3. PERFECTION AND PRIORITY

[SUBPART 1. LAW GOVERNING PERFECTION AND PRIORITY]

9–301. Law Governing Perfection and Priority of Security Interests.

9–302. Law Governing Perfection and Priority of Agricultural Liens.

9–303. Law Governing Perfection and Priority of Security Interests in Goods Covered by a Certificate of Title.

9–304. Law Governing Perfection and Priority of Security Interests in Deposit Accounts.

9–305. Law Governing Perfection and Priority of Security Interests in Investment Property.

9–306. Law Governing Perfection and Priority of Security Interests in Letter-of-Credit Rights.

9–307. Location of Debtor.

[SUBPART 2. PERFECTION]

9–308. When Security Interest or Agricultural Lien Is Perfected; Continuity of Perfection.

9–309. Security Interest Perfected Upon Attachment.

9–310. When Filing Required to Perfect Security Interest or Agricultural Lien; Security Interests and Agricultural Liens to Which Filing Provisions Do Not Apply.

9–311. Perfection of Security Interests in Property Subject to Certain Statutes, Regulations, and Treaties.

9–312. Perfection of Security Interests in Chattel Paper, Deposit Accounts, Documents, Goods Covered by Documents, Instruments, Investment Property, Letter-of-Credit Rights, and Money; Perfection by Permissive Filing; Temporary Perfection Without Filing or Transfer of Possession.

9–313. When Possession by or Delivery to Secured Party Perfects Security Interest Without Filing.

9–314. Perfection by Control.

9–315. Secured Party's Rights on Disposition of Collateral and in Proceeds.

9–316. Effect of Change in Governing Law.

[SUBPART 3. PRIORITY]

9–317. Interests That Take Priority Over or Take Free of Security Interest or Agricultural Lien.

9–318. No Interest Retained in Right to Payment That Is Sold; Rights and Title of Seller of Account or Chattel Paper With Respect to Creditors and Purchasers.

9–319. Rights and Title of Consignee With Respect to Creditors and Purchasers.

9–320. Buyer of Goods.

9–321. Licensee of General Intangible and Lessee of Goods in Ordinary Course of Business.

9–322. Priorities Among Conflicting Security Interests in and Agricultural Liens on Same Collateral.

9–323. Future Advances.

9–324. Priority of Purchase-Money Security Interests.

9–325. Priority of Security Interests in Transferred Collateral.

9–326. Priority of Security Interests Created by New Debtor.

9–327. Priority of Security Interests in Deposit Account.

9–328. Priority of Security Interests in Investment Property.

9–329. Priority of Security Interests in Letter-of-Credit Right.

9–330. Priority of Purchaser of Chattel Paper or Instrument.

9–331. Priority of Rights of Purchasers of Instruments, Documents, and Securities Under Other Articles; Priority of Interests in Financial Assets and Security Entitlements Under Article 8.

9–332. Transfer of Money; Transfer of Funds From Deposit Account.

9–333. Priority of Certain Liens Arising by Operation of Law.

9–334. Priority of Security Interests in Fixtures and Crops.

9–335. Accessions.

9–336. Commingled Goods.

9–337. Priority of Security Interests in Goods Covered by Certificate of Title.

9–338. Priority of Security Interest or Agricultural Lien Perfected by Filed Financing Statement Providing Certain Incorrect Information.

9–339. Priority Subject to Subordination.

ARTICLE 9

[SUBPART 4.   RIGHTS OF BANK]

9–340.   Effectiveness of Right of Recoupment or Set-Off Against Deposit Account.

9–341.   Bank's Rights and Duties With Respect to Deposit Account.

9–342.   Bank's Right to Refuse to Enter Into or Disclose Existence of Control Agreement.

PART 4.   RIGHTS OF THIRD PARTIES

9–401.   Alienability of Debtor's Rights.

9–402.   Secured Party Not Obligated on Contract of Debtor or in Tort.

9–403.   Agreement Not to Assert Defenses Against Assignee.

9–404.   Rights Acquired by Assignee; Claims and Defenses Against Assignee.

9–405.   Modification of Assigned Contract.

9–406.   Discharge of Account Debtor; Notification of Assignment; Identification and Proof of Assignment; Restrictions on Assignment of Accounts, Chattel Paper, Payment Intangibles, and Promissory Notes Ineffective.

9–407.   Restrictions on Creation or Enforcement of Security Interest in Leasehold Interest or in Lessor's Residual Interest.

9–408.   Restrictions on Assignment of Promissory Notes, Health-Care-Insurance Receivables, and Certain General Intangibles Ineffective.

9–409.   Restrictions on Assignment of Letter-of-Credit Rights Ineffective.

PART 5.   FILING

[SUBPART 1. FILING OFFICE; CONTENTS AND EFFECTIVENESS OF FINANCING STATEMENT]

9–501.   Filing Office.

9–502.   Contents of Financing Statement; Record of Mortgage as Financing Statement; Time of Filing Financing Statement.

9–503.   Name of Debtor and Secured Party.

9–504.   Indication of Collateral.

9–505.   Filing and Compliance With Other Statutes and Treaties for Consignments, Leases, Other Bailments, and Other Transactions.

9–506.   Effect of Errors or Omissions.

9–507.   Effect of Certain Events on Effectiveness of Financing Statement.

9–508.   Effectiveness of Financing Statement if New Debtor Becomes Bound by Security Agreement.

9–509.   Persons Entitled to File a Record.

9–510.   Effectiveness of Filed Record.

9–511.   Secured Party of Record.

9–512.   Amendment of Financing Statement.

9–513.   Termination Statement.

9–514.   Assignment of Powers of Secured Party of Record.

9–515.   Duration and Effectiveness of Financing Statement; Effect of Lapsed Financing Statement.

9–516.   What Constitutes Filing; Effectiveness of Filing.

9–517.   Effect of Indexing Errors.

9–518.   Claim Concerning Inaccurate or Wrongfully Filed Record.

[SUBPART 2.   DUTIES AND OPERATION OF FILING OFFICE]

9–519.   Numbering, Maintaining, and Indexing Records; Communicating Information Provided in Records.

9–520.   Acceptance and Refusal to Accept Record.

9–521.   Uniform Form of Written Financing Statement and Amendment.

9–522.   Maintenance and Destruction of Records.

9–523.   Information From Filing Office; Sale or License of Records.

9–524.   Delay by Filing Office.

9–525.   Fees.
9–526.   Filing-Office Rules.
9–527.   Duty to Report.

PART 6.   DEFAULT

[SUBPART 1.   DEFAULT AND ENFORCEMENT OF SECURITY INTEREST]

9–601.   Rights After Default; Judicial Enforcement; Consignor or Buyer of Accounts, Chattel Paper, Payment Intangibles, or Promissory Notes.
9–602.   Waiver and Variance of Rights and Duties.
9–603.   Agreement on Standards Concerning Rights and Duties.
9–604.   Procedure if Security Agreement Covers Real Property or Fixtures.
9–605.   Unknown Debtor or Secondary Obligor.
9–606.   Time of Default for Agricultural Lien.
9–607.   Collection and Enforcement by Secured Party.
9–608.   Application of Proceeds of Collection or Enforcement; Liability for Deficiency and Right to Surplus.
9–609.   Secured Party's Right to Take Possession After Default.
9–610.   Disposition of Collateral After Default.
9–611.   Notification Before Disposition of Collateral.
9–612.   Timeliness of Notification Before Disposition of Collateral.
9–613.   Contents and Form of Notification Before Disposition of Collateral: General.
9–614.   Contents and Form of Notification Before Disposition of Collateral: Consumer-Goods Transaction.
9–615.   Application of Proceeds of Disposition; Liability for Deficiency and Right to Surplus.
9–616.   Explanation of Calculation of Surplus or Deficiency.
9–617.   Rights of Transferee of Collateral.
9–618.   Rights and Duties of Certain Secondary Obligors.
9–619.   Transfer of Record or Legal Title.
9–620.   Acceptance of Collateral in Full or Partial Satisfaction of Obligation; Compulsory Disposition of Collateral.
9–621.   Notification of Proposal to Accept Collateral.
9–622.   Effect of Acceptance of Collateral.
9–623.   Right to Redeem Collateral.
9–624.   Waiver.

[SUBPART 2.   NONCOMPLIANCE WITH ARTICLE]

9–625.   Remedies for Secured Party's Failure to Comply With Article.
9–626.   Action in Which Deficiency or Surplus Is in Issue.
9–627.   Determination of Whether Conduct Was Commercially Reasonable.
9–628.   Nonliability and Limitation on Liability of Secured Party; Liability of Secondary Obligor.

PART 7.   TRANSITION RULES [Omitted]

PART 8.   TRANSITION PROVISIONS FOR 2010 AMENDMENTS [Omitted]

PART 1

GENERAL PROVISIONS

[SUBPART 1. SHORT TITLE, DEFINITIONS, AND GENERAL CONCEPTS]

§ 9–101.   Short Title.

This article may be cited as Uniform Commercial Code-Secured Transactions.

Official Comment

1. **Source.** This Article supersedes former Uniform Commercial Code (UCC) Article 9. As did its predecessor, it provides a comprehensive scheme for the regulation of security interests in personal property and fixtures. For the most part this Article follows the general approach and retains much of the terminology of former Article 9. In addition to describing many aspects of the operation and interpretation of this Article, these Comments explain the material changes that this Article makes to former Article 9. Former Article 9 superseded the wide variety of pre-UCC security devices. Unlike the Comments to former Article 9, however, these Comments dwell very little on the pre-UCC state of the law. For that reason, the Comments to former Article 9 will remain of substantial historical value and interest. They also will remain useful in understanding the background and general conceptual approach of this Article.

Citations to "Bankruptcy Code Section ____" in these Comments are to Title 11 of the United States Code as in effect on July 1, 2010.

2. **Background and History.** In 1990, the Permanent Editorial Board for the UCC with the support of its sponsors, The American Law Institute and the National Conference of Commissioners on Uniform State Laws, established a committee to study Article 9 of the UCC. The study committee issued its report as of December 1, 1992, recommending the creation of a drafting committee for the revision of Article 9 and also recommending numerous specific changes to Article 9. Organized in 1993, a drafting committee met fifteen times from 1993 to 1998. This Article was approved by its sponsors in 1998. This Article was conformed to revised Article 1 in 2001 and to amendments to Article 7 in 2003. The sponsors approved amendments to selected sections of this Article in 2010.

3. **Reorganization and Renumbering; Captions; Style.** This Article reflects a substantial reorganization of former Article 9 and renumbering of most sections. New Part 4 deals with several aspects of third-party rights and duties that are unrelated to perfection and priority. Some of these were covered by Part 3 of former Article 9. Part 5 deals with filing (covered by former Part 4) and Part 6 deals with default and enforcement (covered by former Part 5). Appendix I contains conforming revisions to other articles of the UCC, and Appendix II contains model provisions for production-money priority. [*Note from West Advisory Panel: Appendices I and II are omitted from this volume.*]

This Article also includes headings for the subsections as an aid to readers. Unlike section captions, which are part of the UCC, see Section 1–107, subsection headings are not a part of the official text itself and have not been approved by the sponsors. Each jurisdiction in which this Article is introduced may consider whether to adopt the headings as a part of the statute and whether to adopt a provision clarifying the effect, if any, to be given to the headings. This Article also has been conformed to current style conventions.

4. **Summary of Revisions.** Following is a brief summary of some of the more significant revisions of Article 9 that are included in the 1998 revision of this Article.

a. **Scope of Article 9.** This Article expands the scope of Article 9 in several respects.

Deposit accounts. Section 9–109 includes within this Article's scope deposit accounts as original collateral, except in consumer transactions. Former Article 9 dealt with deposit accounts only as proceeds of other collateral.

Sales of payment intangibles and promissory notes. Section 9–109 also includes within the scope of this Article most sales of "payment intangibles" (defined in Section 9–102 as general intangibles under which an account debtor's principal obligation is monetary) and "promissory notes" (also defined in Section 9–102). Former Article 9 included sales of accounts and chattel paper, but not sales of payment intangibles or promissory notes. In its inclusion of sales of payment intangibles and promissory notes, this Article continues the drafting convention found in former Article 9; it provides that the sale of accounts, chattel paper, payment intangibles, or promissory notes creates a "security interest." The definition of "account" in Section 9–102 also has been expanded to include various rights to payment that were general intangibles under former Article 9.

Health-care-insurance receivables. Section 9–109 narrows Article 9's exclusion of transfers of interests in insurance policies by carving out of the exclusion "health-care-insurance receivables" (defined in Section 9–102). A health-care-insurance receivable is included within the definition of "account" in Section 9–102.

Nonpossessory statutory agricultural liens. Section 9–109 also brings nonpossessory statutory agricultural liens within the scope of Article 9.

Consignments. Section 9–109 provides that "true" consignments-bailments for the purpose of sale by the bailee are security interests covered by Article 9, with certain exceptions. See Section 9–102 (defining "consignment"). Currently, many consignments are subject to Article 9's filing requirements by operation of former Section 2–326.

Supporting obligations and property securing rights to payment. This Article also addresses explicitly (i) obligations, such as guaranties and letters of credit, that support payment or performance of collateral such as accounts, chattel paper, and payment intangibles, and (ii) any property (including real property) that secures a right to payment or performance that is subject to an Article 9 security interest. See Sections 9–203, 9–308.

Commercial tort claims. Section 9–109 expands the scope of Article 9 to include the assignment of commercial tort claims by narrowing the exclusion of tort claims generally. However, this Article continues to exclude tort claims for bodily injury and other non-business tort claims of a natural person. See Section 9–102 (defining "commercial tort claim").

Transfers by States and governmental units of States. Section 9–109 narrows the exclusion of transfers by States and their governmental units. It excludes only transfers covered by another statute (other than a statute generally applicable to security interests) to the extent the statute governs the creation, perfection, priority, or enforcement of security interests.

Nonassignable general intangibles, promissory notes, health-care-insurance receivables, and letter-of-credit rights. This Article enables a security interest to attach to letter-of-credit rights, health-care-insurance receivables, promissory notes, and general intangibles, including contracts, permits, licenses, and franchises, notwithstanding a contractual or statutory prohibition against or limitation on assignment. This Article explicitly protects third parties against any adverse effect of the creation or attempted enforcement of the security interest. See Sections 9–408, 9–409.

Subject to Sections 9–408 and 9–409 and two other exceptions (Sections 9–406, concerning accounts, chattel paper, and payment intangibles, and 9–407, concerning interests in leased goods), Section 9–401 establishes a baseline rule that the inclusion of transactions and collateral within the scope of Article 9 has no effect on non-Article 9 law dealing with the alienability or inalienability of property. For example, if a commercial tort claim is nonassignable under other applicable law, the fact that a security interest in the claim is within the scope of Article 9 does not override the other applicable law's effective prohibition of assignment.

b.   **Duties of Secured Party.** This Article provides for expanded duties of secured parties.

Release of control. Section 9–208 imposes upon a secured party having control of a deposit account, investment property, or a letter-of-credit right the duty to release control when there is no secured obligation and no commitment to give value. Section 9–209 contains analogous provisions when an account debtor has been notified to pay a secured party.

Information. Section 9–210 expands a secured party's duties to provide the debtor with information concerning collateral and the obligations that it secures.

Default and enforcement. Part 6 also includes some additional duties of secured parties in connection with default and enforcement. See, e.g., Section 9–616 (duty to explain calculation of deficiency or surplus in a consumer-goods transaction).

c.   **Choice of Law.** The choice-of-law rules for the law governing perfection, the effect of perfection or nonperfection, and priority are found in Part 3, Subpart 1 (Sections 9–301 through 9–307). See also Section 9–316.

Where to file: Location of debtor. This Article changes the choice-of-law rule governing perfection (i.e., where to file) for most collateral to the law of the jurisdiction where the debtor is located. See Section 9–301. Under former Article 9, the jurisdiction of the debtor's location governed only perfection and priority of a security interest in accounts, general intangibles, mobile goods, and, for purposes of perfection by filing, chattel paper and investment property.

Determining debtor's location. As a baseline rule, Section 9–307 follows former Section 9–103, under which the location of the debtor is the debtor's place of business (or chief executive office, if the debtor has more than one place of business). Section 9–307 contains three major exceptions. First, a "registered organization," such as a corporation or limited liability company, is located in the State under whose law the debtor is organized, e.g., a corporate debtor's State of incorporation. Second, an individual debtor is located at his or her principal residence. Third, there are special rules for determining the location of the United States and registered organizations organized under the law of the United States.

Location of non-U.S. debtors. If, applying the foregoing rules, a debtor is located in a jurisdiction whose law does not require public notice as a condition of perfection of a nonpossessory security interest, the entity is deemed located in the District of Columbia. See Section 9–307. Thus, to the extent that this Article applies to non-U.S. debtors, perfection could be accomplished in many cases by a domestic filing.

Priority. For tangible collateral such as goods and instruments, Section 9–301 provides that the law applicable to priority and the effect of perfection or nonperfection will remain the law of the jurisdiction where the collateral is located, as under former Section 9–103 (but without the confusing "last event" test). For intangible collateral, such as accounts, the applicable law for priority will be that of the jurisdiction in which the debtor is located.

Possessory security interests; agricultural liens. Perfection, the effect of perfection or nonperfection, and priority of a possessory security interest or an agricultural lien are governed by the law of the jurisdiction where the collateral subject to the security interest or lien is located. See Sections 9–301, 9–302.

Goods covered by certificates of title; deposit accounts; letter-of-credit rights; investment property. This Article includes several refinements to the treatment of choice-of-law matters for goods covered by certificates of title. See Section 9–303. It also provides special choice-of-law rules, similar to those for investment property under current Articles 8 and 9, for deposit accounts (Section 9–304), investment property (Section 9–305), and letter-of-credit rights (Section 9–306).

Change in applicable law. Section 9–316 addresses perfection following a change in applicable law.

d. **Perfection.** The rules governing perfection of security interests and agricultural liens are found in Part 3, Subpart 2 (Sections 9–308 through 9–316).

Deposit accounts; letter-of-credit rights. With certain exceptions, this Article provides that a security interest in a deposit account or a letter-of-credit right may be perfected *only* by the secured party's acquiring "control" of the deposit account or letter-of-credit right. See Sections 9–312, 9–314. Under Section 9–104, a secured party has "control" of a deposit account when, with the consent of the debtor, the secured party obtains the depositary bank's agreement to act on the secured party's instructions (including when the secured party becomes the account holder) or when the secured party is itself the depositary bank. The control requirements are patterned on Section 8–106, which specifies the requirements for control of investment property. Under Section 9–107, "control" of a letter-of-credit right occurs when the issuer or nominated person consents to an assignment of proceeds under Section 5–114.

Electronic chattel paper. Section 9–102 includes a new defined term: "electronic chattel paper." Electronic chattel paper is a record or records consisting of information stored in an electronic medium (i.e., it is not written). Perfection of a security interest in electronic chattel paper may be by control or filing. See Sections 9–105 (*sui generis* definition of control of electronic chattel paper), 9–312 (perfection by filing), 9–314 (perfection by control).

Investment property. The perfection requirements for "investment property" (defined in Section 9–102), including perfection by control under Section 9–106, remain substantially unchanged. However, a new provision in Section 9–314 is designed to ensure that a secured party retains control in "repledge" transactions that are typical in the securities markets.

Instruments, agricultural liens, and commercial tort claims. This Article expands the types of collateral in which a security interest may be perfected by filing to include instruments. See Section 9–312. Agricultural liens and security interests in commercial tort claims also are perfected by filing, under this Article. See Sections 9–308, 9–310.

Sales of payment intangibles and promissory notes. Although former Article 9 covered the outright sale of accounts and chattel paper, sales of most other types of receivables also are financing transactions to which Article 9 should apply. Accordingly, Section 9–102 expands the definition of "account" to include many types of receivables (including "health-care-insurance receivables," defined in Section 9–102) that former Article 9 classified as "general intangibles." It thereby subjects to Article 9's filing system sales of more types of receivables than did former Article 9. Certain sales of payment intangibles—primarily bank loan participation transactions—should not be subject to the Article 9 filing rules. These transactions fall in a residual category of collateral, "payment intangibles" (general intangibles under which the account debtor's principal obligation is monetary), the sale of which is exempt from the filing requirements of Article 9. See Sections 9–102, 9–109, 9–309 (perfection upon attachment). The perfection rules for sales of promissory notes are the same as those for sales of payment intangibles.

Possessory security interests. Several provisions of this Article address aspects of security interests involving a secured party or a third party who is in possession of the collateral. In particular, Section 9–313 resolves a number of uncertainties under former Section 9–305. It provides that a security interest in collateral in the possession of a third party is perfected when the third party acknowledges in an authenticated record that it holds for the secured party's benefit. Section 9–313 also provides that a third party need not so acknowledge and that its acknowledgment does not impose any duties on it, unless it otherwise agrees. A special rule in Section 9–313 provides that if a secured party already is in possession of collateral, its security interest remains perfected by possession if it delivers the collateral to a third party and the collateral is accompanied by instructions to hold it for the secured party or to redeliver it to the secured party. Section 9–313 also clarifies the limited circumstances under which a security interest in goods covered by a certificate of title may be perfected by the secured party's taking possession.

Automatic perfection. Section 9–309 lists various types of security interests as to which no public-notice step is required for perfection (e.g., purchase-money security interests in consumer goods other than automobiles). This automatic perfection also extends to a transfer of a health-care-insurance receivable *to* a health-care provider. Those transfers normally will be made by natural persons who receive health-care services; there is little value in requiring filing for perfection in that context. Automatic perfection also applies to security interests created by sales of payment intangibles and promissory notes. Section 9–308 provides that a perfected security interest in collateral supported by a "supporting obligation" (such as an account supported by a guaranty) also is a perfected security interest in the supporting obligation, and that a perfected security interest in an obligation secured by a security interest or lien on property (e.g., a real-property mortgage) also is a perfected security interest in the security interest or lien.

e.   **Priority; Special Rules for Banks and Deposit Accounts.** The rules governing priority of security interests and agricultural liens are found in Part 3, Subpart 3 (Sections 9–317 through 9–342). This Article includes several new priority rules and some special rules relating to banks and deposit accounts (Sections 9–340 through 9–342).

Purchase-money security interests: General; consumer-goods transactions; inventory. Section 9–103 substantially rewrites the definition of purchase-money security interest (PMSI) (although the term is not formally "defined"). The substantive changes, however, apply only to non-consumer-goods transactions. (Consumer transactions and consumer-goods transactions are discussed below in Comment 4.j.) For non-consumer-goods transactions, Section 9–103 makes clear that a security interest in collateral may be (to some extent) both a PMSI as well as a non-PMSI, in accord with the "dual status" rule applied by some courts under former Article 9 (thereby rejecting the "transformation" rule). The definition provides an even broader conception of a PMSI in inventory, yielding a result that accords with private agreements entered into in response to the uncertainty under former Article 9. It also treats consignments as purchase-money security interests in inventory. Section 9–324 revises the PMSI priority rules, but for the most part without material change in substance. Section 9–324 also clarifies the priority rules for competing PMSIs in the same collateral.

Purchase-money security interests in livestock; agricultural liens. Section 9–324 provides a special PMSI priority, similar to the inventory PMSI priority rule, for livestock. Section 9–322 (which contains the baseline first-to-file-or-perfect priority rule) also recognizes special non-Article 9 priority rules for agricultural liens, which can override the baseline first-in-time rule.

Purchase-money security interests in software. Section 9–324 contains a new priority rule for a software purchase-money security interest. (Section 9–102 includes a definition of "software.") Under Section 9–103, a software PMSI includes a PMSI in software that is used in goods that are also subject to a PMSI. (Note also that the definition of "chattel paper" has been expanded to include records that evidence a monetary obligation and a security interest in specific goods and software used in the goods.)

Investment property. The priority rules for investment property are substantially similar to the priority rules found in former Section 9–115, which was added in conjunction with the 1994 revisions to UCC Article 8. Under Section 9–328, if a secured party has control of investment property (Sections 8–106, 9–106), its security interest is senior to a security interest perfected in another manner (e.g., by filing). Also under Section 9–328, security interests perfected by control generally rank according to the time that control is obtained or, in the case of a security entitlement or a commodity contract carried in a commodity account, the time when the control arrangement is entered into. This is a change from former Section 9–115, under which the security interests ranked equally. However, as between a securities intermediary's security interest in a security entitlement that it maintains for the debtor and a security interest held by another secured party, the securities intermediary's security interest is senior.

Deposit accounts. This Article's priority rules applicable to deposit accounts are found in Section 9–327. They are patterned on and are similar to those for investment property in former Section 9–115 and Section 9–328 of this Article. Under Section 9–327, if a secured party has control of a deposit account, its security interest is senior to a security interest perfected in another manner (i.e., as cash proceeds). Also under Section 9–327, security interests perfected by control rank according to the time that control is obtained, but as between a depositary bank's security interest and one held by another secured party, the depositary bank's security interest is senior. A corresponding rule in Section 9–340 makes a depositary bank's right of set-off generally senior to a security interest held by another secured party. However, if the other secured party becomes the depositary bank's customer with respect to the deposit account, then its security interest is senior to the depositary bank's security interest and right of set-off. Sections 9–327, 9–340.

Letter-of-credit rights. The priority rules for security interests in letter-of-credit rights are found in Section 9–329. They are somewhat analogous to those for deposit accounts. A security interest perfected by control has priority over one perfected in another manner (i.e., as a supporting obligation for the collateral in which a security interest is perfected). Security interests in a letter-of-credit right perfected by control rank according to the time that control is obtained. However, the rights of a transferee beneficiary or a nominated person are independent and superior to the extent provided in Section 5–114. See Section 9–109(c)(4).

Chattel paper and instruments. Section 9–330 is the successor to former Section 9–308. As under former Section 9–308, differing priority rules apply to purchasers of chattel paper who give new value and take possession (or, in the case of electronic chattel paper, obtain control) of the collateral depending on whether a conflicting security interest in the collateral is claimed merely as proceeds. The principal change relates to the role of knowledge and the effect of an indication of a previous assignment of the collateral. Section 9–330 also affords priority to purchasers of instruments who take possession in good faith and without knowledge that the purchase violates the rights of the competing secured party. In addition, to qualify for priority, purchasers of chattel paper, but not of instruments, must purchase in the ordinary course of business.

Proceeds. Section 9–322 contains new priority rules that clarify when a special priority of a security interest in collateral continues or does not continue with respect to proceeds of the collateral. Other refinements to the priority rules for proceeds are included in Sections 9–324 (purchase-money security interest priority) and 9–330 (priority of certain purchasers of chattel paper and instruments).

Miscellaneous priority provisions. This Article also includes (i) clarifications of selected good-faith-purchase and similar issues (Sections 9–317, 9–331); (ii) new priority rules to deal with the "double debtor" problem arising when a debtor creates a security interest in collateral acquired by the debtor subject to a security interest created by another person (Section 9–325); (iii) new priority rules to deal with the problems created when a change in corporate structure or the like results in a new entity that has become bound by the original debtor's after-acquired property agreement (Section 9–326); (iv) a provision enabling most transferees of funds from a deposit account or money to take free of a security interest (Section 9–332); (v) substantially rewritten and refined priority rules dealing with accessions and commingled goods (Sections 9–335, 9–336); (vi) revised priority rules for security interests in goods covered by a certificate of title (Section 9–337); and (vii) provisions designed to ensure that security interests in deposit accounts will not extend to most transferees of funds on deposit or payees from deposit accounts and will not otherwise "clog" the payments system (Sections 9–341, 9–342).

Model provisions relating to production-money security interests. Appendix II [*Note from West Advisory Panel: Appendix II is omitted from this volume*] to this Article contains model definitions and priority rules relating to "production-money security interests" held by secured parties who give new value used in the production of crops. Because no consensus emerged on the wisdom of these provisions during the drafting process, the sponsors make no recommendation on whether these model provisions should be enacted.

f. **Proceeds.** Section 9–102 contains an expanded definition of "proceeds" of collateral which includes additional rights and property that arise out of collateral, such as distributions on account of collateral and claims arising out of the loss or nonconformity of, defects in, or damage to collateral. The term also includes collections on account of "supporting obligations," such as guarantees.

g. **Part 4: Additional Provisions Relating to Third-Party Rights.** New Part 4 contains several provisions relating to the relationships between certain third parties and the parties to secured transactions. It contains new Sections 9–401 (replacing former Section 9–311) (alienability of debtor's rights), 9–402 (replacing former Section 9–317) (secured party not obligated on debtor's contracts), 9–403 (replacing former Section 9–206) (agreement not to assert defenses against assignee), 9–404, 9–405, and 9–406 (replacing former Section 9–318) (rights acquired by assignee, modification of assigned contract, discharge of account debtor, restrictions on assignment of account, chattel paper, promissory note, or payment intangible ineffective), 9–407 (replacing some provisions of former Section 2A–303) (restrictions on creation or enforcement of security interest in leasehold interest or lessor's residual interest ineffective). It also contains new Sections 9–408 (restrictions on assignment of promissory notes, health-care-insurance receivables ineffective, and certain general intangibles ineffective) and 9–409 (restrictions on assignment of letter-of-credit rights ineffective), which are discussed above.

      h.   **Filing.** Part 5 (formerly Part 4) of Article 9 has been substantially rewritten to simplify the statutory text and to deal with numerous problems of interpretation and implementation that have arisen over the years.

     Medium-neutrality. This Article is "medium-neutral"; that is, it makes clear that parties may file and otherwise communicate with a filing office by means of records communicated and stored in media other than on paper.

     Identity of person who files a record; authorization. Part 5 is largely indifferent as to the person who effects a filing. Instead, it addresses whose authorization is necessary for a person to file a record with a filing office. The filing scheme does not contemplate that the identity of a "filer" will be a part of the searchable records. This approach is consistent with, and a necessary aspect of, eliminating signatures or other evidence of authorization from the system (except to the extent that filing offices may choose to employ authentication procedures in connection with electronic communications). As long as the appropriate person authorizes the filing, or, in the case of a termination statement, the debtor is entitled to the termination, it is largely insignificant whether the secured party or another person files any given record.

     Section 9–509 collects in one place most of the rules that determine when a record may be filed. In general, the debtor's authorization is required for the filing of an initial financing statement or an amendment that adds collateral. With one further exception, a secured party of record's authorization is required for the filing of other amendments. The exception arises if a secured party has failed to provide a termination statement that is required because there is no outstanding secured obligation or commitment to give value. In that situation, a debtor is authorized to file a termination statement indicating that it has been filed by the debtor.

     Financing statement formal requisites. The formal requisites for a financing statement are set out in Section 9–502. A financing statement must provide the name of the debtor and the secured party and an indication of the collateral that it covers. Sections 9–503 and 9–506 address the sufficiency of a name provided on a financing statement and clarify when a debtor's name is correct and when an incorrect name is insufficient. Section 9–504 addresses the indication of collateral covered. Under Section 9–504, a super-generic description (e.g., "all assets" or "all personal property") in a financing statement is a sufficient indication of the collateral. (Note, however, that a super-generic description is inadequate for purposes of a security agreement. See Sections 9–108, 9–203.) To facilitate electronic filing, this Article does not require that the debtor's signature or other authorization appear on a financing statement. Instead, it prohibits the filing of unauthorized financing statements and imposes liability upon those who violate the prohibition. See Sections 9–509, 9–626.

     Filing-office operations. Part 5 contains several provisions governing filing operations. First, it prohibits the filing office from rejecting an initial financing statement or other record for a reason other than one of the few that are specified. See Sections 9–520, 9–516. Second, the filing office is obliged to link all subsequent records (e.g., assignments, continuation statements, etc.) to the initial financing statement to which they relate. See Section 9–519. Third, the filing office may delete a financing statement and related records from the files no earlier than one year after lapse (lapse normally is five years after the filing date), and then only if a continuation statement has not been filed. See Sections 9–515, 9–519, 9–522. Thus, a financing statement and related records would be discovered by a search of the files even after the filing of a termination statement. This approach helps eliminate filing-office discretion and also eases problems associated with multiple secured parties and multiple partial assignments. Fourth, Part 5 mandates performance standards for filing offices. See Sections 9–519, 9–520, 9–523. Fifth, it provides for the promulgation of filing-office rules to deal with details best left out of the statute and requires the filing office to submit periodic reports. See Sections 9–526, 9–527.

     Defaulting or missing secured parties and fraudulent filings. In some areas of the country, serious problems have arisen from fraudulent financing statements that are filed against public officials and other persons. This Article addresses the fraud problem by providing the opportunity for a debtor to file a termination statement when a secured party wrongfully refuses or fails to provide a termination statement. See Section 9–509. This opportunity also addresses the problem of secured parties that simply disappear through mergers or liquidations. In addition, Section 9–518 affords a statutory method by which a debtor who believes that a filed record is inaccurate or was wrongfully filed may indicate that fact in the files, albeit without affecting the efficacy, if any, of the challenged record.

     Extended period of effectiveness for certain financing statements. Section 9–515 contains an exception to the usual rule that financing statements are effective for five years unless a continuation statement is filed to continue the effectiveness for another five years. Under that section, an initial financing statement filed in connection with a "public-finance transaction" or a "manufactured-home transaction" (terms defined in Section 9–102) is effective for 30 years.

National form of financing statement and related forms. Section 9–521 provides for uniform, national written forms of financing statements and related written records that must be accepted by a filing office that accepts written records.

i. **Default and Enforcement.** Part 6 of Article 9 extensively revises former Part 5. Provisions relating to enforcement of consumer-goods transactions and consumer transactions are discussed in Comment 4.j.

Debtor, secondary obligor; waiver. Section 9–602 clarifies the identity of persons who have rights and persons to whom a secured party owes specified duties under Part 6. Under that section, the rights and duties are enjoyed by and run to the "debtor," defined in Section 9–102 to mean any person with a non-lien property interest in collateral, and to any "obligor." However, with one exception (Section 9–616, as it relates to a consumer obligor), the rights and duties concerned affect non-debtor obligors only if they are "secondary obligors." "Secondary obligor" is defined in Section 9–102 to include one who is secondarily obligated on the secured obligation, e.g., a guarantor, or one who has a right of recourse against the debtor or another obligor with respect to an obligation secured by collateral. However, under Section 9–628, the secured party is relieved from any duty or liability to any person unless the secured party knows that the person is a debtor or obligor. Resolving an issue on which courts disagreed under former Article 9, this Article generally prohibits waiver by a secondary obligor of its rights and a secured party's duties under Part 6. See Section 9–602. However, Section 9–624 permits a secondary obligor or debtor to waive the right to notification of disposition of collateral and, in a non-consumer transaction, the right to redeem collateral, if the secondary obligor or debtor agrees to do so after default.

Rights of collection and enforcement of collateral. Section 9–607 explains in greater detail than former 9–502 the rights of a secured party who seeks to collect or enforce collateral, including accounts, chattel paper, and payment intangibles. It also sets forth the enforcement rights of a depositary bank holding a security interest in a deposit account maintained with the depositary bank. Section 9–607 relates solely to the rights of a secured party vis-a-vis a debtor with respect to collections and enforcement. It does not affect the rights or duties of third parties, such as account debtors on collateral, which are addressed elsewhere (e.g., Section 9–406). Section 9–608 clarifies the manner in which proceeds of collection or enforcement are to be applied.

Disposition of collateral: Warranties of title. Section 9–610 imposes on a secured party who disposes of collateral the warranties of title, quiet possession, and the like that are otherwise applicable under other law. It also provides rules for the exclusion or modification of those warranties.

Disposition of collateral: Notification, application of proceeds, surplus and deficiency, other effects. Section 9–611 requires a secured party to give notification of a disposition of collateral to other secured parties and lienholders who have filed financing statements against the debtor covering the collateral. (That duty was eliminated by the 1972 revisions to Article 9.) However, that section relieves the secured party from that duty when the secured party undertakes a search of the records and a report of the results is unreasonably delayed. Section 9–613, which applies only to non-consumer transactions, specifies the contents of a sufficient notification of disposition and provides that a notification sent 10 days or more before the earliest time for disposition is sent within a reasonable time. Section 9–615 addresses the application of proceeds of disposition, the entitlement of a debtor to any surplus, and the liability of an obligor for any deficiency. Section 9–619 clarifies the effects of a disposition by a secured party, including the rights of transferees of the collateral.

Rights and duties of secondary obligor. Section 9–618 provides that a secondary obligor obtains the rights and assumes the duties of a secured party if the secondary obligor receives an assignment of a secured obligation, agrees to assume the secured party's rights and duties upon a transfer to it of collateral, or becomes subrogated to the rights of the secured party with respect to the collateral. The assumption, transfer, or subrogation is not a disposition of collateral under Section 9–610, but it does relieve the former secured party of further duties. Former Section 9–504(5) did not address whether a secured party was relieved of its duties in this situation.

Transfer of record or legal title. Section 9–619 contains a new provision making clear that a transfer of record or legal title to a secured party is not of itself a disposition under Part 6. This rule applies regardless of the circumstances under which the transfer of title occurs.

Strict foreclosure. Section 9–620, unlike former Section 9–505, permits a secured party to accept collateral in partial satisfaction, as well as full satisfaction, of the obligations secured. This right of strict foreclosure extends to intangible as well as tangible property. Section 9–622 clarifies the effects of an acceptance of collateral on the rights of junior claimants. It rejects the approach taken by some courts—deeming a secured party to have constructively retained collateral in satisfaction of the secured obligations—in the case of a secured party's unreasonable delay in the disposition of collateral. Instead, unreasonable delay is relevant when determining whether a disposition under Section 9–610 is commercially reasonable.

Effect of noncompliance: "Rebuttable presumption" test. Section 9–626 adopts the "rebuttable presumption" test for the failure of a secured party to proceed in accordance with certain provisions of Part 6. (As discussed in Comment 4.j., the test does not necessarily apply to consumer transactions.) Under this approach, the deficiency claim of a noncomplying secured party is calculated by crediting the obligor with the greater of the actual net proceeds of a disposition and the amount of net proceeds that would have been realized if the disposition had been conducted in accordance with Part 6 (e.g., in a commercially reasonable manner). For non-consumer transactions, Section 9–626 rejects the "absolute bar" test that some courts have imposed; that approach bars a noncomplying secured party from recovering any deficiency, regardless of the loss (if any) the debtor suffered as a consequence of the noncompliance.

"Low-price" dispositions: Calculation of deficiency and surplus. Section 9–615(f) addresses the problem of procedurally regular dispositions that fetch a low price. Subsection (f) provides a special method for calculating a deficiency if the proceeds of a disposition of collateral to a secured party, a person related to the secured party, or a secondary obligor are "significantly below the range of proceeds that a complying disposition to a person other than the secured party, a person related to the secured party, or a secondary obligor would have brought." ("Person related to" is defined in Section 9–102.) In these situations there is reason to suspect that there may be inadequate incentives to obtain a better price. Consequently, instead of calculating a deficiency (or surplus) based on the actual net proceeds, the deficiency (or surplus) would be calculated based on the proceeds that would have been received in a disposition to a person other than the secured party, a person related to the secured party, or a secondary obligor.

    j.   **Consumer Goods, Consumer-Goods Transactions, and Consumer Transactions.** This Article (including the accompanying conforming revisions (see Appendix I)) includes several special rules for "consumer goods," "consumer transactions," and "consumer-goods transactions." Each term is defined in Section 9–102. [*Note from West Advisory Panel: Appendix I is omitted from this volume.*]

    (i)   Revised Sections 2–502 and 2–716 provide a buyer of consumer goods with enhanced rights to possession of the goods, thereby accelerating the opportunity to achieve "buyer in ordinary course of business" status under Section 1–201.

    (ii)   Section 9–103(e) (allocation of payments for determining extent of purchase-money status), (f) (purchase-money status not affected by cross-collateralization, refinancing, restructuring, or the like), and (g) (secured party has burden of establishing extent of purchase-money status) do not apply to consumer-goods transactions. Sections 9–103 also provides that the limitation of those provisions to transactions other than consumer-goods transactions leaves to the courts the proper rules for consumer-goods transactions and prohibits the courts from drawing inferences from that limitation.

    (iii)   Section 9–108 provides that in a consumer transaction a description of consumer goods, a security entitlement, securities account, or commodity account "only by [UCC-defined] type of collateral" is not a sufficient collateral description in a security agreement.

    (iv)   Sections 9–403 and 9–404 make effective the Federal Trade Commission's anti-holder-in-due-course rule (when applicable), 16 C.F.R. Part 433, even in the absence of the required legend.

    (v)   The 10–day safe-harbor for notification of a disposition provided by Section 9–612 does not apply in a consumer transaction.

    (vi)   Section 9–613 (contents and form of notice of disposition) does not apply to a consumer-goods transaction.

    (vii)   Section 9–614 contains special requirements for the contents of a notification of disposition and a safe-harbor, "plain English" form of notification, for consumer-goods transactions.

    (viii)   Section 9–616 requires a secured party in a consumer-goods transaction to provide a debtor with a notification of how it calculated a deficiency at the time it first undertakes to collect a deficiency.

    (ix)   Section 9–620 prohibits partial strict foreclosure with respect to consumer goods collateral and, unless the debtor agrees to waive the requirement in an authenticated record after default, in certain cases requires the secured party to dispose of consumer goods collateral which has been repossessed.

(x)   Section 9–626 ("rebuttable presumption" rule) does not apply to a consumer transaction. Section 9–626 also provides that its limitation to transactions other than consumer transactions leaves to the courts the proper rules for consumer transactions and prohibits the courts from drawing inferences from that limitation.

k.   **Good Faith.** Section 9–102 contains a new definition of "good faith" that includes not only "honesty in fact" but also "the observance of reasonable commercial standards of fair dealing." The definition is similar to the ones adopted in connection with other, recently completed revisions of the UCC.

l.   **Transition Provisions.** Part 7 (Sections 9–701 through 9–709) contains transition provisions. Transition from former Article 9 to this Article will be particularly challenging in view of its expanded scope, its modification of choice-of-law rules for perfection and priority, and its expansion of the methods of perfection.

m.   **Conforming and Related Amendments to Other UCC Articles.** Appendix I contains several proposed revisions to the provisions and Comments of other UCC articles. [*Note from West Advisory Panel: Appendix I is omitted from this volume.*] For the most part the revisions are explained in the Comments to the proposed revisions. Cross-references in other UCC articles to sections of Article 9 also have been revised.

Article 1. Revised Section 1–201 contains revisions to the definitions of "buyer in ordinary course of business," "purchaser," and "security interest."

Articles 2 and 2A. Sections 2–210, 2–326, 2–502, 2–716, 2A–303, and 2A–307 have been revised to address the intersection between Articles 2 and 2A and Article 9.

Article 5. New Section 5–118 is patterned on Section 4–210. It provides for a security interest in documents presented under a letter of credit in favor of the issuer and a nominated person on the letter of credit.

Article 8. Revisions to Section 8–106, which deals with "control" of securities and security entitlements, conform it to Section 8–302, which deals with "delivery." Revisions to Section 8–110, which deals with a "securities intermediary's jurisdiction," conform it to the revised treatment of a "commodity intermediary's jurisdiction" in Section 9–305. Sections 8–301 and 8–302 have been revised for clarification. Section 8–510 has been revised to conform it to the revised priority rules of Section 9–328. Several Comments in Article 8 also have been revised.

As amended in 2010.

§ 9–102.   Definitions and Index of Definitions.

(a)   **[Article 9 definitions.]** In this article:

(1)   "Accession" means goods that are physically united with other goods in such a manner that the identity of the original goods is not lost.

(2)   "Account", except as used in "account for", means a right to payment of a monetary obligation, whether or not earned by performance, (i) for property that has been or is to be sold, leased, licensed, assigned, or otherwise disposed of, (ii) for services rendered or to be rendered, (iii) for a policy of insurance issued or to be issued, (iv) for a secondary obligation incurred or to be incurred, (v) for energy provided or to be provided, (vi) for the use or hire of a vessel under a charter or other contract, (vii) arising out of the use of a credit or charge card or information contained on or for use with the card, or (viii) as winnings in a lottery or other game of chance operated or sponsored by a State, governmental unit of a State, or person licensed or authorized to operate the game by a State or governmental unit of a State. The term includes health-care-insurance receivables. The term does not include (i) rights to payment evidenced by chattel paper or an instrument, (ii) commercial tort claims, (iii) deposit accounts, (iv) investment property, (v) letter-of-credit rights or letters of credit, or (vi) rights to payment for money or funds advanced or sold, other than rights arising out of the use of a credit or charge card or information contained on or for use with the card.

(3)   "Account debtor" means a person obligated on an account, chattel paper, or general intangible. The term does not include persons obligated to pay a negotiable instrument, even if the instrument constitutes part of chattel paper.

(4)   "Accounting", except as used in "accounting for", means a record:

(A)   authenticated by a secured party;

(B) indicating the aggregate unpaid secured obligations as of a date not more than 35 days earlier or 35 days later than the date of the record; and

(C) identifying the components of the obligations in reasonable detail.

(5) "Agricultural lien" means an interest in farm products:

    (A) which secures payment or performance of an obligation for:

        (i) goods or services furnished in connection with a debtor's farming operation; or

        (ii) rent on real property leased by a debtor in connection with its farming operation;

    (B) which is created by statute in favor of a person that:

        (i) in the ordinary course of its business furnished goods or services to a debtor in connection with a debtor's farming operation; or

        (ii) leased real property to a debtor in connection with the debtor's farming operation; and

    (C) whose effectiveness does not depend on the person's possession of the personal property.

(6) "As-extracted collateral" means:

    (A) oil, gas, or other minerals that are subject to a security interest that:

        (i) is created by a debtor having an interest in the minerals before extraction; and

        (ii) attaches to the minerals as extracted; or

    (B) accounts arising out of the sale at the wellhead or minehead of oil, gas, or other minerals in which the debtor had an interest before extraction.

(7) "Authenticate" means:

    (A) to sign; or

    (B) with present intent to adopt or accept a record, to attach to or logically associate with the record an electronic sound, symbol, or process.

(8) "Bank" means an organization that is engaged in the business of banking. The term includes savings banks, savings and loan associations, credit unions, and trust companies.

(9) "Cash proceeds" means proceeds that are money, checks, deposit accounts, or the like.

(10) "Certificate of title" means a certificate of title with respect to which a statute provides for the security interest in question to be indicated on the certificate as a condition or result of the security interest's obtaining priority over the rights of a lien creditor with respect to the collateral. The term includes another record maintained as an alternative to a certificate of title by the governmental unit that issues certificates of title if a statute permits the security interest in question to be indicated on the record as a condition or result of the security interest's obtaining priority over the rights of a lien creditor with respect to the collateral.

(11) "Chattel paper" means a record or records that evidence both a monetary obligation and a security interest in specific goods, a security interest in specific goods and software used in the goods, a security interest in specific goods and license of software used in the goods, a lease of specific goods, or a lease of specific goods and license of software used in the goods. In this paragraph, "monetary obligation" means a monetary obligation secured by the goods or owed under a lease of the goods and includes a monetary obligation with respect to software used in the goods. The term does not include (i) charters or other contracts involving the use or hire of a vessel or (ii) records that evidence a right to payment arising out of the use of a credit or charge card or information contained on or for use with the card. If a transaction is evidenced by records that include an instrument or series of instruments, the group of records taken together constitutes chattel paper.

(12) "Collateral" means the property subject to a security interest or agricultural lien. The term includes:

(A) proceeds to which a security interest attaches;

(B) accounts, chattel paper, payment intangibles, and promissory notes that have been sold; and

(C) goods that are the subject of a consignment.

(13) "Commercial tort claim" means a claim arising in tort with respect to which:

(A) the claimant is an organization; or

(B) the claimant is an individual and the claim:

    (i) arose in the course of the claimant's business or profession; and

    (ii) does not include damages arising out of personal injury to or the death of an individual.

(14) "Commodity account" means an account maintained by a commodity intermediary in which a commodity contract is carried for a commodity customer.

(15) "Commodity contract" means a commodity futures contract, an option on a commodity futures contract, a commodity option, or another contract if the contract or option is:

(A) traded on or subject to the rules of a board of trade that has been designated as a contract market for such a contract pursuant to federal commodities laws; or

(B) traded on a foreign commodity board of trade, exchange, or market, and is carried on the books of a commodity intermediary for a commodity customer.

(16) "Commodity customer" means a person for which a commodity intermediary carries a commodity contract on its books.

(17) "Commodity intermediary" means a person that:

(A) is registered as a futures commission merchant under federal commodities law; or

(B) in the ordinary course of its business provides clearance or settlement services for a board of trade that has been designated as a contract market pursuant to federal commodities law.

(18) "Communicate" means:

(A) to send a written or other tangible record;

(B) to transmit a record by any means agreed upon by the persons sending and receiving the record; or

(C) in the case of transmission of a record to or by a filing office, to transmit a record by any means prescribed by filing-office rule.

(19) "Consignee" means a merchant to which goods are delivered in a consignment.

(20) "Consignment" means a transaction, regardless of its form, in which a person delivers goods to a merchant for the purpose of sale and:

(A) the merchant:

    (i) deals in goods of that kind under a name other than the name of the person making delivery;

    (ii) is not an auctioneer; and

    (iii) is not generally known by its creditors to be substantially engaged in selling the goods of others;

(B) with respect to each delivery, the aggregate value of the goods is $1,000 or more at the time of delivery;

(C) the goods are not consumer goods immediately before delivery; and

(D) the transaction does not create a security interest that secures an obligation.

(21) "Consignor" means a person that delivers goods to a consignee in a consignment.

(22) "Consumer debtor" means a debtor in a consumer transaction.

(23) "Consumer goods" means goods that are used or bought for use primarily for personal, family, or household purposes.

(24) "Consumer-goods transaction" means a consumer transaction in which:

    (A) an individual incurs an obligation primarily for personal, family, or household purposes; and

    (B) a security interest in consumer goods secures the obligation.

(25) "Consumer obligor" means an obligor who is an individual and who incurred the obligation as part of a transaction entered into primarily for personal, family, or household purposes.

(26) "Consumer transaction" means a transaction in which (i) an individual incurs an obligation primarily for personal, family, or household purposes, (ii) a security interest secures the obligation, and (iii) the collateral is held or acquired primarily for personal, family, or household purposes. The term includes consumer-goods transactions.

(27) "Continuation statement" means an amendment of a financing statement which:

    (A) identifies, by its file number, the initial financing statement to which it relates; and

    (B) indicates that it is a continuation statement for, or that it is filed to continue the effectiveness of, the identified financing statement.

(28) "Debtor" means:

    (A) a person having an interest, other than a security interest or other lien, in the collateral, whether or not the person is an obligor;

    (B) a seller of accounts, chattel paper, payment intangibles, or promissory notes; or

    (C) a consignee.

(29) "Deposit account" means a demand, time, savings, passbook, or similar account maintained with a bank. The term does not include investment property or accounts evidenced by an instrument.

(30) "Document" means a document of title or a receipt of the type described in Section 7-201(b).

(31) "Electronic chattel paper" means chattel paper evidenced by a record or records consisting of information stored in an electronic medium.

(32) "Encumbrance" means a right, other than an ownership interest, in real property. The term includes mortgages and other liens on real property.

(33) "Equipment" means goods other than inventory, farm products, or consumer goods.

(34) "Farm products" means goods, other than standing timber, with respect to which the debtor is engaged in a farming operation and which are:

    (A) crops grown, growing, or to be grown, including:

        (i)   crops produced on trees, vines, and bushes; and

        (ii) aquatic goods produced in aquacultural operations;

    (B) livestock, born or unborn, including aquatic goods produced in aquacultural operations;

    (C) supplies used or produced in a farming operation; or

    (D) products of crops or livestock in their unmanufactured states.

(35) "Farming operation" means raising, cultivating, propagating, fattening, grazing, or any other farming, livestock, or aquacultural operation.

(36) "File number" means the number assigned to an initial financing statement pursuant to Section 9-519(a).

(37) "Filing office" means an office designated in Section 9-501 as the place to file a financing statement.

(38) "Filing-office rule" means a rule adopted pursuant to Section 9–526.

(39) "Financing statement" means a record or records composed of an initial financing statement and any filed record relating to the initial financing statement.

(40) "Fixture filing" means the filing of a financing statement covering goods that are or are to become fixtures and satisfying Section 9–502(a) and (b). The term includes the filing of a financing statement covering goods of a transmitting utility which are or are to become fixtures.

(41) "Fixtures" means goods that have become so related to particular real property that an interest in them arises under real property law.

(42) "General intangible" means any personal property, including things in action, other than accounts, chattel paper, commercial tort claims, deposit accounts, documents, goods, instruments, investment property, letter-of-credit rights, letters of credit, money, and oil, gas, or other minerals before extraction. The term includes payment intangibles and software.

(43) [Reserved.] ["Good faith" means honesty in fact and the observance of reasonable commercial standards of fair dealing.] [*Note from West Advisory Panel: This subsection will be deleted if the jurisdiction adopts the definition of good faith in revised Article 1 (2001).*]

(44) "Goods" means all things that are movable when a security interest attaches. The term includes (i) fixtures, (ii) standing timber that is to be cut and removed under a conveyance or contract for sale, (iii) the unborn young of animals, (iv) crops grown, growing, or to be grown, even if the crops are produced on trees, vines, or bushes, and (v) manufactured homes. The term also includes a computer program embedded in goods and any supporting information provided in connection with a transaction relating to the program if (i) the program is associated with the goods in such a manner that it customarily is considered part of the goods, or (ii) by becoming the owner of the goods, a person acquires a right to use the program in connection with the goods. The term does not include a computer program embedded in goods that consist solely of the medium in which the program is embedded. The term also does not include accounts, chattel paper, commercial tort claims, deposit accounts, documents, general intangibles, instruments, investment property, letter-of-credit rights, letters of credit, money, or oil, gas, or other minerals before extraction.

(45) "Governmental unit" means a subdivision, agency, department, county, parish, municipality, or other unit of the government of the United States, a State, or a foreign country. The term includes an organization having a separate corporate existence if the organization is eligible to issue debt on which interest is exempt from income taxation under the laws of the United States.

(46) "Health-care-insurance receivable" means an interest in or claim under a policy of insurance which is a right to payment of a monetary obligation for health-care goods or services provided or to be provided.

(47) "Instrument" means a negotiable instrument or any other writing that evidences a right to the payment of a monetary obligation, is not itself a security agreement or lease, and is of a type that in ordinary course of business is transferred by delivery with any necessary indorsement or assignment. The term does not include (i) investment property, (ii) letters of credit, or (iii) writings that evidence a right to payment arising out of the use of a credit or charge card or information contained on or for use with the card.

(48) "Inventory" means goods, other than farm products, which:

    (A) are leased by a person as lessor;

    (B) are held by a person for sale or lease or to be furnished under a contract of service;

    (C) are furnished by a person under a contract of service; or

    (D) consist of raw materials, work in process, or materials used or consumed in a business.

(49) "Investment property" means a security, whether certificated or uncertificated, security entitlement, securities account, commodity contract, or commodity account.

(50) "Jurisdiction of organization", with respect to a registered organization, means the jurisdiction under whose law the organization is formed or organized.

(51) "Letter-of-credit right" means a right to payment or performance under a letter of credit, whether or not the beneficiary has demanded or is at the time entitled to demand payment or performance. The term does not include the right of a beneficiary to demand payment or performance under a letter of credit.

(52) "Lien creditor" means:

    (A)   a creditor that has acquired a lien on the property involved by attachment, levy, or the like;

    (B)   an assignee for benefit of creditors from the time of assignment;

    (C)   a trustee in bankruptcy from the date of the filing of the petition; or

    (D)   a receiver in equity from the time of appointment.

(53) "Manufactured home" means a structure, transportable in one or more sections, which, in the traveling mode, is eight body feet or more in width or 40 body feet or more in length, or, when erected on site, is 320 or more square feet, and which is built on a permanent chassis and designed to be used as a dwelling with or without a permanent foundation when connected to the required utilities, and includes the plumbing, heating, air-conditioning, and electrical systems contained therein. The term includes any structure that meets all of the requirements of this paragraph except the size requirements and with respect to which the manufacturer voluntarily files a certification required by the United States Secretary of Housing and Urban Development and complies with the standards established under Title 42 of the United States Code.

(54) "Manufactured-home transaction" means a secured transaction:

    (A)   that creates a purchase-money security interest in a manufactured home, other than a manufactured home held as inventory; or

    (B)   in which a manufactured home, other than a manufactured home held as inventory, is the primary collateral.

(55) "Mortgage" means a consensual interest in real property, including fixtures, which secures payment or performance of an obligation.

(56) "New debtor" means a person that becomes bound as debtor under Section 9–203(d) by a security agreement previously entered into by another person.

(57) "New value" means (i) money, (ii) money's worth in property, services, or new credit, or (iii) release by a transferee of an interest in property previously transferred to the transferee. The term does not include an obligation substituted for another obligation.

(58) "Noncash proceeds" means proceeds other than cash proceeds.

(59) "Obligor" means a person that, with respect to an obligation secured by a security interest in or an agricultural lien on the collateral, (i) owes payment or other performance of the obligation, (ii) has provided property other than the collateral to secure payment or other performance of the obligation, or (iii) is otherwise accountable in whole or in part for payment or other performance of the obligation. The term does not include issuers or nominated persons under a letter of credit.

(60) "Original debtor", except as used in Section 9–310(c), means a person that, as debtor, entered into a security agreement to which a new debtor has become bound under Section 9–203(d).

(61) "Payment intangible" means a general intangible under which the account debtor's principal obligation is a monetary obligation.

(62) "Person related to", with respect to an individual, means:

    (A)   the spouse of the individual;

    (B)   a brother, brother-in-law, sister, or sister-in-law of the individual;

    (C)   an ancestor or lineal descendant of the individual or the individual's spouse; or

(D) any other relative, by blood or marriage, of the individual or the individual's spouse who shares the same home with the individual.

(63) "Person related to", with respect to an organization, means:

(A) a person directly or indirectly controlling, controlled by, or under common control with the organization;

(B) an officer or director of, or a person performing similar functions with respect to, the organization;

(C) an officer or director of, or a person performing similar functions with respect to, a person described in subparagraph (A);

(D) the spouse of an individual described in subparagraph (A), (B), or (C); or

(E) an individual who is related by blood or marriage to an individual described in subparagraph (A), (B), (C), or (D) and shares the same home with the individual.

(64) "Proceeds", except as used in Section 9–609(b), means the following property:

(A) whatever is acquired upon the sale, lease, license, exchange, or other disposition of collateral;

(B) whatever is collected on, or distributed on account of, collateral;

(C) rights arising out of collateral;

(D) to the extent of the value of collateral, claims arising out of the loss, nonconformity, or interference with the use of, defects or infringement of rights in, or damage to, the collateral; or *see commercial tort claim) 9-102 a 13*

(E) to the extent of the value of collateral and to the extent payable to the debtor or the secured party, insurance payable by reason of the loss or nonconformity of, defects or infringement of rights in, or damage to, the collateral.

(65) "Promissory note" means an instrument that evidences a promise to pay a monetary obligation, does not evidence an order to pay, and does not contain an acknowledgment by a bank that the bank has received for deposit a sum of money or funds.

(66) "Proposal" means a record authenticated by a secured party which includes the terms on which the secured party is willing to accept collateral in full or partial satisfaction of the obligation it secures pursuant to Sections 9–620, 9–621, and 9–622.

(67) "Public-finance transaction" means a secured transaction in connection with which:

(A) debt securities are issued;

(B) all or a portion of the securities issued have an initial stated maturity of at least 20 years; and

(C) the debtor, obligor, secured party, account debtor or other person obligated on collateral, assignor or assignee of a secured obligation, or assignor or assignee of a security interest is a State or a governmental unit of a State.

(68) "Public organic record" means a record that is available to the public for inspection and is:

(A) a record consisting of the record initially filed with or issued by a State or the United States to form or organize an organization and any record filed with or issued by the State or the United States which amends or restates the initial record;

(B) an organic record of a business trust consisting of the record initially filed with a State and any record filed with the State which amends or restates the initial record, if a statute of the State governing business trusts requires that the record be filed with the State; or

(C) a record consisting of legislation enacted by the legislature of a State or the Congress of the United States which forms or organizes an organization, any record amending the legislation, and any record filed with or issued by the State or the United States which amends or restates the name of the organization.

(69) "Pursuant to commitment", with respect to an advance made or other value given by a secured party, means pursuant to the secured party's obligation, whether or not a subsequent event of default or other event not within the secured party's control has relieved or may relieve the secured party from its obligation.

(70) "Record", except as used in "for record", "of record", "record or legal title", and "record owner", means information that is inscribed on a tangible medium or which is stored in an electronic or other medium and is retrievable in perceivable form.

(71) "Registered organization" means an organization formed or organized solely under the law of a single State or the United States by the filing of a public organic record with, the issuance of a public organic record by, or the enactment of legislation by the State or the United States. The term includes a business trust that is formed or organized under the law of a single State if a statute of the State governing business trusts requires that the business trust's organic record be filed with the State.

(72) "Secondary obligor" means an obligor to the extent that:

(A) the obligor's obligation is secondary; or

(B) the obligor has a right of recourse with respect to an obligation secured by collateral against the debtor, another obligor, or property of either.

(73) "Secured party" means:

(A) a person in whose favor a security interest is created or provided for under a security agreement, whether or not any obligation to be secured is outstanding;

(B) a person that holds an agricultural lien;

(C) a consignor;

(D) a person to which accounts, chattel paper, payment intangibles, or promissory notes have been sold;

(E) a trustee, indenture trustee, agent, collateral agent, or other representative in whose favor a security interest or agricultural lien is created or provided for; or

(F) a person that holds a security interest arising under Section 2–401, 2–505, 2–711(3), 2A–508(5), 4–210, or 5–118.

(74) "Security agreement" means an agreement that creates or provides for a security interest.

Does not require a writing! ↑

(75) "Send", in connection with a record or notification, means:

(A) to deposit in the mail, deliver for transmission, or transmit by any other usual means of communication, with postage or cost of transmission provided for, addressed to any address reasonable under the circumstances; or

(B) to cause the record or notification to be received within the time that it would have been received if properly sent under subparagraph (A).

(76) "Software" means a computer program and any supporting information provided in connection with a transaction relating to the program. The term does not include a computer program that is included in the definition of goods.

(77) "State" means a State of the United States, the District of Columbia, Puerto Rico, the United States Virgin Islands, or any territory or insular possession subject to the jurisdiction of the United States.

(78) "Supporting obligation" means a letter-of-credit right or secondary obligation that supports the payment or performance of an account, chattel paper, a document, a general intangible, an instrument, or investment property.

(79) "Tangible chattel paper" means chattel paper evidenced by a record or records consisting of information that is inscribed on a tangible medium.

(80) "Termination statement" means an amendment of a financing statement which:

(A) identifies, by its file number, the initial financing statement to which it relates; and

(B) indicates either that it is a termination statement or that the identified financing statement is no longer effective.

(81) "Transmitting utility" means a person primarily engaged in the business of:

(A) operating a railroad, subway, street railway, or trolley bus;

(B) transmitting communications electrically, electromagnetically, or by light;

(C) transmitting goods by pipeline or sewer; or

(D) transmitting or producing and transmitting electricity, steam, gas, or water.

(b) **[Definitions in other articles.]** "Control" as provided in Section 7–106 and the following definitions in other articles apply to this article:

"Applicant". Section 5–102.
"Beneficiary". Section 5–102.
"Broker". Section 8–102.
"Certificated security". Section 8–102.
"Check". Section 3–104.
"Clearing corporation". Section 8–102.
"Contract for sale". Section 2–106.
"Customer". Section 4–104.
"Entitlement holder". Section 8–102.
"Financial asset". Section 8–102.
"Holder in due course". Section 3–302.
"Issuer" (with respect to a letter of credit or letter-of-credit right). Section 5–102.
"Issuer" (with respect to a security). Section 8–201.
"Issuer" (with respect to a document of title). Section 7–102.
"Lease". Section 2A–103.
"Lease agreement". Section 2A–103.
"Lease contract". Section 2A–103.
"Leasehold interest". Section 2A–103.
"Lessee". Section 2A–103.
"Lessee in ordinary course of business". Section 2A–103.
"Lessor". Section 2A–103.
"Lessor's residual interest". Section 2A–103.
"Letter of credit". Section 5–102.
"Merchant". Section 2–104.
"Negotiable instrument". Section 3–104.
"Nominated person". Section 5–102.
"Note". Section 3–104.
"Proceeds of a letter of credit". Section 5–114.
"Prove". Section 3–103.
"Sale". Section 2–106.
"Securities account". Section 8–501.
"Securities intermediary". Section 8–102.
"Security". Section 8–102.
"Security certificate". Section 8–102.

"Security entitlement". Section 8–102.

"Uncertificated security". Section 8–102.

(c)   **[Article 1 definitions and principles.]** Article 1 contains general definitions and principles of construction and interpretation applicable throughout this article.

As amended in 1999, 2000, 2001, 2003, and 2010.

Official Comment

1.   **Source.** All terms that are defined in Article 9 and used in more than one section are consolidated in this section. Note that the definition of "security interest" is found in Section 1–201, not in this Article, and has been revised. See Appendix I. [*Note from West Advisory Panel: Appendix I is omitted from this volume.*] Many of the definitions in this section are new; many others derive from those in former Section 9–105. The following Comments also indicate other sections of former Article 9 that defined (or explained) terms.

2.   **Parties to Secured Transactions.**

a.   **"Debtor"; "Obligor"; "Secondary Obligor."** Determining whether a person was a "debtor" under former Section 9–105(1)(d) required a close examination of the context in which the term was used. To reduce the need for this examination, this Article redefines "debtor" and adds new defined terms, "secondary obligor" and "obligor." In the context of Part 6 (default and enforcement), these definitions distinguish among three classes of persons: (i) those persons who may have a stake in the proper enforcement of a security interest by virtue of their non-lien property interest (typically, an ownership interest) in the collateral, (ii) those persons who may have a stake in the proper enforcement of the security interest because of their obligation to pay the secured debt, and (iii) those persons who have an obligation to pay the secured debt but have no stake in the proper enforcement of the security interest. Persons in the first class are debtors. Persons in the second class are secondary obligors if any portion of the obligation is secondary or if the obligor has a right of recourse against the debtor or another obligor with respect to an obligation secured by collateral. One must consult the law of suretyship to determine whether an obligation is secondary. The Restatement (3d), Suretyship and Guaranty § 1 (1996), contains a useful explanation of the concept. Obligors in the third class are neither debtors nor secondary obligors. With one exception (Section 9–616, as it relates to a consumer obligor), the rights and duties provided by Part 6 affect non-debtor obligors only if they are "secondary obligors."

By including in the definition of "debtor" all persons with a property interest (other than a security interest in or other lien on collateral), the definition includes transferees of collateral, whether or not the secured party knows of the transfer or the transferee's identity. Exculpatory provisions in Part 6 protect the secured party in that circumstance. See Sections 9–605 and 9–628. The definition renders unnecessary former Section 9–112, which governed situations in which collateral was not owned by the debtor. The definition also includes a "consignee," as defined in this section, as well as a seller of accounts, chattel paper, payment intangibles, or promissory notes.

Secured parties and other lienholders are excluded from the definition of "debtor" because the interests of those parties normally derive from and encumber a debtor's interest. However, if in a *separate* secured transaction a secured party grants, *as debtor*, a security interest in its own interest (i.e., its security interest and any obligation that it secures), the secured party is a debtor *in that transaction*. This typically occurs when a secured party with a security interest in specific goods assigns chattel paper.

Consider the following examples:

Example 1:   Behnfeldt borrows money and grants a security interest in her Miata to secure the debt. Behnfeldt is a debtor and an obligor.

Example 2:   Behnfeldt borrows money and grants a security interest in her Miata to secure the debt. Bruno co-signs a negotiable note as maker. As before, Behnfeldt is the debtor and an obligor. As an accommodation party (see Section 3–419), Bruno is a secondary obligor. Bruno has this status even if the note states that her obligation is a primary obligation and that she waives all suretyship defenses.

Example 3:   Behnfeldt borrows money on an unsecured basis. Bruno co-signs the note and grants a security interest in her Honda to secure her obligation. Inasmuch as Behnfeldt does not have a property interest in the Honda, Behnfeldt is not a debtor. Having granted the security interest, Bruno is the debtor. Because Behnfeldt is a principal obligor, she is not a secondary obligor. Whatever the outcome of enforcement of the security interest against the Honda or Bruno's secondary obligation, Bruno will look to Behnfeldt for her losses. The enforcement will not affect Behnfeldt's aggregate obligations.

When the principal obligor (borrower) and the secondary obligor (surety) each has granted a security interest in different collateral, the status of each is determined by the collateral involved.

Example 4: Behnfeldt borrows money and grants a security interest in her Miata to secure the debt. Bruno co-signs the note and grants a security interest in her Honda to secure her obligation. When the secured party enforces the security interest in Behnfeldt's Miata, Behnfeldt is the debtor, and Bruno is a secondary obligor. When the secured party enforces the security interest in the Honda, Bruno is the "debtor." As in Example 3, Behnfeldt is an obligor, but not a secondary obligor.

If a security interest is granted by a protected series of a limited liability company formed under the Uniform Protected Series Act (2017), the debtor is the protected series. See PEB Commentary No. 23, dated February 24, 2021. The Commentary is available at https://www.ali.org/peb-ucc.

b. **"Secured Party."** The secured party is the person in whose favor the security interest has been created, as determined by reference to the security agreement. This definition controls, among other things, which person has the duties and potential liability that Part 6 imposes upon a secured party. The definition of "secured party" also includes a "consignor," a person to which accounts, chattel paper, payment intangibles, or promissory notes have been sold, and the holder of an agricultural lien.

The definition of "secured party" clarifies the status of various types of representatives. Consider, for example, a multi-bank facility under which Bank A, Bank B, and Bank C are lenders and Bank A serves as the collateral agent. If the security interest is granted to the banks, then they are the secured parties. If the security interest is granted to Bank A as collateral agent, then Bank A is the secured party.

c. **Other Parties.** A "consumer obligor" is defined as the obligor in a consumer transaction. Definitions of "new debtor" and "original debtor" are used in the special rules found in Sections 9–326 and 9–508.

3. **Definitions Relating to Creation of a Security Interest.**

a. **"Collateral."** As under former Section 9–105, "collateral" is the property subject to a security interest and includes accounts and chattel paper that have been sold. It has been expanded in this Article. The term now explicitly includes proceeds subject to a security interest. It also reflects the broadened scope of the Article. It includes property subject to an agricultural lien as well as payment intangibles and promissory notes that have been sold.

b. **"Security Agreement."** The definition of "security agreement" is substantially the same as under former Section 9–105—an agreement that creates or provides for a security interest. However, the term frequently was used colloquially in former Article 9 to refer to the document or writing that contained a debtor's security agreement. This Article eliminates that usage, reserving the term for the more precise meaning specified in the definition.

Whether an agreement creates a security interest depends not on whether the parties intend that the law *characterize* the transaction as a security interest but rather on whether the transaction falls within the definition of "security interest" in Section 1–201. Thus, an agreement that the parties characterize as a "lease" of goods may be a "security agreement," notwithstanding the parties' stated intention that the law treat the transaction as a lease and not as a secured transaction. See Section 1–203.

4. **Goods-Related Definitions.**

a. **"Goods"; "Consumer Goods"; "Equipment"; "Farm Products"; "Farming Operation"; "Inventory."** The definition of "goods" is substantially the same as the definition in former Section 9–105. This Article also retains the four mutually-exclusive "types" of collateral that consist of goods: "consumer goods," "equipment," "farm products," and "inventory." The revisions are primarily for clarification.

The classes of goods are mutually exclusive. For example, the same property cannot simultaneously be both equipment and inventory. In borderline cases—a physician's car or a farmer's truck that might be either consumer goods or equipment—the principal use to which the property is put is determinative. Goods can fall into different classes at different times. For example, a radio may be inventory in the hands of a dealer and consumer goods in the hands of a consumer. As under former Article 9, goods are "equipment" if they do not fall into another category.

The definition of "consumer goods" follows former Section 9–109. The classification turns on whether the debtor uses or bought the goods for use "primarily for personal, family, or household purposes."

Goods are inventory if they are leased by a lessor or held by a person for sale or lease. The revised definition of "inventory" makes clear that the term includes goods leased by the debtor to others as well as goods held for lease. (The same result should have obtained under the former definition.) Goods to be furnished or furnished under a service contract, raw materials, and work in process also are inventory. Implicit in the definition is the criterion that the sales or leases are or will be in the ordinary course of business. For example, machinery used in manufacturing is equipment, not inventory, even though it is the policy of the debtor to sell machinery when it becomes obsolete or worn. Inventory also includes goods that are consumed in a business (e.g., fuel used in operations). In general, goods used in a business are equipment if they are fixed assets or have, as identifiable units, a relatively long period of use, but are inventory, even though not held for sale or lease, if they are used up or consumed in a short period of time in producing a product or providing a service.

Goods are "farm products" if the debtor is engaged in farming operations with respect to the goods. Animals in a herd of livestock are covered whether the debtor acquires them by purchase or as a result of natural increase. Products of crops or livestock remain farm products as long as they have not been subjected to a manufacturing process. The terms "crops" and "livestock" are not defined. The new definition of "farming operations" is for clarification only.

Crops, livestock, and their products cease to be "farm products" when the debtor ceases to be engaged in farming operations with respect to them. If, for example, they come into the possession of a marketing agency for sale or distribution or of a manufacturer or processor as raw materials, they become inventory. Products of crops or livestock, even though they remain in the possession of a person engaged in farming operations, lose their status as farm products if they are subjected to a manufacturing process. What is and what is not a manufacturing operation is not specified in this Article. At one end of the spectrum, some processes are so closely connected with farming—such as pasteurizing milk or boiling sap to produce maple syrup or sugar—that they would not constitute manufacturing. On the other hand an extensive canning operation would be manufacturing. Once farm products have been subjected to a manufacturing operation, they normally become inventory.

The revised definition of "farm products" clarifies the distinction between crops and standing timber and makes clear that aquatic goods produced in aquacultural operations may be either crops or livestock. Although aquatic goods that are vegetable in nature often would be crops and those that are animal would be livestock, this Article leaves the courts free to classify the goods on a case-by-case basis. See Section 9–324, Comment 11.

The definitions of "goods" and "software" are also mutually exclusive. Computer programs usually constitute "software," and, as such, are not "goods" as this Article uses the terms. However, under the circumstances specified in the definition of "goods," computer programs embedded in goods are part of the "goods" and are not "software."

b.   **"Accession"; "Manufactured Home"; "Manufactured-Home Transaction."** Other specialized definitions of goods include "accession" (see the special priority and enforcement rules in Section 9–335), and "manufactured home" (see Section 9–515, permitting a financing statement in a "manufactured-home transaction" to be effective for 30 years). The definition of "manufactured home" borrows from the federal Manufactured Housing Act, 42 U.S.C. §§ 5401 *et seq.*, and is intended to have the same meaning.

c.   **"As-Extracted Collateral."** Under this Article, oil, gas, and other minerals that have not been extracted from the ground are treated as real property, to which this Article does not apply. Upon extraction, minerals become personal property (goods) and eligible to be collateral under this Article. See the definition of "goods," which excludes "oil, gas, and other minerals before extraction." To take account of financing practices reflecting the shift from real to personal property, this Article contains special rules for perfecting security interests in minerals which attach upon extraction and in accounts resulting from the sale of minerals at the wellhead or minehead. See, e.g., Sections 9–301(4) (law governing perfection and priority); 9–501 (place of filing), 9–502 (contents of financing statement), 9–519 (indexing of records). The new term, "as-extracted collateral," refers to the minerals and related accounts to which the special rules apply. The term "at the wellhead" encompasses arrangements based on a sale of the produce at the moment that it issues from the ground and is measured, without technical distinctions as to whether title passes at the "Christmas tree" of a well, the far side of a gathering tank, or at some other point. The term "at . . . the minehead" is comparable.

The following examples explain the operation of these provisions.

Example 5:   Debtor owns an interest in oil that is to be extracted. To secure Debtor's obligations to Lender, Debtor enters into an authenticated agreement granting Lender an interest in the oil. Although Lender may acquire an interest in the oil under real-property law, Lender does not acquire a security interest under this Article until the oil becomes personal property, i.e., until is extracted and becomes "goods" to which this Article applies. Because Debtor had an interest in the oil before extraction and Lender's security interest attached to the oil as extracted, the oil is "as-extracted collateral."

Example 6:   Debtor owns an interest in oil that is to be extracted and contracts to sell the oil to Buyer at the wellhead. In an authenticated agreement, Debtor agrees to sell to Lender the right to payment from

Buyer. This right to payment is an account that constitutes "as-extracted collateral." If Lender then resells the account to Financer, Financer acquires a security interest. However, inasmuch as the debtor-seller in that transaction, Lender, had no interest in the oil before extraction, Financer's collateral (the account it owns) is not "as-extracted collateral."

Example 7:   Under the facts of Example 6, before extraction, Buyer grants a security interest in the oil to Bank. Although Bank's security interest attaches when the oil is extracted, Bank's security interest is not in "as-extracted collateral," inasmuch as its debtor, Buyer, did not have an interest in the oil before extraction.

5.   **Receivables-related Definitions.**

a.   **"Account"; "Health-Care-Insurance Receivable"; "As-Extracted Collateral."** The definition of "account" has been expanded and reformulated. It is no longer limited to rights to payment relating to goods or services. Many categories of rights to payment that were classified as general intangibles under former Article 9 are accounts under this Article. Thus, if they are sold, a financing statement must be filed to perfect the buyer's interest in them. As used in the definition of "account," a right to payment "arising out of the use of a credit or charge card or information contained on or for use with the card" is the right of a card issuer to payment from its cardholder. A credit-card or charge-card transaction may give rise to other rights to payments; however, those other rights do not "arise out of the use" of the card or information contained on or for use with the card. Among the types of property that are expressly excluded from the definition of account is "a right to payment for money or funds advanced or sold." As defined in Section 1–201, "money" is limited essentially to currency. As used in the exclusion from the definition of "account," however, "funds" is a broader concept (although the term is not defined). For example, when a bank-lender credits a borrower's deposit account for the amount of a loan, the bank's advance of funds is not a transaction giving rise to an account.

The definition of "health-care-insurance receivable" is new. It is a subset of the definition of "account." However, the rules generally applicable to account debtors on accounts do not apply to insurers obligated on health-care-insurance receivables. See Sections 9–404(e), 9–405(d), 9–406(i).

Note that certain accounts also are "as-extracted collateral." See Comment 4.c., Examples 6 and 7.

b.   **"Chattel Paper"; "Electronic Chattel Paper"; "Tangible Chattel Paper."** "Chattel paper" consists of a monetary obligation together with a security interest in or a lease of specific goods if the obligation and security interest or lease are evidenced by "a record or records." The definition has been expanded from that found in former Article 9 to include records that evidence a monetary obligation and a security interest in specific goods and software used in the goods, a security interest in specific goods and license of software used in the goods, or a lease of specific goods and license of software used in the goods. The expanded definition covers transactions in which the debtor's or lessee's monetary obligation includes amounts owed with respect to software used in the goods. The monetary obligation with respect to the software need not be owed under a license from the secured party or lessor, and the secured party or lessor need not be a party to the license transaction itself. Among the types of monetary obligations that are included in "chattel paper" are amounts that have been advanced by the secured party or lessor to enable the debtor or lessee to acquire or obtain financing for a license of the software used in the goods. The definition also makes clear that rights to payment arising out of credit-card transactions are not chattel paper.

Charters of vessels are expressly excluded from the definition of chattel paper; they are accounts. The term "charter" as used in this section includes bareboat charters, time charters, successive voyage charters, contracts of affreightment, contracts of carriage, and all other arrangements for the use of vessels. Under former Section 9–105, only if the evidence of an obligation consisted of "a writing or writings" could an obligation qualify as chattel paper. In this Article, traditional, written chattel paper is included in the definition of "tangible chattel paper." "Electronic chattel paper" is chattel paper that is stored in an electronic medium instead of in tangible form.

The concept of an electronic medium should be construed liberally to include electrical, digital, magnetic, optical, electromagnetic, or any other current or similar emerging technologies.

c.   **"Instrument"; "Promissory Note."** The definition of "instrument" includes a negotiable instrument. As under former Section 9–105, it also includes any other right to payment of a monetary obligation that is evidenced by a writing of a type that in ordinary course of business is transferred by delivery (and, if necessary, an indorsement or assignment). Except in the case of chattel paper, the fact that an instrument is secured by a security interest or encumbrance on property does not change the character of the instrument as such or convert the combination of the instrument and collateral into a separate classification of personal property. The definition makes clear that rights to payment arising out of credit-card transactions are not instruments. The definition of "promissory note" is new, necessitated by the inclusion of sales of promissory notes within the scope of Article 9. It explicitly excludes obligations arising out of "orders" to pay (e.g., checks) as opposed to "promises" to pay. See Section 3–104.

    d.   **"General Intangible"; "Payment Intangible."** "General intangible" is the residual category of personal property, including things in action, that is not included in the other defined types of collateral. Examples are various categories of intellectual property and the right to payment of a loan of funds that is not evidenced by chattel paper or an instrument. As used in the definition of "general intangible," "things in action" includes rights that arise under a license of intellectual property, including the right to exploit the intellectual property without liability for infringement. The definition has been revised to exclude commercial tort claims, deposit accounts, and letter-of-credit rights. Each of the three is a separate type of collateral. One important consequence of this exclusion is that tortfeasors (commercial tort claims), banks (deposit accounts), and persons obligated on letters of credit (letter-of-credit rights) are not "account debtors" having the rights and obligations set forth in Sections 9–404, 9–405, and 9–406. In particular, tortfeasors, banks, and persons obligated on letters of credit are not obligated to pay an assignee (secured party) upon receipt of the notification described in Section 9–404(a). See Comment 5.h. Another important consequence relates to the adequacy of the description in the security agreement. See Section 9–108.

    "Payment intangible" is a subset of the definition of "general intangible." The sale of a payment intangible is subject to this Article. See Section 9–109(a)(3). Virtually any intangible right could give rise to a right to payment of money once one hypothesizes, for example, that the account debtor is in breach of its obligation. The term "payment intangible," however, embraces only those general intangibles "under which the account debtor's *principal* obligation is a monetary obligation." (Emphasis added.) A debtor's right to payment from another person of amounts received by the other person on the debtor's behalf, including the right of a merchant in a credit-card, debit-card, prepaid-card, or other payment-card transaction to payment of amounts received by its bank from the card system in settlement of the transaction, is a "payment intangible." (In contrast, the right of a credit-card issuer to payment arising out of the use of a credit card is an "account.")

    In classifying intangible collateral, a court should begin by identifying the particular rights that have been assigned. The account debtor (promisor) under a particular contract may owe several types of monetary obligations as well as other, nonmonetary obligations. If the promisee's right to payment of money is assigned separately, the right is an account or payment intangible, depending on how the account debtor's obligation arose. When all the promisee's rights are assigned together, an account, a payment intangible, and a general intangible all may be involved, depending on the nature of the rights.

    A right to the payment of money is frequently buttressed by ancillary rights, such as rights arising from covenants in a purchase agreement, note, or mortgage requiring insurance on the collateral or forbidding removal of the collateral, rights arising from covenants to preserve the creditworthiness of the promisor, and the lessor's rights with respect to leased goods that arise upon the lessee's default (see Section 2A–523). This Article does not treat these ancillary rights separately from the rights to payment to which they relate. For example, attachment and perfection of an assignment of a right to payment of a monetary obligation, whether it be an account or payment intangible, also carries these ancillary rights. Thus, an assignment of the lessor's right to payment under a lease also transfers the lessor's rights with respect to the leased goods under Section 2A–523. If, taken together, the lessor's rights to payment and with respect to the leased goods are evidenced by chattel paper, then, contrary to *In re Commercial Money Center, Inc.*, 350 B.R. 465 (Bankr. App. 9th Cir. 2006), an assignment of the lessor's right to payment constitutes an assignment of the chattel paper. Although an agreement excluding the lessor's rights with respect to the leased goods from an assignment of the lessor's right to payment may be effective between the parties, the agreement does not affect the characterization of the collateral to the prejudice of creditors of, and purchasers from, the assignor.

    Every "payment intangible" is also a "general intangible." Likewise, "software" is a "general intangible" for purposes of this Article. See Comment 25. Accordingly, except as otherwise provided, statutory provisions applicable to general intangibles apply to payment intangibles and software.

    e.   **"Letter-of-Credit Right."** The term "letter-of-credit right" embraces the rights to payment and performance under a letter of credit (defined in Section 5–102). However, it does not include a beneficiary's right to demand payment or performance. Transfer of those rights to a transferee beneficiary is governed by Article 5. See Sections 9–107, Comment 4, and 9–329, Comments 3 and 4.

    f.   **"Supporting Obligation."** This new term covers the most common types of credit enhancements—suretyship obligations (including guarantees) and letter-of-credit rights that support one of the types of collateral specified in the definition. As explained in Comment 2.a., suretyship law determines whether an obligation is "secondary" for purposes of this definition. Section 9–109 generally excludes from this Article transfers of interests in insurance policies. However, the regulation of a secondary obligation as an insurance product does not necessarily mean that it is a "policy of insurance" for purposes of the exclusion in Section 9–109. Thus, this Article may cover a secondary obligation (as a supporting obligation), even if the obligation is issued by a regulated insurance company and the obligation is subject to regulation as an "insurance" product.

This Article contains rules explicitly governing attachment, perfection, and priority of security interests in supporting obligations. See Sections 9–203, 9–308, 9–310, and 9–322. These provisions reflect the principle that a supporting obligation is an incident of the collateral it supports.

Collections of or other distributions under a supporting obligation are "proceeds" of the supported collateral as well as "proceeds" of the supporting obligation itself. See Section 9–102 (defining "proceeds") and Comment 13.b. As such, the collections and distributions are subject to the priority rules applicable to proceeds generally. See Section 9–322. However, under the special rule governing security interests in a letter-of-credit right, a secured party's failure to obtain control (Section 9–107) of a letter-of-credit right supporting collateral may leave its security interest exposed to a priming interest of a party who does take control. See Section 9–329 (security interest in a letter-of-credit right perfected by control has priority over a conflicting security interest).

g. **"Commercial Tort Claim."** This term is new. A tort claim may serve as original collateral under this Article only if it is a "commercial tort claim." See Section 9–109(d). Although security interests in commercial tort claims are within its scope, this Article does not override other applicable law restricting the assignability of a tort claim. See Section 9–401. A security interest in a tort claim also may exist under this Article if the claim is proceeds of other collateral.

h. **"Account Debtor."** An "account debtor" is a person obligated on an account, chattel paper, or general intangible. The account debtor's obligation often is a monetary obligation; however, this is not always the case. For example, if a franchisee uses its rights under a franchise agreement (a general intangible) as collateral, then the franchisor is an "account debtor." As a general matter, Article 3, and not Article 9, governs obligations on negotiable instruments. Accordingly, the definition of "account debtor" excludes obligors on negotiable instruments constituting part of chattel paper. The principal effect of this change from the definition in former Article 9 is that the rules in Sections 9–403, 9–404, 9–405, and 9–406, dealing with the rights of an assignee and duties of an account debtor, do not apply to an assignment of chattel paper in which the obligation to pay is evidenced by a negotiable instrument. (Section 9–406(d), however, does apply to promissory notes, including negotiable promissory notes.) Rather, the assignee's rights are governed by Article 3. Similarly, the duties of an obligor on a nonnegotiable instrument are governed by non-Article 9 law unless the nonnegotiable instrument is a part of chattel paper, in which case the obligor is an account debtor.

i. **Receivables Under Government Entitlement Programs**. This Article does not contain a defined term that encompasses specifically rights to payment or performance under the many and varied government entitlement programs. Depending on the nature of a right under a program, it could be an account, a payment intangible, a general intangible other than a payment intangible, or another type of collateral. The right also might be proceeds of collateral (e.g., crops).

6. **Investment-Property-Related Definitions: "Commodity Account"; "Commodity Contract"; "Commodity Customer"; "Commodity Intermediary"; "Investment Property."** These definitions are substantially the same as the corresponding definitions in former Section 9–115. "Investment property" includes securities, both certificated and uncertificated, securities accounts, security entitlements, commodity accounts, and commodity contracts. The term investment property includes a "securities account" in order to facilitate transactions in which a debtor wishes to create a security interest in all of the investment positions held through a particular account rather than in particular positions carried in the account. Former Section 9–115 was added in conjunction with Revised Article 8 and contained a variety of rules applicable to security interests in investment property. These rules have been relocated to the appropriate sections of Article 9. See, e.g., Sections 9–203 (attachment), 9–314 (perfection by control), 9–328 (priority).

The terms "security," "security entitlement," and related terms are defined in Section 8–102, and the term "securities account" is defined in Section 8–501. The terms "commodity account," "commodity contract," "commodity customer," and "commodity intermediary" are defined in this section. Commodity contracts are not "securities" or "financial assets" under Article 8. See Section 8–103(f). Thus, the relationship between commodity intermediaries and commodity customers is not governed by the indirect-holding-system rules of Part 5 of Article 8. For securities, Article 9 contains rules on security interests, and Article 8 contains rules on the rights of transferees, including secured parties, on such matters as the rights of a transferee if the transfer was itself wrongful and gives rise to an adverse claim. For commodity contracts, Article 9 establishes rules on security interests, but questions of the sort dealt with in Article 8 for securities are left to other law.

The indirect-holding-system rules of Article 8 are sufficiently flexible to be applied to new developments in the securities and financial markets, where that is appropriate. Accordingly, the definition of "commodity contract" is narrowly drafted to ensure that it does not operate as an obstacle to the application of the Article 8 indirect-holding-system rules to new products. The term "commodity contract" covers those contracts that are traded on or subject to the rules of a designated contract market and foreign commodity contracts that are carried on the books of American commodity intermediaries. The effect of this definition is that the category of commodity contracts that are excluded from Article 8 but governed by Article 9 is essentially the same as the category of contracts that fall within the exclusive regulatory jurisdiction of the federal Commodity Futures Trading Commission.

Commodity contracts are different from securities or other financial assets. A person who enters into a commodity futures contract is not buying an asset having a certain value and holding it in anticipation of increase in value. Rather the person is entering into a contract to buy or sell a commodity at set price for delivery at a future time. That contract may become advantageous or disadvantageous as the price of the commodity fluctuates during the term of the contract. The rules of the commodity exchanges require that the contracts be marked to market on a daily basis; that is, the customer pays or receives any increment attributable to that day's price change. Because commodity customers may incur obligations on their contracts, they are required to provide collateral at the outset, known as "original margin," and may be required to provide additional amounts, known as "variation margin," during the term of the contract.

The most likely setting in which a person would want to take a security interest in a commodity contract is where a lender who is advancing funds to finance an inventory of a physical commodity requires the borrower to enter into a commodity contract as a hedge against the risk of decline in the value of the commodity. The lender will want to take a security interest in both the commodity itself and the hedging commodity contract. Typically, such arrangements are structured as security interests in the entire commodity account in which the borrower carries the hedging contracts, rather than in individual contracts.

One important effect of including commodity contracts and commodity accounts in Article 9 is to provide a clearer legal structure for the analysis of the rights of commodity clearing organizations against their participants and futures commission merchants against their customers. The rules and agreements of commodity clearing organizations generally provide that the clearing organization has the right to liquidate any participant's positions in order to satisfy obligations of the participant to the clearing corporation. Similarly, agreements between futures commission merchants and their customers generally provide that the futures commission merchant has the right to liquidate a customer's positions in order to satisfy obligations of the customer to the futures commission merchant.

The main property that a commodity intermediary holds as collateral for the obligations that the commodity customer may incur under its commodity contracts is not other commodity contracts carried by the customer but the other property that the customer has posted as margin. Typically, this property will be securities. The commodity intermediary's security interest in such securities is governed by the rules of this Article on security interests in securities, not the rules on security interests in commodity contracts or commodity accounts.

Although there are significant analytic and regulatory differences between commodities and securities, the development of commodity contracts on financial products in the past few decades has resulted in a system in which the commodity markets and securities markets are closely linked. The rules on security interests in commodity contracts and commodity accounts provide a structure that may be essential in times of stress in the financial markets. Suppose, for example that a firm has a position in a securities market that is hedged by a position in a commodity market, so that payments that the firm is obligated to make with respect to the securities position will be covered by the receipt of funds from the commodity position. Depending upon the settlement cycles of the different markets, it is possible that the firm could find itself in a position where it is obligated to make the payment with respect to the securities position before it receives the matching funds from the commodity position. If cross-margining arrangements have not been developed between the two markets, the firm may need to borrow funds temporarily to make the earlier payment. The rules on security interests in investment property would facilitate the use of positions in one market as collateral for loans needed to cover obligations in the other market.

7.   **Consumer-Related Definitions: "Consumer Debtor"; "Consumer Goods"; "Consumer-goods transaction"; "Consumer Obligor"; "Consumer Transaction."** The definition of "consumer goods" (discussed above) is substantially the same as the definition in former Section 9-109. The definitions of "consumer debtor," "consumer obligor," "consumer-goods transaction," and "consumer transaction" have been added in connection with

various new (and old) consumer-related provisions and to designate certain provisions that are inapplicable in consumer transactions.

"Consumer-goods transaction" is a subset of "consumer transaction." Under each definition, both the obligation secured and the collateral must have a personal, family, or household purpose. However, "mixed" business and personal transactions also may be characterized as a consumer-goods transaction or consumer transaction. Subparagraph (A) of the definition of consumer-goods transactions and clause (i) of the definition of consumer transaction are primary purposes tests. Under these tests, it is necessary to determine the primary purpose of the obligation or obligations secured. Subparagraph (B) and clause (iii) of these definitions are satisfied if any of the collateral is consumer goods, in the case of a consumer-goods transaction, or "is held or acquired primarily for personal, family, or household purposes," in the case of a consumer transaction. The fact that some of the obligations secured or some of the collateral for the obligation does not satisfy the tests (e.g., some of the collateral is acquired for a business purpose) does not prevent a transaction from being a "consumer transaction" or "consumer-goods transaction."

8. **Filing-Related Definitions: "Continuation Statement"; "File Number"; "Filing Office"; "Filing-office Rule"; "Financing Statement"; "Fixture Filing"; "Manufactured-Home Transaction"; "New Debtor"; "Original Debtor"; "Public-Finance Transaction"; "Termination Statement"; "Transmitting Utility."** These definitions are used exclusively or primarily in the filing-related provisions in Part 5. Most are self-explanatory and are discussed in the Comments to Part 5. A financing statement filed in a manufactured-home transaction or a public-finance transaction may remain effective for 30 years instead of the 5 years applicable to other financing statements. See Section 9–515(b). The definitions relating to medium neutrality also are significant for the filing provisions. See Comment 9.

The definition of "transmitting utility" has been revised to embrace the business of transmitting communications generally to take account of new and future types of communications technology. The term designates a special class of debtors for whom separate filing rules are provided in Part 5, thereby obviating the many local fixture filings that would be necessary under the rules of Section 9–501 for a far-flung public-utility debtor. A transmitting utility will not necessarily be regulated by or operating as such in a jurisdiction where fixtures are located. For example, a utility might own transmission lines in a jurisdiction, although the utility generates no power and has no customers in the jurisdiction.

9. **Definitions Relating to Medium Neutrality.**

a. **"Record."** In many, but not all, instances, the term "record" replaces the term "writing" and "written." A "record" includes information that is in intangible form (e.g., electronically stored) as well as tangible form (e.g., written on paper). Given the rapid development and commercial adoption of modern communication and storage technologies, requirements that documents or communications be "written," "in writing," or otherwise in tangible form do not necessarily reflect or aid commercial practices.

A "record" need not be permanent or indestructible, but the term does not include any oral or other communication that is not stored or preserved by any means. The information must be stored on paper or in some other medium. Information that has not been retained other than through human memory does not qualify as a record. Examples of current technologies commercially used to communicate or store information include, but are not limited to, magnetic media, optical discs, digital voice messaging systems, electronic mail, audio tapes, and photographic media, as well as paper. "Record" is an inclusive term that includes all of these methods of storing or communicating information. Any "writing" is a record. A record may be authenticated. See Comment 9.b. A record may be created without the knowledge or intent of a particular person.

Like the terms "written" or "in writing," the term "record" does not establish the purposes, permitted uses, or legal effect that a record may have under any particular provision of law. Whatever is filed in the Article 9 filing system, including financing statements, continuation statements, and termination statements, whether transmitted in tangible or intangible form, would fall within the definition. However, in some instances, statutes or filing-office rules may require that a paper record be filed. In such cases, even if this Article permits the filing of an electronic record, compliance with those statutes or rules is necessary. Similarly, a filer must comply with a statute or rule that requires a particular type of encoding or formatting for an electronic record.

This Article sometimes uses the terms "for record," "of record," "record or legal title," and "record owner." Some of these are terms traditionally used in real-property law. The definition of "record" in this Article now explicitly excepts these usages from the defined term. Also, this Article refers to a record that is filed or recorded in real-property recording systems to record a mortgage as a "record of a mortgage." This usage recognizes that the defined term "mortgage" means an interest in real property; it does not mean the record that evidences, or is filed or recorded with respect to, the mortgage.

b. **"Authenticate"; "Communicate"; "Send."** The terms "authenticate" and "authenticated" generally replace "sign" and "signed." "Authenticated" replaces and broadens the definition of "signed," in Section 1–201, to encompass authentication of all records, not just writings. (References to authentication of, e.g., an agreement, demand, or notification mean, of course, authentication of a record containing an agreement, demand, or notification.) The terms "communicate" and "send" also contemplate the possibility of communication by nonwritten media. These definitions include the act of transmitting both tangible and intangible records. The definition of "send" replaces, for purposes of this Article, the corresponding term in Section 1–201. The reference to "usual means of communication" in that definition contemplates an inquiry into the appropriateness of the method of transmission used in the particular circumstances involved.

10. **Scope-Related Definitions.**

a. **Expanded Scope of Article: "Agricultural Lien"; "Consignment"; "Payment Intangible"; "Promissory Note."** These new definitions reflect the expanded scope of Article 9, as provided in Section 9–109(a).

b. **Reduced Scope of Exclusions: "Governmental Unit"; "Health-Care-Insurance Receivable"; "Commercial Tort Claims."** These new definitions reflect the reduced scope of the exclusions, provided in Section 9–109(c) and (d), of transfers by governmental debtors and assignments of interests in insurance policies and commercial tort claims.

11. **Choice-of-Law-Related Definitions: "Certificate of Title"; "Governmental Unit"; "Jurisdiction of Organization"; "Public Organic Record"; "Registered Organization"; "State."** These new definitions reflect the changes in the law governing perfection and priority of security interests and agricultural liens provided in Part 3, Subpart 1.

Statutes often require applicants for a certificate of title to identify all security interests on the application and require the issuing agency to indicate the identified security interests on the certificate. Some of these statutes provide that priority over the rights of a lien creditor (i.e., perfection of a security interest) in goods covered by the certificate occurs upon indication of the security interest on the certificate; that is, they provide for the indication of the security interest on the certificate as a "condition" of perfection. Other statutes contemplate that perfection is achieved upon the occurrence of another act, e.g., delivery of the application to the issuing agency, that "results" in the indication of the security interest on the certificate. A certificate governed by either type of statute can qualify as a "certificate of title" under this Article. The statute providing for the indication of a security interest need not expressly state the connection between the indication and perfection. For example, a certificate issued pursuant to a statute that requires applicants to identify security interests, requires the issuing agency to indicate the identified security interests on the certificate, but is silent concerning the legal consequences of the indication would be a "certificate of title" if, under a judicial interpretation of the statute, perfection of a security interest is a legal consequence of the indication. Likewise, a certificate would be a "certificate of title" if another statute provides, expressly or as interpreted, the requisite connection between the indication and perfection.

The first sentence of the definition of "certificate of title" includes certificates consisting of tangible records, of electronic records, and of combinations of tangible and electronic records.

In many States, a certificate of title covering goods that are encumbered by a security interest is delivered to the secured party by the issuing authority. To eliminate the need for the issuance of a paper certificate under these circumstances, several States have revised their certificate-of-title statutes to permit or require a State agency to maintain an electronic record that evidences ownership of the goods and in which a security interest in the goods may be noted. The second sentence of the definition provides that such a record is a "certificate of title" if it is in fact maintained as an alternative to the issuance of a paper certificate of title, regardless of whether the certificate-of-title statute provides that the record is a certificate of title and even if the statute does not expressly state that the record is maintained instead of issuing a paper certificate.

Not every organization that may provide information about itself in the public records is a "registered organization." For example, a general partnership is not a "registered organization," even if it files a statement of partnership authority under Section 303 of the Uniform Partnership Act (1994) or an assumed name ("dba") certificate. This is because such a partnership is not formed or organized by the filing of a record with, or the issuance of a record by, a State or the United States. Likewise, a limited liability partnership, which is a form of general partnership under the Uniform Partnership Act (1997), is not a "registered organization" even if it has filed a record that is a statement of qualification under Section 1001 of the Uniform Partnership Act (1997). The filing of the record does not form or organize the partnership. The filing only provides the partners in the general partnership with a limited liability shield and evidences that the general partnership has limited liability partnership status. See PEB Commentary No. 17. As discussed in PEB Commentary No. 17 the same conclusion

714

would apply to a limited liability partnership formed under the law of state that has not adopted the Uniform Partnership Act (1997) but has adopted for limited liability partnerships similar legislation having the material attributes of that Act. Also as discussed in PEB Commentary No. 17, the same conclusion would apply whether before or after giving effect to the 2010 amendments to this Article. In contrast, corporations, limited liability companies, and limited partnerships ordinarily are "registered organizations."

Not every record concerning a registered organization that is filed with, or issued by, a State or the United States is a "public organic record." For example, a certificate of good standing issued with respect to a corporation or a published index of domestic corporations would not be a "public organic record" because its issuance or publication does not form or organize the corporations named.

When collateral is held in a trust, one must look to non-UCC law to determine whether the trust is a "registered organization." Non-UCC law typically distinguishes between statutory trusts and common-law trusts. A statutory trust is formed by the filing of a record, commonly referred to as a certificate of trust, in a public office pursuant to a statute. See, e.g., Uniform Statutory Trust Entity Act § 201 (2009); Delaware Statutory Trust Act, Del. Code Ann. tit. 12, § 3801 et seq. A statutory trust is a juridical entity, separate from its trustee and beneficial owners, that may sue and be sued, own property, and transact business in its own name. Inasmuch as a statutory trust is a "legal or commercial entity," it qualifies as a "person other than an individual," and therefore as an "organization," under Section 1–201. A statutory trust that is formed by the filing of a record in a public office is a "registered organization," and the filed record is a "public organic record" of the statutory trust, if the filed record is available to the public for inspection. (The requirement that a record be "available to the public for inspection" is satisfied if a copy of the relevant record is available for public inspection.)

Unlike a statutory trust, a common-law trust—whether its purpose is donative or commercial—arises from private action without the filing of a record in a public office. See Uniform Trust Code § 401 (2000); Restatement (Third) of Trusts § 10 (2003). Moreover, under traditional law, a common-law trust is not itself a juridical entity and therefore must sue and be sued, own property, and transact business in the name of the trustee acting in the capacity of trustee. A common-law trust that is a "business trust," i.e., that has a business or commercial purpose, is an "organization" under Section 1–201. However, such a trust would not be a "registered organization" if, as is typically the case, the filing of a public record is not needed to form it.

In some states, however, the trustee of a common-law trust that has a commercial or business purpose is required by statute to file a record in a public office following the trust's formation. See, e.g., Mass. Gen. Laws Ch. 182, § 2; Fla. Stat. Ann. § 609.02. A business trust that is required to file its organic record in a public office is a "registered organization" under the second sentence of the definition if the filed record is available to the public for inspection. Any organic record required to be filed, and filed, with respect to a common-law business trust after the trust is formed is a "public organic record" of the trust. Some statutes require a trust or other organization to file, after formation or organization, a record other than an organic record. See, e.g., N.Y. Gen. Ass'n's Law § 18 (requiring associations doing business within New York to file a certificate designating the secretary of state as an agent upon whom process may be served). This requirement does not render the organization a "registered organization" under the second sentence of the definition, and the record is not a "public organic record."

12. **Deposit-Account-Related Definitions: "Deposit Account"; "Bank."** The revised definition of "deposit account" incorporates the definition of "bank," which is new. The definition derives from the definitions of "bank" in Sections 4–105(1) and 4A–105(a)(2), which focus on whether the organization is "engaged in the business of banking."

Deposit accounts evidenced by Article 9 "instruments" are excluded from the term "deposit account." In contrast, former Section 9–105 excluded from the former definition "an account evidenced by a certificate of deposit." The revised definition clarifies the proper treatment of nonnegotiable or uncertificated certificates of deposit. Under the definition, an uncertificated certificate of deposit would be a deposit account (assuming there is no writing evidencing the bank's obligation to pay) whereas a nonnegotiable certificate of deposit would be a deposit account only if it is not an "instrument" as defined in this section (a question that turns on whether the nonnegotiable certificate of deposit is "of a type that in ordinary course of business is transferred by delivery with any necessary indorsement or assignment.")

A deposit account evidenced by an instrument is subject to the rules applicable to instruments generally. As a consequence, a security interest in such an instrument cannot be perfected by "control" (see Section 9–104), and the special priority rules applicable to deposit accounts (see Sections 9–327 and 9–340) do not apply.

The term "deposit account" does not include "investment property," such as securities and security entitlements. Thus, the term also does not include shares in a money-market mutual fund, even if the shares are redeemable by check.

13. **Proceeds-Related Definitions: "Cash Proceeds"; "Noncash Proceeds"; "Proceeds."** The revised definition of "proceeds" expands the definition beyond that contained in former Section 9–306 and resolves ambiguities in the former section.

a. **Distributions on Account of Collateral.** The phrase "whatever is collected on, or distributed on account of, collateral," in subparagraph (B), is broad enough to cover cash or stock dividends distributed on account of securities or other investment property that is original collateral. Compare former Section 9–306 ("Any payments or distributions made with respect to investment property collateral are proceeds."). This section rejects the holding of *FDIC v. Hastie*, 2 F.3d 1042 (10th Cir. 1993) (postpetition cash dividends on stock subject to a prepetition pledge are not "proceeds" under Bankruptcy Code Section 552(b)), to the extent the holding relies on the Article 9 definition of "proceeds."

b. **Distributions on Account of Supporting Obligations.** Under subparagraph (B), collections on and distributions on account of collateral consisting of various credit-support arrangements ("supporting obligations," as defined in Section 9–102) also are proceeds. Consequently, they are afforded treatment identical to proceeds collected from or distributed by the obligor on the underlying (supported) right to payment or other collateral. Proceeds of supporting obligations also are proceeds of the underlying rights to payment or other collateral.

c. **Proceeds of Proceeds.** The definition of "proceeds" no longer provides that proceeds of proceeds are themselves proceeds. That idea is expressed in the revised definition of "collateral" in Section 9–102. No change in meaning is intended.

d. **Proceeds Received by Person Who Did Not Create Security Interest.** When collateral is sold subject to a security interest and the buyer then resells the collateral, a question arose under former Article 9 concerning whether the "debtor" had "received" what the buyer received on resale and, therefore, whether those receipts were "proceeds" under former Section 9–306(2). This Article contains no requirement that property be "received" by the debtor for the property to qualify as proceeds. It is necessary only that the property be traceable, directly or indirectly, to the original collateral.

e. **Cash Proceeds and Noncash Proceeds.** The definition of "cash proceeds" is substantially the same as the corresponding definition in former Section 9–306. The phrase "and the like" covers property that is functionally equivalent to "money, checks, or deposit accounts," such as some money-market accounts that are securities or part of securities entitlements. Proceeds other than cash proceeds are noncash proceeds.

14. **Consignment-Related Definitions: "Consignee"; "Consignment"; "Consignor."** The definition of "consignment" excludes, in subparagraphs (B) and (C), transactions for which filing would be inappropriate or of insufficient benefit to justify the costs. A consignment excluded from the application of this Article by one of those subparagraphs may still be a true consignment; however, it is governed by non-Article 9 law. The definition also excludes, in subparagraph (D), what have been called "consignments intended for security." These "consignments" are not bailments but secured transactions. Accordingly, all of Article 9 applies to them. See Sections 1–201(b)(35), 9–109(a)(1). The "consignor" is the person who delivers goods to the "consignee" in a consignment.

The definition of "consignment" requires that the goods be delivered "to a merchant for the purpose of sale." If the goods are delivered for another purpose as well, such as milling or processing, the transaction is a consignment nonetheless because a purpose of the delivery is "sale." On the other hand, if a merchant-processor-bailee will not be selling the goods itself but will be delivering to buyers to which the owner-bailor agreed to sell the goods, the transaction would not be a consignment.

Under clause (iii) of subparagraph (A), a transaction is not an Article 9 "consignment" if the consignee is "generally known by its creditors to be substantially engaged in selling the goods of others." Clause (iii) does not apply solely because a particular competing claimant knows that the goods are held on consignment. See PEB Commentary No. 20, dated January 24, 2019.

15. **"Accounting."** This definition describes the record and information that a debtor is entitled to request under Section 9–210.

16. **"Document."** The definition of "document" incorporates both tangible and electronic documents of title. See Section 1–201(b)16 and Comment 16.

18. **"Fixtures."** This definition is unchanged in substance from the corresponding definition in former Section 9–313. See Section 9–334 (priority of security interests in fixtures and crops).

19. **"Good Faith."** This Article expands the definition of "good faith" to include "the observance of reasonable commercial standards of fair dealing." The definition in this section applies when the term is used in

this Article, and the same concept applies in the context of this Article for purposes of the obligation of good faith imposed by Section 1–203 [*unrevised Article 1; see Concordance, p. 22*]. See subsection (c).

20. **"Lien Creditor"** This definition is unchanged in substance from the corresponding definition in former Section 9–301.

21. **"New Value."** This Article deletes former Section 9–108. Its broad formulation of new value, which embraced the taking of after-acquired collateral for a pre-existing claim, was unnecessary, counterintuitive, and ineffective for its original purpose of sheltering after-acquired collateral from attack as a voidable preference in bankruptcy. The new definition derives from Bankruptcy Code Section 547(a). The term is used with respect to temporary perfection of security interests in instruments, certificated securities, or negotiable documents under Section 9–312(e) and with respect to chattel paper priority in Section 9–330.

22. **"Person Related To."** Section 9–615 provides a special method for calculating a deficiency or surplus when "the secured party, a person related to the secured party, or a secondary obligor" acquires the collateral at a foreclosure disposition. Separate definitions of the term are provided with respect to an individual secured party and with respect to a secured party that is an organization. The definitions are patterned on the corresponding definition in Section 1.301(32) of the Uniform Consumer Credit Code (1974).

23. **"Proposal."** This definition describes a record that is sufficient to propose to retain collateral in full or partial satisfaction of a secured obligation. See Sections 9–620, 9–621, 9–622.

24. **"Pursuant to Commitment."** This definition is unchanged in substance from the corresponding definition in former Section 9–105. It is used in connection with special priority rules applicable to future advances. See Section 9–323.

25. **"Software."** The definition of "software" is used in connection with the priority rules applicable to purchase-money security interests. See Sections 9–103, 9–324. Software, like a payment intangible, is a type of general intangible for purposes of this Article. See Comment 4.a., above, regarding the distinction between "goods" and "software."

26. **Terminology: "Assignment" and "Transfer."** In numerous provisions, this Article refers to the "assignment" or the "transfer" of property interests. These terms and their derivatives are not defined. This Article generally follows common usage by using the terms "assignment" and "assign" to refer to transfers of rights to payment, claims, and liens and other security interests. It generally uses the term "transfer" to refer to other transfers of interests in property. Except when used in connection with a letter-of-credit transaction (see Section 9–107, Comment 4), no significance should be placed on the use of one term or the other. Depending on the substance of the transaction, each term as used in this Article refers to the assignment or transfer of an outright ownership interest, to the assignment or transfer of a limited interest, such as a security interest, or both. See Comment 8 to Section 9–401 and PEB Commentary No. 21, dated March 11, 2020.

As amended in 1999, 2000, 2001, 2003, 2010, 2012, 2019, 2020, and 2021.

§ 9–103. Purchase-Money Security Interest; Application of Payments; Burden of Establishing.

(a) **[Definitions.]** In this section:

(1) "purchase-money collateral" means goods or software that secures a purchase-money obligation incurred with respect to that collateral; and

(2) "purchase-money obligation" means an obligation of an obligor incurred as all or part of the price of the collateral or for value given to enable the debtor to acquire rights in or the use of the collateral if the value is in fact so used.

(b) **[Purchase-money security interest in goods.]** A security interest in goods is a purchase-money security interest:

(1) to the extent that the goods are purchase-money collateral with respect to that security interest;

(2) if the security interest is in inventory that is or was purchase-money collateral, also to the extent that the security interest secures a purchase-money obligation incurred with respect to other inventory in which the secured party holds or held a purchase-money security interest; and

(3)   also to the extent that the security interest secures a purchase-money obligation incurred with respect to software in which the secured party holds or held a purchase-money security interest.

(c)   **[Purchase-money security interest in software.]** A security interest in software is a purchase-money security interest to the extent that the security interest also secures a purchase-money obligation incurred with respect to goods in which the secured party holds or held a purchase-money security interest if:

(1)   the debtor acquired its interest in the software in an integrated transaction in which it acquired an interest in the goods; and

(2)   the debtor acquired its interest in the software for the principal purpose of using the software in the goods.

(d)   **[Consignor's inventory purchase-money security interest.]** The security interest of a consignor in goods that are the subject of a consignment is a purchase-money security interest in inventory.

(e)   **[Application of payment in non-consumer-goods transaction.]** In a transaction other than a consumer-goods transaction, if the extent to which a security interest is a purchase-money security interest depends on the application of a payment to a particular obligation, the payment must be applied:

(1)   in accordance with any reasonable method of application to which the parties agree;

(2)   in the absence of the parties' agreement to a reasonable method, in accordance with any intention of the obligor manifested at or before the time of payment; or

(3)   in the absence of an agreement to a reasonable method and a timely manifestation of the obligor's intention, in the following order:

(A)   to obligations that are not secured; and

(B)   if more than one obligation is secured, to obligations secured by purchase-money security interests in the order in which those obligations were incurred.

(f)   **[No loss of status of purchase-money security interest in non-consumer-goods transaction.]** In a transaction other than a consumer-goods transaction, a purchase-money security interest does not lose its status as such, even if:

(1)   the purchase-money collateral also secures an obligation that is not a purchase-money obligation;

(2)   collateral that is not purchase-money collateral also secures the purchase-money obligation; or

(3)   the purchase-money obligation has been renewed, refinanced, consolidated, or restructured.

(g)   **[Burden of proof in non-consumer-goods transaction.]** In a transaction other than a consumer-goods transaction, a secured party claiming a purchase-money security interest has the burden of establishing the extent to which the security interest is a purchase-money security interest.

(h)   **[Non-consumer-goods transactions; no inference.]** The limitation of the rules in subsections (e), (f), and (g) to transactions other than consumer-goods transactions is intended to leave to the court the determination of the proper rules in consumer-goods transactions. The court may not infer from that limitation the nature of the proper rule in consumer-goods transactions and may continue to apply established approaches.

Official Comment

1.   **Source.** Former Section 9–107.

2.   **Scope of This Section.** Under Section 9–309(1), a purchase-money security interest in consumer goods is perfected when it attaches. Sections 9–317 and 9–324 provide special priority rules for purchase-money security interests in a variety of contexts. This section explains when a security interest enjoys purchase-money status.

3.   **"Purchase-Money Collateral"; "Purchase-Money Obligation"; "Purchase-Money Security Interest."** Subsection (a) defines "purchase-money collateral" and "purchase-money obligation." These terms are essential to the description of what constitutes a purchase-money security interest under subsection (b). As used in subsection (a)(2), the definition of "purchase-money obligation," the "price" of collateral or the "value given to

enable" includes obligations for expenses incurred in connection with acquiring rights in the collateral, sales taxes, duties, finance charges, interest, freight charges, costs of storage in transit, demurrage, administrative charges, expenses of collection and enforcement, attorney's fees, and other similar obligations.

The concept of "purchase-money security interest" requires a close nexus between the acquisition of collateral and the secured obligation. Thus, a security interest does not qualify as a purchase-money security interest if a debtor acquires property on unsecured credit and subsequently creates the security interest to secure the purchase price.

4. **Cross-Collateralization of Purchase-Money Security Interests in Inventory.** Subsection (b)(2) deals with the problem of cross-collateralized purchase-money security interests in inventory. Consider a simple example:

> **Example:** Seller (S) sells an item of inventory (Item-1) to Debtor (D), retaining a security interest in Item-1 to secure Item-1's price and all other obligations, existing and future, of D to S. S then sells another item of inventory to D (Item-2), again retaining a security interest in Item-2 to secure Item-2's price as well as all other obligations of D to S. D then pays to S Item-1's price. D then sells Item-2 to a buyer in ordinary course of business, who takes Item-2 free of S's security interest.

Under subsection (b)(2), S's security interest in *Item-1* securing *Item-2's unpaid price* would be a purchase-money security interest. This is so because S has a purchase-money security interest in Item-1, Item-1 secures the price of (a "purchase-money obligation incurred with respect to") Item-2 ("other inventory"), and Item-2 itself was subject to a purchase-money security interest. Note that, to the extent Item-1 secures the price of Item-2, S's security interest in Item-1 would not be a purchase-money security interest under subsection (b)(1). The security interest in Item-1 is a purchase-money security interest under subsection (b)(1) only to the extent that Item-1 is "purchase-money collateral," i.e., only to the extent that Item-1 "secures a purchase-money obligation incurred with respect to that collateral" (i.e., Item-1). See subsection (a)(1).

5. **Purchase-Money Security Interests in Goods and Software.** Subsections (b) and (c) limit purchase-money security interests to security interests in goods, including fixtures, and software. Otherwise, no change in meaning from former Section 9–107 is intended. The second sentence of former Section 9–115(5)(f) made the purchase-money priority rule (former Section 9–312(4)) inapplicable to investment property. This section's limitation makes that provision unnecessary.

Subsection (c) describes the limited circumstances under which a security interest in goods may be accompanied by a purchase-money security interest in software. The software must be acquired by the debtor in a transaction integrated with the transaction in which the debtor acquired the goods, and the debtor must acquire the software for the principal purpose of using the software in the goods. "Software" is defined in Section 9–102.

6. **Consignments.** Under former Section 9–114, the priority of the consignor's interest is similar to that of a purchase-money security interest. Subsection (d) achieves this result more directly, by defining the interest of a "consignor," defined in Section 9–102, to be a purchase-money security interest in inventory for purposes of this Article. This drafting convention obviates any need to set forth special priority rules applicable to the interest of a consignor. Rather, the priority of the consignor's interest as against the rights of lien creditors of the consignee, competing secured parties, and purchasers of the goods from the consignee can be determined by reference to the priority rules generally applicable to inventory, such as Sections 9–317, 9–320, 9–322, and 9–324. For other purposes, including the rights and duties of the consignor and consignee as between themselves, the consignor would remain the owner of goods under a bailment arrangement with the consignee. See Section 9–319.

7. **Provisions Applicable Only to Non-Consumer-Goods Transactions.**

a. **"Dual-Status" Rule.** For transactions other than consumer-goods transactions, this Article approves what some cases have called the "dual-status" rule, under which a security interest may be a purchase-money security interest to some extent and a non-purchase-money security interest to some extent. (Concerning consumer-goods transactions, see subsection (h) and Comment 8.) Some courts have found this rule to be explicit or implicit in the words "to the extent," found in former Section 9–107 and continued in subsections (b)(1) and (b)(2). The rule is made explicit in subsection (e). For non-consumer-goods transactions, this Article rejects the "transformation" rule adopted by some cases, under which any cross-collateralization, refinancing, or the like destroys the purchase-money status entirely.

Consider, for example, what happens when a $10,000 loan secured by a purchase-money security interest is refinanced by the original lender, and, as part of the transaction, the debtor borrows an additional $2,000 secured by the collateral. Subsection (f) resolves any doubt that the security interest remains a purchase-money security interest. Under subsection (b), however, it enjoys purchase-money status only to the extent of $10,000.

b.   **Allocation of Payments.** Continuing with the example, if the debtor makes a $1,000 payment on the $12,000 obligation, then one must determine the extent to which the security interest remains a purchase-money security interest—$9,000 or $10,000. Subsection (e)(1) expresses the overriding principle, applicable in cases other than consumer-goods transactions, for determining the extent to which a security interest is a purchase-money security interest under these circumstances: freedom of contract, as limited by principle of reasonableness. An unconscionable method of application, for example, is not a reasonable one and so would not be given effect under subsection (e)(1). In the absence of agreement, subsection (e)(2) permits the obligor to determine how payments should be allocated. If the obligor fails to manifest its intention, obligations that are not secured will be paid first. (As used in this Article, the concept of "obligations that are not secured" means obligations for which the debtor has not created a security interest. This concept is different from and should not be confused with the concept of an "unsecured claim" as it appears in Bankruptcy Code Section 506(a).) The obligor may prefer this approach, because unsecured debt is likely to carry a higher interest rate than secured debt. A creditor who would prefer to be secured rather than unsecured also would prefer this approach.

After the unsecured debt is paid, payments are to be applied first toward the obligations secured by purchase-money security interests. In the event that there is more than one such obligation, payments first received are to be applied to obligations first incurred. See subsection (e)(3). Once these obligations are paid, there are no purchase-money security interests and no additional allocation rules are needed.

Subsection (f) buttresses the dual-status rule by making it clear that (in a transaction other than a consumer-goods transaction) cross-collateralization and renewals, refinancings, and restructurings do not cause a purchase-money security interest to lose its status as such. The statutory terms "renewed," "refinanced," and "restructured" are not defined. Whether the terms encompass a particular transaction depends upon whether, under the particular facts, the purchase-money character of the security interest fairly can be said to survive. Each term contemplates that an identifiable portion of the purchase-money obligation could be traced to the new obligation resulting from a renewal, refinancing, or restructuring.

c.   **Burden of Proof.** As is the case when the extent of a security interest is in issue, under subsection (g) the secured party claiming a purchase-money security interest in a transaction other than a consumer-goods transaction has the burden of establishing whether the security interest retains its purchase-money status. This is so whether the determination is to be made following a renewal, refinancing, or restructuring or otherwise.

8.   **Consumer-Goods Transactions; Characterization Under Other Law.** Under subsection (h), the limitation of subsections (e), (f), and (g) to transactions other than consumer-goods transactions leaves to the court the determination of the proper rules in consumer-goods transactions. Subsection (h) also instructs the court not to draw any inference from this limitation as to the proper rules for consumer-goods transactions and leaves the court free to continue to apply established approaches to those transactions.

This section addresses only whether a security interest is a "purchase-money security interest" under this Article, primarily for purposes of perfection and priority. See, e.g., Sections 9–317, 9–324. In particular, its adoption of the dual-status rule, allocation of payments rules, and burden of proof standards for non-consumer-goods transactions is not intended to affect or influence characterizations under other statutes. Whether a security interest is a "purchase-money security interest" under other law is determined by that law. For example, decisions under Bankruptcy Code Section 522(f) have applied both the dual-status and the transformation rules. The Bankruptcy Code does not expressly adopt the state law definition of "purchase-money security interest." Where federal law does not defer to this Article, this Article does not, and could not, determine a question of federal law.

§ 9–104.   Control of Deposit Account.   *control for attachment 9-203*

(a)   **[Requirements for control.]** A secured party has control of a deposit account if:

(1)   the secured party is the bank with which the deposit account is maintained;

(2)   the debtor, secured party, and bank have agreed in an authenticated record that the bank will comply with instructions originated by the secured party directing disposition of the funds in the deposit account without further consent by the debtor; or

(3)   the secured party becomes the bank's customer with respect to the deposit account.

(b)   **[Debtor's right to direct disposition.]** A secured party that has satisfied subsection (a) has control, even if the debtor retains the right to direct the disposition of funds from the deposit account.

Official Comment

1. **Source.** New; derived from Section 8–106.

2. **Why "Control" Matters.** This section explains the concept of "control" of a deposit account. "Control" under this section may serve two functions. First, "control . . . pursuant to the debtor's agreement" may substitute for an authenticated security agreement as an element of attachment. See Section 9–203(b)(3)(D). Second, when a deposit account is taken as original collateral, the only method of perfection is obtaining control under this section. See Section 9–312(b)(1).

3. **Requirements for "Control."** This section derives from Section 8–106 of Revised Article 8, which defines "control" of securities and certain other investment property. Under subsection (a)(1), the bank with which the deposit account is maintained has control. The effect of this provision is to afford the bank automatic perfection. No other form of public notice is necessary; all actual and potential creditors of the debtor are always on notice that the bank with which the debtor's deposit account is maintained may assert a claim against the deposit account.

> **Example:** D maintains a deposit account with Bank A. To secure a loan from Banks X, Y, and Z, D creates a security interest in the deposit account in favor of Bank A, as agent for Banks X, Y, and Z. Because Bank A is a "secured party" as defined in Section 9–102, the security interest is perfected by control under subsection (a)(1).

Under subsection (a)(2), a secured party may obtain control by obtaining the bank's authenticated agreement that it will comply with the secured party's instructions without further consent by the debtor. The analogous provision in Section 8–106 does not require that the agreement be authenticated. An agreement to comply with the secured party's instructions suffices for "control" of a deposit account under this section even if the bank's agreement is subject to specified conditions, e.g., that the secured party's instructions are accompanied by a certification that the debtor is in default. (Of course, if the condition is the *debtor's* further consent, the statute explicitly provides that the agreement would *not* confer control.) See revised Section 8–106, Comment 7.

Under subsection (a)(3), a secured party may obtain control by becoming the bank's "customer," as defined in Section 4–104. As the customer, the secured party would enjoy the right (but not necessarily the exclusive right) to withdraw funds from, or close, the deposit account. See Sections 4–401(a), 4–403(a).

As is the case with possession under Section 9–313, in determining whether a particular person has control under subsection (a), the principles of agency apply. See Section 1–103 and Restatement (3d), Agency § 8.12, Comment *b*.

Although the arrangements giving rise to control may themselves prevent, or may enable the secured party at its discretion to prevent, the debtor from reaching the funds on deposit, subsection (b) makes clear that the debtor's ability to reach the funds is not inconsistent with "control."

Perfection by control is not available for bank accounts evidenced by an instrument (e.g., certain certificates of deposit), which by definition are "instruments" and not "deposit accounts." See Section 9–102 (defining "deposit account" and "instrument").

As amended in 2010.

§ 9–105. Control of Electronic Chattel Paper.

(a) **[General rule: control of electronic chattel paper.]** A secured party has control of electronic chattel paper if a system employed for evidencing the transfer of interests in the chattel paper reliably establishes the secured party as the person to which the chattel paper was assigned.

(b) **[Specific facts giving control.]** A system satisfies subsection (a) if the record or records comprising the chattel paper are created, stored, and assigned in such a manner that:

(1) a single authoritative copy of the record or records exists which is unique, identifiable, and, except as otherwise provided in paragraphs (4), (5), and (6), unalterable;

(2) the authoritative copy identifies the secured party as the assignee of the record or records;

(3) the authoritative copy is communicated to and maintained by the secured party or its designated custodian;

(4)   copies or amendments that add or change an identified assignee of the authoritative copy can be made only with the consent of the secured party;

(5)   each copy of the authoritative copy and any copy of a copy is readily identifiable as a copy that is not the authoritative copy; and

(6)   any amendment of the authoritative copy is readily identifiable as authorized or unauthorized.

As amended in 2010.

Official Comment

1.   **Source.** New.

2.   **"Control" of Electronic Chattel Paper.** This Article covers security interests in "electronic chattel paper," a new term defined in Section 9–102. This section governs how "control" of electronic chattel paper may be obtained. Subsection (a), which derives from Section 16 of the Uniform Electronic Transactions Act, sets forth the general test for control. Subsection (b) sets forth a safe harbor test that, if satisfied, establishes control under the general test in subsection (a).

A secured party's control of electronic chattel paper (i) may substitute for an authenticated security agreement for purposes of attachment under Section 9–203, (ii) is a method of perfection under Section 9–314, and (iii) is a condition for obtaining special, non-temporal priority under Section 9–330. Because electronic chattel paper cannot be transferred, assigned, or possessed in the same manner as tangible chattel paper, a special definition of control is necessary. In descriptive terms, this section provides that control of electronic chattel paper is the functional equivalent of possession of "tangible chattel paper" (a term also defined in Section 9–102).

3.   **Development of Control Systems.** This Article leaves to the marketplace the development of systems and procedures, through a combination of suitable technologies and business practices, for dealing with control of electronic chattel paper in a commercial context. Systems that evolve for control of electronic chattel paper may or may not involve a third party custodian of the relevant records. As under UETA, a system must be shown to reliably establish that the secured party is the assignee of the chattel paper. Reliability is a high standard and encompasses the general principles of uniqueness, identifiability, and unalterability found in subsection (b) without setting forth specific guidelines as to how these principles must be achieved. However, the standards applied to determine whether a party is in control of electronic chattel paper should not be more stringent than the standards now applied to determine whether a party is in possession of tangible chattel paper. For example, just as a secured party does not lose possession of tangible chattel paper merely by virtue of the possibility that a person acting on its behalf *could* wrongfully redeliver the chattel paper to the debtor, so control of electronic chattel paper would not be defeated by the possibility that the secured party's interest *could* be subverted by the wrongful conduct of a person (such as a custodian) acting on its behalf.

This section and the concept of control of electronic chattel paper are not based on the same concepts as are control of deposit accounts (Section 9–104), security entitlements, a type of investment property (Section 9–106), and letter-of-credit rights (Section 9–107). The rules for control of those types of collateral are based on existing market practices and legal and regulatory regimes for institutions such as banks and securities intermediaries. Analogous practices for electronic chattel paper are developing nonetheless. The flexible approach adopted by this section, moreover, should not impede the development of these practices and, eventually, legal and regulatory regimes, which may become analogous to those for, e.g., investment property.

4.   **"Authoritative Copy" of Electronic Chattel Paper.** One requirement for establishing control under subsection (b) is that a particular copy be an "authoritative copy." Although other copies may exist, they must be distinguished from the authoritative copy. This may be achieved, for example, through the methods of authentication that are used or by business practices involving the marking of any additional copies. When tangible chattel paper is converted to electronic chattel paper, in order to establish that a copy of the electronic chattel paper is the authoritative copy it may be necessary to show that the tangible chattel paper no longer exists or has been permanently marked to indicate that it is not the authoritative copy.

As amended in 2010.

§ 9–106.   Control of Investment Property.

(a)   **[Control under Section 8–106.]** A person has control of a certificated security, uncertificated security, or security entitlement as provided in Section 8–106.

(b)   **[Control of commodity contract.]** A secured party has control of a commodity contract if:

(1) the secured party is the commodity intermediary with which the commodity contract is carried; or

(2) the commodity customer, secured party, and commodity intermediary have agreed that the commodity intermediary will apply any value distributed on account of the commodity contract as directed by the secured party without further consent by the commodity customer.

(c) **[Effect of control of securities account or commodity account.]** A secured party having control of all security entitlements or commodity contracts carried in a securities account or commodity account has control over the securities account or commodity account.

Official Comment

1. **Source.** Former Section 9–115(e).

2. **"Control" Under Article 8.** For an explanation of "control" of securities and certain other investment property, see Section 8–106, Comments 4 and 7.

3. **"Control" of Commodity Contracts.** This section, as did former Section 9–115(1)(e), contains provisions relating to control of commodity contracts which are analogous to those in Section 8–106 for other types of investment property.

4. **Securities Accounts and Commodity Accounts.** For drafting convenience, control with respect to a securities account or commodity account is defined in terms of obtaining control over the security entitlements or commodity contracts. Of course, an agreement that provides that (without further consent of the debtor) the securities intermediary or commodity intermediary will honor instructions from the secured party concerning a securities account or commodity account described as such is sufficient. Such an agreement necessarily implies that the intermediary will honor instructions concerning all security entitlements or commodity contracts carried in the account and thus affords the secured party control of all the security entitlements or commodity contracts.

§ 9–107. Control of Letter-of-Credit Right.

A secured party has control of a letter-of-credit right to the extent of any right to payment or performance by the issuer or any nominated person if the issuer or nominated person has consented to an assignment of proceeds of the letter of credit under Section 5–114(c) or otherwise applicable law or practice.

Official Comment

1. **Source.** New.

2. **"Control" of Letter-of-Credit Right.** Whether a secured party has control of a letter-of-credit right may determine the secured party's priority as against competing secured parties. See Section 9–329. This section provides that a secured party acquires control of a letter-of-credit right by receiving an assignment if the secured party obtains the consent of the issuer or any nominated person, such as a confirmer or negotiating bank, under Section 5–114 or other applicable law or practice. Because both issuers and nominated persons may give or be obligated to give value under a letter of credit, this section contemplates that a secured party obtains control of a letter-of-credit right with respect to the issuer or a particular nominated person only to the extent that the issuer or that nominated person consents to the assignment. For example, if a secured party obtains control to the extent of an issuer's obligation but fails to obtain the consent of a nominated person, the secured party does not have control to the extent the nominated person gives value. In many cases the person or persons who will give value under a letter of credit will be clear from its terms. In other cases, prudence may suggest obtaining consent from more than one person. The details of the consenting issuer's or nominated person's duties to pay or otherwise render performance to the secured party are left to the agreement of the parties.

3. **"Proceeds of a Letter of Credit."** Section 5–114 follows traditional banking terminology by referring to a letter of credit beneficiary's assignment of its right to receive payment thereunder as an assignment of the "proceeds of a letter of credit." However, as the seller of goods can assign its right to receive payment (an "account") before it has been earned by delivering the goods to the buyer, so the beneficiary of a letter of credit can assign its contingent right to payment before the letter of credit has been honored. See Section 5–114(b). If the assignment creates a security interest, the security interest can be perfected at the time it is created. An assignment of, including the creation of a security interest in, a letter-of-credit right is an assignment of a present interest.

4. **"Transfer" vs. "Assignment."** Letter-of-credit law and practice distinguish the "transfer" of a letter of credit from an "assignment." Under a transfer, the transferee itself becomes the beneficiary and acquires the right to draw. Whether a new, substitute credit is issued or the issuer advises the transferee of its status as such,

the transfer constitutes a novation under which the transferee is the new, substituted beneficiary (but only to the extent of the transfer, in the case of a partial transfer).

Section 5–114(e) provides that the rights of a transferee beneficiary or nominated person are independent of the beneficiary's assignment of the proceeds of a letter of credit and are superior to the assignee's right to the proceeds. For this reason, transfer does not appear in this Article as a means of control or perfection. Section 9–109(c)(4) recognizes the independent and superior rights of a transferee beneficiary under Section 5–114(e); this Article does not apply to the rights of a transferee beneficiary or nominated person to the extent that those rights are independent and superior under Section 5–114.

5.   **Supporting Obligation: Automatic Attachment and Perfection.** A letter-of-credit right is a type of "supporting obligation," as defined in Section 9–102. Under Sections 9–203 and 9–308, a security interest in a letter-of-credit right automatically attaches and is automatically perfected if the security interest in the supported obligation is a perfected security interest. However, unless the secured party has control of the letter-of-credit right or itself becomes a transferee beneficiary, it cannot obtain any rights against the issuer or a nominated person under Article 5. Consequently, as a practical matter, the secured party's rights would be limited to its ability to locate and identify proceeds distributed by the issuer or nominated person under the letter of credit.

§ 9–108.   Sufficiency of Description.

(a)   **[Sufficiency of description.]** Except as otherwise provided in subsections (c), (d), and (e), a description of personal or real property is sufficient, whether or not it is specific, if it reasonably identifies what is described. *general standard of reasonable identification*

(b)   **[Examples of reasonable identification.]** Except as otherwise provided in subsection (d), a description of collateral reasonably identifies the collateral if it identifies the collateral by: *examples of how to identify collateral*

(1)   specific listing;

(2)   category;

(3)   except as otherwise provided in subsection (e), a type of collateral defined in [the Uniform Commercial Code];

(4)   quantity;

(5)   computational or allocational formula or procedure; or

(6)   except as otherwise provided in subsection (c), any other method, if the identity of the collateral is objectively determinable.

(c)   **[Supergeneric description not sufficient.]** A description of collateral as "all the debtor's assets" or "all the debtor's personal property" or using words of similar import does not reasonably identify the collateral.

(d)   **[Investment property.]** Except as otherwise provided in subsection (e), a description of a security entitlement, securities account, or commodity account is sufficient if it describes:

(1)   the collateral by those terms or as investment property; or

(2)   the underlying financial asset or commodity contract.

(e)   **[When description by type insufficient.]** A description only by type of collateral defined in [the Uniform Commercial Code] is an insufficient description of:

(1)   a commercial tort claim; or

(2)   in a consumer transaction, consumer goods, a security entitlement, a securities account, or a commodity account.

Official Comment

1.   **Source.** Former Sections 9–110, 9–115(3).

2.   **General Rules.** Subsection (a) retains substantially the same formulation as former Section 9–110. Subsection (b) expands upon subsection (a) by indicating a variety of ways in which a description might reasonably identify collateral. Whereas a provision similar to subsection (b) was applicable only to investment property under

former Section 9–115(3), subsection (b) applies to all types of collateral, subject to the limitation in subsection (d). Subsection (b) is subject to subsection (c), which follows prevailing case law and adopts the view that an "all assets" or "all personal property" description for purposes of a *security agreement* is *not* sufficient. Note, however, that under Section 9–504, a *financing statement* sufficiently indicates the collateral if it "covers all assets or all personal property."

The purpose of requiring a description of collateral in a security agreement under Section 9–203 is evidentiary. The test of sufficiency of a description under this section, as under former Section 9–110, is that the description do the job assigned to it: make possible the identification of the collateral described. This section rejects any requirement that a description is insufficient unless it is exact and detailed (the so-called "serial number" test).

3.   **After-Acquired Collateral.** Much litigation has arisen over whether a description in a security agreement is sufficient to include after-acquired collateral if the agreement does not explicitly so provide. This question is one of contract interpretation and is not susceptible to a statutory rule (other than a rule to the effect that it is a question of contract interpretation). Accordingly, this section contains no reference to descriptions of after-acquired collateral.

4.   **Investment Property.** Under subsection (d), the use of the wrong Article 8 terminology does not render a description invalid (e.g., a security agreement intended to cover a debtor's "security entitlements" is sufficient if it refers to the debtor's "securities"). Note also that given the broad definition of "securities account" in Section 8–501, a security interest in a securities account also includes all other rights of the debtor against the securities intermediary arising out of the securities account. For example, a security interest in a securities account would include credit balances due to the debtor from the securities intermediary, whether or not they are proceeds of a security entitlement. Moreover, describing collateral as a securities account is a simple way of describing all of the security entitlements carried in the account.

5.   **Consumer Investment Property; Commercial Tort Claims.** Subsection (e) requires greater specificity of description in order to prevent debtors from inadvertently encumbering certain property. Subsection (e) requires that a description by defined "type" of collateral alone of a commercial tort claim or, in a consumer transaction, of a security entitlement, securities account, or commodity account, is not sufficient. For example, "all existing and after-acquired investment property" or "all existing and after-acquired security entitlements," without more, would be insufficient in a consumer transaction to describe a security entitlement, securities account, or commodity account. The reference to "*only* by type" in subsection (e) means that a description is sufficient if it satisfies subsection (a) and contains a descriptive component beyond the "type" alone. Moreover, if the collateral consists of a securities account or commodity account, a description of the account is sufficient to cover all existing and future security entitlements or commodity contracts carried in the account. See Section 9–203(h), (i).

Under Section 9–204, an after-acquired collateral clause in a security agreement will not reach future commercial tort claims. It follows that when an effective security agreement covering a commercial tort claim is entered into the claim already will exist. Subsection (e) does not require a description to be specific. For example, a description such as "all tort claims arising out of the explosion of debtor's factory" would suffice, even if the exact amount of the claim, the theory on which it may be based, and the identity of the tortfeasor(s) are not described. (Indeed, those facts may not be known at the time.)

[SUBPART 2. APPLICABILITY OF ARTICLE]

§ 9–109.   Scope.

(a)   **[General scope of article.]** Except as otherwise provided in subsections (c) and (d), this article applies to:

(1)   a transaction, regardless of its form, that creates a security interest in personal property or fixtures by contract;

(2)   an agricultural lien;

(3)   a sale of accounts, chattel paper, payment intangibles, or promissory notes;

(4)   a consignment;

(5)   a security interest arising under Section 2–401, 2–505, 2–711(3), or 2A–508(5), as provided in Section 9–110; and

(6)   a security interest arising under Section 4–210 or 5–118.

(b)   **[Security interest in secured obligation.]** The application of this article to a security interest in a secured obligation is not affected by the fact that the obligation is itself secured by a transaction or interest to which this article does not apply.

(c)   **[Extent to which article does not apply.]** This article does not apply to the extent that:

(1)   a statute, regulation, or treaty of the United States preempts this article;

(2)   another statute of this State expressly governs the creation, perfection, priority, or enforcement of a security interest created by this State or a governmental unit of this State;

(3)   a statute of another State, a foreign country, or a governmental unit of another State or a foreign country, other than a statute generally applicable to security interests, expressly governs creation, perfection, priority, or enforcement of a security interest created by the State, country, or governmental unit; or

(4)   the rights of a transferee beneficiary or nominated person under a letter of credit are independent and superior under Section 5–114.

(d)   **[Inapplicability of article.]** This article does not apply to:

(1)   a landlord's lien, other than an agricultural lien;

(2)   a lien, other than an agricultural lien, given by statute or other rule of law for services or materials, but Section 9–333 applies with respect to priority of the lien;

(3)   an assignment of a claim for wages, salary, or other compensation of an employee;

(4)   a sale of accounts, chattel paper, payment intangibles, or promissory notes as part of a sale of the business out of which they arose;

(5)   an assignment of accounts, chattel paper, payment intangibles, or promissory notes which is for the purpose of collection only;

(6)   an assignment of a right to payment under a contract to an assignee that is also obligated to perform under the contract;

(7)   an assignment of a single account, payment intangible, or promissory note to an assignee in full or partial satisfaction of a preexisting indebtedness;

(8)   a transfer of an interest in or an assignment of a claim under a policy of insurance, other than an assignment by or to a health-care provider of a health-care-insurance receivable and any subsequent assignment of the right to payment, but Sections 9–315 and 9–322 apply with respect to proceeds and priorities in proceeds;

(9)   an assignment of a right represented by a judgment, other than a judgment taken on a right to payment that was collateral;

(10)   a right of recoupment or set-off, but:

(A)   Section 9–340 applies with respect to the effectiveness of rights of recoupment or set-off against deposit accounts; and

(B)   Section 9–404 applies with respect to defenses or claims of an account debtor;

(11)   the creation or transfer of an interest in or lien on real property, including a lease or rents thereunder, except to the extent that provision is made for:

(A)   liens on real property in Sections 9–203 and 9–308;

(B)   fixtures in Section 9–334;

(C)   fixture filings in Sections 9–501, 9–502, 9–512, 9–516, and 9–519; and

(D)   security agreements covering personal and real property in Section 9–604;

(12) an assignment of a claim arising in tort, other than a commercial tort claim, but Sections 9–315 and 9–322 apply with respect to proceeds and priorities in proceeds; or

(13) an assignment of a deposit account in a consumer transaction, but Sections 9–315 and 9–322 apply with respect to proceeds and priorities in proceeds.

Official Comment

1. **Source.** Former Sections 9–102, 9–104.

2. **Basic Scope Provision.** Subsection (a)(1) derives from former Section 9–102(1) and (2). These subsections have been combined and shortened. No change in meaning is intended. Under subsection (a)(1), all consensual security interests in personal property and fixtures are covered by this Article, except for transactions excluded by subsections (c) and (d). As to which transactions give rise to a "security interest," the definition of that term in Section 1–201 must be consulted. When a security interest is created, this Article applies regardless of the form of the transaction or the name that parties have given to it. Likewise, the subjective intention of the parties with respect to the legal characterization of their transaction is irrelevant to whether this Article applies, as it was to the application of former Article 9 under the proper interpretation of former Section 9–102.

3. **Agricultural Liens.** Subsection (a)(2) is new. It expands the scope of this Article to cover agricultural liens, as defined in Section 9–102.

4. **Sales of Accounts, Chattel Paper, Payment Intangibles, Promissory Notes, and Other Receivables.** Under subsection (a)(3), as under former Section 9–102, this Article applies to sales of accounts and chattel paper. This approach generally has been successful in avoiding difficult problems of distinguishing between transactions in which a receivable secures an obligation and those in which the receivable has been sold outright. In many commercial financing transactions the distinction is blurred.

Subsection (a)(3) expands the scope of this Article by including the sale of a "payment intangible" (defined in Section 9–102 as "a general intangible under which the account debtor's principal obligation is a monetary obligation") and a "promissory note" (also defined in Section 9–102). To a considerable extent, this Article affords these transactions treatment identical to that given sales of accounts and chattel paper. In some respects, however, sales of payment intangibles and promissory notes are treated differently from sales of other receivables. See, e.g., Sections 9–309 (automatic perfection upon attachment), 9–408 (effect of restrictions on assignment). By virtue of the expanded definition of "account" (defined in Section 9–102), this Article now covers sales of (and other security interests in) "health-care-insurance receivables" (also defined in Section 9–102). Although this Article occasionally distinguishes between outright sales of receivables and sales that secure an obligation, neither this Article nor the definition of "security interest" (Section 1–201(37) [*unrevised Article 1; see Concordance, p. 22*]) delineates how a particular transaction is to be classified. That issue is left to the courts.

5. **Transfer of Ownership in Sales of Receivables.** A "sale" of an account, chattel paper, a promissory note, or a payment intangible includes a sale of a right in the receivable, such as a sale of a participation interest. The term also includes the sale of an enforcement right. For example, a "[p]erson entitled to enforce" a negotiable promissory note (Section 3–301) may sell its ownership rights in the instrument. See Section 3–203, Comment 1 ("Ownership rights in instruments may be determined by principles of the law of property, independent of Article 3, which do not depend upon whether the instrument was transferred under Section 3–203."). Also, the right under Section 3–309 to enforce a lost, destroyed, or stolen negotiable promissory note may be sold to a purchaser who could enforce that right by causing the seller to provide the proof required under that section. This Article rejects decisions reaching a contrary result, e.g., *Dennis Joslin Co. v. Robinson Broadcasting*, 977 F. Supp. 491 (D.D.C. 1997).

Nothing in this section or any other provision of Article 9 prevents the transfer of full and complete ownership of an account, chattel paper, an instrument, or a payment intangible in a transaction of sale. However, as mentioned in Comment 4, neither this Article nor the definition of "security interest" in Section 1–201 provides rules for distinguishing sales transactions from those that create a security interest securing an obligation. This Article applies to both types of transactions. The principal effect of this coverage is to apply this Article's perfection and priority rules to these sales transactions. Use of terminology such as "security interest," "debtor," and "collateral" is merely a drafting convention adopted to reach this end, and its use has no relevance to distinguishing sales from other transactions. See PEB Commentary No. 14.

Following a debtor's outright sale and transfer of ownership of a receivable, the debtor-seller retains no legal or equitable rights in the receivable that has been sold. See Section 9–318(a). This is so whether or not the buyer's security interest is perfected. (A security interest arising from the sale of a promissory note or payment intangible is perfected upon attachment without further action. See Section 9–309.) However, if the buyer's interest in accounts or chattel paper is unperfected, a subsequent lien creditor, perfected secured party, or qualified buyer can reach the sold receivable and achieve priority over (or take free of) the buyer's unperfected security interest under Section 9–317. This is so not because the seller of a receivable retains rights in the property sold; it does not. Nor is this so because the seller of a receivable is a "debtor" and the buyer of a receivable is a "secured party" under this Article (they are). It is so for the simple reason that Sections 9–318(b), 9–317, and 9–322 make it so, as did former Sections 9–301 and 9–312. Because the buyer's security interest is unperfected, for purposes of determining the rights of creditors of and purchasers for value from the debtor-seller, under Section 9–318(b) the debtor-seller is deemed to have the rights and title it sold. Section 9–317 subjects the buyer's unperfected interest in accounts and chattel paper to that of the debtor-seller's lien creditor and other persons who qualify under that section.

6. **Consignments.** Subsection (a)(4) is new. This Article applies to every "consignment." The term, defined in Section 9–102, includes many but not all "true" consignments (i.e., bailments for the purpose of sale). If a transaction is a "sale or return," as defined in revised Section 2–326, it is not a "consignment." In a "sale or return" transaction, the buyer becomes the owner of the goods, and the seller may obtain an enforceable security interest in the goods only by satisfying the requirements of Section 9–203.

Under common law, creditors of a bailee were unable to reach the interest of the bailor (in the case of a consignment, the consignor-owner). Like former Section 2–326 and former Article 9, this Article changes the common-law result; however, it does so in a different manner. For purposes of determining the rights and interests of third-party creditors of, and purchasers of the goods from, the consignee, but not for other purposes, such as remedies of the consignor, the consignee is deemed to acquire under this Article whatever rights and title the consignor had or had power to transfer. See Section 9–319. The interest of a consignor is defined to be a security interest under revised Section 1–201(37) [*unrevised Article 1; see Concordance, p. 22*], more specifically, a purchase-money security interest in the consignee's inventory. See Section 9–103(d). Thus, the rules pertaining to lien creditors, buyers, and attachment, perfection, and priority of competing security interests apply to consigned goods. The relationship between the consignor and consignee is left to other law. Consignors also have no duties under Part 6. See Section 9–601(g).

Sometimes parties characterize transactions that secure an obligation (other than the bailee's obligation to returned bailed goods) as "consignments." These transactions are not "consignments" as contemplated by Section 9–109(a)(4). See Section 9–102. This Article applies also to these transactions, by virtue of Section 9–109(a)(1). They create a security interest within the meaning of the first sentence of Section 1–201(37) [*unrevised Article 1; see Concordance, p. 22*].

This Article does not apply to a bailment for sale that falls outside of the definition of "consignment" in Section 9–102. See PEB Commentary No. 20, dated January 24, 2019.

7. **Security Interest in Obligation Secured by Non-Article 9 Transaction.** Subsection (b) is unchanged in substance from former Section 9–102(3). The following example provides an illustration.

Example 1:   O borrows $10,000 from M and secures its repayment obligation, evidenced by a promissory note, by granting to M a mortgage on O's land. This Article does not apply to the creation of the real-property mortgage. However, if M sells the promissory note to X or gives a security interest in the note to secure M's own obligation to X, this Article applies to the security interest thereby created in favor of X. The security interest in the promissory note is covered by this Article even though the note is secured by a real-property mortgage. Also, X's security interest in the note gives X an attached security interest in the mortgage lien that secures the note and, if the security interest in the note is perfected, the security interest in the mortgage lien likewise is perfected. See Sections 9–203, 9–308.

It also follows from subsection (b) that an attempt to obtain or perfect a security interest in a secured obligation by complying with non-Article 9 law, as by an assignment of record of a real-property mortgage, would be ineffective. Finally, it is implicit from subsection (b) that one cannot obtain a security interest in a lien, such as a mortgage on real property, that is not also coupled with an equally effective security interest in the secured obligation. This Article rejects cases such as In re *Maryville Savings & Loan Corp.*, 743 F.2d 413 (6th Cir. 1984), clarified on reconsideration, 760 F.2d 119 (1985).

8. **Federal Preemption.** Former Section 9–104(a) excluded from Article 9 "a security interest subject to any statute of the United States, to the extent that such statute governs the rights of parties to and third parties affected by transactions in particular types of property." Some (erroneously) read the former section to suggest that Article 9 sometimes deferred to federal law even when federal law did not preempt Article 9. Subsection (c)(1) recognizes explicitly that this Article defers to federal law only when and to the extent that it must—i.e., when federal law preempts it.

9. **Governmental Debtors.** Former Section 9–104(e) excluded transfers by governmental debtors. It has been revised and replaced by the exclusions in new paragraphs (2) and (3) of subsection (c). These paragraphs reflect the view that Article 9 should apply to security interests created by a State, foreign country, or a "governmental unit" (defined in Section 9–102) of either except to the extent that another statute governs the issue in question. Under paragraph (2), this Article defers to all statutes of the forum State. (A forum cannot determine whether it should consult the choice-of-law rules in the forum's UCC unless it first determines that its UCC applies to the transaction before it.) Paragraph (3) defers to statutes of another State or a foreign country only to the extent that those statutes contain rules applicable specifically to security interests created by the governmental unit in question.

Example 2: A New Jersey state commission creates a security interest in favor of a New York bank. The validity of the security interest is litigated in New York. The relevant security agreement provides that it is governed by New York law. To the extent that a New Jersey statute contains rules peculiar to creation of security interests by governmental units generally, to creation of security interests by state commissions, or to creation of security interests by this particular state commission, then that law will govern. On the other hand, to the extent that New Jersey law provides that security interests created by governmental units, state commissions, or this state commission are governed by the law generally applicable to secured transactions (i.e., New Jersey's Article 9), then New York's Article 9 will govern.

Example 3: An airline that is an instrumentality of a foreign country creates a security interest in favor of a New York bank. The analysis used in the previous example would apply here. That is, if the matter is litigated in New York, New York law would govern except to the extent that the foreign country enacted a statute applicable to security interests created by governmental units generally or by the airline specifically.

The fact that New York law applies does not necessarily mean that perfection is accomplished by filing in New York. Rather, it means that the court should apply New York's Article 9, including its choice-of-law provisions. Under New York's Section 9–301, perfection is governed by the law of the jurisdiction in which the debtor is located. Section 9–307 determines the debtor's location for choice-of-law purposes.

If a transaction does not bear an appropriate relation to the forum State, then that State's Article 9 will not apply, regardless of whether the transaction would be excluded by paragraph (3).

Example 4: A Belgian governmental unit grants a security interest in its equipment to a Swiss secured party. The equipment is located in Belgium. A dispute arises and, for some reason, an action is brought in a New Mexico state court. Inasmuch as the transaction bears no "appropriate relation" to New Mexico, New Mexico's UCC, including its Article 9, is inapplicable. See Section 1–105(1) [*unrevised Article 1; see Concordance, p. 22*]. New Mexico's Section 9–109(c) on excluded transactions should not come into play. Even if the parties agreed that New Mexico law would govern, the parties' agreement would not be effective because the transaction does not bear a "reasonable relation" to New Mexico. See Section 1–105(1) [*unrevised Article 1; see Concordance, p. 22*].

Conversely, Article 9 will come into play only if the litigation arises in a UCC jurisdiction or if a foreign choice-of-law rule leads a foreign court to apply the law of a UCC jurisdiction. For example, if issues concerning a security interest granted by a foreign airline to a New York bank are litigated overseas, the court may be bound to apply the law of the debtor's jurisdiction and not New York's Article 9.

10. **Certain Statutory and Common-Law Liens; Interests in Real Property.** With few exceptions (nonconsensual agricultural liens being one), this Article applies only to consensual security interests in personal property. Following former Section 9–104(b) and (j), paragraphs (1) and (11) of subsection (d) exclude landlord's liens and leases and most other interests in or liens on real property. These exclusions generally reiterate the limitations on coverage (i.e., "by contract," "in personal property and fixtures") made explicit in subsection (a)(1). Similarly, most jurisdictions provide special liens to suppliers of many types of services and materials, either by statute or by common law. With the exception of agricultural liens, it is not necessary for this Article to provide general codification of this lien structure, which is determined in large part by local conditions and which is far removed from ordinary commercial financing. As under former Section 9–104(c), subsection (d)(2) excludes these suppliers' liens (other than agricultural liens) from this Article. However, Section 9–333 provides a rule for determining priorities between certain possessory suppliers' liens and security interests covered by this Article.

11. **Wage and Similar Claims.** As under former Section 9–104(d), subsection (d)(3) excludes assignments of claims for wages and the like from this Article. These assignments present important social issues that other law addresses. The Federal Trade Commission has ruled that, with some exceptions, the taking of an assignment of wages or other earnings is an unfair act or practice under the Federal Trade Commission Act. See 16 C.F.R. Part 444. State statutes also may regulate such assignments.

12.   **Certain Sales and Assignments of Receivables; Judgments.** In general this Article covers security interests in (including sales of) accounts, chattel paper, payment intangibles, and promissory notes. Paragraphs (4), (5), (6), and (7) of subsection (d) exclude from the Article certain sales and assignments of receivables that, by their nature, do not concern commercial financing transactions. These paragraphs add to the exclusions in former Section 9–104(f) analogous sales and assignments of payment intangibles and promissory notes. For similar reasons, subsection (d)(9) retains the exclusion of assignments of judgments under former Section 9–104(h) (other than judgments taken on a right to payment that itself was collateral under this Article).

13.   **Insurance.** Subsection (d)(8) narrows somewhat the broad exclusion of interests in insurance policies under former Section 9–104(g). This Article now covers assignments by or to a health-care provider of "health-care-insurance receivables" (defined in Section 9–102).

14.   **Set-Off.** Subsection (d)(10) adds two exceptions to the general exclusion of set-off rights from Article 9 under former Section 9–104(i). The first takes account of new Section 9–340, which regulates the effectiveness of a set-off against a deposit account that stands as collateral. The second recognizes Section 9–404, which affords the obligor on an account, chattel paper, or general intangible the right to raise claims and defenses against an assignee (secured party).

15.   **Tort Claims.** Subsection (d)(12) narrows somewhat the broad exclusion of transfers of tort claims under former Section 9–104(k). This Article now applies to assignments of "commercial tort claims" (defined in Section 9–102) as well as to security interests in tort claims that constitute proceeds of other collateral (e.g., a right to payment for negligent destruction of the debtor's inventory). Note that once a claim arising in tort has been settled and reduced to a contractual obligation to pay, the right to payment becomes a payment intangible and ceases to be a claim arising in tort.

This Article contains two special rules governing creation of a security interest in tort claims. First, a description of collateral in a security agreement as "all tort claims" is insufficient to meet the requirement for attachment. See Section 9–108(e). Second, no security interest attaches under an after-acquired property clause to a tort claim. See Section 9–204(b). In addition, this Article does not determine whom the tortfeasor must pay to discharge its obligation. Inasmuch as a tortfeasor is not an "account debtor," the rules governing waiver of defenses and discharge of an obligation by an obligor (Sections 9–403, 9–404, 9–405, and 9–406) are inapplicable to tort-claim collateral.

16.   **Deposit Accounts.** Except in consumer transactions, deposit accounts may be taken as original collateral under this Article. Under former Section 9–104(*l*), deposit accounts were excluded as original collateral, leaving security interests in deposit accounts to be governed by the common law. The common law is nonuniform, often difficult to discover and comprehend, and frequently costly to implement. As a consequence, debtors who wished to use deposit accounts as collateral sometimes were precluded from doing so as a practical matter. By excluding deposit accounts from the Article's scope as original collateral in consumer transactions, subsection (d)(13) leaves those transactions to law other than this Article. However, in both consumer and non-consumer transactions, sections 9–315 and 9–322 apply to deposit accounts as proceeds and with respect to priorities in proceeds.

This Article contains several safeguards to protect debtors against inadvertently encumbering deposit accounts and to reduce the likelihood that a secured party will realize a windfall from a debtor's deposit accounts. For example, because "deposit account" is a separate type of collateral, a security agreement covering general intangibles will not adequately describe deposit accounts. Rather, a security agreement must reasonably identify the deposit accounts that are the subject of a security interest, e.g., by using the term "deposit accounts." See Section 9–108. To perfect a security interest in a deposit account as original collateral, a secured party (other than the bank with which the deposit account is maintained) must obtain "control" of the account either by obtaining the bank's authenticated agreement or by becoming the bank's customer with respect to the deposit account. See Sections 9–312(b)(1), 9–104. Either of these steps requires the debtor's consent.

This Article also contains new rules that determine which State's law governs perfection and priority of a security interest in a deposit account (Section 9–304), priority of conflicting security interests in and set-off rights against a deposit account (Sections 9–327, 9–340), the rights of transferees of funds from an encumbered deposit account (Section 9–332), the obligations of the bank (Section 9–341), enforcement of security interests in a deposit account (Section 9–607(c)), and the duty of a secured party to terminate control of a deposit account (Section 9–208(b)).

As amended in 2000, 2010, and 2019.

730

§ 9–110. Security Interests Arising Under Article 2 or 2A.

A security interest arising under Section 2–401, 2–505, 2–711(3), or 2A–508(5) is subject to this article. However, until the debtor obtains possession of the goods:

(1) the security interest is enforceable, even if Section 9–203(b)(3) has not been satisfied;

(2) filing is not required to perfect the security interest;

(3) the rights of the secured party after default by the debtor are governed by Article 2 or 2A; and

(4) the security interest has priority over a conflicting security interest created by the debtor.

Official Comments

1. **Source.** Former Section 9–113.

2. **Background.** Former Section 9–113, from which this section derives, referred generally to security interests "arising solely under the Article on Sales (Article 2) or the Article on Leases (Article 2A)." Views differed as to the precise scope of that section. In contrast, Section 9–110 specifies the security interests to which it applies.

3. **Security Interests Under Articles 2 and 2A.** Section 2–505 explains how a seller of goods may reserve a security interest in them. Section 2–401 indicates that a reservation of title by the seller of goods, despite delivery to the buyer, is limited to reservation of a security interest. As did former Article 9, this Article governs a security interest arising solely under one of those sections; however, until the buyer obtains possession of the goods, the security interest is enforceable even in the absence of a security agreement, filing is not necessary to perfect the security interest, and the seller-secured party's rights on the buyer's default are governed by Article 2.

Sections 2–711(3) and 2A–508(5) create a security interest in favor of a buyer or lessee in possession of goods that were rightfully rejected or as to which acceptance was justifiably revoked. As did former Article 9, this Article governs a security interest arising solely under one of those sections; however, until the seller or lessor obtains possession of the goods, the security interest is enforceable even in the absence of a security agreement, filing is not necessary to perfect the security interest, and the secured party's (buyer's or lessee's) rights on the debtor's (seller's or lessor's) default are governed by Article 2 or 2A, as the case may be.

4. **Priority.** This section adds to former Section 9–113 a priority rule. Until the debtor obtains possession of the goods, a security interest arising under one of the specified sections of Article 2 or 2A has priority over conflicting security interests created by the debtor. Thus, a security interest arising under Section 2–401 or 2–505 has priority over a conflicting security interest in the buyer's after-acquired goods, even if the goods in question are inventory. Arguably, the same result would obtain under Section 9–322, but even if it would not, a purchase-money-like priority is appropriate. Similarly, a security interest under Section 2–711(3) or 2A–508(5) has priority over security interests claimed by the seller's or lessor's secured lender. This result is appropriate, inasmuch as the payments giving rise to the debt secured by the Article 2 or 2A security interest are likely to be included among the lender's proceeds.

Example: Seller owns equipment subject to a security interest created by Seller in favor of Lender. Buyer pays for the equipment, accepts the goods, and then justifiably revokes acceptance. As long as Seller does not recover possession of the equipment, Buyer's security interest under Section 2–711(3) is senior to that of Lender.

In the event that a security interest referred to in this section conflicts with a security interest that is created by a person other than the debtor, Section 9–325 applies. Thus, if Lender's security interest in the example was created not by Seller but by the person from whom Seller acquired the goods, Section 9–325 would govern.

5. **Relationship to Other Rights and Remedies Under Articles 2 and 2A.** This Article does not specifically address the conflict between (i) a security interest created by a buyer or lessee and (ii) the seller's or lessor's right to withhold delivery under Section 2–702(1), 2–703(a), or 2A–525, the seller's or lessor's right to stop delivery under Section 2–705 or 2A–526, or the seller's right to reclaim under Section 2–507(2) or 2–702(2). These conflicts are governed by the first sentence of Section 2–403(1), under which the buyer's secured party obtains no greater rights in the goods than the buyer had or had power to convey, or Section 2A–307(1), under which creditors of the lessee take subject to the lease contract.

PART 2

EFFECTIVENESS OF SECURITY AGREEMENT; ATTACHMENT OF SECURITY INTEREST; RIGHTS OF PARTIES TO SECURITY AGREEMENT

[SUBPART 1. EFFECTIVENESS AND ATTACHMENT]

§ 9–201.   General Effectiveness of Security Agreement.

(a) **[General effectiveness.]** Except as otherwise provided in [the Uniform Commercial Code], a security agreement is effective according to its terms between the parties, against purchasers of the collateral, and against creditors.

(b) **[Applicable consumer laws and other law.]** A transaction subject to this article is subject to any applicable rule of law which establishes a different rule for consumers and [insert reference to (i) any other statute or regulation that regulates the rates, charges, agreements, and practices for loans, credit sales, or other extensions of credit and (ii) any consumer-protection statute or regulation].

(c) **[Other applicable law controls.]** In case of conflict between this article and a rule of law, statute, or regulation described in subsection (b), the rule of law, statute, or regulation controls. Failure to comply with a statute or regulation described in subsection (b) has only the effect the statute or regulation specifies.

(d) **[Further deference to other applicable law.]** This article does not:

(1) validate any rate, charge, agreement, or practice that violates a rule of law, statute, or regulation described in subsection (b); or

(2) extend the application of the rule of law, statute, or regulation to a transaction not otherwise subject to it.

Official Comment

1. **Source.** Former Sections 9–201, 9–203(4).

2. **Effectiveness of Security Agreement.** Subsection (a) provides that a security agreement is generally effective. With certain exceptions, a security agreement is effective between the debtor and secured party and is likewise effective against third parties. Note that "security agreement" is used here (and elsewhere in this Article) as it is defined in Section 9–102: "an agreement that creates or provides for a security interest." It follows that subsection (a) does not provide that every term or provision contained in a record that contains a security agreement or that is so labeled is effective. Properly read, former Section 9–201 was to the same effect. Exceptions to the general rule of subsection (a) arise where there is an overriding provision in this Article or any other Article of the UCC. For example, Section 9–317 subordinates unperfected security interests to lien creditors and certain buyers, and several provisions in Part 3 subordinate some security interests to other security interests and interests of purchasers.

3. **Law, Statutes, and Regulations Applicable to Certain Transactions.** Subsection (b) makes clear that certain transactions, although subject to this Article, also are subject to other applicable laws relating to consumers or specified in that subsection. Subsection (c) provides that the other law is controlling in the event of a conflict, and that a violation of other law does not *ipso facto* constitute a violation of this Article. Subsection (d) provides that this Article does not validate violations under or extend the application of the other applicable laws.

§ 9–202.   Title to Collateral Immaterial.

Except as otherwise provided with respect to consignments or sales of accounts, chattel paper, payment intangibles, or promissory notes, the provisions of this article with regard to rights and obligations apply whether title to collateral is in the secured party or the debtor.

Official Comment

1. **Source.** Former Section 9–202.

2. **Title Immaterial.** The rights and duties of parties to a secured transaction and affected third parties are provided in this Article without reference to the location of "title" to the collateral. For example, the characteristics of a security interest that secures the purchase price of goods are the same whether the secured party appears to have retained title or the debtor appears to have obtained title and then conveyed title or a lien to the secured party.

3. **When Title Matters.**

a. **Under This Article.** This section explicitly acknowledges two circumstances in which the effect of certain Article 9 provisions turns on ownership (title). First, in some respects sales of accounts, chattel paper, payment intangibles, and promissory notes receive special treatment. See, e.g., Sections 9–207(a), 9–210(b), 9–615(e). Buyers of receivables under former Article 9 were treated specially, as well. See, e.g., former Section 9–502(2). Second, the remedies of a consignor under a true consignment and, for the most part, the remedies of a buyer of accounts, chattel paper, payment intangibles, or promissory notes are determined by other law and not by Part 6. See Section 9–601(g).

b. **Under Other Law.** This Article does not determine which line of interpretation (e.g., title theory or lien theory, retained title or conveyed title) should be followed in cases in which the applicability of another rule of law depends upon who has title. If, for example, a revenue law imposes a tax on the "legal" owner of goods or if a corporation law makes a vote of the stockholders prerequisite to a corporation "giving" a security interest but not if it acquires property "subject" to a security interest, this Article does not attempt to define whether the secured party is a "legal" owner or whether the transaction "gives" a security interest for the purpose of such laws. Other rules of law or the agreement of the parties determines the location and source of title for those purposes.

§ 9–203. Attachment and Enforceability of Security Interest; Proceeds; Supporting Obligations; Formal Requisites.

(a) **[Attachment.]** A security interest attaches to collateral when it becomes enforceable against the debtor with respect to the collateral, unless an agreement expressly postpones the time of attachment.

(b) **[Enforceability.]** Except as otherwise provided in subsections (c) through (i), a security interest is enforceable against the debtor and third parties with respect to the collateral only if: *[handwritten: security agreement PLUS]*

(1) value has been given;

(2) the debtor has rights in the collateral or the power to transfer rights in the collateral to a secured party; and

(3) one of the following conditions is met: *[handwritten: 9-102a7   9-102a(74)   9-108]*

[handwritten: authentication + description] (A) the debtor has authenticated a security agreement that provides a description of the collateral and, if the security interest covers timber to be cut, a description of the land concerned; *[handwritten: (common for attachment since most deals in writing)]*

[handwritten: possession] (B) the collateral is not a certificated security and is in the possession of the secured party under Section 9–313 pursuant to the debtor's security agreement;

[handwritten: delivery] (C) the collateral is a certificated security in registered form and the security certificate has been delivered to the secured party under Section 8–301 pursuant to the debtor's security agreement; or

[handwritten: control] (D) the collateral is deposit accounts, electronic chattel paper, investment property, letter-of-credit rights, or electronic documents, and the secured party has control under Section 7–106, 9–104, 9–105, 9–106, or 9–107 pursuant to the debtor's security agreement.

(c) **[Other UCC provisions.]** Subsection (b) is subject to Section 4–210 on the security interest of a collecting bank, Section 5–118 on the security interest of a letter-of-credit issuer or nominated person, Section 9–110 on a security interest arising under Article 2 or 2A, and Section 9–206 on security interests in investment property.

(d) **[When person becomes bound by another person's security agreement.]** A person becomes bound as debtor by a security agreement entered into by another person if, by operation of law other than this article or by contract:

(1) the security agreement becomes effective to create a security interest in the person's property; or

(2) the person becomes generally obligated for the obligations of the other person, including the obligation secured under the security agreement, and acquires or succeeds to all or substantially all of the assets of the other person.

(e) **[Effect of new debtor becoming bound.]** If a new debtor becomes bound as debtor by a security agreement entered into by another person:

(1) the agreement satisfies subsection (b)(3) with respect to existing or after-acquired property of the new debtor to the extent the property is described in the agreement; and

(2) another agreement is not necessary to make a security interest in the property enforceable.

(f) **[Proceeds and supporting obligations.]** The attachment of a security interest in collateral gives the secured party the rights to proceeds provided by Section 9–315 and is also attachment of a security interest in a supporting obligation for the collateral.

(g) **[Lien securing right to payment.]** The attachment of a security interest in a right to payment or performance secured by a security interest or other lien on personal or real property is also attachment of a security interest in the security interest, mortgage, or other lien.

(h) **[Security entitlement carried in securities account.]** The attachment of a security interest in a securities account is also attachment of a security interest in the security entitlements carried in the securities account.

(i) **[Commodity contracts carried in commodity account.]** The attachment of a security interest in a commodity account is also attachment of a security interest in the commodity contracts carried in the commodity account.

As amended in 2003.

Official Comment

1.   **Source.** Former Sections 9–203, 9–115(2), (6).

2.   **Creation, Attachment, and Enforceability.** Subsection (a) states the general rule that a security interest attaches to collateral only when it becomes enforceable against the debtor. Subsection (b) specifies the circumstances under which a security interest becomes enforceable. Subsection (b) states three basic prerequisites to the existence of a security interest: value (paragraph (1)), rights or power to transfer rights in collateral (paragraph (2)), and agreement plus satisfaction of an evidentiary requirement (paragraph (3)). When all of these elements exist, a security interest becomes enforceable between the parties and attaches under subsection (a). Subsection (c) identifies certain exceptions to the general rule of subsection (b).

3.   **Security Agreement; Authentication.** Under subsection (b)(3), enforceability requires the debtor's security agreement and compliance with an evidentiary requirement in the nature of a Statute of Frauds. Paragraph (3)(A) represents the most basic of the evidentiary alternatives, under which the debtor must authenticate a security agreement that provides a description of the collateral. Under Section 9–102, a "security agreement" is "an agreement that creates or provides for a security interest." Neither that definition nor the requirement of paragraph (3)(A) rejects the deeply rooted doctrine that a bill of sale, although absolute in form, may be shown in fact to have been given as security. Under this Article, as under prior law, a debtor may show by parol evidence that a transfer purporting to be absolute was in fact for security. Similarly, a self-styled "lease" may serve as a security agreement if the agreement creates a security interest. See Section 1–203 (distinguishing security interest from lease).

4.   **Possession, Delivery, or Control Pursuant to Security Agreement.** The other alternatives in subsection (b)(3) dispense with the requirement of an authenticated security agreement and provide alternative evidentiary tests. Under paragraph (3)(B), the secured party's possession substitutes for the debtor's authentication under paragraph (3)(A) if the secured party's possession is "pursuant to the debtor's security agreement." That phrase refers to the debtor's agreement to the secured party's possession for the purpose of creating a security interest. The phrase should not be confused with the phrase "debtor has authenticated a security agreement," used in paragraph (3)(A), which contemplates the debtor's authentication of a record. In the unlikely event that possession is obtained without the debtor's agreement, possession would not suffice as a substitute for an authenticated security agreement. However, once the security interest has become enforceable and has attached, it is not impaired by the fact that the secured party's possession is maintained without the agreement of a subsequent debtor (e.g., a transferee). Possession as contemplated by Section 9–313 is possession

for purposes of subsection (b)(3)(B), even though it may not constitute possession "pursuant to the debtor's agreement" and consequently might not serve as a substitute for an authenticated security agreement under subsection (b)(3)(A). Subsection (b)(3)(C) provides that delivery of a certificated security to the secured party under Section 8–301 pursuant to the debtor's security agreement is sufficient as a substitute for an authenticated security agreement. Similarly, under subsection (b)(3)(D), control of investment property, a deposit account, electronic chattel paper, a letter-of-credit right, or electronic documents satisfies the evidentiary test if control is pursuant to the debtor's security agreement.

5. **Collateral Covered by Other Statute or Treaty.** One evidentiary purpose of the formal requisites stated in subsection (b) is to minimize the possibility of future disputes as to the terms of a security agreement (e.g., as to the property that stands as collateral for the obligation secured). One should distinguish the evidentiary functions of the formal requisites of attachment and enforceability (such as the requirement that a security agreement contain a description of the collateral) from the more limited goals of "notice filing" for financing statements under Part 5, explained in Section 9–502, Comment 2. When perfection is achieved by compliance with the requirements of a statute or treaty described in Section 9–311(a), such as a federal recording act or a certificate-of-title statute, the manner of describing the collateral in a registry imposed by the statute or treaty may or may not be adequate for purposes of this section and Section 9–108. However, the description contained in the security agreement, not the description in a public registry or on a certificate of title, controls for purposes of this section.

6. **Debtor's Rights; Debtor's Power to Transfer Rights.** Subsection (b)(2) conditions attachment on the debtor's having "rights in the collateral or the power to transfer rights in the collateral to a secured party." A debtor's limited rights in collateral, short of full ownership, are sufficient for a security interest to attach. However, in accordance with basic personal property conveyancing principles, the baseline rule is that a security interest attaches only to whatever rights a debtor may have, broad or limited as those rights may be.

Certain exceptions to the baseline rule enable a debtor to transfer, and a security interest to attach to, greater rights than the debtor has. See Part 3, Subpart 3 (priority rules). The phrase, "or the power to transfer rights in the collateral to a secured party," accommodates those exceptions. In some cases, a debtor may have power to transfer another person's rights only to a class of transferees that excludes secured parties. See, e.g., Section 2–403(2) (giving certain merchants power to transfer an entruster's rights to a buyer in ordinary course of business). Under those circumstances, the debtor would not have the power to create a security interest in the other person's rights, and the condition in subsection (b)(2) would not be satisfied.

7. **New Debtors.** Subsection (e) makes clear that the enforceability requirements of subsection (b)(3) are met when a new debtor becomes bound under an original debtor's security agreement. If a new debtor becomes bound as debtor by a security agreement entered into by another person, the security agreement satisfies the requirement of subsection (b)(3) as to the existing and after-acquired property of the new debtor to the extent the property is described in the agreement.

Subsection (d) explains when a new debtor becomes bound. Persons who become bound under paragraph (2) are limited to those who both become primarily liable for the original debtor's obligations and succeed to (or acquire) its assets. Thus, the paragraph excludes sureties and other secondary obligors as well as persons who become obligated through veil piercing and other non-successorship doctrines. In many cases, paragraph (2) will exclude successors to the assets and liabilities of a division of a debtor. See also Section 9–508, Comment 3.

8. **Supporting Obligations.** Under subsection (f), a security interest in a "supporting obligation" (defined in Section 9–102) automatically follows from a security interest in the underlying, supported collateral. This result was implicit under former Article 9. Implicit in subsection (f) is the principle that the secured party's interest in a supporting obligation extends to the supporting obligation only to the extent that it supports the collateral in which the secured party has a security interest. Complex issues may arise, however, if a supporting obligation supports many separate obligations of a particular account debtor and if the supported obligations are separately assigned as security to several secured parties. The problems may be exacerbated if a supporting obligation is limited to an aggregate amount that is less than the aggregate amount of the obligations it supports. This Article does not contain provisions dealing with competing claims to a limited supporting obligation. As under former Article 9, the law of suretyship and the agreements of the parties will control.

9. **Collateral Follows Right to Payment or Performance.** Subsection (g) codifies the common-law rule that a transfer of an obligation secured by a security interest or other lien on personal or real property also transfers the security interest or lien. See Restatement (3d), Property (Mortgages) § 5.4(a) (1997). See also Section 9–308(e) (analogous rule for perfection).

10. **Investment Property.** Subsections (h) and (i) make clear that attachment of a security interest in a securities account or commodity account is also attachment in security entitlements or commodity contracts carried in the accounts.

As amended in 2003 and 2010.

§ 9–204. After-Acquired Property; Future Advances.

(a) **[After-acquired collateral.]** Except as otherwise provided in subsection (b), a security agreement may create or provide for a security interest in after-acquired collateral.

(b) **[When after-acquired property clause not effective.]** A security interest does not attach under a term constituting an after-acquired property clause to:

(1) consumer goods, other than an accession when given as additional security, unless the debtor acquires rights in them within 10 days after the secured party gives value; or

(2) a commercial tort claim.

(c) **[Future advances and other value.]** A security agreement may provide that collateral secures, or that accounts, chattel paper, payment intangibles, or promissory notes are sold in connection with, future advances or other value, whether or not the advances or value are given pursuant to commitment.

Official Comment

1. **Source.** Former Section 9–204.

2. **After-Acquired Property; Continuing General Lien.** Subsection (a) makes clear that a security interest arising by virtue of an after-acquired property clause is no less valid than a security interest in collateral in which the debtor has rights at the time value is given. A security interest in after-acquired property is not merely an "equitable" interest; no further action by the secured party—such as a supplemental agreement covering the new collateral—is required. This section adopts the principle of a "continuing general lien" or "floating lien." It validates a security interest in the debtor's existing and (upon acquisition) future assets, even though the debtor has liberty to use or dispose of collateral without being required to account for proceeds or substitute new collateral. See Section 9–205. Subsection (a), together with subsection (c), also validates "cross-collateral" clauses under which collateral acquired at any time secures advances whenever made.

3. **After-Acquired Consumer Goods.** Subsection (b)(1) makes ineffective an after-acquired property clause covering consumer goods (defined in Section 9–109), except as accessions (see Section 9–335), acquired more than 10 days after the secured party gives value. Subsection (b)(1) is unchanged in substance from the corresponding provision in former Section 9–204(2).

4. **Commercial Tort Claims.** Subsection (b)(2) provides that an after-acquired property clause in a security agreement does not reach future commercial tort claims. In order for a security interest in a tort claim to attach, the claim must be in existence when the security agreement is authenticated. In addition, the security agreement must describe the tort claim with greater specificity than simply "all tort claims." See Section 9–108(e).

5. **Future Advances; Obligations Secured.** Under subsection (c) collateral may secure future as well as past or present advances if the security agreement so provides. This is in line with the policy of this Article toward security interests in after-acquired property under subsection (a). Indeed, the parties are free to agree that a security interest secures any obligation whatsoever. Determining the obligations secured by collateral is solely a matter of construing the parties' agreement under applicable law. This Article rejects the holdings of cases decided under former Article 9 that applied other tests, such as whether a future advance or other subsequently incurred obligation was of the same or a similar type or class as earlier advances and obligations secured by the collateral.

6. **Sales of Receivables.** Subsections (a) and (c) expressly validate after-acquired property and future advance clauses not only when the transaction is for security purposes but also when the transaction is the sale of accounts, chattel paper, payment intangibles, or promissory notes. This result was implicit under former Article 9.

7. **Financing Statements.** The effect of after-acquired property and future advance clauses as components of a security agreement should not be confused with the requirements applicable to financing statements under this Article's system of perfection by notice filing. The references to after-acquired property clauses and future advance clauses in this section are limited to security agreements. There is no need to refer to

after-acquired property or future advances or other obligations secured in a financing statement. See Section 9–502, Comment 2.

As amended in 2000.

§ 9–205.   Use or Disposition of Collateral Permissible.

(a)   **[When security interest not invalid or fraudulent.]** A security interest is not invalid or fraudulent against creditors solely because:

(1)   the debtor has the right or ability to:

(A)   use, commingle, or dispose of all or part of the collateral, including returned or repossessed goods;

(B)   collect, compromise, enforce, or otherwise deal with collateral;

(C)   accept the return of collateral or make repossessions; or

(D)   use, commingle, or dispose of proceeds; or

(2)   the secured party fails to require the debtor to account for proceeds or replace collateral.

(b)   **[Requirements of possession not relaxed.]** This section does not relax the requirements of possession if attachment, perfection, or enforcement of a security interest depends upon possession of the collateral by the secured party.

Official Comment

1.   **Source.** Former Section 9–205.

2.   **Validity of Unrestricted "Floating Lien."** This Article expressly validates the "floating lien" on shifting collateral. See Sections 9–201, 9–204 and Comment 2. This section provides that a security interest is not invalid or fraudulent by reason of the debtor's liberty to dispose of the collateral without being required to account to the secured party for proceeds or substitute new collateral. As did former Section 9–205, this section repeals the rule of *Benedict v. Ratner*, 268 U.S. 353 (1925), and other cases which held such arrangements void as a matter of law because the debtor was given unfettered dominion or control over collateral. The *Benedict* rule did not effectively discourage or eliminate security transactions in inventory and receivables. Instead, it forced financing arrangements to be self-liquidating. Although this section repeals *Benedict*, the filing and other perfection requirements (see Part 3, Subpart 2, and Part 5) provide for public notice that overcomes any potential misleading effects of a debtor's use and control of collateral. Moreover, nothing in this section prevents the debtor and secured party from agreeing to procedures by which the secured party polices or monitors collateral or to restrictions on the debtor's dominion. However, this Article leaves these matters to agreement based on business considerations, not on legal requirements.

3.   **Possessory Security Interests.** Subsection (b) makes clear that this section does not relax the requirements for perfection by possession under Section 9–313. If a secured party allows the debtor access to and control over collateral its security interest may be or become unperfected.

4.   **Permissible Freedom for Debtor to Enforce Collateral.** Former Section 9–205 referred to a debtor's "liberty. . .to collect or compromise accounts or chattel paper." This section recognizes the broader rights of a debtor to "enforce," as well as to "collect" and "compromise" collateral. This section's reference to collecting, compromising, and enforcing "collateral" instead of "accounts or chattel paper" contemplates the many other types of collateral that a debtor may wish to "collect, compromise, or enforce": e.g., deposit accounts, documents, general intangibles, instruments, investment property, and letter-of-credit rights.

§ 9–206.   Security Interest Arising in Purchase or Delivery of Financial Asset.

(a)   **[Security interest when person buys through securities intermediary.]** A security interest in favor of a securities intermediary attaches to a person's security entitlement if:

(1)   the person buys a financial asset through the securities intermediary in a transaction in which the person is obligated to pay the purchase price to the securities intermediary at the time of the purchase; and

(2) the securities intermediary credits the financial asset to the buyer's securities account before the buyer pays the securities intermediary.

(b) **[Security interest secures obligation to pay for financial asset.]** The security interest described in subsection (a) secures the person's obligation to pay for the financial asset.

(c) **[Security interest in payment against delivery transaction.]** A security interest in favor of a person that delivers a certificated security or other financial asset represented by a writing attaches to the security or other financial asset if:

(1) the security or other financial asset:

(A) in the ordinary course of business is transferred by delivery with any necessary indorsement or assignment; and

(B) is delivered under an agreement between persons in the business of dealing with such securities or financial assets; and

(2) the agreement calls for delivery against payment.

(d) **[Security interest secures obligation to pay for delivery.]** The security interest described in subsection (c) secures the obligation to make payment for the delivery.

Official Comment

1. **Source.** Former 9–116.

2. **Codification of "Broker's Lien."** Depending upon a securities intermediary's arrangements with its entitlement holders, the securities intermediary may treat the entitlement holder as entitled to financial assets before the entitlement holder has actually made payment for them. For example, many brokers permit retail customers to pay for financial assets by check. The broker may not receive final payment of the check until several days after the broker has credited the customer's securities account for the financial assets. Thus, the customer will have acquired a security entitlement prior to payment. Subsection (a) provides that, in such circumstances, the securities intermediary has a security interest in the entitlement holder's security entitlement. Under subsection (b) the security interest secures the customer's obligation to pay for the financial asset in question. Subsections (a) and (b) codify and adapt to the indirect holding system the so-called "broker's lien," which has long been recognized. See Restatement, Security § 12.

3. **Financial Assets Delivered Against Payment.** Subsection (c) creates a security interest in favor of persons who deliver certificated securities or other financial assets in physical form, such as money market instruments, if the agreed payment is not received. In some arrangements for settlement of transactions in physical financial assets, the seller's securities custodian will deliver physical certificates to the buyer's securities custodian and receive a time-stamped delivery receipt. The buyer's securities custodian will examine the certificate to ensure that it is in good order, and that the delivery matches a trade in which the buyer has instructed the seller to deliver to that custodian. If all is in order, the receiving custodian will settle with the delivering custodian through whatever funds settlement system has been agreed upon or is used by custom and usage in that market. The understanding of the trade, however, is that the delivery is conditioned upon payment, so that if payment is not made for any reason, the security will be returned to the deliverer. Subsection (c) clarifies the rights of persons making deliveries in such circumstances. It provides the person making delivery with a security interest in the securities or other financial assets; under subsection (d), the security interest secures the seller's right to receive payment for the delivery. Section 8–301 specifies when delivery of a certificated security occurs; that section should be applied as well to other financial assets as well for purposes of this section.

4. **Automatic Attachment and Perfection.** Subsections (a) and (c) refer to attachment of a security interest. Attachment under this section has the same incidents (enforceability, right to proceeds, etc.) as attachment under Section 9–203. This section overrides the general attachment rules in Section 9–203. See Section 9–203(c). A securities intermediary's security interest under subsection (a) is perfected by control without further action. See Section 8–106 (control); 9–314 (perfection). Security interests arising under subsection (c) are automatically perfected. See Section 9–309(9).

Duties of SP in possession §9-207

[SUBPART 2. RIGHTS AND DUTIES]

§ 9-207. Rights and Duties of Secured Party Having Possession or Control of Collateral.

(a) **[Duty of care when secured party in possession.]** Except as otherwise provided in subsection (d), a secured party shall use reasonable care in the custody and preservation of collateral in the secured party's possession. In the case of chattel paper or an instrument, reasonable care includes taking necessary steps to preserve rights against prior parties unless otherwise agreed.

(b) **[Expenses, risks, duties, and rights when secured party in possession.]** Except as otherwise provided in subsection (d), if a secured party has possession of collateral:

(1) reasonable expenses, including the cost of insurance and payment of taxes or other charges, incurred in the custody, preservation, use, or operation of the collateral are chargeable to the debtor and are secured by the collateral;

(2) the risk of accidental loss or damage is on the debtor to the extent of a deficiency in any effective insurance coverage;

(3) the secured party shall keep the collateral identifiable, but fungible collateral may be commingled; and

(4) the secured party may use or operate the collateral:

(A) for the purpose of preserving the collateral or its value;

(B) as permitted by an order of a court having competent jurisdiction; or

(C) except in the case of consumer goods, in the manner and to the extent agreed by the debtor.

(c) **[Duties and rights when secured party in possession or control.]** Except as otherwise provided in subsection (d), a secured party having possession of collateral or control of collateral under Section 7-106, 9-104, 9-105, 9-106, or 9-107:

(1) may hold as additional security any proceeds, except money or funds, received from the collateral;

(2) shall apply money or funds received from the collateral to reduce the secured obligation, unless remitted to the debtor; and

(3) may create a security interest in the collateral.

(d) **[Buyer of certain rights to payment.]** If the secured party is a buyer of accounts, chattel paper, payment intangibles, or promissory notes or a consignor:

(1) subsection (a) does not apply unless the secured party is entitled under an agreement:

(A) to charge back uncollected collateral; or

(B) otherwise to full or limited recourse against the debtor or a secondary obligor based on the nonpayment or other default of an account debtor or other obligor on the collateral; and

(2) subsections (b) and (c) do not apply.

As amended in 2003.

Official Comment

1. **Source.** Former Section 9-207.

2. **Duty of Care for Collateral in Secured Party's Possession.** Like former section 9-207, subsection (a) imposes a duty of care, similar to that imposed on a pledgee at common law, on a secured party in possession of collateral. See Restatement, Security §§ 17, 18. In many cases a secured party in possession of collateral may satisfy this duty by notifying the debtor of action that should be taken and allowing the debtor to take the action itself. If the secured party itself takes action, its reasonable expenses may be added to the secured obligation. The revised definitions of "collateral," "debtor," and "secured party" in Section 9-102 make this section applicable to collateral subject to an agricultural lien if the collateral is in the lienholder's possession. Under Section 1-302 the duty to exercise reasonable care may not be disclaimed by agreement, although under that section the parties

remain free to determine by agreement standards that are not manifestly unreasonable as to what constitutes reasonable care. Unless otherwise agreed, for a secured party in possession of chattel paper or an instrument, reasonable care includes the preservation of rights against prior parties. The secured party's right to have instruments or documents indorsed or transferred to it or its order is dealt with in the relevant sections of Articles 3, 7, and 8. See Sections 3–203(c), 7–506, 8–304(d).

3.   **Specific Rules When Secured Party in Possession or Control of Collateral.** Subsections (b) and (c) provide rules following common-law precedents which apply unless the parties otherwise agree. The rules in subsection (b) apply to typical issues that may arise while a secured party is in possession of collateral, including expenses, insurance, and taxes, risk of loss or damage, identifiable and fungible collateral, and use or operation of collateral. Subsection (c) contains rules that apply in certain circumstances that may arise when a secured party is in either possession or control of collateral. These circumstances include the secured party's receiving proceeds from the collateral and the secured party's creation of a security interest in the collateral.

4.   **Applicability Following Default.** This section applies when the secured party has possession of collateral either before or after default. See Sections 9–601(b), 9–609. Subsection (b)(4)(C) limits agreements concerning the use or operation of collateral to collateral other than consumer goods. Under Section 9–602(1), a debtor cannot waive or vary that limitation.

5.   **"Repledges" and Right of Redemption.** Subsection (c)(3) eliminates the qualification in former Section 9–207 to the effect that the terms of a "repledge" may not "impair" a debtor's "right to redeem" collateral. The change is primarily for clarification. There is no basis on which to draw from subsection (c)(3) any inference concerning the debtor's right to redeem the collateral. The debtor enjoys that right under Section 9–623; this section need not address it. For example, if the collateral is a negotiable note that the secured party (SP-1) repledges to SP-2, nothing in this section suggests that the debtor (D) does not retain the right to redeem the note upon payment to SP-1 of all obligations secured by the note. But, as explained below, the debtor's unimpaired right to redeem as against the debtor's original secured party nevertheless may not be enforceable as against the new secured party.

In resolving questions that arise from the creation of a security interest by SP-1, one must take care to distinguish D's rights against SP-1 from D's rights against SP-2. Once D discharges the secured obligation, D becomes entitled to the note; SP-1 has no legal basis upon which to withhold it. If, as a practical matter, SP-1 is unable to return the note because SP-2 holds it as collateral for SP-1's unpaid debt, then SP-1 is liable to D under the law of conversion.

Whether SP-2 would be liable to D depends on the relative priority of SP-2's security interest and D's interest. By permitting SP-1 to create a security interest in the collateral (repledge), subsection (c)(3) provides a statutory power for SP-1 to give SP-2 a security interest (subject, of course, to any agreement by SP-1 not to give a security interest). In the vast majority of cases where repledge rights are significant, the security interest of the second secured party, SP-2 in the example, will be senior to the debtor's interest. By virtue of the debtor's consent or applicable legal rules, SP-2 typically would cut off D's rights in investment property or be immune from D's claims. See Sections 9–331, 3–306 (holder in due course), 8–303 (protected purchaser), 8–502 (acquisition of a security entitlement), 8–503(e) (action by entitlement holder). Moreover, the expectations and business practices in some markets, such as the securities markets, are such that D's consent to SP-2's taking free of D's rights inheres in D's creation of SP-1's security interest which gives rise to SP-1's power under this section. In these situations, D would have no right to recover the collateral or recover damages from SP-2. Nevertheless, D would have a damage claim against SP-1 if SP-1 had given a security interest to SP-2 in breach of its agreement with D. Moreover, if SP-2's security interest secures an amount that is less than the amount secured by SP-1's security interest (granted by D), then D's exercise of its right to redeem would provide value sufficient to discharge SP-1's obligations to SP-2.

For the most part this section does not change the law under former Section 9–207, although eliminating the reference to the debtor's right of redemption may alter the secured party's right to repledge in one respect. Former Section 9–207 could have been read to limit the secured party's statutory right to repledge collateral to repledge transactions in which the collateral did not secure a greater obligation than that of the original debtor. Inasmuch as this is a matter normally dealt with by agreement between the debtor and secured party, any change would appear to have little practical effect.

6.   **"Repledges" of Investment Property.** The following example will aid the discussion of "repledges" of investment property.

Example. Debtor grants Alpha Bank a security interest in a security entitlement that includes 1000 shares of XYZ Co. stock that Debtor holds through an account with Able & Co. Alpha does not have an account with Able. Alpha uses Beta Bank as its securities custodian. Debtor instructs Able to transfer the shares to Beta, for the account of Alpha, and Able does so. Beta then credits Alpha's account. Alpha has control of the security entitlement for the 1000 shares under Section 8–106(d). (These are the facts of Example 2, Section 8–106, Comment 4.) Although, as between Debtor and Alpha, Debtor may have become the beneficial owner of the new securities entitlement with Beta, Beta has agreed to act on Alpha's entitlement orders because, as between Beta and Alpha, Alpha has become the entitlement holder.

Next, Alpha grants Gamma Bank a security interest in the security entitlement with Beta that includes the 1000 shares of XYZ Co. stock. In order to afford Gamma control of the entitlement, Alpha instructs Beta to transfer the stock to Gamma's custodian, Delta Bank, which credits Gamma's account for 1000 shares. At this point Gamma holds its securities entitlement for its benefit as well as that of its debtor, Alpha. Alpha's derivative rights also are for the benefit of Debtor.

In many, probably most, situations and at any particular point in time, it will be impossible for Debtor or Alpha to "trace" Alpha's "repledge" to any particular securities entitlement or financial asset of Gamma or anyone else. Debtor would retain, of course, a right to redeem the collateral from Alpha upon satisfaction of the secured obligation. However, in the absence of a traceable interest, Debtor would retain only a personal claim against Alpha in the event Alpha failed to restore the security entitlement to Debtor. Moreover, even in the unlikely event that Debtor could trace a property interest, in the context of the financial markets, normally the operation of this section, Debtor's explicit agreement to permit Alpha to create a senior security interest, or legal rules permitting Gamma to cut off Debtor's rights or become immune from Debtor's claims would effectively subordinate Debtor's interest to the holder of a security interest created by Alpha. And, under the shelter principle, all subsequent transferees would obtain interests to which Debtor's interest also would be subordinate.

7. **Buyers of Chattel Paper and Other Receivables; Consignors.** This section has been revised to reflect the fact that a seller of accounts, chattel paper, payment intangibles, or promissory notes retains no interest in the collateral and so is not disadvantaged by the secured party's noncompliance with the requirements of this section. Accordingly, subsection (d) provides that subsection (a) applies only to security interests that secure an obligation and to sales of receivables in which the buyer has recourse against the debtor. (Of course, a buyer of accounts or payment intangibles could not have "possession" of original collateral, but might have possession of proceeds, such as promissory notes or checks.) The meaning of "recourse" in this respect is limited to recourse arising out of the account debtor's failure to pay or other default.

Subsection (d) makes subsections (b) and (c) inapplicable to buyers of accounts, chattel paper, payment intangibles, or promissory notes and consignors. Of course, there is no reason to believe that a buyer of receivables or a consignor could not, for example, create a security interest or otherwise transfer an interest in the collateral, regardless of who has possession of the collateral. However, this section leaves the rights of those owners to law other than Article 9.

As amended in 2000 and 2010.

§ 9–208. Additional Duties of Secured Party Having Control of Collateral.

(a) **[Applicability of section.]** This section applies to cases in which there is no outstanding secured obligation and the secured party is not committed to make advances, incur obligations, or otherwise give value.

(b) **[Duties of secured party after receiving demand from debtor.]** Within 10 days after receiving an authenticated demand by the debtor:

(1) a secured party having control of a deposit account under Section 9–104(a)(2) shall send to the bank with which the deposit account is maintained an authenticated statement that releases the bank from any further obligation to comply with instructions originated by the secured party;

(2) a secured party having control of a deposit account under Section 9–104(a)(3) shall:

(A) pay the debtor the balance on deposit in the deposit account; or

(B) transfer the balance on deposit into a deposit account in the debtor's name;

(3) a secured party, other than a buyer, having control of electronic chattel paper under Section 9–105 shall:

(A) communicate the authoritative copy of the electronic chattel paper to the debtor or its designated custodian;

    (B)   if the debtor designates a custodian that is the designated custodian with which the authoritative copy of the electronic chattel paper is maintained for the secured party, communicate to the custodian an authenticated record releasing the designated custodian from any further obligation to comply with instructions originated by the secured party and instructing the custodian to comply with instructions originated by the debtor; and

    (C)   take appropriate action to enable the debtor or its designated custodian to make copies of or revisions to the authoritative copy which add or change an identified assignee of the authoritative copy without the consent of the secured party;

  (4) a secured party having control of investment property under Section 8–106(d)(2) or 9–106(b) shall send to the securities intermediary or commodity intermediary with which the security entitlement or commodity contract is maintained an authenticated record that releases the securities intermediary or commodity intermediary from any further obligation to comply with entitlement orders or directions originated by the secured party;

  (5) a secured party having control of a letter-of-credit right under Section 9–107 shall send to each person having an unfulfilled obligation to pay or deliver proceeds of the letter of credit to the secured party an authenticated release from any further obligation to pay or deliver proceeds of the letter of credit to the secured party; and

  (6) a secured party having control of an electronic document shall:

    (A)   give control of the electronic document to the debtor or its designated custodian;

    (B)   if the debtor designates a custodian that is the designated custodian with which the authoritative copy of the electronic document is maintained for the secured party, communicate to the custodian an authenticated record releasing the designated custodian from any further obligation to comply with instructions originated by the secured party and instructing the custodian to comply with instructions originated by the debtor; and

    (C)   take appropriate action to enable the debtor or its designated custodian to make copies of or revisions to the authoritative copy which add or change an identified assignee of the authoritative copy without the consent of the secured party.

As amended in 2003.

Official Comment

1.   **Source.** New.

2.   **Scope and Purpose.** This section imposes duties on a secured party who has control of a deposit account, electronic chattel paper, investment property, a letter-of-credit right, or electronic documents of title. The duty to terminate the secured party's control is analogous to the duty to file a termination statement, imposed by Section 9–513. Under subsection (a), it applies only when there is no outstanding secured obligation and the secured party is not committed to give value. The requirements of this section can be varied by agreement under Section 1–102(3) [*unrevised Article 1; see Concordance, p. 22*]. For example, a debtor could by contract agree that the secured party may comply with subsection (b) by releasing control more than 10 days after demand. Also, duties under this section should not be read to conflict with the terms of the collateral itself. For example, if the collateral is a time deposit account, subsection (b)(2) should not require a secured party with control to make an early withdrawal of the funds (assuming that were possible) in order to pay them over to the debtor or put them in an account in the debtor's name.

3.   **Remedy for Failure to Relinquish Control.** If a secured party fails to comply with the requirements of subsection (b), the debtor has the remedy set forth in Section 9–625(e). This remedy is identical to that applicable to failure to provide or file a termination statement under Section 9–513.

4.   **Duty to Relinquish Possession.** Although Section 9–207 addresses directly the duties of a secured party in possession of collateral, that section does not require the secured party to relinquish possession when the secured party ceases to hold a security interest. Under common law, absent agreement to the contrary, the failure to relinquish possession of collateral upon satisfaction of the secured obligation would constitute a conversion. Inasmuch as problems apparently have not surfaced in the absence of statutory duties under former Article 9 and

the common-law duty appears to have been sufficient, this Article does not impose a statutory duty to relinquish possession.

As amended in 2000 and 2003.

§ 9–209. Duties of Secured Party if Account Debtor Has Been Notified of Assignment.

(a) **[Applicability of section.]** Except as otherwise provided in subsection (c), this section applies if:

(1) there is no outstanding secured obligation; and

(2) the secured party is not committed to make advances, incur obligations, or otherwise give value.

(b) **[Duties of secured party after receiving demand from debtor.]** Within 10 days after receiving an authenticated demand by the debtor, a secured party shall send to an account debtor that has received notification of an assignment to the secured party as assignee under Section 9–406(a) an authenticated record that releases the account debtor from any further obligation to the secured party.

(c) **[Inapplicability to sales.]** This section does not apply to an assignment constituting the sale of an account, chattel paper, or payment intangible.

Official Comment

1. **Source.** New.

2. **Scope and Purpose.** Like Sections 9–208 and 9–513, which require a secured party to relinquish control of collateral and to file or provide a termination statement for a financing statement, this section requires a secured party to free up collateral when there no longer is any outstanding secured obligation or any commitment to give value in the future. This section addresses the case in which account debtors have been notified to pay a secured party to whom the receivables have been assigned. It requires the secured party (assignee) to inform the account debtors that they no longer are obligated to make payment to the secured party. See subsection (b). It does not apply to account debtors whose obligations on an account, chattel paper, or payment intangible have been sold. See subsection (c).

§ 9–210. Request for Accounting; Request Regarding List of Collateral or Statement of Account.

(a) **[Definitions.]** In this section:

(1) "Request" means a record of a type described in paragraph (2), (3), or (4).

(2) "Request for an accounting" means a record authenticated by a debtor requesting that the recipient provide an accounting of the unpaid obligations secured by collateral and reasonably identifying the transaction or relationship that is the subject of the request.

(3) "Request regarding a list of collateral" means a record authenticated by a debtor requesting that the recipient approve or correct a list of what the debtor believes to be the collateral securing an obligation and reasonably identifying the transaction or relationship that is the subject of the request.

(4) "Request regarding a statement of account" means a record authenticated by a debtor requesting that the recipient approve or correct a statement indicating what the debtor believes to be the aggregate amount of unpaid obligations secured by collateral as of a specified date and reasonably identifying the transaction or relationship that is the subject of the request.

(b) **[Duty to respond to requests.]** Subject to subsections (c), (d), (e), and (f), a secured party, other than a buyer of accounts, chattel paper, payment intangibles, or promissory notes or a consignor, shall comply with a request within 14 days after receipt:

(1) in the case of a request for an accounting, by authenticating and sending to the debtor an accounting; and

(2) in the case of a request regarding a list of collateral or a request regarding a statement of account, by authenticating and sending to the debtor an approval or correction.

(c)   **[Request regarding list of collateral; statement concerning type of collateral.]** A secured party that claims a security interest in all of a particular type of collateral owned by the debtor may comply with a request regarding a list of collateral by sending to the debtor an authenticated record including a statement to that effect within 14 days after receipt.

(d)   **[Request regarding list of collateral; no interest claimed.]** A person that receives a request regarding a list of collateral, claims no interest in the collateral when it receives the request, and claimed an interest in the collateral at an earlier time shall comply with the request within 14 days after receipt by sending to the debtor an authenticated record:

(1)   disclaiming any interest in the collateral; and

(2)   if known to the recipient, providing the name and mailing address of any assignee of or successor to the recipient's interest in the collateral.

(e)   **[Request for accounting or regarding statement of account; no interest in obligation claimed.]** A person that receives a request for an accounting or a request regarding a statement of account, claims no interest in the obligations when it receives the request, and claimed an interest in the obligations at an earlier time shall comply with the request within 14 days after receipt by sending to the debtor an authenticated record:

(1)   disclaiming any interest in the obligations; and

(2)   if known to the recipient, providing the name and mailing address of any assignee of or successor to the recipient's interest in the obligations.

(f)   **[Charges for responses.]** A debtor is entitled without charge to one response to a request under this section during any six-month period. The secured party may require payment of a charge not exceeding $25 for each additional response.

As amended in 1999.

Official Comment

1.   **Source.** Former Section 9–208.

2.   **Scope and Purpose.** This section provides a procedure whereby a debtor may obtain from a secured party information about the secured obligation and the collateral in which the secured party may claim a security interest. It clarifies and resolves some of the issues that arose under former Section 9–208 and makes information concerning the secured indebtedness readily available to debtors, both before and after default. It applies to agricultural lien transactions (see the definitions of "debtor," "secured party," and "collateral" in Section 9–102), but generally not to sales of receivables. See subsection (b).

3.   **Requests by Debtors Only.** A financing statement filed under Part 5 may disclose only that a secured party may have a security interest in specified types of collateral. In most cases the financing statement will contain no indication of the obligation (if any) secured, whether any security interest actually exists, or the particular property subject to a security interest. Because creditors of and prospective purchasers from a debtor may have legitimate needs for more detailed information, it is necessary to provide a procedure under which the secured party will be required to provide information. On the other hand, the secured party should not be under a duty to disclose any details of the debtor's financial affairs to any casual inquirer or competitor who may inquire. For this reason, this section gives the right to request information to the debtor only. The debtor may submit a request in connection with negotiations with subsequent creditors and purchasers, as well as for the purpose of determining the status of its credit relationship or demonstrating which of its assets are free of a security interest.

4.   **Permitted Types of Requests for Information.** Subsection (a) contemplates that a debtor may request three types of information by submitting three types of "requests" to the secured party. First, the debtor may request the secured party to prepare and send an "accounting" (defined in Section 9–102). Second, the debtor may submit to the secured party a list of collateral for the secured party's approval or correction. Third, the debtor may submit to the secured party for its approval or correction a statement of the aggregate amount of unpaid secured obligations. Inasmuch as a secured party may have numerous transactions and relationships with a debtor, each request must identify the relevant transactions or relationships. Subsections (b) and (c) require the secured party to respond to a request within 14 days following receipt of the request.

5.   **Recipients Claiming No Interest in the Transaction.** A debtor may be unaware that a creditor with whom it has dealt has assigned its security interest or the secured obligation. Subsections (d) and (e) impose

upon recipients of requests under this section the duty to inform the debtor that they claim no interest in the collateral or secured obligation, respectively, and to inform the debtor of the name and mailing address of any known assignee or successor. As under subsections (b) and (c), a response to a request under subsection (d) or (e) is due 14 days following receipt.

6.   **Waiver; Remedy for Failure to Comply.** The debtor's rights under this section may not be waived or varied. See Section 9–602(2). Section 9–625 sets forth the remedies for noncompliance with the requirements of this section.

7.   **Limitation on Free Responses to Requests.** Under subsection (f), during a six-month period a debtor is entitled to receive from the secured party one free response to a request. The debtor is not entitled to a free response to *each* type of request (i.e., three free responses) during a six-month period.

As amended in 2000.

PART 3

PERFECTION AND PRIORITY

[SUBPART 1. LAW GOVERNING PERFECTION AND PRIORITY]

§ 9–301.   Law Governing Perfection and Priority of Security Interests.

Except as otherwise provided in Sections 9–303 through 9–306, the following rules determine the law governing perfection, the effect of perfection or nonperfection, and the priority of a security interest in collateral:

(1)   Except as otherwise provided in this section, while a debtor is located in a jurisdiction, the local law of that jurisdiction governs perfection, the effect of perfection or nonperfection, and the priority of a security interest in collateral.

(2)   While collateral is located in a jurisdiction, the local law of that jurisdiction governs perfection, the effect of perfection or nonperfection, and the priority of a possessory security interest in that collateral.

(3)   Except as otherwise provided in paragraph (4), while tangible negotiable documents, goods, instruments, money, or tangible chattel paper is located in a jurisdiction, the local law of that jurisdiction governs:

(A)   perfection of a security interest in the goods by filing a fixture filing;

(B)   perfection of a security interest in timber to be cut; and

(C)   the effect of perfection or nonperfection and the priority of a nonpossessory security interest in the collateral.

(4)   The local law of the jurisdiction in which the wellhead or minehead is located governs perfection, the effect of perfection or nonperfection, and the priority of a security interest in as-extracted collateral.

As amended in 2003.

Official Comment

1.   **Source.** Former Sections 9–103(1)(a), (b), 9–103(3)(a), (b), 9–103(5), substantially modified.

2.   **Scope of This Subpart.** Part 3, Subpart 1 (Sections 9–301 through 9–307) contains choice-of-law rules similar to those of former Section 9–103. Former Section 9–103 generally addresses which State's law governs "perfection and the effect of perfection or non-perfection of" security interests. See, e.g., former Section 9–103(1)(b). This Article follows the broader and more precise formulation in former Section 9–103(6)(b), which was revised in connection with the promulgation of Revised Article 8 in 1994: "perfection, the effect of perfection or non-perfection, and the priority of" security interests. Priority, in this context, subsumes all of the rules in Part 3, including "cut off" or "take free" rules such as Sections 9–317(b), (c), and (d), 9–320(a), (b), and (d), and 9–332. (The Hague Securities Convention may sometimes modify certain of this subpart's choice-of-law rules, as well as applying them to the requirements for foreclosure and the like, the characterization of a transfer as being outright or by way of security as it affects rights of third parties, and certain other issues. See PEB Commentary No. 19, dated April 11, 2017. The Commentary is available at https://www.ali.org/peb-ucc.)

This subpart does not address choice of law for other purposes. For example, the law applicable to issues such as attachment, validity, characterization of a transaction (e.g., true lease or security interest) as it affects rights between the parties to the transaction, and enforcement is governed by the rules in Section 1–301 ((a) and (b)*); that governing law typically is specified in the same agreement that contains the security agreement. And, another jurisdiction's law may govern other third-party matters addressed in this Article. See Section 9–401, Comment 3. As to the law applicable to characterization, see PEB Commentary No. 24, dated August 12, 2022. The Commentary is available at https://www.ali.org/peb-ucc.

3.   **Scope of Referral.** In designating the jurisdiction whose law governs, this Article directs the court to apply only the substantive ("local") law of a particular jurisdiction and not its choice-of-law rules.

Example 1:   Litigation over the priority of a security interest in accounts arises in State X. State X has adopted the official text of this Article, which provides that priority is determined by the local law of the jurisdiction in which the debtor is located. See Section 9–301(1). The debtor is located in State Y. Even if State Y has retained former Article 9 or enacted a nonuniform choice-of-law rule (e.g., one that provides that perfection is governed by the law of State Z), a State X court should look only to the substantive law of State Y and disregard State Y's choice-of-law rule. State Y's substantive law (e.g., its Section 9–501) provides that financing statements should be filed in a filing office in State Y. Note, however, that if the identical perfection issue were to be litigated in State Y, the court would look to State Y's former Section 9–103 or nonuniform 9–301 and conclude that a filing in State Y is ineffective.

Example 2:   In the preceding Example, assume that State X has adopted the official text of this Article, and State Y has adopted a nonuniform Section 9–301(1) under which perfection is governed by the whole law of State X, including its choice-of-law rules. If litigation occurs in State X, the court should look to the substantive law of State Y, which provides that financing statements are to be filed in a filing office in State Y. If litigation occurs in State Y, the court should look to the law of State X, whose choice-of-law rule requires that the court apply the substantive law of State Y. Thus, regardless of the jurisdiction in which the litigation arises, the financing statement should be filed in State Y.

4.   **Law Governing Perfection: General Rule.** Paragraph (1) contains the general rule: the law governing perfection of security interests in both tangible and intangible collateral, whether perfected by filing or automatically, is the law of the jurisdiction of the debtor's location, as determined under Section 9–307.

Paragraph (1) substantially simplifies the choice-of-law rules. Former Section 9–103 contained different choice-of-law rules for different types of collateral. Under Section 9–301(1), the law of a single jurisdiction governs perfection with respect to most types of collateral, both tangible and intangible. Paragraph (1) eliminates the need for former Section 9–103(1)(c), which concerned purchase-money security interests in tangible collateral that is intended to move from one jurisdiction to the other. It is likely to reduce the frequency of cases in which the governing law changes after a financing statement is properly filed. (Presumably, debtors change their own location less frequently than they change the location of their collateral.) The approach taken in paragraph (1) also eliminates some difficult priority issues and the need to distinguish between "mobile" and "ordinary" goods, and it reduces the number of filing offices in which secured parties must file or search when collateral is located in several jurisdictions.

5.   **Law Governing Perfection: Exceptions.** The general rule is subject to several exceptions. It does not apply to goods covered by a certificate of title (see Section 9–303), deposit accounts (see Section 9–304), investment property (see Section 9–305), or letter-of-credit rights (see Section 9–306). Nor does it apply to possessory security interests, i.e., security interests that the secured party has perfected by taking possession of the collateral (see paragraph (2)), security interests perfected by filing a fixture filing (see subparagraph (3)(A)), security interests in timber to be cut (subparagraph (3)(B)), or security interests in as-extracted collateral (see paragraph (4)).

a.   **Possessory Security Interests.** Paragraph (2) applies to possessory security interests and provides that perfection is governed by the local law of the jurisdiction in which the collateral is located. This is the rule of former Section 9–103(1)(b), except paragraph (2) eliminates the troublesome "last event" test of former law.

---

*   *Note from West Advisory Panel: In the 2010 amendments to Article 9, a reference to unrevised Section 1–105(1) at this point in the Comment was changed to refer to Section 1–301 in revised Article 1. In 2017, the PEB adopted an amendment to the Comment that inadvertently reinstated the reference to unrevised Article 1 and added a reference to revised Section 1–301(a) and (b). An amendment is expected that will conform the two changes and remove entirely the reference to unrevised Section 1–105, leaving the text as shown here.*

The distinction between nonpossessory and possessory security interests creates the potential for the same jurisdiction to apply two different choice-of-law rules to determine perfection in the same collateral. For example, were a secured party in possession of an instrument or a tangible document to relinquish possession in reliance on temporary perfection, the applicable law immediately would change from that of the location of the collateral to that of the location of the debtor. The applicability of two different choice-of-law rules for perfection is unlikely to lead to any material practical problems. The perfection rules of one Article 9 jurisdiction are likely to be identical to those of another. Moreover, under paragraph (3), the relative priority of competing security interests in tangible collateral is resolved by reference to the law of the jurisdiction in which the collateral is located, regardless of how the security interests are perfected.

b. **Fixture Filings.** Under the general rule in paragraph (1), a security interest in fixtures may be perfected by filing in the office specified by Section 9–501(a) as enacted in the jurisdiction in which the debtor is located. However, application of this rule to perfection of a security interest by filing a fixture filing could yield strange results. For example, perfection of a security interest in fixtures located in Arizona and owned by a Delaware corporation would be governed by the law of Delaware. Although Delaware law would send one to a filing office in Arizona for the place to file a financing statement as a fixture filing, see Section 9–501, Delaware law would not take account of local, nonuniform, real-property filing and recording requirements that Arizona law might impose. For this reason, paragraph (3)(A) contains a special rule for security interests perfected by a fixture filing; the law of the jurisdiction in which the fixtures are located governs perfection, including the formal requisites of a fixture filing. Under paragraph (3)(C), the same law governs priority. Fixtures are "goods" as defined in Section 9–102.

The filing of a financing statement to perfect a security interest in collateral of a transmitting utility constitutes a fixture filing with respect to goods that are or become fixtures. See Section 9–501(b). Accordingly, to perfect a security interest in goods of this kind by a fixture filing, a financing statement must be filed in the office specified by Section 9–501(b) as enacted in the jurisdiction in which the goods are located. If the fixtures collateral is located in more than one State, filing in all of those States will be necessary to perfect a security interest in all the fixtures collateral by a fixture filing. Of course, a security interest in nearly all types of collateral (including fixtures) of a transmitting utility may be perfected by filing in the office specified by Section 9–501(b) as enacted in the jurisdiction in which the transmitting utility is located. However, such a filing will not be effective as a fixture filing except with respect to goods that are located in that jurisdiction.

c. **Timber to Be Cut.** Application of the general rule in paragraph (1) to perfection of a security interest in timber to be cut would yield undesirable results analogous to those described with respect to fixtures. Paragraph (3)(B) adopts a similar solution: perfection is governed by the law of the jurisdiction in which the timber is located. As with fixtures, under paragraph (3)(C), the same law governs priority. Timber to be cut also is "goods" as defined in Section 9–102.

Paragraph (3)(B) applies only to "timber to be cut," not to timber that has been cut. Consequently, once the timber is cut, the general choice-of-law rule in paragraph (1) becomes applicable. To ensure continued perfection, a secured party should file in both the jurisdiction in which the timber to be cut is located and in the state where the debtor is located. The former filing would be with the office in which a real property mortgage would be filed, and the latter would be a central filing. See Section 9–501.

d. **As-Extracted Collateral.** Paragraph (4) adopts the rule of former Section 9–103(5) with respect to certain security interests in minerals and related accounts. Like security interests in fixtures perfected by filing a fixture filing, security interests in minerals that are as-extracted collateral are perfected by filing in the office designated for the filing or recording of a mortgage on the real property. For the same reasons, the law governing perfection and priority is the law of the jurisdiction in which the wellhead or minehead is located.

6. **Change in Law Governing Perfection.** When the debtor changes its location to another jurisdiction, the jurisdiction whose law governs perfection under paragraph (1) changes, as well. Similarly, the law governing perfection of a possessory security interest in collateral under paragraph (2) changes when the collateral is removed to another jurisdiction. Nevertheless, these changes will not result in an immediate loss of perfection. See Section 9–316(a), (b).

7. **Law Governing Effect of Perfection and Priority: Goods, Documents, Instruments, Money, Negotiable Documents, and Tangible Chattel Paper.** Under former Section 9–103, the law of a single jurisdiction governed both questions of perfection and those of priority. This Article generally adopts that approach. See paragraph (1). But the approach may create problems if the debtor and collateral are located in different jurisdictions. For example, assume a security interest in equipment located in Pennsylvania is perfected by filing in Illinois, where the debtor is located. If the law of the jurisdiction in which the debtor is located were to

govern priority, then the priority of an execution lien on goods located in Pennsylvania would be governed by rules enacted by the Illinois legislature.

To address this problem, paragraph (3)(C) divorces questions of perfection from questions of "the effect of perfection or nonperfection and the priority of a security interest." Under paragraph (3)(C), the rights of competing claimants to tangible collateral are resolved by reference to the law of the jurisdiction in which the collateral is located. A similar bifurcation applied to security interests in investment property under former Section 9–103(6). See Section 9–305.

Paragraph (3)(C) applies the law of the situs to determine priority only with respect to goods (including fixtures), instruments, money, tangible negotiable documents, and tangible chattel paper. Compare former Section 9–103(1), which applied the law of the location of the collateral to documents, instruments, and "ordinary" (as opposed to "mobile") goods. This Article does not distinguish among types of goods. The ordinary/mobile goods distinction appears to address concerns about where to file and search, rather than concerns about priority. There is no reason to preserve this distinction under the bifurcated approach.

Particularly serious confusion may arise when the choice-of-law rules of a given jurisdiction result in each of two competing security interests in the same collateral being governed by a different priority rule. The potential for this confusion existed under former Section 9–103(4) with respect to chattel paper: Perfection by possession was governed by the law of the location of the paper, whereas perfection by filing was governed by the law of the location of the debtor. Consider the mess that would have been created if the language or interpretation of former Section 9–308 were to differ in the two relevant States, or if one of the relevant jurisdictions (e.g., a foreign country) had not adopted Article 9. The potential for confusion could have been exacerbated when a secured party perfected both by taking possession in the State where the collateral is located (State A) and by filing in the State where the debtor is located (State B)—a common practice for some chattel paper financers. By providing that the law of the jurisdiction in which the collateral is located governs priority, paragraph (3) substantially diminishes this problem.

8.   **Non-U.S. Debtors.** This Article applies the same choice-of-law rules to all debtors, foreign and domestic. For example, it adopts the bifurcated approach for determining the law applicable to security interests in goods and other tangible collateral. See Comment 5.a., above. The Article contains a new rule specifying the location of non-U.S. debtors for purposes of this Part. The rule appears in Section 9–307 and is explained in the Comments to that section. Former Section 9–103(3)(c), which contained a special choice-of-law rule governing security interests created by debtors located in a non-U.S. jurisdiction, proved unsatisfactory and was deleted.

As amended in 2003, 2010, 2017, and 2022.

§ 9–302.   Law Governing Perfection and Priority of Agricultural Liens.

While farm products are located in a jurisdiction, the local law of that jurisdiction governs perfection, the effect of perfection or nonperfection, and the priority of an agricultural lien on the farm products.

Official Comment

1.   **Source.** New.

2.   **Agricultural Liens.** This section provides choice-of-law rules for agricultural liens on farm products. Perfection, the effect of perfection or nonperfection, and priority all are governed by the law of the jurisdiction in which the farm products are located. Other choice-of-law rules, including Section 1–301, determine which jurisdiction's law governs other matters, such as the secured party's rights on default. See Section 9–301, Comment 2. Inasmuch as no agricultural lien on proceeds arises under this Article, this section does not expressly apply to proceeds of agricultural liens. However, if another statute creates an agricultural lien on proceeds, it may be appropriate for courts to apply the choice-of-law rule in this section to determine priority in the proceeds.

As amended in 2010.

§ 9–303.   Law Governing Perfection and Priority of Security Interests in Goods Covered by a Certificate of Title.

(a)   **[Applicability of section.]** This section applies to goods covered by a certificate of title, even if there is no other relationship between the jurisdiction under whose certificate of title the goods are covered and the goods or the debtor.

(b)   **[When goods covered by certificate of title.]** Goods become covered by a certificate of title when a valid application for the certificate of title and the applicable fee are delivered to the appropriate authority. Goods cease to be covered by a certificate of title at the earlier of the time the certificate of title ceases to be effective under the law of the issuing jurisdiction or the time the goods become covered subsequently by a certificate of title issued by another jurisdiction.

(c) **[Applicable law.]** The local law of the jurisdiction under whose certificate of title the goods are covered governs perfection, the effect of perfection or nonperfection, and the priority of a security interest in goods covered by a certificate of title from the time the goods become covered by the certificate of title until the goods cease to be covered by the certificate of title.

Official Comment

1. **Source.** Former Section 9–103(2)(a), (b), substantially revised.

2. **Scope of This Section.** This section applies to "goods covered by a certificate of title." The new definition of "certificate of title" in Section 9–102 makes clear that this section applies not only to certificate-of-title statutes under which perfection occurs upon notation of the security interest on the certificate but also to those that contemplate notation but provide that perfection is achieved by another method, e.g., delivery of designated documents to an official. Subsection (a), which is new, makes clear that this section applies to certificates of a jurisdiction having no other contacts with the goods or the debtor. This result comports with most of the reported cases on the subject and with contemporary business practices in the trucking industry.

3. **Law Governing Perfection and Priority.** Subsection (c) is the basic choice-of-law rule for goods covered by a certificate of title. Perfection and priority of a security interest are governed by the law of the jurisdiction under whose certificate of title the goods are covered from the time the goods become covered by the certificate of title until the goods cease to be covered by the certificate of title.

Normally, under the law of the relevant jurisdiction, the perfection step would consist of compliance with that jurisdiction's certificate-of-title statute and a resulting notation of the security interest on the certificate of title. See Section 9–311(b). In the typical case of an automobile or over-the-road truck, a person who wishes to take a security interest in the vehicle can ascertain whether it is subject to any security interests by looking at the certificate of title. But certificates of title cover certain types of goods in some States but not in others. A secured party who does not realize this may extend credit and attempt to perfect by filing in the jurisdiction in which the debtor is located. If the goods had been titled in another jurisdiction, the lender would be unperfected.

Subsection (b) explains when goods become covered by a certificate of title and when they cease to be covered. Goods may become covered by a certificate of title, even though no certificate of title has issued. Former Section 9–103(2)(b) provided that the law of the jurisdiction issuing the certificate ceases to apply upon "surrender" of the certificate. This Article eliminates the concept of "surrender." However, if the certificate is surrendered in conjunction with an appropriate application for a certificate to be issued by another jurisdiction, the law of the original jurisdiction ceases to apply because the goods became covered subsequently by a certificate of title from another jurisdiction. Alternatively, the law of the original jurisdiction ceases to apply when the certificate "ceases to be effective" under the law of that jurisdiction. Given the diversity in certificate-of-title statutes, the term "effective" is not defined.

4. **Continued Perfection.** The fact that the law of one State ceases to apply under subsection (b) does not mean that a security interest perfected under that law becomes unperfected automatically. In most cases, the security interest will remain perfected. See Section 9–316(d), (e). Moreover, a perfected security interest may be subject to defeat by certain buyers and secured parties. See Section 9–337.

5. **Inventory.** Compliance with a certificate-of-title statute generally is *not* the method of perfecting security interests in inventory. Section 9–311(d) provides that a security interest created in inventory held by a person in the business of selling goods of that kind is subject to the normal filing rules; compliance with a certificate-of-title statute is not necessary or effective to perfect the security interest. Most certificate-of-title statutes are in accord.

The following example explains the subtle relationship between this rule and the choice-of-law rules in Section 9–303 and former Section 9–103(2):

Example: Goods are located in State A and covered by a certificate of title issued under the law of State A. The State A certificate of title is "clean"; it does not reflect a security interest. Owner takes the goods to State B and sells (trades in) the goods to Dealer, who is in the business of selling goods of that kind and is located (within the meaning of Section 9–307) in State B. As is customary, Dealer retains the duly assigned State A certificate of title pending resale of the goods. Dealer's inventory financer, SP, obtains a security interest in the goods under its after-acquired property clause.

Under Section 9–311(d) of both State A and State B, Dealer's inventory financer, SP, must perfect by filing instead of complying with a certificate-of-title statute. If Section 9–303 were read to provide that the law applicable to perfection of SP's security interest is that of State A, because the goods are covered by a State A certificate, then SP would be required to file in State A under State A's Section 9–501. That result would be anomalous, to say the least, since the principle underlying Section 9–311(d) is that the inventory should be treated as ordinary goods.

Section 9–303 (and former Section 9–103(2)) should be read as providing that the law of State B, not State A, applies. A court looking to the forum's Section 9–303(a) would find that Section 9–303 applies only if two conditions are met: (i) the goods are covered by a State as explained in Section 9–303(b), i.e., application had been made for a State (here, State A) to issue a certificate of title covering the goods and (ii) the certificate is a "certificate of title" as defined in Section 9–102, i.e., "a statute provides for the security interest in question to be indicated on the certificate as a condition or result of the security interest's obtaining priority over the rights of a lien creditor." Stated otherwise, Section 9–303 applies only when compliance with a certificate-of-title statute, and not filing, is the appropriate method of perfection. Under the law of State A, *for purposes of perfecting SP's security interest in the dealer's inventory*, the proper method of perfection is filing—not compliance with State A's certificate-of-title statute. For that reason, the goods are not covered by a "certificate of title," and the second condition is not met. Thus, Section 9–303 does not apply to the goods. Instead, Section 9–301 applies, and the applicable law is that of State B, where the debtor (dealer) is located.

6.   **External Constraints on This Section.** The need to coordinate Article 9 with a variety of nonuniform certificate-of-title statutes, the need to provide rules to take account of situations in which multiple certificates of title are outstanding with respect to particular goods, and the need to govern the transition from perfection by filing in one jurisdiction to perfection by notation in another all create pressure for a detailed and complex set of rules. In an effort to minimize complexity, this Article does not attempt to coordinate Article 9 with the entire array of certificate-of-title statutes. In particular, Sections 9–303, 9–311, and 9–316(d) and (e) assume that the certificate-of-title statutes to which they apply do not have relation-back provisions (i.e., provisions under which perfection is deemed to occur at a time earlier than when the perfection steps actually are taken). A Legislative Note to Section 9–311 recommends the elimination of relation-back provisions in certificate-of-title statutes affecting perfection of security interests.

Ideally, at any given time, only one certificate of title is outstanding with respect to particular goods. In fact, however, sometimes more than one jurisdiction issues more than one certificate of title with respect to the same goods. This situation results from defects in certificate-of-title laws and the interstate coordination of those laws, not from deficiencies in this Article. As long as the possibility of multiple certificates of title remains, the potential for innocent parties to suffer losses will continue. At best, this Article can identify clearly which innocent parties will bear the losses in familiar fact patterns.

As amended in 2000.

§ 9–304.   Law Governing Perfection and Priority of Security Interests in Deposit Accounts.

(a)   **[Law of bank's jurisdiction governs.]** The local law of a bank's jurisdiction governs perfection, the effect of perfection or nonperfection, and the priority of a security interest in a deposit account maintained with that bank.

(b)   **[Bank's jurisdiction.]** The following rules determine a bank's jurisdiction for purposes of this part:

(1)   If an agreement between the bank and its customer governing the deposit account expressly provides that a particular jurisdiction is the bank's jurisdiction for purposes of this part, this article, or [the Uniform Commercial Code], that jurisdiction is the bank's jurisdiction.

(2)   If paragraph (1) does not apply and an agreement between the bank and its customer governing the deposit account expressly provides that the agreement is governed by the law of a particular jurisdiction, that jurisdiction is the bank's jurisdiction.

(3)   If neither paragraph (1) nor paragraph (2) applies and an agreement between the bank and its customer governing the deposit account expressly provides that the deposit account is maintained at an office in a particular jurisdiction, that jurisdiction is the bank's jurisdiction.

(4) If none of the preceding paragraphs applies, the bank's jurisdiction is the jurisdiction in which the office identified in an account statement as the office serving the customer's account is located.

(5) If none of the preceding paragraphs applies, the bank's jurisdiction is the jurisdiction in which the chief executive office of the bank is located.

Official Comment

1. **Source.** New; derived from Section 8–110(e) and former Section 9–103(6).

2. **Deposit Accounts.** Under this section, the law of the "bank's jurisdiction" governs perfection and priority of a security interest in deposit accounts. Subsection (b) contains rules for determining the "bank's jurisdiction." The substance of these rules is substantially similar to that of the rules determining the "security intermediary's jurisdiction" under former Section 8–110(e), except that subsection (b)(1) provides more flexibility than the analogous provision in former Section 8–110(e)(1). Subsection (b)(1) permits the parties to choose the law of one jurisdiction to govern perfection and priority of security interests and a different governing law for other purposes. The parties' choice is effective, even if the jurisdiction whose law is chosen bears no relationship to the parties or the transaction. Section 8–110(e)(1) has been conformed to subsection (b)(1) of this section, and Section 9–305(b)(1), concerning a commodity intermediary's jurisdiction, makes a similar departure from former Section 9–103(6)(e)(i).

3. **Change in Law Governing Perfection.** When the bank's jurisdiction changes, the jurisdiction whose law governs perfection under subsection (a) changes, as well. Nevertheless, the change will not result in an immediate loss of perfection. See Section 9–316(f), (g).

§ 9–305. Law Governing Perfection and Priority of Security Interests in Investment Property.

(a) **[Governing law: general rules.]** Except as otherwise provided in subsection (c), the following rules apply:

(1) While a security certificate is located in a jurisdiction, the local law of that jurisdiction governs perfection, the effect of perfection or nonperfection, and the priority of a security interest in the certificated security represented thereby.

(2) The local law of the issuer's jurisdiction as specified in Section 8–110(d) governs perfection, the effect of perfection or nonperfection, and the priority of a security interest in an uncertificated security.

(3) The local law of the securities intermediary's jurisdiction as specified in Section 8–110(e) governs perfection, the effect of perfection or nonperfection, and the priority of a security interest in a security entitlement or securities account.

(4) The local law of the commodity intermediary's jurisdiction governs perfection, the effect of perfection or nonperfection, and the priority of a security interest in a commodity contract or commodity account.

(b) **[Commodity intermediary's jurisdiction.]** The following rules determine a commodity intermediary's jurisdiction for purposes of this part:

(1) If an agreement between the commodity intermediary and commodity customer governing the commodity account expressly provides that a particular jurisdiction is the commodity intermediary's jurisdiction for purposes of this part, this article, or [the Uniform Commercial Code], that jurisdiction is the commodity intermediary's jurisdiction.

(2) If paragraph (1) does not apply and an agreement between the commodity intermediary and commodity customer governing the commodity account expressly provides that the agreement is governed by the law of a particular jurisdiction, that jurisdiction is the commodity intermediary's jurisdiction.

(3) If neither paragraph (1) nor paragraph (2) applies and an agreement between the commodity intermediary and commodity customer governing the commodity account expressly provides that the commodity account is maintained at an office in a particular jurisdiction, that jurisdiction is the commodity intermediary's jurisdiction.

751

(4) If none of the preceding paragraphs applies, the commodity intermediary's jurisdiction is the jurisdiction in which the office identified in an account statement as the office serving the commodity customer's account is located.

(5) If none of the preceding paragraphs applies, the commodity intermediary's jurisdiction is the jurisdiction in which the chief executive office of the commodity intermediary is located.

(c) **[When perfection governed by law of jurisdiction where debtor located.]** The local law of the jurisdiction in which the debtor is located governs:

(1) perfection of a security interest in investment property by filing;

(2) automatic perfection of a security interest in investment property created by a broker or securities intermediary; and

(3) automatic perfection of a security interest in a commodity contract or commodity account created by a commodity intermediary.

Official Comment

1.   **Source.** Former Section 9–103(6).

2.   **Investment Property: General Rules.** This section specifies choice-of-law rules for perfection and priority of security interests in investment property. Subsection (a)(1) covers security interests in certificated securities. Subsection (a)(2) covers security interests in uncertificated securities. Subsection (a)(3) covers security interests in security entitlements and securities accounts, and where the Hague Securities Convention applies it may in occasional instances modify subsection (a)(3)'s results as discussed in Comments 3, 5 and 6 to Section 8–110. Subsection (a)(4) covers security interests in commodity contracts and commodity accounts. The approach of each of these paragraphs is essentially the same. They identify the jurisdiction's law that governs questions of perfection and priority by using the same principles that Article 8 uses to determine other questions concerning that form of investment property. Thus, for certificated securities, the law of the jurisdiction in which the certificate is located governs. Cf. Section 8–110(c). For uncertificated securities, the law of the issuer's jurisdiction governs. Cf. Section 8–110(a). For security entitlements and securities accounts, the law designated by the agreement between the securities intermediary and the entitlement holder governing the securities account generally governs. Cf. Section 8–110(b), (e)(1) and (2) and Convention article 4(1).

For commodity contracts and commodity accounts, the law of the commodity intermediary's jurisdiction governs, though if particular assets of this type qualify as securities held with an intermediary within the meaning of the Convention, the Convention would also apply. Commodity contracts and commodity accounts are not governed by Article 8, and for this reason subsection (b) contains rules that specify the commodity intermediary's jurisdiction that are analogous to the rules in Section 8–110(e) specifying a securities intermediary's jurisdiction. Subsection (b)(1) affords the parties greater flexibility than did former Section 9–103(6)(3). See also Section 9–304(b) (bank's jurisdiction); Revised Section 8–110(e)(1) and (2) (securities intermediary's jurisdiction).

3.   **Investment Property: Exceptions.** Subsection (c) establishes an exception to the general rules discussed in the preceding Comment. It provides that perfection of a security interest by filing, automatic perfection of a security interest in investment property created by a debtor who is a broker or securities intermediary (see Section 9–309(10)), and automatic perfection of a security interest in a commodity contract or commodity account of a debtor who is a commodity intermediary (see Section 9–309(11)) are governed by the law of the jurisdiction in which the debtor is located, as determined under Section 9–307.

The Hague Securities Convention generally preserves these rules for perfection by filing. However, if the debtor is located in a non-U.S. jurisdiction, or if the account agreement designates the law of a non-U.S. jurisdiction, then filing may be appropriate only in a different jurisdiction or altogether unavailable. See Convention articles 12(2)(b) and 4(1), respectively, and PEB Commentary No. 19, dated April 11, 2017, particularly footnote 25.

4.   **Examples:** The following examples illustrate the rules in this section:

Example 1:   A customer residing in New Jersey maintains a securities account with Able & Co. The agreement between the customer and Able specifies that it is governed by Pennsylvania law but expressly provides that California is Able's jurisdiction for purposes of the Uniform Commercial Code. Through the account the customer holds securities of a Massachusetts corporation, which Able holds through a clearing corporation located in New York. The customer obtains a margin loan from Able. Subsection (a)(3) provides that California law—the law of the securities intermediary's jurisdiction—governs perfection and priority of the security interest, even if California has no other relationship to the parties or the transaction. Even if other facts cause the Hague Securities Convention to apply (see Comment 1 to Section 8–110), the Convention does not change this result, provided that the account agreement either was entered into before the Convention's effectiveness in the United States or expressly specifies that the law of California is applicable to all issues specified in Convention article 2(1), and also provided that at the time of the agreement Able had an office in the United States engaged in a regular activity of maintaining securities accounts.

Example 2: A customer residing in New Jersey maintains a securities account with Able & Co. The agreement between the customer and Able specifies that it is governed by Pennsylvania law. Through the account the customer holds securities of a Massachusetts corporation, which Able holds through a clearing corporation located in New York. The customer obtains a loan from a lender located in Illinois. The lender takes a security interest and perfects by obtaining an agreement among the debtor, itself, and Able, which satisfies the requirement of Section 8–106(d)(2) to give the lender control. Subsection (a)(3) provides that Pennsylvania law—the law of the securities intermediary's jurisdiction—governs perfection and priority of the security interest, even if Pennsylvania has no other relationship to the parties or the transaction. Even if other facts cause the Hague Securities Convention to apply, the Convention does not change this result, provided that at the time of the agreement between the customer and Able, Able had an office in the United States engaged in a regular activity of maintaining securities accounts.

Example 3: A customer residing in New Jersey maintains a securities account with Able & Co. The agreement between the customer and Able specifies that it is governed by Pennsylvania law. Through the account, the customer holds securities of a Massachusetts corporation, which Able holds through a clearing corporation located in New York. The customer borrows from SP-1, and SP-1 files a financing statement in New Jersey. Later, the customer obtains a loan from SP-2. SP-2 takes a security interest and perfects by obtaining an agreement among the debtor, itself, and Able, which satisfies the requirement of Section 8–106(d)(2) to give SP-2 control. Subsection (c)(1) provides that perfection of SP-1's security interest by filing is governed by the location of the debtor, so the filing in New Jersey was appropriate. Even if other facts cause the Hague Securities Convention to apply, Convention article 12(2)(b) preserves this result. Subsection (a)(3), however, provides that Pennsylvania law—the law designated by the agreement between the customer and Able—governs all other questions of perfection and priority, and the Convention preserves this result, provided that at the time of the agreement between the customer and Able, Able had an office in the United States engaged in a regular activity of maintaining securities accounts. Thus, Pennsylvania law governs perfection of SP-2's security interest, and Pennsylvania law also governs the priority of the security interests of SP-1 and SP-2.

Example 4: A customer maintains a securities account with Able & Co. The customer is an Ontario, Canada corporation with its chief executive office in Toronto. The agreement between the customer and Able specifies that it is governed by New York law, and at the time of the agreement Able had an office in the United States engaged in a regular activity of maintaining securities accounts. The customer obtains a loan secured by the securities account, and the lender wishes to perfect by filing. Subsection (c)(1) provides that perfection of the security interest by filing is generally governed by the law of the location of the debtor (in this case Ontario, assuming that it has a filing system described by Section 9–307(c)); however, Convention article 12(2)(b) recognizes Article 9's place-of-filing rules only when they designate a U.S. jurisdiction for the filing. As a result, subsection (c)(1) does not govern filing for this transaction, and perfection of the security interest is governed by the substantive law of the jurisdiction designated by the account agreement (in this case New York).

Example 5: A customer maintains a securities account with Able & Co. The customer is a Texas corporation. The agreement between the customer and Able specifies that it is governed by English law, and at the time of the agreement Able had an office in England engaged in a regular activity of maintaining securities accounts. The customer obtains a loan secured by the securities account, and the lender wishes to perfect by filing. Subsection (c)(1), if it applied, would provide that perfection of the security interest by filing is governed by the law of the location of the debtor (in this case Texas); however, under Convention article 4(1), perfection of the security interest is governed by the law of the jurisdiction designated by the account agreement (in this case England), rather than by the law of any UCC jurisdiction.

5. **Change in Law Governing Perfection.** When the issuer's jurisdiction, the securities intermediary's jurisdiction, or commodity intermediary's jurisdiction changes, the jurisdiction whose law governs perfection under subsection (a) changes, as well. Similarly, the law governing perfection of a possessory security interest in a certificated security changes when the collateral is removed to another jurisdiction, see subsection (a)(1), and

the law governing perfection by filing changes when the debtor changes its location. See subsection (c). Nevertheless, under the UCC these changes will not result in an immediate loss of perfection. See Section 9–316(f), (g). Along generally similar lines in cases to which the Hague Securities Convention applies, article 7 provides that when the account agreement is amended to designate a new jurisdiction's law under article 4(1), the new law governs perfection, except that the old law continues to govern the perfection of security or other property interests that arose before the amendment and a limited number of other issues affecting such interests, without limitation as to time.

As amended in 2010 and 2017.

§ 9–306. Law Governing Perfection and Priority of Security Interests in Letter-of-Credit Rights.

(a) **[Governing law: issuer's or nominated person's jurisdiction.]** Subject to subsection (c), the local law of the issuer's jurisdiction or a nominated person's jurisdiction governs perfection, the effect of perfection or nonperfection, and the priority of a security interest in a letter-of-credit right if the issuer's jurisdiction or nominated person's jurisdiction is a State.

(b) **[Issuer's or nominated person's jurisdiction.]** For purposes of this part, an issuer's jurisdiction or nominated person's jurisdiction is the jurisdiction whose law governs the liability of the issuer or nominated person with respect to the letter-of-credit right as provided in Section 5–116.

(c) **[When section not applicable.]** This section does not apply to a security interest that is perfected only under Section 9–308(d).

Official Comment

1. **Source.** New; derived in part from Section 8–110(e) and former Section 9–103(6).

2. *Sui Generis* **Treatment.** This section governs the applicable law for perfection and priority of security interests in letter-of-credit rights, other than a security interest perfected only under Section 9–308(d) (i.e., as a supporting obligation). The treatment differs substantially from that provided in Section 9–304 for deposit accounts. The basic rule is that the law of the issuer's or nominated person's (e.g., confirmer's) jurisdiction, derived from the terms of the letter of credit itself, controls perfection and priority, but only if the issuer's or nominated person's jurisdiction is a State, as defined in Section 9–102. If the issuer's or nominated person's jurisdiction is not a State, the baseline rule of Section 9–301 applies—perfection and priority are governed by the law of the debtor's location, determined under Section 9–307. Export transactions typically involve a foreign issuer and a domestic nominated person, such as a confirmer, located in a State. The principal goal of this section is to reduce the likelihood that perfection and priority would be governed by the law of a foreign jurisdiction in a transaction that is essentially domestic from the standpoint of the debtor-beneficiary, its creditors, and a domestic nominated person.

3. **Issuer's or Nominated Person's Jurisdiction.** Subsection (b) defers to the rules established under Section 5–116 for determination of an issuer's or nominated person's jurisdiction.

Example: An Italian bank issues a letter of credit that is confirmed by a New York bank. The beneficiary is a Connecticut corporation. The letter of credit provides that the issuer's liability is governed by Italian law, and the confirmation provides that the confirmer's liability is governed by the law of New York. Under Sections 9–306(b) and 5–116(a), Italy is the issuer's jurisdiction and New York is the confirmer's (nominated person's) jurisdiction. Because the confirmer's jurisdiction is a State, the law of New York governs perfection and priority of a security interest in the beneficiary's letter-of-credit right against the confirmer. See Section 9–306(a). However, because the issuer's jurisdiction is not a State, the law of that jurisdiction does not govern. See Section 9–306(a). Rather, the choice-of-law rule in Section 9–301(1) applies to perfection and priority of a security interest in the beneficiary's letter-of-credit right against the issuer. Under that section, perfection and priority are governed by the law of the jurisdiction in which the debtor (beneficiary) is located. That jurisdiction is Connecticut. See Section 9–307.

4. **Scope of this Section.** This section specifies only the law governing perfection, the effect of perfection or nonperfection, and priority of security interests. Section 5–116 specifies the law governing the liability of, and Article 5 (or other applicable law) deals with the rights and duties of, an issuer or nominated person. Perfection, nonperfection, and priority have no effect on those rights and duties.

5. **Change in Law Governing Perfection.** When the issuer's jurisdiction, or nominated person's jurisdiction changes, the jurisdiction whose law governs perfection under subsection (a) changes, as well. Nevertheless, this change will not result in an immediate loss of perfection. See Section 9–316(f), (g).

§ 9–307. Location of Debtor.

(a) **["Place of business."]** In this section, "place of business" means a place where a debtor conducts its affairs.

(b) **[Debtor's location: general rules.]** Except as otherwise provided in this section, the following rules determine a debtor's location:

(1) A debtor who is an individual is located at the individual's principal residence.

(2) A debtor that is an organization and has only one place of business is located at its place of business.

(3) A debtor that is an organization and has more than one place of business is located at its chief executive office.

(c) **[Limitation of applicability of subsection (b).]** Subsection (b) applies only if a debtor's residence, place of business, or chief executive office, as applicable, is located in a jurisdiction whose law generally requires information concerning the existence of a nonpossessory security interest to be made generally available in a filing, recording, or registration system as a condition or result of the security interest's obtaining priority over the rights of a lien creditor with respect to the collateral. If subsection (b) does not apply, the debtor is located in the District of Columbia.

(d) **[Continuation of location: cessation of existence, etc.]** A person that ceases to exist, have a residence, or have a place of business continues to be located in the jurisdiction specified by subsections (b) and (c).

(e) **[Location of registered organization organized under State law.]** A registered organization that is organized under the law of a State is located in that State.

(f) **[Location of registered organization organized under federal law; bank branches and agencies.]** Except as otherwise provided in subsection (i), a registered organization that is organized under the law of the United States and a branch or agency of a bank that is not organized under the law of the United States or a State are located:

(1) in the State that the law of the United States designates, if the law designates a State of location;

(2) in the State that the registered organization, branch, or agency designates, if the law of the United States authorizes the registered organization, branch, or agency to designate its State of location, including by designating its main office, home office, or other comparable office; or

(3) in the District of Columbia, if neither paragraph (1) nor paragraph (2) applies.

(g) **[Continuation of location: change in status of registered organization.]** A registered organization continues to be located in the jurisdiction specified by subsection (e) or (f) notwithstanding:

(1) the suspension, revocation, forfeiture, or lapse of the registered organization's status as such in its jurisdiction of organization; or

(2) the dissolution, winding up, or cancellation of the existence of the registered organization.

(h) **[Location of United States.]** The United States is located in the District of Columbia.

(i) **[Location of foreign bank branch or agency if licensed in only one state.]** A branch or agency of a bank that is not organized under the law of the United States or a State is located in the State in which the branch or agency is licensed, if all branches and agencies of the bank are licensed in only one State.

(j) **[Location of foreign air carrier.]** A foreign air carrier under the Federal Aviation Act of 1958, as amended, is located at the designated office of the agent upon which service of process may be made on behalf of the carrier.

(k)   **[Section applies only to this part.]** This section applies only for purposes of this part.

As amended in 2010.

Official Comment

1.   **Source.** Former Section 9–103(3)(d), substantially revised.

2.   **General Rules.** As a general matter, the location of the debtor determines the jurisdiction whose law governs perfection of a security interest. See Sections 9–301(1), 9–305(c). It also governs priority of a security interest in certain types of intangible collateral, such as accounts, electronic chattel paper, and general intangibles. This section determines the location of the debtor for choice-of-law purposes, but not for other purposes. See subsection (k).

Subsection (b) states the general rules: An individual debtor is deemed to be located at the individual's principal residence with respect to both personal and business assets. Any other debtor is deemed to be located at its place of business if it has only one, or at its chief executive office if it has more than one place of business.

As used in this section, a "place of business" means a place where the debtor conducts its affairs. See subsection (a). Thus, every organization, even eleemosynary institutions and other organizations that do not conduct "for profit" business activities, has a "place of business." Under subsection (d), a person who ceases to exist, have a residence, or have a place of business continues to be located in the jurisdiction determined by subsection (b).

The term "chief executive office" is not defined in this Section or elsewhere in the Uniform Commercial Code. "Chief executive office" means the place from which the debtor manages the main part of its business operations or other affairs. This is the place where persons dealing with the debtor would normally look for credit information, and is the appropriate place for filing. With respect to most multi-state debtors, it will be simple to determine which of the debtor's offices is the "chief executive office." Even when a doubt arises, it would be rare that there could be more than two possibilities. A secured party in such a case may protect itself by perfecting under the law of each possible jurisdiction.

Similarly, the term "principal residence" is not defined. If the security interest in question is a purchase-money security interest in consumer goods which is perfected upon attachment, see Section 9–309(1), the choice of law may make no difference. In other cases, when a doubt arises, prudence may dictate perfecting under the law of each jurisdiction that might be the debtor's "principal residence."

Questions sometimes arise about the location of the debtor with respect to collateral held in a common-law trust. A typical common-law trust is not itself a juridical entity capable of owning property and so would not be a "debtor" as defined in Section 9–102. Rather, the debtor with respect to property held in a common-law trust typically is the trustee of the trust acting in the capacity of trustee. (The beneficiary would be a "debtor" with respect to its beneficial interest in the trust, but not with respect to the property held in the trust.) If a common-law trust has multiple trustees located in different jurisdictions, a secured party who perfects by filing would be well advised to file a financing statement in each jurisdiction in which a trustee is located, as determined under Section 9–307. Filing in all relevant jurisdictions would insure perfection and minimize any priority complications that otherwise might arise.

The general rules are subject to several exceptions, each of which is discussed below.

3.   **Non-U.S. Debtors.** Under the general rules of this section, a non-U.S. debtor normally would be located in a foreign jurisdiction and, as a consequence, foreign law would govern perfection. When foreign law affords no public notice of security interests, the general rule yields unacceptable results.

Accordingly, subsection (c) provides that the normal rules for determining the location of a debtor (i.e., the rules in subsection (b)) apply only if they yield a location that is "a jurisdiction whose law generally requires information concerning the existence of a nonpossessory security interest to be made generally available in a filing, recording, or registration system as a condition or result of the security interest's obtaining priority over the rights of a lien creditor with respect to the collateral." The phrase "generally requires" is meant to include legal regimes that generally require notice in a filing or recording system as a condition of perfecting nonpossessory security interests, but which permit perfection by another method (e.g., control, automatic perfection, temporary perfection) in limited circumstances. A jurisdiction that has adopted this Article or an earlier version of this Article is such a jurisdiction. If the rules in subsection (b) yield a jurisdiction whose law does not generally require notice in a filing or registration system and none of the special rules in subsection (e), (f), (i) and (j) applies, the debtor is located in the District of Columbia.

Example 1:   Debtor is an English corporation with 7 offices in the United States and its chief executive office in London, England. Debtor creates a security interest in its accounts. Under subsection (b)(3), Debtor would be located in England. However, subsection (c) provides that subsection (b) applies only if English law generally conditions perfection on giving public notice in a filing, recording, or registration system. Otherwise, Debtor is located in the District of Columbia. Under Section 9–301(1), perfection, the effect of perfection, and priority are governed by the law of the jurisdiction of the debtor's location—here, England or the District of Columbia (depending on the content of English law).

Example 2:   Debtor is an English corporation with 7 offices in the United States and its chief executive office in London, England. Debtor creates a security interest in equipment located in London. Under subsection (b)(3) Debtor would be located in England. However, subsection (c) provides that subsection (b) applies only if English law generally conditions perfection on giving public notice in a filing, recording, or registration system. Otherwise, Debtor is located in the District of Columbia. Under Section 9–301(1), perfection is governed by the law of the jurisdiction of the debtor's location, whereas, under Section 9–301(3), the law of the jurisdiction in which the collateral is located—here, England—governs priority.

The foregoing discussion assumes that each transaction bears an appropriate relation to the forum State. In the absence of an appropriate relation, the forum State's entire UCC, including the choice-of-law provisions in Article 9 (Sections 9–301 through 9–307), will not apply. See Section 9–109, Comment 9.

4.   **Registered Organizations Organized Under Law of a State.** Under subsection (e), a "registered organization" (defined in Section 9–102 so as to ordinarily include corporations, limited partnerships, limited liability companies, and statutory trusts) organized under the law of a "State" (defined in Section 9–102) is located in its State of organization. The term "registered organization" includes a business trust described in the second sentence of the term's definition. See Section 9–102. The trust's public organic record, typically the trust agreement, usually will indicate the jurisdiction under whose law the trust is organized. A protected series formed under the Uniform Protected Series Act (2017) is a registered organization. See PEB Commentary No. 23, dated February 24, 2021. The Commentary is available at https://www.ali.org/peb-ucc.

Determining the registered organization-debtor's location by reference to the jurisdiction of organization could provide some important side benefits for the filing systems. A jurisdiction could structure its filing system so that it would be impossible to make a mistake in a registered organization-debtor's name on a financing statement. For example, a filer would be informed if a filed record designated an incorrect corporate name for the debtor. Linking filing to the jurisdiction of organization also could reduce pressure on the system imposed by transactions in which registered organizations cease to exist—as a consequence of merger or consolidation, for example. The jurisdiction of organization might prohibit such transactions unless steps were taken to ensure that existing filings were refiled against a successor or terminated by the secured party.

5.   **Registered Organizations Organized Under Law of United States; Branches and Agencies of Banks Not Organized Under Law of United States.** Subsection (f) specifies the location of a debtor that is a registered organization organized under the law of the United States. It defers to the law of the United States, to the extent that that law determines, or authorizes the debtor to determine, the debtor's location. Thus, if the law of the United States designates a particular State as the debtor's location, that State is the debtor's location for purposes of this Article's choice-of-law rules. Similarly, if the law of the United States authorizes the registered organization to designate its State of location, the State that the registered organization designates is the State in which it is located for purposes of this Article's choice-of-law rules. In other cases, the debtor is located in the District of Columbia.

In some cases, the law of the United States authorizes the registered organization to designate a main office, home office, or other comparable office. See, e.g., 12 U.S.C. §§ 22 and 1464(a); 12 C.F.R. § 552.3. Designation of such an office constitutes the designation of the State of location for purposes of Section 9–307(f)(2).

Subsection (f) also specifies the location of a branch or agency in the United States of a foreign bank that has one or more branches or agencies in the United States. The law of the United States authorizes a foreign bank (or, on behalf of the bank, a federal agency) to designate a single home state for all of the foreign bank's branches and agencies in the United States. See 12 U.S.C. Section 3103(c) and 12 C.F.R. Section 211.22. As authorized, the designation constitutes the State of location for the branch or agency for purposes of Section 9–307(f), unless all of a foreign bank's branches or agencies that are in the United States are licensed in only one State, in which case the branches and agencies are located in that State. See subsection (i).

In cases not governed by subsection (f) or (i), the location of a foreign bank is determined by subsections (b) and (c).

6. **United States.** To the extent that Article 9 governs (see Sections 1–301, 9–109(c)), the United States is located in the District of Columbia for purposes of this Article's choice-of-law rules. See subsection (h).

7. **Foreign Air Carriers.** Subsection (j) follows former Section 9–103(3)(d). To the extent that it is applicable, the Convention on the International Recognition of Rights in Aircraft (Geneva Convention) supersedes state legislation on this subject, as set forth in Section 9–311(b), but some nations are not parties to that Convention.

As amended in 2010 and 2021.

[SUBPART 2. PERFECTION]

§ 9–308. When Security Interest or Agricultural Lien Is Perfected; Continuity of Perfection.

(a) **[Perfection of security interest.]** Except as otherwise provided in this section and Section 9–309, a security interest is perfected if it has attached and all of the applicable requirements for perfection in Sections 9–310 through 9–316 have been satisfied. A security interest is perfected when it attaches if the applicable requirements are satisfied before the security interest attaches.

(b) **[Perfection of agricultural lien.]** An agricultural lien is perfected if it has become effective and all of the applicable requirements for perfection in Section 9–310 have been satisfied. An agricultural lien is perfected when it becomes effective if the applicable requirements are satisfied before the agricultural lien becomes effective.

(c) **[Continuous perfection; perfection by different methods.]** A security interest or agricultural lien is perfected continuously if it is originally perfected by one method under this article and is later perfected by another method under this article, without an intermediate period when it was unperfected.

(d) **[Supporting obligation.]** Perfection of a security interest in collateral also perfects a security interest in a supporting obligation for the collateral.

(e) **[Lien securing right to payment.]** Perfection of a security interest in a right to payment or performance also perfects a security interest in a security interest, mortgage, or other lien on personal or real property securing the right.

(f) **[Security entitlement carried in securities account.]** Perfection of a security interest in a securities account also perfects a security interest in the security entitlements carried in the securities account.

(g) **[Commodity contract carried in commodity account.]** Perfection of a security interest in a commodity account also perfects a security interest in the commodity contracts carried in the commodity account.

Legislative Note: Any statute conflicting with subsection (e) must be made expressly subject to that subsection.

Official Comment

1. **Source.** Former Sections 9–303, 9–115(2).

2. **General Rule.** This Article uses the term "attach" to describe the point at which property becomes subject to a security interest. The requisites for attachment are stated in Section 9–203. When it attaches, a security interest may be either perfected or unperfected. "Perfected" means that the security interest has attached and the secured party has taken all the steps required by this Article as specified in Sections 9–310 through 9–316. A perfected security interest may still be or become subordinate to other interests. See, e.g., Sections 9–320, 9–322. However, in general, after perfection the secured party is protected against creditors and transferees of the debtor and, in particular, against any representative of creditors in insolvency proceedings instituted by or against the debtor. See, e.g., Section 9–317.

Subsection (a) explains that the time of perfection is when the security interest has attached and any necessary steps for perfection, such as taking possession or filing, have been taken. The "except" clause refers to the perfection-upon-attachment rules appearing in Section 9–309. It also reflects that other subsections of this section, e.g., subsection (d), contain automatic-perfection rules. If the steps for perfection have been taken in advance, as when the secured party files a financing statement before giving value or before the debtor acquires rights in the collateral, then the security interest is perfected when it attaches.

3.   **Agricultural Liens.** Subsection (b) is new. It describes the elements of perfection of an agricultural lien.

4.   **Continuous Perfection.** The following example illustrates the operation of subsection (c):

Example 1:   Debtor, an importer, creates a security interest in goods that it imports and the documents of title that cover the goods. The secured party, Bank, takes possession of a tangible negotiable bill of lading covering certain imported goods and thereby perfects its security interest in the bill of lading and the goods. See Sections 9–313(a), 9–312(c)(1). Bank releases the bill of lading to the debtor for the purpose of procuring the goods from the carrier and selling them. Under Section 9–312(f), Bank continues to have a perfected security interest in the document and goods for 20 days. Bank files a financing statement covering the collateral before the expiration of the 20-day period. Its security interest now continues perfected for as long as the filing is good.

If the successive stages of Bank's security interest succeed each other without an intervening gap, the security interest is "perfected continuously," and the date of perfection is when the security interest first became perfected (i.e., when Bank received possession of the tangible bill of lading). If, however, there is a gap between stages—for example, if Bank does not file until after the expiration of the 20-day period specified in Section 9–312(f) and leaves the collateral in the debtor's possession—then, the chain being broken, the perfection is no longer continuous. The date of perfection would now be the date of filing (after expiration of the 20-day period). Bank's security interest would be vulnerable to any interests arising during the gap period which under Section 9–317 take priority over an unperfected security interest.

5.   **Supporting Obligations.** Subsection (d) is new. It provides for automatic perfection of a security interest in a supporting obligation for collateral if the security interest in the collateral is perfected. This is unlikely to effect any change in the law prior to adoption of this Article.

Example 2:   Buyer is obligated to pay Debtor for goods sold. Buyer's president guarantees the obligation. Debtor creates a security interest in the right to payment (account) in favor of Lender. Under Section 9–203(f), the security interest attaches to Debtor's rights under the guarantee (supporting obligation). Under subsection (d), perfection of the security interest in the account constitutes perfection of the security interest in Debtor's rights under the guarantee.

6.   **Rights to Payment Secured by Lien.** Subsection (e) is new. It deals with the situation in which a security interest is created in a right to payment that is secured by a security interest, mortgage, or other lien.

Example 3:   Owner gives to Mortgagee a mortgage on Blackacre to secure a loan. Owner's obligation to pay is evidenced by a promissory note. In need of working capital, Mortgagee borrows from Financer and creates a security interest in the note in favor of Financer. Section 9–203(g) adopts the traditional view that the mortgage follows the note; i.e., the transferee of the note acquires the mortgage, as well. This subsection adopts a similar principle: perfection of a security interest in the right to payment constitutes perfection of a security interest in the mortgage securing it.

An important consequence of the rules in Section 9–203(g) and subsection (e) is that, by acquiring a perfected security interest in a mortgage (or other secured) note, the secured party acquires a security interest in the mortgage (or other lien) that is senior to the rights of a person who becomes a lien creditor of the mortgagee (Article 9 debtor). See Section 9–317(a)(2). This result helps prevent the separation of the mortgage (or other lien) from the note.

Under this Article, attachment and perfection of a security interest in a secured right to payment do not of themselves affect the obligation to pay. For example, if the obligation is evidenced by a negotiable note, then Article 3 dictates the person whom the maker must pay to discharge the note and any lien securing it. See Section 3–602. If the right to payment is a payment intangible, then Section 9–406 determines whom the account debtor must pay.

Similarly, this Article does not determine who has the power to release a mortgage of record. That issue is determined by real-property law.

7.   **Investment Property.** Subsections (f) and (g) follow former Section 9–115(2).

As amended in 2003.

§ 9–309.   Security Interest Perfected Upon Attachment.

The following security interests are perfected when they attach:

(1)   a purchase-money security interest in consumer goods, except as otherwise provided in Section 9–311(b) with respect to consumer goods that are subject to a statute or treaty described in Section 9–311(a);

(2)   an assignment of accounts or payment intangibles which does not by itself or in conjunction with other assignments to the same assignee transfer a significant part of the assignor's outstanding accounts or payment intangibles;

(3)   a sale of a payment intangible;

(4)   a sale of a promissory note;

(5)   a security interest created by the assignment of a health-care-insurance receivable to the provider of the health-care goods or services;

(6)   a security interest arising under Section 2–401, 2–505, 2–711(3), or 2A–508(5), until the debtor obtains possession of the collateral;

(7)   a security interest of a collecting bank arising under Section 4–210;

(8)   a security interest of an issuer or nominated person arising under Section 5–118;

(9)   a security interest arising in the delivery of a financial asset under Section 9–206(c);

(10) a security interest in investment property created by a broker or securities intermediary;

(11) a security interest in a commodity contract or a commodity account created by a commodity intermediary;

(12) an assignment for the benefit of all creditors of the transferor and subsequent transfers by the assignee thereunder;

(13) a security interest created by an assignment of a beneficial interest in a decedent's estate; and

(14) a sale by an individual of an account that is a right to payment of winnings in a lottery or other game of chance.

Official Comment

1.   **Source.** Derived from former Sections 9–302(1), 9–115(4)(c), (d), 9–116.

2.   **Automatic Perfection.** This section contains the perfection-upon-attachment rules previously located in former Sections 9–302(1), 9–115(4)(c), (d), and 9–116. Rather than continue to state the rule by indirection, this section explicitly provides for perfection upon attachment.

3.   **Purchase-Money Security Interest in Consumer Goods.** Former Section 9–302(1)(d) has been revised and appears here as paragraph (1). No filing or other step is required to perfect a purchase-money security interest in consumer goods, other than goods, such as automobiles, that are subject to a statute or treaty described in Section 9–311(a). However, filing is required to perfect a non-purchase-money security interest in consumer goods and is necessary to prevent a buyer of consumer goods from taking free of a security interest under Section 9–320(b). A fixture filing is required for priority over conflicting interests in fixtures to the extent provided in Section 9–334.

4.   **Rights to Payment.** Paragraph (2) expands upon former Section 9–302(1)(e) by affording automatic perfection to certain assignments of payment intangibles as well as accounts. The purpose of paragraph (2) is to save from *ex post facto* invalidation casual or isolated assignments—assignments which no one would think of filing. Any person who regularly takes assignments of any debtor's accounts or payment intangibles should file. In this connection Section 9–109(d)(4) through (7), which excludes certain transfers of accounts, chattel paper, payment intangibles, and promissory notes from this Article, should be consulted.

Paragraphs (3) and (4), which are new, afford automatic perfection to sales of payment intangibles and promissory notes, respectively. They reflect the practice under former Article 9. Under that Article, filing a financing statement did not affect the rights of a buyer of payment intangibles or promissory notes, inasmuch as the former Article did not cover those sales. To the extent that the exception in paragraph (2) covers outright sales of payment intangibles, which automatically are perfected under paragraph (3), the exception is redundant.

Paragraph (14), which is new, affords automatic perfection to sales by individuals of an "account" (as defined in Section 9–102) consisting of the right to winnings in a lottery or other game of chance. Payments on these accounts typically extend for periods of twenty years or more. It would be unduly burdensome for the secured party, who would have no other reason to maintain contact with the seller, to monitor the seller's whereabouts for such a length of time. This paragraph was added in 2001. It applies to a sale of an account described in it, even if the sale was entered into before the effective date of the paragraph. However, if the relative priorities of conflicting claims to the account were established before the paragraph took effect, Article 9 as in effect immediately prior to the date the paragraph took effect determines priority.

5. **Health-Care-Insurance Receivables.** Paragraph (5) extends automatic perfection to assignments of health-care-insurance receivables if the assignment is made to the health-care provider that provided the health-care goods or services. The primary effect is that, when an individual assigns a right to payment under an insurance policy to the person who provided health-care goods or services, the provider has no need to file a financing statement against the individual. The normal filing requirements apply to other assignments of health-care-insurance receivables covered by this Article, e.g., assignments from the health-care provider to a financer.

6. **Investment Property.** Paragraph (9) replaces the last clause of former Section 9–116(2), concerning security interests that arise in the delivery of a financial asset.

Paragraphs (10) and (11) replace former Section 9–115(4)(c) and (d), concerning secured financing of securities and commodity firms and clearing corporations. The former sections indicated that, with respect to certain security interests created by a securities intermediary or commodity intermediary, "[t]he filing of a financing statement . . . has no effect for purposes of perfection or priority with respect to that security interest." No change in meaning is intended by the deletion of the quoted phrase.

Secured financing arrangements for securities firms are currently implemented in various ways. In some circumstances, lenders may require that the transactions be structured as "hard pledges," where the securities are transferred on the books of a clearing corporation from the debtor's account to the lender's account or to a special pledge account for the lender where they cannot be disposed of without the specific consent of the lender. In other circumstances, lenders are content with so-called "agreement to pledge" or "agreement to deliver" arrangements, where the debtor retains the positions in its own account, but reflects on its books that the positions have been hypothecated and promises that the securities will be transferred to the secured party's account on demand.

The perfection and priority rules of this Article are designed to facilitate current secured financing arrangements for securities firms as well as to provide sufficient flexibility to accommodate new arrangements that develop in the future. Hard pledge arrangements are covered by the concept of control. See Sections 9–314, 9–106, 8–106. Non-control secured financing arrangements for securities firms are covered by the automatic perfection rule of paragraph (10). Before the 1994 revision of Articles 8 and 9, agreement to pledge arrangements could be implemented under a provision that a security interest in securities given for new value under a written security agreement was perfected without filing or possession for a period of 21 days. Although the security interests were temporary in legal theory, the financing arrangements could, in practice, be continued indefinitely by rolling over the loans at least every 21 days. Accordingly, a knowledgeable creditor of a securities firm realizes that the firm's securities may be subject to security interests that are not discoverable from any public records. The automatic-perfection rule of paragraph (10) makes it unnecessary to engage in the purely formal practice of rolling over these arrangements every 21 days.

In some circumstances, a clearing corporation may be the debtor in a secured financing arrangement. For example, a clearing corporation that settles delivery-versus-payment transactions among its participants on a net, same-day basis relies on timely payments from all participants with net obligations due to the system. If a participant that is a net debtor were to default on its payment obligation, the clearing corporation would not receive some of the funds needed to settle with participants that are net creditors to the system. To complete end-of-day settlement after a payment default by a participant, a clearing corporation that settles on a net, same-day basis may need to draw on credit lines and pledge securities of the defaulting participant or other securities pledged by participants in the clearing corporation to secure such drawings. The clearing corporation may be the top-tier securities intermediary for the securities pledged, so that it would not be practical for the lender to obtain control. Even where the clearing corporation holds some types of securities through other intermediaries, however, the clearing corporation is unlikely to be able to complete the arrangements necessary to convey "control" over the securities to be pledged in time to complete settlement in a timely manner. However, the term "securities intermediary" is defined in Section 8–102(a)(14) to include clearing corporations. Thus, the perfection rule of paragraph (10) applies to security interests in investment property granted by clearing corporations.

7.   **Beneficial Interests in Trusts.** Under former Section 9–302(1)(c), filing was not required to perfect a security interest created by an assignment of a beneficial interest in a trust. Because beneficial interests in trusts are now used as collateral with greater frequency in commercial transactions, under this Article filing is required to perfect a security interest in a beneficial interest.

8.   **Assignments for Benefit of Creditors.** No filing or other action is required to perfect an assignment for the benefit of creditors. These assignments are not financing transactions, and the debtor ordinarily will not be engaging in further credit transactions.

§ 9–310.   When Filing Required to Perfect Security Interest or Agricultural Lien; Security Interests and Agricultural Liens to Which Filing Provisions Do Not Apply.

(a)   **[General rule: perfection by filing.]** Except as otherwise provided in subsection (b) and Section 9–312(b), a financing statement must be filed to perfect all security interests and agricultural liens.

(b)   **[Exceptions: filing not necessary.]** The filing of a financing statement is not necessary to perfect a security interest:

(1)   that is perfected under Section 9–308(d), (e), (f), or (g);

(2)   that is perfected under Section 9–309 when it attaches;

(3)   in property subject to a statute, regulation, or treaty described in Section 9–311(a);

(4)   in goods in possession of a bailee which is perfected under Section 9–312(d)(1) or (2);

(5)   in certificated securities, documents, goods, or instruments which is perfected without filing, control, or possession under Section 9–312(e), (f), or (g);

(6)   in collateral in the secured party's possession under Section 9–313;

(7)   in a certificated security which is perfected by delivery of the security certificate to the secured party under Section 9–313;

(8)   in deposit accounts, electronic chattel paper, electronic documents, investment property, or letter-of-credit rights which is perfected by control under Section 9–314;

(9)   in proceeds which is perfected under Section 9–315; or

(10) that is perfected under Section 9–316.

(c)   **[Assignment of perfected security interest.]** If a secured party assigns a perfected security interest or agricultural lien, a filing under this article is not required to continue the perfected status of the security interest against creditors of and transferees from the original debtor.

As amended in 2003.

Official Comment

1.   **Source.** Former Section 9–302(1), (2).

2.   **General Rule.** Subsection (a) establishes a central Article 9 principle: Filing a financing statement is necessary for perfection of security interests and agricultural liens. However, filing is not necessary to perfect a security interest that is perfected by another permissible method, see subsection (b), nor does filing ordinarily perfect a security interest in a deposit account, letter-of-credit right, or money. See Section 9–312(b). Part 5 of the Article deals with the office in which to file, mechanics of filing, and operations of the filing office.

3.   **Exemptions from Filing.** Subsection (b) lists the security interests for which filing is not required as a condition of perfection, because they are perfected automatically upon attachment (subsections (b)(2) and (b)(9)) or upon the occurrence of another event (subsections (b)(1), (b)(5), and (b)(9)), because they are perfected under the law of another jurisdiction (subsection (b)(10)), or because they are perfected by another method, such as by the secured party's taking possession or control (subsections (b)(3), (b)(4), (b)(5), (b)(6), (b)(7), and (b)(8)).

4.   **Assignments of Perfected Security Interests.** Subsection (c) concerns assignment of a perfected security interest or agricultural lien. It provides that no filing is necessary in connection with an assignment by a secured party to an assignee in order to maintain perfection as against creditors of and transferees from the original debtor.

Example 1:   Buyer buys goods from Seller, who retains a security interest in them. After Seller perfects the security interest by filing, Seller assigns the perfected security interest to X. The security interest, in X's hands and without further steps on X's part, continues perfected against *Buyer's* transferees and creditors.

Example 2:   Dealer creates a security interest in specific equipment in favor of Lender. After Lender perfects the security interest in the equipment by filing, Lender assigns the chattel paper (which includes the perfected security interest in Dealer's equipment) to X. The security interest in the equipment, in X's hands and without further steps on X's part, continues perfected against *Dealer's* transferees and creditors. However, regardless of whether Lender made the assignment to secure Lender's obligation to X or whether the assignment was an outright sale of the chattel paper, the assignment creates a security interest in the chattel paper in favor of X. Accordingly, X must take whatever steps may be required for perfection in order to be protected against *Lender's* transferees and creditors with respect to the chattel paper.

Subsection (c) applies not only to an assignment of a security interest perfected by filing but also to an assignment of a security interest perfected by a method other than by filing, such as by control or by possession. Although subsection (c) addresses explicitly only the absence of an additional filing requirement, the same result normally will follow in the case of an assignment of a security interest perfected by a method other than by filing. For example, as long as possession of collateral is maintained by an assignee or by the assignor or another person on behalf of the assignee, no further perfection steps need be taken on account of the assignment to continue perfection as against creditors and transferees of the original debtor. Of course, additional action may be required for perfection of the assignee's interest as against creditors and transferees of the *assignor*.

Similarly, subsection (c) applies to the assignment of a security interest perfected by compliance with a statute, regulation, or treaty under Section 9–311(b), such as a certificate-of-title statute. Unless the statute expressly provides to the contrary, the security interest will remain perfected against creditors of and transferees from the original debtor, even if the assignee takes no action to cause the certificate of title to reflect the assignment or to cause its name to appear on the certificate of title. See PEB Commentary No. 12, which discusses this issue under former Section 9–302(3). Compliance with the statute is "equivalent to filing" under Section 9–311(b).

§ 9–311.   Perfection of Security Interests in Property Subject to Certain Statutes, Regulations, and Treaties.

(a)   **[Security interest subject to other law.]** Except as otherwise provided in subsection (d), the filing of a financing statement is not necessary or effective to perfect a security interest in property subject to:

(1)   a statute, regulation, or treaty of the United States whose requirements for a security interest's obtaining priority over the rights of a lien creditor with respect to the property preempt Section 9–310(a);

(2)   [list any statute covering automobiles, trailers, mobile homes, boats, farm tractors, or the like, which provides for a security interest to be indicated on a certificate of title as a condition or result of perfection, and any non-Uniform Commercial Code central filing statute]; or

(3)   a statute of another jurisdiction which provides for a security interest to be indicated on a certificate of title as a condition or result of the security interest's obtaining priority over the rights of a lien creditor with respect to the property.

(b)   **[Compliance with other law.]** Compliance with the requirements of a statute, regulation, or treaty described in subsection (a) for obtaining priority over the rights of a lien creditor is equivalent to the filing of a financing statement under this article. Except as otherwise provided in subsection (d) and Sections 9–313 and 9–316(d) and (e) for goods covered by a certificate of title, a security interest in property subject to a statute, regulation, or treaty described in subsection (a) may be perfected only by compliance with those requirements, and a security interest so perfected remains perfected notwithstanding a change in the use or transfer of possession of the collateral.

(c)   **[Duration and renewal of perfection.]** Except as otherwise provided in subsection (d) and Section 9–316(d) and (e), duration and renewal of perfection of a security interest perfected by compliance with the requirements prescribed by a statute, regulation, or treaty described in subsection (a) are governed by the statute, regulation, or treaty. In other respects, the security interest is subject to this article.

(d) **[Inapplicability to certain inventory.]** During any period in which collateral subject to a statute specified in subsection (a)(2) is inventory held for sale or lease by a person or leased by that person as lessor and that person is in the business of selling goods of that kind, this section does not apply to a security interest in that collateral created by that person.

Legislative Note: This Article contemplates that perfection of a security interest in goods covered by a certificate of title occurs upon receipt by appropriate State officials of a properly tendered application for a certificate of title on which the security interest is to be indicated, without a relation back to an earlier time. States whose certificate-of-title statutes provide for perfection at a different time or contain a relation-back provision should amend the statutes accordingly.

As amended in 2000 and 2010.

Official Comment

1.   **Source.** Former Section 9–302(3), (4).

2.   **Federal Statutes, Regulations, and Treaties.** Subsection (a)(1) exempts from the filing provisions of this Article transactions as to which a system of filing—state or federal—has been established under federal law. Subsection (b) makes clear that when such a system exists, perfection of a relevant security interest can be achieved only through compliance with that system (i.e., filing under this Article is not a permissible alternative).

An example of the type of federal statute referred to in subsection (a)(1) is 49 U.S.C. §§ 44107–11, for civil aircraft of the United States. The Assignment of Claims Act of 1940, as amended, provides for notice to contracting and disbursing officers and to sureties on bonds but does not establish a national filing system and therefore is not within the scope of subsection (a)(1). An assignee of a claim against the United States may benefit from compliance with the Assignment of Claims Act. But regardless of whether the assignee complies with that Act, the assignee must file under this Article in order to perfect its security interest against creditors and transferees of its assignor.

Subsection (a)(1) provides explicitly that the filing requirement of this Article defers only to federal statutes, regulations, or treaties whose requirements for a security interest's obtaining priority over the rights of a lien creditor preempt Section 9–310(a). The provision eschews reference to the term "perfection," inasmuch as Section 9–308 specifies the meaning of that term and a preemptive rule may use other terminology.

3.   **State Statutes.** Subsections (a)(2) and (3) exempt from the filing requirements of this Article transactions covered by State certificate-of-title statutes covering motor vehicles and the like. The description of certificate-of-title statutes in subsections (a)(2) and (a)(3) tracks the language of the definition of "certificate of title" in Section 9–102. For a discussion of the operation of state certificate-of-title statutes in interstate contexts, see the Comments to Section 9–303.

Some states have enacted central filing statutes with respect to secured transactions in kinds of property that are of special importance in the local economy. Subsection (a)(2) defers to these statutes with respect to filing for that property.

4.   **Inventory Covered by Certificate of Title.** Under subsection (d), perfection of a security interest in the inventory of a person in the business of selling goods of that kind is governed by the normal perfection rules, even if the inventory is subject to a certificate-of-title statute. Compliance with a certificate-of-title statute is both unnecessary and ineffective to perfect a security interest in inventory to which this subsection applies. Thus, a secured party who finances an automobile dealer that is in the business of selling and leasing its inventory of automobiles can perfect a security interest in all the automobiles by filing a financing statement but not by compliance with a certificate-of-title statute.

Subsection (d), and thus the filing and other perfection provisions of this Article, does not apply to inventory that is subject to a certificate-of-title statute and is of a kind that the debtor is not in the business of selling. For example, if goods are subject to a certificate-of-title statute and the debtor is in the business of leasing but not of selling, goods of that kind, the other subsections of this section govern perfection of a security interest in the goods. The fact that the debtor eventually sells the goods does not, of itself, mean that the debtor "is in the business of selling goods of that kind."

The filing and other perfection provisions of this Article apply to goods subject to a certificate-of-title statute only "during any period in which collateral is inventory held for sale or lease or leased." If the debtor takes goods of this kind out of inventory and uses them, say, as equipment, a filed financing statement would not remain effective to perfect a security interest.

5. **Compliance with Perfection Requirements of Other Statute.** Subsection (b) makes clear that compliance with the perfection requirements (i.e., the requirements for obtaining priority over a lien creditor), but not other requirements, of a statute, regulation, or treaty described in subsection (a) is sufficient for perfection under this Article. Perfection of a security interest under such a statute, regulation, or treaty has all the consequences of perfection under this Article.

The interplay of this section with certain certificate-of-title statutes may create confusion and uncertainty. For example, statutes under which perfection does not occur until a certificate of title is issued will create a gap between the time that the goods are covered by the certificate under Section 9–303 and the time of perfection. If the gap is long enough, it may result in turning some unobjectionable transactions into avoidable preferences under Bankruptcy Code Section 547. (The preference risk arises if more than 30 days passes between the time a security interest attaches (or the debtor receives possession of the collateral, in the case of a purchase-money security interest) and the time it is perfected.) Accordingly, the Legislative Note to this section instructs the legislature to amend the applicable certificate-of-title statute to provide that perfection occurs upon receipt by the appropriate State official of a properly tendered application for a certificate of title on which the security interest is to be indicated.

Under some certificate-of-title statutes, including the Uniform Motor Vehicle Certificate of Title and Anti-Theft Act, perfection generally occurs upon delivery of specified documents to a state official but may, under certain circumstances, relate back to the time of attachment. This relation-back feature can create great difficulties for the application of the rules in Sections 9–303 and 9–311(b). Accordingly, the Legislative Note also recommends to legislatures that they remove any relation-back provisions from certificate-of-title statutes affecting security interests.

6. **Compliance with Perfection Requirements of Other Statute as Equivalent to Filing.** Under Subsection (b), compliance with the perfection requirements (i.e., the requirements for obtaining priority over a lien creditor) of a statute, regulation, or treaty described in subsection (a) "is equivalent to the filing of a financing statement."

The quoted phrase appeared in former Section 9–302(3). Its meaning was unclear, and many questions arose concerning the extent to which and manner in which Article 9 rules referring to "filing" were applicable to perfection by compliance with a certificate-of-title statute. This Article takes a variety of approaches for applying Article 9's filing rules to compliance with other statutes and treaties. First, as discussed above in Comment 5, it leaves the determination of some rules, such as the rule establishing time of perfection (Section 9–516(a)), to the other statutes themselves. Second, this Article explicitly applies some Article 9 filing rules to perfection under other statutes or treaties. See, e.g., Section 9–505. Third, this Article makes other Article 9 rules applicable to security interests perfected by compliance with another statute through the "equivalent to . . . filing" provision in the first sentence of Section 9–311(b). The third approach is reflected for the most part in occasional Comments explaining how particular rules apply when perfection is accomplished under Section 9–311(b). See, e.g., Section 9–310, Comment 4; Section 9–315, Comment 6; Section 9–317, Comment 8. The absence of a Comment indicating that a particular filing provision applies to perfection pursuant to Section 9–311(b) does not mean the provision is inapplicable.

7. **Perfection by Possession of Goods Covered by Certificate-of-Title Statute.** A secured party who holds a security interest perfected under the law of State A in goods that subsequently are covered by a State B certificate of title may face a predicament. Ordinarily, the secured party will have four months under State B's Section 9–316(c) and (d) in which to (re)perfect as against a purchaser of the goods by having its security interest noted on a State B certificate. This procedure is likely to require the cooperation of the debtor and any competing secured party whose security interest has been noted on the certificate. Comment 4(e) to former Section 9–103 observed that "that cooperation is not likely to be forthcoming from an owner who wrongfully procured the issuance of a new certificate not showing the out-of-state security interest, or from a local secured party finding himself in a priority contest with the out-of-state secured party." According to that Comment, "[t]he only solution for the out-of-state secured party under present certificate of title statutes seems to be to reperfect by possession, i.e., by repossessing the goods." But the "solution" may not have worked: Former Section 9–302(4) provided that a security interest in property subject to a certificate-of-title statute "can be perfected only by compliance therewith."

Sections 9–316(d) and (e), 9–311(c), and 9–313(b) of this Article resolve the conflict by providing that a security interest that remains perfected solely by virtue of Section 9–316(e) can be (re)perfected by the secured party's taking possession of the collateral. These sections contemplate only that taking possession of goods covered by a certificate of title will work as a method of perfection. None of these sections creates a right to take possession. Section 9–609 and the agreement of the parties define the secured party's right to take possession.

As amended in 2000 and 2010.

§ 9–312. Perfection of Security Interests in Chattel Paper, Deposit Accounts, Documents, Goods Covered by Documents, Instruments, Investment Property, Letter-of-Credit Rights, and Money; Perfection by Permissive Filing; Temporary Perfection Without Filing or Transfer of Possession.

(a) **[Perfection by filing permitted.]** A security interest in chattel paper, negotiable documents, instruments, or investment property may be perfected by filing.

(b) **[Control or possession of certain collateral.]** Except as otherwise provided in Section 9–315(c) and (d) for proceeds:

(1) a security interest in a deposit account may be perfected only by control under Section 9–314;

(2) and except as otherwise provided in Section 9–308(d), a security interest in a letter-of-credit right may be perfected only by control under Section 9–314; and

(3) a security interest in money may be perfected only by the secured party's taking possession under Section 9–313.

(c) **[Goods covered by negotiable document.]** While goods are in the possession of a bailee that has issued a negotiable document covering the goods:

(1) a security interest in the goods may be perfected by perfecting a security interest in the document; and

(2) a security interest perfected in the document has priority over any security interest that becomes perfected in the goods by another method during that time.

(d) **[Goods covered by nonnegotiable document.]** While goods are in the possession of a bailee that has issued a nonnegotiable document covering the goods, a security interest in the goods may be perfected by:

(1) issuance of a document in the name of the secured party;

(2) the bailee's receipt of notification of the secured party's interest; or

(3) filing as to the goods.

(e) **[Temporary perfection: new value.]** A security interest in certificated securities, negotiable documents, or instruments is perfected without filing or the taking of possession or control for a period of 20 days from the time it attaches to the extent that it arises for new value given under an authenticated security agreement.

(f) **[Temporary perfection: goods or documents made available to debtor.]** A perfected security interest in a negotiable document or goods in possession of a bailee, other than one that has issued a negotiable document for the goods, remains perfected for 20 days without filing if the secured party makes available to the debtor the goods or documents representing the goods for the purpose of:

(1) ultimate sale or exchange; or

(2) loading, unloading, storing, shipping, transshipping, manufacturing, processing, or otherwise dealing with them in a manner preliminary to their sale or exchange.

(g) **[Temporary perfection: delivery of security certificate or instrument to debtor.]** A perfected security interest in a certificated security or instrument remains perfected for 20 days without filing if the secured party delivers the security certificate or instrument to the debtor for the purpose of:

(1) ultimate sale or exchange; or

(2) presentation, collection, enforcement, renewal, or registration of transfer.

(h) **[Expiration of temporary perfection.]** After the 20-day period specified in subsection (e), (f), or (g) expires, perfection depends upon compliance with this article.

As amended in 2003.

Official Comment

1. **Source.** Former Section 9–304, with additions and some changes.

2. **Instruments.** Under subsection (a), a security interest in instruments may be perfected by filing. This rule represents an important change from former Article 9, under which the secured party's taking possession of an instrument was the only method of achieving long-term perfection. The rule is likely to be particularly useful in transactions involving a large number of notes that a debtor uses as collateral but continues to collect from the makers. A security interest perfected by filing is subject to defeat by certain subsequent purchasers (including secured parties). Under Section 9–330(d), purchasers for value who take possession of an instrument without knowledge that the purchase violates the rights of the secured party generally would achieve priority over a security interest in the instrument perfected by filing. In addition, Section 9–331 provides that filing a financing statement does not constitute notice that would preclude a subsequent purchaser from becoming a holder in due course and taking free of all claims under Section 3–306.

3. **Chattel Paper; Negotiable Documents.** Subsection (a) further provides that filing is available as a method of perfection for security interests in chattel paper and negotiable documents. Tangible chattel paper is sometimes delivered to the assignee, and sometimes left in the hands of the assignor for collection. Subsection (a) allows the assignee to perfect its security interest by filing in the latter case. Alternatively, the assignee may perfect by taking possession. See Section 9–313(a). An assignee of electronic chattel paper may perfect by taking control. See Sections 9–314(a), 9–105. The security interest of an assignee who takes possession or control may qualify for priority over a competing security interest perfected by filing. See Section 9–330.

Negotiable documents may be, and usually are, delivered to the secured party. See Article 1, Section 1–201 (definition of "delivery"). The secured party's taking possession of a tangible document or control of an electronic document will suffice as a perfection step. See Sections 9–313(a), 9–314 and 7–106. However, as is the case with chattel paper, a security interest in a negotiable document may be perfected by filing.

4. **Investment Property.** A security interest in investment property, including certificated securities, uncertificated securities, security entitlements, and securities accounts, may be perfected by filing. However, security interests created by brokers, securities intermediaries, or commodity intermediaries are automatically perfected; filing is of no effect. See Section 9–309(10), (11). A security interest in all kinds of investment property also may be perfected by control, see Sections 9–314, 9–106, and a security interest in a certificated security also may be perfected by the secured party's taking delivery under Section 8–301. See Section 9–313(a). A security interest perfected only by filing is subordinate to a conflicting security interest perfected by control or delivery. See Section 9–328(1), (5). Thus, although filing is a permissible method of perfection, a secured party who perfects by filing takes the risk that the debtor has granted or will grant a security interest in the same collateral to another party who obtains control. Also, perfection by filing would not give the secured party protection against other types of adverse claims, since the Article 8 adverse claim cut-off rules require control. See Section 8–510.

5. **Deposit Accounts.** Under new subsection (b)(1), the only method of perfecting a security interest in a deposit account as original collateral is by control. Filing is ineffective, except as provided in Section 9–315 with respect to proceeds. As explained in Section 9–104, "control" can arise as a result of an agreement among the secured party, debtor, and bank, whereby the bank agrees to comply with instructions of the secured party with respect to disposition of the funds on deposit, even though the debtor retains the right to direct disposition of the funds. Thus, subsection (b)(1) takes an intermediate position between certain non-UCC law, which conditions the effectiveness of a security interest on the secured party's enjoyment of such dominion and control over the deposit account that the debtor is unable to dispose of the funds, and the approach this Article takes to securities accounts, under which a secured party who is unable to reach the collateral without resort to judicial process may perfect by filing. By conditioning perfection on "control," rather than requiring the secured party to enjoy absolute dominion to the exclusion of the debtor, subsection (b)(1) permits perfection in a wide variety of transactions, including those in which the secured party actually relies on the deposit account in extending credit and maintains some meaningful dominion over it, but does not wish to deprive the debtor of access to the funds altogether.

6. **Letter-of-Credit Rights.** Letter-of-credit rights commonly are "supporting obligations," as defined in Section 9–102. Perfection as to the related account, chattel paper, document, general intangible, instrument, or investment property will perfect as to the letter-of-credit rights. See Section 9–308(d). Subsection (b)(2) provides

that, in other cases, a security interest in a letter-of-credit right may be perfected only by control. "Control," for these purposes, is explained in Section 9–107.

7. **Goods Covered by Document of Title.** Subsection (c) applies to goods in the possession of a bailee who has issued a negotiable document covering the goods. Subsection (d) applies to goods in the possession of a bailee who has issued a nonnegotiable document of title, including a document of title that is "non-negotiable" under Section 7–104. Section 9–313 governs perfection of a security interest in goods in the possession of a bailee who has not issued a document of title.

Subsection (c) clarifies the perfection and priority rules in former Section 9–304(2). Consistently with the provisions of Article 7, subsection (c) takes the position that, as long as a negotiable document covering goods is outstanding, title to the goods is, so to say, locked up in the document. Accordingly, a security interest in goods covered by a negotiable document may be perfected by perfecting a security interest in the document. The security interest also may be perfected by another method, e.g., by filing. The priority rule in subsection (c) governs only priority between (i) a security interest in goods which is perfected by perfecting in the document and (ii) a security interest in the goods which becomes perfected by another method while the goods are covered by the document.

Example 1:   While wheat is in a grain elevator and covered by a negotiable warehouse receipt, Debtor creates a security interest in the wheat in favor of SP-1 and SP-2. SP-1 perfects by filing a financing statement covering "wheat." Thereafter, SP-2 perfects by filing a financing statement describing the warehouse receipt. Subsection (c)(1) provides that SP-2's security interest is perfected. Subsection (c)(2) provides that SP-2's security interest is senior to SP-1's.

Example 2:   The facts are as in Example 1, but SP-1's security interest attached and was perfected before the goods were delivered to the grain elevator. Subsection (c)(2) does not apply, because SP-1's security interest did not become perfected during the time that the wheat was in the possession of a bailee. Rather, the first-to-file-or-perfect priority rule applies. See Sections 9–322 and 7–503.

A secured party may become "a holder to whom a negotiable document of title has been duly negotiated" under Section 7–501. If so, the secured party acquires the rights specified by Article 7. Article 9 does not limit those rights, which may include the right to priority over an earlier-perfected security interest. See Section 9–331(a).

Subsection (d) takes a different approach to the problem of goods covered by a nonnegotiable document. Here, title to the goods is not looked on as being locked up in the document, and the secured party may perfect its security interest directly in the goods by filing as to them. The subsection provides two other methods of perfection: issuance of the document in the secured party's name (as consignee of a straight bill of lading or the person to whom delivery would be made under a non-negotiable warehouse receipt) and receipt of notification of the secured party's interest by the bailee. Perfection under subsection (d) occurs when the bailee receives notification of the secured party's interest in the goods, regardless of who sends the notification. Receipt of notification is effective to perfect, regardless of whether the bailee responds. Unlike former Section 9–304(3), from which it derives, subsection (d) does not apply to goods in the possession of a bailee who has not issued a document of title. Section 9–313(c) covers that case and provides that perfection by possession as to goods not covered by a document requires the bailee's acknowledgment.

8. **Temporary Perfection Without Having First Otherwise Perfected.** Subsection (e) follows former Section 9–304(4) in giving perfected status to security interests in certificated securities, instruments, and negotiable documents for a short period (reduced from 21 to 20 days, which is the time period generally applicable in this Article), although there has been no filing and the collateral is in the debtor's possession or control. The 20-day temporary perfection runs from the date of attachment. There is no limitation on the purpose for which the debtor is in possession, but the secured party must have given "new value" (defined in Section 9–102) under an authenticated security agreement.

9. **Maintaining Perfection After Surrendering Possession.** There are a variety of legitimate reasons—many of them are described in subsections (f) and (g)—why certain types of collateral must be released temporarily to a debtor. No useful purpose would be served by cluttering the files with records of such exceedingly short term transactions.

Subsection (f) affords the possibility of 20-day perfection in negotiable documents and goods in the possession of a bailee but not covered by a negotiable document. Subsection (g) provides for 20-day perfection in certificated securities and instruments. These subsections derive from former Section 9–305(5). However, the period of temporary perfection has been reduced from 21 to 20 days, which is the time period generally applicable in this Article, and "enforcement" has been added in subsection (g) as one of the special and limited purposes for which a secured party can release an instrument or certificated security to the debtor and still remain perfected. The period of temporary perfection runs from the date a secured party who already has a perfected security interest turns over the collateral to the debtor. There is no new value requirement, but the turnover must be for one or more of the purposes stated in subsection (f) or (g). The 20-day period may be extended by perfecting as to the collateral by another method before the period expires. However, if the security interest is not perfected by another method until after the 20-day period expires, there will be a gap during which the security interest is unperfected.

Temporary perfection extends only to the negotiable document or goods under subsection (f) and only to the certificated security or instrument under subsection (g). It does not extend to proceeds. If the collateral is sold, the security interest will continue in the proceeds for the period specified in Section 9–315.

Subsections (f) and (g) deal only with perfection. Other sections of this Article govern the priority of a security interest in goods after surrender of possession or control of the document covering them. In the case of a purchase-money security interest in inventory, priority may be conditioned upon giving notification to a prior inventory financer. See Section 9–324.

As amended in 2003.

POSSESSION — Attachment 9-203

§ 9–313. When Possession by or Delivery to Secured Party Perfects Security Interest Without Filing.

(a) **[Perfection by possession or delivery.]** Except as otherwise provided in subsection (b), a secured party may perfect a security interest in tangible negotiable documents, goods, instruments, money, or tangible chattel paper by taking possession of the collateral. A secured party may perfect a security interest in certificated securities by taking delivery of the certificated securities under Section 8–301.

(b) **[Goods covered by certificate of title.]** With respect to goods covered by a certificate of title issued by this State, a secured party may perfect a security interest in the goods by taking possession of the goods only in the circumstances described in Section 9–316(d).

(c) **[Collateral in possession of person other than debtor.]** With respect to collateral other than certificated securities and goods covered by a document, a secured party takes possession of collateral in the possession of a person other than the debtor, the secured party, or a lessee of the collateral from the debtor in the ordinary course of the debtor's business, when:

(1) the person in possession authenticates a record acknowledging that it holds possession of the collateral for the secured party's benefit; or

(2) the person takes possession of the collateral after having authenticated a record acknowledging that it will hold possession of collateral for the secured party's benefit.

(d) **[Time of perfection by possession; continuation of perfection.]** If perfection of a security interest depends upon possession of the collateral by a secured party, perfection occurs no earlier than the time the secured party takes possession and continues only while the secured party retains possession.

(e) **[Time of perfection by delivery; continuation of perfection.]** A security interest in a certificated security in registered form is perfected by delivery when delivery of the certificated security occurs under Section 8–301 and remains perfected by delivery until the debtor obtains possession of the security certificate.

(f) **[Acknowledgment not required.]** A person in possession of collateral is not required to acknowledge that it holds possession for a secured party's benefit.

(g) **[Effectiveness of acknowledgment; no duties or confirmation.]** If a person acknowledges that it holds possession for the secured party's benefit:

(1) the acknowledgment is effective under subsection (c) or Section 8–301(a), even if the acknowledgment violates the rights of a debtor; and

(2) unless the person otherwise agrees or law other than this article otherwise provides, the person does not owe any duty to the secured party and is not required to confirm the acknowledgment to another person.

(h) **[Secured party's delivery to person other than debtor.]** A secured party having possession of collateral does not relinquish possession by delivering the collateral to a person other than the debtor or

For agents, individuals/SPs

For Bailee

For Bailees but blurry line so do 9-313c

↳ this works best

769

for bulk transfer of mortgage notes but — could — work for other bailee situation

a lessee of the collateral from the debtor in the ordinary course of the debtor's business if the person was instructed before the delivery or is instructed contemporaneously with the delivery:

(1)   to hold possession of the collateral for the secured party's benefit; or

(2)   to redeliver the collateral to the secured party.

(i)   **[Effect of delivery under subsection (h); no duties or confirmation.]** A secured party does not relinquish possession, even if a delivery under subsection (h) violates the rights of a debtor. A person to which collateral is delivered under subsection (h) does not owe any duty to the secured party and is not required to confirm the delivery to another person unless the person otherwise agrees or law other than this article otherwise provides.

As amended in 2003.

Official Comment

1.   **Source.** Former Sections 9–305, 9–115(6).

2.   **Perfection by Possession.** As under the common law of pledge, no filing is required by this Article to perfect a security interest if the secured party takes possession of the collateral. See Section 9–310(b)(6).

This section permits a security interest to be perfected by the taking of possession only when the collateral is goods, instruments, tangible negotiable documents, money, or tangible chattel paper. Accounts, commercial tort claims, deposit accounts, investment property, letter-of-credit rights, letters of credit, and oil, gas, or other minerals before extraction are excluded. (But see Comment 6, below, regarding certificated securities.) A security interest in accounts and payment intangibles—property not ordinarily represented by any writing whose delivery operates to transfer the right to payment—may under this Article be perfected only by filing. This rule would not be affected by the fact that a security agreement or other record described the assignment of such collateral as a "pledge." Section 9–309(2) exempts from filing certain assignments of accounts or payment intangibles which are out of the ordinary course of financing. These exempted assignments are perfected when they attach. Similarly, under Section 9–309(3), sales of payment intangibles are automatically perfected.

3.   **"Possession."** This section does not define "possession." It adopts the general concept as it developed under former Article 9. As under former Article 9, in determining whether a particular person has possession, the principles of agency apply. For example, if the collateral is in possession of an agent of the secured party for the purposes of possessing on behalf of the secured party, and if the agent is not also an agent of the debtor, the secured party has taken actual possession, and subsection (c) does not apply. Sometimes a person holds collateral both as an agent of the secured party and as an agent of the debtor. The fact of dual agency is not of itself inconsistent with the secured party's having taken possession (and thereby having rendered subsection (c) inapplicable). The debtor cannot qualify as an agent for the secured party for purposes of the secured party's taking possession. And, under appropriate circumstances, a court may determine that a person in possession is so closely connected to or controlled by the debtor that the debtor has retained effective possession, even though the person may have agreed to take possession on behalf of the secured party. If so, the person's taking possession would not constitute the secured party's taking possession and would not be sufficient for perfection. See also Section 9–205(b). In a typical escrow arrangement, where the escrowee has possession of collateral as agent for both the secured party and the debtor, the debtor's relationship to the escrowee is not such as to constitute retention of possession by the debtor.

4.   **Goods in Possession of Third Party: Perfection.** Former Section 9–305 permitted perfection of a security interest by notification to a bailee in possession of collateral. This Article distinguishes between goods in the possession of a bailee who has issued a document of title covering the goods and goods in the possession of a third party who has not issued a document. Section 9–312(c) or (d) applies to the former, depending on whether the document is negotiable. Section 9–313(c) applies to the latter. It provides a method of perfection by possession when the collateral is possessed by a third person who is not the secured party's agent.

Notification of a third person does not suffice to perfect under Section 9–313(c). Rather, perfection does not occur unless the third person authenticates an acknowledgment that it holds possession of the collateral for the secured party's benefit. Compare Section 9–312(d), under which receipt of notification of the security party's interest by a bailee holding goods covered by a nonnegotiable document is sufficient to perfect, even if the bailee does not acknowledge receipt of the notification. A third person may acknowledge that it will hold for the secured party's benefit goods to be received in the future. Under these circumstances, perfection by possession occurs when the third person obtains possession of the goods.

Under subsection (c), acknowledgment of notification by a "lessee . . . in . . . ordinary course of . . . business" (defined in Section 2A–103) does not suffice for possession. The section thus rejects the reasoning of *In re Atlantic Systems, Inc.*, 135 B.R. 463 (Bankr. S.D.N.Y. 1992) (holding that notification to debtor-lessor's lessee sufficed to perfect security interest in leased goods). See Steven O. Weise, *Perfection by Possession: The Need for an Objective Test*, 29 Idaho Law Rev. 705 (1992–93) (arguing that lessee's possession in ordinary course of debtor-lessor's business does not provide adequate public notice of possible security interest in leased goods). Inclusion of a per se rule concerning lessees is not meant to preclude a court, under appropriate circumstances, from determining that a third person is so closely connected to or controlled by the debtor that the debtor has retained effective possession. If so, the third person's acknowledgment would not be sufficient for perfection.

In some cases, it may be uncertain whether a person who has possession of collateral is an agent of the secured party or a non-agent bailee. Under those circumstances, prudence might suggest that the secured party obtain the person's acknowledgment to avoid litigation and ensure perfection by possession regardless of how the relationship between the secured party and the person is characterized.

5. **No Relation Back.** Former Section 9–305 provided that a security interest is perfected by possession from the time possession is taken "without a relation back." As the Comment to former Section 9–305 observed, the relation-back theory, under which the taking of possession was deemed to relate back to the date of the original security agreement, has had little vitality since the 1938 revision of the Federal Bankruptcy Act. The theory is inconsistent with former Article 9 and with this Article. See Section 9–313(d). Accordingly, this Article deletes the quoted phrase as unnecessary. Where a pledge transaction is contemplated, perfection dates only from the time possession is taken, although a security interest may attach, unperfected. The only exceptions to this rule are the short, 20-day periods of perfection provided in Section 9–312(e), (f), and (g), during which a debtor may have possession of specified collateral in which there is a perfected security interest.

6. **Certificated Securities.** The second sentence of subsection (a) reflects the traditional rule for perfection of a security interest in certificated securities. Compare Section 9–115(6) (1994 Official Text); Sections 8–321, 8–313(1)(a) (1978 Official Text); Section 9–305 (1972 Official Text). It has been modified to refer to "delivery" under Section 8–301. Corresponding changes appear in Section 9–203(b).

Subsection (e), which is new, applies to a secured party in possession of security certificates or another person who has taken delivery of security certificates and holds them for the secured party's benefit under Section 8–301. See Comment 8.

Under subsection (e), a possessory security interest in a certificated security remains perfected until the debtor obtains possession of the security certificate. This rule is analogous to that of Section 9–314(c), which deals with perfection of security interests in investment property by control. See Section 9–314, Comment 3.

7. **Goods Covered by Certificate of Title.** Subsection (b) is necessary to effect changes to the choice-of-law rules governing goods covered by a certificate of title. These changes are described in the Comments to Section 9–311. Subsection (b), like subsection (a), does not create a right to take possession. Rather, it indicates the circumstances under which the secured party's taking possession of goods covered by a certificate of title is effective to perfect a security interest in the goods: the goods become covered by a certificate of title issued by this State at a time when the security interest is perfected by any method under the law of another jurisdiction.

8. **Goods in Possession of Third Party: No Duty to Acknowledge; Consequences of Acknowledgment.** Subsections (f) and (g) are new and address matters as to which former Article 9 was silent. They derive in part from Section 8–106(g). Subsection (f) provides that a person in possession of collateral is not required to acknowledge that it holds for a secured party. Subsection (g)(1) provides that an acknowledgment is effective even if wrongful as to the debtor. Subsection (g)(2) makes clear that an acknowledgment does not give rise to any duties or responsibilities under this Article. Arrangements involving the possession of goods are hardly standardized. They include bailments for services to be performed on the goods (such as repair or processing), for use (leases), as security (pledges), for carriage, and for storage. This Article leaves to the agreement of the parties and to any other applicable law the imposition of duties and responsibilities upon a person who acknowledges under subsection (c). For example, by acknowledging, a third party does not become obliged to act on the secured party's direction or to remain in possession of the collateral unless it agrees to do so or other law so provides.

9. **Delivery to Third Party by Secured Party.** New subsections (h) and (i) address the practice of mortgage warehouse lenders. These lenders typically send mortgage notes to prospective purchasers under cover of letters advising the prospective purchasers that the lenders hold security interests in the notes. These lenders relied on notification to maintain perfection under former 9–305. Requiring them to obtain authenticated acknowledgments from each prospective purchaser under subsection (c) could be unduly burdensome and disruptive of established practices. Under subsection (h), when a secured party in possession itself delivers the

771

collateral to a third party, instructions to the third party would be sufficient to maintain perfection by possession; an acknowledgment would not be necessary. Under subsection (i), the secured party does not relinquish possession by making a delivery under subsection (h), even if the delivery violates the rights of the debtor. That subsection also makes clear that a person to whom collateral is delivered under subsection (h) does not owe any duty to the secured party and is not required to confirm the delivery to another person unless the person otherwise agrees or law other than this Article provides otherwise.

As amended in 2000 and 2003.

§ 9–314.   Perfection by Control.

(a)   **[Perfection by control.]** A security interest in investment property, deposit accounts, letter-of-credit rights, electronic chattel paper, or electronic documents may be perfected by control of the collateral under Section 7–106, 9–104, 9–105, 9–106, or 9–107.

(b)   **[Specified collateral: time of perfection by control; continuation of perfection.]** A security interest in deposit accounts, electronic chattel paper, letter-of-credit rights, or electronic documents is perfected by control under Section 7–106, 9–104, 9–105, or 9–107 when the secured party obtains control and remains perfected by control only while the secured party retains control.

(c)   **[Investment property: time of perfection by control; continuation of perfection.]** A security interest in investment property is perfected by control under Section 9–106 from the time the secured party obtains control and remains perfected by control until:

(1)   the secured party does not have control; and

(2)   one of the following occurs:

(A)   if the collateral is a certificated security, the debtor has or acquires possession of the security certificate;

(B)   if the collateral is an uncertificated security, the issuer has registered or registers the debtor as the registered owner; or

(C)   if the collateral is a security entitlement, the debtor is or becomes the entitlement holder.

As amended in 2003.

Official Comment

1.   **Source.** Substantially new; derived in part from former Section 9–115(4).

2.   **Control.** This section provides for perfection by control with respect to investment property, deposit accounts, letter-of-credit rights, electronic chattel paper, and electronic documents. For explanations of how a secured party takes control of these types of collateral, see Sections 9–104 through 9–107 and Section 7–106. Subsection (b) explains when a security interest is perfected by control and how long a security interest remains perfected by control. Like Section 9–313(d) and for the same reasons, subsection (b) makes no reference to the doctrine of "relation back." See Section 9–313, Comment 5. As to an electronic document that is reissued in a tangible medium, Section 7–105, a secured party that is perfected by control in the electronic document should file as to the document before relinquishing control in order to maintain continuous perfection in the document. See Section 9–308.

3.   **Investment Property.** Subsection (c) provides a special rule for investment property. Once a secured party has control, its security interest remains perfected by control until the secured party ceases to have control and the debtor receives possession of collateral that is a certificated security, becomes the registered owner of collateral that is an uncertificated security, or becomes the entitlement holder of collateral that is a security entitlement. The result is particularly important in the "repledge" context. See Section 9–207, Comment 5.

In a transaction in which a secured party who has control grants a security interest in investment property or sells outright the investment property, by virtue of the debtor's consent or applicable legal rules, a purchaser from the secured party typically will cut off the debtor's rights in the investment property or be immune from the debtor's claims. See Section 9–207, Comments 5 and 6. If the investment property is a security, the debtor normally would retain no interest in the security following the purchase from the secured party, and a claim of the debtor against the secured party for redemption (Section 9–623) or otherwise with respect to the security would be a purely personal claim. If the investment property transferred by the secured party is a financial asset in which the debtor had a security entitlement credited to a securities account maintained with the secured party as a securities intermediary, the debtor's claim against the secured party could arise as a part of its securities account notwithstanding its personal nature. (This claim would be analogous to a "credit balance" in the securities account, which is a component of the securities account even though it is a personal claim against the intermediary.) In the case in which the debtor may retain an interest in investment property notwithstanding a repledge or sale by the secured party, subsection (c) makes clear that the security interest will remain perfected by control.

As amended in 2003.

§ 9–315. Secured Party's Rights on Disposition of Collateral and in Proceeds.

(a) **[Disposition of collateral: continuation of security interest or agricultural lien; proceeds.]** Except as otherwise provided in this article and in Section 2–403(2):

(1) a security interest or agricultural lien continues in collateral notwithstanding sale, lease, license, exchange, or other disposition thereof unless the secured party authorized the disposition free of the security interest or agricultural lien; and

(2) a security interest attaches to any identifiable proceeds of collateral.

(b) **[When commingled proceeds identifiable.]** Proceeds that are commingled with other property are identifiable proceeds:

(1) if the proceeds are goods, to the extent provided by Section 9–336; and

(2) if the proceeds are not goods, to the extent that the secured party identifies the proceeds by a method of tracing, including application of equitable principles, that is permitted under law other than this article with respect to commingled property of the type involved.

(c) **[Perfection of security interest in proceeds.]** A security interest in proceeds is a perfected security interest if the security interest in the original collateral was perfected.

(d) **[Continuation of perfection.]** A perfected security interest in proceeds becomes unperfected on the 21st day after the security interest attaches to the proceeds unless:

(1) the following conditions are satisfied:

(A) a filed financing statement covers the original collateral;

(B) the proceeds are collateral in which a security interest may be perfected by filing in the office in which the financing statement has been filed; and

(C) the proceeds are not acquired with cash proceeds;

(2) the proceeds are identifiable cash proceeds; or

(3) the security interest in the proceeds is perfected other than under subsection (c) when the security interest attaches to the proceeds or within 20 days thereafter.

(e) **[When perfected security interest in proceeds becomes unperfected.]** If a filed financing statement covers the original collateral, a security interest in proceeds which remains perfected under subsection (d)(1) becomes unperfected at the later of:

(1) when the effectiveness of the filed financing statement lapses under Section 9–515 or is terminated under Section 9–513; or

(2) the 21st day after the security interest attaches to the proceeds.

Official Comment

1. **Source.** Former Section 9–306.

2. **Continuation of Security Interest or Agricultural Lien Following Disposition of Collateral.** Subsection (a)(1), which derives from former Section 9–306(2), contains the general rule that a security interest survives disposition of the collateral. In these cases, the secured party may repossess the collateral from the transferee or, in an appropriate case, maintain an action for conversion. The secured party may claim both any proceeds and the original collateral but, of course, may have only one satisfaction.

In many cases, a purchaser or other transferee of collateral will take free of a security interest, and the secured party's only right will be to proceeds. For example, the general rule does not apply, and a security interest does not continue in collateral, if the secured party authorized the disposition, in the agreement that contains the security agreement or otherwise. Subsection (a)(1) adopts the view of PEB Commentary No. 3 and makes explicit that the authorized disposition to which it refers is an authorized disposition "free of" the security interest or agricultural lien. The secured party's right to proceeds under this section or under the express terms of an agreement does not in itself constitute an authorization of disposition. The change in language from former Section 9–306(2) is not intended to address the frequently litigated situation in which the effectiveness of the secured party's consent to a disposition is conditioned upon the secured party's receipt of the proceeds. In that situation, subsection (a) leaves the determination of authorization to the courts, as under former Article 9.

This Article contains several provisions under which a transferee takes free of a security interest or agricultural lien. For example, Section 9–317 states when transferees take free of unperfected security interests; Sections 9–320 and 9–321 on goods, 9–321 on general intangibles, 9–330 on chattel paper and instruments, and 9–331 on negotiable instruments, negotiable documents, and securities state when purchasers of such collateral take free of a security interest, even though perfected and even though the disposition was not authorized. Section 9–332 enables most transferees (including non-purchasers) of funds from a deposit account and most transferees of money to take free of a perfected security interest in the deposit account or money.

Likewise, the general rule that a security interest survives disposition does not apply if the secured party entrusts goods collateral to a merchant who deals in goods of that kind and the merchant sells the collateral to a buyer in ordinary course of business. Section 2–403(2) gives the merchant the power to transfer all the secured party's rights to the buyer, even if the sale is wrongful as against the secured party. Thus, under subsection (a)(1), an entrusting secured party runs the same risk as any other entruster.

3.   **Secured Party's Right to Identifiable Proceeds.** Under subsection (a)(2), which derives from former Section 9–306(2), a security interest attaches to any identifiable "proceeds," as defined in Section 9–102. See also Section 9–203(f). Subsection (b) is new. It indicates when proceeds commingled with other property are identifiable proceeds and permits the use of whatever methods of tracing other law permits with respect to the type of property involved. Among the "equitable principles" whose use other law may permit is the "lowest intermediate balance rule." See Restatement (2d), Trusts § 202.

4.   **Automatic Perfection in Proceeds: General Rule.** Under subsection (c), a security interest in proceeds is a perfected security interest if the security interest in the original collateral was perfected. This Article extends the period of automatic perfection in proceeds from 10 days to 20 days. Generally, a security interest in proceeds becomes unperfected on the 21st day after the security interest attaches to the proceeds. See subsection (d). The loss of perfected status under subsection (d) is prospective only. Compare, e.g., Section 9–515(c) (deeming security interest unperfected retroactively).

5.   **Automatic Perfection in Proceeds: Proceeds Acquired with Cash Proceeds.** Subsection (d)(1) derives from former Section 9–306(3)(a). It carries forward the basic rule that a security interest in proceeds remains perfected beyond the period of automatic perfection if a filed financing statement covers the original collateral (e.g., inventory) and the proceeds are collateral in which a security interest may be perfected by filing in the office where the financing statement has been filed (e.g., equipment). A different rule applies if the proceeds are acquired with cash proceeds, as is the case if the original collateral (inventory) is sold for cash (cash proceeds) that is used to purchase equipment (proceeds). Under these circumstances, the security interest in the equipment proceeds remains perfected only if the description in the filed financing indicates the type of property constituting the proceeds (e.g., "equipment").

This section reaches the same result but takes a different approach. It recognizes that the treatment of proceeds acquired with cash proceeds under former Section 9–306(3)(a) essentially was superfluous. In the example, had the filing covered "equipment" as well as "inventory," the security interest in the proceeds would have been perfected under the usual rules governing after-acquired equipment (see former Sections 9–302, 9–303); paragraph (3)(a) added only an exception to the general rule. Subsection (d)(1)(C) of this section takes a more direct approach. It makes the general rule of continued perfection inapplicable to proceeds acquired with cash proceeds, leaving perfection of a security interest in those proceeds to the generally applicable perfection rules under subsection (d)(3).

Example 1:   Lender perfects a security interest in Debtor's inventory by filing a financing statement covering "inventory." Debtor sells the inventory and deposits the buyer's check into a deposit account. Debtor draws a check on the deposit account and uses it to pay for equipment. Under the "lowest intermediate balance rule," which is a permitted method of tracing in the relevant jurisdiction, see Comment 3, the funds used to pay for the equipment were identifiable proceeds of the inventory. Because the proceeds (equipment) were acquired with cash proceeds (deposit account), subsection (d)(1) does not extend perfection beyond the 20-day automatic period.

Example 2: Lender perfects a security interest in Debtor's inventory by filing a financing statement covering "all debtor's property." As in Example 1, Debtor sells the inventory, deposits the buyer's check into a deposit account, draws a check on the deposit account, and uses the check to pay for equipment. Under the "lowest intermediate balance rule," which is a permitted method of tracing in the relevant jurisdiction, see Comment 3, the funds used to pay for the equipment were identifiable proceeds of the inventory. Because the proceeds (equipment) were acquired with cash proceeds (deposit account), subsection (d)(1) does not extend perfection beyond the 20-day automatic period. However, because the financing statement is sufficient to perfect a security interest in debtor's equipment, under subsection (d)(3) the security interest in the equipment proceeds remains perfected beyond the 20-day period.

6. **Automatic Perfection in Proceeds: Lapse or Termination of Financing Statement During 20-Day Period; Perfection Under Other Statute or Treaty.** Subsection (e) provides that a security interest in proceeds perfected under subsection (d)(1) ceases to be perfected when the financing statement covering the original collateral lapses or is terminated. If the lapse or termination occurs before the 21st day after the security interest attaches, however, the security interest in the proceeds remains perfected until the 21st day. Section 9–311(b) provides that compliance with the perfection requirements of a statute or treaty described in Section 9–311(a) "is equivalent to the filing of a financing statement." It follows that collateral subject to a security interest perfected by such compliance under Section 9–311(b) is covered by a "filed financing statement" within the meaning of Section 9–315(d) and (e).

7. **Automatic Perfection in Proceeds: Continuation of Perfection in Cash Proceeds.** Former Section 9–306(3)(b) provided that if a filed financing statement covered original collateral, a security interest in identifiable cash proceeds of the collateral remained perfected beyond the ten-day period of automatic perfection. Former Section 9–306(3)(c) contained a similar rule with respect to identifiable cash proceeds of investment property. Subsection (d)(2) extends the benefits of former Sections 9–306(3)(b) and (3)(c) to identifiable cash proceeds of all types of original collateral in which a security interest is perfected by any method. Under subsection (d)(2), if the security interest in the original collateral was perfected, a security interest in identifiable cash proceeds will remain perfected indefinitely, regardless of whether the security interest in the original collateral remains perfected. In many cases, however, a purchaser or other transferee of the cash proceeds will take free of the perfected security interest. See, e.g., Sections 9–330(d) (purchaser of check), 9–331 (holder in due course of check), 9–332 (transferee of money or funds from a deposit account).

8. **Insolvency Proceedings; Returned and Repossessed Goods.** This Article deletes former Section 9–306(4), which dealt with proceeds in insolvency proceedings. Except as otherwise provided by the Bankruptcy Code, the debtor's entering into bankruptcy does not affect a secured party's right to proceeds.

This Article also deletes former Section 9–306(5), which dealt with returned and repossessed goods. Section 9–330, Comments 9 to 11 explain and clarify the application of priority rules to returned and repossessed goods as proceeds of chattel paper.

9. **Proceeds of Collateral Subject to Agricultural Lien.** This Article does not determine whether a lien extends to proceeds of farm products encumbered by an agricultural lien. If, however, the proceeds are themselves farm products on which an "agricultural lien" (defined in Section 9–102) arises under other law, then the agricultural-lien provisions of this Article apply to the agricultural lien on the proceeds in the same way in which they would apply had the farm products not been proceeds.

§ 9–316. Effect of Change in Governing Law.

(a) **[General rule: effect on perfection of change in governing law.]** A security interest perfected pursuant to the law of the jurisdiction designated in Section 9–301(1) or 9–305(c) remains perfected until the earliest of:

(1) the time perfection would have ceased under the law of that jurisdiction;

(2) the expiration of four months after a change of the debtor's location to another jurisdiction; or

(3) the expiration of one year after a transfer of collateral to a person that thereby becomes a debtor and is located in another jurisdiction.

(b) **[Security interest perfected or unperfected under law of new jurisdiction.]** If a security interest described in subsection (a) becomes perfected under the law of the other jurisdiction before the earliest time or event described in that subsection, it remains perfected thereafter. If the security interest does not become perfected under the law of the other jurisdiction before the earliest time or event, it becomes unperfected and is deemed never to have been perfected as against a purchaser of the collateral for value.

(c) **[Possessory security interest in collateral moved to new jurisdiction.]** A possessory security interest in collateral, other than goods covered by a certificate of title and as-extracted collateral consisting of goods, remains continuously perfected if:

(1) the collateral is located in one jurisdiction and subject to a security interest perfected under the law of that jurisdiction;

(2) thereafter the collateral is brought into another jurisdiction; and

(3) upon entry into the other jurisdiction, the security interest is perfected under the law of the other jurisdiction.

(d) **[Goods covered by certificate of title from this state.]** Except as otherwise provided in subsection (e), a security interest in goods covered by a certificate of title which is perfected by any method under the law of another jurisdiction when the goods become covered by a certificate of title from this State remains perfected until the security interest would have become unperfected under the law of the other jurisdiction had the goods not become so covered.

(e) **[When subsection (d) security interest becomes unperfected against purchasers.]** A security interest described in subsection (d) becomes unperfected as against a purchaser of the goods for value and is deemed never to have been perfected as against a purchaser of the goods for value if the applicable requirements for perfection under Section 9–311(b) or 9–313 are not satisfied before the earlier of:

(1) the time the security interest would have become unperfected under the law of the other jurisdiction had the goods not become covered by a certificate of title from this State; or

(2) the expiration of four months after the goods had become so covered.

(f) **[Change in jurisdiction of bank, issuer, nominated person, securities intermediary, or commodity intermediary.]** A security interest in deposit accounts, letter-of-credit rights, or investment property which is perfected under the law of the bank's jurisdiction, the issuer's jurisdiction, a nominated person's jurisdiction, the securities intermediary's jurisdiction, or the commodity intermediary's jurisdiction, as applicable, remains perfected until the earlier of:

(1) the time the security interest would have become unperfected under the law of that jurisdiction; or

(2) the expiration of four months after a change of the applicable jurisdiction to another jurisdiction.

(g) **[Subsection (f) security interest perfected or unperfected under law of new jurisdiction.]** If a security interest described in subsection (f) becomes perfected under the law of the other jurisdiction before the earlier of the time or the end of the period described in that subsection, it remains perfected thereafter. If the security interest does not become perfected under the law of the other jurisdiction before the earlier of that time or the end of that period, it becomes unperfected and is deemed never to have been perfected as against a purchaser of the collateral for value.

(h) **[Effect on filed financing statement of change in governing law.]** The following rules apply to collateral to which a security interest attaches within four months after the debtor changes its location to another jurisdiction:

(1) A financing statement filed before the change pursuant to the law of the jurisdiction designated in Section 9–301(1) or 9–305(c) is effective to perfect a security interest in the collateral if the financing statement would have been effective to perfect a security interest in the collateral had the debtor not changed its location.

(2) If a security interest perfected by a financing statement that is effective under paragraph (1) becomes perfected under the law of the other jurisdiction before the earlier of the time the

financing statement would have become ineffective under the law of the jurisdiction designated in Section 9–301(1) or 9–305(c) or the expiration of the four-month period, it remains perfected thereafter. If the security interest does not become perfected under the law of the other jurisdiction before the earlier time or event, it becomes unperfected and is deemed never to have been perfected as against a purchaser of the collateral for value.

(i)   **[Effect of change in governing law on financing statement filed against original debtor.]** If a financing statement naming an original debtor is filed pursuant to the law of the jurisdiction designated in Section 9–301(1) or 9–305(c) and the new debtor is located in another jurisdiction, the following rules apply:

(1)   The financing statement is effective to perfect a security interest in collateral acquired by the new debtor before, and within four months after, the new debtor becomes bound under Section 9–203(d), if the financing statement would have been effective to perfect a security interest in the collateral had the collateral been acquired by the original debtor.

(2)   A security interest perfected by the financing statement and which becomes perfected under the law of the other jurisdiction before the earlier of the time the financing statement would have become ineffective under the law of the jurisdiction designated in Section 9–301(1) or 9–305(c) or the expiration of the four-month period remains perfected thereafter. A security interest that is perfected by the financing statement but which does not become perfected under the law of the other jurisdiction before the earlier time or event becomes unperfected and is deemed never to have been perfected as against a purchaser of the collateral for value.

As amended in 2010.

Official Comment

1.   **Source.** Former Section 9–103(1)(d), (2)(b), (3)(e), as modified.

2.   **Continued Perfection.** Subsections (a) through (g) deal with continued perfection of security interests that have been perfected under the law of another jurisdiction. The fact that the law of a particular jurisdiction ceases to govern perfection under Sections 9–301 through 9–307 does not necessarily mean that a security interest perfected under that law automatically becomes unperfected. To the contrary: This section generally provides that a security interest perfected under the law of one jurisdiction remains perfected for a fixed period of time (four months or one year, depending on the circumstances), even though the jurisdiction whose law governs perfection changes. However, cessation of perfection under the law of the original jurisdiction cuts short the fixed period. The four-month and one-year periods are long enough for a secured party to discover in most cases that the law of a different jurisdiction governs perfection and to reperfect (typically by filing) under the law of that jurisdiction. If a secured party properly reperfects a security interest before it becomes unperfected under subsection (a), then the security interest remains perfected continuously thereafter. See subsection (b).

Example 1:   Debtor is a general partnership whose chief executive office is in Pennsylvania. Lender perfects a security interest in Debtor's equipment by filing in Pennsylvania on May 15, 2002. On April 1, 2005, without Lender's knowledge, Debtor moves its chief executive office to New Jersey. Lender's security interest remains perfected for four months after the move. See subsection (a)(2).

Example 2:   Debtor is a general partnership whose chief executive office is in Pennsylvania. Lender perfects a security interest in Debtor's equipment by filing in Pennsylvania on May 15, 2002. On April 1, 2007, without Lender's knowledge, Debtor moves its chief executive office to New Jersey. Lender's security interest remains perfected only through May 14, 2007, when the effectiveness of the filed financing statement lapses. See subsection (a)(1). Although, under these facts, Lender would have only a short period of time to discover that Debtor had relocated and to reperfect under New Jersey law, Lender could have protected itself by filing a continuation statement in Pennsylvania before Debtor relocated. By doing so, Lender would have prevented lapse and allowed itself the full four months to discover Debtor's new location and refile there or, if Debtor is in default, to perfect by taking possession of the equipment.

Example 3:   Under the facts of Example 2, Lender files a financing statement in New Jersey before the effectiveness of the Pennsylvania financing statement lapses. Under subsection (b), Lender's security interest is continuously perfected beyond May 14, 2007, for a period determined by New Jersey's Article 9.

Subsection (a)(3) allows a one-year period in which to reperfect. The longer period is necessary, because, even with the exercise of due diligence, the secured party may be unable to discover that the collateral has been transferred to a person located in another jurisdiction. In any event, the period is cut short if the financing statement becomes ineffective under the law of the jurisdiction in which it is filed.

> **Example 4:**   Debtor is a Pennsylvania corporation. On January 1, Lender perfects a security interest in Debtor's equipment by filing in Pennsylvania. Debtor's shareholders decide to "reincorporate" in Delaware. On March 1, they form a Delaware corporation (Newcorp) into which they merge Debtor. The merger effectuates a transfer of the collateral from Debtor to Newcorp, which thereby becomes a debtor and is located in another jurisdiction. Under subsection (a)(3), the security interest remains perfected for one year after the merger. If a financing statement is filed in Delaware against Newcorp within the year following the merger, then the security interest remains perfected thereafter for a period determined by Delaware's Article 9.

Note that although Newcorp is a "new debtor" as defined in Section 9–102, the application of subsection (a)(3) is not limited to transferees who are new debtors. Note also that, under Section 9–507, the financing statement naming Debtor remains effective even though Newcorp has become the debtor.

> Subsection (a) addresses security interests that are perfected (i.e., that have attached and as to which any required perfection step has been taken) before the debtor changes its location. Subsection (h) applies to security interests that have not attached before the location changes. See Comment 7.

3.   **Retroactive Unperfection.** Subsection (b) sets forth the consequences of the failure to reperfect before perfection ceases under subsection (a): the security interest becomes unperfected prospectively and, as against purchasers for value, including buyers and secured parties, but not as against donees or lien creditors, retroactively. The rule applies to agricultural liens, as well. See also Section 9–515 (taking the same approach with respect to lapse). Although this approach creates the potential for circular priorities, the alternative—retroactive unperfection against lien creditors—would create substantial and unjustifiable preference risks.

> **Example 5:**   Under the facts of Example 4, six months after the merger, Buyer bought from Newcorp some equipment formerly owned by Debtor. At the time of the purchase, Buyer took subject to Lender's perfected security interest, of which Buyer was unaware. See Section 9–315(a)(1). However, subsection (b) provides that if Lender fails to reperfect in Delaware within a year after the merger, its security interest becomes unperfected and is deemed never to have been perfected against Buyer. Having given value and received delivery of the equipment without knowledge of the security interest and before it was perfected, Buyer would take free of the security interest. See Section 9–317(b).

> **Example 6:**   Under the facts of Example 4, one month before the merger, Debtor created a security interest in certain equipment in favor of Financer, who perfected by filing in Pennsylvania. At that time, Financer's security interest is subordinate to Lender's. See Section 9–322(a)(1). Financer reperfects by filing in Delaware within a year after the merger, but Lender fails to do so. Under subsection (b), Lender's security interest is deemed never to have been perfected against Financer, a purchaser for value. Consequently, under Section 9–322(a)(2), Financer's security interest is now senior.

Of course, the expiration of the time period specified in subsection (a) does not of itself prevent the secured party from later reperfecting under the law of the new jurisdiction. If the secured party does so, however, there will be a gap in perfection, and the secured party may lose priority as a result. Thus, in Example 6, if Lender perfects by filing in Delaware more than one year under the merger, it will have a new date of filing and perfection for purposes of Section 9–322(a)(1). Financer's security interest, whose perfection dates back to the filing in Pennsylvania under subsection (b), will remain senior.

4.   **Possessory Security Interests.** Subsection (c) deals with continued perfection of possessory security interests. It applies not only to security interests perfected solely by the secured party's having taken possession of the collateral. It also applies to security interests perfected by a method that includes as an element of perfection the secured party's having taken possession, such as perfection by taking delivery of a certificated security in registered form, see Section 9–313(a), and perfection by obtaining control over a certificated security. See Section 9–314(a).

5.   **Goods Covered by Certificate of Title.** Subsections (d) and (e) address continued perfection of a security interest in goods covered by a certificate of title. The following examples explain the operation of those subsections.

> **Example 7:**   Debtor's automobile is covered by a certificate of title issued by Illinois. Lender perfects a security interest in the automobile by complying with Illinois' certificate-of-title statute. Thereafter, Debtor applies for a certificate of title in Indiana. Six months thereafter, Creditor acquires a judicial lien on the automobile. Under Section 9–303(b), Illinois law ceases to govern perfection; rather, once Debtor delivers the application and applicable fee to the appropriate Indiana authority, Indiana law governs. Nevertheless,

under Indiana's Section 9–316(d), Lender's security interest remains perfected until it would become unperfected under Illinois law had no certificate of title been issued by Indiana. (For example, Illinois' certificate-of-title statute may provide that the surrender of an Illinois certificate of title in connection with the issuance of a certificate of title by another jurisdiction causes a security interest noted thereon to become unperfected.) If Lender's security interest remains perfected, it is senior to Creditor's judicial lien.

Example 8:   Under the facts in Example 7, five months after Debtor applies for an Indiana certificate of title, Debtor sells the automobile to Buyer. Under subsection (e)(2), because Lender did not reperfect within the four months after the goods became covered by the Indiana certificate of title, Lender's security interest is deemed never to have been perfected against Buyer. Under Section 9–317(b), Buyer is likely to take free of the security interest. Lender could have protected itself by perfecting its security interest either under Indiana's certificate-of-title statute, see Section 9–311, or, if it had a right to do so under an agreement or Section 9–609, by taking possession of the automobile. See Section 9–313(b).

The results in Examples 7 and 8 do not depend on the fact that the original perfection was achieved by notation on a certificate of title. Subsection (d) applies regardless of the method by which a security interest is perfected under the law of another jurisdiction when the goods became covered by a certificate of title from this State.

Section 9–337 affords protection to a limited class of persons buying or acquiring a security interest in the goods while a security interest is perfected under the law of another jurisdiction but after this State has issued a clean certificate of title.

6.   **Deposit Accounts, Letter-of-Credit Rights, and Investment Property.** Subsections (f) and (g) address changes in the jurisdiction of a bank, issuer of an uncertificated security, issuer of or nominated person under a letter of credit, securities intermediary, and commodity intermediary. The provisions are analogous to those of subsections (a) and (b).

7.   **Security Interests that Attach after Debtor Changes Location.** In contrast to subsections (a) and (b), which address security interests that are perfected (i.e., that have attached and as to which any required perfection step has been taken) before the debtor changes its location, subsection (h) addresses security interests that attach within four months after the debtor changes its location. Under subsection (h), a filed financing statement that would have been effective to perfect a security interest in the collateral if the debtor had not changed its location is effective to perfect a security interest in collateral acquired within four months after the relocation.

Example 9:   Debtor, an individual whose principal residence is in Pennsylvania, grants to Lender a security interest in Debtor's existing and after-acquired inventory. Lender perfects the security interest by filing a proper financing statement in Pennsylvania on January 2, 2014. On March 31, 2014, Debtor's principal residence is relocated to New Jersey. Upon the relocation, New Jersey law governs perfection of a security interest in Debtor's inventory. See Sections 9–301, 9–307. Under New Jersey's Section 9–316(a), Lender's security interest in Debtor's inventory on hand at the time of the relocation remains perfected for four months thereafter. Had Debtor not relocated, the financing statement filed in Pennsylvania would have been effective to perfect Lender's security interest in inventory acquired by Debtor after March 31, 2014. Accordingly, under subsection (h), the financing statement is effective to perfect Lender's security interest in inventory that Debtor acquires within the four months after Debtor's location changed.

In Example 9, Lender's security interest in the inventory acquired within the four months after Debtor's relocation will be perfected when it attaches. It will remain perfected if, before the expiration of the four-month period, the security interest is perfected under the law of New Jersey. Otherwise, the security interest will become unperfected at the end of the four-month period and will be deemed never to have been perfected as against a purchaser for value. See subsection (h)(2).

8.   **Collateral Acquired by New Debtor.** Subsection (i) is similar to subsection (h). Whereas subsection (h) addresses security interests that attach within four months after a debtor changes its location, subsection (i) addresses security interests that attach within four months after a new debtor becomes bound as debtor by a security agreement entered into by another person. Subsection (i) also addresses collateral acquired by the new debtor before it becomes bound.

Example 10:   Debtor, a Pennsylvania corporation, grants to Lender a security interest in Debtor's existing and after-acquired inventory. Lender perfects the security interest by filing a proper financing statement in Pennsylvania on January 2, 2014. On March 31, 2014, Debtor merges into Survivor, a Delaware corporation. Because Survivor is located in Delaware, Delaware law governs perfection of a security interest in Survivor's inventory. See Sections 9–301, 9–307. Under Delaware's Section 9–316(a), Lender's security interest in the inventory that Survivor acquired from Debtor remains perfected for one year after the transfer. See Comment 2. By virtue of the merger, Survivor becomes bound as debtor by Debtor's security agreement. See Section 9–203(d). As a consequence, Lender's security interest attaches to all of Survivor's inventory under Section 9–203, and Lender's collateral now includes inventory in which Debtor never had an interest. The financing statement filed in Pennsylvania against Debtor is effective under Delaware's Section 9–316(i) to perfect Lender's security interest in inventory that Survivor acquired before, and within the four months after, becoming bound as debtor by Debtor's security agreement. This is because the financing statement filed in Pennsylvania would have been effective to perfect Lender's security interest in this collateral had Debtor, rather than Survivor, acquired it.

If the financing statement is effective, Lender's security interest in the collateral that Survivor acquired before, and within four months after, Survivor became bound as debtor will be perfected upon attachment. It will remain perfected if, before the expiration of the four-month period, the security interest is perfected under Delaware law. Otherwise, the security interest will become unperfected at the end of the four-month period and will be deemed never to have been perfected as against a purchaser for value.

Section 9–325 contains special rules governing the priority of competing security interests in collateral that is transferred, by merger or otherwise, to a new debtor or other person who becomes a debtor with respect to the collateral. Section 9–326 contains special rules governing the priority of competing security interests in collateral acquired by a new debtor other than by transfer from the original debtor.

9.   **Agricultural Liens.** This section does not apply to agricultural liens.

Example 11:   Supplier holds an agricultural lien on corn. The lien arises under an Iowa statute. Supplier perfects by filing a financing statement in Iowa, where the corn is located. See Section 9–302. Debtor stores the corn in Missouri. Assume the Iowa agricultural lien survives or an agricultural lien arises under Missouri law (matters that this Article does not govern). Once the corn is located in Missouri, Missouri becomes the jurisdiction whose law governs perfection. See Section 9–302. Thus, the agricultural lien will not be perfected unless Supplier files a financing statement in Missouri.

As amended in 2000 and 2010.

[SUBPART 3. PRIORITY]

§ 9–317.   Interests That Take Priority Over or Take Free of Security Interest or Agricultural Lien.

(a)   **[Conflicting security interests and rights of lien creditors.]** A security interest or agricultural lien is subordinate to the rights of:

(1)   a person entitled to priority under Section 9–322; and

(2)   except as otherwise provided in subsection (e), a person that becomes a lien creditor before the earlier of the time:

(A)   the security interest or agricultural lien is perfected; or

(B)   one of the conditions specified in Section 9–203(b)(3) is met and a financing statement covering the collateral is filed.

(b)   **[Buyers that receive delivery.]** Except as otherwise provided in subsection (e), a buyer, other than a secured party, of tangible chattel paper, tangible documents, goods, instruments, or a certificated security takes free of a security interest or agricultural lien if the buyer gives value and receives delivery of the collateral without knowledge of the security interest or agricultural lien and before it is perfected.

(c)   **[Lessees that receive delivery.]** Except as otherwise provided in subsection (e), a lessee of goods takes free of a security interest or agricultural lien if the lessee gives value and receives delivery of the collateral without knowledge of the security interest or agricultural lien and before it is perfected.

(d)   **[Licensees and buyers of certain collateral.]** A licensee of a general intangible or a buyer, other than a secured party, of collateral other than tangible chattel paper, tangible documents, goods, instruments, or a certificated security takes free of a security interest if the licensee or buyer gives value without knowledge of the security interest and before it is perfected.

(e)   **[Purchase-money security interest.]** Except as otherwise provided in Sections 9–320 and 9–321, if a person files a financing statement with respect to a purchase-money security interest before or within 20 days after the debtor receives delivery of the collateral, the security interest takes priority over the rights of a buyer, lessee, or lien creditor which arise between the time the security interest attaches and the time of filing.

As amended in 2000, 2003, and 2010.

Official Comment

1.   **Source.** Former Sections 9–301, 2A–307(2).

2.   **Scope of This Section.** As did former Section 9–301, this section lists the classes of persons who take priority over, or take free of, an unperfected security interest. Section 9–308 explains when a security interest or agricultural lien is "perfected." A security interest that has attached (see Section 9–203) but as to which a required perfection step has not been taken is "unperfected." Certain provisions have been moved from former Section 9–301. The definition of "lien creditor" now appears in Section 9–102, and the rules governing priority in future advances are found in Section 9–323.

3.   **Competing Security Interests.** Section 9–322 states general rules for determining priority among conflicting security interests and refers to other sections that state special rules of priority in a variety of situations. The security interests given priority under Section 9–322 and the other sections to which it refers take priority in general even over a perfected security interest. *A fortiori* they take priority over an unperfected security interest.

4.   **Filed but Unattached Security Interest vs. Lien Creditor.** Under former Section 9–301(1)(b), a lien creditor's rights had priority over an unperfected security interest. Perfection required attachment (former Section 9–303), and attachment required the giving of value (former Section 9–203). It followed that, if a secured party had filed a financing statement, but the debtor had not entered into a security agreement and value had not yet been given, an intervening lien creditor whose lien arose after filing but before attachment of the security interest acquired rights that are senior to those of the secured party who later gives value. This result comported with the *nemo dat* concept: When the security interest attached, the collateral was already subject to the judicial lien.

On the other hand, this approach treated the first secured advance differently from all other advances, even in circumstances in which a security agreement covering the collateral had been entered into before the judicial lien attached. The special rule for future advances in former Section 9–301(4) (substantially reproduced in Section 9–323(b)) afforded priority to a discretionary advance made by a secured party within 45 days after the lien creditor's rights arose as long as the secured party was "perfected" when the lien creditor's lien arose—i.e., as long as the advance was not the first one and an earlier advance had been made.

Subsection (a)(2) revises former Section 9–301(1)(b) and, in appropriate cases, treats the first advance the same as subsequent advances. More specifically, a judicial lien that arises after the security-agreement condition of Section 9–203(b)(3) is satisfied and a financing statement is filed, but before the security interest attaches and becomes perfected, is subordinate to all advances secured by the security interest, even the first advance, except as otherwise provided in Section 9–323(b). However, if the security interest becomes unperfected (e.g., because the effectiveness of the filed financing statement lapses) before the judicial lien arises, the security interest is subordinate. If a financing statement is filed but a security interest does not attach, then no priority contest arises. The lien creditor has the only enforceable claim to the property.

5.   **Security Interest of Consignor or Receivables Buyer vs. Lien Creditor.** Section 1–201(b)(35) defines "security interest" to include the interest of most true consignors of goods and the interest of most buyers of certain receivables (accounts, chattel paper, payment intangibles, and promissory notes). A consignee of goods or a seller of accounts or chattel paper each is deemed to have rights in the collateral which a lien creditor may reach, as long as the competing security interest of the consignor or buyer is unperfected. This is so even though, as between the consignor and the debtor-consignee, the latter has only limited rights, and, as between the buyer and debtor-seller, the latter does not have any rights in the collateral. See Sections 9–318 (seller), 9–319 (consignee). Security interests arising from sales of payment intangibles and promissory notes are automatically perfected. See Section 9–309. Accordingly, a subsequent judicial lien always would be subordinate to the rights of a buyer of those types of receivables.

6.   **Purchasers Other Than Secured Parties.** Subsections (b), (c), and (d) afford priority over an unperfected security interest to certain purchasers (other than secured parties) of collateral. They derive from former Sections 9–301(1)(c), 2A–307(2), and 9–301(d). Former Section 9–301(1)(c) and (1)(d) provided that

unperfected security interests are "subordinate" to the rights of certain purchasers. But, as former Comment 9 suggested, the practical effect of subordination in this context is that the purchaser takes free of the security interest. To avoid any possible misinterpretation, subsections (b) and (d) of this section use the phrase "takes free."

Subsection (b) governs goods, as well as intangibles of the type whose transfer is effected by physical delivery of the representative piece of paper (tangible chattel paper, tangible documents, instruments, and security certificates). To obtain priority, a buyer must both give value and receive delivery of the collateral without knowledge of the existing security interest and before perfection. Even if the buyer gave value without knowledge and before perfection, the buyer would take subject to the security interest if perfection occurred before physical delivery of the collateral to the buyer. Subsection (c) contains a similar rule with respect to lessees of goods. Note that a lessee of goods in ordinary course of business takes free of all security interests created by the lessor, even if perfected. See Section 9–321.

Normally, there will be no question when a buyer of tangible chattel paper, tangible documents, instruments, or security certificates "receives delivery" of the property. See Section 1–201 (defining "delivery"). However, sometimes a buyer or lessee of goods, such as complex machinery, takes delivery of the goods in stages and completes assembly at its own location. Under those circumstances, the buyer or lessee "receives delivery" within the meaning of subsections (b) and (c) when, after an inspection of the portion of the goods remaining with the seller or lessor, it would be apparent to a potential lender to the seller or lessor that another person might have an interest in the goods.

The rule of subsection (b) obviously is not appropriate where the collateral consists of intangibles and there is no representative piece of paper whose physical delivery is the only or the customary method of transfer. Therefore, with respect to such intangibles (including accounts, electronic chattel paper, electronic documents, general intangibles, and investment property other than certificated securities), subsection (d) gives priority to any buyer who gives value without knowledge, and before perfection, of the security interest. A licensee of a general intangible takes free of an unperfected security interest in the general intangible under the same circumstances. Note that a licensee of a general intangible in ordinary course of business takes rights under a nonexclusive license free of security interests created by the licensor, even if perfected. See Section 9–321.

Unless Section 9–109 excludes the transaction from this Article, a buyer of accounts, chattel paper, payment intangibles, or promissory notes is a "secured party" (defined in Section 9–102), and subsections (b) and (d) do not determine priority of the security interest created by the sale. Rather, the priority rules generally applicable to competing security interests apply. See Section 9–322.

7. **Agricultural Liens.** Subsections (a), (b), and (c) subordinate unperfected agricultural liens in the same manner in which they subordinate unperfected security interests.

8. **Purchase-Money Security Interests.** Subsection (e) derives from former Section 9–301(2). It provides that, if a purchase-money security interest is perfected by filing no later than 20 days after the debtor receives delivery of the collateral, the security interest takes priority over the rights of buyers, lessees, or lien creditors which arise between the time the security interest attaches and the time of filing. Subsection (e) differs from former Section 9–301(2) in two significant respects. First, subsection (e) protects a purchase-money security interest against all buyers and lessees, not just against transferees in bulk. Second, subsection (e) conditions this protection on filing within 20, as opposed to ten, days after delivery.

Section 9–311(b) provides that compliance with the perfection requirements of a statute or treaty described in Section 9–311(a) "is equivalent to the filing of a financing statement." It follows that a person who perfects a security interest in goods covered by a certificate of title by complying with the perfection requirements of an applicable certificate-of-title statute "files a financing statement" within the meaning of subsection(e).

As amended in 1999, 2000, 2003, and 2010.

§ 9–318.   No Interest Retained in Right to Payment That Is Sold; Rights and Title of Seller of Account or Chattel Paper With Respect to Creditors and Purchasers.

(a) **[Seller retains no interest.]** A debtor that has sold an account, chattel paper, payment intangible, or promissory note does not retain a legal or equitable interest in the collateral sold.

(b) **[Deemed rights of debtor if buyer's security interest unperfected.]** For purposes of determining the rights of creditors of, and purchasers for value of an account or chattel paper from, a debtor that has sold an account or chattel paper, while the buyer's security interest is unperfected, the debtor is deemed to have rights and title to the account or chattel paper identical to those the debtor sold.

Official Comment

1. **Source.** New.

2. **Sellers of Accounts, Chattel Paper, Payment Intangibles, and Promissory Notes.** Section 1–201(b)(35) defines "security interest" to include the interest of a buyer of accounts, chattel paper, payment intangibles, or promissory notes. See also Section 9–109(a) and Comment 5. Subsection (a) makes explicit what was implicit, but perfectly obvious, under former Article 9: The fact that a sale of an account or chattel paper gives rise to a "security interest" does not imply that the seller retains an interest in the property that has been sold. To the contrary, a seller of an account or chattel paper retains no interest whatsoever in the property to the extent that it has been sold. Subsection (a) also applies to sales of payment intangibles and promissory notes, transactions that were not covered by former Article 9. Neither this Article nor the definition of "security interest" in Section 1–201 provides rules for distinguishing sales transactions from those that create a security interest securing an obligation.

3. **Buyers of Accounts and Chattel Paper.** Another aspect of sales of accounts and chattel paper also was implicit, and equally obvious, under former Article 9: If the buyer's security interest is unperfected, then for purposes of determining the rights of certain third parties, the seller (debtor) is deemed to have all rights and title that the seller sold. The seller is deemed to have these rights even though, as between the parties, it has sold all its rights to the buyer. Subsection (b) makes this explicit. As a consequence of subsection (b), if the buyer's security interest is unperfected, the seller can transfer, and the creditors of the seller can reach, the account or chattel paper as if it had not been sold.

Example: Debtor sells accounts or chattel paper to Buyer-1 and retains no interest in them. Buyer-1 does not file a financing statement. Debtor then sells the same receivables to Buyer-2. Buyer-2 files a proper financing statement. Having sold the receivables to Buyer-1, Debtor would not have any rights in the collateral so as to permit Buyer-2's security (ownership) interest to attach. Nevertheless, under this section, for purposes of determining the rights of purchasers for value from Debtor, Debtor is deemed to have the rights that Debtor sold. Accordingly, Buyer-2's security interest attaches, is perfected by the filing, and, under Section 9–322, is senior to Buyer-1's interest.

4. **Effect of Perfection.** If the security interest of a buyer of accounts or chattel paper is perfected the usual result would take effect: transferees from and creditors of the seller could not acquire an interest in the sold accounts or chattel paper. The same result generally would occur if payment intangibles or promissory notes were sold, inasmuch as the buyer's security interest is automatically perfected under Section 9–309. However, in certain circumstances a purchaser who takes possession of a promissory note will achieve priority, under Sections 9–330 or 9–331, over the security interest of an earlier buyer of the promissory note. It necessarily follows that the seller in those circumstances retains the power to transfer the promissory note, as if it had not been sold, to a purchaser who obtains priority under either of those sections. See Section 9–203(b)(3), Comment 6.

As amended in 2010.

§ 9–319. Rights and Title of Consignee With Respect to Creditors and Purchasers.

(a) **[Consignee has consignor's rights.]** Except as otherwise provided in subsection (b), for purposes of determining the rights of creditors of, and purchasers for value of goods from, a consignee, while the goods are in the possession of the consignee, the consignee is deemed to have rights and title to the goods identical to those the consignor had or had power to transfer.

(b) **[Applicability of other law.]** For purposes of determining the rights of a creditor of a consignee, law other than this article determines the rights and title of a consignee while goods are in the consignee's possession if, under this part, a perfected security interest held by the consignor would have priority over the rights of the creditor.

Official Comment

1. **Source.** New.

2. **Consignments.** This section takes an approach to consignments similar to that taken by Section 9–318 with respect to buyers of accounts and chattel paper. Revised Section 1–201(b)(35) defines "security interest" to include the interest of a consignor of goods under many true consignments. Section 9–319(a) provides that, for purposes of determining the rights of certain third parties, the consignee is deemed to acquire all rights and title that the consignor had, if the consignor's security interest is unperfected. The consignee acquires these rights even though, as between the parties, it purchases a limited interest in the goods (as would be the case in a true

783

consignment, under which the consignee acquires only the interest of a bailee). As a consequence of this section, creditors of the consignee can acquire judicial liens and security interests in the goods while the goods are in the possession of the consignee.

The termination of a consignment does not *ipso facto* cause the consignee to lose its status as such with respect to the consignee's creditors whose claims to the goods arose before termination. Return of the goods to the consignor causes the consignee to lose its deemed rights and title, but it does not discharge a security interest or judicial lien that attached while the consignee was in possession. See PEB Commentary No. 20, dated January 24, 2019.

Insofar as creditors of the consignee are concerned, this Article to a considerable extent reformulates the former law, which appeared in former Sections 2–326 and 9–114, without changing the results. However, neither Article 2 nor former Article 9 specifically addresses the rights of non-ordinary course buyers from the consignee. Former Section 9–114 contained priority rules applicable to security interests in consigned goods. Under this Article, the priority rules for purchase-money security interests in inventory apply to consignments. See Section 9–103(d). Accordingly, a special section containing priority rules for consignments no longer is needed. Section 9–317 determines whether the rights of a judicial lien creditor are senior to the interest of the consignor, Sections 9–322 and 9–324 govern competing security interests in consigned goods, and Sections 9–317, 9–315, and 9–320 determine whether a buyer takes free of the consignor's interest.

The following example explains the operation of this section:

Example 1:   SP-1 delivers goods to Debtor in a transaction constituting a "consignment" as defined in Section 9–102. SP-1 does not file a financing statement. Debtor then grants a security interest in the goods to SP-2. SP-2 files a proper financing statement. Assuming Debtor is a mere bailee, as in a "true" consignment, Debtor would not have any rights in the collateral (beyond those of a bailee) so as to permit SP-2's security interest to attach to any greater rights. Nevertheless, under this section, for purposes of determining the rights of Debtor's creditors, Debtor is deemed to acquire SP-1's rights. Accordingly, SP-2's security interest attaches, is perfected by the filing, and, under Section 9–322, is senior to SP-1's interest.

3.   **Effect of Perfection.** Subsection (b) contains a special rule with respect to consignments that are perfected. If application of this Article would result in the consignor having priority over a competing creditor, then other law determines the rights and title of the consignee.

Example 2:   SP-1 delivers goods to Debtor in a transaction constituting a "consignment" as defined in Section 9–102. SP-1 files a proper financing statement. Debtor then grants a security interest in the goods to SP-2. Under Section 9–322, SP-1's security interest is senior to SP-2's. Subsection (b) indicates that, for purposes of determining SP-2's rights, other law determines the rights and title of the consignee. If, for example, a consignee obtains only the special property of a bailee, then SP-2's security interest would attach only to that special property.

Example 3:   SP-1 obtains a security interest in all Debtor's existing and after-acquired inventory. SP-1 perfects its security interest with a proper filing. Then SP-2 delivers goods to Debtor in a transaction constituting a "consignment" as defined in Section 9–102. SP-2 files a proper financing statement but does not send notification to SP-1 under Section 9–324(b). Accordingly, SP-2's security interest is junior to SP-1's under Section 9–322(a). Under Section 9–319(a), Debtor is deemed to have the consignor's rights and title, so that SP-1's security interest attaches to SP-2's ownership interest in the goods. Thereafter, Debtor grants a security interest in the goods to SP-3, and SP-3 perfects by filing. Because SP-2's perfected security interest is senior to SP-3's under Section 9–322(a), Section 9–319(b) applies: Other law determines Debtor's rights and title to the goods insofar as SP-3 is concerned, and SP-3's security interest attaches to those rights.

As amended in 2010 and 2019.

§ 9–320.   Buyer of Goods.

(a)   **[Buyer in ordinary course of business.]** Except as otherwise provided in subsection (e), a buyer in ordinary course of business, other than a person buying farm products from a person engaged in farming operations, takes free of a security interest created by the buyer's seller, even if the security interest is perfected and the buyer knows of its existence.

(b)   **[Buyer of consumer goods.]** Except as otherwise provided in subsection (e), a buyer of goods from a person who used or bought the goods for use primarily for personal, family, or household purposes takes free of a security interest, even if perfected, if the buyer buys:

(1)   without knowledge of the security interest;

(2)   for value;

(3)   primarily for the buyer's personal, family, or household purposes; and

(4)   before the filing of a financing statement covering the goods.

(c)   **[Effectiveness of filing for subsection (b).]** To the extent that it affects the priority of a security interest over a buyer of goods under subsection (b), the period of effectiveness of a filing made in the jurisdiction in which the seller is located is governed by Section 9–316(a) and (b).

(d)   **[Buyer in ordinary course of business at wellhead or minehead.]** A buyer in ordinary course of business buying oil, gas, or other minerals at the wellhead or minehead or after extraction takes free of an interest arising out of an encumbrance.

(e)   **[Possessory security interest not affected.]** Subsections (a) and (b) do not affect a security interest in goods in the possession of the secured party under Section 9–313.

Official Comment

1.   **Source.** Former Section 9–307.

2.   **Scope of This Section.** This section states when buyers of goods take free of a security interest even though perfected. Of course, a buyer who takes free of a perfected security interest takes free of an unperfected one. Section 9–317 should be consulted to determine what purchasers, in addition to the buyers covered in this section, take free of an unperfected security interest. Article 2 states general rules on purchase of goods from a seller with defective or voidable title (Section 2–403).

3.   **Buyers in Ordinary Course.** Subsection (a) derives from former Section 9–307(1). The definition of "buyer in ordinary course of business" in Section 1–201 restricts its application to buyers "from a person, other than a pawnbroker, in the business of selling goods of that kind." Thus subsection (a) applies primarily to inventory collateral. The subsection further excludes from its operation buyers of "farm products" (defined in Section 9–102) from a person engaged in farming operations. The buyer in ordinary course of business is defined as one who buys goods "in good faith, without knowledge that the sale violates the rights of another person and in the ordinary course." Subsection (a) provides that such a buyer takes free of a security interest, even though perfected, and even though the buyer knows the security interest exists. Reading the definition together with the rule of law results in the buyer's taking free if the buyer merely knows that a security interest covers the goods but taking subject if the buyer knows, in addition, that the sale violates a term in an agreement with the secured party.

As did former Section 9–307(1), subsection (a) applies only to security interests created by the seller of the goods to the buyer in ordinary course. However, under certain circumstances a buyer in ordinary course who buys goods that were encumbered with a security interest created by a person other than the seller may take free of the security interest, as Example 2 explains. See also Comment 6, below.

Example 1:   Manufacturer, who is in the business of manufacturing appliances, owns manufacturing equipment subject to a perfected security interest in favor of Lender. Manufacturer sells the equipment to Dealer, who is in the business of buying and selling used equipment. Buyer buys the equipment from Dealer. Even if Buyer qualifies as a buyer in the ordinary course of business, Buyer does not take free of Lender's security interest under subsection (a), because Dealer did not create the security interest; Manufacturer did.

Example 2:   Manufacturer, who is in the business of manufacturing appliances, owns manufacturing equipment subject to a perfected security interest in favor of Lender. Manufacturer sells the equipment to Dealer, who is in the business of buying and selling used equipment. Lender learns of the sale but does nothing to assert its security interest. Buyer buys the equipment from Dealer. Inasmuch as Lender's acquiescence constitutes an "entrusting" of the goods to Dealer within the meaning of Section 2–403(3) Buyer takes free of Lender's security interest under Section 2–403(2) if Buyer qualifies as a buyer in ordinary course of business.

4.   **Buyers of Farm Products.** This section does not enable a buyer of farm products to take free of a security interest created by the seller, even if the buyer is a buyer in ordinary course of business. However, a buyer of farm products may take free of a security interest under Section 1324 of the Food Security Act of 1985, 7 U.S.C. § 1631.

5.   **Buyers of Consumer Goods.** Subsection (b), which derives from former Section 9–307(2), deals with buyers of collateral that the debtor-seller holds as "consumer goods" (defined in Section 9–102). Under Section 9–

309(1), a purchase-money interest in consumer goods, except goods that are subject to a statute or treaty described in Section 9–311(a) (such as automobiles that are subject to a certificate-of-title statute), is perfected automatically upon attachment. There is no need to file to perfect. Under subsection (b) a buyer of consumer goods takes free of a security interest, even though perfected, if the buyer buys (1) without knowledge of the security interest, (2) for value, (3) primarily for the buyer's own personal, family, or household purposes, and (4) before a financing statement is filed.

As to purchase money-security interests which are perfected without filing under Section 9–309(1): A secured party may file a financing statement, although filing is not required for perfection. If the secured party does file, all buyers take subject to the security interest. If the secured party does not file, a buyer who meets the qualifications stated in the preceding paragraph takes free of the security interest.

As to security interests for which a perfection step is required: This category includes all non-purchase-money security interests, and all security interests, whether or not purchase-money, in goods subject to a statute or treaty described in Section 9–311(a), such as automobiles covered by a certificate-of-title statute. As long as the required perfection step has not been taken and the security interest remains unperfected, not only the buyers described in subsection (b) but also the purchasers described in Section 9–317 will take free of the security interest. After a financing statement has been filed or the perfection requirements of the applicable certificate-of-title statute have been complied with (compliance is the equivalent of filing a financing statement; see Section 9–311(b)), all subsequent buyers, under the rule of subsection (b), are subject to the security interest.

The rights of a buyer under subsection (b) turn on whether a financing statement has been filed against consumer goods. Occasionally, a debtor changes his or her location after a filing is made. Subsection (c), which derives from former Section 9–103(1)(d)(iii), deals with the continued effectiveness of the filing under those circumstances. It adopts the rules of Sections 9–316(a) and (b). These rules are explained in the Comments to that section.

6. **Authorized Dispositions.** The limitations that subsections (a) and (b) impose on the persons who may take free of a security interest apply of course only to unauthorized sales by the debtor. If the secured party authorized the sale in an express agreement or otherwise, the buyer takes free under Section 9–315(a) without regard to the limitations of this section. (That section also states the right of a secured party to the proceeds of a sale, authorized or unauthorized.) Moreover, the buyer also takes free if the secured party waived or otherwise is precluded from asserting its security interest against the buyer. See Section 1–103.

7. **Oil, Gas, and Other Minerals.** Under subsection (d), a buyer in ordinary course of business of minerals at the wellhead or minehead or after extraction takes free of a security interest created by the seller. Specifically, it provides that qualified buyers take free not only of Article 9 security interests but also of interests "arising out of an encumbrance." As defined in Section 9–102, the term "encumbrance" means "a right, other than an ownership interest, in real property." Thus, to the extent that a mortgage encumbers minerals not only before but also after extraction, subsection (d) enables a buyer in ordinary course of the minerals to take free of the mortgage. This subsection does not, however, enable these buyers to take free of interests arising out of ownership interests in the real property. This issue is significant only in a minority of states. Several of them have adopted special statutes and nonuniform amendments to Article 9 to provide special protections to mineral owners, whose interests often are highly fractionalized in the case of oil and gas. See Terry I. Cross, *Oil and Gas Product Liens— Statutory Security Interests for Producers and Royalty Owners Under the Statutes of Kansas, New Mexico, Oklahoma, Texas and Wyoming,* 50 Consumer Fin. L. Q. Rep. 418 (1996). Inasmuch as a complete resolution of the issue would require the addition of complex provisions to this Article, and there are good reasons to believe that a uniform solution would not be feasible, this Article leaves its resolution to other legislation.

8. **Possessory Security Interests.** Subsection (e) is new. It rejects the holding of *Tanbro Fabrics Corp. v. Deering Milliken, Inc.,* 350 N.E.2d 590 (N.Y. 1976) and, together with Section 9–317(b), prevents a buyer of goods collateral from taking free of a security interest if the collateral is in the possession of the secured party. "The secured party" referred in subsection (e) is the holder of the security interest referred to in subsection (a) or (b). Section 9–313 determines whether a secured party is in possession for purposes of this section. Under some circumstances, Section 9–313 provides that a secured party is in possession of collateral even if the collateral is in the physical possession of a third party.

§ 9–321. Licensee of General Intangible and Lessee of Goods in Ordinary Course of Business.

(a) **["Licensee in ordinary course of business."]** In this section, "licensee in ordinary course of business" means a person that becomes a licensee of a general intangible in good faith, without knowledge that the license violates the rights of another person in the general intangible, and in the ordinary course from a person in the business of licensing general intangibles of that kind. A person becomes a licensee in the ordinary course if the license to the person comports with the usual or customary practices in the kind of business in which the licensor is engaged or with the licensor's own usual or customary practices.

(b) **[Rights of licensee in ordinary course of business.]** A licensee in ordinary course of business takes its rights under a nonexclusive license free of a security interest in the general intangible created by the licensor, even if the security interest is perfected and the licensee knows of its existence.

(c) **[Rights of lessee in ordinary course of business.]** A lessee in ordinary course of business takes its leasehold interest free of a security interest in the goods created by the lessor, even if the security interest is perfected and the lessee knows of its existence.

Official Comment

1. **Source.** Derived from Sections 2A–103(1)(*o*), 2A–307(3).

2. **Licensee in Ordinary Course.** Like the analogous rules in Section 9–320(a) with respect to buyers in ordinary course and subsection (c) with respect to lessees in ordinary course, the new rule in subsection (b) reflects the expectations of the parties and the marketplace: a licensee under a nonexclusive license takes subject to a security interest unless the secured party authorizes the license free of the security interest or other, controlling law such as that of this section (protecting ordinary-course licensees) dictates a contrary result. See Sections 9–201, 9–315. The definition of "licensee in ordinary course of business" in subsection (a) is modeled upon that of "buyer in ordinary course of business."

3. **Lessee in Ordinary Course.** Subsection (c) contains the rule formerly found in Section 2A–307(3). The rule works in the same way as that of Section 9–320(a).

§ 9–322. Priorities Among Conflicting Security Interests in and Agricultural Liens on Same Collateral.

(a) **[General priority rules.]** Except as otherwise provided in this section, priority among conflicting security interests and agricultural liens in the same collateral is determined according to the following rules:

(1) Conflicting perfected security interests and agricultural liens rank according to priority in time of filing or perfection. Priority dates from the earlier of the time a filing covering the collateral is first made or the security interest or agricultural lien is first perfected, if there is no period thereafter when there is neither filing nor perfection.

(2) A perfected security interest or agricultural lien has priority over a conflicting unperfected security interest or agricultural lien.

(3) The first security interest or agricultural lien to attach or become effective has priority if conflicting security interests and agricultural liens are unperfected.

(b) **[Time of perfection: proceeds and supporting obligations.]** For the purposes of subsection (a)(1):

(1) the time of filing or perfection as to a security interest in collateral is also the time of filing or perfection as to a security interest in proceeds; and

(2) the time of filing or perfection as to a security interest in collateral supported by a supporting obligation is also the time of filing or perfection as to a security interest in the supporting obligation.

(c) **[Special priority rules: proceeds and supporting obligations.]** Except as otherwise provided in subsection (f), a security interest in collateral which qualifies for priority over a conflicting security interest under Section 9–327, 9–328, 9–329, 9–330, or 9–331 also has priority over a conflicting security interest in:

(1) any supporting obligation for the collateral; and

(2) proceeds of the collateral if:

787

(A)   the security interest in proceeds is perfected;

(B)   the proceeds are cash proceeds or of the same type as the collateral; and

(C)   in the case of proceeds that are proceeds of proceeds, all intervening proceeds are cash proceeds, proceeds of the same type as the collateral, or an account relating to the collateral.

(d)   **[First-to-file priority rule for certain collateral.]** Subject to subsection (e) and except as otherwise provided in subsection (f), if a security interest in chattel paper, deposit accounts, negotiable documents, instruments, investment property, or letter-of-credit rights is perfected by a method other than filing, conflicting perfected security interests in proceeds of the collateral rank according to priority in time of filing.

(e)   **[Applicability of subsection (d).]** Subsection (d) applies only if the proceeds of the collateral are not cash proceeds, chattel paper, negotiable documents, instruments, investment property, or letter-of-credit rights.

(f)   **[Limitations on subsections (a) through (e).]** Subsections (a) through (e) are subject to:

(1)   subsection (g) and the other provisions of this part;

(2)   Section 4–210 with respect to a security interest of a collecting bank;

(3)   Section 5–118 with respect to a security interest of an issuer or nominated person; and

(4)   Section 9–110 with respect to a security interest arising under Article 2 or 2A.

(g)   **[Priority under agricultural lien statute.]** A perfected agricultural lien on collateral has priority over a conflicting security interest in or agricultural lien on the same collateral if the statute creating the agricultural lien so provides.

Official Comment

1.   **Source.** Former Section 9–312(5), (6).

2.   **Scope of This Section.** In a variety of situations, two or more people may claim a security interest in the same collateral. This section states general rules of priority among conflicting security interests. As subsection (f) provides, the general rules in subsections (a) through (e) are subject to the rule in subsection (g) governing perfected agricultural liens and to the other rules in this Part of this Article. Rules that override this section include those applicable to purchase-money security interests (Section 9–324) and those qualifying for special priority in particular types of collateral. See, e.g., Section 9–327 (deposit accounts); Section 9–328 (investment property); Section 9–329 (letter-of-credit rights); Section 9–330 (chattel paper and instruments); Section 9–334 (fixtures). In addition, the general rules of sections (a) through (e) are subject to priority rules governing security interests arising under Articles 2, 2A, 4, and 5.

3.   **General Rules.** Subsection (a) contains three general rules. Subsection (a)(1) governs the priority of competing perfected security interests. Subsection (a)(2) governs the priority of competing security interests if one is perfected and the other is not. Subsection (a)(3) governs the priority of competing unperfected security interests. The rules may be regarded as adaptations of the idea, deeply rooted at common law, of a race of diligence among creditors. The first two rules are based on precedence in the time as of which the competing secured parties either filed their financing statements or obtained perfected security interests. Under subsection (a)(1), the first secured party who files or perfects has priority. Under subsection (a)(2), which is new, a perfected security interest has priority over an unperfected one. Under subsection (a)(3), if both security interests are unperfected, the first to attach has priority. Note that Section 9–709(b) may affect the application of subsection (a) to a filing that occurred before the effective date of this Article and which would be ineffective to perfect a security interest under former Article 9 but effective under this Article.

4.   **Competing Perfected Security Interests.** When there is more than one perfected security interest, the security interests rank according to priority in time of filing or perfection. "Filing," of course, refers to the filing of an effective financing statement. "Perfection" refers to the acquisition of a perfected security interest, i.e., one that has attached and as to which any required perfection step has been taken. See Sections 9–308 and 9–309.

Example 1:   On February 1, A files a financing statement covering a certain item of Debtor's equipment. On March 1, B files a financing statement covering the same equipment. On April 1, B makes a loan to Debtor and obtains a security interest in the equipment. On May 1, A makes a loan to Debtor and obtains a security interest in the same collateral. A has priority even though B's loan was made earlier and was perfected when made. It makes no difference whether A knew of B's security interest when A made its advance.

The problem stated in Example 1 is peculiar to a notice-filing system under which filing may occur before the security interest attaches (see Section 9–502). The justification for determining priority by order of filing lies in the necessity of protecting the filing system—that is, of allowing the first secured party who has filed to make subsequent advances without each time having to check for subsequent filings as a condition of protection. Note, however, that this first-to-file protection is not absolute. For example, Section 9–324 affords priority to certain purchase-money security interests, even if a competing secured party was the first to file or perfect.

Under a notice-filing system, a filed financing statement indicates to third parties that a person may have a security interest in the collateral indicated. With further inquiry, they may discover the complete state of affairs. When a financing statement that is ineffective when filed becomes effective thereafter, the policy underlying the notice-filing system determines the "time of filing" for purposes of subsection (a)(1). For example, the unauthorized filing of an otherwise sufficient initial financing statement becomes authorized, and the financing statement becomes effective, upon the debtor's post-filing authorization or ratification of the filing. See Section 9–509, Comment 3. Because the notice value of the financing statement is independent of the timing of authorization or ratification, the time of the unauthorized filing is the "time of filing" for purposes of subsection (a)(1). The same policy applies to the other priority rules in this part.

Example 2: A and B make non-purchase-money advances secured by the same collateral. The collateral is in Debtor's possession, and neither security interest is perfected when the second advance is made. Whichever secured party first perfects its security interest (by taking possession of the collateral or by filing) takes priority. It makes no difference whether that secured party knows of the other security interest at the time it perfects its own.

The rule of subsection (a)(1), affording priority to the first to file or perfect, applies to security interests that are perfected by any method, including temporarily (Section 9–312) or upon attachment (Section 9–309), even though there may be no notice to creditors or subsequent purchasers and notwithstanding any common-law rule to the contrary. The form of the claim to priority, i.e., filing or perfection, may shift from time to time, and the rank will be based on the first filing or perfection as long as there is no intervening period without filing or perfection. See Section 9–308(c).

Example 3: On October 1, A acquires a temporarily perfected (20-day) security interest, unfiled, in a tangible negotiable document in the debtor's possession under Section 9–312(e). On October 5, B files and thereby perfects a security interest that previously had attached to the same document. On October 10, A files. A has priority, even after the 20-day period expires, regardless of whether A knows of B's security interest when A files. A was the first to perfect and maintained continuous perfection or filing since the start of the 20-day period. However, the perfection of A's security interest extends only "to the extent it arises for new value given." To the extent A's security interest secures advances made by A beyond the 20-day period, its security interest would be subordinate to B's, inasmuch as B was the first to file.

In general, the rule in subsection (a)(1) does not distinguish among various advances made by a secured party. The priority of every advance dates from the earlier of filing or perfection. However, in rare instances, the priority of an advance dates from the time the advance is made. See Example 3 and Section 9–323.

5. **Priority in After-Acquired Property.** The application of the priority rules to after-acquired property must be considered separately for each item of collateral. Priority does not depend only on time of perfection but may also be based on priority in filing before perfection.

Example 4: On February 1, A makes advances to Debtor under a security agreement covering "all Debtor's machinery, both existing and after-acquired." A promptly files a financing statement. On April 1, B takes a security interest in all Debtor's machinery, existing and after-acquired, to secure an outstanding loan. The following day, B files a financing statement. On May 1, Debtor acquires a new machine. When Debtor acquires rights in the new machine, both A and B acquire security interests in the machine simultaneously. Both security interests are perfected simultaneously. However, A has priority because A filed before B.

When after-acquired collateral is encumbered by more than one security interest, one of the security interests often is a purchase-money security interest that is entitled to special priority under Section 9–324.

6. **Priority in Proceeds: General Rule.** Subsection (b)(1) follows former Section 9–312(6). It provides that the baseline rules of subsection (a) apply generally to priority conflicts in proceeds except where otherwise provided (e.g., as in subsections (c) through (e)). Under Section 9–203, attachment cannot occur (and therefore,

under Section 9–308, perfection cannot occur) as to particular collateral until the collateral itself comes into existence and the debtor has rights in it. Thus, a security interest in proceeds of original collateral does not attach and is not perfected until the proceeds come into existence and the debtor acquires rights in them.

Example 5:   On April 1, Debtor authenticates a security agreement granting to A security interest in all Debtor's existing and after-acquired inventory. The same day, A files a financing statement covering inventory. On May 1, Debtor authenticates a security agreement granting B a security interest in all Debtor's existing and future accounts. On June 1, Debtor sells inventory to a customer on 30-day unsecured credit. When Debtor acquires the account, B's security interest attaches to it and is perfected by B's financing statement. At the very same time, A's security interest attaches to the account as proceeds of the inventory and is automatically perfected. See Section 9–315. Under subsection (b) of this section, for purposes of determining A's priority in the account, the time of filing as to the original collateral (April 1, as to inventory) is also the time of filing as to proceeds (account). Accordingly, A's security interest in the account has priority over B's. Of course, had B filed its financing statement before A filed (e.g., on March 1), then B would have priority in the accounts.

Section 9–324 governs the extent to which a special purchase-money priority in goods or software carries over into the proceeds of the original collateral.

7.   **Priority in Proceeds: Special Rules.** Subsections (c), (d), and (e), which are new, provide additional priority rules for proceeds of collateral in situations where the temporal (first-in-time) rules of subsection (a)(1) are not appropriate. These new provisions distinguish what these Comments refer to as "non-filing collateral" from what they call "filing collateral." As used in these Comments, non-filing collateral is collateral of a type for which perfection may be achieved by a method other than filing (possession or control, mainly) and for which secured parties who so perfect generally do not expect or need to conduct a filing search. More specifically, non-filing collateral is chattel paper, deposit accounts, negotiable documents, instruments, investment property, and letter-of-credit rights. Other collateral—accounts, commercial tort claims, general intangibles, goods, nonnegotiable documents, and payment intangibles—is filing collateral.

8.   **Proceeds of Non-Filing Collateral: Non-Temporal Priority.** Subsection (c)(2) provides a baseline priority rule for proceeds of non-filing collateral which applies if the secured party has taken the steps required for non-temporal priority over a conflicting security interest in non-filing collateral (e.g., control, in the case of deposit accounts, letter-of-credit rights, investment property, and in some cases, electronic negotiable documents, section 9–331). This rule determines priority in proceeds of non-filing collateral whether or not there exists an actual conflicting security interest in the original non-filing collateral. Under subsection (c)(2), the priority in the original collateral continues in proceeds if the security interest in proceeds is perfected and the proceeds are cash proceeds or non-filing proceeds "of the same type" as the original collateral. As used in subsection (c)(2), "type" means a type of collateral defined in the Uniform Commercial Code and should be read broadly. For example, a security is "of the same type" as a security entitlement (i.e., investment property), and a promissory note is "of the same type" as a draft (i.e., an instrument).

Example 6:   SP-1 perfects its security interest in investment property by filing. SP-2 perfects subsequently by taking control of a certificated security. Debtor receives cash proceeds of the security (e.g., dividends deposited into Debtor's deposit account). If the first-to-file-or-perfect rule of subsection (a)(1) were applied, SP-1's security interest in the cash proceeds would be senior, although SP-2's security interest continues perfected under Section 9–315 beyond the 20-day period of automatic perfection. This was the result under former Article 9. Under subsection (c), however, SP-2's security interest is senior.

Note that a different result would obtain in Example 6 (i.e., SP-1's security interest would be senior) if SP-1 were to obtain control of the deposit-account proceeds. This is so because subsection (c) is subject to subsection (f), which in turn provides that the priority rules under subsections (a) through (e) are subject to "the other provisions of this part." One of those "other provisions" is Section 9–327, which affords priority to a security interest perfected by control. See Section 9–327(1).

Example 7:   SP-1 perfects its security interest in investment property by filing. SP-2 perfects subsequently by taking control of a certificated security. Debtor receives proceeds of the security consisting of a new certificated security issued as a stock dividend on the original collateral. Although the new security is of the same type as the original collateral (i.e., investment property), once the 20-day period of automatic perfection expires (see Section 9–315(d)), SP-2's security interest is unperfected. (SP-2 has not filed or taken delivery or control, and no temporary-perfection rule applies.) Consequently, once the 20-day period expires, subsection (c) does not confer priority, and, under subsection (a)(2), SP-1's security interest in the security is senior. This was the result under former Article 9.

Example 8: SP-1 perfects its security interest in investment property by filing. SP-2 perfects subsequently by taking control of a certificated security and also by filing against investment property. Debtor receives proceeds of the security consisting of a new certificated security issued as a stock dividend of the collateral. Because the new security is of the same type as the original collateral (i.e., investment property) and (unlike Example 7) SP-2's security interest is perfected by filing, SP-2's security interest is senior under subsection (c). If the new security were redeemed by the issuer upon surrender and yet another security were received by Debtor, SP-2's security interest would continue to enjoy priority under subsection (c). The new security would be proceeds of proceeds.

Example 9: SP-1 perfects its security interest in investment property by filing. SP-2 subsequently perfects its security interest in investment property by taking control of a certificated security and also by filing against investment property. Debtor receives proceeds of the security consisting of a dividend check that it deposits to a deposit account. Because the check and the deposit account are cash proceeds, SP-1's and SP-2's security interests in the cash proceeds are perfected under Section 9–315 beyond the 20-day period of automatic perfection. However, SP-2's security interest is senior under subsection (c).

Example 10: SP-1 perfects its security interest in investment property by filing. SP-2 perfects subsequently by taking control of a certificated security and also by filing against investment property. Debtor receives an instrument as proceeds of the security. (Assume that the instrument is not cash proceeds.) Because the instrument is not of the same type as the original collateral (i.e., investment property), SP-2's security interest, although perfected by filing, does not achieve priority under subsection (c). Under the first-to-file-or-perfect rule of subsection (a)(1), SP-1's security interest in the proceeds is senior.

The proceeds of proceeds are themselves proceeds. See Section 9–102 (defining "proceeds" and "collateral"). Sometimes competing security interests arise in proceeds that are several generations removed from the original collateral. As the following example explains, the applicability of subsection (c) may turn on the nature of the intervening proceeds.

Example 11: SP-1 perfects its security interest in Debtor's deposit account by obtaining control. Thereafter, SP-2 files against inventory, (presumably) searches, finds no indication of a conflicting security interest, and advances against Debtor's existing and after-acquired inventory. Debtor uses funds from the deposit account to purchase inventory, which SP-1 can trace as identifiable proceeds of its security interest in Debtor's deposit account, and which SP-2 claims as original collateral. The inventory is sold and the proceeds deposited into *another* deposit account, as to which SP-1 has not obtained control. Subsection (c) does not govern priority in this other deposit account. This deposit account is cash proceeds and is also the same type of collateral as SP-1's original collateral, as required by subsections (c)(2)(A) and (B). However, SP-1's security interest does not satisfy subsection (c)(2)(C) because the inventory proceeds, which intervened between the original deposit account and the deposit account constituting the proceeds at issue, are not cash proceeds, proceeds of the same type as the collateral (original deposit account), or an account relating to the collateral. Stated otherwise, once proceeds other than cash proceeds, proceeds of the same type as the original collateral, or an account relating to the original collateral intervene in the chain of proceeds, priority under subsection (c) is thereafter unavailable. The special priority rule in subsection (d) also is inapplicable to this case. See Comment 9, Example 13, below. Instead, the general first-to-file-or-perfect rule of subsections (a) and (b) apply. Under that rule, SP-1 has priority unless its security interest in the inventory proceeds became unperfected under Section 9–315(d). Had SP-2 filed against inventory before SP-1 obtained control of the original deposit account, then SP-2 would have had priority even if SP-1's security interest in the inventory proceeds remained perfected.

If two security interests in the same original collateral are entitled to priority in an item of proceeds under subsection (c)(2), the security interest having priority in the original collateral has priority in the proceeds.

9. **Proceeds of Non-Filing Collateral: Special Temporal Priority.** Under subsections (d) and (e), if a security interest in non-filing collateral is perfected by a method other than filing (e.g., control or possession), it does not retain its priority over a conflicting security interest in proceeds that are filing collateral. Moreover, it is not entitled to priority in proceeds under the first-to file-or-perfect rule of subsections (a)(1) and (b). Instead, under subsection (d), priority is determined by a new first-to-file rule.

Example 12: SP-1 perfects its security interest in Debtor's deposit account by obtaining control. Thereafter, SP-2 files against equipment, (presumably) searches, finds no indication of a conflicting security interest, and advances against Debtor's equipment. SP-1 then files against Debtor's equipment. Debtor uses funds from the deposit account to purchase equipment, which SP-1 can trace as proceeds of its security interest in Debtor's deposit account. If the first-to-file-or-perfect rule were applied, SP-1's security interest would be senior under subsections (a)(1) and (b), because it was the first to perfect in the original collateral and there was no period during which its security interest was unperfected. Under subsection (d), however, SP-2's security interest would be senior because it filed first. This corresponds with the likely expectations of the parties.

Note that under subsection (e), the first-to-file rule of subsection (d) applies only if the proceeds in question are other than non-filing collateral (i.e., if the proceeds are filing collateral). If the proceeds are non-filing collateral, either the first-to-file-or-perfect rule under subsections (a) and (b) or the non-temporal priority rule in subsection (c) would apply, depending on the facts.

Example 13:   SP-1 perfects its security interest in Debtor's deposit account by obtaining control. Thereafter, SP-2 files against inventory, (presumably) searches, finds no indication of a conflicting security interest, and advances against Debtor's existing and after-acquired inventory. Debtor uses funds from the deposit account to purchase inventory, which SP-1 can trace as identifiable proceeds of its security interest in Debtor's deposit account, and which SP-2 claims as original collateral. The inventory is sold and the proceeds deposited into *another* deposit account, as to which SP-1 has not obtained control. As discussed above in Comment 8, Example 11, subsection (c) does not govern priority in this deposit account. Subsection (d) also does not govern, because the proceeds at issue (the deposit account) are cash proceeds. See subsection (e). Rather, the general rules of subsections (a) and (b) govern.

10.   **Priority in Supporting Obligations.** Under subsections (b)(2) and (c)(1), a security interest having priority in collateral also has priority in a supporting obligation for that collateral. However, the rules in these subsections are subject to the special rule in Section 9–329 governing the priority of security interests in a letter-of-credit right. See subsection (f). Under Section 9–329, a secured party's failure to obtain control (Section 9–107) of a letter-of-credit right that serves as supporting collateral leaves its security interest exposed to a priming interest of a party who does take control.

11.   **Unperfected Security Interests.** Under subsection (a)(3), if conflicting security interests are unperfected, the first to attach has priority. This rule may be of merely theoretical interest, inasmuch as it is hard to imagine a situation where the case would come into litigation without either secured party's having perfected its security interest. If neither security interest had been perfected at the time of the filing of a petition in bankruptcy, ordinarily neither would be good against the trustee in bankruptcy under the Bankruptcy Code.

12.   **Agricultural Liens.** Statutes other than this Article may purport to grant priority to an agricultural lien as against a conflicting security interest or agricultural lien. Under subsection (g), if another statute grants priority to an agricultural lien, the agricultural lien has priority only if the same statute creates the agricultural lien and the agricultural lien is perfected. Otherwise, subsection (a) applies the same priority rules to an agricultural lien as to a security interest, regardless of whether the agricultural lien conflicts with another agricultural lien or with a security interest.

Inasmuch as no agricultural lien on proceeds arises under this Article, subsections (b) through (e) do not apply to proceeds of agricultural liens. However, if an agricultural lien has priority under subsection (g) and the statute creating the agricultural lien gives the secured party a lien on proceeds of the collateral subject to the lien, a court should apply the principle of subsection (g) and award priority in the proceeds to the holder of the perfected agricultural lien.

As amended in 2000, 2003, and 2010.

§ 9–323.   Future Advances.

(a)   **[When priority based on time of advance.]** Except as otherwise provided in subsection (c), for purposes of determining the priority of a perfected security interest under Section 9–322(a)(1), perfection of the security interest dates from the time an advance is made to the extent that the security interest secures an advance that:

(1)   is made while the security interest is perfected only:

(A)   under Section 9–309 when it attaches; or

(B)   temporarily under Section 9–312(e), (f), or (g); and

(2)   is not made pursuant to a commitment entered into before or while the security interest is perfected by a method other than under Section 9–309 or 9–312(e), (f), or (g).

[handwritten: no filing]

[handwritten: → Filing]

(b)   **[Lien creditor.]** Except as otherwise provided in subsection (c), a security interest is subordinate to the rights of a person that becomes a lien creditor to the extent that the security interest secures an advance made more than 45 days after the person becomes a lien creditor unless the advance is made:

(1)   without knowledge of the lien; or

(2)   pursuant to a commitment entered into without knowledge of the lien.

(c)   **[Buyer of receivables.]** Subsections (a) and (b) do not apply to a security interest held by a secured party that is a buyer of accounts, chattel paper, payment intangibles, or promissory notes or a consignor.

(d)   **[Buyer of goods.]** Except as otherwise provided in subsection (e), a buyer of goods other than a buyer in ordinary course of business takes free of a security interest to the extent that it secures advances made after the earlier of:

(1)   the time the secured party acquires knowledge of the buyer's purchase; or

(2)   45 days after the purchase.

(e)   **[Advances made pursuant to commitment: priority of buyer of goods.]** Subsection (d) does not apply if the advance is made pursuant to a commitment entered into without knowledge of the buyer's purchase and before the expiration of the 45-day period.

(f)   **[Lessee of goods.]** Except as otherwise provided in subsection (g), a lessee of goods, other than a lessee in ordinary course of business, takes the leasehold interest free of a security interest to the extent that it secures advances made after the earlier of:

(1)   the time the secured party acquires knowledge of the lease; or

(2)   45 days after the lease contract becomes enforceable.

(g)   **[Advances made pursuant to commitment: priority of lessee of goods.]** Subsection (f) does not apply if the advance is made pursuant to a commitment entered into without knowledge of the lease and before the expiration of the 45-day period.

As amended in 1999.

Official Comment

1.   **Source.** Former Sections 9–312(7), 9–301(4), 9–307(3), 2A–307(4).

2.   **Scope of This Section.** A security agreement may provide that collateral secures future advances. See Section 9–204(c). This section collects all of the special rules dealing with the priority of advances made by a secured party after a third party acquires an interest in the collateral. Subsection (a) applies when the third party is a competing secured party. It replaces and clarifies former Section 9–312(7). Subsection (b) deals with lien creditors and replaces former Section 9–301(4). Subsections (d) and (e) deal with buyers and replace former Section 9–307(3). Subsections (f) and (g) deal with lessees and replace former Section 2A–307(4).

3.   **Competing Security Interests.** Under a proper reading of the first-to-file-or-perfect rule of Section 9–322(a)(1) (and former Section 9–312(5)), it is abundantly clear that the time when an advance is made plays no role in determining priorities among conflicting security interests except when a financing statement was not filed and the advance is the giving of value as the last step for attachment and perfection. Thus, a secured party takes subject to all advances secured by a competing security interest having priority under Section 9–322(a)(1). This result generally obtains regardless of how the competing security interest is perfected and regardless of whether the advances are made "pursuant to commitment" (Section 9–102). Subsection (a) of this section states the only other instance when the time of an advance figures in the priority scheme in Section 9–322: when the security interest is perfected only automatically under Section 9–309 or temporarily under Section 9–312(e), (f), or (g), and the advance is not made pursuant to a commitment entered into while the security interest was perfected by another method. Thus, an advance has priority from the date it is made only in the rare case in which it is made without commitment and while the security interest is perfected only temporarily under Section 9–312.

The new formulation in subsection (a) clarifies the result when the initial advance is paid and a new ("future") advance is made subsequently. Under former Section 9–312(7), the priority of the new advance turned on whether it was "made while a security interest is perfected." This section resolves any ambiguity by omitting the quoted phrase.

Example 1:   On February 1, A makes an advance secured by machinery in the debtor's possession and files a financing statement. On March 1, B makes an advance secured by the same machinery and files a financing statement. On April 1, A makes a further advance, under the original security agreement, against the same machinery. A was the first to file and so, under the first-to-file-or-perfect rule of Section 9–322(a)(1), A's security interest has priority over B's, both as to the February 1 and as to the April 1 advance. It makes no difference whether A knows of B's intervening advance when A makes the second advance. Note that, as long as A was the first to file or perfect, A would have priority with respect to both advances if either A or B had perfected by taking possession of the collateral. Likewise, A would have priority if A's April 1 advance was not made under the original agreement with the debtor, but was under a new agreement.

Example 2:   On October 1, A acquires a temporarily perfected (20-day) security interest, unfiled, in a tangible negotiable document in the debtor's possession under Section 9–312(e) or (f). The security interest secures an advance made on that day as well as future advances. On October 5, B files and thereby perfects a security interest that previously had attached to the same document. On October 8, A makes an additional advance. On October 10, A files. Under Section 9–322(a)(1), because A was the first to perfect and maintained continuous perfection or filing since the start of the 20-day period, A has priority, even after the 20-day period expires. See Section 9–322, Comment 4, Example 3. However, under this section, for purposes of Section 9–322(a)(1), to the extent A's security interest secures the October 8 advance, the security interest was perfected on October 8. Inasmuch as B perfected on October 5, B has priority over the October 8 advance.

The rule in subsection (a) is more liberal toward the priority of future advances than the corresponding rules applicable to intervening lien creditors (subsection (b)), buyers (subsections (d) and (e)), and lessees (subsections (f) and (g)).

4.   **Competing Lien Creditors.** Subsection (b) replaces former Section 9–301(4) and addresses the rights of a "lien creditor," as defined in Section 9–102. Under Section 9–317(a)(2), a security interest is senior to the rights of a person who becomes a lien creditor, unless the person becomes a lien creditor before the security interest is perfected and before a financing statement covering the collateral is filed and Section 9–203(b)(3) is satisfied. Subsection (b) of this section provides that a security interest is subordinate to those rights to the extent that the specified circumstances occur. Subsection (b) does not elevate the priority of a security interest that is subordinate to the rights of a lien creditor under Section 9–317(a)(2); it only subordinates.

As under former Section 9–301(4), a secured party's knowledge does not cut short the 45-day period during which future advances can achieve priority over an intervening lien creditor's interest. Rather, because of the impact of the rule in subsection (b) on the question whether the security interest for future advances is "protected" under Section 6323(c)(2) and (d) of the Internal Revenue Code as amended by the Federal Tax Lien Act of 1966, the priority of the security interest for future advances over a lien creditor is made absolute for 45 days regardless of knowledge of the secured party concerning the lien. If, however, the advance is made after the 45 days, the advance will not have priority unless it was made or committed without knowledge of the lien.

5.   **Sales of Receivables; Consignments.** Subsections (a) and (b) do not apply to outright sales of accounts, chattel paper, payment intangibles, or promissory notes, nor do they apply to consignments.

6.   **Competing Buyers and Lessees.** Under subsections (d) and (e), a buyer will not take subject to a security interest to the extent it secures advances made after the secured party has knowledge that the buyer has purchased the collateral or more than 45 days after the purchase unless the advances were made pursuant to a commitment entered into before the expiration of the 45-day period and without knowledge of the purchase. Subsections (f) and (g) provide an analogous rule for lessees. Of course, a buyer in ordinary course who takes free of the security interest under Section 9–320 and a lessee in ordinary course who takes free under Section 9–321 are not subject to any future advances. Subsections (d) and (e) replace former Section 9–307(3), and subsections (f) and (g) replace former Section 2A–307(4). No change in meaning is intended.

As amended in 1999, 2000, and 2003.

§ 9–324.   Priority of Purchase-Money Security Interests.

(a)   **[General rule: purchase-money priority.]** Except as otherwise provided in subsection (g), a perfected purchase-money security interest in goods other than inventory or livestock has priority over a conflicting security interest in the same goods, and, except as otherwise provided in Section 9–327, a perfected security interest in its identifiable proceeds also has priority, if the purchase-money security interest is perfected when the debtor receives possession of the collateral or within 20 days thereafter.

(b) **[Inventory purchase-money priority.]** Subject to subsection (c) and except as otherwise provided in subsection (g), a perfected purchase-money security interest in inventory has priority over a conflicting security interest in the same inventory, has priority over a conflicting security interest in chattel paper or an instrument constituting proceeds of the inventory and in proceeds of the chattel paper, if so provided in Section 9–330, and, except as otherwise provided in Section 9–327, also has priority in identifiable cash proceeds of the inventory to the extent the identifiable cash proceeds are received on or before the delivery of the inventory to a buyer, if:

(1) the purchase-money security interest is perfected when the debtor receives possession of the inventory;

(2) the purchase-money secured party sends an authenticated notification to the holder of the conflicting security interest;

(3) the holder of the conflicting security interest receives the notification within five years before the debtor receives possession of the inventory; and

(4) the notification states that the person sending the notification has or expects to acquire a purchase-money security interest in inventory of the debtor and describes the inventory.

(c) **[Holders of conflicting inventory security interests to be notified.]** Subsections (b)(2) through (4) apply only if the holder of the conflicting security interest had filed a financing statement covering the same types of inventory:

(1) if the purchase-money security interest is perfected by filing, before the date of the filing; or

(2) if the purchase-money security interest is temporarily perfected without filing or possession under Section 9–312(f), before the beginning of the 20-day period thereunder.

(d) **[Livestock purchase-money priority.]** Subject to subsection (e) and except as otherwise provided in subsection (g), a perfected purchase-money security interest in livestock that are farm products has priority over a conflicting security interest in the same livestock, and, except as otherwise provided in Section 9–327, a perfected security interest in their identifiable proceeds and identifiable products in their unmanufactured states also has priority, if:

(1) the purchase-money security interest is perfected when the debtor receives possession of the livestock;

(2) the purchase-money secured party sends an authenticated notification to the holder of the conflicting security interest;

(3) the holder of the conflicting security interest receives the notification within six months before the debtor receives possession of the livestock; and

(4) the notification states that the person sending the notification has or expects to acquire a purchase-money security interest in livestock of the debtor and describes the livestock.

(e) **[Holders of conflicting livestock security interests to be notified.]** Subsections (d)(2) through (4) apply only if the holder of the conflicting security interest had filed a financing statement covering the same types of livestock:

(1) if the purchase-money security interest is perfected by filing, before the date of the filing; or

(2) if the purchase-money security interest is temporarily perfected without filing or possession under Section 9–312(f), before the beginning of the 20-day period thereunder.

(f) **[Software purchase-money priority.]** Except as otherwise provided in subsection (g), a perfected purchase-money security interest in software has priority over a conflicting security interest in the same collateral, and, except as otherwise provided in Section 9–327, a perfected security interest in its identifiable proceeds also has priority, to the extent that the purchase-money security interest in the goods in which the software was acquired for use has priority in the goods and proceeds of the goods under this section.

(g) **[Conflicting purchase-money security interests.]** If more than one security interest qualifies for priority in the same collateral under subsection (a), (b), (d), or (f):

(1) a security interest securing an obligation incurred as all or part of the price of the collateral has priority over a security interest securing an obligation incurred for value given to enable the debtor to acquire rights in or the use of collateral; and

(2) in all other cases, Section 9–322(a) applies to the qualifying security interests.

Official Comment

1. **Source.** Former Section 9–312(3), (4).

2. **Priority of Purchase-Money Security Interests.** This section contains the priority rules applicable to purchase-money security interests, as defined in Section 9–103. It affords a special, non-temporal priority to those purchase-money security interests that satisfy the statutory conditions. In most cases, priority will be over a security interest asserted under an after-acquired property clause. See Section 9–204 on the extent to which security interests in after-acquired property are validated.

A purchase-money security interest can be created only in goods and software. See Section 9–103. Section 9–324(a), which follows former Section 9–312(4), contains the general rule for purchase-money security interests in goods. It is subject to subsections (b) and (c), which derive from former Section 9–312(3) and apply to purchase-money security interests in inventory, and subsections (d) and (e), which apply to purchase-money security interests in livestock that are farm products. Subsection (f) applies to purchase-money security interests in software. Subsection (g) deals with the relatively unusual case in which a debtor creates two purchase-money security interests in the same collateral and both security interests qualify for special priority under one of the other subsections.

Former Section 9–312(2) contained a rule affording special priority to those who provided secured credit that enabled a debtor to produce crops. This rule proved unworkable and has been eliminated from this Article. Instead, model Section 9–324A contains a revised production-money priority rule. That section is a model, not uniform, provision. The sponsors of the UCC have taken no position as to whether it should be enacted, instead leaving the matter for state legislatures to consider if they are so inclined.

3. **Purchase-Money Priority in Goods Other Than Inventory and Livestock.** Subsection (a) states a general rule applicable to all types of goods except inventory and farm-products livestock: the purchase-money interest takes priority if it is perfected when the debtor receives possession of the collateral or within 20 days thereafter. (As to the 20-day "grace period," compare Section 9–317(e). Former Sections 9–312(4) and 9–301(2) contained a 10-day grace period.) The perfection requirement means that the purchase-money secured party either has filed a financing statement before that time or has a temporarily perfected security interest in goods covered by documents under Section 9–312(e) and (f) which is continued in a perfected status by filing before the expiration of the 20-day period specified in that section. A purchase-money security interest qualifies for priority under subsection (a), even if the purchase-money secured party knows that a conflicting security interest has been created and/or that the holder of the conflicting interest has filed a financing statement covering the collateral.

Normally, there will be no question when "the debtor receives possession of the collateral" for purposes of subsection (a). However, sometimes a debtor buys goods and takes possession of them in stages, and then assembly and testing are completed (by the seller or debtor-buyer) at the debtor's location. Under those circumstances, the buyer "takes possession" within the meaning of subsection (a) when, after an inspection of the portion of the goods in the debtor's possession, it would be apparent to a potential lender to the debtor that the debtor has acquired an interest in the goods taken as a whole.

A similar issue concerning the time when "the debtor receives possession" arises when a person acquires possession of goods under a transaction that is not governed by this Article and then later agrees to buy the goods on secured credit. For example, a person may take possession of goods as lessee under a lease contract and then exercise an option to purchase the goods from the lessor on secured credit. Under Section 2A–307(1), creditors of the lessee generally take subject to the lease contract; filing a financing statement against the lessee is unnecessary to protect the lessor's leasehold or residual interest. Once the lease is converted to a security interest, filing a financing statement is necessary to protect the seller's (former lessor's) security interest. Accordingly, the 20-day period in subsection (a) does not commence until the goods become "collateral" (defined in Section 9–102), i.e., until they are subject to a security interest.

4. **Purchase-Money Security Interests in Inventory.** Subsections (b) and (c) afford a means by which a purchase-money security interest in inventory can achieve priority over an earlier-filed security interest in the same collateral. To achieve priority, the purchase-money security interest must be perfected when the debtor receives possession of the inventory. For a discussion of when "the debtor receives possession," see Comment 3, above. The 20-day grace period of subsection (a) does not apply.

The arrangement between an inventory secured party and its debtor typically requires the secured party to make periodic advances against incoming inventory or periodic releases of old inventory as new inventory is received. A fraudulent debtor may apply to the secured party for advances even though it has already given a purchase-money security interest in the inventory to another secured party. For this reason, subsections (b)(2) through (4) and (c) impose a second condition for the purchase-money security interest's achieving priority: the purchase-money secured party must give notification to the holder of a conflicting security interest who filed against the same item or type of inventory before the purchase-money secured party filed or its security interest became perfected temporarily under Section 9–312(e) or (f). The notification requirement protects the non-purchase-money inventory secured party in such a situation: if the inventory secured party has received notification, it presumably will not make an advance; if it has not received notification (or if the other security interest does not qualify as purchase-money), any advance the inventory secured party may make ordinarily will have priority under Section 9–322. Inasmuch as an arrangement for periodic advances against incoming goods is unusual outside the inventory field, subsection (a) does not contain a notification requirement.

5. **Notification to Conflicting Inventory Secured Party: Timing.** Under subsection (b)(3), the perfected purchase-money security interest achieves priority over a conflicting security interest only if the holder of the conflicting security interest receives a notification within five years before the debtor receives possession of the purchase-money collateral. If the debtor never receives possession, the five-year period never begins, and the purchase-money security interest has priority, even if notification is not given. However, where the purchase-money inventory financing began by the purchase-money secured party's possession of a negotiable document of title, to retain priority the secured party must give the notification required by subsection (b) at or before the usual time, i.e., when the debtor gets possession of the inventory, even though the security interest remains perfected for 20 days under Section 9–312(e) or (f).

Some people have mistakenly read former Section 9–312(3)(b) to require, as a condition of purchase-money priority in inventory, that the purchase-money secured party give the notification before it files a financing statement. Read correctly, the "before" clauses compare (i) the time when the holder of the conflicting security interest filed a financing statement with (ii) the time when the purchase-money security interest becomes perfected by filing or automatically perfected temporarily. Only if (i) occurs before (ii) must notification be given to the holder of the conflicting security interest. Subsection (c) has been rewritten to clarify this point.

6. **Notification to Conflicting Inventory Secured Party: Address.** Inasmuch as the address provided as that of the secured party on a filed financing statement is an "address that is reasonable under the circumstances," the holder of a purchase-money security interest may satisfy the requirement to "send" notification to the holder of a conflicting security interest in inventory by sending a notification to that address, even if the address is or becomes incorrect. See Section 9–102 (definition of "send"). Similarly, because the address is "held out by [the holder of the conflicting security interest] as the place for receipt of such communications [i.e., communications relating to security interests]," the holder is deemed to have "received" a notification delivered to that address. See Section 1–202(e).

7. **Consignments.** Subsections (b) and (c) also determine the priority of a consignor's interest in consigned goods as against a security interest in the goods created by the consignee. Inasmuch as a consignment subject to this Article is defined to be a purchase-money security interest, see Section 9–103(d), no inference concerning the nature of the transaction should be drawn from the fact that a consignor uses the term "security interest" in its notice under subsection (b)(4). Similarly, a notice stating that the consignor has delivered or expects to deliver goods, properly described, "on consignment" meets the requirements of subsection (b)(4), even if it does not contain the term "security interest," and even if the transaction subsequently is determined to be a security interest. Cf. Section 9–505 (use of "consignor" and "consignee" in financing statement).

8. **Priority in Proceeds: General.** When the purchase-money secured party has priority over another secured party, the question arises whether this priority extends to the proceeds of the original collateral. Subsections (a), (d), and (f) give an affirmative answer, but only as to proceeds in which the security interest is perfected (see Section 9–315). Although this qualification did not appear in former Section 9–312(4), it was implicit in that provision.

In the case of inventory collateral under subsection (b), where financing frequently is based on the resulting accounts, chattel paper, or other proceeds, the special priority of the purchase-money secured interest carries over into only certain types of proceeds. As under former Section 9–312(3), the purchase-money priority in inventory under subsection (b) carries over into identifiable cash proceeds (defined in Section 9–102) received on or before the delivery of the inventory to a buyer.

As a general matter, also like former Section 9–312(3), the purchase-money priority in inventory does *not* carry over into proceeds consisting of accounts or chattel paper. Many parties financing inventory are quite content to protect their first-priority security interest in the inventory itself. They realize that when the inventory is sold, someone else will be financing the resulting receivables (accounts or chattel paper), and the priority for inventory will not run forward to the receivables constituting the proceeds. Indeed, the cash supplied by the receivables financer often will be used to pay the inventory financing. In some situations, the party financing the inventory on a purchase-money basis makes contractual arrangements that the proceeds of receivables financing by another be devoted to paying off the inventory security interest.

However, the purchase-money priority in inventory *does* carry over to proceeds consisting of chattel paper and its proceeds (and also to instruments) to the extent provided in Section 9–330. Under Section 9–330(e), the holder of a purchase-money security interest in inventory is deemed to give new value for proceeds consisting of chattel paper. Taken together, Sections 9–324(b) and 9–330(e) enable a purchase-money inventory secured party to obtain priority in chattel paper constituting proceeds of the inventory, even if the secured party does not actually give new value for the chattel paper, provided the purchase-money secured party satisfies the other conditions for achieving priority.

When the proceeds of original collateral (goods or software) consist of a deposit account, Section 9–327 governs priority to the extent it conflicts with the priority rules of this section.

9. **Priority in Accounts Constituting Proceeds of Inventory.** The application of the priority rules in subsection (b) is shown by the following examples:

Example 1: Debtor creates a security interest in its existing and after-acquired inventory in favor of SP-1, who files a financing statement covering inventory. SP-2 subsequently takes a purchase-money security interest in certain inventory and, under subsection (b), achieves priority in this inventory over SP-1. This inventory is then sold, producing accounts. Accounts are not cash proceeds, and so the special purchase-money priority in the inventory does not control the priority in the accounts. Rather, the first-to-file-or-perfect rule of Section 9–322(a)(1) applies. The time of SP-1's filing as to the inventory is also the time of filing as to the accounts under Section 9–322(b). Assuming that each security interest in the accounts proceeds remains perfected under Section 9–315, SP-1 has priority as to the accounts.

Example 2: In Example 1, if SP-2 had filed directly against accounts, the date of that filing as to accounts would be compared with the date of SP-1's filing as to the inventory. The first filed would prevail under Section 9–322(a)(1).

Example 3: If SP-3 had filed against accounts in Example 1 before either SP-1 or SP-2 filed against inventory, SP-3's filing against accounts would have priority over the filings of SP-1 and SP-2. This result obtains even though the filings against inventory are effective to continue the perfected status of SP-1's and SP-2's security interest in the accounts beyond the 20-day period of automatic perfection. See Section 9–315. SP-1's and SP-2's position as to the inventory does not give them a claim to accounts (as proceeds of the inventory) which is senior to someone who has filed earlier against accounts. If, on the other hand, either SP-1's or SP-2's filing against the inventory preceded SP-3's filing against accounts, SP-1 or SP-2 would outrank SP-3 as to the accounts.

10. **Purchase-Money Security Interests in Livestock.** New subsections (d) and (e) provide a purchase-money priority rule for farm-products livestock. They are patterned on the purchase-money priority rule for inventory found in subsections (b) and (c) and include a requirement that the purchase-money secured party notify earlier-filed parties. Two differences between subsections (b) and (d) are noteworthy. First, unlike the purchase-money inventory lender, the purchase-money livestock lender enjoys priority in *all* proceeds of the collateral. Thus, under subsection (d), the purchase-money secured party takes priority in accounts over an earlier-filed accounts financer. Second, subsection (d) affords priority in certain products of the collateral as well as proceeds.

11. **Purchase-Money Security Interests in Aquatic Farm Products.** Aquatic goods produced in aquacultural operations (e.g., catfish raised on a catfish farm) are farm products. See Section 9–102 (definition of "farm products"). The definition does not indicate whether aquatic goods are "crops," as to which the model production money security interest priority in Section 9–324A applies, or "livestock," as to which the purchase-money priority in subsection (d) of this section applies. This Article leaves courts free to determine the classification of particular aquatic goods on a case-by-case basis, applying whichever priority rule makes more sense in the overall context of the debtor's business.

12. **Purchase-Money Security Interests in Software.** Subsection (f) governs the priority of purchase-money security interests in software. Under Section 9–103(c), a purchase-money security interest arises in

software only if the debtor acquires its interest in the software for the principal purpose of using the software in goods subject to a purchase-money security interest. Under subsection (f), a purchase-money security interest in software has the same priority as the purchase-money security interest in the goods in which the software was acquired for use. This priority is determined under subsections (b) and (c) (for inventory) or (a) (for other goods).

13. **Multiple Purchase-Money Security Interests.** New subsection (g) governs priority among multiple purchase-money security interests in the same collateral. It grants priority to purchase-money security interests securing the price of collateral (i.e., created in favor of the seller) over purchase-money security interests that secure enabling loans. Section 7.2(c) of the Restatement (3d) of the Law of Property (Mortgages) (1997) adopts this rule with respect to real property mortgages. As Comment *d* to that section explains:

> the equities favor the vendor. Not only does the vendor part with specific real estate rather than money, but the vendor would never relinquish it at all except on the understanding that the vendor will be able to use it to satisfy the obligation to pay the price. This is the case even though the vendor may know that the mortgagor is going to finance the transaction in part by borrowing from a third party and giving a mortgage to secure that obligation. In the final analysis, the law is more sympathetic to the vendor's hazard of losing real estate previously owned than to the third party lender's risk of being unable to collect from an interest in real estate that never previously belonged to it.

The first-to-file-or-perfect rule of Section 9–322 applies to multiple purchase-money security interests securing enabling loans.

As amended in 2010.

§ 9–325.   Priority of Security Interests in Transferred Collateral.

(a) **[Subordination of security interest in transferred collateral.]** Except as otherwise provided in subsection (b), a security interest created by a debtor is subordinate to a security interest in the same collateral created by another person if:

(1) the debtor acquired the collateral subject to the security interest created by the other person;

(2) the security interest created by the other person was perfected when the debtor acquired the collateral; and

(3) there is no period thereafter when the security interest is unperfected.

(b) **[Limitation of subsection (a) subordination.]** Subsection (a) subordinates a security interest only if the security interest:

(1) otherwise would have priority solely under Section 9–322(a) or 9–324; or

(2) arose solely under Section 2–711(3) or 2A–508(5).

Official Comment

1. **Source.** New.

2. **"Double Debtor Problem."** This section addresses the "double debtor" problem, which arises when a debtor acquires property that is subject to a security interest created by another debtor.

3. **Taking Subject to Perfected Security Interest.** Consider the following scenario:

Example 1:   A owns an item of equipment subject to a perfected security interest in favor of SP-A. A sells the equipment to B, not in the ordinary course of business. B acquires its interest subject to SP-A's security interest. See Sections 9–201, 9–315(a)(1). Under this section, if B creates a security interest in the equipment in favor of SP-B, SP-B's security interest is subordinate to SP-A's security interest, even if SP-B filed against B before SP-A filed against A, and even if SP-B took a purchase-money security interest. Normally, SP-B could have investigated the source of the equipment and discovered SP-A's filing before making an advance against the equipment, whereas SP-A had no reason to search the filings against someone other than its debtor, A.

4. **Taking Subject to Unperfected Security Interest.** This section applies only if the security interest in the transferred collateral was perfected when the transferee acquired the collateral. See subsection (a)(2). If this condition is not met, then the normal priority rules apply.

Example 2:   A owns an item of equipment subject to an unperfected security interest in favor of SP-A. A sells the equipment to B, who gives value and takes delivery of the equipment without knowledge of the security interest. B takes free of the security interest. See Section 9–317(b). If B then creates a security interest in favor of SP-B, no priority issue arises; SP-B has the only security interest in the equipment.

Example 3:   The facts are as in Example 2, except that B knows of SP-A's security interest and therefore takes the equipment subject to it. If B creates a security interest in the equipment in favor of SP-B, this section does not determine the relative priority of the security interests. Rather, the normal priority rules govern. If SP-B perfects its security interest, then, under Section 9–322(a)(2), SP-A's unperfected security interest will be junior to SP-B's perfected security interest. The award of priority to SP-B is premised on the belief that SP-A's failure to file could have misled SP-B.

5.   **Taking Subject to Perfected Security Interest that Becomes Unperfected.** This section applies only if the security interest in the transferred collateral did not become unperfected at any time after the transferee acquired the collateral. See subsection (a)(3). If this condition is not met, then the normal priority rules apply.

Example 4:   As in Example 1, A owns an item of equipment subject to a perfected security interest in favor of SP-A. A sells the equipment to B, not in the ordinary course of business. B acquires its interest subject to SP-A's security interest. See Sections 9–201, 9–315(a)(1). B creates a security interest in favor of SP-B, and SP-B perfects its security interest. This section provides that SP-A's security interest is senior to SP-B's. However, if SP-A's financing statement lapses while SP-B's security interest is perfected, then the normal priority rules would apply, and SP-B's security interest would become senior to SP-A's security interest. See Sections 9–322(a)(2), 9–515(c).

6.   **Unusual Situations.** The appropriateness of the rule of subsection (a) is most apparent when it works to subordinate security interests having priority under the basic priority rules of Section 9–322(a) or the purchase-money priority rules of Section 9–324. The rule also works properly when applied to the security interest of a buyer under Section 2–711(3) or a lessee under Section 2A–508(5). However, subsection (a) may provide an inappropriate resolution of the "double debtor" problem in some of the wide variety of other contexts in which the problem may arise. Although subsection (b) limits the application of subsection (a) to those cases in which subordination is known to be appropriate, courts should apply the rule in other settings, if necessary to promote the underlying purposes and policies of the Uniform Commercial Code. See Section 1–103(a).

As amended in 2005.

§ 9–326.   Priority of Security Interests Created by New Debtor.

(a)   **[Subordination of security interest created by new debtor.]** Subject to subsection (b), a security interest that is created by a new debtor in collateral in which the new debtor has or acquires rights and is perfected solely by a filed financing statement that would be ineffective to perfect the security interest but for the application of Section 9–316(i)(1) or 9–508 is subordinate to a security interest in the same collateral which is perfected other than by such a filed financing statement.

(b)   **[Priority under other provisions; multiple original debtors.]** The other provisions of this part determine the priority among conflicting security interests in the same collateral perfected by filed financing statements described in subsection (a). However, if the security agreements to which a new debtor became bound as debtor were not entered into by the same original debtor, the conflicting security interests rank according to priority in time of the new debtor's having become bound.

Official Comment

1.   **Source.** New.

2.   **Subordination of Security Interests Created by New Debtor.** This section addresses the priority contests that may arise when a new debtor becomes bound by the security agreement of an original debtor and each debtor has a secured creditor.

Subsection (a) subordinates the original debtor's secured party's security interest perfected against the new debtor by a filed financing statement that would be ineffective to perfect the security interest but for Section 9–508 or, if the original debtor and new debtor are located in different jurisdictions, Section 9–316(i)(1). The security interest is subordinated to security interests in the same collateral perfected by another method, e.g., by filing against the new debtor. This section does not subordinate a security interest perfected by a new initial financing statement providing the name of the new debtor, even if the initial financing statement is filed to maintain the effectiveness of a financing statement under the circumstances described in Section 9–508(b). Nor does it subordinate a security interest perfected by a financing statement filed against the original debtor which remains effective against collateral transferred by the original debtor to the new debtor. See Section 9–508(c). Concerning priority contests involving transferred collateral, see Sections 9–325 and 9–507.

Example 1: SP-X holds a perfected-by-filing security interest in X Corp's existing and after-acquired inventory, and SP-Z holds a perfected-by-possession security interest in an item of Z Corp's inventory. Both X Corp and Z Corp are located in the same jurisdiction under Section 9–307. Z Corp becomes bound as debtor by X Corp's security agreement (e.g., Z Corp buys X Corp's assets and assumes its security agreement). See Section 9–203(d). But for Section 9–508, SP-X's financing statement would be ineffective to perfect a security interest in the item of inventory in which Z Corp has rights. However, subsection (a) provides that SP-X's perfected security interest is subordinate to SP-Z's, regardless of whether SP-X's financing statement was filed before SP-Z perfected its security interest.

Example 2: SP-X holds a perfected-by-filing security interest in X Corp's existing and after-acquired inventory, and SP-Z holds a perfected-by-filing security interest in Z Corp's existing and after-acquired inventory. Both X Corp and Z Corp are located in the same jurisdiction under Section 9–307. Z Corp becomes bound as debtor by X Corp's security agreement. Immediately thereafter, and before the effectiveness of SP-X's financing statement lapses, Z Corp acquires a new item of inventory. But for Section 9–508, SP-X's financing statement would be ineffective to perfect a security interest in the new item of inventory in which Z Corp has rights. However, because SP-Z's security interest was perfected by a filing whose effectiveness does not depend on Section 9–316(i)(1) or 9–508, subsection (a) subordinates SP-X's perfected security interest to SP-Z's. This would be the case even if SP-Z filed after Z Corp became bound by X Corp's security agreement, and regardless of which financing statement was filed first.

The same result would obtain if X Corp and Z Corp were located in different jurisdictions. SP-X's security interest would be perfected by a financing statement that would be ineffective but for Section 9–316(i)(1), whereas the effectiveness of SP-Z's filing does not depend on Section 9–316(i)(1) or 9–508.

3. **Other Priority Rules.** Subsection (b) addresses the priority among security interests created by the original debtor (X Corp). By invoking the other priority rules of this subpart, as applicable, subsection (b) preserves the relative priority of security interests created by the original debtor.

Example 3: Under the facts of Example 2, SP-Y also holds a perfected-by-filing security interest in X Corp's existing and after-acquired inventory. SP-Y filed after SP-X. Inasmuch as both SP-X's and SP-Y's security interests in inventory acquired by Z Corp after it became bound would be unperfected but for the application of Section 9–508, the normal priority rules determine their relative priorities. Under the "first-to-file-or-perfect" rule of Section 9–322(a)(1), SP-X has priority over SP-Y.

Example 4: Under the facts of Example 3, after Z Corp became bound by X Corp's security agreement, SP-Y promptly filed a new initial financing statement against Z Corp. SP-X's security interest remains perfected only by virtue of its original filing against X Corp which "would be ineffective to perfect the security interest but for the application of Section 9–508." Because SP-Y's security interest is perfected by the filing of a financing statement whose effectiveness does not depend on Section 9–508 or 9–316(i)(1), subsection (a) subordinates SP-X's security interest to SP-Y's. If both SP-X and SP-Y file a new initial financing statement against Z Corp, then the "first-to-file-or-perfect" rule of Section 9–322(a)(1) governs their priority inter se as well as their priority against SP-Z.

The second sentence of subsection (b) effectively limits the applicability of the first sentence to situations in which a new debtor has become bound by more than one security agreement entered into by the *same* original debtor. When the new debtor has become bound by security agreements entered into by *different* original debtors, the second sentence provides that priority is based on priority in time of the new debtor's becoming bound.

Example 5: Under the facts of Example 2, SP-W holds a perfected-by-filing security interest in W Corp's existing and after-acquired inventory. After Z Corp became bound by X Corp's security agreement in favor of SP-X, Z Corp became bound by W Corp's security agreement. Under subsection (b), SP-W's security interest in inventory acquired by Z Corp is subordinate to that of SP-X, because Z Corp became bound under SP-X's security agreement before it became bound under SP-W's security agreement. This is the result regardless of which financing statement (SP-X's or SP-W's) was filed first.

The second sentence of subsection (b) reflects the generally accepted view that priority based on the first-to-file rule is inappropriate for resolving priority disputes when the filings were made against different debtors. Like subsection (a) and the first sentence of subsection (b), however, the second sentence of subsection (b) relates only to priority conflicts among security interests would be unperfected but for the application of Section 9–316(i)(1) or 9–508.

> **Example 6:**   Under the facts of Example 5, after Z Corp became bound by W Corp's security agreement, SP-W promptly filed a new initial financing statement against Z Corp. At that time, SP-X's security interest was perfected only pursuant to its original filing against X Corp which "would be ineffective to perfect the security interest but for the application of Section 9–508." Because SP-W's security interest is perfected by the filing of a financing statement whose effectiveness does not depend on Section 9–316(i)(1) or 9–508, subsection (a) subordinates SP-X's security interest to SP-W's. If both SP-X and SP-W file a new initial financing statement against Z Corp, then the "first-to-file-or-perfect" rule of Section 9–322(a)(1) governs their priority inter se as well as their priority against SP-Z.

As amended in 2010.

§ 9–327.   Priority of Security Interests in Deposit Account.

The following rules govern priority among conflicting security interests in the same deposit account:

(1)   A security interest held by a secured party having control of the deposit account under Section 9–104 has priority over a conflicting security interest held by a secured party that does not have control.

(2)   Except as otherwise provided in paragraphs (3) and (4), security interests perfected by control under Section 9–314 rank according to priority in time of obtaining control.

(3)   Except as otherwise provided in paragraph (4), a security interest held by the bank with which the deposit account is maintained has priority over a conflicting security interest held by another secured party.

(4)   A security interest perfected by control under Section 9–104(a)(3) has priority over a security interest held by the bank with which the deposit account is maintained.

Official Comment

1.   **Source.** New; derived from former Section 9–115(5).

2.   **Scope of This Section.** This section contains the rules governing the priority of conflicting security interests in deposit accounts. It overrides conflicting priority rules. See Sections 9–322(f)(1), 9–324(a), (b), (d), (f). This section does not apply to accounts evidenced by an instrument (e.g., certain certificates of deposit), which by definition are not "deposit accounts."

3.   **Control.** Under paragraph (1), security interests perfected by control (Sections 9–314, 9–104) take priority over those perfected otherwise, e.g., as identifiable cash proceeds under Section 9–315. Secured parties for whom the deposit account is an integral part of the credit decision will, at a minimum, insist upon the right to immediate access to the deposit account upon the debtor's default (i.e., control). Those secured parties for whom the deposit account is less essential will not take control, thereby running the risk that the debtor will dispose of funds on deposit (either outright or for collateral purposes) after default but before the account can be frozen by court order or the secured party can obtain control.

Paragraph (2) governs the case (expected to be very rare) in which a bank enters into a Section 9–104(a)(2) control agreement with more than one secured party. It provides that the security interests rank according to time of obtaining control. If the bank is solvent and the control agreements are well drafted, the bank will be liable to each secured party, and the priority rule will have no practical effect.

4.   **Priority of Bank.** Under paragraph (3), the security interest of the bank with which the deposit account is maintained normally takes priority over all other conflicting security interests in the deposit account, regardless of whether the deposit account constitutes the competing secured party's original collateral or its proceeds. A rule of this kind enables banks to extend credit to their depositors without the need to examine either the public record or their own records to determine whether another party might have a security interest in the deposit account.

A secured party who takes a security interest in the deposit account as original collateral can protect itself against the results of this rule in one of two ways. It can take control of the deposit account by becoming the bank's customer. Under paragraph (4), this arrangement operates to subordinate the bank's security interest. Alternatively, the secured party can obtain a subordination agreement from the bank. See Section 9–339.

A secured party who claims the deposit account as proceeds of other collateral can reduce the risk of becoming junior by obtaining the debtor's agreement to deposit proceeds into a specific cash-collateral account and obtaining the agreement of that bank to subordinate all its claims to those of the secured party. But if the debtor violates its agreement and deposits funds into a deposit account other than the cash-collateral account, the secured party risks being subordinated.

5. **Priority in Proceeds of, and Funds Transferred from, Deposit Account.** The priority afforded by this section does not extend to proceeds of a deposit account. Rather, Section 9–322(c) through (e) and the provisions referred to in Section 9–322(f) govern priorities in proceeds of a deposit account. Section 9–315(d) addresses continuation of perfection in proceeds of deposit accounts. As to funds transferred from a deposit account that serves as collateral, see Section 9–332.

§ 9–328. Priority of Security Interests in Investment Property.

The following rules govern priority among conflicting security interests in the same investment property:

(1) A security interest held by a secured party having control of investment property under Section 9–106 has priority over a security interest held by a secured party that does not have control of the investment property.

(2) Except as otherwise provided in paragraphs (3) and (4), conflicting security interests held by secured parties each of which has control under Section 9–106 rank according to priority in time of:

(A) if the collateral is a security, obtaining control;

(B) if the collateral is a security entitlement carried in a securities account and:

(i) if the secured party obtained control under Section 8–106(d)(1), the secured party's becoming the person for which the securities account is maintained;

(ii) if the secured party obtained control under Section 8–106(d)(2), the securities intermediary's agreement to comply with the secured party's entitlement orders with respect to security entitlements carried or to be carried in the securities account; or

(iii) if the secured party obtained control through another person under Section 8–106(d)(3), the time on which priority would be based under this paragraph if the other person were the secured party; or

(C) if the collateral is a commodity contract carried with a commodity intermediary, the satisfaction of the requirement for control specified in Section 9–106(b)(2) with respect to commodity contracts carried or to be carried with the commodity intermediary.

(3) A security interest held by a securities intermediary in a security entitlement or a securities account maintained with the securities intermediary has priority over a conflicting security interest held by another secured party.

(4) A security interest held by a commodity intermediary in a commodity contract or a commodity account maintained with the commodity intermediary has priority over a conflicting security interest held by another secured party.

(5) A security interest in a certificated security in registered form which is perfected by taking delivery under Section 9–313(a) and not by control under Section 9–314 has priority over a conflicting security interest perfected by a method other than control.

(6) Conflicting security interests created by a broker, securities intermediary, or commodity intermediary which are perfected without control under Section 9–106 rank equally.

(7) In all other cases, priority among conflicting security interests in investment property is governed by Sections 9–322 and 9–323.

Official Comment

1. **Source.** Former Section 9–115(5).

2.   Scope of This Section. This section contains the rules governing the priority of conflicting security interests in investment property. Paragraph (1) states the most important general rule—that a secured party who obtains control has priority over a secured party who does not obtain control. Paragraphs (2) through (4) deal with conflicting security interests each of which is perfected by control. Paragraph (5) addresses the priority of a security interest in a certificated security which is perfected by delivery but not control. Paragraph (6) deals with the relatively unusual circumstance in which a broker, securities intermediary, or commodity intermediary has created conflicting security interests none of which is perfected by control. Paragraph (7) provides that the general priority rules of Sections 9–322 and 9–323 apply to cases not covered by the specific rules in this section. The principal application of this residual rule is that the usual first in time of filing rule applies to conflicting security interests that are perfected only by filing. Because the control priority rule of paragraph (1) provides for the ordinary cases in which persons purchase securities on margin credit from their brokers, there is no need for special rules for purchase-money security interests. See also Section 9–103 (limiting purchase-money collateral to goods and software).

3.   General Rule: Priority of Security Interest Perfected by Control. Under paragraph (1), a secured party who obtains control has priority over a secured party who does not obtain control. The control priority rule does not turn on either temporal sequence or awareness of conflicting security interests. Rather, it is a structural rule, based on the principle that a lender should be able to rely on the collateral without question if the lender has taken the necessary steps to assure itself that it is in a position where it can foreclose on the collateral without further action by the debtor. The control priority rule is necessary because the perfection rules provide considerable flexibility in structuring secured financing arrangements. For example, at the "retail" level, a secured lender to an investor who wants the full measure of protection can obtain control, but the creditor may be willing to accept the greater measure of risk that follows from perfection by filing. Similarly, at the "wholesale" level, a lender to securities firms can leave the collateral with the debtor and obtain a perfected security interest under the automatic perfection rule of Section 9–309(10), but a lender who wants to be entirely sure of its position will want to obtain control. The control priority rule of paragraph (1) is an essential part of this system of flexibility. It is feasible to provide more than one method of perfecting security interests only if the rules ensure that those who take the necessary steps to obtain the full measure of protection do not run the risk of subordination to those who have not taken such steps. A secured party who is unwilling to run the risk that the debtor has granted or will grant a conflicting control security interest should not make a loan without obtaining control of the collateral.

As applied to the retail level, the control priority rule means that a secured party who obtains control has priority over a conflicting security interest perfected by filing without regard to inquiry into whether the control secured party was aware of the filed security interest. Prior to the 1994 revisions to Articles 8 and 9, Article 9 did not permit perfection of security interests in securities by filing. Accordingly, parties who deal in securities never developed a practice of searching the UCC files before conducting securities transactions. Although filing is now a permissible method of perfection, in order to avoid disruption of existing practices in this business it is necessary to give perfection by filing a different and more limited effect for securities than for some other forms of collateral. The priority rules are not based on the assumption that parties who perfect by the usual method of obtaining control will search the files. Quite the contrary, the control priority rule is intended to ensure that, with respect to investment property, secured parties who do obtain control are entirely unaffected by filings. To state the point another way, perfection by filing is intended to affect only general creditors or other secured creditors who rely on filing. The rule that a security interest perfected by filing can be primed by a control security interest, without regard to awareness, is a consequence of the system of perfection and priority rules for investment property. These rules are designed to take account of the circumstances of the securities markets, where filing is not given the same effect as for some other forms of property. No implication is made about the effect of filing with respect to security interests in other forms of property, nor about other Article 9 rules, e.g., Section 9–330, which govern the circumstances in which security interests in other forms of property perfected by filing can be primed by subsequent perfected security interests.

The following examples illustrate the application of the priority rule in paragraph (1):

Example 1:   Debtor borrows from Alpha and grants Alpha a security interest in a variety of collateral, including all of Debtor's investment property. At that time Debtor owns 1000 shares of XYZ Co. stock for which Debtor has a certificate. Alpha perfects by filing. Later, Debtor borrows from Beta and grants Beta a security interest in the 1000 shares of XYZ Co. stock. Debtor delivers the certificate, properly indorsed, to Beta. Alpha and Beta both have perfected security interests in the XYZ Co. stock. Beta has control, see Section 8–106(b)(1), and hence has priority over Alpha.

Example 2:   Debtor borrows from Alpha and grants Alpha a security interest in a variety of collateral, including all of Debtor's investment property. At that time Debtor owns 1000 shares of XYZ Co. stock, held

804

through a securities account with Able & Co. Alpha perfects by filing. Later, Debtor borrows from Beta and grants Beta a security interest in the 1000 shares of XYZ Co. stock. Debtor instructs Able to have the 1000 shares transferred through the clearing corporation to Custodian Bank, to be credited to Beta's account with Custodian Bank. Alpha and Beta both have perfected security interests in the XYZ Co. stock. Beta has control, see Section 8–106(d)(1), and hence has priority over Alpha.

Example 3:   Debtor borrows from Alpha and grants Alpha a security interest in a variety of collateral, including all of Debtor's investment property. At that time Debtor owns 1000 shares of XYZ Co. stock, which is held through a securities account with Able & Co. Alpha perfects by filing. Later, Debtor borrows from Beta and grants Beta a security interest in the 1000 shares of XYZ Co. stock. Debtor, Able, and Beta enter into an agreement under which Debtor will continue to receive dividends and distributions, and will continue to have the right to direct dispositions, but Beta will also have the right to direct dispositions and receive the proceeds. Alpha and Beta both have perfected security interests in the XYZ Co. stock (more precisely, in the Debtor's security entitlement to the financial asset consisting of the XYZ Co. stock). Beta has control, see Section 8–106(d)(2), and hence has priority over Alpha.

Example 4:   Debtor borrows from Alpha and grants Alpha a security interest in a variety of collateral, including all of Debtor's investment property. At that time Debtor owns 1000 shares of XYZ Co. stock, held through a securities account with Able & Co. Alpha perfects by filing. Debtor's agreement with Able & Co. provides that Able has a security interest in all securities carried in the account as security for any obligations of Debtor to Able. Debtor incurs obligations to Able and later defaults on the obligations to Alpha and Able. Able has control by virtue of the rule of Section 8–106(e) that if a customer grants a security interest to its own intermediary, the intermediary has control. Since Alpha does not have control, Able has priority over Alpha under the general control priority rule of paragraph (1).

4.   **Conflicting Security Interests Perfected by Control: Priority of Securities Intermediary or Commodity Intermediary.** Paragraphs (2) through (4) govern the priority of conflicting security interests each of which is perfected by control. The following example explains the application of the rules in paragraphs (3) and (4):

Example 5:   Debtor holds securities through a securities account with Able & Co. Debtor's agreement with Able & Co. provides that Able has a security interest in all securities carried in the account as security for any obligations of Debtor to Able. Debtor borrows from Beta and grants Beta a security interest in 1000 shares of XYZ Co. stock carried in the account. Debtor, Able, and Beta enter into an agreement under which Debtor will continue to receive dividends and distributions and will continue to have the right to direct dispositions, but Beta will also have the right to direct dispositions and receive the proceeds. Debtor incurs obligations to Able and later defaults on the obligations to Beta and Able. Both Beta and Able have control, so the general control priority rule of paragraph (1) does not apply. Compare Example 4. Paragraph (3) provides that a security interest held by a securities intermediary in positions of its own customer has priority over a conflicting security interest of an external lender, so Able has priority over Beta. (Paragraph (4) contains a parallel rule for commodity intermediaries.) The agreement among Able, Beta, and Debtor could, of course, determine the relative priority of the security interests of Able and Beta, see Section 9–339, but the fact that the intermediary has agreed to act on the instructions of a secured party such as Beta does not itself imply any agreement by the intermediary to subordinate.

5.   **Conflicting Security Interests Perfected by Control: Temporal Priority.** Former Section 9–115 introduced into Article 9 the concept of conflicting security interests that rank equally. Paragraph (2) of this section governs priority in those circumstances in which more than one secured party (other than a broker, securities intermediary, or commodity intermediary) has control. It replaces the equal-priority rule for conflicting security interests in investment property with a temporal rule. For securities, both certificated and uncertificated, under paragraph (2)(A) priority is based on the time that control is obtained. For security entitlements carried in securities accounts, the treatment is more complex. Paragraph (2)(B) bases priority on the timing of the steps taken to achieve control. The following example illustrates the application of paragraph (2).

Example 6:   Debtor borrows from Alpha and grants Alpha a security interest in a variety of collateral, including all of Debtor's investment property. At that time Debtor owns a security entitlement that includes 1000 shares of XYZ Co. stock that Debtor holds through a securities account with Able & Co. Debtor, Able, and Alpha enter into an agreement under which Debtor will continue to receive dividends and distributions, and will continue to have the right to direct dispositions, but Alpha will also have the right to direct dispositions and receive the proceeds. Later, Debtor borrows from Beta and grants Beta a security interest in all its investment property, existing and after-acquired. Debtor, Able, and Beta enter into an agreement under which Debtor will continue to receive dividends and distributions, and will continue to have the right to direct dispositions, but Beta will also have the right to direct dispositions and receive the proceeds. Alpha and Beta both have perfected-by-control security interests in the security entitlement to the XYZ Co. stock by virtue of their agreements with Able. See Sections 9–314(a), 9–106(a), 8–106(d)(2). Under paragraph (2)(B)(ii), the priority of each security interest dates from the time of the secured party's agreement with Able. Because Alpha's agreement was first in time, Alpha has priority. This priority applies equally to security entitlements to financial assets credited to the account after the agreement was entered into.

The priority rule is analogous to "first-to-file" priority under Section 9–322 with respect to after-acquired collateral. Paragraphs (2)(B)(i) and (2)(B)(iii) provide similar rules for security entitlements as to which control is obtained by other methods, and paragraph (2)(C) provides a similar rule for commodity contracts carried in a commodity account. Section 8–510 also has been revised to provide a temporal priority conforming to paragraph (2)(B).

6. **Certificated Securities.** A long-standing practice has developed whereby secured parties whose collateral consists of a security evidenced by a security certificate take possession of the security certificate. If the security certificate is in bearer form, the secured party's acquisition of possession constitutes "delivery" under Section 8–301(a)(1), and the delivery constitutes "control" under Section 8–106(a). Comment 5 discusses the priority of security interests perfected by control of investment property.

If the security certificate is in registered form, the secured party will not achieve control over the security unless the security certificate contains an appropriate indorsement or is (re)registered in the secured party's name. See Section 8–106(b). However, the secured party's acquisition of possession constitutes "delivery" of the security certificate under Section 8–301 and serves to perfect the security interest under Section 9–313(a), even if the security certificate has not been appropriately indorsed and has not been (re)registered in the secured party's name. A security interest perfected by this method has priority over a security interest perfected other than by control (e.g., by filing). See paragraph (5).

The priority rule stated in paragraph (5) may seem anomalous, in that it can afford less favorable treatment to purchasers who buy collateral outright that to those who take a security interest in it. For example, a buyer of a security certificate would cut off a security interest perfected by filing only if the buyer achieves the status of a protected purchaser under Section 8–303. The buyer would not be a protected purchaser, for example, if it does not obtain "control" under Section 8–106 (e.g., if it fails to obtain a proper indorsement of the certificate) or if it had notice of an adverse claim under Section 8–105. The apparent anomaly disappears, however, when one understands the priority rule not as one intended to protect careless or guilty parties, but as one that eliminates the need to conduct a search of the public records only insofar as necessary to serve the needs of the securities markets.

7. **Secured Financing of Securities Firms.** Priority questions concerning security interests granted by brokers and securities intermediaries are governed by the general control-beats-non-control priority rule of paragraph (1), as supplemented by the special rules set out in paragraphs (2) (temporal priority—first to control), (3) (special priority for securities intermediary), and (6) (equal priority for non-control). The following examples illustrate the priority rules as applied to this setting. (In all cases it is assumed that the debtor retains sufficient other securities to satisfy all customers' claims. This section deals with the relative rights of secured lenders to a securities firm. Disputes between a secured lender and the firm's own customers are governed by Section 8–511.)

Example 7:   Able & Co., a securities dealer, enters into financing arrangements with two lenders, Alpha Bank and Beta Bank. In each case the agreements provide that the lender will have a security interest in the securities identified on lists provided to the lender on a daily basis, that the debtor will deliver the securities to the lender on demand, and that the debtor will not list as collateral any securities which the debtor has pledged to any other lender. Upon Able's insolvency it is discovered that Able has listed the same securities on the collateral lists provided to both Alpha and Beta. Alpha and Beta both have perfected security interests under the automatic-perfection rule of Section 9–309(10). Neither Alpha nor Beta has control. Paragraph (6) provides that the security interests of Alpha and Beta rank equally, because each of them has a non-control security interest granted by a securities firm. They share pro-rata.

Example 8:   Able enters into financing arrangements, with Alpha Bank and Beta Bank as in Example 7. At some point, however, Beta decides that it is unwilling to continue to provide financing on a non-control basis. Able directs the clearing corporation where it holds its principal inventory of securities to move specified securities into Beta's account. Upon Able's insolvency it is discovered that a list of collateral provided to Alpha includes securities that had been moved to Beta's account. Both Alpha and Beta have perfected security interests; Alpha under the automatic-perfection rule of Section 9–309(10), and Beta under that rule and also the perfection-by-control rule in Section 9–314(a). Beta has control but Alpha does not. Beta has priority over Alpha under paragraph (1).

Example 9: Able & Co. carries its principal inventory of securities through Clearing Corporation, which offers a "shared control" facility whereby a participant securities firm can enter into an arrangement with a lender under which the securities firm will retain the power to trade and otherwise direct dispositions of securities carried in its account, but Clearing Corporation agrees that, at any time the lender so directs, Clearing Corporation will transfer any securities from the firm's account to the lender's account or otherwise dispose of them as directed by the lender. Able enters into financing arrangements with two lenders, Alpha and Beta, each of which obtains such a control agreement from Clearing Corporation. The agreement with each lender provides that Able will designate specific securities as collateral on lists provided to the lender on a daily or other periodic basis, and that it will not pledge the same securities to different lenders. Upon Able's insolvency, it is discovered that Able has listed the same securities on the collateral lists provided to both Alpha and Beta. Both Alpha and Beta have control over the disputed securities. Paragraph (2) awards priority to whichever secured party first entered into the agreement with Clearing Corporation.

8. **Relation to Other Law.** Section 1–103 [*unrevised Article 1; see Concordance, p. 22*] provides that "unless displaced by particular provisions of this Act, the principles of law and equity . . . shall supplement its provisions." There may be circumstances in which a secured party's action in acquiring a security interest that has priority under this section constitutes conduct that is wrongful under other law. Though the possibility of such resort to other law may provide an appropriate "escape valve" for cases of egregious conduct, care must be taken to ensure that this does not impair the certainty and predictability of the priority rules. Whether a court may appropriately look to other law to impose liability upon or estop a secured party from asserting its Article 9 priority depends on an assessment of the secured party's conduct under the standards established by such other law as well as a determination of whether the particular application of such other law is displaced by the UCC.

Some circumstances in which other law is clearly displaced by the UCC rules are readily identifiable. Common law "first in time, first in right" principles, or correlative tort liability rules such as common law conversion principles under which a purchaser may incur liability to a person with a prior property interest without regard to awareness of that claim, are necessarily displaced by the priority rules set out in this section since these rules determine the relative ranking of security interests in investment property. So too, Article 8 provides protections against adverse claims to certain purchasers of interests in investment property. In circumstances where a secured party not only has priority under Section 9–328, but also qualifies for protection against adverse claims under Section 8–303, 8–502, or 8–510, resort to other law would be precluded.

In determining whether it is appropriate in a particular case to look to other law, account must also be taken of the policies that underlie the commercial law rules on securities markets and security interests in securities. A principal objective of the 1994 revision of Article 8 and the provisions of Article 9 governing investment property was to ensure that secured financing transactions can be implemented on a simple, timely, and certain basis. One of the circumstances that led to the revision was the concern that uncertainty in the application of the rules on secured transactions involving securities and other financial assets could contribute to systemic risk by impairing the ability of financial institutions to provide liquidity to the markets in times of stress. The control priority rule is designed to provide a clear and certain rule to ensure that lenders who have taken the necessary steps to establish control do not face a risk of subordination to other lenders who have not done so.

The control priority rule does not turn on an inquiry into the state of a secured party's awareness of potential conflicting claims because a rule under which a person's rights depended on that sort of after-the-fact inquiry could introduce an unacceptable measure of uncertainty. If an inquiry into awareness could provide a complete and satisfactory resolution of the problem in all cases, the priority rules of this section would have incorporated that test. The fact that they do not necessarily means that resort to other law based solely on that factor is precluded, though the question whether a control secured party induced or encouraged its financing arrangement with actual knowledge that the debtor would be violating the rights of another secured party may, in some circumstances, appropriately be treated as a factor in determining whether the control party's action is the kind of egregious conduct for which resort to other law is appropriate.

§ 9–329. Priority of Security Interests in Letter-of-Credit Right.

The following rules govern priority among conflicting security interests in the same letter-of-credit right:

(1)   A security interest held by a secured party having control of the letter-of-credit right under Section 9–107 has priority to the extent of its control over a conflicting security interest held by a secured party that does not have control.

(2)   Security interests perfected by control under Section 9–314 rank according to priority in time of obtaining control.

Official Comment

1.   **Source.** New; loosely modeled after former Section 9–115(5).

2.   **General Rule.** Paragraph (1) awards priority to a secured party who perfects a security interest directly in letter-of-credit rights (i.e., one that takes an assignment of proceeds and obtains consent of the issuer or any nominated person under Section 5–114(c)) over another conflicting security interest (i.e., one that is perfected automatically in the letter-of-credit rights as supporting obligations under Section 9–308(d)). This is consistent with international letter-of-credit practice and provides finality to payments made to recognized assignees of letter-of-credit proceeds. If an issuer or nominated person recognizes multiple security interests in a letter-of-credit right, resulting in multiple parties having control (Section 9–107), under paragraph (2) the security interests rank according to the time of obtaining control.

3.   **Drawing Rights; Transferee Beneficiaries.** Drawing under a letter of credit is personal to the beneficiary and requires the beneficiary to perform the conditions for drawing under the letter of credit. Accordingly, a beneficiary's grant of a security interest in a letter of credit includes the beneficiary's "letter-of-credit right" as defined in Section 9–102 and the right to "proceeds of [the] letter of credit" as defined in Section 5–114(a), but does not include the right to demand payment under the letter of credit.

Section 5–114(e) provides that the "[r]ights of a transferee beneficiary or nominated person are independent of the beneficiary's assignment of the proceeds of a letter of credit and are superior to the assignee's right to the proceeds." To the extent the rights of a transferee beneficiary or nominated person are independent and superior, this Article does not apply. See Section 9–109(c).

Under Article 5, there is in effect a novation upon the transfer with the issuer becoming bound on a new, independent obligation to the transferee. The rights of nominated persons and transferee beneficiaries under a letter of credit include the right to demand payment from the issuer. Under Section 5–114(e), their rights to payment are independent of their obligations to the beneficiary (or original beneficiary) and superior to the rights of assignees of letter-of-credit proceeds (Section 5–114(c)) and others claiming a security interest in the beneficiary's (or original beneficiary's) letter-of-credit rights.

A transfer of drawing rights under a transferable letter of credit establishes independent Article 5 rights in the transferee and does not create or perfect an Article 9 security interest in the transferred drawing rights. The definition of "letter-of-credit right" in Section 9–102 excludes a beneficiary's drawing rights. The exercise of drawing rights by a transferee beneficiary may breach a contractual obligation of the transferee to the original beneficiary concerning when and how much the transferee may draw or how it may use the funds received under the letter of credit. If, for example, drawing rights are transferred to support a sale or loan from the transferee to the original beneficiary, then the transferee would be obligated to the original beneficiary under the sale or loan agreement to account for any drawing and for the use of any funds received. The transferee's obligation would be governed by the applicable law of contracts or restitution.

4.   **Secured Party-Transferee Beneficiaries.** As described in Comment 3, drawing rights under letters of credit are transferred in many commercial contexts in which the transferee is not a secured party claiming a security interest in an underlying receivable supported by the letter of credit. Consequently, a transfer of a letter of credit is not a method of "perfection" of a security interest. The transferee's independent right to draw under the letter of credit and to receive and retain the value thereunder (in effect, priority) is not based on Article 9 but on letter-of-credit law and the terms of the letter of credit. Assume, however, that a secured party does hold a security interest in a receivable that is owned by a beneficiary-debtor and supported by a transferable letter of credit. Assume further that the beneficiary-debtor causes the letter of credit to be transferred to the secured party, the secured party draws under the letter of credit, and, upon the issuer's payment to the secured party-transferee, the underlying account debtor's obligation to the original beneficiary-debtor is satisfied. In this situation, the payment to the secured party-transferee is proceeds of the receivable collected by the secured party-transferee. Consequently, the secured party-transferee would have certain duties to the debtor and third parties under Article 9. For example, it would be obliged to collect under the letter of credit in a commercially reasonable manner and to remit any surplus pursuant to Sections 9–607 and 9–608.

808

This scenario is problematic under letter-of-credit law and practice, inasmuch as a transferee beneficiary collects in its own right arising from its own performance. Accordingly, under Section 5–114, the independent and superior rights of a transferee control over any inconsistent duties under Article 9. A transferee beneficiary may take a transfer of drawing rights to avoid reliance on the original beneficiary's credit and collateral, and it may consider any Article 9 rights superseded by its Article 5 rights. Moreover, it will not always be clear (i) whether a transferee beneficiary has a security interest in the underlying collateral, (ii) whether any security interest is senior to the rights of others, or (iii) whether the transferee beneficiary is aware that it holds a security interest. There will be clear cases in which the role of a transferee beneficiary as such is merely incidental to a conventional secured financing. There also will be cases in which the existence of a security interest may have little to do with the position of a transferee beneficiary as such. In dealing with these cases and less clear cases involving the possible application of Article 9 to a nominated person or a transferee beneficiary, the right to demand payment under a letter of credit should be distinguished from letter-of-credit rights. The courts also should give appropriate consideration to the policies and provisions of Article 5 and letter-of-credit practice as well as Article 9.

§ 9–330. Priority of Purchaser of Chattel Paper or Instrument.

(a) **[Purchaser's priority: security interest claimed merely as proceeds.]** A purchaser of chattel paper has priority over a security interest in the chattel paper which is claimed merely as proceeds of inventory subject to a security interest if:

(1) in good faith and in the ordinary course of the purchaser's business, the purchaser gives new value and takes possession of the chattel paper or obtains control of the chattel paper under Section 9–105; and

(2) the chattel paper does not indicate that it has been assigned to an identified assignee other than the purchaser.

(b) **[Purchaser's priority: other security interests.]** A purchaser of chattel paper has priority over a security interest in the chattel paper which is claimed other than merely as proceeds of inventory subject to a security interest if the purchaser gives new value and takes possession of the chattel paper or obtains control of the chattel paper under Section 9–105 in good faith, in the ordinary course of the purchaser's business, and without knowledge that the purchase violates the rights of the secured party.

(c) **[Chattel paper purchaser's priority in proceeds.]** Except as otherwise provided in Section 9–327, a purchaser having priority in chattel paper under subsection (a) or (b) also has priority in proceeds of the chattel paper to the extent that:

(1) Section 9–322 provides for priority in the proceeds; or

(2) the proceeds consist of the specific goods covered by the chattel paper or cash proceeds of the specific goods, even if the purchaser's security interest in the proceeds is unperfected.

(d) **[Instrument purchaser's priority.]** Except as otherwise provided in Section 9–331(a), a purchaser of an instrument has priority over a security interest in the instrument perfected by a method other than possession if the purchaser gives value and takes possession of the instrument in good faith and without knowledge that the purchase violates the rights of the secured party.

(e) **[Holder of purchase-money security interest gives new value.]** For purposes of subsections (a) and (b), the holder of a purchase-money security interest in inventory gives new value for chattel paper constituting proceeds of the inventory.

(f) **[Indication of assignment gives knowledge.]** For purposes of subsections (b) and (d), if chattel paper or an instrument indicates that it has been assigned to an identified secured party other than the purchaser, a purchaser of the chattel paper or instrument has knowledge that the purchase violates the rights of the secured party.

Official Comment

1. **Source.** Former Section 9–308.

2. **Non-Temporal Priority.** This Article permits a security interest in chattel paper or instruments to be perfected either by filing or by the secured party's taking possession. This section enables secured parties and other purchasers of chattel paper (both electronic and tangible) and instruments to obtain priority over earlier-perfected security interests, thereby promoting the negotiability of these types of receivables.

3. **Chattel Paper.** Subsections (a) and (b) follow former Section 9–308 in distinguishing between earlier-perfected security interests in chattel paper that is claimed merely as proceeds of inventory subject to a security interest and chattel paper that is claimed other than merely as proceeds. Like former Section 9–308, this section does not elaborate upon the phrase "merely as proceeds." For an elaboration, see PEB Commentary No. 8.

This section makes explicit the "good faith" requirement and retains the requirements of "the ordinary course of the purchaser's business" and the giving of "new value" as conditions for priority. Concerning the last, this Article deletes former Section 9–108 and adds to Section 9–102 a completely different definition of the term "new value." Under subsection (e), the holder of a purchase-money security interest in inventory is deemed to give "new value" for chattel paper constituting the proceeds of the inventory. Accordingly, the purchase-money secured party may qualify for priority in the chattel paper under subsection (a) or (b), whichever is applicable, even if it does not make an additional advance against the chattel paper.

If a possessory security interest in tangible chattel paper or a perfected-by-control security interest in electronic chattel paper does not qualify for priority under this section, it may be subordinate to a perfected-by-filing security interest under Section 9–322(a)(1).

4. **Possession and Control.** To qualify for priority under subsection (a) or (b), a purchaser must "take[ ] possession of the chattel paper or obtain[ ] control of the chattel paper under Section 9–105." When chattel paper comprises one or more tangible records and one or more electronic records, a purchaser may satisfy the possession-or-control requirement by taking possession of the tangible records under Section 9–313 and having control of the electronic records under Section 9–105. In determining which of several related records constitutes chattel paper and thus is relevant to possession or control, the form of the records is irrelevant. Rather, the touchstone is whether possession or control of the record would afford the public notice contemplated by the possession and control requirements. For example, because possession or control of an amendment extending the term of a lease would not afford the contemplated public notice, the amendment would not constitute chattel paper regardless of whether the amendment is in tangible form and the lease is in electronic form, the amendment is electronic and the lease is tangible, the amendment and lease are both tangible, or the amendment and lease are both electronic.

Two common practices have raised particular concerns with respect to the possession requirement. First, in some cases the parties create more than one copy or counterpart of chattel paper evidencing a single secured obligation or lease. This practice raises questions as to which counterpart is the "original" and whether it is necessary for a purchaser to take possession of all counterparts in order to "take possession" of the chattel paper. Second, parties sometimes enter into a single "master" agreement. The master agreement contemplates that the parties will enter into separate "schedules" from time to time, each evidencing chattel paper. Must a purchaser of an obligation or lease evidenced by a single schedule also take possession of the master agreement as well as the schedule in order to "take possession" of the chattel paper?

The problem raised by the first practice is easily solved. The parties may in the terms of their agreement and by designation on the chattel paper identify only one counterpart as the original chattel paper for purposes of taking possession of the chattel paper. Concerns about the second practice also are easily solved by careful drafting. Each schedule should provide that it incorporates the terms of the master agreement, not the other way around. This will make it clear that each schedule is a "stand alone" document.

A secured party may wish to convert tangible chattel paper to electronic chattel paper and vice versa. The priority of a security interest in chattel paper under subsection (a) or (b) may be preserved, even if the form of the chattel paper changes. The principle implied in the preceding paragraph, i.e., that not every copy of chattel paper is relevant, applies to "control" as well as to "possession." When there are multiple copies of chattel paper, a secured party may take "possession" or obtain "control" of the chattel paper if it acts with respect to the copy or copies that are reliably identified as the copy or copies that are relevant for purposes of possession or control. This principle applies as well to chattel paper that has been converted from one form to another, even if the relevant copies are not the "original" chattel paper.

5. **Chattel Paper Claimed Merely as Proceeds.** Subsection (a) revises the rule in former Section 9–308(b) to eliminate reference to what the purchaser knows. Instead, a purchaser who meets the possession or control, ordinary course, and new value requirements takes priority over a competing security interest unless the chattel paper itself indicates that it has been assigned to an identified assignee other than the purchaser. Thus subsection (a) recognizes the common practice of placing a "legend" on chattel paper to indicate that it has been assigned. This approach, under which the chattel paper purchaser who gives new value in ordinary course can rely on possession of unlegended, tangible chattel paper without any concern for other facts that it may know, comports with the expectations of both inventory and chattel paper financers.

6.   **Chattel Paper Claimed Other Than Merely as Proceeds.** Subsection (b) eliminates the requirement that the purchaser take without knowledge that the "specific paper" is subject to the security interest and substitutes for it the requirement that the purchaser take "without knowledge that the purchase violates the rights of the secured party." This standard derives from the definition of "buyer in ordinary course of business" in Section 1–201(b)(9). The source of the purchaser's knowledge is irrelevant. Note, however, that "knowledge" means "actual knowledge." Section 1–202(b).

In contrast to a junior secured party in accounts, who may be required in some special circumstances to undertake a search under the "good faith" requirement, see Comment 5 to Section 9–331, a purchaser of chattel paper under this section is not required as a matter of good faith to make a search in order to determine the existence of prior security interests. There may be circumstances where the purchaser undertakes a search nevertheless, either on its own volition or because other considerations make it advisable to do so, e.g., where the purchaser also is purchasing accounts. Without more, a purchaser of chattel paper who has seen a financing statement covering the chattel paper or who knows that the chattel paper is encumbered with a security interest, does not have knowledge that its purchase violates the secured party's rights. However, if a purchaser sees a statement in a financing statement to the effect that a purchase of chattel paper from the debtor would violate the rights of the filed secured party, the purchaser would have such knowledge. Likewise, under new subsection (f), if the chattel paper itself indicates that it had been assigned to an identified secured party other than the purchaser, the purchaser would have wrongful knowledge for purposes of subsection (b), thereby preventing the purchaser from qualifying for priority under that subsection, even if the purchaser did not have actual knowledge. In the case of tangible chattel paper, the indication normally would consist of a written legend on the chattel paper. In the case of electronic chattel paper, this Article leaves to developing market and technological practices the manner in which the chattel paper would indicate an assignment.

7.   **Instruments.** Subsection (d) contains a special priority rule for instruments. Under this subsection, a purchaser of an instrument has priority over a security interest perfected by a method other than possession (e.g., by filing, temporarily under Section 9–312(e) or (g), as proceeds under Section 9–315(d), or automatically upon attachment under Section 9–309(4) if the security interest arises out of a sale of the instrument) if the purchaser gives value and takes possession of the instrument in good faith and without knowledge that the purchase violates the rights of the secured party. Generally, to the extent subsection (d) conflicts with Section 3–306, subsection (d) governs. See Section 3–102(b). For example, notice of a conflicting security interest precludes a purchaser from becoming a holder in due course under Section 3–302 and thereby taking free of all claims to the instrument under Section 3–306. However, a purchaser who takes even with knowledge of the security interest qualifies for priority under subsection (d) if it takes without knowledge that the purchase violates the rights of the holder of the security interest. Likewise, a purchaser qualifies for priority under subsection (d) if it takes for "value" as defined in Section 1–201 [*unrevised Article 1; see Concordance, p. 22*], even if it does not take for "value" as defined in Section 3–303.

Subsection (d) is subject to Section 9–331(a), which provides that Article 9 does not limit the rights of a holder in due course under Article 3. Thus, in the rare case in which the purchaser of an instrument qualifies for priority under subsection (d), but another person has the rights of a holder in due course of the instrument, the other person takes free of the purchaser's claim. See Section 3–306.

The rule in subsection (d) is similar to the rules in subsections (a) and (b), which govern priority in chattel paper. The observations in Comment 6 concerning the requirement of good faith and the phrase "without knowledge that the purchase violates the rights of the secured party" apply equally to purchasers of instruments. However, unlike a purchaser of chattel paper, to qualify for priority under this section a purchaser of an instrument need only give "value" as defined in Section 1–201 [*unrevised Article 1; see Concordance, p. 22*]; it need not give "new value." Also, the purchaser need not purchase the instrument in the ordinary course of its business.

Subsection (d) applies to checks as well as notes. For example, to collect and retain checks that are proceeds (collections) of accounts free of a senior secured party's claim to the same checks, a junior secured party must satisfy the good-faith requirement (honesty in fact and the observance of reasonable commercial standards of fair dealing) of this subsection. This is the same good-faith requirement applicable to holders in due course. See Section 9–331, Comment 5.

8.   **Priority in Proceeds of Chattel Paper.** Subsection (c) sets forth the two circumstances under which the priority afforded to a purchaser of chattel paper under subsection (a) or (b) extends also to proceeds of the chattel paper. The first is if the purchaser would have priority under the normal priority rules applicable to proceeds. The second, which the following Comments discuss in greater detail, is if the proceeds consist of the specific goods covered by the chattel paper. Former Article 9 generally was silent as to the priority of a security interest in proceeds when a purchaser qualifies for priority under Section 9–308 (but see former Section 9–306(5)(b), concerning returned and repossessed goods).

9. **Priority in Returned and Repossessed Goods.** Returned and repossessed goods may constitute proceeds of chattel paper. The following Comments explain the treatment of returned and repossessed goods as proceeds of chattel paper. The analysis is consistent with that of PEB Commentary No. 5, which these Comments replace, and is based upon the following example:

Example: SP-1 has a security interest in all the inventory of a dealer in goods (Dealer); SP-1's security interest is perfected by filing. Dealer sells some of its inventory to a buyer in the ordinary course of business (BIOCOB) pursuant to a conditional sales contract (chattel paper) that does not indicate that it has been assigned to SP-1. SP-2 purchases the chattel paper from Dealer and takes possession of the paper in good faith, in the ordinary course of business, and without knowledge that the purchase violates the rights of SP-1. Subsequently, BIOCOB returns the goods to Dealer because they are defective. Alternatively, Dealer acquires possession of the goods following BIOCOB's default.

10. **Assignment of Non-Lease Chattel Paper.**

a. **Loan by SP-2 to Dealer Secured by Chattel Paper (or Functional Equivalent Pursuant to Recourse Arrangement).**

(1) **Returned Goods.** If BIOCOB returns the goods to Dealer for repairs, Dealer is merely a bailee and acquires thereby no meaningful rights in the goods to which SP-1's security interest could attach. (Although SP-1's security interest could attach to Dealer's interest as a bailee, that interest is not likely to be of any particular value to SP-1.) Dealer is the owner of the *chattel paper* (i.e., the owner of a right to payment secured by a security interest in the goods); SP-2 has a security interest in the chattel paper, as does SP-1 (as proceeds of the goods under Section 9–315). Under Section 9–330, SP-2's security interest in the chattel paper is senior to that of SP-1. SP-2 enjoys this priority regardless of whether, or when, SP-2 filed a financing statement covering the chattel paper. Because chattel paper and goods represent different types of collateral, Dealer does not have any meaningful interest in *goods* to which either SP-1's or SP-2's security interest could attach in order to secure Dealer's obligations to either creditor. See Section 9–102 (defining "chattel paper" and "goods").

Now assume that BIOCOB returns the goods to Dealer under circumstances whereby Dealer once again becomes the owner of the goods. This would be the case, for example, if the goods were defective and BIOCOB was entitled to reject or revoke acceptance of the goods. See Sections 2–602 (rejection), 2–608 (revocation of acceptance). Unless BIOCOB has waived its defenses as against assignees of the chattel paper, SP-1's and SP-2's rights against BIOCOB would be subject to BIOCOB's claims and defenses. See Sections 9–403, 9–404. SP-1's security interest would attach again because the returned goods would be proceeds of the chattel paper. Dealer's acquisition of the goods easily can be characterized as "proceeds" consisting of an "in kind" collection on or distribution on account of the chattel paper. See Section 9–102 (definition of "proceeds"). Assuming that SP-1's security interest is perfected by filing against the goods and that the filing is made in the same office where a filing would be made against the chattel paper, SP-1's security interest in the goods would remain perfected beyond the 20-day period of automatic perfection. See Section 9–315(d).

Because Dealer's newly reacquired interest in the goods is proceeds of the chattel paper, SP-2's security interest also would attach in the goods as proceeds. If SP-2 had perfected its security interest in the chattel paper by filing (again, assuming that filing against the chattel paper was made in the same office where a filing would be made against the goods), SP-2's security interest in the reacquired goods would be perfected beyond 20 days. See Section 9–315(d). However, if SP-2 had relied only on its possession of the chattel paper for perfection and had not filed against the chattel paper or the goods, SP-2's security interest would be unperfected after the 20-day period. See Section 9–315(d). Nevertheless, SP-2's unperfected security interest in the goods would be senior to SP-1's security interest under Section 9–330(c). The result in this priority contest is not affected by SP-2's acquiescence or non-acquiescence in the return of the goods to Dealer.

(2) **Repossessed Goods.** As explained above, Dealer owns the chattel paper covering the goods, subject to security interests in favor of SP-1 and SP-2. In Article 9 parlance, Dealer has an interest in chattel paper, not goods. If Dealer, SP-1, or SP-2 repossesses the goods upon BIOCOB's default, whether the repossession is rightful or wrongful as among Dealer, SP-1, or SP-2, Dealer's interest will not change. The location of goods and the party who possesses them does not affect the fact that Dealer's interest is in chattel paper, not goods. The goods continue to be owned by BIOCOB. SP-1's security interest in the goods does not attach until such time as Dealer reacquires an interest (other than a bare possessory interest) in the goods. For example, Dealer might buy the goods at a foreclosure sale from SP-2 (whose security interest in the chattel paper is senior to that of SP-1); that disposition would cut off BIOCOB's rights in the goods. Section 9–617.

In many cases the matter would end upon sale of the goods to Dealer at a foreclosure sale and there would be no priority contest between SP-1 and SP-2; Dealer would be unlikely to buy the goods under circumstances whereby SP-2 would retain its security interest. There can be exceptions, however. For example, Dealer may be obliged to purchase the goods from SP-2 and SP-2 may be obliged to convey the goods to Dealer, but Dealer may fail to pay SP-2. Or, one could imagine that SP-2, like SP-1, has a general security interest in the inventory of Dealer. In the latter case, SP-2 should not receive the benefit of any special priority rule, since its interest in no way derives from priority under Section 9–330. In the former case, SP-2's security interest in the goods reacquired by Dealer is senior to SP-1's security interest under Section 9–330.

b. **Dealer's Outright Sale of Chattel Paper to SP-2.** Article 9 also applies to a transaction whereby SP-2 buys the chattel paper in an outright sale transaction without recourse against Dealer. Sections 1–201(37) [*unrevised Article 1; see Concordance, p. 22*], 9–109(a). Although Dealer does not, in such a transaction, retain any residual ownership interest in the chattel paper, the chattel paper constitutes proceeds of the goods to which SP-1's security interest will attach and continue following the sale of the goods. Section 9–315(a). Even though Dealer has not retained any interest in the chattel paper, as discussed above BIOCOB subsequently may return the goods to Dealer under circumstances whereby Dealer reacquires an interest in the goods. The priority contest between SP-1 and SP-2 will be resolved as discussed above; Section 9–330 makes no distinction among purchasers of chattel paper on the basis of whether the purchaser is an outright buyer of chattel paper or one whose security interest secures an obligation of Dealer.

11. **Assignment of Lease Chattel Paper.** As defined in Section 9–102, "chattel paper" includes not only writings that evidence security interests in specific goods but also those that evidence true leases of goods.

The analysis with respect to lease chattel paper is similar to that set forth above with respect to non-lease chattel paper. It is complicated, however, by the fact that, unlike the case of chattel paper arising out of a sale, Dealer retains a residual interest in the *goods*. See Section 2A–103(1)(q) (defining "lessor's residual interest"); *In re Leasing Consultants, Inc.*, 486 F.2d 367 (2d Cir. 1973) (lessor's residual interest under true lease is an interest in goods and is a separate type of collateral from lessor's interest in the lease). If Dealer leases goods to a "lessee in ordinary course of business" (LIOCOB), then LIOCOB takes its interest under the lease (i.e., its "leasehold interest") free of the security interest of SP-1. See Sections 2A–307(3), 2A–103(1)(m) (defining "leasehold interest"), (1)(o) (defining "lessee in ordinary course of business"). SP-1 would, however, retain its security interest in the residual interest. In addition, SP-1 would acquire an interest in the lease chattel paper as proceeds. If Dealer then assigns the lease chattel paper to SP-2, Section 9–330 gives SP-2 priority over SP-1 with respect to the chattel paper, *but not* with respect to the residual interest in the *goods*. Consequently, assignees of lease chattel paper typically take a security interest in and file against the lessor's residual interest in goods, expecting their priority in the goods to be governed by the first-to-file-or-perfect rule of Section 9–322.

If the goods are returned to Dealer, other than upon expiration of the lease term, then the security interests of both SP-1 and SP-2 normally would attach to the goods as proceeds of the chattel paper. (If the goods are returned to Dealer at the expiration of the lease term and the lessee has made all payments due under the lease, however, then Dealer no longer has any rights under the chattel paper. Dealer's interest in the goods consists solely of its residual interest, as to which SP-2 has no claim.) This would be the case, for example, when the lessee rescinds the lease or when the lessor recovers possession in the exercise of its remedies under Article 2A. See, e.g., Section 2A–525. If SP-2 enjoyed priority in the chattel paper under Section 9–330, then SP-2 likewise would enjoy priority in the returned goods as proceeds. This does not mean that SP-2 necessarily is entitled to the entire value of the returned goods. The value of the goods represents the sum of the present value of (i) the value of their use for the term of the lease and (ii) the value of the residual interest. SP-2 has priority in the former, but SP-1 ordinarily would have priority in the latter. Thus, an allocation of a portion of the value of the goods to each component may be necessary. Where, as here, one secured party has a security interest in the lessor's residual interest and another has a priority security interest in the chattel paper, it may be advisable for the conflicting secured parties to establish a method for making such an allocation and otherwise to determine their relative rights in returned goods by agreement.

As amended in 2000 and 2010.

§ 9–331. Priority of Rights of Purchasers of Instruments, Documents, and Securities Under Other Articles; Priority of Interests in Financial Assets and Security Entitlements Under Article 8.

(a) **[Rights under Articles 3, 7, and 8 not limited.]** This article does not limit the rights of a holder in due course of a negotiable instrument, a holder to which a negotiable document of title has been duly negotiated, or a protected purchaser of a security. These holders or purchasers take priority over an earlier security interest, even if perfected, to the extent provided in Articles 3, 7, and 8.

(b)   **[Protection under Article 8.]** This article does not limit the rights of or impose liability on a person to the extent that the person is protected against the assertion of a claim under Article 8.

(c)   **[Filing not notice.]** Filing under this article does not constitute notice of a claim or defense to the holders, or purchasers, or persons described in subsections (a) and (b).

Official Comment

1.   **Source.** Former Section 9–309.

2.   **"Priority."** In some provisions, this Article distinguishes between claimants that take collateral free of a security interest (in the sense that the security interest no longer encumbers the collateral) and those that take an interest in the collateral that is senior to a surviving security interest. See, e.g., Section 9–317. Whether a holder or purchaser referred to in this section takes free or is senior to a security interest depends on whether the purchaser is a buyer of the collateral or takes a security interest in it. The term "priority" is meant to encompass both scenarios, as it does in Section 9–330.

3.   **Rights Acquired by Purchasers.** The rights to which this section refers are set forth in Sections 3–305 and 3–306 (holder in due course), 7–502 (holder to whom a negotiable document of title has been duly negotiated), and 8–303 (protected purchaser). The holders and purchasers referred to in this section do not always take priority over a security interest. See, e.g., Section 7–503 (affording paramount rights to certain owners and secured parties as against holder to whom a negotiable document of title has been duly negotiated). Accordingly, this section adds the clause, "to the extent provided in Articles 3, 7, and 8" to former Section 9–309.

4.   **Financial Assets and Security Entitlements.** New subsection (b) provides explicit protection for those who deal with financial assets and security entitlements and who are immunized from liability under Article 8. See, e.g., Sections 8–502, 8–503(e), 8–510, 8–511. The new subsection makes explicit in Article 9 what is implicit in former Article 9 and explicit in several provisions of Article 8. It does not change the law.

5.   **Collections by Junior Secured Party.** Under this section, a secured party with a junior security interest in receivables (accounts, chattel paper, promissory notes, or payment intangibles) may collect and retain the proceeds of those receivables free of the claim of a senior secured party to the same receivables, if the junior secured party is a holder in due course of the proceeds. In order to qualify as a holder in due course, the junior must satisfy the requirements of Section 3–302, which include taking in "good faith." This means that the junior not only must act "honestly" but also must observe "reasonable commercial standards of fair dealing" under the particular circumstances. See Section 9–102(a). Although "good faith" does not impose a general duty of inquiry, e.g., a search of the records in filing offices, there may be circumstances in which "reasonable commercial standards of fair dealing" would require such a search.

Consider, for example, a junior secured party in the business of financing or buying accounts who fails to undertake a search to determine the existence of prior security interests. Because a search, under the usages of trade of that business, would enable it to know or learn upon reasonable inquiry that collecting the accounts violated the rights of a senior secured party, the junior may fail to meet the good-faith standard. See *Utility Contractors Financial Services, Inc. v. Amsouth Bank, NA,* 985 F.2d 1554 (11th Cir. 1993). Likewise, a junior secured party who collects accounts when it knows or should know under the particular circumstances that doing so would violate the rights of a senior secured party, because the debtor had agreed not to grant a junior security interest in, or sell, the accounts, may not meet the good-faith test. Thus, if a junior secured party conducted or should have conducted a search and a financing statement filed on behalf of the senior secured party states such a restriction, the junior's collection would not meet the good-faith standard. On the other hand, if there was a course of performance between the senior secured party and the debtor which placed no such restrictions on the debtor and allowed the debtor to collect and use the proceeds without any restrictions, the junior secured party may then satisfy the requirements for being a holder in due course. This would be more likely in those circumstances where the junior secured party was providing additional financing to the debtor on an on-going basis by lending against or buying the accounts and had no notice of any restrictions against doing so. Generally, the senior secured party would not be prejudiced because the practical effect of such payment to the junior secured party is little different than if the debtor itself had made the collections and subsequently paid the secured party from the debtor's general funds. Absent collusion, the junior secured party would take the funds free of the senior security interests. See Section 9–332. In contrast, the senior secured party is likely to be prejudiced if the debtor is going out of business and the junior secured party collects the accounts by notifying the account debtors to make payments directly to the junior. Those collections may not be consistent with "reasonable commercial standards of fair dealing."

814

Whether the junior secured party qualifies as a holder in due course is fact-sensitive and should be decided on a case-by-case basis in the light of those circumstances. Decisions such as *Financial Management Services, Inc. v. Familian*, 905 P.2d 506 (Ariz. App. Div. 1995) (finding holder in due course status) could be determined differently under this application of the good-faith requirement.

The concepts addressed in this Comment are also applicable to junior secured parties as purchasers of instruments under Section 9–330(d). See Section 9–330, Comment 7.

§ 9–332. Transfer of Money; Transfer of Funds From Deposit Account.

(a) **[Transferee of money.]** A transferee of money takes the money free of a security interest unless the transferee acts in collusion with the debtor in violating the rights of the secured party.

(b) **[Transferee of funds from deposit account.]** A transferee of funds from a deposit account takes the funds free of a security interest in the deposit account unless the transferee acts in collusion with the debtor in violating the rights of the secured party.

Official Comment

1. **Source.** New.

2. **Scope of This Section.** This section affords broad protection to transferees who take funds from a deposit account and to those who take money. The term "transferee" is not defined; however, the debtor itself is not a transferee. Thus this section does not cover the case in which a debtor withdraws money (currency) from its deposit account or the case in which a bank debits an encumbered account and credits another account it maintains for the debtor.

A transfer of funds from a deposit account, to which subsection (b) applies, normally will be made by check, by funds transfer, or by debiting the debtor's deposit account and crediting another depositor's account.

Example 1: Debtor maintains a deposit account with Bank A. The deposit account is subject to a perfected security interest in favor of Lender. Debtor draws a check on the account, payable to Payee. Inasmuch as the check is not the proceeds of the deposit account (it is an order to pay funds from the deposit account), Lender's security interest in the deposit account does not give rise to a security interest in the check. Payee deposits the check into its own deposit account, and Bank A pays it. Unless Payee acted in collusion with Debtor in violating Lender's rights, Payee takes the funds (the credits running in favor of Payee) free of Lender's security interest. This is true regardless of whether Payee is a holder in due course of the check and even if Payee gave no value for the check.

Example 2: Debtor maintains a deposit account with Bank A. The deposit account is subject to a perfected security interest in favor of Lender. At Bank B's suggestion, Debtor moves the funds from the account at Bank A to Debtor's deposit account with Bank B. Unless Bank B acted in collusion with Debtor in violating Lender's rights, Bank B takes the funds (the credits running in favor of Bank B) free from Lender's security interest. See subsection (b). However, inasmuch as the deposit account maintained with Bank B constitutes the proceeds of the deposit account at Bank A, Lender's security interest would attach to that account as proceeds. See Section 9–315.

Subsection (b) also would apply if, in the example, Bank A debited Debtor's deposit account in exchange for the issuance of Bank A's cashier's check. Lender's security interest would attach to the cashier's check as proceeds of the deposit account, and the rules applicable to instruments would govern any competing claims to the cashier's check. See, e.g., Sections 3–306, 9–322, 9–330, 9–331.

If Debtor withdraws money (currency) from an encumbered deposit account and transfers the money to a third party, then subsection (a), to the extent not displaced by federal law relating to money, applies. It contains the same rule as subsection (b).

Subsection (b) applies to *transfers of funds from* a deposit account; it does not apply to *transfers of the deposit account* itself or of an interest therein. For example, this section does not apply to the creation of a security interest in a deposit account. Competing claims to the deposit account itself are dealt with by other Article 9 priority rules. See Sections 9–317(a), 9–327, 9–340, 9–341. Similarly, a corporate merger normally would not result in a transfer of funds from a deposit account. Rather, it might result in a transfer of the deposit account itself. If so, the normal rules applicable to transferred collateral would apply; this section would not.

3. **Policy.** Broad protection for transferees helps to ensure that security interests in deposit accounts do not impair the free flow of funds. It also minimizes the likelihood that a secured party will enjoy a claim to

whatever the transferee purchases with the funds. Rules concerning recovery of payments traditionally have placed a high value on finality. The opportunity to upset a completed transaction, or even to place a completed transaction in jeopardy by bringing suit against the transferee of funds, should be severely limited. Although the giving of value usually is a prerequisite for receiving the ability to take free from third-party claims, where payments are concerned the law is even more protective. Thus, Section 3–418(c) provides that, even where the law of restitution otherwise would permit recovery of funds paid by mistake, no recovery may be had from a person "who in good faith changed position in reliance on the payment." Rather than adopt this standard, this section eliminates all reliance requirements whatsoever. Payments made by mistake are relatively rare, but payments of funds from encumbered deposit accounts (e.g., deposit accounts containing collections from accounts receivable) occur with great regularity. In most cases, unlike payment by mistake, no one would object to these payments. In the vast proportion of cases, the transferee probably would be able to show a change of position in reliance on the payment. This section does not put the transferee to the burden of having to make this proof.

4. **"Bad Actors."** To deal with the question of the "bad actor," this section borrows "collusion" language from Article 8. See, e.g., Sections 8–115, 8–503(e). This is the most protective (i.e., least stringent) of the various standards now found in the UCC. Compare, e.g., Section 1–201(b)(9) ("without knowledge that the sale violates the rights of another person"); Section 1–201(b)(20) ("honesty in fact and the observance of reasonable commercial standards of fair dealing"); Section 3–302(a)(2)(v) ("without notice of any claim").

5. **Transferee Who Does Not Take Free.** This section sets forth the circumstances under which certain transferees of money or funds take free of security interests. It does not determine the rights of a transferee who does not take free of a security interest.

Example 3:   The facts are as in Example 2, but, in wrongfully moving the funds from the deposit account at Bank A to Debtor's deposit account with Bank B, Debtor acts in collusion with Bank B. Bank B does not take the funds free of Lender's security interest under this section. If Debtor grants a security interest to Bank B, Section 9–327 governs the relative priorities of Lender and Bank B. Under Section 9–327(3), Bank B's security interest in the Bank B deposit account is senior to Lender's security interest in the deposit account as proceeds. However, Bank B's senior security interest does not protect Bank B against any liability to Lender that might arise from Bank B's wrongful conduct.

As amended in 2010.

§ 9–333.   Priority of Certain Liens Arising by Operation of Law.

(a)   **["Possessory lien."]** In this section, "possessory lien" means an interest, other than a security interest or an agricultural lien:

(1)   which secures payment or performance of an obligation for services or materials furnished with respect to goods by a person in the ordinary course of the person's business;

(2)   which is created by statute or rule of law in favor of the person; and

(3)   whose effectiveness depends on the person's possession of the goods.

(b)   **[Priority of possessory lien.]** A possessory lien on goods has priority over a security interest in the goods unless the lien is created by a statute that expressly provides otherwise.

Official Comment

1.   **Source.** Former Section 9–310.

2.   **"Possessory Liens."** This section governs the relative priority of security interests arising under this Article and "possessory liens," i.e., common-law and statutory liens whose effectiveness depends on the lienor's possession of goods with respect to which the lienor provided services or furnished materials in the ordinary course of its business. As under former Section 9–310, the possessory lien has priority over a security interest unless the possessory lien is created by a statute that expressly provides otherwise. If the statute creating the possessory lien is silent as to its priority relative to a security interest, this section provides a rule of interpretation that the possessory lien takes priority, even if the statute has been construed judicially to make the possessory lien subordinate.

§ 9–334. Priority of Security Interests in Fixtures and Crops.

(a) **[Security interest in fixtures under this article.]** A security interest under this article may be created in goods that are fixtures or may continue in goods that become fixtures. A security interest does not exist under this article in ordinary building materials incorporated into an improvement on land.

(b) **[Security interest in fixtures under real-property law.]** This article does not prevent creation of an encumbrance upon fixtures under real property law.

(c) **[General rule: subordination of security interest in fixtures.]** In cases not governed by subsections (d) through (h), a security interest in fixtures is subordinate to a conflicting interest of an encumbrancer or owner of the related real property other than the debtor.

(d) **[Fixtures purchase-money priority.]** Except as otherwise provided in subsection (h), a perfected security interest in fixtures has priority over a conflicting interest of an encumbrancer or owner of the real property if the debtor has an interest of record in or is in possession of the real property and:

(1) the security interest is a purchase-money security interest;

(2) the interest of the encumbrancer or owner arises before the goods become fixtures; and

(3) the security interest is perfected by a fixture filing before the goods become fixtures or within 20 days thereafter.

(e) **[Priority of security interest in fixtures over interests in real property.]** A perfected security interest in fixtures has priority over a conflicting interest of an encumbrancer or owner of the real property if:

(1) the debtor has an interest of record in the real property or is in possession of the real property and the security interest:

(A) is perfected by a fixture filing before the interest of the encumbrancer or owner is of record; and

(B) has priority over any conflicting interest of a predecessor in title of the encumbrancer or owner;

(2) before the goods become fixtures, the security interest is perfected by any method permitted by this article and the fixtures are readily removable:

(A) factory or office machines;

(B) equipment that is not primarily used or leased for use in the operation of the real property; or

(C) replacements of domestic appliances that are consumer goods;

(3) the conflicting interest is a lien on the real property obtained by legal or equitable proceedings after the security interest was perfected by any method permitted by this article; or

(4) the security interest is:

(A) created in a manufactured home in a manufactured-home transaction; and

(B) perfected pursuant to a statute described in Section 9–311(a)(2).

(f) **[Priority based on consent, disclaimer, or right to remove.]** A security interest in fixtures, whether or not perfected, has priority over a conflicting interest of an encumbrancer or owner of the real property if:

(1) the encumbrancer or owner has, in an authenticated record, consented to the security interest or disclaimed an interest in the goods as fixtures; or

(2) the debtor has a right to remove the goods as against the encumbrancer or owner.

(g) **[Continuation of paragraph (f)(2) priority.]** The priority of the security interest under paragraph (f)(2) continues for a reasonable time if the debtor's right to remove the goods as against the encumbrancer or owner terminates.

(h) **[Priority of construction mortgage.]** A mortgage is a construction mortgage to the extent that it secures an obligation incurred for the construction of an improvement on land, including the acquisition cost of the land, if a recorded record of the mortgage so indicates. Except as otherwise provided in subsections (e) and (f), a security interest in fixtures is subordinate to a construction mortgage if a record of the mortgage is recorded before the goods become fixtures and the goods become fixtures before the completion of the construction. A mortgage has this priority to the same extent as a construction mortgage to the extent that it is given to refinance a construction mortgage.

(i) **[Priority of security interest in crops.]** A perfected security interest in crops growing on real property has priority over a conflicting interest of an encumbrancer or owner of the real property if the debtor has an interest of record in or is in possession of the real property.

(j) **[Subsection (i) prevails.]** Subsection (i) prevails over any inconsistent provisions of the following statutes:

[List here any statutes containing provisions inconsistent with subsection (i).]

Legislative Note: States that amend statutes to remove provisions inconsistent with subsection (i) need not enact subsection (j).

Official Comment

1.   **Source.** Former Section 9–313.

2.   **Scope of This Section.** This section contains rules governing the priority of security interests in fixtures and crops as against persons who claim an interest in real property. Priority contests with other Article 9 security interests are governed by the other priority rules of this Article. The provisions with respect to fixtures follow those of former Section 9–313. However, they have been rewritten to conform to Section 2A–309 and to prevailing style conventions. Subsections (i) and (j), which apply to crops, are new.

3.   **Security Interests in Fixtures.** Certain goods that are the subject of personal-property (chattel) financing become so affixed or otherwise so related to real property that they become part of the real property. These goods are called "fixtures." See Section 9–102 (definition of "fixtures"). Some fixtures retain their personal-property nature: a security interest under this Article may be created in fixtures and may continue in goods that become fixtures. See subsection (a). However, if the goods are ordinary building materials incorporated into an improvement on land, no security interest in them exists. Rather, the priority of claims to the building materials are determined by the law governing claims to real property. (Of course, the fact that no security interest exists in ordinary building materials incorporated into an improvement on land does not prejudice any rights the secured party may have against the debtor or any other person who violated the secured party's rights by wrongfully incorporating the goods into real property.)

Thus, this section recognizes three categories of goods: (1) those that retain their chattel character entirely and are not part of the real property; (2) ordinary building materials that have become an integral part of the real property and cannot retain their chattel character for purposes of finance; and (3) an intermediate class that has become real property for certain purposes, but as to which chattel financing may be preserved.

To achieve priority under certain provisions of this section, a security interest must be perfected by making a "fixture filing" (defined in Section 9–102) in the real-property records. Because the question whether goods have become fixtures often is a difficult one under applicable real-property law, a secured party may make a fixture filing as a precaution. Courts should not infer from a fixture filing that the secured party concedes that the goods are or will become fixtures.

4.   **Priority in Fixtures: General.** In considering priority problems under this section, one must first determine whether real-property claimants per se have an interest in the crops or fixtures as part of real property. If not, it is immaterial, so far as concerns real property parties as such, whether a security interest arising under this Article is perfected or unperfected. In no event does a real-property claimant (e.g., owner or mortgagee) acquire an interest in a "pure" chattel just because a security interest therein is unperfected. If on the other hand real-property law gives real-property parties an interest in the goods, a conflict arises and this section states the priorities.

5.   **Priority in Fixtures: Residual Rule.** Subsection (c) states the residual priority rule, which applies only if one of the other rules does not: A security interest in fixtures is subordinate to a conflicting interest of an encumbrancer or owner of the related real property other than the debtor.

6. **Priority in Fixtures: First to File or Record.** Subsection (e)(1), which follows former Section 9–313(4)(b), contains the usual priority rule of conveyancing, that is, the first to file or record prevails. In order to achieve priority under this rule, however, the security interest must be perfected by a "fixture filing" (defined in Section 9–102), i.e., a filing for record in the real property records and indexed therein, so that it will be found in a real-property search ... The condition in subsection (e)(1)(B), that the security interest must have had priority over any conflicting interest of a predecessor in title of the conflicting encumbrancer or owner, appears to limit to the first-in-time principle. However, this apparent limitation is nothing other than an expression of the usual rule that a person must be entitled to transfer what he has. Thus, if the fixture security interest is subordinate to a mortgage, it is subordinate to an interest of an assignee of the mortgage, even though the assignment is a later recorded instrument. Similarly if the fixture security interest is subordinate to the rights of an owner, it is subordinate to a subsequent grantee of the owner and likewise subordinate to a subsequent mortgagee of the owner.

7. **Priority in Fixtures: Purchase-Money Security Interests.** Subsection (d), which follows former Section 9–313(4)(a), contains the principal exception to the first-to-file-or-record rule of subsection (e)(1). It affords priority to purchase-money security interests in fixtures as against *prior* recorded real-property interests, provided that the purchase-money security interest is filed as a fixture filing in the real-property records before the goods become fixtures or within 20 days thereafter. This priority corresponds to the purchase-money priority under Section 9–324(a). (Like other 10-day periods in former Article 9, the 10-day period in this section has been changed to 20 days.)

It should be emphasized that this purchase-money priority with the 20-day grace period for filing is limited to rights against real-property interests that arise *before* the goods become fixtures. There is no such priority with the 20-day grace period as against real-property interests that arise subsequently. The fixture security interest can defeat subsequent real-property interests only if it is filed first and prevails under the usual conveyancing rule in subsection (e)(1) or one of the other rules in this section.

8. **Priority in Fixtures: Readily Removable Goods.** Subsection (e)(2), which derives from Section 2A–309 and former Section 9–313(4)(d), contains another exception to the usual first-to-file-or-perfect rule. It affords priority to the holders of security interests in certain types of readily removable goods—factory and office machines, equipment that is not primarily used or leased for use in the operation of the real property, and (as discussed below) certain replacements of domestic appliances. This rule is made necessary by the confusion in the law as to whether certain machinery, equipment, and appliances become fixtures. It protects a secured party who, perhaps in the mistaken belief that the readily removable goods will not become fixtures, makes a UCC filing (or otherwise perfects under this Article) rather than making a fixture filing.

Frequently, under applicable law, goods of the type described in subsection (e)(2) will not be considered to have become part of the real property. In those cases, the fixture security interest does not conflict with a real-property interest, and resort to this section is unnecessary. However, if the goods have become part of the real property, subsection (e)(2) enables a fixture secured party to take priority over a conflicting real-property interest if the fixture security interest is perfected by a fixture filing or by any other method permitted by this Article. If perfection is by fixture filing, the fixture security interest would have priority over subsequently recorded real-property interests under subsection (e)(1) and, if the fixture security interest is a purchase-money security interest (a likely scenario), it would also have priority over most real property interests under the purchase-money priority of subsection (d). Note, however, that unlike the purchase-money priority rule in subsection (d), the priority rules in subsection (e) override the priority given to a construction mortgage under subsection (h).

The rule in subsection (e)(2) is limited to readily removable replacements of domestic appliances. It does not apply to original installations. Moreover, it is limited to appliances that are "consumer goods" (defined in Section 9–102) in the hands of the debtor. The principal effect of the rule is to make clear that a secured party financing occasional replacements of domestic appliances in noncommercial, owner-occupied contexts need not concern itself with real-property descriptions or records; indeed, for a purchase-money replacement of consumer goods, perfection without any filing will be possible. See Section 9–309(1).

9. **Priority in Fixtures: Judicial Liens.** Subsection (e)(3), which follows former Section 9–313(4)(d), adopts a first-in-time rule applicable to conflicts between a fixture security interest and a lien on the real property obtained by legal or equitable proceedings. Such a lien is subordinate to an earlier-perfected security interest, regardless of the method by which the security interest was perfected. Judgment creditors generally are not reliance creditors who search real-property records. Accordingly, a perfected fixture security interest takes priority over a subsequent judgment lien or other lien obtained by legal or equitable proceedings, even if no evidence of the security interest appears in the relevant real-property records. Subsection (e)(3) thus protects a perfected fixture

security interest from avoidance by a trustee in bankruptcy under Bankruptcy Code Section 544(a), regardless of the method of perfection.

10. **Priority in Fixtures: Manufactured Homes.** A manufactured home may become a fixture. New subsection (e)(4) contains a special rule granting priority to certain security interests created in a "manufactured home" as part of a "manufactured-home transaction" (both defined in Section 9–102). Under this rule, a security interest in a manufactured home that becomes a fixture has priority over a conflicting interest of an encumbrancer or owner of the real property if the security interest is perfected under a certificate-of-title statute (see Section 9–311). Subsection (e)(4) is only one of the priority rules applicable to security interests in a manufactured home that becomes a fixture. Thus, a security interest in a manufactured home which does not qualify for priority under this subsection may qualify under another.

11. **Priority in Fixtures: Construction Mortgages.** The purchase-money priority presents a difficult problem in relation to construction mortgages. The latter ordinarily will have been recorded even before the commencement of delivery of materials to the job, and therefore would take priority over fixture security interests were it not for the purchase-money priority. However, having recorded first, the holder of a construction mortgage reasonably expects to have first priority in the improvement built using the mortgagee's advances. Subsection (g) expressly gives priority to the construction mortgage recorded before the filing of the purchase-money security interest in fixtures. A refinancing of a construction mortgage has the same priority as the construction mortgage itself. The phrase "an obligation incurred for the construction of an improvement" covers both optional advances and advances pursuant to commitment. Both types of advances have the same priority under subsection (g).

The priority under this subsection applies only to goods that become fixtures during the construction period leading to the completion of the improvement. The construction priority will not apply to additions to the building made long after completion of the improvement, even if the additions are financed by the real-property mortgagee under an open-end clause of the construction mortgage. In such case, subsections (d), (e), and (f) govern.

Although this subsection affords a construction mortgage priority over a purchase-money security interest that otherwise would have priority under subsection (d), the subsection is subject to the priority rules in subsections (e) and (f). Thus, a construction mortgage may be junior to a fixture security interest perfected by a fixture filing before the construction mortgage was recorded. See subsection (e)(1).

12. **Crops.** Growing crops are "goods" in which a security interest may be created and perfected under this Article. In some jurisdictions, a mortgage of real property may cover crops, as well. In the event that crops are encumbered by both a mortgage and an Article 9 security interest, subsection (i) provides that the security interest has priority. States whose real-property law provides otherwise should either amend that law directly or override it by enacting subsection (j).

§ 9–335.   Accessions.

(a) **[Creation of security interest in accession.]** A security interest may be created in an accession and continues in collateral that becomes an accession.

(b) **[Perfection of security interest.]** If a security interest is perfected when the collateral becomes an accession, the security interest remains perfected in the collateral.

(c) **[Priority of security interest.]** Except as otherwise provided in subsection (d), the other provisions of this part determine the priority of a security interest in an accession.

(d) **[Compliance with certificate-of-title statute.]** A security interest in an accession is subordinate to a security interest in the whole which is perfected by compliance with the requirements of a certificate-of-title statute under Section 9–311(b).

(e) **[Removal of accession after default.]** After default, subject to Part 6, a secured party may remove an accession from other goods if the security interest in the accession has priority over the claims of every person having an interest in the whole.

(f) **[Reimbursement following removal.]** A secured party that removes an accession from other goods under subsection (e) shall promptly reimburse any holder of a security interest or other lien on, or owner of, the whole or of the other goods, other than the debtor, for the cost of repair of any physical injury to the whole or the other goods. The secured party need not reimburse the holder or owner for any diminution in value of the whole or the other goods caused by the absence of the accession removed or by any necessity for replacing it. A person entitled to reimbursement may refuse permission to remove until the secured party gives adequate assurance for the performance of the obligation to reimburse.

Official Comment

1.   **Source.** Former Section 9–314.

2.   **"Accession."** This section applies to an "accession," as defined in Section 9–102, regardless of the cost or difficulty of removing the accession from the other goods, and regardless of whether the original goods have come to form an integral part of the other goods. This section does not apply to goods whose identity has been lost. Goods of that kind are "commingled goods" governed by Section 9–336. Neither this section nor the following one addresses the case of collateral that changes form without the addition of other goods.

3.   **"Accession" vs. "Other Goods."** This section distinguishes among the "accession," the "other goods," and the "whole." The last term refers to the combination of the "accession" and the "other goods." If one person's collateral becomes physically united with another person's collateral, each is an "accession."

Example 1:   SP-1 holds a security interest in the debtor's tractors (which are not subject to a certificate-of-title statute), and SP-2 holds a security interest in a particular tractor engine. The engine is installed in a tractor. From the perspective of SP-1, the tractor becomes an "accession" and the engine is the "other goods." From the perspective of SP-2, the engine is the "accession" and the tractor is the "other goods." The completed tractor—tractor cum engine—constitutes the "whole."

4.   **Scope.** This section governs only a few issues concerning accessions. Subsection (a) contains rules governing continuation of a security interest in an accession. Subsection (b) contains a rule governing continued perfection of a security interest in goods that become an accession. Subsection (d) contains a special priority rule governing accessions that become part of a whole covered by a certificate of title. Subsections (e) and (f) govern enforcement of a security interest in an accession.

5.   **Matters Left to Other Provisions of This Article: Attachment and Perfection.** Other provisions of this Article often govern accession-related issues. For example, this section does not address whether a secured party acquires a security interest in the whole if its collateral becomes an accession. Normally this will turn on the description of the collateral in the security agreement.

Example 2:   Debtor owns a computer subject to a perfected security interest in favor of SP-1. Debtor acquires memory and installs it in the computer. Whether SP-1's security interest attaches to the memory depends on whether the security agreement covers it.

Similarly, this section does not determine whether perfection against collateral that becomes an accession is effective to perfect a security interest in the whole. Other provisions of this Article, including the requirements for indicating the collateral covered by a financing statement, resolve that question.

6.   **Matters Left to Other Provisions of This Article: Priority.** With one exception, concerning goods covered by a certificate of title (see subsection (d)), the other provisions of this Part, including the rules governing purchase-money security interests, determine the priority of most security interests in an accession, including the relative priority of a security interest in an accession and a security interest in the whole. See subsection (c).

Example 3:   Debtor owns an office computer subject to a security interest in favor of SP-1. Debtor acquires memory and grants a perfected security interest in the memory to SP-2. Debtor installs the memory in the computer, at which time (one assumes) SP-1's security interest attaches to the memory. The first-to-file-or-perfect rule of Section 9–322 governs priority in the memory. If, however, SP-2's security interest is a purchase-money security interest, Section 9–324(a) would afford priority in the memory to SP-2, regardless of which security interest was perfected first.

7.   **Goods Covered by Certificate of Title.** This section does govern the priority of a security interest in an accession that is or becomes part of a whole that is subject to a security interest perfected by compliance with a certificate-of-title statute. Subsection (d) provides that a security interest in the whole, perfected by compliance with a certificate-of-title statute, takes priority over a security interest in the accession. It enables a secured party to rely upon a certificate of title without having to check the UCC files to determine whether any components of the collateral may be encumbered. The subsection imposes a corresponding risk upon those who finance goods that may become part of goods covered by a certificate of title. In doing so, it reverses the priority that appeared reasonable to most pre-UCC courts.

Example 4:   Debtor owns an automobile subject to a security interest in favor of SP-1. The security interest is perfected by notation on the certificate of title. Debtor buys tires subject to a perfected-by-filing purchase-money security interest in favor of SP-2 and mounts the tires on the automobile's wheels. If the security interest in the automobile attaches to the tires, then SP-1 acquires priority over SP-2. The same result would obtain if SP-1's security interest attached to the automobile and was perfected after the tires had been mounted on the wheels.

§ 9–336.   Commingled Goods.

(a) **["Commingled goods."]** In this section, "commingled goods" means goods that are physically united with other goods in such a manner that their identity is lost in a product or mass.

(b) **[No security interest in commingled goods as such.]** A security interest does not exist in commingled goods as such. However, a security interest may attach to a product or mass that results when goods become commingled goods.

(c) **[Attachment of security interest to product or mass.]** If collateral becomes commingled goods, a security interest attaches to the product or mass.

(d) **[Perfection of security interest.]** If a security interest in collateral is perfected before the collateral becomes commingled goods, the security interest that attaches to the product or mass under subsection (c) is perfected.

(e) **[Priority of security interest.]** Except as otherwise provided in subsection (f), the other provisions of this part determine the priority of a security interest that attaches to the product or mass under subsection (c).

(f) **[Conflicting security interests in product or mass]** If more than one security interest attaches to the product or mass under subsection (c), the following rules determine priority:

(1) A security interest that is perfected under subsection (d) has priority over a security interest that is unperfected at the time the collateral becomes commingled goods.

(2) If more than one security interest is perfected under subsection (d), the security interests rank equally in proportion to the value of the collateral at the time it became commingled goods.

Official Comment

1. **Source.** Former Section 9–315.

2. **"Commingled Goods."** Subsection (a) defines "commingled goods." It is meant to include not only goods whose identity is lost through manufacturing or production (e.g., flour that has become part of baked goods) but also goods whose identity is lost by commingling with other goods from which they cannot be distinguished (e.g., ball bearings).

3. **Consequences of Becoming "Commingled Goods."** By definition, the identity of the original collateral cannot be determined once the original collateral becomes commingled goods. Consequently, the security interest in the specific original collateral alone is lost once the collateral becomes commingled goods, and no security interest in the original collateral can be created thereafter except as a part of the resulting product or mass. See subsection (b).

Once collateral becomes commingled goods, the secured party's security interest is transferred from the original collateral to the product or mass. See subsection (c). If the security interest in the original collateral was perfected, the security interest in the product or mass is a perfected security interest. See subsection (d). This perfection continues until lapse.

4. **Priority of Perfected Security Interests That Attach Under This Section.** This section governs the priority of competing security interests in a product or mass only when both security interests arise under this section. In that case, if both security interests are perfected by operation of this section (see subsections (c) and (d)), then the security interests rank equally, in proportion to the value of the collateral at the time it became commingled goods. See subsection (f)(2).

Example 1:   SP-1 has a perfected security interest in Debtor's eggs, which have a value of $300 and secure a debt of $400, and SP-2 has a perfected security interest in Debtor's flour, which has a value of $500 and secures a debt of $700. Debtor uses the flour and eggs to make cakes, which have a value of $1000. The two security interests rank equally and share in the ratio of 3:5. Applying this ratio to the entire value of the product, SP-1 would be entitled to $375 (i.e., 3/8 × $1000), and SP-2 would be entitled to $625 (i.e., 5/8 × $1000).

Example 2:   Assume the facts of Example 1, except that SP-1's collateral, worth $300, secures a debt of $200. Recall that, if the cake is worth $1000, then applying the ratio of 3:5 would entitle SP-1 to $375 and SP-2 to $625. However, SP-1 is not entitled to collect from the product more than it is owed. Accordingly, SP-1's share would be only $200, SP-2 would receive the remaining value, up to the amount it is owed ($700).

Example 3:   Assume that the cakes in the previous examples have a value of only $600. Again, the parties share in the ratio of 3:5. If, as in Example 1, SP-1 is owed $400, then SP-1 is entitled to $225 (i.e., 3/8 × $600), and SP-2 is entitled to $375 (i.e., 5/8 × $600). Debtor receives nothing. If, however, as in Example 2, SP-1 is owed only $200, then SP-2 receives $400.

The results in the foregoing examples remain the same, regardless of whether SP-1 or SP-2 (or each) has a purchase-money security interest.

5.   **Perfection: Unperfected Security Interests.** The rule explained in the preceding Comment applies only when both security interests in original collateral are perfected when the goods become commingled goods. If a security interest in original collateral is unperfected at the time the collateral becomes commingled goods, subsection (f)(1) applies.

Example 4:   SP-1 has a perfected security interest in the debtor's eggs, and SP-2 has an unperfected security interest in the debtor's flour. Debtor uses the flour and eggs to make cakes. Under subsection (c), both security interests attach to the cakes. But since SP-1's security interest was perfected at the time of commingling and SP-2's was not, only SP-1's security interest in the cakes is perfected. See subsection (d). Under subsection (f)(1) and Section 9–322(a)(2), SP-1's perfected security interest has priority over SP-2's unperfected security interest.

If both security interests are unperfected, the rule of Section 9–322(a)(3) would apply.

6.   **Multiple Security Interests.** On occasion, a single input may be encumbered by more than one security interest. In those cases, the multiple secured parties should be treated like a single secured party for purposes of determining their collective share under subsection (f)(2). The normal priority rules would determine how that share would be allocated between them. Consider the following example, which is a variation on Example 1 above:

Example 5:   SP-1A has a perfected, first-priority security interest in Debtor's eggs. SP-1B has a perfected, second-priority security interest in the same collateral. The eggs have a value of $300. Debtor owes $200 to SP-1A and $200 to SP-1B. SP-2 has a perfected security interest in Debtor's flour, which has a value of $500 and secures a debt of $600. Debtor uses the flour and eggs to make cakes, which have a value of $1000.

For purposes of subsection (f)(2), SP-1A and SP-1B should be treated like a single secured party. The collective security interest would rank equally with that of SP-2. Thus, the secured parties would share in the ratio of 3 (for SP-1A and SP-1B combined) to 5 (for SP-2). Applying this ratio to the entire value of the product, SP-1A and SP-1B in the aggregate would be entitled to $375 (i.e., 3/8 × $1000), and SP-2 would be entitled to $625 (i.e., 5/8 × $1000).

SP-1A and SP-1B would share the $375 in accordance with their priority, as established under other rules. Inasmuch as SP-1A has first priority, it would receive $200, and SP-1B would receive $175.

7.   **Priority of Security Interests That Attach Other Than by Operation of This Section.** Under subsection (e), the normal priority rules determine the priority of a security interest that attaches to the product or mass other than by operation of this section. For example, assume that SP-1 has a perfected security interest in Debtor's existing and after-acquired baked goods, and SP-2 has a perfected security interest in Debtor's flour. When the flour is processed into cakes, subsections (c) and (d) provide that SP-2 acquires a perfected security interest in the cakes. If SP-1 filed against the baked goods before SP-2 filed against the flour, then SP-1 will enjoy priority in the cakes. See Section 9–322 (first-to-file-or-perfect). But if SP-2 filed against the flour before SP-1 filed against the baked goods, then SP-2 will enjoy priority in the cakes to the extent of its security interest.

§ 9–337.   Priority of Security Interests in Goods Covered by Certificate of Title.

If, while a security interest in goods is perfected by any method under the law of another jurisdiction, this State issues a certificate of title that does not show that the goods are subject to the security interest or contain a statement that they may be subject to security interests not shown on the certificate:

(1)   a buyer of the goods, other than a person in the business of selling goods of that kind, takes free of the security interest if the buyer gives value and receives delivery of the goods after issuance of the certificate and without knowledge of the security interest; and

(2)   the security interest is subordinate to a conflicting security interest in the goods that attaches, and is perfected under Section 9–311(b), after issuance of the certificate and without the conflicting secured party's knowledge of the security interest.

Official Comment

1.   **Source.** Derived from former Section 9–103(2)(d).

2.   **Protection for Buyers and Secured Parties.** This section affords protection to certain good-faith purchasers for value who are likely to have relied on a "clean" certificate of title, i.e., one that neither shows that the goods are subject to a particular security interest nor contains a statement that they may be subject to security interests not shown on the certificate. Under this section, a buyer can take free of, and the holder of a conflicting security interest can acquire priority over, a security interest that is perfected by any method under the law of another jurisdiction. The fact that the security interest has been reperfected by possession under Section 9–313 does not of itself disqualify the holder of a conflicting security interest from protection under paragraph (2).

§ 9–338.   Priority of Security Interest or Agricultural Lien Perfected by Filed Financing Statement Providing Certain Incorrect Information.

If a security interest or agricultural lien is perfected by a filed financing statement providing information described in Section 9–516(b)(5) which is incorrect at the time the financing statement is filed:

(1)   the security interest or agricultural lien is subordinate to a conflicting perfected security interest in the collateral to the extent that the holder of the conflicting security interest gives value in reasonable reliance upon the incorrect information; and

(2)   a purchaser, other than a secured party, of the collateral takes free of the security interest or agricultural lien to the extent that, in reasonable reliance upon the incorrect information, the purchaser gives value and, in the case of tangible chattel paper, tangible documents, goods, instruments, or a security certificate, receives delivery of the collateral.

As amended in 2003.

Official Comment

1.   **Source.** New.

2.   **Effect of Incorrect Information in Financing Statement.** Section 9–520(a) requires the filing office to reject financing statements that do not contain information concerning the debtor as specified in Section 9–516(b)(5). An error in this information does not render the financing statement ineffective. On rare occasions, a subsequent purchaser of the collateral (i.e., a buyer or secured party) may rely on the misinformation to its detriment. This section subordinates a security interest or agricultural lien perfected by an effective, but flawed, financing statement to the rights of a buyer or holder of a perfected security interest to the extent that, in reasonable reliance on the incorrect information, the purchaser gives value and, in the case of tangible collateral, receives delivery of the collateral. A purchaser who has not made itself aware of the information in the filing office with respect to the debtor cannot act in "reasonable reliance" upon incorrect information.

3.   **Relationship to Section 9–507.** This section applies to financing statements that contain information that is incorrect at the time of filing and imposes a small risk of subordination on the filer. In contrast, Section 9–507 deals with financing statements containing information that is correct at the time of filing but which becomes incorrect later. Except as provided in Section 9–507 with respect to changes in the name that is sufficient as the name of the debtor under Section 9–503(a), an otherwise effective financing statement does not become ineffective if the information contained in it becomes inaccurate.

As amended in 2010.

§ 9–339.   Priority Subject to Subordination.

This article does not preclude subordination by agreement by a person entitled to priority.

Official Comment

1. **Source.** Former Section 9–316.

2. **Subordination by Agreement.** The preceding sections deal elaborately with questions of priority. This section makes it entirely clear that a person entitled to priority may effectively agree to subordinate its claim. Only the person entitled to priority may make such an agreement: a person's rights cannot be adversely affected by an agreement to which the person is not a party.

[SUBPART 4. RIGHTS OF BANK]

§ 9–340.   Effectiveness of Right of Recoupment or Set-Off Against Deposit Account.

(a)   **[Exercise of recoupment or set-off.]** Except as otherwise provided in subsection (c), a bank with which a deposit account is maintained may exercise any right of recoupment or set-off against a secured party that holds a security interest in the deposit account.

(b)   **[Recoupment or set-off not affected by security interest.]** Except as otherwise provided in subsection (c), the application of this article to a security interest in a deposit account does not affect a right of recoupment or set-off of the secured party as to a deposit account maintained with the secured party.

(c)   **[When set-off ineffective.]** The exercise by a bank of a set-off against a deposit account is ineffective against a secured party that holds a security interest in the deposit account which is perfected by control under Section 9–104(a)(3), if the set-off is based on a claim against the debtor.

Official Comment

1. **Source.** New; subsection (b) is based on a nonuniform Illinois amendment.

2. **Set-off vs. Security Interest.** This section resolves the conflict between a security interest in a deposit account and the bank's rights of recoupment and set-off.

Subsection (a) states the general rule and provides that the bank may effectively exercise rights of recoupment and set-off against the secured party. Subsection (c) contains an exception: if the secured party has control under Section 9–104(a)(3) (i.e., if it has become the bank's customer), then any set-off exercised by the bank against a debt owed by the debtor (as opposed to a debt owed to the bank by the secured party) is ineffective. The bank may, however, exercise its recoupment rights effectively. This result is consistent with the priority rule in Section 9–327(4), under which the security interest of a bank in a deposit account is subordinate to that of a secured party who has control under Section 9–104(a)(3).

This section deals with rights of set-off and recoupment that a bank may have under other law. It does not create a right of set-off or recoupment, nor is it intended to override any limitations or restrictions that other law imposes on the exercise of those rights.

3. **Preservation of Set-Off Right.** Subsection (b) makes clear that a bank may hold both a right of set-off against, and an Article 9 security interest in, the same deposit account. By holding a security interest in a deposit account, a bank does not impair any right of set-off it would otherwise enjoy. This subsection does not pertain to accounts evidenced by an instrument (e.g., certain certificates of deposit), which are excluded from the definition of "deposit accounts."

§ 9–341.   Bank's Rights and Duties With Respect to Deposit Account.

Except as otherwise provided in Section 9–340(c), and unless the bank otherwise agrees in an authenticated record, a bank's rights and duties with respect to a deposit account maintained with the bank are not terminated, suspended, or modified by:

(1)   the creation, attachment, or perfection of a security interest in the deposit account;

(2)   the bank's knowledge of the security interest; or

(3)   the bank's receipt of instructions from the secured party.

Official Comment

1.   **Source.** New.

2.   **Free Flow of Funds.** This section is designed to prevent security interests in deposit accounts from impeding the free flow of funds through the payment system. Subject to two exceptions, it leaves the bank's rights and duties with respect to the deposit account and the funds on deposit unaffected by the creation or perfection of a security interest or by the bank's knowledge of the security interest. In addition, the section permits the bank to ignore the instructions of the secured party unless it had agreed to honor them or unless other law provides to the contrary. A secured party who wishes to deprive the debtor of access to funds on deposit or to appropriate those funds for itself needs to obtain the agreement of the bank, utilize the judicial process, or comply with procedures set forth in other law. Section 4–303(a), concerning the effect of notice on a bank's right and duty to pay items, is not to the contrary. That section addresses only whether an otherwise effective notice comes too late; it does not determine whether a timely notice is otherwise effective.

3.   **Operation of Rule.** The general rule of this section is subject to Section 9–340(c), under which a bank's right of set-off may not be exercised against a deposit account in the secured party's name if the right is based on a claim against the debtor. This result reflects current law in many jurisdictions and does not appear to have unduly disrupted banking practices or the payments system. The more important function of this section, which is not impaired by Section 9–340, is the bank's right to follow the debtor's (customer's) instructions (e.g., by honoring checks, permitting withdrawals, etc.) until such time as the depository institution is served with judicial process or receives instructions with respect to the funds on deposit from a secured party who has control over the deposit account.

4.   **Liability of Bank.** This Article does not determine whether a bank that pays out funds from an encumbered deposit is liable to the holder of a security interest. Although the fact that a secured party has control over the deposit account and the manner by which control was achieved may be relevant to the imposition of liability, whatever rule applies generally when a bank pays out funds in which a third party has an interest would determine liability to a secured party. Often, this rule is found in a non-UCC adverse claim statute.

5.   **Certificates of Deposit.** This section does not address the obligations of banks that issue instruments evidencing deposits (e.g., certain certificates of deposit).

§ 9–342.   Bank's Right to Refuse to Enter Into or Disclose Existence of Control Agreement.

This article does not require a bank to enter into an agreement of the kind described in Section 9–104(a)(2), even if its customer so requests or directs. A bank that has entered into such an agreement is not required to confirm the existence of the agreement to another person unless requested to do so by its customer.

Official Comment

1.   **Source.** New; derived from Section 8–106(g).

2.   **Protection for Bank.** This section protects banks from the need to enter into agreements against their will and from the need to respond to inquiries from persons other than their customers.

PART 4

RIGHTS OF THIRD PARTIES

§ 9–401.   Alienability of Debtor's Rights.

(a)   **[Other law governs alienability; exceptions.]** Except as otherwise provided in subsection (b) and Sections 9–406, 9–407, 9–408, and 9–409, whether a debtor's rights in collateral may be voluntarily or involuntarily transferred is governed by law other than this article.

(b)   **[Agreement does not prevent transfer.]** An agreement between the debtor and secured party which prohibits a transfer of the debtor's rights in collateral or makes the transfer a default does not prevent the transfer from taking effect.

Official Comment

1. **Source.** Former Section 9–311.

2. **Scope of This Part.** This Part deals with several issues affecting third parties (i.e., parties other than the debtor and the secured party). These issues are not addressed in Part 3, Subpart 3, which deals with priorities. This Part primarily addresses the rights and duties of account debtors and other persons obligated on collateral who are not, themselves, parties to a secured transaction.

3. **Governing Law.** There was some uncertainty under former Article 9 as to which jurisdiction's law (usually, which jurisdiction's version of Article 9) applied to the matters that this Part addresses. Part 3, Subpart 1, does not determine the law governing these matters because they do not relate to perfection, the effect of perfection or nonperfection, or priority. However, it might be inappropriate for a designation of applicable law by a debtor and secured party under Section 1–301 to control the law applicable to an independent transaction or relationship between the debtor and an account debtor.

Consider an example under Section 9–408.

Example 1: State X has adopted this Article; former Article 9 is the law of State Y. A general intangible (e.g., a franchise agreement) between a debtor-franchisee, D, and an account debtor-franchisor, AD, is governed by the law of State Y. D grants to SP a security interest in its rights under the franchise agreement. The franchise agreement contains a term prohibiting D's assignment of its rights under the agreement. D and SP agree that their secured transaction is governed by the law of State X. Under State X's Section 9–408, the restriction on D's assignment is ineffective to prevent the creation, attachment, or perfection of SP's security interest. State Y's former Section 9–318(4), however, does not address restrictions on the creation of security interests in general intangibles other than general intangibles for money due or to become due. Accordingly, it does not address restrictions on the assignment to SP of D's rights under the franchise agreement. The non-Article-9 law of State Y, which does address restrictions, provides that the prohibition on assignment is effective.

This Article does not provide a specific answer to the question of which State's law applies to the restriction on assignment in the example. However, assuming that under non-UCC choice-of-law principles the effectiveness of the restriction would be governed by the law of State Y, which governs the franchise agreement, the fact that State X's Article 9 governs the secured transaction between SP and D would not override the otherwise applicable law governing the agreement. Of course, to the extent that jurisdictions eventually adopt identical versions of this Article and courts interpret it consistently, the inability to identify the applicable law in circumstances such as those in the example may be inconsequential.

4. **Inalienability Under Other Law.** Subsection (a) addresses the question whether property necessarily is transferable by virtue of its inclusion (i.e., its eligibility as collateral) within the scope of Article 9. It gives a negative answer, subject to the identified exceptions. The substance of subsection (a) was implicit under former Article 9.

5. **Negative Pledge Covenant.** Subsection (b) is an exception to the general rule in subsection (a). It makes clear that in secured transactions under this Article the debtor has rights in collateral (whether legal title or equitable) which it can transfer and which its creditors can reach. It is best explained with an example.

Example 2: A debtor, D, grants to SP a security interest to secure a debt in excess of the value of the collateral. D agrees with SP that it will not create a subsequent security interest in the collateral and that any security interest purportedly granted in violation of the agreement will be void. Subsequently, in violation of its agreement with SP, D purports to grant a security interest in the same collateral to another secured party.

Subsection (b) validates D's creation of the subsequent (prohibited) security interest, which might even achieve priority over the earlier security interest. See Comment 7. However, unlike some other provisions of this Part, such as Section 9–406, subsection (b) does not provide that the agreement restricting assignment itself is "ineffective." Consequently, the debtor's breach may create a default.

6. **Rights of Lien Creditors.** Difficult problems may arise with respect to attachment, levy, and other judicial procedures under which a debtor's creditors may reach collateral subject to a security interest. For example, an obligation may be secured by collateral worth many times the amount of the obligation. If a lien creditor has caused all or a portion of the collateral to be seized under judicial process, it may be difficult to determine the amount of the debtor's "equity" in the collateral that has been seized. The section leaves resolution of this problem to the courts. The doctrine of marshaling may be appropriate.

7.   **Sale of Receivables.** If a debtor sells an account, chattel paper, payment intangible, or promissory note outright, as against the buyer the debtor has no remaining rights to transfer. If, however, the buyer fails to perfect its interest, then solely insofar as the rights of certain third parties are concerned, the debtor is deemed to retain its rights and title. See Section 9–318. The debtor has the power to convey these rights to a subsequent purchaser. If the subsequent purchaser (buyer or secured lender) perfects its interest, it will achieve priority over the earlier, unperfected purchaser. See Section 9–322(a)(1).

8.   **Use of the Term "Assignment."** The term "assignment," as used in this Article, refers to both an outright transfer of ownership and a transfer of an interest to secure an obligation. See Comment 26 to Section 9–102 and PEB Commentary No. 21, dated March 11, 2020.

As amended in 2020.

§ 9–402.   Secured Party Not Obligated on Contract of Debtor or in Tort.

The existence of a security interest, agricultural lien, or authority given to a debtor to dispose of or use collateral, without more, does not subject a secured party to liability in contract or tort for the debtor's acts or omissions.

Official Comment

1.   **Source.** Former Section 9–317.

2.   **Nonliability of Secured Party.** This section, like former Section 9–317, rejects theories on which a secured party might be held liable on a debtor's contracts or in tort merely because a security interest exists or because the debtor is entitled to dispose of or use collateral. This section expands former Section 9–317 to cover agricultural liens.

§ 9–403.   Agreement Not to Assert Defenses Against Assignee.

(a)   **["Value."]** In this section, "value" has the meaning provided in Section 3–303(a).

(b)   **[Agreement not to assert claim or defense.]** Except as otherwise provided in this section, an agreement between an account debtor and an assignor not to assert against an assignee any claim or defense that the account debtor may have against the assignor is enforceable by an assignee that takes an assignment:

(1)   for value;

(2)   in good faith;

(3)   without notice of a claim of a property or possessory right to the property assigned; and

(4)   without notice of a defense or claim in recoupment of the type that may be asserted against a person entitled to enforce a negotiable instrument under Section 3–305(a).

(c)   **[When subsection (b) not applicable.]** Subsection (b) does not apply to defenses of a type that may be asserted against a holder in due course of a negotiable instrument under Section 3–305(b).

(d)   **[Omission of required statement in consumer transaction.]** In a consumer transaction, if a record evidences the account debtor's obligation, law other than this article requires that the record include a statement to the effect that the rights of an assignee are subject to claims or defenses that the account debtor could assert against the original obligee, and the record does not include such a statement:

(1)   the record has the same effect as if the record included such a statement; and

(2)   the account debtor may assert against an assignee those claims and defenses that would have been available if the record included such a statement.

(e)   **[Rule for individual under other law.]** This section is subject to law other than this article which establishes a different rule for an account debtor who is an individual and who incurred the obligation primarily for personal, family, or household purposes.

(f)   **[Other law not displaced.]** Except as otherwise provided in subsection (d), this section does not displace law other than this article which gives effect to an agreement by an account debtor not to assert a claim or defense against an assignee.

1. **Source.** Former Section 9–206.

2. **Scope and Purpose.** Subsection (b), like former Section 9–206, generally validates an agreement between an account debtor and an assignor that the account debtor will not assert against an assignee claims and defenses that it may have against the assignor. These agreements are typical in installment sale agreements and leases. However, this section expands former Section 9–206 to apply to all account debtors; it is not limited to account debtors that have bought or leased goods. This section applies only to the obligations of an "account debtor," as defined in Section 9–102. Thus, it does not determine the circumstances under which and the extent to which a person who is obligated on a negotiable instrument is disabled from asserting claims and defenses. Rather, Article 3 must be consulted. See, e.g., Sections 3–305, 3–306. Article 3 governs even when the negotiable instrument constitutes part of chattel paper. See Section 9–102 (an obligor on a negotiable instrument constituting part of chattel paper is not an "account debtor").

3. **Conditions of Validation; Relationship to Article 3.** Subsection (b) validates an account debtor's agreement only if the assignee takes an assignment for value, in good faith, and without notice of conflicting claims to the property assigned or of certain claims or defenses of the account debtor. Like former Section 9–206, this section is designed to put the assignee in a position that is no better and no worse than that of a holder in due course of a negotiable instrument under Article 3. However, former Section 9–206 left open certain issues, e.g., whether the section incorporated the special Article 3 definition of "value" in Section 3–303 or the generally applicable definition in Section 1–201(44) [*unrevised Article 1; see Concordance, p. 22*]. Subsection (a) addresses this question; it provides that "value" has the meaning specified in Section 3–303(a). Similarly, subsection (c) provides that subsection (b) does not validate an agreement with respect to defenses that could be asserted against a holder in due course under Section 3–305(b) (the so-called "real" defenses). In 1990, the definition of "holder in due course" (Section 3–302) and the articulation of the rights of a holder in due course (Sections 3–305 and 3–306) were revised substantially. This section tracks more closely the rules of Sections 3–302, 3–305, and 3–306.

4. **Relationship to Terms of Assigned Property.** Former Section 9–206(2), concerning warranties accompanying the sale of goods, has been deleted as unnecessary. This Article does not regulate the terms of the account, chattel paper, or general intangible that is assigned, except insofar as the account, chattel paper, or general intangible itself creates a security interest (as often is the case with chattel paper). Thus, Article 2, and not this Article, determines whether a seller of goods makes or effectively disclaims warranties, even if the sale is secured. Similarly, other law, and not this Article, determines the effectiveness of an account debtor's undertaking to pay notwithstanding, and not to assert, any defenses or claims against an assignor—e.g., a "hell-or-high-water" provision in the underlying agreement that is assigned. If other law gives effect to this undertaking, then, under principles of *nemo dat,* the undertaking would be enforceable by the assignee (secured party). If other law prevents the assignor from enforcing the undertaking, this section nevertheless might permit the assignee to do so. The right of the assignee to enforce would depend upon whether, under the particular facts, the account debtor's undertaking fairly could be construed as an agreement that falls within the scope of this section and whether the assignee meets the requirements of this section.

5. **Relationship to Federal Trade Commission Rule.** Subsection (d) is new. It applies to rights evidenced by a record that is required to contain, but does not contain, the notice set forth in Federal Trade Commission Rule 433, 16 C.F.R. Part 433 (the "Holder-in-Due-Course Regulations"). Under this subsection, an assignee of such a record takes subject to the consumer account debtor's claims and defenses to the same extent as it would have if the writing had contained the required notice. Thus, subsection (d) effectively renders waiver-of-defense clauses ineffective in the transactions with consumers to which it applies.

6. **Relationship to Other Law.** Like former Section 9–206(1), this section takes no position on the enforceability of waivers of claims and defenses by consumer account debtors, leaving that question to other law. However, the reference to "law other than this article" in subsection (e) encompasses administrative rules and regulations; the reference in former Section 9–206(1) that it replaces ("statute or decision") arguably did not.

This section does not displace other law that gives effect to a non-consumer account debtor's agreement not to assert defenses against an assignee, even if the agreement would not qualify under subsection (b). See subsection (f). It validates, but does not invalidate, agreements made by a non-consumer account debtor. This section also does not displace other law to the extent that the other law permits an assignee, who takes an assignment with notice of a claim of a property or possessory right, a defense, or a claim in recoupment, to enforce an account debtor's agreement not to assert claims and defenses against the assignor (e.g., a "hell-or-high-water" agreement). See Comment 4. It also does not displace an assignee's right to assert that an account debtor is estopped from asserting a claim or defense. Nor does this section displace other law with respect to waivers of potential future claims and defenses that are the subject of an agreement between the account debtor and the assignee. Finally, it does not displace Section 1–107 [*unrevised Article 1; see Concordance, p. 22*], concerning waiver of a breach that allegedly already has occurred.

§ 9–404.   Rights Acquired by Assignee; Claims and Defenses Against Assignee.

(a)   **[Assignee's rights subject to terms, claims, and defenses; exceptions.]** Unless an account debtor has made an enforceable agreement not to assert defenses or claims, and subject to subsections (b) through (e), the rights of an assignee are subject to:

(1)   all terms of the agreement between the account debtor and assignor and any defense or claim in recoupment arising from the transaction that gave rise to the contract; and

(2)   any other defense or claim of the account debtor against the assignor which accrues before the account debtor receives a notification of the assignment authenticated by the assignor or the assignee.

(b)   **[Account debtor's claim reduces amount owed to assignee.]** Subject to subsection (c) and except as otherwise provided in subsection (d), the claim of an account debtor against an assignor may be asserted against an assignee under subsection (a) only to reduce the amount the account debtor owes.

(c)   **[Rule for individual under other law.]** This section is subject to law other than this article which establishes a different rule for an account debtor who is an individual and who incurred the obligation primarily for personal, family, or household purposes.

(d)   **[Omission of required statement in consumer transaction.]** In a consumer transaction, if a record evidences the account debtor's obligation, law other than this article requires that the record include a statement to the effect that the account debtor's recovery against an assignee with respect to claims and defenses against the assignor may not exceed amounts paid by the account debtor under the record, and the record does not include such a statement, the extent to which a claim of an account debtor against the assignor may be asserted against an assignee is determined as if the record included such a statement.

(e)   **[Inapplicability to health-care-insurance receivable.]** This section does not apply to an assignment of a health-care-insurance receivable.

Official Comment

1.   **Source.** Former Section 9–318(1).

2.   **Purpose; Rights of Assignee in General.** Subsection (a), like former Section 9–318(1), provides that an assignee generally takes an assignment subject to defenses and claims of an account debtor. Under subsection (a)(1), if the account debtor's defenses on an assigned claim arise from the transaction that gave rise to the contract with the assignor, it makes no difference whether the defense or claim accrues before or after the account debtor is notified of the assignment. Under subsection (a)(2), the assignee takes subject to other defenses or claims only if they accrue before the account debtor has been notified of the assignment. Of course, an account debtor may waive its right to assert defenses or claims against an assignee under Section 9–403 or other applicable law. Subsection (a) tracks Section 3–305(a)(3) more closely than its predecessor.

3.   **Limitation on Affirmative Claims.** Subsection (b) is new. It limits the claim that the account debtor may assert against an assignee. Borrowing from Section 3–305(a)(3) and cases construing former Section 9–318, subsection (b) generally does not afford the account debtor the right to an affirmative recovery from an assignee.

4.   **Consumer Account Debtors; Relationship to Federal Trade Commission Rule.** Subsections (c) and (d) also are new. Subsection (c) makes clear that the rules of this section are subject to other law establishing special rules for consumer account debtors. An "account debtor who is an individual" as used in subsection (c) includes individuals who are jointly or jointly and severally obligated. Subsection (d) applies to rights evidenced by a record that is required to contain, but does not contain, the notice set forth in Federal Trade Commission Rule 433, 16 C.F.R. Part 433 (the "Holder-in-Due-Course Regulations"). Under subsection (d), a consumer account debtor has the same right to an affirmative recovery from an assignee of such a record as the consumer would have had against the assignee had the record contained the required notice.

5.   **Scope; Application to "Account Debtor."** This section deals only with the rights and duties of "account debtors"—and for the most part only with account debtors on accounts, chattel paper, and payment intangibles. Subsection (e) provides that the obligation of an insurer with respect to a health-care-insurance

receivable is governed by other law. References in this section to an "account debtor" include account debtors on collateral that is proceeds. Neither this section nor any other provision of this Article, including Sections 9–408 and 9–409, provides analogous regulation of the rights and duties of other obligors on collateral, such as the maker of a negotiable instrument (governed by Article 3), the issuer of or nominated person under a letter of credit (governed by Article 5), or the issuer of a security (governed by Article 8). Article 9 leaves those rights and duties untouched; however, Section 9–409 deals with the special case of letters of credit. When chattel paper is composed in part of a negotiable instrument, the obligor on the instrument is not an "account debtor," and Article 3 governs the rights of the assignee of the chattel paper with respect to the issues that this section addresses. See, e.g., Section 3–601 (dealing with discharge of an obligation to pay a negotiable instrument).

§ 9–405.   Modification of Assigned Contract.

(a) **[Effect of modification on assignee.]** A modification of or substitution for an assigned contract is effective against an assignee if made in good faith. The assignee acquires corresponding rights under the modified or substituted contract. The assignment may provide that the modification or substitution is a breach of contract by the assignor. This subsection is subject to subsections (b) through (d).

(b) **[Applicability of subsection (a).]** Subsection (a) applies to the extent that:

(1) the right to payment or a part thereof under an assigned contract has not been fully earned by performance; or

(2) the right to payment or a part thereof has been fully earned by performance and the account debtor has not received notification of the assignment under Section 9–406(a).

(c) **[Rule for individual under other law.]** This section is subject to law other than this article which establishes a different rule for an account debtor who is an individual and who incurred the obligation primarily for personal, family, or household purposes.

(d) **[Inapplicability to health-care-insurance receivable.]** This section does not apply to an assignment of a health-care-insurance receivable.

Official Comment

1. **Source.** Former Section 9–318(2).

2. **Modification of Assigned Contract.** The ability of account debtors and assignors to modify assigned contracts can be important, especially in the case of government contracts and complex contractual arrangements (e.g., construction contracts) with respect to which modifications are customary. Subsections (a) and (b) provide that good-faith modifications of assigned contracts are binding against an assignee to the extent that (i) the right to payment has not been fully earned or (ii) the right to payment has been earned and notification of the assignment has not been given to the account debtor. Former Section 9–318(2) did not validate modifications of fully-performed contracts under any circumstances, whether or not notification of the assignment had been given to the account debtor. Subsection (a) protects the interests of assignees by (i) limiting the effectiveness of modifications to those made in good faith, (ii) affording the assignee with corresponding rights under the contract as modified, and (iii) recognizing that the modification may be a breach of the assignor's agreement with the assignee.

3. **Consumer Account Debtors.** Subsection (c) is new. It makes clear that the rules of this section are subject to other law establishing special rules for consumer account debtors.

4. **Account Debtors on Health-Care-Insurance Receivables.** Subsection (d) also is new. It provides that this section does not apply to an assignment of a health-care-insurance receivable. The obligation of an insurer with respect to a health-care-insurance receivable is governed by other law.

§ 9–406.   Discharge of Account Debtor; Notification of Assignment; Identification and Proof of Assignment; Restrictions on Assignment of Accounts, Chattel Paper, Payment Intangibles, and Promissory Notes Ineffective.

(a) **[Discharge of account debtor; effect of notification.]** Subject to subsections (b) through (i), an account debtor on an account, chattel paper, or a payment intangible may discharge its obligation by paying the assignor until, but not after, the account debtor receives a notification, authenticated by the assignor or the assignee, that the amount due or to become due has been assigned and that payment is to be made to the assignee. After receipt of the notification, the account debtor may discharge its obligation by paying the assignee and may not discharge the obligation by paying the assignor.

(b)   **[When notification ineffective.]** Subject to subsection (h), notification is ineffective under subsection (a):

(1)   if it does not reasonably identify the rights assigned;

(2)   to the extent that an agreement between an account debtor and a seller of a payment intangible limits the account debtor's duty to pay a person other than the seller and the limitation is effective under law other than this article; or

(3)   at the option of an account debtor, if the notification notifies the account debtor to make less than the full amount of any installment or other periodic payment to the assignee, even if:

    (A)   only a portion of the account, chattel paper, or payment intangible has been assigned to that assignee;

    (B)   a portion has been assigned to another assignee; or

    (C)   the account debtor knows that the assignment to that assignee is limited.

(c)   **[Proof of assignment.]** Subject to subsection (h), if requested by the account debtor, an assignee shall seasonably furnish reasonable proof that the assignment has been made. Unless the assignee complies, the account debtor may discharge its obligation by paying the assignor, even if the account debtor has received a notification under subsection (a).

(d)   **[Term restricting assignment generally ineffective.]** Except as otherwise provided in subsections (e) and (k) and Sections 2A–303 and 9–407, and subject to subsection (h), a term in an agreement between an account debtor and an assignor or in a promissory note is ineffective to the extent that it:

(1)   prohibits, restricts, or requires the consent of the account debtor or person obligated on the promissory note to the assignment or transfer of, or the creation, attachment, perfection, or enforcement of a security interest in, the account, chattel paper, payment intangible, or promissory note; or

(2)   provides that the assignment or transfer or the creation, attachment, perfection, or enforcement of the security interest may give rise to a default, breach, right of recoupment, claim, defense, termination, right of termination, or remedy under the account, chattel paper, payment intangible, or promissory note.

(e)   **[Inapplicability of subsection (d) to certain sales.]** Subsection (d) does not apply to the sale of a payment intangible or promissory note, other than a sale pursuant to a disposition under Section 9–610 or as acceptance of collateral under Section 9–620.

(f)   **[Legal restrictions on assignment generally ineffective.]** Except as otherwise provided in subsection (k) and Sections 2A–303 and 9–407 and subject to subsections (h) and (i), a rule of law, statute, or regulation that prohibits, restricts, or requires the consent of a government, governmental body or official, or account debtor to the assignment or transfer of, or creation of a security interest in, an account or chattel paper is ineffective to the extent that the rule of law, statute, or regulation:

(1)   prohibits, restricts, or requires the consent of the government, governmental body or official, or account debtor to the assignment or transfer of, or the creation, attachment, perfection, or enforcement of a security interest in the account or chattel paper; or

(2)   provides that the assignment or transfer or the creation, attachment, perfection, or enforcement of the security interest may give rise to a default, breach, right of recoupment, claim, defense, termination, right of termination, or remedy under the account or chattel paper.

(g)   **[Subsection (b)(3) not waivable.]** Subject to subsection (h), an account debtor may not waive or vary its option under subsection (b)(3).

(h)   **[Rule for individual under other law.]** This section is subject to law other than this article which establishes a different rule for an account debtor who is an individual and who incurred the obligation primarily for personal, family, or household purposes.

(i) **[Inapplicability to health-care-insurance receivable.]** This section does not apply to an assignment of a health-care-insurance receivable.

(j) **[Section prevails over specified inconsistent law.]** This section prevails over any inconsistent provisions of the following statutes, rules, and regulations:

[List here any statutes, rules, and regulations containing provisions inconsistent with this section.]

(k) **[Inapplicability to interests in certain entities.]** Subsections (d), (f), and (j) do not apply to a security interest in an ownership interest in a general partnership, limited partnership, or limited liability company.

Legislative Note: States that amend statutes, rules, and regulations to remove provisions inconsistent with this section need not enact subsection (j).

As amended in 1999, 2000, 2010, and 2018.

Official Comment

1. **Source.** Former Section 9–318(3), (4).

2. **Account Debtor's Right to Pay Assignor Until Notification.** Subsection (a) provides the general rule concerning an account debtor's right to pay the assignor until the account debtor receives appropriate notification. The revision makes clear that once the account debtor receives the notification, the account debtor cannot discharge its obligation by paying the assignor. It also makes explicit that payment to the assignor before notification, or payment to the assignee after notification, discharges the obligation. No change in meaning from former Section 9–318 is intended. Nothing in this section conditions the effectiveness of a notification on the identity of the person who gives it. An account debtor that doubts whether the right to payment has been assigned may avail itself of the procedures in subsection (c). See Comment 4.

An effective notification under subsection (a) must be authenticated. This requirement normally could be satisfied by sending notification on the notifying person's letterhead or on a form on which the notifying person's name appears. In each case the printed name would be a symbol adopted by the notifying person for the purpose of identifying the person and adopting the notification. See Section 9–102 (defining "authenticate").

Subsection (a) applies only to account debtors on accounts, chattel paper, and payment intangibles. (Section 9–102 defines the term "account debtor" more broadly, to include those obligated on all general intangibles.) Although subsection (a) is more precise than its predecessor, it probably does not change the rule that applied under former Article 9. Former Section 9–318(3) referred to the account debtor's obligation to "pay," indicating that the subsection was limited to account debtors on accounts, chattel paper, and other payment obligations.

3. **Limitations on Effectiveness of Notification.** Subsection (b) contains some special rules concerning the effectiveness of a notification under subsection (a).

Subsection (b)(1) tracks former Section 9–318(3) by making ineffective a notification that does not reasonably identify the rights assigned. A reasonable identification need not identify the right to payment with specificity, but what is reasonable also is not left to the arbitrary decision of the account debtor. If an account debtor has doubt as to the adequacy of a notification, it may not be safe in disregarding the notification unless it notifies the assignee with reasonable promptness as to the respects in which the account debtor considers the notification defective.

Subsection (b)(2), which is new, applies only to sales of payment intangibles. It makes a notification ineffective to the extent that other law gives effect to an agreement between an account debtor and a seller of a payment intangible that limits the account debtor's duty to pay a person other than the seller. Payment intangibles are substantially less fungible than accounts and chattel paper. In some (e.g., commercial bank loans), account debtors customarily and legitimately expect that they will not be required to pay any person other than the financial institution that has advanced funds.

It has become common in financing transactions to assign interests in a single obligation to more than one assignee. Requiring an account debtor that owes a single obligation to make multiple payments to multiple assignees would be unnecessarily burdensome. Thus, under subsection (b)(3), an account debtor that is notified to pay an assignee less than the full amount of any installment or other periodic payment has the option to treat the notification as ineffective, ignore the notice, and discharge the assigned obligation by paying the assignor. Some account debtors may not realize that the law affords them the right to ignore certain notices of assignment with impunity. By making the notification ineffective at the account debtor's option, subsection (b)(3) permits an account debtor to pay the assignee in accordance with the notice and thereby to satisfy its obligation *pro tanto*. Under subsection (g), the rights and duties created by subsection (b)(3) cannot be waived or varied.

4. **Proof of Assignment.** Subsection (c) links payment with discharge, as in subsection (a). It follows former Section 9–318(3) in referring to the right of the account debtor to pay the assignor if the requested proof of assignment is not seasonably forthcoming. Even if the proof is not forthcoming, the notification of assignment would remain effective, so that, in the absence of reasonable proof of the assignment, the account debtor could discharge the obligation by paying either the assignee or the assignor. Of course, if the assignee did not in fact receive an assignment, the account debtor cannot discharge its obligation by paying a putative assignee who is a stranger. The observations in Comment 3 concerning the reasonableness of an identification of a right to payment also apply here. An account debtor that questions the adequacy of proof submitted by an assignee would be well advised to promptly inform the assignee of the defects.

An account debtor may face another problem if its obligation becomes due while the account debtor is awaiting reasonable proof of the assignment that it has requested from the assignee. This section does not excuse the account debtor from timely compliance with its obligations. Consequently, an account debtor that has received a notification of assignment and who has requested reasonable proof of the assignment may discharge its obligation by paying the assignor at the time (or even earlier if reasonably necessary to avoid risk of default) when a payment is due, even if the account debtor has not yet received a response to its request for proof. On the other hand, after requesting reasonable proof of the assignment, an account debtor may not discharge its obligation by paying the assignor substantially in advance of the time that the payment is due unless the assignee has failed to provide the proof seasonably.

5. **Contractual Restrictions on Assignment.** Former Section 9–318(4) rendered ineffective an agreement between an account debtor and an assignor which prohibited assignment of an account (whether outright or to secure an obligation) or prohibited a security assignment of a general intangible for the payment of money due or to become due. Subsection (d) essentially follows former Section 9–318(4), but expands the rule of free assignability to chattel paper (subject to Sections 2A–303 and 9–407) and promissory notes and explicitly overrides both restrictions and prohibitions of assignment. The policies underlying the ineffectiveness of contractual restrictions under this section build on common-law developments that essentially have eliminated legal restrictions on assignments of rights to payment as security and other assignments of rights to payment such as accounts and chattel paper. Any that might linger for accounts and chattel paper are addressed by new subsection (f). See Comment 6.

Former Section 9–318(4) did not apply to a sale of a payment intangible (as described in the former provision, "a general intangible for money due or to become due") but did apply to an assignment of a payment intangible for security. Subsection (e) continues this approach and also makes subsection (d) inapplicable to sales of promissory notes. Section 9–408 addresses anti-assignment clauses with respect to sales of payment intangibles and promissory notes.

Like former Section 9–318(4), subsection (d) provides that anti-assignment clauses are "ineffective." The quoted term means that the clause is of no effect whatsoever; the clause does not prevent the assignment from taking effect between the parties and the prohibited assignment does not constitute a default under the agreement between the account debtor and assignor. However, subsection (d) does not override terms that do not directly prohibit, restrict, or require consent to an assignment but which might, nonetheless, present a practical impairment of the assignment. Properly read, however, subsection (d) reaches only covenants that prohibit, restrict, or require consents to assignments; it does not override all terms that might "impair" an assignment in fact.

Example: Buyer enters into an agreement with Seller to buy equipment that Seller is to manufacture according to Buyer's specifications. Buyer agrees to make a series of prepayments during the construction process. In return, Seller agrees to set aside the prepaid funds in a special account and to use the funds solely for the manufacture of the designated equipment. Seller also agrees that it will not assign any of its rights under the sale agreement with Buyer. Nevertheless, Seller grants to Secured Party a security interest in its accounts. Seller's anti-assignment agreement is ineffective under subsection (d); its agreement concerning the use of prepaid funds, which is not a restriction or prohibition on assignment, is not. However, if Secured Party notifies Buyer to make all future payments directly to Secured Party, Buyer will be obliged to do so under subsection (a) if it wishes the payments to discharge its obligation. Unless Secured Party releases the funds to Seller so that Seller can comply with its use-of-funds covenant, Seller will be in breach of that covenant.

In the example, there appears to be a plausible business purpose for the use-of-funds covenant. However, a court may conclude that a covenant with no business purpose other than imposing an impediment to an assignment actually is a direct restriction that is rendered ineffective by subsection (d).

6. **Legal Restrictions on Assignment.** Former Section 9–318(4), like subsection (d) of this section, addressed only contractual restrictions on assignment. The former section was grounded on the reality that legal, as opposed to contractual, restrictions on assignments of rights to payment had largely disappeared. New subsection (f) codifies this principle of free assignability for accounts and chattel paper. For the most part the discussion of contractual restrictions in Comment 5 applies as well to legal restrictions rendered ineffective under subsection (f).

7. **Multiple Assignments.** This section, like former Section 9–318, is not a complete codification of the law of assignments of rights to payment. In particular, it is silent concerning many of the ramifications for an account debtor in cases of multiple assignments of the same right. For example, an assignor might assign the same receivable to multiple assignees (which assignments could be either inadvertent or wrongful). Or, the assignor could assign the receivable to assignee-1, which then might re-assign it to assignee-2, and so forth. The rights and duties of an account debtor in the face of multiple assignments and in other circumstances not resolved in the statutory text are left to the common-law rules. See, e.g., Restatement (2d), Contracts §§ 338(3), 339. The failure of former Article 9 to codify these rules does not appear to have caused problems.

8. **Consumer Account Debtors.** Subsection (h) is new. It makes clear that the rules of this section are subject to other law establishing special rules for consumer account debtors.

9. **Account Debtors on Health-Care-Insurance Receivables.** Subsection (i) also is new. The obligation of an insurer with respect to a health-care-insurance receivable is governed by other law. Section 9–408 addresses contractual and legal restrictions on the assignment of a health-care-insurance receivable.

10. **Inapplicability to Certain Ownership Interests.** This section does not apply to an ownership interest in a limited liability company, limited partnership, or general partnership, regardless of the name of the interest and whether the interest: (i) pertains to economic rights, governance rights, or both; (ii) arises under: (a) an operating agreement, the applicable limited liability company act, or both; or (b) a partnership agreement, the applicable partnership act, or both; or (iii) is owned by: (a) a member of a company or transferee or assignee of a member; or (b) a partner or a transferee or assignee of a partner; or (iv) comprises contractual, property, other rights, or some combination thereof.

As amended in 2018.

§ 9–407. Restrictions on Creation or Enforcement of Security Interest in Leasehold Interest or in Lessor's Residual Interest.

(a) **[Term restricting assignment generally ineffective.]** Except as otherwise provided in subsection (b), a term in a lease agreement is ineffective to the extent that it:

(1) prohibits, restricts, or requires the consent of a party to the lease to the assignment or transfer of, or the creation, attachment, perfection, or enforcement of a security interest in an interest of a party under the lease contract or in the lessor's residual interest in the goods; or

(2) provides that the assignment or transfer or the creation, attachment, perfection, or enforcement of the security interest may give rise to a default, breach, right of recoupment, claim, defense, termination, right of termination, or remedy under the lease.

(b) **[Effectiveness of certain terms.]** Except as otherwise provided in Section 2A–303(7), a term described in subsection (a)(2) is effective to the extent that there is:

(1) a transfer by the lessee of the lessee's right of possession or use of the goods in violation of the term; or

(2) a delegation of a material performance of either party to the lease contract in violation of the term.

(c) **[Security interest not material impairment.]** The creation, attachment, perfection, or enforcement of a security interest in the lessor's interest under the lease contract or the lessor's residual interest in the goods is not a transfer that materially impairs the lessee's prospect of obtaining return performance or materially changes the duty of or materially increases the burden or risk imposed on the lessee within the purview of Section 2A–303(4) unless, and then only to the extent that, enforcement actually results in a delegation of material performance of the lessor.

As amended in 1999.

Official Comment

1.   **Source.** Section 2A–303.

2.   **Restrictions on Assignment Generally Ineffective.** Under subsection (a), as under former Section 2A–303(3), a term in a lease agreement which prohibits or restricts the creation of a security interest generally is ineffective. This reflects the general policy of Section 9–406(d) and former Section 9–318(4). This section has been conformed in several respects to analogous provisions in Sections 9–406, 9–408, and 9–409, including the substitution of "ineffective" for "not enforceable" and the substitution of "assignment or transfer of, or the creation, attachment, perfection, or enforcement of a security interest" for "creation or enforcement of a security interest."

3.   **Exceptions for Certain Transfers and Delegations.** Subsection (b) provides exceptions to the general ineffectiveness of restrictions under subsection (a). A term that otherwise is ineffective under subsection (a)(2) is effective to the extent that a lessee transfers its right to possession and use of goods or if either party delegates material performance of the lease contract in violation of the term. However, under subsection (c), as under former Section 2A–303(3), a lessor's creation of a security interest in its interest in a lease contract or its residual interest in the leased goods is not a material impairment under Section 2A–303(4) (former Section 2A–303(5)), absent an actual delegation of the lessor's material performance. The terms of the lease contract determine whether the lessor, in fact, has any remaining obligations to perform. If it does, it is then necessary to determine whether there has been an actual delegation of "material performance." See Section 2A–303, Comments 3 and 4.

As amended in 1999.

§ 9–408.   Restrictions on Assignment of Promissory Notes, Health-Care-Insurance Receivables, and Certain General Intangibles Ineffective.

(a)   **[Term restricting assignment generally ineffective.]** Except as otherwise provided in subsections (b) and (f), a term in a promissory note or in an agreement between an account debtor and a debtor which relates to a health-care-insurance receivable or a general intangible, including a contract, permit, license, or franchise, and which term prohibits, restricts, or requires the consent of the person obligated on the promissory note or the account debtor to, the assignment or transfer of, or creation, attachment, or perfection of a security interest in, the promissory note, health-care-insurance receivable, or general intangible, is ineffective to the extent that the term:

(1)   would impair the creation, attachment, or perfection of a security interest; or

(2)   provides that the assignment or transfer or the creation, attachment, or perfection of the security interest may give rise to a default, breach, right of recoupment, claim, defense, termination, right of termination, or remedy under the promissory note, health-care-insurance receivable, or general intangible.

(b)   **[Applicability of subsection (a) to sales of certain rights to payment.]** Subsection (a) applies to a security interest in a payment intangible or promissory note only if the security interest arises out of a sale of the payment intangible or promissory note, other than a sale pursuant to a disposition under Section 9–610 or as acceptance of collateral under Section 9–620.

(c)   **[Legal restrictions on assignment generally ineffective.]** Except as otherwise provided in subsection (f), a rule of law, statute, or regulation that prohibits, restricts, or requires the consent of a government, governmental body or official, person obligated on a promissory note, or account debtor to the assignment or transfer of, or creation of a security interest in, a promissory note, health-care-insurance receivable, or general intangible, including a contract, permit, license, or franchise between an account debtor and a debtor, is ineffective to the extent that the rule of law, statute, or regulation:

(1)   would impair the creation, attachment, or perfection of a security interest; or

(2)   provides that the assignment or transfer or the creation, attachment, or perfection of the security interest may give rise to a default, breach, right of recoupment, claim, defense, termination, right of termination, or remedy under the promissory note, health-care-insurance receivable, or general intangible.

(d)   **[Limitation on ineffectiveness under subsections (a) and (c).]** To the extent that a term in a promissory note or in an agreement between an account debtor and a debtor which relates to a health-care-insurance receivable or general intangible or a rule of law, statute, or regulation described in subsection (c) would be effective under law other than this article but is ineffective under subsection (a) or (c), the creation, attachment, or perfection of a security interest in the promissory note, health-care-insurance receivable, or general intangible:

(1)   is not enforceable against the person obligated on the promissory note or the account debtor;

(2)   does not impose a duty or obligation on the person obligated on the promissory note or the account debtor;

(3)   does not require the person obligated on the promissory note or the account debtor to recognize the security interest, pay or render performance to the secured party, or accept payment or performance from the secured party;

(4)   does not entitle the secured party to use or assign the debtor's rights under the promissory note, health-care-insurance receivable, or general intangible, including any related information or materials furnished to the debtor in the transaction giving rise to the promissory note, health-care-insurance receivable, or general intangible;

(5)   does not entitle the secured party to use, assign, possess, or have access to any trade secrets or confidential information of the person obligated on the promissory note or the account debtor; and

(6)   does not entitle the secured party to enforce the security interest in the promissory note, health-care-insurance receivable, or general intangible.

(e)   **[Section prevails over specified inconsistent law.]** This section prevails over any inconsistent provisions of the following statutes, rules, and regulations:

[List here any statutes, rules, and regulations containing provisions inconsistent with this section.]

(f)   **[Inapplicability to interests in certain entities.]** This section does not apply to a security interest in an ownership interest in a general partnership, limited partnership, or limited liability company.

Legislative Note: States that amend statutes, rules, and regulations to remove provisions inconsistent with this section need not enact subsection (e).

As amended in 1999, 2010, and 2018.

Official Comment

1.   **Source.** New.

2.   **Free Assignability.** This section makes ineffective any attempt to restrict the assignment of a general intangible, health-care-insurance receivable, or promissory note, whether the restriction appears in the terms of a promissory note or the agreement between an account debtor and a debtor (subsection (a)) or in a rule of law, including a statute or governmental rule or regulation (subsection (c)). This result allows the creation, attachment, and perfection of a security interest in a general intangible, such as an agreement for the nonexclusive license of software, as well as sales of certain receivables, such as a health-care-insurance receivable (which is an "account"), payment intangible, or promissory note, without giving rise to a default or breach by the assignor or from triggering a remedy of the account debtor or person obligated on a promissory note. This enhances the ability of certain debtors to obtain credit. On the other hand, subsection (d) protects the other party—the "account debtor" on a general intangible or the person obligated on a promissory note—from adverse effects arising from the security interest. It leaves the account debtor's or obligated person's rights and obligations unaffected in all material respects if a restriction rendered ineffective by subsection (a) or (c) would be effective under law other than Article 9.

Example 1:   A term of an agreement for the nonexclusive license of computer software prohibits the licensee from assigning any of its rights as licensee with respect to the software. The agreement also provides that an attempt to assign rights in violation of the restriction is a default entitling the licensor to terminate the license agreement. The licensee, as debtor, grants to a secured party a security interest in its rights under the license and in the computers in which it is installed. Under this section, the term prohibiting assignment and providing for a default upon an attempted assignment is ineffective to prevent the creation, attachment, or perfection of the security interest or entitle the licensor to terminate the license agreement. However, under subsection (d), the secured party (absent the licensor's agreement) is not entitled to enforce the license or to use, assign, or otherwise enjoy the benefits of the licensed software, and the licensor need not recognize (or pay any attention to) the secured party. Even if the secured party takes possession of the computers on the debtor's default, the debtor would remain free to remove the software from the computer, load it on another computer, and continue to use it, if the license so permits. If the debtor does not remove the software, other law may require the secured party to remove it before disposing of the computer. Disposition of the software with the computer could violate an effective prohibition on enforcement of the security interest. See subsection (d).

3.   **Nature of Debtor's Interest.** Neither this section nor any other provision of this Article determines whether a debtor has a property interest. The definition of the term "security interest" provides that it is an "interest in personal property." See Section 1–201(b)(35). Ordinarily, a debtor can create a security interest in collateral only if it has "rights in the collateral." See Section 9–203(b). Other law determines whether a debtor has a property interest ("rights in the collateral") and the nature of that interest. For example, the nonexclusive license addressed in Example 1 may not create any property interest whatsoever in the intellectual property (e.g., copyright) that underlies the license and that effectively enables the licensor to grant the license. The debtor's property interest may be confined solely to its interest in the promises made by the licensor in the license agreement (e.g., a promise not to sue the debtor for its use of the software).

4.   **Scope: Sales of Payment Intangibles and Other General Intangibles; Assignments Unaffected by this Section.** Subsections (a) and (c) render ineffective restrictions on assignments only "to the extent" that the assignments restrict the "creation, attachment, or perfection of a security interest," including sales of payment intangibles and promissory notes. This section does not render ineffective a restriction on an assignment that does not create a security interest. For example, if the debtor in Comment 2, Example 1 purported to assign the license to another entity that would use the computer software itself, other law would govern the effectiveness of the anti-assignment provisions.

Subsection (a) applies to a security interest in payment intangibles only if the security interest arises out of sale of the payment intangibles. Contractual restrictions directed to security interests in payment intangibles which secure an obligation are subject to Section 9–406(d). Subsection (a) also deals with sales of promissory notes which also create security interests. See Section 9–109(a). Subsection (c) deals with all security interests in payment intangibles or promissory notes, whether or not arising out of a sale.

Subsection (a) does not render ineffective any term, and subsection (c) does not render ineffective any law, statute or regulation, that restricts outright sales of general intangibles other than payment intangibles. They deal only with restrictions on security interests. The only sales of general intangibles that create security interests are sales of payment intangibles.

5.   **Terminology: "Account Debtor"; "Person Obligated on a Promissory Note."** This section uses the term "account debtor" as it is defined in Section 9–102. The term refers to the party, other than the debtor, to a general intangible, including a permit, license, franchise, or the like, and the person obligated on a health-care-insurance receivable, which is a type of account. The definition of "account debtor" does not limit the term to persons who are obligated to *pay* under a general intangible. Rather, the term includes all persons who are obligated on a general intangible, including those who are obligated to render performance in exchange for payment. In some cases, e.g., the creation of a security interest in a franchisee's rights under a franchise agreement, the principal payment obligation may be owed *by* the debtor (franchisee) *to* the account debtor (franchisor). This section also refers to a "person obligated on a promissory note," inasmuch as those persons do not fall within the definition of "account debtor."

Example 2:   A licensor and licensee enter into an agreement for the nonexclusive license of computer software. The licensee's interest in the license agreement is a general intangible. If the licensee grants to a secured party a security interest in its rights under the license agreement, the licensee is the debtor and the licensor is the account debtor. On the other hand, if the licensor grants to a secured party a security interest in its right to payment (an account) under the license agreement, the licensor is the debtor and the licensee is the account debtor. (This section applies to the security interest in the general intangible but not to the security interest in the account, which is not a health-care-insurance receivable.)

6.   **Effects on Account Debtors and Persons Obligated on Promissory Notes.** Subsections (a) and (c) affect two classes of persons. These subsections affect account debtors on general intangibles and health-care-insurance receivables and persons obligated on promissory notes. Subsection (c) also affects governmental entities that enact or determine rules of law. *However, subsection (d) ensures that these affected persons are not affected adversely.* That provision removes any burdens or adverse effects on these persons for which any rational basis

could exist to restrict the effectiveness of an assignment or to exercise any remedies. For this reason, the effects of subsections (a) and (c) are immaterial insofar as those persons are concerned.

Subsection (a) does not override terms that do not directly prohibit, restrict, or require consent to an assignment but which might, nonetheless, present a practical impairment of the assignment. Properly read, however, this section, like Section 9–406(d), reaches only covenants that prohibit, restrict, or require consents to assignments; it does not override all terms that might "impair" an assignment in fact.

Example 3:   A licensor and licensee enter into an agreement for the nonexclusive license of valuable business software. The license agreement includes terms (i) prohibiting the licensee from assigning its rights under the license, (ii) prohibiting the licensee from disclosing to anyone certain information relating to the software and the licensor, and (iii) deeming prohibited assignments and prohibited disclosures to be defaults. The licensee wishes to obtain financing and, in exchange, is willing to grant a security interest in its rights under the license agreement. The secured party, reasonably, refuses to extend credit unless the licensee discloses the information that it is prohibited from disclosing under the license agreement. The secured party cannot determine the value of the proposed collateral in the absence of this information. Under this section, the terms of the license prohibiting the assignment (grant of the security interest) and making the assignment a default are ineffective. However, the nondisclosure covenant is not a term that prohibits the assignment or creation of a security interest in the license. Consequently, the nondisclosure term is enforceable even though the *practical* effect is to restrict the licensee's ability to use its rights under the license agreement as collateral.

The nondisclosure term also would be effective in the factual setting of Comment 2, Example 1. If the secured party's possession of the computers loaded with software would put it in a position to discover confidential information that the debtor was prohibited from disclosing, the licensor should be entitled to enforce its rights against the secured party. Moreover, the licensor could have required the debtor to obtain the secured party's agreement that (i) it would immediately return all copies of software loaded on the computers and that (ii) it would not examine or otherwise acquire any information contained in the software. This section does not prevent an account debtor from protecting by agreement its independent interests that are unrelated to the "creation, attachment, or perfection" of a security interest. In Example 1, moreover, the secured party is not in possession of copies of software by virtue of its security interest or in connection with enforcing its security interest *in the debtor's license of the software*. Its possession is incidental to its possession of the computers, in which it has a security interest. Enforcing against the secured party a restriction relating to the software in no way interferes with its security interest in the computers.

7.   **Effect in Assignor's Bankruptcy.** This section could have a substantial effect if the assignor enters bankruptcy. Roughly speaking, Bankruptcy Code Section 552 invalidates security interests in property acquired after a bankruptcy petition is filed, except to the extent that the postpetition property constitutes proceeds of prepetition collateral.

Example 4:   A debtor is the owner of a cable television franchise that, under applicable law, cannot be assigned without the consent of the municipal franchisor. A lender wishes to extend credit to the debtor, provided that the credit is secured by the debtor's "going business" value. To secure the loan, the debtor grants a security interest in all its existing and after-acquired property. The franchise represents the principal value of the business. The municipality refuses to consent to any assignment for collateral purposes. If other law were given effect, the security interest in the franchise would not attach; and if the debtor were to enter bankruptcy and sell the business, the secured party would receive but a fraction of the business's value. Under this section, however, the security interest would attach to the franchise. As a result, the security interest would attach to the proceeds of any sale of the franchise while a bankruptcy is pending. However, this section would protect the interests of the municipality by preventing the secured party from enforcing its security interest to the detriment of the municipality.

8.   **Effect Outside of Bankruptcy.** The principal effects of this section will take place outside of bankruptcy. Compared to the relatively few debtors that enter bankruptcy, there are many more that do not. By making available previously unavailable property as collateral, this section should enable debtors to obtain additional credit. For purposes of determining whether to extend credit, under some circumstances a secured party may ascribe value to the collateral to which its security interest has attached, even if this section precludes the secured party from enforcing the security interest without the agreement of the account debtor or person obligated on the promissory note. This may be the case where the secured party sees a likelihood of obtaining that agreement in the future. This may also be the case where the secured party anticipates that the collateral will give rise to a type of proceeds as to which this section would not apply.

Example 5:   Under the facts of Example 4, the debtor does not enter bankruptcy. Perhaps in exchange for a fee, the municipality agrees that the debtor may transfer the franchise to a buyer. As consideration for the transfer, the debtor receives from the buyer its check for part of the purchase price and its promissory note for the balance. The security interest attaches to the check and promissory note as proceeds. See Section 9–315(a)(2). This section does not apply to the security interest in the check, which is not a promissory note, health-care-insurance receivable, or general intangible. Nor does it apply to the security interest in the promissory note, inasmuch as it was not sold to the secured party.

9.   **Contrary Federal Law.** This section does not override federal law to the contrary. However, it does reflect an important policy judgment that should provide a template for future federal law reforms.

10.   **Inapplicability to Certain Ownership Interests.** This section does not apply to an ownership interest in a limited liability company, limited partnership, or general partnership, regardless of the name of the interest and whether the interest: (i) pertains to economic rights, governance rights, or both; (ii) arises under: (a) an operating agreement, the applicable limited liability company act, or both; or (b) a partnership agreement, the applicable partnership act, or both; or (iii) is owned by: (a) a member of a company or transferee or assignee of a member; or (b) a partner or a transferee or assignee of a partner; or (iv) comprises contractual, property, other rights, or some combination thereof.

As amended in 2010 and 2018.

§ 9–409.   Restrictions on Assignment of Letter-of-Credit Rights Ineffective.

(a)   **[Term or law restricting assignment generally ineffective.]** A term in a letter of credit or a rule of law, statute, regulation, custom, or practice applicable to the letter of credit which prohibits, restricts, or requires the consent of an applicant, issuer, or nominated person to a beneficiary's assignment of or creation of a security interest in a letter-of-credit right is ineffective to the extent that the term or rule of law, statute, regulation, custom, or practice:

(1)   would impair the creation, attachment, or perfection of a security interest in the letter-of-credit right; or

(2)   provides that the assignment or the creation, attachment, or perfection of the security interest may give rise to a default, breach, right of recoupment, claim, defense, termination, right of termination, or remedy under the letter-of-credit right.

(b)   **[Limitation on ineffectiveness under subsection (a).]** To the extent that a term in a letter of credit is ineffective under subsection (a) but would be effective under law other than this article or a custom or practice applicable to the letter of credit, to the transfer of a right to draw or otherwise demand performance under the letter of credit, or to the assignment of a right to proceeds of the letter of credit, the creation, attachment, or perfection of a security interest in the letter-of-credit right:

(1)   is not enforceable against the applicant, issuer, nominated person, or transferee beneficiary;

(2)   imposes no duties or obligations on the applicant, issuer, nominated person, or transferee beneficiary; and

(3)   does not require the applicant, issuer, nominated person, or transferee beneficiary to recognize the security interest, pay or render performance to the secured party, or accept payment or other performance from the secured party.

As amended in 1999.

Official Comment

1.   **Source.** New.

2.   **Purpose and Relevance.** This section, patterned on Section 9–408, limits the effectiveness of attempts to restrict the creation, attachment, or perfection of a security interest in letter-of-credit rights, whether the restriction appears in the letter of credit or a rule of law, custom, or practice applicable to the letter of credit. It protects the creation, attachment, and perfection of a security interest while preventing these events from giving rise to a default or breach by the assignor or from triggering a remedy or defense of the issuer or other person obligated on a letter of credit. Letter-of-credit rights are a type of supporting obligation. See Section 9–102. Under Sections 9–203 and 9–308, a security interest in a supporting obligation attaches and is perfected automatically if the security interest in the supported obligation attaches and is perfected. See Section 9–107, Comment 5. The

automatic attachment and perfection under Article 9 would be anomalous or misleading if, under other law (e.g., Article 5), a restriction on transfer or assignment were effective to block attachment and perfection.

3. **Relationship to Letter-of-Credit Law.** Although restrictions on an assignment of a letter of credit are ineffective to prevent creation, attachment, and perfection of a security interest, subsection (b) protects the issuer and other parties from any adverse effects of the security interest by preserving letter-of-credit law and practice that limits the right of a beneficiary to transfer its right to draw or otherwise demand performance (Section 5–112) and limits the obligation of an issuer or nominated person to recognize a beneficiary's assignment of letter-of-credit proceeds (Section 5–114). Thus, this section's treatment of letter-of-credit rights differs from this Article's treatment of instruments and investment property. Moreover, under Section 9–109(c)(4), this Article does not apply to the extent that the rights of a transferee beneficiary or nominated person are independent and superior under Section 5–114, thereby preserving the "independence principle" of letter-of-credit law.

PART 5

FILING

[SUBPART 1. FILING OFFICE; CONTENTS AND EFFECTIVENESS OF FINANCING STATEMENT]

§ 9–501. Filing Office.

(a) **[Filing offices.]** Except as otherwise provided in subsection (b), if the local law of this State governs perfection of a security interest or agricultural lien, the office in which to file a financing statement to perfect the security interest or agricultural lien is:

   (1) the office designated for the filing or recording of a record of a mortgage on the related real property, if:

      (A) the collateral is as-extracted collateral or timber to be cut; or

      (B) the financing statement is filed as a fixture filing and the collateral is goods that are or are to become fixtures; or

   (2) the office of [ ] [or any office duly authorized by [ ]], in all other cases, including a case in which the collateral is goods that are or are to become fixtures and the financing statement is not filed as a fixture filing.

(b) **[Filing office for transmitting utilities.]** The office in which to file a financing statement to perfect a security interest in collateral, including fixtures, of a transmitting utility is the office of [ ]. The financing statement also constitutes a fixture filing as to the collateral indicated in the financing statement which is or is to become fixtures.

Legislative Note: The State should designate the filing office where the brackets appear. The filing office may be that of a governmental official (e.g., the Secretary of State) or a private party that maintains the State's filing system.

Official Comment

1. **Source.** Derived from former Section 9–401.

2. **Where to File.** Subsection (a) indicates where in a given State a financing statement is to be filed. Former Article 9 afforded each State three alternative approaches, depending on the extent to which the State desires central filing (usually with the Secretary of State), local filing (usually with a county office), or both. As Comment 1 to former Section 9–401 observed, "The principal advantage of state-wide filing is ease of access to the credit information which the files exist to provide. Consider for example the national distributor who wishes to have current information about the credit standing of the thousands of persons he sells to on credit. The more completely the files are centralized on a state-wide basis, the easier and cheaper it becomes to procure credit information; the more the files are scattered in local filing units, the more burdensome and costly." Local filing increases the net costs of secured transactions also by increasing uncertainty and the number of required filings. Any benefit that local filing may have had in the 1950's is now insubstantial. Accordingly, this Article dictates central filing for most situations, while retaining local filing for real-estate-related collateral and special filing provisions for transmitting utilities.

3. **Minerals and Timber.** Under subsection (a)(1), a filing in the office where a record of a mortgage on the related real property would be filed will perfect a security interest in as-extracted collateral. Inasmuch as the security interest does not attach until extraction, the filing continues to be effective after extraction. A different result occurs with respect to timber to be cut, however. Unlike as-extracted collateral, standing timber may be goods before it is cut. See Section 9–102 (defining "goods"). Once cut, however, it is no longer timber *to be* cut, and the filing in the real-property-mortgage office ceases to be effective. The timber then becomes ordinary goods, and filing in the office specified in subsection (a)(2) is necessary for perfection. Note also that after the timber is cut the law of the debtor's location, not the location of the timber, governs perfection under Section 9–301.

4. **Fixtures.** There are two ways in which a secured party may file a financing statement to perfect a security interest in goods that are or are to become fixtures. It may file in the Article 9 records, as with most other goods. See subsection (a)(2). Or it may file the financing statement as a "fixture filing," defined in Section 9–102, in the office in which a record of a mortgage on the related real property would be filed. See subsection(a)(1)(B).

5. **Transmitting Utilities.** The usual filing rules do not apply well for a transmitting utility (defined in Section 9–102). Many pre-UCC statutes provided special filing rules for railroads and in some cases for other public utilities, to avoid the requirements for filing with legal descriptions in every county in which such debtors had property. Former Section 9–401(5) recreated and broadened these provisions, and subsection (b) follows this approach. The nature of the debtor will inform persons searching the record as to where to make a search.

A given State's subsection (b) applies only if the local law of that State governs perfection. As to most collateral, perfection by filing is governed by the law of the jurisdiction in which the debtor is located. See Section 9–301(1). However, the law of the jurisdiction in which goods that are or become fixtures are located governs perfection by filing a fixture filing. See Section 9–301(3)(A). As a consequence, filing in the filing office of more than one State may be necessary to perfect a security interest in fixtures collateral of a transmitting utility by filing a fixture filing. See Section 9–301, Comment 5.b.

As amended in 2010.

§ 9–502. Contents of Financing Statement; Record of Mortgage as Financing Statement; Time of Filing Financing Statement.

(a) **[Sufficiency of financing statement.]** Subject to subsection (b), a financing statement is sufficient only if it:

(1) provides the name of the debtor;

(2) provides the name of the secured party or a representative of the secured party; and

(3) indicates the collateral covered by the financing statement.

(b) **[Real-property-related financing statements.]** Except as otherwise provided in Section 9–501(b), to be sufficient, a financing statement that covers as-extracted collateral or timber to be cut, or which is filed as a fixture filing and covers goods that are or are to become fixtures, must satisfy subsection (a) and also:

(1) indicate that it covers this type of collateral;

(2) indicate that it is to be filed [for record] in the real property records;

(3) provide a description of the real property to which the collateral is related [sufficient to give constructive notice of a mortgage under the law of this State if the description were contained in a record of the mortgage of the real property]; and

(4) if the debtor does not have an interest of record in the real property, provide the name of a record owner.

(c) **[Record of mortgage as financing statement.]** A record of a mortgage is effective, from the date of recording, as a financing statement filed as a fixture filing or as a financing statement covering as-extracted collateral or timber to be cut only if:

(1) the record indicates the goods or accounts that it covers;

(2) the goods are or are to become fixtures related to the real property described in the record or the collateral is related to the real property described in the record and is as-extracted collateral or timber to be cut;

(3) the record satisfies the requirements for a financing statement in this section, but:

    (A) the record need not indicate that it is to be filed in the real property records; and

    (B) the record sufficiently provides the name of a debtor who is an individual if it provides the individual name of the debtor or the surname and first personal name of the debtor, even if the debtor is an individual to whom Section 9–503(a)(4) applies; and

(4) the record is [duly] recorded.

(d) **[Filing before security agreement or attachment.]** A financing statement may be filed before a security agreement is made or a security interest otherwise attaches.

Legislative Note: Language in brackets is optional. Where the State has any special recording system for real property other than the usual grantor-grantee index (as, for instance, a tract system or a title registration or Torrens system) local adaptations of subsection (b) and Section 9–519(d) and (e) may be necessary. See, e.g., Mass. Gen. Laws Chapter 106, Section 9–410.

A State should enact the 2010 amendments to Section 9–502 only if the State enacts Alternative A of the 2010 amendments to Section 9–503.

As amended in 2010.

Official Comment

1. **Source.** Former Section 9–402(1), (5), (6).

2. **"Notice Filing."** This section adopts the system of "notice filing." What is required to be filed is not, as under pre-UCC chattel mortgage and conditional sales acts, the security agreement itself, but only a simple record providing a limited amount of information (financing statement). The financing statement may be filed before the security interest attaches or thereafter. See subsection (d). See also Section 9–308(a) (contemplating situations in which a financing statement is filed before a security interest attaches).

The notice itself indicates merely that a person may have a security interest in the collateral indicated. Further inquiry from the parties concerned will be necessary to disclose the complete state of affairs. Section 9–210 provides a statutory procedure under which the secured party, at the debtor's request, may be required to make disclosure. However, in many cases, information may be forthcoming without the need to resort to the formalities of that section.

Notice filing has proved to be of great use in financing transactions involving inventory, accounts, and chattel paper, because it obviates the necessity of refiling on each of a series of transactions in a continuing arrangement under which the collateral changes from day to day. However, even in the case of filings that do not necessarily involve a series of transactions (e.g., a loan secured by a single item of equipment), a financing statement is effective to encompass transactions under a security agreement not in existence and not contemplated at the time the notice was filed, if the indication of collateral in the financing statement is sufficient to cover the collateral concerned. Similarly, a financing statement is effective to cover after-acquired property of the type indicated and to perfect with respect to future advances under security agreements, regardless of whether after-acquired property or future advances are mentioned in the financing statement and even if not in the contemplation of the parties at the time the financing statement was authorized to be filed.

3. **Debtor's Signature; Required Authorization.** Subsection (a) sets forth the simple formal requirements for an effective financing statement. These requirements are: (1) the debtor's name; (2) the name of a secured party or representative of the secured party; and (3) an indication of the collateral.

Whereas former Section 9–402(1) required the debtor's signature to appear on a financing statement, this Article contains no signature requirement. The elimination of the signature requirement facilitates paperless filing. (However, as PEB Commentary No. 15 indicates, a paperless financing statement was sufficient under former Article 9.) Elimination of the signature requirement also makes the exceptions provided by former Section 9–402(2) unnecessary.

The fact that this Article does not require that an authenticating symbol be contained in the public record does not mean that all filings are authorized. Rather, Section 9–509(a) entitles a person to file an initial financing statement, an amendment that adds collateral, or an amendment that adds a debtor only if the debtor authorizes the filing, and Section 9–509(d) entitles a person other than the debtor to file a termination statement only if the secured party of record authorizes the filing. Of course, a filing has legal effect only to the extent it is authorized. See Section 9–510.

Law other than this Article, including the law with respect to ratification of past acts, generally determines whether a person has the requisite authority to file a record under this Article. See Sections 1–103 and 9–509, Comment 3. However, under Section 9–509(b), the debtor's authentication of (or becoming bound by) a security agreement *ipso facto* constitutes the debtor's authorization of the filing of a financing statement covering the collateral described in the security agreement. The secured party need not obtain a separate authorization.

Section 9–625 provides a remedy for unauthorized filings. Making an unauthorized filing also may give rise to civil or criminal liability under other law. In addition, this Article contains provisions that assist in the discovery of unauthorized filings and the amelioration of their practical effect. For example, Section 9–518 provides a procedure whereby a person may add to the public record a statement to the effect that a financing statement indexed under the person's name was wrongfully filed, and Section 9–509(d) entitles any person to file a termination statement if the secured party of record fails to comply with its obligation to file or send one to the debtor, the debtor authorizes the filing, and the termination statement so indicates. However, the filing office is neither obligated nor permitted to inquire into issues of authorization. See Section 9–520(a).

4. **Certain Other Requirements.** Subsection (a) deletes other provisions of former Section 9–402(1) because they seems unwise (real-property description for financing statements covering crops), unnecessary (adequacy of copies of financing statements), or both (copy of security agreement as financing statement). In addition, the filing office must reject a financing statement lacking certain other information formerly required as a condition of perfection (e.g., an address for the debtor or secured party). See Sections 9–516(b), 9–520(a). However, if the filing office accepts the record, it is effective nevertheless. See Section 9–520(c).

5. **Real-Property-Related Filings.** Subsection (b) contains the requirements for financing statements filed as fixture filings and financing statements covering timber to be cut or minerals and minerals-related accounts constituting as-extracted collateral. A description of the related real property must be sufficient to reasonably identify it. See Section 9–108. This formulation rejects the view that the real property description must be by metes and bounds, or otherwise conforming to traditional real-property practice in conveyancing, but, of course, the incorporation of such a description by reference to the recording data of a deed, mortgage or other instrument containing the description should suffice under the most stringent standards. The proper test is that a description of real property must be sufficient so that the financing statement will fit into the real-property search system and be found by a real-property searcher. Under the optional language in subsection (b)(3), the test of adequacy of the description is whether it would be adequate in a record of a mortgage of the real property. As suggested in the Legislative Note, more detail may be required if there is a tract indexing system or a land registration system.

If the debtor does not have an interest of record in the real property, a real-property-related financing statement must show the name of a record owner, and Section 9–519(d) requires the financing statement to be indexed in the name of that owner. This requirement also enables financing statements covering as-extracted collateral or timber to be cut and financing statements filed as fixture filings to fit into the real-property search system.

6. **Record of Mortgage Effective as Financing Statement.** Subsection (c) explains when a record of a mortgage is effective as a financing statement filed as a fixture filing or to cover timber to be cut or as-extracted collateral. Use of the term "record of a mortgage" recognizes that in some systems the record actually filed is not the record pursuant to which a mortgage is created. Moreover, "mortgage" is defined in Section 9–102 as an "interest in real property," not as the record that creates or evidences the mortgage or the record that is filed in the public recording systems. A record creating a mortgage may also create a security interest with respect to fixtures (or other goods) in conformity with this Article. A single agreement creating a mortgage on real property and a security interest in chattels is common and useful for certain purposes. Under subsection (c), the recording of the record evidencing a mortgage (if it satisfies the requirements for a financing statement) constitutes the filing of a financing statement as to the fixtures (but not, of course, as to other goods). Section 9–515(g) makes the usual five-year maximum life for financing statements inapplicable to mortgages that operate as fixture filings under Section 9–502(c). Such mortgages are effective for the duration of the real-property recording.

Of course, if a combined mortgage covers chattels that are not fixtures, a regular financing statement filing is necessary with respect to the chattels, and subsection (c) is inapplicable. Likewise, a financing statement filed as a "fixture filing" is not effective to perfect a security interest in personal property other than fixtures.

In some cases it may be difficult to determine whether goods are or will become fixtures. Nothing in this Part prohibits the filing of a "precautionary" fixture filing, which would provide protection in the event goods are determined to be fixtures. The fact of filing should not be a factor in the determining whether goods are fixtures. Cf. Section 9–505(b).

§ 9–503. Name of Debtor and Secured Party.

(a) **[Sufficiency of debtor's name.]** A financing statement sufficiently provides the name of the debtor:

(1) except as otherwise provided in paragraph (3), if the debtor is a registered organization or the collateral is held in a trust that is a registered organization, only if the financing statement provides the name that is stated to be the registered organization's name on the public organic record most recently filed with or issued or enacted by the registered organization's jurisdiction of organization which purports to state, amend, or restate the registered organization's name;

(2) subject to subsection (f), if the collateral is being administered by the personal representative of a decedent, only if the financing statement provides, as the name of the debtor, the name of the decedent and, in a separate part of the financing statement, indicates that the collateral is being administered by a personal representative;

(3) if the collateral is held in a trust that is not a registered organization, only if the financing statement:

  (A) provides, as the name of the debtor:

    (i) if the organic record of the trust specifies a name for the trust, the name specified; or

    (ii) if the organic record of the trust does not specify a name for the trust, the name of the settlor or testator; and

  (B) in a separate part of the financing statement:

    (i) if the name is provided in accordance with subparagraph (A)(i), indicates that the collateral is held in a trust; or

    (ii) if the name is provided in accordance with subparagraph (A)(ii), provides additional information sufficient to distinguish the trust from other trusts having one or more of the same settlors or the same testator and indicates that the collateral is held in a trust, unless the additional information so indicates;

[ALTERNATIVE A]

(4) subject to subsection (g), if the debtor is an individual to whom this State has issued a [driver's license] that has not expired, only if the financing statement provides the name of the individual which is indicated on the [driver's license];

(5) if the debtor is an individual to whom paragraph (4) does not apply, only if the financing statement provides the individual name of the debtor or the surname and first personal name of the debtor; and

(6) in other cases:

  (A) if the debtor has a name, only if the financing statement provides the organizational name of the debtor; and

  (B) if the debtor does not have a name, only if it provides the names of the partners, members, associates, or other persons comprising the debtor, in a manner that each name provided would be sufficient if the person named were the debtor.

(b) **[Additional debtor-related information.]** A financing statement that provides the name of the debtor in accordance with subsection (a) is not rendered ineffective by the absence of:

(1) a trade name or other name of the debtor; or

(2) unless required under subsection (a)(6)(B), names of partners, members, associates, or other persons comprising the debtor.

[ALTERNATIVE B]

(4)   if the debtor is an individual, only if the financing statement:

    (A)   provides the individual name of the debtor;

    (B)   provides the surname and first personal name of the debtor; or

    (C)   subject to subsection (g), provides the name of the individual which is indicated on a [driver's license] that this State has issued to the individual and which has not expired; and

(5)   in other cases:

    (A)   if the debtor has a name, only if the financing statement provides the organizational name of the debtor; and

    (B)   if the debtor does not have a name, only if the financing statement provides the names of the partners, members, associates, or other persons comprising the debtor, in a manner that each name provided would be sufficient if the person named were the debtor.

(b)   **[Additional debtor-related information.]** A financing statement that provides the name of the debtor in accordance with subsection (a) is not rendered ineffective by the absence of:

(1)   a trade name or other name of the debtor; or

(2)   unless required under subsection (a)(5)(B), names of partners, members, associates, or other persons comprising the debtor.

[END OF ALTERNATIVES]

(c)   **[Debtor's trade name insufficient.]** A financing statement that provides only the debtor's trade name does not sufficiently provide the name of the debtor.

(d)   **[Representative capacity.]** Failure to indicate the representative capacity of a secured party or representative of a secured party does not affect the sufficiency of a financing statement.

(e)   **[Multiple debtors and secured parties.]** A financing statement may provide the name of more than one debtor and the name of more than one secured party.

(f)   **[Name of decedent.]** The name of the decedent indicated on the order appointing the personal representative of the decedent issued by the court having jurisdiction over the collateral is sufficient as the "name of the decedent" under subsection (a)(2).

[ALTERNATIVE A]

(g)   **[Multiple driver's licenses.]** If this State has issued to an individual more than one [driver's license] of a kind described in subsection (a)(4), the one that was issued most recently is the one to which subsection (a)(4) refers.

[ALTERNATIVE B]

(g)   **[Multiple driver's licenses.]** If this State has issued to an individual more than one [driver's license] of a kind described in subsection (a)(4)(C), the one that was issued most recently is the one to which subsection (a)(4)(C) refers.

[END OF ALTERNATIVES]

(h)   **[Definition.]** In this section, the "name of the settlor or testator" means:

(1)   if the settlor is a registered organization, the name that is stated to be the settlor's name on the public organic record most recently filed with or issued or enacted by the settlor's jurisdiction of organization which purports to state, amend, or restate the settlor's name; or

(2)   in other cases, the name of the settlor or testator indicated in the trust's organic record.

Legislative Note:

    1.   This Act contains two alternative sets of amendments relating to the names of individual debtors. A State should enact the same Alternative, A or B, for both subsections (a) and (i) of Section 9–503. A State that enacts Alternative A of the amendments to this section should also enact the amendments to Section 9–502.

2.   *Both Alternatives refer, in part, to the name as shown on a debtor's driver's license. The Legislature should be aware that, in some States, certain characters that may be used by the State's department of motor vehicles (or similar agency) in the name on a driver's license may not be accepted by the State's central or local UCC filing offices under current regulations or internal protocols. This may occur because of technological limitations of the filing offices or merely as a result of inconsistent procedures. Similar issues may exist for field sizes as well. In these situations, perfection of a security interest granted by a debtor with such a driver's license may be impossible under Alternative A of the amendments and the utility of Alternative B, under which the name on the driver's license is one of the names that is sufficient, may be reduced. Accordingly, the State may wish to determine if one or more of these issues exist and, if so, to make certain that such issues have been resolved. A successful resolution might be accomplished by statute, agency regulation, or technological change effectuated before or as part of the enactment of this Act.*

3.   *Regardless of which Alternative is enacted, in States in which a single agency issues driver's licenses and non-driver identification cards as an alternative to a driver's license, such that at any given time an individual may hold either a driver's license or an identification card but not both, the State should replace each use of the term "driver's license" with a phrase meaning "driver's license or identification card" but containing the analogous terms used in the enacting State. In other States, the State should replace the term "driver's license" with the analogous term used in the enacting State.*

As amended in 2010.

Official Comment

1.   **Source.** Subsections (a)(4)(A), (b), and (c) derive from former Section 9–402(7); otherwise, new.

2.   **Debtor's Name.** The requirement that a financing statement provide the debtor's name is particularly important. Financing statements are indexed under the name of the debtor, and those who wish to find financing statements search for them under the debtor's name. Subsection (a) explains what the debtor's name is for purposes of a financing statement.

a.   **Registered Organizations.** As a general matter, if the debtor is a "registered organization" (defined in Section 9–102 so as to ordinarily include corporations, limited partnerships, limited liability companies, and statutory trusts), then the debtor's name is the name shown on the "public organic record" of the debtor's "jurisdiction of organization" (both also defined in Section 9–102).

b.   **Collateral Held in a Trust.** When a financing statement covers collateral that is held in a trust that is a registered organization, subsection (a)(1) governs the name of the debtor. If, however, the collateral is held in a trust that is not a registered organization, subsection (a)(3) applies. (As used in this Article, collateral "held in a trust" includes collateral as to which the trust is the debtor as well as collateral as to which the trustee is the debtor.) This subsection adopts a convention that generally results in the name of the trust or the name of the trust's settlor being provided as the name of the debtor on the financing statement, even if, as typically is the case with common-law trusts, the "debtor" (defined in Section 9–102) is a trustee acting with respect to the collateral. This convention provides more accurate information and eases the burden for searchers, who otherwise would have difficulty with respect to debtor trustees that are large financial institutions.

More specifically, if a trust's organic record specifies a name for the trust, subsection (a)(3) requires the financing statement to provide, as the name of the debtor, the name for the trust specified in the organic record. In addition, the financing statement must indicate, in a separate part of the financing statement, that the collateral is held in a trust.

If the organic record of the trust does not specify a name for the trust, the name required for the financing statement is the name of the settlor or, in the case of a testamentary trust, the testator, in each case as determined under subsection (h). In addition, the financing statement must provide sufficient additional information to distinguish the trust from other trusts having one or more of the same settlors or the same testator. In many cases an indication of the date on which the trust was settled will satisfy this requirement. If neither the name nor the additional information indicates that the collateral is held in a trust, the financing statement must indicate that fact, but not as part of the debtor's name.

Neither the indication that the collateral is held in a trust nor the additional information that distinguishes the trust from other trusts having one or more of the same settlors or the same testator is part of the debtor's name. Nevertheless, a financing statement that fails to provide, in a separate part of the financing statement, any required indication or additional information does not sufficiently provide the name of the debtor under Sections 9–502(a) and 9–503(a)(3), does not "substantially satisfy[ ] the requirements" of Part 5 within the meaning of Section 9–506(a), and so is ineffective.

     c.   **Collateral Administered by a Personal Representative.** Subsection (a)(2) deals with collateral that is being administered by an executor, administrator, or other personal representative of a decedent. Even if, as often is the case, the representative is the "debtor" (defined in Section 9–102), the financing statement must provide the name of the decedent as the name of the debtor. Subsection (f) provides a safe harbor, under which the name of the decedent indicated on the order appointing the personal representative issued by the court having jurisdiction over the collateral is sufficient as the name of the decedent. If the order indicates more than one name for the decedent, the first name in the list qualifies under subsection (f); however, other names in the list also may qualify as the "name of the decedent" within the meaning of subsection (a)(2). In addition to providing the name of the decedent, the financing statement must indicate, in a separate part of the financing statement, that the collateral is being administered by a personal representative. Although the indication is not part of the debtor's name, a financing statement that fails to provide the indication does not sufficiently provide the name of the debtor under Sections 9–502(a) and 9–503(a)(2), does not "substantially satisfy[ ] the requirements" of Part 5 within the meaning of Section 9–506(a), and so is ineffective.

     d.   **Individuals.** This Article provides alternative approaches towards the requirement for providing the name of a debtor who is an individual.

     Alternative A. Alternative A distinguishes between two groups of individual debtors. For debtors holding an unexpired driver's license issued by the State where the financing statement is filed (ordinarily the State where the debtor maintains the debtor's principal residence), Alternative A requires that a financing statement provide the name indicated on the license. When a debtor does not hold an unexpired driver's license issued by the relevant State, the requirement can be satisfied in either of two ways. A financing statement is sufficient if it provides the "individual name" of the debtor. Alternatively, a financing statement is sufficient if it provides the debtor's surname (i.e., family name) and first personal name (i.e., first name other than the surname).

     Alternative B. Alternative B provides three ways in which a financing statement may sufficiently provide the name of an individual who is a debtor. The "individual name" of the debtor is sufficient, as is the debtor's surname and first personal name. If the individual holds an unexpired driver's license issued by the State where the financing statement is filed (ordinarily the State of the debtor's principal residence), the name indicated on the driver's license also is sufficient.

     Name indicated on the driver's license. A financing statement does not "provide the name of the individual which is indicated" on the debtor's driver's license unless the name it provides is the same as the name indicated on the license. This is the case even if the name indicated on the debtor's driver's license contains an error.

     Example 1:   Debtor, an individual whose principal residence is in Illinois, grants a security interest to SP in certain business equipment. SP files a financing statement with the Illinois filing office. The financing statement provides the name appearing on Debtor's Illinois driver's license, "Joseph Allan Jones." Regardless of which Alternative is in effect in Illinois, this filing would be sufficient under Illinois' Section 9–503(a), even if Debtor's correct middle name is Alan, not Allan.

     A filing against "Joseph A. Jones" or "Joseph Jones" would not "provide the name of the individual which is indicated" on the debtor's driver's license. However, these filings might be sufficient if Alternative A is in effect in Illinois and Jones has no current (i.e., unexpired) Illinois driver's license, or if Illinois has enacted Alternative B.

     Determining the name that should be provided on the financing statement must not be done mechanically. The order in which the components of an individual's name appear on a driver's license differs among the States. Had the debtor in Example 1 obtained a driver's license from a different State, the license might have indicated the name as "Jones Joseph Allan." Regardless of the order on the driver's license, the debtor's surname must be provided in the part of the financing statement designated for the surname.

     Alternatives A and B both refer to a license issued by "this State." Perfection of a security interest by filing ordinarily is determined by the law of the jurisdiction in which the debtor is located. See Section 9–301(1). (Exceptions to the general rule are found in Section 9–301(3) and (4), concerning fixture filings, timber to be cut, and as-extracted collateral.) A debtor who is an individual ordinarily is located at the individual's principal residence. See Section 9–307(b). (An exception appears in Section 9–307(c).) Thus, a given State's Section 9–503 ordinarily will apply during any period when the debtor's principal residence is located in that State, even if during that time the debtor holds or acquires a driver's license from another State.

When a debtor's principal residence changes, the location of the debtor under Section 9–307 also changes and perfection by filing ordinarily will be governed by the law of the debtor's new location. As a consequence of the application of that jurisdiction's Section 9–316, a security interest that is perfected by filing under the law of the debtor's former location will remain perfected for four months after the relocation, and thereafter if the secured party perfects under the law of the debtor's new location. Likewise, a financing statement filed in the former location may be effective to perfect a security interest that attaches after the debtor relocates. See Section 9–316(h).

Individual name of the debtor. Article 9 does not determine the "individual name" of a debtor. Nor does it determine which element or elements in a debtor's name constitute the surname. In some cases, determining the "individual name" of a debtor may be difficult, as may determining the debtor's surname. This is because in the case of individuals, unlike registered organizations, there is no public organic record to which reference can be made and from which the name and its components can be definitively determined.

Names can take many forms in the United States. For example, whereas a surname is often colloquially referred to as a "last name," the sequence in which the elements of a name are presented is not determinative. In some cultures, the surname appears first, while in others it may appear in a location that is neither first nor last. In addition, some surnames are composed of multiple elements that, taken together, constitute a single surname. These elements may or may not be separated by a space or connected by a hyphen, "i," or "y." In other instances, some or all of the same elements may not be part of the surname. In some cases, a debtor's entire name might be composed of only a single element, which should be provided in the part of the financing statement designated for the surname.

In disputes as to whether a financing statement sufficiently provides the "individual name" of a debtor, a court should refer to any non-UCC law concerning names. However, case law about names may have developed in contexts that implicate policies different from those of Article 9. A court considering an individual's name for purposes of determining the sufficiency of a financing statement is not necessarily bound by cases that were decided in other contexts and for other purposes.

Individuals are asked to provide their names on official documents such as tax returns and bankruptcy petitions. An individual may provide a particular name on an official document in response to instructions relating to the document rather than because the name is actually the individual's name. Accordingly, a court should not assume that the name an individual provides on an official document necessarily constitutes the "individual name" for purposes of the sufficiency of the debtor's name on a financing statement. Likewise, a court should not assume that the name as presented on an individual's birth certificate is necessarily the individual's current name.

In applying non-UCC law for purposes of determining the sufficiency of a debtor's name on a financing statement, a court should give effect to the instruction in Section 1–103(a)(1) that the UCC "must be liberally construed and applied to promote its underlying purposes and policies," which include simplifying and clarifying the law governing commercial transactions. Thus, determination of a debtor's name in the context of the Article 9 filing system must take into account the needs of both filers and searchers. Filers need a simple and predictable system in which they can have a reasonable degree of confidence that, without undue burden, they can determine a name that will be sufficient so as to permit their financing statements to be effective. Likewise, searchers need a simple and predictable system in which they can have a reasonable degree of confidence that, without undue burden, they will discover all financing statements pertaining to the debtor in question. The court also should take into account the purpose of the UCC to make the law uniform among the various jurisdictions. See Section 1–103(a)(3).

Of course, once an individual debtor's name has been determined to be sufficient for purposes of Section 9–503, a financing statement that provides a variation of that name, such as a "nickname" that does not constitute the debtor's name, does not sufficiently provide the name of the debtor under this section. Cf. Section 9–503(c) (a financing statement providing only a debtor's trade name is not sufficient).

If there is any doubt about an individual debtor's name, a secured party may choose to file one or more financing statements that provide a number of possible names for the debtor and a searcher may similarly choose to search under a number of possible names.

Note that, even if the name provided in an initial financing statement is correct, the filing office nevertheless must reject the financing statement if it does not identify an individual debtor's surname (e.g., if it is not clear whether the debtor's surname is Perry or Mason). See Section 9–516(b)(3)(C).

3.   **Secured Party's Name.** New subsection (d) makes clear that when the secured party is a representative, a financing statement is sufficient if it names the secured party, whether or not it indicates any representative capacity. Similarly, a financing statement that names a representative of the secured party is sufficient, even if it does not indicate the representative capacity.

> **Example 2:**   Debtor creates a security interest in favor of Bank X, Bank Y, and Bank Z, but not to their representative, the collateral agent (Bank A). The collateral agent is not itself a secured party. See Section 9–102. Under Sections 9–502(a) and 9–503(d), however, a financing statement is effective if it names as secured party Bank A and not the actual secured parties, even if it omits Bank A's representative capacity.

Each person whose name is provided in an initial financing statement as the name of the secured party or representative of the secured party is a secured party of record. See Section 9–511.

4.   **Multiple Names.** Subsection (e) makes explicit what is implicit under former Article 9: a financing statement may provide the name of more than one debtor and secured party. See Section 1–106 (words in the singular include the plural). With respect to records relating to more than one debtor, see Section 9–520(d). With respect to financing statements providing the name of more than one secured party, see Sections 9–509(e) and 9–510(b).

As amended in 2010.

§ 9–504.   Indication of Collateral. *Standard for the Financing Statement*

A financing statement sufficiently indicates the collateral that it covers if the financing statement provides:

(1)   a description of the collateral pursuant to Section 9–108; or

(2)   an indication that the financing statement covers all assets or all personal property.

As amended in 1999.

meaning a description in the FS saves this

Official Comment

1.   **Source.** Former Section 9–402(1).

2.   **Indication of Collateral.** To comply with Section 9–502(a), a financing statement must "indicate" the collateral it covers. A financing statement sufficiently indicates collateral claimed to be covered by the financing statement if it satisfies the purpose of conditioning perfection on the filing of a financing statement, i.e., if it provides notice that a person may have a security interest in the collateral claimed. See Section 9–502, Comment 2. In particular, an indication of collateral that would have satisfied the requirements of former Section 9–402(1) (i.e., "a statement indicating the types, or describing the items, of collateral") suffices under Section 9–502(a). An indication may satisfy the requirements of Section 9–502(a), even if it would not have satisfied the requirements of former Section 9–402(1). A financing statement (including any attachments) that does not itself supply information satisfying Section 9–502(a)(3) or Section 9–504(a), but, rather, refers solely to a record not attached to the financing statement for information seeking to satisfy those provisions, does not satisfy the sufficiency requirement of Section 9–502(a)(3) that the financing statement indicate the collateral that it covers. See PEB Commentary No. 26, dated August 12, 2022. The Commentary is available at https://www.ali.org/peb-ucc.

This section provides two safe harbors. Under paragraph (1), a "description" of the collateral (as the term is explained in Section 9–108) suffices as an indication for purposes of the sufficiency of a financing statement.

Debtors sometimes create a security interest in all, or substantially all, of their assets. To accommodate this practice, paragraph (2) expands the class of sufficient collateral references to embrace "an indication that the financing statement covers all assets or all personal property." If the property in question belongs to the debtor and is personal property, any searcher will know that the property is covered by the financing statement. Of course, regardless of its breadth, a financing statement has no effect with respect to property indicated but to which a security interest has not attached. Note that a broad statement of this kind (e.g., "all debtor's personal property") would not be a sufficient "description" for purposes of a security agreement. See Sections 9–203(b)(3)(A), 9–108. It follows that a somewhat narrower description than "all assets," e.g., "all assets other than automobiles," is sufficient for purposes of this section, even if it does not suffice for purposes of a security agreement.

As amended in 2000 and 2022.

§ 9–505. Filing and Compliance With Other Statutes and Treaties for Consignments, Leases, Other Bailments, and Other Transactions.

(a) **[Use of terms other than "debtor" and "secured party."]** A consignor, lessor, or other bailor of goods, a licensor, or a buyer of a payment intangible or promissory note may file a financing statement, or may comply with a statute or treaty described in Section 9–311(a), using the terms "consignor", "consignee", "lessor", "lessee", "bailor", "bailee", "licensor", "licensee", "owner", "registered owner", "buyer", "seller", or words of similar import, instead of the terms "secured party" and "debtor".

(b) **[Effect of financing statement under subsection (a).]** This part applies to the filing of a financing statement under subsection (a) and, as appropriate, to compliance that is equivalent to filing a financing statement under Section 9–311(b), but the filing or compliance is not of itself a factor in determining whether the collateral secures an obligation. If it is determined for another reason that the collateral secures an obligation, a security interest held by the consignor, lessor, bailor, licensor, owner, or buyer which attaches to the collateral is perfected by the filing or compliance.

Official Comment

1. **Source.** Former Section 9–408.

2. **Precautionary Filing.** Occasionally, doubts arise concerning whether a transaction creates a relationship to which this Article or its filing provisions apply. For example, questions may arise over whether a "lease" of equipment in fact creates a security interest or whether the "sale" of payment intangibles in fact secures an obligation, thereby requiring action to perfect the security interest. This section, which derives from former Section 9–408, affords the option of filing of a financing statement with appropriate changes of terminology but without affecting the substantive question of classification of the transaction.

3. **Changes from Former Section 9–408.** This section expands the rule of Section 9–408 to embrace more generally other bailments and transactions, as well as sales transactions, primarily sales of payment intangibles and promissory notes. It provides the same benefits for compliance with a statute or treaty described in Section 9–311(a) that former Section 9–408 provided for filing, in connection with the use of terms such as "lessor," "consignor," etc. The references to "owner" and "registered owner" are intended to address, for example, the situation where a putative lessor is the registered owner of an automobile covered by a certificate of title and the transaction is determined to create a security interest. Although this section provides that the security interest is perfected, the relevant certificate-of-title statute may expressly provide to the contrary or may be ambiguous. If so, it may be necessary or advisable to amend the certificate-of-title statute to ensure that perfection of the security interest will be achieved.

As did former Section 1–201, former Article 9 referred to transactions, including leases and consignments, "intended as security." This misleading phrase created the erroneous impression that the parties to a transaction can dictate how the law will classify it (e.g., as a bailment or as a security interest) and thus affect the rights of third parties. This Article deletes the phrase wherever it appears. Subsection (b) expresses the principle more precisely by referring to a security interest that "secures an obligation."

4. **Consignments.** Although a "true" consignment is a bailment, the filing and priority provisions of former Article 9 applied to "true" consignments. See former Sections 2–326(3), 9–114. A consignment "intended as security" created a security interest that was in all respects subject to former Article 9. This Article subsumes most true consignments under the rubric of "security interest." See Sections 9–102 (definition of "consignment"), 9–109(a)(4), 1–201(b)(35) (definition of "security interest"). Nevertheless, it maintains the distinction between a (true) "consignment," as to which only certain aspects of Article 9 apply, and a so-called consignment that actually "secures an obligation," to which Article 9 applies in full. The revisions to this section reflect the change in terminology.

As amended in 2010.

§ 9–506. Effect of Errors or Omissions.

(a) **[Minor errors and omissions.]** A financing statement substantially satisfying the requirements of this part is effective, even if it has minor errors or omissions, unless the errors or omissions make the financing statement seriously misleading.

(b)   **[Financing statement seriously misleading.]** Except as otherwise provided in subsection (c), a financing statement that fails sufficiently to provide the name of the debtor in accordance with Section 9–503(a) is seriously misleading.

(c)   **[Financing statement not seriously misleading.]** If a search of the records of the filing office under the debtor's correct name, using the filing office's standard search logic, if any, would disclose a financing statement that fails sufficiently to provide the name of the debtor in accordance with Section 9–503(a), the name provided does not make the financing statement seriously misleading.

(d)   **["Debtor's correct name."]** For purposes of Section 9–508(b), the "debtor's correct name" in subsection (c) means the correct name of the new debtor.

Official Comment

1.   **Source.** Former Section 9–402(8).

2.   **Errors and Omissions.** Like former Section 9–402(8), subsection (a) is in line with the policy of this Article to simplify formal requisites and filing requirements. It is designed to discourage the fanatical and impossibly refined reading of statutory requirements in which courts occasionally have indulged themselves. Subsection (a) provides the standard applicable to indications of collateral. Subsections (b) and (c), which are new, concern the effectiveness of financing statements in which the debtor's name is incorrect. Subsection (b) contains the general rule: a financing statement that fails sufficiently to provide the debtor's name in accordance with Section 9–503(a) is seriously misleading as a matter of law. Subsection (c) provides an exception: If the financing statement nevertheless would be discovered in a search under the debtor's correct name, using the filing office's standard search logic, if any, then as a matter of law the incorrect name does not make the financing statement seriously misleading. A financing statement that is seriously misleading under this section is ineffective even if it is disclosed by (i) using a search logic other than that of the filing office to search the official records, or (ii) using the filing office's standard search logic to search a data base other than that of the filing office. For purposes of subsection (c), any name that satisfies Section 9–503(a) at the time of the search is a "correct name."

This section and Section 9–503 balance the interests of filers and searchers. Searchers are not expected to ascertain nicknames, trade names, and the like by which the debtor may be known and then search under each of them. Rather, it is the secured party's responsibility to provide the name of the debtor sufficiently in a filed financing statement. Subsection (c) sets forth the only situation in which a financing statement that fails sufficiently to provide the name of the debtor is not seriously misleading. As stated in subsection (b), if the name of the debtor provided on a financing statement is insufficient and subsection (c) is not satisfied, the financing statement is seriously misleading. Such a financing statement is ineffective even if the debtor is known in some contexts by the name provided on the financing statement and even if searchers know or have reason to know that the name provided on the financing statement refers to the debtor. Any suggestion to the contrary in a judicial opinion is incorrect.

To satisfy the requirements of Section 9–503(a)(2), a financing statement must indicate that the collateral is being administered by a personal representative. To satisfy the requirements of Section 9–503(a)(3), a financing statement must indicate that the collateral is held in a trust and provide additional information that distinguishes the trust from certain other trusts. The indications and additional information are not part of the debtor's name. Nevertheless, a financing statement that fails to provide an indication or the additional information when required does not sufficiently provide the name of the debtor under Sections 9–502(a) and 9–503(a), does not "substantially satisfy[ ] the requirements" of Part 5 within the meaning of this section and so is ineffective.

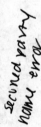

In addition to requiring the debtor's name and an indication of the collateral, Section 9–502(a) requires a financing statement to provide the name of the secured party or a representative of the secured party. Inasmuch as searches are not conducted under the secured party's name, and no filing is needed to continue the perfected status of security interest after it is assigned, an error in the name of the secured party or its representative will not be seriously misleading. However, in an appropriate case, an error of this kind may give rise to an estoppel in favor of a particular holder of a conflicting claim to the collateral. See Section 1–103.

3.   **New Debtors.** Subsection (d) provides that, in determining the extent to which a financing statement naming an original debtor is effective against a new debtor, the sufficiency of the financing statement should be tested against the name of the new debtor.

As amended in 2010.

§ 9–507. Effect of Certain Events on Effectiveness of Financing Statement.

(a) **[Disposition.]** A filed financing statement remains effective with respect to collateral that is sold, exchanged, leased, licensed, or otherwise disposed of and in which a security interest or agricultural lien continues, even if the secured party knows of or consents to the disposition.

(b) **[Information becoming seriously misleading.]** Except as otherwise provided in subsection (c) and Section 9–508, a financing statement is not rendered ineffective if, after the financing statement is filed, the information provided in the financing statement becomes seriously misleading under Section 9–506.

(c) **[Change in debtor's name.]** If the name that a filed financing statement provides for a debtor becomes insufficient as the name of the debtor under Section 9–503(a) so that the financing statement becomes seriously misleading under Section 9–506:

(1) the financing statement is effective to perfect a security interest in collateral acquired by the debtor before, or within four months after, the filed financing statement becomes seriously misleading; and

(2) the financing statement is not effective to perfect a security interest in collateral acquired by the debtor more than four months after the filed financing statement becomes seriously misleading, unless an amendment to the financing statement which renders the financing statement not seriously misleading is filed within four months after the financing statement became seriously misleading.

As amended in 2010.

Official Comment

1. **Source.** Former Section 9–402(7).

2. **Scope of Section.** This section deals with situations in which the information in a proper financing statement becomes inaccurate after the financing statement is filed. Compare Section 9–338, which deals with situations in which a financing statement contains a particular kind of information concerning the debtor (i.e., the information described in Section 9–516(b)(5)) that is incorrect at the time it is filed.

3. **Post-Filing Disposition of Collateral.** Under subsection (a), a financing statement remains effective even if the collateral is sold or otherwise disposed of. This subsection clarifies the third sentence of former Section 9–402(7) by providing that a financing statement remains effective following the disposition of collateral only when the security interest or agricultural lien continues in that collateral. This result is consistent with the conclusion of PEB Commentary No. 3. Normally, a security interest does continue after disposition of the collateral. See Section 9–315(a). Law other than this Article determines whether an agricultural lien survives disposition of the collateral.

As a consequence of the disposition, the collateral may be owned by a person other than the debtor against whom the financing statement was filed. Under subsection (a), the secured party remains perfected even if it does not correct the public record. For this reason, any person seeking to determine whether a debtor owns collateral free of security interests must inquire as to the debtor's source of title and, if circumstances seem to require it, search in the name of a former owner. Subsection (a) addresses only the sufficiency of the information contained in the financing statement. A disposition of collateral may result in loss of perfection for other reasons. See Section 9–316.

Example: Dee Corp. is an Illinois corporation. It creates a security interest in its equipment in favor of Secured Party. Secured Party files a proper financing statement in Illinois. Dee Corp. sells an item of equipment to Bee Corp., a Pennsylvania corporation, subject to the security interest. The security interest continues, see Section 9–315(a), and remains perfected, see Section 9–507(a), notwithstanding that the financing statement is filed under "D" (for Dee Corp.) and not under "B." However, because Bee Corp. is located in Pennsylvania and not Illinois, see Section 9–307, unless Secured Party perfects under Pennsylvania law within one year after the transfer, its security interest will become unperfected and will be deemed to have been unperfected against purchasers of the collateral. See Section 9–316.

4. **Other Post-Filing Changes.** Subsection (b) provides that, as a general matter, post-filing changes that render a financing statement seriously misleading have no effect on a financing statement. The financing statement remains effective. It is subject to two exceptions: Section 9–508 and Section 9–507(c). Section 9–508

addresses the effectiveness of a financing statement filed against an original debtor when a new debtor becomes bound by the original debtor's security agreement. It is discussed in the Comments to that section. Section 9–507(c) addresses cases in which a filed financing statement provides a name that, at the time of filing, satisfies the requirements of Section 9–503(a) with respect to the named debtor but, at a later time, no longer does so.

Example 1:　　Debtor, an individual whose principal residence is in California, grants a security interest to SP in certain business equipment. SP files a financing statement with the California filing office. Alternative A is in effect in California. The financing statement provides the name appearing on Debtor's California driver's license, "James McGinty." Debtor obtains a court order changing his name to "Roger McGuinn" but does not change his driver's license. Even after the court order issues, the name provided for the debtor in the financing statement is sufficient under Section 9–503(a). Accordingly, Section 9–507(c) does not apply.

The same result would follow if Alternative B is in effect in California.

Under Section 9–503(a)(4) (Alternative A), if the debtor holds a current (i.e., unexpired) driver's license issued by the State where the financing statement is filed, the name required for the financing statement is the name indicated on the license that was issued most recently by that State. If the debtor does not have a current driver's license issued by that State, then the debtor's name is determined under subsection (a)(5). It follows that a debtor's name may change, and a financing statement providing the name on the debtor's then-current driver's license may become seriously misleading, if the license expires and the debtor's name under subsection (a)(5) is different. The same consequences may follow if a debtor's driver's license is renewed and the names on the licenses differ.

Example 2:　　The facts are as in Example 1. Debtor's driver's license expires one year after the entry of the court order changing Debtor's name. Debtor does not renew the license. Upon expiration of the license, the name required for sufficiency by Section 9–503(a) is the individual name of the debtor or the debtor's surname and first personal name. The name "James McGinty" has become insufficient.

Example 3:　　The facts are as in Example 1. Before the license expires, Debtor renews the license. The name indicated on the new license is "Roger McGuinn." Upon issuance of the new license, "James McGinty" becomes insufficient as the debtor's name under Section 9–503(a).

The same results would follow if Alternative B is in effect in California (assuming that, following the issuance of the court order, "James McGinty" is neither the individual name of the debtor nor the debtor's surname and first personal name).

Even if the name provided as the name of the debtor becomes insufficient under Section 9–503(a), the filed financing statement does not become seriously misleading, and Section 9–507(c) does not apply, if the financing statement can be found by searching under the debtor's "correct" name, using the filing office's standard search logic. See Section 9–506. Any name that satisfies Section 9–503(a) at the time of the search is a "correct name" for these purposes. Thus, assuming that a search of the records of the California filing office under "Roger McGuinn," using the filing office's standard search logic, would not disclose a financing statement naming "James McGinty," the financing statement in Examples 2 and 3 has become seriously misleading and Section 9–507(c) applies.

If a filed financing statement becomes seriously misleading because the name it provides for a debtor becomes insufficient, the financing statement, unless amended to provide a sufficient name for the debtor, is effective only to perfect a security interest in collateral acquired by the debtor before, or within four months after, the change. If an amendment that provides a sufficient name is filed within four months after the change, the financing statement as amended would be effective also with respect to collateral acquired more than four months after the change. If an amendment that provides a sufficient name is filed more than four months after the change, the financing statement as amended would be effective also with respect to collateral acquired more than four months after the change, but only from the time of the filing of the amendment.

As amended in 2010.

§ 9–508.　Effectiveness of Financing Statement if New Debtor Becomes Bound by Security Agreement.

　　(a)　**[Financing statement naming original debtor.]** Except as otherwise provided in this section, a filed financing statement naming an original debtor is effective to perfect a security interest in collateral in which a new debtor has or acquires rights to the extent that the financing statement would have been effective had the original debtor acquired rights in the collateral.

(b) **[Financing statement becoming seriously misleading.]** If the difference between the name of the original debtor and that of the new debtor causes a filed financing statement that is effective under subsection (a) to be seriously misleading under Section 9–506:

(1) the financing statement is effective to perfect a security interest in collateral acquired by the new debtor before, and within four months after, the new debtor becomes bound under Section 9–203(d); and

(2) the financing statement is not effective to perfect a security interest in collateral acquired by the new debtor more than four months after the new debtor becomes bound under Section 9–203(d) unless an initial financing statement providing the name of the new debtor is filed before the expiration of that time.

(c) **[When section not applicable.]** This section does not apply to collateral as to which a filed financing statement remains effective against the new debtor under Section 9–507(a).

Official Comment

1. **Source.** New.

2. **The Problem.** Section 9–203(d) and (e) and this section deal with situations where one party (the "new debtor") becomes bound as debtor by a security agreement entered into by another person (the "original debtor"). These situations often arise as a consequence of changes in business structure. For example, the original debtor may be an individual debtor who operates a business as a sole proprietorship and then incorporates it. Or, the original debtor may be a corporation that is merged into another corporation. Under both former Article 9 and this Article, collateral that is transferred in the course of the incorporation or merger normally would remain subject to a perfected security interest. See Sections 9–315(a), 9–507(a). Former Article 9 was less clear with respect to whether an after-acquired property clause in a security agreement signed by the original debtor would be effective to create a security interest in property acquired by the new corporation or the merger survivor and, if so, whether a financing statement filed against the original debtor would be effective to perfect the security interest. This section and Sections 9–203(d) and (e) are a clarification.

3. **How New Debtor Becomes Bound.** Normally, a security interest is unenforceable unless the debtor has authenticated a security agreement describing the collateral. See Section 9–203(b). New Section 9–203(e) creates an exception, under which a security agreement entered into by one person is effective with respect to the property of another. This exception comes into play if a "new debtor" becomes bound as debtor by a security agreement entered into by another person (the "original debtor"). (The quoted terms are defined in Section 9–102.) If a new debtor does become bound, then the security agreement entered into by the original debtor satisfies the security-agreement requirement of Section 9–203(b)(3) as to existing or after-acquired property of the new debtor to the extent the property is described in the security agreement. In that case, no other agreement is necessary to make a security interest enforceable in that property. See Section 9–203(e).

Section 9–203(d) explains when a new debtor becomes bound by an original debtor's security agreement. Under Section 9–203(d)(1), a new debtor becomes bound as debtor if, by contract or operation of other law, the security agreement becomes effective to create a security interest in the new debtor's property. For example, if the applicable corporate law of mergers provides that when A Corp merges into B Corp, B Corp becomes a debtor under A Corp's security agreement, then B Corp would become bound as debtor following such a merger. Similarly, B Corp would become bound as debtor if B Corp contractually assumes A's obligations under the security agreement.

Under certain circumstances, a new debtor becomes bound for purposes of this Article even though it would not be bound under other law. Under Section 9–203(d)(2), a new debtor becomes bound when, by contract or operation of other law, it (i) becomes obligated not only for the secured obligation but also generally for the obligations of the original debtor and (ii) acquires or succeeds to substantially all the assets of the original debtor. For example, some corporate laws provide that, when two corporations merge, the surviving corporation succeeds to the assets of its merger partner and "has all liabilities" of both corporations. In the case where, for example, A Corp merges into B Corp (and A Corp ceases to exist), some people have questioned whether A Corp's grant of a security interest in its existing and after-acquired property becomes a "liability" of B Corp, such that B Corp's existing and after-acquired property becomes subject to a security interest in favor of A Corp's lender. Even if corporate law were to give a negative answer, under Section 9–203(d)(2), B Corp would become bound for purposes of Section 9–203(e) and this section. The "substantially all of the assets" requirement of Section 9–203(d)(2) excludes sureties and other secondary obligors as well as persons who become obligated through veil piercing and other non-successorship doctrines. In most cases, it will exclude successors to the assets and liabilities of a division of a debtor.

4.   **When Financing Statement Effective Against New Debtor.** Subsection (a) provides that a filing against the original debtor generally is effective to perfect a security interest in collateral that a new debtor has at the time it becomes bound by the original debtor's security agreement and collateral that it acquires after the new debtor becomes bound. Under subsection (b), however, if the filing against the original debtor is seriously misleading as to the new debtor's name, the filing is effective as to collateral acquired by the new debtor more than four months after the new debtor becomes bound only if a person files during the four-month period an initial financing statement providing the name of the new debtor. Compare Section 9–507(c) (four-month period of effectiveness with respect to collateral acquired by a debtor after the name provided for the debtor becomes insufficient as the name of the debtor). As to the meaning of "initial financing statement" in this context, see Section 9–512, Comment 5.

5.   **Transferred Collateral.** This section does not apply to collateral transferred by the original debtor to a new debtor. See subsection (c). Under those circumstances, the filing against the original debtor continues to be effective until it lapses or perfection is lost for another reason. See sections 9–316, 9–507(a).

6.   **Priority.** Section 9–326 governs the priority contest between a secured creditor of the original debtor and a secured creditor of the new debtor.

As amended in 2000 and 2010.

§ 9–509.   Persons Entitled to File a Record.

(a)   **[Person entitled to file record.]** A person may file an initial financing statement, amendment that adds collateral covered by a financing statement, or amendment that adds a debtor to a financing statement only if:

(1)   the debtor authorizes the filing in an authenticated record or pursuant to subsection (b) or (c); or

(2)   the person holds an agricultural lien that has become effective at the time of filing and the financing statement covers only collateral in which the person holds an agricultural lien.

(b)   **[Security agreement as authorization.]** By authenticating or becoming bound as debtor by a security agreement, a debtor or new debtor authorizes the filing of an initial financing statement, and an amendment, covering:

(1)   the collateral described in the security agreement; and

(2)   property that becomes collateral under Section 9–315(a)(2), whether or not the security agreement expressly covers proceeds.

(c)   **[Acquisition of collateral as authorization.]** By acquiring collateral in which a security interest or agricultural lien continues under Section 9–315(a)(1), a debtor authorizes the filing of an initial financing statement, and an amendment, covering the collateral and property that becomes collateral under Section 9–315(a)(2).

(d)   **[Person entitled to file certain amendments.]** A person may file an amendment other than an amendment that adds collateral covered by a financing statement or an amendment that adds a debtor to a financing statement only if:

(1)   the secured party of record authorizes the filing; or

(2)   the amendment is a termination statement for a financing statement as to which the secured party of record has failed to file or send a termination statement as required by Section 9–513(a) or (c), the debtor authorizes the filing, and the termination statement indicates that the debtor authorized it to be filed.

(e)   **[Multiple secured parties of record.]** If there is more than one secured party of record for a financing statement, each secured party of record may authorize the filing of an amendment under subsection (d).

As amended in 2000.

Official Comment

1.   **Source.** New.

2.   **Scope and Approach of This Section.** This section collects in one place most of the rules determining whether a record may be filed. Section 9–510 explains the extent to which a filed record is effective. Under these sections, the identity of the person who effects a filing is immaterial. The filing scheme contemplated by this Part does not contemplate that the identity of a "filer" will be a part of the searchable records. This is consistent with, and a necessary aspect of, eliminating signatures or other evidence of authorization from the system. (Note that the 1972 amendments to this Article eliminated the requirement that a financing statement contain the signature of the secured party.) As long as the appropriate person authorizes the filing, or, in the case of a termination statement, the debtor is entitled to the termination, it is insignificant whether the secured party or another person files any given record. The question of authorization is one for the court, not the filing office. However, a filing office may choose to employ authentication procedures in connection with electronic communications, e.g., to verify the identity of a filer who seeks to charge the filing fee.

3.   **Unauthorized Filings.** Records filed in the filing office do not require signatures for their effectiveness. Subsection (a)(1) substitutes for the debtor's signature on a financing statement the requirement that the debtor authorize in an authenticated record the filing of an initial financing statement or an amendment that adds collateral. Also, under subsection (a)(1), if an amendment adds a debtor, the debtor who is added must authorize the amendment. A person who files an unauthorized record in violation of subsection (a)(1) is liable under Section 9–625(b) and (e) for actual and statutory damages. Of course, a filed financing statement is ineffective to perfect a security interest if the filing is not authorized. See Section 9–510(a). Law other than this Article, including the law with respect to ratification of past acts, generally determines whether a person has the requisite authority to file a record under this section. See Sections 1–103, 9–502, Comment 3. This Article applies to other issues, such as the priority of a security interest perfected by the filing of a financing statement. See Section 9–322, Comment 4.

4.   **Ipso Facto Authorization.** Under subsection (b), the authentication of a security agreement *ipso facto* constitutes the debtor's authorization of the filing of a financing statement covering the collateral described in the security agreement. The secured party need not obtain a separate authorization. Similarly, a new debtor's becoming bound by a security agreement *ipso facto* constitutes the new debtor's authorization of the filing of a financing statement covering the collateral described in the security agreement by which the new debtor has become bound. And, under subsection (c), the acquisition of collateral in which a security interest continues after disposition under Section 9–315(a)(1) *ipso facto* constitutes an authorization to file an initial financing statement against the person who acquired the collateral. The authorization to file an initial financing statement also constitutes an authorization to file a record covering actual proceeds of the original collateral, even if the security agreement is silent as to proceeds. See Section 9–322, Comment 4.

Example 1:   Debtor authenticates a security agreement creating a security interest in Debtor's inventory in favor of Secured Party. Secured Party files a financing statement covering inventory and accounts. The financing statement is authorized insofar as it covers inventory and unauthorized insofar as it covers accounts. (Note, however, that the financing statement will be effective to perfect a security interest in accounts constituting proceeds of the inventory to the same extent as a financing statement covering only inventory.)

Example 2:   Debtor authenticates a security agreement creating a security interest in Debtor's inventory in favor of Secured Party. Secured Party files a financing statement covering inventory. Debtor sells some inventory, deposits the buyer's payment into a deposit account, and withdraws the funds to purchase equipment. As long as the equipment can be traced to the inventory, the security interest continues in the equipment. See Section 9–315(a)(2). However, because the equipment was acquired with cash proceeds, the financing statement becomes ineffective to perfect the security interest in the equipment on the 21st day after the security interest attaches to the equipment unless Secured Party continues perfection beyond the 20-day period by filing a financing statement against the equipment or amending the filed financing statement to cover equipment. See Section 9–315(d). Debtor's authentication of the security agreement authorizes the filing of an initial financing statement or amendment covering the equipment, which is "property that becomes collateral under Section 9–315(a)(2)." See Section 9–509(b)(2).

5.   **Agricultural Liens.** Under subsection (a)(2), the holder of an agricultural lien may file a financing statement covering collateral subject to the lien without obtaining the debtor's authorization. Because the lien arises as matter of law, the debtor's consent is not required. A person who files an unauthorized record in violation of this subsection is liable under Section 9–625(e) for a statutory penalty and damages.

6.   **Amendments; Termination Statements Authorized by Debtor.** Most amendments may not be filed unless the secured party of record, as determined under Section 9–511, authorizes the filing. See subsection (d)(1). However, under subsection (d)(2), the authorization of the secured party of record is not required for the filing of a termination statement if the secured party of record failed to send or file a termination statement as required by Section 9–513, the debtor authorizes it to be filed, and the termination statement so indicates. An authorization to file a record under subsection (d) is effective even if the authorization is not in an authenticated record. Compare subsection (a)(1). However, both the person filing the record and the person giving the authorization may wish to obtain and retain a record indicating that the filing was authorized.

7.   **Multiple Secured Parties of Record.** Subsection (e) deals with multiple secured parties of record. It permits each secured party of record to authorize the filing of amendments. However, Section 9–510(b) protects the rights and powers of one secured party of record from the effects of filings made by another secured party of record. See Section 9–510, Comment 3.

8.   **Successor to Secured Party of Record.** A person may succeed to the powers of the secured party of record by operation of other law, e.g., the law of corporate mergers. In that case, the successor has the power to authorize filings within the meaning of this section.

As amended in 2010.

§ 9–510.   Effectiveness of Filed Record.

(a)   **[Filed record effective if authorized.]** A filed record is effective only to the extent that it was filed by a person that may file it under Section 9–509.

(b)   **[Authorization by one secured party of record.]** A record authorized by one secured party of record does not affect the financing statement with respect to another secured party of record.

(c)   **[Continuation statement not timely filed.]** A continuation statement that is not filed within the six-month period prescribed by Section 9–515(d) is ineffective.

Official Comment

1.   **Source.** New.

2.   **Ineffectiveness of Unauthorized or Overbroad Filings.** Subsection (a) provides that a filed financing statement is effective only to the extent it was filed by a person entitled to file it.

Example 1:   Debtor authorizes the filing of a financing statement covering inventory. Under Section 9–509, the secured party may file a financing statement covering only inventory; it may not file a financing statement covering other collateral. The secured party files a financing statement covering inventory and equipment. This section provides that the financing statement is effective only to the extent the secured party may file it. Thus, the financing statement is effective to perfect a security interest in inventory but ineffective to perfect a security interest in equipment.

3.   **Multiple Secured Parties of Record.** Section 9–509(e) permits any secured party of record to authorize the filing of most amendments. Subsection (b) of this section prevents a filing authorized by one secured party of record from affecting the rights and powers of another secured party of record without the latter's consent.

Example 2:   Debtor creates a security interest in favor of A and B. The filed financing statement names A and B as the secured parties. An amendment deleting some collateral covered by the financing statement is filed pursuant to B's authorization. Although B's security interest in the deleted collateral becomes unperfected, A's security interest remains perfected in all the collateral.

Example 3:   Debtor creates a security interest in favor of A and B. The financing statement names A and B as the secured parties. A termination statement is filed pursuant to B's authorization. Although the effectiveness of the financing statement terminates with respect to B's security interest, A's rights are unaffected. That is, the financing statement continues to be effective to perfect A's security interest.

4.   **Continuation Statements.** A continuation statement may be filed only within the six months immediately before lapse. See Section 9–515(d). The filing office is obligated to reject a continuation statement that is filed outside the six-month period. See Sections 9–520(a), 9–516(b)(7). Subsection (c) provides that if the filing office fails to reject a continuation statement that is not filed in a timely manner, the continuation statement is ineffective nevertheless.

§ 9–511.   Secured Party of Record.

(a)   **[Secured party of record.]** A secured party of record with respect to a financing statement is a person whose name is provided as the name of the secured party or a representative of the secured party in an initial financing statement that has been filed. If an initial financing statement is filed under Section 9–514(a), the assignee named in the initial financing statement is the secured party of record with respect to the financing statement.

(b)   **[Amendment naming secured party of record.]** If an amendment of a financing statement which provides the name of a person as a secured party or a representative of a secured party is filed, the person named in the amendment is a secured party of record. If an amendment is filed under Section 9–514(b), the assignee named in the amendment is a secured party of record.

(c)   **[Amendment deleting secured party of record.]** A person remains a secured party of record until the filing of an amendment of the financing statement which deletes the person.

Official Comment

1.   **Source.** New.

2.   **Secured Party of Record.** This new section explains how the secured party of record is to be determined. If SP-1 is named as the secured party in an initial financing statement, it is the secured party of record. Similarly, if an initial financing statement reflects a total assignment from SP-0 to SP-1, then SP-1 is the secured party of record. See subsection (a). If, subsequently, an amendment is filed assigning SP-1's status to SP-2, then SP-2 becomes the secured party of record in place of SP-1. The same result obtains if a subsequent amendment deletes the reference to SP-1 and substitutes therefor a reference to SP-2. If, however, a subsequent amendment adds SP-2 as a secured party but does not purport to remove SP-1 as a secured party, then SP-2 and SP-1 each is a secured party of record. See subsection (b). An amendment purporting to remove the only secured party of record without providing a successor is ineffective. See Section 9–512(e). At any point in time, all effective records that comprise a financing statement must be examined to determine the person or persons that have the status of secured party of record.

3.   **Successor to Secured Party of Record.** Application of other law may result in a person succeeding to the powers of a secured party of record. For example, if the secured party of record (A) merges into another corporation (B) and the other corporation (B) survives, other law may provide that B has all of A's powers. In that case, B is authorized to take all actions under this Part that A would have been authorized to take. Similarly, acts taken by a person who is authorized under generally applicable principles of agency to act on behalf of the secured party of record are effective under this Part.

§ 9–512.   Amendment of Financing Statement.

[ALTERNATIVE A]

(a)   **[Amendment of information in financing statement.]** Subject to Section 9–509, a person may add or delete collateral covered by, continue or terminate the effectiveness of, or, subject to subsection (e), otherwise amend the information provided in, a financing statement by filing an amendment that:

(1)   identifies, by its file number, the initial financing statement to which the amendment relates; and

(2)   if the amendment relates to an initial financing statement filed [or recorded] in a filing office described in Section 9–501(a)(1), provides the information specified in Section 9–502(b).

[ALTERNATIVE B]

(a)   **[Amendment of information in financing statement.]** Subject to Section 9–509, a person may add or delete collateral covered by, continue or terminate the effectiveness of, or, subject to subsection (e), otherwise amend the information provided in, a financing statement by filing an amendment that:

(1)   identifies, by its file number, the initial financing statement to which the amendment relates; and

(2)   if the amendment relates to an initial financing statement filed [or recorded] in a filing office described in Section 9–501(a)(1), provides the date [and time] that the initial financing statement was filed [or recorded] and the information specified in Section 9–502(b).

[END OF ALTERNATIVES]

(b) **[Period of effectiveness not affected.]** Except as otherwise provided in Section 9–515, the filing of an amendment does not extend the period of effectiveness of the financing statement.

(c) **[Effectiveness of amendment adding collateral.]** A financing statement that is amended by an amendment that adds collateral is effective as to the added collateral only from the date of the filing of the amendment.

(d) **[Effectiveness of amendment adding debtor.]** A financing statement that is amended by an amendment that adds a debtor is effective as to the added debtor only from the date of the filing of the amendment.

(e) **[Certain amendments ineffective.]** An amendment is ineffective to the extent it:

(1) purports to delete all debtors and fails to provide the name of a debtor to be covered by the financing statement; or

(2) purports to delete all secured parties of record and fails to provide the name of a new secured party of record.

Legislative Note: States whose real-estate filing offices require additional information in amendments and cannot search their records by both the name of the debtor and the file number should enact Alternative B to Sections 9–512(a), 9–518(b), 9–518(d), 9–519(f) and 9–522(a).

As amended in 2010.

Official Comment

1.   **Source.** Former 9–402(4).

2.   **Changes to Financing Statements.** This section addresses changes to financing statements, including addition and deletion of collateral. Although termination statements, assignments, and continuation statements are types of amendment, this Article follows former Article 9 and contains separate sections containing additional provisions applicable to particular types of amendments. See Section 9–513 (termination statements); 9–514 (assignments); 9–515 (continuation statements). One should not infer from this separate treatment that this Article requires a separate amendment to accomplish each change. Rather, a single amendment would be legally sufficient to, e.g., add collateral and continue the effectiveness of the financing statement.

3.   **Amendments.** An amendment under this Article may identify only the information contained in a financing statement that is to be changed; alternatively, it may take the form of an amended and restated financing statement. The latter would state, for example, that the financing statement "is amended and restated to read as follows: . . ." References in this Part to an "amended financing statement" are to a financing statement as amended by an amendment using either technique.

This section revises former Section 9–402(4) to permit secured parties of record to make changes in the public record without the need to obtain the debtor's signature. However, the filing of an amendment that adds collateral or adds a debtor must be authorized by the debtor or it will not be effective. See Sections 9–509(a), 9–510(a).

4.   **Amendment Adding Debtor.** An amendment that adds a debtor is effective, provided that the added debtor authorizes the filing. See Section 9–509(a). However, filing an amendment adding a debtor to a previously filed financing statement affords no advantage over filing an initial financing statement against that debtor and may be disadvantageous. With respect to the added debtor, for purposes of determining the priority of the security interest, the time of filing is the time of the filing of the amendment, not the time of the filing of the initial financing statement. See subsection (d). However, the effectiveness of the financing statement lapses with respect to added debtor at the time it lapses with respect to the original debtor. See subsection (b).

5.   **Amendment Adding Debtor Name.** Many states have enacted statutes governing the "conversion" of one organization organized under the law of that state, e.g., a corporation, into another such organization, e.g., a limited liability company. This Article defers to those statutes to determine whether the resulting organization is the same legal person as the initial, converting organization (albeit with a different name) or whether the resulting organization is a different legal person. When the governing statute does not clearly resolve the question, a secured party whose debtor is the converting organization may wish to proceed as if the statute provides for both results. In these circumstances, an amendment adding to the initial financing statement the name of the resulting organization may be preferable to an amendment substituting that name for the name of the debtor provided on the initial financing statement. In the event the governing statute is construed as providing that the resulting

organization is the same legal person as the converting organization, but with a different name, the timely filing of such an amendment would satisfy the requirement of Section 9–507(c)(2). If, however, the governing statute is construed as providing that the resulting organization is a different legal person, the financing statement (which continues to provide the name of the original debtor) would be effective as to collateral acquired by the resulting organization ("new debtor") before, and within four months after, the conversion. See Section 9–508(b)(1). Inasmuch as it is the first financing statement filed against the resulting organization by the secured party, the record adding the name of the resulting organization as a debtor would constitute "an initial financing statement providing the name of the new debtor" under Section 9–508(b)(2). The secured party also may wish to file another financing statement naming the resulting organization as debtor. See Comment 4.

6. **Deletion of All Debtors or Secured Parties of Record.** Subsection (e) assures that there will be a debtor and secured party of record for every financing statement.

Example: A filed financing statement names A and B as secured parties of record and covers inventory and equipment. An amendment deletes equipment and purports to delete A and B as secured parties of record without adding a substitute secured party. The amendment is ineffective to the extent it purports to delete the secured parties of record but effective with respect to the deletion of collateral. As a consequence, the financing statement, as amended, covers only inventory, but A and B remain as secured parties of record.

As amended in 2010.

§ 9–513.   Termination Statement.

(a)   **[Consumer goods.]** A secured party shall cause the secured party of record for a financing statement to file a termination statement for the financing statement if the financing statement covers consumer goods and:

(1)   there is no obligation secured by the collateral covered by the financing statement and no commitment to make an advance, incur an obligation, or otherwise give value; or

(2)   the debtor did not authorize the filing of the initial financing statement.

(b)   **[Time for compliance with subsection (a).]** To comply with subsection (a), a secured party shall cause the secured party of record to file the termination statement:

(1)   within one month after there is no obligation secured by the collateral covered by the financing statement and no commitment to make an advance, incur an obligation, or otherwise give value; or

(2)   if earlier, within 20 days after the secured party receives an authenticated demand from a debtor.

(c)   **[Other collateral.]** In cases not governed by subsection (a), within 20 days after a secured party receives an authenticated demand from a debtor, the secured party shall cause the secured party of record for a financing statement to send to the debtor a termination statement for the financing statement or file the termination statement in the filing office if:

(1)   except in the case of a financing statement covering accounts or chattel paper that has been sold or goods that are the subject of a consignment, there is no obligation secured by the collateral covered by the financing statement and no commitment to make an advance, incur an obligation, or otherwise give value;

(2)   the financing statement covers accounts or chattel paper that has been sold but as to which the account debtor or other person obligated has discharged its obligation;

(3)   the financing statement covers goods that were the subject of a consignment to the debtor but are not in the debtor's possession; or

(4)   the debtor did not authorize the filing of the initial financing statement.

(d)   **[Effect of filing termination statement.]** Except as otherwise provided in Section 9–510, upon the filing of a termination statement with the filing office, the financing statement to which the termination statement relates ceases to be effective. Except as otherwise provided in Section 9–510, for purposes of Sections 9–519(g), 9–522(a), and 9–523(c), the filing with the filing office of a termination statement relating to a financing statement that indicates that the debtor is a transmitting utility also causes the effectiveness of the financing statement to lapse.

As amended in 2000.

Official Comment

1.   **Source.** Former Section 9–404.

2.   **Duty to File or Send.** This section specifies when a secured party must cause the secured party of record to file or send to the debtor a termination statement for a financing statement. Because most financing statements expire in five years unless a continuation statement is filed (Section 9–515), no compulsion is placed on the secured party to file a termination statement unless demanded by the debtor, except in the case of consumer goods. Because many consumers will not realize the importance to them of clearing the public record, an affirmative duty is put on the secured party in that case. But many purchase-money security interests in consumer goods will not be filed, except for motor vehicles. See Section 9–309(1). Under Section 9–311(b), compliance with a certificate-of-title statute is "equivalent to the filing of a financing statement under this article." Thus, this section applies to a certificate of title unless the section is superseded by a certificate-of-title statute that contains a specific rule addressing a secured party's duty to cause a notation of a security interest to be removed from a certificate of title. In the context of a certificate of title, however, the secured party could comply with this section by causing the removal itself or providing the debtor with documentation sufficient to enable the debtor to effect the removal.

Subsections (a) and (b) apply to a financing statement covering consumer goods. Subsection (c) applies to other financing statements. Subsection (a) and (c) each makes explicit what was implicit under former Article 9: If the debtor did not authorize the filing of a financing statement in the first place, the secured party of record should file or send a termination statement. The liability imposed upon a secured party that fails to comply with subsection (a) or (c) is identical to that imposed for the filing of an unauthorized financing statement or amendment. See Section 9–625(e).

3.   **"Bogus" Filings.** A secured party's duty to send a termination statement arises when the secured party "receives" an authenticated demand from the debtor. In the case of an unauthorized financing statement, the person named as debtor in the financing statement may have no relationship with the named secured party and no reason to know the secured party's address. Inasmuch as the address in the financing statement is "held out by [the person named as secured party in the financing statement] as the place for receipt of such communications [i.e., communications relating to security interests]," the putative secured party is deemed to have "received" a notification delivered to that address. See Section 1–202(e). If a termination statement is not forthcoming, the person named as debtor itself may authorize the filing of a termination statement, which will be effective if it indicates that the person authorized it to be filed. See Sections 9–509(d)(2), 9–510(c).

4.   **Buyers of Receivables.** Applied literally, former Section 9–404(1) would have required many buyers of receivables to file a termination statement immediately upon filing a financing statement because "there is no outstanding secured obligation and no commitment to make advances, incur obligations, or otherwise give value." Subsections (c)(1) and (2) remedy this problem. While the security interest of a buyer of accounts or chattel paper (B-1) is perfected, the debtor is not deemed to retain an interest in the sold receivables and thus could transfer no interest in them to another buyer (B-2) or to a lien creditor (LC). However, for purposes of determining the rights of the debtor's creditors and certain purchasers of accounts or chattel paper from the debtor, while B-1's security interest is unperfected, the debtor-seller is deemed to have rights in the sold receivables, and a competing security interest or judicial lien may attach to those rights. See Sections 9–318, 9–109, Comment 5. Suppose that B-1's security interest in certain accounts and chattel paper is perfected by filing, but the effectiveness of the financing statement lapses. Both before and after lapse, B-1 collects some of the receivables. After lapse, LC acquires a lien on the accounts and chattel paper. B-1's unperfected security interest in the accounts and chattel paper is subordinate to LC's rights. See Section 9–317(a)(2). But collections on accounts and chattel paper are not "accounts" or "chattel paper." Even if B-1's security interest in the accounts and chattel paper is or becomes unperfected, neither the debtor nor LC acquires rights to the collections that B-1 collects (and owns) before LC acquires a lien.

5.   **Effect of Filing.** Subsection (d) states the effect of filing a termination statement: the related financing statement ceases to be effective. If one of several secured parties of record files a termination statement, subsection (d) applies only with respect to the rights of the person who authorized the filing of the termination statement. See Section 9–510(b). The financing statement remains effective with respect to the rights of the others. However, even if a financing statement is *terminated* (and thus no longer is effective) with respect to all secured parties of

862

record, the financing statement, including the termination statement, will remain of record until at least one year after it *lapses* with respect to all secured parties of record. See Section 9–519(g).

As amended in 2010.

§ 9–514. Assignment of Powers of Secured Party of Record.

(a) **[Assignment reflected on initial financing statement.]** Except as otherwise provided in subsection (c), an initial financing statement may reflect an assignment of all of the secured party's power to authorize an amendment to the financing statement by providing the name and mailing address of the assignee as the name and address of the secured party.

(b) **[Assignment of filed financing statement.]** Except as otherwise provided in subsection (c), a secured party of record may assign of record all or part of its power to authorize an amendment to a financing statement by filing in the filing office an amendment of the financing statement which:

(1) identifies, by its file number, the initial financing statement to which it relates;

(2) provides the name of the assignor; and

(3) provides the name and mailing address of the assignee.

(c) **[Assignment of record of mortgage.]** An assignment of record of a security interest in a fixture covered by a record of a mortgage which is effective as a financing statement filed as a fixture filing under Section 9–502(c) may be made only by an assignment of record of the mortgage in the manner provided by law of this State other than [the Uniform Commercial Code].

Official Comment

1. **Source.** Former Section 9–405.

2. **Assignments.** This section provides a permissive device whereby a secured party of record may effectuate an assignment of its power to affect a financing statement. It may also be useful for a secured party who has assigned all or part of its security interest or agricultural lien and wishes to have the fact noted of record, so that inquiries concerning the transaction would be addressed to the assignee. See Section 9–502, Comment 2. Upon the filing of an assignment, the assignee becomes the "secured party of record" and may authorize the filing of a continuation statement, termination statement, or other amendment. Note that under Section 9–310(c) no filing of an assignment is required as a condition of continuing the perfected status of the security interest against creditors and transferees of the original debtor. However, if an assignment is not filed, the assignor remains the secured party of record, with the power (even if not the right) to authorize the filing of effective amendments. See Sections 9–511(c), 9–509(d).

Where a record of a mortgage is effective as a financing statement filed as a fixture filing (Section 9–502(c)), then an assignment of record of the security interest may be made only in the manner in which an assignment of record of the mortgage may be made under local real-property law.

3. **Comparison to Prior Law.** Most of the changes reflected in this section are for clarification or to embrace medium-neutral drafting. As a general matter, this section preserves the opportunity given by former Section 9–405 to assign a security interest of record in one of two different ways. Under subsection (a), a secured party may assign all of its power to affect a financing statement by naming an assignee in the initial financing statement. The secured party of record may accomplish the same result under subsection (b) by making a subsequent filing. Subsection (b) also may be used for an assignment of only some of the secured party of record's power to affect a financing statement, e.g., the power to affect the financing statement as it relates to particular items of collateral or as it relates to an undivided interest in a security interest in all the collateral. An initial financing statement may not be used to change the secured party of record under these circumstances. However, an amendment adding the assignee as a secured party of record may be used.

§ 9–515. Duration and Effectiveness of Financing Statement; Effect of Lapsed Financing Statement.

(a) **[Five-year effectiveness.]** Except as otherwise provided in subsections (b), (e), (f), and (g), a filed financing statement is effective for a period of five years after the date of filing.

(b) **[Public-finance or manufactured-home transaction.]** Except as otherwise provided in subsections (e), (f), and (g), an initial financing statement filed in connection with a public-finance transaction or manufactured-home transaction is effective for a period of 30 years after the date of filing if it indicates that it is filed in connection with a public-finance transaction or manufactured-home transaction.

(c) **[Lapse and continuation of financing statement.]** The effectiveness of a filed financing statement lapses on the expiration of the period of its effectiveness unless before the lapse a continuation statement is filed pursuant to subsection (d). Upon lapse, a financing statement ceases to be effective and any security interest or agricultural lien that was perfected by the financing statement becomes unperfected, unless the security interest is perfected otherwise. If the security interest or agricultural lien becomes unperfected upon lapse, it is deemed never to have been perfected as against a purchaser of the collateral for value.

(d) **[When continuation statement may be filed.]** A continuation statement may be filed only within six months before the expiration of the five-year period specified in subsection (a) or the 30-year period specified in subsection (b), whichever is applicable.

(e) **[Effect of filing continuation statement.]** Except as otherwise provided in Section 9–510, upon timely filing of a continuation statement, the effectiveness of the initial financing statement continues for a period of five years commencing on the day on which the financing statement would have become ineffective in the absence of the filing. Upon the expiration of the five-year period, the financing statement lapses in the same manner as provided in subsection (c), unless, before the lapse, another continuation statement is filed pursuant to subsection (d). Succeeding continuation statements may be filed in the same manner to continue the effectiveness of the initial financing statement.

(f) **[Transmitting utility financing statement.]** If a debtor is a transmitting utility and a filed initial financing statement so indicates, the financing statement is effective until a termination statement is filed.

(g) **[Record of mortgage as financing statement.]** A record of a mortgage that is effective as a financing statement filed as a fixture filing under Section 9–502(c) remains effective as a financing statement filed as a fixture filing until the mortgage is released or satisfied of record or its effectiveness otherwise terminates as to the real property.

As amended in 2010.

Official Comment

1. **Source.** Former Section 9–403(2), (3), (6).

2. **Period of Financing Statement's Effectiveness.** Subsection (a) states the general rule: a financing statement is effective for a five-year period unless its effectiveness is continued under this section or terminated under Section 9–513. Subsection (b) provides that if the financing statement relates to a public-finance transaction or a manufactured-home transaction and so indicates, the financing statement is effective for 30 years. These financings typically extend well beyond the standard, five-year period. Under subsection (f), a financing statement filed against a transmitting utility remains effective indefinitely, until a termination statement is filed. Likewise, under subsection (g), a mortgage effective as a fixture filing remains effective until its effectiveness terminates under real-property law.

3. **Lapse.** When the period of effectiveness under subsection (a) or (b) expires, the effectiveness of the financing statement lapses. The last sentence of subsection (c) addresses the effect of lapse. The deemed retroactive unperfection applies only with respect to purchasers for value; unlike former Section 9–403(2), it does not apply with respect to lien creditors.

Example 1: SP-1 and SP-2 both hold security interests in the same collateral. Both security interests are perfected by filing. SP-1 filed first and has priority under Section 9–322(a)(1). The effectiveness of SP-1's filing lapses. As long as SP-2's security interest remains perfected thereafter, SP-2 is entitled to priority over SP-1's security interest, which is deemed never to have been perfected as against a purchaser for value (SP-2). See Section 9–322(a)(2).

Example 2: SP holds a security interest perfected by filing. On July 1, LC acquires a judicial lien on the collateral. Two weeks later, the effectiveness of the financing statement lapses. Although the security interest becomes unperfected upon lapse, it was perfected when LC acquired its lien. Accordingly, notwithstanding the lapse, the perfected security interest has priority over the rights of LC, who is not a purchaser. See Section 9–317(a)(2).

4. **Effect of Debtor's Bankruptcy.** Under former Section 9–403(2), lapse was tolled if the debtor entered bankruptcy or another insolvency proceeding. Nevertheless, being unaware that insolvency proceedings had been commenced, filing offices routinely removed records from the files as if lapse had not been tolled. Subsection (c) deletes the former tolling provision and thereby imposes a new burden on the secured party: to be sure that a financing statement does not lapse during the debtor's bankruptcy. The secured party can prevent lapse by filing a continuation statement, even without first obtaining relief from the automatic stay. See Bankruptcy Code Section 362(b)(3). Of course, if the debtor enters bankruptcy before lapse, the provisions of this Article with respect to lapse would be of no effect to the extent that federal bankruptcy law dictates a contrary result (e.g., to the extent that the Bankruptcy Code determines rights as of the date of the filing of the bankruptcy petition).

5. **Continuation Statements.** Subsection (d) explains when a continuation statement may be filed. A continuation statement filed at a time other than that prescribed by subsection (d) is ineffective, see Section 9–510(c), and the filing office may not accept it. See Sections 9–520(a), 9–516(b). Subsection (e) specifies the effect of a continuation statement and provides for successive continuation statements.

§ 9–516. What Constitutes Filing; Effectiveness of Filing.

(a) **[What constitutes filing.]** Except as otherwise provided in subsection (b), communication of a record to a filing office and tender of the filing fee or acceptance of the record by the filing office constitutes filing.

(b) **[Refusal to accept record; filing does not occur.]** Filing does not occur with respect to a record that a filing office refuses to accept because:

(1) the record is not communicated by a method or medium of communication authorized by the filing office;

(2) an amount equal to or greater than the applicable filing fee is not tendered;

(3) the filing office is unable to index the record because:

(A) in the case of an initial financing statement, the record does not provide a name for the debtor;

(B) in the case of an amendment or information statement, the record:

(i) does not identify the initial financing statement as required by Section 9–512 or 9–518, as applicable; or

(ii) identifies an initial financing statement whose effectiveness has lapsed under Section 9–515;

(C) in the case of an initial financing statement that provides the name of a debtor identified as an individual or an amendment that provides a name of a debtor identified as an individual which was not previously provided in the financing statement to which the record relates, the record does not identify the debtor's surname; or

(D) in the case of a record filed [or recorded] in the filing office described in Section 9–501(a)(1), the record does not provide a sufficient description of the real property to which it relates;

(4) in the case of an initial financing statement or an amendment that adds a secured party of record, the record does not provide a name and mailing address for the secured party of record;

(5) in the case of an initial financing statement or an amendment that provides a name of a debtor which was not previously provided in the financing statement to which the amendment relates, the record does not:

(A) provide a mailing address for the debtor;

(B) indicate whether the name provided as the name of the debtor is the name of an individual or an organization;

(6) in the case of an assignment reflected in an initial financing statement under Section 9–514(a) or an amendment filed under Section 9–514(b), the record does not provide a name and mailing address for the assignee; or

(7) in the case of a continuation statement, the record is not filed within the six-month period prescribed by Section 9–515(d).

(c) **[Rules applicable to subsection (b).]** For purposes of subsection (b):

(1) a record does not provide information if the filing office is unable to read or decipher the information; and

(2) a record that does not indicate that it is an amendment or identify an initial financing statement to which it relates, as required by Section 9–512, 9–514, or 9–518, is an initial financing statement.

(d) **[Refusal to accept record; record effective as filed record.]** A record that is communicated to the filing office with tender of the filing fee, but which the filing office refuses to accept for a reason other than one set forth in subsection (b), is effective as a filed record except as against a purchaser of the collateral which gives value in reasonable reliance upon the absence of the record from the files.

As amended in 2010.

Official Comment

1.   **Source.** Subsection (a): former Section 9–403(1); the remainder is new.

2.   **What Constitutes Filing.** Subsection (a) deals generically with what constitutes filing of a record, including an initial financing statement and amendments of all kinds (e.g., assignments, termination statements, and continuation statements). It follows former Section 9–403(1), under which either acceptance of a record by the filing office or presentation of the record and tender of the filing fee constitutes filing.

3.   **Effectiveness of Rejected Record.** Subsection (b) provides an exclusive list of grounds upon which the filing office may reject a record. See Section 9–520(a). Although some of these grounds would also be grounds for rendering a filed record ineffective (e.g., an initial financing statement does not provide a name for the debtor), many others would not be (e.g., an initial financing statement does not provide a mailing address for the debtor or secured party of record). Neither this section nor Section 9–520 requires or authorizes the filing office to determine, or even consider, the accuracy of information provided in a record.

A financing statement or other record that is communicated to the filing office but which the filing office refuses to accept provides no public notice, regardless of the reason for the rejection. However, this section distinguishes between records that the filing office rightfully rejects and those that it wrongfully rejects. A filer is able to prevent a rightful rejection by complying with the requirements of subsection (b). No purpose is served by giving effect to records that justifiably never find their way into the system, and subsection (b) so provides.

Subsection (d) deals with the filing office's unjustified refusal to accept a record. Here, the filer is in no position to prevent the rejection and as a general matter should not be prejudiced by it. Although wrongfully rejected records generally are effective, subsection (d) contains a special rule to protect a third-party purchaser of the collateral (e.g., a buyer or competing secured party) who gives value in reliance upon the apparent absence of the record from the files. As against a person who searches the public record and reasonably relies on what the public record shows, subsection (d) imposes upon the filer the risk that a record failed to make its way into the filing system because of the filing office's wrongful rejection of it. (Compare Section 9–517, under which a mis-indexed financing statement is fully effective.) This risk is likely to be small, particularly when a record is presented electronically, and the filer can guard against this risk by conducting a post-filing search of the records. Moreover, Section 9–520(b) requires the filing office to give prompt notice of its refusal to accept a record for filing.

4.   **Method or Medium of Communication.** Rejection pursuant to subsection (b)(1) for failure to communicate a record properly should be understood to mean noncompliance with procedures relating to security, authentication, or other communication-related requirements that the filing office may impose. Subsection (b)(1) does not authorize a filing office to impose additional substantive requirements. See Section 9–520, Comment 2.

5.   **Address for Secured Party of Record.** Under subsection (b)(4) and Section 9–520(a), the lack of a mailing address for the secured party of record requires the filing office to reject an initial financing statement. The failure to include an address for the secured party of record no longer renders a financing statement ineffective. See Section 9–502(a). The function of the address is not to identify the secured party of record but rather to provide an address to which others can send required notifications, e.g., of a purchase-money security interest in inventory or of the disposition of collateral. Inasmuch as the address shown on a filed financing statement is an "address that is reasonable under the circumstances," a person required to send a notification to the secured party may satisfy the requirement by sending a notification to that address, even if the address is or

becomes incorrect. See Section 9–102 (definition of "send"). Similarly, because the address is "held out by [the secured party] as the place for receipt of such communications [i.e., communications relating to security interests]," the secured party is deemed to have received a notification delivered to that address. See Section 1–202(e).

6. **Uncertainty Concerning Individual Debtor's Surname.** Subsection (b)(3)(C) requires the filing office to reject an initial financing statement or amendment adding an individual debtor if the office cannot index the record because it does not identify the debtor's surname (e.g., it is unclear whether the debtor's surname is Elton or John).

7. **Inability of Filing Office to Read or Decipher Information.** Under subsection (c)(1), if the filing office cannot read or decipher information, the information is not provided by a record for purposes of subsection (b).

8. **Classification of Records.** For purposes of subsection (b), a record that does not indicate it is an amendment or identify an initial financing statement to which it relates is deemed to be an initial financing statement. See subsection (c)(2).

9. **Effectiveness of Rejectable But Unrejected Record.** Section 9–520(a) requires the filing office to refuse to accept an initial financing statement for a reason set forth in subsection (b). However, if the filing office accepts such a financing statement nevertheless, the financing statement generally is effective if it complies with the requirements of Section 9–502(a) and (b). See Section 9–520(c). Similarly, an otherwise effective financing statement generally remains so even though the information in the financing statement becomes incorrect. See Section 9–507(b). (Note that if the information required by subsection (b)(5) is incorrect when the financing statement is filed, Section 9–338 applies.)

As amended in 2010.

§ 9–517.   Effect of Indexing Errors.

The failure of the filing office to index a record correctly does not affect the effectiveness of the filed record.

Official Comment

1. **Source.** New.

2. **Effectiveness of Mis-Indexed Records.** This section provides that the filing office's error in mis-indexing a record does not render ineffective an otherwise effective record. As did former Section 9–401, this section imposes the risk of filing-office error on those who search the files rather than on those who file.

§ 9–518.   Claim Concerning Inaccurate or Wrongfully Filed Record.

(a) **[Statement with respect to record indexed under person's name.]** A person may file in the filing office an information statement with respect to a record indexed there under the person's name if the person believes that the record is inaccurate or was wrongfully filed.

[ALTERNATIVE A]

(b) **[Contents of statement under subsection (a).]** An information statement under subsection (a) must:

(1) identify the record to which it relates by the file number assigned to the initial financing statement to which the record relates;

(2) indicate that it is an information statement; and

(3) provide the basis for the person's belief that the record is inaccurate and indicate the manner in which the person believes the record should be amended to cure any inaccuracy or provide the basis for the person's belief that the record was wrongfully filed.

[ALTERNATIVE B]

(b) **[Contents of statement under subsection (a).]** An information statement under subsection (a) must:

(1) identify the record to which it relates by:

(A) the file number assigned to the initial financing statement to which the record relates; and

(B) if the information statement relates to a record filed [or recorded] in a filing office described in Section 9–501(a)(1), the date [and time] that the initial financing statement was filed [or recorded] and the information specified in Section 9–502(b);

(2) indicate that it is an information statement; and

(3) provide the basis for the person's belief that the record is inaccurate and indicate the manner in which the person believes the record should be amended to cure any inaccuracy or provide the basis for the person's belief that the record was wrongfully filed.

[END OF ALTERNATIVES]

(c) **[Statement by secured party of record.]** A person may file in the filing office an information statement with respect to a record filed there if the person is a secured party of record with respect to the financing statement to which the record relates and believes that the person that filed the record was not entitled to do so under Section 9–509(d).

[ALTERNATIVE A]

(d) **[Contents of statement under subsection (c).]** An information statement under subsection (c) must:

(1) identify the record to which it relates by the file number assigned to the initial financing statement to which the record relates;

(2) indicate that it is an information statement; and

(3) provide the basis for the person's belief that the person that filed the record was not entitled to do so under Section 9–509(d).

[ALTERNATIVE B]

(d) **[Contents of statement under subsection (c).]** An information statement under subsection (c) must:

(1) identify the record to which it relates by:

(A) the file number assigned to the initial financing statement to which the record relates; and

(B) if the information statement relates to a record filed [or recorded] in a filing office described in Section 9–501(a)(1), the date [and time] that the initial financing statement was filed [or recorded] and the information specified in Section 9–502(b);

(2) indicate that it is an information statement; and

(3) provide the basis for the person's belief that the person that filed the record was not entitled to do so under Section 9–509(d).

[END OF ALTERNATIVES]

(e) **[Record not affected by information statement.]** The filing of an information statement does not affect the effectiveness of an initial financing statement or other filed record.

Legislative Note: States whose real-estate filing offices require additional information in amendments and cannot search their records by both the name of the debtor and the file number should enact Alternative B to Sections 9–512(a), 9–518(b), 9–518(d), 9–519(f) and 9–522(a).

As amended in 2010.

Official Comment

1. **Source.** New.

2. **Information Statements.** Former Article 9 did not afford a nonjudicial means for a debtor to indicate that a financing statement or other record was inaccurate or wrongfully filed. Subsection (a) affords the debtor the right to file an information statement. Among other requirements, the information statement must provide the basis for the debtor's belief that the public record should be corrected. See subsection (b). These provisions, which

resemble the analogous remedy in the Fair Credit Reporting Act, 15 U.S.C. § 1681i, afford an aggrieved person the opportunity to state its position on the public record. They do not permit an aggrieved person to change the legal effect of the public record. Thus, although a filed information statement becomes part of the "financing statement," as defined in Section 9–102, the filing does not affect the effectiveness of the initial financing statement or any other filed record. See subsection (e).

Sometimes a person files a termination statement or other record relating to a filed financing statement without being entitled to do so. A secured party of record with respect to the financing statement who believes that such a record has been filed may, but need not, file an information statement indicating that the person that filed the record was not entitled to do so. See subsection (c). An information statement has no legal effect. Its sole purpose is to provide some limited public notice that the efficacy of a filed record is disputed. If the person that filed the record was not entitled to do so, the filed record is ineffective, regardless of whether the secured party of record files an information statement. Likewise, if the person that filed the record was entitled to do so, the filed record is effective, even if the secured party of record files an information statement. See Section 9–510(a), 9–518(e). Because an information statement filed under subsection (c) has no legal effect, a secured party of record—even one who is aware of the unauthorized filing of a record—has no duty to file one. Just as searchers bear the burden of determining whether the filing of initial financing statement was authorized, searchers bear the burden of determining whether the filing of every subsequent record was authorized.

Inasmuch as the filing of an information statement has no legal effect, this section does not provide a mechanism by which a secured party can correct an error that it discovers in its own financing statement.

This section does not displace other provisions of this Article that impose liability for making unauthorized filings or failing to file or send a termination statement (see Section 9–625(e)), nor does it displace any available judicial remedies.

3. **Resort to Other Law.** This Article cannot provide a satisfactory or complete solution to problems caused by misuse of the public records. The problem of "bogus" filings is not limited to the UCC filing system but extends to the real-property records, as well. A summary judicial procedure for correcting the public record and criminal penalties for those who misuse the filing and recording systems are likely to be more effective and put less strain on the filing system than provisions authorizing or requiring action by filing and recording offices.

As amended in 2010.

[SUBPART 2. DUTIES AND OPERATION OF FILING OFFICE]

§ 9–519. Numbering, Maintaining, and Indexing Records; Communicating Information Provided in Records.

(a) **[Filing office duties.]** For each record filed in a filing office, the filing office shall:

(1) assign a unique number to the filed record;

(2) create a record that bears the number assigned to the filed record and the date and time of filing;

(3) maintain the filed record for public inspection; and

(4) index the filed record in accordance with subsections (c), (d), and (e).

(b) **[File number.]** A file number [assigned after January 1, 2002,] must include a digit that:

(1) is mathematically derived from or related to the other digits of the file number; and

(2) aids the filing office in determining whether a number communicated as the file number includes a single-digit or transpositional error.

(c) **[Indexing: general.]** Except as otherwise provided in subsections (d) and (e), the filing office shall:

(1) index an initial financing statement according to the name of the debtor and index all filed records relating to the initial financing statement in a manner that associates with one another an initial financing statement and all filed records relating to the initial financing statement; and

(2) index a record that provides a name of a debtor which was not previously provided in the financing statement to which the record relates also according to the name that was not previously provided.

(d) **[Indexing: real-property-related financing statement.]** If a financing statement is filed as a fixture filing or covers as-extracted collateral or timber to be cut, [it must be filed for record and] the filing office shall index it:

(1) under the names of the debtor and of each owner of record shown on the financing statement as if they were the mortgagors under a mortgage of the real property described; and

(2) to the extent that the law of this State provides for indexing of records of mortgages under the name of the mortgagee, under the name of the secured party as if the secured party were the mortgagee thereunder, or, if indexing is by description, as if the financing statement were a record of a mortgage of the real property described.

(e) **[Indexing: real-property-related assignment.]** If a financing statement is filed as a fixture filing or covers as-extracted collateral or timber to be cut, the filing office shall index an assignment filed under Section 9–514(a) or an amendment filed under Section 9–514(b):

(1) under the name of the assignor as grantor; and

(2) to the extent that the law of this State provides for indexing a record of the assignment of a mortgage under the name of the assignee, under the name of the assignee.

[ALTERNATIVE A]

(f) **[Retrieval and association capability.]** The filing office shall maintain a capability:

(1) to retrieve a record by the name of the debtor and by the file number assigned to the initial financing statement to which the record relates; and

(2) to associate and retrieve with one another an initial financing statement and each filed record relating to the initial financing statement.

[ALTERNATIVE B]

(f) **[Retrieval and association capability.]** The filing office shall maintain a capability:

(1) to retrieve a record by the name of the debtor and:

(A) if the filing office is described in Section 9–501(a)(1), by the file number assigned to the initial financing statement to which the record relates and the date [and time] that the record was filed [or recorded]; or

(B) if the filing office is described in Section 9–501(a)(2), by the file number assigned to the initial financing statement to which the record relates; and

(2) to associate and retrieve with one another an initial financing statement and each filed record relating to the initial financing statement.

[END OF ALTERNATIVES]

(g) **[Removal of debtor's name.]** The filing office may not remove a debtor's name from the index until one year after the effectiveness of a financing statement naming the debtor lapses under Section 9–515 with respect to all secured parties of record.

(h) **[Timeliness of filing office performance.]** The filing office shall perform the acts required by subsections (a) through (e) at the time and in the manner prescribed by filing-office rule, but not later than two business days after the filing office receives the record in question.

[(i) **[Inapplicability to real-property-related filing office.]** Subsection[s] [(b)] [and] [(h)] do[es] not apply to a filing office described in Section 9–501(a)(1).]

Legislative Notes:

1. States whose filing offices currently assign file numbers that include a verification number, commonly known as a "check digit," or can implement this requirement before the effective date of this Article should omit the bracketed language in subsection (b).

2. In States in which writings will not appear in the real property records and indices unless actually recorded the bracketed language in subsection (d) should be used.

3. States whose real-estate filing offices require additional information in amendments and cannot search their records by both the name of the debtor and the file number should enact Alternative B to Sections 9–512(a), 9–518(b), 9–518(d), 9–519(f) and 9–522(a).

4. A State that elects not to require real-estate filing offices to comply with either or both of subsections (b) and (h) may adopt an applicable variation of subsection (i) and add "Except as otherwise provided in subsection (i)," to the appropriate subsection or subsections.

As amended in 2010.

Official Comment

1. **Source.** Former Sections 9–403(4), (7), 9–405(2).

2. **Filing Office's Duties.** Subsections (a) through (e) set forth the duties of the filing office with respect to filed records. Subsection (h), which is new, imposes a minimum standard of performance for those duties. Prompt indexing is crucial to the effectiveness of any filing system. An accepted but un-indexed record affords no public notice. Subsection (f) requires the filing office to maintain appropriate storage and retrieval facilities, and subsection (g) contains minimum requirements for the retention of records.

3. **File Number.** Subsection (a)(1) requires the filing office to assign a unique number to each filed record. That number is the "file number" only if the record is an initial financing statement. See Section 9–102.

4. **Time of Filing.** Subsection (a)(2) and Section 9–523 refer to the "date and time" of filing. The statutory text does not contain any instructions to a filing office as to how the time of filing is to be determined. The method of determining or assigning a time of filing is an appropriate matter for filing-office rules to address.

5. **Related Records.** Subsections (c) and (f) are designed to ensure that an initial financing statement and all filed records relating to it are associated with one another, indexed under the name of the debtor, and retrieved together. To comply with subsection (f), a filing office (other than a real-property recording office in a State that enacts subsection (f), Alternative B) must be capable of retrieving records in each of two ways: by the name of the debtor and by the file number of the initial financing statement to which the record relates.

6. **Prohibition on Deleting Names from Index.** This Article contemplates that the filing office will not delete the name of a debtor from the index until at least one year passes after the effectiveness of the financing statement lapses as to all secured parties of record. See subsection (g). This rule applies even if the filing office accepts an amendment purporting to delete or modify the name of a debtor or terminate the effectiveness of the financing statement. If an amendment provides a modified name for a debtor, the amended name should be added to the index, see subsection (c)(2), but the pre-amendment name should remain in the index.

Compared to former Article 9, the rule in subsection (g) increases the amount of information available to those who search the public records. The rule also contemplates that searchers—not the filing office—will determine the significance and effectiveness of filed records.

§ 9–520.   Acceptance and Refusal to Accept Record.

(a)   **[Mandatory refusal to accept record.]** A filing office shall refuse to accept a record for filing for a reason set forth in Section 9–516(b) and may refuse to accept a record for filing only for a reason set forth in Section 9–516(b).

(b)   **[Communication concerning refusal.]** If a filing office refuses to accept a record for filing, it shall communicate to the person that presented the record the fact of and reason for the refusal and the date and time the record would have been filed had the filing office accepted it. The communication must be made at the time and in the manner prescribed by filing-office rule but [, in the case of a filing office described in Section 9–501(a)(2),] in no event more than two business days after the filing office receives the record.

(c)   **[When filed financing statement effective.]** A filed financing statement satisfying Section 9–502(a) and (b) is effective, even if the filing office is required to refuse to accept it for filing under subsection (a). However, Section 9–338 applies to a filed financing statement providing information described in Section 9–516(b)(5) which is incorrect at the time the financing statement is filed.

(d)   **[Separate application to multiple debtors.]** If a record communicated to a filing office provides information that relates to more than one debtor, this part applies as to each debtor separately.

Legislative Note: A State that elects not to require real-property filing offices to comply with subsection (b) should include the bracketed language.

Official Comment

1. **Source.** New.

2. **Refusal to Accept Record for Filing.** In some States, filing offices considered themselves obligated by former Article 9 to review the form and content of a financing statement and to refuse to accept those that they determine are legally insufficient. Some filing offices imposed requirements for or conditions to filing that do not appear in the statute. Under this section, the filing office is not expected to make legal judgments and is not permitted to impose additional conditions or requirements.

Subsection (a) both prescribes and limits the bases upon which the filing office must and may reject records by reference to the reasons set forth in Section 9–516(b). For the most part, the bases for rejection are limited to those that prevent the filing office from dealing with a record that it receives—because some of the requisite information (e.g., the debtor's name) is missing or cannot be deciphered, because the record is not communicated by a method (e.g., it is MIME-rather than UU-encoded) or medium (e.g., it is written rather than electronic) that the filing office accepts, or because the filer fails to tender an amount equal to or greater than the filing fee.

3. **Consequences of Accepting Rejectable Record.** Section 9–516(b) includes among the reasons for rejecting an initial financing statement the failure to give certain information that is not required as a condition of effectiveness. In conjunction with Section 9–516(b)(5), this section requires the filing office to refuse to accept a financing statement that is legally sufficient to perfect a security interest under Section 9–502 but does not contain a mailing address for the debtor or disclose whether the debtor is an individual or an organization. The information required by Section 9–516(b)(5) assists searchers in weeding out "false positives," i.e., records that a search reveals but which do not pertain to the debtor in question. It assists filers by helping to ensure that the debtor's name is correct and that the financing statement is filed in the proper jurisdiction.

If the filing office accepts a financing statement that does not give this information at all, the filing is fully effective. Section 9–520(c). The financing statement also generally is effective if the information is given but is incorrect; however, Section 9–338 affords protection to buyers and holders of perfected security interests who gives value in reasonable reliance upon the incorrect information.

4. **Filing Office's Duties with Respect to Rejected Record.** Subsection (b) requires the filing office to communicate the fact of rejection and the reason therefor within a fixed period of time. Inasmuch as a rightfully rejected record is ineffective and a wrongfully rejected record is not fully effective, prompt communication concerning any rejection is important.

5. **Partial Effectiveness of Record.** Under subsection (d), the provisions of this Part apply to each debtor separately. Thus, a filing office may reject an initial financing statement or other record as to one named debtor but accept it as to the other.

Example: An initial financing statement is communicated to the filing office. The financing statement names two debtors, John Smith and Jane Smith. It contains all of the information described in Section 9–516(b)(5) with respect to John but lacks some of the information with respect to Jane. The filing office must accept the financing statement with respect to John, reject it with respect to Jane, and notify the filer of the rejection.

As amended in 2010.

§ 9–521.   Uniform Form of Written Financing Statement and Amendment.

(a) **[Initial financing statement form.]** A filing office that accepts written records may not refuse to accept a written initial financing statement in the following form and format except for a reason set forth in Section 9–516(b):

UCC FINANCING STATEMENT
FOLLOW INSTRUCTIONS

A. NAME & PHONE OF CONTACT AT FILER (optional)

B. E-MAIL CONTACT AT FILER (optional)

C. SEND ACKNOWLEDGMENT TO: (Name and Address)

THE ABOVE SPACE IS FOR FILING OFFICE USE ONLY

1. DEBTOR'S NAME: Provide only one Debtor name (1a or 1b) (use exact, full name; do not omit, modify, or abbreviate any part of the Debtor's name); if any part of the Individual Debtor's name will not fit in line 1b, leave all of item 1 blank, check here ☐ and provide the Individual Debtor information in item 10 of the Financing Statement Addendum (Form UCC1Ad)

1a. ORGANIZATION'S NAME			

OR

1b. INDIVIDUAL'S SURNAME	FIRST PERSONAL NAME	ADDITIONAL NAME(S)/INITIAL(S)	SUFFIX

1c. MAILING ADDRESS	CITY	STATE	POSTAL CODE	COUNTRY

2. DEBTOR'S NAME: Provide only one Debtor name (2a or 2b) (use exact, full name; do not omit, modify, or abbreviate any part of the Debtor's name); if any part of the Individual Debtor's name will not fit in line 2b, leave all of item 2 blank, check here ☐ and provide the Individual Debtor information in item 10 of the Financing Statement Addendum (Form UCC1Ad)

2a. ORGANIZATION'S NAME			

OR

2b. INDIVIDUAL'S SURNAME	FIRST PERSONAL NAME	ADDITIONAL NAME(S)/INITIAL(S)	SUFFIX

2c. MAILING ADDRESS	CITY	STATE	POSTAL CODE	COUNTRY

3. SECURED PARTY'S NAME (or NAME of ASSIGNEE of ASSIGNOR SECURED PARTY) Provide only one Secured Party name (3a or 3b)

3a. ORGANIZATION'S NAME			

OR

3b. INDIVIDUAL'S SURNAME	FIRST PERSONAL NAME	ADDITIONAL NAME(S)/INITIAL(S)	SUFFIX

3c. MAILING ADDRESS	CITY	STATE	POSTAL CODE	COUNTRY

4. COLLATERAL: This financing statement covers the following collateral

5. Check only if applicable and check only one box: Collateral is ☐ held in a Trust (see UCC1Ad, item 17 and Instructions) ☐ being administered by a Decedent's Personal Representative

6a. Check only if applicable and check only one box   **6b.** Check only if applicable and check only one box

☐ Public-Finance Transaction ☐ Manufactured-Home Transaction ☐ A Debtor is a Transmitting Utility   ☐ Agricultural Lien ☐ Non-UCC Filing

7. ALTERNATIVE DESIGNATION (if applicable): ☐ Lessee/Lessor ☐ Consignee/Consignor ☐ Seller/Buyer ☐ Bailee/Bailor ☐ Licensee/Licensor

8. OPTIONAL FILER REFERENCE DATA:

UCC FINANCING STATEMENT (Form UCC1) (Rev. 04/20/11)

UCC FINANCING STATEMENT ADDENDUM
FOLLOW INSTRUCTIONS

9. NAME OF FIRST DEBTOR: Same as line 1a or 1b on Financing Statement; if line 1b was left blank because Individual Debtor name did not fit, check here ☐

9a. ORGANIZATION'S NAME	

OR

9b. INDIVIDUAL'S SURNAME	
FIRST PERSONAL NAME	
ADDITIONAL NAME(S)/INITIAL(S)	SUFFIX

THE ABOVE SPACE IS FOR FILING OFFICE USE ONLY

10. DEBTOR'S NAME Provide (10a or 10b) only *one* additional Debtor name or Debtor name that did not fit in line 1b or 2b of the Financing Statement (Form UCC1) (use exact, full name; do not omit, modify, or abbreviate any part of the Debtor's name) and enter the mailing address in line 10c

10a. ORGANIZATION'S NAME				

OR

10b. INDIVIDUAL'S SURNAME				
INDIVIDUAL'S FIRST PERSONAL NAME				
INDIVIDUAL'S ADDITIONAL NAME(S)/INITIAL(S)				SUFFIX

10c. MAILING ADDRESS	CITY	STATE	POSTAL CODE	COUNTRY

11. ☐ **ADDITIONAL SECURED PARTY'S NAME** or ☐ **ASSIGNOR SECURED PARTY'S NAME:** Provide only *one* name (11a or 11b)

11a. ORGANIZATION'S NAME			

OR

11b. INDIVIDUAL'S SURNAME	FIRST PERSONAL NAME	ADDITIONAL NAME(S)/INITIAL(S)	SUFFIX
11c. MAILING ADDRESS	CITY	STATE	POSTAL CODE	COUNTRY

12. ADDITIONAL SPACE FOR ITEM 4 (Collateral)

13. ☐ This FINANCING STATEMENT is to be filed [for record] [or recorded] in the REAL ESTATE RECORDS (if applicable)	14. This FINANCING STATEMENT: ☐ covers timber to be cut ☐ covers as-extracted collateral ☐ is filed as a fixture filing
15. Name and address of a RECORD OWNER of real estate described in item 16 (if Debtor does not have a record interest)	16. Description of real estate:

17. MISCELLANEOUS:

UCC FINANCING STATEMENT ADDENDUM (Form UCC1Ad) (Rev. 04/20/11)

(b) [Amendment form.] A filing office that accepts written records may not refuse to accept a written record in the following form and format except for a reason set forth in Section 9–516(b):

UCC FINANCING STATEMENT AMENDMENT
FOLLOW INSTRUCTIONS

A. NAME & PHONE OF CONTACT AT FILER (optional)

B. E-MAIL CONTACT AT FILER (optional)

C. SEND ACKNOWLEDGMENT TO: (Name and Address)

THE ABOVE SPACE IS FOR FILING OFFICE USE ONLY

1a. INITIAL FINANCING STATEMENT FILE NUMBER

1b. ☐ This FINANCING STATEMENT AMENDMENT is to be filed [for record] (or recorded) in the REAL ESTATE RECORDS
Filer: attach Amendment Addendum (Form UCC3Ad) and provide Debtor's name in item 13

2. ☐ **TERMINATION:** Effectiveness of the Financing Statement identified above is terminated with respect to the security interest(s) of Secured Party authorizing this Termination Statement

3. ☐ **ASSIGNMENT** (full or partial): Provide name of Assignee in item 7a or 7b, and address of Assignee in item 7c and name of Assignor in item 9
For partial assignment, complete items 7 and 8 and also indicate affected collateral in item 8

4. ☐ **CONTINUATION:** Effectiveness of the Financing Statement identified above with respect to the security interest(s) of Secured Party authorizing this Continuation Statement is continued for the additional period provided by applicable law

5. ☐ **PARTY INFORMATION CHANGE:**

Check one of these two boxes   **AND** Check one of these three boxes to:

This Change affects ☐ Debtor or ☐ Secured Party of record   ☐ CHANGE name and/or address: Complete item 6a or 6b; and item 7a or 7b and item 7c   ☐ ADD name: Complete item 7a or 7b, and item 7c   ☐ DELETE name: Give record name to be deleted in item 6a or 6b

6. **CURRENT RECORD INFORMATION:** Complete for Party Information Change - provide only one name (6a or 6b)

6a. ORGANIZATION'S NAME

OR 6b. INDIVIDUAL'S SURNAME | FIRST PERSONAL NAME | ADDITIONAL NAME(S)/INITIAL(S) | SUFFIX

7. **CHANGED OR ADDED INFORMATION:** Complete for Assignment or Party Information Change - provide only one name (7a or 7b) (use exact, full name; do not omit, modify, or abbreviate any part of the Debtor's name)

7a. ORGANIZATION'S NAME

OR 7b. INDIVIDUAL'S SURNAME

INDIVIDUAL'S FIRST PERSONAL NAME

INDIVIDUAL'S ADDITIONAL NAME(S)/INITIAL(S) | SUFFIX

7c. MAILING ADDRESS | CITY | STATE | POSTAL CODE | COUNTRY

8. ☐ **COLLATERAL CHANGE:** Also check one of these four boxes: ☐ ADD collateral ☐ DELETE collateral ☐ RESTATE covered collateral ☐ ASSIGN collateral
Indicate collateral:

9. **NAME** OF SECURED PARTY OF RECORD AUTHORIZING THIS AMENDMENT: Provide only one name (9a or 9b) (name of Assignor, if this is an Assignment)
If this is an Amendment authorized by a DEBTOR, check here ☐ and provide name of authorizing Debtor

9a. ORGANIZATION'S NAME

OR 9b. INDIVIDUAL'S SURNAME | FIRST PERSONAL NAME | ADDITIONAL NAME(S)/INITIAL(S) | SUFFIX

10. OPTIONAL FILER REFERENCE DATA:

UCC FINANCING STATEMENT AMENDMENT (Form UCC3) (Rev. 04/20/11)

UCC FINANCING STATEMENT AMENDMENT ADDENDUM
FOLLOW INSTRUCTIONS

11. INITIAL FINANCING STATEMENT FILE NUMBER: Same as item 1a on Amendment form

12. NAME OF PARTY AUTHORIZING THIS AMENDMENT: Same as item 9 on Amendment form

12a. ORGANIZATION'S NAME

OR 12b. INDIVIDUAL'S SURNAME

FIRST PERSONAL NAME

ADDITIONAL NAME(S)/INITIAL(S)   SUFFIX

THE ABOVE SPACE IS FOR FILING OFFICE USE ONLY

13. Name of DEBTOR on related financing statement (Name of a current Debtor of record required for indexing purposes only in some filing offices - see Instruction item 13): Provide only one Debtor name (13a or 13b) (use exact, full name; do not omit, modify, or abbreviate any part of the Debtor's name); see instructions if name does not fit

13a. ORGANIZATION'S NAME

OR 13b. INDIVIDUAL'S SURNAME   FIRST PERSONAL NAME   ADDITIONAL NAME(S)/INITIAL(S)   SUFFIX

14. ADDITIONAL SPACE FOR ITEM 8 (Collateral):

15. This FINANCING STATEMENT AMENDMENT:
☐ covers timber to be cut   ☐ covers as-extracted collateral   ☐ is filed as a fixture filing

16. Name and address of a RECORD OWNER of real estate described in item 17 (if Debtor does not have a record interest):

17. Description of real estate:

18. MISCELLANEOUS:

UCC FINANCING STATEMENT AMENDMENT ADDENDUM (Form UCC3Ad) (Rev. 04/20/11)

As amended in 2010.

Official Comment

1. **Source.** New.

2. **"Safe Harbor" Written Forms.** Although Section 9–520 limits the bases upon which the filing office can refuse to accept records, this section provides sample written forms that must be accepted in every filing office in the country, as long as the filing office's rules permit it to accept written communications. By completing one of the forms in this section, a secured party can be certain that the filing office is obligated to accept it.

The forms in this section are based upon national financing statement forms that were in use under former Article 9. Those forms were developed over an extended period and reflect the comments and suggestions of filing officers, secured parties and their counsel, and service companies. The formatting of those forms and of the ones in this section has been designed to reduce error by both filers and filing offices.

A filing office that accepts written communications may not reject, on grounds of form or format, a filing using these forms. Although filers are not required to use the forms, they are encouraged and can be expected to do so, inasmuch as the forms are well designed and avoid the risk of rejection on the basis of form or format. As their use expands, the forms will rapidly become familiar to both filers and filing-office personnel. Filing offices may and should encourage the use of these forms by declaring them to be the "standard" (but not exclusive) forms for each jurisdiction, albeit without in any way suggesting that alternative forms are unacceptable.

The multi-purpose form in subsection (b) covers changes with respect to the debtor, the secured party, the collateral, and the status of the financing statement (termination and continuation). A single form may be used for several different types of amendments at once (e.g., both to change a debtor's name and continue the effectiveness of the financing statement).

§ 9–522. Maintenance and Destruction of Records.

[ALTERNATIVE A]

(a) **[Post-lapse maintenance and retrieval of information.]** The filing office shall maintain a record of the information provided in a filed financing statement for at least one year after the effectiveness of the financing statement has lapsed under Section 9–515 with respect to all secured parties of record. The record must be retrievable by using the name of the debtor and by using the file number assigned to the initial financing statement to which the record relates.

[ALTERNATIVE B]

(a) **[Post-lapse maintenance and retrieval of information.]** The filing office shall maintain a record of the information provided in a filed financing statement for at least one year after the effectiveness of the financing statement has lapsed under Section 9–515 with respect to all secured parties of record. The record must be retrievable by using the name of the debtor and:

(1) if the record was filed [or recorded] in the filing office described in Section 9–501(a)(1), by using the file number assigned to the initial financing statement to which the record relates and the date [and time] that the record was filed [or recorded]; or

(2) if the record was filed in the filing office described in Section 9–501(a)(2), by using the file number assigned to the initial financing statement to which the record relates.

[END OF ALTERNATIVES]

(b) **[Destruction of written records.]** Except to the extent that a statute governing disposition of public records provides otherwise, the filing office immediately may destroy any written record evidencing a financing statement. However, if the filing office destroys a written record, it shall maintain another record of the financing statement which complies with subsection (a).

Legislative Note: States whose real-estate filing offices require additional information in amendments and cannot search their records by both the name of the debtor and the file number should enact Alternative B to Sections 9–512(a), 9–518(b), 9–518(d), 9–519(f) and 9–522(a).

As amended in 2010.

Official Comment

1. **Source.** Former Section 9–403(3), revised substantially.

2. **Maintenance of Records.** Section 9–523 requires the filing office to provide information concerning certain lapsed financing statements. Accordingly, subsection (a) requires the filing office to maintain a record of the information in a financing statement for at least one year after lapse. During that time, the filing office may not delete any information with respect to a filed financing statement; it may only add information. This approach relieves the filing office from any duty to determine whether to substitute or delete information upon receipt of an amendment. It also assures searchers that they will receive all information with respect to financing statements filed against a debtor and thereby be able themselves to determine the state of the public record.

The filing office may maintain this information in any medium. Subsection (b) permits the filing office immediately to destroy written records evidencing a financing statement, provided that the filing office maintains another record of the information contained in the financing statement as required by subsection (a).

§ 9–523.   Information From Filing Office; Sale or License of Records.

(a)   **[Acknowledgment of filing written record.]** If a person that files a written record requests an acknowledgment of the filing, the filing office shall send to the person an image of the record showing the number assigned to the record pursuant to Section 9–519(a)(1) and the date and time of the filing of the record. However, if the person furnishes a copy of the record to the filing office, the filing office may instead:

(1)   note upon the copy the number assigned to the record pursuant to Section 9–519(a)(1) and the date and time of the filing of the record; and

(2)   send the copy to the person.

(b)   **[Acknowledgment of filing other record.]** If a person files a record other than a written record, the filing office shall communicate to the person an acknowledgment that provides:

(1)   the information in the record;

(2)   the number assigned to the record pursuant to Section 9–519(a)(1); and

(3)   the date and time of the filing of the record.

(c)   **[Communication of requested information.]** The filing office shall communicate or otherwise make available in a record the following information to any person that requests it:

(1)   whether there is on file on a date and time specified by the filing office, but not a date earlier than three business days before the filing office receives the request, any financing statement that:

(A)   designates a particular debtor [or, if the request so states, designates a particular debtor at the address specified in the request];

(B)   has not lapsed under Section 9–515 with respect to all secured parties of record; and

(C)   if the request so states, has lapsed under Section 9–515 and a record of which is maintained by the filing office under Section 9–522(a);

(2)   the date and time of filing of each financing statement; and

(3)   the information provided in each financing statement.

(d)   **[Medium for communicating information.]** In complying with its duty under subsection (c), the filing office may communicate information in any medium. However, if requested, the filing office shall communicate information by issuing [its written certificate] [a record that can be admitted into evidence in the courts of this State without extrinsic evidence of its authenticity].

(e)   **[Timeliness of filing office performance.]** The filing office shall perform the acts required by subsections (a) through (d) at the time and in the manner prescribed by filing-office rule, but not later than two business days after the filing office receives the request.

(f)   **[Public availability of records.]** At least weekly, the [insert appropriate official or governmental agency] [filing office] shall offer to sell or license to the public on a nonexclusive basis, in bulk, copies of all records filed in it under this part, in every medium from time to time available to the filing office.

Legislative Notes:

1.   *States whose filing office does not offer the additional service of responding to search requests limited to a particular address should omit the bracketed language in subsection (c)(1)(A).*

2.   *A State that elects not to require real-estate filing offices to comply with either or both of subsections (e) and (f) should specify in the appropriate subsection(s) only the filing office described in Section 9–501(a)(2).*

Official Comment

1. **Source.** Former Section 9–407; subsections (d) and (e) are new.

2. **Filing Office's Duty to Provide Information.** Former Section 9–407, dealing with obtaining information from the filing office, was bracketed to suggest to legislatures that its enactment was optional. Experience has shown that the method by which interested persons can obtain information concerning the public records should be uniform. Accordingly, the analogous provisions of this Article are not in brackets.

Most of the other changes from former Section 9–407 are for clarification, to embrace medium-neutral drafting, or to impose standards of performance on the filing office.

3. **Acknowledgments of Filing.** Subsections (a) and (b) require the filing office to acknowledge the filing of a record. Under subsection (a), the filing office is required to acknowledge the filing of a written record only upon request of the filer. Subsection (b) requires the filing office to acknowledge the filing of a non-written record even in the absence of a request from the filer.

4. **Response to Search Request.** Subsection (c)(3) requires the filing office to provide "the information contained in each financing statement" to a person who requests it. This requirement can be satisfied by providing copies, images, or reports. The requirement does not in any manner inhibit the filing office from also offering to provide less than all of the information (presumably for a lower fee) to a person who asks for less. Thus, subsection (c) accommodates the practice of providing only the type of record (e.g., initial financing statement, continuation statement), number assigned to the record, date and time of filing, and names and addresses of the debtor and secured party when a requesting person asks for no more (i.e., when the person does not ask for copies of financing statements). In contrast, the filing office's obligation under subsection (b) to provide an acknowledgment containing "the information contained in the record" is not defined by a customer's request. Thus unless the filer stipulates otherwise, to comply with subsection (b) the filing office's acknowledgment must contain all of the information in a record.

Subsection (c) assures that a minimum amount of information about filed records will be available to the public. It does not preclude a filing office from offering additional services.

5. **Lapsed and Terminated Financing Statements.** This section reflects the policy that terminated financing statements will remain part of the filing office's data base. The filing office may remove from the data base only lapsed financing statements, and then only when at least a year has passed after lapse. See Section 9–519(g). Subsection (c)(1)(C) requires a filing office to conduct a search and report as to lapsed financing statements that have not been removed from the data base, when requested.

6. **Search by Debtor's Address.** Subsection (c)(1)(A) contemplates that, by making a single request, a searcher will receive the results of a search of the entire public record maintained by any given filing office. Addition of the bracketed language in subsection (c)(1)(A) would permit a search report limited to financing statements showing a particular address for the debtor, but only if the search request is so limited. With or without the bracketed language, this subsection does not permit the filing office to compel a searcher to limit a request by address.

7. **Medium of Communication; Certificates.** Former Article 9 provided that the filing office respond to a request for information by providing a certificate. The principle of medium-neutrality would suggest that the statute not require a written certificate. Subsection (d) follows this principle by permitting the filing office to respond by communicating "in any medium." By permitting communication "in any medium," subsection (d) is not inconsistent with a system in which persons other than filing office staff conduct searches of the filing office's (computer) records.

Some searchers find it necessary to introduce the results of their search into evidence. Because official written certificates might be introduced into evidence more easily than official communications in another medium, subsection (d) affords States the option of requiring the filing office to issue written certificates upon request. The alternative bracketed language in subsection (d) recognizes that some States may prefer to permit the filing office to respond in another medium, as long as the response can be admitted into evidence in the courts of that State without extrinsic evidence of its authenticity.

8. **Performance Standard.** The utility of the filing system depends on the ability of searchers to get current information quickly. Accordingly, subsection (e) requires that the filing office respond to a request for information no later than two business days after it receives the request. The information contained in the response must be current as of a date no earlier than three business days before the filing office receives the

request. See subsection (c)(1). The failure of the filing office to comply with performance standards, such as subsection (e), has no effect on the private rights of persons affected by the filing of records.

9.   **Sales of Records in Bulk.** Subsection (f), which is new, mandates that the appropriate official or the filing office sell or license the filing records to the public in bulk, on a nonexclusive basis, in every medium available to the filing office. The details of implementation are left to filing-office rules.

§ 9–524.   Delay by Filing Office.

Delay by the filing office beyond a time limit prescribed by this part is excused if:

(1)   the delay is caused by interruption of communication or computer facilities, war, emergency conditions, failure of equipment, or other circumstances beyond control of the filing office; and

(2)   the filing office exercises reasonable diligence under the circumstances.

Official Comment

Source. New; derived from Section 4–109.

§ 9–525.   Fees.

(a)   **[Initial financing statement or other record: general rule.]** Except as otherwise provided in subsection (e), the fee for filing and indexing a record under this part, other than an initial financing statement of the kind described in subsection (b), is [the amount specified in subsection (c), if applicable, plus]:

(1) $[X] if the record is communicated in writing and consists of one or two pages;

(2) $[2X] if the record is communicated in writing and consists of more than two pages; and

(3) $[½X] if the record is communicated by another medium authorized by filing-office rule.

(b)   **[Initial financing statement: public-finance and manufactured-housing transactions.]** Except as otherwise provided in subsection (e), the fee for filing and indexing an initial financing statement of the following kind is [the amount specified in subsection (c), if applicable, plus]:

(1) $_____ if the financing statement indicates that it is filed in connection with a public-finance transaction;

(2) $_____ if the financing statement indicates that it is filed in connection with a manufactured-home transaction.

[ALTERNATIVE A]

(c)   **[Number of names.]** The number of names required to be indexed does not affect the amount of the fee in subsections (a) and (b).

[ALTERNATIVE B]

(c)   **[Number of names.]** Except as otherwise provided in subsection (e), if a record is communicated in writing, the fee for each name more than two required to be indexed is $_____.

[END OF ALTERNATIVES]

(d)   **[Response to information request.]** The fee for responding to a request for information from the filing office, including for [issuing a certificate showing] [communicating] whether there is on file any financing statement naming a particular debtor, is:

(1) $_____ if the request is communicated in writing; and

(2) $_____ if the request is communicated by another medium authorized by filing-office rule.

(e)   **[Record of mortgage.]** This section does not require a fee with respect to a record of a mortgage which is effective as a financing statement filed as a fixture filing or as a financing statement covering as-extracted collateral or timber to be cut under Section 9–502(c). However, the recording and satisfaction fees that otherwise would be applicable to the record of the mortgage apply.

Legislative Notes:

1. To preserve uniformity, a State that places the provisions of this section together with statutes setting fees for other services should do so without modification.

2. A State should enact subsection (c), Alternative A, and omit the bracketed language in subsections (a) and (b) unless its indexing system entails a substantial additional cost when indexing additional names.

As amended in 2000.

Official Comment

1. **Source.** Various sections of former Part 4.

2. **Fees.** This section contains all fee requirements for filing, indexing, and responding to requests for information. Uniformity in the fee structure (but not necessarily in the amount of fees) makes this Article easier for secured parties to use and reduces the likelihood that a filed record will be rejected for failure to pay at least the correct amount of the fee. See Section 9–516(b)(2).

The costs of processing electronic records are less than those with respect to written records. Accordingly, this section mandates a lower fee as an incentive to file electronically and imposes the additional charge (if any) for multiple debtors only with respect to written records. When written records are used, this Article encourages the use of the uniform forms in Section 9–521. The fee for filing these forms should be no greater than the fee for other written records.

To make the relevant information included in a filed record more accessible once the record is found, this section mandates a higher fee for longer written records than for shorter ones. Finally, recognizing that financing statements naming more than one debtor are most often filed against a husband and wife, any additional charge for multiple debtors applies to records filed with respect to more than two debtors, rather than with respect to more than one.

§ 9–526.   Filing-Office Rules.

(a)   **[Adoption of filing-office rules.]** The [insert appropriate governmental official or agency] shall adopt and publish rules to implement this article. The filing-office rules must be[:

(1)]   consistent with this article[; and

(2)   adopted and published in accordance with the [insert any applicable state administrative procedure act]].

(b)   **[Harmonization of rules.]** To keep the filing-office rules and practices of the filing office in harmony with the rules and practices of filing offices in other jurisdictions that enact substantially this part, and to keep the technology used by the filing office compatible with the technology used by filing offices in other jurisdictions that enact substantially this part, the [insert appropriate governmental official or agency], so far as is consistent with the purposes, policies, and provisions of this article, in adopting, amending, and repealing filing-office rules, shall:

(1)   consult with filing offices in other jurisdictions that enact substantially this part; and

(2)   consult the most recent version of the Model Rules promulgated by the International Association of Corporate Administrators or any successor organization; and

(3)   take into consideration the rules and practices of, and the technology used by, filing offices in other jurisdictions that enact substantially this part.

Official Comment

1.   **Source.** New; subsection (b) derives in part from the Uniform Consumer Credit Code (1974).

2.   **Rules Required.** Operating a filing office is a complicated business, requiring many more rules and procedures than this Article can usefully provide. Subsection (a) requires the adoption of rules to carry out the provisions of Article 9. The filing-office rules must be consistent with the provisions of the statute and adopted in accordance with local procedures. The publication requirement informs secured parties about filing-office practices, aids secured parties in evaluating filing-related risks and costs, and promotes regularity of application within the filing office.

3. **Importance of Uniformity.** In today's national economy, uniformity of the policies and practices of the filing offices will reduce the costs of secured transactions substantially. The International Association of Corporate Administrators (IACA), referred to in subsection (b), is an organization whose membership includes filing officers from every State. These individuals are responsible for the proper functioning of the Article 9 filing system and have worked diligently to develop model filing-office rules, with a view toward efficiency and uniformity.

Although uniformity is an important desideratum, subsection (a) affords considerable flexibility in the adoption of filing-office rules. Each State may adopt a version of subsection (a) that reflects the desired relationship between the statewide filing office described in Section 9–501(a)(2) and the local filing offices described in Section 9–501(a)(1) and that takes into account the practices of its filing offices. Subsection (a) need not designate a single official or agency to adopt rules applicable to all filing offices, and the rules applicable to the statewide filing office need not be identical to those applicable to the local filing office. For example, subsection (a) might provide for the statewide filing office to adopt filing-office rules, and, if not prohibited by other law, the filing office might adopt one set of rules for itself and another for local offices. Or, subsection (a) might designate one official or agency to adopt rules for the statewide filing office and another to adopt rules for local filing offices.

§ 9–527.   Duty to Report.

The [insert appropriate governmental official or agency] shall report [annually on or before _____] to the [Governor and Legislature] on the operation of the filing office. The report must contain a statement of the extent to which:

(1)   the filing-office rules are not in harmony with the rules of filing offices in other jurisdictions that enact substantially this part and the reasons for these variations; and

(2)   the filing-office rules are not in harmony with the most recent version of the Model Rules promulgated by the International Association of Corporate Administrators, or any successor organization, and the reasons for these variations.

Official Comment

1. **Source.** New; derived in part from the Uniform Consumer Credit Code (1974).

2. **Duty to Report.** This section is designed to promote compliance with the standards of performance imposed upon the filing office and with the requirement that the filing office's policies, practices, and technology be consistent and compatible with the policies, practices, and technology of other filing offices.

PART 6

DEFAULT

[SUBPART 1. DEFAULT AND ENFORCEMENT OF SECURITY INTEREST]

§ 9–601.   Rights After Default; Judicial Enforcement; Consignor or Buyer of Accounts, Chattel Paper, Payment Intangibles, or Promissory Notes.

(a)   **[Rights of secured party after default.]** After default, a secured party has the rights provided in this part and, except as otherwise provided in Section 9–602, those provided by agreement of the parties. A secured party:

(1)   may reduce a claim to judgment, foreclose, or otherwise enforce the claim, security interest, or agricultural lien by any available judicial procedure; and

(2)   if the collateral is documents, may proceed either as to the documents or as to the goods they cover.

(b)   **[Rights and duties of secured party in possession or control.]** A secured party in possession of collateral or control of collateral under Section 7–106, 9–104, 9–105, 9–106, or 9–107 has the rights and duties provided in Section 9–207.

(c)   **[Rights cumulative; simultaneous exercise.]** The rights under subsections (a) and (b) are cumulative and may be exercised simultaneously.

(d) **[Rights of debtor and obligor.]** Except as otherwise provided in subsection (g) and Section 9–605, after default, a debtor and an obligor have the rights provided in this part and by agreement of the parties.

(e) **[Lien of levy after judgment.]** If a secured party has reduced its claim to judgment, the lien of any levy that may be made upon the collateral by virtue of an execution based upon the judgment relates back to the earliest of:

(1) the date of perfection of the security interest or agricultural lien in the collateral;

(2) the date of filing a financing statement covering the collateral; or

(3) any date specified in a statute under which the agricultural lien was created.

(f) **[Execution sale.]** A sale pursuant to an execution is a foreclosure of the security interest or agricultural lien by judicial procedure within the meaning of this section. A secured party may purchase at the sale and thereafter hold the collateral free of any other requirements of this article.

(g) **[Consignor or buyer of certain rights to payment.]** Except as otherwise provided in Section 9–607(c), this part imposes no duties upon a secured party that is a consignor or is a buyer of accounts, chattel paper, payment intangibles, or promissory notes.

As amended in 2003.

Official Comment

1. **Source.** Former Section 9–501(1), (2), (5).

2. **Enforcement: In General.** The rights of a secured party to enforce its security interest in collateral after the debtor's default are an important feature of a secured transaction. (Note that the term "rights," as defined in Section 1–201, includes "remedies.") This Part provides those rights as well as certain limitations on their exercise for the protection of the defaulting debtor, other creditors, and other affected persons. However, subsections (a) and (d) make clear that the rights provided in this Part do not exclude other rights provided by agreement.

3. **When Remedies Arise.** Under subsection (a) the secured party's rights arise "[a]fter default." As did former Section 9–501, this Article leaves to the agreement of the parties the circumstances giving rise to a default. This Article does not determine whether a secured party's post-default conduct can constitute a waiver of default in the face of an agreement stating that such conduct shall not constitute a waiver. Rather, it continues to leave to the parties' agreement, as supplemented by law other than this Article, the determination whether a default has occurred or has been waived. See Section 1–103.

4. **Possession of Collateral; Section 9–207.** After a secured party takes possession of collateral following a default, there is no longer any distinction between a security interest that before default was nonpossessory and a security interest that was possessory before default, as under a common-law pledge. This Part generally does not distinguish between the rights of a secured party with a nonpossessory security interest and those of a secured party with a possessory security interest. However, Section 9–207 addresses rights and duties with respect to collateral in a secured party's possession. Under subsection (b) of this section, Section 9–207 applies not only to possession before default but also to possession after default. Subsection (b) also has been conformed to Section 9–207, which, unlike former Section 9–207, applies to secured parties having control of collateral.

5. **Cumulative Remedies.** Former Section 9–501(1) provided that the secured party's remedies were cumulative, but it did not explicitly provide whether the remedies could be exercised simultaneously. Subsection (c) permits the simultaneous exercise of remedies if the secured party acts in good faith. The liability scheme of Subpart 2 affords redress to an aggrieved debtor or obligor. Moreover, permitting the simultaneous exercise of remedies under subsection (c) does not override any non-UCC law, including the law of tort and statutes regulating collection of debts, under which the simultaneous exercise of remedies in a particular case constitutes abusive behavior or harassment giving rise to liability.

6. **Judicial Enforcement.** Under subsection (a) a secured party may reduce its claim to judgment or foreclose its interest by any available procedure outside this Article under applicable law. Subsection (e) generally follows former Section 9–501(5). It makes clear that any judicial lien that the secured party may acquire against the collateral effectively is a continuation of the original security interest (if perfected) and not the acquisition of a new interest or a transfer of property on account of a preexisting obligation. Under former Section 9–501(5), the

judicial lien was stated to relate back to the date of perfection of the security interest. Subsection (e), however, provides that the lien relates back to the earlier of the date of filing or the date of perfection. This provides a secured party who enforces a security interest by judicial process with the benefit of the "first-to-file-or-perfect" priority rule of Section 9–322(a)(1).

7. **Agricultural Liens.** Part 6 provides parallel treatment for the enforcement of agricultural liens and security interests. Because agricultural liens are statutory rather than consensual, this Article does draw a few distinctions between these liens and security interests. Under subsection (e), the statute creating an agricultural lien would govern whether and the date to which an execution lien relates back. Section 9–606 explains when a "default" occurs in the agricultural lien context.

8. **Execution Sales.** Subsection (f) also follows former Section 9–501(5). It makes clear that an execution sale is an appropriate method of foreclosure contemplated by this Part. However, the sale is governed by other law and not by this Article, and the limitations under Section 9–610 on the right of a secured party to purchase collateral do not apply.

9. **Sales of Receivables; Consignments.** Subsection (g) provides that, except as provided in Section 9–607(c), the duties imposed on secured parties do not apply to buyers of accounts, chattel paper, payment intangibles, or promissory notes. Although denominated "secured parties," these buyers own the entire interest in the property sold and so may enforce their rights without regard to the seller ("debtor") or the seller's creditors. Likewise, a true consignor may enforce its ownership interest under other law without regard to the duties that this Part imposes on secured parties. Note, however, that Section 9–615 governs cases in which a consignee's secured party (other than a consignor) is enforcing a security interest that is senior to the security interest (i.e., ownership interest) of a true consignor.

§ 9–602. Waiver and Variance of Rights and Duties.

Except as otherwise provided in Section 9–624, to the extent that they give rights to a debtor or obligor and impose duties on a secured party, the debtor or obligor may not waive or vary the rules stated in the following listed sections:

(1) Section 9–207(b)(4)(C), which deals with use and operation of the collateral by the secured party;

(2) Section 9–210, which deals with requests for an accounting and requests concerning a list of collateral and statement of account;

(3) Section 9–607(c), which deals with collection and enforcement of collateral;

(4) Sections 9–608(a) and 9–615(c) to the extent that they deal with application or payment of noncash proceeds of collection, enforcement, or disposition;

(5) Sections 9–608(a) and 9–615(d) to the extent that they require accounting for or payment of surplus proceeds of collateral;

(6) Section 9–609 to the extent that it imposes upon a secured party that takes possession of collateral without judicial process the duty to do so without breach of the peace; *may waive right to notice 9-624*

(7) Sections 9–610(b), 9–611, 9–613, and 9–614, which deal with disposition of collateral;

(8) Section 9–615(f), which deals with calculation of a deficiency or surplus when a disposition is made to the secured party, a person related to the secured party, or a secondary obligor;

(9) Section 9–616, which deals with explanation of the calculation of a surplus or deficiency;

(10) Sections 9–620, 9–621, and 9–622, which deal with acceptance of collateral in satisfaction of obligation; *may waive right to require sale 9-629B*

(11) Section 9–623, which deals with redemption of collateral; *may not waive in consumer trans. 9-624*

(12) Section 9–624, which deals with permissible waivers; and

(13) Sections 9–625 and 9–626, which deal with the secured party's liability for failure to comply with this article.

Official Comment

1.   **Source.** Former Section 9–501(3).

2.   **Waiver: In General.** Section 1–102(3) [*unrevised Article 1; see Concordance, p. 22*] addresses which provisions of the UCC are mandatory and which may be varied by agreement. With exceptions relating to good faith, diligence, reasonableness, and care, immediate parties, as between themselves, may vary its provisions by agreement. However, in the context of rights and duties after default, our legal system traditionally has looked with suspicion on agreements that limit the debtor's rights and free the secured party of its duties. As stated in former Section 9–501, Comment 4, "no mortgage clause has ever been allowed to clog the equity of redemption." The context of default offers great opportunity for overreaching. The suspicious attitudes of the courts have been grounded in common sense. This section, like former Section 9–501(3), codifies this long-standing and deeply rooted attitude. The specified rights of the debtor and duties of the secured party may not be waived or varied except as stated. Provisions that are not specified in this section are subject to the general rules in Section 1–102(3) [*unrevised Article 1; see Concordance, p. 22*].

3.   **Nonwaivable Rights and Duties.** This section revises former Section 9–501(3) by restricting the ability to waive or modify additional specified rights and duties: (i) duties under Section 9–207(b)(4)(C), which deals with the use and operation of consumer goods, (ii) the right to a response to a request for an accounting, concerning a list of collateral, or concerning a statement of account (Section 9–210), (iii) the duty to collect collateral in a commercially reasonable manner (Section 9–607), (iv) the implicit duty to refrain from a breach of the peace in taking possession of collateral under Section 9–609, (v) the duty to apply noncash proceeds of collection or disposition in a commercially reasonable manner (Sections 9–608 and 9–615), (vi) the right to a special method of calculating a surplus or deficiency in certain dispositions to a secured party, a person related to secured party, or a secondary obligor (Section 9–615), (vii) the duty to give an explanation of the calculation of a surplus or deficiency (Section 9–616), (viii) the right to limitations on the effectiveness of certain waivers (Section 9–624), and (ix) the right to hold a secured party liable for failure to comply with this Article (Sections 9–625 and 9–626). For clarity and consistency, this Article uses the term "waive or vary" instead of "renounc[e] or modify[ ]," which appeared in former Section 9–504(3).

This section provides generally that the specified rights and duties "may not be waived or varied." However, it does not restrict the ability of parties to agree to settle, compromise, or renounce claims for past conduct that may have constituted a violation or breach of those rights and duties, even if the settlement involves an express "waiver."

Section 9–610(c) limits the circumstances under which a secured party may purchase at its own private disposition. Transactions of this kind are equivalent to "strict foreclosures" and are governed by Sections 9–620, 9–621, and 9–622. The provisions of these sections can be waived only to the extent provided in Section 9–624(b). See Section 9–602.

4.   **Waiver by Debtors and Obligors.** The restrictions on waiver contained in this section apply to obligors as well as debtors. This resolves a question under former Article 9 as to whether secondary obligors, assuming that they were "debtors" for purposes of former Part 5, were permitted to waive, under the law of suretyship, rights and duties under that Part.

5.   **Certain Post-Default Waivers.** Section 9–624 permits post-default waivers in limited circumstances. These waivers must be made in agreements that are authenticated. Under Section 1–201, an " 'agreement' means the bargain of the parties in fact." In considering waivers under Section 9–624 and analogous agreements in other contexts, courts should carefully scrutinize putative agreements that appear in records that also address many additional or unrelated matters.

As amended in 2010.

§ 9–603.   Agreement on Standards Concerning Rights and Duties.

(a)   **[Agreed standards.]** The parties may determine by agreement the standards measuring the fulfillment of the rights of a debtor or obligor and the duties of a secured party under a rule stated in Section 9–602 if the standards are not manifestly unreasonable.

(b)   **[Agreed standards inapplicable to breach of peace.]** Subsection (a) does not apply to the duty under Section 9–609 to refrain from breaching the peace.

1.   **Source.** Former Section 9–501(3).

2.   **Limitation on Ability to Set Standards.** Subsection (a), like former Section 9–501(3), permits the parties to set standards for compliance with the rights and duties under this Part if the standards are not "manifestly unreasonable." Under subsection (b), the parties are not permitted to set standards measuring fulfillment of the secured party's duty to take collateral without breaching the peace.

§ 9–604.   Procedure if Security Agreement Covers Real Property or Fixtures.

(a)   **[Enforcement: personal and real property.]** If a security agreement covers both personal and real property, a secured party may proceed:

(1)   under this part as to the personal property without prejudicing any rights with respect to the real property; or

(2)   as to both the personal property and the real property in accordance with the rights with respect to the real property, in which case the other provisions of this part do not apply.

(b)   **[Enforcement: fixtures.]** Subject to subsection (c), if a security agreement covers goods that are or become fixtures, a secured party may proceed:

(1)   under this part; or

(2)   in accordance with the rights with respect to real property, in which case the other provisions of this part do not apply.

(c)   **[Removal of fixtures.]** Subject to the other provisions of this part, if a secured party holding a security interest in fixtures has priority over all owners and encumbrancers of the real property, the secured party, after default, may remove the collateral from the real property.

(d)   **[Injury caused by removal.]** A secured party that removes collateral shall promptly reimburse any encumbrancer or owner of the real property, other than the debtor, for the cost of repair of any physical injury caused by the removal. The secured party need not reimburse the encumbrancer or owner for any diminution in value of the real property caused by the absence of the goods removed or by any necessity of replacing them. A person entitled to reimbursement may refuse permission to remove until the secured party gives adequate assurance for the performance of the obligation to reimburse.

1.   **Source.** Former Sections 9–501(4), 9–313(8).

2.   **Real-Property-Related Collateral.** The collateral in many transactions consists of both real and personal property. In the interest of simplicity, speed, and economy, subsection (a), like former Section 9–501(4), permits (but does not require) the secured party to proceed as to both real and personal property in accordance with its rights and remedies with respect to the real property. Subsection (a) also makes clear that a secured party who exercises rights under Part 6 with respect to personal property does not prejudice any rights under real-property law.

This Article does not address certain other real-property-related problems. In a number of States, the exercise of remedies by a creditor who is secured by both real property and non-real property collateral is governed by special legal rules. For example, under some anti-deficiency laws, creditors risk loss of rights against personal property collateral if they err in enforcing their rights against the real property. Under a "one-form-of-action" rule (or rule against splitting a cause of action), a creditor who judicially enforces a real property mortgage and does not proceed in the same action to enforce a security interest in personalty may (among other consequences) lose the right to proceed against the personalty. Although statutes of this kind create impediments to enforcement of security interests, this Article does not override these limitations under other law.

3.   **Fixtures.** Subsection (b) is new. It makes clear that a security interest in fixtures may be enforced either under real-property law or under any of the applicable provisions of Part 6, including sale or other disposition either before or after removal of the fixtures (see subsection (c)). Subsection (b) also serves to overrule cases holding that a secured party's only remedy after default is the removal of the fixtures from the real property. See, e.g., *Maplewood Bank & Trust v. Sears, Roebuck & Co.*, 625 A.2d 537 (N.J. Super. Ct. App. Div. 1993).

Subsection (c) generally follows former Section 9–313(8). It gives the secured party the right to remove fixtures under certain circumstances. A secured party whose security interest in fixtures has priority over owners and encumbrancers of the real property may remove the collateral from the real property. However, subsection (d) requires the secured party to reimburse any owner (other than the debtor) or encumbrancer for the cost of repairing any physical injury caused by the removal. This right to reimbursement is implemented by the last sentence of subsection (d), which gives the owner or encumbrancer a right to security or indemnity as a condition for giving permission to remove.

§ 9–605. Unknown Debtor or Secondary Obligor.

A secured party does not owe a duty based on its status as secured party:

(1)   to a person that is a debtor or obligor, unless the secured party knows:

(A)   that the person is a debtor or obligor;

(B)   the identity of the person; and

(C)   how to communicate with the person; or

(2)   to a secured party or lienholder that has filed a financing statement against a person, unless the secured party knows:

(A)   that the person is a debtor; and

(B)   the identity of the person.

Official Comment

1.   **Source.** New.

2.   **Duties to Unknown Persons.** This section relieves a secured party from duties owed to a debtor or obligor, if the secured party does not know about the debtor or obligor. Similarly, it relieves a secured party from duties owed to a secured party or lienholder who has filed a financing statement against the debtor, if the secured party does not know about the debtor. For example, a secured party may be unaware that the original debtor has sold the collateral subject to the security interest and that the new owner has become the debtor. If so, the secured party owes no duty to the new owner (debtor) or to a secured party who has filed a financing statement against the new owner. This section should be read in conjunction with the exculpatory provisions in Section 9–628. Note that it relieves a secured party not only from duties arising under this Article but also from duties arising under other law by virtue of the secured party's status as such under this Article, unless the other law otherwise provides.

§ 9–606. Time of Default for Agricultural Lien.

For purposes of this part, a default occurs in connection with an agricultural lien at the time the secured party becomes entitled to enforce the lien in accordance with the statute under which it was created.

Official Comment

1.   **Source.** New.

2.   **Time of Default.** Remedies under this Part become available upon the debtor's "default." See Section 9–601. This section explains when "default" occurs in the agricultural-lien context. It requires one to consult the enabling statute to determine when the lienholder is entitled to enforce the lien.

§ 9–607. Collection and Enforcement by Secured Party.

(a)   **[Collection and enforcement generally.]** If so agreed, and in any event after default, a secured party:

(1)   may notify an account debtor or other person obligated on collateral to make payment or otherwise render performance to or for the benefit of the secured party;

(2)   may take any proceeds to which the secured party is entitled under Section 9–315;

(3)   may enforce the obligations of an account debtor or other person obligated on collateral and exercise the rights of the debtor with respect to the obligation of the account debtor or other person obligated on collateral to make payment or otherwise render performance to the debtor, and with

respect to any property that secures the obligations of the account debtor or other person obligated on the collateral;

(4) if it holds a security interest in a deposit account perfected by control under Section 9–104(a)(1), may apply the balance of the deposit account to the obligation secured by the deposit account; and

(5) if it holds a security interest in a deposit account perfected by control under Section 9–104(a)(2) or (3), may instruct the bank to pay the balance of the deposit account to or for the benefit of the secured party.

(b) **[Nonjudicial enforcement of mortgage.]** If necessary to enable a secured party to exercise under subsection (a)(3) the right of a debtor to enforce a mortgage nonjudicially, the secured party may record in the office in which a record of the mortgage is recorded:

(1) a copy of the security agreement that creates or provides for a security interest in the obligation secured by the mortgage; and

(2) the secured party's sworn affidavit in recordable form stating that:

(A) a default has occurred with respect to the obligation secured by the mortgage; and

(B) the secured party is entitled to enforce the mortgage nonjudicially.

(c) **[Commercially reasonable collection and enforcement.]** A secured party shall proceed in a commercially reasonable manner if the secured party:

(1) undertakes to collect from or enforce an obligation of an account debtor or other person obligated on collateral; and

(2) is entitled to charge back uncollected collateral or otherwise to full or limited recourse against the debtor or a secondary obligor.

(d) **[Expenses of collection and enforcement.]** A secured party may deduct from the collections made pursuant to subsection (c) reasonable expenses of collection and enforcement, including reasonable attorney's fees and legal expenses incurred by the secured party.

(e) **[Duties to secured party not affected.]** This section does not determine whether an account debtor, bank, or other person obligated on collateral owes a duty to a secured party.

As amended in 2010.

Official Comment

1. **Source.** Former Section 9–502; subsections (b), (d), and (e) are new.

2. **Collections: In General.** Collateral consisting of rights to payment is not only the most liquid asset of a typical debtor's business but also is property that may be collected without any interruption of the debtor's business This situation is far different from that in which collateral is inventory or equipment, whose removal may bring the business to a halt. Furthermore, problems of valuation and identification, present with collateral that is tangible personal property, frequently are not as serious in the case of rights to payment and other intangible collateral. Consequently, this section, like former Section 9–502, recognizes that financing through assignments of intangibles lacks many of the complexities that arise after default in other types of financing. This section allows the assignee to liquidate collateral by collecting whatever may become due on the collateral, whether or not the method of collection contemplated by the security arrangement before default was direct (i.e., payment by the account debtor to the assignee, "notification" financing) or indirect (i.e., payment by the account debtor to the assignor, "nonnotification" financing).

3. **Scope.** The scope of this section is broader than that of former Section 9–502. It applies not only to collections from account debtors and obligors on instruments but also to enforcement more generally against all persons obligated on collateral. It explicitly provides for the secured party's enforcement of the debtor's rights in respect of the account debtor's (and other third parties') obligations and for the secured party's enforcement of supporting obligations with respect to those obligations. (Supporting obligations are components of the collateral under Section 9–203(f).) The rights of a secured party under subsection (a) include the right to enforce claims that the debtor may enjoy against others. For example, the claims might include a breach-of-warranty claim arising

out of a defect in equipment that is collateral or a secured party's action for an injunction against infringement of a patent that is collateral. Those claims typically would be proceeds of original collateral under Section 9–315.

4. **Collection and Enforcement Before Default.** Like Part 6 generally, this section deals with the rights and duties of secured parties following default. However, as did former Section 9–502 with respect to collection rights, this section also applies to the collection and enforcement rights of secured parties even if a default has not occurred, as long as the debtor has so agreed. It is not unusual for debtors to agree that secured parties are entitled to collect and enforce rights against account debtors prior to default.

5. **Collections by Junior Secured Party.** A secured party who holds a security interest in a right to payment may exercise the right to collect and enforce under this section, even if the security interest is subordinate to a conflicting security interest in the same right to payment. Whether the junior secured party has priority in the collected proceeds depends on whether the junior secured party qualifies for priority as a purchaser of an instrument (e.g., the account debtor's check) under Section 9–330(d), as a holder in due course of an instrument under Sections 3–305 and 9–331(a), or as a transferee of money under Section 9–332(a). See Sections 9–330, Comment 7; 9–331, Comment 5; and 9–332.

6. **Relationship to Rights and Duties of Persons Obligated on Collateral.** This section permits a secured party to collect and enforce obligations included in collateral in its capacity as a secured party. It is not necessary for a secured party first to become the owner of the collateral pursuant to a disposition or acceptance. However, the secured party's rights, as between it and the debtor, to collect from and enforce collateral against account debtors and others obligated on collateral under subsection (a) are subject to Section 9–341, Part 4, and other applicable law. *Neither this section nor former Section 9–502 should be understood to regulate the duties of an account debtor or other person obligated on collateral.* Subsection (e) makes this explicit. For example, the secured party may be unable to exercise the debtor's rights under an instrument if the debtor is in possession of the instrument, or under a non-transferable letter of credit if the debtor is the beneficiary. Unless a secured party has control over a letter-of-credit right and is entitled to receive payment or performance from the issuer or a nominated person under Article 5, its remedies with respect to the letter-of-credit right may be limited to the recovery of any identifiable proceeds from the debtor. This section establishes only the baseline rights of the secured party *vis-a-vis the debtor*—the secured party is entitled to enforce and collect after default or earlier if so agreed.

7. **Deposit Account Collateral.** Subsections (a)(4) and (5) set forth the self-help remedy for a secured party whose collateral is a deposit account. Subsection (a)(4) addresses the rights of a secured party that is the bank with which the deposit account is maintained. That secured party automatically has control of the deposit account under Section 9–104(a)(1). After default, and otherwise if so agreed, the bank/secured party may apply the funds on deposit to the secured obligation.

If a security interest of a third party is perfected by control (Section 9–104(a)(2) or (a)(3)), then after default, and otherwise if so agreed, the secured party may instruct the bank to pay out the funds in the account. If the third party has control under Section 9–104(a)(3), the depositary institution is obliged to obey the instruction because the secured party is its customer. See Section 4–401. If the third party has control under Section 9–104(a)(2), the control agreement determines the depositary institution's obligation to obey.

If a security interest in a deposit account is unperfected, or is perfected by filing by virtue of the proceeds rules of Section 9–315, the depositary institution ordinarily owes no obligation to obey the secured party's instructions. See Section 9–341. To reach the funds without the debtor's cooperation, the secured party must use an available judicial procedure.

8. **Rights Against Mortgagor of Real Property.** Subsection (b) addresses the situation in which the collateral consists of a mortgage note (or other obligation secured by a mortgage on real property). After the debtor's (mortgagee's) default, the secured party (assignee) may wish to proceed with a nonjudicial foreclosure of the mortgage securing the note but may be unable to do so because it has not become the assignee of record. The assignee/secured party may not have taken a recordable assignment at the commencement of the transaction (perhaps the mortgage note in question was one of hundreds assigned to the secured party as collateral). Having defaulted, the mortgagee may be unwilling to sign a recordable assignment. This section enables the secured party (assignee) to become the assignee of record by recording in the applicable real-property records the security agreement and an affidavit certifying default. Of course, the secured party's rights derive from those of its debtor. Subsection (b) would not entitle the secured party to proceed with a foreclosure unless the mortgagor also were in default or the debtor (mortgagee) otherwise enjoyed the right to foreclose.

9. **Commercial Reasonableness.** Subsection (c) provides that the secured party's collection and enforcement rights under subsection (a) must be exercised in a commercially reasonable manner. These rights

include the right to settle and compromise claims against the account debtor. The secured party's failure to observe the standard of commercial reasonableness could render it liable to an aggrieved person under Section 9–625, and the secured party's recovery of a deficiency would be subject to Section 9–626. Subsection (c) does not apply if, as is characteristic of most sales of accounts, chattel paper, payment intangibles, and promissory notes, the secured party (buyer) has no right of recourse against the debtor (seller) or a secondary obligor. However, if the secured party does have a right of recourse, the commercial-reasonableness standard applies to collection and enforcement even though the assignment to the secured party was a "true" sale. The obligation to proceed in a commercially reasonable manner arises because the collection process affects the extent of the seller's recourse liability, not because the seller retains an interest in the sold collateral (the seller does not). Concerning classification of a transaction, see Section 9–109, Comment 4.

10. **Attorney's Fees and Legal Expenses.** The phrase "reasonable attorney's fees and legal expenses," which appears in subsection (d), includes only those fees and expenses incurred in proceeding against account debtors or other third parties. The secured party's right to recover these expenses from the collections arises automatically under this section. The secured party also may incur other attorney's fees and legal expenses in proceeding against the debtor or obligor. Whether the secured party has a right to recover those fees and expenses depends on whether the debtor or obligor has agreed to pay them, as is the case with respect to attorney's fees and legal expenses under Sections 9–608(a)(1)(A) and 9–615(a)(1). The parties also may agree to allocate a portion of the secured party's overhead to collection and enforcement under subsection (d) or Section 9–608(a).

As amended in 2000.

§ 9–608. Application of Proceeds of Collection or Enforcement; Liability for Deficiency and Right to Surplus.

(a) **[Application of proceeds, surplus, and deficiency if obligation secured.]** If a security interest or agricultural lien secures payment or performance of an obligation, the following rules apply:

(1) A secured party shall apply or pay over for application the cash proceeds of collection or enforcement under Section 9–607 in the following order to:

(A) the reasonable expenses of collection and enforcement and, to the extent provided for by agreement and not prohibited by law, reasonable attorney's fees and legal expenses incurred by the secured party;

(B) the satisfaction of obligations secured by the security interest or agricultural lien under which the collection or enforcement is made; and

(C) the satisfaction of obligations secured by any subordinate security interest in or other lien on the collateral subject to the security interest or agricultural lien under which the collection or enforcement is made if the secured party receives an authenticated demand for proceeds before distribution of the proceeds is completed.

(2) If requested by a secured party, a holder of a subordinate security interest or other lien shall furnish reasonable proof of the interest or lien within a reasonable time. Unless the holder complies, the secured party need not comply with the holder's demand under paragraph (1)(C).

(3) A secured party need not apply or pay over for application noncash proceeds of collection and enforcement under Section 9–607 unless the failure to do so would be commercially unreasonable. A secured party that applies or pays over for application noncash proceeds shall do so in a commercially reasonable manner.

(4) A secured party shall account to and pay a debtor for any surplus, and the obligor is liable for any deficiency.

(b) **[No surplus or deficiency in sales of certain rights to payment.]** If the underlying transaction is a sale of accounts, chattel paper, payment intangibles, or promissory notes, the debtor is not entitled to any surplus, and the obligor is not liable for any deficiency.

As amended in 2000.

Official Comment

1.   **Source.** Subsection (a) is new; subsection (b) derives from former Section 9–502(2).

2.   **Modifications of Prior Law.** Subsections (a) and (b) modify former Section 9–502(2) by explicitly providing for the application of proceeds recovered by the secured party in substantially the same manner as provided in Section 9–615(a) and (e) for dispositions of collateral.

3.   **Surplus and Deficiency.** Subsections (a)(4) and (b) omit, as unnecessary, the references contained in former Section 9–502(2) to agreements varying the baseline rules on surplus and deficiency. The parties are always free to agree that an obligor will not be liable for a deficiency, even if the collateral secures an obligation, and that an obligor is liable for a deficiency, even if the transaction is a sale of receivables. For parallel provisions, see Section 9–615(d) and (e).

4.   **Noncash Proceeds.** Subsection (a)(3) addresses the situation in which an enforcing secured party receives noncash proceeds.

Example: An enforcing secured party receives a promissory note from an account debtor who is unable to pay an account when it is due. The secured party accepts the note in exchange for extending the date on which the account debtor's obligation is due. The secured party may wish to credit its debtor (the assignor) with the principal amount of the note upon receipt of the note, but probably will prefer to credit the debtor only as and when the note is paid.

Under subsection (a)(3), the secured party is under no duty to apply the note or its value to the outstanding obligation unless its failure to do so would be commercially unreasonable. If the secured party does apply the note to the outstanding obligation, however, it must do so in a commercially reasonable manner. The parties may provide for the method of application of noncash proceeds by agreement, if the method is not manifestly unreasonable. See Section 9–603. This section does not explain when the failure to apply noncash proceeds would be commercially unreasonable; it leaves that determination to case-by-case adjudication. In the example, the secured party appears to have accepted the account debtor's note in order to increase the likelihood of payment and decrease the likelihood that the account debtor would dispute its obligation. Under these circumstances, it may well be commercially reasonable for the secured party to credit its debtor's obligations only as and when cash proceeds are collected from the account debtor, especially given the uncertainty that attends the account debtor's eventual payment. For an example of a secured party's receipt of noncash proceeds in which it may well be commercially unreasonable for the secured party to delay crediting its debtor's obligations with the value of noncash proceeds, see Section 9–615, Comment 3.

When the secured party is not required to "apply or pay over for application noncash proceeds," the proceeds nonetheless remain collateral subject to this Article. If the secured party were to dispose of them, for example, appropriate notification would be required (see Section 9–611), and the disposition would be subject to the standards provided in this Part (see Section 9–610). Moreover, a secured party in possession of the noncash proceeds would have the duties specified in Section 9–207.

5.   **No Effect on Priority of Senior Security Interest.** The application of proceeds required by subsection (a) does not affect the priority of a security interest in collateral which is senior to the interest of the secured party who is collecting or enforcing collateral under Section 9–607. Although subsection (a) imposes a duty to apply proceeds to the enforcing secured party's expenses and to the satisfaction of the secured obligations owed to it and to subordinate secured parties, that duty applies only among the enforcing secured party and those persons. Concerning the priority of a junior secured party who collects and enforces collateral, see Section 9–607, Comment 5.

§ 9–609.   Secured Party's Right to Take Possession After Default.

(a)   **[Possession; rendering equipment unusable; disposition on debtor's premises.]** After default, a secured party:

(1)   may take possession of the collateral; and

(2)   without removal, may render equipment unusable and dispose of collateral on a debtor's premises under Section 9–610.

(b)   **[Judicial and nonjudicial process.]** A secured party may proceed under subsection (a):

(1)   pursuant to judicial process; or

(2)   without judicial process, if it proceeds without breach of the peace.

(c)   **[Assembly of collateral.]** If so agreed, and in any event after default, a secured party may require the debtor to assemble the collateral and make it available to the secured party at a place to be designated by the secured party which is reasonably convenient to both parties.

Official Comment

1.   **Source.** Former Section 9–503.

2.   **Secured Party's Right to Possession.** This section follows former Section 9–503 and earlier uniform legislation. It provides that the secured party is entitled to take possession of collateral after default.

3.   **Judicial Process; Breach of Peace.** Subsection (b) permits a secured party to proceed under this section without judicial process if it does so "without breach of the peace." Although former Section 9–503 placed the same condition on a secured party's right to take possession of collateral, subsection (b) extends the condition to the right provided in subsection (a)(2) as well. Like former Section 9–503, this section does not define or explain the conduct that will constitute a breach of the peace, leaving that matter for continuing development by the courts. In considering whether a secured party has engaged in a breach of the peace, however, courts should hold the secured party responsible for the actions of others taken on the secured party's behalf, including independent contractors engaged by the secured party to take possession of collateral.

This section does not authorize a secured party who repossesses without judicial process to utilize the assistance of a law-enforcement officer. A number of cases have held that a repossessing secured party's use of a law-enforcement officer without benefit of judicial process constituted a failure to comply with former Section 9–503.

4.   **Damages for Breach of Peace.** Concerning damages that may be recovered based on a secured party's breach of the peace in connection with taking possession of collateral, see Section 9–625, Comment 3.

5.   **Multiple Secured Parties.** More than one secured party may be entitled to take possession of collateral under this section. Conflicting rights to possession among secured parties are resolved by the priority rules of this Article. Thus, a senior secured party is entitled to possession as against a junior claimant. Non-UCC law governs whether a junior secured party in possession of collateral is liable to the senior in conversion. Normally, a junior who refuses to relinquish possession of collateral upon the demand of a secured party having a superior possessory right to the collateral would be liable in conversion.

6.   **Secured Party's Right to Disable and Dispose of Equipment on Debtor's Premises.** In the case of some collateral, such as heavy equipment, the physical removal from the debtor's plant and the storage of the collateral pending disposition may be impractical or unduly expensive. This section follows former Section 9–503 by providing that, in lieu of removal, the secured party may render equipment unusable or may dispose of collateral on the debtor's premises. Unlike former Section 9–503, however, this section explicitly conditions these rights on the debtor's default. Of course, this section does not validate unreasonable action by a secured party. Under Section 9–610, all aspects of a disposition must be commercially reasonable.

7.   **Debtor's Agreement to Assemble Collateral.** This section follows former Section 9–503 also by validating a debtor's agreement to assemble collateral and make it available to a secured party at a place that the secured party designates. Similar to the treatment of agreements to permit collection prior to default under Section 9–607 and former 9–502, however, this section validates these agreements whether or not they are conditioned on the debtor's default. For example, a debtor might agree to make available to a secured party, from time to time, any instruments or negotiable documents that the debtor receives on account of collateral. A court should not infer from this section's validation that a debtor's agreement to assemble and make available collateral would not be enforceable under other applicable law.

8.   **Agreed Standards.** Subject to the limitation imposed by Section 9–603(b), this section's provisions concerning agreements to assemble and make available collateral and a secured party's right to disable equipment and dispose of collateral on a debtor's premises are likely topics for agreement on standards as contemplated by Section 9–603.

§ 9–610.   Disposition of Collateral After Default.

(a)   **[Disposition after default.]** After default, a secured party may sell, lease, license, or otherwise dispose of any or all of the collateral in its present condition or following any commercially reasonable preparation or processing.

(b) **[Commercially reasonable disposition.]** Every aspect of a disposition of collateral, including the method, manner, time, place, and other terms, must be commercially reasonable. If commercially reasonable, a secured party may dispose of collateral by public or private proceedings, by one or more contracts, as a unit or in parcels, and at any time and place and on any terms.

(c) **[Purchase by secured party.]** A secured party may purchase collateral:

(1) at a public disposition; or

(2) at a private disposition only if the collateral is of a kind that is customarily sold on a recognized market or the subject of widely distributed standard price quotations.

(d) **[Warranties on disposition.]** A contract for sale, lease, license, or other disposition includes the warranties relating to title, possession, quiet enjoyment, and the like which by operation of law accompany a voluntary disposition of property of the kind subject to the contract.

(e) **[Disclaimer of warranties.]** A secured party may disclaim or modify warranties under subsection (d):

(1) in a manner that would be effective to disclaim or modify the warranties in a voluntary disposition of property of the kind subject to the contract of disposition; or

(2) by communicating to the purchaser a record evidencing the contract for disposition and including an express disclaimer or modification of the warranties.

(f) **[Record sufficient to disclaim warranties.]** A record is sufficient to disclaim warranties under subsection (e) if it indicates "There is no warranty relating to title, possession, quiet enjoyment, or the like in this disposition" or uses words of similar import.

Official Comment

1. **Source.** Former Section 9–504(1), (3)

2. **Commercially Reasonable Dispositions.** Subsection (a) follows former Section 9–504 by permitting a secured party to dispose of collateral in a commercially reasonable manner following a default. Although subsection (b) permits both public and private dispositions, including public and private dispositions conducted over the Internet, "every aspect of a disposition . . . must be commercially reasonable." This section encourages private dispositions on the assumption that they frequently will result in higher realization on collateral for the benefit of all concerned. Subsection (a) does not restrict dispositions to sales; collateral may be sold, leased, licensed, or otherwise disposed. Section 9–627 provides guidance for determining the circumstances under which a disposition is "commercially reasonable."

3. **Time of Disposition.** This Article does not specify a period within which a secured party must dispose of collateral. This is consistent with this Article's policy to encourage private dispositions through regular commercial channels. It may, for example, be prudent not to dispose of goods when the market has collapsed. Or, it might be more appropriate to sell a large inventory in parcels over a period of time instead of in bulk. Of course, under subsection (b) every aspect of a disposition of collateral must be commercially reasonable. This requirement explicitly includes the "method, manner, time, place and other terms." For example, if a secured party does not proceed under Section 9–620 and holds collateral for a long period of time without disposing of it, and if there is no good reason for not making a prompt disposition, the secured party may be determined not to have acted in a "commercially reasonable" manner. See also Section 1–203 [*unrevised Article 1; see Concordance, p. 22*] (general obligation of good faith).

4. **Pre-Disposition Preparation and Processing.** Former Section 9–504(1) appeared to give the secured party the choice of disposing of collateral either "in its then condition or following any commercially reasonable preparation or processing." Some courts held that the "commercially reasonable" standard of former Section 9–504(3) nevertheless could impose an affirmative duty on the secured party to process or prepare the collateral prior to disposition. Subsection (a) retains the substance of the quoted language. Although courts should not be quick to impose a duty of preparation or processing on the secured party, subsection (a) does not grant the secured party the right to dispose of the collateral "in its then condition" under *all* circumstances. A secured party may not dispose of collateral "in its then condition" when, taking into account the costs and probable benefits of preparation or processing and the fact that the secured party would be advancing the costs at its risk, it would be commercially unreasonable to dispose of the collateral in that condition.

5. **Disposition by Junior Secured Party.** Disposition rights under subsection (a) are not limited to first-priority security interests. Rather, any secured party as to whom there has been a default enjoys the right to dispose of collateral under this subsection. The exercise of this right by a secured party whose security interest is subordinate to that of another secured party does not of itself constitute a conversion or otherwise give rise to liability in favor of the holder of the senior security interest. Section 9–615 addresses application of the proceeds of a disposition by a junior secured party. Under Section 9–615(a), a junior secured party owes no obligation to apply the proceeds of disposition to the satisfaction of obligations secured by a senior security interest. Section 9–615(g) builds on this general rule by protecting certain juniors from claims of a senior concerning cash proceeds of the disposition. Even if a senior were to have a non-Article 9 claim to proceeds of a junior's disposition, Section 9–615(g) would protect a junior that acts in good faith and without knowledge that its actions violate the rights of a senior party. Because the disposition by a junior would not cut off a senior's security interest or other lien (see Section 9–617), in many (probably most) cases the junior's receipt of the cash proceeds would not violate the rights of the senior.

The holder of a senior security interest is entitled, by virtue of its priority, to take possession of collateral from the junior secured party and conduct its own disposition, provided that the senior enjoys the right to take possession of the collateral from the debtor. See Section 9–609. The holder of a junior security interest normally must notify the senior secured party of an impending disposition. See Section 9–611. Regardless of whether the senior receives a notification from the junior, the junior's disposition does not of itself discharge the senior's security interest. See Section 9–617. Unless the senior secured party has authorized the disposition free and clear of its security interest, the senior's security interest ordinarily will survive the disposition by the junior and continue under Section 9–315(a). If the senior enjoys the right to repossess the collateral from the debtor, the senior likewise may recover the collateral from the transferee.

When a secured party's collateral is encumbered by another security interest or other lien, one of the claimants may seek to invoke the equitable doctrine of marshaling. As explained by the Supreme Court, that doctrine "rests upon the principle that a creditor having two funds to satisfy his debt, may not by his application of them to his demand, defeat another creditor, who may resort to only one of the funds." *Meyer v. United States*, 375 U.S. 233, 236 (1963), quoting *Sowell v. Federal Reserve Bank*, 268 U.S. 449, 456–57 (1925). The purpose of the doctrine is "to prevent the arbitrary action of a senior lienor from destroying the rights of a junior lienor or a creditor having less security." Id. at 237. Because it is an equitable doctrine, marshaling "is applied only when it can be equitably fashioned as to all of the parties" having an interest in the property. Id. This Article leaves courts free to determine whether marshaling is appropriate in any given case. See Section 1–103.

6. **Security Interests of Equal Rank.** Sometimes two security interests enjoy the same priority. This situation may arise by contract, e.g., pursuant to "equal and ratable" provisions in indentures, or by operation of law. See Section 9–328(6). This Article treats a security interest having equal priority like a senior security interest in many respects. Assume, for example, that SP-X and SP-Y enjoy equal priority, SP-W is senior to them, and SP-Z is junior. If SP-X disposes of the collateral under this section, then (i) SP-W's and SP-Y's security interests survive the disposition but SP-Z's does not, see Section 9–617, and (ii) neither SP-W nor SP-Y is entitled to receive a distribution of proceeds, but SP-Z is. See Section 9–615(a)(3).

When one considers the ability to obtain possession of the collateral, a secured party with equal priority is unlike a senior secured party. As the senior secured party, SP-W should enjoy the right to possession as against SP-X. See Section 9–609, Comment 5. If SP-W takes possession and disposes of the collateral under this section, it is entitled to apply the proceeds to satisfy its secured claim. SP-Y, however, should not have such a right to take possession from SP-X; otherwise, once SP-Y took possession from SP-X, SP-X would have the right to get possession from SP-Y, which would be obligated to redeliver possession to SP-X, and so on. Resolution of this problem is left to the parties and, if necessary, the courts.

7. **Public vs. Private Dispositions.** This Part maintains two distinctions between "public" and other dispositions: (i) the secured party may buy at the former, but normally not at the latter (Section 9–610(c)), and (ii) the debtor is entitled to notification of "the time and place of a public disposition" and notification of "the time after which" a private disposition or other intended disposition is to be made (Section 9–613(1)(E)). It does not retain the distinction under former Section 9–504(4), under which transferees in a noncomplying public disposition could lose protection more easily than transferees in other noncomplying dispositions. Instead, Section 9–617(b) adopts a unitary standard. Although the term is not defined, as used in this Article, a "public disposition" is one at which the price is determined after the public has had a meaningful opportunity for competitive bidding. "Meaningful opportunity" is meant to imply that some form of advertisement or public notice must precede the sale (or other disposition) and that the public must have access to the sale (disposition).

A secured party's purchase of collateral at its own private disposition is equivalent to a "strict foreclosure" and is governed by Sections 9–620, 9–621, and 9–622. The provisions of these sections can be waived only to the extent provided in Section 9–624(b). See Section 9–602.

8. **Investment Property.** Dispositions of investment property may be regulated by the federal securities laws. Although a "public" disposition of securities under this Article may implicate the registration requirements of the Securities Act of 1933, it need not do so. A disposition that qualifies for a "private placement" exemption under the Securities Act of 1933 nevertheless may constitute a "public" disposition within the meaning of this section. Moreover, the "commercially reasonable" requirements of subsection (b) need not prevent a secured party from conducting a foreclosure sale without the issuer's compliance with federal registration requirements.

9. **"Recognized Market."** A "recognized market," as used in subsection (c) and Section 9–611(d), is one in which the items sold are fungible and prices are not subject to individual negotiation. For example, the New York Stock Exchange is a recognized market. A market in which prices are individually negotiated or the items are not fungible is not a recognized market, even if the items are the subject of widely disseminated price guides or are disposed of through dealer auctions.

10. **Relevance of Price.** While not itself sufficient to establish a violation of this Part, a low price suggests that a court should scrutinize carefully all aspects of a disposition to ensure that each aspect was commercially reasonable. Note also that even if the disposition is commercially reasonable, Section 9–615(f) provides a special method for calculating a deficiency or surplus if (i) the transferee in the disposition is the secured party, a person related to the secured party, or a secondary obligor, and (ii) the amount of proceeds of the disposition is significantly below the range of proceeds that a complying disposition to a person other than the secured party, a person related to the secured party, or a secondary obligor would have brought.

11. **Warranties.** Subsection (d) affords the transferee in a disposition under this section the benefit of any title, possession, quiet enjoyment, and similar warranties that would have accompanied the disposition by operation of non-Article 9 law had the disposition been conducted under other circumstances. For example, the Article 2 warranty of title would apply to a sale of goods, the analogous warranties of Article 2A would apply to a lease of goods, and any common-law warranties of title would apply to dispositions of other types of collateral. See, e.g., Restatement (2d), Contracts § 333 (warranties of assignor).

Subsection (e) explicitly provides that these warranties can be disclaimed either under other applicable law or by communicating a record containing an express disclaimer. The record need not be written, but an oral communication would not be sufficient. See Section 9–102 (definition of "record"). Subsection (f) provides a sample of wording that will effectively exclude the warranties in a disposition under this section, whether or not the exclusion would be effective under non-Article 9 law.

The warranties incorporated by subsection (d) are those relating to "title, possession, quiet enjoyment, and the like." Depending on the circumstances, a disposition under this section also may give rise to other statutory or implied warranties, e.g., warranties of quality or fitness for purpose. Law other than this Article determines whether such other warranties apply to a disposition under this section. Other law also determines issues relating to disclaimer of such warranties. For example, a foreclosure sale of a car by a car dealer could give rise to an implied warranty of merchantability (Section 2–314) unless effectively disclaimed or modified (Section 2–316).

This section's approach to these warranties conflicts with the former Comment to Section 2–312. This Article rejects the baseline assumption that commercially reasonable dispositions under this section are out of the ordinary commercial course or peculiar. The Comment to Section 2–312 has been revised accordingly.

As amended in 2010.

§ 9-611. Notification Before Disposition of Collateral.

(a) **["Notification date."]** In this section, "notification date" means the earlier of the date on which:

(1) a secured party sends to the debtor and any secondary obligor an authenticated notification of disposition; or

(2) the debtor and any secondary obligor waive the right to notification.

(b) **[Notification of disposition required.]** Except as otherwise provided in subsection (d), a secured party that disposes of collateral under Section 9–610 shall send to the persons specified in subsection (c) a reasonable authenticated notification of disposition.

(c)   **[Persons to be notified.]** To comply with subsection (b), the secured party shall send an authenticated notification of disposition to:

(1)   the debtor;

(2)   any secondary obligor; and

(3)   if the collateral is other than consumer goods:

   (A)   any other person from which the secured party has received, before the notification date, an authenticated notification of a claim of an interest in the collateral;

   (B)   any other secured party or lienholder that, 10 days before the notification date, held a security interest in or other lien on the collateral perfected by the filing of a financing statement that:

      (i)   identified the collateral;

      (ii)   was indexed under the debtor's name as of that date; and

      (iii) was filed in the office in which to file a financing statement against the debtor covering the collateral as of that date; and

   (C)   any other secured party that, 10 days before the notification date, held a security interest in the collateral perfected by compliance with a statute, regulation, or treaty described in Section 9–311(a).

(d)   **[Subsection (b) inapplicable: perishable collateral; recognized market.]** Subsection (b) does not apply if the collateral is perishable or threatens to decline speedily in value or is of a type customarily sold on a recognized market.

(e)   **[Compliance with subsection (c)(3)(B).]** A secured party complies with the requirement for notification prescribed by subsection (c)(3)(B) if:

(1)   not later than 20 days or earlier than 30 days before the notification date, the secured party requests, in a commercially reasonable manner, information concerning financing statements indexed under the debtor's name in the office indicated in subsection (c)(3)(B); and

(2)   before the notification date, the secured party:

   (A)   did not receive a response to the request for information; or

   (B)   received a response to the request for information and sent an authenticated notification of disposition to each secured party or other lienholder named in that response whose financing statement covered the collateral.

Official Comment

1.   **Source.** Former Section 9–504(3).

2.   **Reasonable Notification.** This section requires a secured party who wishes to dispose of collateral under Section 9–610 to send "a reasonable authenticated notification of disposition" to specified interested persons, subject to certain exceptions. The notification must be reasonable as to the manner in which it is sent, its timeliness (i.e., a reasonable time before the disposition is to take place), and its content. See Sections 9–612 (timeliness of notification), 9–613 (contents of notification generally), 9–614 (contents of notification in consumer-goods transactions).

3.   **Notification to Debtors and Secondary Obligors.** This section imposes a duty to send notification of a disposition not only to the debtor but also to any secondary obligor. Subsections (b) and (c) resolve an uncertainty under former Article 9 by providing that secondary obligors (sureties) are entitled to receive notification of an intended disposition of collateral, regardless of who created the security interest in the collateral. If the surety created the security interest, it would be the debtor. If it did not, it would be a secondary obligor. (This Article also resolves the question of the secondary obligor's ability to waive, pre-default, the right to notification—waiver generally is not permitted. See Section 9–602.) Section 9–605 relieves a secured party from any duty to send notification to a debtor or secondary obligor unknown to the secured party.

Under subsection (b), the principal obligor (borrower) is not always entitled to notification of disposition.

896

Example: Behnfeldt borrows on an unsecured basis, and Bruno grants a security interest in her car to secure the debt. Behnfeldt is a primary obligor, not a secondary obligor. As such, she is not entitled to notification of disposition under this section.

4. **Notification to Other Secured Parties.** Prior to the 1972 amendments to Article 9, former Section 9–504(3) required the enforcing secured party to send reasonable notification of the disposition:

> except in the case of consumer goods to any other person who has a security interest in the collateral and who has duly filed a financing statement indexed in the name of the debtor in this State or who is known by the secured party to have a security interest in the collateral.

The 1972 amendments eliminated the duty to give notice to secured parties other than those from whom the foreclosing secured party had received written notice of a claim of an interest in the collateral.

Many of the problems arising from dispositions of collateral encumbered by multiple security interests can be ameliorated or solved by informing all secured parties of an intended disposition and affording them the opportunity to work with one another. To this end, subsection (c)(3)(B) expands the duties of the foreclosing secured party to include the duty to notify (and the corresponding burden of searching the files to discover) certain competing secured parties. The subsection imposes a search burden that in some cases may be greater than the pre-1972 burden on foreclosing secured parties but certainly is more modest than that faced by a new secured lender.

To determine who is entitled to notification, the foreclosing secured party must determine the proper office for filing a financing statement as of a particular date, measured by reference to the "notification date," as defined in subsection (a). This determination requires reference to the choice-of-law provisions of Part 3. The secured party must ascertain whether any financing statements covering the collateral and indexed under the debtor's name, as the name existed as of that date, in fact were filed in that office. The foreclosing secured party generally need not notify secured parties whose effective financing statements have become more difficult to locate because of changes in the location of the debtor, proceeds rules, or changes in the name that is sufficient as the name of the debtor under Section 9–503(a).

Under subsection (c)(3)(C), the secured party also must notify a secured party who has perfected a security interest by complying with a statute or treaty described in Section 9–311(a), such as a certificate-of-title statute.

Subsection (e) provides a "safe harbor" that takes into account the delays that may be attendant to receiving information from the public filing offices. It provides, generally, that the secured party will be deemed to have satisfied its notification duty under subsection (c)(3)(B) if it requests a search from the proper office at least 20 but not more than 30 days before sending notification to the debtor and if it also sends a notification to all secured parties (and other lienholders) reflected on the search report. The secured party's duty under subsection (c)(3)(B) also will be satisfied if the secured party requests but does not receive a search report before the notification is sent to the debtor. Thus, if subsection (e) applies, a secured party who is entitled to notification under subsection (c)(3)(B) has no remedy against a foreclosing secured party who does not send the notification. The foreclosing secured party has complied with the notification requirement. Subsection (e) has no effect on the requirements of the other paragraphs of subsection (c). For example, if the foreclosing secured party received a notification from the holder of a conflicting security interest in accordance with subsection (c)(3)(A) but failed to send to the holder a notification of the disposition, the holder of the conflicting security interest would have the right to recover any loss under Section 9–625(b).

5. **Authentication Requirement.** Subsections (b) and (c) explicitly provide that a notification of disposition must be "authenticated." Some cases read former Section 9–504(3) as validating oral notification.

6. **Second Try.** This Article leaves to judicial resolution, based upon the facts of each case, the question whether the requirement of "reasonable notification" requires a "second try," i.e., whether a secured party who sends notification and learns that the debtor did not receive it must attempt to locate the debtor and send another notification.

7. **Recognized Market; Perishable Collateral.** New subsection (d) makes it clear that there is no obligation to give notification of a disposition in the case of perishable collateral or collateral customarily sold on a recognized market (e.g., marketable securities). Former Section 9–504(3) might be read (incorrectly) to relieve the secured party from its duty to notify a debtor but not from its duty to notify other secured parties in connection with dispositions of such collateral.

8. **Failure to Conduct Notified Disposition.** Nothing in this Article prevents a secured party from electing not to conduct a disposition after sending a notification. Nor does this Article prevent a secured party

from electing to send a revised notification if its plans for disposition change. This assumes, however, that the secured party acts in good faith, the revised notification is reasonable, and the revised plan for disposition and any attendant delay are commercially reasonable.

9.   **Waiver.** A debtor or secondary obligor may waive the right to notification under this section only by a post-default authenticated agreement. See Section 9–624(a).

10.   **Other Law.** Other State or federal law may contain requirements concerning notification of a disposition of property by a secured party. For example, federal law imposes notification requirements with respect to the enforcement of mortgages on federally documented vessels. Principles of statutory interpretation and, in the context of federal law, supremacy and preemption determine whether and to what extent law other than this Article supplements, displaces, or is displaced by this Article. See Sections 1–103, 1–104, 9–109(c)(1).

As amended in 2010.

§ 9–612.   Timeliness of Notification Before Disposition of Collateral.

(a)   **[Reasonable time is question of fact.]** Except as otherwise provided in subsection (b), whether a notification is sent within a reasonable time is a question of fact.

(b)   **[10-day period sufficient in non-consumer transaction.]** In a transaction other than a consumer transaction, a notification of disposition sent after default and 10 days or more before the earliest time of disposition set forth in the notification is sent within a reasonable time before the disposition.

Official Comment

1.   **Source.** New.

2.   **Reasonable Notification.** Section 9–611(b) requires the secured party to send a "reasonable authenticated notification." Under that section, as under former Section 9–504(3), one aspect of a reasonable notification is its timeliness. This generally means that the notification must be sent at a reasonable time in advance of the date of a public disposition or the date after which a private disposition is to be made. A notification that is sent so near to the disposition date that a notified person could not be expected to act on or take account of the notification would be unreasonable.

3.   **Timeliness of Notification: Safe Harbor.** The 10-day notice period in subsection (b) is intended to be a "safe harbor" and not a minimum requirement. To qualify for the "safe harbor" the notification must be sent after default. A notification also must be sent in a commercially reasonable manner. See Section 9–611(b) ("reasonable authenticated notification"). These requirements prevent a secured party from taking advantage of the "safe harbor" by, for example, giving the debtor a notification at the time of the original extension of credit or sending the notice by surface mail to a debtor overseas.

§ 9–613.   Contents and Form of Notification Before Disposition of Collateral: General.

Except in a consumer-goods transaction, the following rules apply:

(1)   The contents of a notification of disposition are sufficient if the notification:

(A)   describes the debtor and the secured party;

(B)   describes the collateral that is the subject of the intended disposition;

(C)   states the method of intended disposition;

(D)   states that the debtor is entitled to an accounting of the unpaid indebtedness and states the charge, if any, for an accounting; and

(E)   states the time and place of a public disposition or the time after which any other disposition is to be made.

(2)   Whether the contents of a notification that lacks any of the information specified in paragraph (1) are nevertheless sufficient is a question of fact.

(3)   The contents of a notification providing substantially the information specified in paragraph (1) are sufficient, even if the notification includes:

(A)   information not specified by that paragraph; or

(B) minor errors that are not seriously misleading.

(4) A particular phrasing of the notification is not required.

(5) The following form of notification and the form appearing in Section 9–614(3), when completed, each provides sufficient information:

NOTIFICATION OF DISPOSITION OF COLLATERAL

To: [*Name of debtor, obligor, or other person to which the notification is sent*]

From: [*Name, address, and telephone number of secured party*]

Name of Debtor(s): [*Include only if debtor(s) are not an addressee*]

[*For a public disposition:*]

We will sell [or lease or license, *as applicable*] the [*describe collateral*] [to the highest qualified bidder] in public as follows:

Day and Date: _____

Time: _____

Place: _____

[*For a private disposition:*]

We will sell [or lease or license, *as applicable*] the [*describe collateral*] privately sometime after [*day and date*].

You are entitled to an accounting of the unpaid indebtedness secured by the property that we intend to sell [or lease or license, *as applicable*] [for a charge of $_____]. You may request an accounting by calling us at [*telephone number*]

[End of Form]

As amended in 2000.

Official Comment

1. **Source.** New.

2. **Contents of Notification.** To comply with the "reasonable authenticated notification" requirement of Section 9–611(b), the contents of a notification must be reasonable. Except in a consumer-goods transaction, the contents of a notification that includes the information set forth in paragraph (1) are sufficient as a matter of law, unless the parties agree otherwise. (The reference to "time" of disposition means here, as it did in former Section 9–504(3), not only the hour of the day but also the date.) Although a secured party may choose to include additional information concerning the transaction or the debtor's rights and obligations, no additional information is required unless the parties agree otherwise. A notification that lacks some of the information set forth in paragraph (1) nevertheless may be sufficient if found to be reasonable by the trier of fact, under paragraph (2). A properly completed sample form of notification in paragraph (5) or in Section 9–614(a)(3) is an example of a notification that would contain the information set forth in paragraph (1). Under paragraph (4), however, no particular phrasing of the notification is required.

This section applies to a notification of a public disposition conducted electronically. A notification of an electronic disposition satisfies paragraph (1)(E) if it states the time when the disposition is scheduled to begin and states the electronic location. For example, under the technology current in 2010, the Uniform Resource Locator (URL) or other Internet address where the site of the public disposition can be accessed suffices as an electronic location.

As amended in 2010.

§ 9–614. Contents and Form of Notification Before Disposition of Collateral: Consumer-Goods Transaction.

In a consumer-goods transaction, the following rules apply:

(1) A notification of disposition must provide the following information:

(A)   the information specified in Section 9–613(1);

(B)   a description of any liability for a deficiency of the person to which the notification is sent;

(C)   a telephone number from which the amount that must be paid to the secured party to redeem the collateral under Section 9–623 is available; and

(D)   a telephone number or mailing address from which additional information concerning the disposition and the obligation secured is available.

(2)   A particular phrasing of the notification is not required.

(3)   The following form of notification, when completed, provides sufficient information:

[Name and address of secured party]

[Date]

NOTICE OF OUR PLAN TO SELL PROPERTY

[Name and address of any obligor who is also a debtor]

Subject: [Identification of Transaction]

We have your [describe collateral], because you broke promises in our agreement.

[For a public disposition:]

We will sell [describe collateral] at public sale. A sale could include a lease or license. The sale will be held as follows:

Date: _____

Time: _____

Place: _____

You may attend the sale and bring bidders if you want.

[For a private disposition:]

We will sell [describe collateral] at private sale sometime after [date]. A sale could include a lease or license.

The money that we get from the sale (after paying our costs) will reduce the amount you owe. If we get less money than you owe, you [will or will not, as applicable] still owe us the difference. If we get more money than you owe, you will get the extra money, unless we must pay it to someone else.

You can get the property back at any time before we sell it by paying us the full amount you owe (not just the past due payments), including our expenses. To learn the exact amount you must pay, call us at [telephone number].

If you want us to explain to you in writing how we have figured the amount that you owe us, you may call us at [telephone number] [or write us at [secured party's address]] and request a written explanation. [We will charge you $ for the explanation if we sent you another written explanation of the amount you owe us within the last six months.]

If you need more information about the sale call us at [telephone number] [or write us at [secured party's address]].

We are sending this notice to the following other people who have an interest in [describe collateral] or who owe money under your agreement:

[Names of all other debtors and obligors, if any]

[End of Form]

(4)   A notification in the form of paragraph (3) is sufficient, even if additional information appears at the end of the form.

(5)   A notification in the form of paragraph (3) is sufficient, even if it includes errors in information not required by paragraph (1), unless the error is misleading with respect to rights arising under this article.

(6) If a notification under this section is not in the form of paragraph (3), law other than this article determines the effect of including information not required by paragraph (1).

Official Comment

1. **Source.** New.

2. **Notification in Consumer-Goods Transactions.** Paragraph (1) sets forth the information required for a reasonable notification in a consumer-goods transaction. A notification that lacks any of the information set forth in paragraph (1) is insufficient as a matter of law. Compare Section 9–613(2), under which the trier of fact may find a notification to be sufficient even if it lacks some information listed in paragraph (1) of that section.

3. **Safe-Harbor Form of Notification; Errors in Information.** Although paragraph (2) provides that a particular phrasing of a notification is not required, paragraph (3) specifies a safe-harbor form that, when properly completed, satisfies paragraph (1). Paragraphs (4), (5), and (6) contain special rules applicable to erroneous and additional information. Under paragraph (4), a notification in the safe-harbor form specified in paragraph (3) is not rendered insufficient if it contains additional information at the end of the form. Paragraph (5) provides that non-misleading errors in information contained in a notification are permitted if the safe-harbor form is used *and if the errors are in information not required by paragraph (1)*. Finally, if a notification is in a form other than the paragraph (3) safe-harbor form, other law determines the effect of including in the notification information other than that required by paragraph (1).

§ 9–615. Application of Proceeds of Disposition; Liability for Deficiency and Right to Surplus.

(a) **[Application of proceeds.]** A secured party shall apply or pay over for application the cash proceeds of disposition under Section 9–610 in the following order to:

(1) the reasonable expenses of retaking, holding, preparing for disposition, processing, and disposing, and, to the extent provided for by agreement and not prohibited by law, reasonable attorney's fees and legal expenses incurred by the secured party;

(2) the satisfaction of obligations secured by the security interest or agricultural lien under which the disposition is made;

(3) the satisfaction of obligations secured by any subordinate security interest in or other subordinate lien on the collateral if:

(A) the secured party receives from the holder of the subordinate security interest or other lien an authenticated demand for proceeds before distribution of the proceeds is completed; and

(B) in a case in which a consignor has an interest in the collateral, the subordinate security interest or other lien is senior to the interest of the consignor; and

(4) a secured party that is a consignor of the collateral if the secured party receives from the consignor an authenticated demand for proceeds before distribution of the proceeds is completed.

(b) **[Proof of subordinate interest.]** If requested by a secured party, a holder of a subordinate security interest or other lien shall furnish reasonable proof of the interest or lien within a reasonable time. Unless the holder does so, the secured party need not comply with the holder's demand under subsection (a)(3).

(c) **[Application of noncash proceeds.]** A secured party need not apply or pay over for application noncash proceeds of disposition under Section 9–610 unless the failure to do so would be commercially unreasonable. A secured party that applies or pays over for application noncash proceeds shall do so in a commercially reasonable manner.

(d) **[Surplus or deficiency if obligation secured.]** If the security interest under which a disposition is made secures payment or performance of an obligation, after making the payments and applications required by subsection (a) and permitted by subsection (c):

(1) unless subsection (a)(4) requires the secured party to apply or pay over cash proceeds to a consignor, the secured party shall account to and pay a debtor for any surplus; and

(2) the obligor is liable for any deficiency.

(e)   **[No surplus or deficiency in sales of certain rights to payment.]** If the underlying transaction is a sale of accounts, chattel paper, payment intangibles, or promissory notes:

(1)   the debtor is not entitled to any surplus; and

(2)   the obligor is not liable for any deficiency.

(f)   **[Calculation of surplus or deficiency in disposition to person related to secured party.]** The surplus or deficiency following a disposition is calculated based on the amount of proceeds that would have been realized in a disposition complying with this part to a transferee other than the secured party, a person related to the secured party, or a secondary obligor if:

(1)   the transferee in the disposition is the secured party, a person related to the secured party, or a secondary obligor; and

(2)   the amount of proceeds of the disposition is significantly below the range of proceeds that a complying disposition to a person other than the secured party, a person related to the secured party, or a secondary obligor would have brought.

(g)   **[Cash proceeds received by junior secured party.]** A secured party that receives cash proceeds of a disposition in good faith and without knowledge that the receipt violates the rights of the holder of a security interest or other lien that is not subordinate to the security interest or agricultural lien under which the disposition is made:

(1)   takes the cash proceeds free of the security interest or other lien;

(2)   is not obligated to apply the proceeds of the disposition to the satisfaction of obligations secured by the security interest or other lien; and

(3)   is not obligated to account to or pay the holder of the security interest or other lien for any surplus.

As amended in 2000.

Official Comment

1.   **Source.** Former Section 9–504(1), (2).

2.   **Application of Proceeds.** This section contains the rules governing application of proceeds and the debtor's liability for a deficiency following a disposition of collateral. Subsection (a) sets forth the basic order of application. The proceeds are applied first to the expenses of disposition, second to the obligation secured by the security interest that is being enforced, and third, in the specified circumstances, to interests that are subordinate to that security interest.

Subsections (a) and (d) also address the right of a consignor to receive proceeds of a disposition by a secured party whose interest is senior to that of the consignor. Subsection (a) requires the enforcing secured party to pay excess proceeds first to subordinate secured parties or lienholders whose interests are senior to that of a consignor and, finally, to a consignor. Inasmuch as a consignor is the owner of the collateral, secured parties and lienholders whose interests are junior to the consignor's interest will not be entitled to any proceeds. In like fashion, under subsection (d)(1) the debtor is not entitled to a surplus when the enforcing secured party is required to pay over proceeds to a consignor.

3.   **Noncash Proceeds.** Subsection (c) addresses the application of noncash proceeds of a disposition, such as a note or lease. The explanation in Section 9–608, Comment 4, generally applies to this subsection.

Example: A secured party in the business of selling or financing automobiles takes possession of collateral (an automobile) following its debtor's default. The secured party decides to sell the automobile in a private disposition under Section 9–610 and sends appropriate notification under Section 9–611. After undertaking its normal credit investigation and in accordance with its normal credit policies, the secured party sells the automobile on credit, on terms typical of the credit terms normally extended by the secured party in the ordinary course of its business. The automobile stands as collateral for the remaining balance of the price. The noncash proceeds received by the secured party are chattel paper. The secured party may wish to credit its debtor (the assignor) with the principal amount of the chattel paper or may wish to credit the debtor only as and when the payments are made on the chattel paper by the buyer.

Under subsection (c), the secured party is under no duty to apply the noncash proceeds (here, the chattel paper) or their value to the secured obligation unless its failure to do so would be commercially unreasonable. If a secured

902

party elects to apply the chattel paper to the outstanding obligation, however, it must do so in a commercially reasonable manner. The facts in the example indicate that it would be commercially unreasonable for the secured party to fail to apply the value of the chattel paper to the original debtor's secured obligation. Unlike the example in Comment 4 to Section 9–608, the noncash proceeds received in this example are of the type that the secured party regularly generates in the ordinary course of its financing business in nonforeclosure transactions. The original debtor should not be exposed to delay or uncertainty in this situation. Of course, there will be many situations that fall between the examples presented in the Comment to Section 9–608 and in this Comment. This Article leaves their resolution to the court based on the facts of each case.

One would expect that where noncash proceeds are or may be material, the secured party and debtor would agree to more specific standards in an agreement entered into before or after default. The parties may agree to the method of application of noncash proceeds if the method is not manifestly unreasonable. See Section 9–603.

When the secured party is not required to "apply or pay over for application noncash proceeds," the proceeds nonetheless remain collateral subject to this Article. See Section 9–608, Comment 4.

4. **Surplus and Deficiency.** Subsection (d) deals with surplus and deficiency. It revises former Section 9–504(2) by imposing an explicit requirement that the secured party "pay" the debtor for any surplus, while retaining the secured party's duty to "account." Inasmuch as the debtor may not be an obligor, subsection (d) provides that the obligor (not the debtor) is liable for the deficiency. The special rule governing surplus and deficiency when receivables have been sold likewise takes into account the distinction between a debtor and an obligor. Subsection (d) also addresses the situation in which a consignor has an interest that is subordinate to the security interest being enforced.

5. **Collateral Under New Ownership.** When the debtor sells collateral subject to a security interest, the original debtor (creator of the security interest) is no longer a debtor inasmuch as it no longer has a property interest in the collateral; the buyer is the debtor. See Section 9–102. As between the debtor (buyer of the collateral) and the original debtor (seller of the collateral), the debtor (buyer) normally would be entitled to the surplus following a disposition. Subsection (d) therefore requires the secured party to pay the surplus to the debtor (buyer), not to the original debtor (seller) with which it has dealt. But, because this situation typically arises as a result of the debtor's wrongful act, this Article does not expose the secured party to the risk of determining ownership of the collateral. If the secured party does not know about the buyer and accordingly pays the surplus to the original debtor, the exculpatory provisions of this Article exonerate the secured party from liability to the buyer. See Sections 9–605, 9–628(a), (b). If a debtor sells collateral *free* of a security interest, as in a sale to a buyer in ordinary course of business (see Section 9–320(a)), the property is no longer collateral and the buyer is not a debtor.

6. **Certain "Low-Price" Dispositions.** Subsection (f) provides a special method for calculating a deficiency or surplus when the secured party, a person related to the secured party (defined in Section 9–102), or a secondary obligor acquires the collateral at a foreclosure disposition. It recognizes that when the foreclosing secured party or a related party is the transferee of the collateral, the secured party sometimes lacks the incentive to maximize the proceeds of disposition. As a consequence, the disposition may comply with the procedural requirements of this Article (e.g., it is conducted in a commercially reasonable manner following reasonable notice) but nevertheless fetch a low price.

Subsection (f) adjusts for this lack of incentive. If the proceeds of a disposition of collateral to a secured party, a person related to the secured party, or a secondary obligor are "significantly below the range of proceeds that a complying disposition to a person other than the secured party, a person related to the secured party, or a secondary obligor would have brought," then instead of calculating a deficiency (or surplus) based on the actual net proceeds, the calculation is based upon the amount that would have been received in a commercially reasonable disposition to a person other than the secured party, a person related to the secured party, or a secondary obligor. Subsection (f) thus rejects the view that the secured party's receipt of such a price necessarily constitutes noncompliance with Part 6. However, such a price may suggest the need for greater judicial scrutiny. See Section 9–610, Comment 10.

7. **"Person Related To."** Section 9–102 defines "person related to." That term is a key element of the system provided in subsection (f) for low-price dispositions. One part of the definition applies when the secured party is an individual, and the other applies when the secured party is an organization. The definition is patterned closely on the corresponding definition in Section 1.301(32) of the Uniform Consumer Credit Code.

§ 9–616.   Explanation of Calculation of Surplus or Deficiency.

(a)   **[Definitions.]** In this section:

(1)   "Explanation" means a writing that:

    (A)   states the amount of the surplus or deficiency;

    (B)   provides an explanation in accordance with subsection (c) of how the secured party calculated the surplus or deficiency;

    (C)   states, if applicable, that future debits, credits, charges, including additional credit service charges or interest, rebates, and expenses may affect the amount of the surplus or deficiency; and

    (D)   provides a telephone number or mailing address from which additional information concerning the transaction is available.

(2)   "Request" means a record:

    (A)   authenticated by a debtor or consumer obligor;

    (B)   requesting that the recipient provide an explanation; and

    (C)   sent after disposition of the collateral under Section 9–610.

(b)   **[Explanation of calculation.]** In a consumer-goods transaction in which the debtor is entitled to a surplus or a consumer obligor is liable for a deficiency under Section 9–615, the secured party shall:

(1)   send an explanation to the debtor or consumer obligor, as applicable, after the disposition and:

    (A)   before or when the secured party accounts to the debtor and pays any surplus or first makes written demand on the consumer obligor after the disposition for payment of the deficiency; and

    (B)   within 14 days after receipt of a request; or

(2)   in the case of a consumer obligor who is liable for a deficiency, within 14 days after receipt of a request, send to the consumer obligor a record waiving the secured party's right to a deficiency.

(c)   **[Required information.]** To comply with subsection (a)(1)(B), a writing must provide the following information in the following order:

(1)   the aggregate amount of obligations secured by the security interest under which the disposition was made, and, if the amount reflects a rebate of unearned interest or credit service charge, an indication of that fact, calculated as of a specified date:

    (A)   if the secured party takes or receives possession of the collateral after default, not more than 35 days before the secured party takes or receives possession; or

    (B)   if the secured party takes or receives possession of the collateral before default or does not take possession of the collateral, not more than 35 days before the disposition;

(2)   the amount of proceeds of the disposition;

(3)   the aggregate amount of the obligations after deducting the amount of proceeds;

(4)   the amount, in the aggregate or by type, and types of expenses, including expenses of retaking, holding, preparing for disposition, processing, and disposing of the collateral, and attorney's fees secured by the collateral which are known to the secured party and relate to the current disposition;

(5)   the amount, in the aggregate or by type, and types of credits, including rebates of interest or credit service charges, to which the obligor is known to be entitled and which are not reflected in the amount in paragraph (1); and

(6)   the amount of the surplus or deficiency.

(d) **[Substantial compliance.]** A particular phrasing of the explanation is not required. An explanation complying substantially with the requirements of subsection (a) is sufficient, even if it includes minor errors that are not seriously misleading.

(e) **[Charges for responses.]** A debtor or consumer obligor is entitled without charge to one response to a request under this section during any six-month period in which the secured party did not send to the debtor or consumer obligor an explanation pursuant to subsection (b)(1). The secured party may require payment of a charge not exceeding $25 for each additional response.

Official Comment

1. **Source.** New.

2. **Duty to Send Information Concerning Surplus or Deficiency.** This section reflects the view that, in every consumer-goods transaction, the debtor or obligor is entitled to know the amount of a surplus or deficiency and the basis upon which the surplus or deficiency was calculated. Under subsection (b)(1), a secured party is obligated to provide this information (an "explanation," defined in subsection (a)(1)) no later than the time that it accounts for and pays a surplus or the time of its first written attempt to collect the deficiency. The obligor need not make a request for an accounting in order to receive an explanation. A secured party who does not attempt to collect a deficiency in writing or account for and pay a surplus has no obligation to send an explanation under subsection (b)(1) and, consequently, cannot be liable for noncompliance.

A debtor or secondary obligor need not wait until the secured party commences written collection efforts in order to receive an explanation of how a deficiency or surplus was calculated. Subsection (b)(1)(B) obliges the secured party to send an explanation within 14 days after it receives a "request" (defined in subsection (a)(2)).

3. **Explanation of Calculation of Surplus or Deficiency.** Subsection (c) contains the requirements for how a calculation of a surplus or deficiency must be explained in order to satisfy subsection (a)(1)(B). It gives a secured party some discretion concerning rebates of interest or credit service charges. The secured party may include these rebates in the aggregate amount of obligations secured, under subsection (c)(1), or may include them with other types of rebates and credits under subsection (c)(5). Rebates of interest or credit service charges are the only types of rebates for which this discretion is provided. If the secured party provides an explanation that includes rebates of pre-computed interest, its explanation must so indicate. The expenses and attorney's fees to be described pursuant to subsection (c)(4) are those relating to the most recent disposition, not those that may have been incurred in connection with earlier enforcement efforts and which have been resolved by the parties.

4. **Liability for Noncompliance.** A secured party who fails to comply with subsection (b)(2) is liable for any loss caused plus $500. See Section 9–625(b), (c), (e)(6). A secured party who fails to send an explanation under subsection (b)(1) is liable for any loss caused plus, if the noncompliance was "part of a pattern, or consistent with a practice of noncompliance," $500. See Section 9–625(b), (c), (e)(5). However, a secured party who fails to comply with this section is not liable for statutory minimum damages under Section 9–625(c)(2). See Section 9–628(d).

As amended in 2010.

§ 9–617. Rights of Transferee of Collateral.

(a) **[Effects of disposition.]** A secured party's disposition of collateral after default:

(1) transfers to a transferee for value all of the debtor's rights in the collateral;

(2) discharges the security interest under which the disposition is made; and

(3) discharges any subordinate security interest or other subordinate lien [other than liens created under [cite acts or statutes providing for liens, if any, that are not to be discharged]].

(b) **[Rights of good-faith transferee.]** A transferee that acts in good faith takes free of the rights and interests described in subsection (a), even if the secured party fails to comply with this article or the requirements of any judicial proceeding.

(c) **[Rights of other transferee.]** If a transferee does not take free of the rights and interests described in subsection (a), the transferee takes the collateral subject to:

(1) the debtor's rights in the collateral;

(2)   the security interest or agricultural lien under which the disposition is made; and

(3)   any other security interest or other lien.

Official Comment

1.   **Source.** Former Section 9–504(4).

2.   **Title Taken by Good-Faith Transferee.** Subsection (a) sets forth the rights acquired by persons who qualify under subsection (b)—transferees who act in good faith. Such a person is a "transferee," inasmuch as a buyer at a foreclosure sale does not meet the definition of "purchaser" in Section 1–201 (the transfer is not, vis-a-vis the debtor, "voluntary"). By virtue of the expanded definition of the term "debtor" in Section 9–102, subsection (a) makes clear that the ownership interest of a person who bought the collateral subject to the security interest is terminated by a subsequent disposition under this Part. Such a person is a debtor under this Article. Under former Article 9, the result arguably was the same, but the statute was less clear. Under subsection (a), a disposition normally discharges the security interest being foreclosed and any subordinate security interests and other liens.

A disposition has the effect specified in subsection (a), even if the secured party fails to comply with this Article. An aggrieved person (e.g., the holder of a subordinate security interest to whom a notification required by Section 9–611 was not sent) has a right to recover any loss under Section 9–625(b).

3.   **Unitary Standard in Public and Private Dispositions.** Subsection (b) now contains a unitary standard that applies to transferees in both private and public dispositions—acting in good faith. However, this change from former Section 9–504(4) should not be interpreted to mean that a transferee acts in good faith even though it has knowledge of defects or buys in collusion, standards applicable to public dispositions under the former section. Properly understood, those standards were specific examples of the absence of good faith.

4.   **Title Taken by Nonqualifying Transferee.** Subsection (c) specifies the consequences for a transferee who does not qualify for protection under subsections (a) and (b) (i.e., a transferee who does not act in good faith). The transferee takes subject to the rights of the debtor, the enforcing secured party, and other security interests or other liens. In such a case the disposition is ineffective to the extent that it would otherwise have cut off the debtor's rights in the collateral, and the debtor retains those rights, including the debtor's right of redemption under Section 9–623, albeit subject to the security interest under which the disposition was made and any other security interests or liens. See PEB Commentary No. 22, dated August 24, 2020. The Commentary is available at https://www.ali.org/peb-ucc.

As amended in 2020.

§ 9–618.   Rights and Duties of Certain Secondary Obligors.

(a)   **[Rights and duties of secondary obligor.]** A secondary obligor acquires the rights and becomes obligated to perform the duties of the secured party after the secondary obligor:

(1)   receives an assignment of a secured obligation from the secured party;

(2)   receives a transfer of collateral from the secured party and agrees to accept the rights and assume the duties of the secured party; or

(3)   is subrogated to the rights of a secured party with respect to collateral.

(b)   **[Effect of assignment, transfer, or subrogation.]** An assignment, transfer, or subrogation described in subsection (a):

(1)   is not a disposition of collateral under Section 9–610; and

(2)   relieves the secured party of further duties under this article.

Official Comment

1.   **Source.** Former Section 9–504(5).

2.   **Scope of This Section.** Under this section, assignments of secured obligations and other transactions (regardless of form) that function like assignments of secured obligations are not dispositions to which Part 6 applies. Rather, they constitute assignments of rights and (occasionally) delegations of duties. Application of this section may require an investigation into the agreement of the parties, which may not be reflected in the words of

the repurchase agreement (e.g., when the agreement requires a recourse party to "purchase the collateral" but contemplates that the purchaser will then conduct an Article 9 foreclosure disposition).

This section, like former Section 9–504(5), does not constitute a general and comprehensive rule for allocating rights and duties upon assignment of a secured obligation. Rather, it applies only in situations involving a secondary obligor described in subsection (a). In other contexts, the agreement of the parties and applicable law other than Article 9 determine whether the assignment imposes upon the assignee any duty to the debtor and whether the assignor retains its duties to the debtor after the assignment.

Subsection (a)(1) applies when there has been an assignment of an obligation that is secured at the time it is assigned. Thus, if a secondary obligor acquires the collateral at a disposition under Section 9–610 and simultaneously or subsequently discharges the unsecured deficiency claim, subsection (a)(1) is not implicated. Similarly, subsection (a)(3) applies only when the secondary obligor is subrogated to the secured party's rights with respect to collateral. Thus, this subsection will not be implicated if a secondary obligor discharges the debtor's unsecured obligation for a post-disposition deficiency. Similarly, if the secured party disposes of some of the collateral and the secondary obligor thereafter discharges the remaining obligation, subsection (a) applies only with respect to rights and duties concerning the remaining collateral, and, under subsection (b), the subrogation is not a disposition *of the remaining collateral*.

As discussed more fully in Comment 3, a secondary obligor may receive a transfer of collateral in a disposition under Section 9–610 in exchange for a payment that is applied against the secured obligation. However, a secondary obligor who pays and receives a transfer of collateral does not necessarily become subrogated to the rights of the secured party as contemplated by subsection (a)(3). Only to the extent the secondary obligor makes a payment in satisfaction of its secondary obligation would it become subrogated. To the extent its payment constitutes the price of the collateral in a Section 9–610 disposition by the secured party, the secondary obligor would not be subrogated. Thus, if the amount paid by the secondary obligor for the collateral in a Section 9–610 disposition is itself insufficient to discharge the secured obligation, but the secondary obligor makes an additional payment that satisfies the remaining balance, the secondary obligor would be subrogated to the secured party's deficiency claim. However, the duties of the secured party *as such* would have come to an end with respect to that collateral. In some situations the capacity in which the payment is made may be unclear. Accordingly, the parties should in their relationship provide clear evidence of the nature and circumstances of the payment by the secondary obligor.

3. **Transfer of Collateral to Secondary Obligor.** It is possible for a secured party to transfer collateral to a secondary obligor in a transaction that is a disposition under Section 9–610 and that establishes a surplus or deficiency under Section 9–615. Indeed, this Article includes a special rule, in Section 9–615(f), for establishing a deficiency in the case of some dispositions to, *inter alia*, secondary obligors. This Article rejects the view, which some may have ascribed to former Section 9–504(5), that a transfer of collateral to a recourse party can *never* constitute a disposition of collateral which discharges a security interest. Inasmuch as a secured party could itself buy collateral at its own public sale, it makes no sense to prohibit a recourse party ever from buying at the sale.

4. **Timing and Scope of Obligations.** Under subsection (a), a recourse party acquires rights and incurs obligations only "after" one of the specified circumstances occurs. This makes clear that when a successor assignee, transferee, or subrogee becomes obligated it does not assume any liability for earlier actions or inactions of the secured party whom it has succeeded unless it agrees to do so. Once the successor becomes obligated, however, it is responsible for complying with the secured party's duties thereafter. For example, if the successor is in possession of collateral, then it has the duties specified in Section 9–207.

Under subsection (b), the same event (assignment, transfer, or subrogation) that gives rise to rights to, and imposes obligations on, a successor relieves its predecessor of any further duties under this Article. For example, if the security interest is enforced after the secured obligation is assigned, the assignee—but not the assignor— has the duty to comply with this Part. Similarly, the assignment does not excuse the assignor from liability for failure to comply with duties that arose before the event or impose liability on the assignee for the assignor's failure to comply.

§ 9–619. Transfer of Record or Legal Title.

(a) **["Transfer statement."]** In this section, "transfer statement" means a record authenticated by a secured party stating:

(1) that the debtor has defaulted in connection with an obligation secured by specified collateral;

(2) that the secured party has exercised its post-default remedies with respect to the collateral;

(3)   that, by reason of the exercise, a transferee has acquired the rights of the debtor in the collateral; and

(4)   the name and mailing address of the secured party, debtor, and transferee.

(b)   **[Effect of transfer statement.]** A transfer statement entitles the transferee to the transfer of record of all rights of the debtor in the collateral specified in the statement in any official filing, recording, registration, or certificate-of-title system covering the collateral. If a transfer statement is presented with the applicable fee and request form to the official or office responsible for maintaining the system, the official or office shall:

(1)   accept the transfer statement;

(2)   promptly amend its records to reflect the transfer; and

(3)   if applicable, issue a new appropriate certificate of title in the name of the transferee.

(c)   **[Transfer not a disposition; no relief of secured party's duties.]** A transfer of the record or legal title to collateral to a secured party under subsection (b) or otherwise is not of itself a disposition of collateral under this article and does not of itself relieve the secured party of its duties under this article.

Official Comment

1.   **Source.** New.

2.   **Transfer of Record or Legal Title.** Potential buyers of collateral that is covered by a certificate of title (e.g., an automobile) or is subject to a registration system (e.g., a copyright) typically require as a condition of their purchase that the certificate or registry reflect their ownership. In many cases, this condition can be met only with the consent of the record owner. If the record owner is the debtor and, as may be the case after the default, the debtor refuses to cooperate, the secured party may have great difficulty disposing of the collateral.

Subsection (b) provides a simple mechanism for obtaining record or legal title, for use primarily when other law does not provide one. Of course, use of this mechanism will not be effective to clear title to the extent that subsection (b) is preempted by federal law. Subsection (b) contemplates a transfer of record or legal title to a third party, following a secured party's exercise of its disposition or acceptance remedies under this Part, as well as a transfer by a debtor to a secured party prior to the secured party's exercise of those remedies. Under subsection (c), a transfer of record or legal title (under subsection (b) or under other law) to a secured party prior to the exercise of those remedies merely puts the secured party in a position to pass legal or record title to a transferee at foreclosure. A secured party who has obtained record or legal title retains its duties with respect to enforcement of its security interest, and the debtor retains its rights as well.

3.   **Title-Clearing Systems Under Other Law.** Applicable non-UCC law (e.g., a certificate-of-title statute, federal registry rules, or the like) may provide a means by which the secured party may obtain or transfer record or legal title for the purpose of a disposition of the property under this Article. The mechanism provided by this section is in addition to any title-clearing provision under law other than this Article.

§ 9–620.   Acceptance of Collateral in Full or Partial Satisfaction of Obligation; Compulsory Disposition of Collateral.

(a)   **[Conditions to acceptance in satisfaction.]** Except as otherwise provided in subsection (g), a secured party may accept collateral in full or partial satisfaction of the obligation it secures only if:

(1)   the debtor consents to the acceptance under subsection (c);

(2)   the secured party does not receive, within the time set forth in subsection (d), a notification of objection to the proposal authenticated by:

(A)   a person to which the secured party was required to send a proposal under Section 9–621; or

(B)   any other person, other than the debtor, holding an interest in the collateral subordinate to the security interest that is the subject of the proposal;

(3)   if the collateral is consumer goods, the collateral is not in the possession of the debtor when the debtor consents to the acceptance; and

(4)   subsection (e) does not require the secured party to dispose of the collateral or the debtor waives the requirement pursuant to Section 9–624.

(b)   **[Purported acceptance ineffective.]** A purported or apparent acceptance of collateral under this section is ineffective unless:

(1)   the secured party consents to the acceptance in an authenticated record or sends a proposal to the debtor; and

(2)   the conditions of subsection (a) are met.

(c)   **[Debtor's consent.]** For purposes of this section:

(1)   a debtor consents to an acceptance of collateral in partial satisfaction of the obligation it secures only if the debtor agrees to the terms of the acceptance in a record authenticated after default; and

(2)   a debtor consents to an acceptance of collateral in full satisfaction of the obligation it secures only if the debtor agrees to the terms of the acceptance in a record authenticated after default or the secured party:

(A)   sends to the debtor after default a proposal that is unconditional or subject only to a condition that collateral not in the possession of the secured party be preserved or maintained;

(B)   in the proposal, proposes to accept collateral in full satisfaction of the obligation it secures; and

(C)   does not receive a notification of objection authenticated by the debtor within 20 days after the proposal is sent.

(d)   **[Effectiveness of notification.]** To be effective under subsection (a)(2), a notification of objection must be received by the secured party:

(1)   in the case of a person to which the proposal was sent pursuant to Section 9–621, within 20 days after notification was sent to that person; and

(2)   in other cases:

(A)   within 20 days after the last notification was sent pursuant to Section 9–621; or

(B)   if a notification was not sent, before the debtor consents to the acceptance under subsection (c).

(e)   **[Mandatory disposition of consumer goods.]** A secured party that has taken possession of collateral shall dispose of the collateral pursuant to Section 9–610 within the time specified in subsection (f) if:

(1)   60 percent of the cash price has been paid in the case of a purchase-money security interest in consumer goods; or

(2)   60 percent of the principal amount of the obligation secured has been paid in the case of a non-purchase-money security interest in consumer goods.

(f)   **[Compliance with mandatory disposition requirement.]** To comply with subsection (e), the secured party shall dispose of the collateral:

(1)   within 90 days after taking possession; or

(2)   within any longer period to which the debtor and all secondary obligors have agreed in an agreement to that effect entered into and authenticated after default.

(g)   **[No partial satisfaction in consumer transaction.]** In a consumer transaction, a secured party may not accept collateral in partial satisfaction of the obligation it secures.

Official Comment

1.   **Source.** Former Section 9–505.

2. **Overview.** This section and the two sections following deal with strict foreclosure, a procedure by which the secured party acquires the debtor's interest in the collateral without the need for a sale or other disposition under Section 9–610. Although these provisions derive from former Section 9–505, they have been entirely reorganized and substantially rewritten. The more straightforward approach taken in this Article eliminates the fiction that the secured party always will present a "proposal" for the retention of collateral and the debtor will have a fixed period to respond. By eliminating the need (but preserving the possibility) for proceeding in that fashion, this section eliminates much of the awkwardness of former Section 9–505. It reflects the belief that strict foreclosures should be encouraged and often will produce better results than a disposition for all concerned.

Subsection (a) sets forth the conditions necessary to an effective acceptance (formerly, retention) of collateral in full or partial satisfaction of the secured obligation. Section 9–621 requires in addition that a secured party who wishes to proceed under this section notify certain other persons who have or claim to have an interest in the collateral. Unlike the failure to meet the conditions in subsection (a), under Section 9–622(b) the failure to comply with the notification requirement of Section 9–621 does not render the acceptance of collateral ineffective. Rather, the acceptance can take effect notwithstanding the secured party's noncompliance. A person to whom the required notice was not sent has the right to recover damages under Section 9–625(b). Section 9–622(a) sets forth the effect of an acceptance of collateral.

3. **Conditions to Effective Acceptance.** Subsection (a) contains the conditions necessary to the effectiveness of an acceptance of collateral. Subsection (a)(1) requires the debtor's consent. Under subsections (c)(1) and (c)(2), the debtor may consent by agreeing to the acceptance in writing after default. Subsection (c)(2) contains an alternative method by which to satisfy the debtor's-consent condition in subsection (a)(1). It follows the proposal-and-objection model found in former Section 9–505: The debtor consents if the secured party sends a proposal to the debtor and does not receive an objection within 20 days. Under subsection (c)(1), however, that silence is not deemed to be consent with respect to acceptances in partial satisfaction. Thus, a secured party who wishes to conduct a "partial strict foreclosure" must obtain the debtor's agreement in a record authenticated after default. In all other respects, the conditions necessary to an effective partial strict foreclosure are the same as those governing acceptance of collateral in full satisfaction. (But see subsection (g), prohibiting partial strict foreclosure of a security interest in consumer transactions.)

The time when a debtor consents to a strict foreclosure is significant in several circumstances under this section and the following one. See Sections 9–620(a)(1), (d)(2), 9–621(a)(1), (a)(2), (a)(3). For purposes of determining the time of consent, a debtor's conditional consent constitutes consent.

Subsection (a)(2) contains the second condition to the effectiveness of an acceptance under this section—the absence of a timely objection from a person holding a junior interest in the collateral or from a secondary obligor. Any junior party—secured party or lienholder—is entitled to lodge an objection to a proposal, even if that person was not entitled to notification under Section 9–621. Subsection (d), discussed below, indicates when an objection is timely.

Subsections (a)(3) and (a)(4) contain special rules for transactions in which consumers are involved. See Comment 12.

4. **Proposals.** Section 9–102 defines the term "proposal." It is necessary to send a "proposal" to the debtor only if the debtor does not agree to an acceptance in an authenticated record as described in subsection (c)(1) or (c)(2). Section 9–621(a) determines whether it is necessary to send a proposal to third parties. A proposal need not take any particular form as long as it sets forth the terms under which the secured party is willing to accept collateral in satisfaction. A proposal to accept collateral should specify the amount (or a means of calculating the amount, such as by including a per diem accrual figure) of the secured obligations to be satisfied, state the conditions (if any) under which the proposal may be revoked, and describe any other applicable conditions. Note, however, that a conditional proposal generally requires the debtor's agreement in order to take effect. See subsection (c).

5. **Secured Party's Agreement; No "Constructive" Strict Foreclosure.** The conditions of subsection (a) relate to actual or implied consent by the debtor and any secondary obligor or holder of a junior security interest or lien. To ensure that the debtor cannot unilaterally cause an acceptance of collateral, subsection (b) provides that compliance with these conditions is necessary but not sufficient to cause an acceptance of collateral. Rather, under subsection (b), acceptance does not occur unless, in addition, the secured party consents to the acceptance in an authenticated record or sends to the debtor a proposal. For this reason, a mere delay in collection or disposition of collateral does not constitute a "constructive" strict foreclosure. Instead, delay is a factor relating to whether the secured party acted in a commercially reasonable manner for purposes of Section 9–607 or 9–610. A

debtor's voluntary surrender of collateral to a secured party and the secured party's acceptance of possession of the collateral does not, of itself, necessarily raise an implication that the secured party intends or is proposing to accept the collateral in satisfaction of the secured obligation under this section.

6. **When Acceptance Occurs.** This section does not impose any formalities or identify any steps that a secured party must take in order to accept collateral once the conditions of subsections (a) and (b) have been met. Absent facts or circumstances indicating a contrary intention, the fact that the conditions have been met provides a sufficient indication that the secured party has accepted the collateral on the terms to which the secured party has consented or proposed and the debtor has consented or failed to object. Following a proposal, acceptance of the collateral normally is automatic upon the secured party's becoming bound and the time for objection passing. As a matter of good business practice, an enforcing secured party may wish to memorialize its acceptance following a proposal, such as by notifying the debtor that the strict foreclosure is effective or by placing a written record to that effect in its files. The secured party's agreement to accept collateral is self-executing and cannot be breached. The secured party is bound by its agreement to accept collateral and by any proposal to which the debtor consents.

7. **No Possession Requirement.** This section eliminates the requirement in former Section 9–505 that the secured party be "in possession" of collateral. It clarifies that intangible collateral, which cannot be possessed, may be subject to a strict foreclosure under this section. However, under subsection (a)(3), if the collateral is consumer goods, acceptance does not occur unless the debtor is not in possession.

8. **When Objection Timely.** Subsection (d) explains when an objection is timely and thus prevents an acceptance of collateral from taking effect. An objection by a person to which notification was sent under Section 9–621 is effective if it is received by the secured party within 20 days from the date the notification was sent to that person. Other objecting parties (i.e., third parties who are not entitled to notification) may object at any time within 20 days after the last notification is sent under Section 9–621. If no such notification is sent, third parties must object before the debtor agrees to the acceptance in writing or is deemed to have consented by silence. The former may occur any time after default, and the latter requires a 20-day waiting period. See subsection (c).

9. **Applicability of Other Law.** This section does not purport to regulate all aspects of the transaction by which a secured party may become the owner of collateral previously owned by the debtor. For example, a secured party's acceptance of a motor vehicle in satisfaction of secured obligations may require compliance with the applicable motor vehicle certificate-of-title law. State legislatures should conform those laws so that they mesh well with this section and Section 9–610, and courts should construe those laws and this section harmoniously. A secured party's acceptance of collateral in the possession of the debtor also may implicate statutes dealing with a seller's retention of possession of goods sold.

10. **Accounts, Chattel Paper, Payment Intangibles, and Promissory Notes.** If the collateral is accounts, chattel paper, payment intangibles, or promissory notes, then a secured party's acceptance of the collateral in satisfaction of secured obligations would constitute a sale to the secured party. That sale normally would give rise to a new security interest (the ownership interest) under Sections 1–201(37) [*unrevised Article 1; see Concordance, p. 22*] and 9–109. In the case of accounts and chattel paper, the new security interest would remain perfected by a filing that was effective to perfect the secured party's original security interest. In the case of payment intangibles or promissory notes, the security interest would be perfected when it attaches. See Section 9–309. However, the procedures for acceptance of collateral under this section satisfy all necessary formalities and a new security agreement authenticated by the debtor would not be necessary.

11. **Role of Good Faith.** Section 1–304 imposes an obligation of good faith on a secured party's enforcement under this Article. This obligation may not be disclaimed by agreement. See Section 1–302. Thus, a proposal and acceptance made under this section in bad faith would not be effective. For example, a secured party's proposal to accept marketable securities worth $1,000 in full satisfaction of indebtedness in the amount of $100, made in the hopes that the debtor might inadvertently fail to object, would be made in bad faith. On the other hand, in the normal case proposals and acceptances should be not second-guessed on the basis of the "value" of the collateral involved. Disputes about valuation or even a clear excess of collateral value over the amount of obligations satisfied do not necessarily demonstrate the absence of good faith.

12. **Special Rules in Consumer Cases.** Subsection (e) imposes an obligation on the secured party to dispose of consumer goods under certain circumstances. Subsection (f) explains when a disposition that is required under subsection (e) is timely. An effective acceptance of collateral cannot occur if subsection (e) requires a disposition unless the debtor waives this requirement pursuant to Section 9–624(b). Moreover, a secured party who takes possession of collateral and unreasonably delays disposition violates subsection (e), if applicable, and may also violate Section 9–610 or other provisions of this Part. Subsection (e) eliminates as superfluous the express

statutory reference to "conversion" found in former Section 9–505. Remedies available under other law, including conversion, remain available under this Article in appropriate cases. See Sections 1–103, 1–305.

Subsection (g) prohibits the secured party in consumer transactions from accepting collateral in partial satisfaction of the obligation it secures. If a secured party attempts an acceptance in partial satisfaction in a consumer transaction, the attempted acceptance is void.

As amended in 2010.

§ 9–621.   Notification of Proposal to Accept Collateral.

(a)   **[Persons to which proposal to be sent.]** A secured party that desires to accept collateral in full or partial satisfaction of the obligation it secures shall send its proposal to:

(1)   any person from which the secured party has received, before the debtor consented to the acceptance, an authenticated notification of a claim of an interest in the collateral;

(2)   any other secured party or lienholder that, 10 days before the debtor consented to the acceptance, held a security interest in or other lien on the collateral perfected by the filing of a financing statement that:

(A)   identified the collateral;

(B)   was indexed under the debtor's name as of that date; and

(C)   was filed in the office or offices in which to file a financing statement against the debtor covering the collateral as of that date; and

(3)   any other secured party that, 10 days before the debtor consented to the acceptance, held a security interest in the collateral perfected by compliance with a statute, regulation, or treaty described in Section 9–311(a).

(b)   **[Proposal to be sent to secondary obligor in partial satisfaction.]** A secured party that desires to accept collateral in partial satisfaction of the obligation it secures shall send its proposal to any secondary obligor in addition to the persons described in subsection (a).

Official Comment

1.   **Source.** Former Section 9–505.

2.   **Notification Requirement.** Subsection (a) specifies three classes of competing claimants to whom the secured party must send notification of its proposal: (i) those who notify the secured party that they claim an interest in the collateral, (ii) holders of certain security interests and liens who have filed against the debtor, and (iii) holders of certain security interests who have perfected by compliance with a statute (including a certificate-of-title statute), regulation, or treaty described in Section 9–311(a). With regard to (ii), see Section 9–611, Comment 4. Subsection (b) also requires notification to any secondary obligor if the proposal is for acceptance in partial satisfaction.

Unlike Section 9–611, this section contains no "safe harbor," which excuses an enforcing secured party from notifying certain secured parties and other lienholders. This is because, unlike Section 9–610, which requires that a disposition of collateral be commercially reasonable, Section 9–620 permits the debtor and secured party to set the amount of credit the debtor will receive for the collateral subject only to the requirement of good faith. An effective acceptance discharges subordinate security interests and other subordinate liens. See Section 9–622. If collateral is subject to several liens securing debts much larger than the value of the collateral, the debtor may be disinclined to refrain from consenting to an acceptance by the holder of the senior security interest, even though, had the debtor objected and the senior disposed of the collateral under Section 9–610, the collateral may have yielded more than enough to satisfy the senior security interest (but not enough to satisfy all the liens). Accordingly, this section imposes upon the enforcing secured party the risk of the filing office's errors and delay. The holder of a security interest who is entitled to notification under this section but to whom the enforcing secured party does not send notification has the right to recover under Section 9–625(b) any loss resulting from the secured party's noncompliance with this section.

As amended in 2010.

§ 9–622. Effect of Acceptance of Collateral.

(a) **[Effect of acceptance.]** A secured party's acceptance of collateral in full or partial satisfaction of the obligation it secures:

(1) discharges the obligation to the extent consented to by the debtor;

(2) transfers to the secured party all of a debtor's rights in the collateral;

(3) discharges the security interest or agricultural lien that is the subject of the debtor's consent and any subordinate security interest or other subordinate lien; and

(4) terminates any other subordinate interest.

(b) **[Discharge of subordinate interest notwithstanding noncompliance.]** A subordinate interest is discharged or terminated under subsection (a), even if the secured party fails to comply with this article.

Official Comment

1. **Source.** New.

2. **Effect of Acceptance.** Subsection (a) specifies the effect of an acceptance of collateral in full or partial satisfaction of the secured obligation. The acceptance to which it refers is an effective acceptance. If a purported acceptance is ineffective under Section 9–620, e.g., because the secured party receives a timely objection from a person entitled to notification, then neither this subsection nor subsection (b) applies. Paragraph (1) expresses the fundamental consequence of accepting collateral in full or partial satisfaction of the secured obligation—the obligation is discharged to the extent consented to by the debtor. Unless otherwise agreed, the obligor remains liable for any deficiency. Paragraphs (2) through (4) indicate the effects of an acceptance on various property rights and interests. Paragraph (2) follows Section 9–617(a) in providing that the secured party acquires "all of a debtor's rights in the collateral." Under paragraph (3), the effect of strict foreclosure on holders of junior security interests and other liens is the same regardless of whether the collateral is accepted in full or partial satisfaction of the secured obligation: all junior encumbrances are discharged. Paragraph (4) provides for the termination of other subordinate interests.

Subsection (b) makes clear that subordinate interests are discharged under subsection (a) regardless of whether the secured party complies with this Article. Thus, subordinate interests are discharged regardless of whether a proposal was required to be sent or, if required, was sent. However, a secured party's failure to send a proposal or otherwise to comply with this Article may subject the secured party to liability under Section 9–625.

§ 9–623. Right to Redeem Collateral.

(a) **[Persons that may redeem.]** A debtor, any secondary obligor, or any other secured party or lienholder may redeem collateral.

(b) **[Requirements for redemption.]** To redeem collateral, a person shall tender:

(1) fulfillment of all obligations secured by the collateral; and

(2) the reasonable expenses and attorney's fees described in Section 9–615(a)(1).

(c) **[When redemption may occur.]** A redemption may occur at any time before a secured party:

(1) has collected collateral under Section 9–607;

(2) has disposed of collateral or entered into a contract for its disposition under Section 9–610; or

(3) has accepted collateral in full or partial satisfaction of the obligation it secures under Section 9–622.

Official Comment

1. **Source.** Former Section 9–506.

2. **Redemption Right.** Under this section, as under former Section 9–506, the debtor or another secured party may redeem collateral as long as the secured party has not collected (Section 9–607), disposed of or contracted for the disposition of (Section 9–610), or accepted (Section 9–620) the collateral. Although this section generally follows former Section 9–506, it extends the right of redemption to holders of nonconsensual liens. To

redeem the collateral a person must tender fulfillment of all obligations secured, plus certain expenses. If the entire balance of a secured obligation has been accelerated, it would be necessary to tender the entire balance. A tender of fulfillment obviously means more than a new promise to perform an existing promise. It requires payment in full of all monetary obligations then due and performance in full of all other obligations then matured. If unmatured secured obligations remain, the security interest continues to secure them (i.e., as if there had been no default).

3.   **Redemption of Remaining Collateral Following Partial Enforcement.** Under Section 9–610 a secured party may make successive dispositions of portions of its collateral. These dispositions would not affect the debtor's, another secured party's, or a lienholder's right to redeem the remaining collateral.

4.   **Effect of "Repledging."** Section 9–207 generally permits a secured party having possession or control of collateral to create a security interest in the collateral. As explained in the Comments to that section, the debtor's right (as opposed to its practical ability) to redeem collateral is not affected by, and does not affect, the priority of a security interest created by the debtor's secured party.

§ 9–624.   Waiver.

(a)   **[Waiver of disposition notification.]** A debtor or secondary obligor may waive the right to notification of disposition of collateral under Section 9–611 only by an agreement to that effect entered into and authenticated after default.

(b)   **[Waiver of mandatory disposition.]** A debtor may waive the right to require disposition of collateral under Section 9–620(e) only by an agreement to that effect entered into and authenticated after default.

(c)   **[Waiver of redemption right.]** Except in a consumer-goods transaction, a debtor or secondary obligor may waive the right to redeem collateral under Section 9–623 only by an agreement to that effect entered into and authenticated after default.

Official Comment

1.   **Source.** Former Sections 9–504(3), 9–505, 9–506.

2.   **Waiver.** This section is a limited exception to Section 9–602, which generally prohibits waiver by debtors and obligors. It makes no provision for waiver of the rule prohibiting a secured party from buying at its own private disposition. Transactions of this kind are equivalent to "strict foreclosures" and are governed by Sections 9–620, 9–621, and 9–622.

[SUBPART 2. NONCOMPLIANCE WITH ARTICLE]

§ 9–625.   Remedies for Secured Party's Failure to Comply With Article.

(a)   **[Judicial orders concerning noncompliance.]** If it is established that a secured party is not proceeding in accordance with this article, a court may order or restrain collection, enforcement, or disposition of collateral on appropriate terms and conditions.

(b)   **[Damages for noncompliance.]** Subject to subsections (c), (d), and (f), a person is liable for damages in the amount of any loss caused by a failure to comply with this article. Loss caused by a failure to comply may include loss resulting from the debtor's inability to obtain, or increased costs of, alternative financing.

(c)   **[Persons entitled to recover damages; statutory damages if collateral is consumer goods.]** Except as otherwise provided in Section 9–628:

(1)   a person that, at the time of the failure, was a debtor, was an obligor, or held a security interest in or other lien on the collateral may recover damages under subsection (b) for its loss; and

(2)   if the collateral is consumer goods, a person that was a debtor or a secondary obligor at the time a secured party failed to comply with this part may recover for that failure in any event an amount not less than the credit service charge plus 10 percent of the principal amount of the obligation or the time-price differential plus 10 percent of the cash price.

(d)   **[Recovery when deficiency eliminated or reduced.]** A debtor whose deficiency is eliminated under Section 9–626 may recover damages for the loss of any surplus. However, a debtor or secondary obligor

914

whose deficiency is eliminated or reduced under Section 9–626 may not otherwise recover under subsection (b) for noncompliance with the provisions of this part relating to collection, enforcement, disposition, or acceptance.

(e) **[Statutory damages: noncompliance with specified provisions.]** In addition to any damages recoverable under subsection (b), the debtor, consumer obligor, or person named as a debtor in a filed record, as applicable, may recover $500 in each case from a person that:

(1) fails to comply with Section 9–208;

(2) fails to comply with Section 9–209;

(3) files a record that the person is not entitled to file under Section 9–509(a);

(4) fails to cause the secured party of record to file or send a termination statement as required by Section 9–513(a) or (c);

(5) fails to comply with Section 9–616(b)(1) and whose failure is part of a pattern, or consistent with a practice, of noncompliance; or

(6) fails to comply with Section 9–616(b)(2).

(f) **[Statutory damages: noncompliance with Section 9–210.]** A debtor or consumer obligor may recover damages under subsection (b) and, in addition, $500 in each case from a person that, without reasonable cause, fails to comply with a request under Section 9–210. A recipient of a request under Section 9–210 which never claimed an interest in the collateral or obligations that are the subject of a request under that section has a reasonable excuse for failure to comply with the request within the meaning of this subsection.

(g) **[Limitation of security interest: noncompliance with Section 9–210.]** If a secured party fails to comply with a request regarding a list of collateral or a statement of account under Section 9–210, the secured party may claim a security interest only as shown in the list or statement included in the request as against a person that is reasonably misled by the failure.

As amended in 2000 and 2010.

Official Comment

1. **Source.** Former Section 9–507.

2. **Remedies for Noncompliance; Scope.** Subsections (a) and (b) provide the basic remedies afforded to those aggrieved by a secured party's failure to comply with this Article. Like all provisions that create liability, they are subject to Section 9–628, which should be read in conjunction with Section 9–605. The principal limitations under this Part on a secured party's right to enforce its security interest against collateral are the requirements that it proceed in good faith (Section 1–203) [*unrevised Article 1; see Concordance, p. 22*], in a commercially reasonable manner (Sections 9–607 and 9–610), and, in most cases, with reasonable notification (Sections 9–611 through 9–614). Following former Section 9–507, under subsection (a) an aggrieved person may seek injunctive relief, and under subsection (b) the person may recover damages for losses caused by noncompliance. Unlike former Section 9–507, however, subsections (a) and (b) are not limited to noncompliance with provisions of this Part of Article 9. Rather, they apply to noncompliance with any provision of this Article. The change makes this section applicable to noncompliance with Sections 9–207 (duties of secured party in possession of collateral), 9–208 (duties of secured party having control over deposit account), 9–209 (duties of secured party if account debtor has been notified of an assignment), 9–210 (duty to comply with request for accounting, etc.), 9–509(a) (duty to refrain from filing unauthorized financing statement), and 9–513(a) or (c) (duty to provide termination statement). Subsection (a) also modifies the first sentence of former Section 9–507(1) by adding the references to "collection" and "enforcement." Subsection (c)(2), which gives a minimum damage recovery in consumer-goods transactions, applies only to noncompliance with the provisions of this Part.

Subsection (a) displaces other state law governing availability of the types of relief addressed in that subsection to the extent that the other state law would preclude the availability of injunctive relief in an otherwise appropriate case solely because the aggrieved party would be able to obtain a collectible money judgment for noncompliance with the rules of this Article. Rather, under subsection (a), in an appropriate case the aggrieved party should be able obtain relief of the sort described in that subsection even if it would be possible for the aggrieved party to obtain such a judgment. See PEB Commentary No. 27, dated December 16, 2022, discussing the issue in the context of a noncomplying disposition under Section 9–610. The Commentary is available at https://www.ali.org/peb-ucc.

3.   **Damages for Noncompliance with This Article.** Subsection (b) sets forth the basic remedy for failure to comply with the requirements of this Article: a damage recovery in the amount of loss caused by the noncompliance. Subsection (c) identifies who may recover under subsection (b). It affords a remedy to any aggrieved person who is a debtor or obligor. However, a principal obligor who is not a debtor may recover damages only for noncompliance with Section 9–616, inasmuch as none of the other rights and duties in this Article run in favor of such a principal obligor. Such a principal obligor could not suffer any loss or damage on account of noncompliance with rights or duties of which it is not a beneficiary. Subsection (c) also affords a remedy to an aggrieved person who holds a competing security interest or other lien, regardless of whether the aggrieved person is entitled to notification under Part 6. The remedy is available even to holders of senior security interests and other liens. The exercise of this remedy is subject to the normal rules of pleading and proof. A person who has delegated the duties of a secured party but who remains obligated to perform them is liable under this subsection. The last sentence of subsection (d) eliminates the possibility of double recovery or other over-compensation arising out of a reduction or elimination of a deficiency under Section 9–626, based on noncompliance with the provisions of this Part relating to collection, enforcement, disposition, or acceptance. Assuming no double recovery, a debtor whose deficiency is eliminated under Section 9–626 may pursue a claim for a surplus. Because Section 9–626 does not apply to consumer transactions, the statute is silent as to whether a double recovery or other over-compensation is possible in a consumer transaction.

Damages for violation of the requirements of this Article, including Section 9–609, are those reasonably calculated to put an eligible claimant in the position that it would have occupied had no violation occurred. See Section 1–106 [*unrevised Article 1; see Concordance, p. 22*]. Subsection (b) supports the recovery of actual damages for committing a breach of the peace in violation of Section 9–609, and principles of tort law supplement this subsection. See Section 1–103. However, to the extent that damages in tort compensate the debtor for the same loss dealt with by this Article, the debtor should be entitled to only one recovery.

4.   **Minimum Damages in Consumer-Goods Transactions.** Subsection (c)(2) provides a minimum, statutory, damage recovery for a debtor and secondary obligor in a consumer-goods transaction. It is patterned on former Section 9–507(1) and is designed to ensure that every noncompliance with the requirements of Part 6 in a consumer-goods transaction results in liability, regardless of any injury that may have resulted. Subsection (c)(2) leaves the treatment of statutory damages as it was under former Article 9. A secured party is not liable for statutory damages under this subsection more than once with respect to any one secured obligation (see Section 9–628(e)), nor is a secured party liable under this subsection for failure to comply with Section 9–616 (see Section 9–628(d)).

Following former Section 9–507(1), this Article does not include a definition or explanation of the terms "credit service charge," "principal amount," "time-price differential," or "cash price," as used in subsection (c)(2). It leaves their construction and application to the court, taking into account the subsection's purpose of providing a minimum recovery in consumer-goods transactions.

5.   **Supplemental Damages.** Subsections (e) and (f) provide damages that supplement the recovery, if any, under subsection (b). Subsection (e) imposes an additional $500 liability upon a person who fails to comply with the provisions specified in that subsection, and subsection (f) imposes like damages on a person who, without reasonable excuse, fails to comply with a request for an accounting or a request regarding a list of collateral or statement of account under Section 9–210. However, under subsection (f), a person has a reasonable excuse for the failure if the person never claimed an interest in the collateral or obligations that were the subject of the request.

6.   **Estoppel.** Subsection (g) limits the extent to which a secured party who fails to comply with a request regarding a list of collateral or statement of account may claim a security interest.

As amended in 2022.

§ 9–626.   Action in Which Deficiency or Surplus Is in Issue.

(a)   **[Applicable rules if amount of deficiency or surplus in issue.]** In an action arising from a transaction, other than a consumer transaction, in which the amount of a deficiency or surplus is in issue, the following rules apply:

(1) A secured party need not prove compliance with the provisions of this part relating to collection, enforcement, disposition, or acceptance unless the debtor or a secondary obligor places the secured party's compliance in issue.

(2) If the secured party's compliance is placed in issue, the secured party has the burden of establishing that the collection, enforcement, disposition, or acceptance was conducted in accordance with this part. *The Rebuttable presumption Rule in non consumer transactions*

(3) Except as otherwise provided in Section 9–628, if a secured party fails to prove that the collection, enforcement, disposition, or acceptance was conducted in accordance with the provisions of this part relating to collection, enforcement, disposition, or acceptance, the liability of a debtor or a secondary obligor for a deficiency is limited to an amount by which the sum of the secured obligation, expenses, and attorney's fees exceeds the greater of:

(A) the proceeds of the collection, enforcement, disposition, or acceptance; or

(B) the amount of proceeds that would have been realized had the noncomplying secured party proceeded in accordance with the provisions of this part relating to collection, enforcement, disposition, or acceptance.

(4) For purposes of paragraph (3)(B), the amount of proceeds that would have been realized is equal to the sum of the secured obligation, expenses, and attorney's fees unless the secured party proves that the amount is less than that sum.

(5) If a deficiency or surplus is calculated under Section 9–615(f), the debtor or obligor has the burden of establishing that the amount of proceeds of the disposition is significantly below the range of prices that a complying disposition to a person other than the secured party, a person related to the secured party, or a secondary obligor would have brought.

(b) **[Non-consumer transactions; no inference.]** The limitation of the rules in subsection (a) to transactions other than consumer transactions is intended to leave to the court the determination of the proper rules in consumer transactions. [The court may not infer from that limitation the nature of the proper rule in consumer transactions and may continue to apply established approaches.] *can still use other old rules if you like (depends on the J)*

Official Comment

1. **Source.** New.

2. **Scope.** The basic damage remedy under Section 9–625(b) is subject to the special rules in this section for transactions other than consumer transactions. This section addresses situations in which the amount of a deficiency or surplus is in issue, i.e., situations in which the secured party has collected, enforced, disposed of, or accepted the collateral. It contains special rules applicable to a determination of the amount of a deficiency or surplus. Because this section affects a person's liability for a deficiency, it is subject to Section 9–628, which should be read in conjunction with Section 9–605. The rules in this section apply only to noncompliance in connection with the "collection, enforcement, disposition, or acceptance" under Part 6. For other types of noncompliance with Part 6, the general liability rule of Section 9–625(b)—recovery of actual damages—applies. Consider, for example, a repossession that does not comply with Section 9–609 for want of a default. The debtor's remedy is under Section 9–625(b). In a proper case, the secured party also may be liable for conversion under non-UCC law. If the secured party thereafter disposed of the collateral, however, it would violate Section 9–610 at that time, and this section would apply.

3. **Rebuttable Presumption Rule.** Subsection (a) establishes the rebuttable presumption rule for transactions other than consumer transactions. Under paragraph (1), the secured party need not prove compliance with the relevant provisions of this Part as part of its prima facie case. If, however, the debtor or a secondary obligor raises the issue (in accordance with the forum's rules of pleading and practice), then the secured party bears the burden of proving that the collection, enforcement, disposition, or acceptance complied. In the event the secured party is unable to meet this burden, then paragraph (3) explains how to calculate the deficiency. Under this rebuttable presumption rule, the debtor or obligor is to be credited with the greater of the actual proceeds of the disposition or the proceeds that would have been realized had the secured party complied with the relevant provisions. If a deficiency remains, then the secured party is entitled to recover it. The references to "the secured obligation, expenses, and attorney's fees" in paragraphs (3) and (4) embrace the application rules in Sections 9–608(a) and 9–615(a).

Unless the secured party proves that compliance with the relevant provisions would have yielded a smaller amount, under paragraph (4) the amount that a complying collection, enforcement, or disposition would have yielded is deemed to be equal to the amount of the secured obligation, together with expenses and attorney's fees. Thus, the secured party may not recover any deficiency unless it meets this burden.

4. **Consumer Transactions.** Although subsection (a) adopts a version of the rebuttable presumption rule for transactions other than consumer transactions, with certain exceptions Part 6 does not specify the effect of a secured party's noncompliance in consumer transactions. (The exceptions are the provisions for the recovery of damages in Section 9–625.) Subsection (b) provides that the limitation of subsection (a) to transactions other than consumer transactions is intended to leave to the court the determination of the proper rules in consumer transactions. It also instructs the court not to draw any inference from the limitation as to the proper rules for consumer transactions and leaves the court free to continue to apply established approaches to those transactions.

Courts construing former Section 9–507 disagreed about the consequences of a secured party's failure to comply with the requirements of former Part 5. Three general approaches emerged. Some courts have held that a noncomplying secured party may not recover a deficiency (the "absolute bar" rule). A few courts held that the debtor can offset against a claim to a deficiency all damages recoverable under former Section 9–507 resulting from the secured party's noncompliance (the "offset" rule). A plurality of courts considering the issue held that the noncomplying secured party is barred from recovering a deficiency unless it overcomes a rebuttable presumption that compliance with former Part 5 would have yielded an amount sufficient to satisfy the secured debt. In addition to the nonuniformity resulting from court decisions, some States enacted special rules governing the availability of deficiencies.

5. **Burden of Proof When Section 9–615(f) Applies.** In a non-consumer transaction, subsection (a)(5) imposes upon a debtor or obligor the burden of proving that the proceeds of a disposition are so low that, under Section 9–615(f), the actual proceeds should not serve as the basis upon which a deficiency or surplus is calculated. Were the burden placed on the secured party, then debtors might be encouraged to challenge the price received in every disposition to the secured party, a person related to the secured party, or a secondary obligor.

6. **Delay in Applying This Section.** There is an inevitable delay between the time a secured party engages in a noncomplying collection, enforcement, disposition, or acceptance and the time of a subsequent judicial determination that the secured party did not comply with Part 6. During the interim, the secured party, believing that the secured obligation is larger than it ultimately is determined to be, may continue to enforce its security interest in collateral. If some or all of the secured indebtedness ultimately is discharged under this section, a reasonable application of this section would impose liability on the secured party for the amount of any excess, unwarranted recoveries but would not make the enforcement efforts wrongful.

§ 9–627. Determination of Whether Conduct Was Commercially Reasonable.

(a) **[Greater amount obtainable under other circumstances; no preclusion of commercial reasonableness.]** The fact that a greater amount could have been obtained by a collection, enforcement, disposition, or acceptance at a different time or in a different method from that selected by the secured party is not of itself sufficient to preclude the secured party from establishing that the collection, enforcement, disposition, or acceptance was made in a commercially reasonable manner.

(b) **[Dispositions that are commercially reasonable.]** A disposition of collateral is made in a commercially reasonable manner if the disposition is made:

(1) in the usual manner on any recognized market;

(2) at the price current in any recognized market at the time of the disposition; or

(3) otherwise in conformity with reasonable commercial practices among dealers in the type of property that was the subject of the disposition.

(c) **[Approval by court or on behalf of creditors.]** A collection, enforcement, disposition, or acceptance is commercially reasonable if it has been approved:

(1) in a judicial proceeding;

(2) by a bona fide creditors' committee;

(3) by a representative of creditors; or

(4) by an assignee for the benefit of creditors.

(d)   **[Approval under subsection (c) not necessary; absence of approval has no effect.]** Approval under subsection (c) need not be obtained, and lack of approval does not mean that the collection, enforcement, disposition, or acceptance is not commercially reasonable.

Official Comment

1.   **Source.** Former Section 9–507(2).

2.   **Relationship of Price to Commercial Reasonableness.** Some observers have found the notion contained in subsection (a) (derived from former Section 9–507(2)) (the fact that a better price could have been obtained does not establish lack of commercial reasonableness) to be inconsistent with that found in Section 9–610(b) (derived from former Section 9–504(3)) (every aspect of the disposition, including its terms, must be commercially reasonable). There is no such inconsistency. While not itself sufficient to establish a violation of this Part, a low price suggests that a court should scrutinize carefully all aspects of a disposition to ensure that each aspect was commercially reasonable.

The law long has grappled with the problem of dispositions of personal and real property which comply with applicable procedural requirements (e.g., advertising, notification to interested persons, etc.) but which yield a price that seems low. This Article addresses that issue in Section 9–615(f). That section applies only when the transferee is the secured party, a person related to the secured party, or a secondary obligor. It contains a special rule for calculating a deficiency or surplus in a complying disposition that yields a price that is "significantly below the range of proceeds that a complying disposition to a person other than the secured party, a person related to the secured party, or a secondary obligor would have brought."

3.   **Determination of Commercial Reasonableness; Advance Approval.** It is important to make clear the conduct and procedures that are commercially reasonable and to provide a secured party with the means of obtaining, by court order or negotiation with a creditors' committee or a representative of creditors, advance approval of a proposed method of enforcement as commercially reasonable. This section contains rules that assist in that determination and provides for advance approval in appropriate situations. However, none of the specific methods of disposition specified in subsection (b) is required or exclusive.

4.   **"Recognized Market."** As in Sections 9–610(c) and 9–611(d), the concept of a "recognized market" in subsections (b)(1) and (2) is quite limited; it applies only to markets in which there are standardized price quotations for property that is essentially fungible, such as stock exchanges.

§ 9–628. Nonliability and Limitation on Liability of Secured Party; Liability of Secondary Obligor.

(a)   **[Limitation of liability of secured party for noncompliance with article.]** Unless a secured party knows that a person is a debtor or obligor, knows the identity of the person, and knows how to communicate with the person:

(1)   the secured party is not liable to the person, or to a secured party or lienholder that has filed a financing statement against the person, for failure to comply with this article; and

(2)   the secured party's failure to comply with this article does not affect the liability of the person for a deficiency.

(b)   **[Limitation of liability based on status as secured party.]** A secured party is not liable because of its status as secured party:

(1)   to a person that is a debtor or obligor, unless the secured party knows:

(A)   that the person is a debtor or obligor;

(B)   the identity of the person; and

(C)   how to communicate with the person; or

(2)   to a secured party or lienholder that has filed a financing statement against a person, unless the secured party knows:

(A)   that the person is a debtor; and

(B)   the identity of the person.

(c) **[Limitation of liability if reasonable belief that transaction not a consumer-goods transaction or consumer transaction.]** A secured party is not liable to any person, and a person's liability for a deficiency is not affected, because of any act or omission arising out of the secured party's reasonable belief that a transaction is not a consumer-goods transaction or a consumer transaction or that goods are not consumer goods, if the secured party's belief is based on its reasonable reliance on:

(1) a debtor's representation concerning the purpose for which collateral was to be used, acquired, or held; or

(2) an obligor's representation concerning the purpose for which a secured obligation was incurred.

(d) **[Limitation of liability for statutory damages.]** A secured party is not liable to any person under Section 9–625(c)(2) for its failure to comply with Section 9–616.

(e) **[Limitation of multiple liability for statutory damages.]** A secured party is not liable under Section 9–625(c)(2) more than once with respect to any one secured obligation.

Official Comment

1. **Source.** New.

2. **Exculpatory Provisions.** Subsections (a), (b), and (c) contain exculpatory provisions that should be read in conjunction with Section 9–605. Without this group of provisions, a secured party could incur liability to unknown persons and under circumstances that would not allow the secured party to protect itself. The broadened definition of the term "debtor" underscores the need for these provisions.

If a secured party reasonably, but mistakenly, believes that a consumer transaction or consumer-goods transaction is a non-consumer transaction or non-consumer-goods transaction, and if the secured party's belief is based on its reasonable reliance on a representation of the type specified in subsection (c)(1) or (c)(2), then this Article should be applied as if the facts reasonably believed and the representation reasonably relied upon were true. For example, if a secured party reasonably believed that a transaction was a non-consumer transaction and its belief was based on reasonable reliance on the debtor's representation that the collateral secured an obligation incurred for business purposes, the secured party is not liable to any person, and the debtor's liability for a deficiency is not affected, because of any act or omission of the secured party which arises out of the reasonable belief. Of course, if the secured party's belief is not reasonable or, even if reasonable, is not based on reasonable reliance on the debtor's representation, this limitation on liability is inapplicable.

3. **Inapplicability of Statutory Damages to Section 9–616.** Subsection (d) excludes noncompliance with Section 9–616 entirely from the scope of statutory damage liability under Section 9–625(c)(2).

4. **Single Liability for Statutory Minimum Damages.** Subsection (e) ensures that a secured party will incur statutory damages only once in connection with any one secured obligation.

As amended in 2000.

[PART 7 TRANSITION RULES OMITTED]

[PART 8 TRANSITION PROVISIONS FOR 2010 AMENDMENTS OMITTED]

UCC ARTICLE 12

CONTROLLABLE ELECTRONIC RECORDS

Article 12 was added in 2022. It is presented without <u>underline</u> formatting.

12–101.   Title.
12–102.   Definitions.
12–103.   Relation to Article 9 and Consumer Laws.
12–104.   Rights in Controllable Account, Controllable Electronic Record, and Controllable Payment Intangible.
12–105.   Control of Controllable Electronic Record.
12–106.   Discharge of Account Debtor on Controllable Account or Controllable Payment Intangible.
12–107.   Governing Law.

PREFATORY NOTE TO ARTICLE 12

1.   Introduction to Controllable Electronic Records. Article 12, which deals with controllable electronic records, and the conforming amendments to Articles 1 and 9, in particular, are a major part of the effort to adapt the UCC to emerging technologies as they might affect electronic commerce.

Article 12 creates a legal regime that is meant to apply more broadly than to electronic (intangible) assets that are created using existing technologies such as distributed ledger technology (DLT), including blockchain technology, which records transactions in bitcoin and other digital assets. It also aspires to apply to electronic assets that may be created using technologies that have yet to be developed, or even imagined.

The adoption of DLT has underscored two important trends in electronic commerce. First, people have begun to assign economic value to some electronic records that bear no relationship to extrinsic rights and interests. For example, without any law or legally enforceable agreement, people around the world have agreed to treat virtual currencies such as bitcoin (or, more precisely "transaction outputs" generated by the Bitcoin protocol) as a medium of exchange and store of value. Second, people are using the creation or transfer of electronic records to transfer rights to receive payment, rights to receive performance of other obligations (e.g., services or delivery of goods), and other rights and interests in personal and real property.

These trends will inevitably result in disputes among claimants to electronic records and their related rights and other benefits. Uncertainty as to the criteria for resolving these claims creates commercial risk. The magnitude of these risks will grow as these trends continue.

As explained in more detail below, Article 12 is designed to reduce these risks by providing legal rules governing the transfer—both outright and for security—of interests in some, but not all, electronic records (*controllable electronic records*). These rules specify certain rights in a controllable electronic record that a purchaser would acquire. Many systems for transferring controllable electronic records are pseudonymous, so that the transferee of a controllable electronic record may be unable to verify the identity of the transferor or the source of the transferor's title. Accordingly, the Article 12 rules would make controllable electronic records negotiable, in the sense that a qualifying good faith purchaser for value could take a controllable electronic record free of third-party claims of a property interest in the controllable electronic record.

Experience with DLT and other records-management systems has established some general functions required for electronic records to serve as an effective and reliable means of transferring economic value.

- The electronic record must have some "use" or benefit that one person can enjoy and can exclude all others from enjoying, e.g., the power to "spend" a bitcoin (or, more precisely, the power to include an unspent transaction output (a UTXO) in a message that the Bitcoin protocol will record to its blockchain).

- A person must be able to transfer to another person this exclusive power to use and the exclusive power to transfer the electronic record. To remain exclusive, the transfer must divest the transferor of the power to use the electronic record.

- A person must be able to demonstrate to others that the person has the power to use and transfer control of the electronic record.

As discussed in the Comments to Section 12–105, these functions form the basis of the Article 12 concept of *control*. To receive the benefits of negotiability and take free of third-party claims of a property interest in a controllable electronic record, a person must have control of the controllable electronic record. In addition, control serves as a method of perfection of a security interest in a controllable electronic record and as a condition for achieving a non-temporal priority of a security interest. In this context, it may be useful to think of control as the functional analogue of possession of tangible personal property such as goods. Note that the concept of control allows for certain exceptions to the exclusivity of powers.

Article 12 governs certain rights (primarily property rights) of transacting parties and other persons that might be affected by the transactions. Article 12 does not govern assets other than controllable electronic records except, in coordination with Article 9, controllable accounts and controllable payment intangibles evidenced by controllable electronic records (discussed below). Like the UCC in general, Article 12 is not a regulatory statute. The fact that an asset is or is not a controllable electronic record under the UCC would not necessarily affect the application of laws regulating, for example, banking, securities, commodities, money transmission, and taxation.

2. Scope of Article 12.

Article 12 applies to *controllable electronic records*. Controllable electronic records are a subset of what often are referred to as digital assets. Article 12 is designed to work for both technologies that are known and those that may be developed in the future. Whether an asset is a controllable electronic record (and therefore within the scope of Article 12) depends on whether the characteristics of the asset and the protocols of any system on which the asset is recorded make it suitable for the application of Article 12's substantive rules. The nature of electronic commerce is constantly changing. For this reason, the technology on which an asset depends, the type of asset, and the prevailing use of the asset should all be irrelevant to whether the asset is a controllable electronic record.

To determine whether Article 12 applies to a particular asset, for example, bitcoin, one must determine whether the asset falls within the definition of *controllable electronic record*. A controllable electronic record is a *record*, as the UCC defines the term. A record is information that is retrievable in perceivable form. Section 1–201(b)(31) (defining "record"). A controllable electronic record is a record that is stored in an electronic medium and that can be subjected to *control*, as defined in Section 12–105. Sections 1–201(b)(16A) (defining "electronic"); 12–102(a)(1) (defining "controllable electronic record"). An electronic record that cannot be subjected to control under Section 12–105 is outside the scope of Article 12. As already mentioned, Article 12 addresses primarily certain property rights in controllable electronic records. Of course, that an electronic record is not subject to control does not imply that it does not have commercial utility. Businesses generate and sell or license large quantities of electronic records that do not require the attributes of negotiability that Article 12 affords to controllable electronic records.

The meaning of control in the UCC depends on the type of property involved. See Sections 7–106 (electronic documents of title); 8–106 (four different types of investment property, each with a different definition of "control"); 9–104 (deposit accounts); 9–105 (chattel paper); 9–105A (electronic money). The Comments to Section 12–105 explain the requirements for obtaining control of a controllable electronic record. For present purposes of exposition, it is sufficient to think of bitcoin and other virtual currencies as prototypical controllable electronic records. The provisions under other law that govern control and other matters for other types of electronic records (some of which are modified by these amendments) are not addressed by Article 12.

3. Substantive Provisions of Article 12.

The principal function of Article 12 is to specify certain rights of a *purchaser* of a controllable electronic record. A purchaser is a person that acquires an interest in property by a voluntary transaction, such as a sale. Section 1–201(b)(29) (defining "purchase"), (30) (defining "purchaser"). Purchasers include both buyers and secured parties. Law other than Article 12 would determine whether a person acquires any rights in a controllable electronic record and so would be eligible to be a purchaser. Section 12–104(c).

Section 12–104 adopts the "shelter" principle, under which a purchaser of a controllable electronic record acquires whatever rights the transferor had or had power to transfer. Section 12–104(d). A similar rule appears in Articles 2, 3, 7, and 8. See Sections 2–403(1) (goods); 3–203(b) (negotiable instruments); 7–504(a) (documents of title); 8–302(a) (certificated and uncertificated securities).

The ability to take a controllable electronic record free of third-party property claims appears to be necessary for a controllable electronic record to have commercial utility. As is the case with Articles 2, 3, 7, and 9, Article 12 would facilitate commerce by affording to certain good-faith purchasers for value (buyers as well as secured parties) greater rights than their transferors had or had power to transfer. (Article 8 also provides for certain purchasers for value to take greater rights than their transferors had, but does not contain an explicit good-faith requirement. See Section 8–303.) Article 12 refers to these purchasers as *qualifying purchasers*. Qualifying purchasers are purchasers that obtain control of a controllable electronic record for value, in good faith, and without notice of any claim of a property interest in the controllable electronic record. Section 12–102(a)(2). Like a holder in due course of a negotiable instrument, a qualifying purchaser of a controllable electronic record takes the controllable electronic record free of property claims. Section 12–104(e).

Consider an example in which *B* contracts to buy bitcoin from *S*.

- Law other than Article 12 generally would determine whether *S* is the owner of the bitcoin.

- Law other than Article 12 would resolve issues concerning the formation of the contract of sale between *B* and *S* and the obligations of the parties under the contract.

- Except to the extent provided by Article 12, law other than Article 12 would determine what steps are necessary for *B* to acquire rights in the bitcoin.

- By acquiring rights in the bitcoin by sale, *B* would become a purchaser of the bitcoin within the meaning of UCC Article 1.

- Article 12 provides that if *B* becomes a purchaser, *B* will acquire whatever rights *S* had or had power to transfer. As a general matter, law other than Article 12 would define these rights. *B* would acquire these rights regardless of whether *B* obtained control of the bitcoin.

In this example, law other than Article 12 includes UCC Article 9, which determines the steps necessary for a security interest to attach to a controllable electronic record. More generally, Article 9 governs any conflict between Article 9 and Article 12. Section 12–103(a).

Now assume that *O* is the owner of the bitcoin and that *S* is a hacker, who acquired control of the bitcoin illegally from *O*.

- Just as a buyer of goods can obtain possession from a seller that has no rights in the goods, *B* can obtain control of the bitcoin, even if *S* "stole" it from *O*.

- If *B* obtains control of the bitcoin for value, in good faith, and without notice of any claim of a property interest, *B* would be a qualifying purchaser.

- Even if *B* would not have acquired any rights in the bitcoin under non-Article 12 law (for example, because *S*, a "thief," had no rights to give), as an Article 12 qualifying purchaser, *B* would acquire the bitcoin free of all claims of a property interest in the bitcoin. *S*'s control of the bitcoin gave *S* the power to transfer rights to a qualifying purchaser, such as *B*. Even if *O* could locate *B*, *B* would defeat *O*'s claim of ownership and own the bitcoin free and clear. (The same result would obtain if *B* bought a negotiable instrument from a thief under circumstances where *B* became a holder in due course. This distinguishes "negotiable" property from property such as goods, as to which a buyer from a thief normally obtains no rights.)

4. Rights or Property Linked to a Controllable Electronic Record.

a. General Rules.

Recall that a controllable electronic record is a record, i.e., information. Some records have what one might call "inherent value" solely because the market treats them as having value. Bitcoin would be an example of such a record. Bitcoin can be exchanged (sold) for cash or other valuable assets. Or, the owner of bitcoin can hold the bitcoin as an investment.

The value of many records, however, is as evidence of the rights of the parties to a transaction or of the rights of a party in other property. In these situations, it is essential to differentiate between the *record* and the *rights* that are evidenced by the record.

Suppose, for example, that *S* and *B* enter into a written contract for the sale of 100 air purifiers. The contract provides that at a specified time in the future, *S* is to deliver the goods and *B* is to pay for them. *B* may sell (assign) to *P* the right to receive delivery of the goods from *S*. *P* has acquired a valuable asset, i.e., the right to receive delivery.

In contrast, if *B* sells to *P* only the paper (record) on which the contract is written, *P* might or might not acquire the right to delivery of the goods, depending on whether applicable law treats the sale of the paper as an assignment of the right to delivery (as can be the case with a negotiable document of title under UCC Article 7). *P* would become the owner of the paper in any event, but the paper itself may be of little value.

If the contract for the sale of air purifiers were electronic rather than written, the same analysis would apply. The right evidenced by the electronic record (i.e., *B*'s right to receive delivery from *S*) would be the valuable asset, not the record itself.

Suppose that the contract of sale between *B* and *S* is evidenced by a controllable electronic record that *B* sells to *P*. Under Section 12–104(d), *P* would acquire all rights *in the controllable electronic record* that the transferor (*B*) had or had power to transfer. If *P* obtains control of the controllable electronic record for value, in good faith, and without notice of any claim of a property right in the controllable electronic record, *P* will become a qualifying purchaser and, as such, would acquire its rights *in the controllable electronic record* free of any claim of a property right under Section 12–104.

But the controllable electronic record itself may or may not be a valuable asset. In this example, unlike bitcoin, the record would have value to *P* only if by virtue of acquiring rights in the controllable electronic record, *P* would also acquire the right to receive delivery of the goods from *S*.

Except to the extent provided by Article 12, that Article leaves to other law the question whether *P*'s acquisition of rights in the controllable electronic record gives *P* the right to receive delivery of the goods. Section 12–104(f). We would typically expect that under other law *P* would not acquire the right to receive the goods merely by acquiring rights in the controllable electronic record, any more than *P* would have acquired the right to receive the goods if the record were in paper form, the paper were physically delivered to *P*, and P acquired rights in the paper.

Suppose, however, that other law does provide that, by acquiring the controllable electronic record, *P* would acquire the right to receive delivery of the goods from *S*. Suppose also that *P* becomes a qualifying purchaser of the controllable electronic record. As we have seen, as a qualifying purchaser, *P* would take its rights in the controllable electronic record free of property claims. But even though under non-Article 12 law *P* would (as posited) acquire the right to receive delivery of the goods, *P* would not acquire that right free of property claims unless non-Article 12 law also were to provide otherwise. Section 12–104(f).

b.   Exceptions: Controllable Accounts and Controllable Payment Intangibles.

As a general rule, Article 12 applies to records and not to rights evidenced by records (or to rights that records are purported to evidence). And, in general, law other than Article 12 would govern what steps must be taken or conditions must be satisfied for a person to acquire an interest in a controllable electronic record and the rights, if any, that the person acquires in other property (including a right to payment or performance of an obligation) as a result of acquiring an interest in the record. This "other" law includes UCC Article 9.

Article 12 provides an important exception to this general rule. The exception concerns rights to payment (specifically, accounts and payment intangibles) that are evidenced by a controllable electronic record and as to which the obligor (account debtor) undertakes to pay the person that has control of the controllable electronic record. These rights to payment are referred to as "controllable accounts" and "controllable payment intangibles." See Section 9–102(a)(27A) (defining "controllable account") and (27B) (defining "controllable payment intangible"). A qualifying purchaser of a controllable account or controllable payment intangible takes free of property claims and is protected from certain actions. See Section 12–104(a) through (e), (g), and (h), and Comments 6 through 10. As to the feasibility and rationale for this exception for controllable accounts and controllable payment intangibles, see Section 12–104, Comments 9 and 10.

The 2022 Article 9 Revisions amend several sections of Article 9 to deal with various aspects of security interests in controllable accounts, controllable electronic records, and controllable payment intangibles. See Sections 9–101, Comment 4.a.; 9–102, Comment 5.d.1.

5.   Governing Law for Article 12.

Section 12–107 provides rules on governing law. The general rule under subsection (a) is that the local law of a "controllable electronic record's jurisdiction" governs matters covered by Article 12. The controllable electronic record's jurisdiction is determined by an express provision in the record or in the system in which the record is recorded. If not so designated, it is determined based on the designation of the law governing the record or the system generally. Absent any such designations, at the bottom of this "waterfall" of alternatives, the governing law will be that of the District of Columbia. Subsection (b) provides an exception for the rights and duties of account debtors under Section 12–106 if an agreement between the account debtor and an assignor of the record provides for the law of another jurisdiction to govern those rights and duties.

The law of the controllable electronic record's jurisdiction also governs perfection and priority of security interests in controllable electronic records, controllable accounts, and controllable payment intangibles. Perfection by filing, however, is governed by the law of the location of the debtor. See Section 9–306B.

§ 12–101. Title.

This article may be cited as Uniform Commercial Code—Controllable Electronic Records.

Official Comment

Subsection headings. Subsection headings are not a part of the official text itself and have not been approved by the sponsors. See Section 1–107, Comment 1.

§ 12–102. Definitions.

(a)   [Article 12 definitions.]

In this article:

(1)   "Controllable electronic record" means a record stored in an electronic medium that can be subjected to control under Section 12–105. The term does not include a controllable account, a controllable payment intangible, a deposit account, an electronic copy of a record evidencing chattel paper, an electronic document of title, electronic money, investment property, or a transferable record.

(2)   "Qualifying purchaser" means a purchaser of a controllable electronic record or an interest in a controllable electronic record that obtains control of the controllable electronic record for value, in good faith, and without notice of a claim of a property right in the controllable electronic record.

(3)   "Transferable record" has the meaning provided for that term in:

(A)   Section 201(a)(1) of the Electronic Signatures in Global and National Commerce Act, 15 U.S.C. Section 7021(a)(1)[, as amended]; or

(B)   [cite to Uniform Electronic Transactions Act Section 16(a)].

(4)   "Value" has the meaning provided in Section 3–303(a), as if references in that subsection to an "instrument" were references to a controllable account, controllable electronic record, or controllable payment intangible.

(b)   [Definitions in Article 9.] The definitions in Article 9 of "account debtor", "controllable account", "controllable payment intangible", "chattel paper", "deposit account", "electronic money", and "investment property" apply to this article.

(c)   [Article 1 definitions and principles.] Article 1 contains general definitions and principles of construction and interpretation applicable throughout this article.

Legislative Note: It is the intent of this act to incorporate future amendments to the federal law cited in subsection (a)(3)(A). A state in which the constitution or other law does not permit incorporation of future amendments when a federal statute is incorporated into state law should omit the phrase "[as amended]". A state in which, in the absence of a legislative declaration, future amendments are incorporated into state law also should omit the phrase.

In subsection (a)(3)(B), the state should cite to the state's version of the Uniform Electronic Transactions Act Section 16(a) or comparable state law.

Official Comment

1.   **Source.** Subsection (a)(2), defining "qualifying purchaser," derives from Section 3–302(a)(2), which defines "holder in due course" of a negotiable instrument.

2.   **"Controllable electronic record."** To be a "controllable electronic record" (CER) within the scope of Article 12, an electronic record must be susceptible of control under Section 12–105. Unlike "transferable records" under the Electronic Signatures in Global and National Commerce Act (E-SIGN) or a "transferable record" under the Uniform Electronic Transactions Act (UETA), a record can be a CER under Article 12 in the absence of an agreement to that effect.

This definition uses the term "record," defined in Section 1–201 to include "information . . . that is stored in an electronic or other medium and is retrievable in perceivable form." The term "electronic" also is defined in Section 1–201. These broad definitions of "record" and "electronic" necessarily produce an expansive meaning of "electronic record." An electronic record would include, for example, music stored on compact disks, email messages, digital photos, personal and other information stored on a social media platform, and all types of databases stored on in an electronic medium. But most of these electronic records typically would not fall within the definition of a CER in subsection (a)(1), which includes only those electronic records "that can be subjected to control under Section 12–105." See generally Prefatory Note 2.

Consider, for example, a so-called "page" on a social media platform. Generalizations about social media/social networking platforms are difficult and these systems no doubt will continue to evolve. But these platforms typically involve licensing arrangements with users that do not permit the users (or anyone) to acquire the exclusive powers contemplated by the definition of "control" in Section 12–105. Consequently, these electronic records are not controllable electronic records as defined.

The provisions of Article 12 also do not apply to certain specified types of electronic records, and the definition has been limited accordingly. For example, the definition does not include a "transferable record" under E-SIGN or UETA. It also does not include "investment property," as defined in Section 9–102(a)(49). For this reason, the rights of an entitlement holder in a controllable electronic record that is a financial asset with respect to which the entitlement holder has a security entitlement are excluded from the definition (although the entitlement holder's securities intermediary may hold directly an interest in a controllable electronic record that it has credited to a securities account). See Sections 8–102(a)(9) (defining "financial asset"), (a)(14) (defining "securities intermediary"), (a)(17) (defining "security entitlement"), and Comment 9; 9–102(a)(49) (defining "investment property"). See also Section 8–103(h), clarifying that a controllable electronic record is not a "financial asset" except pursuant to Section 8–102(a)(9)(iii).

A controllable electronic record is not itself a "security," defined in part in Section 8–102(a)(15) as "an obligation of an issuer or a share, participation, or other interest in an issuer or in property or an enterprise of an issuer." It also is not "a share or similar equity interest," an "investment company security," or "an interest in a partnership or limited liability company." See Section 8–103(a), (b), and (c). For a discussion of the roles that controllable electronic records may play in transactions involving uncertificated securities, see Section 8–102, Comment 18.

3. **"Qualifying purchaser."** The conditions for becoming a qualifying purchaser were drawn from Article 3. More specifically, the conditions for becoming a qualifying purchaser were drawn from Section 3–302(a)(2), which defines "holder in due course" of a negotiable instrument. Among these conditions is that a person take the instrument "for value." See subsection (a)(4) (defining "value") and Comment 5. To meet the requirements for a qualifying purchaser under subsection (a)(2) there must be a time at which all of the requirements are satisfied. For example, if a purchaser obtains notice of a claim of a property right before giving value or satisfying the requirements for control, the purchaser cannot be a qualifying purchaser.

Under Section 12–104(a), not only a purchaser of a controllable electronic record but also a purchaser of a controllable account or controllable payment intangible may be a qualifying purchaser. Moreover, a purchaser of a controllable account or a controllable payment intangible may be a qualifying purchaser even if the purchaser does not also purchase the controllable electronic record that evidences the account or payment intangible. For example, a secured party having a security interest in all of a debtor's accounts and payment intangibles would be a purchaser of those rights to payment, which would include the debtor's controllable accounts and payment intangibles. If the secured party were to obtain control of the debtor's controllable account or payment intangible, it would become a qualifying purchaser if it also met the other conditions for that status. However, to obtain control of the controllable account or controllable payment intangible, a requirement for qualifying purchaser status, the purchaser must obtain control of the controllable electronic record evidencing the controllable account or controllable payment intangible. Section 12–104(b); see also Section 9–107A. A person need not be a purchaser, however, to obtain control of a controllable electronic record.

4. **"Transferable record."** This definition facilitates the exclusion of transferable records from the definition of controllable electronic record.

5. **"Value."** This definition adopts the concept of value in Section 3–303, which is narrower than the generally applicable concept in Section 1–204. Comment 10 to Section 12–104 explains the difference between the two concepts.

§ 12–103. Relation to Article 9 and Consumer Laws.

(a) **[Article 9 governs in case of conflict.]** If there is conflict between this article and Article 9, Article 9 governs.

(b) **[Applicable consumer law and other laws.]** A transaction subject to this article is subject to any applicable rule of law that establishes a different rule for consumers and [insert reference to (i) any other statute or regulation that regulates the rates, charges, agreements, and practices for loans, credit sales, or other extensions of credit and (ii) any consumer-protection statute or regulation].

Official Comment

Source. Subsection (a) follows Section 3–102(b). Notwithstanding subsection (a), as is the case with respect to Article 3, Article 9 explicitly defers to Article 12 in some instances. See, e.g., Section 9–331. Subsection (b) is copied from Section 9–201(b). To the extent that Article 9 contains provisions described in subsection (b), subsections (a) and (b) are not mutually exclusive.

§ 12–104. Rights in Controllable Account, Controllable Electronic Record, and Controllable Payment Intangible.

(a) **[Applicability of section to controllable account and controllable payment intangible.]** This section applies to the acquisition and purchase of rights in a controllable account or controllable payment intangible, including the rights and benefits under subsections (c), (d), (e), (g), and (h) of a purchaser and qualifying purchaser, in the same manner this section applies to a controllable electronic record.

(b) **[Control of controllable account and controllable payment intangible.]** To determine whether a purchaser of a controllable account or a controllable payment intangible is a qualifying purchaser, the purchaser obtains control of the account or payment intangible if it obtains control of the controllable electronic record that evidences the account or payment intangible.

(c) **[Applicability of other law to acquisition of rights.]** Except as provided in this section, law other than this article determines whether a person acquires a right in a controllable electronic record and the right the person acquires.

(d) **[Shelter principle and purchase of limited interest.]** A purchaser of a controllable electronic record acquires all rights in the controllable electronic record that the transferor had or had power to transfer, except that a purchaser of a limited interest in a controllable electronic record acquires rights only to the extent of the interest purchased.

(e) **[Rights of qualifying purchaser.]** A qualifying purchaser acquires its rights in the controllable electronic record free of a claim of a property right in the controllable electronic record.

(f) **[Limitation of rights of qualifying purchaser in other property.]** Except as provided in subsections (a) and (e) for a controllable account and a controllable payment intangible or law other than this article, a qualifying purchaser takes a right to payment, right to performance, or other interest in property evidenced by the controllable electronic record subject to a claim of a property right in the right to payment, right to performance, or other interest in property.

(g) **[No-action protection for qualifying purchaser.]** An action may not be asserted against a qualifying purchaser based on both a purchase by the qualifying purchaser of a controllable electronic record and a claim of a property right in another controllable electronic record, whether the action is framed in conversion, replevin, constructive trust, equitable lien, or other theory.

(h) **[Filing not notice.]** Filing of a financing statement under Article 9 is not notice of a claim of a property right in a controllable electronic record.

Official Comment

1. **Source.** Subsection (d) derives from Section 2–403(1) (concerning the rights of a purchaser).

Subsection (e) derives from Sections 3–306 (concerning the rights of a holder in due course of an instrument) and 8–303 (concerning rights of a protected purchaser of a security).

Subsection (g) derives from Section 8–502 (protecting entitlement holders).

Subsection (h) derives from Section 9–331(c) (filing under Article 9 does not provide notice for purposes of protections of purchasers under other articles).

2.   **Applicability of section to controllable accounts and controllable payment intangibles.** Under subsection (a), the provisions of this section apply to controllable accounts and controllable payment intangibles in the same manner that they apply to controllable electronic records. For example, a qualifying purchaser of a controllable account that obtains control of the controllable electronic record that evidences the account (and who thereby obtains control of the account under subsection (b) and Section 9–107A) would take the account free of conflicting claims of a property right in the account under subsection (e). Under subsection (b), for purposes of determining whether a purchaser of a controllable account or controllable payment intangible obtains control, the purchaser obtains control by obtaining control of the controllable electronic record that evidences the account or payment intangible. Unless otherwise specified or the context otherwise requires, references to a controllable electronic record in the official comments in this Article also refer to a controllable account or controllable payment intangible.

3.   **Applicability of other law.** As a general matter, subsection (c) leaves to other law the resolution of questions concerning the transfer of rights in a controllable electronic record, such as the acts that must be taken to effectuate a transfer of rights and the scope of the rights that a transferee acquires. Subsections (d) through (h) contain important exceptions to subsection (c).

> **Example 1:** *A* creates a controllable electronic record. Although the system in which the electronic record is recorded may determine how the electronic record can be used and control may be transferred, other law would determine what rights *A* has in the controllable electronic record. If, for example, A created the electronic record in the scope of its employment, A's rights would be subject to the terms of A's employment contract.
>
> *A* and *B* agree to the sale of the controllable electronic record to *B*. Other law would determine what steps need to be taken for *B* to acquire rights in the controllable electronic record. Once *B* acquires those rights under other law, *B* would be a purchaser (as defined in Section 1–201), whose rights also would be determined by subsection (d) (i.e., the shelter principle, discussed below in Comment 4). However, even if B did not acquire rights under other law, if B met the requirements for a qualifying purchaser, its rights would be determined by subsections (e) and (g). See Comments 7 and 8, below.

The "law other than this article" that may apply to the transfer of rights in a controllable electronic record under subsection (c) includes UCC Article 9. Section 9–203 would apply, for example, to determine whether a purported secured party acquired an enforceable security interest in a controllable electronic record.

4.   **Purchaser and transferor under subsection (d): shelter principle and resulting controllable electronic records.** Subsection (d) sets forth the familiar "shelter" principle, under which a purchaser of a controllable electronic record acquires whatever rights the transferor had or had power to transfer. However, in some cases the controllable electronic record that is acquired by the purchaser will not be the "same" controllable electronic record that was transferred by the transferor. Such a transfer might involve the elimination of a "transferred" controllable electronic record and the resulting and corresponding derivative creation and acquisition of a new controllable electronic record. An example of such a resulting controllable electronic record is the unspent transaction output (UTXO) generated by a transaction in bitcoin. The Bitcoin protocol operates by allowing users to "spend" their UTXOs to create one or more new UTXOs for the same amount of bitcoin, so each transfer produces new UTXOs controlled by the transferees (one of which may be the transferor—spender—of the bitcoin). Subsection (d) should be construed broadly to encompass such transfers and resulting derivative controllable electronic records acquired by a purchaser. Because subsection (d) addresses the rights of a purchaser in the "purchased" asset and not the "transferred" asset, this construction is wholly consistent with the statutory text.

Notwithstanding the broad subsection (d) shelter principle, which provides that a purchaser acquires "all rights" of the transferor, those rights are subject to the reach of Section 1–304. Under that section a contract or duty under the UCC imposes an overarching "obligation of good faith in its performance and enforcement." Section 1–304. In this context, "performance and enforcement" include the exercise of rights under the UCC, such as the rights conferred on a purchaser by the subsection (d) shelter principle. See Section 1–304, Comment 2. For example, consider a qualifying purchaser of a controllable electronic record, controllable account, or controllable payment intangible who then sells that asset to a person who is not a qualifying purchaser. If the second purchaser had previously engaged in fraudulent or illegal activity in connection with the purchased asset or an asset to which the purchased asset is attributable, the purchaser's exercise of rights under subsection (d) as to the purchased asset may be in breach of its obligation of good faith. Section 3–203(b) states this result directly with respect to a transferee of a negotiable instrument if the transferee previously engaged in fraud or illegality with respect to the same instrument. Section 3–203(b). The same result would apply under subsection (d). Subsection (d) relies on the application of the general obligation of good faith under Section 1–304 to reach the appropriate result. However, unlike negotiable instruments, many controllable electronic records are fungible. For this reason, in some cases it might not be possible to establish that an acquired controllable electronic record has a sufficient nexus with a transferee's earlier fraud or illegality.

5. **Nonpurchaser having control.** Under Section 12–105, a person may have control of a controllable electronic record even if the person has no property interest in the controllable electronic record. A person that has control of, but no property interest in, a controllable electronic record would not be a purchaser of the controllable electronic record and so would not be eligible to be a qualifying purchaser under this section.

Example 2: Debtor granted to Secured Party a security interest in all Debtor's existing and after-acquired accounts, chattel paper, and payment intangibles. Secured Party perfected its security interest in a specific controllable account by obtaining control of the controllable electronic record that evidences the controllable account. See Section 9–107A.

Because Debtor's security agreement does not cover controllable electronic records, Secured Party would have no interest in the controllable electronic record. Accordingly, Secured Party would not be a purchaser of the controllable electronic record. However, as a purchaser of the controllable accounts and controllable payment intangibles, Secured Party could benefit from the take-free rule in subsection (e) (discussed in Comment 7).

6. **Distinction between controllable electronic record and controllable account or controllable payment intangible evidenced by the controllable electronic record.** Even though a controllable electronic record evidences a controllable account or controllable payment intangible, the controllable electronic record is distinct from the account or payment intangible that it evidences. The account or payment intangible is connected with (or "tethered" to) the electronic record by virtue of the relevant account debtor's obligation to pay the person in control of the controllable electronic record. Moreover, control of the controllable account or payment intangible is achieved only by obtaining control of the controllable electronic record that evidences the account or payment intangible. Example 2 explains that a purchaser may obtain a property interest in the controllable account or controllable payment intangible even if it does not acquire any interest in the controllable electronic record that evidences the account or payment intangible. (On the other hand, merely obtaining control of a controllable electronic record does not result in the acquisition of an interest in the record.) This approach is intended to avoid a trap for the unwary purchaser that obtains an interest in the account or payment intangible (which is the asset that has stand-alone value) but might fail to acquire an interest in the related controllable electronic record. However, good practice may encourage a purchaser to acquire an interest in the controllable electronic record as well, which would eliminate any potential confusion.

7. **The take-free rule.** Subsection (e) makes controllable electronic records and, under subsection (a), controllable accounts and controllable payment intangibles, highly negotiable. Subsection (e) derives from Section 3–306, under which a holder in due course takes a negotiable instrument free of a claim of a property right in the instrument. A qualifying purchaser of a controllable electronic record, controllable account, or controllable payment intangible takes free of all claims of a property right in the purchased controllable electronic record, account, or payment intangible.

Example 3: Hacker, a thief, "steals" and obtains control of a controllable electronic record. Hacker then sells the controllable electronic record to Buyer, who obtains control and otherwise meets the requirements for a qualifying purchaser (by obtaining control and purchasing for value, in good faith, and without notice of a claim of a property right).

As a general matter, law other than Article 12 would determine whether any particular transaction creates a property interest in a controllable electronic record. Section 12–104(c). However, even if under other applicable law Hacker has no rights in, and no right to transfer, the "stolen" controllable electronic record, subsection (e) enables Buyer, a qualifying purchaser, to take the controllable electronic record (or any purchased controllable account or controllable payment intangible evidenced by the controllable electronic record) free of claims of a property right—including that of the rightful owner.

As Example 3 illustrates, a person in control of a controllable electronic record, such as Hacker, has the power, even if not the right, to transfer rights in the record to a qualifying purchaser. Of course, if the qualifying purchaser is a secured party whose security interest secures an obligation, the purchaser would take free of the conflicting property right only to the extent of the obligation secured. See Section 12–104(d) (purchaser of a limited interest); *cf.* Section 3–302(e). Moreover, even if a secured party were not a qualifying purchaser of a controllable electronic record, controllable account, or controllable payment intangible, its security interest in the collateral over which it obtained control would, however, have priority over a conflicting security interest that was perfected by a method other than control. Section 9–326A.

8.   **Subsection (g)—the "no-action" rule.** Subsection (g) applies in the situation (explained in Comment 4) in which the "resulting" controllable electronic record (or controllable account or controllable payment intangible) purchased by a qualifying purchaser is not the "same" record, account, or payment intangible that was transferred. In such a situation, a person claiming a property right in the transferred asset may assert a claim against a purchaser of the "resulting" asset even though the claimant is *not* asserting a claim of a *property right in* the purchased asset. If the claim is based on both the purchaser's purchase of the acquired asset and the claimant's claim of a property right in the transferred asset, subsection (g) protects the qualifying purchaser from liability to the claimant based on any theory. The qualifying purchaser's protection from the assertion of such a claim does not depend on any proof that the purchased asset is somehow "traceable" to the transferred asset.

If instead, such a claimant were to assert a claim based on a property right in the purchased asset, then the qualifying purchaser would take free of that claim under subsection (e). Subsection (e) applies whether or not the acquired asset is the same asset that was transferred.

9.   **"Tethered" assets.** Certain controllable electronic records may carry with them rights to other assets, for example, goods or rights to payment. By its terms, the take-free rule in subsection (e) applies to controllable electronic records (and, under subsection (a), controllable accounts and controllable payment intangibles evidenced by a controllable electronic record). One might argue that the inclusion of controllable accounts and controllable payment intangibles in the scope of subsection (e) is unnecessary. By taking a controllable electronic record free of property claims, the argument would be that a person takes not only the controllable electronic record itself but also all rights that are "carried" in the controllable electronic record free and clear.

Subsection (f) defeats that argument. It limits the application of the take-free rule in subsection (e) to controllable electronic records and, through the application of subsection (a), controllable accounts and controllable payment intangibles evidenced by a controllable electronic record. Under subsection (f), except as provided in subsections (a) and (e), a qualifying purchaser takes rights to payment (other than controllable accounts and controllable payment intangibles), rights to performance, and interests in property that are evidenced by a controllable electronic record subject to third-party property claims, unless law other than Article 12 provides to the contrary. The reference in subsection (f) to "law other than this article" contemplates that another article of the UCC might provide a contrary rule for some types of property that might be tethered to a controllable electronic record.

The treatment of controllable accounts and controllable payment intangibles in Articles 9 and 12 is feasible because Article 9 already provides the legal framework for assignments of accounts and payment intangibles. In addition, because accounts and payment intangibles are rights to payment of monetary obligations, tethering of an account or payment intangible to a controllable electronic record is straightforward. The account debtor is obligated to pay the person that has control of the relevant controllable electronic record (subject to the qualifications imposed by Section 12–106).

10.   **Creating the functional equivalent of a negotiable instrument.** Two defining characteristics of an Article 3 negotiable instrument are that a holder in due course (i) takes free of claims of a property or possessory right to the instrument (Section 3–306) and (ii) takes free of most defenses and claims in recoupment (Section 3–305). Article 3 applies only to written instruments. Article 12 and the revisions to Article 9 provide a method for reaching a similar result with respect to controllable accounts and controllable payment intangibles.

As regards the first characteristic, a qualifying purchaser could acquire the controllable account or controllable payment intangible free of any claim of a property interest. As regards the second characteristic, the definition of "qualifying purchaser" omits some of the conditions for becoming a holder in due course. For example, to qualify as a holder in due course, a holder must take "without notice that any party has a defense or claim in recoupment . . . ." Section 3–302(a)(2)(vi). A controllable electronic record is information; there are no parties to a controllable electronic record. However, there are parties to a controllable account or controllable payment intangible. Accordingly, Sections 9–404 and 9–403 would determine whether a purchaser of the controllable account or controllable payment intangible takes free of a defense. Section 9–403 ordinarily would give effect to the account debtor's agreement not to assert claims or defenses.

Section 9–403 adopts the meaning of value in Section 3–303, as does Article 12. The concept of value in Section 3–303 is narrower than the concept in Section 1–204, which applies generally to UCC transactions. Under Section 1–204, a person gives value for rights if the person acquires them in return for a promise. However, under

Section 3–303, if a negotiable instrument is issued or transferred for a promise of performance, the instrument is transferred for value only to the extent that the promise has been performed.

§ 12–105. Control of Controllable Electronic Record.

(a) **[General rule: control of controllable electronic record.]** A person has control of a controllable electronic record if the electronic record, a record attached to or logically associated with the electronic record, or a system in which the electronic record is recorded:

(1) gives the person:

(A) power to avail itself of substantially all the benefit from the electronic record; and

(B) exclusive power, subject to subsection (b), to:

(i) prevent others from availing themselves of substantially all the benefit from the electronic record; and

(ii) transfer control of the electronic record to another person or cause another person to obtain control of another controllable electronic record as a result of the transfer of the electronic record; and

(2) enables the person readily to identify itself in any way, including by name, identifying number, cryptographic key, office, or account number, as having the powers specified in paragraph (1).

(b) **[Meaning of exclusive.]** Subject to subsection (c), a power is exclusive under subsection (a)(1)(B)(i) and (ii) even if:

(1) the controllable electronic record, a record attached to or logically associated with the electronic record, or a system in which the electronic record is recorded limits the use of the electronic record or has a protocol programmed to cause a change, including a transfer or loss of control or a modification of benefits afforded by the electronic record; or

(2) the power is shared with another person.

(c) **[When power not shared with another person.]** A power of a person is not shared with another person under subsection (b)(2) and the person's power is not exclusive if:

(1) the person can exercise the power only if the power also is exercised by the other person; and

(2) the other person:

(A) can exercise the power without exercise of the power by the person; or

(B) is the transferor to the person of an interest in the controllable electronic record or a controllable account or controllable payment intangible evidenced by the controllable electronic record.

(d) **[Presumption of exclusivity of certain powers.]** If a person has the powers specified in subsection (a)(1)(B)(i) and (ii), the powers are presumed to be exclusive.

(e) **[Control through another person.]** A person has control of a controllable electronic record if another person, other than the transferor to the person of an interest in the controllable electronic record or a controllable account or controllable payment intangible evidenced by the controllable electronic record:

(1) has control of the electronic record and acknowledges that it has control on behalf of the person; or

(2) obtains control of the electronic record after having acknowledged that it will obtain control of the electronic record on behalf of the person.

(f) **[No requirement to acknowledge.]** A person that has control under this section is not required to acknowledge that it has control on behalf of another person.

(g) **[No duties or confirmation.]** If a person acknowledges that it has or will obtain control on behalf of another person, unless the person otherwise agrees or law other than this article or Article 9 otherwise provides, the person does not owe any duty to the other person and is not required to confirm the acknowledgment to any other person.

Official Comment

1. **Why "control" matters.** Control serves two major functions in Article 12. An electronic record is a "controllable electronic record" and is subject to the provisions of this Article only if it can be subjected to control under this section. See Section 12–102(a)(1) (defining "controllable electronic record"). And only a person having control of a controllable electronic record is eligible to become a qualifying purchaser and so to take free of claims of a property interest in the controllable electronic record, or any controllable account or controllable payment intangible evidenced by the controllable electronic record, and to be protected by the "no-action" rule. See Section 12–104(e) and (g).

Article 9 provides that obtaining control of a controllable electronic record is one method by which to perfect a security interest in the controllable electronic record or in any controllable account or controllable payment intangible evidenced by the controllable electronic record. See Sections 9–107A; 9–314. Moreover, a security interest perfected by control has priority over a conflicting security interest that was perfected by a method other than control and "control . . . pursuant to the debtor's agreement" may substitute for ~~an authenticated~~ a signed security agreement as an element of attachment. See Sections 9–326A; 9–203(b)(3)(D).

2. **Powers and sources of powers; inability to exercise a power.** This section conditions control on a person's having the three powers specified in subsection (a)(1). A person would have the powers described in that subsection if the controllable electronic record, a record attached to or logically associated with the controllable electronic record, or any system in which it is recorded gives the person those powers. This description of the source of the relevant powers should be construed broadly and functionally. For example, a person would have a power even if the characteristics of the particular purchaser disable the person from exercising the power. This would be the case, for example, when the purchaser holds the private key required to access the benefit of the controllable electronic record but lacks the hardware required to use it. In addition, a system in which the person in control is identified is a permissible source of a power even if it is related to but not precisely the "same" system in which the controllable electronic record is recorded. Moreover, this broad and functional construction is particularly important for references to "a record attached to or logically associated with the electronic record, or a system in which the electronic record is recorded," as used in Section 12–105(a) and (b) (and elsewhere). For example, overly literal or technical interpretations of the terminology "attached to" or "logically associated" are inappropriate. The statutory language must be adapted and applied in a functional manner to technology, systems, and infrastructure that may be developed and employed in the future. The goal is to embrace records and systems that are connected to a particular electronic record in such a manner that the information contained in or the functions performed by those "attached" or "associated" records are appropriately and reasonably attributable to and identifiable as connected with the electronic record itself. See also, e.g., Sections 7–106, 9–105, 9–105A, 9–306A, 9–605, 9–628, and 12–107.

3. **"Benefit."** Subsection (a)(1)(A) and (a)(1)(B)(i) condition control of a controllable electronic record on a person's relationship to the benefit of the controllable electronic record.

As used in this section, the "benefit" of a controllable electronic record refers to the rights that are afforded by the controllable electronic record and the uses to which the controllable electronic record can be put. These, in turn, depend on the characteristics of the controllable electronic record in question. For example, the benefit afforded by control of a bitcoin is that it can be held or disposed of (sold or spent). And control of a controllable electronic record evidencing a controllable account or controllable payment intangible affords the benefit of the right to collect from the account debtor (obligor).

The system in which a controllable electronic record is recorded may limit the benefit from the controllable electronic record that is available to those who interact with the system. In determining whether a person has the power to avail itself of substantially all the benefit from a controllable electronic record under subsection (a)(1)(A), or to prevent others from availing themselves of substantially all the benefit from a controllable electronic record under subsection (a)(1)(B)(i), only the benefit that the system makes available (subject to the system's inherent limitations) should be considered.

4. **Power to retrieve information.** By definition, the information constituting an electronic record must be "retrievable in perceivable form." Section 1–201(b)(31) (defining "record"). The power to retrieve the record in perceivable form is included in the benefit of a controllable electronic record. "Perceivable form" means that the contents of the record are intelligible; the ability to perceive the indecipherable jumble of an encrypted record does not give a person the power to retrieve the record in perceivable form.

To have control of a controllable electronic record under subsection (a)(1)(A), a person must have at least the nonexclusive power to avail itself of this benefit. If a person also has the exclusive power to decrypt the encrypted record, the person will have the exclusive power to prevent others from availing themselves of substantially all the benefit from the controllable electronic record and thereby will satisfy the condition in subsection (a)(1)(B)(i).

5. **Exclusive powers.** Unlike the power in subsection (a)(1)(A), the powers in subsection (a)(1)(B)(i) and (a)(1)(B)(ii) must be held exclusively by the person claiming control in order to establish control. However, once it is established that a person has received those powers, subsection (d) provides a presumption of exclusivity. Consequently, a person asserting control need not prove exclusivity in order to make out a *prima facie* case. Application of the presumption will be governed also by Section 1–206 (effects of a presumption under the UCC) and applicable non-UCC law (including rules of procedure and evidence). In addition, subsection (b) contains two qualifications of the term "exclusive" as used in subsection (a)(1)(B). A power can be "exclusive" under subsection (a)(1)(B) even if one or both of these qualifications apply.

Subsection (b)(1) takes account of the fact that the powers of a purchaser of a controllable electronic record necessarily are subject to the attributes of the controllable electronic record, records associated with the controllable electronic record, and the protocols of any system in which the controllable electronic record is recorded. For example, a transfer of control resulting from a program that is a part of a system's protocol is inherent in the controllable electronic record and does not impair the exclusivity of the power of the person in control of the record. Subsection (b)(1) also contemplates that the potential for the system to otherwise modify (or even destroy) controllable electronic records would not impair the exclusivity.

Example 1: Pursuant to the governance apparatus of a system (Propofolium) for a cryptocurrency (propofol), an upgrade to the system was made that modified the consensus mechanism for determining the effectiveness of transfers of propofols within the system. Although this change did not divest any holder of propofols of its control, it prospectively modified the system for all propofols. The adoption of this change and the potential for such a change (or any other change) are functions of the attributes of the system and, consequently, of all propofols. Neither this change nor such potential impaired the exclusivity, for purposes of subsection (a)(1)(B), of the powers of a person in control of propofols.

Subsection (b)(2) allows for a power to be shared with another person without impairing the exclusivity of the power. One effect of subsection (b)(2) is that, under a multi-signature (multi-sig) agreement, any person that is readily identifiable under subsection (a)(2) and shares the relevant power would be eligible to have control, even if the action of another person is a condition for the exercise of the power. For example, a person in control may agree that another person's action on the relevant system would be required to effect a transfer of control without impairing the requisite exclusivity.

Example 2: Pursuant to a multi-sig arrangement, control of propofols (in the system described in Example 1) is shared by Campbell, Elizabeth, Mia, and Natasha. Under the multi-sig arrangement, the exercise of powers over the propofols requires action by three of the four persons having control. None of the participants acting alone has the power to exercise the relevant powers. Subsection (b)(2) makes clear that all four participants have control over the propofols and exclusivity is not impaired by the shared control under the multi-sig arrangement.

Although all four persons in Example 2 have control, that may leave many questions as to the rights of the four as among themselves. For example, if more than one of the four were secured parties, it would be important for them to settle by agreement issues such as relative priorities and enforcement rights. Similar situations can arise in other contexts and with respect to other types of collateral.

A multi-sig arrangement for a controllable electronic record, such as that described in Example 2, may provide enhanced security. For example, if the power of one participant is compromised by a "hacker," the required actions by the other participants would prevent the hacker from exercising unauthorized power over the record. Although the hacker might possess the power along with the remaining multi-sig participants, those participants would continue to have control. A multi-sig structure also may protect against the misuse of a record by ensuring that actions by multiple persons are required for exercising power over the record.

Subsection (c) provides that in certain circumstances a power is not shared within the meaning of subsection (b)(2), the relaxation of the exclusivity requirement provided by subsection (b)(2) does not apply, and, consequently, a person's power is not exclusive. Subsection (c) provides that a person does not share an exclusive power with another person if the person can exercise the power only with the other person's cooperation (subsection (c)(1)) but the other person either (i) can exercise the power without the person's cooperation (subsection (c)(2)(A)) or (ii) is the transferor to the person (transferee) of an interest in the controllable electronic record or a controllable account or controllable payment intangible evidenced by the controllable electronic record (subsection (c)(2)(B)). It follows that a person to which subsection (c) applies does not have control based on its exclusive powers (although it might have control through another person under subsection (e), discussed below, or if another person having control is acting as the person's agent).

Comment 9 addresses the rationale for disqualifying the transferee from a transferor under subsection (c)(2)(B) from the benefit of sharing a power under subsection (b)(2).

The following examples illustrate the application of subsection (c):

Example 3: Under a multi-sig arrangement, exercise by any two of Campbell, Elizabeth, and Mia is required to exercise a power with respect to a controllable electronic record (CER). None of the three can exercise a power without the cooperation of another, so all three have control because they share the power. Even if Campbell were the transferor of the CER to Elizabeth, Elizabeth's power is shared, and therefore treated as exclusive, because Campbell cannot block Elizabeth's exercise of the power if Mia acts with Elizabeth. It follows that subsection (c)(1) does not apply, subsection (b)(2) does apply, and Elizabeth shares the power with Campbell. (The same result would apply with respect to Mia's power if Campbell were the transferor of the CER to Mia.)

Example 4: Under a multi-sig arrangement, exercise by both Campbell and Elizabeth are required to exercise a power, so subsection (c)(1) applies with respect to each person. However, neither Campbell nor Elizabeth can exercise the power without cooperation of the other and neither is the transferor to the other, so subsection (c)(2)(A) and (2)(B) does not apply with respect to either person. It follows that Campbell and Elizabeth each share the power.

Example 5: The facts are the same as in Example 4, but Campbell is the transferor of an interest in the CER to Elizabeth. Elizabeth does not share the power with Campbell and Elizabeth's power is not exclusive because subsection (c)(1) and (2)(B) applies.

Example 6: Under a multi-sig arrangement, Mia or Natasha can exercise a power only with the exercise by Campbell, but Campbell can exercise the power unilaterally without the exercise by either Mia or Natasha. Neither Mia nor Natasha shares the power with Campbell because subsection (c)(1) and (2)(A) apply, so neither Mia's nor Natasha's power is treated as exclusive. Campbell's power is exclusive *in fact* and Campbell need not rely on subsection (b)(2) for shared power.

Example 7: Under a multi-sig arrangement, Mia can exercise a power only with exercise by Elizabeth or Natasha, but Elizabeth and Natasha each can exercise the power unilaterally without the exercise by the other or by Mia. Elizabeth and Natasha share the power, but Mia does not share the power with Elizabeth or Natasha. Mia's power is not exclusive because subsection (c)(1) and (2)(A) applies.

Although the presumption in subsection (d) is not expressly made subject to subsection (c), it is functionally so. Under Section 1–206, once evidence is introduced that subsection (c) applies and that, accordingly, a person relying on the presumption cannot rely on the relaxation of the exclusivity requirement provided by subsection (b)(2), the presumption would no longer apply.

6. **Transfer of control.** The power to transfer control of a controllable electronic record under subsection (a)(1)(B)(ii) includes the power to cause another person to obtain control of another derivative and resulting controllable electronic record that results from the transfer of the controllable electronic record. See Section 12–104, Comment 4.

7. **Readily identify itself.** Subsection (a)(2) provides that a person does not have control of a controllable electronic record unless the controllable electronic record, a record attached to or logically associated with the controllable electronic record, or any system in which the controllable electronic record is recorded enables the person readily to identify itself as the person having the requisite powers. The identification need not be by a "name," but also may be by "identifying number, cryptographic key, office, or account number"—language derived from Section 3–110(c). The reference to "office" means a public office. See Section 3–110, Comment 3. This subsection does not obligate a person to identify itself as having control. However, to prove that it has control, a person would need to prove that the relevant records or any system in which the controllable electronic record is recorded readily identifies the person as such. Consistent with the subsection (d) presumption of exclusivity, proof that a person has the powers specified in section (a)(1) does not require proof of exclusivity—i.e., proof of a negative (that no one else has such powers). The means of identification mentioned in subsection (a)(2) derive from Section 3–110(c). Subsection (a)(2) adds "cryptographic key" as an example of a way in which a person may be identified.

8. **Control through another person.** Neither Article 12 nor any other provision of the UCC would restrict or render ineffective any agreement of a person in control of a controllable electronic record to hold control

on behalf of another person. This result is implicit from subsection (b)(2) dealing with sharing of control. It also would follow under principles of agency. But such an arrangement should be effective regardless of any agency or fiduciary relationship.

This concept is expressly addressed in Section 8–106(d)(3), on control of a security entitlement, which achieves perfection of a security interest under Sections 9–106(a) and 9–314(a). It also applies to perfection by possession under Section 9–313(c) if a person other than the debtor or the secured party (or the secured party's agent) is in possession of collateral. Under those provisions, however, effectiveness is conditioned in some circumstances on an "acknowledgment" by the person in control or possession. Under Section 9–313(c) the acknowledgment must be in a signed record. These provisions appear to derive from practices involving bailees of tangible property, such as goods, chattel paper, and certificated securities. See Section 9–313, Comment 4.

Subsection (e) likewise provides for control by a person through another person's acknowledgment that it has control on behalf of the person. Subsection (e) is patterned on Section 9–313(c), but like Section 8–106(d)(3), subsection (e) omits the requirement in Section 9–313(c) that an acknowledgment be made in a signed record. Although best practices might suggest the wisdom of relying on a signed record to evidence such an acknowledgment, subsection (e) would permit proof by other means. Under subsection (e) for an acknowledgment by another person to be effective to confer control on a person, the other person making the acknowledgment must be one "other than the transferor of an interest in the electronic record" to the person. The rationale for this limitation is discussed in Comment 9. Control based on an acknowledgment under subsection (e) by another person having control continues only while the other person retains control. This result necessarily follows because such control derives solely from the other person's continued control.

The combined operation of subsections (b)(2) and (e) ensure that the continuance of various existing practices would not prevent or cause the loss of control. For example, a person in control may wish to grant another person the power to approve or disapprove a transfer of control on the system. Alternatively, a person in control may wish to permit a system administrator, the system itself, or a prearranged operation to transfer control to another person under specified conditions without participation by the person in control. And, of course, a person in control may wish to delegate the power to transfer control to an agent or fiduciary.

Provisions substantially similar to subsection (e) are included in Section 7–106 (control of electronic documents of title), Section 8–106(d)(3) (control of security entitlement), 9–104 (control of deposit accounts), 9–105 (control of authoritative electronic copies of records evidencing chattel paper), and 9–105A (control of electronic money).

9. **Shared powers under subsection (b)(2) and control through another person under subsection (e): Limitations related to transferors and transferees of interests in controllable electronic records.** Subsection (c)(2)(B) disqualifies a transferee (which includes a secured party in a secured transaction) of an interest in a controllable electronic record (or controllable account or controllable payment intangible) from the benefit of a shared power under subsection (b)(2) when the transferor retains a blocking power (i.e., when the transferee cannot exercise the power unless the transferor also exercises the power). In similar fashion, under subsection (e), an acknowledgment by a transferor of an interest in a controllable electronic record (or controllable account or controllable payment intangible) that the transferor has control for the benefit of a person is ineffective to confer control on the person. Each of these limitations is premised on the view that the transferor has not been divested sufficiently of its powers over the relevant controllable electronic record so as to warrant treating the transferee as a secured party having a security interest perfected by control or as having the requisite control to be a qualifying purchaser.

Subsection (c)(1) and (c)(2)(B) contemplates that the transferor has retained a blocking power over the transferee's exercise of a power. Subsection (e) contemplates that the transferor remains in control and has merely acknowledged that its control is for the transferee's benefit and that the acknowledgment is ineffective to confer control on the transferee. Although the concept of shared control is newly introduced in the UCC, holding possession or control for another is not. Section 9–313(c) expressly provides in this context that an acknowledging person having possession of goods must be a person "other than the debtor" for a secured party to take possession through the acknowledging person. The official comments to Section 8–106 are to the same effect in the context of control of a security entitlement. See Section 8–106(d)(3), Comment 4A and pre-2022 Comment 4. The same policy that underpins the inapplicability of this method of control to an acknowledgment by a debtor applies as well to a transferor that is not an Article 9 debtor. Control is intended to be a proxy for and a functional equivalent of the transfer of physical possession of goods. In general, a person can obtain control through control by an agent, but under subsection (e) an acknowledgment by a debtor or transferor (even "as agent") that acknowledges control on behalf of a secured party or other transferee would be ineffective. This corresponds to the policy underlying Section

935

9–313 that "the debtor cannot qualify as an agent for the secured party for purposes of the secured party's taking possession." Section 9–313, Comment 3.

Notwithstanding these limitations, they would not impair the continued perfection by control upon a secured party's assignment of a perfected-by-control security interest in a controllable electronic record to a successor secured party. The following example illustrates.

Example 8: Debtor (D) buys a CER and obtains control. D then grants a security interest in the CER to Secured Party A (SPA) to secure D's obligation to SPA and transfers to SPA control of the CER (*not* pursuant to shared control with D or pursuant to subsection (e)). SPA then assigns to Secured Party B (SPB) the secured obligation owed by D to SPA.

As to perfection of the security interest granted by D, perfection by control is not affected even if SPA retains powers over the CER (as between SPA and SPB) following the assignment to SPB. The security interest remains perfected. This is consistent with the policy underlying 9–310(c)—an assignment of a security interest should not require the assignee to refile or take an assignment of record of a filed financing statement in favor of the assignor for protection against a debtor's creditors and transferees.

The economic interest being assigned by SPA to SPB in Example 8 is primarily the *right to payment or performance* of the obligation of D that is secured by the CER. If the transfer of the secured obligation by SPA to SPB itself creates a security interest securing an obligation (e.g., owed by SPA to SPB), then SPB should perfect the security interest granted by SPA (which is distinct from the security interest in the CER granted by D and assigned by SPA to SPB). The method of perfection will depend on the nature of the secured obligation—the type of collateral—being assigned. Is the right to payment an instrument, an account, or a payment intangible? Or is performance of the secured obligation pursuant to another type of general intangible? SPB should file a financing statement against SPA, as debtor, or take possession of the instrument, if applicable. However, as to the underlying collateral securing the assigned obligation—the CER—attachment and perfection of SPB's security interest in the obligation of D owed to SPA would also constitute attachment and perfection as to the security interest in the CER securing that obligation. Sections 9–203(g); 9–308(e); see also 1 Restatement (Second) of Contracts § 340, Comment b ("b. Security follows the debt. Where a secured claim is assigned, the collateral is ordinarily assigned as well.").

If the transfer by SPA to SPB is an outright transfer (a sale) of an account, a payment intangible, or a promissory note, the transfer creates a security interest and the analysis in the preceding paragraph applies (except that the security interest arising from the sale of a payment intangible or promissory note is automatically perfected under Section 9–309(a)(3) and (4)). If the transfer is a sale of another type of general intangible or instrument that is secured by the CER, then non-Article 9 law applies to the transfer. However, the same result may occur under the common-law rule that the collateral (the CER) follows a secured obligation that is transferred. See Sections 9–203, Comment 9; 9–308, Comment 6.

For obvious business reasons, SPB may not wish to allow SPA to remain in control of the CER and may require SPA to transfer control to it as a condition to the transaction. Alternatively, SPB may obtain control through sharing powers with SPA or through SPA's acknowledgment pursuant to subsection (e). It is true that SPA's assignment to SPB of D's secured obligation carried with it the collateral—the CER—securing the obligation. But such a derivative acquisition (through the operation of Sections 9–203(g) and 9–308(e)) by SPB would not be a transfer by SPA of "an interest in" the CER within the meaning of the limitations imposed in subsections (c)(2)(B) or (e). The operation of these rules, providing that collateral follows the transfer of a secured obligation, are based on the premise that any necessary public notice provided in connection with the assignment of the obligation provides, in turn, sufficient public notice with respect to the underlying collateral. It follows that the policy to be implemented by subsections (c)(2)(B) and (e) is not implicated by such an assignment.

10. **No requirement to acknowledge, no duties, and no requirement to confirm acknowledgment.** Subsections (f) and (g) derive from Section 9–313(f) and (g). Subsection (f) makes clear that a person that has control under this section has no duty to acknowledge that it has or will obtain control on behalf of another person. Arrangements for a person to acknowledge that it has or will obtain control on behalf of another person are not standardized. Accordingly, subsection (g) leaves to the agreement of the parties and to any other applicable law (other than this Article or Article 9) any duties of a person that does acknowledge that it has or will obtain control on behalf of another person and provides that a person making an acknowledgment is not required to confirm the acknowledgment to another person.

For example, subsection (e) would apply to give control to a person, Alpha, when another person, Beta, has control of a controllable electronic record and acknowledges that it has control on behalf of Alpha. However, under subsection (f), Beta is not required to so acknowledge. And under subsection (g), even if Beta does so acknowledge,

Beta owes no duty to Alpha unless Beta agrees or other law so provides, and Beta is not required to confirm its acknowledgment to any other person.

§ 12–106. Discharge of Account Debtor on Controllable Account or Controllable Payment Intangible.

(a) **[Discharge of account debtor.]** An account debtor on a controllable account or controllable payment intangible may discharge its obligation by paying:

(1) the person having control of the controllable electronic record that evidences the controllable account or controllable payment intangible; or

(2) except as provided in subsection (b), a person that formerly had control of the controllable electronic record.

(b) **[Content and effect of notification.]** Subject to subsection (d), the account debtor may not discharge its obligation by paying a person that formerly had control of the controllable electronic record if the account debtor receives a notification that:

(1) is signed by a person that formerly had control or the person to which control was transferred;

(2) reasonably identifies the controllable account or controllable payment intangible;

(3) notifies the account debtor that control of the controllable electronic record that evidences the controllable account or controllable payment intangible was transferred;

(4) identifies the transferee, in any reasonable way, including by name, identifying number, cryptographic key, office, or account number; and

(5) provides a commercially reasonable method by which the account debtor is to pay the transferee.

(c) **[Discharge following effective notification.]** After receipt of a notification that complies with subsection (b), the account debtor may discharge its obligation by paying in accordance with the notification and may not discharge the obligation by paying a person that formerly had control.

(d) **[When notification ineffective.]** Subject to subsection (h), notification is ineffective under subsection (b):

(1) unless, before the notification is sent, the account debtor and the person that, at that time, had control of the controllable electronic record that evidences the controllable account or controllable payment intangible agree in a signed record to a commercially reasonable method by which a person may furnish reasonable proof that control has been transferred;

(2) to the extent an agreement between the account debtor and seller of a payment intangible limits the account debtor's duty to pay a person other than the seller and the limitation is effective under law other than this article; or

(3) at the option of the account debtor, if the notification notifies the account debtor to:

(A) divide a payment;

(B) make less than the full amount of an installment or other periodic payment; or

(C) pay any part of a payment by more than one method or to more than one person.

(e) **[Proof of transfer of control.]** Subject to subsection (h), if requested by the account debtor, the person giving the notification under subsection (b) seasonably shall furnish reasonable proof, using the method in the agreement referred to in subsection (d)(1), that control of the controllable electronic record has been transferred. Unless the person complies with the request, the account debtor may discharge its obligation by paying a person that formerly had control, even if the account debtor has received a notification under subsection (b).

(f) **[What constitutes reasonable proof.]** A person furnishes reasonable proof under subsection (e) that control has been transferred if the person demonstrates, using the method in the agreement referred to in subsection (d)(1), that the transferee has the power to:

(1) avail itself of substantially all the benefit from the controllable electronic record;

   (2)   prevent others from availing themselves of substantially all the benefit from the controllable electronic record; and

   (3)   transfer the powers specified in paragraphs (1) and (2) to another person.

   (g)   **[Rights not waivable.]** Subject to subsection (h), an account debtor may not waive or vary its rights under subsections (d)(1) and (e) or its option under subsection (d)(3).

   (h)   **[Rule for individual under other law.]** This section is subject to law other than this article which establishes a different rule for an account debtor who is an individual and who incurred the obligation primarily for personal, family, or household purposes.

Official Comment

1.   **Source.** These provisions derive from Section 3–602, which governs the discharge of a person obligated on a negotiable instrument, and Section 9–406(a), (b) and (c), which governs the discharge of an account debtor, including a person obligated on an account or payment intangible.

2.   **The basic rules.** This section applies only to an account debtor that has undertaken to pay the person that has control of the controllable electronic record that evidences the obligation to pay. See Section 9–102 (defining "controllable account" and "controllable payment intangible"). Section 9–406 would continue to apply in other respects and to all other account debtors. As to the relationship between this section and Section 9–406, see Comment 5.

Under subsection (a)(1), an account debtor may discharge its obligation on the controllable account or controllable payment intangible by paying the person that has control of the related controllable electronic record at the time of payment. Subsections (a)(2) and (b) would remove from an account debtor the burden of determining who has control of the related controllable electronic record at any given time—a burden that, with respect to some controllable electronic records, an account debtor may be unable to satisfy. Under subsection (a)(2), subject to subsection (b), an account debtor may discharge its obligation by paying a person that formerly had control of the related controllable electronic record, which presumably would include the initial obligee.

Subsection (b) reflects the fact that a person to which control has been transferred may not wish to take the risk that the account debtor will discharge its obligation by paying the transferor. Subsection (b) protects the transferee by providing that, if the account debtor receives an effective notification that control has been transferred, the account debtor may discharge its obligation by paying in accordance with the notification and may not discharge its obligation by paying a person that formerly had control. The notification must be signed by a person formerly having control or by the transferee.

To be effective under subsection (b), a notification must reasonably identify the controllable account or controllable payment intangible, notify the account debtor that control of the controllable electronic record that evidences the controllable account or controllable payment intangible was transferred, identify the transferee in any reasonable way, and provide a commercially reasonable method by which the account debtor is to make payments to the transferee. A change in the identity of the person to which the account debtor must make payment should not, and typically will not, impose a significant burden on the account debtor. However, one can imagine a method of making payment that would be burdensome, for example, making a payment through a trading platform or payment service with which the account debtor does not have an account. For this reason, the designated method of making payment must be "commercially reasonable."

3.   **"Reasonable proof."** As noted above, this section derives in large part from Section 9–406, which provides for notification that an account or payment intangible has been assigned. Experience suggests that account debtors that have received notification of an assignment under Section 9–406 typically make payments in accordance with the notice. Recognizing that an account debtor may be uncertain whether a notification is legitimate, Section 9–406 affords to an account debtor the right to request proof that the account or payment intangible was assigned. See generally, Section 9–406, Comment 4.

Subsection (e) contains a similar provision. On the account debtor's request, the person giving the notification must seasonably furnish reasonable proof that control of the controllable electronic record has been transferred. If the person does not comply with the request, the account debtor may ignore the notification and discharge its obligation by paying a person formerly in control.

"Reasonable proof" requires evidence that would be understood by a typical account debtor to whom it is proffered as demonstrating to a reasonably high probability that control of the controllable electronic record has been transferred to the transferee. Subsection (f) provides a safe harbor for providing reasonable proof. It enables a person to satisfy the account debtor's request by demonstrating that the transferee has the power to avail itself of substantially all the benefit from the controllable electronic record, to prevent others from availing themselves of substantially all the benefit from the controllable electronic record, and to transfer these powers to another person. This demonstration would not necessarily prove that a person actually has control of a controllable electronic record because it need not show that the transferee held the last two powers exclusively. Nevertheless, such a demonstration would constitute "reasonable proof" under subsection (f). A person that has control should have little difficulty providing this proof, as a person cannot have control unless it can readily identify itself as having the requisite powers. See Section 12–105(a)(2). Reasonable proof that is seasonably furnished by a person other than the person that gave the notification would constitute compliance with the account debtor's request.

Subsection (e) requires that reasonable proof be provided "using the agreed method." Subsection (f) requires that a person use "the agreed method" to demonstrate that the transferee has the specified powers. "Agreed method" refers to the commercially reasonable method to which the parties agreed, in a signed record, before the notification was sent. If parties did not so agree, the notification is ineffective under subsection (d)(1).

An account debtor may agree to participate in a system providing for the control of controllable accounts or controllable payment intangibles. If the system is programmed to provide for notification to the account debtor upon the transfer of control, the account debtor's agreement and the operation of the system may satisfy the requirements of subsections (d)(1), (e), and (f).

4. **Additional considerations for account debtors.** The requirement in subsection (e) that reasonable proof be furnished using the "agreed method" provides considerable protection for account debtors upon receipt of a notification of assignment and making a request for proof. There are, however, other considerations that are of importance to account debtors but are beyond the scope of the frameworks provided by Articles 9 and 12. One such consideration is the potential involvement of pseudonymous payees, which may raise issues such as compliance with anti-money laundering regulations and sanctions compliance. These are examples of issues that a well-structured program for controllable accounts and controllable payment intangibles might address.

5. **Relationship to Section 9–406.** Section 9–406 governs the discharge of the obligation of an account debtor. Section 9–406 carves out of its scope transactions to the extent covered by this section. See Section 9–406(l).

§ 12–107.   Governing Law.

(a)   **[Governing law: general rule.]** Except as provided in subsection (b), the local law of a controllable electronic record's jurisdiction governs a matter covered by this article.

(b)   **[Governing law: Section 12–106.]** For a controllable electronic record that evidences a controllable account or controllable payment intangible, the local law of the controllable electronic record's jurisdiction governs a matter covered by Section 12–106 unless an effective agreement determines that the local law of another jurisdiction governs.

(c)   **[Controllable electronic record's jurisdiction.]** The following rules determine a controllable electronic record's jurisdiction under this section:

(1)   If the controllable electronic record, or a record attached to or logically associated with the controllable electronic record and readily available for review, expressly provides that a particular jurisdiction is the controllable electronic record's jurisdiction for purposes of this article or [the Uniform Commercial Code], that jurisdiction is the controllable electronic record's jurisdiction.

(2)   If paragraph (1) does not apply and the rules of the system in which the controllable electronic record is recorded are readily available for review and expressly provide that a particular jurisdiction is the controllable electronic record's jurisdiction for purposes of this article or [the Uniform Commercial Code], that jurisdiction is the controllable electronic record's jurisdiction.

(3)   If paragraphs (1) and (2) do not apply and the controllable electronic record, or a record attached to or logically associated with the controllable electronic record and readily available for review, expressly provides that the controllable electronic record is governed by the law of a particular jurisdiction, that jurisdiction is the controllable electronic record's jurisdiction.

(4)   If paragraphs (1), (2), and (3) do not apply and the rules of the system in which the controllable electronic record is recorded are readily available for review and expressly provide that the

controllable electronic record or the system is governed by the law of a particular jurisdiction, that jurisdiction is the controllable electronic record's jurisdiction.

(5) If paragraphs (1) through (4) do not apply, the controllable electronic record's jurisdiction is the District of Columbia.

(d) **[Applicability of Article 12.]** If subsection (c)(5) applies and Article 12 is not in effect in the District of Columbia without material modification, the governing law for a matter covered by this article is the law of the District of Columbia as though Article 12 were in effect in the District of Columbia without material modification. In this subsection, "Article 12" means Article 12 of Uniform Commercial Code Amendments (2022).

(e) **[Relation of matter or transaction to controllable electronic record's jurisdiction not necessary.]** To the extent subsections (a) and (b) provide that the local law of the controllable electronic record's jurisdiction governs a matter covered by this article, that law governs even if the matter or a transaction to which the matter relates does not bear any relation to the controllable electronic record's jurisdiction.

(f) **[Rights of purchasers determined at time of purchase.]** The rights acquired under Section 12–104 by a purchaser or qualifying purchaser are governed by the law applicable under this section at the time of purchase.

Official Comment

1.   **Source.** The provisions of Section 12–107 (as well as Sections 9–306A and 9–306B) derive from Sections 8–110 and 9–305 on law governing perfection and priority of security interests in investment property and the relevance of a securities intermediary's jurisdiction and a commodity intermediary's jurisdiction.

2.   **The basic rule: Law governing matters covered by Article 12.** Subsection (a) states the basic rule that the local law of the controllable electronic record's jurisdiction governs the matters covered by this Article. The "matters covered by" this Article are relatively narrow and discrete, albeit enormously important. If the choice-of-law rule provided by this section points to a jurisdiction that has adopted Article 12, those matters would include the interpretation and application of Article 12, including its definitions. In general, issues that would be determined by the provisions of this Article are to be determined under the law that is applicable as determined by this section. These include the rights of purchasers and property claimants more generally with respect to controllable electronic records, controllable accounts, and controllable payment intangibles to the extent dealt with by this Article—issues addressed by section 12–104. The rights and obligations of account debtors, to the extent dealt with by section 12–106, are also matters covered. Matters not covered by this Article, including matters as to which this Article expressly provides are covered by other law, are not within the scope of this section.

3.   **Practical considerations on determination of governing law.** This section relating to the law governing the matters covered by this Article must confront substantial practical considerations. These considerations arise primarily from two factors. First, as described below, this section relies primarily on a "waterfall" of alternatives for determining a controllable electronic record's jurisdiction. The first four elements of the waterfall require for their applicability express provisions of a controllable electronic record, an attached or logically associated record, or the system in which a controllable electronic record is recorded. However, many controllable electronic records and systems existing at the time of the 2022 Amendments do not contain these provisions. As explained in Comment 6, the expectation is that over time electronic records and related systems will adopt these provisions in reliance on this section, thereby satisfying at least one of the first four elements of the waterfall. Second, in the absence of these provisions, at the bottom of the waterfall the controllable electronic record's jurisdiction is the District of Columbia. See Comment 6.

4.   **Governing law for Section 12–106.** Subsection (b) provides an exception to the general rule of subsection (a) that "the local law of a controllable electronic record's jurisdiction governs the matters covered by this Article." The exception recognizes that an account debtor's rights and duties generally are governed by the law applicable to the underlying obligation of the account debtor, and not by the law applicable to the agreement between the assignor (debtor) and the assignee (secured party)—a security agreement. See Section 9–401, Comment 3. Subsection (b) recognizes that an effective agreement (i.e., one effective under Section 1–301(a)) between the account debtor and assignor may choose a different law to cover the matters covered by Section 12–106 (i.e., the account debtor's rights and duties addressed in that section). Such an agreement may, of course, address matters other than those covered by Section 12–106 (for example, an agreement that all obligations of the account debtor are governed by the laws of State X).

940

5. **Determination of controllable electronic record's jurisdiction.** The basic rule that the law of a controllable electronic record's jurisdiction governs the matters covered by Article 12 may be viewed as a rough proxy for the traditional role of the location of tangible asset (e.g., goods) in determining the applicable law (*lex rei sitae*). Drawing on the analogous provisions in Sections 8–110 and 9–305 in the context of a security entitlement or securities account or a commodity contract or commodity account, under subsection (c) it is the controllable electronic record itself, records attached thereto or associated therewith, or the system in which the controllable electronic record is recorded that determines the controllable electronic record's jurisdiction and, thereby, the governing law. Subsection (c) provides a "waterfall" of rules based on provisions that identify a particular jurisdiction as the controllable electronic record's jurisdiction or alternatively that provide the governing law for a controllable electronic record or the system in which the record is recorded. As to subsection (e), see Section 8–110, Comment 5A.

Paragraphs (1) through (4) of the subsection (c) waterfall each relies on information available from a controllable electronic record, an attached or logically associated record, or rules of a system in which the record is recorded. A controllable electronic record's jurisdiction is determined by one of these sources that "expressly provide[s]" that a jurisdiction is the controllable electronic record's jurisdiction or that a particular jurisdiction's law is the governing law. These paragraphs refer to attached or logically associated records or system rules that are "readily available." They also assume that the controllable electronic record is itself readily available to anyone choosing to deal with the record. These provisions are based on the assumption that the relevant express provision will be available to an interested person without the imposition of unreasonable burdens.

6. **Bottom of the waterfall: District of Columbia.** Many controllable electronic records, attached or logically associated records, and systems in which controllable electronic records are recorded that exist at the time of the 2022 Amendments do not identify the "controllable electronic record's jurisdiction" or the governing law (some permissioned systems being exceptions). (It is anticipated that, upon widespread adoption of Article 12 and accompanying amendments, systems will adapt and the first four elements of the waterfall will become more generally applicable for identifying a controllable electronic record's jurisdiction.) Consequently, subsection (c)(5) addresses an issue that does not normally exist in the context of Sections 8–110 and 9–305. It might be thought that the logical choice for the residual rule for designating the controllable electronic record's jurisdiction at bottom of the waterfall would be, the location of the debtor. That approach would follow the role of the location of a debtor under Sections 9–301 and 9–307. However, that location may not readily be determined by parties to a transaction, primarily because in many cases involving controllable electronic records the transferor is not known to or easily discoverable by a purchaser. See Prefatory Note 1 to Article 12. Consequently, Subsection (c)(5) resolves this issue by providing that the controllable electronic record's jurisdiction is the District of Columbia.

7. **District of Columbia as controllable electronic record's jurisdiction.** The designation of the District of Columbia as the controllable electronic record's jurisdiction follows Section 9–307(c), which designates the District of Columbia as the location of a debtor that otherwise would be located in a jurisdiction whose law does not provide for a generally applicable system of public notice (such a filing or registration) for nonpossessory security interests. This designation also assumes that the District of Columbia will have adopted Article 12 and the conforming amendments to Articles 1 and 9 in substantially the uniform version—i.e., without material modification of the official text. This is a plausible assumption based on the history of adoptions in that jurisdiction. Because the controllable electronic record's jurisdiction does not govern perfection of a security interest by filing, the designation of the District of Columbia at the bottom of the waterfall will not confer on that jurisdiction any economic benefits of fees for filing of financing statements. See Section 9–306B(b). Subsection (d) addresses the unlikely situation that the District of Columbia does not adopt Article 12 without material modification of the official text or later adopts materially non-uniform amendments. Subsection (d) is patterned loosely (but as closely as feasible) on the TRADES Regulations, 31 CFR § 357.11(e), for U.S. Treasury securities.

The term "Article 12" is defined in subsection (d) as the officially promulgated 2022 version of Article 12 and conforming amendments. In determining whether the District of Columbia has enacted Article 12 without material modification, a court or other tribunal should consider the materiality of any provision in the context of the issue or issues before it. A modification of a provision that would be material in another context should be disregarded if it has no bearing on the issue or issues before the tribunal. In connection with any future revision of the Article 12 official text, it will be important for transitional provisions to address the situations in which the District of Columbia may or may not have adopted the revised official text.

8. **Relevant time for determination of governing law.** Subsection (f) provides that the rights of purchasers are governed by the applicable law as of the time of purchase. Note that Sections 8–110 and 9–305 do not contain an analogous rule with respect to a securities intermediary's jurisdiction. However, Section 8–110(c) does provide a similar rule for the delivery of a security certificate and adverse claims. As to the timing of the

determination of the governing law for other issues under Article 12, such as the rights and duties of account debtors under Section 12–106, the section does not specify a time. As with most statutory provisions relating to governing law, courts are free to determine the appropriate relevant time taking into account the relevant facts and the nature of the issues involved.

UCC ARTICLE A

TRANSITIONAL PROVISIONS FOR UNIFORM COMMERCIAL CODE AMENDMENTS (2022)

Article A was added in 2022. It is presented without <u>underline</u> formatting.

PART 1. GENERAL PROVISIONS AND DEFINITIONS

A-101.   Short Title.
A-102.   Definitions.

PART 2. GENERAL TRANSITIONAL PROVISION

A-201.   Saving Clause.

PART 3. TRANSITIONAL PROVISIONS FOR ARTICLES 9 AND 12

A-301.   Saving Clause.
A-302.   Security Interest Perfected Before Effective Date.
A-303.   Security Interest Unperfected Before Effective Date.
A-304.   Effectiveness of Actions Taken Before Effective Date.
A-305.   Priority.
A-306.   Priority of Claims When Priority Rules of Article 9 Do Not Apply.

PART 4. EFFECTIVE DATE

A-401.   Effective Date.

PREFATORY NOTE TO ARTICLE A—TRANSITIONAL PROVISIONS

The Uniform Commercial Code Amendments (2022) (2022 Amendments) pose special challenges. The amendments add a new Article 12, covering new classes of property, and provide extensive revisions to Article 9. They also include amendments to every other UCC article (save Article 6). Earlier transitional provisions do not provide an adequate template for addressing such a broad set of amendments. However, this article draws substantially on Article 9, Part 7, the transitional provisions applicable to the 1998 Article 9 Revisions. In particular, the substantial amendments to Article 9 and the new Article 12 contained in the 2022 Amendments require that special attention be given to post-effective date perfection and priority issues.

A uniform law as complex as the 2022 Amendments necessarily gives rise to difficult problems and uncertainties during the transition to the new law. As is customary for uniform laws, these amendments are based on the general assumption that all States will have enacted substantially identical versions. While always important, uniformity is particularly important to the success of these amendments, especially those to Article 9 and the new Article 12 and conforming amendments to other articles relating to each.

Article 9, Part 7, provided that several material changes in the law would be given effect one year after a "uniform" effective date. (As it turned out, all but a few states enacted the 1998 Article 9 Revisions with the uniform effective date.). However, for practical reasons many states may wish to provide an effective date for this act that is consistent with their usual timing for effectiveness of legislation. Consequently, this article does not provide for a uniform effective date but does provide for a uniform adjustment date (Adjustment Date), which is July 1, 2025, on which several material provisions (in particular, new priority rules that would override pre-effective-date established priorities) would apply. However, if the uniform Adjustment Date would be less than one year after the effective date for a state's adoption of these amendments, then the state should adopt an Adjustment Date that is one year after the state's effective date. The minimum of a one-year period between the effective date and the Adjustment Date is important. It is intended primarily to provide sufficient time for a person to achieve perfection or priority of a security interest under the 2022 Amendments following the effective date, or for a person with an established priority in property to protect its priority before the priority might otherwise be lost on the Adjustment Date.

The law, other than the Uniform Commercial Code, of a state adopting the 2022 Amendments determines the time of day on the state's effective date on which the amendments take effect.

Legislative Note: A state should codify Parts 1, 2 and 3 of this article as a part of the state's [Uniform Commercial Code].

In its codification of this article a state should provide a title that is conducive to its usual methods of codification, which is likely to ensure that it is called to the attention of users of the state's [Uniform Commercial Code], and which will avoid misunderstandings as to the relationship of this article to the other provisions of the state's [Uniform Commercial Code]. The designation of "Article" indicates that this article is a part of the state's [Uniform Commercial Code] as are the other articles. A state that uses a designation other than "article" may adopt for this article that other designation (such as "division"). Alternatively, a state may wish to adopt for this article a distinctive designation, such as "annex," which would distinguish its focus on transitional provisions from the content of other articles.

PART 1

GENERAL PROVISIONS AND DEFINITIONS

§ A-101.   Short Title.

This article may be cited as Transitional Provisions for Uniform Commercial Code Amendments (2022).

§ A-102.   Definitions.

(a)   [Article A Definitions.] In this article:

(1)   "Adjustment date" means July 1, 2025, or the date that is one year after [the effective date of this [act]], whichever is later.

(2)   "Article 12" means Article 12 of [the Uniform Commercial Code].

(3)   "Article 12 property" means a controllable account, controllable electronic record, or controllable payment intangible.

(b)   [Definitions in other articles.] The following definitions in other articles of [the Uniform Commercial Code] apply to this article.

"Controllable account". Section 9–102.

"Controllable electronic record". Section 12–102.

"Controllable payment intangible". Section 9–102.

"Electronic money". Section 9–102.

"Financing statement". Section 9–102.

(c)   [Article 1 definitions and principles.] Article 1 contains general definitions and principles of construction and interpretation applicable throughout this article.

Official Comment

Subsection headings. Subsection headings are not a part of the official text itself and have not been approved by the sponsors.

PART 2

GENERAL TRANSITIONAL PROVISION

§ A–201. Saving Clause.

Except as provided in Part 3, a transaction validly entered into before [the effective date of this [act]] and the rights, duties, and interests flowing from the transaction remain valid thereafter and may be terminated, completed, consummated, or enforced as required or permitted by law other than [the Uniform Commercial Code] or, if applicable, [the Uniform Commercial Code], as though this [act] had not taken effect.

Official Comment

1. **Source.** This Section is drawn from pre-2022 Section 10–102(2) (now withdrawn).

2. **In general: Prospective application.** This section is a savings clause that provides in general for the prospective application of the 2022 Amendments and the preservation of the validity of pre-effective-date transactions and the rights, duties, and interests flowing from those transactions. Part 3 provides important exceptions to this prospective application for Articles 9 and new Article 12.

3. **Prospective application: Examples.**

"Conspicuous." 2022 section 1–201(b)(10) provides a revised definition of "conspicuous" and revised Comment 10 provides extensive new commentary. The revised definition applies to a record that becomes a part of the relevant transaction after the effective date.

"Hybrid transaction" and "hybrid lease." The 2022 revisions of Sections 2–102 and 2A–102 address a sale of goods that is a part of a "hybrid transaction" and a lease of goods that is part of a "hybrid lease." See Sections 2–106(5) (defining "hybrid transaction") and 2A–103(1)(h.1) (defining "hybrid lease"). These revisions apply to transactions entered into after the effective date.

4. **Revisions reflecting continuation of pre-effective-date precedents.** Several revisions are intended to clarify and reaffirm understandings of pre-effective-date interpretations of the Uniform Commercial Code and are intended to modify some pre-effective-date judicial interpretations. Examples include (i) the amendment to Section 3–104, which clarifies that neither a choice-of-law nor a choice-of-forum clause prevents a promise from being a negotiable instrument, (ii) the amendments to Section 4A–201, which indicate that a security procedure may impose an obligation on both the receiving bank and the customer and may involve the use of symbols, sounds, or biometrics, (iii) the clarifying revision of Section 5–116, (iv) the new definitions of "assignee" and "assignor" in Section 9–102(a)(7A) and (7B), and (v) clarification in Section 9–204(b.1) as to the attachment of a security interest in consumer goods as proceeds or commingled goods and in a commercial tort claim as proceeds. However, this transitional rule will be important in situations in which the controlling pre-effective-date case law is not consistent with the amended provisions.

PART 3

TRANSITIONAL PROVISIONS FOR ARTICLES 9 AND 12

§ A–301. Saving Clause.

(a) **[Pre-effective-date transaction, lien, or interest.]** Except as provided in this part, Article 9 as amended by this [act] and Article 12 apply to a transaction, lien, or other interest in property, even if the transaction, lien, or interest was entered into, created, or acquired before [the effective date of this [act]].

(b) **[Continuing validity.]** Except as provided in subsection (c) and Sections A–302 through A–306:

(1) a transaction, lien, or interest in property that was validly entered into, created, or transferred before [the effective date of this [act]] and was not governed by [the Uniform Commercial Code], but would be subject to Article 9 as amended by this [act] or Article 12 if it had been entered into, created, or transferred on or after [the effective date of this [act]], including the rights, duties, and interests flowing from the transaction, lien, or interest, remains valid on and after [the effective date of this [act]]; and

(2) the transaction, lien, or interest may be terminated, completed, consummated, and enforced as required or permitted by this [act] or by the law that would apply if this [act] had not taken effect.

(c) **[Pre-effective-date proceeding.]** This [act] does not affect an action, case, or proceeding commenced before [the effective date of this [act]].

Official Comment

1. **Source.** This section derives from Section 9–702.

2. **Pre-effective-date transactions, liens, and interests.** Subsection (a) contains the general rule that Article 9 as amended by this act (2022 Article 9) and Article 12 generally apply to transactions, liens (including security interests), and interests in property, even if entered into, created, or acquired before the effective date. Thus, for example, secured transactions entered into under Article 9 before amendment by this act (as used in these official comments to Article A, "pre-2022 Article 9") must be terminated, completed, consummated, and enforced under this act. However, other provisions in this part provide exceptions to this general rule.

3. **Pre-effective-date transactions not governed by pre-effective-date Uniform Commercial Code.** Subsection (b) is an exception to the general rule. It applies to valid, pre-effective-date transactions, liens, and other interests in property that were not governed by the pre-2022 Uniform Commercial Code but would be governed by this act if they had been entered into or created after this act takes effect. Under subsection (b), these valid transactions, such as the sale of a controllable electronic record, retain their validity under this act and may be terminated, completed, consummated, and enforced as required or permitted by the law that would apply had this act not taken effect or, to the extent not inconsistent with that law, this act.

4. **Judicial proceedings commenced before effective date.** As is usual in transitional provisions, subsection (c) provides that this act does not affect litigation pending on the effective date.

§ A–302.   Security Interest Perfected Before Effective Date.

(a) **[Continuing perfection: perfection requirements satisfied.]** A security interest that is enforceable and perfected immediately before [the effective date of this [act]] is a perfected security interest under this [act] if, on [the effective date of this [act]], the requirements for enforceability and perfection under this [act] are satisfied without further action.

(b) **[Continuing perfection: enforceability or perfection requirements not satisfied.]** If a security interest is enforceable and perfected immediately before [the effective date of this [act]], but the requirements for enforceability or perfection under this [act] are not satisfied on [the effective date of this [act]], the security interest:

(1) is a perfected security interest until the earlier of the time perfection would have ceased under the law in effect immediately before [the effective date of this [act]] or the adjustment date;

(2) remains enforceable thereafter only if the security interest satisfies the requirements for enforceability under Section 9–203, as amended by this [act], before the adjustment date; and

(3) remains perfected thereafter only if the requirements for perfection under this [act] are satisfied before the time specified in paragraph (1).

Official Comment

1. **Source.** This section derives from Section 9–703.

2. **Perfected security interests under pre-2022 Article 9 and 2022 Article 9.** This section deals with security interests that are perfected under pre-2022 Article 9 immediately before this act takes effect. Subsection (a) provides, not surprisingly, that if the security interest would be a perfected security interest under 2022 Article 9 (i.e., if the transaction satisfies 2022 Article 9's requirements for enforceability (attachment) and perfection), no further action need be taken for the security interest to be a perfected security interest.

Example 1. A pre-effective-date security agreement and financing statement covered "all accounts and general intangibles now owned or hereafter acquired." After the effective date the debtor acquired controllable accounts, controllable electronic records, and controllable payment intangibles. The security interest in the after-acquired collateral is enforceable and perfected under both pre-2022 and 2022 Article 9. The controllable accounts are accounts, the controllable electronic records and controllable payment

946

intangibles are general intangibles, and filing is an appropriate method of perfection for that collateral under both versions of Article 9.

Other examples of methods of perfection under pre-2022 Article 9 that also would achieve perfection under 2022 Article 9 include filing a financing statement and perfection by control in electronic documents under pre-2022 and amended Section 7–106, in chattel paper under pre-2022 Section 9–105, and in chattel paper evidenced by authoritative electronic records under 2022 Section 9–105.

3. **Security interests enforceable and perfected under pre-2022 Article 9 but unenforceable or unperfected under 2022 Article 9.** Subsection (b) deals with security interests that are enforceable and perfected under pre-2022 Article 9 immediately before this act takes effect but do not satisfy the requirements for enforceability (attachment) or perfection under 2022 Article 9. These security interests are perfected security interests until the earlier of the time perfection would have ceased under the law in effect immediately before this act takes effect and the adjustment date. If the security interest satisfies the requirements for attachment and perfection within that period, the security interest remains continuously perfected thereafter. If the security interest satisfies only the requirements for attachment within that period, the security interest becomes unperfected on the adjustment date.

Example 2. A pre-effective-date security agreement signed by Debtor in favor of Secured Party covers, among other things, "all money . . . and general intangibles now owned or hereafter acquired." Secured Party filed a proper financing statement in the appropriate filing office covering "All personal property." Debtor owns electronic money, spitcoin, issued by the government of El Cuspidouro. Under pre-2022 Article 9 the electronic money might be characterized as a general intangible if "money" were to be construed (at least for purposes of Article 9) to include only tangible money as to which perfection is possible only by possession. See pre-2022 Section 9–312(b)(3). Alternatively, even if the spitcoin is money, perfection might be possible by filing under the baseline rule of Section 9–310, inasmuch as the spitcoin (an intangible) cannot be possessed. Assume, therefore, that under pre-2022 Article 9 Secured Party's security interest in the spitcoin is perfected by filing. Assume also that spitcoin can be subjected to control under Section 9–105A. As to the spitcoin owned by the debtor before the effective date, under subsection (b) the security interest would remain perfected until the adjustment date but would become unperfected under 2022 Article 9 on the adjustment date unless earlier perfected by control. This is so because a security interest in electronic money that can be subject to control under Section 9–105A, such as spitcoin, may be perfected only by control under 2022 Article 9. Sections 9–312(b)(4); 9–314(a). The security interest in any spitcoin acquired by the debtor after the effective date would be unperfected until the secured party obtains control.

Example 3. Secured Party has a pre-effective-date security interest in a security entitlement perfected by control pursuant to Sections 9–106 and 8–106(d)(3), based on control held by Kontroal Phreeque LLC (KP) on behalf of Secured Party. Even in the highly unlikely event that following the effective date the secured party could not prove that KP acknowledged its control on behalf of the secured party in conformity with 2022 Section 8–106(d)(3), its security interest would nevertheless remain perfected beyond the adjustment date. Perfection by control for a security entitlement under Section 9–106 depends on control under 8–106 and, under Section A–301(a), Part 3 of this article, including subsection (b), does not apply to transactions under Article 8 because Section A–301(a) applies only to Articles 9 and 12. The rules under pre-effective date Article 8 continue to apply to the pre-effective date transaction. As to financial assets acquired and becoming a part of the security entitlement after the effective date, however, 2022 Articles 8 and 9 would apply. Secured Party could perfect its security interest in those financial assets through a complying acknowledgment by KP or by filing. This means for a securities account involving active trading, for example, the secured party should ensure compliance with the 2022 Article 8 control requirements at or before the effective date so as to ensure perfection in post-effective date-acquired financial assets.

4. **Interpretation of pre-effective-date security agreements.** Section 9–102 defines "security agreement" as "an agreement that creates or provides for a security interest." Under Section 1–201(b)(3), an "agreement" is a "bargain of the parties in fact." If parties to a pre-effective-date security agreement describe the collateral by using a term defined in pre-2022 Article 9 in one way and defined in 2022 Article 9 in another way, in most cases it should be presumed that the bargain of the parties contemplated the meaning of the term under pre-2022 Article 9. Definitions of terms relating to collateral which have been amended in 2022 Article 9 are "account," "chattel paper," "instrument," "money," and "general intangible." A different result might be appropriate, for example, if a security agreement explicitly contemplated future changes in the Article 9 definitions of types of collateral–for example, "'Accounts' means 'accounts' as defined in the Uniform Commercial Code Article 9 of [State X], *as that definition may be amended from time to time*." Whether a different interpretive approach is

appropriate in any given case depends on the bargain of the parties, as determined by applying ordinary principles of contract law.

§ A–303.   Security Interest Unperfected Before Effective Date.

A security interest that is enforceable immediately before [the effective date of this [act]] but is unperfected at that time:

(1) remains an enforceable security interest until the adjustment date;

(2) remains enforceable thereafter if the security interest becomes enforceable under Section 9–203, as amended by this [act], on [the effective date of this [act]] or before the adjustment date; and

(3) becomes perfected:

   (A) without further action, on [the effective date of this [act]] if the requirements for perfection under this [act] are satisfied before or at that time; or

   (B) when the requirements for perfection are satisfied if the requirements are satisfied after that time.

Official Comment

1. **Source.** This Section derives from Section 9–704.

2. **Pre-effective-date enforceable but unperfected security interests.** This section deals with security interests that are enforceable but unperfected (i.e., subordinate to the rights of a person who becomes a lien creditor) under pre-2022 Article 9 or other applicable law immediately before this act takes effect. These security interests remain enforceable until the adjustment date, and thereafter if the appropriate steps for attachment under 2022 Article 9 are taken before the adjustment date. See Section A–304(c) (This section's treatment of enforceability is the same as that of Section A–302.) The security interest becomes a perfected security interest on the effective date if, at that time, the security interest satisfies the requirements for perfection (which include the requirements for attachment) under 2022 Article 9. If the security interest does not satisfy the requirements for perfection until sometime thereafter, it becomes a perfected security interest at that later time.

Example 1. Prior to the effective date Debtor obtained a loan from Secured Party and signed a security agreement covering "all cryptocurrencies now owned or hereafter acquired." The security interest attached to various cryptocurrencies owned by Debtor, including 1,000 happicoins held by debtor on the happicoins blockchain platform. Debtor then transferred the 1,000 happicoins to Secured Party on the blockchain. Although the happicoins are general intangibles, Secured Party failed to file a financing statement necessary to perfect its security interest under pre-2022 Article 9.

Under 2022 Article 9, the happicoins would be controllable electronic records and the transfer of the happicoins to Secured Party would give Secured Party "control" of the happicoins as provided in Section 12–105. Before 2022 Article 9 (i.e., including 2022 Sections 9–107A and 9–314) and Article 12 became effective, Secured Party's security interest was unperfected as noted above. Upon the effective date, however, the security interest became perfected by control as a result of the pre-effective-date transfer of control to Secured Party.

Example 2. Prior to the effective date Debtor obtained a loan from Secured Party and signed a security agreement covering certain specified deposit accounts and "all documents and chattel paper now owned or hereafter acquired by Debtor." The security interest attached to the deposit accounts and to various documents and chattel paper owned by Debtor. Persons in control of certain electronic chattel paper, electronic documents, and deposit accounts included in the collateral acknowledged that they had control of that collateral on behalf of Secured Party. Assuming that an agency relationship cannot be established between these acknowledging persons and Secured Party, it is perhaps arguable that Secured Party's security interest in the relevant collateral was unperfected because Secured Party did not have control under pre-2022 Sections 7–106, 9–104, and 9–105. However, because the pre-effective-date acknowledgments would give Secured Party control under the relevant 2022 sections, its security interest, even if not perfected pre-effective date, became perfected by control on the effective date.

§ A–304. Effectiveness of Actions Taken Before Effective Date.

(a) **[Pre-effective-date action; attachment and perfection before adjustment date.]** If action, other than the filing of a financing statement, is taken before [the effective date of this [act]] and the action would have resulted in perfection of the security interest had the security interest become enforceable before [the effective date of this [act]], the action is effective to perfect a security interest that attaches under this [act] before the adjustment date. An attached security interest becomes unperfected on the adjustment date unless the security interest becomes a perfected security interest under this [act] before the adjustment date.

(b) **[Pre-effective-date filing.]** The filing of a financing statement before [the effective date of this [act]] is effective to perfect a security interest on [the effective date of this [act]] to the extent the filing would satisfy the requirements for perfection under this [act].

(c) **[Pre-effective-date enforceability action.]** The taking of an action before [the effective date of this [act]] is sufficient for the enforceability of a security interest on [the effective date of this [act]] if the action would satisfy the requirements for enforceability under this [act].

Official Comment

1. **Source.** Subsections (a) and (b) of this Section derive from Section 9–705. Subsection (c) is new.

2. **General.** This section addresses primarily the situation in which the perfection step or requirement for enforceability is taken under pre-2022 Article 9 or other applicable law before the effective date of this act, but the security interest does not attach until after that date.

3. **Perfection other than by filing.** Subsection (a) applies when the perfection step is a step other than the filing of a financing statement. If the step that would be a valid perfection step under pre-2022 Article 9 or other law is taken before this act takes effect, and if a security interest attaches before the adjustment date, then the security interest becomes a perfected security interest upon attachment. However, the security interest becomes unperfected on the adjustment date unless the requirements for attachment and perfection under 2022 Article 9 are satisfied within that period.

4. **Perfection by filing: ineffective filings made effective.** Subsection (b) deals with financing statements that were filed under pre-2022 Article 9 and which would not have perfected a security interest under the pre-2022 Article, but which would perfect a security interest under 2022 Article 9. Under subsection (b), such a financing statement is effective to perfect a security interest to the extent it complies with 2022 Article 9. Subsection (b) applies regardless of the reason for the filing. When this act takes effect, the filing becomes effective to perfect a security interest assuming the filing satisfies the perfection requirements under 2022 Article 9.

Example 1. Prior to the effective date Debtor obtained a loan from Secured Party and signed a security agreement covering, among other collateral, "money," "accounts," "chattel paper," and "general intangibles." Secured Party filed a financing statement covering "all assets." If, under the applicable pre-2022 Article 9 as interpreted by the courts, electronic currency was "money" as defined in pre-2022 Section 1–201 even though as an intangible it could not be possessed, then under the applicable pre-2022 Section 9–312(b)(3), filing a financing statement was not an effective method of perfection. Assume, however, that under 2022 Articles 1 and 9, the electronic currency is not "money," and is instead a general intangible. Under 2022 Article 9, filing is an effective method of perfection. Upon the effective date of 2022 Article 9, the security interest became perfected by the pre-effective-date filed financing statement.

Example 2. Prior to the effective date Debtor obtained a loan from Secured Party and signed a security agreement covering, among other collateral, "accounts," "chattel paper," and "general intangibles." Secured Party filed a financing statement covering "accounts." Under the applicable pre-2022 Article 9, a certain right to payment was chattel paper because it was a lease of specific goods, even though the transaction also covered, and the lessee's monetary obligation also related to, various other assets and various services. Because the filed financing statement covered only accounts, the security interest in the chattel paper was unperfected. Under 2022 Article 9, however, the right to payment was an "account," and not chattel paper, assuming that the lessee's right to possession and use of the goods was not "the predominant purpose of the transaction." Section 9–102(a)(11)(B)(ii). On that assumption, upon the effective date the security interest became perfected by the pre-effective-date filed financing statement covering accounts.

5.   **Enforceability of security interest: unenforceable security interest made enforceable.**

Example 3. Under the facts of Example 1, Section A–303, Comment 2, instead of signing a security agreement Debtor agreed orally to grant to Secured Party a security interest in the happicoins. It follows that under pre-2022 Article 9 Secured Party's security interest was unenforceable and did not attach to the happicoins for want of a signed security agreement. Pre-2022 Section 9–203(b)(3)(A). However, upon the effective date of 2022 Article 9, Secured Party had control of the happicoins under 2022 Article 9. Sections 12–105. At that time the security interest became enforceable and attached under Sections 9–107A and 9–203(b)(3)(D) and also was perfected by control.

§ A–305.   Priority.

(a)   **[Determination of priority.]** Subject to subsections (b) and (c), this [act] determines the priority of conflicting claims to collateral.

(b)   **[Established priorities.]** Subject to subsection (c), if the priorities of claims to collateral were established before [the effective date of this [act]], Article 9 as in effect before [the effective date of this [act]] determines priority.

(c)   **[Determination of certain priorities on adjustment date.]** On the adjustment date, to the extent the priorities determined by Article 9 as amended by this [act] modify the priorities established before [the effective date of this [act]], the priorities of claims to Article 12 property and electronic money established before [the effective date of this [act]] cease to apply.

Official Comment

1.   **Source.** This section derives from Section 9–709.

2.   **Law governing priority and established priorities.** Ordinarily, 2022 Article 9 determines the priority of conflicting claims to collateral under subsection (a). However, when the relative priorities of the claims were established before the effective date, pre-2022 Article 9 governs under subsection (b). Subsection (c) provides an exception to subsection (b).

Example 1. In 2021, prior to the effective date, Debtor obtained a loan from Secured Party and signed a security agreement covering "all cryptocurrency and money now owned or hereafter acquired." The security interest attached to various cryptocurrencies owned by Debtor, including 1,000 happicoins held by Debtor on the happicoins blockchain platform. Secured Party promptly filed a financing statement covering "all general intangibles, including cryptocurrencies." In 2022, also prior to the effective date, Debtor obtained a loan from Lender and signed a security agreement covering "all cryptocurrency." Although the happicoins are general intangibles, Lender failed to file a financing statement. Because the priorities of the claims were established before the effective date, pre-2022 Article 9 governs. Secured Party's perfected security interest has priority over Lender's unperfected security interest under pre-2022 Section 9–322(a)(2).

Example 2. The facts are the same as in Example 1, except that Debtor transferred control of the 1,000 happicoins to Lender on the blockchain in 2022 *before* the effective date. Because Lender failed to file a financing statement and control was not a method of perfection under pre-2022 Article 9, Lender's security interest was unperfected immediately prior to the effective date. However, because under 2022 Article 9 the happicoins are controllable electronic records and Lender has "control" of the happicoins under Section 12–105, Lender's security interest became perfected on the effective date. Nevertheless, because the priorities of Secured Party's and Lender's security interests were established before the effective date, Secured Party's security interest continues to have priority after the effective date. (However, see Example 4 for the shift of priority on the adjustment date.)

Example 3. The facts are the same as in Example 1, except that in 2023, *after* the effective date, Debtor transferred control of the 1,000 happicoins to Lender on the blockchain. Under 2022 Article 9, the happicoins were controllable electronic records and the transfer of control of the happicoins gave Lender "control" of the happicoins as provided in Section 12–105. The affirmative step of transferring control established anew the relative priority of the conflicting claims after the effective date. 2022 Article 9 determines priority and Lender's security interest has priority under Section 9–326A (without any deferral until the adjustment date). Moreover, Lender also may have priority over other property claims as a qualifying purchaser under Section 12–104(e).

One consequence of the rule on established priorities in subsection (b) is that the mere taking effect of this act does not of itself adversely affect the priority of conflicting claims to collateral, as Example 2 illustrates. However, as Example 3 illustrates, relative priorities that are "established" before the effective date do not necessarily remain unchanged following the effective date. Of course, unlike priority contests among security interests, some priorities are established permanently, for example, the rights of a buyer of property who took free of a security interest under pre-2022 Article 9.

3. **Modification of established priorities on adjustment date.**

Subsection (c) provides an exception to the respect that subsection (b) affords to pre-effective-date established priorities, but only for security interests in Article 12 property—controllable accounts, controllable electronic records, and controllable payment intangibles—and electronic money.

Example 4. The facts are the same as in Example 2. Lender's security interest became perfected by control on the effective date, Secured Party's established priority continued to apply under subsection (b). Under subsection (c), however, on the adjustment date the priorities shifted. Secured Party's established priority ceased to apply and Lender's perfection by control gave Lender priority under 2022 Section 9–326A.

4. **Transfers of collateral after the effective date.**

Example 5. The facts are the same as in Example 2. In 2023, *after* the effective date, Debtor acquired an additional 500 happicoins. The security interests of both Secured Party and Lender attached to the happicoins pursuant to the after-acquired property clauses in their respective security agreements. Secured Party's security interest was perfected by its earlier financing statement filing. Lender then perfected its security interest by Debtor's transfer of control of the happicoins to Lender. Lender's security interest in the additional happicoins perfected by control gave Lender priority as to those happicoins under Section 9–326A. Unlike the situation in Example 2, however, as to the newly acquired happicoins the priorities were not established prior to the effective date. Before the effective date neither creditor could have had a "perfected" security interest in happicoins in which Debtor had not yet acquired rights.

Example 6. The facts are the same as in Example 1. In 2023, *after* the effective date, Debtor transferred 750 spitcoins, an electronic money, to Beier. Beier then obtained control of the spitcoins under Section 9–105A. Secured Party's security interest in the spitcoins, which were either money not capable of being possessed or general intangibles under pre-2022 Article 9, are assumed to be perfected by filing. See Section A–302, Comment 3, Example 2. Because there was no wrongful collusion with Debtor (indeed, Beier had no knowledge or notice of Secured Party's security interest), Beier took the spitcoin free of Secured Party's security interest under Section 9–332(c).

§ A–306. Priority of Claims When Priority Rules of Article 9 Do Not Apply.

(a) **[Determination of priority.]** Subject to subsections (b) and (c), Article 12 determines the priority of conflicting claims to Article 12 property when the priority rules of Article 9 as amended by this [act] do not apply.

(b) **[Established priorities.]** Subject to subsection (c), when the priority rules of Article 9 as amended by this [act] do not apply and the priorities of claims to Article 12 property were established before [the effective date of this [act]], law other than Article 12 determines priority.

(c) **[Determination of certain priorities on adjustment date.]** When the priority rules of Article 9 as amended by this [act] do not apply, to the extent the priorities determined by this [act] modify the priorities established before [the effective date of this [act]], the priorities of claims to Article 12 property established before [the effective date of this [act]] cease to apply on the adjustment date.

Official Comment

1. **Source.** This section derives from Section 9–709 and, in part, from Section 8–510.

2. **Applicability of this section to Article 12 property.** Although this section applies to Article 12 property (controllable accounts, controllable electronic records, and controllable payment intangibles) when the priority rules of Article 9 do not apply, it applies primarily to controllable electronic records. Its application to controllable accounts and controllable payment intangibles is quite limited because Article 9 applies to most sales of accounts and payment intangibles (as well as to the use of that property to secure an obligation). Section 9–109(a)(3). There is a very limited exclusion from the scope of Article 9 for a sale of accounts and payment intangibles in connection with a sale of the business out of which they arose. Section 9–109(d)(4).

3. **Law governing priority and established priorities.** Ordinarily, when the priority rules of Article 9 do not apply, Article 12 determines the priority of conflicting claims to Article 12 property under subsection (a).

However, when the relative priorities of the claims were established before the effective date, under subsection (b) law other than Article 12 governs. Subsection (c) provides an exception to subsection (b).

4. **Law governing priority and established priorities.**

Example 1. In 2021, prior to the effective date, Aiko owned 500 happicoins (a cryptocurrency consisting of controllable electronic records) over which Aiko had control (within the meaning of Section 12–105, which was not yet effective) on the happicoin blockchain. In December 2021 Aiko sold the 500 happicoins to Barbara for $10,000 cash. Aiko provided Barbara with a signed memorandum acknowledging the sale and Aiko's receipt of the purchase price and agreeing to hold the happicoins for Barbara pending Barbara's further instructions.

In January 2022 (also prior to the effective date), Aiko sold the same 500 happicoins to Molly for $12,000 cash. Aiko provided Molly with a signed memorandum similar to the one Aiko had provided to Barbara. Assume that, under the non-Uniform Commercial Code applicable law, Barbara remained the owner of the happicoins and under that law Molly obtained no interest in the happicoins pursuant to the purported sale because Aiko had retained no interest and had nothing to transfer to Molly. Because the priorities of the claims of Aiko, Barbara, and Molly were established before the effective date, under subsection (a) those priorities remained in effect after the effective date and Barbara remains the owner of the happicoins.

Example 2. The facts are the same as in Example 1, except that *before* the effective date, Aiko transferred control of the happicoins to Molly on the happicoins blockchain. Again, assume that under the non-Uniform Commercial Code applicable law that transfer of control had no legal effect. After the effective date the relative priorities are unchanged from those described in Example 1 because the relative priorities were established before the effective date and subsection (b) applies.

Example 3. The facts are the same as in Example 1, except that *after* the effective date, Aiko transferred control of the happicoins to Molly on the happicoins blockchain. Under Article 12, the happicoins were controllable electronic records and the transfer of control of the happicoins gave Molly "control" of the happicoins as provided in Section 12–105. Because (it is assumed) Molly met the requirements for a "qualifying purchaser" under Section 12–104(e), Molly acquired the happicoins free of Barbara's property claim. The affirmative step of transferring control after the effective date established anew the relative priority of the conflicting claims after the effective date. Under Section A–301(a), Article 12 applies to the pre-effective-date transactions and property interests and subsection (a) of this section applies.

5. **Modification of established priorities on adjustment date.** Subsection (c) provides an exception to the respect that subsection (b) affords to pre-effective-date established priorities.

Example 4. The facts are the same as in Example 2. However, on the adjustment date the established priorities change. Because (it is assumed) Molly met the requirements for a "qualifying purchaser" under Section 12–104(e), on the adjustment date Molly acquired the happicoins free of Barbara's property claim. Under Section A–301(a), Article 12 applies to the pre-effective-date transactions and property interests and subsection (a) of this section applies.

6. **Transfers after the effective date.**

Example 5. The facts are the same as in Example 1, except that *after* the effective date Aiko sold the happicoins to Jacob, for value, and also transferred control of the happicoins to Jacob on the happicoins blockchain. Because (it is assumed) Jacob met the requirements for a "qualifying purchaser" under Section 12–104(e), Jacob acquired the happicoins free of both Barbara's and Molly's property claims. Note that Jacob took the happicoins free of conflicting claims in the post-effective date acquisition immediately upon acquisition as a qualifying purchaser. Jacob's priority was established after the effective date and was not deferred until the adjustment date, as was the case for Molly's rights in Example 4.

PART 4

EFFECTIVE DATE

§ A–401.   Effective Date.

This [act] takes effect on . . .

APPENDIX D

PEB COMMENTARIES AND REPORTS ON THE UNIFORM COMMERCIAL CODE [SELECTED PROVISIONS]*

CONTENTS**

PEB Resolution on Purposes, Standards and Procedures for PEB Commentary to the UCC

PEB Commentary No. 8, Section 9–330 (1991)

PEB Commentary No. 10, Section 1–203 (1994)

PEB Commentary No. 11, Suretyship Issues Under Sections 3–116, 3–305, 3–415, 3–419, and 3–605 (1994)

PEB Report, Effect of Non-Uniform Scope Provisions in Revised Article 9 of the UCC (2004)

PEB Report, Application of the UCC to Selected Issues Relating to Mortgage Notes (2011)

PEB Commentary No. 17, Limited Liability Partnerships under the Choice of Law Rules of Article 9 (2012)

PEB Commentary No. 19, Hague Securities Convention's Effect on Determining the Applicable Law for Indirectly Held Securities (2017)

PEB Commentary No. 20, Consignments (2019)

PEB Commentary No. 21, Use of the Term "Assignment" in Article 9 of the Uniform Commercial Code (2020)

PEB Commentary No. 22, Status of a Disposition under Section 9–610 of the Uniform Commercial Code if the Transferee Does Not Act in Good Faith (2020)

PEB Commentary No. 23, Protected Series under the Uniform Protected Series Act (2021)

PEB Commentary No. 24, Scope of Article 9 Choice-Of-Law Rules Regarding Characterization of Transactions (2022)

PEB Commentary No. 26, Indication of Collateral in a Financing Statement (2022)

PEB Commentary No. 27, Injunction Against a Noncomplying Disposition Under Section 9–610 of The Uniform Commercial Code (2022)

CURRENT PERMANENT EDITORIAL BOARD (PEB) FOR THE UCC

Chair

Tim Schnabel

Members

Carl S. Bjerre
Amelia H. Boss
Henry Deeb Gabriel
Teresa Wilton Harmon
Stephanie Heller
Juliet M. Moringiello
H. Kathleen Patchel

Norman M. Powell
Richard L. Revesz
Edwin E. Smith
Steven O. Weise

ABA Liaisons

Kristen D. Adams
Carter H. Klein

Emeritus Members

Boris Auerbach
Patricia Brumfield Fry

William H. Henning
Frederick H. Miller
James. J. White

Director of Research

Neil B. Cohen

Ex Officio

David F. Levi, ALI President
Dan Robbins, ULC President

PEB RESOLUTION ON PURPOSES, STANDARDS AND PROCEDURES FOR PEB COMMENTARY TO THE UCC

1.   The Permanent Editorial Board (PEB), in accordance with the standards and procedures set out in this resolution of March 14, 1987, and the authority given in the agreement between the American Law

---

*   Copyright © 2023 by The American Law Institute and the Uniform Law Commission. Reproduced with the permission of the Permanent Editorial Board for the Uniform Commercial Code. All rights reserved.

**   *Note from West Advisory Panel: We have omitted PEB Commentaries Nos. 2, 3, 5, 6, 7, 9, 12, 14, and 15 because they have been superseded by UCC revisions. Abridged volumes in this series contain only the Commentaries and Reports pertinent to the volume.*

APPENDIX D

Institute and the National Conference of Commissioners on Uniform State Laws dated July 31, 1986, will issue supplemental commentary on the Uniform Commercial Code (UCC) from time to time.

a. The supplemental commentary of the PEB generally will be known as *PEB Commentary,* to distinguish it from the Official Comments to the UCC, and will be preserved separately from the Official Comments.

b. The underlying purposes and policies of the *PEB Commentary* are those specified in UCC § 1–102(2). A *PEB Commentary* should come within one or more of the following specific purposes, which should be made apparent at the inception of the Commentary: (1) to resolve an ambiguity in the UCC by restating more clearly what the PEB considers to be the legal rule; (2) to state a preferred resolution of an issue on which judicial opinion or scholarly writing diverges; (3) to elaborate on the application of the UCC where the statute and/or the Official Comment leaves doubt as to inclusion or exclusion of, or application to, particular circumstances or transactions; (4) consistent with UCC § 1–102(2)(b), to apply the principles of the UCC to new or changed circumstances; (5) to clarify or elaborate upon the operation of the UCC as it relates to other statutes (such as the Bankruptcy Code and various federal and state consumer protection statutes) and general principles of law and equity pursuant to UCC § 1–103; or (6) to otherwise improve the operation of the UCC.

c. The format of the *PEB Commentary* normally will consist of an identification of the issue, a discussion concerning the possible resolutions of the issue to be addressed, and a statement of the view of the PEB as to how the issue should be resolved. On a carefully selected basis supplemental commentary may be issued as an identified supplement to the Official Comments, in which case it generally should take the form of a brief exposition modeled substantially on the form and style of the Official Comments.

d. Topics for *PEB Commentary* will be selected periodically by the PEB from suggestions, accompanied by supporting reasons, made by PEB members and by other persons. *PEB Commentary* may be issued whether or not a perceived issue has been litigated or is in litigation, and whether or not the position taken by the PEB accords with the weight of authority on the issue. The number of topics and topics that are chosen at any given time will be determined by the PEB weighing criteria appropriate under the circumstances, which may include the practical importance of the issue, the absence of other means of resolution, the time and effort to be involved in the preparation of the *PEB Commentary,* the extent to which the *PEB Commentary* is likely to be successful in addressing an issue, whether it is known to the PEB that the topic of the *PEB Commentary* is in specific litigation and, if so, the probable impact upon that litigation, and the availability of resources. However, normally no *PEB Commentary* should be begun with respect to a UCC Article that is undergoing amendment or initial promulgation except upon consultation with and concurrence of the study or drafting committee for such amendment or initial promulgation. Moreover, except in extraordinary cases and in the case of *PEB Commentary* identified as specific supplements to Official Comments, an Official Comment, as opposed to the text of the UCC, should not be the specific subject of *PEB Commentary*.

e. For a variety of reasons, topics initially identified by the PEB for *PEB Commentary* and advisors' drafts of *PEB Commentary* (discussed in paragraph 2 below) may not result in the final approval of *PEB Commentary*. Such reasons might include the failure of a consensus to emerge on the substance of an issue or a conclusion that the issue would better be treated by a change in the UCC Official Text. No inference should be drawn from, and no weight should be accorded to, any withdrawal of an advisor's draft or any failure to proceed with a *PEB Commentary* on any particular topic.

2. The process by which *PEB Commentary* is prepared and issued by the PEB should be flexible, but usually should include:

a. periodic publication of the topics under consideration by the PEB with a request for comment by interested persons by a stated date as to whether any listed topic should be deleted or a related topic added and as to the appropriate resolution of the issues presented by the topics under consideration;

b.   selection of one or more appropriate advisers, who are not members of the PEB, to review any comments submitted by interested persons and other relevant materials and to prepare a tentative adviser's draft of the proposed *PEB Commentary;*

c.   publication of the adviser's draft of the *PEB Commentary,* after supervisory review of the PEB, soliciting comments by interested persons by a stated date on the substance and style of the work;

d.   approval by the PEB of the substance and style of the *PEB Commentary* as finally submitted by the adviser(s) and comments submitted by interested persons or, when warranted, the withdrawal of the proposal with the reasons for withdrawal stated; and

e.   periodic publication of such *PEB Commentary* as is approved by the PEB on a regular schedule.

Approval by the PEB of *PEB Commentary* shall be by three quarters of the members of the PEB voting on the *Commentary.* The manner of publication of *PEB Commentary* by the PEB will be in accordance with procedures formulated under a resolution related to that subject generally.

PEB COMMENTARY NO. 8
SECTION 9–330
(December 10, 1991 as amended to apply to Revised Article 9)*

ISSUE

Section 9–330(a) provides a special priority rule for purchasers of chattel paper who give new value and take possession, or obtain control, of the chattel paper in the ordinary course of their business. Subsection (a) provides that such purchasers take priority over a security interest in the chattel paper "which is claimed merely as proceeds of inventory subject to a security interest . . ."

This Commentary addresses an issue that may arise under § 9–330(a): When is a security interest in chattel paper "claimed merely as proceeds of inventory subject to a security interest" so that the subsequent chattel paper financer who meets the other requirements of § 9–330(a) takes free of it?

INTRODUCTORY DISCUSSION

Most chattel paper is generated by dealers in automobiles, trucks, machinery, and other durable goods of substantial value. Such dealers frequently sell their chattel paper or use it as collateral for loans. Buyers of chattel paper usually take possession of the paper and collect from the debtors thereon themselves. Also, some lenders on chattel paper will take possession and handle collections. (Financers with a security interest in chattel paper covering smaller appliances, television sets, etc., frequently do not take possession of the paper.)

Under the ordinary priority rules of the Code (first to file or perfect has priority) the buyer of, or lender on, chattel paper would have to make a filing search before the transaction to determine whether a prior party has filed a financing statement covering chattel paper or inventory of which the chattel paper might be proceeds. (If a security interest in inventory is perfected by filing, there is also an automatically perfected proceeds security interest in chattel paper which is generated when inventory subject to the security interest is sold.) A filing search requirement before each transaction would entail substantial delays and significant expense even if the search revealed no prior filed financing statement. In the many cases in which there is a prior filed financing statement covering chattel paper or inventory, or both, the application of the general § 9–322 priority rules would always give the first filer priority. Such a system would make it difficult for any buyer or lender other than the first filed secured party to purchase or lend on the security of chattel paper and would make it particularly difficult for a dealer to deal as to chattel paper with anyone other than

---

* PEB Commentary No. 8 was originally issued in 1991, and covered two issues that arose under former UCC Section 9–308. Revised UCC Section 9–330 continues the basic provisions of former Section 9–308 with minor changes. One of the questions addressed in the original Commentary—whether a financer of chattel paper that takes possession of it has a duty to make inquiry or search to determine whether there is an existing security interest in that chattel paper—is answered in the negative by Comment 6 to Revised UCC Section 9–330. The other question dealt with in the original Commentary—when does a secured party have an interest in chattel paper "merely as proceeds"—is not resolved in Revised UCC Section 9–330 or addressed in the Comments to that section. Accordingly, that discussion has been continued in this amended Commentary, modified to conform to the differences between former UCC Section 9–308 and Revised UCC Section 9–330. Unless otherwise indicated, references in this amended Commentary to sections of Article 9 are references to Revised Article 9.

the inventory financer. Prior filings would have to be limited to specific chattel paper or subordination agreements or releases would have to be secured from prior filed inventory or chattel paper financers each time items of chattel paper are transferred to a different financer.

When Article 9 was being drafted in the 1950s, some financers of chattel paper left it with the dealer who had generated it and others took possession of the paper. The drafters of the Code did not want to disrupt those practices. Therefore, the problem presented to the drafters was how to structure priority rules so that both forms of financing could continue efficiently and safely. The Code drafters might have encouraged the practice of purchasing and taking possession of chattel paper by treating chattel paper like instruments and providing that a security interest in chattel paper could be perfected only by taking possession. That rule, however, would have denied perfected status to security interests in chattel paper left with the debtor and would have disrupted that widely used form of financing. Requiring possession for perfection of chattel paper would also have meant that an inventory financer's proceeds interest in chattel paper would be lost after 20 days unless the financer took possession of the paper. On the other hand, as already noted, applying the ordinary Code priority rules to chattel paper would have imposed substantial impediments to the widespread business of buying and taking possession of chattel paper. The drafters, therefore, struck a compromise between the interests of non-possessory financers of chattel paper and inventory financers with a non-possessory proceeds interest in the paper on the one hand, and, on the other hand, competing chattel paper financers who take possession of the paper. Section 9–330 continues that compromise and extends it to protect financers who gain control of electronic chattel paper. (See § 9–105 regarding control of electronic chattel paper.)

Under that compromise a secured party can have a non-possessory security interest in chattel paper perfected through filing (including a proceeds interest therein) which will be good against subsequent non-possessory security interests and judgment creditors including the trustee in bankruptcy, but, under § 9–330, that security interest will frequently be junior to a chattel paper purchaser who gives new value and takes possession, or obtains control, of the paper in the ordinary course of its business. (See also § 9–322(c) regarding proceeds.)

The above discussion has reviewed the basic reason for the adoption of the rules set out in § 9–330. The discussion now turns to the specific issue arising under § 9–330 which this Commentary addresses.

ISSUE

When is a security interest in chattel paper claimed "merely as proceeds of inventory subject to a security interest" so that a chattel paper financer that gives new value and takes possession, or obtains control, of the paper in the ordinary course of its business has priority unless the chattel paper indicates that it has been assigned to an identified assignee other than the financer?

DISCUSSION

Preliminarily, it should be noted that this issue may be of limited importance since, even if the security interest is more than a mere proceeds interest, the chattel paper financer under § 9–330 will take free of the interest unless it has knowledge that the purchase violates the rights of the secured party. The following discussion should be read with this caveat in mind.

A brief description of two common types of inventory secured financing will help put the discussion of the meaning of a "mere proceeds interest" in its business context.

(a)   The first type, which will be called "type A," is inventory financing of automobiles and large items of equipment in which the financing is primarily item by item (each item of inventory secures a precise amount loaned against that item even though there may be a cross-security provision), with a requirement that the associated inventory debt be paid off when the item is sold, or after a maximum period (usually 90 days subject to renewal), whichever first occurs.

(b)   The second ("type B") is a general floating loan secured by inventory *and* receivables (sometimes called an "availability loan") under which the debtor is entitled to borrow from the secured party such amounts as the debtor may desire, subject to a maximum availability determined by a formula, e.g., 50% of cost of saleable inventory plus 80% of the amount of receivables not in default more than 30 days. This type of financing is usually used in situations involving smaller items of inventory as to which it would be too burdensome to account on an individual basis and in which the receivables are accounts rather than chattel paper so that § 9–330 issues do not arise. However, such financing arrangements may sometimes involve larger, more expensive items of inventory which are frequently sold on credit generating chattel paper.

For the reasons stated below, the Board believes that a type A inventory financer will frequently have only a "mere proceeds interest" in chattel paper which is generated when items of inventory subject to its security interest are sold. On the other hand, as noted below, the Board believes that a type B financer has more than a mere proceeds interest in any chattel paper generated on sale of the inventory.

The type A inventory financer having a proceeds claim to the chattel paper must do something more than rest on that proceeds claim in order to prevail against the person described in § 9–330(a)(1), namely, a purchaser who "in good faith and in the ordinary course of the purchaser's business . . . gives new value and takes possession of the chattel paper or obtains control of the chattel paper under Section 9–105." Such an inventory financer takes the chattel paper out of the "mere proceeds" category only by giving value against it in some new transaction. Such a lender gives new value, as it commonly will, by purchasing the chattel paper (or, in some types of transactions, making a specific loan against it). Whether the type A inventory financer will be willing to give value against the chattel paper instead of merely resting on its proceeds claim until payment will depend on the quality of the paper. That quality depends upon such factors as the credit worthiness of the buyer who is the principal obligor on the chattel paper, the amount of the buyer's down payment and hence the amount of the chattel paper debt as compared to the value of the collateral (the former inventory), and the terms under which the dealer (the former inventory debtor) is willing to assume full or limited recourse to support the buyer's obligation under the chattel paper. Not infrequently the financer and the dealer will negotiate a package purchase of several items of chattel paper in which the total price is determined by the quality of the paper, the extent of the recourse, and so on. When the financer buys, or lends against, chattel paper in the way just outlined, there is a "new transaction" by which the financer has acquired an interest in the specific chattel paper which is more than a "mere proceeds interest."

If, however, the type A inventory financer does not by some new transaction give value against specific chattel paper, the fact that the inventory debt is unpaid and that the security agreement specifically claims the chattel paper proceeds as additional collateral does not give the financer more than a mere proceeds interest. Further, while no doubt much inventory financing is carried out with nominal profit to the financer in anticipation that it will be given the opportunity to acquire the chattel paper, in the Board's opinion this anticipation of receiving the chattel paper does not take the case out of the "mere proceeds" phrase of the statute.

As pointed out above, the Board believes that the type B financer at all times has more than a mere proceeds interest in the chattel paper on hand whether or not at any specific time there is sufficient inventory on hand to secure the amount of the loan outstanding at that time. The structure of the deal is such that the chattel paper is part of the primary collateral for the debt. That interest extends to any chattel paper subsequently generated by a sale of inventory whether or not at any particular time the existing inventory is adequate security for the debt actually outstanding.

A number of reported cases under former Article 9 involved priority conflicts between inventory financers and purchasers of chattel paper who took possession, gave new value, and acted in the ordinary course of their business. In those cases, the courts applied the "mere proceeds" rules of former § 9–308, and the chattel paper financer always won.[1] The courts have not always carefully reported the facts, but it is clear that in at least one of the cases, the security agreement did specifically claim an interest in chattel paper and the court did not treat that fact as significant.[2] In most of the cases, the court did not carefully

[1] See e.g. *Aetna Finance Corp. v. Massey-Ferguson, Inc.*, 626 F. Supp. 482, 42 UCC Rep. Serv. (Callaghan) 1501 (S.D. Ind. 1985); *Northwest Acceptance Corp. v. Lynnwood Equipment, Inc.*, 1 UCC Rep.Serv.2d (Callaghan) 980, 1710 (W.D. Wash. 1986); *Rex Financial Corp. v. Great Western Bank & Trust*, 23 Ariz. App. 286, 532 P.2d 558, 16 UCC Rep.Serv. (Callaghan) 1155 (Ariz. App. 1975); *Commercial Credit Corp. v. National Credit Corp.*, 251 Ark. 541, 473 S.W.2d 876, 10 UCC Rep.Serv. (Callaghan) 232 (Ark. 1971); *American State Bank v. Avco Financial Services of the United States, Inc.*, 71 Cal. App. 3d 774, 139 Cal.Rptr. 658, 22 UCC Rep.Serv. (Callaghan) 235 (Cal. App. 1977); *Home Savings Ass'n v. General Electric Credit Corp.*, 101 Nev. 595, 708 P.2d 280, 42 UCC Rep.Serv. (Callaghan) 1489 (Nev. 1985); *Chrysler Credit Corp. v. Sharp*, 56 Misc.2d 261, 288 N.Y.S.2d 525, 5 UCC Rep.Serv. (Callaghan) 226 (N.Y. Sup. Ct. 1968); *Bank of Beulah v. Chase*, 231 N.W.2d 738, 17 UCC Rep.Serv. (Callaghan) 259 (N.D. 1975); *Associates Discount Corp. v. Old Freeport Bank*, 421 Pa. 609, 220 A.2d 621, 3 UCC Rep.Serv. (Callaghan) 481 (Pa. 1966); *Borg-Warner Acceptance Corp. v. C.I.T. Corp.*, 679 S.W.2d 140, 39 UCC Rep.Serv. (Callaghan) 1864 (Tex. Ct. App. 1984).

[2] *Home Savings Ass'n*, *supra* note 1.

consider whether the chattel paper financer had knowledge of the prior interest in the chattel paper, but in several cases the court either assumed that the chattel paper financer had knowledge or the findings of fact show that the chattel paper financer did have knowledge.[3] The results in all those cases are consistent with the position taken in this Commentary.

CONCLUSION

If a financer loans or extends credit for the cost of specific items of inventory and expects to be paid upon the sale of the items, the financer's security interest in chattel paper generated when the items are sold is a mere proceeds interest unless the financer in a new transaction gives value against the specific paper. On the other hand, a lender who agrees to lend up to a specified percentage of the cost of inventory and of receivables has more than a mere proceeds interest in chattel paper which is a part of the receivables covered by the security agreement. In inventory financing transactions which do not fall within the above two categories, whether the financer has more than a mere proceeds interest in chattel paper generated when inventory subject to its secured interest is sold must be determined from an examination of all the facts of the case.

PEB COMMENTARY NO. 10
SECTION 1–203[*]
(February 10, 1994)

ISSUE

Section 1–203 provides that "Every contract or duty within this Act imposes an obligation of good faith in its performance or enforcement."[1] While this concept applies generally to every contract, it finds particular expression throughout the Code. For example, out of over 400 Code provisions, more than 50 sections make specific reference to "good faith."[2]

The meaning of "good faith" varies with the context. Sometimes the context is as a standard of performance or enforcement; other times the context is that of good faith purchase.[3] This Commentary deals only with good faith performance or enforcement of a right or duty under a contract that is within the Code.

In the context in which the obligation of good faith functions as the standard of contract performance or enforcement, can the failure to meet this standard support a cause of action where no other basis for a cause of action exists? This Commentary examines this question in order to promote a uniform understanding of what it means to say that a general obligation of good faith is imposed on every contracting party. In so doing, several principles are discussed.

DISCUSSION

1. *Good Faith, Commercial Expectations, and the Concept of Agreement*

Section 1–201(19) defines good faith as "honesty in fact in the conduct or transaction concerned."[4] Commentators have said that this general requirement of good faith sets a "subjective" standard,[5] while the

---

[3] *American State Bank, Rex Financial Corp.*, both *supra* note 1.

[*] *Note from West Advisory Panel: Referring to unrevised Article 1. See revised § 1–304.*

[1] This does not mean that the obligation of good faith as defined in the Code will necessarily apply to all aspects of the same transaction. As written, the scope of § 1–203 is co-extensive with the Code's coverage. For example, if a loan agreement that provides for an Article 9 security interest also contains financial covenants which are not governed by the Code, § 1–203 would apply to the former and the general law of contracts would apply to the latter. See, e.g., Restatement, Second, Contracts § 205 (1981).

[2] Farnsworth, *Good Faith Performance and Commercial Reasonableness Under the Uniform Commercial Code,* 30 U.Chi.L.Rev. 666, 667 (1963).

[3] See, e.g., UCC §§ 2–403 (good faith purchaser); 3–302 (holder in due course); 9–307 (buyer in the ordinary course of business). On the distinction between the doctrines of good faith performance and good faith purchase, see generally id.

[4] This sparse definition found in Article 1 is expanded elsewhere in the Code for purposes of particular Articles. See, e.g., §§ 2–103(1)(b); 2A–103(2); 3–103(a)(4); 4–104(c); 4A–105(a)(6). This expanded definition "is concerned with the fairness of conduct rather than the care with which an act is performed." UCC § 3–103, Comment 4.

[5] See Aronstein, *Good Faith Performance of Security Agreements: The Liability of Corporate Managers,* 120 U.Pa.L.Rev. 1, 31 (1971) ("Good faith [as] defined in § 1–201(19) . . . [has] been historically construed as applying only to

958

particularized definitions elsewhere also create an additional "objective" standard of the observance of reasonable commercial standards of fair dealing. This Commentary applies with equal force to both standards of good faith.

The principal author of the Code, Karl Llewellyn, recognized that parties develop expectations over time against the background of commercial practices and that if commercial law fails to account for those practices, it will cut against the parties' actual expectations. In an unpublished commentary on the Proposed Final Draft of the Uniform Revised Sales Act, Llewellyn had this to say about good faith:

> No inconsistency of language and background exists merely because the words used mean something different to an outsider than they do to the merchants who used that language in the light of the commercial background against which they contracted. This is the necessary result of applying commercial standards and principles of good faith to the agreement.... Moreover, where the commercial background normally gives to a term in question some breadth of meaning so that it describes a range of acceptable tolerances rather than a sharp-edged single line of action, any attempted narrowing of this meaning by one party is so unusual as not likely to be expected or perceived by the other. Therefore, attention must be called to a desire to contract at material variance from the accepted commercial pattern of contract or use of language. Thus, this Act rejects any "surprise" variation from the fair and normal meaning of the agreement.[6]

Explaining the doctrine of good faith in such terms is thus a recognition that, as expressed in the Code, it serves as a directive to protect the reasonable expectations of the contracting parties. The general imperative that the reasonable expectations of the parties are the measure of the good faith of each suggests that good faith is a concept with conceptual content related to that of agreement.

The Code definition of "Agreement" reads:

> "Agreement" means the bargain of the parties in fact as found in their language or by implication from other circumstances including course of dealing or usage of trade or course of performance as provided in this Act (Sections 1–205 and 2–208).[7]

The agreement of the parties consists of more than their language alone. In elaborating on this theme, Comment 3 to § 1–201 emphasizes that "the word [agreement] is intended to include full recognition of usage of trade, course of dealing, *course of performance* and the surrounding circumstances as effective parts thereof. . . ." (emphasis added).[8]

---

the actor's subjective state of mind."); Braucher, *The Legislative History of the Uniform Commercial Code*, 58 Colum.L.Rev. 798, 812 (1958) (describing the test of good faith in § 1–201(19) as a "subjective" test, sometimes known as the rule of "the pure heart and empty head"); Lawrence, *The Prematurely Reported Demise of the Perfect Tender Rule*, 35 U.Kan.L.Rev. 557, 571 (1987) ("Good faith is a subjective term meaning 'honesty in fact in the contract or transaction concerned.' ").

[6] The Karl Llewellyn Papers, The University of Chicago Law Library, File J.X.2.K. 1, 9, *reprinted in* D. Patterson, *Good Faith and Lender Liability* 217 (1990).

[7] UCC § 1–201(3). Furthermore, Comment 1 to § 1–205 ("Course of Dealing and Usage of Trade") reinforces this definition by stating:

> This Act rejects both the "lay-dictionary" and the "conveyancer's" reading of a commercial agreement. Instead the meaning of the agreement of the parties is to be determined by the language used by them and by their action, read and interpreted in the light of commercial practices and other surrounding circumstances. The measure and background for interpretation are set by the commercial context, which may explain and supplement even the language of a formal or final writing.

[8] This Commentary recognizes the fact that course of performance is defined in Articles 2 and 2A and was originally not a part of the general definition of "Agreement" in Article 1. The concept is included here as an element of the agreement of the parties because there exists no plausible justification for excluding it. This view is strongly supported by Comments 1 and 2 to § 2–208. Comment 2, in particular, emphasizes that "a course of performance is always relevant to determine the meaning of the agreement." See also Westinghouse Credit Corp. v. Shelton, 645 F.2d 869, 31 UCC Rep.Serv. (Callaghan) 410 (10th Cir. 1981) (course of performance may also be used for discerning the meaning of "Agreement" in Article 9).

The Restatement, Second, of Contracts does not reflect the Code's isolation of course of performance in Articles 2 and 2A. The Restatement provides that all four elements—express terms, course of dealing, course of performance, and usage of trade—are all elements of the meaning of "contract." See Restatement, Second, Contracts § 203. In fact, § 202(4) states

APPENDIX D

"Course of dealing" is defined as follows:

A course of dealing is a sequence of previous conduct between the parties to a particular transaction which is fairly to be regarded as establishing a common basis of understanding for interpreting their expressions and other conduct.[9]

"Usage of trade" is defined as follows:

A usage of trade is any practice or method of dealing having such regularity of observance in a place, vocation or trade as to justify an expectation that it will be observed with respect to the transaction in question. The existence and scope of such a usage are to be proved as facts. If it is established that such a usage is embodied in a written trade code or similar writing the interpretation of the writing is for the court.[10]

"Course of performance" is defined as follows:

Where the contract for sale involves repeated occasions for performance by either party with knowledge of the nature of the performance and opportunity for objection to it by the other, any course of performance accepted or acquiesced in without objection shall be relevant to determine the meaning of the agreement.[11]

In addition to two definitional sections, § 1–205 contains two additional methodological sections which direct how express terms, course of dealing, and usage of trade are to be synthesized:

(3)   A course of dealing between parties and any usage of trade in the vocation or trade in which they are engaged or of which they are or should be aware give particular meaning to and supplement or qualify terms of an agreement.

(4)   The express terms of an agreement and an applicable course of dealing or usage of trade shall be construed wherever reasonable as consistent with each other; but when such construction is unreasonable express terms control both course of dealing and usage of trade and course of dealing controls usage of trade.[12]

At this juncture it is important to recognize that one acts in good faith relative to the agreement of the parties. To decide the question whether a party has acted in good faith, a court must first ascertain the substance of the parties' agreement.

The performance and enforcement of agreements in a manner consistent with the reasonable expectations of the parties is in keeping with the broadest understanding of contract doctrine.[13] The Code

---

that "any course of performance accepted or acquiesced in without objection is given great weight in the interpretation of the agreement."

⁹   UCC § 1–205(1).

¹⁰   UCC § 1–205(2).

¹¹   UCC § 2–208(1). This definition is duplicated in § 2A–207(1).

¹²   UCC § 1–205(3)–(4). The connection between § 1–205 and good faith is made explicit in the Comment to § 1–203, wherein it is stated that the obligation of good faith "is further implemented by Section 1–205 on course of dealing and usage of trade."

The interpretational priorities set forth in § 1–205 are, with the added inclusion of course of performance, duplicated in § 2–208(2). That section states as follows:

The express terms of the agreement and any such course of performance, as well as any course of dealing and usage of trade, shall be construed whenever reasonable as consistent with each other; but when such construction is unreasonable, express terms shall control course of performance and course of performance shall control both course of dealing and usage of trade (Section 1–205).

See also UCC § 2A–207(2).

¹³   See 3 A. Corbin, *Corbin on Contracts* § 570 (West Supp. 1993).

If the purpose of contract law is to enforce the reasonable expectations of parties induced by promises, then at some point it becomes necessary for courts to look to the substance rather than to the form of the agreement, and to hold that substance controls over form. What courts are doing here, whether calling the process "implication" of promises, or interpreting the requirements of "good faith," as the current fashion may be, is but a recognition that the parties occasionally have understandings or expectations that were so fundamental that they did not need to negotiate about those expectations. When the court "implies a promise" or holds that "good faith" requires a party not to violate those

is consistent with this tradition of thought. However, the Code's concept of agreement broadens the sources for determining the meaning of the parties' agreement. The concept of agreement is not limited to the terms of the parties' writing: it includes a variety of elements, all of which must be synthesized.

Under § 1–205(4), the initial interpretive effort is to read all the terms as consistent with one another. Only when this is impossible does the interpreter then move to a lexical ordering of the terms, with express terms at the head of the list. Cases which make no attempt to reconcile the various terms before according priority to express terms in the construction of the parties' agreement must be considered to have proceeded improperly.[14] The better application of § 1–205(4), and the issues of interpretation which are central to it, is illustrated in cases like *Nanakuli Paving & Rock Co. v. Shell Oil Co.*, 664 F.2d 772, 32 UCC Rep.Serv. (Callaghan) 1025 (9th Cir. 1981) (upholding a finding that the written price term in an asphalt supply contract was qualified by a trade practice requiring suppliers to delay price increases for jobs on which buyers have already bid). Accordingly, in order to answer the question, "Has a party performed or enforced a contractual right or duty in good faith?", the content of the parties' agreement must first be determined.[15]

2.   UCC § 1–203 Does Not Create an Independent Cause of Action

The inherent flaw in the view that § 1–203 supports an independent cause of action is the belief that the obligation of good faith has an existence which is conceptually separate from the underlying agreement. As the above discussion demonstrates, however, this is an incorrect view of the duty. "A party cannot simply 'act in good faith.' One acts in good faith relative to the agreement of the parties. Thus the real question is 'What is the Agreement of the parties?' "[16] Put differently, good faith merely directs attention to the parties' reasonable expectations; it is not an independent source from which rights and duties evolve.[17] The language of § 1–203 itself makes this quite clear by providing that the obligation to perform or enforce in good faith extends only to the rights and duties resulting from the parties' contract. The term "contract" is, in turn, defined as "the total legal obligation which results from the parties' *agreement*. . . ."[18] Consequently, resort to principles of law or equity outside the Code are not appropriate to create rights, duties, and liabilities inconsistent with those stated in the Code.[19] For example, a breach of a contract or duty within the Code arising from a failure to act in good faith does not give rise to a claim for punitive damages unless specifically permitted.[20]

---

expectations, it is recognizing that sometimes silence says more than words, and it is understanding its duty to the spirit of the bargain is higher than its duty to the technicalities of the language.

Id. Reiter & Swan, Contracts and the Protection of Reasonable Expectations, in *Studies in Contract Law* 1, 11 (B. Reiter & J. Swan eds. 1980) ("[T]hroughout the law of contract, a striving to protect reasonable expectations is visible. . . .").

[14]   See, e.g., Southern Concrete Servs. v. Mableton Contractors, Inc., 407 F.Supp. 581, 19 UCC Rep.Serv. (Callaghan) 79 (N.D.Ga. 1975), *aff'd mem.*, 569 F.2d 1154 (5th Cir. 1978); Division of Triple T Serv. v. Mobil Oil Corp., 304 N.Y.S.2d 191, 6 UCC Rep.Serv. (Callaghan) 1011 (Sup.Ct. 1969).

[15]   For a non-Code decision which is consistent with this approach, see Southwest Savings and Loan Association v. Sunamp Systems, Inc., 838 P.2d 1314 (Ariz.App. 1992) (holding that inquiry does not stop with recognition that lender had general authority in written loan agreement to take the particular action, but inquiry extends to whether lender exercised that authority "for a reason beyond the risks" assumed by borrower in loan agreement, or beyond borrower's "justified expectations," in the context of how a reasonable lender might act).

[16]   Patterson, *supra*, at 143. Good faith is sometimes the basis of an implied term to fill a gap or deal with an omitted case, e.g., the duty of cooperation frequently imposed on a party whose cooperation is essential and not unreasonably burdensome; or, the duty to give notice within a reasonable time of some important fact of which the other party would otherwise be unaware. See § 2–309(3) and Comment 8; 2 Farnsworth on Contracts §§ 7.17, 7.17a (1990). A breach of such duties gives rise to a cause of action for breach of the contract of which the implied term becomes a part. Although such a cause of action arguably has the same practical content as a cause of action based upon a purported breach of § 1–203, there is an important methodological difference in that this Commentary requires, in the case of contracts within the Code, that the focus be upon the Agreement of the parties and their reasonable expectations.

[17]   Cases reaching this conclusion include Management Assistance, Inc. v. Computer Dimensions, Inc., 546 F.Supp. 666 (N.D.Ga. 1982), *aff'd* 747 F.2d 708 (11th Cir. 1984), and Chandler v. Hunter, 340 So.2d 818, 21 UCC Rep.Serv. (Callaghan) 484 (Ala.Civ.App. 1976). A contrary conclusion was reached in Reid v. Key Bank of Southern Maine, Inc., 821 F.2d 9, 3 UCC Rep.Serv.2d (Callaghan) 1665 (1st Cir. 1987).

[18]   UCC § 1–201(11) (emphasis supplied).

[19]   See UCC § 1–103.

[20]   See UCC § 1–106(1).

APPENDIX D

CONCLUSION

Section 1–203 does not support a cause of action where no other basis for a cause of action exists.

The concept of Agreement permeates the entirety of the Code. For example, § 9–105(1)(*l*) incorporates the Article 1 concept of Agreement directly into Article 9. The "agreement of the parties" cannot be read off the face of a document, but must be discerned against the background of actual commercial practice. Not only does the Code recognize "the reasonable practices and standards of the commercial community . . . [as] an appropriate source of legal obligation,"[21] but it also rejects the "premise that the language used [by the parties] has the meaning attributable to [it] by rules of construction existing in the law rather than the meaning which arises out of the commercial context in which it was used."[22] The correct perspective on the meaning of good faith performance and enforcement is the Agreement of the parties. The critical question is, "Has 'X' acted in good faith with respect to the performance or enforcement of some right or duty under the terms of the Agreement?" It is therefore wrong to conclude that as long as the agreement allows a party to do something, it is under all terms and conditions permissible. Such a conclusion overlooks completely the distinction between merely performing or enforcing a right or duty under an agreement on the one hand and, on the other hand, doing so in a way that recognizes that the agreement should be interpreted in a manner consistent with the reasonable expectations of the parties in the light of the commercial conditions existing in the context under scrutiny. The latter is the correct approach. Examples are: (1) Is it reasonable for a buyer in a particular locale or trade to expect that an express quantity term in a contract is "not really" a quantity term, but a mere projection to be adjusted according to market forces?;[23] (2) Does a party to a sales contract that permits discretionary termination have the right to expect that the decision whether to terminate will be made on the basis of sound business criteria?

The Official Comment to § 1–203 is amended by adding the following language at the end of the first paragraph:

> This section does not support an independent cause of action for failure to perform or enforce in good faith. Rather, this section means that a failure to perform or enforce, in good faith, a specific duty or obligation under the contract, constitutes a breach of that contract or makes unavailable, under the particular circumstances, a remedial right or power. This distinction makes it clear that the doctrine of good faith merely directs a court towards interpreting contracts within the commercial context in which they are created, performed, and enforced, and does not create a separate duty of fairness and reasonableness which can be independently breached. See PEB Commentary No. 10, dated February 10, 1994.

PEB COMMENTARY NO. 11
SURETYSHIP ISSUES UNDER SECTIONS 3–116, 3–305, 3–415, 3–419, AND 3–605
(February 10, 1994, as amended to apply to Revised Article 9)*

INTRODUCTION

The promulgation of revised Article 3 of the Uniform Commercial Code has given rise to a number of questions concerning the provisions in that Article governing the rights and duties of accommodation parties. This heightened level of interest results from many factors. In particular, the provisions in revised Article 3 concerning accommodation parties differ significantly from those in former Article 3 in ways that are complex and not always obvious. Application of these rules often raises issues that were not pertinent

---

[21] Kastely, *Stock Equipment for the Bargain in Fact: Trade Usage, "Express Terms," and Consistency Under Section 1–205 of the Uniform Commercial Code,* 64 N.C.L.Rev. 777, 780 (1986).

[22] UCC § 2–202, Comment 1.

[23] See Columbia Nitrogen Corp. v. Royster Co., 451 F.2d 3, 9 UCC Rep.Serv. (Callaghan) 977 (4th Cir. 1971).

* PEB Commentary No. 11, which addresses suretyship issues that arise under Article 3 of the Uniform Commercial Code, was originally issued in 1994. Issue 11 in the original Commentary dealt with the power of an accommodation party on an instrument that is secured by a security interest governed by Uniform Commercial Code Article 9 to waive the rights of that party that were provided for in Part 5 of former Article 9. Since the issuance of the original Commentary, former Article 9 has been replaced with Revised Article 9 and the Restatement of Suretyship and Guaranty, which was in the process of being drafted in 1994, has been promulgated by the American Law Institute. This amended Commentary updates the discussion of Issue 11 to reflect Revised Article 9 and the promulgation of the Restatement of Suretyship and Guaranty.

under prior law. In addition, the promulgation in 1995 of the Restatement of Suretyship and Guaranty by The American Law Institute has generated greater interest in the rights and duties of sureties, including, of course, accommodation parties.

As a result of this heightened interest, the suretyship rules in Article 3 have been the subject of a great deal of scrutiny, which has resulted in a recognition that the treatment of some suretyship issues in revised Article 3 should be clarified. It is the purpose of this Commentary to answer several questions that have arisen concerning the rights and duties of accommodation parties. This Commentary concludes with a series of revisions and additions to the Comments to various sections in Article 3 that govern suretyship issues.

ISSUE 1

If another person agrees to be liable for the obligation of the maker of a note, are the rights and duties of that person determined by the provisions of Article 3 governing accommodation parties, by the general law of suretyship, or both?

DISCUSSION

A person who agrees to be liable for the debt of another is clearly a surety. See Restatement of Suretyship and Guaranty § 1. If the person effectuates the agreement by becoming a party (i.e., a co-maker or indorser) to the same instrument that creates the obligation, the surety is also an accommodation party. In such a case, the rules in §§ 3–116, 3–305, 3–415, 3–419, and 3–605 concerning accommodation parties are applicable. Of course, these sections will not resolve all possible issues concerning the rights and duties of the surety. In the event that a situation is presented that is not resolved by those sections, the resolution may be provided by the general law of suretyship because, pursuant to § 1–103, that law is applicable unless displaced by provisions of this Act. If the surety does not effectuate the obligation by becoming a party to the note, the surety is not an accommodation party. In that case, the surety's rights and duties are determined by the general law of suretyship.

In unusual cases, two parties to an instrument may have a surety relationship that is not governed by Article 3 because the requirements of § 3–419(a) are not fulfilled. For example, assume that the payee of an instrument would like to sell it, but the potential buyer will agree to buy the instrument only if, in the event that the instrument is dishonored, the buyer has recourse not only against the issuer and the payee but also against someone more creditworthy. Accordingly, the payee produces a creditworthy person who agrees to stand behind the payee's obligations with respect to the instrument. The transfer to the buyer is then made after both the payee and the creditworthy person indorse the instrument. The creditworthy person is a party to the instrument as an indorser and is an accommodation party for the issuer who is the accommodated party. The creditworthy person is also a surety with respect to the obligation of both the issuer and the payee as indorser. The creditworthy person, however, is not an accommodation party for the payee and the payee is not an accommodated party under § 3–419(a) inasmuch as the instrument was not issued for value given for the benefit of the payee. Therefore, the general law of suretyship, and not the provisions in Article 3 concerning accommodation parties, provides the rules that govern the suretyship relationship between the creditworthy person and the payee.[1]

ISSUE 2

What are the differences between the rights of an accommodation party with respect to the accommodated party under revised Article 3 and former Article 3?

DISCUSSION

Under the general law of suretyship, as between the principal obligor and the secondary obligor, it is the principal obligor who ought to bear the cost of performance. Restatement of Suretyship and Guaranty § 1. Suretyship law provides three mechanisms to effectuate that cost allocation. First, if the principal obligor is charged with notice of the secondary obligation, the principal obligor owes the secondary obligor a duty of performance; this duty of performance can be enforced by the secondary obligor through the mechanism commonly known as exoneration. Restatement of Suretyship and Guaranty § 21. Second, a secondary obligor who performs may be subrogated to the rights of the obligee against the principal obligor (regardless of whether the principal obligor was charged with notice of the secondary obligation).

---

[1] The revisions to Comment 3 to § 3–419 and Comment 6 to § 3–605 reflect this discussion. See Appendix, par. 3 and par. 10.

APPENDIX D

Restatement of Suretyship and Guaranty § 27. Third, if the principal obligor is charged with notice of the secondary obligation, the principal obligor must reimburse a secondary obligor who performs the obligation. Restatement of Suretyship and Guaranty § 22. If the principal obligor is not charged with notice of the secondary obligation, a secondary obligor who performs is nonetheless entitled to restitution from the principal obligor. Restatement of Suretyship and Guaranty § 26.

An accommodation party is always a surety. Former Article 3 explicitly provided in § 3–415(5) that an accommodation party who paid the instrument was entitled to enforce the instrument against the accommodated party. This right essentially codified the surety's right of subrogation. Other rights of the accommodation party against the accommodated party were left to the general law of suretyship through § 1–103. In § 3–419(e), revised Article 3 also in effect sets forth subrogation rights of accommodation parties by providing that such parties are "entitled to enforce the instrument against the accommodated party." That section also codifies the accommodation party's right to be reimbursed by the accommodated party. Unlike the general law of suretyship, however, that right is not limited to situations in which the accommodated party was charged with notice of the accommodation party's obligation. Thus, it need not be determined whether the accommodated party is charged with notice of the accommodation party's obligation, and the right of restitution that is present in the general law of suretyship is superfluous. Revised Article 3, like former Article 3, leaves the accommodated party's duty of performance and the accommodation party's concomitant right of exoneration to the general law of suretyship through § 1–103.[2]

ISSUE 3

Is an accommodation party entitled to reimbursement if the accommodated party had a defense to its obligation that could have been raised by the accommodation party against the person entitled to enforce the instrument?

DISCUSSION

The juxtaposition of the accommodated party's duty to reimburse the accommodation party (§ 3–419(e)) with the accommodated party's right to raise defenses (§ 3–305(b)) raises important policy issues. If a duty to reimburse exists even when the accommodated party had a defense, that duty could be said to obviate the value of the defense. On the other hand, if no duty to reimburse exists in such circumstances, the cost of performance will be borne ultimately by the accommodation party rather than the accommodated party.

There are a number of different contexts in which the situation may arise. Generally speaking, the accommodation party may raise as a defense to its obligation the defenses of the accommodated party to *its* obligation. See § 3–305(d). There are three exceptions. The accommodated party's defenses of discharge in insolvency proceedings, infancy, and lack of legal capacity are not available to the accommodation party. If the accommodation party pays the instrument when the accommodated party had one of these defenses, the accommodated party has no duty to reimburse the accommodation party. The accommodation party has, in a sense, assumed the risk that such defenses will exist.

Occasionally, an accommodation party will pay an instrument even though the accommodated party has a defense that is available to the accommodation party. In such cases, the existence of the duty to reimburse may depend on whether the accommodation party was aware of the defense at the time it paid the instrument. If the accommodation party was unaware of the defense, there is a duty to reimburse. Thus, there is an incentive for the accommodated party to make the accommodation party aware of any defenses it may have. If the accommodation party pays the instrument while aware of a defense of the accommodated party, however, reimbursement would ordinarily not be justified but might be justified in some circumstances. Resolution of this issue is left to the general law of suretyship through § 1–103.[3]

ISSUE 4

Section 3–415(a) provides that an indorser's obligation to pay the instrument upon dishonor is owed, *inter alia*, to a subsequent indorser who pays the instrument. What if both the prior indorser and subsequent indorser are anomalous indorsers?

---

[2] The revision to Comment 5 to § 3–419 reflects this discussion. See Appendix, par. 5.

[3] The addition of Comments 6 and 7 to § 3–419 reflect this discussion. See Appendix, par. 6.

DISCUSSION

In the general law of suretyship, when there are two secondary obligors for the same underlying obligation, the relationship between those two secondary obligors may be that of co-suretyship or sub-suretyship. In a co-suretyship situation, the two secondary obligors are jointly and severally liable and, as between themselves, have a right of contribution against each other. In a sub-suretyship situation, on the other hand, the second secondary obligor is, in a sense, a surety for the obligation of the first secondary obligor. Thus, as between the two secondary obligors, the first obligor occupies the position of a principal obligor while the later one occupies the position of a secondary obligor. It is often difficult to determine whether the two secondary obligors are co-sureties or sub-sureties, especially in the context of negotiable instruments when the obligations of those parties may be created by a signature alone, unaccompanied by words of explanation.

Article 3 treats successive anomalous indorsers as having joint and several liability on the instrument. See § 3–116(a). If one of the anomalous indorsers pays the instrument, that indorser has a right to receive contribution from the other indorser. See § 3–116(b). Accordingly, the general rule of § 3–415(a), that a subsequent indorser who pays the instrument may recover the full amount of the instrument from a prior indorser, does not apply in such cases. Section 3–116(b) does not recognize a distinction between a co-surety and a sub-surety, but in providing for a right to contribution, § 3–116(b) has the effect of treating anomalous indorsers as though they were co-sureties. Section 3–116(b), however, is subject to "agreement of the affected parties." If the subsequent indorser can prove an agreement with the prior indorser giving the subsequent indorser rights as a sub-surety, that agreement changes the rule of § 3–116(b). If the subsequent indorser pays the instrument and has rights under the agreement as a sub-surety, the subsequent indorser has a right of recourse against the prior indorser for the amount of the payment rather than only a right to contribution; if the prior indorser pays the instrument, there is no right of recourse against the subsequent indorser.[4]

ISSUE 5

What effect do words of guaranty have on the obligation of an indorser to a person entitled to enforce an instrument?

DISCUSSION

Under former § 3–416, the obligation of an indorser who added the words "payment guaranteed" or "collection guaranteed" to the indorsement was different than that of an indorser who did not add those words. The addition of the words "payment guaranteed" (or their equivalent) meant that if the instrument was not paid when due the indorser would pay it without resort to any other party. Thus, an indorser who guaranteed payment could be said to have waived presentment, notice of dishonor, and protest, as well as all demand upon the maker or drawee. In contrast, the addition of the words "collection guaranteed" (or their equivalent) meant that the indorser was required to pay only after the holder reduced its claim against the maker or acceptor to judgment or it was shown that such a proceeding would be useless.

Section 3–419(d) preserves the concept of a guaranty of collection, but no provision is made for a guaranty of payment. Moreover, the preferred treatment given to a guarantor of collection is only applicable when the words accompanying the indorsement indicate "unambiguously that the party is guaranteeing collection rather than payment of the obligation of another party to the instrument." Thus, an indorser who adds the words "payment guaranteed," or the like, to the indorsement has the same liability as an indorser who added no special words to the indorsement. Such an indorser may be entitled, *inter alia*, to notice of dishonor pursuant to § 3–503.[5]

ISSUE 6

May a person entitled to enforce an instrument avoid discharge of an accommodation party pursuant to § 3–605 by "reserving rights" against that party in conjunction with a release, extension, or other modification of the duty of the accommodated party?

---

[4] The addition of Comment 5 to § 3–415 reflects this discussion. See Appendix, par. 2.

[5] The revision to Comment 4 to § 3–419 reflects this discussion. See Appendix, par. 4.

APPENDIX D

DISCUSSION

Under former UCC § 3–606(1)(a), a release, extension, or other modification of the accommodated party's duty accompanied by an express "reservation of rights" against the accommodation party would not discharge that party. This provision paralleled the general law of suretyship in many jurisdictions.

Article 3 rejects the reservation of rights doctrine. The effects of a release, extension, or other modification of the accommodated party's duty cannot be changed by the incantation of a "reservation of rights." Pursuant to § 3–605(b), a release of the accommodated party does not discharge the accommodation party, so there is no need for the person entitled to enforce the instrument to take any action, such as a reservation of rights, to preserve recourse against the accommodation party. Pursuant to § 3–605(c)–(d), an extension or modification of the accommodated party's duty discharges the accommodation party to the extent that the extension or modification would otherwise cause the accommodation party a loss. This discharge cannot be avoided by a "reservation of rights" by the person entitled to enforce the instrument.[6]

ISSUE 7

If a person entitled to enforce an instrument agrees to extend the due date of the accommodated party's performance and, pursuant to § 3–605(c), the extension does not discharge the accommodation party, what is the effect of the extension on the obligation of the accommodation party? In particular, is the due date for the accommodation party's performance extended correspondingly? May the accommodation party perform on the original due date?

DISCUSSION

The person entitled to enforce the instrument will not be able to enforce the instrument against the accommodation party until the extended due date. If the accommodation party is an indorser, this is because an indorser is not liable until dishonor of the instrument, which, under these circumstances, cannot occur until it is unpaid on the extended due date. If the accommodation party is a co-maker, this is because, under § 3–305(d), until the extended due date the accommodation party will be able to assert the accommodated party's defense that, pursuant to the extension agreement, performance is not yet due.

The accommodation party may, however, perform on the original due date. The accommodation party is bound in accordance with the terms of its original engagement. The agreement between the accommodated party and the person entitled to enforce the instrument cannot bind the accommodation party to a change in its obligation without the accommodation party's consent. The effect on the recourse of the accommodation party against the accommodated party of performance by the accommodation party on the original due date is not addressed in § 3–419 and is left to the general law of suretyship.

Even though the accommodation party has the option of paying the instrument on the original due date, the accommodation party is not precluded from asserting its rights to discharge under § 3–605(c) if it does not exercise that option. The critical issue is whether the extension caused the accommodation party a loss by increasing the difference between the accommodation party's cost of performing its obligation on the instrument and the amount recoverable from the accommodated party pursuant to § 3–419(e). The decision by the accommodation party not to exercise its option to pay on the original due date may, under the circumstances, be a factor to be considered in the determination of that issue.[7]

ISSUE 8

What if the person entitled to enforce the instrument agrees, in one transaction, to both an extension of time for the accommodated party's performance and another modification of the accommodation party's obligation? What if there is a dispute as to whether, as a result of these changes, the accommodation party has suffered a loss?

DISCUSSION

This question highlights the difficulties in properly allocating the burden of persuasion when the agreement between the person entitled to enforce the instrument and the accommodated party involves both an extension governed by § 3–605(c) and a modification governed by § 3–605(d). The accommodation party

---

[6] The revision to Comment 3 to § 3–605 reflects this discussion. See Appendix, par. 7.

[7] The revision to Comment 4 to § 3–605 reflects this discussion. See Appendix, par. 8.

has the burden of demonstrating loss from an extension, but the person entitled to enforce the instrument has the burden of overcoming a presumption of loss from other modifications.

If neither party introduces evidence as to loss causation, the result is full discharge of the accommodation party because § 3–605(d) applies. If the person entitled to enforce the instrument seeks to overcome the presumption of loss from the modification, it is entitled to a presumption that the extension alone caused no loss. Thus, the accommodation party will have to introduce evidence as to the effect of the extension, while the person entitled to enforce the instrument will have to introduce evidence as to the effect of the modification. On the basis of this evidence, the court will make an overall determination of the effect of the changes on the accommodation party's right of recourse against the accommodated party.[8]

ISSUE 9

How can § 3–305(d), which provides that the accommodation party can raise defenses of the accommodated party, be reconciled with § 3–605(b), which provides that a release of the accommodated party does not discharge the accommodation party?

DISCUSSION

While § 3–305(d) provides that an accommodation party can raise most defenses of the accommodated party, that section must be read in conjunction with § 3–605, which governs the effect on the obligation of the accommodation party of an act or omission of the person entitled to enforce the instrument. Section 3–605(b) provides that a release of the accommodated party does not discharge the accommodation party. Thus, while examined in isolation, § 3–305(d) might seem to allow the accommodation party to raise, as a defense to *its* obligation, a release of the accommodated party granted by the person entitled to enforce the instrument, the applicability of that section to such a release must be considered in light of § 3–605(b). If the release of the accommodated party is part of a settlement pursuant to which the person entitled to enforce the instrument accepts partial payment from an accommodated party who is financially unable to pay the entire amount of the note, the transaction falls within the scope of § 3–605(b) and the accommodation party cannot escape liability by asserting § 3–305(d) essentially to nullify § 3–605(b). If, on the other hand, the release of the accommodated party is part of an accord and satisfaction settling a dispute as to the obligation of the accommodated party, the accommodation party may utilize § 3–305(d) to assert that release as a defense to its obligation because § 3–605(b) is not intended to apply to settlement of disputed claims.[9]

ISSUE 10

What sort of language is sufficient to waive discharge under § 3–605?

DISCUSSION

Section 3–605(i) provides that a party is not discharged under that section if the instrument or a separate agreement of the party waives such discharge "either specifically or by general language indicating that parties waive defenses based on suretyship or impairment of collateral." Thus, no particular language or form of agreement is required, and the standards for enforcing such a term are the same as the standards for enforcing any other term in an instrument or agreement. There is no requirement of particularity in referring to the four grounds for discharge established by § 3–605 so long as the language used indicates that suretyship defenses are waived. By allowing the use of general language, the rule recognizes that the use of lengthy provisions containing detailed waivers or even separate identification of each ground for discharge does not necessarily promote greater understanding of an instrument's terms. Yet, the requirement that the language indicate that defenses are being waived assures that a diligent indorser or accommodation party will, at the least, not be unjustly surprised when it is asserted that the terms of the instrument or agreement delete protections that would otherwise be available. In adopting this course, § 3–605 is consistent with the general law of suretyship. See Restatement of Suretyship and Guaranty § 48.[10]

---

[8] The revision to Comment 5 to § 3–605 reflects this discussion. See Appendix, par. 9.

[9] The revision to Comment 5 to § 3–305 reflects this discussion. See Appendix, par. 1.

[10] The revision to Comment 8 to § 3–605 reflects this discussion. See Appendix, par. 11.

APPENDIX D

ISSUE 11

As a result of § 3–605(i), may an accommodation party waive whatever protections it may have pursuant to Part 6 of Article 9?

DISCUSSION

Section 3–605(e) provides that impairment of an interest in collateral for the obligation of the accommodated party may discharge the accommodation party. Section 3–605(g) defines impairment of an interest in collateral as including, *inter alia,* failure to comply with applicable law in disposing of collateral. In the case of personal property or fixtures, applicable law includes, of course, Article 9. Thus, failure to comply with the rules in Part 6 of Article 9 concerning disposition of collateral for the accommodated party's obligation constitutes impairment of an interest in collateral. In addition, the accommodation party will qualify as an "obligor" and a "secondary obligor" with respect to that collateral. See § 9–102(a)(59), (71). Obligors and, to a much greater extent, secondary obligors, are provided with substantial protections in Part 6 of Article 9. Section 9–602 provides that, with few exceptions, obligors may not waive these protections. Section 3–605(i), on the other hand, provides that an accommodation party may waive discharge under this section (including discharge for impairment of an interest in collateral pursuant to § 3–605(e)). This does not mean that the accommodation party may waive *all* protections it may have concerning disposition of collateral; rather, it provides for the waiver of protections created by § 3–605. To the extent that Article 9 also provides the accommodation party similar protections, waiver of those protections is governed by Article 9 as interpreted in each jurisdiction.[11]

APPENDIX

1. Comment 5 to § 3–305 is amended by adding an unnumbered paragraph as follows:

Section 3–305(d) must be read in conjunction with Section 3–605, which provides rules (usually referred to as suretyship defenses) for determining when the obligation of an accommodation party is discharged, in whole or in part, because of some act or omission of a person entitled to enforce the instrument. To the extent a rule stated in Section 3–605 is inconsistent with Section 3–305(d), the Section 3–605 rule governs. For example, under Section 3–605(b), discharge under Section 3–604 of the accommodated party does not discharge the accommodation party. As explained in Comment 3 to Section 3–605, discharge of the accommodated party is normally part of a settlement under which the holder of a note accepts partial payment from an accommodated party who is financially unable to pay the entire amount of the note. If the holder then brings an action against the accommodation party to recover the remaining unpaid amount of the note, the accommodation party cannot use Section 3–305(d) to nullify Section 3–605(b) by asserting the discharge of the accommodated party as a defense. On the other hand, suppose the accommodated party is a buyer of goods who issued the note to the seller who took the note for the buyer's obligation to pay for the goods. Suppose the buyer has a claim for breach of warranty with respect to the goods against the seller and the warranty claim may be asserted against the holder of the note. The warranty claim is a claim in recoupment. If the holder and the accommodated party reach a settlement under which the holder accepts payment less than the amount of the note in full satisfaction of the note and the warranty claim, the accommodation party could defend an action on the note by the holder by asserting the accord and satisfaction under Section 3–305(d). There is no conflict with Section 3–605(b) because that provision is not intended to apply to settlement of disputed claims. Other examples of the use of Section 3–305(d) in cases in which Section 3–605 applies are stated in Comment 4 to Section 3–605. See PEB Commentary No. 11, dated February 10, 1994.

2. A new Comment 5 to § 3–415 is added as follows:

5. As stated in subsection (a), the obligation of an indorser to pay the amount due on the instrument is generally owed not only to a person entitled to enforce the instrument but also to a subsequent indorser who paid the instrument. But if the prior indorser and the subsequent indorser are both anomalous indorsers, this rule does not apply. In that case, Section 3–116 applies. Under Section 3–116(a), the anomalous indorsers are jointly and severally liable and if either pays the instrument the indorser who pays has a right of contribution against the other. Section 3–116(b). The

---

[11] The revision to Comment 8 to § 3–605 reflects this discussion. See Appendix, par. 11.

right to contribution in Section 3–116(b) is subject to "agreement of the affected parties." Suppose the subsequent indorser can prove an agreement with the prior indorser under which the prior indorser agreed to treat the subsequent indorser as a guarantor of the obligation of the prior indorser. Rights of the two indorsers between themselves would be governed by the agreement. Under suretyship law, the subsequent indorser under such an agreement is referred to as a sub-surety. Under the agreement, if the subsequent indorser pays the instrument there is a right to reimbursement from the prior indorser; if the prior indorser pays the instrument, there is no right of recourse against the subsequent indorser. See PEB Commentary No. 11, dated February 10, 1994.

3.   Comment 3 to § 3–419 is amended by adding an unnumbered paragraph as follows:

An accommodation party is always a surety. A surety who is not a party to the instrument, however, is not an accommodation party. For example, if M issues a note payable to the order of P, and S signs a separate contract in which S agrees to pay P the amount of the instrument if it is dishonored, S is a surety but is not an accommodation party. In such a case, S's rights and duties are determined under the general law of suretyship. In unusual cases two parties to an instrument may have a surety relationship that is not governed by Article 3 because the requirements of Section 3–419(a) are not met. In those cases the general law of suretyship applies to the relationship. See PEB Commentary No. 11, dated February 10, 1994.

4.   Comment 4 to § 3–419 is amended by adding the following two sentences:

Words added to an anomalous indorsement indicating that payment of the instrument is guaranteed by the indorser do not change the liability of the indorser as stated in Section 3–415. This is a change from former Section 3–416(5). See PEB Commentary No. 11, supra.

5.   Comment 5 to § 3–419 is amended by deleting the struck-out words and adding the underlined words as follows:

5.   Subsection (e) restates subsection (5) of present Section 3–415 like former Section 3–415(5), provides that an accommodation party that pays the instrument is entitled to enforce the instrument against the accommodated party. Since the accommodation party that pays the instrument is entitled to enforce the instrument against the accommodated party, the accommodation party also obtains rights to any security interest or other collateral that secures payment of the instrument. Subsection (e) also provides that an accommodation party that pays the instrument is entitled to reimbursement from the accommodated party. See PEB Commentary No. 11, supra.

6.   A new Comment 6 and a new Comment 7 to § 3–419 are added as follows:

6.   In occasional cases, the accommodation party might pay the instrument even though the accommodated party had a defense to its obligation that was available to the accommodation party under Section 3–305(d). In such cases, the accommodation party's right to reimbursement may conflict with the accommodated party's right to raise its defense. For example, suppose the accommodation party pays the instrument without being aware of the defense. In that case the accommodation party should be entitled to reimbursement. Suppose the accommodation party paid the instrument with knowledge of the defense. In that case, to the extent of the defense, reimbursement ordinarily would not be justified, but under some circumstances reimbursement may be justified depending upon the facts of the case. The resolution of this conflict is left to the general law of suretyship. Section 1–103. See PEB Commentary No. 11, supra.

7.   Section 3–419, along with Section 3–116(a) and (b), Section 3–305(d) and Section 3–605, provides rules governing the rights of accommodation parties. In addition, except to the extent that it is displaced by provisions of this Article, the general law of suretyship also applies to the rights of accommodation parties. Section 1–103. See PEB Commentary No. 11, supra.

7.   Comment 3 to § 3–605 is amended by dividing it into two paragraphs, deleting the struck-out words, and adding the underlined words as follows:

3.   Subsection (b) addresses the effect of discharge under Section 3–604 of the principal debtor. In the hypothetical case stated in Comment 1, release of Borrower by Bank does not release Accommodation Party. As a practical matter, Bank will not gratuitously release Borrower. Discharge of Borrower normally would be part of a settlement with Borrower if Borrower is insolvent or in

APPENDIX D

financial difficulty. If Borrower is unable to pay all creditors, it may be prudent for Bank to take partial payment, but Borrower will normally insist on a release of the obligation. If Bank takes $3,000 and releases Borrower from the $10,000 debt, Accommodation Party is not injured. To the extent of the payment Accommodation Party's obligation to Bank is reduced. The release of Borrower by Bank does not affect the right of Accommodation Party to obtain reimbursement from Borrower <u>or to enforce the note against Borrower</u> if Accommodation Party pays Bank. Section 3–419(e). Subsection (b) is designed to allow a creditor to settle with the principal debtor without risk of losing rights against sureties. Settlement is in the interest of sureties as well as the creditor. <u>Subsection (b), however, is not intended to apply to a settlement of a disputed claim which discharges the obligation.</u>

Subsection (b) changes the law stated in former Section 3–606 but the change relates largely to formalities rather than substance. Under former Section 3–606, Bank <u>in the hypothetical case stated in Comment 1</u> could settle with and release Borrower without releasing Accommodation Party, but to accomplish that result Bank had to either obtain the consent of Accommodation Party or make an express reservation of rights against Accommodation Party at the time it released Borrower. The reservation of rights was made in the agreement between Bank and Borrower by which the release of Borrower was made. There was no requirement in former Section 3–606 that any notice be given to Accommodation Party. ~~The reservation of rights doctrine is abolished in~~ Section 3–605 ~~with respect to rights on instruments~~ <u>eliminates the necessity that Bank formally reserve rights against Accommodation Party in order to retain rights of recourse against Accommodation Party.</u> See PEB Commentary No. 11, dated February 10, 1994.

8. Comment 4 to § 3–605 is amended by adding six unnumbered paragraphs as follows:

Under other provisions of Article 3, what is the effect of an extension agreement between the holder of a note and the maker who is an accommodated party? The question is illustrated by the following case:

Case # 1. A borrows money from Lender and issues a note payable on April 1, 1992. B signs the note for accommodation at the request of Lender. B signed the note either as co-maker or as an anomalous indorser. In either case Lender subsequently makes an agreement with A extending the due date of A's obligation to pay the note to July 1, 1992. In either case B did not agree to the extension.

What is the effect of the extension agreement on B? Could Lender enforce the note against B if the note is not paid on April 1, 1992? A's obligation to Lender to pay the note on April 1, 1992 may be modified by the agreement of Lender. If B is an anomalous indorser Lender cannot enforce the note against B unless the note has been dishonored. Section 3–415(a). Under Section 3–502(a)(3) dishonor occurs if it is not paid on the day it becomes payable. Since the agreement between A and Lender extended the due date of A's obligation to July 1, 1992 there is no dishonor because A was not obligated to pay Lender on April 1, 1992. If B is a co-maker the analysis is somewhat different. Lender has no power to amend the terms of the note without the consent of both A and B. By an agreement with A, Lender can extend the due date of A's obligation to Lender to pay the note but B's obligation is to pay the note according to the terms of the note at the time of issue. Section 3–412. However, B's obligation to pay the note is subject to a defense because B is an accommodation party. B is not obliged to pay Lender if A is not obliged to pay Lender. Under Section 3–305(d), B as an accommodation party can assert against Lender any defense of A. A has a defense based on the extension agreement. Thus, the result is that Lender could not enforce the note against B until July 1, 1992. This result is consistent with the right of B if B is an anomalous indorser.

As a practical matter an extension of the due date will normally occur when the accommodated party is unable to pay on the due date. The interest of the accommodation party normally is to defer payment to the holder rather than to pay right away and rely on an action against the accommodated party that may have little or no value. But in unusual cases the accommodation party may prefer to pay the holder on the original due date. In such cases, the accommodation party may do so. This is because the extension agreement between the accommodated party and the holder cannot bind the accommodation party to a change in its obligation without the accommodation party's consent. The effect on the recourse of the accommodation party against the accommodated party of performance by the accommodation party on the original due date is not addressed in § 3–419 and is left to the general law of suretyship.

Even though X has the option of paying the instrument on the original due date, X is not precluded from asserting its rights to discharge under Section 3–605(c) if it does not exercise that option. The critical issue is whether the extension caused X a loss by increasing the difference between X's cost of performing its obligation on the instrument and the amount recoverable from Corporation pursuant to Section 3–419(e). The decision by X not to exercise its option to pay on the original due date may, under the circumstances, be a factor to be considered in the determination of that issue. See PEB Commentary No. 11, supra.

9.   Comment 5 to § 3–605 is amended by adding seven unnumbered paragraphs as follows:

The following is an illustration of the kind of case to which Section 3–605(d) would apply:

Case # 2. Corporation borrows money from Lender and issues a note payable to Lender. X signs the note as an accommodation party for Corporation. The loan agreement under which the note was issued states various events of default which allow Lender to accelerate the due date of the note. Among the events of default are breach of covenants not to incur debt beyond specified limits and not to engage in any line of business substantially different from that currently carried on by Corporation. Without consent of X, Lender agrees to modify the covenants to allow Corporation to enter into a new line of business that X considers to be risky, and to incur debt beyond the limits specified in the loan agreement to finance the new venture. This modification releases X unless Lender proves that the modification did not cause loss to X or that the loss caused by the modification was less than X's right of recourse.

Sometimes there is both an extension of the due date and some other modification. In that case both subsections (c) and (d) apply. The following is an example:

Case # 3. Corporation was indebted to Lender on a note payable on April 1, 1992 and X signed the note as an accommodation party for Corporation. The interest rate on the note was 12 percent. Lender and Corporation agreed to a six-month extension of the due date of the note to October 1, 1992 and an increase in the interest rate to 14 percent after April 1, 1992. Corporation defaulted on October 1, 1992. Corporation paid no interest during the six-month extension period. Corporation is insolvent and has no assets from which unsecured creditors can be paid. Lender demanded payment from X.

Assume X is an anomalous indorser. First consider Section 3–605(c) alone. If there had been no change in the interest rate, the fact that Lender gave an extension of six months to Corporation would not result in discharge unless X could prove loss with respect to the right of recourse because of the extension. If the financial condition of Corporation on April 1, 1992 would not have allowed any recovery on the right of recourse, X can't show any loss as a result of the extension with respect to the amount due on the note on April 1, 1992. Since the note accrued interest during the six-month extension, is there a loss equal to the accrued interest? Since the interest rate was not raised, only Section 3–605(c) would apply and X probably could not prove any loss. The obligation of X includes interest on the note until the note is paid. To the extent payment was delayed X had the use of the money that X otherwise would have had to pay to Lender. X could have prevented the running of interest by paying the debt. Since X did not do so, X suffered no loss as the result of the extension.

If the interest rate was raised, Section 3–605(d) also must be considered. If X is an anomalous indorser, X's liability is to pay the note according to its terms at the time of indorsement. Section 3–415(a). Thus, X's obligation to pay interest is measured by the terms of the note (12%) rather than by the increased amount of 14 percent. The same analysis applies if X had been a co-maker. Under Section 3–412 the liability of the issuer of a note is to pay the note according to its terms at the time it was issued. Either obligation could be changed by contract and that occurred with respect to Corporation when it agreed to the increase in the interest rate, but X did not join in that agreement and is not bound by it. Thus, the most that X can be required to pay is the amount due on the note plus interest at the rate of 12 percent.

Does the modification discharge X under Section 3–605(d)? Any modification that increases the monetary obligation of X is material. An increase of the interest rate from 12 percent to 14 percent is certainly a material modification. There is a presumption that X is discharged because Section 3–605(d) creates a presumption that the modification caused a loss to X equal to the amount of the right of recourse. Thus, Lender has the burden of proving absence of loss or a loss less than the amount of the right of recourse. Since Corporation paid no interest during the six-month period, the issue is like the issue presented under Section 3–605(c) which we have just discussed. The increase in the interest rate could not have affected the right of recourse because no interest was paid by Corporation. X is in the same position as X would have been in if there had been an extension without an increase in the interest rate.

The analysis with respect to Section 3–605(c) and (d) would have been different if we change the assumptions. Suppose Corporation was not insolvent on April 1, 1992, that Corporation paid interest at the higher rate during the six-month period, and that Corporation was insolvent at the end of the six-month period. In this case it is possible that the extension and the additional burden placed on Corporation by the increased interest rate may have been detrimental to X.

There are difficulties in properly allocating burden of proof when the agreement between Lender and Corporation involves both an extension under Section 3–605(c) and a modification under Section 3–605(d). The agreement may have caused loss to X but it may be difficult to identify the extent to which the loss was caused by the extension or the other modification. If neither Lender nor X introduces evidence on the issue, the result is full discharge because Section 3–605(d) applies. Thus, Lender has the burden of overcoming the presumption in Section 3–605(d). In doing so, Lender should be entitled to a presumption that the extension of time by itself caused no loss. Section 3–605(c) is based on such a presumption and X should be required to introduce evidence on the effect of the extension on the right of recourse. Lender would have to introduce evidence on the effect of the increased interest rate. Thus both sides will have to introduce evidence. On the basis of this evidence the court will have to make a determination of the overall effect of the agreement on X's right of recourse. See PEB Commentary No. 11, supra.

10.   The second paragraph of Comment 6 to § 3–605 is amended to read as follows:

In some states a real property grantee who assumes the obligation of the grantor as maker of a note secured by the real property becomes by operation of law a principal debtor and the grantor becomes a surety. The meager case authority was split on whether former Section 3–606 applied to release the grantor if the holder released or extended the obligation of the grantee. Revised Article 3 takes no position on the effect of the release of the grantee in this case. Section 3–605(b) does not apply because the holder has not discharged the obligation of a "party," a term defined in Section 3–103(a)(8) as "party to an instrument." The assuming grantee is not a party to the instrument. The resolution of this question is governed by general principles of law, including the law of suretyship. See PEB Commentary No. 11, supra.

11.   Comment 8 to § 3–605 is amended by adding the underlined words as follows:

8.   Subsection (i) is a continuation of former law which allowed suretyship defenses to be waived. As the subsection provides, a party is not discharged under this section if the instrument or a separate agreement of the party waives discharge either specifically or by general language indicating that defenses based on suretyship and impairment of collateral are waived. No particular language or form of agreement is required, and the standards for enforcing such a term are the same as the standards for enforcing any other term in an instrument or agreement.

Subsection (i), however, applies only to a "discharge under this section." The right of an accommodation party to be discharged under Section 3–605(e) because of an impairment of collateral can be waived. But with respect to a note secured by personal property collateral, Article 9 also applies. If an accommodation party is a "debtor" under Section 9–105(1)(d) 9–102(a)(28), an "obligor" under Section 9–102(a)(59), or a "secondary obligor" under Section 9–102(a)(71), the accommodation party has rights under Article 9. Under Section 9–501(3)(b) 9–602, many rights of an Article 9 debtor or obligor under Part 6 of Article 9 under Section 9–504(3) and Section 9–505(1), which deal with disposition of collateral, cannot be waived except as provided in Article 9. These Article 9 rights are independent of rights under Section 3–605. Since Section 3–605(i) is specifically limited to discharge under Section 3–605, a waiver of rights with respect to Section 3–605 has no effect on rights under

PEB REPORT

Article 9. With respect to Article 9 rights, Section 9–501(3)(b)9–602 controls. See PEB Commentary No. 11, supra.

PEB REPORT
EFFECT OF NON-UNIFORM SCOPE PROVISIONS IN REVISED ARTICLE 9 OF THE UNIFORM COMMERCIAL CODE
(December 1, 2004)

I. Introduction

Revised Article 9 has now been enacted in all 50 states and in the District of Columbia. As has been the case with other Articles of the Uniform Commercial Code, the various state enactments contain a number of deviations from the Official Text of Revised Article 9.

While some deviations from the Official Text reflect accommodation of uniquely local issues, others represent substantive policy choices by the enacting legislatures to differ from the national model provided by the Official Text of Revised Article 9. While non-uniformities in the latter category are inconsistent with the ideal of a truly *Uniform* Commercial Code, they are, of course, inevitable in a democratic system that entrusts enactment to 51 different legislatures. Moreover, it must be recognized that the Uniform Commercial Code has never been enacted in a truly uniform way. There have been local variations ever since the widespread enactment of the Code, including variations in Article 9. The substantive non-uniformities in the enactment of Revised Article 9 are well-catalogued in two articles by Penelope L. Christophorou, Kenneth C. Kettering, Lynn A. Soukup, and Steven O. Weise: *Under the Surface of Revised Article 9: Selected Variations in State Enactments from the Official Text of Revised Article 9*,[1] and *Analysis of State Variations*.[2]

Such non-uniformities have the potential to be problematic in our national economy, where transactions frequently cross state lines and where more than one jurisdiction can be the forum in which litigation establishing the rights of parties can be instituted. Nonetheless, most of the deviations from the Official Text of Revised Article 9 will not cause serious transactional difficulties so long as the parties involved educate themselves as to the applicable law.

There is one group of non-uniformities, though, that has the potential to cause transactional difficulty and legal uncertainty, because these non-uniformities can create difficult conflict of laws issues. This group of non-uniform enactments relates to the scope provisions of Revised Article 9.

II. Uncertainties Arising from Non-uniformities as to Scope

Uniform Commercial Code Section 9–109(a)[3] provides that, "[e]xcept as otherwise provided in subsections (c) and (d)," Revised Article 9 applies, *inter alia*, to all transactions, regardless of their form, that create a security interest in personal property or fixtures by contract and to sales of accounts, chattel paper, payment intangibles, or promissory notes. Section 9–109(c) excludes application of Revised Article 9 in certain situations *to the extent that* the transactions are governed by other law referred to in that subsection.[4] Section 9–109(d) excludes application of Revised Article 9 altogether to the transactions and interests listed in that subsection.[5] While there are non-uniformities in enactment with respect to subsection

---

[1] 34 Uniform Commercial Code Law Journal 331 (2002).

[2] 34 Uniform Commercial Code Law Journal 358 (2002) (hereinafter referred to as "State Variations").

[3] Unless otherwise noted, all references to Article 9 are to the Official Text of Revised Article 9.

[4] Section 9–109(c) provides:

This article does not apply to the extent that:

    (1) a statute, regulation, or treaty of the United States preempts this article;

    (2) another statute of this State expressly governs the creation, perfection, priority, or enforcement of a security interest created by this State or a governmental unit of this State;

    (3) statute of another State, a foreign country, or a governmental unit of another State or a foreign country, other than a statute generally applicable to security interests, expressly governs creation, perfection, priority, or enforcement of a security interest created by the State, country, or governmental unit; or

    (4) the rights of a transferee beneficiary or nominated person under a letter of credit are independent and superior under Section 5–114.

[5] Section 9–109(d) provides:

APPENDIX D

(c), variations with respect to subsection (d) raise more difficult issues. In most cases, these non-uniform enactments add further exclusions to the 13 listed exclusions in the Official Text of the subsection. Thus, Article 9 as enacted in a state with such a non-uniform enactment does not govern some transactions that are governed by Article 9 in states that have followed the Official Text. In a few states, however, the non-uniform variations delete an exclusion that appears in subsection (d) of the Official Text, with the result that transactions not governed by Article 9 in states that have followed the Official Text are governed by Article 9 of such states.

A. Non-uniform Exclusions

For purposes of this Report, attention is drawn particularly to the most common types of non-uniform enactments of Section 9–109(d)—those that exclude from the scope of Article 9 transactions that are otherwise within the scope of the Official Text of the Article: (i) 18 states exclude from Article 9 transfers by the government of any state,[6] (ii) 18 states exclude from Article 9 transfers of interests in workers compensation and similar programs,[7] and (iii)13 states exclude from Article 9 transfers of interests in special needs trusts.[8] The relatively large number of states with these non-uniform exclusions makes it likely that conflict of laws issues will arise with some frequency.

If a transaction that is the subject of a non-uniform exclusion from Article 9 does not have a relationship to any state other than the state that has excluded that transaction from Article 9, and litigation takes place in a forum in that state, Revised Article 9 would not be applicable to the transaction. However, such a purely local transaction (accompanied by local litigation) may not be the norm. In many

---

This article does not apply to:

    (1)   a landlord's lien, other than an agricultural lien;

    (2)   a lien, other than an agricultural lien, given by statute or other rule of law for services or materials, but Section 9–333 applies with respect to priority of the lien;

    (3)   an assignment of a claim for wages, salary, or other compensation of an employee;

    (4)   a sale of accounts, chattel paper, payment intangibles, or promissory notes as part of a sale of the business out of which they arose;

    (5)   an assignment of accounts, chattel paper, payment intangibles, or promissory notes which is for the purpose of collection only;

    (6)   an assignment of a right to payment under a contract to an assignee that is also obligated to perform under the contract;

    (7)   an assignment of a single account, payment intangible, or promissory note to an assignee in full or partial satisfaction of a preexisting indebtedness;

    (8)   a transfer of an interest in or an assignment of a claim under a policy of insurance, other than an assignment by or to a health-care provider of a health-care-insurance receivable and any subsequent assignment of the right to payment, but Sections 9–315 and 9–322 apply with respect to proceeds and priorities in proceeds;

    (9)   an assignment of a right represented by a judgment, other than a judgment taken on a right to payment that was collateral;

    (10)   a right of recoupment or set-off, but:

        (A) Section 9–340 applies with respect to the effectiveness of rights of recoupment or set-off against deposit accounts; and

        (B) Section 9–404 applies with respect to defenses or claims of an account debtor;

    (11)   the creation or transfer of an interest in or lien on real property, including a lease or rents thereunder, except to the extent that provision is made for:

        (A) liens on real property in Sections 9–203 and 9–308;

        (B) fixtures in Section 9–334;

        (C) fixture filings in Sections 9–501, 9–502, 9–512, 9–516, and 9–519; and

        (D) security agreements covering personal and real property in Section 9–604;

    (12)   an assignment of a claim arising in tort, other than a commercial tort claim, but Sections 9–315 and 9–322 apply with respect to proceeds and priorities in proceeds; or

    (13)   an assignment of a deposit account in a consumer transaction, but Sections 9–315 and 9–322 apply with respect to proceeds and priorities in proceeds.

[6]   See *State Variations* at 361–82. Thirteen other states exclude transfers only by "this state." By their limited nature, these exclusions are likely to cause fewer choice of law problems. See *id.*

[7]   See *id.*

[8]   See *id.*

cases, the parties (or some other aspect of the transaction) may relate to a state that has not excluded the transaction from Article 9, or the litigation may take place in a state that has not excluded the transaction from Article 9. Accordingly, conflict of laws issues must be addressed.

1. Litigation in non-excluding forum

What happens if litigation concerning a security interest excluded from the scope of Article 9 as enacted in State X is instituted in the courts of State Y, which has not excluded the transaction from the scope of Article 9? In such a case, the conflict of laws rules of State Y determine which state's law applies. The Uniform Commercial Code of State Y contains two sets of rules that determine the state whose law will govern secured transactions issues in the litigation. With respect to issues of perfection and priority, UCC Sections 9–301 through 9–307 of State Y provide the rules that determine which state's law governs.[9] With respect to issues of enforceability, attachment, and other rights and duties between debtor and secured party, though, the applicable law is determined by the conflict of laws rules in UCC Article 1 of State Y. Article 1's conflict of laws rules appear in Section 1–301 of Revised Article 1 and Section 1–105 of former Article 1. As the following analysis demonstrates, it is possible for a court in State Y to conclude, by application of that forum's conflict of laws rules, that the law of State Y (or another state that has not excluded the transaction from the scope of Article 9) is applicable, even if the transaction has significant contacts with State X.

a. Enforceability, attachment, and other rights between the parties

If litigation concerning a transaction that is excluded from the scope of Article 9 in State X takes place in the courts of State Y, which has not excluded the transaction from its Article 9, the law that governs enforceability, attachment, and other rights between the parties will be determined by application of Revised Section 1–301 or former Section 1–105, as enacted in the forum state. If application of Revised Section 1–301 or former Section 1–105 directs the State Y court to apply the law of State X, the court will apply that law—which, as a result of the exclusion in State X, will not be Article 9, but, rather, whatever other law of State X governs in light of the fact that the transaction has been excluded from State X's Article 9.[10] It is possible, of course, for Revised Section 1–301 or former Section 1–105 to direct the State Y court to apply the law of State Y (or another state that has not excluded the transaction from Article 9) even though the transaction has some connection to State X. In this regard, it should be noted that both Revised Section 1–301 and former Section 1–105 provide the parties to a transaction with some autonomy as to selection of the governing law.[11]

b. Perfection and priority

If, under the law of the state determined to be applicable pursuant to State Y's enactment of Revised Section 1–301 or former Section 1–105 (whether the applicable law is the non-Article 9 law of State X or Article 9 of State Y), the security interest in question is enforceable and attached, issues of perfection of that security interest and the priority of that security interest are likely to arise. If the litigation concerning these issues takes place in the courts of State Y, those courts must apply the conflict of laws rules in UCC Sections 9–301 through 9–307 to determine which state's law governs issues of perfection and priority. Once again, depending on the situation, the State Y court might be directed by these sections to apply the non-Article 9 law of State X for either or both of these issues, or it might be directed to apply the law of State Y (or another state that has not excluded application of Article 9 to the transaction at hand);[12] in the latter case, the rules in Article 9 of State Y or such other state would apply even though the transaction has some connection with State X.

---

[9] More precisely, these sections govern issues of perfection, the effect of perfection or nonperfection, and the priority of a security interest in collateral.

[10] It is important in this regard to recall that excluding a transaction from the scope of Article 9 is not the same thing as prohibiting that transaction. Exclusion from Article 9 merely means that other law governs the transaction. Only if other law prohibits the transaction is the transaction prohibited. As a practical matter, though, parties may be unwilling to enter into a transaction if the other law that would govern it is uncertain or antiquated.

[11] Section 1–301 provides somewhat greater party autonomy in non-consumer transactions but is also explicitly limited by considerations of public policy. See Revised UCC Section 1–301(f).

[12] The conflict of laws rules in Sections 9–301 through 9–307, unlike those in Revised Section 1–301 and former Section 1–105, do not generally defer to choices made by the parties.

APPENDIX D

2. Litigation in excluding forum

It is also possible for litigation concerning a security interest excluded from the scope of Article 9 in State X to be instituted in the courts of State X, even if the transaction has significant contacts with State Y, which has not excluded the transaction from its enactment of Article 9. In such a case, the conflict of laws rules of State X determine which state's law applies. If all aspects of the transaction relate to no state other than State X, the analysis is likely trivial, resulting in application of the law of State X to all aspects of the transaction; but, as noted above, such a purely local transaction may not be the norm. In cases in which the law of a state other than State X might conceivably apply, the analysis is made much more difficult by the fact that the conflict of laws rules that will determine the applicable law may not be the conflict of laws rules found in the Uniform Commercial Code.

a. Enforceability, attachment, and other rights between the parties

If litigation concerning a transaction that is excluded from the scope of Article 9 in State X takes place in a court of State X, it is not clear which conflict of laws rules the court must apply in order to determine the state whose law governs enforceability, attachment, and other rights between the parties. If no other aspect of the transaction is within the scope of Article 9 of State X or within the scope of another Article of the Uniform Commercial Code of State X, it is likely that the conflict of laws rules in UCC Article 1 do not apply. This result is stated explicitly in Revised UCC Section 1–301(b), and is implicit in former Section 1–105. Thus, the general conflict of laws principles of State X determine whether the non-Article 9 law of State X applies to these issues or, rather, whether the Article 9 of State Y (or another state that has not excluded the transaction from Article 9) applies. Because conflict of laws rules outside the UCC are not uniform in the various states, it may be difficult to predict which state's law would be applied by the courts of a state that has excluded a transaction from Article 9. *It is the view of the Permanent Editorial Board that a court in a state that has excluded from the scope of its Article 9 a transaction that would otherwise be within the scope of that Article should give serious consideration to applying to such a transaction the conflict of laws rules in that state's enactment of Article 1, even though those rules may not, strictly speaking, be binding on the court, on the theory that those rules represent a general statement of legislative policy as to conflict of laws issues in secured transactions.*

b. Perfection and priority

If litigation concerning a transaction that is excluded from the scope of Article 9 in State X takes place in a court of State X, and, under the law applied by that court (whether that law is the non-Article 9 law of State X or Article 9 of State Y), the security interest granted by the debtor to the secured party is enforceable and attached, issues of perfection of that security interest and the priority of that security interest are likely to arise. In such a case, it is also not clear which conflict of laws rules the court must apply in order to determine the state whose law governs issues of perfection and priority. In this situation, UCC Sections 9–301 through 9–307 of State X are not, strictly speaking, applicable to determine which state's law governs issues of perfection and priority. This is because Sections 9–301 through 9–307 are part of Article 9, and, as a result of State X's non-uniform scope provision, Article 9 of State X (including Sections 9–301 through 9–307) does not apply to the transaction. As a result, a State X court will be required to determine (without the explicit legislative guidance in the Uniform Commercial Code) the nature of State X's conflict of laws rule for issues relating to perfection and priority of security interests that are outside the scope of State X's Article 9. A search for such conflict of laws rules might be quite difficult, and the search could conceivably lead to a rule directing the court to apply the law of a state other than the state whose law that would be applicable by virtue of UCC Sections 9–301 through 9–307. Such a result would be unfortunate, because it would necessitate parties to secured transactions that are excluded from the scope of Article 9 in *any* state to consider the possibility that litigation concerning the security interest might take place in such a state, and that the courts of that state might look to the law of a different state for perfection (and, thus, the location of any required filing) than would a state that has enacted the Official Text of Article 9. Requiring parties to perform such complex conflict of laws analyses not based on application of the conflict of laws rules of the Uniform Commercial Code, and to make protective filings in various states in order to be sure of perfection regardless of where litigation takes place, is wasteful. *Accordingly, it is the view of the Permanent Editorial Board that a court in a state that has excluded from the scope of its Article 9 a transaction that would otherwise be within the scope of that Article should give serious consideration to applying to such a transaction the conflict of laws rules in that state's enactment of Sections 9–301 through*

9–307, even though those rules may not, strictly speaking, be binding on the court, on the theory that those rules represent a general statement of legislative policy as to conflict of laws issues in secured transactions.

B. Non-uniform Inclusions

For purposes of this Report, attention is drawn to non-uniform enactments of UCC Section 9–109(d) which delete the exclusion in Section 9–109(d)(13) for "an assignment of a deposit account in a consumer transaction."[13] This exclusion is deleted in the enactment of Revised Article 9 in four states—Idaho, Illinois, Mississippi, and North Dakota. As in the case of non-uniform exclusions from the scope of Article 9, this leads to the possibility of differing determinations of applicable law depending on whether a dispute is litigated in a state that has enacted the Official Text of Article 9 or a state that has enacted this non-uniform inclusion with respect to Article 9.

The basic conflict of laws analysis for this non-uniform inclusion is the same as described in Part A of this Report. If an issue concerning a security interest in a deposit account in a consumer transaction is litigated in a state that has enacted the Official Text of Revised Article 9 and, thus, in which assignments of deposit accounts in consumer transactions are outside the scope of Article 9, neither the conflict of laws rules in Revised Section 1–301 or former Section 1–105 (governing attachment, enforceability, and other bilateral issues) nor the conflict of laws rules in Sections 9–301 through 9–307 (governing perfection and priority) are applicable. This can lead to uncertainty as to the applicability of Article 9 if the transaction also touches upon one of the states that has enacted the non-uniform inclusion of deposit accounts in consumer transactions. *As is the case with respect to non-uniform exclusions from the scope of Article 9, discussed in Part A, it is the view of the Permanent Editorial Board that a court in a state that has followed the Official Text of Revised Article 9 and, accordingly, has enacted the exclusion of assignments of deposit accounts in consumer transactions from the scope of Article 9, should consider its legislature's enactment of the conflict of laws rules in that state's enactment of Article 1 and Sections 9–301 through 9–307 as general statements of legislative policy as to conflict of laws issues in secured transactions and apply the principles of those sections to conflict of laws issues relating to assignments of such deposit accounts even though, strictly speaking, they may not be binding on the court.*

If, on the other hand, an issue concerning a security interest in a deposit account in a consumer transaction is litigated in a state that has enacted the non-uniform inclusion of these transactions in the scope of Article 9, the conflict of laws rules in Revised Section 1–301 and former Section 1–105 (governing attachment, enforceability, and other bilateral issues) and the conflict of laws rules in Sections 9–301 through 9–307 (governing perfection and priority) are applicable.

III. Conclusion

The non-uniform enactments of the scope provisions of Revised Article 9 leads to the possibility of non-uniform determinations of which state's law governs legal issues arising from a secured transaction. As a result, different rules could be applied to a secured transaction depending on the location of the court in which litigation takes place. This situation would impose significant costs and uncertainty on transactions that are the subject of non-uniform scope provisions. This difficulty can be avoided if courts in states with non-uniform scope provisions nonetheless consider their legislatures' enactments of Revised Section 1–301 or former Section 1–105 and Sections 9–301 through 9–307 as general statements of legislative policy as to conflict of laws issues in secured transactions and apply the principles of those sections even though, strictly speaking, they may not be binding on the court. If this practice is followed, all U.S. courts should make the same determination of which state's law governs issues arising under a secured transaction that is within the scope of Article 9 in some, but not all, states.

---

[13] Section 9–109(d)(13) provides, however, that "sections 9–315 and 9–322 apply with respect to proceeds and priorities in proceeds."

APPENDIX D

PEB REPORT
APPLICATION OF THE UNIFORM COMMERCIAL CODE
TO SELECTED ISSUES RELATING TO MORTGAGE NOTES
(November 14, 2011)

Preface

In 1961, the American Law Institute and the Uniform Law Commission, the organizations that jointly sponsor the Uniform Commercial Code, established the Permanent Editorial Board for the Uniform Commercial Code (PEB). One of the charges of the PEB is to issue commentaries "and other articulations as appropriate to reflect the correct interpretation of the [Uniform Commercial] Code and issuing the same in a manner and at times best calculated to advance the uniformity and orderly development of commercial law." Such commentaries and other articulations are issued directly by the PEB rather than by action of the American Law Institute and the Uniform Law Commission.

This Report of the Permanent Editorial Board is such an articulation, addressing the application of the Uniform Commercial Code to issues of legal, economic, and social importance arising from the issuance and transfer of mortgage notes. A draft of this Report was made available to the public for comment on March 29, 2011, and the comments that were received have been taken into account in preparing the final Report.

Introduction

Recent economic developments have brought to the forefront complex legal issues about the enforcement and collection of mortgage debt. Many of these issues are governed by local real property law and local rules of foreclosure procedure, but others are addressed in a uniform way throughout the United States by provisions of the Uniform Commercial Code (UCC).[1] Although the UCC provisions are settled law, it has become apparent that not all courts and attorneys are familiar with them. In addition, the complexity of some of the rules has proved daunting.

The Permanent Editorial Board for the Uniform Commercial Code[2] has prepared this Report in order to further the understanding of this statutory background by identifying and explaining several key rules in the UCC that govern the transfer and enforcement of notes secured by a mortgage[3] on real property. The UCC, of course, does not resolve all issues in this field. Most particularly, as to both substance and procedure, the enforcement of real estate mortgages by foreclosure is primarily the province of a state's real property law (although determinations made pursuant to the UCC are typically relevant under that law). Accordingly, this Report should be understood as providing guidance only as to the issues the Report addresses.[4]

---

[1] The UCC is a uniform law sponsored by the American Law Institute and the Uniform Law Commission. It has been enacted in every state (as well as the District of Columbia, Puerto Rico, and the United States Virgin Islands) in whole or significant part. This Report is based on the current Official Text of the UCC. Some states have enacted some non-uniform provisions that are generally not relevant to the issues discussed in this Report. Of course, the enacted text of the UCC in the state whose law is applicable governs. See note 6, *infra*, regarding the various different versions of Article 3 of the UCC in effect in the states.

[2] In 1961, the American Law Institute and the Uniform Law Commission, the organizations that jointly sponsor the UCC, established the Permanent Editorial Board for the Uniform Commercial Code (PEB). One of the charges of the PEB is to issue commentaries "and other articulations as appropriate to reflect the correct interpretation of the [Uniform Commercial] Code and issuing the same in a manner and at times best calculated to advance the uniformity and orderly development of commercial law."

[3] This Report, like Article 9 of the UCC, uses the term "mortgage" to include a consensual interest in real property to secure an obligation whether created by mortgage, trust deed, or the like. See UCC § 9–102(a)(55) and Official Comment 17 thereto and former UCC § 9–105(1)(j). This Report uses the term "mortgage note" to refer to a note secured by a mortgage, whether or not the note is a negotiable instrument under UCC Article 3.

[4] Of course, the application of the UCC rules to particular factual circumstances depends on the nature of those circumstances. Facts raising legal issues other than those addressed in this Report can result in different rights and obligations than would be the case in the absence of those facts. Accordingly, this Report should not be read as a statement of the total legal implications of any factual scenario. Rather, the Report sets out the UCC rules that are common to the transactions discussed so as to provide a common basis for understanding the application of those rules. The impact of non-UCC law that applies to other aspects of such transactions is beyond the scope of this Report.

PEB REPORT

Background

Issues relating to the transfer, ownership, and enforcement of mortgage notes are primarily governed by two Articles of the UCC:

- In cases in which the mortgage note is a negotiable instrument,[5] Article 3 of the UCC[6] provides rules governing the obligations of parties on the note[7] and the enforcement of those obligations.

- In cases involving either negotiable or non-negotiable notes, Article 9 of the UCC[8] contains important rules governing how ownership of those notes may be transferred, the effect of the transfer of ownership of the notes on the ownership of the mortgages securing those notes, and the right of the transferee, under certain circumstances, to record its interest in the mortgage in the applicable real estate recording office.

This Report explains the application of the rules in both of those UCC Articles to provide guidance in:

- Identifying the person who is entitled to enforce the payment obligation of the maker[9] of a mortgage note, and to whom the maker owes that obligation; and

- Determining who owns the rights represented by the note and mortgage.

Together, the provisions in Articles 3 and 9 of the UCC (along with general principles that appear in Article 1 and that apply to all transactions governed by the UCC) provide legal rules that apply to these questions.[10] Moreover, these rules displace any inconsistent common law rules that might have otherwise previously governed the same questions.[11]

---

[5] The requirements that must be satisfied in order for a note to be a negotiable instrument are set out in UCC § 3–104.

[6] Except for New York, every state (as well as the District of Columbia, Puerto Rico, and the United States Virgin Islands) has enacted either the 1990 Official Text of Article 3 or the newer 2002 Official Text (the latter having been adopted in ten states as of the date of this Report). Unless indicated to the contrary all discussions of provisions in Article 3 apply equally to both versions. Much of the analysis of UCC Article 3 in this Report also applies under the older version of Article 3 in effect in New York, although many section numbers differ. The Report does not address those aspects of New York's Article 3 that are different from the 1990 or 2002 texts.

[7] In this Report, such notes are sometimes referred to as "negotiable notes."

[8] Unlike Article 3 (which has not been enacted in its modern form in New York), the current version of Article 9 has been enacted in all 50 states, the District of Columbia, and the United States Virgin Islands. Some states have enacted non-uniform provisions that are generally not relevant to the issues discussed in this Report (but see note 31 with respect to one relevant non-uniformity). A limited set of amendments to Article 9 was approved by the American Law Institute and the Uniform Law Commission in 2010. Except as noted in this Report, those amendments (which provide for a uniform effective date of July 1, 2013) are not germane to the matters addressed in this Report.

[9] A note can have more than one obligor. In some cases, this is because there is more than one maker (in which case they are jointly and severally liable; see UCC § 3–116(a)). In other cases, there may be an indorser. The obligation of an indorser is different from that of a maker in that the indorser's obligation is triggered by dishonor of the note (see UCC § 3–415) and, unless waived, indorsers have additional procedural protections (such as notice of dishonor; see UCC § 3–503)). These differences do not affect the issues addressed in this Report. For simplicity, this Report uses the term "maker" to refer to both makers and indorsers.

[10] Subject to limitations on the ability to affect the rights of third parties, the effect of these provisions may be varied by agreement. UCC § 1–302. Variation by agreement is not permitted when the variation would disclaim obligations of good faith, diligence, reasonableness, or care prescribed by the UCC or when the UCC otherwise so indicates (see, *e.g.*, UCC § 9–602). But the meaning of the statute itself cannot be varied by agreement. Thus, for example, private parties cannot make a note negotiable unless it complies with UCC § 3–104. See Official Comment 1 to UCC § 1–302. Similarly, parties may not avoid the application of UCC Article 9 to a transaction that falls within its scope. See *id.* and Official Comment 2 to UCC § 9–109.

[11] UCC § 1–103(b). As noted in Official Comment 2 to UCC § 1–103:

The Uniform Commercial Code was drafted against the backdrop of existing bodies of law, including the common law and equity, and relies on those bodies of law to supplement its provisions in many important ways. At the same time, the Uniform Commercial Code is the primary source of commercial law rules in areas that it governs, and its rules represent choices made by its drafters and the enacting legislatures about the appropriate policies to be furthered in the transactions it covers. Therefore, while principles of common law and equity may *supplement* provisions of the Uniform Commercial Code, they may not be used to *supplant* its provisions, or the purposes and policies those provisions reflect, unless a specific provision of the Uniform Commercial Code provides otherwise. In the absence of

APPENDIX D

This Report does not, however, address all of the rules in the UCC relating to enforcement, transfer, and ownership of mortgage notes. Rather, it reviews the rules relating to four specific questions:

- Who is the person entitled to enforce a mortgage note and, correspondingly, to whom is the obligation to pay the note owed?

- How can the owner of a mortgage note effectively transfer ownership of that note to another person or effectively use that note as collateral for an obligation?

- What is the effect of transfer of an interest in a mortgage note on the mortgage securing it?

- May a person to whom an interest in a mortgage note has been transferred, but who has not taken a recordable assignment of the mortgage, take steps to become the assignee of record in the real estate recording system of the mortgage securing the note?[12]

Question One—To Whom is the Obligation to Pay a Mortgage Note Owed?

If the mortgage note is a negotiable instrument,[13] Article 3 of the UCC provides a largely complete set of rules governing the obligations of parties on the note, including how to determine who may enforce those obligations and, thus, to whom those obligations are owed. The following discussion analyzes the application of these rules to that determination in the context of mortgage notes that are negotiable instruments.[14]

In the context of mortgage notes that have been sold or used as collateral to secure an obligation, the central concept for making that determination is identification of the "person entitled to enforce" the note.[15] Several issues are resolved by that determination. Most particularly:

(i)   the maker's obligation on the note is to pay the amount of the note to *the person entitled to enforce the note*,[16]

(ii)   the maker's payment to *the person entitled to enforce the note* results in discharge of the maker's obligation,[17] and

(iii)   the maker's failure to pay, when due, the amount of the note to *the person entitled to enforce the note* constitutes dishonor of the note.[18]

Thus, a person seeking to enforce rights based on the failure of the maker to pay a mortgage note must identify the person entitled to enforce the note and establish that that person has not been paid. This portion of this Report sets out the criteria for qualifying as a "person entitled to enforce" a mortgage note. The

---

such a provision, the Uniform Commercial Code preempts principles of common law and equity that are inconsistent with either its provisions or its purposes and policies.

[12]   The Report does not discuss the application of common law principles, such as the law of agency, that supplement the provisions of the UCC other than to note some situations in which the text or comments of the UCC identify such principles as being relevant. See UCC § 1–103(b).

[13]   See UCC § 3–104 for the requirements that must be fulfilled in order for a payment obligation to qualify as a negotiable instrument. It should not be assumed that all mortgage notes are negotiable instruments. The issue of the negotiability of a particular mortgage note, which requires application of the standards in UCC § 3–104 to the words of the particular note, is beyond the scope of this Report.

[14]   Law other than Article 3, including contract law, governs this determination for non-negotiable mortgage notes. That law is beyond the scope of this Report.

[15]   The concept of "person entitled to enforce" a note is not synonymous with "owner" of the note. See Official Comment 1 to UCC § 3–203. A person need not be the owner of a note to be the person entitled to enforce it, and not all owners will qualify as persons entitled to enforce. Rules that address transfer of ownership of a note are addressed in the discussion of Question 2 below.

[16]   UCC § 3–412. (If the note has been dishonored, and an indorser has paid the note to the person entitled to enforce it, the maker's obligation runs to the indorser.)

[17]   UCC § 3–602. The law of agency is applicable in determining whether a payment has been made to a person entitled to enforce. See *id.*, Official Comment 3. Note that, in states that have enacted the 2002 Official Text of UCC Article 3, UCC § 3–602(b) provides that a maker is also discharged by paying a person formerly entitled to enforce the note if the maker has not received adequate notification that the note has been transferred and that payment is to be made to the transferee. This amendment aligns the protection afforded to makers of notes that have been assigned with comparable protection afforded to obligors on other payment rights that have been assigned. See, *e.g.*, UCC § 9–406(a); Restatement (Second), Contracts § 338(1).

[18]   See UCC § 3–502. See also UCC § 3–602.

discussion of Question Two addresses how ownership of a mortgage note may be effectively transferred from an owner to another person.

UCC Section 3–301 provides only three ways in which a person may qualify as the person entitled to enforce a note, two of which require the person to be in possession of the note (which may include possession by a third party that possesses it for the person):[19]

- The first way that a person may qualify as the person entitled to enforce a note is to be its "holder." This familiar concept, set out in detail in UCC Section 1–201(b)(21)(A), requires that the person be in possession of the note and either (i) the note is payable to that person or (ii) the note is payable to bearer. Determining to whom a note is payable requires examination not only of the face of the note but also of any indorsements. This is because the party to whom a note is payable may be changed by indorsement[20] so that, for example, a note payable to the order of a named payee that is indorsed in blank by that payee becomes payable to bearer.[21]

- The second way that a person may be the person entitled to enforce a note is to be a "nonholder in possession of the [note] who has the rights of a holder."

  o How can a person who is not the holder of a note have the rights of a holder? This can occur by operation of law outside the UCC, such as the law of subrogation or estate administration, by which one person is the successor to or acquires another person's rights.[22] It can also occur if the delivery of the note to that person constitutes a "transfer" (as that term is defined in UCC Section 3–203, see below) because transfer of a note "vests in the transferee any right of the transferor to enforce the instrument."[23] Thus, if a holder (who, as seen above, is a person entitled to enforce a note) transfers the note to another person, that other person (the transferee) obtains from the holder the right to enforce the note even if the transferee does not become the holder (as in the example below). Similarly, a subsequent transfer will result in the subsequent transferee being a person entitled to enforce the note.

  o Under what circumstances does delivery of a note qualify as a transfer? As stated in UCC Section 3–203(a), a note is transferred "when it is delivered by a person other than its issuer for the purpose of giving to the person receiving delivery the right to enforce the instrument." For example, assume that the payee of a note sells it to an assignee, intending to transfer all of the payee's rights to the note, but delivers the note to the assignee without indorsing it. The assignee will not qualify as a holder (because the note is still payable to the payee) but, because the transaction between the payee and the assignee qualifies as a transfer, the assignee now has all of the payee's rights to enforce the note and thereby qualifies as the person entitled to enforce it. Thus, the failure to obtain the indorsement of the payee does not prevent a person in possession of the note from being the person entitled to enforce it, but demonstrating that status is more difficult. This is because the person in possession of

---

[19] See UCC § 1–103(b) (unless displaced by particular provisions of the UCC, the law of, *inter alia*, principal and agent supplements the provisions of the UCC). See also UCC § 3–420, Comment 1 ("Delivery to an agent [of a payee] is delivery to the payee."). Note that "delivery" of a negotiable instrument is defined in UCC § 1–201(b)(15) as voluntary transfer of possession. This Report does not address the determination of whether a particular person is an agent of another person under the law of agency and the agency law implications of such a determination.

[20] "Indorsement," as defined in UCC § 3–204(a), requires the signature of the indorser. The law of agency determines whether a signature made by a person purporting to act as a representative binds the represented person. UCC § 3–402(a); see note 12, supra. An indorsement may appear either on the instrument or on a separate piece of paper (usually referred to as an *allonge*) affixed to the instrument. See UCC § 3–204(a) and Comment 1, par. 4.

[21] UCC Section 3–205 contains the rules concerning the effect of various types of indorsement on the party to whom a note is payable. Either a "special indorsement" (see UCC § 3–205(a)) or a "blank indorsement" (see UCC § 3–205(b)) can change the identity of the person to whom the note is payable. A special indorsement is an indorsement that identifies the person to whom it makes the note payable, while a blank indorsement is an indorsement that does not identify such a person and results in the instrument becoming payable to bearer. When an instrument is indorsed in blank (and, thus, is payable to bearer), it may be negotiated by transfer of possession alone until specially indorsed. UCC § 3–205(b).

[22] See Official Comment to UCC § 3–301.

[23] UCC § 3–203(b).

the note must also demonstrate the purpose of the delivery of the note to it in order to qualify as the person entitled to enforce.[24]

- There is a third method of qualifying as a person entitled to enforce a note that, unlike the previous two methods, does not require possession of the note. This method is quite limited—it applies only in cases in which "the person cannot reasonably obtain possession of the instrument because the instrument was destroyed, its whereabouts cannot be determined, or it is in the wrongful possession of an unknown person or a person that cannot be found or is not amenable to service of process."[25] In such a case, a person qualifies as a person entitled to enforce the note if the person demonstrates not only that one of those circumstances is present but also demonstrates that the person was formerly in possession of the note and entitled to enforce it when the loss of possession occurred and that the loss of possession was not as a result of transfer (as defined above) or lawful seizure. If the person proves those facts, as well as the terms of the note, the person is a person entitled to enforce the note and may seek to enforce it even though it is not in possession of the note,[26] but the court may not enter judgment in favor of the person unless the court finds that the maker is adequately protected against loss that might occur if the note subsequently reappears.[27]

Illustrations:

1. Maker issued a negotiable mortgage note payable to the order of Payee. Payee is in possession of the note, which has not been indorsed. Payee is the holder of the note and, therefore, is the person entitled to enforce it. UCC §§ 1–201(b)(21)(A), 3–301(i).

2. Maker issued a negotiable mortgage note payable to the order of Payee. Payee indorsed the note in blank and gave possession of it to Transferee. Transferee is the holder of the note and, therefore, is the person entitled to enforce it. UCC §§ 1–201(b)(21)(A), 3–301(i).

3. Maker issued a negotiable mortgage note payable to the order of Payee. Payee sold the note to Transferee and gave possession of it to Transferee for the purpose of giving Transferee the right to enforce the note. Payee did not, however, indorse the note. Transferee is not the holder of the note because, while Transferee is in possession of the note, it is payable neither to bearer nor to Transferee. UCC § 1–201(b)(21)(A). Nonetheless, Transferee is a person entitled to enforce the note. This is because the note was transferred to Transferee and the transfer vested in Transferee Payee's right to enforce the note. UCC § 3–203(a)–(b). As a result, Transferee is a nonholder in possession of the note with the rights of a holder and, accordingly, a person entitled to enforce the note. UCC § 3–301(ii).

4. Same facts as Illustrations 2 and 3, except that (i) under the law of agency, Agent is the agent of Transferee for purposes of possessing the note and (ii) it is Agent, rather than Transferee, to whom actual physical possession of the note is given by Payee. In the facts of Illustration 2, Transferee is a holder of the note and a person entitled to enforce it. In the context of Illustration 3, Transferee is a person entitled to enforce the note. Whether Agent may enforce the note or mortgage on behalf of Transferee depends in part on the law of agency and, in the case of the mortgage, real property law.

---

[24] If the note was transferred for value and the transferee does not qualify as a holder because of the lack of indorsement by the transferor, "the transferee has a specifically enforceable right to the unqualified indorsement of the transferor." See UCC § 3–203(c).

[25] UCC § 3–309(a)(iii) (1990 text), 3–309(a)(3) (2002 text). The 2002 text goes on to provide that a transferee from the person who lost possession of a note may also qualify as a person entitled to enforce it. See UCC § 3–309(a)(1)(B) (2002). This point was thought to be implicit in the 1990 text, but was rejected in some cases in which the issue was raised. The reasoning of those cases was rejected in Official Comment 5 to UCC § 9–109 and the point was made explicit in the 2002 text of Article 3.

[26] To prevail the person must establish not only that the person is a person entitled to enforce the note but also the other elements of the maker's obligation to pay such a person. See generally UCC §§ 3–309(b), 3–412. Moreover, as is the case with respect to the enforcement of all rights under the UCC, the person enforcing the note must act in good faith in enforcing the note. UCC § 1–304.

[27] See *id.* UCC § 3–309(b) goes on to state that "Adequate protection may be provided by any reasonable means."

5. Same facts as Illustration 2, except that after obtaining possession of the note, Transferee lost the note and its whereabouts cannot be determined. Transferee is a person entitled to enforce the note even though Transferee does not have possession of it. UCC § 3–309(a). If Transferee brings an action on the note against Maker, Transferee must establish the terms of the note and the elements of Maker's obligation on it. The court may not enter judgment in favor of Transferee, however, unless the court finds that Maker is adequately protected against loss that might occur by reason of a claim of another person (such as the finder of the note) to enforce the note. UCC § 3–309(b).

Question Two—What Steps Must be Taken for the Owner of a Mortgage Note to Transfer Ownership of the Note to Another Person or Use the Note as Collateral for an Obligation?

In the discussion of Question One, this Report addresses identification of the person who is entitled to enforce a note. That discussion does not address who "owns" the note. While, in many cases, the person entitled to enforce a note is also its owner, this need not be the case. The rules that determine whether a person is a person entitled to enforce a note do not require that person to be the owner of the note,[28] and a change in ownership of a note does not necessarily bring about a concomitant change in the identity of the person entitled to enforce the note. This is because the rules that determine who is entitled to enforce a note and the rules that determine whether the note, or an interest in it, have been effectively transferred serve different functions:

- The rules that determine who is entitled to enforce a note are concerned primarily with the maker of the note, providing the maker with a relatively simple way of determining to whom his or her obligation is owed and, thus, whom to pay in order to be discharged.

- The rules concerning transfer of ownership and other interests in a note, on the other hand, primarily relate to who, among competing claimants, is entitled to the economic value of the note.

In a typical transaction, when a note is issued to a payee, the note is initially owned by that payee. If that payee seeks either to use the note as collateral or sell the note outright, Article 9 of the UCC governs that transaction and determines whether the creditor or buyer has obtained a property right in the note. As is generally known, Article 9 governs transactions in which property is used as collateral for an obligation.[29] In addition, however, Article 9 governs the sale of most payment rights, including the sale of both negotiable and non-negotiable notes.[30] With very few exceptions, the same Article 9 rules that apply to transactions in which a payment right is collateral for an obligation also apply to transactions in which a payment right is sold. Rather than contain two parallel sets of rules—one for transactions in which payment rights are collateral and the other for sales of payment rights—Article 9 uses nomenclature conventions to apply one set of rules to both types of transactions. This is accomplished primarily by defining the term "security interest" to include not only an interest in property that secures an obligation but also the right of a buyer of a payment right in a transaction governed by Article 9.[31] Similarly, definitional conventions denominate the seller of such a payment right as the "debtor," the buyer as the "secured party," and the sold payment right as the "collateral."[32] As a result, for purposes of Article 9, the buyer of a promissory note is a "secured party" that has acquired a "security interest" in the note from the "debtor," and the rules that apply to

---

[28] See UCC § 3–301, which provides, in relevant part, that "A person may be a person entitled to enforce the instrument even though the person is not the owner of the instrument. . . ."

[29] UCC § 9–109(a)(1).

[30] With certain limited exceptions not germane to this Report, Article 9 governs the sale of accounts, chattel paper, payment intangibles, and promissory notes. UCC § 9–109(a)(3). The term "promissory note" includes not only notes that fulfill the requirements of a negotiable instrument under UCC § 3–104 but also notes that do not fulfill those requirements but nonetheless are of a "type that in ordinary business is transferred by delivery with any necessary indorsement or assignment." See UCC §§ 9–102(a)(65) (definition of "promissory note") and 9–102(a)(47) (definition of "instrument" as the term is used in Article 9).

[31] See UCC § 1–201(b)(35) [UCC § 1–201(37) in states that have not yet enacted the 2001 revised text of UCC Article 1]. (For reasons that are not apparent, when South Carolina enacted the 1998 revised text of UCC Article 9, which included an amendment to UCC § 1–201 to expand the definition of "security interest" to include the right of a buyer of a promissory note, it did not enact the amendment to § 1–201. This Report does not address the effect of that omission.) The limitation to transactions governed by Article 9 refers to the exclusion, in cases not germane to this Report, of certain assignments of payment rights from the reach of Article 9.

[32] UCC §§ 9–102(a)(28)(B); 9–102(a)(72)(D); 9–102(a)(12)(B).

security interests that secure an obligation generally also apply to transactions in which a promissory note is sold.

Section 9–203(b) of the Uniform Commercial Code provides that three criteria must be fulfilled in order for the owner of a mortgage note effectively to create a "security interest" (either an interest in the note securing an obligation or the outright sale of the note to a buyer) in it.

- The first two criteria are straightforward—"value" must be given[33] and the debtor/seller must have rights in the note or the power to transfer rights in the note to a third party.[34]

- The third criterion may be fulfilled in either one of two ways. Either the debtor/seller must "authenticate"[35] a "security agreement"[36] that describes the note[37] or the secured party must take possession[38] of the note pursuant to the debtor's security agreement.[39]

  o Thus, if the secured party (including a buyer) takes possession of the mortgage note pursuant to the security agreement of the debtor (including a seller), this criterion is satisfied even if that agreement is oral or otherwise not evidenced by an authenticated record.

  o Alternatively, if the debtor authenticates a security agreement describing the note, this criterion is satisfied even if the secured party does *not* take possession of the note. (Note that in this situation, in which the seller of a note may retain possession of it, the owner of a note may be a different person than the person entitled to enforce the note.)[40]

---

[33] UCC § 9–203(b)(1). UCC § 1–204 provides that giving "value" for rights includes not only acquiring them for consideration but also acquiring them in return for a binding commitment to extend credit, as security for or in complete or partial satisfaction of a preexisting claim, or by accepting delivery of them under a preexisting contract for their purchase.

[34] UCC § 9–203(b)(2). Limited rights that are short of full ownership are sufficient for this purpose. See Official Comment 6 to UCC § 9–203.

[35] This term is defined to include signing and its electronic equivalent. See UCC § 9–102(a)(7).

[36] A "security agreement" is an agreement that creates or provides for a security interest (including the rights of a buyer arising upon the outright sale of a payment right). See UCC § 9–102(a)(73).

[37] Article 9's criteria for descriptions of property in a security agreement are quite flexible. Generally speaking, any description suffices, whether or not specific, if it reasonably identifies the property. See UCC § 9–108(a)–(b). A "supergeneric" description consisting solely of words such as "all of the debtor's assets" or "all of the debtor's personal property" is not sufficient, however. UCC § 9–108(c). A narrower description, limiting the property to a particular category or type, such as "all notes," is sufficient. For example, a description that refers to "all of the debtor's notes" is sufficient.

[38] See UCC § 9–313. As noted in Official Comment 3 to UCC § 9–313, "in determining whether a particular person has possession, the principles of agency apply." In addition, UCC § 9–313 also contains two special rules under which possession by a non-agent may constitute possession by the secured party. First, if a person who is not an agent is in possession of the collateral and the person authenticates a record acknowledging that the person holds the collateral for the secured party's benefit, possession by that person constitutes possession by the secured party. UCC § 9–313(c). Second, a secured party that has possession of collateral does not relinquish possession by delivering the collateral to another person (other than the debtor or a lessee of the collateral from the debtor in the ordinary course of the debtor's business) if the delivery is accompanied by instructions to that person to hold possession of the collateral for the benefit of the secured party or redeliver it to the secured party. UCC § 9–313(h). See also Official Comment 9 to UCC § 9–313 ("New subsections (h) and (i) address the practice of mortgage warehouse lenders.") Possession as contemplated by UCC § 9–313 is also possession for purposes of UCC § 9–203. See UCC § 9–203, Comment 4.

[39] UCC §§ 9–203(b)(3)(A)–(B).

[40] As noted in the discussion of Question One, payment by the maker of a negotiable note to the person entitled to enforce it discharges the maker's obligations on the note. UCC § 3–602. This is the case even if the person entitled to enforce the note is not its owner. As between the person entitled to enforce the note and the owner of the note, the right to the money paid by the maker is determined by the UCC and other applicable law, such as the law of contract and the law of restitution, as well as agency law. See, e.g., UCC §§ 3–306 and 9–315(a)(2). As noted in comment 3 to UCC § 3–602, "if the original payee of the note transfers ownership of the note to a third party but continues to service the obligation, the law of agency might treat payments made to the original payee as payments made to the third party."

Satisfaction of these three criteria of Section 9–203(b) results in the secured party (including a buyer of the note) obtaining a property right (whether outright ownership or a security interest to secure an obligation) in the note from the debtor (including a seller of the note).[41]

Illustrations:

6. Maker issued a mortgage note payable to the order of Payee.[42] Payee borrowed money from Funder and, to secure Payee's repayment obligation, Payee and Funder agreed that Funder would have a security interest in the note. Simultaneously with the funding of the loan, Payee gave possession of the note to Funder. Funder has an attached and enforceable security interest in the note. UCC § 9–203(b). This is the case even if Payee's agreement is oral or otherwise not evidenced by an authenticated record. Payee is no longer a person entitled to enforce the note (because Payee is no longer in possession of it and it has not been lost, stolen, or destroyed). UCC § 3–301. Funder is a person entitled to enforce the note if either (i) Payee indorsed the note by blank indorsement or by a special indorsement identifying Funder as the person to whom the indorsement makes the note payable (because, in such cases, Funder would be the holder of the note), or (ii) the delivery of the note from Payee to Funder constitutes a transfer of the note under UCC § 3–203 (because, in such case, Funder would be a nonholder in possession of the note with the rights of a holder). See also UCC §§ 1–201(b)(21)(A), 3–205(a)–(b), and 3–301(i)–(ii).

7. Maker issued a mortgage note payable to the order of Payee. Payee borrowed money from Funder and, in a signed writing that reasonably identified the note (whether specifically or as part of a category or a type of property defined in the UCC), granted Funder a security interest in the note to secure Payee's repayment obligation. Payee, however, retained possession of the note. Funder has an attached and enforceable security interest in the note. UCC § 9–203(b). If the note is negotiable, Payee remains the holder and the person entitled to enforce the note because Payee is in possession of it and it is payable to the order of Payee. UCC §§ 1–201(b)(21)(A), 3–301(i).

8. Maker issued a mortgage note payable to the order of Payee. Payee sold the note to Funder, giving possession of the note to Funder in exchange for the purchase price. The sale of the note is governed by Article 9 and the rights of Funder as buyer constitute a "security interest." UCC §§ 9–109(a)(3), 1–201(b)(35). The security interest is attached and is enforceable. UCC § 9–203(b). This is the case even if the sales agreement was oral or otherwise not evidenced by an authenticated record. If the note is negotiable, Funder is also a person entitled to enforce the note, whether or not Payee indorsed it, because either (i) Funder is a holder of the note (if Payee indorsed it by blank indorsement or by a special indorsement identifying Funder as the person to whom the indorsement makes the note payable) or (ii) Funder is a nonholder in possession of the note (if there is no such indorsement) who has obtained the rights of Payee by transfer of the note pursuant to UCC § 3–203. See also UCC §§ 1–201(b)(21)(A), 3–205(a)–(b), and 3–301(i)–(ii).

9. Maker issued a mortgage note payable to the order of Payee. Pursuant to a signed writing that reasonably identified the note (whether specifically or as part of a category or a type of property defined in the UCC), Payee sold the note to Funder. Payee, however, retained possession of the note. The sale of the note is governed by Article 9 and the rights of Funder as buyer constitute a "security interest." UCC § 1–201(b)(35). The security interest is attached and is enforceable. UCC § 9–203(b). If the note is negotiable, Payee remains the holder and the person entitled to enforce

---

[41] For cases in which another person claims an interest in the note (whether as a result of another voluntary transfer by the debtor or otherwise), reference to Article 9's rules governing perfection and priority of security interests may be required in order to rank order those claims (and, in some cases, determine whether a party has taken the note free of competing claims to the note). In the case of notes that are negotiable instruments, the Article 3 concept of "holder in due course" (see UCC § 3–302) should be considered as well, because a holder in due course takes its rights in an instrument free of competing property claims to it (as well as free of most defenses to obligations on it). See UCC §§ 3–305 and 3–306. With respect to determining whether the owner of a note has effectively transferred a property interest to a transferee, however, the perfection and priority rules are largely irrelevant. (The application of the perfection and priority rules can result in the rights of the transferee either being subordinate to the rights of a competing claimant or being extinguished by the rights of the competing claimant. See, e.g., UCC §§ 9–317(b), 9–322(a), 9–330(d), and 9–331(a).)

[42] For this Illustration, as well as Illustrations 7–11, the analysis under UCC Article 9 is the same whether the mortgage note is negotiable or non-negotiable. This is because, in either case, the mortgage note will qualify as a "promissory note" and, therefore, an "instrument" under UCC Article 9. See UCC §§ 9–102(a)(47), (65).

the note (even though, as between Payee and Funder, Funder owns the note) because Payee is in possession of it and it is payable to the order of Payee. UCC §§ 1–201(b)(21)(A), 3–301(i).

Question Three—What is the Effect of Transfer of an Interest in a Mortgage Note on the Mortgage Securing It?

What if a note secured by a mortgage is sold (or the note is used as collateral to secure an obligation), but the parties do not take any additional actions to assign the mortgage that secures payment of the note, such as execution of a recordable assignment of the mortgage? UCC Section 9–203(g) explicitly provides that, in such cases, the assignment of the interest of the seller or other grantor of a security interest in the note automatically transfers a corresponding interest in the mortgage to the assignee: "The attachment of a security interest in a right to payment or performance secured by a security interest or other lien on personal or real property is also attachment of a security interest in the security interest, mortgage, or other lien." (As noted previously, a "security interest" in a note includes the right of a buyer of the note.)

While this question has provoked some uncertainty and has given rise to some judicial analysis that disregards the impact of Article 9,[43] the UCC is unambiguous: the sale of a mortgage note (or other grant of a security interest in the note) not accompanied by a separate conveyance of the mortgage securing the note does not result in the mortgage being severed from the note.[44]

It is important to note in this regard, however, that UCC Section 9–203(g) addresses only whether, as between the seller of a mortgage note (or a debtor who uses it as collateral) and the buyer or other secured party, the interest of the seller (or debtor) in the mortgage has been correspondingly transferred to the secured party. UCC Section 9–308(e) goes on to state that, if the secured party's security interest in the note is perfected, the secured party's security interest in the mortgage securing the note is also perfected,[45] with result that the right of the secured party is senior to the rights of a person who then or later becomes a lien creditor of the seller of (or other grantor of a security interest in) the note. Neither of these rules, however, determines the ranking of rights in the underlying real property itself, or the effect of recordation or non-recordation in the real property recording system on enforcement of the mortgage.[46]

Illustration:

10. Same facts as Illustration 9. The signed writing was silent with respect to the mortgage securing the note and the parties made no other agreement with respect to the mortgage. The attachment of Funder's interest in the rights of Payee in the note also constitutes attachment of an interest in the rights of Payee in the mortgage. UCC § 9–203(g).

---

[43] *See, e.g.,* the discussion of this issue in *U.S. Bank v. Ibanez,* 458 Mass. 637 at 652–53, 941 N.E.2d 40 at 53–54 (2011). In that discussion, the court cited Massachusetts common law precedents pre-dating the enactment of the current text of Article 9 to the effect that a mortgage does not follow a note in the absence of a separate assignment of the mortgage, but did not address the effect of Massachusetts's subsequent enactment of UCC § 9–203(g) on those precedents. Under the rule in UCC § 9–203(g), if the holder of the note in question demonstrated that it had an attached security interest (including the interest of a buyer) in the note, the holder of the note in question would also have a security interest in the mortgage securing the note even in the absence of a separate assignment of the mortgage. (This Report does not address whether, under the facts of the *Ibanez* case, the holder of the note had an attached security interest in the note and, thus, qualified for the application of UCC § 9–203(g). Moreover, even if the holder had an attached security interest in the note and, thus, had a security interest in the mortgage, this would not, of itself, mean that the holder could enforce the mortgage without a recordable assignment of the mortgage to the holder. Whatever steps are required in order to enforce a mortgage in the absence of a recordable assignment are the province of real property law. The matter is addressed, in part, in the discussion of Question 4 below.)

[44] Official Comment 9 to UCC § 9–203 confirms this point: "Subsection (g) codifies the common-law rule that a transfer of an obligation secured by a security interest or other lien on personal or real property also transfers the security interest or lien." Pursuant to UCC § 1–302(a), the parties to the transaction may agree that an interest in the mortgage securing the note does not accompany the note, but such an agreement is unlikely. See, *e.g.,* Restatement (3d), Property (Mortgages) § 5.4, comment *a* ("It is conceivable that on rare occasions a mortgagee will wish to disassociate the obligation and the mortgage, but that result should follow only upon evidence that the parties to the transfer so agreed.").

[45] See Official Comment 6 to UCC § 9–308, which also observes that "this result helps prevent the separation of the mortgage (or other lien) from the note." Note also that, as explained in Official Comment 7 to UCC § 9–109, "It also follows from [UCC § 9–109(b)] that an attempt to obtain or perfect a security interest in a secured obligation by complying with non-Article 9 law, as by an assignment of record of a real-property mortgage, would be ineffective."

[46] Similarly, Official Comment 6 to UCC § 9–308 states that "this Article does not determine who has the power to release a mortgage of record. That issue is determined by real-property law."

PEB REPORT

Question Four—What Actions May a Person to Whom an Interest in a Mortgage Note Has Been Transferred, but Who Has not Taken a Recordable Assignment of the Mortgage, Take in Order to Become the Assignee of Record of the Mortgage Securing the Note?

In some states, a party without a recorded interest in a mortgage may not enforce the mortgage non-judicially. In such states, even though the buyer of a mortgage note (or a creditor to whom a security interest in the note has been granted to secure an obligation) automatically obtains corresponding rights in the mortgage,[47] this may be insufficient as a matter of applicable real estate law to enable that buyer or secured creditor to enforce the mortgage upon default of the maker if the buyer or secured creditor does not have a recordable assignment. The buyer or other secured party may attempt to obtain such a recordable assignment from the seller or debtor at the time it seeks to enforce the mortgage, but such an attempt may be unsuccessful.[48]

Article 9 of the UCC provides such a buyer or secured creditor a mechanism by which it can record its interest in the realty records in order to conduct a non-judicial foreclosure. UCC Section 9–607(b) provides that "if necessary to enable a secured party [including the buyer of a mortgage note] to exercise . . . the right of [its transferor]to enforce a mortgage nonjudicially," the secured party may record in the office in which the mortgage is recorded (i) a copy of the security agreement transferring an interest in the note to the secured party and (ii) the secured party's sworn affidavit in recordable form stating that default has occurred[49] and that the secured party is entitled to enforce the mortgage non-judicially.[50]

Illustration:

11. Same facts as Illustration 10. Maker has defaulted on the note and mortgage and Funder would like to enforce the mortgage non-judicially. In the relevant state, however, only a party with a recorded interest in a mortgage may enforce it non-judicially. Funder may record in the relevant mortgage recording office a copy of the signed writing pursuant to which the note was sold to Funder and a sworn affidavit stating that Maker has defaulted and that Funder is entitled to enforce the mortgage non-judicially. UCC § 9–607(b).

Summary

The Uniform Commercial Code provides four sets of rules that determine matters that are important in the context of enforcement of mortgage notes and the mortgages that secure them:

- First, in the case of a mortgage note that is a negotiable instrument, Article 3 of the UCC determines the identity of the person who is entitled to enforce the note and to whom the maker owes its payment obligation; payment to the person entitled to enforce the note discharges the maker's obligation, but failure to pay that party when the note is due constitutes dishonor.

- Second, for both negotiable and non-negotiable mortgage notes, Article 9 of the UCC determines whether a transferee of the note from its owner has obtained an attached property right in the note.

- Third, Article 9 of the UCC provides that a transferee of a mortgage note whose property right in the note has attached also automatically has an attached property right in the mortgage that secures the note.

- Finally, Article 9 of the UCC provides a mechanism by which the owner of a note and the mortgage securing it may, upon default of the maker of the note, record its interest in the mortgage in the realty records in order to conduct a non-judicial foreclosure.

---

[47] See discussion of Question Three, *supra*.

[48] In some cases, the seller or debtor may no longer be in business. In other cases, it may simply be unresponsive to requests for execution of documents with respect to a transaction in which it no longer has an economic interest. Moreover, in cases in which mortgage note was collateral for an obligation owed to the secured party, the defaulting debtor may simply be unwilling to assist its secured party. See Official Comment 8 to UCC § 9–607.

[49] The 2010 amendments to Article 9 (see fn. 8, *supra*) add language to this provision to clarify that "default," in this context, means default with respect to the note or other obligation secured by the mortgage.

[50] UCC § 9–607(b) does not address other conditions that must be satisfied for judicial or non-judicial enforcement of a mortgage.

As noted previously, these UCC rules do not resolve all issues in this field. The enforcement of real estate mortgages by foreclosure is primarily the province of a state's real property law, but legal determinations made pursuant to the four sets of UCC rules described in this Report will, in many cases, be central to administration of that law. In such cases, proper application of real property law requires proper application of the UCC rules discussed in this Report.

PEB COMMENTARY NO. 17
LIMITED LIABILITY PARTNERSHIPS UNDER
THE CHOICE OF LAW RULES OF ARTICLE 9
(June 29, 2012)

BACKGROUND

The location of an organization,[1] as "location" is determined under U.C.C. § 9–307, plays an important role in determining the local law that governs perfection, the effect of perfection or nonperfection, and the priority of a security interest. See U.C.C. § 9–301(1). As a general matter, a "registered organization" is located, as determined under U.C.C. § 9–307(e), in the State under whose laws the organization is organized while an organization that is not a registered organization is considered under U.C.C. § 9–307(b)(2) to be located in the State in which the organization has its place of business.[2]

The 2010 amendments to Article 9 clarified and expanded the definition of "registered organization" by providing in relevant part that the term "means an organization formed or organized solely under the law of a single State . . . by the filing of a public organic record with . . . the State. . . ." See U.C.C. § 9–102(a)(71)(2010).

The 2010 amendments also added a new definition of "public organic record." The term in relevant part means "a record that is available to the public for inspection and is . . . a record consisting of the record initially filed with . . . a State . . . to form or organize an organization and any record filed with . . . the State . . . which amends or restates the initial record." See U.C.C. § 9–102(a)(68)(2010).

ISSUE

Under the 2010 amendments to Article 9, should a limited liability partnership organized under the law of a State be considered a registered organization or an organization that is not a registered organization?

ANALYSIS

A full survey of the limited liability partnership law of each State is beyond the scope of this Commentary. This Commentary focuses upon the Uniform Partnership Act promulgated by the Uniform Law Commission in 1997 (the "1997 UPA") as a typical example of a State's limited liability partnership law.[3]

Under the 1997 UPA a general partnership is formed from the association of the partners and not from any public filing with the State. See 1997 UPA § 202. Under Section 1001 of the 1997 UPA a general partnership may become a limited liability partnership by obtaining a vote of its partners to become a limited liability partnership and by filing with the State a statement of qualification. The already existing partnership becomes a limited liability partnership on the date of the filing of the statement or on such later date as is designated in the statement. See 1997 UPA § 1001(e). Once the statement of qualification becomes effective, Section 306(c) of the 1997 UPA establishes a liability shield that protects the partnership's partners from vicarious personal liability for all partnership obligations incurred while the partnership is a

---

[1] The term "organization" is defined in U.C.C. § 1–201(b)(25) as a "person" other than an individual. The term "person" is defined in U.C.C. § 1–201(b)(27) to include not only an individual but also a corporation, partnership or other legal or commercial entity.

[2] If an organization that is not a registered organization has more than one place of business, it is considered under U.C.C. § 9–307(b)(3) to be located where its chief executive office is located.

[3] The reasoning and conclusions of this Commentary would also apply to legislation similar to the 1997 UPA that has the material attributes of the 1997 UPA discussed in this Commentary, including those provisions (discussed later in the text) that state that a limited liability partnership is a continuation of the pre-existing general partnership.

limited liability partnership. The partnership's status as a limited liability partnership remains in effect until the statement is canceled or revoked. *See* 1997 UPA §§ 105(d), 1001(e), and 1003.

Under the 1997 UPA a limited liability partnership is not a new entity; rather, the original partnership, formed by the association of the partners, continues as a partnership, albeit with the liability shield for its partners. Section 201(b) of the 1997 UPA states categorically: "A limited liability partnership continues to be the same entity that existed before the filing of a statement of qualification under Section 1001." An official comment elaborates:

[T]he filing of a statement of qualification does not create a "new" partnership. The filing partnership continues to be the same partnership entity that existed before the filing. Similarly, the amendment or cancellation of a statement of qualification under Section 105(d) or the revocation of a statement of qualification under Section 1003(c) does not terminate the partnership and create a "new" partnership. See Section 1003(d). Accordingly, a partnership remains the same entity regardless of a filing, cancellation, or revocation of a statement of qualification.

It follows that the statement of qualification filed with the State and by which a partnership becomes a limited liability partnership under the 1997 UPA is not a "public organic record" under the 2010 amendments to Article 9. The statement of qualification is not a record filed with the State to "form or organize" the partnership. It is the association of the partners that forms the partnership, not any record publicly filed with the State. Both conceptually and legally, a partnership is formed wholly apart from the filing of a statement of qualification with the State.

Because a limited liability partnership is not formed or organized by the filing of a public organic record, it cannot be a "registered organization" under the 2010 amendments to Article 9.[4]

The forgoing analysis does not suggest that a change of law for the characterization of a limited liability partnership, as discussed in this Commentary, was effected by the 2010 amendments to Article 9. Even before giving effect to the 2010 amendments, a limited liability partnership would not be considered a "registered organization." That is because the public filing of a statement of qualification would not be a record that "the State . . . must maintain . . . showing the organization to have been organized." *See* U.C.C. § 9–102(a)(70)(2009). The statement of qualification maintained by the State would show only that the partners have the benefit of the liability shield, not that the partnership itself has been organized.

CONCLUSION

The 2010 amendments to Article 9 did not change the law on whether a limited liability partnership should be characterized as a registered organization under Article 9. Whether before or after giving effect to the 2010 amendments to Article 9, a limited liability partnership organized under the law of a State that has adopted the 1997 UPA, or similar legislation having the material attributes of the 1997 UPA discussed in this Commentary, is an organization that is not a "registered organization" as defined by U.C.C. § 9–102(a).

Official Comment 11 to U.C.C. § 9–102 is amended by adding at the end of the penultimate sentence of the second paragraph of the Official Comment (the fifth paragraph after giving effect to the changes to the Official Comment made in connection with the 2010 amendments to Article 9):

Likewise, a limited liability partnership, which is a form of general partnership under the Uniform Partnership Act (1997), is not a "registered organization" even if it has filed a record that is a statement of qualification under Section 1001 of the Uniform Partnership Act (1997). The filing of the record does not form or organize the partnership. The filing only provides the partners in the general partnership with a limited liability shield and evidences that the general partnership has limited liability partnership status. See PEB Commentary No. 17. As discussed in PEB Commentary No. 17 the same conclusion would apply to a limited liability partnership formed under the law of state that has not adopted the Uniform Partnership Act (1997) but has adopted for limited liability partnerships similar legislation having the material attributes of that Act. Also as discussed in PEB Commentary No. 17, the same conclusion would apply whether before or after giving effect to the 2010 amendments to this Article.

---

[4] A limited liability partnership should be distinguished from a limited partnership. This Commentary does not address a limited partnership. A limited partnership is ordinarily considered to be a registered organization. *See* U.C.C. § 9–102 cmt. 11.

APPENDIX D

PEB COMMENTARY NO. 19
HAGUE SECURITIES CONVENTION'S EFFECT ON DETERMINING
THE APPLICABLE LAW FOR INDIRECTLY HELD SECURITIES
(April 11, 2017)

ISSUE

How does the Convention on the Law Applicable to Certain Rights in Respect of Securities Held with an Intermediary, concluded on July 5, 2006 (the "Hague Securities Convention" or "Convention") affect UCC Articles 8 and 9's determination of the applicable law for investment securities in the indirect holding system?

BACKGROUND AND GENERAL ASSESSMENT

The Hague Securities Convention meshes very well with UCC Articles 8 and 9, and in most instances will not lead to different results. The Convention carries certain complexities in determining the applicable law, and in some instances it may designate the law of a jurisdiction different from that designated by UCC Articles 8 and 9 alone, but difficulties of this nature are inevitable in any instrument affecting intermediated securities and designed to apply across multiple national systems.

The resolution of commercial law questions often depends as much on the applicable choice of law rules as it does on the substantive law of the jurisdiction that those choice of law rules designate. For questions concerning indirectly held securities the United States choice of law rules are provided primarily by UCC sections 8–110 and 9–305, which depending on the circumstances may designate either a jurisdiction that has enacted the substantive law of UCC Articles 8 and 9 or another jurisdiction. Other nations' choice of law rules differ, of course, and this diversity of choice of law rules with its corresponding diversity of possibly applicable substantive law may cause substantial difficulties in planning transactions and resolving disputes. To help ameliorate these problems, the Hague Securities Convention provides uniform choice of law rules among nations adhering to the Convention ("Contracting States"). The Convention has effect as a matter of United States law beginning on April 1, 2017 (the "Effective Date").[1]

This Commentary explains the Convention's primary interactions with the UCC.[2] Where the Convention applies, it prevails to that extent over a contrary UCC rule because of the Supremacy Clause of the Constitution; but otherwise the applicable UCC provisions continue in full force and effect. The Convention's text is available at the Web site of the Hague Conference on Private International Law, http://hcch.e-vision.nl.

I. Overview of the Convention

The Convention applies to a broad range of issues affecting securities held with an intermediary, in any case or transaction involving a choice between the law of different nations. The Convention may apply to transactions that are not obviously or initially international in character. It applies even to transactions completed before the Effective Date, but it takes care to preserve the intended effect of pre-Effective Date account agreements under most circumstances.

---

[1] See Convention art. 19(1) (Convention enters into force on the first day of the month following the expiration of three months after the deposit of the third instrument of ratification, acceptance, approval or accession). All article and paragraph references are to the Convention unless otherwise indicated, and all section and subsection references are to the 2014–2015 Official Text of the UCC.

The United States is implementing the Convention on a "self-executing" basis, so that the Convention itself will be controlling law within the United States with respect to cases or transactions to which it applies. See Senate Exec. Rept. 114–15, at 7 (2016) (Report of Senate Committee on Foreign Relations, setting forth a resolution that the Senate advises and consents to ratification of the Convention, with a declaration that the Convention is self-executing). No other declarations were made as a part of the United States ratification.

[2] Useful further sources on the Convention include Christophe Bernasconi and Harry C. Sigman, The Hague Convention on the Law Applicable to Certain Rights in Respect of Securities held with an Intermediary (Hague Securities Convention), 2005 Uniform L. Rev. 117; James S. Rogers, Conflict of Laws for Transactions in Securities Held Through Intermediaries, 39 Cornell Int'l L.J. 285 (2006); and Carl S. Bjerre and Sandra M. Rocks, A Transactional Approach to the Hague Securities Convention, 3 Capital Markets L. J. 109 (2008). A uniquely official and exhaustive resource is Roy Goode, Hideki Kanda, and Karl Kreuzer, with the assistance of Christophe Bernasconi (Permanent Bureau), Explanatory Report on the Hague Convention on the Law Applicable to Certain Rights in Respect of Securities Held with an Intermediary (2005) (hereinafter "Explanatory Report").

Under the Convention's primary rule the applicable law is determined by either of two provisions appearing in the account agreement between a securities intermediary and its entitlement holder, namely a general governing law clause or a specialized clause that focuses directly on the group of commercial law issues in question. The Convention's primary rule is thus very similar to UCC subsections 8–110(b), (e)(1) and (2), and 9–305(a)(3). However this primary rule unlike the UCC rules operates only if the intermediary has, at the time of the agreement, an office in the applicable jurisdiction that is engaged in a regular activity of maintaining securities accounts (usually called a "Qualifying Office"). If the account agreement contains neither of the two above provisions, or if the Qualifying Office requirement is not met, the Convention provides a series of fall-back rules somewhat different from those of the UCC. For perfection of security interests by filing, the Convention accommodates UCC Article 9's choice of law rule designating the substantive law of the location of the debtor, with certain exceptions.

Though overall the Convention meshes very well with UCC Articles 8 and 9, in some instances it may designate the law of a different jurisdiction (whether a different nation or a different U.S. state). In addition to differences arising from the Qualifying Office requirement (see Part II for further discussion), differences could notably arise regarding the jurisdiction in which to perfect a security interest by filing when the account agreement designates the law of a non-U.S. jurisdiction, or when the debtor is located in a non-U.S. jurisdiction (see Part III), and regarding the continued perfection of a security interest following an amendment to the account agreement's designation of governing law (see Part IV). As indicated above, such instances are generally manageable by sound transactional planning.

II.   The Convention's Scope and Primary Rule

The Convention applies to "securities held with an intermediary,"[3] a scope generally comparable in UCC terms to security entitlements created by a securities intermediary's book-entry credit of a security under section 8–501(b)(1).[4] The Convention applies broadly to all instances "involving a choice between the laws of different States" (i.e. nations),[5] and can accordingly apply by reason of any of many elements, including without limitation a non-U.S. location of a party involved in the transaction, a non-U.S. party asserting an adverse claim, non-U.S. securities being credited to the securities account, or non-U.S. law being specified by the account agreement or other transaction document. Indeed one may wish to plan all indirect holding system transactions with the Convention as well as UCC Article 8 in mind, because even in transactions that appear wholly domestic, international factors may in fact be present (for example, if the securities intermediary holds securities for the entitlement holder through a non-U.S. intermediary) or may later become present (for example, if a non-U.S. party acquires an interest in or asserts an adverse claim to assets credited to the account).

---

[3]   Convention arts. 2(1), 1(1)(f).

[4]   However, the definition of security may differ as between the UCC and the Convention. Compare section 8–102(a)(15) with Convention art. 1(1)(a) (defining security as "any shares, bonds, or other financial instruments or financial assets (other than cash), or any interest therein." The Convention definition is "intentionally drawn in very broad terms so as to accommodate changes in market practice"; the test is "a fluid one which is to be determined by reference to the practice and perception of the relevant market at the material time." Explanatory Report ¶ 1–2, 1–3. The Explanatory Report suggests that financial futures and options, which may be commodity contracts under the UCC, are securities within the scope of the Convention. Id. ¶ 1–2.

There is no doubt that the Convention, like UCC Article 8, applies to multiple tier holding arrangements, such as where the account holder holds through a broker which in turn holds through a clearing corporation. See Explanatory Report ¶ 1–4 ("in light of the intermediated holding system, which may involve a chain of intermediaries between the account holder and the issuer, [the phrase 'or any interest therein' in article 1(1)(a)'s definition of securities] also refers to the interest which the account holder's intermediary (or any other intermediary in the chain) has in securities held with its intermediary").

On a related point, UCC Article 8 provides for security entitlements not only to securities (defined relatively narrowly in section 8–102(a)(15)) but also to a broad range of other financial assets, including "any property . . . held . . . in a securities account if the securities intermediary has expressly agreed . . . that the property is to be treated as a financial asset . . . ." Section 8–102(a)(9)(iii). The Convention's above-noted definition of security expressly includes financial assets and to that extent may be somewhat more expansive than UCC Article 8's definition of security, but it is important to note that the Convention neither defines financial asset nor permits the parties' agreement alone to be determinative.

[5]   Convention art. 3. The Convention refers to "cases" rather than "instances," but the Convention's term should not be misunderstood as suggesting that the Convention applies only in litigation.

APPENDIX D

The Convention applies regardless of whether the law that it designates is that of a Contracting State, though of course the Convention itself is the law only of Contracting States.[6] The Convention law applies to events that have occurred before an insolvency proceeding, notwithstanding the opening of the proceeding.[7] As is standard in international instruments, the Convention is to be interpreted in light of the need to promote uniformity in its application.[8] Contracting States may refuse the Convention's choice of law rules only in very rare cases.[9]

For securities held with an intermediary the Convention determines the choice of law for a broad range of issues specified in article 2(1). These include all of the issues specified by sections 8–110(b), 9–305(a)(3) and the applicable portions of 9–305(c), relating to acquisition or disposition of interests, perfection and priority of security interests, and taking free of adverse claims. The table below shows the correlations between these two sets of issues, as well as highlighting other issues covered by Convention article 2(1) that reach further than those UCC sections. In this connection it is also important to note that the Convention's issues affecting a "disposition" are not limited to security interests, because Convention article 1(h) defines that term as also including other transfers of limited interests plus outright transfers.

UCC provision	*Convention provision(s)*
subsection 8–110(b)(1): acquisition of a security entitlement from the securities intermediary	article 2(1)(a): legal nature and effects against the intermediary and third parties of the rights resulting from a credit of securities to a securities account
subsection 8–110(b)(2): rights and duties of the securities intermediary and entitlement holder arising out of a security entitlement	article 2(1)(a): legal nature and effects against the intermediary and third parties of the rights resulting from a credit of securities to a securities account (emphasis added)
subsection 8–110(b)(3): whether the securities intermediary owes any duties to an adverse claimant to a security entitlement	article 2(1)(e): duties, if any, of an intermediary to a person other than the account holder who asserts in competition with the account holder or another person an interest in securities held with that intermediary
subsection 8–110(b)(4): whether an adverse claim can be asserted against a person who acquires a security entitlement from the securities intermediary or a person who purchases a security entitlement or interest therein from an entitlement holder	article 2(1)(a): legal nature and effects against the intermediary and third parties of the rights resulting from a credit of securities to a securities account (emphasis added)
	article 2(1)(d): whether a person's interest in securities held with an intermediary extinguishes or has priority over another person's interest

---

[6] Convention art. 9.

[7] Convention art. 8. On the other hand, the Convention is not otherwise an insolvency choice of law convention. Except for the issues referred to in article 2(1), the Convention does not determine which jurisdiction's law applies to insolvency issues such as the ranking of claims or the avoidability of transfers.

[8] Convention art. 13. This may mean avoiding purely United States canons of interpretation and taking into account decisions of courts of other Contracting States. Cf. section 1–103(a)(3) (UCC to be applied to promote underlying purpose and policy of "mak[ing] uniform the law among the various jurisdictions").

[9] Convention art. 11(1) ("manifestly contrary to the public policy of the forum"), 11(2) (substantive provisions of the forum which, "irrespective of rules of conflict of laws, must be applied even to international situations"). Even these narrow exceptions are further limited by article 11(3).

UCC provision	Convention provision(s)
subsection 9–305(a)(3): perfection, the effect of perfection or nonperfection, and the priority of a security interest in a security entitlement or securities account	article 2(1)(b): legal nature and effects against the intermediary and third parties of a disposition of securities held with an intermediary (emphasis added)
subsection 9–201(a): the third-party rather than strictly bilateral effects of attachment of a security interest	article 2(1)(c): requirements, if any, for perfection of a disposition of securities held with an intermediary
not statutorily addressed: the characterization of a transfer as being outright or by way of security	article 2(1)(d): whether a person's interest in securities held with an intermediary extinguishes or has priority over another person's interest
subsection 9–305(c)(1): perfection of a security interest in investment property by filing	article 2(1)(c): requirements, if any, for perfection of a disposition of securities held with an intermediary
subsection 9–305(c)(2): automatic perfection of a security interest in investment property created by a broker or securities intermediary	article 2(1)(c): requirements, if any, for perfection of a disposition of securities held with an intermediary
subsection 1–301(a): requirements for foreclosure and the like of security interests and other dispositions	article 2(1)(f): requirements, if any, for the realisation of an interest in securities held with an intermediary
subsection 1–301(a): transferee's rights to proceeds and the like as against transferor	article 2(1)(g): whether a disposition of securities held with an intermediary extends to entitlements to dividends, income, or other distributions, or to redemption, sale or other proceeds

The Convention does not cover issues under UCC Article 8's direct holding system, and does not cover rights or duties of the issuer even in the indirect holding system.[10] The Convention also does not cover purely contractual matters between the securities intermediary and its entitlement holder, such as the enforceability of an arbitration clause in the account agreement, or the purely two-party aspects of attachment of a security interest.[11]

The Convention's primary choice of law rule for the issues above is highly parallel to that of the UCC, because under both bodies of law the rule depends directly on either of two provisions of the account agreement.[12] Under Convention article 4(1), just as under UCC sections 8–110(e)(2) and 9–305(a)(3), if the agreement contains an express governing law clause, then the law specified by that clause is also the law designated by the Convention.[13] Alternatively, under Convention article 4(1) similarly to UCC sections 8–110(e)(1) and 9–305(a)(3), if the agreement contains a specialized clause expressly designating a certain jurisdiction's law for the group of commercial law issues in question, then that jurisdiction's law will control,

---

[10]   Convention art. 2(3)(c).

[11]   Convention art. 2(3)(a).

[12]   The account agreement in question is the one between the account holder and the intermediary with which the account holder has its account, rather than another intermediary at a higher tier. See Convention article 1(1)(e) (agreement with "relevant intermediary") and (g) (defining relevant intermediary as "the intermediary that maintains the securities account for the account holder"); subsections 8–110(e)(1) and (2) (agreement between the entitlement holder and "its" intermediary); cf. subsection 8–112(c) (directing creditor process to "the securities intermediary with whom the debtor's securities account is maintained" as a matter of substantive law). If an original account agreement is later amended, for example by a control agreement providing that the account is now governed by a law different from that originally designated, then the term "account agreement" refers to the original agreement as amended. See Explanatory Report ¶ 1–15 ("The definition [of account agreement] does not require that the account agreement fulfil any formal requirements. . . . [I]f in writing [it] may consist of one or more documents."). Amendments to an account agreement changing the governing law are further discussed in Part IV below.

[13]   Convention art. 4(1), first sentence ("The law applicable to all the issues specified in Article 2(1) is the law in force in the State expressly agreed in the account agreement as the State whose law governs the account agreement . . . "). However, with respect to the Convention, the Qualifying Office test must also be met, as discussed below.

even if the jurisdiction is different from the one specified in the governing law clause.[14] Both bodies of law accommodate agreement provisions designating the law of either a nation (called a "State" in the Convention) or a U.S. state, Canadian province or the like (called a "territorial unit of a Multi-unit State" in the Convention).[15] Both bodies of law also generally eliminate renvoi, meaning that only the jurisdiction's substantive law applies, not its conflicts of law rules.[16]

The only notable exception to this parallelism between the Convention and the UCC is that the Convention's primary rule applies only if the intermediary has, at the time of the agreement, a Qualifying Office in the applicable jurisdiction engaged in a regular activity of maintaining securities accounts.[17] The Convention clarifies this requirement by specifying safe-harbor activities that satisfy the requirement[18] and by also specifying certain mechanical functions that do not in and of themselves satisfy it.[19] Of importance to agreements designating the law of a U.S. state, the Qualifying Office requirement is applied broadly to Multi-unit States, so that the office may be located in any territorial unit of the same Multi-unit State, rather than necessarily in the particular territorial unit designated by the agreement.[20] Thus an account agreement expressly governed by the law of New York and specifying no other jurisdiction as governing the Convention's article 2(1) issues effectively designates New York law under the Convention even if the intermediary has a Qualifying Office only in New Jersey.

---

[14] Convention art. 4(1), first sentence (" . . . or, if the account agreement expressly provides that another law is applicable to all such issues, that other law."). Here too, with respect to the Convention, the Qualifying Office test must also be met, as discussed below.

Because of the Convention's reference to "all such issues," a clause is ineffective if it singles out only certain issues for treatment under this choice of law rule.

In U.S. account agreements these specialized clauses will presumably be the exception rather than the rule, with parties usually using only the governing law clause just discussed. However when the account agreement uses the specialized clause to designate a jurisdiction different from that of the governing law clause (or for some reason uses the specialized clause without a governing law clause at all), drafters should note that a clause simply tracking the language of section 8–110(e)(1) might not satisfy the present provision of article 4(1), or vice versa. Under section 8–110(e)(1) the specialized clause should provide that a particular jurisdiction is the securities intermediary's jurisdiction, while under article 4(1) the specialized clause should provide that the particular jurisdiction's law is applicable to all issues specified in article 2(1). A clause satisfying both the UCC and Convention provisions might read, for example, "The parties hereto agree that the State of New York is the securities intermediary's jurisdiction for purposes of UCC Article 8 and that the law in force therein is applicable to all the issues specified in Article 2(1) of the Hague Securities Convention."

Nevertheless for account agreements entered into before the Effective Date a clause tracking the language of section 8–110(e)(1) does suffice under article 4(1), as discussed in Part IV below.

[15] Convention arts. 1(1)(m) (defining Multi-unit State as "a State within which two or more territorial units of that State, or both the State and one or more of its territorial units, have their own rules of law in respect of any of the issues specified in Article 2(1)"), 12(1)(a) ("If the account holder and the relevant intermediary have agreed on the law of a specified territorial unit of a Multi-unit State . . . the references to "State" in the first sentence of Article 4(1) are to that territorial unit"); section 8–110(e)(1), (2) ("the law of a particular jurisdiction").

To the extent that U.S. federal law applies to the article 2(1) issues, the Convention recognizes that an account agreement designating the law of a particular U.S. state also incorporates that federal law. See Convention arts. 12(2)(a) (applying "the law of the Multi-unit State itself"), 4(1), first sentence (designating "the law in force in" the jurisdiction rather than the law "of" the jurisdiction). For example, the TRADES Regulations governing book-entry interests in Treasury securities, 31 C.F.R. 357, contain substantive provisions addressing the perfection and super-priority of security interests in favor of the United States in security entitlements of Federal Reserve Bank participants. Such provisions are included within article 12(2)(a), as are the parallel provisions contained in regulations governing securities issued by various government-sponsored entities.

[16] Convention art. 10 (" 'law' means the law in force in a State other than its choice of law rules"); sections 8–110(b), 9–305(a)(3) and 9–305(c)(3) ("local law"). For perfection of security interests by filing, the Convention provides a rule on choice of law among the states of the United States that in most instances accommodates UCC Article 9's usual location-of-the-debtor filing rule. See Part III below.

[17] Convention art. 4(1), second sentence.

[18] The Qualifying Office requirement is conclusively met if the office either "effects or monitors entries to securities accounts" or "administers payments or corporate actions relating to securities held with the intermediary". Id. The securities accounts maintained by the office need not necessarily include the particular securities accounts to which the account agreement in question relates.

[19] Convention art. 4(2) (mere location of technology supporting bookkeeping or data processing; mere operation of call centers for communication with account holders, etc.).

[20] Convention art. 12(1)(b).

If the account agreement contains neither of the express clauses contemplated by the primary rule, or if the Qualifying Office test is not satisfied with respect to such a clause, the Convention provides certain fallback rules that differ in their details from the fallback rules of section 8–110(e).[21]

III. Preservation of UCC Article 9's Location-of-Debtor Rule for Perfection of Security Interests by Filing

Though the Convention generally eliminates renvoi, it generally preserves UCC Article 9's own choice of law rule for perfection of a security interest in indirectly held securities by the filing of a financing statement. This UCC Article 9 rule designates the law of the location of the debtor,[22] which keeps the jurisdiction for filing for this type of collateral the same as that for virtually all other types of personal property.[23] Convention article 12(2)(b)'s preservation of the UCC Article 9 rule may be explained by example:

> Debtor is using the Japanese securities credited to its securities account with Intermediary as collateral for a loan from Lender; Debtor is a registered organization organized solely under the law of Texas; and the account agreement between Debtor and Intermediary provides that the agreement is governed by the law of New York. If Lender wished to perfect by, for example, obtaining control by agreement under sections 8–106(d)(2) and 9–106, then the Convention's primary rule would designate the applicable law as New York (assuming that the Qualifying Office requirement is met); but if Lender wishes to perfect by filing a financing statement (perhaps because the value of other personal property collateral in the transaction makes the securities account of secondary importance), then Convention article 12(2)(b) accommodates the UCC Article 9 location-of-debtor rule designating the applicable law for filing as Texas.[24] Accordingly Lender should file in Texas, in the office designated by section 9–501(a) as enacted in Texas, and should follow the substantive rules for financing statements set forth in part 5 of Article 9 as enacted in Texas.

It is important to note, however, that the Convention provision also narrows the UCC Article 9 rule somewhat. Specifically, the Convention provision does not apply to cases in which the account agreement

---

[21] The two sets of fallback rules are as follows:

	UCC § 8–110(e)	Convention
First fallback	subsection (e)(3): jurisdiction of an office at which the securities account is maintained, as expressly provided in the account agreement.	article 5(1): State of a particular office through which the intermediary entered into the account agreement, as expressly and unambiguously stated in the account agreement, if Qualifying Office requirement is met with respect to that office.
Second fallback	subsection (e)(4): jurisdiction in which the office serving the entitlement holder's account is located, as identified in an account statement.	article 5(2): State in which the intermediary is organized.
Third fallback	subsection (e)(5): jurisdiction of the chief executive office of the intermediary.	article 5(3): State in which the intermediary has its principal place of business.

Seeking an abundance of clarity the Convention also enumerates criteria that do not determine the applicable law, just as UCC Article 8 does. See Convention art. 6; cf. section 8–110(f).

[22] Section 9–305(c)(1).

[23] See generally section 9–301(1). The location of the debtor is determined under section 9–307.

[24] Convention article 12(2)(b) provides: "In applying this Convention [i.e. in following the account agreement's and article 4(1)'s designation of New York law] . . . if the law in force in a territorial unit of a Multi-unit State [i.e. New York's section 9–305(c)(1)] designates the law of another territorial unit of that State [i.e. Texas as the location of the debtor under section 9–307(e)] to govern perfection by public filing, recording or registration, the law of that other territorial unit [i.e. Texas's filing-office and substantive filing law] governs that issue."

designates the law of, or the debtor is located for UCC Article 9 purposes in, a jurisdiction other than a territorial unit of the United States.[25]

It was noted above that the Qualifying Office rule applies broadly to Multi-unit States, and this same breadth applies when article 4(1) is applied with the overlay of article 12(2)(b). On the facts of the example above, the Convention designates Texas as the applicable law for filing even if Intermediary's only Qualifying Office is in New Jersey and not in Texas or New York.[26]

IV. Pre-Convention Account Agreements and Other Change of Law Matters

The Convention generally applies as described above to all account agreements even if they were entered into before the Effective Date.[27] However, most pre-Convention transactions do not need to be amended or renegotiated in order to retain their intended effects. To illustrate, suppose that an account agreement, entered into before the Effective Date, provides "This agreement shall be governed by the law of New York." Until the Effective Date, New York was the applicable law under the UCC alone because of the agreement's governing law clause under subsection 8–110(e)(2). From the Effective Date forward (provided only that the Convention's usual Qualifying Office requirement is satisfied), New York continues to be the applicable law for Convention purposes under articles 16(1) and 4(1).

A slightly more complex variation is dealt with by Convention article 16(3). Suppose that the pre-Effective Date account agreement provides "This agreement shall be governed by the law of New York, except that California is the securities intermediary's jurisdiction for purposes of the Uniform Commercial Code." In this case, until the Effective Date, California was the applicable law under the UCC alone because of the agreement's securities intermediary clause under subsection 8–110(e)(1). From the Effective Date forward (provided only that the Convention's usual Qualifying Office requirement is satisfied), California

---

[25] This is illustrated by two variations on the main example above. First, suppose that the account agreement designates the law of England rather than New York, with Debtor being located in Texas as in the main example. On these facts, UCC Article 9 standing alone formerly called for filing in Texas, but under the Convention English law applies, including any filing provisions thereunder. UCC section 9–305(c)(1)'s provision for filing in Texas is irrelevant because the Convention's primary rule does not in the first instance designate the law of any UCC jurisdiction and hence article 12(2)(b) is not triggered. The Convention's place-of-filing provision is limited by Convention articles 4 and 5 and UCC Article 9's place-of-filing provision is not similarly limited by sections 8–110 or 9–305(a)(3).

Second, suppose that the account agreement designates the law of New York as in the main example, but that Debtor is a non-U.S. corporation with its chief executive office in Ontario, Canada, and that the law of Ontario generally requires filing, recordation or the like as specified in UCC section 9–307(c). For Article 9 purposes Debtor is thus located in Ontario under section 9–307(b). On these facts, UCC Article 9 standing alone formerly caused Ontario law (including Ontario's substantive filing provisions) to apply; but under the Convention New York law applies, including New York's substantive filing provisions, and most notably New York's designation in § 9–501 of a New York filing office. The key to this result is that Convention article 12(2)(b) has no application here, because Ontario is not "another territorial unit of [the same] State [agreed upon in the account agreement]," and as a result the transaction is governed by the substantive law designated by Convention article 4(1) alone.

Many otherwise non-U.S. debtors are located in the District of Columbia under section 9–307(c)'s exception to section 9–307(b), and such cases are fully accommodated by Convention article 12(2)(b) so that the District of Columbia is the jurisdiction for perfection by filing (not unlike the main Texas example in the text above). But section 9–307(c) has no bearing on the Ontario example just discussed, because it applies only "[i]f subsection (b) does not apply," which is not the case here. That is, the fact that filing in Ontario is not effective as a matter of U.S. law results from the limitations of Convention article 12(2)(b) itself, rather than from any aspect of Ontario law addressed by section 9–307(c).

Separately from its limitations on section 9–305(c)(1), the Convention also does not preserve section 9–305(c)(2)'s choice of law rule for automatic perfection of a security interest in investment property created by a broker or securities intermediary, but this is of little practical importance because the rule is uniform across U.S. jurisdictions and by its nature requires no location-directed action such as filing.

[26] Convention art. 12(1)(b).

[27] Convention art. 16(1) ("References in this Convention to an account agreement include an account agreement entered into before this Convention entered into force in accordance with Article 19(1)"). The rules described are inapplicable to account agreements that expressly refer to the Convention. Convention art. 16(2).

continues to be the applicable law for Convention purposes under article 16(3).[28] Note that California would not be the applicable law for Convention purposes under articles 16(1) and 4(1) alone.[29]

Convention article 15 addresses conflicts between a party that acquires rights before the Effective Date under the law that applies at that time, and another party that acquires rights after the Effective Date under the law designated by the Convention. Convention article 15 provides that such a conflict is to be resolved under the law designated by the Convention. This rule should rarely be disruptive to the first party, particularly in light of article 16 as just discussed. The rule promotes a quite substantial interest in the clarity of results that arises from the Convention's prompt and broad application.

Change of law matters can also arise after the Effective Date when an amendment to the account agreement designates a new applicable law. For example, if a securities account initially governed by English law is used as collateral for a U.S. lender that wishes to perfect the security interest using a control agreement under New York law, then the lender might build into the control agreement an amendment to the account agreement changing its governing law clause, with the debtor's and intermediary's consent to that amendment of course being necessary. Assuming such an amendment satisfies Convention article 4(1), including the Qualifying Office requirement applied at the time of the amendment, then article 7(3) provides for the law designated by the amendment to govern most of the Convention's article 2(1) issues. However, to protect pre-amendment interests of third parties, article 7(4) provides for the pre-amendment law to continue governing a handful of issues,[30] without limitation as to time. UCC Article 9 is broadly similar, with the law designated by the amendment generally governing,[31] and protections for pre-amendment interests being a subject for the new jurisdiction's substantive law.[32]

V. Amendment to Official Comments

Amendments to some of the Official Comments to the UCC sections affected by the Convention are appropriate in order to make better known the interactions discussed above. The Official Comments to section 8–110, 9–305, 9–301 and 1–301 are hereby amended as shown in Appendix A, effective on the Effective Date.

Appendix A [to PEB Commentary 19]

Amendments to Official Comments

Section 8–110:

1. This section deals with applicability and choice of law issues concerning Article 8. The distinction between the direct and indirect holding systems plays a significant role in determining the governing law. An investor in the direct holding system is registered on the books of the issuer and/or has possession of a

---

[28] Convention article 16(3) provides in pertinent part: "Any express terms of an account agreement which would have the effect, under the rules of the State whose law governs that agreement, that the law in force in a particular State, or a territorial unit of a particular Multi-unit State, applies to any of the issues specified in Article 2(1), shall have the effect that such law governs all the issues specified in Article 2(1), provided that the relevant intermediary had, at the time the agreement was entered into, an office in that State which satisfied the condition specified in the second sentence of Article 4(1)." As applied to the example in the text, under New York law alone, the quoted clause would have the effect that California law governs the section 8–110(b) issues that are also included in article 2(1), and as a result (again subject to the Qualifying Office requirement) the clause is bootstrapped so as to govern all of the other issues in article 2(1) as well.

This rule does not apply to pre-Convention account agreements that contain an express reference to the Convention, and its scope may be further limited by declaration. See arts. 16(2) and (3). The United States is not making any such declaration, though of course on this point as elsewhere in the Convention, account should be taken of declarations made by a non-U.S. Contracting State to the extent enforcement in that Contracting State is foreseeable.

[29] After all, the reference to California satisfies neither of article 4(1)'s alternatives: it is not a governing law clause, and it does not "expressly provide that another law is applicable to all [the] issues [specified in article 2(1)]".

[30] The pre-amendment law notably continues to govern perfection of pre-amendment interests, and most issues of their priority as against competing pre-amendment interests. However these protections do not apply to a party that has consented to the amendment. Convention art. 7(4), (5).

[31] See section 9–305(a)(3).

[32] When the new jurisdiction's substantive law is the UCC, a party with a security interest perfected under the pre-amendment law has a limited grace period, usually of four months, within which the interest remains perfected and the secured party can re-perfect under the law of the new jurisdiction. Section 9–316(f), (g). The UCC has no explicit provision protecting pre-amendment interests other than security interests.

APPENDIX D

security certificate. Accordingly, the jurisdiction of incorporation of the issuer or location of the certificate determine the applicable law. By contrast, an investor in the indirect holding system has a security entitlement, which is a bundle of rights against the securities intermediary with respect to a security, rather than a direct interest in the underlying security. Accordingly, in the rules for the indirect holding system, the jurisdiction of incorporation of the issuer of the underlying security or the location of any certificates that might be held by the intermediary or a higher tier intermediary, do not determine the applicable law.

For securities in the indirect holding system, but not the direct holding system, this section's provisions are subject to the Convention on the Law Applicable to Certain Rights in Respect of Securities Held with an Intermediary (the "Convention" or "Hague Securities Convention"), to which the United States is a party. The Convention's primary rule is highly similar to this section, though there are potential differences as well. See Comments 3 and 5 through 7 below and PEB Commentary No. 19, dated April 11, 2017.

The Hague Securities Convention applies broadly to all instances "involving a choice between the laws of different [nations]", and can accordingly apply by reason of any of many elements, including without limitation a non-U.S. location of a party involved in the transaction, a non-U.S. party asserting an adverse claim, non-U.S. securities being credited to the securities account, or non-U.S. law being specified by the account agreement or other transaction document. Indeed one may wish to plan all indirect holding system transactions with the Hague Securities Convention as well as UCC Article 8 in mind, because even in transactions that appear wholly domestic, international factors may in fact be present (for example, if the securities intermediary holds securities for the entitlement holder through a non-U.S. intermediary) or may later become present (for example, if a non-U.S. party acquires an interest in or asserts an adverse claim to assets credited to the account).

In each of subsections (a), (b) and (c), the phrase "local law" refers to the law of a jurisdiction other than its conflict of laws rules. See Restatement (Second) of Conflict of Laws § 4.

2.   [. . .]

Although subsection (a) provides that the issuer's rights and duties concerning registration of transfer are governed by the law of the issuer's jurisdiction, other matters related to registration of transfer, such as appointment of a guardian for a registered owner or the existence of agency relationships, might be governed by another jurisdiction's law. Neither this section nor Section 1–105 (Revised Section 1–301) deals with what law governs the appointment of the administrator or executor; that question is determined under generally applicable choice of law rules.

3.   Subsection (b) ~~provides~~and, where the Hague Securities Convention applies, article 2(1) thereof provide that the law ~~of the securities intermediary's jurisdiction governs~~governing the issues concerning the indirect holding system that are dealt with in Article 8~~.~~ are principally determined by the agreement between the securities intermediary and the entitlement holder governing the securities account.

Paragraphs (1) and (2) and Hague Securities Convention article 2(1)(a) cover the matters dealt with in the Article 8 rules defining the concept of security entitlement and specifying the duties of securities intermediaries. Paragraph (3) ~~provides that the law of the security intermediary's jurisdiction determines~~and Convention article 2(1)(e) cover whether the intermediary owes any duties to an adverse claimant. Paragraph (4) ~~provides that the law of the security intermediary's jurisdiction determines~~and Convention article 2(1)(a) and (d) cover whether adverse claims can be asserted against entitlement holders and others.

~~Subsection (e) determines what is a "securities intermediary's jurisdiction." The policy of subsection (b)~~Subsection (e) and Hague Securities Convention article 4 provide that the account agreement may effectively determine the applicable law for the foregoing issues in either of two ways. Most directly and doubtless most frequently, under both subsection (e)(2) and article 4(1), the law chosen by the parties to govern the account agreement determines the applicable law. Alternatively, subsection (e)(1) and article 4(1) provide mutually comparable rules that require slightly different phrasing in the agreement. Under subsection (e)(1), if the account agreement expressly provides that a particular jurisdiction is the securities intermediary's jurisdiction for purposes of UCC Article 8, then that provision determines the applicable law, even if the agreement's overall governing law clause (if any) is different. Under Convention article 4(1)'s comparable rule, if the account agreement expressly provides that a particular jurisdiction's law is applicable to all the issues specified in article 2(1) of the Hague Securities Convention, then that provision determines the applicable law, even if the agreement's overall governing law clause (if any) is different. The policy is to ensure that a securities intermediary and all of its entitlement holders can look to a single, readily-identifiable body of law to determine their rights and duties. ~~Accordingly, subsection (e) sets out a sequential series of tests to facilitate identification of that body of law. Paragraph (1) of subsection (e) permits specification of the securities intermediary's jurisdiction by agreement. In the absence of such a specification, the law chosen by the parties to govern the securities account determines the securities intermediary's jurisdiction. See paragraph (2). Because the policy of this section~~

Where the Hague Securities Convention applies, the foregoing provisions of an account agreement effectively determine the applicable law only if the intermediary, at the time of the agreement, had an office in the designated jurisdiction (which may be anywhere in the United States if the account agreement specifies a state of the United States) that is engaged in a regular activity of maintaining securities accounts (a "Qualifying Office"). However, because the policy of this section and the Convention is to enable parties to determine, in advance and with certainty, what law will apply to transactions governed by this Article, the validation of the parties' selection of governing law by agreement is not conditioned upon a determination that the jurisdiction whose law is chosen bear a "reasonable relation" to the transaction. See Section 4A-507; compare Section 1-105(1) (Revised Section 1-301(a)). That is also true with respect to the similar provisions in subsection (d) of this section and in Section 9-305. The remaining paragraphs in subsection (e) and Convention article 5 contain additional default rules for determining the ~~securities intermediary's jurisdiction~~applicable law.

The Hague Securities Convention applies regardless of whether the law that it designates is that of a nation adhering thereto, though of course the Convention itself is the law only of adhering nations. The Convention applies to account agreements entered into before as well as after the Convention's effectiveness in the United States. However, for pre-Convention agreements that specify that a state of the United States is the securities intermediary's jurisdiction for purposes of UCC Article 8 and that do not expressly refer to the Convention, article 16(3) preserves the agreements' intended effect, by treating them as providing that the specified state's law is applicable to all the issues specified in article 2(1), if the Qualifying Office test is met. There is no doubt that the Convention, like UCC Article 8, applies to multiple tier holding arrangements, such as where the account holder holds through a broker which in turn holds through a clearing corporation.

Subsection (f) makes explicit a point that is implicit in the UCC Article 8 description of a security entitlement as a bundle of rights against the intermediary with respect to a security or other financial asset, rather than as a direct interest in the underlying security or other financial asset. The governing law for relationships in the indirect holding system is not determined by such matters as the jurisdiction of incorporation of the issuer of the securities held through the intermediary, or the location of any physical certificates held by the intermediary or a higher tier intermediary. Hague Securities Convention article 6 is in accord.

[4. . . .]

5. The following examples illustrate how a ~~court in a jurisdiction which has enacted this section~~forum applying these rules would determine the governing law:

Example 1: John Doe, a resident of Kansas, maintains a securities account with Able & Co. Able is incorporated in Delaware. Its chief executive offices are located in Illinois. The office where Doe transacts business with Able is located in Missouri. The agreement between Doe and Able ~~specifies~~provides that it is generally governed by the law of New York but also that Illinois is the securities intermediary's (Able's) jurisdiction for purposes of UCC Article 8 and that Illinois law is applicable to all the issues specified in article 2(1) of the Hague Securities Convention. Through the account, Doe holds securities of a Colorado corporation, which Able holds through Clearing Corporation. The rules of Clearing Corporation provide that the rights and duties of Clearing Corporation and its participants are governed by New York law. Subsection (a) specifies that a controversy concerning the rights and duties as between the issuer and Clearing Corporation is governed by Colorado law. Subsections (b) and (e) specify that a controversy concerning the rights and duties as between the Clearing Corporation and Able is governed by New York law, and that a controversy concerning the rights and duties as between Able and Doe is governed by Illinois law. Even if other facts cause the Hague Securities Convention to apply (see Comment 1), the Convention does not change the subsection (b) and (e) results, if at the time of the respective agreements Clearing Corporation and Able had offices in the United States engaged in a regular activity of maintaining securities accounts. The Convention does not apply to the subsection (a) result.

Example 2: Same facts as to Doe and Able as in Example 1. Through the account, Doe holds securities of a Senegalese corporation, which Able holds through Clearing Corporation. Clearing Corporation's operations are located in Belgium, and its rules and agreements with its participants provide that they are governed by Belgian law. Clearing Corporation holds the securities through a custodial account at the Paris branch office of Global Bank, which is organized under English law. The agreement between Clearing Corporation and Global Bank provides that it is governed by French law. Subsection (a) specifies that a controversy concerning the rights and duties as between the issuer and Global Bank is governed by Senegalese law. ~~Subsections (b) and (e) specify~~Prior to United States implementation of the Hague Securities Convention, subsections (b) and (e) had the effect in a U.S. forum that a controversy concerning the rights and duties as between Global Bank and Clearing Corporation ~~is~~was governed by French law, that a controversy concerning the rights and duties as between Clearing Corporation and Able ~~is~~was governed by Belgian law, and that a controversy concerning the rights and duties as between Able and Doe ~~is governed by Illinois law~~was governed by Illinois law. Under the Convention, the subsection (b) and (e) results are unchanged, if at the time of the respective agreements Global Bank, Clearing Corporation and Able had offices in France, Belgium and the United States, respectively, engaged in a regular activity of maintaining securities accounts. The Convention does not apply to the subsection (a) result.

Example 3: John Doe, a resident of Kansas, maintains a securities account with Able & Co. Able is organized in Switzerland and has its chief executive offices there. The agreement between Doe and Able provides that New York is the securities intermediary's jurisdiction for purposes of UCC Article 8. The agreement was entered into before the Hague Securities Convention's effectiveness in the United States, does not expressly provide that New York or any other law is applicable to all the issues specified in article 2(1) of the Hague Securities Convention, and does not otherwise expressly refer to the Convention. Through the account, Doe holds securities of a Japanese issuer. Roe, who lives in Japan, claims ownership of the securities and seeks to hold Able liable for not transferring the asset to Roe. Because the agreement between Doe and Able was entered into before the Convention's effectiveness in the United States, Convention article 16(3) specifies that the controversy between Roe and Able is governed by the law of New York, but only if at the time of the agreement between Doe and Able, Able had an office in the United States engaged in a regular activity of maintaining securities accounts.

6. To the extent that this section ~~does not~~ or the Hague Securities Convention do not specify the governing law, general choice of law rules apply. For example, suppose that in ~~either of the e~~Examples 1 or 2 in the preceding Comment, Doe enters into an agreement with Roe, ~~also a resident of Kansas,~~ in which Doe agrees to transfer all of his interests in the securities held through Able to Roe. Neither UCC Article 8 ~~does not deal~~nor the Convention deals with whether such an agreement is enforceable or whether it gives Roe some interest in Doe's security entitlement. This section ~~specifies~~and the Convention specify what jurisdiction's law governs the issues that are dealt with in UCC Article 8. or listed in Convention article 2(1) respectively. UCC Article 8, however, does specify that securities intermediaries have only limited duties with respect to adverse claims. See Section 8–115. Subsection (b)(3) of this section ~~provides~~and Convention article 2(1)(e) provide that Illinois law governs whether Able owes any duties to an adverse claimant. Thus, ~~if~~because Illinois has adopted Revised Article 8, Section 8–115 as enacted in Illinois determines whether Roe has any rights against Able.

7. The UCC choice of law provisions concerning security interests in securities and security entitlements are set out in Section 9–305., and within its scope the Hague Securities Convention also applies to such transactions.

* * *

Section 9–305:

[1. . . .]

2. Investment Property: General Rules. This section specifies choice-of-law rules for perfection and priority of security interests in investment property. Subsection (a)(1) covers security interests in certificated securities. Subsection (a)(2) covers security interests in uncertificated securities. Subsection (a)(3) covers security interests in security entitlements and securities accounts~~.~~, and where the Hague Securities Convention applies it may in occasional instances modify subsection (a)(3)'s results as discussed in Comments 3, 5 and 6 to Section 8–110. Subsection (a)(4) covers security interests in commodity contracts and commodity accounts. The approach of each of these paragraphs is essentially the same. They identify the jurisdiction's law that governs questions of perfection and priority by using the same principles that Article 8 uses to determine other questions concerning that form of investment property. Thus, for certificated securities, the law of the jurisdiction in which the certificate is located governs. Cf. Section 8–110(c). For uncertificated securities, the law of the issuer's jurisdiction governs. Cf. Section 8–110(a). For security entitlements and securities accounts, the law ~~of~~designated by the ~~securities intermediary's jurisdiction~~agreement between the securities intermediary and the entitlement holder governing the securities account generally governs. Cf. Section 8–110(b), (e)(1) and (2) and Convention article 4(1).

For commodity contracts and commodity accounts, the law of the commodity intermediary's jurisdiction governs, though if particular assets of this type qualify as securities held with an intermediary within the meaning of the Convention, the Convention would also apply. ~~Because commodity~~Commodity contracts and commodity accounts are not governed by Article 8, and for this reason subsection (b) contains rules that specify the commodity intermediary's jurisdiction~~. These~~ that are analogous to the rules in Section 8–110(e) specifying a securities intermediary's jurisdiction. Subsection (b)(1) affords the parties greater flexibility than did former Section 9–103(6)(3). See also Section 9–304(b) (bank's jurisdiction); Revised Section 8–110(e)(1) and (2) (securities intermediary's jurisdiction).

3. Investment Property: Exceptions. Subsection (c) establishes an exception to the general rules ~~set out in subsection (a).~~discussed in the preceding Comment. It provides that perfection of a security interest by filing, automatic perfection of a security interest in investment property created by a debtor who is a broker or securities intermediary (see Section 9–309(10)), and automatic perfection of a security interest in a commodity contract or commodity account of a debtor who is a commodity intermediary (see Section 9–309(11)) are governed by the law of the jurisdiction in which the debtor is located, as determined under Section 9–307.

The Hague Securities Convention generally preserves these rules for perfection by filing. However, if the debtor is located in a non-U.S. jurisdiction, or if the account agreement designates the law of a non-U.S. jurisdiction, then filing may be appropriate only in a different jurisdiction or altogether unavailable. See Convention articles 12(2)(b) and 4(1), respectively, and PEB Commentary No. 19, dated April 11, 2017, particularly footnote 25.

4. Examples: The following examples illustrate the rules in this section:

Example 1: A customer residing in New Jersey maintains a securities account with Able & Co. The agreement between the customer and Able specifies that it is governed by Pennsylvania law but expressly provides that ~~the law of~~California is Able's jurisdiction for purposes of the Uniform Commercial Code. Through the account the customer holds securities of a Massachusetts corporation, which Able holds through a clearing corporation located in New York. The customer obtains a margin loan from Able. Subsection (a)(3) provides that California law—the law of the securities intermediary's jurisdiction—governs perfection and priority of the security interest, even if California has no other relationship to the parties or the transaction. Even if other facts cause the Hague Securities Convention to apply (see Comment 1 to Section 8–110), the Convention does not change this result, provided that the account agreement either was entered into before the Convention's effectiveness in the United States or expressly specifies that the law of California is applicable to all issues specified in Convention article 2(1), and also provided that at the time of the agreement Able had an office in the United States engaged in a regular activity of maintaining securities accounts.

Example 2: A customer residing in New Jersey maintains a securities account with Able & Co. The agreement between the customer and Able specifies that it is governed by Pennsylvania law. Through the account the customer holds securities of a Massachusetts corporation, which Able holds through a clearing corporation located in New York. The customer obtains a loan from a lender located in Illinois. The lender takes a security interest and perfects by obtaining an agreement among the debtor, itself, and Able, which satisfies the requirement of Section 8–106(d)(2) to give the lender control. Subsection (a)(3) provides that Pennsylvania law—the law of the securities intermediary's jurisdiction—governs perfection and priority of the security interest, even if Pennsylvania has no other relationship to the parties or the transaction. Even if other facts cause the Hague Securities Convention to apply, the Convention does not change this result, provided that at the time of the agreement between the customer and Able, Able had an office in the United States engaged in a regular activity of maintaining securities accounts.

Example 3:   A customer residing in New Jersey maintains a securities account with Able & Co. The agreement between the customer and Able specifies that it is governed by Pennsylvania law. Through the account, the customer holds securities of a Massachusetts corporation, which Able holds through a clearing corporation located in New York. The customer borrows from SP-1, and SP-1 files a financing statement in New Jersey. Later, the customer obtains a loan from SP-2. SP-2 takes a security interest and perfects by obtaining an agreement among the debtor, itself, and Able, which satisfies the requirement of Section 8–106(d)(2) to give the SP-2 control. Subsection (c)(1) provides that perfection of SP-1's security interest by filing is governed by the location of the debtor, so the filing in New Jersey was appropriate. Even if other facts cause the Hague Securities Convention to apply, Convention article 12(2)(b) preserves this result. Subsection (a)(3), however, provides that Pennsylvania law—the law of the securities intermediary's jurisdiction designated by the agreement between the customer and Able—governs all other questions of perfection and priority, and the Convention preserves this result, provided that at the time of the agreement between the customer and Able, Able had an office in the United States engaged in a regular activity of maintaining securities accounts. Thus, Pennsylvania law governs perfection of SP-2's security interest, and Pennsylvania law also governs the priority of the security interests of SP-1 and SP-2.

Example 4:   A customer maintains a securities account with Able & Co. The customer is an Ontario, Canada corporation with its chief executive office in Toronto. The agreement between the customer and Able specifies that it is governed by New York law, and at the time of the agreement Able had an office in the United States engaged in a regular activity of maintaining securities accounts. The customer obtains a loan secured by the securities account, and the lender wishes to perfect by filing. Subsection (c)(1) provides that perfection of the security interest by filing is generally governed by the law of the location of the debtor (in this case Ontario, assuming that it has a filing system described by Section 9–307(c)); however, Convention article 12(2)(b) recognizes Article 9's place-of-filing rules only when they designate a U.S. jurisdiction for the filing. As a result, subsection (c)(1) does not govern filing for this transaction, and perfection of the security interest is governed by the substantive law of the jurisdiction designated by the account agreement (in this case New York).

Example 5:   A customer maintains a securities account with Able & Co. The customer is a Texas corporation. The agreement between the customer and Able specifies that it is governed by English law, and at the time of the agreement Able had an office in England engaged in a regular activity of maintaining securities accounts. The customer obtains a loan secured by the securities account, and the lender wishes to perfect by filing. Subsection (c)(1), if it applied, would provide that perfection of the security interest by filing is governed by the law of the location of the debtor (in this case Texas); however, under Convention article 4(1), perfection of the security interest is governed by the law of the jurisdiction designated by the account agreement (in this case England), rather than by the law of any UCC jurisdiction.

5.   Change in Law Governing Perfection. When the issuer's jurisdiction, the securities intermediary's jurisdiction, or commodity intermediary's jurisdiction changes, the jurisdiction whose law governs perfection under subsection (a) changes, as well. Similarly, the law governing perfection of a possessory security interest in a certificated security changes when the collateral is removed to another jurisdiction, see subsection (a)(1), and the law governing perfection by filing changes when the debtor changes its location. See subsection (c). Nevertheless, under the UCC these changes will not result in an immediate loss of perfection. See Section 9–316. Along generally similar lines in cases to which the Hague Securities Convention applies, article 7 provides that when the account agreement is amended to designate a new jurisdiction's law under article 4(1), the new law governs perfection, except that the old law continues to govern the perfection of security or other property interests that arose before the amendment and a limited number of other issues affecting such interests, without limitation as to time.

PEB COMMENTARY NO. 20

*   *   *

Section 9–301:

[. . .]

2.   Scope of This Subpart. Part 3, Subpart 1 (Sections 9–301 through 9–307) contains choice-of-law rules similar to those of former Section 9–103. Former Section 9–103 generally addresses which State's law governs "perfection and the effect of perfection or non-perfection of" security interests. See, e.g., former Section 9–103(1)(b). This Article follows the broader and more precise formulation in former Section 9–103(6)(b), which was revised in connection with the promulgation of Revised Article 8 in 1994: "perfection, the effect of perfection or non-perfection, and the priority of" security interests. Priority, in this context, subsumes all of the rules in Part 3, including "cut off" or "take free" rules such as Sections 9–317(b), (c), and (d), 9–320(a), (b), and (d), and 9–332. This subpart does not address choice of law for other purposes. For example, the law applicable to issues such as attachment, validity, characterization (e.g., true lease or security interest), and enforcement is governed by the rules in Section 1–105(1) (Revised Section 1–301(a) and (b)); that governing law typically is specified in the same agreement that contains the security agreement. In transactions to which the Hague Securities Convention applies, the requirements for foreclosure and the like, the characterization of a transfer as being outright or by way of security, and certain other issues will generally be governed by the law specified in the account agreement. See PEB Commentary No. 19, dated April 11, 2017. And, another jurisdiction's law may govern other third-party matters addressed in this Article. See Section 9–401, Comment 3.

[. . .]

*   *   *

Section 1–301:

[. . .]

4.   Subsection (c) spells out essential limitations on the parties' right to choose the applicable law. Especially in Article 9 parties taking a security interest or asked to extend credit which may be subject to a security interest must have sure ways to find out whether and where to file and where to look for possible existing filings.

5.   Sections 9–301 through 9–307 should be consulted as to the rules for perfection of security interests and agricultural liens and the effect of perfection and nonperfection and priority. In transactions to which the Hague Securities Convention applies, the requirements for foreclosure and the like, the characterization of a transfer as being outright or by way of security, and certain other issues will generally be governed by the law specified in the account agreement. See PEB Commentary No. 19, dated April 11, 2017.

[. . .]

PEB COMMENTARY NO. 20
CONSIGNMENTS
(January 24, 2019)

INTRODUCTION

Before the 1998 revision of Article 9 and its attendant revision of § 2–326, many believed that "[t]he Uniform Commercial Code's provisions regarding consignments [were] not models of draftsmanship."[1] Before the revision, most of the rules governing consignments were found in § 2–326. That section provided that goods that were sold on a "sale or return" basis were subject to claims of the buyer's creditors while the goods were in the buyer's possession. That provision, standing alone, would have no effect on consignments but for § 2–326(3), which indicated that, for purposes of determining the rights of creditors of the consignee in the consigned goods,[2] the goods were deemed to be "sale or return" and, thus, subject to claims of the

---

[1]   In re State Street Auto Sales, Inc., 81 B.R. 215, 216 (Bankr. D. Mass. 1988).

[2]   Former U.C.C. § 2–326 did not use the words "consignor" and "consignee." Rather, it referred to situations in which "goods are delivered to a person for sale and such person maintains a place of business at which he deals in goods of the kind involved, under a name other than the name of the person making delivery." Former U.C.C. § 2–326(3).

consignee's creditors. A consignor could avoid the application of the deemed-sale-or-return rule by complying with the filing provisions of Article 9.[3] Former § 9–114 added additional rules for these situations. This statutory scheme proved difficult for attorneys and judges to follow.

The 1998 revision rewrote the rules governing consignments and situated all of them in Article 9 (rather than continuing the bifurcation of the rules between Article 2 and Article 9). The purpose of the revised statute was to clarify these provisions, in most cases without changing the rights of the creditors of the consignee.[4] However, some reported cases and articles suggest that, despite this clarification, the law of consignments remains puzzling to some of the lawyers and judges who have grappled with it. In an effort to improve the understanding of these rules, this Commentary reiterates the proper legal treatment of consignments and explains where some commentators and courts have interpreted the statute in a manner inconsistent with the proper result.

The legal rules governing consignments can have a significant effect on the rights of the consignor and the rights of the other creditors of the consignee. A creditor generally has recourse only to the property rights that its debtor has. As explained below in part (1) of the Discussion, a consignee is a bailee. Under general legal principles, a consignee, like other bailees, would have only a special interest (or special property) in the consigned goods limited to the purposes of the bailment (consignment). Ownership of the bailed goods would be retained by the bailor (consignor) and could not be subjected to the claims of the bailee's (consignee's) creditors.[5] Article 9 significantly changes this result with respect to the consignments that it governs: Article 9 treats the consignor's interest in the goods as a "security interest"[6] and, therefore, contemplates that a creditor of a consignee will be able to reach the consignor's rights in consigned goods if the consignor's security interest is unperfected.[7] In that case a judicial lien that the creditor acquires on the consigned goods would be senior to the consignor's unperfected security interest.[8] To allow for this result, § 9–319(a) provides that "for purposes of determining the rights of creditors of, and purchasers for value of goods from, a consignee, . . . the consignee is deemed to have rights and title to the goods identical to those the consignor had or had power to transfer."[9] The consignee's creditors benefit from these deemed rights "while the goods are in the possession of the consignee."[10]

In the case of consignments not governed by Article 9, non-UCC law determines the rights of creditors of the consignee. The deemed-sale-or-return rule in former § 2–326 has been deleted.

DISCUSSION

This Commentary focuses on three issues: (1) How to distinguish a "consignment" (as § 9–102(a)(20) defines the term) from other transactions; (2) Whether "generally known by its creditors," (as used in Article 9's definition of "consignment") refers to the knowledge of creditors generally or to the knowledge of a particular competing creditor; and (3) The effect of the limitation, "while the goods are in the possession of the consignee," in § 9–319(a).

---

[3] Alternatively, a consignor could have (i) complied with an applicable law providing for a consignor's interest or the like to be evidenced by a sign or (ii) established that the consignee was generally known by its creditors to be substantially engaged in selling the goods of others,

[4] U.C.C. § 9–319 cmt. 2.

[5] This Commentary assumes that the consignor was the owner of the goods when they were delivered to the consignee, as is typically the case.

[6] See U.C.C. § 1–201(b)(35) (defining "security interest" to include "any interest of a consignor . . . in a transaction that is subject to Article 9").

[7] U.C.C. § 9–319. Even a consignor that perfects its security interest may need to send a purchase-money notification pursuant to § 9–324(b) in order for its security interest to achieve priority over a conflicting security interest in the consigned goods after giving effect to U.C.C. § 9–319(a). See U.C.C. § 9–319 cmt. 2, ex. 3.

[8] U.C.C. § 9–317(a)(2); see U.C.C. § 9–102(a)(52) (defining "lien creditor" to include a person that has acquired a lien "by attachment, levy, or the like").

[9] U.C.C. § 9–319(a). This rule is subject to an important exception: Law other than Article 9 determines the rights of a creditor of the consignee if, under Article 9, "a perfected security interest held by the consignor would have priority over the rights of the creditor." U.C.C. § 9–319(b).

[10] U.C.C. § 9–319(a).

PEB COMMENTARY NO. 20

(1) Distinguishing among types of transactions

Although the term "consignment" is sometimes used to refer to other transactions, a consignment is properly understood to be a bailment, *i.e.*, a transaction in which one person (the bailor) delivers goods to another (the bailee) for a limited purpose.[11] As in every bailment, the consignor-bailor retains ownership of the delivered goods. The law governing a bailment depends on the limited purpose for which the goods are delivered. A consignment is a delivery of goods to a bailee for the purpose of sale, but is not a sale to the bailee. The person making delivery is a "consignor," and the person taking delivery is a "consignee."

Certain consignments are governed by Article 9.[12] They are the "consignments" defined in § 9–102(a)(20), which are sometimes referred to as "Article 9 consignments."[13] An Article 9 consignment does not secure payment or other performance of an obligation. Nevertheless, for purposes of Article 9, the consignor's ownership interest in goods that are the subject of an Article 9 consignment is treated as a purchase-money security interest in inventory.[14]

Consignments (*i.e.*, bailments for the purpose of sale) that fall outside the definition of "consignment" in § 9–102 are not governed by Article 9.[15] In these non-Article 9 consignments, the consignor's ownership interest in the consigned goods is not an Article 9 security interest. Rather, these transactions are governed by non-UCC law, which typically is the common law, as modified by any applicable non-UCC statutes.[16]

Consignments, which are bailments for the purpose of sale, are different from other bailments, including bailments for hire (leases), which are governed by Article 2A; bailments for storage, as to which Article 7 or non-UCC law may apply; and bailments for processing, which are governed by non-UCC law.[17]

Consignments, in which the consignor retains its ownership interest in the goods after delivery, are different from sales, which are transfers of ownership.[18] In some sales, the parties agree that the seller retains an interest in the sold goods until the buyer pays the price. Regardless of whether the agreement characterizes the interest retained by the seller as a security interest or as title, and regardless of whether the agreement purports to be a consignment, the seller's interest is limited to a security interest that secures

---

[11] Consignments that are bailments for sale often are called "true consignments," to distinguish them from non-bailment transactions that the parties refer to as "consignments." For example, the parties may refer to a transaction as a "consignment" when it actually creates a security interest that secures an obligation or when the person receiving delivery has agreed to pay for the goods.

[12] U.C.C. § 9–109(a)(4). Not all Article 9 rules apply to a consignment governed by Article 9. For example, as a general matter, Part 6 of Article 9 does not apply to consignments. U.C.C. § 9–601(g).

[13] U.C.C. § 9–102(a)(20) defines "consignment" to mean:

> a transaction, regardless of its form, in which a person delivers goods to a merchant for the purpose of sale and:
>   (A) the merchant:
>   (i) deals in goods of that kind under a name other than the name of the person making delivery;
>   (ii) is not an auctioneer; and
>   (iii) is not generally known by its creditors to be substantially engaged in selling the goods of others;
>   (B) with respect to each delivery, the aggregate value of the goods is $1,000 or more at the time of delivery;
>   (C) the goods are not consumer goods immediately before delivery; and
>   (D) the transaction does not create a security interest that secures an obligation.

[14] U.C.C. § 9–103(d).

[15] Nor are they governed by Article 2's "sale or return" rules discussed below.

[16] U.C.C. § 9–102 cmt. 14 ("A consignment excluded from the application of this Article by [§ 9–102(a)(20)(B) or (C)] may still be a true consignment; however, it is governed by non-Article 9 law."). Non-Article 9 law may be provided by another statute or by a rule of common law. For example, many states have non-UCC statutes governing the relationship between artists and art dealers. *See, e.g.*, N.Y. Arts & Cult. Aff. Law §§ 12.01, 12.03 (McKinney 2011 & Supp. 2015). Some of these statutes govern all consignments within their scope, including those that are governed by Article 9.

[17] For an example of an opinion that fails to recognize that the law does not treat all bailments alike, see *In re Mississippi Valley Livestock, Inc.*, 745 F.3d 299 (7th Cir. 2014). Cattle were delivered to a cattle merchant that agreed to sell them on the owner's behalf. Instead of analyzing the transaction as a consignment, the court erroneously treated the transaction as if it were a simple bailment for storage: "Had Mississippi Valley sent the very same cattle back to J & R (as when a theater-goer retrieves her own car from a parking garage after the show), the case would be easy." *Id.* at 304.

[18] *See* U.C.C. § 2–106(1) ("A 'sale' consists in the passing of title from the seller to the buyer for a price . . . .").

an obligation, *i.e.*, the buyer's promise to pay.[19] As such, it is governed by Article 9 in the same manner as any other security interest that secures an obligation. It is not an Article 9 "consignment."[20]

Sometimes, when goods are sold and delivered to a buyer primarily for resale, the buyer and seller agree that that the buyer may return the goods even though they conform to the contract. A transaction of this kind is a "sale or return."[21] Although both a consignment and a sale or return may allow for the return of delivered goods, the transactions are fundamentally different and are mutually exclusive.[22] A consignment is a bailment, and the consignor remains the owner of the consigned goods. A sale or return is, as the name suggests, a sale, pursuant to which the buyer becomes the owner of the goods. Absent an agreement otherwise, the seller does not retain any interest in goods delivered to the buyer.[23] The buyer becomes the owner of the goods, even though it has a right to return the goods and to transfer ownership back to the seller.[24] A sale or return is not a consignment; a consignment is not a sale or return.[25] The link between these concepts in former § 2–326 was not carried forward in revised Article 9.

(1)   "Generally known by its creditors"

If the consignee is "generally known by its creditors to be substantially engaged in selling the goods of others," the transaction is not an Article 9 "consignment."[26] By its terms, the quoted language refers to the knowledge[27] of the consignee's creditors generally. It makes no reference to the knowledge of a particular competing claimant.

The quoted language should be read in accordance with its terms. The Article 9 definition of "consignment" determines which bailments for sale are governed by Article 9's perfection and priority rules and which are not. Consignments in which a consignee is "generally known by its creditors" to be substantially engaged in selling the goods of others are thus excluded from Article 9 and are governed by non-UCC law.[28]

---

[19] U.C.C. § 1–201(b)(35) (defining "security interest"); U.C.C. § 2–401(1); U.C.C. § 9–109(a)(1). In these transactions, the buyer becomes the owner of the goods, even if the agreement designates the buyer as a "consignee."

[20] "[A] security interest that secures an obligation" is excluded from the definition of consignment. U.C.C. § 9–102(a)(20)(D). For example, if the consignee has the obligation to pay for the consigned goods that are not sold, the transaction would be a sale of the goods to the consignee with a retention or reservation of title by the consignor until payment and, hence, a security interest securing an obligation.

[21] "Unless otherwise agreed, if delivered goods may be returned by the buyer even though they conform to the contract, the transaction is . . . a 'sale or return' if the goods are delivered primarily for resale." U.C.C. § 2–326(1)(b).

[22] Some courts and commentators have missed this essential point. For example, in one case, a merchant took delivery of goods under a contract that provided that the merchant, "as the exclusive agent for Consignor, will offer [the consigned goods] for sale." *In re Morgansen's Ltd.*, 302 B.R. 784, 790 (Bankr. E.D.N.Y. 2003). The merchant's only written obligation was to pay to the consignor the net proceeds of sale, less a commission. *Id.* at 789. The court, however, mistakenly believed that a person who is considered a consignee is a " 'buyer' for resale." *Id.* Having found that the consignors failed to prove that the transactions were not excluded from the definition of "consignment" by § 9–102(a)(20)(A)(ii) and (A)(iii) (*i.e.*, that the merchant was not an auctioneer and was not generally known by its creditors to be substantially engaged in selling the goods of others), the court nevertheless found that the transactions were not "consignments" as defined in Article 9. Rather than applying the common law, the court erroneously turned to § 2–326 and concluded that "the goods consigned to the debtor clearly were delivered on a 'sale or return' basis." *Id. See also* Hilary Jay, Note, *A Picture Imperfect: The Rights of Art Consignor-Collectors When Their Art Dealer Files for Bankruptcy*, 58 Duke L.J. 1859 (2009) (proceeding on the erroneous premise that a consignment as defined in Article 9 can also be a sale or return).

[23] *See* U.C.C. § 2–401(1) (providing that "[a]ny retention or reservation by the seller of the title (property) in goods shipped or delivered to the buyer is limited in effect to a reservation of a security interest."); U.C.C. § 1–201(b)(35) (providing to the same effect).

[24] *See* U.C.C. § 2–326(1) cmt. 1 (stating that a sale or return "is a present sale of goods which may be undone at the buyer's option").

[25] Some of the confusion may have arisen from former § 2–326, whose caption included the words "Consignment Sales" and whose subsection (3) deemed certain goods that were delivered for sale (*i.e.*, that were the subject of a consignment) to be held on sale or return. To conform § 2–326 with Revised Article 9, the caption was amended and former subsection (3) was deleted.

[26] U.C.C. § 9–102(a)(20)(A)(iii).

[27] "Knowledge" means "actual knowledge." U.C.C. § 1–202(b).

[28] Under non-UCC law, the goods of a consignor typically would not be subject to the claims of the consignee's creditors. *See* U.C.C. § 9–109 cmt. 6. This would be the case for a consignment that is excluded from Article 9, whether

Some authorities have misconstrued the condition contained in § 9–102(a)(20)(A)(iii) by interpreting "generally known by its creditors" to mean "known by the competing claimant."[29] Under this misinterpretation, a given transaction would be a consignment subject to Article 9's perfection and priority rules vis-à-vis creditors without knowledge that the person in possession is "substantially engaged in selling the goods of others" and would be excluded from Article 9 as to creditors with that knowledge. This anomalous result could lead to difficult priority disputes without promoting any Article 9 policy.

A proper reading of "generally known by its creditors" does not allow for such a result and is consistent with the Article 9 policy that limits the role of knowledge in priority disputes. The priority between competing security interests in goods (including purchase-money security interests) is not affected by what the competing claimants know,[30] nor is the priority between a security interest and a judicial lien.[31] Just as an unperfected security interest that secures an obligation is subordinate to the rights of a particular competing lien creditor or perfected secured party whether or not the lien creditor or perfected secured party has knowledge of the security interest, so an unperfected security interest held by a consignor is subordinate to the rights of a particular lien creditor or perfected secured party whether or not the lien creditor or perfected secured party has knowledge of the consignment.[32]

This is not to say that the knowledge of the competing claimant is irrelevant. In determining whether the consignee is "generally known by its creditors," the competing creditor with knowledge would be included in the group of all creditors of the consignee.

(2) "While the goods are in the possession of the consignee"

As explained in the Introduction, for purposes of determining the rights of creditors of the consignee (and purchasers for value from the consignee), a consignee generally is deemed to have rights and title identical to those that the consignor had or had power to transfer, in which case creditors of the consignee have recourse to the consigned goods.[33] The general rule applies, and the consignee's creditors benefit from these deemed rights and title, "while the goods are in the possession of the consignee."[34] Upon returning the goods to the consignor, the consignee loses all deemed rights to the goods. After that time, the consignee cannot encumber the goods with a security interest, nor can the consignee's creditors acquire a judicial lien on the goods.

The result differs when the consignee creates an enforceable security interest in consigned goods while they are in the consignee's possession and then returns the unsold goods to the consignor. The fact that the goods no longer are in the possession of the consignee, which is no longer deemed to have the consignor's rights and title, does not strip the consignee's secured party of its security interest. Under § 9–319(a), while the goods were in the possession of the consignee the consignee was deemed to have had rights in and the power to transfer the consigned goods. Once the other requirements of § 9–203(b) were satisfied, the security interest became "enforceable against the debtor [the consignee] and third parties."[35] If the consignee was then to sell the goods to a non-ordinary-course buyer, the security interest of the consignee's secured party

---

because the consignee is generally known by its creditors to be substantially engaged in selling the goods of others (§ 9–102(a)(20)(A)(iii)), the aggregate value of the goods is less than $1000 (§ 9–102(a)(20)(B)), or the goods were consumer goods immediately before delivery (§ 9–102(a)(20)(C)). *See In re Haley & Steele, Inc.*, 20 Mass. L. Rptr. 204, 58 UCC Rep. Serv. 2d 394 (Mass. Super. 2005) (goods of consignor that were consumer goods before delivery to the consignee were not subject to the claims of the consignee's creditors). The filing of a financing statement by a consignor whose consignment is excluded from Article 9 would be a meaningless act under Article 9.

[29] *See, e.g., Fariba v. Dealer Servs. Corp.*, 100 Cal. Rptr. 3d 219 (Cal. Ct. App. 2009) and authorities cited therein.

[30] *See* U.C.C. § 9–322(a) & cmt. 4 ex. 1 & 2; § 9–324.

[31] *See* U.C.C. § 9–317(a), (e).

[32] Knowledge may be relevant to the priority of buyers and lessees as against an unperfected security interest. *See* U.C.C. § 9–317(b), (c). But inasmuch as consigned goods are held for sale by a merchant that "deals in goods of that kind," U.C.C. § 9–102(a)(20)(A)(i), a buyer of the goods almost invariably will qualify as a buyer in ordinary course of business and, as such, will take free of the consignor's security interest, even if the buyer knows of its existence. See U.C.C. § 1–201(b)(9) (defining "buyer in ordinary course of business" to include only buyers that buy from "a person, other than a pawnbroker, in the business of selling goods of that kind"); U.C.C. § 9–320(a). This result also follows from U.C.C. § 2–403(2).

[33] U.C.C. § 9–319.

[34] U.C.C. § 9–319(a).

[35] U.C.C. § 9–203(b).

ordinarily would continue in the sold goods, even though the consignee would no longer have any deemed rights in, or deemed title to, them.[36] Likewise, if the consignee returns collateral (goods) to the owner, an enforceable security interest in the collateral would continue, unless the consignee's secured party authorized the return free of its security interest.[37]

The same logic follows if the consignment is terminated. " 'Consignee' means a merchant to which goods are delivered in a consignment."[38] The termination of a consignment does not *ipso facto* cause a "consignee" to lose its status as such with respect to consigned goods remaining in the possession of the consignee as against the consignee's creditors whose claims to the goods arose before termination.[39]

However, there may be circumstances in which the consignee lacks sufficient rights in consigned goods to create a security interest in them while they are in the consignee's possession. For example, if the consignor has perfected its security interest in the consigned goods such that the consignor would achieve priority over a competing secured party claiming a security interest in the after-acquired inventory of the consignee ("inventory secured party"), then under § 9–319(b) the rights of the inventory secured party with respect to the consigned goods are determined under other law. (This is the case despite § 9–319(a) because § 9–319(b) is an exception to § 9–319(a).) Other law may provide that the consignee has no rights in or power to transfer rights in the consigned goods. If so, no security interest granted to the inventory secured party by the consignee would attach to the consigned goods under § 9–203(b). Inasmuch as no security interest was created in favor of the inventory secured party, any return of the consigned goods to the consignor would not be subject to a security interest held by the inventory secured party.[40]

AMENDMENTS TO OFFICIAL COMMENTS

With the discussion in this Commentary in mind the Official Comments are amended as follow.

Official Comment 4 to § 2–326 is amended to read:

4.   The transactions governed by this section are sales; the persons to whom the goods are delivered are buyers. This section has no application to transactions in which goods are delivered to a person who has neither bought the goods nor contracted to buy them. See PEB Commentary No. 20, dated January 24, 2019. Transactions in which a non-buyer takes delivery of goods for the purpose of selling them are bailments called consignments and are not "sale on approval" or "sale or return" transactions. Certain consignment transactions were dealt with in former Sections 2–326(3) and 9–114. These provisions have been deleted and have been replaced by new provisions in Article 9. See, e.g., Sections 9–109(a)(4); 9–103(d); 9–319.

Official Comment 14 to § 9–102 is amended by adding at the end the following new paragraph:

Under clause (iii) of subparagraph (A), a transaction is not an Article 9 "consignment" if the consignee is "generally known by its creditors to be substantially engaged in selling the goods of others." Clause (iii) does not apply solely because a particular competing claimant knows that the goods are held on consignment. See PEB Commentary No. 20, dated January 24, 2019.

The final paragraph of Official Comment 6 to § 9–109 is amended to read:

---

[36] *See* U.C.C. § 9–315(a)(1) (providing that, with some exceptions, a security interest continues in collateral notwithstanding a sale or other disposition thereof). It is incorrect to read § 9–319(a) itself as cutting off the security interest of the consignee's secured party after the security interest has attached, even if the goods are subsequently sold or otherwise disposed of by the consignee. As § 9–315(a)(1) provides, the security interest would be cut off if the secured party authorized the disposition free of the security interest or if the security interest was cut off under § 2–403(2) or another provision of Article 9, such as § 9–320(a).

[37] *See* U.C.C. § 9–315(a)(1). Any suggestion to the contrary, as in *Fariba, supra* note 29, is incorrect. This Commentary does not address whether in a particular case the secured party may have authorized the return free of the security interest.

[38] U.C.C. § 9–102(a)(19).

[39] This Commentary does not address whether the consignee loses its status as such with respect to creditors of the consignee whose claims to the goods arose *after* termination of the consignment and while the consigned goods were still in the possession of the consignee.

[40] A similar result would obtain if, as in Example 2 of comment 3 to § 9–319, other law provides that, as a bailee, a consignee has a special property in respect of consigned goods in its possession. SP-2's security interest could attach only to those limited rights and so would be of no practical value.

This Article does not apply to a bailment for sale that falls outside of the definition of "consignment" in § 9–102. See PEB Commentary No. 20, dated January 24, 2019.

The first paragraph of Official Comment 2 to § 9–319 is amended to read as follows, with the second paragraph added:

2. **Consignments.** This section takes an approach to consignments similar to that taken by Section 9–318 with respect to buyers of accounts and chattel paper. Revised Section 1–201(b)(35) defines "security interest" to include the interest of a consignor of goods under many true consignments. Section 9–319(a) provides that, for purposes of determining the rights of certain third parties, the consignee is deemed to acquire all rights and title that the consignor had, if the consignor's security interest is unperfected. The consignee acquires these rights even though, as between the parties, it purchases a limited interest in the goods (as would be the case in a true consignment, under which the consignee acquires only the interest of a bailee). As a consequence of this section, creditors of the consignee can acquire judicial liens and security interests in the goods while the goods are in the possession of the consignee.

The termination of a consignment does not *ipso facto* cause the consignee to lose its status as such with respect to the consignee's creditors whose claims to the goods arose before termination. Return of the goods to the consignor causes the consignee to lose its deemed rights and title, but it does not discharge a security interest or judicial lien that attached while the consignee was in possession. See PEB Commentary No. 20, dated January 24, 2019.

PEB COMMENTARY NO. 21
USE OF THE TERM "ASSIGNMENT" IN ARTICLE 9 OF THE UNIFORM COMMERCIAL CODE
(March 11, 2020)

INTRODUCTION

Article 9 of the Uniform Commercial Code (the "UCC") addresses in Part 4 the rights of third parties in secured transactions. The third parties are typically "account debtors,"[1] i.e., persons obligated on accounts,[2] chattel paper,[3] or general intangibles[4] (including payment intangibles[5]). However, many of the provisions of Part 4, instead of referring to a "debtor,"[6] "secured party,"[7] and "security interest,"[8] all of which terms are defined in the UCC, refer to an "assignor," an "assignee," and an "assignment," or sometimes to an "assigned contract," none of which terms are defined in the UCC.[9]

This Commentary explains what constitutes an "assignment" and the scope of the terms "assignor" and "assignee" in relation to the statutory scheme of Article 9.

DISCUSSION

Article 9 applies to both a sale of certain payment rights—accounts, chattel paper, payment intangibles, and promissory notes (for convenience, referred to herein as "specified payment rights")—and

---

[1] U.C.C. § 9–102(a)(3) (defining "account debtor").

[2] U.C.C. § 9–102(a)(2) (defining "account").

[3] U.C.C. § 9–102(a)(11) (defining "chattel paper").

[4] U.C.C. § 9–102(a)(42) (defining "general intangible").

[5] U.C.C. § 9–102(a)(61) (defining "payment intangible").

[6] U.C.C. § 9–102(a)(28) (defining "debtor").

[7] U.C.C. § 9–102(a)(73) (defining "secured party").

[8] U.C.C. § 1–201(b)(35) (defining "security interest").

[9] Section 9–403 addresses an agreement of an account debtor not to assert claims or defenses against an "assignee." Section 9–404 addresses the rights acquired by an "assignee" and certain claims and defenses that an account debtor can assert against an "assignee." Section 9–405 focuses on modifications to an "assigned contract." Section 9–406 sets forth the rights of an account debtor when notified of an "assignment." Sections 9–406, 9–407, 9–408, and 9–409 generally address certain contractual and legal restrictions on "assignment." Section 9–209 describes certain duties of a secured party if an account debtor has been notified of an "assignment."

to the grant of an interest in specified payment rights to secure an obligation.[10] Put another way, Article 9 applies both to an outright assignment of ownership of specified payment rights and to an assignment of specified payment rights for security. The terms "debtor" and "secured party" are defined to include the participants in both types of transactions.[11]

For ease of reference, we refer in this Commentary to a security interest that secures an obligation as a "SISO."

Article 9's use of the term "assignment," and the correlative terms "assignor" and "assignee," is largely historical. Former versions of Article 9 used these terms as they were used in general contract law.[12] In that context, it was understood that an "assignment" could be either an outright transfer of ownership of a specified payment right or a SISO in a specified payment right.[13] The 1999 revisions of Article 9 retained that terminology to avoid any suggestion that the scope or substance of the applicable rules had been changed. Although revised Article 9 does not define the terms "assignment," "assignor," and "assignee," Comment 26 to Section 9–102 states that "[d]epending on the context, [the term "assignment"] may refer to the assignment . . . of an outright ownership interest or to the assignment . . . of a limited interest, such as a security interest." Accordingly, unless there is good reason for any of these terms to apply more narrowly, each applies, as appropriate, both to an outright assignment of ownership and to a SISO.

Some courts have interpreted the term "assignment," especially in the context of Section 9–406(a),[14] as referring only to an outright assignment of ownership. This narrow reading of the term "assignment" is contrary to the use of the term in Article 9 and the holdings of other courts[15] and is incorrect.

Section 9–406(a) provides that, when an account debtor receives a notification from an assignor or an assignee that a specified payment right has been assigned to the assignee and an instruction to pay the assignee, the account debtor may thereafter discharge its obligation to make the payment owed by paying the assignee. After receipt of the notification and payment instruction, the account debtor may not discharge the account debtor's payment obligation by paying the assignor. Under some courts' erroneously narrow interpretation, Section 9–406(a) applies only when the assignment is a sale of the specified payment right and does not apply when the assignment is a SISO.[16]

---

[10] *See* U.C.C. § 9–109(a)(1), (3).

[11] Section 9–102(a)(28) states that a "debtor" includes both "a person having an interest, other than a security interest or other lien, in the collateral, whether or not the person is an obligor" and "a seller of accounts, chattel paper, payment intangibles, or promissory notes." Section 9–102(a)(73) states that a "secured party" includes both "a person in whose favor a security interest is created or provided for under a security agreement" and "a person to which accounts, chattel paper, payment intangibles, or promissory notes have been sold." U.C.C. § 9–102(a)(73). In addition, Section 1–201(b)(35) defines a "security interest" to include both "an interest in personal property . . . which secures payment or performance of an obligation" and "any interest of . . . a buyer of accounts, chattel paper, a payment intangible, or a promissory note in a transaction that is subject to Article 9." U.C.C. § 1–201(b)(35).

[12] *See generally* RESTATEMENT (SECOND) OF CONTRACTS ch. 15, "Assignment and Delegation" (AM. LAW INST. 1981) (using "assignment" to refer interchangeably to the outright transfer of a right under a contract and to the creation of a security interest in a right under a contract).

[13] *See* U.C.C. § 9–406, cmt. 5 ("Former Section 9–318(4) rendered ineffective an agreement between an account debtor and an assignor which prohibited assignment of an account (whether outright or to secure an obligation) . . . ."); 7 THOMAS M. QUINN, QUINN'S UNIFORM COMMERCIAL CODE COMMENTARY AND LAW DIGEST (Rev. 2d ed. 2011), at 961–62 (discussing former U.C.C. § 9–318). Case law under former U.C.C. § 9–318 was consistent with the broad interpretation of the term "assignment" to include both an outright transfer and a SISO. *See, e.g., First Nat'l Bank of Boston v. Thomson Consumer Elecs., Inc.*, 84 F.3d 397, 399 (11th Cir. 1996); *Bank of Waunakee v. Rochester Cheese Sales, Inc.*, 906 F.2d 1185, 1190 (7th Cir. 1990); *In re Johnson*, 439 B.R. 416, 432 (Bankr. E.D. Mich. 2010), *aff'd on other grounds*, No. 10–14292, 2011 WL 1983339 (E.D. Mich. May 23, 2011).

[14] *See, e.g., Durham Capital Corporation v. Ocwen Loan Servicing, LLC*, 777 F. App'x 952 (11th Cir. 2019), citing *IIG Capital LLC v. Archipelago, L.L.C.*, 36 A.D.3d 401, 404 (N.Y. App. Div. 2007).

[15] *See, e.g., ARA Inc. v. City of Glendale*, 360 F. Supp. 3d 957 (D. Ariz. 2019); *Nisbet, Inc. v. Wells Fargo Bank*, No. SA–14–CV–00469–RP, 2015 WL 1408839 (W.D. Tex. Mar. 26, 2015) (order denying motion to dismiss for failure to state a claim); *Swift Energy Operating, L.L.C. v. Plemco-South, Inc.*, 157 So. 3d 1154 (La. Ct. App. 2015).

[16] Presumably, under the narrow interpretation, if the assignment is a SISO in a specified payment right and is therefore outside of the scope of Section 9–406(a), other law determines whether an account debtor may discharge the account debtor's payment obligation by paying the assignee or by continuing to pay the assignor after receipt of the notification and instruction.

There is no policy reason to limit the term "assignment" in Section 9–406, or elsewhere in Article 9, to an outright transfer of ownership. Doing so would place a burden on the account debtor to determine whether the assignment was a sale or a SISO in order to know whether, for example, the obligations and rights in Part 4 apply to the account debtor. That burden is both heavy and unjustifiable. The account debtor is not a party to the assignment transaction and typically has no basis for making that determination. Nor does it make sense to require the account debtor to obtain the assignment documentation from the assignor or the assignee, and then to analyze the transaction between the assignor and the assignee to ascertain whether the transaction is actually a sale, merely to be confident that the account debtor may discharge its payment obligation by paying the assignee or to have other rights, claims, duties, and defenses of an account debtor under Part 4. Given the difficulty that courts often have in determining whether an assignment of a payment right is a sale or a SISO,[17] an account debtor should not be expected to make that determination.[18] In the context of Section 9–406(a), for example, all that should matter to the account debtor is to know whom the account debtor may pay in order to discharge the account debtor's payment obligation.[19] Similarly, an assignee often would not have certainty on whether Part 4 of Article 9 applies to its rights or whether the common law of contracts applies. This lack of certainty would have a negative effect on the availability of financing.

One court has expressed the view that the narrow interpretation of the term "assignment" is consistent with Article 9's "legislative scheme." According to the court, because a secured party's right to enforce a SISO in a specified payment right is addressed in Section 9–607, there is no need for Section 9–406(a) to afford to such a secured party a "parallel" right.[20] However, the court failed to consider subsection (e) of Section 9–607. That subsection states, in relevant part, that "[t]his section does not determine whether an account debtor . . . owes a duty to a secured party." In other words, Sections 9–607 and 9–406 address different rights. Section 9–607 addresses the rights of a secured party *vis-à-vis the debtor* to collect a specified payment right. Section 9–406 addresses a secured party's rights *against the account debtor* to collect a specified payment right. If Section 9–406—and Part 4 of Article 9 more generally—did not apply to an assignment constituting a SISO, there would be a gap in Article 9: nothing in Article 9 would address the rights, claims, duties, and defenses of an account debtor with respect to that type of assignment.

As explained in Section 1–103(a)(2), one of the purposes of the UCC is "to permit the continued expansion of commercial practices through custom, usage, and agreement of the parties." The narrow interpretation of the term "assignment" in Part 4 would undermine that purpose. Suppose, for example, that pursuant to Section 9–406(a), a debtor who has granted a SISO in a specified payment right notifies the account debtor that the right has been assigned and instructs the account debtor that payment is to be made to a particular assignee. The narrow interpretation would leave to other law whether the account debtor may discharge the account debtor's payment obligation by paying the debtor or by paying the secured party. The broader interpretation makes clear when the account debtor may discharge the account debtor's payment obligation by paying the debtor and when the account debtor may discharge the obligation by

---

[17] "In many commercial financing transactions the distinction is blurred." U.C.C. § 9–109, cmt. 4.

[18] Similarly, an assignor should not have to make these judgments to determine if Part 4 applies to rights that the assignor may have under Part 4, such as the assignor's right under U.C.C. § 9–405 to make good faith modifications to an assigned contract that bind the assignee.

[19] *See* U.C.C. § 9–406, cmt. 5 (applying U.C.C. § 9–406(a) to an account debtor's right to a discharge on an account that secures an obligation). Likewise, there is no reason to limit the term "assignment" in the opposite direction, i.e., to a SISO in a specified payment right to the exclusion of a sale of the specified payment right, as the court apparently did in *Contrarian Funds, LLC v. Woodbridge Group of Companies (In re Woodbridge Group of Companies)*, 606 B.R. 201 (D. Del. 2019). In this decision dealing *inter alia* with the anti-assignment provisions in Section 9–406 and 9–408, the court incorrectly held that Section 9–408(a), rather than Section 9–406(d), applied to the assignment of a promissory note that secured an obligation and that neither Section applied to the sale of a promissory note. The court misunderstood Section 9–406(e). That section provides that Section 9–406(d) does not apply to the sale of a promissory note, and Section 9–408(b), which provides that Section 9–408(a) specifically does apply to the sale of a promissory note. For a critique of the *Woodbridge* decision, *see* Bruce A. Markell, *The Road to Perdition: 180 Equipment, Woodbridge and Liddle Pave the Way*, 39 BANKRUPTCY LAW LETTER 1 (Nov. 2019); *see also* Stephen L. Sepinuck, *Personal Property Secured Transactions*, 74 THE BUSINESS LAWYER, 1291, 1297–98, and Carl S. Bjerre and Stephen L. Sepinuck, *Spotlight*, 9 THE TRANSACTIONAL LAWYER (Feb. 2019), each of which critiques the bankruptcy court's decision upheld by the district court.

[20] *Durham*, 777 F. App'x at 956.

paying the secured party.[21] The broader interpretation creates greater certainty for both the secured party and the account debtor and is consistent with expectations in commercial practice.[22]

The broader interpretation of the term "assignment" is relevant not only for Section 9–406(a) but also for other provisions of Article 9 in which the term "assignment" is used, such as in the balance of the provisions of Part 4 and in Section 9–209. Likewise, the term "assignor" in those provisions includes a debtor who grants a SISO, and the term "assignee" includes the secured party in whose favor such a security interest is granted.

AMENDMENTS TO OFFICIAL COMMENTS

With the discussion in this Commentary in mind, the Official Comments to Section 9–401 are amended to add the following new Official Comment:

8. **Use of the Term "Assignment."** The term "assignment," as used in this Article, refers to both an outright transfer of ownership and a transfer of an interest to secure an obligation. See Comment 26 to Section 9–102 and PEB Commentary No. 21, dated March 11, 2020.

In addition, Official Comment 26 to Section 9–102 is amended as follows:

26. **Terminology: "Assignment" and "Transfer."** In numerous provisions, this Article refers to the "assignment" or the "transfer" of property interests. These terms and their derivatives are not defined. This Article generally follows common usage by using the terms "assignment" and "assign" to refer to transfers of rights to payment, claims, and liens and other security interests. It generally uses the term "transfer" to refer to other transfers of interests in property. Except when used in connection with a letter-of-credit transaction (see Section 9–107, Comment 4), no significance should be placed on the use of one term or the other. Depending on the ~~context~~ substance of the transaction, each term as used in this Article ~~may~~ refers to the assignment or transfer of an outright ownership interest, ~~or~~ to the assignment or transfer of a limited interest, such as a security interest, or both. See Comment 8 to Section 9–401 and PEB Commentary No. 21, dated March 11, 2020.

PEB COMMENTARY NO. 22
STATUS OF A DISPOSITION UNDER SECTION 9–610 OF THE UNIFORM COMMERCIAL CODE IF THE TRANSFEREE DOES NOT ACT IN GOOD FAITH
(August 24, 2020)

INTRODUCTION

Article 9 of the Uniform Commercial Code provides several statutory rights available to a secured party if the debtor defaults on obligations secured by a security interest in collateral within the scope of Article 9.[1] One of those rights is the right of the secured party to dispose of the collateral under Section 9–610. That section is supplemented by Section 9–617, which describes the rights in the collateral that a transferee obtains following a disposition of the collateral to the transferee under Section 9–610. A "transferee that acts in good faith takes free"[2] of "all of the debtor's rights in the collateral."[3] Among other things, Section 9–617(c)(1) states that a transferee that does not act in good faith takes subject to "the debtor's rights in the collateral."

---

[21] Some courts have expressed skepticism that a secured party is entitled to sue an account debtor whose payment obligation to the debtor has not been discharged under U.C.C. § 9–406(a). *See, e.g., Forest Capital, LLC v. BlackRock, Inc.,* 658 F. App'x 675 (4th Cir. 2016). However, if the account debtor has not been discharged under U.C.C. § 9–406(a) on its contractual obligation to the debtor, the account debtor remains liable to the debtor. Article 9 gives the secured party the right to enforce the debtor's rights against the account debtor. *See* U.C.C. § 9–607.

[22] *See, e.g.,* FORMS UNDER ARTICLE 9 OF THE UCC, AMERICAN BAR ASSOCIATION BUSINESS LAW SECTION UNIFORM COMMERCIAL CODE COMMITTEE (3d ed. 2016) at 595–96. Form 4.6 is a form of "Demand for Payment on Account Debtor of Borrower." The form, invoking U.C.C. § 9–406, assumes that the account debtor is obligated on collateral that secures a loan by the secured party to a debtor who is the "borrower."

[1] *See, e.g.,* U.C.C. §§ 9–609 (peaceful possession), 9–607 (collection), 9–610 (disposition), and 9–620 (acceptance of collateral).

[2] U.C.C. § 9–617(b).

[3] U.C.C. § 9–617(a)(1).

PEB COMMENTARY NO. 22

This Commentary explains the effect of a transferee taking subject to the debtor's rights in the collateral.

DISCUSSION

The debtor's "rights" include whatever ownership rights that the debtor has in the collateral, along with statutory rights under Article 9.[4] The debtor has certain rights under Article 9 when a secured party seeks to enforce its statutory remedy of disposition under Section 9–610. One of those rights is the right of the debtor to redeem the collateral under Section 9–623 by satisfying the obligations secured by the secured party's security interest in the collateral. The right of redemption enables the debtor to "buy back" the secured party's security interest in the collateral by paying the secured party what it is owed on the secured obligations or by otherwise performing the secured obligations.

The importance of the debtor's right of redemption in particular is reflected in Article 9's limits on the debtor's ability to waive the right. In a transaction other than a consumer-goods transaction, the debtor's right of redemption may be waived only by the debtor's agreement to that effect entered into and authenticated by the debtor after default.[5] In a consumer-goods transaction, the debtor's right of redemption may not be waived at all.[6]

Even so, Sections 9–617(a) and (b) provide that a "transferee that acts in good faith"[7] in connection with a "secured party's disposition of collateral after default"[8] "takes free of"[9] "all of the debtor's rights in the collateral."[10] This is the case "even if the secured party fails to comply with [Article 9] or the requirements of any judicial proceeding."[11]

The transferee will not "take free" if the transferee fails to "act in good faith."[12] In that case, subsection (c) of Section 9–617 makes explicit the negative implication of subsections (a) and (b): "the transferee [not acting in good faith] takes the collateral subject to . . . the debtor's rights in the collateral. . . ."[13]

To be sure, Section 9–623 cuts off the debtor's right of redemption when the secured party "has disposed of collateral or entered into a contract for its disposition under Section 9–610 . . . ."[14] The question then arises whether, if the secured party disposes of collateral, a transferee who is not acting in good faith takes the collateral subject to the debtor's right of redemption in the collateral or, alternatively, whether, because the right of redemption is cut off by a Section 9–610 disposition, the transferee takes the collateral free of the right.

This Commentary concludes that a transferee who has not acted in good faith does take subject to the debtor's right of redemption in addition to other rights of the debtor in the collateral. Section 9–617(c)(1) states that the transferee in a Section 9–610 disposition who is not acting in good faith takes subject to the debtor's rights in the collateral. A natural reading of the phrase "debtor's rights in the collateral" is that those rights include the debtor's right of redemption. Indeed, nothing in Article 9 suggests that "the debtor's rights in the collateral" do not include the debtor's right of redemption. It follows that the right of redemption is not cut off if the transferee does not act in good faith. It would be anomalous in that circumstance for

---

[4] *See* U.C.C. § 9–203(b)(2).

[5] U.C.C. § 9–624(c).

[6] *See* U.C.C. § 9–602(11).

[7] U.C.C. § 9–617(b).

[8] U.C.C. § 9–617(a).

[9] U.C.C. § 9–617(b).

[10] U.C.C. § 9–617(a).

[11] U.C.C. § 9–617(b). The policy rationale for "taking free" is to incentivize prospective transferees to bid for the collateral and to do so at prices that minimize economic loss to the secured party, the debtor, and others who have an interest in the collateral.

[12] *See* U.C.C. § 9–617(b) and cmt. 4 to U.C.C. § 9–617. "Good faith" requires that the transferee act with honesty in fact and in the observance of reasonable commercial standards of fair dealing. U.C.C. § 1–201(b)(20).

[13] U.C.C. § 9–617(c)(1). This Commentary does not address under what circumstances a transferee, such as a transferee who knows that the secured party is failing to comply with Article 9, is still considered to be acting in good faith. The resolution of that matter may depend on the specific facts and circumstances of the disposition and on the transferee's relationship to the secured party and is best left to the courts.

[14] U.C.C. § 9–623(c)(2).

Section 9–617(c)(1) to provide that a transferee not acting in good faith takes the collateral subject to the debtor's rights in the collateral if the disposition cuts off one of the debtor's key rights in the collateral, the right of redemption.

If the debtor retains the debtor's right of redemption and other rights in the collateral on account of the transferee not acting in good faith, those rights could not have been transferred to the transferee nor would the transferee take free of those rights (as would have been the case had the transferee acted in good faith).[15] In other words, the disposition is ineffective to the extent that it would otherwise have cut off the debtor's right of redemption[16] and other rights in the collateral. Absent a permitted and effective waiver by the debtor, the debtor retains whatever rights the debtor had in the collateral before the disposition including the right of redemption, albeit subject to the security interest under which the disposition was made and any other security interest or other lien.[17]

For this reason, this Commentary disagrees with the decision in *Atlas MF Mezzanine Borrower, LLC v. Macquarie Texas Loan Holder LLC*, 174 A.D.3d 150 (2019). In that case the debtor alleged that the disposition transferee had not acted in good faith and that therefore the disposition should be set aside. The court, citing a policy against disturbing foreclosure sales in the interest of commercial certainty, rejected the debtor's argument that the sale should be set aside and instead explained its view that the debtor's remedy was to seek monetary damages. Although the debtor may indeed be entitled to seek monetary damages for a disposition that did not comply with Section 9–610,[18] the debtor is also entitled to the debtor's right of redemption and other rights in the collateral when the transferee has not acted in good faith. A bad faith transferee may not rely on the "take free" rule. Any policy based on commercial certainty is subordinate to the policy of not rewarding those that do not act in good faith.

AMENDMENTS TO OFFICIAL COMMENTS

With the discussion in this Commentary in mind, Official Comment 4 to Section 9–617 is amended as follows:

4. **Title Taken by Nonqualifying Transferee.** Subsection (c) specifies the consequences for a transferee who does not qualify for protection under subsections (a) and (b) (i.e., a transferee who does not act in good faith). The transferee takes subject to the rights of the debtor, the enforcing secured party, and other security interests or other liens. In such a case the disposition is ineffective to the extent that it would otherwise have cut off the debtor's rights in the collateral, and the debtor retains those rights, including the debtor's right of redemption under Section 9–623, albeit subject to the security interest under which the disposition was made and any other security interests or liens. See PEB Commentary No. 22, dated August 24, 2020. The Commentary is available at https://www.ali.org/peb-ucc.

PEB COMMENTARY NO. 23
PROTECTED SERIES UNDER THE UNIFORM
PROTECTED SERIES ACT (2017)
(February 24, 2021)

INTRODUCTION

In 2017, the Uniform Law Commission promulgated the Uniform Protected Series Act ("UPSA"). This Commentary clarifies aspects of the relationship between UPSA and the Uniform Commercial Code (the "UCC").

---

[15] U.C.C. § 9–617(a)(1).

[16] *See* U.C.C. § 9–623(c)(2).

[17] *See* U.C.C. § 9–617(c).

[18] *See* U.C.C. § 9–625(b).

PEB COMMENTARY NO. 23

A number of states have enacted statutes that provide for protected series[1] within a limited liability company.[2] A protected series is generally empowered by such a statute to conduct its own activities under its own name, and it has the rights and duties provided in the statute. It is contemplated that the protected series will keep the assets associated with it separate from those of the limited liability company and other protected series of the limited liability company.[3] Moreover, under such a statute, the protected series generally is obligated solely to creditors whose obligations arose from interaction with the protected series; the creditors of a protected series have no claim against the assets associated with the limited liability company or of another protected series of the limited liability company. A public filing indicating the creation or existence of any particular protected series may or may not be required under the relevant statute. UPSA will, where enacted, provide for protected series of limited liability companies organized under the laws of those states.

A protected series under the existing state statutes and under UPSA is not a subsidiary of the limited liability company. Rather, a protected series exists within a limited liability company, typically the company that established the protected series. However, UPSA and several other statutes expressly refer to a protected series as a "person,"[4] and, under UPSA and most, if not all, other statutes, a protected series has the essential characteristics which, since at least the early 19th century, are typically associated with the construct of a person for purposes of legal recognition of personhood.[5] Nonetheless, as noted below, a protected series has a few atypical attributes. Moreover, as explained in the Prefatory Note to UPSA, "in some regulatory environments, [w]ith the approval of the relevant regulator, a series limited liability

---

[1] A protected series is sometimes referred to as a "series." *See* UNIF. PROTECTED SERIES ACT (2017), prefatory note, pt. 2. This Commentary refers to a series as a "protected series" to be consistent with the use of that term in the Uniform Protected Series Act (2017) and to avoid confusion with other so-called "series" in the marketplace, such as series of bonds or equity securities. Effective August 1, 2019, the Delaware Limited Liability Company Act refers to both a "protected series," and a "registered series." *See* DEL. CODE ANN. tit 6, §§ 18–215, –218 (West 2019). The former term is a new name for what the statute previously labeled as a "series." The latter term refers to a series established through the filing of a "certificate of registered series" in the office of the Delaware Secretary of State. Thus, a "registered series" under the Delaware act resembles a "protected series" under the UPSA.

[2] As of Aug. 6, 2019, the following statutes provide for protected series within a limited liability company. ALA. CODE §§ 10A–5A–11.01 to –.16 (2018); DEL. CODE ANN. tit. 6, § 18–215 (West 2019); D.C. CODE § 29–802.06 (2013); 805 ILL. COMP. STAT. ANN. 180/37–40 (West 2010 & Supp. | 2019); IND. CODE ANN. §§ 23–18.1–1–1 to –7–4 (West 2011); IOWA CODE §§ 489.1201–1206 (2019); KAN. STAT. ANN. § 17–76, 143 (West 2008 & Supp. | 2015); MO. REV. STAT. § 347.186. (2016); MONT. CODE ANN. § 35–8–304 (2017); NEV. REV. STAT. § 86.296 (2018); OKLA. STAT. ANN. tit. 18, §§ 2005(B), 2054.4 (West 2012); TENN. CODE ANN. § 48–249–309 (West 2010); TEX. BUS. ORGS. CODE ANN. §§ 101.601–622 (West 2012); UTAH CODE ANN. §§ 48–3a–1201 to 1209 (West 2014); P.R. LAWS ANN. tit. 14, § 3967 (2011).

[3] Even with regard to tangible, fungible assets, the separation need not be physical. UPSA § 301(d) (stating that "[t]he records and recordkeeping" "separating the assets may be organized by specific listing, category, type, quantity, or computational or allocational formula or procedure, *including a percentage or share of any asset*, or in any other reasonable manner) (emphasis added).

[4] In Delaware, the reference appears in the limited liability company statute's definition of a person. DEL. CODE ANN. tit. 6, § 18–101(14) (West 2019) (defining "person" to include a "limited liability company" and a range of other entities "or series thereof"). UPSA makes the reference in two places. UPSA § 102(7) (relying generally on the definition of "person" in the underlying LLC act while adding that " '[p]erson' includes a protected series"); § 104 (stating that "[a] limited liability company is a person"). The lead-in language to UPSA § 102 ("In this [act] . . .)" indicates that the UPSA definition of "person" applies only to UPSA itself and not necessarily to other law of the enacting state, let alone to the law of another jurisdiction which may not have enacted UPSA.

[5] A "person" is "a subject of legal rights and duties" conferred by the sovereign. JOHN CHIPMAN GRAY, THE NATURE AND SOURCES OF THE LAW 27 (Roland Gray rev., 2d ed., The MacMillan Co. 1931) ("a 'person' is a subject of legal rights and duties"); JOHN SALMOND, JURISPRUDENCE 318 (Glanville L. Williams ed., 10th ed. 1947) (a person is "capable of rights [and] duties"); Bryant Smith, *Legal Personality*, 37 YALE L.J. 283, 283 (1928) (a person is "the subject of rights and duties"); *Corporations—Right to Prefer Creditors*, 11 HARV. L. REV. 550 (1898) (referring to the by-then well-recognized "idea of a corporation as a legal person having powers similar to those of an individual"); *see generally* Trs. of Dartmouth Coll. v. Woodward, 17 U.S. 518 (1819). For a more recent discussion of the meaning of "person," see Elvia Arcelia Quintana Adriano, *The Natural Person, Legal Entity or Juridical Person and Juridical Personality*, 4 PENN STATE J.L. & INT'L AFFS. 363 (2015) ("A subject of law is any being capable to act as holder of powers, or liable with obligations in a juridical relationship"). For a more recent case supporting the same proposition, see People ex rel. Nonhuman Rts. Project, Inc. v. Lavery, 998 N.Y.S.2d 248, 124 A.D.3d 148 (2014) (". . . legal personhood has consistently been defined in terms of both rights *and duties* . . ." (emphasis in original)).

company makes one regulatory filing or holds a single license, and the various protected series of the company function under the aegis of that filing or license."[6]

Because a protected series is expected to enter into transactions for itself and in its own name, a party might enter into a transaction within the scope of the UCC with a protected series. For example, a lender might extend credit to a protected series secured by a security interest governed by Article 9 of the UCC in existing and after-acquired personal property assets associated with the protected series. Lawyers in such transactions are often uncertain as to whether the Article 9 "debtor" in such a transaction is the protected series or the limited liability company itself and, if the protected series is the debtor, whether that debtor is a registered organization. Uncertainty with respect to these legal issues creates uncertainty as to how Article 9 rules apply to such extensions of credit, affecting the availability and cost of credit.

Similar determinations are necessary if the protected series is a seller of certain payment rights—accounts, chattel paper, payment intangibles or promissory notes—or is a consignee of goods under a consignment within the scope of Article 9.

DISCUSSION

This Commentary focuses on five issues in transactions with a protected series: (1) Is a protected series a "person" as defined in Article 1 of the UCC? (2) Who is the "debtor" if a security interest within the scope of Article 9 is granted by a protected series to secure an obligation? (3) Who is the debtor if the security interest within the scope of Article 9 is the interest of a buyer of accounts, chattel paper, payment intangibles, or promissory notes from a protected series? (4) Who is the Article 9 debtor if the security interest is the interest of a consignor in a transaction that is a consignment within the scope of Article 9 to a protected series as consignee? (5) If the debtor is a protected series, is the debtor a "registered organization" for purposes of Article 9?

This Commentary addresses these issues for protected series established under UPSA, which was drafted with the status of a protected series under the UCC in mind. This Commentary does not address protected series statutes containing provisions that vary from the relevant provisions of UPSA.[7] Nevertheless, as a general matter, this Commentary does not preclude application of its analysis to an issue concerning a protected series of a limited liability company established under law other than UPSA, or a protected series of any other alternative business entity or organization statute, if the statute contains the substance of the provisions of UPSA relevant to the issue discussed. Accordingly, the analysis contained in this Commentary may be useful in resolving these issues under another protected series statute to the extent that the statute's relevant provisions are the same as or substantially similar to those of UPSA.

(1)   Is a protected series a "person" under the UCC?

This Commentary concludes that, under Article 1 of the UCC, a protected series established under UPSA is a "person."

Section 1–201(b)(27) defines the term "person" as follows:

"Person" means an individual, corporation, business trust, estate, trust, partnership, limited liability company, association, joint venture, government, governmental subdivision, agency, or instrumentality, public corporation, or any other legal or commercial entity.

Reasonable minds might differ as to which of the organizations specified in the definition best describes a protected series. A protected series might be considered to be an "association."[8] Or a protected series might be considered to be some other, unspecified, type of "legal or commercial entity." Article 1 does not define the term "association." Nor does it further explain the phrase "other legal or commercial entity." However,

---

[6]   UPSA prefatory note, pt. 4.

[7]   For example, the discussion below on whether a protected series is a "registered organization" under Section 9–102(a)(71) will not be applicable if the relevant limited liability company statute does not provide for a protected series of the company to be established by a public filing.

[8]   Indeed, Delaware has declared that a "protected series" under its Limited Liability Company Act is an "association" not only under the act itself but also "[[f]or all purposes of the laws of the State of Delaware." *See* DEL. CODE ANN. tit. 6, § 18–215(b)(12) (West 2019).

that phrase is a residual category, what might be described as a "catch-all" term for other legal or commercial entities that have the attributes of a "person," as further discussed below.

This analysis proceeds by focusing on the "catch-all" term. If a protected series is an "association," then it is clearly a "person" under Section 1–201(b)(27). If a protected series is not an association, however, the question becomes whether a protected series fits within the "catch-all" phrase "other legal or commercial entity."

That a protected series may be either another "legal" entity or another "commercial" entity is consistent with both the historical formulation of the term "person" in the context of Section 1–201(b)(27) and the interpretative canon of *ejusdem generis*.[9] Together, the history and the canon identify a set of characteristics associated with personhood, notwithstanding that every person might not necessarily possess each characteristic.

The definition of the term "person," through its definition of the term "organization," had been part of the Official Text of the UCC issued in 1952. Although predecessor uniform acts had used similar terms, the definition of the terms in the predecessor uniform acts did not include the phrase "any other legal or commercial entity," and it is unclear why that phrase was added to the UCC definition.

Nevertheless, the later deliberations of the Uniform Law Commission's Committee on Style are instructive. As early as 1989, the Committee on Style proposed a standardized definition of "person" for other acts promulgated by the Uniform Law Commission.[10] As initially proposed, the definition read:

"Person" means an individual, corporation, business trust, estate, trust, partnership, association, joint venture, government, governmental subdivision or agency, or any other legal or commercial entity."[11]

An accompanying footnote references the emergence of a new construct—the limited liability company—which "of course, would be included in the *catchall* 'any other legal or commercial entity' " (emphasis added).[12] Shortly thereafter, noting that the forthcoming Uniform Statutory Construction Act explicitly includes the term "limited liability company" within its definition of the term "person," it was suggested that the standardized definition should explicitly include it, notwithstanding its inclusion by the "catchall phrase 'any other legal or commercial entity.' "[13]

The deliberations of the Committee on Style strongly suggest that the phrase "or any other legal or commercial entity" was intended as a "catch-all" so that the definition of "person" not only includes individuals and the full range of then-recognized and emerging non-individuals that might enjoy the ability to hold assets or contract but also what its advocates described as a "catch-all" for any not-yet-recognized non-individuals that might enjoy the ability to hold assets or contract.

At the same time, the canon places limits on an overly broad interpretation of the term "person." According to the canon, "where general words follow specific words in a statutory enumeration, the general words are construed to embrace only objects similar to those enumerated by the specific words."[14] *Ejusdem generis* gives effect to both the general and specific terms by "treating the particular words as indicating the class, and the general words as extending the provisions of the statute to everything embraced in that class, though not specifically named by the particular words. In light of the specific terms, the general term is

---

[9]   *Ejusdem Generis*, BLACK'S LAW DICTIONARY (11th ed. 2019) ("A canon of construction holding that when a general word or phrase follows a list of specifics, the general word or phrase will be interpreted to include only items of the same class as those listed.").

[10]   *See* Eugene A. Burdick, Chairman, Comm. on Style, Proposed Standardized Definitions for Consideration of Executive Committee (Oct. 18, 1989).

[11]   *Id.*

[12]   *Id.* n.3.

[13]   *See* Memorandum from Eugene A. Burdick, Chairman of the Comm. on Style, and James C. McKay, Jr., Chairman of the Comm. on Liaison with Legis. Drafting Agencies, to the Exec. Comm. of the Unif. L. Comm'n, n.1 (May 16, 1991).

[14]   Washington State Dep't of Soc. & Health Servs. v. Guardianship Est. of Keffeler, 537 U.S. 371, 372, 123 S. Ct. 1017, 1019, 154 L. Ed. 2d 972 (2003).

restricted to include only things of the same kind, class, character, or nature as those specifically enumerated."[15]

A protected series does have a few attributes not generally associated with personhood. A protected series exists under the aegis of the limited liability company that established the protected series and cannot exist on its own.[16] Furthermore, as a general matter, a protected series necessarily ceases to exist when the limited liability company itself ceases to exist.[17]

However, a protected series under UPSA has many other attributes that strongly suggest that a protected series is a "person."[18] A protected series is distinct from its associated members, the limited liability company, and any other protected series of the limited liability company.[19] A protected series generally possesses the same powers as the limited liability company including the power to own its own assets and to sue and be sued in its own name.[20] A protected series is not liable for the debts of the limited liability company or another protected series of the limited liability company merely because it is a protected series,[21] nor are its assets generally available to creditors of the limited liability company or another protected series of the limited liability company, so long as its assets are "associated" with the protected series.[22] A protected series has its own members[23] which are distinct from the protected series[24] and which are generally entitled to vertical liability shields for acts of the protected series.[25]

Despite those few attributes to the contrary, the other attributes indicate, for purposes of the canon, that a protected series is of "the same kind, class, character, or nature" as those specifically enumerated in the definition of the term "person" in Section 1–201(b)(27).

Given the historical formulation of the term "person" with its "catch-all" phrase and even after giving effect to the canon, it would be anomalous for a protected series to have all of these attributes under the common law definition of "person" and yet fall outside of the definition of "person" under the UCC. This conclusion is further supported by the clear intent of UPSA's drafters to establish the "personhood" of a protected series under UPSA by expressly including a protected series under UPSA's own definition of "person"[26] and stating categorically that:

A protected series of a series limited liability company is a person distinct from:

(1) the company, subject to Sections 104(c), 501(1), and 502(d); (2) another protected series of the company; (3) a member of the company, whether or not the member is an associated member of the protected series; (4) a protected-series transferee of a protected series of the company; and (5) a transferee of a transferable interest of the company.[27]

---

[15] Huggett v. Dep't of Nat. Res., 464 Mich. 711, 718–19, 629 N.W.2d 915, 920 (2001) (citations and internal quotations omitted).

[16] UPSA § 103 cmt.; UPSA § 104 cmt. to subsec. (c).

[17] The one exception is in the case of the very limited form of merger permitted under the UPSA, UPSA § 104(c). *See also* UPSA§ 607(1)(A) (permitting a protected series of a series limited liability company that does not survive a merger to be relocated to the series limited liability company that does survive).

[18] See *supra* note 5, referring generally to the power, rights and duties of a "person."

[19] UPSA § 103.

[20] UPSA § 104(a), (b).

[21] UPSA § 401(b).

[22] UPSA § 404; see UPSA § 301 for determining when an asset of a protected series is "associated" with the protected series.

[23] The members of a protected series are referred to as "associated members" under UPSA. UPSA § 102(3). An associated member must be a member of the limited liability company itself. UPSA § 302(a).

[24] UPSA § 103(3).

[25] UPSA § 401(a).

[26] UPSA § 102(7).

[27] UPSA § 103. The cited sections pertain to the characteristics noted *supra* at note 17. UPSA itself leaves open the possibility that a protected series is a "commercial entity" if not a "legal" entity. UPSA § 102(7) cmt. UPSA is designed to work in conjunction with the enacting state's limited liability company statute under a construct referred to as "extrapolation." *See* UPSA, prefatory note, pt. 6. Under that construct, UPSA uses terms defined by reference in the limited liability company statute. *See* UPSA § 102 legis. note. That statute may be the Uniform Limited Liability

Of course, ultimately whether a non-individual is a "person" as that term is used in the UCC is determined by the definition of the term "person" in the UCC itself, *i.e.*, by Section 1–201(b)(27). However, UPSA's denomination of a protected series as a "person" for purposes of UPSA is suggestive of the result under the UCC for consistency, where appropriate, among uniform state laws. More fundamentally, a protected series under UPSA has most of the attributes reflected in the specific organizations listed in Section 1–201(b)(27) and is consistent with the meaning of "person" as reflected in the historical formulation of the term in Section 1–201(b)(27).

In sum, this Commentary concludes that a protected series falls within the contours of the "catch-all" phrase "any other legal or commercial entity" in the definition of person in Section 1–201(b)(27).

(2)   Who is the "debtor" if a security interest is granted by a protected series to secure an obligation?

This Commentary concludes that, if a protected series grants a security interest in collateral to secure an obligation, the protected series is the "debtor" as that term is used in Article 9. Section 9–102(a)(28) defines the term "debtor" to include "a *person* having an interest, other than a security interest or lien, in the collateral. . ." (emphasis added).[28] If a protected series is a "person" as defined in Section 1–201(b)(27), as this Commentary concludes, it follows that, if a protected series grants a security interest in collateral to secure an obligation, the protected series is the debtor.

(3)   Who is the "debtor" if the security interest within the scope of Article 9 is the interest of a buyer of accounts, chattel paper, payment intangibles, or promissory notes from a protected series?

Likewise, this Commentary concludes that if a security interest within the scope of Article 9[29] is the interest of a buyer of accounts, chattel paper, payment intangibles, or promissory notes from a protected series,[30] the protected series is the "debtor" as that term is used in Article 9. Section 9–102(a)(28) defines the term "debtor" to include "a seller of accounts, chattel paper, payment intangibles or promissory notes. . . ."[31] Even though the definition of "debtor" does not use the term "person" when referring to a "seller," Article 9 incorporates Article 2's definition of "sale"[32] (and the corresponding meaning of "seller") from Article 2, which refers to a "person."[33] If a protected series is a "person," as this Commentary concludes, it follows that the protected series can qualify as a "seller" and, accordingly, as a "debtor."

(4)   Who is the "debtor" if the security interest is the interest of a consignor in a transaction that is a "consignment" (as defined in Article 9) as to which a protected series is the consignee?

For similar reasons, this Commentary concludes that if a security interest is the interest of a consignor in a transaction that is a "consignment" within the scope of Article 9 to a protected series as consignee,[34] the protected series is the "debtor."[35] Section 9–102(a)(28) defines the term "debtor" to include "a consignee." Even though the definition of "consignee" does not use the term "person," nevertheless the definition does use the term "merchant."[36] And the term "merchant" has the same meaning in Article 9 as it does in Article 2.[37] Under Article 2, a "merchant" is a "person."[38] Accordingly, a consignee must be a "person" in order to be

---

Company Act (2006) (Last Amended 2013). *Id.* Section 102(15) of that Act, like U.C.C. § 1–201(b)(27), does define the term "person" to include an "other . . . commercial entity."

[28]   U.C.C. § 9–102(a)(28)(A).

[29]   Pursuant to U.C.C. § 9–109(a)(3), sales of accounts, chattel paper, payment intangibles and promissory notes are generally within the scope of Article 9, subject to some exclusions found in subsections (c) and (d) of that section.

[30]   See U.C.C. § 1–201(b)(35) defining the term "security interest" to include any interest of a buyer of accounts, chattel paper, payment intangibles or promissory notes in a transaction subject to Article 9.

[31]   U.C.C. § 9–102(a)(28)(B).

[32]   U.C.C. § 9–102(b), providing a cross-reference" to the term "sale" as defined in U.C.C. § 2–106.

[33]   Cf. U.C.C. § 2–103(1)(d) defining a "seller" as "a *person* who sells goods or contracts to sell goods." (emphasis added). It would be anomalous if a debtor that granted a security interest in collateral to secure an obligation must be a "person" but a seller of accounts, chattel paper, payment intangibles or promissory notes need not be a "person."

[34]   See U.C.C. § 9–102(a)(20) defining the term "consignment."

[35]   See U.C.C. § 9–102(a)(35) defining the term "security interest" to include any interest of a consignor in a transaction subject to Article 9.

[36]   See U.C.C. § 9–102(a)(20) referring to a person delivering goods to a "merchant."

[37]   See U.C.C. § 9–102(b) providing a cross-reference" to the term "merchant" as defined in U.C.C. § 2–104.

[38]   See U.C.C. § 2–104(1) defining "a merchant" as "a *person* who deals in goods. . . ." (emphasis added).

a consignee just as a seller must be a "person" in order to be a seller. If a protected series is a "person," as this Commentary concludes, it follows that the protected series can qualify as a "consignee" and, accordingly, as a "debtor."

(5) *If the debtor with respect to a security interest is a protected series, is that debtor a registered organization for purposes of Article 9?*

Regardless of whether a security interest secures an obligation, or arises from a sale of accounts, chattel paper, payment intangibles, or promissory notes, or from a consignment within the scope of Article 9, important Article 9 rules depend on whether the debtor with respect to that security interest is a "registered organization." For one thing, the rules in Section 9–307 that determine the jurisdiction in which a debtor is located are different for registered organizations than for other debtors; this has a major effect on the application of the conflict of laws rules in Sections 9–301 *et seq.* Second, the rules in Section 9–503 that determine whether a financing statement sufficiently provides the name of a debtor are different for debtors that are registered organizations than for other debtors.

This Commentary concludes that a debtor that is a protected series is a "registered organization." This conclusion follows from the definitions of "organization" in Section 1–201(b)(25) and "registered organization" in Section 9–102(a)(71). Section 1–201(b)(25) defines the term "organization" to mean "a person other than an individual." Because a protected series is a "person" as defined in § 1–201(b)(27) and is not an individual, a protected series must be an "organization."

Section 9–102(a)(71) defines the term "registered organization" to include an organization organized solely under the law of a single State . . . by the filing of a public organic record with . . . the State . . . ." The term "public organic record" is defined in Section 9–102(a)(68) to include:

a record that is available to the public for inspection and is:

(A) a record consisting of the record initially filed with or issued by a State . . . to form or organize an organization . . .;

. . . .

Under UPSA, a protected series of a limited liability company is established when the limited liability company delivers to the Secretary of State of the state in which the limited liability company is organized a "protected series designation" signed by the company and providing the name of the protected series and the protected series designation takes effect.[39] The protected series designation, when filed, is available for public inspection so as to provide transparency to the public of the existence of the protected series.[40]

It follows that, because under UPSA the protected series designation is filed with the Secretary of State to establish the protected series and is available to the public for inspection, the protected series designation is a "public organic record" as defined in Section 9–102(a)(68). It also follows that, because the protected series is an organization formed under the law of a single state—the state of organization of the limited liability company—by the filing of the protected series designation, the protected series is a "registered organization" as defined in Section 9–102(a)(71).

AMENDMENTS TO OFFICIAL COMMENTS

With the discussion in this Commentary in mind, the Official Comments are amended as follows:

The Official Comments to § 1–201 are amended by adding the following sentences at the end of the comment on the term "person" in clause 27:

A protected series formed under the Uniform Protected Series Act (2017) is a "person." See PEB Commentary No. 23, dated February 24, 2021. The Commentary is available at https://www.ali.org/peb-ucc.

Official Comment 2.a to § 9–102 is amended to add the following new paragraph at the end of the comment:

---

[39] UPSA § 201(b)–(c).

[40] UPSA § 202 cmt. to subsec. (b)(1).

PEB COMMENTARY NO. 24

If a security interest is granted by a protected series of a limited liability company formed under the Uniform Protected Series Act (2017), the debtor is the protected series. See PEB Commentary No. 23, dated February 24, 2021. The Commentary is available at https://www.ali.org/peb-ucc.

Official Comment 4 to § 9–307 is amended to add the following sentences at the end of the first paragraph of the comment:

A protected series formed under the Uniform Protected Series Act (2017) is a registered organization. See PEB Commentary No. 23, dated February 24, 2021. The Commentary is available at https://www. ali.org/peb-ucc.

PEB COMMENTARY NO. 24
SCOPE OF ARTICLE 9 CHOICE-OF-LAW RULES REGARDING CHARACTERIZATION OF TRANSACTIONS
(August 12, 2022)

INTRODUCTION

Secured transactions frequently relate to more than one jurisdiction. Accordingly, choice- of-law rules that determine the jurisdiction whose law applies to a particular aspect of a secured transaction are an important part of secured transactions law. Depending on the issue, secured transactions governed by Article 9 of the Uniform Commercial Code may be subject to two different sets of choice-of-law rules—those in Article 1 and those in Article 9. Some uncertainty has arisen as to which of those choice-of-law rules is applicable for determining whether a transaction creates a security interest governed by Article 9.

DISCUSSION

Consistently since the enactment of the Uniform Commercial Code, two different sets of choice-of-law rules have governed secured transactions. The Code's general choice-of-law rule in Article 1, now codified in Section 1–301 but largely unchanged in substance from previous versions in effect since before the promulgation of Revised Article 9,[1] provides parties to a transaction substantial autonomy to choose the law governing their rights and duties with respect to that transaction. The current text of the provision states, in part, that "Except as otherwise provided in this section, when a transaction bears a reasonable relation to this state and also to another state or nation the parties may agree that the law either of this state or of such other state or nation shall govern their rights and duties."[2] This autonomy yields, however, to mandatory choice-of-law rules in Article 9. More specifically, the general choice-of-law rule in Section 1–301 states that it does not apply to, *inter alia*, matters governed by Sections 9–301 through 9–307.[3] Those sections, like their predecessors in earlier versions of Article 9, determine the law governing perfection, the effect of perfection or non-perfection, and priority.[4] While the content of those rules has changed significantly since the pre-2001 version of Article 9, their scope—essentially determining the law governing perfection and priority and leaving other matters to the Article 1 choice-of-law rules—has remained unchanged.

Case Law Under Pre-2001 UCC

In the 1980s and 1990s, there were several judicial decisions about transactions in the form of a lease (or, in one case, a conditional sale) that (i) would likely create a security interest under the UCC in effect in the state in which the leased goods were located, but (ii) were stated to be governed by the laws of a jurisdiction

---

[1] The 2001 Official Text of U.C.C. § 1–301 contained significant changes to this general rule but was enacted only in the U.S. Virgin Islands. Those changes were subsequently removed from the Official Text and replaced with text substantively identical to the rules in former U.C.C. § 1–105.

[2] U.C.C. § 1–301(a). (As with other U.C.C. provisions, construction and application of this provision is guided by U.C.C. § 1–103(a), and the applicability of supplemental principles of law is guided by U.C.C. § 1–103(b).)

[3] *See* U.C.C. § 1–301(c)(8).

[4] *See* U.C.C. § 9–301. Prior to the Article 9 amendments that went into effect in 2001, the Article 9 rules were stated as determining the law governing "perfection and the effect of perfection or non-perfection of a security interest in collateral." See the former U.C.C. § 9–103(1)(b) (1994). The reference to "the effect of perfection or non-perfection" was understood as including priority; the addition of the explicit reference to priority in the 2001 text was intended only for clarity and not to expand the scope of the Article 9 choice-of-law rules.

that would not characterize the transaction as creating a security interest.[5] In each of these cases, the lessor or conditional seller took no actions that would constitute perfection of a security interest, and a competing claimant (a bankruptcy trustee or competing secured creditor) argued that the transaction should be treated as creating a security interest, with the consequence that the security interest was unperfected and would be subordinate to the competing claimant. Thus, resolution of each case required determination of which jurisdiction's law governed whether the transaction did or not create a security interest. Was the issue governed by the law of the jurisdiction selected by the parties to govern their transaction (a determination made by applying the Article 1 choice-of-law rule) or by the law of the jurisdiction in which the goods were located (a determination made by applying the Article 9 choice-of-law rules for perfection then in effect)? Each case concluded that the Article 9 choice-of-law rules should be applied to these characterization issues.

In the most well-known case, *In re Eagle Enterprises, Inc.*, 237 B.R. 269 (E.D. Pa. 1999), the "lessor" was a German company, the "lessee" was apparently located in Pennsylvania, and the equipment that was the subject of the transaction was located in Pennsylvania. The "lease," which would be a security interest under Article 1,[6] provided that it was governed by the law of Germany, and the German "lessor" did not file a financing statement. The German lessor argued that no financing statement was necessary because the choice of German law meant that German law controlled the issue of characterization, and German law would characterize the transaction as a lease. The court disagreed, stating:

> Under [the lessor's] theory, sellers of business equipment could routinely characterize sales transactions as leases or select the law of a jurisdiction which would so treat them, although they have an option to purchase for token consideration at the end of the lease term and, even without filing a financing statement, would be able to assert a claim to the equipment superior to that of the trustee if the "lessee" declares bankruptcy. This would completely undermine the Uniform Commercial Code requirement that holders of purchase money security interests in business equipment file financing statements to perfect their security interests, the purpose of which is to provide potential creditors with notice that another party in fact owns an interest in a potential debtor's business equipment.

Id. at 272–73 (citation omitted).

The same issue previously arose in a domestic context in *Carlson v. Tandy Computer Leasing*, 803 F.2d 391 (8th Cir. 1986). In *Carlson*, the lessor argued for the application of Texas law (the law specified in the agreement) to the characterization issue, believing that that law would have resulted in the "lease" being treated as a lease and not as a security interest governed by Article 9's perfection and priority rules. On the other hand, the lessee's trustee argued that the law of Missouri (where the lessee and the equipment were located) should control, believing that Missouri law would treat the lessor's interest as a security interest governed by Article 9's perfection and priority rules. The court rejected the lessor's argument that the choice-of-law clause in the "lease" agreement should determine the characterization for purposes of determining the consequences of the lessor's failure to file a financing statement:

> The policy behind section 1–105(2) [the predecessor of current UCC Section 1–301(a)], especially as it relates to the scope of Article 9 of the Missouri U.C.C., is to prohibit choice of law agreements when the rights of third parties are at stake. If we applied Texas law to determine whether a security interest existed here, this would violate a fundamental purpose of Article 9: to create commercial certainty and predictability by allowing third party creditors to rely on the specific perfection and priority rules that govern collateral within the scope of Article 9. In order to prevent the constant unilateral expansion and contraction of the scope of Missouri's Article 9, a Missouri court would apply Missouri law to determine the scope of Article 9 of the Missouri U.C.C.[7]

---

[5] At that time, under former Article 9, perfection of a security interest in goods, and the effect of perfection or non-perfection of that security interest, were generally governed by the law of the jurisdiction in which the goods were located, while other issues relating to secured transactions were subject to the rule in Article 1 providing parties with significant autonomy to select by agreement the law governing their transaction.

[6] At that time, the U.C.C. definition of "security interest" was codified in U.C.C. § 1–201(37). Currently, the definition is codified in U.C.C. §§ 1–201(b)(35) and 1–203.

[7] Ironically, after rejecting the choice-of-law clause in the lease and applying Missouri law to the characterization issue, the court concluded that Missouri law would not characterize the lessor's interest as a security interest.

Id. at 394 (citation omitted).

The *Carlson* court also distinguished its choice-of-law analysis from situations in which only rights of the parties to the transaction *inter se* were at stake:

> The present case is unlike those situations where only the rights of parties privy to the initial choice of law agreement are implicated. In those situations, no policy is furthered by refusing to allow the parties to select the law governing their rights alone. Nor is this a case where, despite the existence of a secured transaction, no issues concerning the scope or matters within the scope of Article 9 are raised. Instead, the question here concerns the scope of Article 9 of the Missouri U.C.C. Section 1–105(2) of the Missouri U.C.C. requires that we apply Missouri law.

Id. (citations omitted).

As noted above, the characterization issue has also arisen at least once in the context of a transaction characterized by the parties as a sale of goods with title retained by the seller until the buyer pays the entire purchase price. *Hong Kong and Shanghai Banking Corp. v. HFH USA Corp.*, 805 F.Supp. 133 (W.D.N.Y. 1992), cited *Carlson* in rejecting the application of a clause choosing the law of Germany to the question of whether such a retention-of-title credit sale should be characterized as creating a security interest.[8]

Revised Article 9

As noted above, revised Article 9 substantially changed the *content* of the Article 9 choice of rules in Sections 9–301 through 9–307 that determine the law that governs perfection, the effect of perfection or non-perfection, and priority of a security interest.[9] The statutory text of revised Article 9 made no change, however, with respect to the border between the applicability of the Article 1 choice-of-law rules and the applicability of the Article 9 choice-of-law rules. As before, the UCC continues to state that the Article 1 rules apply except for matters addressed by the choice- of-law rules governing perfection, the effect of perfection or non-perfection, and priority.[10]

Nonetheless, as part of the promulgation of revised Article 9, a comment was added to Section 9–301 (the section stating the general choice-of-law rule for perfection). Comment 2 to Section 9–301 states, in relevant part, that the choice-of-law rules in Part 3 of Article 9 address perfection, the effect of perfection or non-perfection, and priority but

> [do] not address choice of law for other purposes. For example, the law applicable to issues such as attachment, validity, characterization (e.g., true lease or security interest), and enforcement is governed by the rules in Section 1–301; that governing law typically is specified in the same agreement that contains the security agreement.

There is no indication that the intent of the revisions to the Article 9 choice-of-law rules was to change the pre-2001 status quo under which those rules governed matters related to perfection and priority of security interests (including, as found by the cases such as *Eagle Enterprises* and *Carlson*, whether a transaction creates a security interest that, if not perfected, would be subordinate to most competing claimants) while the general Article 1 choice-of-law rules governed matters relating to rights and duties between the parties to the transaction. Yet, the reference to characterization in the text of Comment 2 might be read as unintentionally changing that status quo so as to apply the Article 1 choice-of-law rules to all matters related to characterization of the transaction, even when characterization would affect the rights of persons who are not parties to the transaction. Such a reading would be inconsistent with the intent of Section 9–301, would undermine UCC perfection rules as stated in the *Eagle Enterprises* opinion, and would erode the distinction noted in the *Carlson* opinion between situations relating to perfection and priority,

---

[8]   In this case, the law of New York, the state in which the goods were located, would have treated the "conditional sale" as creating a security interest, while the law of Germany would not have done so.

[9]   Most relevant for the purpose of the issue at hand, revised Article 9 generally changes the law governing perfection of a security interest in goods from that of the jurisdiction in which the goods are located to that of the jurisdiction in which the debtor is located.

[10]   As noted above, the reference to priority was added in 2001 for clarity but priority was generally understood previously has having been included in the concept of "the effect of perfection or non-perfection." *See supra* text accompanying note 4.

which have an impact on third parties, and "those situations where only the rights of parties privy to the initial choice of law agreement are implicated."[11]

Accordingly, the reference in Comment 2 to characterization of a transaction should be read as referring that issue to Section 1–301 only insofar as characterization affects rights between the parties to the transaction. Nonetheless, because the current text of Comment 2 is not as precise as it should be with respect to this point, the Permanent Editorial Board has concluded that the comment should be amended to make the point clearly.

AMENDMENTS TO OFFICIAL COMMENT

Official Comment 2 to Section 9–301 is hereby amended to add clarifying language as follows:

2.   **Scope of This Subpart**. Part 3, Subpart 1 (Sections 9–301 through 9–307) contains choice-of-law rules similar to those of former Section 9–103. Former Section 9–103 generally addresses which State's law governs "perfection and the effect of perfection or non-perfection of" security interests. See, e.g., former Section 9–103(1)(b). This Article follows the broader and more precise formulation in former Section 9–103(6)(b), which was revised in connection with the promulgation of Revised Article 8 in 1994: "perfection, the effect of perfection or non-perfection, and the priority of" security interests. Priority, in this context, subsumes all of the rules in Part 3, including "cut off" or "take free" rules such as Sections 9–317(b), (c), and (d), 9–320(a), (b), and (d), and 9–332. (The Hague Securities Convention may sometimes modify certain of this subpart's choice-of-law rules, as well as applying them to the requirements for foreclosure and the like, the characterization of a transfer as being outright or by way of security as it affects rights of third parties, and certain other issues. See PEB Commentary No. 19, dated April 11, 2017. The Commentary is available at https://www.ali.org/peb-ucc.)

This subpart does not address choice of law for other purposes. For example, the law applicable to issues such as attachment, validity, characterization of a transaction (e.g., true lease or security interest) as it affects rights between the parties to the transaction, and enforcement is governed by the rules in Section 1–301; that governing law typically is specified in the same agreement that contains the security agreement. ~~In transactions to which the Hague Securities Convention applies, the requirements for foreclosure and the like, the characterization of a transfer as being outright or by way of security, and certain other issues will generally be governed by the law specified in the account agreement. See PEB Commentary No. 19, dated April 11, 2017.~~ And, another jurisdiction's law may govern other third-party matters addressed in this Article. See Section 9–401, Comment 3. As to the law applicable to characterization, see PEB Commentary No. 24, dated August 12, 2022. The Commentary is available at https://www.ali.org/peb-ucc.

PEB COMMENTARY NO. 26
INDICATION OF COLLATERAL IN A FINANCING STATEMENT
(August 12, 2022)

ISSUE

Does a financing statement[2] that indicates the collateral solely by reference in the financing statement to the security agreement or other record not attached to[3] the financing statement "indicate" the collateral that it covers, as required for the sufficiency of a financing statement under Section 9–502(a)(3) of the Uniform Commercial Code?

---

[11]   As to the inappropriateness of allowing parties to select the governing law for issues that have an impact on third parties, *see* Matter of First River Energy, L.L.C., 986 F.3d 914, 927–28 (5th Cir. 2021); Fishback Nursery, Inc. v. PNC Bank, Nat'l Ass'n, 920 F.3d 932, 938 (5th Cir. 2019).

[2]   The term "financing statement" includes "an initial financing statement and any filed record related to the initial financing statement." U.C.C. § 9–102(a)(39).

[3]   In deference to common parlance, and for ease of comprehension, this Commentary speaks of records that are "attached to" a financing statement to refer to records that are included in the filed records comprising an initial financing statement or amendment that adds collateral, as applicable. The term "record" means "information that is inscribed on a tangible medium or which is stored in an electronic or other medium and is retrievable in perceivable form." U.C.C. § 9–102(a)(70).

PEB COMMENTARY NO. 26

DISCUSSION

Introduction. Sections 9–308 to 9–316 of the UCC set forth the methods by which security interests can be perfected. Section 9–310(a) establishes the default rule: unless otherwise provided in Section 9–310(b) or 9–312(b), a financing statement must be filed to perfect a security interest.[4] Under Section 9–502(a)(3), a financing statement is sufficient only if, among other things, it "indicates the collateral covered by the financing statement." Section 9–504 states that a financing statement is sufficient if it "provides" a "description" of the collateral pursuant to Section 9–108[5] or "provides" an "indication" that the financing statement covers all assets or all personal property of the debtor.[6]

This Commentary concludes that a financing statement does not satisfy Section 9–504 when the financing statement does not itself (including any attachments) contain a collateral description sufficient under Section 9–108 or an indication that the security interest covers "all assets" or "all personal property." The financing statement does not satisfy the requirement if the financing statement indicates the collateral covered by the financing statement solely by referring to a record not attached to the financing statement (even if that record contains information that, if it were contained in the financing statement or an attachment, would satisfy the statutory standard).

This conclusion follows both from the text of the UCC and its underlying purposes and policies.

The text of the UCC. Section 9–502(a)(3) states that a financing statement is sufficient only if it *indicates* the collateral covered by the financing statement. That requirement is satisfied, according to Section 9–504, if the financing statement "provides" either a description of the collateral that would be sufficient under Section 9–108 or an indication that the financing statement covers "all assets" or "all personal property" of the debtor. Section 9–504 is one of several sections in which Article 9 refers to a record "providing" certain information to be sufficient. Section 9–502(a)(1) states that a financing statement is sufficient only if it "provides" the name of the debtor. When Article 9 requires a record such as a financing statement to "provide" certain information and states what is a sufficient provision of that information, the plain meaning of the text, and context and purposes of Article 9, requires the information to be in that record.

The purposes and policy of the UCC. Article 9 is but one article of the UCC. Article 1 (General Provisions) "applies to a transaction to the extent that it is governed by another article."[7] Section 1–103 provides as follows:

> (a) The Uniform Commercial Code must be liberally construed and applied to promote its underlying purposes and policies, which are:
>
> (1) To simplify, clarify, and modernize the law governing commercial transactions;
>
> (2) To permit the continued expansion of commercial practices through custom, usage, and agreement of the parties; and
>
> (3) To make uniform the law among the various jurisdictions.

As stated, among the purposes and policies of the UCC are simplicity, clarity, and uniformity in the law as enacted in various jurisdictions.

---

[4] The actions described in Section 9–310 and the other sections to which it refers will suffice to perfect a security interest that has attached. If the actions described in those sections occur before attachment of the security interest, the security interest becomes perfected when it attaches. U.C.C. § 9–308(a).

[5] U.C.C. § 9–504(1). Section 9–108 generally requires that, to be sufficient, the collateral description must "reasonably identify" what is described. This Commentary addresses only whether a financing statement "provides" a sufficient description of the collateral under Section 9–108, or "provides" an indication that the financing statement covers all assets or all personal property, if the words of that description or indication are not in the records constituting the financing statement but instead are in a record that is not attached to the financing statement.

[6] U.C.C. § 9–504(2). Such "supergeneric" indications of collateral were not sufficient under former Article 9. *See* former U.C.C. § 9–402(1) ("financing statement is sufficient if it . . . contains a statement indicating the types, or describing the items, of collateral").

[7] U.C.C. § 1–102.

Comment 1 to Section 1–103 elaborates:

The Uniform Commercial Code should be construed in accordance with its underlying purposes and policies. The text of each section should be read in the light of the purpose and policy of the rule or principle in question, as also of the Uniform Commercial Code as a whole, and the application of the language should be construed narrowly or broadly, as the case may be, in conformity with the purposes and policies involved.

Publicly searchable financing statements efficiently, reliably, and inexpensively provide to third parties the information necessary for assessment of the risk that others have certain rights in the personal property indicated in the financing statement. The Comments to Sections 9–502 and 9–504 state the purpose served by use of a financing statement (emphasis added):

The *notice* itself indicates merely that a person may have a security interest *in the collateral indicated.* . . .

. . . However, even in the case of filings that do not necessarily involve a series of transactions (e.g., a loan secured by a single item of equipment), a financing statement is effective to encompass transactions under a security agreement not in existence and not contemplated at the time the notice was filed, if the indication of collateral *in the financing statement* is sufficient to cover the collateral concerned.[8]

A financing statement sufficiently indicates collateral claimed to be covered by the financing statement if it satisfies the *purpose* of conditioning perfection on the filing of a financing statement, i.e., if *it provides notice* that a person may have a security interest in the collateral claimed.[9]

The purposes of the UCC § 9–502(a)(3) requirement that a financing statement *indicate* the collateral, like the purposes of the UCC § 9–504(1) provision that a financing statement "provide" an indication of the collateral, are best served if those provisions are interpreted to mean that an adequate collateral description appears in the record or records that are attached to the financing statement, not solely in a record that is not "attached" to the financing statement. If the collateral description is not in the records comprising the financing statement, a searcher would need to make inquiries outside of the records of the filing office to obtain even the most basic information about the collateral covered. Such inquiries are inherently inefficient.[10] Moreover, those inquiries might not yield the needed information.[11] The court in *In re Financial Oversight and Management Board for Puerto Rico*,[12] considering the comparable rule in former Article 9, adopted this analysis:

[K]ey goals of the UCC and its filing system . . . include fair notice to other creditors and the public of a security interest. . . .

. . . Requiring interested parties to contact debtors at their own expense about encumbered collateral, with no guarantee of a timely or accurate answer, would run counter to the notice purpose of the UCC.[13]

---

8   U.C.C. § 9–501, cmt. 2 (emphasis added).

9   U.C.C. § 9–504, cmt. 2 (emphasis added).

10   Requiring that an adequate indication appear in the record or records that are attached to the financing statement reduces the cost of credit for borrowers because an efficient, inexpensive, and reliable notice system makes financing less expensive in a holistic sense for lenders.

11   While Section 9–210 requires a secured party to provide its debtor with information about collateral in which the secured party claims a security interest when requested, the section generally allows the secured party up to 14 days in which to do so. The section does not require a secured party to provide the information to a third party such as a searcher. *See* U.C.C. § 9–210, cmt. 3. As stated in *In re* Financial Oversight and Management Board for Puerto Rico, 914 F.3d 694 (1st Cir. 2019) (discussed below), this statutory right is not an efficient or timely alternative to requiring the filer to attach the indication to the financing statement. Nor would it be reliable, as the searcher would not have assurance that any record not attached to the financing statement is the latest version of that record or that the record may not be subsequently amended.

12   914 F.3d 694 (1st Cir. 2019).

13   *Id.* at 711 (citations and footnote omitted).

The court held that a financing statement did not provide a sufficient indication of collateral where the only indication was in a document not attached to the financing statement.[14]

However, any concern about a searcher needing to make inquiries outside of the records of the filing office goes only so far. The inquiry burden on the searcher is balanced against the burden on the filer of providing a sufficient collateral indication in or attached to the financing statement. That balance is evident in that a financing statement with a collateral description on its face providing sufficient information to "reasonably identify" the collateral or an "all assets" indication, which indication in either case *also* refers to information not attached to the financing statement for *additional* information, may be sufficient. When a financing statement that provides information that meets the standard for sufficient indication under Section 9–504(1) *also* refers to additional information in an unattached record, this does not cause the financing statement to fail the standards for sufficient indication.

For example, consider a financing statement that describes the collateral as "all inventory supplied by secured party to debtor under a supply agreement between debtor and secured party." This description of the collateral would be sufficient because the description of the collateral as inventory alone would be sufficient[15] under Sections 9–108 and 9–504(1). This language puts the searcher on notice that a security interest may be claimed in certain inventory even though a determination of the particular inventory encumbered may require further due diligence by the searcher, or even the implementation of intercreditor arrangements, if the searcher is considering extending credit against inventory or its proceeds. The searcher may decide not to inquire further if the searcher is considering extending credit only against non-inventory collateral.[16]

CONCLUSION

A financing statement that supplies information about the collateral that it covers solely by reference to a record not attached to the financing statement is not sufficient because it does not indicate the collateral that it covers as required by UCC § 9–502(a)(3). To the extent that *In re I80 Equipment, LLC*[17] is inconsistent with this conclusion, this Commentary is to the contrary.

AMENDMENT TO OFFICIAL COMMENT

Official Comment 2 to Section 9–504 is hereby amended to add the following at the end of the first paragraph thereof:

A financing statement (including any attachments) that does not itself supply information satisfying Section 9–502(a)(3) or Section 9–504(a), but, rather, refers solely to a record not attached to the financing statement for information seeking to satisfy those provisions, does not satisfy the sufficiency requirement of Section 9–502(a)(3) that the financing statement indicate the collateral that it covers. See PEB Commentary No. 26, dated August 12, 2022. The Commentary is available at https://www.ali. org/peb-ucc.

---

[14] The somewhat different wording in current Section 9–504 does not change the necessity of having the financing statement itself contain sufficient information about the collateral. Section 9–402(1) of former Article 9 required that a financing statement "contain" a statement "*indicating* the types, or *describing* the items, of collateral" (emphasis added). Section 9–502(a)(3) requires that a financing statement "indicate[ ]" (accommodating the wording of 9–504(2)) the collateral covered by the financing statement. This requirement is satisfied by "provid[ing]" a description of the collateral pursuant to Section 9–108. Former Article 9 was generally in effect before July 1, 2001, the effective date of current Article 9.

[15] This assumes that the debtor in fact holds the goods as "inventory" as defined in Section 9–102(a)(48).

[16] The searcher might also consider whether a financing statement might cover inventory as "proceeds" of the collateral indicated in the financing statement. U.C.C. § 9–315.

[17] 938 F.3d. 866 (7th Cir. 2019), *reh'g en banc denied*, (7th Cir. 2019), *cert. denied*, 140 S. Ct. 1125 (2020).

APPENDIX D

PEB COMMENTARY NO. 27
INJUNCTION AGAINST A NONCOMPLYING DISPOSITION UNDER
SECTION 9–610 OF THE UNIFORM COMMERCIAL CODE
(December 16, 2022)

INTRODUCTION

Article 9 of the Uniform Commercial Code (the "UCC") provides several statutory rights to a secured party if the debtor defaults on obligations secured by a security interest.[1] One of those rights is the right of the secured party to dispose of the collateral under Section 9–610. However, that right is subject to corresponding duties on the secured party, such as the duty to act in good faith,[2] the duty to provide the debtor and certain other persons with timely notification of the disposition in advance of disposition,[3] and the duty to conduct all aspects of the disposition in a commercially reasonable manner.[4] If the secured party is not proceeding to conduct the disposition in compliance with these duties, Section 9–625(a) of the UCC provides that a court "may order or restrain . . . disposition of collateral on appropriate terms and conditions."

This Commentary addresses whether a court must deny a request for an order or restraint against a secured party proceeding with a noncomplying Article 9 disposition solely because the party making the request (the "aggrieved party") would be able to bring an action against the secured party that would result in a collectable judgment for money damages.[5]

DISCUSSION

Consider the following situation:

Secured Party makes a loan to Debtor. To secure payment of the loan, Debtor grants to Secured Party a security interest in Debtor's member interest in a limited liability company, which owns a valuable real estate project. Debtor defaults on the loan, and Secured Party, as permitted by the loan documents, declares the loan to be immediately due and payable.

When Debtor does not pay the loan, Secured Party schedules a public sale of the member interest without (a) hiring any professionals to market the interest or otherwise conducting any marketing for the interest, (b) providing available information to potential bidders as to the limited liability company's operating agreement or the finances or operation of the real estate project, or (c) offering available procedures for access to the project for any physical inspection. Secured Party intends to credit bid at the sale to purchase the member interest for Secured Party's own account. Debtor receives a sufficient notification of the method, time and place of the public sale ten days before the sale date.

Debtor brings a lawsuit against Secured Party seeking to restrain the sale of the member interest on the grounds that the disposition does not comply with the requirement in Section 9–610(b) that every aspect of the disposition be commercially reasonable. Secured Party responds that such a restraint may not be ordered by the court. According to Secured Party, this is because (a) under Section 9–625(b), Secured Party would be liable for damages in the amount of any loss caused by a failure to comply with the requirements of Section 9–610(b); (b) any judgment for such liability would be collectable from Secured Party; and (c) under general principles of law and equity in the applicable state, an injunction is unavailable when the aggrieved party can be made whole for any loss by a collectable money judgment.

Section 9–625(a) of the UCC states that "[i]f it is established that a secured party is not proceeding in accordance with this article, a court may order or restrain . . . disposition of collateral on appropriate terms

---

[1] *See, e.g.,* U.C.C. §§ 9–609 (possession without use of judicial process), 9–607 (collection), 9–610 (disposition), 9–620 (acceptance of collateral).

[2] U.C.C. § 1–304.

[3] U.C.C. § 9–611.

[4] U.C.C. § 9–610(b). The requirement of commercial reasonableness may not be waived or otherwise varied by the debtor or an obligor. *See* U.C.C. § 9–602(3), (7). *See also* U.C.C. § 1–302(b).

[5] The analysis contained in this Commentary is equally applicable to a collection on collateral that is not performed by a secured party in a commercially reasonable manner when required by U.C.C. § 9–607(c) and to a collection, enforcement, or disposition if the secured party is failing to comply with other provisions of Article 9.

and conditions." Section 1–103(b) provides that "the principles of law and equity . . . supplement" the provisions of the UCC, unless those principles are "displaced by the particular provisions of the Uniform Commercial Code." The question is whether, notwithstanding the power granted to courts in Section 9–625(a), a court is precluded from granting the relief described in that section if under a state's otherwise-applicable equitable principles the relief would be denied because a collectable money damages remedy is available to the aggrieved party.

For the reasons described below, we conclude that, to the extent that general state law principles governing equitable relief would limit the power granted to courts by Section 9–625(a) by precluding the availability of equitable relief where a collectable money damages remedy is available, Section 9–625(a) displaces those general principles.

While Section 9–625(a) authorizes a court to order or restrain disposition of collateral on appropriate terms and conditions, some courts have rejected requests for such relief, based not on a lack of authority or appropriateness under that section but, rather, by application of general factors limiting equitable relief under other state law when the aggrieved party has a collectable money damages remedy.[6] Under this approach, if the secured party is proceeding to conduct the disposition in violation of its duties under Article 9, the aggrieved party is not entitled to injunctive relief so long as the aggrieved party has available to it a money damages remedy that can be collected from the secured party. The aggrieved party under this approach would not suffer an irreparable harm or would have an adequate remedy at law in the form a collectable money damages remedy under Section 9–625(b). This Commentary concludes that that approach is not consistent with Section 9–625(a) and does not further the Article 9 policy of debtor protection from secured party misbehavior.

First, the approach of courts that deny injunctive relief when it would not be available under the state's general principles of equitable relief would reduce Section 9–625(a) to surplusage. Under general equitable principles, an aggrieved party seeking an injunction may typically obtain it if the party shows that it is more likely than not to prevail on the merits of its claim, will be irreparably harmed if the action to be enjoined is taken, and has no adequate remedy at law and the party's hands are sufficiently "clean" to merit equitable relief.[7] A reading of Section 9–625(a) as being limited by factors that reject relief whenever there is a collectable money damages remedy would be logically equivalent to Section 9–625(a) not being included in the UCC. In fact, nothing in Section 9–625(a) refers to the unavailability of a collectable money damages remedy as a condition of obtaining equitable relief, and the better reading of Section 9–625(a) is that, under Section 1–103(b), the UCC provision displaces any general rule of law and equity that imposes such a condition.

Moreover, requiring the denial of relief under Section 9–625(a) solely because of the availability of a collectable money damages remedy would ignore the difficulty in proving the existence and amount of damages that follow from violation of the Section 9–610 rules in many cases. A theoretical remedy that founders as a result of the impracticability of proof can hardly be said to be adequate. The fact that an aggrieved party would be able to collect a money judgment from a non-complying secured party provides scant protection to the aggrieved party against violation of Article 9 and the resulting consequences. Indeed, this is recognized by Article 9 in some contexts by reallocating burdens of persuasion[8] or providing for statutory damages that need not be proved to have been suffered as actual damages.[9]

This is not to say that Section 9–625(a) requires a court to order or restrain a disposition whenever it is established that the secured party is acting inconsistently with Article 9. As stated previously, the

---

[6]   See, e.g., Shelbourne BRF LLC v. SR 677 Bway LLC, 139 N.Y.S.3d 799, 800 (App. Div. 2021) (noting that "plaintiffs failed to demonstrate the requisite irreparable harm"); 1248 Associates Mezz II LLC v. 12E48 Mezz II LLC, No. 651812/2020, 2020 WL 2569405, at *1 (N.Y. Sup. Ct. May 18, 2020) (citing Atlas MF Mezzanine Borrower, LLC v. Macquarie Tex. Loan Holder LLC, 105 N.Y.S.3d 59 (App. Div. 2019)); cf. Broadway 500 West Monroe Mezz II LLC v. Transwestern Mezzanine Realty Partners II, LLC, 915 N.Y.S.2d 248 (App. Div. 2011) (denying an injunction request against a foreclosure of a mortgage on non-residential real property on the basis that damages are always an adequate remedy at law for collateral held by a debtor as an investment and that, therefore, there can be no irreparable harm in such a case).

[7]   See, e.g., 11A CHARLES ALAN WRIGHT & ARTHUR R. MILLER, FEDERAL PRACTICE AND PROCEDURE §§ 2941–2950 (3d ed. 2010) (analyzing principles applicable in federal court actions).

[8]   E.g., U.C.C. § 9–626(a)(4).

[9]   E.g., U.C.C. § 9–625(c)(2), (e), (f).

APPENDIX D

language of Section 9–625(a) is permissive rather than mandatory. A court may take into account factors that are typically considered when deciding whether to grant equitable relief, such as irreparable harm, the availability of an adequate remedy at law and "unclean hands," and this Commentary should not be read as taking a position as to the appropriateness or inappropriateness of an order or restraint in any particular case. A court is not required, however, to deny relief under Section 9–625(a) in a case in which the relief is otherwise appropriate solely because of the availability of a collectable money damages remedy. Under a proper reading of Section 9–625(a), a court has flexibility in fashioning an order or restraint notwithstanding the availability of the collectable money damages remedy, because Section 9–625(a) gives the court the power to base any restraint on "appropriate terms and conditions."

This effect of Section 9–625(a) is contemplated by Article 1 of the UCC. Section 1–305(b) states: "Any right or obligation declared by [the Uniform Commercial Code] is enforceable by action unless the provision declaring it specifies a different and limited effect." Comment 2 to Section 1–305 then explains: "Whether . . . equitable relief is available is determined not by this section but by specific provisions *and* by supplemental principles. Cf. Sections 1–103, 2–716."[10] So, in the context of this Commentary, whether an order or restraint is available to an aggrieved party to prevent a secured party from proceeding with a non-complying Article 9 disposition is determined by a combination of Section 9–625(a) and traditional principles on which injunctive relief may be granted, rather than on those traditional principles alone.

The discretion of the court to grant the injunction on the basis that it is established that the secured party is not proceeding in accordance with Article 9 in conducting the disposition notwithstanding the availability of the collectable money damages remedy also furthers the purpose under Article 9 of protecting the debtor and other parties against secured party misbehavior. A focus by the court solely on the availability of the collectable money damages remedy as a reason to deny an order or restraint preventing a noncomplying Section 9–610 disposition may fail sufficiently to create incentives for a secured party to conform its behavior to the requirements of Article 9. In determining whether to structure the disposition to comply with Article 9, the secured party may well take into account the burdens on the aggrieved party to (a) bring a post-disposition lawsuit against the secured party, (b) prove the amount of money damages, and (c) pay the expenses of the lawsuit. Because of those burdens, the possibility of a post- disposition lawsuit for money damages alone may fail to encourage the secured party to be as diligent in insuring that the disposition complies with Article 9 as it might otherwise be.

Section 9–625(a) follows former Section 9–507(1).[11] As Official Comment 1 to former Section 9–507 then explained:

In the case where [the secured party] proceeds, or is about to proceed, [without complying with the requirements of goods faith and commercial reasonableness], it is vital both to the debtor and other creditors to provide a remedy for the failure to comply with the statutory duty. *This remedy will be of particular importance when it is applied prospectively before the unreasonable disposition has been concluded.* This section therefore provides that a secured party proposing to dispose of collateral in an unreasonable manner, may, by court order, be restrained from doing so, and such an order might appropriately provide . . . that [the secured party] proceed with the sale or other disposition under specified terms and conditions[12]

Nothing in Section 9–625(a) suggests that the remedy of restraint or judicial order to prevent a disposition not complying with Article 9 is of any less importance today than it was under former Section 9–507(1).[13]

Finally, it is not unusual that a statute, like Section 9–625(a), might modify traditional equitable principles, including the availability of injunctive relief, that would apply in the absence of the statute.[14]

---

[10] U.C.C. § 1–305, cmt. 2 (emphasis added).

[11] U.C.C. § 9–625, cmt. 1.

[12] U.C.C. § 9–507, cmt. 1 (rev. 2001) (emphasis added).

[13] The Comment may be traced back to the 1952 Official Text of the UCC.

[14] *See, e.g.,* 11A CHARLES ALAN WRIGHT & ARTHUR R. MILLER, FEDERAL PRACTICE AND PROCEDURE § 942 (3d ed. 2010) (citing federal statutes modifying rights to injunctive relief); FLA. STAT. ANN. § 39.504 (West 2022) (injunction to prevent child abuse); ME. REV. STAT. ANN. tit. 5, § 209 (West 2022) (injunction against unfair and deceptive practices).

Indeed, other provisions in the UCC itself modify otherwise applicable rights to injunctive relief.[15] Moreover, courts have recognized that, as a general matter, when evidence shows that the defendants are engaged in, or are about to be engaged in, acts or practices prohibited by a statute and the statute provides for injunctive relief to prevent such violations (without referring to traditional equitable grounds for injunctive relief), otherwise applicable equitable grounds for injunctive relief need not be shown.[16]

AMENDMENTS TO OFFICIAL COMMENTS

Official Comment 2 to Section 9–625 is amended by adding the following new paragraph at the end of the comment:

Subsection (a) displaces other state law governing availability of the types of relief addressed in that subsection to the extent that the other state law would preclude the availability of injunctive relief in an otherwise appropriate case solely because the aggrieved party would be able to obtain a collectible money judgment for noncompliance with the rules of this Article. Rather, under subsection (a), in an appropriate case the aggrieved party should be able obtain relief of the sort described in that subsection even if it would be possible for the aggrieved party to obtain such a judgment. See PEB Commentary No. 27, dated December 16, 2022, discussing the issue in the context of a noncomplying disposition under Section 9–610. The Commentary is available at https://www.ali.org/peb-ucc.

Official Comment 2 to Section 1–305 is amended by changing its last sentence to read as follows:

Cf. Sections 1–103, 2–716, 9–625.

---

[15] *See* U.C.C. § 4A–503 (limiting persons against whom an injunction to prevent executing or completing a payment order may be obtained); U.C.C. § 5–109(b) (establishing mandatory criteria for an injunction to prevent an issuer from honoring a drawing under a letter of credit).

[16] Burlington N. R.R. Co. v. Dep't of Revenue of State of Wash., 934 F.2d 1064, 1074 (9th Cir. 1991) (quoting Atchison, Topeka & Santa Fe R.R. Co. v. Lennen, 640 F.2d 255, 259–260 (10th Cir. 1981). *See also, e.g.*, Shadid v. Fleming, 160 F.2d 752, 753 (10th Cir. 1947) (noting that "where an injunction is authorized by statute it is unnecessary for plaintiff to plead and prove the existence of the usual equitable grounds, irreparable injury and absence of an adequate remedy at law. It is enough if the requirements of the statute are satisfied"); Henderson v. Burd, 133 F.2d 515, 517 (2d Cir. 1943) ("The contention that the plaintiff failed to prove the existence of the usual equitable grounds for relief, such as irreparable damage, is plainly irrelevant. Where an injunction is authorized by statute it is enough if the statutory conditions are satisfied.").

APPENDIX E

PREFATORY NOTE TO 2022
UCC AMENDMENTS

---

1.   **Background.** In 2019, the Uniform Law Commission and The American Law Institute (the Sponsors) appointed a Joint Committee to consider whether changes to the UCC are advisable to accommodate emerging technologies, such as artificial intelligence, distributed ledger technology, and virtual currency. The Joint Committee was initially formed as a study committee, but subsequently was constituted as the Drafting Committee to prepare amendments to the UCC.

The Drafting Committee held 18 meetings from October 2019 to March 2022. It also met with ULC commissioners in advance of the ULC Annual Meetings in 2021 and 2022. Several informal working groups were formed and these groups provided substantial input to the Drafting Committee. More than 300 observers to the Drafting Committee participated in the process. During the process members of the Drafting Committee and observers reached out to industry groups and other stakeholders for input and also participated in many CLE presentations and meetings to educate members of the bar and other interested constituencies.

The work of the Drafting Committee focused primarily on the following areas concerning the UCC: digital assets (controllable electronic records), electronic money, chattel paper, "bundled" or "hybrid" transactions (consisting of the sale or lease of goods together with the sale, lease, or licensing of other property and the provision of services as an integrated transaction), documents of title, payment systems, miscellaneous UCC amendments, and consumer issues.

The ALI approved Tentative Draft No. 1 (April 2022) of the Uniform Commercial Code and Emerging Technologies draft, subject to the usual caveats, at its annual meeting in May 2022. The ULC approved the Uniform Commercial Code Amendments (2022) (2022 Amendments) at its annual meeting in July 2022.

2.   **Overview of 2022 Amendments.**

a.   **New UCC Article 12—Controllable electronic records, controllable accounts, controllable payment intangibles.** The 2022 Amendments include a new UCC Article 12 that governs the transfer of property rights in certain intangible digital assets ("controllable electronic records") that have been or may be created and may involve the use of new technologies. These assets include, for example, certain types of (non-fiat) virtual currency and nonfungible tokens (NFTs). "Control" of controllable electronic records is a central organizing concept under Article 12. Controllable electronic records are defined to include only those electronic records that can be subjected to control. Control is best understood in a general sense as a functional equivalent of "possession" of a controllable electronic record and a necessary condition for protection as a good faith purchaser for value (a "qualifying purchaser") of a controllable electronic record. Article 12 confers an attribute of negotiability on controllable electronic records because a qualifying purchaser takes its interest free of conflicting property claims to the record.

Controllable electronic records also provide a mechanism for evidencing certain rights to payment— controllable accounts and controllable payment intangibles. An account debtor (obligor) on such a right to payment agrees to make payments to the person that has control of the controllable electronic record that evidences the right to payment. Assignments and other aspects of these rights to payment are governed by revisions to UCC Article 9, discussed below, as well as Article 12. Because a qualifying purchaser of a controllable account or controllable payment intangible will take free of competing property claims, these rights to payment also would have this attribute of negotiability. Article 12 provides special rules with respect to the payment obligations and conditions of discharge of account debtors on controllable accounts and controllable payment obligations.

Article 12 includes a choice-of-law rule for the matters that it covers in connection with transactions in controllable electronic records.

b.   **Secured transactions amendments—UCC Article 9.**

Article 12 conforming and other amendments. The 2022 Amendments include extensive amendments to UCC Article 9. Several of these amendments address security interests in controllable electronic records and in the

APPENDIX E

rights to payment that are embedded in, or tethered to, controllable electronic records—controllable accounts and controllable payment intangibles. Perfection (i.e., essentially, enforceability against third parties) of security interests in these assets may be achieved by a secured party obtaining control of the asset or filing a financing statement in the appropriate jurisdiction's filing office. A security interest perfected by control has priority over a security interest perfected by filing. The amendments also provide special rules for the law governing perfection and priority for security interests in controllable electronic records, controllable accounts, and controllable payment intangibles. These rules draw on the Article 12 choice-of-law rule.

Chattel paper. UCC Article 9 affords special treatment to "chattel paper" (e.g., installment sale contracts and personal property leases). The amendments redefine "chattel paper" and update the relevant Article 9 provisions. The revised definition resolves uncertainty that has arisen under the previous definition and more accurately reflects the distinction between the seller's or lessor's right to payment and the record (e.g., installment sale contract or lease) evidencing that right. The revised definition also resolves uncertainty that has arisen when goods are leased as part of a hybrid transaction involving services or non-goods property as well as specific goods. The amendments address additional issues relating to hybrid transactions, mentioned in 2.d., below, and provide an amended definition of "control" of an authoritative electronic copy of a record evidencing chattel paper, which reflects a more accurate and technologically flexible approach than the previous definition.

Money. The amendments include a revised definition of "money" in Article 1, which applies throughout the UCC unless otherwise provided. They also include amendments that define "electronic money" and provide a definition of "control" of electronic money that tracks the corresponding definition for control of controllable electronic records. Perfection of a security interest in electronic money (a subset of money) as original collateral must be by control, not filing. The amendments provide a revised Article 9 definition of "money" that excludes deposit accounts (which could in the future be adopted by a government as money) and money in an electronic form that cannot be subjected to control. The amendments also update and clarify the take-free rules for transferees of money—both electronic money and tangible money—and transferees of funds from deposit accounts.

Control through another person. Revisions to the provisions on control in Sections 9–104 (control of deposit accounts), 9–105 (control of authoritative electronic copy of record evidencing chattel paper), and 9–105A (control of electronic money) and a conforming modification to Section 8–106(d)(3) (control of security entitlement) address control through the acknowledgment of a person in control. For similar provisions, see Sections 7–106 (control of electronic document of title) and 12–105 (control of controllable electronic record). For a discussion relevant to these revisions, see Section 12–105, Comment 8.

Assignments. The amendments contain new Article 9 definitions of the terms "assignee" and "assignor," which conform to the descriptions in the pre-2022 official comments.

c.   **Payments amendments—UCC Articles 3 (negotiable instruments), 4 (bank deposits and collections), and 4A (funds transfers).** The amendments include several revisions to Articles 3, 4 and 4A or their official comments. The amendments relate to negotiability, remote deposit capture, statements of account, the scope of Article 4A (definition of payment order), and security procedures. The amendments also replace references to a "writing" with references to a "record." Many of the changes are to the official comments and are intended to further clarify the statutory text.

d.   **Other emerging technologies-related amendments.** The amendments contain a revised definition of "conspicuous" in Article 1 and a revised and an updated official comment on that term. They also add to Article 1 the standard definition of "electronic" used by the ULC and adopt revised Article 1 definitions of "send" and "sign," which address records other than writings.

The amendments also amend Sections 2–102 and 2A–102 and related definitions to clarify the scope of Articles 2 and 2A with respect to hybrid transactions. They also include amendments to several provisions of Articles 2 and 2A to change previous references to a "writing" or "written" communication to refer instead to a "record."

The amendments include a revised Section 7–106, defining "control" for electronic documents of title. The revised section retains the general rule and the safe harbor under the previous provision and adds an additional safe harbor along the lines of the revised section on control of chattel paper. The amendments also include revisions to the official comments to several provisions of Articles 7 and 9, in particular to clarify the treatment of nonnegotiable documents of title.

Finally, the amendments include several revisions to the official comments to Article 8 (investment securities), in particular to make clear that a controllable electronic record may be a "financial asset" credited to a securities account.

e. **Miscellaneous amendments**. The Article 1 definition of "person" is amended to include a protected series established under non-UCC law.

Amendments to Section 5–116 cure an ambiguity relating to the separate status of bank branches in the former provision and to reject incorrectly decided case law arising from that ambiguity.

f. **Official Comments**. The amendments include additional revisions of the official comments to many sections. The amended official comments remove certain references to obsolete and withdrawn UCC provisions and other uniform laws except as may be necessary or useful to explain particular issues.

APPENDIX F

2022 AMENDMENTS TO UCC ARTICLE 9

In ~~strikeout~~/<u>underline</u> format.

9–101.   Short Title.

9–102.   Definitions and Index of Definitions.

9–104.   Control of Deposit Account.

9–105.   ~~Control of Electronic Chattel Paper~~<u>Control of Electronic Copy of Record Evidencing Chattel Paper</u>.

<u>9–105A.   Control of Electronic Money.</u>

<u>9–107A.   Control of Controllable Electronic Record, Controllable Account, or Controllable Payment Intangible.</u>

<u>9–107B.   No Requirement to Acknowledge or Confirm; No Duties.</u>

9–108.   Sufficiency of Description.

9–109.   Scope.

9–203.   Attachment and Enforceability of Security Interest; Proceeds; Supporting Obligations; Formal Requisites.

9–204.   After-Acquired Property; Future Advances.

9–207.   Rights and Duties of Secured Party Having Possession or Control of Collateral.

9–208.   Additional Duties of Secured Party Having Control of Collateral.

9–209.   Duties of Secured Party if Account Debtor Has Been Notified of Assignment.

9–210.   Request for Accounting; Request Regarding List of Collateral or Statement of Account.

9–301.   Law Governing Perfection and Priority of Security Interests.

9–304.   Law Governing Perfection and Priority of Security Interests in Deposit Accounts.

9–305.   Law Governing Perfection and Priority of Security Interests in Investment Property.

<u>9–306A.   Law Governing Perfection and Priority of Security Interests in Chattel Paper.</u>

<u>9–306B.   Law Governing Perfection and Priority of Security Interests in Controllable Accounts, Controllable Electronic Records, and Controllable Payment Intangibles.</u>

9–310.   When Filing Required to Perfect Security Interest or Agricultural Lien; Security Interests and Agricultural Liens to Which Filing Provisions Do Not Apply.

9–312.   Perfection of Security Interests in Chattel Paper, <u>Controllable Accounts, Controllable Electronic Records, Controllable Payment Intangibles,</u> Deposit Accounts, <u>Negotiable</u> Documents, Goods Covered by Documents, Instruments, Investment Property, Letter-of-Credit Rights, and Money; Perfection by Permissive Filing; Temporary Perfection Without Filing or Transfer of Possession.

9–313.   When Possession by or Delivery to Secured Party Perfects Security Interest Without Filing.

9–314.   Perfection by Control.

<u>9–314A.   Perfection by Possession and Control of Chattel Paper.</u>

9–316.   Effect of Change in Governing Law.

9–317.   Interests That Take Priority Over or Take Free of Security Interest or Agricultural Lien.

9–322.   Priorities Among Conflicting Security Interests in and Agricultural Liens on Same Collateral.

9–323.   Future Advances.

9–324.   Priority of Purchase-Money Security Interests.

<u>9–326A.   Priority of Security Interest in Controllable Account, Controllable Electronic Record, and Controllable Payment Intangible.</u>

9–330.   Priority of Purchaser of Chattel Paper or Instrument.

9–331.   Priority of Rights of Purchasers of <u>Controllable Accounts, Controllable Electronic Records, Controllable Payment Intangibles,</u>~~Instruments,~~ Documents, <u>Instruments,</u> and Securities Under Other

1037

Articles; Priority of Interests in Financial Assets and Security Entitlements and Protection Against Assertion of Claim Under ~~Article 8~~Articles 8 and 12.

9–332.   Transfer of Money; Transfer of Funds From Deposit Account.

9–334.   Priority of Security Interests in Fixtures and Crops.

9–341.   Bank's Rights and Duties With Respect to Deposit Account.

9–401.   Alienability of Debtor's Rights.

9–403.   Agreement Not to Assert Defenses Against Assignee.

9–404.   Rights Acquired by Assignee; Claims and Defenses Against Assignee.

9–406.   Discharge of Account Debtor; Notification of Assignment; Identification and Proof of Assignment; Restrictions on Assignment of Accounts, Chattel Paper, Payment Intangibles, and Promissory Notes Ineffective.

9–408.   Restrictions on Assignment of Promissory Notes, Health-Care-Insurance Receivables, and Certain General Intangibles Ineffective.

9–502.   Contents of Financing Statement; Record of Mortgage as Financing Statement; Time of Filing Financing Statement.

9–508.   Effectiveness of Financing Statement if New Debtor Becomes Bound by Security Agreement.

9–509.   Persons Entitled to File a Record.

9–513.   Termination Statement.

9–516.   What Constitutes Filing; Effectiveness of Filing.

9–601.   Rights After Default; Judicial Enforcement; Consignor or Buyer of Accounts, Chattel Paper, Payment Intangibles, or Promissory Notes.

9–602.   Waiver and Variance of Rights and Duties.

9–605.   Unknown Debtor or Secondary Obligor.

9–608.   Application of Proceeds of Collection or Enforcement; Liability for Deficiency and Right to Surplus.

9–610.   Disposition of Collateral After Default.

9–611.   Notification Before Disposition of Collateral.

9–612.   Timeliness of Notification Before Disposition of Collateral.

9–613.   Contents and Form of Notification Before Disposition of Collateral: General.

9–614.   Contents and Form of Notification Before Disposition of Collateral: Consumer-Goods Transaction.

9–615.   Application of Proceeds of Disposition; Liability for Deficiency and Right to Surplus.

9–616.   Explanation of Calculation of Surplus or Deficiency.

9–619.   Transfer of Record or Legal Title.

9–620.   Acceptance of Collateral in Full or Partial Satisfaction of Obligation; Compulsory Disposition of Collateral.

9–621.   Notification of Proposal to Accept Collateral.

9–624.   Waiver.

9–627.   Determination of Whether Conduct Was Commercially Reasonable.

9–628.   Nonliability and Limitation on Liability of Secured Party; Liability of Secondary Obligor.

§ 9–101.   Short Title.

* * *

Official Comment

~~1. Source. This Article supersedes former Uniform Commercial Code (UCC) Article 9. As did its predecessor, it provides a comprehensive scheme for the regulation of security interests in personal property and fixtures. For the most part this Article follows the general approach and retains much of the terminology of former Article 9. In addition to describing many aspects of the operation and interpretation of this Article, these Comments explain the material changes that this Article makes to former Article 9. Former Article 9 superseded the wide variety of pre-UCC security devices. Unlike the Comments to former Article 9, however, these Comments dwell very little on the pre-UCC state of the law. For that reason, the Comments to former Article 9 will remain of substantial historical value and interest. They also will remain useful in understanding the background and general conceptual approach of this Article.~~

~~Citations to "Bankruptcy Code Section "in these Comments are to Title 11 of the United States Code as in effect on July 1, 2010.~~

~~2.~~ 1. **Source, Background, and History.** In 1990, the Permanent Editorial Board for the UCC with the support of its sponsors, The American Law Institute and the National Conference of Commissioners on Uniform State Laws, established a committee to study <u>Uniform Commercial Code (UCC)</u> Article 9 ~~of the UCC~~. The study committee issued its report as of December 1, 1992, recommending the creation of a drafting committee for the revision of Article 9 and also recommending numerous specific changes to Article 9. Organized in 1993, a drafting committee met fifteen times from 1993 to 1998. ~~This~~ <u>Extensive revisions of this</u> Article ~~was~~ <u>were</u> approved by its sponsors in 1998 <u>(1998 Revisions)</u>. ~~This~~ <u>The</u> Article was conformed to revised Article 1 in 2001 and to amendments to Article 7 in 2003. The sponsors approved amendments to selected sections of this Article in 2010.

<u>The 1998 Revisions superseded former Article 9 (pre-1998 Article 9) and, as did their predecessor, provided a comprehensive scheme for the regulation of security interests in personal property and fixtures. For the most part the 1998 Article 9 followed the general approach and retains much of the terminology of pre-1998 Article 9. Comment 3 describes the material changes made by the 1998 Revisions. Pre-1998 Article 9 superseded the wide variety of pre-UCC security devices. Unlike the Comments to pre-1998 Article 9, however, these Comments dwell very little on the pre-UCC state of the law. For that reason, the Comments to pre-1998 Article 9 will remain of substantial historical value and interest. They also will remain useful in understanding the background and general conceptual approach of this Article.</u>

<u>Article 9 was again extensively revised in 2022 (2022 Article 9 Revisions) pursuant to the Uniform Commercial Code Amendments (2022) (2022 Amendments). In particular, the 2022 Article 9 Revisions conform and adapt Article 9 to Article 12, covering controllable electronic records and rights to payment that are tethered to controllable electronic records—controllable accounts and controllable payment intangibles. For a brief summary of the 2022 Article 9 Revisions, see Comment 4, below. *Except as noted in Comments 3 and 4 below, the 1998 Article 9 remains substantially unchanged following the 2022 Article 9 Revisions.*</u>

<u>Note also that citations to "Bankruptcy Code Section" in these Comments are to Title 11 of the United States Code as in effect on July 1, 2022.</u>

~~3~~ 2. **1998 Revisions: Reorganization and Renumbering; Captions; Style.** ~~This Article reflects a~~ <u>The 1998 Revisions embraced</u> a substantial reorganization of former Article 9 and renumbering of most sections <u>of Article 9,</u> ~~New~~ <u>including a new</u> Part 4 ~~deals~~ <u>dealing</u> with several aspects of third-party rights and duties that are unrelated to perfection and priority. Some of these were covered by Part 3 of ~~former~~ <u>pre-1998</u> Article 9. <u>Also added was a</u> new Part 5, ~~deals~~ <u>dealing</u> with filing (formerly covered by ~~former~~ <u>pre-1998</u> Part 4), and Part 6, ~~deals~~ <u>dealing</u> with default and enforcement (formerly covered by ~~former~~ <u>pre-1998</u> Part 5). ~~Appendix I contains conforming revisions to other articles of the UCC, and Appendix II contains model provisions for production money priority.~~ ~~This Article~~ <u>The 1998 Revisions</u> also ~~includes~~ <u>include</u> headings for the subsections as an aid to readers. Unlike section captions, which are part of the UCC, see Section 1–107, subsection headings are not a part of the official text itself and have not been approved by the sponsors. ~~Each jurisdiction in which this Article is introduced may consider whether to adopt the headings as a part of the statute and whether to adopt a provision clarifying the effect, if any, to be given to the headings. This Article also has been conformed to current style conventions.~~

~~4~~ 3. **Summary of** <u>1998</u> **Revisions.** Following is a brief summary of some of the more significant ~~revisions~~ <u>features of the 1998 Revisions</u> of Article 9 ~~that are included in the 1998 revision of this Article~~.

a. **Scope of Article 9.** ~~This Article expands~~ <u>The 1998 Revisions expanded</u> the scope of Article 9 in several respects.

Deposit accounts. Section 9–109 includes within this Article's scope deposit accounts as original collateral, except in consumer transactions. ~~Former~~ <u>Pre-1998</u> Article 9 dealt with deposit accounts only as proceeds of other collateral.

Sales of payment intangibles and promissory notes. Section 9–109 also includes within the scope of this Article most sales of "payment intangibles" (defined in Section 9–102 as general intangibles under which an account debtor's principal obligation is monetary) and "promissory notes" (also defined in Section 9–102). ~~Former~~ <u>Pre-1998</u> Article 9 included sales of accounts and chattel paper, but not sales of payment intangibles or promissory notes. In its inclusion of sales of payment intangibles and promissory notes, this Article continues the drafting convention found in ~~former~~ <u>pre-1998</u> Article 9; ~~it provides that~~ the sale of accounts, chattel paper, payment intangibles, or promissory notes creates a "security interest." The definition of "account" in Section 9–102 also ~~has been~~ <u>was</u> expanded to include various rights to payment that were general intangibles under ~~former~~ <u>pre-1998</u> Article 9.

* * *

Consignments. Section 9–109 ~~provides that~~ added "true" consignments–bailments for the purpose of sale by the bailee ~~are security interests covered by~~ to the scope of Article 9, with certain exceptions. See Section 9–102 (defining "consignment"). ~~Currently~~ Under the pre-1998 UCC, many consignments ~~are~~ were subject to Article 9's filing requirements by operation of ~~former~~ pre-1998 Section 2–326.

Supporting obligations and property securing rights to payment. ~~This Article~~ The 1998 Revisions also ~~addresses~~ addressed explicitly (i) obligations, such as guaranties and letters of credit, that support payment or performance of collateral such as accounts, chattel paper, and payment intangibles, and (ii) any property (including real property) that secures a right to payment or performance that is subject to an Article 9 security interest. See Sections 9–203, 9–308.

Commercial tort claims. Section 9–109 expands the scope of Article 9 to include the assignment of commercial tort claims by narrowing the exclusion of tort claims generally. However, ~~this Article continues~~ Article 9 continues to exclude tort claims for bodily injury and other non-business tort claims of a natural person. See Section 9–102 (defining "commercial tort claim").

Transfers by States and governmental units of States. Section 9–109 narrows the exclusion of transfers by States and their governmental units. ~~It excludes~~ by excluding only transfers covered by another statute (other than a statute generally applicable to security interests) to the extent the statute governs the creation, perfection, priority, or enforcement of security interests.

Nonassignable general intangibles, promissory notes, health-care-insurance receivables, and letter-of-credit rights. ~~This Article enables~~ The 1998 Revisions enabled a security interest to attach to letter-of-credit rights, health-care-insurance receivables, promissory notes, and general intangibles, including contracts, permits, licenses, and franchises, notwithstanding a contractual or statutory prohibition against or limitation on assignment. ~~This~~ The revised Article explicitly protects third parties against any adverse effect of the creation or attempted enforcement of the security interest. See Sections 9–408, 9–409.

* * *

b. **Duties of Secured Party.** ~~This Article provides~~ The 1998 Revisions provided for expanded duties of secured parties.

* * *

c. **Choice of Law.** The choice-of-law rules included in the 1998 Revisions for the law governing perfection, the effect of perfection or nonperfection, and priority are found in Part 3, Subpart 1 (Sections 9–301 through 9–307). See also Section 9–316.

Where to file: Location of debtor. ~~This Article changes~~ The 1998 Revisions changed the choice-of-law rule governing perfection (i.e., where to file) for most collateral to the law of the jurisdiction where the debtor is located. See Section 9–301. Under ~~former~~ pre-1998 Article 9, the jurisdiction of the debtor's location governed only perfection and priority of a security interest in accounts, general intangibles, mobile goods, and, for purposes of perfection by filing, chattel paper and investment property.

Determining debtor's location. As a baseline rule, Section 9–307 follows ~~former~~ pre-1998 Section 9–103, under which the location of the debtor is the debtor's place of business (or chief executive office, if the debtor has more than one place of business). Section 9–307 contains three major exceptions. First, a "registered organization," such as a corporation or limited liability company, is located in the State under whose law the debtor is organized, e.g., a corporate debtor's State of incorporation. Second, an individual debtor is located at his or her principal residence. Third, there are special rules for determining the location of the United States and registered organizations organized under the law of the United States.

* * *

Priority. For tangible collateral such as goods and instruments, Section 9–301 provides that the law applicable to priority and the effect of perfection or nonperfection will remain the law of the jurisdiction where the collateral is located, as under ~~former~~ pre-1998 Section 9–103 (but without the confusing "last event" test). For intangible collateral, such as accounts, the applicable law for priority ~~will be~~ is that of the jurisdiction in which the debtor is located.

* * *

Goods covered by certificates of title; deposit accounts; letter-of-credit rights; investment property. ~~This Article includes~~ The 1998 Revisions to Article 9 included several refinements to the treatment of choice-of-law matters for goods covered by certificates of title. See Section 9–303. ~~It~~ The revision also ~~provides~~ provided special choice-of-law rules, similar to those for investment property under Articles 8 and 9, for deposit accounts (Section 9–304), investment property (Section 9–305), and letter-of-credit rights (Section 9–306).

* * *

d. **Perfection.** The 1998 revised rules governing perfection of security interests and agricultural liens are found in Part 3, Subpart 2 (Sections 9–308 through 9–316).

Deposit accounts; letter-of-credit rights. With certain exceptions, ~~this Article provides~~ the 1998 Revisions provided that a security interest in a deposit account or a letter-of-credit right may be perfected *only* by the secured party's acquiring "control" of the deposit account or letter-of-credit right. See Sections 9–312, 9–314. Under Section 9–104, a secured party has "control" of a deposit account when, with the consent of the debtor, the secured party obtains the depositary bank's agreement to act on the secured party's instructions (including when the secured party becomes the account holder) or when the secured party is itself the depositary bank. The control requirements are patterned on Section 8–106, which specifies the requirements for control of certain investment property. Under Section 9–107, "control" of a letter-of-credit right occurs when the issuer or nominated person consents to an assignment of proceeds under Section 5–114.

Electronic chattel paper and tangible chattel paper definitions deleted in 2022 Article 9 Revisions. Section 9–102 ~~includes~~ of the 1998 Revisions included ~~a~~ new defined ~~term~~ terms: "electronic chattel ~~paper.~~ paper" and "tangible chattel paper." ~~Electronic chattel paper is a record or records consisting of information stored in an electronic medium (i.e., it is not written). Perfection of a security interest in electronic chattel paper may be by control or filing. See Sections 9–105 (*sui generis* definition of control of electronic chattel paper), 9–312 (perfection by filing), 9–314 (perfection by control).~~ However, the 2022 Article 9 Revisions deleted those terms and modified the definition of "chattel paper" and the rules for chattel paper evidenced by electronic records, as discussed in Comment 4 and Section 9–102, Comment 5.b.

Investment property. The 1998 Revisions left the perfection requirements for "investment property" (defined in Section 9–102), including perfection by control under Section 9–106, ~~remain~~ substantially unchanged. However, a new provision in Section 9–314 is designed to ensure that a secured party retains control in "repledge" transactions that are typical in the securities markets.

Instruments, ~~agricultural liens,~~ and commercial tort claims. ~~This Article expands~~ The 1998 Revisions expanded the types of collateral in which a security interest may be perfected by filing to include instruments. See Section 9–312. ~~Agricultural~~ Under the revised Article ~~liens and~~ security interests in commercial tort claims also are perfected by filing ~~under this Article~~. See Sections 9–308, 9–310.

Sales of payment intangibles and promissory notes. Although ~~former~~ pre-1998 Article 9 covered the outright sale of accounts and chattel paper, under the revised Article sales of most other types of receivables also are financing transactions to which Article 9 should apply. Accordingly, Section 9–102 expanded the definition of "account" to include many types of receivables (including "health-care-insurance receivables," defined in Section 9–102) that ~~former~~ pre-1998 Article 9 classified as "general intangibles." It thereby subjects to Article 9's filing system sales of more types of receivables than did ~~former~~ pre-1998 Article 9. Certain sales of payment intangibles–primarily bank loan participation transactions–should not be subject to the Article 9 filing rules. These transactions ~~fall~~ are placed in a residual category of collateral, "payment intangibles" (general intangibles under which the account debtor's principal obligation is monetary), the sale of which is exempt from the filing requirements of Article 9. See Sections 9–102, 9–109, 9–309 (perfection upon attachment). The perfection rules for sales of promissory notes are the same as those for sales of payment intangibles.

Possessory security interests. Several provisions of 1998 Article 9 address aspects of security interests involving a secured party or a third party who is in possession of ~~the~~ collateral. In particular, Section 9–313 resolves a number of uncertainties under ~~former~~ pre-1998 Section 9–305. It provides that a security interest in collateral in the possession of a third party is perfected when the third party acknowledges in ~~an authenticated~~ a signed record that it holds for the secured party's benefit. Section 9–313 also provides that a third party need not so acknowledge and that its acknowledgment does not impose any duties on it, unless it otherwise agrees. A special rule in Section 9–313 provides that if a secured party already is in possession of collateral, its security interest remains perfected by possession if it delivers the collateral to a third party and the collateral is accompanied by instructions to hold it for the secured party or to redeliver it to the secured party. Section 9–313 also clarifies the limited circumstances under which a security interest in goods covered by a certificate of title may be perfected by the secured party's taking possession.

Automatic perfection. The 1998 Revisions added Section 9–309, which lists various types of security interests as to which no public-notice step is required for perfection (e.g., purchase-money security interests in consumer goods other than automobiles). This automatic perfection also extends to a transfer of a health-care-insurance receivable *to* a health-care provider. Those transfers normally will be made by natural persons who receive health-care services; there is little value in requiring filing for perfection in that context. Automatic perfection also applies to security interests created by sales of payment intangibles and promissory notes. Section 9–308 provides that a perfected security interest in collateral supported by a "supporting obligation" (such as an account supported by a guaranty) also is a perfected security interest in the supporting obligation, and that a perfected security interest in an obligation secured by a security interest or lien on property (e.g., a real-property mortgage) also is a perfected security interest in the security interest or lien.

e. **Priority; Special Rules for Banks and Deposit Accounts.** The rules governing priority of security interests and agricultural liens under the 1998 Revisions are found in Part 3, Subpart 3 (Sections 9–317 through 9–342). ~~This~~ The revised Article includes several new priority rules and some special rules relating to banks and deposit accounts (Sections 9–340 through 9–342).

Purchase-money security interests: General; consumer-goods transactions; inventory. Section 9–103 substantially rewrites the definition of purchase-money security interest (PMSI) (although the term is not formally "defined"). The substantive changes, however, apply only to non-consumer-goods transactions. (Consumer transactions and consumer-goods transactions are discussed below in Comment 4.j.) For non-consumer-goods transactions, Section 9–103 makes clear that a security interest in collateral may be (to some extent) both a PMSI as well as a non-PMSI, in accord with the "dual status" rule applied by some courts under ~~former~~ pre-1998 Article 9 (thereby rejecting the "transformation" rule). The revised definition provides an even broader conception of a PMSI in inventory, yielding a result that accords with private agreements entered into in response to the uncertainty under ~~former~~ pre-1998 Article 9. It also treats consignments as purchase-money security interests in inventory. Section 9–324 ~~revises~~ clarifies the PMSI priority rules, but for the most part without material change in substance. Section 9–324 also clarifies the priority rules for competing PMSIs in the same collateral.

Purchase-money security interests in livestock; agricultural liens. Section 9–324 provides a special PMSI priority, similar to the inventory PMSI priority rule, for livestock. Section 9–322 (~~which contains~~ the baseline first-to-file-or-perfect priority rule) also recognizes special non-Article 9 priority rules for agricultural liens, which can override the baseline first-in-time rule.

Purchase-money security interests in software. Section 9–324 contains a new priority rule for a software purchase-money security interest. (Section 9–102 includes a definition of "software.") Under Section 9–103, a software PMSI includes a PMSI in software that is used in goods that are also subject to a PMSI. ~~(Note also that the definition of "chattel paper" has been also is expanded to include records that evidence a monetary obligation and a security interest in specific goods and software used in the goods.)~~

Investment property. The 1998 priority rules for investment property are substantially similar to the priority rules found in ~~former~~ pre-1998 Section 9–115, which was added in conjunction with the 1994 revisions to UCC Article 8. Under Section 9–328, if a secured party has control of investment property (Sections 8–106, 9–106), its security interest is senior to a security interest perfected in another manner (e.g., by filing). Also under Section 9–328, security interests perfected by control generally rank according to the time that control is obtained or, in the case of a security entitlement or a commodity contract carried in a commodity account, the time when the control arrangement is entered into. ~~This is~~ That was a change from ~~former~~ pre-1998 Section 9–115, under which the security interests ranked equally. However, as between a securities intermediary's security interest in a security entitlement that it maintains for the debtor and a security interest held by another secured party, the securities intermediary's security interest is senior.

Deposit accounts. ~~This Article's~~ The 1998 priority rules applicable to deposit accounts are found in Section 9–327. ~~They~~ and are patterned on and ~~are~~ similar to those for investment property in ~~former~~ pre-1998 Section 9–115 and Section 9–328 ~~of this Article~~. Under Section 9–327, if a secured party has control of a deposit account, its security interest is senior to a security interest perfected in another manner (i.e., as cash proceeds). Also under Section 9–327, security interests perfected by control rank according to the time that control is obtained, but as between a depositary bank's security interest and one held by another secured party, the depositary bank's security interest is senior. A corresponding rule in Section 9–340 makes a depositary bank's right of set-off generally senior to a security interest held by another secured party. However, if the other secured party becomes the depositary bank's customer with respect to the deposit account, then its security interest is senior to the depositary bank's security interest and right of set-off. Sections 9–327, 9–340.

Letter-of-credit rights. The 1998 priority rules for security interests in letter-of-credit rights are ~~found~~ set out in Section 9–329. They are somewhat analogous to those for deposit accounts. A security interest perfected by control has priority over one perfected in another manner (i.e., as a supporting obligation for the collateral in which a security interest is perfected). Security interests in a letter-of-credit right perfected by control rank according to the time that control is obtained. However, the rights of a transferee beneficiary or a nominated person are independent and superior to the extent provided in Section 5–114. See Section 9–109(c)(4).

Chattel paper and instruments. Section 9–330 is the 1998 successor to ~~former~~ pre-1998 Section 9–308. As under ~~former~~ pre-1998 Section 9–308, under the 1998 Revisions differing priority rules apply to purchasers of chattel paper who give new value and take possession (or, in the case of electronic chattel paper, obtain control) of the collateral—depending on whether a conflicting security interest in the collateral is claimed merely as proceeds. The principal change ~~relates~~ related to the role of knowledge and the effect of an indication of a previous assignment of the collateral. 1998 Section 9–330 also ~~affords~~ afforded priority to purchasers of instruments who take possession in good faith and without knowledge that the purchase violates the rights of the competing secured party. In addition, to qualify for priority, purchasers of chattel paper, but not of instruments, must purchase in the ordinary course of business. The 2022 Article 9 Revisions eliminated the defined terms "electronic chattel paper" and "tangible chattel paper," revised the definition of "chattel paper" in Section 9–102 and modified the Section 9–330 priority rule accordingly. See Comment 4.b. and Section 9–102, Comment 5.b.

Proceeds. 1998 Section 9–322 contains new priority rules that clarify when a special priority of a security interest in collateral continues or does not continue with respect to proceeds of the collateral. Other 1998 refinements to the priority rules for proceeds are included in Sections 9–324 (purchase-money security interest priority) and 9–330 (priority of certain purchasers of chattel paper and instruments).

Miscellaneous priority provisions. ~~This Article also includes~~ The 1998 Revisions to Article 9 also included (i) clarifications of selected good-faith-purchase and similar issues (Sections 9–317, 9–331); (ii) new priority rules to deal with the "double debtor" problem arising when a debtor creates a security interest in collateral acquired by the debtor subject to a security interest created by another person (Section 9–325); (iii) new priority rules to deal with the problems created when a change in corporate structure or the like results in a new entity that has become bound by the original debtor's after-acquired property agreement (Section 9–326); (iv) a provision enabling most transferees of funds from a deposit account or money to take free of a security interest (Section 9–332); (v) substantially rewritten and refined priority rules dealing with accessions and commingled goods (Sections 9–335, 9–336); (vi) revised priority rules for security interests in goods covered by a certificate of title (Section 9–337); and (vii) provisions designed to ensure that security interests in deposit accounts will not extend to most transferees of funds on deposit or payees from deposit accounts and will not otherwise "clog" the payments system (Sections 9–341, 9–342).

Model provisions relating to production-money security interests. Appendix II to ~~this Article contains~~ the 1998 Revisions contained model definitions and priority rules relating to "production-money security interests" held by secured parties who give new value used in the production of crops. Because no consensus emerged on the wisdom of these provisions during the drafting process, the sponsors ~~make~~ made no recommendation on whether these model provisions should be enacted.

f. **Proceeds.** Revised Section 9–102 ~~contains~~ provides an expanded definition of "proceeds" of collateral, which includes additional rights and property that arise out of collateral, such as distributions on account of collateral and claims arising out of the loss or nonconformity of, defects in, or damage to collateral. The ~~term also includes~~ revised definition of "proceeds" also includes collections on account of "supporting obligations," such as guarantees.

g. **Part 4: Additional Provisions Relating to Third-Party Rights.** ~~New~~ The 1998 Revisions added a new Part 4 ~~contains~~ that includes several provisions relating to the relationships between certain third parties and the parties to secured transactions. ~~It contains~~ Part 4 contains new Sections 9–401 (replacing ~~former~~ pre-1998 Section 9–311) (alienability of debtor's rights), 9–402 (replacing ~~former~~ pre-1998 Section 9–317) (secured party not obligated on debtor's contracts), 9–403 (replacing ~~former~~ pre-1998 Section 9–206) (agreement not to assert defenses against assignee), 9–404, 9–405, and 9–406 (replacing ~~former~~ pre-1998 Section 9–318) (rights acquired by assignee, modification of assigned contract, discharge of account debtor, restrictions on assignment of account, chattel paper, promissory note, or payment intangible ineffective), 9–407 (replacing some provisions of ~~former~~ pre-1998 Section 2A–303) (restrictions on creation or enforcement of security interest in leasehold interest or lessor's residual interest ineffective). ~~It~~ New Part 4 also ~~contains~~ added new Sections 9–408 (restrictions on assignment of promissory notes, health-care-insurance receivables ineffective, and certain general intangibles ineffective) and 9–409 (restrictions on assignment of letter-of-credit rights ineffective)~~, which are discussed above~~. See Comment 3.a.

h.   **Filing.** New Part 5 (~~formerly~~ replacing pre-1998 Part 4) of Article 9 ~~has been~~ was substantially rewritten to simplify the statutory text and to deal with numerous problems of interpretation and implementation that have arisen over the years.

Medium-neutrality. ~~This Article~~ Part 5 is "medium-neutral"; that is, it makes clear that parties may file and otherwise communicate with a filing office by means of records communicated and stored in media other than on paper.

Identity of person who files a record; authorization. Part 5 also is largely indifferent as to the person who effects a filing. Instead, it addresses whose authorization is necessary for a person to file a record with a filing office. The filing scheme does not contemplate that the identity of a "filer" will be a part of the searchable records. This approach is consistent with, and a necessary aspect of, eliminating signatures or other evidence of authorization from the system (except to the extent that filing offices may choose to employ authentication procedures in connection with electronic communications). As long as the appropriate person authorizes the filing, or, in the case of a termination statement, the debtor is entitled to the termination, it is largely insignificant whether the secured party or another person files any given record.

* * *

Financing statement formal requisites. The formal requisites for a financing statement under the 1998 Revisions are set out in Section 9–502. A financing statement must provide the name of the debtor and the secured party and an indication of the collateral that it covers. Sections 9–503 and 9–506 address the sufficiency of a name provided on a financing statement and clarify when a debtor's name is correct and when an incorrect name is insufficient. Section 9–504 addresses the indication of collateral covered. Under Section 9–504, a super-generic description (e.g., "all assets" or "all personal property") in a financing statement is a sufficient indication of the collateral. (Note, however, that a super-generic description is inadequate for purposes of a security agreement. See Sections 9–108, 9–203.) To facilitate electronic filing, this Article does not require that the debtor's signature or other authorization appear on a financing statement. Instead, it prohibits the filing of unauthorized financing statements and imposes liability upon those who violate the prohibition. See Sections 9–509, 9–626.

Filing-office operations. The 1998 Part 5 ~~contains~~ introduced several provisions governing filing operations. First, it prohibits the filing office from rejecting an initial financing statement or other record for a reason other than one of the few that are specified. See Sections 9–520, 9–516. Second, the filing office is obliged to link all subsequent records (e.g., assignments, continuation statements, etc.) to the initial financing statement to which they relate. See Section 9–519. Third, the filing office may delete a financing statement and related records from the files no earlier than one year after lapse (lapse normally is five years after the filing date), and then only if a continuation statement has not been filed. See Sections 9–515, 9–519, 9–522. Thus, a financing statement and related records would be discovered by a search of the files even after the filing of a termination statement. This approach helps eliminate filing-office discretion and also eases problems associated with multiple secured parties and multiple partial assignments. Fourth, Part 5 mandates performance standards for filing offices. See Sections 9–519, 9–520, 9–523. Fifth, it provides for the promulgation of filing-office rules to deal with details best left out of the statute and requires the filing office to submit periodic reports. See Sections 9–526, 9–527.

Defaulting or missing secured parties and fraudulent filings. In some areas of the country, serious problems ~~have~~ had arisen from fraudulent financing statements ~~that are~~ filed against public officials and other persons. ~~This~~ The 1998 Article 9 ~~addresses~~ addressed the fraud problem by providing the opportunity for a debtor to file a termination statement when a secured party wrongfully refuses or fails to provide a termination statement. See Section 9–509. This opportunity also addresses the problem of secured parties that simply disappear through mergers or liquidations. In addition, Section 9–518 ~~affords~~ provides a statutory method by which a debtor who believes that a filed record is inaccurate or was wrongfully filed may indicate that fact in the files, albeit without affecting the efficacy, if any, of the challenged record.

* * *

i.   **Default and Enforcement.** Part 6 of the 1998 Revisions to Article 9 extensively ~~revises~~ revised and replaced ~~former~~ pre-1998 Part 5. Provisions relating to enforcement of consumer-goods transactions and consumer transactions are discussed in Comment 4.j.

Debtor, secondary obligor; waiver. Section 9–602 clarifies the identity of persons who have rights and persons to whom a secured party owes specified duties under Part 6. Under that section, the rights and duties are enjoyed by and run to the "debtor," defined in Section 9–102 to mean any person with a non-lien property interest in collateral, and to any "obligor." However, with one exception (Section 9–616, as it relates to a consumer obligor), the rights and duties concerned affect non-debtor obligors only if they are "secondary obligors." "Secondary obligor" is defined in Section 9–102 to include one who is secondarily obligated on the secured obligation, e.g., a guarantor, or one who has a right of recourse against the debtor or another obligor with respect to an obligation secured by collateral. However, under ~~Section~~ Sections 9–605 and 9–628, the secured party is relieved from any ~~duty or liability~~ duties and liabilities to any person unless the secured party knows that the person is a debtor or obligor. (The 2022 Article 9 Revisions have modified Sections 9–605 and 9–628. See 2022 Section 9–605, Comments 2 and 3.) Resolving an issue on which courts disagreed under ~~former~~ pre-1998 Article 9, ~~this Article~~ revised Article 9 generally prohibits waiver by a secondary obligor of its rights and a secured party's duties under Part 6. See Section 9–602. However, Section 9–624 permits a secondary obligor or debtor to waive the right to notification of disposition of collateral and, in a non-consumer transaction, the right to redeem collateral, if the secondary obligor or debtor agrees to do so after default.

Rights of collection and enforcement of collateral. Section 9–607 explains in greater detail than ~~former~~ pre-1998 Section 9–502 the rights of a secured party who seeks to collect or enforce collateral, including accounts, chattel paper, and payment intangibles. It also sets forth the enforcement rights of a depositary bank holding a security interest in a deposit account maintained with the depositary bank. Section 9–607 relates solely to the rights of a secured party vis-a-vis a debtor with respect to collections and enforcement. It does not affect the rights or duties of third parties, such as account debtors on collateral, which are addressed elsewhere (e.g., new Section 9–406). Section 9–608 clarifies the manner in which proceeds of collection or enforcement are to be applied.

* * *

Rights and duties of secondary obligor. Section 9–618 provides that a secondary obligor obtains the rights and assumes the duties of a secured party if the secondary obligor receives an assignment of a secured obligation, agrees to assume the secured party's rights and duties upon a transfer to it of collateral, or becomes subrogated to the rights of the secured party with respect to the collateral. The assumption, transfer, or subrogation is not a disposition of collateral under Section 9–610, but it does relieve the former secured party of further duties. ~~Former~~ Pre-1998 Section 9–504(5) did not address whether a secured party was relieved of its duties in this situation.

* * *

Strict foreclosure. Section 9–620, unlike ~~former~~ pre-1998 Section 9–505, permits a secured party to accept collateral in partial satisfaction, as well as full satisfaction, of the obligations secured. This right of strict foreclosure extends to intangible as well as tangible property. Section 9–622 clarifies the effects of an acceptance of collateral on the rights of junior claimants. It rejects the approach taken by some courts–deeming a secured party to have constructively retained collateral in satisfaction of the secured obligations–in the case of a secured party's unreasonable delay in the disposition of collateral. Instead, unreasonable delay is relevant when determining whether a disposition under Section 9–610 is commercially reasonable.

* * *

j. **Consumer Goods, Consumer-Goods Transactions, and Consumer Transactions.** ~~This Article~~ The 1998 Revisions (including the accompanying conforming revisions (see Appendix I)) ~~includes~~ included several special rules for "consumer goods," "consumer transactions," and "consumer-goods transactions." Each term is defined in Section 9–102.

(i) Revised Sections 2–502 and 2–716 provide a buyer of consumer goods with enhanced rights to possession of the goods, thereby accelerating and enhancing the opportunity to achieve "buyer in ordinary course of business" status under Section 1–201.

(ii) Section 9–103(e) (allocation of payments for determining extent of purchase-money status), (f) (purchase-money status not affected by cross-collateralization, refinancing, restructuring, or the like), and (g) (secured party has burden of establishing extent of purchase-money status) do not apply to consumer-goods transactions. ~~Sections~~ Section 9–103 also provides that the limitation of those provisions to transactions other than consumer-goods transactions leaves to the courts the proper rules for consumer-goods transactions and prohibits the courts from drawing inferences from that limitation.

* * *

(ix) Section 9–620 prohibits partial strict foreclosure with respect to consumer goods collateral and, unless the debtor agrees to waive the requirement in ~~an authenticated~~ a signed record after default, in certain cases requires the secured party to dispose of consumer goods collateral which has been repossessed.

* * *

k.   **Good Faith.** ~~Section 9–102 contains~~ The 1998 Revisions added in Section 9–102 a new definition of "good faith" that ~~includes~~ included not only "honesty in fact" but also "the observance of reasonable commercial standards of fair dealing." ~~The definition is similar to the ones adopted in connection with other, recently completed revisions of the UCC.~~ That definition was deleted by the conforming amendments to the 2001 revision of Article 1 as unnecessary, given the revised definition in Section 1–201(b)(20).

l.   ~~**Transition Provisions.** Part 7 (Sections 9–701 through 9–709) contains transition provisions. Transition from former Article 9 to this Article will be particularly challenging in view of its expanded scope, its modification of choice-of-law rules for perfection and priority, and its expansion of the methods of perfection. Amendment approved by the Permanent Editorial Board for Uniform Commercial Code December 31, 2001.~~ [Reserved.]

m.   **Conforming and Related Amendments to Other UCC Articles.** Appendix I to the 1998 Revisions ~~contains~~ contained several revisions to the provisions and Comments of other UCC articles. For the most part ~~the~~ those revisions are explained in the Comments to the ~~proposed revisions~~ 1998 Revisions. ~~Cross-references in other UCC articles to sections of Article 9 also have been revised.~~

Article 1. Revised Section 1–201 ~~contains~~ provides revisions to the definitions of "buyer in ordinary course of business," "purchaser," and "security interest."

Articles 2 and 2A. Sections 2–210, 2–326, 2–502, 2–716, 2A–303, and 2A–307 ~~have been~~ are revised to address the intersection between Articles 2 and 2A and Article 9.

* * *

Article 8. Revisions to Section 8–106, which deals with "control" of securities and security entitlements, conform it to Section 8–302, which deals with "delivery." Revisions to Section 8–110, which deals with a "securities intermediary's jurisdiction," conform it to the revised treatment of a "commodity intermediary's jurisdiction" in Section 9–305. Sections 8–301 and 8–302 ~~have been~~ are revised for clarification. Section 8–510 ~~has been~~ is revised to conform it to the revised priority rules of Section 9–328. Several Comments in Article 8 also ~~have been~~ are revised.

4.   **Summary of 2022 Article 9 Revisions.** Following is a brief summary of some of the more significant revisions that are included in the 2022 Article 9 Revisions. The 2022 amendments to Article 9 are extensive. Many of the amendments are necessary to conform Article 9 to new Article 12, which (along with its Comments) should be read along with the Article 9 amendments and Comments. Other material amendments include those relating to chattel paper and money, among other matters.

a.   **Article 12-Related Revisions.** Article 12-related amendments to Article 9 include the addition of two new kinds of collateral under Article 9: controllable account (a subset of account) and controllable payment intangible (a subset of payment intangible, which is a subset of general intangible). A controllable account or controllable payment intangible is created when the account or payment intangible is evidenced by a controllable electronic record (defined in Section 12–102(a)(1), and a subset of general intangible), which results if the account debtor obligated on the account or payment intangible has agreed to pay the person in control of the controllable electronic record. Perfection of a security interest in a controllable electronic record, controllable account, or controllable payment intangible may be by control or by filing a financing statement. Control of a controllable electronic record is determined under Section 12–105. Control of a controllable account or controllable payment intangible is achieved by obtaining control of the controllable electronic record that evidences the account or payment intangible. Section 9–107A(b). A security interest in a controllable account, controllable electronic record, or controllable payment intangible which is perfected by control has priority over a security interest held by a secured party that does not have control. Section 9–326A.

As is the case for secured parties protected by take-free rules under other articles, the rights of a secured party that takes free of competing property interests under Section 12–104(e) or that is protected from certain actions under Section 12–104(g), as a qualifying purchaser of a controllable account, controllable electronic record, or controllable payment intangible, are respected under Article 9. Section 9–331.

The law of the controllable electronic record's jurisdiction under Section 12–107 governs perfection by control and priority of a security interest in a controllable account, controllable electronic record, or controllable payment intangible. Section 9–306B(a). The law of the jurisdiction in which a debtor is located governs perfection by filing (but not priority) for such collateral. Section 9–306B(b).

The 2022 Article 9 Revisions also contain several other Article 12-related conforming amendments to Article 9.

b.   **Chattel Paper-Related Amendments**. These amendments primarily address two issues that have arisen under the pre-2022 Article 9 with respect to transactions in chattel paper.

First, the definition of "chattel paper" created uncertainty in "bundled" or "hybrid" transactions in which monetary obligations exist not only under a lease of goods but also with respect to other property and services relating to the leased goods. Frequently, the value of the non-goods aspect of a transaction is substantially greater than the value of the lessee's rights under the lease of goods. Uncertainty existed among those who finance chattel paper and other rights to payment as to whether these transactions give rise to chattel paper. The revisions resolve this issue by treating only those transactions whose predominant purpose was to give the obligor (lessee) the right to possession and use of the goods as giving rise to "chattel paper." Some similar issues arise in connection with chattel paper that includes a security interest securing specific goods. See Section 9–102, Comment 5.b.

Second, the pre-2022 statutory distinction between "tangible chattel paper" and "electronic chattel paper" caused practical problems. As to tangible chattel paper (i.e., evidenced by writings), problems arose in the case of multiple originals of writings and situations in which separate writings covered different components of chattel paper. Official comments issued in connection with the 1998 Revisions addressed, but did not entirely resolve, these issues. As to electronic chattel paper, the safe harbor for control was based on a "single authoritative copy" of the chattel paper. Moreover, in some situations tangible chattel paper is converted to electronic form and electronic chattel paper is converted to tangible form. Additional uncertainty existed when one or more records comprised one or more authoritative tangible copies of the records that evidenced the right to payment and rights in related property and one or more authoritative electronic copies of those records also existed.

The 2022 Article 9 Revisions provide a single rule, under which a security interest in chattel paper can be perfected by taking possession of the authoritative tangible copies, if any, and obtaining control of the electronic authoritative copies, if any. This single rule addresses cases where some records evidencing chattel paper are electronic and some are tangible or where a record in one medium is replaced by a record in another.

The 2022 Article 9 Revisions also define chattel paper more accurately, as the right to payment of a monetary obligation that is secured by a security interest in specific goods or owed under a lease of specific goods, if the right to payment and interest in the goods are evidenced by a record.

Finally, the 2022 Article 9 Revisions provide a new choice-of-law rule for perfection and priority of security interests in chattel paper that is evidenced by authoritative electronic copies of records or by such electronic copies and authoritative tangible copies. For such chattel paper, Section 9–306A provides that perfection by control and possession of authoritative copies and priority are governed by the law of the "chattel paper's jurisdiction," based loosely on Sections 8–110 and 9–305. For chattel paper evidenced only by authoritative tangible copies, Section 9–306A(d) provides that perfection by possession and priority are governed by the law of the location of the authoritative tangible copies. Perfection by filing continues to be governed by the law of the location of the debtor for all chattel paper.

c.   **Money-Related Amendments.**

Section 1–201(b)(24) defines "money" as including "a medium of exchange currently authorized or adopted by a domestic or foreign government . . . ." There is no way of knowing how money in an intangible form might develop, but there are indications that some countries might authorize or adopt intangible tokens as a medium of exchange and others might authorize or adopt deposit accounts with a central bank as money. (These tokens or accounts sometimes are referred to as central bank digital currency or CBDC.) For many purposes, there is no need for the UCC to distinguish among types of money. For Article 9 purposes, however, distinctions must be drawn. Only tangible money is susceptible of perfection by possession. And the steps needed for perfection by control with respect to intangible tokens, such as controllable electronic records, will not work for deposit accounts with a central bank, and vice versa. For this reason, the revisions provide an Article 9 definition of "money" that is narrower than the Article 1 definition. The Article 9 definition expressly excludes deposit accounts (but not CBDC that is a token). Thus, "electronic money," defined in Section 9–102 as "money in an electronic form," would not include deposit accounts. The Article 9 definition of "money" also excludes money in an electronic form that cannot be subjected to control under Section 9–105A.

The Article 9 provisions governing "deposit accounts" would remain suitable for accounts with a central bank, even if a government has adopted these accounts as money. The revisions leave Article 9's treatment of deposit accounts largely unchanged. Under the revisions, a security interest in electronic money as original collateral can be perfected only by control. The requirements for obtaining control of electronic money under Section 9–105A are essentially the same as those for obtaining control of a controllable electronic record under Article 12.

The 2022 Article 9 Revisions also make changes to Section 9–332, the take-free rules for transferees of money, including the addition of a new rule applicable to electronic money, and transferees of funds from deposit accounts.

d.   **Transitional Rules.** Article A to the 2022 Amendments provides important transitional rules. These rules are designed to protect the expectations of parties to transactions entered into before the effective date of a state's enactment of the revisions. They also provide for an adequate period of time for parties to pre-effective date transactions to make adjustments so as to preserve certain pre-effective date priorities.

§ 9–102.   Definitions and Index of Definitions.

(a)   [Article 9 definitions.] In this article:

* * *

(2)   "Account", except as used in "account for", "account statement", "account to", "commodity account" in paragraph (14), "customer's account", "deposit account" in paragraph (29), "on account of", and "statement of account", means a right to payment of a monetary obligation, whether or not earned by performance, (i) for property that has been or is to be sold, leased, licensed, assigned, or otherwise disposed of, (ii) for services rendered or to be rendered, (iii) for a policy of insurance issued or to be issued, (iv) for a secondary obligation incurred or to be incurred, (v) for energy provided or to be provided, (vi) for the use or hire of a vessel under a charter or other contract, (vii) arising out of the use of a credit or charge card or information contained on or for use with the card, or (viii) as winnings in a lottery or other game of chance operated or sponsored by a State, governmental unit of a State, or person licensed or authorized to operate the game by a State or governmental unit of a State. The term includes controllable accounts and health-care-insurance receivables. The term does not include (i) ~~rights to payment evidenced by chattel paper or an instrument~~ chattel paper, (ii) commercial tort claims, (iii) deposit accounts, (iv) investment property, (v) letter-of-credit rights or letters of credit, ~~or~~ (vi) rights to payment for money or funds advanced or sold, other than rights arising out of the use of a credit or charge card or information contained on or for use with the ~~card~~ card, or (vii) rights to payment evidenced by an instrument.

(3)   "Account debtor" means a person obligated on an account, chattel paper, or general intangible. The term does not include persons obligated to pay a negotiable instrument, even if the negotiable instrument ~~constitutes part of~~ evidences chattel paper.

(4)   "Accounting", except as used in "accounting for", means a record:

   (A)   ~~authenticated~~ signed by a secured party;

   (B)   indicating the aggregate unpaid secured obligations as of a date not more than 35 days earlier or 35 days later than the date of the record; and

   (C)   identifying the components of the obligations in reasonable detail.

* * *

(7)   ~~"Authenticate" means:~~

   (A)   ~~to sign; or~~

   (B)   ~~with present intent to adopt or accept a record, to attach to or logically associate with the record an electronic sound, symbol, or process.~~ [Reserved.]

(7A)   "Assignee", except as used in "assignee for benefit of creditors", means a person (i) in whose favor a security interest that secures an obligation is created or provided for under a security agreement, whether or not the obligation is outstanding or (ii) to which an account, chattel paper, payment intangible, or promissory note has been sold. The term includes a person to which a security interest has been transferred by a secured party.

(7B)   "Assignor" means a person that (i) under a security agreement creates or provides for a security interest that secures an obligation or (ii) sells an account, chattel paper, payment intangible, or promissory note. The term includes a secured party that has transferred a security interest to another person.

* * *

(11) ~~"Chattel paper" means a record or records that evidence both a monetary obligation and a security interest in specific goods, a security interest in specific goods and software used in the goods, a security interest in specific goods and license of software used in the goods, a lease of specific goods, or a lease of specific goods and license of software used in the goods. In this paragraph, "monetary obligation" means a monetary obligation secured by the goods or owed under a lease of the goods and includes a monetary obligation with respect to software used in the goods. The term does not include (i) charters or other contracts involving the use or hire of a vessel or (ii) records that evidence a right to payment arising out of the use of a credit or charge card or information contained on or for use with the card. If a transaction is evidenced by records that include an instrument or series of instruments, the group of records taken together constitutes chattel paper.~~

(11) "Chattel paper" means:

  (A) a right to payment of a monetary obligation secured by specific goods, if the right to payment and security agreement are evidenced by a record; or

  (B) a right to payment of a monetary obligation owed by a lessee under a lease agreement with respect to specific goods and a monetary obligation owed by the lessee in connection with the transaction giving rise to the lease, if:

   (i)   the right to payment and lease agreement are evidenced by a record; and

   (ii) the predominant purpose of the transaction giving rise to the lease was to give the lessee the right to possession and use of the goods.

  The term does not include a right to payment arising out of a charter or other contract involving the use or hire of a vessel or a right to payment arising out of the use of a credit or charge card or information contained on or for use with the card.

* * *

(27A) "Controllable account" means an account evidenced by a controllable electronic record that provides that the account debtor undertakes to pay the person that has control under Section 12–105 of the controllable electronic record.

(27B) "Controllable payment intangible" means a payment intangible evidenced by a controllable electronic record that provides that the account debtor undertakes to pay the person that has control under Section 12–105 of the controllable electronic record.

* * *

(31) ~~"Electronic chattel paper" means chattel paper evidenced by a record or records consisting of information stored in an electronic medium.~~ [Reserved.]

(31A) "Electronic money" means money in an electronic form.

* * *

(42) "General intangible" means any personal property, including things in action, other than accounts, chattel paper, commercial tort claims, deposit accounts, documents, goods, instruments, investment property, letter-of-credit rights, letters of credit, money, and oil, gas, or other minerals before extraction. The term includes controllable electronic records, payment intangibles, and software.

(43) [Reserved.] ["Good faith" means honesty in fact and the observance of reasonable commercial standards of fair dealing.]

* * *

(47) "Instrument" means a negotiable instrument or any other writing that evidences a right to the payment of a monetary obligation, is not itself a security agreement or lease, and is of a type that in ordinary course of business is transferred by delivery with any necessary indorsement or assignment. The term does not include (i) investment property, (ii) letters of credit, ~~or~~ (iii) writings

that evidence a right to payment arising out of the use of a credit or charge card or information contained on or for use with the card, or (iv) writings that evidence chattel paper.

* * *

(54A) "Money" has the meaning in Section 1–201(b)(24), but does not include (i) a deposit account or (ii) money in an electronic form that cannot be subjected to control under Section 9–105A.

* * *

(61) "Payment intangible" means a general intangible under which the account debtor's principal obligation is a monetary obligation. The term includes a controllable payment intangible.

* * *

(66) "Proposal" means a record ~~authenticated~~ signed by a secured party which includes the terms on which the secured party is willing to accept collateral in full or partial satisfaction of the obligation it secures pursuant to Sections 9–620, 9–621, and 9–622.

* * *

(75) ~~"Send", in connection with a record or notification, means:~~

(A) ~~to deposit in the mail, deliver for transmission, or transmit by any other usual means of communication, with postage or cost of transmission provided for, addressed to any address reasonable under the circumstances; or~~

(B) ~~to cause the record or notification to be received within the time that it would have been received if properly sent under subparagraph (A).~~ [Reserved.]

* * *

(79) ~~"Tangible chattel paper" means chattel paper evidenced by a record or records consisting of information that is inscribed on a tangible medium.~~ [Reserved.]

(79A) "Tangible money" means money in a tangible form.

* * *

(b) **[Definitions in other articles.]** "Control" as provided in Section 7–106 and the following definitions in other articles apply to this article:

* * *

"Controllable electronic record". Section 12–102.

* * *

"Protected purchaser". Section 8–303.

* * *

"Qualifying purchaser". Section 12–102.

* * *

Legislative Note: Replicate the formatting of the tabulated material in subsection (a)(11) exactly to ensure that the meaning of the material is preserved.

The definition of "good faith" in subsection (a)(43) was deleted from subsection (a) pursuant to a conforming amendment accompanying the 2001 amendments of Article 1. However, any jurisdiction that has not adopted the revised definition of "good faith" in Section 1–201(b)(20) should retain the definition of "good faith" in subsection (a)(43).

Official Comment

1.   **Source.** All terms that are defined in Article 9 and used in more than one section are consolidated in this section. Note that the definition of "security interest" is found in Section 1–201, not in this Article, ~~and has been revised. See Appendix I.~~ Many of the definitions in this section ~~are new; many others~~ derive from those in ~~former~~ pre-1998 Section 9–105. ~~The following Comments also indicate other sections of former Article 9 that~~

defined (or explained) terms. Other definitions were added by the 1998 Revisions or modified or added by the 2022 Article 9 Revisions.

2. **Parties to Secured Transactions.**

a. **"Debtor"; "Obligor"; "Secondary Obligor."** Determining whether a person was a "debtor" under former pre-1998 Section 9–105(1)(d) required a close examination of the context in which the term was used. To reduce the need for this examination, this Article redefines the 1998 Revisions redefined "debtor" and adds added new defined terms, "secondary obligor" and "obligor." In the context of Part 6 (default and enforcement), these definitions distinguish among three classes of persons: (i) those persons who may have a stake in the proper enforcement of a security interest by virtue of their non-lien property interest (typically, an ownership interest) in the collateral, (ii) those persons who may have a stake in the proper enforcement of the security interest because of their obligation to pay the secured debt, and (iii) those persons who have an obligation to pay the secured debt but have no stake in the proper enforcement of the security interest. Persons in the first class are debtors. Persons in the second class are secondary obligors if any portion of the obligation is secondary or if the obligor has a right of recourse against the debtor or another obligor with respect to an obligation secured by collateral. One must consult the law of suretyship to determine whether an obligation is secondary. The Restatement (3d), Suretyship and Guaranty § 1 (1996), contains a useful explanation of the concept. Obligors in the third class are neither debtors nor secondary obligors. With one exception (Section 9–616, as it relates to a consumer obligor), the rights and duties provided by Part 6 affect non-debtor obligors only if they are "secondary obligors."

By including in the definition of "debtor" all persons with a property interest (other than a security interest in or other lien on collateral), the definition includes transferees of collateral, whether or not the secured party knows of the transfer or the transferee's identity. Exculpatory provisions in Part 6 protect the secured party in that circumstance. See Sections 9–605 and 9–628. The definition renders unnecessary former pre-1998 Section 9–112, which governed situations in which collateral was not owned by the debtor. The definition also includes a "consignee," as defined in this section, as well as a seller of accounts, chattel paper, payment intangibles, or promissory notes.

* * *

If a security interest is granted by a protected series of a limited liability company formed, for example, under the Uniform Protected Series Act (2017), the debtor is the protected series. See PEB Commentary No. 23, dated February 24, 2021. The Commentary is available at https://www.ali.org/peb-ucc. The 2022 definition of "person" in Section 1–201(b)(27) includes a protected series.

b. **"Secured Party."** * * *

* * *

b.1. **"Assignee"; "Assignor."** Instead of referring to a "debtor," "secured party," and "security interest," all of which are defined terms, several provisions of Article 9, including Part 4, refer to the "assignment" or the "transfer" of property interests and some refer to an "assignor," "assignee," or "assigned contract." None of those terms are defined in the UCC. Some courts have read the undefined terms in an unduly narrow way. In 2020, the Permanent Editorial Board for the UCC issued a Commentary clarifying the meanings of these terms and amended the official comments accordingly. PEB Commentary No. 21. This Article generally follows common usage by using the terms "assignment" and "assign" to refer to transfers of rights to payment, claims, and liens and other security interests. It generally uses the term "transfer" to refer to other transfers of interests in property. Except when used in connection with a letter-of-credit transaction (see Section 9–107, Comment 4), no significance should be placed on the use of one term or the other. Depending on the substance of the transaction, each term as used in this Article refers to the assignment or transfer of an outright ownership interest or to the assignment or transfer of a limited interest, such as a security interest, or both.

The 2022 Article 9 Revisions added new definitions of "assignee" and "assignor." Paragraph 7A defines "assignee" as a person in whose favor a security interest securing an obligation is created or to which an account, chattel paper, a payment intangible, or a promissory note has been sold. Paragraph 7B defines "assignor" as creating a security interest securing an obligation or that sells an account, chattel paper, a payment intangible, or a promissory note. These definitions incorporate the essence of the 2020 PEB Commentary into the statutory text. The definitions also specify that an "assignor" includes a secured party that transfers a security interest to another person and an "assignee" includes a person to which a security interest has been transferred by a secured party. By their terms, the defined terms "assignee" and "assignor" contemplate assignments in particular contexts. However, several references in this article to "assigned," "assignment" and "assignee" include transfers in broader contexts than those addressed in the defined terms. See, e.g., subsection (a)(2) ("assigned," in definition of "account") and (a)(47) ("assignment," in definition of "instrument") and Sections 9–109, 9–408, 9–409, and 9–519.

Absent a contrary agreement, an assignee obtains the rights and powers of an assignor as against an account debtor on assigned collateral (e.g., under Section 9–406) and as between the assignee and the assignor (debtor) (e.g., under Section 9–607). See also Restatement (Second) of Contracts § 317(1) (1981) (emphasis added):

> An assignment of a right is a manifestation of the assignor's intention to transfer it *by virtue of which* the assignor's right to performance by the obligor is extinguished in whole or in part and *the assignee acquires a right to such performance.*

Several provisions of this Article and its official comments also refer to the "transfer" of property interests. Although that term and its cognates are not defined, depending on the context it may include an "assignment." Moreover, a transfer of property is not limited to transactions of "purchase" and may include the transfer of a limited interest. See also Section 9–332, Comment 2A.

* * *

3.   **Definitions Relating to Creation of a Security Interest.**

a.   **"Collateral."** As under ~~former~~ pre-1998 Section 9–105, "collateral" is the property subject to a security interest and includes accounts, ~~and~~ chattel paper, payment intangibles, and promissory notes that have been sold. ~~It has been expanded in this Article.~~ The 1998 Revisions expanded the term ~~now explicitly includes~~ to include proceeds subject to a security interest. ~~It also reflects the~~ and also broadened the scope of the Article. ~~It includes~~ to include as collateral property subject to an agricultural lien as well as payment intangibles and promissory notes that have been sold.

b.   **"Security Agreement."** The definition of "security agreement" is substantially the same as under ~~former~~ pre-1998 Section 9–105–an agreement that creates or provides for a security interest. However, the term frequently was used colloquially in ~~former~~ pre-1998 Article 9 to refer to the document or writing that contained a debtor's security agreement. ~~This Article eliminates~~ The 1998 Article 9 eliminated that usage, reserving the term for the more precise meaning specified in the definition.

* * *

4.   **Goods-Related Definitions.**

a.   **"Goods"; "Consumer Goods"; "Equipment"; "Farm Products"; "Farming Operation"; "Inventory."** The definition of "goods" is substantially the same as the definition in ~~former~~ pre-1998 Section 9–105. This Article also retains the four mutually-exclusive "types" of collateral that consist of goods: "consumer goods," "equipment," "farm products," and "inventory." The revisions are primarily for clarification.

The classes of goods are mutually exclusive. For example, the same property cannot simultaneously be both equipment and inventory. In borderline cases–a physician's car or a farmer's truck that might be either consumer goods or equipment–the principal use to which the property is put is determinative. Goods can fall into different classes at different times. For example, a radio may be inventory in the hands of a dealer and consumer goods in the hands of a consumer. As under ~~former~~ pre-1998 Article 9, goods are "equipment" if they do not fall into another category.

The definition of "consumer goods" follows ~~former~~ pre-1998 Section 9–109. The classification turns on whether the debtor uses or bought the goods for use "primarily for personal, family, or household purposes."

Goods are inventory if they are leased by a lessor or held by a person for sale or lease. The revised definition of "inventory" makes clear that the term includes goods leased by the debtor to others as well as goods held for lease. (The same result should have obtained under the ~~former~~ pre-1998 definition.) Goods to be furnished or furnished under a service contract, raw materials, and work in process also are inventory. Implicit in the definition is the criterion that the sales or leases are or will be in the ordinary course of business. For example, machinery used in manufacturing is equipment, not inventory, even though it is the policy of the debtor to sell machinery when it becomes obsolete or worn. Inventory also includes goods that are consumed in a business (e.g., fuel used in operations). In general, goods used in a business are equipment if they are fixed assets or have, as identifiable units, a relatively long period of use, but are inventory, even though not held for sale or lease, if they are used up or consumed in a short period of time in producing a product or providing a service.

* * *

Crops, livestock, and their products cease to be "farm products" when the debtor ceases to be engaged in farming operations with respect to them. If, for example, they come into the possession of a marketing agency for sale or distribution or of a manufacturer or processor as raw materials, they become inventory. Products of crops or livestock, even though they remain in the possession of a person engaged in farming operations, lose their status as farm products if they are subjected to a manufacturing process. What is and what is not a manufacturing operation process is not specified in this Article. At one end of the spectrum, some processes are so closely connected with farming–such as pasteurizing milk or boiling sap to produce maple syrup or sugar–that they would not constitute manufacturing. On the other hand an extensive canning operation would be manufacturing. Once farm products have been subjected to a manufacturing operation process, they normally become inventory.

* * *

c.   **"As-Extracted Collateral."** Under this Article, oil, gas, and other minerals that have not been extracted from the ground are treated as real property, to which this Article does not apply. Upon extraction, minerals become personal property (goods) and eligible to be collateral under this Article. See the definition of "goods," which excludes "oil, gas, and other minerals before extraction." To take account of financing practices reflecting the shift from real to personal property, this Article contains special rules for perfecting security interests in minerals which attach upon extraction and in accounts resulting from the sale of minerals at the wellhead or minehead. See, e.g., Sections 9–301(4) (law governing perfection and priority); 9–501 (place of filing), 9–502 (contents of financing statement), 9–519 (indexing of records). The new term, "as-extracted collateral," added by the 1998 Revisions, refers to the minerals and related accounts to which the special rules apply. The term "at the wellhead" encompasses arrangements based on a sale of the produce product (goods) at the moment that it issues from the ground and is measured, without technical distinctions as to whether title passes at the "Christmas tree" of a well, the far side of a gathering tank, or at some other point. The term "at . . . the minehead" is comparable.

The following examples explain the operation of these provisions.

Example 5: Debtor owns an interest in oil that is to be extracted. To secure Debtor's obligations to Lender, Debtor enters into an authenticated a signed agreement granting Lender an interest in the oil. Although Lender may acquire an interest in the oil under real-property law, Lender does not acquire a security interest under this Article until the oil becomes personal property, i.e., until it is extracted and becomes "goods" to which this Article applies. Because Debtor had an interest in the oil before extraction and Lender's security interest attached to the oil as extracted, the oil is "as-extracted collateral."

Example 6: Debtor owns an interest in oil that is to be extracted and contracts to sell the oil to Buyer at the wellhead. In an authenticated a signed agreement, Debtor agrees to sell to Lender the right to payment from Buyer. This right to payment is an account that constitutes "as-extracted collateral." If Lender then resells the account to Financer, Financer acquires a security interest. However, inasmuch as the debtor-seller in that transaction, Lender, had no interest in the oil before extraction, Financer's collateral (the account it owns) is not "as-extracted collateral."

* * *

5.   **Receivables-related Definitions.**

a.   **"Account"; "Health-Care-Insurance Receivable"; "As-Extracted Collateral."** The definition of "account" has been expanded and reformulated. It is no longer limited to rights to payment relating to goods or services. Many categories of rights to payment that were classified as general intangibles under former pre-1998 Article 9 are accounts under this Article. Thus, if they are sold, a financing statement must be filed to perfect the buyer's interest in them. As used in the definition of "account," a right to payment "arising out of the use of a credit or charge card or information contained on or for use with the card" is the right of a card issuer to payment from its cardholder. A credit-card or charge-card transaction may give rise to other rights to payments; however, those other rights do not "arise out of the use" of the card or information contained on or for use with the card. Among the types of property that are expressly excluded from the definition is "a right to payment for money or funds advanced or sold." As defined in Section 1–201, "money" is limited essentially to currency. As used in the exclusion from the definition of "account," however, "funds" is a broader concept than money (although the term is not defined). For example, when a bank-lender credits a borrower's deposit account for the amount of a loan, the bank's advance of funds is not a transaction giving rise to an account. The 2022 Article 9 Revisions amended the definition of "money" in Section 1–201(b)(24) and added a new, more narrow, definition of "money" in Section 9–102(a)(54A). See Comment 12A.

* * *

The 2022 Article 9 Revisions amended the definition of "account" to reflect the 2022 revised definition of "chattel paper," discussed in Comment 5.b. The revised definition of "account" also includes some additional exceptions that accommodate the use of the term "account" in other provisions. These new exceptions were implicit in the former definition. Moreover, the exceptions for the defined terms "commodity account" and "deposit account" implicitly apply to all uses of those terms in this Article.

b. **"Chattel Paper.";** ~~"Electronic Chattel Paper"; "Tangible Chattel Paper."~~ "Chattel paper" ~~consists of a monetary obligation together with a security interest in or a lease of specific goods if the obligation and security interest or lease are evidenced by "a record or records.". The definition has been expanded from that found in former Article 9 to include records that evidence a monetary obligation and a security interest in specific goods and software used in the goods, a security interest in specific goods and license of software used in the goods, or a lease of specific goods and license of software used in the goods. The expanded definition covers transactions in which the debtor's or lessee's monetary obligation includes amounts owed with respect to software used in the goods. The monetary obligation with respect to the software need not be owed under a license from the secured party or lessor, and the secured party or lessor need not be a party to the license transaction itself. Among the types of monetary obligations that are included in "chattel paper" are amounts that have been advanced by the secured party or lessor to enable the debtor or lessee to acquire or obtain financing for a license of the software used in the goods. The definition also makes clear that rights to payment arising out of credit-card transactions are not chattel paper.~~ "Chattel paper" consists of a monetary obligation that is either secured by specific goods or arises in connection with a lease of specific goods, in each case if the obligation and security interest or lease is evidenced by a record. The monetary obligation itself need not be related to the goods. For example, a loan secured by specific goods and evidenced by one or more records creates chattel paper regardless of the purpose of the loan.

Rights to payment arising out of ~~Charters~~ charters of vessels or the use of credit or charge cards are expressly excluded from the definition of chattel paper; they are accounts. The term "charter" as used in this section includes bareboat charters, time charters, successive voyage charters, contracts of affreightment, contracts of carriage, and all other arrangements for the use of vessels. ~~Under former Section 9–105, only if the evidence of an obligation consisted of "a writing or writings" could an obligation qualify as chattel paper. In this Article, traditional, written chattel paper is included in the definition of "tangible chattel paper." "Electronic chattel paper" is chattel paper that is stored in an electronic medium instead of in tangible form.~~

~~The concept of an electronic medium should be construed liberally to include electrical, digital, magnetic, optical, electromagnetic, or any other current or similar emerging technologies.~~

What distinguishes chattel paper from other rights to payment is the fact that creditor has an interest in specific goods to enforce the right to payment. For example, the fact that a secured party also has an interest in other property does not prevent the right to payment from being chattel paper, provided that the specific goods are the primary collateral.

Example 8. To secure a loan, Borrower grants Lender a security interest in a specified item of equipment and a deposit account. The loan and the security interest are evidenced by one or more records. The right to payment is chattel paper, assuming the equipment is the primary collateral.

In Example 8, the inclusion of some incidental collateral, such as a deposit account, does not prevent characterization of the right to payment as chattel paper. Another typical example would be the inclusion of after-acquired replacement parts to be installed on the specific goods. On the other hand, to be chattel paper, a right to payment must be accompanied by a security interest in *specific* goods or a lease of *specific* goods. A right to payment secured by a security interest in rotating collateral is not chattel paper.

Example 9. To secure a loan, Borrower grants Lender a security interest in all of Borrower's existing and after-acquired inventory. The loan and the security interest are evidenced by one or more records. The right to payment is not chattel paper.

Example 10. To secure a loan, Borrower grants Lender a security interest in a specifically described item of equipment, which is not the primary collateral, and also in all of Borrower's existing and after-acquired equipment. The loan and the security interest are evidenced by one or more records. The right to payment is not chattel paper.

Example 9 is the easy case because no "specific goods" are identified. As to Example 10, it is true that the monetary obligation is secured by "specific goods" and the definition of chattel paper does not specify that the obligation must be secured *only* by specific goods. However, if the right to payment in Example 10 were to be characterized as chattel paper, it would be possible to convert virtually any monetary obligation evidenced by records and secured by any collateral into chattel paper merely by including as collateral a specific item of goods (whether inventory, equipment, consumer goods, or farm products). The special rules for chattel paper contemplate that specific goods are the primary collateral, even if some incidental property also might be included. If additional goods or other property are included and the specific goods are not the primary collateral, then classification as chattel paper would not be appropriate. Of course, there may be close cases. In those situations, parties should take appropriate precautions.

A right to payment arising from a lease of specific goods gives rise to chattel paper only if the predominant purpose of the transaction is to provide the lessee the right to possession and use of the goods. Therefore, under paragraph (11)(B)(ii), when a lease of specific goods is combined with an obligation to provide or right to receive other property or services, the resulting right to payment will be chattel paper only if the goods aspect of the transaction predominates.

Example 11. Customer and Car Dealer enter into a transaction, evidenced by one or more records, pursuant to which, in exchange for a payment of $2,000 per month: (i) Customer is entitled to possession of a specific vehicle for 36 months; (ii) Car Dealer will provide round-the-clock monitoring of the vehicle's location and condition, and alert authorities to provide road-side assistance in the event of a malfunction or accident; and (iii) Car Dealer will, from time to time, remotely update the vehicle's operating system. The value of the right to possess and use the vehicle is significantly greater than the value of the monitoring service and updates. Because the goods aspect of the transaction predominates, under paragraph (11)(B)(ii) Customer's monetary obligation, including the portion attributable to Car Dealer's obligation to provide monitoring and updates, constitutes chattel paper.

Example 12. Customer and Cableco enter into a transaction, evidenced by one or more records, pursuant to which, in exchange for a payment of $200 per month, Cableco will provide Customer with specified television programming and a device needed to access the programming (a "lease" of the device). If the components of the transaction were priced separately, the price for the programming would be substantially more than the price for possession and use of the device. Because the goods aspect of this transaction does not predominate, under paragraph (11)(B)(ii) Customer's monetary obligation does not constitute chattel paper.

The 2022 revision to the definition of chattel paper omits the references to "software used in the goods" and a "license of software used in the goods" as superfluous, inasmuch as there is no reason to single out software. Other types of property may secure an obligation or be included in a transaction involving a lease, as discussed above. See also Sections 2–102 (scope of Article 2); 2–106(5) (defining "hybrid transaction"); 2A–102 (scope of Article 2A); 2A–103(1)(h.1) (definition of "hybrid lease"). These references were omitted from the definition of chattel paper for clarification and did not result in any change in the scope of the definition.

The 2022 revision to the definition of "chattel paper" also changed the language from "a record or records that evidence a monetary obligation" to "a right to payment of a monetary obligation . . . evidenced by a record." This semantic change was for clarification purposes only; it does not imply a change in meaning. Chattel paper is and has always been a right to payment of a monetary obligation. Because the revised definition is based on the obligation, rather than the record, the definition no longer includes the following statement, which was included in the previous definition: "If a transaction is evidenced by records that include an instrument or series of instruments, the group of records taken together constitutes chattel paper." The omission of that statement also does not imply a change in meaning, except that writings evidencing chattel paper are excluded from the definition of "instrument" under Section 9–102(a)(47). Although the definition refers to "a record," chattel paper can be evidenced by one or more records because, under Section 1–106, unless the statutory context otherwise requires, words in the singular number include the plural.

Finally, the revised definition of "chattel paper" and the approach to perfection of a security interest by possession and control under Section 9–314A have eliminated the need to have separate definitions of "electronic chattel paper" and "tangible chattel paper" in Section 9–102. Consequently, those definitions have been deleted.

c.   **"Instrument"; "Promissory Note."** The definition of "instrument" includes a negotiable instrument. As under ~~former~~ pre-1998 Section 9–105, it also includes any other right to payment of a monetary obligation that is evidenced by a writing of a type that in ordinary course of business is transferred by delivery (and, if necessary, an indorsement or assignment). The 2022 revised definition of "instrument" explicitly excludes a writing that evidences a right to payment that is chattel paper. This revision clarifies and makes explicit the understanding before the revision that an obligation on an instrument that evidences chattel paper is to be treated (e.g., under Section 9–330) as an obligation on chattel paper and not on an instrument. ~~Except in the case of chattel paper~~ With that exception, the fact that an instrument is secured by a security interest or encumbrance on property does not change the character of the instrument as such or convert the combination of the instrument and collateral into a separate classification of personal property. The definition also makes clear that rights to payment arising out of credit-card transactions are not instruments. The definition of "promissory note," added in the 1998 Revisions, is new, was necessitated by the inclusion of sales of promissory notes within the scope of Article 9. It explicitly excludes obligations arising out of "orders" to pay (e.g., checks) as opposed to "promises" to pay. See Section 3–104. Under the 2022 Article 9 Revisions, Sections 9–406(d) and 9–408(g) adopt a modified meaning of "promissory note" as that term is used in Sections 9–406(d) and 9–408(a) through (d). See Comment 5.h.; see also Sections 9–406, Comment 5; 9–408, Comment 11.

d.   **"General Intangible"; "Payment Intangible."** "General intangible" is the residual category of personal property, including things in action, that is not included in the other defined types of collateral. Examples are various categories of intellectual property and the right to payment of a loan of funds that is not evidenced by chattel paper or an instrument. As used in the definition of "general intangible," "things in action" includes rights that arise under a license of intellectual property, including the right to exploit the intellectual property without liability for infringement. The definition has been revised was revised in 1998 to exclude commercial tort claims, deposit accounts, and letter-of-credit rights. Each of the three is a separate type of collateral. One important consequence of this exclusion is that tortfeasors (commercial tort claims), banks (deposit accounts), and persons obligated on letters of credit (letter-of-credit rights) are not "account debtors" having the rights and obligations set forth in Sections 9–404, 9–405, and 9–406. In particular, tortfeasors, banks, and persons obligated on letters of credit are not obligated to pay an assignee (secured party) upon receipt of the notification described in Section 9–404(a). See Comment 5.h. Another important consequence relates to the adequacy of the description in the security agreement. See Section 9–108.

"Payment intangible" is a subset of the definition of "general intangible" The sale of a payment intangible is subject to this Article. See Section 9–109(a)(3). Virtually any intangible right could give rise to a right to payment of money once one hypothesizes, for example, that the account debtor is in breach of its obligation. The term "payment intangible," however, embraces only those general intangibles "under which the account debtor's *principal* obligation is a monetary obligation." (Emphasis added.) A debtor's right to payment from another person of amounts received by the other person on the debtor's behalf, including the right of a merchant in a credit-card, debit-card, prepaid-card, or other payment-card transaction to payment of amounts received by its bank from the card system in settlement of the transaction, is a "payment intangible." (In contrast, the right of a credit-card issuer to payment arising out of the use of a credit card is an "account.") If a bank is the obligor on a monetary obligation not evidenced by an instrument or chattel paper, the obligation or the right to payment of the obligation may be a deposit account, an account, a payment intangible, or another type of collateral depending on the facts and circumstances. Of course, the classification of a monetary obligation or a right to payment of the obligation for purposes of this Article would not necessarily affect the application of laws regulating, for example, banking, securities, commodities, money transmission, and taxation.

* * *

d.1.   **"Controllable Account"; "Controllable Payment Intangible."** Article 9 affords special treatment for security interests in controllable accounts and controllable payment intangibles, i.e., those accounts and payment intangibles that are evidenced by a controllable electronic record and as to which the account debtor (obligor) undertakes to pay the person having control of the controllable electronic record. Of course, a person would be an account debtor only if it were actually obligated on the account or payment intangible evidenced by the controllable electronic record. Although the definitions refer to a controllable electronic record that "provides" for an account debtor's undertaking, an account debtor's promise to pay normally would arise and be evidenced apart from the controllable electronic record itself. However, the definitions contemplate that a controllable electronic record evidencing an account or payment intangible (or an associated record) would indicate in some fashion an account debtor's obligation and that the controllable electronic record evidences the account or payment intangible. If a bank is the obligor on a monetary obligation payable to the person in control of a controllable electronic record, the obligation or the right to payment of the obligation may be a deposit account, a controllable account, a controllable payment intangible, or another type of collateral depending on the facts and circumstances. The classification of a monetary obligation or a right to payment of the obligation for purposes of this Article would not necessarily affect the application of laws regulating, for example, banking, securities, commodities, money transmission, and taxation.

An undertaking to pay the "person that has control" means an undertaking to pay the person that has control at the time payment is made. However, an undertaking to pay Smith, even though Smith happens to have control of the relevant controllable electronic record at the time the undertaking was made, is not an undertaking to pay the person that has control.

The special treatment for controllable accounts and controllable payment intangibles includes the following:

- Perfection of a security interest in a controllable account or controllable payment intangible can be achieved by filing a financing statement or by obtaining control of the controllable electronic record that evidences the controllable account or controllable payment intangible. Sections 9–312(a); 9–314(a); 9–107A(b).

- A security interest in a controllable electronic record, controllable account, or controllable payment intangible that is perfected by control has priority over a conflicting security interest that is perfected by another method. Section 9–326A.

- The benefit of the take-free and no-action rules for qualifying purchasers (including secured parties) of controllable electronic records also extends to qualifying purchasers of controllable accounts and controllable payment intangibles, whether or not the qualifying purchaser also purchases the related controllable electronic record. See Section 12–104(a) and Comments 5 through 8.

* * *

g. **"Commercial Tort Claim."** ~~This term is new.~~ A tort claim may serve as original collateral under this Article only if it is a "commercial tort claim." See Section 9–109(d). Although security interests in commercial tort claims are within its scope, this Article does not override other applicable law restricting the assignability of a tort claim. See Section 9–401. A security interest in a tort claim also may exist under this Article if the claim is proceeds of other collateral. See Section 9–204(b.1) and Comment 4A.

h. **"Account Debtor."** An "account debtor" is a person obligated on an account, chattel paper, or general intangible. The account debtor's obligation often is a monetary obligation; however, this is not always the case. For example, if a franchisee uses its rights under a franchise agreement (a general intangible) as collateral, then the franchisor is an "account debtor." As a general matter, Article 3, and not Article 9, governs obligations on negotiable instruments. Accordingly, the definition of "account debtor" excludes obligors on negotiable instruments constituting part of chattel paper. The principal effect of this change from the definition in ~~former~~ pre-1998 Article 9 is that the rules in Sections 9–403, 9–404, 9–405, and 9–406, dealing with the rights of an assignee and duties of an account debtor, do not apply to an assignment of chattel paper in which the obligation to pay is evidenced by a negotiable instrument. (Section 9–406(d), however, does apply to ~~promissory notes, including negotiable promissory notes~~ a negotiable instrument that is a "promissory note," as that term is used in the 2022 revision of subsection (d). See Comment 5.c.) Rather, the ~~assignee's~~ rights of an assignee of a negotiable instrument are governed by Article 3. Similarly, the duties of an obligor on a nonnegotiable instrument are governed by non-Article 9 law unless the nonnegotiable instrument is a part of chattel paper, in which case the obligor is an account debtor.

The definition of "account debtor" was revised in 2022 to add the modifier "negotiable" to the second reference to "instrument," making it clear that an obligor on a negotiable instrument is not an account debtor. This amendment (which is intended to clarify and not to change the meaning of the definition) is useful because the definition of "instrument" has been revised to exclude writings that evidence chattel paper. However, the definition of "negotiable instrument" in Section 1–201 continues to apply under Article 9. See Section 9–102(a)(47) and (b); Comment 5.c. Of course, a record or records evidencing chattel paper must evidence either a security agreement or lease agreement in addition to a right to payment of a monetary obligation.

* * *

6. **Investment-Property-Related Definitions: "Commodity Account"; "Commodity Contract"; "Commodity Customer"; "Commodity Intermediary"; "Investment Property."** These definitions are substantially the same as the corresponding definitions in ~~former~~ pre-1998 Section 9–115. "Investment property" includes securities, both certificated and uncertificated, securities accounts, security entitlements, commodity accounts, and commodity contracts. The term investment property includes a "securities account" in order to facilitate transactions in which a debtor wishes to create a security interest in all of the investment positions held through a particular account rather than in particular positions carried in the account. ~~Former~~ Pre-1998 Section 9–115 was added in conjunction with Revised Article 8 and contained a variety of rules applicable to security interests in investment property. ~~These rules have been~~ The 1998 Revisions relocated these rules to the appropriate sections of Article 9. See, e.g., Sections 9–203 (attachment), 9–314 (perfection by control), 9–328 (priority).

The terms "security," "security entitlement," and related terms are defined in Section 8–102, and the term "securities account" is defined in Section 8–501. The terms "commodity account," "commodity contract," "commodity customer," and "commodity intermediary" are defined in this section. Commodity contracts are not "securities" or "financial assets" under Article 8. See Section 8–103(f). Thus, the relationship between commodity intermediaries and commodity customers is not governed by the indirect-holding-system rules of Part 5 of Article 8. For securities, Article 9 contains rules on security interests, and Article 8 contains rules on the rights of transferees, including secured parties, on such matters as the rights of a transferee if the transfer was itself wrongful and gives rise to an adverse claim. For commodity contracts, Article 9 establishes rules on security interests, but questions <u>relating to commodity contracts</u> of the sort dealt with in Article 8 for securities are left to other law.

* * *

7. **Consumer-Related Definitions: "Consumer Debtor"; "Consumer Goods"; "Consumer-goods transaction"; "Consumer Obligor"; "Consumer Transaction."** The definition of "consumer goods" (discussed above) is substantially the same as the definition in ~~former~~ <u>pre-1998</u> Section 9–109. The <u>1998 Revisions added the</u> definitions of "consumer debtor," "consumer obligor," "consumer-goods transaction," and "consumer transaction" ~~have been added~~ in connection with various ~~new (and old)~~ <u>1998 and pre-1998</u> consumer-related provisions and to designate certain provisions that are inapplicable in consumer transactions.

* * *

8. **Filing-Related Definitions: "Continuation Statement"; "File Number"; "Filing Office"; "Filing-office Rule"; "Financing Statement"; "Fixture Filing"; "Manufactured-Home Transaction"; "New Debtor"; "Original Debtor"; "Public-Finance Transaction"; "Termination Statement"; "Transmitting Utility."** * * *

The definition of "transmitting utility" ~~has been revised to embrace~~ <u>embraces</u> the business of transmitting communications generally to take account of new and future types of communications technology. The term designates a special class of debtors for whom separate filing rules are provided in Part 5, thereby obviating the many local fixture filings that would be necessary under the rules of Section 9–501 for a far-flung public-utility debtor. A transmitting utility will not necessarily be regulated by or operating as such in a jurisdiction where fixtures are located. For example, a utility might own transmission lines in a jurisdiction, although the utility generates no power and has no customers in the jurisdiction. <u>Of course, the definition applies only for purposes of this Article and not for purposes of any other law, regulation, or rule.</u>

9. **Definitions Relating to Medium Neutrality.**

a. **"Record."** In ~~many, but not all, instances,~~ <u>general</u> the term "record" replaces the term "writing" and "written." A "record" includes information that is in intangible form (e.g., electronically stored) as well as tangible form (e.g., written on paper). <u>Section 9–102(a)(70).</u> Given the rapid development and commercial adoption of modern communication and storage technologies, requirements that documents or communications be "written," "in writing," or otherwise in tangible form do not necessarily reflect or aid commercial practices.

A "record" need not be permanent or indestructible, but the term does not include any oral or other communication that is not stored or preserved by any means. The information must be stored on paper or in some other medium. Information that has not been retained other than through human memory does not qualify as a record. Examples of modern technologies commercially used to communicate or store information include, but are not limited to, magnetic media, optical discs, digital voice messaging systems, electronic mail, audio tapes, and photographic media, as well as paper. "Record" is an inclusive term that includes all of these methods of storing or communicating information. Any "writing" is a record. A record may be ~~authenticated~~ <u>signed</u>. See Comment 9.b. A record may be created without the knowledge or intent of a particular person.

* * *

b. **"Authenticate"; "Sign"; "Communicate"; "Send."** The ~~terms~~ <u>defined term</u> "authenticate" <u>has been deleted in the 2022 Article 9 Revisions. That term</u> and "authenticated" <u>were</u> generally ~~replace~~ <u>used in Article 9 instead of</u> "sign" and "signed." ~~"Authenticated" replaces and broadens the definition of "signed."~~ <u>However, the 2022 revised definition of "sign"</u> in Section 1–201 ~~, to encompass~~ <u>encompasses</u> authentication of all records, not just writings. <u>Accordingly, "sign" and "signed" are now used in Article 9.</u> (References to ~~authentication~~ <u>signing</u> of, e.g., an agreement, demand, or notification mean, of course, ~~authentication~~ <u>signing</u> of a record containing an agreement, demand, or notification.) The terms "communicate" and "send" also contemplate the possibility of communication by nonwritten media. These definitions include the act of transmitting both tangible and intangible records. The <u>2022 Amendments deleted the</u> definition of "send" ~~replaces, for purposes of this Article, the corresponding term in Section 1–201. The reference to "usual means of communication" in that definition contemplates an inquiry into the appropriateness of the method of transmission used in the particular circumstances involved~~ <u>in this section and added a corresponding definition to Section 1–201, replacing the pre-2022 definition in that section.</u>

10. **Scope-Related Definitions.**

a. **Expanded Scope of Article: "Agricultural Lien"; "Consignment"; "Payment Intangible"; "Promissory Note."** These ~~new~~ definitions reflect the expanded scope of <u>1998</u> Article 9, as provided in Section 9–109(a).

b. **Reduced Scope of Exclusions: "Governmental Unit"; "Health-Care-Insurance Receivable"; "Commercial Tort Claims."** These ~~new~~ definitions reflect the reduced scope of the <u>1998</u> exclusions, provided in Section 9–109(c) and (d), of transfers by governmental debtors and assignments of interests in insurance policies and commercial tort claims.

11. **Choice-of-Law-Related Definitions: "Certificate of Title"; "Governmental Unit"; "Jurisdiction of Organization"; "Public Organic Record;" "Registered Organization"; "State."** These ~~new~~ definitions reflect the changes in the law governing perfection and priority of security interests and agricultural liens provided in Part 3, Subpart 1 <u>of the 1998 Revisions</u>.

* * *

12. **Deposit-Account-Related Definitions: "Deposit Account"; "Bank."** The <u>1998</u> revised definition of "deposit account" incorporates the definition of "bank," which is new. The <u>new</u> definition derives from the definitions of "bank" in Sections 4–105(1) and 4A–105(a)(2), which focus on whether the organization is "engaged in the business of banking."

Deposit accounts evidenced by Article 9 "instruments" are excluded from the term "deposit account." In contrast, ~~former~~ <u>pre-1998</u> Section 9–105 excluded from the definition "an account evidenced by a certificate of deposit." The revised definition clarifies the proper treatment of nonnegotiable or uncertificated certificates of deposit. Under the definition, an uncertificated certificate of deposit would be a deposit account (assuming there is no writing evidencing the bank's obligation to pay) whereas a nonnegotiable certificate of deposit would be a deposit account only if it is not an "instrument" as defined in this section (a question that turns on whether the nonnegotiable certificate of deposit is "of a type that in ordinary course of business is transferred by delivery with any necessary indorsement or assignment.")

A deposit account evidenced by an instrument is subject to the rules applicable to instruments generally. As a consequence, a security interest in such an instrument cannot be perfected by "control" (see Section 9–104), and the special priority rules applicable to deposit accounts (see Sections 9–327 and 9–340) do not apply. <u>If a bank is the obligor on a monetary obligation not evidenced by an instrument or chattel paper, the obligation or the right to payment of the obligation may be a deposit account, an account, a payment intangible, or another type of collateral depending on the facts and circumstances. Of course, the classification of a monetary obligation or a right to payment of the obligation for purposes of this Article would not necessarily affect the application of laws regulating, for example, banking, securities, commodities, money transmission, and taxation.</u>

* * *

<u>12A. **Money-Related Definitions and Terms: "Money"; "Electronic Money"; "Tangible Money"; "Funds"; "Monetary Obligation."** The Article 9 definition of "money" in subsection (a)(54A), added by the 2022 Article 9 Revisions, is a subset of the definition of "money" as defined in Section 1–201(b)(24). It follows that cryptocurrencies, such as bitcoin, that are not "money" as defined in Section 1–201 because they were in existence and used before adoption by a government, also are not Article 9 money. An obligation to pay in such cryptocurrencies would not be an account, chattel paper, or a payment intangible or an obligation on an instrument because the obligation would not be a "monetary obligation" or an obligation to pay money. One purpose of the Article 9 definition is to ensure that even if some deposit accounts were to become "money" as defined in Article 1, the provisions relating to perfection and priority for security interests in deposit accounts, and not those for money, will apply to that collateral. Some countries may authorize or adopt deposit accounts with a central bank as a form of "money." See Section 9–101, Comment 4.c. However, the Article 9 provisions governing "deposit accounts" would remain suitable for such accounts with a central bank, even if a government has adopted these accounts as money. The 2022 Article 9 Revisions leave Article 9's treatment of deposit accounts largely unchanged. However, for purposes of Article 9 and in the interest of clarity, the definition of "money" in Section 9–102(a)(31A) excludes deposit accounts. Under this definition, deposit accounts would not be money for Article 9 purposes even if they were to become money under the Article 1 definition. Another purpose of the Article 9 definition of "money" is to exclude from that definition money (as defined in Section 1–201(b)(24)) in an electronic form that cannot be subjected to control under Section 9–105A. Such property would be a general intangible, governed by the perfection and priority rules for that type of collateral.</u>

Some countries may authorize or adopt intangible tokens as a medium of exchange that would be "money" as defined in both Article 1 and Article 9. See Section 9–101, Comment 4.c. Such intangible tokens would be "electronic money," as defined in Section 9–102(a)(31A). A security interest in electronic money as original collateral can be perfected only by control. Sections 9–312(b)(4); 9–314; 9–105A. The requirements for obtaining control of electronic money are essentially the same as those for obtaining control of a controllable electronic record under Article 12. Sections 9–105A; 12–105. The definition of "tangible money" in Section 9–102(a)(79A) uses the word "tangible" with its normal meaning (as something that has physical or corporeal existence, such as goods).

"Monetary obligation" as used in the Uniform Commercial Code (including in Article 9) is not a defined term. The term contemplates an obligation to pay "money" as defined in Section 1–201(b)(24). Consequently, for example, a right to payment of money in an electronic form that cannot be subjected to control, excluded from the Article 9 definition of "money" in subsection (a)(54A), would be a monetary obligation. It follows that such a right to payment could be an account, chattel paper, a payment intangible, or an instrument—including a negotiable instrument, which is defined to include a promise to pay "money" as the term is defined in Section 1–201. See Section 3–104(a) (defining "negotiable instrument"). Also, the term "funds" (like "monetary obligation," an undefined term), as used in the Uniform Commercial Code includes a right to payment of money as defined in Section 1–201(b)(24). As mentioned above, because cryptocurrencies such as bitcoin are not "money" as defined in Section 1–201 (unless they were not in existence and used before adoption by a government), a cryptocurrency or an obligation to pay in cryptocurrency would not be a "monetary obligation" or "funds."

13. **Proceeds-Related Definitions: "Cash Proceeds"; "Noncash Proceeds"; "Proceeds."** The revised definition of "proceeds" ~~expands~~ expanded the definition beyond that contained in ~~former~~ pre-1998 Section 9–306 and resolves ambiguities in the former ~~section~~ definition.

a. **Distributions on Account of Collateral.** The phrase "whatever is collected on, or distributed on account of, collateral," in subparagraph (B), is broad enough to cover cash or stock dividends distributed on account of securities or other investment property that is original collateral. Compare ~~former~~ pre-1998 Section 9–306 ("Any payments or distributions made with respect to investment property collateral are proceeds."). This section rejects the holding of *Hastie v. FDIC*, 2 F.3d 1042 (10th Cir. 1993) (postpetition cash dividends on stock subject to a prepetition pledge are not "proceeds" under Bankruptcy Code Section 552(b)), to the extent the holding relies on the Article 9 definition of "proceeds."

* * *

d. **Proceeds Received by Person Who Did Not Create Security Interest.** When collateral is sold subject to a security interest and the buyer then resells the collateral, a question arose under ~~former~~ pre-1998 Article 9 concerning whether the "debtor" had "received" what the buyer received on resale and, therefore, whether those receipts were "proceeds" under ~~former~~ pre-1998 Section 9–306(2). This Article contains no requirement that property be "received" by the debtor for the property to qualify as proceeds. It is necessary only that the property be traceable, directly or indirectly, to the original collateral.

e. **Cash Proceeds and Noncash Proceeds.** The definition of "cash proceeds" is substantially the same as the corresponding definition in ~~former~~ pre-1998 Section 9–306. The phrase "and the like" covers property that is functionally equivalent to "money, checks, or deposit accounts," such as some money-market accounts that are securities or part of securities entitlements. Proceeds other than cash proceeds are noncash proceeds.

f. **Forks and Airdrops for Controllable Electronic Records.** Sometimes there occurs a change in the software (code) of a system (sometimes referred to as a "protocol" or "platform") in which a controllable electronic record is recorded. When such a change occurs in a blockchain platform, the blockchain may remain intact, no new blockchain may result, and the change sometimes is colloquially referred to as a "soft fork." If, instead, such a change results in a new, separate blockchain that exists alongside the original blockchain and a new controllable electronic record is created, the change is sometimes referred to as a "hard fork." But the terms "fork," "soft fork," and "hard fork" are ambiguous and not used consistently. Even in a hard fork situation the pre-fork controllable electronic record typically would remain intact (although its value might be affected). A person in control of the original record may not automatically obtain control of a new record. Additional steps may be required for the person in control of the original record to obtain control of the new record.

Depending on the nature and structure of the fork, a new controllable electronic record arising under a hard fork may be property "distributed on account of" the original record or "rights arising out of" the original record, thereby constituting proceeds of the original record under subparagraph (B) or (C), or both, of the definition of "proceeds." If the new record is identifiable "proceeds," then the rules on attachment, perfection, priority under Sections 9–203(f), 9–315, and 9–322 would apply. If a security interest in the original record is perfected by control, the creation of the new record in connection with a hard fork typically results in the secured party obtaining control (or having the opportunity to obtain control) of the new record. If that is not the case and perfection of the security interest in the original record is only by control, however, then perfection would continue in the new record only until the 21st day after the security interest attaches to the new record, unless one of the exceptions under subsection (d) applies. Section 9–315(c), (d). For this reason, a secured party may wish also to perfect its security interest by filing so that the perfection would continue thereafter in any proceeds under Section 9–315(d)(1). A secured party that does so may, to ensure the priority of its perfected security interest, also wish to consider obtaining a release or subordination from any earlier filed secured party whose financing statement covers the same type of property. Even if that is achieved, a security interest in the record that is perfected by control (even if control is later obtained) would have priority over a security interest perfected only by filing. Section 9–326A.

New controllable electronic records also may be provided to persons in control of existing records by way of an "airdrop" that does not involve a fork in an existing blockchain. Depending on the circumstances, these new records may or may not be proceeds of the existing, original record.

If the original record were a financial asset credited to a securities account, the new record might become proceeds of a security entitlement for the reasons described above. Concerning the duties, if any, of a securities intermediary with respect to such a distribution, see Section 8–505, Comment 4.

This discussion focuses on forks and airdrops related to controllable electronic records in the context of blockchain technology, the prevailing relevant technology in 2022. In determining whether property may be proceeds of collateral in the contexts of other and future technologies, the principles and policies reflected in this discussion should be considered.

14. **Consignment-Related Definitions: "Consignee"; "Consignment"; "Consignor."** The definition of "consignment," added by the 1998 Revisions, excludes, in subparagraphs (B) and (C), transactions for which filing would be inappropriate or of insufficient benefit to justify the costs. A consignment excluded from the application of this Article by one of those subparagraphs may still be a true consignment; however, it is governed by non-Article 9 law. The definition also excludes, in subparagraph (D), what have been called "consignments intended for security." These "consignments" are not bailments but secured transactions. Accordingly, all of Article 9 applies to them. See Sections 1–201(b)(35), 9–109(a)(1). The "consignor" is the person who delivers goods to the "consignee" in a consignment.

* * *

Under clause (iii) of subparagraph (A), a transaction is not an Article 9 "consignment" if the consignee is "generally known by its creditors to be substantially engaged in selling the goods of others." Clause (iii) does not apply solely because a particular competing claimant knows that the goods are held on consignment. See PEB Commentary No. 20, dated January 24, 2019.

15. **"Accounting."** This definition describes the record and information that a debtor is entitled to request under Section 9–210. Consistent with the revised definition of "sign" in Section 1–201, the cognate term "signed" replaces the reference to "authenticated" in the pre-2022 text of this definition.

* * *

17. **"Encumbrance"; "Mortgage."** The definitions of "encumbrance" and "mortgage" are unchanged in substance from the corresponding definitions in former pre-1998 Section 9–105. They are used primarily in the special real-property-related priority and other provisions relating to crops, fixtures, and accessions.

18. **"Fixtures."** This definition is unchanged in substance from the corresponding definition in former pre-1998 Section 9–313. See Section 9–334 (priority of security interests in fixtures and crops).

19. **"Good Faith."** This Article expands the definition of "good faith" to include "the observance of reasonable commercial standards of fair dealing." The definition in this section applies when the term is used in this Article, and the same concept applies in the context of this Article for purposes of the obligation of good faith imposed by Section 1–203. See subsection (c). The definition of "good faith" added by the 1998 Revisions, which incorporated the concept of "reasonable commercial standards of fair dealing," was deleted by the conforming amendments to the 2001 revision of Article 1. The definition is unnecessary given the revised definition in Section 1–201(b)(20).

20. **"Lien Creditor."** This definition is unchanged in substance from the corresponding definition in former pre-1998 Section 9–301.

21. **"New Value."** This Article deletes The 1998 Revisions deleted former pre-1998 Section 9–108. Its broad formulation of new value, which embraced the taking of after-acquired collateral for a pre-existing claim, was

unnecessary, counterintuitive, and ineffective for its original purpose of sheltering after-acquired collateral from attack as a voidable preference in bankruptcy. The new definition of "new value" derives from Bankruptcy Code Section 547(a). The term is used with respect to temporary perfection of security interests in instruments, certificated securities, or negotiable documents under Section 9–312(e) and with respect to chattel paper priority in Section 9–330.

* * *

23.   **"Proposal."** This definition describes a record that is sufficient to propose to retain collateral in full or partial satisfaction of a secured obligation. See Sections 9–620, 9–621, 9–622. Consistent with the revised definition of "sign" in Section 1–201, the 2022 revision of the definition adopts the cognate term "signed" to replace the term "authenticated" used in the pre-2022 text.

24.   **"Pursuant to Commitment."** This definition is unchanged in substance from the corresponding definition in ~~former~~ pre-1998 Section 9–105. It is used in connection with special priority rules applicable to future advances. See Section 9–323.

* * *

~~26.   **Terminology: "Assignment" and "Transfer."** In numerous provisions, this Article refers to the "assignment" or the "transfer" of property interests. These terms and their derivatives are not defined. This Article generally follows common usage by using the terms "assignment" and "assign" to refer to transfers of rights to payment, claims, and liens and other security interests. It generally uses the term "transfer" to refer to other transfers of interests in property. Except when used in connection with a letter-of-credit transaction (see Section 9–107, Comment 4), no significance should be placed on the use of one term or the other. Depending on the substance of the transaction, each term as used in this Article refers to the assignment or transfer of an outright ownership interest or to the assignment or transfer of a limited interest, such as a security interest, or both.~~

§ 9–104.   Control of Deposit Account.

(a)   **[Requirements for control.]** A secured party has control of a deposit account if:

* * *

(2)   the debtor, secured party, and bank have agreed in ~~an authenticated~~ a signed record that the bank will comply with instructions originated by the secured party directing disposition of the funds in the deposit account without further consent by the debtor; ~~or~~

(3)   the secured party becomes the bank's customer with respect to the deposit account ~~.~~; or

(4)   another person, other than the debtor:

  (A)   has control of the deposit account and acknowledges that it has control on behalf of the secured party; or

  (B)   obtains control of the deposit account after having acknowledged that it will obtain control of the deposit account on behalf of the secured party.

* * *

Official Comment

1.   **Source.** ~~New; derived~~ Derived from Section 8–106.

2.   **Why "Control" Matters.** This section explains the concept of "control" of a deposit account. "Control" under this section may serve two functions. First, "control . . . pursuant to the debtor's agreement" may substitute for ~~an authenticated~~ a signed security agreement as an element of attachment. See Section 9–203(b)(3)(D). Second, when a deposit account is taken as original collateral, the only method of perfection is obtaining control under this section. See Section 9–312(b)(1).

3.   **Requirements for "Control: In General."** * * *

* * *

Under subsection (a)(2), a secured party may obtain control by obtaining the bank's ~~authenticated~~ signed agreement that it will comply with the secured party's instructions without further consent by the debtor. The analogous provision in Section 8–106 does not require that the agreement be ~~authenticated~~ signed. An agreement to comply with the secured party's instructions suffices for "control" of a deposit account under this section even if the bank's agreement is subject to specified conditions, e.g., that the secured party's instructions are accompanied by a certification that the debtor is in default. (Of course, if the condition is the *debtor's* further consent, the statute explicitly provides that the agreement would *not* confer control.) See ~~revised~~ Section 8–106, Comment 7.

* * *

4. **Control on behalf of another person.** Subsection (a)(4) provides for a secured party to obtain control of a deposit account by virtue of the acknowledgment by another person, other than the debtor, in control of the deposit account. It generally follows revisions to the corresponding provisions for control of electronic documents of title (Section 7–106(g)), control of a security entitlement (8–106(d)), control of an electronic copy of a record evidencing chattel paper (Section 9–105(g)), control of electronic money (Section 9–105A(e)), and control of controllable electronic records (Section 12–105(e)). For a brief discussion, see Section 12–105, Comments 8 and 9.

An acknowledgment by a person in control under subsection (a)(4) would not impose any duties on the bank with which the deposit account is maintained. Indeed, the bank may have no knowledge or involvement whatsoever with a control person's acknowledgment under that subsection. On the other hand, subsection (a)(4) should not be construed to permit the bank with which the deposit account is maintained to short-circuit subsection (a)(2), which provides for control through a control agreement among the debtor, the bank, and the control person. However, it would be possible for the bank, acting in a capacity other than as the depositary bank (for example, as a secured party) to acknowledge that it has control on behalf of another purchaser under subsection (a)(4).

Section 9–107B(a) makes clear that a person that has control under this section has no duty to acknowledge that it has or will obtain control on behalf of another person. Arrangements for a person to acknowledge that it has or will obtain control on behalf of another person are not standardized. Accordingly, Section 9–107B(b) leaves to the agreement of the parties and to any other applicable law any duties of a person that does acknowledge that it has or will obtain control on behalf of another person and provides that a person making an acknowledgment is not required to confirm the acknowledgment to another person.

§ 9–105. ~~Control of Electronic Chattel Paper~~ Control of Electronic Copy of Record Evidencing Chattel Paper.

~~(a) [General rule: control of electronic chattel paper.] A secured party has control of electronic chattel paper if a system employed for evidencing the transfer of interests in the chattel paper reliably establishes the secured party as the person to which the chattel paper was assigned.~~

~~(b) [Specific facts giving control.] A system satisfies subsection (a) if the record or records comprising the chattel paper are created, stored, and assigned in such a manner that:~~

~~(1) a single authoritative copy of the record or records exists which is unique, identifiable, and, except as otherwise provided in paragraphs (4), (5), and (6), unalterable;~~

~~(2) the authoritative copy identifies the secured party as the assignee of the record or records;~~

~~(3) the authoritative copy is communicated to and maintained by the secured party or its designated custodian;~~

~~(4) copies or amendments that add or change an identified assignee of the authoritative copy can be made only with the consent of the secured party;~~

~~(5) each copy of the authoritative copy and any copy of a copy is readily identifiable as a copy that is not the authoritative copy; and~~

~~(6) any amendment of the authoritative copy is readily identifiable as authorized or unauthorized.~~

(a) **[General rule: control of electronic copy of record evidencing chattel paper.]** A purchaser has control of an authoritative electronic copy of a record evidencing chattel paper if a system employed for evidencing the assignment of interests in the chattel paper reliably establishes the purchaser as the person to which the authoritative electronic copy was assigned.

(b) **[Single authoritative copy.]** A system satisfies subsection (a) if the record or records evidencing the chattel paper are created, stored, and assigned in a manner that:

(1) a single authoritative copy of the record or records exists which is unique, identifiable, and, except as otherwise provided in paragraphs (4), (5), and (6), unalterable;

(2)　the authoritative copy identifies the purchaser as the assignee of the record or records;

(3)　the authoritative copy is communicated to and maintained by the purchaser or its designated custodian;

(4)　copies or amendments that add or change an identified assignee of the authoritative copy can be made only with the consent of the purchaser;

(5)　each copy of the authoritative copy and any copy of a copy is readily identifiable as a copy that is not the authoritative copy; and

(6)　any amendment of the authoritative copy is readily identifiable as authorized or unauthorized.

(c)　**[One or more authoritative copies.]** A system satisfies subsection (a), and a purchaser has control of an authoritative electronic copy of a record evidencing chattel paper, if the electronic copy, a record attached to or logically associated with the electronic copy, or a system in which the electronic copy is recorded:

(1)　enables the purchaser readily to identify each electronic copy as either an authoritative copy or a nonauthoritative copy;

(2)　enables the purchaser readily to identify itself in any way, including by name, identifying number, cryptographic key, office, or account number, as the assignee of the authoritative electronic copy; and

(3)　gives the purchaser exclusive power, subject to subsection (d), to:

(A)　prevent others from adding or changing an identified assignee of the authoritative electronic copy; and

(B)　transfer control of the authoritative electronic copy.

(d)　**[Meaning of exclusive.]** Subject to subsection (e), a power is exclusive under subsection (c)(3)(A) and (B) even if:

(1)　the authoritative electronic copy, a record attached to or logically associated with the authoritative electronic copy, or a system in which the authoritative electronic copy is recorded limits the use of the authoritative electronic copy or has a protocol programmed to cause a change, including a transfer or loss of control; or

(2)　the power is shared with another person.

(e)　**[When power not shared with another person.]** A power of a purchaser is not shared with another person under subsection (d)(2) and the purchaser's power is not exclusive if:

(1)　the purchaser can exercise the power only if the power also is exercised by the other person; and

(2)　the other person:

(A)　can exercise the power without exercise of the power by the purchaser; or

(B)　is the transferor to the purchaser of an interest in the chattel paper.

(f)　**[Presumption of exclusivity of certain powers.]** If a purchaser has the powers specified in subsection (c)(3)(A) and (B), the powers are presumed to be exclusive.

(g)　**[Obtaining control through another person.]** A purchaser has control of an authoritative electronic copy of a record evidencing chattel paper if another person, other than the transferor to the purchaser of an interest in the chattel paper:

(1)　has control of the authoritative electronic copy and acknowledges that it has control on behalf of the purchaser; or

(2)　obtains control of the authoritative electronic copy after having acknowledged that it will obtain control of the electronic copy on behalf of the purchaser.

Official Comment

1.　~~Source.~~ New.

~~2. **"Control" of Electronic Chattel Paper.** This Article covers security interests in "electronic chattel paper," a new term defined in Section 9–102. This section governs how "control" of electronic chattel paper may be obtained. Subsection (a), which derives from Section 16 of the Uniform Electronic Transactions Act, sets forth the general test for control. Subsection (b) sets forth a safe harbor test that, if satisfied, establishes control under the general test in subsection (a).~~

~~A secured party's control of electronic chattel paper (i) may substitute for an authenticated security agreement for purposes of attachment under Section 9–203, (ii) is a method of perfection under Section 9–314, and (iii) is a condition for obtaining special, non-temporal priority under Section 9–330. Because electronic chattel paper cannot be transferred, assigned, or possessed in the same manner as tangible chattel paper, a special definition of control is necessary. In descriptive terms, this section provides that control of electronic chattel paper is the functional equivalent of possession of "tangible chattel paper" (a term also defined in Section 9–102).~~

~~3. **Development of Control Systems.** This Article leaves to the marketplace the development of systems and procedures, through a combination of suitable technologies and business practices, for dealing with control of electronic chattel paper in a commercial context. Systems that evolve for control of electronic chattel paper may or may not involve a third party custodian of the relevant records. As under UETA, a system must be shown to reliably establish that the secured party is the assignee of the chattel paper. Reliability is a high standard and encompasses the general principles of uniqueness, identifiability, and unalterability found in subsection (b) without setting forth specific guidelines as to how these principles must be achieved. However, the standards applied to determine whether a party is in control of electronic chattel paper should not be more stringent than the standards now applied to determine whether a party is in possession of tangible chattel paper. For example, just as a secured party does not lose possession of tangible chattel paper merely by virtue of the possibility that a person acting on its behalf *could* wrongfully redeliver the chattel paper to the debtor, so control of electronic chattel paper would not be defeated by the possibility that the secured party's interest *could* be subverted by the wrongful conduct of a person (such as a custodian) acting on its behalf.~~

~~This section and the concept of control of electronic chattel paper are not based on the same concepts as are control of deposit accounts (Section 9–104), security entitlements, a type of investment property (Section 9–106), and letter-of-credit rights (Section 9–107). The rules for control of those types of collateral are based on existing market practices and legal and regulatory regimes for institutions such as banks and securities intermediaries. Analogous practices for electronic chattel paper are developing nonetheless. The flexible approach adopted by this section, moreover, should not impede the development of these practices and, eventually, legal and regulatory regimes, which may become analogous to those for, e.g., investment property.~~

~~4. **"Authoritative Copy" of Electronic Chattel Paper.** One requirement for establishing control under subsection (b) is that a particular copy be an "authoritative copy." Although other copies may exist, they must be distinguished from the authoritative copy. This may be achieved, for example, through the methods of authentication that are used or by business practices involving the marking of any additional copies. When tangible chattel paper is converted to electronic chattel paper, in order to establish that a copy of the electronic chattel paper is the authoritative copy it may be necessary to show that the tangible chattel paper no longer exists or has been permanently marked to indicate that it is not the authoritative copy.~~

1. **The Functions of Control.** A secured party can perfect a security interest in chattel paper by filing. *See* Section 9–312(a). Alternatively, a secured party can perfect a security interest in chattel paper by taking possession of all authoritative tangible copies of the record evidencing the chattel paper and obtaining control of all authoritative electronic copies of the record evidencing chattel paper. Section 9–314A. Possession and control also are conditions for achieving priority under Section 9–330(a), (b), and (c). A secured party's possession or control of chattel paper also may substitute for a signed security agreement for purposes of attachment under Section 9–203.

2. **Conditions for Obtaining Control: In General.** This section provides the requirements for obtaining control of chattel paper. As explained in the comment to the definition of "chattel paper," the definitions of "electronic chattel paper" and "tangible chattel paper" have been deleted as unnecessary. See Section 9–102, Comment 5.b.

Subsections (a) and (b) are substantially unchanged under the 2022 Article 9 Revisions. Subsection (a), which derives from Section 16 of the Uniform Electronic Transactions Act, sets forth the general test for control. (The amendments to subsection (a) primarily reflect the changes to the definition of chattel paper in Section 9–102.) Subsections (b) and (c) set forth safe harbor tests that, if satisfied, establish control under the general test in subsection (a). *It is important to note that compliance with the conditions for control in subsection (c) would satisfy the conditions provided in subsection (b).* However, subsection (b) has been retained out of an abundance of caution and to provide assurances of the continuing viability of pre-2022 systems for control of chattel paper evidenced by electronic records.

3. **Development of Control Systems and Application of Subsection (b).** This Article leaves to the marketplace the development of systems and procedures, through a combination of suitable technologies and business practices, for dealing with control of chattel paper in a commercial context. As under UETA and under the general standard for control under subsection (a), for control under subsection (b), as supplemented by subsection (g), a system must be shown to reliably establish that the secured party is the assignee of the chattel paper. Reliability is a high standard and encompasses the general principle of identifiability of an assignee of an authoritative copy as found in subsection (b), but without setting forth specific guidelines as to how compliance with this principle must be achieved. Under subsection (b), at any point in time, a party should be able to identify the single authoritative copy of the record or records evidencing the chattel paper which is unique and identifiable as the authoritative copy. This does not mean that once created the authoritative copy need be static and never moved or copied from its original location. To the extent that backup systems exist which result in multiple copies, the key to this idea is that at any point in time, the one authoritative copy needs to be unique and identifiable. However, the standards applied to determine whether a party is in control of chattel paper should not be more stringent than the pre-2022 standards applied to determine whether a party is in possession of tangible chattel paper. For example, just as a secured party does not lose possession of tangible chattel paper merely by virtue of the possibility that a person acting on its behalf *could* wrongfully redeliver the chattel paper to the debtor, so control of chattel paper evidenced by an electronic copy of a record or records would not be defeated by the possibility that the secured party's control *could* be subverted by the wrongful conduct of a person (such as a custodian) acting on its behalf.

4. **Subsection (c) Safe Harbor: In General.** The subsection (c) "safe harbor" generally follows Section 12–105 for control of controllable electronic records. See generally Section 12–105 and Comments. It differs from subsection (b), which (as explained above) is based on a "single authoritative copy" of an electronic record or records. Subsection (b) would be inapplicable when the relevant record is maintained on a blockchain or another distributed ledger. The utility of distributed ledger technology depends on there being multiple authoritative copies of a record. However, as with subsection (b), control under subsection (c) also meets the high standard of reliability under subsection (a) as to the identifiability of an assignee of authoritative copies. The conditions for "control" in subsection (c) are meant to reflect the functions that possession serves with respect to writings, but in a more accurate and technologically flexible way than does the definition in subsection (b).

Subsection (c), as supplemented by subsections (d) through (g), sets forth the requirements for a purchaser to have "control of an authoritative electronic copy of a record evidencing chattel paper." However, for purposes of perfection of a security interest in the chattel paper under Section 9–314A and qualification for non-temporal priority under Section 9–330, the purchaser must obtain control of *each* authoritative electronic copy (i.e., *all* of the copies) of a record evidencing the chattel paper and take possession of each tangible copy (if any) of the record evidencing the chattel paper.

5. **Control of Electronic Copy of Record Evidencing Chattel Paper under Subsection (c).** Under subsection (c), to obtain control of an electronic copy of a record evidencing chattel paper a purchaser must be able to identify each electronic copy as authoritative or nonauthoritative and identify itself as the assignee of the authoritative copy. As to the means of identification, see Section 12–105, Comment 7. In addition, the purchaser must have the exclusive power to prevent others from adding or changing an identified assignee and to transfer control of the authoritative copy. However, once it is established that a person has received those powers, subsection (f) provides a presumption of exclusivity. Consequently, a person asserting control need not prove exclusivity in order to make out a *prima facie* case. Application of the presumption will be governed also by Section 1–206 (effects of a presumption under the UCC) and applicable non-UCC law (including rules of procedure and evidence). See generally Section 12–105, Comment 5. Subsection (d) contains two qualifications of the term "exclusive" as used in subsection (c)(3). A power can be "exclusive" under subsection (c)(3) even if one or both of these qualifications apply.

Subsection (e) provides that in certain circumstances a power is not shared within the meaning of subsection (d)(2), the relaxation of the exclusivity requirement provided by subsection (d)(2) does not apply, and, consequently, a purchaser's power is not exclusive. Subsection (e) provides that a purchaser does not share an exclusive power with another person if the purchaser can exercise the power only with the other person's cooperation (subsection (e)(1)) but the other person either (i) can exercise the power without the purchaser's cooperation (subsection (e)(2)(A)) or (ii) is the transferor to the purchaser of an interest in the chattel paper (subsection (e)(2)(B)). It follows that a purchaser to which subsection (e) applies does not have control based on its exclusive powers (although it might have control through another person under subsection (g), discussed below, or if another person having control is acting as the person's agent). As to the rationale for disqualifying a purchaser (which includes a secured party in a secured transaction) from sharing powers with a transferor to the purchaser, as provided in subsection (e)(2)(B), and from the benefit of shared control under subsection (d)(2), and for examples of the operation of subsection (e) (in the context of the similar provision in Section 12–105), see Section 12–105, Comments 5 and 9.

6. **Control Through Another Person.** Subsection (g) provides for a purchaser to obtain control of an electronic copy by virtue of the acknowledgment by another person in control of the electronic copy. It follows revisions to the corresponding provisions for control of electronic documents of title (Section 7–106(g)), control of a security entitlement (Section 8–106(d)(3)), control of deposit accounts (Section 9–104(a)(4)), control of electronic money (Section 9–105A(e)), and control of controllable electronic records (Section 12–105(e)). For a brief discussion, see Section 12–105, Comment 8. For an acknowledgment by another person to be effective to confer control on a purchaser under subsection (g), the other person making the acknowledgment must be one "other than the transferor to the purchaser of an interest in the chattel paper." The rationale for this limitation is discussed in Section 12–105, Comment 9.

Section 9–107B(a) makes clear that a person that has control under this section has no duty to acknowledge that it has or will obtain control on behalf of another person. Arrangements for a person to acknowledge that it has or will obtain control on behalf of another person are not standardized. Accordingly, Section 9–107B(b) leaves to the agreement of the parties and to any other applicable law any duties of a person that does acknowledge that it has or will obtain control on behalf of another person and provides that a person making an acknowledgment is not required to confirm the acknowledgment to another person. For example, subsection (g) would apply to give control to a person, Alpha, when another person, Beta, has control of each authoritative electronic copy of a record evidencing chattel paper and acknowledges that it has control on behalf of Alpha. However, under Section 9–107B(a), Beta is not required to so acknowledge. And under Section 9–107B(b), even if Beta does so acknowledge, Beta owes no duty to Alpha unless Beta agrees or other law so provides and Beta is not required to confirm its acknowledgment to any other person.

7. **References to "Secured Party" Changed to "Purchaser."** References to a "secured party" in the pre-2022 text of this section have been changed to refer to a "purchaser." This change aligns the text with the priority rules of Section 9–330(a), (b), and (c).

§ 9–105A. Control of Electronic Money.

(a) **[General rule: control of electronic money.]** A person has control of electronic money if:

(1) the electronic money, a record attached to or logically associated with the electronic money, or a system in which the electronic money is recorded gives the person:

(A) power to avail itself of substantially all the benefit from the electronic money; and

(B) exclusive power, subject to subsection (b), to:

(i) prevent others from availing themselves of substantially all the benefit from the electronic money; and

(ii) transfer control of the electronic money to another person or cause another person to obtain control of other electronic money as a result of the transfer of the electronic money; and

(2) the electronic money, a record attached to or logically associated with the electronic money, or a system in which the electronic money is recorded enables the person readily to identify itself in any way, including by name, identifying number, cryptographic key, office, or account number, as having the powers under paragraph (1).

(b) **[Meaning of exclusive.]** Subject to subsection (c), a power is exclusive under subsection (a)(1)(B)(i) and (ii) even if:

(1) the electronic money, a record attached to or logically associated with the electronic money, or a system in which the electronic money is recorded limits the use of the electronic money or has a protocol programmed to cause a change, including a transfer or loss of control; or

(2) the power is shared with another person.

(c)   **[When power not shared with another person.]** A power of a person is not shared with another person under subsection (b)(2) and the person's power is not exclusive if:

(1)   the person can exercise the power only if the power also is exercised by the other person; and

(2)   the other person:

(A)   can exercise the power without exercise of the power by the person; or

(B)   is the transferor to the person of an interest in the electronic money.

(d)   **[Presumption of exclusivity of certain powers.]** If a person has the powers specified in subsection (a)(1)(B)(i) and (ii), the powers are presumed to be exclusive.

(e)   **[Control through another person.]** A person has control of electronic money if another person, other than the transferor to the person of an interest in the electronic money:

(1)   has control of the electronic money and acknowledges that it has control on behalf of the person; or

(2)   obtains control of the electronic money after having acknowledged that it will obtain control of the electronic money on behalf of the person.

Official Comment

1.   **"Control" of Electronic Money: In General.** A security interest in electronic money as original collateral may be perfected only by control pursuant to this section. Section 9–312(b)(4). These requirements for obtaining control generally track those in Section 12–105 for controllable electronic records. See generally Section 12–105, Comments.

2.   **Control on Behalf of Another Person.** Subsection (e) provides for a person to obtain control of electronic money by virtue of the acknowledgment by another person in control of the electronic money. It follows revisions to the corresponding provisions for control of electronic documents of title (Section 7–106(g)), control of a security entitlement (Section 8–106(d)(3)), control of deposit accounts (Section 9–104(a)(4)), control of an electronic copy of a record evidencing chattel paper (Section 9–105(g)), and control of controllable electronic records (Section 12–105(e)). For a brief discussion, see Section 12–105, Comment 8.

Section 9–107B(a) makes clear that a person that has control under this section has no duty to acknowledge that it has or will obtain control on behalf of another person. Arrangements for a person to acknowledge that it has or will obtain control on behalf of another person are not standardized. Accordingly, Section 9–107B(b) leaves to the agreement of the parties and to any other applicable law any duties of a person that does acknowledge that it has or will obtain control on behalf of another person and provides that a person making an acknowledgment is not required to confirm the acknowledgment to another person.

§ 9–107A. Control of Controllable Electronic Record, Controllable Account, or Controllable Payment Intangible.

(a)   **[Control under Section 12–105.]** A secured party has control of a controllable electronic record as provided in Section 12–105.

(b)   **[Control of controllable account and controllable payment intangible.]** A secured party has control of a controllable account or controllable payment intangible if the secured party has control of the controllable electronic record that evidences the controllable account or controllable payment intangible.

Official Comment

1.   **Perfection by Control or Filing and Priority for Controllable Electronic Records.** Perfection by filing and perfection by control are alternative methods of perfection for a controllable electronic record. See Sections 9–312, 9–314. Under this section, a secured party has control of a controllable electronic record as provided in Section 12–105. Under Section 9–326A, a security interest in a controllable electronic record that is perfected by control has priority over a security interest perfected by another method.

2.   **Perfection by Control or Filing and Priority for Controllable Account or Controllable Payment Intangible.** Perfection by filing and perfection by control also are alternative methods of perfection for a controllable account or controllable payment intangible. See Sections 9–312, 9–314. Under this section, a secured party would obtain control of a controllable account or controllable payment intangible by obtaining control of the

controllable electronic record that evidences the controllable account or controllable payment intangible. Under Section 9–326A, a security interest in a controllable account or controllable payment intangible that is perfected by control has priority over a security interest perfected by another method.

By definition, a controllable account would be an Article 9 "account," and a controllable payment intangible would be an Article 9 "payment intangible." Section 9–102. The fact that an account or payment intangible is a controllable account or controllable payment intangible does not affect a secured party's alternative of perfection by filing. Moreover, that fact does not affect the applicability of other provisions of Article 9, including the provisions governing an account debtor's agreement not to assert defenses (Section 9–403) and the statutory overrides of legal and contractual restrictions on the assignability of accounts and payment intangibles (Sections 9–406 and 9–408).

§ 9–107B. No Requirement to Acknowledge or Confirm; No Duties.

(a) **[No requirement to acknowledge.]** A person that has control under Section 9–104, 9–105, or 9–105A is not required to acknowledge that it has control on behalf of another person.

(b) **[No duties or confirmation.]** If a person acknowledges that it has or will obtain control on behalf of another person, unless the person otherwise agrees or law other than this article otherwise provides, the person does not owe any duty to the other person and is not required to confirm the acknowledgment to any other person.

Official Comment

1. **Source.** Section 9–107B derives from Sections 8–106(g) and 9–313(f) and (g).

2. **Purpose.** Subsection (a) makes clear that a person that has control under the specified sections has no duty to acknowledge that it has or will obtain control on behalf of another person. Arrangements for a person to acknowledge that it has control on behalf of another person are not standardized. Accordingly, subsection (b) leaves to the agreement of the parties and to any other applicable law any duties of a person that does acknowledge that it has or will obtain control on behalf of any other person.

§ 9–108.   Sufficiency of Description.

* * *

Official Comment

* * *

5. **Consumer Investment Property; Commercial Tort Claims.** Subsection (e) requires greater specificity of description in order to prevent debtors from inadvertently encumbering certain property. Subsection (e) ~~requires~~ provides that a description by defined "type" of collateral alone of a commercial tort claim or, in a consumer transaction, of a security entitlement, securities account, or commodity account, is not sufficient. For example, "all existing and after-acquired investment property" or "all existing and after-acquired security entitlements," without more, would be insufficient in a consumer transaction to describe a security entitlement, securities account, or commodity account. The reference to "*only* by type" in subsection (e) means that a description is sufficient if it satisfies subsection (a) and also contains a descriptive component beyond the "type" alone. For example, a description such as "all goods now or hereafter sold by secured party to debtor" would suffice, but note that Section 9–204(b)(1) would apply except in the case of a purchase-money security interest. See Section 9–204, Comment 3. Moreover, if the collateral consists of a securities account or commodity account, a description of the account is sufficient to cover all existing and future security entitlements or commodity contracts carried in the account. See Section 9–203(h), (i).

Under Section 9–204, an after-acquired collateral clause in a security agreement will not reach future commercial tort claims. It follows that when an effective security agreement (or amendment) covering a commercial tort claim as original collateral is entered into the claim already will exist. Subsection (e) does not require a description to be ~~specific.~~ specific, so long as it extends beyond the "type." For example, a description such as "all tort claims arising out of the explosion of debtor's factory" would suffice, even if the exact amount of the claim, the theory on which it may be based, and the identity of the tortfeasor(s) are not described. (Indeed, those facts may not be known at the time.)

The enhanced specificity (beyond the "type") that subsection (e) requires does not apply to the attachment of security interests in commercial tort claims or collateral in consumer transactions that are identifiable proceeds of other collateral. A security interest automatically attaches to such property under Sections 9–203(f) and 9–315(a)(2). This point is confirmed by Section 9–204(b.1).

§ 9–109. Scope.

* * *

Official Comment

* * *

4. **Sales of Accounts, Chattel Paper, Payment Intangibles, Promissory Notes, and Other Receivables.** * * *

Subsection (a)(3), ~~expands~~ added by the 1998 Revisions, expanded the scope of this Article by including the sale of a "payment intangible" (defined in Section 9–102 as "a general intangible under which the account debtor's principal obligation is a monetary obligation") and a "promissory note" (also defined in Section 9–102). To a considerable extent, this Article affords these transactions treatment identical to that given sales of accounts and chattel paper. In some respects, however, sales of payment intangibles and promissory notes are treated differently from sales of other receivables. See, e.g., Sections 9–309 (automatic perfection upon attachment), 9–408 (effect of restrictions on assignment). By virtue of the 1998 expanded definition of "account" (defined in Section 9–102), this Article ~~now~~ covers sales of (and other security interests in) "health-care-insurance receivables" (also defined in Section 9–102). Although this Article occasionally distinguishes between outright sales of receivables and sales that secure an obligation, neither this Article nor the definition of "security interest" (Section ~~1–201(37)~~ 1–201(b)(35)) delineates how a particular transaction is to be classified. That issue is left to the courts.

* * *

6. **Consignments.** Subsection (a)(4) ~~is new~~ was added by the 1998 Revisions. * * *

* * *

Sometimes parties characterize transactions that secure an obligation (other than the bailee's obligation to return bailed goods) as "consignments." These transactions are not "consignments" as contemplated by Section 9–109(a)(4). See Section 9–102. This Article applies also to these transactions, by virtue of Section 9–109(a)(1). They create a security interest within the meaning of the first sentence of Section ~~1–201(37)~~ 1–201(b)(35).

* * *

16. **Deposit Accounts.** * * *

* * * To perfect a security interest in a deposit account as original collateral, a secured party (other than the bank with which the deposit account is maintained) must obtain "control" of the account either by obtaining the bank's ~~authenticated~~ signed agreement or by becoming the bank's customer with respect to the deposit account. See Sections 9–312(b)(1), 9–104. Either of these steps requires the debtor's consent.

* * *

§ 9–203. Attachment and Enforceability of Security Interest; Proceeds; Supporting Obligations; Formal Requisites.

* * *

(b) **[Enforceability.]** Except as otherwise provided in subsections (c) through (i), a security interest is enforceable against the debtor and third parties with respect to the collateral only if:

* * * *security agreement PLUS*

(3) one of the following conditions is met:

9-102a1 *9-102a(74)* *9-108*

authentication w/ description

(A) the debtor has ~~authenticated~~ signed a security agreement that provides a description of the collateral and, if the security interest covers timber to be cut, a description of the land concerned;

possession * * *B. *collateral is not certificated security and is in the possession of the secured party under 9-313 pursuant to the debtor's security agreement.*

delivery
– OR –

(C) the collateral is a certificated security in registered form and the security certificate has been delivered to the secured party under Section 8–301 pursuant to the debtor's security agreement; ~~or~~

control

(D) the collateral is controllable accounts, controllable electronic records, controllable payment intangibles, deposit accounts, ~~electronic chattel paper,~~ electronic documents, electronic money, investment property, or letter-of-credit rights, ~~or electronic documents,~~ and the secured party has control under Section 7–106, 9–104, ~~9–105,~~ 9–105A, 9–106, ~~or~~ 9–107, or 9–107A pursuant to the debtor's security agreement; or

(E) the collateral is chattel paper and the secured party has possession and control under Section 9–314A pursuant to the debtor's security agreement.

* * *

Official Comment

* * *

3. **Security Agreement; Signed.** Under subsection (b)(3), enforceability requires the debtor's security agreement and compliance with an evidentiary requirement in the nature of a Statute of Frauds. Paragraph (3)(A) represents the most basic of the evidentiary alternatives, under which the debtor must ~~authenticate~~ sign a security agreement that provides a description of the collateral. Under Section 9–102, a "security agreement" is "an agreement that creates or provides for a security interest." Neither that definition nor the requirement of paragraph (3)(A) rejects the deeply rooted doctrine that a bill of sale, although absolute in form, may be shown in fact to have been given as security. Under this Article, as under prior law, a debtor may show by parol evidence that a transfer purporting to be absolute was in fact for security. Similarly, a self-styled "lease" may serve as a security agreement if the agreement creates a security interest. See Section 1–203 (distinguishing security interest from lease). Consistent with the revised definition of "sign" in Section 1–201, the cognate terms "signed" and "signing" replace the references to "authenticated" and "authentication" in the pre-2022 text of this Section.

4. **Possession, Delivery, or Control Pursuant to Security Agreement.** The other alternatives in subsection (b)(3) dispense with the requirement of ~~an authenticated~~ a signed security agreement and provide alternative evidentiary tests. Under paragraph (3)(B), the secured party's possession substitutes for the debtor's ~~authentication~~ signed security agreement under paragraph (3)(A) if the secured party's possession is "pursuant to the debtor's security agreement." That phrase refers to the debtor's agreement to the secured party's possession ~~for the purpose of creating~~ in connection with the creation of a security interest. The phrase should not be confused with the phrase "debtor has ~~authenticated~~ signed a security agreement," used in paragraph (3)(A), which contemplates the debtor's ~~authentication~~ signing of a record. In the unlikely event that possession is obtained without the debtor's agreement, possession would not suffice as a substitute for ~~an authenticated~~ a signed security agreement. However, once the security interest has become enforceable and has attached, it is not impaired by the fact that the secured party's possession is maintained without the agreement of a subsequent debtor (e.g., a transferee). Possession as contemplated by Section 9–313 is possession for purposes of subsection (b)(3)(B), even though it may not constitute possession "pursuant to the debtor's agreement" and consequently might not serve as a substitute for ~~an authenticated~~ a signed security agreement under subsection (b)(3)(A). Subsection (b)(3)(C) provides that delivery of a certificated security to the secured party under Section 8–301 pursuant to the debtor's security agreement is sufficient as a substitute for ~~an authenticated~~ a signed security agreement. Similarly, under subsection (b)(3)(D), control of controllable accounts, controllable electronic records, controllable payment intangibles, deposit accounts, electronic documents, electronic money, investment property, ~~a deposit account, electronic chattel paper,~~ or a letter-of-credit ~~right, or electronic documents~~ rights satisfies the evidentiary test if control is pursuant to the debtor's security agreement, and under subsection (b)(3)(E), possession and control of chattel paper under Section 9–314A satisfies the evidentiary test if pursuant to the debtor's security agreement.

* * *

8. **Proceeds and Supporting Obligations.** Under subsection (f), attachment of a security interest in original collateral also is attachment of a security interest in identifiable proceeds as provided in Section 9–315(a)(2). It is not necessary for a security agreement to mention "proceeds" or otherwise to describe collateral consisting of proceeds. See also Section 9–108, Comment 5. Also under subsection (f), a security interest in a "supporting obligation" (defined in Section 9–102) automatically follows from a security interest in the underlying, supported collateral. This result was implicit under ~~former~~ pre-1998 Article 9. Implicit in subsection (f) is the principle that the secured party's interest in a supporting obligation extends to the supporting obligation only to the extent that it supports the collateral in which the secured party has a security interest. Complex issues may

arise, however, if a supporting obligation supports many separate obligations of a particular account debtor and if the supported obligations are separately assigned as security to several secured parties. The problems may be exacerbated if a supporting obligation is limited to an aggregate amount that is less than the aggregate amount of the obligations it supports. This Article does not contain provisions dealing with competing claims to a limited supporting obligation. As under ~~former~~ pre-1998 Article 9, other law, including the law of suretyship, and the agreements of the parties will control.

* * *

§ 9–204.   After-Acquired Property; Future Advances.

* * *

(b)   **[When after-acquired property clause not effective.]** ~~A~~ Subject to subsection (b.1), a security interest does not attach under a term constituting an after-acquired property clause to:

* * *

(b.1) **[Limitation on subsection (b).]** Subsection (b) does not prevent a security interest from attaching:

(1)   to consumer goods as proceeds under Section 9–315(a) or commingled goods under Section 9–336(c);

(2)   to a commercial tort claim as proceeds under Section 9–315(a); or

(3)   under an after-acquired property clause to property that is proceeds of consumer goods or a commercial tort claim.

* * *

Official Comment

* * *

3.   **After-Acquired Consumer Goods.** Subsection (b)(1) makes ineffective an after-acquired property clause covering consumer goods (defined in Section ~~9–109~~ 9–102(a)(23)), except as accessions (see Section 9–335), acquired more than 10 days after the secured party gives value. Subsection (b)(1) is unchanged in substance from the corresponding provision in ~~former~~ pre-1998 Section 9–204(2). However, a term granting a security interest in consumer goods that will be purchase-money collateral in the transaction is not "a term constituting an after-acquired property clause." Consequently, subsection (b)(1) does not prevent the security interest from attaching to the purchase-money collateral even if the collateral is not an accession and the debtor acquires rights in the collateral more than 10 days after the secured party gives value.

4.   **Commercial Tort Claims.** Subsection (b)(2) provides that an after-acquired property clause in a security agreement does not reach future commercial tort claims. In order for a security interest in a tort claim as original collateral to attach, the claim must be in existence when the security agreement is ~~authenticated~~ signed. In addition, the security agreement must describe the tort claim with greater specificity than simply "all tort claims." See Section 9–108(e).

4A.   **Proceeds and Commingled Goods.** Subsection (b.1) clarifies and makes explicit what is implicit in the pre-2022 text of subsection (b). Subsection (b) does not prevent a security interest from attaching to consumer goods as proceeds or as commingled goods, to commercial tort claims as proceeds, or under an after-acquired property clause to proceeds of consumer goods or commercial tort claims. This clarification corrects and rejects the erroneous holdings of several cases addressing commercial tort claims that are proceeds. As to proceeds, this result also follows from Section 9–203(f).

* * *

§ 9–207.   Rights and Duties of Secured Party Having Possession or Control of Collateral.

* * *

(c) **[Duties and rights when secured party in possession or control.]** Except as otherwise provided in subsection (d), a secured party having possession of collateral or control of collateral under Section 7–106, 9–104, 9–105, 9–105A, 9–106, ~~or~~ 9–107, or 9–107A:

* * *

§ 9–208. Additional Duties of Secured Party Having Control of Collateral.

* * *

(b) **[Duties of secured party after receiving demand from debtor.]** Within 10 days after receiving ~~an authenticated~~ a signed demand by the debtor:

(1) a secured party having control of a deposit account under Section 9–104(a)(2) shall send to the bank with which the deposit account is maintained ~~an authenticated statement~~ a signed record that releases the bank from any further obligation to comply with instructions originated by the secured party;

* * *

(3) ~~a secured party, other than a buyer, having control of electronic chattel paper under Section 9–105 shall:~~

    (A) ~~communicate the authoritative copy of the electronic chattel paper to the debtor or its designated custodian;~~

    (B) ~~if the debtor designates a custodian that is the designated custodian with which the authoritative copy of the electronic chattel paper is maintained for the secured party, communicate to the custodian an authenticated record releasing the designated custodian from any further obligation to comply with instructions originated by the secured party and instructing the custodian to comply with instructions originated by the debtor; and~~

    (C) ~~take appropriate action to enable the debtor or its designated custodian to make copies of or revisions to the authoritative copy which add or change an identified assignee of the authoritative copy without the consent of the secured party; and~~

(3) a secured party, other than a buyer, having control under Section 9–105 of an authoritative electronic copy of a record evidencing chattel paper shall transfer control of the electronic copy to the debtor or a person designated by the debtor;

(4) a secured party having control of investment property under Section 8–106(d)(2) or 9–106(b) shall send to the securities intermediary or commodity intermediary with which the security entitlement or commodity contract is maintained ~~an authenticated~~ a signed record that releases the securities intermediary or commodity intermediary from any further obligation to comply with entitlement orders or directions originated by the secured party;

(5) a secured party having control of a letter-of-credit right under Section 9–107 shall send to each person having an unfulfilled obligation to pay or deliver proceeds of the letter of credit to the secured party ~~an authenticated~~ a signed release from any further obligation to pay or deliver proceeds of the letter of credit to the secured party; ~~and~~

(6) ~~a secured party having control of an electronic document shall:~~

    (A) ~~give control of the electronic document to the debtor or its designated custodian;~~

    (B) ~~if the debtor designates a custodian that is the designated custodian with which the authoritative copy of the electronic document is maintained for the secured party, communicate to the custodian an authenticated record releasing the designated custodian from any further obligation to comply with instructions originated by the secured party and instructing the custodian to comply with instructions originated by the debtor; and~~

    (C) ~~take appropriate action to enable the debtor or its designated custodian to make copies of or revisions to the authoritative copy which add or change an identified assignee of the authoritative copy without the consent of the secured party.~~

(6) a secured party having control under Section 7–106 of an authoritative electronic copy of an electronic document shall transfer control of the electronic copy to the debtor or a person designated by the debtor;

(7) a secured party having control under Section 9–105A of electronic money shall transfer control of the electronic money to the debtor or a person designated by the debtor; and

(8) a secured party having control under Section 12–105 of a controllable electronic record, other than a buyer of a controllable account or controllable payment intangible evidenced by the controllable electronic record, shall transfer control of the controllable electronic record to the debtor or a person designated by the debtor.

Official Comment

* * *

2. **Scope and Purpose.** This section imposes duties on a secured party who has control of a deposit account, an electronic copy of a record evidencing chattel paper, investment property, a letter-of-credit right, or an electronic documents document of title, electronic money, or a controllable electronic record. The duty to terminate the secured party's control is analogous to the duty to file a termination statement, imposed by Section 9–513. Under subsection (a), it applies only when there is no outstanding secured obligation and the secured party is not committed to give value. The requirements of this section can be varied by agreement under Section 1–102(3). For example, a debtor could by contract agree that the secured party may comply with subsection (b) by releasing control more than 10 days after demand. Also, duties under this section should not be read to conflict with the terms of the collateral itself. For example, if the collateral is a time deposit account, subsection (b)(2) should not require a secured party with control to make an early withdrawal of the funds (assuming that were possible) in order to pay them over to the debtor or put them in an account in the debtor's name.

Note that subsection (b)(8) addresses secured parties that have control of a controllable electronic record. That control may have been obtained for the purpose of perfecting a security interest in a controllable account or controllable payment intangible evidenced by the controllable electronic record, even if the secured party did not have a security interest in the controllable electronic record itself.

This section does not explicitly impose duties on a secured party whose control is based on the acknowledgment under Section 7–106(g), 9–104(a)(4), or 9–105A(e) or under 9–107A and 12–105(e) by another person having control. Such a secured party would have control only while the other, acknowledging person retains control. This result necessarily follows because such a secured party's control derives solely from the other person's continued control. See, e.g., Section 9–314, Comment 2. Upon compliance with this section by an acknowledging person having control, the control of a person having control through such person's acknowledgment would cease.

* * *

5. **"Signed" Replaces "Authenticated."** Consistent with the revised definition of "sign" in Section 1–201, the cognate term "signed" replaces references to "authenticated" in the pre-2022 text of this section.

§ 9–209. Duties of Secured Party if Account Debtor Has Been Notified of Assignment.

* * *

(b) **[Duties of secured party after receiving demand from debtor.]** Within 10 days after receiving an authenticated a signed demand by the debtor, a secured party shall send to an account debtor that has received notification under Section 9–406(a) or 12–106(b) of an assignment to the secured party as assignee under Section 9–406(a) an authenticated a signed record that releases the account debtor from any further obligation to the secured party.

* * *

Official Comment

* * *

3. **"Signed" Replaces "Authenticated."** Consistent with the revised definition of "sign" in Section 1–201, the cognate term "signed" replaces references to "authenticated" in the pre-2022 text of this section.

§9–210. Request for Accounting; Request Regarding List of Collateral or Statement of Account.

(a) **[Definitions.]** In this section:

* * *

(2) "Request for an accounting" means a record ~~authenticated~~ <u>signed</u> by a debtor requesting that the recipient provide an accounting of the unpaid obligations secured by collateral and reasonably identifying the transaction or relationship that is the subject of the request.

(3) "Request regarding a list of collateral" means a record ~~authenticated~~ <u>signed</u> by a debtor requesting that the recipient approve or correct a list of what the debtor believes to be the collateral securing an obligation and reasonably identifying the transaction or relationship that is the subject of the request.

(4) "Request regarding a statement of account" means a record ~~authenticated~~ <u>signed</u> by a debtor requesting that the recipient approve or correct a statement indicating what the debtor believes to be the aggregate amount of unpaid obligations secured by collateral as of a specified date and reasonably identifying the transaction or relationship that is the subject of the request.

(b) **[Duty to respond to requests.]** Subject to subsections (c), (d), (e), and (f), a secured party, other than a buyer of accounts, chattel paper, payment intangibles, or promissory notes or a consignor, shall comply with a request within 14 days after receipt:

(1) in the case of a request for an accounting, by ~~authenticating~~ <u>signing</u> and sending to the debtor an accounting; and

(2) in the case of a request regarding a list of collateral or a request regarding a statement of account, by ~~authenticating~~ <u>signing</u> and sending to the debtor an approval or correction.

(c) **[Request regarding list of collateral; statement concerning type of collateral.]** A secured party that claims a security interest in all of a particular type of collateral owned by the debtor may comply with a request regarding a list of collateral by sending to the debtor ~~an authenticated~~ <u>a signed</u> record including a statement to that effect within 14 days after receipt.

(d) **[Request regarding list of collateral; no interest claimed.]** A person that receives a request regarding a list of collateral, claims no interest in the collateral when it receives the request, and claimed an interest in the collateral at an earlier time shall comply with the request within 14 days after receipt by sending to the debtor ~~an authenticated~~ <u>a signed</u> record:

* * *

(e) **[Request for accounting or regarding statement of account; no interest in obligation claimed.]** A person that receives a request for an accounting or a request regarding a statement of account, claims no interest in the obligations when it receives the request, and claimed an interest in the obligations at an earlier time shall comply with the request within 14 days after receipt by sending to the debtor ~~an authenticated~~ <u>a signed</u> record:

* * *

Official Comment

* * *

8. **"Signed" and "Signing" Replaces "Authenticated" and "Authenticating."** Consistent with the revised definition of "sign" in Section 1–201, the cognate terms "signed" and "signing" replace references to "authenticated" and "authenticating" in the pre-2022 text of this section.

§9–301. Law Governing Perfection and Priority of Security Interests.

Except as otherwise provided in Sections 9–303 through ~~9–306~~ <u>9–306B</u>, the following rules determine the law governing perfection, the effect of perfection or nonperfection, and the priority of a security interest in collateral:

* * *

(3)   Except as otherwise provided in paragraph (4), while negotiable <u>tangible</u> documents, goods, instruments, <u>or tangible</u> money, ~~or tangible chattel paper~~ is located in a jurisdiction, the local law of that jurisdiction governs:

    (A)   perfection of a security interest in the goods by filing a fixture filing;

    (B)   perfection of a security interest in timber to be cut; and

    (C)   the effect of perfection or nonperfection and the priority of a nonpossessory security interest in the collateral.

* * *

Official Comment

* * *

2.   Scope of This Subpart. * * * In transactions to which the Hague Securities Convention applies, the requirements for foreclosure and the like, the characterization of a transfer as being outright or by way of security, and certain other issues will generally be governed by the law specified in the account agreement. See PEB Commentary No. 19~~, dated April 11, 2017~~. And, another jurisdiction's law may govern other third-party matters addressed in this Article. See Section 9–401, Comment 3.

* * *

5.   Law Governing Perfection: Exceptions. The general rule is subject to several exceptions. It does not apply to goods covered by a certificate of title (see Section 9–303), deposit accounts (see Section 9–304), investment property (see Section 9–305), ~~or~~ letter-of-credit rights (see Section 9–306)<u>, chattel paper (see Section 9–306A), or controllable accounts, controllable electronic records, or controllable payment intangibles (see Section 9–306B)</u>. Nor does it apply to possessory security interests, i.e., security interests that the secured party has perfected by taking possession of the collateral (see paragraph (2)), security interests perfected by filing a fixture filing (see subparagraph (3)(A)), security interests in timber to be cut (subparagraph (3)(B)), or security interests in as-extracted collateral (see paragraph (4)). <u>No exception is made for electronic money and the general rule applies (unless preempted by federal law).</u>

    a.   Possessory Security Interests. Paragraph (2) applies to possessory security interests and provides that perfection <u>and priority</u> is governed by the local law of the jurisdiction in which the collateral is located. This is the rule of ~~former~~ <u>pre-1998</u> Section 9–103(1)(b), except paragraph (2) eliminates the troublesome "last event" test of former law.

* * *

§ 9–304.   Law Governing Perfection and Priority of Security Interests in Deposit Accounts.

    (a)   **[Law of bank's jurisdiction governs.]** The local law of a bank's jurisdiction governs perfection, the effect of perfection or nonperfection, and the priority of a security interest in a deposit account maintained with that bank <u>even if the transaction does not bear any relation to the bank's jurisdiction</u>.

* * *

Official Comment

* * *

4.   **No Relation to Bank's Jurisdiction Required.** <u>As to the final clause of subsection (a), see Section 8–110, Comment 5A.</u>

§ 9–305.   Law Governing Perfection and Priority of Security Interests in Investment Property.

    (a)   **[Governing law: general rules.]** Except as otherwise provided in subsection (c), the following rules apply:

* * *

(5)   Paragraphs (2), (3), and (4) apply even if the transaction does not bear any relation to the jurisdiction.

* * *

Official Comment

* * *

3.   Investment Property: Exceptions. * * *

The Hague Securities Convention generally preserves these rules for perfection by filing. However, if the debtor is located in a non-U.S. jurisdiction, or if the account agreement designates the law of a non-U.S. jurisdiction, then filing may be appropriate only in a different jurisdiction or altogether unavailable. See Convention articles 12(2)(b) and 4(1), respectively, and PEB Commentary No. 19, dated April 11, 2017, particularly footnote 25.

* * *

6.   No Relation of Transaction to Issuer's, Securities Intermediary's, or Commodity Intermediary's Jurisdiction Required. As to subsection (a)(5), see Section 8–110, Comment 5A.

§ 9–306A.   Law Governing Perfection and Priority of Security Interests in Chattel Paper.

(a)   **[Chattel paper evidenced by authoritative electronic copy.]** Except as provided in subsection (d), if chattel paper is evidenced only by an authoritative electronic copy of the chattel paper or is evidenced by an authoritative electronic copy and an authoritative tangible copy, the local law of the chattel paper's jurisdiction governs perfection, the effect of perfection or nonperfection, and the priority of a security interest in the chattel paper, even if the transaction does not bear any relation to the chattel paper's jurisdiction.

(b)   **[Chattel paper's jurisdiction.]** The following rules determine the chattel paper's jurisdiction under this section:

(1)   If the authoritative electronic copy of the record evidencing chattel paper, or a record attached to or logically associated with the electronic copy and readily available for review, expressly provides that a particular jurisdiction is the chattel paper's jurisdiction for purposes of this part, this article, or [the Uniform Commercial Code], that jurisdiction is the chattel paper's jurisdiction.

(2)   If paragraph (1) does not apply and the rules of the system in which the authoritative electronic copy is recorded are readily available for review and expressly provide that a particular jurisdiction is the chattel paper's jurisdiction for purposes of this part, this article, or [the Uniform Commercial Code], that jurisdiction is the chattel paper's jurisdiction.

(3)   If paragraphs (1) and (2) do not apply and the authoritative electronic copy, or a record attached to or logically associated with the electronic copy and readily available for review, expressly provides that the chattel paper is governed by the law of a particular jurisdiction, that jurisdiction is the chattel paper's jurisdiction.

(4)   If paragraphs (1), (2), and (3) do not apply and the rules of the system in which the authoritative electronic copy is recorded are readily available for review and expressly provide that the chattel paper or the system is governed by the law of a particular jurisdiction, that jurisdiction is the chattel paper's jurisdiction.

(5)   If paragraphs (1) through (4) do not apply, the chattel paper's jurisdiction is the jurisdiction in which the debtor is located.

(c)   **[Chattel paper evidenced by authoritative tangible copy.]** If an authoritative tangible copy of a record evidences chattel paper and the chattel paper is not evidenced by an authoritative electronic copy, while the authoritative tangible copy of the record evidencing chattel paper is located in a jurisdiction, the local law of that jurisdiction governs:

(1)   perfection of a security interest in the chattel paper by possession under Section 9–314A; and

(2)   the effect of perfection or nonperfection and the priority of a security interest in the chattel paper.

(d)   **[When perfection governed by law of jurisdiction where debtor located.]** The local law of the jurisdiction in which the debtor is located governs perfection of a security interest in chattel paper by filing.

Official Comment

1.   **Source.** Section 9–306A(a) and (b) derive from Sections 8–110(e) and 9–305 on law governing perfection and priority of security interests in investment property (as do Sections 9–306B and 12–107).

2.   **Applicability of this Section.** This section determines the law governing perfection and priority of security interests in chattel paper. Subsections (a) and (b) apply to chattel paper that is evidenced only by an authoritative electronic copy of the chattel paper or by an authoritative electronic copy and an authoritative tangible copy. Subsection (c) applies to chattel paper that is evidenced by an authoritative tangible copy but not evidenced by an authoritative electronic copy. Subsection (d) applies to perfection by filing for all chattel paper.

3.   **Authoritative Electronic Copy: Chattel Paper's Jurisdiction.** Subsection (a) specifies the law governing perfection and priority of security interests in chattel paper evidenced by an authoritative electronic copy of the chattel paper, even if it is also evidenced by an authoritative tangible copy. Subject to subsection (d) on perfection by filing, the law governing perfection and priority is the local law of the chattel paper's jurisdiction. Drawing on Sections 8–110 and 9–305, it is the authoritative electronic copy itself, records attached thereto or associated therewith, or the system in which the authoritative electronic copy is recorded that determines the chattel paper's jurisdiction and, therefore, the governing law. Subsection (b) provides a "waterfall" of rules based on provisions that identify a particular jurisdiction as the chattel paper's jurisdiction or alternatively that provide the governing law of the chattel paper or of the system in which the electronic copy is recorded. When no such identification or provision is made, it is the debtor's location, determined under Section 9–307, that is the chattel paper's jurisdiction. As to the final clause of subsection (a), see Section 8–110, Comment 5A.

4.   **Rationale for Subsection (a).** A buyer of, or secured lender against, chattel paper may arrange for authoritative electronic copies of chattel paper that it wishes to have assigned to it to be originated in or submitted into a system for the control and assignment of the chattel paper. The secured parties and lessors that will be assigning the chattel paper may be located in many different jurisdictions. As to assignments of the chattel paper by these secured parties and lessors (assignor-debtors), but for this section perfection and priority would be governed by the law of each assignor-debtor's location under Section 9–301(1). Under this section, however, the law of a single jurisdiction—the chattel paper's jurisdiction—could govern perfection and priority with respect to all of the assignments. By avoiding the application of the laws of multiple jurisdictions to perfection and priority, this rule could substantially reduce transaction costs.

5.   **Authoritative tangible copy.** Subsection (c) ties the choice-of-law rules to the location of the authoritative tangible copy when no authoritative electronic copy exists. In that circumstance, the local law of the jurisdiction where the authoritative tangible copy is physically located governs perfection of a security interest in the chattel paper by possession, under Section 9–314A, and priority. Like its predecessor, subsection (c) assumes that all the authoritative tangible copies are located in the same jurisdiction. However, assuming the secured party is in possession of all the tangible copies, even if the copies are located in more than one jurisdiction the situation is unlikely to be problematic.

6.   **Perfection by filing.** Subsection (d) provides that the local law of the jurisdiction where the debtor is located governs perfection by filing for all chattel paper.

§ 9–306B. Law Governing Perfection and Priority of Security Interests in Controllable Accounts, Controllable Electronic Records, and Controllable Payment Intangibles.

(a)   **[Governing law: general rules.]** Except as provided in subsection (b), the local law of the controllable electronic record's jurisdiction specified in Section 12–107(c) and (d) governs perfection, the effect of perfection or nonperfection, and the priority of a security interest in a controllable electronic record and a security interest in a controllable account or controllable payment intangible evidenced by the controllable electronic record.

(b)   **[When perfection governed by law of jurisdiction where debtor located.]** The local law of the jurisdiction in which the debtor is located governs:

    (1)   perfection of a security interest in a controllable account, controllable electronic record, or controllable payment intangible by filing; and

(2)   automatic perfection of a security interest in a controllable payment intangible created by a sale of the controllable payment intangible.

Official Comment

1.   **Perfection by control and priority.** Subsection (a) deals with perfection of a security interest in a controllable account, controllable electronic record, or controllable payment intangible other than by filing—i.e., perfection by control under Section 12–105—and priority. For these purposes the governing law is that of the controllable electronic record's jurisdiction under Section 12–107(c) and (d).

2.   **Perfection by filing.** Under subsection (b) the local law of the jurisdiction of the debtor's location governs perfection of a security interest in a controllable account, controllable electronic record, or controllable payment intangible by filing (but not priority, as to which subsection (a) would apply). Because controllable electronic records are general intangibles and controllable accounts and controllable payment intangibles are subsets of accounts and payment intangibles, this provision does not change prior law.

§ 9–310.   When Filing Required to Perfect Security Interest or Agricultural Lien; Security Interests and Agricultural Liens to Which Filing Provisions Do Not Apply.

* * *

(b)   **[Exceptions: filing not necessary.]** The filing of a financing statement is not necessary to perfect a security interest:

* * *

(8)   in <u>controllable accounts, controllable electronic records, controllable payment intangibles,</u> deposit accounts, ~~electronic chattel paper,~~ electronic documents, investment property, or letter-of-credit rights which is perfected by control under Section 9–314;

<u>(8.1) in chattel paper which is perfected by possession and control under Section 9–314A;</u>

* * *

Official Comment

* * *

3.   **Exemptions from Filing.** Subsection (b) lists the security interests for which filing is not required as a condition of perfection, because they are perfected automatically upon attachment (subsections (b)(2) and (b)(9)) or upon the occurrence of another event (subsections (b)(1), (b)(5), and (b)(9)), because they are perfected under the law of another jurisdiction (subsection (b)(10)), or because they are perfected by another method, such as by the secured party's taking possession or control (subsections (b)(3), (b)(4), (b)(5), (b)(6), (b)(7), ~~and~~ (b)(8)<u>, and (b)(8.1)</u>)).

* * *

§ 9–312.   Perfection of Security Interests in Chattel Paper, <u>Controllable Accounts, Controllable Electronic Records, Controllable Payment Intangibles,</u> Deposit Accounts, Negotiable Documents, Goods Covered by Documents, Instruments, Investment Property, Letter-of-Credit Rights, and Money; Perfection by Permissive Filing; Temporary Perfection Without Filing or Transfer of Possession.

(a)   **[Perfection by filing permitted.]** A security interest in chattel paper, ~~negotiable documents,~~ <u>controllable accounts, controllable electronic records, controllable payment intangibles,</u> instruments, ~~or~~ investment property<u>, or negotiable documents</u> may be perfected by filing.

(b)   **[Control or possession of certain collateral.]** Except as otherwise provided in Section 9–315(c) and (d) for proceeds:

* * *

(2)   except as otherwise provided in Section 9–308(d), a security interest in a letter-of-credit right may be perfected only by control under Section 9–314; ~~and~~

(3) a security interest in <u>tangible</u> money may be perfected only by the secured party's taking possession under Section 9–313<u>; and</u>

<u>(4)   a security interest in electronic money may be perfected only by control under Section 9–314.</u>

* * *

(e) **[Temporary perfection: new value.]** A security interest in certificated securities, negotiable documents, or instruments is perfected without filing or the taking of possession or control for a period of 20 days from the time it attaches to the extent that it arises for new value given under ~~an authenticated~~ <u>a</u> <u>signed</u> security agreement.

* * *

Official Comment

* * *

<u>4A</u>. **Controllable Accounts, Controllable Electronic Records, and Controllable Payment Intangibles.** <u>Consistent with the treatment of chattel paper, instruments, investment property, and negotiable documents, under subsection (a) a security interest in controllable accounts, controllable electronic records, and controllable payment intangibles may be perfected by filing. A security interest in that collateral also may be perfected by control. Section 9–314.</u>

* * *

<u>6A</u>. **Money.** <u>Under subsection (b)(3), a security interest in tangible money may be perfected only by possession under Section 9–313. Similarly, under subsection (b)(4), a security interest in electronic money may be perfected only by control under Section 9–314.</u>

7.   **Goods Covered by Document of Title.** * * *.

* * *

Subsection (d) takes a different approach to the problem of goods covered by a nonnegotiable document. Here, title to the goods is not looked on as being locked up in the document~~,~~<u>. For example, a transferee that takes delivery of a nonnegotiable document receives, under Section 7–504(a), "the title and rights" of the transferor, but the transferee would not thereby become a "person entitled under the document" with a right to receive delivery of the goods from the bailee.</u> ~~and the~~ <u>The</u> secured party may perfect its security interest directly in the goods by filing as to them. The subsection provides two other methods of perfection: issuance of the document in the secured party's name (as consignee of a straight bill of lading or the person to whom delivery would be made under a non-negotiable warehouse receipt) and receipt of notification of the secured party's interest by the bailee. <u>Issuance (or reissuance) of the nonnegotiable document in the secured party's name would allow the secured party to become a "person entitled under the document." However, the bailee's receipt of notification would not confer on the secured party the status of a person entitled unless the notification resulted from an instruction under the document. See Section 7–102(a)(9) (defining "person entitled under the document") and Comment 6.</u> Perfection under subsection (d) occurs when the bailee receives notification of the secured party's interest in the goods, regardless of who sends the notification. Receipt of notification is effective to perfect, regardless of whether the bailee responds. Unlike ~~former~~ <u>pre-1998</u> Section 9–304(3), from which it derives, subsection (d) does not apply to goods in the possession of a bailee who has not issued a document of title. Section 9–313(c) covers that case and provides that perfection by possession as to goods not covered by a document requires the bailee's acknowledgment.

<u>Subsection (a) makes clear that a security interest in negotiable documents (and other collateral mentioned there) may be perfected by filing, but it makes no mention of nonnegotiable documents. However, under the general rule of Section 9–310, a security interest in a nonnegotiable document can be perfected by filing. A security interest in an electronic document, negotiable or nonnegotiable, can be perfected by control under Section 7–106. Section 9–314(a). But a security interest in a nonnegotiable tangible document cannot be perfected by possession. Section 9–313(a). Although a perfected security interest in a nonnegotiable document might provide useful benefits for the secured party, it would not perfect a security interest in the goods. And by perfecting a security interest in the nonnegotiable document the secured party would not thereby become a "person entitled under the document." Indeed, unless the secured party also took delivery of the document (i.e., possession or control under Section 1–201(b)(15)), it would not obtain the rights of a transferee under Section 7–504(a).</u>

8.   **Temporary Perfection Without Having First Otherwise Perfected.** Subsection (e) follows ~~former~~ <u>pre-1998</u> Section 9–304(4) in giving perfected status to security interests in certificated securities, instruments,

and negotiable documents for a short period (reduced from 21 to 20 days, which is the time period generally applicable in this Article), although there has been no filing and the collateral is in the debtor's possession or control. The 20-day temporary perfection runs from the date of attachment. There is no limitation on the purpose for which the debtor is in possession, but the secured party must have given "new value" (defined in Section 9–102) under ~~an authenticated~~ a signed security agreement.

* * *

10. **"Signed" Replaces "Authenticated."** Consistent with the revised definition of "sign" in Section 1–201, the cognate term "signed" replaces the reference to "authenticated" in the pre-2022 text of this section.

§ 9–313. When Possession by or Delivery to Secured Party Perfects Security Interest Without Filing.

(a) **[Perfection by possession or delivery.]** Except as otherwise provided in subsection (b), a secured party may perfect a security interest in ~~tangible negotiable documents,~~ goods, instruments, negotiable tangible documents, or tangible money, ~~or tangible chattel paper~~ by taking possession of the collateral. A secured party may perfect a security interest in certificated securities by taking delivery of the certificated securities under Section 8–301.

* * *

(c) **[Collateral in possession of person other than debtor.]** With respect to collateral other than certificated securities and goods covered by a document, a secured party takes possession of collateral in the possession of a person other than the debtor, the secured party, or a lessee of the collateral from the debtor in the ordinary course of the debtor's business, when:

(1) the person in possession ~~authenticates~~ signs a record acknowledging that it holds possession of the collateral for the secured party's benefit; or

(2) the person takes possession of the collateral after having ~~authenticated~~ signed a record acknowledging that it will hold possession of the collateral for the secured party's benefit.

(d) **[Time of perfection by possession; continuation of perfection.]** If perfection of a security interest depends upon possession of the collateral by a secured party, perfection occurs ~~no~~ not earlier than the time the secured party takes possession and continues only while the secured party retains possession.

* * *

Official Comment

* * *

2. **Perfection by Possession.** * * *

This section permits a security interest to be perfected by the taking of possession only when the collateral is goods, instruments, ~~tangible~~ negotiable tangible documents, or tangible money, ~~or tangible chattel paper~~. Accounts, commercial tort claims, deposit accounts, investment property, letter-of-credit rights, letters of credit, and oil, gas, or other minerals before extraction are excluded. (But see Comment 6, below, regarding certificated securities.) A security interest in accounts and payment intangibles—property not ordinarily represented by any writing whose delivery operates to transfer the right to payment—may under this Article be perfected only by filing. This rule would not be affected by the fact that a security agreement or other record described the assignment of such collateral as a "pledge." Section 9–309(2) exempts from filing certain assignments of accounts or payment intangibles which are out of the ordinary course of financing. These exempted assignments are perfected when they attach. Similarly, under Section 9–309(3), sales of payment intangibles are automatically perfected.

Perfection by possession of chattel paper evidenced by an authoritative tangible record (formerly defined as "tangible chattel paper") has been removed from this section. Instead, perfection by possession and control of chattel paper is governed by Section 9–314A.

* * *

4. **Goods in Possession of Third Party: Perfection.** * * *

Notification of a third person does not suffice to perfect under Section 9–313(c). Rather, perfection does not occur unless the third person ~~authenticates~~ signs an acknowledgment that it holds possession of the collateral for the secured party's benefit. Compare Section 9–312(d), under which receipt of notification of the security party's interest by a bailee holding goods covered by a nonnegotiable document is sufficient to perfect, even if the bailee does not acknowledge receipt of the notification. A third person may acknowledge that it will hold for the secured party's benefit goods to be received in the future. Under these circumstances, perfection by possession occurs when the third person obtains possession of the goods.

* * *

5. **No Relation Back; time of perfection and continuation of perfection.** Former Section 9–305 provided that a security interest is perfected by possession from the time possession is taken "without a relation back." As the Comment to ~~former~~ pre-1998 Section 9–305 observed, the relation-back theory, under which the taking of possession was deemed to relate back to the date of the original security agreement, has had little vitality since the 1938 revision of the Federal Bankruptcy Act. The theory is inconsistent with ~~former~~ pre-1998 Article 9 and with this Article. See Section 9–313(d). Accordingly, this Article deletes the quoted phrase as unnecessary. ~~Where~~ Under subsection (d), where a pledge (perfection by possession) transaction is contemplated, perfection dates only from the time possession is taken~~, although a security interest may attach, unperfected~~. The only exceptions to this rule are the short, 20-day periods of perfection provided in Section 9–312(e), (f), and (g), during which a debtor may have possession of specified collateral in which there is a perfected security interest. Also under subsection (d), perfection continues only while the secured party retains possession. However, if a secured party's possession is based on an acknowledgment under Section 9–313(c) by another person in possession, the secured party remains perfected by possession only while the other person retains possession. This result necessarily follows because such a secured party's possession derives solely from the other person's continued possession.

* * *

9. **Delivery to Third Party by Secured Party.** ~~New subsections~~ Subsections (h) and (i) address the practice of mortgage warehouse lenders. These lenders typically send mortgage notes to prospective purchasers under cover of letters advising the prospective purchasers that the lenders hold security interests in the notes. These lenders relied on notification to maintain perfection under ~~former~~ pre-1998 9–305. Requiring them to obtain ~~authenticated~~ signed acknowledgments from each prospective purchaser under subsection (c) could be unduly burdensome and disruptive of established practices. Under subsection (h), when a secured party in possession itself delivers the collateral to a third party, instructions to the third party would be sufficient to maintain perfection by possession; an acknowledgment would not be necessary. Under subsection (i), the secured party does not relinquish possession by making a delivery under subsection (h), even if the delivery violates the rights of the debtor. That subsection also makes clear that a person to whom collateral is delivered under subsection (h) does not owe any duty to the secured party and is not required to confirm the delivery to another person unless the person otherwise agrees or law other than this Article provides otherwise.

10. **"Signs" and "Signed" Replaces "Authenticates" and "Authenticated."** Consistent with the revised definition of "sign" in Section 1–201, the cognate terms "signs" and "signed" replace the references to "authenticates" and "authenticated" in the pre-2022 text of this section.

§ 9–314. Perfection by Control.

(a) **[Perfection by control.]** A security interest in ~~investment property, deposit accounts, letter-of-credit rights, electronic chattel paper, or electronic documents~~ controllable accounts, controllable electronic records, controllable payment intangibles, deposit accounts, electronic documents, electronic money, investment property, or letter-of-credit rights may be perfected by control of the collateral under Section 7–106, 9–104, ~~9–105,~~ 9–105A, 9–106, ~~or~~ 9–107, or 9–107A.

(b) **[Specified collateral: time of perfection by control; continuation of perfection.]** A security interest in ~~deposit accounts, electronic chattel paper, letter-of-credit rights, or electronic documents,~~ controllable accounts, controllable electronic records, controllable payment intangibles, deposit accounts, electronic documents, electronic money, or letter-of-credit rights is perfected by control under Section 7–106, 9–104, ~~9–105,~~ 9–105A, ~~or~~ 9–107, or 9–107A ~~when~~ not earlier than the time the secured party obtains control and remains perfected by control only while the secured party retains control.

(c) **[Investment property: time of perfection by control; continuation of perfection.]** A security interest in investment property is perfected by control under Section 9–106 ~~from~~ not earlier than the time the secured party obtains control and remains perfected by control until:

* * *

Official Comment

* * *

2.   **Control.** This section provides for perfection by control with respect to ~~investment property, deposit accounts,~~ controllable accounts, controllable electronic records, controllable payment intangibles, deposit accounts, electronic documents, electronic money, investment property, and letter-of-credit rights, ~~electronic chattel paper, and electronic documents~~. ~~For explanations of~~ Concerning how a secured party takes control of these types of collateral, see Sections 7–106, 9–104, 9–105A, ~~through~~ 9–107, and 9–107A, and ~~Section 7–106~~ Comments. Subsection (b) explains when a security interest is perfected by control and how long a security interest remains perfected by control. Like Section 9–313(d) and for the same reasons, subsection (b) makes no reference to the doctrine of "relation back." See Section 9–313, Comment 5. As to an electronic document that is reissued in a tangible medium~~,~~ (see Section 7–105), a secured party that is perfected by control in the electronic document should file as to the document before relinquishing control in order to maintain continuous perfection in the document. See Section 9–308. If a secured party's control is based on an acknowledgment under Section 7–106(g), 9–104(a)(4), or 9–105A(e) or under 9–107A and 12–105(e) by another person having control, the secured party remains perfected by control only while the other person retains control. This result necessarily follows because such a secured party's control derives solely from the other person's continued control.

Perfection by control of chattel paper evidenced by an authoritative electronic record (formerly defined as "electronic chattel paper") has been removed from this section. Instead, perfection by possession and control of chattel paper is governed by Section 9–314A.

3.   **Investment Property.** Subsection (c) provides a special rule for investment property. Once a secured party has control, its security interest remains perfected by control until the secured party ceases to have control and the debtor receives possession of collateral that is a certificated security, becomes the registered owner of collateral that is an uncertificated security, or becomes the entitlement holder of collateral that is a security entitlement. The result is particularly important in the "repledge" context. See Section 9–207, Comment 5. In a transaction in which a secured party who has control grants a security interest in investment property or sells outright the investment property, by virtue of the debtor's consent or applicable legal rules, a purchaser from the secured party typically will cut off the debtor's rights in the investment property or be immune from the debtor's claims. See Section 9–207, Comments 5 and 6. If the investment property is a security, the debtor normally would retain no interest in the security following the purchase from the secured party, and a claim of the debtor against the secured party for redemption (Section 9–623) or otherwise with respect to the security would be a purely personal claim.

If the investment property transferred by the secured party is a financial asset in which the debtor had a security entitlement credited to a securities account maintained with the secured party as a securities intermediary, the debtor's claim against the secured party could arise as a part of its securities account notwithstanding its personal nature. (This claim would be analogous to a "credit balance" in the securities account, which is a component of the securities account even though it is a personal claim against the intermediary.) In the case in which the debtor may retain an interest in investment property notwithstanding a repledge or sale by the secured party, subsection (c) makes clear that the security interest will remain perfected by control. Notwithstanding subsection (c), if a secured party's control is based on an acknowledgment under Section 8–106(d)(3) by another person having control, the secured party remains perfected by control only while the other person retains control. This result necessarily follows because such a secured party's control derives solely from the other person's continued control. Although Section 8–106(d)(3) was amended by the 2022 Article 9 Revisions, this result also applied to a secured party in control under pre-2022 subsection (d)(3).

3A.   **Shared control between debtor and secured party (and other transferor and transferee) and control through another person.** Sections 7–106 (control of electronic documents), 9–105 (control of authoritative electronic records evidencing chattel paper), 9–105A (control of electronic money), and 12–105 (control of controllable electronic records, on which control of controllable accounts and controllable payment intangibles under Section 9–107A depends) contemplate the possibility that both a debtor and a secured party may have control of the relevant collateral by sharing an exclusive power. Such shared control between a debtor and secured party does not *necessarily* impair perfection of a security interest under this section or Section 9–314A. On shared exclusive powers, see generally Section 12–105, Comment 5. However, if a secured party can exercise a power only if the power is exercised also by the debtor, the power would not be shared and, consequently, the secured party would not have control based on the exclusive power. This result follows from Section 12–105(c) and corresponding subsections in the other provisions on control cited above. Under Section 12–105(c), because a

1083

debtor would be a "transferor of an interest" in a controllable electronic record or a controllable account or payment intangible evidenced by the record, the debtor's "blocking power" (i.e., the secured party can exercise the power only if the debtor also exercises the power) with respect to the secured party's exercise of the power would disqualify the secured party from sharing (and, consequently, enjoying) the exclusive power and perfection by control based on exclusive powers. Similarly, a purchaser in that situation would be disqualified from having control and thereby from enjoying the status and benefits of a qualifying purchaser (Section 12–102(a)(2)) under Section 12–104(e) and (g) if the purchaser takes from a transferor of an interest and the transferor has such a blocking power (whether or not the transferor is a debtor).

Section 12–105(e) contains a similar limitation in connection with control through another person. An acknowledging person must be one "other than the transferor of an interest in the electronic record." The same or a similar limitation is found in the other provisions relating to control through another person. See Sections 7–106(g) (control of electronic document of title); 8–106(d)(3) (control of a security entitlement); 9–104(a)(4) (control of deposit accounts); 9–105(g) (control of authoritative electronic copy of record evidencing chattel paper); 9–105A)(e) (control of electronic money).

For a discussion of the rationale for these limitations on sharing exclusive control and control through another person, see Section 12–105, Comment 9.

* * *

§ 9–314A. Perfection by Possession and Control of Chattel Paper.

(a) **[Perfection by possession and control.]** A secured party may perfect a security interest in chattel paper by taking possession of each authoritative tangible copy of the record evidencing the chattel paper and obtaining control of each authoritative electronic copy of the electronic record evidencing the chattel paper.

(b) **[Time of perfection; continuation of perfection.]** A security interest is perfected under subsection (a) not earlier than the time the secured party takes possession and obtains control and remains perfected under subsection (a) only while the secured party retains possession and control.

(c) **[Application of Section 9–313 to perfection by possession of chattel paper.]** Section 9–313(c) and (f) through (i) applies to perfection by possession of an authoritative tangible copy of a record evidencing chattel paper.

Official Comment

1. **"Authoritative copy."** To perfect a security interest in chattel paper other than by filing, this section provides that a secured party must obtain control of all authoritative electronic copies and take possession of all authoritative tangible copies.

Like the pre-2022 text, Section 9–105(b) distinguishes between authoritative and nonauthoritative copies of electronic chattel paper and refers to copies that are "authoritative." And, like its predecessor, Section 9–105(b) does not define the term "authoritative." However, it also applies this concept to tangible records that evidence chattel paper.

To show that it has possession of all authoritative tangible copies of a record evidencing chattel paper and all authoritative electronic copies of a record evidencing chattel paper, a purchaser can produce the tangible copies in its possession and prove control of the electronic copies and provide evidence that these are authoritative copies. The purchaser need not prove a negative—i.e., that no other tangible or electronic authoritative copies exist—to make a prima facie case. The purchaser's possession of the authoritative tangible copies and control of the authoritative electronic copies gives the purchaser the power to prevent others from taking possession or control of the copies and the power to transfer possession and control of the copies.

Perfection of a security interest in chattel paper by taking possession of the collateral generally has been understood to mean taking possession of the wet-ink "original." Experience has shown that the concept of an original breaks down when one allows for the possibility of the same monetary obligation being evidenced by different media over time, such as where electronic records evidencing the chattel paper are "papered out" (replaced with tangible records evidencing the same chattel paper) or tangible records are "converted" to electronic records.

Whether an electronic or tangible copy of a record evidencing chattel paper is authoritative depends on the facts and circumstances. The determination should turn on whether the copy provides reasonable notice to third parties that it is one that must be subject to control or possession for purposes of perfection and priority. To accommodate current practices and future technology, parties are allowed considerable flexibility in determining the method used to establish whether a particular copy is authoritative, provided that third parties are able to reasonably identify the authoritative copies that must be possessed or controlled to achieve perfection. For example, the parties could develop a system or protocol where each tangible or electronic copy is "watermarked" as authoritative or nonauthoritative or where the terms of the records themselves describe how to determine which copies are authoritative and which are not.

2. **Time of perfection; continuation of perfection.** Subsection (b) is modeled on Sections 9–313(d) and 9–314(b). If a secured party's possession or control is based on the acknowledgment under Section 9–313(c) or 9–105(g) by another person in possession or control, the secured party remains perfected by possession or control only while the other person retains possession or control. This result necessarily follows because such a secured party's possession or control derives solely from the other person's continued possession or control.

3. **Applicability of Section 9–313.** Subsection (c) makes specified subsections of Section 9–313 applicable to possession of authoritative tangible copies of records evidencing chattel paper.

4. **Shared control.** As to the sharing of powers over an authoritative electronic copy of a record evidencing chattel paper (see Section 9–105(c)(2)) by a debtor and a secured party (or by another transferor and transferee) and control through another person (see Section 9–105(g)), see Sections 9–314, Comment 3A; 12–105, Comment 9.

§ 9–316. Effect of Change in Governing Law.

(a) **[General rule: effect on perfection of change in governing law.]** A security interest perfected pursuant to the law of the jurisdiction designated in Section 9–301(1), ~~or~~ 9–305(c), 9–306A(d), or 9–306B(b) remains perfected until the earliest of:

* * *

(f) **[Change in jurisdiction of chattel paper, controllable electronic record, bank, issuer, nominated person, securities intermediary, or commodity intermediary.]** A security interest in chattel paper, controllable accounts, controllable electronic records, controllable payment intangibles, deposit accounts, letter-of-credit rights, or investment property which is perfected under the law of the chattel paper's jurisdiction, the controllable electronic record's jurisdiction, the bank's jurisdiction, the issuer's jurisdiction, a nominated person's jurisdiction, the securities intermediary's jurisdiction, or the commodity intermediary's jurisdiction, as applicable, remains perfected until the earlier of:

* * *

Official Comment

* * *

4. **Possessory Security Interests.** Subsection (c) deals with continued perfection of possessory security interests. It applies not only to security interests perfected solely by the secured party's having taken possession of the collateral. It also applies to security interests perfected by a method that includes as an element of perfection the secured party's having taken possession, such as perfection by taking delivery of a certificated security in registered form, see Section 9–313(a), ~~and~~ perfection by obtaining control over a certificated security. ~~See,~~ see Section 9–314(a), and perfection by taking possession of and control over authoritative copies of records evidencing chattel paper, see Section 9–314A(a).

* * *

6. **Controllable Accounts, Controllable Electronic Records, Controllable Payment Intangibles, Chattel Paper, Deposit Accounts, Letter-of-Credit Rights, and Investment Property.** Subsections (f) and (g) address changes in the jurisdiction of a bank, controllable electronic record, chattel paper, issuer of an uncertificated security, issuer of or nominated person under a letter of credit, securities intermediary, and commodity intermediary. The provisions are analogous to those of subsections (a) and (b).

* * *

§ 9–317. Interests That Take Priority Over or Take Free of Security Interest or Agricultural Lien.

* * *

(b) **[Buyers that receive delivery.]** Except as otherwise provided in subsection (e), a buyer, other than a secured party, ~~of tangible chattel paper, tangible documents,~~ of goods, instruments, tangible documents, or a security certificate takes free of a security interest or agricultural lien if the buyer gives value and receives delivery of the collateral without knowledge of the security interest or agricultural lien and before it is perfected.

* * *

(d) **[Licensees and buyers of certain collateral.]** ~~A~~ Subject to subsections (f) through (i), a licensee of a general intangible or a buyer, other than a secured party, of collateral other than ~~tangible chattel paper,~~ electronic money, ~~tangible documents,~~ goods, instruments, tangible documents, or a certificated security takes free of a security interest if the licensee or buyer gives value without knowledge of the security interest and before it is perfected.

* * *

(f) **[Buyers of chattel paper.]** A buyer, other than a secured party, of chattel paper takes free of a security interest if, without knowledge of the security interest and before it is perfected, the buyer gives value and:

(1) receives delivery of each authoritative tangible copy of the record evidencing the chattel paper; and

(2) if each authoritative electronic copy of the record evidencing the chattel paper can be subjected to control under Section 9–105, obtains control of each authoritative electronic copy.

(g) **[Buyers of electronic documents.]** A buyer of an electronic document takes free of a security interest if, without knowledge of the security interest and before it is perfected, the buyer gives value and, if each authoritative electronic copy of the document can be subjected to control under Section 7–106, obtains control of each authoritative electronic copy.

(h) **[Buyers of controllable electronic records.]** A buyer of a controllable electronic record takes free of a security interest if, without knowledge of the security interest and before it is perfected, the buyer gives value and obtains control of the controllable electronic record.

(i) **[Buyers of controllable accounts and controllable payment intangibles.]** A buyer, other than a secured party, of a controllable account or a controllable payment intangible takes free of a security interest if, without knowledge of the security interest and before it is perfected, the buyer gives value and obtains control of the controllable account or controllable payment intangible.

Official Comment

* * *

6. **Purchasers Other Than Secured Parties.** Subsections (b), (c), ~~and~~ (d), and (f) through (i) afford priority over an unperfected security interest to certain ~~purchasers~~ buyers (other than secured parties) of collateral. They derive in part from ~~former~~ pre-1998 Sections 9–301(1)(c), 2A–307(2), and 9–301(d). ~~Former~~ Pre-1998 Section 9–301(1)(c) and (1)(d) provided that unperfected security interests are "subordinate" to the rights of certain purchasers. But, as ~~former~~ pre-1998 Comment 9 suggested, the practical effect of subordination in this context is that the purchaser takes free of the security interest. To avoid any possible misinterpretation these subsections ~~(b) and (d) of this section~~ now use the phrase "takes free."

Subsection (b) governs goods, as well as intangibles of the type whose transfer is effected by physical delivery of the representative piece of paper (~~tangible chattel paper,~~ tangible documents, instruments, and security certificates). To obtain priority, a buyer must both give value and receive delivery of the collateral without knowledge of the existing security interest and before perfection. Even if the buyer gave value without knowledge and before perfection, the buyer would take subject to the security interest if perfection occurred before physical delivery of the collateral to the buyer. Subsection (c) contains a similar rule with respect to lessees of goods. Note that a lessee of goods in ordinary course of business takes free of all security interests created by the lessor, even if perfected. See Section 9–321.

* * *

Subsection (b) no longer applies to chattel paper. The take-free rule in subsection (f) for buyers of chattel paper reflects the corresponding 2022 changes in the definition of chattel paper and in the methods of perfection. *See* Sections 9–102(a)(11) (defining "chattel paper"); 9–314A (perfection by possession and control). Note that subsection (f) applies only to a buyer of chattel paper "other than a secured party" and most buyers of chattel paper are secured parties. See Sections 9–102(a)(73) (defining "secured party" as including a person to which chattel paper has been sold); 9–109(a)(3) (Article 9 applies to a sale of chattel paper); 1–201(b)(35) (defining "security interest" to include the interest of a buyer of chattel paper). However, Article 9 does not apply to "a sale of . . . chattel paper . . . as part of a sale of the business out of which . . . [the chattel paper] arose" and, accordingly, subsection (f) could apply to a buyer of chattel paper in such a sale-of-business transaction. Subsection (f) provides that such a buyer of chattel paper takes free of a security interest if, without knowledge of the security interest and before it is perfected, the buyer gives value and receives delivery of each authoritative tangible copy of the record evidencing the chattel paper and, if the chattel paper can be subjected to control, the buyer obtains control of each authoritative electronic copy.

Although chattel paper has been removed from subsection (b), the phrase "other than a secured party" has been retained because buyers of instruments that are promissory notes, but not buyers of other instruments, are secured parties. See Sections 9–109(a)(3) (Article 9 applies to a sale of a promissory note); 1–201(b)(35) (defining "security interest" to include the interest of a buyer of a promissory note).

The rule of subsection (b) obviously is not appropriate where the collateral consists of intangibles and there is no representative piece of paper whose physical delivery is the only or the customary method of transfer or no means of taking control of the collateral as a functional equivalent of a delivery. Therefore, with respect to such intangibles (including accounts other than controllable accounts, ~~electronic chattel paper,~~ electronic documents not subject to control, general intangibles other than controllable payment intangibles, and investment property other than certificated securities), subsection (d) gives priority to any buyer who gives value without knowledge, and before perfection, of the security interest. Buyers of electronic money also are excluded from the application of subsection (d) because transferees of electronic money which obtain control take free of security interests under Section 9–332(c), which provides a standard more generous to transferees than subsection (d). A licensee of a general intangible takes free of an unperfected security interest in the general intangible under the same circumstances (to the extent of the licensee's rights under the license). Note that a licensee of a general intangible in ordinary course of business takes rights under a nonexclusive license free of security interests created by the licensor, even if perfected. See Section 9–321.

Unless Section 9–109 excludes the transaction from this Article, a buyer of accounts, ~~chattel paper,~~ payment intangibles, or promissory notes is a "secured party" (defined in Section 9–102), and ~~subsections (b) and (d) do~~ subsection (d) does not determine priority of the security interest created by the sale. Rather, the priority rules generally applicable to competing security interests apply. See, e.g., Section 9–322.

6A. [Buyers of Electronic Documents, Controllable Electronic Records, Controllable Accounts, and Controllable Payment Intangibles.] Subsection (g) provides a take-free rule for electronic documents, subsection (h) so provides for controllable electronic records, and subsection (i) so provides for controllable accounts and controllable payment intangibles. Subsection (g) conditions the take-free rule on the buyer obtaining control of authoritative electronic copies of the document only if the authoritative electronic copies can be subjected to control. Subsection (h) conditions the take-free rule for a buyer of a controllable electronic record on the buyer's obtaining control of the electronic record. Similarly, under subsection (i), the take-free rule for a buyer, other than a secured party, of a controllable account or controllable payment intangible is conditioned on the buyer's obtaining control of the account or payment intangible. Although in general a buyer of an account or a payment intangible is a secured party, there are limited exceptions. See Sections 1–201(b)(35) ("security interest" includes interest of buyer of accounts or payment intangibles); 9–109(d)(4) (inapplicability of Article 9 to sale of accounts or payment intangibles as a part of the sale of a business).

* * *

§ 9–322. Priorities Among Conflicting Security Interests in and Agricultural Liens on Same Collateral.

* * *

Official Comment

* * *

6. **Priority in Proceeds: General Rule.** * * *

Example 5: On April 1, Debtor ~~authenticates~~ signs a security agreement granting to A a security interest in all Debtor's existing and after-acquired inventory. The same day, A files a financing statement covering inventory. On May 1, Debtor ~~authenticates~~ signs a security agreement granting B a security interest in all Debtor's existing and future accounts. The same day, B files a financing statement covering accounts. On June 1, Debtor sells inventory to a customer on 30-day unsecured credit. When Debtor acquires the account, B's security interest attaches to it and is perfected by B's financing statement. At the very same time, A's security interest attaches to the account as proceeds of the inventory and is automatically perfected. See Section 9–315. Under subsection (b) of this section, for purposes of determining A's priority in the account, the time of filing as to the original collateral (April 1, as to inventory) is also the time of filing as to proceeds (account). Accordingly, A's security interest in the account has priority over B's. Of course, had B filed its financing statement before A filed (e.g., on March 1), then B would have priority in the accounts.

* * *

§ 9–323. Future Advances.

* * *

(d) **[Buyer of goods.]** Except as otherwise provided in subsection (e), a buyer of goods ~~other than a buyer in ordinary course of business~~ takes free of a security interest to the extent that it secures advances made after the earlier of:

* * *

(f) **[Lessee of goods.]** Except as otherwise provided in subsection (g), a lessee of goods~~, other than a lessee in ordinary course of business,~~ takes the leasehold interest free of a security interest to the extent that it secures advances made after the earlier of:

* * *

Official Comment

* * *

6. **Competing Buyers and Lessees.** Under subsections (d) and (e), a buyer will not take subject to a security interest to the extent it secures advances made after the secured party has knowledge that the buyer has purchased the collateral or more than 45 days after the purchase unless the advances were made pursuant to a commitment entered into before the expiration of the 45-day period and without knowledge of the purchase. Subsections (f) and (g) provide an analogous rule for lessees. Subsections (d) and (e) replace pre-1998 Section 9–307(3), and subsections (f) and (g) replace pre-1998 Section 2A–307(4). No change in meaning is intended.

Of course, a buyer in ordinary course who takes free of the security interest under Section 9–320 and a lessee in ordinary course who takes free under Section 9–321 are not subject to any future advances. However, the exceptions for a buyer in ordinary course of business and a lessee in ordinary course of business in the 1998 text of subsections (d) and (f) have been deleted. Even if such a buyer or lessee does not meet the requirements under Section 9–320 or 9–321 to take free of a security interest, it should be entitled to the benefits of those subsections, which apply to buyers generally. This change is consistent with the intended result under the 1998 text. ~~Subsections (d) and (e) replace former Section 9–307(3), and subsections (f) and (g) replace former Section 2A–307(4). No change in meaning is intended.~~

§ 9–324. Priority of Purchase-Money Security Interests.

* * *

(b) **[Inventory purchase-money priority.]** Subject to subsection (c) and except as otherwise provided in subsection (g), a perfected purchase-money security interest in inventory has priority over a conflicting security interest in the same inventory, has priority over a conflicting security interest in chattel paper or an instrument constituting proceeds of the inventory and in proceeds of the chattel paper, if so provided in Section 9–330, and, except as otherwise provided in Section 9–327, also has priority in identifiable cash proceeds of the inventory to the extent the identifiable cash proceeds are received on or before the delivery of the inventory to a buyer, if:

* * *

(2) the purchase-money secured party sends ~~an authenticated~~ a signed notification to the holder of the conflicting security interest;

* * *

(d) [**Livestock purchase-money priority.**] Subject to subsection (e) and except as otherwise provided in subsection (g), a perfected purchase-money security interest in livestock that are farm products has priority over a conflicting security interest in the same livestock, and, except as otherwise provided in Section 9–327, a perfected security interest in their identifiable proceeds and identifiable products in their unmanufactured states also has priority, if:

* * *

(2) the purchase-money secured party sends ~~an authenticated~~ a signed notification to the holder of the conflicting security interest;

* * *

Official Comment

* * *

14. **"Signed" Replaces "Authenticated."** Consistent with the revised definition of "sign" in Section 1–201, the cognate term "signed" replaces the references to "authenticated" in the pre-2022 text of this section.

§ 9–326A. Priority of Security Interest in Controllable Account, Controllable Electronic Record, and Controllable Payment Intangible.

A security interest in a controllable account, controllable electronic record, or controllable payment intangible held by a secured party having control of the account, electronic record, or payment intangible has priority over a conflicting security interest held by a secured party that does not have control.

Official Comment

1. [**Control priority.**] This section adopts an approach to priority in controllable accounts, controllable electronic records, and controllable payment intangibles that is similar to the approach of Sections 9–327 (deposit accounts) and 9–328 (investment property): A security interest perfected by control has priority over conflicting security interests that are not perfected by control.

2. [**Multiple persons having control.**] This section does not apply if more than one secured party has control of a controllable account, controllable electronic record, or controllable payment intangible, which may occur through shared control or a person in control acknowledging that it has control on behalf of another person. See Section 12–105(b)(2) (shared control), (e) (control through another person). In those situations, the residual first-to-file-or-perfect rule of Section 9–322(a)(1) would apply. However, affected persons may believe that the application of that first-in-time rule is not appropriate in some circumstances.

Example: A person (A) has a security interest in a controllable electronic record perfected by control (other than through an acknowledgment by another person under Section 12–105(e)) and A acknowledges that it has control on behalf of another person (B). B has a security interest perfected by a financing statement filed before A obtained control. Under Section 9–322(a) (the first-to-file-or-perfect rule), by obtaining control through A's acknowledgment B's security interest would have priority over A's previously senior security interest. To avoid that result, A might insist on B's subordination as a condition to A's acknowledgment. See Section 9–339 (subordination by agreement). In cases of multiple persons having control, it will be important for interested persons to adjust priorities by agreement, when appropriate. See also Section 12–105, Comment 5.

A secured party that relies on perfection by control resulting from the acknowledgment of another person under Section 12–105(e) need not prove a formal agency relationship with the acknowledging person. This is a principal rationale underlying the various provisions in Articles 7, 8, 9, and 12 which provide for a person to obtain control through another person's control and acknowledgment. However, a person obtaining control through an acknowledgment necessarily must rely on the integrity of the acknowledging person. In the case of perfection by control in the Example, the acknowledging person presumably also has control for the benefit of the debtor. The secured party's (B's) control, and perfection, depends on the acknowledging person's (A's) continued control. The secured party's (B's) perfection would be lost if the acknowledging person (A) were to lose or give up control, as by transferring control to the debtor or any other person. See, e.g., Section 9–314, Comment 2.

An acknowledging person also might serially acknowledge over time that it holds for the benefit of multiple purchasers (secured parties or buyers). Putting aside perfection by filing as in the Example, secured parties so perfected would have priority based on priority of timing of control under Section 9–322(a). However, a transfer of control by the acknowledging person to a qualifying purchaser, or an acknowledgment by that the person that it has control on behalf of a buyer or secured party that is a qualifying purchaser, would allow the qualifying purchaser to take free of (or have priority over) earlier security interests or other interests. It follows that a first-to-control priority rule for security interests would not protect a secured party having control through another person's acknowledgment from having its interest cut off or subordinated by a later-in-time qualifying purchaser. Such a "first-to-control" priority rule would be illusory inasmuch as purchasers relying on control through another person's acknowledgment would have no reliable method of determining priority over subsequent transferees other than reliance on the acknowledging person's integrity.

§ 9–330. Priority of Purchaser of Chattel Paper or Instrument.

(a) **[Purchaser's priority: security interest claimed merely as proceeds.]** A purchaser of chattel paper has priority over a security interest in the chattel paper which is claimed merely as proceeds of inventory subject to a security interest if:

(1) in good faith and in the ordinary course of the purchaser's business, the purchaser gives new value, and takes possession of each authoritative tangible copy of the record evidencing the chattel paper, or and obtains control of under Section 9–105 of each authoritative electronic copy of the record evidencing the chattel paper under Section 9–105; and

(2) the chattel paper does authoritative copies of the record evidencing the chattel paper do not indicate that it the chattel paper has been assigned to an identified assignee other than the purchaser.

(b) **[Purchaser's priority: other security interests.]** A purchaser of chattel paper has priority over a security interest in the chattel paper which is claimed other than merely as proceeds of inventory subject to a security interest if the purchaser gives new value, and takes possession of each authoritative tangible copy of the record evidencing the chattel paper, or and obtains control of under Section 9–105 of each authoritative electronic copy of the record evidencing the chattel paper under Section 9–105 in good faith, in the ordinary course of the purchaser's business, and without knowledge that the purchase violates the rights of the secured party.

* * *

(f) **[Indication of assignment gives knowledge.]** For purposes of subsections (b) and (d), if the authoritative copies of the record evidencing chattel paper or an instrument indicates indicate that it the chattel paper or instrument has been assigned to an identified secured party other than the purchaser, a purchaser of the chattel paper or instrument has knowledge that the purchase violates the rights of the secured party.

Official Comment

* * *

2. **Non-Temporal Priority.** This Article permits a security interest to be perfected in chattel paper either by filing or by the secured party's possession and control under Section 9–314A and in or instruments to be perfected either by filing or by the secured party's taking possession under Sections 9–312 and 9–313. This section enables secured parties and other purchasers of chattel paper (both evidenced by either or both authoritative electronic and tangible records) and instruments to obtain priority over earlier-perfected security interests, thereby promoting the negotiability of these types of receivables.

3. **Chattel Paper.** Subsections (a) and (b) follow former pre-1998 Section 9–308 in distinguishing between earlier-perfected security interests in chattel paper that is claimed merely as proceeds of inventory subject to a security interest and chattel paper that is claimed other than merely as proceeds. Like former pre-1998 Section 9–308, this section does not elaborate upon the phrase "merely as proceeds." For an elaboration, see PEB Commentary No. 8.

This section makes explicit the "good faith" requirement and retains the pre-1998 requirements of "the ordinary course of the purchaser's business" and the giving of "new value" as conditions for priority. Concerning the last, this Article deletes former pre-1998 Section 9–108 and adds to Section 9–102 a completely different definition of the term "new value." See Section 9–102, Comment 21 (discussing "new value"). Under subsection (e), the holder of a purchase-money security interest in inventory is deemed to give "new value" for chattel paper constituting the proceeds of the inventory. Accordingly, the purchase-money secured party may qualify for priority in the chattel paper under subsection (a) or (b), whichever is applicable, even if it does not make an additional advance against the chattel paper.

If a ~~possessory~~ security interest in ~~tangible~~ chattel paper ~~or a~~ that is perfected ~~by control security interest in electronic chattel paper~~ by possession and control under Section 9–314A does not qualify for priority under this section, it may be subordinate to a perfected-by-filing security interest under Section 9–322(a)(1).

4.   **Possession and Control.** To qualify for priority under subsection (a) or (b), a purchaser must "take[ ] possession of each authoritative tangible copy of the record evidencing the chattel paper ~~or~~ and obtain[ ] control ~~of~~ under Section 9–105 of each authoritative electronic copy of the record evidencing the chattel paper." ~~When chattel paper comprises one or more tangible records and one or more electronic records, a purchaser may satisfy the possession or control~~ this requirement ~~by taking possession of the tangible records under Section 9–313 and having control of the electronic records under Section 9–105.~~ Note that possession and control are methods of perfection under Section 9–314A. In determining which of several related records constitutes chattel paper and thus is relevant to possession or control, the form of the records is irrelevant. Rather, the ~~touchstone is whether possession or control of the record would afford the~~ possession-and-control requirement is based on the premise that it affords public notice ~~contemplated by the possession and control requirements~~. For example, because possession or control of an amendment extending the term of a lease would not afford the contemplated public notice, the amendment would not constitute a record evidencing chattel paper regardless of whether the amendment is in tangible form and the lease is in electronic form, the amendment is electronic and the lease is tangible, the amendment and lease are both tangible, or the amendment and lease are both electronic.

Two common practices have raised particular concerns with respect to the possession requirement. First, in some cases the parties create more than one copy or counterpart of chattel paper evidencing a single secured obligation or lease. This practice raises questions as to which counterpart is the "original" and whether it is necessary for a purchaser to take possession of all counterparts in order to "take possession" of the chattel paper. Second, parties sometimes enter into a single "master" agreement. The master agreement contemplates that the parties will enter into separate "schedules" from time to time, each evidencing chattel paper. Must a purchaser of an obligation or lease evidenced by a single schedule also take possession of the record evidencing the master agreement as well as the record evidencing the schedule in order to "take possession[ ]" of each authoritative tangible copy of the record evidencing the chattel paper"?

The problem raised by the first practice is easily solved. The parties may in the terms of their agreement and by designation on the chattel paper identify only one counterpart as the original, authoritative tangible copy of the chattel paper for purposes of ~~taking~~ the possession ~~of the chattel paper~~ requirement. Concerns about the second practice also are easily solved by careful drafting. Each schedule should provide that it incorporates the terms of the master agreement, not the other way around. This will make it clear that each schedule is a "stand alone" document.

A secured party may wish to convert ~~tangible~~ chattel paper evidenced by authoritative tangible copies to ~~electronic~~ chattel paper evidenced by electronic copies and vice versa. The priority of a security interest in chattel paper under subsection (a) or (b) may be preserved, even if the form of the chattel paper changes. The principle implied in the preceding paragraph, i.e., that not every copy of chattel paper is relevant, applies to "control" as well as to "possession." When there are multiple copies of chattel paper, a secured party may take "possession" or obtain "control" of the chattel paper if it acts with respect to the copy or copies that are reliably identified as the authoritative copy or copies ~~that are relevant for purposes of possession or control~~. Concerning the identification of copies as authoritative or nonauthoritative, see Section 9–105(c) and Comment 3. ~~This principle applies as well to chattel paper that has been converted from one form to another, even if the relevant copies are not the "original" chattel paper.~~

5.   **Chattel Paper Claimed Merely as Proceeds.** ~~Subsection (a) revises the rule in former Section 9–308(b) to eliminate reference to what the purchaser knows. Instead~~ Under subsection (a), a purchaser who meets the ~~possession or control~~ possession-and-control, good faith, ordinary course, and new value requirements takes priority over a competing security interest claimed merely as proceeds of inventory unless the authoritative copies of the record evidencing the chattel paper ~~itself indicates~~ indicate that ~~it~~ the chattel paper has been assigned to an identified assignee other than the purchaser. Thus subsection (a) recognizes the common practice of placing a "legend" on chattel paper to indicate that it has been assigned. This approach, under which the chattel paper purchaser who gives new value in ordinary course can rely on possession and control of unlegended, ~~tangible~~

chattel paper without any concern for other facts that it may know, comports with the expectations of both inventory and chattel paper financers.

6. **Chattel Paper Claimed Other Than Merely as Proceeds.** ~~Subsection (b) eliminates the requirement that the purchaser take without knowledge that the "specific paper" is subject to the security interest and substitutes for it the requirement that the purchaser take~~ Under subsection (b), a purchaser who meets the possession-and-control, good faith, ordinary course, and new value requirements takes priority over a competing security interest claimed other than merely as proceeds of inventory if it takes "without knowledge that the purchase violates the rights of the secured party." This standard derives from the definition of "buyer in ordinary course of business" in Section 1–201(b)(9). The source of the purchaser's knowledge is irrelevant. Note, however, that "knowledge" means "actual knowledge." Section 1–202(b).

In contrast to a junior secured party in accounts, who may be required in some special circumstances to undertake a search under the "good faith" requirement, see Comment 5 to Section 9–331, a purchaser of chattel paper under this section is not required as a matter of good faith to make a search in order to determine the existence of prior security interests. There may be circumstances where the purchaser undertakes a search nevertheless, either on its own volition or because other considerations make it advisable to do so, e.g., where the purchaser also is purchasing accounts. Without more, a purchaser of chattel paper who has seen a financing statement covering the chattel paper or who knows that the chattel paper is encumbered with a security interest, does not have knowledge that its purchase violates the secured party's rights. However, if a purchaser sees a statement in a financing statement to the effect that a purchase of chattel paper from the debtor would violate the rights of the filed secured party, the purchaser would have such knowledge. Likewise, under ~~new~~ subsection (f), if the authoritative copies of the chattel paper ~~itself indicates~~ indicate that ~~it~~ the chattel paper had been assigned to an identified secured party other than the purchaser, the purchaser would have wrongful knowledge for purposes of subsection (b), thereby preventing the purchaser from qualifying for priority under that subsection, even if the purchaser did not have actual knowledge. In the case of authoritative tangible copies of a record evidencing chattel paper, the indication normally would consist of a written legend on the copies ~~chattel paper~~. In the case of authoritative electronic copies of the record evidencing chattel paper, this Article leaves to developing market and technological practices the manner in which the ~~chattel paper~~ copies would indicate an assignment.

Subsections (a) and (f) each refer to the possibility that authoritative copies of records evidencing chattel paper may indicate that the chattel paper has been assigned to an identified assignee. Those subsections should be read and interpreted in a manner consistent with Section 9–105 on control of authoritative electronic copies of records evidencing chattel paper. Accordingly, references in subsections (a) and (f) to an indication in a record evidencing chattel paper also embrace, for authoritative electronic copies of such records, records attached to or logically associated with the authoritative electronic copies and systems in which the authoritative electronic copies are recorded. See Section 9–105(c) and (d)(1).

7. **Instruments.** * * *

* * *

The rule in subsection (d) is similar to the rules in subsections (a) and (b), which govern priority in chattel paper. The observations in Comment 6 concerning the requirement of good faith and the phrase "without knowledge that the purchase violates the rights of the secured ~~party"~~ party," including the operation of subsection (f) if an instrument indicates that it has been assigned to an identified secured party, apply equally to purchasers of instruments. However, unlike a purchaser of chattel paper, to qualify for priority under ~~this section~~ subsection (d) a purchaser of an instrument need only give "value" as defined in Section ~~1–201~~ 1–204; it need not give "new value." Also, the purchaser need not purchase the instrument in the ordinary course of its business.

* * *

10. **Assignment of Non-Lease Chattel Paper.**

* * *

b. **Dealer's Outright Sale of Chattel Paper to SP-2.** Article 9 also applies to a transaction whereby SP-2 buys the chattel paper in an outright sale transaction without recourse against Dealer. Sections ~~1–201(37)~~ 1–201(b)(35), 9–109(a). Although Dealer does not, in such a transaction, retain any residual ownership interest in the chattel paper, the chattel paper constitutes proceeds of the goods to which SP-1's security interest will attach and continue following the sale of the goods. Section 9–315(a). Even though Dealer has not retained any interest in the chattel paper, as discussed above BIOCOB subsequently may return the goods to Dealer under circumstances whereby Dealer reacquires an interest in the goods. The priority contest between SP–1 and SP–2 will be resolved as discussed above; Section 9–330 makes no distinction among purchasers of chattel paper on the basis of whether the purchaser is an outright buyer of chattel paper or one whose security interest secures an obligation of Dealer.

11. **Assignment of Lease Chattel Paper.** As defined in Section 9–102, "chattel paper" includes not only ~~writings that evidence security interests in~~ rights to payment secured by specific goods but also ~~those that evidence~~ rights to payment owed by a lessee under a true ~~leases~~ lease of goods.

* * *

§ 9–331.   Priority of Rights of Purchasers of <u>Controllable Accounts, Controllable Electronic Records, Controllable Payment Intangibles,</u>~~Instruments,~~ Documents, Instruments, and Securities Under Other Articles; Priority of Interests in Financial Assets and Security Entitlements <u>and Protection Against Assertion of Claim</u> Under ~~Article 8~~ <u>Articles 8 and 12.</u>

(a)   **[Rights under Articles 3, 7, ~~and~~ 8<u>, and 12</u> not limited.]** This article does not limit the rights of a holder in due course of a negotiable instrument, a holder to which a negotiable document of title has been duly negotiated, ~~or~~ a protected purchaser of a security<u>, or a qualifying purchaser of a controllable account, controllable electronic record, or controllable payment intangible</u>. These holders or purchasers take priority over an earlier security interest, even if perfected, to the extent provided in Articles 3, 7, ~~and~~ 8<u>, and 12</u>.

(b)   **[Protection under ~~Article 8~~ <u>Articles 8 and 12</u>.]** This article does not limit the rights of or impose liability on a person to the extent that the person is protected against the assertion of a claim under Article 8 <u>or 12</u>.

* * *

Official Comment

* * *

3.   * * *

<u>The state-law Uniform Electronic Transactions Act (UETA) and the federal Electronic Signature in Global and National Commerce Act, 15 U.S.C. §§ 7001 *et seq.* (E-SIGN), provide certain rules for records referred to and defined as "transferable records." See UETA Section 16 and E-SIGN, 15 U.S.C. § 7021. When certain conditions have been met, those acts confer on a person the status of a "holder" (as defined in 1–201(b)(21), formerly Section 1–201(20)) of an "equivalent record" under pre-1998 Section 9–308 (now, in part, Section 9–330) and the rights and defenses of a "purchaser" under that section, among other effects. E-SIGN also refers to the rights and defenses of a purchaser under Section 9–330. As a matter of the application of the Uniform Commercial Code, those are not the only sections of the Uniform Commercial Code that would logically be affected by UETA and E-SIGN. For example, the rights of a holder in due course under Section 9–331(a) would also be covered by the application of those acts, when the conditions for applicability have been satisfied.</u>

* * *

§ 9–332.   Transfer of Money; Transfer of Funds from Deposit Account.

(a)   **[Transferee of <u>tangible</u> money.]** A transferee of <u>tangible</u> money takes the money free of a security interest ~~unless the transferee acts~~ <u>if the transferee receives possession of the money without acting</u> in collusion with the debtor in violating the rights of the secured party.

(b)   **[Transferee of funds from deposit account.]** A transferee of funds from a deposit account takes the funds free of a security interest in the deposit account ~~unless the transferee acts~~ <u>if the transferee receives the funds without acting</u> in collusion with the debtor in violating the rights of the secured party.

(c)   **[Transferee of electronic money.]** <u>A transferee of electronic money takes the money free of a security interest if the transferee obtains control of the money without acting in collusion with the debtor in violating the rights of the secured party.</u>

Official Comment

* * *

2.   **Scope of this Section.** This section affords broad protection ~~to~~ for transferees ~~who take~~ of money and of funds from a deposit account ~~and to those who take money.~~ to take free of a security interest.

2A.   **Meaning of "Transfer."** The term "transferee" is not defined; however, the debtor itself is not a transferee. Thus this section does not cover the case in which a debtor withdraws money (currency) from its deposit account or the case in which a bank debits an encumbered account and credits another account it maintains for the debtor.

A "transfer" of property occurs when the transferee has obtained a property interest in the relevant property. See Section 9–102, Comment 2.b.1 ("Several provisions of this Article and its official comments also refer to the 'transfer' of *property* interests." (emphasis added)). Other law determines when the transferee has acquired a property interest. See Section 9–408, Comment 3 ("Other law determines whether a debtor has a property interest ('rights in the collateral') and the nature of that interest."). Although the terms "transfer" and "transferee" are not defined in the UCC, the term "transfer" is broader in scope than "purchase," which requires taking in a "voluntary transaction creating an interest in property." Section 1–201(b)(29). For example, "transfer" includes an involuntary transfer such as the acquisition of a judicial lien by a lien creditor. See Section 9–102(a)(52) (defining "lien creditor"). However, many references to a "transfer" in the UCC and official comments relate to a voluntary transfer to a purchaser, as indicated by the context.

2B.   **Transferees of Tangible Money.** Subsection (a) conditions the take-free rule on the transferee's receipt of possession of tangible money. This reflects what had always been assumed under the pre-2022 text— that a transfer of an interest in tangible money which is not accompanied by a physical transfer of possession would not impair the rights of third parties.

2C.   **Transferees of Funds from Deposit Account.** Subsection (b) reflects the corresponding change for a transfer of funds from a deposit account. To qualify for the take-free protection under subsection (b), the transferee must "receive[] the funds without acting in collusion . . ." The amendments to subsections (a) and (b) clarify what was implicit under the original text. Although "funds" is not defined in the UCC, if deposit accounts with a central bank or another bank were to become money, as defined in Section 1–201(b)(24), transfers from such deposit accounts would be covered by subsection (b) and not subsection (c) (discussed in Comment 2.D.). See Section 9–102(a)(54A) (defining "money," for purposes of Article 9, to exclude deposit accounts).

* * *

Example 2: Debtor maintains a deposit account with Bank A. The deposit account is subject to a perfected security interest in favor of Lender. At Bank B's suggestion, Debtor moves the funds from the account at Bank A to Debtor's deposit account with Bank B. Unless Bank B acted in collusion with Debtor in violating Lender's rights, Bank B takes the funds (the credits running in favor of Bank B) free from Lender's security interest. See subsection (b). However, inasmuch as the deposit account maintained with Bank B constitutes the proceeds of the deposit account at Bank A, Lender's security interest would attach to that account as proceeds. See Section 9–315.

Subsection (b) also would apply if, in ~~the example~~ these examples, Bank A debited Debtor's deposit account in exchange for the issuance of Bank A's cashier's check. Lender's security interest would attach to the cashier's check as proceeds of the deposit account, and the rules applicable to instruments would govern any competing claims to the cashier's check. See, e.g., Sections 3–306, 9–322, 9–330, 9–331.

If Debtor withdraws ~~money (currency)~~ funds from an encumbered deposit account, receives the funds in the form of tangible money, and transfers the money to a third party, then subsection (a), to the extent not displaced by federal law relating to money, applies to the transfer. It contains substantially the same rule as subsection (b).

Subsection (b) applies to *transfers of funds from* a deposit account; it does not apply to *transfers of the deposit account* itself or of an interest therein. Because a deposit account is a monetary obligation (debt) of the depositary bank to its depositor, a transfer of the deposit account itself does not transfer the funds credited to the deposit account. For example, this section does not apply to the creation of a security interest in a deposit account. Competing claims to the deposit account itself are dealt with by other Article 9 priority rules. See Sections 9–317(a), 9–327, 9–340, 9–341. Similarly, a corporate merger normally would not result in a transfer of funds from a deposit account. Rather, it might result in a transfer of the deposit account itself. If so, the normal rules applicable to transferred collateral would apply; this section would not.

The depositor's creditors (whether secured parties or lien creditors) do not have any interest in any *funds* (or any other assets of the depositary bank) as a result of having an interest in the deposit account (the right to payment of the bank's obligation). Consequently, a transferee of funds that takes free of a security interest under subsection (b) does so whether the security interest in the deposit account from which the funds were transferred arises as original collateral or as proceeds.

A transferee of *an interest in the deposit account*, such as a garnishing lien creditor, does not take free of a security interest in a deposit account under subsection (b). A transferee takes free under subsection (b) only upon the actual receipt of *funds* from the deposit account. The proper construction of subsection (b) rejects cases that treat garnishment of a deposit account as an immediate transfer of funds or an interest in funds credited to the deposit account.

The last event that provides a recovery for a creditor in a garnishment action virtually always would be a transfer of funds from a deposit account. However, this does not mean that a perfected security interest will always be cut off by a garnishing creditor. By intervening in the garnishment proceeding to assert its senior security interest before funds are disbursed, the secured party might assert and retain its priority. However, the relevant procedural law may not provide the secured party with adequate advance notice. In some cases, a control agreement that perfects a security interest in the deposit account may require the garnished bank to provide prompt notice to the secured party. But not all control agreements will so provide. Moreover, the secured party's priority is not absolute. See, e.g., Section 9–401, Comment 6 (explaining that the equitable doctrine of marshaling may be appropriate in the case of a lien creditor's interest in collateral when a senior secured party is oversecured).

2D. **Transferees of Electronic Money.** Because "electronic money" is new, no pattern of past practices or understandings exists. However, subsection (c) provides a take-free rule for electronic money that complements subsection (a) by conditioning the take-free rule on the transferee's obtaining control.

2E. **Temporal Aspect of Collusion Test.** For a transferee to take free of a security interest under this section the transferee must receive delivery of tangible money, receive funds from a deposit account, or obtain control of electronic money without acting in collusion. Whether the transferee is acting without collusion is determined as of the time of delivery to the transferee or receipt of funds or obtaining control by the transferee.

* * *

4. **"Bad Actors."** To deal with the question of the "bad actor," this section borrows "collusion" language from Article 8. See, e.g., Sections 8–115, 8–503(e). This is the most protective (i.e., least stringent) of the various standards now found in the UCC. Compare, e.g., Section 1–201(b)(9) ("without knowledge that the sale violates the rights of another person," in the definition of "buyer in ordinary course of business"); Section 1–201(b)(20) (defining "good faith" as "honesty in fact and the observance of reasonable commercial standards of fair dealing"); Section 3–302(a)(2)(v) ("without notice of any claim").

* * *

§ 9–334. Priority of Security Interests in Fixtures and Crops.

* * *

(f) [**Priority based on consent, disclaimer, or right to remove.**] A security interest in fixtures, whether or not perfected, has priority over a conflicting interest of an encumbrancer or owner of the real property if:

(1) the encumbrancer or owner has, in ~~an authenticated~~ a signed record, consented to the security interest or disclaimed an interest in the goods as fixtures; or

* * *

Official Comment

* * *

13. **"Signed" Replaces "Authenticated."** Consistent with the revised definition of "sign" in Section 1–201, the cognate term "signed" replaces the reference to "authenticated" in the pre-2022 text of this section.

§ 9–341. Bank's Rights and Duties with Respect to Deposit Account.

Except as otherwise provided in Section 9–340(c), and unless the bank otherwise agrees in ~~an authenticated~~ a signed record, a bank's rights and duties with respect to a deposit account maintained with the bank are not terminated, suspended, or modified by:

* * *

Official Comment

* * *

6.   **"Signed" Replaces "Authenticated."** Consistent with the revised definition of "sign" in Section 1–201, the cognate term "signed" replaces the reference to "authenticated" in the pre-2022 text of this section.

§ 9–401.   Alienability of Debtor's Rights.

* * *

Official Comment

* * *

8.   Use of the Term "Assignment." The term "assignment," as used in this Article, refers to both an outright transfer of ownership and a transfer of an interest to secure an obligation. See ~~Section~~ Section 9–102, Comment ~~26~~ 2.b.1; ~~to Section 9–102 and~~ PEB Commentary No. 21~~, dated March 11, 2020~~.

§ 9–403.   Agreement Not to Assert Defenses Against Assignee.

* * *

Official Comment

* * *

3.   **Conditions of Validation; Relationship to Article 3.** Subsection (b) validates an account debtor's agreement only if the assignee takes an assignment for value, in good faith, and without notice of conflicting claims to the property assigned or of certain claims or defenses of the account debtor. Like ~~former~~ pre-1998 Section 9–206, this section is designed to put the assignee in a position that is no better and no worse than that of a holder in due course of a negotiable instrument under Article 3. However, ~~former~~ pre-1998 Section 9–206 left open certain issues, e.g., whether the section incorporated the special Article 3 definition of "value" in Section 3–303 or the generally applicable definition in ~~Section 1–201(44)~~ Article 1 (Section 1–204). Subsection (a) addresses this question; it provides that "value" has the meaning specified in Section 3–303(a). Similarly, subsection (c) provides that subsection (b) does not validate an agreement with respect to defenses that could be asserted against a holder in due course under Section 3–305(b) (the so-called "real" defenses). In 1990, the definition of "holder in due course" (Section 3–302) and the articulation of the rights of a holder in due course (Sections 3–305 and 3–306) were revised substantially. This section tracks more closely the rules of Sections 3–302, 3–305, and 3–306.

* * *

§ 9–404.   Rights Acquired by Assignee; Claims and Defenses Against Assignee.

(a)   **[Assignee's rights subject to terms, claims, and defenses; exceptions.]** Unless an account debtor has made an enforceable agreement not to assert defenses or claims, and subject to subsections (b) through (e), the rights of an assignee are subject to:

* * *

(2)   any other defense or claim of the account debtor against the assignor which accrues before the account debtor receives a notification of the assignment ~~authenticated~~ signed by the assignor or the assignee.

* * *

Official Comment

* * *

6.   **"Signed" Replaces "Authenticated."** Consistent with the revised definition of "sign" in Section 1–201, the cognate term "signed" replaces the reference to "authenticated" in the pre-2022 text of this section.

§ 9–406. Discharge of Account Debtor; Notification of Assignment; Identification and Proof of Assignment; Restrictions on Assignment of Accounts, Chattel Paper, Payment Intangibles, and Promissory Notes Ineffective.

(a) **[Discharge of account debtor; effect of notification.]** Subject to subsections (b) through (i) and (*l*), an account debtor on an account, chattel paper, or a payment intangible may discharge its obligation by paying the assignor until, but not after, the account debtor receives a notification, ~~authenticated~~ signed by the assignor or the assignee, that the amount due or to become due has been assigned and that payment is to be made to the assignee. After receipt of the notification, the account debtor may discharge its obligation by paying the assignee and may not discharge the obligation by paying the assignor.

(b) **[When notification ineffective.]** Subject to ~~subsection~~ subsections (h) and (*l*), notification is ineffective under subsection (a):

* * *

(c) **[Proof of assignment.]** Subject to ~~subsection~~ subsections (h) and (*l*), if requested by the account debtor, an assignee shall seasonably furnish reasonable proof that the assignment has been made. Unless the assignee complies, the account debtor may discharge its obligation by paying the assignor, even if the account debtor has received a notification under subsection (a).

(d) **[Term restricting assignment generally ineffective.]** In this subsection, "promissory note" includes a negotiable instrument that evidences chattel paper. Except as otherwise provided in subsections (e) and (k) and Sections 2A–303 and 9–407, and subject to subsection (h), a term in an agreement between an account debtor and an assignor or in a promissory note is ineffective to the extent that it:

* * *

(g) **[Subsection (b)(3) not waivable.]** Subject to ~~subsection~~ subsections (h) and (*l*), an account debtor may not waive or vary its option under subsection (b)(3).

* * *

(*l*) **[Inapplicability of certain subsections.]** Subsections (a), (b), (c), and (g) do not apply to a controllable account or controllable payment intangible.

Legislative Note:

In 2018, a new subsection (k) was added to Section 9–406. A state that has not previously enacted that subsection should consider doing so in connection with the enactment of the 2022 Amendments.

Official Comment

* * *

2. **Account Debtor's Right to Pay Assignor Until Notification.** Subsection (a) provides the general rule concerning an account debtor's right to pay the assignor until the account debtor receives appropriate notification. The revision makes clear that once the account debtor receives the notification, the account debtor cannot discharge its obligation by paying the assignor. It also makes explicit that payment to the assignor before notification, or payment to the assignee after notification, discharges the obligation. No change in meaning from ~~former~~ pre-1998 Section 9–318 is intended. Nothing in this section conditions the effectiveness of a notification on the identity of the person who gives it. An account debtor that doubts whether the right to payment has been assigned may avail itself of the procedures in subsection (c). See Comment 4. As to the rights and powers of an assignee generally, see Section 9–102(a)(7A) (defining "assignee"), (7B) (defining "assignor"), and Comment 2.b.1.

An effective notification under subsection (a) must be ~~authenticated~~ signed. This requirement normally could be satisfied by sending notification on the notifying person's letterhead or on a form on which the notifying person's name appears. In each case the printed name would be a symbol adopted by the notifying person for the purpose of identifying the person and adopting the notification. See Section ~~9–102~~ 1–201(b)(37) (defining ~~"authenticate"~~ "sign").

* * *

5. **Contractual Restrictions on Assignment.** ~~Former~~ Pre-1998 Section 9–318(4) rendered ineffective an agreement between an account debtor and an assignor which prohibited assignment of an account (whether outright or to secure an obligation) or prohibited a security assignment of a general intangible for the payment of

money due or to become due. Subsection (d) essentially follows ~~former~~ pre-1998 Section 9–318(4), but expands the rule of free assignability to chattel paper (subject to Sections 2A–303 and 9–407) and promissory notes and explicitly overrides both restrictions and prohibitions of assignment. The policies underlying the ineffectiveness of contractual restrictions under this section build on common-law developments that essentially have eliminated legal restrictions on assignments of rights to payment as security and other assignments of rights to payment such as accounts and chattel paper. Any that might linger for accounts and chattel paper are addressed by ~~new~~ subsection (f). See Comment 6.

The first sentence of subsection (d) ensures that the subsection applies to a negotiable instrument that would be a promissory note but for (i) the exclusion of writings that evidence chattel paper from the definition of "instrument" (Section 9–102(a)(47), as revised in 2022) and (ii) the definition of "promissory note" (Section 9–102(a)(65)) as a subset of "instrument." That sentence also ensures that subsection (d) applies to an obligor on such a negotiable instrument, even though the obligor is not an "account debtor" (Section 9–102(a)(3)). The sentence restores the scope of subsection (d) to apply to all obligations and obligors on chattel paper, as was the case prior to the revision of the definition of "instrument".

* * *

10. **Inapplicability to Certain Ownership Interests.** ~~This section does~~ Subsection (k) provides that subsections (d), (f), and (j) do not apply to a security interest in an ownership interest in a limited liability company, limited partnership, or general partnership, regardless of the name of the interest and whether the interest: (i) pertains to economic rights, governance rights, or both; (ii) arises under: (a) an operating agreement, the applicable limited liability company act, or both; or (b) a partnership agreement, the applicable partnership act, or both; or (iii) is owned by: (a) a member of a company or transferee or assignee of a member; or (b) a partner or a transferee or assignee of a partner; or (iv) comprises contractual, property, other rights, or some combination thereof. Ownership interests referred to in subsection (k) include interests in a series of a limited liability company, limited partnership, or general partnership, if the series is a "person" (Section 1–201(b)(27)).

11. **Controllable Accounts and Controllable payment intangibles.** For controllable accounts and controllable payment intangibles, subsection (*l*) recognizes that subsections (a), (b), (c) and (g) are replaced by analogous provisions in Section 12–106.

12. **"Signed" Replaces "Authenticated."** Consistent with the revised definition of "sign" in Section 1–201, the cognate term "signed" replaces the reference to "authenticated" in the pre-2022 text of this section.

§ 9–408.   Restrictions on Assignment of Promissory Notes, Health-Care-Insurance Receivables, and Certain General Intangibles Ineffective.

* * *

(g)   **["Promissory note."]** In this section, "promissory note" includes a negotiable instrument that evidences chattel paper.

* * *

Legislative Note: * * *

In 2018, a new subsection (f) was added to Section 9–408. A state that has not previously enacted that subsection should consider doing so in connection with the enactment of the 2022 Amendments.

Official Comment

* * *

11.   Subsection (g) ensures that this section applies to a negotiable instrument that would be a promissory note but for (i) the exclusion of writings that evidence chattel paper from the definition of "instrument" (Section 9–102(a)(47), as revised in 2022) and (ii) the definition of "promissory note" (Section 9–102(a)(65)) as a subset of "instrument." See Section 9–406, Comment 5.

§ 9–502.   Contents of Financing Statement; Record of Mortgage as Financing Statement; Time of Filing Financing Statement.

* * *

Official Comment

* * *

3.   **Debtor's Signature; Required Authorization.** * * *

* * *

Law other than this Article, including the law with respect to ratification of past acts, generally determines whether a person has the requisite authority to file a record under this Article. See Sections 1–103 and 9–509, Comment 3. However, under Section 9–509(b), the debtor's ~~authentication~~ signing of (or becoming bound by) a security agreement *ipso facto* constitutes the debtor's authorization of the filing of a financing statement covering the collateral described in the security agreement. The secured party need not obtain a separate authorization. *Amendment approved by the Permanent Editorial Board for Uniform Commercial Code December 31, 2001.*

* * *

§ 9–508.   Effectiveness of Financing Statement if New Debtor Becomes Bound by Security Agreement.

* * *

Official Comment

* * *

3.   **How New Debtor Becomes Bound.** Normally, a security interest is unenforceable unless the debtor has ~~authenticated~~ signed a security agreement describing the collateral. See Section 9–203(b). ~~New~~ Section 9–203(e) creates an exception, under which a security agreement entered into by one person is effective with respect to the property of another. This exception comes into play if a "new debtor" becomes bound as debtor by a security agreement entered into by another person (the "original debtor"). (The quoted terms are defined in Section 9–102.) If a new debtor does become bound, then the security agreement entered into by the original debtor satisfies the security-agreement requirement of Section 9–203(b)(3) as to existing or after-acquired property of the new debtor to the extent the property is described in the security agreement. In that case, no other agreement is necessary to make a security interest enforceable in that property. See Section 9–203(e).

* * *

§ 9–509.   Persons Entitled to File a Record.

(a)   **[Person entitled to file record.]** A person may file an initial financing statement, amendment that adds collateral covered by a financing statement, or amendment that adds a debtor to a financing statement only if:

(1)   the debtor authorizes the filing in ~~an authenticated~~ a signed record or pursuant to subsection (b) or (c); or

* * *

(b)   **[Security agreement as authorization.]** By ~~authenticating~~ signing or becoming bound as debtor by a security agreement, a debtor or new debtor authorizes the filing of an initial financing statement, and an amendment, covering:

* * *

Official Comment

* * *

3.   **Unauthorized Filings.** Records filed in the filing office do not require signatures for their effectiveness. Subsection (a)(1) substitutes for the debtor's signature on a financing statement the requirement that the debtor authorize in ~~an authenticated~~ a signed record the filing of an initial financing statement or an amendment that adds collateral. Also, under subsection (a)(1), if an amendment adds a debtor, the debtor who is added must authorize the amendment. A person who files an unauthorized record in violation of subsection (a)(1) is liable under Section 9–625(b) and (e) for actual and statutory damages. Of course, a filed financing statement

is ineffective to perfect a security interest if the filing is not authorized. See Section 9–510(a). Law other than this Article, including the law with respect to ratification of past acts, generally determines whether a person has the requisite authority to file a record under this section. See Sections 1–103, 9–502, Comment 3. This Article applies to other issues, such as the priority of a security interest perfected by the filing of a financing statement. See Section 9–322, Comment 4. *Amendment approved by the Permanent Editorial Board for Uniform Commercial Code December 31, 2001.*

4.   *Ipso Facto* **Authorization.** Under subsection (b), the ~~authentication~~ signing of a security agreement *ipso facto* constitutes the debtor's authorization of the filing of a financing statement covering the collateral described in the security agreement. The secured party need not obtain a separate authorization. Similarly, a new debtor's becoming bound by a security agreement *ipso facto* constitutes the new debtor's authorization of the filing of a financing statement covering the collateral described in the security agreement by which the new debtor has become bound. And, under subsection (c), the acquisition of collateral in which a security interest continues after disposition under Section 9–315(a)(1) *ipso facto* constitutes an authorization to file an initial financing statement against the person who acquired the collateral. The authorization to file an initial financing statement also constitutes an authorization to file a record covering actual proceeds of the original collateral, even if the security agreement is silent as to proceeds.

Example 1: Debtor ~~authenticates~~ signs a security agreement creating a security interest in Debtor's inventory in favor of Secured Party. Secured Party files a financing statement covering inventory and accounts. The financing statement is authorized insofar as it covers inventory and unauthorized insofar as it covers accounts. (Note, however, that the financing statement will be effective to perfect a security interest in accounts constituting proceeds of the inventory to the same extent as a financing statement covering only inventory.)

Example 2: Debtor ~~authenticates~~ signs a security agreement creating a security interest in Debtor's inventory in favor of Secured Party. Secured Party files a financing statement covering inventory. Debtor sells some inventory, deposits the buyer's payment into a deposit account, and withdraws the funds to purchase equipment. As long as the equipment can be traced to the inventory, the security interest continues in the equipment. See Section 9–315(a)(2). However, because the equipment was acquired with cash proceeds, the financing statement becomes ineffective to perfect the security interest in the equipment on the 21st day after the security interest attaches to the equipment unless Secured Party continues perfection beyond the 20-day period by filing a financing statement against the equipment or amending the filed financing statement to cover equipment. See Section 9–315(d). Debtor's ~~authentication~~ signing of the security agreement authorizes the filing of an initial financing statement or amendment covering the equipment, which is "property that becomes collateral under Section 9–315(a)(2)." See Section 9–509(b)(2).

* * *

6.   **Amendments; Termination Statements Authorized by Debtor.** Most amendments may not be filed unless the secured party of record, as determined under Section 9–511, authorizes the filing. See subsection (d)(1). However, under subsection (d)(2), the authorization of the secured party of record is not required for the filing of a termination statement if the secured party of record failed to send or file a termination statement as required by Section 9–513, the debtor authorizes it to be filed, and the termination statement so indicates. An authorization to file a record under subsection (d) is effective even if the authorization is not in ~~an authenticated~~ a signed record. Compare subsection (a)(1). However, both the person filing the record and the person giving the authorization may wish to obtain and retain a record indicating that the filing was authorized.

* * *

9.   <u>**"Signed" and "Signing" Replace "Authenticated" and "Authenticating."** Consistent with the revised definition of "sign" in Section 1–201, the cognate terms "signed" and "signing" replace the references to "authenticated" and "authenticating" in the pre-2022 text of this section.</u>

§ 9–513.   Termination Statement.

* * *

(b)   **[Time for compliance with subsection (a).]** To comply with subsection (a), a secured party shall cause the secured party of record to file the termination statement:

* * *

(2)   if earlier, within 20 days after the secured party receives ~~an authenticated~~ a signed demand from a debtor.

(c)   **[Other collateral.]** In cases not governed by subsection (a), within 20 days after a secured party receives ~~an authenticated~~ a signed demand from a debtor, the secured party shall cause the secured party of record for a financing statement to send to the debtor a termination statement for the financing statement or file the termination statement in the filing office if:

* * *

Official Comment

* * *

2.   **Duty to File or Send.** * * *

* * *

References to a "termination statement" in this section and in Part 5 generally should be interpreted functionally, based on the purposes of the termination. A termination statement includes any amendment that meets the definition of that term by containing an indication that the amendment "is a termination statement" or that the identified financing statement "is no longer effective." Section 9–102(a)(80). The amendment may terminate the effectiveness of a financing statement in whole or in part. For example, if a person did not authorize the filing of a financing statement against it as debtor, under subsection (a)(2) and (c)(4) the person may demand that the financing statement be terminated *as to that person*, even if the financing statement remains of record and effective as to one or more other persons named as debtors in the financing statement. Such a termination statement may take the form of an amendment that deletes the person as a debtor. Similarly, if a person authorized the filing of a financing statement as to some collateral but not as to other property identified as collateral on the financing statement, the person may demand that the financing statement be terminated *as to the unauthorized identified collateral*, even if the financing statement remains of record and effective as to other identified collateral. Such a termination statement may take the form of an amendment that deletes the unauthorized identified collateral from coverage of the financing statement. Even if such amendments do not indicate explicitly that they are termination statements, they would nonetheless indicate that the financing statement "is no longer effective" to the extent specified and fall within the definition of "termination statement."

3.   **"Bogus" Filings.** A secured party's duty to send a termination statement arises when the secured party "receives" ~~an authenticated~~ a signed demand from the debtor. In the case of an unauthorized financing statement, the person named as debtor in the financing statement may have no relationship with the named secured party and no reason to know the secured party's address. Inasmuch as the address in the financing statement is "held out by [the person named as secured party in the financing statement] as the place for receipt of such communications [i.e., communications relating to security interests]," the putative secured party is deemed to have "received" a notification delivered to that address. See Section 1–202(e). If a termination statement is not forthcoming, the person named as debtor itself may authorize the filing of a termination statement, which will be effective if it indicates that the person authorized it to be filed. See Sections 9–509(d)(2), ~~9–510(c)~~ 9–510(a).

* * *

6.   **"Signed" Replaces "Authenticated."** Consistent with the revised definition of "sign" in Section 1–201, the cognate term "signed" replaces the references to "authenticated" in the pre-2022 text of this section.

§ 9–516.   What Constitutes Filing; Effectiveness of Filing.

* * *

Official Comment

* * *

4.   Method or Medium of Communication. Rejection pursuant to subsection (b)(1) for failure to communicate a record properly should be understood to mean noncompliance with procedures relating to security, ~~authentication~~ signing, or other communication-related requirements that the filing office may impose. Subsection (b)(1) does not authorize a filing office to impose additional substantive requirements. See Section 9–520, Comment 2.

* * *

APPENDIX F

§ 9–601. Rights After Default; Judicial Enforcement; Consignor or Buyer of Accounts, Chattel Paper, Payment Intangibles, or Promissory Notes.

* * *

(b) **[Rights and duties of secured party in possession or control.]** A secured party in possession of collateral or control of collateral under Section 7–106, 9–104, 9–105, 9–105A, 9–106, or 9–107, or 9–107A has the rights and duties provided in Section 9–207.

* * *

§ 9–602. Waiver and Variance of Rights and Duties.

* * *

Official Comment

* * *

5. **Certain Post-Default Waivers.** Section 9–624 permits post-default waivers in limited circumstances. These waivers must be made in agreements that are ~~authenticated~~ signed. Under Section 1–201, an "'agreement' means the bargain of the parties in fact." In considering waivers under Section 9–624 and analogous agreements in other contexts, courts should carefully scrutinize putative agreements that appear in records that also address many additional or unrelated matters.

§ 9–605. Unknown Debtor or Secondary Obligor.

A (a) **[In general: No duty owed by secured party.]** Except as provided in subsection (b), a secured party does not owe a duty based on its status as secured party:

* * *

(b) **[Exception: Secured party owes duty to debtor or obligor.]** A secured party owes a duty based on its status as a secured party to a person if, at the time the secured party obtains control of collateral that is a controllable account, controllable electronic record, or controllable payment intangible or at the time the security interest attaches to the collateral, whichever is later:

(1) the person is a debtor or obligor; and

(2) the secured party knows that the information in subsection (a)(1)(A), (B), or (C) relating to the person is not provided by the collateral, a record attached to or logically associated with the collateral, or the system in which the collateral is recorded.

Official Comment

* * *

2. **Duties to Unknown Persons and Limitation of Liability.** This section relieves a secured party from duties owed to a debtor or obligor if the secured party does not know about the debtor or obligor. Similarly, it relieves a secured party from duties owed to a secured party or lienholder who has filed a financing statement against the debtor if the secured party does not know about the debtor. Section 9–628(a) and (b) provide analogous limitations of liability. For example, a secured party may be unaware that the original debtor has sold the collateral subject to the security interest and that the new owner has become the debtor. If so, the secured party owes no duty to the new owner (debtor) or to a secured party who has filed a financing statement against the new owner. ~~This section should be read in conjunction with the exculpatory provisions in Section 9–628.~~ Note that this section relieves a secured party not only from duties arising under this Article but also from duties arising under other law by virtue of the secured party's status as such under this Article, unless the other law otherwise provides.

This section should be read in conjunction with the limitations on liability contained in the exculpatory provisions in subsections (a), (b), and (c) of Section 9–628. Without this group of provisions, a secured party could incur liability to unknown persons and under circumstances that would not allow the secured party to protect itself. The broadened definition of the term "debtor" underscores the need for these provisions. For example, as noted above, a debtor may dispose of collateral subject to a security interest, resulting in the transferee becoming a debtor, but the secured party may have no knowledge of the disposition or that the transferee has become a debtor. In that situation the secured party will have no means of giving notice to or accounting to the transferee debtor. Sections 9–605 and 9–628 contemplate such situations by relieving the secured party of its duties to the debtor and limiting the secured party's liability to the debtor.

3. **Exceptions to Relief from Duties and Limitation of Liability.** In some cases, lenders may extend secured credit without knowing, or having the ability to discover, the identity of their borrowers. Pre-2022 Sections 9–605(a) and 9–628(a) and (b) would excuse these secured parties from having duties to their debtors and obligors, including, for example, the duty to notify the debtor or secondary obligor before disposing of the collateral and the duty to account to the debtor for any surplus arising from a disposition, and would limit the secured parties' liability to their debtors and obligors. In many cases these debtors and obligors may be aware that their identities are unknown to their secured parties. By failing to make their identities and contact information known, these debtors and obligors may be impairing the ability of their secured parties to comply with their duties under Article 9. However, such debtor complicity notwithstanding, if secured parties were relieved of their duties in these circumstances, it would conflict with the policy of Section 9–602, which prohibits a waiver or variance of many rights of debtors and obligors and duties of secured parties.

Sections 9–605(b) and 9–628(f) reflect the policy that a secured party should not be free to avoid statutory duties or absolve itself from liability to a debtor or obligor when the secured party knows that the collateral, records attached to or logically associated with the collateral, and the system in which the collateral is recorded do not provide the secured party with the information necessary to fulfill its statutory duties. As discussed in the following paragraph, the secured party's knowledge that it may not be able to comply with its duties enables the secured party to protect itself from being in breach of these duties. (A person has knowledge of or knows a fact if it has "actual knowledge." Section 1–202(b).) The exceptions from the exculpatory protections otherwise afforded to secured parties are determined by the secured party's knowledge at the later of the time the secured party obtains control of a controllable account, controllable electronic record, or controllable payment intangible or the time that the security interest attaches to the collateral.

Obtaining control or attachment of the security interest serves as a rough proxy for the context in which a secured party may know that it may be unable to comply with its duties, usually because the transferor is pseudonymous. The carve-out from the exculpatory protection is limited to duties owed to and liability to a debtor—the transferor of a controllable account, controllable electronic record, or controllable payment intangible over which the secured party obtains control—or obligor. The secured party in such situations could protect itself by choosing not to enter into a transaction in which it might be unable to comply with its statutory duties or by conditioning its participation on disclosure of the debtor's or obligor's identity and contact information. Ideally, systems providing for the transfer of controllable electronic records would provide mechanisms that would permit compliance with such duties (such as methods of communication and making payments that would preserve a debtor's or obligor's pseudonymity, where that is desired). The amendments to Sections 9–605 and 9–628 provide incentives for system design that would allow for compliance with Article 9 duties.

Secured parties that enter into transactions with knowledge that they may not be able to comply with their Article 9 duties do so at their own peril. Of course, if a secured party possesses, or can obtain, the information necessary to comply with its duties, there is no need for the exculpation from those duties. Note, however, that the limitation on a secured party's relief from duties and liability relates only to secured transactions involving controllable accounts, controllable electronic records, or controllable payment intangibles. Designing systems for these assets that would afford secured parties with opportunities to comply with their Article 9 duties, as suggested above, could eliminate the risks to secured parties and also provide for the protection of debtors' and obligors' rights.

§ 9–608. Application of Proceeds of Collection or Enforcement; Liability for Deficiency and Right to Surplus.

(a) **[Application of proceeds, surplus, and deficiency if obligation secured.]** If a security interest or agricultural lien secures payment or performance of an obligation, the following rules apply:

(1) A secured party shall apply or pay over for application the cash proceeds of collection or enforcement under Section 9–607 in the following order to:

(A) the reasonable expenses of collection and enforcement and, to the extent provided for by agreement and not prohibited by law, reasonable attorney's fees and legal expenses incurred by the secured party;

(B) the satisfaction of obligations secured by the security interest or agricultural lien under which the collection or enforcement is made; and

(C)   the satisfaction of obligations secured by any subordinate security interest in or other lien on the collateral subject to the security interest or agricultural lien under which the collection or enforcement is made if the secured party receives ~~an authenticated~~ a signed demand for proceeds before distribution of the proceeds is completed.

* * *

Official Comment

* * *

6.   **"Signed" Replaces "Authenticated."** Consistent with the revised definition of "sign" in Section 1–201, the cognate term "signed" replaces the reference to "authenticated" in the pre-2022 text of this section.

§ 9–610.   Disposition of Collateral After Default.

* * *

Official Comment

* * *

9.   **"Recognized Market."** A "recognized market," as used in subsection (c)(2), ~~and~~ Section 9–611(d), and Section 9–627(b)(1) and (2), is one in which the items sold are fungible and ~~prices are not subject to individual negotiation. For example, the New York Stock Exchange is a recognized market. A market in which prices are individually negotiated or the items are not fungible is not a recognized market, even if the items are the subject of widely disseminated price guides or are disposed of through dealer auctions.~~ which generally produces market prices that are not lower than those that would be expected to result from, as applicable, (i) commercially reasonable dispositions to persons other than the secured party, (ii) commercially reasonable dispositions made with otherwise required notifications to the debtor or other affected persons, or (iii) dispositions otherwise made in a commercially reasonable manner. (As used here, "fungible" items are those that are considered interchangeable in the relevant market and not only items that are strictly "identical" to the other items.) The intended goals of the recognized market exceptions are to ensure that neither the debtor nor other affected parties would be disadvantaged by the special treatment given to recognized markets and to facilitate the efficiencies and cost savings that the special treatment may provide. The purpose of including in subsection (c)(2) collateral that is "the subject of widely distributed standard price quotations" and the criteria for determining whether price quotations meet this standard in subsection (c)(2) are the same as for a recognized market, although the availability of such standard price quotations may be based on, but distributed independently of, a "market" in which acquisitions and dispositions are made. Although a recognized market need not be subject to direct or indirect (e.g., self-regulatory) regulation or supervision, the existence of regulatory requirements or guidelines that are designed to arrive at prices consistent with those contemplated by subsection (c)(2) may provide useful guidance for applying the regulated market standard.

Traditionally, it has been understood that a market in which prices are individually negotiated is not a recognized market, even if the items are the subject of widely disseminated price guides (such as the Kelly Blue Book for automobiles) or are disposed of through specialized auctions (such as those conducted for dealers in livestock and automobiles). However, this does not suggest that, for example, dispositions at prices reflected in such guides or of livestock or automobiles at such auctions could not be commercially reasonable.

The New York Stock Exchange, NASDAQ, the Chicago Mercantile Exchange, and ICE Futures U.S., Inc. are examples of recognized markets. Such exchanges match buy and sell orders submitted by or on behalf of buyers and sellers that are not typically known to each other and do not involve individual negotiations. Other parties, such as inter-dealer brokers in the on-the-run U.S. Treasury market and broker-dealers in the equities market, often operate similar trading facilities that would likewise not involve known buyers or sellers or individual negotiations and may constitute recognized markets. These markets provide for robust trading with active bidding on fungible assets. There is no reason to believe that prices obtained on these markets would be less favorable to debtors, other obligors, and other interested persons than if collateral were disposed of in an off-market public or private disposition.

Trading environments generally referred to as "over-the-counter" or "OTC" markets, however, typically have involved prospective buyers and sellers that can know each other and have direct communication in order to make trades. Unlike typical exchanges, OTC markets normally do involve the individual negotiation of a price. See Carl S. Bjerre, *Investment Securities*, 71 Bus. Law. 1311, 1316–17 (2016) (contrasting exchanges and typical OTC markets for equity securities and explaining that OTC markets have tended to feature thinner markets with less liquidity and more variability of pricing).

In considering the recognized market exceptions, it is important to appreciate that recognized markets and other systems that produce equivalent "widely distributed standard price quotations" are not limited to traditional exchanges, such as those mentioned above. In particular, the exchange-OTC dichotomy no longer offers such a reliable, bright-line test for determining status as a recognized market or as a source of widely distributed standard price quotations. To be sure, some OTC markets do not qualify for the exceptions. However, recent years have witnessed a variety of new trading platforms, the use of new technologies, and new sources of providing and consuming information. There now exist markets, in particular for debt securities (including United States Treasury securities), that might be classified as OTC markets under the traditional taxonomy, but which qualify for the exceptions as recognized markets or as sources of data for widely distributed standard price quotations. Market participants rely on prices provided by these markets to the same extent and for the same purposes (including in connection with default and enforcement of security interests) as they rely on prices generated by traditional securities and commodities exchanges. These prices are widely available from business publications and online sources as well as from private subscription-based service providers. It can safely be assumed that these financial markets and the data that they provide to the public will continue to evolve. The touchstone for determining whether a market structure is a recognized market or one that produces equivalent price quotations is a functional one. It is not based on the "type" of market (e.g., "exchange," "OTC," or other classification). It is based on whether the market or distribution of price quotations provides reliable and trusted data on prices consistent with the purposes of subsection (c)(2) and the corresponding provisions of Sections 9–611 and 9–627.

§ 9–611. Notification Before Disposition of Collateral.

(a) **["Notification date."]** In this section, "notification date" means the earlier of the date on which:

(1) a secured party sends to the debtor and any secondary obligor ~~an authenticated~~ a signed notification of disposition; or

* * *

(b) **[Notification of disposition required.]** Except as otherwise provided in subsection (d), a secured party that disposes of collateral under Section 9–610 shall send to the persons specified in subsection (c) a reasonable ~~authenticated~~ signed notification of disposition.

(c) **[Persons to be notified.]** To comply with subsection (b), the secured party shall send ~~an authenticated~~ a signed notification of disposition to:

* * *

(3) if the collateral is other than consumer goods:

(A) any other person from which the secured party has received, before the notification date, ~~an authenticated~~ a signed notification of a claim of an interest in the collateral;

(B) any other secured party or lienholder that, 10 days before the notification date, held a security interest in or other lien on the collateral perfected by the filing of a financing statement that:

(i) identified the collateral;

(ii) was indexed under the debtor's name as of that date; and

(iii) was filed in the office in which to file a financing statement against the debtor covering the collateral as of that date; and

(C) any other secured party that, 10 days before the notification date, held a security interest in the collateral perfected by compliance with a statute, regulation, or treaty described in Section 9–311(a).

* * *

(e) **[Compliance with subsection (c)(3)(B).]** A secured party complies with the requirement for notification prescribed by subsection (c)(3)(B) if:

* * *

(2)   before the notification date, the secured party:

    (A)   did not receive a response to the request for information; or

    (B)   received a response to the request for information and sent ~~an authenticated~~ a signed notification of disposition to each secured party or other lienholder named in that response whose financing statement covered the collateral.

Official Comment

* * *

2.   **Reasonable Notification.** This section requires a secured party who wishes to dispose of collateral under Section 9–610 to send "a reasonable ~~authenticated~~ signed notification of disposition" to specified interested persons, subject to certain exceptions. The notification must be reasonable as to the manner in which it is sent, its timeliness (i.e., a reasonable time before the disposition is to take place), and its content. See Sections 9–612 (timeliness of notification), 9–613 (contents of notification generally), 9–614 (contents of notification in consumer-goods transactions).

* * *

5.   ~~**Authentication**~~ **Signature Requirement.** Subsections (b), ~~and~~ (c), and (e) explicitly provide that ~~a notification of disposition~~ notifications must be ~~"authenticated."~~ "signed." Some cases read ~~former~~ pre-1998 Section 9–504(3) as validating oral notification. Consistent with the revised definition of "sign" in Section 1–201, the cognate term "signed" replaces the references to "authenticated" in the pre-2022 text of this section.

* * *

7.   **Recognized Market; Perishable Collateral.** ~~New subsection~~ Subsection (d) makes it clear that there is no obligation to give notification of a disposition in the case of perishable collateral or collateral customarily sold on a recognized market (e.g., marketable securities). ~~Former Section 9–504(3) might be read (incorrectly) to relieve the secured party from its duty to notify a debtor but not from its duty to notify other secured parties in connection with dispositions of such collateral.~~ As to what constitutes a recognized market, see Section 9–610, Comment 9.

* * *

9.   **Waiver.** A debtor or secondary obligor may waive the right to notification under this section only by a post-default ~~authenticated~~ signed agreement. See Section 9–624(a).

* * *

§ 9–612.   Timeliness of Notification Before Disposition of Collateral.

* * *

Official Comment

* * *

2.   **Reasonable Notification.** Section 9–611(b) requires the secured party to send a "reasonable ~~authenticated~~ signed notification." Under that section, as under ~~former~~ pre-1998 Section 9–504(3), one aspect of a reasonable notification is its timeliness. This generally means that the notification must be sent at a reasonable time in advance of the date of a public disposition or the date after which a private disposition is to be made. A notification that is sent so near to the disposition date that a notified person could not be expected to act on or take account of the notification would be unreasonable.

3.   **Timeliness of Notification: Safe Harbor.** The 10-day notice period in subsection (b) is intended to be a "safe harbor" and not a minimum requirement. To qualify for the "safe harbor" the notification must be sent after default. A notification also must be sent in a commercially reasonable manner. See Section 9–611(b) ("reasonable ~~authenticated~~ signed notification"). These requirements prevent a secured party from taking advantage of the "safe harbor" by, for example, giving the debtor a notification at the time of the original extension of credit or sending the notice by surface mail to a debtor overseas.

§ 9–613. Contents and Form of Notification Before Disposition of Collateral: General.

(a) [Contents and form of notification.] Except in a consumer-goods transaction, the following rules apply:

(1) The contents of a notification of disposition are sufficient if the notification:

    (A) describes the debtor and the secured party;

    (B) describes the collateral that is the subject of the intended disposition;

    (C) states the method of intended disposition;

    (D) states that the debtor is entitled to an accounting of the unpaid indebtedness and states the charge, if any, for an accounting; and

    (E) states the time and place of a public disposition or the time after which any other disposition is to be made.

(2) Whether the contents of a notification that lacks any of the information specified in paragraph (1) are nevertheless sufficient is a question of fact.

(3) The contents of a notification providing substantially the information specified in paragraph (1) are sufficient, even if the notification includes:

    (A) information not specified by that paragraph; or

    (B) minor errors that are not seriously misleading.

(4) A particular phrasing of the notification is not required.

(5) The following form of notification and the form appearing in Section ~~9–614(3)~~ 9–614(a)(3), when completed in accordance with the instructions in subsection (b) and Section 9–614(b), each provides sufficient information:

NOTIFICATION OF DISPOSITION OF COLLATERAL

~~To: [*Name of debtor, obligor, or other person to which he notification is sent*]~~

~~From: [*Name, address, and telephone number of secured party*]~~

~~Name of Debtor(s): [*Include only if debtor(s) are not an addressee*]~~

  ~~[*For a public disposition:*]~~

  ~~We will sell [or lease or license, as applicable] the [*describe collateral*] [to the highest qualified bidder] in public as follows:~~

  ~~Day and Date: ____~~

  ~~Time: ____~~

  ~~Place: ____~~

  ~~[*For a private disposition:*]~~

  ~~We will sell [or lease or license, *as applicable*] the [*describe collateral*] privately sometime after [*day and date*].~~

  ~~You are entitled to an accounting of the unpaid indebtedness secured by the property that we intend to sell [or lease or license, *as applicable*] [for a charge of $____]. You may request an accounting by calling us at [*telephone number*]~~

~~**[End of Form]**~~

NOTIFICATION OF DISPOSITION OF COLLATERAL

To: (Name of debtor, obligor, or other person to which the notification is sent)

From: (Name, address, and telephone number of secured party)

  {1}   Name of any debtor that is not an addressee: (Name of each debtor)

{2}　We will sell (describe collateral) (to the highest qualified bidder) at public sale. A sale could include a lease or license. The sale will be held as follows:

(Date)

(Time)

(Place)

{3}　We will sell (describe collateral) at private sale sometime after (date). A sale could include a lease or license.

{4}　You are entitled to an accounting of the unpaid indebtedness secured by the property that we intend to sell or, as applicable, lease or license.

{5}　If you request an accounting you must pay a charge of $ (amount).

{6}　You may request an accounting by calling us at (telephone number).

[End of Form]

(b)　**[Instructions for form of notification.]** The following instructions apply to the form of notification in subsection (a)(5):

(1)　The instructions in this subsection refer to the numbers in braces before items in the form of notification in subsection (a)(5). Do not include the numbers or braces in the notification. The numbers and braces are used only for the purpose of these instructions.

(2)　Include and complete item {1} only if there is a debtor that is not an addressee of the notification and list the name or names.

(3)　Include and complete either item {2}, if the notification relates to a public disposition of the collateral, or item {3}, if the notification relates to a private disposition of the collateral. If item {2} is included, include the words "to the highest qualified bidder" only if applicable.

(4)　Include and complete items {4} and {6}.

(5)　Include and complete item {5} only if the sender will charge the recipient for an accounting.

Official Comment

* * *

2.　**Contents of Notification.** To comply with the "reasonable ~~authenticated~~ signed notification" requirement of Section 9–611(b), the contents of a notification must be reasonable. * * *

* * *

3.　**[Style Changes in Safe-Harbor Form and Medium Neutrality]** No change in substance is intended by the changes in style to the form provided in paragraph (5) of the pre-2022 text of this section. However, the presentation and explanation of how to use the form has been simplified and clarified.

§ 9–614.　Contents and Form of Notification Before Disposition of Collateral: Consumer-Goods Transaction.

(a)　**[Contents and form of notification.]** In a consumer-goods transaction, the following rules apply:

(1)　A notification of disposition must provide the following information:

(A)　the information specified in Section ~~9–613(1)~~ 9–613(a)(1);

(B)　a description of any liability for a deficiency of the person to which the notification is sent;

(C)　a telephone number from which the amount that must be paid to the secured party to redeem the collateral under Section 9–623 is available; and

(D)　a telephone number or mailing address from which additional information concerning the disposition and the obligation secured is available.

(2) A particular phrasing of the notification is not required.

(3) The following form of notification, when completed <u>in accordance with the instructions in subsection (b)</u>, provides sufficient information:

[Name and address of secured party]

[Date]

NOTICE OF OUR PLAN TO SELL PROPERTY

[*Name and address of any obligor who is also a debtor*]

Subject: [*Identification of Transaction*]

We have your [*describe collateral*], because you broke promises in our agreement.

[*For a public disposition:*]

We will sell [*describe collateral*] at public sale. A sale could include a lease or license. The sale will be held as follows:

 Date: ____

 Time: ____

 Place: ____

You may attend the sale and bring bidders if you want.

[*For a private disposition:*]

We will sell [*describe collateral*] at private sale sometime after [*date*]. A sale could include a lease or license.

The money that we get from the sale (after paying our costs) will reduce the amount you owe. If we get less money than you owe, you [*will or will not, as applicable*] still owe us the difference. If we get more money than you owe, you will get the extra money, unless we must pay it to someone else.

You can get the property back at any time before we sell it by paying us the full amount you owe (not just the past due payments), including our expenses. To learn the exact amount you must pay, call us at [telephone number].

If you want us to explain to you in writing how we have figured the amount that you owe us, you may call us at [*telephone number*] [or write us at [*secured party's address*]] and request a written explanation. [We will charge you $____ for the explanation if we sent you another written explanation of the amount you owe us within the last six months.]

If you need more information about the sale call us at [*telephone number*]] [or write us at [*secured party's address*]].

We are sending this notice to the following other people who have an interest in [*describe collateral*] or who owe money under your agreement:

[*Names of all other debtors and obligors, if any*]

[End of Form]

(Name and address of secured party)

(Date)

NOTICE OF OUR PLAN TO SELL PROPERTY

(Name and address of any obligor who is also a debtor)

Subject: (Identify transaction)

 We have your (describe collateral), because you broke promises in our agreement.

 {1} We will sell (describe collateral) at public sale. A sale could include a lease or license. The sale will be held as follows:

(Date)

(Time)

(Place)

You may attend the sale and bring bidders if you want.

{2} We will sell (describe collateral) at private sale sometime after (date). A sale could include a lease or license.

{3} The money that we get from the sale, after paying our costs, will reduce the amount you owe. If we get less money than you owe, you (will or will not, as applicable) still owe us the difference. If we get more money than you owe, you will get the extra money, unless we must pay it to someone else.

{4} You can get the property back at any time before we sell it by paying us the full amount you owe, not just the past due payments, including our expenses. To learn the exact amount you must pay, call us at (telephone number).

{5} If you want us to explain to you in (writing) (writing or in (description of electronic record)) (description of electronic record) how we have figured the amount that you owe us, {6} call us at (telephone number) (or) (write us at (secured party's address)) (or contact us by (description of electronic communication method)) {7} and request (a written explanation) (a written explanation or an explanation in (description of electronic record)) (an explanation in (description of electronic record)).

{8} We will charge you $ (amount) for the explanation if we sent you another written explanation of the amount you owe us within the last six months.

{9} If you need more information about the sale (call us at (telephone number)) (or) (write us at (secured party's address)) (or contact us by (description of electronic communication method)).

{10} We are sending this notice to the following other people who have an interest in (describe collateral) or who owe money under your agreement:

(Names of all other debtors and obligors, if any)

[End of Form]

* * *

(b) **[Instructions for form of notification.]** The following instructions apply to the form of notification in subsection (a)(3):

(1) The instructions in this subsection refer to the numbers in braces before items in the form of notification in subsection (a)(3). Do not include the numbers or braces in the notification. The numbers and braces are used only for the purpose of these instructions.

(2) Include and complete either item {1}, if the notification relates to a public disposition of the collateral, or item {2}, if the notification relates to a private disposition of the collateral.

(3) Include and complete items {3}, {4}, {5}, {6}, and {7}.

(4) In item {5}, include and complete any one of the three alternative methods for the explanation—writing, writing or electronic record, or electronic record.

(5) In item {6}, include the telephone number. In addition, the sender may include and complete either or both of the two additional alternative methods of communication—writing or electronic communication—for the recipient of the notification to communicate with the sender. Neither of the two additional methods of communication is required to be included.

(6) In item {7}, include and complete the method or methods for the explanation—writing, writing or electronic record, or electronic record—included in item {5}.

(7) Include and complete item {8} only if a written explanation is included in item {5} as a method for communicating the explanation and the sender will charge the recipient for another written explanation.

(8) In item {9}, include either the telephone number or the address or both the telephone number and the address. In addition, the sender may include and complete the additional method of communication—electronic communication—for the recipient of the notification to communicate with the sender. The additional method of electronic communication is not required to be included.

(9) If item {10} does not apply, insert "None" after "agreement:".

Official Comment

* * *

4. **[Style Changes in Safe-Harbor Form and Medium Neutrality]** No change in substance is intended by the changes in style to the form provided in paragraph (3) of the pre-2022 text of this section, except that in furtherance of medium neutrality references to "electronic record" and "electronic communication method" have been added to the form. However, the presentation and explanation of how to use the form has been simplified and clarified.

§ 9–615. Application of Proceeds of Disposition; Liability for Deficiency and Right to Surplus.

(a) **[Application of proceeds.]** A secured party shall apply or pay over for application the cash proceeds of disposition under Section 9–610 in the following order to:

* * *

(3) the satisfaction of obligations secured by any subordinate security interest in or other subordinate lien on the collateral if:

(A) the secured party receives from the holder of the subordinate security interest or other lien ~~an authenticated~~ a signed demand for proceeds before distribution of the proceeds is completed; and

(B) in a case in which a consignor has an interest in the collateral, the subordinate security interest or other lien is senior to the interest of the consignor; and

(4) a secured party that is a consignor of the collateral if the secured party receives from the consignor ~~an authenticated~~ a signed demand for proceeds before distribution of the proceeds is completed.

* * *

Official Comment

* * *

8. **"Signed" Replaces "Authenticated."** Consistent with the revised definition of "sign" in Section 1–201, the cognate term "signed" replaces the reference to "authenticated" in the pre-2022 text of this section.

§ 9–616. Explanation of Calculation of Surplus or Deficiency.

(a) **[Definitions.]** In this section:

(1) "Explanation" means a ~~writing~~ record that:

(A) states the amount of the surplus or deficiency;

(B) provides an explanation in accordance with subsection (c) of how the secured party calculated the surplus or deficiency;

(C) states, if applicable, that future debits, credits, charges, including additional credit service charges or interest, rebates, and expenses may affect the amount of the surplus or deficiency; and

(D) provides a telephone number or mailing address from which additional information concerning the transaction is available.

(2) "Request" means a record:

(A)   ~~authenticated~~ <u>signed</u> by a debtor or consumer obligor;

(B)   requesting that the recipient provide an explanation; and

(C)   sent after disposition of the collateral under Section 9–610.

(b)   **[Explanation of calculation.]** In a consumer-goods transaction in which the debtor is entitled to a surplus or a consumer obligor is liable for a deficiency under Section 9–615, the secured party shall:

(1)   send an explanation to the debtor or consumer obligor, as applicable, after the disposition and:

(A)   before or when the secured party accounts to the debtor and pays any surplus or first makes ~~written~~ demand <u>in a record</u> on the consumer obligor after the disposition for payment of the deficiency; and

(B)   within 14 days after receipt of a request; or

* * *

(c)   **[Required information.]** To comply with subsection (a)(1)(B), ~~a writing~~ <u>an explanation</u> must provide the following information in the following order:

* * *

Official Comment

* * *

2.   **Duty to Send Information Concerning Surplus or Deficiency.** This section reflects the view that, in every consumer-goods transaction, the debtor or obligor is entitled to know the amount of a surplus or deficiency and the basis upon which the surplus or deficiency was calculated. Under subsection (b)(1), a secured party is obligated to provide this information (an "explanation," defined in subsection (a)(1)) no later than the time that it accounts for and pays a surplus or the time of its first ~~written attempt~~ <u>demand in a record in an attempt</u> to collect the deficiency. The obligor need not make a request for an accounting in order to receive an explanation. A secured party who does not attempt to collect a deficiency in ~~writing~~ <u>a demand in a record</u> or account for and pay a surplus has no obligation to send an explanation under subsection (b)(1) and, consequently, cannot be liable for noncompliance.

A debtor or secondary obligor need not wait until the secured party commences ~~written~~ collection efforts in <u>a demand in a record in</u> order to receive an explanation of how a deficiency or surplus was calculated. Subsection (b)(1)(B) obliges the secured party to send an explanation within 14 days after it receives a "request" (defined in subsection (a)(2)).

* * *

5.   **"Signed" Replaces "Authenticated"; Medium Neutrality.** <u>Consistent with the revised definition of "sign" in Section 1–201, the cognate term "signed" replaces the reference to "authenticated" in the pre-2022 text of this section. In furtherance of medium neutrality, the reference in the pre-2022 text of this section to a "written demand" has been replaced by a reference to a "demand in a record" and the reference to a "writing" has been replaced by a reference to a "record."</u>

§ 9–619.   Transfer of Record or Legal Title.

(a)   **["Transfer statement."]** In this section, "transfer statement" means a record ~~authenticated~~ <u>signed</u> by a secured party stating:

* * *

Official Comment

* * *

4.   **"Signed" Replaces "Authenticated."** <u>Consistent with the revised definition of "sign" in Section 1–201, the cognate term "signed" replaces the reference to "authenticated" in the pre-2022 text of this section.</u>

§ 9–620. **Acceptance of Collateral in Full or Partial Satisfaction of Obligation; Compulsory Disposition of Collateral.**

(a) **[Conditions to acceptance in satisfaction.]** Except as otherwise provided in subsection (g), a secured party may accept collateral in full or partial satisfaction of the obligation it secures only if:

* * *

(2) the secured party does not receive, within the time set forth in subsection (d), a notification of objection to the proposal ~~authenticated~~ signed by:

(A) a person to which the secured party was required to send a proposal under Section 9–621; or

(B) any other person, other than the debtor, holding an interest in the collateral subordinate to the security interest that is the subject of the proposal;

* * *

(b) **[Purported acceptance ineffective.]** A purported or apparent acceptance of collateral under this section is ineffective unless:

(1) the secured party consents to the acceptance in ~~an authenticated~~ a signed record or sends a proposal to the debtor; and

* * *

(c) **[Debtor's consent.]** For purposes of this section:

(1) a debtor consents to an acceptance of collateral in partial satisfaction of the obligation it secures only if the debtor agrees to the terms of the acceptance in a record ~~authenticated~~ signed after default; and

(2) a debtor consents to an acceptance of collateral in full satisfaction of the obligation it secures only if the debtor agrees to the terms of the acceptance in a record ~~authenticated~~ signed after default or the secured party:

(A) sends to the debtor after default a proposal that is unconditional or subject only to a condition that collateral not in the possession of the secured party be preserved or maintained;

(B) in the proposal, proposes to accept collateral in full satisfaction of the obligation it secures; and

(C) does not receive a notification of objection ~~authenticated~~ signed by the debtor within 20 days after the proposal is sent.

* * *

(f) **[Compliance with mandatory disposition requirement.]** To comply with subsection (e), the secured party shall dispose of the collateral:

* * *

(2) within any longer period to which the debtor and all secondary obligors have agreed in an agreement to that effect entered into and ~~authenticated~~ signed after default.

* * *

Official Comment

* * *

3. **Conditions to Effective Acceptance.** Subsection (a) contains the conditions necessary to the effectiveness of an acceptance of collateral. Subsection (a)(1) requires the debtor's consent. Under subsections (c)(1) and (c)(2), the debtor may consent by agreeing to the acceptance in writing after default. Subsection (c)(2) contains an alternative method by which to satisfy the debtor's-consent condition in subsection (a)(1). It follows the proposal-and-objection model found in ~~former~~ pre-1998 Section 9–505: The debtor consents if the secured party

1113

sends a proposal to the debtor and does not receive an objection within 20 days. Under subsection (c)(1), however, that silence is not deemed to be consent with respect to acceptances in partial satisfaction. Thus, a secured party who wishes to conduct a "partial strict foreclosure" must obtain the debtor's agreement in a record ~~authenticated~~ signed after default. In all other respects, the conditions necessary to an effective partial strict foreclosure are the same as those governing acceptance of collateral in full satisfaction. (But see subsection (g), prohibiting partial strict foreclosure of a security interest in consumer transactions.)

* * *

4. **Proposals.** Section 9–102 defines the term "proposal." It is necessary to send a "proposal" to the debtor only if the debtor does not agree to an acceptance in ~~an authenticated~~ a signed record as described in subsection (c)(1) or (c)(2). Section 9–621(a) determines whether it is necessary to send a proposal to third parties. A proposal need not take any particular form as long as it sets forth the terms under which the secured party is willing to accept collateral in satisfaction. A proposal to accept collateral should specify the amount (or a means of calculating the amount, such as by including a per diem accrual figure) of the secured obligations to be satisfied, state the conditions (if any) under which the proposal may be revoked, and describe any other applicable conditions. Note, however, that a conditional proposal generally requires the debtor's agreement in order to take effect. See subsection (c).

5. **Secured Party's Agreement; No "Constructive" Strict Foreclosure.** The conditions of subsection (a) relate to actual or implied consent by the debtor and any secondary obligor or holder of a junior security interest or lien. To ensure that the debtor cannot unilaterally cause an acceptance of collateral, subsection (b) provides that compliance with these conditions is necessary but not sufficient to cause an acceptance of collateral. Rather, under subsection (b), acceptance does not occur unless, in addition, the secured party consents to the acceptance in ~~an authenticated~~ a signed record or sends to the debtor a proposal. For this reason, a mere delay in collection or disposition of collateral does not constitute a "constructive" strict foreclosure. Instead, delay is a factor relating to whether the secured party acted in a commercially reasonable manner for purposes of Section 9–607 or 9–610. A debtor's voluntary surrender of collateral to a secured party and the secured party's acceptance of possession of the collateral does not, of itself, necessarily raise an implication that the secured party intends or is proposing to accept the collateral in satisfaction of the secured obligation under this section.

* * *

10. **Accounts, Chattel Paper, Payment Intangibles, and Promissory Notes.** If the collateral is accounts, chattel paper, payment intangibles, or promissory notes, then a secured party's acceptance of the collateral in satisfaction of secured obligations would constitute a sale to the secured party. That sale normally would give rise to a new security interest (the ownership interest) under Sections ~~1–201(37)~~ 1–201(b)(35) and 9–109. In the case of accounts and chattel paper, the new security interest would remain perfected by a filing that was effective to perfect the secured party's original security interest. In the case of payment intangibles or promissory notes, the security interest would be perfected when it attaches. See Section 9–309. However, the procedures for acceptance of collateral under this section satisfy all necessary formalities and a new security agreement ~~authenticated~~ signed by the debtor would not be necessary.

* * *

13. <u>**"Signed" Replaces "Authenticated."** Consistent with the revised definition of "sign" in Section 1–201, the cognate term "signed" replaces the references to "authenticated" in the pre-2022 text of this section.</u>

§ 9–621.   Notification Of Proposal to Accept Collateral.

(a) **[Persons to which proposal to be sent.]** A secured party that desires to accept collateral in full or partial satisfaction of the obligation it secures shall send its proposal to:

(1) any person from which the secured party has received, before the debtor consented to the acceptance, ~~an authenticated~~ a signed notification of a claim of an interest in the collateral;

* * *

Official Comment

* * *

3. <u>**"Signed" Replaces "Authenticated."** Consistent with the revised definition of "sign" in Section 1–201, the cognate term "signed" replaces the reference to "authenticated" in the pre-2022 text of this section.</u>

§ 9–624.   Waiver.

(a)   **[Waiver of disposition notification.]** A debtor or secondary obligor may waive the right to notification of disposition of collateral under Section 9–611 only by an agreement to that effect entered into and ~~authenticated~~ signed after default.

(b)   **[Waiver of mandatory disposition.]** A debtor may waive the right to require disposition of collateral under Section 9–620(e) only by an agreement to that effect entered into and ~~authenticated~~ signed after default.

(c)   **[Waiver of redemption right.]** Except in a consumer-goods transaction, a debtor or secondary obligor may waive the right to redeem collateral under Section 9–623 only by an agreement to that effect entered into and ~~authenticated~~ signed after default.

Official Comment

* * *

3.   **"Signed" Replaces "Authenticated."** Consistent with the revised definition of "sign" in Section 1–201, the cognate term "signed" replaces the references to "authenticated" in the pre-2022 text of this section.

§ 9–627.   Determination of Whether Conduct Was Commercially Reasonable.

* * *

Official Comment

* * *

4.   **"Recognized Market."** As in Sections 9–610(c) and 9–611(d), the concept of a "recognized market" in subsections (b)(1) and (2) is quite limited; it applies only to markets in which there are standardized price quotations for property that is essentially fungible, such as (but not limited to) ~~stock~~ securities and commodities exchanges. See Section 9–610, Comment 9 (discussing standards for a "recognized market").

§ 9–628.   Nonliability and Limitation on Liability of Secured Party; Liability of Secondary Obligor.

(a)   **[Limitation of liability of secured party for noncompliance with article.]** ~~Unless~~ Subject to subsection (f), unless a secured party knows that a person is a debtor or obligor, knows the identity of the person, and knows how to communicate with the person:

* * *

(b)   **[Limitation of liability based on status as secured party.]** A Subject to subsection (f), a secured party is not liable because of its status as secured party:

* * *

(f)   **[Exception: Limitation of liability under subsections (a) and (b) does not apply.]** Subsections (a) and (b) do not apply to limit the liability of a secured party to a person if, at the time the secured party obtains control of collateral that is a controllable account, controllable electronic record, or controllable payment intangible or at the time the security interest attaches to the collateral, whichever is later:

(1)   the person is a debtor or obligor; and

(2)   the secured party knows that the information in subsection (b)(1)(A), (B), or (C) relating to the person is not provided by the collateral, a record attached to or logically associated with the collateral, or the system in which the collateral is recorded.

Official Comment

* * *

2. **Exculpatory Provisions.** ~~Subsections (a), (b), and (c) contain exculpatory provisions that should be read in conjunction with Section 9–605 and Comments. Without this group of provisions, a secured party could incur liability to unknown persons and under circumstances that would not allow the secured party to protect itself. The broadened definition of the term "debtor" underscores the need for these provisions.~~ <u>With respect to subsection (f), see Section 9–605, Comments 2 and 3.</u>

* * *

UNIFORM VOIDABLE TRANSACTIONS ACT*

Promulgated in 1984 as the Uniform Fraudulent Transfer Act; amended and renamed in 2014.

Current through April 2023

For updates, see www.uniformlaws.org

---

1.   Definitions.
2.   Insolvency.
3.   Value.
4.   Transfer or Obligation Voidable as to Present or Future Creditor.
5.   Transfer or Obligation Voidable as to Present Creditor.
6.   When Transfer Is Made or Obligation Is Incurred.
7.   Remedies of Creditor.
8.   Defenses, Liability, and Protection of Transferee or Obligee.
9.   Extinguishment of Claim for Relief.
10.   Governing Law.
11.   Application to Series Organization.
12.   Supplementary Provisions.
13.   Uniformity of Application and Construction.
14.   Relation to Electronic Signatures in Global and National Commerce Act.
15.   Short Title.
16.   Repeals; Conforming Amendments.

---

§ 1.   Definitions.

As used in this [Act]:

(1)   "Affiliate" means:

(i)   a person that directly or indirectly owns, controls, or holds with power to vote, 20 percent or more of the outstanding voting securities of the debtor, other than a person that holds the securities:

(A)   as a fiduciary or agent without sole discretionary power to vote the securities; or

(B)   solely to secure a debt, if the person has not in fact exercised the power to vote;

(ii)   a corporation 20 percent or more of whose outstanding voting securities are directly or indirectly owned, controlled, or held with power to vote, by the debtor or a person that directly or indirectly owns, controls, or holds, with power to vote, 20 percent or more of the outstanding voting securities of the debtor, other than a person that holds the securities:

(A)   as a fiduciary or agent without sole discretionary power to vote the securities; or

(B)   solely to secure a debt, if the person has not in fact exercised the power to vote;

(iii)   a person whose business is operated by the debtor under a lease or other agreement, or a person substantially all of whose assets are controlled by the debtor; or

*   Copyright © 2014 by The American Law Institute and the Uniform Law Commission. Reproduced with permission. All rights reserved.

    (iv)   a person that operates the debtor's business under a lease or other agreement or controls substantially all of the debtor's assets.

  (2) "Asset" means property of a debtor, but the term does not include:

    (i)   property to the extent it is encumbered by a valid lien;

    (ii)   property to the extent it is generally exempt under nonbankruptcy law; or

    (iii)   an interest in property held in tenancy by the entireties to the extent it is not subject to process by a creditor holding a claim against only one tenant.

  (3) "Claim", except as used in "claim for relief", means a right to payment, whether or not the right is reduced to judgment, liquidated, unliquidated, fixed, contingent, matured, unmatured, disputed, undisputed, legal, equitable, secured, or unsecured.

  (4) "Creditor" means a person that has a claim.

  (5) "Debt" means liability on a claim.

  (6) "Debtor" means a person that is liable on a claim.

  (7) "Electronic" means relating to technology having electrical, digital, magnetic, wireless, optical, electromagnetic, or similar capabilities.

  (8) "Insider" includes:

    (i)   if the debtor is an individual:

      (A)   a relative of the debtor or of a general partner of the debtor;

      (B)   a partnership in which the debtor is a general partner;

      (C)   a general partner in a partnership described in clause (B); or

      (D)   a corporation of which the debtor is a director, officer, or person in control;

    (ii)   if the debtor is a corporation:

      (A)   a director of the debtor;

      (B)   an officer of the debtor;

      (C)   a person in control of the debtor;

      (D)   a partnership in which the debtor is a general partner;

      (E)   a general partner in a partnership described in clause (D); or

      (F)   a relative of a general partner, director, officer, or person in control of the debtor;

    (iii)   if the debtor is a partnership:

      (A)   a general partner in the debtor;

      (B)   a relative of a general partner in, a general partner of, or a person in control of the debtor;

      (C)   another partnership in which the debtor is a general partner;

      (D)   a general partner in a partnership described in clause (C); or

      (E)   a person in control of the debtor;

    (iv)   an affiliate, or an insider of an affiliate as if the affiliate were the debtor; and

    (v)   a managing agent of the debtor.

  (9) "Lien" means a charge against or an interest in property to secure payment of a debt or performance of an obligation, and includes a security interest created by agreement, a judicial lien obtained by legal or equitable process or proceedings, a common-law lien, or a statutory lien.

  (10) "Organization" means a person other than an individual.

(11) "Person" means an individual, estate, partnership, association, trust, business or nonprofit entity, public corporation, government or governmental subdivision, agency, or instrumentality, or other legal or commercial entity.

(12) "Property" means anything that may be the subject of ownership.

(13) "Record" means information that is inscribed on a tangible medium or that is stored in an electronic or other medium and is retrievable in perceivable form.

(14) "Relative" means an individual related by consanguinity within the third degree as determined by the common law, a spouse, or an individual related to a spouse within the third degree as so determined, and includes an individual in an adoptive relationship within the third degree.

(15) "Sign" means, with present intent to authenticate or adopt a record:

(i) to execute or adopt a tangible symbol; or

(ii) to attach to or logically associate with the record an electronic symbol, sound, or process.

(16) "Transfer" means every mode, direct or indirect, absolute or conditional, voluntary or involuntary, of disposing of or parting with an asset or an interest in an asset, and includes payment of money, release, lease, license, and creation of a lien or other encumbrance.

(17) "Valid lien" means a lien that is effective against the holder of a judicial lien subsequently obtained by legal or equitable process or proceedings.

§ 2. Insolvency.

(a) A debtor is insolvent if, at a fair valuation, the sum of the debtor's debts is greater than the sum of the debtor's assets.

(b) A debtor that is generally not paying the debtor's debts as they become due other than as a result of a bona fide dispute is presumed to be insolvent. The presumption imposes on the party against which the presumption is directed the burden of proving that the nonexistence of insolvency is more probable than its existence.

(c) Assets under this section do not include property that has been transferred, concealed, or removed with intent to hinder, delay, or defraud creditors or that has been transferred in a manner making the transfer voidable under this [Act].

(d) Debts under this section do not include an obligation to the extent it is secured by a valid lien on property of the debtor not included as an asset.

§ 3. Value.

(a) Value is given for a transfer or an obligation if, in exchange for the transfer or obligation, property is transferred or an antecedent debt is secured or satisfied, but value does not include an unperformed promise made otherwise than in the ordinary course of the promisor's business to furnish support to the debtor or another person.

(b) For the purposes of Section 4(a)(2) and Section 5, a person gives a reasonably equivalent value if the person acquires an interest of the debtor in an asset pursuant to a regularly conducted, noncollusive foreclosure sale or execution of a power of sale for the acquisition or disposition of the interest of the debtor upon default under a mortgage, deed of trust, or security agreement.

(c) A transfer is made for present value if the exchange between the debtor and the transferee is intended by them to be contemporaneous and is in fact substantially contemporaneous.

§ 4. Transfer or Obligation Voidable as to Present or Future Creditor.

(a) A transfer made or obligation incurred by a debtor is voidable as to a creditor, whether the creditor's claim arose before or after the transfer was made or the obligation was incurred, if the debtor made the transfer or incurred the obligation:

(1)   with actual intent to hinder, delay, or defraud any creditor of the debtor; or

(2)   without receiving a reasonably equivalent value in exchange for the transfer or obligation, and the debtor:

    (i)   was engaged or was about to engage in a business or a transaction for which the remaining assets of the debtor were unreasonably small in relation to the business or transaction; or

    (ii)   intended to incur, or believed or reasonably should have believed that the debtor would incur, debts beyond the debtor's ability to pay as they became due.

(b)   In determining actual intent under subsection (a)(1), consideration may be given, among other factors, to whether:

(1)   the transfer or obligation was to an insider;

(2)   the debtor retained possession or control of the property transferred after the transfer;

(3)   the transfer or obligation was disclosed or concealed;

(4)   before the transfer was made or obligation was incurred, the debtor had been sued or threatened with suit;

(5)   the transfer was of substantially all the debtor's assets;

(6)   the debtor absconded;

(7)   the debtor removed or concealed assets;

(8)   the value of the consideration received by the debtor was reasonably equivalent to the value of the asset transferred or the amount of the obligation incurred;

(9)   the debtor was insolvent or became insolvent shortly after the transfer was made or the obligation was incurred;

(10)   the transfer occurred shortly before or shortly after a substantial debt was incurred; and

(11)   the debtor transferred the essential assets of the business to a lienor who transferred the assets to an insider of the debtor.

(c)   A creditor making a claim for relief under subsection (a) has the burden of proving the elements of the claim for relief by a preponderance of the evidence.

§ 5.   Transfer or Obligation Voidable as to Present Creditor.

(a)   A transfer made or obligation incurred by a debtor is voidable as to a creditor whose claim arose before the transfer was made or the obligation was incurred if the debtor made the transfer or incurred the obligation without receiving a reasonably equivalent value in exchange for the transfer or obligation and the debtor was insolvent at that time or the debtor became insolvent as a result of the transfer or obligation.

(b)   A transfer made by a debtor is voidable as to a creditor whose claim arose before the transfer was made if the transfer was made to an insider for an antecedent debt, the debtor was insolvent at that time, and the insider had reasonable cause to believe that the debtor was insolvent.

(c)   Subject to Section 2(b), a creditor making a claim for relief under subsection (a) or (b) has the burden of proving the elements of the claim for relief by a preponderance of the evidence.

§ 6.   When Transfer Is Made or Obligation Is Incurred.

For the purposes of this [Act]:

(1)   a transfer is made:

    (i)   with respect to an asset that is real property other than a fixture, but including the interest of a seller or purchaser under a contract for the sale of the asset, when the transfer is so far perfected that a good-faith purchaser of the asset from the debtor against which applicable law permits the transfer to be perfected cannot acquire an interest in the asset that is superior to the interest of the transferee; and

    (ii)   with respect to an asset that is not real property or that is a fixture, when the transfer is so far perfected that a creditor on a simple contract cannot acquire a judicial lien otherwise than under this [Act] that is superior to the interest of the transferee;

(2)   if applicable law permits the transfer to be perfected as provided in paragraph (1) and the transfer is not so perfected before the commencement of an action for relief under this [Act], the transfer is deemed made immediately before the commencement of the action;

(3)   if applicable law does not permit the transfer to be perfected as provided in paragraph (1), the transfer is made when it becomes effective between the debtor and the transferee;

(4)   a transfer is not made until the debtor has acquired rights in the asset transferred; and

(5)   an obligation is incurred:

    (i)   if oral, when it becomes effective between the parties; or

    (ii)   if evidenced by a record, when the record signed by the obligor is delivered to or for the benefit of the obligee.

§ 7.   Remedies of Creditor.

(a)   In an action for relief against a transfer or obligation under this [Act], a creditor, subject to the limitations in Section 8, may obtain:

(1)   avoidance of the transfer or obligation to the extent necessary to satisfy the creditor's claim;

(2)   an attachment or other provisional remedy against the asset transferred or other property of the transferee if available under applicable law; and

(3)   subject to applicable principles of equity and in accordance with applicable rules of civil procedure:

    (i)   an injunction against further disposition by the debtor or a transferee, or both, of the asset transferred or of other property;

    (ii)   appointment of a receiver to take charge of the asset transferred or of other property of the transferee; or

    (iii)   any other relief the circumstances may require.

(b)   If a creditor has obtained a judgment on a claim against the debtor, the creditor, if the court so orders, may levy execution on the asset transferred or its proceeds.

§ 8.   Defenses, Liability, and Protection of Transferee or Obligee.

(a)   A transfer or obligation is not voidable under Section 4(a)(1) against a person that took in good faith and for a reasonably equivalent value given the debtor or against any subsequent transferee or obligee.

(b)   To the extent a transfer is avoidable in an action by a creditor under Section 7(a)(1), the following rules apply:

(1)   Except as otherwise provided in this section, the creditor may recover judgment for the value of the asset transferred, as adjusted under subsection (c), or the amount necessary to satisfy the creditor's claim, whichever is less. The judgment may be entered against:

    (i)   the first transferee of the asset or the person for whose benefit the transfer was made; or

    (ii)   an immediate or mediate transferee of the first transferee, other than:

        (a)   a good-faith transferee that took for value; or

        (b)   an immediate or mediate good-faith transferee of a person described in clause (A).

(2)   Recovery pursuant to Section 7(a)(1) or (b) of or from the asset transferred or its proceeds, by levy or otherwise, is available only against a person described in paragraph 1(i) or (ii).

(c)   If the judgment under subsection (b) is based upon the value of the asset transferred, the judgment must be for an amount equal to the value of the asset at the time of the transfer, subject to adjustment as the equities may require.

(d)   Notwithstanding voidability of a transfer or an obligation under this [Act], a good-faith transferee or obligee is entitled, to the extent of the value given the debtor for the transfer or obligation, to:

(1)   a lien on or a right to retain an interest in the asset transferred;

(2)   enforcement of an obligation incurred; or

(3)   a reduction in the amount of the liability on the judgment.

(e)   A transfer is not voidable under Section 4(a)(2) or Section 5 if the transfer results from:

(1)   termination of a lease upon default by the debtor when the termination is pursuant to the lease and applicable law; or

(2)   enforcement of a security interest in compliance with Article 9 of the Uniform Commercial Code, other than acceptance of collateral in full or partial satisfaction of the obligation it secures.

(f)   A transfer is not voidable under Section 5(b):

(1)   to the extent the insider gave new value to or for the benefit of the debtor after the transfer was made, except to the extent the new value was secured by a valid lien;

(2)   if made in the ordinary course of business or financial affairs of the debtor and the insider; or

(3)   if made pursuant to a good-faith effort to rehabilitate the debtor and the transfer secured present value given for that purpose as well as an antecedent debt of the debtor.

(g)   The following rules determine the burden of proving matters referred to in this section:

(1)   A party that seeks to invoke subsection (a), (d), (e), or (f) has the burden of proving the applicability of that subsection.

(2)   Except as otherwise provided in paragraphs (3) and (4), the creditor has the burden of proving each applicable element of subsection (b) or (c).

(3)   The transferee has the burden of proving the applicability to the transferee of subsection (b)(1)(ii)(A) or (B).

(4)   A party that seeks adjustment under subsection (c) has the burden of proving the adjustment.

(h)   The standard of proof required to establish matters referred to in this section is preponderance of the evidence.

§ 9.   Extinguishment of Claim for Relief.

A claim for relief with respect to a transfer or obligation under this [Act] is extinguished unless action is brought:

(a)   under Section 4(a)(1), not later than four years after the transfer was made or the obligation was incurred or, if later, not later than one year after the transfer or obligation was or could reasonably have been discovered by the claimant;

(b)   under Section 4(a)(2) or 5(a), not later than four years after the transfer was made or the obligation was incurred; or

(c)   under Section 5(b), not later than one year after the transfer was made.

§ 10. Governing Law.

(a) In this section, the following rules determine a debtor's location:

(1) A debtor who is an individual is located at the individual's principal residence.

(2) A debtor that is an organization and has only one place of business is located at its place of business.

(3) A debtor that is an organization and has more than one place of business is located at its chief executive office.

(b) A claim for relief in the nature of a claim for relief under this [Act] is governed by the local law of the jurisdiction in which the debtor is located when the transfer is made or the obligation is incurred.

§ 11. Application to Series Organization.

(a) In this section:

(1) "Protected series" means an arrangement, however denominated, created by a series organization that, pursuant to the law under which the series organization is organized, has the characteristics set forth in paragraph (2).

(2) "Series organization" means an organization that, pursuant to the law under which it is organized, has the following characteristics:

(i) The organic record of the organization provides for creation by the organization of one or more protected series, however denominated, with respect to specified property of the organization, and for records to be maintained for each protected series that identify the property of or associated with the protected series.

(ii) Debt incurred or existing with respect to the activities of, or property of or associated with, a particular protected series is enforceable against the property of or associated with the protected series only, and not against the property of or associated with the organization or other protected series of the organization.

(iii) Debt incurred or existing with respect to the activities or property of the organization is enforceable against the property of the organization only, and not against the property of or associated with a protected series of the organization.

(b) A series organization and each protected series of the organization is a separate person for purposes of this [Act], even if for other purposes a protected series is not a person separate from the organization or other protected series of the organization.

Legislative Note: This section should be enacted even if the enacting jurisdiction does not itself have legislation enabling the creation of protected series. For example, in such an enacting jurisdiction this section will apply if a protected series of a series organization organized under the law of a different jurisdiction makes a transfer to another protected series of that organization and, under applicable choice of law rules, the voidability of the transfer is governed by the law of the enacting jurisdiction.

§ 12. Supplementary Provisions.

Unless displaced by the provisions of this [Act], the principles of law and equity, including the law merchant and the law relating to principal and agent, estoppel, laches, fraud, misrepresentation, duress, coercion, mistake, insolvency, or other validating or invalidating cause, supplement its provisions.

§ 13. Uniformity of Application and Construction.

This [Act] shall be applied and construed to effectuate its general purpose to make uniform the law with respect to the subject of this [Act] among states enacting it.

§ 14. Relation to Electronic Signatures in Global and National Commerce Act.

This [Act] modifies, limits, or supersedes the Electronic Signatures in Global and National Commerce Act, 15 U.S.C. Section 7001 et seq., but does not modify, limit, or supersede Section 101(c) of that act, 15 U.S.C. Section 7001(c), or authorize electronic delivery of any of the notices described in Section 103(b) of that act, 15 U.S.C. Section 7003(b).

§ 15. Short Title.

This [Act], which was formerly cited as the Uniform Fraudulent Transfer Act, may be cited as the Uniform Voidable Transactions Act.

§ 16. Repeals; Conforming Amendments.

(a) ...

(b) ...

(c) ...

FOOD SECURITY ACT OF 1985

7 U.S.C. § 1631

Current through April 10, 2023; P.L. 118–3

For updates, see http://uscode.house.gov

§ 1631. Protection for purchasers of farm products

(a) Congressional findings

Congress finds that—

(1) certain State laws permit a secured lender to enforce liens against a purchaser of farm products even if the purchaser does not know that the sale of the products violates the lender's security interest in the products, lacks any practical method for discovering the existence of the security interest, and has no reasonable means to ensure that the seller uses the sales proceeds to repay the lender;

(2) these laws subject the purchaser of farm products to double payment for the products, once at the time of purchase, and again when the seller fails to repay the lender;

(3) the exposure of purchasers of farm products to double payment inhibits free competition in the market for farm products; and

(4) this exposure constitutes a burden on and an obstruction to interstate commerce in farm products.

(b) Declaration of purpose

The purpose of this section is to remove such burden on and obstruction to interstate commerce in farm products.

(c) Definitions

For the purposes of this section—

(1) The term "buyer in the ordinary course of business" means a person who, in the ordinary course of business, buys farm products from a person engaged in farming operations who is in the business of selling farm products.

(2) The term "central filing system" means a system for filing effective financing statements or notice of such financing statements on a statewide basis and which has been certified by the Secretary of the United States Department of Agriculture; the Secretary shall certify such system if the system complies with the requirements of this section; specifically under such system—

(A) effective financing statements or notice of such financing statements are filed with the office of the Secretary of State of a State;

(B) the Secretary of State records the date and hour of the filing of such statements;

(C) the Secretary of State compiles all such statements into a master list—

(i) organized according to farm products;

(ii) arranged within each such product—

(I) in alphabetical order according to the last name of the individual debtors, or, in the case of debtors doing business other than as individuals, the first word in the name of such debtors; and

(II) in numerical order according to the social security number, or other approved unique identifier, of the individual debtors or, in the case of debtors doing business other than as individuals, the Internal Revenue Service taxpayer identification number, or other approved unique identifier, of such debtors, except that the numerical list containing social security or taxpayer identification numbers may be encrypted for security purposes if the Secretary of State provides a method by which an effective search of the encrypted numbers may be conducted to determine whether the farm product at issue is subject to 1 or more liens; and

(III) geographically by county or parish; and

(IV) by crop year;

(iii) containing the information referred to in paragraph (4)(D);

(D) the Secretary of State maintains a list of all buyers of farm products, commission merchants, and selling agents who register with the Secretary of State, on a form indicating—

(i) the name and address of each buyer, commission merchant and selling agent;

(ii) the interest of each buyer, commission merchant, and selling agent in receiving the lists described in subparagraph (E); and

(iii) the farm products in which each buyer, commission merchant, and selling agent has an interest;

(E) the Secretary of State distributes regularly as prescribed by the State to each buyer, commission merchant, and selling agent on the list described in subparagraph (D) a copy in written or printed form of those portions of the master list described in subparagraph (C) that cover the farm products in which such buyer, commission merchant, or selling agent has registered an interest except that—

(i) the distribution of the portion of the master list may be in electronic, written, or printed form; and

(ii) if social security or taxpayer identification numbers on the master list are encrypted, the Secretary of State may distribute the master list only—

(I) by compact disc or other electronic media that contains—

(aa) the recorded list of debtor names; and

(bb) an encryption program that enables the buyer, commission merchant, and selling agent to enter a social security number for matching against the recorded list of encrypted social security or taxpayer identification numbers; and

(II) on the written request of the buyer, commission merchant, or selling agent, by paper copy of the list to the requestor;

(F) the Secretary of State furnishes to those who are not registered pursuant to (2)(D) of this section[1] oral confirmation within 24 hours of any effective financing statement on request followed by written confirmation to any buyer of farm products buying from a debtor, or commission merchant or selling agent selling for a seller covered by such statement.

(3) The term "commission merchant" means any person engaged in the business of receiving any farm product for sale, on commission, or for or on behalf of another person.

(4) The term "effective financing statement" means a statement that—

(A) is an original or reproduced copy of the statement, or, in the case of a State which (under the applicable State law provisions of the Uniform Commercial Code) allows the electronic

---

[1] So in original. Probably should be "pursuant to subparagraph (D)". [*Note from West Advisory Panel: the revisor's note refers to (c)(2)(D).*]

filing of financing statements without the signature of the debtor, is an electronically reproduced copy of the statement;

(B) other than in the case of an electronically reproduced copy of the statement, is signed, authorized, or otherwise authenticated by the debtor, and filed with the Secretary of State of a State by the secured party;

(C) contains,

(i) the name and address of the secured party;

(ii) the name and address of the person indebted to the secured party;

(iii) the social security number, or other approved unique identifier, of the debtor or, in the case of a debtor doing business other than as an individual, the Internal Revenue Service taxpayer identification number, or other approved unique identifier, of such debtor; and

(iv) a description of the farm products subject to the security interest created by the debtor, including the amount of such products where applicable, and the name of each county or parish in which the farm products are produced or located;

(D) must be amended in writing, within 3 months, similarly signed, authorized, or otherwise authenticated by the debtor and filed, to reflect material changes;

(E) remains effective for a period of 5 years from the date of filing, subject to extensions for additional periods of 5 years each by refiling or filing a continuation statement within 6 months before the expiration of the initial 5 year period;

(F) lapses on either the expiration of the effective period of the statement or the filing of a notice signed, authorized, or otherwise authenticated by the secured party that the statement has lapsed, whichever occurs first;

(G) is accompanied by the requisite filing fee set by the Secretary of State; and

(H) substantially complies with the requirements of this subparagraph even though it contains minor errors that are not seriously misleading.

(5)[2] The term "farm product" means an agricultural commodity such as wheat, corn, soybeans, or a species of livestock such as cattle, hogs, sheep, horses, or poultry used or produced in farming operations, or a product of such crop or livestock in its unmanufactured state (such as ginned cotton, wool-clip, maple syrup, milk, and eggs), that is in the possession of a person engaged in farming operations.

(6) The term "knows" or "knowledge" means actual knowledge.

(7) The term "security interest" means an interest in farm products that secures payment or performance of an obligation.

(8) The term "selling agent" means any person, other than a commission merchant, who is engaged in the business of negotiating the sale and purchase of any farm product on behalf of a person engaged in farming operations.

(9) The term "State" means each of the 50 States, the District of Columbia, the Commonwealth of Puerto Rico, Guam, the Virgin Islands of the United States, American Samoa, the Commonwealth of the Northern Mariana Islands, or the Trust Territory of the Pacific Islands.

(10) The term "person" means any individual, partnership, corporation, trust, or any other business entity.

(11) The term "Secretary of State" means the Secretary of State or the designee of the State.

---

[2] So in original. Another par. (5) follows par. (11).

(5)[3] The term "approved unique identifier" means a number, combination of numbers and letters, or other identifier selected by the Secretary of State using a selection system or method approved by the Secretary of Agriculture.

(d) Purchases free of security interest

Except as provided in subsection (e) of this section and notwithstanding any other provision of Federal, State, or local law, a buyer who in the ordinary course of business buys a farm product from a seller engaged in farming operations shall take free of a security interest created by the seller, even though the security interest is perfected; and the buyer knows of the existence of such interest.

(e) Purchases subject to security interest

A buyer of farm products takes subject to a security interest created by the seller if—

(1)(A)   within 1 year before the sale of the farm products, the buyer has received from the secured party or the seller written notice of the security interest organized according to farm products that—

(i)   is an original or reproduced copy thereof;

(ii)   contains,

(I)   the name and address of the secured party;

(II)   the name and address of the person indebted to the secured party;

(III)   the social security number, or other approved unique identifier, of the debtor or, in the case of a debtor doing business other than as an individual, the Internal Revenue Service taxpayer identification number, or other approved unique identifier, of such debtor; and

(IV)   a description of the farm products subject to the security interest created by the debtor, including the amount of such products where applicable, crop year, and the name of each county or parish in which the farm products are produced or located;

(iii)   must be amended in writing, within 3 months, similarly signed, authorized, or otherwise authenticated and transmitted, to reflect material changes;

(iv)   will lapse on either the expiration period of the statement or the transmission of a notice signed, authorized, or otherwise authenticated by the secured party that the statement has lapsed, whichever occurs first; and

(v)   contains any payment obligations imposed on the buyer by the secured party as conditions for waiver or release of the security interest; and

(B)   the buyer has failed to perform the payment obligations, or

(2)   in the case of a farm product produced in a State that has established a central filing system—

(A)   the buyer has failed to register with the Secretary of State of such State prior to the purchase of farm products; and

(B)   the secured party has filed an effective financing statement or notice that covers the farm products being sold; or

(3)   in the case of a farm product produced in a State that has established a central filing system, the buyer—

(A)   receives from the Secretary of State of such State written notice as provided in subsection (c)(2)(E) or (c)(2)(F) that specifies both the seller and the farm product being sold by such seller as being subject to an effective financing statement or notice; and

---

[3]   So in original. Another par. (5) follows par. (4).

(B) does not secure a waiver or release of the security interest specified in such effective financing statement or notice from the secured party by performing any payment obligation or otherwise.

(f) Law governing "receipt"

What constitutes receipt, as used in this section, shall be determined by the law of the State in which the buyer resides.

(g) Commission merchants or selling agents: sales free of or subject to security interest; law governing "receipt"

(1) Except as provided in paragraph (2) and notwithstanding any other provision of Federal, State, or local law, a commission merchant or selling agent who sells, in the ordinary course of business, a farm product for others, shall not be subject to a security interest created by the seller in such farm product even though the security interest is perfected and even though the commission merchant or selling agent knows of the existence of such interest.

(2) A commission merchant or selling agent who sells a farm product for others shall be subject to a security interest created by the seller in such farm product if—

(A) within 1 year before the sale of such farm product the commission merchant or selling agent has received from the secured party or the seller written notice of the security interest; organized according to farm products, that—

(i) is an original or reproduced copy thereof;

(ii) contains,

(I) the name and address of the secured party;

(II) the name and address of the person indebted to the secured party;

(III) the social security number, or other approved unique identifier, of the debtor or, in the case of a debtor doing business other than as an individual, the Internal Revenue Service taxpayer identification number, or other approved unique identifier, of such debtor; and

(IV) a description of the farm products subject to the security interest created by the debtor, including the amount of such products, where applicable, crop year, and the name of each county or parish in which the farm products are produced or located;

(iii) must be amended in writing, within 3 months, similarly signed, authorized, or otherwise authenticated and transmitted, to reflect material changes;

(iv) will lapse on either the expiration period of the statement or the transmission of a notice signed, authorized, or otherwise authenticated by the secured party that the statement has lapsed, whichever occurs first; and

(v) contains any payment obligations imposed on the commission merchant or selling agent by the secured party as conditions for waiver or release of the security interest; and

(B) the commission merchant or selling agent has failed to perform the payment obligations;

(C) in the case of a farm product produced in a State that has established a central filing system—

(i) the commission merchant or selling agent has failed to register with the Secretary of State of such State prior to the purchase of farm products; and

(ii) the secured party has filed an effective financing statement or notice that covers the farm products being sold; or

(D) in the case of a farm product produced in a State that has established a central filing system, the commission merchant or selling agent—

(i) receives from the Secretary of State of such State written notice as provided in subsection (c)(2)(E) or (c)(2)(F) of this section that specifies both the seller and the farm products being sold by such seller as being subject to an effective financing statement or notice; and

(ii) does not secure a waiver or release of the security interest specified in such effective financing statement or notice from the secured party by performing any payment obligation or otherwise.

(3) What constitutes receipt, as used in this section, shall be determined by the law of the State in which the buyer resides.

(h) Security agreements; identity lists; notice of identity or accounting for proceeds; violations

(1) A security agreement in which a person engaged in farming operations creates a security interest in a farm product may require the person to furnish to the secured party a list of the buyers, commission merchants, and selling agents to or through whom the person engaged in farming operations may sell such farm product.

(2) If a security agreement contains a provision described in paragraph (1) and such person engaged in farming operations sells the farm product collateral to a buyer or through a commission merchant or selling agent not included on such list, the person engaged in farming operations shall be subject to paragraph (3) unless the person—

(A) has notified the secured party in writing of the identity of the buyer, commission merchant, or selling agent at least 7 days prior to such sale; or

(B) has accounted to the secured party for the proceeds of such sale not later than 10 days after such sale.

(3) A person violating paragraph (2) shall be fined $5,000 or 15 per centum of the value or benefit received for such farm product described in the security agreement, whichever is greater.

(i) Regulations

The Secretary of Agriculture shall prescribe regulations not later than 90 days after December 23, 1985, to aid States in the implementation and management of a central filing system.

(j) Effective date

This section shall become effective 12 months after December 23, 1985.

(Pub. L. 99–198, Title XIII, § 1324, Dec. 23, 1985, 99 Stat. 1535; Pub. L. 104–127, Title VI, § 662, Apr. 4, 1996, 110 Stat. 1107; Pub. L. 107–171, Title X, § 10604, May 13, 2002, 116 Stat. 512; Pub. L. 108–447, Div. A, Title VII, § 776, Dec. 8, 2004, 118 Stat. 2849; Pub. L. 110–234, Title XIV, § 14215, May 22, 2008, 122 Stat. 1466; Pub. L. 110–246, § 4(a), Title XIV, § 14215, June 18, 2008, 122 Stat. 1664, 2228.)

FEDERAL TRADE COMMISSION
CREDIT PRACTICES REGULATIONS

---

16 C.F.R. Part 444

Current through April 12, 2023; 88 F.R. 22350

For updates, see www.ecfr.gov

444.1   Definitions.

444.2   Unfair credit practices.

444.3   Unfair or deceptive cosigner practices.

444.4   Late charges.

444.5   State exemptions.

---

§ 444.1   Definitions.

(a)   Lender. A person who engages in the business of lending money to consumers within the jurisdiction of the Federal Trade Commission.

(b)   Retail installment seller. A person who sells goods or services to consumers on a deferred payment basis or pursuant to a lease-purchase arrangement within the jurisdiction of the Federal Trade Commission.

(c)   Person. An individual, corporation, or other business organization.

(d)   Consumer. A natural person who seeks or acquires goods, services, or money for personal, family, or household use.

(e)   Obligation. An agreement between a consumer and a lender or retail installment seller.

(f)   Creditor. A lender or a retail installment seller.

(g)   Debt. Money that is due or alleged to be due from one to another.

(h)   Earnings. Compensation paid or payable to an individual or for his or her account for personal services rendered or to be rendered by him or her, whether denominated as wages, salary, commission, bonus, or otherwise, including periodic payments pursuant to a pension, retirement, or disability program.

(i)   Household goods. Clothing, furniture, appliances, one radio and one television, linens, china, crockery, kitchenware, and personal effects (including wedding rings) of the consumer and his or her dependents, provided that the following are not included within the scope of the term household goods:

    (1)   Works of art;

    (2)   Electronic entertainment equipment (except one television and one radio);

    (3)   Items acquired as antiques; and

    (4)   Jewelry (except wedding rings).

(j)   Antique. Any item over one hundred years of age, including such items that have been repaired or renovated without changing their original form or character.

(k)   Cosigner. A natural person who renders himself or herself liable for the obligation of another person without compensation. The term shall include any person whose signature is requested as a condition to granting credit to another person, or as a condition for forbearance on collection of another person's obligation that is in default. The term shall not include a spouse whose signature is required on a credit obligation to perfect a security interest pursuant to State law. A person who does not receive goods, services, or money in return for a credit obligation does not receive compensation within the meaning of this definition. A person is a cosigner within the meaning of this definition whether or not he or she is designated as such on a credit obligation.

§ 444.2 Unfair credit practices.

(a) In connection with the extension of credit to consumers in or affecting commerce, as commerce is defined in the Federal Trade Commission Act, it is an unfair act or practice within the meaning of Section 5 of that Act for a lender or retail installment seller directly or indirectly to take or receive from a consumer an obligation that:

(1) Constitutes or contains a cognovit or confession of judgment (for purposes other than executory process in the State of Louisiana), warrant of attorney, or other waiver of the right to notice and the opportunity to be heard in the event of suit or process thereon.

(2) Constitutes or contains an executory waiver or a limitation of exemption from attachment, execution, or other process on real or personal property held, owned by, or due to the consumer, unless the waiver applies solely to property subject to a security interest executed in connection with the obligation.

(3) Constitutes or contains an assignment of wages or other earnings unless:

(i) The assignment by its terms is revocable at the will of the debtor, or

(ii) The assignment is a payroll deduction plan or preauthorized payment plan, commencing at the time of the transaction, in which the consumer authorizes a series of wage deductions as a method of making each payment, or

(iii) The assignment applies only to wages or other earnings already earned at the time of the assignment.

(4) Constitutes or contains a nonpossessory security interest in household goods other than a purchase money security interest.

(b) [Reserved.]

§ 444.3 Unfair or deceptive cosigner practices.

(a) In connection with the extension of credit to consumers in or affecting commerce, as commerce is defined in the Federal Trade Commission Act, it is:

(1) A deceptive act or practice within the meaning of Section 5 of that Act for a lender or retail installment seller, directly or indirectly, to misrepresent the nature or extent of cosigner liability to any person.

(2) An unfair act or practice within the meaning of Section 5 of that Act for a lender or retail installment seller, directly or indirectly, to obligate a cosigner unless the cosigner is informed prior to becoming obligated, which in the case of open end credit shall mean prior to the time that the agreement creating the cosigner's liability for future charges is executed, of the nature of his or her liability as cosigner.

(b) Any lender or retail installment seller who complies with the preventive requirements in paragraph (c) of this section does not violate paragraph (a) of this section.

(c) To prevent these unfair or deceptive acts or practices, a disclosure, consisting of a separate document that shall contain the following statement and no other, shall be given to the cosigner prior to becoming obligated, which in the case of open end credit shall mean prior to the time that the agreement creating the cosigner's liability for future charges is executed:

Notice to Cosigner

You are being asked to guarantee this debt. Think carefully before you do. If the borrower doesn't pay the debt, you will have to. Be sure you can afford to pay if you have to, and that you want to accept this responsibility.

You may have to pay up to the full amount of the debt if the borrower does not pay. You may also have to pay late fees or collection costs, which increase this amount.

The creditor can collect this debt from you without first trying to collect from the borrower. The creditor can use the same collection methods against you that can be used against the borrower, such as suing you, garnishing your wages, etc. If this debt is ever in default, that fact may become a part of your credit record.

This notice is not the contract that makes you liable for the debt.

§ 444.4   Late charges.

(a)   In connection with collecting a debt arising out of an extension of credit to a consumer in or affecting commerce, as commerce is defined in the Federal Trade Commission Act, it is an unfair act or practice within the meaning of section 5 of that Act for a creditor, directly or indirectly, to levy or collect any delinquency charge on a payment, which payment is otherwise a full payment for the applicable period and is paid on its due date or within an applicable grace period, when the only delinquency is attributable to late fee(s) or delinquency charge(s) assessed on earlier installment(s).

(b)   For purposes of this section, collecting a debt means any activity other than the use of judicial process that is intended to bring about or does bring about repayment of all or part of a consumer debt.

§ 444.5   State exemptions.

(a)   If, upon application to the Federal Trade Commission by an appropriate State agency, the Federal Trade Commission determines that:

(1)   There is a State requirement or prohibition in effect that applies to any transaction to which a provision of this rule applies; and

(2)   The State requirement or prohibition affords a level of protection to consumers that is substantially equivalent to, or greater than, the protection afforded by this rule;

Then that provision of the rule will not be in effect in that State to the extent specified by the Federal Trade Commission in its determination, for as long as the State administers and enforces the State requirement or prohibition effectively.

(b)   [Reserved.]

FEDERAL TAX LIEN STATUTE

INTERNAL REVENUE CODE

26 U.S.C. §§ 6321–6323

Current through April 10, 2023; P.L. 118–3

For updates, see http://uscode.house.gov

§ 6321.　Lien for taxes

If any person liable to pay any tax neglects or refuses to pay the same after demand, the amount (including any interest, additional amount, addition to tax, or assessable penalty, together with any costs that may accrue in addition thereto) shall be a lien in favor of the United States upon all property and rights to property, whether real or personal, belonging to such person.

§ 6322.　Period of lien

Unless another date is specifically fixed by law, the lien imposed by section 6321 shall arise at the time the assessment is made and shall continue until the liability for the amount so assessed (or a judgment against the taxpayer arising out of such liability) is satisfied or becomes unenforceable by reason of lapse of time.

§ 6323.　Validity and priority against certain persons

(a) **Purchasers, holders of security interests, mechanic's lienors, and judgment lien creditors.**—The lien imposed by section 6321 shall not be valid as against any purchaser, holder of a security interest, mechanic's lienor, or judgment lien creditor until notice thereof which meets the requirements of subsection (f) has been filed by the Secretary.

(b) **Protection for certain interests even though notice filed.**—Even though notice of a lien imposed by section 6321 has been filed, such lien shall not be valid—

(1) **Securities.**—With respect to a security (as defined in subsection (h)(4))—

(A) as against a purchaser of such security who at the time of purchase did not have actual notice or knowledge of the existence of such lien; and

(B) as against a holder of a security interest in such security who, at the time such interest came into existence, did not have actual notice or knowledge of the existence of such lien.

(2) **Motor vehicles.**—With respect to a motor vehicle (as defined in subsection (h)(3)), as against a purchaser of such motor vehicle, if—

(A) at the time of the purchase such purchaser did not have actual notice or knowledge of the existence of such lien, and

(B) before the purchaser obtains such notice or knowledge, he has acquired possession of such motor vehicle and has not thereafter relinquished possession of such motor vehicle to the seller or his agent.

(3) **Personal property purchased at retail.**—With respect to tangible personal property purchased at retail, as against a purchaser in the ordinary course of the seller's trade or business, unless at the time of such purchase such purchaser intends such purchase to (or knows such purchase will) hinder, evade, or defeat the collection of any tax under this title.

1135

(4) Personal property purchased in casual sale.—With respect to household goods, personal effects, or other tangible personal property described in section 6334(a) purchased (not for resale) in a casual sale for less than $1,000, as against the purchaser, but only if such purchaser does not have actual notice or knowledge (A) of the existence of such lien, or (B) that this sale is one of a series of sales.

(5) Personal property subject to possessory lien.—With respect to tangible personal property subject to a lien under local law securing the reasonable price of the repair or improvement of such property, as against a holder of such a lien, if such holder is, and has been, continuously in possession of such property from the time such lien arose.

(6) Real property tax and special assessment liens.—With respect to real property, as against a holder of a lien upon such property, if such lien is entitled under local law to priority over security interests in such property which are prior in time, and such lien secures payment of—

　(A) a tax of general application levied by any taxing authority based upon the value of such property;

　(B) a special assessment imposed directly upon such property by any taxing authority, if such assessment is imposed for the purpose of defraying the cost of any public improvement; or

　(C) charges for utilities or public services furnished to such property by the United States, a State or political subdivision thereof, or an instrumentality of any one or more of the foregoing.

(7) Residential property subject to a mechanic's lien for certain repairs and improvements.—With respect to real property subject to a lien for repair or improvement of a personal residence (containing not more than four dwelling units) occupied by the owner of such residence, as against a mechanic's lienor, but only if the contract price on the contract with the owner is not more than $5,000.

(8) Attorneys' liens.—With respect to a judgment or other amount in settlement of a claim or of a cause of action, as against an attorney who, under local law, holds a lien upon or a contract enforceable against such judgment or amount, to the extent of his reasonable compensation for obtaining such judgment or procuring such settlement, except that this paragraph shall not apply to any judgment or amount in settlement of a claim or of a cause of action against the United States to the extent that the United States offsets such judgment or amount against any liability of the taxpayer to the United States.

(9) Certain insurance contracts.—With respect to a life insurance, endowment, or annuity contract, as against the organization which is the insurer under such contract, at any time—

　(A) before such organization had actual notice or knowledge of the existence of such lien;

　(B) after such organization had such notice or knowledge, with respect to advances required to be made automatically to maintain such contract in force under an agreement entered into before such organization had such notice or knowledge; or

　(C) after satisfaction of a levy pursuant to section 6332(b), unless and until the Secretary delivers to such organization a notice, executed after the date of such satisfaction, of the existence of such lien.

(10) Deposit-secured loans.—With respect to a savings deposit, share, or other account, with an institution described in section 581 or 591, to the extent of any loan made by such institution without actual notice or knowledge of the existence of such lien, as against such institution, if such loan is secured by such account.

(c) Protection for certain commercial transactions financing agreements, etc.—

　(1) In general.—To the extent provided in this subsection, even though notice of a lien imposed by section 6321 has been filed, such lien shall not be valid with respect to a security interest which came into existence after tax lien filing but which—

　　(A) is in qualified property covered by the terms of a written agreement entered into before tax lien filing and constituting—

(i) a commercial transactions financing agreement,

(ii) a real property construction or improvement financing agreement, or

(iii) an obligatory disbursement agreement, and

(B) is protected under local law against a judgment lien arising, as of the time of tax lien filing, out of an unsecured obligation.

(2) Commercial transactions financing agreement.—For purposes of this subsection—

(A) Definition.—The term "commercial transactions financing agreement" means an agreement (entered into by a person in the course of his trade or business)—

(i) to make loans to the taxpayer to be secured by commercial financing security acquired by the taxpayer in the ordinary course of his trade or business, or

(ii) to purchase commercial financing security (other than inventory) acquired by the taxpayer in the ordinary course of his trade or business;

but such an agreement shall be treated as coming within the term only to the extent that such loan or purchase is made before the 46th day after the date of tax lien filing or (if earlier) before the lender or purchaser had actual notice or knowledge of such tax lien filing.

(B) Limitation on qualified property.—The term "qualified property", when used with respect to a commercial transactions financing agreement, includes only commercial financing security acquired by the taxpayer before the 46th day after the date of tax lien filing.

(C) Commercial financing security defined.—The term "commercial financing security" means (i) paper of a kind ordinarily arising in commercial transactions, (ii) accounts receivable, (iii) mortgages on real property, and (iv) inventory.

(D) Purchaser treated as acquiring security interest.—A person who satisfies subparagraph (A) by reason of clause (ii) thereof shall be treated as having acquired a security interest in commercial financing security.

(3) Real property construction or improvement financing agreement.—For purposes of this subsection—

(A) Definition.—The term "real property construction or improvement financing agreement" means an agreement to make cash disbursements to finance—

(i) the construction or improvement of real property,

(ii) a contract to construct or improve real property, or

(iii) the raising or harvesting of a farm crop or the raising of livestock or other animals.

For purposes of clause (iii), the furnishing of goods and services shall be treated as the disbursement of cash.

(B) Limitation on qualified property.—The term "qualified property", when used with respect to a real property construction or improvement financing agreement, includes only—

(i) in the case of subparagraph (A)(i), the real property with respect to which the construction or improvement has been or is to be made,

(ii) in the case of subparagraph (A)(ii), the proceeds of the contract described therein, and

(iii) in the case of subparagraph (A)(iii), property subject to the lien imposed by section 6321 at the time of tax lien filing and the crop or the livestock or other animals referred to in subparagraph (A)(iii).

(4) Obligatory disbursement agreement.—For purposes of this subsection—

(A) Definition.—The term "obligatory disbursement agreement" means an agreement (entered into by a person in the course of his trade or business) to make disbursements, but such an agreement shall be treated as coming within the term only to the extent of disbursements which are required to be made by reason of the intervention of the rights of a person other than the taxpayer.

(B) Limitation on qualified property.—The term "qualified property", when used with respect to an obligatory disbursement agreement, means property subject to the lien imposed by section 6321 at the time of tax lien filing and (to the extent that the acquisition is directly traceable to the disbursements referred to in subparagraph (A)) property acquired by the taxpayer after tax lien filing.

(C) Special rules for surety agreements.—Where the obligatory disbursement agreement is an agreement ensuring the performance of a contract between the taxpayer and another person—

(i) the term "qualified property" shall be treated as also including the proceeds of the contract the performance of which was ensured, and

(ii) if the contract the performance of which was ensured was a contract to construct or improve real property, to produce goods, or to furnish services, the term "qualified property" shall be treated as also including any tangible personal property used by the taxpayer in the performance of such ensured contract.

(d) 45-day period for making disbursements.—Even though notice of a lien imposed by section 6321 has been filed, such lien shall not be valid with respect to a security interest which came into existence after tax lien filing by reason of disbursements made before the 46th day after the date of tax lien filing, or (if earlier) before the person making such disbursements had actual notice or knowledge of tax lien filing, but only if such security interest—

(1) is in property (A) subject, at the time of tax lien filing, to the lien imposed by section 6321, and (B) covered by the terms of a written agreement entered into before tax lien filing, and

(2) is protected under local law against a judgment lien arising, as of the time of tax lien filing, out of an unsecured obligation.

(e) Priority of interest and expenses.—If the lien imposed by section 6321 is not valid as against a lien or security interest, the priority of such lien or security interest shall extend to—

(1) any interest or carrying charges upon the obligation secured,

(2) the reasonable charges and expenses of an indenture trustee or agent holding the security interest for the benefit of the holder of the security interest,

(3) the reasonable expenses, including reasonable compensation for attorneys, actually incurred in collecting or enforcing the obligation secured,

(4) the reasonable costs of insuring, preserving, or repairing the property to which the lien or security interest relates,

(5) the reasonable costs of insuring payment of the obligation secured, and

(6) amounts paid to satisfy any lien on the property to which the lien or security interest relates, but only if the lien so satisfied is entitled to priority over the lien imposed by section 6321,

to the extent that, under local law, any such item has the same priority as the lien or security interest to which it relates.

(f) Place for filing notice; form.—

(1) Place for filing.—The notice referred to in subsection (a) shall be filed—

(A) Under State laws.—

(i) **Real property.**—In the case of real property, in one office within the State (or the county, or other governmental subdivision), as designated by the laws of such State, in which the property subject to the lien is situated; and

(ii) **Personal property.**—In the case of personal property, whether tangible or intangible, in one office within the State (or the county, or other governmental subdivision), as designated by the laws of such State, in which the property subject to the lien is situated, except that State law merely conforming to or reenacting Federal law establishing a national filing system does not constitute a second office for filing as designated by the laws of such State; or

(B) **With clerk of district court.**—In the office of the clerk of the United States district court for the judicial district in which the property subject to the lien is situated, whenever the State has not by law designated one office which meets the requirements of subparagraph (A); or

(C) **With Recorder of Deeds of the District of Columbia.**—In the office of the Recorder of Deeds of the District of Columbia, if the property subject to the lien is situated in the District of Columbia.

(2) **Situs of property subject to lien.**—For purposes of paragraphs (1) and (4), property shall be deemed to be situated—

(A) **Real property.**—In the case of real property, at its physical location; or

(B) **Personal property.**—In the case of personal property, whether tangible or intangible, at the residence of the taxpayer at the time the notice of lien is filed.

For purposes of paragraph (2)(B), the residence of a corporation or partnership shall be deemed to be the place at which the principal executive office of the business is located, and the residence of a taxpayer whose residence is without the United States shall be deemed to be in the District of Columbia.

(3) **Form.**—The form and content of the notice referred to in subsection (a) shall be prescribed by the Secretary. Such notice shall be valid notwithstanding any other provision of law regarding the form or content of a notice of lien.

(4) **Indexing required with respect to certain real property.**—In the case of real property, if—

(A) under the laws of the State in which the real property is located, a deed is not valid as against a purchaser of the property who (at the time of purchase) does not have actual notice or knowledge of the existence of such deed unless the fact of filing of such deed has been entered and recorded in a public index at the place of filing in such a manner that a reasonable inspection of the index will reveal the existence of the deed, and

(B) there is maintained (at the applicable office under paragraph (1)) an adequate system for the public indexing of Federal tax liens,

then the notice of lien referred to in subsection (a) shall not be treated as meeting the filing requirements under paragraph (1) unless the fact of filing is entered and recorded in the index referred to in subparagraph (B) in such a manner that a reasonable inspection of the index will reveal the existence of the lien.

(5) **National filing systems.**—The filing of a notice of lien shall be governed solely by this title and shall not be subject to any other Federal law establishing a place or places for the filing of liens or encumbrances under a national filing system.

(g) **Refiling of notice.**—For purposes of this section—

(1) **General rule.**—Unless notice of lien is refiled in the manner prescribed in paragraph (2) during the required refiling period, such notice of lien shall be treated as filed on the date on which it is filed (in accordance with subsection (f)) after the expiration of such refiling period.

(2) **Place for filing.**—A notice of lien refiled during the required refiling period shall be effective only—

(A) if—

(i)   such notice of lien is refiled in the office in which the prior notice of lien was filed, and

(ii)   in the case of real property, the fact of refiling is entered and recorded in an index to the extent required by subsection (f)(4); and

(B)   in any case in which, 90 days or more prior to the date of a refiling of notice of lien under subparagraph (A), the Secretary received written information (in the manner prescribed in regulations issued by the Secretary) concerning a change in the taxpayer's residence, if a notice of such lien is also filed in accordance with subsection (f) in the State in which such residence is located.

(3)   Required refiling period.—In the case of any notice of lien, the term "required refiling period" means—

(A)   the one-year period ending 30 days after the expiration of 10 years after the date of the assessment of the tax, and

(B)   the one-year period ending with the expiration of 10 years after the close of the preceding required refiling period for such notice of lien.

(4)   Transitional rule.—Notwithstanding paragraph (3), if the assessment of the tax was made before January 1, 1962, the first required refiling period shall be the calendar year 1967.

(h)   Definitions.—For purposes of this section and section 6324—

(1)   Security interest.—The term "security interest" means any interest in property acquired by contract for the purpose of securing payment or performance of an obligation or indemnifying against loss or liability. A security interest exists at any time (A) if, at such time, the property is in existence and the interest has become protected under local law against a subsequent judgment lien arising out of an unsecured obligation, and (B) to the extent that, at such time, the holder has parted with money or money's worth.

(2)   Mechanic's lienor.—The term "mechanic's lienor" means any person who under local law has a lien on real property (or on the proceeds of a contract relating to real property) for services, labor, or materials furnished in connection with the construction or improvement of such property. For purposes of the preceding sentence, a person has a lien on the earliest date such lien becomes valid under local law against subsequent purchasers without actual notice, but not before he begins to furnish the services, labor, or materials.

(3)   Motor vehicle.—The term "motor vehicle" means a self-propelled vehicle which is registered for highway use under the laws of any State or foreign country.

(4)   Security.—The term "security" means any bond, debenture, note, or certificate or other evidence of indebtedness, issued by a corporation or a government or political subdivision thereof, with interest coupons or in registered form, share of stock, voting trust certificate, or any certificate of interest or participation in, certificate of deposit or receipt for, temporary or interim certificate for, or warrant or right to subscribe to or purchase, any of the foregoing; negotiable instrument; or money.

(5)   Tax lien filing.—The term "tax lien filing" means the filing of notice (referred to in subsection (a)) of the lien imposed by section 6321.

(6)   Purchaser.—The term "purchaser" means a person who, for adequate and full consideration in money or money's worth, acquires an interest (other than a lien or security interest) in property which is valid under local law against subsequent purchasers without actual notice. In applying the preceding sentence for purposes of subsection (a) of this section, and for purposes of section 6324—

(A)   a lease of property,

(B)   a written executory contract to purchase or lease property,

(C)   an option to purchase or lease property or any interest therein, or

(D)   an option to renew or extend a lease of property,

which is not a lien or security interest shall be treated as an interest in property.

(i) Special rules.—

(1) Actual notice or knowledge.—For purposes of this subchapter, an organization shall be deemed for purposes of a particular transaction to have actual notice or knowledge of any fact from the time such fact is brought to the attention of the individual conducting such transaction, and in any event from the time such fact would have been brought to such individual's attention if the organization had exercised due diligence. An organization exercises due diligence if it maintains reasonable routines for communicating significant information to the person conducting the transaction and there is reasonable compliance with the routine. Due diligence does not require an individual acting for the organization to communicate information unless such communication is part of his regular duties or unless he has reason to know of the transaction and that the transaction would be materially affected by the information.

(2) Subrogation.—Where, under local law, one person is subrogated to the rights of another with respect to a lien or interest, such person shall be subrogated to such rights for purposes of any lien imposed by section 6321 or 6324.

(3) Forfeitures.—For purposes of this subchapter, a forfeiture under local law of property seized by a law enforcement agency of a State, county, or other local governmental subdivision shall relate back to the time of seizure, except that this paragraph shall not apply to the extent that under local law the holder of an intervening claim or interest would have priority over the interest of the State, county, or other local governmental subdivision in the property.

(4) Cost-of-living adjustment.—In the case of notices of liens imposed by section 6321 which are filed in any calendar year after 1998, each of the dollar amounts under paragraph (4) or (7) of subsection (b) shall be increased by an amount equal to.—

    (A) such dollar amount, multiplied by

    (B) the cost-of-living adjustment determined under section 1(f)(3) for the calendar year, determined by substituting "calendar year 1996" for "calendar year 2016" in subparagraph (A)(ii) thereof.

    If any amount as adjusted under the preceding sentence is not a multiple of $10, such amount shall be rounded to the nearest multiple of $10.

(j) Withdrawal of notice in certain circumstances.—

(1) In general.—The Secretary may withdraw a notice of a lien filed under this section and this chapter shall be applied as if the withdrawn notice had not been filed, if the Secretary determines that—

    (A) the filing of such notice was premature or otherwise not in accordance with administrative procedures of the Secretary,

    (B) the taxpayer has entered into an agreement under section 6159 to satisfy the tax liability for which the lien was imposed by means of installment payments, unless such agreement provides otherwise,

    (C) the withdrawal of such notice will facilitate the collection of the tax liability, or

    (D) with the consent of the taxpayer or the National Taxpayer Advocate, the withdrawal of such notice would be in the best interests of the taxpayer (as determined by the National Taxpayer Advocate) and the United States.

Any such withdrawal shall be made by filing notice at the same office as the withdrawn notice. A copy of such notice of withdrawal shall be provided to the taxpayer.

(2) Notice to credit agencies, etc.—Upon written request by the taxpayer with respect to whom a notice of a lien was withdrawn under paragraph (1), the Secretary shall promptly make reasonable efforts to notify credit reporting agencies, and any financial institution or creditor whose name and address is specified in such request, of the withdrawal of such notice. Any such request shall be in such form as the Secretary may prescribe.

BANKRUPTCY CODE

11 U.S.C. §§ 101–1530

Current through April 10, 2023; P.L. 118–3

For updates, see http://uscode.house.gov

Chapter

1.   General Provisions
3.   Case Administration
5.   Creditors, the Debtor, and the Estate
7.   Liquidation
9.   Adjustment of Debts of a Municipality
11.   Reorganization
12.   Adjustment of Debts of a Family Farmer or Fisherman With Regular Annual Income
13.   Adjustment of Debts of an Individual With Regular Income
15.   Ancillary and Other Cross-Border Cases

CHAPTER 1—GENERAL PROVISIONS

101.   Definitions
102.   Rules of construction
103.   Applicability of chapters
104.   Adjustment of dollar amounts
105.   Power of court
106.   Waiver of sovereign immunity
107.   Public access to papers
108.   Extension of time
109.   Who may be a debtor
110.   Penalty for persons who negligently or fraudulently prepare bankruptcy petitions
111.   Nonprofit budget and credit counseling agencies; financial management instructional courses
112.   Prohibition on disclosure of name of minor children

§ 101. Definitions

In this title the following definitions shall apply:

(1)   The term "accountant" means accountant authorized under applicable law to practice public accounting, and includes professional accounting association, corporation, or partnership, if so authorized.

(2)   The term "affiliate" means—

(A)   entity that directly or indirectly owns, controls, or holds with power to vote, 20 percent or more of the outstanding voting securities of the debtor, other than an entity that holds such securities—

(i)   in a fiduciary or agency capacity without sole discretionary power to vote such securities; or

1143

(ii)   solely to secure a debt, if such entity has not in fact exercised such power to vote;

(B)   corporation 20 percent or more of whose outstanding voting securities are directly or indirectly owned, controlled, or held with power to vote, by the debtor, or by an entity that directly or indirectly owns, controls, or holds with power to vote, 20 percent or more of the outstanding voting securities of the debtor, other than an entity that holds such securities—

(i)   in a fiduciary or agency capacity without sole discretionary power to vote such securities; or

(ii)   solely to secure a debt, if such entity has not in fact exercised such power to vote;

(C)   person whose business is operated under a lease or operating agreement by a debtor, or person substantially all of whose property is operated under an operating agreement with the debtor; or

(D)   entity that operates the business or substantially all of the property of the debtor under a lease or operating agreement.

(3)   The term "assisted person" means any person whose debts consist primarily of consumer debts and the value of whose nonexempt property is less than $226,850.

(4)   The term "attorney" means attorney, professional law association, corporation, or partnership, authorized under applicable law to practice law.

(4A)   The term "bankruptcy assistance" means any goods or services sold or otherwise provided to an assisted person with the express or implied purpose of providing information, advice, counsel, document preparation, or filing, or attendance at a creditors' meeting or appearing in a case or proceeding on behalf of another or providing legal representation with respect to a case or proceeding under this title.

(5)   The term "claim" means—

(A)   right to payment, whether or not such right is reduced to judgment, liquidated, unliquidated, fixed, contingent, matured, unmatured, disputed, undisputed, legal, equitable, secured, or unsecured; or

(B)   right to an equitable remedy for breach of performance if such breach gives rise to a right to payment, whether or not such right to an equitable remedy is reduced to judgment, fixed, contingent, matured, unmatured, disputed, undisputed, secured, or unsecured.

(6)   The term "commodity broker" means futures commission merchant, foreign futures commission merchant, clearing organization, leverage transaction merchant, or commodity options dealer, as defined in section 761 of this title, with respect to which there is a customer, as defined in section 761 of this title.

(7)   The term "community claim" means claim that arose before the commencement of the case concerning the debtor for which property of the kind specified in section 541(a)(2) of this title is liable, whether or not there is any such property at the time of the commencement of the case.

(7A)   The term "commercial fishing operation" means—

(A)   the catching or harvesting of fish, shrimp, lobsters, urchins, seaweed, shellfish, or other aquatic species or products of such species; or

(B)   for purposes of section 109 and chapter 12, aquaculture activities consisting of raising for market any species or product described in subparagraph (A).

(7B)   The term "commercial fishing vessel" means a vessel used by a family fisherman to carry out a commercial fishing operation.

(8)   The term "consumer debt" means debt incurred by an individual primarily for a personal, family, or household purpose.

(9)   The term "corporation"—

(A)   includes—

    (i) association having a power or privilege that a private corporation, but not an individual or a partnership, possesses;

    (ii) partnership association organized under a law that makes only the capital subscribed responsible for the debts of such association;

    (iii) joint-stock company;

    (iv) unincorporated company or association; or

    (v) business trust; but

  (B) does not include limited partnership.

(10) The term "creditor" means—

  (A) entity that has a claim against the debtor that arose at the time of or before the order for relief concerning the debtor;

  (B) entity that has a claim against the estate of a kind specified in section 348(d), 502(f), 502(g), 502(h) or 502(i) of this title; or

  (C) entity that has a community claim.

(10A)   The term "current monthly income"—

  (A) means the average monthly income from all sources that the debtor receives (or in a joint case the debtor and the debtor's spouse receive) without regard to whether such income is taxable income, derived during the 6-month period ending on—

    (i) the last day of the calendar month immediately preceding the date of the commencement of the case if the debtor files the schedule of current income required by section 521(a)(1)(B)(ii); or

    (ii) the date on which current income is determined by the court for purposes of this title if the debtor does not file the schedule of current income required by section 521(a)(1)(B)(ii); and

  (B)(i)   includes any amount paid by any entity other than the debtor (or in a joint case the debtor and the debtor's spouse), on a regular basis for the household expenses of the debtor or the debtor's dependents (and in a joint case the debtor's spouse if not otherwise a dependent); and

    (ii) excludes—

      (I) benefits received under the Social Security Act (42 U.S.C. 301 et seq.);

      (II) payments to victims of war crimes or crimes against humanity on account of their status as victims of such crimes;

      (III) payments to victims of international terrorism or domestic terrorism, as those terms are defined in section 2331 of title 18, on account of their status as victims of such terrorism; and

      (IV) any monthly compensation, pension, pay, annuity, or allowance paid under title 10, 37, or 38 in connection with a disability, combat-related injury or disability, or death of a member of the uniformed services, except that any retired pay excluded under this subclause shall include retired pay paid under chapter 61 of title 10 only to the extent that such retired pay exceeds the amount of retired pay to which the debtor would otherwise be entitled if retired under any provision of title 10 other than chapter 61 of that title.

(11) The term "custodian" means—

  (A) receiver or trustee of any of the property of the debtor, appointed in a case or proceeding not under this title;

  (B) assignee under a general assignment for the benefit of the debtor's creditors; or

(C) trustee, receiver, or agent under applicable law, or under a contract, that is appointed or authorized to take charge of property of the debtor for the purpose of enforcing a lien against such property, or for the purpose of general administration of such property for the benefit of the debtor's creditors.

(12) The term "debt" means liability on a claim.

(12A) The term "debt relief agency" means any person who provides any bankruptcy assistance to an assisted person in return for the payment of money or other valuable consideration, or who is a bankruptcy petition preparer under section 110, but does not include—

(A) any person who is an officer, director, employee, or agent of a person who provides such assistance or of the bankruptcy petition preparer;

(B) a nonprofit organization that is exempt from taxation under section 501(c)(3) of the Internal Revenue Code of 1986;

(C) a creditor of such assisted person, to the extent that the creditor is assisting such assisted person to restructure any debt owed by such assisted person to the creditor;

(D) a depository institution (as defined in section 3 of the Federal Deposit Insurance Act) or any Federal credit union or State credit union (as those terms are defined in section 101 of the Federal Credit Union Act), or any affiliate or subsidiary of such depository institution or credit union; or

(E) an author, publisher, distributor, or seller of works subject to copyright protection under title 17, when acting in such capacity.

(13) The term "debtor" means person or municipality concerning which a case under this title has been commenced.

(13A) The term "debtor's principal residence"—

(A) means a residential structure if used as the principal residence by the debtor, including incidental property, without regard to whether that structure is attached to real property; and

(B) includes an individual condominium or cooperative unit, a mobile or manufactured home, or trailer if used as the principal residence by the debtor.

(14) The term "disinterested person" means a person that—

(A) is not a creditor, an equity security holder, or an insider;

(B) is not and was not, within 2 years before the date of the filing of the petition, a director, officer, or employee of the debtor; and

(C) does not have an interest materially adverse to the interest of the estate or of any class of creditors or equity security holders, by reason of any direct or indirect relationship to, connection with, or interest in, the debtor, or for any other reason.

(14A) The term "domestic support obligation" means a debt that accrues before, on, or after the date of the order for relief in a case under this title, including interest that accrues on that debt as provided under applicable nonbankruptcy law notwithstanding any other provision of this title, that is—

(A) owed to or recoverable by—

(i) a spouse, former spouse, or child of the debtor or such child's parent, legal guardian, or responsible relative; or

(ii) a governmental unit;

(B) in the nature of alimony, maintenance, or support (including assistance provided by a governmental unit) of such spouse, former spouse, or child of the debtor or such child's parent, without regard to whether such debt is expressly so designated;

(C) established or subject to establishment before, on, or after the date of the order for relief in a case under this title, by reason of applicable provisions of—

(i) a separation agreement, divorce decree, or property settlement agreement;

(ii) an order of a court of record; or

(iii) a determination made in accordance with applicable nonbankruptcy law by a governmental unit; and

(D) not assigned to a nongovernmental entity, unless that obligation is assigned voluntarily by the spouse, former spouse, child of the debtor, or such child's parent, legal guardian, or responsible relative for the purpose of collecting the debt.

(15) The term "entity" includes person, estate, trust, governmental unit, and United States trustee.

(16) The term "equity security" means—

(A) share in a corporation, whether or not transferable or denominated "stock", or similar security;

(B) interest of a limited partner in a limited partnership; or

(C) warrant or right, other than a right to convert, to purchase, sell, or subscribe to a share, security, or interest of a kind specified in subparagraph (A) or (B) of this paragraph.

(17) The term "equity security holder" means holder of an equity security of the debtor.

(18) The term "family farmer" means—

(A) individual or individual and spouse engaged in a farming operation whose aggregate debts do not exceed $11,097,350 and not less than 50 percent of whose aggregate noncontingent, liquidated debts (excluding a debt for the principal residence of such individual or such individual and spouse unless such debt arises out of a farming operation), on the date the case is filed, arise out of a farming operation owned or operated by such individual or such individual and spouse, and such individual or such individual and spouse receive from such farming operation more than 50 percent of such individual's or such individual and spouse's gross income for—

(i) the taxable year preceding; or

(ii) each of the 2d and 3d taxable years preceding;

the taxable year in which the case concerning such individual or such individual and spouse was filed; or

(B) corporation or partnership in which more than 50 percent of the outstanding stock or equity is held by one family, or by one family and the relatives of the members of such family, and such family or such relatives conduct the farming operation, and

(i) more than 80 percent of the value of its assets consists of assets related to the farming operation;

(ii) its aggregate debts do not exceed $11,097,350 and not less than 50 percent of its aggregate noncontingent, liquidated debts (excluding a debt for one dwelling which is owned by such corporation or partnership and which a shareholder or partner maintains as a principal residence, unless such debt arises out of a farming operation), on the date the case is filed, arise out of the farming operation owned or operated by such corporation or such partnership; and

(iii) if such corporation issues stock, such stock is not publicly traded.

(19) The term "family farmer with regular annual income" means family farmer whose annual income is sufficiently stable and regular to enable such family farmer to make payments under a plan under chapter 12 of this title.

(19A) The term "family fisherman" means—

(A) an individual or individual and spouse engaged in a commercial fishing operation—

(i) whose aggregate debts do not exceed $2,268,550 and not less than 80 percent of whose aggregate noncontingent, liquidated debts (excluding a debt for the principal residence of such individual or such individual and spouse, unless such debt arises out of a commercial fishing operation), on the date the case is filed, arise out of a commercial fishing operation owned or operated by such individual or such individual and spouse; and

(ii) who receive from such commercial fishing operation more than 50 percent of such individual's or such individual's and spouse's gross income for the taxable year preceding the taxable year in which the case concerning such individual or such individual and spouse was filed; or

(B) a corporation or partnership—

(i) in which more than 50 percent of the outstanding stock or equity is held by—

(I) 1 family that conducts the commercial fishing operation; or

(II) 1 family and the relatives of the members of such family, and such family or such relatives conduct the commercial fishing operation; and

(ii)(I) more than 80 percent of the value of its assets consists of assets related to the commercial fishing operation;

(II) its aggregate debts do not exceed $2,268,550 and not less than 80 percent of its aggregate noncontingent, liquidated debts (excluding a debt for 1 dwelling which is owned by such corporation or partnership and which a shareholder or partner maintains as a principal residence, unless such debt arises out of a commercial fishing operation), on the date the case is filed, arise out of a commercial fishing operation owned or operated by such corporation or such partnership; and

(III) if such corporation issues stock, such stock is not publicly traded.

(19B) The term "family fisherman with regular annual income" means a family fisherman whose annual income is sufficiently stable and regular to enable such family fisherman to make payments under a plan under chapter 12 of this title.

(20) The term "farmer" means (except when such term appears in the term "family farmer") person that received more than 80 percent of such person's gross income during the taxable year of such person immediately preceding the taxable year of such person during which the case under this title concerning such person was commenced from a farming operation owned or operated by such person.

(21) The term "farming operation" includes farming, tillage of the soil, dairy farming, ranching, production or raising of crops, poultry, or livestock, and production of poultry or livestock products in an unmanufactured state.

(21A) The term "farmout agreement" means a written agreement in which—

(A) the owner of a right to drill, produce, or operate liquid or gaseous hydrocarbons on property agrees or has agreed to transfer or assign all or a part of such right to another entity; and

(B) such other entity (either directly or through its agents or its assigns), as consideration, agrees to perform drilling, reworking, recompleting, testing, or similar or related operations, to develop or produce liquid or gaseous hydrocarbons on the property.

(21B) The term "Federal depository institutions regulatory agency" means—

(A) with respect to an insured depository institution (as defined in section 3(c)(2) of the Federal Deposit Insurance Act) for which no conservator or receiver has been appointed, the appropriate Federal banking agency (as defined in section 3(q) of such Act);

(B) with respect to an insured credit union (including an insured credit union for which the National Credit Union Administration has been appointed conservator or liquidating agent), the National Credit Union Administration;

(C) with respect to any insured depository institution for which the Resolution Trust Corporation has been appointed conservator or receiver, the Resolution Trust Corporation; and

(D) with respect to any insured depository institution for which the Federal Deposit Insurance Corporation has been appointed conservator or receiver, the Federal Deposit Insurance Corporation.

(22) The term "financial institution" means—

(A) a Federal reserve bank, or an entity that is a commercial or savings bank, industrial savings bank, savings and loan association, trust company, federally-insured credit union, or receiver, liquidating agent, or conservator for such entity and, when any such Federal reserve bank, receiver, liquidating agent, conservator or entity is acting as agent or custodian for a customer (whether or not a "customer", as defined in section 741) in connection with a securities contract (as defined in section 741) such customer; or

(B) in connection with a securities contract (as defined in section 741) an investment company registered under the Investment Company Act of 1940.

(22A) The term "financial participant" means—

(A) an entity that, at the time it enters into a securities contract, commodity contract, swap agreement, repurchase agreement, or forward contract, or at the time of the date of the filing of the petition, has one or more agreements or transactions described in paragraph (1), (2), (3), (4), (5), or (6) of section 561(a) with the debtor or any other entity (other than an affiliate) of a total gross dollar value of not less than $1,000,000,000 in notional or actual principal amount outstanding (aggregated across counterparties) at such time or on any day during the 15-month period preceding the date of the filing of the petition, or has gross mark-to-market positions of not less than $100,000,000 (aggregated across counterparties) in one or more such agreements or transactions with the debtor or any other entity (other than an affiliate) at such time or on any day during the 15-month period preceding the date of the filing of the petition; or

(B) a clearing organization (as defined in section 402 of the Federal Deposit Insurance Corporation Improvement Act of 1991).

(23) The term "foreign proceeding" means a collective judicial or administrative proceeding in a foreign country, including an interim proceeding, under a law relating to insolvency or adjustment of debt in which proceeding the assets and affairs of the debtor are subject to control or supervision by a foreign court, for the purpose of reorganization or liquidation.

(24) The term "foreign representative" means a person or body, including a person or body appointed on an interim basis, authorized in a foreign proceeding to administer the reorganization or the liquidation of the debtor's assets or affairs or to act as a representative of such foreign proceeding.

(25) The term "forward contract" means—

(A) a contract (other than a commodity contract, as defined in section 761) for the purchase, sale, or transfer of a commodity, as defined in section 761(8) of this title, or any similar good, article, service, right, or interest which is presently or in the future becomes the subject of dealing in the forward contract trade, or product or byproduct thereof, with a maturity date more than two days after the date the contract is entered into, including, but not limited to, a repurchase or reverse repurchase transaction (whether or not such repurchase or reverse repurchase transaction is a "repurchase agreement", as defined in this section)[1] consignment, lease, swap, hedge transaction, deposit, loan, option, allocated transaction, unallocated transaction, or any other similar agreement;

---

[1] So in original. Probably should be followed by a comma.

(B) any combination of agreements or transactions referred to in subparagraphs (A) and (C);

(C) any option to enter into an agreement or transaction referred to in subparagraph (A) or (B);

(D) a master agreement that provides for an agreement or transaction referred to in subparagraph (A), (B), or (C), together with all supplements to any such master agreement, without regard to whether such master agreement provides for an agreement or transaction that is not a forward contract under this paragraph, except that such master agreement shall be considered to be a forward contract under this paragraph only with respect to each agreement or transaction under such master agreement that is referred to in subparagraph (A), (B), or (C); or

(E) any security agreement or arrangement, or other credit enhancement related to any agreement or transaction referred to in subparagraph (A), (B), (C), or (D), including any guarantee or reimbursement obligation by or to a forward contract merchant or financial participant in connection with any agreement or transaction referred to in any such subparagraph, but not to exceed the damages in connection with any such agreement or transaction, measured in accordance with section 562.

(26) The term "forward contract merchant" means a Federal reserve bank, or an entity the business of which consists in whole or in part of entering into forward contracts as or with merchants in a commodity (as defined in section 761) or any similar good, article, service, right, or interest which is presently or in the future becomes the subject of dealing in the forward contract trade.

(27) The term "governmental unit" means United States; State; Commonwealth; District; Territory; municipality; foreign state; department, agency, or instrumentality of the United States (but not a United States trustee while serving as a trustee in a case under this title), a State, a Commonwealth, a District, a Territory, a municipality, or a foreign state; or other foreign or domestic government.

(27A) The term "health care business"—

(A) means any public or private entity (without regard to whether that entity is organized for profit or not for profit) that is primarily engaged in offering to the general public facilities and services for—

(i) the diagnosis or treatment of injury, deformity, or disease; and

(ii) surgical, drug treatment, psychiatric, or obstetric care; and

(B) includes—

(i) any—

(I) general or specialized hospital;

(II) ancillary ambulatory, emergency, or surgical treatment facility;

(III) hospice;

(IV) home health agency; and

(V) other health care institution that is similar to an entity referred to in subclause (I), (II), (III), or (IV); and

(ii) any long-term care facility, including any—

(I) skilled nursing facility;

(II) intermediate care facility;

(III) assisted living facility;

(IV) home for the aged;

(V) domiciliary care facility; and

(VI) health care institution that is related to a facility referred to in subclause (I), (II), (III), (IV), or (V), if that institution is primarily engaged in offering room, board, laundry, or personal assistance with activities of daily living and incidentals to activities of daily living.

(27B) The term "incidental property" means, with respect to a debtor's principal residence—

(A) property commonly conveyed with a principal residence in the area where the real property is located;

(B) all easements, rights, appurtenances, fixtures, rents, royalties, mineral rights, oil or gas rights or profits, water rights, escrow funds, or insurance proceeds; and

(C) all replacements or additions.

(28) The term "indenture" means mortgage, deed of trust, or indenture, under which there is outstanding a security, other than a voting-trust certificate, constituting a claim against the debtor, a claim secured by a lien on any of the debtor's property, or an equity security of the debtor.

(29) The term "indenture trustee" means trustee under an indenture.

(30) The term "individual with regular income" means individual whose income is sufficiently stable and regular to enable such individual to make payments under a plan under chapter 13 of this title, other than a stockbroker or a commodity broker.

(31) The term "insider" includes—

(A) if the debtor is an individual—

(i) relative of the debtor or of a general partner of the debtor;

(ii) partnership in which the debtor is a general partner;

(iii) general partner of the debtor; or

(iv) corporation of which the debtor is a director, officer, or person in control;

(B) if the debtor is a corporation—

(i) director of the debtor;

(ii) officer of the debtor;

(iii) person in control of the debtor;

(iv) partnership in which the debtor is a general partner;

(v) general partner of the debtor; or

(vi) relative of a general partner, director, officer, or person in control of the debtor;

(C) if the debtor is a partnership—

(i) general partner in the debtor;

(ii) relative of a general partner in, general partner of, or person in control of the debtor;

(iii) partnership in which the debtor is a general partner;

(iv) general partner of the debtor; or

(v) person in control of the debtor;

(D) if the debtor is a municipality, elected official of the debtor or relative of an elected official of the debtor;

(E) affiliate, or insider of an affiliate as if such affiliate were the debtor; and

(F) managing agent of the debtor.

(32) The term "insolvent" means—

(A) with reference to an entity other than a partnership and a municipality, financial condition such that the sum of such entity's debts is greater than all of such entity's property, at a fair valuation, exclusive of—

(i) property transferred, concealed, or removed with intent to hinder, delay, or defraud such entity's creditors; and

(ii) property that may be exempted from property of the estate under section 522 of this title;

(B) with reference to a partnership, financial condition such that the sum of such partnership's debts is greater than the aggregate of, at a fair valuation—

(i) all of such partnership's property, exclusive of property of the kind specified in subparagraph (A)(i) of this paragraph; and

(ii) the sum of the excess of the value of each general partner's nonpartnership property, exclusive of property of the kind specified in subparagraph (A) of this paragraph, over such partner's nonpartnership debts; and

(C) with reference to a municipality, financial condition such that the municipality is—

(i) generally not paying its debts as they become due unless such debts are the subject of a bona fide dispute; or

(ii) unable to pay its debts as they become due.

(33) The term "institution-affiliated party"—

(A) with respect to an insured depository institution (as defined in section 3(c)(2) of the Federal Deposit Insurance Act), has the meaning given it in section 3(u) of the Federal Deposit Insurance Act; and

(B) with respect to an insured credit union, has the meaning given it in section 206(r) of the Federal Credit Union Act.

(34) The term "insured credit union" has the meaning given it in section 101(7) of the Federal Credit Union Act.

(35) The term "insured depository institution"—

(A) has the meaning given it in section 3(c)(2) of the Federal Deposit Insurance Act; and

(B) includes an insured credit union (except in the case of paragraphs (21B) and (33)(A) of this subsection).

(35A) The term "intellectual property" means—

(A) trade secret;

(B) invention, process, design, or plant protected under title 35;

(C) patent application;

(D) plant variety;

(E) work of authorship protected under title 17; or

(F) mask work protected under chapter 9 of title 17;

to the extent protected by applicable nonbankruptcy law.

(36) The term "judicial lien" means lien obtained by judgment, levy, sequestration, or other legal or equitable process or proceeding.

(37) The term "lien" means charge against or interest in property to secure payment of a debt or performance of an obligation.

(38) The term "margin payment" means, for purposes of the forward contract provisions of this title, payment or deposit of cash, a security or other property, that is commonly known in the forward contract trade as original margin, initial margin, maintenance margin, or variation margin, including mark-to-market payments, or variation payments.

(38A) The term "master netting agreement"—

(A) means an agreement providing for the exercise of rights, including rights of netting, setoff, liquidation, termination, acceleration, or close out, under or in connection with one or more contracts that are described in any one or more of paragraphs (1) through (5) of section 561(a), or any security agreement or arrangement or other credit enhancement related to one or more of the foregoing, including any guarantee or reimbursement obligation related to 1 or more of the foregoing; and

(B) if the agreement contains provisions relating to agreements or transactions that are not contracts described in paragraphs (1) through (5) of section 561(a), shall be deemed to be a master netting agreement only with respect to those agreements or transactions that are described in any one or more of paragraphs (1) through (5) of section 561(a).

(38B) The term "master netting agreement participant" means an entity that, at any time before the date of the filing of the petition, is a party to an outstanding master netting agreement with the debtor.

(39) The term "mask work" has the meaning given it in section 901(a)(2) of title 17.

(39A) The term "median family income" means for any year—

(A) the median family income both calculated and reported by the Bureau of the Census in the then most recent year; and

(B) if not so calculated and reported in the then current year, adjusted annually after such most recent year until the next year in which median family income is both calculated and reported by the Bureau of the Census, to reflect the percentage change in the Consumer Price Index for All Urban Consumers during the period of years occurring after such most recent year and before such current year.

(40) The term "municipality" means political subdivision or public agency or instrumentality of a State.

(40A) The term "patient" means any individual who obtains or receives services from a health care business.

(40B) The term "patient records" means any record relating to a patient, including a written document or a record recorded in a magnetic, optical, or other form of electronic medium.

(41) The term "person" includes individual, partnership, and corporation, but does not include governmental unit, except that a governmental unit that—

(A) acquires an asset from a person—

(i) as a result of the operation of a loan guarantee agreement; or

(ii) as receiver or liquidating agent of a person;

(B) is a guarantor of a pension benefit payable by or on behalf of the debtor or an affiliate of the debtor; or

(C) is the legal or beneficial owner of an asset of—

(i) an employee pension benefit plan that is a governmental plan, as defined in section 414(d) of the Internal Revenue Code of 1986; or

(ii) an eligible deferred compensation plan, as defined in section 457(b) of the Internal Revenue Code of 1986;

shall be considered, for purposes of section 1102 of this title, to be a person with respect to such asset or such benefit.

(41A)   The term "personally identifiable information" means—

(A)   if provided by an individual to the debtor in connection with obtaining a product or a service from the debtor primarily for personal, family, or household purposes—

    (i)   the first name (or initial) and last name of such individual, whether given at birth or time of adoption, or resulting from a lawful change of name;

    (ii)   the geographical address of a physical place of residence of such individual;

    (iii) an electronic address (including an e-mail address) of such individual;

    (iv) a telephone number dedicated to contacting such individual at such physical place of residence;

    (v)   a social security account number issued to such individual; or

    (vi) the account number of a credit card issued to such individual; or

(B)   if identified in connection with 1 or more of the items of information specified in subparagraph (A)—

    (i)   a birth date, the number of a certificate of birth or adoption, or a place of birth; or

    (ii)   any other information concerning an identified individual that, if disclosed, will result in contacting or identifying such individual physically or electronically.

(42) The term "petition" means petition filed under section 301, 302, 303, and[2] 1504 of this title, as the case may be, commencing a case under this title.

(42A)   The term "production payment" means a term overriding royalty satisfiable in cash or in kind—

(A)   contingent on the production of a liquid or gaseous hydrocarbon from particular real property; and

(B)   from a specified volume, or a specified value, from the liquid or gaseous hydrocarbon produced from such property, and determined without regard to production costs.

(43) The term "purchaser" means transferee of a voluntary transfer, and includes immediate or mediate transferee of such a transferee.

(44) The term "railroad" means common carrier by railroad engaged in the transportation of individuals or property or owner of trackage facilities leased by such a common carrier.

(45) The term "relative" means individual related by affinity or consanguinity within the third degree as determined by the common law, or individual in a step or adoptive relationship within such third degree.

(46) The term "repo participant" means an entity that, at any time before the filing of the petition, has an outstanding repurchase agreement with the debtor.

(47) The term "repurchase agreement" (which definition also applies to a reverse repurchase agreement)—

(A)   means—

    (i)   an agreement, including related terms, which provides for the transfer of one or more certificates of deposit, mortgage related securities (as defined in section 3 of the Securities Exchange Act of 1934), mortgage loans, interests in mortgage related securities or mortgage loans, eligible bankers' acceptances, qualified foreign government securities (defined as a security that is a direct obligation of, or that is fully guaranteed by, the central government of a member of the Organization for Economic Cooperation and Development), or securities that are direct obligations of, or that are fully guaranteed by, the United States or any agency of the United States against the transfer of funds by the transferee of such

---

[2]   So in original. Probably should be "or".

certificates of deposit, eligible bankers' acceptances, securities, mortgage loans, or interests, with a simultaneous agreement by such transferee to transfer to the transferor thereof certificates of deposit, eligible bankers' acceptance, securities, mortgage loans, or interests of the kind described in this clause, at a date certain not later than 1 year after such transfer or on demand, against the transfer of funds;

> **(ii)** any combination of agreements or transactions referred to in clauses (i) and (iii);

> **(iii)** an option to enter into an agreement or transaction referred to in clause (i) or (ii);

> **(iv)** a master agreement that provides for an agreement or transaction referred to in clause (i), (ii), or (iii), together with all supplements to any such master agreement, without regard to whether such master agreement provides for an agreement or transaction that is not a repurchase agreement under this paragraph, except that such master agreement shall be considered to be a repurchase agreement under this paragraph only with respect to each agreement or transaction under the master agreement that is referred to in clause (i), (ii), or (iii); or

> **(v)** any security agreement or arrangement or other credit enhancement related to any agreement or transaction referred to in clause (i), (ii), (iii), or (iv), including any guarantee or reimbursement obligation by or to a repo participant or financial participant in connection with any agreement or transaction referred to in any such clause, but not to exceed the damages in connection with any such agreement or transaction, measured in accordance with section 562 of this title; and

(B) does not include a repurchase obligation under a participation in a commercial mortgage loan.

(48) The term "securities clearing agency" means person that is registered as a clearing agency under section 17A of the Securities Exchange Act of 1934, or exempt from such registration under such section pursuant to an order of the Securities and Exchange Commission, or whose business is confined to the performance of functions of a clearing agency with respect to exempted securities, as defined in section 3(a)(12) of such Act for the purposes of such section 17A.

(48A) The term "securities self regulatory organization" means either a securities association registered with the Securities and Exchange Commission under section 15A of the Securities Exchange Act of 1934 or a national securities exchange registered with the Securities and Exchange Commission under section 6 of the Securities Exchange Act of 1934.

(49) The term "security"—

> **(A)** includes—

> > **(i)** note;

> > **(ii)** stock;

> > **(iii)** treasury stock;

> > **(iv)** bond;

> > **(v)** debenture;

> > **(vi)** collateral trust certificate;

> > **(vii)** pre-organization certificate or subscription;

> > **(viii)** transferable share;

> > **(ix)** voting-trust certificate;

> > **(x)** certificate of deposit;

> > **(xi)** certificate of deposit for security;

> > **(xii)** investment contract or certificate of interest or participation in a profit-sharing agreement or in an oil, gas, or mineral royalty or lease, if such contract or interest is required

to be the subject of a registration statement filed with the Securities and Exchange Commission under the provisions of the Securities Act of 1933, or is exempt under section 3(b) of such Act from the requirement to file such a statement;

(**xiii**) interest of a limited partner in a limited partnership;

(**xiv**) other claim or interest commonly known as "security"; and

(**xv**) certificate of interest or participation in, temporary or interim certificate for, receipt for, or warrant or right to subscribe to or purchase or sell, a security; but

(**B**) does not include—

(**i**) currency, check, draft, bill of exchange, or bank letter of credit;

(**ii**) leverage transaction, as defined in section 761 of this title;

(**iii**) commodity futures contract or forward contract;

(**iv**) option, warrant, or right to subscribe to or purchase or sell a commodity futures contract;

(**v**) option to purchase or sell a commodity;

(**vi**) contract or certificate of a kind specified in subparagraph (A)(xii) of this paragraph that is not required to be the subject of a registration statement filed with the Securities and Exchange Commission and is not exempt under section 3(b) of the Securities Act of 1933 from the requirement to file such a statement; or

(**vii**) debt or evidence of indebtedness for goods sold and delivered or services rendered.

(**50**) The term "security agreement" means agreement that creates or provides for a security interest.

(**51**) The term "security interest" means lien created by an agreement.

(**51A**) The term "settlement payment" means, for purposes of the forward contract provisions of this title, a preliminary settlement payment, a partial settlement payment, an interim settlement payment, a settlement payment on account, a final settlement payment, a net settlement payment, or any other similar payment commonly used in the forward contract trade.

(**51B**) The term "single asset real estate" means real property constituting a single property or project, other than residential real property with fewer than 4 residential units, which generates substantially all of the gross income of a debtor who is not a family farmer and on which no substantial business is being conducted by a debtor other than the business of operating the real property and activities incidental thereto.

(**51C**) The term "small business case" means a case filed under chapter 11 of this title in which the debtor is a small business debtor and has not elected that subchapter V of chapter 11 of this title shall apply.

(**51D**) The term "small business debtor"—

(**A**) subject to subparagraph (B), means a person engaged in commercial or business activities (including any affiliate of such person that is also a debtor under this title and excluding a person whose primary activity is the business of owning single asset real estate) that has aggregate noncontingent liquidated secured and unsecured debts as of the date of the filing of the petition or the date of the order for relief in an amount not more than $3,024,725 (excluding debts owed to 1 or more affiliates or insiders) not less than 50 percent of which arose from the commercial or business activities of the debtor; and

(**B**) does not include—

(**i**) any member of a group of affiliated debtors under this title that has aggregate noncontingent liquidated secured and unsecured debts in an amount greater than $3,024,725 (excluding debt owed to 1 or more affiliates or insiders);

(ii) any debtor that is a corporation subject to the reporting requirements under section 13 or 15(d) of the Securities Exchange Act of 1934 (15 U.S.C. 78m, 78o(d)); or

(iii) any debtor that is an affiliate of a corporation described in clause (ii).

(52) The term "State" includes the District of Columbia and Puerto Rico, except for the purpose of defining who may be a debtor under chapter 9 of this title.

(53) The term "statutory lien" means lien arising solely by force of a statute on specified circumstances or conditions, or lien of distress for rent, whether or not statutory, but does not include security interest or judicial lien, whether or not such interest or lien is provided by or is dependent on a statute and whether or not such interest or lien is made fully effective by statute.

(53A) The term "stockbroker" means person—

(A) with respect to which there is a customer, as defined in section 741 of this title; and

(B) that is engaged in the business of effecting transactions in securities—

(i) for the account of others; or

(ii) with members of the general public, from or for such person's own account.

(53B) The term "swap agreement"—

(A) means—

(i) any agreement, including the terms and conditions incorporated by reference in such agreement, which is—

(I) an interest rate swap, option, future, or forward agreement, including a rate floor, rate cap, rate collar, cross-currency rate swap, and basis swap;

(II) a spot, same day-tomorrow, tomorrow-next, forward, or other foreign exchange, precious metals, or other commodity agreement;

(III) a currency swap, option, future, or forward agreement;

(IV) an equity index or equity swap, option, future, or forward agreement;

(V) a debt index or debt swap, option, future, or forward agreement;

(VI) a total return, credit spread or credit swap, option, future, or forward agreement;

(VII) a commodity index or a commodity swap, option, future, or forward agreement;

(VIII) a weather swap, option, future, or forward agreement;

(IX) an emissions swap, option, future, or forward agreement; or

(X) an inflation swap, option, future, or forward agreement;

(ii) any agreement or transaction that is similar to any other agreement or transaction referred to in this paragraph and that—

(I) is of a type that has been, is presently, or in the future becomes, the subject of recurrent dealings in the swap or other derivatives markets (including terms and conditions incorporated by reference therein); and

(II) is a forward, swap, future, option, or spot transaction on one or more rates, currencies, commodities, equity securities, or other equity instruments, debt securities or other debt instruments, quantitative measures associated with an occurrence, extent of an occurrence, or contingency associated with a financial, commercial, or economic consequence, or economic or financial indices or measures of economic or financial risk or value;

(iii) any combination of agreements or transactions referred to in this subparagraph;

(iv) any option to enter into an agreement or transaction referred to in this subparagraph;

(v) a master agreement that provides for an agreement or transaction referred to in clause (i), (ii), (iii), or (iv), together with all supplements to any such master agreement, and without regard to whether the master agreement contains an agreement or transaction that is not a swap agreement under this paragraph, except that the master agreement shall be considered to be a swap agreement under this paragraph only with respect to each agreement or transaction under the master agreement that is referred to in clause (i), (ii), (iii), or (iv); or

(vi) any security agreement or arrangement or other credit enhancement related to any agreements or transactions referred to in clause (i) through (v), including any guarantee or reimbursement obligation by or to a swap participant or financial participant in connection with any agreement or transaction referred to in any such clause, but not to exceed the damages in connection with any such agreement or transaction, measured in accordance with section 562; and

(B) is applicable for purposes of this title only, and shall not be construed or applied so as to challenge or affect the characterization, definition, or treatment of any swap agreement under any other statute, regulation, or rule, including the Gramm-Leach-Bliley Act, the Legal Certainty for Bank Products Act of 2000, the securities laws (as such term is defined in section 3(a)(47) of the Securities Exchange Act of 1934) and the Commodity Exchange Act.

(53C)   The term "swap participant" means an entity that, at any time before the filing of the petition, has an outstanding swap agreement with the debtor.

(56A)[3]   The term "term overriding royalty" means an interest in liquid or gaseous hydrocarbons in place or to be produced from particular real property that entitles the owner thereof to a share of production, or the value thereof, for a term limited by time, quantity, or value realized.

(53D)   The term "timeshare plan" means and shall include that interest purchased in any arrangement, plan, scheme, or similar device, but not including exchange programs, whether by membership, agreement, tenancy in common, sale, lease, deed, rental agreement, license, right to use agreement, or by any other means, whereby a purchaser, in exchange for consideration, receives a right to use accommodations, facilities, or recreational sites, whether improved or unimproved, for a specific period of time less than a full year during any given year, but not necessarily for consecutive years, and which extends for a period of more than three years. A "timeshare interest" is that interest purchased in a timeshare plan which grants the purchaser the right to use and occupy accommodations, facilities, or recreational sites, whether improved or unimproved, pursuant to a timeshare plan.

(54) The term "transfer" means—

(A) the creation of a lien;

(B) the retention of title as a security interest;

(C) the foreclosure of a debtor's equity of redemption; or

(D) each mode, direct or indirect, absolute or conditional, voluntary or involuntary, of disposing of or parting with—

(i) property; or

(ii) an interest in property.

(54A)   The term "uninsured State member bank" means a State member bank (as defined in section 3 of the Federal Deposit Insurance Act) the deposits of which are not insured by the Federal Deposit Insurance Corporation.

---

[3]   So in original.

(55) The term "United States", when used in a geographical sense, includes all locations where the judicial jurisdiction of the United States extends, including territories and possessions of the United States.

§ 102. Rules of construction

In this title—

(1) "after notice and a hearing", or a similar phrase—

(A) means after such notice as is appropriate in the particular circumstances, and such opportunity for a hearing as is appropriate in the particular circumstances; but

(B) authorizes an act without an actual hearing if such notice is given properly and if—

(i) such a hearing is not requested timely by a party in interest; or

(ii) there is insufficient time for a hearing to be commenced before such act must be done, and the court authorizes such act;

(2) "claim against the debtor" includes claim against property of the debtor;

(3) "includes" and "including" are not limiting;

(4) "may not" is prohibitive, and not permissive;

(5) "or" is not exclusive;

(6) "order for relief" means entry of an order for relief;

(7) the singular includes the plural;

(8) a definition, contained in a section of this title that refers to another section of this title, does not, for the purpose of such reference, affect the meaning of a term used in such other section; and

(9) "United States trustee" includes a designee of the United States trustee.

§ 103. Applicability of chapters

(a) Except as provided in section 1161 of this title, chapters 1, 3, and 5 of this title apply in a case under chapter 7, 11, 12, or 13 of this title, and this chapter, sections 307, 362(*o*), 555 through 557, and 559 through 562 apply in a case under chapter 15.

(b) Subchapters I and II of chapter 7 of this title apply only in a case under such chapter.

(c) Subchapter III of chapter 7 of this title applies only in a case under such chapter concerning a stockbroker.

(d) Subchapter IV of chapter 7 of this title applies only in a case under such chapter concerning a commodity broker.

(e) Scope of Application.—Subchapter V of chapter 7 of this title shall apply only in a case under such chapter concerning the liquidation of an uninsured State member bank, or a corporation organized under section 25A of the Federal Reserve Act, which operates, or operates as, a multilateral clearing organization pursuant to section 409 of the Federal Deposit Insurance Corporation Improvement Act of 1991.

(f) Except as provided in section 901 of this title, only chapters 1 and 9 of this title apply in a case under such chapter 9.

(g) Except as provided in section 901 of this title, subchapters I, II, and III of chapter 11 of this title apply only in a case under such chapter.

(h) Subchapter IV of chapter 11 of this title applies only in a case under such chapter concerning a railroad.

(i) Subchapter V of chapter 11 of this title applies only in a case under chapter 11 in which a debtor (as defined in section 1182) elects that subchapter V of chapter 11 shall apply.

(j) Chapter 13 of this title applies only in a case under such chapter.

(k) Chapter 12 of this title applies only in a case under such chapter.

(l) Chapter 15 applies only in a case under such chapter, except that—

    (1) sections 1505, 1513, and 1514 apply in all cases under this title; and

    (2) section 1509 applies whether or not a case under this title is pending.

§ 104. Adjustment of dollar amounts

(a) On April 1, 1998, and at each 3-year interval ending on April 1 thereafter, each dollar amount in effect under sections 101(3), 101(18), 101(19A), 101(51D), 109(e), 303(b), 507(a), 522(d), 522(f)(3) and 522(f)(4), 522(n), 522(p), 522(q), 523(a)(2)(C), 541(b), 547(c)(9), 707(b), 1182(1), 1322(d), 1325(b), and 1326(b)(3) of this title and section 1409(b) of title 28 immediately before such April 1 shall be adjusted—

    (1) to reflect the change in the Consumer Price Index for All Urban Consumers, published by the Department of Labor, for the most recent 3-year period ending immediately before January 1 preceding such April 1, and

    (2) to round to the nearest $25 the dollar amount that represents such change.

(b) Not later than March 1, 1998, and at each 3-year interval ending on March 1 thereafter, the Judicial Conference of the United States shall publish in the Federal Register the dollar amounts that will become effective on such April 1 under sections 101(3), 101(18), 101(19A), 101(51D), 109(e), 303(b), 507(a), 522(d), 522(f)(3) and 522(f)(4), 522(n), 522(p), 522(q), 523(a)(2)(C), 541(b), 547(c)(9), 707(b), 1182(1), 1322(d), 1325(b), and 1326(b)(3) of this title and section 1409(b) of title 28.

(c) Adjustments made in accordance with subsection (a) shall not apply with respect to cases commenced before the date of such adjustments.

§ 105. Power of court

(a) The court may issue any order, process, or judgment that is necessary or appropriate to carry out the provisions of this title. No provision of this title providing for the raising of an issue by a party in interest shall be construed to preclude the court from, sua sponte, taking any action or making any determination necessary or appropriate to enforce or implement court orders or rules, or to prevent an abuse of process.

(b) Notwithstanding subsection (a) of this section, a court may not appoint a receiver in a case under this title.

(c) The ability of any district judge or other officer or employee of a district court to exercise any of the authority or responsibilities conferred upon the court under this title shall be determined by reference to the provisions relating to such judge, officer, or employee set forth in title 28. This subsection shall not be interpreted to exclude bankruptcy judges and other officers or employees appointed pursuant to chapter 6 of title 28 from its operation.

(d) The court, on its own motion or on the request of a party in interest—

    (1) shall hold such status conferences as are necessary to further the expeditious and economical resolution of the case; and

    (2) unless inconsistent with another provision of this title or with applicable Federal Rules of Bankruptcy Procedure, may issue an order at any such conference prescribing such limitations and conditions as the court deems appropriate to ensure that the case is handled expeditiously and economically, including an order that—

        (A) sets the date by which the trustee must assume or reject an executory contract or unexpired lease; or

        (B) in a case under chapter 11 of this title—

            (i) sets a date by which the debtor, or trustee if one has been appointed, shall file a disclosure statement and plan;

(ii) sets a date by which the debtor, or trustee if one has been appointed, shall solicit acceptances of a plan;

(iii) sets the date by which a party in interest other than a debtor may file a plan;

(iv) sets a date by which a proponent of a plan, other than the debtor, shall solicit acceptances of such plan;

(v) fixes the scope and format of the notice to be provided regarding the hearing on approval of the disclosure statement; or

(vi) provides that the hearing on approval of the disclosure statement may be combined with the hearing on confirmation of the plan.

§ 106. Waiver of sovereign immunity

(a) Notwithstanding an assertion of sovereign immunity, sovereign immunity is abrogated as to a governmental unit to the extent set forth in this section with respect to the following:

(1) Sections 105, 106, 107, 108, 303, 346, 362, 363, 364, 365, 366, 502, 503, 505, 506, 510, 522, 523, 524, 525, 542, 543, 544, 545, 546, 547, 548, 549, 550, 551, 552, 553, 722, 724, 726, 744, 749, 764, 901, 922, 926, 928, 929, 944, 1107, 1141, 1142, 1143, 1146, 1201, 1203, 1205, 1206, 1227, 1231, 1301, 1303, 1305, and 1327 of this title.

(2) The court may hear and determine any issue arising with respect to the application of such sections to governmental units.

(3) The court may issue against a governmental unit an order, process, or judgment under such sections or the Federal Rules of Bankruptcy Procedure, including an order or judgment awarding a money recovery, but not including an award of punitive damages. Such order or judgment for costs or fees under this title or the Federal Rules of Bankruptcy Procedure against any governmental unit shall be consistent with the provisions and limitations of section 2412(d)(2)(A) of title 28.

(4) The enforcement of any such order, process, or judgment against any governmental unit shall be consistent with appropriate nonbankruptcy law applicable to such governmental unit and, in the case of a money judgment against the United States, shall be paid as if it is a judgment rendered by a district court of the United States.

(5) Nothing in this section shall create any substantive claim for relief or cause of action not otherwise existing under this title, the Federal Rules of Bankruptcy Procedure, or nonbankruptcy law.

(b) A governmental unit that has filed a proof of claim in the case is deemed to have waived sovereign immunity with respect to a claim against such governmental unit that is property of the estate and that arose out of the same transaction or occurrence out of which the claim of such governmental unit arose.

(c) Notwithstanding any assertion of sovereign immunity by a governmental unit, there shall be offset against a claim or interest of a governmental unit any claim against such governmental unit that is property of the estate.

§ 107. Public access to papers

(a) Except as provided in subsections (b) and (c) of this section and subject to section 112, a paper filed in a case under this title and the dockets of a bankruptcy court are public records and open to examination by an entity at reasonable times without charge.

(b) On request of a party in interest, the bankruptcy court shall, and on the bankruptcy court's own motion, the bankruptcy court may—

(1) protect an entity with respect to a trade secret or confidential research, development, or commercial information; or

(2) protect a person with respect to scandalous or defamatory matter contained in a paper filed in a case under this title.

(c)(1) The bankruptcy court, for cause, may protect an individual, with respect to the following types of information to the extent the court finds that disclosure of such information would create undue risk of identity theft or other unlawful injury to the individual or the individual's property:

(A) Any means of identification (as defined in section 1028(d) of title 18) contained in a paper filed, or to be filed, in a case under this title.

(B) Other information contained in a paper described in subparagraph (A).

(2) Upon ex parte application demonstrating cause, the court shall provide access to information protected pursuant to paragraph (1) to an entity acting pursuant to the police or regulatory power of a domestic governmental unit.

(3) The United States trustee, bankruptcy administrator, trustee, and any auditor serving under section 586(f) of title 28—

(A) shall have full access to all information contained in any paper filed or submitted in a case under this title; and

(B) shall not disclose information specifically protected by the court under this title.

§ 108. Extension of time

(a) If applicable nonbankruptcy law, an order entered in a nonbankruptcy proceeding, or an agreement fixes a period within which the debtor may commence an action, and such period has not expired before the date of the filing of the petition, the trustee may commence such action only before the later of—

(1) the end of such period, including any suspension of such period occurring on or after the commencement of the case; or

(2) two years after the order for relief.

(b) Except as provided in subsection (a) of this section, if applicable nonbankruptcy law, an order entered in a nonbankruptcy proceeding, or an agreement fixes a period within which the debtor or an individual protected under section 1201 or 1301 of this title may file any pleading, demand, notice, or proof of claim or loss, cure a default, or perform any other similar act, and such period has not expired before the date of the filing of the petition, the trustee may only file, cure, or perform, as the case may be, before the later of—

(1) the end of such period, including any suspension of such period occurring on or after the commencement of the case; or

(2) 60 days after the order for relief.

(c) Except as provided in section 524 of this title, if applicable nonbankruptcy law, an order entered in a nonbankruptcy proceeding, or an agreement fixes a period for commencing or continuing a civil action in a court other than a bankruptcy court on a claim against the debtor, or against an individual with respect to which such individual is protected under section 1201 or 1301 of this title, and such period has not expired before the date of the filing of the petition, then such period does not expire until the later of—

(1) the end of such period, including any suspension of such period occurring on or after the commencement of the case; or

(2) 30 days after notice of the termination or expiration of the stay under section 362, 922, 1201, or 1301 of this title, as the case may be, with respect to such claim.

§ 109. Who may be a debtor

(a) Notwithstanding any other provision of this section, only a person that resides or has a domicile, a place of business, or property in the United States, or a municipality, may be a debtor under this title.

(b) A person may be a debtor under chapter 7 of this title only if such person is not—

(1) a railroad;

(2) a domestic insurance company, bank, savings bank, cooperative bank, savings and loan association, building and loan association, homestead association, a New Markets Venture Capital company as defined in section 351 of the Small Business Investment Act of 1958, a small business investment company licensed by the Small Business Administration under section 301 of the Small Business Investment Act of 1958, credit union, or industrial bank or similar institution which is an insured bank as defined in section 3(h) of the Federal Deposit Insurance Act, except that an uninsured State member bank, or a corporation organized under section 25A of the Federal Reserve Act, which operates, or operates as, a multilateral clearing organization pursuant to section 409 of the Federal Deposit Insurance Corporation Improvement Act of 1991 may be a debtor if a petition is filed at the direction of the Board of Governors of the Federal Reserve System; or

(3)(A) a foreign insurance company, engaged in such business in the United States; or

(B) a foreign bank, savings bank, cooperative bank, savings and loan association, building and loan association, or credit union, that has a branch or agency (as defined in section 1(b) of the International Banking Act of 1978) in the United States.

(c) An entity may be a debtor under chapter 9 of this title if and only if such entity—

(1) is a municipality;

(2) is specifically authorized, in its capacity as a municipality or by name, to be a debtor under such chapter by State law, or by a governmental officer or organization empowered by State law to authorize such entity to be a debtor under such chapter;

(3) is insolvent;

(4) desires to effect a plan to adjust such debts; and

(5)(A) has obtained the agreement of creditors holding at least a majority in amount of the claims of each class that such entity intends to impair under a plan in a case under such chapter;

(B) has negotiated in good faith with creditors and has failed to obtain the agreement of creditors holding at least a majority in amount of the claims of each class that such entity intends to impair under a plan in a case under such chapter;

(C) is unable to negotiate with creditors because such negotiation is impracticable; or

(D) reasonably believes that a creditor may attempt to obtain a transfer that is avoidable under section 547 of this title.

(d) Only a railroad, a person that may be a debtor under chapter 7 of this title (except a stockbroker or a commodity broker), and an uninsured State member bank, or a corporation organized under section 25A of the Federal Reserve Act, which operates, or operates as, a multilateral clearing organization pursuant to section 409 of the Federal Deposit Insurance Corporation Improvement Act of 1991 may be a debtor under chapter 11 of this title.

(e) Only an individual with regular income that owes, on the date of the filing of the petition, noncontingent, liquidated debts of less than $2,750,000 or an individual with regular income and such individual's spouse, except a stockbroker or a commodity broker, that owe, on the date of the filing of the petition, noncontingent, liquidated debts that aggregate less than $2,750,000 may be a debtor under chapter 13 of this title.

[*Note from West Advisory Panel:* Congress amended § 109(e) to eliminate the separate unsecured and secured debt limits previously required for eligibility to file for chapter 13. The amendment creating a single $2.75M debt limit expires on June 21, 2024, at which point § 109(e) will read as it did on June 20, 2022. *See* 136 Stat. 1300.]

(f) Only a family farmer or family fisherman with regular annual income may be a debtor under chapter 12 of this title.

(g) Notwithstanding any other provision of this section, no individual or family farmer may be a debtor under this title who has been a debtor in a case pending under this title at any time in the preceding 180 days if—

(1) the case was dismissed by the court for willful failure of the debtor to abide by orders of the court, or to appear before the court in proper prosecution of the case; or

(2) the debtor requested and obtained the voluntary dismissal of the case following the filing of a request for relief from the automatic stay provided by section 362 of this title.

(h)(1) Subject to paragraphs (2) and (3), and notwithstanding any other provision of this section other than paragraph (4) of this subsection, an individual may not be a debtor under this title unless such individual has, during the 180-day period ending on the date of filing of the petition by such individual, received from an approved nonprofit budget and credit counseling agency described in section 111(a) an individual or group briefing (including a briefing conducted by telephone or on the Internet) that outlined the opportunities for available credit counseling and assisted such individual in performing a related budget analysis.

(2)(A) Paragraph (1) shall not apply with respect to a debtor who resides in a district for which the United States trustee (or the bankruptcy administrator, if any) determines that the approved nonprofit budget and credit counseling agencies for such district are not reasonably able to provide adequate services to the additional individuals who would otherwise seek credit counseling from such agencies by reason of the requirements of paragraph (1).

(B) The United States trustee (or the bankruptcy administrator, if any) who makes a determination described in subparagraph (A) shall review such determination not later than 1 year after the date of such determination, and not less frequently than annually thereafter. Notwithstanding the preceding sentence, a nonprofit budget and credit counseling agency may be disapproved by the United States trustee (or the bankruptcy administrator, if any) at any time.

(3)(A) Subject to subparagraph (B), the requirements of paragraph (1) shall not apply with respect to a debtor who submits to the court a certification that—

(i) describes exigent circumstances that merit a waiver of the requirements of paragraph (1);

(ii) states that the debtor requested credit counseling services from an approved nonprofit budget and credit counseling agency, but was unable to obtain the services referred to in paragraph (1) during the 7-day period beginning on the date on which the debtor made that request; and

(iii) is satisfactory to the court.

(B) With respect to a debtor, an exemption under subparagraph (A) shall cease to apply to that debtor on the date on which the debtor meets the requirements of paragraph (1), but in no case may the exemption apply to that debtor after the date that is 30 days after the debtor files a petition, except that the court, for cause, may order an additional 15 days.

(4) The requirements of paragraph (1) shall not apply with respect to a debtor whom the court determines, after notice and hearing, is unable to complete those requirements because of incapacity, disability, or active military duty in a military combat zone. For the purposes of this paragraph, incapacity means that the debtor is impaired by reason of mental illness or mental deficiency so that he is incapable of realizing and making rational decisions with respect to his financial responsibilities; and "disability" means that the debtor is so physically impaired as to be unable, after reasonable effort, to participate in an in person, telephone, or Internet briefing required under paragraph (1).

§ 110. Penalty for persons who negligently or fraudulently prepare bankruptcy petitions

(a) In this section—

(1) "bankruptcy petition preparer" means a person, other than an attorney for the debtor or an employee of such attorney under the direct supervision of such attorney, who prepares for compensation a document for filing; and

(2) "document for filing" means a petition or any other document prepared for filing by a debtor in a United States bankruptcy court or a United States district court in connection with a case under this title.

(b)(1) A bankruptcy petition preparer who prepares a document for filing shall sign the document and print on the document the preparer's name and address. If a bankruptcy petition preparer is not an individual, then an officer, principal, responsible person, or partner of the bankruptcy petition preparer shall be required to—

(A) sign the document for filing; and

(B) print on the document the name and address of that officer, principal, responsible person, or partner.

(2)(A) Before preparing any document for filing or accepting any fees from or on behalf of a debtor, the bankruptcy petition preparer shall provide to the debtor a written notice which shall be on an official form prescribed by the Judicial Conference of the United States in accordance with rule 9009 of the Federal Rules of Bankruptcy Procedure.

(B) The notice under subparagraph (A)—

(i) shall inform the debtor in simple language that a bankruptcy petition preparer is not an attorney and may not practice law or give legal advice;

(ii) may contain a description of examples of legal advice that a bankruptcy petition preparer is not authorized to give, in addition to any advice that the preparer may not give by reason of subsection (e)(2); and

(iii) shall—

(I) be signed by the debtor and, under penalty of perjury, by the bankruptcy petition preparer; and

(II) be filed with any document for filing.

(c)(1) A bankruptcy petition preparer who prepares a document for filing shall place on the document, after the preparer's signature, an identifying number that identifies individuals who prepared the document.

(2)(A) Subject to subparagraph (B), for purposes of this section, the identifying number of a bankruptcy petition preparer shall be the Social Security account number of each individual who prepared the document or assisted in its preparation.

(B) If a bankruptcy petition preparer is not an individual, the identifying number of the bankruptcy petition preparer shall be the Social Security account number of the officer, principal, responsible person, or partner of the bankruptcy petition preparer.

(d) A bankruptcy petition preparer shall, not later than the time at which a document for filing is presented for the debtor's signature, furnish to the debtor a copy of the document.

(e)(1) A bankruptcy petition preparer shall not execute any document on behalf of a debtor.

(2)(A) A bankruptcy petition preparer may not offer a potential bankruptcy debtor any legal advice, including any legal advice described in subparagraph (B).

(B) The legal advice referred to in subparagraph (A) includes advising the debtor—

(i) whether—

(I) to file a petition under this title; or

(II) commencing a case under chapter 7, 11, 12, or 13 is appropriate;

(ii) whether the debtor's debts will be discharged in a case under this title;

(iii) whether the debtor will be able to retain the debtor's home, car, or other property after commencing a case under this title;

(iv) concerning—

(I) the tax consequences of a case brought under this title; or

(II) the dischargeability of tax claims;

(v) whether the debtor may or should promise to repay debts to a creditor or enter into a reaffirmation agreement with a creditor to reaffirm a debt;

(vi) concerning how to characterize the nature of the debtor's interests in property or the debtor's debts; or

(vii) concerning bankruptcy procedures and rights.

(f) A bankruptcy petition preparer shall not use the word "legal" or any similar term in any advertisements, or advertise under any category that includes the word "legal" or any similar term.

(g) A bankruptcy petition preparer shall not collect or receive any payment from the debtor or on behalf of the debtor for the court fees in connection with filing the petition.

(h)(1) The Supreme Court may promulgate rules under section 2075 of title 28, or the Judicial Conference of the United States may prescribe guidelines, for setting a maximum allowable fee chargeable by a bankruptcy petition preparer. A bankruptcy petition preparer shall notify the debtor of any such maximum amount before preparing any document for filing for the debtor or accepting any fee from or on behalf of the debtor.

(2) A declaration under penalty of perjury by the bankruptcy petition preparer shall be filed together with the petition, disclosing any fee received from or on behalf of the debtor within 12 months immediately prior to the filing of the case, and any unpaid fee charged to the debtor. If rules or guidelines setting a maximum fee for services have been promulgated or prescribed under paragraph (1), the declaration under this paragraph shall include a certification that the bankruptcy petition preparer complied with the notification requirement under paragraph (1).

(3)(A) The court shall disallow and order the immediate turnover to the bankruptcy trustee any fee referred to in paragraph (2)—

(i) found to be in excess of the value of any services rendered by the bankruptcy petition preparer during the 12-month period immediately preceding the date of the filing of the petition; or

(ii) found to be in violation of any rule or guideline promulgated or prescribed under paragraph (1).

(B) All fees charged by a bankruptcy petition preparer may be forfeited in any case in which the bankruptcy petition preparer fails to comply with this subsection or subsection (b), (c), (d), (e), (f), or (g).

(C) An individual may exempt any funds recovered under this paragraph under section 522(b).

(4) The debtor, the trustee, a creditor, the United States trustee (or the bankruptcy administrator, if any) or the court, on the initiative of the court, may file a motion for an order under paragraph (3).

(5) A bankruptcy petition preparer shall be fined not more than $500 for each failure to comply with a court order to turn over funds within 30 days of service of such order.

(i)(1) If a bankruptcy petition preparer violates this section or commits any act that the court finds to be fraudulent, unfair, or deceptive, on the motion of the debtor, trustee, United States trustee (or the bankruptcy administrator, if any), and after notice and a hearing, the court shall order the bankruptcy petition preparer to pay to the debtor—

(A) the debtor's actual damages;

(B) the greater of—

(i) $2,000; or

(ii) twice the amount paid by the debtor to the bankruptcy petition preparer for the preparer's services; and

(C) reasonable attorneys' fees and costs in moving for damages under this subsection.

(2) If the trustee or creditor moves for damages on behalf of the debtor under this subsection, the bankruptcy petition preparer shall be ordered to pay the movant the additional amount of $1,000 plus reasonable attorneys' fees and costs incurred.

(j)(1) A debtor for whom a bankruptcy petition preparer has prepared a document for filing, the trustee, a creditor, or the United States trustee in the district in which the bankruptcy petition preparer resides, has conducted business, or the United States trustee in any other district in which the debtor resides may bring a civil action to enjoin a bankruptcy petition preparer from engaging in any conduct in violation of this section or from further acting as a bankruptcy petition preparer.

(2)(A) In an action under paragraph (1), if the court finds that—

(i) a bankruptcy petition preparer has—

(I) engaged in conduct in violation of this section or of any provision of this title;

(II) misrepresented the preparer's experience or education as a bankruptcy petition preparer; or

(III) engaged in any other fraudulent, unfair, or deceptive conduct; and

(ii) injunctive relief is appropriate to prevent the recurrence of such conduct,

the court may enjoin the bankruptcy petition preparer from engaging in such conduct.

(B) If the court finds that a bankruptcy petition preparer has continually engaged in conduct described in subclause (I), (II), or (III) of clause (i) and that an injunction prohibiting such conduct would not be sufficient to prevent such person's interference with the proper administration of this title, has not paid a penalty imposed under this section, or failed to disgorge all fees ordered by the court the court may enjoin the person from acting as a bankruptcy petition preparer.

(3) The court, as part of its contempt power, may enjoin a bankruptcy petition preparer that has failed to comply with a previous order issued under this section. The injunction under this paragraph may be issued on the motion of the court, the trustee, or the United States trustee (or the bankruptcy administrator, if any).

(4) The court shall award to a debtor, trustee, or creditor that brings a successful action under this subsection reasonable attorneys' fees and costs of the action, to be paid by the bankruptcy petition preparer.

(k) Nothing in this section shall be construed to permit activities that are otherwise prohibited by law, including rules and laws that prohibit the unauthorized practice of law.

(*l*)(1) A bankruptcy petition preparer who fails to comply with any provision of subsection (b), (c), (d), (e), (f), (g), or (h) may be fined not more than $500 for each such failure.

(2) The court shall triple the amount of a fine assessed under paragraph (1) in any case in which the court finds that a bankruptcy petition preparer—

(A) advised the debtor to exclude assets or income that should have been included on applicable schedules;

(B) advised the debtor to use a false Social Security account number;

(C) failed to inform the debtor that the debtor was filing for relief under this title; or

(D) prepared a document for filing in a manner that failed to disclose the identity of the bankruptcy petition preparer.

(3) A debtor, trustee, creditor, or United States trustee (or the bankruptcy administrator, if any) may file a motion for an order imposing a fine on the bankruptcy petition preparer for any violation of this section.

(4)(A) Fines imposed under this subsection in judicial districts served by United States trustees shall be paid to the United States trustees, who shall deposit an amount equal to such fines in the United States Trustee Fund.

(B) Fines imposed under this subsection in judicial districts served by bankruptcy administrators shall be deposited as offsetting receipts to the fund established under section 1931 of title 28, and shall remain available until expended to reimburse any appropriation for the amount paid out of such appropriation for expenses of the operation and maintenance of the courts of the United States.

§ 111. Nonprofit budget and credit counseling agencies; financial management instructional courses

(a) The clerk shall maintain a publicly available list of—

(1) nonprofit budget and credit counseling agencies that provide 1 or more services described in section 109(h) currently approved by the United States trustee (or the bankruptcy administrator, if any); and

(2) instructional courses concerning personal financial management currently approved by the United States trustee (or the bankruptcy administrator, if any), as applicable.

(b) The United States trustee (or bankruptcy administrator, if any) shall only approve a nonprofit budget and credit counseling agency or an instructional course concerning personal financial management as follows:

(1) The United States trustee (or bankruptcy administrator, if any) shall have thoroughly reviewed the qualifications of the nonprofit budget and credit counseling agency or of the provider of the instructional course under the standards set forth in this section, and the services or instructional courses that will be offered by such agency or such provider, and may require such agency or such provider that has sought approval to provide information with respect to such review.

(2) The United States trustee (or bankruptcy administrator, if any) shall have determined that such agency or such instructional course fully satisfies the applicable standards set forth in this section.

(3) If a nonprofit budget and credit counseling agency or instructional course did not appear on the approved list for the district under subsection (a) immediately before approval under this section, approval under this subsection of such agency or such instructional course shall be for a probationary period not to exceed 6 months.

(4) At the conclusion of the applicable probationary period under paragraph (3), the United States trustee (or bankruptcy administrator, if any) may only approve for an additional 1-year period, and for successive 1-year periods thereafter, an agency or instructional course that has demonstrated during the probationary or applicable subsequent period of approval that such agency or instructional course—

(A) has met the standards set forth under this section during such period; and

(B) can satisfy such standards in the future.

(5) Not later than 30 days after any final decision under paragraph (4), an interested person may seek judicial review of such decision in the appropriate district court of the United States.

(c)(1) The United States trustee (or the bankruptcy administrator, if any) shall only approve a nonprofit budget and credit counseling agency that demonstrates that it will provide qualified counselors, maintain adequate provision for safekeeping and payment of client funds, provide adequate counseling with respect to client credit problems, and deal responsibly and effectively with other matters relating to the quality, effectiveness, and financial security of the services it provides.

(2) To be approved by the United States trustee (or the bankruptcy administrator, if any), a nonprofit budget and credit counseling agency shall, at a minimum—

(A) have a board of directors the majority of which—

(i) are not employed by such agency; and

(ii) will not directly or indirectly benefit financially from the outcome of the counseling services provided by such agency;

(B) if a fee is charged for counseling services, charge a reasonable fee, and provide services without regard to ability to pay the fee;

(C) provide for safekeeping and payment of client funds, including an annual audit of the trust accounts and appropriate employee bonding;

(D) provide full disclosures to a client, including funding sources, counselor qualifications, possible impact on credit reports, and any costs of such program that will be paid by such client and how such costs will be paid;

(E) provide adequate counseling with respect to a client's credit problems that includes an analysis of such client's current financial condition, factors that caused such financial condition, and how such client can develop a plan to respond to the problems without incurring negative amortization of debt;

(F) provide trained counselors who receive no commissions or bonuses based on the outcome of the counseling services provided by such agency, and who have adequate experience, and have been adequately trained to provide counseling services to individuals in financial difficulty, including the matters described in subparagraph (E);

(G) demonstrate adequate experience and background in providing credit counseling; and

(H) have adequate financial resources to provide continuing support services for budgeting plans over the life of any repayment plan.

(d) The United States trustee (or the bankruptcy administrator, if any) shall only approve an instructional course concerning personal financial management—

(1) for an initial probationary period under subsection (b)(3) if the course will provide at a minimum—

(A) trained personnel with adequate experience and training in providing effective instruction and services;

(B) learning materials and teaching methodologies designed to assist debtors in understanding personal financial management and that are consistent with stated objectives directly related to the goals of such instructional course;

(C) adequate facilities situated in reasonably convenient locations at which such instructional course is offered, except that such facilities may include the provision of such instructional course by telephone or through the Internet, if such instructional course is effective;

(D) the preparation and retention of reasonable records (which shall include the debtor's bankruptcy case number) to permit evaluation of the effectiveness of such instructional course, including any evaluation of satisfaction of instructional course requirements for each debtor attending such instructional course, which shall be available for inspection and evaluation by the Executive Office for United States Trustees, the United States trustee (or the bankruptcy administrator, if any), or the chief bankruptcy judge for the district in which such instructional course is offered; and

(E) if a fee is charged for the instructional course, charge a reasonable fee, and provide services without regard to ability to pay the fee; and

(2) for any 1-year period if the provider thereof has demonstrated that the course meets the standards of paragraph (1) and, in addition—

(A) has been effective in assisting a substantial number of debtors to understand personal financial management; and

(B) is otherwise likely to increase substantially the debtor's understanding of personal financial management.

(e) The district court may, at any time, investigate the qualifications of a nonprofit budget and credit counseling agency referred to in subsection (a), and request production of documents to ensure the integrity and effectiveness of such agency. The district court may, at any time, remove from the approved list under subsection (a) a nonprofit budget and credit counseling agency upon finding such agency does not meet the qualifications of subsection (b).

(f) The United States trustee (or the bankruptcy administrator, if any) shall notify the clerk that a nonprofit budget and credit counseling agency or an instructional course is no longer approved, in which case the clerk shall remove it from the list maintained under subsection (a).

(g)(1) No nonprofit budget and credit counseling agency may provide to a credit reporting agency information concerning whether a debtor has received or sought instruction concerning personal financial management from such agency.

(2) A nonprofit budget and credit counseling agency that willfully or negligently fails to comply with any requirement under this title with respect to a debtor shall be liable for damages in an amount equal to the sum of—

(A) any actual damages sustained by the debtor as a result of the violation; and

(B) any court costs or reasonable attorneys' fees (as determined by the court) incurred in an action to recover those damages.

§ 112. Prohibition on disclosure of name of minor children

The debtor may be required to provide information regarding a minor child involved in matters under this title but may not be required to disclose in the public records in the case the name of such minor child. The debtor may be required to disclose the name of such minor child in a nonpublic record that is maintained by the court and made available by the court for examination by the United States trustee, the trustee, and the auditor (if any) serving under section 586(f) of title 28, in the case. The court, the United States trustee, the trustee, and such auditor shall not disclose the name of such minor child maintained in such nonpublic record.

CHAPTER 3—CASE ADMINISTRATION

SUBCHAPTER I—COMMENCEMENT OF A CASE

301.   Voluntary cases.
302.   Joint cases.
303.   Involuntary cases.
304.   [Repealed.]
305.   Abstention.
306.   Limited appearance.
307.   United States trustee.
308.   Debtor reporting requirements.

SUBCHAPTER II—OFFICERS

321.   Eligibility to serve as trustee.
322.   Qualification of trustee.
323.   Role and capacity of trustee.
324.   Removal of trustee or examiner.
325.   Effect of vacancy.
326.   Limitation on compensation of trustee.
327.   Employment of professional persons.
328.   Limitation on compensation of professional persons.
329.   Debtor's transactions with attorneys.
330.   Compensation of officers.

331.   Interim compensation.
332.   Consumer privacy ombudsman.
333.   Appointment of patient care ombudsman.

SUBCHAPTER III—ADMINISTRATION

341.   Meetings of creditors and equity security holders.
342.   Notice.
343.   Examination of the debtor.
344.   Self-incrimination; immunity.
345.   Money of estates.
346.   Special provisions related to the treatment of State and local taxes.
347.   Unclaimed property.
348.   Effect of conversion.
349.   Effect of dismissal.
350.   Closing and reopening cases.
351.   Disposal of patient records.

SUBCHAPTER IV—ADMINISTRATIVE POWERS

361.   Adequate protection.
362.   Automatic stay.
363.   Use, sale, or lease of property.
364.   Obtaining credit.
365.   Executory contracts and unexpired leases.
366.   Utility service.

SUBCHAPTER I—COMMENCEMENT OF A CASE

§ 301. Voluntary cases

(a) A voluntary case under a chapter of this title is commenced by the filing with the bankruptcy court of a petition under such chapter by an entity that may be a debtor under such chapter.

(b) The commencement of a voluntary case under a chapter of this title constitutes an order for relief under such chapter.

§ 302. Joint cases

(a) A joint case under a chapter of this title is commenced by the filing with the bankruptcy court of a single petition under such chapter by an individual that may be a debtor under such chapter and such individual's spouse. The commencement of a joint case under a chapter of this title constitutes an order for relief under such chapter.

(b) After the commencement of a joint case, the court shall determine the extent, if any, to which the debtors' estates shall be consolidated.

§ 303. Involuntary cases

(a) An involuntary case may be commenced only under chapter 7 or 11 of this title, and only against a person, except a farmer, family farmer, or a corporation that is not a moneyed, business, or commercial corporation, that may be a debtor under the chapter under which such case is commenced.

(b) An involuntary case against a person is commenced by the filing with the bankruptcy court of a petition under chapter 7 or 11 of this title—

(1) by three or more entities, each of which is either a holder of a claim against such person that is not contingent as to liability or the subject of a bona fide dispute as to liability or amount, or an indenture trustee representing such a holder, if such noncontingent, undisputed claims aggregate at least $18,600 more than the value of any lien on property of the debtor securing such claims held by the holders of such claims;

(2) if there are fewer than 12 such holders, excluding any employee or insider of such person and any transferee of a transfer that is voidable under section 544, 545, 547, 548, 549, or 724(a) of this title, by one or more of such holders that hold in the aggregate at least $18,600 of such claims;

(3) if such person is a partnership—

    (A) by fewer than all of the general partners in such partnership; or

    (B) if relief has been ordered under this title with respect to all of the general partners in such partnership, by a general partner in such partnership, the trustee of such a general partner, or a holder of a claim against such partnership; or

(4) by a foreign representative of the estate in a foreign proceeding concerning such person.

(c) After the filing of a petition under this section but before the case is dismissed or relief is ordered, a creditor holding an unsecured claim that is not contingent, other than a creditor filing under subsection (b) of this section, may join in the petition with the same effect as if such joining creditor were a petitioning creditor under subsection (b) of this section.

(d) The debtor, or a general partner in a partnership debtor that did not join in the petition, may file an answer to a petition under this section.

(e) After notice and a hearing, and for cause, the court may require the petitioners under this section to file a bond to indemnify the debtor for such amounts as the court may later allow under subsection (i) of this section.

(f) Notwithstanding section 363 of this title, except to the extent that the court orders otherwise, and until an order for relief in the case, any business of the debtor may continue to operate, and the debtor may continue to use, acquire, or dispose of property as if an involuntary case concerning the debtor had not been commenced.

(g) At any time after the commencement of an involuntary case under chapter 7 of this title but before an order for relief in the case, the court, on request of a party in interest, after notice to the debtor and a hearing, and if necessary to preserve the property of the estate or to prevent loss to the estate, may order the United States trustee to appoint an interim trustee under section 701 of this title to take possession of the property of the estate and to operate any business of the debtor. Before an order for relief, the debtor may regain possession of property in the possession of a trustee ordered appointed under this subsection if the debtor files such bond as the court requires, conditioned on the debtor's accounting for and delivering to the trustee, if there is an order for relief in the case, such property, or the value, as of the date the debtor regains possession, of such property.

(h) If the petition is not timely controverted, the court shall order relief against the debtor in an involuntary case under the chapter under which the petition was filed. Otherwise, after trial, the court shall order relief against the debtor in an involuntary case under the chapter under which the petition was filed, only if—

(1) the debtor is generally not paying such debtor's debts as such debts become due unless such debts are the subject of a bona fide dispute as to liability or amount; or

(2) within 120 days before the date of the filing of the petition, a custodian, other than a trustee, receiver, or agent appointed or authorized to take charge of less than substantially all of the property of the debtor for the purpose of enforcing a lien against such property, was appointed or took possession.

(i) If the court dismisses a petition under this section other than on consent of all petitioners and the debtor, and if the debtor does not waive the right to judgment under this subsection, the court may grant judgment—

(1) against the petitioners and in favor of the debtor for—

    (A) costs; or

    (B) a reasonable attorney's fee; or

  (2) against any petitioner that filed the petition in bad faith, for—

    (A) any damages proximately caused by such filing; or

    (B) punitive damages.

(j) Only after notice to all creditors and a hearing may the court dismiss a petition filed under this section—

  (1) on the motion of a petitioner;

  (2) on consent of all petitioners and the debtor; or

  (3) for want of prosecution.

(k)(1) If—

    (A) the petition under this section is false or contains any materially false, fictitious, or fraudulent statement;

    (B) the debtor is an individual; and

    (C) the court dismisses such petition,

the court, upon the motion of the debtor, shall seal all the records of the court relating to such petition, and all references to such petition.

  (2) If the debtor is an individual and the court dismisses a petition under this section, the court may enter an order prohibiting all consumer reporting agencies (as defined in section 603(f) of the Fair Credit Reporting Act (15 U.S.C. 1681a(f))) from making any consumer report (as defined in section 603(d) of that Act) that contains any information relating to such petition or to the case commenced by the filing of such petition.

  (3) Upon the expiration of the statute of limitations described in section 3282 of title 18, for a violation of section 152 or 157 of such title, the court, upon the motion of the debtor and for good cause, may expunge any records relating to a petition filed under this section.

§ 304. [Repealed.]

§ 305. Abstention

(a) The court, after notice and a hearing, may dismiss a case under this title, or may suspend all proceedings in a case under this title, at any time if—

  (1) the interests of creditors and the debtor would be better served by such dismissal or suspension; or

  (2)(A) a petition under section 1515 for recognition of a foreign proceeding has been granted; and

    (B) the purposes of chapter 15 of this title would be best served by such dismissal or suspension.

(b) A foreign representative may seek dismissal or suspension under subsection (a)(2) of this section.

(c) An order under subsection (a) of this section dismissing a case or suspending all proceedings in a case, or a decision not so to dismiss or suspend, is not reviewable by appeal or otherwise by the court of appeals under section 158(d), 1291, or 1292 of title 28 or by the Supreme Court of the United States under section 1254 of title 28.

§ 306. Limited appearance

An appearance in a bankruptcy court by a foreign representative in connection with a petition or request under section 303 or 305 of this title does not submit such foreign representative to the jurisdiction of any court in the United States for any other purpose, but the bankruptcy court may condition any order under section 303 or 305 of this title on compliance by such foreign representative with the orders of such bankruptcy court.

§ 307. United States trustee

The United States trustee may raise and may appear and be heard on any issue in any case or proceeding under this title but may not file a plan pursuant to section 1121(c) of this title.

§ 308. Debtor reporting requirements

(a) For purposes of this section, the term "profitability" means, with respect to a debtor, the amount of money that the debtor has earned or lost during current and recent fiscal periods.

(b) A debtor in a small business case shall file periodic financial and other reports containing information including—

(1) the debtor's profitability;

(2) reasonable approximations of the debtor's projected cash receipts and cash disbursements over a reasonable period;

(3) comparisons of actual cash receipts and disbursements with projections in prior reports;

(4) whether the debtor is—

(A) in compliance in all material respects with postpetition requirements imposed by this title and the Federal Rules of Bankruptcy Procedure; and

(B) timely filing tax returns and other required government filings and paying taxes and other administrative expenses when due;

(5) if the debtor is not in compliance with the requirements referred to in paragraph (4)(A) or filing tax returns and other required government filings and making the payments referred to in paragraph (4)(B), what the failures are and how, at what cost, and when the debtor intends to remedy such failures; and

(6) such other matters as are in the best interests of the debtor and creditors, and in the public interest in fair and efficient procedures under chapter 11 of this title.

SUBCHAPTER II—OFFICERS

§ 321. Eligibility to serve as trustee

(a) A person may serve as trustee in a case under this title only if such person is—

(1) an individual that is competent to perform the duties of trustee and, in a case under chapter 7, 12, or 13 of this title, resides or has an office in the judicial district within which the case is pending, or in any judicial district adjacent to such district; or

(2) a corporation authorized by such corporation's charter or bylaws to act as trustee, and, in a case under chapter 7, 12, or 13 of this title, having an office in at least one of such districts.

(b) A person that has served as an examiner in the case may not serve as trustee in the case.

(c) The United States trustee for the judicial district in which the case is pending is eligible to serve as trustee in the case if necessary.

§ 322. Qualification of trustee

(a) Except as provided in subsection (b)(1), a person selected under section 701, 702, 703, 1104, 1163, 1183, 1202, or 1302 of this title to serve as trustee in a case under this title qualifies if before seven days after such selection, and before beginning official duties, such person has filed with the court a bond in favor of the United States conditioned on the faithful performance of such official duties.

(b)(1) The United States trustee qualifies wherever such trustee serves as trustee in a case under this title.

(2) The United States trustee shall determine—

(A) the amount of a bond required to be filed under subsection (a) of this section; and

(B) the sufficiency of the surety on such bond.

(c) A trustee is not liable personally or on such trustee's bond in favor of the United States for any penalty or forfeiture incurred by the debtor.

(d) A proceeding on a trustee's bond may not be commenced after two years after the date on which such trustee was discharged.

§ 323. Role and capacity of trustee

(a) The trustee in a case under this title is the representative of the estate.

(b) The trustee in a case under this title has capacity to sue and be sued.

§ 324. Removal of trustee or examiner

(a) The court, after notice and a hearing, may remove a trustee, other than the United States trustee, or an examiner, for cause.

(b) Whenever the court removes a trustee or examiner under subsection (a) in a case under this title, such trustee or examiner shall thereby be removed in all other cases under this title in which such trustee or examiner is then serving unless the court orders otherwise.

§ 325. Effect of vacancy

A vacancy in the office of trustee during a case does not abate any pending action or proceeding, and the successor trustee shall be substituted as a party in such action or proceeding.

§ 326. Limitation on compensation of trustee

(a) In a case under chapter 7 or 11, other than a case under subchapter V of chapter 11, the court may allow reasonable compensation under section 330 of this title of the trustee for the trustee's services, payable after the trustee renders such services, not to exceed 25 percent on the first $5,000 or less, 10 percent on any amount in excess of $5,000 but not in excess of $50,000, 5 percent on any amount in excess of $50,000 but not in excess of $1,000,000, and reasonable compensation not to exceed 3 percent of such moneys in excess of $1,000,000, upon all moneys disbursed or turned over in the case by the trustee to parties in interest, excluding the debtor, but including holders of secured claims.

(b) In a case under subchapter V of chapter 11 or chapter 12 or 13 of this title, the court may not allow compensation for services or reimbursement of expenses of the United States trustee or of a standing trustee appointed under section 586(b) of title 28, but may allow reasonable compensation under section 330 of this title of a trustee appointed under section 1202(a) or 1302(a) of this title for the trustee's services, payable after the trustee renders such services, not to exceed five percent upon all payments under the plan.

(c) If more than one person serves as trustee in the case, the aggregate compensation of such persons for such service may not exceed the maximum compensation prescribed for a single trustee by subsection (a) or (b) of this section, as the case may be.

(d) The court may deny allowance of compensation for services or reimbursement of expenses of the trustee if the trustee failed to make diligent inquiry into facts that would permit denial of allowance under section 328(c) of this title or, with knowledge of such facts, employed a professional person under section 327 of this title.

§ 327. Employment of professional persons

(a) Except as otherwise provided in this section, the trustee, with the court's approval, may employ one or more attorneys, accountants, appraisers, auctioneers, or other professional persons, that do not hold or represent an interest adverse to the estate, and that are disinterested persons, to represent or assist the trustee in carrying out the trustee's duties under this title.

(b) If the trustee is authorized to operate the business of the debtor under section 721, 1202, or 1108 of this title, and if the debtor has regularly employed attorneys, accountants, or other professional persons on salary, the trustee may retain or replace such professional persons if necessary in the operation of such business.

(c) In a case under chapter 7, 12, or 11 of this title, a person is not disqualified for employment under this section solely because of such person's employment by or representation of a creditor, unless there is objection by another creditor or the United States trustee, in which case the court shall disapprove such employment if there is an actual conflict of interest.

(d) The court may authorize the trustee to act as attorney or accountant for the estate if such authorization is in the best interest of the estate.

(e) The trustee, with the court's approval, may employ, for a specified special purpose, other than to represent the trustee in conducting the case, an attorney that has represented the debtor, if in the best interest of the estate, and if such attorney does not represent or hold any interest adverse to the debtor or to the estate with respect to the matter on which such attorney is to be employed.

(f) The trustee may not employ a person that has served as an examiner in the case.

§ 328. Limitation on compensation of professional persons

(a) The trustee, or a committee appointed under section 1102 of this title, with the court's approval, may employ or authorize the employment of a professional person under section 327 or 1103 of this title, as the case may be, on any reasonable terms and conditions of employment, including on a retainer, on an hourly basis, on a fixed or percentage fee basis, or on a contingent fee basis. Notwithstanding such terms and conditions, the court may allow compensation different from the compensation provided under such terms and conditions after the conclusion of such employment, if such terms and conditions prove to have been improvident in light of developments not capable of being anticipated at the time of the fixing of such terms and conditions.

(b) If the court has authorized a trustee to serve as an attorney or accountant for the estate under section 327(d) of this title, the court may allow compensation for the trustee's services as such attorney or accountant only to the extent that the trustee performed services as attorney or accountant for the estate and not for performance of any of the trustee's duties that are generally performed by a trustee without the assistance of an attorney or accountant for the estate.

(c) Except as provided in section 327(c), 327(e), or 1107(b) of this title, the court may deny allowance of compensation for services and reimbursement of expenses of a professional person employed under section 327 or 1103 of this title if, at any time during such professional person's employment under section 327 or 1103 of this title, such professional person is not a disinterested person, or represents or holds an interest adverse to the interest of the estate with respect to the matter on which such professional person is employed.

§ 329. Debtor's transactions with attorneys

(a) Any attorney representing a debtor in a case under this title, or in connection with such a case, whether or not such attorney applies for compensation under this title, shall file with the court a statement of the compensation paid or agreed to be paid, if such payment or agreement was made after one year before the date of the filing of the petition, for services rendered or to be rendered in contemplation of or in connection with the case by such attorney, and the source of such compensation.

(b) If such compensation exceeds the reasonable value of any such services, the court may cancel any such agreement, or order the return of any such payment, to the extent excessive, to—

    (1) the estate, if the property transferred—

        (A) would have been property of the estate; or

        (B) was to be paid by or on behalf of the debtor under a plan under chapter 11, 12, or 13 of this title; or

    (2) the entity that made such payment.

§ 330. Compensation of officers

    (a)(1) After notice to the parties in interest and the United States Trustee and a hearing, and subject to sections 326, 328, and 329, the court may award to a trustee, a consumer privacy ombudsman appointed under section 332, an examiner, an ombudsman appointed under section 333, or a professional person employed under section 327 or 1103—

        (A) reasonable compensation for actual, necessary services rendered by the trustee, examiner, ombudsman, professional person, or attorney and by any paraprofessional person employed by any such person; and

        (B) reimbursement for actual, necessary expenses.

    (2) The court may, on its own motion or on the motion of the United States Trustee, the United States Trustee for the District or Region, the trustee for the estate, or any other party in interest, award compensation that is less than the amount of compensation that is requested.

    (3) In determining the amount of reasonable compensation to be awarded to an examiner, trustee under chapter 11, or professional person, the court shall consider the nature, the extent, and the value of such services, taking into account all relevant factors, including—

        (A) the time spent on such services;

        (B) the rates charged for such services;

        (C) whether the services were necessary to the administration of, or beneficial at the time at which the service was rendered toward the completion of, a case under this title;

        (D) whether the services were performed within a reasonable amount of time commensurate with the complexity, importance, and nature of the problem, issue, or task addressed;

        (E) with respect to a professional person, whether the person is board certified or otherwise has demonstrated skill and experience in the bankruptcy field; and

        (F) whether the compensation is reasonable based on the customary compensation charged by comparably skilled practitioners in cases other than cases under this title.

    (4)(A) Except as provided in subparagraph (B), the court shall not allow compensation for—

        (i) unnecessary duplication of services; or

        (ii) services that were not—

            (I) reasonably likely to benefit the debtor's estate; or

            (II) necessary to the administration of the case.

    (B) In a chapter 12 or chapter 13 case in which the debtor is an individual, the court may allow reasonable compensation to the debtor's attorney for representing the interests of the debtor in connection with the bankruptcy case based on a consideration of the benefit and necessity of such services to the debtor and the other factors set forth in this section.

    (5) The court shall reduce the amount of compensation awarded under this section by the amount of any interim compensation awarded under section 331, and, if the amount of such interim compensation exceeds the amount of compensation awarded under this section, may order the return of the excess to the estate.

(6) Any compensation awarded for the preparation of a fee application shall be based on the level and skill reasonably required to prepare the application.

(7) In determining the amount of reasonable compensation to be awarded to a trustee, the court shall treat such compensation as a commission, based on section 326.

(b)(1) There shall be paid from the filing fee in a case under chapter 7 of this title $45 to the trustee serving in such case, after such trustee's services are rendered.

(2) The Judicial Conference of the United States—

(A) shall prescribe additional fees of the same kind as prescribed under section 1914(b) of title 28; and

(B) may prescribe notice of appearance fees and fees charged against distributions in cases under this title;

to pay $15 to trustees serving in cases after such trustees' services are rendered. Beginning 1 year after the date of the enactment of the Bankruptcy Reform Act of 1994, such $15 shall be paid in addition to the amount paid under paragraph (1).

(c) Unless the court orders otherwise, in a case under chapter 12 or 13 of this title the compensation paid to the trustee serving in the case shall not be less than $5 per month from any distribution under the plan during the administration of the plan.

(d) In a case in which the United States trustee serves as trustee, the compensation of the trustee under this section shall be paid to the clerk of the bankruptcy court and deposited by the clerk into the United States Trustee System Fund established by section 589a of title 28.

(e)(1) There is established a fund in the Treasury of the United States, to be known as the "Chapter 7 Trustee Fund", which shall be administered by the Director of the Administrative Office of the United States Courts.

(2) Deposits into the Chapter 7 Trustee Fund under section 589a(f)(1)(C) of title 28 shall be available until expended for the purposes described in paragraph (3).

(3) For fiscal years 2021 through 2026, the Chapter 7 Trustee Fund shall be available to pay the trustee serving in a case that is filed under chapter 7 or a case that is converted to a chapter 7 case in the most recent fiscal year (referred to in this subsection as a "chapter 7 case") the amount described in paragraph (4) for the chapter 7 case in which the trustee has rendered services.

(4) The amount described in this paragraph shall be the lesser of—

(A) $60; or

(B) a pro rata share, for each chapter 7 case, of the fees collected under section 1930(a)(6) of title 28 and deposited to the United States Trustee System Fund under section 589a(f)(1) of title 28, less the amounts specified in section 589a(f)(1)(A) and (B) of title 28.

(5) The payment received by a trustee under paragraph (3) shall be paid in addition to the amount paid under subsection (b).

(6) Not later than September 30, 2021, the Director of the Administrative Office of the United States Courts shall promulgate regulations for the administration of this subsection.

§ 331. Interim compensation

A trustee, an examiner, a debtor's attorney, or any professional person employed under section 327 or 1103 of this title may apply to the court not more than once every 120 days after an order for relief in a case under this title, or more often if the court permits, for such compensation for services rendered before the date of such an application or reimbursement for expenses incurred before such date as is provided under section 330 of this title. After notice and a hearing, the court may allow and disburse to such applicant such compensation or reimbursement.

§ 332. Consumer privacy ombudsman

(a) If a hearing is required under section 363(b)(1)(B), the court shall order the United States trustee to appoint, not later than 7 days before the commencement of the hearing, 1 disinterested person (other than the United States trustee) to serve as the consumer privacy ombudsman in the case and shall require that notice of such hearing be timely given to such ombudsman.

(b) The consumer privacy ombudsman may appear and be heard at such hearing and shall provide to the court information to assist the court in its consideration of the facts, circumstances, and conditions of the proposed sale or lease of personally identifiable information under section 363(b)(1)(B). Such information may include presentation of—

(1) the debtor's privacy policy;

(2) the potential losses or gains of privacy to consumers if such sale or such lease is approved by the court;

(3) the potential costs or benefits to consumers if such sale or such lease is approved by the court; and

(4) the potential alternatives that would mitigate potential privacy losses or potential costs to consumers.

(c) A consumer privacy ombudsman shall not disclose any personally identifiable information obtained by the ombudsman under this title.

§ 333. Appointment of patient care ombudsman

(a)(1) If the debtor in a case under chapter 7, 9, or 11 is a health care business, the court shall order, not later than 30 days after the commencement of the case, the appointment of an ombudsman to monitor the quality of patient care and to represent the interests of the patients of the health care business unless the court finds that the appointment of such ombudsman is not necessary for the protection of patients under the specific facts of the case.

(2)(A) If the court orders the appointment of an ombudsman under paragraph (1), the United States trustee shall appoint 1 disinterested person (other than the United States trustee) to serve as such ombudsman.

(B) If the debtor is a health care business that provides long-term care, then the United States trustee may appoint the State Long-Term Care Ombudsman appointed under the Older Americans Act of 1965 for the State in which the case is pending to serve as the ombudsman required by paragraph (1).

(C) If the United States trustee does not appoint a State Long-Term Care Ombudsman under subparagraph (B), the court shall notify the State Long-Term Care Ombudsman appointed under the Older Americans Act of 1965 for the State in which the case is pending, of the name and address of the person who is appointed under subparagraph (A).

(b) An ombudsman appointed under subsection (a) shall—

(1) monitor the quality of patient care provided to patients of the debtor, to the extent necessary under the circumstances, including interviewing patients and physicians;

(2) not later than 60 days after the date of appointment, and not less frequently than at 60-day intervals thereafter, report to the court after notice to the parties in interest, at a hearing or in writing, regarding the quality of patient care provided to patients of the debtor; and

(3) if such ombudsman determines that the quality of patient care provided debtor is declining significantly or is otherwise being materially compromised motion or a written report, with notice to the parties in interest immedi determination.

(c)(1)   An ombudsman appointed under subsection (a) shall maintain any information obtained by such ombudsman under this section that relates to patients (including information relating to patient records) as confidential information. Such ombudsman may not review confidential patient records unless the court approves such review in advance and imposes restrictions on such ombudsman to protect the confidentiality of such records.

(2)   An ombudsman appointed under subsection (a)(2)(B) shall have access to patient records consistent with authority of such ombudsman under the Older Americans Act of 1965 and under non-Federal laws governing the State Long-Term Care Ombudsman program.

SUBCHAPTER III—ADMINISTRATION

§ 341. Meetings of creditors and equity security holders

(a)   Within a reasonable time after the order for relief in a case under this title, the United States trustee shall convene and preside at a meeting of creditors.

(b)   The United States trustee may convene a meeting of any equity security holders.

(c)   The court may not preside at, and may not attend, any meeting under this section including any final meeting of creditors. Notwithstanding any local court rule, provision of a State constitution, any otherwise applicable nonbankruptcy law, or any other requirement that representation at the meeting of creditors under subsection (a) be by an attorney, a creditor holding a consumer debt or any representative of the creditor (which may include an entity or an employee of an entity and may be a representative for more than 1 creditor) shall be permitted to appear at and participate in the meeting of creditors in a case under chapter 7 or 13, either alone or in conjunction with an attorney for the creditor. Nothing in this subsection shall be construed to require any creditor to be represented by an attorney at any meeting of creditors.

(d)   Prior to the conclusion of the meeting of creditors or equity security holders, the trustee shall orally examine the debtor to ensure that the debtor in a case under chapter 7 of this title is aware of—

    (1)   the potential consequences of seeking a discharge in bankruptcy, including the effects on credit history;

    (2)   the debtor's ability to file a petition under a different chapter of this title;

    (3)   the effect of receiving a discharge of debts under this title; and

    (4)   the effect of reaffirming a debt, including the debtor's knowledge of the provisions of section 524(d) of this title.

(e)   Notwithstanding subsections (a) and (b), the court, on the request of a party in interest and after notice and a hearing, for cause may order that the United States trustee not convene a meeting of creditors or equity security holders if the debtor has filed a plan as to which the debtor solicited acceptances prior to the commencement of the case.

§ 342. Notice

(a)   There shall be given such notice as is appropriate, including notice to any holder of a community claim, of an order for relief in a case under this title.

(b)   Before the commencement of a case under this title by an individual whose debts are primarily consumer debts, the clerk shall give to such individual written notice containing—

    (1)   a brief description of—

        (A)   chapters 7, 11, 12, and 13 and the general purpose, benefits, and costs of proceeding under each of those chapters; and

        (B)   the types of services available from credit counseling agencies; and

    (2)   statements specifying that—

(A) a person who knowingly and fraudulently conceals assets or makes a false oath or statement under penalty of perjury in connection with a case under this title shall be subject to fine, imprisonment, or both; and

(B) all information supplied by a debtor in connection with a case under this title is subject to examination by the Attorney General.

(c)(1) If notice is required to be given by the debtor to a creditor under this title, any rule, any applicable law, or any order of the court, such notice shall contain the name, address, and last 4 digits of the taxpayer identification number of the debtor. If the notice concerns an amendment that adds a creditor to the schedules of assets and liabilities, the debtor shall include the full taxpayer identification number in the notice sent to that creditor, but the debtor shall include only the last 4 digits of the taxpayer identification number in the copy of the notice filed with the court.

(2)(A) If, within the 90 days before the commencement of a voluntary case, a creditor supplies the debtor in at least 2 communications sent to the debtor with the current account number of the debtor and the address at which such creditor requests to receive correspondence, then any notice required by this title to be sent by the debtor to such creditor shall be sent to such address and shall include such account number.

(B) If a creditor would be in violation of applicable nonbankruptcy law by sending any such communication within such 90-day period and if such creditor supplies the debtor in the last 2 communications with the current account number of the debtor and the address at which such creditor requests to receive correspondence, then any notice required by this title to be sent by the debtor to such creditor shall be sent to such address and shall include such account number.

(d) In a case under chapter 7 of this title in which the debtor is an individual and in which the presumption of abuse arises under section 707(b), the clerk shall give written notice to all creditors not later than 10 days after the date of the filing of the petition that the presumption of abuse has arisen.

(e)(1) In a case under chapter 7 or 13 of this title of a debtor who is an individual, a creditor at any time may both file with the court and serve on the debtor a notice of address to be used to provide notice in such case to such creditor.

(2) Any notice in such case required to be provided to such creditor by the debtor or the court later than 7 days after the court and the debtor receive such creditor's notice of address, shall be provided to such address.

(f)(1) An entity may file with any bankruptcy court a notice of address to be used by all the bankruptcy courts or by particular bankruptcy courts, as so specified by such entity at the time such notice is filed, to provide notice to such entity in all cases under chapters 7 and 13 pending in the courts with respect to which such notice is filed, in which such entity is a creditor.

(2) In any case filed under chapter 7 or 13, any notice required to be provided by a court with respect to which a notice is filed under paragraph (1), to such entity later than 30 days after the filing of such notice under paragraph (1) shall be provided to such address unless with respect to a particular case a different address is specified in a notice filed and served in accordance with subsection (e).

(3) A notice filed under paragraph (1) may be withdrawn by such entity.

(g)(1) Notice provided to a creditor by the debtor or the court other than in accordance with this section (excluding this subsection) shall not be effective notice until such notice is brought to the attention of such creditor. If such creditor designates a person or an organizational subdivision of such creditor to be responsible for receiving notices under this title and establishes reasonable procedures so that such notices receivable by such creditor are to be delivered to such person or such subdivision, then a notice provided to such creditor other than in accordance with this section (excluding this subsection) shall not be considered to have been brought to the attention of such creditor until such notice is received by such person or such subdivision.

(2) A monetary penalty may not be imposed on a creditor for a violation of a stay in effect under section 362(a) (including a monetary penalty imposed under section 362(k)) or for failure to comply with section 542 or 543 unless the conduct that is the basis of such violation or of such failure occurs after such creditor receives notice effective under this section of the order for relief.

§ 343. Examination of the debtor

The debtor shall appear and submit to examination under oath at the meeting of creditors under section 341(a) of this title. Creditors, any indenture trustee, any trustee or examiner in the case, or the United States trustee may examine the debtor. The United States trustee may administer the oath required under this section.

§ 344. Self-incrimination; immunity

Immunity for persons required to submit to examination, to testify, or to provide information in a case under this title may be granted under part V of title 18.

§ 345. Money of estates

(a) A trustee in a case under this title may make such deposit or investment of the money of the estate for which such trustee serves as will yield the maximum reasonable net return on such money, taking into account the safety of such deposit or investment.

(b) Except with respect to a deposit or investment that is insured or guaranteed by the United States or by a department, agency, or instrumentality of the United States or backed by the full faith and credit of the United States, the trustee shall require from an entity with which such money is deposited or invested—

(1) a bond—

(A) in favor of the United States;

(B) secured by the undertaking of a corporate surety approved by the United States trustee for the district in which the case is pending; and

(C) conditioned on—

(i) a proper accounting for all money so deposited or invested and for any return on such money;

(ii) prompt repayment of such money and return; and

(iii) faithful performance of duties as a depository; or

(2) the deposit of securities of the kind specified in section 9303 of title 31;

unless the court for cause orders otherwise.

(c) An entity with which such moneys are deposited or invested is authorized to deposit or invest such moneys as may be required under this section.

§ 346. Special provisions related to the treatment of State and local taxes

(a) Whenever the Internal Revenue Code of 1986 provides that a separate taxable estate or entity is created in a case concerning a debtor under this title, and the income, gain, loss, deductions, and credits of such estate shall be taxed to or claimed by the estate, a separate taxable estate is also created for purposes of any State and local law imposing a tax on or measured by income and such income, gain, loss, deductions, and credits shall be taxed to or claimed by the estate and may not be taxed to or claimed by the debtor. The preceding sentence shall not apply if the case is dismissed. The trustee shall make tax returns of income required under any such State or local law.

(b) Whenever the Internal Revenue Code of 1986 provides that no separate taxable estate shall be created in a case concerning a debtor under this title, and the income, gain, loss, deductions, and credits of an estate shall be taxed to or claimed by the debtor, such income, gain, loss, deductions, and credits shall be taxed to or claimed by the debtor under a State or local law imposing a tax on or measured by income and may not be taxed to or claimed by the estate. The trustee shall make such tax returns of income of corporations and of partnerships as are required under any State or local law, but with respect to partnerships, shall make such returns only to the extent such returns are also required to be made under such Code. The estate shall be liable for any tax imposed on such corporation or partnership, but not for any tax imposed on partners or members.

(c) With respect to a partnership or any entity treated as a partnership under a State or local law imposing a tax on or measured by income that is a debtor in a case under this title, any gain or loss resulting from a distribution of property from such partnership, or any distributive share of any income, gain, loss, deduction, or credit of a partner or member that is distributed, or considered distributed, from such partnership, after the commencement of the case, is gain, loss, income, deduction, or credit, as the case may be, of the partner or member, and if such partner or member is a debtor in a case under this title, shall be subject to tax in accordance with subsection (a) or (b).

(d) For purposes of any State or local law imposing a tax on or measured by income, the taxable period of a debtor in a case under this title shall terminate only if and to the extent that the taxable period of such debtor terminates under the Internal Revenue Code of 1986.

(e) The estate in any case described in subsection (a) shall use the same accounting method as the debtor used immediately before the commencement of the case, if such method of accounting complies with applicable nonbankruptcy tax law.

(f) For purposes of any State or local law imposing a tax on or measured by income, a transfer of property from the debtor to the estate or from the estate to the debtor shall not be treated as a disposition for purposes of any provision assigning tax consequences to a disposition, except to the extent that such transfer is treated as a disposition under the Internal Revenue Code of 1986.

(g) Whenever a tax is imposed pursuant to a State or local law imposing a tax on or measured by income pursuant to subsection (a) or (b), such tax shall be imposed at rates generally applicable to the same types of entities under such State or local law.

(h) The trustee shall withhold from any payment of claims for wages, salaries, commissions, dividends, interest, or other payments, or collect, any amount required to be withheld or collected under applicable State or local tax law, and shall pay such withheld or collected amount to the appropriate governmental unit at the time and in the manner required by such tax law, and with the same priority as the claim from which such amount was withheld or collected was paid.

(i)(1) To the extent that any State or local law imposing a tax on or measured by income provides for the carryover of any tax attribute from one taxable period to a subsequent taxable period, the estate shall succeed to such tax attribute in any case in which such estate is subject to tax under subsection (a).

(2) After such a case is closed or dismissed, the debtor shall succeed to any tax attribute to which the estate succeeded under paragraph (1) to the extent consistent with the Internal Revenue Code of 1986.

(3) The estate may carry back any loss or tax attribute to a taxable period of the debtor that ended before the date of the order for relief under this title to the extent that—

(A) applicable State or local tax law provides for a carryback in the case of the debtor; and

(B) the same or a similar tax attribute may be carried back by the estate to such a taxable period of the debtor under the Internal Revenue Code of 1986.

(j)(1) For purposes of any State or local law imposing a tax on or measured by income, income is not realized by the estate, the debtor, or a successor to the debtor by reason of discharge of indebtedness in a case under this title, except to the extent, if any, that such income is subject to tax under the Internal Revenue Code of 1986.

(2) Whenever the Internal Revenue Code of 1986 provides that the amount excluded from gross income in respect of the discharge of indebtedness in a case under this title shall be applied to reduce the tax attributes of the debtor or the estate, a similar reduction shall be made under any State or local law imposing a tax on or measured by income to the extent such State or local law recognizes such attributes. Such State or local law may also provide for the reduction of other attributes to the extent that the full amount of income from the discharge of indebtedness has not been applied.

(k)(1)   Except as provided in this section and section 505, the time and manner of filing tax returns and the items of income, gain, loss, deduction, and credit of any taxpayer shall be determined under applicable nonbankruptcy law.

(2)   For Federal tax purposes, the provisions of this section are subject to the Internal Revenue Code of 1986 and other applicable Federal nonbankruptcy law.

§ 347.   Unclaimed property

(a)   Ninety days after the final distribution under section 726, 1194, 1226, or 1326 of this title in a case under chapter 7, subchapter V of chapter 11, 12, or 13 of this title, as the case may be, the trustee shall stop payment on any check remaining unpaid, and any remaining property of the estate shall be paid into the court and disposed of under chapter 129 of title 28.

(b)   Any security, money, or other property remaining unclaimed at the expiration of the time allowed in a case under chapter 9, 11, or 12 of this title for the presentation of a security or the performance of any other act as a condition to participation in the distribution under any plan confirmed under section 943(b), 1129, 1173, 1191, or 1225 of this title, as the case may be, becomes the property of the debtor or of the entity acquiring the assets of the debtor under the plan, as the case may be.

§ 348.   Effect of conversion

(a)   Conversion of a case from a case under one chapter of this title to a case under another chapter of this title constitutes an order for relief under the chapter to which the case is converted, but, except as provided in subsections (b) and (c) of this section, does not effect a change in the date of the filing of the petition, the commencement of the case, or the order for relief.

(b)   Unless the court for cause orders otherwise, in sections 701(a), 727(a)(10), 727(b), 1102(a), 1110(a)(1), 1121(b), 1121(c), 1141(d)(4), 1201(a), 1221, 1228(a), 1301(a), and 1305(a) of this title, "the order for relief under this chapter" in a chapter to which a case has been converted under section 706, 1112, 1208, or 1307 of this title means the conversion of such case to such chapter.

(c)   Sections 342 and 365(d) of this title apply in a case that has been converted under section 706, 1112, 1208, or 1307 of this title, as if the conversion order were the order for relief.

(d)   A claim against the estate or the debtor that arises after the order for relief but before conversion in a case that is converted under section 1112, 1208, or 1307 of this title, other than a claim specified in section 503(b) of this title, shall be treated for all purposes as if such claim had arisen immediately before the date of the filing of the petition.

(e)   Conversion of a case under section 706, 1112, 1208, or 1307 of this title terminates the service of any trustee or examiner that is serving in the case before such conversion.

(f)(1)   Except as provided in paragraph (2), when a case under chapter 13 of this title is converted to a case under another chapter under this title—

    (A)   property of the estate in the converted case shall consist of property of the estate, as of the date of filing of the petition, that remains in the possession of or is under the control of the debtor on the date of conversion;

    (B)   valuations of property and of allowed secured claims in the chapter 13 case shall apply only in a case converted to a case under chapter 11 or 12, but not in a case converted to a case under chapter 7, with allowed secured claims in cases under chapters 11 and 12 reduced to the extent that they have been paid in accordance with the chapter 13 plan; and

    (C)   with respect to cases converted from chapter 13—

        (i)   the claim of any creditor holding security as of the date of the filing of the petition shall continue to be secured by that security unless the full amount of such claim determined under applicable nonbankruptcy law has been paid in full as of the date of conversion, notwithstanding any valuation or determination of the amount of an allowed secured claim made for the purposes of the case under chapter 13; and

(ii) unless a prebankruptcy default has been fully cured under the plan at the time of conversion, in any proceeding under this title or otherwise, the default shall have the effect given under applicable nonbankruptcy law.

(2) If the debtor converts a case under chapter 13 of this title to a case under another chapter under this title in bad faith, the property of the estate in the converted case shall consist of the property of the estate as of the date of conversion.

§ 349. Effect of dismissal

(a) Unless the court, for cause, orders otherwise, the dismissal of a case under this title does not bar the discharge, in a later case under this title, of debts that were dischargeable in the case dismissed; nor does the dismissal of a case under this title prejudice the debtor with regard to the filing of a subsequent petition under this title, except as provided in section 109(g) of this title.

(b) Unless the court, for cause, orders otherwise, a dismissal of a case other than under section 742 of this title—

(1) reinstates—

(A) any proceeding or custodianship superseded under section 543 of this title;

(B) any transfer avoided under section 522, 544, 545, 547, 548, 549, or 724(a) of this title, or preserved under section 510(c)(2), 522(i)(2), or 551 of this title; and

(C) any lien voided under section 506(d) of this title;

(2) vacates any order, judgment, or transfer ordered, under section 522(i)(1), 542, 550, or 553 of this title; and

(3) revests the property of the estate in the entity in which such property was vested immediately before the commencement of the case under this title.

§ 350. Closing and reopening cases

(a) After an estate is fully administered and the court has discharged the trustee, the court shall close the case.

(b) A case may be reopened in the court in which such case was closed to administer assets, to accord relief to the debtor, or for other cause.

§ 351. Disposal of patient records

If a health care business commences a case under chapter 7, 9, or 11, and the trustee does not have a sufficient amount of funds to pay for the storage of patient records in the manner required under applicable Federal or State law, the following requirements shall apply:

(1) The trustee shall—

(A) promptly publish notice, in 1 or more appropriate newspapers, that if patient records are not claimed by the patient or an insurance provider (if applicable law permits the insurance provider to make that claim) by the date that is 365 days after the date of that notification, the trustee will destroy the patient records; and

(B) during the first 180 days of the 365-day period described in subparagraph (A), promptly attempt to notify directly each patient that is the subject of the patient records and appropriate insurance carrier concerning the patient records by mailing to the most recent known address of that patient, or a family member or contact person for that patient, and to the appropriate insurance carrier an appropriate notice regarding the claiming or disposing of patient records.

(2) If, after providing the notification under paragraph (1), patient records are not claimed during the 365-day period described under that paragraph, the trustee shall mail, by certified mail, at the end of such 365-day period a written request to each appropriate Federal agency to request permission from that agency to deposit the patient records with that agency, except that no Federal agency is required to accept patient records under this paragraph.

(3) If, following the 365-day period described in paragraph (2) and after providing the notification under paragraph (1), patient records are not claimed by a patient or insurance provider, or request is not granted by a Federal agency to deposit such records with that agency, the trustee shall destroy those records by—

    (A) if the records are written, shredding or burning the records; or

    (B) if the records are magnetic, optical, or other electronic records, by otherwise destroying those records so that those records cannot be retrieved.

SUBCHAPTER IV—ADMINISTRATIVE POWERS

§ 361. Adequate protection

When adequate protection is required under section 362, 363, or 364 of this title of an interest of an entity in property, such adequate protection may be provided by—

(1) requiring the trustee to make a cash payment or periodic cash payments to such entity, to the extent that the stay under section 362 of this title, use, sale, or lease under section 363 of this title, or any grant of a lien under section 364 of this title results in a decrease in the value of such entity's interest in such property;

(2) providing to such entity an additional or replacement lien to the extent that such stay, use, sale, lease, or grant results in a decrease in the value of such entity's interest in such property; or

(3) granting such other relief, other than entitling such entity to compensation allowable under section 503(b)(1) of this title as an administrative expense, as will result in the realization by such entity of the indubitable equivalent of such entity's interest in such property.

§ 362. Automatic stay

(a) Except as provided in subsection (b) of this section, a petition filed under section 301, 302, or 303 of this title, or an application filed under section 5(a)(3) of the Securities Investor Protection Act of 1970, operates as a stay, applicable to all entities, of—

(1) the commencement or continuation, including the issuance or employment of process, of a judicial, administrative, or other action or proceeding against the debtor that was or could have been commenced before the commencement of the case under this title, or to recover a claim against the debtor that arose before the commencement of the case under this title;

(2) the enforcement, against the debtor or against property of the estate, of a judgment obtained before the commencement of the case under this title;

(3) any act to obtain possession of property of the estate or of property from the estate or to exercise control over property of the estate;

(4) any act to create, perfect, or enforce any lien against property of the estate;

(5) any act to create, perfect, or enforce against property of the debtor any lien to the extent that such lien secures a claim that arose before the commencement of the case under this title;

(6) any act to collect, assess, or recover a claim against the debtor that arose before the commencement of the case under this title;

(7) the setoff of any debt owing to the debtor that arose before the commencement of the case under this title against any claim against the debtor; and

(8) the commencement or continuation of a proceeding before the United States Tax Court concerning a tax liability of a debtor that is a corporation for a taxable period the bankruptcy court may determine or concerning the tax liability of a debtor who is an individual for a taxable period ending before the date of the order for relief under this title.

(b) The filing of a petition under section 301, 302, or 303 of this title, or of an application under section 5(a)(3) of the Securities Investor Protection Act of 1970, does not operate as a stay—

(1) under subsection (a) of this section, of the commencement or continuation of a criminal action or proceeding against the debtor;

(2) under subsection (a)—

(A) of the commencement or continuation of a civil action or proceeding—

(i) for the establishment of paternity;

(ii) for the establishment or modification of an order for domestic support obligations;

(iii) concerning child custody or visitation;

(iv) for the dissolution of a marriage, except to the extent that such proceeding seeks to determine the division of property that is property of the estate; or

(v) regarding domestic violence;

(B) of the collection of a domestic support obligation from property that is not property of the estate;

(C) with respect to the withholding of income that is property of the estate or property of the debtor for payment of a domestic support obligation under a judicial or administrative order or a statute;

(D) of the withholding, suspension, or restriction of a driver's license, a professional or occupational license, or a recreational license, under State law, as specified in section 466(a)(16) of the Social Security Act;

(E) of the reporting of overdue support owed by a parent to any consumer reporting agency as specified in section 466(a)(7) of the Social Security Act;

(F) of the interception of a tax refund, as specified in sections 464 and 466(a)(3) of the Social Security Act or under an analogous State law; or

(G) of the enforcement of a medical obligation, as specified under title IV of the Social Security Act;

(3) under subsection (a) of this section, of any act to perfect, or to maintain or continue the perfection of, an interest in property to the extent that the trustee's rights and powers are subject to such perfection under section 546(b) of this title or to the extent that such act is accomplished within the period provided under section 547(e)(2)(A) of this title;

(4) under paragraph (1), (2), (3), or (6) of subsection (a) of this section, of the commencement or continuation of an action or proceeding by a governmental unit or any organization exercising authority under the Convention on the Prohibition of the Development, Production, Stockpiling and Use of Chemical Weapons and on Their Destruction, opened for signature on January 13, 1993, to enforce such governmental unit's or organization's police and regulatory power, including the enforcement of a judgment other than a money judgment, obtained in an action or proceeding by the governmental unit to enforce such governmental unit's or organization's police or regulatory power;

[(5) Repealed.]

(6) under subsection (a) of this section, of the exercise by a commodity broker, forward contract merchant, stockbroker, financial institution, financial participant, or securities clearing agency of any contractual right (as defined in section 555 or 556) under any security agreement or arrangement or other credit enhancement forming a part of or related to any commodity contract, forward contract or securities contract, or of any contractual right (as defined in section 555 or 556) to offset or net out any termination value, payment amount, or other transfer obligation arising under or in connection with 1 or more such contracts, including any master agreement for such contracts;

(7) under subsection (a) of this section, of the exercise by a repo participant or financial participant of any contractual right (as defined in section 559) under any security agreement or arrangement or other credit enhancement forming a part of or related to any repurchase agreement, or of any contractual right (as defined in section 559) to offset or net out any termination value, payment amount, or other transfer obligation arising under or in connection with 1 or more such agreements, including any master agreement for such agreements;

(8) under subsection (a) of this section, of the commencement of any action by the Secretary of Housing and Urban Development to foreclose a mortgage or deed of trust in any case in which the mortgage or deed of trust held by the Secretary is insured or was formerly insured under the National Housing Act and covers property, or combinations of property, consisting of five or more living units;

(9) under subsection (a), of—

(A) an audit by a governmental unit to determine tax liability;

(B) the issuance to the debtor by a governmental unit of a notice of tax deficiency;

(C) a demand for tax returns; or

(D) the making of an assessment for any tax and issuance of a notice and demand for payment of such an assessment (but any tax lien that would otherwise attach to property of the estate by reason of such an assessment shall not take effect unless such tax is a debt of the debtor that will not be discharged in the case and such property or its proceeds are transferred out of the estate to, or otherwise revested in, the debtor).

(10) under subsection (a) of this section, of any act by a lessor to the debtor under a lease of nonresidential real property that has terminated by the expiration of the stated term of the lease before the commencement of or during a case under this title to obtain possession of such property;

(11) under subsection (a) of this section, of the presentment of a negotiable instrument and the giving of notice of and protesting dishonor of such an instrument;

(12) under subsection (a) of this section, after the date which is 90 days after the filing of such petition, of the commencement or continuation, and conclusion to the entry of final judgment, of an action which involves a debtor subject to reorganization pursuant to chapter 11 of this title and which was brought by the Secretary of Transportation under section 31325 of title 46 (including distribution of any proceeds of sale) to foreclose a preferred ship or fleet mortgage, or a security interest in or relating to a vessel or vessel under construction, held by the Secretary of Transportation under chapter 537 of title 46 or section 109(h) of title 49, or under applicable State law;

(13) under subsection (a) of this section, after the date which is 90 days after the filing of such petition, of the commencement or continuation, and conclusion to the entry of final judgment, of an action which involves a debtor subject to reorganization pursuant to chapter 11 of this title and which was brought by the Secretary of Commerce under section 31325 of title 46 (including distribution of any proceeds of sale) to foreclose a preferred ship or fleet mortgage in a vessel or a mortgage, deed of trust, or other security interest in a fishing facility held by the Secretary of Commerce under chapter 537 of title 46;

(14) under subsection (a) of this section, of any action by an accrediting agency regarding the accreditation status of the debtor as an educational institution;

(15) under subsection (a) of this section, of any action by a State licensing body regarding the licensure of the debtor as an educational institution;

(16) under subsection (a) of this section, of any action by a guaranty agency, as defined in section 435(j) of the Higher Education Act of 1965 or the Secretary of Education regarding the eligibility of the debtor to participate in programs authorized under such Act;

(17) under subsection (a) of this section, of the exercise by a swap participant or financial participant of any contractual right (as defined in section 560) under any security agreement or arrangement or other credit enhancement forming a part of or related to any swap agreement, or of any contractual right (as defined in section 560) to offset or net out any termination value, payment amount, or other transfer obligation arising under or in connection with 1 or more such agreements, including any master agreement for such agreements;

(18) under subsection (a) of the creation or perfection of a statutory lien for an ad valorem property tax, or a special tax or special assessment on real property whether or not ad valorem, imposed by a governmental unit, if such tax or assessment comes due after the date of the filing of the petition;

(19) under subsection (a), of withholding of income from a debtor's wages and collection of amounts withheld, under the debtor's agreement authorizing that withholding and collection for the benefit of a pension, profit-sharing, stock bonus, or other plan established under section 401, 403, 408, 408A, 414, 457, or 501(c) of the Internal Revenue Code of 1986, that is sponsored by the employer of the debtor, or an affiliate, successor, or predecessor of such employer—

(A) to the extent that the amounts withheld and collected are used solely for payments relating to a loan from a plan under section 408(b)(1) of the Employee Retirement Income Security Act of 1974 or is subject to section 72(p) of the Internal Revenue Code of 1986; or

(B) a loan from a thrift savings plan permitted under subchapter III of chapter 84 of title 5, that satisfies the requirements of section 8433(g) of such title;

but nothing in this paragraph may be construed to provide that any loan made under a governmental plan under section 414(d), or a contract or account under section 403(b), of the Internal Revenue Code of 1986 constitutes a claim or a debt under this title;

(20) under subsection (a), of any act to enforce any lien against or security interest in real property following entry of the order under subsection (d)(4) as to such real property in any prior case under this title, for a period of 2 years after the date of the entry of such an order, except that the debtor, in a subsequent case under this title, may move for relief from such order based upon changed circumstances or for other good cause shown, after notice and a hearing;

(21) under subsection (a), of any act to enforce any lien against or security interest in real property—

(A) if the debtor is ineligible under section 109(g) to be a debtor in a case under this title; or

(B) if the case under this title was filed in violation of a bankruptcy court order in a prior case under this title prohibiting the debtor from being a debtor in another case under this title;

(22) subject to subsection (*l*), under subsection (a)(3), of the continuation of any eviction, unlawful detainer action, or similar proceeding by a lessor against a debtor involving residential property in which the debtor resides as a tenant under a lease or rental agreement and with respect to which the lessor has obtained before the date of the filing of the bankruptcy petition, a judgment for possession of such property against the debtor;

(23) subject to subsection (m), under subsection (a)(3), of an eviction action that seeks possession of the residential property in which the debtor resides as a tenant under a lease or rental agreement based on endangerment of such property or the illegal use of controlled substances on such property, but only if the lessor files with the court, and serves upon the debtor, a certification under penalty of perjury that such an eviction action has been filed, or that the debtor, during the 30-day period preceding the date of the filing of the certification, has endangered property or illegally used or allowed to be used a controlled substance on the property;

(24) under subsection (a), of any transfer that is not avoidable under section 544 and that is not avoidable under section 549;

(25) under subsection (a), of—

(A) the commencement or continuation of an investigation or action by a securities self regulatory organization to enforce such organization's regulatory power;

(B) the enforcement of an order or decision, other than for monetary sanctions, obtained in an action by such securities self regulatory organization to enforce such organization's regulatory power; or

(C) any act taken by such securities self regulatory organization to delist, delete, or refuse to permit quotation of any stock that does not meet applicable regulatory requirements;

(26) under subsection (a), of the setoff under applicable nonbankruptcy law of an income tax refund, by a governmental unit, with respect to a taxable period that ended before the date of the order for relief against an income tax liability for a taxable period that also ended before the date of the order for relief, except that in any case in which the setoff of an income tax refund is not permitted under applicable nonbankruptcy law because of a pending action to determine the amount or legality of a tax liability, the governmental unit may hold the refund pending the resolution of the action, unless the court, on the motion of the trustee and after notice and a hearing, grants the taxing authority adequate protection (within the meaning of section 361) for the secured claim of such authority in the setoff under section 506(a);

(27) under subsection (a) of this section, of the exercise by a master netting agreement participant of any contractual right (as defined in section 555, 556, 559, or 560) under any security agreement or arrangement or other credit enhancement forming a part of or related to any master netting agreement, or of any contractual right (as defined in section 555, 556, 559, or 560) to offset or net out any termination value, payment amount, or other transfer obligation arising under or in connection with 1 or more such master netting agreements to the extent that such participant is eligible to exercise such rights under paragraph (6), (7), or (17) for each individual contract covered by the master netting agreement in issue;

(28) under subsection (a), of the exclusion by the Secretary of Health and Human Services of the debtor from participation in the medicare program or any other Federal health care program (as defined in section 1128B(f) of the Social Security Act pursuant to title XI or XVIII of such Act); and

(29) under subsection (a)(1) of this section, of any action by—

    (A) an amateur sports organization, as defined in section 220501(b) of title 36, to replace a national governing body, as defined in that section, under section 220528 of that title, or

    (B) the corporation, as defined in section 2201501b) of title 36, to revoke the certification of a national governing body, as defined in that section, under section 220521 of that title.

The provisions of paragraphs (12) and (13) of this subsection shall apply with respect to any such petition filed on or before December 31, 1989.

(c) Except as provided in subsections (d), (e), (f), and (h) of this section—

(1) the stay of an act against property of the estate under subsection (a) of this section continues until such property is no longer property of the estate;

(2) the stay of any other act under subsection (a) of this section continues until the earliest of—

    (A) the time the case is closed;

    (B) the time the case is dismissed; or

    (C) if the case is a case under chapter 7 of this title concerning an individual or a case under chapter 9, 11, 12, or 13 of this title, the time a discharge is granted or denied;

(3) if a single or joint case is filed by or against a debtor who is an individual in a case under chapter 7, 11, or 13, and if a single or joint case of the debtor was pending within the preceding 1-year period but was dismissed, other than a case refiled under a chapter other than chapter 7 after dismissal under section 707(b)—

    (A) the stay under subsection (a) with respect to any action taken with respect to a debt or property securing such debt or with respect to any lease shall terminate with respect to the debtor on the 30th day after the filing of the later case;

    (B) on the motion of a party in interest for continuation of the automatic stay and upon notice and a hearing, the court may extend the stay in particular cases as to any or all creditors (subject to such conditions or limitations as the court may then impose) after notice and a hearing completed before the expiration of the 30-day period only if the party in interest demonstrates that the filing of the later case is in good faith as to the creditors to be stayed; and

(C) for purposes of subparagraph (B), a case is presumptively filed not in good faith (but such presumption may be rebutted by clear and convincing evidence to the contrary)—

(i) as to all creditors, if—

(I) more than 1 previous case under any of chapters 7, 11, and 13 in which the individual was a debtor was pending within the preceding 1-year period;

(II) a previous case under any of chapters 7, 11, and 13 in which the individual was a debtor was dismissed within such 1-year period, after the debtor failed to—

(aa) file or amend the petition or other documents as required by this title or the court without substantial excuse (but mere inadvertence or negligence shall not be a substantial excuse unless the dismissal was caused by the negligence of the debtor's attorney);

(bb) provide adequate protection as ordered by the court; or

(cc) perform the terms of a plan confirmed by the court; or

(III) there has not been a substantial change in the financial or personal affairs of the debtor since the dismissal of the next most previous case under chapter 7, 11, or 13 or any other reason to conclude that the later case will be concluded—

(aa) if a case under chapter 7, with a discharge; or

(bb) if a case under chapter 11 or 13, with a confirmed plan that will be fully performed; and

(ii) as to any creditor that commenced an action under subsection (d) in a previous case in which the individual was a debtor if, as of the date of dismissal of such case, that action was still pending or had been resolved by terminating, conditioning, or limiting the stay as to actions of such creditor; and

(4)(A)(i) if a single or joint case is filed by or against a debtor who is an individual under this title, and if 2 or more single or joint cases of the debtor were pending within the previous year but were dismissed, other than a case refiled under a chapter other than Chapter 7 after dismissal under section 707(b), the stay under subsection (a) shall not go into effect upon the filing of the later case; and

(ii) on request of a party in interest, the court shall promptly enter an order confirming that no stay is in effect;

(B) if, within 30 days after the filing of the later case, a party in interest requests the court may order the stay to take effect in the case as to any or all creditors (subject to such conditions or limitations as the court may impose), after notice and a hearing, only if the party in interest demonstrates that the filing of the later case is in good faith as to the creditors to be stayed;

(C) a stay imposed under subparagraph (B) shall be effective on the date of the entry of the order allowing the stay to go into effect; and

(D) for purposes of subparagraph (B), a case is presumptively filed not in good faith (but such presumption may be rebutted by clear and convincing evidence to the contrary)—

(i) as to all creditors if—

(I) 2 or more previous cases under this title in which the individual was a debtor were pending within the 1-year period;

(II) a previous case under this title in which the individual was a debtor was dismissed within the time period stated in this paragraph after the debtor failed to file or amend the petition or other documents as required by this title or the court without substantial excuse (but mere inadvertence or negligence shall not be substantial excuse unless the dismissal was caused by the negligence of the debtor's attorney), failed to provide adequate protection as ordered by the court, or failed to perform the terms of a plan confirmed by the court; or

(III) there has not been a substantial change in the financial or personal affairs of the debtor since the dismissal of the next most previous case under this title, or any other reason to conclude that the later case will not be concluded, if a case under chapter 7, with a discharge, and if a case under chapter 11 or 13, with a confirmed plan that will be fully performed; or

(ii) as to any creditor that commenced an action under subsection (d) in a previous case in which the individual was a debtor if, as of the date of dismissal of such case, such action was still pending or had been resolved by terminating, conditioning, or limiting the stay as to such action of such creditor.

(d) On request of a party in interest and after notice and a hearing, the court shall grant relief from the stay provided under subsection (a) of this section, such as by terminating, annulling, modifying, or conditioning such stay—

(1) for cause, including the lack of adequate protection of an interest in property of such party in interest;

(2) with respect to a stay of an act against property under subsection (a) of this section, if—

(A) the debtor does not have an equity in such property; and

(B) such property is not necessary to an effective reorganization;

(3) with respect to a stay of an act against single asset real estate under subsection (a), by a creditor whose claim is secured by an interest in such real estate, unless, not later than the date that is 90 days after the entry of the order for relief (or such later date as the court may determine for cause by order entered within that 90-day period) or 30 days after the court determines that the debtor is subject to this paragraph, whichever is later—

(A) the debtor has filed a plan of reorganization that has a reasonable possibility of being confirmed within a reasonable time; or

(B) the debtor has commenced monthly payments that—

(i) may, in the debtor's sole discretion, notwithstanding section 363(c)(2), be made from rents or other income generated before, on, or after the date of the commencement of the case by or from the property to each creditor whose claim is secured by such real estate (other than a claim secured by a judgment lien or by an unmatured statutory lien); and

(ii) are in an amount equal to interest at the then applicable nondefault contract rate of interest on the value of the creditor's interest in the real estate; or

(4) with respect to a stay of an act against real property under subsection (a), by a creditor whose claim is secured by an interest in such real property, if the court finds that the filing of the petition was part of a scheme to delay, hinder, or defraud creditors that involved either—

(A) transfer of all or part ownership of, or other interest in, such real property without the consent of the secured creditor or court approval; or

(B) multiple bankruptcy filings affecting such real property.

If recorded in compliance with applicable State laws governing notices of interests or liens in real property, an order entered under paragraph (4) shall be binding in any other case under this title purporting to affect such real property filed not later than 2 years after the date of the entry of such order by the court, except that a debtor in a subsequent case under this title may move for relief from such order based upon changed circumstances or for good cause shown, after notice and a hearing. Any Federal, State, or local governmental unit that accepts notices of interests or liens in real property shall accept any certified copy of an order described in this subsection for indexing and recording.

(e)(1) Thirty days after a request under subsection (d) of this section for relief from the stay of any act against property of the estate under subsection (a) of this section, such stay is terminated with respect to the party in interest making such request, unless the court, after notice and a hearing, orders such stay continued in effect pending the conclusion of, or as a result of, a final hearing and determination under subsection (d) of this section. A hearing under this subsection may be a preliminary hearing, or may be consolidated with the final hearing under subsection (d) of this section. The court shall order such stay continued in effect pending the conclusion of the final hearing under subsection (d) of this section if there is a reasonable likelihood that the party opposing relief from such stay will prevail at the conclusion of such final hearing. If the hearing under this subsection is a preliminary hearing, then such final hearing shall be concluded not later than thirty days after the conclusion of such preliminary hearing, unless the 30-day period is extended with the consent of the parties in interest or for a specific time which the court finds is required by compelling circumstances.

(2) Notwithstanding paragraph (1), in a case under chapter 7, 11, or 13 in which the debtor is an individual, the stay under subsection (a) shall terminate on the date that is 60 days after a request is made by a party in interest under subsection (d), unless—

(A) a final decision is rendered by the court during the 60-day period beginning on the date of the request; or

(B) such 60-day period is extended—

(i) by agreement of all parties in interest; or

(ii) by the court for such specific period of time as the court finds is required for good cause, as described in findings made by the court.

(f) Upon request of a party in interest, the court, with or without a hearing, shall grant such relief from the stay provided under subsection (a) of this section as is necessary to prevent irreparable damage to the interest of an entity in property, if such interest will suffer such damage before there is an opportunity for notice and a hearing under subsection (d) or (e) of this section.

(g) In any hearing under subsection (d) or (e) of this section concerning relief from the stay of any act under subsection (a) of this section—

(1) the party requesting such relief has the burden of proof on the issue of the debtor's equity in property; and

(2) the party opposing such relief has the burden of proof on all other issues.

(h)(1) In a case in which the debtor is an individual, the stay provided by subsection (a) is terminated with respect to personal property of the estate or of the debtor securing in whole or in part a claim, or subject to an unexpired lease, and such personal property shall no longer be property of the estate if the debtor fails within the applicable time set by section 521(a)(2)—

(A) to file timely any statement of intention required under section 521(a)(2) with respect to such personal property or to indicate in such statement that the debtor will either surrender such personal property or retain it and, if retaining such personal property, either redeem such personal property pursuant to section 722, enter into an agreement of the kind specified in section 524(c) applicable to the debt secured by such personal property, or assume such unexpired lease pursuant to section 365(p) if the trustee does not do so, as applicable; and

(B) to take timely the action specified in such statement, as it may be amended before expiration of the period for taking action, unless such statement specifies the debtor's intention to reaffirm such debt on the original contract terms and the creditor refuses to agree to the reaffirmation on such terms.

(2) Paragraph (1) does not apply if the court determines, on the motion of the trustee filed before the expiration of the applicable time set by section 521(a)(2), after notice and a hearing, that such personal property is of consequential value or benefit to the estate, and orders appropriate adequate protection of the creditor's interest, and orders the debtor to deliver any collateral in the debtor's possession to the trustee. If the court does not so determine, the stay provided by subsection (a) shall terminate upon the conclusion of the hearing on the motion.

(i) If a case commenced under chapter 7, 11, or 13 is dismissed due to the creation of a debt repayment plan, for purposes of subsection (c)(3), any subsequent case commenced by the debtor under any such chapter shall not be presumed to be filed not in good faith.

(j) On request of a party in interest, the court shall issue an order under subsection (c) confirming that the automatic stay has been terminated.

(k)(1) Except as provided in paragraph (2), an individual injured by any willful violation of a stay provided by this section shall recover actual damages, including costs and attorneys' fees, and, in appropriate circumstances, may recover punitive damages.

(2) If such violation is based on an action taken by an entity in the good faith belief that subsection (h) applies to the debtor, the recovery under paragraph (1) of this subsection against such entity shall be limited to actual damages.

(l)(1) Except as otherwise provided in this subsection, subsection (b)(22) shall apply on the date that is 30 days after the date on which the bankruptcy petition is filed, if the debtor files with the petition and serves upon the lessor a certification under penalty of perjury that—

(A) under nonbankruptcy law applicable in the jurisdiction, there are circumstances under which the debtor would be permitted to cure the entire monetary default that gave rise to the judgment for possession, after that judgment for possession was entered; and

(B) the debtor (or an adult dependent of the debtor) has deposited with the clerk of the court, any rent that would become due during the 30-day period after the filing of the bankruptcy petition.

(2) If, within the 30-day period after the filing of the bankruptcy petition, the debtor (or an adult dependent of the debtor) complies with paragraph (1) and files with the court and serves upon the lessor a further certification under penalty of perjury that the debtor (or an adult dependent of the debtor) has cured, under nonbankruptcy law applicable in the jurisdiction, the entire monetary default that gave rise to the judgment under which possession is sought by the lessor, subsection (b)(22) shall not apply, unless ordered to apply by the court under paragraph (3).

(3)(A) If the lessor files an objection to any certification filed by the debtor under paragraph (1) or (2), and serves such objection upon the debtor, the court shall hold a hearing within 10 days after the filing and service of such objection to determine if the certification filed by the debtor under paragraph (1) or (2) is true.

(B) If the court upholds the objection of the lessor filed under subparagraph (A)—

(i) subsection (b)(22) shall apply immediately and relief from the stay provided under subsection (a)(3) shall not be required to enable the lessor to complete the process to recover full possession of the property; and

(ii) the clerk of the court shall immediately serve upon the lessor and the debtor a certified copy of the court's order upholding the lessor's objection.

(4) If a debtor, in accordance with paragraph (5), indicates on the petition that there was a judgment for possession of the residential rental property in which the debtor resides and does not file a certification under paragraph (1) or (2)—

(A) subsection (b)(22) shall apply immediately upon failure to file such certification, and relief from the stay provided under subsection (a)(3) shall not be required to enable the lessor to complete the process to recover full possession of the property; and

(B) the clerk of the court shall immediately serve upon the lessor and the debtor a certified copy of the docket indicating the absence of a filed certification and the applicability of the exception to the stay under subsection (b)(22).

(5)(A) Where a judgment for possession of residential property in which the debtor resides as a tenant under a lease or rental agreement has been obtained by the lessor, the debtor shall so indicate on the bankruptcy petition and shall provide the name and address of the lessor that obtained that pre-petition judgment on the petition and on any certification filed under this subsection.

(B) The form of certification filed with the petition, as specified in this subsection, shall provide for the debtor to certify, and the debtor shall certify—

(i) whether a judgment for possession of residential rental housing in which the debtor resides has been obtained against the debtor before the date of the filing of the petition; and

(ii) whether the debtor is claiming under paragraph (1) that under nonbankruptcy law applicable in the jurisdiction, there are circumstances under which the debtor would be permitted to cure the entire monetary default that gave rise to the judgment for possession, after that judgment of possession was entered, and has made the appropriate deposit with the court.

(C) The standard forms (electronic and otherwise) used in a bankruptcy proceeding shall be amended to reflect the requirements of this subsection.

(D) The clerk of the court shall arrange for the prompt transmittal of the rent deposited in accordance with paragraph (1)(B) to the lessor.

(m)(1) Except as otherwise provided in this subsection, subsection (b)(23) shall apply on the date that is 15 days after the date on which the lessor files and serves a certification described in subsection (b)(23).

(2)(A) If the debtor files with the court an objection to the truth or legal sufficiency of the certification described in subsection (b)(23) and serves such objection upon the lessor, subsection (b)(23) shall not apply, unless ordered to apply by the court under this subsection.

(B) If the debtor files and serves the objection under subparagraph (A), the court shall hold a hearing within 10 days after the filing and service of such objection to determine if the situation giving rise to the lessor's certification under paragraph (1) existed or has been remedied.

(C) If the debtor can demonstrate to the satisfaction of the court that the situation giving rise to the lessor's certification under paragraph (1) did not exist or has been remedied, the stay provided under subsection (a)(3) shall remain in effect until the termination of the stay under this section.

(D) If the debtor cannot demonstrate to the satisfaction of the court that the situation giving rise to the lessor's certification under paragraph (1) did not exist or has been remedied—

(i) relief from the stay provided under subsection (a)(3) shall not be required to enable the lessor to proceed with the eviction; and

(ii) the clerk of the court shall immediately serve upon the lessor and the debtor a certified copy of the court's order upholding the lessor's certification.

(3) If the debtor fails to file, within 15 days, an objection under paragraph (2)(A)—

(A) subsection (b)(23) shall apply immediately upon such failure and relief from the stay provided under subsection (a)(3) shall not be required to enable the lessor to complete the process to recover full possession of the property; and

(B) the clerk of the court shall immediately serve upon the lessor and the debtor a certified copy of the docket indicating such failure.

(n)(1) Except as provided in paragraph (2), subsection (a) does not apply in a case in which the debtor—

(A) is a debtor in a small business case pending at the time the petition is filed;

(B) was a debtor in a small business case that was dismissed for any reason by an order that became final in the 2-year period ending on the date of the order for relief entered with respect to the petition;

(C) was a debtor in a small business case in which a plan was confirmed in the 2-year period ending on the date of the order for relief entered with respect to the petition; or

(D) is an entity that has acquired substantially all of the assets or business of a small business debtor described in subparagraph (A), (B), or (C), unless such entity establishes by a preponderance of the evidence that such entity acquired substantially all of the assets or business of such small business debtor in good faith and not for the purpose of evading this paragraph.

(2) Paragraph (1) does not apply—

    (A) to an involuntary case involving no collusion by the debtor with creditors; or

    (B) to the filing of a petition if—

        (i) the debtor proves by a preponderance of the evidence that the filing of the petition resulted from circumstances beyond the control of the debtor not foreseeable at the time the case then pending was filed; and

        (ii) it is more likely than not that the court will confirm a feasible plan, but not a liquidating plan, within a reasonable period of time.

    (*o*) The exercise of rights not subject to the stay arising under subsection (a) pursuant to paragraph (6), (7), (17), or (27) of subsection (b) shall not be stayed by any order of a court or administrative agency in any proceeding under this title.

§ 363.   Use, sale, or lease of property

    (a) In this section, "cash collateral" means cash, negotiable instruments, documents of title, securities, deposit accounts, or other cash equivalents whenever acquired in which the estate and an entity other than the estate have an interest and includes the proceeds, products, offspring, rents, or profits of property and the fees, charges, accounts or other payments for the use or occupancy of rooms and other public facilities in hotels, motels, or other lodging properties subject to a security interest as provided in section 552(b) of this title, whether existing before or after the commencement of a case under this title.

    (b)(1) The trustee, after notice and a hearing, may use, sell, or lease, other than in the ordinary course of business, property of the estate, except that if the debtor in connection with offering a product or a service discloses to an individual a policy prohibiting the transfer of personally identifiable information about individuals to persons that are not affiliated with the debtor and if such policy is in effect on the date of the commencement of the case, then the trustee may not sell or lease personally identifiable information to any person unless—

    (A) such sale or such lease is consistent with such policy; or

    (B) after appointment of a consumer privacy ombudsman in accordance with section 332, and after notice and a hearing, the court approves such sale or such lease—

        (i) giving due consideration to the facts, circumstances, and conditions of such sale or such lease; and

        (ii) finding that no showing was made that such sale or such lease would violate applicable nonbankruptcy law.

    (2) If notification is required under subsection (a) of section 7A of the Clayton Act in the case of a transaction under this subsection, then—

    (A) notwithstanding subsection (a) of such section, the notification required by such subsection to be given by the debtor shall be given by the trustee; and

    (B) notwithstanding subsection (b) of such section, the required waiting period shall end on the 15th day after the date of the receipt, by the Federal Trade Commission and the Assistant Attorney General in charge of the Antitrust Division of the Department of Justice, of the notification required under such subsection (a), unless such waiting period is extended—

        (i) pursuant to subsection (e)(2) of such section, in the same manner as such subsection (e)(2) applies to a cash tender offer;

        (ii) pursuant to subsection (g)(2) of such section; or

        (iii) by the court after notice and a hearing.

(c)(1) If the business of the debtor is authorized to be operated under section 721, 1108, 1183, 1184, 1203, 1204, or 1304 of this title and unless the court orders otherwise, the trustee may enter into transactions, including the sale or lease of property of the estate, in the ordinary course of business, without notice or a hearing, and may use property of the estate in the ordinary course of business without notice or a hearing.

(2) The trustee may not use, sell, or lease cash collateral under paragraph (1) of this subsection unless—

(A) each entity that has an interest in such cash collateral consents; or

(B) the court, after notice and a hearing, authorizes such use, sale, or lease in accordance with the provisions of this section.

(3) Any hearing under paragraph (2)(B) of this subsection may be a preliminary hearing or may be consolidated with a hearing under subsection (e) of this section, but shall be scheduled in accordance with the needs of the debtor. If the hearing under paragraph (2)(B) of this subsection is a preliminary hearing, the court may authorize such use, sale, or lease only if there is a reasonable likelihood that the trustee will prevail at the final hearing under subsection (e) of this section. The court shall act promptly on any request for authorization under paragraph (2)(B) of this subsection.

(4) Except as provided in paragraph (2) of this subsection, the trustee shall segregate and account for any cash collateral in the trustee's possession, custody, or control.

(d) The trustee may use, sell, or lease property under subsection (b) or (c) of this section—

(1) In the case of a debtor that is a corporation or trust that is not a moneyed business, commercial corporation, or trust, only in accordance with nonbankruptcy law applicable to the transfer of property by a debtor that such a corporation or trust; and

(2) only to the extent not inconsistent with any relief granted under subsection (c), (d), (e), or (f) of section 362.

(e) Notwithstanding any other provision of this section, at any time, on request of an entity that has an interest in property used, sold, or leased, or proposed to be used, sold, or leased, by the trustee, the court, with or without a hearing, shall prohibit or condition such use, sale, or lease as is necessary to provide adequate protection of such interest. This subsection also applies to property that is subject to any unexpired lease of personal property (to the exclusion of such property being subject to an order to grant relief from the stay under section 362).

(f) The trustee may sell property under subsection (b) or (c) of this section free and clear of any interest in such property of an entity other than the estate, only if—

(1) applicable nonbankruptcy law permits sale of such property free and clear of such interest;

(2) such entity consents;

(3) such interest is a lien and the price at which such property is to be sold is greater than the aggregate value of all liens on such property;

(4) such interest is in bona fide dispute; or

(5) such entity could be compelled, in a legal or equitable proceeding, to accept a money satisfaction of such interest.

(g) Notwithstanding subsection (f) of this section, the trustee may sell property under subsection (b) or (c) of this section free and clear of any vested or contingent right in the nature of dower or curtesy.

(h) Notwithstanding subsection (f) of this section, the trustee may sell both the estate's interest, under subsection (b) or (c) of this section, and the interest of any co-owner in property in which the debtor had, at the time of the commencement of the case, an undivided interest as a tenant in common, joint tenant, or tenant by the entirety, only if—

(1) partition in kind of such property among the estate and such co-owners is impracticable;

(2)   sale of the estate's undivided interest in such property would realize significantly less for the estate than sale of such property free of the interests of such co-owners;

(3)   the benefit to the estate of a sale of such property free of the interests of co-owners outweighs the detriment, if any, to such co-owners; and

(4)   such property is not used in the production, transmission, or distribution, for sale, of electric energy or of natural or synthetic gas for heat, light, or power.

(i)   Before the consummation of a sale of property to which subsection (g) or (h) of this section applies, or of property of the estate that was community property of the debtor and the debtor's spouse immediately before the commencement of the case, the debtor's spouse, or a co-owner of such property, as the case may be, may purchase such property at the price at which such sale is to be consummated.

(j)   After a sale of property to which subsection (g) or (h) of this section applies, the trustee shall distribute to the debtor's spouse or the co-owners of such property, as the case may be, and to the estate, the proceeds of such sale, less the costs and expenses, not including any compensation of the trustee, of such sale, according to the interests of such spouse or co-owners, and of the estate.

(k)   At a sale under subsection (b) of this section of property that is subject to a lien that secures an allowed claim, unless the court for cause orders otherwise the holder of such claim may bid at such sale, and, if the holder of such claim purchases such property, such holder may offset such claim against the purchase price of such property.

(l)   Subject to the provisions of section 365, the trustee may use, sell, or lease property under subsection (b) or (c) of this section, or a plan under chapter 11, 12, or 13 of this title may provide for the use, sale, or lease of property, notwithstanding any provision in a contract, a lease, or applicable law that is conditioned on the insolvency or financial condition of the debtor, on the commencement of a case under this title concerning the debtor, or on the appointment of or the taking possession by a trustee in a case under this title or a custodian, and that effects, or gives an option to effect, a forfeiture, modification, or termination of the debtor's interest in such property.

(m)   The reversal or modification on appeal of an authorization under subsection (b) or (c) of this section of a sale or lease of property does not affect the validity of a sale or lease under such authorization to an entity that purchased or leased such property in good faith, whether or not such entity knew of the pendency of the appeal, unless such authorization and such sale or lease were stayed pending appeal.

(n)   The trustee may avoid a sale under this section if the sale price was controlled by an agreement among potential bidders at such sale, or may recover from a party to such agreement any amount by which the value of the property sold exceeds the price at which such sale was consummated, and may recover any costs, attorneys' fees, or expenses incurred in avoiding such sale or recovering such amount. In addition to any recovery under the preceding sentence, the court may grant judgment for punitive damages in favor of the estate and against any such party that entered into such an agreement in willful disregard of this subsection.

(o)   Notwithstanding subsection (f), if a person purchases any interest in a consumer credit transaction that is subject to the Truth in Lending Act or any interest in a consumer credit contract (as defined in section 433.1 of title 16 of the Code of Federal Regulations (January 1, 2004), as amended from time to time), and if such interest is purchased through a sale under this section, then such person shall remain subject to all claims and defenses that are related to such consumer credit transaction or such consumer credit contract, to the same extent as such person would be subject to such claims and defenses of the consumer had such interest been purchased at a sale not under this section.

(p)   In any hearing under this section—

(1)   the trustee has the burden of proof on the issue of adequate protection; and

(2)   the entity asserting an interest in property has the burden of proof on the issue of the validity, priority, or extent of such interest.

§ 364. Obtaining credit

(a) If the trustee is authorized to operate the business of the debtor under section 721, 1108, 1183, 1184, 1203, 1204, or 1304 of this title, unless the court orders otherwise, the trustee may obtain unsecured credit and incur unsecured debt in the ordinary course of business allowable under section 503(b)(1) of this title as an administrative expense.

(b) The court, after notice and a hearing, may authorize the trustee to obtain unsecured credit or to incur unsecured debt other than under subsection (a) of this section, allowable under section 503(b)(1) of this title as an administrative expense.

(c) If the trustee is unable to obtain unsecured credit allowable under section 503(b)(1) of this title as an administrative expense, the court, after notice and a hearing, may authorize the obtaining of credit or the incurring of debt—

    (1) with priority over any or all administrative expenses of the kind specified in section 503(b) or 507(b) of this title;

    (2) secured by a lien on property of the estate that is not otherwise subject to a lien; or

    (3) secured by a junior lien on property of the estate that is subject to a lien.

(d)(1) The court, after notice and a hearing, may authorize the obtaining of credit or the incurring of debt secured by a senior or equal lien on property of the estate that is subject to a lien only if—

    (A) the trustee is unable to obtain such credit otherwise; and

    (B) there is adequate protection of the interest of the holder of the lien on the property of the estate on which such senior or equal lien is proposed to be granted.

    (2) In any hearing under this subsection, the trustee has the burden of proof on the issue of adequate protection.

(e) The reversal or modification on appeal of an authorization under this section to obtain credit or incur debt, or of a grant under this section of a priority or a lien, does not affect the validity of any debt so incurred, or any priority or lien so granted, to an entity that extended such credit in good faith, whether or not such entity knew of the pendency of the appeal, unless such authorization and the incurring of such debt, or the granting of such priority or lien, were stayed pending appeal.

(f) Except with respect to an entity that is an underwriter as defined in section 1145(b) of this title, section 5 of the Securities Act of 1933, the Trust Indenture Act of 1939, and any State or local law requiring registration for offer or sale of a security or registration or licensing of an issuer of, underwriter of, or broker or dealer in, a security does not apply to the offer or sale under this section of a security that is not an equity security.

[*Note from West Advisory Panel.* Pub. L. 116–260 created a temporary subsection (g) to § 364, which expired on December 27, 2022, except for any case commenced before December 27, 2022. See 134 Stat. 2015, 2016, 2017. For the text of subsection (g), see Title 11, Chapter 3, Subchapter IV, § 364 Editorial Notes, Amendments, 2020 at http://uscode.house.gov]

§ 365. Executory contracts and unexpired leases

(a) Except as provided in sections 765 and 766 of this title and in subsections (b), (c), and (d) of this section, the trustee, subject to the court's approval, may assume or reject any executory contract or unexpired lease of the debtor.

(b)(1) If there has been a default in an executory contract or unexpired lease of the debtor, the trustee may not assume such contract or lease unless, at the time of assumption of such contract or lease, the trustee—

    (A) cures, or provides adequate assurance that the trustee will promptly cure, such default other than a default that is a breach of a provision relating to the satisfaction of any provision (other than a penalty rate or penalty provision) relating to a default arising from any failure to perform nonmonetary obligations under an unexpired lease of real property, if it is impossible for

BANKRUPTCY CODE

the trustee to cure such default by performing nonmonetary acts at and after the time of assumption, except that if such default arises from a failure to operate in accordance with a nonresidential real property lease, then such default shall be cured by performance at and after the time of assumption in accordance with such lease, and pecuniary losses resulting from such default shall be compensated in accordance with the provisions of this paragraph;

(B) compensates, or provides adequate assurance that the trustee will promptly compensate, a party other than the debtor to such contract or lease, for any actual pecuniary loss to such party resulting from such default; and

(C) provides adequate assurance of future performance under such contract or lease.

(2) Paragraph (1) of this subsection does not apply to a default that is a breach of a provision relating to—

(A) the insolvency or financial condition of the debtor at any time before the closing of the case;

(B) the commencement of a case under this title;

(C) the appointment of or taking possession by a trustee in a case under this title or a custodian before such commencement; or

(D) the satisfaction of any penalty rate or penalty provision relating to a default arising from any failure by the debtor to perform nonmonetary obligations under the executory contract or unexpired lease.

(3) For the purposes of paragraph (1) of this subsection and paragraph (2)(B) of subsection (f), adequate assurance of future performance of a lease of real property in a shopping center includes adequate assurance—

(A) of the source of rent and other consideration due under such lease, and in the case of an assignment, that the financial condition and operating performance of the proposed assignee and its guarantors, if any, shall be similar to the financial condition and operating performance of the debtor and its guarantors, if any, as of the time the debtor became the lessee under the lease;

(B) that any percentage rent due under such lease will not decline substantially;

(C) that assumption or assignment of such lease is subject to all the provisions thereof, including (but not limited to) provisions such as a radius, location, use, or exclusivity provision, and will not breach any such provision contained in any other lease, financing agreement, or master agreement relating to such shopping center; and

(D) that assumption or assignment of such lease will not disrupt any tenant mix or balance in such shopping center.

(4) Notwithstanding any other provision of this section, if there has been a default in an unexpired lease of the debtor, other than a default of a kind specified in paragraph (2) of this subsection, the trustee may not require a lessor to provide services or supplies incidental to such lease before assumption of such lease unless the lessor is compensated under the terms of such lease for any services and supplies provided under such lease before assumption of such lease.

(c) The trustee may not assume or assign any executory contract or unexpired lease of the debtor, whether or not such contract or lease prohibits or restricts assignment of rights or delegation of duties, if—

(1)(A) applicable law excuses a party, other than the debtor, to such contract or lease from accepting performance from or rendering performance to an entity other than the debtor or the debtor in possession, whether or not such contract or lease prohibits or restricts assignment of rights or delegation of duties; and

(B) such party does not consent to such assumption or assignment; or

(2) such contract is a contract to make a loan, or extend other debt financing or financial accommodations, to or for the benefit of the debtor, or to issue a security of the debtor; or

(3) such lease is of nonresidential real property and has been terminated under applicable nonbankruptcy law prior to the order for relief.

(d)(1) In a case under chapter 7 of this title, if the trustee does not assume or reject an executory contract or unexpired lease of residential real property or of personal property of the debtor within 60 days after the order for relief, or within such additional time as the court, for cause, within such 60-day period, fixes, then such contract or lease is deemed rejected.

(2) In a case under chapter 9, 11, 12, or 13 of this title, the trustee may assume or reject an executory contract or unexpired lease of residential real property or of personal property of the debtor at any time before the confirmation of a plan but the court, on the request of any party to such contract or lease, may order the trustee to determine within a specified period of time whether to assume or reject such contract or lease.

(3) The trustee shall timely perform all the obligations of the debtor, except those specified in section 365(b)(2), arising from and after the order for relief under any unexpired lease of nonresidential real property, until such lease is assumed or rejected, notwithstanding section 503(b)(1) of this title. The court may extend, for cause, the time for performance of any such obligation that arises within 60 days after the date of the order for relief, but the time for performance shall not be extended beyond such 60-day period. This subsection shall not be deemed to affect the trustee's obligations under the provisions of subsection (b) or (f) of this section. Acceptance of any such performance does not constitute waiver or relinquishment of the lessor's rights under such lease or under this title.

[*Note from West Advisory Panel.* Pub. L 116–260 temporarily amended § 365(d)(3) for cases under subchapter V of chapter 11. That amendment expired on December 27, 2022, *except* for subchapter V cases commenced before December 27, 2022. *See* 134 Stat. 3219. For a description of the temporary amendment, *see* Title 11, Chapter 3, Subchapter IV, § 365 Editorial Notes, Amendments, 2020 at http://uscode.house.gov]

(4)(A) Subject to subparagraph (B), an unexpired lease of nonresidential real property under which the debtor is the lessee shall be deemed rejected, and the trustee shall immediately surrender that nonresidential real property to the lessor, if the trustee does not assume or reject the unexpired lease by the earlier of—

(i) the date that is 120 days after the date of the order for relief; or

(ii) the date of the entry of an order confirming a plan.

(B)(i) The court may extend the period determined under subparagraph (A), prior to the expiration of the 120-day period, for 90 days on the motion of the trustee or lessor for cause.

(ii) If the court grants an extension under clause (i), the court may grant a subsequent extension only upon prior written consent of the lessor in each instance.

[*Note from West Advisory Panel.* For subchapter V cases under chapter 11 commenced before December 27, 2022, the time period in § 365(d)(4)(A)(i), (B)(i) is 210, not 120, days. *See* 134 Stat. 3219.]

(5) The trustee shall timely perform all of the obligations of the debtor, except those specified in section 365(b)(2), first arising from or after 60 days after the order for relief in a case under chapter 11 of this title under an unexpired lease of personal property (other than personal property leased to an individual primarily for personal, family, or household purposes), until such lease is assumed or rejected notwithstanding section 503(b)(1) of this title, unless the court, after notice and a hearing and based on the equities of the case, orders otherwise with respect to the obligations or timely performance thereof. This subsection shall not be deemed to affect the trustee's obligations under the provisions of subsection (b) or (f). Acceptance of any such performance does not constitute waiver or relinquishment of the lessor's rights under such lease or under this title.

(e)(1) Notwithstanding a provision in an executory contract or unexpired lease, or in applicable law, an executory contract or unexpired lease of the debtor may not be terminated or modified, and any right or obligation under such contract or lease may not be terminated or modified, at any time after the commencement of the case solely because of a provision in such contract or lease that is conditioned on—

(A)   the insolvency or financial condition of the debtor at any time before the closing of the case;

(B)   the commencement of a case under this title; or

(C)   the appointment of or taking possession by a trustee in a case under this title or a custodian before such commencement.

(2)   Paragraph (1) of this subsection does not apply to an executory contract or unexpired lease of the debtor, whether or not such contract or lease prohibits or restricts assignment of rights or delegation of duties, if—

(A)(i)   applicable law excuses a party, other than the debtor, to such contract or lease from accepting performance from or rendering performance to the trustee or to an assignee of such contract or lease, whether or not such contract or lease prohibits or restricts assignment of rights or delegation of duties; and

(ii)   such party does not consent to such assumption or assignment; or

(B)   such contract is a contract to make a loan, or extend other debt financing or financial accommodations, to or for the benefit of the debtor, or to issue a security of the debtor.

(f)(1)   Except as provided in subsections (b) and (c) of this section, notwithstanding a provision in an executory contract or unexpired lease of the debtor, or in applicable law, that prohibits, restricts, or conditions the assignment of such contract or lease, the trustee may assign such contract or lease under paragraph (2) of this subsection.

(2)   The trustee may assign an executory contract or unexpired lease of the debtor only if—

(A)   the trustee assumes such contract or lease in accordance with the provisions of this section; and

(B)   adequate assurance of future performance by the assignee of such contract or lease is provided, whether or not there has been a default in such contract or lease.

(3)   Notwithstanding a provision in an executory contract or unexpired lease of the debtor, or in applicable law that terminates or modifies, or permits a party other than the debtor to terminate or modify, such contract or lease or a right or obligation under such contract or lease on account of an assignment of such contract or lease, such contract, lease, right, or obligation may not be terminated or modified under such provision because of the assumption or assignment of such contract or lease by the trustee.

(g)   Except as provided in subsections (h)(2) and (i)(2) of this section, the rejection of an executory contract or unexpired lease of the debtor constitutes a breach of such contract or lease—

(1)   if such contract or lease has not been assumed under this section or under a plan confirmed under chapter 9, 11, 12, or 13 of this title, immediately before the date of the filing of the petition; or

(2)   if such contract or lease has been assumed under this section or under a plan confirmed under chapter 9, 11, 12, or 13 of this title—

(A)   if before such rejection the case has not been converted under section 1112, 1208, or 1307 of this title, at the time of such rejection; or

(B)   if before such rejection the case has been converted under section 1112, 1208, or 1307 of this title—

(i)   immediately before the date of such conversion, if such contract or lease was assumed before such conversion; or

(ii)   at the time of such rejection, if such contract or lease was assumed after such conversion.

(h)(1)(A)   If the trustee rejects an unexpired lease of real property under which the debtor is the lessor and—

(i) if the rejection by the trustee amounts to such a breach as would entitle the lessee to treat such lease as terminated by virtue of its terms, applicable nonbankruptcy law, or any agreement made by the lessee, then the lessee under such lease may treat such lease as terminated by the rejection; or

(ii) if the term of such lease has commenced, the lessee may retain its rights under such lease (including rights such as those relating to the amount and timing of payment of rent and other amounts payable by the lessee and any right of use, possession, quiet enjoyment, subletting, assignment, or hypothecation) that are in or appurtenant to the real property for the balance of the term of such lease and for any renewal or extension of such rights to the extent that such rights are enforceable under applicable nonbankruptcy law.

(B) If the lessee retains its rights under subparagraph (A)(ii), the lessee may offset against the rent reserved under such lease for the balance of the term after the date of the rejection of such lease and for the term of any renewal or extension of such lease, the value of any damage caused by the nonperformance after the date of such rejection, of any obligation of the debtor under such lease, but the lessee shall not have any other right against the estate or the debtor on account of any damage occurring after such date caused by such nonperformance.

(C) The rejection of a lease of real property in a shopping center with respect to which the lessee elects to retain its rights under subparagraph (A)(ii) does not affect the enforceability under applicable nonbankruptcy law of any provision in the lease pertaining to radius, location, use, exclusivity, or tenant mix or balance.

(D) In this paragraph, "lessee" includes any successor, assign, or mortgagee permitted under the terms of such lease.

(2)(A) If the trustee rejects a timeshare interest under a timeshare plan under which the debtor is the timeshare interest seller and—

(i) if the rejection amounts to such a breach as would entitle the timeshare interest purchaser to treat the timeshare plan as terminated under its terms, applicable nonbankruptcy law, or any agreement made by timeshare interest purchaser, the timeshare interest purchaser under the timeshare plan may treat the timeshare plan as terminated by such rejection; or

(ii) if the term of such timeshare interest has commenced, then the timeshare interest purchaser may retain its rights in such timeshare interest for the balance of such term and for any term of renewal or extension of such timeshare interest to the extent that such rights are enforceable under applicable nonbankruptcy law.

(B) If the timeshare interest purchaser retains its rights under subparagraph (A), such timeshare interest purchaser may offset against the moneys due for such timeshare interest for the balance of the term after the date of the rejection of such timeshare interest, and the term of any renewal or extension of such timeshare interest, the value of any damage caused by the nonperformance after the date of such rejection, of any obligation of the debtor under such timeshare plan, but the timeshare interest purchaser shall not have any right against the estate or the debtor on account of any damage occurring after such date caused by such nonperformance.

(i)(1) If the trustee rejects an executory contract of the debtor for the sale of real property or for the sale of a timeshare interest under a timeshare plan, under which the purchaser is in possession, such purchaser may treat such contract as terminated, or, in the alternative, may remain in possession of such real property or timeshare interest.

(2) If such purchaser remains in possession—

(A) such purchaser shall continue to make all payments due under such contract, but may,* offset against such payments any damages occurring after the date of the rejection of such contract caused by the nonperformance of any obligation of the debtor after such date, but such

---

* So in original. The comma probably should not appear.

purchaser does not have any rights against the estate on account of any damages arising after such date from such rejection, other than such offset; and

  (B) the trustee shall deliver title to such purchaser in accordance with the provisions of such contract, but is relieved of all other obligations to perform under such contract.

  (j) A purchaser that treats an executory contract as terminated under subsection (i) of this section, or a party whose executory contract to purchase real property from the debtor is rejected and under which such party is not in possession, has a lien on the interest of the debtor in such property for the recovery of any portion of the purchase price that such purchaser or party has paid.

  (k) Assignment by the trustee to an entity of a contract or lease assumed under this section relieves the trustee and the estate from any liability for any breach of such contract or lease occurring after such assignment.

  (l) If an unexpired lease under which the debtor is the lessee is assigned pursuant to this section, the lessor of the property may require a deposit or other security for the performance of the debtor's obligations under the lease substantially the same as would have been required by the landlord upon the initial leasing to a similar tenant.

  (m) For purposes of this section 365 and sections 541(b)(2) and 362(b)(10), leases of real property shall include any rental agreement to use real property.

  (n)(1) If the trustee rejects an executory contract under which the debtor is a licensor of a right to intellectual property, the licensee under such contract may elect—

  (A) to treat such contract as terminated by such rejection if such rejection by the trustee amounts to such a breach as would entitle the licensee to treat such contract as terminated by virtue of its own terms, applicable nonbankruptcy law, or an agreement made by the licensee with another entity; or

  (B) to retain its rights (including a right to enforce any exclusivity provision of such contract, but excluding any other right under applicable nonbankruptcy law to specific performance of such contract) under such contract and under any agreement supplementary to such contract, to such intellectual property (including any embodiment of such intellectual property to the extent protected by applicable nonbankruptcy law), as such rights existed immediately before the case commenced, for—

  (i) the duration of such contract; and

  (ii) any period for which such contract may be extended by the licensee as of right under applicable nonbankruptcy law.

  (2) If the licensee elects to retain its rights, as described in paragraph (1)(B) of this subsection, under such contract—

  (A) the trustee shall allow the licensee to exercise such rights;

  (B) the licensee shall make all royalty payments due under such contract for the duration of such contract and for any period described in paragraph (1)(B) of this subsection for which the licensee extends such contract; and

  (C) the licensee shall be deemed to waive—

  (i) any right of setoff it may have with respect to such contract under this title or applicable nonbankruptcy law; and

  (ii) any claim allowable under section 503(b) of this title arising from the performance of such contract.

  (3) If the licensee elects to retain its rights, as described in paragraph (1)(B) of this subsection, then on the written request of the licensee the trustee shall—

(A) to the extent provided in such contract, or any agreement supplementary to such contract, provide to the licensee any intellectual property (including such embodiment) held by the trustee; and

(B) not interfere with the rights of the licensee as provided in such contract, or any agreement supplementary to such contract, to such intellectual property (including such embodiment) including any right to obtain such intellectual property (or such embodiment) from another entity.

(4) Unless and until the trustee rejects such contract, on the written request of the licensee the trustee shall—

(A) to the extent provided in such contract or any agreement supplementary to such contract—

(i) perform such contract; or

(ii) provide to the licensee such intellectual property (including any embodiment of such intellectual property to the extent protected by applicable nonbankruptcy law) held by the trustee; and

(B) not interfere with the rights of the licensee as provided in such contract, or any agreement supplementary to such contract, to such intellectual property (including such embodiment), including any right to obtain such intellectual property (or such embodiment) from another entity.

(o) In a case under chapter 11 of this title, the trustee shall be deemed to have assumed (consistent with the debtor's other obligations under section 507), and shall immediately cure any deficit under, any commitment by the debtor to a Federal depository institutions regulatory agency (or predecessor to such agency) to maintain the capital of an insured depository institution, and any claim for a subsequent breach of the obligations thereunder shall be entitled to priority under section 507. This subsection shall not extend any commitment that would otherwise be terminated by any act of such an agency.

(p)(1) If a lease of personal property is rejected or not timely assumed by the trustee under subsection (d), the leased property is no longer property of the estate and the stay under section 362(a) is automatically terminated.

(2)(A) If the debtor in a case under chapter 7 is an individual, the debtor may notify the creditor in writing that the debtor desires to assume the lease. Upon being so notified, the creditor may, at its option, notify the debtor that it is willing to have the lease assumed by the debtor and may condition such assumption on cure of any outstanding default on terms set by the contract.

(B) If, not later than 30 days after notice is provided under subparagraph (A), the debtor notifies the lessor in writing that the lease is assumed, the liability under the lease will be assumed by the debtor and not by the estate.

(C) The stay under section 362 and the injunction under section 524(a)(2) shall not be violated by notification of the debtor and negotiation of cure under this subsection.

(3) In a case under chapter 11 in which the debtor is an individual and in a case under chapter 13, if the debtor is the lessee with respect to personal property and the lease is not assumed in the plan confirmed by the court, the lease is deemed rejected as of the conclusion of the hearing on confirmation. If the lease is rejected, the stay under section 362 and any stay under section 1301 is automatically terminated with respect to the property subject to the lease.

§ 366. Utility service

(a) Except as provided in subsections (b) and (c) of this section, a utility may not alter, refuse, or discontinue service to, or discriminate against, the trustee or the debtor solely on the basis of the commencement of a case under this title or that a debt owed by the debtor to such utility for service rendered before the order for relief was not paid when due.

(b) Such utility may alter, refuse, or discontinue service if neither the trustee nor the debtor, within 20 days after the date of the order for relief, furnishes adequate assurance of payment, in the form of a deposit or other security, for service after such date. On request of a party in interest and after notice and a hearing, the court may order reasonable modification of the amount of the deposit or other security necessary to provide adequate assurance of payment.

(c)(1)(A) For purposes of this subsection, the term "assurance of payment" means—

    (i) a cash deposit;

    (ii) a letter of credit;

    (iii) a certificate of deposit;

    (iv) a surety bond;

    (v) a prepayment of utility consumption; or

    (vi) another form of security that is mutually agreed on between the utility and the debtor or the trustee.

    (B) For purposes of this subsection an administrative expense priority shall not constitute an assurance of payment.

(2) Subject to paragraphs (3) and (4), with respect to a case filed under chapter 11, a utility referred to in subsection (a) may alter, refuse, or discontinue utility service, if during the 30-day period beginning on the date of the filing of the petition, the utility does not receive from the debtor or the trustee adequate assurance of payment for utility service that is satisfactory to the utility.

(3)(A) On request of a party in interest and after notice and a hearing, the court may order modification of the amount of an assurance of payment under paragraph (2).

    (B) In making a determination under this paragraph whether an assurance of payment is adequate, the court may not consider—

    (i) the absence of security before the date of the filing of the petition;

    (ii) the payment by the debtor of charges for utility service in a timely manner before the date of the filing of the petition; or

    (iii) the availability of an administrative expense priority.

(4) Notwithstanding any other provision of law, with respect to a case subject to this subsection, a utility may recover or set off against a security deposit provided to the utility by the debtor before the date of the filing of the petition without notice or order of the court.

CHAPTER 5—CREDITORS, THE DEBTOR, AND THE ESTATE

SUBCHAPTER I—CREDITORS AND CLAIMS

501.   Filing of proofs of claims or interests.
502.   Allowance of claims or interests.
503.   Allowance of administrative expenses.
504.   Sharing of compensation.
505.   Determination of tax liability.
506.   Determination of secured status.
507.   Priorities.
508.   Effect of distribution other than under this title.
509.   Claims of codebtors.
510.   Subordination.
511.   Rate of interest on tax claims.

SUBCHAPTER II—DEBTOR'S DUTIES AND BENEFITS

521. Debtor's duties.
522. Exemptions.
523. Exceptions to discharge.
524. Effect of discharge.
525. Protection against discriminatory treatment.
526. Restrictions on debt relief agencies.
527. Disclosures.
528. Requirements for debt relief agencies.

SUBCHAPTER III—THE ESTATE

541. Property of the estate.
542. Turnover of property to the estate.
543. Turnover of property by a custodian.
544. Trustee as lien creditor and as successor to certain creditors and purchasers.
545. Statutory liens.
546. Limitations on avoiding powers.
547. Preferences.
548. Fraudulent transfers and obligations.
549. Postpetition transactions.
550. Liability of transferee of avoided transfer.
551. Automatic preservation of avoided transfer.
552. Postpetition effect of security interest.
553. Setoff.
554. Abandonment of property of the estate.
555. Contractual right to liquidate, terminate, or accelerate a securities contract.
556. Contractual right to liquidate, terminate, or accelerate a commodities contract or forward contract.
557. Expedited determination of interests in, and abandonment or other disposition of grain assets.
558. Defenses of the estate.
559. Contractual right to liquidate, terminate, or accelerate a repurchase agreement.
560. Contractual right to liquidate, terminate, or accelerate a swap agreement.
561. Contractual right to terminate, liquidate, accelerate, or offset under a master netting agreement and across contracts; proceedings under chapter 15.
562. Timing of damage measurement in connection with swap agreements, securities contracts, forward contracts, commodity contracts, repurchase agreements, and master netting agreements.

SUBCHAPTER I—CREDITORS AND CLAIMS

§ 501. Filing of proofs of claims or interests

(a) A creditor or an indenture trustee may file a proof of claim. An equity security holder may file a proof of interest.

(b) If a creditor does not timely file a proof of such creditor's claim, an entity that is liable to such creditor with the debtor, or that has secured such creditor, may file a proof of such claim.

(c) If a creditor does not timely file a proof of such creditor's claim, the debtor or the trustee may file a proof of such claim.

(d) A claim of a kind specified in section 502(e)(2), 502(f), 502(g), 502(h) or 502(i) of this title may be filed under subsection (a), (b), or (c) of this section the same as if such claim were a claim against the debtor and had arisen before the date of the filing of the petition.

(e) A claim arising from the liability of a debtor for fuel use tax assessed consistent with the requirements of section 31705 of title 49 may be filed by the base jurisdiction designated pursuant to the International Fuel Tax Agreement (as defined in section 31701 of title 49) and, if so filed, shall be allowed as a single claim.

§ 502. Allowance of claims or interests

(a) A claim or interest, proof of which is filed under section 501 of this title, is deemed allowed, unless a party in interest, including a creditor of a general partner in a partnership that is a debtor in a case under chapter 7 of this title, objects.

(b) Except as provided in subsections (e)(2), (f), (g), (h) and (i) of this section, if such objection to a claim is made, the court, after notice and a hearing, shall determine the amount of such claim in lawful currency of the United States as of the date of the filing of the petition, and shall allow such claim in such amount, except to the extent that—

(1) such claim is unenforceable against the debtor and property of the debtor, under any agreement or applicable law for a reason other than because such claim is contingent or unmatured;

(2) such claim is for unmatured interest;

(3) if such claim is for a tax assessed against property of the estate, such claim exceeds the value of the interest of the estate in such property;

(4) if such claim is for services of an insider or attorney of the debtor, such claim exceeds the reasonable value of such services;

(5) such claim is for a debt that is unmatured on the date of the filing of the petition and that is excepted from discharge under section 523(a)(5) of this title;

(6) if such claim is the claim of a lessor for damages resulting from the termination of a lease of real property, such claim exceeds—

(A) the rent reserved by such lease, without acceleration, for the greater of one year, or 15 percent, not to exceed three years, of the remaining term of such lease, following the earlier of—

(i) the date of the filing of the petition; and

(ii) the date on which such lessor repossessed, or the lessee surrendered, the leased property; plus

(B) any unpaid rent due under such lease, without acceleration, on the earlier of such dates;

(7) if such claim is the claim of an employee for damages resulting from the termination of an employment contract, such claim exceeds—

(A) the compensation provided by such contract, without acceleration, for one year following the earlier of—

(i) the date of the filing of the petition; or

(ii) the date on which the employer directed the employee to terminate, or such employee terminated, performance under such contract; plus

(B) any unpaid compensation due under such contract, without acceleration, on the earlier of such dates;

(8) such claim results from a reduction, due to late payment, in the amount of an otherwise applicable credit available to the debtor in connection with an employment tax on wages, salaries, or commissions earned from the debtor; or

(9) proof of such claim is not timely filed, except to the extent tardily filed as permitted under paragraph (1), (2), or (3) of section 726(a) or under the Federal Rules of Bankruptcy Procedure, except that—

(A) a claim of a governmental unit shall be timely filed if it is filed before 180 days after the date of the order for relief or such later time as the Federal Rules of Bankruptcy Procedure may provide; and

(B) in a case under chapter 13, a claim of a governmental unit for a tax with respect to a return filed under section 1308 shall be timely if the claim is filed on or before the date that is 60 days after the date on which such return was filed as required.

(c) There shall be estimated for purpose of allowance under this section—

(1) any contingent or unliquidated claim, the fixing or liquidation of which, as the case may be, would unduly delay the administration of the case; or

(2) any right to payment arising from a right to an equitable remedy for breach of performance.

(d) Notwithstanding subsections (a) and (b) of this section, the court shall disallow any claim of any entity from which property is recoverable under section 542, 543, 550, or 553 of this title or that is a transferee of a transfer avoidable under section 522(f), 522(h), 544, 545, 547, 548, 549, or 724(a) of this title, unless such entity or transferee has paid the amount, or turned over any such property, for which such entity or transferee is liable under section 522(i), 542, 543, 550, or 553 of this title.

(e)(1) Notwithstanding subsections (a), (b), and (c) of this section and paragraph (2) of this subsection, the court shall disallow any claim for reimbursement or contribution of an entity that is liable with the debtor on or has secured the claim of a creditor, to the extent that—

(A) such creditor's claim against the estate is disallowed;

(B) such claim for reimbursement or contribution is contingent as of the time of allowance or disallowance of such claim for reimbursement or contribution; or

(C) such entity asserts a right of subrogation to the rights of such creditor under section 509 of this title.

(2) A claim for reimbursement or contribution of such an entity that becomes fixed after the commencement of the case shall be determined, and shall be allowed under subsection (a), (b), or (c) of this section, or disallowed under subsection (d) of this section, the same as if such claim had become fixed before the date of the filing of the petition.

(f) In an involuntary case, a claim arising in the ordinary course of the debtor's business or financial affairs after the commencement of the case but before the earlier of the appointment of a trustee and the order for relief shall be determined as of the date such claim arises, and shall be allowed under subsection (a), (b), or (c) of this section or disallowed under subsection (d) or (e) of this section, the same as if such claim had arisen before the date of the filing of the petition.

(g)(1) A claim arising from the rejection, under section 365 of this title or under a plan under chapter 9, 11, 12, or 13 of this title, of an executory contract or unexpired lease of the debtor that has not been assumed shall be determined, and shall be allowed under subsection (a), (b), or (c) of this section or disallowed under subsection (d) or (e) of this section, the same as if such claim had arisen before the date of the filing of the petition.

(2) A claim for damages calculated in accordance with section 562 shall be allowed under subsection (a), (b), or (c), or disallowed under subsection (d) or (e), as if such claim had arisen before the date of the filing of the petition.

(h) A claim arising from the recovery of property under section 522, 550, or 553 of this title shall be determined, and shall be allowed under subsection (a), (b), or (c) of this section, or disallowed under subsection (d) or (e) of this section, the same as if such claim had arisen before the date of the filing of the petition.

(i) A claim that does not arise until after the commencement of the case for a tax entitled to priority under section 507(a)(8) of this title shall be determined, and shall be allowed under subsection (a), (b), or (c) of this section, or disallowed under subsection (d) or (e) of this section, the same as if such claim had arisen before the date of the filing of the petition.

(j) A claim that has been allowed or disallowed may be reconsidered for cause. A reconsidered claim may be allowed or disallowed according to the equities of the case. Reconsideration of a claim under this subsection does not affect the validity of any payment or transfer from the estate made to a holder of an allowed claim on account of such allowed claim that is not reconsidered, but if a reconsidered claim is allowed and is of the same class as such holder's claim, such holder may not receive any additional payment or transfer from the estate on account of such holder's allowed claim until the holder of such reconsidered and allowed claim receives payment on account of such claim proportionate in value to that already received by such other holder. This subsection does not alter or modify the trustee's right to recover from a creditor any excess payment or transfer made to such creditor.

(k)(1) The court, on the motion of the debtor and after a hearing, may reduce a claim filed under this section based in whole on an unsecured consumer debt by not more than 20 percent of the claim, if—

(A) the claim was filed by a creditor who unreasonably refused to negotiate a reasonable alternative repayment schedule proposed on behalf of the debtor by an approved nonprofit budget and credit counseling agency described in section 111;

(B) the offer of the debtor under subparagraph (A)—

(i) was made at least 60 days before the date of the filing of the petition; and

(ii) provided for payment of at least 60 percent of the amount of the debt over a period not to exceed the repayment period of the loan, or a reasonable extension thereof; and

(C) no part of the debt under the alternative repayment schedule is nondischargeable.

(2) The debtor shall have the burden of proving, by clear and convincing evidence, that—

(A) the creditor unreasonably refused to consider the debtor's proposal; and

(B) the proposed alternative repayment schedule was made prior to expiration of the 60-day period specified in paragraph (1)(B)(i).

§ 503. Allowance of administrative expenses

(a) An entity may timely file a request for payment of an administrative expense, or may tardily file such request if permitted by the court for cause.

(b) After notice and a hearing, there shall be allowed administrative expenses, other than claims allowed under section 502(f) of this title, including—

(1)(A) the actual, necessary costs and expenses of preserving the estate including—

(i) wages, salaries, and commissions for services rendered after the commencement of the case; and

(ii) wages and benefits awarded pursuant to a judicial proceeding or a proceeding of the National Labor Relations Board as back pay attributable to any period of time occurring after commencement of the case under this title, as a result of a violation of Federal or State law by the debtor, without regard to the time of the occurrence of unlawful conduct on which such award is based or to whether any services were rendered, if the court determines that payment of wages and benefits by reason of the operation of this clause will not substantially increase the probability of layoff or termination of current employees, or of nonpayment of domestic support obligations, during the case under this title;

(B) any tax—

(i) incurred by the estate, whether secured or unsecured, including property taxes for which liability is in rem, in personam, or both, except a tax of a kind specified in section 507(a)(8) of this title; or

(ii) attributable to an excessive allowance of a tentative carryback adjustment that the estate received, whether the taxable year to which such adjustment relates ended before or after the commencement of the case;

(C) any fine, penalty, or reduction in credit relating to a tax of a kind specified in subparagraph (B) of this paragraph; and

(D) notwithstanding the requirements of subsection (a), a governmental unit shall not be required to file a request for the payment of an expense described in subparagraph (B) or (C), as a condition of its being an allowed administrative expense;

(2) compensation and reimbursement awarded under section 330(a) of this title;

(3) the actual, necessary expenses, other than compensation and reimbursement specified in paragraph (4) of this subsection, incurred by—

(A) a creditor that files a petition under section 303 of this title;

(B) a creditor that recovers, after the court's approval, for the benefit of the estate any property transferred or concealed by the debtor;

(C) a creditor in connection with the prosecution of a criminal offense relating to the case or to the business or property of the debtor;

(D) a creditor, an indenture trustee, an equity security holder, or a committee representing creditors or equity security holders other than a committee appointed under section 1102 of this title, in making a substantial contribution in a case under chapter 9 or 11 of this title;

(E) a custodian superseded under section 543 of this title, and compensation for the services of such custodian; or

(F) a member of a committee appointed under section 1102 of this title, if such expenses are incurred in the performance of the duties of such committee;

(4) reasonable compensation for professional services rendered by an attorney or an accountant of an entity whose expense is allowable under subparagraph (A), (B), (C), (D), or (E) of paragraph (3) of this subsection, based on the time, the nature, the extent, and the value of such services, and the cost of comparable services other than in a case under this title, and reimbursement for actual, necessary expenses incurred by such attorney or accountant;

(5) reasonable compensation for services rendered by an indenture trustee in making a substantial contribution in a case under chapter 9 or 11 of this title, based on the time, the nature, the extent, and the value of such services, and the cost of comparable services other than in a case under this title;

(6) the fees and mileage payable under chapter 119 of title 28;

(7) with respect to a nonresidential real property lease previously assumed under section 365, and subsequently rejected, a sum equal to all monetary obligations due, excluding those arising from or relating to a failure to operate or a penalty provision, for the period of 2 years following the later of the rejection date or the date of actual turnover of the premises, without reduction or setoff for any reason whatsoever except for sums actually received or to be received from an entity other than the debtor, and the claim for remaining sums due for the balance of the term of the lease shall be a claim under section 502(b)(6);

(8) the actual, necessary costs and expenses of closing a health care business incurred by a trustee or by a Federal agency (as defined in section 551(1) of title 5) or a department or agency of a State or political subdivision thereof, including any cost or expense incurred—

(A) in disposing of patient records in accordance with section 351; or

(B) in connection with transferring patients from the health care business that is in the process of being closed to another health care business; and

(9) the value of any goods received by the debtor within 20 days before the date of commencement of a case under this title in which the goods have been sold to the debtor in the ordinary course of such debtor's business.

[*Note from West Advisory Panel*. Pub. L. 116–260 created a temporary § 503(b)(10), which expired on December 27, 2022, *except* for cases commenced before December 27, 2022. *See* 134 Stat. 2015, 2016, 2017. For the text of temporary § 503(b)(10), *see* Title 11, Chapter 5, Subchapter I, § 503, Editorial Notes, Amendments, 2020 at http://uscode.house.gov]

(c) Notwithstanding subsection (b), there shall neither be allowed, nor paid—

    (1) a transfer made to, or an obligation incurred for the benefit of, an insider of the debtor for the purpose of inducing such person to remain with the debtor's business, absent a finding by the court based on evidence in the record that—

        (A) the transfer or obligation is essential to retention of the person because the individual has a bona fide job offer from another business at the same or greater rate of compensation;

        (B) the services provided by the person are essential to the survival of the business; and

        (C) either—

            (i) the amount of the transfer made to, or obligation incurred for the benefit of, the person is not greater than an amount equal to 10 times the amount of the mean transfer or obligation of a similar kind given to nonmanagement employees for any purpose during the calendar year in which the transfer is made or the obligation is incurred; or

            (ii) if no such similar transfers were made to, or obligations were incurred for the benefit of, such nonmanagement employees during such calendar year, the amount of the transfer or obligation is not greater than an amount equal to 25 percent of the amount of any similar transfer or obligation made to or incurred for the benefit of such insider for any purpose during the calendar year before the year in which such transfer is made or obligation is incurred;

    (2) a severance payment to an insider of the debtor, unless—

        (A) the payment is part of a program that is generally applicable to all full-time employees; and

        (B) the amount of the payment is not greater than 10 times the amount of the mean severance pay given to nonmanagement employees during the calendar year in which the payment is made; or

    (3) other transfers or obligations that are outside the ordinary course of business and not justified by the facts and circumstances of the case, including transfers made to, or obligations incurred for the benefit of, officers, managers, or consultants hired after the date of the filing of the petition.

§ 504. Sharing of compensation

    (a) Except as provided in subsection (b) of this section, a person receiving compensation or reimbursement under section 503(b)(2) or 503(b)(4) of this title may not share or agree to share—

    (1) any such compensation or reimbursement with another person; or

    (2) any compensation or reimbursement received by another person under such sections.

    (b)(1) A member, partner, or regular associate in a professional association, corporation, or partnership may share compensation or reimbursement received under section 503(b)(2) or 503(b)(4) of this title with another member, partner, or regular associate in such association, corporation, or partnership, and may share in any compensation or reimbursement received under such sections by another member, partner, or regular associate in such association, corporation, or partnership.

    (2) An attorney for a creditor that files a petition under section 303 of this title may share compensation and reimbursement received under section 503(b)(4) of this title with any other attorney contributing to the services rendered or expenses incurred by such creditor's attorney.

    (c) This section shall not apply with respect to sharing, or agreeing to share, compensation with a bona fide public service attorney referral program that operates in accordance with non-Federal law regulating attorney referral services and with rules of professional responsibility applicable to attorney acceptance of referrals.

§ 505. Determination of tax liability

(a)(1)   Except as provided in paragraph (2) of this subsection, the court may determine the amount or legality of any tax, any fine or penalty relating to a tax, or any addition to tax, whether or not previously assessed, whether or not paid, and whether or not contested before and adjudicated by a judicial or administrative tribunal of competent jurisdiction.

(2)   The court may not so determine—

(A)   the amount or legality of a tax, fine, penalty, or addition to tax if such amount or legality was contested before and adjudicated by a judicial or administrative tribunal of competent jurisdiction before the commencement of the case under this title;

(B)   any right of the estate to a tax refund, before the earlier of—

(i)   120 days after the trustee properly requests such refund from the governmental unit from which such refund is claimed; or

(ii)   a determination by such governmental unit of such request; or

(C)   the amount or legality of any amount arising in connection with an ad valorem tax on real or personal property of the estate, if the applicable period for contesting or redetermining that amount under applicable nonbankruptcy law has expired.

(b)(1)(A) The clerk shall maintain a list under which a Federal, State, or local governmental unit responsible for the collection of taxes within the district may—

(i)   designate an address for service of requests under this subsection; and

(ii)   describe where further information concerning additional requirements for filing such requests may be found.

(B)   If such governmental unit does not designate an address and provide such address to the clerk under subparagraph (A), any request made under this subsection may be served at the address for the filing of a tax return or protest with the appropriate taxing authority of such governmental unit.

(2)   A trustee may request a determination of any unpaid liability of the estate for any tax incurred during the administration of the case by submitting a tax return for such tax and a request for such a determination to the governmental unit charged with responsibility for collection or determination of such tax at the address and in the manner designated in paragraph (1). Unless such return is fraudulent, or contains a material misrepresentation, the estate, the trustee, the debtor, and any successor to the debtor are discharged from any liability for such tax—

(A)   upon payment of the tax shown on such return, if—

(i)   such governmental unit does not notify the trustee, within 60 days after such request, that such return has been selected for examination; or

(ii)   such governmental unit does not complete such an examination and notify the trustee of any tax due, within 180 days after such request or within such additional time as the court, for cause, permits;

(B)   upon payment of the tax determined by the court, after notice and a hearing, after completion by such governmental unit of such examination; or

(C)   upon payment of the tax determined by such governmental unit to be due.

(c)   Notwithstanding section 362 of this title, after determination by the court of a tax under this section, the governmental unit charged with responsibility for collection of such tax may assess such tax against the estate, the debtor, or a successor to the debtor, as the case may be, subject to any otherwise applicable law.

§ 506. Determination of secured status

(a)(1)   An allowed claim of a creditor secured by a lien on property in which the estate has an interest, or that is subject to setoff under section 553 of this title, is a secured claim to the extent of the value of such creditor's interest in the estate's interest in such property, or to the extent of the amount subject to setoff, as the case may be, and is an unsecured claim to the extent that the value of such creditor's interest or the amount so subject to setoff is less than the amount of such allowed claim. Such value shall be determined in light of the purpose of the valuation and of the proposed disposition or use of such property, and in conjunction with any hearing on such disposition or use or on a plan affecting such creditor's interest.

(2)   If the debtor is an individual in a case under chapter 7 or 13, such value with respect to personal property securing an allowed claim shall be determined based on the replacement value of such property as of the date of the filing of the petition without deduction for costs of sale or marketing. With respect to property acquired for personal, family, or household purposes, replacement value shall mean the price a retail merchant would charge for property of that kind considering the age and condition of the property at the time value is determined.

(b)   To the extent that an allowed secured claim is secured by property the value of which, after any recovery under subsection (c) of this section, is greater than the amount of such claim, there shall be allowed to the holder of such claim, interest on such claim, and any reasonable fees, costs, or charges provided for under the agreement or State statute under which such claim arose.

(c)   The trustee may recover from property securing an allowed secured claim the reasonable, necessary costs and expenses of preserving, or disposing of, such property to the extent of any benefit to the holder of such claim, including the payment of all ad valorem property taxes with respect to the property.

(d)   To the extent that a lien secures a claim against the debtor that is not an allowed secured claim, such lien is void, unless—

(1)   such claim was disallowed only under section 502(b)(5) or 502(e) of this title; or

(2)   such claim is not an allowed secured claim due only to the failure of any entity to file a proof of such claim under section 501 of this title.

§ 507. Priorities

(a)   The following expenses and claims have priority in the following order:

(1)   First:

(A)   Allowed unsecured claims for domestic support obligations that, as of the date of the filing of the petition in a case under this title, are owed to or recoverable by a spouse, former spouse, or child of the debtor, or such child's parent, legal guardian, or responsible relative, without regard to whether the claim is filed by such person or is filed by a governmental unit on behalf of such person, on the condition that funds received under this paragraph by a governmental unit under this title after the date of the filing of the petition shall be applied and distributed in accordance with applicable nonbankruptcy law.

(B)   Subject to claims under subparagraph (A), allowed unsecured claims for domestic support obligations that, as of the date of the filing of the petition, are assigned by a spouse, former spouse, child of the debtor, or such child's parent, legal guardian, or responsible relative to a governmental unit (unless such obligation is assigned voluntarily by the spouse, former spouse, child, parent, legal guardian, or responsible relative of the child for the purpose of collecting the debt) or are owed directly to or recoverable by a governmental unit under applicable nonbankruptcy law, on the condition that funds received under this paragraph by a governmental unit under this title after the date of the filing of the petition be applied and distributed in accordance with applicable nonbankruptcy law.

(C)   If a trustee is appointed or elected under section 701, 702, 703, 1104, 1202, or 1302, the administrative expenses of the trustee allowed under paragraphs (1)(A), (2), and (6) of section 503(b) shall be paid before payment of claims under subparagraphs (A) and (B), to the extent that the trustee administers assets that are otherwise available for the payment of such claims.

(2) Second, administrative expenses allowed under section 503(b) of this title, unsecured claims of any Federal reserve bank related to loans made through programs or facilities authorized under section 13(3) of the Federal Reserve Act (12 U.S.C. 343), and any fees and charges assessed against the estate under chapter 123 of title 28.

(3) Third, unsecured claims allowed under section 502(f) of this title.

(4) Fourth, allowed unsecured claims, but only to the extent of $15,150 for each individual or corporation, as the case may be, earned within 180 days before the date of the filing of the petition or the date of the cessation of the debtor's business, whichever occurs first, for—

    (A) wages, salaries, or commissions, including vacation, severance, and sick leave pay earned by an individual; or

    (B) sales commissions earned by an individual or by a corporation with only 1 employee, acting as an independent contractor in the sale of goods or services for the debtor in the ordinary course of the debtor's business if, and only if, during the 12 months preceding that date, at least 75 percent of the amount that the individual or corporation earned by acting as an independent contractor in the sale of goods or services was earned from the debtor.

(5) Fifth, allowed unsecured claims for contributions to an employee benefit plan—

    (A) arising from services rendered within 180 days before the date of the filing of the petition or the date of the cessation of the debtor's business, whichever occurs first; but only

    (B) for each such plan, to the extent of—

        (i) the number of employees covered by each such plan multiplied by $15,150; less

        (ii) the aggregate amount paid to such employees under paragraph (4) of this subsection, plus the aggregate amount paid by the estate on behalf of such employees to any other employee benefit plan.

(6) Sixth, allowed unsecured claims of persons—

    (A) engaged in the production or raising of grain, as defined in section 557(b) of this title, against a debtor who owns or operates a grain storage facility, as defined in section 557(b) of this title, for grain or the proceeds of grain, or

    (B) engaged as a United States fisherman against a debtor who has acquired fish or fish produce from a fisherman through a sale or conversion, and who is engaged in operating a fish produce storage or processing facility—

but only to the extent of $7,475 for each such individual.

(7) Seventh, allowed unsecured claims of individuals, to the extent of $3,350 for each such individual, arising from the deposit, before the commencement of the case, of money in connection with the purchase, lease, or rental of property, or the purchase of services, for the personal, family, or household use of such individuals, that were not delivered or provided.

(8) Eighth, allowed unsecured claims of governmental units, only to the extent that such claims are for—

    (A) a tax on or measured by income or gross receipts for a taxable year ending on or before the date of the filing of the petition—

        (i) for which a return, if required, is last due, including extensions, after three years before the date of the filing of the petition;

        (ii) assessed within 240 days before the date of the filing of the petition, exclusive of—

            (I) any time during which an offer in compromise with respect to that tax was pending or in effect during that 240-day period, plus 30 days; and

            (II) any time during which a stay of proceedings against collections was in effect in a prior case under this title during that 240-day period, plus 90 days; or

(iii) other than a tax of a kind specified in section 523(a)(1)(B) or 523(a)(1)(C) of this title, not assessed before, but assessable, under applicable law or by agreement, after, the commencement of the case;

(B) a property tax incurred before the commencement of the case and last payable without penalty after one year before the date of the filing of the petition;

(C) a tax required to be collected or withheld and for which the debtor is liable in whatever capacity;

(D) an employment tax on a wage, salary, or commission of a kind specified in paragraph (4) of this subsection earned from the debtor before the date of the filing of the petition, whether or not actually paid before such date, for which a return is last due, under applicable law or under any extension, after three years before the date of the filing of the petition;

(E) an excise tax on—

(i) a transaction occurring before the date of the filing of the petition for which a return, if required, is last due, under applicable law or under any extension, after three years before the date of the filing of the petition; or

(ii) if a return is not required, a transaction occurring during the three years immediately preceding the date of the filing of the petition;

(F) a customs duty arising out of the importation of merchandise—

(i) entered for consumption within one year before the date of the filing of the petition;

(ii) covered by an entry liquidated or reliquidated within one year before the date of the filing of the petition; or

(iii) entered for consumption within four years before the date of the filing of the petition but unliquidated on such date, if the Secretary of the Treasury certifies that failure to liquidate such entry was due to an investigation pending on such date into assessment of antidumping or countervailing duties or fraud, or if information needed for the proper appraisement or classification of such merchandise was not available to the appropriate customs officer before such date; or

(G) a penalty related to a claim of a kind specified in this paragraph and in compensation for actual pecuniary loss.

An otherwise applicable time period specified in this paragraph shall be suspended for any period during which a governmental unit is prohibited under applicable nonbankruptcy law from collecting a tax as a result of a request by the debtor for a hearing and an appeal of any collection action taken or proposed against the debtor, plus 90 days; plus any time during which the stay of proceedings was in effect in a prior case under this title or during which collection was precluded by the existence of 1 or more confirmed plans under this title, plus 90 days.

(9) Ninth, allowed unsecured claims based upon any commitment by the debtor to a Federal depository institutions regulatory agency (or predecessor to such agency) to maintain the capital of an insured depository institution.

(10) Tenth, allowed claims for death or personal injury resulting from the operation of a motor vehicle or vessel if such operation was unlawful because the debtor was intoxicated from using alcohol, a drug, or another substance.

(b) If the trustee, under section 362, 363, or 364 of this title, provides adequate protection of the interest of a holder of a claim secured by a lien on property of the debtor and if, notwithstanding such protection, such creditor has a claim allowable under subsection (a)(2) of this section arising from the stay of action against such property under section 362 of this title, from the use, sale, or lease of such property under section 363 of this title, or from the granting of a lien under section 364(d) of this title, then such creditor's claim under such subsection shall have priority over every other claim allowable under such subsection.

(c)   For the purpose of subsection (a) of this section, a claim of a governmental unit arising from an erroneous refund or credit of a tax has the same priority as a claim for the tax to which such refund or credit relates.

(d)   An entity that is subrogated to the rights of a holder of a claim of a kind specified in subsection (a)(1), (a)(4), (a)(5), (a)(6), (a)(7), (a)(8), or (a)(9) is not subrogated to the right of the holder of such claim to priority under such subsection.

§ 508.   Effect of distribution other than under this title

If a creditor of a partnership debtor receives, from a general partner that is not a debtor in a case under chapter 7 of this title, payment of, or a transfer of property on account of, a claim that is allowed under this title and that is not secured by a lien on property of such partner, such creditor may not receive any payment under this title on account of such claim until each of the other holders of claims on account of which such holders are entitled to share equally with such creditor under this title has received payment under this title equal in value to the consideration received by such creditor from such general partner.

§ 509.   Claims of codebtors

(a)   Except as provided in subsection (b) or (c) of this section, an entity that is liable with the debtor on, or that has secured, a claim of a creditor against the debtor, and that pays such claim, is subrogated to the rights of such creditor to the extent of such payment.

(b)   Such entity is not subrogated to the rights of such creditor to the extent that—

(1)   a claim of such entity for reimbursement or contribution on account of such payment of such creditor's claim is—

(A)   allowed under section 502 of this title;

(B)   disallowed other than under section 502(e) of this title; or

(C)   subordinated under section 510 of this title; or

(2)   as between the debtor and such entity, such entity received the consideration for the claim held by such creditor.

(c)   The court shall subordinate to the claim of a creditor and for the benefit of such creditor an allowed claim, by way of subrogation under this section, or for reimbursement or contribution, of an entity that is liable with the debtor on, or that has secured, such creditor's claim, until such creditor's claim is paid in full, either through payments under this title or otherwise.

§ 510.   Subordination

(a)   A subordination agreement is enforceable in a case under this title to the same extent that such agreement is enforceable under applicable nonbankruptcy law.

(b)   For the purpose of distribution under this title, a claim arising from rescission of a purchase or sale of a security of the debtor or of an affiliate of the debtor, for damages arising from the purchase or sale of such a security, or for reimbursement or contribution allowed under section 502 on account of such a claim, shall be subordinated to all claims or interests that are senior to or equal the claim or interest represented by such security, except that if such security is common stock, such claim has the same priority as common stock.

(c)   Notwithstanding subsections (a) and (b) of this section, after notice and a hearing, the court may—

(1)   under principles of equitable subordination, subordinate for purposes of distribution all or part of an allowed claim to all or part of another allowed claim or all or part of an allowed interest to all or part of another allowed interest; or

(2)   order that any lien securing such a subordinated claim be transferred to the estate.

§ 511.   Rate of interest on tax claims

(a)   If any provision of this title requires the payment of interest on a tax claim or on an administrative expense tax, or the payment of interest to enable a creditor to receive the present value of the allowed amount of a tax claim, the rate of interest shall be the rate determined under applicable nonbankruptcy law.

(b)   In the case of taxes paid under a confirmed plan under this title, the rate of interest shall be determined as of the calendar month in which the plan is confirmed.

SUBCHAPTER II—DEBTOR'S DUTIES AND BENEFITS

§ 521.   Debtor's duties

(a)   The debtor shall—

     (1)   file—

         (A)   a list of creditors; and

         (B)   unless the court orders otherwise—

             (i)   a schedule of assets and liabilities;

             (ii)   a schedule of current income and current expenditures;

             (iii)   a statement of the debtor's financial affairs and, if section 342(b) applies, a certificate—

                 (I)   of an attorney whose name is indicated on the petition as the attorney for the debtor, or a bankruptcy petition preparer signing the petition under section 110(b)(1), indicating that such attorney or the bankruptcy petition preparer delivered to the debtor the notice required by section 342(b); or

                 (II)   if no attorney is so indicated, and no bankruptcy petition preparer signed the petition, of the debtor that such notice was received and read by the debtor;

             (iv)   copies of all payment advices or other evidence of payment received within 60 days before the date of the filing of the petition, by the debtor from any employer of the debtor;

             (v)   a statement of the amount of monthly net income, itemized to show how the amount is calculated; and

             (vi)   a statement disclosing any reasonably anticipated increase in income or expenditures over the 12-month period following the date of the filing of the petition;

     (2)   if an individual debtor's schedule of assets and liabilities includes debts which are secured by property of the estate—

         (A)   within thirty days after the date of the filing of a petition under chapter 7 of this title or on or before the date of the meeting of creditors, whichever is earlier, or within such additional time as the court, for cause, within such period fixes, file with the clerk a statement of his intention with respect to the retention or surrender of such property and, if applicable, specifying that such property is claimed as exempt, that the debtor intends to redeem such property, or that the debtor intends to reaffirm debts secured by such property; and

         (B)   within 30 days after the first date set for the meeting of creditors under section 341(a), or within such additional time as the court, for cause, within such 30-day period fixes, perform his intention with respect to such property, as specified by subparagraph (A) of this paragraph;

except that nothing in subparagraphs (A) and (B) of this paragraph shall alter the debtor's or the trustee's rights with regard to such property under this title, except as provided in section 362(h);

(3) if a trustee is serving in the case or an auditor is serving under section 586(f) of title 28, cooperate with the trustee as necessary to enable the trustee to perform the trustee's duties under this title;

(4) if a trustee is serving in the case or an auditor is serving under section 586(f) of title 28, surrender to the trustee all property of the estate and any recorded information, including books, documents, records, and papers, relating to property of the estate, whether or not immunity is granted under section 344 of this title;

(5) appear at the hearing required under section 524(d) of this title;

(6) in a case under chapter 7 of this title in which the debtor is an individual, not retain possession of personal property as to which a creditor has an allowed claim for the purchase price secured in whole or in part by an interest in such personal property unless the debtor, not later than 45 days after the first meeting of creditors under section 341(a), either—

(A) enters into an agreement with the creditor pursuant to section 524(c) with respect to the claim secured by such property; or

(B) redeems such property from the security interest pursuant to section 722; and

(7) unless a trustee is serving in the case, continue to perform the obligations required of the administrator (as defined in section 3 of the Employee Retirement Income Security Act of 1974) of an employee benefit plan if at the time of the commencement of the case the debtor (or any entity designated by the debtor) served as such administrator.

If the debtor fails to so act within the 45-day period referred to in paragraph (6), the stay under section 362(a) is terminated with respect to the personal property of the estate or of the debtor which is affected, such property shall no longer be property of the estate, and the creditor may take whatever action as to such property as is permitted by applicable nonbankruptcy law, unless the court determines on the motion of the trustee filed before the expiration of such 45-day period, and after notice and a hearing, that such property is of consequential value or benefit to the estate, orders appropriate adequate protection of the creditor's interest, and orders the debtor to deliver any collateral in the debtor's possession to the trustee.

(b) In addition to the requirements under subsection (a), a debtor who is an individual shall file with the court—

(1) a certificate from the approved nonprofit budget and credit counseling agency that provided the debtor services under section 109(h) describing the services provided to the debtor; and

(2) a copy of the debt repayment plan, if any, developed under section 109(h) through the approved nonprofit budget and credit counseling agency referred to in paragraph (1).

(c) In addition to meeting the requirements under subsection (a), a debtor shall file with the court a record of any interest that a debtor has in an education individual retirement account (as defined in section 530(b)(1) of the Internal Revenue Code of 1986), an interest in an account in a qualified ABLE program (as defined in section 529A(b) of such Code,[1] or under a qualified State tuition program (as defined in section 529(b)(1) of such Code).

(d) If the debtor fails timely to take the action specified in subsection (a)(6) of this section, or in paragraphs (1) and (2) of section 362(h), with respect to property which a lessor or bailor owns and has leased, rented, or bailed to the debtor or as to which a creditor holds a security interest not otherwise voidable under section 522(f), 544, 545, 547, 548, or 549, nothing in this title shall prevent or limit the operation of a provision in the underlying lease or agreement that has the effect of placing the debtor in default under such lease or agreement by reason of the occurrence, pendency, or existence of a proceeding under this title or the insolvency of the debtor. Nothing in this subsection shall be deemed to justify limiting such a provision in any other circumstance.

(e)(1) If the debtor in a case under chapter 7 or 13 is an individual and if a creditor files with the court at any time a request to receive a copy of the petition, schedules, and statement of financial affairs

---

[1] So in original. A closing parenthesis probably should precede the comma.

filed by the debtor, then the court shall make such petition, such schedules, and such statement available to such creditor.

(2)(A)   The debtor shall provide—

(i)   not later than 7 days before the date first set for the first meeting of creditors, to the trustee a copy of the Federal income tax return required under applicable law (or at the election of the debtor, a transcript of such return) for the most recent tax year ending immediately before the commencement of the case and for which a Federal income tax return was filed; and

(ii)   at the same time the debtor complies with clause (i), a copy of such return (or if elected under clause (i), such transcript) to any creditor that timely requests such copy.

(B)   If the debtor fails to comply with clause (i) or (ii) of subparagraph (A), the court shall dismiss the case unless the debtor demonstrates that the failure to so comply is due to circumstances beyond the control of the debtor.

(C)   If a creditor requests a copy of such tax return or such transcript and if the debtor fails to provide a copy of such tax return or such transcript to such creditor at the time the debtor provides such tax return or such transcript to the trustee, then the court shall dismiss the case unless the debtor demonstrates that the failure to provide a copy of such tax return or such transcript is due to circumstances beyond the control of the debtor.

(3)   If a creditor in a case under chapter 13 files with the court at any time a request to receive a copy of the plan filed by the debtor, then the court shall make available to such creditor a copy of the plan—

(A)   at a reasonable cost; and

(B)   not later than 7 days after such request is filed.

(f)   At the request of the court, the United States trustee, or any party in interest in a case under chapter 7, 11, or 13, a debtor who is an individual shall file with the court—

(1)   at the same time filed with the taxing authority, a copy of each Federal income tax return required under applicable law (or at the election of the debtor, a transcript of such tax return) with respect to each tax year of the debtor ending while the case is pending under such chapter;

(2)   at the same time filed with the taxing authority, each Federal income tax return required under applicable law (or at the election of the debtor, a transcript of such tax return) that had not been filed with such authority as of the date of the commencement of the case and that was subsequently filed for any tax year of the debtor ending in the 3-year period ending on the date of the commencement of the case;

(3)   a copy of each amendment to any Federal income tax return or transcript filed with the court under paragraph (1) or (2); and

(4)   in a case under chapter 13—

(A)   on the date that is either 90 days after the end of such tax year or 1 year after the date of the commencement of the case, whichever is later, if a plan is not confirmed before such later date; and

(B)   annually after the plan is confirmed and until the case is closed, not later than the date that is 45 days before the anniversary of the confirmation of the plan;

a statement, under penalty of perjury, of the income and expenditures of the debtor during the tax year of the debtor most recently concluded before such statement is filed under this paragraph, and of the monthly income of the debtor, that shows how income, expenditures, and monthly income are calculated.

(g)(1)   A statement referred to in subsection (f)(4) shall disclose—

(A)   the amount and sources of the income of the debtor;

(B) the identity of any person responsible with the debtor for the support of any dependent of the debtor; and

(C) the identity of any person who contributed, and the amount contributed, to the household in which the debtor resides.

(2) The tax returns, amendments, and statement of income and expenditures described in subsections (e)(2)(A) and (f) shall be available to the United States trustee (or the bankruptcy administrator, if any), the trustee, and any party in interest for inspection and copying, subject to the requirements of section 315(c) of the Bankruptcy Abuse Prevention and Consumer Protection Act of 2005.

(h) If requested by the United States trustee or by the trustee, the debtor shall provide—

(1) a document that establishes the identity of the debtor, including a driver's license, passport, or other document that contains a photograph of the debtor; or

(2) such other personal identifying information relating to the debtor that establishes the identity of the debtor.

(i)(1) Subject to paragraphs (2) and (4) and notwithstanding section 707(a), if an individual debtor in a voluntary case under chapter 7 or 13 fails to file all of the information required under subsection (a)(1) within 45 days after the date of the filing of the petition, the case shall be automatically dismissed effective on the 46th day after the date of the filing of the petition.

(2) Subject to paragraph (4) and with respect to a case described in paragraph (1), any party in interest may request the court to enter an order dismissing the case. If requested, the court shall enter an order of dismissal not later than 7 days after such request.

(3) Subject to paragraph (4) and upon request of the debtor made within 45 days after the date of the filing of the petition described in paragraph (1), the court may allow the debtor an additional period of not to exceed 45 days to file the information required under subsection (a)(1) if the court finds justification for extending the period for the filing.

(4) Notwithstanding any other provision of this subsection, on the motion of the trustee filed before the expiration of the applicable period of time specified in paragraph (1), (2), or (3), and after notice and a hearing, the court may decline to dismiss the case if the court finds that the debtor attempted in good faith to file all the information required by subsection (a)(1)(B)(iv) and that the best interests of creditors would be served by administration of the case.

(j)(1) Notwithstanding any other provision of this title, if the debtor fails to file a tax return that becomes due after the commencement of the case or to properly obtain an extension of the due date for filing such return, the taxing authority may request that the court enter an order converting or dismissing the case.

(2) If the debtor does not file the required return or obtain the extension referred to in paragraph (1) within 90 days after a request is filed by the taxing authority under that paragraph, the court shall convert or dismiss the case, whichever is in the best interests of creditors and the estate.

§ 522. Exemptions

(a) In this section—

(1) "dependent" includes spouse, whether or not actually dependent; and

(2) "value" means fair market value as of the date of the filing of the petition or, with respect to property that becomes property of the estate after such date, as of the date such property becomes property of the estate.

(b)(1) Notwithstanding section 541 of this title, an individual debtor may exempt from property of the estate the property listed in either paragraph (2) or, in the alternative, paragraph (3) of this subsection. In joint cases filed under section 302 of this title and individual cases filed under section 301 or 303 of this title by or against debtors who are husband and wife, and whose estates are ordered to be jointly administered under Rule 1015(b) of the Federal Rules of Bankruptcy Procedure, one debtor may not elect to exempt property listed in paragraph (2) and the other debtor elect to exempt property listed in paragraph (3) of this subsection. If the parties cannot agree on the alternative to be elected, they shall be deemed to elect paragraph (2), where such election is permitted under the law of the jurisdiction where the case is filed.

(2)   Property listed in this paragraph is property that is specified under subsection (d), unless the State law that is applicable to the debtor under paragraph (3)(A) specifically does not so authorize.

(3)   Property listed in this paragraph is—

    (A)   subject to subsections (*o*) and (p), any property that is exempt under Federal law, other than subsection (d) of this section, or State or local law that is applicable on the date of the filing of the petition to the place in which the debtor's domicile has been located for the 730 days immediately preceding the date of the filing of the petition or if the debtor's domicile has not been located in a single State for such 730-day period, the place in which the debtor's domicile was located for 180 days immediately preceding the 730-day period or for a longer portion of such 180-day period than in any other place;

    (B)   any interest in property in which the debtor had, immediately before the commencement of the case, an interest as a tenant by the entirety or joint tenant to the extent that such interest as a tenant by the entirety or joint tenant is exempt from process under applicable nonbankruptcy law; and

    (C)   retirement funds to the extent that those funds are in a fund or account that is exempt from taxation under section 401, 403, 408, 408A, 414, 457, or 501(a) of the Internal Revenue Code of 1986.

If the effect of the domiciliary requirement under subparagraph (A) is to render the debtor ineligible for any exemption, the debtor may elect to exempt property that is specified under subsection (d).

(4)   For purposes of paragraph (3)(C) and subsection (d)(12), the following shall apply:

    (A)   If the retirement funds are in a retirement fund that has received a favorable determination under section 7805 of the Internal Revenue Code of 1986, and that determination is in effect as of the date of the filing of the petition in a case under this title, those funds shall be presumed to be exempt from the estate.

    (B)   If the retirement funds are in a retirement fund that has not received a favorable determination under such section 7805, those funds are exempt from the estate if the debtor demonstrates that—

        (i)   no prior determination to the contrary has been made by a court or the Internal Revenue Service; and

        (ii)(I)   the retirement fund is in substantial compliance with the applicable requirements of the Internal Revenue Code of 1986; or

            (II)   the retirement fund fails to be in substantial compliance with the applicable requirements of the Internal Revenue Code of 1986 and the debtor is not materially responsible for that failure.

    (C)   A direct transfer of retirement funds from 1 fund or account that is exempt from taxation under section 401, 403, 408, 408A, 414, 457, or 501(a) of the Internal Revenue Code of 1986, under section 401(a)(31) of the Internal Revenue Code of 1986, or otherwise, shall not cease to qualify for exemption under paragraph (3)(C) or subsection (d)(12) by reason of such direct transfer.

    (D)(i)   Any distribution that qualifies as an eligible rollover distribution within the meaning of section 402(c) of the Internal Revenue Code of 1986 or that is described in clause (ii) shall not cease to qualify for exemption under paragraph (3)(C) or subsection (d)(12) by reason of such distribution.

        (ii)   A distribution described in this clause is an amount that—

(I) has been distributed from a fund or account that is exempt from taxation under section 401, 403, 408, 408A, 414, 457, or 501(a) of the Internal Revenue Code of 1986; and

(II) to the extent allowed by law, is deposited in such a fund or account not later than 60 days after the distribution of such amount.

(c) Unless the case is dismissed, property exempted under this section is not liable during or after the case for any debt of the debtor that arose, or that is determined under section 502 of this title as if such debt had arisen, before the commencement of the case, except—

(1) a debt of a kind specified in paragraph (1) or (5) of section 523(a) (in which case, notwithstanding any provision of applicable nonbankruptcy law to the contrary, such property shall be liable for a debt of a kind specified in such paragraph);

(2) a debt secured by a lien that is—

(A)(i) not avoided under subsection (f) or (g) of this section or under section 544, 545, 547, 548, 549, or 724(a) of this title; and

(ii) not void under section 506(d) of this title; or

(B) a tax lien, notice of which is properly filed;

(3) a debt of a kind specified in section 523(a)(4) or 523(a)(6) of this title owed by an institution-affiliated party of an insured depository institution to a Federal depository institutions regulatory agency acting in its capacity as conservator, receiver, or liquidating agent for such institution; or

(4) a debt in connection with fraud in the obtaining or providing of any scholarship, grant, loan, tuition, discount, award, or other financial assistance for purposes of financing an education at an institution of higher education (as that term is defined in section 101 of the Higher Education Act of 1965 (20 U.S.C. 1001)).

(d) The following property may be exempted under subsection (b)(2) of this section:

(1) The debtor's aggregate interest, not to exceed $27,900 in value, in real property or personal property that the debtor or a dependent of the debtor uses as a residence, in a cooperative that owns property that the debtor or a dependent of the debtor uses as a residence, or in a burial plot for the debtor or a dependent of the debtor.

(2) The debtor's interest, not to exceed $4,450 in value, in one motor vehicle.

(3) The debtor's interest, not to exceed $700 in value in any particular item or $14,875 in aggregate value, in household furnishings, household goods, wearing apparel, appliances, books, animals, crops, or musical instruments, that are held primarily for the personal, family, or household use of the debtor or a dependent of the debtor.

(4) The debtor's aggregate interest, not to exceed $1,875 in value, in jewelry held primarily for the personal, family, or household use of the debtor or a dependent of the debtor.

(5) The debtor's aggregate interest in any property, not to exceed in value $1,475 plus up to $13,950 of any unused amount of the exemption provided under paragraph (1) of this subsection.

(6) The debtor's aggregate interest, not to exceed $2,800 in value, in any implements, professional books, or tools, of the trade of the debtor or the trade of a dependent of the debtor.

(7) Any unmatured life insurance contract owned by the debtor, other than a credit life insurance contract.

(8) The debtor's aggregate interest, not to exceed in value $14,875 less any amount of property of the estate transferred in the manner specified in section 542(d) of this title, in any accrued dividend or interest under, or loan value of, any unmatured life insurance contract owned by the debtor under which the insured is the debtor or an individual of whom the debtor is a dependent.

(9) Professionally prescribed health aids for the debtor or a dependent of the debtor.

(10) The debtor's right to receive—

    (A) a social security benefit, unemployment compensation, or a local public assistance benefit;

    (B) a veterans' benefit;

    (C) a disability, illness, or unemployment benefit;

    (D) alimony, support, or separate maintenance, to the extent reasonably necessary for the support of the debtor and any dependent of the debtor;

    (E) a payment under a stock bonus, pension, profitsharing, annuity, or similar plan or contract on account of illness, disability, death, age, or length of service, to the extent reasonably necessary for the support of the debtor and any dependent of the debtor, unless—

        (i) such plan or contract was established by or under the auspices of an insider that employed the debtor at the time the debtor's rights under such plan or contract arose;

        (ii) such payment is on account of age or length of service; and

        (iii) such plan or contract does not qualify under section 401(a), 403(a), 403(b), or 408 of the Internal Revenue Code of 1986.

(11) The debtor's right to receive, or property that is traceable to—

    (A) an award under a crime victim's reparation law;

    (B) a payment on account of the wrongful death of an individual of whom the debtor was a dependent, to the extent reasonably necessary for the support of the debtor and any dependent of the debtor;

    (C) a payment under a life insurance contract that insured the life of an individual of whom the debtor was a dependent on the date of such individual's death, to the extent reasonably necessary for the support of the debtor and any dependent of the debtor;

    (D) a payment, not to exceed $27,900, on account of personal bodily injury, not including pain and suffering or compensation for actual pecuniary loss, of the debtor or an individual of whom the debtor is a dependent; or

    (E) a payment in compensation of loss of future earnings of the debtor or an individual of whom the debtor is or was a dependent, to the extent reasonably necessary for the support of the debtor and any dependent of the debtor.

(12) Retirement funds to the extent that those funds are in a fund or account that is exempt from taxation under section 401, 403, 408, 408A, 414, 457, or 501(a) of the Internal Revenue Code of 1986.

    (e) A waiver of an exemption executed in favor of a creditor that holds an unsecured claim against the debtor is unenforceable in a case under this title with respect to such claim against property that the debtor may exempt under subsection (b) of this section. A waiver by the debtor of a power under subsection (f) or (h) of this section to avoid a transfer, under subsection (g) or (i) of this section to exempt property, or under subsection (i) of this section to recover property or to preserve a transfer, is unenforceable in a case under this title.

    (f)(1) Notwithstanding any waiver of exemptions but subject to paragraph (3), the debtor may avoid the fixing of a lien on an interest of the debtor in property to the extent that such lien impairs an exemption to which the debtor would have been entitled under subsection (b) of this section, if such lien is—

    (A) a judicial lien, other than a judicial lien that secures a debt of a kind that is specified in section 523(a)(5); or

    (B) a nonpossessory, nonpurchase-money security interest in any—

        (i) household furnishings, household goods, wearing apparel, appliances, books, animals, crops, musical instruments, or jewelry that are held primarily for the personal, family, or household use of the debtor or a dependent of the debtor;

        (ii) implements, professional books, or tools, of the trade of the debtor or the trade of a dependent of the debtor; or

(iii) professionally prescribed health aids for the debtor or a dependent of the debtor.

(2)(A) For the purposes of this subsection, a lien shall be considered to impair an exemption to the extent that the sum of—

(i) the lien;

(ii) all other liens on the property; and

(iii) the amount of the exemption that the debtor could claim if there were no liens on the property;

exceeds the value that the debtor's interest in the property would have in the absence of any liens.

(B) In the case of a property subject to more than 1 lien, a lien that has been avoided shall not be considered in making the calculation under subparagraph (A) with respect to other liens.

(C) This paragraph shall not apply with respect to a judgment arising out of a mortgage foreclosure.

(3) In a case in which State law that is applicable to the debtor—

(A) permits a person to voluntarily waive a right to claim exemptions under subsection (d) or prohibits a debtor from claiming exemptions under subsection (d); and

(B) either permits the debtor to claim exemptions under State law without limitation in amount, except to the extent that the debtor has permitted the fixing of a consensual lien on any property or prohibits avoidance of a consensual lien on property otherwise eligible to be claimed as exempt property;

the debtor may not avoid the fixing of a lien on an interest of the debtor or a dependent of the debtor in property if the lien is a nonpossessory, nonpurchase-money security interest in implements, professional books, or tools of the trade of the debtor or a dependent of the debtor or farm animals or crops of the debtor or a dependent of the debtor to the extent the value of such implements, professional books, tools of the trade, animals, and crops exceeds $7,575.

(4)(A) Subject to subparagraph (B), for purposes of paragraph (1)(B), the term "household goods" means—

(i) clothing;

(ii) furniture;

(iii) appliances;

(iv) 1 radio;

(v) 1 television;

(vi) 1 VCR;

(vii) linens;

(viii) china;

(ix) crockery;

(x) kitchenware;

(xi) educational materials and educational equipment primarily for the use of minor dependent children of the debtor;

(xii) medical equipment and supplies;

(xiii) furniture exclusively for the use of minor children, or elderly or disabled dependents of the debtor;

(xiv) personal effects (including the toys and hobby equipment of minor dependent children and wedding rings) of the debtor and the dependents of the debtor; and

        (xv)   1 personal computer and related equipment.

    (B)   The term "household goods" does not include—

        (i)   works of art (unless by or of the debtor, or any relative of the debtor);

        (ii)   electronic entertainment equipment with a fair market value of more than $800 in the aggregate (except 1 television, 1 radio, and 1 VCR);

        (iii)   items acquired as antiques with a fair market value of more than $800 in the aggregate;

        (iv)   jewelry with a fair market value of more than $800 in the aggregate (except wedding rings); and

        (v)   a computer (except as otherwise provided for in this section), motor vehicle (including a tractor or lawn tractor), boat, or a motorized recreational device, conveyance, vehicle, watercraft, or aircraft.

  (g)   Notwithstanding sections 550 and 551 of this title, the debtor may exempt under subsection (b) of this section property that the trustee recovers under section 510(c)(2), 542, 543, 550, 551, or 553 of this title, to the extent that the debtor could have exempted such property under subsection (b) of this section if such property had not been transferred, if—

    (1)(A)   such transfer was not a voluntary transfer of such property by the debtor; and

    (B)   the debtor did not conceal such property; or

    (2)   the debtor could have avoided such transfer under subsection (f)(1)(B) of this section.

  (h)   The debtor may avoid a transfer of property of the debtor or recover a setoff to the extent that the debtor could have exempted such property under subsection (g)(1) of this section if the trustee had avoided such transfer, if—

    (1)   such transfer is avoidable by the trustee under section 544, 545, 547, 548, 549, or 724(a) of this title or recoverable by the trustee under section 553 of this title; and

    (2)   the trustee does not attempt to avoid such transfer.

  (i)(1)   If the debtor avoids a transfer or recovers a setoff under subsection (f) or (h) of this section, the debtor may recover in the manner prescribed by, and subject to the limitations of, section 550 of this title, the same as if the trustee had avoided such transfer, and may exempt any property so recovered under subsection (b) of this section.

    (2)   Notwithstanding section 551 of this title, a transfer avoided under section 544, 545, 547, 548, 549, or 724(a) of this title, under subsection (f) or (h) of this section, or property recovered under section 553 of this title, may be preserved for the benefit of the debtor to the extent that the debtor may exempt such property under subsection (g) of this section or paragraph (1) of this subsection.

  (j)   Notwithstanding subsections (g) and (i) of this section, the debtor may exempt a particular kind of property under subsections (g) and (i) of this section only to the extent that the debtor has exempted less property in value of such kind than that to which the debtor is entitled under subsection (b) of this section.

  (k)   Property that the debtor exempts under this section is not liable for payment of any administrative expense except—

    (1)   the aliquot share of the costs and expenses of avoiding a transfer of property that the debtor exempts under subsection (g) of this section, or of recovery of such property, that is attributable to the value of the portion of such property exempted in relation to the value of the property recovered; and

    (2)   any costs and expenses of avoiding a transfer under subsection (f) or (h) of this section, or of recovery of property under subsection (i)(1) of this section, that the debtor has not paid.

  (*l*)   The debtor shall file a list of property that the debtor claims as exempt under subsection (b) of this section. If the debtor does not file such a list, a dependent of the debtor may file such a list, or may claim property as exempt from property of the estate on behalf of the debtor. Unless a party in interest objects, the property claimed as exempt on such list is exempt.

(m) Subject to the limitation in subsection (b), this section shall apply separately with respect to each debtor in a joint case.

(n) For assets in individual retirement accounts described in section 408 or 408A of the Internal Revenue Code of 1986, other than a simplified employee pension under section 408(k) of such Code or a simple retirement account under section 408(p) of such Code, the aggregate value of such assets exempted under this section, without regard to amounts attributable to rollover contributions under section 402(c), 402(e)(6), 403(a)(4), 403(a)(5), and 403(b)(8) of the Internal Revenue Code of 1986, and earnings thereon, shall not exceed $1,512,350 in a case filed by a debtor who is an individual, except that such amount may be increased if the interests of justice so require.

(o) For purposes of subsection (b)(3)(A), and notwithstanding subsection (a), the value of an interest in—

(1) real or personal property that the debtor or a dependent of the debtor uses as a residence;

(2) a cooperative that owns property that the debtor or a dependent of the debtor uses as a residence;

(3) a burial plot for the debtor or a dependent of the debtor; or

(4) real or personal property that the debtor or a dependent of the debtor claims as a homestead;

shall be reduced to the extent that such value is attributable to any portion of any property that the debtor disposed of in the 10-year period ending on the date of the filing of the petition with the intent to hinder, delay, or defraud a creditor and that the debtor could not exempt, or that portion that the debtor could not exempt, under subsection (b), if on such date the debtor had held the property so disposed of.

(p)(1) Except as provided in paragraph (2) of this subsection and sections 544 and 548, as a result of electing under subsection (b)(3)(A) to exempt property under State or local law, a debtor may not exempt any amount of interest that was acquired by the debtor during the 1215-day period preceding the date of the filing of the petition that exceeds in the aggregate $189,050 in value in—

(A) real or personal property that the debtor or a dependent of the debtor uses as a residence;

(B) a cooperative that owns property that the debtor or a dependent of the debtor uses as a residence;

(C) a burial plot for the debtor or a dependent of the debtor; or

(D) real or personal property that the debtor or dependent of the debtor claims as a homestead.

(2)(A) The limitation under paragraph (1) shall not apply to an exemption claimed under subsection (b)(3)(A) by a family farmer for the principal residence of such farmer.

(B) For purposes of paragraph (1), any amount of such interest does not include any interest transferred from a debtor's previous principal residence (which was acquired prior to the beginning of such 1215-day period) into the debtor's current principal residence, if the debtor's previous and current residences are located in the same State.

(q)(1) As a result of electing under subsection (b)(3)(A) to exempt property under State or local law, a debtor may not exempt any amount of an interest in property described in subparagraphs (A), (B), (C), and (D) of subsection (p)(1) which exceeds in the aggregate $189,050 if—

(A) the court determines, after notice and a hearing, that the debtor has been convicted of a felony (as defined in section 3156 of title 18), which under the circumstances, demonstrates that the filing of the case was an abuse of the provisions of this title; or

(B) the debtor owes a debt arising from—

(i) any violation of the Federal securities laws (as defined in section 3(a)(47) of the Securities Exchange Act of 1934), any State securities laws, or any regulation or order issued under Federal securities laws or State securities laws;

(ii) fraud, deceit, or manipulation in a fiduciary capacity or in connection with the purchase or sale of any security registered under section 12 or 15(d) of the Securities Exchange Act of 1934 or under section 6 of the Securities Act of 1933;

(iii) any civil remedy under section 1964 of title 18; or

(iv) any criminal act, intentional tort, or willful or reckless misconduct that caused serious physical injury or death to another individual in the preceding 5 years.

(2) Paragraph (1) shall not apply to the extent the amount of an interest in property described in subparagraphs (A), (B), (C), and (D) of subsection (p)(1) is reasonably necessary for the support of the debtor and any dependent of the debtor.

§ 523.   Exceptions to discharge

(a) A discharge under section 727, 1141, 1192, 1228(a), 1228(b), or 1328(b) of this title does not discharge an individual debtor from any debt—

(1) for a tax or a customs duty—

(A) of the kind and for the periods specified in section 507(a)(3) or 507(a)(8) of this title, whether or not a claim for such tax was filed or allowed;

(B) with respect to which a return, or equivalent report or notice, if required—

(i) was not filed or given; or

(ii) was filed or given after the date on which such return, report, or notice was last due, under applicable law or under any extension, and after two years before the date of the filing of the petition; or

(C) with respect to which the debtor made a fraudulent return or willfully attempted in any manner to evade or defeat such tax;

(2) for money, property, services, or an extension, renewal, or refinancing of credit, to the extent obtained by—

(A) false pretenses, a false representation, or actual fraud, other than a statement respecting the debtor's or an insider's financial condition;

(B) use of a statement in writing—

(i) that is materially false;

(ii) respecting the debtor's or an insider's financial condition;

(iii) on which the creditor to whom the debtor is liable for such money, property, services, or credit reasonably relied; and

(iv) that the debtor caused to be made or published with intent to deceive; or

(C)(i) for purposes of subparagraph (A)—

(I) consumer debts owed to a single creditor and aggregating more than $800 for luxury goods or services incurred by an individual debtor on or within 90 days before the order for relief under this title are presumed to be nondischargeable; and

(II) cash advances aggregating more than $1,100 that are extensions of consumer credit under an open end credit plan obtained by an individual debtor on or within 70 days before the order for relief under this title, are presumed to be nondischargeable; and

(ii) for purposes of this subparagraph—

(I) the terms "consumer", "credit", and "open end credit plan" have the same meanings as in section 103 of the Truth in Lending Act; and

(II) the term "luxury goods or services" does not include goods or services reasonably necessary for the support or maintenance of the debtor or a dependent of the debtor;

(3) neither listed nor scheduled under section 521(a)(1) of this title, with the name, if known to the debtor, of the creditor to whom such debt is owed, in time to permit—

(A) if such debt is not of a kind specified in paragraph (2), (4), or (6) of this subsection, timely filing of a proof of claim, unless such creditor had notice or actual knowledge of the case in time for such timely filing; or

(B) if such debt is of a kind specified in paragraph (2), (4), or (6) of this subsection, timely filing of a proof of claim and timely request for a determination of dischargeability of such debt under one of such paragraphs, unless such creditor had notice or actual knowledge of the case in time for such timely filing and request;

(4) for fraud or defalcation while acting in a fiduciary capacity, embezzlement, or larceny;

(5) for a domestic support obligation;

(6) for willful and malicious injury by the debtor to another entity or to the property of another entity;

(7) to the extent such debt is for a fine, penalty, or forfeiture payable to and for the benefit of a governmental unit, and is not compensation for actual pecuniary loss, other than a tax penalty—

(A) relating to a tax of a kind not specified in paragraph (1) of this subsection; or

(B) imposed with respect to a transaction or event that occurred before three years before the date of the filing of the petition;

(8) unless excepting such debt from discharge under this paragraph would impose an undue hardship on the debtor and the debtor's dependents, for—

(A)(i) an educational benefit overpayment or loan made, insured, or guaranteed by a governmental unit, or made under any program funded in whole or in part by a governmental unit or nonprofit institution; or

(ii) an obligation to repay funds received as an educational benefit, scholarship, or stipend; or

(B) any other educational loan that is a qualified education loan, as defined in section 221(d)(1) of the Internal Revenue Code of 1986, incurred by a debtor who is an individual;

(9) for death or personal injury caused by the debtor's operation of a motor vehicle, vessel, or aircraft if such operation was unlawful because the debtor was intoxicated from using alcohol, a drug, or another substance;

(10) that was or could have been listed or scheduled by the debtor in a prior case concerning the debtor under this title or under the Bankruptcy Act in which the debtor waived discharge, or was denied a discharge under section 727(a)(2), (3), (4), (5), (6), or (7) of this title, or under section 14c(1), (2), (3), (4), (6), or (7) of such Act;

(11) provided in any final judgment, unreviewable order, or consent order or decree entered in any court of the United States or of any State, issued by a Federal depository institutions regulatory agency, or contained in any settlement agreement entered into by the debtor, arising from any act of fraud or defalcation while acting in a fiduciary capacity committed with respect to any depository institution or insured credit union;

(12) for malicious or reckless failure to fulfill any commitment by the debtor to a Federal depository institutions regulatory agency to maintain the capital of an insured depository institution, except that this paragraph shall not extend any such commitment which would otherwise be terminated due to any act of such agency;

(13) for any payment of an order of restitution issued under title 18, United States Code;

(14) incurred to pay a tax to the United States that would be nondischargeable pursuant to paragraph (1);

(14A) incurred to pay a tax to a governmental unit, other than the United States, that would be nondischargeable under paragraph (1);

(14B) incurred to pay fines or penalties imposed under Federal election law;

(15) to a spouse, former spouse, or child of the debtor and not of the kind described in paragraph (5) that is incurred by the debtor in the course of a divorce or separation or in connection with a separation agreement, divorce decree or other order of a court of record, or a determination made in accordance with State or territorial law by a governmental unit;

(16) for a fee or assessment that becomes due and payable after the order for relief to a membership association with respect to the debtor's interest in a unit that has condominium ownership, in a share of a cooperative corporation, or a lot in a homeowners association, for as long as the debtor or the trustee has a legal, equitable, or possessory ownership interest in such unit, such corporation, or such lot, but nothing in this paragraph shall except from discharge the debt of a debtor for a membership association fee or assessment for a period arising before entry of the order for relief in a pending or subsequent bankruptcy case;

(17) for a fee imposed on a prisoner by any court for the filing of a case, motion, complaint, or appeal, or for other costs and expenses assessed with respect to such filing, regardless of an assertion of poverty by the debtor under subsection (b) or (f)(2) of section 1915 of title 28 (or a similar non-Federal law), or the debtor's status as a prisoner, as defined in section 1915(h) of title 28 (or a similar non-Federal law);

(18) owed to a pension, profit-sharing, stock bonus, or other plan established under section 401, 403, 408, 408A, 414, 457, or 501(c) of the Internal Revenue Code of 1986, under—

(A) a loan permitted under section 408(b)(1) of the Employee Retirement Income Security Act of 1974, or subject to section 72(p) of the Internal Revenue Code of 1986; or

(B) a loan from a thrift savings plan permitted under subchapter III of chapter 84 of title 5, that satisfies the requirements of section 8433(g) of such title;

but nothing in this paragraph may be construed to provide that any loan made under a governmental plan under section 414(d), or a contract or account under section 403(b), of the Internal Revenue Code of 1986 constitutes a claim or a debt under this title; or

(19) that—

(A) is for—

(i) the violation of any of the Federal securities laws (as that term is defined in section 3(a)(47) of the Securities Exchange Act of 1934), any of the State securities laws, or any regulation or order issued under such Federal or State securities laws; or

(ii) common law fraud, deceit, or manipulation in connection with the purchase or sale of any security; and

(B) results, before, on, or after the date on which the petition was filed, from—

(i) any judgment, order, consent order, or decree entered in any Federal or State judicial or administrative proceeding;

(ii) any settlement agreement entered into by the debtor; or

(iii) any court or administrative order for any damages, fine, penalty, citation, restitutionary payment, disgorgement payment, attorney fee, cost, or other payment owed by the debtor.

For purposes of this subsection, the term "return" means a return that satisfies the requirements of applicable nonbankruptcy law (including applicable filing requirements). Such term includes a return prepared pursuant to section 6020(a) of the Internal Revenue Code of 1986, or similar State or local law, or a written stipulation to a judgment or a final order entered by a nonbankruptcy tribunal, but does not include a return made pursuant to section 6020(b) of the Internal Revenue Code of 1986, or a similar State or local law.

(b) Notwithstanding subsection (a) of this section, a debt that was excepted from discharge under subsection (a)(1), (a)(3), or (a)(8) of this section, under section 17a(1), 17a(3), or 17a(5) of the Bankruptcy Act, under section 439A of the Higher Education Act of 1965, or under section 733(g) of the Public Health Service Act in a prior case concerning the debtor under this title, or under the Bankruptcy Act, is dischargeable in a case under this title unless, by the terms of subsection (a) of this section, such debt is not dischargeable in the case under this title.

(c)(1) Except as provided in subsection (a)(3)(B) of this section, the debtor shall be discharged from a debt of a kind specified in paragraph (2), (4), or (6) of subsection (a) of this section, unless, on request of the creditor to whom such debt is owed, and after notice and a hearing, the court determines such debt to be excepted from discharge under paragraph (2), (4), or (6), as the case may be, of subsection (a) of this section.

(2) Paragraph (1) shall not apply in the case of a Federal depository institutions regulatory agency seeking, in its capacity as conservator, receiver, or liquidating agent for an insured depository institution, to recover a debt described in subsection (a)(2), (a)(4), (a)(6), or (a)(11) owed to such institution by an institution-affiliated party unless the receiver, conservator, or liquidating agent was appointed in time to reasonably comply, or for a Federal depository institutions regulatory agency acting in its corporate capacity as a successor to such receiver, conservator, or liquidating agent to reasonably comply, with subsection (a)(3)(B) as a creditor of such institution-affiliated party with respect to such debt.

(d) If a creditor requests a determination of dischargeability of a consumer debt under subsection (a)(2) of this section, and such debt is discharged, the court shall grant judgment in favor of the debtor for the costs of, and a reasonable attorney's fee for, the proceeding if the court finds that the position of the creditor was not substantially justified, except that the court shall not award such costs and fees if special circumstances would make the award unjust.

(e) Any institution-affiliated party of an insured depository institution shall be considered to be acting in a fiduciary capacity with respect to the purposes of subsection (a)(4) or (11).

§ 524. Effect of discharge

(a) A discharge in a case under this title—

(1) voids any judgment at any time obtained, to the extent that such judgment is a determination of the personal liability of the debtor with respect to any debt discharged under section 727, 944, 1141, 1192, 1228, or 1328 of this title, whether or not discharge of such debt is waived;

(2) operates as an injunction against the commencement or continuation of an action, the employment of process, or an act, to collect, recover or offset any such debt as a personal liability of the debtor, whether or not discharge of such debt is waived; and

(3) operates as an injunction against the commencement or continuation of an action, the employment of process, or an act, to collect or recover from, or offset against, property of the debtor of the kind specified in section 541(a)(2) of this title that is acquired after the commencement of the case, on account of any allowable community claim, except a community claim that is excepted from discharge under section 523, 1192, 1228(a)(1), or 1328(a)(1), or that would be so excepted, determined in accordance with the provisions of sections 523(c) and 523(d) of this title, in a case concerning the debtor's spouse commenced on the date of the filing of the petition in the case concerning the debtor, whether or not discharge of the debt based on such community claim is waived.

(b) Subsection (a)(3) of this section does not apply if—

(1)(A) the debtor's spouse is a debtor in a case under this title, or a bankrupt or a debtor in a case under the Bankruptcy Act, commenced within six years of the date of the filing of the petition in the case concerning the debtor; and

(B)   the court does not grant the debtor's spouse a discharge in such case concerning the debtor's spouse; or

(2)(A)   the court would not grant the debtor's spouse a discharge in a case under chapter 7 of this title concerning such spouse commenced on the date of the filing of the petition in the case concerning the debtor; and

(B)   a determination that the court would not so grant such discharge is made by the bankruptcy court within the time and in the manner provided for a determination under section 727 of this title of whether a debtor is granted a discharge.

(c)   An agreement between a holder of a claim and the debtor, the consideration for which, in whole or in part, is based on a debt that is dischargeable in a case under this title is enforceable only to any extent enforceable under applicable nonbankruptcy law, whether or not discharge of such debt is waived, only if—

(1)   such agreement was made before the granting of the discharge under section 727, 1141, 1192, 1228, or 1328 of this title;

(2)   the debtor received the disclosures described in subsection (k) at or before the time at which the debtor signed the agreement;

(3)   such agreement has been filed with the court and, if applicable, accompanied by a declaration or an affidavit of the attorney that represented the debtor during the course of negotiating an agreement under this subsection, which states that—

(A)   such agreement represents a fully informed and voluntary agreement by the debtor;

(B)   such agreement does not impose an undue hardship on the debtor or a dependent of the debtor; and

(C)   the attorney fully advised the debtor of the legal effect and consequences of—

(i)   an agreement of the kind specified in this subsection; and

(ii)   any default under such an agreement;

(4)   the debtor has not rescinded such agreement at any time prior to discharge or within sixty days after such agreement is filed with the court, whichever occurs later, by giving notice of rescission to the holder of such claim;

(5)   the provisions of subsection (d) of this section have been complied with; and

(6)(A)   in a case concerning an individual who was not represented by an attorney during the course of negotiating an agreement under this subsection, the court approves such agreement as—

(i)   not imposing an undue hardship on the debtor or a dependent of the debtor; and

(ii)   in the best interest of the debtor.

(B)   Subparagraph (A) shall not apply to the extent that such debt is a consumer debt secured by real property.

(d)   In a case concerning an individual, when the court has determined whether to grant or not to grant a discharge under section 727, 1141, 1192, 1228, or 1328 of this title, the court may hold a hearing at which the debtor shall appear in person. At any such hearing, the court shall inform the debtor that a discharge has been granted or the reason why a discharge has not been granted. If a discharge has been granted and if the debtor desires to make an agreement of the kind specified in subsection (c) of this section and was not represented by an attorney during the course of negotiating such agreement, then the court shall hold a hearing at which the debtor shall appear in person and at such hearing the court shall—

(1)   inform the debtor—

(A)   that such an agreement is not required under this title, under nonbankruptcy law, or under any agreement not made in accordance with the provisions of subsection (c) of this section; and

(B)   of the legal effect and consequences of—

(i) an agreement of the kind specified in subsection (c) of this section; and

(ii) a default under such an agreement; and

(2) determine whether the agreement that the debtor desires to make complies with the requirements of subsection (c)(6) of this section, if the consideration for such agreement is based in whole or in part on a consumer debt that is not secured by real property of the debtor.

(e) Except as provided in subsection (a)(3) of this section, discharge of a debt of the debtor does not affect the liability of any other entity on, or the property of any other entity for, such debt.

(f) Nothing contained in subsection (c) or (d) of this section prevents a debtor from voluntarily repaying any debt.

(g)(1)(A) After notice and hearing, a court that enters an order confirming a plan of reorganization under chapter 11 may issue, in connection with such order, an injunction in accordance with this subsection to supplement the injunctive effect of a discharge under this section.

(B) An injunction may be issued under subparagraph (A) to enjoin entities from taking legal action for the purpose of directly or indirectly collecting, recovering, or receiving payment or recovery with respect to any claim or demand that, under a plan of reorganization, is to be paid in whole or in part by a trust described in paragraph (2)(B)(i), except such legal actions as are expressly allowed by the injunction, the confirmation order, or the plan of reorganization.

(2)(A) Subject to subsection (h), if the requirements of subparagraph (B) are met at the time an injunction described in paragraph (1) is entered, then after entry of such injunction, any proceeding that involves the validity, application, construction, or modification of such injunction, or of this subsection with respect to such injunction, may be commenced only in the district court in which such injunction was entered, and such court shall have exclusive jurisdiction over any such proceeding without regard to the amount in controversy.

(B) The requirements of this subparagraph are that—

(i) the injunction is to be implemented in connection with a trust that, pursuant to the plan of reorganization—

(I) is to assume the liabilities of a debtor which at the time of entry of the order for relief has been named as a defendant in personal injury, wrongful death, or property-damage actions seeking recovery for damages allegedly caused by the presence of, or exposure to, asbestos or asbestos-containing products;

(II) is to be funded in whole or in part by the securities of 1 or more debtors involved in such plan and by the obligation of such debtor or debtors to make future payments, including dividends;

(III) is to own, or by the exercise of rights granted under such plan would be entitled to own if specified contingencies occur, a majority of the voting shares of—

(aa) each such debtor;

(bb) the parent corporation of each such debtor; or

(cc) a subsidiary of each such debtor that is also a debtor; and

(IV) is to use its assets or income to pay claims and demands; and

(ii) subject to subsection (h), the court determines that—

(I) the debtor is likely to be subject to substantial future demands for payment arising out of the same or similar conduct or events that gave rise to the claims that are addressed by the injunction;

(II) the actual amounts, numbers, and timing of such future demands cannot be determined;

(III) pursuit of such demands outside the procedures prescribed by such plan is likely to threaten the plan's purpose to deal equitably with claims and future demands;

(IV) as part of the process of seeking confirmation of such plan—

(aa) the terms of the injunction proposed to be issued under paragraph (1)(A), including any provisions barring actions against third parties pursuant to paragraph (4)(A), are set out in such plan and in any disclosure statement supporting the plan; and

(bb) a separate class or classes of the claimants whose claims are to be addressed by a trust described in clause (i) is established and votes, by at least 75 percent of those voting, in favor of the plan; and

(V) subject to subsection (h), pursuant to court orders or otherwise, the trust will operate through mechanisms such as structured, periodic, or supplemental payments, pro rata distributions, matrices, or periodic review of estimates of the numbers and values of present claims and future demands, or other comparable mechanisms, that provide reasonable assurance that the trust will value, and be in a financial position to pay, present claims and future demands that involve similar claims in substantially the same manner.

(3)(A)   If the requirements of paragraph (2)(B) are met and the order confirming the plan of reorganization was issued or affirmed by the district court that has jurisdiction over the reorganization case, then after the time for appeal of the order that issues or affirms the plan—

(i)   the injunction shall be valid and enforceable and may not be revoked or modified by any court except through appeal in accordance with paragraph (6);

(ii)   no entity that pursuant to such plan or thereafter becomes a direct or indirect transferee of, or successor to any assets of, a debtor or trust that is the subject of the injunction shall be liable with respect to any claim or demand made against such entity by reason of its becoming such a transferee or successor; and

(iii)   no entity that pursuant to such plan or thereafter makes a loan to such a debtor or trust or to such a successor or transferee shall, by reason of making the loan, be liable with respect to any claim or demand made against such entity, nor shall any pledge of assets made in connection with such a loan be upset or impaired for that reason;

(B)   Subparagraph (A) shall not be construed to—

(i)   imply that an entity described in subparagraph (A)(ii) or (iii) would, if this paragraph were not applicable, necessarily be liable to any entity by reason of any of the acts described in subparagraph (A);

(ii)   relieve any such entity of the duty to comply with, or of liability under, any Federal or State law regarding the making of a fraudulent conveyance in a transaction described in subparagraph (A)(ii) or (iii); or

(iii)   relieve a debtor of the debtor's obligation to comply with the terms of the plan of reorganization, or affect the power of the court to exercise its authority under sections 1141 and 1142 to compel the debtor to do so.

(4)(A)(i) Subject to subparagraph (B), an injunction described in paragraph (1) shall be valid and enforceable against all entities that it addresses.

(ii)   Notwithstanding the provisions of section 524(e), such an injunction may bar any action directed against a third party who is identifiable from the terms of such injunction (by name or as part of an identifiable group) and is alleged to be directly or indirectly liable for the conduct of, claims against, or demands on the debtor to the extent such alleged liability of such third party arises by reason of—

(I)   the third party's ownership of a financial interest in the debtor, a past or present affiliate of the debtor, or a predecessor in interest of the debtor;

(II) the third party's involvement in the management of the debtor or a predecessor in interest of the debtor, or service as an officer, director or employee of the debtor or a related party;

(III) the third party's provision of insurance to the debtor or a related party; or

(IV) the third party's involvement in a transaction changing the corporate structure, or in a loan or other financial transaction affecting the financial condition, of the debtor or a related party, including but not limited to—

(aa) involvement in providing financing (debt or equity), or advice to an entity involved in such a transaction; or

(bb) acquiring or selling a financial interest in an entity as part of such a transaction.

(iii) As used in this subparagraph, the term "related party" means—

(I) a past or present affiliate of the debtor;

(II) a predecessor in interest of the debtor; or

(III) any entity that owned a financial interest in—

(aa) the debtor;

(bb) a past or present affiliate of the debtor; or

(cc) a predecessor in interest of the debtor.

(B) Subject to subsection (h), if, under a plan of reorganization, a kind of demand described in such plan is to be paid in whole or in part by a trust described in paragraph (2)(B)(i) in connection with which an injunction described in paragraph (1) is to be implemented, then such injunction shall be valid and enforceable with respect to a demand of such kind made, after such plan is confirmed, against the debtor or debtors involved, or against a third party described in subparagraph (A)(ii), if—

(i) as part of the proceedings leading to issuance of such injunction, the court appoints a legal representative for the purpose of protecting the rights of persons that might subsequently assert demands of such kind, and

(ii) the court determines, before entering the order confirming such plan, that identifying such debtor or debtors, or such third party (by name or as part of an identifiable group), in such injunction with respect to such demands for purposes of this subparagraph is fair and equitable with respect to the persons that might subsequently assert such demands, in light of the benefits provided, or to be provided, to such trust on behalf of such debtor or debtors or such third party.

(5) In this subsection, the term "demand" means a demand for payment, present or future, that—

(A) was not a claim during the proceedings leading to the confirmation of a plan of reorganization;

(B) arises out of the same or similar conduct or events that gave rise to the claims addressed by the injunction issued under paragraph (1); and

(C) pursuant to the plan, is to be paid by a trust described in paragraph (2)(B)(i).

(6) Paragraph (3)(A)(i) does not bar an action taken by or at the direction of an appellate court on appeal of an injunction issued under paragraph (1) or of the order of confirmation that relates to the injunction.

(7) This subsection does not affect the operation of section 1144 or the power of the district court to refer a proceeding under section 157 of title 28 or any reference of a proceeding made prior to the date of the enactment of this subsection.

(h) Application to Existing Injunctions.—For purposes of subsection (g)—

(1) subject to paragraph (2), if an injunction of the kind described in subsection (g)(1)(B) was issued before the date of the enactment of this Act, as part of a plan of reorganization confirmed by an order entered before such date, then the injunction shall be considered to meet the requirements of subsection (g)(2)(B) for purposes of subsection (g)(2)(A), and to satisfy subsection (g)(4)(A)(ii), if—

     (A) the court determined at the time the plan was confirmed that the plan was fair and equitable in accordance with the requirements of section 1129(b);

     (B) as part of the proceedings leading to issuance of such injunction and confirmation of such plan, the court had appointed a legal representative for the purpose of protecting the rights of persons that might subsequently assert demands described in subsection (g)(4)(B) with respect to such plan; and

     (C) such legal representative did not object to confirmation of such plan or issuance of such injunction; and

(2) for purposes of paragraph (1), if a trust described in subsection (g)(2)(B)(i) is subject to a court order on the date of the enactment of this Act staying such trust from settling or paying further claims—

     (A) the requirements of subsection (g)(2)(B)(ii)(V) shall not apply with respect to such trust until such stay is lifted or dissolved; and

     (B) if such trust meets such requirements on the date such stay is lifted or dissolved, such trust shall be considered to have met such requirements continuously from the date of the enactment of this Act.

(i) The willful failure of a creditor to credit payments received under a plan confirmed under this title, unless the order confirming the plan is revoked, the plan is in default, or the creditor has not received payments required to be made under the plan in the manner required by the plan (including crediting the amounts required under the plan), shall constitute a violation of an injunction under subsection (a)(2) if the act of the creditor to collect and failure to credit payments in the manner required by the plan caused material injury to the debtor.

(j) Subsection (a)(2) does not operate as an injunction against an act by a creditor that is the holder of a secured claim, if—

(1) such creditor retains a security interest in real property that is the principal residence of the debtor;

(2) such act is in the ordinary course of business between the creditor and the debtor; and

(3) such act is limited to seeking or obtaining periodic payments associated with a valid security interest in lieu of pursuit of in rem relief to enforce the lien.

(k)(1) The disclosures required under subsection (c)(2) shall consist of the disclosure statement described in paragraph (3), completed as required in that paragraph, together with the agreement specified in subsection (c), statement, declaration, motion and order described, respectively, in paragraphs (4) through (8), and shall be the only disclosures required in connection with entering into such agreement.

(2) Disclosures made under paragraph (1) shall be made clearly and conspicuously and in writing. The terms "Amount Reaffirmed" and "Annual Percentage Rate" shall be disclosed more conspicuously than other terms, data or information provided in connection with this disclosure, except that the phrases "Before agreeing to reaffirm a debt, review these important disclosures" and "Summary of Reaffirmation Agreement" may be equally conspicuous. Disclosures may be made in a different order and may use terminology different from that set forth in paragraphs (2) through (8), except that the terms "Amount Reaffirmed" and "Annual Percentage Rate" must be used where indicated.

(3) The disclosure statement required under this paragraph shall consist of the following:

(A) The statement: "Part A: Before agreeing to reaffirm a debt, review these important disclosures:";

(B) Under the heading "Summary of Reaffirmation Agreement", the statement: "This Summary is made pursuant to the requirements of the Bankruptcy Code";

(C) The "Amount Reaffirmed", using that term, which shall be—

(i) the total amount of debt that the debtor agrees to reaffirm by entering into an agreement of the kind specified in subsection (c), and

(ii) the total of any fees and costs accrued as of the date of the disclosure statement, related to such total amount.

(D) In conjunction with the disclosure of the "Amount Reaffirmed", the statements—

(i) "The amount of debt you have agreed to reaffirm"; and

(ii) "Your credit agreement may obligate you to pay additional amounts which may come due after the date of this disclosure. Consult your credit agreement.".

(E) The "Annual Percentage Rate", using that term, which shall be disclosed as—

(i) if, at the time the petition is filed, the debt is an extension of credit under an open end credit plan, as the terms "credit" and "open end credit plan" are defined in section 103 of the Truth in Lending Act, then—

(I) the annual percentage rate determined under paragraphs (5) and (6) of section 127(b) of the Truth in Lending Act, as applicable, as disclosed to the debtor in the most recent periodic statement prior to entering into an agreement of the kind specified in subsection (c) or, if no such periodic statement has been given to the debtor during the prior 6 months, the annual percentage rate as it would have been so disclosed at the time the disclosure statement is given to the debtor, or to the extent this annual percentage rate is not readily available or not applicable, then

(II) the simple interest rate applicable to the amount reaffirmed as of the date the disclosure statement is given to the debtor, or if different simple interest rates apply to different balances, the simple interest rate applicable to each such balance, identifying the amount of each such balance included in the amount reaffirmed, or

(III) if the entity making the disclosure elects, to disclose the annual percentage rate under subclause (I) and the simple interest rate under subclause (II); or

(ii) if, at the time the petition is filed, the debt is an extension of credit other than under an open end credit plan, as the terms "credit" and "open end credit plan" are defined in section 103 of the Truth in Lending Act, then—

(I) the annual percentage rate under section 128(a)(4) of the Truth in Lending Act, as disclosed to the debtor in the most recent disclosure statement given to the debtor prior to the entering into an agreement of the kind specified in subsection (c) with respect to the debt, or, if no such disclosure statement was given to the debtor, the annual percentage rate as it would have been so disclosed at the time the disclosure statement is given to the debtor, or to the extent this annual percentage rate is not readily available or not applicable, then

(II) the simple interest rate applicable to the amount reaffirmed as of the date the disclosure statement is given to the debtor, or if different simple interest rates apply to different balances, the simple interest rate applicable to each such balance, identifying the amount of such balance included in the amount reaffirmed, or

(III) if the entity making the disclosure elects, to disclose the annual percentage rate under (I) and the simple interest rate under (II).

(F) If the underlying debt transaction was disclosed as a variable rate transaction on the most recent disclosure given under the Truth in Lending Act, by stating "The interest rate on

1237

your loan may be a variable interest rate which changes from time to time, so that the annual percentage rate disclosed here may be higher or lower."

(G) If the debt is secured by a security interest which has not been waived in whole or in part or determined to be void by a final order of the court at the time of the disclosure, by disclosing that a security interest or lien in goods or property is asserted over some or all of the debts the debtor is reaffirming and listing the items and their original purchase price that are subject to the asserted security interest, or if not a purchase-money security interest then listing by items or types and the original amount of the loan.

(H) At the election of the creditor, a statement of the repayment schedule using 1 or a combination of the following—

    (i) by making the statement: "Your first payment in the amount of $___ is due on ___ but the future payment amount may be different. Consult your reaffirmation agreement or credit agreement, as applicable.", and stating the amount of the first payment and the due date of that payment in the places provided;

    (ii) by making the statement: "Your payment schedule will be:", and describing the repayment schedule with the number, amount, and due dates or period of payments scheduled to repay the debts reaffirmed to the extent then known by the disclosing party; or

    (iii) by describing the debtor's repayment obligations with reasonable specificity to the extent then known by the disclosing party.

(I) The following statement: "Note: When this disclosure refers to what a creditor 'may' do, it does not use the word 'may' to give the creditor specific permission. The word 'may' is used to tell you what might occur if the law permits the creditor to take the action. If you have questions about your reaffirming a debt or what the law requires, consult with the attorney who helped you negotiate this agreement reaffirming a debt. If you don't have an attorney helping you, the judge will explain the effect of your reaffirming a debt when the hearing on the reaffirmation agreement is held.".

(J)(i) The following additional statements:

"Reaffirming a debt is a serious financial decision. The law requires you to take certain steps to make sure the decision is in your best interest. If these steps are not completed, the reaffirmation agreement is not effective, even though you have signed it.

"1. Read the disclosures in this Part A carefully. Consider the decision to reaffirm carefully. Then, if you want to reaffirm, sign the reaffirmation agreement in Part B (or you may use a separate agreement you and your creditor agree on).

"2. Complete and sign Part D and be sure you can afford to make the payments you are agreeing to make and have received a copy of the disclosure statement and a completed and signed reaffirmation agreement.

"3. If you were represented by an attorney during the negotiation of your reaffirmation agreement, the attorney must have signed the certification in Part C.

"4. If you were not represented by an attorney during the negotiation of your reaffirmation agreement, you must have completed and signed Part E.

"5. The original of this disclosure must be filed with the court by you or your creditor. If a separate reaffirmation agreement (other than the one in Part B) has been signed, it must be attached.

"6. If you were represented by an attorney during the negotiation of your reaffirmation agreement, your reaffirmation agreement becomes effective upon filing with the court unless the reaffirmation is presumed to be an undue hardship as explained in Part D.

"7. If you were not represented by an attorney during the negotiation of your reaffirmation agreement, it will not be effective unless the court approves it. The court will notify you of the hearing on your reaffirmation agreement. You must attend this hearing in bankruptcy court where the judge will review your reaffirmation agreement. The bankruptcy court must approve your reaffirmation agreement as consistent with your best interests, except that no court approval is required if your reaffirmation agreement is for a consumer debt secured by a mortgage, deed of trust, security deed, or other lien on your real property, like your home.

"Your right to rescind (cancel) your reaffirmation agreement. You may rescind (cancel) your reaffirmation agreement at any time before the bankruptcy court enters a discharge order, or before the expiration of the 60-day period that begins on the date your reaffirmation agreement is filed with the court, whichever occurs later. To rescind (cancel) your reaffirmation agreement, you must notify the creditor that your reaffirmation agreement is rescinded (or canceled).

"What are your obligations if you reaffirm the debt? A reaffirmed debt remains your personal legal obligation. It is not discharged in your bankruptcy case. That means that if you default on your reaffirmed debt after your bankruptcy case is over, your creditor may be able to take your property or your wages. Otherwise, your obligations will be determined by the reaffirmation agreement which may have changed the terms of the original agreement. For example, if you are reaffirming an open end credit agreement, the creditor may be permitted by that agreement or applicable law to change the terms of that agreement in the future under certain conditions.

"Are you required to enter into a reaffirmation agreement by any law? No, you are not required to reaffirm a debt by any law. Only agree to reaffirm a debt if it is in your best interest. Be sure you can afford the payments you agree to make.

"What if your creditor has a security interest or lien? Your bankruptcy discharge does not eliminate any lien on your property. A 'lien' is often referred to as a security interest, deed of trust, mortgage or security deed. Even if you do not reaffirm and your personal liability on the debt is discharged, because of the lien your creditor may still have the right to take the property securing the lien if you do not pay the debt or default on it. If the lien is on an item of personal property that is exempt under your State's law or that the trustee has abandoned, you may be able to redeem the item rather than reaffirm the debt. To redeem, you must make a single payment to the creditor equal to the amount of the allowed secured claim, as agreed by the parties or determined by the court.".

(ii) In the case of a reaffirmation under subsection (m)(2), numbered paragraph 6 in the disclosures required by clause (i) of this subparagraph shall read as follows:

"6. If you were represented by an attorney during the negotiation of your reaffirmation agreement, your reaffirmation agreement becomes effective upon filing with the court.".

(4) The form of such agreement required under this paragraph shall consist of the following:

"Part B: Reaffirmation Agreement. I (we) agree to reaffirm the debts arising under the credit agreement described below.

"Brief description of credit agreement:

"Description of any changes to the credit agreement made as part of this reaffirmation agreement:

"Signature: Date:

"Borrower:

"Co-borrower, if also reaffirming these debts:

"Accepted by creditor:

"Date of creditor acceptance:".

(5)   The declaration shall consist of the following:

(A)   The following certification:

"Part C: Certification by Debtor's Attorney (If Any).

"I hereby certify that (1) this agreement represents a fully informed and voluntary agreement by the debtor; (2) this agreement does not impose an undue hardship on the debtor or any dependent of the debtor; and (3) I have fully advised the debtor of the legal effect and consequences of this agreement and any default under this agreement.

"Signature of Debtor's Attorney: Date:".

(B)   If a presumption of undue hardship has been established with respect to such agreement, such certification shall state that, in the opinion of the attorney, the debtor is able to make the payment.

(C)   In the case of a reaffirmation agreement under subsection (m)(2), subparagraph (B) is not applicable.

(6)(A)   The statement in support of such agreement, which the debtor shall sign and date prior to filing with the court, shall consist of the following:

"Part D: Debtor's Statement in Support of Reaffirmation Agreement.

"1.   I believe this reaffirmation agreement will not impose an undue hardship on my dependents or me. I can afford to make the payments on the reaffirmed debt because my monthly income (take home pay plus any other income received) is \$___, and my actual current monthly expenses including monthly payments on post-bankruptcy debt and other reaffirmation agreements total \$___, leaving \$___ to make the required payments on this reaffirmed debt. I understand that if my income less my monthly expenses does not leave enough to make the payments, this reaffirmation agreement is presumed to be an undue hardship on me and must be reviewed by the court. However, this presumption may be overcome if I explain to the satisfaction of the court how I can afford to make the payments here: ___.

"2.   I received a copy of the Reaffirmation Disclosure Statement in Part A and a completed and signed reaffirmation agreement.".

(B)   Where the debtor is represented by an attorney and is reaffirming a debt owed to a creditor defined in section 19(b)(1)(A)(iv) of the Federal Reserve Act, the statement of support of the reaffirmation agreement, which the debtor shall sign and date prior to filing with the court, shall consist of the following:

"I believe this reaffirmation agreement is in my financial interest. I can afford to make the payments on the reaffirmed debt. I received a copy of the Reaffirmation Disclosure Statement in Part A and a completed and signed reaffirmation agreement.".

(7)   The motion that may be used if approval of such agreement by the court is required in order for it to be effective, shall be signed and dated by the movant and shall consist of the following:

"Part E: Motion for Court Approval (To be completed only if the debtor is not represented by an attorney.). I (we), the debtor(s), affirm the following to be true and correct:

"I am not represented by an attorney in connection with this reaffirmation agreement.

"I believe this reaffirmation agreement is in my best interest based on the income and expenses I have disclosed in my Statement in Support of this reaffirmation agreement, and because (provide any additional relevant reasons the court should consider):

"Therefore, I ask the court for an order approving this reaffirmation agreement.".

(8)   The court order, which may be used to approve such agreement, shall consist of the following:

"Court Order: The court grants the debtor's motion and approves the reaffirmation agreement described above.".

(*l*)   Notwithstanding any other provision of this title the following shall apply:

(1)   A creditor may accept payments from a debtor before and after the filing of an agreement of the kind specified in subsection (c) with the court.

(2)   A creditor may accept payments from a debtor under such agreement that the creditor believes in good faith to be effective.

(3)   The requirements of subsections (c)(2) and (k) shall be satisfied if disclosures required under those subsections are given in good faith.

(m)(1)   Until 60 days after an agreement of the kind specified in subsection (c) is filed with the court (or such additional period as the court, after notice and a hearing and for cause, orders before the expiration of such period), it shall be presumed that such agreement is an undue hardship on the debtor if the debtor's monthly income less the debtor's monthly expenses as shown on the debtor's completed and signed statement in support of such agreement required under subsection (k)(6)(A) is less than the scheduled payments on the reaffirmed debt. This presumption shall be reviewed by the court. The presumption may be rebutted in writing by the debtor if the statement includes an explanation that identifies additional sources of funds to make the payments as agreed upon under the terms of such agreement. If the presumption is not rebutted to the satisfaction of the court, the court may disapprove such agreement. No agreement shall be disapproved without notice and a hearing to the debtor and creditor, and such hearing shall be concluded before the entry of the debtor's discharge.

(2)   This subsection does not apply to reaffirmation agreements where the creditor is a credit union, as defined in section 19(b)(1)(A)(iv) of the Federal Reserve Act.

§ 525.   Protection against discriminatory treatment

(a)   Except as provided in the Perishable Agricultural Commodities Act, 1930, the Packers and Stockyards Act, 1921, and section 1 of the Act entitled "An Act making appropriations for the Department of Agriculture for the fiscal year ending June 30, 1944, and for other purposes," approved July 12, 1943, a governmental unit may not deny, revoke, suspend, or refuse to renew a license, permit, charter, franchise, or other similar grant to, condition such a grant to, discriminate with respect to such a grant against, deny employment to, terminate the employment of, or discriminate with respect to employment against, a person that is or has been a debtor under this title or a bankrupt or a debtor under the Bankruptcy Act, or another person with whom such bankrupt or debtor has been associated, solely because such bankrupt or debtor is or has been a debtor under this title or a bankrupt or debtor under the Bankruptcy Act, has been insolvent before the commencement of the case under this title, or during the case but before the debtor is granted or denied a discharge, or has not paid a debt that is dischargeable in the case under this title or that was discharged under the Bankruptcy Act.

(b)   No private employer may terminate the employment of, or discriminate with respect to employment against, an individual who is or has been a debtor under this title, a debtor or bankrupt under the Bankruptcy Act, or an individual associated with such debtor or bankrupt, solely because such debtor or bankrupt—

(1)   is or has been a debtor under this title or a debtor or bankrupt under the Bankruptcy Act;

(2)   has been insolvent before the commencement of a case under this title or during the case but before the grant or denial of a discharge; or

(3)   has not paid a debt that is dischargeable in a case under this title or that was discharged under the Bankruptcy Act.

(c)(1)   A governmental unit that operates a student grant or loan program and a person engaged in a business that includes the making of loans guaranteed or insured under a student loan program may not deny a student grant, loan, loan guarantee, or loan insurance to a person that is or has been a debtor under this title or a bankrupt or debtor under the Bankruptcy Act, or another person with whom the debtor or bankrupt has been associated, because the debtor or bankrupt is or has been a debtor under this title or a bankrupt or debtor under the Bankruptcy Act, has been insolvent before the commencement of a case under this title or during the pendency of the case but before the debtor is granted or denied a discharge, or has not paid a debt that is dischargeable in the case under this title or that was discharged under the Bankruptcy Act.

  (2) In this section, "student loan program" means any program operated under title IV of the Higher Education Act of 1965 or a similar program operated under State or local law.

§ 526. Restrictions on debt relief agencies

  (a) A debt relief agency shall not—

  (1) fail to perform any service that such agency informed an assisted person or prospective assisted person it would provide in connection with a case or proceeding under this title;

  (2) make any statement, or counsel or advise any assisted person or prospective assisted person to make a statement in a document filed in a case or proceeding under this title, that is untrue or misleading, or that upon the exercise of reasonable care, should have been known by such agency to be untrue or misleading;

  (3) misrepresent to any assisted person or prospective assisted person, directly or indirectly, affirmatively or by material omission, with respect to—

    (A) the services that such agency will provide to such person; or

    (B) the benefits and risks that may result if such person becomes a debtor in a case under this title; or

  (4) advise an assisted person or prospective assisted person to incur more debt in contemplation of such person filing a case under this title or to pay an attorney or bankruptcy petition preparer a fee or charge for services performed as part of preparing for or representing a debtor in a case under this title.

  (b) Any waiver by any assisted person of any protection or right provided under this section shall not be enforceable against the debtor by any Federal or State court or any other person, but may be enforced against a debt relief agency.

  (c)(1) Any contract for bankruptcy assistance between a debt relief agency and an assisted person that does not comply with the material requirements of this section, section 527, or section 528 shall be void and may not be enforced by any Federal or State court or by any other person, other than such assisted person.

  (2) Any debt relief agency shall be liable to an assisted person in the amount of any fees or charges in connection with providing bankruptcy assistance to such person that such debt relief agency has received, for actual damages, and for reasonable attorneys' fees and costs if such agency is found, after notice and a hearing, to have—

    (A) intentionally or negligently failed to comply with any provision of this section, section 527, or section 528 with respect to a case or proceeding under this title for such assisted person;

    (B) provided bankruptcy assistance to an assisted person in a case or proceeding under this title that is dismissed or converted to a case under another chapter of this title because of such agency's intentional or negligent failure to file any required document including those specified in section 521; or

    (C) intentionally or negligently disregarded the material requirements of this title or the Federal Rules of Bankruptcy Procedure applicable to such agency.

  (3) In addition to such other remedies as are provided under State law, whenever the chief law enforcement officer of a State, or an official or agency designated by a State, has reason to believe that any person has violated or is violating this section, the State—

    (A) may bring an action to enjoin such violation;

    (B) may bring an action on behalf of its residents to recover the actual damages of assisted persons arising from such violation, including any liability under paragraph (2); and

(C) in the case of any successful action under subparagraph (A) or (B), shall be awarded the costs of the action and reasonable attorneys' fees as determined by the court.

(4) The district courts of the United States for districts located in the State shall have concurrent jurisdiction of any action under subparagraph (A) or (B) of paragraph (3).

(5) Notwithstanding any other provision of Federal law and in addition to any other remedy provided under Federal or State law, if the court, on its own motion or on the motion of the United States trustee or the debtor, finds that a person intentionally violated this section, or engaged in a clear and consistent pattern or practice of violating this section, the court may—

(A) enjoin the violation of such section; or

(B) impose an appropriate civil penalty against such person.

(d) No provision of this section, section 527, or section 528 shall—

(1) annul, alter, affect, or exempt any person subject to such sections from complying with any law of any State except to the extent that such law is inconsistent with those sections, and then only to the extent of the inconsistency; or

(2) be deemed to limit or curtail the authority or ability—

(A) of a State or subdivision or instrumentality thereof, to determine and enforce qualifications for the practice of law under the laws of that State; or

(B) of a Federal court to determine and enforce the qualifications for the practice of law before that court.

§ 527. Disclosures

(a) A debt relief agency providing bankruptcy assistance to an assisted person shall provide—

(1) the written notice required under section 342(b)(1); and

(2) to the extent not covered in the written notice described in paragraph (1), and not later than 3 business days after the first date on which a debt relief agency first offers to provide any bankruptcy assistance services to an assisted person, a clear and conspicuous written notice advising assisted persons that—

(A) all information that the assisted person is required to provide with a petition and thereafter during a case under this title is required to be complete, accurate, and truthful;

(B) all assets and all liabilities are required to be completely and accurately disclosed in the documents filed to commence the case, and the replacement value of each asset as defined in section 506 must be stated in those documents where requested after reasonable inquiry to establish such value;

(C) current monthly income, the amounts specified in section 707(b)(2), and, in a case under chapter 13 of this title, disposable income (determined in accordance with section 707(b)(2)), are required to be stated after reasonable inquiry; and

(D) information that an assisted person provides during their case may be audited pursuant to this title, and that failure to provide such information may result in dismissal of the case under this title or other sanction, including a criminal sanction.

(b) A debt relief agency providing bankruptcy assistance to an assisted person shall provide each assisted person at the same time as the notices required under subsection (a)(1) the following statement, to the extent applicable, or one substantially similar. The statement shall be clear and conspicuous and shall be in a single document separate from other documents or notices provided to the assisted person:

"IMPORTANT INFORMATION ABOUT BANKRUPTCY ASSISTANCE SERVICES FROM AN ATTORNEY OR BANKRUPTCY PETITION PREPARER.

"If you decide to seek bankruptcy relief, you can represent yourself, you can hire an attorney to represent you, or you can get help in some localities from a bankruptcy petition preparer who is not an attorney. THE LAW REQUIRES AN ATTORNEY OR BANKRUPTCY PETITION PREPARER TO GIVE YOU A WRITTEN CONTRACT SPECIFYING WHAT THE ATTORNEY OR BANKRUPTCY PETITION PREPARER WILL DO FOR YOU AND HOW MUCH IT WILL COST. Ask to see the contract before you hire anyone.

"The following information helps you understand what must be done in a routine bankruptcy case to help you evaluate how much service you need. Although bankruptcy can be complex, many cases are routine.

"Before filing a bankruptcy case, either you or your attorney should analyze your eligibility for different forms of debt relief available under the Bankruptcy Code and which form of relief is most likely to be beneficial for you. Be sure you understand the relief you can obtain and its limitations. To file a bankruptcy case, documents called a Petition, Schedules, and Statement of Financial Affairs, and in some cases a Statement of Intention, need to be prepared correctly and filed with the bankruptcy court. You will have to pay a filing fee to the bankruptcy court. Once your case starts, you will have to attend the required first meeting of creditors where you may be questioned by a court official called a 'trustee' and by creditors.

"If you choose to file a chapter 7 case, you may be asked by a creditor to reaffirm a debt. You may want help deciding whether to do so. A creditor is not permitted to coerce you into reaffirming your debts.

"If you choose to file a chapter 13 case in which you repay your creditors what you can afford over 3 to 5 years, you may also want help with preparing your chapter 13 plan and with the confirmation hearing on your plan which will be before a bankruptcy judge.

"If you select another type of relief under the Bankruptcy Code other than chapter 7 or chapter 13, you will want to find out what should be done from someone familiar with that type of relief.

"Your bankruptcy case may also involve litigation. You are generally permitted to represent yourself in litigation in bankruptcy court, but only attorneys, not bankruptcy petition preparers, can give you legal advice.".

(c) Except to the extent the debt relief agency provides the required information itself after reasonably diligent inquiry of the assisted person or others so as to obtain such information reasonably accurately for inclusion on the petition, schedules or statement of financial affairs, a debt relief agency providing bankruptcy assistance to an assisted person, to the extent permitted by nonbankruptcy law, shall provide each assisted person at the time required for the notice required under subsection (a)(1) reasonably sufficient information (which shall be provided in a clear and conspicuous writing) to the assisted person on how to provide all the information the assisted person is required to provide under this title pursuant to section 521, including—

    (1) how to value assets at replacement value, determine current monthly income, the amounts specified in section 707(b)(2) and, in a chapter 13 case, how to determine disposable income in accordance with section 707(b)(2) and related calculations;

    (2) how to complete the list of creditors, including how to determine what amount is owed and what address for the creditor should be shown; and

    (3) how to determine what property is exempt and how to value exempt property at replacement value as defined in section 506.

(d) A debt relief agency shall maintain a copy of the notices required under subsection (a) of this section for 2 years after the date on which the notice is given the assisted person.

§ 528. Requirements for debt relief agencies

(a) A debt relief agency shall—

    (1) not later than 5 business days after the first date on which such agency provides any bankruptcy assistance services to an assisted person, but prior to such assisted person's petition under this title being filed, execute a written contract with such assisted person that explains clearly and conspicuously—

    (A) the services such agency will provide to such assisted person; and

    (B) the fees or charges for such services, and the terms of payment;

  (2) provide the assisted person with a copy of the fully executed and completed contract;

  (3) clearly and conspicuously disclose in any advertisement of bankruptcy assistance services or of the benefits of bankruptcy directed to the general public (whether in general media, seminars or specific mailings, telephonic or electronic messages, or otherwise) that the services or benefits are with respect to bankruptcy relief under this title; and

  (4) clearly and conspicuously use the following statement in such advertisement: "We are a debt relief agency. We help people file for bankruptcy relief under the Bankruptcy Code." or a substantially similar statement.

(b)(1) An advertisement of bankruptcy assistance services or of the benefits of bankruptcy directed to the general public includes—

  (A) descriptions of bankruptcy assistance in connection with a chapter 13 plan whether or not chapter 13 is specifically mentioned in such advertisement; and

  (B) statements such as "federally supervised repayment plan" or "Federal debt restructuring help" or other similar statements that could lead a reasonable consumer to believe that debt counseling was being offered when in fact the services were directed to providing bankruptcy assistance with a chapter 13 plan or other form of bankruptcy relief under this title.

  (2) An advertisement, directed to the general public, indicating that the debt relief agency provides assistance with respect to credit defaults, mortgage foreclosures, eviction proceedings, excessive debt, debt collection pressure, or inability to pay any consumer debt shall—

  (A) disclose clearly and conspicuously in such advertisement that the assistance may involve bankruptcy relief under this title; and

  (B) include the following statement: "We are a debt relief agency. We help people file for bankruptcy relief under the Bankruptcy Code." or a substantially similar statement.

SUBCHAPTER III—THE ESTATE

§ 541. Property of the estate

  (a) The commencement of a case under section 301, 302, or 303 of this title creates an estate. Such estate is comprised of all the following property, wherever located and by whomever held:

  (1) Except as provided in subsections (b) and (c)(2) of this section, all legal or equitable interests of the debtor in property as of the commencement of the case.

  (2) All interests of the debtor and the debtor's spouse in community property as of the commencement of the case that is—

  (A) under the sole, equal, or joint management and control of the debtor; or

  (B) liable for an allowable claim against the debtor, or for both an allowable claim against the debtor and an allowable claim against the debtor's spouse, to the extent that such interest is so liable.

  (3) Any interest in property that the trustee recovers under section 329(b), 363(n), 543, 550, 553, or 723 of this title.

  (4) Any interest in property preserved for the benefit of or ordered transferred to the estate under section 510(c) or 551 of this title.

  (5) Any interest in property that would have been property of the estate if such interest had been an interest of the debtor on the date of the filing of the petition, and that the debtor acquires or becomes entitled to acquire within 180 days after such date—

  (A) by bequest, devise, or inheritance;

(B) as a result of a property settlement agreement with the debtor's spouse, or of an interlocutory or final divorce decree; or

(C) as a beneficiary of a life insurance policy or of a death benefit plan.

(6) Proceeds, product, offspring, rents, or profits of or from property of the estate, except such as are earnings from services performed by an individual debtor after the commencement of the case.

(7) Any interest in property that the estate acquires after the commencement of the case.

(b) Property of the estate does not include—

(1) any power that the debtor may exercise solely for the benefit of an entity other than the debtor;

(2) any interest of the debtor as a lessee under a lease of nonresidential real property that has terminated at the expiration of the stated term of such lease before the commencement of the case under this title, and ceases to include any interest of the debtor as a lessee under a lease of nonresidential real property that has terminated at the expiration of the stated term of such lease during the case;

(3) any eligibility of the debtor to participate in programs authorized under the Higher Education Act of 1965 (20 U.S.C. 1001 et seq.; 42 U.S.C. 2751 et seq.), or any accreditation status or State licensure of the debtor as an educational institution;

(4) any interest of the debtor in liquid or gaseous hydrocarbons to the extent that—

(A)(i) the debtor has transferred or has agreed to transfer such interest pursuant to a farmout agreement or any written agreement directly related to a farmout agreement; and

(ii) but for the operation of this paragraph, the estate could include the interest referred to in clause (i) only by virtue of section 365 or 544(a)(3) of this title; or

(B)(i) the debtor has transferred such interest pursuant to a written conveyance of a production payment to an entity that does not participate in the operation of the property from which such production payment is transferred; and

(ii) but for the operation of this paragraph, the estate could include the interest referred to in clause (i) only by virtue of section 365 or 542 of this title;

(5) funds placed in an education individual retirement account (as defined in section 530(b)(1) of the Internal Revenue Code of 1986) not later than 365 days before the date of the filing of the petition in a case under this title, but—

(A) only if the designated beneficiary of such account was a child, stepchild, grandchild, or stepgrandchild of the debtor for the taxable year for which funds were placed in such account;

(B) only to the extent that such funds—

(i) are not pledged or promised to any entity in connection with any extension of credit; and

(ii) are not excess contributions (as described in section 4973(e) of the Internal Revenue Code of 1986); and

(C) in the case of funds placed in all such accounts having the same designated beneficiary not earlier than 720 days nor later than 365 days before such date, only so much of such funds as does not exceed $7,575;

(6) funds used to purchase a tuition credit or certificate or contributed to an account in accordance with section 529(b)(1)(A) of the Internal Revenue Code of 1986 under a qualified State tuition program (as defined in section 529(b)(1) of such Code) not later than 365 days before the date of the filing of the petition in a case under this title, but—

(A) only if the designated beneficiary of the amounts paid or contributed to such tuition program was a child, stepchild, grandchild, or stepgrandchild of the debtor for the taxable year for which funds were paid or contributed;

(B) with respect to the aggregate amount paid or contributed to such program having the same designated beneficiary, only so much of such amount as does not exceed the total contributions permitted under section 529(b)(6) of such Code with respect to such beneficiary, as adjusted beginning on the date of the filing of the petition in a case under this title by the annual increase or decrease (rounded to the nearest tenth of 1 percent) in the education expenditure category of the Consumer Price Index prepared by the Department of Labor; and

(C) in the case of funds paid or contributed to such program having the same designated beneficiary not earlier than 720 days nor later than 365 days before such date, only so much of such funds as does not exceed $7,575;

(7) any amount—

(A) withheld by an employer from the wages of employees for payment as contributions—

(i) to—

(I) an employee benefit plan that is subject to title I of the Employee Retirement Income Security Act of 1974 or under an employee benefit plan which is a governmental plan under section 414(d) of the Internal Revenue Code of 1986;

(II) a deferred compensation plan under section 457 of the Internal Revenue Code of 1986; or

(III) a tax-deferred annuity under section 403(b) of the Internal Revenue Code of 1986;

except that such amount under this subparagraph shall not constitute disposable income as defined in section 1325(b)(2); or

(ii) to a health insurance plan regulated by State law whether or not subject to such title; or

(B) received by an employer from employees for payment as contributions—

(i) to—

(I) an employee benefit plan that is subject to title I of the Employee Retirement Income Security Act of 1974 or under an employee benefit plan which is a governmental plan under section 414(d) of the Internal Revenue Code of 1986;

(II) a deferred compensation plan under section 457 of the Internal Revenue Code of 1986; or

(III) a tax-deferred annuity under section 403(b) of the Internal Revenue Code of 1986;

except that such amount under this subparagraph shall not constitute disposable income, as defined in section 1325(b)(2); or

(ii) to a health insurance plan regulated by State law whether or not subject to such title;

(8) subject to subchapter III of chapter 5, any interest of the debtor in property where the debtor pledged or sold tangible personal property (other than securities or written or printed evidences of indebtedness or title) as collateral for a loan or advance of money given by a person licensed under law to make such loans or advances, where—

(A) the tangible personal property is in the possession of the pledgee or transferee;

(B) the debtor has no obligation to repay the money, redeem the collateral, or buy back the property at a stipulated price; and

(C) neither the debtor nor the trustee have exercised any right to redeem provided under the contract or State law, in a timely manner as provided under State law and section 108(b);

    (9) any interest in cash or cash equivalents that constitute proceeds of a sale by the debtor of a money order that is made—

        (A) on or after the date that is 14 days prior to the date on which the petition is filed; and

        (B) under an agreement with a money order issuer that prohibits the commingling of such proceeds with property of the debtor (notwithstanding that, contrary to the agreement, the proceeds may have been commingled with property of the debtor),

unless the money order issuer had not taken action, prior to the filing of the petition, to require compliance with the prohibition; or

    (10) funds placed in an account of a qualified ABLE program (as defined in section 529A(b) of the Internal Revenue Code of 1986) not later than 365 days before the date of the filing of the petition in a case under this title, but—

        (A) only if the designated beneficiary of such account was a child, stepchild, grandchild, or stepgrandchild of the debtor for the taxable year for which funds were placed in such account;

        (B) only to the extent that such funds—

            (i) are not pledged or promised to any entity in connection with any extension of credit; and

            (ii) are not excess contributions (as described in section 4973(h) of the Internal Revenue Code of 1986); and

        (C) in the case of funds placed in all such accounts having the same designated beneficiary not earlier than 720 days nor later than 365 days before such date, only so much of such funds as does not exceed $7,575.

Paragraph (4) shall not be construed to exclude from the estate any consideration the debtor retains, receives, or is entitled to receive for transferring an interest in liquid or gaseous hydrocarbons pursuant to a farmout agreement.

    (c)(1) Except as provided in paragraph (2) of this subsection, an interest of the debtor in property becomes property of the estate under subsection (a)(1), (a)(2), or (a)(5) of this section notwithstanding any provision in an agreement, transfer instrument, or applicable nonbankruptcy law—

        (A) that restricts or conditions transfer of such interest by the debtor; or

        (B) that is conditioned on the insolvency or financial condition of the debtor, on the commencement of a case under this title, or on the appointment of or taking possession by a trustee in a case under this title or a custodian before such commencement, and that effects or gives an option to effect a forfeiture, modification, or termination of the debtor's interest in property.

    (2) A restriction on the transfer of a beneficial interest of the debtor in a trust that is enforceable under applicable nonbankruptcy law is enforceable in a case under this title.

    (d) Property in which the debtor holds, as of the commencement of the case, only legal title and not an equitable interest, such as a mortgage secured by real property, or an interest in such a mortgage, sold by the debtor but as to which the debtor retains legal title to service or supervise the servicing of such mortgage or interest, becomes property of the estate under subsection (a)(1) or (2) of this section only to the extent of the debtor's legal title to such property, but not to the extent of any equitable interest in such property that the debtor does not hold.

    (e) In determining whether any of the relationships specified in paragraph (5)(A) or (6)(A) of subsection (b) exists, a legally adopted child of an individual (and a child who is a member of an individual's household, if placed with such individual by an authorized placement agency for legal adoption by such individual), or a foster child of an individual (if such child has as the child's principal place of abode the home of the debtor and is a member of the debtor's household) shall be treated as a child of such individual by blood.

(f) Notwithstanding any other provision of this title, property that is held by a debtor that is a corporation described in section 501(c)(3) of the Internal Revenue Code of 1986 and exempt from tax under section 501(a) of such Code may be transferred to an entity that is not such a corporation, but only under the same conditions as would apply if the debtor had not filed a case under this title.

§ 542. Turnover of property to the estate

(a) Except as provided in subsection (c) or (d) of this section, an entity, other than a custodian, in possession, custody, or control, during the case, of property that the trustee may use, sell, or lease under section 363 of this title, or that the debtor may exempt under section 522 of this title, shall deliver to the trustee, and account for, such property or the value of such property, unless such property is of inconsequential value or benefit to the estate.

(b) Except as provided in subsection (c) or (d) of this section, an entity that owes a debt that is property of the estate and that is matured, payable on demand, or payable on order, shall pay such debt to, or on the order of, the trustee, except to the extent that such debt may be offset under section 553 of this title against a claim against the debtor.

(c) Except as provided in section 362(a)(7) of this title, an entity that has neither actual notice nor actual knowledge of the commencement of the case concerning the debtor may transfer property of the estate, or pay a debt owing to the debtor, in good faith and other than in the manner specified in subsection (d) of this section, to an entity other than the trustee, with the same effect as to the entity making such transfer or payment as if the case under this title concerning the debtor had not been commenced.

(d) A life insurance company may transfer property of the estate or property of the debtor to such company in good faith, with the same effect with respect to such company as if the case under this title concerning the debtor had not been commenced, if such transfer is to pay a premium or to carry out a nonforfeiture insurance option, and is required to be made automatically, under a life insurance contract with such company that was entered into before the date of the filing of the petition and that is property of the estate.

(e) Subject to any applicable privilege, after notice and a hearing, the court may order an attorney, accountant, or other person that holds recorded information, including books, documents, records, and papers, relating to the debtor's property or financial affairs, to turn over or disclose such recorded information to the trustee.

§ 543. Turnover of property by a custodian

(a) A custodian with knowledge of the commencement of a case under this title concerning the debtor may not make any disbursement from, or take any action in the administration of, property of the debtor, proceeds, product, offspring, rents, or profits of such property, or property of the estate, in the possession, custody, or control of such custodian, except such action as is necessary to preserve such property.

(b) A custodian shall—

　(1)　deliver to the trustee any property of the debtor held by or transferred to such custodian, or proceeds, product, offspring, rents, or profits of such property, that is in such custodian's possession, custody, or control on the date that such custodian acquires knowledge of the commencement of the case; and

　(2)　file an accounting of any property of the debtor, or proceeds, product, offspring, rents, or profits of such property, that, at any time, came into the possession, custody, or control of such custodian.

(c) The court, after notice and a hearing, shall—

　(1)　protect all entities to which a custodian has become obligated with respect to such property or proceeds, product, offspring, rents, or profits of such property;

　(2)　provide for the payment of reasonable compensation for services rendered and costs and expenses incurred by such custodian; and

(3) surcharge such custodian, other than an assignee for the benefit of the debtor's creditors that was appointed or took possession more than 120 days before the date of the filing of the petition, for any improper or excessive disbursement, other than a disbursement that has been made in accordance with applicable law or that has been approved, after notice and a hearing, by a court of competent jurisdiction before the commencement of the case under this title.

(d) After notice and hearing, the bankruptcy court—

(1) may excuse compliance with subsection (a), (b), or (c) of this section if the interests of creditors and, if the debtor is not insolvent, of equity security holders would be better served by permitting a custodian to continue in possession, custody, or control of such property, and

(2) shall excuse compliance with subsections (a) and (b)(1) of this section if the custodian is an assignee for the benefit of the debtor's creditors that was appointed or took possession more than 120 days before the date of the filing of the petition, unless compliance with such subsections is necessary to prevent fraud or injustice.

§ 544. Trustee as lien creditor and as successor to certain creditors and purchasers

(a) The trustee shall have, as of the commencement of the case, and without regard to any knowledge of the trustee or of any creditor, the rights and powers of, or may avoid any transfer of property of the debtor or any obligation incurred by the debtor that is voidable by—

(1) a creditor that extends credit to the debtor at the time of the commencement of the case, and that obtains, at such time and with respect to such credit, a judicial lien on all property on which a creditor on a simple contract could have obtained such a judicial lien, whether or not such a creditor exists;

(2) a creditor that extends credit to the debtor at the time of the commencement of the case, and obtains, at such time and with respect to such credit, an execution against the debtor that is returned unsatisfied at such time, whether or not such a creditor exists; or

(3) a bona fide purchaser of real property, other than fixtures, from the debtor, against whom applicable law permits such transfer to be perfected, that obtains the status of a bona fide purchaser and has perfected such transfer at the time of the commencement of the case, whether or not such a purchaser exists.

(b)(1) Except as provided in paragraph (2), the trustee may avoid any transfer of an interest of the debtor in property or any obligation incurred by the debtor that is voidable under applicable law by a creditor holding an unsecured claim that is allowable under section 502 of this title or that is not allowable only under section 502(e) of this title.

(2) Paragraph (1) shall not apply to a transfer of a charitable contribution (as that term is defined in section 548(d)(3)) that is not covered under section 548(a)(1)(B), by reason of section 548(a)(2). Any claim by any person to recover a transferred contribution described in the preceding sentence under Federal or State law in a Federal or State court shall be preempted by the commencement of the case.

§ 545. Statutory liens

The trustee may avoid the fixing of a statutory lien on property of the debtor to the extent that such lien—

(1) first becomes effective against the debtor—

(A) when a case under this title concerning the debtor is commenced;

(B) when an insolvency proceeding other than under this title concerning the debtor is commenced;

(C) when a custodian is appointed or authorized to take or takes possession;

(D) when the debtor becomes insolvent;

(E) when the debtor's financial condition fails to meet a specified standard; or

(F) at the time of an execution against property of the debtor levied at the instance of an entity other than the holder of such statutory lien;

(2) is not perfected or enforceable at the time of the commencement of the case against a bona fide purchaser that purchases such property at the time of the commencement of the case, whether or not such a purchaser exists, except in any case in which a purchaser is a purchaser described in section 6323 of the Internal Revenue Code of 1986, or in any other similar provision of State or local law;

(3) is for rent; or

(4) is a lien of distress for rent.

§ 546. Limitations on avoiding powers

(a) An action or proceeding under section 544, 545, 547, 548, or 553 of this title may not be commenced after the earlier of—

(1) the later of—

(A) 2 years after the entry of the order for relief; or

(B) 1 year after the appointment or election of the first trustee under section 702, 1104, 1163, 1202, or 1302 of this title if such appointment or such election occurs before the expiration of the period specified in subparagraph (A); or

(2) the time the case is closed or dismissed.

(b)(1) The rights and powers of a trustee under sections 544, 545, and 549 of this title are subject to any generally applicable law that—

(A) permits perfection of an interest in property to be effective against an entity that acquires rights in such property before the date of perfection; or

(B) provides for the maintenance or continuation of perfection of an interest in property to be effective against an entity that acquires rights in such property before the date on which action is taken to effect such maintenance or continuation.

(2) If—

(A) a law described in paragraph (1) requires seizure of such property or commencement of an action to accomplish such perfection, or maintenance or continuation of perfection of an interest in property; and

(B) such property has not been seized or such an action has not been commenced before the date of the filing of the petition;

such interest in such property shall be perfected, or perfection of such interest shall be maintained or continued, by giving notice within the time fixed by such law for such seizure or such commencement.

(c)(1) Except as provided in subsection (d) of this section and in section 507(c), and subject to the prior rights of a holder of a security interest in such goods or the proceeds thereof, the rights and powers of the trustee under sections 544(a), 545, 547, and 549 are subject to the right of a seller of goods that has sold goods to the debtor, in the ordinary course of such seller's business, to reclaim such goods if the debtor has received such goods while insolvent, within 45 days before the date of the commencement of a case under this title, but such seller may not reclaim such goods unless such seller demands in writing reclamation of such goods—

(A) not later than 45 days after the date of receipt of such goods by the debtor; or

(B) not later than 20 days after the date of commencement of the case, if the 45-day period expires after the commencement of the case.

(2) If a seller of goods fails to provide notice in the manner described in paragraph (1), the seller still may assert the rights contained in section 503(b)(9).

(d) In the case of a seller who is a producer of grain sold to a grain storage facility, owned or operated by the debtor, in the ordinary course of such seller's business (as such terms are defined in section 557 of this title) or in the case of a United States fisherman who has caught fish sold to a fish processing facility owned or operated by the debtor in the ordinary course of such fisherman's business, the rights and powers of the trustee under sections 544(a), 545, 547, and 549 of this title are subject to any statutory or common law right of such producer or fisherman to reclaim such grain or fish if the debtor has received such grain or fish while insolvent, but—

    (1) such producer or fisherman may not reclaim any grain or fish unless such producer or fisherman demands, in writing, reclamation of such grain or fish before ten days after receipt thereof by the debtor; and

    (2) the court may deny reclamation to such a producer or fisherman with a right of reclamation that has made such a demand only if the court secures such claim by a lien.

(e) Notwithstanding sections 544, 545, 547, 548(a)(1)(B), and 548(b) of this title, the trustee may not avoid a transfer that is a margin payment, as defined in section 101, 741, or 761 of this title, or settlement payment, as defined in section 101 or 741 of this title, made by or to (or for the benefit of) a commodity broker, forward contract merchant, stockbroker, financial institution, financial participant, or securities clearing agency, or that is a transfer made by or to (or for the benefit of) a commodity broker, forward contract merchant, stockbroker, financial institution, financial participant, or securities clearing agency, in connection with a securities contract, as defined in section 741(7), commodity contract, as defined in section 761(4), or forward contract, that is made before the commencement of the case, except under section 548(a)(1)(A) of this title.

(f) Notwithstanding sections 544, 545, 547, 548(a)(1)(B), and 548(b) of this title, the trustee may not avoid a transfer made by or to (or for the benefit of) a repo participant or financial participant, in connection with a repurchase agreement and that is made before the commencement of the case, except under section 548(a)(1)(A) of this title.

(g) Notwithstanding sections 544, 545, 547, 548(a)(1)(B) and 548(b) of this title, the trustee may not avoid a transfer, made by or to (or for the benefit of) a swap participant or financial participant, under or in connection with any swap agreement and that is made before the commencement of the case, except under section 548(a)(1)(A) of this title.

(h) Notwithstanding the rights and powers of a trustee under sections 544(a), 545, 547, 549, and 553, if the court determines on a motion by the trustee made not later than 120 days after the date of the order for relief in a case under chapter 11 of this title and after notice and a hearing, that a return is in the best interests of the estate, the debtor, with the consent of a creditor and subject to the prior rights of holders of security interests in such goods or the proceeds of such goods, may return goods shipped to the debtor by the creditor before the commencement of the case, and the creditor may offset the purchase price of such goods against any claim of the creditor against the debtor that arose before the commencement of the case.

(i)(1) Notwithstanding paragraphs (2) and (3) of section 545, the trustee may not avoid a warehouseman's lien for storage, transportation, or other costs incidental to the storage and handling of goods.

    (2) The prohibition under paragraph (1) shall be applied in a manner consistent with any State statute applicable to such lien that is similar to section 7–209 of the Uniform Commercial Code, as in effect on the date of enactment of the Bankruptcy Abuse Prevention and Consumer Protection Act of 2005, or any successor to such section 7–209.

(j) Notwithstanding sections 544, 545, 547, 548(a)(1)(B), and 548(b) the trustee may not avoid a transfer made by or to (or for the benefit of) a master netting agreement participant under or in connection with any master netting agreement or any individual contract covered thereby that is made before the commencement of the case, except under section 548(a)(1)(A) and except to the extent that the trustee could otherwise avoid such a transfer made under an individual contract covered by such master netting agreement.

§ 547. Preferences

(a) In this section—

(1) "inventory" means personal property leased or furnished, held for sale or lease, or to be furnished under a contract for service, raw materials, work in process, or materials used or consumed in a business, including farm products such as crops or livestock, held for sale or lease;

(2) "new value" means money or money's worth in goods, services, or new credit, or release by a transferee of property previously transferred to such transferee in a transaction that is neither void nor voidable by the debtor or the trustee under any applicable law, including proceeds of such property, but does not include an obligation substituted for an existing obligation;

(3) "receivable" means right to payment, whether or not such right has been earned by performance; and

(4) a debt for a tax is incurred on the day when such tax is last payable without penalty, including any extension.

(b) Except as provided in subsections (c) and (i) of this section, the trustee may, based on reasonable due diligence in the circumstances of the case and taking into account a party's known or reasonably knowable affirmative defenses under subsection (c), avoid any transfer of an interest of the debtor in property—

(1) to or for the benefit of a creditor;

(2) for or on account of an antecedent debt owed by the debtor before such transfer was made;

(3) made while the debtor was insolvent;

(4) made—

(A) on or within 90 days before the date of the filing of the petition; or

(B) between ninety days and one year before the date of the filing of the petition, if such creditor at the time of such transfer was an insider; and

(5) that enables such creditor to receive more than such creditor would receive if—

(A) the case were a case under chapter 7 of this title;

(B) the transfer had not been made; and

(C) such creditor received payment of such debt to the extent provided by the provisions of this title.

(c) The trustee may not avoid under this section a transfer—

(1) to the extent that such transfer was—

(A) intended by the debtor and the creditor to or for whose benefit such transfer was made to be a contemporaneous exchange for new value given to the debtor; and

(B) in fact a substantially contemporaneous exchange;

(2) to the extent that such transfer was in payment of a debt incurred by the debtor in the ordinary course of business or financial affairs of the debtor and the transferee, and such transfer was—

(A) made in the ordinary course of business or financial affairs of the debtor and the transferee; or

(B) made according to ordinary business terms;

(3) that creates a security interest in property acquired by the debtor—

(A) to the extent such security interest secures new value that was—

(i) given at or after the signing of a security agreement that contains a description of such property as collateral;

    (ii) given by or on behalf of the secured party under such agreement;

    (iii) given to enable the debtor to acquire such property; and

    (iv) in fact used by the debtor to acquire such property; and

  (B) that is perfected on or before 30 days after the debtor receives possession of such property;

(4) to or for the benefit of a creditor, to the extent that, after such transfer, such creditor gave new value to or for the benefit of the debtor—

  (A) not secured by an otherwise unavoidable security interest; and

  (B) on account of which new value the debtor did not make an otherwise unavoidable transfer to or for the benefit of such creditor;

(5) that creates a perfected security interest in inventory or a receivable or the proceeds of either, except to the extent that the aggregate of all such transfers to the transferee caused a reduction, as of the date of the filing of the petition and to the prejudice of other creditors holding unsecured claims, of any amount by which the debt secured by such security interest exceeded the value of all security interests for such debt on the later of—

  (A)(i) with respect to a transfer to which subsection (b)(4)(A) of this section applies, 90 days before the date of the filing of the petition; or

  (ii) with respect to a transfer to which subsection (b)(4)(B) of this section applies, one year before the date of the filing of the petition; or

  (B) the date on which new value was first given under the security agreement creating such security interest;

(6) that is the fixing of a statutory lien that is not avoidable under section 545 of this title;

(7) to the extent such transfer was a bona fide payment of a debt for a domestic support obligation;

(8) if, in a case filed by an individual debtor whose debts are primarily consumer debts, the aggregate value of all property that constitutes or is affected by such transfer is less than $625; or

(9) if, in a case filed by a debtor whose debts are not primarily consumer debts, the aggregate value of all property that constitutes or is affected by such transfer is less than $7,575.

(d) The trustee may avoid a transfer of an interest in property of the debtor transferred to or for the benefit of a surety to secure reimbursement of such a surety that furnished a bond or other obligation to dissolve a judicial lien that would have been avoidable by the trustee under subsection (b) of this section. The liability of such surety under such bond or obligation shall be discharged to the extent of the value of such property recovered by the trustee or the amount paid to the trustee.

(e)(1) For the purposes of this section—

  (A) a transfer of real property other than fixtures, but including the interest of a seller or purchaser under a contract for the sale of real property, is perfected when a bona fide purchaser of such property from the debtor against whom applicable law permits such transfer to be perfected cannot acquire an interest that is superior to the interest of the transferee; and

  (B) a transfer of a fixture or property other than real property is perfected when a creditor on a simple contract cannot acquire a judicial lien that is superior to the interest of the transferee.

(2) For the purposes of this section, except as provided in paragraph (3) of this subsection, a transfer is made—

  (A) at the time such transfer takes effect between the transferor and the transferee, if such transfer is perfected at, or within 30 days after, such time, except as provided in subsection (c)(3)(B);

    (B) at the time such transfer is perfected, if such transfer is perfected after such 30 days; or

    (C) immediately before the date of the filing of the petition, if such transfer is not perfected at the later of—

        (i) the commencement of the case; or

        (ii) 30 days after such transfer takes effect between the transferor and the transferee.

    (3) For the purposes of this section, a transfer is not made until the debtor has acquired rights in the property transferred.

    (f) For the purposes of this section, the debtor is presumed to have been insolvent on and during the 90 days immediately preceding the date of the filing of the petition.

    (g) For the purposes of this section, the trustee has the burden of proving the avoidability of a transfer under subsection (b) of this section, and the creditor or party in interest against whom recovery or avoidance is sought has the burden of proving the nonavoidability of a transfer under subsection (c) of this section.

    (h) The trustee may not avoid a transfer if such transfer was made as a part of an alternative repayment schedule between the debtor and any creditor of the debtor created by an approved nonprofit budget and credit counseling agency.

    (i) If the trustee avoids under subsection (b) a transfer made between 90 days and 1 year before the date of the filing of the petition, by the debtor to an entity that is not an insider for the benefit of a creditor that is an insider, such transfer shall be considered to be avoided under this section only with respect to the creditor that is an insider.

[*Note from West Advisory Panel.* Pub. L. 116–260 created a temporary § 547(j), which expired on December 27, 2022, *except* for cases commenced before December 27, 2022. *See* 134 Stat. 3219, 3220, 3221. For a description of the temporary amendment, *see* Title 11, Chapter 5, Subchapter III, § 547 Editorial Notes, Amendments, 2020 at http://uscode.house.gov]

§ 548. Fraudulent transfers and obligations

    (a)(1) The trustee may avoid any transfer (including any transfer to or for the benefit of an insider under an employment contract) of an interest of the debtor in property, or any obligation (including any obligation to or for the benefit of an insider under an employment contract) incurred by the debtor, that was made or incurred on or within 2 years before the date of the filing of the petition, if the debtor voluntarily or involuntarily—

    (A) made such transfer or incurred such obligation with actual intent to hinder, delay, or defraud any entity to which the debtor was or became, on or after the date that such transfer was made or such obligation was incurred, indebted; or

    (B)(i) received less than a reasonably equivalent value in exchange for such transfer or obligation; and

        (ii)(I) was insolvent on the date that such transfer was made or such obligation was incurred, or became insolvent as a result of such transfer or obligation;

        (II) was engaged in business or a transaction, or was about to engage in business or a transaction, for which any property remaining with the debtor was an unreasonably small capital;

        (III) intended to incur, or believed that the debtor would incur, debts that would be beyond the debtor's ability to pay as such debts matured; or

        (IV) made such transfer to or for the benefit of an insider, or incurred such obligation to or for the benefit of an insider, under an employment contract and not in the ordinary course of business.

(2)   A transfer of a charitable contribution to a qualified religious or charitable entity or organization shall not be considered to be a transfer covered under paragraph (1)(B) in any case in which—

   (A)   the amount of that contribution does not exceed 15 percent of the gross annual income of the debtor for the year in which the transfer of the contribution is made; or

   (B)   the contribution made by a debtor exceeded the percentage amount of gross annual income specified in subparagraph (A), if the transfer was consistent with the practices of the debtor in making charitable contributions.

(b)   The trustee of a partnership debtor may avoid any transfer of an interest of the debtor in property, or any obligation incurred by the debtor, that was made or incurred on or within 2 years before the date of the filing of the petition, to a general partner in the debtor, if the debtor was insolvent on the date such transfer was made or such obligation was incurred, or became insolvent as a result of such transfer or obligation.

(c)   Except to the extent that a transfer or obligation voidable under this section is voidable under section 544, 545, or 547 of this title, a transferee or obligee of such a transfer or obligation that takes for value and in good faith has a lien on or may retain any interest transferred or may enforce any obligation incurred, as the case may be, to the extent that such transferee or obligee gave value to the debtor in exchange for such transfer or obligation.

(d)(1)   For the purposes of this section, a transfer is made when such transfer is so perfected that a bona fide purchaser from the debtor against whom applicable law permits such transfer to be perfected cannot acquire an interest in the property transferred that is superior to the interest in such property of the transferee, but if such transfer is not so perfected before the commencement of the case, such transfer is made immediately before the date of the filing of the petition.

(2)   In this section—

   (A)   "value" means property, or satisfaction or securing of a present or antecedent debt of the debtor, but does not include an unperformed promise to furnish support to the debtor or to a relative of the debtor;

   (B)   a commodity broker, forward contract merchant, stockbroker, financial institution, financial participant, or securities clearing agency that receives a margin payment, as defined in section 101, 741, or 761 of this title, or settlement payment, as defined in section 101 or 741 of this title, takes for value to the extent of such payment;

   (C)   a repo participant or financial participant that receives a margin payment, as defined in section 741 or 761 of this title, or settlement payment, as defined in section 741 of this title, in connection with a repurchase agreement, takes for value to the extent of such payment;

   (D)   a swap participant or financial participant that receives a transfer in connection with a swap agreement takes for value to the extent of such transfer; and

   (E)   a master netting agreement participant that receives a transfer in connection with a master netting agreement or any individual contract covered thereby takes for value to the extent of such transfer, except that, with respect to a transfer under any individual contract covered thereby, to the extent that such master netting agreement participant otherwise did not take (or is otherwise not deemed to have taken) such transfer for value.

(3)   In this section, the term "charitable contribution" means a charitable contribution, as that term is defined in section 170(c) of the Internal Revenue Code of 1986, if that contribution—

   (A)   is made by a natural person; and

   (B)   consists of—

      (i)   a financial instrument (as that term is defined in section 731(c)(2)(C) of the Internal Revenue Code of 1986); or

      (ii)   cash.

(4) In this section, the term "qualified religious or charitable entity or organization" means—

(A) an entity described in section 170(c)(1) of the Internal Revenue Code of 1986; or

(B) an entity or organization described in section 170(c)(2) of the Internal Revenue Code of 1986.

(e)(1) In addition to any transfer that the trustee may otherwise avoid, the trustee may avoid any transfer of an interest of the debtor in property that was made on or within 10 years before the date of the filing of the petition, if—

(A) such transfer was made to a self-settled trust or similar device;

(B) such transfer was by the debtor;

(C) the debtor is a beneficiary of such trust or similar device; and

(D) the debtor made such transfer with actual intent to hinder, delay, or defraud any entity to which the debtor was or became, on or after the date that such transfer was made, indebted.

(2) For the purposes of this subsection, a transfer includes a transfer made in anticipation of any money judgment, settlement, civil penalty, equitable order, or criminal fine incurred by, or which the debtor believed would be incurred by—

(A) any violation of the securities laws (as defined in section 3(a)(47) of the Securities Exchange Act of 1934 (15 U.S.C. 78c(a)(47))), any State securities laws, or any regulation or order issued under Federal securities laws or State securities laws; or

(B) fraud, deceit, or manipulation in a fiduciary capacity or in connection with the purchase or sale of any security registered under section 12 or 15(d) of the Securities Exchange Act of 1934 (15 U.S.C. 78*l* and 78*o*(d)) or under section 6 of the Securities Act of 1933 (15 U.S.C. 77f).

§ 549. Postpetition transactions

(a) Except as provided in subsection (b) or (c) of this section, the trustee may avoid a transfer of property of the estate—

(1) that occurs after the commencement of the case; and

(2)(A) that is authorized only under section 303(f) or 542(c) of this title; or

(B) that is not authorized under this title or by the court.

(b) In an involuntary case, the trustee may not avoid under subsection (a) of this section a transfer made after the commencement of such case but before the order for relief to the extent any value, including services, but not including satisfaction or securing of a debt that arose before the commencement of the case, is given after the commencement of the case in exchange for such transfer, notwithstanding any notice or knowledge of the case that the transferee has.

(c) The trustee may not avoid under subsection (a) of this section a transfer of an interest in real property to a good faith purchaser without knowledge of the commencement of the case and for present fair equivalent value unless a copy or notice of the petition was filed, where a transfer of an interest in such real property may be recorded to perfect such transfer, before such transfer is so perfected that a bona fide purchaser of such real property, against whom applicable law permits such transfer to be perfected, could not acquire an interest that is superior to such interest of such good faith purchaser. A good faith purchaser without knowledge of the commencement of the case and for less than present fair equivalent value has a lien on the property transferred to the extent of any present value given, unless a copy or notice of the petition was so filed before such transfer was so perfected.

(d) An action or proceeding under this section may not be commenced after the earlier of—

(1) two years after the date of the transfer sought to be avoided; or

(2) the time the case is closed or dismissed.

§ 550. Liability of transferee of avoided transfer

(a) Except as otherwise provided in this section, to the extent that a transfer is avoided under section 544, 545, 547, 548, 549, 553(b), or 724(a) of this title, the trustee may recover, for the benefit of the estate, the property transferred, or, if the court so orders, the value of such property, from—

(1) the initial transferee of such transfer or the entity for whose benefit such transfer was made; or

(2) any immediate or mediate transferee of such initial transferee.

(b) The trustee may not recover under section[1] (a)(2) of this section from—

(1) a transferee that takes for value, including satisfaction or securing of a present or antecedent debt, in good faith, and without knowledge of the voidability of the transfer avoided; or

(2) any immediate or mediate good faith transferee of such transferee.

(c) If a transfer made between 90 days and one year before the filing of the petition—

(1) is avoided under section 547(b) of this title; and

(2) was made for the benefit of a creditor that at the time of such transfer was an insider;

the trustee may not recover under subsection (a) from a transferee that is not an insider.

(d) The trustee is entitled to only a single satisfaction under subsection (a) of this section.

(e)(1) A good faith transferee from whom the trustee may recover under subsection (a) of this section has a lien on the property recovered to secure the lesser of—

(A) the cost, to such transferee, of any improvement made after the transfer, less the amount of any profit realized by or accruing to such transferee from such property; and

(B) any increase in the value of such property as a result of such improvement, of the property transferred.

(2) In this subsection, "improvement" includes—

(A) physical additions or changes to the property transferred;

(B) repairs to such property;

(C) payment of any tax on such property;

(D) payment of any debt secured by a lien on such property that is superior or equal to the rights of the trustee; and

(E) preservation of such property.

(f) An action or proceeding under this section may not be commenced after the earlier of—

(1) one year after the avoidance of the transfer on account of which recovery under this section is sought; or

(2) the time the case is closed or dismissed.

§ 551. Automatic preservation of avoided transfer

Any transfer avoided under section 522, 544, 545, 547, 548, 549, or 724(a) of this title, or any lien void under section 506(d) of this title, is preserved for the benefit of the estate but only with respect to property of the estate.

---

[1] So in original. Probably should be "subsection".

§ 552. Postpetition effect of security interest

(a) Except as provided in subsection (b) of this section, property acquired by the estate or by the debtor after the commencement of the case is not subject to any lien resulting from any security agreement entered into by the debtor before the commencement of the case.

(b)(1) Except as provided in sections 363, 506(c), 522, 544, 545, 547, and 548 of this title, if the debtor and an entity entered into a security agreement before the commencement of the case and if the security interest created by such security agreement extends to property of the debtor acquired before the commencement of the case and to proceeds, products, offspring, or profits of such property, then such security interest extends to such proceeds, products, offspring, or profits acquired by the estate after the commencement of the case to the extent provided by such security agreement and by applicable nonbankruptcy law, except to any extent that the court, after notice and a hearing and based on the equities of the case, orders otherwise.

(2) Except as provided in sections 363, 506(c), 522, 544, 545, 547, and 548 of this title, and notwithstanding section 546(b) of this title, if the debtor and an entity entered into a security agreement before the commencement of the case and if the security interest created by such security agreement extends to property of the debtor acquired before the commencement of the case and to amounts paid as rents of such property or the fees, charges, accounts, or other payments for the use or occupancy of rooms and other public facilities in hotels, motels, or other lodging properties, then such security interest extends to such rents and such fees, charges, accounts, or other payments acquired by the estate after the commencement of the case to the extent provided in such security agreement, except to any extent that the court, after notice and a hearing and based on the equities of the case, orders otherwise.

§ 553. Setoff

(a) Except as otherwise provided in this section and in sections 362 and 363 of this title, this title does not affect any right of a creditor to offset a mutual debt owing by such creditor to the debtor that arose before the commencement of the case under this title against a claim of such creditor against the debtor that arose before the commencement of the case, except to the extent that—

   (1) the claim of such creditor against the debtor is disallowed;

   (2) such claim was transferred, by an entity other than the debtor, to such creditor—

      (A) after the commencement of the case; or

      (B)(i) after 90 days before the date of the filing of the petition; and

        (ii) while the debtor was insolvent (except for a setoff of a kind described in section 362(b)(6), 362(b)(7), 362(b)(17), 362(b)(27), 555, 556, 559, 560, or 561); or

   (3) the debt owed to the debtor by such creditor was incurred by such creditor—

      (A) after 90 days before the date of the filing of the petition;

      (B) while the debtor was insolvent; and

      (C) for the purpose of obtaining a right of setoff against the debtor (except for a setoff of a kind described in section 362(b)(6), 362(b)(7), 362(b)(17), 362(b)(27), 555, 556, 559, 560, or 561).

(b)(1) Except with respect to a setoff of a kind described in section 362(b)(6), 362(b)(7), 362(b)(17), 362(b)(27), 555, 556, 559, 560, 561, 365(h), 546(h), or 365(i)(2) of this title, if a creditor offsets a mutual debt owing to the debtor against a claim against the debtor on or within 90 days before the date of the filing of the petition, then the trustee may recover from such creditor the amount so offset to the extent that any insufficiency on the date of such setoff is less than the insufficiency on the later of—

      (A) 90 days before the date of the filing of the petition; and

      (B) the first date during the 90 days immediately preceding the date of the filing of the petition on which there is an insufficiency.

(2)   In this subsection, "insufficiency" means amount, if any, by which a claim against the debtor exceeds a mutual debt owing to the debtor by the holder of such claim.

(c)   For the purposes of this section, the debtor is presumed to have been insolvent on and during the 90 days immediately preceding the date of the filing of the petition.

§ 554.   Abandonment of property of the estate

(a)   After notice and a hearing, the trustee may abandon any property of the estate that is burdensome to the estate or that is of inconsequential value and benefit to the estate.

(b)   On request of a party in interest and after notice and a hearing, the court may order the trustee to abandon any property of the estate that is burdensome to the estate or that is of inconsequential value and benefit to the estate.

(c)   Unless the court orders otherwise, any property scheduled under section 521(a)(1) of this title not otherwise administered at the time of the closing of a case is abandoned to the debtor and administered for purposes of section 350 of this title.

(d)   Unless the court orders otherwise, property of the estate that is not abandoned under this section and that is not administered in the case remains property of the estate.

§ 555.   Contractual right to liquidate, terminate, or accelerate a securities contract

The exercise of a contractual right of a stockbroker, financial institution, financial participant, or securities clearing agency to cause the liquidation, termination, or acceleration of a securities contract, as defined in section 741 of this title, because of a condition of the kind specified in section 365(e)(1) of this title shall not be stayed, avoided, or otherwise limited by operation of any provision of this title or by order of a court or administrative agency in any proceeding under this title unless such order is authorized under the provisions of the Securities Investor Protection Act of 1970 or any statute administered by the Securities and Exchange Commission. As used in this section, the term "contractual right" includes a right set forth in a rule or bylaw of a derivatives clearing organization (as defined in the Commodity Exchange Act), a multilateral clearing organization (as defined in the Federal Deposit Insurance Corporation Improvement Act of 1991), a national securities exchange, a national securities association, a securities clearing agency, a contract market designated under the Commodity Exchange Act, a derivatives transaction execution facility registered under the Commodity Exchange Act, or a board of trade (as defined in the Commodity Exchange Act), or in a resolution of the governing board thereof, and a right, whether or not in writing, arising under common law, under law merchant, or by reason of normal business practice.

§ 556.   Contractual right to liquidate, terminate, or accelerate a commodities contract or forward contract

The contractual right of a commodity broker, financial participant, or forward contract merchant to cause the liquidation, termination, or acceleration of a commodity contract, as defined in section 761 of this title, or forward contract because of a condition of the kind specified in section 365(e)(1) of this title, and the right to a variation or maintenance margin payment received from a trustee with respect to open commodity contracts or forward contracts, shall not be stayed, avoided, or otherwise limited by operation of any provision of this title or by the order of a court in any proceeding under this title. As used in this section, the term "contractual right" includes a right set forth in a rule or bylaw of a derivatives clearing organization (as defined in the Commodity Exchange Act), a multilateral clearing organization (as defined in the Federal Deposit Insurance Corporation Improvement Act of 1991), a national securities exchange, a national securities association, a securities clearing agency, a contract market designated under the Commodity Exchange Act, a derivatives transaction execution facility registered under the Commodity Exchange Act, or a board of trade (as defined in the Commodity Exchange Act) or in a resolution of the governing board thereof and a right, whether or not evidenced in writing, arising under common law, under law merchant or by reason of normal business practice.

§ 557. Expedited determination of interests in, and abandonment or other disposition of grain assets

(a) This section applies only in a case concerning a debtor that owns or operates a grain storage facility and only with respect to grain and the proceeds of grain. This section does not affect the application of any other section of this title to property other than grain and proceeds of grain.

(b) In this section—

(1) "grain" means wheat, corn, flaxseed, grain sorghum, barley, oats, rye, soybeans, other dry edible beans, or rice;

(2) "grain storage facility" means a site or physical structure regularly used to store grain for producers, or to store grain acquired from producers for resale; and

(3) "producer" means an entity which engages in the growing of grain.

(c)(1) Notwithstanding sections 362, 363, 365, and 554 of this title, on the court's own motion the court may, and on the request of the trustee or an entity that claims an interest in grain or the proceeds of grain the court shall, expedite the procedures for the determination of interests in and the disposition of grain and the proceeds of grain, by shortening to the greatest extent feasible such time periods as are otherwise applicable for such procedures and by establishing, by order, a timetable having a duration of not to exceed 120 days for the completion of the applicable procedure specified in subsection (d) of this section. Such time periods and such timetable may be modified by the court, for cause, in accordance with subsection (f) of this section.

(2) The court shall determine the extent to which such time periods shall be shortened, based upon—

(A) any need of an entity claiming an interest in such grain or the proceeds of grain for a prompt determination of such interest;

(B) any need of such entity for a prompt disposition of such grain;

(C) the market for such grain;

(D) the conditions under which such grain is stored;

(E) the costs of continued storage or disposition of such grain;

(F) the orderly administration of the estate;

(G) the appropriate opportunity for an entity to assert an interest in such grain; and

(H) such other considerations as are relevant to the need to expedite such procedures in the case.

(d) The procedures that may be expedited under subsection (c) of this section include—

(1) the filing of and response to—

(A) a claim of ownership;

(B) a proof of claim;

(C) a request for abandonment;

(D) a request for relief from the stay of action against property under section 362(a) of this title;

(E) a request for determination of secured status;

(F) a request for determination of whether such grain or the proceeds of grain—

(i) is property of the estate;

(ii) must be turned over to the estate; or

(iii) may be used, sold, or leased; and

    (G)   any other request for determination of an interest in such grain or the proceeds of grain;

    (2)   the disposition of such grain or the proceeds of grain, before or after determination of interests in such grain or the proceeds of grain, by way of—

    (A)   sale of such grain;

    (B)   abandonment;

    (C)   distribution; or

    (D)   such other method as is equitable in the case;

    (3)   subject to sections 701, 702, 703, 1104, 1183, 1202, and 1302 of this title, the appointment of a trustee or examiner and the retention and compensation of any professional person required to assist with respect to matters relevant to the determination of interests in or disposition of such grain or the proceeds of grain; and

    (4)   the determination of any dispute concerning a matter specified in paragraph (1), (2), or (3) of this subsection.

    (e)(1)   Any governmental unit that has regulatory jurisdiction over the operation or liquidation of the debtor or the debtor's business shall be given notice of any request made or order entered under subsection (c) of this section.

    (2)   Any such governmental unit may raise, and may appear and be heard on, any issue relating to grain or the proceeds of grain in a case in which a request is made, or an order is entered, under subsection (c) of this section.

    (3)   The trustee shall consult with such governmental unit before taking any action relating to the disposition of grain in the possession, custody, or control of the debtor or the estate.

    (f)   The court may extend the period for final disposition of grain or the proceeds of grain under this section beyond 120 days if the court finds that—

    (1)   the interests of justice so require in light of the complexity of the case; and

    (2)   the interests of those claimants entitled to distribution of grain or the proceeds of grain will not be materially injured by such additional delay.

    (g)   Unless an order establishing an expedited procedure under subsection (c) of this section, or determining any interest in or approving any disposition of grain or the proceeds of grain, is stayed pending appeal—

    (1)   the reversal or modification of such order on appeal does not affect the validity of any procedure, determination, or disposition that occurs before such reversal or modification, whether or not any entity knew of the pendency of the appeal; and

    (2)   neither the court nor the trustee may delay, due to the appeal of such order, any proceeding in the case in which such order is issued.

    (h)(1)   The trustee may recover from grain and the proceeds of grain the reasonable and necessary costs and expenses allowable under section 503(b) of this title attributable to preserving or disposing of grain or the proceeds of grain, but may not recover from such grain or the proceeds of grain any other costs or expenses.

    (2)   Notwithstanding section 326(a) of this title, the dollar amounts of money specified in such section include the value, as of the date of disposition, of any grain that the trustee distributes in kind.

    (i)   In all cases where the quantity of a specific type of grain held by a debtor operating a grain storage facility exceeds ten thousand bushels, such grain shall be sold by the trustee and the assets thereof distributed in accordance with the provisions of this section.

§ 558. Defenses of the estate

The estate shall have the benefit of any defense available to the debtor as against any entity other than the estate, including statutes of limitation, statutes of frauds, usury, and other personal defenses. A waiver of any such defense by the debtor after the commencement of the case does not bind the estate.

§ 559. Contractual right to liquidate, terminate, or accelerate a repurchase agreement

The exercise of a contractual right of a repo participant or financial participant to cause the liquidation, termination, or acceleration of a repurchase agreement because of a condition of the kind specified in section 365(e)(1) of this title shall not be stayed, avoided, or otherwise limited by operation of any provision of this title or by order of a court or administrative agency in any proceeding under this title, unless, where the debtor is a stockbroker or securities clearing agency, such order is authorized under the provisions of the Securities Investor Protection Act of 1970 or any statute administered by the Securities and Exchange Commission. In the event that a repo participant or financial participant liquidates one or more repurchase agreements with a debtor and under the terms of one or more such agreements has agreed to deliver assets subject to repurchase agreements to the debtor, any excess of the market prices received on liquidation of such assets (or if any such assets are not disposed of on the date of liquidation of such repurchase agreements, at the prices available at the time of liquidation of such repurchase agreements from a generally recognized source or the most recent closing bid quotation from such a source) over the sum of the stated repurchase prices and all expenses in connection with the liquidation of such repurchase agreements shall be deemed property of the estate, subject to the available rights of setoff. As used in this section, the term "contractual right" includes a right set forth in a rule or bylaw of a derivatives clearing organization (as defined in the Commodity Exchange Act), a multilateral clearing organization (as defined in the Federal Deposit Insurance Corporation Improvement Act of 1991), a national securities exchange, a national securities association, a securities clearing agency, a contract market designated under the Commodity Exchange Act, a derivatives transaction execution facility registered under the Commodity Exchange Act, or a board of trade (as defined in the Commodity Exchange Act) or in a resolution of the governing board thereof and a right, whether or not evidenced in writing, arising under common law, under law merchant or by reason of normal business practice.

§ 560. Contractual right to liquidate, terminate, or accelerate a swap agreement

The exercise of any contractual right of any swap participant or financial participant to cause the liquidation, termination, or acceleration of one or more swap agreements because of a condition of the kind specified in section 365(e)(1) of this title or to offset or net out any termination values or payment amounts arising under or in connection with the termination, liquidation, or acceleration of one or more swap agreements shall not be stayed, avoided, or otherwise limited by operation of any provision of this title or by order of a court or administrative agency in any proceeding under this title. As used in this section, the term "contractual right" includes a right set forth in a rule or bylaw of a derivatives clearing organization (as defined in the Commodity Exchange Act), a multilateral clearing organization (as defined in the Federal Deposit Insurance Corporation Improvement Act of 1991), a national securities exchange, a national securities association, a securities clearing agency, a contract market designated under the Commodity Exchange Act, a derivatives transaction execution facility registered under the Commodity Exchange Act, or a board of trade (as defined in the Commodity Exchange Act) or in a resolution of the governing board thereof and a right, whether or not evidenced in writing, arising under common law, under law merchant, or by reason of normal business practice.

§ 561. Contractual right to terminate, liquidate, accelerate, or offset under a master netting agreement and across contracts; proceedings under chapter 15

(a) Subject to subsection (b), the exercise of any contractual right, because of a condition of the kind specified in section 365(e)(1), to cause the termination, liquidation, or acceleration of or to offset or net termination values, payment amounts, or other transfer obligations arising under or in connection with one or more (or the termination, liquidation, or acceleration of one or more)—

(1) securities contracts, as defined in section 741(7);

(2) commodity contracts, as defined in section 761(4);

(3) forward contracts;

(4) repurchase agreements;

(5) swap agreements; or

(6) master netting agreements,

shall not be stayed, avoided, or otherwise limited by operation of any provision of this title or by any order of a court or administrative agency in any proceeding under this title.

(b)(1) A party may exercise a contractual right described in subsection (a) to terminate, liquidate, or accelerate only to the extent that such party could exercise such a right under section 555, 556, 559, or 560 for each individual contract covered by the master netting agreement in issue.

(2) If a debtor is a commodity broker subject to subchapter IV of chapter 7—

(A) a party may not net or offset an obligation to the debtor arising under, or in connection with, a commodity contract traded on or subject to the rules of a contract market designated under the Commodity Exchange Act or a derivatives transaction execution facility registered under the Commodity Exchange Act against any claim arising under, or in connection with, other instruments, contracts, or agreements listed in subsection (a) except to the extent that the party has positive net equity in the commodity accounts at the debtor, as calculated under such subchapter; and

(B) another commodity broker may not net or offset an obligation to the debtor arising under, or in connection with, a commodity contract entered into or held on behalf of a customer of the debtor and traded on or subject to the rules of a contract market designated under the Commodity Exchange Act or a derivatives transaction execution facility registered under the Commodity Exchange Act against any claim arising under, or in connection with, other instruments, contracts, or agreements listed in subsection (a).

(3) No provision of subparagraph (A) or (B) of paragraph (2) shall prohibit the offset of claims and obligations that arise under—

(A) a cross-margining agreement or similar arrangement that has been approved by the Commodity Futures Trading Commission or submitted to the Commodity Futures Trading Commission under paragraph (1) or (2) of section 5c(c) of the Commodity Exchange Act and has not been abrogated or rendered ineffective by the Commodity Futures Trading Commission; or

(B) any other netting agreement between a clearing organization (as defined in section 761) and another entity that has been approved by the Commodity Futures Trading Commission.

(c) As used in this section, the term "contractual right" includes a right set forth in a rule or bylaw of a derivatives clearing organization (as defined in the Commodity Exchange Act), a multilateral clearing organization (as defined in the Federal Deposit Insurance Corporation Improvement Act of 1991), a national securities exchange, a national securities association, a securities clearing agency, a contract market designated under the Commodity Exchange Act, a derivatives transaction execution facility registered under the Commodity Exchange Act, or a board of trade (as defined in the Commodity Exchange Act) or in a resolution of the governing board thereof, and a right, whether or not evidenced in writing, arising under common law, under law merchant, or by reason of normal business practice.

(d) Any provisions of this title relating to securities contracts, commodity contracts, forward contracts, repurchase agreements, swap agreements, or master netting agreements shall apply in a case under chapter 15, so that enforcement of contractual provisions of such contracts and agreements in accordance with their terms will not be stayed or otherwise limited by operation of any provision of this title or by order of a court in any case under this title, and to limit avoidance powers to the same extent as in a proceeding under chapter 7 or 11 of this title (such enforcement not to be limited based on the presence or absence of assets of the debtor in the United States).

§ 562. Timing of damage measurement in connection with swap agreements, securities contracts, forward contracts, commodity contracts, repurchase agreements, and master netting agreements

(a) If the trustee rejects a swap agreement, securities contract (as defined in section 741), forward contract, commodity contract (as defined in section 761), repurchase agreement, or master netting agreement pursuant to section 365(a), or if a forward contract merchant, stockbroker, financial institution, securities clearing agency, repo participant, financial participant, master netting agreement participant, or swap participant liquidates, terminates, or accelerates such contract or agreement, damages shall be measured as of the earlier of—

(1) the date of such rejection; or

(2) the date or dates of such liquidation, termination, or acceleration.

(b) If there are not any commercially reasonable determinants of value as of any date referred to in paragraph (1) or (2) of subsection (a), damages shall be measured as of the earliest subsequent date or dates on which there are commercially reasonable determinants of value.

(c) For the purposes of subsection (b), if damages are not measured as of the date or dates of rejection, liquidation, termination, or acceleration, and the forward contract merchant, stockbroker, financial institution, securities clearing agency, repo participant, financial participant, master netting agreement participant, or swap participant or the trustee objects to the timing of the measurement of damages—

(1) the trustee, in the case of an objection by a forward contract merchant, stockbroker, financial institution, securities clearing agency, repo participant, financial participant, master netting agreement participant, or swap participant; or

(2) the forward contract merchant, stockbroker, financial institution, securities clearing agency, repo participant, financial participant, master netting agreement participant, or swap participant, in the case of an objection by the trustee,

has the burden of proving that there were no commercially reasonable determinants of value as of such date or dates.

CHAPTER 7—LIQUIDATION

SUBCHAPTER I—OFFICERS AND ADMINISTRATION

701. Interim trustee.
702. Election of trustee.
703. Successor trustee.
704. Duties of trustee.
705. Creditors' committee.
706. Conversion.
707. Dismissal of a case or conversion to a case under chapter 11 or 13.

SUBCHAPTER II—COLLECTION, LIQUIDATION, AND DISTRIBUTION OF THE ESTATE

721. Authorization to operate business.
722. Redemption.
723. Rights of partnership trustee against general partners.
724. Treatment of certain liens.
725. Disposition of certain property.
726. Distribution of property of the estate.
727. Discharge.

SUBCHAPTER III—STOCKBROKER LIQUIDATION

741. Definitions for this subchapter.
742. Effect of section 362 of this title in this subchapter.
743. Notice.
744. Executory contracts.
745. Treatment of accounts.
746. Extent of customer claims.
747. Subordination of certain customer claims.
748. Reduction of securities to money.
749. Voidable transfers.
750. Distribution of securities.
751. Customer name securities.
752. Customer property.
753. Stockbroker liquidation and forward contract merchants, commodity brokers, stockbrokers, financial institutions, financial participants, securities clearing agencies, swap participants, repo participants, and master netting agreement participants.

SUBCHAPTER IV—COMMODITY BROKER LIQUIDATION

761. Definitions for this subchapter.
762. Notice to the Commission and right to be heard.
763. Treatment of accounts.
764. Voidable transfers.
765. Customer instructions.
766. Treatment of customer property.
767. Commodity broker liquidation and forward contract merchants, commodity brokers, stockbrokers, financial institutions, financial participants, securities clearing agencies, swap participants, repo participants, and master netting agreement participants.

SUBCHAPTER V—CLEARING BANK LIQUIDATION

781. Definitions.
782. Selection of trustee.
783. Additional powers of trustee.
784. Right to be heard.

SUBCHAPTER I—OFFICERS AND ADMINISTRATION

§ 701. Interim trustee

(a)(1)   Promptly after the order for relief under this chapter, the United States trustee shall appoint one disinterested person that is a member of the panel of private trustees established under section 586(a)(1) of title 28 or that is serving as trustee in the case immediately before the order for relief under this chapter to serve as interim trustee in the case.

(2)   If none of the members of such panel is willing to serve as interim trustee in the case, then the United States trustee may serve as interim trustee in the case.

(b)   The service of an interim trustee under this section terminates when a trustee elected or designated under section 702 of this title to serve as trustee in the case qualifies under section 322 of this title.

(c)   An interim trustee serving under this section is a trustee in a case under this title.

§ 702. Election of trustee

(a) A creditor may vote for a candidate for trustee only if such creditor—

(1) holds an allowable, undisputed, fixed, liquidated, unsecured claim of a kind entitled to distribution under section 726(a)(2), 726(a)(3), 726(a)(4), 752(a), 766(h), or 766(i) of this title;

(2) does not have an interest materially adverse, other than an equity interest that is not substantial in relation to such creditor's interest as a creditor, to the interest of creditors entitled to such distribution; and

(3) is not an insider.

(b) At the meeting of creditors held under section 341 of this title, creditors may elect one person to serve as trustee in the case if election of a trustee is requested by creditors that may vote under subsection (a) of this section, and that hold at least 20 percent in amount of the claims specified in subsection (a)(1) of this section that are held by creditors that may vote under subsection (a) of this section.

(c) A candidate for trustee is elected trustee if—

(1) creditors holding at least 20 percent in amount of the claims of a kind specified in subsection (a)(1) of this section that are held by creditors that may vote under subsection (a) of this section vote; and

(2) such candidate receives the votes of creditors holding a majority in amount of claims specified in subsection (a)(1) of this section that are held by creditors that vote for a trustee.

(d) If a trustee is not elected under this section, then the interim trustee shall serve as trustee in the case.

§ 703. Successor trustee

(a) If a trustee dies or resigns during a case, fails to qualify under section 322 of this title, or is removed under section 324 of this title, creditors may elect, in the manner specified in section 702 of this title, a person to fill the vacancy in the office of trustee.

(b) Pending election of a trustee under subsection (a) of this section, if necessary to preserve or prevent loss to the estate, the United States trustee may appoint an interim trustee in the manner specified in section 701(a).

(c) If creditors do not elect a successor trustee under subsection (a) of this section or if a trustee is needed in a case reopened under section 350 of this title, then the United States trustee—

(1) shall appoint one disinterested person that is a member of the panel of private trustees established under section 586(a)(1) of title 28 to serve as trustee in the case; or

(2) may, if none of the disinterested members of such panel is willing to serve as trustee, serve as trustee in the case.

§ 704. Duties of trustee

(a) The trustee shall—

(1) collect and reduce to money the property of the estate for which such trustee serves, and close such estate as expeditiously as is compatible with the best interests of parties in interest;

(2) be accountable for all property received;

(3) ensure that the debtor shall perform his intention as specified in section 521(a)(2)(B) of this title;

(4) investigate the financial affairs of the debtor;

(5) if a purpose would be served, examine proofs of claims and object to the allowance of any claim that is improper;

(6) if advisable, oppose the discharge of the debtor;

(7) unless the court orders otherwise, furnish such information concerning the estate and the estate's administration as is requested by a party in interest;

(8) if the business of the debtor is authorized to be operated, file with the court, with the United States trustee, and with any governmental unit charged with responsibility for collection or determination of any tax arising out of such operation, periodic reports and summaries of the operation of such business, including a statement of receipts and disbursements, and such other information as the United States trustee or the court requires;

(9) make a final report and file a final account of the administration of the estate with the court and with the United States trustee;

(10) if with respect to the debtor there is a claim for a domestic support obligation, provide the applicable notice specified in subsection (c);

(11) if, at the time of the commencement of the case, the debtor (or any entity designated by the debtor) served as the administrator (as defined in section 3 of the Employee Retirement Income Security Act of 1974) of an employee benefit plan, continue to perform the obligations required of the administrator; and

(12) use all reasonable and best efforts to transfer patients from a health care business that is in the process of being closed to an appropriate health care business that—

    (A) is in the vicinity of the health care business that is closing;

    (B) provides the patient with services that are substantially similar to those provided by the health care business that is in the process of being closed; and

    (C) maintains a reasonable quality of care.

(b)(1) With respect to a debtor who is an individual in a case under this chapter—

    (A) the United States trustee (or the bankruptcy administrator, if any) shall review all materials filed by the debtor and, not later than 10 days after the date of the first meeting of creditors, file with the court a statement as to whether the debtor's case would be presumed to be an abuse under section 707(b); and

    (B) not later than 7 days after receiving a statement under subparagraph (A), the court shall provide a copy of the statement to all creditors.

(2) The United States trustee (or bankruptcy administrator, if any) shall, not later than 30 days after the date of filing a statement under paragraph (1), either file a motion to dismiss or convert under section 707(b) or file a statement setting forth the reasons the United States trustee (or the bankruptcy administrator, if any) does not consider such a motion to be appropriate, if the United States trustee (or the bankruptcy administrator, if any) determines that the debtor's case should be presumed to be an abuse under section 707(b) and the product of the debtor's current monthly income, multiplied by 12 is not less than—

    (A) in the case of a debtor in a household of 1 person, the median family income of the applicable State for 1 earner; or

    (B) in the case of a debtor in a household of 2 or more individuals, the highest median family income of the applicable State for a family of the same number or fewer individuals.

(c)(1) In a case described in subsection (a)(10) to which subsection (a)(10) applies, the trustee shall—

    (A)(i) provide written notice to the holder of the claim described in subsection (a)(10) of such claim and of the right of such holder to use the services of the State child support enforcement agency established under sections 464 and 466 of the Social Security Act for the State in which such holder resides, for assistance in collecting child support during and after the case under this title;

(ii) include in the notice provided under clause (i) the address and telephone number of such State child support enforcement agency; and

(iii) include in the notice provided under clause (i) an explanation of the rights of such holder to payment of such claim under this chapter;

(B)(i) provide written notice to such State child support enforcement agency of such claim; and

(ii) include in the notice provided under clause (i) the name, address, and telephone number of such holder; and

(C) at such time as the debtor is granted a discharge under section 727, provide written notice to such holder and to such State child support enforcement agency of—

(i) the granting of the discharge;

(ii) the last recent known address of the debtor;

(iii) the last recent known name and address of the debtor's employer; and

(iv) the name of each creditor that holds a claim that—

(I) is not discharged under paragraph (2), (4), or (14A) of section 523(a); or

(II) was reaffirmed by the debtor under section 524(c).

(2)(A) The holder of a claim described in subsection (a)(10) or the State child support enforcement agency of the State in which such holder resides may request from a creditor described in paragraph (1)(C)(iv) the last known address of the debtor.

(B) Notwithstanding any other provision of law, a creditor that makes a disclosure of a last known address of a debtor in connection with a request made under subparagraph (A) shall not be liable by reason of making such disclosure.

§ 705. Creditors' committee

(a) At the meeting under section 341(a) of this title, creditors that may vote for a trustee under section 702(a) of this title may elect a committee of not fewer than three, and not more than eleven, creditors, each of whom holds an allowable unsecured claim of a kind entitled to distribution under section 726(a)(2) of this title.

(b) A committee elected under subsection (a) of this section may consult with the trustee or the United States trustee in connection with the administration of the estate, make recommendations to the trustee or the United States trustee respecting the performance of the trustee's duties, and submit to the court or the United States trustee any question affecting the administration of the estate.

§ 706. Conversion

(a) The debtor may convert a case under this chapter to a case under chapter 11, 12, or 13 of this title at any time, if the case has not been converted under section 1112, 1208, or 1307 of this title. Any waiver of the right to convert a case under this subsection is unenforceable.

(b) On request of a party in interest and after notice and a hearing, the court may convert a case under this chapter to a case under chapter 11 of this title at any time.

(c) The court may not convert a case under this chapter to a case under chapter 12 or 13 of this title unless the debtor requests or consents to such conversion.

(d) Notwithstanding any other provision of this section, a case may not be converted to a case under another chapter of this title unless the debtor may be a debtor under such chapter.

§ 707. Dismissal of a case or conversion to a case under chapter 11 or 13

(a) The court may dismiss a case under this chapter only after notice and a hearing and only for cause, including—

(1)   unreasonable delay by the debtor that is prejudicial to creditors;

(2)   nonpayment of any fees or charges required under chapter 123 of title 28; and

(3)   failure of the debtor in a voluntary case to file, within fifteen days or such additional time as the court may allow after the filing of the petition commencing such case, the information required by paragraph (1) of section 521(a), but only on a motion by the United States trustee.

(b)(1)   After notice and a hearing, the court, on its own motion or on a motion by the United States trustee, trustee (or bankruptcy administrator, if any), or any party in interest, may dismiss a case filed by an individual debtor under this chapter whose debts are primarily consumer debts, or, with the debtor's consent, convert such a case to a case under chapter 11 or 13 of this title, if it finds that the granting of relief would be an abuse of the provisions of this chapter. In making a determination whether to dismiss a case under this section, the court may not take into consideration whether a debtor has made, or continues to make, charitable contributions (that meet the definition of "charitable contribution" under section 548(d)(3)) to any qualified religious or charitable entity or organization (as that term is defined in section 548(d)(4)).

(2)(A)(i)   In considering under paragraph (1) whether the granting of relief would be an abuse of the provisions of this chapter, the court shall presume abuse exists if the debtor's current monthly income reduced by the amounts determined under clauses (ii), (iii), and (iv), and multiplied by 60 is not less than the lesser of—

         (I)   25 percent of the debtor's nonpriority unsecured claims in the case, or $9,075, whichever is greater; or

         (II) $15,150.

     (ii)(I)   The debtor's monthly expenses shall be the debtor's applicable monthly expense amounts specified under the National Standards and Local Standards, and the debtor's actual monthly expenses for the categories specified as Other Necessary Expenses issued by the Internal Revenue Service for the area in which the debtor resides, as in effect on the date of the order for relief, for the debtor, the dependents of the debtor, and the spouse of the debtor in a joint case, if the spouse is not otherwise a dependent. Such expenses shall include reasonably necessary health insurance, disability insurance, and health savings account expenses for the debtor, the spouse of the debtor, or the dependents of the debtor. Notwithstanding any other provision of this clause, the monthly expenses of the debtor shall not include any payments for debts. In addition, the debtor's monthly expenses shall include the debtor's reasonably necessary expenses incurred to maintain the safety of the debtor and the family of the debtor from family violence as identified under section 302 of the Family Violence Prevention and Services Act, or other applicable Federal law. The expenses included in the debtor's monthly expenses described in the preceding sentence shall be kept confidential by the court. In addition, if it is demonstrated that it is reasonable and necessary, the debtor's monthly expenses may also include an additional allowance for food and clothing of up to 5 percent of the food and clothing categories as specified by the National Standards issued by the Internal Revenue Service.

         (II)   In addition, the debtor's monthly expenses may include, if applicable, the continuation of actual expenses paid by the debtor that are reasonable and necessary for care and support of an elderly, chronically ill, or disabled household member or member of the debtor's immediate family (including parents, grandparents, siblings, children, and grandchildren of the debtor, the dependents of the debtor, and the spouse of the debtor in a joint case who is not a dependent) and who is unable to pay for such reasonable and necessary expenses. Such monthly expenses may include, if applicable, contributions to an account of a qualified ABLE program to the extent such contributions are not excess contributions (as described in Section 4973(h) of the Internal Revenue Code of 1986) and if the designated beneficiary of each account is a child, stepchild, grandchild, or stepgrandchild of the debtor.

         (III) In addition, for a debtor eligible for chapter 13, the debtor's monthly expenses may include the actual administrative expenses of administering a chapter 13 plan for the district in which the debtor resides, up to an amount of 10 percent of the projected plan payments, as determined under schedules issued by the Executive Office for United States Trustees.

(IV) In addition, the debtor's monthly expenses may include the actual expenses for each dependent child less than 18 years of age, not to exceed $2,275 per year per child, to attend a private or public elementary or secondary school if the debtor provides documentation of such expenses and a detailed explanation of why such expenses are reasonable and necessary, and why such expenses are not already accounted for in the National Standards, Local Standards, or Other Necessary Expenses referred to in subclause (I).

(V) In addition, the debtor's monthly expenses may include an allowance for housing and utilities, in excess of the allowance specified by the Local Standards for housing and utilities issued by the Internal Revenue Service, based on the actual expenses for home energy costs if the debtor provides documentation of such actual expenses and demonstrates that such actual expenses are reasonable and necessary.

(iii) The debtor's average monthly payments on account of secured debts shall be calculated as the sum of—

(I) the total of all amounts scheduled as contractually due to secured creditors in each month of the 60 months following the date of the filing of the petition; and

(II) any additional payments to secured creditors necessary for the debtor, in filing a plan under chapter 13 of this title, to maintain possession of the debtor's primary residence, motor vehicle, or other property necessary for the support of the debtor and the debtor's dependents, that serves as collateral for secured debts;

divided by 60.

(iv) The debtor's expenses for payment of all priority claims (including priority child support and alimony claims) shall be calculated as the total amount of debts entitled to priority, divided by 60.

(B)(i) In any proceeding brought under this subsection, the presumption of abuse may only be rebutted by demonstrating special circumstances, such as a serious medical condition or a call or order to active duty in the Armed Forces, to the extent such special circumstances that justify additional expenses or adjustments of current monthly income for which there is no reasonable alternative.

(ii) In order to establish special circumstances, the debtor shall be required to itemize each additional expense or adjustment of income and to provide—

(I) documentation for such expense or adjustment to income; and

(II) a detailed explanation of the special circumstances that make such expenses or adjustment to income necessary and reasonable.

(iii) The debtor shall attest under oath to the accuracy of any information provided to demonstrate that additional expenses or adjustments to income are required.

(iv) The presumption of abuse may only be rebutted if the additional expenses or adjustments to income referred to in clause (i) cause the product of the debtor's current monthly income reduced by the amounts determined under clauses (ii), (iii), and (iv) of subparagraph (A) when multiplied by 60 to be less than the lesser of—

(I) 25 percent of the debtor's nonpriority unsecured claims, or $9,075, whichever is greater; or

(II) $15,150.

(C) As part of the schedule of current income and expenditures required under section 521, the debtor shall include a statement of the debtor's current monthly income, and the calculations that determine whether a presumption arises under subparagraph (A)(i), that show how each such amount is calculated.

(D) Subparagraphs (A) through (C) shall not apply, and the court may not dismiss or convert a case based on any form of means testing—

    (i) if the debtor is a disabled veteran (as defined in section 3741(1) of title 38), and the indebtedness occurred primarily during a period during which he or she was—

        (I) on active duty (as defined in section 101(d)(1) of title 10); or

        (II) performing a homeland defense activity (as defined in section 901(1) of title 32); or

    (ii) with respect to the debtor, while the debtor is—

        (I) on, and during the 540-day period beginning immediately after the debtor is released from, a period of active duty (as defined in section 101(d)(1) of title 10) of not less than 90 days; or

        (II) performing, and during the 540-day period beginning immediately after the debtor is no longer performing, a homeland defense activity (as defined in section 901(1) of title 32) performed for a period of not less than 90 days;

if after September 11, 2001, the debtor while a member of a reserve component of the Armed Forces or a member of the National Guard, was called to such active duty or performed such homeland defense activity.

(3) In considering under paragraph (1) whether the granting of relief would be an abuse of the provisions of this chapter in a case in which the presumption in paragraph (2)(A)(i) does not arise or is rebutted, the court shall consider—

    (A) whether the debtor filed the petition in bad faith; or

    (B) the totality of the circumstances (including whether the debtor seeks to reject a personal services contract and the financial need for such rejection as sought by the debtor) of the debtor's financial situation demonstrates abuse.

(4)(A) The court, on its own initiative or on the motion of a party in interest, in accordance with the procedures described in rule 9011 of the Federal Rules of Bankruptcy Procedure, may order the attorney for the debtor to reimburse the trustee for all reasonable costs in prosecuting a motion filed under section 707(b), including reasonable attorneys' fees, if—

    (i) a trustee files a motion for dismissal or conversion under this subsection; and

    (ii) the court—

        (I) grants such motion; and

        (II) finds that the action of the attorney for the debtor in filing a case under this chapter violated rule 9011 of the Federal Rules of Bankruptcy Procedure.

(B) If the court finds that the attorney for the debtor violated rule 9011 of the Federal Rules of Bankruptcy Procedure, the court, on its own initiative or on the motion of a party in interest, in accordance with such procedures, may order—

    (i) the assessment of an appropriate civil penalty against the attorney for the debtor; and

    (ii) the payment of such civil penalty to the trustee, the United States trustee (or the bankruptcy administrator, if any).

(C) The signature of an attorney on a petition, pleading, or written motion shall constitute a certification that the attorney has—

    (i) performed a reasonable investigation into the circumstances that gave rise to the petition, pleading, or written motion; and

 (ii) determined that the petition, pleading, or written motion—

  (I) is well grounded in fact; and

  (II) is warranted by existing law or a good faith argument for the extension, modification, or reversal of existing law and does not constitute an abuse under paragraph (1).

 (D) The signature of an attorney on the petition shall constitute a certification that the attorney has no knowledge after an inquiry that the information in the schedules filed with such petition is incorrect.

 (5)(A) Except as provided in subparagraph (B) and subject to paragraph (6), the court, on its own initiative or on the motion of a party in interest, in accordance with the procedures described in rule 9011 of the Federal Rules of Bankruptcy Procedure, may award a debtor all reasonable costs (including reasonable attorneys' fees) in contesting a motion filed by a party in interest (other than a trustee or United States trustee (or bankruptcy administrator, if any)) under this subsection if—

  (i) the court does not grant the motion; and

  (ii) the court finds that—

   (I) the position of the party that filed the motion violated rule 9011 of the Federal Rules of Bankruptcy Procedure; or

   (II) the attorney (if any) who filed the motion did not comply with the requirements of clauses (i) and (ii) of paragraph (4)(C), and the motion was made solely for the purpose of coercing a debtor into waiving a right guaranteed to the debtor under this title.

 (B) A small business that has a claim of an aggregate amount less than $1,525 shall not be subject to subparagraph (A)(ii)(I).

 (C) For purposes of this paragraph—

  (i) the term "small business" means an unincorporated business, partnership, corporation, association, or organization that—

   (I) has fewer than 25 full-time employees as determined on the date on which the motion is filed; and

   (II) is engaged in commercial or business activity; and

  (ii) the number of employees of a wholly owned subsidiary of a corporation includes the employees of—

   (I) a parent corporation; and

   (II) any other subsidiary corporation of the parent corporation.

 (6) Only the judge or United States trustee (or bankruptcy administrator, if any) may file a motion under section 707(b), if the current monthly income of the debtor, or in a joint case, the debtor and the debtor's spouse, as of the date of the order for relief, when multiplied by 12, is equal to or less than—

 (A) in the case of a debtor in a household of 1 person, the median family income of the applicable State for 1 earner;

 (B) in the case of a debtor in a household of 2, 3, or 4 individuals, the highest median family income of the applicable State for a family of the same number or fewer individuals; or

 (C) in the case of a debtor in a household exceeding 4 individuals, the highest median family income of the applicable State for a family of 4 or fewer individuals, plus $825 per month for each individual in excess of 4.

 (7)(A) No judge, United States trustee (or bankruptcy administrator, if any), trustee, or other party in interest may file a motion under paragraph (2) if the current monthly income of the debtor, including a veteran (as that term is defined in section 101 of title 38), and the debtor's spouse combined, as of the date of the order for relief when multiplied by 12, is equal to or less than—

    (i)   in the case of a debtor in a household of 1 person, the median family income of the applicable State for 1 earner;

    (ii)   in the case of a debtor in a household of 2, 3, or 4 individuals, the highest median family income of the applicable State for a family of the same number or fewer individuals; or

    (iii)   in the case of a debtor in a household exceeding 4 individuals, the highest median family income of the applicable State for a family of 4 or fewer individuals, plus $825 per month for each individual in excess of 4.

    (B)   In a case that is not a joint case, current monthly income of the debtor's spouse shall not be considered for purposes of subparagraph (A) if—

    (i)(I)   the debtor and the debtor's spouse are separated under applicable nonbankruptcy law; or

    (II)   the debtor and the debtor's spouse are living separate and apart, other than for the purpose of evading subparagraph (A); and

    (ii)   the debtor files a statement under penalty of perjury—

    (I)   specifying that the debtor meets the requirement of subclause (I) or (II) of clause (i); and

    (II)   disclosing the aggregate, or best estimate of the aggregate, amount of any cash or money payments received from the debtor's spouse attributed to the debtor's current monthly income.

(c)(1)   In this subsection—

    (A)   the term "crime of violence" has the meaning given such term in section 16 of title 18; and

    (B)   the term "drug trafficking crime" has the meaning given such term in section 924(c)(2) of title 18.

    (2)   Except as provided in paragraph (3), after notice and a hearing, the court, on a motion by the victim of a crime of violence or a drug trafficking crime, may when it is in the best interest of the victim dismiss a voluntary case filed under this chapter by a debtor who is an individual if such individual was convicted of such crime.

    (3)   The court may not dismiss a case under paragraph (2) if the debtor establishes by a preponderance of the evidence that the filing of a case under this chapter is necessary to satisfy a claim for a domestic support obligation.

SUBCHAPTER II—COLLECTION, LIQUIDATION, AND DISTRIBUTION OF THE ESTATE

§ 721. Authorization to operate business

The court may authorize the trustee to operate the business of the debtor for a limited period, if such operation is in the best interest of the estate and consistent with the orderly liquidation of the estate.

§ 722. Redemption

An individual debtor may, whether or not the debtor has waived the right to redeem under this section, redeem tangible personal property intended primarily for personal, family, or household use, from a lien securing a dischargeable consumer debt, if such property is exempted under section 522 of this title or has been abandoned under section 554 of this title, by paying the holder of such lien the amount of the allowed secured claim of such holder that is secured by such lien in full at the time of redemption.

§ 723. Rights of partnership trustee against general partners

(a) If there is a deficiency of property of the estate to pay in full all claims which are allowed in a case under this chapter concerning a partnership and with respect to which a general partner of the partnership is personally liable, the trustee shall have a claim against such general partner to the extent that under applicable nonbankruptcy law such general partner is personally liable for such deficiency.

(b) To the extent practicable, the trustee shall first seek recovery of such deficiency from any general partner in such partnership that is not a debtor in a case under this title. Pending determination of such deficiency, the court may order any such partner to provide the estate with indemnity for, or assurance of payment of, any deficiency recoverable from such partner, or not to dispose of property.

(c) The trustee has a claim against the estate of each general partner in such partnership that is a debtor in a case under this title for the full amount of all claims of creditors allowed in the case concerning such partnership. Notwithstanding section 502 of this title, there shall not be allowed in such partner's case a claim against such partner on which both such partner and such partnership are liable, except to any extent that such claim is secured only by property of such partner and not by property of such partnership. The claim of the trustee under this subsection is entitled to distribution in such partner's case under section 726(a) of this title the same as any other claim of a kind specified in such section.

(d) If the aggregate that the trustee recovers from the estates of general partners under subsection (c) of this section is greater than any deficiency not recovered under subsection (b) of this section, the court, after notice and a hearing, shall determine an equitable distribution of the surplus so recovered, and the trustee shall distribute such surplus to the estates of the general partners in such partnership according to such determination.

§ 724. Treatment of certain liens

(a) The trustee may avoid a lien that secures a claim of a kind specified in section 726(a)(4) of this title.

(b) Property in which the estate has an interest and that is subject to a lien that is not avoidable under this title (other than to the extent that there is a properly perfected unavoidable tax lien arising in connection with an ad valorem tax on real or personal property of the estate) and that secures an allowed claim for a tax, or proceeds of such property, shall be distributed—

    (1) first, to any holder of an allowed claim secured by a lien on such property that is not avoidable under this title and that is senior to such tax lien;

    (2) second, to any holder of a claim of a kind specified in section 507(a)(1)(C) or 507(a)(2) (except that such expenses under each such section, other than claims for wages, salaries, or commissions that arise after the date of the filing of the petition, shall be limited to expenses incurred under this chapter and shall not include expenses incurred under chapter 11 of this title), 507(a)(1)(A), 507(a)(1)(B), 507(a)(3), 507(a)(4), 507(a)(5), 507(a)(6), or 507(a)(7) of this title, to the extent of the amount of such allowed tax claim that is secured by such tax lien;

    (3) third, to the holder of such tax lien, to any extent that such holder's allowed tax claim that is secured by such tax lien exceeds any amount distributed under paragraph (2) of this subsection;

    (4) fourth, to any holder of an allowed claim secured by a lien on such property that is not avoidable under this title and that is junior to such tax lien;

    (5) fifth, to the holder of such tax lien, to the extent that such holder's allowed claim secured by such tax lien is not paid under paragraph (3) of this subsection; and

    (6) sixth, to the estate.

(c) If more than one holder of a claim is entitled to distribution under a particular paragraph of subsection (b) of this section, distribution to such holders under such paragraph shall be in the same order as distribution to such holders would have been other than under this section.

(d) A statutory lien the priority of which is determined in the same manner as the priority of a tax lien under section 6323 of the Internal Revenue Code of 1986 shall be treated under subsection (b) of this section the same as if such lien were a tax lien.

(e) Before subordinating a tax lien on real or personal property of the estate, the trustee shall—

    (1) exhaust the unencumbered assets of the estate; and

    (2) in a manner consistent with section 506(c), recover from property securing an allowed secured claim the reasonable, necessary costs and expenses of preserving or disposing of such property.

(f) Notwithstanding the exclusion of ad valorem tax liens under this section and subject to the requirements of subsection (e), the following may be paid from property of the estate which secures a tax lien, or the proceeds of such property:

    (1) Claims for wages, salaries, and commissions that are entitled to priority under section 507(a)(4).

    (2) Claims for contributions to an employee benefit plan entitled to priority under section 507(a)(5).

§ 725. Disposition of certain property

After the commencement of a case under this chapter, but before final distribution of property of the estate under section 726 of this title, the trustee, after notice and a hearing, shall dispose of any property in which an entity other than the estate has an interest, such as a lien, and that has not been disposed of under another section of this title.

§ 726. Distribution of property of the estate

(a) Except as provided in section 510 of this title, property of the estate shall be distributed—

    (1) first, in payment of claims of the kind specified in, and in the order specified in, section 507 of this title, proof of which is timely filed under section 501 of this title or tardily filed on or before the earlier of—

        (A) the date that is 10 days after the mailing to creditors of the summary of the trustee's final report; or

        (B) the date on which the trustee commences final distribution under this section;

    (2) second, in payment of any allowed unsecured claim, other than a claim of a kind specified in paragraph (1), (3), or (4) of this subsection, proof of which is—

        (A) timely filed under section 501(a) of this title;

        (B) timely filed under section 501(b) or 501(c) of this title; or

        (C) tardily filed under section 501(a) of this title, if—

            (i) the creditor that holds such claim did not have notice or actual knowledge of the case in time for timely filing of a proof of such claim under section 501(a) of this title; and

            (ii) proof of such claim is filed in time to permit payment of such claim;

    *(3) third, in payment of any allowed unsecured claim proof of which is tardily filed under section 501(a) of this title, other than a claim of the kind specified in paragraph (2)(C) of this subsection;

    (4) fourth, in payment of any allowed claim, whether secured or unsecured, for any fine, penalty, or forfeiture, or for multiple, exemplary, or punitive damages, arising before the earlier of the order for relief or the appointment of a trustee, to the extent that such fine, penalty, forfeiture, or damages are not compensation for actual pecuniary loss suffered by the holder of such claim;

    (5) fifth, in payment of interest at the legal rate from the date of the filing of the petition, on any claim paid under paragraph (1), (2), (3), or (4) of this subsection; and

    (6) sixth, to the debtor.

(b) Payment on claims of a kind specified in paragraph (1), (2), (3), (4), (5), (6), (7), (8), (9), or (10) of section 507(a) of this title, or in paragraph (2), (3), (4), or (5) of subsection (a) of this section, shall be made pro rata among claims of the kind specified in each such particular paragraph, except that in a case that has been converted to this chapter under section 1112, 1208, or 1307 of this title, a claim allowed under section 503(b) of this title incurred under this chapter after such conversion has priority over a claim allowed under section 503(b) of this title incurred under any other chapter of this title or under this chapter before such conversion and over any expenses of a custodian superseded under section 543 of this title.

(c) Notwithstanding subsections (a) and (b) of this section, if there is property of the kind specified in section 541(a)(2) of this title, or proceeds of such property, in the estate, such property or proceeds shall be segregated from other property of the estate, and such property or proceeds and other property of the estate shall be distributed as follows:

(1) Claims allowed under section 503 of this title shall be paid either from property of the kind specified in section 541(a)(2) of this title, or from other property of the estate, as the interest of justice requires.

(2) Allowed claims, other than claims allowed under section 503 of this title, shall be paid in the order specified in subsection (a) of this section, and, with respect to claims of a kind specified in a particular paragraph of section 507 of this title or subsection (a) of this section, in the following order and manner:

(A) First, community claims against the debtor or the debtor's spouse shall be paid from property of the kind specified in section 541(a)(2) of this title, except to the extent that such property is solely liable for debts of the debtor.

(B) Second, to the extent that community claims against the debtor are not paid under subparagraph (A) of this paragraph, such community claims shall be paid from property of the kind specified in section 541(a)(2) of this title that is solely liable for debts of the debtor.

(C) Third, to the extent that all claims against the debtor including community claims against the debtor are not paid under subparagraph (A) or (B) of this paragraph such claims shall be paid from property of the estate other than property of the kind specified in section 541(a)(2) of this title.

(D) Fourth, to the extent that community claims against the debtor or the debtor's spouse are not paid under subparagraph (A), (B), or (C) of this paragraph, such claims shall be paid from all remaining property of the estate.

§ 727. Discharge

(a) The court shall grant the debtor a discharge, unless—

(1) the debtor is not an individual;

(2) the debtor, with intent to hinder, delay, or defraud a creditor or an officer of the estate charged with custody of property under this title, has transferred, removed, destroyed, mutilated, or concealed, or has permitted to be transferred, removed, destroyed, mutilated, or concealed—

(A) property of the debtor, within one year before the date of the filing of the petition; or

(B) property of the estate, after the date of the filing of the petition;

(3) the debtor has concealed, destroyed, mutilated, falsified, or failed to keep or preserve any recorded information, including books, documents, records, and papers, from which the debtor's financial condition or business transactions might be ascertained, unless such act or failure to act was justified under all of the circumstances of the case;

(4) the debtor knowingly and fraudulently, in or in connection with the case—

(A) made a false oath or account;

(B) presented or used a false claim;

(C) gave, offered, received, or attempted to obtain money, property, or advantage, or a promise of money, property, or advantage, for acting or forbearing to act; or

(D) withheld from an officer of the estate entitled to possession under this title, any recorded information, including books, documents, records, and papers, relating to the debtor's property or financial affairs;

(5) the debtor has failed to explain satisfactorily, before determination of denial of discharge under this paragraph, any loss of assets or deficiency of assets to meet the debtor's liabilities;

(6) the debtor has refused, in the case—

(A) to obey any lawful order of the court, other than an order to respond to a material question or to testify;

(B) on the ground of privilege against self-incrimination, to respond to a material question approved by the court or to testify, after the debtor has been granted immunity with respect to the matter concerning which such privilege was invoked; or

(C) on a ground other than the properly invoked privilege against self-incrimination, to respond to a material question approved by the court or to testify;

(7) the debtor has committed any act specified in paragraph (2), (3), (4), (5), or (6) of this subsection, on or within one year before the date of the filing of the petition, or during the case, in connection with another case, under this title or under the Bankruptcy Act, concerning an insider;

(8) the debtor has been granted a discharge under this section, under section 1141 of this title, or under section 14, 371, or 476 of the Bankruptcy Act, in a case commenced within 8 years before the date of the filing of the petition;

(9) the debtor has been granted a discharge under section 1228 or 1328 of this title, or under section 660 or 661 of the Bankruptcy Act, in a case commenced within six years before the date of the filing of the petition, unless payments under the plan in such case totaled at least—

(A) 100 percent of the allowed unsecured claims in such case; or

(B)(i) 70 percent of such claims; and

(ii) the plan was proposed by the debtor in good faith, and was the debtor's best effort;

(10) the court approves a written waiver of discharge executed by the debtor after the order for relief under this chapter;

(11) after filing the petition, the debtor failed to complete an instructional course concerning personal financial management described in section 111, except that this paragraph shall not apply with respect to a debtor who is a person described in section 109(h)(4) or who resides in a district for which the United States trustee (or the bankruptcy administrator, if any) determines that the approved instructional courses are not adequate to service the additional individuals who would otherwise be required to complete such instructional courses under this section (The United States trustee (or the bankruptcy administrator, if any) who makes a determination described in this paragraph shall review such determination not later than 1 year after the date of such determination, and not less frequently than annually thereafter.); or

(12) the court after notice and a hearing held not more than 10 days before the date of the entry of the order granting the discharge finds that there is reasonable cause to believe that—

(A) section 522(q)(1) may be applicable to the debtor; and

(B) there is pending any proceeding in which the debtor may be found guilty of a felony of the kind described in section 522(q)(1)(A) or liable for a debt of the kind described in section 522(q)(1)(B).

(b) Except as provided in section 523 of this title, a discharge under subsection (a) of this section discharges the debtor from all debts that arose before the date of the order for relief under this chapter, and any liability on a claim that is determined under section 502 of this title as if such claim had arisen before the commencement of the case, whether or not a proof of claim based on any such debt or liability is filed under section 501 of this title, and whether or not a claim based on any such debt or liability is allowed under section 502 of this title.

(c)(1) The trustee, a creditor, or the United States trustee may object to the granting of a discharge under subsection (a) of this section.

(2) On request of a party in interest, the court may order the trustee to examine the acts and conduct of the debtor to determine whether a ground exists for denial of discharge.

(d) On request of the trustee, a creditor, or the United States trustee, and after notice and a hearing, the court shall revoke a discharge granted under subsection (a) of this section if—

(1) such discharge was obtained through the fraud of the debtor, and the requesting party did not know of such fraud until after the granting of such discharge;

(2) the debtor acquired property that is property of the estate, or became entitled to acquire property that would be property of the estate, and knowingly and fraudulently failed to report the acquisition of or entitlement to such property, or to deliver or surrender such property to the trustee;

(3) the debtor committed an act specified in subsection (a)(6) of this section; or

(4) the debtor has failed to explain satisfactorily—

(A) a material misstatement in an audit referred to in section 586(f) of title 28; or

(B) a failure to make available for inspection all necessary accounts, papers, documents, financial records, files, and all other papers, things, or property belonging to the debtor that are requested for an audit referred to in section 586(f) of title 28.

(e) The trustee, a creditor, or the United States trustee may request a revocation of a discharge—

(1) under subsection (d)(1) of this section within one year after such discharge is granted; or

(2) under subsection (d)(2) or (d)(3) of this section before the later of—

(A) one year after the granting of such discharge; and

(B) the date the case is closed.

SUBCHAPTER III—STOCKBROKER LIQUIDATION

§ 741. Definitions for this subchapter

In this subchapter—

(1) "Commission" means Securities and Exchange Commission;

(2) "customer" includes—

(A) entity with whom a person deals as principal or agent and that has a claim against such person on account of a security received, acquired, or held by such person in the ordinary course of such person's business as a stockbroker, from or for the securities account or accounts of such entity—

(i) for safekeeping;

(ii) with a view to sale;

(iii) to cover a consummated sale;

(iv) pursuant to a purchase;

(v) as collateral under a security agreement; or

(vi) for the purpose of effecting registration of transfer; and

(B) entity that has a claim against a person arising out of—

    (i) a sale or conversion of a security received, acquired, or held as specified in subparagraph (A) of this paragraph; or

    (ii) a deposit of cash, a security, or other property with such person for the purpose of purchasing or selling a security;

  (3) "customer name security" means security—

    (A) held for the account of a customer on the date of the filing of the petition by or on behalf of the debtor;

    (B) registered in such customer's name on such date or in the process of being so registered under instructions from the debtor; and

    (C) not in a form transferable by delivery on such date;

  (4) "customer property" means cash, security, or other property, and proceeds of such cash, security, or property, received, acquired, or held by or for the account of the debtor, from or for the securities account of a customer—

    (A) including—

      (i) property that was unlawfully converted from and that is the lawful property of the estate;

      (ii) a security held as property of the debtor to the extent such security is necessary to meet a net equity claim of a customer based on a security of the same class and series of an issuer;

      (iii) resources provided through the use or realization of a customer's debit cash balance or a debit item includible in the Formula for Determination of Reserve Requirement for Brokers and Dealers as promulgated by the Commission under the Securities Exchange Act of 1934; and

      (iv) other property of the debtor that any applicable law, rule, or regulation requires to be set aside or held for the benefit of a customer, unless including such property as customer property would not significantly increase customer property; but

    (B) not including—

      (i) a customer name security delivered to or reclaimed by a customer under section 751 of this title; or

      (ii) property to the extent that a customer does not have a claim against the debtor based on such property;

  (5) "margin payment" means payment or deposit of cash, a security, or other property, that is commonly known to the securities trade as original margin, initial margin, maintenance margin, or variation margin, or as a mark-to-market payment, or that secures an obligation of a participant in a securities clearing agency;

  (6) "net equity" means, with respect to all accounts of a customer that such customer has in the same capacity—

    (A)(i) aggregate dollar balance that would remain in such accounts after the liquidation, by sale or purchase, at the time of the filing of the petition, of all securities positions in all such accounts, except any customer name securities of such customer; minus

      (ii) any claim of the debtor against such customer in such capacity that would have been owing immediately after such liquidation; plus

    (B) any payment by such customer to the trustee, within 60 days after notice under section 342 of this title, of any business related claim of the debtor against such customer in such capacity;

  (7) "securities contract"—

    (A) means—

(i) a contract for the purchase, sale, or loan of a security, a certificate of deposit, a mortgage loan, any interest in a mortgage loan, a group or index of securities, certificates of deposit, or mortgage loans or interests therein (including an interest therein or based on the value thereof), or option on any of the foregoing, including an option to purchase or sell any such security, certificate of deposit, mortgage loan, interest, group or index, or option, and including any repurchase or reverse repurchase transaction on any such security, certificate of deposit, mortgage loan, interest, group or index, or option (whether or not such repurchase or reverse repurchase transaction is a "repurchase agreement", as defined in section 101);

(ii) any option entered into on a national securities exchange relating to foreign currencies;

(iii) the guarantee (including by novation) by or to any securities clearing agency of a settlement of cash, securities, certificates of deposit, mortgage loans or interests therein, group or index of securities, or mortgage loans or interests therein (including any interest therein or based on the value thereof), or option on any of the foregoing, including an option to purchase or sell any such security, certificate of deposit, mortgage loan, interest, group or index, or option (whether or not such settlement is in connection with any agreement or transaction referred to in clauses (i) through (xi));

(iv) any margin loan;

(v) any extension of credit for the clearance or settlement of securities transactions;

(vi) any loan transaction coupled with a securities collar transaction, any prepaid forward securities transaction, or any total return swap transaction coupled with a securities sale transaction;

(vii) any other agreement or transaction that is similar to an agreement or transaction referred to in this subparagraph;

(viii) any combination of the agreements or transactions referred to in this subparagraph;

(ix) any option to enter into any agreement or transaction referred to in this subparagraph;

(x) a master agreement that provides for an agreement or transaction referred to in clause (i), (ii), (iii), (iv), (v), (vi), (vii), (viii), or (ix), together with all supplements to any such master agreement, without regard to whether the master agreement provides for an agreement or transaction that is not a securities contract under this subparagraph, except that such master agreement shall be considered to be a securities contract under this subparagraph only with respect to each agreement or transaction under such master agreement that is referred to in clause (i), (ii), (iii), (iv), (v), (vi), (vii), (viii), or (ix); or

(xi) any security agreement or arrangement or other credit enhancement related to any agreement or transaction referred to in this subparagraph, including any guarantee or reimbursement obligation by or to a stockbroker, securities clearing agency, financial institution, or financial participant in connection with any agreement or transaction referred to in this subparagraph, but not to exceed the damages in connection with any such agreement or transaction, measured in accordance with section 562; and

(B) does not include any purchase, sale, or repurchase obligation under a participation in a commercial mortgage loan;

(8) "settlement payment" means a preliminary settlement payment, a partial settlement payment, an interim settlement payment, a settlement payment on account, a final settlement payment, or any other similar payment commonly used in the securities trade; and

(9) "SIPC" means Securities Investor Protection Corporation.

§ 742. Effect of section 362 of this title in this subchapter

Notwithstanding section 362 of this title, SIPC may file an application for a protective decree under the Securities Investor Protection Act of 1970. The filing of such application stays all proceedings in the case under this title unless and until such application is dismissed. If SIPC completes the liquidation of the debtor, then the court shall dismiss the case.

§ 743. Notice

The clerk shall give the notice required by section 342 of this title to SIPC and to the Commission.

§ 744. Executory contracts

Notwithstanding section 365(d)(1) of this title, the trustee shall assume or reject, under section 365 of this title, any executory contract of the debtor for the purchase or sale of a security in the ordinary course of the debtor's business, within a reasonable time after the date of the order for relief, but not to exceed 30 days. If the trustee does not assume such a contract within such time, such contract is rejected.

§ 745. Treatment of accounts

(a) Accounts held by the debtor for a particular customer in separate capacities shall be treated as accounts of separate customers.

(b) If a stockbroker or a bank holds a customer net equity claim against the debtor that arose out of a transaction for a customer of such stockbroker or bank, each such customer of such stockbroker or bank shall be treated as a separate customer of the debtor.

(c) Each trustee's account specified as such on the debtor's books, and supported by a trust deed filed with, and qualified as such by, the Internal Revenue Service, and under the Internal Revenue Code of 1986, shall be treated as a separate customer account for each beneficiary under such trustee account.

§ 746. Extent of customer claims

(a) If, after the date of the filing of the petition, an entity enters into a transaction with the debtor, in a manner that would have made such entity a customer had such transaction occurred before the date of the filing of the petition, and such transaction was entered into by such entity in good faith and before the qualification under section 322 of this title of a trustee, such entity shall be deemed a customer, and the date of such transaction shall be deemed to be the date of the filing of the petition for the purpose of determining such entity's net equity.

(b) An entity does not have a claim as a customer to the extent that such entity transferred to the debtor cash or a security that, by contract, agreement, understanding, or operation of law, is—

   (1) part of the capital of the debtor; or

   (2) subordinated to the claims of any or all creditors.

§ 747. Subordination of certain customer claims

Except as provided in section 510 of this title, unless all other customer net equity claims have been paid in full, the trustee may not pay in full or pay in part, directly or indirectly, any net equity claim of a customer that was, on the date the transaction giving rise to such claim occurred—

   (1) an insider;

   (2) a beneficial owner of at least five percent of any class of equity securities of the debtor, other than—

      (A) nonconvertible stock having fixed preferential dividend and liquidation rights; or

      (B) interests of limited partners in a limited partnership;

   (3) a limited partner with a participation of at least five percent in the net assets or net profits of the debtor; or

(4) an entity that, directly or indirectly, through agreement or otherwise, exercised or had the power to exercise control over the management or policies of the debtor.

§ 748. Reduction of securities to money

As soon as practicable after the date of the order for relief, the trustee shall reduce to money, consistent with good market practice, all securities held as property of the estate, except for customer name securities delivered or reclaimed under section 751 of this title.

§ 749. Voidable transfers

(a) Except as otherwise provided in this section, any transfer of property that, but for such transfer, would have been customer property, may be avoided by the trustee, and such property shall be treated as customer property, if and to the extent that the trustee avoids such transfer under section 544, 545, 547, 548, or 549 of this title. For the purpose of such sections, the property so transferred shall be deemed to have been property of the debtor and, if such transfer was made to a customer or for a customer's benefit, such customer shall be deemed, for the purposes of this section, to have been a creditor.

(b) Notwithstanding sections 544, 545, 547, 548, and 549 of this title, the trustee may not avoid a transfer made before seven days after the order for relief if such transfer is approved by the Commission by rule or order, either before or after such transfer, and if such transfer is—

(1) a transfer of a securities contract entered into or carried by or through the debtor on behalf of a customer, and of any cash, security, or other property margining or securing such securities contract; or

(2) the liquidation of a securities contract entered into or carried by or through the debtor on behalf of a customer.

§ 750. Distribution of securities

The trustee may not distribute a security except under section 751 of this title.

§ 751. Customer name securities

The trustee shall deliver any customer name security to or on behalf of the customer entitled to such security, unless such customer has a negative net equity. With the approval of the trustee, a customer may reclaim a customer name security after payment to the trustee, within such period as the trustee allows, of any claim of the debtor against such customer to the extent that such customer will not have a negative net equity after such payment.

§ 752. Customer property

(a) The trustee shall distribute customer property ratably to customers on the basis and to the extent of such customers' allowed net equity claims and in priority to all other claims, except claims of the kind specified in section 507(a)(2) of this title that are attributable to the administration of such customer property.

(b)(1) The trustee shall distribute customer property in excess of that distributed under subsection (a) of this section in accordance with section 726 of this title.

(2) Except as provided in section 510 of this title, if a customer is not paid the full amount of such customer's allowed net equity claim from customer property, the unpaid portion of such claim is a claim entitled to distribution under section 726 of this title.

(c) Any cash or security remaining after the liquidation of a security interest created under a security agreement made by the debtor, excluding property excluded under section 741(4)(B) of this title, shall be apportioned between the general estate and customer property in the same proportion as the general estate of the debtor and customer property were subject to such security interest.

§ 753. Stockbroker liquidation and forward contract merchants, commodity brokers, stockbrokers, financial institutions, financial participants, securities clearing agencies, swap participants, repo participants, and master netting agreement participants

Notwithstanding any other provision of this title, the exercise of rights by a forward contract merchant, commodity broker, stockbroker, financial institution, financial participant, securities clearing agency, swap participant, repo participant, or master netting agreement participant under this title shall not affect the priority of any unsecured claim it may have after the exercise of such rights.

SUBCHAPTER IV—COMMODITY BROKER LIQUIDATION

§ 761. Definitions for this subchapter

In this subchapter—

(1) "Act" means Commodity Exchange Act;

(2) "clearing organization" means a derivatives clearing organization registered under the Act;

(3) "Commission" means Commodity Futures Trading Commission;

(4) "commodity contract" means—

(A) with respect to a futures commission merchant, contract for the purchase or sale of a commodity for future delivery on, or subject to the rules of, a contract market or board of trade;

(B) with respect to a foreign futures commission merchant, foreign future;

(C) with respect to a leverage transaction merchant, leverage transaction;

(D) with respect to a clearing organization, contract for the purchase or sale of a commodity for future delivery on, or subject to the rules of, a contract market or board of trade that is cleared by such clearing organization, or commodity option traded on, or subject to the rules of, a contract market or board of trade that is cleared by such clearing organization;

(E) with respect to a commodity options dealer, commodity option;

(F)(i) any other contract, option, agreement, or transaction that is similar to a contract, option, agreement, or transaction referred to in this paragraph; and

(ii) with respect to a futures commission merchant or a clearing organization, any other contract, option, agreement, or transaction, in each case, that is cleared by a clearing organization;

(G) any combination of the agreements or transactions referred to in this paragraph;

(H) any option to enter into an agreement or transaction referred to in this paragraph;

(I) a master agreement that provides for an agreement or transaction referred to in subparagraph (A), (B), (C), (D), (E), (F), (G), or (H), together with all supplements to such master agreement, without regard to whether the master agreement provides for an agreement or transaction that is not a commodity contract under this paragraph, except that the master agreement shall be considered to be a commodity contract under this paragraph only with respect to each agreement or transaction under the master agreement that is referred to in subparagraph (A), (B), (C), (D), (E), (F), (G), or (H); or

(J) any security agreement or arrangement or other credit enhancement related to any agreement or transaction referred to in this paragraph, including any guarantee or reimbursement obligation by or to a commodity broker or financial participant in connection with any agreement or transaction referred to in this paragraph, but not to exceed the damages in connection with any such agreement or transaction, measured in accordance with section 562;

(5) "commodity option" means agreement or transaction subject to regulation under section 4c(b) of the Act;

(6) "commodity options dealer" means person that extends credit to, or that accepts cash, a security, or other property from, a customer of such person for the purchase or sale of an interest in a commodity option;

(7) "contract market" means a registered entity;

(8) "contract of sale", "commodity", "derivatives clearing organization", "future delivery", "board of trade", "registered entity", and "futures commission merchant" have the meanings assigned to those terms in the Act;

(9) "customer" means—

(A) with respect to a futures commission merchant—

(i) entity for or with whom such futures commission merchant deals and that holds a claim against such futures commission merchant on account of a commodity contract made, received, acquired, or held by or through such futures commission merchant in the ordinary course of such futures commission merchant's business as a futures commission merchant from or for the commodity futures account of such entity; or

(ii) entity that holds a claim against such futures commission merchant arising out of—

(I) the making, liquidation, or change in the value of a commodity contract of a kind specified in clause (i) of this subparagraph;

(II) a deposit or payment of cash, a security, or other property with such futures commission merchant for the purpose of making or margining such a commodity contract; or

(III) the making or taking of delivery on such a commodity contract;

(B) with respect to a foreign futures commission merchant—

(i) entity for or with whom such foreign futures commission merchant deals and that holds a claim against such foreign futures commission merchant on account of a commodity contract made, received, acquired, or held by or through such foreign futures commission merchant in the ordinary course of such foreign futures commission merchant's business as a foreign futures commission merchant from or for the foreign futures account of such entity; or

(ii) entity that holds a claim against such foreign futures commission merchant arising out of—

(I) the making, liquidation, or change in value of a commodity contract of a kind specified in clause (i) of this subparagraph;

(II) a deposit or payment of cash, a security, or other property with such foreign futures commission merchant for the purpose of making or margining such a commodity contract; or

(III) the making or taking of delivery on such a commodity contract;

(C) with respect to a leverage transaction merchant—

(i) entity for or with whom such leverage transaction merchant deals and that holds a claim against such leverage transaction merchant on account of a commodity contract engaged in by or with such leverage transaction merchant in the ordinary course of such leverage transaction merchant's business as a leverage transaction merchant from or for the leverage account of such entity; or

(ii) entity that holds a claim against such leverage transaction merchant arising out of—

(I) the making, liquidation, or change in value of a commodity contract of a kind specified in clause (i) of this subparagraph;

(II) a deposit or payment of cash, a security, or other property with such leverage transaction merchant for the purpose of entering into or margining such a commodity contract; or

(III) the making or taking of delivery on such a commodity contract;

(D) with respect to a clearing organization, clearing member of such clearing organization with whom such clearing organization deals and that holds a claim against such clearing organization on account of cash, a security, or other property received by such clearing organization to margin, guarantee, or secure a commodity contract in such clearing member's proprietary account or customers' account; or

(E) with respect to a commodity options dealer—

(i) entity for or with whom such commodity options dealer deals and that holds a claim on account of a commodity contract made, received, acquired, or held by or through such commodity options dealer in the ordinary course of such commodity options dealer's business as a commodity options dealer from or for the commodity options account of such entity; or

(ii) entity that holds a claim against such commodity options dealer arising out of—

(I) the making of, liquidation of, exercise of, or a change in value of, a commodity contract of a kind specified in clause (i) of this subparagraph; or

(II) a deposit or payment of cash, a security, or other property with such commodity options dealer for the purpose of making, exercising, or margining such a commodity contract;

(10) "customer property" means cash, a security, or other property, or proceeds of such cash, security, or property, received, acquired, or held by or for the account of the debtor, from or for the account of a customer—

(A) including—

(i) property received, acquired, or held to margin, guarantee, secure, purchase, or sell a commodity contract;

(ii) profits or contractual or other rights accruing to a customer as a result of a commodity contract;

(iii) an open commodity contract;

(iv) specifically identifiable customer property;

(v) warehouse receipt or other document held by the debtor evidencing ownership of or title to property to be delivered to fulfill a commodity contract from or for the account of a customer;

(vi) cash, a security, or other property received by the debtor as payment for a commodity to be delivered to fulfill a commodity contract from or for the account of a customer;

(vii) a security held as property of the debtor to the extent such security is necessary to meet a net equity claim based on a security of the same class and series of an issuer;

(viii) property that was unlawfully converted from and that is the lawful property of the estate; and

(ix) other property of the debtor that any applicable law, rule, or regulation requires to be set aside or held for the benefit of a customer, unless including such property as customer property would not significantly increase customer property; but

(B) not including property to the extent that a customer does not have a claim against the debtor based on such property;

(11) "foreign future" means contract for the purchase or sale of a commodity for future delivery on, or subject to the rules of, a board of trade outside the United States;

(12) "foreign futures commission merchant" means entity engaged in soliciting or accepting orders for the purchase or sale of a foreign future or that, in connection with such a solicitation or acceptance, accepts cash, a security, or other property, or extends credit to margin, guarantee, or secure any trade or contract that results from such a solicitation or acceptance;

(13) "leverage transaction" means agreement that is subject to regulation under section 19 of the Commodity Exchange Act, and that is commonly known to the commodities trade as a margin account, margin contract, leverage account, or leverage contract;

(14) "leverage transaction merchant" means person in the business of engaging in leverage transactions;

(15) "margin payment" means payment or deposit of cash, a security, or other property, that is commonly known to the commodities trade as original margin, initial margin, maintenance margin, or variation margin, including mark-to-market payments, settlement payments, variation payments, daily settlement payments, and final settlement payments made as adjustments to settlement prices;

(16) "member property" means customer property received, acquired, or held by or for the account of a debtor that is a clearing organization, from or for the proprietary account of a customer that is a clearing member of the debtor; and

(17) "net equity" means, subject to such rules and regulations as the Commission promulgates under the Act, with respect to the aggregate of all of a customer's accounts that such customer has in the same capacity—

(A) the balance remaining in such customer's accounts immediately after—

(i) all commodity contracts of such customer have been transferred, liquidated, or become identified for delivery; and

(ii) all obligations of such customer in such capacity to the debtor have been offset; plus

(B) the value, as of the date of return under section 766 of this title, of any specifically identifiable customer property actually returned to such customer before the date specified in subparagraph (A) of this paragraph; plus

(C) the value, as of the date of transfer, of—

(i) any commodity contract to which such customer is entitled that is transferred to another person under section 766 of this title; and

(ii) any cash, security, or other property of such customer transferred to such other person under section 766 of this title to margin or secure such transferred commodity contract.

§ 762. Notice to the Commission and right to be heard

(a) The clerk shall give the notice required by section 342 of this title to the Commission.

(b) The Commission may raise and may appear and be heard on any issue in a case under this chapter.

§ 763. Treatment of accounts

(a) Accounts held by the debtor for a particular customer in separate capacities shall be treated as accounts of separate customers.

(b) A member of a clearing organization shall be deemed to hold such member's proprietary account in a separate capacity from such member's customers' account.

(c)   The net equity in a customer's account may not be offset against the net equity in the account of any other customer.

§ 764.   Voidable transfers

(a)   Except as otherwise provided in this section, any transfer by the debtor of property that, but for such transfer, would have been customer property, may be avoided by the trustee, and such property shall be treated as customer property, if and to the extent that the trustee avoids such transfer under section 544, 545, 547, 548, 549, or 724(a) of this title. For the purpose of such sections, the property so transferred shall be deemed to have been property of the debtor, and, if such transfer was made to a customer or for a customer's benefit, such customer shall be deemed, for the purposes of this section, to have been a creditor.

(b)   Notwithstanding sections 544, 545, 547, 548, 549, and 724(a) of this title, the trustee may not avoid a transfer made before seven days after the order for relief, if such transfer is approved by the Commission by rule or order, either before or after such transfer, and if such transfer is—

(1)   a transfer of a commodity contract entered into or carried by or through the debtor on behalf of a customer, and of any cash, securities, or other property margining or securing such commodity contract; or

(2)   the liquidation of a commodity contract entered into or carried by or through the debtor on behalf of a customer.

§ 765.   Customer instructions

(a)   The notice required by section 342 of this title to customers shall instruct each customer—

(1)   to file a proof of such customer's claim promptly, and to specify in such claim any specifically identifiable security, property, or commodity contract; and

(2)   to instruct the trustee of such customer's desired disposition, including transfer under section 766 of this title or liquidation, of any commodity contract specifically identified to such customer.

(b)   The trustee shall comply, to the extent practicable, with any instruction received from a customer regarding such customer's desired disposition of any commodity contract specifically identified to such customer. If the trustee has transferred, under section 766 of this title, such a commodity contract, the trustee shall transmit any such instruction to the commodity broker to whom such commodity contract was so transferred.

§ 766.   Treatment of customer property

(a)   The trustee shall answer all margin calls with respect to a specifically identifiable commodity contract of a customer until such time as the trustee returns or transfers such commodity contract, but the trustee may not make a margin payment that has the effect of a distribution to such customer of more than that to which such customer is entitled under subsection (h) or (i) of this section.

(b)   The trustee shall prevent any open commodity contract from remaining open after the last day of trading in such commodity contract, or into the first day on which notice of intent to deliver on such commodity contract may be tendered, whichever occurs first. With respect to any commodity contract that has remained open after the last day of trading in such commodity contract or with respect to which delivery must be made or accepted under the rules of the contract market on which such commodity contract was made, the trustee may operate the business of the debtor for the purpose of—

(1)   accepting or making tender of notice of intent to deliver the physical commodity underlying such commodity contract;

(2)   facilitating delivery of such commodity; or

(3)   disposing of such commodity if a party to such commodity contract defaults.

(c)   The trustee shall return promptly to a customer any specifically identifiable security, property, or commodity contract to which such customer is entitled, or shall transfer, on such customer's behalf, such security, property, or commodity contract to a commodity broker that is not a debtor under this title, subject to such rules or regulations as the Commission may prescribe, to the extent that the value of such security, property, or commodity contract does not exceed the amount to which such customer would be entitled under subsection (h) or (i) of this section if such security, property, or commodity contract were not returned or transferred under this subsection.

(d) If the value of a specifically identifiable security, property, or commodity contract exceeds the amount to which the customer of the debtor is entitled under subsection (h) or (i) of this section, then such customer to whom such security, property, or commodity contract is specifically identified may deposit cash with the trustee equal to the difference between the value of such security, property, or commodity contract and such amount, and the trustee then shall—

(1) return promptly such security, property, or commodity contract to such customer; or

(2) transfer, on such customer's behalf, such security, property, or commodity contract to a commodity broker that is not a debtor under this title, subject to such rules or regulations as the Commission may prescribe.

(e) Subject to subsection (b) of this section, the trustee shall liquidate any commodity contract that—

(1) is identified to a particular customer and with respect to which such customer has not timely instructed the trustee as to the desired disposition of such commodity contract;

(2) cannot be transferred under subsection (c) of this section; or

(3) cannot be identified to a particular customer.

(f) As soon as practicable after the commencement of the case, the trustee shall reduce to money, consistent with good market practice, all securities and other property, other than commodity contracts, held as property of the estate, except for specifically identifiable securities or property distributable under subsection (h) or (i) of this section.

(g) The trustee may not distribute a security or other property except under subsection (h) or (i) of this section.

(h) Except as provided in subsection (b) of this section, the trustee shall distribute customer property ratably to customers on the basis and to the extent of such customers' allowed net equity claims, and in priority to all other claims, except claims of a kind specified in section 507(a)(2) of this title that are attributable to the administration of customer property. Such distribution shall be in the form of—

(1) cash;

(2) the return or transfer, under subsection (c) or (d) of this section, of specifically identifiable customer securities, property, or commodity contracts; or

(3) payment of margin calls under subsection (a) of this section.

Notwithstanding any other provision of this subsection, a customer net equity claim based on a proprietary account, as defined by Commission rule, regulation, or order, may not be paid either in whole or in part, directly or indirectly, out of customer property unless all other customer net equity claims have been paid in full.

(i) If the debtor is a clearing organization, the trustee shall distribute—

(1) customer property, other than member property, ratably to customers on the basis and to the extent of such customers' allowed net equity claims based on such customers' accounts other than proprietary accounts, and in priority to all other claims, except claims of a kind specified in section 507(a)(2) of this title that are attributable to the administration of such customer property; and

(2) member property ratably to customers on the basis and to the extent of such customers' allowed net equity claims based on such customers' proprietary accounts, and in priority to all other claims, except claims of a kind specified in section 507(a)(2) of this title that are attributable to the administration of member property or customer property.

(j)(1) The trustee shall distribute customer property in excess of that distributed under subsection (h) or (i) of this section in accordance with section 726 of this title.

(2) Except as provided in section 510 of this title, if a customer is not paid the full amount of such customer's allowed net equity claim from customer property, the unpaid portion of such claim is a claim entitled to distribution under section 726 of this title.

§ 767. Commodity broker liquidation and forward contract merchants, commodity brokers, stockbrokers, financial institutions, financial participants, securities clearing agencies, swap participants, repo participants, and master netting agreement participants

Notwithstanding any other provision of this title, the exercise of rights by a forward contract merchant, commodity broker, stockbroker, financial institution, financial participant, securities clearing agency, swap participant, repo participant, or master netting agreement participant under this title shall not affect the priority of any unsecured claim it may have after the exercise of such rights.

SUBCHAPTER V—CLEARING BANK LIQUIDATION

§ 781. Definitions

For purposes of this subchapter, the following definitions shall apply:

(1) Board.—The term "Board" means the Board of Governors of the Federal Reserve System.

(2) Depository Institution.—The term "depository institution" has the same meaning as in section 3 of the Federal Deposit Insurance Act.

(3) Clearing Bank.—The term "clearing bank" means an uninsured State member bank, or a corporation organized under section 25A of the Federal Reserve Act, which operates, or operates as, a multilateral clearing organization pursuant to section 409 of the Federal Deposit Insurance Corporation Improvement Act of 1991.

§ 782. Selection of trustee

(a) In General.—

(1) Appointment.—Notwithstanding any other provision of this title, the conservator or receiver who files the petition shall be the trustee under this chapter, unless the Board designates an alternative trustee.

(2) Successor.—The Board may designate a successor trustee if required.

(b) Authority of Trustee.—Whenever the Board appoints or designates a trustee, chapter 3 and sections 704 and 705 of this title shall apply to the Board in the same way and to the same extent that they apply to a United States trustee.

§ 783. Additional powers of trustee

(a) Distribution of Property Not of the Estate.—The trustee under this subchapter has power to distribute property not of the estate, including distributions to customers that are mandated by subchapters III and IV of this chapter.

(b) Disposition of Institution.—The trustee under this subchapter may, after notice and a hearing—

(1) sell the clearing bank to a depository institution or consortium of depository institutions (which consortium may agree on the allocation of the clearing bank among the consortium);

(2) merge the clearing bank with a depository institution;

(3) transfer contracts to the same extent as could a receiver for a depository institution under paragraphs (9) and (10) of section 11(e) of the Federal Deposit Insurance Act;

(4)   transfer assets or liabilities to a depository institution; and

(5)   transfer assets and liabilities to a bridge depository institution as provided in paragraphs (1), (3)(A), (5), and (6) of section 11(n) of the Federal Deposit Insurance Act, paragraphs (9) through (13) of such section, and subparagraphs (A) through (H) and subparagraph (K) of paragraph (4) of such section 11(n), except that—

(A)   the bridge depository institution to which such assets or liabilities are transferred shall be treated as a clearing bank for the purpose of this subsection; and

(B)   any references in any such provision of law to the Federal Deposit Insurance Corporation shall be construed to be references to the appointing agency and that references to deposit insurance shall be omitted.

(c)   **Certain Transfers Included.**—Any reference in this section to transfers of liabilities includes a ratable transfer of liabilities within a priority class.

§ 784.   Right to be heard

The Board or a Federal reserve bank (in the case of a clearing bank that is a member of that bank) may raise and may appear and be heard on any issue in a case under this subchapter.

CHAPTER 9—ADJUSTMENT OF DEBTS OF A MUNICIPALITY

SUBCHAPTER I—GENERAL PROVISIONS

901.   Applicability of other sections of this title.
902.   Definitions for this chapter.
903.   Reservation of State power to control municipalities.
904.   Limitation on jurisdiction and powers of court.

SUBCHAPTER II—ADMINISTRATION

921.   Petition and proceedings relating to petition.
922.   Automatic stay of enforcement of claims against the debtor.
923.   Notice.
924.   List of creditors.
925.   Effect of list of claims.
926.   Avoiding powers.
927.   Limitation on recourse.
928.   Post petition effect of security interest.
929.   Municipal leases.
930.   Dismissal.

SUBCHAPTER III—THE PLAN

941.   Filing of plan.
942.   Modification of plan.
943.   Confirmation.
944.   Effect of confirmation.
945.   Continuing jurisdiction and closing of the case.
946.   Effect of exchange of securities before the date of the filing of the petition.

SUBCHAPTER I—GENERAL PROVISIONS

§ 901.   Applicability of other sections of this title

   (a)   Sections 301, 333, 344, 347(b), 349, 350(b) 351,,[1] 361, 362, 364(c), 364(d), 364(e), 364(f), 365, 366, 501, 502, 503, 504, 506, 507(a)(2), 509, 510, 524(a)(1), 524(a)(2), 544, 545, 546, 547, 548, 549(a), 549(c), 549(d), 550, 551, 552, 553, 555, 556, 557, 559, 560, 561, 562, 1102, 1103, 1109, 1111(b), 1122, 1123(a)(1), 1123(a)(2), 1123(a)(3), 1123(a)(4), 1123(a)(5), 1123(b), 1123(d), 1124, 1125, 1126(a), 1126(b), 1126(c), 1126(e), 1126(f), 1126(g), 1127(d), 1128, 1129(a)(2), 1129(a)(3), 1129(a)(6), 1129(a)(8), 1129(a)(10), 1129(b)(1), 1129(b)(2)(A), 1129(b)(2)(B), 1142(b), 1143, 1144, and 1145 of this title apply in a case under this chapter.

   (b)   A term used in a section of this title made applicable in a case under this chapter by subsection (a) of this section or section 103(e) of this title has the meaning defined for such term for the purpose of such applicable section, unless such term is otherwise defined in section 902 of this title.

   (c)   A section made applicable in a case under this chapter by subsection (a) of this section that is operative if the business of the debtor is authorized to be operated is operative in a case under this chapter.

§ 902.   Definitions for this chapter

In this chapter—

   (1)   "property of the estate", when used in a section that is made applicable in a case under this chapter by section 103(e) or 901 of this title, means property of the debtor;

   (2)   "special revenues" means—

      (A)   receipts derived from the ownership, operation, or disposition of projects or systems of the debtor that are primarily used or intended to be used primarily to provide transportation, utility, or other services, including the proceeds of borrowings to finance the projects or systems;

      (B)   special excise taxes imposed on particular activities or transactions;

      (C)   incremental tax receipts from the benefited area in the case of tax-increment financing;

      (D)   other revenues or receipts derived from particular functions of the debtor, whether or not the debtor has other functions; or

      (E)   taxes specifically levied to finance one or more projects or systems, excluding receipts from general property, sales, or income taxes (other than tax-increment financing) levied to finance the general purposes of the debtor;

   (3)   "special tax payer" means record owner or holder of legal or equitable title to real property against which a special assessment or special tax has been levied the proceeds of which are the sole source of payment of an obligation issued by the debtor to defray the cost of an improvement relating to such real property;

   (4)   "special tax payer affected by the plan" means special tax payer with respect to whose real property the plan proposes to increase the proportion of special assessments or special taxes referred to in paragraph (2) of this section assessed against such real property; and

   (5)   "trustee", when used in a section that is made applicable in a case under this chapter by section 103(e) or 901 of this title, means debtor, except as provided in section 926 of this title.

§ 903.   Reservation of State power to control municipalities

   This chapter does not limit or impair the power of a State to control, by legislation or otherwise, a municipality of or in such State in the exercise of the political or governmental powers of such municipality, including expenditures for such exercise, but—

   (1)   a State law prescribing a method of composition of indebtedness of such municipality may not bind any creditor that does not consent to such composition; and

---

   [1]   So in original. The second comma probably should follow "350(b)".

(2) a judgment entered under such a law may not bind a creditor that does not consent to such composition.

§ 904. Limitation on jurisdiction and powers of court

Notwithstanding any power of the court, unless the debtor consents or the plan so provides, the court may not, by any stay, order, or decree, in the case or otherwise, interfere with—

(1) any of the political or governmental powers of the debtor;

(2) any of the property or revenues of the debtor; or

(3) the debtor's use or enjoyment of any income-producing property.

SUBCHAPTER II—ADMINISTRATION

§ 921. Petition and proceedings relating to petition

(a) Notwithstanding sections 109(d) and 301 of this title, a case under this chapter concerning an unincorporated tax or special assessment district that does not have such district's own officials is commenced by the filing under section 301 of this title of a petition under this chapter by such district's governing authority or the board or body having authority to levy taxes or assessments to meet the obligations of such district.

(b) The chief judge of the court of appeals for the circuit embracing the district in which the case is commenced shall designate the bankruptcy judge to conduct the case.

(c) After any objection to the petition, the court, after notice and a hearing, may dismiss the petition if the debtor did not file the petition in good faith or if the petition does not meet the requirements of this title.

(d) If the petition is not dismissed under subsection (c) of this section, the court shall order relief under this chapter notwithstanding section 301(b).

(e) The court may not, on account of an appeal from an order for relief, delay any proceeding under this chapter in the case in which the appeal is being taken; nor shall any court order a stay of such proceeding pending such appeal. The reversal on appeal of a finding of jurisdiction does not affect the validity of any debt incurred that is authorized by the court under section 364(c) or 364(d) of this title.

§ 922. Automatic stay of enforcement of claims against the debtor

(a) A petition filed under this chapter operates as a stay, in addition to the stay provided by section 362 of this title, applicable to all entities, of—

(1) the commencement or continuation, including the issuance or employment of process, of a judicial, administrative, or other action or proceeding against an officer or inhabitant of the debtor that seeks to enforce a claim against the debtor; and

(2) the enforcement of a lien on or arising out of taxes or assessments owed to the debtor.

(b) Subsections (c), (d), (e), (f), and (g) of section 362 of this title apply to a stay under subsection (a) of this section the same as such subsections apply to a stay under section 362(a) of this title.

(c) If the debtor provides, under section 362, 364, or 922 of this title, adequate protection of the interest of the holder of a claim secured by a lien on property of the debtor and if, notwithstanding such protection such creditor has a claim arising from the stay of action against such property under section 362 or 922 of this title or from the granting of a lien under section 364(d) of this title, then such claim shall be allowable as an administrative expense under section 503(b) of this title.

(d) Notwithstanding section 362 of this title and subsection (a) of this section, a petition filed under this chapter does not operate as a stay of application of pledged special revenues in a manner consistent with section 927 of this title to payment of indebtedness secured by such revenues.

§ 923. Notice

There shall be given notice of the commencement of a case under this chapter, notice of an order for relief under this chapter, and notice of the dismissal of a case under this chapter. Such notice shall also be published at least once a week for three successive weeks in at least one newspaper of general circulation published within the district in which the case is commenced, and in such other newspaper having a general circulation among bond dealers and bondholders as the court designates.

§ 924. List of creditors

The debtor shall file a list of creditors.

§ 925. Effect of list of claims

A proof of claim is deemed filed under section 501 of this title for any claim that appears in the list filed under section 924 of this title, except a claim that is listed as disputed, contingent, or unliquidated.

§ 926. Avoiding powers

(a) If the debtor refuses to pursue a cause of action under section 544, 545, 547, 548, 549(a), or 550 of this title, then on request of a creditor, the court may appoint a trustee to pursue such cause of action.

(b) A transfer of property of the debtor to or for the benefit of any holder of a bond or note, on account of such bond or note, may not be avoided under section 547 of this title.

§ 927. Limitation on recourse

The holder of a claim payable solely from special revenues of the debtor under applicable nonbankruptcy law shall not be treated as having recourse against the debtor on account of such claim pursuant to section 1111(b) of this title.

§ 928. Post petition effect of security interest

(a) Notwithstanding section 552(a) of this title and subject to subsection (b) of this section, special revenues acquired by the debtor after the commencement of the case shall remain subject to any lien resulting from any security agreement entered into by the debtor before the commencement of the case.

(b) Any such lien on special revenues, other than municipal betterment assessments, derived from a project or system shall be subject to the necessary operating expenses of such project or system, as the case may be.

§ 929. Municipal leases

A lease to a municipality shall not be treated as an executory contract or unexpired lease for the purposes of section 365 or 502(b)(6) of this title solely by reason of its being subject to termination in the event the debtor fails to appropriate rent.

§ 930. Dismissal

(a) After notice and a hearing, the court may dismiss a case under this chapter for cause, including—

    (1) want of prosecution;

    (2) unreasonable delay by the debtor that is prejudicial to creditors;

    (3) failure to propose a plan within the time fixed under section 941 of this title;

    (4) if a plan is not accepted within any time fixed by the court;

    (5) denial of confirmation of a plan under section 943(b) of this title and denial of additional time for filing another plan or a modification of a plan; or

    (6) if the court has retained jurisdiction after confirmation of a plan—

(A) material default by the debtor with respect to a term of such plan; or

(B) termination of such plan by reason of the occurrence of a condition specified in such plan.

(b) The court shall dismiss a case under this chapter if confirmation of a plan under this chapter is refused.

SUBCHAPTER III—THE PLAN

§ 941. Filing of plan

The debtor shall file a plan for the adjustment of the debtor's debts. If such a plan is not filed with the petition, the debtor shall file such a plan at such later time as the court fixes.

§ 942. Modification of plan

The debtor may modify the plan at any time before confirmation, but may not modify the plan so that the plan as modified fails to meet the requirements of this chapter. After the debtor files a modification, the plan as modified becomes the plan.

§ 943. Confirmation

(a) A special tax payer may object to confirmation of a plan.

(b) The court shall confirm the plan if—

(1) the plan complies with the provisions of this title made applicable by sections 103(e) and 901 of this title;

(2) the plan complies with the provisions of this chapter;

(3) all amounts to be paid by the debtor or by any person for services or expenses in the case or incident to the plan have been fully disclosed and are reasonable;

(4) the debtor is not prohibited by law from taking any action necessary to carry out the plan;

(5) except to the extent that the holder of a particular claim has agreed to a different treatment of such claim, the plan provides that on the effective date of the plan each holder of a claim of a kind specified in section 507(a)(2) of this title will receive on account of such claim cash equal to the allowed amount of such claim;

(6) any regulatory or electoral approval necessary under applicable nonbankruptcy law in order to carry out any provision of the plan has been obtained, or such provision is expressly conditioned on such approval; and

(7) the plan is in the best interests of creditors and is feasible.

§ 944. Effect of confirmation

(a) The provisions of a confirmed plan bind the debtor and any creditor, whether or not—

(1) a proof of such creditor's claim is filed or deemed filed under section 501 of this title;

(2) such claim is allowed under section 502 of this title; or

(3) such creditor has accepted the plan.

(b) Except as provided in subsection (c) of this section, the debtor is discharged from all debts as of the time when—

(1) the plan is confirmed;

(2) the debtor deposits any consideration to be distributed under the plan with a disbursing agent appointed by the court; and

(3) the court has determined—

(A) that any security so deposited will constitute, after distribution, a valid legal obligation of the debtor; and

(B) that any provision made to pay or secure payment of such obligation is valid.

(c) The debtor is not discharged under subsection (b) of this section from any debt—

(1) excepted from discharge by the plan or order confirming the plan; or

(2) owed to an entity that, before confirmation of the plan, had neither notice nor actual knowledge of the case.

§ 945. Continuing jurisdiction and closing of the case

(a) The court may retain jurisdiction over the case for such period of time as is necessary for the successful implementation of the plan.

(b) Except as provided in subsection (a) of this section, the court shall close the case when administration of the case has been completed.

§ 946. Effect of exchange of securities before the date of the filing of the petition

The exchange of a new security under the plan for a claim covered by the plan, whether such exchange occurred before or after the date of the filing of the petition, does not limit or impair the effectiveness of the plan or of any provision of this chapter. The amount and number specified in section 1126(c) of this title include the amount and number of claims formerly held by a creditor that has participated in any such exchange.

CHAPTER 11—REORGANIZATION

SUBCHAPTER I—OFFICERS AND ADMINISTRATION

1101.   Definitions for this chapter.
1102.   Creditors' and equity security holders' committees.
1103.   Powers and duties of committees.
1104.   Appointment of trustee or examiner.
1105.   Termination of trustee's appointment.
1106.   Duties of trustee and examiner.
1107.   Rights, powers, and duties of debtor in possession.
1108.   Authorization to operate business.
1109.   Right to be heard.
1110.   Aircraft equipment and vessels.
1111.   Claims and interests.
1112.   Conversion or dismissal.
1113.   Rejection of collective bargaining agreements.
1114.   Payment of insurance benefits to retired employees.
1115.   Property of the estate.
1116.   Duties of trustee or debtor in possession in small business cases.

SUBCHAPTER II—THE PLAN

1121.   Who may file a plan.
1122.   Classification of claims or interests.
1123.   Contents of plan.
1124.   Impairment of claims or interests.
1125.   Postpetition disclosure and solicitation.
1126.   Acceptance of plan.
1127.   Modification of plan.

1128.   Confirmation hearing.
1129.   Confirmation of plan.

SUBCHAPTER III—POSTCONFIRMATION MATTERS

1141.   Effect of confirmation.
1142.   Implementation of plan.
1143.   Distribution.
1144.   Revocation of an order of confirmation.
1145.   Exemption from securities laws.
1146.   Special tax provisions.

SUBCHAPTER IV—RAILROAD REORGANIZATION

1161.   Inapplicability of other sections.
1162.   Definition.
1163.   Appointment of trustee.
1164.   Right to be heard.
1165.   Protection of the public interest.
1166.   Effect of subtitle IV of title 49 and of Federal, State, or local regulations.
1167.   Collective bargaining agreements.
1168.   Rolling stock equipment.
1169.   Effect of rejection of lease of railroad line.
1170.   Abandonment of railroad line.
1171.   Priority claims.
1172.   Contents of plan.
1173.   Confirmation of plan.
1174.   Liquidation.

SUBCHAPTER V—SMALL BUSINESS DEBTOR REORGANIZATION

1181.   Inapplicability of other sections.
1182.   Definitions.
1183.   Trustee.
1184.   Rights and powers of a debtor in possession.
1185.   Removal of debtor in possession.
1186.   Property of the estate.
1187.   Duties and reporting requirements of debtors.
1188.   Status conference.
1189.   Filing of the plan.
1190.   Contents of plan.
1191.   Confirmation of plan.
1192.   Discharge.
1193.   Modification of plan.
1194.   Payments.
1195.   Transactions with professionals.

SUBCHAPTER I—OFFICERS AND ADMINISTRATION

§ 1101.   Definitions for this chapter

In this chapter—

(1)   "debtor in possession" means debtor except when a person that has qualified under section 322 of this title is serving as trustee in the case;

(2)   "substantial consummation" means—

(A)   transfer of all or substantially all of the property proposed by the plan to be transferred;

(B)   assumption by the debtor or by the successor to the debtor under the plan of the business or of the management of all or substantially all of the property dealt with by the plan; and

(C)   commencement of distribution under the plan.

§ 1102.   Creditors' and equity security holders' committees

(a)(1)   Except as provided in paragraph (3), as soon as practicable after the order for relief under chapter 11 of this title, the United States trustee shall appoint a committee of creditors holding unsecured claims and may appoint additional committees of creditors or of equity security holders as the United States trustee deems appropriate.

(2)   On request of a party in interest, the court may order the appointment of additional committees of creditors or of equity security holders if necessary to assure adequate representation of creditors or of equity security holders. The United States trustee shall appoint any such committee.

(3)   Unless the court for cause orders otherwise, a committee of creditors may not be appointed in a small business case or a case under subchapter V of this chapter.

(4)   On request of a party in interest and after notice and a hearing, the court may order the United States trustee to change the membership of a committee appointed under this subsection, if the court determines that the change is necessary to ensure adequate representation of creditors or equity security holders. The court may order the United States trustee to increase the number of members of a committee to include a creditor that is a small business concern (as described in section 3(a)(1) of the Small Business Act), if the court determines that the creditor holds claims (of the kind represented by the committee) the aggregate amount of which, in comparison to the annual gross revenue of that creditor, is disproportionately large.

(b)(1)   A committee of creditors appointed under subsection (a) of this section shall ordinarily consist of the persons, willing to serve, that hold the seven largest claims against the debtor of the kinds represented on such committee, or of the members of a committee organized by creditors before the commencement of the case under this chapter, if such committee was fairly chosen and is representative of the different kinds of claims to be represented.

(2)   A committee of equity security holders appointed under subsection (a)(2) of this section shall ordinarily consist of the persons, willing to serve, that hold the seven largest amounts of equity securities of the debtor of the kinds represented on such committee.

(3)   A committee appointed under subsection (a) shall—

(A)   provide access to information for creditors who—

(i)   hold claims of the kind represented by that committee; and

(ii)   are not appointed to the committee;

(B)   solicit and receive comments from the creditors described in subparagraph (A); and

(C)   be subject to a court order that compels any additional report or disclosure to be made to the creditors described in subparagraph (A).

§ 1103.   Powers and duties of committees

(a)   At a scheduled meeting of a committee appointed under section 1102 of this title, at which a majority of the members of such committee are present, and with the court's approval, such committee may select and authorize the employment by such committee of one or more attorneys, accountants, or other agents, to represent or perform services for such committee.

(b)   An attorney or accountant employed to represent a committee appointed under section 1102 of this title may not, while employed by such committee, represent any other entity having an adverse interest in connection with the case. Representation of one or more creditors of the same class as represented by the committee shall not per se constitute the representation of an adverse interest.

(c)   A committee appointed under section 1102 of this title may—

> **(1)**   consult with the trustee or debtor in possession concerning the administration of the case;

> **(2)**   investigate the acts, conduct, assets, liabilities, and financial condition of the debtor, the operation of the debtor's business and the desirability of the continuance of such business, and any other matter relevant to the case or to the formulation of a plan;

> **(3)**   participate in the formulation of a plan, advise those represented by such committee of such committee's determinations as to any plan formulated, and collect and file with the court acceptances or rejections of a plan;

> **(4)**   request the appointment of a trustee or examiner under section 1104 of this title; and

> **(5)**   perform such other services as are in the interest of those represented.

(d)   As soon as practicable after the appointment of a committee under section 1102 of this title, the trustee shall meet with such committee to transact such business as may be necessary and proper.

§ 1104.   Appointment of trustee or examiner

(a)   At any time after the commencement of the case but before confirmation of a plan, on request of a party in interest or the United States trustee, and after notice and a hearing, the court shall order the appointment of a trustee—

> **(1)**   for cause, including fraud, dishonesty, incompetence, or gross mismanagement of the affairs of the debtor by current management, either before or after the commencement of the case, or similar cause, but not including the number of holders of securities of the debtor or the amount of assets or liabilities of the debtor; or

> **(2)**   if such appointment is in the interests of creditors, any equity security holders, and other interests of the estate, without regard to the number of holders of securities of the debtor or the amount of assets or liabilities of the debtor.

(b)(1)   Except as provided in section 1163 of this title, on the request of a party in interest made not later than 30 days after the court orders the appointment of a trustee under subsection (a), the United States trustee shall convene a meeting of creditors for the purpose of electing one disinterested person to serve as trustee in the case. The election of a trustee shall be conducted in the manner provided in subsections (a), (b), and (c) of section 702 of this title.

> **(2)(A)**   If an eligible, disinterested trustee is elected at a meeting of creditors under paragraph (1), the United States trustee shall file a report certifying that election.

>> **(B)**   Upon the filing of a report under subparagraph (A)—

>>> **(i)**   the trustee elected under paragraph (1) shall be considered to have been selected and appointed for purposes of this section; and

>>> **(ii)**   the service of any trustee appointed under subsection (a) shall terminate.

>> **(C)**   The court shall resolve any dispute arising out of an election described in subparagraph (A).

(c)   If the court does not order the appointment of a trustee under this section, then at any time before the confirmation of a plan, on request of a party in interest or the United States trustee, and after notice and a hearing, the court shall order the appointment of an examiner to conduct such an investigation of the debtor as is appropriate, including an investigation of any allegations of fraud, dishonesty, incompetence, misconduct, mismanagement, or irregularity in the management of the affairs of the debtor of or by current or former management of the debtor, if—

(1) such appointment is in the interests of creditors, any equity security holders, and other interests of the estate; or

(2) the debtor's fixed, liquidated, unsecured debts, other than debts for goods, services, or taxes, or owing to an insider, exceed $5,000,000.

(d) If the court orders the appointment of a trustee or an examiner, if a trustee or an examiner dies or resigns during the case or is removed under section 324 of this title, or if a trustee fails to qualify under section 322 of this title, then the United States trustee, after consultation with parties in interest, shall appoint, subject to the court's approval, one disinterested person other than the United States trustee to serve as trustee or examiner, as the case may be, in the case.

(e) The United States trustee shall move for the appointment of a trustee under subsection (a) if there are reasonable grounds to suspect that current members of the governing body of the debtor, the debtor's chief executive or chief financial officer, or members of the governing body who selected the debtor's chief executive or chief financial officer, participated in actual fraud, dishonesty, or criminal conduct in the management of the debtor or the debtor's public financial reporting.

§ 1105. Termination of trustee's appointment

At any time before confirmation of a plan, on request of a party in interest or the United States trustee, and after notice and a hearing, the court may terminate the trustee's appointment and restore the debtor to possession and management of the property of the estate and of the operation of the debtor's business.

§ 1106. Duties of trustee and examiner

(a) A trustee shall—

(1) perform the duties of the trustee, as specified in paragraphs (2), (5), (7), (8), (9), (10), (11), and (12) of section 704(a);

(2) if the debtor has not done so, file the list, schedule, and statement required under section 521(a)(1) of this title;

(3) except to the extent that the court orders otherwise, investigate the acts, conduct, assets, liabilities, and financial condition of the debtor, the operation of the debtor's business and the desirability of the continuance of such business, and any other matter relevant to the case or to the formulation of a plan;

(4) as soon as practicable—

(A) file a statement of any investigation conducted under paragraph (3) of this subsection, including any fact ascertained pertaining to fraud, dishonesty, incompetence, misconduct, mismanagement, or irregularity in the management of the affairs of the debtor, or to a cause of action available to the estate; and

(B) transmit a copy or a summary of any such statement to any creditors' committee or equity security holders' committee, to any indenture trustee, and to such other entity as the court designates;

(5) as soon as practicable, file a plan under section 1121 of this title, file a report of why the trustee will not file a plan, or recommend conversion of the case to a case under chapter 7, 12, or 13 of this title or dismissal of the case;

(6) for any year for which the debtor has not filed a tax return required by law, furnish, without personal liability, such information as may be required by the governmental unit with which such tax return was to be filed, in light of the condition of the debtor's books and records and the availability of such information;

(7) after confirmation of a plan, file such reports as are necessary or as the court orders; and

(8) if with respect to the debtor there is a claim for a domestic support obligation, provide the applicable notice specified in subsection (c).

(b) An examiner appointed under section 1104(d) of this title shall perform the duties specified in paragraphs (3) and (4) of subsection (a) of this section, and, except to the extent that the court orders otherwise, any other duties of the trustee that the court orders the debtor in possession not to perform.

(c)(1)   In a case described in subsection (a)(8) to which subsection (a)(8) applies, the trustee shall—

(A)(i)   provide written notice to the holder of the claim described in subsection (a)(8) of such claim and of the right of such holder to use the services of the State child support enforcement agency established under sections 464 and 466 of the Social Security Act for the State in which such holder resides, for assistance in collecting child support during and after the case under this title; and

(ii) include in the notice required by clause (i) the address and telephone number of such State child support enforcement agency;

(B)(i)   provide written notice to such State child support enforcement agency of such claim; and

(ii) include in the notice required by clause (i) the name, address, and telephone number of such holder; and

(C) at such time as the debtor is granted a discharge under section 1141, provide written notice to such holder and to such State child support enforcement agency of—

(i)   the granting of the discharge;

(ii)   the last recent known address of the debtor;

(iii) the last recent known name and address of the debtor's employer; and

(iv) the name of each creditor that holds a claim that—

(I)   is not discharged under paragraph (2), (4), or (14A) of section 523(a); or

(II)   was reaffirmed by the debtor under section 524(c).

(2)(A)   The holder of a claim described in subsection (a)(8) or the State child enforcement support agency of the State in which such holder resides may request from a creditor described in paragraph (1)(C)(iv) the last known address of the debtor.

(B) Notwithstanding any other provision of law, a creditor that makes a disclosure of a last known address of a debtor in connection with a request made under subparagraph (A) shall not be liable by reason of making such disclosure.

§ 1107.   Rights, powers, and duties of debtor in possession

(a) Subject to any limitations on a trustee serving in a case under this chapter, and to such limitations or conditions as the court prescribes, a debtor in possession shall have all the rights, other than the right to compensation under section 330 of this title, and powers, and shall perform all the functions and duties, except the duties specified in sections 1106(a)(2), (3), and (4) of this title, of a trustee serving in a case under this chapter.

(b) Notwithstanding section 327(a) of this title, a person is not disqualified for employment under section 327 of this title by a debtor in possession solely because of such person's employment by or representation of the debtor before the commencement of the case.

§ 1108.   Authorization to operate business

Unless the court, on request of a party in interest and after notice and a hearing, orders otherwise, the trustee may operate the debtor's business.

§ 1109.   Right to be heard

(a) The Securities and Exchange Commission may raise and may appear and be heard on any issue in a case under this chapter, but the Securities and Exchange Commission may not appeal from any judgment, order, or decree entered in the case.

(b) A party in interest, including the debtor, the trustee, a creditors' committee, an equity security holders' committee, a creditor, an equity security holder, or any indenture trustee, may raise and may appear and be heard on any issue in a case under this chapter.

§ 1110.   Aircraft equipment and vessels

(a)(1) Except as provided in paragraph (2) and subject to subsection (b), the right of a secured party with a security interest in equipment described in paragraph (3), or of a lessor or conditional vendor of such equipment, to take possession of such equipment in compliance with a security agreement, lease, or conditional sale contract, and to enforce any of its other rights or remedies, under such security agreement, lease, or conditional sale contract, to sell, lease, or otherwise retain or dispose of such equipment, is not limited or otherwise affected by any other provision of this title or by any power of the court.

(2) The right to take possession and to enforce the other rights and remedies described in paragraph (1) shall be subject to section 362 if—

(A) before the date that is 60 days after the date of the order for relief under this chapter, the trustee, subject to the approval of the court, agrees to perform all obligations of the debtor under such security agreement, lease, or conditional sale contract; and

(B) any default, other than a default of a kind specified in section 365(b)(2), under such security agreement, lease, or conditional sale contract—

(i) that occurs before the date of the order is cured before the expiration of such 60-day period;

(ii) that occurs after the date of the order and before the expiration of such 60-day period is cured before the later of—

(I) the date that is 30 days after the date of the default; or

(II) the expiration of such 60-day period; and

(iii) that occurs on or after the expiration of such 60-day period is cured in compliance with the terms of such security agreement, lease, or conditional sale contract, if a cure is permitted under that agreement, lease, or contract.

(3) The equipment described in this paragraph—

(A) is—

(i) an aircraft, aircraft engine, propeller, appliance, or spare part (as defined in section 40102 of title 49) that is subject to a security interest granted by, leased to, or conditionally sold to a debtor that, at the time such transaction is entered into, holds an air carrier operating certificate issued pursuant to chapter 447 of title 49 for aircraft capable of carrying 10 or more individuals or 6,000 pounds or more of cargo; or

(ii) a vessel documented under chapter 121 of title 46 that is subject to a security interest granted by, leased to, or conditionally sold to a debtor that is a water carrier that, at the time such transaction is entered into, holds a certificate of public convenience and necessity or permit issued by the Department of Transportation; and

(B) includes all records and documents relating to such equipment that are required, under the terms of the security agreement, lease, or conditional sale contract, to be surrendered or returned by the debtor in connection with the surrender or return of such equipment.

(4) Paragraph (1) applies to a secured party, lessor, or conditional vendor acting in its own behalf or acting as trustee or otherwise in behalf of another party.

(b) The trustee and the secured party, lessor, or conditional vendor whose right to take possession is protected under subsection (a) may agree, subject to the approval of the court, to extend the 60-day period specified in subsection (a)(1).

(c)(1) In any case under this chapter, the trustee shall immediately surrender and return to a secured party, lessor, or conditional vendor, described in subsection (a)(1), equipment described in subsection (a)(3), if at any time after the date of the order for relief under this chapter such secured party, lessor, or conditional vendor is entitled pursuant to subsection (a)(1) to take possession of such equipment and makes a written demand for such possession to the trustee.

(2) At such time as the trustee is required under paragraph (1) to surrender and return equipment described in subsection (a)(3), any lease of such equipment, and any security agreement or conditional sale contract relating to such equipment, if such security agreement or conditional sale contract is an executory contract, shall be deemed rejected.

(d) With respect to equipment first placed in service on or before October 22, 1994, for purposes of this section—

(1) the term "lease" includes any written agreement with respect to which the lessor and the debtor, as lessee, have expressed in the agreement or in a substantially contemporaneous writing that the agreement is to be treated as a lease for Federal income tax purposes; and

(2) the term "security interest" means a purchase-money equipment security interest.

§ 1111.   Claims and interests

(a) A proof of claim or interest is deemed filed under section 501 of this title for any claim or interest that appears in the schedules filed under section 521(a)(1) or 1106(a)(2) of this title, except a claim or interest that is scheduled as disputed, contingent, or unliquidated.

(b)(1)(A) A claim secured by a lien on property of the estate shall be allowed or disallowed under section 502 of this title the same as if the holder of such claim had recourse against the debtor on account of such claim, whether or not such holder has such recourse, unless—

(i) the class of which such claim is a part elects, by at least two-thirds in amount and more than half in number of allowed claims of such class, application of paragraph (2) of this subsection; or

(ii) such holder does not have such recourse and such property is sold under section 363 of this title or is to be sold under the plan.

(B) A class of claims may not elect application of paragraph (2) of this subsection if—

(i) the interest on account of such claims of the holders of such claims in such property is of inconsequential value; or

(ii) the holder of a claim of such class has recourse against the debtor on account of such claim and such property is sold under section 363 of this title or is to be sold under the plan.

(2) If such an election is made, then notwithstanding section 506(a) of this title, such claim is a secured claim to the extent that such claim is allowed.

§ 1112.   Conversion or dismissal

(a) The debtor may convert a case under this chapter to a case under chapter 7 of this title unless—

(1) the debtor is not a debtor in possession;

(2) the case originally was commenced as an involuntary case under this chapter; or

(3) the case was converted to a case under this chapter other than on the debtor's request.

(b)(1) Except as provided in paragraph (2) and subsection (c), on request of a party in interest, and after notice and a hearing, the court shall convert a case under this chapter to a case under chapter 7 or dismiss a case under this chapter, whichever is in the best interests of creditors and the estate, for cause unless the court determines that the appointment under section 1104(a) of a trustee or an examiner is in the best interests of creditors and the estate.

(2) The court may not convert a case under this chapter to a case under chapter 7 or dismiss a case under this chapter if the court finds and specifically identifies unusual circumstances establishing that converting or dismissing the case is not in the best interests of creditors and the estate, and the debtor or any other party in interest establishes that—

(A) there is a reasonable likelihood that a plan will be confirmed within the timeframes established in sections 1121(e) and 1129(e) of this title, or if such sections do not apply, within a reasonable period of time; and

(B) the grounds for converting or dismissing the case include an act or omission of the debtor other than under paragraph (4)(A)—

(i) for which there exists a reasonable justification for the act or omission; and

(ii) that will be cured within a reasonable period of time fixed by the court.

(3) The court shall commence the hearing on a motion under this subsection not later than 30 days after filing of the motion, and shall decide the motion not later than 15 days after commencement of such hearing, unless the movant expressly consents to a continuance for a specific period of time or compelling circumstances prevent the court from meeting the time limits established by this paragraph.

(4) For purposes of this subsection, the term "cause" includes—

(A) substantial or continuing loss to or diminution of the estate and the absence of a reasonable likelihood of rehabilitation;

(B) gross mismanagement of the estate;

(C) failure to maintain appropriate insurance that poses a risk to the estate or to the public;

(D) unauthorized use of cash collateral substantially harmful to 1 or more creditors;

(E) failure to comply with an order of the court;

(F) unexcused failure to satisfy timely any filing or reporting requirement established by this title or by any rule applicable to a case under this chapter;

(G) failure to attend the meeting of creditors convened under section 341(a) or an examination ordered under rule 2004 of the Federal Rules of Bankruptcy Procedure without good cause shown by the debtor;

(H) failure timely to provide information or attend meetings reasonably requested by the United States trustee (or the bankruptcy administrator, if any);

(I) failure timely to pay taxes owed after the date of the order for relief or to file tax returns due after the date of the order for relief;

(J) failure to file a disclosure statement, or to file or confirm a plan, within the time fixed by this title or by order of the court;

(K) failure to pay any fees or charges required under chapter 123 of title 28;

(L) revocation of an order of confirmation under section 1144;

(M) inability to effectuate substantial consummation of a confirmed plan;

(N) material default by the debtor with respect to a confirmed plan;

(O) termination of a confirmed plan by reason of the occurrence of a condition specified in the plan; and

(P) failure of the debtor to pay any domestic support obligation that first becomes payable after the date of the filing of the petition.

(c) The court may not convert a case under this chapter to a case under chapter 7 of this title if the debtor is a farmer or a corporation that is not a moneyed, business, or commercial corporation, unless the debtor requests such conversion.

(d) The court may convert a case under this chapter to a case under chapter 12 or 13 of this title only if—

> **(1)** the debtor requests such conversion;

> **(2)** the debtor has not been discharged under section 1141(d) of this title; and

> **(3)** if the debtor requests conversion to chapter 12 of this title, such conversion is equitable.

(e) Except as provided in subsections (c) and (f), the court, on request of the United States trustee, may convert a case under this chapter to a case under chapter 7 of this title or may dismiss a case under this chapter, whichever is in the best interest of creditors and the estate if the debtor in a voluntary case fails to file, within fifteen days after the filing of the petition commencing such case or such additional time as the court may allow, the information required by paragraph (1) of section 521(a), including a list containing the names and addresses of the holders of the twenty largest unsecured claims (or of all unsecured claims if there are fewer than twenty unsecured claims), and the approximate dollar amounts of each of such claims.

(f) Notwithstanding any other provision of this section, a case may not be converted to a case under another chapter of this title unless the debtor may be a debtor under such chapter.

§ 1113. Rejection of collective bargaining agreements

(a) The debtor in possession, or the trustee if one has been appointed under the provisions of this chapter, other than a trustee in a case covered by subchapter IV of this chapter and by title I of the Railway Labor Act, may assume or reject a collective bargaining agreement only in accordance with the provisions of this section.

(b)(1) Subsequent to filing a petition and prior to filing an application seeking rejection of a collective bargaining agreement, the debtor in possession or trustee (hereinafter in this section "trustee" shall include a debtor in possession), shall—

> **(A)** make a proposal to the authorized representative of the employees covered by such agreement, based on the most complete and reliable information available at the time of such proposal, which provides for those necessary modifications in the employees benefits and protections that are necessary to permit the reorganization of the debtor and assures that all creditors, the debtor and all of the affected parties are treated fairly and equitably; and

> **(B)** provide, subject to subsection (d)(3), the representative of the employees with such relevant information as is necessary to evaluate the proposal.

> **(2)** During the period beginning on the date of the making of a proposal provided for in paragraph (1) and ending on the date of the hearing provided for in subsection (d)(1), the trustee shall meet, at reasonable times, with the authorized representative to confer in good faith in attempting to reach mutually satisfactory modifications of such agreement.

(c) The court shall approve an application for rejection of a collective bargaining agreement only if the court finds that—

> **(1)** the trustee has, prior to the hearing, made a proposal that fulfills the requirements of subsection (b)(1);

> **(2)** the authorized representative of the employees has refused to accept such proposal without good cause; and

> **(3)** the balance of the equities clearly favors rejection of such agreement.

(d)(1) Upon the filing of an application for rejection the court shall schedule a hearing to be held not later than fourteen days after the date of the filing of such application. All interested parties may appear and be heard at such hearing. Adequate notice shall be provided to such parties at least ten days before the date of such hearing. The court may extend the time for the commencement of such hearing for a period not exceeding seven days where the circumstances of the case, and the interests of justice require such extension, or for additional periods of time to which the trustee and representative agree.

(2) The court shall rule on such application for rejection within thirty days after the date of the commencement of the hearing. In the interests of justice, the court may extend such time for ruling for such additional period as the trustee and the employees' representative may agree to. If the court does not rule on such application within thirty days after the date of the commencement of the hearing, or within such additional time as the trustee and the employees' representative may agree to, the trustee may terminate or alter any provisions of the collective bargaining agreement pending the ruling of the court on such application.

(3) The court may enter such protective orders, consistent with the need of the authorized representative of the employee to evaluate the trustee's proposal and the application for rejection, as may be necessary to prevent disclosure of information provided to such representative where such disclosure could compromise the position of the debtor with respect to its competitors in the industry in which it is engaged.

(e) If during a period when the collective bargaining agreement continues in effect, and if essential to the continuation of the debtor's business, or in order to avoid irreparable damage to the estate, the court, after notice and a hearing, may authorize the trustee to implement interim changes in the terms, conditions, wages, benefits, or work rules provided by a collective bargaining agreement. Any hearing under this paragraph shall be scheduled in accordance with the needs of the trustee. The implementation of such interim changes shall not render the application for rejection moot.

(f) No provision of this title shall be construed to permit a trustee to unilaterally terminate or alter any provisions of a collective bargaining agreement prior to compliance with the provisions of this section.

§ 1114.   Payment of insurance benefits to retired employees

(a) For purposes of this section, the term "retiree benefits" means payments to any entity or person for the purpose of providing or reimbursing payments for retired employees and their spouses and dependents, for medical, surgical, or hospital care benefits, or benefits in the event of sickness, accident, disability, or death under any plan, fund, or program (through the purchase of insurance or otherwise) maintained or established in whole or in part by the debtor prior to filing a petition commencing a case under this title.

(b)(1) For purposes of this section, the term "authorized representative" means the authorized representative designated pursuant to subsection (c) for persons receiving any retiree benefits covered by a collective bargaining agreement or subsection (d) in the case of persons receiving retiree benefits not covered by such an agreement.

(2) Committees of retired employees appointed by the court pursuant to this section shall have the same rights, powers, and duties as committees appointed under sections 1102 and 1103 of this title for the purpose of carrying out the purposes of sections 1114 and 1129(a)(13) and, as permitted by the court, shall have the power to enforce the rights of persons under this title as they relate to retiree benefits.

(c)(1) A labor organization shall be, for purposes of this section, the authorized representative of those persons receiving any retiree benefits covered by any collective bargaining agreement to which that labor organization is signatory, unless (A) such labor organization elects not to serve as the authorized representative of such persons, or (B) the court, upon a motion by any party in interest, after notice and hearing, determines that different representation of such persons is appropriate.

(2) In cases where the labor organization referred to in paragraph (1) elects not to serve as the authorized representative of those persons receiving any retiree benefits covered by any collective bargaining agreement to which that labor organization is signatory, or in cases where the court, pursuant to paragraph (1) finds different representation of such persons appropriate, the court, upon a motion by any party in interest, and after notice and a hearing, shall appoint a committee of retired employees if the debtor seeks to modify or not pay the retiree benefits or if the court otherwise determines that it is appropriate, from among such persons, to serve as the authorized representative of such persons under this section.

(d) The court, upon a motion by any party in interest, and after notice and a hearing, shall order the appointment of a committee of retired employees if the debtor seeks to modify or not pay the retiree benefits or if the court otherwise determines that it is appropriate, to serve as the authorized representative, under this section, of those persons receiving any retiree benefits not covered by a collective bargaining agreement. The United States trustee shall appoint any such committee.

(e)(1) Notwithstanding any other provision of this title, the debtor in possession, or the trustee if one has been appointed under the provisions of this chapter (hereinafter in this section "trustee" shall include a debtor in possession), shall timely pay and shall not modify any retiree benefits, except that—

> **(A)** the court, on motion of the trustee or authorized representative, and after notice and a hearing, may order modification of such payments, pursuant to the provisions of subsections (g) and (h) of this section, or

> **(B)** the trustee and the authorized representative of the recipients of those benefits may agree to modification of such payments,

after which such benefits as modified shall continue to be paid by the trustee.

(2) Any payment for retiree benefits required to be made before a plan confirmed under section 1129 of this title is effective has the status of an allowed administrative expense as provided in section 503 of this title.

(f)(1) Subsequent to filing a petition and prior to filing an application seeking modification of the retiree benefits, the trustee shall—

> **(A)** make a proposal to the authorized representative of the retirees, based on the most complete and reliable information available at the time of such proposal, which provides for those necessary modifications in the retiree benefits that are necessary to permit the reorganization of the debtor and assures that all creditors, the debtor and all of the affected parties are treated fairly and equitably; and

> **(B)** provide, subject to subsection (k)(3), the representative of the retirees with such relevant information as is necessary to evaluate the proposal.

(2) During the period beginning on the date of the making of a proposal provided for in paragraph (1), and ending on the date of the hearing provided for in subsection (k)(1), the trustee shall meet, at reasonable times, with the authorized representative to confer in good faith in attempting to reach mutually satisfactory modifications of such retiree benefits.

(g) The court shall enter an order providing for modification in the payment of retiree benefits if the court finds that—

> **(1)** the trustee has, prior to the hearing, made a proposal that fulfills the requirements of subsection (f);

> **(2)** the authorized representative of the retirees has refused to accept such proposal without good cause; and

> **(3)** such modification is necessary to permit the reorganization of the debtor and assures that all creditors, the debtor, and all of the affected parties are treated fairly and equitably, and is clearly favored by the balance of the equities;

except that in no case shall the court enter an order providing for such modification which provides for a modification to a level lower than that proposed by the trustee in the proposal found by the court to have complied with the requirements of this subsection and subsection (f): *Provided, however,* That at any time after an order is entered providing for modification in the payment of retiree benefits, or at any time after an agreement modifying such benefits is made between the trustee and the authorized representative of the recipients of such benefits, the authorized representative may apply to the court for an order increasing those benefits which order shall be granted if the increase in retiree benefits sought is consistent with the standard set forth in paragraph (3): *Provided further,* That neither the trustee nor the authorized representative is precluded from making more than one motion for a modification order governed by this subsection.

(h)(1) Prior to a court issuing a final order under subsection (g) of this section, if essential to the continuation of the debtor's business, or in order to avoid irreparable damage to the estate, the court, after notice and a hearing, may authorize the trustee to implement interim modifications in retiree benefits.

(2) Any hearing under this subsection shall be scheduled in accordance with the needs of the trustee.

(3) The implementation of such interim changes does not render the motion for modification moot.

(i) No retiree benefits paid between the filing of the petition and the time a plan confirmed under section 1129 of this title becomes effective shall be deducted or offset from the amounts allowed as claims for any benefits which remain unpaid, or from the amounts to be paid under the plan with respect to such claims for unpaid benefits, whether such claims for unpaid benefits are based upon or arise from a right to future unpaid benefits or from any benefits not paid as a result of modifications allowed pursuant to this section.

(j) No claim for retiree benefits shall be limited by section 502(b)(7) of this title.

(k)(1) Upon the filing of an application for modifying retiree benefits, the court shall schedule a hearing to be held not later than fourteen days after the date of the filing of such application. All interested parties may appear and be heard at such hearing. Adequate notice shall be provided to such parties at least ten days before the date of such hearing. The court may extend the time for the commencement of such hearing for a period not exceeding seven days where the circumstances of the case, and the interests of justice require such extension, or for additional periods of time to which the trustee and the authorized representative agree.

(2) The court shall rule on such application for modification within ninety days after the date of the commencement of the hearing. In the interests of justice, the court may extend such time for ruling for such additional period as the trustee and the authorized representative may agree to. If the court does not rule on such application within ninety days after the date of the commencement of the hearing, or within such additional time as the trustee and the authorized representative may agree to, the trustee may implement the proposed modifications pending the ruling of the court on such application.

(3) The court may enter such protective orders, consistent with the need of the authorized representative of the retirees to evaluate the trustee's proposal and the application for modification, as may be necessary to prevent disclosure of information provided to such representative where such disclosure could compromise the position of the debtor with respect to its competitors in the industry in which it is engaged.

(l) If the debtor, during the 180-day period ending on the date of the filing of the petition—

(1) modified retiree benefits; and

(2) was insolvent on the date such benefits were modified;

the court, on motion of a party in interest, and after notice and a hearing, shall issue an order reinstating as of the date the modification was made, such benefits as in effect immediately before such date unless the court finds that the balance of the equities clearly favors such modification.

(m) This section shall not apply to any retiree, or the spouse or dependents of such retiree, if such retiree's gross income for the twelve months preceding the filing of the bankruptcy petition equals or exceeds $250,000, unless such retiree can demonstrate to the satisfaction of the court that he is unable to obtain health, medical, life, and disability coverage for himself, his spouse, and his dependents who would otherwise be covered by the employer's insurance plan, comparable to the coverage provided by the employer on the day before the filing of a petition under this title.

§ 1115.   Property of the estate

(a) In a case in which the debtor is an individual, property of the estate includes, in addition to the property specified in section 541—

(1) all property of the kind specified in section 541 that the debtor acquires after the commencement of the case but before the case is closed, dismissed, or converted to a case under chapter 7, 12, or 13, whichever occurs first; and

(2) earnings from services performed by the debtor after the commencement of the case but before the case is closed, dismissed, or converted to a case under chapter 7, 12, or 13, whichever occurs first.

(b) Except as provided in section 1104 or a confirmed plan or order confirming a plan, the debtor shall remain in possession of all property of the estate.

§ 1116.   Duties of trustee or debtor in possession in small business cases

In a small business case, a trustee or the debtor in possession, in addition to the duties provided in this title and as otherwise required by law, shall—

(1) append to the voluntary petition or, in an involuntary case, file not later than 7 days after the date of the order for relief—

(A) its most recent balance sheet, statement of operations, cash-flow statement, and Federal income tax return; or

(B) a statement made under penalty of perjury that no balance sheet, statement of operations, or cash-flow statement has been prepared and no Federal tax return has been filed;

(2) attend, through its senior management personnel and counsel, meetings scheduled by the court or the United States trustee, including initial debtor interviews, scheduling conferences, and meetings of creditors convened under section 341 unless the court, after notice and a hearing, waives that requirement upon a finding of extraordinary and compelling circumstances;

(3) timely file all schedules and statements of financial affairs, unless the court, after notice and a hearing, grants an extension, which shall not extend such time period to a date later than 30 days after the date of the order for relief, absent extraordinary and compelling circumstances;

(4) file all postpetition financial and other reports required by the Federal Rules of Bankruptcy Procedure or by local rule of the district court;

(5) subject to section 363(c)(2), maintain insurance customary and appropriate to the industry;

(6)(A) timely file tax returns and other required government filings; and

(B) subject to section 363(c)(2), timely pay all taxes entitled to administrative expense priority except those being contested by appropriate proceedings being diligently prosecuted; and

(7) allow the United States trustee, or a designated representative of the United States trustee, to inspect the debtor's business premises, books, and records at reasonable times, after reasonable prior written notice, unless notice is waived by the debtor.

SUBCHAPTER II—THE PLAN

§ 1121.   Who may file a plan

(a) The debtor may file a plan with a petition commencing a voluntary case, or at any time in a voluntary case or an involuntary case.

(b) Except as otherwise provided in this section, only the debtor may file a plan until after 120 days after the date of the order for relief under this chapter.

(c)   Any party in interest, including the debtor, the trustee, a creditors' committee, an equity security holders' committee, a creditor, an equity security holder, or any indenture trustee, may file a plan if and only if—

    (1)   a trustee has been appointed under this chapter;

    (2)   the debtor has not filed a plan before 120 days after the date of the order for relief under this chapter; or

    (3)   the debtor has not filed a plan that has been accepted, before 180 days after the date of the order for relief under this chapter, by each class of claims or interests that is impaired under the plan.

(d)(1)   Subject to paragraph (2), on request of a party in interest made within the respective periods specified in subsections (b) and (c) of this section and after notice and a hearing, the court may for cause reduce or increase the 120-day period or the 180-day period referred to in this section.

    (2)(A)   The 120-day period specified in paragraph (1) may not be extended beyond a date that is 18 months after the date of the order for relief under this chapter.

        (B)   The 180-day period specified in paragraph (1) may not be extended beyond a date that is 20 months after the date of the order for relief under this chapter.

(e)   In a small business case—

    (1)   only the debtor may file a plan until after 180 days after the date of the order for relief, unless that period is—

        (A)   extended as provided by this subsection, after notice and a hearing; or

        (B)   the court, for cause, orders otherwise;

    (2)   the plan and a disclosure statement (if any) shall be filed not later than 300 days after the date of the order for relief; and

    (3)   the time periods specified in paragraphs (1) and (2), and the time fixed in section 1129(e) within which the plan shall be confirmed, may be extended only if—

        (A)   the debtor, after providing notice to parties in interest (including the United States trustee), demonstrates by a preponderance of the evidence that it is more likely than not that the court will confirm a plan within a reasonable period of time;

        (B)   a new deadline is imposed at the time the extension is granted; and

        (C)   the order extending time is signed before the existing deadline has expired.

§ 1122.   Classification of claims or interests

(a)   Except as provided in subsection (b) of this section, a plan may place a claim or an interest in a particular class only if such claim or interest is substantially similar to the other claims or interests of such class.

(b)   A plan may designate a separate class of claims consisting only of every unsecured claim that is less than or reduced to an amount that the court approves as reasonable and necessary for administrative convenience.

§ 1123.   Contents of plan

(a)   Notwithstanding any otherwise applicable nonbankruptcy law, a plan shall—

    (1)   designate, subject to section 1122 of this title, classes of claims, other than claims of a kind specified in section 507(a)(2), 507(a)(3), or 507(a)(8) of this title, and classes of interests;

    (2)   specify any class of claims or interests that is not impaired under the plan;

    (3)   specify the treatment of any class of claims or interests that is impaired under the plan;

(4) provide the same treatment for each claim or interest of a particular class, unless the holder of a particular claim or interest agrees to a less favorable treatment of such particular claim or interest;

(5) provide adequate means for the plan's implementation, such as—

(A) retention by the debtor of all or any part of the property of the estate;

(B) transfer of all or any part of the property of the estate to one or more entities, whether organized before or after the confirmation of such plan;

(C) merger or consolidation of the debtor with one or more persons;

(D) sale of all or any part of the property of the estate, either subject to or free of any lien, or the distribution of all or any part of the property of the estate among those having an interest in such property of the estate;

(E) satisfaction or modification of any lien;

(F) cancellation or modification of any indenture or similar instrument;

(G) curing or waiving of any default;

(H) extension of a maturity date or a change in an interest rate or other term of outstanding securities;

(I) amendment of the debtor's charter; or

(J) issuance of securities of the debtor, or of any entity referred to in subparagraph (B) or (C) of this paragraph, for cash, for property, for existing securities, or in exchange for claims or interests, or for any other appropriate purpose;

(6) provide for the inclusion in the charter of the debtor, if the debtor is a corporation, or of any corporation referred to in paragraph (5)(B) or (5)(C) of this subsection, of a provision prohibiting the issuance of nonvoting equity securities, and providing, as to the several classes of securities possessing voting power, an appropriate distribution of such power among such classes, including, in the case of any class of equity securities having a preference over another class of equity securities with respect to dividends, adequate provisions for the election of directors representing such preferred class in the event of default in the payment of such dividends;

(7) contain only provisions that are consistent with the interests of creditors and equity security holders and with public policy with respect to the manner of selection of any officer, director, or trustee under the plan and any successor to such officer, director, or trustee; and

(8) in a case in which the debtor is an individual, provide for the payment to creditors under the plan of all or such portion of earnings from personal services performed by the debtor after the commencement of the case or other future income of the debtor as is necessary for the execution of the plan.

(b) Subject to subsection (a) of this section, a plan may—

(1) impair or leave unimpaired any class of claims, secured or unsecured, or of interests;

(2) subject to section 365 of this title, provide for the assumption, rejection, or assignment of any executory contract or unexpired lease of the debtor not previously rejected under such section;

(3) provide for—

(A) the settlement or adjustment of any claim or interest belonging to the debtor or to the estate; or

(B) the retention and enforcement by the debtor, by the trustee, or by a representative of the estate appointed for such purpose, of any such claim or interest;

(4) provide for the sale of all or substantially all of the property of the estate, and the distribution of the proceeds of such sale among holders of claims or interests;

(5) modify the rights of holders of secured claims, other than a claim secured only by a security interest in real property that is the debtor's principal residence, or of holders of unsecured claims, or leave unaffected the rights of holders of any class of claims; and

(6) include any other appropriate provision not inconsistent with the applicable provisions of this title.

(c) In a case concerning an individual, a plan proposed by an entity other than the debtor may not provide for the use, sale, or lease of property exempted under section 522 of this title, unless the debtor consents to such use, sale, or lease.

(d) Notwithstanding subsection (a) of this section and sections 506(b), 1129(a)(7), and 1129(b) of this title, if it is proposed in a plan to cure a default the amount necessary to cure the default shall be determined in accordance with the underlying agreement and applicable nonbankruptcy law.

§ 1124.   Impairment of claims or interests

Except as provided in section 1123(a)(4) of this title, a class of claims or interests is impaired under a plan unless, with respect to each claim or interest of such class, the plan—

(1) leaves unaltered the legal, equitable, and contractual rights to which such claim or interest entitles the holder of such claim or interest; or

(2) notwithstanding any contractual provision or applicable law that entitles the holder of such claim or interest to demand or receive accelerated payment of such claim or interest after the occurrence of a default—

(A) cures any such default that occurred before or after the commencement of the case under this title, other than a default of a kind specified in section 365(b)(2) of this title or of a kind that section 365(b)(2) expressly does not require to be cured;

(B) reinstates the maturity of such claim or interest as such maturity existed before such default;

(C) compensates the holder of such claim or interest for any damages incurred as a result of any reasonable reliance by such holder on such contractual provision or such applicable law;

(D) if such claim or such interest arises from any failure to perform a nonmonetary obligation, other than a default arising from failure to operate a nonresidential real property lease subject to section 365(b)(1)(A), compensates the holder of such claim or such interest (other than the debtor or an insider) for any actual pecuniary loss incurred by such holder as a result of such failure; and

(E) does not otherwise alter the legal, equitable, or contractual rights to which such claim or interest entitles the holder of such claim or interest.

§ 1125.   Postpetition disclosure and solicitation

(a) In this section—

(1) "adequate information" means information of a kind, and in sufficient detail, as far as is reasonably practicable in light of the nature and history of the debtor and the condition of the debtor's books and records, including a discussion of the potential material Federal tax consequences of the plan to the debtor, any successor to the debtor, and a hypothetical investor typical of the holders of claims or interests in the case, that would enable such a hypothetical investor of the relevant class to make an informed judgment about the plan, but adequate information need not include such information about any other possible or proposed plan and in determining whether a disclosure statement provides adequate information, the court shall consider the complexity of the case, the benefit of additional information to creditors and other parties in interest, and the cost of providing additional information; and

(2) "investor typical of holders of claims or interests of the relevant class" means investor having—

(A) a claim or interest of the relevant class;

(B) such a relationship with the debtor as the holders of other claims or interests of such class generally have; and

(C) such ability to obtain such information from sources other than the disclosure required by this section as holders of claims or interests in such class generally have.

(b) An acceptance or rejection of a plan may not be solicited after the commencement of the case under this title from a holder of a claim or interest with respect to such claim or interest, unless, at the time of or before such solicitation, there is transmitted to such holder the plan or a summary of the plan, and a written disclosure statement approved, after notice and a hearing, by the court as containing adequate information. The court may approve a disclosure statement without a valuation of the debtor or an appraisal of the debtor's assets.

(c) The same disclosure statement shall be transmitted to each holder of a claim or interest of a particular class, but there may be transmitted different disclosure statements, differing in amount, detail, or kind of information, as between classes.

(d) Whether a disclosure statement required under subsection (b) of this section contains adequate information is not governed by any otherwise applicable nonbankruptcy law, rule, or regulation, but an agency or official whose duty is to administer or enforce such a law, rule, or regulation may be heard on the issue of whether a disclosure statement contains adequate information. Such an agency or official may not appeal from, or otherwise seek review of, an order approving a disclosure statement.

(e) A person that solicits acceptance or rejection of a plan, in good faith and in compliance with the applicable provisions of this title, or that participates, in good faith and in compliance with the applicable provisions of this title, in the offer, issuance, sale, or purchase of a security, offered or sold under the plan, of the debtor, of an affiliate participating in a joint plan with the debtor, or of a newly organized successor to the debtor under the plan, is not liable, on account of such solicitation or participation, for violation of any applicable law, rule, or regulation governing solicitation of acceptance or rejection of a plan or the offer, issuance, sale, or purchase of securities.

(f) Notwithstanding subsection (b), in a small business case—

(1) the court may determine that the plan itself provides adequate information and that a separate disclosure statement is not necessary;

(2) the court may approve a disclosure statement submitted on standard forms approved by the court or adopted under section 2075 of title 28; and

(3)(A) the court may conditionally approve a disclosure statement subject to final approval after notice and a hearing;

(B) acceptances and rejections of a plan may be solicited based on a conditionally approved disclosure statement if the debtor provides adequate information to each holder of a claim or interest that is solicited, but a conditionally approved disclosure statement shall be mailed not later than 25 days before the date of the hearing on confirmation of the plan; and

(C) the hearing on the disclosure statement may be combined with the hearing on confirmation of a plan.

(g) Notwithstanding subsection (b), an acceptance or rejection of the plan may be solicited from a holder of a claim or interest if such solicitation complies with applicable nonbankruptcy law and if such holder was solicited before the commencement of the case in a manner complying with applicable nonbankruptcy law.

§ 1126. Acceptance of plan

(a) The holder of a claim or interest allowed under section 502 of this title may accept or reject a plan. If the United States is a creditor or equity security holder, the Secretary of the Treasury may accept or reject the plan on behalf of the United States.

(b) For the purposes of subsections (c) and (d) of this section, a holder of a claim or interest that has accepted or rejected the plan before the commencement of the case under this title is deemed to have accepted or rejected such plan, as the case may be, if—

    (1) the solicitation of such acceptance or rejection was in compliance with any applicable nonbankruptcy law, rule, or regulation governing the adequacy of disclosure in connection with such solicitation; or

    (2) if there is not any such law, rule, or regulation, such acceptance or rejection was solicited after disclosure to such holder of adequate information, as defined in section 1125(a) of this title.

(c) A class of claims has accepted a plan if such plan has been accepted by creditors, other than any entity designated under subsection (e) of this section, that hold at least two-thirds in amount and more than one-half in number of the allowed claims of such class held by creditors, other than any entity designated under subsection (e) of this section, that have accepted or rejected such plan.

(d) A class of interests has accepted a plan if such plan has been accepted by holders of such interests, other than any entity designated under subsection (e) of this section, that hold at least two-thirds in amount of the allowed interests of such class held by holders of such interests, other than any entity designated under subsection (e) of this section, that have accepted or rejected such plan.

(e) On request of a party in interest, and after notice and a hearing, the court may designate any entity whose acceptance or rejection of such plan was not in good faith, or was not solicited or procured in good faith or in accordance with the provisions of this title.

(f) Notwithstanding any other provision of this section, a class that is not impaired under a plan, and each holder of a claim or interest of such class, are conclusively presumed to have accepted the plan, and solicitation of acceptances with respect to such class from the holders of claims or interests of such class is not required.

(g) Notwithstanding any other provision of this section, a class is deemed not to have accepted a plan if such plan provides that the claims or interests of such class do not entitle the holders of such claims or interests to receive or retain any property under the plan on account of such claims or interests.

§ 1127.   Modification of plan

    (a) The proponent of a plan may modify such plan at any time before confirmation, but may not modify such plan so that such plan as modified fails to meet the requirements of sections 1122 and 1123 of this title. After the proponent of a plan files a modification of such plan with the court, the plan as modified becomes the plan.

    (b) The proponent of a plan or the reorganized debtor may modify such plan at any time after confirmation of such plan and before substantial consummation of such plan, but may not modify such plan so that such plan as modified fails to meet the requirements of sections 1122 and 1123 of this title. Such plan as modified under this subsection becomes the plan only if circumstances warrant such modification and the court, after notice and a hearing, confirms such plan as modified, under section 1129 of this title.

    (c) The proponent of a modification shall comply with section 1125 of this title with respect to the plan as modified.

    (d) Any holder of a claim or interest that has accepted or rejected a plan is deemed to have accepted or rejected, as the case may be, such plan as modified, unless, within the time fixed by the court, such holder changes such holder's previous acceptance or rejection.

    (e) If the debtor is an individual, the plan may be modified at any time after confirmation of the plan but before the completion of payments under the plan, whether or not the plan has been substantially consummated, upon request of the debtor, the trustee, the United States trustee, or the holder of an allowed unsecured claim, to—

        (1) increase or reduce the amount of payments on claims of a particular class provided for by the plan;

        (2) extend or reduce the time period for such payments; or

(3)   alter the amount of the distribution to a creditor whose claim is provided for by the plan to the extent necessary to take account of any payment of such claim made other than under the plan.

(f)(1)   Sections 1121 through 1128 and the requirements of section 1129 apply to any modification under subsection (e).

(2)   The plan, as modified, shall become the plan only after there has been disclosure under section 1125 as the court may direct, notice and a hearing, and such modification is approved.

§ 1128.   Confirmation hearing

(a)   After notice, the court shall hold a hearing on confirmation of a plan.

(b)   A party in interest may object to confirmation of a plan.

§ 1129.   Confirmation of plan

(a)   The court shall confirm a plan only if all of the following requirements are met:

(1)   The plan complies with the applicable provisions of this title.

(2)   The proponent of the plan complies with the applicable provisions of this title.

(3)   The plan has been proposed in good faith and not by any means forbidden by law.

(4)   Any payment made or to be made by the proponent, by the debtor, or by a person issuing securities or acquiring property under the plan, for services or for costs and expenses in or in connection with the case, or in connection with the plan and incident to the case, has been approved by, or is subject to the approval of, the court as reasonable.

(5)(A)(i)   The proponent of the plan has disclosed the identity and affiliations of any individual proposed to serve, after confirmation of the plan, as a director, officer, or voting trustee of the debtor, an affiliate of the debtor participating in a joint plan with the debtor, or a successor to the debtor under the plan; and

(ii)   the appointment to, or continuance in, such office of such individual, is consistent with the interests of creditors and equity security holders and with public policy; and

(B)   the proponent of the plan has disclosed the identity of any insider that will be employed or retained by the reorganized debtor, and the nature of any compensation for such insider.

(6)   Any governmental regulatory commission with jurisdiction, after confirmation of the plan, over the rates of the debtor has approved any rate change provided for in the plan, or such rate change is expressly conditioned on such approval.

(7)   With respect to each impaired class of claims or interests—

(A)   each holder of a claim or interest of such class—

(i)   has accepted the plan; or

(ii)   will receive or retain under the plan on account of such claim or interest property of a value, as of the effective date of the plan, that is not less than the amount that such holder would so receive or retain if the debtor were liquidated under chapter 7 of this title on such date; or

(B)   if section 1111(b)(2) of this title applies to the claims of such class, each holder of a claim of such class will receive or retain under the plan on account of such claim property of a value, as of the effective date of the plan, that is not less than the value of such holder's interest in the estate's interest in the property that secures such claims.

(8)   With respect to each class of claims or interests—

(A)   such class has accepted the plan; or

(B)   such class is not impaired under the plan.

(9) Except to the extent that the holder of a particular claim has agreed to a different treatment of such claim, the plan provides that—

    (A) with respect to a claim of a kind specified in section 507(a)(2) or 507(a)(3) of this title, on the effective date of the plan, the holder of such claim will receive on account of such claim cash equal to the allowed amount of such claim;

    (B) with respect to a class of claims of a kind specified in section 507(a)(1), 507(a)(4), 507(a)(5), 507(a)(6), or 507(a)(7) of this title, each holder of a claim of such class will receive—

        (i) if such class has accepted the plan, deferred cash payments of a value, as of the effective date of the plan, equal to the allowed amount of such claim; or

        (ii) if such class has not accepted the plan, cash on the effective date of the plan equal to the allowed amount of such claim;

    (C) with respect to a claim of a kind specified in section 507(a)(8) of this title, the holder of such claim will receive on account of such claim regular installment payments in cash—

        (i) of a total value, as of the effective date of the plan, equal to the allowed amount of such claim;

        (ii) over a period ending not later than 5 years after the date of the order for relief under section 301, 302, or 303; and

        (iii) in a manner not less favorable than the most favored nonpriority unsecured claim provided for by the plan (other than cash payments made to a class of creditors under section 1122(b)); and

    (D) with respect to a secured claim which would otherwise meet the description of an unsecured claim of a governmental unit under section 507(a)(8), but for the secured status of that claim, the holder of that claim will receive on account of that claim, cash payments, in the same manner and over the same period, as prescribed in subparagraph (C).

(10) If a class of claims is impaired under the plan, at least one class of claims that is impaired under the plan has accepted the plan, determined without including any acceptance of the plan by any insider.

(11) Confirmation of the plan is not likely to be followed by the liquidation, or the need for further financial reorganization, of the debtor or any successor to the debtor under the plan, unless such liquidation or reorganization is proposed in the plan.

(12) All fees payable under section 1930 of title 28, as determined by the court at the hearing on confirmation of the plan, have been paid or the plan provides for the payment of all such fees on the effective date of the plan.

(13) The plan provides for the continuation after its effective date of payment of all retiree benefits, as that term is defined in section 1114 of this title, at the level established pursuant to subsection (e)(1)(B) or (g) of section 1114 of this title, at any time prior to confirmation of the plan, for the duration of the period the debtor has obligated itself to provide such benefits.

(14) If the debtor is required by a judicial or administrative order, or by statute, to pay a domestic support obligation, the debtor has paid all amounts payable under such order or such statute for such obligation that first become payable after the date of the filing of the petition.

(15) In a case in which the debtor is an individual and in which the holder of an allowed unsecured claim objects to the confirmation of the plan—

    (A) the value, as of the effective date of the plan, of the property to be distributed under the plan on account of such claim is not less than the amount of such claim; or

    (B) the value of the property to be distributed under the plan is not less than the projected disposable income of the debtor (as defined in section 1325(b)(2)) to be received during the 5-year period beginning on the date that the first payment is due under the plan, or during the period for which the plan provides payments, whichever is longer.

(16) All transfers of property under the plan shall be made in accordance with any applicable provisions of nonbankruptcy law that govern the transfer of property by a corporation or trust that is not a moneyed, business, or commercial corporation or trust.

(b)(1)   Notwithstanding section 510(a) of this title, if all of the applicable requirements of subsection (a) of this section other than paragraph (8) are met with respect to a plan, the court, on request of the proponent of the plan, shall confirm the plan notwithstanding the requirements of such paragraph if the plan does not discriminate unfairly, and is fair and equitable, with respect to each class of claims or interests that is impaired under, and has not accepted, the plan.

(2)   For the purpose of this subsection, the condition that a plan be fair and equitable with respect to a class includes the following requirements:

(A) With respect to a class of secured claims, the plan provides—

(i)(I)   that the holders of such claims retain the liens securing such claims, whether the property subject to such liens is retained by the debtor or transferred to another entity, to the extent of the allowed amount of such claims; and

(II)   that each holder of a claim of such class receive on account of such claim deferred cash payments totaling at least the allowed amount of such claim, of a value, as of the effective date of the plan, of at least the value of such holder's interest in the estate's interest in such property;

(ii)   for the sale, subject to section 363(k) of this title, of any property that is subject to the liens securing such claims, free and clear of such liens, with such liens to attach to the proceeds of such sale, and the treatment of such liens on proceeds under clause (i) or (iii) of this subparagraph; or

(iii)   for the realization by such holders of the indubitable equivalent of such claims.

(B) With respect to a class of unsecured claims—

(i)   the plan provides that each holder of a claim of such class receive or retain on account of such claim property of a value, as of the effective date of the plan, equal to the allowed amount of such claim; or

(ii)   the holder of any claim or interest that is junior to the claims of such class will not receive or retain under the plan on account of such junior claim or interest any property, except that in a case in which the debtor is an individual, the debtor may retain property included in the estate under section 1115, subject to the requirements of subsection (a)(14) of this section.

(C) With respect to a class of interests—

(i)   the plan provides that each holder of an interest of such class receive or retain on account of such interest property of a value, as of the effective date of the plan, equal to the greatest of the allowed amount of any fixed liquidation preference to which such holder is entitled, any fixed redemption price to which such holder is entitled, or the value of such interest; or

(ii)   the holder of any interest that is junior to the interests of such class will not receive or retain under the plan on account of such junior interest any property.

(c)   Notwithstanding subsections (a) and (b) of this section and except as provided in section 1127(b) of this title, the court may confirm only one plan, unless the order of confirmation in the case has been revoked under section 1144 of this title. If the requirements of subsections (a) and (b) of this section are met with respect to more than one plan, the court shall consider the preferences of creditors and equity security holders in determining which plan to confirm.

(d)   Notwithstanding any other provision of this section, on request of a party in interest that is a governmental unit, the court may not confirm a plan if the principal purpose of the plan is the avoidance of taxes or the avoidance of the application of section 5 of the Securities Act of 1933. In any hearing under this subsection, the governmental unit has the burden of proof on the issue of avoidance.

(e) In a small business case, the court shall confirm a plan that complies with the applicable provisions of this title and that is filed in accordance with section 1121(e) not later than 45 days after the plan is filed unless the time for confirmation is extended in accordance with section 1121(e)(3).

SUBCHAPTER III—POSTCONFIRMATION MATTERS

§ 1141.   Effect of confirmation

(a) Except as provided in subsections (d)(2) and (d)(3) of this section, the provisions of a confirmed plan bind the debtor, any entity issuing securities under the plan, any entity acquiring property under the plan, and any creditor, equity security holder, or general partner in the debtor, whether or not the claim or interest of such creditor, equity security holder, or general partner is impaired under the plan and whether or not such creditor, equity security holder, or general partner has accepted the plan.

(b) Except as otherwise provided in the plan or the order confirming the plan, the confirmation of a plan vests all of the property of the estate in the debtor.

(c) Except as provided in subsections (d)(2) and (d)(3) of this section and except as otherwise provided in the plan or in the order confirming the plan, after confirmation of a plan, the property dealt with by the plan is free and clear of all claims and interests of creditors, equity security holders, and of general partners in the debtor.

(d)(1) Except as otherwise provided in this subsection, in the plan, or in the order confirming the plan, the confirmation of a plan—

    (A) discharges the debtor from any debt that arose before the date of such confirmation, and any debt of a kind specified in section 502(g), 502(h), or 502(i) of this title, whether or not—

        (i) a proof of the claim based on such debt is filed or deemed filed under section 501 of this title;

        (ii) such claim is allowed under section 502 of this title; or

        (iii) the holder of such claim has accepted the plan; and

    (B) terminates all rights and interests of equity security holders and general partners provided for by the plan.

(2) A discharge under this chapter does not discharge a debtor who is an individual from any debt excepted from discharge under section 523 of this title.

(3) The confirmation of a plan does not discharge a debtor if—

    (A) the plan provides for the liquidation of all or substantially all of the property of the estate;

    (B) the debtor does not engage in business after consummation of the plan; and

    (C) the debtor would be denied a discharge under section 727(a) of this title if the case were a case under chapter 7 of this title.

(4) The court may approve a written waiver of discharge executed by the debtor after the order for relief under this chapter.

(5) In a case in which the debtor is an individual—

    (A) unless after notice and a hearing the court orders otherwise for cause, confirmation of the plan does not discharge any debt provided for in the plan until the court grants a discharge on completion of all payments under the plan;

    (B) at any time after the confirmation of the plan, and after notice and a hearing, the court may grant a discharge to the debtor who has not completed payments under the plan if—

        (i) the value, as of the effective date of the plan, of property actually distributed under the plan on account of each allowed unsecured claim is not less than the amount that would have been paid on such claim if the estate of the debtor had been liquidated under chapter 7 on such date;

  (ii) modification of the plan under section 1127 is not practicable; and

  (iii) subparagraph (C) permits the court to grant a discharge; and

 (C) the court may grant a discharge if, after notice and a hearing held not more than 10 days before the date of the entry of the order granting the discharge, the court finds that there is no reasonable cause to believe that—

  (i) section 522(q)(1) may be applicable to the debtor; and

  (ii) there is pending any proceeding in which the debtor may be found guilty of a felony of the kind described in section 522(q)(1)(A) or liable for a debt of the kind described in section 522(q)(1)(B);

and if the requirements of subparagraph (A) or (B) are met.

 (6) Notwithstanding paragraph (1), the confirmation of a plan does not discharge a debtor that is a corporation from any debt—

 (A) of a kind specified in paragraph (2)(A) or (2)(B) of section 523(a) that is owed to a domestic governmental unit, or owed to a person as the result of an action filed under subchapter III of chapter 37 of title 31 or any similar State statute; or

 (B) for a tax or customs duty with respect to which the debtor—

  (i) made a fraudulent return; or

  (ii) willfully attempted in any manner to evade or to defeat such tax or such customs duty.

§ 1142.   Implementation of plan

 (a) Notwithstanding any otherwise applicable nonbankruptcy law, rule, or regulation relating to financial condition, the debtor and any entity organized or to be organized for the purpose of carrying out the plan shall carry out the plan and shall comply with any orders of the court.

 (b) The court may direct the debtor and any other necessary party to execute or deliver or to join in the execution or delivery of any instrument required to effect a transfer of property dealt with by a confirmed plan, and to perform any other act, including the satisfaction of any lien, that is necessary for the consummation of the plan.

§ 1143.   Distribution

 If a plan requires presentment or surrender of a security or the performance of any other act as a condition to participation in distribution under the plan, such action shall be taken not later than five years after the date of the entry of the order of confirmation. Any entity that has not within such time presented or surrendered such entity's security or taken any such other action that the plan requires may not participate in distribution under the plan.

§ 1144.   Revocation of an order of confirmation

 On request of a party in interest at any time before 180 days after the date of the entry of the order of confirmation, and after notice and a hearing, the court may revoke such order if and only if such order was procured by fraud. An order under this section revoking an order of confirmation shall—

 (1) contain such provisions as are necessary to protect any entity acquiring rights in good faith reliance on the order of confirmation; and

 (2) revoke the discharge of the debtor.

§ 1145.   Exemption from securities laws

(a)   Except with respect to an entity that is an underwriter as defined in subsection (b) of this section, section 5 of the Securities Act of 1933 and any State or local law requiring registration for offer or sale of a security or registration or licensing of an issuer of, underwriter of, or broker or dealer in, a security do not apply to—

(1)   the offer or sale under a plan of a security of the debtor, of an affiliate participating in a joint plan with the debtor, or of a successor to the debtor under the plan—

(A)   in exchange for a claim against, an interest in, or a claim for an administrative expense in the case concerning, the debtor or such affiliate; or

(B)   principally in such exchange and partly for cash or property;

(2)   the offer of a security through any warrant, option, right to subscribe, or conversion privilege that was sold in the manner specified in paragraph (1) of this subsection, or the sale of a security upon the exercise of such a warrant, option, right, or privilege;

(3)   the offer or sale, other than under a plan, of a security of an issuer other than the debtor or an affiliate, if—

(A)   such security was owned by the debtor on the date of the filing of the petition;

(B)   the issuer of such security is—

(i)   required to file reports under section 13 or 15(d) of the Securities Exchange Act of 1934; and

(ii)   in compliance with the disclosure and reporting provision of such applicable section; and

(C)   such offer or sale is of securities that do not exceed—

(i)   during the two-year period immediately following the date of the filing of the petition, four percent of the securities of such class outstanding on such date; and

(ii)   during any 180-day period following such two-year period, one percent of the securities outstanding at the beginning of such 180-day period; or

(4)   a transaction by a stockbroker in a security that is executed after a transaction of a kind specified in paragraph (1) or (2) of this subsection in such security and before the expiration of 40 days after the first date on which such security was bona fide offered to the public by the issuer or by or through an underwriter, if such stockbroker provides, at the time of or before such transaction by such stockbroker, a disclosure statement approved under section 1125 of this title, and, if the court orders, information supplementing such disclosure statement.

(b)(1)   Except as provided in paragraph (2) of this subsection and except with respect to ordinary trading transactions of an entity that is not an issuer, an entity is an underwriter under section 2(a)(11) of the Securities Act of 1933, if such entity—

(A)   purchases a claim against, interest in, or claim for an administrative expense in the case concerning, the debtor, if such purchase is with a view to distribution of any security received or to be received in exchange for such a claim or interest;

(B)   offers to sell securities offered or sold under the plan for the holders of such securities;

(C)   offers to buy securities offered or sold under the plan from the holders of such securities, if such offer to buy is—

(i)   with a view to distribution of such securities; and

(ii)   under an agreement made in connection with the plan, with the consummation of the plan, or with the offer or sale of securities under the plan; or

(D)   is an issuer, as used in such section 2(a)(11), with respect to such securities.

(2) An entity is not an underwriter under section 2(a)(11) of the Securities Act of 1933 or under paragraph (1) of this subsection with respect to an agreement that provides only for—

(A)(i) the matching or combining of fractional interests in securities offered or sold under the plan into whole interests; or

(ii) the purchase or sale of such fractional interests from or to entities receiving such fractional interests under the plan; or

(B) the purchase or sale for such entities of such fractional or whole interests as are necessary to adjust for any remaining fractional interests after such matching.

(3) An entity other than an entity of the kind specified in paragraph (1) of this subsection is not an underwriter under section 2(a)(11) of the Securities Act of 1933 with respect to any securities offered or sold to such entity in the manner specified in subsection (a)(1) of this section.

(c) An offer or sale of securities of the kind and in the manner specified under subsection (a)(1) of this section is deemed to be a public offering.

(d) The Trust Indenture Act of 1939 does not apply to a note issued under the plan that matures not later than one year after the effective date of the plan.

§ 1146. Special tax provisions

(a) The issuance, transfer, or exchange of a security, or the making or delivery of an instrument of transfer under a plan confirmed under section 1129 or 1191 of this title, may not be taxed under any law imposing a stamp tax or similar tax.

(b) The court may authorize the proponent of a plan to request a determination, limited to questions of law, by a State or local governmental unit charged with responsibility for collection or determination of a tax on or measured by income, of the tax effects, under section 346 of this title and under the law imposing such tax, of the plan. In the event of an actual controversy, the court may declare such effects after the earlier of—

(1) the date on which such governmental unit responds to the request under this subsection; or

(2) 270 days after such request.

SUBCHAPTER IV—RAILROAD REORGANIZATION

§ 1161. Inapplicability of other sections

Sections 341, 343, 1102(a)(1), 1104, 1105, 1107, 1129(a)(7), and 1129(c) of this title do not apply in a case concerning a railroad.

§ 1162. Definition

In this subchapter, "Board" means the "Surface Transportation Board".

§ 1163. Appointment of trustee

As soon as practicable after the order for relief the Secretary of Transportation shall submit a list of five disinterested persons that are qualified and willing to serve as trustees in the case. The United States trustee shall appoint one of such persons to serve as trustee in the case.

§ 1164. Right to be heard

The Board, the Department of Transportation, and any State or local commission having regulatory jurisdiction over the debtor may raise and may appear and be heard on any issue in a case under this chapter, but may not appeal from any judgment, order, or decree entered in the case.

§ 1165.   Protection of the public interest

In applying sections 1166, 1167, 1169, 1170, 1171, 1172, 1173, and 1174 of this title, the court and the trustee shall consider the public interest in addition to the interests of the debtor, creditors, and equity security holders.

§ 1166.   Effect of subtitle IV of title 49 and of Federal, State, or local regulations

Except with respect to abandonment under section 1170 of this title, or merger, modification of the financial structure of the debtor, or issuance or sale of securities under a plan, the trustee and the debtor are subject to the provisions of subtitle IV of title 49 that are applicable to railroads, and the trustee is subject to orders of any Federal, State, or local regulatory body to the same extent as the debtor would be if a petition commencing the case under this chapter had not been filed, but—

(1) any such order that would require the expenditure, or the incurring of an obligation for the expenditure, of money from the estate is not effective unless approved by the court; and

(2) the provisions of this chapter are subject to section 601(b) of the Regional Rail Reorganization Act of 1973.

§ 1167.   Collective bargaining agreements

Notwithstanding section 365 of this title, neither the court nor the trustee may change the wages or working conditions of employees of the debtor established by a collective bargaining agreement that is subject to the Railway Labor Act except in accordance with section 6 of such Act.

§ 1168.   Rolling stock equipment

(a)(1) The right of a secured party with a security interest in or of a lessor or conditional vendor of equipment described in paragraph (2) to take possession of such equipment in compliance with an equipment security agreement, lease, or conditional sale contract, and to enforce any of its other rights or remedies under such security agreement, lease, or conditional sale contract, to sell, lease, or otherwise retain or dispose of such equipment, is not limited or otherwise affected by any other provision of this title or by any power of the court, except that right to take possession and enforce those other rights and remedies shall be subject to section 362, if—

(A) before the date that is 60 days after the date of commencement of a case under this chapter, the trustee, subject to the court's approval, agrees to perform all obligations of the debtor under such security agreement, lease, or conditional sale contract; and

(B) any default, other than a default of a kind described in section 365(b)(2), under such security agreement, lease, or conditional sale contract—

(i) that occurs before the date of commencement of the case and is an event of default therewith is cured before the expiration of such 60-day period;

(ii) that occurs or becomes an event of default after the date of commencement of the case and before the expiration of such 60-day period is cured before the later of—

(I) the date that is 30 days after the date of the default or event of the default; or

(II) the expiration of such 60-day period; and

(iii) that occurs on or after the expiration of such 60-day period is cured in accordance with the terms of such security agreement, lease, or conditional sale contract, if cure is permitted under that agreement, lease, or conditional sale contract.

(2) The equipment described in this paragraph—

(A) is rolling stock equipment or accessories used on rolling stock equipment, including superstructures or racks, that is subject to a security interest granted by, leased to, or conditionally sold to a debtor; and

(B) includes all records and documents relating to such equipment that are required, under the terms of the security agreement, lease, or conditional sale contract, that is to be surrendered or returned by the debtor in connection with the surrender or return of such equipment.

(3) Paragraph (1) applies to a secured party, lessor, or conditional vendor acting in its own behalf or acting as trustee or otherwise in behalf of another party.

(b) The trustee and the secured party, lessor, or conditional vendor whose right to take possession is protected under subsection (a) may agree, subject to the court's approval, to extend the 60-day period specified in subsection (a)(1).

(c)(1) In any case under this chapter, the trustee shall immediately surrender and return to a secured party, lessor, or conditional vendor, described in subsection (a)(1), equipment described in subsection (a)(2), if at any time after the date of commencement of the case under this chapter such secured party, lessor, or conditional vendor is entitled pursuant to subsection (a)(1) to take possession of such equipment and makes a written demand for such possession of the trustee.

(2) At such time as the trustee is required under paragraph (1) to surrender and return equipment described in subsection (a)(2), any lease of such equipment, and any security agreement or conditional sale contract relating to such equipment, if such security agreement or conditional sale contract is an executory contract, shall be deemed rejected.

(d) With respect to equipment first placed in service on or prior to October 22, 1994, for purposes of this section—

(1) the term "lease" includes any written agreement with respect to which the lessor and the debtor, as lessee, have expressed in the agreement or in a substantially contemporaneous writing that the agreement is to be treated as a lease for Federal income tax purposes; and

(2) the term "security interest" means a purchase-money equipment security interest.

(e) With respect to equipment first placed in service after October 22, 1994, for purposes of this section, the term "rolling stock equipment" includes rolling stock equipment that is substantially rebuilt and accessories used on such equipment.

§ 1169. Effect of rejection of lease of railroad line

(a) Except as provided in subsection (b) of this section, if a lease of a line of railroad under which the debtor is the lessee is rejected under section 365 of this title, and if the trustee, within such time as the court fixes, and with the court's approval, elects not to operate the leased line, the lessor under such lease, after such approval, shall operate the line.

(b) If operation of such line by such lessor is impracticable or contrary to the public interest, the court, on request of such lessor, and after notice and a hearing, shall order the trustee to continue operation of such line for the account of such lessor until abandonment is ordered under section 1170 of this title, or until such operation is otherwise lawfully terminated, whichever occurs first.

(c) During any such operation, such lessor is deemed a carrier subject to the provisions of subtitle IV of title 49 that are applicable to railroads.

§ 1170. Abandonment of railroad line

(a) The court, after notice and a hearing, may authorize the abandonment of all or a portion of a railroad line if such abandonment is—

(1)(A) in the best interest of the estate; or

(B) essential to the formulation of a plan; and

(2) consistent with the public interest.

(b) If, except for the pendency of the case under this chapter, such abandonment would require approval by the Board under a law of the United States, the trustee shall initiate an appropriate application for such abandonment with the Board. The court may fix a time within which the Board shall report to the court on such application.

(c) After the court receives the report of the Board, or the expiration of the time fixed under subsection (b) of this section, whichever occurs first, the court may authorize such abandonment, after notice to the Board, the Secretary of Transportation, the trustee, any party in interest that has requested notice, any affected shipper or community, and any other entity prescribed by the court, and a hearing.

(d)(1) Enforcement of an order authorizing such abandonment shall be stayed until the time for taking an appeal has expired, or, if an appeal is timely taken, until such order has become final.

(2) If an order authorizing such abandonment is appealed, the court, on request of a party in interest, may authorize suspension of service on a line or a portion of a line pending the determination of such appeal, after notice to the Board, the Secretary of Transportation, the trustee, any party in interest that has requested notice, any affected shipper or community, and any other entity prescribed by the court, and a hearing. An appellant may not obtain a stay of the enforcement of an order authorizing such suspension by the giving of a supersedeas bond or otherwise, during the pendency of such appeal.

(e)(1) In authorizing any abandonment of a railroad line under this section, the court shall require the rail carrier to provide a fair arrangement at least as protective of the interests of employees as that established under section 11326(a) of title 49.

(2) Nothing in this subsection shall be deemed to affect the priorities or timing of payment of employee protection which might have existed in the absence of this subsection.

§ 1171. Priority claims

(a) There shall be paid as an administrative expense any claim of an individual or of the personal representative of a deceased individual against the debtor or the estate, for personal injury to or death of such individual arising out of the operation of the debtor or the estate, whether such claim arose before or after the commencement of the case.

(b) Any unsecured claim against the debtor that would have been entitled to priority if a receiver in equity of the property of the debtor had been appointed by a Federal court on the date of the order for relief under this title shall be entitled to the same priority in the case under this chapter.

§ 1172. Contents of plan

(a) In addition to the provisions required or permitted under section 1123 of this title, a plan—

(1) shall specify the extent to and the means by which the debtor's rail service is proposed to be continued, and the extent to which any of the debtor's rail service is proposed to be terminated; and

(2) may include a provision for—

(A) the transfer of any or all of the operating railroad lines of the debtor to another operating railroad; or

(B) abandonment of any railroad line in accordance with section 1170 of this title.

(b) If, except for the pendency of the case under this chapter, transfer of, or operation of or over, any of the debtor's rail lines by an entity other than the debtor or a successor to the debtor under the plan would require approval by the Board under a law of the United States, then a plan may not propose such a transfer or such operation unless the proponent of the plan initiates an appropriate application for such a transfer or such operation with the Board and, within such time as the court may fix, not exceeding 180 days, the Board, with or without a hearing, as the Board may determine, and with or without modification or condition, approves such application, or does not act on such application. Any action or order of the Board approving, modifying, conditioning, or disapproving such application is subject to review by the court only under sections 706(2)(A), 706(2)(B), 706(2)(C), and 706(2)(D) of title 5.

(c)(1) In approving an application under subsection (b) of this section, the Board shall require the rail carrier to provide a fair arrangement at least as protective of the interests of employees as that established under section 11326(a) of title 49.

(2) Nothing in this subsection shall be deemed to affect the priorities or timing of payment of employee protection which might have existed in the absence of this subsection.

§ 1173. Confirmation of plan

(a) The court shall confirm a plan if—

(1) the applicable requirements of section 1129 of this title have been met;

(2) each creditor or equity security holder will receive or retain under the plan property of a value, as of the effective date of the plan, that is not less than the value of property that each such creditor or equity security holder would so receive or retain if all of the operating railroad lines of the debtor were sold, and the proceeds of such sale, and the other property of the estate, were distributed under chapter 7 of this title on such date;

(3) in light of the debtor's past earnings and the probable prospective earnings of the reorganized debtor, there will be adequate coverage by such prospective earnings of any fixed charges, such as interest on debt, amortization of funded debt, and rent for leased railroads, provided for by the plan; and

(4) the plan is consistent with the public interest.

(b) If the requirements of subsection (a) of this section are met with respect to more than one plan, the court shall confirm the plan that is most likely to maintain adequate rail service in the public interest.

§ 1174. Liquidation

On request of a party in interest and after notice and a hearing, the court may, or, if a plan has not been confirmed under section 1173 of this title before five years after the date of the order for relief, the court shall, order the trustee to cease the debtor's operation and to collect and reduce to money all of the property of the estate in the same manner as if the case were a case under chapter 7 of this title.

SUBCHAPTER V—SMALL BUSINESS DEBTOR REORGANIZATION

§ 1181. Inapplicability of other sections

(a) In General.—Sections 105(d), 1101(1), 1104, 1105, 1106, 1107, 1108, 1115, 1116, 1121, 1123(a)(8), 1123(c), 1127, 1129(a)(15), 1129(b), 1129(c), 1129(e), and 1141(d)(5) of this title do not apply in a case under this subchapter.

(b) Court Authority.—Unless the court for cause orders otherwise, paragraphs (1), (2), and (4) of section 1102(a) and sections 1102(b), 1103, and 1125 of this title do not apply in a case under this subchapter.

(c) Special Rule for Discharge.—If a plan is confirmed under section 1191(b) of this title, section 1141(d) of this title shall not apply, except as provided in section 1192 of this title.

§ 1182. Definitions

In this subchapter:

(1) Debtor.—The term 'debtor'—

(A) subject to subparagraph (B), means a person engaged in commercial or business activities (including any affiliate of such person that is also a debtor under this title and excluding a person whose primary activity is the business of owning single asset real estate) that has aggregate noncontingent liquidated secured and unsecured debts as of the date of the filing of the petition or the date of the order for relief in an amount not more than $7,500,000 (excluding debts owed to 1 or more affiliates or insiders) not less than 50 percent of which arose from the commercial or business activities of the debtor; and

(B) does not include—

(i) any member of a group of affiliated debtors under this title that has aggregate noncontingent liquidated secured and unsecured debts in an amount greater than $7,500,000 (excluding debt owed to 1 or more affiliates or insiders);

(ii) any debtor that is a corporation subject to the reporting requirements under section 13 or 15(d) of the Securities Exchange Act of 1934 (15 U.S.C. 78m, 78o(d)); or

(iii) any debtor that is an affiliate of a corporation described in clause (ii).

(2) **Debtor in possession.**—The term 'debtor in possession' means the debtor, unless removed as debtor in possession under section 1185(a) of this title.

[*Note from West Advisory Panel:* Congress amended § 1182(1) to increase the debt limit for subchapter V to $7.5M. The amendment expires on June 21, 2024, at which point the term "debtor" in § 1182(1) will mean a small business debtor. *See* 136 Stat. 1298, 1299, 1300.]

§ 1183.   Trustee

(a) **In General**—If the United States trustee has appointed an individual under section 586(b) of title 28 to serve as standing trustee in cases under this subchapter, and if such individual qualifies as a trustee under section 322 of this title, then that individual shall serve as trustee in any case under this subchapter. Otherwise, the United States trustee shall appoint one disinterested person to serve as trustee in the case or the United States trustee may serve as trustee in the case, as necessary.

(b) **Duties**—The trustee shall—

(1) perform the duties specified in paragraphs (2), (5), (6), (7), and (9) of section 704(a) of this title;

(2) perform the duties specified in paragraphs (3), (4), and (7) of section 1106(a) of this title, if the court, for cause and on request of a party in interest, the trustee, or the United States trustee, so orders;

(3) appear and be heard at the status conference under section 1188 of this title and any hearing that concerns—

(A) the value of property subject to a lien;

(B) confirmation of a plan filed under this subchapter;

(C) modification of the plan after confirmation; or

(D) the sale of property of the estate;

(4) ensure that the debtor commences making timely payments required by a plan confirmed under this subchapter;

(5) if the debtor ceases to be a debtor in possession—

(A) perform the duties specified in section 704(a)(8) and paragraphs (1), (2), and (6) of section 1106(a) of this title; and

(B) be authorized to operate the business of the debtor;

(6) if there is a claim for a domestic support obligation with respect to the debtor, perform the duties specified in section 704(c) of this title; and

(7) facilitate the development of a consensual plan of reorganization.

(c) Termination of Trustee Service.—

(1) **In General**.—If the plan of the debtor is confirmed under section 1191(a) of this title, the service of the trustee in the case shall terminate when the plan has been substantially consummated, except that the United States trustee may reappoint a trustee as needed for performance of duties under subsection (b)(3)(C) of this section and section 1185(a) of this title.

(2) Service of notice of substantial consummation.—Not later than 14 days after the plan of the debtor is substantially consummated, the debtor shall file with the court and serve on the trustee, the United States trustee, and all parties in interest notice of such substantial consummation

§ 1184. Rights and powers of a debtor in possession

Subject to such limitations or conditions as the court may prescribe, a debtor in possession shall have all the rights, other than the right to compensation under section 330 of this title, and powers, and shall perform all functions and duties, except the duties specified in paragraphs (2), (3), and (4) of section 1106(a) of this title, of a trustee serving in a case under this chapter, including operating the business of the debtor.

§ 1185. Removal of a debtor in possession

(a) In General.—On request of a party in interest, and after notice and a hearing, the court shall order that the debtor shall not be a debtor in possession for cause, including fraud, dishonesty, incompetence, or gross mismanagement of the affairs of the debtor, either before or after the date of commencement of the case, or for failure to perform the obligations of the debtor under a plan confirmed under this subchapter.

(b) Reinstatement.—On request of a party in interest, and after notice and a hearing, the court may reinstate the debtor in possession.

§ 1186. Property of the estate

(a) Inclusions.—If a plan is confirmed under section 1191(b) of this title, property of the estate includes, in addition to the property specified in section 541 of this title—

(1) all property of the kind specified in that section that the debtor acquires after the date of commencement of the case but before the case is closed, dismissed, or converted to a case under chapter 7, 12, or 13 of this title, whichever occurs first; and

(2) earnings from services performed by the debtor after the date of commencement of the case but before the case is closed, dismissed, or converted to a case under chapter 7, 12, or 13 of this title, whichever occurs first.

(b) Debtor Remaining in Possession.—Except as provided in section 1185 of this title, a plan confirmed under this subchapter, or an order confirming a plan under this subchapter, the debtor shall remain in possession of all property of the estate.

§ 1187. Duties and reporting requirements of debtors

(a) Filing Requirements.—Upon electing to be a debtor under this subchapter, the debtor shall file the documents required by subparagraphs (A) and (B) of section 1116(1) of this title.

(b) Other Applicable Provisions.—A debtor, in addition to the duties provided in this title and as otherwise required by law, shall comply with the requirements of section 308 and paragraphs (2), (3), (4), (5), (6), and (7) of section 1116 of this title.

(c) Separate Disclosure Statement Exemption.—If the court orders under section 1181(b) of this title that section 1125 of this title applies, section 1125(f) of this title shall apply.

§ 1188. Status conference

(a) In General.—Except as provided in subsection (b), not later than 60 days after the entry of the order for relief under this chapter, the court shall hold a status conference to further the expeditious and economical resolution of a case under this subchapter.

(b) Exception.—The court may extend the period of time for holding a status conference under subsection (a) if the need for an extension is attributable to circumstances for which the debtor should not justly be held accountable.

(c) **Report**.—Not later than 14 days before the date of the status conference under subsection (a), the debtor shall file with the court and serve on the trustee and all parties in interest a report that details the efforts the debtor has undertaken and will undertake to attain a consensual plan of reorganization.

§ 1189. Filing of the plan

(a) **Who May File a Plan**.—Only the debtor may file a plan under this subchapter.

(b) **Deadline**.—The debtor shall file a plan not later than 90 days after the order for relief under this chapter, except that the court may extend the period if the need for the extension is attributable to circumstances for which the debtor should not justly be held accountable

§ 1190. Contents of plan

A plan filed under this subchapter—

(1) shall include—

(A) a brief history of the business operations of the debtor;

(B) a liquidation analysis; and

(C) projections with respect to the ability of the debtor to make payments under the proposed plan of reorganization;

(2) shall provide for the submission of all or such portion of the future earnings or other future income of the debtor to the supervision and control of the trustee as is necessary for the execution of the plan; and

(3) notwithstanding section 1123(b)(5) of this title, may modify the rights of the holder of a claim secured only by a security interest in real property that is the principal residence of the debtor if the new value received in connection with the granting of the security interest was—

(A) not used primarily to acquire the real property; and

(B) used primarily in connection with the small business of the debtor.

§ 1191. Confirmation of plan

(a) **Terms**.—The court shall confirm a plan under this subchapter only if all of the requirements of section 1129(a), other than paragraph (15) of that section, of this title are met.

(b) **Exception**.—Notwithstanding section 510(a) of this title, if all of the applicable requirements of section 1129(a) of this title, other than paragraphs (8), (10), and (15) of that section, are met with respect to a plan, the court, on request of the debtor, shall confirm the plan notwithstanding the requirements of such paragraphs if the plan does not discriminate unfairly, and is fair and equitable, with respect to each class of claims or interests that is impaired under, and has not accepted, the plan.

(c) **Rule of Construction**.—For purposes of this section, the condition that a plan be fair and equitable with respect to each class of claims or interests includes the following requirements:

(1) With respect to a class of secured claims, the plan meets the requirements of section 1129(b)(2)(A) of this title.

(2) As of the effective date of the plan—

(A) the plan provides that all of the projected disposable income of the debtor to be received in the 3-year period, or such longer period not to exceed 5 years as the court may fix, beginning on the date that the first payment is due under the plan will be applied to make payments under the plan; or

(B) the value of the property to be distributed under the plan in the 3-year period, or such longer period not to exceed 5 years as the court may fix, beginning on the date on which the first distribution is due under the plan is not less than the projected disposable income of the debtor.

(3)(A) The debtor will be able to make all payments under the plan; or

(B)(i) there is a reasonable likelihood that the debtor will be able to make all payments under the plan; and

(ii) the plan provides appropriate remedies, which may include the liquidation of nonexempt assets, to protect the holders of claims or interests in the event that the payments are not made.

(d) Disposable Income.—For purposes of this section, the term 'disposable income' means the income that is received by the debtor and that is not reasonably necessary to be expended—

(1) for—

(A) the maintenance or support of the debtor or a dependent of the debtor; or

(B) a domestic support obligation that first becomes payable after the date of the filing of the petition; or

(2) for the payment of expenditures necessary for the continuation, preservation, or operation of the business of the debtor.

(e) Special Rule.—Notwithstanding section 1129(a)(9)(A) of this title, a plan that provides for the payment through the plan of a claim of a kind specified in paragraph (2) or (3) of section 507(a) of this title may be confirmed under subsection (b) of this section.

[*Note from West Advisory Panel.* Pub. L. 116–260 created a temporary § 1191(f), which expired on December 27, 2022, *except* for cases commenced before December 27, 2022. *See* 134 Stat. 2015, 2016, 2017. For the text of temporary § 1191(f), *see* Title 11, Chapter 11, Subchapter V, § 1191, Editorial Notes, Amendments, 2020 at http://uscode.house.gov]

§ 1192. Discharge

If the plan of the debtor is confirmed under section 1191(b) of this title, as soon as practicable after completion by the debtor of all payments due within the first 3 years of the plan, or such longer period not to exceed 5 years as the court may fix, unless the court approves a written waiver of discharge executed by the debtor after the order for relief under this chapter, the court shall grant the debtor a discharge of all debts provided in section 1141(d)(1)(A) of this title, and all other debts allowed under section 503 of this title and provided for in the plan, except any debt—

(1) on which the last payment is due after the first 3 years of the plan, or such other time not to exceed 5 years fixed by the court; or

(2) of the kind specified in section 523(a) of this title.

§ 1193. Modification of plan

(a) Modification Before Confirmation.—The debtor may modify a plan at any time before confirmation, but may not modify the plan so that the plan as modified fails to meet the requirements of sections 1122 and 1123 of this title, with the exception of subsection (a)(8) of such section 1123. After the modification is filed with the court, the plan as modified becomes the plan.

(b) Modification After Confirmation.—If a plan has been confirmed under section 1191(a) of this title, the debtor may modify the plan at any time after confirmation of the plan and before substantial consummation of the plan, but may not modify the plan so that the plan as modified fails to meet the requirements of sections 1122 and 1123 of this title, with the exception of subsection (a)(8) of such section 1123. The plan, as modified under this subsection, becomes the plan only if circumstances warrant the modification and the court, after notice and a hearing, confirms the plan as modified under section 1191(a) of this title.

(c) Certain Other Modifications.—If a plan has been confirmed under section 1191(b) of this title, the debtor may modify the plan at any time within 3 years, or such longer time not to exceed 5 years, as fixed by the court, but may not modify the plan so that the plan as modified fails to meet the requirements of section 1191(b) of this title. The plan as modified under this subsection becomes the plan only if circumstances warrant such modification and the court, after notice and a hearing, confirms such plan, as modified, under section 1191(b) of this title.

    (d) Holders of a Claim or Interest.—If a plan has been confirmed under section 1191(a) of this title, any holder of a claim or interest that has accepted or rejected the plan is deemed to have accepted or rejected, as the case may be, the plan as modified, unless, within the time fixed by the court, such holder changes the previous acceptance or rejection of the holder

§ 1194.   Payments

    (a) Retention and Distribution by Trustee.—Payments and funds received by the trustee shall be retained by the trustee until confirmation or denial of confirmation of a plan. If a plan is confirmed, the trustee shall distribute any such payment in accordance with the plan. If a plan is not confirmed, the trustee shall return any such payments to the debtor after deducting—

        (1) any unpaid claim allowed under section 503(b) of this title;

        (2) any payment made for the purpose of providing adequate protection of an interest in property due to the holder of a secured claim; and

        (3) any fee owing to the trustee.

    (b) Other Plans.—If a plan is confirmed under section 1191(b) of this title, except as otherwise provided in the plan or in the order confirming the plan, the trustee shall make payments to creditors under the plan.

    (c) Payments Prior to Confirmation.—Prior to confirmation of a plan, the court, after notice and a hearing, may authorize the trustee to make payments to the holder of a secured claim for the purpose of providing adequate protection of an interest in property.

§ 1195.   Transactions with professionals

    Notwithstanding section 327(a) of this title, a person is not disqualified for employment under section 327 of this title, by a debtor solely because that person holds a claim of less than $10,000 that arose prior to commencement of the case.

CHAPTER 12—ADJUSTMENT OF DEBTS OF A FAMILY FARMER OR FISHERMAN WITH REGULAR ANNUAL INCOME

SUBCHAPTER I—OFFICERS, ADMINISTRATION, AND THE ESTATE

1201.   Stay of action against codebtor.
1202.   Trustee.
1203.   Rights and powers of debtor.
1204.   Removal of debtor as debtor in possession.
1205.   Adequate protection.
1206.   Sales free of interests.
1207.   Property of the estate.
1208.   Conversion or dismissal.

SUBCHAPTER II—THE PLAN

1221.   Filing of plan.
1222.   Contents of plan.
1223.   Modification of plan before confirmation.
1224.   Confirmation hearing.
1225.   Confirmation of plan.
1226.   Payments.
1227.   Effect of confirmation.

1228.   Discharge.
1229.   Modification of plan after confirmation.
1230.   Revocation of an order of confirmation.
1231.   Special tax provisions.
1232.   Claim by a governmental unit based on the disposition of property used in a farming operation.

SUBCHAPTER I—OFFICERS, ADMINISTRATION, AND THE ESTATE

§ 1201.   Stay of action against codebtor

(a)   Except as provided in subsections (b) and (c) of this section, after the order for relief under this chapter, a creditor may not act, or commence or continue any civil action, to collect all or any part of a consumer debt of the debtor from any individual that is liable on such debt with the debtor, or that secured such debt, unless—

(1)   such individual became liable on or secured such debt in the ordinary course of such individual's business; or

(2)   the case is closed, dismissed, or converted to a case under chapter 7 of this title.

(b)   A creditor may present a negotiable instrument, and may give notice of dishonor of such an instrument.

(c)   On request of a party in interest and after notice and a hearing, the court shall grant relief from the stay provided by subsection (a) of this section with respect to a creditor, to the extent that—

(1)   as between the debtor and the individual protected under subsection (a) of this section, such individual received the consideration for the claim held by such creditor;

(2)   the plan filed by the debtor proposes not to pay such claim; or

(3)   such creditor's interest would be irreparably harmed by continuation of such stay.

(d)   Twenty days after the filing of a request under subsection (c)(2) of this section for relief from the stay provided by subsection (a) of this section, such stay is terminated with respect to the party in interest making such request, unless the debtor or any individual that is liable on such debt with the debtor files and serves upon such party in interest a written objection to the taking of the proposed action.

§ 1202.   Trustee

(a)   If the United States trustee has appointed an individual under section 586(b) of title 28 to serve as standing trustee in cases under this chapter and if such individual qualifies as a trustee under section 322 of this title, then such individual shall serve as trustee in any case filed under this chapter. Otherwise, the United States trustee shall appoint one disinterested person to serve as trustee in the case or the United States trustee may serve as trustee in the case if necessary.

(b)   The trustee shall—

(1)   perform the duties specified in sections 704(a)(2), 704(a)(3), 704(a)(5), 704(a)(6), 704(a)(7), and 704(a)(9) of this title;

(2)   perform the duties specified in section 1106(a)(3) and 1106(a)(4) of this title if the court, for cause and on request of a party in interest, the trustee, or the United States trustee, so orders;

(3)   appear and be heard at any hearing that concerns—

(A)   the value of property subject to a lien;

(B)   confirmation of a plan;

(C)   modification of the plan after confirmation; or

(D)   the sale of property of the estate;

(4) ensure that the debtor commences making timely payments required by a confirmed plan;

(5) if the debtor ceases to be a debtor in possession, perform the duties specified in sections 704(a)(8), 1106(a)(1), 1106(a)(2), 1106(a)(6), 1106(a)(7), and 1203; and

(6) if with respect to the debtor there is a claim for a domestic support obligation, provide the applicable notice specified in subsection (c).

(c)(1) In a case described in subsection (b)(6) to which subsection (b)(6) applies, the trustee shall—

(A)(i) provide written notice to the holder of the claim described in subsection (b)(6) of such claim and of the right of such holder to use the services of the State child support enforcement agency established under sections 464 and 466 of the Social Security Act for the State in which such holder resides, for assistance in collecting child support during and after the case under this title; and

(ii) include in the notice provided under clause (i) the address and telephone number of such State child support enforcement agency;

(B)(i) provide written notice to such State child support enforcement agency of such claim; and

(ii) include in the notice provided under clause (i) the name, address, and telephone number of such holder; and

(C) at such time as the debtor is granted a discharge under section 1228, provide written notice to such holder and to such State child support enforcement agency of—

(i) the granting of the discharge;

(ii) the last recent known address of the debtor;

(iii) the last recent known name and address of the debtor's employer; and

(iv) the name of each creditor that holds a claim that—

(I) is not discharged under paragraph (2), (4), or (14A) of section 523(a); or

(II) was reaffirmed by the debtor under section 524(c).

(2)(A) The holder of a claim described in subsection (b)(6) or the State child support enforcement agency of the State in which such holder resides may request from a creditor described in paragraph (1)(C)(iv) the last known address of the debtor.

(B) Notwithstanding any other provision of law, a creditor that makes a disclosure of a last known address of a debtor in connection with a request made under subparagraph (A) shall not be liable by reason of making that disclosure.

§ 1203.   Rights and powers of debtor

Subject to such limitations as the court may prescribe, a debtor in possession shall have all the rights, other than the right to compensation under section 330, and powers, and shall perform all the functions and duties, except the duties specified in paragraphs (3) and (4) of section 1106(a), of a trustee serving in a case under chapter 11, including operating the debtor's farm or commercial fishing operation.

§ 1204.   Removal of debtor as debtor in possession

(a) On request of a party in interest, and after notice and a hearing, the court shall order that the debtor shall not be a debtor in possession for cause, including fraud, dishonesty, incompetence, or gross mismanagement of the affairs of the debtor, either before or after the commencement of the case.

(b) On request of a party in interest, and after notice and a hearing, the court may reinstate the debtor in possession.

§1205.   Adequate protection

(a)   Section 361 does not apply in a case under this chapter.

(b)   In a case under this chapter, when adequate protection is required under section 362, 363, or 364 of this title of an interest of an entity in property, such adequate protection may be provided by—

(1)   requiring the trustee to make a cash payment or periodic cash payments to such entity, to the extent that the stay under section 362 of this title, use, sale, or lease under section 363 of this title, or any grant of a lien under section 364 of this title results in a decrease in the value of property securing a claim or of an entity's ownership interest in property;

(2)   providing to such entity an additional or replacement lien to the extent that such stay, use, sale, lease, or grant results in a decrease in the value of property securing a claim or of an entity's ownership interest in property;

(3)   paying to such entity for the use of farmland the reasonable rent customary in the community where the property is located, based upon the rental value, net income, and earning capacity of the property; or

(4)   granting such other relief, other than entitling such entity to compensation allowable under section 503(b)(1) of this title as an administrative expense, as will adequately protect the value of property securing a claim or of such entity's ownership interest in property.

§1206.   Sales free of interests

After notice and a hearing, in addition to the authorization contained in section 363(f), the trustee in a case under this chapter may sell property under section 363(b) and (c) free and clear of any interest in such property of an entity other than the estate if the property is farmland, farm equipment, or property used to carry out a commercial fishing operation (including a commercial fishing vessel), except that the proceeds of such sale shall be subject to such interest.

§1207.   Property of the estate

(a)   Property of the estate includes, in addition to the property specified in section 541 of this title—

(1)   all property of the kind specified in such section that the debtor acquires after the commencement of the case but before the case is closed, dismissed, or converted to a case under chapter 7 of this title, whichever occurs first; and

(2)   earnings from services performed by the debtor after the commencement of the case but before the case is closed, dismissed, or converted to a case under chapter 7 of this title, whichever occurs first.

(b)   Except as provided in section 1204, a confirmed plan, or an order confirming a plan, the debtor shall remain in possession of all property of the estate.

§1208.   Conversion or dismissal

(a)   The debtor may convert a case under this chapter to a case under chapter 7 of this title at any time. Any waiver of the right to convert under this subsection is unenforceable.

(b)   On request of the debtor at any time, if the case has not been converted under section 706 or 1112 of this title, the court shall dismiss a case under this chapter. Any waiver of the right to dismiss under this subsection is unenforceable.

(c)   On request of a party in interest, and after notice and a hearing, the court may dismiss a case under this chapter for cause, including—

(1)   unreasonable delay, or gross mismanagement, by the debtor that is prejudicial to creditors;

(2)   nonpayment of any fees and charges required under chapter 123 of title 28;

(3)   failure to file a plan timely under section 1221 of this title;

(4)　failure to commence making timely payments required by a confirmed plan;

(5)　denial of confirmation of a plan under section 1225 of this title and denial of a request made for additional time for filing another plan or a modification of a plan;

(6)　material default by the debtor with respect to a term of a confirmed plan;

(7)　revocation of the order of confirmation under section 1230 of this title, and denial of confirmation of a modified plan under section 1229 of this title;

(8)　termination of a confirmed plan by reason of the occurrence of a condition specified in the plan;

(9)　continuing loss to or diminution of the estate and absence of a reasonable likelihood of rehabilitation; and

(10)　failure of the debtor to pay any domestic support obligation that first becomes payable after the date of the filing of the petition.

(d)　On request of a party in interest, and after notice and a hearing, the court may dismiss a case under this chapter or convert a case under this chapter to a case under chapter 7 of this title upon a showing that the debtor has committed fraud in connection with the case.

(e)　Notwithstanding any other provision of this section, a case may not be converted to a case under another chapter of this title unless the debtor may be a debtor under such chapter.

SUBCHAPTER II—THE PLAN

§ 1221.　　Filing of plan

The debtor shall file a plan not later than 90 days after the order for relief under this chapter, except that the court may extend such period if the need for an extension is attributable to circumstances for which the debtor should not justly be held accountable.

§ 1222.　　Contents of plan

(a)　The plan shall—

(1)　provide for the submission of all or such portion of future earnings or other future income of the debtor to the supervision and control of the trustee as is necessary for the execution of the plan;

(2)　provide for the full payment, in deferred cash payments, of all claims entitled to priority under section 507, unless the holder of a particular claim agrees to a different treatment of that claim;

(3)　if the plan classifies claims and interests, provide the same treatment for each claim or interest within a particular class unless the holder of a particular claim or interest agrees to less favorable treatment; and

(4)　notwithstanding any other provision of this section, a plan may provide for less than full payment of all amounts owed for a claim entitled to priority under section 507(a)(1)(B) only if the plan provides that all of the debtor's projected disposable income for a 5-year period beginning on the date that the first payment is due under the plan will be applied to make payments under the plan.

(b)　Subject to subsections (a) and (c) of this section, the plan may—

(1)　designate a class or classes of unsecured claims, as provided in section 1122 of this title, but may not discriminate unfairly against any class so designated; however, such plan may treat claims for a consumer debt of the debtor if an individual is liable on such consumer debt with the debtor differently than other unsecured claims;

(2)　modify the rights of holders of secured claims, or of holders of unsecured claims, or leave unaffected the rights of holders of any class of claims;

(3)　provide for the curing or waiving of any default;

(4) provide for payments on any unsecured claim to be made concurrently with payments on any secured claim or any other unsecured claim;

(5) provide for the curing of any default within a reasonable time and maintenance of payments while the case is pending on any unsecured claim or secured claim on which the last payment is due after the date on which the final payment under the plan is due;

(6) subject to section 365 of this title, provide for the assumption, rejection, or assignment of any executory contract or unexpired lease of the debtor not previously rejected under such section;

(7) provide for the payment of all or part of a claim against the debtor from property of the estate or property of the debtor;

(8) provide for the sale of all or any part of the property of the estate or the distribution of all or any part of the property of the estate among those having an interest in such property;

(9) provide for payment of allowed secured claims consistent with section 1225(a)(5) of this title, over a period exceeding the period permitted under section 1222(c);

(10) provide for the vesting of property of the estate, on confirmation of the plan or at a later time, in the debtor or in any other entity;

(11) provide for the payment of interest accruing after the date of the filing of the petition on unsecured claims that are nondischargeable under section 1228(a), except that such interest may be paid only to the extent that the debtor has disposable income available to pay such interest after making provision for full payment of all allowed claims; and

(12) include any other appropriate provision not inconsistent with this title.

(c) Except as provided in subsections (b)(5) and (b)(9), the plan may not provide for payments over a period that is longer than three years unless the court for cause approves a longer period, but the court may not approve a period that is longer than five years.

(d) Notwithstanding subsection (b)(2) of this section and sections 506(b) and 1225(a)(5) of this title, if it is proposed in a plan to cure a default, the amount necessary to cure the default, shall be determined in accordance with the underlying agreement and applicable nonbankruptcy law.

§ 1223. Modification of plan before confirmation

(a) The debtor may modify the plan at any time before confirmation, but may not modify the plan so that the plan as modified fails to meet the requirements of section 1222 of this title.

(b) After the debtor files a modification under this section, the plan as modified becomes the plan.

(c) Any holder of a secured claim that has accepted or rejected the plan is deemed to have accepted or rejected, as the case may be, the plan as modified, unless the modification provides for a change in the rights of such holder from what such rights were under the plan before modification, and such holder changes such holder's previous acceptance or rejection.

§ 1224. Confirmation hearing

After expedited notice, the court shall hold a hearing on confirmation of the plan. A party in interest, the trustee, or the United States trustee may object to the confirmation of the plan. Except for cause, the hearing shall be concluded not later than 45 days after the filing of the plan.

§ 1225. Confirmation of plan

(a) Except as provided in subsection (b), the court shall confirm a plan if—

(1) the plan complies with the provisions of this chapter and with the other applicable provisions of this title;

(2) any fee, charge, or amount required under chapter 123 of title 28, or by the plan, to be paid before confirmation, has been paid;

(3)   the plan has been proposed in good faith and not by any means forbidden by law;

(4)   the value, as of the effective date of the plan, of property to be distributed under the plan on account of each allowed unsecured claim is not less than the amount that would be paid on such claim if the estate of the debtor were liquidated under chapter 7 of this title on such date;

(5)   with respect to each allowed secured claim provided for by the plan—

(A)   the holder of such claim has accepted the plan;

(B)(i)   the plan provides that the holder of such claim retain the lien securing such claim; and

(ii)   the value, as of the effective date of the plan, of property to be distributed by the trustee or the debtor under the plan on account of such claim is not less than the allowed amount of such claim; or

(C)   the debtor surrenders the property securing such claim to such holder;

(6)   the debtor will be able to make all payments under the plan and to comply with the plan; and

(7)   the debtor has paid all amounts that are required to be paid under a domestic support obligation and that first become payable after the date of the filing of the petition if the debtor is required by a judicial or administrative order, or by statute, to pay such domestic support obligation.

(b)(1)   If the trustee or the holder of an allowed unsecured claim objects to the confirmation of the plan, then the court may not approve the plan unless, as of the effective date of the plan—

(A)   the value of the property to be distributed under the plan on account of such claim is not less than the amount of such claim;

(B)   the plan provides that all of the debtor's projected disposable income to be received in the three-year period, or such longer period as the court may approve under section 1222(c), beginning on the date that the first payment is due under the plan will be applied to make payments under the plan; or

(C)   the value of the property to be distributed under the plan in the 3-year period, or such longer period as the court may approve under section 1222(c), beginning on the date that the first distribution is due under the plan is not less than the debtor's projected disposable income for such period.

(2)   For purposes of this subsection, "disposable income" means income which is received by the debtor and which is not reasonably necessary to be expended—

(A)   for the maintenance or support of the debtor or a dependent of the debtor or for a domestic support obligation that first becomes payable after the date of the filing of the petition; or

(B)   for the payment of expenditures necessary for the continuation, preservation, and operation of the debtor's business.

(c)   After confirmation of a plan, the court may order any entity from whom the debtor receives income to pay all or any part of such income to the trustee.

[*Note from West Advisory Panel.* Pub. L. 116–260 created a temporary § 1225(d), which expired on December 27, 2022, *except* for cases commenced before December 27, 2022. *See* 134 Stat. 2016, 2017. For the text of temporary § 1225(d), *see* Title 11, Chapter 12, Subchapter II, § 1225, Editorial Notes, Amendments, 2020 at http://uscode.house.gov]

§ 1226.   Payments

(a)   Payments and funds received by the trustee shall be retained by the trustee until confirmation or denial of confirmation of a plan. If a plan is confirmed, the trustee shall distribute any such payment in accordance with the plan. If a plan is not confirmed, the trustee shall return any such payments to the debtor, after deducting—

    (1) any unpaid claim allowed under section 503(b) of this title; and

    (2) if a standing trustee is serving in the case, the percentage fee fixed for such standing trustee.

  (b) Before or at the time of each payment to creditors under the plan, there shall be paid—

    (1) any unpaid claim of the kind specified in section 507(a)(2) of this title; and

    (2) if a standing trustee appointed under section 1202(c) of this title is serving in the case, the percentage fee fixed for such standing trustee under section 1202(d) of this title.

  (c) Except as otherwise provided in the plan or in the order confirming the plan, the trustee shall make payments to creditors under the plan.

§1227. Effect of confirmation

  (a) Except as provided in section 1228(a) of this title, the provisions of a confirmed plan bind the debtor, each creditor, each equity security holder, and each general partner in the debtor, whether or not the claim of such creditor, such equity security holder, or such general partner in the debtor is provided for by the plan, and whether or not such creditor, such equity security holder, or such general partner in the debtor has objected to, has accepted, or has rejected the plan.

  (b) Except as otherwise provided in the plan or the order confirming the plan, the confirmation of a plan vests all of the property of the estate in the debtor.

  (c) Except as provided in section 1228(a) of this title and except as otherwise provided in the plan or in the order confirming the plan, the property vesting in the debtor under subsection (b) of this section is free and clear of any claim or interest of any creditor provided for by the plan.

§1228. Discharge

  (a) Subject to subsection (d), as soon as practicable after completion by the debtor of all payments under the plan, and in the case of a debtor who is required by a judicial or administrative order, or by statute, to pay a domestic support obligation, after such debtor certifies that all amounts payable under such order or such statute that are due on or before the date of the certification (including amounts due before the petition was filed, but only to the extent provided for by the plan) have been paid, other than payments to holders of allowed claims provided for under section 1222(b)(5) or 1222(b)(9) of this title, unless the court approves a written waiver of discharge executed by the debtor after the order for relief under this chapter, the court shall grant the debtor a discharge of all debts provided for by the plan, allowed under section 503 of this title, or disallowed under section 502 of this title, except any debt—

    (1) provided for under section 1222(b)(5) or 1222(b)(9) of this title; or

    (2) of a kind specified in section 523(a) of this title, except as provided in section 1232(c).

  (b) Subject to subsection (d), at any time after the confirmation of the plan and after notice and a hearing, the court may grant a discharge to a debtor that has not completed payments under the plan only if—

    (1) the debtor's failure to complete such payments is due to circumstances for which the debtor should not justly be held accountable;

    (2) the value, as of the effective date of the plan, of property actually distributed under the plan on account of each allowed unsecured claim is not less than the amount that would have been paid on such claim if the estate of the debtor had been liquidated under chapter 7 of this title on such date; and

    (3) modification of the plan under section 1229 of this title is not practicable.

  (c) A discharge granted under subsection (b) of this section discharges the debtor from all unsecured debts provided for by the plan or disallowed under section 502 of this title, except any debt—

    (1)   provided for under section 1222(b)(5) or 1222(b)(9) of this title; or

    (2)   of a kind specified in section 523(a) of this title, except as provided in section 1232(c).

  (d)   On request of a party in interest before one year after a discharge under this section is granted, and after notice and a hearing, the court may revoke such discharge only if—

    (1)   such discharge was obtained by the debtor through fraud; and

    (2)   the requesting party did not know of such fraud until after such discharge was granted.

  (e)   After the debtor is granted a discharge, the court shall terminate the services of any trustee serving in the case.

  (f)   The court may not grant a discharge under this chapter unless the court after notice and a hearing held not more than 10 days before the date of the entry of the order granting the discharge finds that there is no reasonable cause to believe that—

    (1)   section 522(q)(1) may be applicable to the debtor; and

    (2)   there is pending any proceeding in which the debtor may be found guilty of a felony of the kind described in section 522(q)(1)(A) or liable for a debt of the kind described in section 522(q)(1)(B).

§ 1229.   Modification of plan after confirmation

  (a)   At any time after confirmation of the plan but before the completion of payments under such plan, the plan may be modified, on request of the debtor, the trustee, or the holder of an allowed unsecured claim, to—

    (1)   increase or reduce the amount of payments on claims of a particular class provided for by the plan;

    (2)   extend or reduce the time for such payments; or

    (3)   alter the amount of the distribution to a creditor whose claim is provided for by the plan to the extent necessary to take account of any payment of such claim other than under the plan.

    (4)   provide for the payment of a claim described in section 1232(a) that arose after the date on which the petition was filed.

  (b)(1)   Sections 1222(a), 1222(b), and 1223(c) of this title and the requirements of section 1225(a) of this title apply to any modification under subsection (a) of this section.

    (2)   The plan as modified becomes the plan unless, after notice and a hearing, such modification is disapproved.

  (c)   A plan modified under this section may not provide for payments over a period that expires after three years after the time that the first payment under the original confirmed plan was due, unless the court, for cause, approves a longer period, but the court may not approve a period that expires after five years after such time.

  (d)   A plan may not be modified under this section—

    (1)   to increase the amount of any payment due before the plan as modified becomes the plan;

    (2)   by anyone except the debtor, based on an increase in the debtor's disposable income, to increase the amount of payments to unsecured creditors required for a particular month so that the aggregate of such payments exceeds the debtor's disposable income for such month; or

    (3)   in the last year of the plan by anyone except the debtor, to require payments that would leave the debtor with insufficient funds to carry on the farming operation after the plan is completed.

§ 1230.   Revocation of an order of confirmation

  (a)   On request of a party in interest at any time within 180 days after the date of the entry of an order of confirmation under section 1225 of this title, and after notice and a hearing, the court may revoke such order if such order was procured by fraud.

(b) If the court revokes an order of confirmation under subsection (a) of this section, the court shall dispose of the case under section 1207 of this title, unless, within the time fixed by the court, the debtor proposes and the court confirms a modification of the plan under section 1229 of this title.

§ 1231.   Special tax provisions

(a) The issuance, transfer, or exchange of a security, or the making or delivery of an instrument of transfer under a plan confirmed under section 1225 of this title, may not be taxed under any law imposing a stamp tax or similar tax.

(b) The court may authorize the proponent of a plan to request a determination, limited to questions of law, by any governmental unit charged with responsibility for collection or determination of a tax on or measured by income, of the tax effects, under section 346 of this title and under the law imposing such tax, of the plan. In the event of an actual controversy, the court may declare such effects after the earlier of—

    (1) the date on which such governmental unit responds to the request under this subsection; or

    (2) 270 days after such request.

§ 1232.   Claim by a governmental unit based on the disposition of property used in a farming operation

(a) Any unsecured claim of a governmental unit against the debtor or the estate that arises before the filing of the petition, or that arises after the filing of the petition and before the debtor's discharge under section 1228, as a result of the sale, transfer, exchange, or other disposition of any property used in the debtor's farming operation—

    (1) shall be treated as an unsecured claim arising before the date on which the petition is filed;

    (2) shall not be entitled to priority under section 507;

    (3) shall be provided for under a plan; and

    (4) shall be discharged in accordance with section 1228.

(b) For purposes of applying sections 1225(a)(4), 1228(b)(2), and 1229(b)(1) to a claim described in subsection (a) of this section, the amount that would be paid on such claim if the estate of the debtor were liquidated in a case under chapter 7 of this title shall be the amount that would be paid by the estate in a chapter 7 case if the claim were an unsecured claim arising before the date on which the petition was filed and were not entitled to priority under section 507.

(c) For purposes of applying sections 523(a), 1228(a)(2), and 1228(c)(2) to a claim described in subsection (a) of this section, the claim shall not be treated as a claim of a kind specified in subparagraph (A) or (B) of section 523(a)(1).

    (d)(1) A governmental unit may file a proof of claim for a claim described in subsection (a) that arises after the date on which the petition is filed.

    (2) If a debtor files a tax return after the filing of the petition for a period in which a claim described in subsection (a) arises, and the claim relates to the tax return, the debtor shall serve notice of the claim on the governmental unit charged with the responsibility for the collection of the tax at the address and in the manner designated in section 505(b)(1). Notice under this paragraph shall state that the debtor has filed a petition under this chapter, state the name and location of the court in which the case under this chapter is pending, state the amount of the claim, and include a copy of the filed tax return and documentation supporting the calculation of the claim.

    (3) If notice of a claim has been served on the governmental unit in accordance with paragraph (2), the governmental unit may file a proof of claim not later than 180 days after the date on which such notice was served. If the governmental unit has not filed a timely proof of the claim, the debtor or trustee may file proof of the claim that is consistent with the notice served under paragraph (2). If a proof of claim is filed by the debtor or trustee under this paragraph, the governmental unit may not amend the proof of claim.

(4) A claim filed under this subsection shall be determined and shall be allowed under subsection (a), (b), or (c) of section 502, or disallowed under subsection (d) or (e) of section 502, in the same manner as if the claim had arisen immediately before the date of the filing of the petition.

CHAPTER 13—ADJUSTMENT OF DEBTS OF AN INDIVIDUAL WITH REGULAR INCOME

SUBCHAPTER I—OFFICERS, ADMINISTRATION, AND THE ESTATE

1301.　Stay of action against codebtor.
1302.　Trustee.
1303.　Rights and powers of debtor.
1304.　Debtor engaged in business.
1305.　Filing and allowance of postpetition claims.
1306.　Property of the estate.
1307.　Conversion or dismissal.
1308.　Filing of prepetition tax returns.

SUBCHAPTER II—THE PLAN

1321.　Filing of plan.
1322.　Contents of plan.
1323.　Modification of plan before confirmation.
1324.　Confirmation hearing.
1325.　Confirmation of plan.
1326.　Payments.
1327.　Effect of confirmation.
1328.　Discharge.
1329.　Modification of plan after confirmation.
1330.　Revocation of an order of confirmation.

SUBCHAPTER I—OFFICERS, ADMINISTRATION, AND THE ESTATE

§ 1301.　Stay of action against codebtor

(a) Except as provided in subsections (b) and (c) of this section, after the order for relief under this chapter, a creditor may not act, or commence or continue any civil action, to collect all or any part of a consumer debt of the debtor from any individual that is liable on such debt with the debtor, or that secured such debt, unless—

(1) such individual became liable on or secured such debt in the ordinary course of such individual's business; or

(2) the case is closed, dismissed, or converted to a case under chapter 7 or 11 of this title.

(b) A creditor may present a negotiable instrument, and may give notice of dishonor of such an instrument.

(c) On request of a party in interest and after notice and a hearing, the court shall grant relief from the stay provided by subsection (a) of this section with respect to a creditor, to the extent that—

(1) as between the debtor and the individual protected under subsection (a) of this section, such individual received the consideration for the claim held by such creditor;

(2) the plan filed by the debtor proposes not to pay such claim; or

(3) such creditor's interest would be irreparably harmed by continuation of such stay.

(d) Twenty days after the filing of a request under subsection (c)(2) of this section for relief from the stay provided by subsection (a) of this section, such stay is terminated with respect to the party in interest making such request, unless the debtor or any individual that is liable on such debt with the debtor files and serves upon such party in interest a written objection to the taking of the proposed action.

§ 1302. Trustee

(a) If the United States trustee appoints an individual under section 586(b) of title 28 to serve as standing trustee in cases under this chapter and if such individual qualifies under section 322 of this title, then such individual shall serve as trustee in the case. Otherwise, the United States trustee shall appoint one disinterested person to serve as trustee in the case or the United States trustee may serve as a trustee in the case.

(b) The trustee shall—

(1) perform the duties specified in sections 704(a)(2), 704(a)(3), 704(a)(4), 704(a)(5), 704(a)(6), 704(a)(7), and 704(a)(9) of this title;

(2) appear and be heard at any hearing that concerns—

(A) the value of property subject to a lien;

(B) confirmation of a plan; or

(C) modification of the plan after confirmation;

(3) dispose of, under regulations issued by the Director of the Administrative Office of the United States Courts, moneys received or to be received in a case under chapter XIII of the Bankruptcy Act;

(4) advise, other than on legal matters, and assist the debtor in performance under the plan;

(5) ensure that the debtor commences making timely payments under section 1326 of this title; and

(6) if with respect to the debtor there is a claim for a domestic support obligation, provide the applicable notice specified in subsection (d).

(c) If the debtor is engaged in business, then in addition to the duties specified in subsection (b) of this section, the trustee shall perform the duties specified in sections 1106(a)(3) and 1106(a)(4) of this title.

(d)(1) In a case described in subsection (b)(6) to which subsection (b)(6) applies, the trustee shall—

(A)(i) provide written notice to the holder of the claim described in subsection (b)(6) of such claim and of the right of such holder to use the services of the State child support enforcement agency established under sections 464 and 466 of the Social Security Act for the State in which such holder resides, for assistance in collecting child support during and after the case under this title; and

(ii) include in the notice provided under clause (i) the address and telephone number of such State child support enforcement agency;

(B)(i) provide written notice to such State child support enforcement agency of such claim; and

(ii) include in the notice provided under clause (i) the name, address, and telephone number of such holder; and

(C) at such time as the debtor is granted a discharge under section 1328, provide written notice to such holder and to such State child support enforcement agency of—

(i) the granting of the discharge;

(ii) the last recent known address of the debtor;

(iii) the last recent known name and address of the debtor's employer; and

(iv) the name of each creditor that holds a claim that—

        (I)   is not discharged under paragraph (2) or (4) of section 523(a); or

        (II)   was reaffirmed by the debtor under section 524(c).

    (2)(A)   The holder of a claim described in subsection (b)(6) or the State child support enforcement agency of the State in which such holder resides may request from a creditor described in paragraph (1)(C)(iv) the last known address of the debtor.

    (B)   Notwithstanding any other provision of law, a creditor that makes a disclosure of a last known address of a debtor in connection with a request made under subparagraph (A) shall not be liable by reason of making that disclosure.

§ 1303.   Rights and powers of debtor

    Subject to any limitations on a trustee under this chapter, the debtor shall have, exclusive of the trustee, the rights and powers of a trustee under sections 363(b), 363(d), 363(e), 363(f), and 363(*l*), of this title.

§ 1304.   Debtor engaged in business

    (a)   A debtor that is self-employed and incurs trade credit in the production of income from such employment is engaged in business.

    (b)   Unless the court orders otherwise, a debtor engaged in business may operate the business of the debtor and, subject to any limitations on a trustee under sections 363(c) and 364 of this title and to such limitations or conditions as the court prescribes, shall have, exclusive of the trustee, the rights and powers of the trustee under such sections.

    (c)   A debtor engaged in business shall perform the duties of the trustee specified in section 704(a)(8) of this title.

§ 1305.   Filing and allowance of postpetition claims

    (a)   A proof of claim may be filed by any entity that holds a claim against the debtor—

    (1)   for taxes that become payable to a governmental unit while the case is pending; or

    (2)   that is a consumer debt, that arises after the date of the order for relief under this chapter, and that is for property or services necessary for the debtor's performance under the plan.

    (b)   Except as provided in subsection (c) of this section, a claim filed under subsection (a) of this section shall be allowed or disallowed under section 502 of this title, but shall be determined as of the date such claim arises, and shall be allowed under section 502(a), 502(b), or 502(c) of this title, or disallowed under section 502(d) or 502(e) of this title, the same as if such claim had arisen before the date of the filing of the petition.

    (c)   A claim filed under subsection (a)(2) of this section shall be disallowed if the holder of such claim knew or should have known that prior approval by the trustee of the debtor's incurring the obligation was practicable and was not obtained.

§ 1306.   Property of the estate

    (a)   Property of the estate includes, in addition to the property specified in section 541 of this title—

    (1)   all property of the kind specified in such section that the debtor acquires after the commencement of the case but before the case is closed, dismissed, or converted to a case under chapter 7, 11, or 12 of this title, whichever occurs first; and

    (2)   earnings from services performed by the debtor after the commencement of the case but before the case is closed, dismissed, or converted to a case under chapter 7, 11, or 12 of this title, whichever occurs first.

    (b)   Except as provided in a confirmed plan or order confirming a plan, the debtor shall remain in possession of all property of the estate.

§ 1307.   Conversion or dismissal

(a) The debtor may convert a case under this chapter to a case under chapter 7 of this title at any time. Any waiver of the right to convert under this subsection is unenforceable.

(b) On request of the debtor at any time, if the case has not been converted under section 706, 1112, or 1208 of this title, the court shall dismiss a case under this chapter. Any waiver of the right to dismiss under this subsection is unenforceable.

(c) Except as provided in subsection (f) of this section, on request of a party in interest or the United States trustee and after notice and a hearing, the court may convert a case under this chapter to a case under chapter 7 of this title, or may dismiss a case under this chapter, whichever is in the best interests of creditors and the estate, for cause, including—

    (1) unreasonable delay by the debtor that is prejudicial to creditors;

    (2) nonpayment of any fees and charges required under chapter 123 of title 28;

    (3) failure to file a plan timely under section 1321 of this title;

    (4) failure to commence making timely payments under section 1326 of this title;

    (5) denial of confirmation of a plan under section 1325 of this title and denial of a request made for additional time for filing another plan or a modification of a plan;

    (6) material default by the debtor with respect to a term of a confirmed plan;

    (7) revocation of the order of confirmation under section 1330 of this title, and denial of confirmation of a modified plan under section 1329 of this title;

    (8) termination of a confirmed plan by reason of the occurrence of a condition specified in the plan other than completion of payments under the plan;

    (9) only on request of the United States trustee, failure of the debtor to file, within fifteen days, or such additional time as the court may allow, after the filing of the petition commencing such case, the information required by paragraph (1) of section 521(a);

    (10) only on request of the United States trustee, failure to timely file the information required by paragraph (2) of section 521(a); or

    (11) failure of the debtor to pay any domestic support obligation that first becomes payable after the date of the filing of the petition.

(d) Except as provided in subsection (f) of this section, at any time before the confirmation of a plan under section 1325 of this title, on request of a party in interest or the United States trustee and after notice and a hearing, the court may convert a case under this chapter to a case under chapter 11 or 12 of this title.

(e) Upon the failure of the debtor to file a tax return under section 1308, on request of a party in interest or the United States trustee and after notice and a hearing, the court shall dismiss a case or convert a case under this chapter to a case under chapter 7 of this title, whichever is in the best interest of the creditors and the estate.

(f) The court may not convert a case under this chapter to a case under chapter 7, 11, or 12 of this title if the debtor is a farmer, unless the debtor requests such conversion.

(g) Notwithstanding any other provision of this section, a case may not be converted to a case under another chapter of this title unless the debtor may be a debtor under such chapter.

§ 1308.   Filing of prepetition tax returns

(a) Not later than the day before the date on which the meeting of the creditors is first scheduled to be held under section 341(a), if the debtor was required to file a tax return under applicable nonbankruptcy law, the debtor shall file with appropriate tax authorities all tax returns for all taxable periods ending during the 4-year period ending on the date of the filing of the petition.

(b)(1)   Subject to paragraph (2), if the tax returns required by subsection (a) have not been filed by the date on which the meeting of creditors is first scheduled to be held under section 341(a), the trustee may hold open that meeting for a reasonable period of time to allow the debtor an additional period of time to file any unfiled returns, but such additional period of time shall not extend beyond—

(A)   for any return that is past due as of the date of the filing of the petition, the date that is 120 days after the date of that meeting; or

(B)   for any return that is not past due as of the date of the filing of the petition, the later of—

(i)   the date that is 120 days after the date of that meeting; or

(ii)   the date on which the return is due under the last automatic extension of time for filing that return to which the debtor is entitled, and for which request is timely made, in accordance with applicable nonbankruptcy law.

(2)   After notice and a hearing, and order entered before the tolling of any applicable filing period determined under paragraph (1), if the debtor demonstrates by a preponderance of the evidence that the failure to file a return as required under paragraph (1) is attributable to circumstances beyond the control of the debtor, the court may extend the filing period established by the trustee under paragraph (1) for—

(A)   a period of not more than 30 days for returns described in paragraph (1)(A); and

(B)   a period not to extend after the applicable extended due date for a return described in paragraph (1)(B).

(c)   For purposes of this section, the term "return" includes a return prepared pursuant to subsection (a) or (b) of section 6020 of the Internal Revenue Code of 1986, or a similar State or local law, or a written stipulation to a judgment or a final order entered by a nonbankruptcy tribunal.

SUBCHAPTER II—THE PLAN

§ 1321.   Filing of plan

The debtor shall file a plan.

§ 1322.   Contents of plan

(a)   The plan—

(1)   shall provide for the submission of all or such portion of future earnings or other future income of the debtor to the supervision and control of the trustee as is necessary for the execution of the plan;

(2)   shall provide for the full payment, in deferred cash payments, of all claims entitled to priority under section 507 of this title, unless the holder of a particular claim agrees to a different treatment of such claim;

(3)   if the plan classifies claims, shall provide the same treatment for each claim within a particular class; and.

(4)   notwithstanding any other provision of this section, may provide for less than full payment of all amounts owed for a claim entitled to priority under section 507(a)(1)(B) only if the plan provides that all of the debtor's projected disposable income for a 5-year period beginning on the date that the first payment is due under the plan will be applied to make payments under the plan.

(b)   Subject to subsections (a) and (c) of this section, the plan may—

(1)   designate a class or classes of unsecured claims, as provided in section 1122 of this title, but may not discriminate unfairly against any class so designated; however, such plan may treat claims for a consumer debt of the debtor if an individual is liable on such consumer debt with the debtor differently than other unsecured claims;

(2) modify the rights of holders of secured claims, other than a claim secured only by a security interest in real property that is the debtor's principal residence, or of holders of unsecured claims, or leave unaffected the rights of holders of any class of claims;

(3) provide for the curing or waiving of any default;

(4) provide for payments on any unsecured claim to be made concurrently with payments on any secured claim or any other unsecured claim;

(5) notwithstanding paragraph (2) of this subsection, provide for the curing of any default within a reasonable time and maintenance of payments while the case is pending on any unsecured claim or secured claim on which the last payment is due after the date on which the final payment under the plan is due;

(6) provide for the payment of all or any part of any claim allowed under section 1305 of this title;

(7) subject to section 365 of this title, provide for the assumption, rejection, or assignment of any executory contract or unexpired lease of the debtor not previously rejected under such section;

(8) provide for the payment of all or part of a claim against the debtor from property of the estate or property of the debtor;

(9) provide for the vesting of property of the estate, on confirmation of the plan or at a later time, in the debtor or in any other entity;

(10) provide for the payment of interest accruing after the date of the filing of the petition on unsecured claims that are nondischargeable under section 1328(a), except that such interest may be paid only to the extent that the debtor has disposable income available to pay such interest after making provision for full payment of all allowed claims; and

(11) include any other appropriate provision not inconsistent with this title.

(c) Notwithstanding subsection (b)(2) and applicable nonbankruptcy law—

(1) a default with respect to, or that gave rise to, a lien on the debtor's principal residence may be cured under paragraph (3) or (5) of subsection (b) until such residence is sold at a foreclosure sale that is conducted in accordance with applicable nonbankruptcy law; and

(2) in a case in which the last payment on the original payment schedule for a claim secured only by a security interest in real property that is the debtor's principal residence is due before the date on which the final payment under the plan is due, the plan may provide for the payment of the claim as modified pursuant to section 1325(a)(5) of this title.

(d)(1) If the current monthly income of the debtor and the debtor's spouse combined, when multiplied by 12, is not less than—

(A) in the case of a debtor in a household of 1 person, the median family income of the applicable State for 1 earner;

(B) in the case of a debtor in a household of 2, 3, or 4 individuals, the highest median family income of the applicable State for a family of the same number or fewer individuals; or

(C) in the case of a debtor in a household exceeding 4 individuals, the highest median family income of the applicable State for a family of 4 or fewer individuals, plus $825 per month for each individual in excess of 4,

the plan may not provide for payments over a period that is longer than 5 years.

(2) If the current monthly income of the debtor and the debtor's spouse combined, when multiplied by 12, is less than—

(A) in the case of a debtor in a household of 1 person, the median family income of the applicable State for 1 earner;

(B) in the case of a debtor in a household of 2, 3, or 4 individuals, the highest median family income of the applicable State for a family of the same number or fewer individuals; or

(C) in the case of a debtor in a household exceeding 4 individuals, the highest median family income of the applicable State for a family of 4 or fewer individuals, plus $825 per month for each individual in excess of 4,

the plan may not provide for payments over a period that is longer than 3 years, unless the court, for cause, approves a longer period, but the court may not approve a period that is longer than 5 years.

(e) Notwithstanding subsection (b)(2) of this section and sections 506(b) and 1325(a)(5) of this title, if it is proposed in a plan to cure a default, the amount necessary to cure the default, shall be determined in accordance with the underlying agreement and applicable nonbankruptcy law.

(f) A plan may not materially alter the terms of a loan described in section 362(b)(19) and any amounts required to repay such loan shall not constitute "disposable income" under section 1325.

§ 1323.   Modification of plan before confirmation

(a) The debtor may modify the plan at any time before confirmation, but may not modify the plan so that the plan as modified fails to meet the requirements of section 1322 of this title.

(b) After the debtor files a modification under this section, the plan as modified becomes the plan.

(c) Any holder of a secured claim that has accepted or rejected the plan is deemed to have accepted or rejected, as the case may be, the plan as modified, unless the modification provides for a change in the rights of such holder from what such rights were under the plan before modification, and such holder changes such holder's previous acceptance or rejection.

§ 1324.   Confirmation hearing

(a) Except as provided in subsection (b) and after notice, the court shall hold a hearing on confirmation of the plan. A party in interest may object to confirmation of the plan.

(b) The hearing on confirmation of the plan may be held not earlier than 20 days and not later than 45 days after the date of the meeting of creditors under section 341(a), unless the court determines that it would be in the best interests of the creditors and the estate to hold such hearing at an earlier date and there is no objection to such earlier date.

§ 1325.   Confirmation of plan

(a) Except as provided in subsection (b), the court shall confirm a plan if—

(1) the plan complies with the provisions of this chapter and with the other applicable provisions of this title;

(2) any fee, charge, or amount required under chapter 123 of title 28, or by the plan, to be paid before confirmation, has been paid;

(3) the plan has been proposed in good faith and not by any means forbidden by law;

(4) the value, as of the effective date of the plan, of property to be distributed under the plan on account of each allowed unsecured claim is not less than the amount that would be paid on such claim if the estate of the debtor were liquidated under chapter 7 of this title on such date;

(5) with respect to each allowed secured claim provided for by the plan—

(A) the holder of such claim has accepted the plan;

(B)(i) the plan provides that—

(I) the holder of such claim retain the lien securing such claim until the earlier of—

(aa) the payment of the underlying debt determined under nonbankruptcy law; or

(bb) discharge under section 1328; and

(II) if the case under this chapter is dismissed or converted without completion of the plan, such lien shall also be retained by such holder to the extent recognized by applicable nonbankruptcy law;

(ii) the value, as of the effective date of the plan, of property to be distributed under the plan on account of such claim is not less than the allowed amount of such claim; and

(iii) if—

(I) property to be distributed pursuant to this subsection is in the form of periodic payments, such payments shall be in equal monthly amounts; and

(II) the holder of the claim is secured by personal property, the amount of such payments shall not be less than an amount sufficient to provide to the holder of such claim adequate protection during the period of the plan; or

(C) the debtor surrenders the property securing such claim to such holder;

(6) the debtor will be able to make all payments under the plan and to comply with the plan;

(7) the action of the debtor in filing the petition was in good faith;

(8) the debtor has paid all amounts that are required to be paid under a domestic support obligation and that first become payable after the date of the filing of the petition if the debtor is required by a judicial or administrative order, or by statute, to pay such domestic support obligation; and

(9) the debtor has filed all applicable Federal, State, and local tax returns as required by section 1308.

For purposes of paragraph (5), section 506 shall not apply to a claim described in that paragraph if the creditor has a purchase money security interest securing the debt that is the subject of the claim, the debt was incurred within the 910-day period preceding the date of the filing of the petition, and the collateral for that debt consists of a motor vehicle (as defined in section 30102 of title 49) acquired for the personal use of the debtor, or if collateral for that debt consists of any other thing of value, if the debt was incurred during the 1-year period preceding that filing.

(b)(1) If the trustee or the holder of an allowed unsecured claim objects to the confirmation of the plan, then the court may not approve the plan unless, as of the effective date of the plan—

(A) the value of the property to be distributed under the plan on account of such claim is not less than the amount of such claim; or

(B) the plan provides that all of the debtor's projected disposable income to be received in the applicable commitment period beginning on the date that the first payment is due under the plan will be applied to make payments to unsecured creditors under the plan.

(2) For purposes of this subsection, the term "disposable income" means current monthly income received by the debtor (other than child support payments, foster care payments, or disability payments for a dependent child made in accordance with applicable nonbankruptcy law to the extent reasonably necessary to be expended for such child) less amounts reasonably necessary to be expended—

(A)(i) for the maintenance or support of the debtor or a dependent of the debtor, or for a domestic support obligation, that first becomes payable after the date the petition is filed; and

(ii) for charitable contributions (that meet the definition of "charitable contribution" under section 548(d)(3)) to a qualified religious or charitable entity or organization (as defined in section 548(d)(4)) in an amount not to exceed 15 percent of gross income of the debtor for the year in which the contributions are made; and

(B) if the debtor is engaged in business, for the payment of expenditures necessary for the continuation, preservation, and operation of such business.

(3) Amounts reasonably necessary to be expended under paragraph (2), other than subparagraph (A)(ii) of paragraph (2), shall be determined in accordance with subparagraphs (A) and (B) of section 707(b)(2), if the debtor has current monthly income, when multiplied by 12, greater than—

(A) in the case of a debtor in a household of 1 person, the median family income of the applicable State for 1 earner;

(B) in the case of a debtor in a household of 2, 3, or 4 individuals, the highest median family income of the applicable State for a family of the same number or fewer individuals; or

(C) in the case of a debtor in a household exceeding 4 individuals, the highest median family income of the applicable State for a family of 4 or fewer individuals, plus $825 per month for each individual in excess of 4.

(4) For purposes of this subsection, the "applicable commitment period"—

(A) subject to subparagraph (B), shall be—

(i) 3 years; or

(ii) not less than 5 years, if the current monthly income of the debtor and the debtor's spouse combined, when multiplied by 12, is not less than—

(I) in the case of a debtor in a household of 1 person, the median family income of the applicable State for 1 earner;

(II) in the case of a debtor in a household of 2, 3, or 4 individuals, the highest median family income of the applicable State for a family of the same number or fewer individuals; or

(III) in the case of a debtor in a household exceeding 4 individuals, the highest median family income of the applicable State for a family of 4 or fewer individuals, plus $825 per month for each individual in excess of 4; and

(B) may be less than 3 or 5 years, whichever is applicable under subparagraph (A), but only if the plan provides for payment in full of all allowed unsecured claims over a shorter period.

(c) After confirmation of a plan, the court may order any entity from whom the debtor receives income to pay all or any part of such income to the trustee.

[*Note from West Advisory Panel.* Pub. L. 116–260 created a temporary § 1325(d), which expired on December 27, 2022, *except* for cases commenced before December 27, 2022. *See* 134 Stat. 2016, 2017. For the text of temporary § 1325(d), *see* Title 11, Chapter 13, Subchapter II, § 1325, Editorial Notes, Amendments, 2020 at http://uscode.house.gov]

§ 1326.   Payments

(a)(1) Unless the court orders otherwise, the debtor shall commence making payments not later than 30 days after the date of the filing of the plan or the order for relief, whichever is earlier, in the amount—

(A) proposed by the plan to the trustee;

(B) scheduled in a lease of personal property directly to the lessor for that portion of the obligation that becomes due after the order for relief, reducing the payments under subparagraph (A) by the amount so paid and providing the trustee with evidence of such payment, including the amount and date of payment; and

(C) that provides adequate protection directly to a creditor holding an allowed claim secured by personal property to the extent the claim is attributable to the purchase of such property by the debtor for that portion of the obligation that becomes due after the order for relief, reducing the payments under subparagraph (A) by the amount so paid and providing the trustee with evidence of such payment, including the amount and date of payment.

(2) A payment made under paragraph (1)(A) shall be retained by the trustee until confirmation or denial of confirmation. If a plan is confirmed, the trustee shall distribute any such payment in accordance with the plan as soon as is practicable. If a plan is not confirmed, the trustee shall return any such payments not previously paid and not yet due and owing to creditors pursuant to paragraph (3) to the debtor, after deducting any unpaid claim allowed under section 503(b).

(3) Subject to section 363, the court may, upon notice and a hearing, modify, increase, or reduce the payments required under this subsection pending confirmation of a plan.

(4) Not later than 60 days after the date of filing of a case under this chapter, a debtor retaining possession of personal property subject to a lease or securing a claim attributable in whole or in part to the purchase price of such property shall provide the lessor or secured creditor reasonable evidence of the maintenance of any required insurance coverage with respect to the use or ownership of such property and continue to do so for so long as the debtor retains possession of such property.

(b) Before or at the time of each payment to creditors under the plan, there shall be paid—

(1) any unpaid claim of the kind specified in section 507(a)(2) of this title;

(2) if a standing trustee appointed under section 586(b) of title 28 is serving in the case, the percentage fee fixed for such standing trustee under section 586(e)(1)(B) of title 28; and

(3) if a chapter 7 trustee has been allowed compensation due to the conversion or dismissal of the debtor's prior case pursuant to section 707(b), and some portion of that compensation remains unpaid in a case converted to this chapter or in the case dismissed under section 707(b) and refiled under this chapter, the amount of any such unpaid compensation, which shall be paid monthly—

(A) by prorating such amount over the remaining duration of the plan; and

(B) by monthly payments not to exceed the greater of—

(i) $25; or

(ii) the amount payable to unsecured nonpriority creditors, as provided by the plan, multiplied by 5 percent, and the result divided by the number of months in the plan.

(c) Except as otherwise provided in the plan or in the order confirming the plan, the trustee shall make payments to creditors under the plan.

(d) Notwithstanding any other provision of this title—

(1) compensation referred to in subsection (b)(3) is payable and may be collected by the trustee under that paragraph, even if such amount has been discharged in a prior case under this title; and

(2) such compensation is payable in a case under this chapter only to the extent permitted by subsection (b)(3).

§ 1327. Effect of confirmation

(a) The provisions of a confirmed plan bind the debtor and each creditor, whether or not the claim of such creditor is provided for by the plan, and whether or not such creditor has objected to, has accepted, or has rejected the plan.

(b) Except as otherwise provided in the plan or the order confirming the plan, the confirmation of a plan vests all of the property of the estate in the debtor.

(c) Except as otherwise provided in the plan or in the order confirming the plan, the property vesting in the debtor under subsection (b) of this section is free and clear of any claim or interest of any creditor provided for by the plan.

§ 1328. Discharge

(a) Subject to subsection (d), as soon as practicable after completion by the debtor of all payments under the plan, and in the case of a debtor who is required by a judicial or administrative order, or by statute, to pay a domestic support obligation, after such debtor certifies that all amounts payable under such order or such statute that are due on or before the date of the certification (including amounts due before the petition was filed, but only to the extent provided for by the plan) have been paid, unless the court approves a written waiver of discharge executed by the debtor after the order for relief under this chapter, the court shall grant the debtor a discharge of all debts provided for by the plan or disallowed under section 502 of this title, except any debt—

    (1)   provided for under section 1322(b)(5);

    (2)   of the kind specified in section 507(a)(8)(C) or in paragraph (1)(B), (1)(C), (2), (3), (4), (5), (8), or (9) of section 523(a);

    (3)   for restitution, or a criminal fine, included in a sentence on the debtor's conviction of a crime; or

    (4)   for restitution, or damages, awarded in a civil action against the debtor as a result of willful or malicious injury by the debtor that caused personal injury to an individual or the death of an individual.

  (b)   Subject to subsection (d), at any time after the confirmation of the plan and after notice and a hearing, the court may grant a discharge to a debtor that has not completed payments under the plan only if—

    (1)   the debtor's failure to complete such payments is due to circumstances for which the debtor should not justly be held accountable;

    (2)   the value, as of the effective date of the plan, of property actually distributed under the plan on account of each allowed unsecured claim is not less than the amount that would have been paid on such claim if the estate of the debtor had been liquidated under chapter 7 of this title on such date; and

    (3)   modification of the plan under section 1329 of this title is not practicable.

  (c)   A discharge granted under subsection (b) of this section discharges the debtor from all unsecured debts provided for by the plan or disallowed under section 502 of this title, except any debt—

    (1)   provided for under section 1322(b)(5) of this title; or

    (2)   of a kind specified in section 523(a) of this title.

  (d)   Notwithstanding any other provision of this section, a discharge granted under this section does not discharge the debtor from any debt based on an allowed claim filed under section 1305(a)(2) of this title if prior approval by the trustee of the debtor's incurring such debt was practicable and was not obtained.

  (e)   On request of a party in interest before one year after a discharge under this section is granted, and after notice and a hearing, the court may revoke such discharge only if—

    (1)   such discharge was obtained by the debtor through fraud; and

    (2)   the requesting party did not know of such fraud until after such discharge was granted.

  (f)   Notwithstanding subsections (a) and (b), the court shall not grant a discharge of all debts provided for in the plan or disallowed under section 502, if the debtor has received a discharge—

    (1)   in a case filed under chapter 7, 11, or 12 of this title during the 4-year period preceding the date of the order for relief under this chapter, or

    (2)   in a case filed under chapter 13 of this title during the 2-year period preceding the date of such order.

  (g)(1)   The court shall not grant a discharge under this section to a debtor unless after filing a petition the debtor has completed an instructional course concerning personal financial management described in section 111.

    (2)   Paragraph (1) shall not apply with respect to a debtor who is a person described in section 109(h)(4) or who resides in a district for which the United States trustee (or the bankruptcy administrator, if any) determines that the approved instructional courses are not adequate to service the additional individuals who would otherwise be required to complete such instructional course by reason of the requirements of paragraph (1).

(3) The United States trustee (or the bankruptcy administrator, if any) who makes a determination described in paragraph (2) shall review such determination not later than 1 year after the date of such determination, and not less frequently than annually thereafter.

(h) The court may not grant a discharge under this chapter unless the court after notice and a hearing held not more than 10 days before the date of the entry of the order granting the discharge finds that there is no reasonable cause to believe that—

(1) section 522(q)(1) may be applicable to the debtor; and

(2) there is pending any proceeding in which the debtor may be found guilty of a felony of the kind described in section 522(q)(1)(A) or liable for a debt of the kind described in section 522(q)(1)(B).

§ 1329. Modification of plan after confirmation

(a) At any time after confirmation of the plan but before the completion of payments under such plan, the plan may be modified, upon request of the debtor, the trustee, or the holder of an allowed unsecured claim, to—

(1) increase or reduce the amount of payments on claims of a particular class provided for by the plan;

(2) extend or reduce the time for such payments;

(3) alter the amount of the distribution to a creditor whose claim is provided for by the plan to the extent necessary to take account of any payment of such claim other than under the plan; or

(4) reduce amounts to be paid under the plan by the actual amount expended by the debtor to purchase health insurance for the debtor (and for any dependent of the debtor if such dependent does not otherwise have health insurance coverage) if the debtor documents the cost of such insurance and demonstrates that—

(A) such expenses are reasonable and necessary;

(B)(i)   if the debtor previously paid for health insurance, the amount is not materially larger than the cost the debtor previously paid or the cost necessary to maintain the lapsed policy; or

(ii) if the debtor did not have health insurance, the amount is not materially larger than the reasonable cost that would be incurred by a debtor who purchases health insurance, who has similar income, expenses, age, and health status, and who lives in the same geographical location with the same number of dependents who do not otherwise have health insurance coverage; and

(C) the amount is not otherwise allowed for purposes of determining disposable income under section 1325(b) of this title;

and upon request of any party in interest, files proof that a health insurance policy was purchased.

(b)(1)   Sections 1322(a), 1322(b), and 1323(c) of this title and the requirements of section 1325(a) of this title apply to any modification under subsection (a) of this section.

(2) The plan as modified becomes the plan unless, after notice and a hearing, such modification is disapproved.

(c) A plan modified under this section may not provide for payments over a period that expires after the applicable commitment period under section 1325(b)(1)(B) after the time that the first payment under the original confirmed plan was due, unless the court, for cause, approves a longer period, but the court may not approve a period that expires after five years after such time.

§ 1330.   Revocation of an order of confirmation

(a)   On request of a party in interest at any time within 180 days after the date of the entry of an order of confirmation under section 1325 of this title, and after notice and a hearing, the court may revoke such order if such order was procured by fraud.

(b)   If the court revokes an order of confirmation under subsection (a) of this section, the court shall dispose of the case under section 1307 of this title, unless, within the time fixed by the court, the debtor proposes and the court confirms a modification of the plan under section 1329 of this title.

CHAPTER 15—ANCILLARY AND OTHER CROSS-BORDER CASES

1501.   Purpose and scope of application.

SUBCHAPTER I—GENERAL PROVISIONS

1502.   Definitions.
1503.   International obligations of the United States.
1504.   Commencement of ancillary case.
1505.   Authorization to act in a foreign country.
1506.   Public policy exception.
1507.   Additional assistance.
1508.   Interpretation.

SUBCHAPTER II—ACCESS OF FOREIGN REPRESENTATIVES AND CREDITORS TO THE COURT

1509.   Right of direct access.
1510.   Limited jurisdiction.
1511.   Commencement of case under section 301, 302, or 303.
1512.   Participation of a foreign representative in a case under this title.
1513.   Access of foreign creditors to a case under this title.
1514.   Notification to foreign creditors concerning a case under this title.

SUBCHAPTER III—RECOGNITION OF A FOREIGN PROCEEDING AND RELIEF

1515.   Application for recognition.
1516.   Presumptions concerning recognition.
1517.   Order granting recognition.
1518.   Subsequent information.
1519.   Relief that may be granted upon filing petition for recognition.
1520.   Effects of recognition of a foreign main proceeding.
1521.   Relief that may be granted upon recognition.
1522.   Protection of creditors and other interested persons.
1523.   Actions to avoid acts detrimental to creditors.
1524.   Intervention by a foreign representative.

SUBCHAPTER IV—COOPERATION WITH FOREIGN COURTS AND FOREIGN REPRESENTATIVES

1525.   Cooperation and direct communication between the court and foreign courts or foreign representatives.
1526.   Cooperation and direct communication between the trustee and foreign courts or foreign representatives.
1527.   Forms of cooperation.

SUBCHAPTER V—CONCURRENT PROCEEDINGS

1528.   Commencement of a case under this title after recognition of a foreign main proceeding.

1529.   Coordination of a case under this title and a foreign proceeding.

1530.   Coordination of more than 1 foreign proceeding.

1531.   Presumption of insolvency based on recognition of a foreign main proceeding.

1532.   Rule of payment in concurrent proceedings.

---

§ 1501.   Purpose and scope of application

(a) The purpose of this chapter is to incorporate the Model Law on Cross-Border Insolvency so as to provide effective mechanisms for dealing with cases of cross-border insolvency with the objectives of—

    (1) cooperation between—

        (A) courts of the United States, United States trustees, trustees, examiners, debtors, and debtors in possession; and

        (B) the courts and other competent authorities of foreign countries involved in cross-border insolvency cases;

    (2) greater legal certainty for trade and investment;

    (3) fair and efficient administration of cross-border insolvencies that protects the interests of all creditors, and other interested entities, including the debtor;

    (4) protection and maximization of the value of the debtor's assets; and

    (5) facilitation of the rescue of financially troubled businesses, thereby protecting investment and preserving employment.

(b) This chapter applies where—

    (1) assistance is sought in the United States by a foreign court or a foreign representative in connection with a foreign proceeding;

    (2) assistance is sought in a foreign country in connection with a case under this title;

    (3) a foreign proceeding and a case under this title with respect to the same debtor are pending concurrently; or

    (4) creditors or other interested persons in a foreign country have an interest in requesting the commencement of, or participating in, a case or proceeding under this title.

(c) This chapter does not apply to—

    (1) a proceeding concerning an entity, other than a foreign insurance company, identified by exclusion in section 109(b);

    (2) an individual, or to an individual and such individual's spouse, who have debts within the limits specified in section 109(e) and who are citizens of the United States or aliens lawfully admitted for permanent residence in the United States; or

    (3) an entity subject to a proceeding under the Securities Investor Protection Act of 1970, a stockbroker subject to subchapter III of chapter 7 of this title, or a commodity broker subject to subchapter IV of chapter 7 of this title.

(d) The court may not grant relief under this chapter with respect to any deposit, escrow, trust fund, or other security required or permitted under any applicable State insurance law or regulation for the benefit of claim holders in the United States.

SUBCHAPTER I—GENERAL PROVISIONS

§ 1502.　Definitions

For the purposes of this chapter, the term—

　(1)　"debtor" means an entity that is the subject of a foreign proceeding;

　(2)　"establishment" means any place of operations where the debtor carries out a nontransitory economic activity;

　(3)　"foreign court" means a judicial or other authority competent to control or supervise a foreign proceeding;

　(4)　"foreign main proceeding" means a foreign proceeding pending in the country where the debtor has the center of its main interests;

　(5)　"foreign nonmain proceeding" means a foreign proceeding, other than a foreign main proceeding, pending in a country where the debtor has an establishment;

　(6)　"trustee" includes a trustee, a debtor in possession in a case under any chapter of this title, or a debtor under chapter 9 of this title;

　(7)　"recognition" means the entry of an order granting recognition of a foreign main proceeding or foreign nonmain proceeding under this chapter; and

　(8)　"within the territorial jurisdiction of the United States", when used with reference to property of a debtor, refers to tangible property located within the territory of the United States and intangible property deemed under applicable nonbankruptcy law to be located within that territory, including any property subject to attachment or garnishment that may properly be seized or garnished by an action in a Federal or State court in the United States.

§ 1503.　International obligations of the United States

To the extent that this chapter conflicts with an obligation of the United States arising out of any treaty or other form of agreement to which it is a party with one or more other countries, the requirements of the treaty or agreement prevail.

§ 1504.　Commencement of ancillary case

A case under this chapter is commenced by the filing of a petition for recognition of a foreign proceeding under section 1515.

§ 1505.　Authorization to act in a foreign country

A trustee or another entity (including an examiner) may be authorized by the court to act in a foreign country on behalf of an estate created under section 541. An entity authorized to act under this section may act in any way permitted by the applicable foreign law.

§ 1506.　Public policy exception

Nothing in this chapter prevents the court from refusing to take an action governed by this chapter if the action would be manifestly contrary to the public policy of the United States.

§ 1507.　Additional assistance

　(a)　Subject to the specific limitations stated elsewhere in this chapter the court, if recognition is granted, may provide additional assistance to a foreign representative under this title or under other laws of the United States.

　(b)　In determining whether to provide additional assistance under this title or under other laws of the United States, the court shall consider whether such additional assistance, consistent with the principles of comity, will reasonably assure—

(1)   just treatment of all holders of claims against or interests in the debtor's property;

(2)   protection of claim holders in the United States against prejudice and inconvenience in the processing of claims in such foreign proceeding;

(3)   prevention of preferential or fraudulent dispositions of property of the debtor;

(4)   distribution of proceeds of the debtor's property substantially in accordance with the order prescribed by this title; and

(5)   if appropriate, the provision of an opportunity for a fresh start for the individual that such foreign proceeding concerns.

§ 1508.   Interpretation

In interpreting this chapter, the court shall consider its international origin, and the need to promote an application of this chapter that is consistent with the application of similar statutes adopted by foreign jurisdictions.

SUBCHAPTER II—ACCESS OF FOREIGN REPRESENTATIVES AND CREDITORS TO THE COURT

§ 1509.   Right of direct access

(a)   A foreign representative may commence a case under section 1504 by filing directly with the court a petition for recognition of a foreign proceeding under section 1515.

(b)   If the court grants recognition under section 1517, and subject to any limitations that the court may impose consistent with the policy of this chapter—

(1)   the foreign representative has the capacity to sue and be sued in a court in the United States;

(2)   the foreign representative may apply directly to a court in the United States for appropriate relief in that court; and

(3)   a court in the United States shall grant comity or cooperation to the foreign representative.

(c)   A request for comity or cooperation by a foreign representative in a court in the United States other than the court which granted recognition shall be accompanied by a certified copy of an order granting recognition under section 1517.

(d)   If the court denies recognition under this chapter, the court may issue any appropriate order necessary to prevent the foreign representative from obtaining comity or cooperation from courts in the United States.

(e)   Whether or not the court grants recognition, and subject to sections 306 and 1510, a foreign representative is subject to applicable nonbankruptcy law.

(f)   Notwithstanding any other provision of this section, the failure of a foreign representative to commence a case or to obtain recognition under this chapter does not affect any right the foreign representative may have to sue in a court in the United States to collect or recover a claim which is the property of the debtor.

§ 1510.   Limited jurisdiction

The sole fact that a foreign representative files a petition under section 1515 does not subject the foreign representative to the jurisdiction of any court in the United States for any other purpose.

§ 1511.   Commencement of case under section 301, 302, or 303

(a)   Upon recognition, a foreign representative may commence—

(1)   an involuntary case under section 303; or

(2) a voluntary case under section 301 or 302, if the foreign proceeding is a foreign main proceeding.

(b) The petition commencing a case under subsection (a) must be accompanied by a certified copy of an order granting recognition. The court where the petition for recognition has been filed must be advised of the foreign representative's intent to commence a case under subsection (a) prior to such commencement.

§ 1512. Participation of a foreign representative in a case under this title

Upon recognition of a foreign proceeding, the foreign representative in the recognized proceeding is entitled to participate as a party in interest in a case regarding the debtor under this title.

§ 1513. Access of foreign creditors to a case under this title

(a) Foreign creditors have the same rights regarding the commencement of, and participation in, a case under this title as domestic creditors.

(b)(1) Subsection (a) does not change or codify present law as to the priority of claims under section 507 or 726, except that the claim of a foreign creditor under those sections shall not be given a lower priority than that of general unsecured claims without priority solely because the holder of such claim is a foreign creditor.

    (2)(A) Subsection (a) and paragraph (1) do not change or codify present law as to the allowability of foreign revenue claims or other foreign public law claims in a proceeding under this title.

    (B) Allowance and priority as to a foreign tax claim or other foreign public law claim shall be governed by any applicable tax treaty of the United States, under the conditions and circumstances specified therein.

§ 1514. Notification to foreign creditors concerning a case under this title

(a) Whenever in a case under this title notice is to be given to creditors generally or to any class or category of creditors, such notice shall also be given to the known creditors generally, or to creditors in the notified class or category, that do not have addresses in the United States. The court may order that appropriate steps be taken with a view to notifying any creditor whose address is not yet known.

(b) Such notification to creditors with foreign addresses described in subsection (a) shall be given individually, unless the court considers that, under the circumstances, some other form of notification would be more appropriate. No letter or other formality is required.

(c) When a notification of commencement of a case is to be given to foreign creditors, such notification shall—

    (1) indicate the time period for filing proofs of claim and specify the place for filing such proofs of claim;

    (2) indicate whether secured creditors need to file proofs of claim; and

    (3) contain any other information required to be included in such notification to creditors under this title and the orders of the court.

(d) Any rule of procedure or order of the court as to notice or the filing of a proof of claim shall provide such additional time to creditors with foreign addresses as is reasonable under the circumstances.

SUBCHAPTER III—RECOGNITION OF A FOREIGN PROCEEDING AND RELIEF

§ 1515. Application for recognition

(a) A foreign representative applies to the court for recognition of a foreign proceeding in which the foreign representative has been appointed by filing a petition for recognition.

(b) A petition for recognition shall be accompanied by—

(1) a certified copy of the decision commencing such foreign proceeding and appointing the foreign representative;

(2) a certificate from the foreign court affirming the existence of such foreign proceeding and of the appointment of the foreign representative; or

(3) in the absence of evidence referred to in paragraphs (1) and (2), any other evidence acceptable to the court of the existence of such foreign proceeding and of the appointment of the foreign representative.

(c) A petition for recognition shall also be accompanied by a statement identifying all foreign proceedings with respect to the debtor that are known to the foreign representative.

(d) The documents referred to in paragraphs (1) and (2) of subsection (b) shall be translated into English. The court may require a translation into English of additional documents.

§ 1516.   Presumptions concerning recognition

(a) If the decision or certificate referred to in section 1515(b) indicates that the foreign proceeding is a foreign proceeding and that the person or body is a foreign representative, the court is entitled to so presume.

(b) The court is entitled to presume that documents submitted in support of the petition for recognition are authentic, whether or not they have been legalized.

(c) In the absence of evidence to the contrary, the debtor's registered office, or habitual residence in the case of an individual, is presumed to be the center of the debtor's main interests.

§ 1517.   Order granting recognition

(a) Subject to section 1506, after notice and a hearing, an order recognizing a foreign proceeding shall be entered if—

(1) such foreign proceeding for which recognition is sought is a foreign main proceeding or foreign nonmain proceeding within the meaning of section 1502;

(2) the foreign representative applying for recognition is a person or body; and

(3) the petition meets the requirements of section 1515.

(b) Such foreign proceeding shall be recognized—

(1) as a foreign main proceeding if it is pending in the country where the debtor has the center of its main interests; or

(2) as a foreign nonmain proceeding if the debtor has an establishment within the meaning of section 1502 in the foreign country where the proceeding is pending.

(c) A petition for recognition of a foreign proceeding shall be decided upon at the earliest possible time. Entry of an order recognizing a foreign proceeding constitutes recognition under this chapter.

(d) The provisions of this subchapter do not prevent modification or termination of recognition if it is shown that the grounds for granting it were fully or partially lacking or have ceased to exist, but in considering such action the court shall give due weight to possible prejudice to parties that have relied upon the order granting recognition. A case under this chapter may be closed in the manner prescribed under section 350.

§ 1518.   Subsequent information

From the time of filing the petition for recognition of a foreign proceeding, the foreign representative shall file with the court promptly a notice of change of status concerning—

(1) any substantial change in the status of such foreign proceeding or the status of the foreign representative's appointment; and

(2) any other foreign proceeding regarding the debtor that becomes known to the foreign representative.

§ 1519.   Relief that may be granted upon filing petition for recognition

(a) From the time of filing a petition for recognition until the court rules on the petition, the court may, at the request of the foreign representative, where relief is urgently needed to protect the assets of the debtor or the interests of the creditors, grant relief of a provisional nature, including—

(1) staying execution against the debtor's assets;

(2) entrusting the administration or realization of all or part of the debtor's assets located in the United States to the foreign representative or another person authorized by the court, including an examiner, in order to protect and preserve the value of assets that, by their nature or because of other circumstances, are perishable, susceptible to devaluation or otherwise in jeopardy; and

(3) any relief referred to in paragraph (3), (4), or (7) of section 1521(a).

(b) Unless extended under section 1521(a)(6), the relief granted under this section terminates when the petition for recognition is granted.

(c) It is a ground for denial of relief under this section that such relief would interfere with the administration of a foreign main proceeding.

(d) The court may not enjoin a police or regulatory act of a governmental unit, including a criminal action or proceeding, under this section.

(e) The standards, procedures, and limitations applicable to an injunction shall apply to relief under this section.

(f) The exercise of rights not subject to the stay arising under section 362(a) pursuant to paragraph (6), (7), (17), or (27) of section 362(b) or pursuant to section 362(*o*) shall not be stayed by any order of a court or administrative agency in any proceeding under this chapter.

§ 1520.   Effects of recognition of a foreign main proceeding

(a) Upon recognition of a foreign proceeding that is a foreign main proceeding—

(1) sections 361 and 362 apply with respect to the debtor and the property of the debtor that is within the territorial jurisdiction of the United States;

(2) sections 363, 549, and 552 apply to a transfer of an interest of the debtor in property that is within the territorial jurisdiction of the United States to the same extent that the sections would apply to property of an estate;

(3) unless the court orders otherwise, the foreign representative may operate the debtor's business and may exercise the rights and powers of a trustee under and to the extent provided by sections 363 and 552; and

(4) section 552 applies to property of the debtor that is within the territorial jurisdiction of the United States.

(b) Subsection (a) does not affect the right to commence an individual action or proceeding in a foreign country to the extent necessary to preserve a claim against the debtor.

(c) Subsection (a) does not affect the right of a foreign representative or an entity to file a petition commencing a case under this title or the right of any party to file claims or take other proper actions in such a case.

§ 1521.   Relief that may be granted upon recognition

(a) Upon recognition of a foreign proceeding, whether main or nonmain, where necessary to effectuate the purpose of this chapter and to protect the assets of the debtor or the interests of the creditors, the court may, at the request of the foreign representative, grant any appropriate relief, including—

(1) staying the commencement or continuation of an individual action or proceeding concerning the debtor's assets, rights, obligations or liabilities to the extent they have not been stayed under section 1520(a);

(2) staying execution against the debtor's assets to the extent it has not been stayed under section 1520(a);

(3) suspending the right to transfer, encumber or otherwise dispose of any assets of the debtor to the extent this right has not been suspended under section 1520(a);

(4) providing for the examination of witnesses, the taking of evidence or the delivery of information concerning the debtor's assets, affairs, rights, obligations or liabilities;

(5) entrusting the administration or realization of all or part of the debtor's assets within the territorial jurisdiction of the United States to the foreign representative or another person, including an examiner, authorized by the court;

(6) extending relief granted under section 1519(a); and

(7) granting any additional relief that may be available to a trustee, except for relief available under sections 522, 544, 545, 547, 548, 550, and 724(a).

(b) Upon recognition of a foreign proceeding, whether main or nonmain, the court may, at the request of the foreign representative, entrust the distribution of all or part of the debtor's assets located in the United States to the foreign representative or another person, including an examiner, authorized by the court, provided that the court is satisfied that the interests of creditors in the United States are sufficiently protected.

(c) In granting relief under this section to a representative of a foreign nonmain proceeding, the court must be satisfied that the relief relates to assets that, under the law of the United States, should be administered in the foreign nonmain proceeding or concerns information required in that proceeding.

(d) The court may not enjoin a police or regulatory act of a governmental unit, including a criminal action or proceeding, under this section.

(e) The standards, procedures, and limitations applicable to an injunction shall apply to relief under paragraphs (1), (2), (3), and (6) of subsection (a).

(f) The exercise of rights not subject to the stay arising under section 362(a) pursuant to paragraph (6), (7), (17), or (27) of section 362(b) or pursuant to section 362(o) shall not be stayed by any order of a court or administrative agency in any proceeding under this chapter.

§ 1522. Protection of creditors and other interested persons

(a) The court may grant relief under section 1519 or 1521, or may modify or terminate relief under subsection (c), only if the interests of the creditors and other interested entities, including the debtor, are sufficiently protected.

(b) The court may subject relief granted under section 1519 or 1521, or the operation of the debtor's business under section 1520(a)(3), to conditions it considers appropriate, including the giving of security or the filing of a bond.

(c) The court may, at the request of the foreign representative or an entity affected by relief granted under section 1519 or 1521, or at its own motion, modify or terminate such relief.

(d) Section 1104(d) shall apply to the appointment of an examiner under this chapter. Any examiner shall comply with the qualification requirements imposed on a trustee by section 322.

§ 1523. Actions to avoid acts detrimental to creditors

(a) Upon recognition of a foreign proceeding, the foreign representative has standing in a case concerning the debtor pending under another chapter of this title to initiate actions under sections 522, 544, 545, 547, 548, 550, 553, and 724(a).

(b) When a foreign proceeding is a foreign nonmain proceeding, the court must be satisfied that an action under subsection (a) relates to assets that, under United States law, should be administered in the foreign nonmain proceeding.

§ 1524.   Intervention by a foreign representative

Upon recognition of a foreign proceeding, the foreign representative may intervene in any proceedings in a State or Federal court in the United States in which the debtor is a party.

SUBCHAPTER IV—COOPERATION WITH FOREIGN COURTS AND FOREIGN REPRESENTATIVES

§ 1525.   Cooperation and direct communication between the court and foreign courts or foreign representatives

(a) Consistent with section 1501, the court shall cooperate to the maximum extent possible with a foreign court or a foreign representative, either directly or through the trustee.

(b) The court is entitled to communicate directly with, or to request information or assistance directly from, a foreign court or a foreign representative, subject to the rights of a party in interest to notice and participation.

§ 1526.   Cooperation and direct communication between the trustee and foreign courts or foreign representatives

(a) Consistent with section 1501, the trustee or other person, including an examiner, authorized by the court, shall, subject to the supervision of the court, cooperate to the maximum extent possible with a foreign court or a foreign representative.

(b) The trustee or other person, including an examiner, authorized by the court is entitled, subject to the supervision of the court, to communicate directly with a foreign court or a foreign representative.

§ 1527.   Forms of cooperation

Cooperation referred to in sections 1525 and 1526 may be implemented by any appropriate means, including—

    (1) appointment of a person or body, including an examiner, to act at the direction of the court;

    (2) communication of information by any means considered appropriate by the court;

    (3) coordination of the administration and supervision of the debtor's assets and affairs;

    (4) approval or implementation of agreements concerning the coordination of proceedings; and

    (5) coordination of concurrent proceedings regarding the same debtor.

SUBCHAPTER V—CONCURRENT PROCEEDINGS

§ 1528.   Commencement of a case under this title after recognition of a foreign main proceeding

After recognition of a foreign main proceeding, a case under another chapter of this title may be commenced only if the debtor has assets in the United States. The effects of such case shall be restricted to the assets of the debtor that are within the territorial jurisdiction of the United States and, to the extent necessary to implement cooperation and coordination under sections 1525, 1526, and 1527, to other assets of the debtor that are within the jurisdiction of the court under sections 541(a) of this title, and 1334(e) of title 28, to the extent that such other assets are not subject to the jurisdiction and control of a foreign proceeding that has been recognized under this chapter.

§ 1529.   Coordination of a case under this title and a foreign proceeding

If a foreign proceeding and a case under another chapter of this title are pending concurrently regarding the same debtor, the court shall seek cooperation and coordination under sections 1525, 1526, and 1527, and the following shall apply:

(1)   If the case in the United States is pending at the time the petition for recognition of such foreign proceeding is filed—

(A)   any relief granted under section 1519 or 1521 must be consistent with the relief granted in the case in the United States; and

(B)   section 1520 does not apply even if such foreign proceeding is recognized as a foreign main proceeding.

(2)   If a case in the United States under this title commences after recognition, or after the date of the filing of the petition for recognition, of such foreign proceeding—

(A)   any relief in effect under section 1519 or 1521 shall be reviewed by the court and shall be modified or terminated if inconsistent with the case in the United States; and

(B)   if such foreign proceeding is a foreign main proceeding, the stay and suspension referred to in section 1520(a) shall be modified or terminated if inconsistent with the relief granted in the case in the United States.

(3)   In granting, extending, or modifying relief granted to a representative of a foreign nonmain proceeding, the court must be satisfied that the relief relates to assets that, under the laws of the United States, should be administered in the foreign nonmain proceeding or concerns information required in that proceeding.

(4)   In achieving cooperation and coordination under sections 1528 and 1529, the court may grant any of the relief authorized under section 305.

§ 1530.   Coordination of more than 1 foreign proceeding

In matters referred to in section 1501, with respect to more than 1 foreign proceeding regarding the debtor, the court shall seek cooperation and coordination under sections 1525, 1526, and 1527, and the following shall apply:

(1)   Any relief granted under section 1519 or 1521 to a representative of a foreign nonmain proceeding after recognition of a foreign main proceeding must be consistent with the foreign main proceeding.

(2)   If a foreign main proceeding is recognized after recognition, or after the filing of a petition for recognition, of a foreign nonmain proceeding, any relief in effect under section 1519 or 1521 shall be reviewed by the court and shall be modified or terminated if inconsistent with the foreign main proceeding.

(3)   If, after recognition of a foreign nonmain proceeding, another foreign nonmain proceeding is recognized, the court shall grant, modify, or terminate relief for the purpose of facilitating coordination of the proceedings.

§ 1531.   Presumption of insolvency based on recognition of a foreign main proceeding

In the absence of evidence to the contrary, recognition of a foreign main proceeding is, for the purpose of commencing a proceeding under section 303, proof that the debtor is generally not paying its debts as such debts become due.

§ 1532.   Rule of payment in concurrent proceedings

Without prejudice to secured claims or rights in rem, a creditor who has received payment with respect to its claim in a foreign proceeding pursuant to a law relating to insolvency may not receive a payment for the same claim in a case under any other chapter of this title regarding the debtor, so long as the payment to other creditors of the same class is proportionately less than the payment the creditor has already received.

OFFICIAL BANKRUPTCY FORMS

For the current version of the Official Bankruptcy Forms, go to http://www.uscourts.gov/forms/
bankruptcy-forms, where the forms can be filled in electronically and either saved or printed.
The forms are updated annually to reflect changes in the statute and bankruptcy rules.

Recollections of the Civil War

With Many Original Diary Entries and Letters
Written from the Seat of War, and with
Annotated References

By

Mason Whiting Tyler

Late Lieut.-Colonel and Brevet-Colonel, 37th Reg't Mass. Vols.

Edited by

William S. Tyler

With Maps and Illustrations

G. P. Putnam's Sons
New York and London
The Knickerbocker Press
1912

MIL
E601
T98

MILITARY
COLLECTION

Copyright, 1912

BY

WILLIAM S. TYLER

DISCARDED
PENNSYLVANIA MILITARY COLLEGE
CHESTER, PENNSYLVANIA
WIDENER UNIVERSITY
LIBRARY

232 52

The Knickerbocker Press, New York

PREFACE

A T the time of his death, my father was nearing the completion of a first draft of his manuscript, which, if he had lived, would have been continued to the conclusion of the war, and then carefully revised in the light of his lifelong study of the historical events. In the loss of a more perfect historical whole, we have gained much that might not have survived a careful revision.

In this first written expression of his recollections and studies of the War time, while as yet he had not a perspective of the book as a whole, his reminiscent moods have led him back over those paths primarily, where his interest was most intense, and the depth of the impressions and intensity of the feelings have been the impulses which for the most part determined what the subjects should be and how much should be said of them. While not a history as a whole, events so selected and so related have a peculiar historical value of their own. There are many histories of the war and autobiographies of great generals, but autobiographies of the soldier in the camp and in the ranks are few. The life of the nation has overshadowed for the time the lives of the men who saved the nation; but it is the men for whom the nation is worth saving, and whose lives in the war are mere incidents of histories, who are the subject of this unfinished story by one of the soldiers.

In fairness to the author who did not live to correct and perfect his work, an effort has been made to verify each event. The task has been arduous and difficult, and the results, which in some cases are unsatisfactory, and for which the author is in no way responsible, are shown by references in foot-notes to the authorities.

Chapter XIII. concludes the manuscript, as he wrote it, and the remaining chapters continue the story as told in his letters, written during the war in the midst of the scenes which they relate, on the march and on the battle-field. The style is quite different, and the language, which is not always approved, is retained for the sake of the freshness and vigor of the story as the soldier told it, at the time, to his family and friends at home. As these letters have their own historical value and peculiar interest, free use of them has been made also in the footnotes in the earlier chapters.

The historical introductions to the later chapters, and many of the connecting links of historical explanation therein, were written by the author's college classmate and lifelong friend, the Reverend Calvin Stebbins, who has bestowed time and labor unsparingly upon all parts of the work.

W. S. T.

NEW YORK,
April, 1912.

BIOGRAPHICAL NOTE[1]

MASON WHITING TYLER was born at Amherst, Massachusetts, June 17, 1840. His father, William Seymour Tyler, was for over sixty years Professor of Greek at Amherst College and was a man of great learning and industry. He taught every member of fifty-one successive classes. Harvard University conferred upon him both the degrees of D.D. and LL.D., although in only two other instances had that university honored one man with both degrees. The latter degree was conferred upon him at the celebration of Harvard's 250th anniversary in 1886.

Colonel Tyler's ancestry is interesting, as it covered the earliest period of New England Colonial history. Among his ancestors may be mentioned the *Mayflower* pilgrim, William Bradford, second Governor of Plymouth Colony; Thomas Hinckley, Governor of Plymouth Colony from 1680 to 1692; Thomas Welles, Colonial Governor of Connecticut, 1655 to 1656 and 1658 to 1659; Major-General John Mason, the hero of the Pequot War and Commander-in-Chief of the Colonial forces in Connecticut; Thomas Willet, in 1647 the successor of Miles Standish as Captain of the Military Company of Plymouth Colony, and in 1665 first Mayor of the city of New York. Of the grantees named in the Royal Charter of Connecticut, 1662, Colonel Tyler was

[1] Extract from Report of the New York State Bar Association, vol. xxxi., 1908, p. 459.

v

descended from four: John Mason, Richard Treat, Anthony Hawkins, and Thomas Welles. Twenty of Colonel Tyler's New England ancestors were Puritan ministers, among them Rev. Thomas Hooker, called by Mather in his *Magnalia*, "The light of the western churches"; Rev. Thomas Thacher, first pastor of the Old South Church, Boston; Rev. Jonathan Edwards, whom John Fiske calls "Probably the greatest intelligence that the western hemisphere has yet seen"; Rev. James Pierpont, one of the founders of Yale College; Rev. Samuel Whiting, the first minister of Lynn, and his wife, Elizabeth St. John, who was the sister of Oliver St. John, Lord Chief Justice of England under Cromwell, of whom Campbell says in his lives of Chief Justices, "With the exception of Oliver Cromwell he had more influence on the events which marked the great constitutional struggle of the 17th century than any leader who appeared on the side of Parliament. He was the first Englishman who ever seriously planned the establishment of a Republican form of government in this country."

Six of Colonel Tyler's ancestors were Revolutionary patriots: Robert Ogden, speaker of the New Jersey Colonial Assembly; Timothy Edwards; Dr. William Whiting, who was prominent for his services and experiments in the manufacture of gunpowder for the Continental Army; Lieutenant Jonathan Seymour; Captain John Tyler, and Deacon John Tyler, Jr. Other ancestors of interest might be mentioned such as Cornelis Melyn, in 1642 made Patroon of Staten Island under the Dutch.

Colonel Tyler was brought up in the college town of Amherst. His father was widely known as a teacher and scholar, and most of the distinguished visitors of the college were at one time or another entertained at the old home, which was in this and many other ways possessed of rare advantages for the sons of whom Colonel Tyler was the oldest. He prepared for college at Amherst Academy and at Williston Seminary, East-hampton, Mass. He entered college in 1858. He was a member of the Psi Upsilon Fraternity, to which his father, his three brothers, and his two sons have also belonged, and in which he always took the greatest interest, being prominent in its councils, and earnestly active in its welfare. In scholarship he stood well. He was Commencement orator, and a member of the Phi Beta Kappa Society. From 1860 to 1862 he was also Class President. On July 10, 1862, he was graduated with the degree of A.B., and three years later received the degree of A.M. [1]

At the close of the war he returned to civil life and took up the study of law in Columbia College Law School, 1865-66, was admitted to the bar in 1866, and then practised three years in the law office of Evarts, Southmayd & Choate. In 1869 he formed a partner-ship with General Henry E. Tremain, under the firm name of Tremain & Tyler. In 1893 he formed a new partnership under the name of Tyler & Durand, and in 1903 that of Tyler & Tyler, consisting of himself and his two sons.

He conducted many important cases, one of the most famous of which was the suit of Marie *v.* Garrison,

[1] His enlistment and service in the Civil War, covering the three years immediately after his graduation from college in July, 1862, are the subject of the story contained in this volume.

resulting in the recovery of over a million dollars. Tremain & Tyler were the attorneys for the importers in the famous "hat trimmings" cases, Hartranft *v.* Langfeld (125 U.S., 128), Robertson *v.* Edelhoff (132 U.S., 614), and others, resulting in the recovery by his firm of several million dollars from the government. They were counsel in the sugar importation cases, Whitney *v.* Robertson (124 U.S., 190). He was also prominent in the removal cases (100 U.S., 457), and as counsel in Pacific Railroad *v.* Ketchum (101 U.S., 289). He was connected with important business enterprises; President of the Cumberland Coal and Iron Company, and director of the Columbus and Hocking Coal and Iron Company, and was many years director and Vice-President of the Rossendale-Reddaway Belting and Hose Company. But he was most active in public enterprises and benevolences. Instrumental in founding the Plainfield Public Library and Reading Room in 1880, the second to be founded in the State of New Jersey, he was its President until his death; was promoter and first President of the Organized Aid Association of Plainfield and North Plainfield; was also one of the early Trustees of the Muhlenberg Hospital; President of the Music Hall Association, and President of the Anti-Racetrack Association of New Jersey. No worthy cause of public interest in Plainfield went without his support. He was also one of the Trustees of Amherst College, 1901–1907. He became a member of the New York State Bar Association in 1890. He was also a member of the Society of the Mayflower Descendants in New York and New Jersey, and Governor of the New Jersey Society; a member of the New Jersey Historical Society, and of the Societies of the Sons of the Revolution, Colonial Wars, and Colonial Governors, and a

MASON W. TYLER IN 1907.

From a photograph by Gessford.

member of the New York Commandery of the Military
Order of the Loyal Legion, and numerous other societies
and clubs.

Colonel Tyler married on December 29, 1869, Eliza
Margaret Schroeder, of New Milford, Conn., a woman
of rare beauty of person and character, with whom he
lived most happily until her death, only nine months
before his own. She was the daughter of Rev. John
Frederick Schroeder, D.D., of Trinity Parish, New York
City, from 1823 to 1839, who won for himself a reputation of being one of the most learned and able preachers
in New York City. Mrs. Tyler's grandfather was
Elijah Boardman, a Revolutionary soldier and one of
the early United States Senators from Connecticut.
Colonel Tyler's sons William S. and Cornelius B. Tyler
are both members of the New York Bar.

Colonel Tyler died suddenly July 2, 1907, in the
Presbyterian Hospital, New York, three weeks after
an operation from which he was supposed to have
recovered.

General Tremain, his law partner for twenty-four
years, said of him: "His was one of those rare natures
who, in business or in social life, radiate the benevolences of humanity and goodness and peace that dispel
the shadows of evil. He was a patriotic soldier, an
honored citizen, a beloved husband and father."

CONTENTS

	PAGE
Biographical Note of Mason Whiting Tyler .	v
Introduction	1

CHAPTER

I.—Early Recollections, and the First Weeks of Civil War . . . 4

II.—First Fifteen Months of War, April, 1861–July, 1862 13

III.—Going to War, July–October, 1862 . 26

IV.—With the Army of the Potomac under McClellan and Burnside, October, 1862–January, 1863 44

V.—The Army of the Potomac under Gen. Hooker, January 26–June 27, 1863 . 73

VI.—Gettysburg, July 1, 2, and 3, 1863 . 98

VII.—The Thirty-Seventh Helps to Enforce the Draft in New York City, July 30–October 14, 1863 112

VIII.—From Fairfax Court-House to Brandy Station, October 16, 1863–March 10, 1864 121

IX.—The Wilderness, May 4, 5, and 6, 1864 . 139

X.—The Sixth Corps at Spottsylvania, May 7–20, 1864 161

Contents

CHAPTER   PAGE

XI.—THE SIGNIFICANCE OF THE BATTLES OF THE WILDERNESS AND SPOTTSYLVANIA . . 200

XII.—AFTER SPOTTSYLVANIA, NORTH ANNA AND COLD HARBOR, MAY 13–JUNE 12, 1864 . 203

XIII.—FROM COLD HARBOR TO PETERSBURG, JUNE 12–17, 1864 216

XIV.—THE RICHMOND CAMPAIGN, PETERSBURG, JUNE 17–JULY 7, 1864 222

XV.—TO THE DEFENCE OF WASHINGTON . 240

XVI.—FROM WASHINGTON TO HALLTOWN, TO FREDERICK AND BACK TO HALLTOWN, JULY 25–SEPTEMBER 18, 1864 . . 253

XVII.—THE BATTLE OF WINCHESTER, SEPTEMBER 19, 1864 274

XVIII.—AT WINCHESTER, SEPTEMBER 20–DECEMBER 12, 1864 284

XIX.—PETERSBURG, DECEMBER 7, 1864–JULY 2, 1865 315

CONCLUSION 343

APPENDIX—SIXTH CORPS AT THE BLOODY ANGLE

1ST BRIGADE, 1ST DIVISION (1ST N. J.) . . 349

2ND " 1ST " (UPTON'S) . . 352

3RD " 1ST " (RUSSELL'S) . . 355

4TH " 1ST " (SHALER'S OR CROSS'S) 357

Contents

APPENDIX—*Continued*

		PAGE
1ST BRIGADE, 2ND DIVISION (WHEATON'S) .		358
2ND " 2ND " (VERMONT) .		361
3RD " 2ND " (BIDWELL'S) .		362
4TH " 2ND " (EUSTIS'S OR EDWARDS'S)		364
1ST " 3RD " (MORRIS'S) .		365
2ND " 3RD " (SMITH'S OR KEIFER'S)		366
INDEX		369

ILLUSTRATIONS

OPPOSITE PAGE

COLONEL MASON WHITING TYLER, . *Frontispiece*
From a photograph, 1888.

MASON W. TYLER viii
From a photograph, 1907.

SAMUEL C. VANCE, RUFUS P. LINCOLN, AND MASON
W. TYLER (*group*) 78
From a tintype, March, 1863.

CAPTAIN MASON W. TYLER 120
From a photograph, 1863 or 1864.

CAPTAIN MASON W. TYLER 318
From a photograph, 1864.

MAPS

THE SALIENT AT SPOTTSYLVANIA 198

THE BATTLEFIELD OF SPOTTSYLVANIA COURT HOUSE *At End*

THE FIELD OF OPERATIONS OF THE 37TH MASS.
REGIMENT AS FAR SOUTH AS SPOTTSYLVANIA
COURT HOUSE . . . . . . *At End*

THE FIELD OF OPERATIONS OF THE 37TH MASS.
REGIMENT FROM SPOTTSYLVANIA TO PETERS-
BURG . . . . *At End*

BOOKS REFERRED TO: ABBREVIATIONS

"O. R.": "War of The Rebellion. Official Records of the Union and Confederate Armies." Government Printing Office, Washington. 130 volumes.

"War Maps": Atlas to accompany the Official Records (above). 3 volumes.

Grant's Memoirs and Sheridan's Memoirs are the "Personal Memoirs" of the two generals, published by Charles L. Webster & Co., N. Y., the one 1886 and the other 1888.

"Bowen": "History of the Thirty-seventh Regiment Mass. Volunteers," by James L. Bowen, 1884.

"Rhodes": "History of the United States," in seven volumes. Harper & Bros., 1893.

Recollections of the Civil War

INTRODUCTION

I HAVE frequently been asked by members of my family and by personal friends to put into some permanent form the story of my experience in the great Civil War, usually called the War of·the Rebellion. I am fully aware that in that struggle there were hundreds, perhaps thousands, of young men, who had just as interesting experiences as I had, and hundreds, perhaps, thousands, of others who passed through much more thrilling experiences. In fact, mine was not an exceptional, but a very common experience.

The war was, however, a very extraordinary war. Nothing like it ever occurred before, and I doubt if anything like it will ever happen again. It was a war between the respective champions of free and slave labor, living under the only successful experiment in republican government which up to that time the world had seen. Their ancestors had taken possession of this continent and occupied different portions of it for the purpose of exploiting the institutions of constitutional liberty. Together they had achieved independence from foreign control. Together they had built a great and powerful nation.

But two civilizations had grown up, one in the North, the other in the South; one based on free labor, the other on slave labor; one devoted to commerce and manufactures, the other to agriculture; one, under the influence of Northern skies, developed a race cold and phlegmatic; and in the other, under Southern influences, an impulsive and domineering people was developed. Originally they both agreed that slavery was wrong. But in the North slave labor was always unprofitable, while in the South, after the invention of the cotton gin, it became exceedingly profitable, and as the North had largely shared in the profits of the slave trade, which was mainly responsible for the rapid growth of slavery in the South, the South naturally felt that if slavery was wrong, it did not lie in the mouths of their Northern neighbors and fellow-countrymen to reproach them on account of it.   Further than this, when slave labor became profitable it was very easy for them to convince themselves that human slavery was not wrong, and they soon began to defend it as a divinely ordained institution, and to claim for it supremacy in the government and throughout the United States.   They were not satisfied with having it simply a domestic institution limited to the Southern States; they wanted to make it a national institution, and to spread it over all the States.   They exultantly boasted that Cotton was King, and entitled to rule the world.   So great did their influence become that Congress passed an act compelling the Northerner to catch and return the Southerner's fugitive slaves, and finally the Supreme Court came under its power and handed down a decision declaring that the black man was a chattel.   In accomplishing this the South acted as a unit, while the North was divided.

The cotton mills of the North depended on the South for supplies, and Northern merchants sold goods in the South, bought and shipped the cotton, the sugar, and the turpentine of the South abroad. Many of them were dealers in slaves, and they and their ancestors had made fortunes in the slave-trade and in furnishing supplies for the slave population and market. These elements, united with a solid South, served to keep the political powers of the country in the control of the party that sympathized with the South and was much the smaller section. Thus, during the greater part of the first sixty years of the nineteenth century, the government of the United States was controlled by the South and its allies from the North, and during the last half of that period the Southern leaders were struggling like Titans to acquire new territory and add distinctively slave States to the Union, that they might increase their vote in Congress and in the Electoral College.

In 1856, the Republican party planted itself squarely on the platform, "No more slave territory," and two years later, in 1858, Abraham Lincoln announced that "a house divided against itself cannot stand," and proclaimed that the vital question before the American people was, "Whether the United States should be all slave or all free." No middle ground was possible. In 1860, Lincoln was elected President on the Republican platform and his own proclaimed prophecy. The South at once seceded, and fired on Fort Sumter. It was the beginning of a war which in four years filled six hundred thousand graves with men in the prime of life.

CHAPTER I

EARLY RECOLLECTIONS, AND THE FIRST WEEKS OF CIVIL WAR

I WAS born June 17, 1840, at Amherst, Massachusetts. My father was at the head of the Greek Department in Amherst College for nearly sixty years. It would be hard to find a more quiet and peaceful hamlet of twenty-five hundred inhabitants than Amherst was in my boyhood days. There was not a public bar nor a drinking saloon in the town. There was not a man in the town worth one hundred thousand dollars. They mostly owned the houses they lived in, and if the houses had mortgages on them they were gradually paying them off. No family had more than one servant; most of them, not any servants. One of the principal industries of the place was furnishing board to the students of the college. There were few wealthy students. Many of the students were working their way through college to become ministers or missionaries. The price of board ranged from seventy-five cents to two dollars and a quarter a week.

The climate in winter was very severe. For three or four months deep snows and ice held sway. Furnaces even in public buildings were unknown in those days. Huge cast-iron stoves heated large rooms, while smaller rooms trusted to the efficiency of open fireplaces, and later to the sheet iron air-tight stoves. The halls and the sleeping-rooms (except the room called the nursery) were as cold as the outer atmosphere. Wood was the only fuel.

As my father's salary was small, every member of the family was expected to contribute his or her share towards carrying on the domestic establishment. My three brothers and I worked the garden in summer (which comprised nearly an acre of ground), raised vegetables and fruit, harvested the hay, took care of a horse, a cow, and the chickens, sawed the wood and piled it, and at all seasons carried it by armfuls into the house until the wood-boxes were filled, built and fed the fires, and, if occasion required, helped about the cooking, the bed-making, the dish-washing, and the other domestic employments. Many hands made light work, and we were adepts in the art of despatching work. Our hours for play were short and few in the week, but they were appreciated and made the most of.

Of course the college attacted a great many distinguished strangers and visitors from all over the world, and as accommodations at the hotels were very uncomfortable, such persons were generally entertained by some member of the college faculty, who in such cases exercised a very simple but charming hospitality. I have seen under my father's roof and at his table governors of States, United States Senators, and members of the House of Representatives, justices of the courts, foreign ministers, distinguished preachers, orators, and teachers, from my own country and from foreign lands, and professors connected with foreign universities, altogether too numerous to mention. They came to do honor to Amherst College and its neighboring institutions, to see and admire the beauty of the scenery, to study and explore. Such an institution is always a centre of mental activity and curiosity.

New England was at this time the storm-centre of anti-slavery sentiment. Webster, Everett, Choate, many of the orthodox clergy in Boston, and many of the faculty of Harvard College were leaders of the conservatives, and strongly influenced sentiment in Boston and vicinity; while Garrison, Phillips, Theodore Parker, and the Beechers were typical abolitionists, and had a strong following throughout New England, particularly in the interior towns and communities. They appealed to the Puritan conscience of the North, and the Anglo-Saxon worship of manhood and liberty as manifested in the Declaration of Independence, and in the growth of free, republican institutions in Europe and America. The South answered by such acts as the Fugitive Slave Bill, by compelling the rendition of Anthony Burns into slavery from Boston, by attempting to compel the admission of Kansas into the Union as a slave State against the will of the inhabitants, and by striking down Senator Sumner of Massachusetts in the Senate-chamber.

All this time the South was threatening to secede from the Union if her demands were not complied with, and it was unsafe for a citizen of a Northern State to travel or be seen in one of the Southern States. The President of the United States, Mr. Buchanan, with his Cabinet, were in substantial sympathy with the South, and were using their official positions to aid the South, rather than the North, in the event of secession. After January 1, 1861, Buchanan's back was slightly stiffened by the substitution of four Northern Democrats in the place of the same number of Southern sympathizers as members of his Cabinet. In the meantime, the

Southern States were arming and drilling and actually
erecting batteries and siege guns for the overthrow or
capture of the national fortresses situated on Southern
soil. In fact, all was doubt and uncertainty in the
North, while the South was full of confidence and
decision.

After Mr. Lincoln's election, and before he was inaugurated, South Carolina and five other States passed
ordinances of secession and established a Confederate
States government. Still not a move was made by the
North. Then there were rumors that the South would
prevent Mr. Lincoln's inauguration by capturing or
assassinating him, and still President Buchanan discouraged any movement of troops looking towards the
protection of Washington, for fear of exciting the South.

Lincoln clandestinely entered the capital and was
inaugurated, and immediately took measures peaceably
to provision our forts. He equipped a steamer with
food supplies and sent her to Fort Sumter. Then the
Southern batteries opened, and Fort Sumter surrendered within thirty-four hours. War had begun.

Yet up to this time the idea of the possibility of war
had hardly entered the Northern mind. Now all was
changed. The North was on fire to avenge the insult
to the flag. All individual differences of opinion generated by self-interest, by timidity, by religious scruples,
or by any other of the thousand and one influences that
divide minute conflicting parties, were fused in the
tremendous heat of patriotism, enthusiasm, and rage,
aroused by the fact that a blow had been struck at the
nation's life. Mr. Rhodes says:

The sentiment of patriotism rose supreme in all hearts.
The service of the country superseded bread-winning labor

and business, and called for the sacrifice on its altar of
parental feeling and wifely tenderness.   It was the uprising
of a great people. . . . Men who had never dreamed of a
soldier's life hurried to enlist.   Laborers, mechanics, clerks,
students and professors of the colleges, many sons of
wealthy and influential families, enrolled themselves for the
common cause.[1]

On Friday, the 19th day of April, 1861, the Sixth
Regiment of Massachusetts Volunteers, while passing
through Baltimore to go to the rescue of the national
capital, was fired upon by Southern sympathizers in
that city, and for several days after, communication
between the North and Washington was closed, and the
fate of the capital was in suspense.   The excitement in
the North, and particularly in Massachusetts, was most
intense.

On the following Sunday afternoon, April 21st, my
father preached a rousing sermon in the college chapel
at Amherst, "On themes suited to the circumstances,
and in a strain intended to inspire courage, heroism, and
self-sacrificing devotion."   We filed out of the chapel
after the service, and our Professor of Chemistry, afterward Colonel Clark, said that he would go with a company of one hundred men if they would be enlisted, and
in less than half an hour, one hundred of the college
students had given their names.   Professor Clark telegraphed at once to Governor Andrew that he had a full
company of students ready to start at his call.   Governor Andrew replied that he could not equip all the men
who had offered their services.   The students' services
would be required later; meanwhile, let them pursue
their studies.   I was one of the one hundred young men

[1] Vol. iii., p. 358.

who tendered their services on this occasion, and were refused.

In the autumn of 1858, I entered college as a member of the class of 1862. Of course, collegians, like other young men of the country, were deeply interested and stirred by what was happening in the political history of the country, but until Sumter was fired upon, and even until Virginia and the border slave States actually seceded, vast masses, perhaps a majority, of the people in the North could not bring themselves to believe that the South would secede and establish a separate government. The political leaders of the South had threatened so long and so much that there was a very general feeling that they were playing a desperate game of bluff. The men who actually believed in secession were supposed to constitute a small minority of the people of the Southern States. They were described as "fire-eaters," and were, for the most part, citizens of the so-called Cotton States. In territory and in the numbers of their inhabitants these States constituted a small portion of the United States. The border States did not raise cotton, and, outside of the property interest in the preservation of the institution of slavery, they were as closely allied with the North as with the South, and, as to slavery, its perpetuation in the States where it already existed was guaranteed by the Constitution, and reasonably secure. Only its extension over additional territory and into new States was assailed by the Republican party, and in 1860 the Republican party succeeded through divisions in the Democratic party, rather than through its ability to control sufficient votes to elect its own candidates.

Under these circumstances it was very easy for a Northern man to persuade himself that there was no real danger of secession on the part of the Southern States. In fact, there seemed to be no reasonable argument in favor of secession and numberless sound arguments against it. The fact that the North believed in the impossibility of secession is indicated by the utter refusal to make any provision against it, or even to prepare for national self-preservation, while the South was carrying off arms, planning to seize forts, organizing and drilling an army, passing ordinances of secession, and actually establishing a rival government. When Sumter fell, and while our flag was trailing in the dust, we rubbed our eyes to find out whether we were awake. It took us forty-eight hours to recover from our amazement, and then all was excitement and anger.

But what a condition existed for undertaking a great war! Our regular army, consisting of about sixteen thousand men, was scattered from Maine on the east to California and Texas on the west and south. Out of one hundred and ninety-eight companies, one hundred and eighty-three were stationed on the frontier or were en route to distant points west of the Mississippi. The remaining fifteen companies were stationed along the Canadian frontier, and on the Atlantic coast from Maine to the Gulf of Mexico. Outside of the regular army, our Northern citizens had for three generations been devoted to the arts and employments of peace. In the War of 1812, they had disgraced themselves by a cowardly surrender of the national capital, and by losing every battle between land forces fought on Northern soil, with perhaps the single exception of the battle of the Thames.

The Mexican War was waged for Southern aggrandizement, and was mainly a school of instruction for the Southern soldier, from which the North derived very little benefit. Our Northern armories and arsenals had been robbed during Buchanan's administration for the benefit of the South. At the very beginning of the struggle, the most distinguished and leading officers of the regular army, such as Lee, the two Johnstons, Bragg, Beauregard, Hardee, and others, resigned their commissions and espoused the cause of the South. But beyond all this, while the men of the North were commercial in habit and spirit, those of the South were of a decided military caste. They were trained in the use of arms; they practised duelling; were good horsemen; and cultivated all the manly sports which gave nerve and dash and inured them to hardship.

Most of our arms that were available were in the hands of the militia. They were of the musket type— not rifles. Until we could buy or manufacture more guns, we could not equip an army of adequate size. Our finances in 1860 had been so mismanaged that the government had not money enough to pay the salaries of its Senators and Representatives, let alone the extraordinary war expenses. Buchanan's administration had done its utmost to wreck the Treasury as well as the army and navy. The public credit was so low that the obligations of the United States were already selling at a discount of fifteen per cent. Congress had not provided a way for meeting such an emergency. There were no laws authorizing the raising or sustaining a larger army than the existing regular army. We had no precedent for such an army, no experience in organizing such an army, no officers whom we knew to be capable of handling it. The military establishment and the financial establishment to pay for it had both to be created anew. It was a large school without teachers.

No wonder that Mr. Lincoln began with great

moderation.   On April 15, 1861, forty-two days after his inauguration, by proclamation he called upon the governors of the several States to furnish 75,000 militia *for three months'* service to be used to suppress unlawful combinations and to cause the laws to be executed, and summoned both houses of Congress to assemble on the next Fourth of July, "to consider and determine such measures as in their wisdom the public safety and interest may seem to demand."[1]   This much he could do under an act of Congress passed in 1795.   On May 3, 1861, he issued an additional proclamation calling for 42,034 volunteers to serve for three years in the army, and 18,000 seamen to serve not less than one nor more than three years in the navy.

Up to this time President Lincoln had not expressed nor declared any intention of waging war upon the South.   He would do his utmost to repossess the property of the United States, and enforce the laws.

[1] *Works* (Federal Ed.), vol. v., p. 284.

CHAPTER II

THE FIRST FIFTEEN MONTHS OF WAR

FROM APRIL, 1861, TO JULY, 1862

ON April 17, 1861, the Commonwealth of Virginia passed an act rescinding the vote by which it became one of the United States, and on April 24th entered into an offensive and defensive alliance with the Confederate States. On April 18th Robert E. Lee said to Francis P. Blair that secession was anarchy, that if he owned all the negroes in the South he would sacrifice them for the Union; but on the 20th he tendered the resignation of his commission in the United States Army and accepted a commission from the Commonwealth of Virginia as Major-General and commander-in-chief of their forces.[1]

On April 18th, 460 Pennsylvania volunteers without arms, and a company of regulars from Minnesota, reached Washington from Harrisburg; on April 19th, the Sixth Massachusetts Volunteers arrived[2]; on the 20th the Gosport Navy Yard near Norfolk was partially destroyed by the Union forces and abandoned.[3]

On the 25th, the isolation of Washington and the anxiety of the North were relieved by the arrival, after

---

[1] Rhodes's *History*, iii., p. 365; *Recollections and Letters of General Lee*, p. 25, etc.; and *Abraham Lincoln*, by Nicolay and Hay, vol. iv., p. 159.

[2] Rhodes, iii., p. 362.　　　　　　　　　　[3] *Id.*, p. 364.

days of delay at Annapolis, of the Seventh New York and the Eighth Massachusetts regiments,[1] and on May 13th communications between Philadelphia and the capital by way of Baltimore were re-established. On April 24th in answer to an inquiry from Reverdy Johnson as to whether he meditated invasion or subjugation of the South, President Lincoln wrote: "I have no objection to declare a thousand times that I have no purpose to invade Virginia or any other State, but I do not mean to let them invade us without striking back."[2]

The border States of Missouri, Kentucky, Tennessee, and Maryland were threatening secession if the United States attempted to coerce, or in any way used force against the South.

The Confederate Congress met at Montgomery, Alabama, on the 29th of April,[3] and on the 6th of May passed an act recognizing the existence of war between the United States and the Confederate States, and at the suggestion of President Davis to raise an army of 100,000 men, immediately authorized him to accept without limit volunteers "to serve for or during the existing war."[4]

While the United States was enlisting its soldiers for thirty days, three months, nine months, or for one, two, or three years, and constantly mustering and discharging them, the Confederate States pursued one consistent course, and enlisted its men for the war. This gave the South an immense advantage in the war. Many mistakes of a similar character will call for mention as our story progresses. Congress met pursuant to the call of the President on July 4th, and

[1] Rhodes, p. 374.   [2] Nicolay and Hay, *Complete Works*, ii., p. 38.
[3] Rhodes, iii., p. 395.   [4] *Id.*, p. 396.

authorized the President to accept the services of 500,-
000 volunteers, and directed the issue of $250,000,000
of bonds.[1]

On May 24th, the Federal troops crossed the Potomac and occupied Alexandria and the Heights of
Arlington.[2]   At Alexandria, Major Ellsworth was shot
and killed in the act of hauling down the Confederate
flag from the cupola of the main hotel of the city.   It
was an inglorious end to a brief but rather promising
career of one of our young soldiers who had achieved
fame by drilling a company of Zouaves in Chicago, and
exhibiting them in the Eastern States.

Public clamor and political impatience now demanded
an advance of the army.   The newspapers talked of
occupying Richmond in twenty days.   There were
75,000 men called into the service in April by President
Lincoln, whose terms of service would expire about
August 1st.   They had been drilled as regiments and
organized into brigades for a week or a fortnight, but
had never been manœuvred in brigade formation,
and as they could no longer be retained in the service
a battle must be fought to give the government the full
benefit of these short enlistments.   It mattered not
that the army had never been manœuvred together
and was essentially a rabble.

The battle of Bull Run was fought on the 21st day of
July.[3]   About 29,000 Confederates met 28,000 Federals.
It ended in a panic and the rout of the Union forces,
with the loss of about 1500 men.   After fighting bravely
for several hours, they ran without a rally until they
reached Washington.

I well remember the excitement at Amherst when we
received the news of this disaster.   We had been fed

---

[1] Rhodes iii., p. 437.   [2] *Id.*, p. 435.   [3] *Id.*, p. 446.

on enthusiasm after Sumter fell, created by Lincoln's call for 75,000 volunteers, and it was a common rumor that in all the States there were more volunteers than could be supplied with arms. The North was once more unanimous. How could we fail! It was the first great setback of the war. We had taken a lesson in the hard school of experience. We had to take many more before we were graduated from the college of war. This first lesson was humiliating and very disappointing; but we set our teeth and went to work to enlist half a million men and organize them into an army. General Scott was retired and General McClellan, who had been successful in a small way in West Virginia, was brought to Washington and made commander-in-chief. During the Crimean War he had been sent abroad as member of a commission to gather military information, and had witnessed the operation of the armies there engaged. He applied himself with intelligence and energy to his great task of forming an army out of the great mass of ignorant and inexperienced men, officered by equally untrained men, who were gathering at Washington in answer to their country's call.

At the call of the President, the several States assembled the regiments. An influential man, very likely a politician, would be authorized by the governor to raise a regiment. He would promise other influential citizens positions as captains or lieutenants if they would assist by raising companies. After the regiment was raised, theoretically the men had the right to choose their own officers. They usually selected the persons who had been active in securing their enlistment, and in this way the promises of the higher regimental officers were made good; but the fact that the final right of election rested with the enlisted men led to much familiarity of a political or love-making character between the men and the office-seekers which was not conducive to good order or discipline.   The result was that every regiment had to go through a weeding-out process among its officers before it was fit for duty.

All the officers of the army having a higher rank than colonel were appointed by the President, who, in addition to his civil office, was by the Constitution made commander-in-chief of the army and navy of the United States.   As our Presidents, with one or two exceptions, were not soldiers or men of military education or training, this resulted in subordinating the army and navy to the civil authorities.   This was all very well in time of peace, but in time of war was a most hazardous arrangement.   Politicians controlled the armies and largely managed and controlled the campaigns.   The disasters of the War of 1812 were probably due to the incompetence of our commanders, who were none other than our President and Secretary of War, who were both civilians, and tried to direct things from their headquarters at Washington.   The same arrangement was undoubtedly responsible for the misfortunes of the Army of the Potomac in its early campaigns.

The President was the constitutional commander. He was a civilian fully occupied with his civil and political duties.   Therefore, he devolved his military duties upon his Secretary of War.   He too was a civilian, and he appointed his favorites, who in many instances were only politicians, to responsible army positions, and constantly meddled with the control of the army and the plans of the military leaders in the field.

General McClellan was a good engineer.   He encircled Washington with a cordon of forts and earthworks of the most improved pattern.   He was a skilful organizer.   By the month of October, 1861, he reported an effective force of 169,000 men divided into five divisions of three brigades each.   We now know that in the Confederate army opposed to him there were but 41,000 men.   But he always insisted that he was outnumbered by the force opposed to him, and was never quite ready to move.

During the late summer and autumn of 1861, the Twenty-first and Twenty-seventh Regiments of Massachusetts Volunteers were recruited from the vicinity of Amherst.   Our Professor of Chemistry, William S. Clark, went as Major of the Twenty-first and took with him as the Adjutant of the regiment, Frazer Stearns, the son of our President, and several students or graduates.   Several of these men were among those who had been enrolled and tendered their services to go with Clark on April 21st.[1]

At Amherst College the period between the fall of Sumter and my graduation in July of the following year was spent in pursuing the usual college curriculum, supplemented by a half-hour's drill four days in each week, under a militia officer, Luke Lyman, afterwards Colonel of the Twenty-seventh Massachusetts Volunteers, who came over from Northampton three or four times a week and drilled and disciplined us in manœuvres and tactics.   We used poles for guns.   Real muskets were too scarce to admit of their being supplied to schools or colleges.   Each class became a company and every man was expected to attend the drills.   In the absence of Colonel Lyman the class captain acted as drill-master.   During the winter and spring months the drill was suspended on account of the want of a proper hall or drill-room.

[1] *Supra*, p. 8.

The class of 1862 was more fortunate than the other classes in having for their captain a very enthusiastic member, who before he came to college had attended a military school, and was regarded by us as a very accomplished soldier. We were very proud of our Captain Vance, and in October, 1861, when Colonel Lyman organized the Twenty-seventh Regiment of Massachusetts Volunteers, he made Vance Captain of one of its companies, and took him with him to the war. Vance afterwards became Colonel of an Indiana regiment.

Major Clark was my father's next-door neighbor, and Frazer Stearns had been my playmate and schoolmate for years before he entered college. Major Francis A. Walker, afterwards Assistant Adjutant-General of the Second Corps, was graduated at Amherst in 1860. He was a man of amazing energy, of handsome person, fine address, and was distinguished in every department of life which he entered. He was a brilliant writer, a fine soldier, a great political economist, a remarkable statistician, and he has left the Massachusetts Institute of Technology at Boston as a monument to his administrative genius and executive force in the department of technical instruction. He was two years in advance of me in college, but I knew him intimately, and greatly admired him. After graduation, he entered the law office of Devens & Hoar, in Worcester, Massachusetts, as a student. When Devens was made Colonel of the Fifteenth Regiment of Massachusetts Volunteers, he took Walker with him as the Sergeant-Major of the regiment. He was with his regiment at Ball's Bluff when, on October 20th, the Twenty-first, with fragments of the Twentieth Massachusetts and the Forty-second New York regiments, was baptized in blood and fire, and by the criminal mismanagement of their commanders,

nearly one half of those engaged were lost. The North
was profoundly stirred, and Massachusetts was horrified
at the wanton sacrifice of her young men.

The Twenty-first and Twenty-seventh Regiments
were assigned to General Burnside, and went with him
to North Carolina. I have spoken of Clark and Stearns
and many fellow-students as being members of the
Twenty-first; in the Twenty-seventh was Vance in
command of the Northampton Company A, and Company D was largely composed of men from Amherst
and vicinity. Early in March, 1862, Adjutant Stearns
was killed at the battle of Newbern.[1] It was a daily
occurrence to see in the papers among the lists of killed
or wounded the name of some acquaintance or friend,
or to meet them on crutches, or bandaged, or with an
arm in a sling. The death of Adjutant Stearns produced a profound impression. The prominence of his
family, his Christian character, and his heroic death so
soon after enlistment united to give him fame and to
enroll him with Ellsworth, Winthrop, and Shaw, among
the martyred dead.

During the spring of my sophomore year, I had suffered from a severe attack of what the doctors then
called lung-fever; I suppose now they would call it
pneumonia. For the last two years of my college
course, I was supposed to be marked for consumption.
I was six feet in height, and when I was graduated I
weighed 128 pounds. I was urged to leave college for
a year, but I preferred to graduate with my class. The
condition on which I was allowed to continue in college
was that after graduation I should take a year and
devote it to recreation. My mother and father had
planned for me a long sea voyage.

[1] O. R., ix., p. 222.

As yet there was no lack of volunteers for the army and navy, although the system of stimulating enlistments by bounties had already begun, but instead of keeping the old and experienced regiments full, they followed the practice of forming new regiments, with officers for the most part green and untried. It was a pernicious system, because in this way old and tried regiments that had made a name for themselves, and were provided with a full complement of trained and experienced officers who knew how to take care of those under them in every emergency, would become skeletons, while the full regiments were composed entirely of green recruits, and were mainly handled and manœuvred by equally unskilled citizens. On the other hand, the Confederate government had, during the winter, met with a series of reverses which roused them to much greater exertion. On the coast they had lost Roanoke Island,[1] Port Royal,[2] and the mouth of the Mississippi.[3] In the interior they were beaten at Mill Spring,[4] Forts Henry,[5] and Donelson,[6] and Island Number 10,[7] and were driven out of Missouri.[8] Early in April, McClellan transferred his army to Fortress Monroe,[9] and threatened to approach Richmond from the south. The Confederate army opposed to McClellan numbered 53,000 men,[10] that of McClellan, about 158,000.[11] The Southern capital was in danger. While Yorktown was besieged for a month,[12] the government in its des-

[1] Feb. 7, 1862, Rhodes, iii., p. 581.   [2] Nov. 7, 1861, *id.*, p. 490.
[3] Apr. 27, 1862, *id.*, p. 629.   [4] Jan. 19, 1862, *id.*, p. 581.
[5] Feb. 6, 1862, *id.*, p. 582.   [6] Feb. 16, 1862, *id.*, p. 593.
[7] Apl. 7, 1862, *id.*, p. 628.   [8] *Id.*, p. 617.   [9] *Id.*, p. 615.
[10] Apl. 17, 1862, *Johnston's Narrative*, p. 117.
[11] Not all available. See *McClellan's Own Story*, pp. 163-4, and telegram and letter from President Lincoln to McClellan April 6 and 9, 1862.
[12] Rhodes, iii., p. 617.

peration put forth its reserve strength. General Lee was military adviser to President Davis, and General Johnston was at the head of the army of defence.[1] General Upton, in his *Military Policy of the United States*, says of this period (page 315):

It was during this month so lost [April] that the Confederate Congress abandoned voluntary enlistments, adopted conscription, and took away from the governors the power to commission Confederate officers; it was during this month when the Army of the Potomac should have been at the doors of Richmond, that almost every regiment of the Confederate army was reorganized; it was during this month that Confederate conscripts began to pour into the old regiments instead of being formed into new organizations; it was during this and the two succeeding months, while McDowell was held back, that these conscripts, associated with veteran comrades, acquired courage and discipline, and it was by concentration during the last month that the Confederate army was made to equal its opponent. The loss of battles was but a trifle compared with the other consequences of this one month's delay. It arrayed against us a military system which enabled the Confederate government to call out the last man and the last dollar as against a system based on voluntary enlistment and the consent of the States.

On May 31st and on June 1st the battle of Fair Oaks, or Seven Pines, was fought.[2] It was a repulse for the Confederates, but McClellan retreated. General Johnston was wounded on the first day, *i.e.*, May 31st, and on June 1st General Lee was assigned to the command of the Confederate army. At this time the Army of the Potomac was within four miles of Richmond. If

[1] Apl. 17, 1862, *Johnston's Narrative.*, p. 117.
[2] Rhodes, iv., p. 24.

General Grant had then been in command he probably would have captured it. But McClellan delayed, and Lee at once commenced to fortify, and in three weeks he pronounced the city safe. At this time, McClellan's army numbered 105,000 and Lee's 64,000.[1]

Now Lee summoned Jackson from the Shenandoah Valley,[2] where, by the rapidity of his movements and the fierceness of his attacks, he had inspired the North with terror.

Thus was ushered in "the Seven Days' Fight," during which Lee, with the loss of a little over 20,000 men in all, compelled the Army of the Potomac to give up its base of supplies on the York River at West Point, and to fall back upon the James River, with a loss of less than 16,000 men. Between armies of the size of these and for seven days of fighting, these losses were small. Lee's losses were much heavier than McClellan's, both absolutely and relatively; but the latter's loss of prestige and morale was awful. McClellan's published correspondence shows that at the time he was overwhelmed with fear. He believed that he was outnumbered two to one. Misleading stories for the purpose of deceiving him as to the number of troops in Lee's and Jackson's armies were published in Richmond and were accepted by him as true. The rebel scouts and spies obtained accurate information about the numbers in our armies, but both at Manassas and before Richmond, McClellan received most exaggerated reports of the numbers of the forces opposed to him, and he never questioned them. He kept promising to move, and all the time fever and disease were making havoc with his army, and yet he was never ready. Even now his army was not so much

[1] Rhodes, p. 24, note 1, and p. 33, note 1.
[2] *Id.*, p. 33.

damaged as Grant's army was after the second day of fighting in the Wilderness. But there was this difference, Grant was not whipped, McClellan was.

The country never knew darker days than the first half of August, 1861.[1] It took several days to find out what had happened. McClellan was ominously silent. It was the end of a period of magnificent promises built upon a lavish expenditure of money, human blood, and the nation's vital resources. All was wasted owing to the lack of competent military leadership. President Lincoln feared to call for further volunteers lest in the general discouragement and gloom the people should fail to respond. No popular leader ever felt the public pulse more accurately than he did. It ended in his secretly getting the governors of the several States to offer him their proportions of an additional levy of 300,000 men for three years' service, and within a month he asked for 300,000 more men for nine months' service.

Commencement exercises at Amherst for that summer began on Sunday, July 6th, and ended Thursday, July 10th. It was a week of the deepest gloom. McClellan was reported to be safe on a gunboat on the James. Where the Army of the Potomac was, nobody knew. Yet the people were not discouraged. They were beginning to appreciate that it was a life-and-death struggle, to be waged until one side or the other was exhausted. Governor Andrew, as was then the custom of the Governor of the Commonwealth, attended at Amherst Commencement Day, and after the public exercises were over, I had a conversation with him in which I told him I had thought of travelling for my health, but had concluded to go to the war, and he

[1] So in original. Probably meant 1862.

replied by offering me a commission if I would raise a company.

A town meeting was held, at which a bounty of $100 to be paid to each enlisted man was voted, and Mr. William F. Stearns, son of our President, who resided in India and was temporarily in this country, offered a further gift of $25 to every man who would enlist from Cambridgeport or Amherst. On the evening of Commencement, we had a public meeting, and I enlisted, and the next day I began the work of enlisting a company for the war.

CHAPTER III

GOING TO THE WAR

JULY TO OCTOBER, 1862

ENTHUSIASM had spent its force. The glamour and tinsel of a soldier's life no longer lured to enlistment. Everybody recognized that it was a most serious business. My work was to travel about the country hunting for men of proper age and build to serve as soldiers, appealing to their patriotism and sense of duty to induce them to enlist. It often required several visits to secure one man. If they were willing to go themselves, family, sweethearts, and friends had to be consulted. One day I would go to Hadley, another to North Hadley, a third to Hatfield, a fourth to Sunderland, a fifth to Shutesbury, etc. I worked evenings as well as in the daytime, because I could get the men together. During the day they were at work. Henry Hills, a genial, wholesouled merchant of Amherst, with a large acquaintance in our neighborhood, sometimes went with me, but more frequently I went alone. By the first of August I had sixty names on my list, and I went down to Boston and reported to the Governor, who commissioned me a Second Lieutenant in the Thirty-sixth Massachusetts Volunteers; and I was on that day mustered into the service of the United States.

The rendezvous of the Thirty-sixth was Camp Wool,

Worcester, but by order of the Governor, the Thirty-second, Thirty-third, Thirty-fourth, and Thirty-fifth Regiments must first be filled, and no assignments of recruits to the Thirty-sixth were made until after August 1st. At that time the unassigned fragments of companies not required to complete these four regiments were divided,—those coming from the eastern part of the State going to the Thirty-sixth at Worcester, and those from the western part of the State to the Thirty-seventh at Camp Briggs, Pittsfield. I was ordered to report with my men at Pittsfield, which I did on August 11th.

The company streets had been laid out, but all was confusion when we arrived. The camp was delightfully located on a level field one mile to the east of Pittsfield, one thousand feet above sea-level, with the beautiful Berkshire Hills and Hoosac Mountains in plain view. Colonel Raymond Lee of the Twentieth Massachusetts was in command of the camp. Two or three wall tents were erected for the accommodation of the regimental officers. A board structure, much like a barn, was occupied by the quartermaster, and a smaller structure of the same character was erected by the sutler for his own use. The first four nights after our arrival, I slept on the floor of the quartermaster's building. This was the main lodging-house for the officers, and Quartermaster Dodge was a very hospitable host. There was a small number of A-tents for so many of the rank and file as could be crowded into them. A full supply of tents did not arrive until August 23d. Uniforms and blankets were distributed to the companies on their arrival. We had a few muskets for guard purposes, and on the 3d of September the regiment was fully armed with the new Springfield rifles.

On August 12th, Major Oliver Edwards, our future Colonel, arrived and relieved Colonel Lee as commander of the camp. He had been in the service for a year, first as Adjutant of the Tenth Massachusetts, subsequently as senior aide on the staff of General Couch. He was twenty-seven years of age, keen eyed and quick in his motions. He acted while other men were making up their minds. He was a rigid disciplinarian, and inspired those under him with respect, buttressed by fear. He was kind and sympathetic with the suffering and the sick, but very severe towards any man who shirked in the performance of duty, or was shiftless. He was an unusually good volunteer officer, and the Thirty-seventh owed much of the good reputation that it acquired and sustained to the soldierly qualities of its Colonel.

Our company was soon filled by adding to the men coming with me, the recruits from South Hadley, South Hadley Falls, and Ware. When completed it was a fine body of men, largely composed of the yeomanry or the old Bay State. It had in its ranks several men of college education, a number of mechanics and machinists, a large number of young men from the farms, with two or three Germans, two Frenchmen, and four or five Irishmen. They could all read and write, and all had at least a common-school education. We were designated Company F in the regiment.

George L. Montague, afterwards Major and Lieutenant-Colonel of the Thirty-seventh, came with the recruits from South Hadley and South Hadley Falls, and immediately entered the lists as a candidate for the captain's position in Company F. He had been a year in the service, first in the Sixth Wisconsin, and afterwards on the military staff of the Governor of that State, with whom he remained until the Governor was accidentally killed at Pittsburg Landing, and he then returned to his native State. He was born and brought up in South Hadley, was a capable man, of engaging manners, and had had experience both in the field and on staff. At that time I did not want to be captain of Company F, first, on account of the precarious condition of my health, and second, because I felt that it was better for the company, as well as myself, that we should have a captain of experience.

I was attacked with camp diarrhœa and symptoms of dysentery on August 14th, and as we had no hospital, the surgeon sent me to the Berkshire Hotel, where I remained until the 18th, when I returned to the regiment, although I was still very weak. On the 20th, Montague was elected Captain. I was elected First Lieutenant of Company F, and our commissions were dated August 13th. Captain Montague was twenty-eight, and I was twenty-two years of age. On the 30th, Company F, being full, was, with five other companies, mustered into the service of the United States.

On the morning after our arrival in camp, we were aroused and the roll was called at 5 o'clock, and on that day we had four hours of drill. Guard-mounting and dress-parade were introduced as soon as we had a sufficient number of companies to make a fair appearance. From this time until we started for Washington we had daily drills of at least four hours a day, first in squads, then in platoons and companies, and these were supplemented the latter part of the time by battalion drills and by marches of greater or less length. Regular army rations were issued to the companies, and the men were learning to cook their food, to keep clean, to take care of their clothing, and to have everything in order to pass inspection. The officers were fed in a mess by the sutler.

In consideration of the fact that we were so soon to be separated by long distances from home, with great uncertainties of future return, the men and officers were indulged, as far as was consistent with the performance of their duties as soldiers, with facilities for seeing and visiting with their relatives and friends. They were allowed to have them in camp from early dawn until nine o'clock at night, and the officers were given leaves of absence and the men furloughs to visit their homes for two or three days. My father and brothers and several of my college classmates came down and visited me for longer or shorter periods, and I remember that such men as Dr. Humphrey, then residing in Pittsfield, but formerly President of Amherst College, and Dr. F. D. Huntington, afterwards Bishop of Central New York, a summer resident of North Hadley, and a graduate of Amherst College, came and called upon me in camp. On Friday, August 29th, I was given leave of absence until Monday noon, and I went home and spent Sunday with my family.

Colonel Edwards announced that he would give the colors to the company that would attain to the greatest proficiency in drill and discipline. Company "F" carried off the prize, and Sergeant Charles S. Bardwell, a splendid specimen of a six-footer from Whately, was selected as color-bearer, and very proudly did he carry the flag until he was promoted to a lieutenancy in the summer of 1863.

On August 22d, I had my first experience as officer of the day. It was a rainy day. Between the rain and my detail, we made the camp shine. On August 27th, Edwards got his commission as Colonel, and he

immediately appointed Captain Montague to fill the
vacancy in the office of Major, and as I still did not feel
equal to the captaincy, Eugene A. Allen, who had served
a year as Sergeant in the Tenth Massachusetts, was
recommended by Colonel Edwards for the place and
duly appointed and commissioned.   He was an admirable officer, and added much to the efficiency of the
regiment.

The last three days of August and the early days of
September were a period of great anxiety in the North.
The battles of Manassas, Second Bull Run, and Chantilly were fought on August 29th, 30th, and September
1st, respectively.[1]   Lee and Jackson penetrated almost
to the defences of Washington.   It was a repetition of
the experiences of the Seven Days' Fight, with the scene
transferred from Richmond to Washington.   To be
compelled to retreat miles in the face of the enemy and
submit to a second thrashing on the field of their dishonor of the previous year was a humiliation which it
would seem the Army of the Potomac might have been
spared.

The most pitiable sight of all was to see our beloved
President, after he had fulfilled the titanic duties
devolved upon him as the civil chief of the nation,
struggling to make up for the deficiencies of his military
advisers and leaders.   He was fully aware of his own
lack of experience and capacity in this department of
the government.   But he could see that the army and
the capital were safer if they were not so widely separated.   Therefore, while he was settling the question
of who should be the next commander to be tried, he
listened to the advice of those who counselled the retreat
of the army from the James to the Potomac.   It was

[1] See Rhodes., vi., pp. 127, 129, 135.

made at a terrible sacrifice in the morale of his army.
The Army of the Potomac never fully recovered from
these early disastrous experiences. The atmosphere
of that army was ever after charged with them.

The Twenty-first Massachusetts was one of those
that suffered very severely at the battle of Chantilly.
Colonel Clark[1] was reported among the killed, and for
days his fate was unknown. The newspapers were full
of exaggerated reports of losses, and my letters from
home spoke of discouragement and mourning. In
camp all was hurry and bustle with daily rumors of our
departure for the seat of war. On September 6th, the
ladies of Pittsfield presented Colonel Edwards with a
beautiful regimental flag of silk, the staff being of oak
from Mount Greylock. The presentation took place
at dress-parade, and at its close, orders were read directing departure for Washington on the morrow.

Sunday, September 7th, was a very hot day. Reveille
was sounded at 4 A.M., and we took a soldier's breakfast
and packed our baggage. We sent home what we
thought we could spare, and still our knapsacks and
haversacks bulged like hay loads on farm wagons. It
was afternoon when we started and marched to the
public square in the town where a religious service was
held. Rev. Dr. Todd prayed for us most earnestly
and impressively. Crowds thronged the streets, flags
were everywhere displayed, and we marched through
them led by a band of music to the depot of the Boston
& Albany (then the Western) Railroad, where we were
loaded on twenty-five cars, and amid resounding cheers
were started for the city of Hudson, where we arrived
about 6 o'clock, and were escorted by the fire department and the local militia from the Hudson depot a

[1] See p. 18.

mile across the city, and embarked on board the steamer *Oregon*, for New York.

After the heat and excitement of the day, it was a great relief to experience the cool breezes and refreshing surroundings of the river. We were too tired, and darkness would not permit us, to see the magnificent scenery through which we were passing. But we enjoyed its effect and slept as only tired, healthy men can sleep. [1]

At 5 A.M. of the next day, Monday, September 8th, we were landed in Jersey City at the wharf of the New Jersey R. R. & Transportation Co., and there waited three hours. An uncle and cousins of mine met me with a basket of provisions, and after the regiment landed, we had a picnic on the dock. About nine o'clock we were again loaded into cars which did not get outside the boundary line of Jersey City until noon, and then the train loitered around on its way to Philadelphia all the afternoon, and arrived there about seven o'clock in the evening.

During the whole war, Philadelphia was famous for the hospitality with which it treated the Union soldiers. Never a regiment went through the city that was not most bountifully fed at its Cooper shop, or at some other equally good place of entertainment. The Thirty-seventh, during its term of service, passed through that city six times, and on each occasion received the same generous treatment at the hands of the Quaker City authorities. On the particular occasion of which I am now writing, the soldiers were unaccustomed to the hard and coarse fare which was usually dealt out to the

[1] "Officers had state-rooms, men slept as they could. A collation was served by the people of Hudson. Liquor clandestinely smuggled aboard was thrown overboard."—M. W. T.'s MS. card diary.

3

men in the ranks by purveyors who were hired to feed them wholesale, and the diet that they had in camp was none too good for human beings. Therefore, when they reached Philadelphia, they had a hearty appetite for the dainty supplies given them, and some of the wags in Company F remarked that they ate enough to last them through their entire term of service.

At midnight we were loaded on freight cars, and started on our way southward, with most of the men asleep on the floor of the cars.[1] A few miles out of Philadelphia, our train crashed into a passenger train mostly filled with soldiers returning to Washington from hospitals, on their way to rejoin their regiments. The train run into was halted between the stations, and was telescoped by our train, which received no injury because it was composed of freight cars, while the passenger train into which we ran was wrecked from end to end. During the next two or three hours we rescued out of the wreckage the mangled remains and corpses of more than thirty victims of the collision. A third train ran into the rear of our train while it was standing on the tracks. I speak of this to show how dangerous the railroad service of that time was. We were detained by this accident until eleven o'clock on the following day, when we were put on board a new train and moved slowly southward. We reached Wilmington, Delaware, in the early afternoon.

Whenever we stopped the farmers and country people brought generous supplies of fruit, peaches, pears, plums, and grapes, and emptied them into our cars. At Wilmington the train stopped, but we were fed on board the cars with nearly as much generosity and bounty as the regiment had received at the hands of

[1] M. W. T.'s card diary says, "I slept on the floor of a car."

the authorities in Philadelphia. Wilmington was only second to Philadelphia in its generous treatment of the soldiers of the Union army when they passed through that city. They seemed to believe it their duty to make up for the deficiency of hospitality shown by the people of Baltimore to the soldiers of the North. A little later in the afternoon, after leaving Wilmington, we crossed the Susquehanna on the ferry-boat *Maryland.* At Havre de Grace, we began to realize that we were in a State where the sentiment in favor of the South distinctly asserted itself. Wherever we went the people glared at us as if we were wolves. There was no sympathy either in their looks or in their actions.

We reached Baltimore about 8 o'clock in the evening. No sign of welcome greeted us here. We marched to a rude frame building, were fed as if we were animals, and then proceeded through dark and deserted streets across the city to the Washington depot of the Baltimore & Ohio Railroad. It was the same route followed by the Sixth Massachusetts on the occasion of their famous trip through Baltimore. Here we spent the night and waited for transportation until the middle of the next afternoon, September 10th. Late in the morning we were loaded again into freight cars and without further incidents we slowly wended our way to Washington, which city we reached about 5 P.M. At Washington we were fed at the Soldiers' Relief Barracks in much the same way as in Baltimore.

That night my company and I slept in the yards of the Baltimore & Ohio Railroad, just outside the old Washington depot. There was hardly room to lie down, and the night was wet and rainy. We had occupied four days and three nights in going from camp at Pittsfield to the city of Washington. This is a fair specimen of the way regiments travelled during the war.

Washington was at this time crowded with wounded and convalescent soldiers, and overwhelmed with recruits coming from the North to fill the vacancies caused by battle and defeat. Everywhere on the streets you saw blue uniforms discolored by service, here and there a soldier limping on crutches or a cane or with his arm in a sling, or his head or some part of his body bandaged. It was very depressing to those just entering the service.

Thursday, September 11th, we breakfasted at the Soldiers' Relief Barracks, and before noon we moved up Pennsylvania Avenue and down Seventh Street over Long Bridge to "the sacred soil of Virginia," to what was known as Camp Chase, the rendezvous of the troops coming from the North to the city of Washington, where they remained until they could be allotted to brigades or divisions in the Army of the Potomac, or some other army or post in the service. Camp Chase was situated to the east of Arlington Heights, near the fortification known as Fort Albany, and overlooked Washington, the Capitol, and most of the public buildings.[1]

On my way through Washington I was followed by a young boy, named James McHugh, who wanted me to hire him as my servant. Up to that time I had carried my own luggage, which consisted of a knapsack and haversack, because no one had offered to serve me in the capacity of a servant, and this boy looked so small that I at first treated him contemptuously, and as entirely unable and unfit for such employment. He

[1] M. W. T.'s card diary says: "It was our first real march, and was very trying and uncomfortable. I had no servant and started with my own knapsack strapped on my back."

followed me so persistently and urged me so hard to
try him that I finally consented and turned over to him
my knapsack; and he proved himself so tough and
strong that I finally employed him, and he remained
with me two years in that capacity.

After our halt at Camp Chase we laid out a camp.
We were without tents, which were not issued to us
until several days later. The road leading to and bor-
dering our camp was lined with cedars. It took very
little time for the soldiers to strip those cedars of their
boughs and transform them into beds. As such they
served an excellent purpose.

From September 12th to 30th we were very busy
becoming a little better acquainted with the various
drills and occupations of the soldier's life in camp.
Previous to this time the Thirty-seventh had been by
itself. Now we were temporarily assigned to a brigade
commanded by General H. L. Briggs (former Colonel of
the Tenth Massachusetts), and in a division commanded by General Casey, a regular army officer, then
and afterwards stationed at Washington. There were
five regiments in all in our brigade and fifteen regiments
in our division.

On September 12th the first detail from the Thirty-
seventh was made for picket duty. Ten men from each
company were detailed, with similar detachments from
each of the other regiments, to report at brigade headquarters, and the brigade detail thus collected went to
division headquarters, and with the details from the
other brigades, were marched by a staff officer out a
mile or two to the front, where the picket line had
previously been located, and we there took our first
lesson in doing picket duty. We were told that bodies
of Rebel cavalry or scouts were lurking in the neighbor-

hood and might attack us and attempt to break through
the line, if we were not watchful. I happened to be
one of the officers detailed on that occasion, and did not
get much sleep or rest that night. It was a tedious
vigil. The night was rainy and in the darkness I
imagined I could hear sounds and almost see the enemy
advancing to attack. I think we stayed out twenty-four
hours. Our line was near Fairfax Court House. Next
day we returned to camp, and drill commenced in earnest. On this occasion it was company drill, and I
devoted the most of the afternoon to it.

September 14th was Sunday, and Sunday in the
army, particularly in the morning, is devoted to a
thorough inspection of the men, their equipments,
accoutrements, tents, and the camp. Every gun is
handled by one of the officers, and if a particle of dirt
or rust or any defect is found in the weapon, the soldier
to whom it belongs is sent to his quarters to put it in
perfect order. The same rule applies to the equipments
and clothing, and after the men are thus inspected, the
company's quarters are gone through in the same thorough manner to see that they are clean and in order,
and woe betide the soldier that is negligent and slovenly
on Sunday morning. When engaged in the active
duties of the campaign, it often happens that inspection
cannot be held, and in stormy weather the routine had
to be somewhat modified, but the officers of every well
regulated and disciplined regiment make thorough
work of the Sunday inspections, and on occasions the
inspector-general from brigade or division headquarters
appears and inspects the regiments and makes a report.

By the 16th of September we began to feel the effect
of the fight that was going on between the Army of the
Potomac and the Confederate army at Crampton's

Pass, and the next day at Antietam in Maryland. We were under orders to march on both these days, and at times by putting our ears to the ground we could recognize the sound of distant cannonading, very dimly, but with sufficient distinctness to convince us that a battle was in progress; and we soon learned from the newspapers of the terrible fighting between the two armies on the latter day. Antietam is generally recognized as the bloodiest single day's battle of the war. It was claimed as a victory by the Army of the Potomac because they held the field. It is now generally conceded that it was a drawn battle, but at the time the Northern forces got some encouragement from it under their claim of victory. Amherst College had cause to mourn over the battle of Antietam, because the Professor of Chemistry, Dr. Manross, was killed on that day. He was a noble man and a very popular teacher.

From this time until the end of the month we were very busily engaged in regimental drills and in brigade and division reviews, which latter events took place as often as every other day to familiarize the men and the officers with the movements of the troops in large bodies.

On September 29th, Monday, we were under marching orders all day. Everything was packed, and we waited until evening for the order to fall in, when an order came directing us to be in battalion line the next morning at daylight, ready to start for Frederick, Maryland. By this order twenty regiments, under command of General Briggs, were ordered to join the Army of the Potomac, and the Thirty-seventh Massachusetts was assigned to General Devens's brigade in the Third Division of the Sixth Corps, commanded by General Couch.[1]

[1] O. R., xix., Part 2, pp. 368, 373.

The Thirty-seventh started the next morning at six o'clock in accordance with this order. Just as the regiment was starting I was detailed with fifty men to take charge of the brigade camps and turn over the government property, tents, etc., and store in Washington the regimental property that could not be carried. The soldiers were allowed to take blankets, overcoats, and only one change of undergarments. The regiment spent the night in the Capitol grounds at Washington, and were allowed to visit the public buildings. In the afternoon of October 1st, they again started on cars, but the next morning found them only a dozen miles beyond the Relay House. They reached Frederick late that afternoon,[1] and from there commenced their march over the Catoctin Mountains towards Sharpsburg. On October 5th, Sunday, they arrived at their destination,[2] and received a hearty welcome from their brothers and neighbors of the Tenth Massachusetts, with whom they were to be brigaded for the next two years.

I did not fancy being separated from my regiment, but as I was not consulted, I immediately went to Washington and it was arranged at General Casey's headquarters that I should be furnished with a horse and the necessary equipment to enable me to go back and forth from Camp Chase to the city. My detail of fifty men felt very much as I did, and they wanted to get through with their work as soon as possible and rejoin their regiments. Accordingly, they worked with a will, and in a couple of days had all the brigade property ready to be transported to Washington.

[1] Oct. 2d, Bowen, p. 76.
[2] Near Downsville, where they joined the Army of the Potomac. Compare Bowen, pp. 81, 88. See War Map 27 (1).

Upon my reporting this fact to General Casey he directed me to take charge of all the other camps of his division, and care for the property in the same way that I had for those of the brigade with which I was connected. This put us back somewhat, but it gave me an opportunity to see something of General Casey. I found him very communicative. I take the following entry from one of my letters written at the time:

The other day while waiting, I had a long conversation with General Casey lasting about two hours. The discussion ranged through the realms of morals, ethics, politics, and war. He is a great admirer of New England, and is particularly proud of his native State, Rhode Island. He said he would not swap a regiment from New England for one from the Middle States with any amount of boot. He particularly inquired about the feeling in Massachusetts in reference to the President's proclamation, which he entirely approved. He was outspoken in his criticism of the military handling of our armies. He said that General McClellan and his clique were growing fat on the lean ribs of the government. He classed Burnside with McClellan, and said he was overestimated by the public. He approved of Banks and Hooker. He asked me about my education and said mathematics was the highest of sciences. He quoted passages from the Greek Testament.

The interview ended with his giving me twenty-five six-mule teams to move my stuff from Camp Chase to Washington, which I accomplished by the morning of October 6th. I then reported to him that my work was done, and turned over my vouchers, and with the necessary transportation for my detail started for Frederick, carrying two large bags[1] of regimental mail which we

[1] Weighing about sixty pounds. Letter to his mother Oct. 9, 1862.

got from the Post-office at Washington and agreed to deliver to the regiments.

Before leaving Washington we visited the Capitol, and found all of its halls and many of its rooms occupied by cots and filled with wounded soldiers.

At 11 P.M., we started for Frederick on a freight train and arrived at 5 A.M., October 7th. We took our mail bags to a vacant lot near by and began the work of assorting and did enough to find several letters for ourselves. Then we visited the hospital and talked with the wounded soldiers and also with some of the citizens. Everybody that we saw was friendly. The Thirty-seventh was reported as encamped near Harper's Ferry. We slept that night in a saloon on the floor. I had no money, and had lived by borrowing for several days past.

Wednesday, October 8th, we started for Harper's Ferry about 11 o'clock, and arrived there about 2.30 P.M. We visited the engine house where John Brown made his stand. We were told the Thirty-seventh might be at Sandy Hook, about two miles distant, so we went there. We called on Colonel Kam of the Pennsylvania Bucktails, and learned from him that the Thirty-seventh was assigned to Couch's division, Franklin's corps, Devens's brigade, and were encamped eighteen miles over the hills. We started on foot at 5.30 P.M. I had only three men of my detail belonging to the Thirty-seventh. So we four got a pole and strung our mail bags on it, and by turns carried it between us, in addition to our knapsacks and arms. It was a beautiful moonlight night. Our route lay along the base of the Maryland hills with the Potomac on our left, but soon left the river to climb the hills. At 10 P.M. we had made only three miles of progress, and were tired enough to halt by a mountain stream that crossed the road and get a night's sleep.

On Thursday, October 9th, we arose at daylight after a refreshing sleep, breakfasted on pork and bread, and then started on our tramp. We very soon found an army wagon going to Sharpsburg, and made an arrangement with the driver to take our mail bags, and deliver them at Sharpsburg. We could then move more rapidly. It was a very picturesque road and country, high wooded mountains and beautiful outlooks, but the roads were rough and bad.

As I was descending a hill, I heard some one call: "Hallo! Mase Tyler," and looking up recognized Frank Walker, then Major on General Couch's staff. He was mounted and followed by a troop of orderlies, and was very cordial in his greeting to me. General Couch had moved his headquarters to take command of the Second Corps. He told me where to find the Thirty-seventh. After leaving him I pushed on, and arrived at Sharpsburg at 11.30 A.M. We had yet seven miles to go before reaching our destination. We found our mail bags, and arranged for their transportation to the camp of the Thirty-seventh, and then got something to eat and went forward over Antietam battle-ground, which showed the effects of the late battle by its destroyed fences, trampled fields, prostrate crops, broken down artillery caissons, and the decomposed bodies of horses, scattered among the graves of the dead. We arrived at the camp of the Thirty-seventh near Williamsport late in the afternoon, October 9th, Thursday, and were most heartily welcomed, especially as we brought the first mail they had received since they left Camp Chase.

CHAPTER IV

WITH THE ARMY OF THE POTOMAC UNDER McCLELLAN AND BURNSIDE

OCTOBER, 1862, TO JANUARY, 1863

THE Thirty-seventh now numbered 971 men. They were assigned to a brigade composed of the Second Rhode Island, the Thirty-sixth New York, and the Seventh and Tenth Massachusetts. The Second Rhode Island was originally commanded by Colonel Sloane, who was killed at Bull Run, and at present was commanded by Colonel Frank Wheaton, a regular army officer and native of Rhode Island. The Thirty-sixth New York was a two years regiment, largely composed of Irishmen, and was commanded by Colonel W. H. Brown. The Seventh Massachusetts was originally commanded by Colonel Darius N. Couch, a West Point graduate, and afterwards commander of the Second Corps, and was now commanded by Colonel David A. Russell, also a West Point graduate, and one of the best soldiers in the Army of the Potomac. The Tenth Massachusetts was originally commanded by Colonel Henry L. Briggs, of Pittsfield, of sterling New England stock, and upon Colonel Briggs's promotion to be a Brigadier-General, for his gallantry at Fair Oaks, he was succeeded by General H. L. Eustis.

The brigade had already made for itself a name for

44

gallantry and distinguished service on the fields of Fair
Oaks and Malvern Hill.   It was now also the most
distinctively Massachusetts brigade in the Army of
the Potomac, and its commander, Brigadier-General
Charles Devens, was a Massachusetts man of rare gifts,
distinguished at the bar, and afterwards on the field
of battle.   He was later Attorney-General of the
United States, and on the Supreme Court Bench of his
native State, and declined an appointment as one of the
Justices of the Supreme Court of the United States.

The Sixth Corps was organized May 18, 1862, by
uniting Franklin's division with W. F. Smith's division
of the Fourth Corps, and after the battle of Antietam,
Couch's division of the Fourth Corps was also transferred and became the Third Division of the Sixth
Corps.   General Franklin was in command of the
corps, and General Couch was promoted to the command of the Second Corps, and General Newton to the
command of our (the Third) Division.   At this time
General Slocum commanded the First Division, and
General Hancock had just been promoted from the
command of a brigade in the Sixth Corps to that of a
division in the Second Corps.

Among the corps of the Army of the Potomac, the
Sixth probably stood next to the Second in the number
and importance of the battles in which it was engaged.
Colonel Fox, in his book entitled *Regimental Losses*, at
page 79, says:

The history of the Sixth Corps, more than any other, is
replete with fascinating interest.   Its record is invested
with more of the romance and brilliancy of war.   There
was the successful assault of Marye's Heights; the brilliant
dash into the rifle-pits at Rappahannock Station; the deadly
hand-to-hand fighting in the gloomy thickets of Spottsyl-

vania; the breathless interest which attaches to their lone
fight at Fort Stevens, where, under the eye of the President,
they saved the National Capitol from the hand of the
invader; the victories in the Valley, with the dramatic
incident at Cedar Creek; and the crowning success at the
storming of Petersburg. Over all these scenes the Greek
Cross waved proudly on the banners of the corps, while its
veteran legions wrought deeds which linked that badge with
an unfading glory and renown.

The camp of the Thirty-seventh was situated near a
small village named Downsville in a beautiful grove
of oak, chestnut, and walnut trees, with a green sward
of grass underneath. The heavy soft turf was very
grateful as a substitute for bedding, because at this
time the men were for the most part obliged to spread
their rubber blankets upon the ground and sleep in the
open air, with their woollen blankets wrapped around
them, as they had no tents. The quartermaster of our
regiment had managed, as he went through Harper's
Ferry, to obtain four or five wall tents with four or five
extra flies, and the wall tents were used for the accommodation of the officers at headquarters, and the flies
were distributed to the officers of the various companies,
each taking one. The fly was simply like a large, long
sheet stretched over a pole with the sides and ends
open, and until we were able to enclose them in the rear
by a brush wall, they only protected us from above.
The weather was cold, especially at night, and we all
found it rather difficult to keep warm. There was
plenty of wood in the vicinity, but for the most part it
consisted of very large trees, which could not be easily
cut up or made into firewood or material for houses
with the tools we had. After a while we managed to
cover the rear of our officers' quarters with brush and

to build large fires in front, which enabled us to live in tolerable comfort.   When, however, it rained and the wind blew, these tents were not much protection.

On October 10th, the regiment was under marching orders all day.   Stuart, the famous cavalry leader of the South, had started on his raid around the Army of the Potomac.   He crossed the Potomac River a few miles above Williamsport, and with 2000 followers rode entirely around our army, recrossing at White's Ford below Harper's Ferry.[1]

General Pleasonton with our cavalry tried to overtake them, but was unable to do so, although in one day he rode eighty miles.   Our orders to march were countermanded that same night, and during the next week we were drilled very energetically, having company drills in the morning, and battalion drills in the afternoon.

My diary states that the army was exceedingly well fed at this time.   We had a company mess with a man hired to cook for us, and the bill of fare consisted of beefsteak, sweet soft bread, butter, battercakes, syrup, fried eggs, and potatoes, and sometimes apples and other fruit.   In order to provide against the dangers of smallpox, the surgeons undertook at this time to vaccinate all who had not recently been vaccinated, and a large number of men in the Thirty-seventh were subjected to this ordeal, and some of them were made pretty sick by it.

In a letter dated October 17th written home, I find the following account of some of our camp experiences:

Captain Allen's boy and mine are quietly deciding who shall wash the dinner dishes by the toss of a penny.   These

[1] See p. 51, footnote 2, relating to White's Ford.

boys are pretty tough specimens. They each have only one garment of a kind. When that gets dirty, they will take it off and wash it and either wait until it dries, or wear it and let it dry on them. It don't matter much which. My boy was running around naked yesterday while he washed his clothes and waited for them to dry, and as they did not dry fast enough to suit him, he concluded to put them on and dry them in that way. At this season he sleeps on the bare ground with anything or nothing over him as it happens. He is now only fourteen. I have one rubber blanket which I need to spread on the ground when I am on the march, or out on picket duty, and in order to provide a proper covering I have just purchased a rubber overcoat, which I can use also as a blanket and spread it over my woollen blanket to keep off the wet and the rain. It only weighs one pound. I was lucky in securing it. Although our sutler brought into camp a large number of them he disposed of them almost immediately.

On the 18th of October, after a hard day's work in drilling and in preparation for inspection of the next day, which was Sunday, at 6 P.M. we were ordered to pack up and march. We started and marched until midnight, reaching Clear Spring, at a distance of fifteen miles from where we started. We made a short stop at Williamsport for the purpose of being reinforced by a squadron of cavalry and a battery. The next morning (October 19th), after an early call and breakfast, we started at 7 o'clock and marched an additional fifteen miles with a halt of only two or three hours at midday, to Hancock, where we arrived at 4 P.M. This was a pretty hard march for an unseasoned regiment—thirty miles in less than twenty-four hours. Almost everybody was complaining of blistered feet and some of the men limped very badly. We were comforted by the report that the Thirty-seventh had fewer stragglers in proportion to its numbers than any of the other regiments.

That night after a short rest at Hancock, Company F was detailed to perform picket duty, and in order to reach the ground, had to march two or three miles farther up the Potomac. Our picket line was along the bank of the Potomac in a picturesque, grandly beautiful country. We enjoyed the scenery and were stimulated by the mountain air, but it was very cold. We suffered a good deal from lack of proper protection against the weather. We were relieved from the picket line by Company E of our regiment, at four o'clock of the next afternoon (October 20th), and returned to camp near Hancock. With an abundant supply of firewood gathered from the surrounding forests, and thoroughly wearied with our long march and our night duty, we slept soundly that night, rested the next day, and retired early with the expectation of a good second night's rest. Just before midnight, however, the camp was aroused by orders to pack up and fall into line, and we marched the rest of the night, arriving at Cherry Run, ten miles below Hancock on the Potomac, in the morning (October 22d). By this time our rations had given out, but the train met us from Williamsport, and rations were immediately issued, and the troops breakfasted on the simple fare of the army—hard-tack and coffee. After two hours of rest we moved back a mile from the river and encamped.

We were in the midst of a good farming region, and one of our servants obtained a turkey from one of the farmers nearby and our mess feasted. Our camp was situated in a beautiful forest which was warm and peaceful in the protection it gave us from the wind and cold. From the river bank half a mile distant, we over-looked a large area of country, which, however, seemed to be commanded by the heights on the southern banks. To be sure that no enemy occupied these heights, a detachment from the Second Rhode Island crossed over and reconnoitred the banks, but found no trace of a hostile force.

Thursday, October 23d, early in the morning, brought us marching orders, and after breakfast we started eastward, apparently bound for our old camp, but after proceeding a short distance we were halted by new orders, and with knapsacks packed, loaded with accoutrements, and with guns stacked, so as to be ready to fall in at a moment's notice, we waited until the middle of the afternoon. We were to have hundreds of such experiences in subsequent campaigns. These long and tedious waits under arms and loads in utter igno-rance of what was the cause of the delay were exceed-ingly trying to the patience of officers and men, and particularly exhausting to the soldiers. There was never a march without more or less of it. On this occa-sion, after a long wait, we were allowed to return to our camp of the previous night, where we remained until Monday, October 27th.

Those four days were days of great discomfort because of rain, but we were to some extent protected by the forest in which we were encamped, and we were able to keep warm by building large fires. The men were without tents, everything they touched was wet, and their clothes were so soaked with moisture that they exhaled steam.

On the 27th, we received orders to return to Williams-port, which we reached about nightfall after a hard march over muddy roads and wet by occasional

showers.   The next day was spent in getting rested
and thoroughly dried.   The air was full of rumors that
the Army of the Potomac was going to move.   The sick
had been ordered into permanent hospitals.   On October 29th, at 2 P.M., we left Williamsport, and after a
march of five miles, reached our old camp near Downsville, where we slept once more under our flies.

This excursion to Hancock was probably undertaken
in anticipation of further raids by General Stuart or
other cavalry leaders into Pennsylvania.   On October
10th, General Stuart with 2000 cavalrymen had crossed
the Potomac above Williamsport, and repeated his
feat of the previous June of going around the Army of
the Potomac, and returning to Lee's army without the
loss of a man.[1]

This raid differed from the former one because it was
from start to finish on Northern soil, and besides living
off the country, he was enabled to obtain fresh remounts
for his entire cavalry force at the expense of his enemies.
He started on October 10th, and recrossed the Potomac
at White's Ford[2] below Harper's Ferry on October 13th.
It was so profitable to the Southern army, and so dis-
graceful and aggravating to the North, that McClellan,
after the horse was stolen, determined to fasten the
barn door, and sent Couch's division on its hurried
march to Hancock, and when the army was ready to
move called us back.

Personally I derived much encouragement from my
own experience in connection with this excursion.   I

---

[1] See War Map 25 (6), showing route in detail.

[2] Swinton says Stuart "recrossed the Potomac below the mouth of the
Monocacy" (*Army of the Potomac*, p. 226).   The place referred to
may be White's Ferry, which exactly fits this description. See p. 247,
infra, and note.

bore the marching very well, and although I had been suffering with camp ailments more or less, both at Washington and at Downsville, the trouble all ended with me after the march to Hancock. The exposure and the hard work of the march thoroughly agreed with me, and from that time I steadily gained in strength and in health. My weight increased, and within six months I had gained over thirty pounds, and during the remainder of the season only on very rare occasions, and then very slightly, was I troubled with anything resembling a cold.

On Thursday, October 30th, our regiment was subjected to a thorough inspection, and during the afternoon we received orders to be ready to march at 4 o'clock the next morning. In pursuance of such orders, on the following day we started at early dawn, and marched twelve miles over rough roads and through a hilly region by way of Keedysville to Rohrersville, where we went into camp in a picturesque basin among the hills and mountains. Encamped on a side of this basin the Army of the Potomac with its bright campfires presented a particularly picturesque scene in the evening.

On Saturday, November 1st, we started at 5 A.M. and marched to Berlin on the Potomac,[1] where we arrived at 2 P.M. Here we were encouraged by the prospect of receiving our first pay for services as soldiers. The regiment was formed in line and mustered; the paymaster with the muster roll in his hands went to each company and called from the muster roll the name of each man to be paid. The muster rolls with his

[1] Six or seven miles east of Harper's Ferry. See War Map 27 (1), which shows all the places named on their line of march as far as White Plains, where they arrived November 6th.

memoranda upon them were then returned to the regimental officers and by them completed, and sent to Washington, and we were told that the regiment would probably be paid sometime within the next two weeks.

Our march to-day was through Compton's Gap[1] and over the South Mountain Pass near the scene of the battle of that name in which General Reno was killed on the 14th of last September. We had supper that night of bread, butter, and fried eggs. Eggs forty cents a dozen, butter forty-five cents a pound, chickens $1.50 a pair. Our camp in the vicinity of Berlin was quite near to General McClellan's headquarters.

On the next day, Sunday, after the usual inspection the men were allowed to make the most of their day of rest until the afternoon. I spent the day below Berlin between the Chesapeake and Ohio Canal and the Potomac. We heard distant cannonading during the day. In the afternoon the quartermaster announced that he had just received a large supply of clothing for the soldiers, and was ready to partially fill the requisitions which we had sent in for needed articles while we were in camp at Downsville. With the cold weather rapidly coming on, and the prospect of an autumn or winter campaign before us, this announcement from the quartermaster was greedily welcomed, and the men were supplied with winter overcoats, which they especially needed, and with such other articles by way of renewals as their requisitions had called for.

On Monday, November 3d, the regiment was formed

[1] Apparently a mistake copied from his original letter home November 1, 1862, and not corrected. See War Map 27 (3) showing road from Rohrersville southeast must take them through Crampton's Gap, but not over the South Mountain Pass, which is five miles farther north, where General Reno was killed September 14, 1862. (See Ropes, ii., 344.)

in line at 9 A.M. with the expectation of crossing the
Potomac on the pontoon bridge at once.   After waiting
four hours for the way to be clear, we took our turn,
and at 1 P.M. were conscious of being once more on
"the sacred soil of Virginia."   The experience of crossing the stream on a pontoon bridge for the first time was
a novelty, and of much interest to the members of the
regiment.   The men were cautioned against keeping
step on the bridge, lest by the rhythm of their motion
they should cause a sufficient swing of the bridge to
break it from its moorings.   Once upon the Virginia
shore, they started off at a good gait, and by nightfall
had marched thirteen miles, and went into camp in a
piece of woods by the roadside, sufficiently weary and
hungry to have a good appetite for supper, and to
sleep soundly without waking until the next morning.

At 4 o'clock Tuesday (November 4th), reveille was
sounded, and by 6 o'clock the men had breakfasted
and were in line, but the road was blocked by artillery
and other troops, and our progress was much delayed.
That night, however, we halted after a march of twelve
miles at or near a small village known as Union.

The country between the Potomac and the Rappahannock rivers in Virginia is intersected by numerous
narrow and very poor roads, which are here and there
crossed by small streams, and usually these streams
are without bridges.   The movement of an army
through such a country and over such highways was a
difficult undertaking, because the roads were hardly
wide enough to allow the passing of the troops, the
wagons, or the artillery, separately; and it took no little
planning and ingenuity to move an army of a hundred
thousand men with its trains of supplies and camp
equipage through such roads and over so many

unbridged streams. If possible, the artillery and the wagons would be given the roads and the men marched through the lots or through the woods by the sides of the roads. The wagons and men crossing the streams would soon churn the river bottoms, and the opposite banks would become soaked with the water which was carried from the stream by the wheels of the wagons and by the feet of the men and horses for hundreds of yards beyond the farther banks. Virginia soil when wet makes an article of mud that is without a rival. If possible, in order to avoid creating such mud-holes, the engineers were called and temporary bridges built to accommodate the marching troops, but very frequently the men were compelled to wade through the streams and make their way as best they could through the muddy banks.

On November 5th, Wednesday, we began to see the marks of the skirmishes, artillery and cavalry fights, indicated by dead horses and here and there an exploded artillery caisson, as well as by marks of the bullets and shot upon the trees, and noted the tracks of the Rebels two days ahead of us all the way. On this day we only progressed five miles towards Ashby's Gap to a point a little beyond Upperville.

On Thursday, November 6th, we started at 6 A.M. and marched eighteen miles to White Plains, where, for the first time in Virginia, we encountered a railroad cut and dismantled track.[1] No cars had been run since June 1st. It was the coldest day we had yet experienced, and as we had not yet received our tents we were sleeping every night in the open air. The next morning (November 7th) we had our first snowstorm, and as no orders to march were received the men

[1] There is no mention in letters of tracks being dismantled.

devoted themselves to keeping warm. It so happened
that we were out of rations, and during the day the
report that there was a large and a well stocked farm in
the near neighborhood led the men to organize parties,
and to supply themselves with sheep and turkeys during
that night. As a consequence the next day the army
was well supplied with fresh mutton and fowls. Such
raiding was forbidden, and usually the order was
strictly enforced. But for some reason, which I never
fully understood, on this occasion the disobedience of
orders was overlooked, and no one was punished. I
have always supposed that it was because everybody
was hungry, and all officers and men had a taste of the
mutton or the fowls.

We afterwards learned that by order of the President
signed and dated November 5th, and delivered November 7th, General McClellan was relieved from the
command of the Army of the Potomac, and General
Burnside appointed to take command. This probably
accounts for the absence of movement by the Army of
the Potomac on this day, and the next day, and on the
9th of November we only moved seven miles to New
Baltimore,[1] where we went into camp.

On November 10th the troops were formed in lines,
and the order relieving McClellan was promulgated.
General McClellan and his staff, with Burnside following in the rear, rode bareheaded through the army
from right to left. The air resounded with cheers,
banners waved, and saluting swords and presented arms
were all significant of the rare devotion and enthusiasm
felt by the army for its commander. It was more like
a triumph than a dismissal. No other commander of
that army ever had to the same degree its enthusiastic

[2] See War Map 74 (1).

admiration and attachment.   On that 10th of November the feeling in the army was unanimous in his favor, and against the authorities in Washington.   They felt that he was a much wronged man, and had been treated very unfairly, and many of them verged on mutiny in expressing their sympathy with him, and devotion to him.   But the sober second thought and sound sense of even those who were his strongest friends raised loyalty to country far above personal devotion to their leader. Burnside felt and acknowledged his own unfitness for the position.   But the army fought with the same resolution and courage at Fredericksburg as at Antietam, although they did not meet with the same measure of success.

From the 11th to the 16th of November we remained at or near New Baltimore.   Our camp was located on the top of a hill.   All the water that we used had to be brought three quarters of a mile.   Wood was scarce and small and the weather was raw, emphasized by bleak and chilly winds.   Manassas Plain was visible for thirty miles.   On the 11th, I had a call from Frank Walker. In a letter dated the 12th I wrote home: "I think I never saw such universal gloom as the removal of McClellan has caused over this army.   I had never before in any degree appreciated the popularity of McClellan with his army.   The army had never succeeded under any other commander.   McClellan organized and made it what it is and the talk among the officers and men is almost mutinous.   It makes me feel very blue.   The first report was that McClellan was promoted to the command of all the armies.   When they [the soldiers] found that he was removed instead of being promoted, there was a tremendous revulsion of feeling in his favor."

On Saturday evening, November 15th, we received orders to be ready to move in the morning, and pursuant to such orders the next morning saw us with baggage packed and in line ready for the march at an early hour. Our route lay through a wild and desolate country with very imperfect roads and almost no human habitations or cultivated lands. Here and there was a woodman's hut or a cabin in the midst of a small clearing. We passed no villages, no court-houses, schools, or churches, but at the end of the first day's march we were said to be near Catlett's Station.[1]

On Monday, November 17th, the country through which we passed was of much the same character. We wandered through the woods, across roads all day, apparently lost, so far as civilized or cultivated surroundings were concerned, and progressed so slowly that at the end of the day we found we had made only eight miles from our starting point.

On Tuesday, November 18th, we acted as guard for the wagon train, which is always a very exhausting service, and at night reached a temporary camp near Stafford Court-House. Our camp was located on low, wet ground, and to add to our misery we ran out of rations. On the evening of the 19th of November, while we were still in this camp, rain set in and our teams got stuck in the mud and required a detail of two hundred men from our regiment to help pull them out. The men were still without tents. If we stood still we sank in the mud. We awoke in the middle of the night to find that we were lying in pools of water. We tried

[1] Letter of November 19, 1862, says: "The first night we halted at Catlett's Station, or rather at Weaversville near there." See War Map 22, Plates 5 and 7. A large map of the whole country as far as Fredericksburg is shown in War Map 8.

to sleep, but could n't, and finally got up and devoted ourselves to getting dry, with only partial success.

On the 21st the trains arrived and whiskey rations were served to the men. On Saturday, the 22d of November, the rain ceased during the morning. I was sent out a half-mile from camp to guard the ammunition train. The weather was still threatening and raw. I got warm by boxing with Joe Taylor. On the following day, Sunday, November 23d, I was relieved from guard duty at 1 P.M., and returned to camp with my detail. We found that we were encamped on the highway from Aquia Creek Landing to Fredericksburg. The Chaplain held services at 2 P.M.—the first time for more than a month. The mail was then distributed, and I was made happy by the receipt of five letters. I also received a copy of the New York *Independent*, and during the afternoon entertained the boys of my company by reading one of Beecher's sermons which seemed to be much enjoyed.

On November 25th, the entire regiment was ordered out five miles from camp to do picket duty. On the 26th, Wednesday, we returned to camp in the afternoon, and during the evening were greatly rejoiced by the arrival of Mr. Birnie from Springfield with boxes and bundles from home for the regiment. I was lieutenant of the guard on that day, and it was part of my duty to receive those boxes and to take care of them until they could be distributed.

Thursday, November 27th, Thanksgiving Day. In the morning after religious services the battalion was formed in the shape of a hollow square, Colonel Edwards read the Governor's proclamation, and under my command the guards brought in and unpacked the boxes, and Mr. Birnie distributed their contents to the various companies and individuals entitled.

My Thanksgiving dinner was hardtack and beefsteak, and for supper we had rice and hardtack, but it was a busy day, crowded with thoughts and memories of home. During the evening the knapsacks left by the regiment at Washington on September 30th, and which I had stored for the regiment, were returned and delivered to the men.

On November 29th, the paymaster arrived and commenced to pay the regiments in our brigade. The Thirty-seventh was not reached until November 30th, and I was passed on that day on account of my second lieutenancy in the Thirty-sixth.

To a certain extent we had by this time begun the erection of log cabins with large open fireplaces and barrels for chimneys. The older regiments of the army had learned to make them during the previous winter, and we very soon copied the example, and to a certain extent were sheltered in such houses. The men in the ranks had to use their rubber blankets for coverings of the roofs, because as yet we had not received our tents, and in this respect the officers were not much better off than the men. The difference was in the fact that they had more rubber blankets.

The paymaster finished his task of paying the regiments of our brigade on the 2d day of December. During our money famine, which to this time had been continuous, our sutler's tent looked like a deserted house. With the advent of the paymaster, wagons loaded with all kinds of temptation for the officers and men seemed to come out of the woods in every direction. During the periods intervening between the paymaster's visits, orders on the paymaster were given by the soldiers, and taken by the sutler in payment for his wares to a moderate extent. At these times he did not suggest purchases by display of goods, but when they had cash in their pockets, his tent was a department store.

On December 3d, Colonel Edwards invited Captain Allen and me to accompany him in a call upon General Devens. The General received us very cordially. I was particularly impressed with the clearness and deliberation with which he expressed his opinions. He was a good specimen of a sturdy New Englander.

On December 4th, we received orders to march, after the companies which were detailed for picket duty had returned to camp. We started at 10 A.M., but made slow progress owing to the narrowness of the road and its occupation by teams. Evening found us in the vicinity of Belle Plain after a march of ten miles, where we bivouacked for the night in a forest where wood and water were plenty. The next morning (December 5th), we started at 6, and after marching six miles went into camp at 11 o'clock, in the vicinity of King George's County Court-House,[1] in an oak forest which in its location and surroundings seemed well adapted for a winter camp. An envious fate refused to let us enjoy it. After a two hours' stay we started again in the rain, moved a mile, and went into camp on a hillside covered with a growth of young pines unfit for fuel, and yet there was no other at hand. We tried to build fires,

---

[1] This is probably an error based on letter of December 6th dated "Camp near King George Court-House," which was corrected in his next letter dated "Camp near White Oak Church, December 9, 1862," where he explains, "The last time I wrote I dated my letter from another place because I did not know exactly where we were. I have however since found out and date accordingly." As King George C. H. was many miles out of their course, the camp on December 5th was more probably near White Oak Church. See War Map 100 (1).

but the fuel would not burn, while it filled the air with a pungent smoke that was painful to the eyes and disagreeable to breathe.   It rained all day, finally changing into a cold, dismal snow-storm, which cleared off in the night, and this was followed by several days of bitterly cold weather, during which the only way we could keep warm was by exercise.   We found a distant piece of woods where we cut down the trees and made them into four-foot logs, which the soldiers would carry on their shoulders a half-mile or more to feed their fires to keep them warm.   We stayed in this uncomfortable camp until December 11th.   It was appropriately named by the soldiers "Camp Misery on Smoky Hill."

During that winter I became quite expert in the use of an axe.   I felled trees and cut and split them into logs and fuel lengths, and thus got warmth and exercise during the period when we were without tents or huts.

On Thursday, December 11th, we were aroused at 3.30, left camp at 5 A.M., and after a rapid march, arrived at 11 o'clock at a point on the north bank of the Rappahannock River near Franklin's Crossing. We filed into a depressed meadow between two hills and stacked arms, and the men took off their knapsacks and waited.

Two pontoon bridges were being built at Franklin's Crossing,[1] and to Devens's brigade was assigned the honor of leading the way across the river.   The Second Rhode Island was selected to cross on the upper bridge, while the Thirty-seventh Massachusetts was to cross at the same time on the lower bridge, and they were to be followed by the left grand division, consisting of the First and Sixth Corps of the Army of the Potomac

[1] See War Map 33 (1).   The location of the pontoons is shown on Map 63 (7).

under the command of General Franklin. Meanwhile, in front of Fredericksburg, General Burnside had been engaged from early morning in an abortive attempt to build two other pontoons, with the result that Rebel sharpshooters occupying the basements of the buildings upon the opposite banks in defiance of all the artillery that he could train upon these buildings shot the pontooners as fast as they appeared to build the bridges.

While my regiment was waiting in the meadow I ascended a neighboring hill and watched the bombardment of the city. The Federal guns were pouring shot and shell into the city with apparent effect, but the moment bridge building was renewed the deadly bullets flew. Later in the day a number of pontoons were launched and selected soldiers sprang into them and were rowed across the river and they drove out the sharpshooters from their hiding places, and occupied the streets in that part of the city until the bridges were laid.

At about 5 P.M., the Thirty-seventh Massachusetts and Second Rhode Island simultaneously started across the bridges at Franklin's Crossing. General Devens and Colonel Edwards led the way on the lower bridge, closely followed by Company F of the Thirty-seventh. The Second Rhode Island deployed a skirmish line on reaching the farther bank. The coast had been cleared by a searching artillery fire, and the bend of the river selected for the bridges was favorable to the control of the farther shore from our side. The result was that the crossing was not opposed, and in a very short time we were in line upon the plain,—a division strong. Then the powers in control decided to trust the keeping of the south bank at that point to the unaided possession of Devens's brigade, and the other brigades of the division were withdrawn for the night to the north bank. It was bitterly cold, and we could have no fires, and our position in line did not allow of much motion. We found an enormous pile of straw near by, and the men wrapped it around their feet and took turns in lying down upon it or in it. But it was a weary night, and Jackson's corps was in our front. What rest we got was with arms in hand. Morning finally came and was never more welcome.

Friday, December 12th, was devoted to getting the Army of the Potomac across the river and into position on its south side. It was a very awkward field on which to fight a battle. In our front was a wooded ridge rising one or two hundred feet, which bends away from the river and leaves a wide and fertile plain at the point where we were; while farther north and back of the city of Fredericksburg, the slope was gradual from the city's edge to the foot of a high terrace. This terrace was surmounted by sightly residences, and at its base, skirting it for a long distance, was a sunken road with a solid stone wall, which here and there protected the road from attack and hid it from sight of those approaching the city. Between the city and the plain where Franklin's left grand division was deployed ran two considerable streams, one of them named Deep Run, and the other Hazel Run. The latter was called fordable, the former was not. The practical effect of this was to divide our forces into two armies. Sumner's right grand division, with four divisions from Hooker's centre grand division, was to assault the heights back of the city, and Franklin's left grand division, with Hooker's two other divisions, was to attack the fortified hills opposite the plains below the city. While the armies were getting into position on the 12th we rested, and watched the long lines file across the river and take their places on the plain.

About 11 A.M., on December 13th, the fighting began in earnest. On the right Sumner struggled all day long to drive the Rebels from the sunken road, but his heroic endeavors were unable to effect a lodgment, and at night his losses numbered toward 9000 men, with very little to show in return, save the honor of having faithfully tried to accomplish the impossible.

On the left, near noon, the First Corps of Franklin's army, assisted by two divisions of the Third Corps, made a fruitless attempt to seize or break through Jackson's line with a loss of 4000 men. The Sixth Corps, with Newton's division in reserve, formed the right of Franklin's army.[1] They lost some men on the skirmish line and listened to the whistle of the bullets and the scream of the shells over their heads for two or three hours. At length, about 3 P.M., our (Newton's) division was formed in line, and we were double-quicked to the left about a mile, where we lay closely hugging the ground amid the furrows of a last year's cornfield, while shot and shell at intervals during two hours shrieked and tore through the air just over our prostrate bodies. We were in the second or third line of battle, and once were ordered forward, but for some reason the order was countermanded before we had proceeded far. After dark we were withdrawn to the rear about a mile, and passed the night in comparative quiet with a fair amount of sleep.

---

[1] Newton's division was the Third, of which the Second Brigade, Brigadier-General Charles Devens, Jr., commanding, comprised the Seventh, Tenth, Thirty-seventh Massachusetts, Thirty-sixth New York, and Second Rhode Island (O. R., xxi., pp. 59, 60).

5

On Sunday, December 14th, we remained all day where we bivouacked the previous evening. Our principal occupation was watching the troops cross the river and go to the front. A feeling of gloom pervaded the army; but we knew nothing of the particulars of the battle already fought. In the evening there was a general disposition to sing hymns. The movement started and spread through the part of the army where we were encamped.

On Monday, December 15th, we were aroused at 2 A.M., and at 4 we moved forward and supported a New Jersey battery near the Richmond Road, and were there all day. After dark the troops were withdrawn and recrossed the Rappahannock. I was detailed to take charge of the "alarm picket." We were stationed in front of the line occupied by our troops. At 11 P.M., I was recalled and with my detail rejoined my regiment, and with the brigade we stood in line while the balance of the grand division marched through us and across the river. About 2 A.M. of the 16th of December, our brigade recrossed; the Thirty-seventh being the last to cross on one of the bridges. The engineers then took up the bridges and the pickets were brought over in the boats.[1]

[1] In a letter dated "Left Bank of the Rappahannock, 8 A.M. Wednesday, December 17th, 1862," he wrote to his parents an account of this Sunday and Monday: "We spent a very quiet Sunday. . . . In the afternoon I read. . . . In the evening I went down with the captain to hear him and one or two of the singers of the regiment sing for awhile. Captain has great taste for music, and a very nice voice, and it is a great pleasure to hear him sing with our other amateurs, among whom we number some superb singers. . . . We retired about ten o'clock and then were awakened at two in the morning . . . and at four were on the move to the front, where we arrived about five, and arranged ourselves so as to support the batteries on our line of battle. We lay there all day without anything of importance occurring, except in the afternoon it was

General Newton, in his official report, says: "My obligations are due to all according to their opportunities, but especially to Brigadier-General Charles Devens, who commanded the advance and rear guard in the crossing and recrossing of the river. . . . The division was never seriously engaged, but manifested a becoming readiness for action, and great fortitude and steadiness under the shelling of the enemy."[1]

The Thirty-seventh had one man killed, and one man wounded, in this, its baptismal battle.[2]

Rain set in before midnight, and added much to the gloom of the occasion. After crossing the river, we marched a mile to the rear and slept in a drenching rain the rest of the night.

It took us several days to recover the full possession of our faculties, and an unusual number from the regi-

---

discovered that the rebels were attempting to entrench about a mile to the front in a piece of woods.

"We shelled them immediately, and they skedaddled quick, a whole regiment of them, I should say.   After shelling about a half an hour, we resumed our quiet again, and lay there until evening, when I was sent with some dozen men from our right wing as an alarm picket.   So I went to my work supposing I had an all night's job before me, but about eleven o'clock I was ordered to draw in my pickets as quietly as possible. I was so astonished that I hardly knew what to do, but I obeyed, and on returning found the regiment drawn up ready for a move, where, I then knew not, but we quietly moved away first to our left, so that I had an idea for the moment that we were merely going to take a position farther to the left, but I was soon undeceived by the turning of the regiment to the rear again.   So back we went to the river's bank and drew up in line of battle until all the other divisions and brigades had passed, and then our regiment crossed while the rest of the brigade waited for the drawing in of the outer line of pickets.   So we were the first to cross, and almost the last to recross (our brigade was the last.)

"We then came up here about half a mile or a mile, and encamped. But we had run almost all the way clear from the front, and were decidedly tired when we halted for the night about 3 o'clock A.M., and then

[1] O. R. vol. xxi., p. 535.   [2] O. R., vol. xxi., p. 142.

ment went to the hospital. We moved camp once or twice, and the greater part of our time and energy was absorbed in procuring fuel and keeping the fires burning. Drilling was resumed on December 22d, and on the 23d Rev. Mr. Cooke appeared in camp as the bearer of Christmas cheer to the boys of the Thirty-seventh, although his boxes did not arrive until January 5th, and meanwhile, Mr. Cooke had to return to Washington with our regimental quartermaster to assist him in securing transportation for his boxes.

My only diversion, beyond ordinary camp life, that I enjoyed on Christmas Day was due to a call from Frank Walker, who dropped in to see me in the afternoon, and I subsequently learned that my father left home on that afternoon, and after a brief stay in New York, Philadelphia, Baltimore, and Washington, in each

---

we slept in a drenching rain until the morning. Yesterday we pitched our tents again and are now waiting further orders. Such is the part we acted in the famous passage of the Rappahannock. I little expected to get out of it with so little harm, only one killed and two wounded. . . .

"I saw a good deal of the battle, and heard more of it, and I don't think the rebels drove us at any one point, certainly on the left. But their front line of batteries was certainly very strong and nobody knew what they had to the rear. We however hear it reported that in the balloon reconnoissance made by General Burnside their line of battalions to the rear was found to be perfectly impregnable, and we knew that if we stayed there another day we should be shelled most terrifically, and so our generals thought it best to retire. It was, I think, however, a disheartening step to the troops, they looked upon it as bad as defeat. It is reported that General Newton, the commander of our division, was so chagrined that he told General Franklin that he would take his division and go to the top of those hills in spite of everything, and hold them too! We rather expected to move down the river the same night to effect a flank movement, but our generals did not see fit, and where we are going next I am sure I don't know, although I should like to very well. I however have gained one thing. I have seen the Rebs, and seen a battle, and almost been in it. Indeed, some of the old regiments told us when we lay up in the left Saturday afternoon and evening that they never had been under severer shelling than that was."

of which cities he called on friends, he arrived in camp on January 2d. I spent New Year's Day and the three succeeding days on picket. Our picket line extended from Pollock's mill on the left, to a point on the river bank near where our pontoon bridges were laid in December.

On board the boat from Washington to Aquia Creek, father made the acquaintance of General Shaler, and he kindly escorted him to our camp. It was very aggravating to me to be on duty at that time, but father improved the time by calling on General Caldwell, Colonel Frank Walker, and Colonel Clark, and I returned to camp on the 4th, and enjoyed three happy days of visiting with him. On the afternoon of the 5th of January, Mr. Cooke returned from Washington with our Christmas boxes, and we feasted on home dainties for several days. All my home neighbors had contributed to my box, and it was rich in cake, preserved meats, fruits, pickles, and a large number of articles made by the ladies intended for my comfort in camp.

On January 7th, father and Mr. Cooke left for home, and we settled down to the dull routine of camp life. Meanwhile, our shelter tents had arrived, greatly to the joy of the whole regiment. The weather was too unsettled to allow our drilling with much regularity. Our camp was poorly situated on rather low ground, and the feeling was pretty general in the regiment that much of the prevailing sickness was due to this fact.

On January 16th, Lieutenant-Colonel Goodrich was discharged from the service by the acceptance of his resignation as lieutenant-colonel. The experience that he had had in the campaign convinced him that he was too old to bear the privations and hardships incident to that life. This produced a vacancy, and Major Montague was recommended immediately for promotion, and Captain Allen of Company F was recommended to take the vacancy created by Colonel Montague's promotion. General Devens insisted upon his right of examining the candidates for promotion before their names were sent forward to Governor Andrew, and with one or two other first lieutenants, whose names were suggested by Colonel Edwards, I was directed to appear before General Devens for such examination. With the experience that I had already had, I felt that I was equal to the exposures and hardships of field service. After submitting to the examination required by General Devens I was very happy to receive his recommendation for my promotion to the captaincy of my own company, which I accordingly received.

Forty-three years afterwards on the occasion of the dedication of the monument erected by the Commonwealth of Massachusetts and the city of Worcester to the memory of General Devens, and dedicated on the 4th of July of that year, it was my privilege to command the survivors of General Devens's old brigade, who were present to participate in the dedicatory exercises. It brought very vividly to mind my slight acquaintance with him, and in particular the courteous and cordial way in which he treated me on the occasion in January, 1863, when I appeared before him as a candidate for promotion to the captaincy of Company F in the Thirty-seventh.

On January 19th we were ordered out on picket duty, and on the 20th were, suddenly and unexpectedly to us, recalled to camp to join the movement inaugurated on that day by General Burnside, and which in history is known as "The Mud Campaign." We started about noon. The skies and the atmosphere portended as

favorable conditions as we could possibly have desired
if Providence had given us the ordering.   The air was
balmy and the sun shone bright.   We marched up the
river seven miles, and about 5 P.M. halted in a beautiful
piece of pine woods.   As we lighted our evening fires in
the forest the scene was worthy of the fairies, and as we
knew very little of our destination there was no disposition to doubt or to fear.   Before midnight the rain
set in and increased in amount all night.   By morning
it was a flood.   The ground on which we slept was
soaked, and our rubber blankets and coats did not protect us from the pelting storm.   Our start had been so
unexpected that very little provision had been made for
the march, so we had hardtack, but very little else.

They attempted to move us across lots so as not to
interfere with the movement of the teams and our
artillery.   We started early in the morning, but by
ten o'clock we found that the roads were full of wagons,
artillery and pontoons which were stuck in the mud
and could not be moved, while the army moving by the
side of the roads was gradually churning the soil into
sloughs which were growing deeper and deeper and
threatening to engulf us.   Finally, after we had advanced only two or three miles, we filed into a woods
and details were made of the men to help pull the
wheeled conveyances of the army out of the mire.   At
this we made very little progress.   They seemed to be
sinking deeper and deeper, and the rain showed little
inclination to cease.   Sixteen horses could not move one
pontoon with men to help.   We went into camp near
the river, and established a picket line.   While the
Confederates laughed and jeered at us, our only resource
was to build fires and try to get dry and wait for the
storm to subside.   The men were soaked, and as an

antidote whiskey rations were issued, and as the soldiers had eaten a very light breakfast, the whiskey was effective enough to make many of them very drowsy.

I was actually soaked to my knees and plastered with mud above my hips. During the afternoon the rain lessened in quantity. We built huge fires and dried ourselves as well as we could, and then lay down in our camp clothes and slept most peacefully. The next day (22d) we got thoroughly dried, and on January 23d, under marching orders at daybreak—destination unknown,—we started, faced towards our old camp, and after plodding for many miles through woods and fields for the purpose of avoiding the muddy roads, we reached there at 2 P.M. to find that in our absence it had been pilfered and sacked; but the huts were there, and in our disconsolate condition we welcomed them as if they were homes.

Burnside was relieved from the command of the army, and the ever hopeful soldiers girded themselves for further struggles.

CHAPTER V

THE ARMY OF THE POTOMAC UNDER GENERAL HOOKER

JANUARY 26 TO JUNE 27, 1863

ONCE more the War Department and the President were called upon to select a commander for the Army of the Potomac. Stanton was at the head of the War Department. He was an excellent man to watch over the expenses, but he had neither military education nor experience. Halleck was still acting as adviser, but he was only a theorist. General Scott had retired. McDowell had failed at Bull Run. McClellan was an excellent organizer and engineer, but too slow to compete with Lee and Jackson in the field. Banks, Sigel, and Pope had been slaughtered in quick succession by Jackson. Burnside had proved the worst failure of all. The question was who next should be tried, and the lot fell upon General Hooker.

Hooker had proved himself brave and aggressive as a division and a corps commander at Williamsburg and Antietam, but he was suspected of disloyalty to his chief at Fredericksburg. In the military and political councils at Washington, his chief backer was Secretary Chase, while all the rest of the Presidential Cabinet, and the corps commanders in the Army of the Potomac, pronounced him incapable of the task devolving upon

73

the commander of the Army of the Potomac at this juncture. No one else was in sight, and President Lincoln finally wrote him a stinging letter of reproach for his faults in the past, and appointed him commander of the Army of the Potomac.[1] Meanwhile, the Army of Northern Virginia, under Lee and his able subordinates, was educating a body of corps, division, and brigade commanders, who, already possessed of natural aptitude and experience, were making of that army a unified force that could be handled with consummate skill by its great leader, General Robert E. Lee. The commander-in-chief understood his corps commanders, who in turn were as thoroughly and ably sustained and re-enforced by their division, brigade, and regimental commanders as any who ever took the field. In the Army of the Potomac these elements had constantly changed, while in the Army of Northern Virginia, they had been educated into unified and co-operating forces. In the Army of the Potomac distinguished officers were few. In the Army of Northern Virginia they were legion.

At the time General Hooker was made the commander of the Army of the Potomac, General Sedgwick was assigned to the command of the Sixth Corps. His name is more thoroughly identified with that of the Sixth Corps than the name of any other officer. He had had a large experience in army life, was brave to a fault, decided in his views, cautious and judicious in his leadership, and he particularly endeared himself to the soldiers of his command by his tender and considerate care for their lives and for their comfort.

General Hooker took command of the army on the 26th day of January, 1863, and immediately went to

[1] *Complete Works*, Nicolay and Hay, vol. ii., p. 306.

work to reorganize the army and to bind it into an efficient whole. He reorganized the cavalry and the artillery; trained and drilled them into much more efficient bodies than they had ever been before. The organization into three grand divisions he abandoned, strengthened the corps organizations, and adopted emblems for each corps and department of the army to be worn by the soldiers in a prominent position upon their caps, and thereby show at a glance to what part of the service they belonged, as well as to what corps, division, or brigade. He saw that the army was well clothed and well fed, and encouraged it, by giving each man or officer a furlough or leave of absence for ten or fifteen days, to return home and get a new supply of health and courage. [1]

[1] In letter dated "White Oak Church, February 2, 1863," M. W. T. wrote: "They are going to give furloughs to one private in each company and to two line officers and one staff officer, of ten days' duration each, and I have been settling who should go in my company by lot this afternoon. . . . Married men have the preference in these furloughs, so that my chances are small. . . ."

The following interesting glimpse behind the scenes of the great conflict at this time is contained in the same letter: "I have just returned from a three days' picket tour. . . . This is the pleasantest tour of picket we have enjoyed yet. I had something of a chance to communicate with the Rebs this time, and improved it by talking with them across the river some ten minutes twice. We found the Forty-eighth Alabama regiment doing picket on the opposite side of the river, and a very polite, affable young man came down and conversed with several of us officers. He asked us what we thought of peace over on this side, said they wanted it much. I asked them if they were willing to come back into the Union, he said he was willing to, but he did not suppose their side were. He said they had plenty of rations of flour and such, but no tea or coffee. They wanted very much to get hold of our papers and of their own accord every day sent over their Richmond dailies. They came over one day of their own accord and played euchre with some of the regiment above us, and were very anxious to trade tobacco and sugar for coffee, etc. They were very polite indeed, and before our departure to-day they announced the sinking of our iron-clads in Charles-

Inspections were frequent, discipline was strict, and the army was subjected to constant and severe drills and exercises by regiments, brigades, and divisions. The numbers and strength of the regiments were also reinforced by recruits and by compelling the soldiers that were detailed for special duties to return and take their places in the ranks. In fact, the whole army was impressed with the feeling that strength, energy, and intelligence were all working together at headquarters and producing lasting results in the line of efficiency.

The Thirty-seventh at first returned to the camp which they had occupied just before their departure on the "Mud Campaign," but after remaining there a month, a new camp was selected by Colonel Edwards, laid out, and built upon well-devised and improved plans. Early in March we moved into it, and under the influence of the generally improved conditions our camp was put into better shape than any camp we had previously occupied. It was ornamented with arches and evergreen bowers and attractive enclosures. The huts and streets were constantly cleaned and every attention was paid to the health of the men and the care of the camp. During the spring, Captain Lincoln and I had frequent opportunities of seeing soldiers from Amherst in other regiments, and called now at the Second Corps on General Walker and General Caldwell,

---

ton Harbor, and the opening of the port. Whether this is true or not we are as yet in the dark, but hope it may prove a canard. I hear that Hooker has issued most stringent orders against having any communication with the Reb pickets. So that I suppose in the future we shall be unable to either receive or give papers, and shall have to live in the dark. I felt some inclination to go over and talk with them awhile, as they invited us to, but thought it would be running too much risk, as we had orders not to communicate with them, even through papers, and they said they had the same."

and now at the Fifth Corps on Captain Shepard of the Class of 1860, Amherst College, and again at the Ninth Corps on our friends of the Twenty-first Massachusetts who enlisted with Colonel Clark.

Among the other luxuries that were provided under General Hooker's direction was soft bread for the whole army, which was baked in brick ovens erected especially for that purpose, and which, with the abundance of vegetables and fresh meat, also provided by his orders, made us think that we were living in great luxury. During the latter part of February the good people of Amherst and vicinity provided us with a fresh box of dainties, which were very gratefully received and appreciated. By the latter part of February, under the fuel requirements of so many men, the whole country in the neighborhood of the army was pretty thoroughly cleared of everything in the shape of wood, and the result was that the army teams were kept busy going to distant points with details and bringing in supplies of wood for the use of the different regiments. Stumps were visible here and there, but the forest had all disappeared as far as the eye could see.

During the latter part of March it became my turn to go on leave of absence. Captain Lincoln and I arranged so that we could be in Amherst together part of our time, and it so happened that our classmate Vance had just been promoted from captaincy to a majority in an Indiana regiment, and we three met in Amherst and spent a very pleasant ten days.

Of course, we were entertained and lionized as the returning soldiers were at that time. We were full of hope and the buoyancy of youth, and we did not allow the shadows of our adversities or the prospect of the hard campaign for which we were preparing, to render us otherwise than cheerful and happy. We had a delightful vacation crowded with many pleasures, and when the time for our return arrived we bade our families and friends a cheerful good-by and started for the front. The train on which I started from New York to Philadelphia met with an accident which delayed me some four or five hours.

When I reached Philadelphia I was troubled with a toothache, and concluded to stop over and obtain the services of a dentist, which I accordingly did with the aid of my college friend, Horace Binny, 3d. This delayed me for one afternoon. At midnight I again started for Washington, but arrived there just too late to take the Aquia Creek boat for that day, and consequently was obliged to remain in Washington until the morrow.

However, I reached camp at 3 o'clock in the afternoon of April 6th.[1]   I found that the army was preparing for a grand review to be held on the next day, before the President of the United States. This review was on a grander scale than any military pageant in which we had previously participated. Four corps were reviewed and the Sixth Corps was in the lead. No pains were spared by the commander-in-chief to make

[1] An incident of the camp life at this time is found in a letter to his mother of this date: "When I arrived this afternoon I found the officers with Colonel Edwards at their head all out playing ball. Games are all the rage now in the Army of the Potomac." And again on the 10th of the same month: "To-day the sun shines very bright and the air is beautifully clear and the wind is fast drying up the mud. Our camp is alive with ball-players, almost every street having its game. My boy Jimmie is so busy playing that he hardly knows how to stop to do my errands. He can play ball with the best of them, and pitching quoits he can beat anybody in my company, captain and all. . . . General Sedgwick was over here yesterday looking through our camp, and said it was the best he had seen."

SAMUEL C. VANCE.

RUFUS P. LINCOLN.

MASON W. TYLER.

From a tintype taken probably during their furlough in Amherst, in March, 1863.

it a perfect success. The different corps got into line without delay and they succeeded each other in their march before the reviewing stand with rapidity and regularity. The generals and their staffs, equipped in their fine regalia, blazing with gilt and gold, were in constant motion all over the field. Cannons fired a salute, and the President, followed by General Hooker and his staff, rode down the line. We saluted, and the President tried to manage his tall hat and make it do duty by way of returning the salute, and considering his awkwardness, he succeeded fairly well. We started at 7.30 in the morning, and returning reached our camp about 1 o'clock in the afternoon. Such reviews well and successfully conducted are very inspiring to the soldiers, and on this occasion every man and officer seemed to feel, as we never had felt before, that we had grown to be a fine army, and that we were bound to give a good account of ourselves. I never knew the Army of the Potomac to be so inspired with confidence in its future as it was at this time. Furloughs and leaves of absence now ceased, and every available man was called back to join his command.[1]

[1] In a letter dated "White Oak Church, Va., April 14, 1863," he wrote: "The enthusiasm of the troops is very high at the present time, and all hands agree in declaring that the army was never in so fine a condition before, not even when we went on to the Peninsula with full ranks. The cavalry marched Monday, and the artillery followed yesterday. Zenas Bliss dropped in suddenly upon us Monday. He is reporting for the *Boston Journal* just at present, and of course is looking out for a fight. He stayed with me last night. . . ."

April 19, 1863, he wrote: "Zenas Bliss came back night before last and spent the night and part of the day yesterday with me. The day before that he spent at General Hooker's headquarters, and took supper, spending the evening in company with Senator Wilson and General Joe, sleeping that night in the bed occupied by President Lincoln when here, and remaining for breakfast. He told me a good many things that he heard General Hooker say, although he was pretty close-mouthed, and

On April 14th orders were issued to furnish eight days' rations in the haversacks of the army, with sixty rounds of ammunition to each man, and everything not absolutely needed upon the march was sent to the rear. It looked like an immediate move, but one of those hard Virginia rains set in that night which soaked the ground and made it impossible for the army to move for at least ten days, unless they wished to repeat the experience of the Burnside "Mud Campaign." We therefore returned to our drills and work of preparation.

During the spring the commanders of the different regiments had been directed to hold classes of instruction for their officers, and each regimental headquarters was more or less of a school of military science. While we were waiting for the waters to dry up and the roads to settle, on the 21st of April General Devens announced that he had been promoted to the command of a division in the Eleventh Corps, and in a brief address of farewell to his old brigade, his eloquence drew tears to the eyes of his comrades. In fact, I doubt if there was a dry eye in the brigade when he announced his farewell. He was succeeded in the command by Colonel William H. Brown of the Thirty-sixth New York. A succession of rainy days held us

---

did not like to tell all he knew. He says General Hooker remarked that he expected the eight days' rations the soldiers now have would carry them to Richmond. He knew to a man how many soldiers the Rebs had opposed to him. His plans had been deranged somewhat by the rain of the past week, and his cavalry was somewhat disorganized by losing horses by drowning, all which might have been saved had the commanders exercised discretion. The greatest difficulty he experienced was in finding subordinates that would exercise proper discretion and were equal to every emergency. This and a lot more he told me of 'Fighting Joe.' All seemed to him very fine, and he left impressed with the power of the man."

fast until the 27th of April. Meanwhile, the whole army had been held in readiness to move as soon as the weather conditions were favorable.[1]

By feigning that he intended to cross the Rappa-hannock at Port Royal ten miles below Fredericksburg and to attack Lee's army on its right flank, by a mas-terly secret movement over blind and wooded roads at a distance from the river, Hooker, between the 27th of April and the 2d of May, succeeded in transferring all of his army, excepting the Sixth Corps and Gibbon's division of the Second Corps, around Lee's left wing, and in locating it in the vicinity of Chancellorsville. This gave him control of the United States Ford some thirteen miles above Fredericksburg on the Rappa-hannock. He had intended to post his army a few miles farther down the river and give it the control of Banks's Ford, which was only six miles from Fredericks-burg. This would have brought him within supporting distance of the Sixth Corps and practically united his army. Just as this part of the plan was about to be realized by the advance of his troops within sight of Banks's Ford, a strange and unaccountable lack of reso-lution took possession of General Hooker, and in spite of the protests of his corps commanders and his staff, he insisted upon withdrawing his army to Chancellorsville and fighting a defensive battle there. This practically prevented him from using his artillery and tied the feet of the left wing of his army, so that they could neither attack in their front, nor move to the assistance of the rest of the army on the right, because they were shut up in an almost impenetrable jungle, which pre-vented a move by that part of his force.

[1] A comprehensive map of the campaign which follows will be found in War Map 41 (1).

General Lee with an army of 58,000 men saw that his adversary was in a net, and disposed his force so as to hold him there with 30,000 men while he sent Jackson with the remainder of his army, amounting to 26,000 men, by a long detour around the right flank of the Army of the Potomac in an endeavor to cut that army off from its line of retreat over the United States Ford. He succeeded in crushing the right wing of the Army of the Potomac, consisting of the Eleventh and Twelfth Corps, and producing such disorder and confusion in the arrangement of its lines of battle that it was practically paralyzèd as an army.

Stonewall Jackson was killed just as he was organizing his troops in one last desperate attempt to seize the United States Ford and cut off the only line open for the retreat of the Federal army. Hooker was stunned. His Third Corps was miles away in the woods. His cavalry was half-way to Richmond. His left wing was snarled up in that terrible Wilderness which a year later came so near to being the burial-place of Grant and his army. He had 37,000 men in his army that never fired a shot, and yet when Stonewall Jackson crushed his right wing on that fateful night of the 2d of May, he had no available reserve at hand. All that saved him was the confusion that prevailed in Jackson's charging column. It was the same thing that saved Lee a year later at Spottsylvania. The charging columns in each case had to halt and re-form their lines. This gave time for a rally. At Chancellorsville, night too intervened.

At this juncture, at 9 P.M. (May 2d), Hooker issued a hurry call to Sedgwick, who was thirteen miles away, three miles below Fredericksburg. At this time Early held the heights back of Fredericksburg with six brigades, or a total of nine thousand men. Hooker ordered Sedgwick to march three miles to Fredericksburg, carry the heights, capture or drive away Early, march ten miles, and at daylight attack Lee's army in the rear and relieve the pressure of Lee's army on that of Hooker. As the despatch was not dated until 9 o'clock in the evening, and the messenger bearing it had to pursue a circuitous route by the north bank of the river to reach Sedgwick, it was near midnight when he received his orders. It was an ablebodied proposition, but Sedgwick tackled it without a murmur. Soon after midnight he was under way groping through the darkness. It was a blind, tedious march through roads lined by woods and over two unbridged streams, but by a favoring fortune, we reached the rear of Fredericksburg between three and four o'clock of that Sunday morning, and waited for the dawn. As we approached the city, we startled a few weary pickets, but they got away in the darkness.

At daylight the Rebel batteries from Marye's and the neighboring heights opened on us, but they found difficulty in depressing their guns enough to do us any injury, and as we were on the outskirts of the city, they could not fire on us without damaging the city. About 10 o'clock we moved into a railroad cut half-way between the edge of the city and the sunken road at the foot of the terrace of Marye's Heights. Here we were pretty well protected from the Rebel fire; but a little in front of us was the sunken road at the foot of Marye's Heights which, in the previous December, was held by a mere handful of men against all the forces that General Burnside could bring into line against it; and on the other side of the road, Marye's Heights, surmounted by a fortified redoubt, bristling with cannon, and occupied by Confederate riflemen, rose defiantly, and seemed to be ready to welcome us to hospitable graves. After two abortive attempts (one by Gibbon on the right, and the other by Howe on the left of our line) to carry the heights, General Sedgwick organized five columns of assault: three under the direction of General Howe, and commanded, respectively, by General Neil, Colonel Grant, and Colonel Seaver, to capture Lee and Cemetery Hills, and starting from the banks of Hazel Creek; and the other two under the direction of General Newton, and commanded, respectively, by Colonels Johns and Spear, to capture Marye's Heights, and starting from the southern edge of the city. Colonel Johns's column consisted of the Seventh Masachusetts and Thirty-sixth New York in the front line, supported by four regiments of Colonel Burnham's Light Division of the Sixth Corps; while Colonel Spear's column consisted of the Sixty-first Pennsylvania and Forty-third New York, supported by Colonel Shaler's brigade.[1]

All five columns were successful in capturing the works they attacked, and were closely followed by the rest of the corps. They lost a thousand men, but they captured more than a thousand prisoners, and the force that carried the "sunken road" at the point of the bayonet, and then poured over Marye's Heights, was led by two regiments of our brigade. Colonel Johns was seriously wounded, and Colonel Spear was killed. The Thirty-seventh reached the summit of the hill just in time to see the surrender and to aid in some of the captures. But the larger part of Early's forces succeeded in making their escape, and were in the fight against us at Salem Heights that afternoon.

It was now 11.30 o'clock, and messengers were

[1] O. R., vol. xxv., pt. 1, p. 559.

immediately despatched by Early to General Lee announcing the capture of Fredericksburg heights by the Sixth Corps. Lee at once called a halt in his attacks upon Hooker and sent McLaws's division with one brigade of Anderson's division to assist Early in staying Sedgwick's advance. Meanwhile, Sedgwick had spent nearly two hours in assembling his corps and resuming his march. Brooks's (First) Division was in advance, "formed in a column of brigade fronts with an extended line of skirmishers in the front and flank." "General Newton followed, marching by the flank along the road." Howe brought up the rear.

Our progress was somewhat delayed by the enemy's skirmishers, who from the outset took advantage of every fence or tree or grove to annoy and harass our column, and for a time gave us considerable trouble. They afterwards withdrew, and we had no further trouble until we approached Salem Heights, so called, about three miles from our starting point. The country here is slightly undulating, and wooded in spots on the right of the plank road. It was bordered on the left a half-mile back from the road by quite a forest, which curved around to the road in our front, and hid from our view a sizable brick building known by the name of Salem Church. A half-mile this side of the church the Confederate lines of battle came into view at scattered intervals, and opened fire with their batteries. Brooks's division was deployed to the left of the road, and Newton partly to the left and partly to the right, and for a couple of hours a fierce conflict of the forces ensued, in which at first the Federal forces were successful, but after driving the Confederates a considerable distance, reinforcements enabled them to force us back nearly to our original line.

The left wing of the Thirty-seventh, of which my company was a part, was detached from the right wing and sent to the assistance of the First (Brooks's) Division and arrived just in time to render substantial aid in checking the Confederate advance by delivering a well directed fire at close range into a part of the advancing line.   Darkness finally intervened, and our regiment was reunited and rested with arms in hand on the front line of battle on the left of the plank road.   The lines of battle were in our front so close to each other that there was very little room to deploy skirmish lines, and between the lines we could hear shrieks and cries from the wounded calling for help. Relief parties were finally organized to bring in such of the wounded as could be reached.   It was a warm spring night, and the mournful notes of the whippoorwill were mingled with the cries of the suffering, and as I remember were audible the greater part of the night.   We slept very little.

With the dawn of the morning, we found the enemy had withdrawn their lines of battle into the edge of the woods about a half-mile to our front, and were moving around our left through the woods at about the same distance.   This led to the re-arrangement of our lines. Brooks's First Division was placed in line nearly parallel to the plank road, but crossing it a mile southwest from Fredericksburg, it united with Howe's division, which then formed a right angle with Brooks's line and extended that line until later it rested its left on a bend in the river.   The Confederates extended their lines so that they occupied Fredericksburg heights early in the day, and cut off our line of retreat in that direction, and all day long we could see them moving their troops into position, and tightening their coils around us·

When we lost our connection with the heights of Fredericksburg, General Sedgwick took possession of the south shore of the river from Banks's Ford to the point where Howe rested the left flank of his division. Newton's division formed a right angle with the right of Brooks's division, and crossed the plank road with his right resting on the river above Banks's Ford.[1]

Thus we were virtually occupying three sides of a hollow square, with our right and left flanks resting on the Rappahannock River, which constituted what would have been the fourth side of the square if it had been complete. It was a long drawn out line some four miles in length, with the batteries of artillery advantageously posted at different points in the line where they could render the most service. We had no reserve and no second line of battle. Our brigade was stationed on the west side of the angle formed by the union of Brooks's and Newton's divisions. All the afternoon we watched the Rebels moving through the woods on our front, and every now and then uttering the Rebel yell, at times apparently forming into lines of battle and preparing for attack. It was one of the most anxious six or seven hours that I ever spent.

About three o'clock in the afternoon I was detailed to take charge of two companies from our regiment, F and H, on the skirmish lines. Our skirmish line was located with its headquarters in the rear of a small house which was surrounded by a garden and orchard, and part of the way by a low hedge behind which the men could lie down; but I was kept moving up and down the line the greater part of the time, watching the movements of the enemy in the opposite woods, with the bullets whistling around me, and every now and then striking

[1] See War Map 135 (6).

with a stinging noise or a thud on the earth by my side. Of course I was at times sheltered by the house and at times was under the cover of a bush or a tree. Every little while when the movements in the woods indicated a gathering of the troops in any locality, our artillery shelled them with great effect, but they were too far away to be effectively reached with rifle or musket balls, and I suppose it was to this that we owed the fact that our skirmish line escaped with very small loss.

As the evening shades set in, we received orders to hold on to the skirmish line until word was sent to us, and then to withdraw as rapidly as possible to the river bank near the ford. Meanwhile, immediately after dark, the withdrawal of the troops was commenced as silently as possible, and by nine o'clock in the evening we got word to withdraw the skirmish lines, and under the leadership of a staff officer sent to guide us, to go as rapidly as possible to the vicinity of Banks's Ford, selected by General Sedgwick as a rendezvous from which the corps would cross the river. It is said that General Sedgwick on the night of the retreat expected to sacrifice our brigade to save the rest of the corps, but although we were the very last to leave the field, we applied the feet so nimbly that we got away from them.[1] One man dropped dead from exhaus-

---

[1] A manuscript note, in M. W. T.'s handwriting, in the margin of his copy of Bowen's *History of the Thirty-seventh Regiment*, at page 154, records his vivid recollection of the exciting experience:

"The race when the order was given to withdraw this skirmish line exceeded in speed all the rapid movements I ever saw executed by a military force. We ran two miles on the keen jump, and sank down exhausted on reaching the regiment at the ford."

An extract from the *Daily Republican* (Springfield) of Monday, May 18, 1863, attests the interest at home in following the exploits of the soldiers in the field:

"Capt. M. W. Tyler of the 37th Regiment, son of Prof. Tyler of

tion. The Rebels were firing shells and were supposed to be close behind us. We crossed the river on pontoon bridges at two o'clock the next morning. The entire loss of the regiment in killed, wounded, and captured was twenty-seven men, during these two days.

The following letter from General Newton to Governor Andrew was forwarded after our return to camp:

HEADQUARTERS THIRD DIVISION, SIXTH CORPS,
OFFICE ADJUTANT-GENERAL, May 15th, 1863.

HIS EXCELLENCY JOHN A. ANDREW,
    Governor of Massachusetts.
SIR:

Permit me to call your attention to the excellent conduct of the Massachusetts regiments under my command during the late operations of the Sixth Corps. The Seventh Massachusetts stormed the Heights of Fredericksburg in columns without firing a shot and suffered severely. To Lieutenant-Colonel Harlow who commanded the regiment after the wounding of Colonel Johns, I mainly attribute this fortunate result. Colonel Harlow proved himself a hero, as this was a charge not exceeded in brilliancy and daring by any operation of the war. The Seventh ough. to receive adequate praise. The Tenth and Thirty-seventh, though under fire in Fredericksburg on the morning of May 3d, rendered their principal service in the afternoon and the following day at Salem Heights. Their coolness under fire and admirable discipline merit the warmest acknowledgments. The Tenth was under command of Major Parker during the most important period of their operations,

---

Amherst College, did himself great credit in the recent battles of Fredericksburg and Chancellorsville. His company was particularly exposed during the re-crossing of the river, and all speak in the highest terms of the coolness of Capt. Tyler. Glad of it. Should n't expect any other report from a man who rejected an offer of a year of foreign travel, free of expense, that he might join the army."

Colonel H. L. Eustis having command of the brigade. The conduct of all these regiments at such critical juncture has been an ample return for all the care bestowed upon their organization and discipline.

I have the honor to be,

Your obedient servant,

JOHN NEWTON, *Major-General.*

General Russell, in his report of the battle, says:

During all of Monday the enemy made repeated attempts in our front to advance his line of skirmishers, but every attempt was foiled through the vigilance and stubborn resistance of the men of this command and through the sharp and precise firing of Lieutenant Butler's battery stationed directly in our rear. Our position here was strengthened by two regiments from the Third Division, the Thirty-sixth New York Volunteers, Lieutenant-Colonel Walsh commanding, and the Thirty-seventh Massachusetts Volunteers, Colonel Edwards, both of whom rendered material assistance in holding and defending the position. Late in the afternoon of Monday, orders were received to draw in our pickets and to cover the withdrawal to Banks's Ford following the Second Division of this Corps. This was effected just at dusk, under cover of a very hot and accurate shelling of the woods in our front from Hexamer's and Butler's batteries. This brigade reached Banks's Ford about nine o'clock in the evening of Monday in good order, and crossed the river in safety at two o'clock in the morning of Tuesday, May 5th.[1]

After crossing we moved back one half mile from the ford and halted for the night, and slept the sleep of exhaustion due to our going without sleep the previous night and our long waiting and watching on the skirmish

[1] O. R., xxv., pt. 1, p. 592.

lines during the afternoon.   About 9 A.M. they roused
us from our slumbers and told us that we must move
farther back beyond reach of the Confederate guns.
So we marched to the rear two miles, and bivouacked in
a piece of woods.   About 4 P.M. it began to rain, and the
rain continued on the 6th and 7th, with signs of clearing
on the 8th.

Meanwhile, General Hooker had crossed with the
rest of the Army of the Potomac at United States Ford
on the night of May 5th, and orders were received on
the evening of the 7th for the army to return to their
old camps at the north side of the Rappahannock, and
accordingly, on the morning of the 8th, we marched
nine miles back to our old camp in mud and rain.   My
diary says, mud almost as bad as that in the "mud
march."   In a letter dated the 9th, written to my
parents, I say:

Here we are back again in our old camp and quarters
after almost a fortnight's absence.   We have made a reconnoissance in force, taken the heights, advanced five miles
into the enemy's country, fought a battle, and accomplished
nothing except that we have given one more crushing blow
to the Army of the Potomac, and promoted the feeling that
we cannot drive the enemy beyond the lines of the Rappahannock River.   As yet we know nothing of what the state
of things is in General Hooker's army.   How badly he was
whipped and what was the reason of his failure are matters
of pure conjecture with us.

I received some credit from the field officers of the
regiment for the way in which I handled the two companies on the picket line during the retreat.   Although
the movement was very rapid, I succeeded in keeping
the men together, which, owing to the darkness of the

night, it was rather difficult to do. Some 200 knapsacks were thrown away by the regiment on the retreat, while of these Company F lost only five. We were the last to leave the field, and were the nearest of any of our troops to the enemy's line. [1]

After our return to camp we resumed the same routine of duties and occupations as before our movement across the river. Daily drills, varied with an occasional detail for picket duty, an occasional review, and frequent thorough inspections by the regimental, brigade, and division inspectors, kept us very busy. The army very soon recovered its confidence and its courage. The feeling among the officers and the men was that General Hooker ought to have succeeded; that the campaign was well planned and admirably executed up to the time that General Hooker withdrew the army into the woods about Chancellorsville. After that he failed utterly both in handling and in fighting his troops, and at the critical moment was himself injured and picked up for dead, leaving the army practically without a commander during the battle. We felt that the organization of the army as a whole was more complete, that the rank and file were in better fighting mood and condition, than they had ever been before, and that if they could only be well commanded the army would give a good account of itself.

During the month of May we moved our camp from

---

[1] Bowen, at page 153, says: "The safety of the Thirty-seventh evoked the most lively satisfaction at corps headquarters, since from its peculiarly exposed position it had been feared that it must be cut off, but the most remarkable fact was that the skirmish line had been able to do so valiant work in delaying the advance of the enemy and still bring away every man. The admirable steadiness and efficiency of Company F had been closely watched and warmly praised by their comrades in the regimental line."

the position we had occupied during the previous March and April to a grove five miles nearer Aquia Creek, where we had a good water supply and plenty of wood for fires and for making an attractive camp. This condition of preparation and camp routine continued until the 4th of June, when we began to receive orders looking toward a movement of the army. On the 6th we broke camp and marched down the Rappahannock to the familiar grounds selected by General Franklin for laying pontoon bridges in the previous December, pitched our tents, and awaited further orders. A pontoon bridge had been laid across the river, and Howe's division of our corps was already on the other side.

Sunday, the 7th, the weather was hot, but relieved by showers in the afternoon. Our camp was on a plantation or farm owned by a Dr. Morson, whose house was situated on the river bank with the cabins of his negroes located around it. The doctor had 1500 acres of land, and the previous summer had had fifty-eight negroes, he told me, but then had only ten left, and they said they would stay only as long as the army stayed. They were staying at Dr. M.'s urgent solicitation, but feared that if the army should leave, they might be sold south. I talked with the negroes, and found their ideas of slavery rather hard. They were carrying on a profitable trade with the soldiers, selling hoe-cakes at twenty-five cents apiece. These cakes consisted of a mixture of cornmeal and water, with a little salt, baked on the hot hearthstones, and were liked by the soldiers because they varied the usual hard-tack diet. We could also sometimes induce the darkies to sell us a little milk at twenty-five cents a quart.

On the 10th of June our brigade crossed the river and went into line behind the rifle-pits in front of the Barnard house where we stayed until the 13th doing guard and picket duty. Occasionally the monotony of the scene would be varied by a few shells from the batteries occupied by the Rebels on the heights, but they never succeeded in doing us any injury by their shell-firing while we were there.[1]

On the night of June 13th we recrossed the Rappahannock and the whole army was put in march toward the north. It was very hot, and all extra accumulations in the shape of underclothing and overcoats and extra suits were thrown away, until the whole country seemed to be covered with the discarded garments of the army.

We reached Stafford Court-House on that day at four o'clock in the afternoon, and then halted until ten o'clock at night, when we started again and marched all night, but made slow progress because there were not roads enough in which the troops could be moved, and

[1] In a letter to his parents, dated June 12, 1863, M. W. T. speaks of the Barnard house as a mass of ruins with "many splendid trees around it, and under one of these I am sitting and writing to-day." "I rather enjoy writing letters when I have the accommodations, but out here it is a task. To begin back where I last left off. Wednesday morning we were relieved from picket duty and returned to support a battery of siege guns that lay on the plain back of our picket ground. There I lay all day. About four P.M. I took it into my head to go in swimming, and had a very nice time. I swam the Rappahannock—some thirty rods wide. . . . That night our division moved across the river, and we started about nine o'clock and got into position on this side in some rifle-pits in front of the famous Barnard house (General Franklin's old headquarters), and where General Bayard was killed. About twelve we were allowed to lie down on the ground with our arms in our hands, but could not undo our blankets. I slept right on the ground for the first time in my life. We were all aroused the next morning a little before day began to dawn, a quarter of three, to stand at arms and be ready for the enemy in case of an attack. We did the same last night. So you see we are gradually turning night into day."

those that we had were largely occupied by the trains and the artillery.

On June 15th we marched sixteen miles to Dumfries, and then rested during the evening until midnight, when we started again and marched eighteen miles on the 16th, reaching the Occoquan at twelve o'clock, and rested there until three in the afternoon, when we again took up our line of march and reached Fairfax Station at six in the evening, having made twenty miles during the day. Rumor told us at this time that Lee was already in Maryland, and marching to the north.

On June 17th we rested, and resumed our march on the 18th, starting at three-thirty in the morning, but after proceeding a short distance beyond Fairfax Court-House, we halted, and pitched our tents and remained until the 24th of June, when we once more received marching orders, and moved to within about five miles of Centreville, and went into camp in a very picturesque country, with the mountains in full view to the west and the plains of Manassas, covered with the verdure of spring, stretching in long distances before us to the south and east. We remained there until the 26th of June, when we moved by Chantilly to Dranesville, making a march of eighteen miles.

On June 27th we started at five in the morning, and marched three miles to Edwards Ferry, where we crossed the Potomac, proceeded two miles farther to the village of Poolsville, and on June 28th we started at four A.M. and marched through Barnesville to the vicinity of Newmarket, a distance of eighteen miles. While here we received the announcement that General Hooker was relieved from the command of the army, and that General Meade had been appointed his successor.

The reason for our march north, which I have here described, was the discovery by General Hooker that Lee was preparing to invade the North. By his victories at Fredericksburg and Chancellorsville he was encouraged to believe that the Army of Northern Virginia was more than a match for the Army of the Potomac on any field. His army was stronger by the addition of Longstreet's corps[1] than it was at Chancellorsville; while the Army of the Potomac was weakened by the expiration of the terms of service of its two years' men, numbering nearly thirty thousand. The North had not yet found a competent commander for the Army of the Potomac; while the South believed that they had an invincible army, led by a genius of war. In Richmond nothing less than the subjugation of the North would satisfy the people. The latter part of May, General Lee began to move his forces towards the upper Rappahannock, and on the 4th of June, when we crossed the river once more, Ewell and Stuart were in the neighborhood of Culpeper. On the 13th they appeared at Winchester, and on the 15th captured a large part of Milroy's army, and the Rebel cavalry pushed on and occupied Chambersburg.[2] On the 27th Ewell encamped within four miles of Harrisburg,[3] the capital of Pennsylvania.

The North once more was panic-stricken. On the 15th President Lincoln issued a proclamation[4] calling upon three Eastern border States and Ohio for 100,000 militia to serve for six months unless sooner discharged, and other States, noticeably New York, volunteered

[1] Swinton, pp. 309–10.
[2] Swinton, pp. 314, 317, 319; Rhodes, iv., p. 273.
[3] Rhodes, iv., p. 273.
[4] O. R., xxvii., pt. 3, p. 136.

aid, and the celebrated Seventh Regiment again took the field, and went to the relief of the sister State of Pennsylvania.   The crisis of the war was at hand, and the battle was to be fought on Northern soil.

CHAPTER VI

GETTYSBURG

JULY 1–3, 1863

THE situation of the two armies when General Meade succeeded to the command of the Army of the Potomac was as follows:

General Hooker had substantially succeeded in keeping the Confederate army west of the Blue Ridge, and General Lee had, therefore, been obliged to cross the Potomac River above Harper's Ferry and was moving his army through the Cumberland Valley[1] into the heart of Pennsylvania. As stated above, Ewell and his corps were in the neighborhood of Harrisburg at Carlisle and York.[2] Lee and Longstreet were at Chambersburg, and Hill and his corps were at Fayetteville,[3] while Stuart and his cavalry corps, who had just started upon one of their raids around the Army of the Potomac, were at Hood's Mill[4] on the Baltimore & Ohio Railroad within a short distance of Baltimore.

The Union army was on the east side of the South Mountain and the Catoctin Range in the vicinity of Frederick, Maryland. On the night of the 28th of June, Lee sent word to his different commands to concentrate at Gettysburg.[5] This recall of Ewell's army

---

[1] O. R., xxvii., pt. 1, p. 114.   [2] O. R., xxvii., pt. 2, p. 298.
[3] Id., p. 606.   [4] Id., pp. 694–5.
[5] Id., p. 307. See Rhodes, iv., 282; Swinton's *Army of the Potomac*, pp. 326, 327.

from its invasion of the southern part of Pennsylvania was due to the fact that Lee was surprised to find the Army of the Potomac so closely in his rear, and that he began to fear they might intercept his line of communications, which he was obliged to keep open to insure a continued supply of ammunition for his army.[1] He moved across the mountain in order to threaten Baltimore and prevent Meade from attacking his rear.

The Union army was anxious to protect the cities of Washington, Baltimore, and Philadelphia, and at this time Meade had in mind to make his line of defence at Pipe Creek, an affluent of the Monocacy River, about twenty miles southeast of Gettysburg. With this in view, on the 29th he moved the First and Eleventh Corps to Emmitsburg, and the Third and Twelfth to Middleburg, and the Fifth Corps to Taneytown, the Second to Union Town,[2] and the Sixth to New Windsor, with cavalry brigades covering his right and left flanks.[3] In the Southern army, Heth's division of Hill's corps was moved to Cashtown,[4] within eight miles of Gettysburg. Longstreet joined the rest of Hill's corps at Fayetteville.[5] At York, Early received the order to return to Gettysburg on the afternoon of the 29th, and prepared to start the next morning.[6] Rodes's and Johnson's divisions started from Carlisle and moved toward Gettysburg, but they were loaded down with plunder and had to move slowly.[7]

[1] Rhodes, iv., p. 282.   [2] Or Union.

[3] See itinerary of the Army of the Potomac, compiled by Mr. Joseph W. Kirkley, O. R., xxvii., pt. 1, p. 144. Also War Map 27 (1).

[4] O. R., xxvii., pt. 2, p. 607. See War Map 43 (7).

[5] See Longstreet's report, O. R., xxvii., pt. 2, p. 358.

[6] O. R., xxvii., pt. 2, p. 467, bottom, General Early's report of the battle of Gettysburg.

[7] The 30th. See report of Major-General R. E. Rodes, O. R., xxvii., pt. 2, p. 551, bot., and top of p. 552.

On June 30th the Union army extended from the
Emmitsburg Road, with the First Corps on its left at
Marsh Creek and the Sixth Corps on its right at Manchester,[1] while of the Confederate army, Ewell's corps
had reached Heidlersburg,[2] nine miles north of Gettysburg.   Longstreet was still at Fayetteville,[3] while the
main part of Hill's corps was at Cashtown,[4] eight miles
west of Gettysburg.   In fact, at the close of the 30th of
June, two thirds of Lee's army was within eight miles
of Gettysburg, while only two sevenths of Meade's
army was within twelve miles of the same place; but
there was this difference: Lee's whole army was under
orders to assemble there, and was actually on its way to
that destination, while one seventh of Meade's army,
viz., the First Corps, was moving in that direction,
while the other corps were waiting for orders.   Stuart's
cavalry had met with obstacles at Hanover and at
Carlisle on this day, but avoided them by making wide
detours which exhausted the strength of his men and
horses.[5]

By evening Meade was aware that the Confederate
forces were gathering at Gettysburg.   Reynolds, at
Marsh Creek with the First Corps, was only separated
by six miles from Hill at Cashtown.   Meade and Reynolds were both from the State of Pennsylvania, and
were both fired with an ardent desire to rid their State
of the insolent invasion of the Southern army at the
earliest practicable moment.   Meade declined to give
Reynolds any orders on the night of the 30th, but the
next morning he told him to advance and hold Gettys-

[1] O. R., xxvii., pt. 1, pp. 114, 144.
[2] O. R., xxvii., pt. 2, p. 444, top, Ewell's report.
[3] See Longstreet's report, *id*., p. 358.
[4] *Id*., p. 607.   See War Map 43 (7).
[5] See Stuart's report, O. R., xxvii., pt. 2, pp. 695–6.

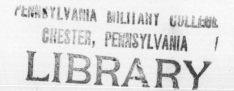
PENNSYLVANIA MILITARY COLLEGE
CHESTER, PENNSYLVANIA
LIBRARY

burg, and directed the Eleventh Corps to support him, and requested the Third Corps to do the same.[1]

Buford, with two cavalry brigades, was in the environs of Gettysburg that night.[2] On the morning of July 1st, a momentous day, Buford, with his cavalry brigades, was in possession of Seminary Ridge, to the west of Gettysburg, and of the country in front of it to Willoughby Run. Hill and his corps were approaching from the west, and Ewell and his corps were approaching from the north.[3] Reynolds and the First Corps of the Union army were coming to his assistance from the south, and Howard with the Eleventh Corps from a still farther starting point,[4] Reynolds being distant three hours, and Howard about six. Back a half-mile from Seminary Ridge, and partially parallel to it, was Cemetery Ridge, which extended three miles towards the south, and there terminated in two famous hills— Round Top and Little Round Top,—and towards the north, the same ridge curved first to the northeast and then to the east and southeast, and terminated in another rugged eminence known to history by the name of Culp's Hill. This was the famous battlefield of Gettysburg.[5] The village of Gettysburg was a short distance north of the point where the ridge curved to the northeast. It was a peaceful hamlet devoted to education and the study of theology, and gave its name to the greatest battle ever fought upon the North American continent.

Buford and his cavalry used every device known to cavalry tactics to delay the progress of the enemy until the arrival of the Union infantry. Meanwhile, Rey-

---

[1] O. R., xxvii., pt. 1, p. 114.   [2] See Buford's report, *id.*, p. 923, top.

[3] See reports of General Lee, O. R., xxvii., pt. 2, pp. 298 and 307.

[4] See report of General Meade, O. R., xxvii., pt. 1, p. 114.

[5] See War Maps 40 (2), 43 (1), 95 (1), 116 (2).

nolds arrived and recognized the advantages of the
Cemetery Ridge for a defensive line of battle, and offered his life as a sacrifice to save it for the Union army.
The First and Eleventh Corps numbered ten thousand
killed, wounded, and captured, in the same cause, but at
the end of the day Lee's army was occupying Seminary
Ridge, while three and a half corps of the Army of the
Potomac were gathered on Cemetery Ridge, and Meade
had concluded to bring his other corps to Gettysburg
and accept the gauge of battle with Lee's invading and
triumphant army there.[1] It was a momentous decision,
and made Gettysburg the American Waterloo.

The Second Corps was already within ten miles of
the battlefield, and Meade sent word to the Fifth, which
was twenty-three miles distant, and to the Sixth,
thirty-six miles distant at Manchester,[2] to hurry forward and join the rest of the army.[3]

It was a hot summer night,[4] and we had retired by
nine o'clock, and suddenly, a little after ten o'clock, we
were aroused by the order to pack, get into line, and
move,—we in the ranks knew not whither or why. In
their hurry they led us ten miles out of our way, and we
had to retrace our steps, but all night long, with never a
halt longer than ten minutes, we trudged away. Morning came, and they allowed us only thirty minutes to
get our breakfast. As we went on, rumors of a great
battle with dubious result reached our ears, but the
farmers along the route brought us words of cheer, and
fed us with cherries and milk and cooked food of great
variety. Still we kept moving. It was a very hot day,

[1] See report of General Meade, O. R., xxvii., pt. 1, p. 115.

[2] About twenty-two miles air-line distance, besides which they went
ten miles out of their way.

[3] See Itinerary by Kirkley, O. R., xxvii., pt. 1, p. 144.

[4] 1st of July.

and as we pressed on the heat told upon the marching men. Many fell out, and when we got within four miles of our destination, orders were issued to halt and get our forces together. It was nearly two hours before we started again, but about two o'clock in the afternoon we arrived on the banks of Rock Creek, a short distance back of Little Round Top. At the point where the Thirty-seventh halted, the stream had been dammed, and there was a small mill. Within a very few minutes the soldiers had stripped off their clothing and hundreds of them were in the pond struggling for a bath. The water was full of blood-suckers; I never saw so many on any other occasion of my life. One or more was ornamenting every soldier as he emerged from the water.

Ours was the last corps of the Army of the Potomac to arrive on the field of battle. The Fifth Corps started at 7 P.M., and by a night march escaped the hot sun and reached its destination a little after 5 o'clock of the morning of the 2d. The day was one of preparation on both sides until 4 o'clock in the afternoon. Our line was shaped like a fishhook, with our right at the point of the hook. The Twelfth Corps was stationed on that flank called Culp's Hill; next, in the order named, were the Eleventh, First, Second, and Third Corps, with the Fifth and Sixth in reserve.[1]

In an endeavor to secure possession or control of the

---

[1] See report of General Meade, O. R., xxvii., pt. 1, p. 115, bottom, and top of 116, which shows the First Corps on the right of the Eleventh instead of on the left. War Map 43 (1) shows the position of the several corps on the 2d of July, with the Sixth in reserve on the right on Cemetery Hill. On the arrival of the Sixth Corps, the Fifth was ordered by General Meade "to move over to our extreme left, and the Sixth to occupy its place as a reserve for the right." [Meade's report (*supra*), p. 116.]

Emmitsburg Road, as well as of the Round Tops and the rocky field in their front called the Devil's Garden, General Sickles of the Third Corps had bent the Union line of battle to the front, and at the Peach Orchard it nearly made a right angle, and was then prolonged to the Devil's Den on its left flank. The two Round Tops were at this time only occupied for signal stations. On the Confederate side Ewell was opposite to our right flank, Hill to our centre, and Longstreet to our left.[1] Their line was five miles long, while ours was only four.[2]

After examination and consideration, General Lee decided to attack the right and left flanks, and at 4 o'clock in the afternoon, General Longstreet, under instructions from General Lee, assaulted General Sickles's exposed angle at the Peach Orchard, at the same time sending a column around our extreme left to secure possession of the two Round Tops. The attack of the Peach Orchard was overwhelming, and for two succeeding hours a terrific combat was waged between the contending forces for the supreme control of that part of the field. Longstreet succeeded in forcing our line back to the foot of Little Round Top and at one time his men had possession of Round Top— and his column pressing forward to occupy Little Round Top, met the Fifth Corps, whom General Warren had diverted from other assigned directions,[3] on the summit of the hill, and in a face-to-face, hand-to-hand grapple, with bayonets, musket butts, and deadly short-range bullets, the Union men strewed the ground with Confederate gray, and drove the shattered remnant of

[1] O. R., xxvii., pt. 2, p. 308.
[2] Position is shown on War Map 43 (1).
[3] See latter part of note, p. 103 *supra*.

the force down the precipitous sides of the hills into the plain.

The Sixth Corps was summoned to assist in driving back Longstreet's assaulting columns, and went into position at the foot of Little Round Top about five o'clock on that afternoon. While there, waiting our turn to join the deadly fray, my recollection is that our brigade was suddenly called upon to join the rescue forces on Little Round Top, and that we started on the double-quick to ascend the hill, but had not gone very far when we were halted, and after a brief delay returned to our former place with the corps.[1]

The different histories of this event speak of "two brigades of the Sixth Corps" participating in this rescue. For instance, General Walker, in his *History of the Second Army Corps*, at page 281, says, "But from Little Round Top, now firmly held by the good troops which first won it, reinforced by the Pennsylvania Reserves and two brigades of the Sixth Corps, coming in from their continuous march of thirty hours, Longstreet recoils." And later, on page 285, he says: "The brigades of Wheaton and Nevin, of the Sixth Corps, arriving from their long march, at the same time come into view alongside of Little Round Top, while Crawford's Pennsylvanians advance from the extreme left of our line. This suffices for Longstreet."

On General Reynolds's death, General Newton, our division commander, was appointed to the command of the First Corps.[2] General Wheaton succeeded him in the command of our (the Third) division, and Colonel Nevin succeeded General Wheaton in command of his (the Third) brigade. Wheaton's and Nevin's brigade

[1] See Meade's report (*supra*), p. 116.
[2] See O. R., xxvii., pt. 1, p. 155, footnote (§).

was one and the same brigade, and the brigade called
Wheaton's, which in these accounts was associated with
Nevin's, was that of General Eustis (the Second), of
which the Thirty-seventh was a member.[1] This corresponds exactly with the account given by Bowen in
his *History of the Thirty-seventh Regiment.* At page
183 he says in speaking of the culmination of Longstreet's attack and fight: "It was at this time that the
Sixth Corps—never more welcome—began to reach the
scene. Nevin's brigade (lately Wheaton's), which had
led the corps in that memorable march, swept over the
hill, pushed the Confederates back, and held the ground.
Close in their wake Eustis's brigade was in line of battle
ready to test its mettle, but it was not needed."

In Doubleday's *Chancellorsville and Gettysburg,*[2]
page 173, in writing of the advance of Ayres's division
of regulars at the "Wheatfield," it is recorded: "His
[Ayres's] return was aided by the artillery on Little
Round Top, and by the advance of part of the Sixth
Corps"; and on page 174, "As Crawford charged, two
brigades of Sedgwick's division [corps?], those of Nevin
and Wheaton [Eustis?], formed on the right and below
Little Round Top. The sight of the firm front presented by these fresh troops discouraged Longstreet,
who went forward to reconnoitre, and he gave up all
attempts at making any farther advance."

It is certain that when Longstreet's attack culminated,

---

[1] The corps organization is given in O. R., xxvii., pt. 1, p. 163:

Third Division: Maj.-Gen. John Newton. Brig.-Gen. Frank Wheaton.
First Brigade: Brig.-Gen. Alexander Shaler.
Second Brigade: Col. Henry L. Eustis (7th, 10th, and 37th Mass. and
2d R. I.).
Third Brigade: Brig.-Gen. Frank Wheaton. Col. David J. Nevin.
[2] *Campaigns of Civil War* (series), Charles Scribner's Sons, 1882.

three of his brigades, namely, those of Wofford, Kershaw,[1] and Anderson, had reached the rear of the
Wheatfield, and were close to the base of Little Round
Top. The Sixth Corps was massed there, and Wheaton's division was in the front of that corps line. Upon
Batchelder's maps of Gettysburg (second day), Nevin's
brigade is located slightly north and west of the ridge
line of Little Round Top, while the other two brigades,
to wit, Eustis's and Shaler's, of that division are located
back of the ridge line and at some distance in a southeasterly direction from Nevin's brigade. I think the
brigades were together and in the position assigned on
the map to Nevin's brigade. I distinctly remember
that our view to the front was not obstructed by trees
as it would have been had we been located where
Batchelder's map puts us. This also accords with the
position assigned to us in the accounts from which I
have above quoted. We did not fire a gun, but we
were ready to go in to the limit of our strength, if our
commanders had but given the word. When the firing
ceased and Longstreet's attack was stayed, we lay down
with muskets and swords in hand, upon a thick mat of
moss of nature's bountiful providing, which furnished
us a bed of oriental or even celestial luxury, and we slept
soundly until dawn of the 3d of July.

Meanwhile Ewell's attack on the right of our line at
Culp's Hill had so far succeeded as to capture a part of
our works, which they held during the night. General
Shaler's brigade of our division and corps was ordered
during the night to report to General Slocum of the
Twelfth Corps, and to co-operate in an attempt to dislodge the enemy. Later, during the morning of the
3d, Eustis's brigade was ordered to aid in the movement,

[1] See Kershaw's Report of the Battle, O. R., xxvii., pt. 2, p. 369.

and made the march to the right of our line, but arrived just in time to find that Culp's Hill had been recaptured and that their services were not needed.

July 3d was a day of excessive heat, and as the Sixth Corps was in reserve, it was their lot to detach brigades or regiments, as they were needed, to go to any part of the line that required strengthening or assistance, and stay until the emergency was past. In this way the corps was much scattered and divided during the day, and it did a great deal of hard work in answer to hurry calls which sent them on long errands at the double-quick. While the regiments were actually engaged or in line of battle, the regimental officers dismounted and sent their horses to a place of safety in the rear. As they were unaccustomed to foot service, these expeditions to different parts of the field on foot and at double-quick, in such a heat, bore particularly hard on them. The result was that an unusually large number of regimental officers were prostrated by the heat on that day, Colonel Edwards and Lieutenant-Colonel Montague of the Thirty-seventh among the number. As stated before, Eustis's brigade was sent to the right of the line early in the day. They returned to their position with the corps a little after one o'clock.

General Lee, finding that his two flank attacks, from which he had anticipated large and decisive results, had both proved failures, now decided to mass his artillery and to launch a selected column of fifteen thousand men into the very heart of the Union army, and by one supreme effort to conquer the North. By noon he had one hundred and forty-five guns in position ready to pour death and destruction into our lines, and for two hours the very earth shrieked and groaned with the cries of the wounded and the agonies of the dying. We were

returning from the right of the line as this *feu d'enfer*
struck us, and in less time than I can tell it we had
twenty-three men killed and wounded by their shells.
We hurried on to join our corps, but had hardly reached
them when our brigade was ordered to return to General Meade's headquarters, which we also did at the
double-quick, and we had the good fortune to reach
there just as Pickett's charge culminated.

We stood in line of battle ready to move forward to
the attack and saw thousands of Pickett's men throw
down their arms and surrender to the Union forces. It
was an inspiring scene. It was one of the few triumphs
the Army of the Potomac was permitted to enjoy.
They could only inscribe Gettysburg and Appomattox
on their banners, while the Army of Northern Virginia
boasted of triumphs from Bull Run to Petersburg. But
it was the dogged pertinacity of the North that would
not give way to discouragement, which out of disaster
wrought the final crown of success, and achieved a
victory that saved the life of the nation. We slept in
peace that night. The next day was given to quiet
and repose. It was the Fourth of July, but the silence of death reigned supreme on the battlefield.
North and South were burying their dead, and had no
thought of celebrating the anniversary of the Nation's
birth.

It was Saturday morning and the Thirty-seventh was
detailed for picket duty. The Confederates were resting under the cover of the trees. Aside from the occasional glimmer of their muskets through the foliage,
there was nothing to indicate their presence. In the
afternoon we moved back into line with the rest of the
army and built rifle-pits for our protection against a
surprise. We were located on a ledge of rocks that

made a hollow place where water accumulated and formed something of a pond. A heavy shower occurred in the middle of the night, and we found ourselves afloat, and were compelled to spend the balance of the night standing in the water. The losses of the Thirty-seventh in the battle of Gettysburg were two enlisted men killed, and twenty-six wounded and nineteen captured or missing.

When we awoke on Sunday morning, July 5th, we were startled by the intelligence that the Confederate army had gone from our front. It did not take long for us to get under way, but the weather was warm and our march very slow.

General Lee went directly west from Gettysburg, and General Meade concluded to go south and avoid a collision with Lee in the mountains. His route lay through Emmitsburg, and from there we climbed over the Catoctin Mountains and passed through Middletown and over the South Mountain Pass back of Middletown into the Valley of the Potomac.[1] It was a wild and picturesque country that we were traversing. The climb up the mountains back of Middletown was very hard. We encountered a heavy rain on the mountain-top, which cleared the atmosphere and gave us a beautiful view of the valley when we started the next morning. Lee went directly to Williamsport, where he had left a pontoon bridge to be used upon his return into Virginia, but when he got there he found that the pontoons had been destroyed by General French of the Union army,[2] and he was obliged to wait for several days before he was able to cross into Virginia. General Meade halted his army opposite that of Lee at Williams-

[1] See War Map 116 (2).
[2] O. R., xxvii., pt. 1, p. 489, top.

port and for two or three days it looked very much as if a general engagement would ensue.

At Funkstown my regiment skirmished with the Rebel army all of one day, and in the course of our pursuit of the Confederates I personally had a very narrow escape. I was directed by Colonel Edwards to explore a hill behind which the Rebels had just disappeared, and we were anxious to know whether the hill was occupied by them or had been vacated. In my explorations I had a rifle ball pass through my hat, and came very near being shot at short range with two other members of my company who were with me on the picket line at the time.

General Lee crossed the Potomac on the 14th of July, and we immediately followed the movement of his column, going down the east side of the Potomac River, while he went down the west side into the Shenandoah Valley.

On July 16th we crossed the Potomac at Berlin, and from there proceeded into Virginia on the east side of the Blue Mountain range. We made eleven miles in our first day's march into Virginia, July 19th, and on the 20th we went as far as Union, where we halted for the night. From Union we moved through Upperville on the 22d of July, and from there went to Rectortown and Salem. The whole country in this part of Virginia at this season of the year was most bountifully supplied with blackberries, sufficient to feed the Army of the Potomac. I never saw blackberries in such quantity and of such fine quality. We feasted upon them for days. We remained in this neighborhood until the end of the month.

CHAPTER VII

THE THIRTY-SEVENTH HELPS TO ENFORCE THE DRAFT IN NEW YORK CITY

JULY 30 TO OCTOBER 14, 1863

JUST at this juncture a peculiar condition of affairs existed in the metropolitan city of New York. Throughout the State, and more especially in the city of New York, there was a lawless element which had a very decided inclination at this time to sympathize with the Rebel armies in the field. New York was the most populous and wealthy State in the Union. It had a large foreign population, and that population, particularly the Irish part of it, was hostile to the negroes, and opposed to the war because they thought it was an abolition movement. Horatio Seymour was the Governor, and the constitutional commander-in-chief of its military forces. He was a popular orator, a plausible demagogue, a man of much force and ability, and a leading Democratic politician, having great influence both in the State and in the national councils of his party.

In the early part of 1863, the Federal government had decided to make an effort to add to the strength of its armies by a compulsory draft. Steps were being taken to enforce such a draft throughout the United States at the very time that the battle of Gettysburg was being fought.   Governor Seymour and the State of New York resisted the draft and threw obstacles in the way of its enforcement.

It was of great importance to the Northern armies and to the national government that the draft should be a success.   Volunteering had ceased, and we had resorted to bounties to fill our ranks.   Owing to the terrible havoc and distress of the war, appeals to patriotism no longer availed.   Once let the army in the field get the idea that they could not depend upon further re-enforcement, and they would become discouraged, and the war would come to a speedy end.   This was the crisis we were facing.   President Lincoln had ordered that the draft be enforced in the City of New York on the 13th of July, 1863.

At the appointed hour, seven o'clock, the provost marshal and his deputies were on hand with the appliances of their office to begin the work.   There was no secrecy about it.   Any citizen could attend and watch the proceedings and see that the business was honestly conducted.   The lists were transferred to slips of paper, put into a large wheel, and after the wheel had been sufficiently revolved to thoroughly stir and mix the slips, a blindfolded man drew from the wheel the names of those whom the law said must serve as soldiers, or furnish a substitute, unless they could prove themselves disqualified for service by age or other incapacity. The poor man immediately said he was discriminated against because he could not pay for a substitute, and suddenly swarms of angry women and infuriated men began to gather in the streets and with bricks, paving stones, and clubs to assault the offices of the provost marshal.   Windows were smashed, the furniture was destroyed, the officers fled for their lives, the buildings were fired, and for four days the city was delivered over to the drunken fury of the mob. The police were powerless. The city militia had gone to Gettysburg in answer to the Governor's call. Colored orphan asylums were set on fire. Negroes were hunted like wild beasts. The houses and homes of the abolitionists and the offices of the newspapers were threatened with destruction, and in many instances barricaded and guarded by armed men. Volunteers and veterans protected the armories and the arsenals, and a few gunboats were anchored in the river to warn the mob of impending retribution at the hands of the national government. Meanwhile the militia began to return, and President Lincoln agreed to postpone the enforcement of the draft until the 19th of August.

On July 30th the order from which the following is extracted was issued:

HEADQUARTERS ARMY OF THE POTOMAC,
July 30, 1863.

Special Orders, No. 202.

VII. Pursuant to instructions which have been received from the general-in-chief, four regiments of this army will immediately proceed to New York Harbor, and, on arriving there, will be reported to Brig.-Gen. E. R. S. Canby. Two of these regiments will be taken from the Third Corps and two from the Sixth Corps, and will be selected preferably from Western and New England regiments. No New York or Pennsylvania troops will be sent. The corps commanders named will detach for duty strong and efficient regiments, and will have them march to-morrow morning, in season to reach Warrenton Junction by 11 A.M.

By command of Major-General Meade:
S. WILLIAMS, *Assistant Adjutant-General.*[1]

[1] O. R., xxvii., pt. 3, p. 787.

On July 31st General Meade reported to General Halleck that the First and Thirty-seventh Massachusetts, Fifth Wisconsin, and Twentieth Indiana were ordered to New York Harbor; aggregate present for duty 1643 men, Colonel Edwards in command.[1]

At midnight of July 30th we were awakened by the startling announcement that we were to start for New York at three o'clock A.M. to assist in enforcing the draft. No more sleep for us that night. We began to pack immediately, and got our breakfast and were ready to start at three A.M., but as usual, on such occasions, the movement was delayed and we did not start until five. Then we marched to Warrenton Junction, ten miles, arriving there at ten-thirty in the morning. We were loaded on freight cars and taken to Alexandria, where we arrived at three o'clock that afternoon. We devoured what pies and cakes we could find at hand in the streets of Alexandria during our short stay there, and then went forward to Washington, where we arrived at five o'clock, and had more pies and cakes. In addition to this we were taken to some barracks and fed on the same kind of rations which were served to us on the occasion of our first visit to Washington. They tasted a little better than they had on the first occasion, because we had become accustomed to that kind of fare, but they did not taste half as good as the street pies and cakes that we picked up along the highway.

We left Washington at midnight and reached Baltimore at eight o'clock the next morning. Here we were fed on lemonade and cake on the streets, which again tasted wonderfully good to our starved stomachs. We left Baltimore at noon and passed through Havre de Grace and reached Philadelphia at eight o'clock that

[1] O. R., xxvii., pt. 1, p. 108.

night, where as usual we had a feast that was fit for the
gods.   From Philadelphia we rode in passenger cars,
which made us feel that we were once more in the country where we were recognized as human beings.   From
there they carried us over the old Camden and Amboy
route to Amboy, where we arrived at eight o'clock
Sunday morning, August 2d, and by nine o'clock were
on board a boat sailing up the magnificent harbor of
New York.   We landed at the Battery at ten o'clock of
that day.

To breathe the sea air and enjoy the refreshing sights
and scenes of a civilized city like New York seemed
like Elysium.   We looked like tramps, but we did not
mind that.   We knew we were welcome, and never
before had the Battery looked so beautiful.   We
marched up Broadway to the City Hall Park, dined at
the Massachusetts Relief rooms just opposite, and then
marched back to the Battery.   There we learned that
our destination was Fort Hamilton, which we reached
at five o'clock that afternoon, and drew tents and
pitched camp as rapidly as possible.   We were prepared
to find any spot attractive after the experiences which
we had passed through, but this seemed like a visit to a
watering place in the midst of the heat of summer, and
all at Uncle Sam's expense.   Good bathing privileges
were given us on the shore a short distance from our
camp, and the next few days we luxuriated in sea bathing.   But it was not all as fine as it looked.   We had
not been there many days before the regiments began
to be afflicted with fever and ague, and as a consequence
we suffered from fever and ague for years afterwards.
The camp was located on the borders of a muddy marsh,
and malaria became epidemic.

Of course we managed to communicate at once with

our friends and let them know that we had unexpectedly come to New York. My father and mother and brothers at the time were making a visit to Binghamton, New York, and they were as much surprised when they received my telegram announcing my presence in New York City as I was at being there. It did not take them very long to come to the city and look me over and see that I was veritably in the flesh, and during the next fortnight we had much pleasant visiting, not only from our relatives, but from friends who happened to know of our presence and took occasion to call upon us. We were allowed more or less liberty in going to the city and in making calls and visits upon our friends there. Of course we were treated with great consideration and had every attention that heart could desire or love bestow.

At Fort Hamilton we were encamped with a company of regulars, and our drill and dress-parade were consequently brought into comparison with theirs. This put us upon our mettle and we did our best to maintain the reputation of the Thirty-seventh for military proficiency.

August 6th was celebrated as a day of special thanksgiving appointed by President Lincoln[1] in recognition of the blessings vouchsafed to the national arms in the victories at Gettysburg and Vicksburg. We celebrated the day as a sort of thanksgiving festival, which the presence of our friends made an occasion of thorough enjoyment. Thus the happy days passed until on the 18th day of August, after dress parade, we received the announcement that our presence would be required in the city on the following day to see that the draft was duly and regularly made.

[1] *Complete Works* (Nicolay and Hay), vol. ii., p. 370.

We at once exchanged our dress suits for our rough campaign suits, were embarked on board a steamboat at the wharf, carried to New York, and disembarked at the Battery, with sixty rounds of ammunition in our cartridge boxes. We passed the night at the Battery, and in the early morning marched up Broadway to Washington Square, where the regiment went into camp and details were made from the various companies and sent to the drafting places to enforce the draft.

Everything was as quiet and orderly as a New England Sabbath. No disturbance occurred anywhere, and in the evening the various details were gathered again in the park and we slept with our guards and pickets thrown out as if we were in the enemy's country, and on the following afternoon the regiment again marched down Broadway to the Battery and embarked on the boat and returned to Fort Hamilton, where our drills and inspections and guard-mountings and parades under the eye of the regulars were resumed.

Colonel Edwards thought this a good time for him to be married and accordingly left us to our own devices, went west to Illinois, and very soon returned with his bride, a charming lady, full of Western vivacity and life. She was immediately adopted by the regiment, and from time to time made us very pleasant visits.

We remained at Fort Hamilton until the 12th of September, when we received orders to pack and to go into camp in the city of New York. The ground selected as a camp for us to occupy was located on Fifth Avenue, between 48th and 49th Streets, near the Catholic Cathedral. Think of residing on Fifth Avenue even for a short space of time after having wallowed in the mud of Virginia! It was like dreamland.

Our camp was immediately the centre of interest there and the ladies of the neighborhood feasted us with all the delicacies that heart could desire. We had daily guard-mountings and dress-parades, attended by large audiences from Fifth Avenue and its vicinity, and long lines of carriages stood waiting on the avenue in front of our quarters, occupied by fair maidens who daily resorted there to witness our proficiency and to encourage us by their presence.

On September 15th, I was sent with a detail, composed of my own company and another company from the regiment, to report to police headquarters at 300 Mulberry Street. My duty there was to receive and take charge of deserters and conscripts who were arrested and brought in by the police each day, and to return them to their regiments in the neighborhood of Washington. I had a large room assigned to me for my office at police headquarters with the two companies lodged in the building to act under my orders. I felt very much like a New York police commissioner with an independent police force. My time was very largely my own, so that I could call on friends or occasionally go to the theatre, always provided I was on hand when the General sent for me to report at his headquarters, which circumstance did not occur more than twice while I was there. This lasted until the 6th of October, when the detail at police headquarters was discontinued, and we rejoined the regiment at Fifth Avenue.

On October 10th I went home to Amherst on leave of absence for ten days, and during my absence the regiment received orders from Washington directing its return to Virginia, which was accordingly undertaken on the 14th of October, 1863. Breaking camp at 8 o'clock in the morning and marching down Fifth

Avenue and Broadway to the foot of Murray Street, they embarked on a steamer and took the cars for Philadelphia. The cause of their return was General Lee's movement against the Army of the Potomac, which resulted in the battle of Bristoe Station, on October 14th.

This New York episode in our career was always remembered as an experience of unusual pleasure such as is rarely accorded to a soldier. We were gratified at being selected for the service, as it was regarded as a special compliment to our reliability as soldiers. It was a picnic that lasted two months and a half, and aside from the fever and ague which we contracted at Fort Hamilton and which stayed with us during the remainder of our term of service, no more enjoyable trip could have been furnished us.

CAPTAIN MASON W. TYLER.

From a photograph taken in 1863 or 1864.

CHAPTER VIII

FROM FAIRFAX COURT-HOUSE TO BRANDY STATION

OCTOBER 16, 1863, TO MARCH 10, 1864

A FTER such an outing, it was hard work to settle down again to hardtack and salt pork, but every feast has its day of retribution. We now had to give up Fifth Avenue and return to the mud huts of Virginia. We reached Fairfax Station about noon, October 16th. It was raining hard. We disembarked and marched to Fairfax Court-House and went to bed in the mud. During the night it cleared and we resumed our march in the morning, going as far as Chantilly, where we rejoined the Sixth Corps and pursued our route to Gainesville and Warrenton. These are classic names in the history of the Army of the Potomac. It was from Warrenton that we left the Army of the Potomac to go to New York. So we were once more back at our starting point after a three months' absence, and our usual routine of picket and inspections and the making of returns commenced, and kept us busy.

In one of my letters, dated November 1st, from the vicinity of Warrenton, I write:

We are stationed on one of the highest hills in the neighborhood. We overlook the surrounding country for miles.

It is a fine prospect.   Hills covered with a beautiful variegated foliage, now in the last stages of their summer glory,
lie in all directions about us, except to the west, where the
Blue Ridge commands a superior homage on account of its
heights.   This is a hilly country, and prettily situated farmhouses dot almost every mountain notch.   The houses are
small and the farms neglected.   My company is scattered
over half a mile of territory, and every little while I am
interrupted by some one wanting to pass through the lines
or a countryman desiring to sell something to the boys.
Wood is scarce; we have to go a mile for our camp supply.
Water also is scarce.

At the time of his advance to Bristoe Station, General
Lee had done all that he could to destroy the railroad
between Warrenton Junction and the Rapidan.   He
had burned the ties, taken up the rails and carried them
away.   Evidently General Meade had decided to
winter his army upon the Rapidan.   It would be
strategically well situated for watching both the Valley
of the Shenandoah on the west and the approaches to
Washington east of the Blue Ridge.   It was about
sixty miles southwest of Washington and was connected by this one line of single-track railway.   Near
the point where the railroad crossed the Rappahannock,
the Confederates had erected a fort, two redoubts,
and several lines of rifle trenches, and these were held
by two thousand men belonging to Early's division of
Ewell's corps.

On Saturday, November 7th, the Sixth Corps left
their camp near Warrenton at five o'clock in the morning, and marched fourteen miles to Rappahannock
Station.   Upon their arrival there they at once formed
line of battle, and our division, under the command of
General Terry, assaulted the redoubt and works and

carried them by storm.   The assaulting column was
led by Brigadier-Generals Russell and Upton, of the
Sixth Corps, who in the most gallant manner conducted
their men over the escarpment of the fort.   By the
free use of the bayonet and with clubbed muskets they
overpowered the garrison, and captured more than
1700 men and seven pieces of artillery.   The Second
Rhode Island and Thirty-seventh Massachusetts were
with Wheaton's brigade on the right of the line supporting the skirmish line composed of the Tenth and
Seventh Massachusetts regiments.[1]

On November 8th we were awakened at four-thirty
A.M., and marched at six, going with the Fifth Corps
to Kelly's Ford, eight miles below Rappahannock
Station on the river.   We remained here until the 12th,
and then returned to Rappahannock Station, crossed
the river, and advanced to where we went into winter
quarters.[2]

---

[1] See General Terry's report, O. R., xxix., pt. 1, p. 605.

In a letter to his parents dated November 8, 1863, M. W. T. wrote
of the advance to Rappahannock Station: "We marched beside the
track of the Culpeper Railroad a good deal of the way.   Such a complete destruction as the Rebs have effected I never saw nor realized
before.   The rails are all carried off and the sleepers are burned.   Four
o'clock found us formed in line of battle, and the contest raged until
long after dark, when the final charge was made into the Rebel works,
taking their first breastworks, seventeen hundred men, and seven pieces
of artillery, rumor says.   It was quite a spirited little affair for a couple
of hours, although most of the firing and fighting was done by the skirmishers, who were very strong.   We lay on the right of the line supporting the Tenth and Seventh, who were on the skirmish line, but too far
to the right to get the heaviest of it.   We, however, could see the most
of it, and the cheers of the combatants told us how the conflict was raging, and we knew very soon of our success after it was achieved."

[2] In a letter to his brother Henry, November 13, 1863, he wrote from
Brandy Station: "I have been reading pretty much all day on 'Military
Law and Courts-Martial.'   Too much reading out here stretched on
your back in your shelter low tents is not the best thing in the world to

General Sedgwick occupied a house owned by John Minor Botts[1] for his headquarters.   I built my own house with a stone chimney this year; heretofore our chimneys had been of wood, thickly plastered with mud on the inside, and with a wooden barrel on top. They sometimes caught fire, but not often.   At this time we belonged to the Second Brigade, Third Division, Sixth Corps.[2]   My diary indicates an unusual amount

take.   It is rather too apt to produce headache, etc.   To be sure, writing sitting on the floor is not much more comfortable, but by varying the two I manage to get along.   We have got into a miserable camp this time.   It is so low where the company streets are situated that if it should rain a single day we should be swamped.   Meanwhile, the boys are busy at work building log huts.   The great trouble is that wood is so scarce that, like the Egyptians of old, it is making bricks without straw. . . .

"The Rebs had got all ready to go into winter quarters.   They had built nice houses in this immediate vicinity that are now occupied by the First Division of our corps.   They evidently were very much surprised at our coming on this side of the Rappahannock.   The railroad is not destroyed, but left entire on this side, and every indication shows that they had settled down to a winter's quiet.   I think it a great pity, now that we have got started, that we don't push right on to Richmond and drive them before us, and trust to the railroad, either this route or the Aquia Creek Line, to supply our wants after we get there.   But that is not Meade, you know.   He never risks anything, but often loses good opportunities by his caution.   The army is in prime condition now, and would like to fight a decisive battle here. . . .

"You must excuse my writing with a pencil, but I have no ink, and I have to borrow so much for my government writing that I hate to borrow when I can help it.   The drums are just beating for retreat.   If you had to be drummed out to the notes of that infernal drum three or ten times a day, according as it happens, you would growl, I know, when you heard it beat.   Accordingly, as I have just been out and attended roll call, I think I have done my duty by the drum this time, and may afford to be cool once more.

"After supper.   I have just been feasting off from a big plate of cakes. They went right to the spot, I assure you.   It is getting rather dark and I must close."

Another letter reads: "Brandy Station, November 15, 1863.

[1] Shown on War Map 87 (2) and (3).   [2] O. R., xxix., pt. 2, p. 605.

of calling and sociability in the regiment during this month. One day I had a visit from Horace Binny, who was a captain on General Neill's staff. Another day Captain Hutchinson of the Forty-ninth Pennsylvania called. Captain Lincoln and I usually spent our evenings together either at his tent or at mine. On November 20th there was a baseball game between the Tenth and Thirty-seventh, and the Thirty-seventh won.

We kept hearing rumors that there was to be a move

My dear Parents: We have had rather an excited, uncertain sort of a Sunday. In the first place, it stormed so hard last night that our camp is all flooded, and the tents are mostly pitched in the midst of the many mud puddles that form our camp. It rained very hard until about ten o'clock this morning, up to which time we had all we could do to keep from being carried off bodily. Then it suddenly cleared off with a rainbow. Just as it cleared off, cannonading commenced over to the east of us, and within twenty minutes we received orders to pack and be ready to move at a moment's notice. So we packed, but hearing nothing further from the Rebs and their supposed attack we got orders to move camp, so we pitched on the side hill, rather than in the mud. By this time it was noon, and we received notice from the quartermaster's department that they had clothing ready to issue to the regiment. So we got our clothing, and ate dinner, and now I have managed to get time enough to write my Sunday letter. I have managed to read the *Independent* and *Congregationalist* at odd spells, while waiting for things to progress, and standing over the fire drying myself. Last night at sundown, the real old Saturday night feeling came over me, and I lay in my tent a good share of the evening, thinking in the dark, while outside it was raining hard. I thought of you gathered around your cheerful fireside, and with your work all laid aside for the pleasant Sunday books, and the papers in each and all of your hands. I could see you perfectly. I thought you looked very comfortable. I only wished I could step in on you for a moment, and a second thought told me I should disturb all that quiet repose, and as it was, we were both very peacefully enjoying ourselves. So perhaps it was best as it was. At any rate, I comforted myself with the thought. It is after dark. It seems as if the days grow dark earlier out here than they used to at home. My present accommodations are not conducive to long letters. If I had a desk to write on I should feel like writing another sheet, but as it is I have to sit like a Turk—cross-legged—and it is not very comfortable, so good-night. Ever your affectionate son, Mason."

of some sort.   We had never attempted a winter campaign, and of course we were very incredulous about the possibility of such a thing, but it was finally attempted.   On November 26th, Thanksgiving Day, we suddenly received marching orders.   We were awakened at four A.M., breakfasted, packed and started at eight.   We moved a half-mile, then we were halted, and the news of Grant's success at Chattanooga was promulgated to the army.   Hooker and Thomas were also mentioned.   We then proceeded on our way, but as it had recently rained, we were much troubled by muddy roads.   Our Thanksgiving dinner was bread and butter.   We made very slow progress, but kept at it persistently, and at ten that evening we found ourselves at Jacob's Mill Ford—having marched a distance of twelve miles.   We remained over the next day at Jacob's Mill Ford to superintend the passage of the trains across the river.

On Saturday, the 28th, we started at one A.M., got under way at two, and overtook the rest of the corps at seven A.M. at Robertson's Tavern, where we united with the left of the Second Corps.   The greater part of the day on Saturday was devoted to the making of a reconnoissance, conducted in the rain, which with the wind greatly delayed our operations.   On Sunday, the 29th, we were awakened at four-thirty A.M., and our division was directed to go with the Second Corps and make a detour around the right of the Rebel position.   We marched some ten or twelve miles through the woods until we struck the Plank Road.   Meanwhile, the rain had ceased and it had cleared off cold.   Our movements had been delayed so seriously by various mishaps that we were obliged to abandon all hope of surprising the enemy, and on Monday morning after a

careful survey of the situation made by Generals Warren and Sedgwick, it was decided to return to camp.
At dark we moved back three miles and encamped in
the woods.[1]

[1] This was the Mine Run campaign. Lee's army was "found to be
spread out for some 20 miles over the country beyond the Rapidan, with
the fords of that river imperfectly guarded. Meade's plan of operations
contemplated a rapid movement of his own army by different routes,
penetrating between the separated corps of his antagonist and fighting
and defeating them in detail" (Bowen, p. 235).

At page 240, Bowen continues: "Having advanced as far as practicable without a conflict, General Meade disposed his army in front of
the Run. . . . General Sedgwick with his First and Second Divisions
was thrown well to the right, while his Third Division [Terry's] . . .
was detached to co-operate with the Second Corps in feeling for a more
vulnerable point to the left.

"Accordingly the men of the Thirty-seventh found themselves
aroused at 1 o'clock in the morning of Sunday, the 29th, drew a small
additional supply of rations, and before daylight were on their way,
passing Robertson's Tavern, through to the plank road and beyond it,
around the head of Mine Run, the advance skirmishing continually with
the enemy's outposts and driving them back till near night, when General Warren, believing that he had found a comparatively weak point,
so reported to Meade and disposed his forces for the attack whenever it
should be ordered. General Sedgwick from the right also reported that
he deemed an assault in his front practicable. General Warren was
strengthened with two divisions from the Third Corps and directed to
attack at 8 o'clock next morning in connection with a heavy artillery
fire from the centre, while Sedgwick was to 'go in' an hour later.

"The Thirty-seventh were in reserve during the night of the 29th,
lying on their arms and sleeping as much as possible in the intense cold,
which had now become so intolerable that men were frozen to death on
the picket line. Early in the morning the regiment was moved forward
to the front line, taking position on the extreme left. It was terribly
uncomfortable lying upon the frozen ground hour after hour waiting for
the signal to spring to their feet and dash forward into the face of death,
and the men would almost have welcomed the command, since it would
have stirred the blood and warmed the benumbed limbs, but it did not
come. The morning's inspection of the works in his front revealed to
Warren that his intention to attack had been anticipated. . . . The
plan of attack which on the previous afternoon had seemed feasible was
now seen to be hazardous to the degree of rashness, . . . and reluctantly

We rested in a forest of pine the next day.   It was a wild November scene; God's canopy overhead, the sighing of the pine branches in the chill autumnal winds, make it memorable through the long years that have intervened.

Frank Walker dropped in upon me that morning, and was cheery as usual.   On Wednesday, we resumed our march.   In a letter written home at this time I say:

I suppose we are somewhere in the vicinity of Verdier-ville, fourteen miles from Orange Court-House.   But I know nothing except as I judge from the distance and direc-tion we have marched.   In fact, no one in the brigade seems to know exactly where we are.   The fact is, we have moved all ways, north, south, east, and west, until even our brigade commanders are at a loss to know our whereabouts. Day before yesterday General Eustis could n't tell within ten miles of where we were.[1]

the orders were issued which should record upon the movement the verdict of 'failure.'

"All day the Thirty-seventh remained in their uncomfortable position, the skirmishers and sharpshooters in front keeping up an incessant fusillade, though by rare good fortune the loss was only one or two men wounded."

The advanced position of the Third Division, Sixth Corps, is shown on War Map 87 (1).

[1] The letter here referred to, dated "Camp-in-the-Woods, December 1, 1863," is addressed to his parents, and continues: "I have not writ-ten since we started because there has been no chance to send or to write. Thanksgiving morning we started and moved through mud very slowly until about ten P.M. when we crossed the Rapidan at Jacob's Ford. We stopped at the ford Friday.   Friday afternoon the Third Corps, rein-forced by one division of our corps, had a small fight with the Rebs, about three miles from where we were, and we, meanwhile, were in line of battle ready to fight if called on.   Friday night we started about twelve o'clock, and marched until about eleven o'clock Saturday through the rain and mud, when we came up with the enemy, confronted by the Second Corps, in the immediate vicinity of Mine Run, as near as I can find out.   We stayed there Saturday.   Sunday morning our division

On Tuesday, December 1st, after we had nice large fires going and were thinking of being very comfortable for the night, we received orders at about eight-thirty P.M. to very quietly pack up and move.   In five minutes we were on our way, and during the next three hours we made between ten and twelve miles.   We were on the double-quick most of the time.   It was very cold, hence running only warmed us.   We crossed the Rapidan at Ely's Ford at seven A.M., December 2d.   Then we rested.   I slept two hours.   We started again at noon and marched until dark twelve miles to Brandy Station, which was only four miles from our camp, where we arrived early the next day.   We were tired and footsore, and very glad to get home; no rations that day, and only one meal the day before.   The Mine Run campaign was the most vexatious we had experienced up to this time.

The Thirty-seventh had two men wounded during this expedition.[1]   But if the orders to attack Lee in his entrenchments had not been countermanded, I fear that it would have been classed with Fredericksburg and Cold Harbor, among the blunders of the Army of the Potomac.

---

was ordered to join the Second Corps, and with them we marched all day Sunday, moving about twelve miles, around the right flank of the Rebs.   When we halted for the night we were said to be only two miles distant from our starting point.   We made a wide detour.

"We stopped yesterday in line of battle all day, within a mile of where we halted Sunday night, expecting an attack every moment.   There was some cannonading going on all day, and occasionally a stray shot would come whizzing over our heads.   Now and then there was a man wounded.   There was only one man wounded in our regiment.   At night they moved us back three miles, and here we are this terribly cold morning 'in the woods,' making big fires and trying to keep warm.   I am in tip-top health and spirits.   I carry my own knapsack, weighing about twenty-five pounds."

[1] O. R., xxix., pt. 1, p. 684.

We were hardly settled in camp when we began to hear rumors of further movements. The fear of such movements perpetually haunted us. This was the army bugaboo. We lived in constant expectation of orders to move. And I don't believe there is any place where rumors start so easily and grow so fast as they do in the army. The air was full of them the greater part of the time. As was usually the case, this particular rumor of a movement did not materialize. It was not many days, however, before we did move our camp a short distance, and we were informed that we might build with the expectation of spending the winter. I had already built two houses with that expectation, and now went to work to build a third.

December 8th, Tuesday, was very cold. I was up early to move timbers and build a winter hut. I built the best chimney in camp. Axes were scarce, everybody was building. That night I slept on poles, took cold, and was sore and stiff for several days. To be sure, these houses were not very elaborate, but we found them very comfortable. They were twelve feet long by seven wide, and made of split logs with the cracks filled with mud, with a chimney made of stones or wood at one end. The roofs were made of the shelter tents which we used for tents when we were engaged in the campaign. Our beds were in the form of bunks, two tiers in height, with poles to sleep on. They were located at the end of the house opposite the fireplace, and the poles when covered with blankets made comfortable beds. In the middle of one side of the house there was a table improvised from cracker boxes, and in front of it a bench made from a log and used for a settee.[1] I

[1] In a letter to his parents, dated "Camp near Brandy Station, November 19, 1863," he wrote: "I have built myself a very cozy house

sent home and had them send me a volume of Black-
stone, with which I whiled away some of my leisure
hours, and they also sent me *Les Miserables*, a copy of
Corinne, Charles O'Malley, and Napier's *Peninsular War*,
so that I had no lack of good literature. [1]

During the month of December I had an attack of
malarial fever, which sent me to the hospital for a few
days. But aside from this, I was able to perform all
the duties that were required of me. We lived very
comfortably this winter. My diary speaks of large
supplies of oysters being sent to the army from Wash-

---

with a stone fireplace at one end, and a small table, at which I am writing, and a good bed that occupies nearly half the tent. We built the
bed for three in anticipation of Lieutenant Harris's return."

[1] In a letter to his mother, from Brandy Station, January 31, 1864,
he wrote: "It has been a pretty busy week to me. Busy not with my
military labors, but with self-imposed labors and pleasures. I have
read two stories. Early in the week I began *The Old Curiosity Shop*,
and finished it Thursday. Then yesterday I finished *The Last Days
of Pompeii*, which I consider one of the best and most powerful stories
I have ever read. I am accomplishing a good deal this winter in the
reading line, and enjoying it much, too. The fact is, I sit in my tent
and read the most of the day, except when I am occupied with my camp
duties, which only occupy me two or three hours a day. I rarely go to
bed before twelve o'clock, because if I do I am sure to lie awake in the
morning. So this makes me quite a long day. Sometimes we get up a
game of ball, and now we have some apparatus for gymnastics, that
occupies some of my time.

"Quite often, the early part of the evening, I engage in a game of
chess or checkers or whist, until about nine o'clock, when I go to reading
again.

"So I have given you a pretty good account of how I spend my time.
You can imagine that I devote some time of each day to writing letters.
That I usually do in the evening.

"Last evening about eight o'clock we received the summons from the
colonel to repair to his tent, and going over found his table spread with
all sorts of delicacies from home, and he invited us to partake in com-
memoration of his birthday. So we spent a jolly hour with the colonel,
and then returned to our tents."

ington.   We always had an abundant supply of soft
bread furnished by our commissaries when we were in
winter quarters.   Borden's condensed milk in cans was
one of the luxuries invented at this time for our delec-
tation and comfort.

During the month of January I spent a few days in
Washington, and while there I was taken to the White
House by Mr. Washburn, our representative in Congress, and presented to President Lincoln.   I have no
recollection of what was said at the interview, but the
fact that I saw him during that visit is indelibly stamped
upon my memory, as it was the only occasion when I
shook hands with him.   During this visit I met General Caldwell at the Metropolitan Hotel, and he invited
me to dine with him.   The General was very free in his
criticisms of men and measures.   He was a man of
superior literary tastes.   Among other things he advised me to read Austin's *Jurisprudence*, for the mental
and legal training that the book afforded.

As the winter progressed, wood for camp use grew
very scarce.   Every cord that we used had to be drawn
by teams from two to four miles.   Under these circumstances we had to be very economical in making fires,
and sometimes we were cold.   Our picket line was six
miles distant from our camp, and the picket details were
made for a week each, so that the men might not have
to go out too many times in the season.   I think I was
not detailed for picket duty more than twice during the
entire winter.   The rules applicable to picket duty were
very strictly enforced, and every precaution was taken
to avoid a surprise.   The corps officer of the day was in
the habit of spending a good deal of time during his
tour of duty on the lines, and woe betide the sentinel
that was inclined to be lax in the performance of his

duties. No effort was spared to make the pickets alert, and as a consequence there was little rest for either the officers or the men during the week that they were detailed for such service.[1]

Three times during this season I was favored with a box of dainties from home, and the men in the company were also remembered and favored in the same way. We had a thirty-pound turkey sent down to us, which was the wonder of the camp. And no dish that was ever concocted was quite so palatable as the mince pies which, during that winter, they sent us from home.

Our camp amusements also were some of them very homelike. Our chaplain used to hold spelling contests, and we had a debating club that was very well patronized. The chaplain had a small building which, after the fashion of New England, he used for both church and school purposes. Here the voice of prayer and song were heard. Music exercises a strange spell over

[1] In a letter to his parents from Brandy Station, February 5, 1864, he wrote:

"I have been out on picket during the last week, so that you have not got your accustomed supply of letters this week, and I am afraid I shall not write a very long one this time, because I am very tired with being up a good deal nights, and marching six miles in coming back to camp. For our picket line is out some six miles. . . . The first day I was out there, there was a very heavy mist, and that night we had quite a severe thunder storm, the first of the season. We had no tents up, and nothing but rails over us to keep the rain off. I, however, kept dry by dint of my rubber overcoat. I slept passably well that night, and at three in the morning, when I had to take my turn at watching, the rain had ceased, and the wind begun to spring up quite cold. Wednesday it was sunny, but cold and windy. We built enormous fires from the oak and maple trees around us, and kept very warm indeed, in fact at our fire alone we kept one good chopper busy cutting down timber and piling it onto the fire. We burned at the rate of about a cord and a half a day. The line that I had command of was almost two miles long, so that it gave me something of a job to go through the length of it once a day. While out on picket I read Bulwer Lytton's *Rienzi*."

the soldier. We had many fine bands which cheered and inspired our life in camp. A man named Stearns in Company F, who usually answered to the sobriquet of the "old hoss," had a wonderfully clear and penetrating voice, and often when everybody was exhausted, in the loneliness of our night and forest marches, he would make the woods ring with a strain of music that seemed to be audible for miles, and gave new life and encouragement to the weary soldier.

During this winter the officers in the regiment drew lots to determine the order in which they would take their leaves of absence, and my lot gave me the eighteenth turn. It looked very doubtful whether I could get my leave, and finally I went without it. During March and April I was engaged in court-martial, and most of the time was acting as Judge Advocate. I was glad to have this experience, as I had decided to make the law my profession, and the experience that I acquired in trying these cases was of some value to me in after years. It gave me some experience in examining witnesses and eliciting testimony. It also brought me in contact with the field officers of other regiments, and enabled me to make many pleasant acquaintances. Our court-martial sat at the headquarters of the Vermont brigade, and there was no better brigade in the army.

Several of our classmates took advantage of Captain Lincoln's and my presence in the army to get a taste of army life. Dr. Shepard was studying dentistry, and to get a little experience in the line of his profession, he came down to the army and made us a visit, and we got the quartermaster to furnish him a tent and he practised on our teeth for nearly a month. He thus did us a favor and benefited himself, at the same time.

M. F. Dickinson[1] promised to come down and spend a couple of weeks with us, but he delayed so long that when he arrived at Washington the army was ready to move, and the government officers at Washington were refusing passes to all applicants who wanted to visit the Army of the Potomac. We finally made an arrangement with our sutler to go to Washington and bring Dickinson down in the guise of a sutler's clerk. Another classmate of ours, by the name of Houghton, came to Washington about the same time, and he got through the lines as an employee of the Christian Commission. We five classmates spent our evenings together at either Lincoln's or my quarters during the greater part of the month of April, and had very jolly times.

From February 28th to March 4th, the Sixth Corps were engaged with the cavalry under General Kilpatrick in an unsuccessful attempt to release the Union prisoners held at Richmond. General Kilpatrick crossed the Rapidan at Ely's Ford, and then despatched Colonel Dahlgren with a picked force of five hundred men to try to enter the defences of Richmond and release the prisoners, while the Sixth Corps kept Lee's army occupied by a feigned attack on his lines in front of the Army of the Potomac. The following lines in my diary refer to our part in this fiasco:

February 27, 1864. Six A.M. arose and packed. Started at 9 A.M. Marched by John Minor Botts' house through Culpeper, and reached James City near Thoroughfare Mountain at 4.30 P.M. I saw an old man and three ladies who lived in a house near the picket line. They told me that flour was $250 a barrel.

My boots were very bad and out of shape, and the consequence was by the time we got to Culpeper, I had two

[1] A college classmate.

good blisters, one on each heel, and each as large as a walnut. But I stuck to it until we arrived at James City, where we stopped for the night. There, by means of bathing and soaking my feet and stockings, I slightly improved my condition. Just as I got settled supposedly for the night, I was detailed with one hundred men for picket duty. It required all my grit to submit and not to shirk or ask to be excused. So I limped up and down that picket line all that weary night.

February 28, 1864. Slept four or five hours last night. Am very lame this morning. Returned to the regiment about 8 o'clock and started to march at 9.30. Reached Robertson's River (a distance of eight miles) about one, and stopped to build a bridge. About 2 P.M. we crossed and bivouacked for the night. Torbert's brigade was in the advance, and occupied Madison Court-House. All the rest of the corps, with the exception of our brigade, stayed on the other side of the river.

Monday, February 29th, we rested, and found it pleasant. Early in the morning, Custer with his cavalry started out and we were to wait for his return before we could turn our faces homeward. Monday night it commenced to rain. I took no shelter tent with me on the reconnoissance, and so had to lie in the open and take it as it came down, filtered by some rails which we put over us.

March 1st, Tuesday, was a very disagreeable day. Rain and mud with a cold air beat pitilessly on man and beast. About 5.30 P.M. Custer and his cavalry appeared, and we waded and ploughed through the mud and the dark until we found a proper place on the north side of the river, and there encamped for the night. We kept up good fires and managed to be tolerably comfortable. We could hear distant firing. But the wagons that had our blankets were not to be found.

Consequently, the officers in our brigade spent a sleepless night. We gathered around large fires and told stories, and the drinkers drank whiskey, and we waited for the dawn. It cleared off during the night, and became cold.

March 2, 1864. Some twenty or thirty darkies passed by us this morning in all sorts of rigs, and in all sorts of sizes, with a great variety of property. Our marching column started about 7. We marched very rapidly. About 3 P.M. we reached Culpeper. Marched through the town to music. Arrived at our camp about 5 P.M., having made twenty-three miles. You can hardly imagine how good a log cabin feels after such an expedition. Words cannot describe how hard I slept that night. Two almost sleepless nights and a long hard march in the mud made me unusually tired, and I went to sleep and slept eleven hours.[1]

Meanwhile, on March 10th, General U. S. Grant had been promoted to the rank of lieutenant-general, and appointed commander-in-chief of all armies in the field. He had the prestige of success in the West, and he brought with him to his new field of operations the reputation of being always ready to fight, of having won Vicksburg by his brilliant strategy, and conquered at Chattanooga by his indomitable courage. He was now to be matched against the ablest commander that the war had produced. We knew that it meant a battle royal, but we had no conception of what was before us. The past was mere child's play in comparison with what we were now to encounter. Little

---

[1] A note in M. W. T.'s handwriting on the margin of his copy of Bowen's history remarks: "I marched on this expedition with a blistered heel, and the scar still remains. My boots did not fit well, and chafed my heel, until the last day I limped on my toe the twenty miles."

did we reck that within thirty days after the campaign opened fifty thousand of our comrades would be numbered among the killed and wounded.

General Grant commenced by reorganizing the Army of the Potomac in three infantry corps, to wit, the Second, Fifth, and Sixth, and one cavalry corps under command of General Sheridan, and maintained the Ninth Corps as a separate organization under command of General Burnside. The First and Third Corps organizations were discontinued, and the regiments from these corps were transferred to the corps whose organizations were retained. By this operation Eustis's brigade became the Fourth Brigade of the Second Division of the Sixth Corps, and General George W. Getty became the commander of that division.

CHAPTER IX

THE WILDERNESS

MAY 4, 5, AND 6, 1864

THE Thirty-seventh had now been in the service twenty-one months. Considering the fact that it had borne its part in five such battles as First and Second Fredericksburg, Salem Heights, Gettysburg, and Rappahannock Station, its percentage of loss had been remarkably low. We began to regard ourselves as favorites of fortune. We were exposed for hours at Salem Heights, yet bullets seemed to avoid us. At Gettysburg, on the afternoon of the second day, we were waiting for the order to wade into the bloody shambles of the Wheatfield, when the firing ceased; and on the third day, we arrived at the point of danger just in time to see the enemy throw down their arms and submit to capture without our firing a gun. Now, however, we were to bear our full share of the losses, to see our regiment dwindle in twelve months from a body of 650 men until it could scarcely muster 150 men for service in the ranks.

It is a singular circumstance that Grant should have been caught in the trap that had proved such a fatal snare to all the hopes of Hooker. If ever a net was spread in the sight of a bird, Lee did it at the Wilderness, and Grant was the bird. The problem that Grant had to solve was the transfer of his army, with its immense trains of ammunition and reserve supplies, from the line of the Orange & Alexandria Railroad to that of the Richmond & Fredericksburg Railroad. The latter road was easily protected and defended; the former was open to attack, and difficult of defence. But on the south side of the Rappahannock, for a distance of thirty miles above Fredericksburg, and with a uniform width of nearly thirty miles south of the river, lies the impenetrable jungle which we call the Wilderness. It is a country cut by deep ravines and sluggish streams. Here and there are cleared spaces, but for the most part it is tangled thicket, a wild, luxuriant forest growth, with a few narrow roads intersecting it, and concealed pathways hidden within its secret depths, known only to the natives of the region. Cavalry were useless here. Artillery could only be used in spots. The trains were an incumbrance because they occupied the roads and interfered with the movement of the troops.

In the recesses of the forest lurked our foes, using all the tricks and devices of savage warfare, crawling through the brush, shooting at us from concealed thickets, springing at us from trees and bushes, while the bullets from unseen guns and masked batteries prostrated our soldiers by the thousand. Human nerves were not made to stand the strain of such a warfare as this. A man can be brave as long as he can see his foe, but will quail and tremble in the presence of darkness and the goblins of the air. It was these unseen, imaginary forces that Lee was now summoning to his assistance. His army numbered a little over seventy thousand men, while Grant had a hundred and twenty thousand. He staked his all on winning with the smaller number against the greater number. He had

made it a drawn battle at Chancellorsville; now he was
going to achieve victory. He had seen Hooker paralyzed by the mighty influence of fear. Why should not
Grant succumb to the same potent force? He came
very near proving that his judgment was sound.

Colonel Long, in his memoirs of Robert E. Lee, at
page 327, writes:

The writer spent the night of the 4th at Lee's headquarters, and breakfasted with him the next morning. The
General displayed the cheerfulness which he usually exhibited at meals, and indulged in a few pleasant jests at the
expense of his staff officers, as was his custom on such
occasions. In the course of the conversation that attended
the meal he expressed himself surprised that his new adversary had placed himself in the same predicament as "Fighting Joe" had done the previous spring. He hoped the
result would be even more disastrous to Grant than that
which Hooker had experienced. He was, indeed, in the
best of spirits, and expressed much confidence in the result—
a confidence which was well founded, for there was much
reason to believe that his antagonist would be at his mercy
while entangled in these pathless and entangled thickets, in
whose intricacies disparity of numbers lost much of its
importance.

When Lee saw Grant starting for the fords of the
Rapidan, he knew that he would very soon be enmeshed
in the heart of the Wilderness, and he hurried his forces
from their various encampments on the line of the
Orange & Alexandria Railroad, and brought them up in
front of the Army of the Potomac to drive it back to the
Rapidan, as he had previously done when Hooker was
in command.

The Second Corps had crossed the Rapidan at Ely's
Ford, and was advancing on Chancellorsville. The

Fifth and Sixth Corps had crossed at Germanna Ford, and were moving towards Wilderness Tavern. The important thing was to keep possession of the roads. Once entangled in the Wilderness the army could neither march nor fight. In many places you could not see the length of a company. The main roads running east and west were the Orange Turnpike and the Orange Plank Road. These were crossed by the Germanna Ford Plank Road, the Brock Road, and several other small byways whose general direction was north and south.

At midday of May 5th, the situation of the contending forces was as follows: South of Wilderness Tavern, Ewell attacked Warren's corps on the turnpike, and the First and Third Divisions with Neill's brigade of the Sixth Corps went to the assistance of Warren, and these two forces fought fiercely with each other the most of the afternoon. A few miles farther to the southeast, Hancock was recalled from Todd's Tavern to meet three brigades of Getty's division of the Sixth Corps[1] at the junction of the Brock Road with the Orange Plank Road, and stop Hill's advance. Longstreet was still many miles away at Gordonsville.

The following extracts from the Official Records will explain the happenings to our division. General Getty says in his report, dated May 5, 1864 (O. R., vol. xxxvi., pt. 1, p. 676):

About 12 M., orders being received from Major-General Meade, commanding Army of the Potomac, to hasten out to the junction of the Orange Court-House and Germanna Plank Roads to support the cavalry, who were being driven

[1] On May 5, 1864, the Thirty-seventh Massachusetts Regiment was in the Fourth (Eustis's) Brigade, of the Second (Getty's) Division, of the Sixth (Sedgwick's) Corps. (See O. R., xxxvi., pt. 1, p. 112.)

in from Parker's Store, the division marched rapidly out on the plank road for a mile and then took the Brock Road, which crossed the Orange Court-House Plank Road a mile in advance of the Germanna Plank Road, instead of the latter. On approaching the crossroads our cavalry was found hastily retiring. Hastening forward, with my staff, I reached the crossroads just as the enemy's skirmishers appeared rapidly advancing to gain possession of this point. The presence of my small retinue, consisting of my staff and orderlies, standing firmly at the point in dispute, although under fire, served to delay their advance for a few minutes, during which Wheaton's brigade (the First) was brought up at the double-quick, faced to the front, and a volley poured in, which drove back the enemy's advance. Skirmishers were then immediately deployed, and advanced a few hundred yards, until they encountered the enemy's skirmishers. The Rebel dead and wounded were found within 30 yards of the crossroads, so nearly had they obtained possession of it. Prisoners taken here reported Hill's corps with Heth's division in advance on the Orange Court-House Plank Road, advancing. I immediately forwarded this information to Major-General Sedgwick, then commanding the corps. The division was formed in two lines at right angles to the Orange Court-House Plank Road, with Wheaton's brigade on both sides of the road, Eustis on the right and Grant's (Vermont) brigade on the left. In obedience to orders several attempts were now made to establish connection with the left of the Fifth Corps, but without success, owing to the fact that the enemy were in force between the division and that corps. For two hours now, save the constant fire of the skirmishers, everything was quiet. Enemy were evidently getting into position and forming their lines.

At 3.30 P.M. the head of Hancock's column (the Second Corps) came up on my left by the Brock Road, and as rapidly as possible were forming on the left of the division. Wheaton's brigade was now placed wholly on the right of

the road. At this juncture orders were received from
Major-General Meade, commanding the Army of the
Potomac, to attack at once without waiting for the Second
Corps. This order was reiterated by Colonel Lyman, of
General Meade's staff, in person. Accordingly the division
advanced at once. A section of artillery from the Second
Corps, under Captain Ricketts, was planted on the plank
road, advanced with the lines, and did good service. Enemy
were found in strong force immediately in front. Their
lines outflanked the division, and though forced back some
distance in the centre, they held in the main their ground
and repulsed every attack. The fighting was very heavy.
About 5.30 P.M. the enemy charged and forced back our
line some fifty yards, when they were checked and repulsed.
On the plank road they got up to, and planted a color at,
one of the guns of Ricketts' section, which, the horses being
killed, could not be withdrawn, but were immediately driven
back, and the gun retaken by a charge of portions of Grant's
and Wheaton's brigades. It was with the utmost difficulty
and only by the most stubborn fighting and tenacity that
the division could hold its ground, outnumbered and outflanked as they were by the whole corps of A. P. Hill. But
the Second Corps, at length getting into position, advanced
on the left and to a great extent relieved the pressure on my
lines. Very heavy fighting, however, without either gaining
or losing ground, was kept up until after dark. The division
was then relieved by troops from the Second Corps and
withdrawn from the front lines.

General Meade, in his official report (O. R., xxxvi.,
pt. 1, p. 189), says:

One division (Getty's) of the Sixth was sent to the Orange
Plank Road, where the Brock road intersects it, to hold this
crossing at all hazards till the arrival of the Second Corps,
ordered up from Todd's Tavern. About noon Major-
General Warren had gotten into position on the pike and

attacked vigorously with the divisions of Griffin and Wadsworth. This attack was at first quite successful, Griffin driving the enemy (Ewell's corps) some distance back on the pike, but, as, owing to the dense thicket and want of roads, the Sixth Corps had not been able to get into position, Griffin's flank was exposed as he advanced, which the enemy taking advantage of, Griffin was compelled partially to withdraw, having to abandon two pieces of artillery. Wadsworth was also driven back. In the meantime Crawford's division, which had the advance in the morning, was withdrawn to the right towards the pike and was formed on the left of Wadsworth, one brigade advancing with Wadsworth. When Wadsworth was compelled to retire Crawford was for a time isolated, but was drawn in, not, however, without the loss of many prisoners. Getty, on arriving on the Orange Plank Road, found our cavalry being driven in by Hill's corps, and had just time to deploy on each side of the road, delivering a volley into the advancing enemy, which checked his progress until the arrival of the head of Hancock's column at about 2 P.M. So soon as Hancock arrived he was directed to attack with Getty, which was done at first successfully, the enemy, however, offering stubborn resistance. Mott's division, Second Corps, gave way, when Brig.-Gen. Alexander Hays, in going to repair the break in the line, was shot dead while gallantly leading his command in the thickest of the fight. The enemy's columns being seen moving over to the Orange Plank Road, Wadsworth's division and Baxter's brigade of the Fifth Corps were sent in that direction to take position and attack in conjunction with Hancock. They did not arrive, however, in time before dark to do more than drive in the enemy's skirmishers and confront him. Toward evening the Sixth Corps made its way through the dense thicket and formed connection with the Fifth, but nothing decisive was accomplished by either corps.

That night of May 5th we slept in the woods in a

thickly wooded ravine a short distance in front of the place that we had occupied for a line of battle during the afternoon. Colonel Edwards was very uneasy because we were on the right of the line occupied by our division, and we had not as yet found out the position of the Fifth Corps; he directed me to take a file of five men, and find out the location of the Sixth Corps in its relation to the Fifth Corps and report at once, so that the regular picket lines could be established, covering our whole front.

I selected Sergeant Graves of Company F, who was an experienced backwoodsman and surveyor, to go with me, and with four others, we slowly and carefully felt our way through the woods until we came in contact with the Fifth Corps encampments. We then went back and made our report to Colonel Edwards, and pickets were established connecting our lines with theirs. Fortunately we did not run into the enemy's line, and owing largely to Sergeant Graves's experience as a woodsman, we were entirely successful in accomplishing what we had undertaken. Sergeant Graves was killed the next day. A braver soldier or a truer patriot than he was did not exist. He left his home and family to serve his country, and at a good deal of sacrifice to his own personal interests. He was a man of education and culture, and he gave it all to his country. I suppose that I was selected to establish this connection between the Fifth Corps and our division because of the fact that I had achieved some reputation of keeping watch of our movements and calculating where we were. I always carried a compass, and always had good maps, and by watching the direction of our various marches with my compass, and marking them out upon the maps, I could generally tell with tolerable accuracy where we were at any given time.

The next morning, May 6th, we arose at four and breakfasted and were ready to move by half-past five. As we had held the advance on the previous day, we were placed in the second line of battle, and the Second Corps were in front of us. Our business was to follow the advance and be ready to take our place in the first line of battle, if at any time the first line needed assistance or support. During the next two hours our progress was steady and sometimes rapid. We drove the enemy before us for a distance of a mile and a half and everything seemed favorable to a complete success on our part, when suddenly the first line of battle gave way and came rushing to the rear. We lay down and let the line pass over us and then arose and poured volley after volley into the woods in our front. We could not see the foe. They were hidden in the thickets and behind the trees. A short distance to our left we saw General Wadsworth rally his division of the Fifth Corps, and meet his death in the same blind passages of the forest. At the same time we saw the Fifty-seventh Massachusetts, with their intrepid leader, Colonel W. F. Bartlett, at their head, throw off their knapsacks and charge rapidly into the woods on our left. General Wadsworth had called on one or two regiments, not of his division, the Thirty-seventh being one, and the Twentieth Massachusetts another, to go forward with him and his division and try to check the Rebel advance upon our left flank. General Wadsworth afterwards personally thanked Colonel Edwards for his efficient support. But in rendering this assistance, the Thirty-seventh got separated from the rest of Eustis's brigade, and when Wadsworth fell, we

were deserted by his division, which fled in great disorder.

Our losses were heavy. In a very short time something like 134 officers and men from our regiment were
numbered among the killed and wounded, and we could
scarcely see where the bullets came from or where the
foe was hidden. In a very short time the firing ceased,
but the enemy's advance was checked and our regiment
was alone, unsupported. The balance of Getty's division seemed to have retreated with the Second Corps.
The only Federal troops in our immediate vicinity
were a brigade belonging to the Second Corps, commanded by General Joshua T. Owen. As the firing in
our front seemed to have ceased for the time, General
Owen and Colonel Edwards held a consultation and
decided that they did not want to withdraw from their
advanced position without orders, and as General
Owen was the ranking officer and had lost his entire
staff, I was detailed at his request to act as his staff officer, and directed to go back through the woods to the
headquarters of the Second Corps and report the position of these two commanders and ask for instructions.

I had a long and tedious ramble, but after wandering
back through the woods a mile and a half, I finally
succeeded in finding the headquarters of the Second
Corps, and reported to General Hancock the situation
of General Owen's brigade and of Colonel Edwards's
regiment. I met there my friend Colonel Walker.
As I was on foot, he immediately dismounted an orderly
and gave me his horse, and sent me to report to General
Birney, because General Owen belonged to his division.
I got to General Birney's headquarters, and made my
report, and Birney immediately detailed one of his staff
officers to go with me and bring out General Owen's

brigade and the Thirty-seventh, and place them in their appointed position with the rest of the corps.

I started back with General Birney's staff officer, but before we had gone a great way, the bullets were so thick that we decided it was safer for us to leave our horses in charge of an orderly and go on foot to the position where the regiment was. One of Berdan's sharpshooters who was lost in the woods joined us here, and we picked up guns and acted as skirmishers advancing through the woods. I finally got to the place where I had left the regiment, but there was no regiment there, and after a consultation with General Birney's staff officer, we concluded to proceed a little farther to the right where we could hear firing, thinking that possibly the brigades for which we were searching might be there. We had only gone a short distance through the woods when we came upon the Rebel skirmish line advancing, who shouted at us to throw down our arms and surrender. I was a few feet farther to the right and immediately turned on my heel and sprang through the woods at a very rapid pace, losing my hat at the first jump, and escaping without further injury than a stiffened finger joint, caused by a musket ball which grazed my hand.

In July, 1865, after my return from the war, I picked up a copy of *Harper's Magazine* for that month, and my eye fell upon an article entitled "Eleven Months in a Rebel Prison," and upon reading it I found that it told the story of my unfortunate comrade, and his subsequent imprisonment. He took the chances of capture and prison: I preferred those of escape.

I ran until I was out of breath, and finally found that General Owen and Colonel Edwards had concluded not to wait for my return, but after a short stay, during which they noticed a movement to surround them, they had returned to the line on the Brock Road, where the rest of the corps were already building earthworks and preparing for their last stand in the battle of the Wilderness. My return, hatless and somewhat dishevelled, to my regiment produced quite an excitement. They thought me captured or dead.[1]

[1] Colonel Edwards, in his memoir entitled "My Recollections of the Civil War" (manuscript, page 74), writes of these experiences:

"The Thirty-seventh in pursuance to General Wadsworth's orders charged to the rear until we had extricated ourselves from the embrace of the enemy, when we marched to the point where he had left the brigade.

"Though the history of modern war cannot show a more heroic charge, though color bearers fell dead and men dropped like dead forest leaves, though the charge was so determined that it was difficult to save the regiment, so reluctant were they to retreat,—yet it was only an episode of the three terrible days' struggle in the Wilderness, and it has never been duly chronicled save by Bowen in his masterly history of the war, entitled *History of the Thirty-seventh Regiment Massachusetts Volunteers*. The enemy out of respect to the dead hero sent his body into our lines under a flag of truce.

"After the charge we formed on the left of Owen's brigade, our left connecting with Mott's division. Owing to the surprise and shock of the charge of the Thirty-seventh the enemy did not attack in front of Owen's brigade, or of our brigade, and the brigade on our left, but the lines farther to our left were broken and Hancock changed front to his rear on his left and resumed his position on the Plank Road. This left our brigade and Owen's isolated, and the enemy were moving so as to cut us entirely off. I urged our brigade commander to move our brigade through the woods to join Hancock on the Plank Road, but he seemed paralyzed and asked me to command the brigade, which I did, retiring the brigade by the right of companies to the rear until the enemy pressed too close on our rear, when we reformed and repulsed the enemy. Owen then assumed command by virtue of seniority and asked me if I would communicate with General Hancock for orders. Captain Mason Tyler —always ready for heroic service—volunteered for this hazardous duty, and though the enemy were between us and Hancock, Captain Tyler reported to General Hancock, who ordered us to report at once to him on the Plank Road. General Hancock mounted Captain Tyler and also sent one of his staff with him. On their way to us Hancock's aid was

In the latter part of the afternoon, after due preparations had been made by the Federals to receive them, the Confederates came sweeping through the woods like a whirlwind. They captured a small part of our line, but were unable to hold it, and they were driven back with heavy loss.

Colonel Fox, in his *Regimental Losses*, p. 115, says: "The heaviest loss sustained by any division in any one battle, occurred in Getty's (2d) Division, Sixth Corps, at the Wilderness, where that division lost 480 killed, 2318 wounded, and 196 missing; total of 2994 men."

General Getty, in his report quoted above, describes the part taken by our division in the battle of the 6th of May, in the following language (O. R., xxxvi., part 1, page 677):

At 6 A.M., May 6th, the Second Corps attacked. This division formed in two lines on both sides of the Plank Road, Eustis on the right, Wheaton in the centre, crossing the Plank Road, and Grant on the left, advanced in support to Birney's division, Second Corps. The enemy were again encountered immediately in front, but after a short struggle were forced back. The troops pushed forward with renewed vigor. The enemy lost ground rapidly, and hundreds of prisoners came pouring in. A mile and a half in advance of the crossroads, Wadsworth's division, of the Fifth Corps, came sweeping in from the right, driving the enemy in great confusion and forming a junction with the troops which had advanced on the Orange Court-House Plank Road. All pressed on after the almost routed army. Having advanced three fourths of a mile farther a heavy

---

captured and Tyler, ordered to surrender, charged through the enemy and reported to me. The two brigades then moved in line towards the Plank Road. The enemy gave way before us and we reported to Hancock without further loss."

artillery fire was encountered from batteries on the left of the road, but masked by thick shrubs and pines.   In compliance with orders from Major-General Birney, the division was moved wholly to the left of the Plank Road, but soon after, perceiving that there were but few troops on the right of the road, and that the enemy threatened to attack from that quarter, I moved Wheaton's and Eustis's brigades back to the right of the road.   All this time we were steadily advancing, driving the enemy in some disorder, and capturing many prisoners, and had reached the point within half a mile of Parker's Store.

The threatened attack on the right now burst with great fury, the lines in front gave way, Wheaton and Eustis stepped into the gap, and by hard fighting held the enemy. Soon the extreme left was forced back.   The enemy, it appeared, had brought up all of Longstreet's corps, and before the onset of these fresh troops, our men, fatigued and disordered by their long advance in line of battle through the dense and almost impenetrable thicket which covers all this tract, gave ground.   This division was soon in the front line, but being outflanked by the breaking of the troops on the left, were forced back with the rest.   Here I received a severe wound through the shoulder, and was compelled to leave the field, turning over the command of the division to Brig.-Gen. Frank Wheaton, the senior brigade commander present, Brigadier-General Neill, with his brigade, having been detached. . . . After a severe contest of some ten hours' duration our troops were forced back to their original position at the crossroads.   The division, throughout all this fighting and falling back, held well together. Not a single regiment or organization was broken up.   The brigade reoccupied nearly their original positions.   Breastworks were hastily thrown up, and preparations made to resist the enemy's farther advance.   At 4 P.M. he attacked, and made the most desperate efforts to break our lines, but was handsomely repulsed, and after a struggle of half an hour withdrew, leaving the ground in

front of our lines covered with the dead and wounded. Late
in the evening the First and Fourth Brigades rejoined the
corps, on the right of the army. . . . In wresting the possession of the crossing of the Orange Court-House and
Brock Roads from Hill's corps, when already occupied by
his skirmishers, it is not claiming too much to say, that the
Second Division saved the army from disastrous defeat,
for that point was of vital importance to us, and its falling
into the hands of the enemy would have cut our army in
two, separating the Second Corps from the Fifth and Sixth,
and would have exposed to capture the Artillery Reserve,
then moving up from Chancellorsville, on the Orange Plank
Road. Throughout the terrible struggle that ensued, this
division held the key-point of the battle-field—the Plank
Road. Their losses, all from killed and wounded, and few
or none, prisoners, show how tenaciously they fought.

In General Meade's report of the battle of the 6th
of May, occurs the following (O. R., xxxvi., part 1, p.
190):

On the 6th, the attacks were made as ordered, but without any particular success on the part of either the Fifth
or Sixth Corps. On the plank road the attack of Wadsworth's and Getty's divisions and Hancock's corps was
quite successful, and the enemy was driven up the road in
confusion and disorder for more than a mile, when, Longstreet's corps coming up, the tide of battle was turned, and
our victorious line was forced back to its former position on
the Brock Road, the gallant Wadsworth falling mortally
wounded while exerting himself to rally the retiring columns. The brave Getty was also severely wounded early
in the action, though refusing for some time to leave the
field.

The cause of Hancock's retreat in the morning was

the arrival of Longstreet and his corps, after an all-night march from Gordonsville, and his sudden appearance through the leafy foliage of the forest, by an abandoned railroad cut in Hancock's rear.   It was like an army of ghosts rising out of the earth.   Such an apparition will unsettle the stoutest nerves.

The Second Corps was at this time the best seasoned and least likely to be panic-stricken of any corps in the Army of the Potomac, yet at the cry that Longstreet was in the brush on their flank, they ran to the rear like sheep, and to the best of my belief, they did not stop until they had reached the position on the Brock Road from which they had started in the morning.   There they could see something, there they could move without being tangled in briars, there they had solid ground to stand on and could fight, and when the Rebels got there they found the Federals were not to be driven out, and in particular did not mean to be driven into the woods.

In going into the details of the panicky behavior of our comrades of the Second and Fifth Corps, I do not mean to claim any special exemption from the same influences producing in the Thirty-seventh the same results under like conditions, although I do claim that the Thirty-seventh was composed of men of unusual intelligence and was especially well disciplined for a volunteer regiment.   I only remember one instance of their career as soldiers when they manifested any dis- position to yield to a panic-stricken fear.   That was on the afternoon of May 6th, when General Longstreet's corps moved forward to attack the Second Corps and Getty's division in the works which they had erected on the Brock Road, after being driven back from the morning's advance.

That afternoon's attack was preceded by a sudden, tremulous rustling of the leaves and boughs in the woods on the front, long before the enemy could be seen, which sounded like a mighty rushing wind, and I presume it was magnified by the condition of our nerves, and for the instant every man in the ranks behind the breastworks seized his gun and started for the rear, and only by the most strenuous exertions on the part of the officers was a rout prevented. It extended to the regiments on our right and left, and I presume was more or less continuous through the whole line, but in our case was stopped before the regiment had gone thirty feet to the rear of the works. The men were prevailed upon to let reason resume its sway and to return to their places behind the earthworks, and when the attack culminated they fought like heroes. In addition I may justly claim that the Sixth Corps was hardly ever in its entire history stampeded, nor did it yield to the terror of panic. The only instance which I can remember where it came very near to being panic-stricken was at Cedar Creek, where it was surprised by General Early and driven back some distance from its camp before it was able to rally, but it was never then beyond the control of its officers as were the soldiers of the Nineteenth and Eighth Corps on the same occasion.

Two or three of the brigades that belonged to the Sixth Corps came very near being routed on the evening of that same 6th of May, 1864, when General Gordon and General Johnston, with their brigades, surprised the brigades of General Shaler and General Seymour on the extreme right of the Sixth Corps and of the Army of the Potomac, just as the shades of evening were gathering, and captured the two brigadiers, and for the time succeeded in stampeding the brigades. The stampede was, however, completely checked and controlled by the commanding presence and restraint exercised by General Sedgwick and General Wright, who promptly succeeded in stopping the rout and in restoring order in the corps.

On that very day, in the afternoon, Mott's division of the Second Corps had manifested a most unaccountable fright and refusal to be controlled, which is thus described by Colonel Swan in his account of the battle of the Wilderness (*The Wilderness Campaign*, Military Historical Society of Massachusetts, vol. iv., page 142):

Till near night our troops as a general thing did all that could be expected of them, maintaining their advanced ground when they found they could do no more, although they knew of their substantial breastworks just in the rear. Then for some unaccountable reason Mott's division gave way.   Colonel McAllister, who afterwards commanded the 1st brigade of that division, says "that to his great astonishment the line began to give way on the left.   It is said first the Excelsior brigade, then my left regiment, the 1st Massachusetts, and regiment after regiment, like a rolling wave, fell back, and all efforts to rally them were in vain."   "To assign a cause for it," he goes on to say, "would be impossible, unless it was from the fact that a large number of the troops were about to leave the service.   I think this had much to do with it."

But here let me observe that in *all* this wood fighting our troops seem to have been greatly alarmed whenever the noise of a contest to the right or the left told them that there was fighting in the rear of a prolongation of their own line.   Such noises seem to have caused more disturbance than a foe directly in front.   And I think it was the same with the enemy's troops.   However, the enemy at this time was not aware of our confusion.

It will be noticed that the instances here cited of panics are for the most part taken from experiences in the Wilderness, and the panic of the Eleventh and Twelfth Corps at Chancellorsville is another instance of the same kind, and due to similar causes. One of those causes is the tendency of the human mind to magnify dangers that cannot be seen or measured by human senses. If you can see a danger and actually apply the human reason to it you will be satisfied to use the best means and methods that your mind can suggest to meet the emergency, but if you cannot see it and you cannot reason about it, your only recourse is to run away from it, and where a crowd is involved it means a race for life.

The Confederate army had this advantage over the Northern army in dealing with such a situation. They were at home in their own country, and very large numbers of them knew every byway and path in the Wilderness, to say nothing of its roads, and knew just where to hide, and where to force the fight, and we were more or less subject to their control on account of this knowledge. It was this that made General Lee so confident that, if he could hold General Grant in the Wilderness, he could double the strength of his own army.

The writer whom I have quoted above further says, in reference to that part of the battle of the Wilderness which was fought upon the Brock Road (page 144):

There are but one or two square miles upon this continent that have been more saturated with blood than was the square mile which lay in front of the Brock Road, and had the Orange Plank Road as a central avenue, in the two days of the Battle of the Wilderness. And this bloody field

differs much from those which have been its rivals as scenes
of slaughter. Within a very limited compass in other
battles thousands have fallen by the fire generally of artillery, not less than of infantry, as they pressed forward to
take some fortified line; and the line once reached, the car-
nage has been awful. But here, although both parties had
breastworks, the fighting was far from being confined to
those breastworks. Nearly every square yard had its fill
of blood, and on nearly every square yard was Northern and
Southern blood intermingled.

And although the battle was fought with the hot sun of
the month of May in Virginia glaring overhead, it was,
as it were, fought in the night. Excepting the roads,
the dense wood rendered it impossible for any soldier to
see what was going on three rods from where he stood.

There was more at stake in the battle of the Wilderness than in any other battle between the Northern
and Southern armies in the War of the Rebellion, with
perhaps the single exception of the battle of Gettysburg.
The Army of the Potomac had never won a decisive victory on Southern soil. McDowell, McClellan,
Burnside, and Hooker in succession, and in each instance commanding a larger army with superior equipment, suffered humiliation and defeat from Southern
generals commanding a ragged and half-starved army
on Southern soil. The Army of Northern Virginia
felt that under the leadership of Lee, backed by
Longstreet, Stuart, and Hill, there was no Southern
position they could not successfully defend, and no
Northern army they could not defeat. They had implicit confidence in their leaders, and in fact, they
had reason for their faith. Against great odds they
had achieved victory after victory, and hardly tasted
defeat.

On the other hand, the Army of the Potomac had suffered a long series of reverses, and were much discouraged by repeated defeats. In their whole career they had hardly tasted the joy of victory. Their leaders had disappointed them, and uselessly wasted their life blood and their vital energies. General Grant had achieved signal victories in the West. The national government in its straits now assigned to him the task of redeeming the reputation of the Army of the Potomac. It was a battle on Southern soil between Lee, with his skilled lieutenants and triumphant army on the one side, and Grant with the much larger Army of the Potomac, disheartened by repeated defeat, on the other side. The stake was the continuance of the United States as one nation if Grant won, or its division into two nations if Lee won. Gettysburg had marked the turn in the tide of the war in favor of the United States. Now Lee and his generals were going to make the supreme effort of their lives in an attempt to stop the flow of that tide southward and drive it back to the Potomac. They believed they could do it; and the North was so tired of the war, with enlistments stopped, the draft a failure, and the party of Peace-at-any-price constantly increasing, that in their dreams of success, the established and recognized Southern Confederacy loomed into sight behind the clouds. If they had succeeded in the Wilderness I cannot say that it would have ended as they anticipated, but it would have given the Union cause a terrible setback, and no man can say what might have resulted. The battle of the Wilderness was fought to a standstill on that square mile where the Brock and the Orange Plank Roads join.

The Thirty-seventh was for two days in the very thick of that fight. It never faltered. When lines of battle were rushing wildly over them to the rear, they opened to let them pass, and then closed their ranks and moved forward against the foe, and stopped the advance. Amidst general disorder and wild dismay they stood or marched in solid ranks and obeyed orders as if they were on parade. That was the character of the regiment. They were soldiers drilled to act as a unit, and to obey, and if Colonel Edwards had ordered them to stand their ground at the farthest point of their advance on the Orange Plank Road, I believe they would have fired their last cartridge and sacrificed their last man.

CHAPTER X

THE SIXTH CORPS AT SPOTTSYLVANIA

MAY 7 TO 20, 1864

AFTER the terrible experiences of the last two days, we were tired enough to sleep, but no such good fortune awaited us. The Sixth Corps met with a serious loss early in the evening through the capture of two of its brigadiers and several hundred officers and men, and General Sedgwick demanded the return of the five brigades of his command which had been detached for duty at different points in the battlefield of the Wilderness. Three of these brigades under Getty were on the Brock Road. After Longstreet's last repulse we tried to secure a little rest behind the earthworks, but it was with guns in our hands, and almost in line of battle.

At ten P.M., May 6th, orders came returning us to the Sixth Corps. It was a dark night, and we stumbled along through the woods, dodging camps, corrals for horses, teams, and the camp followers, who are always in the rear of every army, and a little after midnight concluded we had better wait for the dawn rather than take chances of losing our way. So we dropped down in the woods where we were. We were up with the dawn, and by four o'clock had reached the place in the Sixth Corps assigned to us on the extreme right of the line.

At the place where we halted the country was slightly

elevated above the surrounding woods, but the woods were so dense and the trees so large, that the elevation was of little assistance in enabling us to see our environment. Everything in our front was so quiet that it gave rise to the report that the enemy had retreated in the night, but upon our attempt to advance our skirmish line, the Rebels were developed in force. We hardly had time to get breakfast before our regiment was sent to the right centre of the Sixth Corps to support a battery. It was posted on a hill, but the outlook was very limited in extent. However, they did not allow us to remain here long.

At two P.M., we returned to our position on the right and devoted ourselves to the delightful but arduous occupation of erecting earthworks; by night we had some fine ones, but we were then told that the army would move soon after dark. At ten P.M. we were ordered into line, and Spottsylvania was our goal. Lee and his army were still in our front; we had failed in our endeavor to drive them out of our way, now we were trying the efficiency of a flank movement.

Spottsylvania was fifteen miles distant in a southeasterly direction from where we were. Our orders, therefore, contemplated an oblique movement southeast and around the right flank of the hostile army. The transportation trains (supplies, hospital stores, equipment and ammunition) were started in the afternoon and sent in advance. The Fifth Corps was directed to go by the Brock Road, from which the enemy had apparently withdrawn their forces after the terrific fighting of the 5th and 6th instant, march to Todd's Tavern, and if practicable, proceed and occupy Spottsylvania Court-House.[1] They were to be followed by

[1] See War Map 81 (1).

the Second Corps by the same route. The Sixth and the Ninth Corps were to care for the trains and go by way of Chancellorsville, Aldrich's and Piney Branch Church, and the Sixth was to rendezvous with the Fifth Corps at or near Alsop's, northwest from the Court-House.

It was a night of sweltering heat. No rain had fallen for several days, and the many wheels and feet of horses and men pounded the dry soil into impalpable dust, which rose hundreds of feet into the air, and notified General Lee that our trains were under way in the afternoon, and of the direction of our movement. He immediately sent his cavalry to obstruct our progress over the Brock Road, and Longstreet's corps by a cross-road, to get in front of us and preoccupy the Court-House.

Both armies were badly fagged from want of sleep. The choking dust and the heat greatly aggravated their exhaustion. The Rebel army had this advantage, they were on their own soil, fighting for their homes, and were inspired with an almost superhuman energy, while our army, although they fully believed in the right-eousness of their cause, were conscious that they were invaders, and had met with repeated defeats in all their previous attempts at invasion. Even the iron will of Grant could not overcome the influence of this fact. The result was that the Rebel cavalry succeeded in delaying our Fifth Corps, and Longstreet's corps got between our army and Spottsylvania Court-House, although they started a little later and had to march a little farther than our advance corps.

We of the Sixth Corps had a much longer distance to go, and the trains delayed us. Through the long watches of the night we shuffled a few feet at a time, being choked with dust, stifled by the heat, and weary from lack of sleep. With the dawn (of the 8th), we halted at Chancellorsville for breakfast. Here we left the trains in charge of the Ninth Corps, and after a brief rest pushed on until three o'clock in the afternoon, when we joined the Fifth Corps near Alsop's.

Meanwhile, the last named corps had pushed forward, and two of its divisions had a fierce fight with Longstreet's corps, but failed in their attempt to reach the Court-House, and were driven back a mile or more, meeting the Sixth Corps at Alsop's.

General Sedgwick now took command of the field at this point, and towards evening made an attempt with the First and Second Divisions of the Sixth Corps and Crawford's division, the Pennsylvania Reserves of the Fifth Corps, to clear the obstructions in our front. Our lines were advanced from half to three quarters of a mile, and the enemy developed in such strong force that, owing to the approach of darkness, and the weariness of his men, he concluded it best not to force the fight, and withdrew his attacking lines a short distance. We lay down on our arms and passed the night (of May 8th).

During the night, Lee's entire army arrived and were arranged in a line of battle curving towards the north on the easterly side of the Brock Road so as to occupy a ridge of high land commanding the valley of the Ny, and facing north and east. This formed the famous Salient of Spottsylvania. The line, after curving towards the north, was bent until it ran towards the west, and again towards the south, crossing the Fredericksburg road a short distance north of the Court-House. It was half a mile across the Salient from east to west, and a mile in depth from its northernmost point

or apex to the line drawn across its base in extension of
Lee's main line of defences.

This entire line of the enemy ran through the woods,
with here and there an opening, but for the most part
was hidden from view, except as our columns of attack,
driving in the enemy's pickets, discovered a continuous
heavily fortified line of breastworks, bristling here and
there with cannon, and crowned with log protections
for their heads and with loopholes underneath the
logs for their guns, while in front a network of abatis and
slashings tangled and delayed their assailants, and in
many instances consigned them to a merciless doom.
West of the Brock Road the enemy's line fronted on the
River Po, and did not require such heavy defensive
works.   The Po, with its marshy and thicket-covered
borderlands, was a sufficient protection against an
attack.

In front of the line during May 9th, and at distances
varying at different points from half a mile to a mile,
was deployed the Army of the Potomac with its Second
Corps at the right of its line; the Fifth Corps continuing
the line to the Brock Road on its westerly side about a
mile south of Alsop's; and the Sixth Corps continuing
the line from the Brock Road in a northeasterly direction to a point in the woods three quarters of a mile
northwesterly from the apex of the Salient.   As I
remember it, the Sixth Corps line on that day was
mostly in the woods, and there was hardly a point on
that line where the enemy's line of fortifications could
be seen.   Possibly some parts of it were visible from
the Brock Road.

The point on that road where the Fifth and Sixth
Corps lines joined, is a historic spot.   It was there
that General Sedgwick was killed at 9.30 o'clock of

this very morning of May 9th by the bullet of a sharp-shooter fired from a distant tree. He was engaged in locating a battery when he was shot, and the bullet struck him under the eye, causing instant death. His death was a serious loss to the Sixth Corps, and to the Army of the Potomac. He was one of those solid men that everybody respected. His superior officers and associates leaned upon him; his subordinates had implicit confidence in him; his soldiers loved him. He was "Uncle John" to them. No one ever charged him with disloyalty to his commander; he was modest and unselfish. He was repeatedly asked to accept the command of the Army of the Potomac, but he always declined the honor. He exposed himself recklessly if the occasion required it, but when it came to the lives and the health of his men, he would not waste them, and he was always solicitous for their welfare, both on the march and in the camp. The day of his death was the saddest day the Sixth Corps ever knew, and the other corps recognized that the Army of the Potomac had lost a model soldier and corps commander.

To clear the woods as far as possible of sharpshooters in the trees, our artillery opened fire for a couple of hours, and vigorously shelled the woods all along the line. The shrieking of the shells, the crashing and tearing of the trees and limbs in the forest made a terrific noise. The cannonading seemed to me louder and heavier than that at Gettysburg. Meanwhile, during the day, we were fortifying and building earthworks of a formidable character for our protection.

General Wright of our First Division succeeded to the command of the Sixth Corps, and General David A. Russell (of the Third Brigade, First Division) was promoted to the command of the First Division in

General Wright's place. General Eustis was transferred and placed in command of the brigade lately commanded by General Russell, and Colonel Edwards was promoted to the command of our brigade, and Lieutenant-Colonel Montague to the command of the Thirty-seventh.[1]

Late in the afternoon, the Second Corps crossed the Po. The movement began with an attempt by Barlow's division to capture a wagon train, and developed into a flank attack by three divisions of the Second Corps. They spent the night on the south side of the Po, and in the morning of the 10th made such encouraging progress that they thought it might open the way to Spottsylvania Court-House.

Just then Hancock was ordered by Meade to recross the Po with two of his divisions, and with the Fifth Corps take charge of an assault to be made in front of the Fifth Corps line on the enemy's works. This assault failed, but in the meantime Hancock was obliged to return to the rescue of Barlow's division, which he had left south of the Po when he obeyed General Meade's order, and which, when deserted by the other two divisions, had been assailed by the force that Lee sent to drive back the Second Corps. This accomplished, at seven o'clock in the evening, he renewed his assault with the Fifth Corps, but accomplished nothing.

On that same day the Sixth Corps, under orders from army headquarters, had explored the enemy's fortified line in their front, so far as they were able to do so, and General Russell and Colonel Upton reported that they had found a place in the west face of the Salient opposite their front which they believed could be successfully

[1] See note at p. 142 above.

assailed. With the approval of army headquarters, General Wright had directed Generals Russell and Upton to select twelve regiments from the whole Sixth Corps for the assaulting column, to be led by Upton, and to be supported by General Mott's (Fourth) Division of the Second Corps, temporarily assigned to the Sixth Corps, and under General Wright's command. Colonel Upton selected three regiments from his own Second Brigade of the First Division, four regiments from the Third Brigade, First Division (this was Hancock's original brigade, and recently was commanded by Russell, and particularly distinguished itself at Rappahannock Station), three regiments of the famous Vermont Second Brigade, Second Division, and two regiments of Neill's Third Brigade, Second Division. Under cover of the skirmish line, General Russell, Colonel Upton, and the several regimental commanders carefully examined the ground and received exact instructions as to their respective parts and duties.

At the appointed hour, 6.10 P.M., Colonel Upton had his column formed in four lines under cover of the edge of the woods, and on a concerted signal, they marched and rushed across the intervening fields, drove in the pickets, and in almost solid array went over the fortifications, and after a desperate hand-to-hand fight, compelled the surrender of twelve hundred prisoners with six pieces of artillery and several stands of colors. They also captured an interior line of works which in a measure protected them from attack on the west and south. They made a breach in the enemy's lines of defence nearly a mile long. They held those lines until after dark, momentarily expecting the arrival of the supporting column under Mott, but for some unaccountable reason, it did not come.

I never fully understood why the other regiments of the Sixth Corps in this emergency were not sent to Upton's support. I know that the Thirty-seventh and our brigade started to go to their relief, although, at the time, we did not know of Upton's success or our destination, and after proceeding a half-mile or more, we were halted and shortly after returned to our starting point.

Finally, after three hours of occupation and most desperate fighting, Colonel Upton concluded that without assistance upon failure of ammunition, retreat or capture of his force was inevitable, and with General Russell's approval he withdrew. If he had been sustained, the terrible losses of May 12th might have been avoided. It was a better planned and better executed assault than that of the Second Corps on May 12th, and bitter were the reproaches to which both Russell and Upton gave utterance when upon Upton's return he gained the shelter of the woods. He had most successfully accomplished what he had undertaken, but at a heavy sacrifice of life, while those who were to support him had left him unaided to work out his own salvation and compelled him to surrender all the fruits of his achievement. For his gallantry on this occasion, he was promoted to the rank of brigadier-general.

The night of the 10th was one of restless wakefulness. We remained in the works with arms close at hand. There was desultory firing between the pickets in front of the respective lines. Four times during the night we were roused by alarms, and stood to arms. Not much rest in this; but we were so exhausted that we would drop asleep the moment they allowed us to lie down. It was an anxious night.

Wednesday, May 11th, was a day of comparative

rest and preparation.   General Grant considering that
the failure of Upton's assault was due to lack of cooperation, determined to renew the attempt on a much
larger scale, and gave his directions accordingly to
General Meade.   The Second Corps was to be brought
over from the right of the line in the rear of the Fifth
and Sixth Corps after dark that night to an open space
around the Brown and Landrum houses north of the
Salient,[1] and with the assistance of the Sixth and Ninth
Corps to attempt the capture of the Salient and the
decisive defeat of the Rebel army at the dawn of the
following day.

The historian of the Twentieth Regiment Massachusetts Volunteers, George A. Bruce, at page 368
of his history, says of this order: "These few words of
command resulted in one of the bloodiest battles in history, unique in character, sublime in the heroism displayed by the combatants of either side, which covered
a small space of earth thicker with dead and wounded
men than was ever seen on any battle-field in modern
times."

It commenced to rain in the middle of the afternoon,
and by evening it settled down into a storm which
soaked the earth and drenched the foliage of the forest
and enveloped the scene with a thick covering of mist
and fog, which added much to the gloom and distress
of the occasion.

General Hancock made such examinations as he
could of the field of his action and of the works which
were to be attacked, but he added little to his information in this way, and he was obliged largely to depend
upon the reports of his guides and of the officers who
viewed the works at close quarters on the skirmish line

[1] See War Maps 91 (1), 96 (3).

or in connection with Upton's attack.   He directed the
divisions of his corps, that had been given the opportunity to rest as far as it was possible during the day, to
start from their camps under the lead of guides detailed
for that purpose, in time to report at the Brown house,
which General Hancock had selected as his headquarters, by 10 o'clock in the evening or very soon thereafter.

It was an awful march through the slimy, muddy soil
of Virginia, the difficulties of which can only be appreciated by those who have experienced it under similar
conditions.   But before midnight the three divisions of
the Second Corps had assembled in the vicinity of the
Brown house, and were formed into two columns of
attack, the one under General Barlow, and the other
under General Birney, the latter supported by Mott's
division, while Gibbon and his division were held in
reserve.

The following graphic account of the assault on the
12th of May is taken from the History of the Twentieth
Massachusetts Regiment above referred to (page 372):

For a long time this great column stood waiting for the
word to advance.   It was the largest body of men ever
organized on the continent to be launched for a single blow.
In it were twenty thousand men,—partly in solid mass, and
partly in line,—five thousand more than Pickett led up
Cemetery Hill at Gettysburg.   Seventy-two regiments,
representing the youth and manhood of ten States, the
best that each could furnish, stood arrayed in battle order,
upholding seventy-two battle-flags that had been borne
in honor on many a field, and none of which had ever been
touched by the hands of the enemy.   These flags had been
rent by shot and shell, and now, tattered and torn and wet
with rain, were drooping around their shafts like the be-

draggled wings of a fowl.   For twenty-four hours not one of these twenty thousand men had enjoyed a moment of sleep. Some of the strongest and bravest in the Twentieth dropped to the ground and were unconscious before their bodies touched it.   Most, however, stood up in the ranks, swaying restlessly backward and forward, pulling their feet out of the mud and putting them back again, fretful, complaining, and ill at ease.   From right to left they covered half a mile, in places twenty ranks in depth, and nowhere less than eight.   The exact direction of the Salient from the Brown house had been ascertained on the previous day by the use of the compass, and the first division was so formed that it would strike the projecting point, provided it was able to go forward without deviation from the given course.

A great battle was about to be ushered in without the aid of artillery.   There was neither drum to beat the charge nor bugle to sound the call.   None of the accessories that usually accompany warlike forces and give to them a pomp and circumstance to fill the eye and feed the imagination were here.   There were no officers on horseback, hurrying hither and thither, in front or on either flank, giving life, color, and animation to the field with their clattering sabres, waving plumes, and brilliant uniforms; neither were there any picturesque groups of them in the background. Every one was on foot, for all horses were left behind the lines.   Barlow was in the centre of his massed division, while Birney, Mott, and Gibbon were stationed in the midst of their troops.   So slight was the information given to General Barlow of the character of the ground over which he was to pass, that he inquired of Colonel Comstock, of General Grant's staff, whether or not there was a ravine a thousand feet in depth in front; and receiving no satisfactory answer, he concluded that he was about to lead a forlorn hope and gave his valuables and some messages to a friend.

After a delay of half an hour on account of the fog and darkness, at 4.30 the word was given for the movement to

begin. Until the Salient was captured no other command
was given. The great column became its own commander-
in-chief, for brigade and division generals being buried in
the mass, it was impossible for them to give it directions by
further orders. Still their presence was felt, for the men
were conscious that their leaders were with them to share
every danger. This alone was of no small value. When it
grew lighter, and one could look around, and objects became
visible, it was seen that the corps had been marched all night
through mud and rain for something out of the common
experience. The Second Corps had never before been
massed into a solid body to move against the enemy, and
never in such form as that in which it was now arrayed.
Great events have a power of self-proclamation; and
although nothing had been communicated to the troops as
to what was expected of them, the feeling ran through the
ranks that they were near to momentous happenings. All
thought of what had gone before—want of sleep, fatigue,
untold discomforts—was forgotten, and the manner in
which the drama was to unfold and close was now the
question of supreme interest. The warlike spirit was rising
and became plainly visible. When half a mile out, the
front line of Birney's division perceived that it was somewhat behind Barlow's column, and without orders quick-
ened step and soon came up to a proper alignment. Near
the Landrum house the enemy's pickets opened fire upon
the flanking regiment, but without noticing them it passed
along. As the woods on either side became visible, these
landmarks showed that the true course had been kept, and
the lines had been well preserved. When the column had
ascended a low ridge that crossed its path, the Salient burst
into view, with frowning forts and connecting rifle-pits,
spaced off with traverses rising high above them. Down
the slope in front was a line of abatis, formed of interlacing
trees, whose branches had been cut and sharpened at the
ends, presenting a formidable obstacle. But to men now
wrought to a high pitch of enthusiasm and animated by a

sudden presentiment of victory, obstacles were not considered.

With loud cheering, the troops rushed forward, broke down and burst through the abatis, and in a moment the first wave of this human tide swept over the crest and dropped down on the farther side of the intrenchments. The men had seen much close and hard fighting, but now they were in the midst of the enemy and for the first time were making quick and sharp use of the bayonet and clubbed musket. But these were brave men that they sought to conquer, men who would not willingly drop their flag. They were the same who had been led by Stonewall Jackson; the same who broke through the line at Culp's Hill and held their ground for many hours with fierce tenacity; the same who met and held Warren's men in check on the 5th of May in the Wilderness. The contest was quick, sharp, and decisive. Many were killed and more were wounded; but being surrounded on every side by determined men, Johnson and his whole division, except a few that escaped, surrendered. Twenty guns, thirty flags, and four thousand prisoners were the substantial trophies of this assault. The Second Corps never had a prouder hour, unless it was at Gettysburg, where, holding a defensive position, the action was the reverse of this day's triumph.

There has always been much contention between the divisions as to which planted its flag upon the parapet first, but the difference in time was so slight that each was entitled to share alike in the honor.

Gibbon had been directed to remain in reserve; but either by new orders or a spontaneous impulse (probably the latter), the division followed close in the rear of Barlow and went over the works with his men. Carroll's and Owen's brigades were to the left of Barlow and broke in on Stuart's brigade, which was captured entire with its commander. Webb's brigade marched up into the space between Barlow and Birney and shared with the others in the capture of Walker's and York's brigades.

A gap in the centre of Lee's army had been made, a mile in extent, which gave promise for a time of a complete rout and overthrow of his forces.   And now became manifest, at once, the effect of a condition deemed essential for the initiatory success of the movement, which rendered further direction difficult and unsuccessful.   The hundred or more staff officers, who on their fleet horses would have been able to carry the necessary instructions quickly over a widely extended line, and, with their long experience and high intelligence, would have been so powerful a factor in bringing the troops into order, and arranging them for a further effective advance, were all afoot.   Here in a small space in front of the captured works were twenty thousand men (less the killed, wounded, and a few stragglers), disordered somewhat by the march, more by the assault, now carried away by a sudden victory of unlooked-for proportions and thrown into confusion that required the promptest action to disentangle and reduce to an ordered array.   The enthusiasm of a broken line resulting from a victory is only a little more efficient than the despondency of one broken by defeat.   The officers commanding the divisions were capable men and knew what the situation demanded, but they were almost powerless.   There was no one to carry their orders quickly or assist much in executing them.   At such times as well as during a flight, one might well offer a kingdom for a horse, for he that is thus borne carries with him a dignity and authority that commands respect and wins obedience to his voice.   The most potent and effective arm of the service being thus paralyzed or nearly so, the great corps, which we have seen acting as its own commander-in-chief during the assault, continued to follow its own impulse, which carried it forward in tumultuous pursuit of the enemy.   Forward into the brush and woods the men went, and meeting part of Gordon's reserve division at the McCool house, they put Johnson's brigade to flight and followed on until the fortified line at the base of the Salient was reached.   Here were two fresh brigades and the rallied troops of Johnson. It would have been impossible for the disorganized pursuing force to carry it, and such an action was not attempted.

During this hour, so critical to the Army of Northern Virginia, men on horseback were swiftly flying to various parts of the line to bring up fresh and organized troops to meet the greatest danger that had ever yet threatened it. From Rodes's division came Ramseur; from Mahone's division, Perrin and Harris; and from Wilcox's division, McGowan; these, with Gordon's division, made eight fresh brigades which were soon ready to contest with the Second Corps the conquest of the Salient. By eight o'clock they had forced our wearied and disorganized forces to the outer face of the captured line, around which was waged, until three o'clock the following morning, the fiercest battle of modern times.

The accompanying diagram is a rough sketch of the outline of the Salient and its auxiliary earthworks. They were as well built and as scientifically laid out as any extemporized earthworks I ever saw. They were about five feet high on the inside, faced with logs, and topped with a large log to protect the head, raised so as to leave room enough under the log to handle and aim the muskets. The top of the earthworks outside of the head logs sloped gradually for three feet, and then made a steep descent to the ground.

The outlines of the earthworks on the west front of the Salient were so planned that each separate face (from A to H on the diagram) was enfiladed by the fire from some other part of the line. For this reason the Federal troops were unable to hold possession of the exterior faces of the west front of the Salient, unless they first secured possession of the interior works on that front. For instance, the fronts on G—H and

E—F were enfiladed from B—C. That on C—D from D—E, and so on. In addition to this on the interior fronts of H—I, G—H, F—G, and E—F, they had built strong traverses, extending twelve or fifteen feet perpendicularly, or nearly so, from lines of those faces. These traverses served a double purpose: they prevented us from enfilading those interior faces, and each traverse formed with the front line from which it projected a little fortress, behind which the enemy gathered in groups and poured a deadly fire into our ranks on the westerly front, who were hanging with a deadly grip to the exterior fronts or faces between H and I, and I and K.

In front of the works from A to C, the woods were close to the works. From C to I, they were at different distances, but nowhere more than a thousand feet. The line of earthworks built and occupied by the Sixth Corps extended back of this woods from the point on the Brock Road where Sedgwick was killed, north nearly three quarters of a mile.[1]

G shows the central point of Upton's attack on May 10th, and the lines from F to R indicate the outlines of the interior earthworks captured by Upton, which enabled him to resist the repeated assaults made by the enemy to recapture the lines which he held for nearly three hours.

It is very difficult to determine the exact times when the movements of the different organizations on that day occurred, as well as to trace the movements themselves.

The historian of the Twentieth Massachusetts Regiment says, in the closing sentence above quoted: "By eight o'clock they [the enemy] had forced our wearied

[1] War Maps 55 (2), 96 (3).

and disorganized forces to the outer face of the captured line. . . ."

Returning now to the night of the 11th, General Wright, commanding the Sixth Corps, ordered the Third Division to occupy the entire line of earthworks of the corps, and to release the First and Second Divisions for the support of the Second Corps. At 4.30 o'clock on the morning of the 12th the Second Division took their position northwest of the Brown house in an opening a short distance to the rear of where the assaulting columns of the Second Corps had massed for their attack on the Salient. At the same hour (4.30), the Second Corps began to move forward. At 5 o'clock General Hancock sent the following despatch to General Meade:

> SECOND ARMY CORPS,
> May 12, 1864—5 A.M.
>
> GENERAL MEADE: Our men have the works, with some hundred prisoners; impossible to say how many; whole line moving up. This part of the line was held by Ewell.
>
> WINF'D S. HANCOCK, *Major-General.*

At 5.55 the following despatch was sent:

> HEADQUARTERS SECOND CORPS,
> May 12, 1864—5.55 A.M.
>
> [GENERAL MEADE:]   It is necessary that General Wright should attack at once. All of my troops are engaged.
>
> WINF'D S. HANCOCK.

and subsequently the following was sent and received:

> HEADQUARTERS ARMY OF THE POTOMAC,
> May 12, 1864—6 A.M.
>
> GENERAL HANCOCK: General Wright has been ordered to attack at once vigorously on your right.
>
> S. WILLIAMS,
> *Assistant Adjutant-General.*[1]

[1] See O. R., xxxvi., pt. 2, pp. 656, 657.

According to my recollection, at 6 o'clock of that morning or a little after, Colonel Edwards rushed our brigade, which was in front of the Second Division, through the woods which separated us from the northerly front of the Salient, and we there relieved troops of the Second Corps who occupied a portion of the exterior of the works they had captured from the enemy at dawn.   On our left we joined a regiment belonging to the Tammany Brigade of Mott's division of the Second Corps at a point in the line of earthworks one or two hundred feet west of the apex or east angle of the Salient (see K on diagram).   The Thirty-seventh occupied on this line, from the point of contact with the Second Corps, to a point within one or two hundred feet of the west or Bloody Angle (I on the diagram). We were joined by the Second Rhode Island on our right at the latter point in the same way.   The Tenth Massachusetts joined the right of the Second Rhode Island, and these two regiments extended our line of occupation to a point between G and H as indicated on the diagram.   The Seventh Massachusetts of our brigade was on that day detailed to do picket duty, and was not engaged at the Salient.   Bidwell's brigade, (Third Brigade, Second Division, Sixth Corps) followed us and was put into the fight on our right, next to the Tenth Massachusetts.   The exterior of the earthworks in this part of the line was enfiladed by the enemy's fire so that our troops were unable to occupy the exterior earthworks.   In fact, the enemy's works in front of Bidwell's brigade, and where they were occupied by the Tenth Massachusetts and part of the Second Rhode Island, from I to D on the diagram, were the most bitterly contested part of the field.

If our troops could have got possession of the works

at that point, they would have stopped the deadly fire
from the traverses, and held the interior fortress from
F to R, which enabled Upton, on May 10th, to hold the
captured works against the repeated attempts of the
Confederate forces to dislodge him.   My reasons for
stating that Bidwell's brigade was at this early hour
(between 6 and 9.30 A.M.) located as I have described,
are that Edwards's, Bidwell's, and Wheaton's brigades
were at that hour sent to that part of the field.
Edwards's occupied the works from K to H, and Wheaton's in front of the works from D to A.   It is fair to
presume that Bidwell's brigade connected the other two
brigades and occupied in front of the works from H to
D, as those points are shown on the diagram.

The official reports are consistent with this statement,
although those relating to Bidwell's brigade are very
meagre.   He says:

On the morning of the 12th we were moved to the rear of
the position just captured by General Hancock, and ordered
to support a brigade of this division, commanded by Colonel
Edwards, at the Angle.   The brigade was deployed in line
and moved to this point, and two of the regiments, the
Forty-ninth and Seventy-seventh New York, charged the
Angle and took possession of the crest commanding it,
which they held until relieved."[1]

I suppose this is a euphemistic way of describing the
failure to hold the works.

General Wheaton, in his report, says:

May 12, 6 A.M., ordered to the left and south a mile to
support the Second Corps, who occupied works captured
at daylight.   Advanced under a heavy artillery fire to

[1] O. R., xxxvi., pt. 1, p. 720.

within 50 yards of that part of the works still in the enemy's possession, generally known as the Angle or Slaughter Pen. Here we were exposed to a terrible musketry fire, losing heavily, including many valuable officers. [1]

General Brooke, in his report, same volume, page 411, says that General Wheaton was on the right of the Sixth Corps line (point A on the diagram).

The following despatch from General Hancock to General Meade appears in O. R., xxxvi., pt. 2, page 657:

May 12, 1864—7 A.M.

GENERAL MEADE: General Wright, of Sixth Army Corps, slightly wounded, but still in command.

WINF'D S. HANCOCK,
Major-General.

From the foregoing it appears that at 5.55 A.M. General Hancock was hard pressed, and asked that the Sixth Corps be sent to assist him. At 6 o'clock General Wright was ordered to attack vigorously. His Second Division, which was close at hand, was sent at once into the works. Heavy fighting began along the whole line from the "Apex" of the Salient to the right of the Sixth Corps. The losses in our divisions were heavy. Before 7 o'clock General Wright was listed among the wounded. In a despatch, at 7.15, General Hancock says, "My troops are in great disorder," and in another at 8.50, he says, "The enemy have been attacking us with great vehemence," and at 7.30 Meade sends word to Warren, "Wright says his right is attacked strongly and wants support . . . you must also support him." [2]

---

[1] O. R., xxxvi., pt. 1, p. 684.

[2] See O. R., xxxvi., pt. 2, pp. 657, 658, 662.

It was a foggy, misty morning, with rain at intervals, and I remember that at least three successive columns of the enemy before nine o'clock emerged from the mist, but at close range under our musketry fire were dissolved and swept away. I refer to these proofs now to show that during the three hours and a half between 6 and 9.30, when three brigades of the Second Division of the Sixth Corps were alone on the front of that part of the Salient, where the battle of the "Bloody Angle" was chiefly fought, most desperate fighting was then in progress. You will notice that I say "three brigades of the Second Division." This calls for explanation. This division at that time was composed of four brigades, and the one thus far not accounted for, was the most famous of all its brigades; probably as famous as any brigade in the army. I refer to the Second, commonly known as the Vermont Brigade of the Second Division, Sixth Corps. It was very conspicuous in the fighting of that day; but in the early morning it reported to General Hancock, and was by him "ordered to the extreme left of the Second Corps (which was the extreme left of the Army of the Potomac)," where the brigade formed in two lines, threw out skirmishers and fortified.[1] (See M in the diagram.)

Let us now see what had happened within the enemy's lines during these early morning hours. Under the impression that the attack was to be renewed upon his left flank, General Lee, on the afternoon of the 11th, withdrew his artillery from the Salient, and sent it to his left. During the night General Johnson heard from his picket line in front of the Salient that sounds of activity, indicating possibility of an attack on the

[1] Report of General L. A. Grant, O. R., xxxvi., pt. i, page 703.

Salient, were in the air, and communicated the report to headquarters; whereupon General Lee ordered the immediate return of his artillery, and the batteries came galloping up just as the Second Corps columns of attack sprang into the works and compelled the surrender of Johnson and his defending forces, including his artillery. After securing their prisoners and sending them to the rear, the Second Corps surged forward to the earthworks,—marked S—T on the diagram. At this time they were in the disorganized and confused condition described in the foregoing quotation. General Gordon's division was behind the earthwork. In the then condition of the Second Corps, it was an armed mob attacking a fortified line, defended by the best troops in the Southern army. The result was, our forces were driven back in rout, but rallied on the reverse side of the earthworks.

General Gordon, in his *Reminiscences of the Civil War*, after describing in rather exaggerated phrase his gathering of forces to meet Hancock's advancing host; General Lee's inspiring presence and determination to personally lead them, overcome by the appeals and assurances of his officers and men that if he would go to the rear they would drive back the invaders; the resistless rush under cover of the fog of his organized lines upon the disorganized Second Corps;—closes the paragraph with this remark (page 280), "Every foot of the lost Salient and earthworks was retaken, except that small stretch which the Confederate line was too short to cover." Later on he continues (at page 284):

As soon as it was ascertained that the Confederate lines had been too short to stretch across the whole of the wide-spreading crescent, and that the outer slope of a portion of

Lee's works was still held by Grant's stalwart fighters, the third and last act of that memorable performance was opened. Under my orders, and under cover of the intrench-ment, my men began to slip to the left a few feet at a time, in order to occupy, unobserved if possible, that still open space. The ditch along which they slowly glided, and from which the earth had been thrown to form the embank-ment, favored them; but immediately opposite to them and within a few feet of them on the outer side stood their keen-eyed, alert foemen, holding to their positions with a relent-less grip. This noiseless sliding process had not proceeded far before it was discovered by the watchful men in blue. The discovery was made at the moment when Lee and Grant began to hurl their columns against that portion of the works held by both. Thus was inaugurated that roll of musketry which is likely to remain without a parallel, at least in the length of time it lasted.

Mounting to the crest of the embankment, the Union men poured upon the Confederates a galling fire. To the support of the latter other Confederate commands quickly came, crowding into the ditches, clambering up the embank-ment's side, and returning volley for volley. Then followed the mighty rush from both armies, filling the entire disputed space. Firing into one another's faces, beating one another down with clubbed muskets, the front ranks fought across the embankment's crest almost within an arm's reach, the men behind passing up to them freshly loaded rifles as their own were emptied. As those in front fell, others quickly sprang forward to take their places. On both sides the dead men were piled in heaps. As Confederates fell, their bodies rolled into the ditch, and upon their bleeding forms, their living comrades stood, beating back Grant's furiously charging columns. The bullets seemed to fly in sheets. Be-fore the pelting hail and withering blast the standing timber fell. The breastworks were literally drenched in blood. The coming of the darkness failed to check the raging battle. It only served to increase the awful terror of the scene.

In an address by Colonel Joseph N. Brown, [1] who, after the wounding of General McGowan at the Bloody Angle, on May 12th, had command of what was known as McGowan's (South Carolina) brigade, and which brigade for nineteen hours, from 9 in the morning of the 12th until 4 o'clock on the morning of the 13th, occupied the traverses at the Bloody Angle, and with Harris's Mississippi Brigade did some of the most desperate fighting at the Bloody Angle, it is stated:

On the morning of the 12th of May, the brigade was in front or north of Spottsylvania court-house. Gen. Ewell's corps was on the left or west of us. It was scarcely light when we heard firing along Gen. Ewell's lines and the direction soon indicated that his troops were being driven back. A feeling of unrest among officers of high rank indicated disaster. Gen. Harris's Mississippi Brigade of A. P. Hill's corps was ordered to move in that direction. Soon after 9 o'clock McGowan's brigade was also ordered there. Gen. Grant had massed his troops and assaulted the lines held by Gen. Ewell, capturing Gen. Edward Johnson and over 3000 prisoners. It was to recapture these works and repair the disaster that Harris's and McGowan's brigades were sent forward. Gen. John B. Gordon by a brilliant charge and some other commands of Gen. Ewell's corps had already recaptured part of the works. But the strongest and most ably defended portion including the Angle and the works to the left of it, was still held by the Federal troops. Gen. Harris's brigade had captured part of the line to the right of Gen. Gordon, but did not reach to the Angle. This left the Angle and the works to the right of Gen. Harris for the assault and capture by McGowan's brigade.

[1] Pamphlet printed by The Advocate Publishing Co. (1900), Anderson, S. C., "An Address delivered by Col. Joseph N. Brown, at the November (1900) meeting of the R. E. Lee Chapter of the Daughters of the Confederacy on the Battle of the 'Bloody Angle.'"

It was here that the celebrated incident of Gen. Gordon inducing Gen. Lee to go to the rear occurred. The Angle was not an inverted V nor a horse-shoe as sometimes called in the reports, and in fact was an obtuse instead of an acute angle in the works. These works were on the highest ground or crest at this place, sloping down-hill in front and rear and were in the edge of oak woods on our side and an old field of pines in our front, rather thin nearest the works and thicker farther into the Federal lines in our front. This depression was such a formation as afforded protection to the Federals. From the Angle westward to be occupied by us were traverses or short breastworks some twelve or fifteen feet long running back or south from the front and about the same distance apart and open to the rear. These traverses had been constructed for defence from an enfilading or flank fire to which the troops might be subjected from the enemy on the right of the Angle in case they held it. [A diagram exhibited, the blue lines representing the Federal forces, the black lines the Confederates.]

The brigade on reaching the battle ground was rapidly formed in line of battle, the Twelfth on the right, which would be for the Angle, and the Fourteenth on the left, farthest from the Angle, and the other regiments between. Through some fault of some officers of Gen. Ewell or Gen. Rodes we were not properly directed so as to reach the objective point, and the right of the brigade, the Twelfth Regiment, did not reach as far as the Angle and the other regiments toward the left had to go through the terrible ordeal of a flank movement led by the Twelfth, and it was one of the fiercest and most bloody struggles of the war, but succeeded in reaching and holding the Angle while the Federal troops still held the right of the Angle on the opposite side almost lapping our lines. Thus both sides claimed to hold the Angle. Besides the heavy loss of men there was a greater proportion in loss of officers for the number engaged. We had lost so heavily in officers in the Wilderness that we had perhaps not half our usual number and of these very few escaped being killed or wounded. The charge was made facing a terrific fire in front and a more terrific and deadly fire in flank from the enemy on the right of the Angle. It is only the soldier familiar with battle that knows the fatal effect of a flank fire. But it was met and the works carried, but with it the severe wounding of Gen. McGowan, our brigade commander. Col. B. T. Brockman, the second in command, was mortally wounded; Cols. McCreary of the First and Miller of Orr's Rifles wounded; Lieut.-Col. W. P. Shooter of the First killed, and many line officers wounded, and Adjutant D. E. Brown of the Fourteenth mortally wounded. In the wounding of Gen. McGowan and Col. Brockman, the command of the brigade devolved on me as third in command, being next in rank to Col. Brockman, but my regiment, the Fourteenth, being on the left, and Lieut.-Col. Isaac F. Hunt of the Thirteenth Regiment being near the Angle to the right, he conducted the battle for awhile with the right regiments, being the ranking officer on that part of the line. He soon informed me of the state of affairs and I assumed command, going with him to the right, near the Angle, and at once took in the situation and entered upon the work of holding the Angle during the next succeeding seventeen hours under the most terrific rain of minie balls recorded in the history of warfare. During that seventeen hours the oak woods along our line and to our rear were riddled with bullets; one red oak, near 18 inches in diameter, and a hickory, 8 inches, were cut down by the minie balls in our lines, in the fourth traverse from the Angle, and many others stripped largely of the bark and leaves. The hickory fell late in the afternoon and the oak early in the night.

On arriving at this point and assuming command it became apparent from the few officers left with us, that in order to successfully hold the Angle another officer was needed to forward men to the right to take the places of their comrades as they fell killed or wounded, and to forward ammunition to replenish the cartridge boxes, while the

brigade commander should take his station near the right
and be ready for emergencies as they might arise.   At my
request Col. Hunt took charge of the forwarding of the men
and ammunition as needed, and with almost superhuman
strength performed that duty during the long, deadly
struggle.   Without this efficient service it would seem impossible to have held the lines.   Any weakening of the lines,
or any scarcity of ammunition would have been fatal.   The
brave men towards our left moved with haste to the right
as called upon, and never for a moment did we lack for men
to hold the Angle and traverses to its left, though frequently
the enemy crossed rifles and bayonets across the works and
at times crossed over themselves, when a hand-to-hand
conflict ensued most deadly in its character.   Our men in
the traverses to the left would charge in with the Rebel
yell to the aid of their overpowered comrades, recapture the
position with some prisoners, and drive the others across to
their own side.   Except when the conflict was raging at
such close quarters, the whole fire of the Federals was concentrated from all points and their lines were also heavily
concentrated, and quadrupled, upon our front and that of
Harris, but more than doubly so on the Angle and traverses
in our brigade, heavier at the oak tree on the fourth traverse
above described.   Late in the day it was observed that
quite a number of Harris's brigade were being brought to
the right with our men by Col. Hunt, and the number
increased later, so that by night every part of our brigade,
and especially on the right, was intermingled with the brave
Mississippians.

With one short intermission hereinafter referred to, the
conflict raged every hour and every minute until midnight
with the greatest fury, and from midnight until 4 A.M. on
the 13th it only slackened from the exhaustion and weakness
of our brave soldiers and by the withdrawal of part of the
Union forces in our front.   I say part of them, for by Gen.
Hancock's official report he states that he withdrew his
forces at midnight, but my personal knowledge of the

sweeping bullets along our lines all the night long, impels me to construe his report as withdrawing his corps but leaving other commands to contest the point until morning. At all events soldiers were there and firing continually, closely, and at short range. And to the last our men fell pierced by their bullets. The Mississippians like us had very few officers and in many of the traverses had not an officer with them, nor did they seem to need them for all along the lines they had special orders to move rapidly to any point of greatest danger. This they did every time the enemy secured any footing on the right and drove them out, recovering the lost ground. The lines on the left of the brigade of course became thinner in order to mass on the right and to fill the places of our dead and wounded, and so did the lines of Harris's brigade, for by night we had a large body of them with us on the right. They responded nobly to Col. Hunt's demand on them, for he did not deem it prudent to make the lines of our brigade any weaker. He went still farther to the west into Gen. S. D. Ramseur's brigade, but under orders his officers could not weaken their line. No immediate firing was in their front, but a cross fire from the right of the Angle threw some balls among them to which they could not reply in safety to us. It was a rainy day and water stood in the trenches, reddened with the blood of our wounded and dead comrades, and before dark the dead were so thick in the traverses toward the right that the living had not standing room without trampling on them and they laid them in heaps to make room. Night came on and our men still held every foot of ground which had been captured. The Angle was still ours, and no attempt to cross it was again made. But the deadly fire continued from front and flank, and scores of men fell during the night whose names could not be known and on the roll-call next day were added to the list of missing. It was in the dark of the moon and a drizzling rain fell all night, and the darkness was only broken by the flashing of the guns to light up the horrid scene. After midnight the fire of the enemy slackened but continued dangerous and fatal all night and ceased only as we lvoluntarily left the place at 4 A.M. on the 13th. We quietly left with only a few stray bullets following. We withdrew because a better and stronger line had been formed in our rear, as being better than sending in reinforcements.

At 9.30 o'clock on the morning of the 12th, the enemy had succeeded in taking possession of the interior lines of the works on the west side of the Salient from the point designated as A in the diagram, to a point about 150 feet southwest of the so-called Bloody Angle, designated as I on the diagram, and from that point the Fourth Brigade of the Second Division occupied the exterior line of the earthworks of the Salient to a point within 150 feet of the apex of the Salient, where for a distance of several hundred feet, the enemy had succeeded in dislodging a portion of Mott's division of the Second Corps, and driving them out of their possession of the works. Later in the day this portion of the line was recaptured by the Second Corps.

Until the arrival of the First Division of the Sixth Corps, about 9.30 o'clock, the Fourth Brigade was mainly employed with the other brigades of the Second Division in replying to the almost constant fusillade kept up by the enemy from behind the impenetrable fog in which they were concealed, and repelling three separate assaults of their columns of attack, by which they attempted to compel the Sixth Corps to withdraw entirely from its possession of the works connected with the Salient. For an hour or two after 9.30, the Fourth Brigade was alone in its occupancy of the exterior of the works on that portion of the line, and on both flanks of the brigade, where we occupied the exterior of the works, the enemy occupied the interior at a distance of only four or five feet between the lines.

A little beyond the right of the line occupied by us the enemy had built, in order to prevent the enfilading of their lines by our artillery, a series of traverses which extended perpendicularly from the interior of the earthworks twelve or fifteen feet, at distances of fifteen or twenty feet apart. The whole number of these traverses, so far as they were visible from our line, did not exceed ten. These were occupied by the enemy and used as fortresses, from which they kept up a constant fire upon all of our lines within their vision. On the other hand, a great part of our time was occupied in watching for the appearance of heads above or outside of these fortresses or under the head logs, in order to get shots at their marksmen and silence their fire. As the fog was much of the time so heavy that nothing could be seen but the dim outlines of the works, we kept up a constant fire in order to prevent them from showing themselves, or using the openings under the head logs as port-holes. They used the same tactics in trying to silence our fire.

Thus it continued from 6 o'clock on the morning of the 12th until 4 o'clock on the morning of the 13th, the soldiers of the Fourth Brigade firing during that time about 500 rounds of ammunition to the man. They brought us ammunition by the box. Our guns got hot and we would send them to the rear and receive other guns in exchange, and when our guns were cooled and cleaned they were returned to us. The operation was repeated several times during the day. They did not dare to relieve us because they were afraid that when we were moving out and other regiments were coming in, the enemy would seize the interior of the lines and accomplish the end they had been fighting for. At one time after dark, about 9 o'clock in the evening, an attempt was made to withdraw our line and to substitute another brigade for ours, but in the midst of it the cry was raised that the enemy were occupying the works and we were speedily rushed back into our former position and the attempt to relieve us was given up.

On several occasions during the day undertakings were organized with a view of storming the traverses and getting possession of the interior works. In the morning, between 10 and 11 o'clock, Colonel Edwards was authorized to organize a detail of fifty men who were expected to carry the first traverses at the point of the bayonet. Accordingly he called for volunteers from the Thirty-seventh Massachusetts, and fifty men stepped forward, and I was assigned to the duty of leading them. We withdrew from the works to a protected point just under the crest in the rear of the line and made our plans. I examined, as carefully as I could, from the different standpoints the traverses that were to be assaulted, and agreed with Colonel Edwards as to the line of our attack. When we were all ready to start, orders were received from the headquarters of the corps countermanding the authority to make the attempt. I have the impression that the results of the various assaults attempted by General Upton and General Russell, and in particular by the New Jersey Brigade, had convinced the officers at the headquarters of the corps that it would be a useless slaughter.

If the New Jersey Brigade failed to hold this portion of the works after getting inside of them on the 10th, and were compelled to retire with the loss of 789 men, what could our little handful of fifty men hope to accomplish in their effort to seize and hold the same position? If we had made the attempt there is every probability that the whole detachment would have been sacrificed.

Later in the day Cutler's division of the Fifth Corps was ordered to make an assault on the same part of the enemy's lines, backed if necessary by the other divisions of the Fifth Corps.

General Humphrey in his *Virginia Campaign of '64 and '65*,[1] says of this assault:

> It appearing probable that the enemy's intrenchments in the vicinity of the west angle could be carried if assaulted by the whole Fifth Corps, General Warren was directed to withdraw from his front and move with his whole corps to the designated point and attack. Griffin's division followed Cutler's closely. The other troops of the Fifth Corps were following except Crawford's division, when the project of further assault was given up, as it did not appear to promise a complete success.

The Fourth Brigade did succeed in stopping any advance of the enemy north of the first traverse in the interior of their works. Our guns were trained on that point with instructions to shoot down and annihilate every live thing that appeared on that part of the field. The result was that nothing could live there. Hundreds of muskets were trained ready to shoot if any attempt was made to advance their occupation at that point, and after dark when we could no longer see any such movement a constant fire was kept up to prevent any possible attempt on their part to seize and occupy the Angle. Several such attempts were made during the day, but they had to be abandoned.

General Humphrey further says at page 98:

> It is apparent from these statements that the outer **face**

[1] "Campaigns of the War Series" (Scribner), vol. xii., p. 101.

13

of the captured intrenchments in this part of the field was held by our troops, as they were from there around to the apex of the west angle and *some distance on the west face of the Salient.*

Thus hour after hour we kept up our weary vigil. Every other regiment or brigade of the Sixth Corps that was on the firing line was relieved during the afternoon or early evening.   In volume iv. of the Papers of the Military Historical Society of Massachusetts, on the Wilderness Campaign, at page 66, it is sta ted in the note that all Grant's toilers in the ditch were relieved except the Thirty-seventh Massachusetts.   My understanding is that none of the regiments of the Fourth Brigade, Second Division, was relieved, but of this I am not absolutely certain.   Possibly the Tenth Massachusetts and Second Rhode Island were withdrawn from the firing line at 9 o'clock in the evening, when the attempt was made to relieve the Thirty-seventh Massachusetts, which failed, as I have before described.[1]

[1] General Edwards, of the Thirty-seventh Massachusetts regiment, in his unpublished memoir entitled, "My Recollections of the Civil War" (manuscript, pages 85–7), concludes his account of the battle as follows: "My command was engaged in close, hot fighting from about 5 A.M., May 12th, to 3 A.M., May 13th (22 hours).   This shows that my front was the main point of attack.   The heavy traverses, and enfilading fire, also showed my front to have been the crown or apex of the Angle.   The line of the enemy's enfilading fire across Upton's front, and down the line of the Tenth Massachusetts to the Second Company to the right of the Second Rhode Island passed then to the rear of the Second Rhode Island and Thirty-seventh Massachusetts until opposite the left of the Thirty-seventh Massachusetts the enfilading fire was about 50 yards in their rear.   These facts certainly prove the location of the Angle. As the battle of the Angle (after Hancock's magnificent charge) was no part of the plans of General Grant, it was not considered of much importance by us, but the Richmond *Whig* of May 18th, 1864, showed that the enemy considered it of very great importance, and that the defence

Between three and four o'clock in the morning of May
13th, the enemy withdrew their forces from the Salient
to the earthworks which they had built during the
previous day at its base. We waited for the dawn and
then cautiously peered over the earthworks. They
had so quietly stolen away that we were not aware that
they had gone, and expected to see them rise from
behind their traverses and renew the fight, but it did
not take us long to discover the fact that they had
vacated the Salient.

Such a scene as we there witnessed is beyond the
power of pen to describe. The bodies of the fallen lay
all over the field. Horses and men chopped into hash
by the bullets, and appearing more like piles of jelly
than the distinguishable forms of human life, were
scattered all over the plain. Caissons and artillery
carriages were cut into slivers. Trees large and small
were cut down. It had rained much of the twenty-

---

was the most heroic they had ever met on the part of the Yanks. The
survivors of the Thirty-seventh Massachusetts and the Second Rhode
Island, Tenth Massachusetts, and the regiments of the brigade of the
Second Corps, will recognize the truth of what I have written of the
battle of the Angle. I refrain from mentioning names of those of my
command who were especially brave and efficient as nearly all of the
command did such heroic fighting. In giving this version of the Angle
proper, I have carefully reviewed all the data in my possession, and while
I recognize how nearly impossible it is to give an entirely correct account
of any battle, yet I am confident that what I have written herein is as
correct as it is possible to be, so far as it concerns my own command and
those commands immediately on my right, and left. And this I write
as the honor of the defence of the Angle has been claimed for Upton's
brigade, which might as well have been at the bottom of a well firing
up at the sky for all the loss they did or could inflict upon the enemy,
from the position they occupied. Throughout that long night Captain
T. G. Colt was the only one of my staff able to do duty. His great
heart and intense will kept him up while the other brave men slept like
the dead in the mud and rain. There was no artillery used on our side
at or near the Angle save a section (two guns) on the front of the Second

four hours, and the surface of the plain was torn with the trampling of the armed hosts and the struggles of the combatants. The ground was soaked with blood and water, with here and there pools deeply dyed with the same ingredients.

Among the wounded were Lieutenant-Colonel Montague, Captains Lincoln and Pease, First Lieutenants Champney and Wellman, Second Lieutenants Sparks, Follansbee, and Cooke. The latter was of my company, and in his case and that of Follansbee the wounds proved fatal. Both were recently promoted and commissioned and had excellent records as soldiers. George Cooke was my acquaintance from boyhood, and our relations in the regiment were very intimate. Toward Lincoln I felt like a brother, and as rumor at first reported him as mortally wounded, I had a deep sense of depression as if I were being deserted and left alone. My weariness added much to the force of this impression.

Rhode Island. As the fire of these guns was less effective than the infantry fire owing to the enemy's being entirely protected from our fire until they were within a few yards from us, I requested the officer commanding them to withdraw the guns which he did, the guns being in action but a short time. Two oak trees of considerable size were cut down by bullets in front of my command and a battle flag was captured by the Thirty-seventh Massachusetts. The Vermont Brigade to the right of Wheaton had some hard fighting and drove the enemy from their front and Birney's division to my left repulsed any attempt made by the enemy in their front, but the Angle proper was defended by my command of the Thirty-seventh and Tenth Massachusetts and Second Rhode Island of my own brigade, and what I understand to have been the Excelsior Brigade of the Second Corps, assisted by the effective cross fire of the Tenth New Jersey (after 5 P.M.). The longest and severest fighting was sustained by the Thirty-seventh and Tenth Massachusetts and the Second Rhode Island. My account of the defence of the Angle is mainly limited to the defence of the Angle proper; of the honorable part borne by other commands I could attempt to write only what I saw myself or heard of at the time."

Returning now to the First Division of the Sixth Corps, Upton's official report indicates that, in the early morning, that division was sent to or towards the right of the Army of the Potomac. General Upton there states: "Early on the 12th it [Upton's Second Brigade, First Division] *moved with the division* toward the right flank of the army, but to the left again at 7 A.M., arriving in rear of the Second Corps at 9.30 A.M." (O. R., xxxvi., pt. 1, page 669). In Haines's *History of the Fifteenth New Jersey Regiment*, which regiment belonged to the First (or New Jersey) Brigade and First Division of the Sixth Corps, the following facts appear. General Sedgwick on May 9th, just before he was killed, ordered the First New Jersey Brigade from an exposed position on the Brock Road to a place in the rear near Alsop's house on the same road. On page 174 Haines says:

We had been drawn in, during the night of the 10th, from the position before the Salient, to one behind a work which had been constructed to the left and rear of the position of the morning of the 9th and *to which we had been ordered by General Sedgwick* just before he fell. *On the 11th after the manœuvers in front of this position, we were brought back to this point, where we again spent the night.*

This fixes the position of the New Jersey Brigade and probably of the First Division on the night of the 11th of May, to-wit: at Alsop's, which was one mile west of the Salient. Mr. Haines continues:

When the works at the Salient were taken, we were at once hurried *still further to the right* [N. B. the exact movement described by General Upton as made at the time *by his brigade with the division*] south of the position of the morning of the 9th, *with the view of strengthening the right flank of our army, in case an attack should be made upon it by the enemy, who might naturally suppose we had weakened our line there by the forces taken to the left.* [After stating the success of the Second Corps attack:] The brigade was then double-quicked to the north, to the camp of the night before, from which we had started; then east, . . . and southward to the Bloody Angle."

General Upton states the fact of this digressive movement and Haines's History gives the details and the reasons for the same. The result was that the First Division did not reach the battle-ground until 9.30 A.M., and the Second Division had then been desperately fighting with varying fortunes for three and a half hours.

Under General Russell's direction, the First (or New Jersey) Brigade was put into position opposite the point where Upton made his successful assault on May 10th, the Second (or Upton's) Brigade supported by the Third (or Russell's old) Brigade established the left of its line about two hundred feet south of the west (or "Bloody") angle, in the exterior of the earthworks, extending a little north of west (see O—P on diagram), and the Fourth (or Shaler's) Brigade was put in at various points to fill gaps as they were found to exist in the line, and in particular relieved a portion of Mott's division, Second Corps, at the east angle.

The part taken by each of the commands will more fully appear when the story of each is told. Of course, it is imperfect, but I give it so far as I have been able to gather it from the official records and regimental and brigade histories. Parts of some of these reports have already been quoted, but at the risk of repetition whatever relates to these specific commands will be given in full under headings naming the commands to which they relate.[1]

[1] The story here referred to of the part taken and the positions occupied by each brigade of the Sixth Corps, separately told, will be found in the Appendix, at page 349.

CHAPTER XI

THE SIGNIFICANCE OF THE BATTLES OF THE WILDERNESS AND SPOTTSYLVANIA

THE Wilderness and Spottsylvania were in reality one long drawn battle. Grant started out to administer a decisive defeat to the Army of Northern Virginia. Lee countered, as he had done, so successfully at Chancellorsville, when the Army of the Potomac attempted to advance against him in Virginia, by checking the advance in its beginnings, and then striking a quick, decisive blow in return. He succeeded remarkably at Chancellorsville with these tactics and in the Wilderness he tried it with the assurance of success that he had derived from his experience at Chancellorsville.

His biographers are unanimous in declaring that Lee fully believed that he had Grant in a trap, and would be able to overwhelm him or drive him back as he had Hooker and Burnside. In fact against any other commander of the Army of the Potomac than Grant, after the 6th of May the movement would have ended in a retreat across the Rappahannock. Lee himself was much astonished on the 7th of May when he found that Grant was moving around his right flank and advancing instead of retreating. This was a bitter disappointment to Lee, and at Spottsylvania he summoned all the resources of his great nature in one final supreme effort to stop Grant's advance, and to compel the retreat of the Northern army. This accounts for the terrible conflict that was waged at Spottsylvania. It was the last desperate effort of the Army of Northern Virginia aggressively to check our advance by the right flank and if possible cut us off from our base at Fredericksburg.

After Spottsylvania, Lee fought a defensive fight, although at North Anna, where he was prostrated by sickness, he is quoted by one of his staff as saying, "We must strike them a blow, we must never let them pass us again." The will was still there, but both he and his army were too weak to put it into execution. They were saving their strength for the defensive tactics adopted at Cold Harbor.

It is reported that as Lee rode away from Spottsylvania, he remarked, "We wish no more Salients."

That the pace which General Lee established for the Army of Northern Virginia in the Wilderness and maintained at Spottsylvania was too hot to be kept up, was indicated by what had happened to its leaders. By the time that he reached North Anna, not only was Lee himself prostrated by an alarming sickness, but his great cavalry commander Stuart was killed on the 10th of May, at the Yellow Tavern, a few miles north of Richmond.[1] Two out of three of his corps commanders were disabled, Longstreet by wounds, and A. P. Hill by sickness. These men could not be replaced.

Swinton, in his *History of the Army of the Potomac*, at page 458, sums up the situation of the Northern army in the following language:

Before the lines of Spottsylvania the Army of the

[1] See Long's *Memoirs of R. E. Lee*, page 343.

Potomac had for twelve days and nights engaged in a fierce wrestle, in which it had done all that valor may do to carry a position, by nature and art impregnable.

In this contest, unparalleled in its continuous fury, and swelling to the proportions of a campaign, language is inadequate to convey an impression of the labors, fatigues, and sufferings of the troops, who fought by day only to march by night, from point to point of the long line, and renew the fight on the morrow. Above forty thousand men had already fallen in the bloody encounters of the Wilderness and Spottsylvania, and the exhausted army began to lose its spirit. It was with joy, therefore, that it at length turned its back upon the lines of Spottsylvania.

The Southern losses were proportionately less than the Northern, but the resources of the North were vastly greater than those of the South.

Who can doubt that General Lee, as he turned his back upon the lines of his army at Spottsylvania and thought of his dwindling numbers and his irreparable losses, recognized the fact that the era of great battles between the Army of Northern Virginia and the Army of the Potomac had passed? Henceforth he was on the defensive.

CHAPTER XII

AFTER SPOTTSYLVANIA. NORTH ANNA AND COLD HARBOR

MAY 13 TO JUNE 12, 1864

WHEN the Fourth Brigade, Second Division, were relieved at the Bloody Angle, at 5 o'clock of the morning of May 13th, and allowed to go to the rear, they were so exhausted, that when they were withdrawn to the vicinity of the Landrum house, they could hardly wait for their breakfast of crackers and coffee, until they dropped in their tracks and fell asleep in the soft spongy Virginia soil. They slept without interruption during that day and until evening, when the Sixth Corps was ordered to follow the Fifth Corps in a movement through the woods in the rear of Burnside (Ninth Corps) to the extreme left of the line southeast from Spottsylvania Court-House.

The night was horribly dark, and at times the rain fell in torrents. An attempt had been made to mark the route by building fires at intervals through the woods, and guides supposed to be familiar with the byways and paths of that region were used; but the fires gradually burned out, the guides even got lost, and before daylight we were obliged to halt because of inability to make any progress. With the dawn of day we were started again and moved two or three miles to the left, through the mud, where we rested from 9 o'clock in the morning until 3 o'clock in the afternoon of May 14th. At 3 o'clock in the afternoon we were moved still farther to the left, halted and formed lines of battle with the Third Division of the Sixth Corps thrown across the Po River. After moving our lines three separate times, we were finally allowed to spend the night in a ploughed field, sleeping as we could between the furrows with our arms in our hands.

May 15th was Sunday, and after being awakened at 5 o'clock in the morning and standing in line for an hour, the regiments were allowed to stack arms and to eventually spend the day and the night in attempted rest with one or two interruptions in the shape of orders to move, which were countermanded. Our chaplain even held service at 1 o'clock and preached a sermon.

The weather was threatening and all night the rain fell in heavy showers. This was the beginning of a period of five days of rain, during which General Grant writes that the "roads became so bad that ambulances with wounded men could not move between the Army and Fredericksburg."

On the night of the 17th, the Second and Sixth Corps were suddenly ordered to march back to their old positions at the Salient and to assault at 4 A.M. of the next morning. We marched all night, a step at a time, and in the morning found ourselves near the famous Angle of May 12th.

General Wheaton's brigade was massed for an assault, and we were part of the supports. The attack was made at 4.30 in the morning, but we did not succeed in surprising the enemy, and their works were too strong to be carried by assault. After being subjected to a severe fire of shell, grape, and canister, the Sixth Corps was withdrawn, the Thirty-seventh having suffered a loss of twenty-one men.

During the afternoon of the 18th we returned to our position on the left of the army from which we had started the previous day. That night I was detailed with 100 men to perform picket duty. Our picket line ran through heavily timbered woods. I had great difficulty in establishing the line and making connections at both ends. The forest was so thick and dark that I saw it would be impossible to relieve the line at night. I therefore put three men on each post with instructions that they should relieve each other, and I planted these posts at proper intervals. But as the Confederate picket line was so close in our front that we could hear them moving about and talking, we spent a very anxious night. We were withdrawn at daylight and returned to the regiment, and the corps was moved about a mile to the right and formed line of battle in anticipation of an attack. The day passed without any special occurrence in our front or on our part of the line. General Grant was occupied during this and the next two days with preparations to move the army around the Confederate right flank, which resulted in bringing the two armies face to face on the south bank of the North Anna River on May 24th.

During May 20th I received the following order:

HEADQUARTERS SECOND DIV., 6TH CORPS,
May 19th, 1864.

Special Orders.

No. 81.   [Extract]

Captain M. W. Tyler, 37th Massachusetts Volunteers, is hereby detailed as A. A. D. C. to Brig.-Gen. Neill, Com'd'g 2d Division. He will report with the least possible delay.

By order of

Brig.-Gen. NEILL.

(Signed), WILLIAM H. LONG,
Capt. & A. A. G.

I received the order on the 20th, and reported on the 21st to General Neill at 12 o'clock.

General Thomas H. Neill, who had honored me with an appointment on his staff, was a graduate of West Point in the Class of 1847, had served in the Mexican War and in the Indian campaigns on the frontier. He was brevetted for conspicuous gallantry at Malvern Hill, received four other brevets during the war, and at its close was a brevet major-general of volunteers. When General Getty was wounded on May 6th in the Wilderness, General Neill was assigned to the command of the Second Division, Sixth Corps. He was a man of fine personal presence, very cultivated in his tastes and manners, and in the regular army was generally known as "Beau Neill." It was a rare privilege for me to serve on the staff of such an experienced and capable division commander. My associates on the staff were Captain William H. Long, assistant adjutant-general, Captain Hazard Stevens, division inspector-general, and Captains Horace Binney and Andrew J. Smith, personal aides-de-camp. It was an efficient staff. Excepting myself they were all experienced and seasoned staff officers.

When I reported for duty I was pretty well fagged out. We had fought by day and marched by night until it seemed as if I could hardly put one foot before the other. It was a great relief to mount a horse, although I was so tired that during the first two or three nights it seemed as if I would fall asleep and roll off my horse in spite of myself.

At 3 o'clock on the morning of May 21st, we were ordered out to stand in line. The details for picket and fatigue duty were so large that there were hardly men enough left to man the works. At 9 o'clock we moved back into a new line of works where my regiment spent the rest of the day. During the afternoon the Sixth Corps, which had been selected to cover the final withdrawal of the army from the Spottsylvania lines, was ordered to be in readiness for a move at dark. We were concentrated on high ground, in the vicinity of the Gayle house[1] on the Fredericksburg road. Late in the day, General Hill made a reconnoissance in force to see if we were still in the lines, but was driven back in confusion. The artillery firing was especially effective under the direction of Colonel C. H. Tompkins. The Sixth Corps suffered a loss of a few men, and of these the Thirty-seventh Massachusetts contributed one man killed, and six wounded. I was busy during the engagement carrying orders.

After dark we started and marched slowly, and all the next day, halting briefly for meals. Our route was by Guinea Station,[2] where Stonewall Jackson died,[3] and from thence along the railroad to Milford Point Station. The distance marched was something over twenty miles. We halted at 6.30 P.M., at Calker's Station, very much fatigued, but formed line of battle and spent the night in that array.

The next morning, May 23d, at 5 o'clock we were awake, and I was sent with an engineer officer to find the "Telegraph Road," and see if there were any traces of the Confederate army. I succeeded in finding the road, but no Confederates were in sight, and I reported accordingly, and upon my return had breakfast. For some reason, to me unknown, our march was not resumed until ten o'clock, when we crossed the Ta

[1] See War Map 91 (1) about two miles N. E. of the court-house.
[2] See War Map 81 (2).
[3] See *Life and Letters*, by his wife, p. 453.

River, halted and distributed rations, and then crossed the Polecat River and formed line of battle.

Soon after noon we received word that Warren had reached the North Anna River, and was there engaged with the enemy. We pushed forward and reached the river about 7.30 P.M. The roads were bad, and marching difficult. Warren had crossed the river at Jericho Ford, while the Second Corps had crossed four miles below, at Chesterfield Bridge, and the two corps were trying to connect on the south bank of the river. It was a critical situation, because the Northern army was divided, while the Southern army could concentrate its whole strength against either wing without fear of reinforcement from the other wing. Heavy artillery firing from the north bank upon the part of the enemy's line which separated our wings was kept up the most of the night. At 3 o'clock in the morning of the 24th, the Sixth Corps was awakened and crossed and went into position on the right of the Fifth Corps, and in a short time were protected by a strong line of works.

I spent most of the day in the works with orders to report to headquarters any signs of a movement in our front. On the 25th we were occupied in moving our lines to the left and in supporting the Fifth Corps in an attempt to connect with the Second Corps, and in the afternoon I was charged with the duty of seeing that the division picket line was properly posted. We had occasional bursts of musketry fire on the picket line.

On the 26th, General Russell was moved from our right and sent to the support of Griffin (Fifth Corps), and we had to occupy the line he had vacated. Heavy showers occurred during the afternoons of the 24th, 25th, and 26th. Orders to be ready to move were received at 6 P.M., and at 9 we started on our return across the river.   Between the darkness and the mud it was very difficult to keep the troops in the line of march and over the bridges.   It took us until 3 o'clock in the morning to reach Chesterfield Station, a distance of only five miles, where we halted and rations were issued.

At 6 A.M. on the 27th we started anew, and after a slow muddy march of fifteen miles on a sultry day, we reached Taylor's Ford on the Pamunkey River, where line of battle was formed and we halted for the night.

On May 28th we were aroused at 3 A.M. and started at daylight.   We crossed the Pamunkey at Nelson's Ford, which we reached at 8 o'clock and crossed on pontoons.   After an hour's halt, we moved out a couple of miles and formed line of battle on a ridge of hills.   We were now near Hanovertown,[1] which is thirty-two miles from Chesterfield Station and seventeen miles from Richmond.

May 29th was devoted to reconnoissances in force by the different corps of Meade's army.   The Sixth Corps went towards Hanover Court-House, a partially retrograde movement some ten miles to the northwest of Hanovertown.   No enemy was developed, and on the 30th, in trying to join the Second Corps to the south of us, we got entangled in a swamp which delayed our arrival until it was too late for the Second Corps to attack.   We were a short distance from Haw's shop, and fourteen miles from Richmond.

On May 31st we were in line at daylight, and, under General Neill's direction, I was sent to explore the picket line and report what was in our front.   From this and other reports, the corps and division commanders came to the conclusion that the line occupied by

[1] See War Map 81 (3).

14

the Confederates in our front was too strong by nature and art to be successfully attacked in front. Sheridan had been directed to occupy and hold Old Cold Harbor, and the Sixth and Eighteenth Corps were ordered from the right of the line at Haw's store to go to Sheridan's support at Old Cold Harbor.

It was towards midnight when the corps began to move. The weather was oppressively hot. Our division was to follow the wagon trains, and about midnight I was sent with an orderly to watch and report when the trains had passed, so that we could begin our march. This occupied me the rest of the night, and it was daylight before the roads were sufficiently clear for the Second Division to start.

June 1st was a day of oppressive heat. The soil, pulverized and kicked into the air by the thousands of feet of horses and men who for hours were marching by us, made the atmosphere in the rear of the column almost suffocating. I never knew a more uncomfortable day's march than that of our division on June 1, 1864. The distance we had to go was fifteen miles. The roads were blind and unfamiliar, and the movement of the two advance divisions and of the trains was very slow and very exhausting. The prize for which we were contending was Old Cold Harbor, which, on account of the large number of roads that centred there, was a strategic point of much importance.

The First and Third Divisions of the Sixth Corps arrived at the rendezvous about 10 o'clock in the morning. The Second Division was so delayed by the wagon trains that it was 2 o'clock before they joined the rest of the corps. The Eighteenth Corps had been marching for twenty-four hours, and had made twenty-five miles, and reached the rendezvous shortly after

our arrival.   By 5 o'clock our line of battle was formed.
The Sixth Corps was on the left.   General Ricketts's
(Third) division formed the right of the corps line,
resting on the road running from Old to New Cold
Harbor.   Russell's (First) division was on his left and
Neill's (Second) division was in reserve, with its left
refused to protect the left flank of the corps.   North
of the road the Eighteenth Corps was formed, with
Devens's (Third) division on its left resting on the road
and Brooke's (First) division extending their line
towards the north, and Martindale's (Second) division
in reserve, with its right refused to protect the right
flank of that corps.

The battle opened with artillery, and both the Sixth
and the Eighteenth Corps advanced to the attack with
much spirit, and succeeded in capturing the first line
of works, but were repulsed at the second line.   The
Sixth Corps captured five hundred prisoners, and the
Eighteenth, two hundred and fifty.   But the two corps
accomplished what they were sent there for.   They
held Old Cold Harbor.   The loss of the Sixth Corps in
killed and wounded exceeded twelve hundred men.
The Thirty-seventh Massachusetts had one man killed
and six wounded.   Personally I was very busy carrying
orders and reporting to General Neill the conditions
in the different parts of the line.   During the evening
General Neill directed me to make a personal examination of our division lines the next morning at daylight
and to report to him, which I accordingly did.

During the morning, the Second Corps was brought
from the right of the line at Haw's store and placed on
our left, a march of twelve miles.   This relieved Neill's
division, which was transferred from the reserve to the
part of the line held by Ricketts's division on the pre-

vious day. The Eighteenth Corps extended their line
on the right to connect with Warren (Fifth Corps),
and farther north was the Ninth Corps under Burnside,
in rather attenuated line to cover our base at West
Point. Sheridan, with two divisions of cavalry, covered the left flank of the army, while Wilson, with one
division, performed a similar service on our right flank.
These various changes occupied the second day of June.
An early morning attack had been planned and ordered
by General Grant, but between the heat and the exhausted condition of the soldiers, the army could not be
made ready, and it was postponed until 5 o'clock in the
evening, and then again until 4.30 the next day.

By that time, of course, the Confederate army had
duplicated the defences of Spottsylvania. Barlow's
division of the Second Corps on the left of the Union
line succeeded in taking a part of the Confederate
line in their front. The first line, which effected the
capture, was not supported by the second line of the
division, and consequently had to withdraw, but they
stubbornly fortified and held the ground closely in front.
The other divisions of the Second Corps did not pene-
trate the enemy's lines, although Gibbons's division made
a stubborn fight, and the corps lost three thousand men.

The following description of the part taken by the
Sixth Corps is taken from vol. iv., Military Historical
Society of Massachusetts, page 335:

The Sixth Corps at the appointed time instantly moved
to the front. This corps was formed in two lines of battle,
in the same order as on June 1—Ricketts on the right,
Russell in the centre, and Neill in support. These troops
advanced with great intrepidity. All that courage and
soldierly bearing could accomplish these gallant men did.

At 6 A.M. news was received that Ricketts had carried the line in his front, but Russell was repulsed. It was up the gentle slope from the east face of Watt's Hill and ridge to the northward that Wright had to take his men. The gallant soldiers of the Army of Northern Virginia were too well intrenched to have any trouble in resisting these assaults. The ground over which our men advanced was strewn with dead, dying, and wounded, and in less than half an hour Wright was repulsed at all points.

The corps lost about 1700 men in this attack. The Eighteenth Corps had a similar experience, and lost about 2000 men, and the Ninth Corps told the same tale. In fact, it was the culminating experience of the Army of the Potomac in its series of attacks on strongly fortified works, defended by an ably led and theretofore victorious army, fighting against invasion. They fought desperately, but with little hope. They lost in the neighborhood of ten thousand men,[1] and inflicted a loss of from a third to a half that number on their antagonists. The loss fell on the best and most seasoned material in our army. Furthermore, the enlistment of some of our three years' men now began to expire, and this meant an additional loss to the Army of the Potomac of from six to ten thousand of its choicest soldiers.

It was a sober day for the tired, twice-decimated and whipped army, when, at eventide, they sat down and counted their woes. They had gained a few rods in their advance on Richmond, and they resolutely set to work to hold it. The lines were so near in front of the Second and Sixth Corps that there was no room for pickets, so the main works became fortresses, frowning

---

[1] Fox in his *Regimental Losses*, at p. 541, states the loss of the Union army at Cold Harbor, 12,737.

at each other across a narrow gulf. Elaborate earth-works, with covered ways and traverses for the protection of the men, and embrasures and loopholes for our guns and muskets, were constructed. The firing was constant. If a head appeared above the parapet, the air in that vicinity was alive with bullets, and every now and then a shell would come crashing through the heaped-up earth. The men in front had to be constantly relieved. The air was foul with the stenches arising from unburied bodies of the fallen between the lines.

It was a part of my daily duty to inspect the lines, and I well remember the sickening odors that greeted my nostrils on the second or third day after the battle. Then a truce was arranged, and for two or three hours the men of the two armies mingled while each attended to the burial of their dead. Afterwards, a series of approaches outside of our lines with zigzag trenches leading to parallels were constructed, which exercised the ingenuity of our engineers and interested our soldiers, and drew from the enemy some mortar shells, as well as a good deal of ammunition, with which we were better acquainted. Fusillades of musketry fire at night now became very frequent, and kept us in constant expectation of an attack.

During this period, several shells burst uncomfortably near our headquarters, in fact one shell went through Captain Binney's tent. From June 2d to 15th, the Thirty-seventh had five killed and thirty wounded. The term of service of the Second Rhode Island expired on June 5th, and its battalion of three companies of re-enlisted men was attached to the Thirty-seventh.

Although the regiments in the front line of works were relieved every twenty-four hours, they were only retired to a second or third line a short distance to the rear, where they remained forty-eight hours, when they returned to the front line; yet in the rear lines they were subjected to so many alarms, and were so crowded behind earthworks, that they got very little rest, and when, on the afternoon of June 12th, the army received orders to be ready to move that night, a sense of relief seemed to possess every one, and for the time officers and men forgot the gloom that had possessed them all since the battle of the 3d of June, and exhibited a spirit of cheerfulness.

CHAPTER XIII

FROM COLD HARBOR TO PETERSBURG

FROM JUNE 12 TO 17, 1864

IT, was Sunday evening, June 12th, when we bade a glad adieu to the fateful field of Cold Harbor. At first we moved back about a mile and waited for the roads to be clear of the troops which were to precede us, and finally got under way about ten o'clock. I was charged with the duty of seeing that the different brigades followed each other in due order. It was after midnight before I was able to rejoin the staff at the head of the column. Our progress was slow because we were not familiar with the country. At best, marching an army in the dark is slow business, and when about six o'clock the next morning we halted an hour for breakfast, we found we had progressed only ten miles. After our halt we started again and crossed the Richmond and York Railroad at Summit Station,[1] where the old soldiers of my brigade recognized a camp they had occupied for a fortnight two years before.

Thence we moved by Hopkins Mill,[2] and crossed the Chickahominy at Jones's (or Forge) Bridge,[3] and, after

[1] War Map 20.

[2] About three miles due west of Tunstall's Station on the R. & Y. R. R. See War Map 92 (1).

[3] Compare War Map 17 (1).

crossing, formed line of battle and rested for the night.
During the twenty hours since we started, we had covered a distance of twenty-five miles and had gone without sleep. We were very tired and slept hard that
night.

The next morning we were aroused very early and
commenced our march at four o'clock, and before noon
had reached a place in the vicinity of Charles City Court-
House, where we were halted and went into camp. We
pitched our headquarters tents near a very comfortable
farmhouse. It proved to be the overseer's house on a
large plantation. Rich farm lands lay before us in every
direction as far as the eye could see, but they were
sparsely cultivated. Chickens and cherries were very
abundant, and upon these we feasted. Ex-President
John Tyler had his country residence in this vicinity.

After we got settled in camp, two or three of our staff
mounted horses and went in search of the distinguished
Virginian's home. The house was in charge of negro
servants, who tried faithfully to keep watch and ward,
but the soldiers soon invaded the premises, and upon
being admitted into the rear, forced their way into the
front of the house. It was a plain, comfortable habita-
tion, on a slightly elevated plateau, surrounded by
stately trees, with abundant bookshelves and many
books, and indications of literary work by its recent
occupants. Some books were carried off by the soldiers,
and not a few letters from prominent leaders in the
Confederacy to the ex-President were discovered and
appropriated. Aside from this, I do not think much
harm was done. The next day the place was protected
by a guard.

We were encamped about a mile from Wilcox Landing[1]

[1] South of the Charles City Court-House. See War Map 92 (1).

on the James River, which was selected by our engineers
for the location of a pontoon bridge, the construction of
which they commenced on the afternoon of our arrival
and completed at midnight. It consisted of 104 pontoon boats, each anchored in its place in the river and
connected by beams, and the whole steadied by being
connected at intervals with larger boats, also anchored.
It was 2100 feet long. The Second Corps arrived at
Wilcox Landing on Monday evening, June 13th, and,
on Wednesday morning at daylight, they and their
artillery had been transported on boats to the south
side of the James. After daylight, the bridge was used
to transfer the immense trains with the remainder of
artillery and the cavalry from the north to the south
side of the river. This occupied all day Wednesday,
and a good part of Thursday, the 16th of June.

Meanwhile, we had moved our camp to the river bank,
and were feasting on a fine view from the bluff over-
looking the river and the surrounding country. During
the morning of the 16th, the Fifth Corps was carried
across the river on transports above and below the
bridge. Finally orders came to embark the First and
Third Divisions of the Sixth Corps on transports, and
to land them at City Point, while the Second Division
was to follow the teams and the artillery.

We finally crossed on the bridge at seven o'clock in
the evening, and by a night march followed the trains
towards Petersburg. It was a hot night. The dust
beaten into powder by the hosts of horses and men
ahead of us filled the air with a choking, stifling mixture
that was hardly breathable. Our only relief was to
wash out our mouths with water from our canteens;
and unfortunately the supply of this was both poor
and short. But after a march of sixteen miles, morning

found us in the vicinity of City Point. We expected here to rejoin the other two divisions of the Sixth Corps, but they were detained by General Butler. We rested a couple of hours and pushed forward, and after the issue of rations, joined the Ninth and Second Corps.

At four o'clock in the afternoon we moved forward and relieved the Eighteenth Corps in the front line of battle. Meanwhile, a most unfortunate misunderstanding of orders by the commanders of the Second and Eighteen Corps had resulted, during the afternoon and evening of June 15th, in the loss of an opportunity to capture Petersburg. The Eighteenth Corps, on leaving Cold Harbor, marched back to White House, and from there were transferred in transports down the York River and up the James to Bermuda Hundred, where they landed, and on June 14th they crossed the Appomattox River on pontoons, seven miles below Petersburg.

No wonder that Lee was greatly mystified by these movements of General Grant, and as his particular anxiety was the safety of Richmond, he was constantly on the lookout for an attack at some point on the defences of that city. He never dreamed of an attempt by Grant to capture Petersburg by way of reducing Richmond, until Wednesday morning, when word was brought to him that the Federal army was advancing on Petersburg from Bermuda Hundred, and that the Army of the Potomac was crossing the James River. During Wednesday the defences of Petersburg were occupied by less than five thousand Confederate soldiers, while the Eighteenth Corps was all day within five miles of the heart of the city, and the Second Corps could easily have joined the Eighteenth Corps by four o'clock in the afternoon of that day, while the earliest reinforcements from Lee's army did not reach the Petersburg lines until sunset.

Failure to furnish rations to the Second Corps, as promised, in time for an early start in its march to Petersburg on Wednesday morning, together with a blind order that did not inform General Hancock that he was expected to capture Petersburg that afternoon, and an inaccurate map that carried him away from the intended rendezvous, combined to delay his final arrival until it was too late to attack. During the night Lee's army had begun to arrive, and the chance to capture by assault had vanished.

It looks very much as if Grant and Meade, one or both of them, on that Wednesday morning failed to see and comprehend the possible capture of Petersburg before nightfall, as clearly as they did later, when they learned how completely Lee was deceived by Grant's movement across the James, and how small was the force in front of Petersburg during the whole of that day. When they learned these facts they, of course, recognized that they had lost an opportunity to capture Petersburg, apparently through the delay of the Second Corps in arriving at its destination. For this they were inclined to blame General Hancock. Then the facts about the delayed rations and the imperfect order and misleading map came to light. But Hancock was sensitive and demanded an official investigation, and General Grant responded as follows:

The reputation of the Second Corps and its commander is so high, both with the public and in the army, that an investigation could not add to it. It cannot be tarnished by newspaper articles or scribblers. No official despatch has ever been sent from these headquarters which by any construction could cast blame on the Second Corps or its commander for the part they have played in this campaign.

A doubt has occurred to me in this connection whether Petersburg would have been captured on that Wednesday if rations had been issued and the Second Corps had started as ordered, and if General Hancock's map had located Harrison's Creek in the right place, and his marching orders had indicated an attack that afternoon with the support of the Eighteenth Corps. The weather was oppressively hot. The Second Corps was exhausted by its long march of thirty-five miles from Cold Harbor to Wilcox Landing on Sunday night and all day Monday, and again had no opportunity to sleep on Tuesday night, when it was being transported across the James. The corps was then expected to march seventeen miles through a new and unfamiliar country over dusty roads, and on approaching Petersburg to reconnoitre through a country intersected by deep ravines, more or less protected by woods and several lines of hastily constructed entrenchments, which the Eighteenth Corps had already spent two days in exploring and attacking with indifferent success. The men would have been too tired, and the time too short before dark, to accomplish anything.

CHAPTER XIV

THE RICHMOND CAMPAIGN—PETERSBURG

FROM JUNE 17 TO JULY 7, 1864

NOTE.—The introductions to the chapters in brackets, the notes marked "C. S.," and the conclusion, were contributed, by the author's college classmate and lifelong friend, the Reverend Calvin Stebbins, who has bestowed much time and labor upon all parts of the work.—*W. S. T.*

[INTRODUCTION.—With the arrival of the Second Division of the Sixth Corps at Petersburg on the afternoon of June 17th, the story of his army experience as written out by Colonel Tyler comes to an end. What follows is made up of letters written at the time, and extracts from his diary. This diary he had written out himself in the form of a card catalogue, giving in chronological order the events of every day, with occasional reference to official reports to assist him in writing his story. The reader will miss the reflections of the historical student writing in the quiet of after years, but without doubt will find compensation in the freshness and vigor of letters written in the hurry and excitement of a soldier's life while in active service.

Perhaps it may be well to describe the situation on the 17th of June, 1864.[1] The objective of the Army of the

[1] For the main line of the enemy's works before Petersburg, June 18th, see War Map 105 (7). I cannot locate the road by which the Second Division of the Sixth Corps came up from City Point to Petersburg on the 17th of June, 1864. But the War Maps 65 (1) and (9) show the route taken by the Eighteenth Corps and the works they captured. The Second Division relieved them in the lines on their arrival. It should

Potomac, after the withdrawal from Cold Harbor on the
12th of June, was the communications south of Richmond.
The lieutenant-general was a firm believer in the utility of
railroads in war, and felt that if he could get possession of
the railroads south of Richmond, the position of the Rebel
army would be untenable.   By a masterly movement, he
withdrew his army from Cold Harbor, and swung it around
to Petersburg, some twenty miles south of Richmond.

Petersburg stands on the south bank of the Appomattox
River.   The general course of the river is from west to
east, but a little below Petersburg it turns to the north,
and in a few miles takes an easterly direction and flows into
the James just above City Point.   Petersburg was a railroad centre of great importance.   It was connected by railroads with Richmond, City Point, and Norfolk.   The
terminals of the last two railroads were already in the hands
of the Union army.   But the Weldon Railroad, connecting
with the Carolinas and with tidewater at Wilmington; the
South Side Railroad, connecting with Lynchburg and the
Valley of the Shenandoah; and the Richmond and Danville
Railroad, which intersected the South Side Railroad at
Burkeville, were all in the hands of the enemy, and Petersburg was connected on the south and west with the whole
Southern Confederacy.   There were also several wagon
roads of importance which are often mentioned in the story
of the siege.   There was the Jerusalem Plank Road running
two or three miles east of the Weldon Railroad and parallel
to it; and along the westerly side of the Weldon Railroad
was the Halifax Road running in the same direction; and
still farther on, coming in from the southwest, was the Boyd-

---

be remembered that, owing to imperfect maps, General Grant made a
mistake in his order to General Hancock of the Second Corps, ordering
him to take a position west of Harrison's Creek.   This rivulet was a local
affair, and no one knew anything about it.   When found, it was within
the enemy's lines.   The Second Division was at first on the east side of
the creek to the extreme left.   The position they occupied may also be
seen on War Map 77 (2).—C. S.

ton Plank Road. Over these roads to the west of the
Weldon were hauled large quantities of produce for Lee's
army. For forty-two weeks to come these roads and railroads will be the object of contention.[1]

We may now look at the situation from another point of
view. The Confederate government had appointed General
Beauregard to the command of the military department of
North Carolina and Southern Virginia. He saw at once
the importance of Petersburg, and divined with surer
instinct than his chief what movement General Grant was
likely to make after Cold Harbor, and at once strengthened
the fortifications about Petersburg, which consisted at this
time of a series of redoubts running from the Appomattox
below the city to the river above, a distance of about
seven miles. On the east side, where the Union army was
likely to approach, was a line of thirteen redoubts on
commanding hills about two miles from the city, and running out some three miles from the river. These redoubts
were connected by infantry parapets with high profiles and
ditches. They were very strong and a few men could
defend them against many times their number.

It was not General Grant's intention that the Army of
the Potomac should have anything to do with the capture
of Petersburg. Before leaving Cold Harbor, he sent General Smith with the Eighteenth Corps to White House, and
then by water to Bermuda Hundred, where his command
was reinforced to about eighteen thousand men, from the
Army of the James. At 1.30 on the afternoon of June 15th,
General Smith, in pursuance of orders, came upon the outer
defences of Petersburg, and at seven in the evening ordered
an assault which was successful; but it was found that in
the rear of the line captured were some heavy profile works,
which kept up a galling artillery fire. The Second Division
of the Eighteenth Corps (colored) was ordered to carry the
works by assault, which they gallantly did, capturing five

[1] See War Maps 93 (1), 40 (1), 17 (1), 56 (1).

of the redans, Nos. 7, 8, 9, 10, and 11,[1] with guns, prisoners and ammunition.

The way into Petersburg was now open. It was late, but there was a full moon, and there was no great risk of a disastrous defeat, for at 6.30 that evening General Hancock came up with two divisions of the Second Corps. But General Smith had not the courage to follow up his success and seize the prize within his reach, and deferred the advance until the next morning. In the meantime, troops had been poured into Petersburg, and a new line of fortifications had been built. Speaking of this delay, General Grant, who felt that he had made ample provision for the work to be done, says, "I do not think there is any doubt that Petersburg itself could have been carried without much loss; . . . This would have given us control of both the Weldon and South Side Railroads." (*Personal Memoirs*, ii., 298). He was hurrying forward troops in case of disaster, but remained at Bermuda Hundred to be there in person to direct operations in case Lee should throw his whole army upon Butler. At ten o'clock on the morning of the 16th, General Burnside, with the Ninth Corps, came up and took position on the left. At three o'clock on the morning of the 17th, the First and Second Brigades of the Second Division, under General Potter, dashed forward, and in a most gallant manner carried two redoubts, capturing guns, prisoners, colors, and a large quantity of small arms. There was much hard fighting all day.[2]

In the afternoon, General Neill, commanding the Second Division of the Sixth Corps, sent the assistant adjutant-general of the Army of the Potomac the following despatch: "June 17, 1864—2 P.M. Am at the fingerpost pointing to Ninth Corps, on main road, with my Second Division, Artillery Brigade, Colonel Tompkins, Sixth Corps, and proper complement of ammunition wagons and ambulances

---

[1] See War Map 105 (7).   [2] O. R., xl., pt. 1, p. 545.

15

of the corps.   My men have been marching all night and morning." [1]

In reply to this despatch, a staff officer was sent from headquarters to conduct General Neill and his command to a place not indicated in the report.   But at 4 P.M., General Meade ordered him to relieve the troops of the Eighteenth Corps, and, at 11 P.M., inquired if he had obeyed the order, and received reply that his division was in line of battle, and had relieved Brooks's division, Eighteenth Corps; was unable to do more. [2]

It will be remembered that Captain Tyler was at this time acting on the staff of General Neill, and that the Thirty-seventh Regiment was in the Fourth Brigade of this division.   Before the Army of the Potomac had crossed the James, they received rumors that General Smith with the Eighteenth Corps had carried the works before Petersburg, but on arriving there they found the old enemy confronting them.   Let us now turn to the diary.—C. S.]

AT about 2 o'clock, Friday, June 17th, we moved forward until within a mile of General Smith's line of battle at Mrs. Bailey's house.   At 4 o'clock we relieved the Eighteenth Corps.   Our line ran along the crest of a line of hills.   The Ninth, Second, and Fifth Corps charged to the left of us and drove the enemy back towards the city to our left.   The Thirty-seventh started at 9 P.M., and moved to the vicinity of the Jordan house, [3] but were not engaged that night.

Saturday, June 18th.   An attack was ordered at 4 A.M.; the line was formed and advanced to find that the enemy had evacuated their first line.   We formed for an attack on their second line.   At 12 M. advanced a half mile and were checked.   General Wheaton (First

[1] O. R., xl., pt. 2, p. 132.   [2] Id., p. 133.
[3] See War Map 40 (1).

Brigade, Second Division, Sixth Corps) on the front line advanced to a point within three-fourths of a mile of the city. We could see the church spires very plainly. About 11 o'clock, the Thirty-seventh recrossed the railroad [the railroad to City Point], occupied the vacant works and connected with Wheaton's brigade on their right. Moved forward and attacked at 12 M. Got mixed with Wheaton's brigade. At 3 o'clock, advanced some four hundred yards, but were not supported by the Second Corps on our left. The Thirty-seventh lost four men killed.[1]

Sunday, June 19th. Up at 5 o'clock, and made a tour of the lines. Found things quiet. We occupy a hill which overlooks the plain and commands a fine view of the city. General Grant and staff and our corps commanders have all been over here at times during the afternoon. Brady photographed Meade and his staff.[2] The First and Third Divisions of the Sixth Corps which had been with Butler came up this evening. The Vermont Brigade relieved the First and Fourth this evening

---

[1] The location of the Second Division at 7.15 A.M. is indicated by the despatch of an aide-de-camp from General Neill's headquarters to General Meade: "General Neill's advance has reached Harrison's Creek, [See War Map 65 (9)] and is extended along it, with his right running some distance along the Appomattox. The enemy are seen in position, with their left on the Appomattox. Our force is still on the north bank of the creek." (O.R., xl., pt. 2, p. 191.) The battles of the 17th and 18th were fought by General Meade, and were terrible battles on account of the persistency and the losses. General Grant, writing from City Point at 10 P.M., says: "I am perfectly satisfied that all has been done that could be done, and that the assaults to-day were called for by all the appearances and information that could be obtained. Now we will rest the men and use the spade for their protection until a new vein can be struck." (O. R., xl., pt. 2, p. 157.)—C. S.

[2] Brady's photographs have recently been published by the Review of Reviews Company in ten volumes, entitled *Photographic History of the Civil War.* (1911).

in the lines.   The term of service of the Tenth Massachusetts expired, and they started for home.   One
hundred and sixty men whose terms had not expired
were temporarily attached to the Thirty-seventh.   The
Thirty-seventh to-day lost one man killed.   At dark
we were relieved by the Vermont Brigade.

Letter to his mother, June 19, 1864:

I don't know how long I shall be able to write to you this
morning, but I will begin, and write until I am interrupted,
and then send what I have written.

Last Thursday night we crossed the James and marched
all night, and the next day guarded the trains until 1 P.M.,
when we came upon the Tenth Army Corps, and in the
course of the afternoon we relieved the Eighteenth Army
Corps.   The other two divisions went by transports to
City Point, and were detailed by General Butler at Bermuda
Hundred.   So that was the way I spent my birthday.   It
was awfully hot and I felt about as badly as a man could and
live.

We got our troops into a magnificent position and
were not engaged in the attack that night, so that I slept
and felt better.   Saturday we commenced fighting at four
o'clock in the morning, and kept at it at intervals all day.
We gained about a mile, and took some pretty strong works
without much resistance, and evening found us where we
could look right into the city of Petersburg, some three
quarters of a mile distant.   Our regiment was not engaged,
and I think lost no men.   Yesterday brought me two
letters from home, the latest written last Sunday and
Monday from you.   They were very welcome, I assure you.   You ask me about General Neill.   He is a
very agreeable gentleman, but is not a religious man.
My relations with him are very pleasant, and I am on
pleasant terms with the staff.   My duties are not very
arduous, consisting mostly of carrying orders and seeing

them executed, and the various duties of an aide-de-camp.

General Meade has just been here sitting in my tent for half an hour, and consequently I had to vacate. I heard him talk, but was not introduced to him. He with several other general officers was busy talking over military matters.

My Sundays have usually been very quiet, but to-day it has been an incessant hubbub at our headquarters. The general officers of the army have congregated here for consultation, consequently our tents have been crowded with staff officers. The coast, however, is now almost clear, and we are enjoying comparative quiet. Things are generally quiet on the lines, and the men seem to be resting.

So we have a checkered career out here in the army. All sorts of experiences attend us. The men, however, look rather haggard after their terrible campaigning experience, and they don't have the same amount of spirit they had when they started out. The charges made yesterday lacked spirit, and the organizations of the army are so thinned out that it is not to be wondered at. I must close.

Monday, June 20th. Visited the lines in the mist this morning. No changes. About 9 o'clock the enemy commenced throwing shells from the hills across the Appomattox on our right flank, which burst uncomfortably near our headquarters, wounding two of our soldiers. We moved to corps headquarters and the shells followed us. Captain Young had a narrow escape. At night we were ordered to relieve the Second Division of the Second Corps.[1]

[1] At 8 o'clock on the morning of the 20th, the right of the Sixth Corps rested on the Appomattox. Two divisions, the First and Second, were in line, and the Third (Ricketts's) was in reserve. At 8.30, General Wright received orders from General Meade to relieve one of Hancock's divisions, and hold from the Hare house to the river. The Hare house stood just to the right of where Fort Stedman was afterwards built. One division was to watch the river to the right and he was ordered to

Letter to his classmate, M. F. Dickinson, June 20, 1864:
Your welcome letter reached me yesterday and the
same mail brought me one from Ruf [Captain Rufus P.
Lincoln], so I had a double portion of pleasure. If ever a
man would appreciate letters, it is at such a time as this,
in the midst of a severe campaign with all its fatigues and
anxieties upon you. Then when you feel downhearted and
almost discouraged, there is nothing like a friendly letter to
cheer you up. We are here within a mile of the centre of
Petersburg, apparently full tilt once more against the Army
of Northern Virginia. We can at any time most certainly
destroy the city, and the possibility is that we could take
the city, but whether we could occupy it after we have possessed ourselves of it is another question. The trouble
seems to be just now that their cannon on the crest on the
other side of the Appomattox command everything on this
side. So what we have to do is to wait and see. We had a
fierce little fight on Saturday, and drove the Rebs more
than a mile, occupying works really much stronger than
any that I have seen since we left Washington. They were
not fully defended, and we lost very few men in the assault.
The works and position that the Eighteenth Corps took
from Beauregard, however, on the Thursday previous were
magnificent. I have never seen better, and properly
defended, the whole Army of the Potomac could not have
taken them by assault. But fortunately for us we had
militia to contend with, and gained an easy victory. The
darkies are as thick as pebble stones around us, and it
would amuse you to see some of our big talkers, stragglers
(members of Haversack's Brigade, as we call them),
standing in the midst of these groups of negroes, and telling
them all sorts of frightful yarns. The darkies are growing

---

intrench as strongly as possible. At 8.30 in the evening, General
Wright reported that the corps had taken the position indicated and
that a working party was ordered for 4 o'clock the next morning to complete a work for guns.—C. S. (See O. R., xl., pt. 2, p. 249.)

pale by contact with the Army of the Potomac. I really believe they would demoralize them (the darkies) if they stayed here long. A negro was hanged near our headquarters this morning, by order of the President, for an attempted rape. It drew so large a crowd that the Rebs commenced shelling. Consequently two of our men here at headquarters got wounded. The Tenth Massachusetts has started on its homeward trip this morning. This leaves the Thirty-seventh the last representative of our brigade. We have detachments of from fifty to one hundred men each from other regiments, but our whole brigade to-day numbers 407 men. The Thirty-seventh has, I believe, only a little over 200. We started out in this campaign with over 600 strong. Last week was Class Day at Amherst. How I should have liked to be there and enjoy it with you and Ruf. Binney has just perpetrated a joke that I must put on paper for your edification. He says that the works of Shelley are prevalent among us these days. They are just bringing up some 30-pounder Parrott guns to be mounted on some of these commanding crests. So I suppose we shall have music now. . . . I should like to see you for a little while. How we would talk![1]

[1] After the ineffectual assaults of the 18th, there was little fighting for several days, although there was a good deal of firing especially at night to prevent surprise. The Union lines were extended to the Jerusalem Plank Road, and so strengthened that they could be held by a few men. Butler was ordered to extend his lines to the point on the Appomattox held by the Sixth Corps.

On the 21st, General Grant intimated to General Meade that he desired to envelop Petersburg, as far as possible without attacking fortifications, and without bringing on a battle unless the enemy exposed himself equally; he suggested a movement to the left of Warren who, with the Fifth Corps, held the left of the Union army. Arrangements were immediately made for a movement to the left. The Sixth and Second Corps were relieved by the Ninth, and the Eighteenth and Second were ordered to advance to the left of the Fifth Corps and pivot on that, keeping its right in connection with the left of the Fifth. The Sixth Corps was to pass in the rear of the Second and connect with its left. The country through which the Sixth had to move was densely

Tuesday, June 21st.. Very hot. President Lincoln rode by.

Letter of the 23d says:
I commenced a letter to you Tuesday P.M., but was called away to go to corps headquarters. There we found President Lincoln and Generals Grant and Meade being serenaded by a band of music. That afternoon General Neill was relieved of his command in the Sixth Corps, and ordered to report to the Eighteenth Corps. He invited me to remain on his staff, and said that I should go with him anyway, but on talking to Colonel Edwards, I found that he was very much opposed to it. So after staying over night with the general, I declined.

General Neill was a most agreeable officer to serve with, very gentlemanly and considerate of everybody, an experienced officer and an intelligent man. The Thirty-seventh lost one man to-day, F. B. Crocker, of Company F. Relieved by Martindale's division and moved to the left in an attempt to capture the Weldon and South Side Railroads. Slow and tedious. No sleep for two nights. The Second and Sixth Corps were directed to move independently.

Wednesday, June 22d. Spent a restless night. Bade General Neill good-by, and rode back to rejoin the corps five or six miles on the left of the line. General Wheaton invited me to retain my position on his staff while he was in command. The Second Corps was repulsed while attempting to extend our lines to the left, and we retreated a short distance. At 7 P.M. we advanced a

---

wooded with a thick underbrush, and as progress was slow, General Meade became impatient and ordered the corps to move independently. As a result they became separated, and the enemy taking advantage of it, attacked the unprotected left flank of the Second Corps, capturing four guns and seventeen hundred prisoners.—C. S.

half mile beyond our original position early in the day. We protected the left flank. The Second Corps, Gibbon's division, lost 1700 men and four guns. Great confusion prevailed at headquarters. The Thirty-seventh was on the extreme left of the corps. Two companies, F and G, were sent to guard a bridge running across a swamp.

Thursday, June 23d. The order to attack at 3.30 was for some reason postponed.[1] We lay in a scorching hot sun all day. Captain Beattie with sixty sharp-shooters and a battalion of infantry (Fourth and Eleventh Vermont) penetrated one and one-half miles to the Weldon Railroad. At 2 P.M. he was driven back, and A. P. Hill's corps went around our left flank and captured 500 men from the Vermont Brigade, and killed and wounded quite a number more. The fight was sharp while it lasted. Captain William C. Tracy, a brother of J. Evarts Tracy, was killed. I was out on the field with Major Long, assistant adjutant-general of our division, endeavoring to bring up reinforcements.[2]

Letter to his mother, June 26, 1864:

This awfully hot Sunday morning I am going to try to write a letter home. We have been sweltering in this hot Virginia sun with the thermometer at 102 in the shade now for three days. It seems as if the perspiration runs in streams all the time and brings no relief. Wednesday and Thursday they kept us trotting back and forth in line of

[1] It was found that the enemy had withdrawn.—C. S.

[2] See O. R., xl., pt. 1, pp. 495, 502, and 503. Captain William C. Tracy of the Fourth Vermont was a man of great courage. General L. A. Grant in his report of the day's doings says: "His dead body was found on the field next day, surrounded by the muskets of his men lying on the ground, giving evidence that he had rallied around him the men of his command, and that they surrendered only when their gallant leader had fallen," p. 503.—C. S.

battle over a mile of ground according as our flank was
menaced or the enemy disappeared in our front.   In the
fight of Thursday afternoon, they came down on our flank
and gobbled up some five hundred men belonging to our
splendid Vermont Brigade, which formed a very heavy
skirmish line in front of the left flank of the army.   They
cut through the Third Division skirmish line on our right
and got to the rear of the Vermont boys and took a good
portion of two battalions.   This was very provoking, as we
probably inflicted little loss in return, and we were afraid to
rush out to attack them, as we were formed in a single line
and there was danger of their turning our flank.   So we
had to lie still and let them gobble up our men, and it was
done so quietly that we hardly knew we had suffered any
loss. . . . I ought to be happy that I am well and able to
endure, and have been saved from sickness and wounds
during this terrible campaign.

Tuesday, June 28th.   I played chess with Stevens.

A letter of this date says:
I thought I would write you a line before I leave division
headquarters.   General Getty has arrived this afternoon
and takes immediate command of the division, and as he has
a sufficient staff of his own, there is no longer any need of my
service here, so I am going back to the regiment.   I enjoyed
my experience of staff life very much, and it was profitable
to me in several ways.   It improved me physically, and
broadened my view of military life.   I made acquaintances
and saw the army officers of higher rank that I never should
have seen or known had I remained on duty with the
regiment.   I was enabled to go through this terribly severe
campaign with comparative comfort, and I am not sure
that I could have stood it had I been on foot and in line.

The same letter relates that I was expecting to be
very busy at the end of the month, being also the end

of the quarter on July 1st, when I should have both my monthly and quarterly returns to prepare and forward.

At the house where we are staying now, there are any quantity of old family documents scattered around, and the other day one of the officers picked up a deed of this place dated 1665, and the bargain was that it should be paid for in tobacco. So you see that we are among the early settlements of Virginia.

Letter to his father, July 1, 1864:

Well, I am sitting here beneath a wide-spreading mulberry tree somewhere in Virginia, the exact locality it would be hard to describe. We are some three miles lower on the railroad than we were the last time I wrote. Tuesday afternoon I returned to the regiment on the arrival of General Getty. Wednesday I took an early start and went down to our old camp at Petersburg to get some of my company papers out of my valise. I saw Binney and General Neill. General Neill is very busy organizing the inspector-general's department in the Eighteenth Corps, and Binney is helping him. The general seemed very glad to see me, although I only saw him for a moment. . . .

Well, I got back to our camp about 2 P.M., and in about an hour we were under orders to go to the support of Wilson's cavalry.[1] So off we started, and went to Reams Station, seven miles. Formed line of battle, stayed there

[1] General Wilson, with about 5000 horses and twelve guns, had been sent on the 21st of June around the right of the enemy to destroy the Danville and South Side Railroads. He did a hard bit of work. He marched between the 21st of June and the 1st of July 335 miles, and destroyed more than sixty miles of railway, every railroad station, depot, water-tank, woodpile, bridge, trestle-work, tool-house, and sawmill, from fifteen miles of Petersburg to the Roanoke River. But he was intercepted on his return by a force he could not break through at Reams Station, and the Sixth Corps was sent to his assistance, but arrived too late as he was obliged to find another way out. (O. R., xl., pt. 1, p. 620.)—C. S.

yesterday and tore up some four miles of track, and last night returned to this place, where we have been lying to-day. It is awfully hot this afternoon. I am at present acting as major of the regiment under Lieutenant Colonel Montague, and am very pleasantly situated. I have no news to tell from the boys, except that they are all well— what there is left of them.[1]

Saturday, July 2d.   Mother writes that she has inaugurated and is preparing a festival for July 4th for the benefit of the soldiers. They are to have tableaux, ice cream, gypsies and fortune-telling; music and sports at the gymnasium, and suppers at the hall under the church. All the town is aiding.

Sunday, July 3d. Spent a quiet day. Hot and suffocating. Service in the evening after dress parade.

Monday, July 4th. Very quiet all the morning. Paid in the afternoon. Finished my muster rolls this morning.

Tuesday, July 5th. We started to build a new line of works, in front of our old line, with a very strong heavy relief. Mother writes results of festival to date $437— expects $112 more will come in.[2]

[1] An outline of the movements of the Second Division from June 12th to July 9th is given in the report of General Getty, O. R. xl., pt. 1, p. 494.

[2] The line of works here referred to may be seen on War Map 77 (2). It is the upper dark line running east and west and connecting the fortifications in front with those in the rear. Bowen at page 346 says that the brigade at this time mustered about five hundred of officers and men.

For some days General Wright had been reporting to headquarters that nothing of importance had transpired in front of the lines of the Sixth Corps, and it is no wonder that under the circumstances the soldier would find little to record. But at noon on the 5th, General Grant informed General Meade that the enemy under General Early, who had been advancing down the Shenandoah Valley, had arrived at the Balti-

Wednesday, July 6th. An order was issued that the Fourth Brigade of the Second Division be discontinued, and that the Thirty-seventh, with attached companies of the Seventh and Tenth Massachusetts, be transferred to the Third Brigade, First Division.[1]

The Third Brigade, First Division, was composed of the Forty-ninth, Eighty-second, and One Hundred Nineteenth Pennsylvania, Fifth Wisconsin Battalion, Twenty-third Pennsylvania Veterans and Thirty-seventh Massachusetts with attachments. Colonel Edwards commanded the brigade. This was the brigade that was originally commanded by General Hancock, and consisted of the Forty-third New York, Forty-ninth Pennsylvania, Fifth Wisconsin, and Sixth Maine. Under him it achieved distinction at the battle of Williamsburg, May 5, 1862, where it defeated the Confederate column commanded by two of the ablest generals in the Army of Northern Virginia—Hill and Early. It was one of the brigades making up the famous light division of the Sixth Corps. In November, 1863, this brigade, under the command of General D. A. Russell, charged over the parapet of the fort at Rappahannock Station, and with bayonets and muskets used as clubs, compelled the surrender of seventeen hundred men. When General Upton was allowed to select twelve regiments from the Sixth Corps for his column of attack on the Salient at Spottsylvania on the 10th of May, 1864, four of them were selected from the Third Brigade, to wit: The Fifth

---

more and Ohio Railroad, and ordered him to send a division of good troops to Baltimore. General Meade at once ordered General Wright to send a division of the Sixth Corps, and he selected the Third Division, General Ricketts, which started immediately for City Point.—C. S.

[1] O. R. xl., pt. 3, p. 46.

Wisconsin, Sixth Maine, and the One Hundred Forty-eighth and the One Hundred Nineteenth Pennsylvania.

Thursday, July 7th. This morning at six o'clock we moved into our new camp, in a beautiful piece of woods. Our headquarters are the best of the season. We donned the red cross on our caps and thought to have a little rest.

The same day he wrote to his brother:

Colonel Montague has gone to attend a court martial, and I have seated myself at his table and am going to take my ease with my pen. Since my return to the regiment I have been kept pretty busy making up back accounts, forwarding my papers, etc. We have been building a new line of rifle-pits, or rather breastworks, and now, just as we are ready to occupy them, the order comes transferring us to the First Division.

We have been expecting this for some time, and it gives Colonel Edwards command of General Russell's old brigade, the brigade that did so splendidly at Rappahannock Station. General Russell now commands the division, and we are all great admirers of him and willing to be under his command, although we have the greatest confidence in General Getty. . . .

We have a mighty stiff medical director on our corps, and yesterday he came out with an order driving the Sanitary and Christian Commissions from the corps. I think it is outrageous. They have been very zealous in furnishing the troops with all sorts of vegetables and many other things of which there is the greatest need, and now for him, through a mere whim, to drive them away, I think is too bad. I have been living on lemonade for the past fortnight. There is nothing that tastes so good, but as we have to buy lemons at sutler's prices, it would ruin us to keep it up a great while. One week from to-morrow is Commencement at Amherst. How I should like to be present to hear you speak! We are having very agreeable rest and were surely in need of it.

The Third Division of our corps started this morning for Baltimore. It reminded us of our start a little later than this a year ago for New York. We almost wished we were in their place. But it would not be strange if they found something to do up there before their return. No telling!

CHAPTER XV

TO THE DEFENCE OF WASHINGTON

JULY 8 TO 24, 1864

[INTRODUCTION.—While General Grant was engaged with the siege of Petersburg, things were going very badly in the Valley of the Shenandoah. This valley was of great importance to the enemy. It furnished their army with an almost unlimited supply of grain, beeves, sheep, and horses, and it afforded a convenient avenue for the invasion of the North; and, in case of defeat, its mountain barriers on the east afforded protection to a retreating column whether great or small. It had been the scene of many a humiliation to the national arms. General Sigel had been appointed to the command of the Department of West Virginia, and when the great campaign began by order of the lieutenant-general along all lines on the 4th of May, Sigel was already advancing up the valley; but he was disastrously defeated on the 15th of May at Newmarket. He was relieved at once, and General Hunter was selected for the command. Hunter received his orders from General Grant to advance to Gordonsville, Charlottesville, or Lynchburg, and to destroy the railroads and the James River Canal. Hunter advanced rapidly and made a very brilliant campaign, but was tempted to go to Lynchburg, a point of very great importance, where he was confronted by a large force drawn from Lee's army. He had not ammunition enough to risk a battle, and retired

without loss to the Ohio, and thus the valley was left open
to an invasion of the North.   General Lee had sent General
Early into the valley with a strong force, and as there was
nothing now between the Confederate general and Washington, he went on by rapid marches until his course was
checked for a day by General Wallace in Maryland, who led
against him a much smaller force and was defeated at the
Monocacy, thirty miles from Washington (July 9th).   But
the defeat was in reality a great victory, for the delay he
caused the enemy saved the capital.   The Third Division of
the Sixth Corps covered General Wallace's retreat, and in
his report he speaks in high terms of their steady courage
and discipline, and adds: "The men of the Third Division
were not whipped, but retired reluctantly, under my orders.
They bore the brunt of the battle with a coolness and
steadiness which I venture to say has not been exceeded
in any battle during the war."[1]

General Grant had already ordered the Nineteenth Corps,
just arriving at Fortress Monroe from Louisiana, to proceed
to Washington, and on the evening of the 9th, Major-General Wright received an order, dated at 8.50, directing him
with his corps to proceed at once to City Point, embark
there and report to Major-General Halleck on arriving at
Washington.   Ten minutes after, at 9 o'clock, in a requisition on the chief quartermaster, General Wright says: "I
am ordered to march my corps to City Point.   There will
be about 11,000 men and they will start within an hour."[2]

In the campaign which is about to commence, the Sixth
Corps will render signal service to the country in saving
Washington from the hands of the enemy.   Their first
campaign in the Shenandoah Valley was a failure, but it
will be followed by another which will rank among the most
brilliant campaigns of the war.

On the evening of the 10th, after the Sixth Corps had
embarked for Washington, General Grant telegraphed President Lincoln: "I have sent a whole corps, commanded by an

[1] O. R., xxxvii., pt. 1, p. 191.   [2] *Id.*, xl., pt. 3, p. 106.

excellent officer,"[1] and on the 12th he telegraphed General Halleck: "Give orders assigning Maj.-Gen. Wright to supreme command of all troops moving out against the enemy regardless of the rank of other commanders."[2] The next day the order was issued by the President and General Wright was informed of his position.[3]

It was General Grant's wish to unite the forces under General Wright and those under General Hunter who were at Harper's Ferry, cut off the Confederate column, and either capture or cripple it. But Early, by rapid movements, slipped between the two Union armies and made his escape. General Grant did not see the Sixth Corps again until it was time to go into winter quarters. He could not press the siege of Petersburg with the vigor he wished, but he held on with superb tenacity and patience, although the Rebel army which confronted him was sometimes almost equal in numbers to his own.

The Thirty-seventh is now called to a new field of experience, and we may turn to the card diary.—C. S.]

FRIDAY, July 8th. Petersburg. We are occupying the quarters vacated by General Hamblin. I have been very busy all day making out returns and have completed my quartermaster's returns.

Saturday, July 9th. Quiet all day. About 10 P.M., we received orders to pack and start for City Point; got under way and kept moving all night.

Sunday, July 10th. We reached City Point at 5 A.M. Lay in the hot sun all day, and embarked on board the propeller, *Perit*, for Washington at 7 P.M. Letter of 11th says: "We got on board our boat at seven last night and have been sailing since. My eyes trouble me so much that I am going to give up writing and reading entirely."[4]

[1] O. R., xxxvii., pt. 2, p. 155.   [2] *Id.*, p. 222.   [3] *Id.*, pp. 261, 284.
[4] The command was shipped on board of transports. O. R., xxxvii., pt. I, p. 271.

Monday, July 11th. Passed Fortress Monroe this morning at 9. A French man-of-war was drilling its marines in the harbor. The seamen running over the masts looked like rats. Enjoyed a shower, the first we have experienced for forty days. The trip was enlivened by singing in the afternoon. In the evening the wind blew almost a gale.[1]

Tuesday, July 12th. We passed Aquia Creek, Mathias Point, and Mount Vernon, and this morning reached Washington at noon, and found the "Rebs" within four miles of the city. We marched out Fourteenth Street by Brightwood, through the heavily timbered gates near Fort Stevens. President Lincoln, General Wright and others were visible on the parapet of the fort as we passed through the gates. We formed a part of a line of battle on the right, and moved forward

[1] A portion of the Second Division of the Sixth Corps arrived at Washington about noon on the 11th and found all in confusion. Rumors had hardened down into facts, and it was believed that a greater part of Lee's army was in front of the capital. There were several major-generals and a score or more of brigadiers in the city, but each had a separate command, and there was no head either to organize a defence or plan an attack upon the enemy. Orders were issued rapidly, and as rapidly countermanded. General Wright on arrival in the city received orders from General Halleck to go into camp between Chain Bridge and the line of defences near the river. (O. R., xxxvii., pt. 2, p. 207.) At 1.40 P.M. he received another order through Major-General Augur from General Halleck: "Please stop General Wright's movement up the Potomac and send his command up Seventh Street to rendezvous near the Military Asylum." (*Id.*, p. 209.) Later in the afternoon came another order, commanding him to report with his command to General McCook at Crystal Spring, near Fourteenth Street. At 4.10 P.M., General Wright, from Fort Stevens, reports to General Augur: "The head of my column has nearly reached the front, and, at the suggestion of Major-General McCook, I have directed them to bivouac at Crystal Spring, about half a mile in rear." (*Id.*, p. 208.) General Wright was of the opinion that there was only a thin skirmish line in front of the fort, and offered to put his veterans in and clean them out, but the offer was declined.—C. S.

nearly a mile, the enemy retiring before us. We were not heavily engaged, but four or five men in the regiment were wounded. William H. Shaw,[1] in his *War Dairy*, at page 48, says, "The Thirty-seventh was put on the skirmish line and we had a few shots at the Johnnies; we drove them about two miles, and as it was growing dark, we lay on picket at night."

General Wheaton says, in his report of the battle before Fort Stevens:

Upon arrival at Washington, July 11, at 12 M., I was directed by General Wright to move toward Chain Bridge. While marching up Pennsylvania Avenue was halted by Colonel Taylor, chief of staff, Department of Washington, and informed by him that the enemy was driving in our picket line and seriously threatening Fort Stevens on Seventh street, and received through him General Augur's instructions to march at once in that direction instead of Chain Bridge, as first ordered. I turned my brigade up Eleventh street, and while on the march to Fort Stevens was passed by General Wright, commanding the corps, and received his verbal instructions to mass near Crystal Spring, in the neighborhood of Fort Stevens, where we arrived at 4 o'clock in the P.M.

At 5 P.M., a portion of the Veteran Reserve Corps was driven in towards Fort Stevens by Early's forces and I was ordered to move 500 men of my brigade out to recover the line held in the afternoon. This was successfully accomplished before seven, and the enemy's advance was driven back to their main lines. The position was strengthened at dark and extended from a point opposite the centre of the line between Forts Stevens and Reno to the west and to a point opposite Fort Slocum to the east, a distance of

[1] Of Company D. In 1904 he printed 100 copies of his diary kept during the war.

about two miles.   Skirmishing continued through the night and following day.

At 5 P.M. of the 12th, while in charge of the division, I was ordered to drive in the enemy's skirmish line, and occupy, if successful, two strong wooded hills in our front, the possession of which gave the enemy great advantage of position near our intrenched line.   I ordered Colonel Bid-well, commanding the Third Brigade, to move his command outside the fort, and under cover of a ravine and woods, at trail arms, and every precaution taken to prevent the enemy discovering the movement, from two lines in the rear of my brigade (which was all deployed as skirmishers), and about 300 yards on the right of the Rockville pike, the position being covered by scrub timber and underbrush. Colonel Bidwell was then directed to select three of his very best regiments at an indicated point a few paces in rear of our skirmish line and fronting the strong wooded position held by the enemy.   The attack was ordered to be made by the whole skirmish line of the First (my own) Brigade, and these three regiments from the Third Brigade were to assault and carry the strong position referred to, the remain-der of the Third Brigade to be held ready to support the general movement.   A preconcerted signal was made when these regiments were in position, at which time the batteries from Forts Stevens and Slocum opened fire upon certain indicated points strongly held by the enemy.   As had been previously arranged, after the thirty-sixth shot from Fort Stevens had been fired, a signal was made from the parapet of that work and the commander of the skirmish line and three assaulting regiments dashed forward, surprising and hotly engaging the enemy, who was found to be much stronger than had been supposed.   It became necessary to deploy immediately the three remaining regiments.

The enemy's stubborn resistance showed that a farther advance than already made would require more troops, and two regiments were sent for.   Before their arrival, however (the Thirty-seventh Massachusetts and Second

Rhode Island), an aide-de-camp from General Wright directed me not to attempt more than the holding of the position I had gained, as the object of the attack had been accomplished, and the important points captured and held.

The last shot was fired about 10 o'clock and the remainder of the night was occupied in strengthening the position, burying the dead, and caring for the wounded.[1]

Wednesday, July 13th. During the night we were relieved on the front line by the Eleventh Vermont, and were sent to support the pickets on the extreme right. This morning the darkies cut down all the trees and orchards around us. Transportation was reduced so that each regiment in our brigade had one wagon. Ordered to march at 2 P.M. Moved through Tennally-town to Offutt's Cross-Roads,[2] a distance of fifteen miles—a hard march. Halted for the night at 7 P.M. Our horses did not come up, so all the officers of the regiment were afoot.[3]

Thursday, July 14th. Ordered to move at daylight. The Thirty-seventh was detailed as wagon guard, and therefore started late. Here we were equipped with Spencer rifles. It was esteemed a special compliment to the discipline and good reputation of the regiment.

[1] (O. R., xxxvii., pt. 1, p. 275.) These excerpts from the report of General Wheaton (in temporary command of the Second Division, Sixth Corps, in absence of General Getty) are found in the card diary.

[2] See War Map 7 (1). For another good general map of this region, see War Map 27 (1).

[3] On the afternoon of the 13th, General Wright sent a despatch from Fort Reno to the Secretary of War: "The head of my column is passing this point, and will be pushed forward to the limits of the endurance of the men. . . . I can assure yourself and the President that there will be no delay on my part to head off the enemy, and that the men I have will do all that the number of men can do. They have been well tried and never found wanting." (O. R., xxxvii., pt. 1, p. 265.)—C. S.

We waited until 2 P.M., and then started behind the teams, moved very slowly eight miles and stopped for the night near Seneca Mills. This evening the horses arrived in charge of hostlers. They were shipped in different boats. The slow progress made by the teams was due to the fact that the teamsters were green hands, and did not know how to handle the mules.

On the 14th, General Wright telegraphed General Halleck: "The march is rather a severe one, the men straggling badly. The teams are green, and the trains consequently move much less rapidly than the infantry."[1] Later in the day (6 P.M.) he reports from Poolesville:

Most of the infantry of this corps and a part of the artillery have come up. The train is stretched along the road for a great distance and will not be all up by midnight, if so soon. . . . The enemy had, and kept, about twenty-four hours the start of us, which gave him full time to secure his crossing of the river. . . . My troops have marched over thirty miles in about twenty-four hours, over bad roads and under excessive heat.[2]

Friday, July 15th. Started at 11 to join the division at Poolesville, and arrived there at 3.30 P.M. Blackberries in abundance. Hanged a spy. I visited the town in the afternoon. The Rebs took fifteen thousand dollars' worth of goods from our store, also a very long train of cattle and carriages. Our baggage arrived.

Saturday, July 16th. Started at 5 to go by White's Ford[3] on the Potomac, and found a few of the enemy's cavalry guarding the opposite shore, but a few shells

[1] O. R., xxvii., pt. 1, p. 266.   [2] *Id.*, p. 267.
[3] See footnote at pages 47 and 51, and notes.

scattered them.[1] We waded across. The water was about three feet deep. We pushed on to Leesburg and formed a line of battle on a fine crest. The Rebs passed here this afternoon. General Hunter is coming up to join us. General Getty is in command of the corps.

Sunday, July 17th. We are encamped three miles beyond Leesburg at Clark's Gap.[2] Nothing doing to-day; we are resting. Ricketts's (Third) division[3] returned and joined the corps to-day. General Hunter is at Snicker's Gap, and General Howe is in command of Sigel's forces.[4] The Thirty-seventh attended religious services with the Fifteenth New Jersey. General Crook has followed Early across the Shenandoah, and General Wright has been ordered to be sure that Early is moving south, and return speedily with the Sixth and Nineteenth Corps to Petersburg.

A letter of this date says:

We forded the Potomac yesterday at White's Ford and came to Leesburg, following in the track of the Rebs most of the way. We are waiting for General Hunter to come[5] when I suppose we shall push on. Leesburg is a beautiful place. My eyes are a little better, but I do not dare to use them yet. Am under the doctor's care.

[1] Lieutenant Lamb of Battery C, First Rhode Island Light Artillery, reports that at White's Ford he went into position and fired twenty rounds at the enemy's cavalry. (O. R., xxxvii., pt. 1, p. 281.)

[2] See *id.*, p. 271.

[3] It had been with General Lew Wallace and covered his retreat at the battle of Monocacy. (Bowen, p. 349.)

[4] General A. P. Howe was assigned to the command of the Military District of Harper's Ferry by the President on the 7th of July. O. R., xxxvii., pt. 2, p. 104.)

[5] A detachment of General Hunter's command, under General Crook, arrived at Purcellville, about six miles in advance of Clark's Gap, on the evening of the 16th, and on the evening of the 17th, General Wright reports: "The cavalry of General Crook's command, under General

Monday, July 18th.   Received orders to march at 4 A.M.   Our route was through Hamilton (where flags and handkerchiefs were waved as we passed), then on through Purcellville and Snickersville and through Snicker's Gap.   The march was slow with frequent halts.   General Hunter's command crossed the Shenandoah, had a skirmish with the Rebs and then retired. Macomber[1] stayed with me over night.   Our brigade was detailed for picket duty.

Itinerary: "Moved again, crossing the mountains at Snicker's Gap; came up with the enemy on the bank of the Shenandoah; brigade on picket; so remained until the 20th."[2]

Tuesday, July 19th.   On picket during the day.   The boys tried their Spencer rifles.   Several Rebs shot. Ordered to be ready to move at noon.   Bowen (page 363) says: "There was a lively interchange of shots by the picket lines during the 19th."

Wednesday, July 20th.   Moved the line forward into the woods at sunrise.   Ordered to move at 10 A.M.   The

---

Duffie, more fortunate than the rest, struck the rear of the enemy on the Snickersville pike, capturing 117 mules and horses, 82 wagons, and 62 prisoners, besides killing and wounding a good many."   (O. R., xxxvii., pt. 1, p. 268.)—C. S.

[1] A classmate at Amherst.

[2] O. R., *id.*, p. 272.   In the evening, General Wright ordered General Crook, commanding a division of General Hunter's command, who coming in from the North had struck the Snickersville pike six miles in advance of the Sixth Corps, to send out a cavalry force supported by infantry to harass the rear of the enemy's column.   They found that the enemy had already crossed the Shenandoah and held the opposite bank. On the 18th, General Crook came up with the remainder of his command, and moving about a mile and a half to the right of Snicker's Ford, effected a crossing.   He was hardly in position when he was made the object of several vigorous attacks by the enemy which were successfully repulsed.   While this was going on, the Sixth Corps came up, but as it was rumored that Early's whole force was in their front, General

Thirty-seventh led the crossing and deployed as skirmishers at once, and found several wounded Federal soldiers at a house near by. Order to proceed to Berryville; Captain Young took three companies out to scout with him; sheep, pigs, poultry, colts, and horses abundant. We only advanced three miles from the river, when, owing to a thunderstorm, we were halted and General Wright changed his plans, and at 10 P.M. we started on our return march to Washington.

Itinerary: "With the rest of the corps it forded the Shenandoah and marched to within two miles of Berryville. That night commenced the return march to Washington; continued the march all night and the next day."[1]

Thursday, July 21st. We marched all night, recrossed the Shenandoah, passed through Snicker's Gap, down the eastern slope of Blue Ridge, breakfasted at or near Hamilton (seventeen miles from the start), and reached Leesburg at 2 P.M. Roads rough, people sullen and threatening as we marched through the town with flying colors. At 5 P.M. we halted for the night across Goose Creek, four miles beyond Leesburg. Mosby charged the rear of our column, and took some prisoners at Leesburg. The soldiers bathed and washed in Goose Creek. The water was clear and this the first oppor-

---

Ricketts, then commanding the Sixth Corps, did not think it prudent to cross his men and General Crook withdrew, having lost something like four hundred men and inflicted a loss of over six hundred upon the enemy. (O. R., xxxvii., pt. 1, pp. 287, 290.)—C. S.

[1] O. R., *id.*, p. 272. On the 17th, General Halleck received the following despatch from General Grant, written the day before: "There can be no use in Wright following the enemy with the latter a day ahead, after he has passed entirely beyond (south of) all our communications. I want, if possible, to get the Sixth and Nineteenth Corps here, to use them here before the enemy can get Early back. . . . As soon as the Rebel

tunity to bathe they had had for a month. We heard that Ramseur's division attacked Averell north of Winchester and was defeated and driven to Strasburg.[1]

Friday, July 22d. Started at 8, and marched through Dranesville, where we halted for two hours at noon for refreshments. Crossed Difficult Creek in the afternoon, and were then fifteen miles from Washington. It was a hard march—Shaw says twenty miles.[2]

Saturday, July 23d. Marched at 3.30 A.M. Passed though Falls Church over Chain Bridge, and encamped a mile and a half beyond on the Tennallytown road in the rear of Fort Gaines just west of Washington.[3] Made requisition on the quartermaster to fill wants. Just at night Dr. Hitchcock and my brother Henry called and gave me a genuine surprise. Captain Lincoln was in town.

Bowen (page 365), says: "The next day was Sunday, the 24th, and after an inspection by Captain Tyler, officers and men devoted much of the time to perusing

---

army is known to have passed Hunter's forces, recall Wright and send him back here with all despatch, and also send the Nineteenth Corps. If the enemy have any notion of returning, the fact will be developed before Wright can start back." (O. R., xxxvii., pt. 2, p. 350.) This despatch was sent to General Wright.—C. S.

[1] See Bowen, p. 366. Averell had been trying to communicate with General Wright of the Sixth Corps, but found that he was already on his way back to Washington. Hearing that the enemy was within about three miles of Winchester, he determined to give battle and made a vigorous assault, drove the enemy from the field, and found that they had left four guns, seventy-three killed and one hundred and thirty wounded men on the field. Seventeen officers and two hundred and fifty men were captured. The next day he occupied Winchester where he was joined on the 22d by General Crook. (O. R., xxxvii., pt. 1, p. 326).—C. S.

[2] *War Diary*, p. 50

[3] All these places appear clearly on War Map 7 (1). See Bowen, p. 365; O. R., xxxvii., pt. 1, p. 272 (itinerary).

the large mail which had been brought in and to writing
letters." A generous rain fell, continuing through the
night, and the wind blew strong, but they issued clothing
in the rain as we were ordered to embark that night
(for Petersburg), but it was postponed apparently on
account of the storm.

CHAPTER XVI

FROM WASHINGTON TO HALLTOWN, TO FREDERICK AND BACK TO HALLTOWN

JULY 25 TO SEPTEMBER 18, 1864

[INTRODUCTION.—General Grant had need of the Sixth Corps and was anxious to keep the Army of the Potomac together, and he ordered it on arriving at Washington to proceed at once to Petersburg. The order was communicated to General Wright on the 24th, and preparations were being made for the immediate embarkation of his command. But before the day was over, General Grant sent a telegram to General Halleck: "You can retain Wright until I learn positively what has become of Early. I would prefer a complete smash-up of the enemy's roads about Gordonsville and Charlottesville to having the same force here. If Wright and Hunter can do the job, let them do it." [1]

The pursuit of Early was given up near Barryville, but the Rebel general was not aware of the fact until he arrived at Strasburg, some forty miles up the valley. He immediately turned back, drove General Crook out of Winchester, and pushed on to the Potomac. The Sixth Corps and the commands associated with it were ordered to Halltown, in the Valley of Shenandoah, about four miles west of Harper's Ferry. The position was an admirable one, but they had

[1] O. R., xxxvii., pt. 2, p. 426. The operations of General Sheridan in the Valley of the Shenandoah are given in War Maps 69: (1) represents his first advance and retreat, (2) his second advance after Grant's order, "Go in."—C. S.

253

hardly arrived there when General Halleck ordered them to Frederick, Maryland. The result was that they were put out of connection with the enemy and lost sight of the invading army altogether.

The section of country exposed to invasion was then divided into four military departments, each under a separate commander, and it was not easy for them to unite for joint action. General Grant now proposed to unite these departments under one commander, and nominated General Franklin for the position, and afterwards General Meade, but the authorities at Washington did not agree with him. Something must be done, and he telegraphed to General Halleck on the 1st of August that he had appointed General Sheridan to the temporary command in the field.[1]

On arriving in Washington, General Sheridan called with Secretary Stanton on the President, and Mr. Lincoln with his usual frankness told Sheridan of the Secretary's opposition to him, and that he himself shared the feelings of the Secretary. "But," said the President, "as General Grant has ploughed round the difficulties, I am satisfied."

We may now go back to Washington and resume the story.—C. S.]

MONDAY, July 25th. Rained and blew hard last night. We were ordered to embark for Petersburg at night, but it was postponed apparently on account of the storm. They issued clothing last night in the rain. I was suffering from malaria, and by the surgeon's directions I was moved down to the city. My brother Henry called a carriage and took me to a hotel. Professor Seelye called to see me.

Tuesday, July 26th. This morning Stebbins [a classmate] called to see me. Our corps moved at 11 to Rockville. I tried to find some conveyance with which to reach them, but was unable to do so.

[1] O. R., xxxvii., pt. 2, p. 558.

Wednesday, July 27th. I reported to the provost Marshal, and got transportation to Frederick. I had improved rapidly, but Henry persuaded me to wait and go with him.

In a letter from Binghamton, August 4th, his father wrote:

Henry wrote us, the day after your return to the army, a full and most entertaining account of his finding you, bringing you to Washington, nursing you and visiting with you for five days, till at length you set out refreshed and invigorated for the service. We little thought, when we planned for Henry's employment in the service of the Christian Commission, that almost his first service would be nursing and ministering to you.

Saw Captain Loomis and Lieutenant Chandley, and Stebbins called on me in the evening.

Thursday, July 28th. Stebbins and I circulated about the city; went to the Patent Office in the morning and to the Capitol in the afternoon.

In the meantime, the army had moved very rapidly. On Tuesday the regiment marched by way of Tennally-town and Rockville, and went into camp at 9 P.M. five miles beyond the latter place, some fifteen miles from Washington.[1] The next day they marched thirteen miles and halted early in the afternoon near Hyatts-town. On Thursday the regiment started at 7, passed through Hyattstown and Urbana, halted at noon near Monocacy Creek, the scene of the recent battle between Wallace and Early, rested until 5 P.M., then forded the creek, and leaving Frederick on the right, halted at midnight near Jefferson.

[1] Bowen, p. 365.

After a brief rest, they started again, and marched
to Knoxville on the Potomac, thence up the river, and
across the pontoon bridge at Harper's Ferry, and four
miles beyond to Halltown, where a halt in line of battle
was made.   The distance made was only fifteen miles,
but it was said that thirty men died of sunstroke.   Here
General Crook joined his forces to those of General
Wright.[1]

About 6 P.M. (the 28th,) I started with our sutler,
May, to go to the regiment, and went within fifteen
miles of Rockville.   At midnight we halted and slept
the rest of the night in a barn.

Friday, July 29th.   We made an early start.   Met
some stragglers from the Sixth Corps not behaving
creditably.   We stopped within a mile of Urbana, put
up at an old-fashioned country tavern, and I slept in
the garret.

Saturday, July 30th.   Breakfasted on bread and
milk, and started at 6 A.M.   The country was hilly.
We crossed the Monocacy, and arrived at Frederick
at 10 A.M.; moved on, met some of Mosby's men, and
stopped at a farmhouse over night.

Sunday, July 31st.   Started at 4.30 in pursuit of the
regiment, and overtook them within a mile.   The regiment started at 10 and marched until 2.   The excessive
heat prostrated many men.   We rested until 4.30 and
then resumed the march.   Marched through Jefferson to the beat of the drum, then through Petersville,

[1] Bowen, p. 367; O. R., xxxvii., pt. 1, p. 272.   General George Crook's
command was known as the Army of West Virginia, and consisted of two
divisions, although Sheridan says that there were not men enough to
make more than one fair-sized division (*Memoirs*, vol. i., p. 472).   It
may be interesting to note that the Second Division was commanded
by Colonel R. B. Hayes, afterwards President of the United States.
—C. S.

and encamped in a beautiful grove within a mile of Frederick.[1]

Monday, August 1st. Rested all day. Heard the news from Petersburg and Malvern Hill. Chambersburg reported burned.[2]   W. F. Merrill[3] called.

From camp near Frederick, Md., he wrote to his mother, August 1st:

I don't know as I told you in my last that my regiment went off and left me in Washington sick.   They sent me down to the city to stay until the regiment passed through on its way to City Point, and then when they got orders to proceed up into Maryland, they did not have time to send for me, so I was left.   I there had a nice visit with Hen, and

---

[1] The organization of the Department of West Virginia under General Hunter, July 31, 1864, given in O. R., xxxvii., pt. 2, p. 550, shows:

Sixth Corps, Maj.-Gen. Horatio G. Wright.
First Division, Brig.-Gen. David A. Russell.
Third Brigade, Col. Oliver Edwards.
37th Mass., Lieut.-Col. Geo. L. Montague.
6th Me. (battalion), Maj. Geo. Fuller.
23d Penn., Col. John F. Glenn.
49th Penn., Maj. Arnor W. Wakefield.
82d Penn., Lieut.-Col. John M. Wetherill.
119th Penn., Lieut.-Col. Gideon Clark.
5th Wis. (battalion), Capt. Chas. W. Kempf.

[2] The reference to Petersburg is to the explosion of the mine under the Rebel fortification known as Elliott's salient, on the morning of the 30th; that to Malvern Hill to the operations of the Second Corps under General Hancock north of the James, known to history as the Deep Bottom Campaign.   It was undertaken to draw the Confederate troops from the defences of Petersburg to the defences of Richmond, and thus weaken the enemy's line at the time of the explosion of the mine.   Early had sent forward his cavalry to demand a ransom of some of the towns on the border, and Chambersburg was the first to suffer.   On the 30th, the demand was made for five hundred thousand dollars in currency or one hundred thousand in gold, on threat of immediately burning the town.   As it was impossible to raise such a sum, the torch was applied, and three thousand people saw their homes reduced to ashes.—C. S.

[3] Of the Class of '63, Amherst College.

17

Steb, and Thursday afternoon I started with the sutler to find the regiment. They had marched very fast and had got to Harper's Ferry, some sixty miles, before we overtook them. They recrossed to this side of the river night before last, and I rejoined them yesterday morning.

A great many of the men have fallen sick and given out on these last two campaigns. They can't endure fatigue as they could at the beginning of the campaign, and they don't seem to rally as they did formerly. I pity them.

The troops have been marched on this trip without the slightest consideration. Day before yesterday some ninety boys in our regiment got heated and had spasms, and the trouble is that if they once melt they don't get over it all summer.[1] The marching was terribly hot yesterday and we made only ten miles. I went without the bandage on my eyes while in Washington, and for two or three days my eyes have been very sore to pay for it. I don't know but what I shall have to resign, if my eyes don't grow better. I found letters from Will, Father, and you when I arrived here. I should like to write as much in reply, but I can't do it this morning, and when I tell you what a delight your splendid long letters, so full of incidents and particulars, are to me, I hope you will feel that I appreciate them—although I would pay you in the other coin if I could. Love to Grandma and all the cousins—I must close.

The itinerary says that during the month of July

[1] The march from Washington to Halltown was exhausting in the extreme, and when they were ordered on the 30th to proceed to Frederick, Maryland, General Wright remonstrated and reported his corps "so much fatigued and scattered as to be unable to move this morning." (O. R., xxxvii., pt. 2, p. 511.) A staff officer reported to General Halleck at midnight: "The men are very tired; some of the Sixth Corps stragglers were half-way between Frederick and Harper's Ferry this afternoon." (*Id.*, p. 512.) But the move was insisted upon and orders were issued to start the next morning at daylight. So exhausted were the men and so oppressive was the heat that in twenty-four hours one half of the Sixth Corps had fallen out by the wayside, many of them never to join the ranks again.—C. S.

the regiment marched about two hundred and thirty-nine miles.[1]

Tuesday, August 2d.   Ordered to march, packed, started about 10 A.M., proceeded a few rods, and the orders were countermanded.   Returned and issued rations and rested the remainder of the day.   Large mail.

The following is a letter of this date to his father from camp near Frederick:

I believe about once in so often I sit down and write you a letter on business of some kind or other, and this morning I have come to the conclusion that I had better write you a letter of that kind.   I want to write you about Colonel Edwards.   He has been recommended for promotion by General Russell, who commands our division and is one of the ablest brigadiers in the army.   He had also a very strong recommendation from General Getty, the commander of the Second Division.   These recommendations are backed by Generals Wright and Meade, and approved by General Grant.   These papers are all on file in the War Department, and it would seem as if such papers ought to be sufficient of themselves, and yet it is a fact that such is the character of our Government, that mere military papers, unless they are supported by political influence, are not worth a cent.

Now as to Colonel Edwards's merits, I don't think there is a brigade commander in the corps that has behaved more gallantly, or handled his men in better shape during this entire campaign.   There are few commanders in the army that have more complete control, and can bring their troops up to that pitch of discipline which he effects in whatever he commands.   I don't believe there is a regiment in the service that has shown more steadiness and better soldierly qualities than the Thirty-seventh.

[1] O. R., xxxvii., pt. I, p. 272.

When old regiments like the Tenth Massachusetts and Second Rhode Island, considered among the best regiments in the service, were wavering and shaky, I never during the whole campaign have seen the slightest sign of a waver or of unsteadiness in the Thirty-seventh. They would go anywhere they were ordered without the slightest hesitation.

This perfection of discipline is due in a great measure to Colonel Edwards. Now such a commander, in these times when we have so many mean, cowardly, sneaking commanders, and when we so pre-eminently need good ones; when lack of discipline is the curse of our army, and we have so few that are capable of bringing troops to a proper degree of discipline; when such a man is so much needed, I say he ought to be rewarded. The good opinion of his corps and division commanders has placed him in command of one of the largest brigades in the army, and if General Sedgwick had lived, his best efforts would have been used in his favor. One of General Sedgwick's last acts was to transfer General Eustis to another division, so as to give Colonel Edwards command of a brigade, and he told Colonel E., after the battle in the Wilderness, that he should send forward his name for promotion at the first opportunity. His death prevented. Colonel Edwards is perfectly aware that he is not likely to receive his promotion unless he procures political influence, and yet such is his delicacy of feeling that he says that if his papers, backed by such military commanders, are not sufficient, they may fall through; and yet I know he would feel grateful if they were pushed through. Now I have taken it upon myself to write Mr. Washburn to secure if possible Mr. Sumner's influence in his behalf. I think they ought for the sake of old Massachusetts, for the sake of the cause and the country, to take an interest in the matter. I think all it would need would be for Mr. Sumner to interest himself a little in the case, and, with the aforesaid recommendations, it would go on of itself.

I have written warmly because I feel warmly, and I have

seen so many poor commanders promoted that, when I see a deserving one likely to get the go-by, I feel interested, as a patriot ought to be.

Wednesday, August 3d.   Called at 4, and marched at 4.30, through Buckeyeville[1]; crossed the Monocacy and encamped.   Had a bath, a swim, and a quiet rest. Rations of flour, meal, and soft bread.

Thursday, August 4th.   National fast day.[2]

A letter to his parents from "Buckeyeville," of this date, says:

As we are resting to-day and I am likely to have a little more time than usual, I think I will commence a letter to you bright and early this morning and then I shall be sure to finish it during the day.   I have just written a letter to Hen, so you see I am trying to keep my end of the rope straight with all the family.   I wrote Will yesterday. After several ineffectual attempts to move from the camp where I last wrote you, and where report ordered us to all parts of the globe, we moved yesterday morning some five miles and encamped ourselves, it is said, for a stay of three or four days on the banks of the Monocacy, some five miles from Frederick City.   So the boys are enjoying their stay and improving their time by bathing, fishing, and feeding on the products of Maryland soil.   They keep the farmers' wives busy throughout this whole neighborhood baking the much coveted soft bread, which they buy at fabulous prices (75 cents or $1.00 a loaf).   You would think soldiers' wages would hardly hold out at such rates.   They, however, don't mind prices if they can only get the articles.   Soldiers are

[1] Probably Buckeystown, five miles south of Frederick.   See Bowen p. 369; War Map 27 (1).

[2] This day was the result of a concurrent resolution of Congress, approved July 7th, requesting the President to appoint "a day of humiliation and prayer," and cordially concurring, the President in a proclamation appointed the first Thursday in August "for a day of prayer."—C. S.

utterly regardless of expense when they see anything they want, especially after they have been campaigning awhile.

One of the best officers in our corps died very suddenly this morning, so suddenly that they supposed it must be heart disease. He was wounded in the Spottsylvania fight of May 12th by a ramrod passing through his arm after it had grazed his side. A small piece of the ramrod, it seems, remained in his side and it worked its way in until this morning it pierced his heart and killed him. He was all right yesterday. The post-mortem examination elicited these facts. He was Major Ellis of the Forty-ninth New York, and was the inspector-general of our division. The division was paraded in his honor as his remains were carried to the depot on their way home.

I received the last number of the *Round Table*. I am sorry that they had to give that enterprise up. I hope Charley[1] won't suffer from the failure. I have received one letter from you. Father at Hartford and Mother at Binghamton. Our mails are not very regular.

Friday, August 5th. General Grant visited General Hunter at headquarters. Hunter asked to be relieved, and Sheridan was assigned to the command of the Middle Military Department or Division.[2]

[1] Charles H. Sweetser, the publisher, a classmate.

[2] In the despatch notifying General Halleck of General Sheridan's appointment to temporary duty in the field, General Grant had added: "I want Sheridan put in command of all the troops in the field, with instructions to put himself south of the enemy and follow him to the death. Wherever the enemy goes, let our troops go also." (O. R., xxxvii., pt. 2, p. 558.) President Lincoln happened to see this and it pleased him. He telegraphed General Grant his approval but added: "This, I think, is exactly right as to how our forces should move, but please look over the despatches you may have received from here even since you made that order, and discover, if you can, that there is any idea in the head of any one here of 'putting our army south of the enemy,' or of 'following him to the death' in any direction. I repeat to you, it will neither be done nor attempted, unless you watch it every day and hour and force it." (*Id.*, p. 582.) On the receipt of this, General

On Friday, the Thirty-seventh rested all day. In the evening, received orders to move to Middletown. Assigned to guard the trains, which did not start until the next morning, so we slept all night. It rained.

Saturday, August 6th. Crossed the Monocacy River and camped on the farther side. It rained merrily until 8 o'clock. Moved through Jefferson and Whitmore. The sight of a jail called forth from one of the soldiers the remark, "Oh! for thirteen months within thy peaceful walls." A hard march. Halted at 5.30 for dinner and supper. Went through the culvert under the canal, onto the towpath, and marched two miles in four hours. Halted for the night at 11.30. Mother is anxious about my eyes and sends me a shade.

Sunday, August 7th. Up at 5 o'clock, moved forward and crossed the Potomac River, and halted after four miles at Halltown. The views from these hills are very beautiful. General Sheridan takes command of this military division. To-day at or near Moorfield, Mc-Causland and his cavalry force, fresh from Chambers-

---

Grant informed the President that he would start for Washington in two hours. He did not stop, however, at the capital, but went direct to Monocacy Junction, where he found General Hunter. He asked him where the enemy was, and he replied that he had been so embarrassed by orders from Washington that he had lost all track of the enemy. "Well," said General Grant, "I will find out where the enemy is," and he ordered steam got up, and trains made up, and gave directions to push for Halltown. The army went by rail on the night of the 5th, except those detailed to guard the trains. General Grant immediately telegraphed to General Halleck to send Sheridan to Harper's Ferry, and that he should call at Monocacy Junction. Sheridan came by special train, and on arrival at the Junction found General Grant at the station, had an hour's talk with him, received his orders, and went at once to Harper's Ferry. The position at Halltown was very embarrassing to General Early.—C. S.

burg, were attacked by Averell and badly defeated. Most of his command were captured.[1]

Monday, August 8th.   No news this morning. Rested all day.   Paymaster arrived to-night.

Letter to his classmate, M. F. Dickinson:
FOUR MILES BEYOND HARPER'S FERRY,
August 8, 1864.

DEAR DICK:

I think of you during this hot summer weather as indulging in the luxury of sea bathing, enjoying all the pleasures of the devotee of a fashionable watering-place at this most fashionable season.   I should not object myself to a short sojourn at one of those Long Island beaches, but I have been wonderfully favored, when so many others have fared worse.   So, my dear old fellow, don't believe me complaining.   I am as happy as a lark.   Ruf is back again and that is pleasant.   I missed him very much during the summer months, and am proportionately glad to see him back. . . .

I suppose you will want to know what I am at.   Well, I wish I could tell you.   I suppose, however, we are watching Rebs.   We started from Washington in a terrible flurry and marched at the rate of seventy miles in four days,

[1] Bowen, p. 367.   General Sheridan reported to General Halleck that, on the morning of the 7th, "General Averell overtook the enemy's cavalry under General McCausland, at whose command Chambersburg was burnt; captured three battle-flags, four pieces of artillery, 420 prisoners, a large amount of small arms, and four hundred horses, and scattered the forces."   (O. R., xliii., pt. 1, p. 726.)

As soon as General Early heard that the Union troops were being concentrated at Halltown, he withdrew his forces from the north side of the Potomac and took a position at Martinsburg, about twenty miles to the west and a little to the north of the Union position.   A good macadamized road ran from Martinsburg up through the valley connecting the principal towns, which afforded him a ready means of guarding his communications.—C. S.

crossing the Potomac at Harper's Ferry, and proceeding a short distance into Virginia, until we heard that the Rebs were in Maryland. So back we hurried to the defence of Maryland. We stopped in the vicinity of Frederick several days, and last Saturday crossed the Potomac again, and have rested yesterday and to-day on Virginia soil, waiting, I suppose, for something to turn up. . . .

Yours affectionately,

MASE.

Tuesday, August 9th. The news of the capture of Mobile Bay by Farragut received. Torbert's cavalry arrived to-day.[1]

In a letter to his parents dated Camp near Harper's Ferry, August 9, 1864, he writes:

Here we are within seventy miles of Washington, and not a mail for a week. Somehow or other our regiment seems to have been counted out when they distributed the mails for this corps. . . .

After halting for several days on the banks of the Monocacy, and luxuriating in its cool waters, sudden orders came Friday night for us to pack up and proceed to Harper's Ferry. Our brigade was afterwards detailed as wagon guard, and so we did not start until Saturday morning, about 9 o'clock. However, we slept Friday night with our things all packed, supposing every moment we should be called on. Saturday night we slept on the tow-path of the canal, and Sunday morning marched over to our present camp, about four miles beyond Harper's Ferry. Since then we have been waiting, hardly knowing, I suppose, whether it was best to push into Virginia, or to run back to the defence of Maryland.

[1] The cavalry here referred to was a division of three brigades sent by General Grant from the Army of the Potomac, and Torbert was made the chief of cavalry of the Army of the Shenandoah (O. R., xliii. pt. 1, p. 501).—C. S.

Last night the paymaster came down upon us quite suddenly, but very agreeably. The boys have been sadly in want of money. It was more than five months since they had received any. The paymaster, however, did not do me a great deal of good, except the satisfaction I derived of seeing others happy. We have expected every hour to-day to be off from here, and still we are waiting. I should not complain much if they should leave us here a month. I think we could improve the time faithfully.

General Sheridan's appointment to the command of the troops in this Department, I think, gives great satisfaction. Although General Hunter may be a very good soldier, I don't believe he is a great commander. We have rumors that Lee is coming up this way with his whole army, and that all the Army of the Potomac, except the Second Corps, is coming around by way of Fortress Monroe and Washington to meet him. They seem to have made a most outrageous failure in their attempts upon Petersburg. I am not so much surprised at it, however, from what I saw. The condition of the army, with bad generalship, was enough to ruin the most feasible of undertakings. I don't believe Meade co-operates with Grant to the full extent of his power. No news of any consequence here. My love to all the friends.

Wednesday, August 10th. Aroused at 4.30 to start at 5.30. Passed through Charlestown, the county-seat made famous by the conviction and execution of John Brown in December, 1859. As the several drum corps entered the village, they each, regardless of the terrible heat, took up the air of " John Brown. [1]" Found the railroad torn up. Marched within twelve miles of Winchester. In a forest near Clifton, halted at 5 for the night. Much straggling. Many prostrated by the heat, which was at its worst as we were passing through

[1] Bowen, p. 370.

a cornfield.   Fine shower to-night.   Marched sixteen miles.

He wrote to his parents, August 12th, from Winchester:
I don't know as we shall have a chance to send a mail for a month to come, but as we are resting this afternoon, I think I will improve the opportunity to drop you a line. We left our camp near Harper's Ferry Wednesday, and have marched pretty hard since.   We have suffered more because they have marched us in the heat of the day, or, rather, all day long, and the sun has been terribly scorching. Many a poor fellow has been struck down.

Last night we spent below here somewhere near Berry-ville.   But this morning our corps pushed on to Front Royal, and we were detached to go back to Winchester and convoy a train on to the rest of the troops, so we marched only seven miles this morning and have been resting since.[1]   When we shall go on, I do not learn; probably not before to-morrow, at any rate.   I have not as yet been down into the town, only as we marched through it this morning.   There were so many more anxious to go than I was that I waived my claims.   It is said, however, by those who have been down, that they find a good many strong Union people, and that they have secreted some of our prisoners here and ministered to our wounded.   The Rebs have been here and occupied the ground for the past week or two, so that the country is pretty well cleared of everything that is good.   They tell us that there are some one hundred bushwhackers lurking around here ready to pounce upon all our stragglers.

Saturday morning.   We are under marching orders this morning and expect every minute to go.   Some men from Early's corps came in last night and say that his corps is at

[1] General Sheridan on the 12th ordered General Wright to send a brigade of the Sixth Corps via the Millwood pike to Winchester, to occupy the place until the arrival of the trains (O. R., xliii., pt. 1, p. 775).   The Third Brigade, First Division, was selected.—C. S.

Strasburg, and that he intends to stop there and fight us. There was quite a fight day before yesterday between our cavalry and the Rebs. We attacked their rear guard as they were going out of the town. The wounded of both sides are here now.

Sunday morning. We made a fifteen mile march yesterday at 11 from Winchester to Cedar Creek, down beyond Middletown where we are now encamped. I have been sleeping all the morning until Henry came in with a big pile of letters and woke me up, and I went to reading and have been reading ever since. Your shade came among the rest, and I am sitting here writing to you with it on. It is just the thing. I enjoyed my stay at Winchester very much. I used to feast two or three times a day on bread and milk, and oh! how good it did taste! The weather has been awfully hot the past few days, and we have had to march through the heat of the whole of it. I am in good condition, however, and enjoying myself as much as a man can in this sort of life. I shall write Father and answer his questions soon. I don't dare to use my eyes much more to-day. I got the $10 Father sent me in Washington.

Saturday, August 13th. Moved out on the Strasburg road at 11. Moved in the rear of the trains at 2, through Kernstown, Newtown, Middletown, on to Cedar Creek. Miss Kitty Scan reclaimed her stolen horse and cows. Covered about nineteen miles.

On August 20th, Saturday, he wrote from Charlestown to his mother:

I thought I would muster up courage to drop you a line this afternoon, although I don't feel like the smartest man in the world. I have been suffering from a severe attack of fever and ague for the past three days, and to-day I am suffering from the crazing effects of whiskey and quinine taken to counteract the fever.   We left Middletown Tuesday night, and marched all night; rested near Winchester from 7 until 11, and then moved out five miles on the Berryville road.[1]   That day I marched all day, but my legs would not have carried me an inch farther than they did.

That night the Rebs were coming down upon us about midnight and so they sent our regiment out on picket.   The fact is, we have to do about all the picket duty and skirmish duty for the corps when there is any danger, because we are armed with Spencer rifles.   We started the next morning and marched to Charlestown.   The last two miles I had to get into an ambulance, the first time I ever got into an ambulance since I have been in the service.   May it be the last! We have rested here since.   Where we shall go next, I don't know.   I was very badly off all day yesterday; had a severe shake and a violent fever.   To-day I have kept them off with the doctor's aid, but I am a good deal like a rag.

I was appointed Judge Advocate of a court sitting in this division just before we left Middletown, and had tried one case.   I accepted the position with a good deal of hesitation but I found I could use my eyes with a shade, and as I considered the experience valuable, and the additional pay something of a consideration, I decided to try it.   But I am afraid now I shall have to give it up.

Sunday, August 21st.   I am feeling a little better this

[1] Early, at this time, occupied a strong position at Fisher's Hill, and, on the 14th, Sheridan ordered the Sixth Corps to cross Cedar Creek and occupy the heights at Strasburg.   But while this movement was in progress, he received a despatch from General Halleck, signed by General Grant: "Inform Sheridan that it is now certain two divisions of infantry have gone to Early, and some cavalry and twenty pieces of artillery. . . . He must be cautious and act now on the defensive until movements here force them to detach to send this way" (O. R., xliii., pt. i, p. 43). To accomplish this, he immediately moved a strong force north of the James to menace Richmond.   This despatch led General Sheridan to move back to Halltown.—C. S.

morning. About 8 o'clock the Rebs attacked our
picket line. The Thirty-seventh was at once detailed for
duty, and Companies A, F, and G were sent to the
skirmish line, while the rest of the regiment was held
in reserve. The surgeon sent an ambulance to take
me to the hospital. Although I had eaten nothing for
forty-eight hours, and was very weak, I insisted upon
going with the regiment, and was detailed to command
the skirmishers. I swallowed a tumbler of whiskey,
and mounted my horse, and during the day lived on
whiskey. I was on the skirmish line all day. We had
twenty men killed and wounded out of about seventy-
five on the skirmish line. Of these, three were from
Company A, one each from Companies B, E, and I, six
from Company F, and four from Company G. This
is sometimes called the skirmish at Summit Point. [1]

Sheridan's retreat from Cedar Creek was accounted
for. Early was reinforced by Kershaw's division from
Longstreet's corps and two brigades of cavalry under
Lee.

At nightfall, I was able to get some fresh milk and
bread, and I ate heartily the first meal I had enjoyed
for seventy-two hours. After dark we were withdrawn
from the skirmish line, packed up and retreated to the
vicinity of Harper's Ferry, where we occupied a strong
defensive position between the Potomac and Shenandoah rivers.

Monday, August 22d. Last night moved back to

---

[1] In the affair here referred to, the Second Rhode Island and the
Thirty-seventh Massachusetts were engaged, and General Sheridan
reports to General Grant on the 22d: "The skirmishing was at one
time yesterday rather sharp in front of the latter command [Sixth Corps],
as the line was pressed forward and drove the enemy from a crest in our
front which they occupied early in the day" (O. R., xliii., pt. 1, p. 880).
See War Map 82 (6).—C. S.

Harper's Ferry, and resumed the lines which we occupied from August 7th to 10th, near Halltown. About 11 A.M., our division was ordered out on a reconnoissance. I was too much used up to go, and remained in camp at brigade headquarters. The division went out one and a half miles and halted, and there was no further movement. In the afternoon we had fine showers. I stayed over night at brigade headquarters.

Tuesday, August 23d. I rejoined the regiment this morning, and found them encamped in a beautiful grove on a hill, commanding a fine view of the Valley of the Shenandoah. The Twenty-third Pennsylvania Volunteers went home, their term of service having expired. Colonel Montague is in command of the brigade.

Thursday, August 25th. Made our ordnance returns for the second quarter of 1864. A reconnoissance made this afternoon showed the Rebs still in force in our front.

In a letter of this date to his classmate, M. F. Dickinson, he wrote from Camp near Halltown, Va.:

I have just eaten breakfast, if so I may dignify my frugal meal of hardtack and pork, and to settle it I know of no better recipe than a half hour's conversation with you. I wish I could do it in the good old-fashioned way, in a large arm chair slightly tipped back, with feet upon the stove or mantel. How we would sit and talk! But as I am allowed no such luxury, the best substitute I have is by letter.

We have had a pleasant little trip up the valley as far as Cedar Creek, and spent one day pleasantly at Winchester on the way down. The officers at brigade headquarters had a delightful time with the Winchester ladies. They found one or two very agreeable Union families, and all the officers agreed that the Winchester young ladies were beautiful and charming. Last Sunday we had a brisk little fight at Charlestown. I was in the skirmish line with three companies from our regiment. I lost six men from about twenty-five that I took in from my company—Jo Taylor, Eben Wiley, John and Pat Briton among them. I have not a sergeant left in my company.

Last night I had a pleasant chat with Macomber. He is just as full of fun and humor as he always was, and has any quantity of yarns to tell about his numerous campaignings, and tells them in his own amusing way. Colonel Edwards has gone home to Springfield for a visit with his wife, and this leaves Lieutenant-Colonel Montague in command of the brigade. For although we have six regiments in our brigade, we have no officers higher than lieutenant-colonel. What is to be the end of all this marching and countermarching up and down the Shenandoah Valley, I cannot imagine. It is a question in my mind whether Washington or Richmond is really in the most danger. It is most vexatious to a soldier to be compelled to work so hard and see no results.

Ruf is doing very finely these days and does not seem to suffer much from his wounds. He is waiting very quietly for that commission to turn up. . . . Tell Goodell he owes me a letter. If he does not write me pretty soon, he will owe me another.

Oh! if this cruel war was over, how I would enjoy engaging in some civilized pursuit as you and Goodell are! I am sick to death of this business. It sometimes seems as if I could not possibly stay another year. Still I suppose I shall await the decisions of time. I must go to work on my company papers. I miss George Cook here. He always used to help me at such times.[1]

[1] The Thirty-seventh Regiment remained at Halltown until the 31st of August, when with the whole army it moved to Charlestown, where it remained until the 3d of September, when it marched to Clifton, where the position was intrenched, and the command remained until the 19th. There is little in the diary of interest, and no letters; and the happenings

In a letter to his brother Will, dated Clifton, September 16th, he wrote:

The War Department has just issued the order consolidating the Tenth and Seventh Massachusetts Detachments (the veterans of those regiments) with our regiment. So that will fill us up to the minimum number so that we can have second lieutenants in our regiment, and it will make room for ten or twelve promotions.

It will be rather good once more to have a full complement of officers. Now if they would only give us recruits enough to fill us up full, we should feel as if we amounted to something. There are so many away from these regiments at present that it will not in reality add much to our martial strength. Captain Lincoln has gone to Washington on business for the corps to see about the forwarding of recruits and convalescents to this department. He will be gone some four or five days, and have quite a pleasant little recreation, get paid, etc. We are living on the fat of the land these days. Foraging parties go out almost every day and bring in sheep, lambs, cows, pigs, fruit, and honey. This Shenandoah Valley is the richest country we ever campaigned in. A great many of the officers have provided themselves with cows, and keep them, and have fresh milk continually.

We don't have our baggage out here because we are liable to a fight at any time, and don't wish to be encumbered in that event. This is rather an inconvenience, as at this time there is a good deal of writing to be done.

---

were of so little interest to Captain Tyler that some days he has made no entries in the diary. All that is recorded pertains to the ordinary routine of camp life, such as the making out of returns, picket duty, acting as officers of the day, the results of foraging parties, an account of rain and shine, receiving letters, and visits to and from friends.—C. S.

CHAPTER XVII

THE BATTLE OF WINCHESTER[1]

SEPTEMBER 19, 1864

[INTRODUCTION.—The campaign in the valley had not been satisfactory to the lieutenant-general, and had been the theme of a great deal of criticism in the Northern papers. The siege of Petersburg could not be pressed with the vigor the chief desired because of the absence in the valley of the troops detached from his army, and on the 17th he paid a visit to General Sheridan at Charlestown.

In the opinion of some military critics, General Early had up to this time conducted his affairs with consummate skill and judgment, but not without a boldness that sometimes approached rashness. Two or three times he had given Sheridan an opportunity to strike, rarely offered an opposing general. This led General Early to say in a report to the Confederate government that "the events of the last month had satisfied him that the commander opposed to him was without enterprise and possessed of an excessive caution which amounted to timidity." But while making a rather perilous move to prevent the repairing of the Baltimore and Ohio Railroad, he heard at the telegraph office at Martinsburg that Grant was at Charlestown with Sheridan, and he divined at once that something was likely to take place, and acted accordingly.

General Grant had warned General Sheridan almost every

---

[1] For maps of the battle of Winchester, see War Map 99 (1), and *Sheridan's Memoirs*, vol. ii., p. 26, map.

day since he took command of the Department to be cautious, but he usually encouraged him to strike if it was practicable. He now listened to Sheridan's plans, kept his own carefully written order in his pocket, as he found that only two words of instructions were necessary: "Go in." The laconic order of the lieutenant-general was soon felt through the army, and we find in the diary indications of the coming struggle. General Grant had hardly left Charlestown when orders were issued by Sheridan for an advance.

The Union lines on the morning of the 18th extended from Summit Point on the right to White Post on the left, a distance of some fifteen miles, but the infantry was massed between Clifton and Berryville, and was about seven or eight miles from the battlefield of the next day.

The account of the battle of Winchester was written out quite fully by Colonel Tyler. It would be interesting to know what part Colonel Tyler took at the critical moment in this fight, but he has quoted Official Records to show the part—which was an important one—taken by his regiment, and, as will be seen hereafter, his own conduct was such as to attract the attention of his commanding officers.

The plan on which the battle of Winchester was fought was not the plan which General Sheridan had submitted to the lieutenant-general and which received his approval. This plan proposed to march the Union army south of Winchester, and put it across the enemy's line of retreat. But from the position of the Rebel army, as Sheridan saw it upon his return from Charlestown, he thought it best to fight the enemy in divisions. He thought he could by a rapid movement, crush Ramseur at Winchester before he could be reinforced by Gordon and Rodes, who were some distance to the north. There is a deep gorge or woody ravine about two miles long through which his army had to pass. Wilson, with the cavalry, dashed through it in the morning and carried the earthworks which had been erected to defend it. He should have been supported by the Sixth and Nineteenth Corps, but their progress was impeded in the gorge by ambulance and ammunition wagons. The Sixth Corps was seven hours in making as many miles. The consequence was that Early was reinforced by the divisions of Gordon and Rodes before the battle began, and Sheridan had to fight the whole Rebel army occupying an advantageous position.[1]

It is noted in the diary that the wagon train came up and distributed rations, and was ordered to the rear; that marching orders were issued and countermanded at 5 o'clock.

From Clifton, on Sunday morning, September 18th, he wrote to his parents, and the letter is a striking illustration of how little, at the time, even an intelligent soldier knows of the movements of the army of which he is a member.— C. S.]

Letter of September 16th:

I have just an hour to write you a letter this morning during which I presume I shall have more than a dozen interruptions, as even on this Sunday morning they are issuing rations, making out requisitions, etc. General Grant was here this week, and it is predicted that he was here to some purpose. This morning the teams have come up with our valises and allowed us to put on a clean shirt, and are going right back, it is said. So things look a little as if we were on the eve of a move. Whether we chase Early or go to Petersburg is a question. For the past few days we have been busy with the consolidation of the detachments of the Seventh and Tenth with our regiment.

MONDAY, September 19th. We were up at 2 A.M., with orders to march at 3, and we started promptly, but progress was slow after we crossed the Opequon, owing to the narrow roads, which were badly blocked with troops and ammunition wagons. We reached the field

[1] *Sheridan's Memoirs*, vol. ii., pp. 9–31.

selected for the deployment of the troops, and immediately got into line. The Second and Third Divisions formed the front or first line of battle, and the First Division (ours) was in reserve or second line of battle, separated from them by the Berryville turnpike.[1] Our brigade was on the right of the turnpike.[2]

Cannonading was heard in the morning. But the fight commenced about noon, and the advance for a while was rapid. A gap developed between the Third Division and the Nineteenth Corps to our right, because the Third Division was ordered to maintain its connection on the left with the turnpike, and this obliged them to oblique to the left. The enemy attacked our line at this gap, and attempted to break through. General Russell ordered Upton into the breach, and led the brigade with Upton by his side. Russell had been previously shot through the body, but maintained his seat in his saddle until he was killed at the head of the charging column by the explosion of a shell. He was a gallant soldier and idolized by his followers.[3]

A portion of the Thirty-seventh supported the Fifth Maine battery, which was pouring canister into the advancing Rebel column. But when summoned by Russell, the Thirty-seventh advanced into the gap, and with their Spencer rifles rendered very efficient service in stopping the breach made by the Rebels at the point where the Sixth Corps and the Nineteenth Corps should have joined. Rebel prisoners captured in this advance

---

[1] See War Map 99 (1), showing the positions occupied at the battle of Winchester. For larger environs, see War Map 27 (1). The same positions are stated by Sheridan in vol. ii. of his *Memoirs*, at the top of page 20.

[2] This is explained in General Dalton's report, below. See p. 281.

[3] *Sheridan's Memoirs*, vol. ii., pp. 22–23.

asked what kind of a gun we had that could be loaded all night and fired all day. We blocked their advance and drove them back into their proper line. Upton was wounded in this charge, and Sheridan improved the opportunity to reform his lines. We rested two hours; meanwhile a division of cavalry arrived,[1] and the Eighth Corps was placed in position on the right of our line.

Sheridan started the cavalry and the Eighth Corps turned the Confederate left flank, and then rode with his staff at a full gallop, waving his sword, just in the rear of our advancing line of battle. It was a most inspiring scene. We were not used to seeing a commanding general on the front line of battle, and the exploding shells and the whistling bullets added excitement to the scene. We went forward at double quick, drove the Rebels out of their intrenchments, which, in our front, consisted of fences and thickets on the edge of a field, half wooded and half cleared, and in spots turned into rifle-pits. It was in this charge that Charley Bardwell was shot through the body.

It was now a lively chase. We were in hot pursuit and they were running to the rear as fast as they could, and in the distance we could see our cavalry gradually sweeping around their left flank. We drove them back on Winchester, and they escaped through the town and over the turnpike to the South. We captured some 2500 prisoners, crowding as many of the privates as we could into the court-house and yard and confining the officers in the jail yard.

[1] The cavalry here referred to were "Merritt's brigades led by Custer, Lovell, and Devin," who had just come in on the Martinsburg pike from the North. When they got the word to go, Sheridan says, they "literally rode down a battery of five guns and took about 1200 prisoners" (*Sheridan's Memoirs*, vol. ii., pp. 11, 24, and 26).—C. S.

The Thirty-seventh went into the fight with 276 muskets, and lost twelve enlisted men killed, and seven officers and seventy-two men wounded—a total of ninety-one.[1] It was our largest percentage loss in any single battle. I was wounded by a piece of shell which just grazed my chin and cut it to the bone, passing very close to the jugular vein.

The ladies of Winchester turned out in large numbers, and brought food and dainties to the prisoners. Colonel Edwards was appointed commander of the post, with headquarters at Winchester. His brigade was detailed for garrison duty. Lieutenant-Colonel Montague was made provost marshal, and the Thirty-seventh Regiment became the provost guard. The Thirty-seventh was lodged in the city and the other regiments of the brigade were encamped around the city, on different sides. The Thirty-seventh really did police duty; the other regiments performed picket and guard duty. I took possession of one of the offices in the building opposite the court-house. It was a desolate, windowless, dirty place, but we fixed up some benches along the walls of our room, and spread our blankets upon them, and by day they were lounges, and at night they were beds.

Col. Edwards reports:

This brigade [Third Brigade, First Division, Sixth Corps] with the rest of the corps left its camp near Clifton, Va., on the morning of the 19th instant. Shortly after 3 o'clock reached the Opequon and crossed not long after sunrise. The enemy were met in force about two miles southwest of that stream. The brigade was placed in position on the left of the turnpike, in columns of battalions at full distance, at right angles with the line of battle, with instructions to

[1] O. R., xliii., pt. 1, p. 112.

move by the right flank and keep 300 yards in rear of the line and move forward when the first line advanced. In this position the command suffered severely from a hot and continuous fire from the enemy's artillery.

At 11.40 the column commenced to move forward, coming into line of battle immediately after passing through the first belt of woods. Thus the brigade continued its forward movement under quite a severe fire until ordered to move double quick to the right of the road, as the enemy had broken through the line of the Nineteenth Corps. Seeing the enemy had got to the rear and right of us, I ordered Lieutenant-Colonel Montague, commanding the Thirty-seventh Massachusetts Volunteers, to attack them at that point. At the same time the enemy came out of the woods in front of us in two lines of battle and charged. I advanced my brigade with bayonets at the charge, forcing the fugitives in front to lie down as we passed over them. We opened fire at 150 yards range and drove the enemy back handsomely. At the same time, Lieutenant-Colonel Montague drove the enemy back from the rear and right, taking 150 prisoners and inflicting severe loss upon the enemy, though I regret to say the Thirty-seventh Massachusetts lost over one third its number. Nothing but their Spencer rifles enabled them to defeat more than five times their number.

Capt. H. H. Young, brigade inspector, and Lieutenant Colt, seeing the battery on the left of the road in danger of capture, placed the Forty-ninth Pennsylvania Volunteers in support, who handsomely repulsed the enemy and flanked that part of their line that was in front of the balance of the brigade on the right of the turnpike. General Russell was killed at this time charging with my brigade.

As soon as the lines were reformed on our right, an advance was ordered. We moved steadily forward, driving the enemy before us. General Upton was wounded, and turned over the command of the division to me. Again the advance was ordered and the division charged across the open country in magnificent line and order up to the heights of Winchester. The enemy broke before us and were routed. The Forty-ninth Pennsylvania Volunteers saved Cowan's battery, and the Thirty-seventh Massachusetts Volunteers saved Stevens's. The officers of these two artillery organizations acknowledged that these regiments succeeded in preventing the enemy from capturing their pieces. The Thirty-seventh Massachusetts Volunteers also captured the battle-flag of the Second Virginia Infantry, and the Forty-ninth Pennsylvania the headquarters flag of General Fitzhugh Lee.[1]

General Upton, commanding Second Brigade, First Division, in his report says: "On the left of the brigade, the Thirty-seventh Massachusetts Volunteers rendered invaluable service in supporting Stevens's battery."[2]

The report says General Upton was called to the command of the brigade at 12:30. This must have been the hour of General Russell's death.

Report of Henry R. Dalton, assistant adjutant-general, First Division, Sixth Corps, says:

On Monday, the 19th instant, the division broke camp at 2 A.M.; moved across country to the Berryville pike; from thence via the pike to within three miles of Winchester, when it went in position in support of the other divisions of the corps—the First Brigade, Lieut.-Col. E. L. Campbell, Fifteenth New Jersey Volunteers, commanding, supporting the Third Division on the left of the pike; the Third Brigade, Col. O. Edwards, Thirty-seventh Massachusetts Volunteers, commanding, on the left of the pike, supporting the Second Division; the Second Brigade [General Upton] moving by the flank up the pike.

The enemy, having pushed back the Second Division of

the Nineteenth Corps and a portion of the Third Division of this corps, moved down toward the pike, delivering a severe fire of musketry from the woods and cornfields on the right. The Third Brigade (Edwards's) was now rapidly moved by the flank to the right of the pike, then forward, with the First Brigade, under a heavy fire, to a crest commanding the woods and field through which the enemy moved. This advance was very much assisted by the First New York Battery (Cowan's), commanded by Lieutenant Johnson, which did splendid execution, and was fought with gallantry under a very annoying musketry fire.

At this time, General Upton moved his brigade into line to the right of the pike at an oblique angle to it, thence forward into the woods, delivering heavy volleys into masses of the enemy, who were coming up. This fresh fire from the Second Brigade soon caused the enemy to fall back, so that the whole line moved forward to a position which was easily held till the latter part of the afternoon, though occasionally sharp musketry fire was interchanged.

While personally superintending the advance of the First and Third Brigades to the crest previously referred to, and which he considered of the utmost importance, General Russell was killed by a piece of shell which passed through his heart. He had just before received a bullet wound in the left breast, but had not mentioned this to any of his staff, continuing to urge forward his troops. In this advance, Capt. A. M. Tyler, commissary of musters of the division, was severely wounded in the hand while leading the Thirty-seventh Massachusetts Volunteers belonging to the Third Brigade.

On the death of General Russell, Brig.-Gen. Emory Upton assumed command by order of Maj.-Gen. H. G. Wright, but there being necessarily some delay in giving information of General Russell's death to General Wright, and transmitting the order of General Wright to General Upton to take command, Col. O. Edwards superintended the movements of his own and the First Brigade, carrying out the design of General Russell, which he did, fighting his troops with great gallantry and coolness.

The formation of the division, after the engagement of the morning, being from left to right, Third Brigade, First Brigade, Second Brigade—the left resting near the house on or near the pike—the right brigade crotcheted to the rear and one regiment on its right at right angles, making a connection with the general line of the Nineteenth Corps, Brigadier-General Grover's division, though in advance of it some 150 yards.

At 4 P.M. the enemy, having been routed on the right by the charge of General Crook's troops, moved down in some confusion along the front of the Nineteenth Corps and that of the Second Brigade. This being observed, General Upton ordered the right regiment, mentioned above, to move forward "double quick" to a crest some 200 yards in advance, which it did under an annoying musketry fire; from this crest a well-directed fire on the enemy caused him to continue his flight in still greater confusion than before. The remainder of this brigade was then swung round and forwarded, the left being the pivot, and a connection was formed with General Crook's command, Col. George D. Wells's brigade, when a general advance was made from crest to crest, the enemy giving way without serious opposition.

During this general advance, Brigadier-General Upton was wounded by a shell while urging forward the troops. The command then devolved upon Col. O. Edwards, Thirty-seventh Massachusetts Volunteers, under whose superintendence the division made its final forward movement, carrying the last crest contested for by the enemy.[1]

---

[1] O. R., xliii., pt. 1, pp. 163–4. See War Map 69 (2), and *Sheridan's Personal Memoirs*, ii., 26, map.

CHAPTER XVIII

AT WINCHESTER

FROM SEPTEMBER 20 TO DECEMBER 12, 1864

[INTRODUCTION.—The night after the battle of Winchester, General Early retired in hot haste to a strong position at Fisher's Hill. At five o'clock the next morning, General Sheridan moved rapidly up the Valley pike, and at one o'clock the Sixth Corps were crossing Cedar Creek, and the cavalry, under General Merritt, were occupying the heights of Strasburg, about two miles north of the enemy's position.

The Union general occupied the 21st in examining the enemy's position, and the next day, the 22d, dealt him a very damaging blow, inflicting upon him heavy losses in killed, wounded, and captured. The Third Brigade, Second Division, Sixth Corps, did not take part in the battle of Fisher's Hill, as they had been detailed for guard duty at Winchester, where the Thirty-seventh remained until the 12th of December. From the nature of the case, the situation was not always an easy or a pleasant one.

Unfortunately, the notes in the diary give very little idea of what was going on at Winchester for a few days after the battle. They would probably have brought to the mind of the writer many things that would be exceedingly interesting, for it was a time of intense activity. While General Sheridan was fighting the battle of Fisher's Hill, Colonel Edwards was clearing up the battlefield at Winchester,

284

picking up the scattered arms and various implements of war, burying the dead, bringing in the wounded of both sides, providing for their wants, and sending off prisoners to Harper's Ferry.

Colonel Edwards reports: "All wagons that could be seized have been impressed into the service for the purpose of collecting and bringing in the wounded. . . . I have had all the wagons belonging to my brigade unloaded, and they are now arduously at work on this duty. One hundred wagons in all . . . reported to the medical director by my order at daylight this morning."[1]

The medical director on the 24th reports: "I sent yesterday 700 wounded to Sandy Hook hospital. There are still 3800 here, including 700 Rebels. I learn that more wounded men are on their way to this place from the front. I must send to Harper's Ferry the slightly wounded as rapidly as possible.[2]

On the 28th, Col. Edwards reports: "The medical director has about 2500 wounded here; they will not bear removal for six weeks, that is, with the exception of about 500.[3]—C. S.]

TUESDAY, September 20th. Received more prisoners, making 1500. Sent the officers to the Winchester jail. Had no rations for them.[4] The citizens are very attentive. The air is full of rumors. Our brigade occupies the city and the rest of the corps have gone on with Sheridan in pursuit of the enemy. I called on Major Davis and Captain Drew in the prison yard and took them some whiskey. I was busy all day making

---

[1] O. R., xliii., pt. 2, p. 146.   [2] Id., p. 163.
[3] Id., 2, p. 201.
[4] On the 20th, General Sheridan telegraphed General Stevenson at Harper's Ferry: "Send in addition to the eight days' rations ordered last night for the troops, 20,000 rations to Winchester for our prisoners and wounded" (Id., 2, p. 125).—C. S.

out lists of the prisoners, and watching them to see that none escaped.

Wednesday, September 21st.   Colonel Edwards returned from the front where he temporarily commanded the division.   He sets to work to reorganize things with a strong hand.   The hospitals here, especially the Rebel hospital, are in very bad condition. General Neill returned to-day.[1]

Thursday, September 22d.   Started the prisoners this morning to the rear, and we went to work to police the camp and the city as thoroughly as we could.   Our baggage arrived to-day.   At Fisher's Hill, Sheridan drove Early's forces from their intrenched camp by a flank movement, executed by the Eighth Corps (General Crook's),[2] and captured 1000 prisoners and twenty guns.   Great rejoicing in the North over our victory of the 19th.   One hundred guns fired in each of the military departments.

On the 23d of September, 1864, Professor William S. Tyler wrote from Amherst to his son at Winchester something of the anxieties of the families and friends at home:
I had hoped to learn whether you are yet in the land of the living or have fallen among the hundreds of dead and thousands of wounded in the late glorious battle—before writing you again.   But we hear nothing from you since

---

[1] It will be remembered that Captain Tyler was at one time a member of General Neill's official family.   On the 20th, the order sending General Neill to report for duty to General Wright was "rescinded and he was ordered to proceed to Martinsburg and assume command of the post there" (O. R., xliii., pt. 2, p. 119).—C. S.

[2] Crook's corps was joined by the Sixth, which seems to have had an equal share in the victory.   See Sheridan's reports, O. R., *id.*, pp. 152, 162, and *Memoirs*, pp. 37, 38.   This explains the reference to the Sixth in the letter of the 23d, at page 288 below.—C. S.

the battle—your last date received being Sunday, the 18th,
and we get as yet very meagre reports of the casualties.
From the correspondent of the *Herald* of to-day, however,
I glean enough to show that the Thirty-seventh has not
escaped without serious losses—the names of Captain
Loomis, Captain Pierce, Lieutenant Harris, Lieutenant
Cozens, Lieutenant Bardwell, the last to our great sorrow
reported "dangerous." We derive some encouragement
from the fact that your name does not appear in a list
which gives so many casualties in your regiment. . . .
Dr. Hackett, in a letter just received, adds a postscript,
saying: "I often think of your son in the army, and trust
his life has been preserved, and that he will return to you
in safety." A recent letter from Grandpa Tyler and one
from Grandma Whiting both express a similar interest in
you, and everybody I meet down town inquires if I have
heard from you since the battle.

By the way, the battle is knocking down gold and goods,
etc., faster than even the fall of Atlanta. Gold is reported
this noon at 213, and goods and produce are falling quite as
rapidly, as I fondly hope not to rise again.

*A letter to his brother dated September 23, 1864, refers
to the battle of Winchester:*

I have just written Hen and I will try and drop you a line,
although, as the mail goes very soon, I don't know as I shall
be able to get it off this morning. We have had a big fight
and whipped old Early soundly. The Thirty-seventh
Regiment did splendidly. They lost one third of their men,
but took more prisoners than they lost men. We got the
battle-flag of the famous Stonewall Regiment, the Second
Virginia. It was stamped with the names of thirteen battles
that they had figured prominently in. I received a slight
scratch under my chin, but it did not take me from duty a
moment. Charley Bardwell did splendidly, and was very
severely wounded through the body just at the close of the

action. He is comfortable now, but we watch him very carefully and with great anxiety.

I have a Colt's revolver, navy size, which I picked up on the field. I think I will send it to you at the first opportunity, or I may keep it through the campaign, and then let you have it to keep until I get through the war at least. It will amuse you in some of your leisure time.

This Winchester is a beautiful place, or rather, has been. I think it must have had six or eight thousand inhabitants, and is very compactly built. Now the stores and public buildings are all deserted, and there are very few male inhabitants that are not over sixty years of age. They have some of the prettiest girls here I ever saw, and any quantity of them.

This morning has just brought the news that Sheridan has driven the enemy from Fisher's Hill, and has pursued them beyond Woodstock. The Sixth Corps flanked them and took sixteen guns and 1000 prisoners.[1] I did not tell you why I am here in Winchester. Colonel Edwards is military governor of the place and our brigade occupies the town. Colonel Montague is provost marshal and our regiment is provost guard. Until yesterday morning we had some 1500 Reb prisoners under our charge. We occupy some of the offices that surround the court-house and have very pleasant quarters.

I picked up a little darkey that was taken prisoner in this fight and shall keep him as my servant. I think he will make a first-rate one. He has been a slave, and was with his master who was a captain in a Georgia regiment.

You had better believe everybody is in high glee. The good news cheers them up, and then the thought that we should gain such victories in the place where we have so often suffered defeat makes success doubly welcome. I have picked up a horse, saddle, and bridle since I have been in this march. I don't know as I shall be able to keep him, but I shall try for a while at least. It is too late for this

[1] See p. 286.

morning's mail, so I shall not send this until to-morrow. If I have time I shall add a little more.

On a fragment of a letter without date (probably written the day after the above letter as he refers to the letter), he wrote:

We are living on the fat of the land these days. We keep a cow and a horse, so that I can have bread and milk for supper every night, and milk in my coffee and tea. Then I can indulge in the pleasure of an occasional ride on horseback. In my peregrinations to hunt up the Rebs, I have found it very pleasant to ride sometimes. I also have a darkey who is quite a specimen. I got him out of this lot of Reb prisoners. He is rather slow, but I think will learn to move quickly in time, and he seems to be as faithful as the day is long. I think I shall like him as soon as we become acquainted. . . .

Did you know that it is very probable that the Thirty-seventh sharpshooters shot General Rodes in the battle of Monday? As near as we can find out from Rebel statements, he was engaged in putting the battery that we silenced into position, when he was struck by the ball of a sharpshooter. At the time he is said to have been killed, our regiment was almost the only one that was doing any firing. It was about 12.30 when we advanced alone and drove the Rebs before us, and this battery was brought up to oppose us. That was the time that I got scratched.

Sunday, September 25th. I attended the Episcopal church this morning. It is the only one of the local churches that was open.

Monday, September 26th. Devoted the day to taking lists of all the attendants on the Rebel wounded in the city of Winchester.

Wednesday, September 28th. Very busy day in preparing muster rolls and working on lists covering

Rebel hospitals. Had a pleasant talk with Dr. Love, in charge of Rebel hospitals, this afternoon. In front of Petersburg, two divisions from each of the Fifth and Ninth Corps extended our lines about two miles to the left and held the ground, afterwards fortified by Fort Fisher.

Thursday, September 29th. Paymaster arrived last evening and paid us this morning. Charley Bardwell comfortable.

WINCHESTER, Oct. 2, 1864.

MY DEAR PARENTS:

I have just arisen from the breakfast table, and the news has come that Grant has thrown his army between Petersburg and Richmond, capturing several guns and some prisoners. What is the exact amount of damage done to Rebel lines we are as yet unable to learn, as the newspapers that were to bring us the account of these movements were captured by Mosby. But what we do hear is so cheering that we are all jubilant this morning, and feel that something is being done towards plucking out the heart of the Rebel Confederacy, viz., Richmond. May the Ruler of all things grant that this day our armies may rest with the satisfaction of having done that work. For I believe Richmond has already fallen. I supposed last summer that Grant intended to cut the road between Petersburg and Richmond, and then take his choice whether he would take Petersburg or Richmond. But he decided differently and I presume wisely at the time. I hear that Grant has received since the second battle on the Weldon Railroad, 70,000 reinforcements. In that case he has something of an army.

I have been busy all the week paroling Rebs in the hospitals in this place. It is something of a job, and I am not quite through with it. There are some 800 wounded Rebs and about 200 attendants taking care of them. I have charge of this department of the business in the provost marshal's office, and if any of these come to the office and wish anything, they are referred to me.

Captain Lincoln, you know, has been up to Washington, and brought down some 1300 recruits, convalescents, etc., to our corps. He took them up to the front at Harrisonburg, and delivered them over to the proper authorities, and returned Friday afternoon. He reports that they were almost out of rations when he left, and the trains could not be up for three days; so they cannot support our army at that distance from its base a great while at this season.[1] They have got to do one of two things, change on to the Culpeper line and open that railroad again, or starve it through on what rations they can get from our trains and the country, until they have accomplished their errand up the valley. For undoubtedly we have an important part to play in the drama that is enacting before Richmond.

I have President Hopkins's baccalaureate sermon preached at Williamstown this last Commencement, and have promised myself the treat of reading it to-day. Our chaplain, I understand, has returned, although I have not seen him. So maybe we shall have service to-day for ourselves.

I have just returned from our service. Mr. Lane arrived last night and was rejoiced to find Charley Bardwell very comfortable. This afternoon he gave us the best sermon that I have heard for a year, from the first verse of the twelfth chapter of Romans. His remarks were practical, pointed, and well suited to the occasion. We have plenty of room here, so Mr. Morse has taken as his chapel a nice room a short distance from here on the opposite side of the street. This afternoon two ladies, delegates from the Christian Commission, were present to aid the singing. One, Mrs. Harris, claims to have been the first field agent of the Christian Commission. The other, a Mrs. Beck, is a

[1] The diary remarks Harrisonburg is eighty miles from the base of the army at Martinsburg which makes it difficult to provision and supply the army.

good deal younger than Mrs. Harris, and has been a shorter time at the work, I think. She tells me that she spent some time at Mrs. Tuckerman's this summer, and was there during Commencement. So I had quite a pleasant chat with her about Amherst.

These two ladies are very devoted in their attentions to the soldiers, and spend most of their time in the hospital.

This morning I attended the Episcopal church again, as it is the only church in the place that is open. After the service they administered the sacrament. The ceremony was beautiful and the occasion a very solemn one. It was the first time I ever saw the sacrament as administered by the Episcopalians. . . .

Ever your affec. son,

Mase.

The same day, he wrote to his classmate, M. F. Dickinson:

It is some days since I received your last. To me they have been days of busy occupation. In fact, ever since the battle we have been in one continuous bustle of excitement. We have had some 3000 prisoners to guard at one time or another, and now that we have only the care of the city upon our shoulders, it gives us no slight labor. My special charge has been the enrolling and paroling of the attendants upon the Reb hospitals in the city. There are some 200 attendants upon 800 wounded here in the city. . . . Ruf has been up to the front with some 1300 convalescents and has just got back last Friday afternoon. He is tough and hearty. So yesterday afternoon, while it was raining hard, I sat down and beat him a rubber of cribbage. I am reading *John Halifax* greatly to my delight.

Wednesday, October 5th. General Sheridan began his retreat down the valley. The cavalry were ordered to devastate the valley—mills, storehouses, barns, and crops were to be burned.[1]

Thursday, October 6th. Charley Bardwell died this morning.

[1] During the months of October, November, and December, the record in the diary is meagre, and the letters seem to have taken its place in the mind of the writer. Indeed, most that is recorded in the diary is reported in the letters. The position of the soldier doing guard duty in so important a place as Winchester, situated in a very disloyal section of the country, was not a bed of roses. Mosby and Gilmor were ever on the alert, with every advantage of information and knowledge of the country in their favor, and made the post one of constant anxiety and wearing vigilance.

The Union army had occupied Harrisonburg on the 30th of September but the cavalry had been pushed on to Staunton and Charlottesville, and the valley was now virtually clear of Rebel troops. Bushwhackers were, however, abundant, and made it necessary for every train of two hundred wagons to have an escort of a thousand infantry and five hundred cavalry. The trains often contained five hundred wagons, and deliberate murders of Union soldiers were not infrequent. It was the wish of General Grant that Sheridan should proceed to Gordonsville and Charlottesville, and destroy the railroad connections there, and if practicable threaten Richmond. But Sheridan had fears about the movement, and they were so strong that the lieutenant-general adopted his suggestion and consented to the return of the Sixth and Nineteenth Corps to Petersburg. There was, however, one order of the lieutenant-general that Sheridan carried out in the letter and the spirit. Here is the order together with his own enforcing it, to which reference is made in the diary:

"In pushing up the Shenandoah Valley, as it is expected you will have to go first or last, it is desirable that nothing should be left to invite the enemy to return. Take all provisions, forage, and stock wanted for the use of your command. Such as cannot be consumed, destroy. It is not desirable that buildings should be destroyed—they should, rather, be protected; but the people should be informed that, so long as an army can subsist among them, recurrences of these raids must be expected, and we are determined to stop them at all hazards. Bear in mind the object is to drive the enemy south; and to do this you want to keep him always in sight. Be guided in your course by the course he takes. Make your own arrangements for supplies of all kinds, giving regular vouchers for such as may be taken from loyal citizens."

General Sheridan's order to his chief of cavalry was: "No houses will

WINCHESTER, Oct. 9, 1864.

MY DEAR PARENTS:

While waiting for the time for church, I may as well begin my usual Sunday letter. We are having very cold weather these days. In fact, it takes considerable management to keep warm either night or day. This morning the ground is frozen and the wind blows a bleak November chill, while the clouds are so thick that the sun is hardly able to peer through at all. We have a good fireplace in our room, but the scarcity of wood in this neighborhood renders it rather difficult to keep the fireplace warm, to say nothing of the room. The lights were pretty much all smashed out of the windows when we came here, but by picking up new sashes around the town and making them double, we have managed to stop a little of the circulation of the air, and now for almost the first time in two years, while sleeping in a building, I have taken a real old-fashioned cold, and am suffering from sore throat and snuffles in my nose. Still, I am better this morning than I was yesterday. Yesterday I sat in the house pretty much all day and read Hayne's and Webster's great speeches. I think they made me appreciate more fully the greatness of the contest in which we are engaged, the worth of union and the principles for which we are contending. . . .

I have had a very pleasant Sabbath to-day. In fact, the privilege that we have here of spending a Christian Sabbath in something like a Christian neighborhood is more like home than any military experience we have previously had. The chaplain has a regimental service in the afternoon and in the morning I usually attend church in the city, and the rest of the day the quiet of my own room affords me a place for reading, meditation, and prayer. The quiet

---

be burned, and officers in charge of this delicate but necessary duty must inform the people that the object is to make this valley untenable for the raiding parties of the Rebel army " (*Sheridan's Memoirs*, vol. i., pp. 484 and 485).—C. S.

is as marked here Sunday as in our own New England village. But the churches are too many of them occupied as hospitals for all to attend public worship, and I don't know but that the clergymen have all gone south. At any rate, there is no business transacted and every facility is afforded them for worship within the power of the post commandant. The rest of the week, Winchester is a very lively business place.

Monday morning. Last night quite a train came in from the front bringing a great many refugees; and to see the babies, little girls and boys and half-clad mothers shivering this bleak, cold night, in their shells of buildings, is a sight pitiable to behold. Sheridan has retreated to Fisher's Hill and burnt everything from there to Staunton. We hardly know what to make of the movements. I suppose, however, he knows what he is about, and very likely is obeying orders. It was so cold last night I could not sleep well. I wish I had my overcoat.

Ever your son,

MASON.

Sunday, October 9th. We hear this evening that Custer and Merritt have defeated Rosser at Tom's Brook and chased him twenty miles. Tom's Brook is crossed by the Valley pike some four or five miles south of Fisher's Hill.[1]

[1] General Early was reinforced on the 5th by a brigade of cavalry under the dashing General Rosser. He was hailed as "the saviour of the valley," and his men "were bedecked with laurel branches." He caused the Union army a good deal of trouble and became very bold in his operations. On the 8th, General Sheridan decided to "have Rosser chastised," and halting his infantry, gave orders to General Torbert, his chief of cavalry, to attack the enemy the next morning, "and whip him or get whipped yourself" (*Sheridan's Memoirs*, ii., 56). General Torbert at once made up his command, which consisted of the First and Third Divisions of cavalry, Generals Custer and Merritt, and early the next morning was in front of the enemy who numbered between four and five thousand. General Sheridan made his headquarters that morning

Monday, October 10th. Sheridan retreated to Cedar
Creek. The Eighth Corps encamped on the east of the
turnpike, the Nineteenth on the west of it. The Sixth
Corps marched to the Shenandoah opposite Ashby's
Gap under orders to return to the Army of the Potomac
at Petersburg.

Thursday, October 13th. Early having been reinforced by Kershaw's division (recalled from its return
to General Lee), suddenly appeared at Fisher's Hill, and
repulsed an attack made by a portion of the Eighth
Corps (Thoburn's division). The Thirty-fourth Massachusetts suffered a heavy loss in this fight. The Sixth
Corps, after having made a day's march toward Front
Royal, were ordered back to Cedar Creek, and on arriving went into camp in the rear of the Eighth and Nineteenth Corps.[1]

Tuesday, October 18th. General Sheridan[2] arrived
at our headquarters late in the afternoon and spent the
night.[3] I was present and heard him talk a while.

Wednesday, October 19th. I was awakened long
before dawn by the sound of distant cannonading, and
after listening for a long time concluded it was serious,
and arose and got something to eat and went to head-

---

on Round Top, a hill that overlooked the battlefield just to the south.
The battle was a peculiar one. It was fought with sabres and was stubbornly contested. General Sheridan's account of what he saw, in a
despatch to General Grant, is vivid. "It was a square cavalry fight,
in which the enemy was routed beyond my power to describe. He lost
everything carried on wheels except one piece of artillery, and when last
seen it was passing over Rude's Hill near New Market, on the keen run,
twenty-six miles from the battlefield, to which point the pursuit was
kept up" (O. R., xliii., pt. 2, p. 339.)—C. S.

[1] See *Sheridan's Memoirs*, vol. ii., p. 61.

[2] He has been on a short visit to Washington.

[3] See *Sheridan's Memoirs*, vol. ii., p. 67.

quarters. Found General Sheridan just starting with his staff and escort for the front.

Colonel Edwards appointed me officer of the day. The stragglers of the Nineteenth Army Corps were coming in in large numbers, and I was directed to halt all soldiers on our picket line and form them into companies and battalions. Our brigade was assembled on the south side of the city, and formed in line to be a nucleus of a line of battle in case the army retreated to Winchester, and the picket line was strengthened by large additional details. We stopped a large number of stragglers, and by noon they had ceased. Some teams were parked near the city, but not very many. At evening we received the news that the rout had been turned into a signal victory, and that Sheridan had recaptured all the prisoners and guns taken by Early in the morning, and added to them twenty-four guns and 1200 Rebels. Custer and the cavalry had made the most of the captures. Great enthusiasm prevailed in our camp upon the receipt of this intelligence.[1]

Saturday, October 22d. A despatch of this date, from the headquarters of the Sixth Corps, reads:

[1] The story of the battle of Cedar Creek to which reference is here made, and Sheridan's account of his famous ride from Winchester, "twenty miles away," are given in his *Memoirs*, vol. ii., commencing at page 66, and continuing through the chapter. General Early, having gathered all the strength he could through the return to his army of convalescents and other absentees, had moved quietly from Fisher's Hill in the night of the 18th and early on the morning of the 19th, to surprise Sheridan's army on the north bank of Cedar Creek before Sheridan could get back from Washington. The surprise was so complete a success that the Union army was thrown into confusion, and driven from its camps in disorder back in the direction of Winchester. Sheridan's arrival among the retreating soldiers was made the signal for a return to the front, which culminated in the victory mentioned in the diary.

LIEUT.-COL. C. KINGSBURY, JR.,
   Asst. Adjt.-Gen., Headquarters Middle Military
     Division.

COLONEL:

   I have the honor to request that if not incompatible
with the interests of the service, the Third Brigade,
First Division, Col. O. Edwards commanding, now at Winchester, be returned to duty with the corps. The division
to which the brigade belongs numbers without it only 1550
enlisted men for duty with only one field officer. The
brigade is an excellent one, and might, it is suggested, be
replaced by troops who having seen less service would not
be so valuable in the field, while they could perform the
duty at Winchester as well.

Very respectfully, your obedient servant,

H. G. WRIGHT,

Major-General, Commanding.[1]

WINCHESTER, Oct. 23, 1864.

MY DEAR PARENTS:

   Yesterday, I was on as officer of the day, and kept
quite busy attending to all the business of the city. Last
night they brought in nearly a thousand of our wounded
in army wagons. It was terribly cold, and the poor fellows, besides all the tortures of their wounds, had to suffer
the awful effects of the cold. The Sanitary and Christian
Commissions turned out and supplied them with hot soup,
coffee, tea, and hot whiskey punch, and what blankets they
could find. Still they had to lie in the wagons over night
and were carried on to-day. Luckily the weather modera-
ted towards morning or many of them would have frozen
to death. I am afraid as it was many of them got their
death chill.

   The order has just been issued by General Sheridan for

[1] O. R., xliii., pt. 2, p. 445.

the arrest of all male citizens in the Valley, between the ages of eighteen and forty-five, who are capable of bearing arms.[1] It will cause such a commotion in this town as has not been seen since the war commenced. The papers came this morning with very incomplete accounts of Sheridan's latest great victory.[2]

The Rebs curse the Sixth Corps, and the Unionists are extravagant in their eulogies of it. We enjoy both the curses and the eulogies. One is as great praise as the other. General Sheridan, I understand, credits the victory and the decisive charge to the Second Division of our corps.[3] We are proud of the fact. We used to belong to the Second. The Third Division, as usual, broke. They originally belonged to the old Third Corps; we don't think much of them. The Eighth and Nineteenth Corps have been rather inclined to think that they could whip anything that ever saw light, but they don't say much now. There is very little doubt that the First and Second Divisions behaved splendidly during the whole fight.

I have been to church this morning—the old-school Presbyterian church. They opened for the first time to-day. The minister is quite an able man, I should think, and a very good man. His sermon this morning was on glorifying the Lord, and was one of condolence to the people at this particular time. He spoke of Northern fanatics and Southern demagogues subverting the Constitution. Their people had suffered enormously, and still he glorified the Lord for it all. He quoted Scriptures very freely and was exceedingly earnest in his prayers for peace, but said nothing about the restoration of the Union. Still I liked him for his plain speaking, and his out-and-out frankness bore a very strong contrast to the milk-and-water secessionism of the Episcopalian minister. Yet he made me a little mad

[1] The diary says they were ordered to be sent to Fort McHenry.
[2] Cedar Creek.
[3] This statement in a letter written four days after the battle is confirmed by Sheridan's maturer view in his *Memoirs*, vol. ii., at page 82.

once or twice, and I felt like appointing the service this afternoon and preaching myself. . . .

Two or three weeks ago when we had some hundreds of prisoners in the court-house I was very much interested to see them one Sunday night separate off in squads and hold religious services. They sang and prayed with all the fervor of the Southern heart. I thought then that they were more devout than we were, for all seemed to unite in presence, if not in taking part.

Your affectionate son, MASE.

In a letter to a brother, dated October 25, 1864, from Winchester, he wrote:

We have decided to-day to go out to board. My present chum (Capt. Robinson) and I thought we would try to live in a civilized way for a little while. So we have engaged a boarding place and to-day move in. If possible we shall try to get a few nights' rest in a civilized bed. We have been sleeping on boards and under very few blankets ever since we have been here, and find the weather mighty cold. I have been roaming around very busily this evening. Several of the officers have been busily engaged arresting disloyal citizens. One of my friends on the corps staff was wounded in the last fight and is lying here at Colonel Edwards's headquarters. One or two of his ribs are broken, and there is great danger of his not recovering. I have been up to see him and find him quite feeble. He can read, however, and so I have just sent him up my last *Harper*. As I write there is quite a cannonading going on in our rear towards Martinsburg. There is quite a train expected in to-day, and I am afraid the guerillas have attacked it. I hope it will get through safe and bring my coat. I should not, however, care to have my coat on board if the train is destroyed by guerillas. . . .

I have got to go on as officer of the day to-morrow and a pleasant job I shall have of it, attending to the widows and orphans, calling for their husbands and fathers that we have shut up. They will be sent off soon, however, so that it won't last long.

October 26th, he wrote to his mother:

We have been having quite a scare over a rumor that announced an immediate march to the front for us. It spread like wildfire yesterday afternoon. Colonel Montague got hold of it and sent up to brigade headquarters and found that it all originated with the fact that General Wheaton, who now commands our division, had made an application to General Sheridan for our return. We would thank General Wheaton to keep his applications at home, if that is the tenor of them.

I have just got nicely situated in a very pleasant boarding place here in town. Mrs. O'Bannon is a lady whose acquaintance I made while paroling Rebs. She is a widow, and her husband was an officer in the United States employ. She has lived many years in the best society of Washington, and is an exceedingly cultivated lady. She has two nieces living with her. Captain Hopkins, Captain Robinson, and myself are together there.[1]

[1] Mrs. O'Bannon lived in Kent Street. It was at her house that the notorious Major Harry Gilmor had found shelter after he was wounded at Bunker Hill on the 3d of September, and where he remained until noon of the memorable 19th of September. His hand in burning Chambersburg, in wrecking trains and robbing the passengers, made him very anxious not to fall into the hands of General Sheridan, whose guns were now thundering in his ears. "The three weeks of physical suffering," he wrote afterwards, "I spent in that house were among the happiest in my life" (*Four Years in the Saddle*, p. 271). It is not often that a lady has the grace to extend her courtesies in such opposite directions. The other ladies referred to were Miss Fanny Dickens and Miss Kate Reilly.

At the house of Mrs. O'Bannon, Captain Tyler found an exceedingly pleasant home during his stay at Winchester, and although he saw them but once afterwards, friendly relations with the family were kept up for many years.—C. S.

WINCHESTER, Oct. 27 [1864].

MY DEAR BROTHER:

I have been very busy for twenty four hours as officer of the day. Yesterday and day before we arrested nearly one hundred citizens of disloyal tendencies, and at present have them confined in the building opposite to our quarters.

Of course it has kicked up a terrible muss, and I, as officer of the day, was beset with the entreaties of men and women of the place wishing to see their husbands and fathers. Some old men sixty or seventy years of age and much broken down with the infirmities of old age are there. It is my private opinion that the conscription has been *too* relentless and I am afraid it will overshoot the mark. Still, as I am not consulted, I have no right to express an opinion. After yesterday's experiences, I am in that uneasy, nervous state which is natural after a day of excitement. Therefore you must not expect a very heavy letter this morning. I am not in the condition to write one.

Yesterday afternoon they had a flag presentation in the Forty-ninth Regiment Pennsylvania Volunteers. They are the best regiment from Pennsylvania I have ever seen and re-enlisted almost to a man. The colors were sent on yesterday from the State Department. In the absence of the governor, Colonel Edwards presented them to the regiment with a neat little speech.

In a day or two now we shall be hard at work making out papers for this month. Time really passes so rapidly here that I hardly appreciate that we have been here nearly six weeks. Yet such is the fact. Yesterday afternoon the rumor reached us that we were to be relieved and that the Maryland Brigade was to relieve us. I tell you if there was n't a stir among the boys! The rumor spread in less than ten minutes all over the regiment. It turned out that General Wheaton had made application for us to be sent back to the division. I hope that General Sheridan will decide differently.

Your brother,

MASE.

On October 29th, he wrote to his mother:
The regiment is every man of it on duty. Fifty men have gone off to hunt for Mosby. Then General Sheridan is here taking a survey of the ground and to meet some engineers from Washington. A guard of seventy-five men from our regiment has been detailed to take care of him. This, with our regular duty, takes every man we have. General Sheridan visited all the hospitals here in the city yesterday, and spoke a cheering word to all the wounded. If they don't remember him it will be because they are very forgetful. We think there is nothing like General Sheridan. It has been decided, I understand, to retain our regiment here in the city as long as Colonel Edwards stays. How long that will be remains to be seen.

I have a fine account of General Russell in the Boston *Advertiser*, in which it speaks of our regiment doing very well in the battle of Winchester on the 19th of September. Our regiment was a great favorite of General Russell, and he always relied on us for his tough jobs. Next to General Sedgwick, he was the greatest loss our corps has sustained.

HDQRS. MIDDLE MILITARY DIVISION,
October 27, 1864.
Special Orders No. 67.

. . . .

13. Colonel Heine, commanding Provisional Division, will proceed to Winchester to-morrow morning at 6 o'clock, with his division, and report to Colonel Edwards, commanding that post, for duty. On Colonel Heine, arriving at Winchester, Colonel Edwards will place en route for this point his own brigade, and order it to report to commanding

officer Sixth Corps.[1] By command of Major-General
Sheridan.

C. KINGSBURY, JR.,
Assistant Adjutant-General.[2]

PROVOST MARSHAL'S OFFICE,
WINCHESTER, VA., Nov. 5, 1864.

MY DEAR PARENTS:

I have been so busy the past week that I have had no
time to write letters.   Colonel Montague has gone north,

[1] Organization of troops in the Middle Military Division, commanded
by Maj.-Gen. Philip H. Sheridan, October 31, 1864:

> Sixth Corps, Maj.-Gen. Horatio Wright.
> First Div., Brig.-Gen. Frank Wheaton.
> Third Brig., Col. Thomas S. Allen.
> 37th Mass. (detached at Winchester), Capt. Hugh Donnelly.

O. R., xliii., pt. 2, p. 511.

[2] *Id.*, p. 475.   Colonel Tyler, at this point in his card diary,
has copied the report of Colonel Edwards, commanding the Third
Brigade, First Division, Sixth Corps, under date October 27, 1864:
"On the 9th day of August, my brigade, with the rest of the corps,
commenced the movement up the Valley.   On the 12th, the brigade
was detached from the rest of the division and ordered to garrison Winchester.   Relieved by General Kenly's troops on the 13th; marched as
guard to the trains as far as Middletown, rejoining the division at Cedar
Creek, where remained until night of the 16th, when the command
marched, reaching the Opequon the following afternoon; left on the
morning of the 18th and marched to the vicinity of Charlestown.   On
the 21st the enemy attacked our picket line, the Thirty-seventh Massachusetts and Second Rhode Island Volunteers on the line.   That night
moved back as far as Halltown.   On the afternoon of the 22d, ordered
to support of the army of West Virginia; remained in this position until
the 28th, when the command moved as far as Charlestown, taking up
its old position.   On the 3d of September moved from camp near
Charlestown, Va., and marched as far as Clifton, where the position
was intrenched and the command remained in it until the morning of
the 19th, when, with the rest of the corps, it moved out to the Opequon,
crossed that stream shortly after daylight, and participated in the
engagement of that day, losing sixteen commissioned officers and 228 enlisted men.   On the morning of the 20th the command was assigned to
duty at Winchester, where it has remained as a garrison to the post up
to the present time" (O. R., xliii., pt. 1, p. 186.)—C. S.

and Colonel Edwards put me into the office of the provost
marshal until his return. We have heard this morning
that Colonel Montague has met with an accident and
would not return for some time at least. This, I suppose,
will detain us here for some time to come. I had hoped
to be home by Thanksgiving, but I am afraid it will be
later than that now before I get home. Still, as long as I
am busy and well occupied, I don't care.

Yesterday we had quite an excitement here; General
Sheridan came down from headquarters and stopped with
Colonel Edwards over dinner. He was on his way to
inspect the railroad between here and Harper's Ferry.
They ate some cheese while at Colonel Edwards's, and after
they had got fairly out in the country, the general and several of his staff were taken deadly sick. Captain Moore,
indeed, for a while was thought to be dying, but he finally
rallied, and is to-day very comfortable. I understand
Colonel Edwards and his staff had eaten of the cheese the
night before, and been affected a good deal in the same
way, but not so severely. You can imagine that an affair
of this kind would produce some excitement, because we
did not know but that there might be foul play, and General Sheridan's life endangered. As it was, they had to
send out an ambulance and bring the general and one or
two of his staff in.

Colonel Edwards thinks there is a prospect that we may
stay here during the winter. They are making preparations apparently to rebuild the railroad to Harper's Ferry,
and this would look very much as if they intended to hold
this place during the winter, and in that case they may keep
us here. Still we don't build any hopes on the prospect.
We are happy in the idea that the campaign is so near the
end.

I see a rumor in the paper of to-day that General Rose-
crans has been ordered to the command of the Army of the
Potomac. I should be perfectly satisfied if this were the
case. For although I like General Meade and believe in his

ability, I don't think he supports Grant as he ought to. I
hardly know what to think of the campaign, whether it is
finished or not, for this reason: they have commenced giving
leaves of absence and furloughs in this department, and it
hardly seems as if they would do that if they expected more
fighting immediately, and since Grant's last move proved
nothing, I don't know but that they intend to wait for the
spring campaign before they attempt to do much. The
Army of the Potomac must suffer terribly from want of
proper organization.

Sunday morning. . . . Our regiment, the most of it, went
out last night in search of Mosby. A report was received
here that he was lying in wait for General Sheridan some
eight miles from here; so Colonel Edwards ordered out the
regiment in pursuit. But for infantry to catch Mosby
mounted is not easy. They were gone all night and came
back this morning without any booty, having had nothing
but their tramp. It was exceedingly cold last night and
those out had to suffer. The regiment is worked very hard
here. Colonel Edwards seems to think that he can rely on
nothing else but the Thirty-seventh, so they have to do all
his jobs, and since they have been here, the men have been
on duty two nights out of three a good deal of the time.
This is too much for flesh and blood to endure.

I have been at church this morning and heard our chaplain preach. He has taken the Episcopal church, and is
going to occupy it hereafter for his service. He had a very
respectable audience of soldiers and one or two ladies. His
sermon was upon "Faith that worketh," a very good practical discourse upon the Christian faith, and what it should
bring out in our lives.

Ever your son,
MASE.

WINCHESTER, Nov. 9, 1864.

MY DEAR FATHER:

I guess you will think it about time that you heard

from me again. The fact is, that I hardly have ten minutes in the day that I can call my own, and if I sit down for that length of time, something is sure to come to disturb my repose. This is not the kind of a life to write letters you know. I, however, enjoy my occupation much. It gives me something to think about and to do, and the responsibility is just enough to be agreeable. The work is not hard, it is simply incessant, calling for this or that by somebody all day long. Yesterday was election day with you at the North. I should like to have been with you and seen the fun. Here the day passed unnoticed, except that we were all somewhat weary.

Monday night some one brought word that Fitzhugh Lee with some four thousand cavalry was over to the west of Winchester, either threatening a raid upon the Baltimore and Ohio Railroad, or else an attack upon Winchester. Colonel Edwards acted with his usual determination, and before nine o'clock had us all up in line of battle, and there the regiment stayed waiting in a drizzling rain until morning. I went out with the regiment, but when I saw there was not much chance of a fight, I concluded to return and get a little rest by virtue of my provost-marshal's berth, and so about 12 I returned to my room, and slept the rest of the night. The regiment did not come in until yesterday at noon.

I see considerable of Colonel Edwards these days, and he often wishes to be remembered to you. The colonel is expecting his wife on here shortly. I shall be mighty glad to see her genial face here. Colonel Edwards occupied a beautiful house for his headquarters, and has two large rooms for his own accommodation, except when General Sheridan is here, when he occupies one of them. Rumor says to-day that the army of General Sheridan has fallen back to Kernstown, and is there intending to intrench and go into rather more permanent quarters. Some reports say that they have been expecting every day to have a fight up at the front. They are said to have been reinforced strongly, and Longstreet is said to be in command.   This rumor is old, and not to be relied upon.[1]

Ever your son,

MASON.

WINCHESTER, Nov. 13, 1864.

MY DEAR MOTHER:

Sunday has come around again with its seasonable rest and quiet.   To be sure there is now and then an order, but it is not an incessant drive as during the rest of the week.

This morning an underground mail communication with the Rebs has been discovered, and I have just received orders to ferret it out.   Yesterday there was quite sharp skirmishing with the Reb cavalry all day.   This morning we hear that we took three guns and something like two hundred prisoners.   The prisoners report that Early crossed Cedar Creek with his whole force and retired again last night.   It was lucky for him that General Sheridan did not know it, he would have pounced upon him again.

As I get tired of writing so much the earlier part of the day, I find that I need recreation much in the afternoon, and, as at present I am allowed a horse, I usually try the efficacy of a ride.   There are a great many pleasant views around Winchester, and I am fast making myself acquainted with them.   There is fine hunting (quail and partridges) by going just outside the picket line, and several of our officers

[1] About the 9th of November, General Sheridan took up his headquarters at Kernstown, and began the withdrawal of his forces to that point, and finally decided that a defensive line should be held to enable him to send troops to Petersburg.   But hardly had he withdrawn from the upper valley, when Early, with what he could collect of his shattered army, began to advance and make a show of assuming the offensive.   Sheridan launched at him a force of cavalry under Merritt, Custer, and Powell, which resulted in the usual misfortune to the Rebel cavalry, and Sheridan reported to General Grant: "There has been none of the enemy's forces within reach in my front for a distance of forty miles since the last advance of Early and his hasty retreat."   (O. R., xliii., pt. 2, p. 649.)—C. S.

are fond of indulging their sportsman tastes in this pleasant vale. I have not been out myself as yet, but have intended to go almost any day.

The army has moved back to within five miles of Winchester and they are kept on the *qui vive* pretty much all the time because their position, which can be flanked on either side, is rather a precarious one. . . .

This morning I attended church at the old-school Presbyterian church and heard their pastor, Mr. Graham, preach. The sermon was on the depth of Christ's love—a plain, simple discourse. The congregation was mostly composed of women, and the most of them, mourning for their friends, were dressed in black. The marks of war are indelibly written in the appearance of every family in this town.

Col. Edwards is expecting his wife by every train, and as there is a train coming up to-night, we shall probably have a mail. We are happy over the election news. Massachusetts has done herself credit by her enormous majority.

With much love,

Ever your son,

Mason.

Winchester, Nov. 16, 1864.

My dear Mother:

. . . . To-day is a beautiful day, and the sun is as bright and warm as an October sun usually is. The most of the officers have taken horses and gone out to ride and to enjoy themselves in such glorious air, but I don't feel very much like riding this P.M., and consequently am communing with you. A foraging party went out from here this morning, escorted by Seventeenth Pennsylvania Cavalry, and four of them have just been brought in wounded. The rest were all killed or captured by Mosby. The affair has produced quite an excitement here in the street, and knots of men are talking it over on the corners now.[1] Colonel Edwards went out hunting this morning but came rushing back as soon as he heard the firing. He, however, succeeded in getting some four quails and two rabbits. Mrs. Edwards does not come yet. They are expecting her to-day, I understand. General Sheridan was down from the front yesterday afternoon, and stayed some five hours with Colonel Edwards.

I am invited to sup out to-night with one of the promi-

---

[1] These occurrences appear to have been frequent.

"HEADQUARTERS U. S. FORCES,
"WINCHESTER, VA., November 7, 1864.
"LIEUT.-COL. C. KINGSBURY, Jr.,
"*Assistant Adjutant-General*, Middle Military Division.
"COLONEL:

"I have the honor to state that G. H. Soule, Company G, Fifth Michigan Cavalry, this day entered our lines from the direction of Berryville, and reported as follows: He was taken prisoner by soldiers of Mosby's command on the macadamized road near Newtown, and by them taken to a camp on the Winchester and Berryville turnpike. There he was placed with a squad of Federal prisoners numbering about twenty-two, and with them compelled to draw lots for the purpose of determining upon a certain number who should be hung. Of the twenty-three prisoners, seven were to be executed in retaliation for a like number of Mosby's command who were hung by General Custer. Of the seven upon whom the lot fell, three were hung, two shot, and two escaped. The wounded men—one of them escaped alive by feigning death—are being cared for by Union families in the vicinity of the camp. The men who escaped have reported at this post. The accompanying note was found by a citizen who cut down and buried the bodies, pinned to the clothing of one of the men who were hanged. Captain Brewster, commissary of subsistence of General Custer's command, was among the parties captured. The name of one of the men hanged was ascertained to be George L. Prouty. He was a member of Company L, Fifth Michigan Cavalry.

"Very respectfully, your obedient servant,
"O. EDWARDS,
"*Colonel, Commanding Post.*
"(Inclosure)

"These men have been hung in retaliation for an equal number of Colonel Mosby's men hung by order of General Custer, at Front Royal. Measure for measure." (O. R., vol., xliii., pt. 2, p. 566.) See another like instance, O. R., vol., xliii., pt. 1, p. 186.

nent Union men here. He has been accustomed to flee
whenever the Rebs occupied the town, and his descriptions
of his attempts and successes in running the Reb pickets
are interesting. Your fears of my being poisoned were
most amusing to me. The people with whom we are boarding are among the most aristocratic and cultured people of
the town. They are cousins of the Blairs of Cabinet fame,
and, before the war, were very well off in this world's goods.
They had according to their say some forty or fifty servants
(negroes). It has surprised me to see how easily they adapted themselves to their new position. They never allow
themselves to be idle two consecutive minutes, but their
fingers are flying from early morning to late night. They
cook, wait on the table and attend to our comfort, with all
the grace of old housekeepers. Almost the only recreation
I have seen them take is in the evening, sometimes, when
we ask them to sing for us, and they sit down at the piano
and delight us with the sweetest music.

I shall be mighty busy to-morrow examining into some
pilfering that has been carried on rather extensively here
in town of late. The provost marshal has to be court, judge,
and jury all at once. Good-night for to-night.

Your affec. son,

MASE.

Saturday, November 19th. Captain Lincoln left on
fifteen days' leave, to be present at M. F. Dickinson's
wedding. I could not get away at this time.

November 20th, he wrote to his father from Winchester:
We are expecting to have the railroad finished through to
this place within a few days now. They have sent so large
a force down from here to guard it that it leaves a very
small force within the town. Still, the army is so near that
nothing very disastrous could happen. It is now said that
the principal depot is not to be at Winchester, but at Summit Point, some ten miles from here. In that event, Win-

chester will be held as a kind of an outpost, much as Culpeper was for the army last year. Then the question arises whether we shall stay here. I think we shall as long as Colonel Edwards stays, at least, and Colonel Edwards seems to be high in favor with General Sheridan, and if his wife comes on, General Sheridan will hardly be so ungallant as to send the Colonel off before he has had a nice visit with her. Rumor has had it for several days that our corps was to be ordered off on some special service, where no one knew. Our corps is very small, and hardly amounts to enough to do anything by itself. It can muster only about 8000 men now, and they probably have had 40,000 all told during this summer—four fifths gone.

We are hoping that General Sherman is going to do something towards helping the downfall of Richmond. It does seem as if it was absolutely necessary that we should have that place before the army goes into winter quarters. Where Sherman will turn up I have not the slightest idea. Still, I should not wonder if Mobile attracted his attention. It is quite important that they should have the control of that river.

Wednesday, November 23d.   *In a letter to his brother Henry, he says:*

I have been out and made a call upon one of the ladies of Winchester, who is a native of Frederick City, Maryland, and is well acquainted with the friends of Mr. Schroeder there, the Goldboroughs, and also Mrs. Albert of Baltimore. So I had a pleasant chat with her about them. This lady, although she pretends to be Southern in her feeling and sympathies, still has so many ties with the North that she is very friendly to our officers. There are some people here who boast that they have never spoken to a Yankee soldier or officer since the war commenced, unless they were obliged to, and they won't acknowledge that there are any gentlemen in the Yankee army. They boast that they hope to say at the end of the war that they have uniformly been governed by this principle. They won't be introduced to a Yankee officer. If one happens to come into a room where they are calling or visiting, they will get up and leave. If any of their friends are guilty of any communication with Yankees, they discard them at once, and pronounce them traitors to the Rebel cause. Such is the intolerant spirit that prevails among many of the high-toned Southern chivalry.

Thursday, November 24th. Thanksgiving Day! Our dinner was a success. Everything was nicely cooked. The ladies were very agreeable and did all in their power to make our feast conform to the requirements of a New England Thanksgiving dinner. (M. F. D., Jr., was married to-day, and R. P. L. was best man.)

WINCHESTER, VA.,
Dec. 1, [1864.]

MY DEAR BROTHER HEN:

Our corps is under marching orders this morning, and is said to be on its way to Petersburg. In fact, the First Division has just passed through the city. The Second Division, I understand, will go to-morrow, and the Third Division will go by land with the trains to Alexandria. Of course they are somewhat disgusted at going back to Petersburg. They would rather go almost anywhere else. Their associations with Petersburg are not of the pleasantest. I suppose our regiment will be relieved from this post in a day or two and go with them. We are hardly willing to leave the old Sixth Corps even for the privilege of staying here all winter. We are bound to them by too many ties.

We are all hoping (almost against hope, however) that the corps is going somewhere else than Petersburg, perhaps to Wilmington, Savannah, or Charlestown. The first was said to have been our destination, when we started before, and were ordered back because of Early's attack. Some of

the boys are rather disposed to hope that Early's interference may prove successful again in bringing us back.   In
fact, they would like to have him attack every time they
attempt to move us from the Valley.   Still I think General
Sheridan would have pride enough to show them that he
could whip them, Sixth Corps or no Sixth Corps.   It is now
reported that Colonel Edwards is to remain in command
of the post, and that we are to go with the corps.   That is
rather compromising affairs.   Colonel Edwards has been
quite unwell for a week now, but is said to be improving
under the devoted care of his wife.   Mrs. Edwards is as
pleasant as ever.   She is, however, slightly worried by the
Colonel's illness. . . .

Your affec. brother,
MASE.

Friday, December 2d.   R. P. Lincoln mustered as
Major.

Saturday, December 3d.   The Third Division, Sixth
Corps, passed through Winchester on its way to rejoin
the Army of the Potomac to-day.

Wednesday, December 7th.   I got leave of absence
for twenty days and went home to Amherst.

CHAPTER XIX

PETERSBURG

DECEMBER 7, 1864, TO JULY 2, 1865

[INTRODUCTION.—During his leave of absence which commenced on December 7th and lasted twenty days, Captain Tyler kept in touch with his regiment and with the corps, and made a few notes from which we are enabled to follow their movements. By order of General Sheridan, December 9th, Colonel Edwards was assigned to the command of the Provisional District in addition to his duties as post commander at Winchester.[1]

On Monday, the 12th, the Thirty-seventh Regiment received orders to join the corps at Petersburg. They left Winchester the next day,[2] Tuesday, the 13th, marched to Stephenson's Depot about six miles, took freight cars for Harper's Ferry, where they changed to the Baltimore & Ohio Railroad, and arrived in Washington early Wednesday morning, the 14th.

Captain Donnelly, who was in command, reported to General Halleck at once, and during the afternoon they embarked on the transport, *Lizzie Baker*, for City Point, where they arrived on the afternoon of Thursday, and were transported over the United States military railroad to Parke's Station. There they disembarked and "spent the night shivering in the cold and with very few facilities for keeping warm or comfortable." On Friday, the 16th, after a short march, they rejoined their brigade.

[1] O. R., xliii., pt. 2, p. 765.   [2] See *id.*, p. 779.

The division had already been there for some days. General Grant had informed General Meade that the Sixth Corps was about to leave the Valley, and had suggested "that it relieve the Fifth Corps in the lines." Accordingly, on December 4th, General Meade had ordered General Wheaton, commanding the First Division, Sixth Corps, to report at the army headquarters, near Parke's Station, and near the Aiken house.[1] General Wheaton had replied the same day, "I have the honor to report the arrival of my division—fifty-six hours from Winchester, . . . Your order to relieve Crawford's division, Fifth Corps, received. Will report in person, taking 8 A.M. train to-morrow.[2]

The line occupied by the Sixth Corps extended from Battery 24 on the right to Fort Wadsworth on the left, a distance of about two miles, but they had also to defend a strong line of fortifications in their rear. Fort Wadsworth was situated just west of the Weldon Railroad, and covered the Halifax road near its junction with the Vaughan road.

The position of the Third Brigade, First Division, was just to the right of the fort, almost directly south of Petersburg, which was four or five miles distant. They were in a swamp, and communication was mostly by corduroy paths and roads. The camp of the Thirty-seventh was located on the field which was the scene of the battle of the Fifth Corps for the possession of the Weldon Railroad, on the 18th of August last.[3]

The record of his own experience at home is confined to the relations of family and friends. On December 14th, he attended the Amherst Alumni dinner at Boston, was called upon to speak and responded. He spent Christmas at New Milford, Connecticut. On December 27th, his leave of absence was extended twenty days, on a certificate from Dr. Smith of Amherst. We may now follow the diary.—C. S.]

[1] O. R., xlii., pt. 3, p. 798. The Aiken house was about a mile east of Fort Wadsworth, directly south of the city of Petersburg. See War Map 77 (2).

[2] O. R., xlii., pt. 3, p. 798.   [3] See also War Maps 67 (9), 79 (1).

THURSDAY, January 12, 1865. I came from Amherst to Binghamton, New York, where I was most heartily and enthusiastically entertained.

Friday, January 13th. I came from Binghamton last night to New York, went to Taylor's International Hotel for breakfast, and after a day of visiting with friends, took the night train for Washington.

Saturday, January 14th. Arrived in Washington this morning. In letter of the 15th, I write:

At Washington, they attempted to send me to Camp Distribution to take charge of a body of men made up of stragglers, conscripts, convalescents, etc. As this is the most disagreeable and irksome duty that any officer can be assigned to, and it would necessarily delay me some days in a filthy camp, I demurred, and finally got off through the kindly intervention of General Abner Doubleday in my behalf. I was detained in Washington until 3 P.M. . . . As I had this time in Washington, I called on Mr. William Swinton, the distinguished war correspondent of the New York *Times*. He was the first French teacher I ever had and for a long time lived in my father's family. He treated me very cordially.

I afterwards called on Mr. Washburn, the representative in Congress from the district in which Amherst is situated, and he proposed to take me to the White House to shake hands with President and Mrs. Lincoln. It was a new experience to me, and I was glad to avail myself of the opportunity to go to the White House and attend a reception. Mr. Lincoln shook my hand rather mechanically but treated me graciously, either on account of Mr. W. or because I was a soldier. . . . I found friends on the boat, and we had a merry sail to City Point.

Sunday, January 15th. We sailed through Chesapeake Bay by Fortress Monroe, and up the James River, a very enjoyable trip. The same letter continues:

Five o'clock found me at home once more with my regiment, and the first greeting I received was, "How do you
do, Major!" I was recommended for the brevet of major
for conduct in the battle of Winchester, on September 19th
last. I did not know that the recommendation had been
made or confirmed until they showed me the newspaper report announcing it this afternoon. So you see a pleasant
surprise awaited me.[1]

[1] The recommendation for promotion to which he refers was in the
following language:

"HEADQUARTERS FIRST DIVISION, SIXTH CORPS,
"December 17, 1864.

"MAJ. C. A. WHITTIER,
   "*Acting Assistant Adjutant-General, Sixth Corps.*
"MAJOR: In forwarding the accompanying recommendations made by
the commanders of the First, Second, and Third Brigades of this division
for brevet promotions in their respective commands, I have the honor
to call the attention of the major-general commanding to the distinguished services of the brigade commanders, and to recommend the
following promotions by brevet:

.   .   .   .

"Col. Oliver Edwards, Thirty-seventh Massachusetts Volunteers,
commanding Third Brigade, to be brigadier-general U. S. Volunteers
by brevet for gallantry and distinguished service in the battle of Spottsylvania Court-House, Va., May 12, 1864, and for meritorious conduct
in the battle of Winchester, Va., September 19, 1864. . . .

"One regiment of this division is now on detached service at Winchester, Va., and no recommendations for that regiment have been forwarded
by the commander of the brigade to which it belongs, the Thirty-seventh
Massachusetts Volunteers, and I have the honor to make the following
recommendations, as the facts referred to are personally known to me:
Lieut.-Col. George L. Montague, commanding Thirty-seventh Massachusetts Volunteers, to be colonel by brevet for distinguished gallantry
in the battle of Spottsylvania Court-House, Va., May 12, 1864, in which
battle he was severely wounded. Capt. Mason W. Tyler, Thirty-
seventh Massachusetts Volunteers, to be major by brevet for distinguished gallantry in the battle of Winchester, Va., September 19, 1864,
in which battle he was wounded.

"Very respectfully, your obedient servant,
"FRANK WHEATON,
"*Brevet Major-General, U. S. Volunteers.*"

(O. R., xlii., pt. 3, p. 1028–9.)

CAPTAIN MASON W. TYLER.

From a photograph taken in December, 1864.

In a letter dated Warren Station, January 19, 1865, he wrote to his brother Henry:

Colonel Edwards has been relieved from the command of the brigade, after spending a twenty days' leave with his wife. He is now in the West. He has been brevetted brigadier-general, but hesitates some, I understand, about accepting it.

I have been quite busy the last day or two building on an addition to my house. I have now got quite a grand house, a real palace, so to speak. It is fifteen feet long and some six and a half broad, five feet high at the sides, and seven in the centre. Two of us occupy it. It grieves me very much, however, that we cannot have a fireplace, because wood is so scarce in this neighborhood that it is impossible to get enough to supply a fireplace. Therefore we have to satisfy ourselves with little air-tight box stoves, which we have procured of the sutler. Captain Robinson and I are tenting together as of old. It is very convenient, as his company is next to mine. We have a mess of four persons, and we manage to live very comfortably. This morning we had corned beef hash, and to-morrow morning we expect to have fried pudding. Last night we had scalloped oysters. Our sutler has not come up yet, so that we have had to run hither and yon to buy what we wanted. We expect him now, however, in a day or two.

General Grant says that he expects to be in Richmond within six weeks, so they tell us at corps headquarters— and they ought to know. I hope it may prove so. We are rather expecting that Sherman or Thomas will happen down somewhere in this neighborhood. They will undoubtedly have something to do in solving the problem.

CAMP WARREN STATION,
January 23, 1865.

MY DEAR MOTHER:

I am somewhat fatigued to-night, as I was up all last night and on picket duty. But I can't let this mail go off without dropping you a line.   I meant to have written you a long letter to-day, but I have had one continual stream of interruptions all day long.   I was detailed for picket yesterday morning, and after thirty-six hours of incessant hard rain, I went out, wading in mud all the way to get there, and sitting or standing in mud all the time I was there.   It is the worst line I ever was on.[1]   The country is pretty much all marsh between us and the Rebs, and at this time nearly all overflowed.   There is very little firing on our part of the lines.   In fact, we live on quite amicable terms with our neighbors across the way.   Whenever they intend to fire, they will give us warning by crying "Down-Yanks!" and we sometimes engage in quite spirited conversations with them.   They are very rarely willing to exchange papers with us now, partly because they have had men take that opportunity to desert, and partly because they don't want us to have their papers.   Desertions from their lines are quite frequent, and are now at the rate of one or two a day on our brigade front.   They however are watched very closely, and have to run great risks to get away, so that they are not as frequent as they otherwise would be.   We send over on every opportunity General Grant's orders in regard to deserters.[2]

[1] In another letter of the same date he wrote: "The lines are so close and the danger of a surprise so great that during the twenty-four hours of detail duty we are not allowed to sleep.   Every man has to be on the alert."

[2] The subject of desertion will be frequently referred to in the letters that follow, and it may be well to explain the condition of affairs.   The fear of the Rebel soldier that, if he deserted to the Union side, he would be compelled to take arms against his old companions, was laid at rest by an order of General Grant issued from the War Department at Washington, under date August 31, 1864, entitled Circular No. 31, and reading: "Deserters from the Rebel army are not subject to enrolment or draft, nor are they acceptable as substitutes or recruits."

But there were some questions which had to be settled.   Should the deserter bring his arms with him, and if he did, were they his own property, or did they belong to the United States?   Neither party knew.   And then there was the all-important question: What was to become of

There is a Captain Young who is famous as a Rebel scout
and always goes attended by a large white dog, who is a
terror to their men. He spends his nights between the lines,
and has caught many of their attempted deserters. He

---

those who deserted? General Wright reports on the 18th of February:
"The enemy's pickets have several times recently called to our men,
requesting that some one who was a Mason come out to meet one of
their number, with a view of their ascertaining, in what they conceive
to be a reliable way, what disposition is made of men deserting to our
lines." General Meade authorized the communication to be held with
the enemy's pickets for the purpose proposed (O. R., xlvi., pt. 2, p.
587). This whole matter was settled by Special Order No. 3:

"HEADQUARTERS ARMIES OF THE UNITED STATES,
"IN THE FIELD, VA., January 4, 1865.

"Hereafter deserters from the Confederate Army, who deliver themselves up to the U. S. forces, will, on taking an oath that they will not
again take up arms during the present rebellion, be furnished subsistence and free transportation to their homes, if the same are within the
lines of Federal occupation. If their homes are not within such lines,
they will be furnished subsistence and free transportation to any point
in the Northern States.

"All deserters who take the oath of allegiance will, if they desire it,
be given employment in the Quartermaster's and other departments of
the Army, and the same remuneration paid them as is given to civilian
employees for similar services.

"Military duty, or service endangering them to capture by the Confederate forces, will not be exacted from such as give themselves up to
the U. S. military authorities.

"Deserters who bring arms, horses, mules, or other property into our
lines with them will, on delivering the same to the Quartermaster's
department, receive in money the highest price such arms, horses, mules,
and other property are worth.

"Railroad employees, telegraph operators, mechanics, and other civilians employed by the Confederate authorities, who desert from their
present employment and come into the Federal lines, will be entitled to
all the benefits and immunities of this order.

"By command of Lieutenant-General Grant:
"T. S. BOWERS,
"Assistant Adjutant-General."

(O. R., id., pp. 828, 829.)

On March 4th, this order was republished for the information and
guidance of all concerned, and that very day General Wright reports
that sixteen deserters had come within the lines of the Sixth Corps, eight

spends his time spying out our lines, and General Meade, it is said, has offered a large reward for his capture. Last night the dog, who is his sure precursor, was seen by two of our pickets. I immediately took five of our men, and set out in pursuit. We prowled around between the lines an hour or so, and not meeting him or finding any trace, we had to give it up as a bad job.[1] I did not expect to catch him, but I thought there was no harm in trying. We had an Indian with us who went up within a rod of the Rebel lines. We are not allowed to sleep one minute while on our tour of duty for fear of surprise. The Rebs did surprise a portion of our line a week or two since, and took some fifteen or twenty men prisoners. Since then we have had to be doubly guarded.   Your affec. son,
                                                    MASE.

In a letter written January 25, 1865, he refers to one of the most exciting episodes in the siege of Petersburg:

bringing their arms (*id.*, p. 829). On the 27th of January, General Lee called the attention of his government to the alarming number of desertions. He states that fifty-six men had deserted from General Hill's corps in three days. The cause of this, he thinks, is that the rations are too small. On the 11th of February, he issued a circular exhorting his men to stand by their colors, and deserters to return to their respective commands, and by the authority of the President of the Confederacy, he promises pardon to all who would return within a given time. But many of his men were not only hungry, they were discouraged, and not a few saw what must be the result of the fight in the not distant future, and resorted to all sorts of devices to make their escape.—C. S.

[1] This prowling between the lines was dangerous business. But it was characteristic of the man. When he saw a duty, however dangerous, and thought the cause for which he fought would be advanced by any exposure of himself, he never hesitated. At the battle of Fort Stevens in front of Washington, Colonel Edwards said, "I wish I knew what was behind that hill." Lieutenant Tyler replied, "I will find out," and taking a revolver in each hand he advanced. Just as he reached the top of the hill, a musket appeared and blazed away. He dropped on his face, but the ball passed through his hat, and he beat a speedy retreat. He always felt that the Reb did not intend to kill him and would not have come so near if he had stood on his feet.—C. S.

We have had quite an excitement here for a day or two past over this Rebel gunboat affair. Night before last we were aroused from our slumbers by a terrific cannonading. Very heavy guns were booming in the distance on our right, and little guns seemed to be firing an accompaniment the whole length of the line. They kept us awake the most of the night. Yesterday we heard that four Rebel gunboats had broken from their moorings in the James and been swept down the river, and coming below Fort Darling had engaged our heavy batteries and forts there; that three out of the four had been disabled by our fire, and one had passed down the river comparatively uninjured. As we had no ironclads in the river at the time, and this vessel was said to be a strong type of a monitor, fears were expressed all day yesterday that our shipping at City Point would be destroyed before our monitors could come from Fortress Monroe, and our ears were strained all day expecting to hear heavy guns announcing the opening of the battle. Night came and no guns were heard, and we were somewhat relieved. This morning, however, about 3 o'clock, the renewal of the firing told us that the fight had commenced. But we are still in the dark as to the actual facts and as to the result.[1]

---

[1] The incident here referred to caused a good deal of excitement and great anxiety to the general-in-chief. All but one of the Union ironclads had gone with General Terry on the second Fort Fisher expedition. General Grant, fearing lest the Confederate gunboats anchored in the James just below Richmond might make a dash at his base of supplies at City Point, suggested that a naval officer be sent, on the night of the 23d of January, to plant torpedoes in the river at Trent's Reach. That very night the officer sent back word that the fleet was already coming down the stream. It consisted of six ships three of which grounded on some obstructions in the river. The others came on and were engaged by the shore batteries. The *Onondaga*, a two-turreted monitor that ought to have sunk them all, withdrew and steamed down the river. General Grant's indignation knew no bounds. He telegraphed to the commander that "it would be better to obstruct the channel of the river with sunken gunboats than that a Rebel ram should reach City Point" (O. R., xlvi., pt. 2, p. 225). But at daybreak the *Onondaga* moved up

The next letter contains indications that the lieutenant-general is putting his army in order:

CAMP THIRTY-SEVENTH MASS. VOLS.,
Jan. 29 [1865].

MY DEAR MOTHER:

We are having a terribly cold Sunday. In fact, for a week we have had all that we could do to keep warm, night and day, and in spite of fire, two feet from the stove our tent has been as cold as a barn. The Potomac is frozen over so that we have received mail and provisions only every other day, and we have not had a potato for a week. In spite of cold weather, however, they had the Sunday morning inspection. They are making every effort to bring up the condition and the discipline of the troops, and consequently they make their weekly inspections very rigid. We had to stand out in this terrible cold air two mortal hours this morning (from 10 to 12), while the inspector went through the regiment. To be sure, the most of the time they stacked arms and allowed the men to move around. But they could not go to their houses and were exposed all the time to the merciless wind and cold air. I came pretty near freezing, and went in and warmed myself once or twice. It was so cold I did not rise this morning until after 8 o'clock, and had breakfast at 8.30. This, you will understand, is pretty late for me and my bones did ache before I got up. But I could stand it full as well as the cold. . . .

We have not yet got our chapel started, but the chaplain is intending to build one at the earliest opportunity. At present we have hardly teams enough to supply us with wood to burn. In fact the men bring all their wood nearly two miles, and it is becoming scarce at that distance. Our

---

and opened fire upon the Confederate flagship, the *Virginia*, and with the shore batteries gave her a hard pounding. With the flood tide the enemy succeeded in getting their ships afloat and all retired up the river. During the day General Grant got up some heavy guns, and that night the Rebel fleet came down again, and a terrific artillery battle was kept up for hours, with disastrous results to the enemy.—C. S.

regimental surgeon returned last night. He has been home and got married and brought his wife back with him as far as Washington, where she expects to spend the winter and hopes to see him once or twice before the spring campaign opens. . . .

We don't see the papers now very often. They are not to be depended on these days. The last paper that I saw told us of the burning of Smithsonian Institute. I hope it is going to moderate. The air seems a little warmer to-night.

Your affec. son,
MASE.

The diary continues: During the month of February, we worked a good deal on Fort Fisher, which stands at the point where our lines turn to the south. In the immediate neighborhood, the Fiftieth New York Engineers built a beautiful Gothic church, which they called Poplar Grove Church, and at a little distance built a signal tower one hundred and fifty feet high.[1]

CAMP NEAR WARREN STATION,
Feb. 2, 1865.

MY DEAR FATHER:

. . . Colonel Edwards has lost his brigade, which causes something of a stir among us. It happens after this wise: You know the colonel has not yet returned, and General Wright, who is not friendly to the colonel, has taken advantage of his absence to have some one assigned, by virtue of his brevet rank, to the command of this brigade. So General Hamblin, a younger colonel than we have in our brigade, and who was brevetted at the same time as Colonel Edwards, is assigned by the President to the command at General Wright's solicitation. You know these brevet appointments confer no real rank unless especially assigned to duty in accordance with them by the President. Colonel Edwards, therefore, when he

[1] See Bowen, p. 403.

comes back will find him self superseded by a man whom he really outranks, and who is not one half as worthy of the place as he is.   I don't think the colonel will stand it, and he will probably have to get out of the service as he would otherwise come back to the command of his regiment.   They all say here that he will resign.   I feel very sorry for the colonel, but fear that he can't get around it now.

Colonel Montague is here.   He returned to the regiment last Monday, but is so unwell that he says he shall retire as soon as he can.   His side is not perfectly healed, and the doctors tell him that there is danger of inflammation of the lungs if he exposes himself. . . . Did I tell you that General Sheridan offered to make Colonel Edwards provost marshal of the Middle Military Division if he would stay with him? But the colonel declined and chose to return to his brigade. He will be disappointed when he comes back to find that gone.

Ever your affec. son,
MASON.

Sunday, February 5th.   Under marching orders from five this morning.   Chaplain Morse has succeeded in fitting up a chapel, and held his dedication services this afternoon.   We were packed up all day.   At 7 P.M. we marched to the extreme left of the line, and one half mile beyond, outside the pits, threw up breastworks and spent the night.

During the day he wrote a short letter to his mother:
We are under marching orders, expecting every minute to move.   The orders came suddenly about 5 o'clock this morning.   They woke us out of a sound slumber, and we have been on the jump since.   We shall probably leave our camp standing, as we have received no orders to take our tents down.   We go provided with six days' rations, so that

we shall probably be back in a week. Rumor says that Grant is at Wilmington and Meade in command here.[1]

Monday, February 6th. We lay still all the morning doing nothing. About 3 P.M., we were ordered to move to the left, and proceeded along the Squirrel Level Road. The wounded of the Fifth Corps and cavalry were returning. We crossed Hatcher's Run. The Fifth Corps were driven back in confusion, and massed and moved into the pits. The Second Brigade of our division was engaged. The Fifth Corps, Third Division, fled and behaved very badly. It was nearly dark when we got into line, and after waiting two hours we were withdrawn and went into camp a mile in the rear. It was bitterly cold, and we were soaked with rain, which froze and stiffened our clothes under the influence of the wind. We built fires, but they were of little avail. The rain changed into snow, and we finally rolled up in our blankets and slept the sleep of exhaustion, wet as we were.

[1] This was but a rumor. On the 26th of January, General Grant went down the coast to Cape Fear, on a tour of inspection with General Schofield, but was back at headquarters when the order to march was given.

The lieutenant-general had a peculiar enmity towards all roads, highways as well as railroads, over which supplies could be brought to the enemy. When the Sixth Corps arrived at Petersburg, they relieved the Fifth in the lines, and the Fifth was immediately sent to destroy the Weldon Railroad for forty miles below Petersburg. But it was rumored that the enemy were bringing in supplies by wagons over the Boydton Plank Road. He immediately ordered a movement to put a stop to this. General Lee was very sensitive about his right flank, and could easily move troops from any part of his lines to defend it. When, therefore, a move was made to the left of the Union lines, it had to be in force. In this case, the Second and Fifth Corps were sent out, and the whole army was prepared to go to their assistance. There was much hard fighting during the day, and at night General Humphreys found himself hard pressed, having on his front a part of Hill's and Gordon's corps, and the First Division of the Sixth Corps was sent to his relief. The rest of the story is told in the diary.—C. S.

Tuesday, February 7th.   We waited all day, expecting
to go into action, but no orders came.   The cold
increased.   The earth was stiffened to a solid surface
by the frost.   Wood was plenty, and we made large
fires.   About 1 o'clock, we received orders to return to
camp, and reached our old quarters about 4 o'clock in
the morning.   We had three men wounded.   Otherwise
there was no loss.

*In a letter, February 9th, to his brother William, from
Camp Warren Station, he wrote:*

I returned yesterday from our raid across Hatcher's Run.
We had a most dismal time.   It rained hard and blew very
cold all day Tuesday, and we were both wet through and
frozen stiff, and we only had one night's sleep out of three.
Consequently, I came back slightly wearied with my exertions, and yesterday I felt dull enough.   To-day, however, I
feel brighter and have been reading quietly.   I have at last
got hold of Napier's *Peninsular War*, and am reading it with
a great deal of pleasure.   If they will only give me time
enough to finish it before we have to enter upon the spring
campaign, I shall think I have not entirely misspent my
winter.   Still, I don't do as much as I might if I only had the
proper tools here to work with.   Books are pretty scarce,
and then we cannot get the proper accompaniment for a
full appreciation of them.   For instance, we need, in reading
such a history as this, a good atlas for reference.   Of course
we have here no access to anything of the sort.   I see by the
papers to-day that Harry Gilmor is captured.[1]   I should

[1] This is the Major Gilmor previously referred to, who left Mrs.
O'Bannon's house at Winchester when he heard General Sheridan's
guns, on the 19th of September.   He was a Marylander, and one of the
boldest and most successful partisan chiefs in the valley.   He drew
many of his recruits from his native State, and was very expert in his
operations.   Sheridan determined to get him, and put his scouts after
him.   It was found that he was expecting some recruits from Maryland
and was awaiting them at a house about four miles from Moorfield, a

like to hear what my Rebel friends say to this if it is a fact. You know he was a paragon of excellence in their eyes. I must close to send this by to-night's mail.

CAMP 37TH MASS. VOLS., Feb. 13, '65.

MY DEAR BROTHER HEN:

I believe I am your debtor for one or two letters. I meant to have written you last week, but the first part of the week I was off on that raid, and since my return I have been occupied a portion of the time by court-martial duty, and the rest of the time it has taken all my energies to keep warm. I think yesterday and to-day have been the coldest days of the season, and last night the wind blew so that it tore our tents pretty much all to pieces, and came near leaving us looking through bare poles into the face of heaven which, in the existing state of the temperature, was not so nice. Still we survived the night by dint of close snugging and drifts of clothes.

We have been very much amused with the newspaper accounts of our last move across Hatcher's Run. The correspondents of the Fifth Corps have tried to cover up the bad behavior of a certain portion of the troops of that

very disloyal district. The general ordered Major Young, his scout-master, to take twenty of his best men, put them in Confederate uniforms, represent himself as taking recruits to Gilmore and go to Moorfield, and he told him he would send a squad of Federal cavalry in pursuit of him. Major Young's representations that he had this body of recruits for Gilmore, and was hard pressed by the Union cavalry, secured for him accurate information and a ready access to the house. On arriving he said he must report at once, and going to the guerilla's room he covered him with his cocked six-shooter, and awaking him, imparted to him the information that he was a prisoner to one of General Sheridan's staff officers. Gilmore says, in his *Four Years in the Saddle*, that he remarked, "I suppose that you want me to go with you." To which the officer replied, "I shall be happy to have your company to Winchester, as General Sheridan wishes to consult you about some important military matters." Sheridan sent him to Fort Warren in Boston Harbor, where he remained until the war was over. It was a neat little job, well done, and caused a good deal of fun for those who had a right to laugh. (See *Sheridan's Memoirs*, ii., pp. 105–107).—C. S.

corps by all manner of excuses. One claims that they behaved most gallantly; another correspondent allows that there was slight confusion, but that they were overpowered by vastly superior numbers, and still another that the Sixth Corps, coming up in their rear, fired into them, producing confusion.

The facts in the case were simply these: The Third Division of the Fifth Corps was repulsed, and a causeless panic seized them and they ran more than a mile, and, more than that, they had no enemy of any consequence following them, and those who were nearest to their rear turned and fired upon those who were tardier in their flight and many were thus killed. One brigade of our division was rushed on the double-quick to their support, and the first they knew while they were moving by the flank, before they had had time to deploy, this frightened, rushing tide of men came back upon them, and for the moment threw them into confusion. But General Wheaton soon formed line, and after he had his brigade formed into line, it suffered more from shots fired by our own men in the rear than from the enemy.[1]

This was the brigade which General Warren told General Wheaton saved the day. We rallied several regiments and made them form just in our rear, but some were so frightened that they ran clear into Sixth Corps headquarters before they could be persuaded to halt, a distance of six miles. General Meade sent out his cavalry and arrested 2000 of them along the road who were putting for the rear as fast as they could go. I never saw such a rout, and it made me so mad I wanted to shoot some of the officers, who were as bad as the men—scared to death.

---

[1] See report of Major-General Wheaton, commanding First Division, Sixth Corps, O. R., xlvi., pt. 1, p. 297. At page 299, he says: "While we were being fired upon, Major R. P. Lincoln, the division inspector, had been despatched to General Warren (Fifth Corps), who was close at hand, and informed him of our danger from his men, and through General Warren's exertions the firing was stopped."

It seems that the Rebs were behaving about as badly as our men, and General Lee's official report is much more favorable for us than our generals could publish, and it was circulated among our troops for their encouragement. I see by the papers that Major Shepard is among the missing. I am sorry to hear that, and hope he will turn up all safe yet.

I see Major Young of General Sheridan's scouts has captured Harry Gilmor and has taken him over to Fort Warren. I know Major Young as well as I do you almost. He was on Colonel Edwards's staff all summer and belongs to the Second Rhode Island Regiment of our brigade. I am mighty glad he has met with this success, for I think he is one of the bravest little fellows I ever saw in my life. He has been hunting after Mosby all the fall while we were in the valley. I should like to hear what my Winchester friends would say to Harry Gilmor's capture. If I were there I should laugh at them a little.

Colonel Montague has gone to Washington, and this leaves Captain Hopkins in command of the regiment. Colonel Edwards is expected back this week.

Yr. affec. brother,

Mase.

CAMP WARREN STATION, Feb. 15, 1865.

MY DEAR MOTHER:

Albert Kellogg started for home this morning, and I sent a couple of military pamphlets and some letters home by him. I was very glad the boy could get a chance to go. His mother has wanted so long to see him, and has been so long separated from him, that I hope it will relieve her anxieties.

I have a miserable cold to-day that makes my head feel bigger than a bushel basket. The day also has been one of those murky, stormy days that are well calculated to encourage such feelings. It is cold and rainy and muddy out of doors, and if you stay in, your stove smokes from disgust at the idea of associating its eruptions with such an

atmosphere as this weather affords. I have stayed in my
tent pretty much all day, but I have been nearly suffocated
several times with the smoke. I have managed, however,
to read some fifty pages of Napier, and this afternoon I have
written a letter to Carrie Tyler. So I have not been altogether idle. . . . There is some prospect that we may get
paid up to January 1st next week. That is to say, some one
announced that the paymasters are coming down to pay
the army at that time. I hope and sincerely trust it is so.

Mr. Cutter brought me your box last Saturday night,
and I ate a piece of pie, some currants, and a piece of cake,
and tasted the honey before it had been here five minutes,
and before the next night it was all gone. Much obliged.
I should have said, however, that the bottle of honey, that
is, two thirds of it, stands before me now as I write, and
usually adorns the centre of my table, and is quite an object
of curiosity to the uninitiated. I tell them it is Greek honey.
Whether they fully appreciate that there should be any
special merit in honey from the classic land, I am unable to
say. But they appreciate it as coming from Greece full as
well, I guess, as if I told them it came to them from Mount
Hymettus.

Four deserters came in last night from the Rebs on our
brigade line. They were said by those that saw them to be
splendid-looking fellows, and were from North Carolina
regiments. Almost all the deserters that we get now seem
to be from the Old North State. They say that their State
and their soldiers want to come back into the Union, and
they individually believe it their duty to encourage it by
setting the example.

Mr. Cutter came back, and now he has been detailed as
nurse in the Sixth Corps hospital at City Point. He is unfit
for field duty, and the hospital is the only place that he
ought to serve. I think our Sixth Corps hospital here in
the field is the most tastefully arranged camp that I have
seen since I have been in the army. It is in the form of a
cross and has a beautiful fence made of rough hewn timber,

and this fence describes all sorts of fantastic curves, and all the entrances are adorned with beautiful arches formed of fresh evergreens.   There is some firing on the line to-night, the pickets seem to be having a lively time.   I have sent my watch home by Albert Kellogg.   I want it cleaned, and asked him to bring it back with him.

CAMP WARREN STATION, Feb. 22, 1865.

MY DEAR BROTHER HENRY:

. . . This is Washington's Birthday, and I suppose there will be a good deal of celebrating in the army as well as at home on account of the good news received yesterday.   A hundred guns were fired yesterday in our line in honor of the victory. [1]   You never saw anything like the desertions that are occurring among the Rebs these days. We average about twenty a night on our division line, and on the Ninth Corps I understand they have about one hundred a night.   They tell large stories saying that what come this way are not a circumstance to what are going the other, and they all declare that, as soon as their men fully understand that there is no chance for peace, they will throw down their arms and come in *en masse*, and that they won't be led into any such struggle as they had last summer.   Their very best and most substantial material seems to be deserting.   Some of them are as intelligent men as you often see.

General Grant seems slightly apprehensive of an attack, as he has ordered one tenth of the command to be under arms at all hours of the day and night. [2]   There seems to be

[1] The news of the evacuation of Fort Sumter reached the army on the 21st and a hundred guns were fired by order of General Grant.   The Secretary of War ordered a hundred guns fired on the 22d in honor of the event, and it was done.—C. S.

[2] General Meade had been called away to attend the funeral of his son, and General Parke, commanding the Ninth Corps, was in command of the Army of the Potomac, when the following characteristic letter was written:

an impression that Lee has got to do something desperate, and that very soon. But I hardly think his army is in any condition for such undertaking at the present time.

I am having a chimney put up for my tent. I could not stand the stove any longer. . . .

We have just received orders to look out for an attack, so I must close for this time.

Your affec. brother,

MASE.

Friday, February 24. We heard to-day of the capture of Wilmington, North Carolina. [1]

"CITY POINT, VA., Feb. 22, 1865.

"MAJOR-GENERAL PARKE,

"*Commanding Army of the Potomac:*

"As there is a possibility of an attack from the enemy at any time, and especially an attempt to break your centre, extra vigilance should be kept up both by the pickets and the troops on the line. Let commanders understand that no time is to be lost awaiting orders, if an attack is made, in bringing all their reserves to the point of danger. With proper alacrity in this respect I would have no objection to seeing the enemy get through.

"U. S. GRANT, *Lieutenant-General.*"

(O. R., xli., pt. 2, p. 631.)—C. S.

"CITY POINT, Feb. 24th.

" MAJOR-GENERAL PARKE:

"Announce to your troops the capture of Wilmington on the 22d instant by the troops under Schofield and Terry. Fire a shotted salute in honor of the event at 4 o'clock this afternoon.

"U. S. GRANT, *Lieutenant-General.*"

(O. R. xlvi., pt. 2, p. 670.)

The following circular by General Wright to the officers and soldiers of the Sixth Corps, dated February 25th, will explain a reference in a letter written the next day. " As any movement on the enemy's part is at once to be followed up, the entire corps, without striking tents, will be held ready to move in pursuit at a moment's warning. The major-general commanding deems the utmost vigilance on the part of the pickets, and readiness on the part of the whole command to move promptly, as of first importance, and trusts that the corps will not be behind the others in the army in these particulars." (O. R., *ibid.*, p. 695.)—C. S.

MY DEAR MOTHER:

We have been pretty much all excitement this past week. First the fall of Charlestown, then the capture of Fort Anderson, then, Friday, we received the announcement of the capture of Wilmington. For two or three days here we have been expecting the evacuation of Petersburg to take place. Four days ago, as we learned from deserters, General Lee gave the order to prepare for evacuation. The middle of the week we thought he was going to assault and attempt to break through our lines, and we were up betimes and ready for him, but no General Lee came. Last night we received the order to be ready to move at any hour in the night, as it was thought the Rebs were moving across the river. We were not, however, disturbed, so I suppose they have not yet gone from our front.

Deserters are coming in at the rate of about seventy a night on our corps line. They keep us pretty well informed in regard to the movements of the enemy. Night before last a whole company of South Carolina troops came in. It is not often that we get them from that State.[1] We occasionally see a Richmond paper a day later than we get from the North. Some of them are very blustering, and others do nothing but grumble and find fault.

Amid all the gloom and desperation of the Southern cause, however, I must say I cannot but admire the calm, placid language of General Lee's despatches and letters. Not a word of boastfulness or even enthusiasm that would lead you to think that he was overdoing the matter to inspire hope among the people, and on the other hand there is not one sign of despondency, but every letter bears the impress of resolution and even of confidence in the result. He must be a great man.

Colonel Edwards returned Friday morning and is at present in command of the regiment. He has decided to

[1] General Wright reports that seventy-six deserters came in, about two-thirds with arms (O. R., xlvi., pt. 2, p. 674).

remain in the service. They offer him a brigade in the Second Corps and also one in the Second Division of our corps. He rather expects to go to the Second Corps. Letters from Montague last night state that he expects to be out of the service soon. I was in command of the regiment for a day or two, while Captain Hopkins was officer of the picket line. It is so stormy this morning that our inspection has been postponed. I am officer of the day and consequently on duty, and have to look out for a surprise in case of an attack on our line. One tenth of our command is under arms all the time now. It has cleared off beautifully this afternoon, although the wind blows roughly and makes our tent flap. I think that our large chapel will be rather airy. The church bells have just sounded and I must cease my writing.

Time passes rather stupidly for me these days, in that my eyes deny me the privilege of reading or writing to any great extent. My tent mate reads the papers to me and sometimes other things.

Your affec. son,
MASE.

In a letter to his brother, dated Warren Station, February 26th, he wrote:

Yesterday I was very busy, as I had to muster the regiment. I am not half through my work yet, as I still have more than fifty rolls to look over and correct, which all devolves upon me, as Colonel Edwards is sick and Captain Hopkins is sitting at court martial. We are, however, waiting a day or two for the arrival of the paymaster before we finish our rolls, trusting that we shall be paid up to December 31st.

Monday I was detailed to take charge of a party of 300 men from our division who are at work building Fort Fisher. This fort occupies the nearest point of our lines to the South Side Railroad, and is a large, bastioned work capable of holding 3000 men. Our corps has been at work on it over a month, and it is now nearly completed and is one of the strongest works on our lines. The Rebs have two strong works opposite to it, about 2000 yards distant. Just below Fort Fisher the opposing lines are so near together that the men from both sides chop wood from the same trees and are on perfectly good terms. Now, however, for a week past they are very chary of our men. They are watched much more strictly by their officers on account of the great number of desertions that have taken place. On this account, desertions are not quite as frequent as they have been. Those that do come in, however, report that General Lee has gone to North Carolina, and Johnston is in command of the army. . . .

I have a splendid new fireplace and am enjoying the comfort of it amazingly. Colonel Edwards is talking of taking command of a negro division in Weitzel's corps. [1]

[The month of March was an exceedingly anxious time for the lieutenant-general, but until the last of the month nothing transpired of interest to the outside world. Inspections grew more and more rigid, a vigilant watch was kept on the movements of the enemy to prevent surprise, for General Grant had made up his mind that Lee would try to break the Union lines. But his greatest anxiety was lest he should wake up some morning and find the Rebel army gone. [2] Against both these contingencies he made ample provision. In the meantime, the daily report of the corps commanders was, "Nothing of importance in front of my lines during the last twenty-four hours." This was followed by a statement of the number of deserters who had come in. On the 24th, General Grant issued his orders for an advance on the 29th. [3]

---

[1] Weitzel was, at this time, at Bermuda Hundred, with the rest of the Army of the James. See *Grant's Memoirs*, vol. ii., p. 434.

[2] See O. R., xlvi., pt. i, p. 52; *Grant's Memoirs*, vol. ii., p. 430.

[3] *Grant's Memoirs*, vol. ii., p. 434; O. R., xlvi., pt. i, p. 50.

During this period, the diary was almost entirely neglected, and the letters were given up to personal and domestic matters. Major Tyler during this time had to be very careful about the use of his eyes, and did not read or write more than he was obliged to. Saturday, March 4th, he records the fact that he was this day commissioned major, under date of February 14th.

But General Grant's expectation about an attack in force was realized. On the night of the 24th, General Gordon, with his corps reinforced by Bushrod Johnson's division, made an attempt to break the Union lines between Fort Stedman and Battery No. 10, in front of the Ninth Corps.[1] "The plan," says General Grant, "was well conceived and the execution of it very well done indeed, up to the point of carrying a portion of our line."[2] They succeeded in capturing the fort and several batteries, but the Union army was on the alert and, without orders from General Meade who was at City Point, troops were hurried from all points along the lines to the point of danger. But before they arrived, General Parke, commanding the Ninth Corps, had recaptured the fort and batteries. The attack cost Lee four thousand men and the Union army about two thousand. The Sixth and Second Corps were commanded by General Meade to feel the enemy's strength in their front and to take advantage of any weakness. The next entry in the diary refers to this attack.—C. S.]

Saturday, March 25th. The Rebs attacked and captured Fort Stedman. Our division was ordered to go and aid in its recapture. But the Ninth Corps recaptured it before we got there. We were then ordered back and made a charge and captured the Rebel picket line in front of Fort Wadsworth about 4 o'clock. President and Mrs. Lincoln, General and Mrs. Grant,

[1] See War Map 77 (2), on the east side of the city of Petersburg.
[2] *Memoirs*, vol. ii, p. 431.

and General Meade visited Fort Wadsworth and watched the movement of the troops.[1] I was wounded in the charge while in command of the regiment.[2]

Sunday, March 26th. Our division returned to camp this morning at 4 o'clock.

In a letter from Warren Station he wrote to his parents:
I drop you a line this afternoon to relieve your anxieties, as you will probably hear that I am wounded before this reaches you. I was scratched yesterday afternoon in the fight that our corps had with A. P. Hill's troops. The ball glanced from a tree, and just grazed my knee at the joint. I thought at first the joint was shattered all to pieces, but soon found that I could move it. I stayed on the field mounted on my horse until nine in the evening, and then returned to camp. To-day I am very stiff.

P. S.—Fred Allen[3] has just come in and is to stay six weeks in the service of the Christian Commission. It seems good to see him. The ball, you understand, did not pierce the flesh, but merely grazed it, producing a contusion, and on that particular spot it is rather uncomfortable. The doctors say that I may be around in a week and may not in a month.

[Fred Allen adds:] I write this at Mason's side. I am here to-day, and hearing of Mason's being hurt, hunted him up immediately and am delighted to find that his injury is so slight. I am settled down for six weeks within

[1] It is possible that this was a camp rumor only, as no mention of the visit has been found in the historical authorities.

[2] See itinerary of this date, O. R., xlvi., pt. 1, p. 100. Colonel Edwards, commanding the Third Brigade, First Division, Sixth Corps, in his report of the affair of the 25th, says: "The brigade behaved entirely to my satisfaction, and I would particularly mention the Fifth Wisconsin Volunteers, Colonel Allen, and the Thirty-seventh Massachusetts Volunteers, Major Tyler commanding" (O. R., xlvi., pt. 1, p. 301).

[3] The Rev. Frederick B. Allen.

300 feet of him at the Christian Commission quarters, and shall see a good deal of him. You may be assured I shall do whatever I can for him.

Monday, March 27th. Major Young called.[1]

[Major Tyler was not destined to have a hand in the great campaign which was about to commence—the campaign of the Appomattox. On the 24th of March, General Grant issued his order for an advance of both the Army of the Potomac and the Army of the James, to commence on the 29th, "for the double purpose of turning the enemy out of his present position around Petersburg, and to insure the success of the cavalry under General Sheridan, which will start at the same time, in its effort to reach and destroy the South Side and Danville Railroads."[2]

The desperate attempt of General Lee, on the morning of the 25th, to break the Union lines did not delay the movement ordered by the lieutenant-general, but rather prepared the way for it. Fort Stedman had hardly been recaptured when orders were sent to the corps commanders "to feel the strength of the enemy's lines in their front and to take advantage of any weakness." The Sixth Corps was advanced at once and after some hard fighting succeeded in capturing the enemy's rifle-pits. Several determined but unsuccessful efforts were made to recapture them. It was in this struggle for the rifle-pits that Major Tyler was wounded while in command of his regiment. The result of the fight was the advance of the Union lines something like half a mile. This proved to be a great advantage, for it was on this very ground that the Sixth Corps formed in line of battle when ordered to storm, on the morning of the 2d of April, the fortifications in their front.

Major Tyler's wound proved to be more serious than

[1] This is the Major Young who caught Gilmor. See pages 328 and 331, above.

[2] O. R., xlvi., pt. 1, p. 50.

was at first anticipated, and the army doctors advised him that amputation was necessary. He had seen so much of reckless haste in such cases in the army that he concluded to ask for a furlough and have the advice of a city specialist. The surgeon in Boston also advised amputation; but the family physician in Amherst undertook to save the leg by special treatment. His advice was followed, and in the end proved effectual. But the healing process was slow and excessively painful, and it was several months before he was able to return to his regiment.

After the surrender of the Rebel army at Appomattox, the Sixth Corps was retained for service in Virginia and was not present at the grand review of the Army of the Potomac at Washington on the 23d of May. It was arranged to have a review of the Sixth Corps at Richmond on the 24th. That afternoon they started on their homeward march, and on June 2d the Thirty-seventh went into camp at Bailey's Cross Roads about five miles from Washington. It was at this place on June 6th that Major Tyler rejoined his regiment, as he was able to do by the use of a cane. On the 8th, the corps was reviewed in Washington by the President and his Cabinet, with Generals Grant and Meade and many other officers.

The historian of the regiment thus describes the scene: "For this event, the command was roused very early in the morning, crossing Long Bridge to the vicinity of the Capitol, where the corps was massed. At 9.30 the advance guard, the First Connecticut Cavalry, cleared the way, and at 10 the column began to move. The brigades and divisions proceeded in numerical order, the artillery following the Third Division, and the rear being composed of 200 New York engineers, with a pontoon train. The Third Brigade, First Division, General Edwards, moved in the following order: Eighty-second Pennsylvania Veterans, 960 men, Brevet Brigadier-General Bassett; Second Rhode Island Veterans, 450 men, Lieutenant-Colonel Rhodes; Forty-ninth Pennsylvania Veterans, 305 men, Colonel Hickman;

Thirty-seventh Massachusetts, 300 men, Major Tyler; Fifth Wisconsin, 400 men, Colonel Allen. As the Thirty-seventh passed the reviewing-stand by company front, fewer in numbers than any of its sister organizations, the waste of the terrible campaigns it had passed through was vividly realized. Company K, the color company, proudly bore the tattered standards before the cheering multitudes with scarcely eight files to guard the priceless treasures."[1] The diary records only a few facts and dates.—C. S.]

Wednesday, June 21st. The Thirty-seventh Regiment was mustered out to-day.

Thursday, June 22d. Reveille sounded at 3, broke camp at 5 under General Edwards and marched to Washington; took cars at 11 A.M., reached Baltimore at 3 P.M., started again at 5, reaching Philadelphia after midnight, and were feasted as usual at the Cooper shop.

Friday, June 23d. At daylight took cars for Amboy, and by transport from there reached New York at noon. After dinner marched up Broadway, and at 6 P.M., boarded steamboat *Traveller* for Hudson, which place we reached at daylight of the 24th, and at 5.30 breakfasted.

Saturday, June 24th. Reached Pittsfield by train at 10 o'clock. Twenty-seven cars took us out in 1862; we only required six cars when we returned. We were welcomed by Henry L. Dawes, United States Senator, and E. H. Kellogg. Reached Springfield by train at 2.30 P.M., were taken to the City Hall and feasted. Very enthusiastically received. Reached Readville that evening, and went into camp.

Monday, June 26th. Regimental colors were delivered to the care of the Commonwealth at the State-house.

[1] Bowen, p. 427.

Sunday, July 2d. Payment of men and officers completed, men discharged and regiment disbanded.

CONCLUSION

[It was a great experience to have been associated for nearly three years with such a body of men as composed the Sixth Corps of the Army of the Potomac. Colonel Tyler[1] was very proud of his regiment and of the corps to which it belonged. The nature of the service rendered by the Thirty-seventh is clearly indicated in the fact that the regiment lost in killed and mortally wounded 169 men, besides twelve who died in Rebel prisons. The character of the men in his company is well illustrated by the fact that not one of them deserted.

The Sixth Corps had a great record. Its name will ever be associated with that of Sheridan and the brilliant campaign in the Valley of the Shenandoah. But the last few days of its service were the most remarkable of all. Agreeable to the orders of the lieutenant-general, Sheridan, with the cavalry and the Fifth Corps, moved out on the 29th of March to the left, and on the 31st, he sent word to General Grant: "If the ground would permit, I believe I could, with the Sixth Corps, turn the enemy's left or break through his lines, but I would not like the Fifth Corps to make such an attempt." General Grant replied the same day: "It will be impossible to give you the Sixth Corps for the operation by our left. It is in the centre of our line between Hatcher's Run and the Appomattox. Besides, Wright thinks he can go through the line where he is, and it is advisable to have troops and a commander there who feel so, to co-operate with you when you get around."[2]

---

[1] He was appointed May 4, 1865, Lieutenant-Colonel, and June 26, 1865, Colonel, of the regiment by brevet. He could not be commissioned as Colonel, although in command of the regiment, because the losses in the service had depleted the ranks of the regiment below the numbers required by law for a commissioned officer of that rank.

[2] O. R., xlvi., pt. 3, p. 380.

General Sheridan with the cavalry and the Fifth Corps, on the 1st of April, gained a decisive victory at Five Forks, cutting off the right wing of Lee's army from the main body. When the news reached General Grant's headquarters, about 9 o'clock, the corps commanders were immediately informed and asked as to their condition. At 11 P.M., General Wright, commanding the Sixth Corps, replied: "Everything will be ready. The corps will go in solid, and I am sure will make the fur fly. The general plan being understood well by the various commanders, there will be no hesitation from want of knowledge of what is expected. If the corps does half as well as I expect, we will have broken through the Rebel lines fifteen minutes from the word 'go.'"[1] This despatch was sent by General Meade to General Grant, who replied, "I like the way Wright talks; it argues success. I heartily approve."[2] Orders were immediately issued for an advance at 4 o'clock the next morning.

The Sixth Corps was formed in line of battle at 1 o'clock on the morning of the 2d, on the ground captured by them on the 25th where Major Tyler was wounded, and a little after four the charge was made. An eye-witness standing on the parapet of Fort Welch thus described the scene to Brigadier-General Hazard Stevens, assistant adjutant-general, serving on the staff of General Getty, commanding the Second Division, Sixth Corps: "He related to me, not long afterwards, that he was standing on the parapet when the advance was ordered, and was anxiously peering into the darkness and awaiting the result in doubt and apprehensive of disaster. He could hear the muffled tramp and rustle of the moving host, but could discern nothing. He saw the flashes of the first volley; he heard the mighty shout of ten thousand throats, and then he saw, stretching across the front for half a mile a line of flashing fire, crackling, blazing, and sparkling in the darkness, vividly lightened up here and there by the heavier and

[1] O. R., xlvi., pt. 3, p. 423.   [2] Id., p. 399.

deeper flash of artillery, while shells with their fiery trail sped forward through the gloom in every direction. Although missiles hurtled overhead, and stray bullets went hissing past, he could not leave, but stood intently watching that deadly line of fire. Suddenly in the middle of it there appeared a tiny black spot, a narrow gap, which spread and widened, inch by inch and moment by moment, to the right and left, and then he knew the works were carried, even before the exulting cheers of our troops proclaimed the fact."[1]

The centre of Lee's army was shattered. In vain were his desperate efforts to stay the victorious column. The position he had so long held had become untenable, and that day he ordered the evacuation of Richmond. The lieutenant-general did not forget the wish of General Sheridan, and says: "When the move towards Amelia Court-House had commenced that morning, I ordered Wright's corps, which was on the extreme right, to be moved to the left past the whole army, to take the place of Griffin's, and ordered the latter at the same time to move by and place itself on the right. The object of this movement was to get the Sixth Corps, Wright's, next to the cavalry, with which they had formerly served so harmoniously and so efficiently in the valley of Virginia."[2]

Late in the afternoon of April 6th, the rear guard of the Rebel army made a stand at Sailor's Creek. The Sixth Corps had now to face about ten thousand of Lee's veterans, but not even the fatigue of this strenuous campaign had dampened their ardor. As a result, they took or put *hors de combat* some six thousand of the enemy, and among those taken prisoners were Lieutenant-General Ewald and Briga-dier-General Custis Lee (son of General Robert E. Lee), the latter being captured by Corporal David White of Company E of the Thirty-seventh Massachusetts Regiment.

The next morning presented a scene unparalleled in

[1] Papers of the Historical Society of Massachusetts, vol. vi., p. 426.
[2] *Personal Memoirs*, vol. ii., p. 473.

history. Two great opposing armies rushing through a country as yet unvisited by war, in the full beauty of early spring, without firing a gun, both the pursued and the pursuers exerting all the strength that it was possible for men to exert. At 7 o'clock in the evening of April 7th, General Grant hinted to General Lee that "he felt that further resistance on his part was useless." On the morning of the 9th of April, the Rebels found Sheridan with his cavalry standing across their path, and while they were preparing to attack him, the cavalry withdrew from right to left, and disclosed the Fifth Corps and Ord's Army of the James.

With two army corps and the cavalry in front, and two army corps pressing upon his rear, the great general with his brave soldiers who had so long baffled the Army of the Potomac was now between the upper and nether millstones. "To fight would have been a crime equal to deliberate murder," to surrender was honorable, and never, up to that time certainly, had a foe won or received more generous terms.

Major-General Wright, commanding the Sixth Corps, thus describes the spirit of the corps during the last few days of the war: "In this battle of Sailor's Creek, the corps nobly sustained its previous well-earned reputation. It made the forced march which preceded that battle with great cheerfulness and enthusiasm, and went into the fight with a determination to be successful seldom evinced by the best troops, and by its valor made the battle of Sailor's Creek the most important of the last and crowning contests against the Rebel Army of Northern Virginia. To it had fallen the opportunity of striking the decisive blows, not only at Petersburg, on the 2d of April, but at Sailor's Creek, on the 6th, and most gallantly did it vindicate the confidence reposed in it by its own officers and the commander of the Army of the Potomac. The corps has always fought well, but never better than in the assault at Petersburg, and at Sailor's Creek four days after."[1]

[1] O. R., xlvi., pt. 1, p. 907.

But the Sixth Corps won not only the commendations
of its own commander, but also those of the major-general,
commanding the Army of the Potomac. On April 17th,
General Meade addressed the officers and soldiers presenting
battle-flags captured by the Sixth Corps:

"Officers and soldiers of the Sixth Corps: I thank you
very much for these numerous proofs of your valor captured
during the recent campaign. I do not wish to make any
invidious distinctions between your own and the other corps
of this army. They performed with valor and courage the
part assigned to them. But candor compels me to say that
in my opinion the decisive movement of this campaign
which resulted in the capture of the Army of Northern
Virginia was the gallant and successful assault of the Sixth
Corps on the morning of the 2d of April. It was with
much pleasure I had received a despatch from your commander assuring me his confidence in your courage was so
great that he felt confident of his ability to break through
the enemy's lines. I finally ordered the charge to be made
at 4 o'clock on the morning of the 2d, and it was with still
greater satisfaction that a few hours afterward I had the
pleasure of transmitting a despatch to the general-in-chief
telling him the confidence of your brave commander had
been fully borne out.

"To you, brave men, I return the thanks of the country
and of the army. To each of you a furlough of thirty days
will be granted to enable you to present these proofs of your
valor to the War Department. Let us all hope that the
work upon which we have been engaged for nearly four years
is over, that the South will return to its allegiance, and that
our beloved flag will once more float in triumph over a
peaceful and undivided country extending from the Atlantic
to the Pacific and from the Saint Lawrence to the Gulf of
Mexico."—C. S.][1]

[1] O. R., xlvi., pt. I, p. 909.

APPENDIX

Account of the Parts Taken and the Positions Occupied by the Several Brigades of the Sixth Corps at the Battle of the Bloody Angle at Spottsylvania Court-House

First Brigade of the First Division of the Sixth Corps, Usually Known as the First New Jersey Brigade

THIS brigade was composed of the following regiments: First, Second, Third, Fourth, Tenth, and Fifteenth New Jersey Volunteers.

It was commanded at this time by Colonel Henry W. Brown. Upon the arrival of the brigade with the balance of the First Division of the Sixth Corps at 9.30 o'clock on the morning of the 12th in front of the works at Spottsylvania, the brigade was assigned a position in front of the point assaulted and captured by General Upton on the 10th of May, as heretofore described. They were at once formed into a column of attack in which the First, Fourth, and Fifteenth Regiments constituted the first line, and four companies of the Second Regiment (the other six being on picket), and the Third and Tenth constituted the second line.

By 10 o'clock the column was ready to move, and the order was given to advance and charge.

349

The following description of that charge is given in Haines's *History of the Fifteenth Regiment New Jersey Volunteers*, at pages 174 and 176:

Colonel Penrose led his command [the Fifteenth Regiment] with great steadiness, forbidding his men to fire a musket until they saw the enemy, and every shot should tell. We had first to break our way through a thicket of scraggy pines with dead limbs. Then, as we emerged from the cover, there was a piece of open ground to cross. Beyond this were fallen trees making the abatis; and then the works. These were formed with a bank of earth and logs upon the top, with an opening three inches wide through which our foes could fire with little exposure to themselves. As soon as we appeared, charging over the open plain, they poured upon us their deadly, concentrated fire. Our direction brought us obliquely upon their works. For a long distance to our right, the enemy's rifle-pits could be seen, and their occupants, having no attacking enemy on their front, poured an enfilading fire upon our ranks. In the short space of time required to cross the flat, two hundred men were stretched lifeless, or helpless with wounds, upon the ground.

The Fifteenth did not falter, but dashed on through the abatis and over a portion of the breastworks, some of our numbers falling dead upon the other side. We captured about one hundred prisoners, and a flag belonging to the Fourteenth Georgia, which was seized and borne away by Jacob Stutz, Company B. We drove out or bayoneted those who tenaciously clung to their works. Some threw down their muskets and lifted their hands in token of surrender, and lay crouching in the ditch, only, however, to resume their weapons when their captors were more hardly pressed. . . .

The tenure of our part of the captured works was brief. An enfilading fire from each side poured into our thin ranks. The enemy from the second line of works sent a continuous shower of bullets. It was impossible to hold the captured bank so long as it was swept by works untaken. Accordingly, the men were ordered by Colonel Penrose to fall back, and when Colonel Campbell gathered his shattered battalion beneath the hill, scarce an hundred could be counted.

The following is the list of the losses in this brigade from the 8th to the 21st of May, as given in the Official Reports, xxxvi., pt. 1, p. 144. This includes the killed, wounded, and missing.

The First New Jersey lost 62; Second New Jersey, 68; Third New Jersey, 148; Fourth New Jersey, 89; Tenth New Jersey, 149; Fifteenth New Jersey, 272; Total, 788.

I have not been able to find any official records or any report of the part taken by this brigade, and the only regimental report is that of the Fourth New Jersey contained in the O. R., xxxvi., pt. 1, p. 664. But in this account no particulars are given, although the charge is described, and desperate fighting by the command spoken of.

In Foster's history,[1] in which the designated numbers of the regiments engaged are mentioned, no mention is made of the Tenth New Jersey. That the Tenth was present in the engagement, and bore its share of the fighting, is indicated by the loss that it incurred as given in the above table. In fact, this brigade for about half an hour was engaged in as severe a hand-to-hand, life-and-death struggle as occurred upon the field. After they were driven out from the works, they apparently resumed their position at or near the point where they formed for the attack, and continued there during the day.

[1] *New Jersey and the Rebellion*, by John Y. Foster, is probably the book here referred to.

SECOND BRIGADE OF THE FIRST DIVISION, SIXTH CORPS,
COMMONLY KNOWN AS UPTON'S BRIGADE

This brigade was comprised of four regiments, to wit:
Fifth Maine, One Hundred Twenty-first New York,
Ninety-fifth and Ninety-sixth Pennsylvania.

As before stated, Upton's brigade arrived on the field
at 9.30 o'clock in the morning, and was immediately
ordered forward to the point where the fight was raging
at its hottest, about two hundred feet to the south of the
west or Bloody Angle.

General Upton, in his report, describes his movements
as follows:

The right flank of this corps being threatened, General
Russell directed me to move to the right at double-quick to
support it.   Before we could arrive it gave way.   As the
Ninety-fifth Pennsylvania Volunteers reached an elevated
point of the enemy's works, about 600 yards to the right of
the Landrum house, it received a heavy volley from the
second line of works.   Seeing that the position was of vital
importance to hold, and that all the troops had given way
up to this point, I halted the Ninety-fifth Pennsylvania
Volunteers, faced to the front, and caused it to lie down.

Its left rested near the works connecting with the Second
Corps, while its right, refused, lay behind a crest, oblique
to the works.   Had it given way, the whole line of intrenchments would have been recaptured, and the fruit of the
morning's victory lost, but it held the ground till the Fifth
Maine and One Hundred and Twenty-first New York came
to its support, while the Ninety-sixth Pennsylvania Volunteers passed on to its right.   Shortly after, the Third and
Vermont Brigades arrived.   A section of Gilliss's battery of
the Fifth U. S. artillery, under Lieutenant Metcalf, came
up and opened fire, but was immediately charged and lost
nearly every horse, driver, and cannoneer.   The enemy

charged up to his works within 100 feet of the guns, but a well-directed fire from the infantry behind the crest prevented his farther advance. At the point where our line diverged from the works, the opposing line came in contact, but neither would give ground, and for eighteen hours raged the most sanguinary conflict of the war. The point remained in our possession at the close of the struggle, and is known as the Angle. The brigade was relieved at 5. 30 P.M. by Colonel McLaughlen's of the Second Corps.

. . . After being relieved, the brigade was held in reserve, and after dark was marched to the right of General Rickett's line, near the position occupied on the 9th. [1]

The position referred to as the one occupied on the 9th was in the vicinity of the Alsop house.

Three regiments of this brigade, the Fifth Maine, One Hundred Twenty-first New York, and the Ninety-sixth Pennsylvania, were in the forefront of the assault made on May 10th, under General Upton's lead, upon the same works which were captured by the Second Corps on the 12th of May.

The losses of the twelve regiments involved in Upton's assault are usually stated as amounting to one thousand, killed, wounded, and missing. What proportion of this was borne by the three regiments from Upton's brigade, I do not know. The losses incurred by the three Vermont regiments that participated in that assault are stated in Benedict's history[2] to have been eighty-eight. This should leave a loss of over 900 to be apportioned to the nine other participating regiments, or an average loss to each regiment of 100. So far as Upton's brigade is concerned, the probability is that their loss in the assault of the 10th of May was over 300 rather than under that figure. The losses of

[1] O. R., xxxvi., pt. 1, p. 669.
[2] *Vermont in the Civil War.* See page 451.

Upton's brigade from May 8th to 21st, as given in the Official War Records, are as follows: Fifth Maine, 131; One Hundred Twenty-first New York, 155; Ninety-fifth Pennsylvania, 135; Ninety-sixth Pennsylvania, 178; Total, 599.

If we deduct from this their estimated losses on the 10th, to wit, 300, and the losses incurred by this brigade at Myers's Hill on the 14th, which General Upton, in his report, figures at 100, and which must be included in the foregoing total, the losses of each of the four regiments of the brigade on May 12th would be 99 killed, wounded, and missing.

The foregoing report of General Upton requires explanation in several particulars. There is no doubt that the point where General Upton halted the Ninety-fifth Pennsylvania, with its left resting near the works, etc., was a point in the earthworks about 200 feet south of the west or Bloody Angle. They did not connect there with the Second Corps. They did connect with Edwards's brigade, and the nearest troops of the Second Corps at that point, at the time, were portions of regiments of Mott's division which joined on the left of the Thirty-seventh near the east angle, as I have already stated. These portions of the regiments were driven out of the earthworks about 10 o'clock of May 12th.

The Thirty-seventh Massachusetts held its position on the exterior of those works continuously from 6 o'clock in the morning of May 12th until 4 o'clock of the morning of the next day, as will more clearly appear when I come to describe the part taken in this battle by Edwards's brigade.

As to the position of Upton's and Edwards's brigades, I speak from personal knowledge, because I was there. This is consistent with General Upton's statement above quoted in his report to the effect that "at a point where our line diverged from the works, the opposing lines came in contact, but neither would give ground, and for eighteen hours raged the most sanguinary conflict of the war." This latter statement is not consistent with the previous statement that "all the troops had given way up to this point." I suppose that General Upton's earlier statement that the right flank of the Second Corps gave way before he arrived, refers to the giving way of Mott's troops on the left of Edwards's brigade, to which I have just referred.

Although Upton's brigade was not protected by earthworks when they first went into position, yet at the place where their line of battle was formed there was a natural ridge, behind which they could lie down, and it did not take them long to convert this into rifle-pits which gave them adequate protection. But for this their losses would have been much greater.

THIRD BRIGADE OF THE FIRST DIVISION, SIXTH CORPS, COMMONLY KNOWN AS RUSSELL'S BRIGADE

This brigade consisted of four regiments, to wit: Sixth Maine, Forty-ninth and One Hundred Nineteenth Pennsylvania, and the Fifth Wisconsin.

At the time of General Sedgwick's death, when General Russell was promoted to the command of the First Brigade, Sixth Corps, General Eustis was transferred from our brigade and put in command of this Third Brigade, filling the vacancy caused by General Russell's promotion, and at the same time Colonel Edwards was given command of our brigade.

During the summer of 1864, when Edwards's brigade was transferred from the Second to the First Division, it was consolidated with Russell's old brigade, and in this way it happens that the report found in the Official Records, vol. xxxvi., pt. I, p. 672, was signed by Colonel Edwards, as the commander of that brigade. This would account for the exceedingly brief and formal character of that report. It was not made by any of the officers who commanded the brigade at the time to which the report referred, to wit, May, 1864, and as a consequence there is on record no adequate report of the part taken by this famous brigade in this campaign. All four regiments of this brigade participated in Upton's assault of May 10th, and it was the same brigade that General Russell led to such complete and glorious victory at Rappahannock Station in November, 1863.

On May 12th it was put into position to the right and possibly to the rear of Upton's brigade, and I have no doubt it did, with Upton's brigade, a full share of the fighting which devolved upon that part of the line during that eventful morning. But I have not been able to discover from the reports or regimental histories just what part was borne by Upton's brigade, and what by Russell's, any further than appears from extracts already quoted from the Official Records. But the fact that heavy losses were incurred by Russell's brigade during this period conclusively proves that the brigade was on the front line of battle, and giving and receiving sturdy blows.

The losses of this brigade from May 8th to the 21st, as given in the Official Records (p. 143), show the following: Sixth Maine, 135; Forty-ninth Pennsylvania, 274; One Hundred Nineteenth Pennsylvania, 145; Fifth Wisconsin, 149; Total, 703.

I have not been able to find any separate statement

of the losses borne by this brigade in Upton's assault
of the 10th of May, but if we allow the same average
made in the case of Upton's brigade, to wit, 100 to each
regiment, the losses of the four regiments would amount
to 400, which, deducted from the above total amount
would make the loss of Russell's brigade, on May 12th,
number 303 killed, wounded, and missing. Colonel
Fox, in his *Regimental Losses*, p. 268, states that the
Forty-ninth Pennsylvania lost 260 men in Upton's
assault on May 10th. This would indicate that the
proportion of losses by the brigade in the above total,
chargeable to May 12th, should be still further reduced.

FOURTH BRIGADE OF THE FIRST DIVISION, SIXTH CORPS, COMMONLY KNOWN AS SHALER'S OR CROSS'S BRIGADE

This brigade consisted of five regiments, more particularly described as follows: Sixty-fifth, Sixty-seventh
and One Hundred Twenty-second New York, and
Twenty-third and Eighty-second Pennsylvania.

General Shaler was captured on the 6th of May, in
the battle of the Wilderness, and the command of the
brigade was thereupon devolved upon Colonel Nelson
Cross.

In the report of Major H. R. Dalton, Assistant
Adjutant-General of the First Division, Sixth Corps,
given in O. R., xxxvi., pt. 1, p. 661, the following
reference is made to this brigade. After speaking of
the order of General Russell to put in his division on
the right of the Second Corps, and after disposing of
Upton's and Russell's brigades, the report mentions
"the Fourth Brigade being put in at various points to
fill up gaps along the whole line." Part of this brigade,
under the command of Colonel Joseph E. Hamblin, was

sent to report to General [Wheaton, and General Wheaton refers to it in his report[1] in the following language:

At the same time [10 A.M.] I sent the One Hundred Thirty-ninth Pennsylvania Volunteers to the right and front to relieve a part of the Second [Vermont] Brigade, General Grant, and a part of the Fourth Brigade, First Division, under Col. Joseph E. Hamblin, which had exhausted their ammunition, and the One Hundred and Second Pennsylvania Veteran Volunteers on the right and rear of them as a support and to guard against a flank attack.

I have not been able to discover which regiments were detailed for this duty.

In addition to what I have mentioned above from Major Dalton's report, he mentioned the fact that "the Fourth Brigade buried 480 Rebel dead in our front."

The losses of the brigade from May 8th to the 21st, as given in the Official Records, show the following: Sixty-fifth New York, 97; Sixty-seventh New York, 48; One Hundred Twenty-second New York, 24; Eighty-second Pennsylvania (detachment) 2; Total, 171.[2] These figures would seem to indicate that the two Pennsylvania regiments were not engaged at the Angle.

FIRST BRIGADE OF THE SECOND DIVISION, SIXTH CORPS, KNOWN AS WHEATON'S BRIGADE

This brigade consisted of the following five regiments: Sixty-second New York, Ninety-third Pennsylvania, Ninety-eighth Pennsylvania, One Hundred and Second Pennsylvania, and One Hundred Thirty-ninth Pennsylvania.

[1] O. R., xxxvi., pt. 1, p. 684.   [2] Id., p. 145.

In General Wheaton's official report[1] he describes his movements as follows: "May 12, 6 A.M., ordered to the left and south a mile to support the Second Corps. . . . Advanced . . . within 50 yards of that part of the works . . . known as the Angle or Slaughter Pen." This is a good illustration of what was considered by the officers on that field as "supporting the Second Corps" at the Angle. Both the Bloody Angle and the Second Corps were from a quarter to a half mile distant from the part of the field where General Wheaton's brigade was located. He was in front of the position indicated on the diagram by the letters B, C, and D, and the Second Corps troops were at that time located in the lines between K and L.

At 10 A.M. that part of the line in front of my left which was greatly exposed to the enemy's fire from the pits still held by them, gave way, and I was obliged to send up the Ninety-third Pennsylvania Veteran Volunteers, from my second line, to drive them back and retain the position. At the same time I sent the One Hundred and Thirty-ninth Pennsylvania Volunteers to the right and front to relieve a part of the Second [Vermont] Brigade, General Grant, and a part of the Fourth [Cross's] Brigade, First Division, under Col. Joseph E. Hamblin, which had exhausted their ammunition, and the One Hundred and Second Pennsylvania Veteran Volunteers on the right and rear of them as a support to guard against a flank attack. The One Hundred and Thirty-ninth Pennsylvania Volunteers lost severely in this position, . . . All the regiments of my brigade behaved excellently well and fought with great spirit, although holding ground most disadvantageously opposed to an enemy strongly intrenched and close in our front, the distance in some places being less than sixty yards. At 12 M. the Sixty-second New York Veteran Volunteers and two

[1] O. R., xxxvi., pt. 1, p. 684.

companies of the Ninety-eighth Pennsylvania Veteran Volunteers (the balance of that regiment being on picket a mile to the right), which had been in reserve, although in range of musketry and artillery fire, were ordered to relieve a part of the Second (Vermont) Brigade, on the left of the Ninety-third Pennsylvania. This was accomplished in good order, and these regiments, including the Ninety-third Pennsylvania Volunteers, held this position until relieved by a brigade of the Fifth Corps, under Colonel Bragg, at 3 o'clock in the afternoon. At 1 P.M. the One Hundred Thirty-ninth and One Hundred and Second Pennsylvania Volunteers were relieved by a portion of the brigade of Colonel Smith, of the Third Division of this corps. The balance of the brigade was relieved by a portion of the Fifth Corps at 3 P.M., when I retired my whole command to the opening east of the enemy's works (the part still occupied by them), where they were somewhat shielded by the crest in front from the enemy's fire and they could rest and be supplied with ammunition. At 5 P.M. I was ordered to build a line of rifle-pits on the crest immediately in front, connecting with General Russell on the left and General Ricketts on the right, as a reserve line for defence, which was nearly completed, when, at 8 P.M., I was ordered, by a circuitous and tedious route, through the darkness, mud, rain, and woods, to the right of General Ricketts, which we did not reach until 11 P.M.

It thus appears that General Wheaton and his brigade were actively engaged in fighting the enemy in their works on the extreme right of the Sixth Corps lines from 6 A.M. to 3 P.M., and during that time they were assisted by portions of the Fourth Brigade, First Division (Cross's) and of the Second (Vermont) Brigade, Second Division, and were finally relieved by the Fifth Corps. How desperate the fighting appeared to the commander of the Vermont Brigade will more fully appear when we come to the account of the part taken by that brigade in the battle.

At 5 P.M. General Wheaton's command was put into position between Ricketts's and Russell's divisions, with directions to fortify, after they had been withdrawn from the fighting line and were resting in the rear near Alsop's.

The losses of the brigade from May 8th to the 21st, as given in the Official Records, show the following: Sixty-second New York, 12; Ninety-third Pennsylvania, 79; Ninety-eighth Pennsylvania, 20; One Hundred and Second Pennsylvania, 44; One Hundred Thirty-ninth Pennsylvania, 116; Total, 271, distributed among five regiments.[1]

SECOND BRIGADE OF THE SECOND DIVISION, SIXTH CORPS, COMMONLY KNOWN AS THE VERMONT BRIGADE

This brigade consisted at this time of five regiments: The Second, Third, Fourth, Fifth, and Sixth Vermont Volunteers. These were under the command of Colonel Lewis A. Grant. Colonel Grant, in his official report[2] gives the following account of the part taken by his brigade in the battle of the Angle.

When the Second Corps was driven back, his command was ordered to the extreme left of the Second Corps which was at that time at the extreme left of the Army of the Potomac. The brigade was formed in two lines, threw out skirmishers, and fortified. From the Bloody Angle to the left the Federal troops held the Rebel works, and from the Angle to the right the enemy held them. General Russell commanded the division in the centre and was hard pressed. Colonel Grant was ordered to go to the support of General Russell. Accord-

[1] O. R., xxxvi., pt. 1, p. 145.   [2] O. R., xxxvi., pt. 1, p. 702.

ingly he took regiments of the rear line of the brigade to
the Angle and was then ordered to the support of General Wheaton, commanding a brigade farther to the
right.   He found General Wheaton trying to advance
amidst thick brush, and in the face of a deadly fire
from Rebel rifle-pits.   It was impossible to carry the
works on the right by direct attack, and the enemy were
gaining advantage at the Angle.   Leaving the Fourth
Vermont in command of General Wheaton, he went
back to the Angle, and Colonel Seaver came up from
the left with the balance of the brigade, and it was all
put into the engagement at that point except the Sixth
Regiment, which was held in reserve in the rear of
a swell of ground.   This was the key-point to both
armies and the fighting was of the most desperate and
determined character.   This point held, and the whole
line of works must necessarily fall into the hands of the
victorious party.

Three regiments from this brigade took part in
Upton's assault of May 10th, and according to Benedict's *History of Vermont in the Civil War*, their loss in
that assault was eighty-eight men.

The losses from May 8th to the 21st of said brigade,
as given in the Official War Records, show the following:
Second Vermont, 123; Third Vermont, 74; Fourth Vermont, 42; Fifth Vermont, 75; Sixth Vermont, 37; Total,
351.   Subtracting losses in Upton's assault, 88, will
leave 263, killed, wounded, and missing, as the number
from the brigade chargeable against the fight of the 12th
of May.

THIRD BRIGADE OF THE SECOND DIVISION, SIXTH CORPS,
COMMONLY KNOWN AS BIDWELL'S BRIGADE

This brigade consisted of the five following regiments:

The Seventh Maine, Forty-third New York, Forty-ninth New York, Seventy-seventh New York, and Sixty-first Pennsylvania.

Colonel Bidwell succeeded General Neill in command of the brigade when General Neill was promoted to the command of the division at the time of General Sedgwick's death.

Colonel Bidwell's report [1] gives the following account of the part taken by his brigade in the battle:

On the morning of the 12th we were moved to the rear of the position just captured by General Hancock, and ordered to support a brigade of this division, commanded by Colonel Edwards, at the Angle. The brigade was deployed in line and moved to this point, and two of the regiments, the Forty-ninth and Seventy-seventh New York, charged the Angle and took possession of the crest commanding it, which they held until relieved. The Forty-third New York, Sixty-first Pennsylvania Volunteers, and Seventh Maine were deployed on the right of this position, supporting General Upton's brigade. The first line losing heavily and closing to the left caused a vacancy, which these three regiments moved into and where they remained two hours, delivering a musketry fire, and were relieved and moved to the left to the support of a brigade of the Second Corps. The troops which relieved the Forty-ninth and Seventy-seventh New York were driven back, and those two regiments, with a portion of the Vermont Brigade, formed and retook the crest. About dark the whole line was withdrawn about 300 yards and went into bivouac for the night.

My understanding is that this brigade in the early morning, from 6 to 9.30 o'clock, occupied the exterior line of the enemy's earthworks, between G and D on the diagram, but owing to the enfilading fire was unable

[1] O. R., xxxvi., pt. 1, p. 720.

to retain such possession, meeting the same fate that
befell the Vermont Brigade and the New Jersey Brigade
in their attempts to hold that part of the enemy's
exterior line, and a portion of the brigade was then put
into position in the line of the crest occupied by Upton's
brigade. Subsequently a portion of the Forty-ninth
and Seventy-seventh New York joined with the Vermont Brigade in its attempt to capture the enemy's
works, in which attempt they failed. The brigade was
actively engaged most of the time between 6 in the
morning and 8 in the evening.

Two regiments from this brigade participated in
Upton's assault on the 10th of May and bore their
proportionate share of the losses of that engagement.
The average of such losses to each regiment I have estimated at 100, making the loss of the brigade on that
occasion 200.

The losses from May 8th to the 21st of this brigade, as
given in the Official War Records, show the following:
Seventh Maine, 126; Forty-third New York, 51; Forty-
ninth New York, 131; Seventy-seventh New York, 107;
Sixty-first Pennsylvania, 139; Total, 554, or, after deducting 200 for Upton's charge, there still remained a
loss of 354 to be distributed among the five regiments.

FOURTH BRIGADE OF THE SECOND DIVISION, SIXTH CORPS, COMMONLY KNOWN AS EUSTIS'S OR EDWARDS'S BRIGADE

This brigade consisted of four regiments, the Seventh,
Tenth, and Thirty-seventh Massachusetts, and the
Second Rhode Island.

The Seventh was detailed to do picket duty in front
of the Sixth Corps line on the 12th of May, and was not
actively engaged in the battle at the Bloody Angle.

The three other regiments above mentioned numbered about 900 men present for duty. The brigade was commanded by Brigadier-General Henry L. Eustis until May 9th, when General Eustis was transferred to the command of the Third Brigade, First Division, Sixth Corps, and Colonel Edwards succeeded him in command of the Fourth Brigade, Second Division. The parts taken by the regiments of this brigade at the Salient have already been described.

The losses from May 8th to 21st of these three regiments, as given in the Official Records, show the following: Tenth Massachusetts, 92; Thirty-seventh Massachusetts, 91; Second Rhode Island, 53; Total, 236.

Some of this loss was incurred by these regiments in an attempt which the Sixth and Second Corps made to surprise and capture a portion of the Spottsylvania works at the base of the Salient on the morning of May 18th, which attempt was unsuccessful and was abandoned as soon as it was found that the enemy were in the works in full force. But I can safely say that the loss of the three regiments who participated in the battle of the Angle on May 12th exceeded 200 in number, to be distributed among the three regiments.

By Lieutenant-Colonel Montague's wounds the command of the regiment was devolved upon Captain Donnelly.

FIRST BRIGADE OF THE THIRD DIVISION, SIXTH ARMY CORPS

This brigade was composed of five regiments as follows: Tenth Vermont, One Hundred and Sixth and One Hundred and Fifty-first New York, Fourteenth New Jersey, Eighty-seventh Pennsylvania, and was commanded by Brigadier-General William H. Morris.

As already mentioned, the Third Division was left in charge of the Sixth Corps works in the vicinity of the Alsop house, when the First and Second were ordered to go to the assistance of the Second Corps, and they so remained until about 10 o'clock of the morning of May 12th, when the Third Division was ordered to join the rest of the corps in the vicinity of the Angle.

I think this brigade was posted during the day in the rear of Upton's line of battle, and in the afternoon was with the Second Division returned to the vicinity of the Alsop house, where it was joined by Wheaton's brigade and the First Division of the Sixth Corps as before related.[1]

The losses from May 8th to the 21st of this brigade, as given in the Official Records, show the following: Tenth Vermont, 24; One Hundred and Sixth New York, 38; One Hundred and Fifty-first New York, 23; Fourteenth New Jersey, 28; Eighty-seventh Pennsylvania, 35; Total loss, 148.

What portion of this loss, if any, was incurred through participation in the other engagements in and about Spottsylvania I am unable to state.

SECOND BRIGADE OF THE THIRD DIVISION, SIXTH CORPS

This brigade was composed of six regiments as follows: Sixty-seventh and One Hundred Thirty-eighth Pennsylvania, Sixth Maryland, One hundred Tenth and One Hundred Twenty-second and One hundred Twenty-sixth Ohio.

It was commanded successively in this campaign by Colonel Benjamin F. Smith and by Colonel J. W. Keifer, afterwards Speaker of the House of Representatives.

Colonel Keifer in his official report[2] states as follows:

[1] See O. R., xxxvi., pt. 1, p. 725.   [2] O. R., xxxvi., pt. 1, p.733.

"On the 12th the brigade with the division was formed one mile to the left,[1] about 11 A.M., in support of the First and Second Divisions, Sixth Army Corps, but was not heavily engaged." At page 749 of the same volume, the commander of the One Hundred Twenty-sixth Ohio reports that his "regiment was detached from the division and sent to support Brigadier-General Wheaton's brigade of the Second Division, Sixth Army Corps." It was marched to the front line and engaged the enemy. Fifty rounds of ammunition were exhausted before the regiment was withdrawn.

The report of Colonel Otho H. Brinkley of the One Hundred Tenth Ohio,[2] states:

On the 12th, although not actually engaged, we were constantly manœuvring, and during the whole of the day and until 10 o'clock at night were exposed to a destructive fire of musketry and artillery. During the early part of the day we occupied a position between the enemy's artillery and our own, and being protected by light earthworks but little harm was done us.

The losses from May 8th to the 21st of the brigade, as given in the Official Records, show the following: Sixty-seventh Pennsylvania, 15; One Hundred Thirty-eighth Pennsylvania, 12; Sixth Maryland, 6; One Hundred Tenth Ohio, 34; One Hundred Twenty-second Ohio, 12; One Hundred Twenty-sixth Ohio, 78; Total, 157.

There were only two brigades in the Third Division of the Sixth Corps at this time.

[1] Of their place in the Sixth Corps lines.   [2] *Id.*, p. 742.

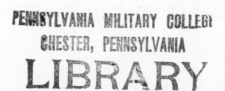

PENNSYLVANIA MILITARY COLLEGE
CHESTER, PENNSYLVANIA
LIBRARY

INDEX

Allen, Col., of 5th Wisconsin, 339
Allen, Rev. F. B., 339
Anderson's division, 85, 107
Amherst, excitement at, 15; Gov.
  Andrew at, 24; Class Day, 231;
  Alumni Dinner, 316
Andrew, Gov., 8; at Amherst, 24;
  letter from Gen. Newton to, 89
Alexandria occupied by Federals, 15
Antietam, Battle of, 39
Aiken House, 316
Arlington occupied by Federals, 15
Anti-Racetrack Ass'n, viii
Appomattox River, crossing at,
  219; Appomattox, campaign of,
  340
Aquia Creek Landing, 59
Austin's *Jurisprudence*, 132
Alsop's, 163, 164
Army of Potomac, the, 39 103,
  154, 155, 158, 159, 165, 197, 200,
  202, 213; review in Washington,
  341
Army of No. Virginia, 158, 200
Army Corps: First, 62, 65, 99,
  100, 103, 105, 138; Second, 45,
  81, 99, 102, 112, 126, 138, 141,
  143, 147, 148, 154, 156, 163, 165,
  170, 178, 182, 190, 197, 204,
  208, 218, 226, 232; Third, 65,
  82, 99, 104, 127, 138; Fourth, 45;
  Fifth, 77, 99, 102, 123, 138, 142,
  146, 154, 163, 167, 170, 193, 203,
  218, 226, 290, 316, 327, 330, 344,
  346; Sixth, 74, 99, 121, 124,
  135, 138, 142, 151, 155, 161, 163,
  169, 177, 181, 190, 194, 197, 203,
  207, 213, 222, 237, 241, 247, 249,
  261, 276, 284, 295, 311, 314, 322,
  332, 341, 349, 352, 355, 358,
  361, 364, 365; Eighth, 155, 278,
  286, 296; Ninth, 77, 138, 163,

203, 212, 219, 226, 290, 333, 338;
  Tenth, 228; Eleventh, 80, 99,
  101, 102, 157, 233; Twelfth, 82,
  99, 103, 107, 157; Eighteenth,
  164, 210, 219, 221, 224, 226, 228;
  Nineteenth, 155, 241, 248, 275,
  277, 283, 296
Ayres's Regulars, 106
Ashby's Gap, 55

Bradford, Wm., Governor of Plymouth, v
Brady Photographs Meade and
  Staff, 227
Bragg, Col., 11, 360
Bailey's house, Mrs., 226
Blair, F. P., 13
Ball's Bluff, Battle of, 19
Banks's Ford, 87
Bardwell, Charley, 290, 293; death
  of, 278
Barlow, Gen., 171
Barnesville, 95
Barryville, 253
Bassett, Bt. Brig.-Gen., 341
Batchelder's map, 107
Bartlett, Col. W. F., 147
Battery No. 10., 338
Baxter's Brigade, 145
Bermuda Hundred, 219
Beattie, Capt., 233
Beauregard, Gen., 11; commands
  No. C. and So. Va., 224
Beck, Mrs., 291
Beechers, the, 6
Beecher's sermons, 59
Belle Plain, 61
Benedict's *Vermont in the Civil
  War*, 353, 362
Berdan's Sharpshooters, 149
Berkshire Hotel, Tyler ill at, 29
Berlin, Crossing at, 111
Bidwell's brigade, 179, 362
Briggs, Gen. H. L., 37, 44

369

Binny, Horace, Capt., 125; Binny's joke, 231
Brinkley, Col. O. H., 367
Birney, Gen., 148, 171
Birnie, Mr., 59
Bristoe Station, Battle of, 120
Boardman, Elijah, grandfather of Mrs. Tyler, ix
Brock Road, 154, 159, 161, 163, 164, 177, 197
Bloody Angle, the, 179, 182, 185, 190, 193, 198, 203, 349, 352, 361
Brown House, 170, 171
Borden's Condensed Milk, 132
Brooke, Gen., checks advance, 86; joins Howe, 86; at Spottsylvania, 181; at Cold Harbor, 211
Botts, John Minor, 124, 135
Brown, Col. H. W., 349
Brown, John, 42
Brown, Col. J. N., commands brigade, 185; address by, 185
Brown, Col. W. H., 44; succeeds Devens, 80
Bowen's History of the 37th Mass. Vols., 150, 251, 325, 342
Bowers, T. S., Ass't Adj. Gen., 321
Boydton Plank Road, 224
Bruce, G. A., 170
Buchanan, President, 6
Buford at Gettysburg, 101
Bull Run, Battle of, 15; Second Battle of, 31
Burnham, Col., Light Division, 84
Burnside, Gen., goes to No. Carolina, 20; commands army, 56; relieved of command, 72; " Mud Campaign," 80;
Butler's battery, 90
Butler, Gen., 219

Caldwell, Gen., 69, 76, 132
Calker's Station, halt at, 207
Chambersburg, 96; reported burned, 257
Campbell, Lives of Chief Justices, vi
Campbell, Col., 351
Camp Briggs at Pittsfield, 27
Camp Chase, 36
Camp Distribution, 317
Camp Misery on Smoky Hill, 62

Camp Warren Station, 319
Crampton's Pass, 38
Chancellorsville, 141, 163, 164, 200
Chantilly, Battle of, 31, 95, 121
Clark, Col. W. S., 8; commander of 21st Mass., 18; reported killed, 32
Charles City C.-H., halt at, 217
Charlottesville, 240, 253
Cashtown, hill at, 100
Catlett's Station, 58
Catoctin Mountains, 40
Chattanooga, 137
Canby, Gen. E. R. S., 114
Chase, Secretary, 73
Casey, Gen., 37
Crawford's charge, 106; Crawford's division, 316
Cedar Creek, 155
Cemetery Ridge, 84, 101
Centreville, 95
Chesterfield Bridge, 208
Cherry Run, 49
Chickahominy River, 216
Christian Commission, 339
City Point, Va., 218; Grant at, 334
Choate, 6
Crocker, F. B., death of, 232
Columbus and Hocking Coal and Iron Co., viii
Cold Harbor, 201
Compton's Pass, 53
Cromwell, Oliver, vi
Confederacy, dreams of success, 159
Confederate Congress, 14; Confederate deserters, 321; Confederate government, 7
Crook, Gen., at Shenandoah, 248; at Winchester, 253; at Fisher's Hill, 286
Cross's brigade, 357
Cooke, Rev. Mr., 68
Cooper shop, feast at, 342
Couch, Gen., 39
Culpeper, 96
Culp's Hill, 101
Cumberland Coal and Iron Co., viii
Custer, Gen., and his cavalry, 136; defeats Rosser, 295; captures by, 297
Cutler's division, 193, 203
Cutter, Mr., 332

Draft in New York, 112
Dahlgren, Col., 135
Dalton, H. R., Adj.-Gen., report by, 281; on 4th brigade, 357
Dranesville, 95
Danville Railroad, 340
Davis, J., calls for volunteers, 14; advised by Lee, 22
Davis, Major, 285
Dawes, Senator H. L., 342
Deep Run, 64
Deserters, Confederate, 321
Devens, Gen., 39, 45; visited by Edwards and Tyler, 61; Monument to, 70; commands division, 80; at Cold Harbor, 211;
Devens and Hoar, 19
Devil's Den, the, 104; Devil's Garden, 104
Drew, Capt., 285
Dickinson, M. F., 135; letters to, 230, 232, 264, 271, 292, 294
Donnelly, Capt., 365
Doubleday, Gen. A., 317
Doubleday's *History of Chancellorsville and Gettysburg*, 106
Downsville, 46
Dumfries, march to, 95

Ewald, Lt.-Gen., capture of, 345
Edwards, Rev. J., vi
Edwards, Col. Oliver, at Pittsfield, 28; prostrated by heat, 108; at N. Y. draft, 115; at Wilderness, 146; faith in, 160; commands brigade, 167; at Spottsylvania, 179; commands 3rd brigade, 237; at Winchester, 279; clearing battlefield, 284; prisoners, 285; returns from front, 286; commands Provisional District, 315; made Brig.-General, 318; relieved, 319; commands regiment, 335; praises 37th Mass., 339; brigade, 364
Edwards, *My Recollections of the Civil War*, 150
Edwards Ferry, 95
Edwards, Timothy, vi
Early, Gen., escapes, 84; erects fort, 122; at Cedar Creek, 155; at Shenandoah, 236; escapes Union Army, 241; reinforced by Kershaw, 270; attacked by Sheridan, 274; report, 274; reinforced by

Gordon, 276; at Fisher's Hill, 284, 296
Evarts, Southmayd & Choate, vii
Ewell, Gen., at Harrisburg, 98; attacks Warren, 142; Ewell's corps, 122
Eleven Months in a Rebel Prison, 149
Everett, 6
Emmitsburg Road, 104
Ellsworth, Major, killed at Alexandria, 15
Eustis, Gen. H. L., commands brigade, 106; in 4th brigade, 138; succeeds Russell, 167; succeeded by Edwards, 365
Ely's Ford, 129, 141

Fair Oaks, Battle o', 22
Fairfax Court-House, 38
Fairfax Station, 95, 121
Franklin's Corps, 42, 45, 63
Franklin's Crossing, 62
Farragut, Admiral, captures Mobile Bay, 265
Frederick, Md., 40
Fredericksburg, Battle of, 57; Sedgwick at, 83; capture by Sixth Corps, 85
Fredericksburg Road, 207
French, Gen., 110
First N. J. Brigade, 349
Fisher's Hill, Sheridan at, 286; Fort Fisher, work on, 325
Five Forks, victory at, 344
Fort Darling, gunboats at, 323
Fort Fisher, 290
Forge at Jones Bridge, 216
Fort Albany, 36
Fort Hamilton, 37th Mass. at, 116
Fortress Monroe, 317
Fort Sumter, surrender of, 7; evacuated, 333
Fort Stevens, 243; Edwards at, 322
Fort Stedman, 229, 338
Fort Wadsworth, 316; visited by Lincoln, 338
Fort Welch, 344
Foster's *New Jersey and the Rebellion*, 351
Four Years in the Saddle, by Gilmore, 329
Fourteenth Georgia, prisoners captured, 350

Fox, *Regimental Losses*, 45, 151, 213, 357
Fugitive Slave Bill, 6
Funkstown, 111

Gainesville, 121
Garrison, 6
Graves, Sergeant, 146
Grant, Col. L. A., 361
Grant, Gen. U. S., praise of, 23; at Chattanooga, 126; made Lieut.-General, 137; at Wilderness, 82, 141; victories in the West, 159; at Spottsylvania, 170; puzzles Gen. Lee, 200; orders attack, 212; exonerates Hancock, 221; *Memoirs* quoted, 225, 337; at Petersburg, 240; unites forces, 242; nominates Franklin and Meade, 254; at Richmond, 319; on deserters, 320; at Cape Fear, 326; extra vigilance of, 334
Gayle house, 207
Germanna Ford, 142
Getty, Gen. G. W., commands 2d Division, 138; supports Hancock, 142; at Wilderness, 151; on Brock Road, 161; wounded, 206; commands division, 234; commands Sixth Corps, 248
Gettysburg, Battle of, 158, 159; Lee at, 98
Gibbon, Gen., 171, 212, 233
Griffin, Gen., 145, 208
Gilliss's battery, 352
Gilmore, Maj. H., capture of, 328
Goodrich, Lt.-Col., resigns, 69
Gordon, Gen., surprises Shaler and Seymour, 155; at "Bloody Angle," 183; *Reminiscences of the Civil War* by, 183; reinforces Early, 276; attack at Fort Stedman, 338
Gordonsville, 142, 240, 253
Gosport Navy Yard partially destroyed, 13
Grover, Brig.-Gen., 283
Guinea Station, 207

Hackett, Dr., 287
Halifax Road, 316
Halleck, Gen., 115, 241, 315
Haines's *History of the 15th N. J. Regt.*, 197, 350

Hamblin, Gen., 242; commands Edwards's brigade, 325
Hamblin, Col. J. E., 357
Hancock, Gen., stops Hill's advance, 142; Tyler reports to, 148; at Wilderness, 153; rescues Barlow, 167; at the Salient, 178; at Bloody Angle, 181; demands an investigation, 220; exonerated, 221; commands 3d brigade, 237
Hancock, camp at, 49
Hanovertown, 209
Hardee, Gen., 11
Hare House, 229
Harlow, Lt.-Col., 89
Harper's Ferry, 42, 47
Harris, Mrs., 291
Harrisburg, 96
Harrison's Creek, 221
Harris, Lieut., 131
Harvard College, 6
Hatcher's Run, raid at, 328, 343
Haversack's brigade, 230
Hawkins, Anthony, vi
Haw's shop, 209
Hays, Brig.-Gen. Alexander, 145
Hazel Run, 64
Hexamer's battery, 90
Hill, Henry, merchant of Amherst, 26
Hill, Gen., Southern confidence in, 158; driven back by Sixth Corps, 207; defeated at Williamsburg, 237; wounded, 201
Hill's Corps, 233, 322, 339
Hinckley, Thos., Gov. of Plymouth, v
Hitchcock, Dr., 251
Hood's Mill, 98
Hooker, Gen., 64; commands army, 74; visited by Lincoln, 79; at Chancellorsville, 81; calls Sedgwick, 82; attacks Lee, 83; at United States Ford, 91; relieved of command, 95
Hooker, Rev. Thos., v
Hopkins, Capt., on picket duty, 336
Hopkins, President, 291
Hopkins's Mill, 216
Houghton, classmate, 135
Howe, Gen., 85; commands Sigel's forces, 248
Humphrey, Dr., President of Amherst, 30

Humphrey, Gen., *Virginia Campaign of '64 and '65*, 193; hard pressed, 327

Hunter, Gen., succeeds Sigel, 240; joins Getty, 248; at Snicker's Gap, 248; succeeded by Sheridan, 262

Huntington, Dr. F. D., Bishop of Central N. Y., 30

Hutchinson, Capt., 125

Ironclads, Union, 323

Jackson, Gen., *Life and Letters*, 207

Jackson, Gen. Stonewall, at United States Ford, 82; faith in, 158; death of, 207

Jacob's Mill Ford, 126

James River Canal, 240

Jerusalem Plank-Road, 223, 231

Jericho Ford, Warren crosses, 208

Johnson, Reverdy, 14

Johnston, Gen., wounded, 22; surprises Gen. Shaler, 155; commands Confederates, 337

Johns, Col., at Marye's Heights, 84; wounded, 89

Jones Bridge, 216

Jordan house, the, 226

Kam, Col., 42

Keedysville, 52

Kellogg, Albert, 331

Kellogg, E. H., 342

Kelly's Ford, 123

Keifer, Col. J. W., 366

Kershaw's brigade, 107

Kilpatrick, Gen., 135

King George's County Court-House, 61

Landrum House, 170, 203, 352

Lee. Brig-Gen. C., capture of, 345

Lee, Gen. Fitzhugh, 281

Lee, Col. R., of 20th Mass. Vols., 27

Lee, Gen. R. E., on secession, 13; commands army, 22; summons Jackson, 23; near Washington, 31; prepares to invade, 96; at Rappahannock, 96; attack at Gettysburg, 104; crosses Potomac, 111; at Wilderness, 140; confidence in, 158; obstructs progress, 163; at the Salient, 182; at Spottsylvania, 200; mystified by Grant, 219; alarm at desertions, 322; plans to evacuate, 335; losses at Fort Stedman, 338; at Fort Welch, 345

Lee, R. E., Chapter of the Daughters of the Confederacy, 185

Leesburg, 248

Lincoln, Abraham, President, 6; election of, 7; inaugurated, 7; calls for volunteers, 14; reviews army, 79; calls for 100,000 men, 96; enforces draft, 113; Thanksgiving day, 117; at Fort Stevens, 243; visit to, 317; at Fort Wadsworth, 338

Lincoln, Capt. R. P., 77, 230, 251, 330; on leave, 311; mustered Major, 314; wounded, 195

Little Round Top, 101, 103

Lizzie Baker, steamer, 315

Long, Capt. W. H., 206

Long's *Memoirs of R. E. Lee*, 141, 201

Long, Maj., 233

Long Bridge, 341

Longstreet, Gen., corps, 96; at Fayetteville, 99; march from Gordonsville, 154; backs Lee, 158; wounded, 201

Love, Dr., 290

Loyal Legion, N. Y. Commandery, ix

Lyman, Luke, Col., 27th Mass. Vols., 18

Lynchburg, 240

McCausland, Gen., attacked by Averell, 264

Macomber, classmate, 249

McCool house, 175

McHugh, James, 36, 47

McLaughlen, Col., 353

McLaws's division, 85

Madison Court-House, 136

Manross, Dr., killed at Antietam, 39

Manassas, Battle of, 31, 95

Manassas Plain, 57

Martindale's division, 211, 232

Marye's Heights, 83; Rebels open fire, 84; capture of, 84

Mason, Maj.-Gen. John, v

Massachusetts Institute of Technology, 19

Mather, *Magnalia*, vi

Maryland, ferry-boat, 35

Massachusetts Military Historical Society, 156, 194, 212
Manchester, Sixth Corps at, 102
Meade, Gen., succeeds Hooker, 95; commands army, 98, 110; at the Rapidan 122; report of, 144; reconnoitres, 209; at Petersburg, 316; capture of Young, 321; at Fort Wadsworth, 338
Melyn, C., Patroon of Staten Island, vi
McClellan, Gen. G. B., commands army, 16; transfers army, 21; opposed by Confederates, 21; retreat, 22; relieved of command, 56
Merrill, W. F., 257
Merritt, Gen., at Strasburg, 284; defeats Rosser, 295
Metcalf, Lieut., 352
Mexican War, 10
Middle Military Division, 326
Milford Point Station, 207
Milroy's army, 96
Mine Run Campaign, 127
Monocacy Creek, 241, 255
Montague, Lt.-Col., prostrated by heat, 108; commands 37th Mass., 167; commands brigade, 271; brevetted Colonel, 318; at Camp Warren, 325; at Washington 331; retires, 335
Moorfield, 328
Morse, Chaplain, fits up chapel, 326
Morson, Dr., 93
Mosby, Col., attack by, 250; search for, 306, 331
Morris, Brig-Gen. W. H., 365
Mott's division, 145, 156, 168, 171; Tammany Brigade, 179, 190
McDowell, Gen., 158
Muhlenberg Hospital, viii
Music Hall Ass'n, viii
Myer's Hill, 354
My Recollections of the Civil War, 150

Napier's Peninsular War, 328
Negroes abused in N. Y., 114
Neill, Gen. T. H., assists Warren, 142; in Mexican War, 206; in 2d Division, 225; ordered to 18th Corps, 232; at Winchester,

286; succeeded by Bidwell, 363
Nelson's Ford, 209
Nevin, Col., succeeds Wheaton, 105
New Baltimore, camp at, 57
Newbern, Battle of, 20
New Cold Harbor, 211
Newmarket, 95
Newton, Gen., 67; letter to Gov. Andrews, 89; commands 1st Corps, 105
New England, sentiment against slavery in, 6
N. J. Brigade, 192, 197, 198
N. J. Society, viii
N. J. Historical Society, viii
N. Y. Independent, 59
N. Y. State Bar Association, viii
North Anna River, 201, 205
North Carolina wishes to rejoin the Union, 332

Occoquan, the, 95
Orange & Alexandria R.R., 140
Orange Court-House, 128
Orange Plank Road, 142, 159, 160
O'Bannan, Mrs., house at Winchester, 328
Organized Aid Ass'n of Plainfield, viii
Ord's Army of the James, 346
Oregon, steamer, 33
Ogden, Robert, vi
Owen, Gen. J. T., 148
Old Cold Harbor, 210; departure from, 216
Onondaga, gunboat, 323
Offutt's Cross-Roads, 246

Plainfield Public Library, viii
Pamunkey River, 208
Parke, Gen., commands Army of Potomac, 333; captures Fort Stedman, 338
Parke's Station on Military Road, 315
Parker, Major, 89
Parker's store, 143
Parker, Theodore, 6
Peach Orchard, the, 104
Pleasonton, Gen., 47
Pennsylvania Bucktails, 42
Penrose, Col., at Spottsylvania, 350
Perit, propeller, 242
Presbyterian Hospital, ix

Petersville, 256
Petersburg, 230, 240, 242, 272, 340; march to, 218; episode at, 322
Phillips, 6
Pollock's mill, 69
Poolesville, 95, 247
Polecat River, crossing at, 208
Poplar Grove Church, 325
Photographic History of the Civil War, 227
Potomac frozen over, 324
Provisional District, Col. Edwards commands, 315
Pickett's charge, 109
Pierpont, Rev. Jas., vi
Pipe Creek, defense at, 98
Phi Beta Kappa Society, vii
Psi Upsilon Fraternity, vii
Purcellville, 249

Ramseur, Gen., 189, 275
Rappahannock, 123, 140, 200; charge at, 237; Rappahannock Station, 356
Readville, camp at, 342
Ream's Station, 235
Rebel gunboat affair, 323
Rectortown, 111
Regiments: 1st Conn., 341; 20th Indiana, 115; 5th Maine, 277, 352; 6th Maine, 237, 355; 7th Maine, 363; 6th Maryland, 366; 1st Mass., 115; 6th Mass., 8, 13; 7th Mass., 44, 84, 123, 179, 237, 364; 8th Mass., 14; 10th Mass., 28, 31, 37, 41, 123, 125, 179, 194, 228, 237, 364; 15th Mass., 19; 20th Mass., 19, 147, 170, 171, 177; 21st Mass., 18, 20; 27th Mass., 18, 20; 32d Mass., 27; 33d Mass., 27; 34th Mass., 27, 296; 35th Mass., 27; 36th Mass., 26, 27, 60; 37th Mass., 28, 37, 39, 40, 42, 44, 46, 60, 66, 76, 84, 103, 109, 115, 123, 139, 147, 154, 159, 167, 179, 192, 204, 226, 277, 283, 289, 364; 57th Mass., 147; 1st N. J., 197, 349, 351; 2d N. J., 349, 351; 3d N. J., 349, 351; 4th N. J., 349, 351; 10th N. J., 349, 351; 14th N. J., 349, 351; 15th N. J., 248, 349, 351; 7th N. Y., 14, 97; 36th N. Y., 44, 80, 84; 42d N. Y., 19; 43d N. Y., 84, 237, 363;
49th N. Y., 363; 62d N. Y., 358; 65th N. Y., 357; 66th N. Y., 357; 77th N. Y., 180, 363; 106th N. Y., 365; 121st N. Y., 352; 122d N. Y., 357; 151st N. Y., 365; 50th N. Y. Engineers, 325; 110th Ohio, 366; 122d Ohio, 366; 126th Ohio, 366; 23d Penn., 237, 271, 357; 49th Penn., 125, 237, 341, 355; 61st Penn., 84, 363; 67th Penn., 366; 82d Penn., 237, 341, 357; 87th Penn., 365; 93d Penn., 358; 95th Penn., 352; 96th Penn., 352; 98th Penn., 358; 102d Penn., 358; 119th Penn., 237, 355; 138th Penn., 366; 139th Penn., 358; 148th Penn., 238; 2d R. I., 44, 63, 123, 179, 194, 214, 331, 341; 2d Vermont, 361; 3d Vermont, 361; 4th Vermont, 233, 361; 5th Vermont, 361; 6th Vermont, 361; 10th Vermont, 365; 11th Vermont, 246; 5th Wisconsin, 115, 237, 238, 339, 342, 355; 5th U. S. Artillery, 352
Relay House, 40
Reno, Gen., killed, 53
Review of Reviews Co., 227
Reynolds, Gen., at Marsh Creek, 100; death of, 105
Richmond & Fredericksburg R.R., 140
Richmond & York R.R., 216
Richmond, advance on, 201, 213; Grant at, 319; evacuation of, 345
Ricketts, Capt., Artillery, 144
Ricketts's division, Gen., 211, 229
Robertson's River, 136
Robertson's Tavern, 126
Robinson, Capt., 300, 319
Rock Creek, 103
Rodes, Gen., 275, 289
Rhodes's *History*, quoted, 7
Rhodes, Lt.-Col., 341
Rohrersville, 52
Rosser, Gen., defeated by Custer, 295
Rossendale-Reddaway Belting and Hose Co., viii
Round Top, 101
Royal Charter of Conn., v
Russell, Gen. D. A., at Fredericksburg, 90; commands 1st Divi-

Russell, Gen. D. A.—*Continued*
sion, 166; assaults by, 192, 198;
supports Griffin, 208; at Rappahannock, 237; death of, 277
Russell's brigade, 355

Sailor's Creek, 345
Shaler, Gen., at Gettysburg, 107;
surprised by Gordon, 155; capture of, 357
Salient, the, 164, 170, 173, 176, 180,
190, 195, 201, 237, 365
Sandy Hook, 42
Stafford Court-House, 58, 94
Sharpsburg, 40, 43
St. John, Elizabeth, vi
Salem, 111; Salem Heights, 85,
139
Scan, Miss Kitty, 268
Sanitary and Christian Commissions, 238
Swan, Col., at Battle of Wilderness, 156
Strasburg, Gen. Early at, 253
Stanton, Secretary, 254
Shaw, W. H., *War Diary*, 243
Stearns, Frazer, Adjutant, 18;
killed at Newbern, 20
Stearns, Wm. F., gifts to volunteers, 25
Stebbins, Rev. C., contributes
introductions, 222
Spear, Col., at Marye's Heights,
84
Seaver, Col., 84
Second Army Corps, Warren's
History of, 105
Second Bull Run, 31
Sedgwick, Gen., commands Sixth
Corps, 74; at Marye's Heights,
84; at Banks's Ford, 87; in winter quarters, 124; stops rout, 156;
takes command, 164; death of,
165; concerning, 197; commands 3d brigade, 355
Seminary Ridge, 101
Shenandoah Valley, 111, 241; campaign of, 343
Shepard, Capt., of class of 1860, 71
Shepard, Dr., 134
Shepard, Maj., among missing,
331
Stephenson's depot, 315
Sheridan, Gen., holds Old Cold
Harbor, 210; appointed temporary command, 254; at Washington, 254; calls on President, 254;
commands Middle Military
Dep't., 262; takes command,
263; retreat at Cedar Creek, 270;
visited by Lieut.-General, 274;
warned by Grant, 275; fought
Rebel army, 276; moves up Valley, 284; battle at Fisher's Hill,
284; drives Early from camp,
286; retreat down Valley, 292;
at Cedar Creek, 296; at headquarters, 296; starts for the
front, 297; recaptures prisoners and guns, 297; captures
Maj. Gilmore, 328; cavalry,
340; victory at Five Forks,
344
Sheridan's *Memoirs* quoted, 274,
329
Sherman, Gen., 312
Stevens, Capt. H., 206, 344
"Seven Days' Fight," the, 23
Seven Pines, Battle of, 22
Seymour, Lieut. J., vi
Seymour, Horatio, Governor of
New York, 112
Seymour, Gen., 155
Snicker's Gap, 249
Snickersville, 249
Sickles, Gen., 104
Sigel, Gen., commands Dept. of
W. Va., 240; defeat at Newmarket, 240
Swinton, Wm., correspondent of
N. Y. *Times*, 317
Swinton's *History of the Army of
the Potomac*, 201
Smith, A. J., 206
Smith, Col. B. F., 366
Smith, W. F., Gen., 45
Smith, Gen., sent to White House,
224
Smith, Dr., of Amherst, 316
Smithsonian Institute, burning
of, 325
Sixth Army Corps: Gen. Sedgwick
commands, 74; reviewed by
President, 78; Col. Johns's column, 84; at New Windsor, 99;
at Little Round Top, 105; at
Chantilly, 121; to Rappahannock, 122; attempts to release
prisoners, 135; at Germanna
Ford, 142; losses at Wilderness,
151; never stampeded, 155; loses
officers, 161; at Alsop's, 163; at

Sixth Army Corps—*Continued*
the Salient, 178; Bloody Angle,
182; at Spottsylvania, 203;
losses, 207; entangled in swamp,
209; at Old Cold Harbor, 210;
losses, 213; at Petersburg, 222;
attack on Salient, 237; saving
Washington, 241; to Petersburg,
253; at Cedar Creek, 285; deserters from Rebels, 322; hospital,
332; at Fort Stedman, 340; held
for service in Va., 341; reviewed
by Lincoln, 341; great record,
343; brigades of, 349; 1st Brig.,
1st Div., 349; 2d Brig., 1st Div.,
352; 3d Brig., 1st Div., 355;
1st. Brig., 2d Div., 358; 2d
Brig., 2d Div., 361; 3d Brig.,
2d Div., 362; 2d Brig., 2d
Div., 364; 1st Brig., 3d Div.,
365; 2d Brig., 3d Div., 366
Sloane, Col., killed at Bull Run,
44
Society of Colonial Governors, ix
Society of *Mayflower* Descend-
ants, viii
Society of Sons of the Revolution,
viii
Society of Colonial Wars, ix
Schroeder, Eliza M., married M.
W. Tyler, ix
Soldiers' Relief Barracks, 36
Schofield, Gen., at Cape Fear, 327
Schofield and Terry capture Wil-
mington, 334
Scott, Gen., retired, 16
Spottsylvania Court-House, 163,
167, 200, 203, 207
Spottsylvania, Salient of, 164;
Confederate defenses at, 212
South Mountain Pass, 53; 110
South threatens to secede, 6
South Side Railroad, 336
Stuart, Gen., 51; cavalry, 98, 100;
under Lee, 158; death of, 201
Summit Point, skirmish at, 270;
Union lines at, 275
Summit Station, 216
Sumner, Gen., 64
Sumner, Senator, from Mass., 6
Stutz, Jacob, 350

Ta River, halt at, 207
Thacher, Rev. Thos., pastor
Old South Church, vi
Tracy, Capt. W. C., death of, 233

Tracy, J. Evarts, 233
Traveller, steamer, 342
Taylor, Joe, 59
Taylor's International Hotel, 317
Taylor's Ford, 209
Treat, Richard, vi
"Telegraph Road," the, 207
Tremain, Gen., partner of M. W.
Tyler, ix
Tennallytown, 246, 255
Twentieth Mass., History of, 170
Terry, Gen., at Rappahannock,
122; Fort River Expedition, 323
Thirty-Seventh Regt., Bowen's *His-
tory of*, 106
Thirty-Seventh Mass. Vols.: at
Camp Briggs, 27; at Jersey
City, 33; reach Washington, 35;
picket duty, 37; in Capitol
grounds, 40; joins Sixth Corps,
45; to Williamsport, 50; in
Virginia, 54; picket duty, 59;
"Camp Misery," 62; crosses
Rappahannock, 65; at Marye's
Heights, 83; checks Confederate
advance, 86; praised by Gen.
Newton, 90; at Little Round
Top, 103; at Gettysburg, 110;
sent to New York, 115; at Fort
Hamilton, 117; ordered to
Washington, 119; with Wheaton's brigade, 123; win at baseball, 125; to Brandy Station,
129; at Wilderness, 139; check
Rebel advance, 147; Col. Montague commands, 167; losses,
207; at Old Cold Harbor, 211; 2d
Rhode Island attached to, 214;
receives men of 10th Mass.,
228; transferred to 3d Brigade,
237; Shenandoah Valley, 241;
to Washington, 241; to City
Point, 242; on skirmish line, 244;
relieved by 11th Vermont, 246;
at Poolesville, 247; at Clark's
Gap, 248; recross Shenandoah,
250; attack by Mosby, 250;
inspection by Capt. Tyler, 251;
to Halltown, 253; at Frederick, 256; to Buckeyeville, 261;
Monocacy River, 263; through
Charlestown, 266; Cedar Creek,
268; at Shenandoah, 271; Col.
Montague commands, 272; at
Cedar Creek, 284; at Winchester, 284; sent to Petersburg, 315;

Thirty-Seventh Mass. Vols.
        Continued
Donnelly commands, 315;
praised by Col. Edwards, 339;
review at Washington, 342;
mustered out, 342; praised by
Meade, 347
Todd, Rev. Dr., 32
Thomas, Gen., 126
Tompkins, Col. C. H., 207, 225
Torbert's brigade, 136
Tuckerman, Mrs., 292
Tyler, John, Capt., vi
Tyler, President John, residence
of, 217
Tyler, John, Jr., Revolutionary
patriot, vi
Tyler, Carrie, 332
Tyler, Henry, letters to, 123, 238,
302, 312, 313, 319, 329, 333
Tyler, Mason W.; birthplace, 4;
enters college, 9; threatened
with consumption, 20; appointed 2d Lieut., 26; appeals for
volunteers, 26; joins 37th Mass.
Vols., 27; starts for Washington,
32; reaches Washington, 35;
joins Devens's brigade, 39;
meets Gen. Casey, 41; picket
duty, 49; Thanksgiving dinner,
60; at Camp Misery, 62; visited
by father, 69; appointed Captain, 70; commands Devens's
brigade, 70; dainties from home,
77; at Marye's Heights, 83;
praised by officers, 91; at Gettysburg, 103; Pickett's men surrender, 109; escapes bullet, 111;
at New York draft, 116; visits
Amherst, 119; Police Commissioner, 119; at Warrenton, 122;
meets Lincoln, 132; Judge Advocate, 134; attempts to release
prisoners, 135; acts as scout,
149; escape at Wilderness, 149;
at Chancellorsville, 164; at the
Salient, 176; Bloody Angle, 190;
joins Gen. Neill, 206; at Cold
Harbor, 220; praises Gen. Neill,
232; joins Col. Edwards, 232;
reaches Washington, 243; suffers from malaria, 254; appointed Judge Advocate, 269; at
Winchester, 277; wounded, 282;
meets Sheridan, 296; goes to
Amherst, 314; at Binghamton,

316; Christmas at New Milford,
316; at Washington, 317; visits
Lincoln, 317; brevetted Major,
318; admires Lee, 335; commands regiment, 336; com-
missioned Major, 338; wounded,
339; returns to Amherst, 341;
feast at Springfield, 342; letters
to brothers, 123, 238, 273, 287,
300, 302, 312, 313, 319, 328,
329, 333, 336; letters to M. F.
Dickinson, 230, 232, 264, 271,
292, 294; letters from father,
255, 286; letters from mother,
236; letters from White Oak
Church, 75, 79; letters to father,
235, 259, 306, 311, 325; letters
to mother, 41, 78, 131, 228, 233,
234, 257, 268, 301, 303, 308, 309,
319, 320, 324, 326, 331, 335;
letters to parents, 47, 57, 66, 91,
94, 123, 125, 128, 130, 133, 261,
265, 267, 276, 290, 294, 298,
304, 339
Tyler, William, letters to, 273,
287, 302, 328
Tyler, Mrs. W. S., letter of July
2, 1864, 236; letter of July
5, 1864, 236; letters to, 41, 66,
78, 91, 94, 123, 125, 128, 130,
131, 133, 228, 233, 234, 257, 261,
265, 267, 268, 276, 290, 294, 298,
301, 304, 308, 309, 319, 320, 324,
326, 331, 335, 339
Tyler, W. S., at Amherst, v; letter
from Binghamton, 255; letter
from Amherst, 286; letters to,
66, 91, 94, 123, 125, 128, 130,
133, 235, 259, 261, 265, 267, 276,
290, 294, 298, 304, 306, 311, 325,
389
Tyler & Durand, vii
Tyler & Tyler, vii

Upperville, 5, 111
Union Army, near Frederick, 98
Union, village of, 54; halt at, 111
Upton, Gen., at the Salient, 167,
192; attack on Salient, 237;
wounded, 278; reports by, 197,
281, 352

Vance, Col., Indiana regiment, 19,
77
Vaughan Road, 316
Verdierville, 128

Vermont Brigade, 134, 182, 227, 234, 361
Vicksburg, 137
Virginia, flagship, 324

Wadsworth's division, 145
Walker, Frank, 19, 43, 57, 68, 128
Wallace, Gen., in Maryland, 241
Warrenton Junction, 114; letter from, 121
Warren's *History of Second Army Corps*, 105
Warren, Gen., at Round Top, 104; at the Salient, 181; at North Anna River, 208
Washburn, Mr., 317
Washington's Birthday at Camp Warren, 333
Watts's Hill, 213
Wheaton, F. W., letter to Maj. Whittier, 318
Webster, Daniel, 6
Wheaton, Gen., at Round Top, 105; at the Salient, 180; reports battle, 244; saves the day, 330; report by, 358
Wheaton's brigade, 113, 204, 227, 358
"Wheatfield," the, 106, 139
Wilderness, Battle of, 139, 151, 156, 158, 194, 200
Williamsport, 43, 50
White Plains, Va., 55
White's Ford, 47
Weitzel's corps, 337
Weldon Railroad, 223, 232
Wells, Col. Geo. D., 283
Welles, Thos., Governor of Conn., v; ancestor of M. W. Tyler, vi
Wright, Gen., at Wilderness, 156;

commands Sixth Corps, 166; wounded, 181; at City Point, 241; at Fort Stevens, 243; receives orders from Grant, 253; report on deserters, 321; displaces Edwards, 325; circular to Sixth Corps, 334; praised by Grant, 344
Wilcox Landing, camp at, 217
Wilderness Tavern, 142
Willet, Thomas, first Mayor New York, v
Willoughby Run, 101
Williamsburg, Battle of, 237
Williamsport, 110
Williams, S., Ass't Adj.-Gen., 114
Wilmington, N. C., capture of, 334
Wilson, Gen., 275
Wilson's division, 212
Wilson's cavalry, 235
Winchester, Battle of, 275; Sheridan at, 297
White Oak Church, letters from, 75, 79
Whiting, Rev. S., vi
Whiting, Dr., W. experiments in gunpowder, vi
Whittier, Maj. C. A., letter from Wheaton, 318
White, Corporal David, capture by, 345
White Post, 275
Wofford's brigade, 107

Yorktown besieged, 21
Young, Capt., escape of, 229; leads scouts, 250; captures scout, 321

1379 YA MC 98 LBC

10-28-94 33060